Classics
of
Western Philosophy

Classics of Western Philosophy

Eighth Edition

Edited by

Steven M. Cahn

Hackett Publishing Company, Inc.
Indianapolis/Cambridge

To Marilyn

Printed in the United States of America

24 23 22 21 20 19 1 2 3 4 5 6

For further information, please address:
Hackett Publishing Company, Inc.
P.O. Box 44937
Indianapolis, IN 46244-0937
www.hackettpublishing.com

Cover design by Brian Rak
Text design by Meera Dash

Library of Congress Cataloging-in-Publication Data

Classics of Western philosophy / edited by Steven M. Cahn. — Eighth Edition.
pages cm
Includes bibliographical references.
ISBN 978-1-60384-743-8 (pbk.) — ISBN 978-1-60384-744-5 (cloth)
1. Philosophy. I. Cahn, Steven M.
B29.C536 2012
190—dc23 2012007912

Contents

Preface ix

Plato 1

Laches 3
Euthyphro 18
Apology 27
Crito 40
Phaedo 47
Meno 80
Symposium 97
Republic (selections) 128

Aristotle 193

Categories (Chapters 1–5) 195
On Interpretation (selections) 199
Posterior Analytics (selections) 205
Physics (selections) 212
On the Soul (selections) 229
Metaphysics (selections) 243
Nicomachean Ethics (selections) 275

Epicurus 330

Letter to Menoeceus 332
The Principal Doctrines 335

Epictetus 338

Encheiridion 340

Sextus Empiricus 352

Outlines of Pyrrhonism (selections) 354

Augustine 372

On Free Choice of the Will (selections) 374
Confessions (Book XI) 390

Plotinus 403

Enneads (selections) 405

Boethius 417

Consolation of Philosophy (selections) 419

Anselm 428

Proslogion 430
Gaunilo's Reply on Behalf of the Fool 442
Anselm's Reply to Gaunilo 445

Moses Maimonides 451

The Guide of the Perplexed (selections) 453

Thomas Aquinas 457

Summa Theologiae (selections) 459

Levi Gersonides 479

The Wars of the Lord (selections) 481

William of Ockham 490

Summa Logicae (selections) 492

René Descartes 499

Discourse on Method 501
Meditations on First Philosophy 527

Thomas Hobbes 560

Leviathan (selections) 562

Baruch Spinoza 592

Ethics (Parts I, II) 594

Gottfried Leibniz 639

Discourse on Metaphysics 641
Monadology 662

John Locke 670

An Essay Concerning Human Understanding (selections) 672

George Berkeley 741

A Treatise Concerning the Principles of Human Knowledge 743
Three Dialogues between Hylas and Philonous 786

David Hume 832

An Enquiry Concerning Human Understanding 834
A Treatise of Human Nature (selections) 900
Dialogues Concerning Natural Religion 927

Immanuel Kant 974

Prolegomena to Any Future Metaphysics 976
Critique of Pure Reason (selections) 1034
Grounding for the Metaphysics of Morals 1110

G.W.F Hegel 1150

Phenomenology of Spirit (selections) 1152

Arthur Schopenhauer 1167

The World as Will and Representation (selections) 1169

Søren Kierkegaard 1177

Concluding Unscientific Postscript (selections) 1179

John Stuart Mill 1185

Utilitarianism 1187
On Liberty (selections) 1220

Friedrich Nietzsche 1227

Twilight of the Idols (selections) 1229

Charles Sanders Peirce 1244

The Fixation of Belief 1246
How to Make Our Ideas Clear 1255

William James 1266

What Pragmatism Means 1268
The Will to Believe 1278

Bertrand Russell 1290

The Problems of Philosophy (Chapters I–V) 1292

Edmund Husserl 1310

Paris Lectures (selections) 1312

Jean-Paul Sartre 1319

The Humanism of Existentialism 1321

Ludwig Wittgenstein 1334

Philosophical Investigations (selections) 1336

J. L. Austin 1351

Sense and Sensibilia (Chapters I–III, V) 1353

Preface

Here in one volume are the complete texts or substantial selections from sixty philosophical masterpieces. Thirty-three of the world's greatest philosophers are represented, their writings spanning more than two millennia. Crucial fields of philosophy are explored in depth: metaphysics, epistemology, ethics, and philosophy of religion. An introduction to each author contains biographical data, philosophical commentary, and bibliographical guides. Annotations are provided to clarify textual references.

• • •

The eighth edition contains five major additions: Plato's *Laches;* Aristotle's *Nicomachean Ethics,* III, 6–9; Descartes' *Discourse on Method;* Berkeley's *A Treatise Concerning the Principles of Human Knowledge* (previously included only in part), and Kant's *Prolegomena to Any Future Metaphysics.*

I very much appreciate the assistance of Richard Bett, Meredith Williams, and Michael Williams of Johns Hopkins University; Kathleen Higgins of the University of Texas; Ruth Anna Putnam of Wellesley College; Sara Ahbel-Rappe of the University of Michigan; Israel Scheffler of Harvard University; David Shatz of Yeshiva University; David Sherman of the University of Montana; Jonathan Vogel of Amherst College; and past and present faculty members at the University of Vermont: Charles Guignon (now of the University of South Florida), Patricia Kitcher and Philip Kitcher (both now of Columbia University), William E. Mann, Derk Pereboom (now of Cornell University), and George Sher (now of Rice University). They have contributed most of the introductions, thereby providing expert commentary on the writings of each philosopher.

I benefited greatly from advice by Professor Guignon regarding the selections from Nietzsche; Professor Higgins regarding the selections from Schopenhauer; Professor Pereboom regarding the selections from Kant and Kierkegaard; Professor Ahbel-Rappe regarding the selections from Plotinus; and Professor Meredith Williams regarding the selections from Wittgenstein. I especially appreciated the advice from Professor Andrea Tschemplik of American University regarding the selections from Hegel and her willingness and that of James H. Stam to give permission for use of their translation of sections from the *Phenomenology of Spirit.* Professor Mann, with whom I consulted on a variety of editorial matters, furnished many of the translations of Latin textual references. For additional suggestions regarding the contents of the book, I am grateful to my friends of many years John O'Connor, David Rosenthal, and the late James Rachels, as well as to the numerous philosophers who have taken the time and effort to write and offer counsel.

Editing and production of the eighth edition were overseen by Brian Rak and Liz Wilson. I appreciate their conscientiousness and sound judgment.

I also wish to thank Jay Hullett and the late Frances Hackett, who have led Hackett Publishing Company and remained true to the values of its late founder, William H. Y. Hackett. Thirty-five years have passed since this work first appeared, and the kind reception it continues to enjoy is a testament to the power of William Hackett's publishing vision.

Steven M. Cahn
Professor of Philosophy
The Graduate Center
The City University of New York
April 2012

Plato

Plato (427–347 B.C.) is surely the most famous of all philosophers. Little is known of his early life, except that he was born into a noble Athenian family and at some time in his late teens came under the philosophical spell of Socrates (469–399 B.C.), about whom valuable information is contained in Plato's *Apology.* The events leading up to and culminating in the Athenian government's trial and execution of Socrates, when Plato was twenty-eight, soured Plato on the idea of embarking on a life in politics and resulted in his leaving Athens to travel for a number of years in the Mediterranean region. Plato returned to Athens in 387 and founded his school, the Academy, in the belief that such an institution was necessary for the education of political leaders who would be morally excellent. The Academy attracted many of the finest contemporary minds, including Aristotle. Plato twice visited Syracuse in a futile attempt to inculcate his moral and political ideas in Syracuse's young tyrant, Dionysius II.

Socrates wrote nothing: It is fortunate that his most illustrious follower did not follow that example. At least twenty-six of Plato's dialogues have survived, ranging in length from the brief *Crito* to the voluble *Laws,* which is longer than the *Republic.* The dialogues are customarily divided into three periods of Plato's literary career: early, middle, and late. The early dialogues—of which the *Laches, Euthyphro, Apology,* and *Crito* are examples—are taken to be accurate if not verbatim portrayals of Socrates in philosophical action. The middle dialogues, represented here by the *Meno, Phaedo,* and *Republic,* display Plato at the height of his literary abilities, seeking to further the projects inspired by Socrates while at the same time introducing doctrines that are extremely unlikely to have been Socrates' own. The late dialogues are dialogues in name only, quite often technically demanding in nature. They appear to represent Plato's efforts to grapple with the critical issues raised by the doctrines enunciated in the middle dialogues and most likely raised by others in the Academy.

As the *Apology* makes clear, Socrates professed to be ignorant of all matters philosophical, although not disputing the Delphic oracle's pronouncement that he was the wisest of all men. He concluded that his "wisdom," compared to the pretenses of others, lay in knowing the extent of his ignorance. Taking his mission to be to show others the magnitude of their ignorance about the most important matters of their lives, Socrates relentlessly grilled his fellow Athenian citizens, using rigorous argumentation to demonstrate that uncritically accepted opinions about philosophically important matters could lead to logical catastrophe: The *Laches, Euthyphro* and the early pages of the *Meno* provide excellent examples of Socrates' technique.

Yet for all his professed ignorance, Socrates clung to several distinctive philosophical doctrines. First, one cannot have genuine knowledge about moral matters unless one can give a rationally defensible account of such notions as courage (*Laches*), piety (*Euthyphro*), justice (*Republic*), and virtue or human excellence in general (*Meno*). Socrates thus pitted himself against the Sophists, a contemporary group of itinerant professional teachers, many of whom fostered the belief in their students that no objective knowledge was to be had in ethics. Socrates believed that moral knowledge is possible but difficult to acquire, and that his method of exposing ignorance in others was a necessary first step to their acquiring it. Second, as the *Meno* intimates, in some way or other virtue (or excellence in humans) is knowledge. The *Laches,* for example, probes the hypothesis that courage is knowledge. That the dialogue's participants do not succeed in identifying what kind of knowledge courage might be illustrates the difficulty in acquiring moral knowledge and the importance of becoming aware of one's ignorance The remarkable corollary of the claim that virtue is knowledge is the thesis that all wrongdoing is the result of ignorance. Third, as illustrated in the *Crito* and argued for in the *Republic,* Socrates believed that it is better for one to suffer injustice than to do injustice.

Plato came to believe that, if ethics is something more than the product of arbitrary convention, and if moral judgments are objective, then ethics must be grounded in objects that are unchanging in character and accessible to human minds. These objects are the Forms, the perfect, abstract objects discussed in the *Phaedo, Symposium,* and *Republic.* Humans can have knowledge of the Forms by recollection, a process that Plato describes in the *Meno,* alludes to in the *Phaedo,* and presupposes in the *Republic.* The importance Plato assigns to the Form of the Good in the *Republic* is designed to show how the acquisition of knowledge of the Forms provides one with the motivation to be virtuous. The connection between intellectual knowledge and moral motivation is also underscored in the Symposium, where Plato argues that love, rationally pursued, will lead the lover to its ultimate object, the Form of Beauty. The doctrine of Recollection in turn presupposes that humans have existed before their present lives. From there it seems a small step to the thesis that the soul is immortal. In the *Phaedo,* whose dramatic setting is the day of Socrates' execution, Plato has Socrates present several arguments for the immortality of the soul. If the soul is immortal, then care for it should be more important than care for the body: One of the major themes of the *Republic* is that behaving justly is at least as valuable for the care of the soul, as well as for the care of the state, as physical health is for the care of the body.

• • •

The amount of excellent philosophical writings on Socrates and Plato is far too large to list here but certainly includes the following. On Socrates in general, see Gregory Vlastos, *Socrates: Ironist and Moral Philosopher* (Ithaca, N.Y.: Cornell University Press, 1991) along with two collections of essays, Hugh Benson, ed., *Essays on the Philosophy of Socrates* (New York: Oxford University Press, 1992) and Gregory Vlastos, ed., *The Philosophy of Socrates* (Garden City, N.J.: Doubleday, 1971). Two studies on early dialogues appearing here are C. D. C. Reeve, *Socrates in the Apology* (Indianapolis, Ind.: Hackett Publishing Company, 1989) and, on the *Crito*, Richard Kraut, *Socrates and the State* (Princeton, N.J.: Princeton University Press, 1984).

Although somewhat demanding, the following works on Plato are superb: R. E. Allen, ed., *Studies in Plato's Metaphysics* (London: Routledge & Kegan Paul, 1965); Gail Fine, ed., *Plato 1: Metaphysics and Epistemology,* and *Plato 2: Ethics, Politics, Religion, and the Soul* (Oxford: Oxford University Press, 1999); Terence Irwin, *Plato's Ethics* (New York: Oxford University Press, 1995); Richard Kraut, ed., *The Cambridge Companion to Plato* (Cambridge: Cambridge University Press, 1992); Gregory Vlastos, ed., *Plato: A Collection of Critical Essays: I: Metaphysics and Epistemology,* and *II: Ethics, Politics, and Philosophy of Art and Religion* (Garden City, N.J.: Doubleday, 1970 and 1971); and Gregory Vlastos, *Platonic Studies,* second edition (Princeton, N.J.: Princeton University Press, 1981). Two books devoted to the *Republic* are Julia Annas, *An Introduction to Plato's Republic* (Oxford: Clarendon Press, 1981) and Richard Kraut, ed., *Plato's Republic* (Lanham, Md.: Rowman & Littlefield, 1997).

William E. Mann

Laches

LYSIMACHUS: You have seen the man fighting in armor, Nicias and Laches. When Melesias and I invited you to see him with us, we neglected to give the reason why, but now we shall explain, because we think it especially right to be frank with you. Now there are some people who make fun of frankness and if anyone asks their advice, they don't say what they think, but they make a shot at what the other man would like to hear and say something different from their own opinion. But you we considered capable not only of forming a judgment but also, having formed one, of saying exactly what you think, and this is why we have taken you into our confidence about what we are going to communicate to you. Now the matter about which I have been making such a long preamble is this: we have these two sons here—this one is the son of my friend Melesias here, and he is called Thucydides after his grandfather, and this one is my son, who also goes by his grandfather's name—we call him Aristides after my father. We have made up our minds to take as good care of them as we possibly can and not to behave like most parents, who, when their children start to grow up, permit them to do whatever they wish. No, we think that now is the time to make a real beginning, so far as we can. Since we knew that both of you had sons too, we thought that you, if anyone, would have been concerned about the sort of training that would make the best men of them. And if by any chance you have not turned your attention to this kind of thing very often, let us remind you that you ought not to neglect it, and let us invite you to care for your sons along with ours. How we reached this conclusion, Nicias and Laches, you must hear, even if it means my talking a bit longer. Now you must know that Melesias and I take our meals together, and the boys eat with us. We shall be frank with you, exactly as I said in the beginning: each of us has a great many fine things to say to the young men about his own father, things they achieved both in war and in peace in their management of the affairs both of their allies and of the city here. But neither of us has a word to say about his own accomplishments. This is what shames us in front of them, and we blame our fathers for allowing us to take things easy when we were growing up, while they were busy with other peoples' affairs. And we point these same things out to the young people here, saying that if they are careless of themselves and disobedient to us, they will turn out to be nobodies, but if they take pains, perhaps they may become worthy of the names they bear. Now the boys promise to be obedient, so we are looking into the question what form of instruction or practise would make them turn out best. Somebody suggested this form of instruction to us, saying that it would be a fine thing for a young man to learn fighting in armor. And he praised this particular man whom you have just seen giving a display and proceeded to encourage us to see him. So we thought we ought to go to see the man and to take you with us, not only as fellow-spectators but also as fellow-counsellors and partners, if you should be willing, in the care of our sons. This is what we wanted to share with you. So now is the time for you to give us your advice, not only about this form of instruction—whether you think it should be learned or not—but also about any other sort of study or pursuit for a young man which you admire. Tell us too, what part you will take in our joint enterprise.

NICIAS: I, for one, Lysimachus and Melesias, applaud your plan and am ready to take part in it. And I think Laches here is ready too.

LACHES: You are quite right, Nicias. As for what Lysimachus said just now about his father and Melesias' father, I think that what he said applied very well to them and to us and to everyone engaged in public affairs, because this is pretty generally what happens to them—that they neglect their private affairs, children as well as everything else, and manage them carelessly. So you were right on this

178a b 179a b c d e 180a b

Reprinted from Plato, *Laches and Charmides*, translated by Rosamond Kent Sprague (Indianapolis: Hackett Publishing Company, 1992), by permission of the publisher.

c point, Lysimachus. But I am astonished that you are inviting us to be your fellow-counsellors in the education of the young men and are not inviting Socrates here! In the first place, he comes from your own deme, and in the second, he is always spending his time in places where the young men engage in any study or noble pursuit of the sort you are looking for.

LYSIMACHUS: What do you mean, Laches? Has our friend Socrates concerned himself with any things of this kind?

LACHES: Certainly, Lysimachus.

NICIAS: This is a point I can vouch for no less than Laches, since he only recently recommended *d* a man to me as music teacher for my son. The man's name is Damon, a pupil of Agathocles, and he is the most accomplished of men, not only in music, but in all the other pursuits in which you would think it worthwhile for boys of his age to spend their time.

LYSIMACHUS: People at my time of life, Socrates, Nicias, and Laches, are no longer familiar with the young because our advancing years keep us at home *e* so much of the time. But if you, son of Sophroniscus, have any good advice to give your fellow-demesman, you ought to give it. And you have a duty to do so, because you are my friend through your father. He and I were always comrades and friends, and he died without our ever having had a single difference. And this present conversation reminds me of something—when the boys here are talking to each other at home, they often mention Socrates and praise him highly, but I've never though to ask if they were speaking *181a* of the son of Sophroniscus. Tell me, boys, is this the Socrates you spoke of on those occasions?

BOYS: Certainly, father, this is the one.

LYSIMACHUS: I am delighted, Socrates, that you keep up your father's good reputation, for he was the best of men, and I am especially pleased at the idea that the close ties between your family and mine will be renewed.

LACHES: Don't under any circumstances let the man get away, Lysimachus—because I have seen him elsewhere keeping up not only his father's reputation *b* but that of his country. He marched with me in the retreat from Delium,[1] and I can tell you that if the rest had been willing to behave in the same manner, our city would be safe and we would not then have suffered a disaster of that kind.

LYSIMACHUS: Socrates, the praise you are receiving is certainly of a high order, both because it comes from men who are to be trusted and because of the qualities for which they praise you. Be assured that I am delighted to hear that you are held in such esteem, and please consider me among those most kindly disposed towards you. You yourself ought to have visited us long before and considered us your *c* friends—that would have been the right thing to do. Well, since we have recognized each other, resolve now, starting today, to associate both with us and the young men here and to make our acquaintance, so that you may preserve the family friendship. So do what I ask, and we in turn shall keep you in mind of your promise. But what have you all to say about our original question? What is your opinion? Is fighting in armor a useful subject for young men to learn or not?

SOCRATES: Well, I shall try to advise you about these things as best I can, Lysimachus, in addition to *d* performing all the things to which you call my attention. However, it seems to me to be more suitable, since I am younger that the others and more inexperienced in these matters, for me to listen first to what they have to say and to learn from them. But if I should have something to add to what they say, then will be the time for me to teach and persuade both you and the others. Come, Nicias, why doesn't one of you two begin?

NICIAS: Well, there is no reason why not, Socrates. I think that knowledge of this branch of study is beneficial for the young in all sorts of ways. *e* For one thing, it is a good idea for the young not to spend their time in the pursuits in which they normally do like to spend it when they are at leisure, but rather in this one, which necessarily improves *182a* their bodies, since it is in no way inferior to gymnastic exercises and no less strenuous, and, at the same time, this and horsemanship are forms of exercise especially suited to a free citizen. For in the contest in which

1. [The Athenians were defeated by the Boeotians under Pagondas at Delium in November of 424, the eighth year of the Peloponnesian War. —R.K.S.]

we are the contestants and in the matters on which our struggle depends,[2] only those are practised who know how to use the instruments of war. And again, there is a certain advantage in this form of instruction even in an actual battle, whenever one has to fight in line with a number of others. But the greatest advantage of it comes when the ranks are broken and it then becomes necessary for a man to fight in *b* single combat, either in pursuit when he has to attack a man who is defending himself, or in flight, when he has to defend himself against another person who is attacking him. A man who had this skill would suffer no harm at the hands of a single opponent, nor even perhaps at the hands of a larger number, but he would have the advantage in every way. Then again, such a study arouses in us the desire for another fine form of instruction, since every man who learns to fight in armor will want to learn the subject that comes next, that is, the science of tactics; and when he has *c* mastered this and taken pride in it, he will press on to the whole art of the general. So it has already become clear that what is connected with this latter art, all the studies and pursuits which are fine and of great value for a man to learn and to practise, have this study as a starting-point. And we shall add to this an advantage which is not at all negligible, that this knowledge will make every man much bolder and braver in war that he was before. And let us not omit to mention, even if to some it might seem a point not worth making, that this art will give a man a finer-looking appearance at the very moment when he needs to have it, and *d* when he will appear more frightening to the enemy because of the way he looks. So my opinion, Lysimachus, is just as I say, that young men should be taught these things, and I have given the reasons why I think so. But if Laches has anything to say on the other side, I would be glad to hear it.

LACHES: But the fact is, Nicias, that it is difficult to maintain of any study whatsoever that it ought not to be learned, because it seems to be a good idea to learn everything. So as far as this fighting in armor *e* is concerned, if it is a genuine branch of study, as those who teach it claim, and as Nicias says, then it ought to be learned, but if it is not a real subject and the people who propose to teach it are deceiving us, or if it is a real subject but not a very important one, what need is there to learn it? The reason I say these things about it is that I consider that, if there were anything in it, it would not have escaped the attention of the Lacedaemonians, who have no other concern in life than to look for and engage in whatever studies and pursuits will increase their superiority in war. *183a* And if the Lacedaemonians had overlooked the art, the teachers of it would certainly not have overlooked this fact, that the Lacedaemonians are the most concerned with such matters of any of the Greeks and that anyone who was honored among them in these matters would make a great deal of money just as is the case when a tragic poet is honored among us. The result is that whenever anyone fancies himself as a good writer of tragedy, he does not go about exhib- *b* iting his plays in the other cities round about Athens but comes straight here and shows his work to our people, as is the natural thing to do. But I observe that those who fight in armor regard Lacedaemon as forbidden ground and keep from setting foot in it. They give it a wide berth and prefer to exhibit to anyone rather than the Spartans—in fact they take pains to select people who themselves admit that plenty of others surpass them in warfare. Then again, *c* Lysimachus, I have encountered quite a few of these gentlemen on the actual field of battle and I have seen what they are like. This makes it possible for us to consider the matter at first hand. In a manner which seems almost deliberate, not a single practitioner of the art of fighting in armor has ever become renowned in war. And yet in all the other arts, those who are well-known in each are those who have practised the various ones. But the men who practise this art seem to be those who have the worst luck at it. For instance, this very man Stesilaus, whom you and I have witnessed giving a display before such a large *d* crowd and praising himself the way he did, I once saw in the quite different circumstances of actual warfare giving a much finer demonstration against his will. On an occasion when a ship on which he was serving as a marine[3] rammed a transport-vessel, he was armed with a combination scythe and spear, as singular a weapon as he was singular a man. His other peculiarities are not worth relating, but let me tell you how his

2. [Nicias presumably refers to the Peloponnesian War.]

3. [That is, as a hoplite on a trireme.]

invention of a scythe plus a spear turned out. In the *e* course of the fight it somehow got entangled in the rigging of the other ship and there it stuck. So Stesilaus dragged at the weapon in an attempt to free it, but he could not, and meanwhile his ship was going by the other ship. For a time he kept running along the deck holding fast to the spear. But when the other ship was actually passing his and was dragging him after it while he still held onto the weapon, he let it *184a* slide through his hand until he just had hold of the ferule at the end. There was laughter and applause from the men on the transport at the sight of him, and when somebody hit the deck at his feet with a stone and he let go the shaft, then even the men on the trireme could no longer keep from laughing when they saw that remarkable scythe-spear dangling from the transport. Now perhaps these things may be of value, as Nicias maintains, but my own experience has been of the sort I describe. So, as I said in the *b* beginning, either it is an art but has little value, or it is not an art but people say and pretend that it is, but in any case it is not worth trying to learn. And then it seems to me that if a cowardly man should imagine he had mastered the art, he would, because of his increasing rashness, show up more clearly the sort of man he was, whereas in the case of a brave man, everyone would be watching him and if he made the smallest mistake, he would incur a great deal of criti- *c* cism. The reason for this is that a man who pretends to knowledge of this sort is the object of envy, so that unless he is outstandingly superior to the rest, there is no way in which he can possibly avoid becoming a laughingstock when he claims to have this knowledge. So the study of this art seems to me to be of this sort, Lysimachus. But, as I said before, we ought not to let Socrates here escape, but we ought to consult him as to his opinion on the matter in hand.

LYSIMACHUS: Well, I do ask your opinion, Socrates, since what might be called our council seems to me to be still in need of someone to cast the *d* deciding vote. If these two had agreed, there would be less necessity of such a procedure, but as it is, you perceive that Laches has voted in opposition to Nicias. So we would do well to hear from you too, and find out with which of them you plan to vote.

SOCRATES: What's that, Lysimachus? Do you intend to cast your vote for whatever position is approved by the majority of us?

LYSIMACHUS: Why, what else could a person do, Socrates?

SOCRATES: And do you, Melesias, plan to act in the same way? Suppose there should be a *e* council to decide whether your son ought to practise a particular kind of gymnastic exercise, would you be persuaded by the greater number or by whoever has been educated and exercised under a good trainer?

MELESIAS: Probably by the latter, Socrates.

SOCRATES: And you would be persuaded by him rather than by the four of us?

MELESIAS: Probably.

SOCRATES: So I think it is by knowledge that one ought to make decisions, if one is to make them well, and not by majority rule.

MELESIAS: Certainly.

SOCRATES: So in this present case it is also necessary to investigate first of all whether any one of us is an expert in the subject we are debating, or not. *185a* And if one of us is, then we should listen to him even if he is only one, and disregard the others. But if no one of us is an expert, then we must look for someone who is. Or do you and Lysimachus suppose that the subject in question is some small thing and not the greatest of all our possessions? The question is really, I suppose, that of whether your sons turn out to be worthwhile persons or the opposite—and the father's whole estate will be managed in accordance with the way the sons turn out.

MELESIAS: You are right.

SOCRATES: So we ought to exercise great forethought in the matter.

MELESIAS: Yes, we should.

SOCRATES: Then, in keeping with what I said *b* just now, how would we investigate if we wanted to find out which of us was the most expert with regard to gymnastics? Wouldn't it be the man who had studied and practised the art and who had had good teachers in that particular subject?

MELESIAS: I should think so.

SOCRATES: And even before that, oughtn't we to investigate what art it is of which we are looking for the teachers?

MELESIAS: What do you mean?

SOCRATES: Perhaps it will be more clear if I put it this way: I do not think we have reached any preliminary agreement as to what in the world we are consulting about and investigating when we ask which of us is expert in it and has acquired teachers c for this purpose, and which of us is not.

NICIAS: But, Socrates, aren't we investigating the art of fighting in armor and discussing whether young men ought to learn it or not?

SOCRATES: Quite so, Nicias. But when a man considers whether or not he should use a certain medicine to anoint his eyes, do you think he is at that moment taking counsel about the medicine or about the eyes?

NICIAS: About the eyes.

SOCRATES: Then too, whenever a man d considers whether or not and when he should put a bridle on a horse, I suppose he is at that moment taking counsel about the horse and not about the bridle?

NICIAS: That is true.

SOCRATES: So, in a word, whenever a man considers a thing for the sake of another thing, he is taking counsel about that thing for the sake of which he was considering, and not about what he was investigating for the sake of something else.

NICIAS: Necessarily so.

SOCRATES: Then the question we ought to ask with respect to the man who gives us advice, is whether he is expert in the care of that thing for the sake of which we are considering when we consider.

NICIAS: Certainly.

SOCRATES: So do we now declare that we are e considering a form of study for the sake of the souls of young men?

NICIAS: Yes.

SOCRATES: Then the question whether any one of us is expert in the care of the soul and is capable of caring for it well, and has had good teachers, is the one we ought to investigate.

LACHES: What's that, Socrates? Haven't you ever noticed that in some matters people become more expert without teachers than with them?

SOCRATES: Yes, I have, Laches, but you would not want to trust them when they said they were good craftsmen unless they should have some well-186a executed product of their art to show you—and not just one but more than one.

LACHES: What you say is true.

SOCRATES: Then what we ought to do, Laches and Nicias, since Lysimachus and Melesias called us in to give them advice about their two sons out of a desire that the boys' souls should become as good as possible—if we say we have teachers to show, is to point out to them the ones who in the first place are good themselves and have tended the souls of many young men, and in the second place have manifestly b taught us. Or, if any one of us says that he himself has had no teacher but has works of his own to tell of, then he ought to show which of the Athenians or foreigners, whether slave or free, is recognized to have become good through his influence. But if this is not the case with any of us, we should give orders that a search be made for others and should not run the risk of ruining the sons of our friends and thus incurring the greatest reproach from their nearest relatives. Now I, Lysimachus and Melesias, am the first to say, concerning myself, that I have had no teacher in this c subject. And yet I have longed after it from my youth up. But I did not have any money to give the sophists, who were the only ones who professed to be able to make a cultivated man of me, and I myself, on the other hand, am unable to discover the art even now. If Nicias or Laches had discovered it or learned it, I would not be surprised, because they are richer than I and so may have learned it from others, and also older, so they may have discovered it already. Thus they seem to me to be capable of educating a man, d because they would never have given their opinions so fearlessly on the subject of pursuits which are beneficial and harmful for the young if they had not believed themselves to be sufficiently informed on the subject. In other matters I have confidence in them, but that they should differ with each other surprises me. So I make this counter-request of you, Lysimachus: just as Laches was urging you just now not to let me go but to ask me questions, so I now call on you not to let Laches go, or Nicias, but to question them, saying that Socrates denies having any knowledge of the matter or being competent to decide which of e you speaks the truth, because he denies having been a discoverer of such things or having been anyone's pupil in them. So, Laches and Nicias, each of you tell us who is the cleverest person with whom you have associated in this matter of educating young men, and whether you acquired your knowledge of the art from another person or found it out for yourselves, and, if you learned it from some one, who were your respective teachers, and what other persons share the 187a same art with them. My reason for saying all this is that, if you are too busy because of your civic responsibilities, we can go to these men and persuade them, either by means of gifts or favors or both, to look after both our boys and yours too so that they won't put their ancestors to shame by turning out to be worthless. But if you yourselves have been the discoverers of such an art, give us an example of what other persons your have already made into fine men by your care when they were originally worthless. Because if you are about to begin educating people now for the first *b* time, you ought to watch out in case the risk is being run, not by a guinea-pig, but by your own sons and the children of your friends, and you should keep from doing just what the proverb says not to do—to begin pottery on a wine jar. So state which of these alternatives you would select as being appropriate and fitting for you and which you would reject. Find out these things from them, Lysimachus, and don't let the men escape.

LYSIMACHUS: I like what Socrates has said, *c* gentlemen. But whether you are willing to be questioned about such matters and to give account of them, you must decide for yourselves, Nicias and Laches. As far as Melesias here and I are concerned, we would certainly be pleased if the two of you were willing to give complete answers to all of Socrates' questions. Because, as I started to say right at the beginning, the reason we invited you to advise us on these matters was that we supposed that you would naturally have given some thought to such things—especially so since your sons, like ours, are very nearly *d* of an age to be educated. So, if you have no objection, speak up and look into the subject along with Socrates, exchanging arguments with each other. Because he is right in saying that it is about the most important of our affairs that we are consulting. So decide if you think this is what ought to be done.

NICIAS: It is quite clear to me, Lysimachus, that your knowledge of Socrates is limited to your acquaintance with his father and that you have had no contact with the man himself, except when he was *e* a child—I suppose he may have mingled with you and your fellow demesmen, following along with his father at the temple or at some other public gathering. But you are obviously still unacquainted with the man as he is now he has grown up.

LYSIMACHUS: What exactly do you mean, Nicias?

NICIAS: You don't appear to me to know that whoever comes into close contact with Socrates and associates with him in conversation must necessarily, even if he began by conversing about something quite different in the first place, keep on being led about by the man's arguments until he submits to answering questions about himself concerning both his present manner of life and the life he had lived hitherto. And when he does submit to this question- *188a* ing, you don't realize that Socrates will not let him go before he has well and truly tested every last detail. I personally am accustomed to the man and know that one has to put up with this kind of treatment from him, and further, I know perfectly well that I myself will have to submit to it. I take pleasure in the man's company, Lysimachus, and don't regard it as at all a bad thing to have it brought to our attention that we have done or are doing wrong. Rather I think that a *b* man who does not run away from such treatment but is willing, according to the saying of Solon, to value learning as long as he lives,[4] not supposing that old age brings him wisdom of itself, will necessarily pay more attention to the rest of his life. For me there is nothing unusual or unpleasant in being examined by Socrates, but I realized some time ago that the *c* conversation would not be about the boys but about ourselves, if Socrates were present. As I say, I don't myself mind talking with Socrates in whatever way he likes—but find out how Laches here feels about such things.

LACHES: I have just one feeling about discussions, Nicias, or, if you like, not one but two, because to some I might seem to be a discussion-lover and to others a discussion-hater. Whenever I hear a man discussing virtue or some kind of wisdom, then, if he really is a man and worthy of the words he utters, *d* I am completely delighted to see the appropriateness and harmony existing between the speaker and his words. And such a man seems to me to be genuinely musical, producing the most beautiful harmony, not on the lyre or some other pleasurable instrument, but actually rendering his own life harmonious by fitting his deeds to his words in a truly Dorian mode, not in the Ionian, nor even, I think, in the Phrygian or Lydian, but in the only harmony that is genuinely

4. [Solon is the Athenian poet and lawgiver of the early sixth century.]

Greek. The discourse of such a man gladdens my heart and makes everyone think that I am a discus- *e* sion-lover because of the enthusiastic way in which I welcome what is said; but the man who acts in the opposite way distresses me, and the better he speaks, the worse I feel, so that his discourse makes me look like a discussion-hater. Now I have no acquaintance with the words of Socrates, but before now, I believe, I have had experience of his deeds, and there I found him a person privileged to speak fair words and to indulge in every kind of frankness. So if he possesses *189a* this ability too, I am in sympathy with the man, and I would submit to being examined by such a person with the greatest pleasure, nor would I find learning burdensome, because I too agree with Solon, though with one reservation—I wish to grow old learning many things, but from good men only. Let Solon grant me this point, that the teacher should himself be good, so that I may not show myself a stupid pupil taking no delight in learning. Whether my teacher is to be younger than I am or not yet famous or has any other such peculiarity troubles me not at all. To *b* you then, Socrates, I present myself as someone for you to teach and to refute in whatever manner you please, and, on the other hand, you are welcome to any knowledge I have myself. Because this has been my opinion of your character since that day on which we shared a common danger and you gave me a sample of your valor—the sort a man must give if he is to render a good account of himself. So say whatever you like and don't let the difference in our ages concern you at all.

c SOCRATES: We certainly can't find fault with you for not being ready both to give advice and to join in the common search.

LYSIMACHUS: But the task is clearly ours, Socrates (for I count you as one of ourselves), so take my place and find out on behalf of the young men what we need to learn from these people, and then, by talking to the boys, join us in giving them advice. Because, on account of my age, I very often forget what questions I was going to ask, and I forget the answers as well. Then, if fresh arguments start up *d* in the middle, my memory is not exactly good. So you do the talking and examine among yourselves the topics we proposed. And I will listen, and when I have heard your conversation, I will do whatever you people think best and so will Melesias here.

SOCRATES: Let us do what Lysimachus and Melesias suggest, Nicias and Laches. Perhaps it won't be a bad idea to ask ourselves the sort of question which we proposed to investigate just now: what teachers have we had in this sort of instruction, and what other persons have we made better? However, I *e* think there is another sort of inquiry that will bring us to the same point and is perhaps one that begins somewhat more nearly from the beginning. Suppose we know, about anything whatsoever, that if it is added to another thing, it makes that thing better, and furthermore, we are able to make the addition, then clearly we know the very thing about which we should be consulting as to how one might obtain it most easily and best. Perhaps you don't understand what I mean, but will do so more easily this way: suppose we know *190a* that sight, when added to the eyes, makes better those eyes to which it is added, and furthermore, we are able to add it to the eyes, then clearly we know what this very thing sight is, about which we should be consulting as to how one might obtain it most easily and best. Because if we didn't know what sight in itself was, nor hearing, we would hardly be worthy counsellors and doctors about either the eyes or the ears as to the manner in which either sight or hearing *b* might best be obtained.

LACHES: You are right, Socrates.

SOCRATES: Well then, Laches, aren't these two now asking our advice as to the manner in which virtue might be added to the souls of their sons to make them better?

LACHES: Yes, indeed.

SOCRATES: Then isn't it necessary for us to start out knowing what virtue is? Because if we are not absolutely certain what it is, how are we going to *c* advise anyone as to the best method of obtaining it?

LACHES: I do not think that there is any way in which we can do this, Socrates.

SOCRATES: We say then, Laches, that we know what it is.

LACHES: Yes, we do say so.

SOCRATES: And what we know, we must, I suppose, be able to state?

LACHES: Of course.

SOCRATES: Let us not, O best of men, begin straightaway with an investigation of the whole of virtue—that would perhaps be too great a task—but let us first see if we have a sufficient knowledge of a *d* part. Then it is likely that the investigation will be easier for us.

LACHES: Yes, let's do it the way you want, Socrates.

SOCRATES: Well, which one of the parts of virtue should we choose? Or isn't it obvious that we ought to take the one to which the technique of fighting in armor appears to lead? I suppose everyone would think it leads to courage, wouldn't they?

LACHES: I think they certainly would.

SOCRATES: Then let us undertake first of all, Laches, to state what courage is. Then after this we will go on to investigate in what way it could be added *e* to the young, to the extent that the addition can be made through occupations and studies. But try to state what I ask, namely, what courage is.

LACHES: Good heavens, Socrates, there is no difficulty about that: if a man is willing to remain at his post and to defend himself against the enemy without running away, then you may rest assured that he is a man of courage.

SOCRATES: Well spoken, Laches. But perhaps I am to blame for not making myself clear; the result is that you did not answer the question I had in mind but a different one.

LACHES: What do you mean, Socrates?

191a SOCRATES: I will tell you if I can. That man, I suppose, is courageous whom you yourself mention, that is, the man who fights the enemy while remaining at his post?

LACHES: Yes, that is my view.

SOCRATES: And I agree. But what about this man, the one who fights with the enemy, not holding his ground, but in retreat?

LACHES: What did you mean, in retreat?

SOCRATES: Why, I mean the way the Scythians are said to fight, as much retreating as pursuing; and then I imagine that Homer is praising the horses of Aeneas when he says they know how "to pursue and *b* fly quickly this way and that", and he praises Aeneas himself for his knowledge of fear and he calls him "counsellor of fright."[5]

LACHES: And Homer is right, Socrates, because he was speaking of chariots, and it was the Scythian horsemen to which you referred. Now cavalry do fight in this fashion, but the hoplites in the manner I describe.

SOCRATES: Except perhaps the Spartan hoplites, Laches. Because they say that at Plataea the Spar- *c* tans, when they were up against the soldiers carrying wicker shields, were not willing to stand their ground and fight against them but ran away. Then when the ranks of the Persians were broken, they turned and fought, just like cavalrymen, and so won that particular battle.[6]

LACHES: You are right.

SOCRATES: So as I said just now, my poor questioning is to blame for your poor answer, because I wanted to learn from you not only what constitutes courage for a hoplite but for a horseman as well and *d* for every sort of warrior. And I wanted to include not only those who are courageous in warfare but also those who are brave in dangers at sea, and the ones who show courage in illness and poverty and affairs of state; and then again I wanted to include not only those who are brave in the face of pain and fear but also those who are clever at fighting desire and pleasure, whether by standing their ground or running *e* away—because there are some men, aren't there, Laches, who are brave in matters like these?

LACHES: Very much so, Socrates.

SOCRATES: So all these men are brave, but some possess courage in pleasures, some in pains, some in desires, and some in fears. And others, I think, show cowardice in the same respects.

LACHES: Yes, they do.

SOCRATES: Then what are courage and cowardice? This is what I wanted to find out. So try again to state first what is the courage that is the same in all these cases. Or don't you yet have a clear understanding of what I mean?

LACHES: Not exactly.

SOCRATES: Well, I mean something like this: *192a* suppose I asked what speed was, which we find in running and in playing the lyre and in speaking and in learning and in many other instances—in fact we may say we display the quality, so far as it is worth mentioning, in movements of the arms or legs or

5. [*Iliad* V, 222–23 and VIII, 106–108.]

6. [The battle of Plataea (in Boeotia) was fought at the end of August 479. The Greeks under Pausanias defeated the Persians under Mardonius.]

tongue or voice or thought? Or isn't this the way you too would express it?

LACHES: Yes, indeed.

SOCRATES: Then if anyone should ask me, "Socrates, what do you say it is which you call swiftness in all these cases," I would answer him that what I call swiftness is the power of accomplishing a great deal in a short time, whether in speech or in running or all the other cases.

LACHES: And you would be right.

SOCRATES: Then make an effort yourself, Laches, to speak in the same way about courage. What faculty is it which, because it is the same in pleasure and in pain and in all the other cases in which we were just saying it occurred, is therefore called courage?

LACHES: Well then, I think it is a sort of endurance of the soul, if it is necessary to say what its nature is in all these cases.

SOCRATES: But it is necessary, at any rate if we are to give an answer to our question. Now this is what appears to me: I think that you don't regard every kind of endurance as courage. The reason I think so is this: I am fairly sure, Laches, that you regard courage as a very fine thing.

LACHES: One of the finest, you may be sure.

SOCRATES: And you would say that endurance accompanied by wisdom is a fine and noble thing?

LACHES: Very much so.

SOCRATES: Suppose it is accompanied by folly? Isn't it just the opposite, harmful and injurious?

LACHES: Yes.

SOCRATES: And you are going to call a thing fine which is of the injurious and harmful sort?

LACHES: No, that wouldn't be right, Socrates.

SOCRATES: Then you won't allow this kind of endurance to be courage, since it is not fine, whereas courage *is* fine.

LACHES: You are right.

SOCRATES: Then, according to your view, it would be wise endurance which would be courage.

LACHES: So it seems.

SOCRATES: Let us see then in what respect it is wise—is it so with respect to everything both great and small? For instance, if a man were to show endurance in spending his money wisely, knowing that by spending it he would get more, would you call this man courageous?

LACHES: Heavens no, not I.

SOCRATES: Well, suppose a man is a doctor, and his son or some other patient is ill with inflammation of the lungs and begs him for something to eat or drink, and the man doesn't give in but perseveres in refusing?

LACHES: No, this would certainly not be courage either, not at all.

SOCRATES: Well, suppose a man endures in battle, and his willingness to fight is based on wise calculation because he knows that others are coming to his aid and that he will be fighting men who are fewer than those on his side, and inferior to them, and in addition his position is stronger: would you say that this man, with his kind of wisdom and preparation, endures more courageously or a man in the opposite camp who is willing to remain and hold out?

LACHES: The one in the opposite camp, Socrates, I should say.

SOCRATES: But surely the endurance of this man is more foolish than that of the other.

LACHES: You are right.

SOCRATES: And you would say that the man who shows endurance in a cavalry attack and had knowledge of horsemanship is less courageous than the man who lacks this knowledge.

LACHES: Yes, I would.

SOCRATES: And the one who endures with knowledge of slinging or archery or some other art is the less courageous.

LACHES: Yes indeed.

SOCRATES: And as many as would be willing to endure in diving down into wells without being skilled, or to endure in any other similar situation, you say are braver than those who are skilled in these things.

LACHES: Why, what else would anyone say, Socrates?

SOCRATES: Nothing, if that is what he thought.

LACHES: Well, this is what I think at any rate.

SOCRATES: And certainly, Laches, such people run risks and endure more foolishly than those who do a thing with art.

LACHES: They clearly do.

SOCRATES: Now foolish daring and endurance

was found by us to be not only disgraceful but harmful, in what we said earlier.

LACHES: Quite so.

SOCRATES: But courage was agreed to be a noble thing.

LACHES: Yes, it was.

SOCRATES: But now, on the contrary, we are saying that a disgraceful thing, foolish endurance, is courage.

LACHES: Yes, we seem to be.

SOCRATES: And do you think we are talking sense?

LACHES: Heavens no, Socrates, I certainly don't.

SOCRATES: Then I don't suppose, Laches, that *e* according to your statement you and I are tuned to the Dorian mode, because our deeds are not harmonizing with our words. In deeds I think anyone would say that we partook of courage, but in words I don't suppose he would, if he were to listen to our present discussion.

LACHES: You are absolutely right.

SOCRATES: Well then: is it good for us to be in such a state?

LACHES: Certainly not, in no way whatsoever.

SOCRATES: But are you willing that we should agree with our statement to a certain extent?

LACHES: To what extent and with what statement?

SOCRATES: With the one that commands us to *194a* endure. If you are willing, let us hold our ground in the search and let us endure, so that courage itself won't make fun of us for not searching for it courageously—if endurance should perhaps be courage after all.

LACHES: I am ready not to give up, Socrates, although I am not really accustomed to arguments of this kind. But an absolute desire for victory has seized me with respect to our conversation, and I am really *b* getting annoyed and being unable to express what I think in this fashion. I still think I know what courage is, but I can't understand how it has escaped me just now so that I can't pin it down in words and say what it is.

SOCRATES: Well, my friend, a good hunter ought to pursue the trail and not give up.

LACHES: Absolutely.

SOCRATES: Then, if you agree, let's also summon Nicias here to the hunt—he might get on much better.

LACHES: I am willing—why not? *c*

SOCRATES: Come along then, Nicias, and, if you can, rescue your friends who are storm-tossed by the argument and find themselves in trouble. You see, of course, that our affairs are in a bad way, so state what you think courage is and get us out of our difficulties as well as confirming your own view by putting it into words.

NICIAS: I have been thinking for some time that you are not defining courage in the right way, Socrates. And you are not employing the excellent observation I have heard you make before now.

SOCRATES: What one was that, Nicias?

NICIAS: I have often heard you say that every *d* one of us is good with respect to that in which he is wise and bad in respect to that in which he is ignorant.

SOCRATES: By heaven, you are right, Nicias.

NICIAS: Therefore, if a man is really courageous, it is clear that he is wise.

SOCRATES: You hear that, Laches?

LACHES: I do, but I don't understand exactly what he means.

SOCRATES: Well, I think I understand him, and the man seems to me to be saying that courage is some kind of wisdom.

LACHES: Why, what sort of wisdom is he talking about, Socrates?

SOCRATES: Why don't you ask him? *e*

LACHES: All right.

SOCRATES: Come, Nicias, tell him what sort of wisdom courage would be according to your view. I don't suppose it is skill in flute playing.

NICIAS: Of course not.

SOCRATES: And not in lyre playing either.

NICIAS: Far from it.

SOCRATES: But what is this knowledge and of what?

LACHES: You are questioning him in just the right way.

SOCRATES: Let him state what kind of knowledge it is.

NICIAS: What I say, Laches, is that it is the knowledge of the fearful and the hopeful in war and *195a* in every other situation.

LACHES: How strangely he talks, Socrates.

SOCRATES: What do you have in mind when you say this, Laches?

LACHES: What do I have in mind? Why, I take wisdom to be quite a different thing from courage.

SOCRATES: Well, Nicias, at any rate, says it isn't.

LACHES: He certainly does—that's the nonsense he talks.

SOCRATES: Well, let's instruct him instead of making fun of him.

NICIAS: Very well, but it strikes me, Socrates, that Laches wants to prove that I am talking nonsense simply because he was shown to be that sort of person *b* himself a moment ago.

LACHES: Quite so, Nicias, and I shall try to demonstrate that very thing, because you *are* talking nonsense. Take an immediate example: in cases of illness, aren't the doctors the ones who know what is to be feared? Or do you think the courageous are the people who know? Perhaps you call the doctors the courageous?

NICIAS: No, of course not.

LACHES: And I don't imagine you mean the farmers either, even though I do suppose they are the ones who know what is to be feared in farming. And all the other craftsmen know what is to be feared and *c* hoped for in their particular arts. But these people are in no way courageous all the same.

SOCRATES: What does Laches mean, Nicias? Because he does seem to be saying something.

NICIAS: Yes, he is saying something, but what he says is not true.

SOCRATES: How so?

NICIAS: He thinks a doctor's knowledge of the sick amounts to something more than being able to describe health and disease, whereas I think their knowledge is restricted to just this. Do you suppose, Laches, that when a man's recovery is more to be feared than his illness, the doctors know this? Or don't you think there are many cases in which it would be better not to get up from an illness? Tell me this: do *d* you maintain that in all cases to live is preferable? In many cases, is it not better to die?

LACHES: Well, I agree with you on this point at least.

NICIAS: And do you suppose that the same things are to be feared by those for whom it is an advantage to die as by those for whom it is an advantage to live?

LACHES: No, I don't.

NICIAS: But do you grant this knowledge to the doctors or to any other craftsmen except the one who knows what is and what is not to be feared, who is the one I call courageous?

SOCRATES: Do you understand what he is saying, Laches?

LACHES: Yes I do—he is calling the seers the *e* courageous.[7] Because who else will know for whom it is better to live than to die? What about you, Nicias—do you admit to being a seer, or, if you are not a seer, to not being courageous?

NICIAS: Well, what of it? Don't you, for your part, think it is appropriate for a seer to know what is to be feared and what is to be hoped?

LACHES: Yes, I do, because I don't see for what other person it would be.

NICIAS: Much more for the man I am talking about, my friend, because the seer needs to know only the signs of what is to be, whether a man will experience death or illness or loss of property, or will experience victory or defeat, in battle or in any other sort of *196a* contest. But why is it more suitable for the seer than for anyone else to judge for whom it is better to suffer or not to suffer these things?

LACHES: It isn't clear to me from this, Socrates, what he is trying to say. Because he doesn't select either the seer or the doctor or anyone else as the man he calls courageous, unless some god is the person he means. Nicias appears to me unwilling to make a gentlemanly admission that he is talking nonsense, *b* but he twists this way and that in an attempt to cover up his difficulty. Even you and I could have executed a similar twist just now if we had wanted to avoid the appearance of contradicting ourselves. If we were making speeches in a court of law, there might be some point in doing this, but as things are, why should anyone adorn himself senselessly with empty words in a gathering like this?

7. [Plato's readers could not fail to be reminded here that Nicias' superstitious reliance on seers was a major factor in the failure of the Athenian expedition to Sicily.]

c SOCRATES: I see no reason why he should, Laches. But let us see if Nicias thinks he is saying something and is not just talking for the sake of talking. Let us find out from him more clearly what it is he means, and if he is really saying something, we will agree with him, but if not, we will instruct him.

LACHES: You go ahead and question him, Socrates, if you want to find out. I think perhaps I have asked enough.

SOCRATES: I have no objection, since the inquiry will be a joint effort on behalf of us both.

LACHES: Very well.

SOCRATES: Then tell me, Nicias, or rather tell *d* *us*, because Laches and I are sharing the argument: you say that courage is knowledge of the grounds of fear and hope?

NICIAS: Yes, I do.

SOCRATES: Then this knowledge is something possessed by very few indeed if, as you say, neither the doctor nor the seer will have it and won't be courageous without acquiring this particular knowledge. Isn't that what you're saying?

NICIAS: Just so.

SOCRATES: Then, as the proverb says, it is true that this is not something "every sow would know,"[8] and she would not be courageous?

NICIAS: I don't think so.

e SOCRATES: Then it is obvious, Nicias that you do not regard the Crommyon sow[9] as having been courageous. I say this not as a joke, but because I think that anyone taking this position must necessarily deny courage to any wild beast or else admit that some wild beast, a lion or a leopard or some sort of wild bar, is wise enough to know what is so difficult that very few men understand it. And, similarly, the man who defines courage as you define it would have to assert that a lion and a stag, a bull and a monkey are all naturally courageous.

197a LACHES: By heaven, you talk well, Socrates. Give us an honest answer to this, Nicias—whether you say that these wild beasts, whom we all admit to be courageous, are wiser than we in these respects, or whether you dare to oppose the general view and say that they are not courageous.

NICIAS: By no means, Laches, do I call courageous wild beasts or anything else that, for lack of understanding, does not fear what should be feared. Rather, I would call them rash and mad. Or do you really suppose I call all children courageous, who fear nothing because they have no sense? On the contrary, *b* I think that rashness and courage are not the same thing. My view is that very few have a share of courage and foresight, but that a great many, men and women and children and wild animals, partake in boldness and audacity and rashness and lack of foresight. These cases, which you and the man in the street call courageous, I call rash, whereas the courageous ones are the sensible people I was talking about. *c*

LACHES: You see, Socrates, how the man decks himself out in words and does it well in his own opinion. Those whom everyone agrees to be courageous he attempts to deprive of that distinction.

NICIAS: I'm not depriving you of it, Laches, so cheer up. I declare that you are wise, and Lamachus[10] too, so long as you are courageous, and I say the same of a great many other Athenians.

LACHES: I shan't say anything about that—though I could—in case you should call me a typical Aexonian.[11]

SOCRATES: Never mind him, Laches. I don't *d* think you realize that he has procured this wisdom from our friend Damon, and Damon spends most of his time with Prodicus,[12] who has the reputation of being best among the sophists at making such verbal distinctions.

LACHES: Well, Socrates, it is certainly more fitting for a sophist to make such clever distinctions than for a man the city thinks worthy to be its leader.

SOCRATES: Well, I suppose it would be fitting, *e* my good friend, for the man in charge of the greatest affairs to have the greatest share of wisdom. But I think it worthwhile to ask Nicias what he has in mind when he defines courage in this way.

LACHES: Well then, you ask him, Socrates.

8. [To the Greek, the pig usually connotes stupidity rather than dirtiness or greed.]

9. [The famous sow of Crommyon (near Corinth) was killed by Theseus.]

10. [Lamachus shared the command of the Sicilian expedition with Nicias and Alcibiades; he died at Syracuse.]

11. [The people of the deme Aexone were regarded as abusive speakers.]

12. [The sophist Prodicus usually appears in Plato as a proponent of nice distinctions in words.]

Socrates: This is just what I intend to do, my good friend. But don't therefore suppose that I shall let you out of your share of the argument. Pay attention and join me in examining what is being said.

Laches: Very well, if that seems necessary.

Socrates: Yes, it does. And you, Nicias, tell us *198a* again from the beginning—you know that when we were investigating courage at the beginning of the argument, we were investigating it as a part of virtue?

Nicias: Yes, we were.

Socrates: And didn't you give your answer supposing that it was a part, and, as such, one among a number of other parts, all of which taken together were called virtue?

Nicias: Yes, why not?

Socrates: And do you also speak of the same parts that I do? In addition to courage, I call temperance and justice and everything else of this kind parts of virtue. Don't you?

b Nicias: Yes, indeed.

Socrates: Stop there. We are in agreement on these points, but let us investigate the grounds of fear and confidence to make sure that you don't regard them in one way and we in another. We will tell you what we think about them, and if you do not agree, you shall instruct us. We regard as fearful things those that produce fear, and as hopeful things those that do not produce fear; and fear is produced not by evils which have happened or are happening but by those which are anticipated. Because fear is the expectation of a future evil—or isn't this your opinion too, Laches?

c Laches: Very much so, Socrates.

Socrates: You hear what we have to say, Nicias: that fearful things are future evils, and the ones inspiring hope are either future non-evils or future goods. Do you agree with this or have you some other view on the subject?

Nicias: I agree with this one.

Socrates: And you declare that knowledge of just these things is courage?

Nicias: Exactly so.

Socrates: Let us find out if we all agree on still a third point.

Nicias: What one is that?

Socrates: I will explain. It seems to me and *d* my friend here that of the various things with which knowledge is concerned, there is not one kind of knowledge by which we know how things have happened in the past, and another by which we know how they are happening at the present time, and still another by which we know how what has not yet happened might best come to be in the future, but that the knowledge is the same in each case. For instance, in the case of health, there is no other art related to the past, the present, and the future except that of medicine, which, although it is a single art, surveys what is, what was, and what is likely to be in the future. Again, in the case of the fruits of the earth, the art of farming conforms *e* to the same pattern. And I suppose that both of you could bear witness that, in the case of the affairs of war, the art of generalship is that which best foresees the future and the other times—nor does this art consider it necessary to be ruled by the art of the seer, but to rule *it*, as being better acquainted with *199a* both present and future in the affairs of war. In fact, the law decrees, not that the seer should command the general, but that the general should command the seer. Is this what we shall say, Laches?

Laches: Yes, it is.

Socrates: Well then, do you agree with us, Nicias, that the same knowledge has understanding of the same things, whether future, present, or past?

Nicias: Yes, that is how it seems to me, Socrates.

Socrates: Now, my good friend, you say that courage is the knowledge of the fearful and the *b* hopeful, isn't that so?

Nicias: Yes, it is.

Socrates: And it was agreed that fearful and hopeful things were future goods and future evils.

Nicias: Yes, it was.

Socrates: And that the same knowledge is of the same things—future ones and all other kinds.

Nicias: Yes, that is the case.

Socrates: Then courage is not knowledge of the fearful and the hopeful only, because it understands not simply future goods and evils, but those of *c* the present and the past and all times, just as is the case with the other kinds of knowledge.

Nicias: So it seems, at any rate.

SOCRATES: Then you have told us about what amounts to a third part of courage, Nicias, whereas we asked you what the whole of courage was. And now it appears, according to your view, that courage is the knowledge not just of the fearful and the hopeful, but in your own opinion, it would be the knowledge *d* of practically all goods and evils put together. Do you agree to this new change, Nicias, or what do you say?

NICIAS: That seems right to me, Socrates.

SOCRATES: Then does a man with this kind of knowledge seem to depart from virtue in any respect if he really knows, in the case of all goods whatsoever, what they are and will be and have been, and similarly in the case of evils? And do you regard that man as lacking in temperance or justice and holiness to whom alone belongs the ability to deal circumspectly with both gods and men with respect to both the fearful and its opposite, and to provide himself with good *e* things through his knowledge of how to associate with them correctly?

NICIAS: I think you have a point, Socrates.

SOCRATES: Then the thing you are now talking about, Nicias, would not be a part of virtue but rather virtue entire.

NICIAS: So it seems.

SOCRATES: And we have certainly stated that courage is one of the parts of virtue.

NICIAS: Yes, we have.

SOCRATES: Then what we are saying now does not appear to hold good.

NICIAS: Apparently not.

SOCRATES: Then we have not discovered, Nicias, what courage is.

NICIAS: We don't appear to.

LACHES: But I, my dear Nicias, felt sure you would make the discovery after you were so scorn- *200a* ful of me while I was answering Socrates. In fact, I had great hopes that with the help of Damon's wisdom you would solve the whole problem.

NICIAS: That's a fine attitude of yours, Laches, to think it no longer to be of any importance that you yourself were just now shown to be a person who knows nothing about courage. What interests you is whether I will turn out to be a person of the same kind. Apparently it will make no difference to you to be ignorant of those things which a man of any pretensions ought to know, so long as you include me in your ignorance. Well, you seem to me to be *b* acting in a thoroughly human fashion by noticing everybody except yourself. As far as I am concerned I think enough has been said on the topic for the present, and if any point has not been covered sufficiently, then later on I think we can correct it both with the help of Damon—whom you think it right to laugh at, though you have never seen the man—and with that of others. And when I feel secure on these points, I will instruct you too and won't begrudge the effort—because you seem to me to be sadly in need of *c* learning.

LACHES: You are a clever man, Nicias, I know. All the same, I advise Lysimachus here and Melesias to say good-bye to you and me as teachers of the young men and to retain the services of this man Socrates, as I said in the beginning. If my boys were the same age, this is what I would do.

NICIAS: And I agree: if Socrates is really willing to undertake the supervision of the boys, then don't look for anyone else. In fact I would gladly entrust Niceratus to him, if he is willing. But when- *d* ever I bring up the subject in any way, he always recommends other people to me but is unwilling to take on the job himself. But see if Socrates might be more willing to listen to you, Lysimachus.

LYSIMACHUS: Well, he should, Nicias, since I myself would be willing to do a great many things for him which I would not be willing to do for practically anyone else. What do you say, Socrates? Will you comply with our request and take an active part with us in helping the young men to become as good as possible?

SOCRATES: Well, it would be a terrible thing, *e* Lysimachus, to be unwilling to join in assisting any man to become as good as possible. If in the conversations we have just had I had seemed to be knowing and the other two had not, then it would be right to issue a special invitation to me to perform this task; but as the matter stands, we were all in the same difficulty. Why then should anybody choose one of us in preference to another? What I think is that he ought *201a* to choose none of us. But as things are, see whether the suggestion I am about to make may not be a good one: what I say we ought to do, my friends—since this is just between ourselves—is to join in searching for the best possible teacher, first for ourselves—we really need one—and then for the young men, sparing neither money nor anything else. What I don't advise is that we remain as we are. And if anyone laughs at us because we think it worthwhile to spend our time *b* in school at our age, then I think we should confront him with the saying of Homer, "Modesty is not a good mate for a needy man."[13] And, not paying any attention to what anyone may say, let us join together in looking after both our own interests and those of the boys.

LYSIMACHUS: I like what you say, Socrates, and the fact that I am the oldest makes me the most eager to go to school along with the boys. Just do this for me: come to my house early tomorrow—don't refuse—so that we may make plans about these matters, but let *c* us make an end of our present conversation.

SOCRATES: I shall do what you say, Lysimachus, and come to you tomorrow, God willing.

13. [*Odyssey* XVII, 347.]

Euthyphro

2 EUTHYPHRO:[1] What's new, Socrates, to make you leave your usual haunts in the Lyceum and spend your time here by the king-archon's court? Surely you are not prosecuting anyone before the king-archon as I am?

SOCRATES: The Athenians do not call this a prosecution but an indictment, Euthyphro.

b E: What is this you say? Someone must have indicted you, for you are not going to tell me that you have indicted someone else.

S: No indeed.

E: But someone else has indicted you?

S: Quite so.

E: Who is he?

S: I do not really know him myself, Euthyphro. He is apparently young and unknown. They call him Meletus, I believe. He belongs to the Pitthean deme, if you know anyone from that deme called Meletus, with long hair, not much of a beard, and a rather aquiline nose.

E: I don't know him, Socrates. What charge does he bring against you?

c S: What charge? A not ignoble one I think, for it is no small thing for a young man to have knowledge of such an important subject. He says he knows how our young men are corrupted and who corrupts them. He is likely to be wise, and when he sees my ignorance corrupting his contemporaries, he pro- d ceeds to accuse me to the city as to their mother. I think he is the only one of our public men to start out the right way, for it is right to care first that the young should be as good as possible, just as a good farmer is likely to take care of the young plants first, and of the others later. So, too, Meletus first gets rid of us who corrupt the young shoots, as he says, 3 and then afterwards he will obviously take care of the older ones and become a source of great blessings for the city, as seems likely to happen to one who started out this way.

E: I could wish this were true, Socrates, but I fear the opposite may happen. He seems to me to start out by harming the very heart of the city by attempting to wrong you. Tell me, what does he say you do to corrupt the young?

S: Strange things, to hear him tell it, for he says b that I am a maker of gods, and on the ground that I create new gods while not believing in the old gods, he has indicted me for their sake, as he puts it.

E: I understand, Socrates. This is because you say that the divine sign keeps coming to you.[2] So he has written this indictment against you as one who makes innovations in religious matters, and he comes to court to slander you, knowing that such things are easily misrepresented to the crowd. The same is true in my case. Whenever I speak of divine matters in c the assembly and foretell the future, they laugh me down as if I were crazy; and yet I have foretold nothing that did not happen. Nevertheless, they envy all of us who do this. One need not worry about them, but meet them head on.

S: My dear Euthyphro, to be laughed at does not matter perhaps, for the Athenians do not mind anyone they think clever, as long as he does not teach his own wisdom, but if they think that he makes others to be like himself they get angry, whether through envy, as you say, or for some other reason. d

Reprinted from *The Trial and Death of Socrates*, translated by G.M.A. Grube (Indianapolis: Hackett Publishing Company, 1975), by permission of the publisher.

1. [We know nothing about Euthyphro except what we can gather from this dialogue. He is obviously a professional priest who considers himself an expert on ritual and on piety generally, and, it seems, is generally so considered. One Euthyphro is mentioned in Plato's *Cratylus* (396d) who is given to *enthousiasmos*, inspiration or possession, but we cannot be sure that it is the same person.—G.M.A.G.]

2. [In Plato, Socrates always speaks of his divine sign or voice as intervening to prevent him from doing or saying something (e.g., *Apology* 31d), but never positively. The popular view was that it enabled him to foretell the future, and Euthyphro here represents that view. Note, however, that Socrates dissociates himself from "you prophets" (3e).]

E: I have certainly no desire to test their feelings towards me in this matter.

S: Perhaps you seem to make yourself but rarely available, and not be willing to teach your own wisdom, but I'm afraid that my liking for people makes them think that I pour out to anybody anything I have to say, not only without charging a fee but even glad to reward anyone who is willing to listen. If then they were intending to laugh at me, as you say they laugh at you, there would be nothing unpleasant in their spending their time in court laughing and jesting, but if they are going to be serious, the outcome *e* is not clear except to you prophets.

E: Perhaps it will come to nothing, Socrates, and you will fight your case as you think best, as I think I will mine.

S: What is your case, Euthyphro? Are you the defendant or the prosecutor?

E: The prosecutor.

S: Whom do you prosecute?

4 E: One whom I am thought crazy to prosecute.

S: Are you pursuing someone who will easily escape you?

E: Far from it, for he is quite old.

S: Who is it?

E: My father.

S: My dear sir! Your own father?

E: Certainly.

S: What is the charge? What is the case about?

E: Murder, Socrates.

S: Good heavens! Certainly, Euthyphro, most *b* men would not know how they could do this and be right. It is not the part of anyone to do this, but of one who is far advanced in wisdom.

E: Yes, by Zeus, Socrates, that is so.

S: Is then the man your father killed one of your relatives? Or is that obvious, for you would not prosecute your father for the murder of a stranger.

E: It is ridiculous, Socrates, for you to think that it makes any difference whether the victim is a stranger or a relative. One should only watch whether the killer acted justly or not; if he acted justly, let him go, but if not, one should prosecute, if, that is *c* to say, the killer shares your hearth and table. The pollution is the same if you knowingly keep company with such a man and do not cleanse yourself and him by bringing him to justice. The victim was a dependent of mine, and when we were farming in Naxos he was a servant of ours. He killed one of our household slaves in drunken anger, so my father bound him hand and foot and threw him in a ditch, then sent a man here to inquire from the priest what *d* should be done. During that time he gave no thought or care to the bound man, as being a killer, and it was no matter if he died, which he did. Hunger and cold and his bonds caused his death before the messenger came back from the seer. Both my father and my other relatives are angry that I am prosecuting my father for murder on behalf of a murderer when he hadn't even killed him, they say, and even if he had, the dead man does not deserve a thought, since he was a killer. For, *e* they say, it is impious for a son to prosecute his father for murder. But their ideas of the divine attitude to piety and impiety are wrong, Socrates.

S: Whereas, by Zeus, Euthyphro, you think that your knowledge of the divine, and of piety and impiety, is so accurate that, when those things happened as you say, you have no fear of having acted impiously in bringing your father to trial?

E: I should be of no use, Socrates, and Euthyphro would not be superior to the majority of men, if I *5* did not have accurate knowledge of all such things.

S: It is indeed most important, my admirable Euthyphro, that I should become your pupil, and as regards this indictment challenge Meletus about these very things and say to him: that in the past too I considered knowledge about the divine to be most important, and that now that he says that I am guilty of improvising and innovating about the gods I have *b* become your pupil. I would say to him: "If, Meletus, you agree that Euthyphro is wise in these matters, consider me, too, to have the right beliefs and do not bring me to trial. If you do not think so, then prosecute that teacher of mine, not me, for corrupting the older men, me and his own father, by teaching me and by exhorting and punishing him." If he is not convinced, and does not discharge me or indict you instead of me, I shall repeat the same challenge in court.

E: Yes, by Zeus, Socrates, and, if he should try to indict me, I think I would find his weak spots and the *c* talk in court would be about him rather than about me.

S: It is because I realize this that I am eager to become your pupil, my dear friend. I know that other people as well as this Meletus do not even seem to notice you, whereas he sees me so sharply and clearly that he indicts me for ungodliness. So tell me now, by Zeus, what you just now maintained you clearly knew: what kind of thing do you say that godliness and ungodliness are, both as regards murder and other *d* things; or is the pious not the same and alike in every action, and the impious the opposite of all that is pious and like itself, and everything that is to be impious presents us with one form[3] or appearance insofar as it is impious?

E: Most certainly, Socrates.

S: Tell me then, what is the pious, and what the impious, do you say?

E: I say that the pious is to do what I am doing now, to prosecute the wrongdoer, be it about murder or temple robbery or anything else, whether the *e* wrongdoer is your father or your mother or anyone else; not to prosecute is impious. And observe, Socrates, that I can cite powerful evidence that the law is so. I have already said to others that such actions are right, not to favor the ungodly, whoever they are. These people themselves believe that Zeus is the best 6 and most just of the gods, yet they agree that he bound his father because he unjustly swallowed his sons, and that he in turn castrated his father for similar reasons. But they are angry with me because I am prosecuting my father for his wrongdoing. They contradict themselves in what they say about the gods and about me.

S: Indeed, Euthyphro, this is the reason why I am a defendant in the case, because I find it hard to accept things like that being said about the gods, and it is likely to be the reason why I shall be told I do wrong. Now, however, if you, who have full knowl- *b* edge of such things, share their opinions, then we must agree with them, too, it would seem. For what are we to say, we who agree that we ourselves have no knowledge of them? Tell me, by the god of friendship, do you really believe these things are true?

E: Yes, Socrates, and so are even more surprising things, of which the majority has no knowledge.

S: And do you believe that there really is war among the gods, and terrible enmities and battles, and other such things as are told by the poets, and *c* other sacred stories such as are embroidered by good writers and by representations of which the robe of the goddess is adorned when it is carried up to the Acropolis? Are we to say these things are true, Euthyphro?

E: Not only these, Socrates, but, as I was saying just now, I will, if you wish, relate many other things about the gods which I know will amaze you.

S: I should not be surprised, but you will tell me these at leisure some other time. For now, try to tell me more clearly what I was asking just now, for, my friend, you did not teach me adequately when I asked *d* you what the pious was, but you told me that what you are doing now, in prosecuting your father for murder, is pious.

E: And I told the truth, Socrates.

S: Perhaps. You agree, however, that there are many other pious actions.

E: There are.

S: Bear in mind then that I did not bid you tell me one or two of the many pious actions but that form itself that makes all pious actions pious, for you agreed that all impious actions are impious and all pious actions pious through one form, or don't you re- *e* member?

E: I do.

S: Tell me then what this form itself is, so that I may look upon it, and using it as a model, say that any action of yours or another's that is of that kind is pious, and if it is not that it is not.

E: If that is how you want it, Socrates, that is how I will tell you.

S: That is what I want.

E: Well then, what is dear to the gods is pious, 7 what is not is impious.

S: Splendid, Euthyphro! You have now answered in the way I wanted. Whether your answer is true I do not know yet, but you will obviously show me that what you say is true.

E: Certainly.

S: Come then, let us examine what we mean.

3. [This is the kind of passage that makes it easier for us to follow the transition from Socrates' universal definitions to the Platonic theory of separately existent eternal universal Forms. The words *eidos* and *idea*, the technical terms for the Platonic Forms, commonly mean physical stature or bodily appearance. As we apply a common epithet, in this case pious, to different actions or things, these must have a common characteristic, present a common appearance or form, to justify the use of the same term; but in the early dialogues, as here, it seems to be thought of as immanent in the particulars and without separate existence. The same is true of 6d where the word "Form" is also used.]

An action or a man dear to the gods is pious, but an action or a man hated by the gods is impious. They are not the same, but quite opposite, the pious and the impious. Is that not so?

E: It is indeed.

S: And that seems to be a good statement?

b E: I think so, Socrates.

S: We have also stated that the gods are in a state of discord, that they are at odds with each other, Euthyphro, and that they are at enmity with each other. Has that, too, been said?

E: It has.

S: What are the subjects of difference that cause hatred and anger? Let us look at it this way. If you and I were to differ about numbers as to which is the greater, would this difference make us enemies and angry with each other, or would we proceed to count c and soon resolve our difference about this?

E: We would certainly do so.

S: Again, if we differed about the larger and the smaller, we would turn to measurement and soon cease to differ.

E: That is so.

S: And about the heavier and the lighter, we would resort to weighing and be reconciled.

E: Of course.

S: What subject of difference would make us angry and hostile to each other if we were unable to come to a decision? Perhaps you do not have an d answer ready, but examine as I tell you whether these subjects are the just and the unjust, the beautiful and the ugly, the good and the bad. Are these not the subjects of difference about which, when we are unable to come to a satisfactory decision, you and I and other men become hostile to each other whenever we do?

E: That is the difference, Socrates, about those subjects.

S: What about the gods, Euthyphro? If indeed they have differences, will it not be about these same subjects?

E: It certainly must be so.

e S: Then according to your argument, my good Euthyphro, different gods consider different things to be just, beautiful, ugly, good, and bad, for they would not be at odds with one another unless they differed about these subjects, would they?

E: You are right.

S: And they like what each of them considers beautiful, good, and just, and hate the opposites of these?

E: Certainly.

S: But you say that the same things are considered just by some gods and unjust by others, and as they 8 dispute about these things they are at odds and at war with each other. Is that not so?

E: It is.

S: The same things then are loved by the gods and hated by the gods, and would be both god-loved and god-hated.

E: It seems likely.

S: And the same things would be both pious and impious, according to this argument?

E: I'm afraid so.

S: So you did not answer my question, you surprising man. I did not ask you what same thing is both pious and impious, and it appears that what is loved by the gods is also hated by them. So it is in no way b surprising if your present action, namely punishing your father, may be pleasing to Zeus but displeasing to Cronus and Uranus, pleasing to Hephaestus but displeasing to Hera, and so with any other gods who differ from each other on this subject.

E: I think, Socrates, that on this subject no gods would differ from one another, that whoever has killed anyone unjustly should pay the penalty.

S: Well now, Euthyphro, have you ever heard c any man maintaining that one who has killed or done anything else unjustly should not pay the penalty?

E: They never cease to dispute on this subject, both elsewhere and in the courts, for when they have committed many wrongs they do and say anything to avoid the penalty.

S: Do they agree they have done wrong, Euthyphro, and in spite of so agreeing do they nevertheless say they should not be punished?

E: No, they do not agree on that point.

S: So they do not say or do just anything. For they do not venture to say this, or dispute that they must not pay the penalty if they have done wrong, d but I think they deny doing wrong. Is that not so?

E: That is true.

S: Then they do not dispute that the wrongdoer must be punished, but they may disagree as to who the wrongdoer is, what he did and when.

E: You are right.

S: Do not the gods have the same experience, if indeed they are at odds with each other about the just and the unjust, as your argument maintains? Some assert that they wrong one another, while others deny it, but no one among gods or men ventures to *e* say that the wrongdoer must not be punished.

E: Yes, that is true, Socrates, as to the main point.

S: And those who disagree, whether men or gods, dispute about each action, if indeed the gods disagree. Some say it is done justly, others unjustly. Is that not so?

E: Yes, indeed.

9 S: Come now, my dear Euthyphro, tell me, too, that I may become wiser, what proof you have that all the gods consider that man to have been killed unjustly who became a murderer while in your service, was bound by the master of his victim, and died in his bonds before the one who bound him found out from the seers what was to be done with him, and that it is right for a son to denounce and to prosecute his father on behalf of such a man. Come, *b* try to show me a clear sign that all the gods definitely believe this action to be right. If you can give me adequate proof of this, I shall never cease to extol your wisdom.

E: This is perhaps no light task, Socrates, though I could show you very clearly.

S: I understand that you think me more dull-witted than the jury, as you will obviously show them that these actions were unjust and that all the gods hate such actions.

E: I will show it to them clearly, Socrates, if only they will listen to me.

c S: They will listen if they think you show them well. But this thought came to me as you were speaking, and I am examining it, saying to myself: "If Euthyphro shows me conclusively that all the gods consider such a death unjust, to what greater extent have I learned from him the nature of piety and impiety? This action would then, it seems, be hated by the gods, but the pious and the impious were not thereby now defined, for what is hated by the gods has also been shown to be loved by them." So I will not insist on this point; let us assume, if you wish, that all the gods consider this unjust and that they *d* all hate it. However, is this the correction we are making in our discussion, that what all the gods hate is impious, and what they all love is pious, and that what some gods love and others hate is neither or both? Is that how you now wish us to define piety and impiety?

E: What prevents us from doing so, Socrates?

S: For my part nothing, Euthyphro, but you look whether on your part this proposal will enable you to teach me most easily what you promised.

E: I would certainly say that the pious is what all *e* the gods love, and the opposite, what all the gods hate, is the impious.

S: Then let us again examine whether that is a sound statement, or do we let it pass, and if one of us, or someone else, merely says that something is so, do we accept that it is so? Or should we examine what the speaker means?

E: We must examine it, but I certainly think that this is now a fine statement.

S: We shall soon know better whether it is. Con- *10* sider this: Is the pious being loved by the gods because it is pious, or is it pious because it is being loved by the gods?

E: I don't know what you mean, Socrates.

S: I shall try to explain more clearly: we speak of something carried[4] and something carrying, of something led and something leading, of something seen and something seeing, and you understand that these things are all different from one another and how they differ?

E: I think I do.

S: So there is also something loved and—a different thing—something loving.

E: Of course.

S: Tell me then whether the thing carried is a *b*

4. [This is the present participle form of the verb *pherome-non*, literally *being-carried*. The following passage is somewhat obscure, especially in translation, but the general meaning is clear. Plato points out that this participle simply indicates the object of an action of carrying, seeing, loving, etc. It follows from the action and adds nothing new, the action being prior to it, not following from it, and a thing is said to be loved because someone loves it, not vice versa. To say therefore that the pious is being loved by the gods says no more than that the gods love it. Euthyphro, however, also agrees that the pious is loved by the gods because of its nature (because it is pious), but the fact of its being loved by the gods does not define that nature, and as a definition is therefore unsatisfactory. It only indicates a quality or affect of the pious, and the pious is therefore still to be defined (11a7).]

carried thing because it is being carried, or for some other reason?

E: No, that is the reason.

S: And the thing led is so because it is being led, and the thing seen because it is being seen?

E: Certainly.

S: It is not being seen because it is a thing seen but on the contrary it is a thing seen because it is being seen; nor is it because it is something led that it is being led but because it is being led that it is something led; nor is something being carried because it is something carried, but it is something *c* carried because it is being carried. Is what I want to say clear, Euthyphro? I want to say this, namely, that if anything is being changed or is being affected in any way, it is not being changed because it is something changed, but rather it is something changed because it is being changed; nor is it being affected because it is something affected, but it is something affected because it is being affected. Or you not agree?

E: I do.

S: Is something loved either something changed or something affected by something?

E: Certainly.

S: So it is in the same case as the things just mentioned; it is not being loved by those who love it because it is something loved, but it is something loved because it is being loved by them?

E: Necessarily.

d S: What then do we say about the pious, Euthyphro? Surely that it is being loved by all the gods, according to what you say?

E: Yes.

S: Is it being loved because it is pious, or for some other reason?

E: For no other reason.

S: It is being loved then because it is pious, but it is not pious because it is being loved?[5]

E: Apparently.

S: And yet it is something loved and god-loved because it is being loved by the gods?

E: Of course.

S: Then the god-loved is not the same as the pious, Euthyphro, nor the pious the same as the god-loved, as you say it is, but one differs from the other.

E: How so, Socrates? *e*

S: Because we agree that the pious is being loved for this reason, that it is pious, but it is not pious because it is being loved. Is that not so?

E: Yes.

S: And that the god-loved, on the other hand, is so because it is being loved by the gods, by the very fact of being loved, but it is not being loved because it is god-loved.

E: True.

S: But if the god-loved and the pious were the same, my dear Euthyphro, then if the pious was being loved because it was pious, the god-loved would also be being loved because it was god-loved; and if the *11* god-loved was god-loved because it was being loved by the gods, then the pious would also be pious because it was being loved by the gods. But now you see that they are in opposite cases as being altogether different from each other: the one is such as to be loved because it is being loved, the other is being loved because it is such as to be loved. I'm afraid, Euthyphro, that when you were asked what piety is, you did not wish to make its nature clear to me, but you told me an affect or quality of it, that the pious has the quality of being loved by all the gods, but you have not yet *b* told me what the pious is. Now, if you will, do not hide things from me but tell me again from the beginning what piety is, whether being loved by the gods or having some other quality—we shall not quarrel about that—but be keen to tell me what the pious and the impious are.

E: But Socrates, I have no way of telling you what I have in mind, for whatever proposition we put forward goes around and refuses to stay put where we establish it.

5. [I quote an earlier comment of mine on this passage: "It gives in a nutshell a point of view from which Plato never departed. Whatever the gods may be, they must by their very nature love the right because it is right." They have no choice in the matter. "This separation of the dynamic power of the gods from the ultimate reality, this setting up of absolute values above the gods themselves was not as unnatural to a Greek as it would be to us. . . . The gods who ruled on Olympus . . . were not creators but created beings. As in Homer, Zeus must obey the balance of Necessity, so the Platonic gods must conform to an eternal scale of values. They did not create them, cannot alter them, cannot indeed wish to do so." (*Plato's Thought*, Boston: Beacon Press, 1958, pp. 152–3.)]

S: Your statements, Euthyphro, seem to belong *c* to my ancestor, Daedalus. If I were stating them and putting them forward, you would perhaps be making fun of me and say that because of my kinship with him my conclusions in discussion run away and will not stay where one puts them. As these propositions are yours, however, we need some other jest, for they will not stay put for you, as you say yourself.

E: I think the same jest will do for our discussion, Socrates, for I am not the one who makes them go round and not remain in the same place; it is you *d* who are the Daedalus; for as far as I am concerned they would remain as they were.

S: It looks as if I was cleverer than Daedalus in using my skill, my friend, insofar as he could only cause to move the things he made himself, but I can make other people's move as well as my own. And the smartest part of my skill is that I am clever without wanting to be, for I would rather have your statements *e* to me remain unmoved than possess the wealth of Tantalus as well as the cleverness of Daedalus. But enough of this. Since I think you are making unnecessary difficulties, I am as eager as you are to find a way to teach me about piety, and do not give up before you do. See whether you think all that is pious is of necessity just.

E: I think so.

S: And is then all that is just pious? Or is all that *12* is pious just, but not all that is just pious, but some of it is and some is not?

E: I do not follow what you are saying, Socrates.

S: Yet you are younger than I by as much as you are wiser. As I say, you are making difficulties because of your wealth of wisdom. Pull yourself together, my dear sir, what I am saying is not difficult to grasp. I am saying the opposite of what the poet said who wrote:

> You do not wish to name Zeus, who had done it, and who made all things grow, for where there is fear *b* there is also shame.

I disagree with the poet. Shall I tell you why?

E: Please do.

S: I do not think that "where there is fear there is also shame," for I think that many people who fear disease and poverty and many other such things feel fear, but are not ashamed of the things they fear. Do you not think so?

E: I do indeed.

S: But where there is shame there is also fear. For is there anyone who, in feeling shame and embar- *c* rassment at anything, does not also at the same time fear and dread a reputation for wickedness?

E: He is certainly afraid.

S: It is then not right to say "where there is fear there is also shame," but that where there is shame there is also fear, for fear covers a larger area than shame. Shame is a part of fear just as odd is a part of number, with the result that it is not true that where there is number there is also oddness, but that where there is oddness there is also number. Do you follow me now?

E: Surely.

S: This is the kind of thing I was asking before, whether where there is piety there is also justice, but where there is justice there is not always piety, for *d* the pious is a part of justice. Shall we say that, or do you think otherwise?

E: No, but like that, for what you say appears to be right.

S: See what comes next: if the pious is a part of the just, we must, it seems, find out what part of the just it is. Now if you asked me something of what we mentioned just now, such as what part of number is the even, and what number that is, I would say it is the number that is divisible into two equal, not unequal, parts. Or do you not think so?

E: I do.

S: Try in this way to tell me what part of the just *e* the pious is, in order to tell Meletus not to wrong us anymore and not to indict me for ungodliness, since I have learned from you sufficiently what is godly and pious and what is not.

E: I think, Socrates, that the godly and pious is the part of the just that is concerned with the care of the gods, while that concerned with the care of men is the remaining part of justice.

S: You seem to me to put that very well, but I still need a bit of information. I do not know yet what *13* you mean by care, for you do not mean the care of the gods in the same sense as the care of other things, as, for example, we say, don't we, that not everyone knows how to care for horses, but the horse breeder does.

E: Yes, I do mean it that way.

S: So horse breeding is the care of horses.

E: Yes.

S: Nor does everyone know how to care for dogs, but the hunter does.

E: That is so.

S: So hunting is the care of dogs.

b E: Yes.

S: And cattle raising is the care of cattle.

E: Quite so.

S: While piety and godliness is the care of the gods, Euthyphro. Is that what you mean?

E: It is.

S: Now care in each case has the same effect; it aims at the good and the benefit of the object cared for, as you can see that horses cared for by horse breeders are benefited and become better. Or do you not think so?

E: I do.

S: So dogs are benefited by dog breeding, cattle *c* by cattle raising, and so with all the others. Or do you think that care aims to harm the object of its care?

E: By Zeus, no.

S: It aims to benefit the object of its care?

E: Of course.

S: Is piety then, which is the care of the gods, also to benefit the gods and make them better? Would you agree that when you do something pious you make some one of the gods better?

E: By Zeus, no.

S: Nor do I think that this is what you mean—far from it—but that is why I asked you what you *d* meant by the care of gods, because I did not believe you meant this kind of care.

E: Quite right, Socrates, that is not the kind of care I mean.

S: Very well, but what kind of care of the gods would piety be?

E: The kind of care, Socrates, that slaves take of their masters.

S: I understand. It is likely to be a kind of service of the gods.

E: Quite so.

S: Could you tell me to the achievement of what goal service to doctors tends? Is it not, do you think, to achieving health?

E: I think so.

e S: What about service to shipbuilders? To what achievement is it directed?

E: Clearly, Socrates, to the building of a ship.

S: And service to housebuilders to the building of a house?

E: Yes.

S: Tell me then, my good sir, to the achievement of what aim does service to the gods tend? You obviously know since you say that you, of all men, have the best knowledge of the divine.

E: And I am telling the truth, Socrates.

S: Tell me then, by Zeus, what is that excellent aim that the gods achieve, using us as their servants?

E: Many fine things, Socrates.

S: So do generals, my friend. Nevertheless you *14* could easily tell me their main concern, which is to achieve victory in war, is it not?

E: Of course.

S: The farmers too, I think, achieve many fine things, but the main point of their efforts is to produce food from the earth.

E: Quite so.

S: Well then, how would you sum up the many fine things that the gods achieve?

E: I told you a short while ago, Socrates, that it is a considerable task to acquire any precise knowl- *b* edge of these things, but, to put it simply, I say that if a man knows how to say and do what is pleasing to the gods at prayer and sacrifice, those are pious actions such as preserve both private houses and public affairs of state. The opposite of these pleasing actions are impious and overturn and destroy everything.

S: You could tell me in far fewer words, if you were willing, the sum of what I asked, Euthyphro, *c* but you are not keen to teach me, that is clear. You were on the point of doing so, but you turned away. If you had given that answer, I should now have acquired from you sufficient knowledge of the nature of piety. As it is, the lover of inquiry must follow his beloved wherever it may lead him. Once more then, what do you say that piety and the pious are? Are they a knowledge of how to sacrifice and pray?

E: They are.

S: To sacrifice is to make a gift to the gods, whereas to pray is to beg from the gods?

E: Definitely, Socrates.

S: It would follow from this statement that piety *d* would be a knowledge of how to give to, and beg from, the gods.

E: You understood what I said very well, Socrates.

S: That is because I am so desirous of your wisdom, and I concentrate my mind on it, so that no word of yours may fall to the ground. But tell me, what is this service to the gods? You say it is to beg from them and to give to them?

E: I do.

S: And to beg correctly would be to ask from them things that we need?

E: What else?

e S: And to give correctly is to give them what they need from us, for it would not be skillful to bring gifts to anyone that are in no way needed.

E: True, Socrates.

S: Piety would then be a sort of trading skill between gods and men?

E: Trading yes, if you prefer to call it that.

S: I prefer nothing, unless it is true. But tell me, what benefit do the gods derive from the gifts they *15* receive from us? What they give us is obvious to all. There is for us no good that we do not receive from them, but how are they benefited by what they receive from us? Or do we have such an advantage over them in the trade that we receive all our blessings from them and they receive nothing from us?

E: Do you suppose, Socrates, that the gods are benefited by what they receive from us?

S: What could those gifts from us to the gods be, Euthyphro?

E: What else, do you think, than honor, reverence, and what I mentioned just now, gratitude.

b S: The pious is then, Euthyphro, pleasing to the gods, but not beneficial or dear to them?

E: I think it is of all things most dear to them.

S: So the pious is once again what is dear to the gods.

E: Most certainly.

S: When you say this, will you be surprised if your arguments seem to move about instead of staying put? And will you accuse me of being Daedalus who makes them move, though you are yourself much more skillful than Daedalus and make them go round in a circle? Or do you not realize that our argument has moved around and come again to the same place? *c* You surely remember that earlier the pious and the god-loved were shown not to be the same but different from each other. Or do you not remember?

E: I do.

S: Do you then not realize now that you are saying that what is dear to the gods is the pious? Is this not the same as the god-loved? Or is it not?

E: It certainly is.

S: Either we were wrong when we agreed before, or, if we were right then, we are wrong now.

E: That seems to be so.

S: So we must investigate again from the beginning what piety is, as I shall not willingly give up before I learn this. Do not think me unworthy, but concentrate your attention and tell the truth. For you *d* know it, if any man does, and I must not let you go, like Proteus, before you tell me. If you had no clear knowledge of piety and impiety you would never have ventured to prosecute your old father for murder on behalf of a servant. For fear of the gods you would have been afraid to take the risk lest you should not be acting rightly, and would have been ashamed before men, but now I know well that you believe you have *e* clear knowledge of piety and impiety. So tell me, my good Euthyphro, and do not hide what you think it is.

E: Some other time, Socrates, for I am in a hurry now, and it is time for me to go.

S: What a thing to do, my friend! By going you have cast me down from a great hope I had, that I would learn from you the nature of the pious and the impious *16* and so escape Meletus' indictment by showing him that I had acquired wisdom in divine matters from Euthyphro, and my ignorance would no longer cause me to be careless and inventive about such things, and that I would be better for the rest of my life.

Apology[1]

17 I do not know, men of Athens, how my accusers affected you; as for me, I was almost carried away in spite of myself, so persuasively did they speak. And yet, hardly anything of what they said is true. Of the many lies they told, one in particular surprised me, namely that you should be careful not to be deceived b by an accomplished speaker like me. That they were not ashamed to be immediately proved wrong by the facts, when I show myself not to be an accomplished speaker at all, that I thought was most shameless on their part—unless indeed they call an accomplished speaker the man who speaks the truth. If they mean that, I would agree that I am an orator, but not after their manner, for indeed, as I say, practically nothing c they said was true. From me you will hear the whole truth, though not, by Zeus, gentlemen, expressed in embroidered and stylized phrases like theirs, but things spoken at random and expressed in the first words that come to mind, for I put my trust in the justice of what I say, and let none of you expect anything else. It would not be fitting at my age, as it might be for a young man, to toy with words when I appear before you.

One thing I do ask and beg of you, gentlemen: if you hear me making my defense in the same kind of language as I am accustomed to use in the marketplace by the bankers' tables,[2] where many of you have heard me, and elsewhere, do not be surprised or d create a disturbance on that account. The position is this: this is my first appearance in a lawcourt, at the age of seventy; I am therefore simply a stranger to the manner of speaking here. Just as if I were really a stranger, you would certainly excuse me if I spoke in that dialect and manner in which I had been 18 brought up, so too my present request seems a just one, for you to pay no attention to my manner of speech—be it better or worse—but to concentrate your attention on whether what I say is just or not, for the excellence of a judge lies in this, as that of a speaker lies in telling the truth.

It is right for me, gentlemen, to defend myself first against the first lying accusations made against me and my first accusers, and then against the later accusations and the later accusers. There have been many who b have accused me to you for many years now, and none of their accusations are true. These I fear much more than I fear Anytus and his friends, though they too are formidable. These earlier ones, however, are more so, gentlemen; they got hold of most of you from childhood, persuaded you and accused me quite falsely, saying that there is a man called Socrates, a wise man, a student of all things in the sky and below the earth, who c makes the worse argument the stronger. Those who spread that rumor, gentlemen, are my dangerous accusers, for their hearers believe that those who study these things do not even believe in the gods. Moreover, these accusers are numerous, and have been at it a long time; also, they spoke to you at an age when you would most readily believe them, some of you being children and adolescents, and they won their case by default, as there was no defense.

What is most absurd in all this is that one cannot even know or mention their names unless one of them is a writer of comedies.[3] Those who maliciously d and slanderously persuaded you—who also, when persuaded themselves then persuaded others—all those are most difficult to deal with: one cannot bring one of them into court or refute him; one must simply fight with shadows, as it were, in making one's defense, and cross-examine when no one answers. I

Reprinted from *The Trial and Death of Socrates*, translated by G.M.A. Grube (Indianapolis: Hackett Publishing Company, 1975), by permission of the publisher.

1. [The word *apology* is a transliteration, not a translation, of the Greek *apologia* which means defense. There is certainly nothing apologetic about the speech.—G.M.A.G.]

2. [The bankers or money-changers had their counters in the marketplace. It seems that this was a favorite place for gossip.]

3. [This refers in particular to Aristophanes, whose comedy, *The Clouds*, produced in 425 B.C., ridiculed the (imaginary) school of Socrates.]

want you to realize too that my accusers are of two kinds: those who have accused me recently, and the old ones I mention; and to think that I must first defend myself against the latter, for you have also heard their accusations first, and to a much greater extent than the more recent.

Very well then. I must surely defend myself and attempt to uproot from your minds in so short a time the slander that has resided there so long. I wish this may happen, if it is in any way better for you and me, and that my defense may be successful, but I think this is very difficult and I am fully aware of how difficult it is. Even so, let the matter proceed as the god may wish, but I must obey the law and make my defense.

Let us then take up the case from its beginning. What is the accusation from which arose the slander in which Meletus trusted when he wrote out the charge against me? What did they say when they slandered me? I must, as if they were my actual prosecutors, read the affidavit they would have sworn. It goes something like this: Socrates is guilty of wrongdoing in that he busies himself studying things in the sky and below the earth; he makes the worse into the stronger argument, and he teaches these same things to others. You have seen this yourself in the comedy of Aristophanes, a Socrates swinging about there, saying he was walking on air and talking a lot of other nonsense about things of which I know nothing at all. I do not speak in contempt of such knowledge, if someone is wise in these things—lest Meletus bring more cases against me—but, gentlemen, I have no part in it, and on this point I call upon the majority of you as witnesses. I think it right that all those of you who have heard me conversing, and many of you have, should tell each other if anyone of you has ever heard me discussing such subjects to any extent at all. From this you will learn that the other things said about me by the majority are of the same kind.

Not one of them is true. And if you have heard from anyone that I undertake to teach people and charge a fee for it, that is not true either. Yet I think it a fine thing to be able to teach people as Gorgias of Leontini does, and Prodicus of Ceos, and Hippias of Elis.[4] Each of these men can go to any city and persuade the young, who can keep company with anyone of their own fellow citizens they want without paying, to leave the company of these, to join with themselves, pay them a fee, and be grateful to them besides. Indeed, I learned that there is another wise man from Paros who is visiting us, for I met a man who has spent more money on Sophists than everybody else put together, Callias, the son of Hipponicus. So I asked him—he has two sons—"Callias," I said, "if your sons were colts or calves, we could find and engage a supervisor for them who would make them excel in their proper qualities, some horse breeder or farmer. Now since they are men, whom do you have in mind to supervise them? Who is an expert in this kind of excellence, the human and social kind? I think you must have given thought to this since you have sons. Is there such a person," I asked, "or is there not?" "Certainly there is," he said. "Who is he?" I asked, "What is his name, where is he from, and what is his fee?" "His name, Socrates, is Evenus, he comes from Paros, and his fee is five minas." I thought Evenus a happy man, if he really possesses this art, and teaches for so moderate a fee. Certainly I would pride and preen myself if I had this knowledge, but I do not have it, gentlemen.

One of you might perhaps interrupt me and say: "But Socrates, what is your occupation? From where have these slanders come? For surely if you did not busy yourself with something out of the common, all these rumors and talk would not have arisen unless you did something other than most people. Tell us what it is, that we may not speak inadvisedly about you." Anyone who says that seems to be right, and I will try to show you what has caused this reputation and slander. Listen then. Perhaps some of you will think I am jesting, but be sure that all that I shall say is true. What has caused my reputation is none other than a certain kind of wisdom. What kind of wisdom? Human wisdom, perhaps. It may be that I really possess this, while those whom I mentioned just now are

4. [These were all well-known Sophists. Gorgias, after whom Plato named one of his dialogues, was a celebrated rhetorician and teacher of rhetoric. He came to Athens in 427 B.C., and his rhetorical tricks took the city by storm. Two dialogues, the authenticity of which has been doubted, are named after Hippias, whose knowledge was encyclopedic. Prodicus was known for his insistence on the precise meaning of words. Both he and Hippias are characters in the *Protagoras* (named after another famous Sophist).]

e wise with a wisdom more than human; else I cannot explain it, for I certainly do not possess it, and whoever says I do is lying and speaks to slander me. Do not create a disturbance, gentlemen, even if you think I am boasting, for the story I shall tell does not originate with me, but I will refer you to a trustworthy source. I shall call upon the god at Delphi as witness to the *21* existence and nature of my wisdom, if it be such. You know Chaerephon. He was my friend from youth, and the friend of most of you, as he shared your exile and your return. You surely know the kind of man he was, how impulsive in any course of action. He went to Delphi at one time and ventured to ask the oracle—as I say, gentlemen, do not create a disturbance—he asked if any man was wiser than I, and the Pythian replied that no one was wiser. Chaerephon is dead, but his brother will testify to you about this.

b Consider that I tell you this because I would inform you about the origin of the slander. When I heard of this reply I asked myself: "Whatever does the god mean? What is his riddle? I am very conscious that I am not wise at all; what then does he mean by saying that I am the wisest? For surely he does not lie; it is not legitimate for him to do so." For a long time I was at a loss as to his meaning; then I very reluctantly turned to some such investigation as this; *c* I went to one of those reputed wise, thinking that there, if anywhere, I could refute the oracle and say to it: "This man is wiser than I, but you said I was." Then, when I examined this man—there is no need for me to tell you his name, he was one of our public men—my experience was something like this: I thought that he appeared wise to many people and especially to himself, but he was not. I then tried to *d* show him that he thought himself wise, but that he was not. As a result he came to dislike me, and so did many of the bystanders. So I withdrew and thought to myself: "I am wiser than this man; it is likely that neither of us knows anything worthwhile, but he thinks he knows something when he does not, whereas when I do not know, neither do I think I know; so I am likely to be wiser than he to this small extent, that I do not think I know what I do not know." After this I approached another man, one of those *e* thought to be wiser than he, and I thought the same thing, and so I came to be disliked both by him and by many others.

After that I proceeded systematically. I realized, to my sorrow and alarm, that I was getting unpopular, but I thought that I must attach the greatest importance to the god's oracle, so I must go to all those who had any reputation for knowledge to examine its meaning. And by the dog,[5] gentlemen of the jury— *22* for I must tell you the truth—I experienced something like this: in my investigation in the service of the god I found that those who had the highest reputation were nearly the most deficient, while those who were thought to be inferior were more knowledgeable. I must give you an account of my journeyings as if they were labors I had undertaken to prove the oracle irrefutable. After the politicians, I went to the poets, the writers of tragedies and dithyrambs and the others, *b* intending in their case to catch myself being more ignorant than they. So I took up those poems with which they seemed to have taken most trouble and asked them what they meant, in order that I might at the same time learn something from them. I am ashamed to tell you the truth, gentlemen, but I must. Almost all the bystanders might have explained the poems better than their authors could. I soon realized *c* that poets do not compose their poems with knowledge, but by some inborn talent and by inspiration, like seers and prophets who also say many fine things without any understanding of what they say. The poets seemed to me to have had a similar experience. At the same time I saw that, because of their poetry, they thought themselves very wise men in other respects, which they were not. So there again I withdrew, thinking that I had the same advantage over them as I had over the politicians.

Finally I went to the craftsmen, for I was conscious of knowing practically nothing, and I knew that I *d* would find that they had knowledge of many fine things. In this I was not mistaken; they knew things I did not know, and to that extent they were wiser than I. But, gentlemen of the jury, the good craftsmen seemed to me to have the same fault as the poets: each of them, because of his success at his craft, thought himself very wise in other most important pursuits, and this error of theirs overshadowed the *e* wisdom they had, so that I asked myself, on behalf of the oracle, whether I should prefer to be as I am,

5. [A curious oath, occasionally used by Socrates, it appears in a longer form in the *Gorgias* (482b) as "by the dog, the god of the Egyptians."]

with neither their wisdom nor their ignorance, or to have both. The answer I gave myself and the oracle was that it was to my advantage to be as I am.

As a result of this investigation, gentlemen of the jury, I acquired much unpopularity, of a kind that is hard to deal with and is a heavy burden; many slanders came from these people and a reputation for wisdom, for in each case the bystanders thought that I myself possessed the wisdom that I proved that my interlocutor did not have. What is probable, gentlemen, is that in fact the god is wise and that his oracular response meant that human wisdom is worth little or nothing, and that when he says this man, Socrates, he is using my name as an example, as if he said: "This man among you, mortals, is wisest who, like Socrates, understands that his wisdom is worthless." So even now I continue this investigation as the god bade me—and I go around seeking out anyone, citizen or stranger, whom I think wise. Then if I do not think he is, I come to the assistance of the god and show him that he is not wise. Because of this occupation, I do not have the leisure to engage in public affairs to any extent, nor indeed to look after my own, but I live in great poverty because of my service to the god.

Furthermore, the young men who follow me around of their own free will, those who have most leisure, the sons of the very rich, take pleasure in hearing people questioned; they themselves often imitate me and try to question others. I think they find an abundance of men who believe they have some knowledge but know little or nothing. The result is that those whom they question are angry, not with themselves but with me. They say: "That man Socrates is a pestilential fellow who corrupts the young." If one asks them what he does and what he teaches to corrupt them, they are silent, as they do not know, but, so as not to appear at a loss, they mention those accusations that are available against all philosophers, about "things in the sky and things below the earth," about "not believing in the gods" and "making the worse the stronger argument"; they would not want to tell the truth, I'm sure, that they have been proved to lay claim to knowledge when they know nothing. These people are ambitious, violent and numerous; they are continually and convincingly talking about me; they have been filling your ears for a long time with vehement slanders against me. From them Meletus attacked me, and Anytus and Lycon, Meletus being vexed on behalf of the poets, Anytus on behalf of the craftsmen and the politicians, Lycon on behalf of the orators, so that, as I started out by saying, I should be surprised if I could rid you of so much slander in so short a time. That, gentlemen of the jury, is the truth for you. I have hidden or disguised nothing. I know well enough that this very conduct makes me unpopular, and this is proof that what I say is true, that such is the slander against me, and that such are its causes. If you look into this either now or later, this is what you will find.

Let this suffice as a defense against the charges of my earlier accusers. After this I shall try to defend myself against Meletus, that good and patriotic man, as he says he is, and my later accusers. As these are a different lot of accusers, let us again take up their sworn deposition. It goes something like this: Socrates is guilty of corrupting the young and of not believing in the gods in whom the city believes, but in other new spiritual things? Such is their charge. Let us examine it point by point.

He says that I am guilty of corrupting the young, but I say that Meletus is guilty of dealing frivolously with serious matters, of irresponsibly bringing people into court, and of professing to be seriously concerned with things about none of which he has ever cared, and I shall try to prove that this is so. Come here and tell me, Meletus. Surely you consider it of the greatest importance that our young men be as good as possible?[6]—Indeed I do.

Come then, tell the jury who improves them. You obviously know, in view of your concern. You say you have discovered the one who corrupts them, namely me, and you bring me here and accuse me to the jury. Come, inform the jury and tell them who it is. You see, Meletus, that you are silent and know not what to say. Does this not seem shameful to you and a sufficient proof of what I say, that you have not been concerned with any of this? Tell me, my good sir, who improves our young men?—The laws.

That is not what I am asking, but what person who has knowledge of the laws to begin with?—These jurymen, Socrates.

6. [Socrates here drops into his usual method of discussion by question and answer. This, no doubt, is what Plato had in mind, at least in part, when he made him ask the indulgence of the jury if he spoke "in his usual manner."]

How do you mean, Meletus? Are these able to educate the young and improve them?—Certainly.

All of them, or some but not others?—All of them.

Very good, by Hera. You mention a great abun- 25 dance of benefactors. But what about the audience? Do they improve the young or not?—They do, too.

What about the members of Council?—The Councillors, also.

But, Meletus, what about the assembly? Do members of the assembly corrupt the young, or do they all improve them?—They improve them.

All the Athenians, it seems, make the young into fine good men, except me, and I alone corrupt them. Is that what you mean?—That is most definitely what I mean.

b You condemn me to a great misfortune. Tell me: does this also apply to horses do you think? That all men improve them and one individual corrupts them? Or is quite the contrary true, one individual is able to improve them, or very few, namely, the horse breeders, whereas the majority, if they have horses and use them, corrupt them? Is that not the case, Meletus, both with horses and all other animals? Of course it is, whether you and Anytus say so or not. It would be a very happy state of affairs if only one person corrupted our youth, while the others improved them.

c You have made it sufficiently obvious, Meletus, that you have never had any concern for our youth; you show your indifference clearly; that you have given no thought to the subjects about which you bring me to trial.

And by Zeus, Meletus, tell us also whether it is better for a man to live among good or wicked fellow citizens. Answer, my good man, for I am not asking a difficult question. Do not the wicked do some harm to those who are ever closest to them, whereas good people benefit them?—Certainly.

d And does the man exist who would rather be harmed than benefited by his associates? Answer, my good sir, for the law orders you to answer. Is there any man who wants to be harmed?—Of course not.

Come now, do you accuse me here of corrupting the young and making them worse deliberately or unwillingly?—Deliberately.

What follows, Meletus? Are you so much wiser at your age than I am at mine that you understand that wicked people always do some harm to their closest *e* neighbors while good people do them good, but I have reached such a pitch of ignorance that I do not realize this, namely that if I make one of my associates wicked I run the risk of being harmed by him so that I do such a great evil deliberately, as you say? I do not believe you, Meletus, and I do not think anyone else will. Either I do not corrupt the young or, if I 26 do, it is unwillingly, and you are lying in either case. Now if I corrupt them unwillingly, the law does not require you to bring people to court for such unwilling wrongdoings, but to get hold of them privately, to instruct them and exhort them; for clearly, if I learn better, I shall cease to do what I am doing unwillingly. You, however, have avoided my company and were unwilling to instruct me, but you bring me here, where the law requires one to bring those who are in need of punishment, not of instruction.

And so, gentlemen of the jury, what I said is clearly true: Meletus has never been at all concerned with *b* these matters. Nonetheless tell us, Meletus, how you say that I corrupt the young; or is it obvious from your deposition that it is by teaching them not to believe in the gods in whom the city believes but in other new spiritual things? Is this not what you say I teach and so corrupt them?—That is most certainly what I do say.

Then by those very gods about whom we are talking, Meletus, make this clearer to me and to the jury: *c* I cannot be sure whether you mean that I teach the belief that there are some gods—and therefore I myself believe that there are gods and am not altogether an atheist, nor am I guilty of that—not, however, the gods in whom the city believes, but others, and that this is the charge against me, that they are others. Or whether you mean that I do not believe in gods at all, and that this is what I teach to others. —This is what I mean, that you do not believe in gods at all.

You are a strange fellow, Meletus. Why do you say *d* this? Do I not believe, as other men do, that the sun and the moon are gods?—No, by Zeus, jurymen, for he says that the sun is stone, and the moon earth.

My dear Meletus, do you think you are prosecuting Anaxagoras? Are you so contemptuous of the jury and think them so ignorant of letters as not to know that the books of Anaxagoras[7] of Clazomenae are full of those theories, and further, that the young men learn from me what they can buy from time to time for a drachma, at most, in the bookshops, and ridicule Socrates if he pretends that these theories are his own, especially as they are so absurd? Is that, by Zeus, what you think of me, Meletus, that I do not believe that there are any gods?—That is what I say, that you do not believe in the gods at all.

You cannot be believed, Meletus, even, I think, by yourself. The man appears to me, gentlemen of the jury, highly insolent and uncontrolled. He seems to have made this deposition out of insolence, violence and youthful zeal. He is like one who composed a riddle and is trying it out: "Will the wise Socrates realize that I am jesting and contradicting myself, or shall I deceive him and others?" I think he contradicts himself in the affidavit, as if he said: "Socrates is guilty of not believing in gods but believing in gods," and surely that is the part of a jester!

Examine with me, gentlemen, how he appears to contradict himself, and you, Meletus, answer us. Remember, gentlemen, what I asked you when I began, not to create a disturbance if I proceed in my usual manner.

Does any man, Meletus, believe in human activities who does not believe in humans? Make him answer, and not again and again create a disturbance. Does any man who does not believe in horses believe in horsemen's activities? Or in flute-playing activities but not in fluteplayers? No, my good sir, no man could. If you are not willing to answer, I will tell you and the jury. Answer the next question, however. Does any man believe in spiritual activities who does not believe in spirits?—No one.

Thank you for answering, if reluctantly, when the jury made you. Now you say that I believe in spiritual things and teach about them, whether new or old, but at any rate spiritual things according to what you say, and to this you have sworn in your deposition. But if I believe in spiritual things I must quite inevitably believe in spirits. Is that not so? It is indeed. I shall assume that you agree, as you do not answer. Do we not believe spirits to be either gods or the children of gods? Yes or no?—Of course.

Then since I do believe in spirits, as you admit, if spirits are gods, this is what I mean when I say you speak in riddles and in jest, as you state that I do not believe in gods and then again that I do, since I do believe in spirits. If on the other hand the spirits are children of the gods, bastard children of the gods by nymphs or some other mothers, as they are said to be, what man would believe children of the gods to exist, but not gods? That would be just as absurd as to believe the young of horses and asses, namely mules, to exist, but not to believe in the existence of horses and asses. You must have made this deposition, Meletus, either to test us or because you were at a loss to find any true wrongdoing of which to accuse me. There is no way in which you could persuade anyone of even small intelligence that it is possible for one and the same man to believe in spiritual but not also in divine things, and then again for that same man to believe neither in spirits nor in gods nor in heroes.

I do not think, gentlemen of the jury, that it requires a prolonged defense to prove that I am not guilty of the charges in Meletus' deposition, but this is sufficient. On the other hand, you know that what I said earlier is true, that I am very unpopular with many people. This will be my undoing, if I am undone, not Meletus or Anytus but the slanders and envy of many people. This has destroyed many other good men and will, I think, continue to do so. There is no danger that it will stop at me.

Someone might say: "Are you not ashamed, Socrates, to have followed the kind of occupation that has led to your being now in danger of death?" However, I should be right to reply to him: "You are wrong, sir, if you think that a man who is any good at all should take into account the risk of life or death; he should look to this only in his actions, whether what he does is right or wrong, whether he is acting like a good or a bad man." According to your view, all the heroes who died at Troy were inferior people, especially the son of Thetis who was so contemptuous of danger compared with disgrace.[8] When he was

7. [Anaxagoras of Clazomenae, born about the beginning of the fifth century, came to Athens as a young man and spent time in the pursuit of natural philosophy. He claimed that the universe was directed by Nous (Mind), and that matter was indestructible but always combining in various ways. He left Athens after being prosecuted for impiety.]

8. [The scene between Thetis and Achilles is from the *Iliad* (18, 94 ff.).]

eager to kill Hector, his goddess mother warned him, as I believe, in some such words as these: "My child, if you avenge the death of your comrade, Patroclus, and you kill Hector, you will die yourself, for your death is to follow immediately after Hector's." Hearing this, he despised death and danger and was much more afraid to live a coward who did not avenge his friends. "Let me die at once," he said, "when once I have given the wrongdoer his deserts, rather than remain here, a laughingstock by the curved ships, a burden upon the earth." Do you think he gave thought to death and danger?

This is the truth of the matter, gentlemen of the jury: wherever a man has taken a position that he believes to be best, or has been placed by his commander, there he must I think remain and face danger, without a thought for death or anything else, rather than disgrace. It would have been a dreadful way to behave, gentlemen of the jury, if, at Potidaea, Amphipolis and Delium, I had, at the risk of death, like anyone else, remained at my post where those you had elected to command had ordered me, and then, when the god ordered me, as I thought and believed, to live the life of a philosopher, to examine myself and others, I had abandoned my post for fear of death or anything else. That would have been a dreadful thing, and then I might truly have justly been brought here for not believing that there are gods, disobeying the oracle, fearing death, and thinking I was wise when I was not. To fear death, gentlemen, is no other than to think oneself wise when one is not, to think one knows what one does not know. No one knows whether death may not be the greatest of all blessings for a man, yet men fear it as if they knew that it is the greatest of evils. And surely it is the most blameworthy ignorance to believe that one knows what one does not know. It is perhaps on this point and in this respect, gentlemen, that I differ from the majority of men, and if I were to claim that I am wiser than anyone in anything, it would be in this, that, as I have no adequate knowledge of things in the underworld, so I do not think I have. I do know, however, that it is wicked and shameful to do wrong, to disobey one's superior, be he god or man. I shall never fear or avoid things of which I do not know, whether they may not be good rather than things that I know to be bad. Even if you acquitted me now and did not believe Anytus, who said to you that either I should not have been brought here in the first place, or that now I am here, you cannot avoid executing me, for if I should be acquitted, your sons would practice the teachings of Socrates and all be thoroughly corrupted; if you said to me in this regard: "Socrates, we do not believe Anytus now; we acquit you, but only on condition that you spend no more time on this investigation and do not practice philosophy, and if you are caught doing so you will die"; if, as I say, you were to acquit me on those terms, I would say to you: "Gentlemen of the jury, I am grateful and I am your friend, but I will obey the god rather than you, and as long as I draw breath and am able, I shall not cease to practice philosophy, to exhort you and in my usual way to point out to any one of you whom I happen to meet: Good Sir, you are an Athenian, a citizen of the greatest city with the greatest reputation for both wisdom and power; are you not ashamed of your eagerness to possess as much wealth, reputation and honors as possible, while you do not care for nor give thought to wisdom or truth, or the best possible state of your soul?" Then, if one of you disputes this and says he does care, I shall not let him go at once or leave him, but I shall question him, examine him and test him, and if I do not think he has attained the goodness that he says he has, I shall reproach him because he attaches little importance to the most important things and greater importance to inferior things. I shall treat in this way anyone I happen to meet, young and old, citizen and stranger, and more so the citizens because you are more kindred to me. Be sure that this is what the god orders me to do, and I think there is no greater blessing for the city than my service to the god. For I go around doing nothing but persuading both young and old among you not to care for your body or your wealth in preference to or as strongly as for the best possible state of your soul, as I say to you: "Wealth does not bring about excellence, but excellence makes wealth and everything else good for men, both individually and collectively."

Now if by saying this I corrupt the young, this advice must be harmful, but if anyone says that I give different advice, he is talking nonsense. On this point I would say to you, gentlemen of the jury: "Whether you believe Anytus or not, whether you acquit me or not, do so on the understanding that this is my course of action, even if I am to face death many times."

Do not create a disturbance, gentlemen, but abide by my request not to cry out at what I say but to listen, for I think it will be to your advantage to listen, and I am about to say other things at which you will perhaps cry out. By no means do this. Be sure that if you kill the sort of man I say I am, you will not harm me more than yourselves. Neither Meletus nor *d* Anytus can harm me in any way; he could not harm me, for I do not think it is permitted that a better man be harmed by a worse; certainly he might kill me, or perhaps banish or disfranchise me, which he and maybe others think to be great harm, but I do not think so. I think he is doing himself much greater harm doing what he is doing now, attempting to have a man executed unjustly. Indeed, gentlemen of the jury, I am far from making a defense now on my own behalf, as might be thought, but on yours, to prevent *e* you from wrongdoing by mistreating the god's gift to you by condemning me; for if you kill me you will not easily find another like me. I was attached to this city by the god—though it seems a ridiculous thing to say—as upon a great and noble horse which was somewhat sluggish because of its size and needed to be stirred up by a kind of gadfly. It is to fulfill some such function that I believe the god has placed me in the city. I never cease to rouse each and every one *31* of you, to persuade and reproach you all day long and everywhere I find myself in your company.

Another such man will not easily come to be among you, gentlemen, and if you believe me you will spare me. You might easily be annoyed with me as people are when they are aroused from a doze, and strike out at me; if convinced by Anytus you could easily kill me, and then you could sleep on for the rest of your days, unless the god, in his care for you, sent you someone else. That I am the kind of person to be a gift of the god to the city you might realize from *b* the fact that it does not seem like human nature for me to have neglected all my own affairs and to have tolerated this neglect now for so many years while I was always concerned with you, approaching each one of you like a father or an elder brother to persuade you to care for virtue. Now if I profited from this by charging a fee for my advice, there would be some sense to it, but you can see for yourselves that, for all their shameless accusations, my accusers have not *c* been able in their impudence to bring forward a witness to say that I have ever received a fee or ever asked for one. I, on the other hand, have a convincing witness that I speak the truth, my poverty.

It may seem strange that while I go around and give this advice privately and interfere in private affairs, I do not venture to go to the assembly and there advise the city. You have heard me give the reason for this in many places. I have a divine or spiritual sign which Meletus has ridiculed in his deposition. This began *d* when I was a child. It is a voice, and whenever it speaks it turns me away from something I am about to do, but it never encourages me to do anything. This is what has prevented me from taking part in public affairs, and I think it was quite right to prevent me. Be sure, gentlemen of the jury, that if I had long ago attempted to take part in politics, I should have died long ago, and benefited neither you nor myself. *e* Do not be angry with me for speaking the truth; no man will survive who genuinely opposes you or any other crowd and prevents the occurrence of many unjust and illegal happenings in the city. A man who *32* really fights for justice must lead a private, not a public, life if he is to survive for even a short time.

I shall give you great proofs of this, not words but what you esteem, deeds. Listen to what happened to me, that you may know that I will not yield to any man contrary to what is right, for fear of death, even if I should die at once for not yielding. The things I shall tell you are commonplace and smack of the lawcourts, but they are true. I have never held any *b* other office in the city, but I served as a member of the Council, and our tribe Antiochis was presiding at the time when you wanted to try as a body the ten generals who had failed to pick up the survivors of the naval battle.[9] This was illegal, as you all recognized later. I was the only member of the presiding committee to oppose your doing something contrary to the laws, and I voted against it. The orators were

9. [This was the battle of Arginusae (south of Lesbos) in 406 B.C., the last Athenian victory of the war. A violent storm prevented the Athenian generals from rescuing their survivors. For this they were tried in Athens and sentenced to death by the assembly. They were tried in a body, and it is this to which Socrates objected in the Council's presiding committee, which prepared the business of the assembly. He obstinately persisted in his opposition, in which he stood alone, and was overruled by the majority. Six generals who were in Athens were executed.]

ready to prosecute me and take me away, and your shouts were egging them on, but I thought I should *c* run any risk on the side of law and justice rather than join you, for fear of prison or death, when you were engaged in an unjust course.

This happened when the city was still a democracy. When the oligarchy was established, the Thirty[10] summoned me to the Hall, along with four others, and ordered us to bring Leon from Salamis, that he might be executed. They gave many such orders to many *d* people, in order to implicate as many as possible in their guilt. Then I showed again, not in words but in action, that, if it were not rather vulgar to say so, death is something I couldn't care less about, but that my whole concern is not to do anything unjust or impious. That government, powerful as it was, did not frighten me into any wrongdoing. When we left the Hall, the other four went to Salamis and brought in Leon, but I went home. I might have been put to *e* death for this, had not the government fallen shortly afterwards. There are many who will witness to these events.

Do you think I would have survived all these years if I were engaged in public affairs and, acting as a good man must, came to the help of justice and considered this the most important thing? Far from it, gentlemen of the jury, nor would any other man. 33 Throughout my life, in any public activity I may have engaged in, I am the same man as I am in private life. I have never come to an agreement with anyone to act unjustly, neither with anyone else nor with any one of those who they slanderously say are my pupils. I have never been anyone's teacher. If anyone, young or old, desires to listen to me when I am talking and dealing with my own concerns, I have never begrudged this to anyone, but I do not converse when *b* I receive a fee and not when I do not. I am equally ready to question the rich and the poor if anyone is willing to answer my questions and listen to what I say. And I cannot justly be held responsible for the good or bad conduct of these people, as I never promised to teach them anything and have not done so. If anyone says that he has learned anything from me, or that he heard anything privately that the others did not hear, be assured that he is not telling the truth.

Why then do some people enjoy spending consid- *c* erable time in my company? You have heard why, gentlemen of the jury, I have told you the whole truth. They enjoy hearing those being questioned who think they are wise, but are not. And this is not unpleasant. To do this has, as I say, been enjoined upon me by the god, by means of oracles and dreams, and in every other way that a divine manifestation has ever ordered a man to do anything. This is true, gentlemen, and can easily be established.

If I corrupt some young men and have corrupted *d* others, then surely some of them who have grown older and realized that I gave them bad advice when they were young should now themselves come up here to accuse me and avenge themselves. If they were unwilling to do so themselves, then some of their kindred, their fathers or brothers or other relations should recall it now if their family had been harmed by me. I see many of these present here, first Crito, my contemporary and fellow demesman, the *e* father of Critobulus here; next Lysanias of Sphettus, the father of Aeschines here; also Antiphon the Cephisian, the father of Epigenes; and others whose brothers spent their time in this way; Nicostratus, the son of Theozotides, brother of Theodotus, and Theodotus has died so he could not influence him; Paralius here, son of Demodocus, whose brother was Theages; 34 there is Adeimantus, son of Ariston, brother of Plato here; Acantidorus, brother of Apollodorus here.

I could mention many others, some one of whom surely Meletus should have brought in as witness in his own speech. If he forgot to do so, then let him do it now; I will yield time if he has anything of the kind to say. You will find quite the contrary, gentlemen. These men are all ready to come to the help of the corruptor, the man who has harmed their *b* kindred, as Meletus and Anytus say. Now those who were corrupted might well have reason to help me, but the uncorrupted, their kindred who are older men, have no reason to help me except the right and proper one, that they know that Meletus is lying and that I am telling the truth.

Very well, gentlemen of the jury. This, and maybe other similar things, is what I have to say in my defense. Perhaps one of you might be angry as he *c* recalls that when he himself stood trial on a less

10. [This was the harsh oligarchy that was set up after the final defeat of Athens in 404 B.C. and that ruled Athens for some nine months in 404–403 before the democracy was restored.]

dangerous charge, he begged and implored the jury with many tears, that he brought his children and many of his friends and family into court to arouse as much pity as he could, but that I do none of these things, even though I may seem to be running the *d* ultimate risk. Thinking of this, he might feel resentful toward me and, angry about this, cast his vote in anger. If there is such a one among you—I do not deem there is, but if there is—I think it would be right to say in reply: My good sir, I too have a household and, in Homer's phrase, I am not born "from oak or rock" but from men, so that I have a family, indeed three sons, gentlemen of the jury, of whom one is an adolescent while two are children. Nevertheless, I will not beg you to acquit me by bringing them here. Why do I do none of these things? Not through *e* arrogance, gentlemen, nor through lack of respect for you. Whether I am brave in the face of death is another matter, but with regard to my reputation and yours and that of the whole city, it does not seem right to me to do these things, especially at my age and with my reputation. For it is generally believed, whether it be true or false, that in certain respects 35 Socrates is superior to the majority of men. Now if those of you who are considered superior, be it in wisdom or courage or whatever other virtue makes them so, are seen behaving like that, it would be a disgrace. Yet I have often seen them do this sort of thing when standing trial, men who are thought to be somebody, doing amazing things as if they thought it a terrible thing to die, and as if they were to be immortal if you did not execute them. I think these *b* men bring shame upon the city so that a stranger, too, would assume that those who are outstanding in virtue among the Athenians, whom they themselves select from themselves to fill offices of state and receive other honors, are in no way better than women. You should not act like that, gentlemen of the jury, those of you who have any reputation at all, and if we do, you should not allow it. You should make it very clear that you will more readily convict a man who performs these pitiful dramatics in court and so makes the city a laughingstock, than a man who keeps quiet.

Quite apart from the question of reputation, gentle- *c* men, I do not think it right to supplicate the jury and to be acquitted because of this, but to teach and persuade them. It is not the purpose of a juryman's office to give justice as a favor to whoever seems good to him, but to judge according to law, and this he has sworn to do. We should not accustom you to perjure yourselves, nor should you make a habit of it. This is irreverent conduct for either of us.

Do not deem it right for me, gentlemen of the jury, that I should act towards you in a way that I do *d* not consider to be good or just or pious, especially, by Zeus, as I am being prosecuted by Meletus here for impiety; clearly, if I convinced you by my supplication to do violence to your oath of office, I would be teaching you not to believe that there are gods, and my defense would convict me of not believing in them. This is far from being the case, gentlemen, for I do believe in them as none of my accusers do. I leave it to you and the god to judge me in the way that will be best for me and for you.

[The jury now gives its verdict of guilty, and Meletus asks for the penalty of death.]

There are many other reasons for my not being *e* angry with you for convicting me, gentlemen of the jury, and what happened was not unexpected. I am 36 much more surprised at the number of votes cast on each side for I did not think the decision would be by so few votes but by a great many. As it is, a switch of only thirty votes would have acquitted me. I think myself that I have been cleared on Meletus' charges, *b* and not only this, but it is clear to all that, if Anytus and Lycon had not joined him in accusing me, he would have been fined a thousand drachmas for not receiving a fifth of the votes.

He assesses the penalty at death. So be it. What counter-assessment should I propose to you, gentlemen of the jury? Clearly it should be a penalty I deserve, and what do I deserve to suffer or to pay because I have deliberately not led a quiet life but have neglected what occupies most people: wealth, household affairs, the position of general or public orator or the other offices, the political clubs and factions that exist in the city? I thought myself too honest to survive if I occupied myself with those *c* things. I did not follow that path that would have made me of no use either to you or to myself, but I went to each of you privately and conferred upon him what I say is the greatest benefit, by trying to persuade him not to care for any of his belongings before caring that he himself should be as good and as wise as possible, not to care for the city's possessions more than for the city itself, and to care for other *d* things in the same way. What do I deserve for being such a man? Some good, gentlemen of the jury, if I must truly make an assessment according to my deserts, and something suitable. What is suitable for a poor benefactor who needs leisure to exhort you? Nothing is more suitable, gentlemen, than for such a man to be fed in the Prytaneum,[11] much more suitable for him than for any one of you who has won a victory at Olympia with a pair or a team of *e* horses. The Olympian victor makes you think yourself happy; I make you be happy. Besides, he does not need food, but I do. So if I must make a just assessment 37 of what I deserve, I assess it as this: free meals in the Prytaneum.

When I say this you may think, as when I spoke of appeals to pity and entreaties, that I speak arrogantly, but that is not the case, gentlemen of the jury; rather it is like this: I am convinced that I never willingly wrong anyone, but I am not convincing you of this, for we have talked together but a short time. *b* If it were the law with us, as it is elsewhere, that a trial for life should not last one but many days, you would be convinced, but now it is not easy to dispel great slanders in a short time. Since I am convinced that I wrong no one, I am not likely to wrong myself, to say that I deserve some evil and to make some such assessment against myself. What should I fear? That I should suffer the penalty Meletus has assessed against me, of which I say I do not know whether it is good or bad? Am I then to choose in preference to this something that I know very well to be an evil *c* and assess the penalty at that? Imprisonment? Why should I live in prison, always subjected to the ruling magistrates, the Eleven? A fine, and imprisonment until I pay it? That would be the same thing for me, as I have no money. Exile? for perhaps you might accept that assessment.

I should have to be inordinately fond of life, gentlemen of the jury, to be so unreasonable as to suppose that other men will easily tolerate my company and *d* conversation when you, my fellow citizens, have been unable to endure them, but found them a burden and resented them so that you are now seeking to get rid of them. Far from it, gentlemen. It would be a fine life at my age to be driven out of one city after another, for I know very well that wherever I go the young men will listen to my talk as they do here. If *e* I drive them away, they will themselves persuade their elders to drive me out; if I do not drive them away, their fathers and relations will drive me out on their behalf.

Perhaps someone might say: But Socrates, if you leave us will you not be able to live quietly, without talking? Now this is the most difficult point on which to convince some of you. If I say that it is impossible 38 for me to keep quiet because that means disobeying the god, you will not believe me and will think I am being ironical. On the other hand, if I say that it is the greatest good for a man to discuss virtue every day and those other things about which you hear me conversing and testing myself and others, for the unexamined life is not worth living for men, you will believe me even less.

What I say is true, gentlemen, but it is not easy to convince you. At the same time, I am not accustomed *b* to think that I deserve any penalty. If I had money, I would assess the penalty at the amount I could pay, for that would not hurt me, but I have none, unless you are willing to set the penalty at the amount I can pay, and perhaps I could pay you one mina of silver.[12] So that is my assessment.

Plato here, gentlemen of the jury, and Crito and Critobulus and Apollodorus bid me put the penalty at thirty minae, and they will stand surety for the money. Well then, that is my assessment, and they will be sufficient guarantee of payment.

[The jury now votes again and sentences Socrates to death.]

It is for the sake of a short time, gentlemen of the *c* jury, that you will acquire the reputation and the guilt, in the eyes of those who want to denigrate the city, of having killed Socrates, a wise man, for they who

11. [The Prytaneum was the magistrates' hall or town hall of Athens in which public entertainments were given, particularly to Olympian victors on their return home.]

12. [One mina was 100 drachmas, equivalent to, say, twenty-five dollars, though in purchasing power probably five times greater. In any case, a ridiculously small sum under the circumstances.]

want to revile you will say that I am wise even if I am not. If you had waited but a little while, this would have happened of its own accord. You see my age, *d* that I am already advanced in years and close to death. I am saying this not to all of you but to those who condemned me to death, and to these same jurors I say: Perhaps you think that I was convicted for lack of such words as might have convinced you, if I thought I should say or do all I could to avoid my sentence. Far from it. I was convicted because I lacked not words but boldness and shamelessness and the willingness to say to you what you would most gladly have heard from me, lamentations and tears and my *e* saying and doing many things that I say are unworthy of me but that you are accustomed to hear from others. I did not think then that the danger I ran should make me do anything mean, nor do I now regret the nature of my defense. I would much rather die after this kind of defense than live after making the other kind. Neither I nor any other man should, 39 on trial or in war, contrive to avoid death at any cost. Indeed it is often obvious in battle that one could escape death by throwing away one's weapons and by turning to supplicate one's pursuers, and there are many ways to avoid death in every kind of danger if one will venture to do or say anything to avoid it. It is not difficult to avoid death, gentlemen of the jury; *b* it is much more difficult to avoid wickedness, for it runs faster than death. Slow and elderly as I am, I have been caught by the slower pursuer, whereas my accusers, being clever and sharp, have been caught by the quicker, wickedness. I leave you now, condemned to death by you, but they are condemned by truth to wickedness and injustice. So I maintain my assessment, and they maintain theirs. This perhaps had to happen, and I think it is as it should be.

c Now I want to prophesy to those who convicted me, for I am at the point when men prophesy most, when they are about to die. I say gentlemen, to those who voted to kill me, that vengeance will come upon you immediately after my death, a vengeance much harder to bear than that which you took in killing me. You did this in the belief that you would avoid giving an account of your life, but I maintain that quite the opposite will happen to you. There will be *d* more people to test you, whom I now held back, but you did not notice it. They will be more difficult to deal with as they will be younger and you will resent them more. You are wrong if you believe that by killing people you will prevent anyone from reproaching you for not living in the right way. To escape such tests is neither possible nor good, but it is best and easiest not to discredit others but to prepare oneself to be as good as possible. With this prophecy to you who convicted me, I part from you.

I should be glad to discuss what has happened with *e* those who voted for my acquittal during the time that the officers of the court are busy and I do not yet have to depart to my death. So, gentlemen, stay with me awhile, for nothing prevents us from talking to each other while it is allowed. To you, as being my 40 friends, I want to show the meaning of what has occurred. A surprising thing has happened to me, judges—you I would rightly call judges. At all previous times my familiar prophetic power, my spiritual manifestation, frequently opposed me, even in small matters, when I was about to do something wrong, but now that, as you can see for yourselves, I was faced with what one might think, and what is generally thought to be, the worst of evils, my divine sign has not opposed me, either when I left home at dawn, *b* or when I came into court, or at any time that I was about to say something during my speech. Yet in other talks it often held me back in the middle of my speaking, but now it has opposed no word or deed of mine. What do I think is the reason for this? I will tell you. What has happened to me may well be a good thing, and those of us who believe death to be an evil are certainly mistaken. I have convincing proof *c* of this, for it is impossible that my familiar sign did not oppose me if I was not about to do what was right.

Let us reflect in this way, too, that there is good hope that death is a blessing, for it is one of two things: either the dead are nothing and have no perception of anything, or it is, as we are told, a change and a relocating for the soul from here to another place. If *d* it is complete lack of perception, like a dreamless sleep, then death would be a great advantage. For I think that if one had to pick out that night during which a man slept soundly and did not dream, put beside it the other nights and days of his life, and then see how many days and nights had been better and more pleasant than that night, not only a private person but the great king would find them easy to count compared with the other days and nights. If *e* death is like this I say it is an advantage, for all eternity would then seem to be no more than a single night. If, on the other hand, death is a change from here to another place, and what we are told is true and all who have died are there, what greater blessing 41 could there be, gentlemen of the jury? If anyone arriving in Hades will have escaped from those who call themselves judges here, and will find those true judges who are said to sit in judgment there, Minos and Rhadamanthus and Aeacus and Triptolemus and the other demi-gods who have been upright in their own life, would that be a poor kind of change? Again, what would one of you give to keep company with Orpheus and Musaeus, Hesiod and Homer? I am willing to die many times if that is true. It would be *b* a wonderful way for me to spend my time whenever I met Palamedes and Ajax, the son of Telamon, and any other of the men of old who died through an unjust conviction, to compare my experience with theirs. I think it would be pleasant. Most important, I could spend my time testing and examining people there, as I do here, as to who among them is wise, and who thinks he is, but is not.

What would one not give, gentlemen of the jury, for the opportunity to examine the man who led *c* the great expedition against Troy, or Odysseus, or Sisyphus, and innumerable other men and women one could mention. It would be an extraordinary happiness to talk with them, to keep company with them and examine them. In any case, they would certainly not put one to death for doing so. They are happier there than we are here in other respects, and for the rest of time they are deathless, if indeed what we are told is true.

You too must be of good hope as regards death, gentlemen of the jury, and keep this one truth in mind, that a good man cannot be harmed either in *d* life or in death, and that his affairs are not neglected by the gods. What has happened to me now has not happened of itself, but it is clear to me that it was better for me to die now and to escape from trouble. That is why my divine sign did not oppose me at any point. So I am certainly not angry with those who convicted me, or with my accusers. Of course that was not their purpose when they accused and convicted me, but they thought they were hurting me, and for this they deserve blame. This much I ask *e* from them: when my sons grow up, avenge yourselves by causing them the same kind of grief that I caused you, if you think they care for money or anything else more than they care for virtue, or if they think they are somebody when they are nobody. Reproach them as I reproach you, that they do not care for the right things and think they are worthy when they are not worthy of anything. If you do this, I shall have 42 been justly treated by you, and my sons also.

Now the hour to part has come. I go to die, you go to live. Which of us goes to the better lot is known to no one, except the god.

Crito

43 SOCRATES: Why have you come so early, Crito? Or is it not still early?

CRITO: It certainly is.

S: How early?

C: Early dawn.

S: I am surprised that the warder was willing to listen to you.

C: He is quite friendly to me by now, Socrates. I have been here often and I have given him something.

S: Have you just come, or have you been here for some time?

C: A fair time.

b S: Then why did you not wake me right away but sit there in silence?

C: By Zeus no, Socrates. I would not myself want to be in distress and awake so long. I have been surprised to see you so peacefully asleep. It was on purpose that I did not wake you, so that you should spend your time most agreeably. Often in the past throughout my life, I have considered the way you live happy, and especially so now that you bear your present misfortune so easily and lightly.

S: It would not be fitting at my age to resent the fact that I must die now.

c C: Other men of your age are caught in such misfortunes, but their age does not prevent them resenting their fate.

S: That is so. Why have you come so early?

C: I bring bad news, Socrates, not for you, apparently, but for me and all your friends the news is bad and hard to bear. Indeed, I would count it among the hardest.

d S: What is it? Or has the ship arrived from Delos, at the arrival of which I must die?

C: It has not arrived yet, but it will, I believe, arrive today, according to a message some men brought from Sunium, where they left it. This makes it obvious that it will come today, and that your life must end tomorrow.

S: May it be for the best. If it so please the gods, so be it. However, I do not think it will arrive today.

44 C: What indication have you of this?

S: I will tell you. I must die the day after the ship arrives.

C: That is what those in authority say.

S: Then I do not think it will arrive on this coming day, but on the next. I take to witness of this a dream I had a little earlier during this night. It looks as if it was the right time for you not to wake me.

C: What was your dream?

S: I thought that a beautiful and comely woman dressed in white approached me. She called me and said: "Socrates, may you arrive at fertile Phthia[1] on b the third day."

C: A strange dream, Socrates.

S: But it seems clear enough to me, Crito.

C: Too clear it seems, my dear Socrates, but listen to me even now and be saved. If you die, it will not be a single misfortune for me. Not only will I be deprived of a friend, the like of whom I shall never find again, but many people who do not know you or me very well will think that I could have saved c you if I were willing to spend money, but that I did not care to do so. Surely there can be no worse reputation than to be thought to value money more highly than one's friends, for the majority will not believe that you yourself were not willing to leave prison while we were eager for you to do so.

S: My good Crito, why should we care so much

Reprinted from *The Trial and Death of Socrates*, translated by G.M.A. Grube (Indianapolis: Hackett Publishing Company, 1975), by permission of the publisher.

1. [A quotation from the ninth book of the *Iliad* (363). Achilles has rejected all the presents of Agamemnon for him to return to the battle, and threatens to go home. He says his ships will sail in the morning, and with good weather he might arrive on the third day "in fertile Phthia" (which is his home). The dream means, obviously, that on the third day Socrates' soul, after death, will find its home. As always, counting the first member of a series, the third day is the day after tomorrow.—G.M.A.G.]

for what the majority think? The most reasonable people, to whom one should pay more attention, will believe that things were done as they were done.

d C: You see, Socrates, that one must also pay attention to the opinion of the majority. Your present situation makes clear that the majority can inflict not the least but pretty well the greatest evils if one is slandered among them.

S: Would that the majority could inflict the greatest evils, for they would then be capable of the greatest good, and that would be fine, but now they cannot do either. They cannot make a man either wise or foolish, but they inflict things haphazardly.

e C: That may be so. But tell me this, Socrates, are you anticipating that I and your other friends would have trouble with the informers if you escape from here, as having stolen you away, and that we should be compelled to lose all our property or pay *45* heavy fines and suffer other punishment besides? If you have any such fear, forget it. We would be justified in running this risk to save you, and worse, if necessary. Do follow my advice, and do not act differently.

S: I do have these things in mind, Crito, and also many others.

C: Have no such fear. It is not much money that some people require to save you and get you out of here. Further, do you not see that those informers are cheap, and that not much money would be needed to deal with them? My money is available and is, I think, *b* sufficient. If, because of your affection for me, you feel you should not spend any of mine, there are those strangers here ready to spend money. One of them, Simmias the Theban, has brought enough for this very purpose. Cebes, too, and a good many others. So, as I say, do not let this fear make you hesitate to save yourself, nor let what you said in court trouble you, that you would not know what to do with yourself *c* if you left Athens, for you would be welcomed in many places to which you might go. If you want to go to Thessaly, I have friends there who will greatly appreciate you and keep you safe, so that no one in Thessaly will harm you.

Besides, Socrates, I do not think that what you are doing is just, to give up your life when you can save it, and to hasten your fate as your enemies would hasten it, and indeed have hastened it in their wish to destroy you. Moreover, I think you are betraying *d* your sons by going away and leaving them, when you could bring them up and educate them. You thus show no concern for what their fate may be. They will probably have the usual fate of orphans. Either one should not have children, or one should share with them to the end the toil of upbringing and education. You seem to me to choose the easiest path, whereas one should choose the path a good and courageous man would choose, particularly when one claims throughout one's life to care for virtue.

I feel ashamed on your behalf and on behalf of us, *e* your friends, lest all that has happened to you be thought due to cowardice on our part: the fact that your trial came to court when it need not have done so, the handling of the trial itself, and now this absurd ending which will be thought to have got beyond our control through some cowardice and unmanliness on *46* our part, since we did not save you, or you save yourself, when it was possible and could be done if we had been of the slightest use. Consider, Socrates, whether this is not only evil, but shameful, both for you and for us. Take counsel with yourself, or rather the time for counsel is past and the decision should have been taken, and there is no further opportunity, for this whole business must be ended tonight. If we delay now, then it will no longer be possible; it will be too late. Let me persuade you on every count, Socrates, and do not act otherwise.

S: My dear Crito, your eagerness is worth much *b* if it should have some right aim; if not, then the greater your keenness the more difficult it is to deal with. We must therefore examine whether we should act in this way or not, as not only now but at all times I am the kind of man who listens only to the argument that on reflection seems best to me. I cannot, now that this fate has come upon me, discard the arguments I used; they seem to me much the same. I value and *c* respect the same principles as before, and if we have no better arguments to bring up at this moment, be sure that I shall not agree with you, not even if the power of the majority were to frighten us with more bogeys, as if we were children, with threats of incarcerations and executions and confiscation of property. How should we examine this matter most reasonably? Would it be by taking up first your argument about the opinions of men, whether it is sound in every *d* case that one should pay attention to some opinions, but not to others? Or was that well-spoken before the necessity to die came upon me, but now it is clear that this was said in vain for the sake of argument, that it was in truth play and nonsense? I am eager to examine together with you, Crito, whether this argument will appear in any way different to me in my present circumstances, or whether it remains the same, whether we are to abandon it or believe it. It was said on every occa- *e* sion by those who thought they were speaking sensibly, as I have just now been speaking, that one should greatly value some people's opinions, but not others. Does that seem to you a sound statement?

You, as far as a human being can tell, are exempt from the likelihood of dying tomorrow, so the present *47* misfortune is not likely to lead you astray. Consider then, do you not think it a sound statement that one must not value all the opinions of men, but some and not others, nor the opinions of all men, but those of some and not of others? What do you say? Is this not well said?

C: It is.

S: One should value the good opinions, and not the bad ones?

C: Yes.

S: The good opinions are those of wise men, the bad ones those of foolish men?

C: Of course.

S: Come then, what of statements such as this: *b* Should a man professionally engaged in physical training pay attention to the praise and blame and opinion of any man, or to those of one man only, namely a doctor or trainer?

C: To those of one only.

S: He should therefore fear the blame and welcome the praise of that one man, and not those of the many?

C: Obviously.

S: He must then act and exercise, eat and drink in the way the one, the trainer and the one who knows, thinks right, not all the others?

C: That is so.

c S: Very well. And if he disobeys the one, disregards his opinion and his praises while valuing those of the many who have no knowledge, will he not suffer harm?

C: Of course.

S: What is that harm, where does it tend, and what part of the man who disobeys does it affect?

C: Obviously the harm is to his body, which it ruins.

S: Well said. So with other matters, not to enumerate them all, and certainly with actions just and unjust, shameful and beautiful, good and bad, about which we are now deliberating, should we follow the *d* opinion of the many and fear it, or that of the one, if there is one who has knowledge of these things and before whom we feel fear and shame more than before all the others? If we do not follow his directions, we shall harm and corrupt that part of ourselves that is improved by just actions and destroyed by unjust actions. Or is there nothing in this?

C: I think there certainly is, Socrates.

S: Come now, if we ruin that which is improved by health and corrupted by disease by not following the opinions of those who know, is life worth living *e* for us when that is ruined? And that is the body, is it not?

C: Yes.

S: And is life worth living with a body that is corrupted and in bad condition?

C: In no way.

S: And is life worth living for us with that part of us corrupted that unjust action harms and just action benefits? Or do we think that part of us, whatever it is, that is concerned with justice and injustice, is inferior to the body? *48*

C: Not at all.

S: It is more valuable?

C: Much more.

S: We should not then think so much of what the majority will say about us, but what he will say who understands justice and injustice, the one, that is, and the truth itself. So that, in the first place, you were wrong to believe that we should care for the opinion of the many about what is just, beautiful, good, and their opposites. "But," someone might say, "the many are able to put us to death."

C: That too is obvious, Socrates, and someone *b* might well say so.

S: And, my admirable friend, that argument that we have gone through remains, I think, as before. Examine the following statement in turn as to whether it stays the same or not, that the most important thing is not life, but the good life.

C: It stays the same.

S: And that the good life, the beautiful life, and the just life are the same; does that still hold, or not?

C: It does hold.

S: As we have agreed so far, we must examine c next whether it is just for me to try to get out of here when the Athenians have not acquitted me. If it is seen to be just, we will try to do so; if it is not, we will abandon the idea. As for those questions you raise about money, reputation, the upbringing of children, Crito, those considerations in truth belong to those people who easily put men to death and would bring them to life again if they could, without thinking; I mean the majority of men. For us, however, since our argument leads to this, the only valid consideration, as we were saying just now, is whether we should be acting rightly in giving money and gratitude to those d who will lead me out of here, and ourselves helping with the escape, or whether in truth we shall do wrong in doing all this. If it appears that we shall be acting unjustly, then we have no need at all to take into account whether we shall have to die if we stay here and keep quiet, or suffer in another way, rather than do wrong.

C: I think you put that beautifully, Socrates, but see what we should do.

e S: Let us examine the question together, my dear friend, and if you can make any objection while I am speaking, make it and I will listen to you, but if you have no objection to make, my dear Crito, then stop now from saying the same thing so often, that I must leave here against the will of the Athenians. I think it important to persuade you before I act, and not to act against your wishes. See whether the start 49 of our inquiry is adequately stated, and try to answer what I ask you in the way you think best.

C: I shall try.

S: Do we say that one must never in any way do wrong willingly, or must one do wrong in one way and not in another? Is to do wrong never good or admirable, as we have agreed in the past, or have all these former agreements been washed out during the b last few days? Have we at our age failed to notice for some time that in our serious discussions we were no different from children? Above all, is the truth such as we used to say it was, whether the majority agree or not, and whether we must still suffer worse things than we do now, or will be treated more gently, that nonetheless, wrongdoing is in every way harmful and shameful to the wrongdoer? Do we say so or not?

C: We do.

S: So one must never do wrong.

C: Certainly not.

S: Nor must one, when wronged, inflict wrong in return, as the majority believe, since one must never do wrong.

C: That seems to be the case. c

S: Come now, should one injure anyone or not, Crito?

C: One must never do so.

S: Well then, if one is oneself injured, is it right, as the majority say, to inflict an injury in return, or is it not?

C: It is never right.

S: Injuring people is no different from wrongdoing.

C: That is true.

S: One should never do wrong in return, nor injure any man, whatever injury one has suffered at his hands. And Crito, see that you do not agree to d this, contrary to your belief. For I know that only a few people hold this view or will hold it, and there is no common ground between those who hold this view and those who do not, but they inevitably despise each other's views. So then consider very carefully whether we have this view in common, and whether you agree, and let this be the basis of our deliberation, that neither to do wrong or to return a wrong is ever right, not even to injure in return for an injury received. Or do you disagree and do not share this view as a basis for discussion? I have held it for a e long time and still hold it now, but if you think otherwise, tell me now. If, however, you stick to our former opinion, then listen to the next point.

C: I stick to it and agree with you. So say on.

S: Then I state the next point, or rather I ask you: when one has come to an agreement that is just with someone, should one fulfill it or cheat on it?

C: One should fulfill it.

S: See what follows from this: if we leave here without the city's permission, are we injuring people 50 whom we should least injure? And are we sticking to a just agreement, or not?

C: I cannot answer your question, Socrates. I do not know.

S: Look at it this way. If, as we were planning to run away from here, or whatever one should call it, the laws and the state came and confronted us and asked: "Tell me, Socrates, what are you intending to do? Do you not by this action you are attempting *b* intend to destroy us, the laws, and indeed the whole city, as far as you are concerned? Or do you think it possible for a city not to be destroyed if the verdicts of its courts have no force but are nullified and set at naught by private individuals?" What shall we answer to this and other such arguments? For many things could be said, especially by an orator on behalf of this law we are destroying, which orders that the *c* judgments of the courts shall be carried out. Shall we say in answer, "The city wronged me, and its decision was not right"? Shall we say that, or what?

C: Yes, by Zeus, Socrates, that is our answer.

S: Then what if the laws said: "Was that the agreement between us, Socrates, or was it to respect the judgments that the city came to?" And if we wondered at their words, they would perhaps add: "Socrates, do not wonder at what we say but answer, *d* since you are accustomed to proceed by question and answer. Come now, what accusation do you bring against us and the city, that you should try to destroy us? Did we not, first, bring you to birth, and was it not through us that your father married your mother and begat you? Tell you, do you find anything to criticize in those of us who are concerned with marriage?" And I would say that I do not criticize them. "Or in those of us concerned with the nurture of babies and the education that you too received? Were those assigned to that subject not right to instruct *e* your father to educate you in the arts and in physical culture?" And I would say that they were right. "Very well," they would continue, "and after you were born and nurtured and educated, could you, in the first place, deny that you are our offspring and servant, both you and your forefathers? If that is so, do you think that we are on an equal footing as regards the right, and that whatever we do to you it is right for you to do to us? You were not on an equal footing with your father as regards the right, nor with your 51 master if you had one, so as to retaliate for anything they did to you, to revile them if they reviled you, to beat them if they beat you, and so with many other things. Do you think you have this right to retaliation against your country and its laws? That if we undertake to destroy you and think it right to do so, you can undertake to destroy us, as far as you can, in return? And will you say that you are right to do so, you who truly care for virtue? Is your wisdom such as not to realize that your country is to be honored more than your mother, your father, and all your ancestors, that it is more to be revered and more sacred, and that it *b* counts for more among the gods and sensible men, that you must worship it, yield to it, and placate its anger more than your father's? You must either persuade it or obey its orders, and endure in silence whatever it instructs you to endure, whether blows or bonds, and if it leads you into war to be wounded or killed, you must obey. To do so is right, and one must not give way or retreat or leave one's post, but both in war and in courts and everywhere else, one must obey the commands of one's city and country, *c* or persuade it as to the nature of justice. It is impious to bring violence to bear against your mother or father; it is much more so to use it against your country." What shall we say in reply, Crito, that the laws speak the truth, or not?

C: I think they do.

S: "Reflect now, Socrates," the laws might say, "that if what we say is true, you are not treating us rightly by planning to do what you are planning. We have given you birth, nurtured you, educated you; we have given you and all other citizens a share of *d* all the good things we could. Even so, by giving every Athenian the opportunity, after he has reached manhood and observed the affairs of the city and us the laws, we proclaim that if we do not please him, he can take his possessions and go wherever he pleases. Not one of our laws raises any obstacle or forbids him, if he is not satisfied with us or the city, if one of you wants to go and live in a colony or wants to go anywhere else, and keep his property. We say, *e* however, that whoever of you remains, when he sees how we conduct our trials and manage the city in other ways, has in fact come to an agreement with us to obey our instructions. We say that the one who disobeys does wrong in three ways, first because in us he disobeys his parents, also those who brought him up, and because, in spite of his agreement, he neither obeys us nor, if we do something wrong, does 52 he try to persuade us to do better. Yet we only propose things, we do not issue savage commands to do whatever we order; we give two alternatives, either to persuade us or to do what we say. He does neither. We do say that you too, Socrates, are open to those charges if you do what you have in mind; you would be among, not the least, but the most guilty of the Athenians." And if I should say "Why so?" they might well be right to upbraid me and say that I am among the Athenians who most definitely came to that agree- *b* ment with them. They might well say: "Socrates, we have convincing proofs that we and the city were congenial to you. You would not have dwelt here most consistently of all the Athenians if the city had not been exceedingly pleasing to you. You have never left the city, even to see a festival, nor for any other reason except military service; you have never gone to stay in any other city, as people do; you have had *c* no desire to know another city or other laws; we and our city satisfied you.

"So decisively did you choose us and agree to be a citizen under us. Also, you have had children in this city, thus showing that it was congenial to you. Then at your trial you could have assessed your penalty at exile if you wished, and you are now attempting to do against the city's wishes what you could then have done with her consent. Then you prided yourself that you did not resent death, but you chose, as you said, death in preference to exile. Now, however, those words do not make you ashamed, and you pay *d* no heed to us, the laws, as you plan to destroy us, and you act like the meanest type of slave by trying to run away, contrary to your commitments and your agreement to live as a citizen under us. First then, answer us on this very point, whether we speak the truth when we say that you agreed, not only in words but by your deeds, to live in accordance with us." What are we to say to that, Crito? Must we not agree?

C: We must, Socrates.

S: "Surely," they might say, "you are breaking the commitments and agreements that you made with *e* us without compulsion or deceit, and under no pressure of time for deliberation. You have had seventy years during which you could have gone away if you did not like us, and if you thought our agreements *53* unjust. You did not choose to go to Sparta or to Crete, which you are always saying are well governed, nor to any other city, Greek or foreign. You have been away from Athens less than the lame or the blind or other handicapped people. It is clear that the city has been outstandingly more congenial to you than to other Athenians, and so have we, the laws, for what city can please without laws? Will you then not now stick to our agreements? You will, Socrates, if we can persuade you, and not make yourself a laughingstock by leaving the city.

"For consider what good you will do yourself or your friends by breaking our agreements and committing such a wrong. It is pretty obvious that your friends will themselves be in danger of exile, disfranchisement and loss of property. As for yourself, if you go *b* to one of the nearby cities—Thebes or Megara, both are well governed—you will arrive as an enemy to their government; all who care for their city will look on you with suspicion, as a destroyer of the laws. You will also strengthen the conviction of the jury that they passed the right sentence on you, for anyone *c* who destroys the laws could easily be thought to corrupt the young and the ignorant. Or will you avoid cities that are well governed and men who are civilized? If you do this, will your life be worth living? Will you have social intercourse with them and not be ashamed to talk to them? And what will you say? The same as you did here, that virtue and justice are man's most precious possession, along with lawful *d* behavior and the laws? Do you not think that Socrates would appear to be an unseemly kind of person? One must think so. Or will you leave those places and go to Crito's friends in Thessaly? There you will find the greatest license and disorder, and they may enjoy hearing from you how absurdly you escaped from prison in some disguise, in a leather jerkin or some other things in which escapees wrap themselves, thus altering your appearance. Will there be no one to say that you, likely to live but a short time more, were so greedy for life that you transgressed the most impor- *e* tant laws? Possibly, Socrates, if you do not annoy anyone, but if you do, many disgraceful things will be said about you.

"You will spend your time ingratiating yourself with all men, and be at their beck and call. What will you do in Thessaly but feast, as if you had gone to a banquet in Thessaly? As for those conversations of yours about justice and the rest of virtue, where will they be? You say you want to live for the sake of your *54* children, that you may bring them up and educate them. How so? Will you bring them up and educate them by taking them to Thessaly and making strangers of them, that they may enjoy that too? Or not so, but they will be better brought up and educated here, while you are alive, though absent? Yes, your friends will look after them. Will they look after them if you go and live in Thessaly, but not if you go away to the underworld? If those who profess themselves your friends are any good at all, one must assume that they will.

b "Be persuaded by us who have brought you up, Socrates. Do not value either your children or your life or anything else more than goodness, in order that when you arrive in Hades you may have all this as your defense before the rulers there. If you do this deed, you will not think it better or more just or more pious here, nor will any one of your friends, nor will it be better for you when you arrive yonder. As it is, you depart, if you depart, after being wronged not by *c* us, the laws, but by men; but if you depart after shamefully returning wrong for wrong and injury for injury, after breaking your agreements and commitments with us, after injuring those you should injure least—yourself, your friends, your country and us—we shall be angry with you while you are still alive, and our brothers, the laws of the underworld, will not receive you kindly, knowing that you tried to destroy us as far as you could. Do not let Crito persuade you, rather than us, to do what he says." *d*

Crito, my dear friend, be assured that these are the words I seem to hear, as the Corybants seem to hear the music of their flutes, and the echo of these words resounds in me, and makes it impossible for me to hear anything else. As far as my present beliefs go, if you speak in opposition to them, you will speak in vain. However, if you think you can accomplish anything, speak.

C: I have nothing to say, Socrates.

S: Let it be then, Crito, and let us act in this way, since this is the way the god is leading us. *e*

Phaedo

57 ECHECRATES: Were you with Socrates yourself, Phaedo,[1] on the day when he drank the poison in prison, or did someone else tell you about it?

PHAEDO: I was there myself, Echecrates.

E: What are the things he said before he died? And how did he die? I should be glad to hear this. Hardly anyone from Phlius[2] visits Athens nowadays, nor has *b* any stranger come from Athens for some time who could give us a clear account of what happened, except that he drank the poison and died, but nothing more.

58 P: Did you not even hear how the trial went?

E: Yes, someone did tell us about that, and we wondered that he seems to have died a long time after the trial took place. Why was that, Phaedo?

P: That was by chance, Echecrates. The day before the trial, as it happened, the prow of the ship that the Athenians send to Delos had been crowned with garlands.

E: What ship is that?

P: It is the ship in which, the Athenians say, Theseus once sailed to Crete, taking with him the *b* two lots of seven victims.[3] He saved them and was himself saved. They vowed then to Apollo, so the story goes, that if they were saved they would send a mission to Delos every year. And from that time to this they send such an annual mission to the god. They have a law to keep the city pure while it lasts, and no execution may take place once the mission has begun until the ship has made its journey to Delos and returned to Athens, and this can sometimes take a long time if the winds delay it. The mission begins when the priest of Apollo crowns the prow of *c* the ship, and this happened, as I say, the day before Socrates' trial. That is why Socrates was in prison a long time between this trial and his execution.

E: What about his actual death, Phaedo? What did he say? What did he do? Who of his friends were with him? Or did the authorities not allow them to be present and he died with no friends present?

P: By no means. Some were present, in fact, a *d* good many.

E: Please be good enough to tell us all that occurred as fully as possible, unless you have some pressing business.

P: I have the time and I will try to tell you the whole story, for nothing gives me more pleasure than to call Socrates to mind, whether talking about him myself, or listening to someone else do so.

E: Your hearers will surely be like you in this, Phaedo. So do try to tell us every detail as exactly as you can.

P: I certainly found being there an astonishing experience. Although I was witnessing the death of *e* one who was my friend, I had no feeling of pity, for the man appeared happy in both manner and words as he died nobly and without fear, Echecrates, so that it struck me that even in going down to the underworld he was going with the gods' blessing and that 59 he would fare well when he got there, if anyone ever does. That is why I had no feeling of pity, such as would seem natural in my sorrow, nor indeed of pleasure, as we engaged in philosophical discussion as we were accustomed to do—for our arguments were of that sort—but I had a strange feeling, an

Reprinted from Plato's *Phaedo*, translated by G.M.A. Grube (Indianapolis: Hackett Publishing Company, 1977), by permission of the publisher. The translation follows Burnet's Oxford text except in rare instances. The only liberty taken is where the answers to Socrates' questions are very brief, merely indicating assent or the like. In such instances, "he said," the so-frequent repetition of which reads awkwardly in English, has been replaced by a dash, to indicate a change of speaker.

1. [Phaedo was a young friend of Socrates who later founded a school of philosophy at Elis.—G.M.A.G.]

2. [Phlius was a community in the northeastern part of the Peloponnesus where a Pythagorean society flourished about this time. We are told by Diogenes Laërtius (early third century A.D.) that Echecrates was a member of that society.]

3. [Legend says that Minos, king of Crete, compelled the Athenians to send seven youths and seven maidens every year to be sacrificed to the Minotaur until Theseus saved them and killed the monster.]

unaccustomed mixture of pleasure and pain at the same time as I reflected that he was just about to die. All of us present were affected in much the same way, sometimes laughing, then weeping; especially one of us, Apollodorus—you know the man and his ways.

b E: Of course I do.

P: He was quite overcome; but I was myself disturbed, and so were the others.

E: Who, Phaedo, were those present?

P: Among the local people there was Apollodorus, whom I mentioned, Critobulus and his father,[4] also Hermogenes, Epigenes, Aeschines and Antisthenes. Ctesippus of Paeania was there, Menexenus and some others. Plato, I believe, was ill.[5]

E: Were there some strangers present?

c P: Yes, Simmias from Thebes with Cebes and Phaedondes, and from Megara, Euclides and Terpsion.

E: What about Aristippus and Cleombrotus? Were they there?

P: No. They were said to be in Aegina.

E: Was there anyone else?

P: I think these were about all.

E: Well then, what do you say the conversation was about?

P: I will try to tell you everything from the beginning. On the previous days also both the others and I used to visit Socrates. We foregathered at daybreak d at the court where the trial took place, for it was close to the prison, and each day we used to wait around talking until the prison should open, for it did not open early. When it opened we used to go in to Socrates and spend most of the day with him. On this day we gathered rather early, because when we left the prison on the previous evening we were in- e formed that the ship from Delos had arrived, and so we told each other to come to the usual place as early as possible. When we arrived the gatekeeper who used to answer our knock came out and told us to wait and not go in until he told us to. "The Eleven,"[6] he said, "are freeing Socrates from his bonds and telling him how his death will take place today." After a short time he came and told us to go in. We found 60 Socrates recently released from his chains, and Xanthippe—you know her—sitting by him, holding their baby. When she saw us, she cried out and said the sort of thing that women usually say: "Socrates, this is the last time your friends will talk to you and you to them." Socrates looked at Crito. "Crito," he said, "let someone take her home." And some of Crito's people led her away lamenting and beating b her breast.

Socrates sat up on the bed, bent his leg and rubbed it with his hand, and as he rubbed he said: "What a strange thing that which men call pleasure seems to be, and how astonishing the relation it has with what is thought to be its opposite, namely pain! A man cannot have both at the same time. Yet if he pursues and catches the one, he is almost always bound to catch the other also, like two creatures with one head. I think that if Aesop had noted this he would have composed a fable that a god wished to reconcile their c opposition but could not do so, so he joined their two heads together, and therefore when a man has the one, the other follows later. This seems to be happening to me. My bonds caused pain in my leg, and now pleasure seems to be following."

Cebes intervened and said: "By Zeus, yes, Socrates, you did well to remind me. Evenus[7] asked me the day before yesterday, as others had done before, what d induced you to write poetry after you came to prison,

4. [The father of Critobulus is Crito, who in the dialogue named after him tries to persuade Socrates to escape from jail. He is also mentioned in *Apology* 33e and plays a prominent part in the death scene at the end of this dialogue. Several of the other friends of Socrates mentioned here also appear in other dialogues. Hermogenes is one of the speakers in the *Cratylus*. Epigenes is mentioned in *Apology* 33e, as is Aeschines. Aeschines was a writer of Socratic dialogues. Menexenus has a part in the *Lysis* and has a dialogue named after him. Simmias and Cebes are mentioned in the *Crito*, 45b, as having come to Athens with enough money to secure Socrates' escape.]

5. [It is interesting to note that Plato makes it clear that he was *not* present on the last day of Scorates' life, whereas in the *Apology* he twice mentions (34a and 38b) that he *was* present at the trial. Whether this has any significance as regards the historical accuracy of the two works is anyone's guess. Probably it just happened to be so, but these are the only instances in which Plato mentions himself in all his works.]

6. [The Eleven were the police commissioners of Athens.]

7. [Socrates refers to Evenus as a Sophist and teacher of the young in *Apology* 20a–b.]

you who had never composed any poetry before, putting the fables of Aesop into verse and composing the hymn to Apollo. If it is of any concern to you that I should have an answer to give to Evenus when he repeats his question, as I know he will, tell me what to say to him."

Tell him the truth, Cebes, he said, that I did not do this with the idea of rivalling him or his poems, for I knew that would not be easy, but I tried to find out the meaning of certain dreams and to satisfy my *e* conscience in case it was this kind of art they were frequently bidding me to practice. The dreams were something like this: the same dream often came to me in the past, now in one shape now in another, but saying the same thing: "Socrates," it said, "practice and cultivate the arts." In the past I imagined that it was instructing and advising me to do what I was doing, such as those who encourage runners in a *61* race, that the dream was thus bidding me do the very thing I was doing, namely, to practice the art of philosophy, this being the highest kind of art, and I was doing that.

But now, after my trial took place, and the festival of the god was preventing my execution, I thought that, in case my dream was bidding me to practice this popular art, I should not disobey it but compose poetry. I thought it safer not to leave here until I had *b* satisfied my conscience by writing poems in obedience to the dream. So I first wrote in honor of the god of the present festival. After that I realized that a poet, if he is to be a poet, must compose fables, not arguments. Being no teller of fables myself, I took the stories I knew and had at hand, the fables of Aesop, and I versified the first ones I came across. Tell this to Evenus, Cebes, wish him well and bid him farewell, and tell him, if he is wise, to follow me *c* as soon as possible. I am leaving today, it seems, as the Athenians so order it.

Said Simmias: "What kind of advice is this you are giving to Evenus, Socrates? I have met him many times, and from my observation he is not at all likely to follow it willingly."

How so, said he, is Evenus not a philosopher?

I think so, Simmias said.

Then Evenus will be willing, like every man who partakes worthily of philosophy. Yet perhaps he will not take his own life, for that, they say, is not right. As he said this, Socrates put his feet on the ground and remained in this position during the rest of the *d* conversation.

Then Cebes asked: "How do you mean Socrates, that it is not right to do oneself violence, and yet that the philosopher will be willing to follow one who is dying?"

Come now, Cebes, have you and Simmias, who keep company with Philolaus,[8] not heard about such things?

Nothing definite, Socrates.

Indeed, I too speak about this from hearsay, but I do not mind telling you what I have heard, for it is perhaps most appropriate for one who is about to depart yonder to tell and examine tales about what we believe that journey to be like. What else could *e* one do in the time we have until sunset?

But whatever is the reason, Socrates, for people to say that it is not right to kill oneself? As to your question just now, I have heard Philolaus say this when staying in Thebes and I have also heard it from others, but I have never heard anyone give a clear account of the matter.

Well, he said, we must do our best, and you may yet hear one. And it may well astonish you if this *62* subject, alone of all things, is simple, and it is never, as with everything else, better at certain times and for certain people to die than to live. And if this is so, you may well find it astonishing that those for whom it is better to die are wrong to help themselves, and that they must wait for someone else to benefit them.

And Cebes, lapsing into his own dialect, laughed quietly and said: "Zeus knows it is."

Indeed, said Socrates, it does seem unreasonable when put like that, but perhaps there is reason to it. *b* There is the explanation that is put in the language of the mysteries, that we men are in a kind of prison, and that one must not free oneself or run away. That seems to me an impressive doctrine and one not easy to understand fully. However, Cebes, this seems to

8. [Philolaus was a contemporary Pythagorean. The reference to him here, as well as the fact that the story is told to Echecrates at Phlius, gives the whole dialogue a Pythagorean background, and this seems a recognition on Plato's part of Pythagorean influence regarding the theories that follow, in particular, the theory of Forms and the purification of man's eternal soul through intellectual activity.]

me well expressed, that the gods are our guardians and that men are one of their possessions. Or do you not think so?

I do, said Cebes.

And would you not be angry if one of your posses- *c* sions killed itself when you had not given any sign that you wished it to die, and if you had any punishment you could inflict, you would inflict it?

Certainly, he said.

Perhaps then, put in this way, it is not unreasonable that one should not kill oneself before a god had indicated some necessity to do so, like the necessity now put upon us.

That seems likely, said Cebes. As for what you were *d* saying, that philosophers should be willing and ready to die, that seems strange, Socrates, if what we said just now is reasonable, namely, that a god is our protector and that we are his possessions. It is not logical that the wisest of men should not resent leaving this service in which they are governed by the best of masters, the gods, for a wise man cannot believe that he will look after himself better when he is free. A foolish man might easily think so, that he must *e* escape from his master; he would not reflect that one must not escape from a good master but stay with him as long as possible, because it would be foolish to escape. But the sensible man would want always to remain with one better than himself. So, Socrates, the opposite of what was said before is likely to be true; the wise would resent dying, whereas the foolish would rejoice at it.

I thought that when Socrates heard this he was pleased by Cebes' argumentation. Glancing at us, he *63* said: "Cebes is always on the track of some arguments; he is certainly not willing to be at once convinced by what one says."

Said Simmias: "But actually, Socrates, I think myself that Cebes has a point now. Why should truly wise men want to avoid the service of masters better than themselves, and leave them easily? And I think Cebes is aiming his argument at you, because you are bearing leaving us so lightly, and leaving those good masters, as you say yourself, the gods."

b You are both justified in what you say, and I think you mean that I must make a defense against this, as if I were in court.

You certainly must, said Simmias.

Come then, he said, let me try to make my defense to you more convincing than it was to the jury. For, Simmias and Cebes, I should be wrong not to resent dying if I did not believe that I should go first to other wise and good gods, and then to men who have died and are better than men are here. Be assured that, as it is, I expect to join the company of good men. *c* This last I would not altogether insist on, but if I insist on anything at all in these matters, it is that I shall come to gods who are very good masters. That is why I am not so resentful, because I have good hope that some future awaits men after death, as we have been told for years, a much better future for the good than for the wicked.

Well now, Socrates, said Simmias, do you intend to keep this belief to yourself as you leave us, or would you share it with us? I certainly think it would be a *d* blessing for us too, and at the same time it would be your defense if you convince us of what you say.

I will try, he said, but first let us see what it is that Crito here has, I think, been wanting to say for quite a while.

What else, Socrates, said Crito, but what the man who is to give you the poison has been telling me for some time, that I should warn you to talk as little as possible. People get heated when they talk, he says, and one should not be heated when taking the poison, *e* as those who do must sometimes drink it two or three times.

Socrates replied: "Take no notice of him; only let him be prepared to administer it twice or, if necessary, three times."

I was rather sure you would say that, Crito said, but he has been bothering me for some time.

Let him be, he said. I want to make my argument before you, my judges, as to why I think that a man who has truly spent his life in philosophy is probably right to be of good cheer in the face of death and to be very hopeful that after death he will attain the greatest blessings yonder. I will try to tell you, Simmias *64* and Cebes, how this may be so. I am afraid that other people do not realize that the one aim of those who practice philosophy in the proper manner is to practice for dying and death. Now if this is true, it would be strange indeed if they were eager for this all their lives and then resent it when what they have wanted and practiced for a long time comes upon them.

Simmias laughed and said: "By Zeus, Socrates, you made me laugh, though I was in no laughing mood b just now. I think that the majority, on hearing this, will think that it describes the philosophers very well, and our people in Thebes would thoroughly agree that philosophers are nearly dead and that the majority of men is well aware that they deserve to be."

And they would be telling the truth, Simmias, except for their being aware. They are not aware of the way true philosophers are nearly dead, nor of the way c they deserve to be, nor of the sort of death they deserve. But never mind them, he said, let us talk among ourselves. Do we believe that there is such a thing as death?

Certainly, said Simmias.

Is it anything else than the separation of the soul from the body? Do we believe that death is this, namely, that the body comes to be separated by itself apart from the soul, and the soul comes to be separated by itself apart from the body? Is death anything else than that?

No, that is what it is, he said.

Consider then, my good sir, whether you share my opinion, for this will lead us to a better knowledge d of what we are investigating. Do you think it is the part of a philosopher to be concerned with such so-called pleasures as those of food and drink?

By no means.

What about the pleasures of sex?

Not at all.

What of the other pleasures concerned with the service of the body? Do you think such a man prizes them greatly, the acquisition of distinguished clothes and shoes and the other bodily ornaments? Do you think he values these or despises them, except in so e far as one cannot do without them?

I think the true philosopher despises them.

Do you not think, he said, that in general such a man's concern is not with the body but that, as far as he can, he turns away from the body towards the soul?

I do.

So in the first place, such things show clearly that 65 the philosopher more than other men frees the soul from association with the body as much as possible?

Apparently.

A man who finds no pleasure in such things and has no part in them is thought by the majority not to deserve to live and to be close to death; the man, that is, who does not care for the pleasures of the body.

What you say is certainly true.

Then what about the actual acquiring of knowledge? Is the body an obstacle when one associates with it in the search for knowledge? I mean, for example, b do men find any truth in sight or hearing, or are not even the poets[9] forever telling us that we do not see or hear anything accurately, and surely if those two physical senses are not clear or precise, our other senses can hardly be accurate, as they are all inferior to these. Do you not think so?

I certainly do, he said.

When then, he asked, does the soul grasp the truth? For whenever it attempts to examine anything with the body, it is clearly deceived by it.

True. c

Is it not in reasoning if anywhere that any reality becomes clear to the soul?

Yes.

And indeed the soul reasons best when none of these senses troubles it, neither hearing nor sight, nor pain nor pleasure, but when it is most by itself, taking leave of the body and as far as possible having no contact or association with it in its search for reality.

That is so.

And it is then that the soul of the philosopher most disdains the body, flees from it and seeks to be d by itself?

It appears so.

What about the following, Simmias? Do we say that there is such a thing as the Just itself, or not?

We do say so, by Zeus.

And the Beautiful, and the Good?

Of course.

And have you ever seen any of these things with your eyes?

In no way, he said.

Or have you ever grasped them with any of your bodily senses? I am speaking of all things such as Size, Health, Strength and, in a word, the reality of all other things, that which each of them essentially is. Is what is most true in them contemplated through e the body, or is this the position: whoever of us prepares himself best and most accurately to grasp that thing

9. ["Even the poets" because poetry concerns itself with the world of sense and appeals to the passions and emotions of the lowest part of the soul (*Republic* 595a ff.), whereas in the *Phaedo* passions and emotions are attributed to the body.]

itself which he is investigating will come closest to the knowledge of it?

Obviously.

Then he will do this most perfectly who approaches the object with thought alone, without associating 66 any sight with his thought, or dragging in any sense perception with his reasoning, but who, using pure thought alone, tries to track down each reality pure and by itself, freeing himself as far as possible from eyes and ears, and in a word, from the whole body, because the body confuses the soul and does not allow it to acquire truth and wisdom whenever it is associated with it. Will not that man reach reality, Simmias, if anyone does?

What you say, said Simmias, is indeed true.

b All these things will necessarily make the true philosophers believe and say to each other something like this: "There is likely to be something such as a path to guide us out of our confusion, because as long as we have a body and our soul is fused with such an evil we shall never adequately attain what we desire, which we affirm to be the truth. The body keeps us busy in a thousand ways because of its need for nurture. Moreover, if certain diseases befall it, c they impede our search for the truth. It fills us with wants, desires, fears, all sorts of illusions and much nonsense, so that, as it is said, in truth and in fact no thought of any kind ever comes to us from the body. Only the body and its desires cause war, civil discord and battles, for all wars are due to the desire to acquire d wealth, and it is the body and the care of it, to which we are enslaved, which compel us to acquire wealth, and all this makes us too busy to practice philosophy. Worst of all, if we do get some respite from it and turn to some investigation, everywhere in our investigations the body is present and makes for confusion and fear, so that it prevents us from seeing the truth.

"It really has been shown to us that, if we are ever to have pure knowledge, we must escape from the e body and observe things in themselves with the soul by itself. It seems likely that we shall, only then, when we are dead, attain that which we desire and of which we claim to be lovers, namely, wisdom, as our argument shows, not while we live; for if it is impossible to attain any pure knowledge with the body, then one of two things is true: either we can never attain knowledge or we can do so after death. Then and 67 not before, the soul is by itself apart from the body. While we live, we shall be closest to knowledge if we refrain as much as possible from association with the body and do not join with it more than we must, if we are not infected with its nature but purify ourselves from it until the god himself frees us. In this way we shall escape the contamination of the body's folly; we shall be likely to be in the company of people of the same kind, and by our own efforts we shall know all that is pure, which is presumably the truth, for it b is not permitted to the impure to attain the pure."

Such are the things, Simmias, that all those who love learning in the proper manner must say to one another and believe. Or do you not think so?

I certainly do, Socrates.

And if this is true, my friend, said Socrates, there is good hope that on arriving where I am going, if anywhere, I shall acquire what has been our chief preoccupation in our past life, so that the journey that is now ordered for me is full of good hope, as it c is also for any other man who believes that his mind has been prepared and, as it were, purified.

It certainly is, said Simmias.

And does purification not turn out to be what we mentioned in our argument some time ago, namely, to separate the soul as far as possible from the body and accustom it to gather itself and collect itself out of every part of the body and to dwell by itself as far as it can both now and in the future, freed, as it were, d from the bonds of the body?

Certainly, he said.

And that freedom and separation of the soul from the body is called death?

That is altogether so.

It is only those who practice philosophy in the right way, we say, who always most want to free the soul; and this release and separation of the soul from the body is the preoccupation of the philosophers?

So it appears.

Therefore, as I said at the beginning, it would be ridiculous for a man to train himself in life to live in a state as close to death as possible, and then to resent it when it comes? e

Ridiculous, of course.

In fact, Simmias, he said, those who practice philosophy in the right way are in training for dying and they fear death least of all men. Consider it from this point of view: if they are altogether estranged from the body and desire to have their soul by itself, would it not be quite absurd for them to be afraid and resentful when this happens? If they did not gladly set out for a place, where, on arrival, they may hope to attain that for which they had yearned during their 68 lifetime, that is, wisdom, and where they would be rid of the presence of that from which they are estranged?

Many men, at the death of their lovers, wives or sons, were willing to go to the underworld, driven by the hope of seeing there those for whose company they longed, and being with them. Will then a true lover of wisdom, who has a similar hope and knows that he will never find it to any extent except in Hades, be resentful of dying and not gladly undertake the journey thither? One must surely think so, my friend, if he is a true philosopher, for he is firmly *b* convinced that he will not find pure knowledge anywhere except there. And if this is so, then, as I said just now, would it not be highly unreasonable for such a man to fear death?

It certainly would, by Zeus, he said.

Then you have sufficient indication, he said, that any man whom you see resenting death was not a *c* lover of wisdom but a lover of the body, and also a lover of wealth or of honors, either or both.

It is certainly as you say.

And, Simmias, he said, does not what is called courage belong especially to men of this disposition?

Most certainly.

And the quality of moderation which even the majority call by that name, that is, not to get swept off one's feet by one's passions, but to treat them with disdain and orderliness, is this not suited only to those *d* who most of all despise the body and live the life of philosophy?

Necessarily so, he said.

If you are willing to reflect on the courage and moderation of other people, you will find them strange.

In what way, Socrates?

You know that they all consider death a great evil?

Definitely, he said.

And the brave among them face death, when they do, for fear of greater evils?

That is so.

Therefore, it is fear and terror that make all men brave, except the philosophers. Yet it is illogical to be brave through fear and cowardice.

e It certainly is.

What of the moderate among them? Is their experience not similar? Is it license of a kind that makes them moderate? We say this is impossible, yet their experience of this unsophisticated moderation turns out to be similar: they fear to be deprived of other pleasures which they desire, so they keep away from some pleasures because they are overcome by others. Now to be mastered by pleasure is what they call license, but what happens to them is that they master certain pleasures because they are mastered by others. 69 This is like what we mentioned just now, that in some way it is a kind of license that has made them moderate.

That seems likely.

My good Simmias, I fear this is not the right exchange to attain virtue, to exchange pleasures for pleasures, pains for pains, and fears for fears, the greater for the less like coins, but that the only valid currency for which all these things should be exchanged is *b* wisdom. With this we have real courage and moderation and justice and, in a word, true virtue, with wisdom, whether pleasures and fears and all such things be present or absent. When these are exchanged for one another in separation from wisdom, such virtue is only an illusory appearance of virtue; it is in fact fit for slaves, without soundness or truth, whereas, in truth, moderation and courage and justice are a purging away of all such things, and wisdom itself is a kind of cleans- *c* ing or purification. It is likely that those who established the mystic rites for us were not inferior persons but were speaking in riddles long ago when they said that whoever arrives in the underworld uninitiated and unsanctified will wallow in the mire, whereas he who arrives there purified and initiated will dwell with the gods. There are indeed, as those concerned with the mysteries say, many who carry the thyrsus but the Bacchants *d* are few.[10] These latter are, in my opinion, no other than those who have practiced philosophy in the right way. I have in my life left nothing undone in order to be counted among these as far as possible, as I have been eager to be in every way. Whether my eagerness was right and we accomplished anything we shall, I think, know for certain in a short time, god willing, on arriving yonder.

This is my defense, Simmias and Cebes, that I am

10. [That is, the true worshippers of Dionysus, as opposed to those who only carry the external symbols of his worship.]

likely to be right to leave you and my masters here *e* without resentment or complaint, believing that there, as here, I shall find good masters and good friends. If my defense is more convincing to you than to the Athenian jury, it will be well.

When Socrates finished, Cebes intervened: Socrates, he said, everything else you said is excellent, I *70* think, but men find it very hard to believe what you said about the soul. They think that after it has left the body it no longer exists anywhere, but that it is destroyed and dissolved on the day the man dies, as soon as it leaves the body; and that, on leaving it, it is dispersed like breath or smoke, has flown away and gone and is no longer anything anywhere. If indeed it gathered itself together and existed by itself and escaped those evils you were recently enumerating, there would then be much good hope, Socrates, that *b* what you say is true; but to believe this requires a good deal of faith and persuasive argument, to believe that the soul still exists after a man has died and that it still possesses some capability and intelligence.

What you say is true, Cebes, Socrates said, but what shall we do? Do you want to discuss whether this is likely to be true or not?

Personally, said Cebes, I should like to hear your opinion on the subject.

I do not think, said Socrates, that anyone who heard me now, not even a comic poet, could say that I am *c* babbling and discussing things that do not concern me, so we must examine the question thoroughly, if you think we should do so. Let us examine it in some such a manner as this: whether the souls of men who have died exist in the underworld or not. We recall an ancient theory that souls arriving there come from here, and then again that they arrive here and are born here from the dead. If that is true, that the living come back from the dead, then surely our souls must *d* exist there, for they could not come back if they did not exist, and this is a sufficient proof that these things are so if it truly appears that the living never come from any other source than from the dead. If this is not the case we should need another argument.

Quite so, said Cebes.

Do not, he said, confine yourself to humanity if you want to understand this more readily, but take all animals and all plants into account, and, in short, *e* for all things which come to be, let us see whether they come to be in this way, that is, from their opposites if they have such, as the beautiful is the opposite of the ugly and the just of the unjust, and a thousand other things of the kind. Let us examine whether those that have an opposite must necessarily come to be from their opposite and from nowhere else, as for example when something comes to be larger it must necessarily become larger from having been smaller before.

Yes.

Then if something smaller comes to be, it will come from something larger before, which became smaller? *71*

That is so, he said.

And the weaker comes to be from the stronger, and the swifter from the slower?

Certainly.

Further, if something worse comes to be, does it not come from the better, and the juster from the more unjust?

Of course.

So we have sufficiently established that all things come to be in this way, opposites from opposites?

Certainly.

There is a further point, something such as this, about these opposites: between each of those pairs of opposites there are two processes: from the one to *b* the other and then again from the other to the first; between the larger and the smaller there is increase and decrease, and we call the one increasing and the other decreasing?

Yes, he said.

And so too there is separation and combination, cooling and heating, and all such things, even if sometimes we do not have a name for the process, but in fact it must be everywhere that they come to be from one another, and that there is a process of becoming from each into the other?

Assuredly, he said.

Well then, is there an opposite to living, as sleeping is the opposite of being awake? *c*

Quite so, he said.

What is it?

Being dead, he said.

Therefore, if these are opposites, they come to be from one another, and there are two processes of generation between the two?

Of course.

I will tell you, said Socrates, one of the two pairs I was just talking about, the pair itself and the two processes, and you will tell me the other. I mean, to sleep and to be awake; to be awake comes from sleeping, and to sleep comes from being awake. Of the two processes one is going to sleep, the other is waking up. Do you accept that, or not?

Certainly.

You tell me in the same way about life and death. Do you not say that to be dead is the opposite of being alive?

I do.

And they come to be from one another?

Yes.

What comes to be from being alive?

Being dead.

And what comes to be from being dead?

One must agree that it is being alive.

Then, Cebes, living creatures and things come to be from the dead?

So it appears, he said.

Then our souls exist in the underworld?

That seems likely.

Then in this case one of the two processes of becoming is clear, for dying is clear enough, is it not?

It certainly is.

What shall we do then? Shall we not supply the opposite process of becoming? Is nature to be lame in this case? Or must we provide a process of becoming opposite to dying?

We surely must.

And what is that?

Coming to life again.

Therefore, he said, if there is such a thing as coming to life again, it would be a process of coming from the dead to the living?

Quite so.

It is agreed between us then that the living come from the dead in this way no less than the dead from the living and, if that is so, it seems to be a sufficient proof that the souls of the dead must be somewhere whence they can come back again.

I think, Socrates, he said, that this follows from what we have agreed on.

Consider in this way, Cebes, he said, that, as I think, we were not wrong to agree. If the two processes of becoming did not always balance each other as if they were going round in a circle, but generation proceeded from one point to its opposite in a straight line and it did not turn back again to the other opposite or take any turning, do you realize that all things would ultimately have the same form, be affected in the same way, and cease to become?

How do you mean? he said.

It is not hard to understand what I mean. If, for example, there was such a process as going to sleep, but no corresponding process of waking up, you realize that in the end everything would show the story of Endymion[11] to have no meaning. There would be no point to it because everything would have the same experience as he and be asleep. And if everything were combined and nothing separated, the saying of Anaxagoras[12] would soon be true, "that all things were mixed together." In the same way, my dear Cebes, if everything that partakes of life were to die and remain in that state and not come to life again, would not everything ultimately have to be dead and nothing alive? Even if the living came from some other source, and all that lived died, how could all things avoid being absorbed in death?

It could not be, Socrates, said Cebes, and I think what you say is altogether true.

I think, Cebes, said he, that this is very definitely the case and that we were not deceived when we agreed on this: coming to life again in truth exists, the living come to be from the dead, and the souls of the dead exist.

Furthermore, Socrates, Cebes rejoined, such is also the case if that theory is true that you are accustomed to mention frequently, that for us learning is no other than recollection. According to this, we must at some previous time have learned what we now recollect. This is possible only if our soul existed somewhere before it took on this human shape. So according to this theory too, the soul is likely to be something immortal.

Cebes, Simmias interrupted, what are the proofs of this? Remind me, for I do not quite recall them at the moment.

11. [Endymion was granted eternal sleep by Zeus, in some versions at the request of Selene (the moon).]

12. [Anaxagoras of Clazomenae was born at the beginning of the fifth century B.C. He came to Athens as a young man and spent most of his life there in the study of natural philosophy. He is quoted later in the dialogue as claiming that the universe is directed by Mind (Nous). See 97c ff. The reference here is to his statement that in the original state of the world all its elements were thoroughly commingled.]

There is one excellent argument, said Cebes, namely that when men are interrogated in the right manner, they always give the right answer of their own accord, and they could not do this if they did not possess the knowledge and the right explanation *b* inside them. Then if one shows them a diagram or something else of that kind, this will show most clearly that such is the case.[13]

If this does not convince you, Simmias, said Socrates, see whether you agree if we examine it in some such way as this, for you doubt that what we call learning is recollection.

It is not that I doubt, said Simmias, but I want to experience the very thing we are discussing, recollection, and from what Cebes undertook to say, I am now remembering and am pretty nearly convinced. Nevertheless, I should like to hear now the way you were intending to explain it.

This way, he said. We surely agree that if anyone *c* recollects anything, he must have known it before.

Quite so, he said.

Do we not also agree that when knowledge comes to mind in this way, it is recollection? What way do I mean? Like this: When a man sees or hears or in some other way perceives one thing and not only knows that thing but also thinks of another thing of which the knowledge is not the same but different, are we not right to say that he recollects the second thing that comes into his mind?

d How do you mean?

Things such as this: To know a man is surely a different knowledge from knowing a lyre.

Of course.

Well, you know what happens to lovers: whenever they see a lyre, a garment, or anything else that their beloved is accustomed to use, they know the lyre, and the image of the boy to whom it belongs comes into their mind. This is recollection, just as someone, on seeing Simmias, often recollects Cebes, and there are thousands of other such occurrences.

Thousands indeed, said Simmias.

Is this kind of thing not recollection of a kind, he said, especially so when one experiences it about *e* things that one had forgotten, because one had not seen them for some time?—Quite so.

Further, he said, can a man seeing the picture of a horse or a lyre recollect a man, or seeing a picture of Simmias recollect Cebes?—Certainly.

Or seeing a picture of Simmias recollect Simmias himself?—He certainly can.

In all these cases the recollection is occasioned by things that are similar, but it can also be occasioned *74* by things that are dissimilar?—It can.

When the recollection is caused by similar things, must one not of necessity also experience this: to consider whether the similarity to that which one recollects is deficient in any respect or complete?—One must.

Consider, he said, whether this is the case: we say that there is something that is equal. I do not mean a stick equal to a stick or a stone to a stone, or anything of that kind, but something else beyond all these, the Equal itself. Shall we say that this exists or not?

Indeed we shall, by Zeus, said Simmias, most defi- *b* nitely.

And do we know what this is?—Certainly.

Whence have we acquired the knowledge of it? Is it not from the things we mentioned just now, from seeing sticks or stones or some other things that are equal we come to think of that other which is different from them? Or doesn't it seem to you to be different? Look at it also this way: do not equal stones and sticks sometimes, while remaining the same, appear to one to be equal and to another to be unequal?—Certainly they do.

But what of the equals themselves?[14] Have they ever appeared unequal to you, or Equality to be In- *c* equality?

Never, Socrates.

13. [In the *Meno* Socrates does precisely that. By means of a geometical diagram and merely by asking Meno's slave questions, he elicits from him the answer that the square on the diagonal of a square is double the original square. There, too, this is taken to prove that knowledge is recollection.]

14. [The plural is puzzling, as only the Form of Equality, on the one hand, and the (imperfectly) equal "sticks and stones" have been mentioned. Commentators suggest that the plural here refers to mathematical equals such as the angles at the base of an isosceles triangle. Plato must have something of the kind in mind, but it is hard to see how he expects a reader who could not be familiar with his later work to realize it, especially as the "equal things" in the next line again refer to the particulars.]

These equal things and the Equal itself are therefore not the same?

I do not think they are the same at all, Socrates.

But it is definitely from the equal things, though they are different from that Equal, that you have derived and grasped the knowledge of equality?

Very true, Socrates.

Whether it be like them or unlike them?

Certainly.

It makes no difference. As long as the sight of one thing makes you think of another, whether it be similar or dissimilar, this must of necessity be *d* recollection?

Quite so.

Well then, he said, do we experience something like this in the case of equal sticks and the other equal objects we just mentioned? Do they seem to us to be equal in the same sense as what is Equal itself? Is there some deficiency in their being such as the Equal, or is there not?

A considerable deficiency, he said.

Whenever someone, on seeing something, realizes that that which he now sees wants to be like some *e* other reality but falls short and cannot be like that other since it is inferior, do we agree that the one who thinks this must have prior knowledge of that to which he says it is like, but deficiently so?

Necessarily.

Well, do we also feel this about the equal objects and the Equal itself, or do we not?

Very definitely.

We must then possess knowledge of the Equal before that time when we first saw the equal objects *75* and realized that all these objects strive to be like the Equal but are deficient in this.

That is so.

Then surely we also agree that this conception of ours derives from seeing or touching or some other sense perception, and cannot come into our mind in any other way, for all these senses, I say, are the same.

They are the same, Socrates, at any rate in respect to that which our argument wishes to make plain.

b Our sense perceptions must surely make us realize that all that we perceive through them is striving to reach that which is Equal but falls short of it; or how do we express it?

Like that.

Then before we began to see or hear or otherwise perceive, we must have possessed knowledge of the Equal itself if we were about to refer our sense perceptions of equal objects to it, and realized that all of them were eager to be like it, but were inferior.

That follows from what has been said, Socrates.

But we began to see and hear and otherwise perceive right after birth?

Certainly.

We must then have acquired the knowledge of *c* equality before this.

Yes.

It seems then that we must have possessed it before birth.

It seems so.

Therefore, if we had this knowledge, we knew before birth and immediately after not only the Equal, but the Greater and the Smaller and all such things, for our present argument is no more about the Equal than about the Beautiful itself, the Good itself, the Just, the Pious, and, as I say, about all those things *d* to which we can attach the word "itself," both when we are putting questions and answering them. So we must have acquired knowledge of them all before we were born.

That is so.

If, having acquired this knowledge in each case, we have not forgotten it, we remain knowing and have knowledge throughout our life, for to know is to acquire knowledge, keep it and not lose it. Do we not call the losing of knowledge forgetting?

Most certainly, Socrates, he said. *e*

But, I think, if we acquired this knowledge before birth, then lost it at birth, and then later by the use of our senses in connection with those objects we mentioned, we recovered the knowledge we had before, would not what we call learning be the recovery of our own knowledge, and we are right to call this recollection?

Certainly.

It was seen to be possible for someone to see or *76* hear or otherwise perceive something, and by this to be put in mind of something else which he had forgotten and which is related to it by similarity or difference. One of two things follows, as I say: either we were born with the knowledge of it, and all of us know it throughout life, or those who later, we say, are learning, are only recollecting, and learning would be recollection.

That is certainly the case, Socrates.

Which alternative do you choose, Simmias? That *b* we are born with this knowledge or that we recollect later the things of which we had knowledge previously?

I have no means of choosing at the moment, Socrates.

Well, can you make this choice? What is your opinion about it? A man who has knowledge would be able to give an account of what he knows, or would he not?

He must certainly be able to do so, Socrates, he said.

And do you think everybody can give an account of the things we were mentioning just now?

I wish they could, said Simmias, but I'm afraid it is much more likely that by this time tomorrow there will be no one left who can do so adequately.

c So you do not think that everybody has knowledge of those things?

No indeed.

So they recollect what they once learned?

They must.

When did our souls acquire the knowledge of them? Certainly not since we were born as men.

Indeed no.

Before that then?

Yes.

So then, Simmias, our souls also existed apart from the body before they took on human form, and they had intelligence.

Unless we acquire the knowledge at the moment of birth, Socrates, for that time is still left to us.

d Quite so, my friend, but at what other time do we lose it? We just now agreed that we are not born with that knowledge. Do we then lose it at the very time we acquire it, or can you mention any other time?

I cannot, Socrates. I did not realize that I was talking nonsense.

So this is our position, Simmias? he said. If those realities we are always talking about exist, the Beautiful and the Good and all that kind of reality, and we refer all the things we perceive to that reality, discovering that it existed before and is ours, and we *e* compare these things with it, then, just as they exist, so our soul must exist before we are born. If these realities do not exist, then this argument is altogether futile. Is this the position, that there is an equal necessity for those realities to exist, and for our souls to exist before we were born? If the former do not exist, neither do the latter?

I do not think, Socrates, said Simmias, that there is any possible doubt that it is equally necessary for both to exist, and it is opportune that our argument comes to the conclusion that our soul exists before **77** we are born, and equally so that reality of which you are now speaking. Nothing is so evident to me personally as that all such things must certainly exist, the Beautiful, the Good, and all those you mentioned just now. I also think that sufficient proof of this has been given.

Then what about Cebes? said Socrates, for we must persuade Cebes also.

He is sufficiently convinced I think, said Simmias, though he is the most difficult of men to persuade by argument, but I believe him to be fully convinced that our soul existed before we were born. I do not think myself, however, that it has been proved that *b* the soul continues to exist after death; the opinion of the majority which Cebes mentioned still stands, that when a man dies his soul is dispersed and this is the end of its existence. What is to prevent the soul coming to be and being constituted from some other source, existing before it enters a human body and then, having done so and departed from it, itself dying and being destroyed?

You are right, Simmias, said Cebes. Half of what *c* needed proof has been proved, namely, that our soul existed before we were born, but further proof is needed that it exists no less after we have died, if the proof is to be complete.

It has been proved even now, Simmias and Cebes, said Socrates, if you are ready to combine this argument with the one we agreed on before, that every living thing must come from the dead. If the soul exists before, it must, as it comes to life and birth, come from nowhere else than death and being dead, *d* so how could it avoid existing after death since it must be born again? What you speak of has then even now been proved. However, I think you and Simmias would like to discuss the argument more fully. You seem to have this childish fear that the wind would really dissolve and scatter the soul, as it leaves the body, especially if one happens to die in a high wind *e* and not in calm weather.

Cebes laughed and said: "Assuming that we were afraid, Socrates, try to change our minds, or rather do not assume that we are afraid, but perhaps there is a child in us who has these fears; try to persuade him not to fear death like a bogey."

You should, said Socrates, sing a charm over him every day until you have charmed away his fears.

78 Where shall we find a good charmer for these fears, Socrates, he said, now that you are leaving us?

Greece is a large country, Cebes, he said, and there are good men in it; the tribes of foreigners are also numerous. You should search for such a charmer among them all, sparing neither trouble nor expense, for there is nothing on which you could spend your money to greater advantage. You must also search among yourselves, for you might not easily find people who could do this better than yourselves.

That shall be done, said Cebes, but let us, if it *b* pleases you, go back to the argument where we left it.

Of course it pleases me.

Splendid, he said.

We must then ask ourselves something like this: what kind of thing is likely to be scattered? On behalf of what kind of thing should one fear this, and for what kind of thing should one not fear it? We should then examine to which class the soul belongs, and as a result either fear for the soul or be of good cheer.

What you say is true.

c Is not anything that is composite and a compound by nature liable to be split up into its component parts, and only that which is noncomposite, if anything, is not likely to be split up?

I think that is the case, said Cebes.

Are not the things that always remain the same and in the same state most likely not to be composite, whereas those that vary from one time to another and are never the same are composite?

I think that is so.

Let us then return to those same things with which *d* we were dealing earlier, to that reality of whose existence we are giving an account in our questions and answers; are they ever the same and in the same state, or do they vary from one time to another; can the Equal itself, the Beautiful itself, each thing in itself, the real, ever be affected by any change whatever? Or does each of them that really is, being uniform by itself, remain the same and never in any way tolerate any change whatever?

It must remain the same, said Cebes, and in the same state, Socrates.

What of the many beautiful particulars, be they men, horses, clothes, or other such things, or the *e* many equal particulars, and all those which bear the same name as those others? Do they remain the same or, in total contrast to those other realities, one might say, never in any way remain the same as themselves or in relation to each other?

The latter is the case; they are never in the same state.

These latter you could touch and see and perceive *79* with the other senses, but those that always remain the same can be grasped only by the reasoning power of the mind? They are not seen but are invisible?

That is altogether true, he said.

Do you then want us to assume two kinds of existences, the visible and the invisible?

Let us assume this.

And the invisible always remains the same, whereas the visible never does?

Let us assume that too.

Now one part of ourselves is the body, another part *b* is the soul?

Quite so.

To which class of existence do we say the body is more alike and akin?

To the visible, as anyone can see.

What about the soul? Is it visible or invisible?

It is not visible to men, Socrates, he said.

Well, we meant visible and invisible to human eyes; or to any others, do you think?

To human eyes.

Then what do we say about the soul? Is it visible or not visible?

Not visible.

So it is invisible?—Yes.

So the soul is more like the invisible than the body, and the body more like the visible?—Without any *c* doubt, Socrates.

Haven't we also said some time ago that when the soul makes use of the body to investigate something, be it through hearing or seeing or some other sense—for to investigate something through the body is to do it through the senses—it is dragged by the body to the things that are never the same, and the soul itself strays and is confused and dizzy, as if it were drunk, in so far as it is in contact with that kind of thing?

Certainly.

d But when the soul investigates by itself it passes into the realm of what is pure, ever existing, immortal and unchanging, and being akin to this, it always stays with it whenever it is by itself and can do so; it ceases to stray and remains in the same state as it is in touch with things of the same kind, and its experience then is what is called wisdom?

Altogether well said and very true, Socrates, he said.

Judging from what we have said before and what *e* we are saying now, to which of these two kinds do you think that the soul is more alike and more akin?

I think, Socrates, he said, that on this line of argument any man, even the dullest, would agree that the soul is altogether more like that which always exists in the same state rather than like that which does not.

What of the body?

That is like the other.

Look at it also this way: when the soul and the *80* body are together, nature orders the one to be subject and to be ruled, and the other to rule and be master. Then again, which do you think is like the divine and which like the mortal? Do you not think that the nature of the divine is to rule and to lead, whereas it is that of the mortal to be ruled and be subject?

I do.

Which does the soul resemble?

Obviously, Socrates, the soul resembles the divine, and the body resembles the mortal.

Consider then, Cebes, whether it follows from all that has been said that the soul is most like the divine, *b* deathless, intelligible, uniform, indissoluble, always the same as itself, whereas the body is most like that which is human, mortal, multiform, unintelligible, soluble, and never consistently the same. Have we anything else to say to show, my dear Cebes, that this is not the case?

We have not.

Well then, that being so, is it not natural for the body to dissolve easily, and for the soul to be altogether indissoluble, or nearly so?

c Of course.

You realize, he said, that when a man dies, the visible part, the body, which exists in the visible world, and which we call the corpse, whose natural lot it would be to dissolve, fall apart and be blown away, does not immediately suffer any of these things but remains for a fair time, in fact, quite a long time if the man dies with his body in a suitable condition and at a favorable season? If the body is emaciated or embalmed, as in Egypt, it remains almost whole for a remarkable length of time, and even if the body decays, some parts of it, namely bones and sinews and *d* the like, are nevertheless, one might say, deathless. Is that not so?—Yes.

Will the soul, the invisible part which makes its way to a region of the same kind, noble and pure and invisible, to Hades in fact, to the good and wise god whither, god willing, my soul must soon be going—will the soul, being of this kind and nature, be scattered and destroyed on leaving the body, as the majority of men say? Far from it, my dear Cebes and *e* Simmias, but what happens is much more like this: if it is pure when it leaves the body and drags nothing bodily with it, as it had no willing association with the body in life, but avoided it and gathered itself together by itself and always practiced this, which is no other than practising philosophy in the right way, *81* in fact, training to die easily. Or is this not training for death?

It surely is.

A soul in this state makes its way to the invisible, which is like itself, the divine and immortal and wise, and arriving there it can be happy, having rid itself of confusion, ignorance, fear, violent desires, and the other human ills and, as is said of the initiates, truly spend the rest of time with the gods. Shall we say this, Cebes, or something different?

This, by Zeus, said Cebes.

But I think that if the soul is polluted and impure *b* when it leaves the body, having always been associated with it and served it, bewitched by physical desires and pleasures to the point at which nothing seems to exist for it but the physical, which one can touch and see or eat and drink or make use of for sexual enjoyment, and if that soul is accustomed to hate and fear and avoid that which is dim and invisible to the eyes but intelligible and to be grasped by philosophy—do you think such a soul will escape pure and by itself?

Impossible, he said. *c*

It is, no doubt, permeated by the physical, which constant intercourse and association with the body, as well as considerable practice, has caused to become ingrained in it?

Quite so.

We must believe, my friend, that this bodily element is heavy, ponderous, earthy, and visible. Through it, such a soul has become heavy and is dragged back to the visible region in fear of the unseen and of Hades. It wanders, as we are told, around *d* graves and monuments, where shadowy phantoms, images that such souls produce, have been seen, souls that have not been freed and purified but share in the visible, and are therefore seen.

That is likely, Socrates.

It is indeed, Cebes. Moreover, these are not the souls of good but of inferior men, which are forced to wander there, paying the penalty for their previous bad upbringing. They wander until their longing for *e* that which accompanies them, the physical, again imprisons them in a body, and they are then, as is likely, bound to such characters as they have practiced in their life.

What kind of characters do you say these are, Socrates?

Those, for example, who have carelessly practiced gluttony, violence and drunkenness are likely to join 82 a company of donkeys or of similar animals. Do you not think so?

Very likely.

Those who have esteemed injustice highly, and tyranny and plunder, will join the tribes of wolves and hawks and kites, or where else shall we say that they go?

Certainly to those, said Cebes.

And clearly, the destination of the others will conform to the way in which they have behaved?

Clearly, of course.

The happiest of these, who will also have the best destination, are those who have practiced popular *b* and social virtue, which they call moderation and justice and which was developed by habit and practice, without philosophy or understanding?

How are they the happiest?

Because it is likely that they will again join a social and gentle group, either of bees or wasps or ants, and then again the same kind of human group, and so be moderate men.

That is likely.

No one may join the company of the gods who has not practiced philosophy and is not completely *c* pure when he departs from life, no one but the lover of learning. It is for this reason, my friends Simmias and Cebes, that those who practice philosophy in the right way keep away from all bodily passions, master them and do not surrender themselves to them; it is not at all for fear of wasting their substance and of poverty, which the majority and the money-lovers fear, nor for fear of dishonor and ill repute, like the ambitious and lovers of honors, that they keep away from them.

That would not be natural for them, Socrates, said Cebes.

By Zeus, no, he said. Those who care for their own *d* soul and do not live for the service of their body dismiss all these things. They do not travel the same road as those who do not know where they are going but, believing that nothing should be done contrary to philosophy and their deliverance and purification, they turn to this and follow wherever philosophy leads.

How so, Socrates?

I will tell you, he said. The lovers of learning know that when philosophy gets hold of their soul, it is imprisoned in and clinging to the body, and that it *e* is forced to examine other things through it as through a cage and not by itself, and that it wallows in every kind of ignorance. Philosophy sees that the worst feature of this imprisonment is that it is due to desires, so that the prisoner himself is contributing to his own incarceration most of all. As I say, the lovers of learning know that philosophy gets hold of their soul 83 when it is in that state, then gently encourages it and tries to free it by showing them that investigation through the eyes is full of deceit, as is that through the ears and the other senses. Philosophy then persuades the soul to withdraw from the senses insofar as it is not compelled to use them and bids the soul to gather itself together by itself, to trust only itself and whatever reality, existing by itself, the soul by itself *b* understands, and not to consider as true whatever it examines by other means, for this is different in different circumstances and is sensible and visible, whereas what the soul itself sees is intelligible and invisible. The soul of the true philosopher thinks that this deliverance must not be opposed and so keeps away from pleasures and desires and pains as far as he can; he reflects that violent pleasure or pain or passion does not cause merely such evils as one might expect, such as one suffers when one has been sick or extravagant *c* through desire, but the greatest and most extreme evil, though one does not reflect on this.

What is that, Socrates? asked Cebes.

That the soul of every man, when it feels violent pleasure or pain in connection with some object, inevitably believes at the same time that what causes such feelings must be very clear and very true, which it is not. Such objects are mostly visible, are they not?

Certainly.

d And doesn't such an experience tie the soul to the body most completely?

How so?

Because every pleasure or pain provides, as it were, another nail to rivet the soul to the body and to weld them together. It makes the soul corporeal, so that it believes that truth is what the body says it is. As it shares the beliefs and delights of the body, I think it inevitably comes to share its ways and manner of life and is unable ever to reach Hades in a pure state; it is always full of body when it departs, so that it soon falls back into another body and grows with it as if *e* it had been sewn into it. Because of this, it can have no part in the company of the divine, the pure and uniform.

What you say is very true, Socrates, said Cebes.

This is why genuine lovers of learning are moderate and brave, or do you think it is for the reasons the majority says they are?

84 I certainly do not.

Indeed no. This is how the soul of a philosopher would reason: it would not think that while philosophy must free it, it should while being freed surrender itself to pleasures and pains and imprison itself again, thus laboring in vain like Penelope at her web. The soul of the philosopher achieves a calm from such emotions; it follows reason and ever stays with it contemplating the true, the divine, which is not the object of opinion. Nurtured by this, it believes that one *b* should live in this manner as long as one is alive and, after death, arrive at what is akin and of the same kind, and escape from human evils. After such nurture there is no danger, Simmias and Cebes, that one should fear that, on parting from the body, the soul would be scattered and dissipated by the winds and no longer be anything anywhere.

c When Socrates finished speaking there was a long silence. He appeared to be concentrating on what had been said, and so were most of us. But Cebes and Simmias were whispering to each other. Socrates observed them and questioned them. "Come," he said, "do you think there is something lacking in my argument? There are still many doubtful points and many objections for anyone who wants a thorough discussion of these matters. If you are discussing some other subject, I have nothing to say, but if you have some difficulty about this one, do not hesitate to speak for yourselves and expound it if you think the argument could be improved, and if you think you will do better, take me along with you in the discussion." *d*

I will tell you the truth, Socrates, said Simmias. Both of us have been in difficulty for some time, and each of us has been urging the other to question you because we wanted to hear what you would say, but we hesitated to bother you, lest it be displeasing to you in your present misfortune.

When Socrates heard this he laughed quietly and said: "Really, Simmias, it would be hard for me to persuade other people that I do not consider my *e* present fate a misfortune if I cannot persuade even you, and you are afraid that it is more difficult to deal with me than before. You seem to think me inferior to the swans in prophecy. They sing before too, but when they realize that they must die they sing most and most beautifully, as they rejoice that they are about to depart to join the god whose servants they *85* are. But men, because of their own fear of death, tell lies about the swans and say that they lament their death and sing in sorrow. They do not reflect that no bird sings when it is hungry or cold or suffers in any other way, neither the nightingale nor the swallow nor the hoopoe, though they do say that these sing laments when in pain. Nor do the swans, but I believe that as they belong to Apollo, they are prophetic, have *b* knowledge of the future and sing of the blessings of the underworld, sing and rejoice on that day beyond what they did before. As I believe myself to be a fellow servant with the swans and dedicated to the same god, and have received from my master a gift of prophecy not inferior to theirs, I am no more despondent than they on leaving life. Therefore, you must speak and ask whatever you want as long as the authorities allow it."

Well spoken, said Simmias. I will tell you my difficulty, and then Cebes will say why he does not accept what was said. I believe, as perhaps you do, that *c* precise knowledge on that subject is impossible or extremely difficult in our present life, but that it surely shows a very poor spirit not to examine thoroughly what is said about it, and to desist before one is exhausted by an all-around investigation. One should achieve one of these things: learn the truth about these things or find it for oneself, or, if that is impossible, *d* adopt the best and most irrefutable of men's theories, and, borne upon this, sail through the dangers of life as upon a raft, unless someone should make that journey safer and less risky upon a firmer vessel of some divine doctrine. So even now, since you have said what you did, I will feel no shame at asking questions, and I will not blame myself in the future because I did not say what I think. As I examine what we said, both by myself and with Cebes, it does not seem to be adequate.

e Said Socrates: "You may well be right, my friend, but tell me how it is inadequate."

In this way, as it seems to me, he said: "One might make the same argument about harmony, lyre and strings, that a harmony is something invisible, without body, beautiful and divine in the attuned lyre, 86 whereas the lyre itself and its strings are physical, bodily, composite, earthy, and akin to what is mortal. Then if someone breaks the lyre, cuts or breaks the strings and then insists, using the same argument as you, that the harmony must still exist and is not destroyed because it would be impossible for the lyre and the strings, which are mortal, still to exist when the strings are broken, and for the harmony, which is akin and of the same nature as the divine and *b* immortal, to be destroyed before that which is mortal; he would say that the harmony itself still must exist and that the wood and the strings must rot before the harmony can suffer. And indeed, Socrates, I think you must have this in mind, that we really do suppose the soul to be something of this kind; as the body is stretched and held together by the hot and the cold, the dry and the moist, and other such things, and *c* our soul is a mixture and harmony of those things when they are mixed with each other rightly and in due measure. If then the soul is a kind of harmony or attunement, clearly, when our body is relaxed or stretched without due measure by diseases and other evils, the soul must immediately be destroyed, even if it be most divine, as are the other harmonies found in music and all the works of artists, and the remains of each body last for a long time until they rot or are *d* burned. Consider what we shall say in answer to one who deems the soul to be a mixture of bodily elements and to be the first to perish in the process we call death."

Socrates looked at us keenly, as was his habit, smiled, and said: "What Simmias says is quite fair. If one of you is more resourceful than I am, why did he not answer him, for he seems to have handled the argument competently. However, I think that before we answer him, we should hear Cebes' objection, in *e* order that we may have time to deliberate on an answer. When we have heard him we should either agree with them, if we think them in tune with us or, if not, defend our own argument. Come then, Cebes. What is troubling you?"

I tell you, said Cebes, the argument seems to me to be at the same point as before and open to the 87 same objection. I do not deny that it has been very elegantly and, if it is not offensive to say so, sufficiently proved that our soul existed before it took on this present form, but I do not believe the same applies to its existing somewhere after our death. Not that I agree with Simmias' objection that the soul is not stronger and much more lasting than the body, for I think it is superior in all these respects. "Why then," the argument might say, "are you still unconvinced? Since you see that when the man dies, the weaker part continues to exist, do you not think that the more lasting part must be preserved during that time?" On *b* this point consider whether what I say makes sense.

Like Simmias, I too need an image, for I think this argument is much as if one said at the death of an old weaver that the man had not perished but was safe and sound somewhere, and offered as proof the fact that the cloak the old man had woven himself and was wearing was still sound and had not perished. *c* If one was not convinced, he would be asked whether a man lasts longer than a cloak which is in use and being worn, and if the answer was that a man lasts much longer, this would be taken as proof that the man was definitely safe and sound, since the more temporary thing had not perished. But Simmias, I do not think that is so, for consider what I say. Anybody could see that the man who said this was talking nonsense. That weaver had woven and worn out many such cloaks. He perished after many of them, but *d* before the last. That does not mean that a man is inferior and weaker than a cloak. The image illustrates, I think, the relationship of the soul to the body, and anyone who says the same thing about them would appear to me to be talking sense, that the soul lasts a long time while the body is weaker and more short-lived. He might say that each soul wears out many bodies, especially if it lives many years. If the body were in a state of flux and perished while the man was still alive, and the soul wove afresh the *e* body that is worn out, yet it would be inevitable that whenever the soul perished it would be wearing the last body it wove and perish only before this last. Then when the soul perished, the body would show the weakness of its nature by soon decaying and disappearing. So we cannot trust this argument and be confident that our soul continues to exist somewhere 88 after our death. For, if one were to concede, even more than you do, to a man using that argument, if one were to grant him not only that the soul exists in the time before we are born, but that there is no reason why the soul of some should not exist and continue to exist after our death, and thus frequently be born and die in turn; if one were to grant him that the soul's nature is so strong that it can survive many bodies, but if, having granted all this, one does not further agree that the soul is not damaged by its many births and is not, in the end, altogether destroyed in one of those deaths, he might say that no *b* one knows which death and dissolution of the body brings about the destruction of the soul, since not one of us can be aware of this. And in that case, any man who faces death with confidence is foolish, unless he can prove that the soul is altogether immortal. If he cannot, a man about to die must of necessity always fear for his soul, lest the present separation of the soul from the body bring about the complete destruction of the soul.

c When we heard what they said we were all depressed, as we told each other afterwards. We had been quite convinced by the previous argument, and they seemed to confuse us again, and to drive us to doubt not only what had already been said but also what was going to be said, lest we be worthless as critics or the subject itself admitted of no certainty.

ECHECRATES: By the gods, Phaedo, you have my sympathy, for as I listen to you now I find myself *d* saying to myself: "What argument shall we trust, now that that of Socrates, which was extremely convincing, has fallen into discredit?" The statement that the soul is some kind of harmony has a remarkable hold on me, now and always, and when it was mentioned it reminded me that I had myself previously thought so. And now I am again quite in need, as if from the beginning, of some other argument to convince me that the soul does not die along with the man. Tell me then, by Zeus, how Socrates tackled the argument. Was he obviously distressed, as you say you people were, or was he not, but quietly came to the rescue *e* of his argument, and did he do so satisfactorily or inadequately? Tell us everything as precisely as you can.

PHAEDO: I have certainly often admired Socrates, Echecrates, but never more than on this occasion. That he had a reply was perhaps not strange. What 89 I wondered at most in him was the pleasant, kind and admiring way he received the young men's argument, and how sharply he was aware of the effect the discussion had on us, and then how well he healed our distress and, as it were, recalled us from our flight and defeat and turned us around to join him in the examination of their argument.

E: How did he do this?

P: I will tell you. I happened to be sitting on his right by the couch on a low stool, so that he was sitting well above me. He stroked my head and pressed *b* the hair on the back of my neck, for he was in the habit of playing with my hair at times. "Tomorrow, Phaedo," he said, "you will probably cut this beautiful hair."

Likely enough, Socrates, I said.

Not if you take my advice, he said.

Why not? said I.

It is today, he said, that I shall cut my hair and you yours, if our argument dies on us, and we cannot revive it. If I were you, and the argument escaped *c* me, I would take an oath, as the Argives[15] did, not to let my hair grow before I fought again and defeated the argument of Simmias and Cebes.

But, I said, they say that not even Heracles could fight two people.

Then call on me as your Iolaus, as long as the daylight lasts.

I shall call on you, but in this case as Iolaus calling on Heracles.

15. [Herodotus (I, 82) tells us that after losing the city of Thyreae to the Spartans, the Argives swore not to let their hair grow again or their women wear golden ornaments until they had recaptured it.]

It makes no difference, he said, but first there is a certain experience we must be careful to avoid.

What is that? I asked.

d That we should not become misologues, as people become misanthropes. There is no greater evil one can suffer than to hate reasonable discourse. Misology and misanthropy arise in the same way. Misanthropy comes when a man without knowledge or skill has placed great trust in someone and believes him to be altogether truthful, sound, and trustworthy; then, a short time afterwards he finds him to be wicked and unreliable, and then this happens in another case; when one has frequently had that experience, espe- *e* cially with those whom one believed to be one's closest friends, then, in the end, after many such blows, one comes to hate all men and to believe that no one is sound in any way at all. Have you not seen this happen?

I surely have, I said.

This is a shameful state of affairs, he said, and obviously due to an attempt to have human relations without any skill in human affairs, for such skill would lead one to believe, what is in fact true, that the very *90* good and the very wicked are both quite rare, and that most men are between those extremes.

How do you mean? said I.

The same as with the very tall and the very short, he said. Do you think anything is rarer than to find an extremely tall man or an extremely short one? Or a dog or anything else whatever? Or again, one extremely swift or extremely slow, ugly or beautiful, white or black? Are you not aware that in all those cases the most extreme at either end are rare and few, but those in between are many and plentiful?

Certainly, I said.

b Therefore, he said, if a contest of wickedness were established, there too the winners, you think, would be very few?

That is likely, said I.

Likely indeed, he said, but arguments are not like men in this particular. I was merely following your lead just now.[16] The similarity lies rather in this: it is as when one who lacks skill in arguments puts his trust in an argument as being true, then shortly afterwards believes it to be false—as sometimes it is and sometimes it is not—and so with another argument and then another. You know how those in particular who spend their time studying contradiction in the end believe themselves to have become very wise and that *c* they alone have understood that there is no soundness or reliability in any object or in any argument, but that all that exists simply fluctuates up and down as if it were in the Euripus[17] and does not remain in the same place for any time at all.

What you say, I said, is certainly true.

It would be pitiable, Phaedo, he said, when there is a true and reliable argument and one that can be understood, if a man who has dealt with such *d* arguments as appear at one time true, at another time untrue, should not blame himself or his own lack of skill but, because of his distress, in the end gladly shift the blame away from himself to the arguments, and spend the rest of his life hating and reviling reasonable discussion and so be deprived of truth and knowledge of reality.

Yes, by Zeus, I said, that would be pitiable indeed.

This then is the first thing we should guard against, he said. We should not allow into our minds the *e* conviction that argumentation has nothing sound about it; much rather we should believe that it is we who are not yet sound and that we must take courage and be eager to attain soundness, you and the others for the sake of your whole life still to come, and I for *91* the sake of death itself. I am in danger at this moment of not having a philosophical attitude about this, but like those who are quite uneducated, I am eager to get the better of you in argument, for the uneducated, when they engage in argument about anything, give no thought to the truth about the subject of discussion but are only eager that those present will accept the position they have set forth. I differ from them only to this extent: I shall not be eager to get the agreement of those present that what I say is true, except incidentally, but I shall be very eager that I should myself be thoroughly convinced that things are so. For I am thinking—see in how contentious a spirit—that if what I say is true, it is a fine thing to be convinced; if, on the other hand, nothing exists after death, at *b*

16. [Socrates presumably means that there are plenty of very bad arguments. It is not clear where he was following Phaedo in the argument.]

17. [The Euripus was the name of the straits between Euboea and Boeotia; its currents were both violent and variable.]

least for this time before I die I shall distress those present less with lamentations and my folly will not continue to exist along with me—that would be a bad thing—but will come to an end in a short time. Thus prepared, Simmias and Cebes, he said, I come to deal with your argument. If you will take my advice, *c* you will give but little thought to Socrates but much more to the truth. If you think that what I say is true, agree with me; if not, oppose it with every argument and take care that in my eagerness I do not deceive myself and you and, like a bee, leave my sting in you when I go.

We must proceed, he said, and first remind me of what you said if I do not appear to remember it. Simmias, as I believe, is in doubt and fear that the soul, *d* though it is more divine and beautiful than the body, yet predeceases it, being a kind of harmony. Cebes, I thought, agrees with me that the soul lasts much longer than the body, but that no one knows whether the soul often wears out many bodies and then, on leaving its last body, is now itself destroyed. This then is death, the destruction of the soul, since the body is always being destroyed. Are these the questions, Simmias and Cebes, which we must investigate?

e They both agreed that they were.

Do you then, he asked, reject all our previous statements, or some but not others?

Some, they both said, but not others.

What, he said, about the statements we made that learning is recollection and that, if this was so, our 92 soul must of necessity exist elsewhere before us, before it was imprisoned in the body?

For myself, said Cebes, I was wonderfully convinced by it at the time and I stand by it now also, more than by any other statement.

That, said Simmias, is also my position, and I should be very surprised if I ever changed my opinion about this.

But you must change your opinion, my Theban friend, said Socrates, if you still believe that a harmony is a composite thing, and that the soul is a kind of harmony of the elements of the body in a state of tension, for surely you will not allow yourself to main- *b* tain that a composite harmony existed before those elements from which it had to be composed, or would you?

Never, Socrates, he said.

Do you realize, he said, that this is what you are in fact saying when you state that the soul exists before it takes on the form and body of a man and that it is composed of elements which do not yet exist? A harmony is not like that to which you compare it; the lyre and the strings and the notes, though still unharmonized, exist; the harmony is composed last *c* of all, and is the first to be destroyed. How will you harmonize this statement with your former one?

In no way, said Simmias.

And surely, he said, a statement about harmony should do so more than any other.

It should, said Simmias.

So your statement is inconsistent? Consider which of your statements you prefer, that learning is recollection or that the soul is a harmony.

I much prefer the former, Socrates. I adopted the *d* latter without proof, because of a certain probability and plausibility, which is why it appeals to most men. I know that arguments of which the proof is based on probability are pretentious and, if one does not guard against them, they certainly deceive one, in geometry and everything else. The theory of recollection and learning, however, was based on an assumption worthy of acceptance, for our soul was said to exist also before it came into the body, just as the reality does that is of the kind that we qualify by the words "which truly is," and I convinced myself that I was quite correct to accept it. Therefore, I cannot *e* accept the theory that the soul is a harmony either from myself or anyone else.

What of this, Simmias? Do you think it natural for a harmony, or any other composite, to be in a different state from that of the elements of which it is composed? 93

Not at all, said Simmias.

Nor, as I think, can it act or be acted upon in a different way than its elements?

He agreed.

One must therefore suppose that a harmony does not direct its components, but is directed by them.

He accepted this.

A harmony is therefore far from making a movement, or uttering a sound, or doing anything else, in a manner contrary to that of its parts.

Far from it indeed, he said.

Does not the nature of each harmony depend on the way it has been harmonized?

I do not understand, he said.

Will it not, if it is more and more fully harmonized,

b be more and more fully a harmony, and if it is less and less fully harmonized, it will be less and less fully a harmony?

Certainly.

Can this be true about the soul, that one soul is more and more fully a soul than another, or is less and less fully a soul, even to the smallest extent?

Not in any way.

Come now, by Zeus, he said. One soul is said to have intelligence and virtue and to be good, another c to have folly and wickedness and to be bad. Are those things truly said?

They certainly are.

What will someone who holds the theory that the soul is a harmony say that those things are which reside in the soul, that is, virtue and wickedness? Are these some other harmony and disharmony? That the good soul is harmonized and, being a harmony, has within itself another harmony, whereas the evil soul is both itself a lack of harmony and has no other within itself?

I don't know what to say, said Simmias, but one who holds that assumption must obviously say something of that kind.

d We have previously agreed, he said, that one soul is not more and not less a soul than another, and this means that one harmony is not more and more fully, or less and less fully, a harmony than another. Is that not so?

Certainly.

Now that which is no more and no less a harmony is not more or less harmonized. Is that so?

It is.

Can that which is neither more nor less harmonized partake more or less of harmony, or does it do so equally?

Equally.

e Then if a soul is neither more nor less a soul than another, it has been harmonized to the same extent?

This is so.

If that is so, it would have no greater share of disharmony or of harmony?

It would not.

That being the case, could one soul have more wickedness or virtue than another, if wickedness is disharmony and virtue harmony?

It could not.

94 But rather, Simmias, according to correct reasoning, no soul, if it is a harmony, will have any share of wickedness, for harmony is surely altogether this very thing, harmony, and would never share in disharmony.

It certainly would not.

Nor would a soul, being altogether this very thing, a soul, share in wickedness?

How could it, in view of what has been said?

So it follows from this argument that all the souls of all living creatures will be equally good, if souls are by nature equally this very thing, souls.

I think so, Socrates.

Does our argument seem right, he said, and does it seem that it should have come to this, if the hypothesis that the soul is a harmony was correct? b

Not in any way, he said.

Further, of all the parts of a man, can you mention any other part that rules him than his soul, especially if it is a wise soul?

I cannot.

Does it do so by following the affections of the body or by opposing them? I mean, for example, that when the body is hot and thirsty the soul draws him to the opposite, to not drinking; when the body is hungry, to not eating, and we see a thousand other examples of the soul opposing the affections of the c body. Is that not so?

It certainly is.

On the other hand we previously agreed that if the soul were a harmony, it would never be out of tune with the stress and relaxation and the striking of the strings or anything else done to its composing elements, but that it would follow and never direct them?

We did so agree, of course.

Well, does it now appear to do quite the opposite, ruling over all the elements of which one says it is d composed, opposing nearly all of them throughout life, directing all their ways, inflicting harsh and painful punishment on them, at times in physical culture and medicine, at other times more gently by threats and exhortations, holding converse with desires and passions and fears as if it were one thing talking to a different one, as Homer wrote somewhere in the *Odyssey* where he says that Odysseus "struck his breast and rebuked his heart saying,

'Endure, my heart, you have endured worse than this' "?

e Do you think that when he composed this the poet thought that his soul was a harmony, a thing to be directed by the affections of the body? Did he not rather regard it as ruling over them and mastering them, itself a much more divine thing than a harmony?

Yes, by Zeus, I think so, Socrates.

Therefore, my good friend, it is quite wrong for us *95* to say that the soul is a harmony, and in saying so we would disagree both with the divine poet Homer and with ourselves.

That is so, he said.

Very well, said Socrates. Harmonia of Thebes seems somehow reasonably propitious to us. How and by what argument, my dear Cebes, can we propitiate Cadmus?[18]

I think, Cebes said, that you will find a way. You dealt with the argument about harmony in a manner that was quite astonishing to me. When Simmias was *b* speaking of his difficulties I was very much wondering whether anyone would be able to deal with his argument, and I was quite dumbfounded when right away he could not resist your argument's first onslaught. I should not wonder therefore if that of Cadmus suffered the same fate.

My good sir, said Socrates, do not boast, lest some malign influence upset the argument we are about to make. However, we leave that to the care of the god, but let us come to grips with it in the Homeric fashion, to see if there is anything in what you say. The sum of your problem is this: you consider that the *c* soul must be proved to be immortal and indestructible before a philosopher on the point of death, who is confident that he will fare much better in the underworld than if he had led any other kind of life, can avoid being foolish and simple-minded in this confidence. To prove that the soul is strong, that it is divine, that it existed before we were born as men, all this, you say, does not show the soul to be immortal but only long-lasting. That it existed for a very long time before, that it knew much and acted much, *d* makes it no more immortal because of that; indeed, its very entering into a human body was the beginning of its destruction, like a disease; it would live that life in distress and would in the end be destroyed in what we call death. You say it makes no difference whether it enters a body once or many times as far as the fear of each of us is concerned, for it is natural for a man who is no fool to be afraid, if he does not know and cannot prove that the soul is immortal. This, I think, is what you maintain, Cebes; I deliberately repeat it often, in order that no point may escape us, and that *e* you may add or subtract something if you wish.

And Cebes said: "There is nothing that I want to add or subtract at the moment. That is what I say."

Socrates paused for a long time, deep in thought. He then said: "This is no unimportant problem that you raise, Cebes, for it requires a thorough investiga- *96* tion of the cause of generation and destruction. I will, if you wish, give you an account of my experience in these matters. Then if something I say seems useful to you, make use of it to persuade us of your position."

I surely do wish that, said Cebes.

Listen then, and I will, Cebes, he said. When I was a young man I was wonderfully keen on that wisdom which they call natural science, for I thought it splendid to know the causes of everything, why it comes to be, why it perishes and why it exists. I was often changing my mind in the investigation, in the *b* first instance, of questions such as these: Are living creatures nurtured when heat and cold produce a kind of putrefaction, as some say? Do we think with our blood, or air, or fire, or none of these, and does the brain provide our senses of hearing and sight and smell, from which come memory and opinion, and from memory and opinion which has become stable, comes knowledge? Then again, as I investigated how these things perish and what happens to things in the sky and on the earth, finally I became convinced that *c* I have no natural aptitude at all for that kind of investigation, and of this I will give you sufficient proof. This investigation made me quite blind even to those things which I and others thought that I clearly knew before, so that I unlearned what I thought I knew before, about many other things and specifically about how men grew. I thought before that it was obvious to anybody that men grew through *d* eating and drinking, for food adds flesh to flesh and bones to bones, and in the same way appropriate parts were added to all other parts of the body, so that the man grew from an earlier small bulk to a large bulk

18. [Harmonia was in legend the wife of Cadmus, the founder of Thebes. Socrates' punning joke is simply that, having dealt with Harmonia (harmony), we must now deal with Cadmus (i.e., Cebes, the other Theban).]

later, and so a small man became big. That is what I thought then. Do you not think it was reasonable?

I do, said Cebes.

Then further consider this: I thought my opinion was satisfactory, that when a large man stood by a e small one he was taller by a head, and so a horse was taller than a horse. Even clearer than this, I thought that ten was more than eight because two had been added, and that a two-cubit length is larger than a cubit because it surpasses it by half its length.

And what do you think now about those things?

That I am far, by Zeus, from believing that I know the cause of any of those things. I will not even allow myself to say that where one is added to one either the one to which it is added or the one that is added becomes two, or that the one added and the one to 97 which it is added become two because of the addition of the one to the other. I wonder that, when each of them is separate from the other, each of them is one, nor are they then two, but that, when they come near to one another, this is the cause of their becoming two, the coming together and being placed closer to one another. Nor can I any longer be persuaded that when one thing is divided, this division is the cause b of its becoming two, for just now the cause of becoming two was the opposite. At that time it was their coming close together and one was added to the other, but now it is because one is taken and separated from the other.

I do not any longer persuade myself that I know why a unit or anything else comes to be, or perishes or exists by the old method of investigation, and I do not accept it, but I have a confused method of my own. One day I heard someone reading, as he said, c from a book of Anaxagoras, and saying that it is Mind that directs and is the cause of everything. I was delighted with this cause and it seemed to me good, in a way, that Mind should be the cause of all. I thought that if this were so, the directing Mind would direct everything and arrange each thing in the way that was best. If then one wished to know the cause of each thing, why it comes to be or perishes or exists, d one had to find what was the best way for it to be, or to be acted upon, or to act. On these premises then it befitted a man to investigate only, about this and other things, what is best. The same man must inevitably also know what is worse, for that is part of the same knowledge. As I reflected on this subject I was glad to think that I had found in Anaxagoras a teacher about the cause of things after my own heart, and that he would tell me, first, whether the earth is e flat or round, and then would explain why it is so of necessity, saying which is better, and that it was better to be so. If he said it was in the middle of the universe, he would go on to show that it was better for it to be in the middle, and if he showed me those things I should be prepared never to desire any other kind of 98 cause. I was ready to find out in the same way about the sun and the moon and the other heavenly bodies, about their relative speed, their turnings and whatever else happened to them, how it is best that each should act or be acted upon. I never thought that Anaxagoras, who said that those things were directed by Mind, would bring in any other cause for them than that it was best for them to be as they are. Once he had b given the best for each as the cause for each and the general cause of all, I thought he would go on to explain the common good for all, and I would not have exchanged my hopes for a fortune. I eagerly acquired his books and read them as quickly as I could in order to know the best and the worst as soon as possible.

This wonderful hope was dashed as I went on reading and saw that the man made no use of Mind, nor gave it any responsibility for the management of things, but mentioned as causes air and ether and water and many other strange things. That seemed c to me much like saying that Socrates' actions are all due to his mind, and then in trying to tell the causes of everything I do, to say that the reason that I am sitting here is because my body consists of bones and sinews, because the bones are hard and are separated by joints, that the sinews are such as to contract and relax, that they surround the bones along with flesh and skin which hold them together, then as the bones d are hanging in their sockets, the relaxation and contraction of the sinews enable me to bend my limbs, and that is the cause of my sitting here with my limbs bent.

Again, he would mention other such causes for my talking to you: sounds and air and hearing, and a thousand other such things, but he would neglect to mention the true causes, that, after the Athenians decided it was better to condemn me, for this reason e it seemed best to me to sit here and more right to remain and to endure whatever penalty they ordered.

For by the dog, I think these sinews and bones could long ago have been in Megara or among the Boeo- 99 tians, taken there by my belief as to the best course, if I had not thought it more right and honorable to endure whatever penalty the city ordered rather than escape and run away. To call those things causes is too absurd. If someone said that without bones and sinews and all such things, I should not be able to do what I decided, he would be right, but surely to say that they are the cause of what I do, and not that I have chosen the best course, even though I act *b* with my mind, is to speak very lazily and carelessly. Imagine not being able to distinguish the real cause from that without which the cause would not be able to act as a cause. It is what the majority appear to do, like people groping in the dark; they call it a cause, thus giving it a name that does not belong to it. That is why one man surrounds the earth with a vortex to make the heavens keep it in place, another *c* makes the air support it like a wide lid. As for their capacity of being in the best place they could possibly be put, this they do not look for, nor do they believe it to have any divine force, but they believe that they will sometime discover a stronger and more immortal Atlas to hold everything together more, and they do not believe that the truly good and "binding" binds and holds them together. I would gladly become the disciple of any man who taught the workings of that kind of cause. However, since I was deprived and could neither discover it myself nor learn it from *d* another, do you wish me to give you an explanation of how, as a second best, I busied myself with the search for the cause, Cebes?

I would wish it above all else, he said.

After this, he said, when I had wearied of investigating things, I thought that I must be careful to avoid the experience of those who watch an eclipse of the sun, for some of them ruin their eyes unless they watch its reflection in water or some such material. *e* A similar thought crossed my mind, and I feared that my soul would be altogether blinded if I looked at things with my eyes and tried to grasp them with each of my senses. So I thought I must take refuge in discussions and investigate the truth of things by means of words. However, perhaps this analogy is 100 inadequate, for I certainly do not admit that one who investigates things by means of words is dealing with images any more than one who looks at facts. However, I started in this manner: taking as my hypothesis in each case the theory that seemed to me the most compelling, I would consider as true, about cause and everything else, whatever agreed with this, and as untrue whatever did not so agree. But I want to put my meaning more clearly for I do not think that you understand me now.

No, by Zeus, said Cebes, not very well.

This, he said, is what I mean. It is nothing new, *b* but what I have never stopped talking about, both elsewhere and in the earlier part of our conversation. I am going to try to show you the kind of cause with which I have concerned myself. I turn back to those oft-mentioned things and proceed from them. I assume the existence of a Beautiful, itself by itself, of a Good and a Great and all the rest. If you grant me these and agree that they exist, I hope to show you the cause as a result, and to find the soul to be immortal.

Take it that I grant you this, said Cebes, and hasten *c* to your conclusion.

Consider then, he said, whether you share my opinion as to what follows, for I think that, if there is anything beautiful besides the Beautiful itself, it is beautiful for no other reason than that it shares in that Beautiful, and I say so with everything. Do you agree to this sort of cause?—I do.

I no longer understand or recognize those other sophisticated causes, and if someone tells me that a *d* thing is beautiful because it has a bright color or shape or any such thing, I ignore these other reasons—for all these confuse me—but I simply, naively and perhaps foolishly cling to this, that nothing else makes it beautiful other than the presence of, or the sharing in, or however you may describe its relationship to that Beautiful we mentioned, for I will not insist on the precise nature of the relationship, but that all beautiful things are beautiful by the Beautiful. That, I think, is the safest answer I can give myself or anyone *e* else. And if I stick to this I think I shall never fall into error. This is the safe answer for me or anyone else to give, namely, that it is through Beauty that beautiful things are made beautiful. Or do you not think so too?—I do.

And that it is through Bigness that big things are big and the bigger are bigger, and that smaller things are made small by Smallness?—Yes.

And you would not accept the statement that one

101 man is taller than another by a head[19] and the shorter man shorter by the same, but you would bear witness that you mean nothing else than that everything that is bigger is made bigger by nothing else than by Bigness, and that is the cause of its being bigger, and the smaller is made smaller only by Smallness, and this is why it is smaller. I think you would be afraid that some opposite argument would confront you if you said that someone is bigger or smaller by a head, first, because the bigger is bigger and the smaller smaller by the same, then because the bigger is bigger b by a head which is small, and this would be strange, namely, that someone is made bigger by something small. Would you not be afraid of this?

I certainly would, said Cebes, laughing.

Then you would be afraid to say that ten is more than eight by two, and that this is the cause of the excess, and not magnitude and because of magnitude, or that two cubits is bigger than one cubit by half and not by Bigness, for this is the same fear.—Certainly.

Then would you not avoid saying that when one c is added to one it is the addition and when it is divided it is the division that is the cause of two? And you would loudly exclaim that you do not know how else each thing can come to be except by sharing in the particular reality in which it shares, and in these cases you do not know of any other cause of becoming two except by sharing in Twoness, and that the things that are to be two must share in this, as that which is to be one must share in Oneness, and you would dismiss these additions and divisions and other such subtleties, and leave them to those wiser than yourself to answer. But you, afraid, as they say, of your own d shadow and your inexperience, would cling to the safety of your own hypothesis and give that answer. If someone then attacked your hypothesis itself, you would ignore him and would not answer until you had examined whether the consequences that follow from it agree with one another or contradict one another. And when you must give an account of your hypothesis itself you will proceed in the same way: you will assume another hypothesis, the one which seems to you best of the higher ones until you come e to something acceptable, but you will not jumble the two as the debaters do by discussing the hypothesis and its consequences at the same time, if you wish to discover any truth. This they do not discuss at all nor give any thought to, but their wisdom enables them to mix everything up and yet to be pleased with themselves, but if you are a philosopher I think you 102 will do as I say.

What you say is very true, said Simmias and Cebes together.

ECHECRATES: Yes, by Zeus, Phaedo, and they were right; I think he made these things wonderfully clear to anyone of even small intelligence.

PHAEDO: Yes indeed, Echecrates, and all those present thought so too.

E: And so do we who were not present but hear of it now. What was said after that?

P: As I recall it, when the above had been accepted, and it was agreed that each of the Forms b existed, and that other things acquired their name by having a share in them, he followed this up by asking: If you say these things are so, when you then say that Simmias is taller than Socrates but shorter than Phaedo, do you not mean that there is in Simmias both tallness and shortness?—I do.

But, he said, do you agree that the words of the statement "Simmias is taller than Socrates" do not express the truth of the matter? It is not, surely, the c nature of Simmias to be taller than Socrates because he is Simmias but because of the tallness he happens to have? Nor is he taller than Socrates because Socrates is Socrates, but because Socrates has smallness compared with the tallness of the other?—True.

Nor is he shorter than Phaedo because Phaedo is Phaedo, but because Phaedo has tallness compared with the shortness of Simmias?—That is so.

So then Simmias is called both short and tall, being between the two, presenting his shortness to be over- d come by the tallness of one, and his tallness to overcome the shortness of the other. He smilingly added, I seem to be going to talk like a book, but it is as I say. The other agreed.

My purpose is that you may agree with me. Now it seems to me that not only Tallness itself is never willing to be tall and short at the same time, but also

19. [This is very puzzling in English. In Greek the confusion is due to the double use of the dative, instrumental and causal, so that it could mean "because of a head," which is nonsense of course, but the ambiguity is there and makes the statement of Socrates possible.]

that the tallness in us[20] will never admit the short or be overcome, but one of two things happens: either e it flees and retreats whenever its opposite, the short, approaches, or it is destroyed by its approach. It is not willing to endure and admit shortness and be other than it was, whereas I admit and endure shortness and still remain the same person and am this short man. But Tallness, being tall, cannot venture to be small. In the same way, the short in us is unwill- 103 ing to become or to be tall ever, nor does any other of the opposites become or be its opposite while still being what it was; either it goes away or is destroyed when that happens.—I altogether agree, said Cebes.

When he heard this, someone of those present—I have no clear memory of who it was—said: "By the gods, did we not agree earlier in our discussion[21] to the very opposite of what is now being said, namely, that the larger came from the smaller and the smaller from the larger, and that this simply was how opposites came to be, from their opposites, but now I think we are saying that this would never happen?"

On hearing this, Socrates inclined his head towards the speaker and said: "You have bravely reminded b us, but you do not understand the difference between what is said now and what was said then, which was that an opposite thing came from an opposite thing; now we say that the opposite itself could never become opposite to itself, neither that in us nor that in nature. Then, my friend, we were talking of things that have opposite qualities and naming these after them, but now we say that these opposites themselves, from the presence of which in them things get their name, never can tolerate the coming to be from one c another." At the same time he looked to Cebes and said: "Does anything of what this man says also disturb you?"

Not at the moment, said Cebes, but I do not deny that many things do disturb me.

We are altogether agreed then, he said, that an opposite will never be opposite to itself.—Entirely agreed.

Consider then whether you will agree to this further point. There is something you call hot and something you call cold.—There is.

Are they the same as what you call snow and fire? d —By Zeus, no.

So the hot is something other than fire, and the cold is something other than snow?—Yes.

You think, I believe, that being snow it will not admit the hot, as we said before, and remain what it was and be both snow and hot, but when the hot approaches it will either retreat before it or be destroyed.—Quite so.

So fire, as the cold approaches, will either go away or be destroyed; it will never venture to admit coldness and remain what it was, fire and cold.—What you e say is true.

It is true then about some of these things that not only the Form itself deserves its own name for all time, but there is something else that is not the Form but has its character whenever it exists. Perhaps I can make my meaning clearer: the Odd must always be given this name we now mention. Is that not so? —Certainly.

Is it the only one of existing things to be called odd—this is my question—or is there something else 104 than the Odd which one must nevertheless also always call odd, as well as by its own name, because it is such by nature as never to be separated from the Odd? I mean, for example, the number three and many others. Consider three: do you not think that it must always be called both by its own name and by that of the Odd, which is not the same as three? That is the nature of three, and of five, and of half of all the numbers; each of them is odd, but it is not b the Odd. Then again, two and four and the whole other column of numbers; each of them, while not being the same as the Even, is always even. Do you not agree?—Of course.

Look now. What I want to make clear is this: not only do those opposites not admit each other, but this is also true of those things which, while not being opposite to each other yet always contain the opposites, and it seems that these do not admit that Form which is opposite to that which is in them; when it approaches them, they either perish or give c way. Shall we not say that three will perish or undergo anything before, while remaining three, becoming even?—Certainly, said Cebes.

20. [The "tallness in us" is not the Form, which is never immanent in the particular, nor need we imagine it to refer to another thing existing between the Form and the particular; it simply refers to the quality of tallness that is clearly inherent in the particulars. The expression could be used without reference to the theory of Forms at all.]

21. [The reference is to 70d–71a above.]

Yet surely two is not the opposite of three?—Indeed it is not.

It is then not only opposite Forms that do not admit each other's approach, but also some other things that do not admit the onset of opposites.—Very true.

Do you then want us, if we can, to define what these are?—I surely do.

d Would they be the things that compel whatever they occupy not only to contain their Form but also always that of some opposite?—How do you mean?

As we were saying just now, you surely know that what the Form of three occupies must be not only three but also odd.—Certainly.

And we say that the opposite Form to the Form that achieves this result could never come to it.—It could not.

Now it is Oddness that has done this?—Yes.

And opposite to this is the Form of the Even?—Yes.

e So then the Form of the Even will never come to three?—Never.

Then three has no share in the Even?—Never.

So three is uneven?—Yes.

As for what I said we must define, that is, what kind of things, while not being opposites to something, yet do not admit the opposite, as, for example, the triad, though it is not the opposite of the Even, yet does not admit it because it always brings along the opposite of 105 the Even, and so the dyad in relation to the Odd, fire to the Cold, and very many other things, see whether you would define it thus: Not only does the opposite not admit its opposite, but that which brings along some opposite into that which it occupies; that which brings this along will not admit the opposite to that which it brings along. Refresh your memory; it is no worse for being heard often. Five does not admit the form of the Even, nor will ten, which is twice five, admit the form of the Odd. It is the opposite of something else, yet it will not admit the form of the Odd. Nor do one-and-a-half and other such b fractions admit the form of the Whole, nor will one-third, and so on, if you follow me and agree to this.

I certainly agree, he said, and I follow you.

Tell me again from the beginning, he said, and do not answer in the words of the question, but do as I do. I say that beyond that safe answer, which I spoke of first, I see another safe answer. If you should ask me what, coming into a body, makes it hot, my reply would not be that safe and ignorant one, that c it is heat, but our present argument provides a more sophisticated answer, namely, fire, and if you ask me what, on coming into a body, makes it sick, I will not say sickness but fever. Nor, if asked the presence of what in a number makes it odd, I will not say oddness but oneness, and so with other things. See if you now sufficiently understand what I want.—Quite sufficiently.

Answer me then, he said, what is it that, present in a body, makes it living?—A soul.

And is that always so?—Of course. d

Whatever the soul occupies, it always brings life to it?—It does.

Is there, or is there not, an opposite to life?—There is.

What is it?—Death.

So the soul will never admit the opposite of that which it brings along, as we agree from what has been said?

Most certainly, said Cebes.

Well, and what do we call that which does not admit the form of the even?—The uneven.

What do we call that which will not admit the just and that which will not admit the musical?

The unmusical, and the other the unjust. e

Very well, what do we call that which does not admit death?

The deathless, he said.

Now the soul does not admit death?—No.

So the soul is deathless?—It is.

Very well, he said. Shall we say that this has been proved, do you think?

Quite adequately proved, Socrates.

Well now, Cebes, he said, if the uneven were of necessity indestructible, surely three would be indestructible?—Of course. 106

And if the non-hot were of necessity indestructible, then whenever anyone brought heat to snow, the snow would retreat safe and unthawed, for it could not be destroyed, nor again could it stand its ground and admit the heat?—What you say is true.

In the same way, if the non-cold were indestructible, then when some cold attacked the fire, it would neither be quenched nor destroyed, but retreat safely.—Necessarily.

Must then the same not be said of the deathless? b If the deathless is also indestructible, it is impossible for the soul to be destroyed when death comes upon it. For it follows from what has been said that it will not admit death or be dead, just as three, we said, will not be even nor will the odd; nor will fire be cold, nor the heat that is in the fire. But, someone might say, what prevents the odd, while not becoming *c* even as has been agreed, from being destroyed, and the even to come to be instead? We could not maintain against the man who said this that it is not destroyed, for the uneven is not indestructible. If we had agreed that it was indestructible we could easily have maintained that at the coming of the even, the odd and the three have gone away and the same would hold for fire and the hot and the other things.—Surely.

And so now, if we are agreed that the deathless is *d* indestructible, the soul, besides being deathless, is indestructible. If not, we need another argument.

There is no need for one as far as that goes, for hardly anything could resist destruction if the deathless, which lasts forever, would admit destruction.

All would agree, said Socrates, that the god, and the Form of life itself, and anything that is deathless, are never destroyed.—All men would agree, by Zeus, to that, and the gods, I imagine, even more so.

e If the deathless is indestructible, then the soul, if it is deathless, would also be indestructible?—Necessarily.

Then when death comes to man, the mortal part of him dies, it seems, but his deathless part goes away safe and indestructible, yielding the place to death.—So it appears.

Therefore the soul, Cebes, he said, is most certainly *107* deathless and indestructible and our souls will really dwell in the underworld.

I have nothing more to say against that, Socrates, said Cebes, nor can I doubt your arguments. If Simmias here or someone else has something to say, he should not remain silent, for I do not know to what further occasion other than the present he could put it off if he wants to say or to hear anything on these subjects.

Certainly, said Simmias, I myself have no remaining grounds for doubt after what has been said; nevertheless, in view of the importance of our subject and my low opinion of human weakness, I am bound *b* still to have some private misgivings about what we have said.

You are not only right to say this, Simmias, Socrates said, but our first hypotheses require clearer examination, even though we find them convincing. And if you analyze them adequately, you will, I think, follow the argument as far as a man can, and if the conclusion is clear, you will look no further.—That is true.

It is right to think then, gentlemen, that if the soul *c* is immortal, it requires our care not only for the time we call our life, but for the sake of all time, and that one is in terrible danger if one does not give it that care. If death were escape from everything, it would be a great boon to the wicked to get rid of the body and of their wickedness together with their soul. But now that the soul appears to be immortal, there is no escape from evil or salvation for it except by becom- *d* ing as good and wise as possible, for the soul goes to the underworld possessing nothing but its education and upbringing, which are said to bring the greatest benefit or harm to the dead right at the beginning of the journey yonder.

We are told that when each person dies, the guardian spirit who was allotted to him in life proceeds to lead him to a certain place, whence those who have been gathered together there must, after being judged, proceed to the underworld with the guide *e* who has been appointed to lead them thither from here. Having there undergone what they must and stayed there the appointed time, they are led back here by another guide after long periods of time. The journey is not as Aeschylus' Telephus[22] describes it. *108* He says that only one single path leads to Hades, but I think it is neither one nor simple, for then there would be no need of guides; one could not make any mistake if there were but one path. As it is, it is likely to have many forks and crossroads; and I base this judgment on the sacred rites and customs here.

The well-ordered and wise soul follows the guide and is not without familiarity with its surroundings, but the soul that is passionately attached to the body, as I said before, hovers around it and the visible world *b* for a long time, struggling and suffering much until it is led away by force and with difficulty by its appointed spirit. When the impure soul which has performed some impure deed joins the others after being involved in unjust killings, or committed other crimes

22. [The *Telephus* of Aeschylus is not extant, and little is known about it.]

which are akin to these and are actions of souls of this kind, everybody shuns it and turns away, unwilling to *c* be its fellow traveller or its guide; such a soul wanders alone completely at a loss until a certain time arrives and it is forcibly led to its proper dwelling place. On the other hand, the soul that has led a pure and moderate life finds fellow travellers and gods to guide it, and each of them dwells in a place suited to it.

There are many strange places upon the earth, and the earth itself is not such as those who are used to discourse upon it believe it to be in nature or size, as someone has convinced me.

d Simmias said: "What do you mean, Socrates? I have myself heard many things said about the earth, but certainly not the things that convince you. I should be glad to hear them."

Indeed, Simmias, I do not think it requires the skill of Glaucus[23] to tell you what they are, but to prove them true requires more than that skill, and I should perhaps not be able to do so. Also, even if I had the knowledge, my remaining time would not *e* be long enough to tell the tale. However, nothing prevents my telling you what I am convinced is the shape of the earth and what its regions are.

Even that is sufficient, said Simmias.

Well then, he said, the first thing of which I am *109* convinced is that if the earth is a sphere in the middle of the heavens, it has no need of air or any other force to prevent it from falling. The homogeneous nature of the heavens on all sides and the earth's own equipoise are sufficient to hold it, for an object balanced in the middle of something homogeneous will have no tendency to incline more in any direction than any other but will remain unmoved. This, he said, is the first point of which I am persuaded.

And rightly so, said Simmias.

Further, the earth is very large, and we live around *b* the sea in a small portion of it between Phasis and the pillars of Heracles, like ants or frogs around a swamp; many other peoples live in many such parts of it. Everywhere about the earth there are numerous hollows of many kinds and shapes and sizes into which the water and the mist and the air have gathered. The earth itself is pure and lies in the pure sky where the stars are situated, which the majority of those who discourse on these subjects call the ether. *c* The water and mist and air are the sediment of the ether and they always flow into the hollows of the earth. We, who dwell in the hollows of it, are unaware of this and we think that we live above, on the surface of the earth. It is as if someone who lived deep down in the middle of the ocean thought he was living on its surface. Seeing the sun and the other heavenly bodies through the water, he would think the sea to *d* be the sky; because he is slow and weak, he has never reached the surface of the sea or risen with his head above the water or come out of the sea to our region here, nor seen how much purer and more beautiful it is than his own region, nor has he ever heard of it from anyone who has seen it.

Our experience is the same: living in a certain hollow of the earth, we believe that we live upon its surface; the air we call the heavens, as if the stars made their way through it; this too is the same: because of our weakness and slowness we are not able to make our way to the upper limit of the air; if anyone got *e* to this upper limit, if anyone came to it or reached it on wings and his head rose above it, then just as fish on rising from the sea see things in our region, he would see things there and, if his nature could endure to contemplate them, he would know that there is the true heaven, the true light and the true earth, for the earth here, these stones and the whole *110* region, are spoiled and eaten away, just as things in the sea are by the salt water.

Nothing worth mentioning grows in the sea, nothing, one might say, is fully developed; there are caves and sand and endless slime and mud wherever there is earth—not comparable in any way with the beauties of our region. So those things above are in their turn far superior to the things we know. Indeed, if this is the moment to tell a tale, Simmias, it is worth hearing *b* about the nature of things on the surface of the earth under the heavens.

At any rate, Socrates, said Simmias, we should be glad to hear this story.

Well then, my friend, in the first place it is said that the earth, looked at from above, looks like those spherical balls made up of twelve pieces of leather; it is multi-colored, and of these colors those used by our painters give us an indication; up there the whole earth has these colors, but much brighter and purer *c*

23. [A proverbial expression meaning that a difficult task required the skill of Glaucus. Its origin is obscure, for there are several explanations given by the Scholiasts.]

than these; one part is sea-green and of marvelous beauty, another is golden, another is white, whiter than chalk or snow; the earth is composed also of the other colors, more numerous and beautiful than any we have seen. The very hollows of the earth, full of water and air, gleaming among the variety of other colors, present a color of their own so that the whole is seen as a continuum of variegated colors. On the surface of the earth the plants grow with corresponding beauty, the trees and the flowers and the fruits, and so with the hills and the stones, more beautiful in their smoothness and transparency and color. Our precious stones here are but fragments, our cornelians, jaspers, emeralds and the rest. All stones there are of that kind, and even more beautiful. The reason is that there they are pure, not eaten away or spoiled by decay and brine, or corroded by the water and air which have flowed into the hollows here and bring ugliness and disease upon earth, stones, the other animals and plants. The earth itself is adorned with all these things, and also with gold and silver and other metals. These stand out, being numerous and massive and occurring everywhere, so that the earth is a sight for the blessed. There are many other living creatures upon the earth, and also men, some living inland, others at the edge of the air, as we live on the edge of the sea, others again live on islands surrounded by air close to the mainland. In a word, what water and the sea are to us, the air is to them, and the ether is to them what the air is to us. The climate is such that they are without disease, and they live much longer than people do here; their eyesight, hearing and intelligence and all such are as superior to ours as air is superior to water and ether to air in purity; they have groves and temples dedicated to the gods, in which the gods really dwell, and they communicate with them by speech and prophecy and by the sight of them; they see the sun and moon and stars as they are, and in other ways their happiness is in accord with this.

This then is the nature of the earth as a whole and of its surroundings; around the whole of it there are many regions in the hollows; some are deeper and more open than that in which we live; others are deeper and have a narrower opening than ours, and there are some that have less depth and more width. All these are connected with each other below the surface of the earth in many places by narrow and broader channels, and thus have outlets through which much water flows from one to another as into mixing bowls; huge rivers of both hot and cold water thus flow beneath the earth eternally, much fire and large rivers of fire, and many of wet mud, both more pure and more muddy, such as those flowing in advance of the lava and the stream of lava itself in Sicily. These streams then fill up every and all regions as the flow reaches each, and all these places move up and down with the oscillating movement of the earth. The natural cause of the oscillation is as follows: One of the hollows of the earth, which is also the biggest, pierces through the whole earth; it is that which Homer mentioned when he said: "Far down where is the deepest pit below the earth . . . ," and which he elsewhere, and many other poets, call Tartarus; into this chasm all the rivers flow together, and again flow out of it, and each river is affected by the nature of the land through which it flows. The reason for their flowing into and out of Tartarus is that this water has no bottom or solid base but it oscillates up and down in waves, and the air and wind about it do the same, for they follow it when it flows to this or that part of the earth. Just as when people breathe, the flow of air goes in and out, so here the air oscillates with the water and creates terrible winds as it goes in and out. Whenever the water retreats to what we call the lower part of the earth, it flows into those parts and fills them up as if the water were pumped in; when it leaves that part for this, it fills these parts again, and the parts filled flow through the channels and through the earth and in each case arrive at the places to which the channels lead and create seas and marshes and rivers and springs. From there the waters flow under the earth again, some flowing around larger and more numerous regions, some around smaller and shallower ones, then flow back into Tartarus, some at a point much lower than where they issued forth, others only a little way, but all of them at a lower point, some of them at the opposite side of the chasm, some on the same side; some flow in a wide circle round the earth once or many times like snakes, then go as far down as possible, then go back into the chasm of Tartarus. From each side it is possible to flow down as far as the center, but not beyond, for this part that faces the river flow from either side is steep.

There are many other large rivers of all kinds, and

among these there are four of note; the biggest which flows on the outside (of the earth) in a circle is called Oceanus; opposite it and flowing in the opposite direction is the Acheron; it flows through many other *113* deserted regions and further underground makes its way to the Acherusian lake to which the souls of the majority come after death and, after remaining there for a certain appointed time, longer for some, shorter for others, they are sent back to birth as living creatures. The third river issues between the first two, and close to its source it falls into a region burning with *b* much fire and makes a lake larger than our sea, boiling with water and mud. From there it goes in a circle, foul and muddy, and winding on its way it comes, among other places, to the edge of the Acherusian lake but does not mingle with its waters; then, coiling many times underground it flows lower down into Tartarus; this is called the Pyriphlegethon, and its lava streams throw off fragments of it in various *c* parts of the earth. Opposite this the fourth river issues forth, which is called Stygion, and it is said to flow first into a terrible and wild region, all of it blue-gray in color, and the lake that this river forms by flowing into it is called the Styx. As its waters fall into the lake they acquire dread powers; then diving below and winding round it flows in the opposite direction from the Pyriphlegethon and into the opposite side of the Acherusian lake; its waters do not mingle with any other; it too flows in a circle and into Tartarus opposite the Pyriphlegethon. The name of that fourth river, the poets tell us, is Cocytus.

d Such is the nature of these things. When the dead arrive at the place to which each has been led by his guardian spirit, they are first judged as to whether they have led a good and pious life. Those who have lived an average life make their way to the Acheron and embark upon such vessels as there are for them and proceed to the lake. There they dwell and are purified by penalties for any wrongdoing they may *e* have committed; they are also suitably rewarded for their good deeds as each deserves. Those who are deemed incurable because of the enormity of their crimes, having committed many great sacrileges or wicked and unlawful murders and other such wrongs—their fitting fate is to be hurled into Tartarus never to emerge from it. Those who are deemed to have committed great but curable crimes, such as doing violence to their father or mother in a fit of temper but who have felt remorse for the rest of their *114* lives, or who have killed someone in a similar manner, these must of necessity be thrown into Tartarus, but a year later the current throws them out, those who are guilty of murder by way of Cocytus, and those who have done violence to their parents by way of the Pyriphlegethon. After they have been carried along to the Acherusian lake, they cry out and shout, some for those they have killed, others for those they have maltreated, and calling them they then pray to them *b* and beg them to allow them to step out into the lake and to receive them. If they persuade them, they do step out and their punishment comes to an end; if they do not, they are taken back into Tartarus and from there into the rivers, and this does not stop until they have persuaded those they have wronged, for this is the punishment which the judges imposed on them.

Those who are deemed to have lived an extremely pious life are freed and released from the regions of *c* the earth as from a prison; they make their way up to a pure dwelling place and live on the surface of the earth. Those who have purified themselves sufficiently by philosophy live in the future altogether without a body; they make their way to even more beautiful dwelling places which it is hard to describe clearly, nor do we now have the time to do so. Because of the things we have enunciated, Simmias, one must make every effort to share in virtue and wisdom in one's life, for the reward is beautiful and the hope is great.

No sensible man would insist that these things are *d* as I have described them, but I think it is fitting for a man to risk the belief—for the risk is a noble one—that this, or something like this, is true about our souls and their dwelling places, since the soul is evidently immortal, and a man should repeat this to himself as if it were an incantation, which is why I have been prolonging my tale. That is the reason why a man should be of good cheer about his own soul, if during life he has ignored the pleasures of the body and its *e* ornamentation as of no concern to him and doing him more harm than good, but has seriously concerned himself with the pleasures of learning, and adorned his soul not with alien but with its own ornaments, namely, moderation, righteousness, courage, freedom *115* and truth, and in that state awaits his journey to the underworld.

Now you, Simmias, Cebes and the rest of you, Socrates continued, will each take that journey at some other time but my fated day calls me now, as a tragic character might say, and it is about time for me to have my bath, for I think it better to have it before I drink the poison and save the women the trouble of washing the corpse.

b When Socrates had said this Crito spoke. Very well, Socrates, what are your instructions to me and the others about your children or anything else? What can we do that would please you most?—Nothing new, Crito, said Socrates, but what I am always saying, that you will please me and mine and yourselves by taking good care of your own selves in whatever you do, even if you do not agree with me now, but if you neglect your own selves, and are unwilling to live *c* following the tracks, as it were, of what we have said now and on previous occasions, you will achieve nothing even if you strongly agree with me at this moment.

We shall be eager to follow your advice, said Crito, but how shall we bury you?

In any way you like, said Socrates, if you can catch me and I do not escape you. And laughing quietly, looking at us, he said: I do not convince Crito that I am this Socrates talking to you here and ordering *d* all I say, but he thinks that I am the thing which he will soon be looking at as a corpse, and so he asks how he shall bury me. I have been saying for some time and at some length that after I have drunk the poison I shall no longer be with you but will leave you to go and enjoy some good fortunes of the blessed, but it seems that I have said all this to him in vain in an attempt to reassure you and myself too. Give a pledge to Crito on my behalf, he said, the opposite pledge to that he gave the jury. He pledged that I *e* would stay, you must pledge that I will not stay after I die, but that I shall go away, so that Crito will bear it more easily when he sees my body being burned or buried and will not be angry on my behalf, as if I were suffering terribly, and so that he should not say at the funeral that he is laying out, or carrying out, or burying Socrates. For know you well, my dear Crito, that to express oneself badly is not only faulty as far as the language goes, but does some harm to the soul. You must be of good cheer, and say you are *116* burying my body, and bury it in any way you like and think most customary.

After saying this he got up and went to another room to take his bath, and Crito followed him and he told us to wait for him. So we stayed, talking among ourselves, questioning what had been said, and then again talking of the great misfortune that had befallen us. We all felt as if we had lost a father and would be orphaned for the rest of our lives. When *b* he had washed, his children were brought to him—two of his sons were small and one was older—and the women of his household came to him. He spoke to them before Crito and gave them what instructions he wanted. Then he sent the women and children away, and he himself joined us. It was now close to sunset, for he had stayed inside for some time. He came and sat down after his bath and conversed for a short while, when the officer of the Eleven came and stood by him and said: "I shall not reproach you *c* as I do the others, Socrates. They are angry with me and curse me when obeying the orders of my superiors, I tell them to drink the poison. During the time you have been here I have come to know you in other ways as the noblest, the gentlest and the best man who has ever come here. So now too I know that you will not make trouble for me; you know who is responsible and you will direct your anger against them. You know what message I bring. Fare you well, and try to endure what you must as easily as possible." *d* The officer was weeping as he turned away and went out. Socrates looked up at him and said: "Fare you well also, we shall do as you bid us." And turning to us he said: "How pleasant the man is! During the whole time I have been here he has come in and conversed with me from time to time, a most agreeable man. And how genuinely he now weeps for me. Come, Crito, let us obey him. Let someone bring the poison if it is ready; if not, let the man prepare it."

But Socrates, said Crito, I think the sun still shines *e* upon the hills and has not yet set. I know that others drink the poison quite a long time after they have received the order, eating and drinking quite a bit, and some of them enjoy intimacy with their loved ones. Do not hurry; there is still some time.

It is natural, Crito, for them to do so, said Socrates, for they think they derive some benefit from doing *117* this, but it is not fitting for me. I do not expect any benefit from drinking the poison a little later, except to become ridiculous in my own eyes for clinging to life, and be sparing of it when there is none left. So do as I ask and do not refuse me.

Hearing this, Crito nodded to the slave who was standing near him; the slave went out and after a time came back with the man who was to administer the poison, carrying it made ready in a cup. When Socrates saw him he said: "Well, my good man, you are an expert in this, what must one do?"—"Just drink *b* it and walk around until your legs feel heavy, and then lie down and it will act of itself." And he offered the cup to Socrates, who took it quite cheerfully, Echecrates, without a tremor or any change of feature or color, but looking at the man from under his eyebrows as was his wont, asked: "What do you say about pouring a libation from this drink? It is allowed?"—"We only mix as much as we believe will suffice," said the man.

c I understand, Socrates said, but one is allowed, indeed one must, utter a prayer to the gods that the journey from here to yonder may be fortunate. This is my prayer and may it be so.

And while he was saying this, he was holding the cup, and then drained it calmly and easily. Most of us had been able to hold back our tears reasonably well up till then, but when we saw him drinking it and after he drank it, we could hold them back no longer; my own tears came in floods against my will. So I covered my face. I was weeping for myself, not *d* for him—for my misfortune in being deprived of such a comrade. Even before me, Crito was unable to restrain his tears and got up. Apollodorus had not ceased from weeping before, and at this moment his noisy tears and anger made everybody present break down, except Socrates. "What is this," he said, "you strange fellows. It is mainly for this reason that I sent the women away, to avoid such unseemliness, for I *e* am told one should die in good omened silence. So keep quiet and control yourselves."

His words made us ashamed, and we checked our tears. He walked around, and when he said his legs were heavy he lay on his back as he had been told to do, and the man who had given him the poison touched his body, and after a while tested his feet and legs, pressed hard upon his foot, and asked him if he felt this, and Socrates said no. Then he pressed *118* his calves, and made his way up his body and showed us that it was cold and stiff. He felt it himself and said that when the cold reached his heart he would be gone. As his belly was getting cold Socrates uncovered his head—he had covered it—and said—these were his last words—"Crito, we owe a cock to Asclepius;[24] make this offering to him and do not forget." —"It shall be done," said Crito, "tell us if there is anything else." But there was no answer. Shortly afterwards Socrates made a movement; the man uncovered him and his eyes were fixed. Seeing this Crito closed his mouth and his eyes.

Such was the end of our comrade, Echecrates, a man who, we would say, was of all those we have known the best, and also the wisest and the most upright.

24. [A cock was sacrificed to Asclepius by the sick people who slept in his temples, hoping for a cure. Socrates obviously means that death is a cure for the ills of life.]

Meno

70 MENO: Can you tell me, Socrates, can virtue[1] be taught? Or is it not teachable but the result of practice, or is it neither of these, but men possess it by nature or in some other way?

SOCRATES: Before now, Meno, Thessalians had a high reputation among the Greeks and were admired for their horsemanship and their wealth, but *b* now, it seems to me, they are also admired for their wisdom, not least the fellow citizens of your friend Aristippus of Larissa. The responsibility for this reputation of yours lies with Gorgias,[2] for when he came to your city he found that the leading Aleuadae, your lover Aristippus among them, loved him for his wisdom, and so did the other leading Thessalians. In particular, he accustomed you to give a bold and grand answer to any question you may be asked, as *c* experts are likely to do. Indeed, he himself was ready to answer any Greek who wished to question him, and every question was answered. But here in Athens, my dear Meno, the opposite is the case, as if there were a dearth of wisdom, and wisdom seems to have departed hence to go to you. If then you want to ask *71* one of us that sort of question, everyone will laugh and say: "Good stranger, you must think me happy indeed if you think I know whether virtue can be taught or how it comes to be; I am so far from knowing whether virtue can be taught or not that I do not even have any knowledge of what virtue itself is."

I myself, Meno, am as poor as my fellow citizens *b* in this matter, and I blame myself for my complete ignorance about virtue. If I do not know what something is, how could I know what qualities it possesses? Or do you think that someone who does not know at all who Meno is could know whether he is good-looking or rich or well-born, or the opposite of these? Do you think that is possible?

M: I do not; but, Socrates, do you really not know what virtue is? Are we to report this to the folk back *c* home about you?

S: Not only that, my friend, but also that, as I believe, I have never yet met anyone else who did know.

M: How so? Did you not meet Gorgias when he was here?

S: I did.

M: Did you then not think that he knew?

S: I do not altogether remember, Meno, so that I cannot tell you now what I thought then. Perhaps he does know; you know what he used to say, so you *d* remind me of what he said. You tell me yourself, if you are willing, for surely you share his views.—I do.

S: Let us leave Gorgias out of it, since he is not here. But Meno, by the gods, what do you yourself say that virtue is? Speak and do not begrudge us, so that I may have spoken a most unfortunate untruth when I said that I had never met anyone who knew, if you and Gorgias are shown to know.

M: It is not hard to tell you, Socrates. First, if *e* you want the virtue of a man, it is easy to say that a man's virtue consists of being able to manage public

Reprinted from Plato's *Meno*, translated by G.M.A. Grube (Indianapolis: Hackett Publishing Company, 1976), by permission of the publisher. The translation follows Burnet's Oxford text. The only liberty taken is where the answers to Socrates' questions are very brief, merely indicating assent or the like. In such instances "he said," the so-frequent repetition of which reads awkwardly in English, has been replaced by a dash, to indicate a change of speaker.

1. [The Greek word is *aretē*. It can refer to specific virtues such as moderation, courage, etc., but it is also used for *the* virtue or conglomeration of virtues that makes a man virtuous or good. In this dialogue it is mostly used in this more general sense. Socrates himself at times (e.g., 93b ff.) uses "good" as equivalent to virtuous.—G.M.A.G.]

2. [Gorgias was perhaps the most famous of the earlier generation of Sophists, those traveling teachers who arose in the late fifth century to fill the need for higher education. They all taught rhetoric, or the art of speaking, but as Meno tells us, Gorgias concentrated on this more than the others and made fewer general claims for his teaching (95c). He visited Athens in 427 B.C., and his rhetorical devices gave him an immediate success. Plato named one of his dialogues after him. Fairly substantive fragments of his writings are extant.]

affairs and in so doing to benefit his friends and harm his enemies and to be careful that no harm comes to himself; if you want the virtue of a woman, it is not difficult to describe: she must manage the home well, preserve its possessions, and be submissive to her husband; the virtue of a child, whether male or female, is different again, and so is that of an elderly man, if you want that, or if you want that of a free 72 man or a slave. And there are very many other virtues, so that one is not at a loss to say what virtue is. There is virtue for every action and every age, for every task of ours and every one of us—and Socrates, the same is true for wickedness.

S: I seem to be in great luck, Meno; while I am looking for one virtue, I have found you to have a whole swarm of them. But, Meno, to follow up the *b* image of swarms, if I were asking you what is the nature of bees, and you said that they are many and of all kinds, what would you answer if I asked you: "Do you mean that they are many and varied and different from one another in so far as they are bees? Or are they no different in that regard, but in some other respect, in their beauty, for example, or their size or in some other such way?" Tell me, what would you answer if thus questioned?

M: I would say that they do not differ from one another in being bees.

S: If I went on to say: "Tell me, what is this very thing, Meno, in which they are all the same and do not *c* differ from one another?" Would you be able to tell me?

M: I would.

S: The same is true in the case of the virtues. Even if they are many and various, all of them have one and the same form[3] which makes them virtues, and it is right to look to this when one is asked to make clear what virtue is. Or do you not understand *d* what I mean?

M: I think I understand, but I certainly do not grasp the meaning of the question as fully as I want to.

S: I am asking whether you think it is only in the case of virtue that there is one for man, another for woman and so on, or is the same true in the case of health and size and strength? Do you think that there is one health for man and another for woman? Or, if it is health, does it have the same form everywhere, whether in man or in anything else whatever? *e*

M: The health of a man seems to me the same as that of a woman.

S: And so with size and strength? If a woman is strong, that strength will be the same and have the same form, for by "the same" I mean that strength is no different as far as being strength, whether in a man or a woman. Or do you think there is a difference?

M: I do not think so.

S: And will there be any difference in the case of virtue, as far as being virtue is concerned, whether it be in a child or an old man, in a woman or in a man? 73

M: I think, Socrates, that somehow this is no longer like those other cases.

S: How so? Did you not say that the virtue of a man consists of managing the city well,[4] and that of a woman of managing the household?—I did.

S: Is it possible to manage a city well, or a household, or anything else, while not managing it moderately and justly?—Certainly not.

S: Then if they manage justly and moderately, *b* they must do so with justice and moderation?—Necessarily.

S: So both the man and the woman, if they are to be good, need the same things, justice and moderation.—So it seems.

S: What about a child and an old man? Can they possibly be good if they are intemperate and unjust?—Certainly not.

3. [The Greek term is *eidos*, which Plato was to use for his separately existing eternal Forms. Its common meaning is stature or appearance. Socrates felt that if we apply the same name or epithet to a number of different things or actions, they must surely have a common characteristic to justify the use of the same term. A definition is then a description of this "form" or appearance, which it presents to the mind's eye. In the earlier dialogues however, as here, this form is not thought of as having a separate existence, but as immanent.]

4. [When discussing goodness or morality, social and political virtues would be more immediately present to the Greek mind than they are to ours. In both Plato and Aristotle a good man is above all a good citizen, whereas the modern mind thinks of goodness mainly in more individual terms, such as sobriety or sexual morals. An extreme example of this occurred in a contemporary judge's summation to the jury in the case of a woman of loose sexual behavior who was accused of murdering her husband. He actually said: "This is a case of murder, not of morals. The morals of the accused have nothing to do with it."]

S: But if they are moderate and just?—Yes.

c S: So all human beings are good in the same way, for they become good by acquiring the same qualities.—It seems so.

S: And they would not be good in the same way if they did not have the same virtue.—They certainly would not be.

S: Since then the virtue of all is the same, try to tell me and to remember what Gorgias, and you with him, said that that same thing is.

d M: What else but to be able to rule over people, if you are seeking one description to fit them all.

S: That is indeed what I am seeking, but Meno, is virtue the same in the case of a child or a slave, namely, for them to be able to rule over a master, and do you think that he who rules is still a slave? —I do not think so at all, Socrates.

S: It is not likely, my good man. Consider this further point: you say that virtue is to be able to rule. Shall we not add to this *justly and not unjustly?*

M: I think so, Socrates, for justice is virtue.

e S: Is it virtue, Meno, or a virtue?—What do you mean?

S: As with anything else. For example, if you wish, take roundness, about which I would say that it is a shape, but not simply that it is shape. I would not so speak of it because there are other shapes.

M: You are quite right. So I too say that not only justice is a virtue but there are many other virtues.

74 S: What are they? Tell me, as I could mention other shapes to you if you bade me do so, so do you mention other virtues.

M: I think courage is a virtue, and moderation, wisdom, and munificence, and very many others.

S: We are having the same trouble again, Meno, though in another way; we have found many virtues while looking for one, but we cannot find the one which covers all the others.

b M: I cannot yet find, Socrates, what you are looking for, one virtue for them all, as in the other cases.

S: That is likely, but I am eager, if I can, that we should make progress, for you understand that the same applies to everything. If someone asked you what I mentioned just now: "What is shape, Meno?" and you told him that it was roundness, and if then he said to you what I did: "Is roundness shape or a shape?" you would surely tell him that it is a shape? —I certainly would.

S: That would be because there are other *c* shapes?—Yes.

S: And if he asked you further what they were, you would tell him?—I would.

S: So too, if he asked you what color is, and you said it is white, and your questioner interrupted you, "Is white color or a color?" you would say that it is a color, because there are also other colors?—I would.

S: And if he bade you mention other colors, you would mention others that are no less colors than white is?—Yes. *d*

S: Then if he pursued the argument as I did and said: "We always arrive at the many; do not talk to me in that way, but since you call all these many by one name, and say that no one of them is not a shape even though they are opposites, tell me what this is which applies as much to the round as to the straight and which you call shape, as you say the *e* round is as much a shape as the straight." Do you not say that?—I do.

S: When you speak like that, do you assert that the round is no more round than it is straight, and that the straight is no more straight than it is round?

M: Certainly not, Socrates.

S: Yet you say that the round is no more a shape than the straight is, nor the one more than the other.—That is true.

S: What then is this to which the name shape applies? Try to tell me. If then you answered the man who was questioning about shape or color: "I do not understand what you want, my man, nor what you 75 mean," he would probably wonder and say: "You do not understand that I am seeking that which is the same in all these cases?" Would you still have nothing to say, Meno, if one asked you: "What is this which applies to the round and the straight and the other things which you call shapes and which is the same in them all?" Try to say, that you may practice for your answer about virtue.

M: No, Socrates, but you tell me. *b*

S: Do you want me to do you this favor?

M: I certainly do.

S: And you will then be willing to tell me about virtue?

M: I will.

S: We must certainly press on. The subject is worth it.

M: It surely is.

S: Come then, let us try to tell you what shape is. See whether you will accept that it is this: Let us say that shape is that which alone of existing things always follows color. Is that satisfactory to you, or do *c* you look for it in some other way? I should be satisfied if you defined virtue in this way.

M: But that is foolish, Socrates.

S: How do you mean?

M: That shape, you say, always follows color. Well then, if someone were to say that he did not know what color is, but that he had the same difficulty as he had about shape, what do you think your answer would be?

S: A true one, surely, and if my questioner was one of those clever and disputatious debaters, I would say to him: "I have given my answer; if it is wrong, it is your job to refute it." Then, if they are friends *d* as you and I are, and want to discuss with each other, they must answer in a manner more gentle and more proper to discussion. By this I mean that the answers must not only be true, but in terms admittedly known to the questioner. I too will try to speak in these terms. *e* Do you call something "the end"? I mean such a thing as a limit or boundary, for all those are, I say, the same thing. Prodicus[5] might disagree with us, but you surely call something "finished" or "completed"—that is what I want to express, nothing elaborate.

M: I do, and I think I understand what you mean.

76 S: Further, you call something a plane, and something else a solid, as in geometry?

M: I do.

S: From this you may understand what I mean by shape, for I say this of every shape, that a shape is that which limits a solid; in a word, a shape is the limit of a solid.

M: And what do you say color is, Socrates?

S: You are outrageous, Meno. You bother an *b* old man to answer questions, but you yourself are not willing to recall and to tell me what Gorgias says that virtue is.

M: After you have answered this, Socrates, I will tell you.

S: Even someone who was blindfolded would know from your conversation that you are handsome and still have lovers.

M: Why so?

S: Because you are forever giving orders in a discussion, as spoiled people do, who behave like tyrants as long as they are young. And perhaps you have recognized that I am at a disadvantage with handsome peo- *c* ple, so I will do you the favor of an answer.

M: By all means do me that favor.

S: Do you want me to answer after the manner of Gorgias, which you would most easily follow?

M: Of course I want that.

S: Do you both say there are effluvia of things, as Empedocles[6] does?—Certainly.

S: And that there are channels through which the effluvia make their way?—Definitely.

S: And some effluvia fit some of the channels, *d* while others are too small or too big?—That is so.

S: And there is something which you call sight?—There is.

S: From this, "comprehend what I state," as Pindar said; for color is an effluvium from shapes which fits the sight and is perceived.

M: That seems to me to be an excellent answer, Socrates.

S: Perhaps it was given in the manner to which you are accustomed. At the same time I think that you can deduce from this answer what sound is, and smell, and many such things.—Quite so. *e*

S: It is a theatrical answer[7] so it pleases you, Meno, more than that about shape.—It does.

S: It is not better, son of Alexidemus, but I am convinced that the other is, and I think you would agree, if you did not have to go away before the

5. [Prodicus was a well-known Sophist who was especially keen on the exact meaning of words, and he was fond of making the proper distinctions between words of similar but not identical meanings. We see him in action in the *Protagoras* of Plato (especially 337a–c) where he appears with two other distinguished Sophists, Protagoras and Hippias. His insistence on the proper definition of words would naturally endear him to Socrates who, in Plato, always treats him with more sympathy than he does the other Sophists. The point here is that Prodicus would object to "end," "limit," and "boundary" being treated as "all the same thing."]

6. [Empedocles (c. 493–433 B.C.) of Acragas in Sicily was a famous physical philosopher. For him there were four eternal elements (earth, water, air, and fire), the intermingling and separation of which produced the physical phenomena. The reference here is to his theories of sense perception.]

7. [Theatrical because it brings in the philosophical theories of Empedocles and a quotation from Pindar, instead of being in simple terms such as Socrates' definition of shape.]

mysteries as you told me yesterday, but could remain and be initiated.

M: I would stay, Socrates, if you could tell me 77 many things like these.

S: I shall certainly not be lacking in eagerness to tell you such things, both for your sake and my own, but I may not be able to tell you many. Come now, you too try to fulfill your promise to me and tell me the nature of virtue as a whole and stop making many out of one, as jokers say whenever someone breaks something; but allow virtue to remain whole *b* and sound, and tell me what it is, for I have given you examples.

M: I think, Socrates, that virtue is, as the poet says, "to find joy in beautiful things and have power." So I say that virtue is to desire beautiful things and have the power to acquire them.

S: Do you mean that the man who desires beautiful things desires good things?—Most certainly.

S: Do you assume that there are people who *c* desire bad things, and others who desire good things? Do you not think, my good man, that all men desire good things?

M: I do not.

S: But some desire bad things?—Yes.

S: Do you mean that they believe the bad things to be good, or that they know they are bad and nevertheless desire them?—I think there are both kinds.

S: Do you think, Meno, that anyone, knowing that bad things are bad, nevertheless desires them? —I certainly do.

S: What do you mean by desiring? Is it to secure for oneself?—What else?

d S: Does he think that the bad things benefit him who possesses them, or does he know they harm him?

M: There are some who believe that the bad things benefit them, others who know that the bad things harm them.

S: And do you think that those who believe that bad things benefit them know that they are bad?

M: No, that I cannot altogether believe.

S: It is clear then that those who do not know *e* things to be bad do not desire what is bad, but they desire those things that they believe to be good but that are in fact bad. It follows that those who have no knowledge of these things and believe them to be good clearly desire good things. Is that not so?—It is likely.

S: Well then, those who you say desire bad things, believing that bad things harm their possessor, know that they will be harmed by them?—Necessarily.

S: And do they not think that those who are 78 harmed are miserable to the extent that they are harmed?—That too is inevitable.

S: And that those who are miserable are unhappy?—I think so.

S: Does anyone wish to be miserable and unhappy?—I do not think so, Socrates.

S: No one then wants what is bad, Meno, unless he wants to be such. For what else is being miserable but to desire bad things and secure them?

M: You are probably right, Socrates, and no one *b* wants what is bad.

S: Were you not saying just now that virtue is to desire good things and have the power to secure them?—Yes, I was.

S: The desiring part of this statement is common to everybody, and one man is no better than another in this?—So it appears.

S: Clearly then, if one man is better than another, he must be better at securing them.—Quite so.

S: This then is virtue according to your argument, the power of securing good things. *c*

M: I think, Socrates, that the case is altogether as you now understand it.

S: Let us see then whether what you say is true, for you may well be right. You say that the capacity to acquire good things is virtue?—I do.

S: And by good things you mean, for example, health and wealth?

M: Yes, and also to acquire gold and silver, also honors and offices in the city.

S: By good things you do not mean other goods than these?

M: No, but I mean all things of this kind.

S: Very well. According to Meno, the hereditary *d* guest friend of the Great King, virtue is the acquisition of gold and silver. Do you add to this acquiring, Meno, the words justly and piously, or does it make no difference to you but even if one secures these things unjustly, you call it virtue none the less?

M: Certainly not, Socrates.

S: You would then call it wickedness?—Indeed I would.

S: It seems then that the acquisition must be accompanied by justice or moderation or piety or *e* some other part of virtue; if it is not, it will not be virtue, even though it provides good things.

M: How could there be virtue without these?

S: Then failing to secure gold and silver, whenever it would not be just to do so, either for oneself or another, is not this failure to secure them also virtue?

M: So it seems.

S: Then to provide these goods would not be virtue any more than not to provide them, but apparently whatever is done with justice will be virtue, and what is done without anything of the kind is wickedness?

M: I think it must necessarily be as you say.

S: We said a little while ago that each of these things was a part of virtue, namely, justice and moderation and all such things?—Yes.

S: Then you are playing with me, Meno.—How so, Socrates?

S: Because I begged you just now not to break up or fragment virtue, and I gave examples of how you should answer. You paid no attention, but you tell me that virtue is to be able to secure good things with justice, and this, you say, is a part of virtue.

M: I do.

S: It follows then from what you agree to, that to act in whatever you do with a part of virtue is virtue, for you say that justice is a part of virtue, as are all such qualities. Why do I say this? Because when I begged you to tell me about virtue as a whole, you are far from telling me what it is. Rather, you say that every action is virtue if it is performed with a part of virtue, as if you had told me what virtue as a whole is, and I would already know that, even if you fragment it into parts.[8] I think you must face the same question from the beginning, my dear Meno, namely, what is virtue, if every action performed with a part of virtue is virtue? For that is what one is saying when he says that every action performed with justice is virtue. Do you not think you should face the same question again, or do you think one knows what a part of virtue is if one does not know virtue itself?—I do not think so.

S: If you remember, when I was answering you about shape, we rejected the kind of answer that tried to answer in terms still being the subject of inquiry and not yet agreed upon.—And we were right to reject them.

S: Then surely, my good sir, you must not think, while the nature of virtue as a whole is still under inquiry, that by answering in terms of the parts of virtue you can make its nature clear to anyone or make anything else clear by speaking in this way, but only that the same question must be put to you again—what do you take the nature of virtue to be when you say what you say? Or do you think there is no point in what I am saying?—I think what you say is right.

S: Answer me again then from the beginning: What do you and your friend say that virtue is?

M: Socrates, before I even met you I used to hear that you are always in a state of perplexity and that you bring others to the same state, and now I think you are bewitching and beguiling me, simply putting me under a spell, so that I am quite perplexed. Indeed, if a joke is in order, you seem, in appearance and in every other way, to be like the broad torpedo fish, for it too makes anyone who comes close and touches it feel numb, and you now seem to have had that kind of effect on me, for both my mind and my tongue are numb, and I have no answer to give you. Yet I have made many speeches about virtue before large audiences on a thousand occasions, very good speeches as I thought, but now I cannot even say what it is. I think you are wise not to sail away from Athens to go and stay elsewhere, for if you were to behave like this as a stranger in another city, you would be driven away for practising sorcery.

S: You are a rascal, Meno, and you nearly deceived me.

M: Why so particularly, Socrates?

S: I know why you drew this image of me.

M: Why do you think I did?

S: So that I should draw an image of you in return. I know that all handsome men rejoice in images of themselves; it is to their advantage, for I think that the images of beautiful people are also beautiful, but I will draw no image of you in turn. Now if the torpedo fish is itself numb and so makes others numb, then I resemble it, but not otherwise, for I myself do not have the answer when I perplex others, but I am more perplexed than anyone when I cause perplexity in others. So now I do not know what virtue is; perhaps you knew before you contacted me, but now you are certainly like one who does not know. Nevertheless, I want to examine and seek together with you what it may be.

8. [That is, Meno is including the term to be defined in the definition.]

M: How will you look for it, Socrates, when you do not know at all what it is? How will you aim to search for something you do not know at all? If you should meet with it, how will you know that this is the thing that you did not know?

e S: I know what you want to say, Meno. Do you realize what a debater's argument you are bringing up, that a man cannot search either for what he knows or for what he does not know? He cannot search for what he knows—since he knows it, there is no need to search—nor for what he does not know, for he does not know what to look for.

M: Does that argument not seem sound to *81* you, Socrates?

S: Not to me.

M: Can you tell me why?

S: I can. I have heard wise men and women talk about divine matters. . . .

M: What did they say?

S: What was, I thought, both true and beautiful.

M: What was it, and who were they?

S: The speakers were among the priests and priestesses whose care it is to be able to give an ac- *b* count of their practices. Pindar too says it, and many others of the divine among our poets. What they say is this; see whether you think they speak the truth: They say that the human soul is immortal; at times it comes to an end, which they call dying, at times it is reborn, but it is never destroyed, and one must therefore live one's life as piously as possible:

> Persephone will return to the sun above in the ninth year the souls of those from whom she will exact punish- *c* ment for old miseries, and from these come noble kings, mighty in strength and greatest in wisdom, and for the rest of time men will call them sacred heroes.

As the soul is immortal, has been born often and has seen all things here and in the underworld, there is nothing which it has not learned; so it is in no way surprising that it can recollect the things it knew *d* before, both about virtue and other things. As the whole of nature is akin, and the soul has learned everything, nothing prevents a man, after recalling one thing only—a process men call learning—discovering everything else for himself, if he is brave and does not tire of the search, for searching and learning are, as a whole, recollection. We must, therefore, not believe that debater's argument, for it would make us idle, and fainthearted men like to hear it, whereas my argument makes them energetic and *e* keen on the search. I trust that this is true, and I want to inquire along with you into the nature of virtue.

M: Yes, Socrates, but how do you mean that we do not learn, but that what we call learning is recollection? Can you teach me that this is so?

S: As I said just now, Meno, you are a rascal. You now ask me if I can teach you, when I say there *82* is no teaching but recollection, in order to show me up at once as contradicting myself.

M: No, by Zeus, Socrates, that was not my intention when I spoke, but just a habit. If you can somehow show me that things are as you say, please do so.

S: It is not easy, but I am nevertheless willing to do my best for your sake. Call one of these many *b* attendants of yours, whichever you like, that I may prove it to you in his case.

M: Certainly. You there, come forward.

S: Is he a Greek? Does he speak Greek?

M: Very much so. He was born in my household.

S: Pay attention then whether you think he is recollecting or learning from me.

M: I will pay attention.

S: Tell me now, boy, you know that a square figure is like this?—I do.

S: A square then is a figure in which all these *c* four sides are equal?—Yes indeed.

S: And it also has these lines through the middle equal?[9]—Yes.

S: And such a figure could be larger or smaller?—Certainly.

S: If then this side were two feet, and this other

9. [Socrates draws a square ABCD. The sides are of course equal, and the "lines through the middle" are the lines joining the middle points of these sides, which also go through the center of the square, namely EF and GH. He then assumes the sides to be two feet.]

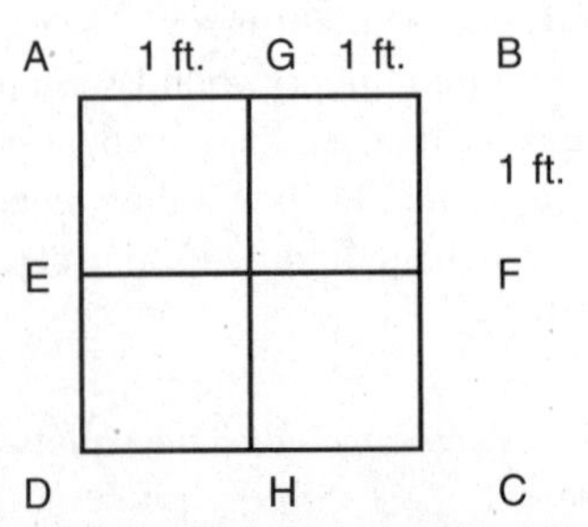

side two feet, how many feet would the whole be? Consider it this way: if it were two feet this way, and only one foot that way, the figure[10] would be once two feet?—Yes.

d S: But if it is two feet also that way, it would surely be twice two feet?—Yes.

S: How many feet is twice two feet? Work it out and tell me.—Four, Socrates.

S: Now we could have another figure twice the size of this one, with the four sides equal like this one.—Yes.

S: How many feet will that be?—Eight.

S: Come now, try to tell me how long each side e of this will be. The side of this is two feet. What about each side of the one which is its double?—Obviously, Socrates, it will be twice the length.

S: You see, Meno, that I am not teaching the boy anything, but all I do is question him. And now he thinks he knows the length of the line on which an eight-foot figure is based. Do you agree?

M: I do.

S: And does he know?

M: Certainly not.

S: He thinks it is a line twice the length?

M: Yes.

S: Watch him now recollecting things in order, as one must recollect. Tell me, boy, do you say that 83 a figure double the size is based on a line double the length? Now I mean such a figure as this, not long on one side and short on the other, but equal in every direction like this one, and double the size, that is, eight feet. See whether you still believe that it will be based on a line double the length.—I do.

S: Now the line becomes double its length if we add another of the same length here?—Yes indeed.

S: And the eight-foot square will be based on it, if there are four lines of that length?—Yes.

b S: Well, let us draw from it four equal lines, and surely that is what you say is the eight-foot square?—Certainly.

S: And within this figure are four squares, each of which is equal to the four-foot square?—Yes.

S: How big is it then? Is it not four times as big?—Of course.

S: Is this square then, which is four times as big, its double?—No, by Zeus.

S: How many times bigger is it?—Four times.

S: Then, my boy, the figure based on a line c twice the length is not double but four times as big?—You are right.

S: And four times four is sixteen, is it not?—Yes.

S: On how long a line should the eight-foot square be based? On *this* line we have a square that is four times bigger, do we not?—Yes.

S: Now this four-foot square is based on this line here, half the length?—Yes.

S: Very well. Is the eight-foot square not double this one and half that one?[11]—Yes.

S: Will it not be based on a line longer than this one and shorter than that one? Is that not so?—I d think so.

S: Good, you answer what you think. And tell me, was this one not two feet long, and that one four feet?—Yes.

S: The line on which the eight-foot square is based must then be longer than this one of two feet, and shorter than that one of four feet?—It must be.

S: Try to tell me then how long a line you say e it is.—Three feet.

S: Then if it is three feet, let us add the half of this one, and it will be three feet? For these are two feet, and the other is one. And here, similarly, these are two feet and that one is one foot, and so the figure you mention comes to be?—Yes.

S: Now if it is three feet this way and three feet that way, will the whole figure be three times three feet?—So it seems.

S: How much is three times three feet?—Nine feet.

S: And the double square was to be how many feet?—Eight.

S: So the eight-foot figure cannot be based on the three-foot line?—Clearly not.

S: But on how long a line? Try to tell us exactly, 84 and if you do not want to work it out, show me from what line.—By Zeus, Socrates, I do not know.

S: You realize, Meno, what point he has reached

10. [That is, the rectangle ABFE, which is obviously two square feet.]

11. [That is, the eight-foot square is double the four-foot square and half the sixteen-foot square, double the square based on a line two feet long, and half the square based on a four-foot side, so it must be based on a line between two and four feet in length. The slave naturally suggests three feet, but that gives a nine-foot square, and is still wrong (83e).]

in his recollection. At first he did not know what the basic line of the eight-foot square was; even now he does not yet know, but then he thought he knew, and answered confidently as if he did know, and he did not think himself at a loss, but now he does think *b* himself at a loss, and as he does not know, neither does he think he knows.

M: That is true.

S: So he is now in a better position with regard to the matter he does not know?

M: I agree with that too.

S: Have we done him any harm by making him perplexed and numb as the torpedo fish does?

M: I do not think so.

S: Indeed, we have probably achieved something relevant to finding out how matters stand, for now, as he does not know, he would be glad to find out, whereas before he thought he could easily make many fine speeches to large audiences about the *c* square of double size and said that it must have a base twice as long.

M: So it seems.

S: Do you think that before he would have tried to find out that which he thought he knew though he did not, before he fell into perplexity and realized he did not know and longed to know?

M: I do not think so, Socrates.

S: Has he then benefitted from being numbed?

M: I think so.

S: Look then how he will come out of his perplexity while searching along with me. I shall do nothing more than ask questions and not teach him. *d* Watch whether you find me teaching and explaining things to him instead of asking for his opinion.

S: You tell me, is this not a four-foot figure? You understand?—I do.

S: We add to it this figure which is equal to it?—Yes.

S: And we add this third figure equal to each of them?—Yes.

S: Could we then fill in the space in the corner?—Certainly.[12]

S: So we have these four equal figures?—Yes.

S: Well then, how many times is the whole figure larger than this one?[13]—Four times. *e*

S: But we should have had one that was twice as large, or do you not remember?—I certainly do.

S: Does not this line from one corner to the other cut each of these figures in two?[14]—Yes. 85

S: So these are four equal lines which enclose this figure?—They are.

S: Consider now: how large is the figure?—I do not understand.

S: Within these four figures, each line cuts off half of each, does it not?—Yes.

S: How many of this size are there in this figure?—Four.

S: How many in this?—Two.

S: What is the relation of four to two?—Double. *b*

S: How many feet in this?—Eight.

S: Based on what line?—This one.

S: That is, on the line that stretches from corner to corner of the four-foot figure?—Yes.—Clever men call this the diagonal, so that if diagonal is its name, you say that the double figure would be that based on the diagonal?—Most certainly, Socrates.

S: What do you think, Meno? Has he, in his answers, expressed any opinion that was not his own? *c*

M: No, they were all his own.

S: And yet, as we said a short time ago, he did not know?—That is true.

S: So these opinions were in him, were they not?—Yes.

S: So the man who does not know has within himself true opinions about the things that he does not know?—So it appears.

S: These opinions have now just been stirred up like a dream, but if he were repeatedly asked these same questions in various ways, you know that in the *d* end his knowledge about these things would be as accurate as anyone's.—It is likely.

S: And he will know it without having been

12. [Socrates now builds up his sixteen-foot square by joining three four-foot squares. Filling "the space in the corner" will give another four-foot square, which completes the sixteen-foot square containing four four-foot squares.]

13. ["This one" is any one of the inside squares of four feet.]

14. [Socrates now draws the diagonals of the four inside squares, namely FH, HE, EG, and GF, which together form the square GFHEG. We should note that Socrates here introduces a new element, which is not the result of a question but of his own knowledge, though the answer to the problem follows from questions. The new square contains four halves of a four-foot square, and is therefore eight feet.]

taught but only questioned, and find the knowledge within himself?—Yes.

S: And is not finding knowledge within oneself recollection?—Certainly.

S: Must he not either have at some time acquired the knowledge he now possesses, or else have always possessed it?—Yes.

S: If he always had it, he would always have *e* known. If he acquired it, he cannot have done so in his present life. Or has someone taught him geometry? For he will perform in the same way about all geometry, and all other knowledge. Has someone taught him everything? You should know, especially as he has been born and brought up in your house.

M: But I know that no one has taught him.

S: Yet he has these opinions, or doesn't he?

M: That seems indisputable, Socrates.

86 S: If he has not acquired them in his present life, is it not clear that he had them and had learned them at some other time?—It seems so.

S: Then that was the time when he was not a human being?—Yes.

S: If then, during the time he exists and is not a human being he will have true opinions which, when stirred by questioning, become knowledge, will not his soul have learned during all time? For it is clear that during all time he exists, either as a man or not.—So it seems.

b S: Then if the truth about reality is always in our soul, the soul would be immortal so that you should always confidently try to seek out and recollect what you do not know at present—that is, what you do not recollect?[15]

M: Somehow, Socrates, I think that what you say is right.

S: I think so too, Meno. I do not insist that my argument is right in all other respects, but I would contend at all costs both in word and deed as far as I could that we will be better men, braver and less idle, if we believe that one must search for the things *c* one does not know, rather than if we believe that it is not possible to find out what we do not know and that we must not look for it.

15. [This is what the whole passage on recollection with the slave is intended to prove, namely, that the sophism introduced by Meno—that one cannot find out what one does not know—is false.]

M: In this too I think you are right, Socrates.

S: Since we are of one mind that one should seek to find out what one does not know, shall we try to find out together what virtue is?

M: Certainly. But Socrates, I should be most pleased to investigate and hear your answer to my original question, whether we should try on the as- *d* sumption that virtue is something teachable, or is a natural gift, or in whatever way it comes to men.

S: If I were directing you, Meno, and not only myself, we would not have investigated whether virtue is teachable or not before we had investigated what virtue itself is. But because you do not even attempt to rule yourself, in order that you may be free, but you try to rule me and do so, I will agree with you—for what can I do? So we must, it appears, inquire into the qualities of something the nature of which *e* we do not yet know. However, please relax your rule a little bit for me and agree to investigate whether it is teachable or not by means of a hypothesis. I mean the way geometers often carry on their investigations. For example, if they are asked whether a specific area 87 can be inscribed in the form of a triangle within a given circle, one of them might say: "I do not yet know whether that area has that property, but I think I have, as it were, a hypothesis that is of use for the problem, namely this: If that area is such that when one has applied it as a rectangle to the given straight line in the circle it is deficient by a figure similar to *b* the very figure which is applied, then I think one alternative results, whereas another results if it is impossible for this to happen. So, by using this hypothesis, I am willing to tell you what results with regard to inscribing it in the circle—that is, whether it is impossible or not." So let us speak about virtue also, since we do not know either what it is or what qualities it possesses, and let us investigate whether it is teachable or not by means of a hypothesis, and say this: Among the things existing in the soul, of what sort is virtue, that it should be teachable or not? First, if it is another sort than knowledge, is it teachable or not, or, as we were just saying, recollectable? Let it *c* make no difference to us which term we use: Is it teachable? Or is it plain to anyone that men cannot be taught anything but knowledge?—I think so.

S: But, if virtue is a kind of knowledge, it is clear that it could be taught.—Of course.

S: We have dealt with that question quickly, that

if it is of one kind it can be taught, if it is of a different kind, it cannot.—We have indeed.

S: The next point to consider seems to be *d* whether virtue is knowledge or something else. —That does seem to be the next point to consider.

S: Well now, do we say that virtue is itself something good, and will this hypothesis stand firm for us, that it is something good?—Of course.

S: If then there is anything else good that is different and separate from knowledge, virtue might well not be a kind of knowledge; but if there is nothing good that knowledge does not encompass, we would be right to suspect that it is a kind of knowledge. —That is so.

e S: Surely virtue makes us good?—Yes.

S: And if we are good, we are beneficent, for all that is good is beneficial. Is that not so?—Yes.

S: So virtue is something beneficial?

M: That necessarily follows from what has been agreed.

S: Let us then examine what kinds of things benefit us, taking them up one by one: health, we say, and strength, and beauty, and also wealth. We say that these things, and others of the same kind, benefit us, do we not?—We do.

S: Yet we say that these same things also some-88 times harm one. Do you agree or not?—I do.

S: Look then, what directing factor determines in each case whether these things benefit or harm us? Is it not the right use of them that benefits us, and the wrong use that harms us?—Certainly.

S: Let us now look at the qualities of the soul. There is something you call moderation, and justice, courage, intelligence, memory, munificence, and all such things?—There is.

b S: Consider whichever of these you believe not to be knowledge but different from it; do they not at times harm us, at other times benefit us? Courage, for example, when it is not wisdom but like a kind of recklessness: when a man is reckless without understanding, he is harmed; when with understanding, he is benefitted.—Yes.

S: The same is true of moderation and mental quickness; when they are learned and disciplined with understanding they are beneficial, but without understanding they are harmful?—Very much so.

c S: Therefore, in a word, all that the soul undertakes and endures, if directed by wisdom, ends in happiness, but if directed by ignorance, it ends in the opposite?—That is likely.

S: If then virtue is something in the soul and it must be beneficial, it must be knowledge, since all the qualities of the soul are in themselves neither *d* beneficial nor harmful, but accompanied by wisdom or folly they become harmful or beneficial. This argument shows that virtue, being beneficial, must be a kind of wisdom.—I agree.

S: Furthermore, those other things we were mentioning just now, wealth and the like, are at times good and at times harmful. Just as for the rest of the soul the direction of wisdom makes things beneficial, but harmful if directed by folly, so in these cases, if the soul *e* uses and directs them right it makes them beneficial, but bad use makes them harmful?—Quite so.

S: The wise soul directs them right, the foolish soul wrongly?—That is so.

S: So one may say this about everything; all other human activities depend on the soul, and those of the soul itself depend on wisdom if they are to be good. 89 According to this argument the beneficial would be wisdom, and we say that virtue is beneficial?—Certainly.

S: Virtue then, as a whole or in part, is wisdom?

M: What you say, Socrates, seems to me quite right.

S: Then, if that is so, the good are not so by nature?—I do not think they are.

S: For if they were, this would follow: if the good *b* were so by nature, we would have people who knew which among the young were by nature good; we would take those whom they had pointed out and guard them in the Acropolis, sealing them up there much more carefully than gold so that no one could corrupt them, and when they reached maturity they would be useful to their cities.—Reasonable enough, Socrates.

S: Since the good are not good by nature, does *c* learning make them so?

M: Necessarily, as I now think, Socrates, and clearly, on our hypothesis, if virtue is knowledge, it can be taught.

S: Perhaps, by Zeus, but may it be that we were not right to agree to this?

M: Yet it seemed to be right at the time.

S: We should not only think it right at the time, but also now and in the future if it is to be at all sound.

d M: What is the difficulty? What do you have in mind that you do not like about it and doubt that virtue is knowledge?

S: I will tell you, Meno. I am not saying that it is wrong to say that virtue is teachable if it is knowledge, but look whether it is reasonable of me to doubt whether it is knowledge. Tell me this: if not only virtue but anything whatever can be taught, should there not be of necessity people who teach it and people who learn it?—I think so.

e S: Then again, if on the contrary there are no teachers or learners of something, we should be right to assume that the subject cannot be taught?

M: Quite so, but do you think that there are no teachers of virtue?

S: I have often tried to find out whether there were any teachers of it, but in spite of all my efforts I cannot find any. And yet I have searched for them with the help of many people, especially those whom I believed to be most experienced in this matter. And now, Meno, Anytus[16] here has opportunely come to sit down by us. Let us share our search with him. It *90* would be reasonable for us to do so, for Anytus, in the first place, is the son of Anthemion, a man of wealth and wisdom, who did not become rich automatically or as the result of a gift like Ismenias the Theban, who recently acquired the possessions of Polycrates, but through his own wisdom and efforts. Further, he did not seem to be an arrogant or puffed up or offensive citizen in other ways, but he was a *b* well-mannered and well-behaved man. Also he gave our friend here a good upbringing and education, as the majority of Athenians believe, for they are electing him to the highest offices. It is right then to look for the teachers of virtue with the help of men such as he, whether there are any and if so who they are. Therefore, Anytus, please join me and your guest friend Meno here, in our inquiry as to who are the teachers of virtue. Look at it in this way: if we wanted *c* Meno to become a good physician, to what teachers would we send him? Would we not send him to the physicians?

A: Certainly.

S: And if we wanted him to be a good shoemaker, to shoemakers?—Yes.

S: And so with other pursuits?—Certainly.

S: Tell me again on this same topic, like this: we say that we would be right to send him to the physicians if we want him to become a physician; whenever we say that, we mean that it would be *d* reasonable to send him to those who practice the craft rather than to those who do not, and to those who exact fees for this very practice and have shown themselves to be teachers of anyone who wishes to come to them and learn. Is it not with this in mind that we would be right to send him?—Yes.

S: And the same is true about flute-playing and the other crafts? It would be very foolish for those *e* who want to make someone a fluteplayer to refuse to send him to those who profess to teach the craft and make money at it, but to send him to make trouble for others by seeking to learn from those who do not claim to be teachers or have a single pupil in that subject which we want the one we send to learn from them? Do you not think it very unreasonable to do so?—By Zeus, I do, and also very ignorant.

S: Quite right. However, you can now deliberate with me about our guest friend Meno here. He has been telling me for some time, Anytus, that he longs *91* to acquire that wisdom and virtue which enables men to manage their households and their cities well, to take care of their parents, to know how to welcome and to send away both citizens and strangers as a good man should. Consider to whom we should be *b* right to send him to learn this virtue. Or is it obvious in view of what was said just now that we should send him to those who profess to be teachers of virtue and have shown themselves to be available to any Greek who wishes to learn, and for this fix a fee and exact it?

A: And who do you say these are, Socrates?

S: You surely know yourself that they are those whom men call sophists.

A: By Heracles, hush, Socrates. May no one of *c* my household or friends, whether citizen or stranger, be mad enough to go to these people and be harmed by them, for they clearly cause the ruin and corruption of their followers.

16. [Anytus was a successful democratic politician in Athens. His success must have come after the restoration of democratic government in Athens in 403 B.C., whereas Meno himself joined the expedition of Cyrus in 401 and never came back to Greece. So the conversation must have taken place about 402. Anytus was one of Socrates' accusers in 399, and Plato obviously expects his readers to have this in mind.]

S: How do you mean, Anytus? Are these people, alone of those who claim the knowledge to benefit one, so different from the others that they not only do not benefit what one entrusts to them but on the *d* contrary corrupt it, even though they obviously expect to make money from the process? I find I cannot believe you, for I know that one man, Protagoras, made more money from this knowledge of his than Phidias who made such notably fine works, and ten other sculptors. Surely what you say is extraordinary, if those who mend old sandals and restore clothes *e* would be found out within the month if they returned the clothes and sandals in a worse state than they received them; if they did this they would soon die of starvation, but the whole of Greece has not noticed for forty years that Protagoras corrupts those who frequent him and sends them away in a worse moral condition than he received them. I believe that he was nearly seventy when he died and had practiced his craft for forty years. During all that time to this very day his reputation has stood high; and not only Protagoras but a great many others, some born before 92 him and some still alive today. Are we to say that you maintain that they deceive and harm the young knowingly, or that they themselves are not aware of it? Are we to deem those whom some people consider the wisest of men to be so mad as that?

A: They are far from being mad, Socrates. It is much rather those among the young who pay their *b* fees who are mad, and even more the relatives who entrust their young to them, and most of all the cities who allow them to come in and do not drive out any citizen or stranger who attempts to behave in this manner.

S: Has some sophist wronged you, Anytus, or why are you so hard on them?

A: No, by Zeus, I have never met one of them, nor would I allow any one of my people to do so.

S: Are you then altogether without any experience of these men?

A: And may I remain so.

c S: How then, my good sir, can you know whether there is any good in their instruction or not, if you are altogether without experience of it?

A: Easily, for I know who they are, whether I have experience of them or not.

S: Perhaps you are a wizard, Anytus, for I wonder, from what you yourself say, how else you know about these things. However, let us not try to find *d* out who the men are whose company would make Meno wicked—let them be the Sophists if you like—but tell us, and benefit your family friend here by telling him, to whom he should go in so large a city to acquire, to any worthwhile degree, the virtue I was just now describing.

A: Why did you not tell him yourself?

S: I did mention those whom I thought to be teachers of it, but you say I am wrong, and perhaps *e* you are right. You tell him in your turn to whom among the Athenians he should go. Tell him the name of anyone you want.

A: Why give him the name of one individual? Any Athenian gentleman he may meet, if he is willing to be persuaded, will make him a better man than the sophists would.

S: And have these gentlemen become virtuous automatically, without learning from anyone, and are 93 they able to teach others what they themselves never learned?

A: I believe that these men have learned from those who were gentlemen before them; or do you not think that there are many good men in this city?

S: I believe, Anytus, that there are many men here who are good at public affairs, and that there have been as many in the past, but have they been good teachers of their own virtue? That is the point we are discussing, not whether there are good men here or not, or whether there have been in the past, *b* but we have been investigating for some time whether virtue can be taught. And in the course of that investigation we are inquiring whether the good men of today and of the past knew how to pass on to another the virtue they themselves possessed, or whether a man cannot pass it on or receive it from another. This is what Meno and I have been investigating for some time. Look at it this way, from what you yourself have said. Would you not say that Themistocles was *c* a good man?—Yes. Even the best of men.

S: And therefore a good teacher of his own virtue if anyone was?

A: I think so, if he wanted to be.

S: But do you think he did not want some other people to be worthy men, and especially his own son? Or do you think he begrudged him this, and *d* deliberately did not pass on to him his own virtue? Have you not heard that Themistocles taught his son Cleophantus to be a good horseman? He could remain standing upright on horseback and shoot javelins from that position and do many other remarkable things which his father had him taught and made skillful at, all of which required good teachers. Have you not heard this from your elders?—I have.

S: So one could not blame the poor natural *e* talents of the son for his failure in virtue?—Perhaps not.

S: But have you ever heard anyone, young or old, say that Cleophantus, the son of Themistocles, was a good and wise man at the same pursuits as his father?—Never.

S: Are we to believe that he wanted to educate his son in those other things but not to do better than his neighbors in that skill which he himself possessed, if indeed virtue can be taught?—Perhaps not, by Zeus.

S: And yet he was, as you yourself agree, among *94* the best teachers of virtue in the past. Let us consider another man, Aristides, the son of Lysimachus. Do you not agree that he was good?—I very definitely do.

S: He too gave his own son Lysimachus the best Athenian education in matters which are the business of teachers, and do you think he made him a better man than anyone else? For you have been in his *b* company and seen the kind of man he is. Or take Pericles, a man of such magnificent wisdom. You know that he brought up two sons, Paralus and Xanthippus?—I know.

S: You also know that he taught them to be as good horsemen as any Athenian, that he educated them in the arts, in gymnastics, and in all else that was a matter of skill not to be inferior to anyone, but did he not want to make them good men? I think he did, but this could not be taught. And lest you think that only a few most inferior Athenians are incapable in this respect, reflect that Thucydides[17] too brought *c* up two sons, Melesias and Stephanus, that he educated them well in all other things. They were the best wrestlers in Athens—he entrusted the one to Xanthias and the other to Eudorus, who were thought to be the best wrestlers of the day, or do you not remember?

A: I remember I have heard that said.

17. [Not the historian but Thucydides, the son of Melesias, an Athenian statesman who was an opponent of Pericles and who was ostracized in 440 B.C.]

S: It is surely clear that he would not have taught *d* his boys what it costs money to teach, but have failed to teach them what costs nothing—making them good men—if that could be taught? Or was Thucydides perhaps an inferior person who had not many friends among the Athenians and the allies? He belonged to a great house; he had great influence in the city and among the other Greeks, so that if virtue could be taught he would have found the man who could make his sons good men, be it a citizen or a stranger, if he himself did not have the time because *e* of his public concerns. But, friend Anytus, virtue can certainly not be taught.

A: I think, Socrates, that you easily speak ill of people. I would advise you, if you will listen to me, to be careful. Perhaps also in another city, and certainly here, it is easier to injure people than to benefit them. I think you know that yourself. *95*

S: I think, Meno, that Anytus is angry, and I am not at all surprised. He thinks, to begin with, that I am slandering those men, and then he believes himself to be one of them. If he ever realizes what slander is, he will cease from anger, but he does not know it now. You tell me, are there not worthy men among your people?—Certainly.

S: Well now, are they willing to offer themselves *b* to the young as teachers? Do they agree they are teachers, and that virtue can be taught?

M: No, by Zeus, Socrates, but sometimes you would hear them say that it can be taught, at other times, that it cannot.

S: Should we say that they are teachers of this subject, when they do not even agree on this point?—I do not think so, Socrates.

S: Further, do you think that these Sophists, who alone profess to be so, are teachers of virtue?

M: I admire this most in Gorgias, Socrates, that *c* you would never hear him promising this. Indeed, he ridicules the others when he hears them making this claim. He thinks one should make people clever speakers.

S: You do not think then that the Sophists are teachers?

M: I cannot tell, Socrates; like most people, at times I think they are, at other times I think that they are not.

S: Do you know that not only you and the other public men at times think that it can be taught, at *d* other times that it cannot, but that the poet Theognis[18] says the same thing?—Where?

S: In his elegiacs: "Eat and drink with these men, and keep their company. Please those whose *e* power is great, for you will learn goodness from the good. If you mingle with bad men you will lose even what wit you possess." You see that here he speaks as if virtue can be taught?—So it appears.

S: Elsewhere, he changes somewhat: "If this could be done" he says, "and intelligence could be instilled," somehow those who could do this "would collect large and numerous fees," and further: "Never would a bad son be born of a good father, for he 96 would be persuaded by wise words, but you will never make a bad man good by teaching." You realize that the poet is contradicting himself on the same subject?—He seems to be.

S: Can you mention any other subject of which those who claim to be teachers not only are not recognized to be teachers of others but are not recognized to have knowledge of it themselves, and are thought to *b* be poor in the very matter which they profess to teach? Or any other subject of which those who are recognized as worthy teachers at one time say it can be taught and at other times that it cannot? Would you say that people who are so confused about a subject can be effective teachers of it?—No, by Zeus, I would not.

S: If then neither the Sophists nor the worthy people themselves are teachers of this subject, clearly there would be no others?—I do not think there are.

c S: If there are no teachers, neither are there pupils?—As you say.

S: And we agreed that a subject that has neither teachers nor pupils is not teachable?—We have so agreed.

S: Now there seem to be no teachers of virtue anywhere?—That is so.

S: If there are no teachers, there are no learners?—That seems so.

S: Then virtue cannot be taught?

d M: Apparently not, if we have investigated this correctly. I certainly wonder, Socrates, whether there are no good men either, or in what way good men come to be.

S: We are probably poor specimens, you and I, Meno. Gorgias has not adequately educated you, nor Prodicus me. We must then at all costs turn our attention to ourselves and find someone who will in some way make us better. I say this in view of our *e* recent investigation, for it is ridiculous that we failed to see that it is not only under the guidance of knowledge that men succeed in their affairs, and that is perhaps why the knowledge of how good men come to be escapes us.

M: How do you mean, Socrates?

S: I mean this: we were right to agree that good men must be beneficent, and that this could not be otherwise. Is that not so?—Yes.

S: And that they will be beneficent if they give us correct guidance in our affairs. To this too we were right to agree?—Yes. 97

S: But that one cannot guide correctly if one does not have knowledge; to this our agreement is likely to be incorrect.—How do you mean?

S: I will tell you. A man who knew the way to Larissa, or anywhere else you like, and went there and guided others would surely lead them well and correctly?—Certainly.

S: What if someone had had a correct opinion *b* as to which was the way but had not gone there nor indeed had knowledge of it, would he not also lead correctly?—Certainly.

S: And as long as he has the right opinion about that of which the other has knowledge, he will not be a worse guide than the one who knows, as he has a true opinion, though not knowledge.—In no way worse.

S: So true opinion is in no way a worse guide to correct action than knowledge. It is this that we omitted in our investigation of the nature of virtue, *c* when we said that only knowledge can lead to correct action, for true opinion can do so also.—So it seems.

S: So correct opinion is no less useful than knowledge?

M: Yes, to this extent, Socrates. But the man who has knowledge will always succeed, whereas he who has true opinion will only succeed at times.

S: How do you mean? Will he who has the right opinion not always succeed, as long as his opinion is right?

M: That appears to be so of necessity, and it makes me wonder, Socrates, this being the case, why *d*

18. [Theognis was a poet of mid-sixth century B.C. A collection of poems is extant (about twelve hundred lines), but the authenticity of a good deal of it is doubtful.]

knowledge is prized far more highly than right opinion, and why they are different.

S: Do you know why you wonder, or shall I tell you?—By all means tell me.

S: It is because you have paid no attention to the statues of Daedalus, but perhaps there are none in Thessaly.

M: What do you have in mind when you say this?

S: That they too run away and escape if one *e* does not tie them down but remain in place if tied down.—So what?

S: To acquire an untied work of Daedalus is not worth much, like acquiring a runaway slave, for it does not remain, but it is worth much if tied down, for his works are very beautiful. What am I thinking of when I say this? True opinions. For true opinions, 98 as long as they remain, are a fine thing and all they do is good, but they are not willing to remain long, and they escape from a man's mind, so that they are not worth much until one ties them down by (giving) an account of the reason why. And that, Meno my friend, is recollection, as we previously agreed. After they are tied down, in the first place they become knowledge, and then they remain in place. That is why knowledge is prized higher than correct opinion, and knowledge differs from correct opinion in being tied down.

M: Yes, by Zeus, Socrates, it seems to be something like that.

b S: Indeed, I too speak as one who does not have knowledge but is guessing. However, I certainly do not think I am guessing that right opinion is a different thing from knowledge. If I claim to know anything else—and I would make that claim about few things—I would put this down as one of the things I know.—Rightly so, Socrates.

S: Well then, is it not correct that when true opinion guides the course of every action, it does no worse than knowledge?—I think you are right in this too.

c S: Correct opinion is then neither inferior to knowledge nor less useful in directing actions, nor is the man who has it less so than he who has knowledge.—That is so.

S: And we agreed that the good man is beneficent?—Yes.

S: Since then it is not only through knowledge but also through right opinion that men are good, and *d* beneficial to their cities when they are, and neither knowledge nor true opinion come to men by nature but are acquired—or do you think either of these comes by nature?—I do not think so.

S: Then if they do not come by nature, men are not so by nature either.—Surely not.

S: As goodness does not come by nature, we inquired next whether it could be taught.—Yes.

S: We thought it could be taught, if it was knowledge?—Yes.

S: And that it was knowledge if it could be taught?—Quite so.

S: And that if there were teachers of it, it could *e* be taught, but if there were not, it was not teachable?—That is so.

S: And then we agreed that there were no teachers of it?—We did.

S: So we agreed that it was neither teachable nor knowledge?—Quite so.

S: But we certainly agree that virtue is a good thing?—Yes.

S: And that which guides correctly is both useful and good?—Certainly.

S: And that only these two things, true belief 99 and knowledge, guide correctly, and that if a man possesses these he gives correct guidance. The things that turn out right by some chance are not due to human guidance, but where there is correct human guidance it is due to two things, true belief or knowledge.—I think that is so.

S: Now because it cannot be taught, virtue no longer seems to be knowledge?—It seems not.

S: So one of the two good and useful things has *b* been excluded, and knowledge is not the guide in public affairs?—I do not think so.

S: So it is not by some kind of wisdom, or by being wise, that such men lead their cities, those such as Themistocles and those mentioned by Anytus just now? That is the reason why they cannot make others be like themselves, because it is not knowledge which makes them what they are.

M: It is likely to be as you say, Socrates.

S: Therefore, if it is not through knowledge, the only alternative is that it is through right opinion that *c* statesmen follow the right course for their cities. As regards knowledge, they are no different from soothsayers and prophets. They too say many true things when inspired, but they have no knowledge of what they are saying.—That is probably so.

S: And so, Meno, is it right to call divine these men who, without any understanding, are right in much that is of importance in what they say and do?—Certainly.

S: We should be right to call divine also those *d* soothsayers and prophets whom we just mentioned, and all the poets, and we should call no less divine and inspired those public men who are no less under the gods' influence and possession, as their speeches lead to success in many important matters, though they have no knowledge of what they are saying.—Quite so.

S: Women too, Meno, call good men divine, and the Spartans, when they eulogize someone, say "This man is divine."

e M: And they appear to be right, Socrates, though perhaps Anytus here will be annoyed with you for saying so.

S: I do not mind that; we shall talk to him again, but if we were right in the way in which we spoke and investigated in this whole discussion, virtue would be neither an inborn quality nor taught, but comes to those who possess it as a gift from the gods which is not accompanied by understanding, unless there *100* is someone among our statesmen who can make another into a statesman. If there were one, he could be said to be among the living as Homer said Teiresias was among the dead, namely, that "he alone retained his wits while the others flitted about like shadows." In the same manner such a man would, as far as virtue is concerned, here also be the only true reality compared, as it were, with shadows.

M: I think that is an excellent way to put it, Socrates. *b*

S: It follows from this reasoning, Meno, that virtue appears to be present in those of us who may possess it as a gift from the gods. We shall have clear knowledge of this when, before we investigate how it comes to be present in men, we first try to find out what virtue in itself is. But now the time has come for me to go. You convince your guest friend Anytus here of these very things of which you have yourself been convinced, in order that he may be more amenable. If you succeed, you will also confer a benefit upon the Athenians.

Symposium

172 APOLLODORUS: In fact, your question does not find me unprepared. Just the other day, as it happens, I was walking to the city from my home in Phaleron when a man I know, who was making his way behind me, saw me and called from a distance:

"The gentleman from Phaleron!" he yelled, trying to be funny. "Hey, Apollodorus, wait!"

So I stopped and waited.

"Apollodorus, I've been looking for you!" he said. *b* "You know there once was a gathering at Agathon's when Socrates, Alcibiades, and their friends had dinner together; I wanted to ask you about the speeches they made on Love. What were they? I heard a version from a man who had it from Phoenix, Philip's son, but it was badly garbled, and he said you were the one to ask. So please, will you tell me all about it? After all, Socrates is your friend—who has a better right than you to report his conversation? But before you begin," he added, "tell me this: were you there yourself?"

c "Your friend must have really garbled his story," I replied, "if you think this affair was so recent that I could have been there."

"I did think that," he said.

"Glaucon, how could you? You know very well Agathon hasn't lived in Athens for many years, while 173 it's been less than three that I've been Socrates' companion and made it my job to know exactly what he says and does each day. Before that, I simply drifted aimlessly. Of course, I used to think that what I was doing was important, but in fact I was the most worthless man on earth—as bad as you are this very moment: I used to think philosophy was the last thing a man should do."

"Stop joking, Apollodorus," he replied. "Just tell me when the party took place."

"When we were still children, when Agathon won the prize with his first tragedy. It was the day after he and his troupe held their victory celebration."

Reprinted from Plato, *Symposium*, translated by Alexander Nehamas and Paul Woodruff (Indianapolis: Hackett Publishing Company, 1989), by permission of the publisher.

"So it really was a long time ago," he said. "Then who told you about it? Was it Socrates himself?"

"Oh, for god's sake, of course not!" I replied. "It *b* was the very same man who told Phoenix, a fellow called Aristodemus, from Cydatheneum, a real runt of a man, who always went barefoot. He went to the party because, I think, he was obsessed with Socrates—one of the worst cases at that time. Naturally, I checked part of his story with Socrates, and Socrates agreed with his account."

"Please tell me, then," he said. "You speak and I'll listen, as we walk to the city. This is the perfect opportunity."

So this is what we talked about on our way; and *c* that's why, as I said before, I'm not unprepared. Well, if I'm to tell *you* about it too—I'll be glad to. After all, my greatest pleasure comes from philosophical conversation, even if I'm only a listener, whether or not I think it will be to my advantage. All other talk, especially the talk of rich businessmen like you, bores me to tears, and I'm sorry for you and your friends because you think your affairs are important when *d* really they're totally trivial. Perhaps, in your turn, you think I'm a failure, and, believe me, I think that what you think is true. But as for all of you, I don't just *think* you are failures—I know it for a fact.

FRIEND: You'll never change, Apollodorus! Always nagging, even at yourself! I do believe you think everybody—yourself first of all—is totally worthless, except, of course, Socrates. I don't know exactly how you came to be called "the maniac," but you certainly talk like one, always furious with everyone, including yourself—but not with Socrates!

APOLLODORUS: Of course, my dear friend, it's *e* perfectly obvious why I have these views about us all: it's simply because I'm a maniac, and I'm raving!

FRIEND: It's not worth arguing about this now, Apollodorus. Please do as I asked: tell me the speeches.

APOLLODORUS: All right . . . Well, the speeches went something like this—but I'd better tell you the 174 whole story from the very beginning, as Aristodemus told it to me.

He said, then, that one day he ran into Socrates, who had just bathed and put on his fancy sandals—both very unusual events. So he asked him where he was going, and why he was looking so good.

Socrates replied, "I'm going to Agathon's for dinner. I managed to avoid yesterday's victory party—I really don't like crowds—but I promised to be there today. So, naturally, I took great pains with my appearance: I'm going to the house of a good-looking man; I had to look my best. But let me ask you this," he added, "I know you haven't been invited to the dinner; *b* how would you like to come anyway?"

And Aristodemus answered, "I'll do whatever you say."

"Come with me, then," Socrates said, "and we shall prove the proverb wrong; the truth is, 'Good men go uninvited to Goodman's feast.'[1] Even Homer himself, when you think about it, did not much like this *c* proverb; he not only disregarded it, he violated it. Agamemnon, of course, is one of his great warriors, while he describes Menelaus as a 'limp spearman.' And yet, when Agamemnon offers a sacrifice and gives a feast, Homer has the weak Menelaus arrive uninvited at his superior's table."[2]

Aristodemus replied to this, "Socrates, I am afraid Homer's description is bound to fit me better than yours. Mine is a case of an obvious inferior arriving uninvited at the table of a man of letters. I think you'd better figure out a good excuse for bringing me along, because, you know, I won't admit I've come *d* without an invitation. I'll say I'm your guest."

"Let's go," he said. "We'll think about what to say 'as we proceed the two of us along the way.' "[3]

With these words, they set out. But as they were walking, Socrates began to think about something, lost himself in thought, and kept lagging behind. Whenever Aristodemus stopped to wait for him, Soc- *e* rates would urge him to go on ahead. When he arrived at Agathon's he found the gate wide open, and that, Aristodemus said, caused him to find himself in a very embarrassing situation: a household slave saw him the moment he arrived and took him immediately to the dining room, where the guests were already lying down on their couches, and dinner was about to be served.

As soon as Agathon saw him, he called:

"Welcome, Aristodemus! What perfect timing! You're just in time for dinner! I hope you're not here for any other reason—if you are, forget it. I looked all over for you yesterday, so I could invite you, but I couldn't find you anywhere. But where is Socrates? How come you didn't bring him along?"

So I turned around (Aristodemus said), and Socrates was nowhere to be seen. And I said that it was actually Socrates who had brought *me* along as his guest.

"I'm delighted he did," Agathon replied. "But *175* where is he?"

"He was directly behind me, but I have no idea where he is now."

"Go look for Socrates," Agathon ordered a slave, "and bring him in. Aristodemus," he added, "you can share Eryximachus' couch."

A slave brought water, and Aristodemus washed himself before he lay down. Then another slave entered and said: "Socrates is here, but he's gone off to the neighbor's porch. He's standing there and won't come in even though I called him several times."

"How strange," Agathon replied. "Go back and bring him in. Don't leave him there."

But Aristodemus stopped him. "No, no," he said. *b* "Leave him alone. It's one of his habits: every now and then he just goes off like that and stands motionless, wherever he happens to be. I'm sure he'll come in very soon, so don't disturb him; let him be."

"Well, all right, if you really think so," Agathon said, and turned to the slaves: "Go ahead and serve the rest of us. What you serve is completely up to you; pretend nobody's supervising you—as if I ever did! Imagine that we are all your own guests, myself *c* included. Give us good reason to praise your service."

So they went ahead and started eating, but there was still no sign of Socrates. Agathon wanted to send for him many times, but Aristodemus wouldn't let him. And, in fact, Socrates came in shortly afterward, as he always did—they were hardly halfway through

1. [Agathon's name could be translated "Goodman." The proverb is, "Good men go uninvited to an inferior man's feast" (Eupolis fr. 289 Kock).—P.W.]

2. [Menelaus calls on Agamemnon at *Iliad* ii.408. Menelaus is called a limp spearman at xvii.587–88.]

3. [An allusion to *Iliad* x.224, "When two go together, one has an idea before the other."]

their meal. Agathon, who, as it happened, was all alone on the farthest couch, immediately called: *d* “Socrates, come lie down next to me. Who knows, if I touch you, I may catch a bit of the wisdom that came to you under my neighbor’s porch. It’s clear *you’ve* seen the light. If you hadn’t, you’d still be standing there.”

Socrates sat down next to him and said, “How wonderful it would be, dear Agathon, if the foolish were filled with wisdom simply by touching the wise. If only wisdom were like water, which always flows *e* from a full cup into an empty one when we connect them with a piece of yarn—well, then I would consider it the greatest prize to have the chance to lie down next to you. I would soon be overflowing with your wonderful wisdom. My own wisdom is of no account—a shadow in a dream—while yours is bright and radiant and has a splendid future. Why, young as you are, you’re so brilliant I could call more than thirty thousand Greeks as witnesses.”

“Now you’ve gone *too* far, Socrates,” Agathon replied. “Well, eat your dinner. Dionysus will soon *176* enough be the judge of our claims to wisdom!”[4]

Socrates took his seat after that and had his meal, according to Aristodemus. When dinner was over, they poured a libation to the god, sang a hymn, and—in short—followed the whole ritual. Then they turned their attention to drinking. At that point Pausanias addressed the group:

“Well, gentlemen, how can we arrange to drink less tonight? To be honest, I still have a terrible hangover from yesterday, and I could really use a break. I daresay most of you could, too, since you were also *b* part of the celebration. So let’s try not to overdo it.”

Aristophanes replied: “Good idea, Pausanias. We’ve got to make a plan for going easy on the drink tonight. I was over my head last night myself, like the others.”

After that, up spoke Eryximachus, son of Acumenus: “Well said, both of you. But I still have one question: How do *you* feel, Agathon? Are you strong enough for serious drinking?”

“Absolutely not,” replied Agathon. “I’ve no strength left for anything.”

c “What a lucky stroke for us,” Eryximachus said, “for me, for Aristodemus, for Phaedrus, and the rest—that you large-capacity drinkers are already exhausted. Imagine how weak drinkers like ourselves feel after last night! Of course I don’t include Socrates in my claims: he can drink or not, and will be satisfied whatever we do. But since none of us seems particularly eager to overindulge, perhaps it would not be amiss for me to provide you with some accurate infor- *d* mation as to the nature of intoxication. If I have learned anything from medicine, it is the following point: inebriation is harmful to everyone. Personally, therefore, I always refrain from heavy drinking; and I advise others against it—especially people who are suffering the effects of a previous night’s excesses.”

“Well,” Phaedrus interrupted him, “I always follow your advice, especially when you speak as a doctor. In this case, if the others know what’s good for them, they too will do just as you say.”

At that point they all agreed not to get drunk that *e* evening; they decided to drink only as much as pleased them.

“It’s settled, then,” said Eryximachus. “We are resolved to force no one to drink more than he wants. I would like now to make a further motion: let us dispense with the flute-girl who just made her entrance; let her play for herself or, if she prefers, for the women in the house. Let us instead spend our evening in conversation. If you are so minded, I would like to propose a subject.” *177*

They all said they were quite willing, and urged him to make his proposal. So Eryximachus said:

“Let me begin by citing Euripides’ *Melanippe*: ‘Not mine the tale.’ What I am about to tell belongs to Phaedrus here, who is deeply indignant on this issue, and often complains to me about it:

“‘Eryximachus,’ he says, ‘isn’t it an awful thing! Our poets have composed hymns in honor of just about any god you can think of; but has a single one of them given one moment’s thought to the god of *b* love, ancient and powerful as he is? As for our fancy intellectuals, they have written volumes praising Heracles and other heroes (as did the distinguished Prodicus). Well, perhaps *that’s* not surprising, but I’ve actually read a book by an accomplished author who saw *c* fit to extol the usefulness of salt! How *could* people pay attention to such trifles and never, not even once, write a proper hymn to Love? How could anyone ignore so great a god?’

4. [Dionysus was the god of wine and drunkenness.]

"Now, Phaedrus, in my judgment, is quite right. I would like, therefore, to take up a contribution, as it were, on his behalf, and gratify his wish. Besides, I *d* think this a splendid time for all of us here to honor the god. If you agree, we can spend the whole evening in discussion, because I propose that each of us give as good a speech in praise of Love as he is capable of giving, in proper order from left to right. And let us begin with Phaedrus, who is at the head of the table and is, in addition, the father of our subject."

"No one will vote against that, Eryximachus," said Socrates. "How could *I* vote 'No,' when the only thing *e* I say I understand is the art of love? Could Agathon and Pausanias? Could Aristophanes, who thinks of nothing but Dionysus and Aphrodite? No one I can see here now could vote against your proposal.

"And though it's not quite fair to those of us who have to speak last, if the first speeches turn out to be good enough and to exhaust our subject, I promise we won't complain. So let Phaedrus begin, with the blessing of Fortune; let's hear his praise of Love."

178 They all agreed with Socrates, and pressed Phaedrus to start. Of course, Aristodemus couldn't remember exactly what everyone said, and I myself don't remember everything he told me. But I'll tell you what he remembered best, and what I consider the most important points.

As I say, he said Phaedrus spoke first, beginning more or less like this:

Love is a great god, wonderful in many ways to gods and men, and most marvelous of all is the way *b* he came into being. We honor him as one of the most ancient gods, and the proof of his great age is this: the parents of Love have no place in poetry or legend. According to Hesiod, the first to be born was Chaos,

> *. . . but then came*
> *Earth, broad-chested, a seat for all, forever safe,*
> *And Love.*[5]

And Acusilaus agrees with Hesiod: after Chaos came Earth and Love, these two.[6] And Parmenides tells of this beginning:

> *The very first god [she] designed was Love.*[7]

All sides agree, then, that Love is one of the most *c* ancient gods. As such, he gives to us the greatest goods. I cannot say what greater good there is for a young boy than a gentle lover, or for a lover than a boy to love. There is a certain guidance each person needs for his whole life, if he is to live well; and nothing imparts this guidance—not high kinship, not public honor, not wealth—nothing imparts this guid- *d* ance as well as Love. What guidance do I mean? I mean a sense of shame at acting shamefully, and a sense of pride in acting well. Without these, nothing fine or great can be accomplished, in public or in private.

What I say is this: if a man in love is found doing something shameful, or accepting shameful treatment because he is a coward and makes no defense, then nothing would give him more pain than being seen by the boy he loves—not even being seen by *e* his father or his comrades. We see the same thing also in the boy he loves, that he is especially ashamed before his lover when he is caught in something shameful. If only there were a way to start a city or an army made up of lovers and the boys they love! Theirs would be the best possible system of society, for they would hold back from all that is shameful, and seek honor in each other's eyes.[8] Even a few of *179* them, in battle side by side, would conquer all the world, I'd say. For a man in love would never allow his loved one, of all people, to see him leaving ranks or dropping weapons. He'd rather die a thousand deaths! And as for leaving the boy behind, or not coming to his aid in danger—why, no one is so base that true Love could not inspire him with courage, *b* and make him as brave as if he'd been born a hero. When Homer says a god "breathes might" into some of the heroes, this is really Love's gift to every lover.[9]

Besides, no one will die for you but a lover, and a lover will do this even if she's a woman. Alcestis is proof to everyone in Greece that what I say is true.[10]

5. [*Theogony* 116–20, 118 omitted.]

6. [Acusilaus was an early–fifth-century writer of genealogies.]

7. [Parmenides, B 13 Diels-Kranz.]

8. [Accepting the deletion of *ē* in e5.]

9. [Cf. *Iliad* x.482, xv.262; *Odyssey* ix.381.]

10. [Alcestis was the self-sacrificing wife of Admetus, whom Apollo gave a chance to live if anyone would go to Hades in his place.]

c Only she was willing to die in place of her husband, although his father and mother were still alive. Because of her love, she went so far beyond his parents in family feeling that she made them look like outsiders, as if they belonged to their son in name only. And when she did this her deed struck everyone, even the gods, as nobly done. The gods were so delighted, in fact, that they gave her the prize they reserve for a handful cho- d sen from the throngs of noble heroes—they sent her soul back from the dead. As you can see, the eager courage of love wins highest honors from the gods.

Orpheus, however, they sent unsatisfied from Hades, after showing him only an image of the woman he came for. They did not give him the woman herself, because they thought he was soft (he was, after all, a cithara-player) and did not dare to die like Alcestis for Love's sake, but contrived to enter living into Hades. So they punished him for that, and made e him die at the hands of women.[11]

The honor they gave to Achilles is another matter. They sent him to the Isles of the Blest because he dared to stand by his lover Patroclus and avenge him, 180 even after he had learned from his mother that he would die if he killed Hector, but that if he chose otherwise he'd go home and end his life as an old man. Instead he chose to die for Patroclus, and more than that, he did it for a man whose life was already over. The gods were highly delighted at this, of course, and gave him special honor, because he made so much of his lover. Aeschylus talks nonsense when he claims Achilles was the lover;[12] he was more beautiful than Patroclus, more beautiful than all the heroes, and still beardless. Besides he was much younger, as Homer says.

In truth, the gods honor virtue most highly when b it belongs to Love. They are more impressed and delighted, however, and are more generous with a loved one who cherishes his lover, than with a lover who cherishes the boy he loves. A lover is more godlike than his boy, you see, since he is inspired by a god. That's why they gave a higher honor to Achilles than to Alcestis, and sent him to the Isles of the Blest.

Therefore I say Love is the most ancient of the gods, the most honored, and the most powerful in helping men gain virtue and blessedness, whether they are alive or have passed away.

That was more or less what Phaedrus said according c to Aristodemus. There followed several other speeches which he couldn't remember very well. So he skipped them and went directly to the speech of Pausanias.

Phaedrus (Pausanias began), I'm not quite sure our subject has been well defined. Our charge has been simple—to speak in praise of Love. This would have been fine if Love himself were simple, too, but as a matter of fact, there are two kinds of Love. In view of this, it might be better to begin by making clear d which kind of Love we are to praise. Let me therefore try to put our discussion back on the right track and explain which kind of Love ought to be praised. Then I shall give him the praise he deserves, as the god he is.

It is a well-known fact that Love and Aphrodite are inseparable. If, therefore, Aphrodite were a single goddess, there could also be a single Love; but, since there are actually two goddesses of that name, there also are two kinds of Love. I don't expect you'll disagree with me about the two goddesses, will you? One is an older deity, the motherless daughter of Uranus, the god of heaven: she is known as Urania, or Heavenly Aphrodite. The other goddess is younger, the daughter of Zeus and Dione: her name is Pande- e mos, or Common Aphrodite. It follows, therefore, that there is a Common as well as a Heavenly Love, depending on which goddess is Love's partner. And although, of course, all the gods must be praised, we must still make an effort to keep these two gods apart.

The reason for this applies in the same way to every type of action: considered in itself, no action is either good or bad, honorable or shameful. Take, for exam- 181 ple, our own case. We had a choice between drinking, singing, or having a conversation. Now, in itself none of these is better than any other: how it comes out depends entirely on how it is performed. If it is done honorably and properly, it turns out to be honorable; if it is done improperly, it is disgraceful. And my point is that exactly this principle applies to being in love: Love is not in himself noble and worthy of praise; that depends on whether the sentiments he produces in us are themselves noble.

11. [Orpheus was a musician of legendary powers, who charmed his way into the underworld in search of his dead wife, Eurydice.]

12. [In his play, *The Myrmidons*. In Homer there is no hint of sexual attachment between Achilles and Patroclus.]

b Now the Common Aphrodite's Love is himself truly common. As such, he strikes wherever he gets a chance. This, of course, is the love felt by the vulgar, who are attached to women no less than to boys, to the body more than to the soul, and to the least intelligent partners, since all they care about is completing the sexual act. Whether they do it honorably or not is of no concern. That is why they do whatever comes their way, sometimes good, sometimes bad; and which one it is is incidental to their purpose. For the Love who moves them belongs to a much younger goddess, who, through her parentage, par- c takes of the nature both of the female and the male.

Contrast this with the Love of Heavenly Aphrodite. This goddess, whose descent is purely male (hence this love is for boys), is considerably older and therefore free from the lewdness of youth. That's why those who are inspired by her Love are attracted to the male: they find pleasure in what is by nature stronger and more intelligent. But, even within the group that is attracted to handsome boys, some are not moved d purely by this Heavenly Love; those who are do not fall in love with little boys; they prefer older ones whose cheeks are showing the first traces of a beard—a sign that they have begun to form minds of their own. I am convinced that a man who falls in love with a young man of this age is generally prepared to share everything with the one he loves—he is eager, in fact, to spend the rest of his own life with him. He certainly does not aim to deceive him—to take advantage of him while he is still young and inexperienced and then, after exposing him to ridicule, to e move quickly on to someone else.

As a matter of fact, there should be a law forbidding affairs with young boys. If nothing else, all this time and effort would not be wasted on such an uncertain pursuit—and what is more uncertain than whether a particular boy will eventually make something of himself, physically or mentally? Good men, of course, are willing to make a law like this for themselves, but those other lovers, the vulgar ones, need external restraint. For just this reason we have placed every 182 possible legal obstacle to their seducing our own wives and daughters. These vulgar lovers are the people who have given love such a bad reputation that some have gone so far as to claim that taking *any* man as a lover is in itself disgraceful. Would anyone make this claim if he weren't thinking of how hasty vulgar lovers are, and therefore how unfair to their loved ones? For nothing done properly and in accordance with our customs would ever have provoked such righteous disapproval.

I should point out, however, that, although the customs regarding Love in most cities are simple and easy to understand, here in Athens (and in Sparta as well) they are remarkably complex. In places where b the people are inarticulate, like Elis or Boeotia, tradition straightforwardly approves taking a lover in every case. No one there, young or old, would ever consider it shameful. The reason, I suspect, is that, being poor speakers, they want to save themselves the trouble of having to offer reasons and arguments in support of their suits.

By contrast, in places like Ionia and almost every other part of the Persian empire, taking a lover is always considered disgraceful. The Persian empire is absolute; that is why it condemns love as well as c philosophy and sport. It is no good for rulers if the people they rule cherish ambitions for themselves or form strong bonds of friendship with one another. That these are precisely the effects of philosophy, sport, and especially of Love is a lesson the tyrants of Athens learned directly from their own experience: Didn't their reign come to a dismal end because of the bonds uniting Harmodius and Aristogiton in love and affection?[13] d

So you can see that plain condemnation of Love reveals lust for power in the rulers and cowardice in the ruled, while indiscriminate approval testifies to general dullness and stupidity.

Our own customs, which, as I have already said, are much more difficult to understand, are also far superior. Recall, for example, that we consider it more honorable to declare your love rather than to keep it a secret, especially if you are in love with a youth of good family and accomplishment, even if he isn't all that beautiful. Recall also that a lover is encouraged in every possible way; this means that what he does is not considered shameful. On the contrary, conquest is deemed noble, and failure shameful. And as for e *attempts* at conquest, our custom is to praise lovers

13. [Harmodius and Aristogiton attempted to overthrow the tyrant Hippias in 514 B.C. Although their attempt failed, the tyranny fell three years later, and the lovers were celebrated as tyrannicides.]

for totally extraordinary acts—so extraordinary, in fact, 183 that if they performed them for any other purpose whatever, they would reap the most profound contempt. Suppose, for example, that in order to secure money, or a public post, or any other practical benefit from another person, a man were willing to do what lovers do for the ones they love. Imagine that in pressing his suit he went to his knees in public view and begged in the most humiliating way, that he swore all sorts of vows, that he spent the night at the other man's doorstep, that he were anxious to provide services even a slave would have refused—well, you can be sure that everyone, his enemies no less than *b* his friends, would stand in his way. His enemies would jeer at his fawning servility, while his friends, ashamed on his behalf, would try everything to bring him back to his senses. But let a lover act in any of these ways, and everyone will immediately say what a charming man he is! No blame attaches to his behavior: custom treats it as noble through and through. And what is even more remarkable is that, at least according to popular wisdom, the gods will forgive a lover even *c* for breaking his vows—a lover's vow, our people say, is no vow at all. The freedom given to the lover by both gods and men according to our custom is immense.

In view of all this, you might well conclude that in our city we consider the lover's desire and the willingness to satisfy it as the noblest things in the world. When, on the other hand, you recall that fathers hire attendants for their sons as soon as they're old enough to be attractive, and that an attendant's main task is to prevent any contact between his charge and his suitors; when you recall how mercilessly a boy's own friends tease him if they catch him at it, and how strongly their elders approve and even *d* encourage such mocking—when you take all this into account, you're bound to come to the conclusion that we Athenians consider such behavior the most shameful thing in the world.

In my opinion, however, the fact of the matter is this. As I said earlier, love is, like everything else, complex: considered simply in itself, it is neither honorable nor a disgrace—its character depends entirely on the behavior it gives rise to. To give oneself to a vile man in a vile way is truly disgraceful behavior; by contrast, it is perfectly honorable to give oneself honorably to the right man. Now you may want to *e* know who counts as vile in this context. I'll tell you: it is the common, vulgar lover, who loves the body rather than the soul, the man whose love is bound to be inconstant, since what he loves is itself mutable and unstable. The moment the body is no longer in bloom, "he flies off and away,"[14] his promises and vows in tatters behind him. How different from this is a man who loves the right sort of character, and who remains its lover for life, attached as he is to something that is permanent. *184*

We can now see the point of our customs: they are designed to separate the wheat from the chaff, the proper love from the vile. That's why we do everything we can to make it as easy as possible for lovers to press their suits and as difficult as possible for young men to comply; it is like a competition, a kind of test to determine to which sort each belongs. This explains two further facts: First, why we consider it shameful to yield too quickly: the passage of time in itself provides a good test in these matters. Second, why we also consider it shameful for a man to be seduced *b* by money or political power, either because he cringes at ill-treatment and will not endure it or because, once he has tasted the benefits of wealth and power, he will not rise above them. None of these benefits is stable or permanent, apart from the fact that no genuine affection can possibly be based upon them.

Our customs, then, provide for only one honorable way of taking a man as a lover. In addition to recognizing that the lover's total and willing subjugation to *c* his beloved's wishes is neither servile nor reprehensible, we allow that there is one—and only one—further reason for willingly subjecting oneself to another which is equally above reproach: that is subjection for the sake of virtue. If someone decides to put himself at another's disposal because he thinks that this will make him better in wisdom or in any other part of virtue, we approve of his voluntary subjection: we consider it neither shameful nor servile. Both these principles—that is, both the principle governing the proper attitude toward the lover of young men and the principle governing the love of wisdom and of *d* virtue in general—must be combined if a young man is to accept a lover in an honorable way. When an older lover and a young man come together and each obeys the principle appropriate to him—when the lover realizes that he is justified in doing anything

14. [*Iliad* ii.71.]

for a loved one who grants him favors, and when the young man understands that he is justified in performing any service for a lover who can make him *e* wise and virtuous—and when the lover *is* able to help the young man become wiser and better, and the young man *is* eager to be taught and improved by his lover—then, and only then, when these two principles coincide absolutely, is it ever honorable for a young man to accept a lover.

Only in this case, we should notice, is it never shameful to be deceived; in every other case it is *185* shameful, both for the deceiver and the person he deceives. Suppose, for example, that someone thinks his lover is rich and accepts him for his money; his action won't be any less shameful if it turns out that he was deceived and his lover was a poor man after all. For the young man has already shown himself to be the sort of person who will do anything for money—and that is far from honorable. By the same token, suppose that someone takes a lover in the mistaken belief that this lover is a good man and likely to make him better himself, while in reality *b* the man is horrible, totally lacking in virtue; even so, it is noble for him to have been deceived. For he too has demonstrated something about himself: that he is the sort of person who will do anything for the sake of virtue—and what could be more honorable than that? It follows, therefore, that giving in to your lover for virtue's sake is honorable, whatever the outcome. And this, of course, is the Heavenly Love of the heavenly goddess. Love's value to the city as a whole and to the citizens is immeasurable, for he compels the *c* lover and his loved one alike to make virtue their central concern. All other forms of love belong to the vulgar goddess.

Phaedrus, I'm afraid this hasty improvisation will have to do as my contribution on the subject of Love.

When Pausanias finally came to a pause (I've learned this sort of fine figure from our clever rhetoricians), it was Aristophanes' turn, according to Aristodemus. But he had such a bad case of the hiccups—he'd probably stuffed himself again, though, of course, it could have been anything—that making a speech was totally out of the question. So he turned *d* to the doctor, Eryximachus, who was next in line, and said to him:

"Eryximachus, it's up to you—as well it should be. Cure me or take my turn."

"As a matter of fact," Eryximachus replied, "I shall do both. I shall take your turn—you can speak in my place as soon as you feel better—and I shall also cure you. While I am giving my speech, you should hold your breath for as long as you possibly can. This may *e* well eliminate your hiccups. If it fails, the best remedy is a thorough gargle. And if even this has no effect, then tickle your nose with a feather. A sneeze or two will cure even the most persistent case."

"The sooner you start speaking, the better," Aristophanes said. "I'll follow your instructions to the letter."

This, then, was the speech of Eryximachus:

Pausanias introduced a crucial consideration in his speech, though in my opinion he did not develop it sufficiently. Let me therefore try to carry his argument to its logical conclusion. His distinction between the *186* two species of Love seems to me very useful indeed. But if I have learned a single lesson from my own field, the science of medicine, it is that Love does not occur only in the human soul; it is not simply the attraction we feel toward human beauty: it is a significantly broader phenomenon. It certainly occurs within the animal kingdom, and even in the world *b* of plants. In fact, it occurs everywhere in the universe. Love is a deity of the greatest importance: he directs everything that occurs, not only in the human domain, but also in that of the gods.

Let me begin with some remarks concerning medicine—I hope you will forgive my giving pride of place to my own profession. The point is that our very bodies manifest the two species of Love. Consider for a moment the marked difference, the radical dissimilarity, between healthy and diseased constitutions and the fact that dissimilar subjects desire and love objects that are themselves dissimilar. Therefore, the love manifested in health is fundamentally distinct from the love manifested in disease. And now recall that, as Pausanias claimed, it is as honorable to yield to a good man as it is shameful to consort with the *c* debauched. Well, my point is that the case of the human body is strictly parallel. Everything sound and healthy in the body must be encouraged and gratified; that is precisely the object of medicine. Conversely, whatever is unhealthy and unsound must be frustrated and rebuffed: that's what it is to be an expert in medicine.

In short, medicine is simply the science of the effects of Love on repletion and depletion of the body, and the hallmark of the accomplished physician is his ability to distinguish the Love that is noble from the Love that is ugly and disgraceful. A good practitioner knows how to affect the body and how to transform its desires; he can implant the proper species of Love when it is absent and eliminate the other sort whenever it occurs. The physician's task is to effect a reconciliation and establish mutual love between the most basic bodily elements. Which are those elements? They are, of course, those that are most opposed to one another, as hot is to cold, bitter to sweet, wet to dry, cases like those. In fact, our ancestor Asclepius first established medicine as a profession when he learned how to produce concord and love between such opposites—that is what those poet fellows say, and—this time—I concur with them.

Medicine, therefore, is guided everywhere by the god of Love, and so are physical education and farming as well. Further, a moment's reflection suffices to show that the case of poetry and music, too, is precisely the same. Indeed, this may have been just what Heraclitus had in mind, though his mode of expression certainly leaves much to be desired. The one, he says, "being at variance with itself is in agreement with itself like the attunement of a bow or a lyre."[15] Naturally, it is patently absurd to claim that an attunement or a harmony is in itself discordant or that its elements are still in discord with one another. Heraclitus probably meant that an expert musician creates a harmony by resolving the prior discord between high and low notes. For surely there can be no harmony so long as high and low are still discordant; harmony, after all, is consonance, and consonance is a species of agreement. Discordant elements, as long as they are still in discord, cannot come to an agreement, and they therefore cannot produce a harmony. Rhythm, for example, is produced only when fast and slow, though earlier discordant, are brought into agreement with each other. Music, like medicine, creates agreement by producing concord and love between these various opposites. Music is therefore simply the science of the effects of Love on rhythm and harmony.

These effects are easily discernible if you consider the constitution of rhythm and harmony in themselves; Love does not occur in both his forms in this domain. But the moment you consider, in their turn, the effects of rhythm and harmony on their audience—either through composition, which creates new verses and melodies, or through musical education, which teaches the correct performance of existing compositions—complications arise directly, and they require the treatment of a good practitioner. Ultimately, the identical argument applies once again: the love felt by good people or by those whom such love might improve in this regard must be encouraged and protected. This is the honorable, heavenly species of Love, produced by the melodies of Urania, the Heavenly Muse. The other, produced by Polyhymnia, the muse of many songs, is common and vulgar. Extreme caution is indicated here: we must be careful to enjoy his pleasures without slipping into debauchery—this case, I might add, is strictly parallel to a serious issue in my own field, namely, the problem of regulating the appetite so as to be able to enjoy a fine meal without unhealthy aftereffects.

In music, therefore, as well as in medicine and in all the other domains, in matters divine as well as in human affairs, we must attend with the greatest possible care to these two species of Love, which are, indeed, to be found everywhere. Even the seasons of the year exhibit their influence. When the elements to which I have already referred—hot and cold, wet and dry—are animated by the proper species of Love, they are in harmony with one another: their mixture is temperate, and so is the climate. Harvests are plentiful; men and all other living things are in good health; no harm can come to them. But when the sort of Love that is crude and impulsive controls the seasons, he brings death and destruction. He spreads the plague and many other diseases among plants and animals; he causes frost and hail and blights. All these are the effects of the immodest and disordered species of Love on the movements of the stars and the seasons of the year, that is, on the objects studied by the science called astronomy.

Consider further the rites of sacrifice and the whole area with which the art of divination is concerned, that is, the interaction between men and gods. Here,

15. [Heraclitus of Ephesus, a philosopher of the early fifth century, was known for his enigmatic sayings. This one is quoted elsewhere in a slightly different form, frg. B 51 Diels-Kranz.]

too, Love is the central concern: our object is to try to maintain the proper kind of Love and to attempt to cure the kind that is diseased. For what is the origin of all impiety? Our refusal to gratify the orderly kind of Love, and our deference to the other sort, when we should have been guided by the former sort of Love in every action in connection with our parents, living or dead, and with the gods. The task of divination is to keep watch over these two species of Love and to doctor them as necessary. Divination, there- *d* fore, is the practice that produces loving affection between gods and men; it is simply the science of the effects of Love on justice and piety.

Such is the power of Love—so varied and great that in all cases it might be called absolute. Yet even so it is far greater when Love is directed, in temperance and justice, toward the good, whether in heaven or on earth: happiness and good fortune, the bonds of human society, concord with the gods above—all these are among his gifts.

Perhaps I, too, have omitted a great deal in this *e* discourse on Love. If so, I assure you, it was quite inadvertent. And if in fact I have overlooked certain points, it is now your task, Aristophanes, to complete the argument—unless, of course, you are planning on a different approach. In any case, proceed; your *189* hiccups seem cured.

Then Aristophanes took over (so Aristodemus said): "The hiccups have stopped all right—but not before I applied the Sneeze Treatment to them. Makes me wonder whether the 'orderly sort of Love' in the body calls for the sounds and itchings that constitute a sneeze, because the hiccups stopped immediately when I applied the Sneeze Treatment."

"You're good, Aristophanes," Eryximachus answered. "But watch what you're doing. You are making jokes before your speech, and you're forcing me to prepare for you to say something funny, and to put *b* up my guard against you, when otherwise you might speak at peace."

Then Aristophanes laughed. "Good point, Eryximachus. So let me 'unsay what I have said.' But don't put up your guard. I'm not worried about saying something funny in my coming oration. That would be pure profit, and it comes with the territory of my Muse. What I'm worried about is that I might say something ridiculous."

"Aristophanes, do you really think you can take a shot at me, and then escape? Use your head! Remember, as you speak, that you will be called upon to give an account. Though perhaps, if I decide to, I'll let *c* you off."

"Eryximachus," Aristophanes said, "indeed I do have in mind a different approach to speaking than the one the two of you used, you and Pausanias. You see, I think people have entirely missed the power of Love, because, if they had grasped it, they'd have built the greatest temples and altars to him and made the greatest sacrifices. But as it is, none of this is done for him, though it should be, more than anything else! For he loves the human race more than any *d* other god, he stands by us in our troubles, and he cures those ills we humans are most happy to have mended. I shall, therefore, try to explain his power to you; and you, please pass my teaching on to everyone else."

First you must learn what Human Nature was in the beginning and what has happened to it since, because long ago our nature was not what it is now, but very different. There were three kinds of human beings, that's my first point—not two as there are *e* now, male and female. In addition to these, there was a third, a combination of those two; its name survives, though the kind itself has vanished. At that time, you see, the word "androgynous" really meant something: a form made up of male and female elements, though now there's nothing but the word, and that's used as an insult. My second point is that the shape of each human being was completely round, with back and sides in a circle; they had four hands each, as many legs as hands, and two faces, exactly *190* alike, on a rounded neck. Between the two faces, which were on opposite sides, was one head with four ears. There were two sets of sexual organs, and everything else was the way you'd imagine it from what I've told you. They walked upright, as we do now, whatever direction they wanted. And whenever they set out to run fast, they thrust out all their eight limbs, the ones they had then, and spun rapidly, the way gymnasts do cartwheels, by bringing their legs around straight.

Now here is why there were three kinds, and why they were as I described them: The male kind was *b* originally an offspring of the sun, the female of the earth, and the one that combined both genders was an offspring of the moon, because the moon shares in both. They were spherical, and so was their motion, because they were like their parents in the sky.

In strength and power, therefore, they were terrible, and they had great ambitions. They made an attempt on the gods, and Homer's story about Ephialtes and Otus was originally about them: how they tried to make an ascent to heaven so as to attack the gods.[16] Then Zeus and the other gods met in council to discuss what to do, and they were sore perplexed. They couldn't wipe out the human race with thunderbolts and kill them all off, as they had the giants, because that would wipe out the worship they receive, along with the sacrifices we humans give them. On the other hand, they couldn't let them run riot. At last, after great effort, Zeus had an idea.

"I think I have a plan," he said, "that would allow human beings to exist and stop their misbehaving: they will give up being wicked when they lose their strength. So I shall now cut each of them in two. At one stroke they will lose their strength and also become more profitable to us, owing to the increase in their number. They shall walk upright on two legs. But if I find they still run riot and do not keep the peace," he said, "I will cut them in two again, and they'll have to make their way on one leg, hopping."

So saying, he cut those human beings in two, the way people cut sorb-apples before they dry them or the way they cut eggs with hairs. As he cut each one, he commanded Apollo to turn its face and half its neck towards the wound, so that each person would see that he'd been cut and keep better order. Then Zeus commanded Apollo to heal the rest of the wound, and Apollo did turn the face around, and he drew skin from all sides over what is now called the stomach, and there he made one mouth, as in a pouch with a drawstring, and fastened it at the center of the stomach. This is now called the navel. Then he smoothed out the other wrinkles, of which there were many, and he shaped the breasts, using some such tool as shoemakers have for smoothing wrinkles out of leather on the form. But he left a few wrinkles around the stomach and the navel, to be a reminder of what happened long ago.

Now, since their natural form had been cut in two, each one longed for its own other half, and so they would throw their arms about each other, weaving themselves together, wanting to grow together. In that condition they would die from hunger and general idleness, because they would not do anything apart from each other. Whenever one of the halves died and one was left, the one that was left still sought another and wove itself together with that. Sometimes the half he met came from a woman, as we'd call her now, sometimes it came from a man; either way, they kept on dying.

Then, however, Zeus took pity on them, and came up with another plan: he moved their genitals around to the front! Before then, you see, they used to have their genitals outside, like their faces, and they cast seed and made children, not in one another, but in the ground, like cicadas. So Zeus brought about this relocation of genitals, and in doing so he invented interior reproduction, *by* the man *in* the woman. The purpose of this was so that, when a man embraced a woman, he would cast his seed and they would have children; but when male embraced male, they would at least have the satisfaction of intercourse, after which they could stop embracing, return to their jobs, and look after their other needs in life. This, then, is the source of our desire to love each other. Love is born into every human being; it calls back the halves of our original nature together; it tries to make one out of two and heal the wound of human nature.

Each of us, then, is a "matching half" of a human whole, because each was sliced like a flatfish, two out of one, and each of us is always seeking the half that matches him. That's why a man who is split from the double sort (which used to be called "androgynous") runs after women. Many lecherous men have come from this class, and so do the lecherous women who run after men. Women who are split from a woman, however, pay no attention at all to men; they are oriented more towards women, and lesbians come from this class. People who are split from a male are male-oriented. While they are boys, because they are chips off the male block, they love men and enjoy lying with men and being embraced by men; those are the best of boys and lads, because they are the most manly in their nature. Of course, some say such boys are shameless, but they're lying. It's not because

16. [*Iliad* v.385, *Odyssey* xi.305 ff.]

they have no shame that such boys do this, you see, but because they are bold and brave and masculine, and they tend to cherish what is like themselves. Do you want me to prove it? Look, these are the only kind of boys who grow up to be real men in politics. *b* When they're grown men, they are lovers of young men, and they naturally pay no attention to marriage or to making babies, except insofar as they are required by local custom. They, however, are quite satisfied to live their lives with one another unmarried. In every way, then, this sort of man grows up as a lover of young men and a lover of Love, always rejoicing in his own kind.

And so, when a person meets the half that is his very own, whatever his orientation, whether it's to young men or not, then something wonderful hap- *c* pens: the two are struck from their senses by love, by a sense of belonging to one another, and by desire, and they don't want to be separated from one another, not even for a moment.

These are the people who finish out their lives together and still cannot say what it is they want from one another. No one would think it is the intimacy of sex—that mere sex is the reason each lover takes *d* so great and deep a joy in being with the other. It's obvious that the soul of every lover longs for something else; his soul cannot say what it is, but like an oracle it has a sense of what it wants, and like an oracle it hides behind a riddle. Suppose two lovers are lying together and Hephaestus[17] stands over them with his mending tools, asking, "What is it you human beings really want from each other?" And suppose they're perplexed, and he asks them again: "Is this your heart's desire, then—for the two of you to become parts of the same whole, as near as can be, and never to separate, day or night? Because if that's your desire, I'd like to weld you together and join you into something that is naturally whole, so that the two of *e* you are made into one. Then the two of you would share one life, as long as you lived, because you would be one being, and by the same token, when you died, you would be one and not two in Hades, having died a single death. Look at your love, and see if this is what you desire: wouldn't this be all the good fortune you could want?"

17. [Cf. *Odyssey* viii.266 ff.]

Surely you can see that no one who received such an offer would turn it down; no one would find anything else that he wanted. Instead, everyone would think he'd found out at last what he had always wanted: to come together and melt together with the one he loves, so that one person emerged from two. Why should this be so? It's because, as I said, we used to be complete wholes in our original nature, and now "Love" is the name for our pursuit of wholeness, for our desire to be complete. *193*

Long ago we were united, as I said; but now the god has divided us as punishment for the wrong we did him, just as the Spartans divided the Arcadians.[18] So there's a danger that if we don't keep order before the gods, we'll be split in two again, and then we'll be walking around in the condition of people carved on gravestones in bas-relief, sawn apart between the nostrils, like half dice. We should encourage all men, therefore, to treat the gods with all due reverence, so *b* that we may escape this fate and find wholeness instead. And we will, if Love is our guide and our commander. Let no one work against him. Whoever opposes Love is hateful to the gods, but if we become friends of the god and cease to quarrel with him, then we shall find the young men that are meant for us and win their love, as very few men do nowadays.

Now don't get ideas, Eryximachus, and turn this speech into a comedy. Don't think I'm pointing this *c* at Pausanias and Agathon. Probably, they both do belong to the group that are entirely masculine in nature. But I am speaking about everyone, men and women alike, and I say there's just one way for the human race to flourish: we must bring love to its perfect conclusion, and each of us must win the favors of his very own young man, so that he can recover his original nature. If that is the ideal, then, of course, the nearest approach to it is best in present circumstances, and that is to win the favor of young men who are naturally sympathetic to us.

If we are to give due praise to the god who can *d* give us this blessing, then, we must praise Love. Love does the best that can be done for the time being:

18. [Arcadia included the city of Mantinea, which opposed Sparta, and was rewarded by having its population divided and dispersed in 385 B.C. Aristophanes seems to be referring anachronistically to those events; such anachronisms are not uncommon in Plato.]

he draws us towards what belongs to us. But for the future, Love promises the greatest hope of all: if we treat the gods with due reverence, he will restore to us our original nature, and by healing us, he will make us blessed and happy.

"That," he said, "is my speech about Love, Eryximachus. It is rather different from yours. As I begged you earlier, don't make a comedy of it. I'd prefer to *e* hear what all the others will say—or, rather, what each of them will say, since Agathon and Socrates are the only ones left."

"I found your speech delightful," said Eryximachus, "so I'll do as you say. Really, we've had such a rich feast of speeches on Love, that if I couldn't vouch for the fact that Socrates and Agathon are masters of the art of love, I'd be afraid that they'd have nothing left to say. But as it is, I have no fears on this score."

194 Then Socrates said, "That's because *you* did beautifully in the contest, Eryximachus. But if you ever get in my position, or rather the position I'll be in after Agathon's spoken so well, then you'll really be afraid. You'll be at your wit's end, as I am now."

"You're trying to bewitch me, Socrates," said Agathon, "by making me think the audience expects great *b* things of my speech, so I'll get flustered."

"Agathon!" said Socrates, "How forgetful do you think I am? I saw how brave and dignified you were when you walked right up to the theater platform along with the actors and looked straight out at that enormous audience. You were about to put your own writing on display, and you weren't the least bit panicked. After seeing that, how could I expect you to be flustered by us, when we are so few?"

"Why, Socrates," said Agathon. "You must think I have nothing but theater audiences on my mind! So you suppose I don't realize that, if you're intelligent, you find a few sensible men much more frightening than a senseless crowd?"

c "No," he said, "It wouldn't be very handsome of me to think you crude in any way, Agathon. I'm sure that if you ever run into people you consider wise, you'll pay more attention to them than to ordinary people. But you can't suppose we're in that class; we were at the theater too, you know, part of the ordinary crowd. Still, if you did run into any wise men, other than yourself, you'd certainly be ashamed at the thought of doing anything ugly in front of them. Is that what you mean?"

"That's true," he said.

"On the other hand, you wouldn't be ashamed to do something ugly in front of ordinary people. Is *d* that it?"

At that point Phaedrus interrupted: "Agathon, my friend, if you answer Socrates, he'll no longer care whether we get anywhere with what we're doing here, so long as he has a partner for discussion. Especially if he's handsome. Now, like you, I enjoy listening to Socrates in discussion, but it is my duty to see to the praising of Love and to exact a speech from every one of this group. When each of you two has made his offering to the god, then you can have your dis- *e* cussion."

"You're doing a beautiful job, Phaedrus," said Agathon. "There's nothing to keep me from giving my speech. Socrates will have many opportunities for discussion later."

I wish first to speak of how I ought to speak, and only then to speak. In my opinion, you see, all those who have spoken before me did not so much celebrate the god as congratulate human beings on the good things that come to them from the god. But who it is who gave these gifts, what he is like—no one has *195* spoken about that. Now, only one method is correct for every praise, no matter whose: you must explain what qualities in the subject of your speech enable him to give the benefits for which we praise him. So now, in the case of Love, it is right for us to praise him first for what he is and afterwards for his gifts.

I maintain, then, that while all the gods are happy, Love—if I may say so without giving offense—is the happiest of them all, for he is the most beautiful and the best. His great beauty lies in this: First, Phaedrus, he is the youngest of the gods.[19] He proves my point *b* himself by fleeing old age in headlong flight, fast-moving though it is (that's obvious—it comes after us faster than it should). Love was born to hate old age and will come nowhere near it. Love always lives with young people and is one of them: the old story holds good that like is always drawn to like. And though on many other points I agree with Phaedrus, I do not agree with this: that Love is more ancient than Cronus and Iapetos. No, I say that he is the *c* youngest of the gods and stays young forever.

19. [Contrast 178b.]

Those old stories Hesiod and Parmenides tell about the gods—those things happened under Necessity, not Love, if what they say is true. For not one of all those violent deeds would have been done—no castrations, no imprisonments—if Love had been present among them. There would have been peace and brotherhood instead, as there has been now as long as Love has been king of the gods.

d So he is young. And besides being young, he is delicate. It takes a poet as good as Homer to show how delicate the god is. For Homer says that Mischief is a god and that she is delicate—well, that her feet are delicate, anyway! He says:

> *. . . hers are delicate feet: not on the ground*
> *Does she draw nigh; she walks instead*
> *upon the heads of men.*[20]

A lovely proof, I think, to show how delicate she is: *e* she doesn't walk on anything hard; she walks only on what is soft. We shall use the same proof about Love, then, to show that he is delicate. For he walks not on earth, not even on people's skulls, which are not really soft at all, but in the softest of all the things that are, there he walks, there he has his home. For he makes his home in the characters, in the souls, of gods and men—and not even in every soul that comes along: when he encounters a soul with a harsh character, he turns away; but when he finds a soft and gentle character, he settles down in it. Always, then, he is touching with his feet and with the whole *196* of himself what is softest in the softest places. He must therefore be most delicate.

He is youngest, then, and most delicate; in addition he has a fluid, supple shape. For if he were hard, he would not be able to enfold a soul completely or escape notice when he first entered it or withdrew. Besides, his graceful good looks prove that he is balanced and fluid in his nature. Everyone knows that Love has extraordinary good looks, and between ugliness and Love there is unceasing war.

And the exquisite coloring of his skin! The way the god consorts with flowers shows that. For he never *b* settles in anything, be it a body or a soul, that cannot flower or has lost its bloom. His place is wherever it is flowery and fragrant; there he settles, there he stays.

Enough for now about the beauty of the god, though much remains still to be said. After this, we should speak of Love's moral character.[21] The main point is that Love is neither the cause nor the victim of any injustice; he does no wrong to gods or men, nor they to him. If anything has an effect on him, it is never by violence, for violence never touches Love. *c* And the effects he has on others are not forced, for every service we give to love we give willingly. And whatever one person agrees on with another, when both are willing, that is right and just; so say "the laws that are kings of society."[22]

And besides justice, he has the biggest share of moderation.[23] For moderation, by common agreement, is power over pleasures and passions, and no pleasure is more powerful than Love! But if they are weaker, they are under the power of Love, and *he* has the power; and because he has power over pleasures and passions, Love is exceptionally moderate.

And as for manly bravery, "Not even Ares can *d* stand up to" Love![24] For Ares has no hold on Love, but Love does on Ares—love of Aphrodite, so runs the tale.[25] But he who has hold is more powerful than he who is held; and so, because Love has power over the bravest of the others, he is bravest of them all.

Now I have spoken about the god's justice, moderation, and bravery; his wisdom remains.[26] I must try

20. [*Iliad* xix.92–93. "Mischief" translates *Atē*.]

21. ["Moral character": *aretē*, i.e., virtue.]

22. [A proverbial expression attributed by Aristotle (*Rhetoric* 1406a17–23) to the fourth-century liberal thinker and rhetorician Alcidamas.]

23. [*Sōphrosunē*. The word can be translated also as "temperance" and, most literally, "sound-mindedness." (Plato and Aristotle generally contrast *sōphrosunē* as a virtue with self-control: the person with *sōphrosunē* is naturally well-tempered in every way and so does not need to control himself, or hold himself back.)]

24. [From Sophocles, fragment 234b Dindorf: "Even Ares cannot withstand Necessity." Ares is the god of war.]

25. [See *Odyssey* viii.266–366. Aphrodite's husband Hephaestus made a snare that caught Ares in bed with Aphrodite.]

26. ["Wisdom" translates *sophia*, which Agathon treats as roughly equivalent to *technē* (professional skill); he refers mainly to the ability to produce things. Accordingly "wis-

not to leave out anything that can be said on this. In the first place—to honor *our* profession as Eryximachus did his[27]—the god is so skilled a poet that he can make others into poets: once Love touches him, *anyone* becomes a poet,

> . . . *howe'er uncultured he had been before.*[28]

This, we may fittingly observe, testifies that Love is a good poet, good, in sum, at every kind of artistic production. For you can't give to another what you don't have yourself, and you can't teach what you don't know.

And as to the production of animals—who will deny that they are all born and begotten through Love's skill?

And as for artisans and professionals—don't we know that whoever has this god for a teacher ends up in the light of fame, while a man untouched by Love ends in obscurity? Apollo, for one, invented archery, medicine, and prophecy when desire and love showed the way. Even he, therefore, would be a pupil of Love, and so would the Muses in music, Hephaestus in bronze work, Athena in weaving, and Zeus in "the governance of gods and men."

That too is how the gods' quarrels were settled, once Love came to be among them—love of beauty, obviously, because love is not drawn to ugliness. Before that, as I said in the beginning, and as the poets say, many dreadful things happened among the gods, because Necessity was king. But once this god was born, all goods came to gods and men alike through love of beauty.

This is how I think of Love, Phaedrus: first, he is himself the most beautiful and the best; after that, if anyone else is at all like that, Love is responsible. I am suddenly struck by a need to say something in poetic meter,[29] that it is he who—

> *Gives peace to men and stillness to the sea,*
> *Lays winds to rest, and careworn men to sleep.*

Love fills us with togetherness and drains all of our divisiveness away. Love calls gatherings like these together. In feasts, in dances, and in ceremonies, he gives the lead. Love moves us to mildness, removes from us wildness. He is giver of kindness, never of meanness. Gracious, kindly[30]—let wise men see and gods admire! Treasure to lovers, envy to others, father of elegance, luxury, delicacy, grace, yearning, desire. Love cares well for good men, cares not for bad ones. In pain, in fear, in desire, or speech, Love is our best guide and guard; he is our comrade and our savior. Ornament of all gods and men, most beautiful leader and the best! Every man should follow Love, sing beautifully his hymns, and join with him in the song he sings that charms the mind of god or man.

This, Phaedrus, is the speech I have to offer. Let it be dedicated to the god, part of it in fun, part of it moderately serious, as best I could manage.

When Agathon finished, Aristodemus said, everyone there burst into applause, so becoming to himself and to the god did they think the young man's speech.

Then Socrates glanced at Eryximachus and said, "Now do you think I was foolish to feel the fear I felt before? Didn't I speak like a prophet a while ago when I said that Agathon would give an amazing speech and I would be tongue-tied?"

"You were prophetic about one thing, I think," said Eryximachus, "that Agathon would speak well. But you, tongue-tied? No, I don't believe that."

"Bless you," said Socrates. "How am I not going to be tongue-tied, I or anyone else, after a speech delivered with such beauty and variety? The other parts may not have been so wonderful, but that at the end! Who would not be struck dumb on hearing the beauty of the words and phrases? Anyway, I was worried that I'd not be able to say anything that came close to them in beauty, and so I would almost have run away and escaped, if there had been a place to go. And, you see, the speech reminded me of Gorgias, so that I actually experienced what Homer describes: I was afraid that Agathon would end by sending the Gorgian head,[31] awesome at speaking in a speech,

dom" translates *sophia* in the first instance; afterward in this passage it is "skill" or "art."]

27. [At 186b.]

28. [Euripides, *Stheneboea* (frg. 666 Nauck).]

29. [After these two lines of poetry, Agathon continues with an extremely poetical prose peroration.]

30. [Accepting the emendation *aganos* at d5.]

31. ["Gorgian head" is a pun on "Gorgon's head." In his peroration Agathon had spoken in the style of Gorgias, and this style was considered to be irresistibly powerful. The sight of a Gorgon's head would turn a man to stone.]

against my speech, and this would turn me to stone by striking me dumb. Then I realized how ridiculous *d* I'd been to agree to join with you in praising Love and to say that I was a master of the art of love, when I knew nothing whatever of this business, of how anything whatever ought to be praised. In my foolishness, I thought you should tell the truth about whatever you praise, that this should be your basis, and that from this a speaker should select the most beautiful truths and arrange them most suitably. I was quite vain, thinking that I would talk well and that I knew the truth about praising anything whatever. But now *e* it appears that this is not what it is to praise anything whatever; rather, it is to apply to the object the grandest and the most beautiful qualities, whether he actually has them or not. And if they are false, that is no objection; for the proposal, apparently, was that everyone here make the rest of us think he is praising Love—and not that he actually praise him. I think that is why you stir up every word and apply it to *199* Love; your description of him and his gifts is designed to make him look better and more beautiful than anything else—to ignorant listeners, plainly, for of course he wouldn't look that way to those who knew. And your praise did seem beautiful and respectful. But I didn't even know the method for giving praise; and it was in ignorance that I agreed to take part in this. So "the tongue" promised, and "the mind" did not.[32] Goodbye to that! I'm not giving another eulogy *b* using that method, not at all—I wouldn't be able to do it!—but, if you wish, I'd like to tell the truth my way. I want to avoid any comparison with your speeches, so as not to give you a reason to laugh at me. So look, Phaedrus, would a speech like this satisfy your requirement? You will hear the truth about Love, and the words and phrasing will take care of themselves."

Then Aristodemus said that Phaedrus and the others urged him to speak in the way he thought was required, whatever it was.

"Well then, Phaedrus," said Socrates, "allow me to ask Agathon a few little questions, so that, once I *c* have his agreement, I may speak on that basis."

"You have my permission," said Phaedrus. "Ask away."

After that, said Aristodemus, Socrates began: "Indeed, Agathon, my friend, I thought you led the way beautifully into your speech when you said that one should first show the qualities of Love himself, and only then those of his deeds. I must admire that beginning. Come, then, since you have beautifully and magnificently expounded his qualities in other *d* ways, tell me this, too, about Love. Is Love such as to be a love of something or of nothing? I'm not asking if he is born *of* some mother or father (for the question whether Love is love of mother or of father would really be ridiculous), but it's as if I'm asking this about a father—whether a father is the father *of* something or not. You'd tell me, of course, if you wanted to give me a good answer, that it's *of* a son or a daughter that a father is the father. Wouldn't you?"

"Certainly," said Agathon.

"Then does the same go for the mother?"

He agreed to that also. *e*

"Well, then," said Socrates, "answer a little more fully, and you will understand better what I want. If I should ask, 'What about this: a brother, just insofar as he *is* a brother, is he the brother of something or not?'"

He said that he was.

"And he's of a brother or a sister, isn't he?"

He agreed.

"Now try to tell me about love," he said. "Is Love the love of nothing or of something?"

"Of something, surely!" *200*

"Then keep this object of love in mind, and remember what it is.[33] But tell me this much: does Love desire that of which it is the love, or not?"

"Certainly," he said.

"At the time he desires and loves something, does he actually have what he desires and loves at that time, or doesn't he?"

"He doesn't. At least, that wouldn't be likely," he said.

"Instead of what's *likely*," said Socrates, "ask yourself whether it's *necessary* that this be so: a thing that desires desires something of which it is in need; *b* otherwise, if it were not in need, it would not desire it. I can't tell you, Agathon, how strongly it strikes me that this is necessary. But how about you?"

32. [The allusion is to Euripides, *Hippolytus* 612.]

33. [Cf. 197b.]

"I think so too."

"Good. Now then, would someone who is tall, want to be tall? Or someone who is strong want to be strong?"

"Impossible, on the basis of what we've agreed."

"Presumably because no one is in need of those things he already has."

"True."

"But maybe a strong man could want to be strong," said Socrates, "or a fast one fast, or a healthy one *c* healthy: in cases like these, you might think people really do want to be things they already are and do want to have qualities they already have—I bring them up so they won't deceive us. But in these cases, Agathon, if you stop to think about them, you will see that these people are what they are at the present time, whether they want to be or not, by a logical necessity. And who, may I ask, would ever bother to desire what's necessary in any event? But when someone says 'I am healthy, but that's just what I want to be,' or 'I am rich, but that's just what I want *d* to be,' or 'I desire the very things that I have,' let us say to him: 'You already have riches and health and strength in your possession, my man, what you want is to possess these things in time to come, since in the present, whether you want to or not, you have them. Whenever you say, *I desire what I already have*, ask yourself whether you don't mean this: *I want the things I have now to be mine in the future as well.*' Wouldn't he agree?"

According to Aristodemus, Agathon said that he would.

So Socrates said, "Then this is what it is to love something which is not at hand, which the lover does not have: it is to desire the preservation of what he *e* now has in time to come, so that he will have it then."

"Quite so," he said.

"So such a man or anyone else who has a desire desires what is not at hand and not present, what he does not have, and what he is not, and that of which he is in need; for such are the objects of desire and love."

"Certainly," he said.

"Come, then," said Socrates. "Let us review the points on which we've agreed. Aren't they, first, that Love is the love of something, and, second, that he *201* loves things of which he has a present need?"

"Yes," he said.

"Now, remember, in addition to these points, what you said in your speech about what it is that Love loves. If you like, I'll remind you. I think you said something like this: that the gods' quarrels were settled by love of beautiful things, for there is no love of ugly ones.[34] Didn't you say something like that?"

"I did," said Agathon.

"And that's a suitable thing to say, my friend," said Socrates. "But if this is so, wouldn't Love have to be a desire for beauty, and never for ugliness?"

He agreed. *b*

"And we also agreed that he loves just what he needs and does not have."

"Yes," he said.

"So Love needs beauty, then, and does not have it."

"Necessarily," he said.

"So! If something needs beauty and has got no beauty at all, would you still say that it is beautiful?"

"Certainly not."

"Then do you still agree that Love is beautiful, if those things are so?"

Then Agathon said, "It turns out, Socrates, I didn't know what I was talking about in that speech." *c*

"It was a beautiful speech, anyway, Agathon," said Socrates. "Now take it a little further. Don't you think that good things are always beautiful as well?"

"I do."

"Then if Love needs beautiful things, and if all good things are beautiful, he will need good things too."

"As for me, Socrates," he said, "I am unable to contradict you. Let it be as you say."

"Then it's the truth, my beloved Agathon, that you are unable to contradict," he said. "It is not hard at all to contradict Socrates."

Now I'll let you go. I shall try to go through for you *d* the speech about Love I once heard from a woman of Mantinea, Diotima—a woman who was wise about many things besides this: once she even put off the plague for ten years by telling the Athenians what sacrifices to make. She is the one who taught me the art of love, and I shall go through her speech as best I can on my own, using what Agathon and I have agreed to as a basis.

34. [197b3–5.]

Following your lead, Agathon, one should first describe who Love is and what he is like, and afterwards *e* describe his works—I think it will be easiest for me to proceed the way Diotima did and tell you how she questioned me.

You see, I had told her almost the same things Agathon told me just now: that Love is a great god and that he belongs to beautiful things.[35] And she used the very same arguments against me that I used against Agathon; she showed how, according to my very own speech, Love is neither beautiful nor good.

So I said, "What do you mean, Diotima? Is Love ugly, then, and bad?"

But she said, "Watch your tongue! Do you really *202* think that, if a thing is not beautiful, it has to be ugly?"

"I certainly do."

"And if a thing's not wise, it's ignorant? Or haven't you found out yet that there's something in between wisdom and ignorance?"

"What's that?"

"It's judging things correctly without being able to give a reason. Surely you see that this is not the same as knowing—for how could knowledge be unreasoning? And it's not ignorance either—for how could what hits the truth be ignorance? Correct judgment, of course, has this character: it is *in between* understanding and ignorance."

b "True," said I, "as you say."

"Then don't force whatever is not beautiful to be ugly, or whatever is not good to be bad. It's the same with Love: when you agree he is neither good nor beautiful, you need not think he is ugly and bad; he could be something in between," she said.

"Yet everyone agrees he's a great god," I said.

"Only those who don't know?" she said. "Is that how you mean 'everyone'? Or do you include those who do know?"

"Oh, everyone together."

And she laughed. "Socrates, how could those who *c* say that he's not a god at all agree that he's a great god?"

"Who says that?" I asked.

"You, for one," she said, "and I for another."

"How can you say this!" I exclaimed.

"That's easy," said she. "Tell me, wouldn't you say that all gods are beautiful and happy? Surely you'd never say a god is not beautiful or happy?"

"Zeus! Not I," I said.

"Well, by calling anyone 'happy,' don't you mean they possess good and beautiful things?"

"Certainly." *d*

"What about Love? You agreed he needs good and beautiful things, and that's why he desires them—because he needs them."

"I certainly did."

"Then how could he be a god if he has no share in good and beautiful things?"

"There's no way he could, apparently."

"Now do you see? You don't believe Love is a god either!"

"Then, what could Love be?" I asked. "A mortal?"

"Certainly not."

"Then, what is he?"

"He's like what we mentioned before," she said. "He is in between mortal and immortal."

"What do you mean, Diotima?"

"He's a great spirit, Socrates. Everything spiritual, *e* you see, is in between god and mortal."

"What is their function?" I asked.

"They are messengers who shuttle back and forth between the two, conveying prayer and sacrifice from men to gods, while to men they bring commands from the gods and gifts in return for sacrifices. Being in the middle of the two, they round out the whole and bind fast the all to all. Through them all divination passes, through them the art of priests in sacrifice *203* and ritual, in enchantment, prophecy, and sorcery. Gods do not mix with men; they mingle and converse with us through spirits instead, whether we are awake or asleep. He who is wise in any of these ways is a man of the spirit, but he who is wise in any other way, in a profession or any manual work, is merely a mechanic. These spirits are many and various, then, and one of them is Love."

"Who are his father and mother?" I asked. *b*

"That's rather a long story," she said. "I'll tell it to you, all the same."

"When Aphrodite was born, the gods held a celebration. Poros, the son of Metis, was there among

35. [The Greek is ambiguous between "Love loves beautiful things" and "Love is one of the beautiful things." Agathon had asserted the former (197b5, 201a5), and this will be a premise in Diotima's argument, but he asserted the latter as well (195a7), and this is what Diotima proceeds to refute.]

them.[36] When they had feasted, Penia came begging, as poverty does when there's a party, and stayed by the gates. Now Poros got drunk on nectar (there was no wine yet, you see) and, feeling drowsy, went into the garden of Zeus, where he fell asleep. Then Penia *c* schemed up a plan to relieve her lack of resources: she would get a child from Poros. So she lay beside him and got pregnant with Love. That is why Love was born to follow Aphrodite and serve her: because he was conceived on the day of her birth. And that's why he is also by nature a lover of beauty, because Aphrodite herself is especially beautiful.

"As the son of Poros and Penia, his lot in life is set to be like theirs. In the first place, he is always poor, and he's far from being delicate and *d* beautiful (as ordinary people think he is); instead, he is tough and shriveled and shoeless and homeless, always lying on the dirt without a bed, sleeping at people's doorsteps and in roadsides under the sky, having his mother's nature, always living with Need. But on his father's side he is a schemer after the beautiful and the good; he is brave, impetuous, and intense, an awesome hunter, always weaving snares, resourceful in his pursuit of intelligence, a lover of wisdom[37] through all his life, a genius with enchantments, potions, and clever pleadings.

e "He is by nature neither immortal nor mortal. But now he springs to life when he gets his way; now he dies—all in the very same day. Because he is his father's son, however, he keeps coming back to life, but then anything he finds his way to always slips away, and for this reason Love is never completely without resources, nor is he ever rich.

204 "He is in between wisdom and ignorance as well. In fact, you see, none of the gods loves wisdom or wants to become wise—for they are wise—and no one else who is wise already loves wisdom; on the other hand, no one who is ignorant will love wisdom either or want to become wise. For what's especially difficult about being ignorant is that you are content with yourself, even though you're neither beautiful and good nor intelligent. If you don't think you need anything, of course you won't want what you don't think you need."

"In that case, Diotima, who *are* the people who love wisdom, if they are neither wise nor igno- *b* rant?"

"That's obvious," she said. "A child could tell you. Those who love wisdom fall in between those two extremes. And Love is one of them, because he is in love with what is beautiful, and wisdom is extremely beautiful. It follows that Love *must* be a lover of wisdom and, as such, is in between being wise and being ignorant. This, too, comes to him from his parentage, from a father who is wise and resourceful and a mother who is not wise and lacks resource.

"My dear Socrates, that, then, is the nature of the Spirit called Love. Considering what you thought *c* about Love, it's no surprise that you were led into thinking of Love as you did. On the basis of what you say, I conclude that you thought Love was *being loved*, rather than *being a lover*. I think that's why Love struck you as beautiful in every way: because it is what is really beautiful and graceful that deserves to be loved, and this is perfect and highly blessed; but being a lover takes a different form, which I have just described."

So I said, "All right then, my friend. What you say about Love is beautiful, but if you're right, what use is Love to human beings?" *d*

"I'll try to teach you that, Socrates, after I finish this. So far I've been explaining the character and the parentage of Love. Now, according to you, he is love for beautiful things. But suppose someone asks us, 'Socrates and Diotima, what is the point of loving beautiful things?'

"It's clearer this way: 'The lover of beautiful things has a desire; what does he desire?' "

"That they become his own," I said.

"But that answer calls for still another question, that is, 'What will this man have, when the beautiful things he wants have become his own?' "

I said there was no way I could give a ready answer to that question. *e*

Then she said, "Suppose someone changes the question, putting 'good' in place of 'beautiful,' and asks you this: 'Tell me, Socrates, a lover of good things has a desire; what does he desire?' "

"That they become his own," I said.

36. [*Poros* means "way," "resource." His mother's name, *Mētis*, means "cunning." *Penia* means "poverty."]

37. [I.e., a philosopher.]

"And what will he have, when the good things he wants have become his own?"

"This time it's easier to come up with the answer," 205 I said. "He'll have happiness."[38]

"That's what makes happy people happy, isn't it—possessing good things. There's no need to ask further, 'What's the point of wanting happiness?' The answer you gave seems to be final."

"True," I said.

"Now this desire for happiness, this kind of love—do you think it is common to all human beings and that everyone wants to have good things forever and ever? What would you say?"

"Just that," I said. "It is common to all."

"Then, Socrates, why don't we say that everyone b is in love," she asked, "since everyone always loves the same things? Instead, we say some people are in love and others not; why is that?"

"I wonder about that myself," I said.

"It's nothing to wonder about," she said. "It's because we divide out a special kind of love, and we refer to it by the word that means the whole—'love'; and for the other kinds of love we use other words."

"What do you mean?" I asked.

"Well, you know, for example, that 'poetry' has a very wide range.[39] After all, everything that is responsi- c ble for creating something out of nothing is a kind of poetry; and so all the creations of every craft and profession are themselves a kind of poetry, and everyone who practices a craft is a poet."

"True."

"Nevertheless," she said, "as you also know, these craftsmen are not called poets. We have other words for them, and out of the whole of poetry we have marked off one part, the part the Muses give us with melody and rhythm, and we refer to this by the word that means the whole. For this alone is called 'poetry,' and those who practice this part of poetry are called poets."

d "True."

"That's also how it is with love. The main point is this: every desire for good things or for happiness is 'the supreme and treacherous love' in everyone. But those who pursue this along any of its many other ways—through making money, or through the love of sports, or through philosophy—we don't say that *these* people are in love, and we don't call them lovers. It's only when people are devoted exclusively to one special kind of love that we use these words that really belong to the whole of it: 'love' and 'in love' and 'lovers.' "

"I am beginning to see your point," I said.

"Now there is a certain story," she said, "according to which lovers are those people who seek their other e halves. But according to my story, a lover does not seek the half or the whole, unless, my friend, it turns out to be good as well. I say this because people are even willing to cut off their own arms and legs if they think they are diseased. I don't think an individual takes joy in what belongs to him personally unless by 'belonging to me' he means 'good' and by 'belonging to another' he means 'bad.' That's because what everyone loves is really nothing other than the good. Do 206 you disagree?"

"Zeus! Not I," I said.

"Now, then," she said. "Can we simply say that people love the good?"

"Yes," I said.

"But shouldn't we add that, in loving it, they want the good to be theirs?"

"We should."

"And not only that," she said. "They want the good to be theirs forever, don't they?"

"We should add that too."

"In a word, then, love is wanting to possess the good forever."

"That's very true," I said. b

"This, then, is the object of love,"[40] she said. "Now, how do lovers pursue it? We'd rightly say that when they are in love they do something with eagerness and zeal. But what is it precisely that they do? Can you say?"

"If I could," I said, "I wouldn't be your student, filled with admiration for your wisdom, and trying to learn these very things."

38. [*Eudaimonia*: no English word catches the full range of this term, which is used for the whole of well-being and the good, flourishing life.]

39. ["Poetry" translates *poiēsis*, lit. 'making,' which can be used for any kind of production or creation. However, the word *poiētēs*, lit. 'maker,' was used mainly for poets—writers of metrical verses that were actually set to music.]

40. [Accepting the emendation *toutou* in b1.]

"Well, I'll tell you," she said. "It is giving birth in beauty,[41] whether in body or in soul."

"It would take divination to figure out what you c mean. I can't."

"Well, I'll tell you more clearly," she said. "All of us are pregnant, Socrates, both in body and in soul, and, as soon as we come to a certain age, we naturally desire to give birth. Now no one can possibly give birth in anything ugly; only in something beautiful. That's because when a man and a woman come together in order to give birth, this is a godly affair. Pregnancy, reproduction—this is an immortal thing for a mortal animal to do, and it cannot occur in d anything that is out of harmony, but ugliness is out of harmony with all that is godly. Beauty, however, is in harmony with the divine. Therefore the goddess who presides at childbirth—she's called Moira or Eilithuia—is really Beauty.[42] That's why, whenever pregnant animals or persons draw near to beauty, they become gentle and joyfully disposed and give birth and reproduce; but near ugliness they are foulfaced and draw back in pain; they turn away and shrink back and do not reproduce, and because they hold on to what they carry inside them, the labor is painful. This is the source of the great excitement about beauty e that comes to anyone who is pregnant and already teeming with life: beauty releases them from their great pain. You see, Socrates," she said, "what Love wants is not beauty, as you think it is."

"Well, what is it, then?"

"Reproduction and birth in beauty."

"Maybe," I said.

"Certainly," she said. "Now, why reproduction? It's because reproduction goes on forever; it is what 207 mortals have in place of immortality. A lover must desire immortality along with the good, if what we agreed earlier was right, that Love wants to possess the good forever. It follows from our argument that Love must desire immortality."

All this she taught me, on those occasions when she spoke on the art of love. And once she asked, "What do you think causes love and desire, Socrates? Don't you see what an awful state a wild animal is in when it wants to reproduce? Footed and winged b animals alike, all are plagued by the disease of Love. First they are sick for intercourse with each other, then for nurturing their young—for their sake the weakest animals stand ready to do battle against the strongest and even to die for them, and they may be racked with famine in order to feed their young. They would do anything for their sake. Human beings, you'd think, would do this because they understand the reason for it; but what causes wild animals to be c in such a state of love? Can you say?"

And I said again that I didn't know.

So she said, "How do you think you'll ever master the art of love, if you don't know that?"

"But that's why I came to you, Diotima, as I just said. I knew I needed a teacher. So tell me what causes this, and everything else that belongs to the art of love."

"If you really believe that Love by its nature aims at what we have often agreed it does, then don't be surprised at the answer," she said. "For among animals d the principle is the same as with us, and mortal nature seeks so far as possible to live forever and be immortal. And this is possible in one way only: by reproduction, because it always leaves behind a new young one in place of the old. Even while each living thing is said to be alive and to be the same—as a person is said to be the same from childhood till he turns into an old man—even then he never consists of the same things, though he is called the same, but he is always being renewed and in other respects passing away, in his hair and flesh and bones and blood and his e entire body. And it's not just in his body, but in his soul, too, for none of his manners, customs, opinions, desires, pleasures, pains, or fears ever remains the same, but some are coming to be in him while others are passing away. And what is still far stranger than that is that not only does one branch of knowledge come to be in us while another passes away and 208 that we are never the same even in respect of our knowledge, but that each single piece of knowledge has the same fate. For what we call *studying* exists

41. [The preposition is ambiguous between "within" and "in the presence of." Diotima may mean that the lover causes the newborn (which may be an idea) to come to be within a beautiful person; or she may mean that he is stimulated to give birth to it in the presence of a beautiful person.]

42. [Moira is known mainly as a Fate, but she was also a birth goddess (*Iliad* xxiv.209), and was identified with the birth goddess Eilithuia (Pindar, *Olympian Odes* vi.42, *Nemean Odes* vii.1).]

because knowledge is leaving us, because forgetting is the departure of knowledge, while studying puts back a fresh memory in place of what went away, thereby preserving a piece of knowledge, so that it seems to be the same. And in that way everything *b* mortal is preserved, not, like the divine, by always being the same in every way, but because what is departing and aging leaves behind something new, something such as it had been. By this device, Socrates," she said, "what is mortal shares in immortality, whether it is a body or anything else, while the immortal has another way. So don't be surprised if everything naturally values its own offspring, because it is for the sake of immortality that everything shows this zeal, which is Love."

Yet when I heard her speech I was amazed, and *c* spoke: "Well," said I, "Most wise Diotima, is this really the way it is?"

And in the manner of a perfect Sophist she said, "Be sure of it, Socrates. Look, if you will, at how human beings seek honor. You'd be amazed at their irrationality, if you didn't have in mind what I spoke about and if you hadn't pondered the awful state of love they're in, wanting to become famous and 'to lay up glory immortal forever,' and how they're ready to brave any danger for the sake of this, much more than they are for their children; and they are prepared *d* to spend money, suffer through all sorts of ordeals, and even die for the sake of glory. Do you really think that Alcestis would have died for Admetus," she asked, "or that Achilles would have died after Patroclus, or that your Codrus would have died so as to preserve the throne for his sons,[43] if they hadn't expected the memory of their virtue—which we still hold in honor—to be immortal? Far from it," she said. "I believe that anyone will do anything for the sake of *e* immortal virtue and the glorious fame that follows; and the better the people, the more they will do, for they are all in love with immortality.

"Now, some people are pregnant in body, and for this reason turn more to women and pursue love in that way, providing themselves through childbirth with immortality and remembrance and happiness, as they think, for all time to come; while others are *209* pregnant in soul—because there surely *are* those who are even more pregnant in their souls than in their bodies, and these are pregnant with what is fitting for a soul to bear and bring to birth. And what is fitting? Wisdom and the rest of virtue, which all poets beget, as well as all the craftsmen who are said to be creative. But by far the greatest and most beautiful part of wisdom deals with the proper ordering of cities and households, and that is called moderation and justice. When someone has been pregnant with these in his *b* soul from early youth, while he is still a virgin, and, having arrived at the proper age, desires to beget and give birth, he too will certainly go about seeking the beauty in which he would beget; for he will never beget in anything ugly. Since he is pregnant, then, he is much more drawn to bodies that are beautiful than to those that are ugly; and if he also has the luck to find a soul that is beautiful and noble and well-formed, he is even more drawn to this combination; such a man makes him instantly teem with ideas and arguments about virtue—the qualities a virtuous *c* man should have and the customary activities in which he should engage; and so he tries to educate him. In my view, you see, when he makes contact with someone beautiful and keeps company with him, he conceives and gives birth to what he has been carrying inside him for ages. And whether they are together or apart, he remembers that beauty. And in common with him he nurtures the newborn; such people, therefore, have much more to share than do the parents of human children, and have a firmer bond of friendship, because the children in whom they have a share are more beautiful and more immortal. Everyone would rather have such children than *d* human ones, and would look up to Homer, Hesiod, and the other good poets with envy and admiration for the offspring they have left behind—offspring, which, because they are immortal themselves, provide their parents with immortal glory and remembrance. For example," she said, "those are the sort of children Lycurgus[44] left behind in Sparta as the saviors of Sparta and virtually all of Greece. Among you the honor goes to Solon for his creation of your laws. Other *e* men in other places everywhere, Greek or barbarian,

43. [Codrus was the legendary last king of Athens. He gave his life to satisfy a prophecy that promised victory to Athens and salvation from the invading Dorians if their king was killed by the enemy.]

44. [Lycurgus was supposed to have been the founder of the oligarchic laws and stern customs of Sparta.]

have brought a host of beautiful deeds into the light and begotten every kind of virtue. Already many shrines have sprung up to honor them for their immortal children, which hasn't happened yet to anyone for human offspring.

"Even you, Socrates, could probably come to be initiated into these rites of love. But as for the purpose of these rites when they are done correctly—that is the final and highest mystery, and I don't know if you are capable of it. I myself will tell you," she said, "and I won't stint any effort. And you must try to follow if you can.

"A lover who goes about this matter correctly must begin in his youth to devote himself to beautiful bodies. First, if the leader[45] leads aright, he should love one body and beget beautiful ideas there; then he should realize that the beauty of any one body is brother to the beauty of any other and that if he is to pursue beauty of form he'd be very foolish not to think that the beauty of all bodies is one and the same. When he grasps this, he must become a lover of all beautiful bodies, and he must think that this wild gaping after just one body is a small thing and despise it.

"After this he must think that the beauty of people's souls is more valuable than the beauty of their bodies, so that if someone is decent in his soul, even though he is scarcely blooming in his body, our lover must be content to love and care for him and to seek to give birth to such ideas as will make young men better. The result is that our lover will be forced to gaze at the beauty of activities and laws and to see that all this is akin to itself, with the result that he will think that the beauty of bodies is a thing of no importance. After customs he must move on to various kinds of knowledge. The result is that he will see the beauty of knowledge and be looking mainly not at beauty in a single example—as a servant would who favored the beauty of a little boy or a man or a single custom (being a slave, of course, he's low and small-minded)—but the lover is turned to the great sea of beauty, and, gazing upon this, he gives birth to many gloriously beautiful ideas and theories, in unstinting love of wisdom,[46] until, having grown and been strengthened there, he catches sight of such knowledge, and it is the knowledge of such beauty. . . .

"Try to pay attention to me," she said, "as best you can. You see, the man who has been thus far guided in matters of Love, who has beheld beautiful things in the right order and correctly, is coming now to the goal of Loving: all of a sudden he will catch sight of something wonderfully beautiful in its nature; that, Socrates, is the reason for all his earlier labors:

"First, it always *is* and neither comes to be nor passes away, neither waxes nor wanes. Second, it is not beautiful this way and ugly that way, nor beautiful at one time and ugly at another, nor beautiful in relation to one thing and ugly in relation to another; nor is it beautiful here but ugly there, as it would be if it were beautiful for some people and ugly for others. Nor will the beautiful appear to him in the guise of a face or hands or anything else that belongs to the body. It will not appear to him as one idea or one kind of knowledge. It is not anywhere in another thing, as in an animal, or in earth, or in heaven, or in anything else, but itself by itself with itself, it is always one in form; and all the other beautiful things share in that, in such a way that when those others come to be or pass away, this does not become the least bit smaller or greater nor suffer any change. So when someone rises by these stages, through loving boys correctly, and begins to see this beauty, he has almost grasped his goal. This is what it is to go aright, or be led by another, into the mystery of Love: one goes always upwards for the sake of this Beauty, starting out from beautiful things and using them like rising stairs: from one body to two and from two to all beautiful bodies, then from beautiful bodies to beautiful customs, and from customs to learning beautiful things, and from these lessons he arrives[47] in the end at this lesson, which is learning of this very Beauty, so that in the end he comes to know just what it is to be beautiful.

"And there in life, Socrates, my friend," said the woman from Mantinea, "there if anywhere should a person live his life, beholding that Beauty. If you once see that, it won't occur to you to measure beauty by gold or clothing or beautiful boys and youths—who, if you see them now, strike you out of your

45. [The leader: Love.]

46. [I.e., philosophy.]

47. [Reading *teleutēsei* at c7.]

senses, and make you, you and many others, eager to be with the boys you love and look at them forever, if there were any way to do that, forgetting food and drink, everything but looking at them and being with *e* them. But how would it be, in our view," she said, "if someone got to see the Beautiful itself, absolute, pure, unmixed, not polluted by human flesh or colors or any other great nonsense of mortality, but if he *212* could see the divine Beauty itself in its one form? Do you think it would be a poor life for a human being to look there and to behold it by that which he ought, and to be with it? Or haven't you remembered," she said, "that in that life alone, when he looks at Beauty in the only way that Beauty can be seen—only then will it become possible for him to give birth not to images of virtue (because he's in touch with no images), but to true virtue (because he is in touch with the true Beauty). The love of the gods belongs to anyone who has given birth to true *b* virtue and nourished it, and if any human being could become immortal, it would be he."

This, Phaedrus and the rest of you, was what Diotima told me. I was persuaded. And once persuaded, I try to persuade others too that human nature can find no better workmate for acquiring this than Love. That's why I say that every man must honor Love, why I honor the rites of Love myself and practice them with special diligence, and why I commend them to others. Now and always I praise the power *c* and courage of Love so far as I am able. Consider this speech, then, Phaedrus, if you wish, a speech in praise of Love. Or if not, call it whatever and however you please to call it.

Socrates' speech finished to loud applause. Meanwhile, Aristophanes was trying to make himself heard over their cheers in order to make a response to something Socrates had said about his own speech.[48] Then, all of a sudden, there was even more noise. A large drunken party had arrived at the courtyard door and they were rattling it loudly, accompanied by the shrieks of some flute-girl they had brought along. Agathon at that point called to his slaves:

d "Go see who it is. If it's people we know, invite them in. If not, tell them the party's over, and we're about to turn in."

A moment later they heard Alcibiades shouting in the courtyard, very drunk and very loud. He wanted to know where Agathon was, he demanded to see Agathon at once. Actually, he was half-carried into the house by the flute-girl and by some other compan- *e* ions of his, but, at the door, he managed to stand by himself, crowned with a beautiful wreath of violets and ivy and ribbons in his hair.

"Good evening, gentlemen. I'm plastered," he announced. "May I join your party? Or should I crown Agathon with this wreath—which is all I came to do, anyway—and make myself scarce? I really couldn't make it yesterday," he continued, "but nothing could stop me tonight! See, I'm wearing the garland myself. I want this crown to come directly from my head to the head that belongs, I don't mind saying, to the cleverest and best looking man in town. Ah, you *213* laugh; you think I'm drunk! Fine, go ahead—I know I'm right anyway. Well, what do you say? May I join you on these terms? Will you have a drink with me or not?"

Naturally they all made a big fuss. They implored him to join them, they begged him to take a seat, and Agathon called him to his side. So Alcibiades, again with the help of his friends, approached Agathon. At the same time, he kept trying to take his ribbons off so that he could crown Agathon with them, but all he succeeded in doing was to push them further down his head until they finally slipped over his eyes. What with the ivy and all, he didn't see Socrates, who had made room for him on the couch as soon as he saw him. So Alcibiades sat down between Socrates and Agathon and, as soon as he did *b* so, he put his arms around Agathon, kissed him, and placed the ribbons on his head.

Agathon asked his slaves to take Alcibiades' sandals off. "We can all three fit on my couch," he said.

"What a good idea!" Alcibiades replied. "But wait a moment! Who's the third?"

As he said this, he turned around, and it was only then that he saw Socrates. No sooner had he seen him than he leaped up and cried:

"Good lord, what's going on here? It's Socrates! *c* You've trapped me again! You always do this to me—all of a sudden you'll turn up out of nowhere where I least expect you! Well, what do you want now? Why did you choose this particular couch? Why aren't you with Aristophanes or anyone else we could tease you

48. [Cf. 205d–e.]

about? But no, you figured out a way to find a place next to the most handsome man in the room!"

"I beg you, Agathon," Socrates said, "protect me *d* from this man! You can't imagine what it's like to be in love with him: from the very first moment he realized how I felt about him, he hasn't allowed me to say two words to anybody else—what am I saying, I can't so much as look at an attractive man but he flies into a fit of jealous rage. He yells; he threatens; he can hardly keep from slapping me around! Please, try to keep him under control. Could you perhaps make him forgive me? And if you can't, if he gets violent, will you defend me? The fierceness of his passion terrifies me!"

"I shall never forgive you!" Alcibiades cried. "I *e* promise you, you'll pay for this! But for the moment," he said, turning to Agathon, "give me some of these ribbons. I'd better make a wreath for him as well—look at that magnificent head! Otherwise, I know, he'll make a scene. He'll be grumbling that, though I crowned you for your first victory, I didn't honor him even though he has never lost an argument in his life."

So Alcibiades took the ribbons, arranged them on Socrates' head, and lay back on the couch. Immediately, however, he started up again:

"Friends, you look sober to me; we can't have that! Let's have a drink! Remember our agreement? We need a master of ceremonies; who should it be? . . . Well, at least till you are all too drunk to care, I elect . . . myself! Who else? Agathon, I want the largest cup around . . . No! Wait! You! Bring me that cooling *214* jar over there!"

He'd seen the cooling jar, and he realized it could hold more than two quarts of wine. He had the slaves fill it to the brim, drained it, and ordered them to fill it up again for Socrates.

"Not that the trick will have any effect on *him*," he told the group. "Socrates will drink whatever you put in front of him, but no one yet has seen him drunk."

The slave filled the jar and, while Socrates was drinking, Eryximachus said to Alcibiades:

b "This is certainly most improper. We cannot simply pour the wine down our throats in silence: we must have some conversation, or at least a song. What we are doing now is hardly civilized."

What Alcibiades said to him was this:

"O Eryximachus, best possible son to the best possible, the most temperate father: Hi!"

"Greetings to you, too," Eryximachus replied. "Now what do you suggest we do?"

"Whatever you say. Ours to obey you, 'For a medical mind is worth a million others.'[49] Please prescribe what you think fit."

"Listen to me," Eryximachus said. "Earlier this evening we decided to use this occasion to offer a *c* series of encomia of Love. We all took our turn—in good order, from left to right—and gave our speeches, each according to his ability. You are the only one not to have spoken yet, though, if I may say so, you have certainly drunk your share. It's only proper, therefore, that you take your turn now. After you have spoken, you can decide on a topic for Socrates on your right; he can then do the same for the man to his right, and we can go around the table once again."

"Well said, O Eryximachus," Alcibiades replied. "But do you really think it's fair to put my drunken ramblings next to your sober orations? And anyway, my dear fellow, I hope you didn't believe a single *d* word Socrates said: the truth is just the opposite! He's the one who will most surely beat me up if I dare praise anyone else in his presence—even a god!"

"Hold your tongue!" Socrates said.

"By god, don't you dare deny it!" Alcibiades shouted. "I would never—*never*—praise anyone else with you around."

"Well, why not just do that, if you want?" Eryximachus suggested. "Why don't you offer an encomium *e* to Socrates?"

"What do you mean?" asked Alcibiades. "Do you really think so, Eryximachus? Should I unleash myself upon him? Should I give him his punishment in front of all of you?"

"Now, wait a minute," Socrates said. "What do you have in mind? Are you going to praise me only in order to mock me? Is that it?"

"I'll only tell the truth—please, let me!"

"I would certainly like to hear the truth from you. By all means, go ahead," Socrates replied.

"Nothing can stop me now," said Alcibiades. "But here's what you can do: if I say anything that's not true, you can just interrupt, if you want, and correct

49. [*Iliad* xi.514.]

215 me; at worst, there'll be mistakes in my speech, not lies. But you can't hold it against me if I don't get everything in the right order—I'll say things as they come to mind. It is no easy task for one in my condition to give a smooth and orderly account of your bizarreness!"

I'll try to praise Socrates, my friends, but I'll have to use an image. And though he may think I'm trying to make fun of him, I assure you my image is no b joke: it aims at the truth. Look at him! Isn't he just like a statue of Silenus? You know the kind of statue I mean; you'll find them in any shop in town. It's a Silenus sitting, his flute[50] or his pipes in his hands, and it's hollow. It's split right down the middle, and inside it's full of tiny statues of the gods. Now look at him again! Isn't he also just like the satyr Marsyas?[51]

Nobody, not even you, Socrates, can deny that you *look* like them. But the resemblance goes beyond appearance, as you're about to hear.

You are impudent, contemptuous, and vile! No? If you won't admit it, I'll bring witnesses. And you're quite a fluteplayer, aren't you? In fact, you're much c more marvelous than Marsyas, who needed instruments to cast his spells on people. And so does anyone who plays his tunes today—for even the tunes Olympus[52] played are Marsyas' work, since Olympus learned everything from him. Whether they are played by the greatest flautist or the meanest flute-girl, his melodies have in themselves the power to possess and so reveal those people who are ready for the god and his mysteries. That's because his melodies are themselves divine. The only difference between you and Marsyas is that you need no instruments; d you do exactly what he does, but with words alone. You know, people hardly ever take a speaker seriously, even if he's the greatest orator; but let anyone—man, woman, or child—listen to you or even to a poor account of what you say—and we are all transported, completely possessed.

If I were to describe for you what an extraordinary effect his words have always had on me (I can feel it this moment even as I'm speaking), you might e actually suspect that I'm drunk! Still, I swear to you, the moment he starts to speak, I am beside myself: my heart starts leaping in my chest, the tears come streaming down my face, even the frenzied Corybantes[53] seem sane compared to me—and, let me tell you, I am not alone. I have heard Pericles and many other great orators, and I have admired their speeches. But nothing like this ever happened to me: they never upset me so deeply that my very own soul started protesting that my life—*my* life!—was no better than the most miserable slave's. And yet that is exactly how this Marsyas here at my side makes me feel all the 216 time: he makes it seem that my life isn't worth living! You can't say that isn't true, Socrates. I know very well that you could make me feel that way this very moment if I gave you half a chance. He always traps me, you see, and he makes me admit that my political career is a waste of time, while all that matters is just what I most neglect: my personal shortcomings, which cry out for the closest attention. So I refuse to listen to him; I stop my ears and tear myself away from him, for, like the Sirens, he could make me b stay by his side till I die.

Socrates is the only man in the world who has made me feel shame—ah, you didn't think I had it in me, did you? Yes, he makes me feel ashamed: I know perfectly well that I can't prove he's wrong when he tells me what I should do; yet, the moment I leave his side, I go back to my old ways: I cave in to my desire to please the crowd. My whole life has become one constant effort to escape from him and keep away, but when I see him, I feel deeply ashamed, because I'm doing nothing about my way of life, though I have c already agreed with him that I should. Sometimes, believe me, I think I would be happier if he were dead. And yet I know that if he dies I'll be even

50. [This is the conventional translation of the word, but the *aulos* was in fact a reed instrument and not a flute. It was held by the ancients to be the instrument that most strongly arouses the emotions.]

51. [Satyrs had the sexual appetites and manners of wild beasts and were usually portrayed with large erections. Sometimes they had horses' tails or ears, sometimes the traits of goats. Marsyas, in myth, dared to compete in music with Apollo and was skinned alive for his impudence.]

52. [Olympus was a legendary musician who was said to be loved by Marsyas (*Minos* 318b5) and to have made music that moved its listeners out of their senses.]

53. [Legendary worshippers of Cybele, who brought about their own derangement through music and dance.]

more miserable. I can't live with him, and I can't live without him! What *can* I do about him?

That's the effect of this satyr's music—on me and many others. But that's the least of it. He's like these creatures in all sorts of other ways; his powers are really extraordinary. Let me tell you about them, be- *d* cause, you can be sure of it, none of you really understands him. But, now I've started, I'm going to show you what he really is.

To begin with, he's crazy about beautiful boys; he constantly follows them around in a perpetual daze. Also, he likes to say he's ignorant and knows nothing. Isn't this just like Silenus? Of course it is! And all this is just on the surface, like the outsides of those statues of Silenus. I wonder, my fellow drinkers, if you have any idea what a sober and temperate man he proves to be once you have looked inside. Believe me, it couldn't matter less to him whether a boy is *e* beautiful. You can't imagine how little he cares whether a person is beautiful, or rich, or famous in any other way that most people admire. He considers all these possessions beneath contempt, and that's exactly how he considers all of us as well. In public, I tell you, his whole life is one big game—a game of irony. I don't know if any of you have seen him when he's really serious. But I once caught him when he was open like Silenus' statues, and I had a glimpse *217* of the figures he keeps hidden within: they were so godlike—so bright and beautiful, so utterly amazing—that I no longer had a choice—I just had to do whatever he told me.

What I thought at the time was that what he really wanted was *me*, and that seemed to me the luckiest coincidence: all I had to do was to let him have his way with me, and he would teach me everything he knew—believe me, I had a lot of confidence in my looks. Naturally, up to that time we'd never been alone together; one of my attendants had always been *b* present. But with this in mind, I sent the attendant away, and met Socrates alone. (You see, in this company I must tell the whole truth: so pay attention. And, Socrates, if I say anything untrue, I want you to correct me.)

So there I was, my friends, alone with him at last. My idea, naturally, was that he'd take advantage of the opportunity to tell me whatever it is that lovers say when they find themselves alone; I relished the moment. But no such luck! Nothing of the sort occurred. Socrates had his usual sort of conversation with me, and at the end of the day he went off. *c*

My next idea was to invite him to the gymnasium with me. We took exercise together, and I was sure that this would lead to something. He took exercise and wrestled with me many times when no one else was present. What can I tell you? I got nowhere. When I realized that my ploy had failed, I decided on a frontal attack. I refused to retreat from a battle I myself had begun, and I needed to know just where matters stood. So what I did was to invite him to dinner, as if *I* were his lover and he my young prey! To tell the truth, it took him quite a while to accept my invitation, but one day he finally arrived. That *d* first time he left right after dinner: I was too shy to try to stop him. But on my next attempt, I started some discussion just as we were finishing our meal and kept him talking late into the night. When he said he should be going, I used the lateness of the hour as an excuse and managed to persuade him to spend the night at my house. He had had his meal on the couch next to mine, so he just made himself *e* comfortable and lay down on it. No one else was there.

Now you must admit that my story so far has been perfectly decent; I could have told it in any company. But you'd never have heard me tell the rest of it, as you're about to do, if it weren't that, as the saying goes, "there's truth in wine when the slaves have left"—and when they're present, too. Also, would it be fair to Socrates for me to praise him and yet to fail to reveal one of his proudest accomplishments? And, furthermore, you know what people say about snakebite—that you'll only talk about it with your *218* fellow victims: only they will understand the pain and forgive you for all the things it made you do. Well, something much more painful than a snake has bitten me in my most sensitive part—I mean my heart, or my soul, or whatever you want to call it, which has been struck and bitten by philosophy, whose grip on young and eager souls is much more vicious than a viper's and makes them do the most amazing things. Now, all you people here, Phaedrus, Agathon, Eryxi- *b* machus, Pausanias, Aristodemus, Aristophanes—I need not mention Socrates himself—and all the rest, have all shared in the madness, the Bacchic frenzy of philosophy. And that's why you will hear the rest of my story; you will understand and forgive both what I did then and what I say now. As for the house slaves and for anyone else who is not an initiate, my story's not for you: block your ears!

c To get back to the story. The lights were out; the slaves had left; the time was right, I thought, to come to the point and tell him freely what I had in mind. So I shook him and whispered:

"Socrates, are you asleep?"

"No, no, not at all," he replied.

"You know what I've been thinking?"

"Well, no, not really."

"I think," I said, "you're the only worthy lover I have ever had—and yet, look how shy you are with me! Well, here's how I look at it. It would be really d stupid not to give you anything you want: you can have me, my belongings, anything my friends might have. Nothing is more important to me than becoming the best man I can be, and no one can help me more than you to reach that aim. With a man like you, in fact, I'd be much more ashamed of what wise people would say if I did *not* take you as my lover, than I would of what all the others, in their foolishness, would say if I did."

He heard me out, and then he said in that absolutely inimitable ironic manner of his:

"Dear Alcibiades, if you are right in what you say e about me, you are already more accomplished than you think. If I really have in me the power to make you a better man, then you can see in me a beauty that is really beyond description and makes your own remarkable good looks pale in comparison. But, then, is this a fair exchange that you propose? You seem to me to want more than your proper share: you offer me the merest appearance of beauty, and in return 219 you want the thing itself, 'gold in exchange for bronze.'[54]

"Still, my dear boy, you should think twice, because you could be wrong, and I may be of no use to you. The mind's sight becomes sharp only when the body's eyes go past their prime—and you are still a good long time away from that."

When I heard this I replied:

"I really have nothing more to say. I've told you exactly what I think. Now it's your turn to consider what you think best for you and me."

b "You're right about that," he answered. "In the future, let's consider things together. We'll always do what seems the best to the two of us."

His words made me think that my own had finally hit their mark, that he was smitten by my arrows. I didn't give him a chance to say another word. I stood up immediately and placed my mantle over the light cloak which, though it was the middle of winter, was his only clothing. I slipped underneath the cloak and c put my arms around this man—this utterly unnatural, this truly extraordinary man—and spent the whole night next to him. Socrates, you can't deny a word of it. But in spite of all my efforts, this hopelessly arrogant, this unbelievably insolent man—he turned me down! He spurned my beauty, of which I was so proud, members of the jury—for this is really what you are: you're here to sit in judgment of Socrates' amazing arrogance and pride. Be sure of it, I swear to you by all the gods and goddesses together, my d night with Socrates went no further than if I had spent it with my own father or older brother!

How do you think I felt after that? Of course, I was deeply humiliated, but also I couldn't help admiring his natural character, his moderation, his fortitude—here was a man whose strength and wisdom went beyond my wildest dreams! How could I bring myself to hate him? I couldn't bear to lose his friendship. e But how could I possibly win him over? I knew very well that money meant much less to him than enemy weapons ever meant to Ajax,[55] and the only trap by means of which I had thought I might capture him had already proved a dismal failure. I had no idea what to do, no purpose in life; ah, no one else has ever known the real meaning of slavery!

All this had already occurred when Athens invaded Potidaea,[56] where we served together and shared the same mess. Now, first, he took the hardships of the campaign much better than I ever did—much better, in fact, than anyone in the whole army. When we were cut off from our supplies, as often happens in 220 the field, no one else stood up to hunger as well as

54. [*Iliad* vi.232–36 tells the famous story of the exchange by Glaucus of golden armor for bronze.]

55. [Ajax, a hero of the Greek army at Troy, carried an enormous shield and so was virtually invulnerable to enemy weapons.]

56. [Potidaea, a city in Thrace allied to Athens, was induced by Corinth to revolt in 432 B.C. The city was besieged by the Athenians and eventually defeated in a bloody local war, 432–430 B.C.]

he did. And yet he was the one man who could really enjoy a feast; and though he didn't much want to drink, when he had to, he could drink the best of us under the table. Still, and most amazingly, no one ever saw him drunk (as we'll straightaway put to the test).

Add to this his amazing resistance to the cold—and, let me tell you, the winter there is something awful. Once, I remember, it was frightfully cold; no one so much as stuck his nose outside. If we absolutely had to leave our tent, we wrapped ourselves in anything we could lay our hands on and tied extra pieces of felt or sheepskin over our boots. Well, Socrates went out in that weather wearing nothing but this same old light cloak, and even in bare feet he made better progress on the ice than the other soldiers did in their boots. You should have seen the looks they gave him; they thought he was only doing it to spite them!

So much for that! But you should hear what else he did during that same campaign,

The exploit our strong-hearted hero dared to do.[57]

One day, at dawn, he started thinking about some problem or other; he just stood outside, trying to figure it out. He couldn't resolve it, but he wouldn't give up. He simply stood there, glued to the same spot. By midday, many soldiers had seen him, and, quite mystified, they told everyone that Socrates had been standing there all day, thinking about something. He was still there when evening came, and after dinner some Ionians moved their bedding outside, where it was cooler and more comfortable (all this took place in the summer), but mainly in order to watch if Socrates was going to stay out there all night. And so he did; he stood on the very same spot until dawn! He only left next morning, when the sun came out, and he made his prayers to the new day.

And if you would like to know what he was like in battle—this is a tribute he really deserves. You know that I was decorated for bravery during that campaign: well, during that very battle, Socrates single-handedly saved my life! He absolutely did! He just refused to leave me behind when I was wounded, and he rescued not only me but my armor as well. For my part, Socrates, I told them right then that the decoration really belonged to you, and you can blame me neither for doing so then nor for saying so now. But the generals, who seemed much more concerned with my social position, insisted on giving the decoration to me, and, I must say, you were more eager than the generals themselves for me to have it.

You should also have seen him at our horrible retreat from Delium.[58] I was there with the cavalry, while Socrates was a foot soldier. The army had already dispersed in all directions, and Socrates was retreating together with Laches. I happened to see them just by chance, and the moment I did I started shouting encouragements to them, telling them I was never going to leave their side, and so on. That day I had a better opportunity to watch Socrates than I ever had at Potidaea, for, being on horseback, I wasn't in very great danger. Well, it was easy to see that he was remarkably more collected than Laches. But when I looked again I couldn't get your words, Aristophanes, out of my mind: in the midst of battle he was making his way exactly as he does around town,

. . . *with swagg'ring gait and roving eye.*[59]

He was observing everything quite calmly, looking out for friendly troops and keeping an eye on the enemy. Even from a great distance it was obvious that this was a very brave man, who would put up a terrific fight if anyone approached him. This is what saved both of them. For, as a rule, you try to put as much distance as you can between yourself and such men in battle; you go after the others, those who run away helter-skelter.

You could say many other marvelous things in praise of Socrates. Perhaps he shares some of his specific accomplishments with others. But, as a whole, he is unique; he is like no one else in the past and no one in the present—this is by far the most amazing thing about him. For we might be able to form an idea of what Achilles was like by comparing him to Brasidas or

57. [*Odyssey* iv.242, 271.]

58. [At Delium, a town on the Boeotian coastline just north of Attica, a major Athenian expeditionary force was routed by a Boeotian army in 424 B.C. For another description of Socrates' action during the retreat, see *Laches* 181b.]

59. [Cf. Aristophanes, *Clouds* 362.]

some other great warrior, or we might compare Pericles with Nestor or Antenor or one of the other great orators.[60] There is a parallel for everyone—everyone else, that is. But this man here is so bizarre, his ways and his ideas are so unusual, that, search as you might, you'll never find anyone else, alive or dead, who's even remotely like him. The best you can do is not to compare him to anything human, but to liken him, as I do, to Silenus and the satyrs, and the same goes for his ideas and arguments.

Come to think of it, I should have mentioned this much earlier: even his ideas and arguments are just like those hollow statues of Silenus. If you were to listen to his arguments, at first they'd strike you as totally ridiculous; they're clothed in words as coarse as the hides worn by the most vulgar satyrs. He's always going on about pack asses, or blacksmiths, or cobblers, or tanners; he's always making the same tired old points in the same tired old words. If you are foolish, or simply unfamiliar with him, you'd find it impossible not to laugh at his arguments. But if you see them when they open up like the statues, if you go behind their surface, you'll realize that no other arguments make any sense. They're truly worthy of a god, bursting with figures of virtue inside. They're of great—no, of the greatest—importance for anyone who wants to become a truly good man.

Well, this is my praise of Socrates, though I haven't spared him my reproach, either; I told you how horribly he treated me—and not only me but also Charmides, Euthydemus, and many others. He has deceived us all: he presents himself as your lover, and, before you know it, you're in love with him yourself! I warn you, Agathon, don't let him fool you! Remember our torments; be on your guard: don't wait, like the fool in the proverb, to learn your lesson from your own misfortune.[61]

Alcibiades' frankness provoked a lot of laughter, especially since it was obvious that he was still in love with Socrates, who immediately said to him:

"You're perfectly sober after all, Alcibiades. Otherwise you could never have concealed your motive so gracefully: how casually you let it drop, almost like an afterthought, at the very end of your speech! As if the real point of all this has not been simply to make trouble between Agathon and me! You think that I should be in love with you and no one else, while you, and no one else, should be in love with Agathon—well, we were *not* deceived; we've seen through your little satyr play. Agathon, my friend, don't let him get away with it: let no one come between us!"

Agathon said to Socrates:

"I'm beginning to think you're right; isn't it proof of that that he literally came between us here on the couch? Why would he do this if he weren't set on separating us? But he won't get away with it; I'm coming right over to lie down next to you."

"Wonderful," Socrates said. "Come here, on my other side."

"My god!" cried Alcibiades. "How I suffer in his hands! He kicks me when I'm down; he never lets me go. Come, don't be selfish, Socrates; at least, let's compromise: let Agathon lie down between us."

"Why, that's impossible," Socrates said. "You have already delivered your praise of me, and now it's my turn to praise whoever's on my right. But if Agathon were next to you, he'd have to praise me all over again instead of having me speak in his honor, as I very much want to do in any case. Don't be jealous; let me praise the boy."

"Oh, marvelous," Agathon cried. "Alcibiades, nothing can make me stay next to you now. I'm moving no matter what. I simply *must* hear what Socrates has to say about me."

"There we go again," said Alcibiades. "It's the same old story: when Socrates is around, nobody else can get close to a good-looking man. Look how smoothly and plausibly he found a reason for Agathon to lie down next to him!"

And then, all of a sudden, while Agathon was changing places, a large drunken group, finding the gates open because someone was just leaving, walked into the room and joined the party. There was noise everywhere, and everyone was made to start drinking again in no particular order.

At that point, Aristodemus said, Eryximachus, Phaedrus, and some others among the original guests

60. [Brasidas, among the most effective Spartan generals during the Peloponnesian War, was mortally wounded while defeating the Athenians at Amphipolis in 422 B.C. Antenor (for the Trojans) and Nestor (for the Greeks) were legendary wise counselors during the Trojan War.]

61. [Cf. *Iliad* xvii.32.]

made their excuses and left. He himself fell asleep and slept for a long time (it was winter, and the nights were quite long). He woke up just as dawn was about to break; the roosters were crowing already. He saw that the others had either left or were asleep on their couches and that only Agathon, Aristophanes, and Socrates were still awake, drinking out of a large cup *d* which they were passing around from left to right. Socrates was talking to them. Aristodemus couldn't remember exactly what they were saying—he'd missed the first part of their discussion, and he was half-asleep anyway—but the main point was that Socrates was trying to prove to them that authors should be able to write both comedy and tragedy: the skillful tragic dramatist should also be a comic poet. He was about to clinch his argument, though, to tell the truth, sleepy as they were, they were hardly able to follow his reasoning. In fact, Aristophanes fell asleep in the middle of the discussion, and very soon thereafter, as day was breaking, Agathon also drifted off.

But after getting them off to sleep, Socrates got up and left, and Aristodemus followed him, as always. He said that Socrates went directly to the Lyceum, washed up, spent the rest of the day just as he always did, and only then, as evening was falling, went home to rest.

Republic

Book I

327 I went down to the Piraeus yesterday with Glaucon, the son of Ariston. I wanted to say a prayer to the goddess,[1] and I was also curious to see how they would manage the festival, since they were holding it for the first time. I thought the procession of the local residents was a fine one and that the one conducted by the Thracians was no less outstanding. After we had said our prayer and seen the procession, we started back *b* towards Athens. Polemarchus saw us from a distance as we were setting off for home and told his slave to run and ask us to wait for him. The slave caught hold of my cloak from behind: Polemarchus wants you to wait, he said. I turned around and asked where Polemarchus was. He's coming up behind you, he said, please wait for him. And Glaucon replied: All right, we will.

c Just then Polemarchus caught up with us. Adeimantus, Glaucon's brother,[2] was with him and so were Niceratus, the son of Nicias, and some others, all of whom were apparently on their way from the procession.

Polemarchus said: It looks to me, Socrates, as if you two are starting off for Athens.

It looks the way it is, then, I said.

Do you see how many we are? he said.

I do.

Well, you must either prove stronger than we are, or you will have to stay here.

Isn't there another alternative, namely, that we persuade you to let us go?

But could you persuade us, if we won't listen?

Certainly not, Glaucon said.

Well, we won't listen; you'd better make up your mind to that.

Don't you know, Adeimantus said, that there is to be a torch race on horseback for the goddess tonight? 328

On horseback? I said. That's something new. Are they going to race on horseback and hand the torches on in relays, or what?

In relays, Polemarchus said, and there will be an all-night festival that will be well worth seeing. After dinner, we'll go out to look at it. We'll be joined there by many of the young men, and we'll talk. So don't go; stay.

It seems, Glaucon said, that we'll have to stay. *b*

If you think so, I said, then we must.

So we went to Polemarchus' house, and there we found Lysias and Euthydemus, the brothers of Polemarchus, Thrasymachus of Chalcedon, Charmantides of Paeania, and Clitophon the son of Aristonymus.[3] Polemarchus' father, Cephalus, was also there, and I thought he looked quite old, as I hadn't seen him for some time. He was sitting on a sort of *c* cushioned chair with a wreath on his head, as he had been offering a sacrifice in the courtyard. There was a circle of chairs, and we sat down by him.

As soon as he saw me, Cephalus welcomed me and said: Socrates, you don't come down to the Piraeus to see us as often as you should. If it were still easy for me to walk to town, you wouldn't have to come here; we'd come to you. But, as it is, you ought to come here more often, for you should know that as the *d* physical pleasures wither away, my desire for conversation and its pleasures grows. So do as I say: Stay with these young men now, but come regularly to see us, just as you would to friends or relatives.

Reprinted from *Plato: Republic*, translated by G.M.A. Grube, revised by C.D.C. Reeve (Indianapolis: Hackett Publishing Company, 1992), by permission of the publisher.

1. [The Thracian goddess Bendis, whose cult had recently been introduced in the Piraeus, the harbor area near Athens.—C.D.C.R.]

2. [Glaucon and Adeimantus were Plato's brothers. They are Socrates' chief interlocutors after Book I.]

3. [Lysias was a well-known writer of speeches for use in legal trials. Socrates discusses a speech attributed to him in the *Phaedrus*. Thrasymachus was a Sophist, a paid teacher of oratory and virtue. The few fragments of his writings that survive are translated in Freeman, *Ancilla to the Pre-Socratic Philosophers* (Cambridge, Mass.: Harvard University Press, 1977). Charmantides is otherwise unknown.]

Indeed, Cephalus, I replied, I enjoy talking with the very old, for we should ask them, as we might ask those who have travelled a road that we too will *e* probably have to follow, what kind of road it is, whether rough and difficult or smooth and easy. And I'd gladly find out from you what you think about this, as you have reached the point in life the poets call "the threshold of old age."[4] Is it a difficult time? What is your report about it?

By god, Socrates, I'll tell you exactly what I think. 329 A number of us, who are more or less the same age, often get together in accordance with the old saying.[5] When we meet, the majority complain about the lost pleasures they remember from their youth, those of sex, drinking parties, feasts, and the other things that go along with them, and they get angry as if they had been deprived of important things and had lived well then but are now hardly living at all. Some others moan about the abuse heaped on old people by their *b* relatives, and because of this they repeat over and over that old age is the cause of many evils. But I don't think they blame the real cause, Socrates, for if old age were really the cause, I should have suffered in the same way and so should everyone else of my age. But as it is, I've met some who don't feel like that in the least. Indeed, I was once present when someone asked the poet Sophocles: "How are you as *c* far as sex goes, Sophocles? Can you still make love with a woman?" "Quiet, man," the poet replied, "I am very glad to have escaped from all that, like a slave who has escaped from a savage and tyrannical master." I thought at the time that he was right, and I still do, for old age brings peace and freedom from all such things. When the appetites relax and cease to importune us, everything Sophocles said comes to pass, and we escape from many mad masters. In these *d* matters and in those concerning relatives, the real cause isn't old age, Socrates, but the way people live. If they are moderate and contented, old age, too, is only moderately onerous; if they aren't, both old age and youth are hard to bear.

I admired him for saying that and I wanted him *e* to tell me more, so I urged him on: When you say things like that, Cephalus, I suppose that the majority of people don't agree, they think that you bear old age more easily not because of the way you live but because you're wealthy, for the wealthy, they say, have many consolations.

That's true; they don't agree. And there is something in what they say, though not as much as they think. Themistocles' retort is relevant here. When someone from Seriphus insulted him by saying that his high reputation was due to his city and not to 330 himself, he replied that, had he been a Seriphian, he wouldn't be famous, but neither would the other even if he had been an Athenian.[6] The same applies to those who aren't rich and find old age hard to bear: A good person wouldn't easily bear old age if he were poor, but a bad one wouldn't be at peace with himself even if he were wealthy.

Did you inherit most of your wealth, Cephalus, I asked, or did you make it for yourself?

What did I make for myself, Socrates, you ask. As a money-maker I'm in a sort of mean between my *b* grandfather and my father. My grandfather and namesake inherited about the same amount of wealth as I possess but multiplied it many times. My father, Lysanias, however, diminished that amount to even less than I have now. As for me, I'm satisfied to leave my sons here not less but a little more than I inherited.

The reason I asked is that you don't seem to love money too much. And those who haven't made their own money are usually like you. But those who have *c* made it for themselves are twice as fond of it as those who haven't. Just as poets love their poems and fathers love their children, so those who have made their own money don't just care about it because it's useful, as other people do, but because it's something they've made themselves. This makes them poor company, for they haven't a good word to say about anything except money.

That's true.

It certainly is. But tell me something else. What's

4. [Homer, *Iliad* 22.60, 24.487; *Odyssey* 25.246, 348, 23.212.]

5. ["God ever draws together like to like" (Homer, *Odyssey* 17.218). See Plato, *Lysis* 214a–215c.]

6. [Themistocles, a fifth-century Athenian statesman, was the chief architect of the Greek victory over Persia. By building up the navy, he secured Athens' future as a naval power and also paved the way for the increased political power of the poorer classes, from which sailors were largely drawn. Seriphus is a small island in the Cyclades.]

d the greatest good you've received from being very wealthy?

What I have to say probably wouldn't persuade most people. But you know, Socrates, that when someone thinks his end is near, he becomes frightened and concerned about things he didn't fear before. It's then that the stories we're told about Hades, about how people who've been unjust here must pay the penalty there—stories he used to make fun of—e twist his soul this way and that for fear they're true. And whether because of the weakness of old age or because he is now closer to what happens in Hades and has a clearer view of it, or whatever it is, he is filled with foreboding and fear, and he examines himself to see whether he has been unjust to anyone. If he finds many injustices in his life, he awakes from sleep in terror, as children do, and lives in anticipation of bad things to come. But someone who knows that 331 he hasn't been unjust has sweet good hope as his constant companion—a nurse to his old age, as Pindar[7] says, for he puts it charmingly, Socrates, when he says that when someone lives a just and pious life

> Sweet hope is in his heart,
> Nurse and companion to his age.
> Hope, captain of the ever-twisting
> Minds of mortal men.

How wonderfully well he puts that. It's in this connection that wealth is most valuable, I'd say, not for every man but for a decent and orderly one. Wealth can b do a lot to save us from having to cheat or deceive someone against our will and from having to depart for that other place in fear because we owe sacrifice to a god or money to a person. It has many other uses, but, benefit for benefit, I'd say that this is how it is most useful to a man of any understanding.

A fine sentiment, Cephalus, but, speaking of this c very thing itself, namely, justice,[8] are we to say unconditionally that it is speaking the truth and paying whatever debts one has incurred? Or is doing these things sometimes just, sometimes unjust? I mean this sort of thing, for example: Everyone would surely agree that if a sane man lends weapons to a friend and then asks for them back when he is out of his mind, the friend shouldn't return them, and wouldn't be acting justly if he did. Nor should anyone be willing to tell the whole truth to someone who is out of his mind.

That's true. d

Then the definition of justice isn't speaking the truth and repaying what one has borrowed.

It certainly is, Socrates, said Polemarchus, interrupting, if indeed we're to trust Simonides at all.[9]

Well, then, Cephalus said, I'll hand over the argument to you, as I have to look after the sacrifice.

So, Polemarchus said, am I then to be your heir in everything?

You certainly are, Cephalus said, laughing, and off he went to the sacrifice.

Then tell us, heir to the argument, I said, just what Simonides stated about justice that you consider e correct.

He stated that it is just to give to each what is owed to him. And it's a fine saying, in my view.

Well, now, it isn't easy to doubt Simonides, for he's a wise and godlike man. But what exactly does he mean? Perhaps you know, Polemarchus, but I don't understand him. Clearly, he doesn't mean what we said a moment ago, that it is just to give back whatever a person has lent to you, even if he's out of his mind when he asks for it. And yet what he has lent to you is surely something that's owed to him, isn't it? 332

Yes.

But it is absolutely not to be given to him when he's out of his mind?

That's true.

Then it seems that Simonides must have meant something different when he says that to return what is owed is just.

Something different indeed, by god. He means that friends owe it to their friends to do good for them, never harm.

7. [Pindar (518–438 B.C.), a lyric poet from Boeotia, was most famous for his poems in celebration of the victors in the games, such as the Olympian and Pythian, held in various parts of Greece.]

8. [Unlike their usual equivalents "just" and "justice," the adjective *dikaios* and the noun *dikaiosunē* are often used in a wider sense, better captured by our words "right" or "correct." The opposite, *adikia*, then has the sense of general wrongdoing.]

9. [Simonides (c. 548–468 B.C.), a lyric and elegiac poet, was born in the Aegean island of Ceos.]

I follow you. Someone doesn't give a lender back what he's owed by giving him gold, if doing so would b be harmful, and both he and the lender are friends. Isn't that what you think Simonides meant?

It is.

But what about this? Should one also give one's enemies whatever is owed to them?

By all means, one should give them what is owed to them. And in my view what enemies owe to each other is appropriately and precisely—something bad.

It seems then that Simonides was speaking in riddles—just like a poet!—when he said what justice is, c for he thought it just to give to each what is appropriate to him, and this is what he called giving him what is owed to him.

What else did you think he meant?

Then what do you think he'd answer if someone asked him: "Simonides, which of the things that are owed or that are appropriate for someone or something to have does the craft[10] we call medicine give, and to whom or what does it give them?"

It's clear that it gives medicines, food, and drink to bodies.

And what owed or appropriate things does the craft we call cooking give, and to whom or what does it give them?

d It gives seasonings to food.

Good. Now, what does the craft we call justice give, and to whom or what does it give it?

If we are to follow the previous answers, Socrates, it gives benefits to friends and does harm to enemies.

Simonides means, then, that to treat friends well and enemies badly is justice?

I believe so.

And who is most capable of treating friends well and enemies badly in matters of disease and health?

A doctor.

e And who can do so best in a storm at sea?

A ship's captain.

What about the just person? In what actions and what work is he most capable of benefiting friends and harming enemies?

In wars and alliances, I suppose.

All right. Now, when people aren't sick, Polemarchus, a doctor is useless to them?

True.

And so is a ship's captain to those who aren't sailing?

Yes.

And to people who aren't at war, a just man is useless?

No, I don't think that at all.

Justice is also useful in peacetime, then?

It is. 333

And so is farming, isn't it?

Yes.

For getting produce?

Yes.

And shoemaking as well?

Yes.

For getting shoes, I think you'd say?

Certainly.

Well, then, what is justice useful for getting and using in peacetime?

Contracts, Socrates.

And by contracts do you mean partnerships, or what?

I mean partnerships.

Is someone a good and useful partner in a game of checkers because he's just or because he's a checkers player? b

Because he's a checkers player.

And in laying bricks and stones, is a just person a better and more useful partner than a builder?

Not at all.

In what kind of partnership, then, is a just person a better partner than a builder or a lyre-player, in the way that a lyre-player is better than a just person at hitting the right notes?

In money matters, I think.

Except perhaps, Polemarchus, in using money, for whenever one needs to buy a horse jointly, I think a horse breeder is a more useful partner, isn't he? c

Apparently.

And when one needs to buy a boat, it's a boatbuilder or a ship's captain?

Probably.

In what joint use of silver or gold, then, is a just person a more useful partner than the others?

10. [The Greek word translated as "craft" here is *technē*. It has the sort of connotation for Socrates and Plato that "science" has for us. Thus fifth-century doctors tried to show that medicine is a craft, much as contemporary psychoanalysts try to convince us that psychoanalysis is a science. For further discussion see Reeve, *Socrates in the Apology*, 37–45.]

When it must be deposited for safekeeping, Socrates.

You mean whenever there is no need to use them but only to keep them?

That's right.

Then it is when money isn't being used that justice is useful for it?

d I'm afraid so.

And whenever one needs to keep a pruning knife safe, but not to use it, justice is useful both in partnerships and for the individual. When you need to use it, however, it is skill at vine pruning that's useful?

Apparently.

You'll agree, then, that when one needs to keep a shield or a lyre safe and not to use them, justice is a useful thing, but when you need to use them, it is soldiery or musicianship that's useful?

Necessarily.

And so, too, with everything else, justice is useless when they are in use but useful when they aren't?

It looks that way.

In that case, justice isn't worth much, since it is *e* only useful for useless things. But let's look into the following point. Isn't the person most able to land a blow, whether in boxing or any other kind of fight, also most able to guard against it?

Certainly.

And the one who is most able to guard against disease is also most able to produce it unnoticed?

So it seems to me, anyway.

And the one who is the best guardian of an army is the very one who can steal the enemy's plans *334* and dispositions?

Certainly.

Whenever someone is a clever guardian, then, he is also a clever thief.

Probably so.

If a just person is clever at guarding money, therefore, he must also be clever at stealing it.

According to our argument, at any rate.

A just person has turned out then, it seems, to be a kind of thief. Maybe you learned this from Homer, for he's fond of Autolycus, the maternal grandfather *b* of Odysseus, whom he describes as better than everyone at lying and stealing.[11] According to you, Homer, and Simonides, then, justice seems to be some sort of craft of stealing, one that benefits friends and harms enemies. Isn't that what you meant?

No, by god, it isn't. I don't know any more what I did mean, but I still believe that to benefit one's friends and harm one's enemies is justice.

Speaking of friends, do you mean those a person believes to be good and useful to him or those who *c* actually are good and useful, even if he doesn't think they are, and similarly with enemies?

Probably, one loves those one considers good and useful and hates those one considers bad and harmful.

But surely people often make mistakes about this, believing many people to be good and useful when they aren't, and making the opposite mistake about enemies?

They do indeed.

And then good people are their enemies and bad ones their friends?

That's right.

And so it's just to benefit bad people and harm good ones? *d*

Apparently.

But good people are just and able to do no wrong?

True.

Then, according to your account, it's just to do bad things to those who do no injustice.

No, that's not just at all, Socrates; my account must be a bad one.

It's just, then, is it, to harm unjust people and benefit just ones?

That's obviously a more attractive view than the other one, anyway.

Then, it follows, Polemarchus, that it is just for the many, who are mistaken in their judgment, to harm their friends, who are bad, and benefit their enemies, who are good. And so we arrive at a conclusion oppo- *e* site to what we said Simonides meant.

That certainly follows. But let's change our definition, for it seems that we didn't define friends and enemies correctly.

How did we define them, Polemarchus?

We said that a friend is someone who is believed to be useful.

And how are we to change that now?

Someone who is both believed to be useful and is useful is a friend; someone who is believed to be useful but isn't, is believed to be a friend but isn't. And the same for the enemy. *335*

11. [The reference is to *Odyssey* 19.392–98.]

According to this account, then, a good person will be a friend and a bad one an enemy.

Yes.

So you want us to add something to what we said before about justice, when we said that it is just to treat friends well and enemies badly. You want us to add to this that it is just to treat well a friend who is good and to harm an enemy who is bad?

b Right. That seems fine to me.

Is it, then, the role of a just man to harm anyone?

Certainly, he must harm those who are both bad and enemies.

Do horses become better or worse when they are harmed?

Worse.

With respect to the virtue[12] that makes dogs good or the one that makes horses good?

The one that makes horses good.

And when dogs are harmed, they become worse in the virtue that makes dogs good, not horses?

Necessarily.

Then won't we say the same about human beings, *c* too, that when they are harmed they become worse in human virtue?

Indeed.

But isn't justice human virtue?

Yes, certainly.

Then people who are harmed must become more unjust?

So it seems.

Can musicians make people unmusical through music?

They cannot.

Or horsemen make people unhorsemanlike through horsemanship?

No.

Well, then, can those who are just make people unjust through justice? In a word, can those who are good make people bad through virtue? *d*

They cannot.

It isn't the function of heat to cool things but of its opposite?

Yes.

Nor the function of dryness to make things wet but of its opposite?

Indeed.

Nor the function of goodness to harm but of its opposite?

Apparently.

And a just person is good?

Indeed.

Then, Polemarchus, it isn't the function of a just person to harm a friend or anyone else, rather it is the function of his opposite, an unjust person?

In my view that's completely true, Socrates.

If anyone tells us, then, that it is just to give to each what he's owed and understands by this that a *e* just man should harm his enemies and benefit his friends, he isn't wise to say it, since what he says isn't true, for it has become clear to us that it is never just to harm anyone?

I agree.

You and I shall fight as partners, then, against anyone who tells us that Simonides, Bias, Pittacus, or any of our other wise and blessedly happy men said this.[13]

I, at any rate, am willing to be your partner in the battle.

Do you know to whom I think the saying belongs that it is just to benefit friends and harm enemies? 336

Who?

I think it belongs to Periander, or Perdiccas, or Xerxes, or Ismenias of Corinth, or some other wealthy man who believed himself to have great power.[14]

12. [If something is a knife (say) or a man, its *aretē* or virtue as a knife or a man is that state or property of it that makes it a good knife or a good man. See *Charmides* 161a8–9; *Euthyphro* 6d6–e1; *Gorgias* 506d2–4; *Protagoras* 332b4–6; *Republic* 353d9–354a2. The *aretē* of a knife might include having a sharp blade; the *aretē* of a man might include being intelligent, well-born, just, or courageous. *Aretē* is thus broader than our notion of moral virtue. It applies to things (such as knives) that are not moral agents. And it applies to aspects of moral agents (such as intelligence or family status) that are not normally considered to be moral aspects of them. For these reasons it is sometimes more appropriate to render *aretē* as "excellence." But "virtue" remains the best overall translation, and once these few facts are borne in mind, it should seldom mislead.]

13. [Bias of Priene in Ionia (now the region of Turkey bordering on the eastern shore of the Aegean) and Pittacus of Mytilene (on the island of Lesbos in the eastern Aegean), both sixth century B.C., were two of the legendary seven sages of Greece.]

14. [Periander was tyrant of the city of Corinth (650–570 B.C.). Perdiccas is probably Perdiccas II, king of Macedon

That's absolutely true.

All right, since it has become apparent that justice and the just aren't what such people say they are, what else could they be?

While we were speaking, Thrasymachus had tried *b* many times to take over the discussion but was restrained by those sitting near him, who wanted to hear our argument to the end. When we paused after what I'd just said, however, he couldn't keep quiet any longer. He coiled himself up like a wild beast about to spring, and he hurled himself at us as if to tear us to pieces.

Polemarchus and I were frightened and flustered as he roared into our midst: What nonsense have you two been talking, Socrates? Why do you act like idiots *c* by giving way to one another? If you truly want to know what justice is, don't just ask questions and then refute the answers simply to satisfy your competitiveness or love of honor. You know very well that it is easier to ask questions than answer them. Give an answer yourself, and tell us what you say the just is. *d* And don't tell me that it's the right, the beneficial, the profitable, the gainful, or the advantageous, but tell me clearly and exactly what you mean; for I won't accept such nonsense from you.

His words startled me, and, looking at him, I was afraid. And I think that if I hadn't seen him before he stared at me, I'd have been dumbstruck. But as it was, I happened to look at him just as our discussion *e* began to exasperate him, so I was able to answer, and, trembling a little, I said: Don't be too hard on us, Thrasymachus, for if Polemarchus and I made an error in our investigation, you should know that we did so unwillingly. If we were searching for gold, we'd never willingly give way to each other, if by doing so we'd destroy our chance of finding it. So don't think that in searching for justice, a thing more valuable than even a large quantity of gold, we'd mindlessly give way to one another or be less than completely serious about finding it. You surely mustn't think that, but rather—as I do—that we're incapable of finding it. Hence it's surely far more appropriate for us to be pitied by you clever people than to be given rough treatment. 337

When he heard that, he gave a loud, sarcastic laugh. By Heracles, he said, that's just Socrates' usual irony.[15] I knew, and I said so to these people earlier, that you'd be unwilling to answer and that, if someone questioned *you*, you'd be ironical and do anything rather than give an answer.

That's because you're a clever fellow, Thrasymachus. You knew very well that if you ask someone how much twelve is, and, as you ask, you warn him by saying "Don't tell me, man, that twelve is twice *b* six, or three times four, or six times two, or four times three, for I won't accept such nonsense," then you'll see clearly, I think, that no one could answer a question framed like that. And if he said to you: "What are you saying, Thrasymachus, am I not to give any of the answers you mention, not even if twelve happens to be one of those things? I'm amazed. Do you want me to say something other than the truth? Or do you mean something else?" What answer would you give him? *c*

Well, so you think the two cases are alike?

Why shouldn't they be alike? But even if they aren't alike, yet seem so to the person you asked, do you think him any less likely to give the answer that seems right to him, whether we forbid him to or not?

Is that what you're going to do, give one of the forbidden answers?

I wouldn't be surprised—provided that it's the one that seems right to me after I've investigated the matter.

What if I show you a different answer about justice than all these—and a better one? What would you *d* deserve then?

What else than the appropriate penalty for one who doesn't know, namely, to learn from the one who does know? Therefore, that's what I deserve.

You amuse me, but in addition to learning, you must pay a fine.

(c. 450–413 B.C.), who is also mentioned in the *Gorgias* 471a–e. Xerxes was the king of Persia who invaded Greece in the second Persian war (begun in 480 B.C.). Ismenias is mentioned in the *Meno* 89e. All four are either notorious tyrants or men famous for their wealth.]

15. [The Greek word *eirōneia*, unlike its usual translation "irony," is correctly applied only to someone who intends to deceive. Thus Thrasymachus is not simply accusing Socrates of saying one thing while meaning another; he is accusing him of trying to deceive those present. See G. Vlastos, "Socratic Irony," *Classical Quarterly* 37 (1987): 79–96.]

I will as soon as I have some money.

He has some already, said Glaucon. If it's a matter of money, speak, Thrasymachus, for we'll all contribute for Socrates.

I know, he said, so that Socrates can carry on as e usual. He gives no answer himself, and then, when someone else does give one, he takes up the argument and refutes it.

How can someone give an answer, I said, when he doesn't know it and doesn't claim to know it, and when an eminent man forbids him to express the opinion he has? It's much more appropriate for you 338 to answer, since you say you know and can tell us. So do it as a favor to me, and don't begrudge your teaching to Glaucon and the others.

While I was saying this, Glaucon and the others begged him to speak. It was obvious that Thrasymachus thought he had a fine answer and that he wanted to earn their admiration by giving it, but he pretended that he wanted to indulge his love of victory by forcing me to answer. However, he agreed in the end, and b then said: There you have Socrates' wisdom; he himself isn't willing to teach, but he goes around learning from others and isn't even grateful to them.

When you say that I learn from others you are right, Thrasymachus, but when you say that I'm not grateful, that isn't true. I show what gratitude I can, but since I have no money, I can give only praise. But just how enthusiastically I give it when someone seems to me to speak well, you'll know as soon as you've answered, for I think that you will speak well.

Listen, then. I say that justice is nothing other than c the advantage of the stronger. Well, why don't you praise me? But then you'd do anything to avoid having to do that.

I must first understand you, for I don't yet know what you mean. The advantage of the stronger, you say, is just. What do you mean, Thrasymachus? Surely you don't mean something like this: Polydamus, the pancratist,[16] is stronger than we are; it is to his advantage to eat beef to build up his physical strength; therefore, this food is also advantageous and just for d us who are weaker than he is?

16. [*Pancration* was a mixture of boxing and wrestling combined with kicking and strangling. Biting and gouging were forbidden, but pretty well everything else, including breaking and dislocating limbs, was permitted.]

You disgust me, Socrates. Your trick is to take hold of the argument at the point where you can do it the most harm.

Not at all, but tell us more clearly what you mean.

Don't you know that some cities are ruled by a tyranny, some by a democracy, and some by an aristocracy?

Of course.

And in each city this element is stronger, namely, the ruler?

Certainly.

And each makes laws to its own advantage. Democracy makes democratic laws, tyranny makes tyrannical e laws, and so on with the others. And they declare what they have made—what is to their own advantage—to be just for their subjects, and they punish anyone who goes against this as lawless and unjust. This, then, is what I say justice is, the same in all cities, the advantage of the established rule. Since the established rule is surely stronger, anyone who reasons 339 correctly will conclude that the just is the same everywhere, namely, the advantage of the stronger.

Now I see what you mean. Whether it's true or not, I'll try to find out. But you yourself have answered that the just is the advantageous, Thrasymachus, whereas you forbade that answer to me. True, you've added "of the stronger" to it.

And I suppose you think that's an insignificant addition. b

It isn't clear yet whether it's significant. But it is clear that we must investigate to see whether or not it's true. I agree that the just is some kind of advantage. But you add that it's *of the stronger*. I don't know about that. We'll have to look into it.

Go ahead and look.

We will. Tell me, don't you also say that it is just to obey the rulers?

I do.

And are the rulers in all cities infallible, or are they liable to error? c

No doubt they are liable to error.

When they undertake to make laws, therefore, they make some correctly, others incorrectly?

I suppose so.

And a law is correct if it prescribes what is to the rulers' own advantage and incorrect if it prescribes what is to their disadvantage? Is that what you mean?

It is.

And whatever laws they make must be obeyed by their subjects, and this is justice?

Of course.

Then, according to your account, it is just to do *d* not only what is to the advantage of the stronger, but also the opposite, what is not to their advantage.

What are you saying?

The same as you. But let's examine it more fully. Haven't we agreed that, in giving orders to their subjects, the rulers are sometimes in error as to what is best for themselves, and yet that it is just for their subjects to do whatever their rulers order? Haven't we agreed to that much?

I think so.

Then you must also think that you have agreed *e* that it is just to do what is disadvantageous to the rulers and those who are stronger, whenever they unintentionally order what is bad for themselves. But you also say that it is just for the others to obey the orders they give. You're terribly clever, Thrasymachus, but doesn't it necessarily follow that it is just to do the opposite of what you said, since the weaker are then ordered to do what is disadvantageous to the stronger?

By god, Socrates, said Polemarchus, that's quite *340* clear.

If you are to be his witness anyway, said Clitophon, interrupting.

Who needs a witness? Polemarchus replied. Thrasymachus himself agrees that the rulers sometimes order what is bad for themselves and that it is just for the others to do it.

That, Polemarchus, is because Thrasymachus maintained that it is just to obey the orders of the rulers.

He also maintained, Clitophon, that the advantage *b* of the stronger is just. And having maintained both principles he went on to agree that the stronger sometimes gives orders to those who are weaker than he is—in other words, to his subjects—that are disadvantageous to the stronger himself. From these agreements it follows that what is to the advantage of the stronger is no more just than what is not to his advantage.

But, Clitophon responded, he said that the advantage of the stronger is what the stronger believes to be his advantage. This is what the weaker must do, and this is what he maintained the just to be.

That isn't what he said, Polemarchus replied.

It makes no difference, Polemarchus, I said. If Thrasymachus wants to put it that way now, let's *c* accept it. Tell me, Thrasymachus, is this what you wanted to say the just is, namely, what the stronger believes to be to his advantage, whether it is in fact to his advantage or not? Is that what we are to say you mean?

Not at all. Do you think I'd call someone who is in error stronger at the very moment he errs?

I did think that was what you meant when you agreed that the rulers aren't infallible but are liable to error.

That's because you are a false witness in arguments, Socrates. When someone makes an error in the treat- *d* ment of patients, do you call him a doctor in regard to that very error? Or when someone makes an error in accounting, do you call him an accountant in regard to that very error in calculation? I think that we express ourselves in words that, taken literally, do say that a doctor is in error, or an accountant, or a grammarian. But each of these, insofar as he is what we call him, never errs, so that, according to the *e* precise account (and you are a stickler for precise accounts), no craftsman ever errs. It's when his knowledge fails him that he makes an error, and in regard to that error he is no craftsman. No craftsman, expert, or ruler makes an error at the moment when he is ruling, even though everyone will say that a physician or a ruler makes errors. It's in this loose way that you must also take the answer I gave earlier. But the most precise answer is this. A ruler, insofar as he is a ruler, *341* never makes errors and unerringly decrees what is best for himself, and this his subject must do. Thus, as I said from the first, it is just to do what is to the advantage of the stronger.

All right, Thrasymachus, so you think I'm a false witness?

You certainly are.

And you think that I asked the questions I did in order to harm you in the argument?

I know it very well, but it won't do you any good. You'll never be able to trick me, so you can't harm *b* me that way, and without trickery you'll never be able to overpower me in argument.

I wouldn't so much as try, Thrasymachus. But in order to prevent this sort of thing from happening again, define clearly whether it is the ruler and stronger in the ordinary sense or in the precise sense whose advantage you said it is just for the weaker to promote as the advantage of the stronger.

I mean the ruler in the most precise sense. Now practice your harm-doing and false witnessing on that if you can—I ask no concessions from you—but you certainly won't be able to.

Do you think that I'm crazy enough to try to shave *c* a lion or to bear false witness against Thrasymachus?

You certainly tried just now, though you were a loser at that too.

Enough of this. Tell me: Is a doctor in the precise sense, whom you mentioned before, a money-maker or someone who treats the sick? Tell me about the one who is really a doctor.

He's the one who treats the sick.

What about a ship's captain? Is a captain in the precise sense a ruler of sailors or a sailor?

A ruler of sailors.

We shouldn't, I think, take into account the fact *d* that he sails in a ship, and he shouldn't be called a sailor for that reason, for it isn't because of his sailing that he is called a ship's captain, but because of his craft and his rule over sailors?

That's true.

And is there something advantageous to each of these, that is, to bodies and to sailors?

Certainly.

And aren't the respective crafts by nature set over them to seek and provide what is to their advantage?

They are.

And is there any advantage for each of the crafts themselves except to be as complete or perfect as possible?

e What are you asking?

This: If you asked me whether our bodies are sufficient in themselves, or whether they need something else, I'd answer: "They certainly have needs. And because of this, because our bodies are deficient rather than self-sufficient, the craft of medicine has now been discovered. The craft of medicine was developed to provide what is advantageous for a body." Do you think that I'm right in saying this or not?

You are right.

342 Now, is medicine deficient? Does a craft need some further virtue, as the eyes are in need of sight, and the ears of hearing, so that another craft is needed to seek and provide what is advantageous to them?[17] Does a craft itself have some similar deficiency, so that each craft needs another, to seek out what is to its advantage? And does the craft that does the seeking need still another, and so on without end? Or does each seek out what is to its own advantage by itself? Or does it need neither itself nor another craft to seek *b* out what is advantageous to it, because of its own deficiencies? Or is it that there is no deficiency or error in any craft? That it isn't appropriate for any craft to seek what is to the advantage of anything except that of which it is the craft? And that, since it is itself correct, it is without either fault or impurity, as long as it is wholly and precisely the craft that it is? Consider this with the preciseness of language you mentioned. Is it so or not?

It appears to be so.

Medicine doesn't seek its own advantage, then, but that of the body? *c*

Yes.

And horse-breeding doesn't seek its own advantage, but that of horses? Indeed, no other craft seeks its own advantage—for it has no further needs—but the advantage of that of which it is the craft?

Apparently so.

Now, surely, Thrasymachus, the crafts rule over and are stronger than the things of which they are the crafts?

Very reluctantly, he conceded this as well.

No kind of knowledge seeks or orders what is advantageous to itself, then, but what is advantageous to the weaker, which is subject to it. *d*

He tried to fight this conclusion, but he conceded it in the end. And after he had, I said: Surely, then, no doctor, insofar as he is a doctor, seeks or orders what is advantageous to himself, but what is advantageous to his patient? We agreed that a doctor in the precise sense is a ruler of bodies, not a money-maker. Wasn't that agreed?

Yes.

17. [Sight is the virtue or excellence of the eyes (see 335b n.12). Without it, the eyes cannot achieve what is advantageous to them, namely, sight. So eyes need some further virtue to seek and provide what is advantageous to them. But Socrates assumes throughout Book I that virtues are crafts (see 332d). Hence he can conclude that the eyes need a further craft to achieve what is advantageous to them.]

So a ship's captain in the precise sense is a ruler of sailors, not a sailor?

e That's what we agreed.

Doesn't it follow that a ship's captain or ruler won't seek and order what is advantageous to himself, but what is advantageous to a sailor?

He reluctantly agreed.

So, then, Thrasymachus, no one in any position of rule, insofar as he is a ruler, seeks or orders what is advantageous to himself, but what is advantageous to his subjects; the ones of whom he is himself the craftsman. It is to his subjects and what is advantageous and proper to them that he looks, and everything he says and does he says and does for them.

When we reached this point in the argument, and 343 it was clear to all that his account of justice had turned into its opposite, instead of answering, Thrasymachus said: Tell me, Socrates, do you still have a wet nurse?

What's this? Hadn't you better answer *my* questions rather than asking *me* such things?

Because she's letting you run around with a snotty nose, and doesn't wipe it when she needs to! Why, for all she cares, you don't even know about sheep and shepherds.

Just what is it I don't know?

You think that shepherds and cowherds seek the b good of their sheep and cattle, and fatten them and take care of them, looking to something other than their master's good and their own. Moreover, you believe that rulers in cities—true rulers, that is—think about their subjects differently than one does about sheep, and that night and day they think of something besides their own advantage. You are so c far from understanding about justice and what's just, about injustice and what's unjust, that you don't realize that justice is really the good of another, the advantage of the stronger and the ruler, and harmful to the one who obeys and serves. Injustice is the opposite, it rules the truly simple and just, and those it rules do what is to the advantage of the other and stronger, and they make the one they serve happy, but themselves not at all. You must look at it as d follows, my most simple Socrates: A just man always gets less than an unjust one. First, in their contracts with one another, you'll never find, when the partnership ends, that a just partner has got more than an unjust one, but less. Second, in matters relating to the city, when taxes are to be paid, a just man pays more on the same property, an unjust one less, but when the city is giving out refunds, a just man gets nothing, while an unjust one makes a large profit. e Finally, when each of them holds a ruling position in some public office, a just person, even if he isn't penalized in other ways, finds that his private affairs deteriorate because he has to neglect them, that he gains no advantage from the public purse because of his justice, and that he's hated by his relatives and acquaintances when he's unwilling to do them an unjust favor. The opposite is true of an unjust man in every respect. Therefore, I repeat what I said before: A person of great power outdoes everyone else.[18] Consider him if you want to figure out how much more 344 advantageous it is for the individual to be just rather than unjust. You'll understand this most easily if you turn your thoughts to the most complete injustice, the one that makes the doer of injustice happiest and the sufferers of it, who are unwilling to do injustice, most wretched. This is tyranny, which through stealth or force appropriates the property of others, whether sacred or profane, public or private, not little by little, but all at once. If someone commits only one part of injustice and is caught, he's punished and greatly b reproached—such partly unjust people are called temple-robbers,[19] kidnappers, housebreakers, robbers, and thieves when they commit these crimes. But when someone, in addition to appropriating their possessions, kidnaps and enslaves the citizens as well, instead of these shameful names he is called happy and blessed, not only by the citizens themselves, but c by all who learn that he has done the whole of injustice. Those who reproach injustice do so because they are afraid not of doing it but of suffering it. So, Socrates, injustice, if it is on a large enough scale, is stronger, freer, and more masterly than justice. And,

18. [Outdoing (*pleonektein*) is an important notion in the remainder of the *Republic*. It is connected to *pleonexia*, which is what one succumbs to when one always wants to outdo everyone else by getting and having more and more. *Pleonexia* is, or is the cause of, injustice (359c), since always wanting to outdo others leads one to try to get what belongs to them, what isn't *one's own*. It is contrasted with *doing or having one's own*, which is, or is the cause of, justice (434a, 441e).]

19. [The temples acted as public treasuries, so that a temple robber is the equivalent of a present-day bank robber.]

as I said from the first, justice is what is advantageous to the stronger, while injustice is to one's own profit and advantage.

Having emptied this great flood of words into our d ears all at once like a bath attendant, Thrasymachus intended to leave. But those present didn't let him and made him stay to give an account of what he had said. I too begged him to stay, and I said to him: After hurling such a speech at us, Thrasymachus, do you intend to leave before adequately instructing us or finding out whether you are right or not? Or do e you think it a small matter to determine which whole way of life would make living most worthwhile for each of us?

Is *that* what I seem to you to think? Thrasymachus said.

Either that, or else you care nothing for us and aren't worried about whether we'll live better or worse lives because of our ignorance of what you say you know. So show some willingness to teach it to us. It wouldn't be a bad investment for you to be the benefactor of a group as large as ours. For my own 345 part, I'll tell you that I am not persuaded. I don't believe that injustice is more profitable than justice, not even if you give it full scope and put no obstacles in its way. Suppose that there *is* an unjust person, and suppose he *does* have the power to do injustice, whether by trickery or open warfare; nonetheless, he doesn't persuade me that injustice is more profitable b than justice. Perhaps someone here, besides myself, feels the same as I do. So come now, and persuade us that we are wrong to esteem justice more highly than injustice in planning our lives.

And how am I to persuade you, if you aren't persuaded by what I said just now? What more can I do? Am I to take my argument and pour it into your very soul?

God forbid! Don't do that! But, first, stick to what you've said, and then, if you change your position, do it openly and don't deceive us. You see, Thrasymachus, that having defined the true doctor—to con- c tinue examining the things you said before—you didn't consider it necessary later to keep a precise guard on the true shepherd. You think that, insofar as he's a shepherd, he fattens sheep, not looking to what is best for the sheep but to a banquet, like a guest about to be entertained at a feast, or to a future sale, like a money-maker rather than a shepherd. Shepherding is concerned only to provide what is best d for the things it is set over, and it is itself adequately provided with all it needs to be at its best when it doesn't fall short in any way of being the craft of shepherding. That's why I thought it necessary for us to agree before[20] that every kind of rule, insofar as it rules, doesn't seek anything other than what is best for the things it rules and cares for, and this is true both of public and private kinds of rule. But do you think that those who rule cities, the true rulers, e rule willingly?

I don't think it, by god, I know it.

But, Thrasymachus, don't you realize that in other kinds of rule no one wants to rule for its own sake, but they ask for pay, thinking that their ruling will benefit not themselves but their subjects? Tell me, doesn't every craft differ from every other in having 346 a different function? Please don't answer contrary to what you believe, so that we can come to some definite conclusion.

Yes, that's what differentiates them.

And each craft benefits us in its own peculiar way, different from the others. For example, medicine gives us health, navigation gives us safety while sailing, and so on with the others?

Certainly.

And wage-earning gives us wages, for this is its function? Or would you call medicine the same as b navigation? Indeed, if you want to define matters precisely, as you proposed, even if someone who is a ship's captain becomes healthy because sailing is advantageous to his health, you wouldn't for that reason call his craft medicine?

Certainly not.

Nor would you call wage-earning medicine, even if someone becomes healthy while earning wages?

Certainly not.

Nor would you call medicine wage-earning, even if someone earns pay while healing?

No. c

We are agreed, then, that each craft brings its own peculiar benefit?

It does.

Then whatever benefit all craftsmen receive in common must clearly result from their joint practice of some additional craft that benefits each of them?

20. [See 341e–342e.]

So it seems.

And we say that the additional craft in question, which benefits the craftsmen by earning them wages, is the craft of wage-earning?

He reluctantly agreed.

Then this benefit, receiving wages, doesn't result *d* from their own craft, but rather, if we're to examine this precisely, medicine provides health, and wage-earning provides wages; house-building provides a house, and wage-earning, which accompanies it, provides a wage; and so on with the other crafts. Each of them does its own work and benefits the things it is set over. So, if wages aren't added, is there any benefit that the craftsman gets from his craft?

Apparently none.

But he still provides a benefit when he works for *e* nothing?

Yes, I think he does.

Then, it is clear now, Thrasymachus, that no craft or rule provides for its own advantage, but, as we've been saying for some time, it provides and orders for its subject and aims at its advantage, that of the weaker, not of the stronger. That's why I said just now, Thrasymachus, that no one willingly chooses to rule and to take other people's troubles in hand and straighten them out, but each asks for wages; for *347* anyone who intends to practice his craft well never does or orders what is best for himself—at least not when he orders as his craft prescribes—but what is best for his subject. It is because of this, it seems, that wages must be provided to a person if he's to be willing to rule, whether in the form of money or honor or a penalty if he refuses.

What do you mean, Socrates? said Glaucon. I know the first two kinds of wages, but I don't understand what penalty you mean or how you can call it a wage.

Then you don't understand the best people's kind of wages, the kind that moves the most decent to rule, when they are willing to rule at all. Don't you know *b* that the love of honor and the love of money are despised, and rightly so?

I do.

Therefore good people won't be willing to rule for the sake of either money or honor. They don't want to be paid wages openly for ruling and get called hired hands, nor to take them in secret from their rule and be called thieves. And they won't rule for the sake of honor, because they aren't ambitious honor-lovers. So, if they're to be willing to rule, some com- *c* pulsion or punishment must be brought to bear on them—perhaps that's why it is thought shameful to seek to rule before one is compelled to. Now, the greatest punishment, if one isn't willing to rule, is to be ruled by someone worse than oneself. And I think that it's fear of this that makes decent people rule when they do. They approach ruling not as something good or something to be enjoyed, but as something necessary, since it can't be entrusted to anyone better *d* than—or even as good as—themselves. In a city of good men, if it came into being, the citizens would fight in order *not to rule*, just as they do now in order to rule. There it would be quite clear that anyone who is really a true ruler doesn't by nature seek his own advantage but that of his subjects. And everyone, knowing this, would rather be benefited by others than take the trouble to benefit them. So I can't at all agree with Thrasymachus that justice is the advantage of the stronger—but we'll look further into that another time. What Thrasymachus is now say- *e* ing—that the life of an unjust person is better than that of a just one—seems to be of far greater importance. Which life would you choose, Glaucon? And which of our views do you consider truer?

I certainly think that the life of a just person is more profitable.

Did you hear all of the good things Thrasymachus listed a moment ago for the unjust life? *348*

I heard, but I wasn't persuaded.

Then, do you want us to persuade him, if we're able to find a way, that what he says isn't true?

Of course I do.

If we oppose him with a parallel speech about the blessings of the just life, and then he replies, and then we do, we'd have to count and measure the good things mentioned on each side, and we'd need a jury to decide the case. But if, on the other hand, *b* we investigate the question, as we've been doing, by seeking agreement with each other, we ourselves can be both jury and advocates at once.

Certainly.

Which approach do you prefer? I asked.

The second.

Come, then, Thrasymachus, I said, answer us from the beginning. You say that complete injustice is more profitable than complete justice?

I certainly do say that, and I've told you why. *c*

Well, then, what do you say about this? Do you call one of the two a virtue and the other a vice?

Of course.

That is to say, you call justice a virtue and injustice a vice?

That's hardly likely, since I say that injustice is profitable and justice isn't.

Then, what exactly do you say?

The opposite.

That justice is a vice?

No, just very high-minded simplicity.

d Then do you call being unjust being low-minded?

No, I call it good judgment.

You consider unjust people, then, Thrasymachus, to be clever and good?

Yes, those who are completely unjust, who can bring cities and whole communities under their power. Perhaps, you think I meant pickpockets? Not that such crimes aren't also profitable, if they're not found out, but they aren't worth mentioning by comparison to what I'm talking about.

I'm not unaware of what you want to say. But I *e* wonder about this: Do you really include injustice with virtue and wisdom, and justice with their opposites?

I certainly do.

That's harder, and it isn't easy now to know what to say. If you had declared that injustice is more profitable, but agreed that it is a vice or shameful, as some others do, we could have discussed the matter on the basis of conventional beliefs. But now, obviously, you'll say that injustice is fine and strong and 349 apply to it all the attributes we used to apply to justice, since you dare to include it with virtue and wisdom.

You've divined my views exactly.

Nonetheless, we mustn't shrink from pursuing the argument and looking into this, just as long as I take you to be saying what you really think. And I believe that you aren't joking now, Thrasymachus, but are saying what you believe to be the truth.

What difference does it make to you, whether *I* believe it or not? It's *my account* you're supposed to be refuting.

It makes no difference. But try to answer this further *b* question: Do you think that a just person wants to outdo[21] someone else who's just?

Not at all, for he wouldn't then be as polite and innocent as he is.

Or to outdo someone who does a just action?

No, he doesn't even want to do that.

And does he claim that he deserves to outdo an unjust person and believe that it is just for him to do so, or doesn't he believe that?

He'd want to outdo him, and he'd claim to deserve to do so, but he wouldn't be able.

That's not what I asked, but whether a just person wants to outdo an unjust person but not a just one, thinking that this is what he deserves? *c*

He does.

What about an unjust person? Does he claim that he deserves to outdo a just person or someone who does a just action?

Of course he does; he thinks he deserves to outdo everyone.

Then will an unjust person also outdo an *unjust* person or someone who does an *unjust* action, and will he strive to get the most he can for himself from everyone?

He will.

Then, let's put it this way: A just person doesn't outdo someone like himself but someone unlike himself, whereas an unjust person outdoes both like and unlike. *d*

Very well put.

An unjust person is clever and good, and a just one is neither?

That's well put, too.

It follows, then, that an unjust person is like clever and good people, while the other isn't?

Of course that's so. How could he fail to be like them when he has their qualities, while the other isn't like them?

Fine. Then each of them has the qualities of the people he's like?

Of course.

All right, Thrasymachus. Do you call one person musical and another nonmusical? *e*

I do.

Which of them is clever in music, and which isn't?

The musical one is clever, of course, and the other isn't.

And the things he's clever in, he's good in, and the things he isn't clever in, he's bad in?

Yes.

21. [*Pleon echein.* See 344a n.18.]

Isn't the same true of a doctor?

It is.

Do you think that a musician, in tuning his lyre and in tightening and loosening the strings, wants to outdo another musician, claiming that this is what he deserves?[22]

I do not.

But he does want to outdo a nonmusician?

Necessarily.

What about a doctor? Does he, when prescribing 350 food and drink, want to outdo another doctor or someone who does the action that medicine prescribes?

Certainly not.

But he does want to outdo a nondoctor?

Yes.

In any branch of knowledge or ignorance, do you think that a knowledgeable person would intentionally try to outdo other knowledgeable people or say something better or different than they do, rather than doing or saying the very same thing as those like him?

Well, perhaps it must be as you say.

And what about an ignorant person? Doesn't he want to outdo both a knowledgeable person and an *b* ignorant one?

Probably.

A knowledgeable person is clever?

I agree.

And a clever one is good?

I agree.

Therefore, a good and clever person doesn't want to outdo those like himself but those who are unlike him and his opposite.

So it seems.

But a bad and ignorant person wants to outdo both his like and his opposite.

Apparently.

Now, Thrasymachus, we found that an unjust person tries to outdo those like him and those unlike him? Didn't you say that?

I did.

And that a just person won't outdo his like but his unlike? *c*

Yes.

Then, a just person is like a clever and good one, and an unjust is like an ignorant and bad one.

It looks that way.

Moreover, we agreed that each has the qualities of the one he resembles.

Yes, we did.

Then, a just person has turned out to be good and clever, and an unjust one ignorant and bad.

Thrasymachus agreed to all this, not easily as I'm telling it, but reluctantly, with toil, trouble, and— *d* since it was summer—a quantity of sweat that was a wonder to behold. And then I saw something I'd never seen before—Thrasymachus blushing. But, in any case, after we'd agreed that justice is virtue and wisdom and that injustice is vice and ignorance, I said: All right, let's take that as established. But we also said that injustice is powerful, or don't you remember that, Thrasymachus?

I remember, but I'm not satisfied with what you're now saying. I could make a speech about it, but, if I did, I know that you'd accuse me of engaging in oratory. So either allow me to speak, or, if you want *e* to ask questions, go ahead, and I'll say, "All right," and nod yes and no, as one does to old wives' tales.

Don't do that, contrary to your own opinion.

I'll answer so as to please you, since you won't let me make a speech. What else do you want?

Nothing, by god. But if that's what you're going to do, go ahead and do it. I'll ask my questions.

Ask ahead.

I'll ask what I asked before, so that we may proceed with our argument about justice and injustice in an *351* orderly fashion, for surely it was claimed that injustice is stronger and more powerful than justice. But, now, if justice is indeed wisdom and virtue, it will easily be shown to be stronger than injustice, since injustice is ignorance (no one could now be ignorant of that). However, I don't want to state the matter so unconditionally, Thrasymachus, but to look into it in some such way as this. Would you say that it is unjust for a city to *b* try to enslave other cities unjustly and to hold them in subjection when it has enslaved many of them?

Of course, that's what the best city will especially do, the one that is most completely unjust.

22. [Socrates' point may seem obscure, but what he has in mind is explained at 350a. All expert musicians try to get the same thing, perfect harmony, so they tighten and loosen their strings to exactly the same degree, namely, the one that will produce the right pitch. In the same way, all doctors who are masters of medicine prescribe the same diet for people with the same diseases, namely, the one that will best restore them to health.]

I understand that's your position, but the point I want to examine is this: Will the city that becomes stronger than another achieve this power without justice, or will it need the help of justice?

If what you said a moment ago stands, and justice *c* is cleverness or wisdom, it will need the help of justice, but if things are as I stated, it will need the help of injustice.

I'm impressed, Thrasymachus, that you don't merely nod yes or no but give very fine answers.

That's because I'm trying to please you.

You're doing well at it, too. So please me some more by answering this question: Do you think that a city, an army, a band of robbers or thieves, or any other tribe with a common unjust purpose would be able to achieve it if they were unjust to each other?

d No, indeed.

What if they weren't unjust to one another? Would they achieve more?

Certainly.

Injustice, Thrasymachus, causes civil war, hatred, and fighting among themselves, while justice brings friendship and a sense of common purpose. Isn't that so?

Let it be so, in order not to disagree with you.

You're still doing well on that front. So tell me this: If the effect of injustice is to produce hatred wherever it occurs, then, whenever it arises, whether among free men or slaves, won't it cause them to hate one another, engage in civil war, and prevent *e* them from achieving any common purpose?

Certainly.

What if it arises between two people? Won't they be at odds, hate each other, and be enemies to one another and to just people?

They will.

Does injustice lose its power to cause dissension when it arises within a single individual, or will it preserve it intact?

Let it preserve it intact.

Apparently, then, injustice has the power, first, to make whatever it arises in—whether it is a city, a family, an army, or anything else—incapable of 352 achieving anything as a unit, because of the civil wars and differences it creates, and, second, it makes that unit an enemy to itself and to what is in every way its opposite, namely, justice. Isn't that so?

Certainly.

And even in a single individual, it has by its nature the very same effect. First, it makes him incapable of achieving anything, because he is in a state of civil war and not of one mind; second, it makes him his own enemy, as well as the enemy of just people. Hasn't it that effect?

Yes.

And the gods too are just?

Let it be so.

So an unjust person is also an enemy of the gods, Thrasymachus, while a just person is their friend? *b*

Enjoy your banquet of words! Have no fear, I won't oppose you. That would make these people hate me.

Come, then, complete the banquet for me by continuing to answer as you've been doing. We have shown that just people are cleverer and more capable of doing things, while unjust ones aren't even able to act together, for when we speak of a powerful achievement by unjust men acting together, what we *c* say isn't altogether true. They would never have been able to keep their hands off each other if they were completely unjust. But clearly there must have been some sort of justice in them that at least prevented them from doing injustice among themselves at the same time as they were doing it to others. And it was this that enabled them to achieve what they did. When they started doing unjust things, they were only halfway corrupted by their injustice (for those who are all bad and completely unjust are completely incapable of accomplishing anything). These are the things I understand to hold, not the ones you first maintained. We must now examine, as we proposed *d* before,[23] whether just people also live better and are happier than unjust ones. I think it's clear already that this is so, but we must look into it further, since the argument concerns no ordinary topic but the way we ought to live.

Go ahead and look.

I will. Tell me, do you think there is such a thing as the function of a horse?

I do. *e*

And would you define the function of a horse or of anything else as that which one can do only with it or best with it?

I don't understand.

23. [See 347e.]

Let me put it this way: Is it possible to see with anything other than eyes?

Certainly not.

Or to hear with anything other than ears?

No.

Then, we are right to say that seeing and hearing are the functions of eyes and ears?

Of course.

What about this? Could you use a dagger or a 353 carving knife or lots of other things in pruning a vine?

Of course.

But wouldn't you do a finer job with a pruning knife designed for the purpose than with anything else?

You would.

Then shall we take pruning to be its function?

Yes.

Now, I think you'll understand what I was asking earlier when I asked whether the function of each thing is what it alone can do or what it does better than anything else.

I understand, and I think that this is the function *b* of each.

All right. Does each thing to which a particular function is assigned also have a virtue?[24] Let's go over the same ground again. We say that eyes have some function?

They do.

So there is also a virtue of eyes?

There is.

And ears have a function?

Yes.

So there is also a virtue of ears?

There is.

And all other things are the same, aren't they?

They are.

And could eyes perform their function well if they *c* lacked their peculiar virtue and had the vice instead?

How could they, for don't you mean if they had blindness instead of sight?

Whatever their virtue is, for I'm not now asking about that but about whether anything that has a function performs it well by means of its own peculiar virtue and badly by means of its vice?

That's true, it does.

So ears, too, deprived of their own virtue, perform their function badly?

That's right.

And the same could be said about everything else? *d*

So it seems.

Come, then, and let's consider this: Is there some function of a soul that you couldn't perform with anything else, for example, taking care of things, ruling, deliberating, and the like? Is there anything other than a soul to which you could rightly assign these, and say that they are its peculiar function?

No, none of them.

What of living? Isn't that a function of a soul?

It certainly is.

And don't we also say that there is a virtue of a soul?

We do.

Then, will a soul ever perform its function well, Thrasymachus, if it is deprived of its own peculiar *e* virtue, or is that impossible?

It's impossible.

Doesn't it follow, then, that a bad soul rules and takes care of things badly and that a good soul does all these things well?

It does.

Now, we agreed that justice is a soul's virtue, and injustice its vice?

We did.

Then, it follows that a just soul and a just man will live well, and an unjust one badly.

Apparently so, according to your argument.

And surely anyone who lives well is blessed and happy, and anyone who doesn't is the opposite. 354

Of course.

Therefore, a just person is happy, and an unjust one wretched.

So be it.

It profits no one to be wretched but to be happy.

Of course.

And so, Thrasymachus, injustice is never more profitable than justice.

Let that be your banquet, Socrates, at the feast of Bendis.

Given by you, Thrasymachus, after you became gentle and ceased to give me rough treatment. Yet I haven't had a fine banquet. But that's my fault not yours. I seem to have behaved like a glutton, snatching *b* at every dish that passes and tasting it before properly savoring its predecessor. Before finding the answer to our first inquiry about what justice is, I let that go and turned to investigate whether it is a kind of vice

24. [See 335b n.12.]

and ignorance or a kind of wisdom and virtue. Then an argument came up about injustice being more profitable than justice, and I couldn't refrain from abandoning the previous one and following up on that. Hence the result of the discussion, as far as I'm *c* concerned, is that I know nothing, for when I don't know what justice is, I'll hardly know whether it is a kind of virtue or not, or whether a person who has it is happy or unhappy.

Book II

357 When I said this, I thought I had done with the discussion, but it turned out to have been only a prelude. Glaucon showed his characteristic courage on this occasion too and refused to accept Thrasymachus' abandonment of the argument. Socrates, he said, do you want to seem to have persuaded us that it is better in every way to be just than unjust, or do *b* you want truly to convince us of this?

I want truly to convince you, I said, if I can.

Well, then, you certainly aren't doing what you want. Tell me, do you think there is a kind of good we welcome, not because we desire what comes from it, but because we welcome it for its own sake—joy, for example, and all the harmless pleasures that have no results beyond the joy of having them?

Certainly, I think there are such things.

And is there a kind of good we like for its own sake *c* and also for the sake of what comes from it—knowing, for example, and seeing and being healthy? We welcome such things, I suppose, on both counts.

Yes.

And do you also see a third kind of good, such as physical training, medical treatment when sick, medicine itself, and the other ways of making money? We'd say that these are onerous but beneficial to us, and we wouldn't choose them for their own sakes, but for the sake of the rewards and other things that *d* come from them.

There is also this third kind. But what of it?

Where do you put justice?

I myself put it among the finest goods, as something 358 to be valued by anyone who is going to be blessed with happiness, both because of itself and because of what comes from it.

That isn't most people's opinion. They'd say that justice belongs to the onerous kind, and is to be practiced for the sake of the rewards and popularity that come from a reputation for justice, but is to be avoided because of itself as something burdensome.

I know that's the general opinion. Thrasymachus faulted justice on these grounds a moment ago and praised injustice, but it seems that I'm a slow learner.

Come, then, and listen to me as well, and see whether you still have that problem, for I think that *b* Thrasymachus gave up before he had to, charmed by you as if he were a snake. But I'm not yet satisfied by the argument on either side. I want to know what justice and injustice are and what power each itself has when it's by itself in the soul. I want to leave out of account their rewards and what comes from each of them. So, if you agree, I'll renew the argument of Thrasymachus. First, I'll state what kind of thing people consider justice to be and what its origins are. *c* Second, I'll argue that all who practice it do so unwillingly, as something necessary, not as something good. Third, I'll argue that they have good reason to act as they do, for the life of an unjust person is, they say, much better than that of a just one.

It isn't, Socrates, that I believe any of that myself. I'm perplexed, indeed, and my ears are deafened listening to Thrasymachus and countless others. But I've yet to hear anyone defend justice in the way I want, proving that it is better than injustice. I want *d* to hear it praised *by itself*, and I think that I'm most likely to hear this from you. Therefore, I'm going to speak at length in praise of the unjust life, and in doing so I'll show you the way I want to hear you praising justice and denouncing injustice. But see whether you want me to do that or not.

I want that most of all. Indeed, what subject could someone with any understanding enjoy discussing more often?

Excellent. Then let's discuss the first subject I mentioned—what justice is and what its origins are. *e*

They say that to do injustice is naturally good and to suffer injustice bad, but that the badness of suffering it so far exceeds the goodness of doing it that those who have done and suffered injustice and tasted both, but who lack the power to do it and avoid suffering it, decide that it is profitable to come to an agreement with each other neither to do injustice nor to suffer 359 it. As a result, they begin to make laws and covenants, and what the law commands they call lawful and just. This, they say, is the origin and essence of justice. It is intermediate between the best and the worst. The best is to do injustice without paying the penalty; the worst is to suffer it without being able to take revenge. Justice is a mean between these two extremes. People value it not as a good but because *b* they are too weak to do injustice with impunity. Someone who has the power to do this, however, and is a true man wouldn't make an agreement with anyone not to do injustice in order not to suffer it. For him that would be madness. This is the nature of justice, according to the argument, Socrates, and these are its natural origins.

We can see most clearly that those who practice justice do it unwillingly and because they lack the power *c* to do injustice, if in our thoughts we grant to a just and an unjust person the freedom to do whatever they like. We can then follow both of them and see where their desires would lead. And we'll catch the just person red-handed travelling the same road as the unjust. The reason for this is the desire to outdo others and get more and more.[1] This is what anyone's nature naturally pursues as good, but nature is forced by law into the perversion of treating fairness with respect.

The freedom I mentioned would be most easily realized if both people had the power they say the ancestor of Gyges of Lydia possessed. The story goes *d* that he was a shepherd in the service of the ruler of Lydia. There was a violent thunderstorm, and an earthquake broke open the ground and created a chasm at the place where he was tending his sheep. Seeing this, he was filled with amazement and went down into it. And there, in addition to many other wonders of which we're told, he saw a hollow bronze horse. There were windowlike openings in it, and, peeping in, he saw a corpse, which seemed to be of more than human size, wearing nothing but a gold *e* ring on its finger. He took the ring and came out of the chasm. He wore the ring at the usual monthly meeting that reported to the king on the state of the flocks. And as he was sitting among the others, he happened to turn the setting of the ring towards himself to the inside of his hand. When he did this, he became invisible to those sitting near him, and they went on talking as if he had gone. He wondered at *360* this, and, fingering the ring, he turned the setting outwards again and became visible. So he experimented with the ring to test whether it indeed had this power—and it did. If he turned the setting inward, he became invisible; if he turned it outward, he became visible again. When he realized this, he at once arranged to become one of the messengers sent to report to the king. And when he arrived there, he seduced the king's wife, attacked the king with her help, killed him, and took over the kingdom. *b*

Let's suppose, then, that there were two such rings, one worn by a just and the other by an unjust person. Now, no one, it seems, would be so incorruptible that he would stay on the path of justice or stay away from other people's property, when he could take whatever he wanted from the marketplace with impunity, go into people's houses and have sex with anyone he wished, kill or release from prison anyone he wished, and do all the other things that would make *c* him like a god among humans. Rather his actions would be in no way different from those of an unjust person, and both would follow the same path. This, some would say, is a great proof that one is never just willingly but only when compelled to be. No one believes justice to be a good when it is kept private, since, wherever either person thinks he can do injustice with impunity, he does it. Indeed, every man believes that injustice is far more profitable to himself than justice. And any exponent of this argument will *d* say he's right, for someone who didn't want to do injustice, given this sort of opportunity, and who didn't touch other people's property would be thought wretched and stupid by everyone aware of the situation, though, of course, they'd praise him in public, deceiving each other for fear of suffering injustice. So much for my second topic.

As for the choice between the lives we're discussing, we'll be able to make a correct judgment about that *e* only if we separate the most just and the most unjust. Otherwise we won't be able to do it. Here's the separation I have in mind. We'll subtract nothing from the injustice of an unjust person and nothing from the justice of a just one, but we'll take each to be complete in his own way of life. First, therefore, we must suppose that an unjust person will act as clever craftsmen

1. [*Pleonexian*. See 344a n.18.]

361 do: A first-rate captain or doctor, for example, knows the difference between what his craft can and can't do. He attempts the first but lets the second go by, and if he happens to slip, he can put things right. In the same way, an unjust person's successful attempts at injustice must remain undetected, if he is to be fully unjust. Anyone who is caught should be thought inept, for the extreme of injustice is to be believed to be just without being just. And our completely unjust person must be given complete injustice; nothing may be subtracted from it. We must allow that, while doing the greatest injustice, he has nonetheless provided himself with the greatest reputation for jus- *b* tice. If he happens to make a slip, he must be able to put it right. If any of his unjust activities should be discovered, he must be able to speak persuasively or to use force. And if force is needed, he must have the help of courage and strength and of the substantial wealth and friends with which he has provided himself.

Having hypothesized such a person, let's now in our argument put beside him a just man, who is simple and noble and who, as Aeschylus says, doesn't want to be believed to be good but to be so.[2] We *c* must take away his reputation, for a reputation for justice would bring him honor and rewards, so that it wouldn't be clear whether he is just for the sake of justice itself or for the sake of those honors and rewards. We must strip him of everything except justice and make his situation the opposite of an unjust person's. Though he does no injustice, he must have the greatest reputation for it, so that his justice may be tested full-strength and not diluted by wrongdoing and what comes from it. Let him stay like that un- *d* changed until he dies—just, but all his life believed to be unjust. In this way, both will reach the extremes, the one of justice and the other of injustice, and we'll be able to judge which of them is happier.

Whew! Glaucon, I said, how vigorously you've scoured each of the men for our competition, just as you would a pair of statues for an art competition.

I do the best I can, he replied. Since the two are as I've described, in any case, it shouldn't be difficult to complete the account of the kind of life that awaits each of them, but it must be done. And if what I say sounds crude, Socrates, remember that it isn't I who *e* speak but those who praise injustice at the expense of justice. They'll say that a just person in such circumstances will be whipped, stretched on a rack, chained, blinded with fire, and, at the end, when he has suffered every kind of evil, he'll be impaled, and will realize then that one shouldn't want to be just but to be believed to be just. Indeed, Aeschylus' words 362 are far more correctly applied to unjust people than to just ones, for the supporters of injustice will say that a really unjust person, having a way of life based on the truth about things and not living in accordance with opinion, doesn't want simply to be believed to be unjust but actually to be so—

> Harvesting a deep furrow in his mind,
> Where wise counsels propagate. *b*

He rules his city because of his reputation for justice; he marries into any family he wishes; he gives his children in marriage to anyone he wishes; he has contracts and partnerships with anyone he wants; and besides benefiting himself in all these ways, he profits because he has no scruples about doing injustice. In any contest, public or private, he's the winner and outdoes[3] his enemies. And by outdoing them, he becomes wealthy, benefiting his friends and harming his enemies. He makes adequate sacrifices to the gods and sets up magnificent offerings to them. *c* He takes better care of the gods, therefore, (and, indeed, of the human beings he's fond of) than a just person does. Hence it's likely that the gods, in turn, will take better care of him than of a just person. That's what they say, Socrates, that gods and humans provide a better life for unjust people than for just ones.

When Glaucon had said this, I had it in mind to respond, but his brother Adeimantus intervened: You *d* surely don't think that the position has been adequately stated?

Why not? I said.

The most important thing to say hasn't been said yet.

2. [In *Seven Against Thebes*, 592–94, it is said of Amphiaraus that "he did not wish to be believed to be the best but to be it." The passage continues with the words Glaucon quotes at 362a–b.]

3. [*Pleonektein*. See 344a n.18.]

Well, then, I replied, a man's brother must stand by him, as the saying goes.[4] If Glaucon has omitted something, you must help him. Yet what he has said is enough to throw me to the canvas and make me unable to come to the aid of justice.

Nonsense, he said. Hear what more I have to say, for we should also fully explore the arguments that are opposed to the ones Glaucon gave, the ones *e* that praise justice and find fault with injustice, so that what I take to be his intention may be clearer.

When fathers speak to their sons, they say that one must be just, as do all the others who have charge of anyone. But they don't praise justice itself, only the 363 high reputations it leads to and the consequences of being thought to be just, such as the public offices, marriages, and other things Glaucon listed. But they elaborate even further on the consequences of reputation. By bringing in the esteem of the gods, they are able to talk about the abundant good things that they themselves and the noble Hesiod and Homer say that the gods give to the pious,[5] for Hesiod says that the *b* gods make the oak trees

> Bear acorns at the top and bees in the middle
> And make fleecy sheep heavy laden with wool

for the just, and tells of many other good things akin to these. And Homer is similar:

> When a good king, in his piety,
> Upholds justice, the black earth bears
> Wheat and barley for him, and his
> *c* trees are heavy with fruit.
> His sheep bear lambs unfailingly,
> and the sea yields up its fish.

Musaeus and his son make the gods give the just more headstrong goods than these.[6] In their stories, they lead the just to Hades, seat them on couches, provide them with a symposium of pious people, crown them with wreaths, and make them spend all their time drinking—as if they thought drunkenness was the finest wage of virtue. Others stretch even *d* further the wages that virtue receives from the gods, for they say that someone who is pious and keeps his promises leaves his children's children and a whole race behind him. In these and other similar ways, they praise justice. They bury the impious and unjust in mud in Hades; force them to carry water in a sieve; bring them into bad repute while they're still alive, and all those penalties that Glaucon gave to the just person they give to the unjust. But they have nothing *e* else to say. This, then, is the way people praise justice and find fault with injustice.

Besides this, Socrates, consider another form of argument about justice and injustice employed both by private individuals and by poets. All go on repeating with one voice that justice and moderation are fine things, but hard and onerous, while licentiousness 364 and injustice are sweet and easy to acquire and are shameful only in opinion and law. They add that unjust deeds are for the most part more profitable than just ones, and, whether in public or private, they willingly honor vicious people who have wealth and other types of power and declare them to be happy. But they dishonor and disregard the weak and the poor, even though they agree that they are better than the others. *b*

But the most wonderful of all these arguments concerns what they have to say about the gods and virtue. They say that the gods, too, assign misfortune and a bad life to many good people, and the opposite fate to their opposites. Begging priests and prophets frequent the doors of the rich and persuade them that they possess a god-given power founded on sacrifices and incantations. If the rich person or any of his ancestors has committed an injustice, they can *c* fix it with pleasant rituals. Moreover, if he wishes to injure some enemy, then, at little expense, he'll be able to harm just and unjust alike, for by means of spells and enchantments they can persuade the gods to serve them. And the poets are brought forward as witnesses to all these accounts. Some harp on the ease of vice, as follows:

> Vice in abundance is easy to get;
> The road is smooth and begins beside you, *d*
> But the gods have put sweat between us and
> virtue,

4. [See Homer, *Odyssey* 16.97–98.]

5. [The two quotations which follow are from Hesiod, *Works and Days* 332–33, and Homer, *Odyssey* 19.109.]

6. [Musaeus was a legendary poet closely associated with the mystery religion of Orphism.]

and a road that is long, rough, and steep.[7] Others quote Homer to bear witness that the gods can be influenced by humans, since he said:

> The gods themselves can be swayed by prayer,
> And with sacrifices and soothing promises,
> Incense and libations, human beings turn
> e them from their purpose
> When someone has transgressed and sinned.[8]

And they present a noisy throng of books by Musaeus and Orpheus, offspring as they say of Selene and the Muses, in accordance with which they perform their rituals.[9] And they persuade not only individuals but whole cities that the unjust deeds of the living or the dead can be absolved or purified through ritual 365 sacrifices and pleasant games. These initiations, as they call them, free people from punishment hereafter, while a terrible fate awaits those who have not performed the rituals.

When all such sayings about the attitudes of gods and humans to virtue and vice are so often repeated, Socrates, what effect do you suppose they have on the souls of young people? I mean those who are clever and are able to flit from one of these sayings to another, so to speak, and gather from them an impression of what sort of person he should be and of how best to travel the road of life. He would surely b ask himself Pindar's question, "Should I by justice or by crooked deceit scale this high wall and live my life guarded and secure?" And he'll answer: "The various sayings suggest that there is no advantage in my being just if I'm not also thought just, while the troubles and penalties of being just are apparent. But they tell me that an unjust person, who has secured for himself a reputation for justice, lives the life of a god. Since, then, 'opinion forcibly overcomes truth' c and 'controls happiness,' as the wise men say, I must surely turn entirely to it.[10] I should create a façade of illusory virtue around me to deceive those who come near, but keep behind it the greedy and crafty fox of the wise Archilochus."[11]

"But surely," someone will object, "it isn't easy for vice to remain always hidden." We'll reply that nothing great is easy. And, in any case, if we're to be happy, we must follow the path indicated in these d accounts. To remain undiscovered we'll form secret societies and political clubs. And there are teachers of persuasion to make us clever in dealing with assemblies and law courts. Therefore, using persuasion in one place and force in another, we'll outdo others[12] without paying a penalty.

"What about the gods? Surely, we can't hide from them or use violent force against them!" Well, if the gods don't exist or don't concern themselves with human affairs, why should we worry at all about hiding from them? If they do exist and do concern themselves with us, we've learned all we know about them e from the laws and the poets who give their genealogies—nowhere else. But these are the very people who tell us that the gods can be persuaded and influenced by sacrifices, gentle prayers, and offerings. Hence, we should believe them on both matters or neither. If we believe them, we should be unjust and offer sacrifices from the fruits of our injustice. If we are just, our only gain is not to be punished by the 366 gods, since we lose the profits of injustice. But if we are unjust, we get the profits of our crimes and transgressions and afterwards persuade the gods by prayer and escape without punishment.

"But in Hades won't we pay the penalty for crimes committed here, either ourselves or our children's children?" "My friend," the young man will say as he does his calculation, "mystery rites have great power and the gods have great power of absolution. The greatest cities tell us this, as do those children of the gods who have become poets and prophets." b

Why, then, should we still choose justice over the greatest injustice? Many eminent authorities agree

7. [*Works and Days* 287–89, with minor alterations.]

8. [*Iliad* 9.497–501, with minor alterations.]

9. [It is not clear whether Orpheus was a real person or a mythical figure. His fame in Greek myth rests on the poems in which the doctrines of the Orphic religion are set forth. These are discussed in W. Burkert, *Greek Religion* (Cambridge, Mass.: Harvard University Press, 1985). Musaeus was a mythical singer closely related to Orpheus. Selene is the Moon.]

10. [The quotation is attributed to Simonides, whom Polemarchus cites in Book I.]

11. [Archilochus of Paros (c. 756–716 B.C.) was an iambic and elegiac poet who composed a famous fable about the fox and the hedgehog.]

12. [*Pleonektountes*. See 344a n.18.]

that, if we practice such injustice with a false façade, we'll do well at the hands of gods and humans, living and dying as we've a mind to. So, given all that has been said, Socrates, how is it possible for anyone of *c* any power—whether of mind, wealth, body, or birth—to be willing to honor justice and not laugh aloud when he hears it praised? Indeed, if anyone can show that what we've said is false and has adequate knowledge that justice is best, he'll surely be full not of anger but of forgiveness for the unjust. He knows that, apart from someone of godlike character who is disgusted by injustice or one who has gained knowl- *d* edge and avoids injustice for that reason, no one is just willingly. Through cowardice or old age or some other weakness, people do indeed object to injustice. But it's obvious that they do so only because they lack the power to do injustice, for the first of them to acquire it is the first to do as much injustice as he can.

And all of this has no other cause than the one that led Glaucon and me to say to you: "Socrates, of all of you who claim to praise justice, from the original heroes of old whose words survive, to the men of the *e* present day, not one has ever blamed injustice or praised justice except by mentioning the reputations, honors, and rewards that are their consequences. No one has ever adequately described what each itself does of its own power by its presence in the soul of the person who possesses it, even if it remains hidden from gods and humans. No one, whether in poetry or in private conversations, has adequately argued that injustice is the worst thing a soul can have in it and that justice is the greatest good. If you had treated the subject in this way and persuaded us from youth, *367* we wouldn't now be guarding against one another's injustices, but each would be his own best guardian, afraid that by doing injustice he'd be living with the worst thing possible."

Thrasymachus or anyone else might say what we've said, Socrates, or maybe even more, in discussing justice and injustice—crudely inverting their powers, in my opinion. And, frankly, it's because I want to *b* hear the opposite from you that I speak with all the force I can muster. So don't merely give us a theoretical argument that justice is stronger than injustice, but tell us what each itself does, because of its own powers, to someone who possesses it, that makes injustice bad and justice good. Follow Glaucon's advice, and don't take reputations into account, for if you don't deprive justice and injustice of their true reputations and attach false ones to them, we'll say that you are not praising them but their reputations and that you're encouraging us to be unjust in secret. In *c* that case, we'll say that you agree with Thrasymachus that justice is the good of another, the advantage of the stronger, while injustice is one's own advantage and profit, though not the advantage of the weaker.

You agree that justice is one of the greatest goods, the ones that are worth getting for the sake of what comes from them, but much more so for their own sake, such as seeing, hearing, knowing, being healthy, *d* and all other goods that are fruitful by their own nature and not simply because of reputation. Therefore, praise justice as a good of that kind, explaining how—because of its very self—it benefits its possessors and how injustice harms them. Leave wages and reputations for others to praise.

Others would satisfy me if they praised justice and blamed injustice in that way, extolling the wages of one and denigrating those of the other. But you, unless you order me to be satisfied, wouldn't, for you've spent your whole life investigating this and *e* nothing else. Don't, then, give us only a theoretical argument that justice is stronger than injustice, but show what effect each has because of itself on the person who has it—the one for good and the other for bad—whether it remains hidden from gods and human beings or not.

While I'd always admired the natures of Glaucon and Adeimantus, I was especially pleased on this occa- *368* sion, and I said: You are the sons of a great man, and Glaucon's lover began his elegy well when he wrote, celebrating your achievements at the battle of Megara,

> Sons of Ariston, godlike offspring of a
> famous man.

That's well said in my opinion, for you must indeed be affected by the divine if you're not convinced that injustice is better than justice and yet can speak on its behalf as you have done. And I believe that you really are unconvinced by your own words. I infer *b* this from the way you live, for if I had only your words to go on, I wouldn't trust you. The more I trust you, however, the more I'm at a loss as to what to do. I don't see how I can be of help. Indeed, I believe I'm incapable of it. And here's my evidence. I thought what I said to Thrasymachus showed that justice is better than injustice, but you won't accept it from me. On the other hand, I don't see how I can refuse my help, for I fear that it may even be impious to have breath in one's body and the ability to speak and yet to stand idly by and not defend justice when it is being prosecuted. So the best course is to give justice any assistance I can.

Glaucon and the others begged me not to abandon the argument but to help in every way to track down what justice and injustice are and what the truth about their benefits is. So I told them what I had in mind: The investigation we're undertaking is not an easy one but requires keen eyesight. Therefore, since we aren't clever people, we should adopt the method of investigation that we'd use if, lacking keen eyesight, we were told to read small letters from a distance and then noticed that the same letters existed elsewhere in a larger size and on a larger surface. We'd consider it a godsend, I think, to be allowed to read the larger ones first and then to examine the smaller ones, to see whether they really are the same.

That's certainly true, said Adeimantus, but how is this case similar to our investigation of justice?

I'll tell you. We say, don't we, that there is the justice of a single man and also the justice of a whole city?

Certainly.

And a city is larger than a single man?

It is larger.

Perhaps, then, there is more justice in the larger thing, and it will be easier to learn what it is. So, if you're willing, let's first find out what sort of thing justice is in a city and afterwards look for it in the individual, observing the ways in which the smaller is similar to the larger.

That seems fine to me.

If we could watch a city coming to be in theory, wouldn't we also see its justice coming to be, and its injustice as well?

Probably so.

And when that process is completed, we can hope to find what we are looking for more easily?

Of course.

Do you think we should try to carry it out, then? It's no small task, in my view. So think it over.

We have already, said Adeimantus. Don't even consider doing anything else.

I think a city comes to be because none of us is self-sufficient, but we all need many things. Do you think that a city is founded on any other principle?

No.

And because people need many things, and because one person calls on a second out of one need and on a third out of a different need, many people gather in a single place to live together as partners and helpers. And such a settlement is called a city.[13] Isn't that so?

It is.

And if they share things with one another, giving and taking, they do so because each believes that this is better for himself?

That's right.

Come, then, let's create a city in theory from its beginnings. And it's our needs, it seems, that will create it.

It is, indeed.

Surely our first and greatest need is to provide food to sustain life.

Certainly.

Our second is for shelter, and our third for clothes and such.

That's right.

How, then, will a city be able to provide all this? Won't one person have to be a farmer, another a builder, and another a weaver? And shouldn't we add a cobbler and someone else to provide medical care?

All right.

So the essential minimum for a city is four or five men?

Apparently.

And what about this? Must each of them contribute his own work for the common use of all? For example, will a farmer provide food for everyone, spending quadruple the time and labor to provide food to be shared by them all? Or will he not bother about that, producing one quarter the food in one quarter the time, and spending the other three quarters, one in building a house, one in the production of clothes, and one in making shoes, not troubling to associate

13. [Notice that a city (*polis*) is a collection of people, not a collection of buildings.]

with the others, but minding his own business on his own?

Perhaps, Socrates, Adeimantus replied, the way you suggested first would be easier than the other.

That certainly wouldn't be surprising, for, even as you were speaking it occurred to me that, in the first place, we aren't all born alike, but each of us differs somewhat in nature from the others, one being suited to one task, another to another. *b* Or don't you think so?

I do.

Second, does one person do a better job if he practices many crafts or—since he's one person himself—if he practices one?

If he practices one.

It's clear, at any rate, I think, that if one misses the right moment in anything, the work is spoiled.

It is.

That's because the thing to be done won't wait on the leisure of the doer, but the doer must of necessity pay close attention to his work rather than treating it *c* as a secondary occupation.

Yes, he must.

The result, then, is that more plentiful and better-quality goods are more easily produced if each person does one thing for which he is naturally suited, does it at the right time, and is released from having to do any of the others.

Absolutely.

Then, Adeimantus, we're going to need more than four citizens to provide the things we've mentioned, for a farmer won't make his own plough, not if it's to be a good one, nor his hoe, nor any of his other *d* farming tools. Neither will a builder—and he, too, needs lots of things. And the same is true of a weaver and a cobbler, isn't it?

It is.

Hence, carpenters, metal workers, and many other craftsmen of that sort will share our little city and make it bigger.

That's right.

Yet it won't be a huge settlement even if we add cowherds, shepherds, and other herdsmen in order *e* that the farmers have cows to do their ploughing, the builders have oxen to share with the farmers in hauling their materials, and the weavers and cobblers have hides and fleeces to use.

It won't be a small one either, if it has to hold all those.

Moreover, it's almost impossible to establish a city in a place where nothing has to be imported.

Indeed it is.

So we'll need yet further people to import from other cities whatever is needed.

Yes.

And if an importer goes empty-handed to another city, without a cargo of the things needed by the city from which he's to bring back what his own city needs, he'll come away empty-handed, won't he? *371*

So it seems.

Therefore our citizens must not only produce enough for themselves at home but also goods of the right quality and quantity to satisfy the requirements of others.

They must.

So we'll need more farmers and other craftsmen in our city.

Yes.

And others to take care of imports and exports. And they're called merchants, aren't they?

Yes.

So we'll need merchants, too.

Certainly.

And if the trade is by sea, we'll need a good many others who know how to sail. *b*

A good many, indeed.

And how will those in the city itself share the things that each produces? It was for the sake of this that we made their partnership and founded their city.

Clearly, they must do it by buying and selling.

Then we'll need a marketplace and a currency for such exchange.

Certainly.

If a farmer or any other craftsman brings some of his products to market, and he doesn't arrive at the *c* same time as those who want to exchange things with him, is he to sit idly in the marketplace, away from his own work?

Not at all. There'll be people who'll notice this and provide the requisite service—in well-organized cities they'll usually be those whose bodies are weakest and who aren't fit to do any other work. They'll stay around the market exchanging money for the goods *d* of those who have something to sell and then exchanging those goods for the money of those who want them.

Then, to fill this need there will have to be retailers in our city, for aren't those who establish themselves in the marketplace to provide this service of buying and selling called retailers, while those who travel between cities are called merchants?

That's right.

There are other servants, I think, whose minds *e* alone wouldn't qualify them for membership in our society but whose bodies are strong enough for labor. These sell the use of their strength for a price called a wage and hence are themselves called wage-earners. Isn't that so?

Certainly.

So wage-earners complete our city?

I think so.

Well, Adeimantus, has our city grown to completeness, then?

Perhaps it has.

Then where are justice and injustice to be found in it? With which of the things we examined did they come in?

I've no idea, Socrates, unless it was somewhere 372 in some need that these people have of one another.

You may be right, but we must look into it and not grow weary. First, then, let's see what sort of life our citizens will lead when they've been provided for in the way we have been describing. They'll produce bread, wine, clothes, and shoes, won't they? They'll build houses, work naked and barefoot in the summer, *b* and wear adequate clothing and shoes in the winter. For food, they'll knead and cook the flour and meal they've made from wheat and barley. They'll put their honest cakes and loaves on reeds or clean leaves, and, reclining on beds strewn with yew and myrtle, they'll feast with their children, drink their wine, and, crowned with wreaths, hymn the gods. They'll enjoy sex with one another but bear no more children than their resources allow, lest they fall into either poverty *c* or war.

It seems that you make your people feast without any delicacies, Glaucon interrupted.

True enough, I said, I was forgetting that they'll obviously need salt, olives, cheese, boiled roots, and vegetables of the sort they cook in the country. We'll give them desserts, too, of course, consisting of figs, chickpeas, and beans, and they'll roast myrtle and acorns before the fire,[14] drinking moderately. And so they'll live in peace and good health, and when they *d* die at a ripe old age, they'll bequeath a similar life to their children.

If you were founding a city for pigs, Socrates, he replied, wouldn't you fatten *them* on the same diet?

Then how should I feed these people, Glaucon? I asked.

In the conventional way. If they aren't to suffer hardship, they should recline on proper couches, dine at a table, and have the delicacies and desserts that people have nowadays. *e*

All right, I understand. It isn't merely the origin of a city that we're considering, it seems, but the origin of a *luxurious* city. And that may not be a bad idea, for by examining it, we might very well see how justice and injustice grow up in cities. Yet the true city, in my opinion, is the one we've described, the healthy one, as it were. But let's study a city with a fever, if that's what you want. There's nothing to stop us. The things I mentioned earlier and the way of life I 373 described won't satisfy some people, it seems, but couches, tables, and other furniture will have to be added, and, of course, all sorts of delicacies, perfumed oils, incense, prostitutes, and pastries. We mustn't provide them only with the necessities we mentioned at first, such as houses, clothes, and shoes, but painting and embroidery must be begun, and gold, ivory, and the like acquired. Isn't that so?

Yes. *b*

Then we must enlarge our city, for the healthy one is no longer adequate. We must increase it in size and fill it with a multitude of things that go beyond what is necessary for a city—hunters, for example, and artists or imitators, many of whom work with shapes and colors, many with music. And there'll be poets and their assistants, actors, choral dancers, contractors, and makers of all kinds of devices, including, among other things, those needed for the adornment of women. And so we'll need more servants, too. Or don't you think that we'll need tutors, wet *c* nurses, nannies, beauticians, barbers, chefs, cooks, and swineherds? We didn't need any of these in our

14. [It seems likely that a sexual pun is intended since myrtle (*murton*) and acorn (*phēgos*) are common slang terms for the female and male genitalia, respectively.]

earlier city, but we'll need them in this one. And we'll also need many more cattle, won't we, if the people are going to eat meat?

Of course.

And if we live like that, we'll have a far greater *d* need for doctors than we did before?

Much greater.

And the land, I suppose, that used to be adequate to feed the population we had then, will cease to be adequate and become too small. What do you think?

The same.

Then we'll have to seize some of our neighbors' land if we're to have enough pasture and ploughland. And won't our neighbors want to seize part of ours as well, if they too have surrendered themselves to the endless acquisition of money and have overstepped the limit of their necessities?

e That's completely inevitable, Socrates.

Then our next step will be war, Glaucon, won't it?

It will.

We won't say yet whether the effects of war are good or bad but only that we've now found the origins of war. It comes from those same desires that are most of all responsible for the bad things that happen to cities and the individuals in them.

That's right.

Then the city must be further enlarged, and not just by a small number, either, but by a whole army, which will do battle with the invaders in defense of 374 the city's substantial wealth and all the other things we mentioned.

Why aren't the citizens themselves adequate for that purpose?

They won't be, if the agreement you and the rest of us made when we were founding the city was a good one, for surely we agreed, if you remember, that it's impossible for a single person to practice many crafts or professions well.

That's true.

Well, then, don't you think that warfare is a pro- *b* fession?

Of course.

Then should we be more concerned about cobbling than about warfare?

Not at all.

But we prevented a cobbler from trying to be a farmer, weaver, or builder at the same time and said that he must remain a cobbler in order to produce fine work. And each of the others, too, was to work all his life at a single trade for which he had a natural aptitude and keep away from all the others, so as not to miss the right moment to practice his own work well. Now, *c* isn't it of the greatest importance that warfare be practiced well? And is fighting a war so easy that a farmer or a cobbler or any other craftsman can be a soldier at the same time? Though no one can become so much as a good player of checkers or dice if he considers it only as a sideline and doesn't practice it from childhood. Or can someone pick up a shield or any other weapon or tool of war and immediately perform adequately in an infantry battle or any other kind? No other *d* tool makes anyone who picks it up a craftsman or champion unless he has acquired the requisite knowledge and has had sufficient practice.

If tools could make anyone who picked them up an expert, they'd be valuable indeed.

Then to the degree that the work of the guardians is most important, it requires most freedom from other *e* things and the greatest skill and devotion.

I should think so.

And doesn't it also require a person whose nature is suited to that way of life?

Certainly.

Then our job, it seems, is to select, if we can, the kind of nature suited to guard the city.

It is.

By god, it's no trivial task that we've taken on. But insofar as we are able, we mustn't shrink from it.

No, we mustn't. 375

Do you think that, when it comes to guarding, there is any difference between the nature of a pedigree young dog and that of a well-born youth?

What do you mean?

Well, each needs keen senses, speed to catch what it sees, and strength in case it has to fight it out with what it captures.

They both need all these things.

And each must be courageous if indeed he's to fight well.

Of course.

And will a horse, a dog, or any other animal be courageous, if he isn't spirited? Or haven't you noticed just how invincible and unbeatable spirit is, so that its pres- *b* ence makes the whole soul fearless and unconquerable?

I have noticed that.

The physical qualities of the guardians are clear, then.

Yes.

And as far as their souls are concerned, they must be spirited.

That too.

But if they have natures like that, Glaucon, won't they be savage to each other and to the rest of the citizens?

By god, it will be hard for them to be anything else.

Yet surely they must be gentle to their own people *c* and harsh to the enemy. If they aren't, they won't wait around for others to destroy the city but will do it themselves first.

That's true.

What are we to do, then? Where are we to find a character that is both gentle and high-spirited at the same time? After all, a gentle nature is the opposite of a spirited one.

Apparently.

If someone lacks either gentleness or spirit, he can't be a good guardian. Yet it seems impossible to combine *d* them. It follows that a good guardian cannot exist.

It looks like it.

I couldn't see a way out, but on reexamining what had gone before, I said: We deserve to be stuck, for we've lost sight of the analogy we put forward.

How do you mean?

We overlooked the fact that there *are* natures of the sort we thought impossible, natures in which these opposites are indeed combined.

Where?

You can see them in other animals, too, but especially in the one to which we compared the guardian, for you know, of course, that a pedigree dog naturally *e* has a character of this sort—he is gentle as can be to those he's used to and knows, but the opposite to those he doesn't know.

I do know that.

So the combination we want is possible after all, and our search for the good guardian is not contrary to nature.

Apparently not.

Then do you think that our future guardian, besides being spirited, must also be by nature philosophical?[15]

How do you mean? I don't understand. 376

It's something else you see in dogs, and it makes you wonder at the animal.

What?

When a dog sees someone it doesn't know, it gets angry before anything bad happens to it. But when it knows someone, it welcomes him, even if it has never received anything good from him. Haven't you ever wondered at that?

I've never paid any attention to it, but obviously that is the way a dog behaves.

Surely this is a refined quality in its nature and one that is truly philosophical. *b*

In what way philosophical?

Because it judges anything it sees to be either a friend or an enemy, on no other basis than that it knows the one and doesn't know the other. And how could it be anything besides a lover of learning, if it defines what is its own and what is alien to it in terms of knowledge and ignorance?

It couldn't.

But surely the love of learning is the same thing as philosophy or the love of wisdom?

It is.

Then, may we confidently assume in the case of a human being, too, that if he is to be gentle toward his own and those he knows, he must be a lover of learning and wisdom? *c*

We may.

Philosophy, spirit, speed, and strength must all, then, be combined in the nature of anyone who is to be a fine and good guardian of our city.

Absolutely.

The natural assets that a good guardian needs and the education he must have to develop them in the best possible way are the next topic. The appropriate basic education for future guardians, Socrates claims, is the traditional one consisting of music and poetry, on the one hand, and physical training, on the other. His discussion of it continues into Book III.

—C.D.C.R.

15. [The word *philosophos* is used here in its general sense to refer to intellectual curiosity or wanting to know things without ulterior motives. Plato is not suggesting (below) that pedigree dogs have the traits that he will attribute to full-blown philosophers in Books V–VII.]

Book III

412b . . . All right, then what's the next thing we have to determine? Isn't it which of these same people will rule and which be ruled?

c Of course.

Now, isn't it obvious that the rulers must be older and the ruled younger?

Yes, it is.

And mustn't the rulers also be the best of them?

That, too.

And aren't the best farmers the ones who are best at farming?

Yes.

Then, as the rulers must be the best of the guardians, mustn't they be the ones who are best at guarding the city?

Yes.

Then, in the first place, mustn't they be knowledgeable and capable, and mustn't they care for the city?

d That's right.

Now, one cares most for what one loves.

Necessarily.

And someone loves something most of all when he believes that the same things are advantageous to it as to himself and supposes that if it does well, he'll do well, and that if it does badly, then he'll do badly too.

That's right.

Then we must choose from among our guardians those men who, upon examination, seem most of all e to believe throughout their lives that they must eagerly pursue what is advantageous to the city and be wholly unwilling to do the opposite.

Such people would be suitable for the job at any rate.

I think we must observe them at all ages to see whether they are guardians of this conviction and make sure that neither compulsion nor magic spells will get them to discard or forget their belief that they must do what is best for the city.

What do you mean by discarding?

I'll tell you. I think the discarding of a belief is either voluntary or involuntary—voluntary when one learns that the belief is false, involuntary in the case 413 of all true beliefs.

I understand voluntary discarding but not involuntary.

What's that? Don't you know that people are voluntarily deprived of bad things, but involuntarily deprived of good ones? And isn't being deceived about the truth a bad thing, while possessing the truth is good? Or don't you think that to believe the things that are is to possess the truth?

That's right, and I do think that people are involuntarily deprived of true opinions.

But can't they also be so deprived by theft, magic spells, and compulsion? b

Now, I don't understand again.

I'm afraid I must be talking like a tragic poet! By "the victims of theft" I mean those who are persuaded to change their minds or those who forget, because time, in the latter case, and argument, in the former, takes away their opinions without their realizing it. Do you understand now?

Yes.

By "the compelled" I mean those whom pain or suffering causes to change their mind.

I understand that, and you're right.

The "victims of magic," I think you'd agree, are those who change their mind because they are under c the spell of pleasure or fear.

It seems to me that everything that deceives does so by casting a spell.

Then, as I said just now, we must find out who are the best guardians of their conviction that they must always do what they believe to be best for the city. We must keep them under observation from childhood and set them tasks that are most likely to make them forget such a conviction or be deceived out of it, and we must select whoever keeps on remem- d bering it and isn't easily deceived, and reject the others. Do you agree?

Yes.

And we must subject them to labors, pains, and contests in which we can watch for these traits.

That's right.

Then we must also set up a competition for the third way in which people are deprived of their convictions, namely, magic. Like those who lead colts into noise and tumult to see if they're afraid, we must expose our young people to fears and pleasures, testing them more thoroughly than gold is tested by fire. If e someone is hard to put under a spell, is apparently gracious in everything, is a good guardian of himself and the music and poetry he has learned, and if he always shows himself to be rhythmical and harmonious, then he is the best person both for himself and for the city. Anyone who is tested in this way as a 414 child, youth, and adult, and always comes out of it untainted, is to be made a ruler as well as a guardian; he is to be honored in life and to receive after his death the most prized tombs and memorials. But anyone who fails to prove himself in this way is to be rejected. It seems to me, Glaucon, that rulers and guardians must be selected and appointed in some such way as this, though we've provided only a general pattern and not the exact details.

It also seems to me that they must be selected in this sort of way.

Then, isn't it truly most correct to call these people *b* complete guardians, since they will guard against external enemies and internal friends, so that the one will lack the power and the other the desire to harm the city? The young people we've hitherto called guardians we'll now call *auxiliaries* and supporters of the guardians' convictions.

I agree.

How, then, could we devise one of those useful falsehoods we were talking about a while ago, one *c* noble falsehood that would, in the best case, persuade even the rulers, but if that's not possible, then the others in the city?

What sort of falsehood?

Nothing new, but a Phoenician story which describes something that has happened in many places. At least, that's what the poets say, and they've persuaded many people to believe it too. It hasn't happened among us, and I don't even know if it could. It would certainly take a lot of persuasion to get people to believe it.

You seem hesitant to tell the story.

When you hear it, you'll realize that I have every reason to hesitate.

Speak, and don't be afraid.

I'll tell it, then, though I don't know where I'll get *d* the audacity or even what words I'll use. I'll first try to persuade the rulers and the soldiers and then the rest of the city that the upbringing and the education we gave them, and the experiences that went with them, were a sort of dream, that in fact they themselves, their weapons, and the other craftsmen's tools were at that time really being fashioned and nurtured *e* inside the earth, and that when the work was completed, the earth, who is their mother, delivered all of them up into the world. Therefore, if anyone attacks the land in which they live, they must plan on its behalf and defend it as their mother and nurse and think of the other citizens as their earthborn brothers.

It isn't for nothing that you were so shy about telling your falsehood.

Appropriately so. Nevertheless, listen to the rest of the story. "All of you in the city are brothers," we'll 415 say to them in telling our story, "but the god who made you mixed some gold into those who are adequately equipped to rule, because they are most valuable. He put silver in those who are auxiliaries and iron and bronze in the farmers and other craftsmen. For the most part you will produce children like yourselves, but, because you are all related, a silver child will occasionally be born from a golden parent, and vice *b* versa, and all the others from each other. So the first and most important command from the god to the rulers is that there is nothing that they must guard better or watch more carefully than the mixture of metals in the souls of the next generation. If an offspring of theirs should be found to have a mixture of iron or bronze, they must not pity him in any way, but give him the rank appropriate to his nature and drive him out to join the craftsmen and farmers. But *c* if an offspring of these people is found to have a mixture of gold or silver, they will honor him and take him up to join the guardians or the auxiliaries, for there is an oracle which says that the city will be ruined if it ever has an iron or a bronze guardian." So, do you have any device that will make our citizens believe this story?

I can't see any way to make them believe it themselves, but perhaps there is one in the case of their *d* sons and later generations and all the other people who come after them.

I understand pretty much what you mean, but even that would help to make them care more for the city and each other. However, let's leave this matter wherever tradition takes it. And let's now arm our earthborn and lead them forth with their rulers in charge. And as they march, let them look for the best place in the city to have their camp, a site from which they can most easily control those within, if anyone is unwilling to obey the laws, or repel any outside *e* enemy who comes like a wolf upon the flock. And when they have established their camp and made the requisite sacrifices, they must see to their sleeping quarters. What do you say?

I agree.

And won't these quarters protect them adequately both in winter and summer?

Of course, for it seems to me that you mean their housing.

Yes, but housing for soldiers, not for money-makers.

How do you mean to distinguish these from one another? *416*

I'll try to tell you. The most terrible and most shameful thing of all is for a shepherd to rear dogs as auxiliaries to help him with his flocks in such a way that, through licentiousness, hunger, or some other bad trait of character, they do evil to the sheep and become like wolves instead of dogs.

That's certainly a terrible thing.

Isn't it necessary, therefore, to guard in every way *b* against our auxiliaries doing anything like that to the citizens because they are stronger, thereby becoming savage masters instead of kindly allies?

It is necessary.

And wouldn't a really good education endow them with the greatest caution in this regard?

But surely they have had an education like that.

Perhaps we shouldn't assert this dogmatically, Glaucon. What we can assert is what we were saying just now, that they must have the right education, whatever it is, if they are to have what will most make them gentle to each other and to those they *c* are guarding.

That's right.

Now, someone with some understanding might say that, besides this education, they must also have the kind of housing and other property that will neither prevent them from being the best guardians nor en- *d* courage them to do evil to the other citizens.

That's true.

Consider, then, whether or not they should live in some such way as this, if they're to be the kind of men we described. First, none of them should possess any private property beyond what is wholly necessary. Second, none of them should have a house or storeroom that isn't open for all to enter at will. Third, whatever sustenance moderate and courageous warrior-athletes require in order to have neither shortfall *e* nor surplus in a given year they'll receive by taxation on the other citizens as a salary for their guardianship. Fourth, they'll have common messes and live together like soldiers in a camp. We'll tell them that they always have gold and silver of a divine sort in their souls as a gift from the gods and so have no further need of human gold. Indeed, we'll tell them that it's impious for them to defile this divine possession by any admixture of such gold, because many impious deeds have been done that involve the currency used by ordinary people, while their own is pure. Hence, *417* for them alone among the city's population, it is unlawful to touch or handle gold or silver. They mustn't be under the same roof as it, wear it as jewelry, or drink from gold or silver goblets. In this way they'd save both themselves and the city. But if they acquire private land, houses, and currency themselves, they'll be household managers and farmers instead of guardians—hostile masters of the other citizens instead of *b* their allies. They'll spend their whole lives hating and being hated, plotting and being plotted against, more afraid of internal than of external enemies, and they'll hasten both themselves and the whole city to almost immediate ruin. For all these reasons, let's say that the guardians must be provided with housing and the rest in this way, and establish this as a law. Or don't you agree?

I certainly do, Glaucon said.

Book IV

427d . . . Well, son of Ariston, your city might now be said to be established. The next step is to get an adequate light somewhere and to call upon your brother as well as Polemarchus and the others, so as to look inside it and see where the justice and the injustice might be in it, what the difference between them is, and which of the two the person who is to be happy should possess, whether its possession is unnoticed by all the gods and human beings or not.

You're talking nonsense, Glaucon said. You promised to look for them yourself because you said it was impious for you not to come to the rescue of justice in every way you could. *e*

That's true, and I must do what I promised, but you'll have to help.

We will.

I hope to find it in this way. I think our city, if indeed it has been correctly founded, is completely good.

Necessarily so.

Clearly, then, it is wise, courageous, moderate, and just.

Clearly.

Then, if we find any of these in it, what's left over will be the ones we haven't found?

428 Of course.

Therefore, as with any other four things, if we were looking for any one of them in something and recognized it first, that would be enough for us, but if we recognized the other three first, this itself would be sufficient to enable us to recognize what we are looking for. Clearly it couldn't be anything other than what's left over.

That's right.

Therefore, since there are four virtues, mustn't we look for them in the same way?

Clearly.

Now, the first thing I think I can see clearly in the city is wisdom, and there seems to be something odd *b* about it.

What's that?

I think that the city we described is really wise. And that's because it has good judgment, isn't it?

Yes.

Now, this very thing, good judgment, is clearly some kind of knowledge, for it's through knowledge, not ignorance, that people judge well.

Clearly.

But there are many kinds of knowledge in the city.

Of course.

Is it because of the knowledge possessed by its carpenters, then, that the city is to be called wise and sound in judgment?

Not at all. It's called skilled in carpentry because *c* of that.

Then it isn't to be called wise because of the knowledge by which it arranges to have the best wooden implements.

No, indeed.

What about the knowledge of bronze items or the like?

It isn't because of any knowledge of that sort.

Nor because of the knowledge of how to raise a harvest from the earth, for it's called skilled in farming because of that.

I should think so.

Then, is there some knowledge possessed by some of the citizens in the city we just founded that doesn't judge about any particular matter but about the city as a whole and the maintenance of good relations, both internally and with other cities? *d*

There is indeed.

What is this knowledge, and who has it?

It is guardianship, and it is possessed by those rulers we just now called complete guardians.

Then, what does this knowledge entitle you to say about the city?

That it has good judgment and is really wise.

Who do you think that there will be more of in our city, metal-workers or these true guardians? *e*

There will be far more metal-workers.

Indeed, of all those who are called by a certain name because they have some kind of knowledge, aren't the guardians the least numerous?

By far.

Then, a whole city established according to nature would be wise because of the smallest class and part in it, namely, the governing or ruling one. And to this class, which seems to be by nature the smallest, belongs a share of the knowledge that alone among 429 all the other kinds of knowledge is to be called wisdom.

That's completely true.

Then we've found one of the four virtues, as well as its place in the city, though I don't know how we found it.

Our way of finding it seems good enough to me.

And surely courage and the part of the city it's in, the part on account of which the city is called courageous, aren't difficult to see.

How is that?

Who, in calling the city cowardly or courageous, would look anywhere other than to the part of it that *b* fights and does battle on its behalf?

No one would look anywhere else.

At any rate, I don't think that the courage or cowardice of its other citizens would cause the city itself to be called either courageous or cowardly.

No, it wouldn't.

The city is courageous, then, because of a part of itself that has the power to preserve through everything its belief about what things are to be feared, namely, that they are the things and kinds of things *c* that the lawgiver declared to be such in the course of educating it. Or don't you call that courage?

I don't completely understand what you mean. Please, say it again.

I mean that courage is a kind of preservation.

What sort of preservation?

That preservation of the belief that has been inculcated by the law through education about what things and sorts of things are to be feared. And by preserving this belief "through everything," I mean preserving *d* it and not abandoning it because of pains, pleasures, desires, or fears. If you like, I'll compare it to something I think it resembles.

I'd like that.

You know that dyers, who want to dye wool purple, first pick out from the many colors of wool the one that is naturally white, then they carefully prepare this in various ways, so that it will absorb the color as well as possible, and only at that point do they apply the purple dye. When something is dyed in *e* this way, the color is fast—no amount of washing, whether with soap or without it, can remove it. But you also know what happens to material if it hasn't been dyed in this way, but instead is dyed purple or some other color without careful preparation.

I know that it looks washed out and ridiculous.

Then, you should understand that, as far as we could, we were doing something similar when we selected our soldiers and educated them in music *430* and physical training. What we were contriving was nothing other than this: That because they had the proper nature and upbringing, they would absorb the laws in the finest possible way, just like a dye, so that their belief about what they should fear and all the rest would become so fast that even such extremely effective detergents as pleasure, pain, fear, and desire wouldn't wash it out—and pleasure is much more *b* potent than any powder, washing soda, or soap. This power to preserve through everything the correct and law-inculcated belief about what is to be feared and what isn't is what I call courage, unless, of course, you say otherwise.

I have nothing different to say, for I assume that you don't consider the correct belief about these same things, which you find in animals and slaves, and which is not the result of education, to be inculcated by law, and that you don't call it courage but something else.

c That's absolutely true.

Then I accept your account of courage.

Accept it instead as my account of *civic* courage, and you will be right. We'll discuss courage more fully some other time, if you like. At present, our inquiry concerns not it but justice. And what we've said is sufficient for that purpose.

You're quite right.

There are now two things left for us to find in the city, namely, moderation[1] and—the goal of our entire inquiry—justice. *d*

That's right.

Is there a way we could find justice so as not to have to bother with moderation any further?

I don't know any, and I wouldn't want justice to appear first if that means that we won't investigate moderation. So if you want to please me, look for the latter first.

I'm certainly willing. It would be wrong not to be. *e*

Look, then.

We will. Seen from here, it is more like a kind of consonance and harmony than the previous ones.

In what way?

Moderation is surely a kind of order, the mastery of certain kinds of pleasures and desires. People indicate as much when they use the phrase "self-control" and other similar phrases. I don't know just what they mean by them, but they are, so to speak, like tracks or clues that moderation has left behind in language. Isn't that so?

Absolutely.

Yet isn't the expression "self-control" ridiculous? The stronger self that does the controlling is the same as the weaker self that gets controlled, so that only one person is referred to in all such expressions. *431*

Of course.

Nonetheless, the expression is apparently trying to indicate that, in the soul of that very person, there is a better part and a worse one and that, whenever the naturally better part is in control of the worse, this is expressed by saying that the person is self-controlled or master of himself. At any rate, one praises someone by calling him self-controlled. But when, on the other hand, the smaller and better part is overpowered by

1. [The Greek term is *sōphrosunē*. It has a very wide meaning: self-control, good sense, reasonableness, temperance, and (in some contexts) chastity. Someone who keeps his head under pressure or temptation possesses *sōphrosunē*.]

the larger, because of bad upbringing or bad com-
b pany, this is called being self-defeated or licentious and is a reproach.

Appropriately so.

Take a look at our new city, and you'll find one of these in it. You'll say that it is rightly called self-controlled, if indeed something in which the better rules the worse is properly called moderate and self-controlled.

I am looking, and what you say is true.

Now, one finds all kinds of diverse desires, plea-
c sures, and pains, mostly in children, women, household slaves, and in those of the inferior majority who are called free.

That's right.

But you meet with the desires that are simple, measured, and directed by calculation in accordance with understanding and correct belief only in the few people who are born with the best natures and receive the best education.

That's true.

Then, don't you see that in your city, too, the desires of the inferior many are controlled by the
d wisdom and desires of the superior few?

I do.

Therefore, if any city is said to be in control of itself and of its pleasures and desires, it is this one.

Absolutely.

And isn't it, therefore, also moderate because of all this?

It is.

And, further, if indeed the ruler and the ruled in
e any city share the same belief about who should rule, it is in this one. Or don't you agree?

I agree entirely.

And when the citizens agree in this way, in which of them do you say moderation is located? In the ruler or the ruled?

I suppose in both.

Then, you see how right we were to divine that moderation resembles a kind of harmony?

How so?

Because, unlike courage and wisdom, each of which resides in one part, making the city brave and wise respectively, moderation spreads throughout the
432 whole. It makes the weakest, the strongest, and those in between—whether in regard to reason, physical strength, numbers, wealth, or anything else—all sing the same song together. And this unanimity, this agreement between the naturally worse and the naturally better as to which of the two is to rule both in the city and in each one, is rightly called moderation.

I agree completely. *b*

All right. We've now found, at least from the point of view of our present beliefs, three out of the four virtues in our city. So what kind of virtue is left, then, that makes the city share even further in virtue? Surely, it's clear that it is justice.

That is clear.

Then, Glaucon, we must station ourselves like hunters surrounding a wood and focus our understanding, so that justice doesn't escape us and vanish into obscurity, for obviously it's around here somewhere. So look and try eagerly to catch sight of it, *c* and if you happen to see it before I do, you can tell me about it.

I wish I could, but you'll make better use of me if you take me to be a follower who can see things when you point them out to him.

Follow, then, and join me in a prayer.

I'll do that, just so long as you lead.

I certainly will, though the place seems to be impenetrable and full of shadows. It is certainly dark and hard to search through. But all the same, we must go on.

Indeed we must. *d*

And then I caught sight of something. Ah ha! Glaucon, it looks as though there's a track here, so it seems that our quarry won't altogether escape us.

That's good news.

Either that, or we've just been stupid.

In what way?

Because what we are looking for seems to have been rolling around at our feet from the very beginning, and we didn't see it, which was ridiculous of us. Just as people sometimes search for the very thing they are holding in their hands, so we didn't look in the right direction but gazed off into the distance, *e* and that's probably why we didn't notice it.

What do you mean?

I mean that, though we've been talking and hearing about it for a long time, I think we didn't understand what we were saying or that, in a way, we were talking about justice.

That's a long prelude for someone who wants to hear the answer.

Then listen and see whether there's anything in 433 what I say. Justice, I think, is exactly what we said must be established throughout the city when we were founding it—either that or some form of it. We stated, and often repeated, if you remember, that everyone must practice one of the occupations in the city for which he is naturally best suited.

Yes, we did keep saying that.

Moreover, we've heard many people say and have often said ourselves that justice is doing one's own b work and not meddling with what isn't one's own.

Yes, we have.

Then, it turns out that this doing one's own work—provided that it comes to be in a certain way—is justice. And do you know what I take as evidence of this?

No, tell me.

I think that this is what was left over in the city when moderation, courage, and wisdom have been found. It is the power that makes it possible for them to grow in the city and that preserves them when c they've grown for as long as it remains there itself. And of course we said that justice would be what was left over when we had found the other three.

Yes, that must be so.

And surely, if we had to decide which of the four will make the city good by its presence, it would be a hard decision. Is it the agreement in belief between the rulers and the ruled? Or the preservation among the soldiers of the law-inspired belief about what is to be feared and what isn't? Or the wisdom and guard- d ianship of the rulers? Or is it, above all, the fact that every child, woman, slave, freeman, craftsman, ruler, and ruled each does his own work and doesn't meddle with what is other people's?

How could this fail to be a hard decision?

It seems, then, that the power that consists in everyone's doing his own work rivals wisdom, moderation, e and courage in its contribution to the virtue of the city.

It certainly does.

And wouldn't you call this rival to the others in its contribution to the city's virtue justice?

Absolutely.

Look at it this way if you want to be convinced. Won't you order your rulers to act as judges in the city's courts?

Of course.

And won't their sole aim in delivering judgments be that no citizen should have what belongs to another or be deprived of what is his own?

They'll have no aim but that.

Because that is just?

Yes.

Therefore, from this point of view also, the having and doing of one's own would be accepted as justice. 434

That's right.

Consider, then, and see whether you agree with me about this. If a carpenter attempts to do the work of a cobbler, or a cobbler that of a carpenter, or they exchange their tools or honors with one another, or if the same person tries to do both jobs, and all other such exchanges are made, do you think that does any great harm to the city?

Not much.

But I suppose that when someone, who is by nature a craftsman or some other kind of money-maker, is puffed up by wealth, or by having a majority of votes, or by his own strength, or by some other such thing, b and attempts to enter the class of soldiers, or one of the unworthy soldiers tries to enter that of the judges and guardians, and these exchange their tools and honors, or when the same person tries to do all these things at once, then I think you'll agree that these exchanges and this sort of meddling bring the city to ruin.

Absolutely.

Meddling and exchange between these three classes, then, is the greatest harm that can happen to the city and would rightly be called the worst thing someone could do to it. c

Exactly.

And wouldn't you say that the worst thing that someone could do to his city is injustice?

Of course.

Then, that exchange and meddling is injustice. Or to put it the other way around: For the money-making, auxiliary, and guardian classes each to do its own work in the city, is the opposite. That's justice, isn't it, and makes the city just?

I agree. Justice is that and nothing else. d

Let's not take that as secure just yet, but if we find that the same form, when it comes to be in each individual person, is accepted as justice there as well, we can assent to it. What else can we say? But if that isn't what we find, we must look for something else to be justice. For the moment, however, let's complete the present inquiry. We thought that, if we first tried to observe justice in some larger thing that possessed it, this would make it easier to observe in a single individual. We agreed that this larger thing is a city, and so we established the best city we could, *e* knowing well that justice would be in one that was good. So, let's apply what has come to light in the city to an individual, and if it is accepted there, all will be well. But if something different is found in the individual, then we must go back and test that on the city. And if we do this, and compare them 435 side by side, we might well make justice light up as if we were rubbing fire-sticks together. And, when it has come to light, we can get a secure grip on it for ourselves.

You're following the road we set, and we must do as you say.

Well, then, are things called by the same name, whether they are bigger or smaller than one another, like or unlike with respect to that to which that name applies?

Alike.

Then a just man won't differ at all from a just city *b* in respect to the form of justice; rather he'll be like the city.

He will.

But a city was thought to be just when each of the three natural classes within it did its own work, and it was thought to be moderate, courageous, and wise because of certain other conditions and states of theirs.

That's true.

Then, if an individual has these same three parts in his soul, we will expect him to be correctly called *c* by the same names as the city if he has the same conditions in them.

Necessarily so.

Then once again we've come upon an easy question, namely, does the soul have these three parts in it or not?

It doesn't look easy to me. Perhaps, Socrates, there's some truth in the old saying that everything fine is difficult.

Apparently so. But you should know, Glaucon, that, in my opinion, we will never get a precise answer *d* using our present methods of argument—although there is another longer and fuller road that does lead to such an answer. But perhaps we can get an answer that's up to the standard of our previous statements and inquiries.

Isn't that satisfactory? It would be enough for me at present.

In that case, it will be fully enough for me too.

Then don't weary, but go on with the inquiry.

Well, then, we are surely compelled to agree that each of us has within himself the same parts and *e* characteristics as the city? Where else would they come from? It would be ridiculous for anyone to think that spiritedness didn't come to be in cities from such individuals as the Thracians, Scythians, and others who live to the north of us who are held to possess spirit, or that the same isn't true of the love of learning, which is mostly associated with our part of the world, or of the love of money, which one might say is 436 conspicuously displayed by the Phoenicians and Egyptians.

It would.

That's the way it is, anyway, and it isn't hard to understand.

Certainly not.

But this *is* hard. Do we do these things with the same part of ourselves, or do we do them with three different parts? Do we learn with one part, get angry with another, and with some third part desire the pleasures of food, drink, sex, and the others that are closely akin to them? Or, when we set out after something, do we act with the whole of our soul, in each case? This is what's hard to determine in a way that's *b* up to the standards of our argument.

I think so too.

Well, then, let's try to determine in that way whether these parts are the same or different.

How?

It is obvious that the same thing will not be willing to do or undergo opposites in the same part of itself, in relation to the same thing, at the same time. So, if we ever find this happening in the soul, we'll know that we aren't dealing with one thing but many. *c*

All right.

Then consider what I'm about to say.

Say on.

Is it possible for the same thing to stand still and move at the same time in the same part of itself?

Not at all.

Let's make our agreement more precise in order to avoid disputes later on. If someone said that a person who is standing still but moving his hands and head is moving and standing still at the same time, we wouldn't consider, I think, that he ought to put it like that. What he ought to say is that one part of the person is standing still and another part is moving. *d* Isn't that so?

It is.

And if our interlocutor became even more amusing and was sophisticated enough to say that whole spinning tops stand still and move at the same time when the peg is fixed in the same place and they revolve, and that the same is true of anything else moving in a circular motion on the same spot, we wouldn't agree, because it isn't with respect to the same parts of themselves that such things both stand still and *e* move. We'd say that they have an axis and a circumference and that with respect to the axis they stand still, since they don't wobble to either side, while with respect to the circumference they move in a circle. But if they do wobble to the left or right, front or back, while they are spinning, we'd say that they aren't standing still in any way.

And we'd be right.

No such statement will disturb us, then, or make us believe that the same thing can be, do, or undergo opposites, at the same time, in the same respect, and 437 in relation to the same thing.

They won't make me believe it, at least.

Nevertheless, in order to avoid going through all these objections one by one and taking a long time to prove them all untrue, let's hypothesize that this is corrrect and carry on. But we agree that if it should ever be shown to be incorrect, all the consequences we've drawn from it will also be lost.

We should agree to that.

Then wouldn't you consider all the following, *b* whether they are doings or undergoings, as pairs of opposites: Assent and dissent, wanting to have something and rejecting it, taking something and pushing it away?

Yes, they are opposites.

What about these? Wouldn't you include thirst, hunger, the appetites as a whole, and wishing and *c* willing somewhere in the class we mentioned? Wouldn't you say that the soul of someone who has an appetite for a thing wants what he has an appetite for and takes to himself what it is his will to have, and that insofar as he wishes something to be given to him, his soul, since it desires this to come about, nods assent to it as if in answer to a question?

I would.

What about not willing, not wishing, and not having an appetite? Aren't these among the very opposites—cases in which the soul pushes and drives things away?

Of course. *d*

Then won't we say that there is a class of things called appetites and that the clearest examples are hunger and thirst?

We will.

One of these is for food and the other for drink?

Yes.

Now, insofar as it is thirst, is it an appetite in the soul for more than that for which we say that it is the appetite? For example, is thirst thirst for hot drink or cold, or much drink or little, or, in a word, for drink of a certain sort? Or isn't it rather that, where heat is present as well as thirst, it causes the appetite to be for something cold as well, and where cold for *e* something hot, and where there is much thirst because of the presence of muchness, it will cause the desire to be for much, and where little for little? But thirst itself will never be for anything other than what it is in its nature to be for, namely, drink itself, and hunger for food.

That's the way it is, each appetite itself is only for its natural object, while the appetite for something of a certain sort depends on additions.

Therefore, let no one catch us unprepared or disturb us by claiming that no one has an appetite for 438 drink but rather good drink, nor food but good food, on the grounds that everyone after all has appetite for good things, so that if thirst is an appetite, it will be an appetite for good drink or whatever, and similarly with the others.[2]

All the same, the person who says that has a point.

But it seems to me that, in the case of all things that are related to something, those that are of a particular sort are related to a particular sort of thing, *b* while those that are merely themselves are related to a thing that is merely itself.

I don't understand.

2. [Plato is here laying the foundations for his rejection of the principle, espoused by Socrates in many earlier dialogues, that weakness of will is impossible.]

Don't you understand that the greater is such as to be greater than something?

Of course.

Than the less?

Yes.

And the much greater than the much less, isn't that so?

Yes.

And the once greater to the once less? And the going-to-be greater than the going-to-be less?

Certainly.

And isn't the same true of the more and the *c* fewer, the double and the half, heavier and lighter, faster and slower, the hot and the cold, and all other such things?

Of course.

And what about the various kinds of knowledge? Doesn't the same apply? Knowledge itself is knowledge of what can be learned itself (or whatever it is that knowledge is of), while a particular sort of knowledge is of a particular sort of thing. For example, when knowledge of building houses came to be, *d* didn't it differ from the other kinds of knowledge, and so was called knowledge of building?

Of course.

And wasn't that because it was a different sort of knowledge from all the others?

Yes.

And wasn't it because it was of a particular sort of thing that it itself became a particular sort of knowledge? And isn't this true of all crafts and kinds of knowledge?

It is.

Well, then, this is what I was trying to say—if you understand it now—when I said that of all things that are related to something, those that are merely themselves are related to things that are merely themselves, while those that are of a particular sort are related to things of a particular sort. However, I don't *e* mean that the sorts in question have to be the same for them both. For example, knowledge of health or disease isn't healthy or diseased, and knowledge of good and bad doesn't itself become good or bad. I mean that, when knowledge became, not knowledge of the thing itself that knowledge is of, but knowledge of something of a particular sort, the result was that it itself became a particular sort of knowledge, and this caused it to be no longer called knowledge without qualification, but—with the addition of the relevant sort—medical knowledge or whatever.

I understand, and I think that that's the way it is.

Then as for thirst, wouldn't you include it among things that are related to something? Surely thirst is related to . . . *439*

I know it's related to drink.

Therefore a particular sort of thirst is for a particular sort of drink. But thirst itself isn't for much or little, good or bad, or, in a word, for drink of a particular sort. Rather, thirst itself is in its nature only for drink itself.

Absolutely.

Hence the soul of the thirsty person, insofar as he's thirsty, doesn't wish anything else but to drink, and it wants this and is impelled towards it. *b*

Clearly.

Therefore, if something draws it back when it is thirsting, wouldn't that be something different in it from whatever thirsts and drives it like a beast to drink? It can't be, we say, that the same thing, with the same part of itself, in relation to the same, at the same time, does opposite things.

No, it can't.

In the same way, I suppose, it's wrong to say of the archer that his hands at the same time push the bow away and draw it towards him. We ought to say that one hand pushes it away and the other draws it towards him.

Absolutely. *c*

Now, would we assert that sometimes there are thirsty people who don't wish to drink?

Certainly, it happens often to many different people.

What, then, should one say about them? Isn't it that there is something in their soul, bidding them to drink, and something different, forbidding them to do so, that overrules the thing that bids?

I think so.

Doesn't that which forbids in such cases come into play—if it comes into play at all—as a result of rational calculation, while what drives and drags them to drink is a result of feelings and diseases? *d*

Apparently.

Hence it isn't unreasonable for us to claim that they are two, and different from one another. We'll call the part of the soul with which it calculates the rational part and the part with which it lusts, hungers, thirsts, and gets excited by other appetites the irrational appetitive part, companion of certain indulgences and pleasures.

e Yes. Indeed, that's a reasonable thing to think.

Then, let these two parts be distinguished in the soul. Now, is the spirited part by which we get angry a third part or is it of the same nature as either of the other two?

Perhaps it's like the appetitive part.

But I've heard something relevant to this, and I believe it. Leontius, the son of Aglaion, was going up from the Piraeus along the outside of the North Wall when he saw some corpses lying at the executioner's feet. He had an appetite to look at them but at the same time he was disgusted and turned away. For a time he struggled with himself and covered his face, but, finally, overpowered by the appetite, he pushed *440* his eyes wide open and rushed towards the corpses, saying, "Look for yourselves, you evil wretches, take your fill of the beautiful sight!"[3]

I've heard that story myself.

It certainly proves that anger sometimes makes war against the appetites, as one thing against another.

Besides, don't we often notice in other cases that when appetite forces someone contrary to rational calculation, he reproaches himself and gets angry *b* with that in him that's doing the forcing, so that of the two factions that are fighting a civil war, so to speak, spirit allies itself with reason? But I don't think you can say that you've ever seen spirit, either in yourself or anyone else, ally itself with an appetite to do what reason has decided must not be done.

No, by god, I haven't.

What happens when a person thinks that he has *c* done something unjust? Isn't it true that the nobler he is, the less he resents it if he suffers hunger, cold, or the like at the hands of someone whom he believes to be inflicting this on him justly, and won't his spirit, as I say, refuse to be aroused?

That's true.

But what happens if, instead, he believes that someone has been unjust to him? Isn't the spirit within him boiling and angry, fighting for what he believes to be just? Won't it endure hunger, cold, and the like and keep on till it is victorious, not ceasing from *d* noble actions until it either wins, dies, or calms down, called to heel by the reason within him, like a dog by a shepherd?

Spirit is certainly like that. And, of course, we made the auxiliaries in our city like dogs obedient to the rulers, who are themselves like shepherds of a city.

You well understand what I'm trying to say. But also reflect on this further point.

What? *e*

The position of the spirited part seems to be the opposite of what we thought before. Then we thought of it as something appetitive, but now we say that it is far from being that, for in the civil war in the soul it aligns itself far more with the rational part.

Absolutely.

Then is it also different from the rational part, or is it some form of it, so that there are two parts in the soul—the rational and the appetitive—instead of three? Or rather, just as there were three classes in the city that held it together, the money-making, the *441* auxiliary, and the deliberative, is the spirited part a third thing in the soul that is by nature the helper of the rational part, provided that it hasn't been corrupted by a bad upbringing?

It must be a third.

Yes, provided that we can show it is different from the rational part, as we saw earlier it was from the appetitive one.

It isn't difficult to show that it is different. Even in small children, one can see that they are full of spirit right from birth, while as far as rational calculation is concerned, some never seem to get a share of it, while the majority do so quite late. *b*

That's really well put. And in animals too one can see that what you say is true. Besides, our earlier quotation from Homer bears it out, where he says,

He struck his chest and spoke to his heart.[4]

For here Homer clearly represents the part that has calculated about better and worse as different from *c* the part that is angry without calculation.

That's exactly right.

Well, then, we've now made our difficult way through a sea of argument. We are pretty much agreed that the same number and the same kinds of classes as are in the city are also in the soul of each individual.

3. [Leontius' desire to look at the corpses is sexual in nature, for a fragment of contemporary comedy tells us that Leontius was known for his love of boys as pale as corpses.]

4. [*Odyssey* 20.27.]

That's true.

Therefore, it necessarily follows that the individual is wise in the same way and in the same part of himself as the city.

That's right.

And isn't the individual courageous in the same *d* way and in the same part of himself as the city? And isn't everything else that has to do with virtue the same in both?

Necessarily.

Moreover, Glaucon, I suppose we'll say that a man is just in the same way as a city.

That too is entirely necessary.

And we surely haven't forgotten that the city was just because each of the three classes in it was doing its own work.

I don't think we could forget that.

Then we must also remember that each one of us in whom each part is doing its own work will himself *e* be just and do his own.

Of course, we must.

Therefore, isn't it appropriate for the rational part to rule, since it is really wise and exercises foresight on behalf of the whole soul, and for the spirited part to obey it and be its ally?

It certainly is.

And isn't it, as we were saying, a mixture of music and poetry, on the one hand, and physical training, on the other, that makes the two parts harmonious, stretching and nurturing the rational part with fine words and learning, relaxing the other part through 442 soothing stories, and making it gentle by means of harmony and rhythm?

That's precisely it.

And these two, having been nurtured in this way, and having truly learned their own roles and been educated in them, will govern the appetitive part, which is the largest part in each person's soul and is by nature most insatiable for money. They'll watch over it to see that it isn't filled with the so-called pleasures of the body and that it doesn't become so big and strong that it no longer does its own work but attempts to enslave and rule over the classes it *b* isn't fitted to rule, thereby overturning everyone's whole life.

That's right.

Then, wouldn't these two parts also do the finest job of guarding the whole soul and body against external enemies—reason by planning, spirit by fighting, following its leader, and carrying out the leader's decisions through its courage?

Yes, that's true.

And it is because of the spirited part, I suppose, that we call a single individual courageous, namely, *c* when it preserves through pains and pleasures the declarations of reason about what is to be feared and what isn't.

That's right.

And we'll call him wise because of that small part of himself that rules in him and makes those declarations and has within it the knowledge of what is advantageous for each part and for the whole soul, which is the community of all three parts.

Absolutely.

And isn't he moderate because of the friendly and harmonious relations between these same parts, namely, when the ruler and the ruled believe in common that the rational part should rule and don't engage in civil war against it? *d*

Moderation is surely nothing other than that, both in the city and in the individual.

And, of course, a person will be just because of what we've so often mentioned, and in that way.

Necessarily.

Well, then, is the justice in us at all indistinct? Does it seem to be something different from what we found in the city?

It doesn't seem so to me.

If there are still any doubts in our soul about this, we could dispel them altogether by appealing to ordinary cases. *e*

Which ones?

For example, if we had to come to an agreement about whether someone similar in nature and training to our city had embezzled a deposit of gold or silver that he had accepted, who do you think would consider him to have done it rather than someone who isn't like him? 443

No one.

And would he have anything to do with temple robberies, thefts, betrayals of friends in private life or of cities in public life?

No, nothing.

And he'd be in no way untrustworthy in keeping an oath or other agreement.

How could he be?

And adultery, disrespect for parents, and neglect of the gods would be more in keeping with every other kind of character than his.

With every one.

And isn't the cause of all this that every part within *b* him does its own work, whether it's ruling or being ruled?

Yes, that and nothing else.

Then, are you still looking for justice to be something other than this power, the one that produces men and cities of the sort we've described?

No, I certainly am not.

Then the dream we had has been completely fulfilled—our suspicion that, with the help of some god, we had hit upon the origin and pattern of justice *c* right at the beginning in founding our city.[5]

Absolutely.

Indeed, Glaucon, the principle that it is right for someone who is by nature a cobbler to practice cobblery and nothing else, for the carpenter to practice carpentry, and the same for the others is a sort of image of justice—that's why it's beneficial.

Apparently.

And in truth justice is, it seems, something of this sort. However, it isn't concerned with someone's doing his own externally, but with what is inside him, *d* with what is truly himself and his own. One who is just does not allow any part of himself to do the work of another part or allow the various classes within him to meddle with each other. He regulates well what is really his own and rules himself. He puts himself in order, is his own friend, and harmonizes the three parts of himself like three limiting notes in a musical scale—high, low, and middle. He binds together those parts and any others there may be in between, and from having been many things he *e* becomes entirely one, moderate and harmonious. Only then does he act. And when he does anything, whether acquiring wealth, taking care of his body, engaging in politics, or in private contracts—in all of these, he believes that the action is just and fine that preserves this inner harmony and helps achieve it, and calls it so, and regards as wisdom the knowledge that oversees such actions. And he believes that the action that destroys this harmony is unjust, and calls it *444* so, and regards the belief that oversees it as ignorance.

5. [See 432c–433b.]

That's absolutely true, Socrates.

Well, then, if we claim to have found the just man, the just city, and what the justice is that is in them, I don't suppose that we'll seem to be telling a complete falsehood.

No, we certainly won't.

Shall we claim it, then?

We shall.

So be it. Now, I suppose we must look for injustice.

Clearly.

Surely, it must be a kind of civil war between the three parts, a meddling and doing of another's work, *b* a rebellion by some part against the whole soul in order to rule it inappropriately. The rebellious part is by nature suited to be a slave, while the other part is not a slave but belongs to the ruling class. We'll say something like that, I suppose, and that the turmoil and straying of these parts are injustice, licentiousness, cowardice, ignorance, and, in a word, the whole of vice.

That's what they are.

So, if justice and injustice are really clear enough to us, then acting justly, acting unjustly, and doing *c* injustice are also clear.

How so?

Because just and unjust actions are no different for the soul than healthy and unhealthy things are for the body.

In what way?

Healthy things produce health, unhealthy ones disease.

Yes.

And don't just actions produce justice in the soul and unjust ones injustice? *d*

Necessarily.

To produce health is to establish the components of the body in a natural relation of control and being controlled, one by another, while to produce disease is to establish a relation of ruling and being ruled contrary to nature.

That's right.

Then, isn't to produce justice to establish the parts of the soul in a natural relation of control, one by another, while to produce injustice is to establish a relation of ruling and being ruled contrary to nature?

Precisely.

Virtue seems, then, to be a kind of health, fine

condition, and well-being of the soul, while vice is *e* disease, shameful condition, and weakness.

That's true.

And don't fine ways of living lead one to the possession of virtue, shameful ones to vice?

Necessarily.

So it now remains, it seems, to inquire whether it *445* is more profitable to act justly, live in a fine way, and be just, whether one is known to be so or not, or to act unjustly and be unjust, provided that one doesn't pay the penalty and become better as a result of punishment.

But, Socrates, this inquiry looks ridiculous to me now that justice and injustice have been shown to be as we have described. Even if one has every kind of food and drink, lots of money, and every sort of power to rule, life is thought to be not worth living when the body's nature is ruined. So even if someone *b* can do whatever he wishes, except what will free him from vice and injustice and make him acquire justice and virtue, how can it be worth living when his soul—the very thing by which he lives—is ruined and in turmoil?

Yes, it is ridiculous. Nevertheless, now that we've come far enough to be able to see most clearly that this is so, we mustn't give up.

That's absolutely the last thing we must do.

Then come here, so that you can see how many *c* forms of vice there are, anyhow that I consider worthy of examination.

I'm following you, just tell me.

Well, from the vantage point we've reached in our argument, it seems to me that there is one form of virtue and an unlimited number of forms of vice, four of which are worth mentioning.

How do you mean?

It seems likely that there are as many types of soul as there are specific types of political constitution.

How many is that?

d Five forms of constitution and five of souls.

What are they?

One is the constitution we've been describing. And it has two names. If one outstanding man emerges among the rulers, it's called a kingship; if more than one, it's called an aristocracy.

That's true.

Therefore, I say that this is one form of constitution. Whether one man emerges or many, none of the significant laws of the city would be changed, if they followed the upbringing and education we described. *e*

Probably not.

Book V

Book V continues the discussion of virtue and vice in souls and cities that was begun at the end of Book IV. But it is immediately interrupted by Polemarchus and the other interlocutors, all of whom want Socrates to explain the remark he made in passing at 423e–424a about the guardians possessing their wives and children in common. Socrates' lengthy response to their request occupies the majority of the book. In it he makes the revolutionary proposal that children should be brought up by the city rather than by their biological parents, and that men and women with the same natural ability should receive the same education and training and do the same kind of work. Hence there will be female guardians and rulers in the kallipolis, as well as male ones.

Glaucon agrees that a city of the sort Socrates has described would be the best one, but he wonders whether or not it could ever really come about. Socrates undertakes to show that it could. The smallest change that would transform an already existing city into the kallipolis is if its kings or rulers become philosophers or if philosophers become its kings or rulers. This proposal, Socrates thinks, is likely to produce even more outrage than those about women and children, but he thinks that outrage will subside when he explains what true philosophers are really like.

Book VI

. . . The subject of women and children has been adequately dealt with, but that of the rulers has to be *e* taken up again from the beginning. We said, if you remember, that they must show themselves to be lovers of their city when tested by pleasure and pain and that they must hold on to their resolve through *503* labors, fears, and all other adversities. Anyone who was incapable of doing so was to be rejected, while anyone who came through unchanged—like gold tested in a fire—was to be made ruler and receive prizes both while he lived and after his death. These were the sort of things we were saying while our argument, afraid of stirring up the very problems that now confront us, veiled its face and slipped by. *b*

That's very true; I do remember it.

We hesitated to say the things we've now dared to say anyway. So let's now also dare to say that those who are to be made our guardians in the most exact sense of the term must be philosophers.

Let's do it.

Then you should understand that there will probably be only a few of them, for they have to have the nature we described, and its parts mostly grow in separation and are rarely found in the same person.

c What do you mean?

You know that ease of learning, good memory, quick wits, smartness, youthful passion, high-mindedness, and all the other things that go along with these are rarely willing to grow together in a mind that will choose an orderly life that is quiet and completely stable, for the people who possess the former traits are carried by their quick wits wherever chance leads them and have no stability at all.

That's true.

On the other hand, people with stable characters, who don't change easily, who aren't easily frightened in battle, and whom one would employ because of their d greater reliability, exhibit similar traits when it comes to learning: They are as hard to move and teach as people whose brains have become numb, and they are filled with sleep and yawning whenever they have to learn anything.

That's so.

Yet we say that someone must have a fine and goodly share of both characters, or he won't receive the truest education, honors, or rule.

That's right.

Then, don't you think that such people will be rare?

Of course.

Therefore they must be tested in the labors, fears, and e pleasures we mentioned previously. But they must also be exercised in many other subjects—which we didn't mention but are adding now—to see whether they can tolerate the most important subjects or will shrink from 504 them like the cowards who shrink from other tests.

It's appropriate to examine them like that. But what do you mean by the most important subjects?

Do you remember when we distinguished three parts in the soul, in order to help bring out what justice, moderation, courage, and wisdom each is?

If I didn't remember that, it wouldn't be just for me to hear the rest.

What about what preceded it?

What was that?

We said, I believe, that, in order to get the finest possible view of these matters, we would need to take b a longer road that would make them plain to anyone who took it but that it was possible to give demonstrations of what they are that would be up to the standard of the previous argument.[1] And you said that that would be satisfactory. So it seems to me that our discussion at that time fell short of exactness, but whether or not it satisfied you is for you to say.

I thought you gave us good measure and so, apparently, did the others.

Any measure of such things that falls short in any way of that which is is not good measure, for nothing c incomplete is the measure of anything, although people are sometimes of the opinion that an incomplete treatment is nonetheless adequate and makes further investigation unnecessary.

Indeed, laziness causes many people to think that.

It is a thought that a guardian of a city and its laws can well do without.

Probably so.

Well, then, he must take the longer road and put as much effort into learning as into physical training, for otherwise, as we were just saying, he will never reach the goal of the most important subject and the d most appropriate one for him to learn.

Aren't these virtues, then, the most important things? he asked. Is there anything even more important than justice and the other virtues we discussed?

There is something more important. However, even for the virtues themselves, it isn't enough to look at a mere sketch, as we did before, while neglecting the most complete account. It's ridiculous, isn't it, to strain every nerve to attain the utmost exactness and clarity about other things of little value and not to consider the most important things worthy of the greatest exactness? e

It certainly is. But do you think that anyone is going to let you off without asking you what this most important subject is and what it concerns?

No, indeed, and you can ask me too. You've certainly heard the answer often enough, but now either you aren't thinking or you intend to make trouble for

1. [See 435d.]

me again by interrupting. And I suspect the latter, 505 for you've often heard it said that the form of the good is the most important thing to learn about and that it's by their relation to it that just things and the others become useful and beneficial. You know very well now that I am going to say this, and, besides, that we have no adequate knowledge of it. And you also know that, if we don't know it, even the fullest possible knowledge of other things is of no benefit to us, any more than if we acquire any possession without the good of it. Or do you think that it is any advantage to have every kind of possession without the good of b it? Or to know everything except the good, thereby knowing nothing fine or good?

No, by god, I don't.

Furthermore, you certainly know that the majority believe that pleasure is the good, while the more sophisticated believe that it is knowledge.

Indeed I do.

And you know that those who believe this can't tell us what sort of knowledge it is, however, but in the end are forced to say that it is knowledge of the good.

And that's ridiculous.

Of course it is. They blame us for not knowing the c good and then turn around and talk to us as if we did know it. They say that it is knowledge of the good—as if we understood what they're speaking about when they utter the word "good."

That's completely true.

What about those who define the good as pleasure? Are they any less full of confusion than the others? Aren't even they forced to admit that there are bad pleasures?

Most definitely.

So, I think, they have to agree that the same things are both good and bad. Isn't that true?

d Of course.

It's clear, then, isn't it, why there are many large controversies about this?

How could it be otherwise?

And isn't this also clear? In the case of just and beautiful things, many people are content with what are believed to be so, even if they aren't really so, and they act, acquire, and form their own beliefs on that basis. Nobody is satisfied to acquire things that are merely believed to be good, however, but everyone wants the things that really *are* good and disdains mere belief here.

That's right.

Every soul pursues the good and does whatever it does for its sake. It divines that the good is something, e but it is perplexed and cannot adequately grasp what it is or acquire the sort of stable beliefs it has about other things, and so it misses the benefit, if any, that even those other things may give. Will we allow the best people in the city, to whom we entrust everything, to be so in the dark about something of this kind and 506 of this importance?

That's the last thing we'd do.

I don't suppose, at least, that just and fine things will have acquired much of a guardian in someone who doesn't even know in what way they are good. And I divine that no one will have adequate knowledge of them until he knows this.

You've divined well.

But won't our constitution be perfectly ordered, if a guardian who knows these things is in charge of it? b

Necessarily. But, Socrates, you must also tell us whether you consider the good to be knowledge or pleasure or something else altogether.

What a man! It's been clear for some time that other people's opinions about these matters wouldn't satisfy you.

Well, Socrates, it doesn't seem right to me for you to be willing to state other people's convictions but not your own, especially when you've spent so much time occupied with these matters. c

What? Do you think it's right to talk about things one doesn't know as if one does know them?

Not as if one knows them, he said, but one ought to be willing to state one's opinions as such.

What? Haven't you noticed that opinions without knowledge are shameful and ugly things? The best of them are blind—or do you think that those who express a true opinion without understanding are any different from blind people who happen to travel the right road?

They're no different.

Do you want to look at shameful, blind, and crooked things, then, when you might hear illuminating and fine ones from other people? d

By god, Socrates, Glaucon said, don't desert us with the end almost in sight. We'll be satisfied if you discuss the good as you discussed justice, moderation, and the rest.

That, my friend, I said, would satisfy me too, but I'm

afraid that I won't be up to it and that I'll disgrace myself and look ridiculous by trying. So let's abandon the quest for what the good itself is for the time being, for *e* even to arrive at my own view about it is too big a topic for the discussion we are now started on. But I am willing to tell you about what is apparently an offspring of the good and most like it. Is that agreeable to you, or would you rather we let the whole matter drop?

It is. The story about the father remains a debt you'll pay another time.

I wish that I could pay the debt in full, and you 507 receive it instead of just the interest. So here, then, is this child and offspring of the good. But be careful that I don't somehow deceive you unintentionally by giving you an illegitimate account of the child.[2]

We'll be as careful as possible, so speak on.

I will when we've come to an agreement and recalled some things that we've already said both here and many other times.

b Which ones?

We say that there are many beautiful things and many good things, and so on for each kind, and in this way we distinguish them in words.

We do.

And beauty itself and good itself and all the things that we thereby set down as many, reversing ourselves, we set down according to a single form of each, believing that there is but one, and call it "the being" of each.[3]

That's true.

And we say that the many beautiful things and the rest are visible but not intelligible, while the forms are intelligible but not visible.

That's completely true.

c With what part of ourselves do we see visible things?

With our sight.

And so audible things are heard by hearing, and with our other senses we perceive all the other perceptible things.

That's right.

Have you considered how lavish the maker of our senses was in making the power to see and be seen?

I can't say I have.

Well, consider it this way. Do hearing and sound need another kind of thing in order for the former to hear and the latter to be heard, a third thing in whose absence the one won't hear or the other be heard? *d*

No, they need nothing else.

And if there are any others that need such a thing, there can't be many of them. Can you think of one?

I can't.

You don't realize that sight and the visible have such a need?

How so?

Sight may be present in the eyes, and the one who has it may try to use it, and colors may be present in things, but unless a third kind of thing is present, which is naturally adapted for this very purpose, you know that sight will see nothing, and the colors will *e* remain unseen.

What kind of thing do you mean?

I mean what you call light.

You're right.

Then it isn't an insignificant kind of link that connects the sense of sight and the power to be seen— 508 it is a more valuable link than any other linked things have got, if indeed light is something valuable.

And, of course, it's very valuable.

Which of the gods in heaven would you name as the cause and controller of this, the one whose light causes our sight to see in the best way and the visible things to be seen?

The same one you and others would name. Obviously, the answer to your question is the sun.

And isn't sight by nature related to that god in this way?

Which way?

Sight isn't the sun, neither sight itself nor that in which it comes to be, namely, the eye. *b*

No, it certainly isn't.

But I think that it is the most sunlike of the senses.

Very much so.

And it receives from the sun the power it has, just like an influx from an overflowing treasury.

Certainly.

The sun is not sight, but isn't it the cause of sight itself and seen by it?

That's right.

Let's say, then, that this is what I called the offspring of the good, which the good begot as its analogue.

2. [Throughout, Socrates is punning on the word *tokos*, which means either a child or the interest on capital.]

3. [The "being" of something is sometimes taken to refer to what we call its essence. Socrates would then be saying that the essence of the fineness present in many things is the form of the fine.]

What the good itself is in the intelligible realm, in relation to understanding and intelligible things, the c sun is in the visible realm, in relation to sight and visible things.

How? Explain a bit more.

You know that, when we turn our eyes to things whose colors are no longer in the light of day but in the gloom of night, the eyes are dimmed and seem nearly blind, as if clear vision were no longer in them.

Of course.

Yet whenever one turns them on things illuminated by the sun, they see clearly, and vision appears in d those very same eyes?

Indeed.

Well, understand the soul in the same way: When it focuses on something illuminated by truth and what is, it understands, knows, and apparently possesses understanding, but when it focuses on what is mixed with obscurity, on what comes to be and passes away, it opines and is dimmed, changes its opinions this way and that, and seems bereft of understanding.

It does seem that way.

So that what gives truth to the things known and e the power to know to the knower is the form of the good. And though it is the cause of knowledge and truth, it is also an object of knowledge. Both knowledge and truth are beautiful things, but the good is other and more beautiful than they. In the visible realm, light and sight are rightly considered sunlike, but it is wrong to think that they are the sun, so here 509 it is right to think of knowledge and truth as goodlike but wrong to think that either of them is the good—for the good is yet more prized.

This is an inconceivably beautiful thing you're talking about, if it provides both knowledge and truth and is superior to them in beauty. You surely don't think that a thing like that could be pleasure.

Hush! Let's examine its image in more detail as follows.

b How?

You'll be willing to say, I think, that the sun not only provides visible things with the power to be seen but also with coming to be, growth, and nourishment, although it is not itself coming to be.

How could it be?

Therefore, you should also say that not only do the objects of knowledge owe their being known to the good, but their being is also due to it, although the good is not being, but superior to it in rank and power.

And Glaucon comically said: By Apollo, what a daemonic superiority! c

It's your own fault; you forced me to tell you my opinion about it.

And I don't want you to stop either. So continue to explain its similarity to the sun, if you've omitted anything.

I'm certainly omitting a lot.

Well, don't, not even the smallest thing.

I think I'll have to omit a fair bit, but, as far as is possible at the moment, I won't omit anything voluntarily.

Don't.

Understand, then, that, as we said, there are these two things, one sovereign of the intelligible kind and d place, the other of the visible (I don't say "of heaven" so as not to seem to you to be playing the Sophist with the name).[4] In any case, you have two kinds of thing, visible and intelligible.

Right.

It is like a line divided into two unequal sections.[5]

4. [The play may be on the similarity of sound between *ouranou* ("of heaven") and *horatou* ("of the visible"). But it is more likely that Socrates is referring to the fact that *ouranou* seems to contain the word *nou*, the genitive case of *nous* ("understanding"), and relative of *noētou* ("of the intelligible"). Hence, if he said that the sun was sovereign of heaven, he might be taken to suggest in sophistical fashion that it was sovereign of the intelligible and that there was no real difference between the good and the sun.]

5. [The line is illustrated below:]

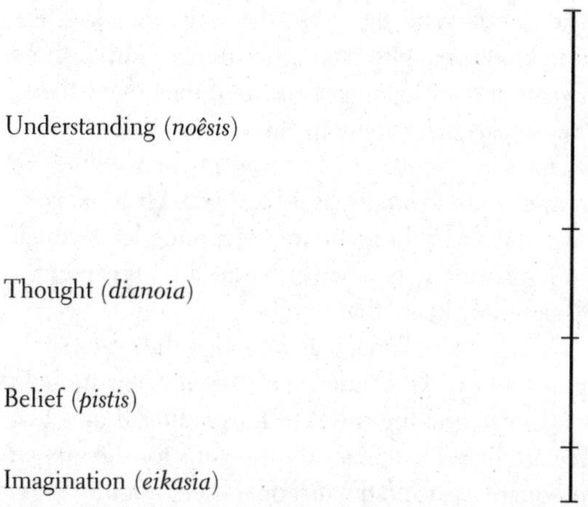

Understanding (*noêsis*)

Thought (*dianoia*)

Belief (*pistis*)

Imagination (*eikasia*)

Then divide each section—namely, that of the visible and that of the intelligible—in the same ratio as the line. In terms now of relative clarity and opacity, one subsection of the visible consists of images. And by images I mean, first, shadows, then reflections in *e* water and in all close-packed, smooth, and shiny ma- *510* terials, and everything of that sort, if you understand.

I do.

In the other subsection of the visible, put the originals of these images, namely, the animals around us, all the plants, and the whole class of manufactured things.

Consider them put.

Would you be willing to say that, as regards truth and untruth, the division is in this proportion: As the opinable is to the knowable, so the likeness is to the thing that it is like?

b Certainly.

Consider now how the section of the intelligible is to be divided.

How?

As follows: In one subsection, the soul, using as images the things that were imitated before, is forced to investigate from hypotheses, proceeding not to a first principle but to a conclusion. In the other subsection, however, it makes its way to a first principle that is *not* a hypothesis, proceeding from a hypothesis but without the images used in the previous subsection, using forms themselves and making its investigation through them.

I don't yet fully understand what you mean.

Let's try again. You'll understand it more easily *c* after the following preamble. I think you know that students of geometry, calculation, and the like hypothesize the odd and the even, the various figures, the three kinds of angles, and other things akin to these in each of their investigations, as if they knew them. They make these their hypotheses and don't think it necessary to give any account of them, either to themselves or to others, as if they were clear to everyone. And going from these first principles through *d* the remaining steps, they arrive in full agreement.

I certainly know that much.

Then you also know that, although they use visible figures and make claims about them, their thought isn't directed to them but to those other things that they are like. They make their claims for the sake of the square itself and the diagonal itself, not the diagonal they draw, and similarly with the others. These figures that they make and draw, of which shadows *e* and reflections in water are images, they now in turn use as images, in seeking to see those others themselves that one cannot see except by means of thought. *511*

That's true.

This, then, is the kind of thing that, on the one hand, I said is intelligible, and, on the other, is such that the soul is forced to use hypotheses in the investigation of it, not travelling up to a first principle, since it cannot reach beyond its hypotheses, but using as images those very things of which images were made in the section below, and which, by comparison to their images, were thought to be clear and to be valued as such.

I understand that you mean what happens in geometry and related sciences. *b*

Then also understand that, by the other subsection of the intelligible, I mean that which reason itself grasps by the power of dialectic. It does not consider these hypotheses as first principles but truly as hypotheses—but as stepping stones to take off from, enabling it to reach the unhypothetical first principle of everything. Having grasped this principle, it reverses itself and, keeping hold of what follows from it, comes down to a conclusion without making use of anything visible at all, but only of forms themselves, moving on from forms to forms, and ending in forms. *c*

I understand, if not yet adequately (for in my opinion you're speaking of an enormous task), that you want to distinguish the intelligible part of that which is, the part studied by the science of dialectic, as clearer than the part studied by the so-called sciences, for which their hypotheses are first principles. And although those who study the objects of these sciences are forced to do so by means of thought rather than sense perception, still, because they do not go back to a genuine first principle, but proceed from hypothe- *d* ses, you don't think that they understand them, even though, given such a principle, they are intelligible. And you seem to me to call the state of the geometers thought but not understanding, thought being intermediate between opinion and understanding.

Your exposition is most adequate. Thus there are four such conditions in the soul, corresponding to the four subsections of our line: Understanding for the highest, thought for the second, belief for the third, and imaging for the last. Arrange them in a *e* ratio, and consider that each shares in clarity to the degree that the subsection it is set over shares in truth.

I understand, agree, and arrange them as you say.

Book VII

514 Next, I said, compare the effect of education and of the lack of it on our nature to an experience like this: Imagine human beings living in an underground, cavelike dwelling, with an entrance a long way up, which is both open to the light and as wide as the cave itself. They've been there since childhood, fixed in the same place, with their necks and legs fettered, able to see only in front of them, because their bonds prevent them from turning their heads around. Light is provided by a fire burning far above and behind *b* them. Also behind them, but on higher ground, there is a path stretching between them and the fire. Imagine that along this path a low wall has been built, like the screen in front of puppeteers above which they show their puppets.

I'm imagining it.

Then also imagine that there are people along the wall, carrying all kinds of artifacts that project above it—statues of people and other animals, made out of *c* stone, wood, and every material. And, as you'd expect, 515 some of the carriers are talking, and some are silent.

It's a strange image you're describing, and strange prisoners.

They're like us. Do you suppose, first of all, that these prisoners see anything of themselves and one another besides the shadows that the fire casts on the wall in front of them?

How could they, if they have to keep their heads *b* motionless throughout life?

What about the things being carried along the wall? Isn't the same true of them?

Of course.

And if they could talk to one another, don't you think they'd suppose that the names they used applied to the things they see passing before them?[1]

They'd have to.

And what if their prison also had an echo from the wall facing them? Don't you think they'd believe that the shadows passing in front of them were talking whenever one of the carriers passing along the wall was doing so?

I certainly do.

Then the prisoners would in every way believe that the truth is nothing other than the shadows of *c* those artifacts.

They must surely believe that.

Consider, then, what being released from their bonds and cured of their ignorance would naturally be like, if something like this came to pass. When one of them was freed and suddenly compelled to stand up, turn his head, walk, and look up toward the light, he'd be pained and dazzled and unable to see the things whose shadows he'd seen before. What do you think he'd say, if we told him that what he'd *d* seen before was inconsequential, but that now—because he is a bit closer to the things that are and is turned towards things that are more—he sees more correctly? Or, to put it another way, if we pointed to each of the things passing by, asked him what each of them is, and compelled him to answer, don't you think he'd be at a loss and that he'd believe that the things he saw earlier were truer than the ones he was now being shown?

Much truer.

And if someone compelled him to look at the light itself, wouldn't his eyes hurt, and wouldn't he turn *e* around and flee towards the things he's able to see, believing that they're really clearer than the ones he's being shown?

He would.

And if someone dragged him away from there by force, up the rough, steep path, and didn't let him go until he had dragged him into the sunlight, wouldn't he be pained and irritated at being treated that way? And when he came into the light, with the 516 sun filling his eyes, wouldn't he be unable to see a single one of the things now said to be true?

He would be unable to see them, at least at first.

I suppose, then, that he'd need time to get adjusted before he could see things in the world above. At first, he'd see shadows most easily, then images of men and other things in water, then the things themselves. Of these, he'd be able to study the things in the sky and the sky itself more easily at night, looking

1. [Reading *parionta autous nomizein onomazein*. I.e., they would think that the name "human being" applied to the shadow of a statue of a human being.]

at the light of the stars and the moon, than during b the day, looking at the sun and the light of the sun.

Of course.

Finally, I suppose, he'd be able to see the sun, not images of it in water or some alien place, but the sun itself, in its own place, and be able to study it.

Necessarily so.

And at this point he would infer and conclude that the sun provides the seasons and the years, governs everything in the visible world, and is in some way c the cause of all the things that he used to see.

It's clear that would be his next step.

What about when he reminds himself of his first dwelling place, his fellow prisoners, and what passed for wisdom there? Don't you think that he'd count himself happy for the change and pity the others?

Certainly.

And if there had been any honors, praises, or prizes among them for the one who was sharpest at identifying the shadows as they passed by and who best remembered which usually came earlier, which later, d and which simultaneously, and who could thus best divine the future, do you think that our man would desire these rewards or envy those among the prisoners who were honored and held power? Instead, wouldn't he feel, with Homer, that he'd much prefer to "work the earth as a serf to another, one without possessions,"[2] and go through any sufferings, rather than share their opinions and live as they do?

e I suppose he would rather suffer anything than live like that.

Consider this too. If this man went down into the cave again and sat down in his same seat, wouldn't his eyes—coming suddenly out of the sun like that—be filled with darkness?

They certainly would.

And before his eyes had recovered—and the adjustment would not be quick—while his vision was still dim, if he had to compete again with the perpetual 517 prisoners in recognizing the shadows, wouldn't he invite ridicule? Wouldn't it be said of him that he'd returned from his upward journey with his eyesight ruined and that it isn't worthwhile even to try to travel upward? And, as for anyone who tried to free them and lead them upward, if they could somehow get their hands on him, wouldn't they kill him?

They certainly would.

This whole image, Glaucon, must be fitted together with what we said before. The visible realm should b be likened to the prison dwelling, and the light of the fire inside it to the power of the sun. And if you interpret the upward journey and the study of things above as the upward journey of the soul to the intelligible realm, you'll grasp what I hope to convey, since that is what you wanted to hear about. Whether it's true or not, only the god knows. But this is how I see it: In the knowable realm, the form of the good is the last thing to be seen, and it is reached only with difficulty. Once one has seen it, however, one must conclude that it is the cause of all that is correct and beautiful in anything, that it produces both light and c its source in the visible realm, and that in the intelligible realm it controls and provides truth and understanding, so that anyone who is to act sensibly in private or public must see it.

I have the same thought, at least as far as I'm able.

Come, then, share with me this thought also: It isn't surprising that the ones who get to this point are unwilling to occupy themselves with human affairs and that their souls are always pressing upwards, eager to spend their time above, for, after all, this is surely what we'd expect, if indeed things fit the image I described before. d

It is.

What about what happens when someone turns from divine study to the evils of human life? Do you think it's surprising, since his sight is still dim, and he hasn't yet become accustomed to the darkness around him, that he behaves awkwardly and appears completely ridiculous if he's compelled, either in the courts or elsewhere, to contend about the shadows of justice or the statues of which they are the shadows and to dispute about the way these things are understood by people who have never seen justice itself? e

That's not surprising at all.

No, it isn't. But anyone with any understanding would remember that the eyes may be confused in 518 two ways and from two causes, namely, when they've come from the light into the darkness *and* when they've come from the darkness into the light. Realizing that the same applies to the soul, when someone

2. [*Odyssey* 11.489–90. The shade of the dead Achilles speaks these words to Odysseus, who is visiting Hades. Plato is, therefore, likening the cave dwellers to the dead.]

sees a soul disturbed and unable to see something, he won't laugh mindlessly, but he'll take into consideration whether it has come from a brighter life and is dimmed through not having yet become accustomed to the dark or whether it has come from greater ignorance into greater light and is dazzled by the increased brilliance. Then he'll declare the first soul happy in its experience and life, and he'll pity the *b* latter—but even if he chose to make fun of it, at least he'd be less ridiculous than if he laughed at a soul that has come from the light above.

What you say is very reasonable.

If that's true, then here's what we must think about these matters: Education isn't what some people declare it to be, namely, putting knowledge into souls *c* that lack it, like putting sight into blind eyes.

They do say that.

But our present discussion, on the other hand, shows that the power to learn is present in everyone's soul and that the instrument with which each learns is like an eye that cannot be turned around from darkness to light without turning the whole body. This instrument cannot be turned around from that which is coming into being without turning the whole soul until it is able to study that which is and the brightest thing that is, namely, the one we call the *d* good. Isn't that right?

Yes.

Then education is the craft concerned with doing this very thing, this turning around, and with how the soul can most easily and effectively be made to do it. It isn't the craft of putting sight into the soul. Education takes for granted that sight is there but that it isn't turned the right way or looking where it ought to look, and it tries to redirect it appropriately.

So it seems.

Now, it looks as though the other so-called virtues of the soul are akin to those of the body, for they really aren't there beforehand but are added later by *e* habit and practice. However, the virtue of reason seems to belong above all to something more divine, which never loses its power but is either useful and beneficial or useless and harmful, depending on the way it is turned. Or have you never noticed this about 519 people who are said to be vicious but clever, how keen the vision of their little souls is and how sharply it distinguishes the things it is turned towards? This shows that its sight isn't inferior but rather is forced to serve evil ends, so that the sharper it sees, the more evil it accomplishes.

Absolutely.

However, if a nature of this sort had been hammered at from childhood and freed from the bonds of kinship with becoming, which have been fastened to it by feasting, greed, and other such pleasures and which, like leaden weights, pull its vision down- *b* wards—if, being rid of these, it turned to look at true things, then I say that the same soul of the same person would see these most sharply, just as it now does the things it is presently turned towards.

Probably so.

And what about the uneducated who have no experience of truth? Isn't it likely—indeed, doesn't it follow necessarily from what was said before—that they will never adequately govern a city? But neither would those who've been allowed to spend their whole lives being educated. The former would fail because they don't have a single goal at which all their actions, *c* public and private, inevitably aim; the latter would fail because they'd refuse to act, thinking that they had settled while still alive in the faraway Isles of the Blessed.[3]

That's true.

It is our task as founders, then, to compel the best natures to reach the study we said before is the most important, namely, to make the ascent and see the good. But when they've made it and looked sufficiently, we mustn't allow them to do what they're *d* allowed to do today.

What's that?

To stay there and refuse to go down again to the prisoners in the cave and share their labors and honors, whether they are of less worth or of greater.

Then are we to do them an injustice by making them live a worse life when they could live a better one?

You are forgetting again that it isn't the law's concern to make any one class in the city outstandingly *e* happy but to contrive to spread happiness throughout the city by bringing the citizens into harmony with each other through persuasion or compulsion and by making them share with each other the benefits that each class can confer on the community. The law

3. [A place where good people are said to live in eternal happiness, normally after death.]

produces such people in the city, not in order to 520 allow them to turn in whatever direction they want, but to make use of them to bind the city together.

That's true, I had forgotten.

Observe, then, Glaucon, that we won't be doing an injustice to those who've become philosophers in our city and that what we'll say to them, when we compel them to guard and care for the others, will be just. We'll say: "When people like you come to be in other cities, they're justified in not sharing in *b* their city's labors, for they've grown there spontaneously, against the will of the constitution. And what grows of its own accord and owes no debt for its upbringing has justice on its side when it isn't keen to pay anyone for that upbringing. But we've made you kings in our city and leaders of the swarm, as it were, both for yourselves and for the rest of the city. You're better and more completely educated than the *c* others and are better able to share in both types of life.[4] Therefore each of you in turn must go down to live in the common dwelling place of the others and grow accustomed to seeing in the dark. When you are used to it, you'll see vastly better than the people there. And because you've seen the truth about fine, just, and good things, you'll know each image for what it is and also that of which it is the image. Thus, for you and for us, the city will be governed, not like the majority of cities nowadays, by people who fight over shadows and struggle against one another in order to rule—as if that were a great good—but by *d* people who are awake rather than dreaming, for the truth is surely this: A city whose prospective rulers are least eager to rule must of necessity be most free from civil war, whereas a city with the opposite kind of rulers is governed in the opposite way."

Absolutely.

Then do you think that those we've nurtured will disobey us and refuse to share the labors of the city, each in turn, while living the greater part of their time with one another in the pure realm?

It isn't possible, for we'll be giving just orders to *e* just people. Each of them will certainly go to rule as to something compulsory, however, which is exactly the opposite of what's done by those who now rule in each city. This is how it is. If you can find a way of life that's better than ruling for the prospective rulers, your well-governed city will become a possibility, for only in it will the truly rich rule—not those 521 who are rich in gold but those who are rich in the wealth that the happy must have, namely, a good and rational life. But if beggars hungry for private goods go into public life, thinking that the good is there for the seizing, then the well-governed city is impossible, for then ruling is something fought over, and this civil and domestic war destroys these people and the rest of the city as well.

That's very true.

Can you name any life that despises political rule besides that of the true philosopher? *b*

No, by god, I can't.

But surely it is those who are not lovers of ruling who must rule, for if they don't, the lovers of it, who are rivals, will fight over it.

Of course.

Then who will you compel to become guardians of the city, if not those who have the best understanding of what matters for good government and who have other honors than political ones, and a better life as well?

No one.

The next topic is the education of the philosopher-kings. (1) Their initial education is in music and poetry, physical training, and elementary mathematics. (2) This is followed by two or three years of compulsory physical training, rather like the military service that some countries still require. (3) Those who are most successful in these studies next receive ten years of education in mathematical science. (4) Those who are again most successful receive five years of training in dialectic. (5) Those who are still most successful receive fifteen years of practical political training. Finally, (6) those who are also successful in practical politics are "compelled to lift up the radiant light of their souls" to the good itself and are equipped to be philosopher-kings.

Book VIII

The description of the kallipolis and of the man whose character resembles it—the philosopher-king—is now complete, and Socrates returns to the argument interrupted at the beginning of Book V. He describes four

4. [That is, the practical life of ruling the city and the theoretical life of studying the good itself.]

individual character types and the four types of constitutions that result when people who possess them rule in a city. He presents these as four stages in the increasing corruption or decline of the kallipolis, and he explains, by appeal to the mathematical myth of the geometrical number, why the kallipolis will decline. However, embedded in the myth is the serious philosophical suggestion that the kallipolis will decline because the philosopher-kings have to rely on sense perception in putting their eugenics policy into practice.

The first of the bad cities Socrates describes is a timocracy. It is ruled by people whose souls are themselves ruled by the spirited part of their soul, in which the desire for honor, victories, and good reputation are located. It is the second-best city to the kallipolis. The third-best city is an oligarchy. It is ruled by people whose souls are ruled by their necessary appetites. The fourth-best city is a democracy. It is ruled by people whose souls are ruled by unnecessary appetites. The worst city of all is a tyranny. It is ruled by someone whose soul is ruled by its lawless and unnecessary appetites.

Book IX

571 It remains, I said, to consider the tyrannical man himself, how he evolves from a democrat, what he is like when he has come into being, and whether he is wretched or blessedly happy.

Yes, he said, he is the one who is still missing.

And do you know what else I think is still missing?

What?

I don't think we have adequately distinguished the kinds and numbers of our desires, and, if that subject isn't adequately dealt with, our entire investigation *b* will be less clear.

Well, isn't now as fine a time as any to discuss the matter?

It certainly is. Consider, then, what I want to know about our desires. It's this: Some of our unnecessary pleasures and desires seem to me to be lawless. They are probably present in everyone, but they are held in check by the laws and by the better desires in alliance with reason. In a few people, they have been eliminated entirely or only a few weak ones remain, while in others they are *c* stronger and more numerous.

What desires do you mean?

Those that are awakened in sleep, when the rest of the soul—the rational, gentle, and ruling part—slumbers. Then the beastly and savage part, full of food and drink, casts off sleep and seeks to find a way to gratify itself. You know that there is nothing it won't dare to do at such a time, free of all control by shame or reason. It doesn't shrink from trying to have sex with a mother, as it supposes, or with anyone else at all, whether man, god, or beast. It will commit *d* any foul murder, and there is no food it refuses to eat. In a word, it omits no act of folly or shamelessness.

That's completely true.

On the other hand, I suppose that someone who is healthy and moderate with himself goes to sleep only after having done the following: First, he rouses his rational part and feasts it on fine arguments and speculations; second, he neither starves nor feasts his *e* appetites, so that they will slumber and not disturb his best part with either their pleasure or their pain, but they'll leave it alone, pure and by itself, to get 572 on with its investigations, to yearn after and perceive something, it knows not what, whether it is past, present, or future; third, he soothes his spirited part in the same way, for example, by not falling asleep with his spirit still aroused after an outburst of anger. And when he has quieted these two parts and aroused the third, in which reason resides, and so takes his rest, you know that it is then that he best grasps the truth and that the visions that appear in his dreams are least lawless. *b*

Entirely so.

However, we've been carried away from what we wanted to establish, which is this: Our dreams make it clear that there is a dangerous, wild, and lawless form of desire in everyone, even in those of us who seem to be entirely moderate or measured. See whether you think I'm talking sense and whether or not you agree with me.

I do agree.

Recall, then, what we said a democratic man is like. He was produced by being brought up from youth by a thrifty father who valued only those desires that make money and who despised the unnecessary *c* ones that aim at frivolity and display. Isn't that right?

Yes.

And by associating with more sophisticated men, who are full of the latter desires, he starts to indulge in every kind of insolence and to adopt their form of behavior, because of his hatred of his father's thrift. But, because he has a better nature than his corrupters, he is pulled in both directions and settles down in the middle between his father's way of life and theirs. And enjoying each in moderation, as he sup- d poses, he leads a life that is neither slavish nor lawless and from having been oligarchic he becomes democratic.

That was and is our opinion about this type of man.

Suppose now that this man has in turn become older and that *he* has a son who is brought up in *his* father's ethos.

All right.

And further suppose that the same things that happened to his father now happen to him. First, he is led to all the kinds of lawlessness that those who are e leading him call freedom. Then his father and the rest of the household come to the aid of the middle desires, while the others help the other ones. Then, when those clever enchanters and tyrant-makers have no hope of keeping hold of the young man in any other way, they contrive to plant in him a powerful erotic love, like a great winged drone, to be the leader of those idle desires that spend whatever is at hand. 573 Or do you think that erotic love is anything other than an enormous drone in such people?

I don't think that it could be anything else.

And when the other desires—filled with incense, myrrh, wreaths, wine, and the other pleasures found in their company—buzz around the drone, nurturing it and making it grow as large as possible, they plant the sting of longing in it. Then this leader of the soul adopts madness as its bodyguard and becomes b frenzied. If it finds any beliefs or desires in the man that are thought to be good or that still have some shame, it destroys them and throws them out, until it's purged him of moderation and filled him with imported madness.

You've perfectly described the evolution of a tyrannical man.

Is this the reason that erotic love has long been called a tyrant?

It looks that way.

Then doesn't a drunken man have something of c a tyrannical mind?

Yes, he has.

And a man who is mad and deranged attempts to rule not just human beings, but gods as well, and expects that he will be able to succeed.

He certainly does.

Then a man becomes tyrannical in the precise sense of the term when either his nature or his way of life or both of them together make him drunk, filled with erotic desire, and mad.

Absolutely.

This, then, it seems, is how a tyrannical man comes to be. But what way does he live?

No doubt *you're* going to tell *me*, just as posers of riddles usually do. d

I am. I think that someone in whom the tyrant of erotic love dwells and in whom it directs everything next goes in for feasts, revelries, luxuries, girlfriends, and all that sort of thing.

Necessarily.

And don't many terrible desires grow up day and night beside the tyrannical one, needing many things to satisfy them?

Indeed they do.

Hence any income someone like that has is soon spent.

Of course.

Then borrowing follows, and expenditure of capital. e

What else?

And when everything is gone, won't the violent crowd of desires that has nested within him inevitably shout in protest? And driven by the stings of the other desires and especially by erotic love itself (which leads all of them as its bodyguard), won't he become frenzied and look to see who possesses anything that he could take, by either deceit or force? 574

He certainly will.

Consequently, he must acquire wealth from every source or live in great pain and suffering.

He must.

And just as the pleasures that are latecomers outdo the older ones and steal away their satisfactions, won't the man himself think that he deserves to outdo his father and mother, even though he is younger than they are—to take and spend his father's wealth when he's spent his own share?

Of course.

And if they won't give it to him, won't he first try
b to steal it from them by deceitful means?

Certainly.

And if that doesn't work, wouldn't he seize it by force?

I suppose so.

And if the old man and woman put up a fight, would he be careful to refrain from acting like a tyrant?

I'm not very optimistic about their fate, if they do.

But, good god, Adeimantus, do you think he'd sacrifice his long-loved and irreplaceable mother for a recently acquired girlfriend whom he can do without? Or that for the sake of a newfound and replace-
c able boyfriend in the bloom of youth, he'd strike his aged and irreplaceable father, his oldest friend? Or that he'd make his parents the slaves of these others, if he brought them under the same roof?

Yes, indeed he would.

It seems to be a very great blessing to produce a tyrannical son!

It certainly does!

What about when the possessions of his father and
d mother give out? With that great swarm of pleasures inside him, won't he first try to break into someone's house or snatch someone's coat late at night? Then won't he try to loot a temple? And in all this, the old traditional opinions that he had held from childhood about what is fine or shameful—opinions that are accounted just—are overcome by the opinions, newly released from slavery, that are now the bodyguard of erotic love and hold sway along with it. When he
e himself was subject to the laws and his father and had a democratic constitution within him, these opinions used only to be freed in sleep. Now, however, under the tyranny of erotic love, he has permanently become while awake what he used to become occasionally while asleep, and he won't hold back from any terrible murder or from any kind of food or act. But, rather, erotic love lives like a tyrant within him, in complete
575 anarchy and lawlessness as his sole ruler, and drives him, as if he were a city, to dare anything that will provide sustenance for itself and the unruly mob around it (some of whose members have come in from the outside as a result of his keeping bad company, while others have come from within, freed and let loose by his own bad habits). Isn't this the life that a tyrannical man leads?

It is indeed.

Now, if there are only a few such men in a city, and the rest of the people are moderate, this mob will leave the city in order to act as a bodyguard to some other tyrant or to serve as mercenaries if there b happens to be a war going on somewhere. But if they chance to live in a time of peace and quiet, they'll remain in the city and bring about lots of little evils.

What sort of evils do you mean?

They steal, break into houses, snatch purses, steal clothes, rob temples, and sell people into slavery. Sometimes, if they are good speakers, they become sycophants and bear false witness and accept bribes.[1]

These evils *are* small, provided that there happen to be only a few such people. c

Yes, for small things are small by comparison to big ones. And when it comes to producing wickedness and misery in a city, all these evils together don't, as the saying goes, come within a mile of the rule of a tyrant. But when such people become numerous and conscious of their numbers, it is they—aided by the foolishness of the people—who create a tyrant. And he, more than any of them, has in his soul the greatest and strongest tyrant of all. d

Naturally, for he'd be the most tyrannical.

That's if the city happens to yield willingly, but if it resists him, then, just as he once chastised his mother and father, he'll now chastise his fatherland, if he can, by bringing in new friends and making his fatherland and his dear old motherland (as the Cretans call it) their slaves and keeping them that way, for this is surely the end at which such a man's desires are directed.

It most certainly is. e

Now, in private life, before a tyrannical man attains power, isn't he this sort of person—one who associates primarily with flatterers who are ready to obey him in everything? Or if he himself happens to need anything from other people, isn't he willing to fawn on them

1. [Athens had nothing corresponding to our public prosecutors. By and large, private citizens prosecuted one another. By the middle of the fifth century, some people began to make a profession of prosecuting others for financial, political, or personal reasons. These people were called sycophants. A vivid sense of their power and importance is conveyed in L. B. Carter, *The Quiet Athenian* (Oxford: Clarendon Press, 1986).]

and make every gesture of friendship, as if he were 576 dealing with his own family? But once he gets what he wants, don't they become strangers again?

Yes, they certainly do.

So someone with a tyrannical nature lives his whole life without being friends with anyone, always a master to one man or a slave to another and never getting a taste of either freedom or true friendship.

That's right.

Wouldn't we be right to call someone like that untrustworthy?

Of course.

And isn't he as unjust as anyone can be? If indeed *b* what we earlier agreed about justice was right.

And it certainly was right.

Then, let's sum up the worst type of man: His waking life is like the nightmare we described earlier.[2]

That's right.

And he evolves from someone by nature most tyrannical who achieves sole rule. And the longer he remains tyrant, the more like the nightmare he becomes.

That's inevitable, said Glaucon, taking over the argument.

Well, then, I said, isn't the man who is clearly most vicious also clearly most wretched? And isn't the one *c* who for the longest time is most of all a tyrant, most wretched for the longest time? If, that is to say, truth rather than majority opinion is to settle these questions.

That much is certain, at any rate.

And isn't a tyrannical man like a city ruled by a tyrant, a democratic man like a city ruled by a democracy, and similarly with the others?

Of course.

And won't the relations between the cities with respect to virtue and happiness be the same as those between the men?

d Certainly.

Then how does the city ruled by a tyrant compare to the city ruled by kings that we described first?

They are total opposites: one is the best, and the other the worst.

I won't ask you which is which, since it's obvious. But is your judgment the same with regard to their happiness and wretchedness? And let's not be dazzled by looking at one man—a tyrant—or at the few who surround him, but since it is essential to go into the city and study the whole of it, let's not give our opinion, till we've gone down and looked into every corner. *e*

That's right, for it's clear to everyone that there is no city more wretched than one ruled by a tyrant and none more happy than one ruled by kings.

Would I be right, then, to make the same challenge about the individuals, assuming, first, that the person who is fit to judge them is someone who in thought 577 can go down into a person's character and examine it thoroughly, someone who doesn't judge from outside, the way a child does, who is dazzled by the façade that tyrants adopt for the outside world to see, but is able to see right through that sort of thing? And, second, that he's someone—since we'd all listen to him if he were—who is competent to judge, because he has lived in the same house with a tyrant and witnessed his behavior at home and his treatment of each member of his household when he is stripped of his theatrical façade, and has also seen how he behaves when in danger from the people? Shouldn't *b* we ask the person who has seen all that to tell us how the tyrant compares to the others in happiness and wretchedness?

That's also right.

Then do you want us to pretend that we are among those who can give such a judgment and that we have already met tyrannical people, so that we'll have someone to answer our questions?

I certainly do.

Come, then, and look at it this way for me: Bearing in mind the resemblance between the city and the *c* man, look at each in turn and describe its condition.

What kinds of things do you want me to describe?

First, speaking of the city, would you say that a tyrannical city is free or enslaved?

It is as enslaved as it is possible to be.

Yet you see in it people who are masters and free.

I do see a few like that, but the whole city, so to speak, and the most decent part of it are wretched, dishonored slaves.

Then, if man and city are alike, mustn't the same structure be in him too? And mustn't his soul be full *d* of slavery and unfreedom, with the most decent parts enslaved and with a small part, the maddest and most vicious, as their master?

2. [See 571c–d.]

It must.

What will you say about such a soul then? Is it free or slave?

Slave, of course.

And isn't the enslaved and tyrannical city least likely to do what it wants?

Certainly.

Then a tyrannical soul—I'm talking about the whole soul—will also be least likely to do what it wants and, forcibly driven by the stings of a dronish *e* gadfly, will be full of disorder and regret.

How could it be anything else?

Is a tyrannically ruled city rich or poor?

Poor.

Then a tyrannical soul, too, must always be poor 578 and unsatisfiable.

That's right.

What about fear? Aren't a tyrannical city and man full of it?

Absolutely.

And do you think that you'll find more wailing, groaning, lamenting, and grieving in any other city?

Certainly not.

Then, are such things more common in anyone besides a tyrannical man, who is maddened by his desires and erotic loves?

How could they be?

It is in view of all these things, I suppose, and *b* others like them, that you judged this to be the most wretched of cities.

And wasn't I right?

Of course you were. But what do you say about a tyrannical man, when you look at these same things?

He's by far the most wretched of all of them.

There you're no longer right.

How is that?

I don't think that this man has yet reached the extreme of wretchedness.

Then who has?

Perhaps you'll agree that this next case is even more wretched.

Which one?

The one who is tyrannical but doesn't live a private *c* life, because some misfortune provides him with the opportunity to become an actual tyrant.

On the basis of what was said before, I assume that what you say is true.

Yes, but in matters of this sort, it isn't enough just to assume these things; one needs to investigate carefully the two men in question by means of argument, for the investigation concerns the most important thing, namely, the good life and the bad one.

That's absolutely right.

Then consider whether I'm talking sense or not, for I think our investigation will be helped by the following examples. *d*

What are they?

We should look at all the wealthy private citizens in our cities who have many slaves, for, like a tyrant, they rule over many, although not over so many as he does.

That's right.

And you know that they're secure and do not fear their slaves.

What have they got to be afraid of?

Nothing. And do you know why?

Yes. It's because the whole city is ready to defend each of its individual citizens.

You're right. But what if some god were to lift one of these men, his fifty or more slaves, and his wife *e* and children out of the city and deposit him with his slaves and other property in a deserted place, where no free person could come to his assistance? How frightened would he be that he himself and his wife and children would be killed by the slaves?

Very frightened indeed.

And wouldn't he be compelled to fawn on some of his own slaves, promise them lots of things, and 579 free them, even though he didn't want to? And wouldn't he himself have become a panderer to slaves?

He'd have to or else be killed.

What if the god were to settle many other neighbors around him, who wouldn't tolerate anyone to claim that he was the master of another and who would inflict the worst punishments on anyone they caught doing it?

I suppose that he'd have even worse troubles, since he'd be surrounded by nothing but vigilant enemies. *b*

And isn't this the kind of prison in which the tyrant is held—the one whose nature is such as we have described it, filled with fears and erotic loves of all kinds? Even though his soul is really greedy for it, he's the only one in the whole city who can't travel abroad or see the sights that other free people want to see. Instead, he lives like a woman, mostly confined to his own house, and envying any other citizen who happens to travel abroad and see something worthwhile.

That's entirely so.

Then, isn't this harvest of evils a measure of the difference between a tyrannical man who is badly governed on the inside—whom you judged to be most wretched just now—and one who doesn't live a private life but is compelled by some chance to be a tyrant, who tries to rule others when he can't even control himself. He's just like an exhausted body without any self-control, which, instead of living privately, is compelled to compete and fight with other bodies all its life.

That's exactly what he's like, Socrates, and what you say is absolutely true.

And so, Glaucon, isn't this a completely wretched condition to be in, and doesn't the reigning tyrant have an even harder life than the one you judged to be hardest?

He certainly does.

In truth, then, and whatever some people may think, a real tyrant is really a slave, compelled to engage in the worst kind of fawning, slavery, and pandering to the worst kind of people. He's so far from satisfying his desires in any way that it is clear—if one happens to know that one must study his whole soul—that he's in the greatest need of most things and truly poor. And, if indeed his state is like that of the city he rules, then he's full of fear, convulsions, and pains throughout his life. And it is like it, isn't it?

Of course it is.

And we'll also attribute to the man what we mentioned before, namely, that he is inevitably envious, untrustworthy, unjust, friendless, impious, host and nurse to every kind of vice, and that his ruling makes him even more so. And because of all these, he is extremely unfortunate and goes on to make those near him like himself.

No one with any understanding could possibly contradict you.

Come, then, and like the judge who makes the final decision,[3] tell me who among the five—the king, the timocrat, the oligarch, the democrat, and the tyrant—is first in happiness, who second, and so on in order.

That's easy. I rank them in virtue and vice, in happiness and its opposite, in the order of their appearance, as I might judge choruses.

Shall we, then, hire a herald, or shall I myself announce that the son of Ariston has given as his verdict that the best, the most just, and the most happy is the most kingly, who rules like a king over himself, and that the worst, the most unjust, and the most wretched is the most tyrannical, who most tyrannizes himself and the city he rules?

Let it be so announced.

And shall I add to the announcement that it holds, whether these things remain hidden from every god and human being or not?

Add it.

Good. Then that is one of our proofs. And there'd be a second, if you happen to think that there is anything in this.

In what?

In the fact that the soul of each individual is divided into three parts, in just the way that a city is, for that's the reason I think that there is another proof.

What is it?

This: it seems to me that there are three pleasures corresponding to the three parts of the soul, one peculiar to each part, and similarly with desires and kinds of rule.

What do you mean?

The first, we say, is the part with which a person learns, and the second the part with which he gets angry. As for the third, we had no one special name for it, since it's multiform, so we named it after the biggest and strongest thing in it. Hence we called it the appetitive part, because of the intensity of its appetites for food, drink, sex, and all the things associated with them, but we also called it the money-loving part, because such appetites are most easily satisfied by means of money.

And rightly so.

Then, if we said that its pleasure and love are for profit, wouldn't that best determine its central feature for the purposes of our argument and insure that we are clear about what we mean when we speak of this part of the soul, and wouldn't we be right to call it money-loving and profit-loving?

That's how it seems to me, at least.

3. [This probably refers to the way in which plays were judged at festivals.]

What about the spirited part? Don't we say that it is wholly dedicated to the pursuit of control, victory, and high repute?

b Certainly.

Then wouldn't it be appropriate for us to call it victory-loving and honor-loving?

It would be most appropriate.

Now, it is clear to everyone that the part with which we learn is always wholly straining to know where the truth lies and that, of the three parts, it cares least for money and reputation.

By far the least.

Then wouldn't it be appropriate for us to call it learning-loving and philosophical?

Of course.

And doesn't this part rule in some people's souls, while one of the other parts—whichever it happens *c* to be—rules in other people's?

That's right.

And isn't that the reason we say that there are three primary kinds of people: philosophic, victory-loving, and profit-loving?

That's it precisely.

And also three forms of pleasure, one assigned to each of them?

Certainly.

And do you realize that, if you chose to ask three such people in turn to tell you which of their lives is most pleasant, each would give the highest praise to his own? Won't a money-maker say that the plea- *d* sure of being honored and that of learning are worthless compared to that of making a profit, if he gets no money from them?

He will.

What about an honor-lover? Doesn't he think that the pleasure of making money is vulgar and that the pleasure of learning—except insofar as it brings him honor—is smoke and nonsense?

He does.

And as for a philosopher, what do you suppose he thinks the other pleasures are worth compared to that *e* of knowing where the truth lies and always being in some such pleasant condition while learning? Won't he think that they are far behind? And won't he call them really necessary, since he'd have no need for them if they weren't necessary for life?

He will: we can be sure of that.

Then, since there's a dispute between the different forms of pleasure and between the lives themselves, not about which way of living is finer or more shameful or better or worse, but about which is more pleasant and less painful, how are we to know which of them is speaking most truly? *582*

Don't ask me.

Look at it this way: How are we to judge things if we want to judge them well? Isn't it by experience, reason, and argument? Or could anyone have better criteria than these?

How could he?

Consider, then: Which of the three men has most experience of the pleasures we mentioned? Does a profit-lover learn what the truth itself is like or acquire more experience of the pleasure of knowing it than a philosopher does of making a profit? *b*

There's a big difference between them. A philosopher has of necessity tasted the other pleasures since childhood, but it isn't necessary for a profit-lover to taste or experience the pleasure of learning the nature of the things that are and how sweet it is. Indeed, even if he were eager to taste it, he couldn't easily do so.

Then a philosopher is far superior to a profit-lover in his experience of both their pleasures.

He certainly is. *c*

What about an honor-lover? Has he more experience of the pleasure of knowing than a philosopher has of the pleasure of being honored?

No, for honor comes to each of them, provided that he accomplishes his aim. A rich man is honored by many people, so is a courageous one and a wise one, but the pleasure of studying the things that are cannot be tasted by anyone except a philosopher.

Then, as far as experience goes, he is the finest judge of the three. *d*

By far.

And he alone has gained his experience in the company of reason.

Of course.

Moreover, the instrument one must use to judge isn't the instrument of a profit-lover or an honor-lover but a philosopher.

What instrument is that?

Arguments, for didn't we say that we must judge by means of them?

Yes.

And argument is a philosopher's instrument most of all.

Of course.

Now, if wealth and profit were the best means of judging things, the praise and blame of a profit-lover *e* would necessarily be truest.

That's right.

And if honor, victory, and courage were the best means, wouldn't it be the praise and blame of an honor-lover?

Clearly.

But since the best means are experience, reason, and argument . . .

The praise of a wisdom-lover and argument-lover is necessarily truest.

Then, of the three pleasures, the most pleasant is 583 that of the part of the soul with which we learn, and the one in whom that part rules has the most pleasant life.

How could it be otherwise? A person with knowledge at least speaks with authority when he praises his own life.

To what life and to what pleasure does the judge give second place?

Clearly, he gives it to those of a warrior and honor-lover, since they're closer to his own than those of a money-maker.

Then the life and pleasure of a profit-lover come last, it seems.

Of course they do.

These, then, are two proofs in a row, and the just *b* person has defeated the unjust one in both. The third is dedicated in Olympic fashion to Olympian Zeus the Savior.[4] Observe then that, apart from those of a knowledgeable person, the other pleasures are neither entirely true nor pure but are like a shadow-painting, as I think I've heard some wise person say. And yet, if this were true, it would be the greatest and most decisive of the overthrows.

It certainly would. But what exactly do you mean?

c I'll find out, if I ask the questions, and you answer.

Ask, then.

Tell me, don't we say that pain is the opposite of pleasure?

Certainly.

And is there such a thing as feeling neither pleasure nor pain?

There is.

Isn't it intermediate between these two, a sort of calm of the soul by comparison to them? Or don't you think of it that way?

I do.

And do you recall what sick people say when they're ill?

Which saying of theirs do you have in mind?

That nothing gives more pleasure than being healthy, but that they hadn't realized that it was most pleasant until they fell ill. *d*

I do recall that.

And haven't you also heard those who are in great pain say that nothing is more pleasant than the cessation of their suffering?

I have.

And there are many similar circumstances, I suppose, in which you find people in pain praising, not enjoyment, but the absence of pain and relief from it as most pleasant.

That may be because at such times a state of calm becomes pleasant enough to content them.

And when someone ceases to feel pleasure, this calm will be painful to him. *e*

Probably so.

Then the calm we described as being intermediate between pleasure and pain will sometimes be both.

So it seems.

Now, is it possible for that which is neither to become both?

Not in my view.

Moreover, the coming to be of either the pleasant or the painful in the soul is a sort of motion, isn't it?

Yes.

And didn't what is neither painful nor pleasant come to light just now as a calm state, intermediate 584 between them?

Yes, it did.

Then, how can it be right to think that the absence of pain is pleasure or that the absence of pleasure is pain?

There's no way it can be.

Then it isn't right. But when the calm is next to the painful it appears pleasant, and when it is next to the pleasant it appears painful. However, there is nothing sound in these appearances as far as the

4. [The first toast at a banquet was to the Olympian Zeus, the third to Zeus the Savior. By combining the two aspects of Zeus in a single form of address, Plato seems to be emphasizing the importance of this final proof.]

truth about pleasure is concerned, only some kind of magic.

That's what the argument suggests, at any rate.

Take a look at the pleasures that don't come out *b* of pains, so that you won't suppose in their case also that it is the nature of pleasure to be the cessation of pain or of pain to be the cessation of pleasure.

Where am I to look? What pleasures do you mean?

The pleasures of smell are especially good examples to take note of, for they suddenly become very intense without being preceded by pain, and when they cease they leave no pain behind. But there are plenty of other examples as well.

That's absolutely true.

Then let no one persuade us that pure pleasure is *c* relief from pain or that pure pain is relief from pleasure.

No, let's not.

However, most of the so-called pleasures that reach the soul through the body, as well as the most intense ones, are of this form—they are some kind of relief from pain.

Yes, they are.

And aren't the pleasures and pains of anticipation, which arise from the expectation of future pleasures or pains, also of this form?

They are.

Do you know what kind of thing they are and what *d* they most resemble?

No, what is it?

Do you believe that there is an up, a down, and a middle in nature?

I do.

And do you think that someone who was brought from down below to the middle would have any other belief than that he was moving upward? And if he stood in the middle and saw where he had come from, would he believe that he was anywhere other than the upper region, since he hasn't seen the one that is truly upper?

By god, I don't see how he could think anything else.

And if he was brought back, wouldn't he suppose that he was being brought down? And wouldn't he *e* be right?

Of course.

Then wouldn't all this happen to him because he is inexperienced in what is really and truly up, down, and in the middle?

Clearly.

Is it any surprise, then, if those who are inexperienced in the truth have unsound opinions about lots of other things as well, or that they are so disposed to pleasure, pain, and the intermediate state that, when they descend to the painful, they believe truly and are really in pain, but that, when they ascend from the painful to the intermediate state, they firmly *585* believe that they have reached fulfillment and pleasure? They are inexperienced in pleasure and so are deceived when they compare pain to painlessness, just as they would be if they compared black to gray without having experienced white.

No, by god, I wouldn't be surprised. In fact, I'd be very surprised if it were any other way.

Think of it this way: Aren't hunger, thirst, and the like some sort of empty states of the body? *b*

They are.

And aren't ignorance and lack of sense empty states of the soul?

Of course.

And wouldn't someone who partakes of nourishment or strengthens his understanding be filled?

Certainly.

Does the truer filling up fill you with that which is less or that which is more?

Clearly, it's with that which is more.

And which kinds partake more of pure being? Kinds of filling up such as filling up with bread or drink or delicacies or food in general? Or the kind of filling up that is with true belief, knowledge, understanding, and, in sum, with all of virtue? Judge it this way: That which is related to what is always the same, immortal, *c* and true, is itself of that kind, and comes to be in something of that kind—this is more, don't you think, than that which is related to what is never the same and mortal, is itself of that kind, and comes to be in something of that kind?

That which is related to what is always the same is far more.

And does the being of what is always the same participate more in being than in knowledge?

Not at all.

Or more than in truth?

Not that either.

And if less in truth, then less in being also?

Necessarily.

And isn't it generally true that the kinds of filling

d up that are concerned with the care of the body share less in truth and being than those concerned with the care of the soul?

Yes, much less.

And don't you think that the same holds of the body in comparison to the soul?

Certainly.

And isn't that which is more, and is filled with things that are more, really more filled than that which is less, and is filled with things that are less?

Of course.

Therefore, if being filled with what is appropriate to our nature is pleasure, that which is more filled with things that are more enjoys more really and truly *e* a more true pleasure, while that which partakes of things that are less is less truly and surely filled and partakes of a less trustworthy and less true pleasure.

That's absolutely inevitable.

Therefore, those who have no experience of reason 586 or virtue, but are always occupied with feasts and the like, are brought down and then back up to the middle, as it seems, and wander in this way throughout their lives, never reaching beyond this to what is truly higher up, never looking up at it or being brought up to it, and so they aren't filled with that which really is and never taste any stable or pure pleasure. Instead, they always look down at the ground like cattle, and, with their heads bent over the dinner table, they feed, fatten, and fornicate. To outdo[5] others in these things, they kick *b* and butt them with iron horns and hooves, killing each other, because their desires are insatiable. For the part that they're trying to fill is like a vessel full of holes, and neither it nor the things they are trying to fill it with are among the things that are.

Socrates, you've exactly described the life of the majority of people, just like an oracle.

Then isn't it necessary for these people to live with pleasures that are mixed with pains, mere images and shadow-paintings of true pleasures? And doesn't the juxtaposition of these pleasures and pains make them *c* appear intense, so that they give rise to mad erotic passions in the foolish, and are fought over in just the way that Stesichorus tells us the phantom of Helen was fought over at Troy by men ignorant of the truth?[6]

Something like that must be what happens.

And what about the spirited part? Mustn't similar things happen to someone who satisfies it? Doesn't his love of honor make him envious and his love of victory make him violent, so that he pursues the satisfaction of his anger and of his desires for honors *d* and victories without calculation or understanding?

Such things must happen to him as well.

Then can't we confidently assert that those desires of even the money-loving and honor-loving parts that follow knowledge and argument and pursue with their help those pleasures that reason approves will attain the truest pleasures possible for them, because they follow truth, and the ones that are most their own, if indeed what is best for each thing is most its *e* own?

And indeed it is best.

Therefore, when the entire soul follows the philosophic part, and there is no civil war in it, each part of it does its own work exclusively and is just, and in particular it enjoys its own pleasures, the best and truest pleasures possible for it. 587

Absolutely.

But when one of the other parts gains control, it won't be able to secure its own pleasure and will compel the other parts to pursue an alien and untrue pleasure.

That's right.

And aren't the parts that are most distant from philosophy and reason the ones most likely to do this sort of compelling?

They're much more likely.

And isn't whatever is most distant from reason also most distant from law and order?

Clearly.

And didn't the erotic and tyrannical desires emerge as most distant from these things? *b*

By far.

And weren't the kingly and orderly ones least distant?

Yes.

Then I suppose that a tyrant will be most distant from a pleasure that is both true and his own and that a king will be least distant.

5. [*Pleonexias*. See 344a n.18.]

6. [According to the story, Stesichorus wrote a poem defaming Helen and was punished by being struck with blindness. His sight was restored when he added a verse to the poem in which he claimed that it was a phantom of Helen and not Helen herself who was at Troy. See *Phaedrus* 243a.]

Necessarily.

So a tyrant will live most unpleasantly, and a king most pleasantly.

Necessarily.

Do you know how much more unpleasant a tyrant's life is than a king's?

I will if you tell me.

There are, it seems, three pleasures, one genuine and two illegitimate, and a tyrant is at the extreme end of the illegitimate ones, since he flees both law *c* and reason and lives with a bodyguard of certain slavish pleasures. But it isn't easy, all the same, to say just how inferior he is to a king, except perhaps as follows. A tyrant is somehow third from an oligarch, for a democrat was between them.

Yes.

Then, if what we said before is true, doesn't he live with an image of pleasure that is third from an oligarch's with respect to truth?[7]

He does.

Now, an oligarch, in turn, is third from a king,[8] if *d* we identify a king and an aristocrat.

Yes, he's third.

So a tyrant is three times three times removed from true pleasure.

Apparently so.

It seems then, on the basis of the magnitude of its number, that the image of tyrannical pleasure is a plane figure.

Exactly.

But then it's clear that, by squaring and cubing it, we'll discover how far a tyrant's pleasure is from that of a king.

It is clear to a mathematician, at any rate.

Then, turning it the other way around, if someone wants to say how far a king's pleasure is from a tyrant's, *e* he'll find, if he completes the calculation, that a king lives 729 times more pleasantly than a tyrant and that a tyrant is the same number of times more wretched.[9]

That's an amazing calculation of the difference between the pleasure and pain of the two men, the just and the unjust. *588*

Yet it's a true one, and one appropriate to human lives, if indeed days, nights, months, and years are appropriate to them.

And of course they are appropriate.

Then, if a good and just person's life is that much more pleasant than the life of a bad and unjust person, won't its grace, fineness, and virtue be incalculably greater?

By god, it certainly will.

All right, then. Since we've reached this point in the argument, let's return to the first things we *b* said, since they are what led us here. I think someone said at some point that injustice profits a completely unjust person who is believed to be just. Isn't that so?

It certainly is.

Now, let's discuss this with him, since we've agreed on the respective powers that injustice and justice have.

How?

By fashioning an image of the soul in words, so that the person who says this sort of thing will know what he is saying.

What sort of image? *c*

One like those creatures that legends tell us used to come into being in ancient times, such as the

---

7. [Third because the Greeks always counted the first as well as the last member of a series, e.g., the day after tomorrow was the third day.]

8. [Because the timocrat is between them.]

9. [Socrates' mathematics is difficult to follow. He seems to have something like this in mind. The tyrant's image of pleasure is two-dimensional, whereas the true pleasure of the philosopher is three-dimensional. Hence, if a one-unit square represents the degree of closeness to true pleasure of an image nine times removed from it, true pleasure should be represented by a nine-unit cube. It follows that the king lives 729 times more pleasantly than the tyrant. However, in order to reach the number 729, which seems to have been significant to Pythagoras and his followers (there were, allegedly, 729 days and nights in the year, and 729 months in the "great year" recognized by the Pythagorean philosopher Philolaus), Socrates has made two fast moves. First, he has illegitimately capitalized on the Greek manner of counting series in order to count the oligarch twice, once as the last term in his first series (tyrant, democrat, oligarch) and again as the first term in his second series (oligarth, timocrat, king). Second, he has *multiplied* the number of times the tyrant is removed from the oligarch by the number of times the oligarch is removed from the king, when he should have *added* them. The tyrant is therefore only five times removed from the king and lives only 125 times less pleasantly!]

Chimera, Scylla, Cerberus,[10] or any of the multitude of others in which many different kinds of things are said to have grown together naturally into one.

Yes, the legends do tell us of such things.

Well, then, fashion a single kind of multicolored beast with a ring of many heads that it can grow and change at will—some from gentle, some from savage animals.

That's work for a clever artist. However, since words *d* are more malleable than wax and the like, consider it done.

Then fashion one other kind, that of a lion, and another of a human being. But make the first much the largest and the other second to it in size.

That's easier—the sculpting is done.

Now join the three of them into one, so that they somehow grow together naturally.

They're joined.

Then, fashion around them the image of one of them, that of a human being so that anyone who sees only the outer covering and not what's inside will *e* think it is a single creature, a human being.

It's done.

Then, if someone maintains that injustice profits this human being and that doing just things brings no advantage, let's tell him that he is simply saying that it is beneficial for him, first, to feed the multiform beast well and make it strong, and also the lion and all that pertains to him; second, to starve and weaken the 589 human being within, so that he is dragged along wherever either of the other two leads; and, third, to leave the parts to bite and kill one another rather than accustoming them to each other and making them friendly.

Yes, that's absolutely what someone who praises injustice is saying.

But, on the other hand, wouldn't someone who maintains that just things are profitable be saying, first, that all our words and deeds should insure that the human being within this human being has the most control; second, that he should take care of the *b* many-headed beast as a farmer does his animals, feeding and domesticating the gentle heads and preventing the savage ones from growing; and, third, that he should make the lion's nature his ally, care for the community of all his parts, and bring them up in such a way that they will be friends with each other and with himself?

Yes, that's exactly what someone who praises justice is saying.

From every point of view, then, anyone who praises justice speaks truly, and anyone who praises injustice speaks falsely. Whether we look at the matter from the point of view of pleasure, good reputation, or advantage, a praiser of justice tells the truth, while *c* one who condemns it has nothing sound to say and condemns without knowing what he is condemning.

In my opinion, at least, he knows nothing about it.

Then let's persuade him gently—for he isn't wrong of his own will—by asking him these questions. Should we say that this is the original basis for the conventions about what is fine and what is shameful? Fine things are those that subordinate the beastlike parts of our nature to the human—or better, perhaps, to the divine; shameful ones are those that enslave *d* the gentle to the savage? Will he agree or what?

He will, if he takes my advice.

In light of this argument, can it profit anyone to acquire gold unjustly if, by doing so, he enslaves the best part of himself to the most vicious? If he got the gold by enslaving his son or daughter to savage and evil men, it wouldn't profit him, no matter how much *e* gold he got. How, then, could he fail to be wretched if he pitilessly enslaves the most divine part of himself to the most godless and polluted one and accepts golden gifts in return for a more terrible destruction than Eriphyle's when she took the necklace in return 590 for her husband's soul?[11]

A much more terrible one, Glaucon said. I'll answer for him.

And don't you think that licentiousness has long been condemned for just these reasons, namely, that because of it, that terrible, large, and multiform beast is let loose more than it should be?

Clearly.

10. [The Chimera was "lion in the front, serpent in the back, and she-goat in the middle" (*Iliad* 6.181). Scylla had six heads, each with three rows of teeth, and twelve feet (see *Odyssey* 12.85 ff., 245 ff.). Cerberus was a huge dog guarding the entrance to Hades; he had three heads and a serpent's tail.]

11. [Eriphyle was bribed by Polynices to persuade her husband, Amphiaraus, to take part in an attack on Thebes. He was killed, and she was murdered by her son in revenge. See *Odyssey* 11.326–27; Pindar, *Nemean* 9.37 ff.]

And aren't stubbornness and irritability condemned because they inharmoniously increase and *b* stretch the lionlike and snakelike[12] part?

Certainly.

And aren't luxury and softness condemned because the slackening and loosening of this same part produce cowardice in it?

Of course.

And aren't flattery and slavishness condemned because they subject the spirited part to the moblike beast, accustoming it from youth on to being insulted for the sake of the money needed to satisfy the beast's insatiable appetites, so that it becomes an ape instead of a lion?

c They certainly are.

Why do you think that the condition of a manual worker is despised? Or is it for any other reason than that, when the best part is naturally weak in someone, it can't rule the beasts within him but can only serve them and learn to flatter them?

Probably so.

Therefore, to insure that someone like that is ruled by something similar to what rules the best person, we say that he ought to be the slave of that best person who has a divine ruler within himself. It isn't to harm *d* the slave that we say he must be ruled, which is what Thrasymachus thought to be true of all subjects, but because it is better for everyone to be ruled by divine reason, preferably within himself and his own, otherwise imposed from without, so that as far as possible all will be alike and friends, governed by the same thing.

Yes, that's right.

This is clearly the aim of the law, which is the ally of everyone. But it's also our aim in ruling our children, we don't allow them to be free until we establish a constitution in them, just as in a city, and—by fostering their best part with our own—equip them with a guardian and ruler similar to our 591 own to take our place. Then, and only then, we set them free.

Clearly so.

12. [The snakelike part hasn't been previously mentioned, although it may be included in "all that pertains to" the lion (588e). It symbolizes some of the meaner components of the spirited part, such as irritability, which it would be unnatural to attribute to the noble lion.]

Then how can we maintain or argue, Glaucon, that injustice, licentiousness, and doing shameful things are profitable to anyone, since, even though he may acquire more money or other sort of power from them, they make him more vicious?

There's no way we can.

Or that to do injustice without being discovered and having to pay the penalty is profitable? Doesn't the one who remains undiscovered become even more vicious, while the bestial part of the one who *b* is discovered is calmed and tamed and his gentle part freed, so that his entire soul settles into its best nature, acquires moderation, justice, and reason, and attains a more valuable state than that of having a fine, strong, healthy body, since the soul itself is more valuable than the body?

That's absolutely certain.

Then won't a person of understanding direct all his efforts to attaining that state of his soul? First, *c* he'll value the studies that produce it and despise the others.

Clearly so.

Second, he won't entrust the condition and nurture of his body to the irrational pleasure of the beast within or turn his life in that direction, but neither will he make health his aim or assign first place to being strong, healthy, and beautiful, unless he happens to acquire moderation as a result. Rather, it's clear that he will always cultivate the harmony of his body for the sake of the consonance in his soul. *d*

He certainly will, if indeed he's to be truly trained in music and poetry.

Will he also keep order and consonance in his acquisition of money, with that same end in view? Or, even though he isn't dazzled by the size of the majority into accepting their idea of blessed happiness, will he increase his wealth without limit and so have unlimited evils?

Not in my view.

Rather, he'll look to the constitution within him and guard against disturbing anything in it, either by *e* too much money or too little. And, in this way, he'll direct both the increase and expenditure of his wealth, as far as he can.

That's exactly what he'll do.

And he'll look to the same thing where honors are concerned. He'll willingly share in and taste those 592 that he believes will make him better, but he'll avoid any public or private honor that might overthrow the established condition of his soul.

If that's his chief concern, he won't be willing to take part in politics.

Yes, by the dog, he certainly will, at least in his own kind of city. But he may not be willing to do so in his fatherland, unless some divine good luck chances to be his.

I understand. You mean that he'll be willing to take part in the politics of the city we were founding and describing, the one that exists in theory, for I *b* don't think it exists anywhere on earth.

But perhaps, I said, there is a model of it in heaven, for anyone who wants to look at it and to make himself its citizen on the strength of what he sees. It makes no difference whether it is or ever will be somewhere, for he would take part in the practical affairs of that city and no other.

Probably so, he said.

Book X

The main argument of the Republic *is now complete. Hence Socrates is in a position to discuss the kind of poetry about human beings that is permitted in the kallipolis, a discussion that had to be postponed in Book III (392a–c). Given the importance Socrates attributes to music and poetry and physical training (424b–425a) and the importance of Homer and Hesiod in Greek education, the return to this topic is hardly an anticlimax. It is rather the moment at which the new philosophy-based education confronts the traditional education based on poetry.*

Central to this discussion is a new account of mimēsis, *or imitation, based on the metaphysical theories introduced in Books V–VII. Earlier in Book III, imitation was something a person did by impersonating a character in a poem (394d ff.); now imitation is something a poem or a painting does.*

Socrates' critique of poetry is extremely subtle. The question on which it focuses is whether what one needs to know in order to be a good poet qualifies one as a teacher of virtue. Socrates argues that it does not. An imitator, in Plato's new technical sense, is someone whose products are third from the truth (597e), because they imitate the sorts of things the craftsman makes, which are themselves only imitations of what the philosopher-king would make (596e–597e). Hence, if poetry is third from the truth, it too will be imitative, and the poet will be an imitator. But Socrates argues that the poet is an imitator in this sense (598d–607a), and consequently he does not even have true belief about virtue. Makers have true belief through associating with users, who alone have knowledge. But imitators don't even have the kind of insight that makers do; they have only opinion—sometimes true, sometimes false—nothing more. Hence they are not reliable teachers of virtue and, because of their disturbing influence even on good people, should not be admitted into the kallipolis. Socrates' ban on imitative poetry is not final, however. He allows for the possibility that someone might be able to construct a defense of poetry that would change his mind (607b–608b).

Having completed his account of poetry, Socrates turns to the topic of the immortality of the soul and to the previously excluded consequences of justice and injustice (609b–612e). He argues, in part by appeal to the Myth of Er, that the good consequences of justice both in this life and in the next far outweigh those of injustice. This completes his argument that justice belongs in the best of the three classes of goods that Glaucon distinguished at the beginning of Book II, since it is choiceworthy both for its own sake and for its consequences.

Aristotle

Aristotle (384–322 B.C.), born in the Ionian colony of Stagira in northern Greece, was the son of a physician to the Macedonian ruler. At eighteen he entered Plato's Academy in Athens, where he remained for two decades until Plato's death. He then taught outside Athens for a dozen years, possibly including three as tutor to the young prince who later became known as Alexander the Great. In 335 Aristotle returned to Athens and founded his own school, the Lyceum, where he did his most productive research. On the death of Alexander in 323, an outbreak of anti-Macedonian feeling swept Athens, and Aristotle withdrew to the city of Calcis, "lest," he reportedly said, "the Athenians should sin twice against philosophy."

A distinguished historian of philosophy once referred to Aristotle as "the greatest mind produced by the Greeks"; even those who might not share this judgment would agree that his intellectual achievements were of enormous magnitude. Virtually singlehanded, he founded the study of logic. His philosophical treatises on metaphysics, ethics, politics, and aesthetics remain more than two thousand years later among the most profound works ever written on these subjects. His scientific studies produced groundbreaking results in biology, psychology, zoology, meteorology, and astronomy. Indeed, his later influence was so profound that during the Middle Ages he was often referred to simply as "the Philosopher."

In his *On Interpretation,* Aristotle explores the varieties of propositions and their possible oppositions. The much-discussed ninth chapter considers the status of statements about future actions. When one person claims that a sea battle will occur tomorrow but another denies this claim, is either claim correct prior to tomorrow? If so, do all events occur by necessity?

As becomes clear in the *Categories,* a treatise on the structure of language with implications about the nature of reality, Aristotle rejected Plato's Theory of Forms, arguing that universals have no subsistence apart from particulars. For example, humanity or redness do not exist independently but only as common elements in specific substances. Thus, whereas Plato viewed knowledge as an a priori inquiry into Ideas, for Aristotle the acquisition of understanding involved an empirical investigation of essential structures shared by individual entities.

The *Posterior Analytics* contains Aristotle's account of the nature of scientific knowledge. His model is geometry, in which theorems are deduced from axioms, although in his own scientific work he realized the importance of empirical research. Nevertheless, his analysis of the logic of science contains numerous points of interest about such matters as definition, argument, and explanation.

He considered every substance a compound of form and matter, a position he maintained in his *Metaphysics,* so named since it came after the *Physics* in a first-century-B.C. edition of his works. In this treatise, after reviewing the opinions of his predecessors, he went on to investigate the study of "being *qua* being," what is true of all things that exist. He maintained that each particular is an embodied essence, a thing with an intelligible structure.

As regards the nature of persons, Aristotle rejected Plato's view of the soul as separate from the body, arguing in *On the Soul* that the soul is the body in action, just as sight is the activity of the eye. The soul, therefore, cannot exist apart from the body, for the processes of being, sensing, and knowing require an organism that lives, senses, and knows.

In the *Physics,* a study of the concepts used in physical science, Aristotle identified four causes or modes of explanation. These have come to be known as the material cause, formal cause, efficient cause, and final cause. In the case of a building, for example, its material cause may be bricks and mortar, its formal cause the architectural blueprints, its efficient cause the builders, and its final cause the providing of shelter. Aristotle stressed the importance of final causes in understanding the world, for in his view nature is teleological, exhibiting purposeful processes.

As to Aristotle's views on the purpose of human life, these are to be found in his *Nicomachean Ethics.* This work (named after Aristotle's son Nicomachus) is universally considered one of the great books of moral philosophy. It ranges from detailed analyses of such concepts as choosing, deliberating, and wishing, to a vision of the highest happiness as a life devoted to the exercise of pure reason. The book possesses some organizational difficulties; like other of Aristotle's treatises, it may consist partly of texts of his lectures as preserved in his students' notes. However, unity is provided by central themes, among which are the commitment to viewing the good as the fulfillment of human nature, the emphasis on a close relationship between ethics and the interests of society, and the need to distinguish moral from intellectual virtue.

This latter distinction provides Aristotle with an answer to the question, raised at the opening of Plato's *Meno,* as to the origin of virtue. According to Aristotle, moral virtue, which we might call "goodness of character," is formed by habit. One becomes good by doing good. Repeated acts of justice and self-control result in a just, self-controlled person who not only performs just and self-controlled actions but does so from a fixed character. Intellectual virtue, on the other hand, which we might refer to as "wisdom," is acquired by teaching and requires foresight and sophisticated intelligence.

In opposition to the Socratic doctrine that a person who knows the good will necessarily do the good, Aristotle insists on our acknowledging the phenomenon of moral weakness: the situation, so easy to recognize and yet so difficult to explain, in which individuals act contrary to what they believe to be for the best. Typically, he emphasizes that a theory which denies the existence of moral weakness is at variance with observed facts.

• • •

A comprehensive guide to Aristotle's thought is Jonathan Barnes, ed., *The Cambridge Companion to Aristotle* (Cambridge: Cambridge University Press, 1995). Detailed analyses of each of Aristotle's major works are provided in the standard commentary by W. D. Ross, *Aristotle: A Complete Exposition of His Works and Thought* (1923; rpt. Cleveland, Ohio: Meridian Books, 1959). For a provocative account of Aristotle's views on propositions about future choices, see Richard Taylor, "The Problem of Future Contingencies," *The Philosophical Review* 66 (1957): 1–28. An incisive discussion of the *Physics* is Sarah Waterlow, *Nature, Change and Agency in Aristotle's Physics* (Oxford: Clarendon Press, 1982). Detailed studies of Aristotle's ethics include Richard Kraut, *Aristotle on the Human Good* (Princeton, N.J.: Princeton University Press, 1989); C. D. C. Reeve, *The Practices of Reason: Aristotle's Nicomachean Ethics* (Oxford: Clarendon Press, 1992); and Nancy Sherman, *The Fabric of Character: Aristotle's Theory of Virtue* (Oxford: Clarendon Press, 1989). Useful articles on the *Ethics* are collected in Nancy Sherman, ed., *Aristotle's Nicomachean Ethics* (Lanham, Md.: Rowman & Littlefield, 1999).

Steven M. Cahn

Categories

1

1a1 If things have only a name in common and the account of the essence corresponding to the name is different for each, they are called homonymous. Both man and the painted animal, for instance, are animals [homonymously]; for these have only a name in common and the account corresponding to the name is different. For if someone says what being an animal 5 is for each of them, he will give a different account for each.

If things have the name in common and also have the same account of the essence corresponding to the name, they are called synonymous. Both man and ox, for instance, are animals synonymously, since each is called animal, by a common name, and the account of the essence is the same. For if someone 10 gives an account of each, saying what being an animal is for each of them, he will give the same account.

Things that are called what they are by having a name from something with a different inflexion are called paronymous; for example, the grammarian is 15 so called from grammar, and the brave person from bravery.

2

Among things said, some involve combination, while others are without combination. Things involving combination are, e.g., man runs, man wins; things without combination are, e.g., man, ox, run, wins.

20 Among beings some are said of a subject but are not in any subject; man, e.g., is said of a subject, an individual man, but is not in any subject. Some are in a subject, but are not said of any subject. (By 'in a subject' I mean what belongs in something, not as 25 a part, and cannot exist separately from what it is in.) An individual [instance of] grammatical knowledge, for example, is in a subject, the soul, but is not said of any subject; and an individual [instance of] white is in a subject, the body (for all color is in body), but is not said of any subject. Some things are both said of a subject and in a subject; knowledge, e.g., is in a 1b subject, the soul, and is said of a subject, grammatical knowledge. Some things are neither in a subject nor said of a subject. This is true, for instance, of an individual man or horse; for nothing of this sort is 5 either in a subject or said of a subject.

Things that are individual and numerically one are, without exception, not said of any subject; but nothing prevents some of them from being in a subject; for an individual [instance of] grammatical knowledge is one of the things in a subject.

3

Whenever one thing is predicated of another as of a 10 subject, everything said of what is predicated is also said of the subject. Man, e.g., is predicated of an individual man, and animal of man; so animal will also be predicated of an individual man; for an indi- 15 vidual man is both man and animal.

Genera which are different and not subordinate to one another have differentiae that are different in species—e.g., the differentiae of animal and of knowledge. For footed, winged, aquatic, and biped are differentiae of animal, but none of them is a differentia of knowledge; for one sort of knowledge is not differ- 20 entiated from another by being biped. But if one genus is subordinate to another, nothing prevents them from having the same differentiae; for the higher genera are predicated of those below them, so that the subject will also have all the differentiae of the thing predicated.

4

Of things said without combination, each signifies 25 either substance or quantity or quality or relative or where or when or being in a position or having or

Reprinted from Aristotle, *Selections*, translated and edited by Terence Irwin and Gail Fine (Indianapolis: Hackett Publishing Company, 1995), by permission of the publisher. The use of brackets within the text indicates insertions not found in the manuscript.

acting on or being affected. To speak in outline, examples of substance are man, horse; of quantity: two feet long, three feet long; of quality: white, grammatical; of relative: double, half, larger; of where: in 2a the Lyceum, in the market place; of when: yesterday, last year; of being in a position: is lying; is sitting; of having: has shoes on, has armor on; of acting on: cutting, burning; of being affected: being cut, being burnt.

5 None of the things just mentioned is said all by itself in any affirmation; an affirmation results from the combination of these things with one another. For every affirmation seems to be either true or false, 10 whereas nothing said without combination—e.g. man, white, runs, wins—is either true or false.

5

What is called substance most fully, primarily, and most of all, is what is neither said of any subject nor in any subject—e.g., an individual man or horse. The 15 species in which the things primarily called substances belong are called secondary substances, and so are their genera. An individual man, e.g., belongs in the species, man, and animal is the genus of the species; these things, then, e.g. man and animal, are called secondary substances.

It is evident from what has been said that if some- 20 thing is said of a subject, then both its name and its account must be predicated of the subject. For instance, man is said of a subject, an individual man, and the name is predicated (since you will predicate man of an individual man); moreover, the account 25 of man will also be predicated of an individual man (since an individual man is also a man). And so both the name and the account will be predicated of the subject.

On the other hand, if something is in a subject, in most cases neither its name nor its account is predicated of the subject. In some cases, however, though 30 nothing prevents the name from being predicated of the subject, the account still cannot be predicated. White, e.g., is in a subject, body, and is predicated of body (for body is said to be white); but the account of white will never be predicated of body.

35 All other things are either said of the primary substances as subjects, or are in them as subjects. This is evident if we examine particular cases. Animal, e.g., is predicated of man, and so also of an individual man; for if it is not predicated of any individual man, neither 2b is it predicated of man at all. Again, colour is in body, and so also in an individual body; for if it is not in any of the particular bodies, neither is it in body at all.

Hence all the other things are either said of the primary substances as subjects, or are in them as 5 subjects. If, then, the primary substances did not exist, neither could any of the other things exist. For all the other things are either said of these as subjects or are in these as subjects, so that if the primary substances did not exist, neither could any of the other things exist.

Among secondary substances, the species is more a substance than the genus, since it is nearer to the primary substance; for if someone says what the primary substance is, it will be more informative and 10 more appropriate if he mentions the species than if he mentions the genus. It will be more informative, for instance, to say that an individual man is a man than to say that he is an animal, since man is more distinctive of an individual man, while animal is more common; and it will be more informative to say that an individual tree is a tree than that it is a plant.

Further, the primary substances are subjects for all 15 the other things, and all the other things are predicated of them or are in them; and this is why they, most of all, are called substances. But as the primary substances are related to other things, so also is the species related to the genus; for the species is a subject for the genus, 20 since the genera are predicated of the species, whereas the species are not reciprocally predicated of the genera. And so for this reason too the species is more a substance than the genus.

Among species themselves, however—those that are not genera—one is no more a substance than another; for it is no more appropriate to say that an individual man is a man than it is to say that an 25 individual horse is a horse. And similarly, among primary substances one is no more a substance than another; for an individual man is no more a substance than an individual ox is.

It is not surprising that, after the primary substances, only their species and genera are said to be secondary 30 substances; for they are the only things predicated that reveal the primary substance. For if one says what an individual man is, it will be appropriate to mention the species or the genus, though it will be more informative to mention man than animal. But it would

35 be inappropriate to mention anything else—e.g. white or runs or any other such thing. Hence it is not surprising that species and genera are the only other things said to be substances.

Further, it is because the primary substances are subjects for everything else that they are said to be 3a substances most fully. But as the primary substances are related to everything else, so also are the species and genera of primary substances related to all the other things; for all the other things are predicated of them. For you will call an individual man grammati- 5 cal, and hence you will call both man and animal grammatical; and the same is true in the other cases.

A feature common to every substance is not being in a subject; for a primary substance is neither said of 10 nor in a subject. In this same way, it is evident that neither are secondary substances in a subject; for man is said of a subject—an individual man—but is not in a subject, since man is not in an individual man. Similarly, animal is said of a subject—an individual 15 man—but animal is not in an individual man.

Further, while things in a subject may sometimes have their name predicated of the subject, their account can never be predicated of it. Secondary substances, on the other hand, have both their account and their name predicated of the subject; for you will 20 predicate both the account of man and the account of animal, of an individual man. Hence no substance is in a subject.

This, however, is not distinctive of substance; the differentia is not in a subject either. For footed and biped are said of a subject—man—but are not in a 25 subject, since neither footed nor biped is in man. Again, the account of the differentia is predicated of whatever subject the differentia is said of; if footed is said of man, e.g., the account of footed will also be predicated of man, since man is footed.

We need not be worried that we will ever be com- 30 pelled to say that the parts of substances, being in a subject (the whole substance), are not substances. For when we spoke of things in a subject, we did not mean things belonging in something as parts.

It is a feature of substances and differentiae that everything called from them is so called synony- 35 mously. For all the predications from these are predicated either of the individuals or of the species. (For there is no predication from a primary substance—since it is not said of any subject—and among secondary substances the species is predicated of an individual, and the genus is predicated both of the species and of an individual. Similarly, differentiae are also 3b predicated both of the species and of the individuals.) Now the primary substances receive the account both of the species and of the genera, and the species receives the account of the genus; for whatever is said of what is predicated will also be said of the subject. 5 Similarly, both the species and the individuals receive the account of the differentiae; and we saw that synonymous things are those that both have the name in common and also have the same account. Hence everything called from substances and differentiae is so called synonymously.

Every substance seems to signify a this. In the case 10 of primary substances, it is indisputably true that each of them signifies a this; for what is revealed is an individual and numerically one. In the case of secondary substances, however, it appears from the character of the name that they also signify a this, whenever one speaks of man or animal; but this is not true. Rather, 15 each signifies a quality; for the subject is not one, as the primary substance is, but man and animal are said of many things. But it does not simply signify a quality as white does; for white signifies nothing other than quality, whereas the species and the genus demarcate 20 the quality of substance—for they signify a substance of a certain quality. One demarcates a wider area with the genus than with the species; for in speaking of animal one encompasses a wider area than in speaking of man.

It is also a feature of substances that nothing is contrary to them. For what could be contrary to a 25 primary substance? Nothing is contrary, for instance, to an individual man; nor is anything contrary to man or animal. This is not distinctive of substance, however, but is also true of many other things—e.g., of quantity, since nothing is contrary to two feet long, 30 nor to ten, nor to anything else of this kind. One might say that many is contrary to few, or large to small; but no definite quantity is contrary to any other.

Substance does not seem to admit of more or less. By this I do not mean that one substance is no more a substance than another—for we have said that it is; 35 rather, I mean that no substance is said to be more or less what it is. For example, if this substance is a man, it will not be more or less a man either than itself or than another. For one man is no more a man than another, in the way that one white thing is whiter than another, or one beautiful thing is more beautiful 4a than another. In some cases a thing is called more or less something than itself—for example, the body which is white is said to be more white now than it was before, and the body which is hot is said to be 5 more or less hot [than it was]. But substance is not spoken of in this way; for a man is not said to be more a man now than before, nor is this said of any other substance. Thus substance does not admit of more or less.

10 It seems most distinctive of substance that numerically one and the same thing is able to receive contraries. In no other case could one cite something numerically one that is able to receive contraries. For example, the color that is numerically one and the 15 same will not be pale and dark; nor will the action which is numerically one and the same be bad and good; and the same is true of anything else that is not a substance. But a substance that is numerically one and the same is able to receive contraries. An individual man, for instance, being one and the same, 20 becomes at one time pale, at another time dark, and hot and cold, and bad and good; nothing of the sort appears in any other case.

Someone might object, however, that statements and beliefs are like this, since the same statement 25 seems to be both true and false. If, e.g., the statement that someone is seated is true, when he has stood up this same statement will be false. The same is true of belief; for if someone were to believe truly that someone is seated, he will believe falsely if he has the same belief about him when he has stood up.

But even if one were to accept this, even so the way in which these receive contraries is different. For in the case of substances, a thing is able to receive 30 contraries by itself changing; for it changed when it became cold from hot (since it altered), or dark from pale, or good from bad, and similarly in the other cases it is able to receive contraries by itself changing. Statements and beliefs, on the other hand, themselves 35 remain completely unmoved in every way; it is because the object [they are about] is moved that the contrary comes to be about them. For the statement that someone is seated remains the same, but it comes 4b to be true at one time, and false at another time, when the object has been moved. The same is true of belief. Hence at least the way in which substance is able to receive contraries—by a change in itself—is distinctive of it, if indeed one were to concede that 5 beliefs and statements are also able to receive contraries.

This, however, is not true. For it is not because they themselves receive something that a statement and a belief are said to be able to receive contraries, but because something else has been affected. For it is because the object is or is not some way that the 10 statement is said to be true or false—not because the statement itself is able to receive contraries; for, without exception, no statement or belief is moved by anything. And so, since nothing comes to be in them, they are not able to receive contraries. But substance is said to be able to receive contraries, because it receives them itself. For it receives sickness and health, or paleness and darkness; and because it 15 itself receives each thing of this sort, it is said to be able to receive contraries.

Hence it is distinctive of substance that numerically one and the same thing is able to receive contraries. So much, then, about substance.

On Interpretation

1

16a We must first establish what names and verbs are, then what negations, affirmations, statements, and sentences are.

Spoken sounds are symbols of affections in the 5 soul, and written marks are symbols of spoken sounds; and just as written marks are not the same for everyone, neither are spoken sounds. But the primary things that these signify (the affections in the soul) are the same for everyone, and what these affections are likenesses of (actual things) are also the same for everyone. We have discussed these questions in *On the Soul*; they belong to another inquiry.

10 Some thoughts in the soul are neither true nor false, while others must be one or the other; the same is true of spoken sounds. For falsity and truth involve combination and division. Names and verbs by them- 15 selves, when nothing is added (for instance, 'man' and 'pale') are like thoughts without combination and separation, since they are not yet either true or false. A sign of this is the fact that 'goatstag' signifies something but is not yet true or false unless 'is' or 'is not' is added, either without qualification or with reference to time.

2

20 A name is a spoken sound that is significant by convention, without time, of which no part is significant in separation. For in 'Grancourt,' the 'court' does not signify anything in itself, as it does in the phrase 'a grand court.' But complex names are not the same 25 as simple ones; for in simple names the part is not at all significant, whereas in complex names the part has some force but does not signify anything in separation—for instance, 'fact' in 'artifact.' I say 'by convention' because nothing is a name by nature; something is a name only if it becomes a symbol. For even inarticulate noises—of beasts, for example—reveal something, but they are not names.

'Not-man' is not a name, nor is any established 30 name rightly applied to it, since neither is it a sentence or a negation. Let us call it an indefinite name.

'Philo's,' 'to-Philo,' and the like are not names but 16b inflections of names. The same account applies to them as to names, except that a name with 'is' or 'was' or 'will be' added is always true or false, whereas an inflection with them added is neither true nor false. For example, in 'Philo's is' or 'Philo's is not' nothing is yet either true or false. 5

3

A verb is [a spoken sound] of which no part signifies separately, and which additionally signifies time; it is a sign of things said of something else. By 'additionally signifies time,' I mean that, for instance, 'recovery' is a name but 'recovers' is a verb; for it additionally signifies something's holding now. And it is always a 10 sign of something's holding, that is to say, of something's holding of a subject.

I do not call 'does not recover' and 'does not ail' verbs; for, although they additionally signify time and always hold of something, there is a difference for which there is no established name. Let us call them indefinite verbs, since they hold of anything whether 15 it is or is not.

Similarly, 'recovered' and 'will-recover' are not verbs, but inflections of verbs. They differ from verbs because verbs additionally signify the present time, whereas inflections of verbs signify times outside the present.

A verb said just by itself is a name and signifies 20 something, since the speaker fixes his thought and the hearer pauses; but it does not yet signify whether something is or is not. For 'being' or 'not being' is not a sign of an object (not even if you say 'what is' without addition); for by itself it is nothing, but it

Reprinted from Aristotle, *Selections*, translated and edited by Terence Irwin and Gail Fine (Indianapolis: Hackett Publishing Company, 1995), by permission of the publisher. The use of brackets within the text indicates insertions not found in the manuscript.

25 additionally signifies some combination, which cannot be thought of without the components.

4

A sentence is a significant spoken sound, of which some part is significant in separation as an expression, not as an affirmation. I mean that 'animal,' for instance, signifies something, but not that it is or is 30 not (but if something is added, there will be an affirmation or negation), whereas the single syllables of 'animal' signify nothing. Nor is the 'ice' in 'mice' significant; here it is only a spoken sound. In the case of double names, as was said, a part signifies, but not by itself.

17a Every sentence is significant, not because it is a [naturally suitable] instrument but, as we said, by convention. But not every sentence is a statement; only those sentences that are true or false are statements. Not every sentence is true or false; a prayer, for instance, is a sentence but it is neither true nor false. Let us set aside these other cases, since inquiry into them is more appropriate for rhetoric or poetics; our present study concerns affirmations.

7

17a38 Some things are universals, others are particulars. By 40 'universal' I mean what is naturally predicated of 17b more than one thing; by 'particular,' what is not. For example, man is a universal, and Callias is a particular.

Necessarily, then, when one says that something does or does not hold of something, one sometimes says this of a universal, sometimes of a particular. Now if one states universally of a universal that something does or does not hold, there will be 5 contrary statements. (By 'stating universally of a universal,' I mean, for instance, 'Every man is pale,' 'No man is pale.') But when one states something of a universal, but not universally, the statements are not contrary, though contrary things may be revealed. (By 'stating of a universal but not univer- 10 sally,' I mean, for instance, 'A man is pale,' 'A man is not pale.' For although man is a universal, it is not used universally in the statement; for 'every' does not signify the universal, but rather signifies that it is used universally.)

In the case of what is predicated, it is not true to predicate a universal universally; for there will be 15 no affirmation in which the universal is predicated universally of what is predicated, as in, for instance, 'Every man is every animal.'

I call an affirmation and a negation contradictory opposites when what one signifies universally the other signifies not universally—for instance, 'Every man is pale' and 'Not every man is pale,' or 'No man is pale' and 'Some man is pale.' But the universal 20 affirmation and the universal negation—for instance, 'Every man is just' and 'No man is just'—are contrary opposites. That is why they cannot both be true at the same time, but their [contradictory] opposites may both be true about the same thing—for instance, 'Not 25 every man is pale' and 'Some man is pale.'

Of contradictory universal statements about a universal, one or the other must be true or false; similarly if they are about particulars—for instance, 'Socrates is pale' and 'Socrates is not pale.' But if they are about universals, but are not universal [statements], it is not always the case that one is true, the other 30 false. For it is true to say at the same time that a man is pale and that a man is not pale, and that a man is handsome and that a man is not handsome; for if ugly, then not handsome. And if something is becoming F, it is also not F. This might seem strange at first sight, since 'A man is not pale' might 35 appear to signify at the same time that no man is pale; but it does not signify the same, nor does it necessarily hold at the same time.

It is clear that a single affirmation has a single negation. For the negation must deny the same thing 40 that the affirmation affirms, and deny it of the same 18a [subject]—either of a particular or of a universal, either universally or not universally, as, for instance, in 'Socrates is pale' and 'Socrates is not pale.' (But if something else is denied, or the same thing is denied of a different [subject], that will not be the opposite statement but a different one.) The opposite of 'Every 5 man is pale' is 'Not every man is pale'; of 'Some man is pale,' 'No man is pale'; of 'A man is pale,' 'A man is not pale.'

We have explained, then, that a single affirmation has a single negation as its contradictory opposite, 10 and which these are; that contrary statements are different, and which these are; and that not all contradictory pairs are true or false, and why and when they are true or false.

9

18a28 In the case of what is and what has been, then, it is 30 necessary that the affirmation or negation be true or false. And in the case of universal statements about universals, it is always [necessary] for one to be true and the other false; and the same is true in the case of particulars, as we have said. But in the case of universals not spoken of universally, this is not necessary; we have also discussed this. But in the case of particulars that are going to be, it is not the same.

For if every affirmation or negation is true or false, 35 then it is also necessary that everything either is the case or is not the case. And so if someone says that something will be and another denies the same thing, clearly it is necessary for one of them to speak truly, if every affirmation is true or false. For both will not be the case at the same time in such cases.

18b For if it is true to say that something is pale or not pale, it is necessary for it to be pale or not pale; and if it is pale or not pale, it was true to affirm or deny this. And if it is not the case, one speaks falsely; and if one speaks falsely, it is not the case. Hence it is necessary for the affirmation or the negation to be true or false.

5 Therefore nothing either is or happens by chance or as chance has it; nor will it be nor not be [thus]. Rather, everything [happens] from necessity and not as chance has it, since either the affirmer or the denier speaks truly. For otherwise, it might equally well happen or not happen; for what happens as chance has it neither is nor will be any more this way than that.

10 Further, if something is pale now, it was true to say previously that it would be pale, so that it was always true to say of any thing that has happened that it would be. But if it was always true to say that it was or would be, it could not not be, or not be going to be. But if something cannot not happen, it is impossible for it not to happen; and what cannot 15 not happen necessarily happens. Everything, then, that will be will be necessarily. Therefore, nothing will be as chance has it or by chance; for if it is by chance it is not from necessity.

But it is not possible to say that neither is true—that, for example, it neither will be nor will not be. For, first, [if this is possible, then] though the affirmation is false, the negation is not true; and though the negation is false, it turns out [on this view] that the 20 affirmation is not true.

Moreover, if it is true to say that it is pale and dark, both must be the case; and if [both] will be the case tomorrow, [both] must be the case tomorrow. But if it neither will nor will not be tomorrow, even so, the sea battle, for instance, will not happen as chance 25 has it; for in this case, the sea battle would have to neither happen nor not happen.

These and others like them are the absurd consequences if in every affirmation and negation (either about universals spoken of universally or about particulars) it is necessary that one of the opposites be true and the other false, and nothing happens as 30 chance has it, but all things are and happen from necessity. Hence there would be no need to deliberate or to take trouble, thinking that if we do this, that will be, and if we do not, it will not be; for it might well be that ten thousand years ago one person said 35 that this would be and another denied it, so that whichever it was true to affirm at that time will be so from necessity.

Nor does it make a difference whether or not anyone made the contradictory statements; for clearly things are thus even if someone did not affirm it and another deny it. For it is not because of the affirming or denying that it will be or will not be the case, nor is this any more so for ten thousand years ago than 19a for any other time.

Hence if in the whole of time things were such that one or the other statement was true, it was necessary for this to happen, and each thing that happened was always such as to happen from necessity. For if someone has said truly that something 5 will happen, it cannot not happen; and it was always true to say of something that has happened that it would be.

But surely this is impossible. For we see that both deliberation and action originate things that will be; and, in general, we see in things that are not always in actuality that there is the possibility both of being 10 and of not being; in these cases both being and not being, and hence both happening and not happening, are possible.

We find that this is clearly true of many things. It is possible, for instance, for this cloak to be cut up, though [in fact] it will not be cut up but will wear out first instead. Similarly, its not being cut up is also

15 possible; for its wearing out first would not have been the case unless its not being cut up were possible. Hence the same is true for other things that happen, since this sort of possibility is ascribed to many of them.

Evidently, then, not everything is or happens from 20 necessity. Rather, some things happen as chance has it, and the affirmation is no more true than the negation. In other cases, one alternative [happens] more than the other and happens usually, but it is still possible for the other to happen and for the first not to happen.

It is necessary for what is, whenever it is, to be, and for what is not, whenever it is not, not to be. But 25 not everything that is necessarily is; and not everything that is not necessarily is not. For everything's being from necessity when it is is not the same as everything's being from necessity without qualification; and the same is true of what is not.

The same argument also applies to contradictories. It is necessary for everything either to be or not to be, and indeed to be going to be or not be going to be. But one cannot divide [the contradictories] and 30 say that one or the other is necessary. I mean that, for instance, it is necessary for there to be or not to be a sea battle tomorrow, but it is not necessary for a sea battle to happen tomorrow, nor is it [necessary] for one not to happen. It is necessary, however, for it either to happen or not to happen.

And so, since the truth of statements corresponds to how things are, it is clear that, for however many 35 things are as chance has it and are such as to admit contraries, it is necessary for the same to be true of the contradictories. This is just what happens with things that neither always are nor always are not. For in these cases it is necessary for one of the contradictories to be true and the other false. It is not, however, [necessary] for this or that one [more than the other one to be true or false]. Rather, [it is true or false] as chance has it; or [in the case of things that happen usually] one is more true than the other, but not thereby true or false [without qualification].

19b Clearly, then, it is not necessary that of every affirmation and negation of opposites, one is true and one false. For what holds for things that are [always] does not also hold for things that are not [always] but are capable of being and of not being; in these cases it is as we have said.

12

Now that we have determined these points, we should 21a34 consider the relation between negations and affirma- 35 tions of *possible to be* and *not possible to be*, and of *admitting of being* and *not admitting of being*, and about what is impossible and what is necessary. For these questions raise some puzzles.

For suppose that complexes are contradictories if they are ordered in accordance with being and not 21b being. For instance, the negation of *being a man* is *not being a man* rather than *being a not-man*, and the negation of *being a pale man* is *not being a pale man*, rather than *being a not-pale man*. For [otherwise] if either the affirmation or the negation [of a given predicate] is true of everything, then it will be 5 true to say that a log is a not-pale man. If this is true, then it follows that in cases where *being* is not added, what is said instead of *being* will have the same effect. For instance, the negation of 'a man walks' is not 'a not-man walks,' but 'a man does not walk'; for there is no difference between saying that a man walks and 10 saying that a man is walking.

And so, if this is true in every case, then it also follows that the negation of *possible to be* is *possible not to be*, rather than *not possible to be*. On the other hand, it seems that whatever is possible to be is also possible not to be; for whatever can be cut up or can walk can also not walk and not be cut up. The reason for this is that whatever can do these things does not 15 always actually do them, so that the negation will also belong to it; for what can walk can also not walk, and what can be seen can also not be seen. But it is impossible for opposite assertions to be true of the same subject. Hence this [—*possible not to be*—] is not the negation [of *possible to be*]. For it follows 20 from what we have said that either the same thing is both said and negated of the same subject at the same time, or affirmation and negation do not result from the addition of *being* and *not being*.

If, then, the first alternative is impossible, the second is to be chosen; hence the negation of *possible to be* is *not possible to be*. The same argument also applies to *admitting of being*; for the negation of this 25 is *not admitting of being*. And this is also true in the same way in the other cases—for instance, *necessary* and *impossible*. In the previous cases *being* and *not being* were additions, and the subjects were pale and man, whereas in this case being counts as a subject, while *possible* and *admitting of being* are additions that determine possibility and impossibility in the case of being, just as in the previous cases *being* or *not being* determined truth.

The negation of *possible not to be* is *not possible not to be*. That is why the [statements] 'it is possible to be' and 'it is possible not to be' might actually seem to follow from each other. For whatever can be can also not be; for these statements do not contradict (22a) each other. But *possible to be* and *not possible to be* never hold at the same time, since they are opposites. Likewise, *possible not to be* and *not possible not to be* never hold at the same time. In the same way, the negation of *necessary to be* is not *necessary not to be*, but *not necessary to be*; and the negation of *necessary not to be* is *not necessary not to be*. Again, the negation of *impossible to be* is not *impossible not to be*, but *not impossible to be*; and the negation of *impossible not to be* is *not impossible not to be*. And in general, as we have said, one must count being and not being as the subjects, and attach these [qualifications] to being and not being to produce affirmation and negation. And one must suppose the opposite expressions to be these: *possible* and *not possible*, *admitting* and *not admitting*, *impossible* and *not impossible*, *necessary* and *not necessary*, *true* and *not true*.

13

On this basis one thing follows from another in a reasonable way. *Admitting of being* follows from *possible to be*, and the latter follows reciprocally from the former. Moreover, both *not impossible to be* and *not necessary to be* follow from *possible to be*. Both *not necessary not to be* and *not impossible not to be* follow from *possible not to be* and *admitting of not being*. *Necessary not to be* and *impossible to be* follow from *not possible to be* and *not admitting of being*. *Necessary to be* and *impossible not to be* follow from *not possible not to be* and from *not admitting of not being*. What we are saying may be studied in the following table:

	A	B
1.	possible to be	not possible to be
2.	admitting of being	not admitting of being
3.	not impossible to be	impossible to be
4.	not necessary to be	necessary not to be

	C	D
1.	possible not to be	not possible not to be
2.	admitting of not being	not admitting of not being
3.	not impossible not to be	impossible not to be
4.	not necessary not to be	necessary to be

Impossible and *not impossible* follow from *admitting* and *possible*, and from *not admitting* and *not possible*, contradictorily, but conversely. For the negation of *impossible* follows from *possible to be*, and the affirmation from the negation, i.e., *impossible to be* from *not possible to be*—for *impossible to be* is an affirmation, whereas *not impossible* is a negation.

But we must see what is true in the case of *necessary*. It is evident, then, that the same does not apply here, but rather the contraries follow, whereas the contra- (22b) dictories are separated. For *not necessary to be* is not the negation of *necessary not to be*, since both of these admit of being true of the same thing—for what is necessary not to be is not necessary to be.

But perhaps this arrangement of the negations of *necessary* is impossible; for what is necessary to be is also possible to be. Otherwise the negation will follow, since it is necessary either to affirm or deny it, so that if it is not possible to be, it is impossible to be; but then what is necessary to be will turn out to be impossible to be, which is absurd. And yet, *not impossible to be* follows from *possible to be*, and *not necessary to be* follows from *not impossible to be*, so that what is necessary to be turns out to be not necessary to be, which is absurd. And yet, neither *necessary to be* nor *necessary not to be* follows from *possible to be*; for in this case [—*possible to be*—], both [being and not being] admit of happening, whereas, whenever one [of *necessary* and *not necessary*] is true, [the conjunction of] those others [—*possible to be* and *possible not to be*—] will no longer be true. For something is possible to be and not to be at the same time, but if it is necessary for it to be or not to be, it will not be possible to be both.

The remaining option, then, is that *not necessary not to be* follows from *possible to be*; for *not necessary not to be* is also true of what is necessary to be. For this also turns out to be the contradictory to what follows from *not possible to be*; for *impossible to be* and *necessary not to be* follow from *not possible to *be*, and the negation of *necessary not to be* is *not necessary not to be*. These contradictories, then, also follow in the way described, and nothing impossible results if they are arranged this way.

b3 The reason these do not follow in the same way 5 as the others is that *impossible* has the same force as *necessary*, when it is applied in the contrary way. For if something is impossible to be, then it is necessary—not necessary to be, but necessary not to be; and if something is impossible not to be, then it is necessary to be. And so if those follow from *possible* and *not possible* in the same way, then these follow in a contrary way, since *necessary* and *impossible* signify the 10 same, except that, as we said, they are applied conversely.

b29 One might be puzzled about whether *possible to be* follows from *necessary to be*. For if it does not follow, then its contradictory—*not possible to be*—will follow; and if one says that this is not the contradictory, then one must say that *possible not to be* is the contradictory; and both of these are false of what is necessary to be. And yet, on the other hand, it seems that whatever can be cut up can also not be 35 cut up, and that whatever can be can also not be, so that what is necessary to be will turn out to admit of not being, which is false.

It is evident, then, that not everything that can be or can walk can also be the opposite, and that there are cases in which this [presence of both opposites] is not true. This is true first of all in the case of things with nonrational potentialities; fire, for instance, has 23a the potentiality to heat, and has a nonrational potentiality. Now in the case of potentialities involving reason, the same potentiality is for more than one thing, and indeed for contraries. This is not true, however, in the case of all nonrational potentialities, but, as we said, fire cannot both heat and not heat. Nor is it true in the case of things that are always in actuality; but some things, even insofar as they have nonrational 5 potentialities, are at the same time capable of producing opposites. Our remark, however, was meant to make it clear that not every potentiality—not even among potentialities of the same kind—is for opposites.

Now some potentialities are homonymous, since things are said to be potentially something in more than one way. In one case [x is said to have a potentiality for F] because it is true [that x is F], in that it is actually [F]; for instance, something is said to have a potentiality for walking because it is walking, and in general something is said to have a potentiality 10 because it is already actualizing the potentiality it is said to have. In another case [x is said to have a potentiality for F] because it might actualize [the potentiality]; for instance, something is said to have a potentiality for walking because it might walk. This second sort of potentiality applies only to things that can be moved; the first sort also applies to immovable things. In both cases it is true to say, both of what is 15 now walking and in actuality and of what might walk, that [if it has the potentiality to walk or be], it is not impossible for it to walk or be. It is not true, then, to ascribe the second sort of potentiality to what is necessary without qualification, but it is true to ascribe the first sort to it.

And so, since the universal follows from the partial, *possible to be*—though not every sort—follows from *necessary to be*. And presumably in fact what is necessary and what is not necessary are the principles of everything's being or not being, and the other cases 20 should be considered as following from these.

It is evident from what has been said, then, that what is necessarily also is in actuality, so that if everlasting things are prior, actuality is also prior to potentiality. Moreover, some things—the primary substances—are actualities without potentiality, while other things have potentiality; these latter are prior in nature [to the potentiality] but posterior in time. Other things are never actualities but are merely potentialities.

Posterior Analytics

BOOK I

1

71a All teaching and all intellectual learning result from previous cognition. This is clear if we examine all the cases; for this is how the mathematical sciences 5 and all crafts arise. This is also true of both deductive and inductive arguments, since they both succeed in teaching because they rely on previous cognition: deductive arguments begin with premisses we are assumed to understand, and inductive arguments prove the universal by relying on the fact that the particular is already clear. Rhetorical arguments also 10 persuade in the same way, since they rely either on examples (and hence on induction) or on argumentations (and hence on deduction).

Previous cognition is needed in two ways. In some cases we must presuppose that something is (for example, that it is true that everything is either asserted or denied truly [of a given subject]). In other cases we must comprehend what the thing spoken of is (for 15 example, that a triangle signifies this); and in other cases we must do both (for example, we must both comprehend what a unit signifies and presuppose that there is such a thing). For something different is needed to make each of these things clear to us.

We may also recognize that *q* by having previously recognized that *p* and acquiring recognition of *q* at the same time [as we acquire recognition of *r*]. This is how, for instance, we acquire recognition of the cases that fall under the universal of which we have cognition; for we previously knew that, say, every 20 triangle has angles equal to two right angles, but we recognize that this figure in the semicircle is a triangle at the same time as we perform the induction [showing that this figure has two right angles]. For in some cases we learn in this way, (rather than recognizing the last term through the middle); this is true when we reach particulars, i.e., things not said of any subject.

Before we perform the induction or the deduction, 25 we should presumably be said to know in one way but not in another. For if we did not know without qualification whether [a given triangle] is, how could we know without qualification that it has two right angles? But clearly we know it insofar as we know it universally, but we do not know it without qualification. Otherwise we will face the puzzle in the *Meno*, since we will turn out to learn either nothing or else 30 nothing but what we [already] know.

For we should not agree with some people's attempted solution to this puzzle. Do you or do you not know that every pair is even? When you say you do, they produce a pair that you did not think existed and hence did not think was even. They solve this puzzle by saying that one does not know that every pair is even, but rather one knows that what one knows to be a pair is even. In fact, however, [contrary to this solution], one knows that of which one has 71b grasped and still possesses the demonstration, and the demonstration one has grasped is not about whatever one knows to be a triangle or a number, but about every number or triangle without qualification; for [in a demonstration] a premiss is not taken to say that what you know to be a triangle or rectangle is so and so, but, on the contrary, it is taken to apply to every case.

But, I think, it is quite possible for us to know in one way what we are learning, while being ignorant of it in another way. For what is absurd is not that we [already] know in some way the very thing we are learning; the absurdity arises only if we already know it to the precise extent and in the precise way in which we are learning it.

2

We think we know a thing without qualification, and not in the sophistic, coincidental way, whenever we 10 think we recognize the explanation because of which

Reprinted from Aristotle, *Selections*, translated and edited by Terence Irwin and Gail Fine (Indianapolis: Hackett Publishing Company, 1995), by permission of the publisher. The use of brackets within the text indicates insertions not found in the manuscript.

the thing is [so], and recognize both that it is the explanation of that thing and that it does not admit of being otherwise. Clearly, then, knowing is something of this sort; for both those who lack knowledge and those who have it think they are in this condition, 15 but those who have the knowledge are really in it. So whatever is known without qualification cannot be otherwise.

We shall say later whether there is also some other way of knowing; but we certainly say that we know through demonstration. By 'demonstration' I mean a deduction expressing knowledge; by 'expressing knowledge' I mean that having the deduction constitutes having knowledge.

20 If, then, knowing is the sort of thing we assumed it is, demonstrative knowledge must also be derived from things that are true, primary, immediate, better known than, prior to, and explanatory of the conclusion; for this will also ensure that the principles are proper to what is being proved. For these conditions are not necessary for a deduction, but they are necessary for a demonstration, since without them a deduc- 25 tion will not produce knowledge.

[The conclusions] must be true, then, because we cannot know what is not [true] (for example, that the diagonal is commensurate). They must be derived from [premisses] that are primary and indemonstrable, because we will have no knowledge unless we have a demonstration of these [premisses]; for to have non-coincidental knowledge of something demonstrable is to have a demonstration of it.

30 They must be explanatory, better known, and prior. They must be explanatory, because we know something whenever we know its explanation. They must be prior if they are indeed explanatory. And they must be previously cognized not only in the sense that we comprehend them, but also in the sense that we know that they are [true]. Things are prior and better known in two ways; for what is prior by 72a nature is not the same as what is prior to us, nor is what is better known [by nature] the same as what is better known to us. By 'what is prior and better known to us' I mean what is closer to perception, and by 'what is prior and better known without qualification' I mean what is further from perception. What is most universal is furthest from perception, 5 and particulars are closest to it; particular and universal are opposite to each other.

Derivation from primary things is derivation from proper principles. (I mean the same by 'primary things' as I mean by 'principles'.) A principle of demonstration is an immediate premiss, and a premiss is immediate if no others are prior to it. A premiss is one or the other part of a contradiction, and it says one thing of one thing. It is dialectical if it takes 10 either part indifferently, demonstrative if it determinately takes one part because it is true. A contradiction is an opposition which, in itself, has nothing in the middle. The part of the contradiction that asserts something of something is an affirmation, and the part that denies something of something is a denial.

By 'thesis' I mean an immediate principle of deduc- 15 tion that cannot be proved, but is not needed if one is to learn anything at all. By 'axiom' I mean a principle one needs in order to learn anything at all; for there are some things of this sort, and it is especially these to which we usually apply the name.

If a thesis asserts one or the other part of a contradiction—for example, that something is or that some- 20 thing is not—it is an assumption; otherwise it is a definition. For a definition is a thesis (since the arithmetician, for example, lays it down that a unit is what is indivisible in quantity), but it is not an assumption (since what it is to be a unit and that a unit is are not the same).

Since our conviction and knowledge about a thing 25 must be based on our having the sort of deduction we call a demonstration, and since we have this sort of deduction when its premisses obtain, not only must we have previous cognition about all or some of the primary things, but we must also know them better. For if *x* makes *y F*, *x* is more *F* than *y*; if, for instance, 30 we love *y* because of *x*, *x* is loved more than *y*. Hence if the primary things produce knowledge and conviction, we must have more knowledge and conviction about them, since they also produce it about subordinate things.

Now if we know *q*, we cannot have greater conviction about *p* than about *q* unless we either know *p* or are in some condition better than knowledge about *p*. This will result, however, unless previous knowl- 35 edge [of the principles] is the basis of conviction produced by demonstration; for we must have greater conviction about all or some of the principles than about the conclusion.

If we are to have knowledge through demonstration, then not only must we know the principles better and have greater conviction about them than about 72b what is proved, but we must also not find anything more convincing or better known that is opposed to the principles and allows us to deduce a mistaken conclusion contrary [to the correct one]. For no one who has knowledge without qualification can be persuaded out of it.

3

5 Some people think that because [knowledge through demonstration] requires knowledge of the primary things, there is no knowledge; others think that there is knowledge, and that everything [knowable] is demonstrable. Neither of these views is either true or necessary.

The first party—those who assume that there is no knowledge at all—claim that we face an infinite regress. They assume that we cannot know posterior things because of prior things, if there are no primary things. Their assumption is correct, since it is impossible to go through an infinite series. If, on the other hand, the regress stops, and there are principles, these are, in their view, unrecognizable, since these principles cannot be demonstrated, and, in these people's view, demonstration is the only way of knowing. But if we cannot know the primary things, then neither can we know without qualification or fully the things 15 derived from them; we can know them only conditionally, on the assumption that we can know the primary things.

The other party agree that knowledge results only from demonstration, but they claim that it is possible to demonstrate everything, since they take circular and reciprocal demonstration to be possible.

We reply that not all knowledge is demonstrative, 20 and in fact knowledge of the immediate premisses is indemonstrable. Indeed, it is evident that this must be so; for if we must know the prior things (i.e., those from which the demonstration is derived), and if eventually the regress stops, these immediate premisses must be indemonstrable. Besides this, we also say that there is not only knowledge but also some origin of knowledge, which gives us cognition of the definitions.

25 Unqualified demonstration clearly cannot be circular, if it must be derived from what is prior and better known. For the same things cannot be both prior and posterior to the same things at the same time, except in different ways (so that, for example, some things are prior relative to us, and others are prior without qualification—this is the way induction makes something known). If this is so, our definition of unquali- 30 fied knowledge will be faulty, and there will be two sorts of knowledge; or [rather] perhaps the second sort of demonstration is not unqualified demonstration, since it is derived from what is [merely] better known to us.

Those who allow circular demonstration must concede not only the previous point, but also that they are simply saying that something is if it is. On these terms it is easy to prove anything. This is clear if we 35 consider three terms—for it does not matter whether we say the demonstration turns back through many or few terms, or through few or two. For suppose that if A is, necessarily B is, and that if B is, necessarily C is; it follows that if A is, C will be. Suppose, then, that if A is, then B necessarily is, and if B is, A is 73a (since this is what circular argument is), and let A be C. In that case, to say that if B is, A is is to say that [if B is,] C is; this [is to say] that if A is, C is. But since C is the same as A, it follows that those who allow circular demonstration simply say that if 5 A is, then A is. On these terms it is easy to prove anything.

But not even this is possible, except for things that are reciprocally predicated, such as distinctive properties. If, then, one thing is laid down, we have proved that it is never necessary for anything else to be the case. (By 'one thing' I mean that neither one term nor one thesis is enough; two theses are the fewest 10 [needed for a demonstration], since they are also the fewest needed for a deduction.) If, then, A follows from B and C, and these follow from each other and from A, then in this way it is possible to prove all the postulates from each other in the first figure, as we proved in the discussion of deduction. We also proved 15 that in the other figures, the result is either no deduction or none relevant to the things assumed. But it is not at all possible to give a circular proof of things that are not reciprocally predicated. And so, since there are few things that are reciprocally predicated in demonstrations, it is clearly empty and impossible to say that demonstration is reciprocal and that for this reason everything is demonstrable. 20

4

Since what is known without qualification cannot be otherwise, what is known by demonstrative knowledge will be necessary. Demonstrative knowledge is what we have by having a demonstration; hence a demonstration is a deduction from things that are necessary. We must, then, find from what and from what sorts of things demonstrations are derived. Let us first determine what we mean by '[belonging] in every case,' 'in its own right,' and 'universal.'

By '[belonging] in every case' I mean what belongs not [merely] in some cases, or at some times, as opposed to others. If, for example, animal belongs to every man, it follows that if it is true to say that this is a man, it is also true to say that he is an animal, and that if he is a man now, he is also an animal now. The same applies if it is true to say that there is a point in every line. A sign of this is the fact that when we are asked whether something belongs in every case, we advance objections by asking whether it fails to belong either in some cases or at some times.

A belongs to B in its own right in the following cases:

(a) A belongs to B in what B is, as, for example, line belongs to triangle, and point to line; for here the essence of B is composed of A, and A is present in the account that says what B is.

(b) A belongs to B, and B itself is present in the account revealing what A is. In this way straight and curved, for instance, belong to line, while odd and even, prime and compound, equilateral and oblong, belong in this way to number. In all these cases either line or number is present in the account saying what [straight or odd, for example,] is. Similarly in other cases, this is what I mean by saying that A belongs to B in its own right. What belongs in neither of these ways I call coincidental—as, for instance, musical or pale belongs to animal.

(c) A is not said of something else B that is the subject of A. A walker or a pale thing, for example, is a walker or a pale thing by being something else; but a substance—i.e., whatever signifies a this—is not what it is by being something else. I say, then, that what is not said of a subject is [a thing] in its own right, whereas what is said of a subject is a coincident.

(d) Moreover, in another way, if A belongs to B because of B itself, then A belongs to B in its own right; if A belongs to B, but not because of B itself, then A is coincidental to B. If, for example, lightning flashed while you were walking, that was coincidental; for the lightning was not caused by your walking but, as we say, was a coincidence. If, however, A belongs to B because of B itself, then it belongs to B in its own right. If, for example, an animal was killed in being sacrificed, the killing belongs to the sacrificing in its own right, since the animal was killed because it was sacrificed, and it was not a coincidence that the animal was killed in being sacrificed.

Hence in the case of unqualified objects of knowledge, whenever A is said to belong to B in its own right, either because B is present in A and A is predicated of B, or because A is present in B, then A belongs to B because of B itself and necessarily. [It belongs necessarily] either because it is impossible for A not to belong to B or because it is impossible for neither A nor its opposite (for example, straight and crooked, or odd and even) to belong to B (for example, a line or a number). For a contrary is either a privation or a contradiction in the same genus; even, for example, is what is not odd among numbers, insofar as this follows. Hence, if it is necessary either to affirm or to deny, then what belongs to a subject in its own right necessarily belongs to that subject.

Let this, then, be our definition of what belongs in every case and of what belongs to something in its own right.

By 'universal' I mean what belongs to its subject in every case and in its own right, and insofar as it is itself. It is evident, then, that what is universal belongs to things necessarily. What belongs to the subject in its own right is the same as what belongs to it insofar as it is itself. A point and straightness, for instance, belong to a line in its own right, since they belong to a line insofar as it is a line. Similarly, two right angles belong to a triangle insofar as it is a triangle, since a triangle is equal in its own right to two right angles.

A universal belongs [to a species] whenever it is proved of an instance that is random and primary. Having two right angles, for instance, is not universal to figure; for though you may prove that some figure has two right angles, you cannot prove it of any random figure, nor do you use any random figure in proving it, since a quadrilateral is a figure but does not have angles equal to two right angles. Again, a random isosceles triangle has angles equal to two right angles, but it is not the primary case, since the triangle is prior. If, then, a random triangle is the 40 primary case that is proved to have two right angles, or whatever it is, then that property belongs universally 74a to this case primarily, and the demonstration holds universally of this case in its own right. It holds of the other cases in a way, but not in their own right; it does not even hold universally of the isosceles triangle, but more widely.

BOOK II

8

93a We must consider over again what is right and what is wrong in what has been said, and what a definition is, and whether or not there is any sort of demonstration of what something is.

Now, we say that knowing what a thing is is the same as knowing the explanation of whether it is. 5 The argument for this is that there is some explanation [of whether a thing is] and this is either the same [as what the thing is] or something else, and if it is something else, then it is either demonstrable or indemonstrable. If, then, it is something else and is demonstrable, the explanation must be a middle term, and must be proved in the first figure, since what is being proved is universal and affirmative.

10 One type of proof, then, would be the one examined just now—proving what something is through something else. For in proofs of what a thing is it is necessary for the middle term to be what [the thing] is, and in proofs of distinctive properties it is necessary for the middle term to be a distinctive property. Hence in one case you will, and in another case you will not, prove the essence of the same object. Now this 15 type of proof, as has been said before, is not a demonstration, but a logical deduction of what something is.

Let us say, then, starting again from the beginning, how a demonstration is possible. In some cases we seek the reason for something when we have already grasped the fact, and in other cases they both become clear at the same time; but it is never possible to recognize the reason before the fact. It is clear, then, that in the same way we cannot recognize the essence of a thing without knowing that the thing is; for it is 20 impossible to know what a thing is if we do not know whether the thing is.

Our grasp of whether a thing is is in some cases [merely] coincidental, while in other cases we grasp whether a thing is by grasping some aspect of the thing itself. We may grasp, for instance, whether thunder is, by grasping that it is some sort of noise in the clouds; whether an eclipse is, by grasping that it is some sort of deprivation of light; whether a man is, by grasping that he is some sort of animal; and whether a soul is, by grasping that it initiates its own motion.

In cases where we know [only] coincidentally that 25 a thing is, we necessarily have no grasp of what the thing is, since we do not even know that the thing is; to inquire into what a thing is when we have not grasped that the thing is is to inquire into nothing. But in the cases where we do grasp some [aspect of the thing itself], it is easier [to inquire into what the thing is]. And so we acquire knowledge of what the thing is to the extent that we know that the thing is.

As a case where we grasp some aspect of what a thing is, let us take first of all the following: Let A 30 be an eclipse, C the moon, and B blocking by the earth. Then to inquire into whether it is eclipsed or not is to inquire into whether B is or not. This question is just the same as the question whether there is an account of [A]; and if there is an account of [A], we also say that [A] is. Or perhaps we ask which of two contradictories—for example, the triangle's having or not having two right angles—satisfies the account. 35

When we find [the account], we know both the fact and the reason at the same time, if [we reach the fact] through immediate [premisses]; if [the premisses are not immediate], then we know the fact, but not the reason. For instance, let C be the moon, A an eclipse, and B the inability to cast a shadow at the full moon when there is nothing apparent between us and it. Suppose, then, that B (inability to cast a 93b shadow when there is nothing between us and it) belongs to C, and that A (being eclipsed) belongs to B. In that case it is clear that the moon has been eclipsed, but it is not thereby clear why it has been eclipsed; we know that there is an eclipse, but we do not know what it is.

If it is clear that A belongs to C, then [to inquire

5 into] why it belongs is to inquire into what B is—whether it is the blocking [by the earth] or the rotation of the moon or its extinguishing. And this is the account of one extreme term—in this case the account of A, since an eclipse is a blocking by the earth.

[Or take another example:] What is thunder? Extinguishing of fire in a cloud. Why does it thunder? Because the fire is extinguished in the cloud. Let C 10 be a cloud, A thunder, B extinguishing of fire. Then B belongs to C, a cloud (since the fire is extinguished in it), and A, the noise, belongs to B; and in fact B is the account of A, the first extreme term. And if there is a further middle term [explaining] B, this 15 will be found from the remaining accounts [of A].

We have said, then, how one grasps the what-it-is, and how it comes to be recognized. And so it turns out that though the what-it-is is neither deduced nor demonstrated, still it is made clear through deduction and demonstration. Hence, in the case where the explanation of a thing is something other than the thing, a demonstration is required for recognition of what the thing is, even though there is no demonstra- 20 tion of what the thing is, as we also said in setting out the puzzles.

9

Some things have something else as their explanation, while other things do not; and so it is clear that in some cases the what-it-is is immediate and a principle. In these cases we must assume (or make evident in some other way) both that it is and what it is—as the 25 students of arithmetic do, since they assume both what the unit is and that it is. In the other cases—those that have a middle term, and where something else is the explanation of their essence—it is possible, as we said, to make clear what something is through demonstration, even though the what-it-is is not demonstrated.

10

Since a definition is said to be an account of the 30 what-it-is, it is evident that one type will be an account of what a name or some other name-like account signifies—for example, what triangle signifies. When we have grasped that [a thing] is [this], we inquire into why it is; but it is difficult to grasp in this way [why a thing is], given that we do not know that the thing is. The reason for this difficulty has been mentioned before: [if we know only what a thing's name signifies], we do not even know whether or not the thing is, unless [we know this] coincidentally. (An account is unified in either of two ways—either by connection, like the *Iliad*, or by revealing one [property] of one [subject] non-coincidentally.)

This, then, is one definition of definition; another sort of definition is an account revealing why something is. Hence the first type of definition signifies but does not prove, whereas the second type will 94a clearly be a sort of demonstration of what something is, but differently arranged—for saying why it thunders is different from saying what thunder is. We will answer the first question by saying 'Because fire is extinguished in the clouds'. And what is thunder? A 5 noise of fire being extinguished in the clouds. These are two different statements, then, of the same account; the first is a continuous demonstration, the second a definition. Moreover, a definition of thunder is noise in the clouds, which is the conclusion of a demonstration of what it is. In contrast to this, the definition of something immediate is an indemonstrable positing of what it is.

One sort of definition, then, is an indemonstrable 10 account of the what-it-is; a second is a deduction of the what-it-is, differing in arrangement from a demonstration; and a third is the conclusion of a demonstration of the what-it-is.

What we have said, then, has made it evident, first, in what way the what-it-is is demonstrable and in 15 what way it is not, and what things are demonstrable and what things are not; secondly, in how many ways a definition is spoken of, in what way it proves the what-it-is and in what way it does not, and what things have definitions and what things do not; and, thirdly, how definition is related to demonstration, and in what way there can be both definition and demonstration of the same thing and in what way there cannot.

19

It is evident, then, what deduction and demonstration 99b are and how they come about; the same holds for demonstrative knowledge, since it is the same [as demonstration]. But how do we come to recognize principles, and what state recognizes them? This will be clear from the following argument, if we first state the puzzles.

20 We said before that we cannot know through demonstration without recognizing the first, immediate principles. But one might be puzzled about whether cognition of the immediate principles is or is not the same [as knowledge of truths derived from them]; whether there is knowledge of each, or knowledge of 25 one but something else of the other; and whether the states are acquired rather than [innately] present in us without our noticing them.

It would be absurd if we had the principles [innately]; for then we would possess cognition that is more exact than demonstration, but without noticing it. If, on the other hand, we acquire the principles and do not previously possess them, how could we recognize and learn them from no prior knowledge? 30 That is impossible, as we also said in the case of demonstration. Evidently, then, we can neither possess the principles [innately] nor acquire them if we are ignorant and possess no state [of knowledge]. Hence we must have some [suitable] potentiality, but not one that is at a level of exactness superior to that of the knowledge we acquire.

35 All animals evidently have [such a potentiality], since they have the innate discriminative potentiality called perception. Some animals that have perception (though not all of them) also retain [in memory] what they perceive; those that do not retain it have no cognition outside perception (either none at all or none about what is not retained), but those that do 100a retain it keep what they have perceived in their souls even after they have perceived. When this has happened many times a [further] difference arises: in some, but not all, cases, a rational account arises from the retention of perceptions.

From perception, then, as we say, memory arises, 5 and from repeated memory of the same thing experience arises; for a number of memories make up one experience. From experience, or [rather] from the whole universal that has settled in the soul—the one apart from the many, whatever is present as one and the same in all of them—arises a principle of craft (if it is about what comes to be) or of science (if it is about what is).

10 Hence the relevant states are not [innate] in us in any determinate character and do not arise from states that have a better grasp on cognition; rather, they arise from perception. It is like what happens in a battle when there is a retreat: first one soldier makes a stand, then a second, then another, until they reach a starting point. The soul's nature gives it a potentiality to be affected in this way.

15 Let us state again, then, what we stated, but not perspicuously, before. When one of the undifferentiated things makes a stand, that is the first universal in the soul; for though one perceives the particular, 100b perception is of the universal—of man, for instance, not of Callias the man. Again, in these [universals something else] makes a stand, until what has no parts and is universal makes a stand—first, for example, a certain sort of animal makes a stand, until animal does, and in this [universal] something else makes a stand in the same way. Clearly, then, we must recog- 5 nize the first things by induction; for that is also how perception produces the universal in us.

Among our intellectual states that grasp the truth, some—knowledge and understanding—are always true, whereas others—for example, belief and reasoning—admit of being false; and understanding is the only sort of state that is more exact than knowledge. Since the principles of demonstration are better known [than the conclusions derived from them], 10 and since all knowledge requires an account, it follows that we can have no knowledge of the principles. Since only understanding can be truer than knowledge, we must have understanding of the principles.

The same conclusion follows from the further point that since the principle of a demonstration is not a demonstration, the principle of knowledge is not knowledge. If, then, the only sort of state besides 15 knowledge that is [always] true is understanding, understanding must be the principle of knowledge. The principle, then, will grasp the principle, and, similarly, all knowledge will grasp its object.

Physics

BOOK I

1

184a In every line of inquiry into something that has principles or causes or elements, we achieve knowledge—that is, scientific knowledge—by cognizing them; for we think we cognize a thing when we know its primary causes and primary principles, all the way to its elements. 15 Clearly, then, it is also true in the science of nature that our first task is to determine the principles.

The natural path is to start from what is better known and more perspicuous to us, and to advance to what is more perspicuous and better known by nature; for what is better known to us is not the same as what is better known without qualification. We must advance in this way, then, from what is less 20 perspicuous by nature but more perspicuous to us, to what is more perspicuous and better known by nature.

The things that, most of all, are initially clear and perspicuous to us are inarticulate wholes; later, as we articulate them, the elements and principles come to be known from them. We must, then, advance from universals to particulars; for the whole is better 25 known in perception, and the universal is a sort of 184b whole, since it includes many things as parts. The same is true, in a way, of names in relation to their accounts. For a name—for instance, 'circle'—signifies a sort of whole and signifies indefinitely, whereas the definition [of a circle] articulates it by stating the particular [properties]. Again, children begin by calling all men 'father' and all women 'mother'; only later do they distinguish different men and different women.

7

30 Let us, then, give our own account of coming to be, in the following way. And first let us deal with all of coming to be; for the natural procedure is to speak first about what is common to every case, and then to study what is special to each case.

When we say that something comes to be one thing from being another and different thing, we are speaking about either simple or compound things. What I mean is this: It is possible that a man comes to be musical, that the not-musical thing comes to 35 be musical, and that the not-musical man comes to 190a be a musical man. By 'simple thing coming to be [*F*]' I mean the man and the not-musical thing; and by 'simple thing that comes into being' I mean the musical thing. By 'compound' I mean both the thing that comes into being and what comes to be that thing, whenever we say that the not-musical man comes to be a musical man. 5

In one type of case we say not only that something comes to be *F*, but also that it comes to be *F from* being *G*; for instance, [the man not only comes to be musical, but also comes to be] musical from being not-musical. But we do not say this for all [properties]; for [the man] did not come to be musical from being a man, but rather the man came to be musical.

When something comes to be *F* (in the sense in which we say a simple thing comes to be [something]), in some cases it remains when it comes to 10 be *F*, and in other cases it does not remain. The man, for instance, remains a man and is still a man when he comes to be musical, whereas the not-musical or unmusical thing, either simple or compound, does not remain.

Now that we have made these distinctions, here is something we can grasp from every case of coming to be, if we look at them all in the way described. In 15 every case there must be some subject that comes to be [something]; even if it is one in number, it is not one in form, since being a man is not the same as being an unmusical thing. (By 'in form' I mean the same as 'in account'.) One thing [that comes to be] remains, and one does not remain. The thing that is

Reprinted from Aristotle, *Selections*, translated and edited by Terence Irwin and Gail Fine (Indianapolis: Hackett Publishing Company, 1995), by permission of the publisher.

The use of brackets within the text indicates insertions not found in the manuscript.

not opposite remains, since the man remains; but the 20 not-musical thing, or the unmusical thing, does not remain. Nor does the thing compounded from both (for instance, the unmusical man) remain.

We say that something comes to be *F* from being *G*, but not that the *G* comes to be *F*, more often in cases where *G* does not remain; for instance, we say that [a man] comes to be musical from being unmusical, but not that [the unmusical comes to be musical] from a man. Still, sometimes we speak 25 in the same way in cases where *G* remains; we say, for instance, that a statue comes to be from bronze, but not that the bronze comes to be a statue. If, however, something comes to be *F* from being *G*, where *G* is opposite to *F* and *G* does not remain, we speak in both ways, saying both that something comes to be *F* from being *G* and that the *G* comes to be *F*; for it is true both that the man comes to be musical from being unmusical and that the unmusical one comes to be musical. That is why we also say the same about the compound: we say 30 both that the musical man comes to be musical from being an unmusical man and that the unmusical man comes to be musical.

Things are said to come to be in many ways, and some things are said not to come to be, but to come to be something; only substances are said to come to be without qualification. In the other cases it is evident that there must be some subject that comes to be [something]; for in fact, when [something] comes 35 to be of some quantity or quality, or relative to another, or somewhere, something is the subject [underlying the change], because a substance is the only 190b thing that is never said of any other subject, whereas everything else is said of a substance.

However, substances—the things that are without qualification—also come to be from some subject. This will become evident if we examine it. For in every case there is something that is a subject from which the thing that comes to be comes to be, as 5 plants and animals come to be from seed.

Some of the things that come to be without qualification do so by change of figure (for instance, a statue); some by addition (for instance, growing things); some by subtraction (for instance, Hermes from the stone); some by composition (for instance, a house); some by alteration (for instance, things changing in accordance with their matter). It is evident that everything that comes to be in this way comes to be from a subject. 10

And so it is clear from what has been said that in every case, what comes to be is composite: there is something that comes into being and something that comes to be this. And this latter thing is of two sorts: either the subject or the opposite. I mean, for instance, that the unmusical is opposite, and the man is subject; and that the lack of figure, shape, and order is the 15 opposite, and the bronze, stone, or gold is the subject.

Suppose, then, that there are indeed causes and principles of natural things, from which they primarily are and have come to be—not come to be coincidentally, but come to be what each thing is called in accordance with its essence. It evidently follows that everything comes to be from the subject and the 20 shape. For in a way the musical man is composed from man and musical, since you will analyze him into their accounts. It is clear, then, that whatever comes to be does so from these things.

The subject is one in number but two in form. Man, gold, and matter in general, is countable, since 25 it is a this more [than the privation is], and what comes to be comes to be from it not coincidentally. The privation—the contrariety—is a coincident. The form is one—for instance, structure, musicality, or anything else predicated in this way.

Hence we should say that in one way there are two principles, and that in another way there are three. 30 In one way they are contraries—if, for instance, one were to speak of the musical and the unmusical, or the hot and the cold, or the ordered and the disordered. But in another way they are not contraries, since contraries cannot be affected by each other. This [puzzle about how becoming is possible] is also solved by the fact that the subject is something different, since it is not a contrary. 35

Hence, in a way the principles are no more numerous than the contraries, but, one might say, they are two in number. On the other hand, because they differ in being, they are not two in every way, but 191a three; for being man is different from being unmusical, and being shapeless is different from being bronze.

We have said, then, how many principles are relevant to the coming to be of natural things, and we have described the different ways they should be counted. And it is clear that some subject must under- 5 lie the contraries, and that there must be two contraries. In another way, however, there need not be two; for just one of the contraries is enough, by its absence or presence, to produce the thing.

The nature that is subject is knowable by analogy. For as bronze is to a statue, or wood is to a bed, or 10 as the shapeless before it acquires a shape is to anything else that has a shape, so the nature that is subject is to a substance, a this, and a being.

This, then, is one principle; it is not one or a being in the way a this is. Another principle is the one specified by the account, and a third is the contrary of this, the privation. The way in which these are 15 two, and the way in which they are more than two, has been stated above.

First, then, it was said that only the contraries were principles. Later we added that something further is needed as subject and that there must be three principles. And from what we have said now it is evident how the contraries differ, how the principles are related to one another, and what the subject is. 20 It is not yet clear, however, whether the form or the subject is substance. Still, it is clear that there are three principles, and in what way there are three, and what sorts of things they are. This, then, should allow us to observe how many principles there are, and what they are.

8

This is also the only solution to the puzzle raised by the earlier philosophers, as we shall now explain. 25 Those who were the first to search for the truth philosophically and for the nature of beings were diverted and, so to speak, pushed off the track by inexperience. They say that nothing that is either comes to be or perishes. For, they say, what comes to be must come to be either from what is or from what is not, and coming to be is impossible in both cases; for what is cannot come to be (since it already is), while nothing can come to be from what is not (since there must be some subject). And then, having reached this result, they make things worse by going on to say that there is no plurality, but only being itself.

They accepted this belief for the reason mentioned. 30 We reply as follows: The claim that something comes to be from what is or from what is not, or that what is or what is not acts on something or is acted on or comes to be anything whatever, is in one way no different from the claim that, for instance, a doctor 191b acts on something or is acted on, or is or comes to be something from being a doctor. We say this about a doctor in two ways; and so, clearly, we also speak in two ways when we say that something is or comes to be something from what is, and that what is is acting on something or being acted on.

Now a doctor builds a house, not insofar as he is a doctor, but insofar as he is a housebuilder; and he 5 becomes pale, not insofar as he is a doctor, but insofar as he is dark. But he practices medicine, or loses his medical knowledge, insofar as he is a doctor. We speak in the fullest sense of a doctor acting on something or being acted on, or coming to be something, from being a doctor, if it is insofar as he is a doctor that he is acted on in this way or produces these things or comes to be these things. So it is also clear that coming to be from what is not signifies this: coming to be from it insofar as it is not. 10

The early philosophers failed to draw this distinction and gave up the question. This ignorance led them into more serious ignorance—so serious that they thought nothing else [besides what already is] either is or comes to be, and so they did away with all coming to be.

We agree with them in saying that nothing comes to be without qualification from what is not, but we say that things come to be in a way—for instance, 15 coincidentally—from what is not. For something comes to be from the privation, which in itself is not and which does not belong to the thing [when it has come to be]. But this causes surprise, and it seems impossible that something should come to be in this way from what is not.

Similarly, there is no coming to be, except coincidentally, from what is, or of what is. But coincidentally what is also comes to be, in the same way as if animal came to be from animal and a certain animal from 20 a certain animal. Suppose, for instance, that a dog came to be from a horse. For the dog would come to be not only from a certain animal, but also from animal, though not insofar as it is animal (for that is already present). But if a certain [sort of] animal is to come to be, not coincidentally, it will not be from animal; and if a certain thing that is [is to come to be], it will not be from what is, nor from what is not. 25 For we have said what 'from what is not' signifies—

i.e., insofar as it is not. Further, we are not doing away with [the principle that] everything is or is not.

This is one way [of solving this puzzle]. Another is [to note] that the same things can be spoken of in accordance with potentiality and actuality; this is discussed more exactly elsewhere.

30 And so, as we have said, we have solved the puzzles that compelled people to do away with some of the things we have mentioned. For this is why earlier thinkers were also diverted from the road leading them to [an understanding of] coming to be, perishing, and change in general. For if they had seen this nature [of the subject], that would have cured all their ignorance.

BOOK II

1

192b Some existing things are natural, while others are due to other causes. Those that are natural are animals 10 and their parts, plants, and the simple bodies, such as earth, fire, air and water; for we say that these things and things of this sort are natural. All these things evidently differ from those that are not naturally constituted, since each of them has within itself a 15 principle of motion and stability in place, in growth and decay, or in alteration.

In contrast to these, a bed, a cloak, or any other [artifact]—insofar as it is described as such, [i.e., as a bed, a cloak, or whatever], and to the extent that it is a product of a craft—has no innate impulse to change; but insofar as it is coincidentally made of 20 stone or earth or a mixture of these, it has an innate impulse to change, and just to that extent. This is because a nature is a type of principle and cause of motion and stability within those things to which it primarily belongs in their own right and not coincidentally. (By 'not coincidentally' I mean, for instance, the following: Someone who is a doctor might cause 25 himself to be healthy, but it is not insofar as he is being healed that he has the medical science; on the contrary, it is coincidental that the same person is a doctor and is being healed, and that is why the two characteristics are sometimes separated from each other.)

The same is true of everything else that is produced, since no such thing has within itself the principle of its own production. In some things (for instance, a 30 house or any other product of handicraft) the principle comes from outside, and it is within other things. In other things (those that might turn out to be coincidental causes for themselves) the principle is within them, but not in their own right.

A nature, then, is what we have said; and the things that have a nature are those that have this sort of principle. All these things are substances; for [a substance] is a sort of subject, and a nature is invariably in a subject. The things that are in accordance with 35 nature include both these and whatever belongs to them in their own right, as traveling upward belongs to fire—for this neither is nor has a nature, but is 193a natural and in accordance with nature. We have said, then, what nature is, and what is natural and in accordance with nature.

To attempt to prove that there is such a thing as nature would be ridiculous; for it is evident that there are many things of the sort we have described. To prove what is evident from what is not evident betrays 5 an inability to discriminate what is known because of itself from what is not. (It is clearly possible to suffer from this inability: someone blind from birth might still make deductions about colors.) And so such people are bound to argue about [mere] names and to understand nothing.

Some people think that the nature and substance 10 of a natural thing is the primary constituent present in it, having no order in its own right, so that the nature of a bed, for instance, [would be] the wood, and the nature of a statue [would be] the bronze. A sign of this, according to Antiphon,[1] is the fact that, if you were to bury a bed and the rotting residue were to become able to sprout, the result would be wood, not a bed. He thinks that this is because the conven- 15 tional arrangement, i.e., the craft [making the wood into a bed], is a [mere] coincident of the wood, whereas the substance is what remains continuously while it is affected in these ways. And if each of these things is related to something else in the same way (bronze and gold, for instance, to water; bones and wood to earth; and so on with anything else), that 20 thing is their nature and substance.

This is why some people say that fire or earth or

1. [Antiphon (c. 479–411 B.C.) was an Athenian orator.—S.M.C.]

air or water is the nature of the things that exist; some say it is some of these, others say it is all of them. For whenever any of these people supposed one, or more than one, of these things to be [the primary constituent], he takes this or these to be all the sub- 25 stance there is, and he takes everything else to be attributes, states, and conditions of these things; and each of these is held to be everlasting, since they do not change from themselves, but the other things come to be and are destroyed an unlimited number of times.

This, then, is one way we speak of a nature: as the primary matter that is a subject for each thing that 30 has within itself a principle of motion and change.

In another way the nature is the shape, i.e., the form in accordance with the account. For just as we speak of craftsmanship in what is in accordance with craft and is crafted, so also we speak of nature in what is in accordance with nature and is natural. But if something were only potentially a bed and still lacked 35 the form of a bed, we would not yet speak of craftsmanship or of a product in accordance with craft; nor would we say the corresponding thing about anything that is constituted naturally. For what is only poten- 193b tially flesh or bone does not have its nature, and is not naturally flesh or bone, until it acquires the form in accordance with the account by which we define flesh or bone and say what it is. In another way, then, the nature is the shape and form of things that have within themselves a principle of motion; this form is 5 not separable except in account. (What is composed of form and matter—for instance, a man—is not a nature, but is natural.)

Indeed, the form is the nature more than the matter is. For something is called [flesh, bone, and so on] when it is actually so, more than when it is only potentially so. Further, a man comes to be from a man, but not a bed from a bed. In fact that is why some say that the nature of the bed is not the shape 10 but the wood, because if it were to sprout the result would be wood, not a bed. If this shows that the wood is the nature, then the shape is also the nature, since a man comes to be from a man. Further, nature, as applied to coming to be, is really a road towards nature; it is not like medical treatment, which is a road not towards medical science, but towards health. 15 For medical treatment necessarily proceeds *from* medical science, not *towards* medical science. But nature [as coming to be] is not related to nature in this way; rather, what is growing, insofar as it is growing, proceeds from something towards something [else]. What is it, then, that grows? Not what it is growing from, but what it is growing into. Therefore, the shape is the nature.

Shape and nature are spoken of in two ways; for the privation is also form in a way. We must consider 20 later whether or not there is a privation and a contrary in unqualified coming to be.

2

Since we have distinguished the different ways we speak of nature, we should next consider how the mathematician differs from the student of nature; for natural bodies certainly have surfaces, solids, lengths, and points, which are what the mathematician stud- 25 ies. We should also consider whether astronomy is different from or a part of the study of nature; for it would be absurd if a student of nature ought to know what the sun or moon is but need not know any of their coincidents in their own right—especially since it is evident that students of nature also discuss the shape of the sun and moon, and specifically whether 30 or not the earth and heaven are spherical.

These things are certainly the concern of both the mathematician and the student of nature. But the mathematician is not concerned with them insofar as each is the limit of a natural body, and he does not study the coincidents of a natural body insofar as they belong to a natural body. That is why he also separates these coincidents; for they are separable in thought from motion, and his separating them makes 35 no difference and results in no falsehood.

Those who say there are Ideas do not notice that they do this too; for they separate natural objects, though these are less separable than mathematical 194a objects. This would be clear if one tried to state the formulae of both natural and mathematical objects—of the things themselves and of their coincidents. For odd and even, straight and curved, and also number, line, and point do not involve motion, whereas flesh, 5 bones, and man do—we speak of them as we speak of the snub nose, not as we speak of the curved.

This is also clear from the parts of mathematics that are more related to the study of nature—for instance, optics, harmonics, and astronomy. These

10 are in a way the reverse of geometry; for geometry investigates natural lines, but not insofar as they are natural, whereas optics investigates mathematical lines, but insofar as they are natural, not insofar as they are mathematical.

Since we speak of nature in two ways—both as form and as matter—we should study it as though we were investigating what snubness is, and so we should study natural objects neither independently 15 of their matter nor [simply] insofar as they have matter. For indeed, since there are these two types of nature, there might be a puzzle about which one the student of nature should study. Perhaps the compound of the two? If so, then also each of them. Then is it the same or a different discipline that knows each one of them?

If we judge by the early thinkers, the student of 20 nature would seem to study [only] matter, since Empedocles[2] and Democritus[3] touched only slightly on form and essence. Craft, however, imitates nature, and the same science knows both the form and the matter up to a point. The doctor, for instance, knows health, and also the bile and phlegm in which health [is realized]; similarly, the housebuilder knows both 25 the form of the house and that its matter is bricks and wood; and the same is true in the other cases. The science of nature, therefore, must also know both types of nature.

Moreover the same discipline studies both what something is for—i.e., the end—and whatever is for the end. Nature is an end and what something is for; 30 for whenever a continuous motion has some end this sort of terminus is also what the motion is for. That is why it was ludicrous for the poet to say 'He has reached the end he was born for'; it was ludicrous because by 'end' we mean not every terminus but only the best one.

For crafts produce their matter (some by producing it without qualification, others by making it suitable for their work); and we use all [matter] as being for 35 our sake, since we are also an end in a way. (For what something is for is of two sorts, as we said in *On Philosophy*.)

There are two crafts that control the matter and 194b involve knowledge: the craft that uses [the matter] and the craft that directs this productive craft. Hence the using craft also directs in a way, but with the difference that the directing craft knows the form, whereas the productive craft knows the matter. For 5 instance, the pilot knows what sort of form the rudder has, and he prescribes [how to produce it], whereas the boatbuilder knows what sort of wood and what sorts of motions are needed to make it. With products of a craft, then, we produce the matter for the sake of the product; with natural things, the matter is already present.

Further, matter is relative; for there is one [sort of] matter for one form, and another for another.

How much, then, must the student of nature know 10 about form and what-it-is? Perhaps as much as the doctor knows about sinews, or the smith about bronze—enough to know what something is for. And he must confine himself to things that are separable in form but are in matter—for a man is born from a man and the sun. But it is a task for first philosophy 15 to determine what is separable and what the separable is like.

3

Now that we have determined these points, we should consider how many and what sorts of causes there are. For our inquiry aims at knowledge; and we think we know something only when we find the reason why it is so, i.e., when we find its primary cause. 20 Clearly, then, we must also find the reason why in the case of coming to be, perishing, and every sort of natural change, so that when we know their principles we can try to refer whatever we are searching for to these principles.

In one way, then, that from which, as a [constituent] present in it, a thing comes to be is said to be that thing's cause—for instance, the bronze and silver, 25 and their genera, are causes of the statue and the bowl.

In another way, the form—i.e., the pattern—is a cause. The form is the account (and the genera of the account) of the essence (for instance, the cause of an octave is the ratio two to one, and in general number), and the parts that are in the account.

Further, the source of the primary principle of change or stability is a cause. For instance, the adviser 30

2. [Regarding Empedocles, see Plato's *Meno*, n.6.]

3. [Democritus (c. 460–c. 370 B.C.) was a Greek philosopher who held that all things were composed of unchangeable atoms.]

is a cause [of the action], and a father is a cause of his child; and in general the producer is a cause of the product, and the initiator of the change is a cause of what is changed.

Further, something's end—i.e., what it is for—is its cause, as health is of walking. For why does he 35 walk? We say, 'To be healthy'; and in saying this we think we have provided the cause. The same is true of all the intermediate steps that are for the end, where something else has initiated the motion, as, 195a for example, slimming, purging, drugs, or instruments are for health; all of these are for the end, though they differ in that some are activities, while others are instruments.

We may take these, then, to be the ways we speak of causes.

5 Since causes are spoken of in many ways, there are many non-coincidental causes of the same thing. Both the sculpting craft and the bronze, for instance, are causes of the statue, not insofar as it is something else, but insofar as it is a statue. But they are not causes in the same way: the bronze is a cause as matter, the sculpting craft as the source of the motion. Some things are causes of each other: hard work, for instance, is the cause of fitness, and fitness of 10 hard work. But they are not causes in the same way: fitness is what the hard work is for, whereas hard work is the principle of motion. Further, the same thing is the cause of contraries; for sometimes if a thing's presence causes *F*, that thing is also, by its absence, taken to cause the contrary of *F*, so that, for instance, if a pilot's presence would have caused the safety of a ship, we take his absence to have 15 caused the shipwreck.

All the causes just mentioned are of four especially evident types: (1) Letters are the cause of syllables, matter of artifacts, fire and such things of bodies, parts of the whole, and the assumptions of the conclusion, as that out of which. In each of these 20 cases one thing—for instance, the parts—is cause as subject, while (2) the other thing—the whole, the composition, and the form—is cause as essence. (3) The seed, the doctor, the adviser and, in general, the producer, are all sources of the principle of change or stability. (4) In other cases, one thing is a cause of other things by being the end and the good. For what the other things are for is taken to 25 be the best and their end—it does not matter [for present purposes] whether we call it the good or the apparent good. These, then, are the number of kinds of causes there are.

Although there are many types of causes, they are fewer when they are arranged under heads. For causes are spoken of in many ways, and even among causes of the same type, some are prior and others posterior. For example, the cause of health is a doctor and 30 [speaking more generally] a craftsman, and the cause of an octave is the double and [speaking more generally] number; in every case the inclusive causes are posterior to the particular.

Further, some things and their genera are coincidental causes. Polycleitus[4] and the sculptor, for instance, are causes of the statue in different ways, because being Polycleitus is coincidental to the sculp- 35 tor. What includes the coincident is also a cause—if, for example, the man or, quite generally, the animal is a cause of the statue. Some coincidental causes are 195b more remote or more proximate than others; if, for instance, the pale man or the musician were said to be the cause of the statue [it would be a more remote cause than Polycleitus is].

We may speak of any [moving] cause, whether proper or coincidental, either as having a potentiality or as actualizing it; for instance, we may say either that 5 the housebuilder, or that the housebuilder actually building, is causing the house to be built.

Similar things may also be said about the things of which the causes are causes. For example, we may speak of the cause of this statue, or of a statue, or of an image in general; or of this bronze, or of bronze, or of matter in general. The same is true of coincidents. We may speak in this same way of combina- 10 tions—of Polycleitus the sculptor, for instance, instead of Polycleitus or a sculptor.

Still, all these ways amount to six, each spoken of in two ways. For there is (1) the particular and (2) the genus, and (3) the coincident and (4) the genus of the coincident; and these may be spoken of either 15 (5) in combination or (6) simply. Each of these may be either active or potential. The difference is the following. Active and particular causes exist and cease to exist simultaneously with the things they cause, so that, for instance, this one practicing medicine exists

4. [Polycleitus was a fifth-century-B.C. Greek sculptor.]

simultaneously with this one being made healthy, 20 and in the same way this one housebuilding exists simultaneously with this thing being built into a house. But this is not true of every cause that is potential; for the house and the housebuilder do not perish simultaneously.

Here as elsewhere, we must always seek the most precise cause. A man, for example, is building because he is a builder, and he is a builder insofar as he has the building craft; his building craft, then, is 25 the prior cause, and the same is true in all cases. Further, we must seek genera as causes of genera, and particulars as causes of particulars; a sculptor, for instance, is the cause of a statue, but this sculptor of this statue. And we must seek a potentiality as the cause of a potential effect, and something actualizing a potentiality as the cause of an actual effect.

This, then, is an adequate determination of the number of causes, and of the ways in which they are causes.

4

30 Luck and chance are also said to be causes, and many things are said to be and to come to be because of them. We must, then, investigate how luck and chance are included in the causes we have mentioned, whether luck is or is not the same as chance, 35 and, in general, what they are.

Some people even wonder whether luck and 196a chance exist. For they say that nothing results from luck; rather, everything that is said to result from chance or luck has some definite cause. If, for instance, as a result of luck someone comes to the market place and finds the person he wanted to meet but did not expect, they say the cause is his wanting 5 to go to market. Similarly, for every other supposed result of luck, they say it is possible to find some cause other than luck. For if there were such a thing as luck, it would appear truly strange and puzzling that none of the early philosophers who discussed the 10 causes of coming to be and perishing ever determined anything about luck; in fact it would seem that they also thought that nothing results from luck. But this too is surprising; for surely many things come to be and exist as a result of luck and chance. Though people know perfectly well that everything that comes to be can be referred to some cause, as the old argument doing away with luck says, everyone nonetheless 15 says that some of these things result from luck and that others do not.

That is why the early philosophers should have mentioned luck in some way or other. But they certainly did not think luck was among the causes they recognized—for instance, love or strife or mind or fire or anything else of that sort. In either case, then, it is strange, whether they supposed there was no such thing as luck, or supposed there was such a thing but omitted to discuss it. It is especially strange consider- 20 ing that they sometimes appeal to luck. Empedocles, for example, appeals to luck when he says that air is separated out on top, not always but as luck has it; at least, he says in his cosmogony that 'it happened to run that way at that time, but often otherwise'. And he says that most of the parts of animals result from luck.

Other people make chance the cause of our heaven 25 and of all worlds. For they say that the vortex, and the motion that dispersed and established everything in its present order, resulted from chance. And this is certainly quite amazing. For animals and plants, they say, neither are nor come to be from luck, but 30 rather nature or mind or something of that sort is the cause, since it is not just any old thing that comes to be from a given type of seed, but an olive-tree comes from one type, and a man from another; and yet they say that the heaven and the most divine of visible things result from chance and have no cause of the sort that animals and plants have. 35

If this is so, it deserves attention, and something might well have been said about it. For in addition 196b to the other strange aspects of what they say, it is even stranger to say all this when they see that nothing in the heavens results from chance, whereas many things happen as a result of luck to things whose existence is not itself a result of luck. Surely the contrary would 5 have been likely.

Other people[5] suppose that luck is a cause, but they take it to be divine and superhuman, and therefore obscure to the human mind.

And so we must consider chance and luck, and determine what each is, and whether they are the same or different, and see how they fit into the causes we have distinguished.

5. [The reference is to Democritus.]

5

10 First, then, we see that some things always, others usually, come about in the same way. Evidently neither luck nor anything that results from luck is said to be the cause of either of these things—either of what is of necessity and always or of what is usually. But since besides these there is a third sort of event 15 which everyone says results from luck, it is evident that there is such a thing as luck and chance; for we know that this third sort of event results from luck and that the results of luck are of this sort.

Further, some events are for something and others are not. Among the former, some are in accordance with a decision while others are not, but both sorts 20 are for something. And so it is clear that even among events that are neither necessary nor usual there are some that admit of being for something. (Events that are for something include both the actions that result from thought and also the results of nature.) This, then, is the sort of event that we regard as a result of luck, whenever an event of that sort comes about coincidentally. For just as some things are something 25 in their own right, and others are something coincidentally, so also it is possible for a cause to be of either sort. For example, the cause of a house is, in its own right, the housebuilder, but coincidentally the pale or musical thing. Hence the cause in its own right is determinate, but the coincidental cause is indeterminate, since one thing might have an unlimited number of coincidents.

30 As has been said, then, whenever this [coincidental causation] occurs among events of the sort that are for something the events [that have these coincidental causes] are said to result from chance and luck. The difference between chance and luck will be determined later; we may take it as evident for the moment that both are found among events of the sort that are for something.

For instance, A would have come when B was collecting subscriptions, in order to recover the debt from B, if A had known [B would be there]. In fact, 35 however, A did not come in order to do this; it was a coincidence that A came [when B happened to be there], and so met B in order to collect the debt— 197a given that A neither usually nor of necessity frequents the place [for that purpose]. The end—collecting the debt—is not a cause [of A's action] in A, but it is the sort of thing that one decides to do and that results from thought. And in this case A's coming is said to result from luck; but if A always or usually frequented the place because he had decided to and for the purpose of collecting the debt, then [A's being there 5 when B was there] would not result from luck.

Clearly, then, luck is a coincidental cause found among events of the sort that are for something, and specifically among those of the sort that are in accordance with a decision. Hence thought (since decision requires thought) and luck concern the same things.

Now the causes whose results might be matters of luck are bound to be indeterminate. That is why luck also seems to be something indeterminate and 10 obscure to human beings, and why, in one way, it might seem that nothing results from luck. For, as we might reasonably expect, all these claims are correct. For in one way things do result from luck, since they are coincidental results and luck is a coincidental cause. But luck is not the unqualified [and hence non-coincidental] cause of anything. The [unqualified] cause of a house, for instance, is a housebuilder, and the coincidental cause a fluteplayer; and the 15 man's coming and collecting the debt, without having come to collect it, has an indefinite number of coincidental causes—he might have come because he wished to see someone, or was going to court or to the theatre.

It is also correct to say that luck is contrary to reason. For rational judgment tells us what is always or usually the case, whereas luck is found in events 20 that happen neither always nor usually. And so, since causes of this sort are indeterminate, luck is also indeterminate.

Still, in some cases one might be puzzled about whether just any old thing might be a cause of a lucky outcome. Surely the wind or the sun's warmth, but not someone's haircut, might be the cause of his health; for some coincidental causes are closer than others to what they cause.

Luck is called good when something good results, 25 bad when something bad results; it is called good and bad fortune when the results are large. That is why someone who just misses great evil or good as well [as someone who has it is] fortunate or unfortunate; for we think of him as already having [the great evil or good], since the near miss seems 30 to us to be no distance. Further, it is reasonable that good fortune is unstable; for luck is unstable, since no result of luck can be either always or usually the case.

As we have said, then, both luck and chance are coincidental causes, found in events of the sort that are neither without exception nor usual, and specifically in events of this sort that might be for something.

6

Chance is not the same as luck, since it extends more widely; for results of luck also result from chance, but not all results of chance result from luck. For luck and its results are found in things that are capable of being fortunate and in general capable of action, and that is why luck must concern what is achievable by action. A sign of this is the fact that good fortune seems to be the same or nearly the same as being happy, and being happy is a sort of action, since it is doing well in action. Hence what cannot act cannot do anything by luck either. Hence neither inanimate things nor beasts nor children do anything by luck, because they are incapable of decision. Nor do they have good or bad fortune, except by a [mere] similarity—as Protarchus[6] said that the stones from which altars are made are fortunate, because they are honored, while their fellows are trodden underfoot. Still, even these things are affected by the results of luck in a way, whenever an agent affects them by some lucky action; but otherwise they are not.

Chance, on the other hand, applies both to animals other than man and to many inanimate things. We say, for instance, that the horse came by chance, since it was saved because it came but did not come in order to be saved. And the tripod fell by chance, because it did not fall in order to be sat on, although it was left standing in order to be sat on.

Hence it is evident that among types of events that are for something (speaking without qualification), we say that a particular event of such a type results from chance if it has an external cause and the actual result is not what it is for; and we say that it results from luck if it results from chance and is an event of the sort that is decided on by an agent who is capable of decision. A sign of this is the fact that we say an event is pointless if it [is of the sort that] is for some result but [in this case] that result is not what it is for. If, for instance, walking is for evacuating the bowels, but when he walked on this occasion it was not [for that reason], then we say that he walked pointlessly and that his walking is pointless. We assume that an event is pointless if it is naturally for something else, but does not succeed in [being for] what it is naturally for. For if someone said that his washing himself was pointless because the sun was not eclipsed, he would be ridiculous, since washing is not for producing eclipses. So also, then, an event happens by chance (as the name suggests) whenever it is pointless. For the stone did not fall in order to hit someone; it fell by chance, because it might have fallen because someone threw it to hit someone.

The separation of chance from luck is sharpest in natural events. For if an event is contrary to nature, we regard it as a result of chance, not of luck. But even this is different from [other cases of chance; the other cases] have an external cause, but [events contrary to nature] have an internal cause.

We have said, then, what chance and luck are and how they differ. Each of them falls under the sort of cause that is the source of the principle of motion. For in every case they are either among natural causes or among those resulting from thought, and the number of these is indeterminate.

Chance and luck are causes of events [of the sort] that mind or nature might have caused, in cases where [particular] events [of this sort] have some coincidental cause. Now nothing coincidental is prior to anything that is in its own right; hence clearly no coincidental cause is prior to something that is a cause in its own right. Chance and luck are therefore posterior to mind and nature. And so however true it might be that chance is the cause of the heavens, still it is necessary for mind and nature to be prior causes of this universe and of many other things.

7

It is clear, then, that there are causes, and that there are as many different types as we say there are; for the reason why something is so includes all these

6. [Protarchus was a student of Gorgias, regarding whom see Plato's *Meno*, n.2.]

different types [of causes]. For we refer the ultimate reason why (1) in the case of unmoved things, to the what-it-is (for instance, in mathematics; for there we refer ultimately to the definition of straight or commensurate or something else), or (2) to what first initiated the motion (for instance, why did they go 20 to war?—because the other side raided them), or (3) to what it is for (for instance, in order to set themselves up as rulers), or (4) in the case of things that come to be, to the matter.

It is evident, then, that these are the causes and that this is their number. Since there are four of them, the student of nature ought to know them all; and in order to give the sort of reason that is appropriate for the study of nature, he must trace it back to all the causes—to the matter, the form, what initiated the motion, and what something is for. The last three 25 often amount to one; for what something is and what it is for are one, and the first source of the motion is the same in species as these, since a man generates a man; and the same is true generally of things that initiate motion by being in motion.

Things that initiate motion without being in motion are outside the scope of the study of nature. For although they initiate motion, they do not do so by having motion or a principle of motion within themselves, but they are unmoved. Hence there are three 30 inquiries: one about what is unmoved, one about what is in motion but imperishable, and one about what is perishable.

And so the reason why is given by referring to the matter, to the what-it-is, and to what first initiated the motion. For in cases of coming to be, this is the normal way of examining the causes—by asking what 35 comes to be after what, and what first acted or was acted on, and so on in order in every case.

Two sorts of principles initiate motion naturally. 198b One of these principles is not itself natural, since it has no principle of motion within itself; this is true of whatever initiates motion without itself being in motion—for instance, what is entirely without motion (i.e., the first of all beings) and also the what-it-is (i.e., the form), since this is the end and what something is for. And so, since natural processes are for something, this cause too must be known.

5 The reason why should be stated in all these ways. For instance, (1) this necessarily results from that (either without exception or usually); (2) if this is to be (as the conclusion from the premisses); (3) that this is the essence; and (4) because it is better thus—not unqualifiedly better, but better in relation to the essence of a given thing.

8

We must first say why nature is among the causes 10 that are for something, and then how necessity applies to natural things. For everyone refers things to necessity, saying that since the hot, the cold, and each element have a certain nature, certain other things are and come to be of necessity. For if they mention 15 any cause other than necessity (as one thinker[7] mentions love or strife, and another[8] mentions mind), they just touch on it, then let it go.

A puzzle now arises: why not suppose that nature acts not for something or because it is better, but of necessity? Zeus's rain does not fall in order to make the grain grow, but of necessity. For it is necessary that what has been drawn up is cooled, and that what has been cooled and become water comes down, 20 and it is coincidental that this makes the grain grow. Similarly, if someone's grain is spoiled on the threshing floor, it does not rain in order to spoil the grain, and the spoilage is coincidental.

Why not suppose, then, that the same is true of the parts of natural organisms? On this view, it is of necessity that, for example, the front teeth grow sharp 25 and well adapted for biting, and the back ones broad and useful for chewing food; this [useful] result was coincidental, not what they were for. The same will be true of all the other parts that seem to be for something. On this view, then, whenever all the parts came about coincidentally as though they were for something, these animals survived, since their constitution, 30 though coming about by chance, made them suitable [for survival]. Other animals, however, were differently constituted and so were destroyed; indeed they are still being destroyed, as Empedocles says of the man-headed calves.

This argument, then, and others like it, might puzzle someone. In fact, however, it is impossible for things to be like this. For these [teeth and other parts]

7. [The reference is to Empedocles.]

8. [The reference is to Anaxagoras, regarding whom see Plato's *Apology*, n.7.]

35 and all natural things come to be as they do either always or usually, whereas no result of luck or chance 199a comes to be either always or usually. (For we do not regard frequent winter rain or a summer heat wave, but only summer rain or a winter heat wave, as a result of luck or coincidence.) If, then, these seem either to be coincidental results or to be for some- 5 thing, and they cannot be coincidental or chance results, they are for something. Now surely all such things are natural, as even those making these claims [about necessity] would agree. We find, then, among things that come to be and are by nature, things that are for something.

Further, whenever [some sequence of actions] has an end, the whole sequence of earlier and later actions is directed towards the end. Surely what is true of 10 action is also true of nature, and what is true of nature is true of each action, if nothing prevents it. Now actions are for something; therefore, natural sequences are for something. For example, if a house came to be naturally, it would come to be just as it actually does by craft, and if natural things came to 15 be not only naturally but also by craft, they would come to be just as they do naturally; one thing, then, is what the other is for. In general, craft either completes the work that nature is unable to complete or imitates nature. If, then, the products of a craft are for something, clearly the products of nature are also for something; for there is the same relation of later stages to earlier in productions of a craft and in productions of nature.

20 This is most evident in the case of animals other than man, since they use neither craft nor inquiry nor deliberation in producing things—indeed this is why some people are puzzled about whether spiders, ants, and other such things operate by understanding or in some other way. If we advance little by little along the same lines, it is evident that even 25 in plants things come to be that promote the end—leaves, for instance, grow for the protection of the fruit. If, then, a swallow makes its nest and a spider its web both naturally and for some end, and if plants grow leaves for the sake of the fruit, and send roots down rather than up for the sake of nourishment, it evidently follows that this sort of 30 cause is among things that come to be and are by nature. And since nature is of two sorts, nature as matter and nature as form, and the form is the end, and since everything else is for the end, the form must be what things are for.

Errors occur even in productions of craft; grammarians, for instance, have written incorrectly, and doctors have given the wrong medicine. Clearly, then, 35 errors are also possible in productions of nature. 199b

In some productions by crafts, the correct action is for something, and in cases of error the attempt is for something but misses the mark. The same will be true, then, of natural things; freaks will be errors, missing what they are for. Hence in the original for- 5 mations of things, a defective principle would also have brought the [man-headed] calves into being, if they were unable to reach any definite term and end—just as, in the actual state of things, [freaks] come to be when the seed is defective. Further, it is necessary for the seed to come into being first, and not the animal straightaway; in fact the 'all-natured first' was seed.

Further, in plants as well as in animals things hap- 10 pen for something, though in a less articulate way. Then what about plants? Did olive-headed vines keep coming into being, as he says [man-headed] calves did? Surely not—that is absurd—but surely they would have to have come into being, if the animals did.

Further, [on Empedocles' view] coming to be would also have to be merely a matter of chance among seeds. But whoever says this does away entirely with nature and natural things. For things are natural 15 when they are moved continuously from some principle in themselves and so arrive at some end. From each principle comes, not the same thing in each case, but not just any old thing either; in every case it proceeds to the same [end], if nothing prevents it.

Now certainly both the end that a process is for and the process that is for this end might also result from luck. We say, for instance, that a friend in a 20 foreign country came by luck and paid the ransom and then went away, when he did the action as though he had come in order to do it, though in fact that was not what he came to do. This end is achieved coincidentally, since (as we said before) luck is one of the coincidental causes. But whenever the end results always or usually, it is neither coinci- 25 dental nor a result of luck. And in natural things that is how it is in every case, unless something prevents it.

Besides, it is strange for people to think there is no end unless they see an agent initiating the motion by deliberation. Even crafts do not deliberate. Moreover, if the shipbuilding craft were in the wood, it would produce a ship in the same way that nature 30 would. And so if what something is for is present in craft, it is also present in nature. This is clearest when a doctor applies medical treatment to himself—that is what nature is like.

It is evident, then, that nature is a cause, and in fact the sort of cause that is for something.

9

Is the necessity present [in nature only] conditional, 35 or is it also unqualified?

200a The sort of necessity that is ascribed nowadays to things that come to be is the sort there would be if someone supposed that a wall came into being of necessity. On this view, heavy things naturally move downwards, and light things upwards, and that is why the stones and the foundations are below, while the earth is above because of its lightness, and the 5 wooden logs are on the very top because they are lightest of all.

Nonetheless, though the wall certainly requires these things, it did not come to be because of them (except insofar as they are its material cause), but in order to give shelter and protection.

The same is true in all other cases that are for something: although they require things that have a necessary nature, they do not come to be because of these things (except insofar as they are the material 10 cause), but for some end. For instance, why does a saw have such and such features? In order to perform this function, and for this end. But this end cannot come to be unless the saw is made of iron; and so it is necessary for it to be made of iron if there is to be a saw performing its function. What is necessary, then, is conditional, but not [necessary] as an end; for necessity is in the matter, whereas the end is in 15 the form.

Necessity is found both in mathematics and in things that come to be naturally, and to some extent the two cases are similar. For instance, since the straight is what it is, it is necessary for a triangle to have angles equal to two right angles. It is not because the triangle has angles equal to two right angles that the straight is what it is; but if the triangle does not have angles equal to two right angles, the straight will not be what it is either.

The reverse is true in the case of things that come to be for an end: if the end is or will be, then the 20 previous things are or will be too. Just as, in the mathematical case, if the conclusion [about the triangle] is false, the principle [about the straight] will not be true either, so also in nature if the [materials] do not exist, the end that the process is for will not come about either. For the end is also a principle; it is a principle not of the action, but of the reasoning. (In the mathematical case [also] the principle is the principle of the reasoning, since in this case there is no action.)

And so, if there is to be a house, it is necessary for these things to come to be or to be present; and in 25 general, the matter that is for something must exist (for example, bricks and stones if there is to be a house). The end, however, does not exist because of these things, except insofar as they are the material cause, nor will it come about because of them; still, in general, the end (the house or the saw) requires them (the stones or the iron). Similarly, in the mathematical case the principles require the triangle to 30 have two right angles.

Evidently, then, necessity in natural things belongs to the material cause and to the motions of matter. The student of nature should mention both causes, but more especially what something is for, since this is the cause of the matter, whereas the matter is not the cause of the end. The end is what something is for, and the principle comes from the definition and 35 the form.

The same is true in productions of craft. For in- 200b stance, since a house is this sort of thing, these things must come to be and be present of necessity; and since health is this, these things must come to be and be present of necessity. In the same way, if a man is this, these things must come to be and be present of necessity; and if these, then these.

But presumably necessity is present in the form as well [as in the matter]. Suppose, for instance, that 5 we define the function of sawing as a certain sort of cutting; this sort of cutting requires a saw with teeth of a certain sort, and these require a saw made of iron. For the form, as well as the matter, has parts in it as matter of the form.

BOOK III

1

200b Since nature is a principle of motion and change, and since our line of inquiry is about nature, we must find out what motion is; for if we do not know what 15 it is, neither can we know what nature is. Once we have determined what motion is, we should try the same approach to the things that come next in order.

Motion seems to be continuous, and the first thing discerned in the continuous is the infinite. That is why those who define the continuous often turn out to be relying on the account of the infinite as well, 20 since they assume that what is infinitely divisible is continuous. Moreover, it seems impossible for there to be motion without place, void, and time.

It is clear, then, both because of these [connections] and because these things are common to everything and universal, that we should undertake a discussion of each of them, since the study of special 25 topics comes after the study of common topics; and first, as we said, we should discuss motion.

Some things are only in actuality, and others are in potentiality and in actuality—thises, or quantities, or qualities, or one of the other predications of being. Among relatives, some are spoken of with reference 30 to excess and deficiency, and others with reference to acting and being affected, and in general with reference to initiating motion and to being moved—for what initiates motion initiates it in what is moved, and what is moved is moved by what initiates motion.

There is no motion apart from things [that are moved]. For what changes always does so either in substance or in quantity or in quality or in place, and 35 we claim that there is nothing that is common and 201a applies to all of these—i.e., is neither a this nor a quantity nor a quality nor any of the other things predicated. Hence there is no motion or change of anything apart from the things mentioned, since there is nothing apart from these things.

Each of these things belongs to everything in [one of] two ways. This is true, for instance, of the this, 5 which in some cases is form and in other cases privation; of quality, which in some cases is pale and in other cases dark; and of quantity, which in some cases is complete and in other cases incomplete. It is true in the same way of local motion, which in some cases is upward and in other cases is downward, or [in other words] where some things are light and others heavy. Hence there are as many kinds of motion and change as there are of being.

In each kind of thing we distinguish what is actually 10 *F* from what is potentially *F*. Hence the actuality of what is *F* potentially, insofar as it is *F* potentially, is motion. The actuality of the alterable, for instance, insofar as it is alterable, is alteration; the actuality of what is capable of growing or its opposite, decaying (since there is no name that covers both), is growing or decaying; the actuality of what is capable of coming to be or perishing is coming to be or perishing; the 15 actuality of what is capable of local movement is local movement. That this is what motion is is clear from the following. Whenever the buildable, insofar as we say it is buildable, is in actuality, it is being built, and this is building. The same applies to learning, curing, rolling, jumping, ripening, and ageing.

In some cases, the same things are both in potentiality 20 and in actuality, though not at the same time or in the same way, but rather they are, for instance, actually hot and potentially cold. It follows that many things will both act on and be affected by each other, since everything of this sort will be capable both of acting and of being affected. Hence what naturally initiates motion is also moveable; for everything of this sort initiates motion by itself being moved. Hence 25 some people even believe that whatever initiates motion is itself moved. The truth about this, however, will be clear from other considerations; for in fact there is something that initiates motion without being moveable. In any case, the actuality of what is potentially *F*, whenever, being in actuality, it is active—not insofar as it is itself, but insofar as it is moveable—is motion.

By 'insofar as' I mean the following: Though bronze is potentially a statue, it is not the actuality of bronze, 30 insofar as it is bronze, that is motion. For being bronze is not the same as being potentially something; for if they were the same without qualification, i.e., in definition, the actuality of bronze insofar as it is bronze would be motion, but in fact, as we have said, they are not the same. This point is clear in the case 35 of contraries. For being potentially healthy is not the same as being potentially ill; if they were the same, 201b then being ill and being healthy would also be the same. Rather, the subject (whether it is moisture or blood) that is healthy and ill [at different times] is one and the same. The two potentialities, therefore, [of *F* insofar as it is *F*, and of *F* insofar as it is moveable] are not the same, just as color and the visible are not the same; and so it is evident that the actuality of what is potentially *F*, insofar as it is potentially *F*, is motion.

It is clear, then, that this actuality is motion, and that something is in fact in motion just when the actuality is this one, and neither earlier nor later. For it is possible for something—for instance, the buildable—to be at one time actual and at another not, and the actuality of the buildable, insofar as it is buildable, is building. For the actuality is either the [process of] building or the house; but when the house exists, it is no longer buildable, whereas what is being built is something buildable; necessarily, then, the actuality is [the process of] building. Now, building is a type of motion; moreover, the same account will also fit the other cases of motion.

2

That this account is correct is clear both from what other people say about motion and from the fact that it is not easy to define it in any other way. For motion and change cannot be assigned to any other genus, as is clear if we examine what some people assign them to. They assert that motion is difference, or inequality, or what is not; but none of these—different things or unequal things or things that are not—is necessarily in motion, and change is no more into these or from these than it is from their opposites.

The reason why they assign motion to these genera is that motion seems to be something indefinite, and the principles in the second column are indefinite because they are privative; for none of them is a this, or of any quality, or any of the other predications. The reason why motion seems to be indefinite is that it cannot be assigned either to the potentiality or to the actuality of beings. For neither what potentially has a given quantity nor what actually has it is necessarily in motion. Moreover, motion seems to be some sort of actuality, but an incomplete one; this is because the potential, of which motion is an actuality, is incomplete. This, then, is why it is difficult to grasp what motion is; for it has to be assigned either to privation or to potentiality or to unqualified actuality, but none of these appears possible.

202a The remaining option, then, is the way [of understanding motion] that we have described: to say that it is a sort of actuality, and, in fact, the sort we have mentioned, which is difficult to notice but possible to be.

As we have said, everything that initiates motion is also moved, provided that it has a potentiality to be moved and that its lack of motion is rest (for, in the case of things that undergo motion, lack of motion is rest). For to act on this sort of thing [i.e., something moveable], insofar as it is of this sort, is just what it is to move it. [The agent] does this by contact, so that it is itself acted on at the same time. That is why motion is the actuality of the moveable insofar as it is moveable; this comes about by contact with the mover, so that [the mover] is also acted on at the same time. In each case the mover will bring some form—either a this or of this quality or of this quantity—that will be the principle and cause of motion whenever the mover initiates motion; for instance, an actual man makes something else actually a man from being potentially a man.

3

It is also evident how to answer the puzzle, by saying that the motion is in the thing moved. For it is the actuality of the thing moved, brought about by the agency of the mover. The actuality of the mover is not different from this; for there must be an actuality of both mover and thing moved, since the mover is an initiator of motion by its potentiality, and it initiates motion by its actuality, but it is the thing moved that it brings to actuality. And so both mover and moved have one actuality, in the way in which the same interval is the interval from one to two and the interval from two to one, and [the same road] is the uphill and the downhill [road]. For these things are one, but their account is not one; and the same applies to the mover and the thing moved.

This, however, raises a logical puzzle. For presumably there must be some actuality of the agent and of what is acted on. The former actuality is *acting on* something, and the latter actuality is *being acted on*; and the achievement and end of the former is an action, and of the latter a way of being acted on. Both of these actualities, then, are motions; if, then, they are different, what are they in?

Either both are in the thing that is affected and moved, or else the acting is in the agent and the being acted on is in the thing acted on. (If this being acted on is [also] to be called acting, then acting will be homonymous.) But now, if this is so, then the motion will be in the mover, since the same account 30 applies to the mover and to the thing moved [as applies to the agent and to the thing acted on]. And so either the mover will be moved or it will have motion and yet not be moved.

Suppose that, on the contrary, both the acting and the being acted on are in the thing that is moved and acted on, and that both teaching and learning, being two [motions], are in the learner. In that case, first of all, the actuality of a given [subject] will not be in that [subject]. Secondly, it is absurd that [the thing acted on] should undergo two motions at the same 35 time. For what will be the two alterations of one [subject] into one form? That is impossible.

Suppose, then, that the actuality [of the mover and 202b the thing moved] are one. But it is unreasonable for two things that are different in form to have one and the same actuality. Moreover if [the processes of] teaching and learning, or [the processes of] acting and being acted on, are the same, then to teach will be the same as to learn, and to act will be the same as to be acted on, so that it will be necessary for the 5 one teaching to be learning [everything that he is teaching], and for the agent to be acted on [by its own action].

Perhaps, however, it is not absurd for the actuality of one thing to be in another thing; for teaching is the actuality of what is capable of teaching, but in some subject [acted on]. It is not cut off, but is the actuality of this [agent] in this [thing acted on]. And perhaps it is not impossible for two things to have one and the same actuality—not in such a way that the actuality is one in being, but in the way in which 10 the potential is related to the actual.

Nor is it necessary for the one teaching to be learning, even if acting and being acted on are the same, given that they are not the same in such a way that one and the same account states the essence of both, as it does for cape and cloak; rather, they are the same in the way in which the road from Thebes to Athens is the same as the road from Athens to Thebes, 15 as has been said before. For if things are [merely] the same in some way, it does not follow that all the same things belong to them; this follows only if their being is the same.

Moreover, even if [the process of] teaching is the same thing as learning, it does not follow that to teach is the same as to learn, just as, even if there is one interval between the two things separated by it, it does not follow that to be separated by the interval from here to there is one and the same as to be separated by the interval from there to here. And, to speak generally, [the process of teaching] is not the same thing in the full sense as learning, nor is acting 20 the same [in the full sense] as being acted on. What is one is the motion to which both the properties [of being a teaching and being a learning] belong. For being the actuality of this [subject] in that one is different in account from being the actuality of that [subject] by the agency of this one.

We have said, then, what motion is, both in general and in particular cases. For it is clear how each species of it will be defined. Alteration, for instance, will be 25 the actuality of the alterable insofar as it is alterable. To make it still better known: [Motion will be] the actuality of what has the potentiality for acting and being acted on, insofar as it has that potentiality. This is true without qualification, and again in particular cases—for instance in building or healing. The same account will be given of each of the other types of motion.

BOOK VIII

6

258b Since motion must be everlasting and must never fail, there must be some everlasting first mover, one or more than one. The question whether each of the unmoved movers is everlasting is irrelevant to this argument; but it will be clear in the following way that there must be something that is itself unmoved and outside all change, either unqualified or coinci- 15 dental, but initiates motion in something else.

Let us suppose, then, if you like, that in the case of some things it is possible for them to be at one time and not to be at another without any coming to be or perishing—for if something has no parts, but it is at one time and is not at another time, perhaps it is necessary for it to be at one time and not to be 20 at another without changing. Let us also suppose that, among the principles that are unmoved but initiate motion, it is possible for some to be at one time and not to be at another time.

Still, this is not possible for every principle of that sort; for it is clear that there is something that causes the self-movers to be at one time and not to be at 25 another time. For every self-mover necessarily has some magnitude, if nothing that lacks parts is moved; but from what we have said it is not necessary for every mover to have magnitude. Hence the cause explaining why some things come to be and other things perish, and in a continuous sequence, cannot be any of the things that are unmoved but do not always exist; nor can some things be the cause of some [parts of the sequence] and other things the 30 cause of other [parts]; for neither any one of them nor all of them together is the cause explaining why the sequence is everlasting and continuous. For the sequence is everlasting and necessary, whereas all these movers are infinitely many and they do not all exist at the same time.

It is clear, then, that however many unmoved mov- 259a ers and self-movers perish and are succeeded by others, so that one unmoved mover moves one thing and another moves another, still there is something that embraces them all and is apart from each of them, which is the cause explaining why some exist and 5 some do not exist, and why the change is continuous. This is the cause of motion in these [other movers], and these are the cause of motion in the other things.

If, then, motion is everlasting, the first mover is also everlasting, if there is just one; and if there are many, there are many everlasting movers. But we must suppose there is one rather than many, and a finite rather than an infinite number. For in every case where the results [of either assumption] are the same, we should assume a finite number [of causes]; 10 for among natural things what is finite and better must exist rather [than its opposite] if this is possible. And one mover is sufficient; it will be first and everlasting among the unmoved things, and the principle of 15 motion for the other things.

On the Soul

BOOK I

1

402a We suppose that knowing is fine and honorable, and that one type of knowing is finer and more honorable than another either because it is more exact or because it is concerned with better and more wonderful things. On both grounds, we might reasonably place 5 inquiry into the soul in the first rank. Moreover, knowledge of it seems to make an important contribution to [knowledge of] the truth as a whole, and especially to the [knowledge of] nature, since the soul is a sort of principle of animals. We seek to study and know the nature and essence of the soul, and then all of its coincidental properties; some of these seem to be distinctive attributes of the soul, while others also 10 seem to belong to animals because they have souls.

And yet it is altogether in every way a most difficult task to reach any conviction about the soul. For, as in many other areas of study, we are seeking the essence and the what-it-is; and so someone might perhaps think some single line of inquiry is appropriate for every case where we want to know the 15 substance—just as demonstration suits all coincidental properties that are distinctive of a given subject. On this view, then, we should seek this single line of inquiry. If, however, no single line of inquiry is suitable for the what-it-is, our task turns out to be still more difficult, since in that case we must discover how to study each area. But even if it is evident 20 whether demonstration or division or some further line of inquiry is the right one, the question of where to begin our investigation causes many puzzles and confusions; for different things—for instance, numbers and surfaces—have different principles.

First of all, presumably, we must determine the soul's genus and what it is. Is it, in other words, a this and a substance, or a quality, or a quantity, or something in one of the other predications that we 25 have distinguished? Further, is it something potential or is it more of an actuality? That makes quite a bit 402b of difference. We should also examine whether it is divisible into parts or has no parts. Do all souls belong to the same species or not? If not, do they differ in species, or in genus? As things are, those who discuss and inquire into the soul would seem to examine only the human soul. Nor should we forget to ask 5 whether there is just one account of the soul, as there is of animal, or a different account for each type of soul—for instance, of horse, dog, man, god—so that the universal animal either is nothing or else is posterior to these. The same will apply to any other common thing predicated.

Further, if there are not many types of soul, but [one type of soul with many] parts, must we begin 10 by inquiring into the whole soul, or by inquiring into the parts? It is also difficult to determine which parts differ in nature from each other and whether we should begin by inquiring into the parts or for their functions. Should we, for instance, begin with understanding, perceiving, and so on, or with the part that understands and the part that perceives? And if we should begin with the functions, we might be puzzled 15 anew about whether we should investigate the corresponding objects before the functions—the object of perception, for instance, before perceiving, and the object of understanding before understanding.

It would indeed seem useful to know the what-it-is, in order to study the causes of the coincidental properties of substances. In mathematics, for instance, it is useful to know what straight and curved are or what a line and a surface are, in order to notice how 20 many right angles the angles of a triangle are equal to. Conversely, however, the [knowledge of the] coincidental properties also is also very important for knowing the what-it-is. For we can state the essence best once we can describe how all or most of the coincidental properties appear to be; for since the 25

Reprinted from Aristotle, *Selections*, translated and edited by Terence Irwin and Gail Fine (Indianapolis: Hackett Publishing Company, 1995), by permission of the publisher. The use of brackets within the text indicates insertions not found in the manuscript.

what-it-is is the principle of all demonstration, a definition will clearly be dialectical and empty unless it results in knowledge, or at least in ready conjecture, about the coincidental properties.

A further puzzle arises about whether all the affections of the soul also belong to what has the soul or there is also some affection that is distinctive of the soul itself. We must find the answer, but it is not easy.

In most cases (for instance, being angry or confident, having an appetite, or perceiving in general), it appears that without the body the soul neither is affected nor acts. Understanding, more than the other affections, would seem to be distinctive *of the soul*; but if it is also some sort of appearance or requires appearance, then understanding also requires a body. And so if some function or affection of the soul is distinctive of it, then the soul would be separable; but if not, then it would not be separable. Similarly, the straight, insofar as it is straight, has many coincidental properties—for instance, that it touches a bronze sphere at a point—but if it is separated, it will not touch the sphere in this way; for it is inseparable, given that in every case it requires some body.

In fact, all the affections of the soul—emotion, gentleness, fear, pity, confidence, and, further, joy, loving, and hating—would seem to require a body, since whenever we have them the body is affected in some way. An indication of this is the fact that sometimes, though something severe and obvious affects us, we are not provoked or frightened; and sometimes we are moved by something small and faint, if the body is swelling and in the condition that accompanies anger. It is still more evident that sometimes, though nothing frightening is happening, people are affected just as a frightened person is.

If this is so, then clearly affections are forms that involve matter. Hence the formulae will be, for instance: 'Being angry is a certain motion of this sort of body or part or capacity by this agency for this end.' Hence study of the soul—either every sort or this sort—turns out to be a task for the student of nature.

The student of nature and the dialectician would give different definitions of each of these affections—of anger, for instance. The dialectician would define it as a desire to inflict pain in return for pain, or something of that sort, whereas the student of nature would define it as a boiling of the blood and of the hot [element] around the heart. The student of nature describes the matter, whereas the dialectician describes the form and the account: for desire, for instance, is the form of the thing, but its existence requires this sort of matter. Similarly, the account of a house is of this sort—that it is a shelter preventing destruction by wind, rain, or heat; someone else will say that it is stones, bricks, and timber; and someone else will say that it is the form in these [stones, for instance], for the sake of this end. Who, then, is the [real] student of nature—the one who is concerned with the matter but is ignorant of the account, or the one who is concerned only with the account? Or is the [real] student of nature more properly the one who mentions both form and matter? If so, then what is each of the first two?

Perhaps in fact there is no one who is concerned with the inseparable affections of matter but not concerned with them insofar as they are separable. Rather, the student of nature is concerned with all the actions and affections of this sort of body and this sort of matter; what is not of this sort concerns someone else, perhaps a craftsman (for instance, a carpenter or a doctor). Inseparable affections, insofar as they are not affections of this sort of body but [are considered] by abstraction, concern the mathematician; insofar as they are separated, they concern first philosophy.

We should return to where our discussion began. We were saying, then, that the affections of the soul (for instance, emotion and fear) are, insofar as they are affections of the soul, inseparable (unlike surface and line) from the natural matter of animals.

BOOK II

1

So much for the views on the soul that our predecessors have handed down. Let us now return and make a new start, trying to determine what the soul is and what account of it best applies to all souls in common.

We say, then, that one kind of being is substance. One sort of substance is matter, which is not a this in its own right; another sort is shape or form, which makes [matter] a this; and the third sort is the compound of matter and form. Matter is potentiality, and form is actuality; actuality is either, for instance, [the state of] knowing or [the activity of] attending [to what one knows].

What seem to be substances most of all are bodies, and especially natural bodies, since these are the sources of the others. Some natural bodies are alive and some are not—by 'life' I mean self-nourishment, 15 growth, and decay.

It follows that every living natural body is a substance and, [more precisely,] substance as compound. But since every such body is also this sort of body—i.e., the sort that is alive—the soul cannot be a body, since the body [is substance] as subject and matter and is not said 20 of a subject. The soul, then, must be substance as the form of a natural body that is potentially alive. Now, substance is actuality; hence the soul will be the actuality of this specific sort of body.

Actuality is spoken of in two ways—one corresponding to [the state of] knowing and the other to attending to [what one knows]. Evidently, then, the soul is the same sort of actuality that knowing is. For both being asleep and being awake require the 25 presence of the soul; being awake corresponds to attending and being asleep to the state of inactive knowing. Moreover, in the same subject the state of knowing precedes the activity. Hence the soul is the first actuality of a natural body that is potentially alive.

412b The sort of natural body that is potentially alive is an organic one. The parts of plants are also organs, though altogether simple ones; the leaf, for instance, is a shelter for the shell, and the shell for the fruit, and similarly the roots correspond to a mouth, since both draw in food. And so, if we must give an account 5 common to every sort of soul, we will say that the soul is the first actuality of a natural organic body.

Hence we need not ask whether the soul and body are one, any more than we need to ask this about the wax and the seal or, in general, about the matter and the thing of which it is the matter. For while one and being are spoken of in several ways, the actuality [and what it actualizes] are fully one.

10 We have said in general, then, that the soul is substance that corresponds to the account; and this [sort of substance] is the essence of this sort of body. Suppose some instrument—an axe, for instance—were a natural body; then being an axe would be its substance, and its soul would also be this [i.e., being an axe]; and if this substance were separated from it, it would no longer be an axe, except homonymously. 15 In fact, however, it is an axe; for the soul is not the essence and form of this sort of body but of the specific sort of natural body that has in itself a principle of motion and rest.

We must also study this point by applying it to the parts [of living things]. If the eye, for instance, were an animal, sight would be its soul. For sight is the eye's substance that corresponds to the account, while 20 the eye is the matter of sight; if an eye loses its sight, it is no longer an eye, except homonymously, as a stone eye or a painted eye is. We must apply this point about the part to the whole living body; for what holds for the relation of part [of the faculty of perception] to part [of the body] holds equally for the relation of the whole *faculty of* perception to the whole perceptive body, insofar as it is perceptive. The 25 sort of body that is potentially alive is not the one that has lost its soul but the one that has it; and the seed or the fruit is potentially this sort of body.

Being awake, then, is a [second] actuality, corresponding to cutting or seeing. The soul is [a first] actuality, corresponding to [the faculty of] sight and 413a to the potentiality of the instrument [to cut]; and the body is potentially this. And as an eye is the pupil plus sight, so an animal is soul plus body.

It is clear, then, that the soul is not separable from the body. At least, some parts of it are not, if it is divisible into parts; for the actuality of some [parts of 5 the soul] is [the actuality] of the parts [of the body] themselves. Still, some [parts of the soul] might well not be actualities of any body and might therefore be separable. Moreover, it is still unclear whether the soul is the actuality of the body in the way a sailor is of a ship.

Let this, then, be our outline definition and sketch 10 of the soul.

2

Since what is perspicuous and better known from the point of view of reason emerges from what is less perspicuous but more evident, we must start again and apply this approach to the soul. For the defining account must not confine itself, as most definitions do, to showing the fact; it must also contain and 15 indicate its cause. The accounts that are customarily stated in formulae are like conclusions, so that if we ask, for instance, what squaring is, we are told that it is making an equilateral rectangle equal to an oblong rectangle. This sort of formula is an account of the conclusion, whereas the one that defines squaring as 20 the finding of the mean states the cause of the fact.

To begin our inquiry, then, we say that living is what distinguishes things with souls from things without souls. Living is spoken of in several ways—for instance, understanding, perception, locomotion, and 25 rest, and also the motion involved in nourishment, and decay and growth. And so whatever has even one of these is said to be alive.

This is why all plants as well [as animals] seem to be alive, since they evidently have an internal potentiality and principle through which they both grow and decay in contrary directions. For they grow up and down and in all directions alike, not just up 30 rather than down; they are continually nourished, and they stay alive as long as they can absorb nourishment. This [sort of life] can be separated from the others, but in mortal things the others cannot be separated from it. This is evident in the case of plants, since they have no other potentiality of the soul.

413b This principle, then, is what makes something alive. What makes something an animal is primarily perception; for whatever has perception, even without motion or locomotion, is said to be an animal, not simply to be alive. Touch is the primary type of 5 perception belonging to all animals, and it can be separated from the other senses, just as the nutritive [potentiality] can be separated from touch and the other senses.

The part of the soul that belongs to plants as well as to animals is called nutritive; and all animals evidently 10 have the sense of touch. Later we will state the explanation of each of these facts. For now let us confine ourselves to saying that the soul is the principle of the [potentialities] we have mentioned—for nutrition, perception, understanding, and motion—and is defined by them.

Is each of these a soul or a part of a soul? And if 15 a part, is it the sort that is separable only in account, or is it also separable in place? In some cases the answer is easily seen, but some parts raise a puzzle. For some plants are evidently still alive when they are cut [from one plant] and are separated from each other; for, we assume, the soul in each plant is actually one but potentially more than one. And we see that the same is also true of other differentiae of the soul. 20 [This is clear] in the case of insects that are cut in two. For each part has both perception and locomotion; if it has perception, then it also has appearance and desire. For if it has perception, then it has pain and pleasure, and if it has these, then it necessarily also has appetite.

So far, however, nothing is evident about under- 25 standing and the potentiality for theoretical study. It would seem to be a different kind of soul, and the only part that can be separated, in the way in which the everlasting can be separated from the perishable.

It evidently follows, however, that the other parts of the soul are not separable, as some say they are. But they evidently differ in account; for perceiving 30 is different from believing, and hence being the perceptive part is different from being the believing part, and so on for each of the other parts mentioned.

Further, animals are differentiated by the fact that some of them have all of these parts, some have some of them, and some have only one; we should 414a investigate the reason for this later. Practically the same is true of the senses; some animals have all of them, some have some of them, and some have only the most necessary one, touch.

When we say we live and perceive by something, 5 we speak in two ways, just as we do when we say we know by something. For we say we know either by knowledge or by the soul, since we say we know by each of these; and similarly, we are healthy in one way by health, in another way by some part or the whole of the body. In these cases, knowledge or health is a sort of shape and form, i.e., an account and a sort of actuality of what is receptive of knowledge or 10 health; for the actuality of the agent seems to occur in the thing that is acted on and suitably disposed.

Now the soul is that by which we primarily live, perceive, and think, and so it will be an account and a form, not matter and subject. For substance, as we said, 15 is spoken of in three ways, as form, matter, and the compound of both; of these, matter is potentiality, form actuality. Since, therefore, the compound of body and soul is ensouled, body is not the actuality of soul, but the soul is the actuality of some sort of body.

This vindicates the view of those who think that the soul is not a body but requires a body; for it is 20 not a body, but it belongs to a body, and for that reason it is present in a body, and in this sort of body.

Our predecessors were wrong, then, in trying to fit the soul into a body without further determining the proper sort of body, even though it appears that not 25 just any old thing receives any old thing. Our view, however, is quite reasonable, since a thing's actuality naturally comes to be in what has the potentiality for it, i.e., in the proper matter.

It is evident from this, then, that the soul is a certain sort of actuality and form of what has the potentiality to be of this sort.

3

As we said, some things have all the potentialities of 30 the soul that were previously mentioned, while other things have some of these potentialities, and others have only one. The potentialities we mentioned were those for nutrition, perception, desire, locomotion, and understanding. Now, plants have only the nutri- *414b* tive part. Other things have the nutritive part and also the perceptive part, and if they have the perceptive part, they also have the desiring part. For desire includes appetite, emotion, and wish; but all animals have at least the sense of touch, and whatever has 5 any perception has pleasure and pain and finds things pleasant or painful. Whatever finds things pleasant and painful also has appetite, since appetite is desire for what is pleasant.

Further, animals have the perception of nourishment; for touch is perception of nourishment, since all living things are nourished by things that are dry and wet and hot and cold, and touch is the perception of these. Animals are nourished by other objects of 10 perception only coincidentally, since neither sound nor color nor smell contributes anything to nourishment, and flavor is an object of touch. Now, hunger and thirst are appetites for the dry and hot, and the wet and cold, respectively, while flavor is a sort of pleasant relish belonging to these.

We must make these points clear later on. For now 15 let us confine ourselves to saying that living things that have touch also have desire. Whether they all have appearance is not clear, and must be considered later.

Besides these parts, some things have the locomotive part. Other—human beings, for instance, and any thinking being that is different from, or superior to, a human being—also have the thinking part and intellect.

Clearly, then, soul will have one single account in 20 the same way that figure has; for just as figure is nothing besides the triangle and the figures that follow in order, so equally the soul is nothing besides those [potentialities] we have mentioned. Still, in the case of figures we can find a common account that fits all of them and is distinctive of none; the same is true for the souls we have mentioned. It is ridiculous, 25 then, in these and other such cases, to seek a common account that is not distinctive of any being and does not fit the proper and indivisible species, if we neglect this [distinctive] account. Hence we must ask what the 32 soul of each particular [kind of thing]—for instance, a plant, a human being, or a beast—is. 33

What is true of the soul is similar to what is true of figure; for in both cases the earlier is invariably 38 present potentially in its successor—for instance, the triangle in the square, and the nutritive in the perceptive. We must consider why they are in this order. *415a* For the perceptive part requires the nutritive, but in plants the nutritive is separated from the perceptive. Again, each of the other senses requires touch, whereas touch is found without the other senses, since 5 many animals lack sight, hearing, and smell. Among things that perceive, some but not all have the locomotive part. Finally and most rarely, some have reasoning and understanding. For perishable things that have reasoning also have all the other parts of the soul; but not all of those that have each of the other 10 parts also have reasoning—on the contrary, some animals lack appearance, while some live by appearance alone. Theoretical intellect requires a different account.

Clearly, then, the account of each of these parts of the soul is also the most proper account of [each type of] soul.

4

If we are to investigate these [parts of the soul] we must find what each of them is and then inquire into 15 the next questions and those that follow. And if we ought to say what, for instance, the understanding or the perceptive or the nutritive part is, we should first say what it is to understand or perceive, since actualities and actions are prior in account to potentialities. 20 If this is so, and if in addition the objects corresponding to the actualities are prior to them and so must be studied first, then we must, for the same reason, begin by determining the objects corresponding to nutrition, sense, and understanding. And so we should first discuss nourishment and generation; for the nutritive soul belongs to other living things as well as 25 [to plants], and it is the first and most widely shared potentiality of the soul, the one that makes all living things alive.

Its functions are generation and the use of nourishment. For the most natural of all functions for a living thing, if it is complete and not defective and does not come to be by chance, is to produce another thing of the same sort as itself (an animal, if it is an animal, and a plant, if it is a plant), in order to share 415b as far as it can in the everlasting and divine. For this is the end they all strive for, and for its sake they do every action that accords with nature. (What something is for is of two types—the goal and the beneficiary.) These living things cannot share in the everlasting and divine by continuously existing, since no perishable thing can remain numerically one and 5 the same; hence they share in it as far as they can, to different degrees, and what remains is not the [parent] itself, but something else of the same sort as [the parent]—something that is specifically, not numerically, one with [the parent].

The soul is the cause and principle of the living body. Now, causes are spoken of in many ways, and 10 the soul is a cause in three of the ways distinguished—as the source of motion, as what something is for, and as the substance of ensouled bodies.

It is clearly the cause as substance; for a thing's substance is the cause of its being, and the being of living things is their living, the cause and principle of which is soul. Moreover, the actuality is the form of what is potentiality.

15 The soul is evidently also a cause by being what something is for. For just as productive thought aims at something, so does nature, and what it aims at is its end. In living things the natural end is the soul; for all natural bodies, of plants no less than of animals, 20 are organs of the soul, since they are for the sake of the soul. (The end for the sake of which is of two types, either the goal or the beneficiary.)

Moreover, the soul is also the source of locomotion, though not all living things have this potentiality. Alteration and growth also depend on the soul; for 25 perception seems to be some kind of alteration, and nothing that lacks a soul perceives. The same applies to growth and decay; for nothing either decays or grows naturally without being nourished, and nothing that has no share of life is nourished.

Empedocles is wrong when he adds that plants grow by putting down roots because earth naturally 416a moves downwards, and that plants grow by extending upwards because fire naturally moves upwards. His conception of up and down is wrong. For up and down are not the same for each particular [sort of] thing as they are for the universe as a whole; in fact, 5 if we ought to call organs the same or different in accordance with their functions, a plant's roots correspond to an animal's head. Besides, what is it that holds the fire and earth together when they are moving in contrary directions? For they will be torn apart unless something prevents it; whatever prevents it will be the soul, the cause of growing and being nourished.

Some think the nature of fire is the unqualified 10 cause of nourishment and growth, since it is the only body that is evidently nourished and grows, and hence one might suppose that it also performs this function in both plants and animals. In fact, however, fire is a sort of joint cause, but not the unqualified cause; 15 it is the soul, rather than fire, that is the unqualified cause. For while fire grows without limit, as long as there is fuel, the size and growth of everything naturally constituted has a limit and form, which are characteristic of soul, not of fire—i.e., of the form rather than of the matter.

Since one and the same potentiality of the soul is both nutritive and generative, we must first determine 20 the facts about nutrition; for this is the function that distinguishes the nutritive potentiality from others.

Contrary seems to nourish contrary, not in every case, but only when they not only come to be but also grow from each other; for many things come to be from each other (healthy from sick, for instance) 25 without gaining any quantity. And not even those contraries that grow seem to nourish each other in the same way; water, for instance, nourishes fire, but fire does not nourish water. It seems to be true, then, of the simple bodies more than of other things, that one thing nourishes and the other is nourished.

A puzzle arises: while some say that like nourishes 30 like, just as (they say) like grows by like, others, as we have said, hold the opposite view, that contrary nourishes contrary; for, they say, like is unaffected by like, but nourishment changes and is digested, and everything changes into its opposite or into the inter- 35 mediate. Moreover, nourishment is affected by the thing nourished, whereas the thing nourished is unaf- 416b fected by the nourishment—just as the matter is affected by the carpenter, who is unaffected by it and merely changes from inactivity to activity.

It matters for this question whether nourishment 5 is the first or last thing added. Perhaps it is both, if undigested nourishment is added first, and digested nourishment last. If so, then it would be possible to speak of nourishment in both ways; for in so far as nourishment is undigested, contrary nourishes contrary, and in so far as it has been digested, like nourishes like. Evidently, then, each view is in a way both correct and incorrect.

Since nothing is nourished except what has a share 10 of life, the ensouled body, in so far as it is ensouled, is what is nourished. Nourishment, therefore, is also relative, not coincidentally, to an ensouled thing. However, nourishing something is not the same as making it grow; for an ensouled thing is caused to grow in so far as it has some quantity, but it is nourished in so far as it is a this and a substance. For 15 it preserves its substance and exists as long as it is nourished; and what it generates is not itself, but something else of the same sort—for its own substance already exists, and a thing does not generate, but preserves, itself.

Hence this sort of principle in the soul is a potentiality of the sort that preserves the ensouled thing, in so far as it is ensouled, and nourishment equips it for its actuality; and so if it has been deprived of 23 nourishment it cannot exist. Further, since a thing's end rightly determines what we should call it, and in this case the end is the generation of another thing 25 of the same sort, this first soul will be the generative soul, generating another thing of the same sort.

We must distinguish three things—what is nourished, what it is nourished by, and what nourishes. What nourishes is this first soul, what is nourished is the ensouled body, and what it is nourished by is the nourishment. What the soul nourishes by is of two types—just as what we steer by is both the hand and the rudder: The first both initiates motion and undergoes it, and the second simply undergoes it. Since all nourishment must be digestible and the hot element produces digestion, every ensouled thing contains heat.

This, then, is an outline of what nutrition is; we 30 should describe it more clearly later in the discussions proper to it.

5

Now that we have determined this, let us discuss perception in general. Perception occurs in being moved and affected, as we have said, since it seems to be a type of alteration. Some also say that like is 35 affected by like; we have said in our general discussion 417a of acting and being affected how this is or is not possible.

A puzzle arises about why we do not perceive the senses themselves, and about why they do not produce perception without external objects, despite the presence of fire, earth, and the other elements, whose 5 intrinsic or coincidental properties are the things that are perceived. Clearly, then, the perceptive part is [what it is] by merely potential, not actual, [perceiving], and so it does not perceive [without an external object]—just as what is combustible is not burnt all by itself without something to burn it, since otherwise it would burn itself with no need of actual fire.

We speak of perceiving in two ways; for we say that 10 something sees or hears both in the case of something that has the potentiality for seeing or hearing, even though it is asleep at the time, and in the case of something that is actually seeing or hearing at the time. It follows that perception is also spoken of in two ways, as potential and as actual, and in the same way both what is potentially perceived and what is actually perceived are called objects of perception.

First, then, let us speak as though the actuality 15 were the same as being affected and moved—for motion is in fact a sort of actuality, though an incomplete one, as we have said elsewhere. Now, everything is affected and moved by an agent that has the relevant property in actuality, so that in a way like is affected by like, and in a way unlike by unlike—for what is 20 being affected is unlike the agent, but when it has been affected it is like the agent.

We must also distinguish types of potentiality and actuality, since just now we were speaking of them without qualification. One way in which someone might know is the way we have in mind in saying that a man knows because man is a kind of thing 25 that knows and has knowledge; another way is the way we have in mind in saying that someone who has grammatical knowledge knows. These knowers have different sorts of potentiality—the first has a potentiality because he has the right sort of genus and matter, whereas the second has a potentiality because he has the potentiality to attend to something when he wishes, if nothing external prevents it. A third sort [of knower] is someone who is attending to something at the time, actualizing his knowledge 30 and fully knowing (for instance) this A. In the first and second case we pass from potentially to actually knowing; but in the first case we do so by being altered through learning, and by frequent changes from the contrary state, while in the second case—where we 417b pass from having arithmetical or grammatical knowledge without actualizing it, to actualizing it—we do so in another way.

Further, there is not just one way of being affected. On the contrary, one way of being affected is a destruction of contrary by contrary, while the other way is more properly preservation, not destruction, of a potential *F* by an actual *F*, when the potential *F* is 5 [not contrary, but] like the actual *F*, in the way that a potentiality is like its actuality. For the second case—where the possessor of knowledge comes to attend to what he knows—either is not a case of alteration at all (since the addition leads to [the knowledge] itself and to the actuality) or is a different kind of alteration. That is why we should not say that the intelligent subject is altered in exercising his intelligence, just as we should not say that the builder is altered in [actually] building.

10 First, then, when an understanding and intelligent subject is led from potentiality to actuality, we should not call this teaching but give it some other name. Again, if a subject with potential knowledge learns and acquires knowledge from a teacher with actual knowledge, then we should say either, as we said, that this is not a case of being affected, or that there 15 are two ways of being altered, one of which is a change into a condition of deprivation, and the other of which is a change into possession of a state and into [the fulfillment of the subject's] nature.

In the perceiver, the first change is produced by its parent; and at birth it possesses perception corresponding to [the second type of] knowledge. We speak of actual perceiving in a way that corresponds to attending, except that the visible, audible, and other 20 perceptible objects that produce the actuality are external. This is because actual perception is of particulars, while knowledge is of universals, which are, in a way, in the soul itself; hence it is up to us to think whenever we want to, but it is not up to us to perceive 25 whenever we want to, since perception requires the presence of its object. The same is true for the types of knowledge that are about perceptible things, and for the same reason—namely that perceptible things are particulars and external.

There may be an opportunity to explain these points more perspicuously another time, but for the 30 moment let us be content with the distinctions we have made. There are different types of potentiality: One is what is meant in saying that a child is potentially a general. A second is what is meant in attributing the potentiality to someone of the right age, and [this second type] applies to the perceptive part. Since 418a the difference between these cases has no name, though our distinctions have shown that they are different, and in what ways, we have to use 'being affected' and 'being altered' as though they were the strictly correct names.

The perceiver is potentially what the perceptible object actually is already, as we have said. When it 5 is being affected, then, it is unlike the object; but when it has been affected it has been made like the object and has acquired its quality.

6

We should first discuss the objects of perception, taking each sense in turn. An object of perception is spoken of in three ways: Two types are perceived intrinsically, and one coincidentally. One type of in- 10 trinsic object is proper to each sense, and the other type of intrinsic object is common to all the senses.

By 'proper object' I mean the one that cannot be perceived by another sense and about which we cannot be deceived. Sight, for instance, is of color; hearing of sound; taste of flavor; and touch has a number of different objects. At any rate, each sense discriminates 15 among its proper objects, and a sense is not deceived about whether, for instance, something is a color or a sound, but can be deceived about whether or where the colored or sounding thing is. These objects, then, are said to be proper to each sense.

Motion, rest, number, shape, and size are the common objects, since they are not proper to any one sense, but are common to them all—a certain sort 20 of motion, for instance, is perceptible by both touch and sight.

Something is said to be coincidentally perceptible if, for instance, the pale [thing] is the son of Diares. For we perceive the son of Diares coincidentally, since he coincides with the pale thing we perceive, and hence we are not affected at all by the perceptible object in so far as it is [the son of Diares].

Among the intrinsic objects of perception, the 25 proper objects are most properly perceptible, and the essence of each sense is by nature relative to these. . . .

11

423b27. . . The objects of touch are the differentiae of body in so far as it is body, i.e., those that distinguish the elements—hot, cold, dry, and wet; we have discussed 30 these earlier in what we said about the elements. Their tactile sense-organ, the primary seat of the sense called touch, is the part that has these qualities poten-424a tially. For perceiving is a way of being affected; hence the agent causes the thing that is affected, which potentially has the quality that the agent has, to have that quality actually.

Hence we do not perceive anything that is as dry or wet, or hard or soft, [as the organ,] but only the excesses in either direction, because the sense is a 5 sort of intermediate condition between the contraries in objects of perception. And that is why a sense discriminates among its objects; for what is intermediate discriminates, since in relation to each extreme it becomes the other extreme. And just as what is going to perceive both pale and dark must be actually neither pale nor dark but potentially both, and simi-10 larly in the other cases, so also in the case of touch, [what is going to perceive the contraries] must be neither hot nor cold.

Further, just as we found that sight in a way perceives both the visible and the invisible, and similarly the other senses perceive the opposites, so also touch perceives the tangible and the intangible. What is intangible is either something that either has altogether very few of the differentiating properties of tangibles—air, for instance—or has an excess of tangible qualities—for instance, things that destroy *the* 15 *sense*.

We have spoken in outline, then, of the senses, one by one.

12

A general point to be grasped is that each sense receives the perceptible forms without the matter. Wax, for instance, receives the design on a signet-ring without the iron or gold; it acquires the design in the 20 gold or bronze, but not insofar as the design is gold or bronze. Similarly, each sense is affected by the thing that has color or flavor or sound, but not insofar as it is said to be that thing [for instance, a horse], but insofar as it has a given quality [for instance, color] and in accordance with the form [of the sense].

The primary sense-organ is the seat of this sort of 25 potentiality. Hence the organ and the capacity are one, but their being is different. For though [the sense-organ] that perceives is of some magnitude, being perceptive is not, and [so] the sense is not something with magnitude but is a [specific sort of] form and potentiality of the organ.

It is also evident from this why excesses in objects of perception destroy the sense-organs. For if the mo- 30 tion is too strong for the sense-organ, then the form, i.e., the sense, is destroyed, just as the harmony and tension are destroyed if the strings of an instrument are struck heavily.

This also makes it evident why plants do not perceive, even though they have one part of soul, and are affected in some ways by objects of touch, since they are chilled and heated. The reason is that they 424b lack a [suitable] intermediate condition and a principle suitable for receiving the form of perceptible things; instead, they are affected [by the form] with the matter.

A puzzle arises about whether something that cannot smell can be at all affected by odor, or something 5 that cannot see can be affected by color, and so on for the other cases. If the object of smell is odor, then anything produced by odor must be [the act of] smelling; hence nothing that is incapable of smelling anything can be affected by odor (the same applies to the other cases), and any such thing must be affected in so far as it is a perceiver. A further argument 10 makes the same conclusion clear. For a body is affected neither by light and darkness nor by sound nor by odor, but only by their subject, as, for instance, the air that comes with the thunder splits the log.

On the other hand, tangible [qualities] and flavors affect bodies; otherwise, what would affect and alter soulless things? Then will the other objects of perception also affect bodies? Perhaps not every body is 15 liable to be affected by odor and sound, and those that are affected are indefinite and impermanent—air, for instance, since it acquires an odor as though affected in some way.

Then what is there to smelling, besides being affected? Perhaps smelling is [not only being affected, but] also perceiving, while air that is affected [by odor], by contrast, soon becomes an object of perception [not a perceiver].

BOOK III

2

425b12 Since we perceive that we are seeing and hearing, it must be either sight or a different sense by which we perceive that we are seeing. [In the second case] the same sense will perceive both sight and the color that is the [external] subject, so that either there will be two senses perceiving the same thing, or else the sense 15 will perceive itself. Again, if the sense that perceives sight is different [from sight itself], then either it will go on without limit or there will be some sense that perceives itself, so that one ought to make this claim about the first sense.

Still, a puzzle arises. If perceiving by sight is seeing and if what we see is color or something colored, then if we are seeing, the first case of seeing will be colored.

20 It is evident, then, that perceiving by sight is not just one thing; for indeed, whenever we are not seeing, we discriminate light and darkness, but not in the same way. Moreover what sees is in fact colored in a way; for a sense-organ receives the object of perception without its matter. That is why, even when the objects of perception have gone away, perceptions 25 and appearances are still present in the sense-organs.

The actuality of the object of perception and of the sense are one and the same, but their being is not the same. I mean, for instance, that the actual sound and the actual hearing [are one and the same]; for it is possible to have [the sense of] hearing without 30 [actually] hearing, and what has sound is not always making a sound. But whenever what has the potentiality to hear is actually hearing, and what has the potentiality to sound is sounding, then actual hearing and actual sounding occur at the same time, so that we would say that one thing is a case of hearing and the 426a other a case of sounding.

If, then, the motion and the action are in the thing affected, both the sounding and the actual hearing must be in the [sense] that has the potentiality. For the actuality of what acts on something and initiates motion in it comes to be in the thing affected—that 5 is why what initiates motion need not be set in motion itself. Now, the actuality of what has the potentiality to sound is sound or sounding, while the actuality of what has a potentiality for hearing is hearing or listening for hearing is of two sorts, and so is sound.

The same account applies to the other senses and their objects. For just as both acting on something 10 and being affected are in the thing affected, not in the thing acting on it, so also both the actuality of the object of perception and the actuality of the perceiver are in the perceiver. In some cases, however, the two actualities have different names, as sounding and hearing have, while in other cases one of them has no name; for the actuality of sight is called seeing, whereas the actuality of color has 15 no name, and the actuality of what has the potentiality to taste is called tasting, whereas the actuality of flavor has no name.

And since the actuality of the object of perception and of what has the potentiality of perceiving are one, but their being is different, it follows that hearing and sounding (spoken of in this way), flavor and tasting, and so on, must all perish or remain in being at the same time. But this is not necessary for the things said to have the relevant potentiality.

In fact the earlier naturalists were wrong on this 20 point, in supposing that nothing was pale or dark without sight, and that there was no flavor without taste. For in a way they were correct, but in a way incorrect. For perception and its object are spoken of in two ways, as potential and as actual; in the case 25 [of the actuality] what they say is correct, but in the case [of the potentiality] it is not. They, however, spoke without qualification about things that are not spoken of without qualification. . . .

3

428a1 . . . If appearance is that in virtue of which some object appears to us, in contrast to what is so called metaphorically, then is it one of those potentialities or states in virtue of which we discriminate and attain *5* truth or falsity? These are perception, belief, knowledge, and understanding.

It is clear as follows that appearance is not the same as perception. For perception is either a potentiality, such as sight, or an actuality, such as seeing; but we have appearances when we have neither of these—in dreams, for instance. Moreover, perception is present in every [animal], but appearance is not. If they *10* were the same in actuality, then it would be possible for all beasts to have appearance, whereas in fact it does not seem possible [for all]; ants or bees, for instance, and grubs [do not have it]. Further, perceptions are always true, whereas most appearances are false. Again, whenever we are actually perceiving accurately, we do not say that this appears to us [to be] a man; we are more inclined to say [that something *15* appears to be so] in cases where we do not see clearly whether something is true or false. Further, as we were saying before, sights appear to us even when we have our eyes closed.

The remaining question is whether appearance is *20* belief; for belief may also be either true or false. Belief, however, implies conviction—since one cannot believe things if one does not find them convincing—whereas no beasts have conviction, though many have appearance. Further, belief implies conviction, conviction implies being persuaded, and persuasion implies reason, whereas no beasts have reason, though some have appearance.

25 It is evident, then, that appearance is neither belief that involves perception, nor belief that is produced through perception, nor a combination of belief and perception. This is so both for the reasons given and also because [on this view] belief will not be about anything other than the thing, if there is one, that is the object of perception.

I mean, for instance, that the combination of a belief about the pale and a perception of the pale will turn out to be appearance; for surely it will not *30* be the combination of a belief about the good and a perception of the pale—for appearance will be hav- *428b* ing a belief non-coincidentally about the very thing one perceives. In fact, however, we sometimes have false appearances about the same things at the same time as we have a true supposition about them, as when, for instance, the sun appears a foot across, even though we are convinced that it is bigger than the inhabited world.

It turns out, then, [on the view being considered] *5* that either we have lost the true belief we had, even though the thing still exists and we have neither forgotten our belief nor been persuaded to change it, or else, if we still have the true belief, the same belief must at the same time be both true and false. But in fact it could have become false only if the thing changed without our noticing it. It follows, then, that appearance cannot be any of these things, nor a product of them.

It is possible, however, when one thing has been *10* set in motion, for a second thing to be set in motion by the first. Moreover, appearance seems to be a sort of motion, to involve perception, to be present in things that have perception, and to be about the objects of perception. Now, it is also possible for motion to result from actual perception, and this motion must be similar to the perception.

Hence this motion cannot occur without percep- *15* tion or in things that do not have perception. Things that have appearance act and are affected in many ways in accordance with it, and it can be either true or false. . . .

4

Now we must consider the part by which the soul *429a10* has knowledge and intelligence, and ask whether it is separable, or it is not separable in magnitude but only in account; and what its differentia is, and how understanding comes about.

Now, if understanding is like perceiving, it consists either in being affected by the object of intellect or in something else of the same sort. Hence the intellect *15* must be unaffected, but receptive of the form; it must have the quality [of the object] potentially, not actually; and it must be related to its object as the perceiving part is related to the objects of perception.

Hence the intellect, since it understands all things, must be unmixed, in order, as Anaxagoras says, to 20 'master' them (i.e., to know them); for the intrusion of any foreign thing would hinder and obstruct it. And so it has no nature except this—that it is potential. Hence the part of the soul called intellect (by which I mean that by which the soul thinks and supposes) is not actually, before it understands, any of the things 25 there are. It is also unreasonable, then, for intellect to be mixed with the body, since it would then acquire some quality (for instance, hot or cold) or even, like the perceiving part, have some organ, whereas in fact it has none.

And so those who say that the soul is a place of forms are right, except that it is the intellectual soul, not the whole soul, which is—potentially, not actually—the forms.

30 The condition of the sense-organ and of the faculty of perception makes it evident that the perceiving part and the intellectual part are unaffected in differ- 429b ent ways. For after a sense perceives something very perceptible, it cannot perceive; after hearing very loud sounds, for instance, it cannot hear sound, and after seeing vivid colors or smelling strong odors, it cannot see or smell. But whenever intellect understands something that is very intelligible, it understands 5 more, not less, about inferior objects; for intellect is separable, whereas the perceiving part requires a body.

When the intellect becomes each thing [that it understands], as it does when someone is said to have actual knowledge (this comes about whenever someone is able to actualize his knowledge through himself), even then it is still potential in a way, though not in the same way as before it learnt or discovered; and then it is capable of understanding itself.

10 Magnitude is different from being magnitude and water from being water; and the same applies in many other cases too, though not in all, since in some cases the thing is the same as its being. It follows that to discriminate being flesh we use something different, or something in a different state, from what we use in discriminating flesh; for flesh requires matter, and, 15 like the snub, it is this [form] in this [matter]. Hence to discriminate the hot and the cold and the things of which flesh is some sort of form, we use the perceptive part; but to discriminate being flesh, we use something else that is either separable [from body] or related to it as a formerly bent line is related to the straight line it has become.

Further, if we turn to things whose being depends on abstraction, the straight is similar to the snub, since it requires something continuous. But if being 20 straight is different from the straight, then so is the essence of straight (duality, let us say) different from the straight, and therefore to discriminate it we use something different, or something in a different state. In general, then, the [separability] of intellect corresponds to the way in which objects are separable from matter.

A puzzle arises. If intellect is simple and unaffected, having, as Anaxagoras says, nothing in common with anything, then how can it understand, if understand- 25 ing consists in being affected? For it seems that two things must have something in common if one is to affect the other. Again, is intellect itself an object of intellect? For if nothing other [than itself] makes it an object of intellect, and if all objects of intellect are one in species, then the other objects of intellect will also be intellect; alternatively, it will need something mixed into it, to make it an object of intellect in the same way as the other objects of intellect are. 30

On the other hand, our previous discussion of ways of being affected because of something in common has shown that the intellect is in a way potentially the objects of intellect, but before it understands them, it is none of them actually. Its potentiality is that of a 430a writing tablet with nothing actually written on it—which is also true of intellect.

Further, intellect itself is an object of intellect in the same way as its objects are. For in the case of things without matter, the understanding part and its object are one, since actual knowledge and its object 5 are the same. (We should investigate why it is not [engaged in the activity of] understanding all the time.) In things that have matter, each object of intellect is potentially present; hence intellect will not be in them (since it is a potentiality for being such things without their matter), but it will be an object of intellect.

5

In the whole of nature each kind of thing has some- 10 thing as its matter, which is potentially all the things in the kind, and something else as the cause and producer, which produces them all—for instance, the craft in relation to its matter. These differences, then, must also be found in the soul. One sort of intellect 15 corresponds to matter, since it becomes all things. Another sort corresponds to the producer by producing all things in the way that a state, such as light, produces things—for in a way light makes potential colors into actual colors. This second sort of intellect is separable, unaffected, and unmixed, since its essence is actuality.

For in every case the producer is more valuable than the thing affected, and the principle is more 20 valuable than the matter. Actual knowledge is the same as its object; potential knowledge is temporally prior in an individual [knower], but in general it is not even temporally prior. But [productive intellect] does not understand at one time and not at another.

Only when it has been separated is it precisely what it is, all by itself. And this alone is immortal and everlasting. But [when it is separated] we do not remember, because this [productive intellect] is 25 unaffected, whereas the intellect that is affected is perishable. And without this [productive intellect] nothing understands. . . .

10

433a9 There are apparently two parts that move us—both 10 intellect and desire, if we take appearance to be a kind of understanding. For many people follow their appearances against their knowledge, and the other animals have appearance but lack understanding and reasoning. Both intellect and desire, then, move us from place to place. This is the intellect that reasons 15 for some goal and is concerned with action; its [concern with an] end distinguishes it from theoretical intellect. All desire also aims at some goal; for the object of desire is the starting point of intellect concerned with action, and the last stage [of our reasoning] is the starting point of action.

Hence it is reasonable to regard these two things—desire, and thought concerned with action—as the movers. For the object of desire moves us, and thought 20 moves us because its starting point is the object of desire. Moreover, whenever appearance moves us, it requires desire.

And so there is one mover, the desiring part. For if there were two—intellect and desire—they would move us insofar as they had a common form. In fact, however, intellect evidently does not move anything without desire, since wish is desire, and any motion in accordance with reasoning is in accordance with wish; desire, on the other hand, also moves us against 25 reasoning, since appetite is a kind of desire. Now, intellect is always correct, but desire and appearance may be either correct or incorrect. Hence in every case the mover is the object of desire, but the object of desire is either the good or the apparent good—not every sort of good, but the good that is achievable in action. What is achievable in action admits of 30 being otherwise.

Evidently, then, the potentiality of the soul that moves us is the one called desire. People who divide *433b* the soul into parts, if they divide it into separate parts corresponding to the different potentialities, will find very many of them—the nutritive, perceptive, intellectual, and deliberative parts, and, moreover, the desiring part; for the difference between these parts is wider than the one between the appetitive and emotional parts.

Desires that are contrary to each other arise, how- 5 ever, when reason and appetite are contrary, which happens in subjects that perceive time. For intellect urges us to draw back because of what is to come, while appetite [urges us on] because of what is present; for the pleasant thing that is present appears both unqualifiedly pleasant and unqualifiedly good, 10 because we do not see what is to come.

Hence the mover is one in species—the desiring part, in so far as it is desiring. Indeed, the first mover of all is the object of desire, since it moves us without being moved, by being present to understanding or appearance. But the movers are numerically more than one.

We must distinguish three things—the mover, its instrument, and the subject moved. There are two types of movers: the unmoved mover and the moved 15 mover. The unmoved mover is the good achievable in action, and the moved mover is the desiring part; for the thing that is moved is moved insofar as it desires, and desire, insofar as it is actual, is a sort of motion. The thing moved is the animal. When we reach the instrument by which desire moves, we reach something bodily, and so we should study it when 20 we study the functions common to soul and body.

To summarize for the present: What moves something as an instrument is found where the same thing is both the starting point and the last stage. In the hinge-joint, for instance, the convex is last, and hence at rest, while the concave is the starting point, and 25 hence is moved. These are different in account, though they are spatially inseparable. For since everything is moved by pushing and pulling, something must remain at rest, as in a circle, and the motion must originate from this.

In general, then, as we have said, an animal moves itself insofar as it has desire. For desire it needs appearance; and appearance is either rational appearance 30 or the perceptual appearance that other animals share [with human beings].

11

We should also consider what it is that moves incom- 434a plete animals, whose only form of perception is touch. Can they have appearance and appetite, or not? For they evidently have pleasure and pain; if they have these, they must have appetite. But how could they have appearance? Well, perhaps, just as they are 5 moved indeterminately, so also they have appearance and appetite, but have them indeterminately.

Now, the other animals as well [as man] also have perceptual appearance, as we have said, but [only] reasoning animals have deliberative appearance. For when we come to the question whether one is to do this or that, we come to a task for reasoning. And [in this case] one must measure by one [standard], since one pursues the greater [good]. And so one is able 10 to make one object of appearance out of many. And this is why [non-rational animals] do not seem to have belief; it is because they lack the [appearance] resulting from reasoning.

That is why desire lacks the deliberative part. And sometimes one desire overcomes and moves another, while sometimes the second overcomes and moves the first, like one sphere moving another, whenever incontinence occurs. By nature the [desire] that is 15 superior is dominant in every case and moves [the agent], and so it turns out that three motions are initiated [in the agent]. The part that has knowledge stays at rest and is not moved.

Now, one sort of supposition and statement is universal, while another is about what is particular; for the first says that this sort of agent ought to do this sort of thing, and the second says that this is this sort of thing and I am this sort of agent. Hence the second 20 belief, not the universal belief, initiates motion; or [rather] both initiate motion, but the first does so by being more at rest, in contrast to the second.

Metaphysics

BOOK I

1

980a21 All human beings by nature desire to know. A sign of this is our liking for the senses; for even apart from their usefulness we like them for themselves—especially the sense of sight, since we choose seeing above practically all the others, not only as an aid to action, but also when we have no intention of acting. 25 The reason is that sight, more than any of the other senses, gives us knowledge of things and clarifies many differences between them.

Animals possess sense-perception by nature at birth. In some but not all of these, perception results in 980b memory, making them more intelligent and better at learning than those that cannot remember. Some animals that cannot hear sounds (for instance, bees and similar kinds of animal) are intelligent but do 25 not learn; those that both perceive sounds and have memory also learn.

Non-human animals live by appearances and memories but have little share in experience, whereas human beings also live by craft and reasoning. In human beings experience results from memory, since 981a many memories of the same thing result in the capacity for a single experience. Experience seems to be quite like science and craft, and indeed human beings attain science and craft through experience; for, as 5 Polus[1] correctly says, experience has produced craft, but inexperience only luck.

A craft arises when many thoughts that arise from experience result in one universal judgment about similar things. For the judgment that in this illness this treatment benefited Callias, Socrates, and others, in many particular cases, is characteristic of experience, but the judgment that it benefited everyone of 10 a certain sort (marked out by a single kind) suffering from a certain disease (for instance, phlegmatic or bilious people when burning with fever) is characteristic of craft.

For practical purposes, experience seems no worse than craft; indeed we even see that experienced people are actually more successful than those who have a rational account but lack experience. The reason 15 is that experience is cognition of particulars, whereas craft is cognition of universals. Moreover, each action and event concerns a particular; in medical treatment, for instance, we do not heal man (except coincidentally) but Callias or Socrates or some other individual 20 who is coincidentally a man. If, then, someone has a rational account but lacks experience, and recognizes the universal but not the particular falling under it, he will often give the wrong treatment, since treatment is applied to the particular.

Nonetheless, we attribute knowing and compre- 25 hending to craft more than to experience, and we judge that craftsmen are wiser than experienced people, on the assumption that in every case knowledge, rather than experience, implies wisdom. This is because craftsmen know the cause, but [merely] experienced people do not; for experienced people know the fact that something is so but not the reason why it is so, whereas craftsmen recognize the reason why, i.e., the cause. 30

That is why we believe that the master craftsmen in a given craft are more honorable, know more, and are wiser than the manual craftsmen, because they 981b know the causes of what is produced. The manual craftsmen, we think, are like inanimate things that produce without knowing what they produce, in the way that, for instance, fire burns; the latter produce their products by a natural tendency, while the manual craftsmen produce theirs because of habit. We assume, then, that some craftsmen are wiser than others not because they are better in practice, but 5

Reprinted from Aristotle, *Selections*, translated and edited by Terence Irwin and Gail Fine (Indianapolis: Hackett Publishing Company, 1995), by permission of the publisher. The use of brackets within the text indicates insertions not found in the manuscript.

1. [Polus, who lived in the fifth century B.C., was a student of the Sophist Gorgias, regarding whom see Plato's *Meno*, n.2.—S.M.C.]

because they have a rational account and recognize the causes.

And in general, a sign that distinguishes those who know from those who do not is their ability to teach. Hence we think craft, rather than experience, is 10 knowledge, since craftsmen can teach, while merely experienced people cannot.

Further, we do not think any of the senses is wisdom, even though they are the most authoritative ways of recognizing particulars. They do not tell us why anything is so; for instance, they do not tell us why fire is hot, but only that it is hot.

It is not surprising, then, that in the earliest times 15 anyone who discovered any craft that went beyond the perceptions common to all was admired not only because he discovered something useful, but also for being a wise person, superior to others. Later on, as more crafts were discovered—some related to necessities, others to [leisure-time] pursuits—those who discovered these latter crafts were in every case judged 20 to be wiser than the others, because their sciences did not aim at practical utility. Hence, finally, after all these crafts had been established, the sciences that aim neither at pleasure nor at necessities were discovered, initially in the places where people had leisure. This is why mathematical crafts arose first in 25 Egypt; for there the priestly class were allowed to be at leisure.

The difference between craft and science and other similar sorts of things has been discussed in the Ethics. The point of our present discussion is to show that in everyone's judgment any discipline deserving the name of wisdom must describe the first causes, 30 i.e., the principles. And so, as we said earlier, the experienced person seems to be wiser than those who have just any old perception; the craftsman seems to 982*a* be wiser than those with nothing more than experience; the master craftsman wiser than the manual craftsman; and the purely theoretical sciences wiser than the productive sciences. It is clear, then, that wisdom is knowledge of certain sorts of principles and causes.

2

5 Since this is the science we are looking for, we should consider what sorts of causes and principles wisdom is the science of. Perhaps this will become clearer if we consider our judgments about the wise person. First, we judge that he has knowledge about all things as far as possible, without, however, having it about 10 each particular [kind of thing]. Next, the one who is capable of knowing difficult things, i.e., things not easily known by human beings, is the wise person; for sense-perception is common to everyone, and that is why it is easy and not characteristic of wisdom. Further, someone is wiser in a given science if he is more exact, and a better teacher of the causes. Again, 15 if one of two sciences is choiceworthy for itself—[purely] for the sake of knowing it—and the other is choiceworthy [only] for the sake of its results, the first has a better claim to be wisdom than the second. Moreover, the superior science has a better claim than the subordinate science; for the wise person must give orders, not take them, and those who are 20 less wise must follow his orders, not he theirs. These, then, are our judgments about wisdom and wise people.

Of these features, we judge that knowledge about everything necessarily belongs to the one who has the best claim to universal science; for he in a way knows everything that is a subject for a science. These most universal things are also just about the most difficult for human beings to know, since they are furthest from perceptions. Further, the most exact 25 sciences are those that, more than the others, study the first things; for the sciences that are derived from fewer principles—for instance, arithmetic—are more exact than those—for instance, geometry—that require further principles. Moreover, the science that studies the causes is more of a teacher, since teachers are those who state something's causes. Besides, 30 knowledge and science for their own sake are most characteristic of the science of the most appropriate object of knowledge. For one who chooses knowledge for its own sake will choose above all the science that 982*b* is a science to the highest degree. This science is the science of the most appropriate objects of knowledge; these objects are the first things, i.e., the causes, since we know the subordinate things because of these and from these, not the other way round. Further, the most superior science—the one that is superior to 5 any subordinate science—is the one that knows the end for which a given thing should be done; this end is something's good, and in general the end is what is best in every sort of nature.

From everything that has been said, then, we find that the name under discussion, [i.e., 'wisdom'], applies to the same science; for we find that wisdom 10 must study the first principles and causes, and the good, the end, is one of the causes.

The fact that this science is not productive is also clearer from those who first engaged in philosophy. For human beings originally began philosophy, as they do now, because of wonder, at first because they wondered at the strange things in front of them, and later because, advancing little by little, they found 15 greater things puzzling—what happens to the moon, the sun and the stars, how the universe comes to be. Someone who wonders and is puzzled thinks he is ignorant (this is why the myth-lover is also a philoso- 20 pher in a way, since myth is composed of wonders); since, then, they engaged in philosophy to escape ignorance, they were evidently pursuing scientific knowledge [simply] for the sake of knowing, not for any further use.

What actually happened is evidence for this view. For it was only when practically everything required for necessities and for ease and [leisure-time] pursuits was supplied that they began to seek this sort of under- 25 standing; clearly, then, we do not seek it for some further use. Just as we describe a free person as one who exists for his own sake and not for someone else's, so we also describe this as the only free science, since it is the only one that exists for its own sake.

Hence the possession of this science might justifi- 30 ably be thought to be beyond human capacity. For in many ways human nature is in slavery, so that, as Simonides says, 'the god alone would have this privilege,' and it is unfitting for human beings to transgress their own level in their search for the science.[2] If there actually is something in what the poets 983a say, and the divine nature is spiteful, divine spite would be likely in this case, and all those who go too far would suffer misfortunes. The divine nature, however, cannot be spiteful; as the proverb says, 'Poets tell many lies.'

Nor ought we to take any science to be more honor- 5 able than this one, since the most divine science is also the most honorable, and this science that we are describing is the most divine. It alone is most divine in two ways: for the divine science [may be understood] as (i) the one that a god more than anyone else would be expected to have, or as (ii) the science of divine things. Only this science [of first causes] satisfies both conditions [for being divine]. For (i) the god seems to be among the causes of all things, and to be some sort of principle, and (ii) this is the sort of science that the god, alone or more than anyone 10 else, would be expected to have. Hence all the other sciences are more necessary than this one, but none is better.

However, the possession of this science must in a way leave us in a condition contrary to the one we were in when we began our search. For, as we said, everyone begins from wonder that something is the way it is, as they wonder at toys that move spontane- 15 ously, or the turnings of the sun, or the incommensurability of the diagonal (for people who have not yet studied the cause are filled with wonder that there is something that is not measured by the smallest length). But we must end up in the contrary and (according to the proverb) the better state, the one that people achieve by learning [the cause] in these 20 other cases as well—for nothing would be more amazing to a geometer than if the diagonal turned out to be commensurable.

We have described, then, the nature of the science we are seeking, and the goal that our search and our whole line of inquiry must reach.

3

It is evident, then, that we must acquire knowledge of the original causes, since we say we know a thing 25 whenever we think we recognize its primary cause. Causes are spoken of in four ways. One of these, we say, is the being and essence; for the reason why is traced back ultimately to the account, and the primary reason why is the cause and principle. Another is the matter and subject. A third is the source of the 30 principle of motion. The fourth is what something is for, i.e., the good—the opposite to the third cause, since it is the end of all coming to be and motion.

We have studied these causes adequately in our 983b work on nature. Still, let us also enlist those who previously took up the investigation of beings and pursued philosophical study about the truth; for it is clear that they also mention causes and principles of

2. [Regarding Simonides, see Plato's *Republic*, Bk. I, n.9.]

some sort. A discussion of their views, then, will ad-
5 vance our present line of inquiry; for either we shall find some other kind of cause or we shall be more convinced about those we have just mentioned.

Most of the first philosophers, then, thought that the only principles of all things were material. For, they say, there is some [subject] that all beings come from, the first thing they come to be from and the
10 last thing they perish into, the substance remaining throughout but changing in respect of its attributes. This, they say, is the element and the principle of beings. And for this reason they think that nothing either comes to be or is destroyed, on the assumption that this nature [that is the subject] persists in every change, just as we say that Socrates does not come to be without qualification when he comes to be good
15 or musical, and that he is not destroyed when he loses these states (because the subject, Socrates himself, remains)—so also they say that nothing else either comes to be or perishes without qualification (for there must be some nature, either one or more than one, that persists while everything else comes to be from it).

But they do not all agree about the number or type of this material principle. Thales,[3] the originator of
20 this sort of philosophy, says it is water (that is why he also declared that the earth rests on water). Presumably he reached this judgment from seeing that what nourishes all things is wet and that the hot itself comes from the wet and is kept alive by it (and what all
25 things come to be from is there principle). He also reached this judgment because he thought that the seeds of all things have a wet nature (and water is the principle of the nature of wet things).

Some people think that even those who first gave accounts of the gods in very ancient times, long before the present, accepted this judgment about nature. For
30 the ancients made Oceanus and Tethys the parents of coming to be and described the oath of the gods as water, which they called Styx; for what is oldest is most honored, and what is most honored is the oath.
984a It is perhaps unclear whether this belief about nature is in fact old or even ancient, but at any rate this is what Thales is said to have declared about the first cause. (No one would think of including Hippon[4] among these philosophers, given the triviality of his thought.) 5

Anaximenes[5] and Diogenes[6] take air to be both prior to water and also the primary principle of all the simple bodies, while Hippasus of Metapontium[7] and Heraclitus of Ephesus[8] say this about fire. Empedocles[9] takes the four bodies to be principles, adding earth as a fourth to the ones mentioned. These, he says, always remain and do not come to be, except 10 insofar as they come to be more or fewer, being combined into one and dispersed from one into many.

Anaxagoras of Clazomenae,[10] who was older than Empedocles but wrote later, says that the principles are unlimited; for he says that practically all the uniform things (for instance, water or fire) come to be and are destroyed only in the ways we have mentioned, by 15 being combined and dispersed; they do not come to be or get destroyed in any other way, but always remain.

If one went by these views, one might judge that the material cause is the only sort of cause. But as people thus advanced, reality itself showed them the way and compelled them to search. For however true 20 it might be that all coming to be and perishing is from one (or more than one) thing, still, why does this happen, and what is the cause? For certainly the subject does not produce change in itself. I mean, for instance, neither the wood nor the bronze causes itself to change, nor does the wood itself produce a

3. [Thales of Miletus (c. 636–c. 546 B.C.), the earliest Pre-Socratic philosopher, maintained that everything in nature is composed of water.]

4. [Hippon was a philosopher of nature who lived during the fifth century B.C.]

5. [Anaximenes was a sixth-century-B.C. Pre-Socratic philosopher who maintained that air was the basic element of nature.]

6. [Diogenes was a fifth-century-B.C. philosopher who revived the teaching of Anaximenes.]

7. [Hippasus was an early Pythagorean, one of the followers of Pythagoras, the sixth-century-B.C. philosopher who founded a religious order that believed in reincarnation and considered numbers the essence of the world.]

8. Heraclitus (c. 535–c. 475 B.C.) was an influential Pre-Socratic philosopher who viewed the world-order as a continuous flux and considered any claim to permanence an illusion of the human senses.]

9. [Regarding Empedocles, see Plato's *Meno*, n.6.]

10. [Regarding Anaxagoras, see Plato's *Phaedo*, n.12.]

25 bed, or the bronze a statue, but something else causes the change. And to search for this is (in our view) to search for the second principle—the source of the principle of motion.

Those who were the very first to undertake this line of inquiry into nature, who said that the subject is one, were quite satisfied with this. But at least some 30 of those who said that the subject is one, as though defeated by this search [for an explanation of change], said that the one, i.e., nature as a whole, is immobile, not only as regards coming to be and perishing (that was an old belief agreed on by all), but also as regards every other sort of change. This view is distinctive 984*b* of them.

Of those who said that the universe is one element, none managed to notice this [second] cause, unless Parmenides[11] did; he noticed it only insofar as he 5 posited not only one cause, but also in a way two causes. Indeed those who recognize more than one element—for instance, hot and cold, or fire and earth—make it easier to state [the cause that initiates motion], since they regard fire as having a nature that initiates motion, and water, earth, and other such things as having natures contrary to this.

After these sorts of principles were proposed by these people, other people found them inadequate to generate the nature of beings; once again, as we said, it was as though the truth itself compelled them, 10 and so they began to search for the next sort of principle. For presumably it is unlikely that fire or earth or anything else of that sort would cause some things to be in a good and fine state and would cause other things to come to be in that state, and unlikely that people would think so; still, it was unsatisfactory to 15 entrust so great a result to chance and luck. And so when one of them said that mind is present (in nature just as in animals) as the cause of the world order and of all its arrangement, he seemed like a sober person, and his predecessors seemed like babblers in comparison. We know that Anaxagoras evidently 20 made a start on giving such accounts, but an earlier statement of them is ascribed to Hermotimus of Clazomenae.[12] Those who held this view posited a principle of beings that is at once both the cause of things turning out well and the sort of cause that is the source of motion for beings.

4

One might suspect that the first to search for this sort of cause was Hesiod[13] and anyone else who counted desire or appetite among beings as a principle, as 25 Parmenides, for instance, also did. For he too, in describing the coming to be of the whole universe, says: 'Desire was the first of all the gods she devised.' And Hesiod says: 'Before everything else that came to be, there was chaos, and then the broad-fronted earth, and desire, preeminent among all the immortals.' He assumes that there must be some cause 30 among beings to initiate motion in things and to bring them together. Let us leave it till later to determine which of these people was the first [to discover this sort of cause].

Moreover, the contraries of good things (i.e., disorder and ugliness no less than order and beauty) were also apparent in nature, and bad things were appar- 985*a* ently more numerous than good things, and base things more numerous than beautiful things. For this reason someone else introduced love and strife so that each of them would be the cause of one of these two sorts of things. For if we follow Empedocles' argument, and do not confine ourselves to his mumbling way of expressing it, but attend to what he has 5 in mind, we will find that love is the cause of good things, and strife of bad. And so, if one were to claim that in a way Empedocles said—indeed was the first to say—that the good and the bad are principles, one would perhaps be right, if the cause of all goods is the good itself. 10

These people, then, as we say, evidently made this much progress in fastening on two of the four causes that we distinguished in our work on nature—the matter and the principle of motion. But they did so dimly and not at all perspicuously. They were like unskilled boxers in fights, who, in the course of moving around, often land good punches, but are not 15

11. [Parmenides, who lived in the late sixth century B.C. and at least half of the fifth century, was an influential Pre-Socratic philosopher who viewed the world-order as composed of being itself and considered any claim to change an illusion of the human senses.]

12. [No other information is known about Hermotimus.]

13. [Hesiod was an eighth-century-B.C. Greek poet whose works are a rich source of mythology.]

guided by knowledge; in the same way these thinkers would seem not to know what they are saying, since they evidently make practically no use of these causes, except to a slight degree.

Anaxagoras, for instance, uses mind as an ad hoc device 20 for the production of the universe; it is when he is puzzled about the cause of something's being necessarily as it is that he drags in mind, but in other cases he recognizes anything but mind as the cause of things that come to be. Empedocles, admittedly, uses these causes more than Anaxagoras does, but he too still makes insufficient use of them, and he does not succeed 25 in using them consistently. At any rate, he often makes love draw things apart, and strife draw them together. For whenever strife scatters the universe into its elements, all the fire is gathered into one, and so is each of the other elements; and whenever love brings things back together again into one, the parts from each element are necessarily scattered again.

30 Empedocles, then, went beyond his predecessors. He was the first to distinguish this cause and to introduce it; he did not take the principle of motion to be one, but assumed different and contrary principles. Moreover, he was the first to say that there are four material elements. In fact, though, he does not use 985b all four, but treats them as two, treating fire in its own right as one nature, and its opposites—earth, air, and water—as together constituting another; this may be gathered from studying his poems. As we say, then, this is how many principles he recognized, and this is what he said about them.

5 Leucippus[14] and his colleague Democritus,[15] on the other hand, say that the elements are the full and the empty, and that, of these, the full and solid is what is, and the empty is what is not. That is why they also say that what is no more of a being than what is not, because body is no more of a being than 10 the empty is. They take these to be the material causes of beings.

Those who take the substance that is the subject to be one explain how everything else comes to be by referring to the ways in which the subject is affected, taking the rare and the dense to be the principle of the ways it is affected. In the same way, Leucippus and Democritus take the differentiae to be the causes of the other things. They say, however, that there are three of these differentiae—shape, order, and position. 15 For they say that what is is differentiated only by rhythm, touching, and turning. Of these rhythm is shape, touching is order, and turning is position; for A differs from N in shape. AN from NA in order, 20 and Z from N in position. Like the other people, however, they were too lazy to take up the question about motion and to ask from what source and in what way it arises in beings.

This, then, would seem to be the extent, as we say, of the earlier thinkers' search for these two causes.

6

987a29 Plato's work came after the philosophical views we have mentioned; it agreed with them in most ways, but it also had distinctive features setting it apart 30 from the philosophy of the Italians. For in his youth Plato first became familiar with Cratylus[16] and with the Heraclitean beliefs that all perceptible things are always flowing and that there is no knowledge of them; he held these views later too. 987b Socrates, on the other hand, was concerned with ethics and not at all with nature as a whole; he was seeking the universal in ethics and was the first to turn his thought to definitions. Plato agreed with Socrates, 5 but because of his Heraclitean views he took these definitions to apply not to perceptible things but to other things; for, he thought, the common formula could not be of any of the perceptible things, since they are always changing. Beings of this sort [that definitions are of], then, he called Ideas, and he said that perceptible things are apart from these, and are all called after them, since the things with the same names as the Forms are what they are by participation in them. 10

In speaking of 'participation' he changed only the name; for the Pythagoreans[17] say that things are what

14. [Leucippus was a fifth-century-B.C. philosopher who developed the theory that the world is composed of solid, invisible atoms.]

15. [Regarding Democritus, see Aristotle's *Physics*, n.3.]

16. [Cratylus, a young contemporary of Socrates, carried the teachings of Heraclitus to their extreme, maintaining that not only can you not step twice in the same river, you cannot step in the same river even once, since the river is changing as you step.]

17. [Regarding the Pythagoreans, see n.7.]

they are by imitating numbers, and Plato (changing the name) said they are what they are by participating [in Forms]. But they left it to others to investigate what it is to participate in or to imitate Forms.

15 Further, he says that, apart from perceptible things and Forms, there are also mathematical objects in between. These differ from perceptible things in being everlasting and immobile; they differ from Forms in that there are many of the same kind, whereas there is only one Form for each kind of thing.

Since the Forms are the causes of other things, he thought that their elements are the elements of all beings. The great and the small, then, as matter, and *20* the one, as substance, are principles; for Forms come from these, by participating in the one. And yet he said, agreeing with the Pythagoreans, that the one is substance, and that it is not said to be one by being *25* something else. He also agreed with them in saying that numbers are the causes of the being of other things; but in positing a duality instead of treating the indeterminate as one, and in taking the great and small to constitute the indeterminate, he held a distinctive view of his own. Moreover, in his view numbers exist apart from perceptible things; whereas the Pythagoreans take the objects themselves to be numbers, and do not place mathematical objects between perceptible things and Forms.

30 His claim that the one and numbers exist apart from the other objects (in contrast to the Pythagorean view) and his introduction of the Forms were the result of his investigation of arguments; for none of his predecessors engaged in dialectic. He made the other nature [besides the One] a duality because he thought that numbers (except the primes) could be *988a* neatly produced from the duality, as though from something malleable.

What actually happens, though, is the contrary of this, and it is implausible to think it would happen in the way they [the Platonists] say. For in their view many things are made out of the matter, but the Form generates only once; in fact, however, only one table is apparently made out of one [bit of] matter, whereas the agent who applies the form, though he is one, *5* makes many tables. Similarly, in the case of male and female, the female is impregnated from one copulation, whereas the male impregnates many females. And yet these things are imitations of those principles [that they believe in].

This, then, was what Plato determined about the questions we are investigating. It is evident from what has been said that he used only two causes, the cause involving the what-it-is and the material cause; for *10* the Forms are causes of the what-it-is of the other things, and the one is the cause of the what-it-is of Forms. The nature of the matter that is the subject for the Forms (in the case of perceptible things) and for the one (in the case of Forms) is also evident: it is the duality, the great and the small. Further, he has assigned the cause of good and bad to the elements, one to each, as we say some earlier philoso- *15* phers, such as Empedocles and Anaxagoras, also sought to do.

9

. . . As for those who posited Ideas, the first objection *990a34* is that in seeking to grasp the causes of the beings in this world, they introduced different things, equal *990b* in number to them. It is as though someone wanted to count things and thought he could not do it if there were fewer of them, but could do it if he added more. For the Forms they resorted to in their *5* search for the causes of things in this world are practically equal in number to—or at any rate are no fewer than—the things in this world. For take each [kind of] thing that has a one over many, both substances and non-substances, both things in this world and everlasting things; in each case there is some [one over many] that has the same name [as the many].

Further, none of the proofs we offer to show that there are Forms appears to succeed; for some of them are invalid, while some also yield Forms of *10* things that we think have no Forms. For the arguments from the sciences yield Forms of all the things of which there are sciences; the one over many yields Forms even of negations; and the argument *15* from thinking about something that has perished yields Forms of things that perish, since there is an appearance of these. Further, among the more accurate arguments, some produce Ideas of relatives, whereas we deny that these are a kind of things that are in their own right; others introduce the Third Man.

And in general the arguments for Forms undermine the existence of things that matter more to us than the existence of the Ideas does. For they imply that number, not duality, is first and that what is relative is prior to what is in its own right, and they lead to all the other [unacceptable] conclusions that some people have been led to believe by following the beliefs about the Ideas, even though these beliefs conflict with their own principles.

Further, the reasoning that leads us to say that there are Ideas also yields Forms of many other things as well as of substances. For a thought is one not only in the case of substances but also in other cases; there are sciences of other things as well as of substance; and thousands of other such difficulties arise.

On the other hand, it is necessary, and follows from the beliefs about Forms, that if things can participate in Forms, only substances can have Ideas; for a thing does not participate in a Form coincidentally, but insofar as it is not said of a subject. (If, for instance, something participates in the Double itself, it also participates in the Everlasting, but coincidentally, since it is coincidental that the Double is everlasting.) Hence the Forms will be substances. But the same things signify substances among the Forms as in this world—otherwise what will the claim that there is something apart from these things, the one over many, amount to? And if the Idea and the things participating in it have the same form, they will have something in common—for why should [what it is to be] two be one and the same thing in all the perishable twos and in all of the many everlasting twos, but not one and the same thing in the Two itself and in some particular two? But if they do not have the same form, they will be [merely] homonymous; it will be like calling both Callias and a wooden [statue] a man, when one has observed no common [nature] that they share.

One might be especially puzzled about what on earth Forms contribute to perceptible things, either to those that are everlasting or to those that come to be and perish; for they cause neither motion nor any change in them. Nor do they contribute to knowledge of other things, since they are not their substance—if they were, they would be in the other things. Nor do they contribute to the being of other things, since Forms are not present in the things that participate in them. For if they were present, they might perhaps be thought to be causes, as white is if it is mixed in a white object. This argument was first stated by Anaxagoras and then by Eudoxus[18] and certain others. It is easily upset, since it is easy to collect many impossible consequences that challenge such a belief.

Nor can the other things be from Forms in any of the ways things are normally said to be from something. And to say that Forms are patterns and that other things participate in them is empty talk, mere poetic metaphors. For what is it that looks to the Ideas when it produces things? And it is possible for one thing to be, or to come to be, like another without being copied from it, so that whether or not Socrates exists someone like Socrates might come to be; and clearly the same would be true even if Socrates were everlasting. Further, there will be many patterns of the same thing, hence many Forms; the Forms of man, for instance, will be Animal and Biped as well as Man-itself. Further, the Forms will be patterns not only of perceptible things, but also of themselves—the genus, for instance, of its species—so that the same thing will be both pattern and copy.

Further, it would seem impossible for a substance to be separate from what it is the substance of. How, then, if the Ideas are the substances of things, could they be separate from them?

According to the *Phaedo*, the Forms are the causes both of being and of coming to be. But what participates in the Forms does not come to be, even if the Forms exist, unless something initiates the motion. And in addition to these [natural things], many things—for instance, a house or a ring—which in our view have no Forms, come to be. Hence it is clearly also possible for the [natural] things to be and to come to be because of causes of the sort just mentioned.

Further, if the Forms are numbers, how can they be causes? Is it because beings are other numbers, so that one number, for instance, is man, another is Socrates, and another is Callias? If so, why are one lot of numbers causes of the other lot? It makes no difference if the Forms are everlasting and the other things are not. But if it is because things in this world—for instance, a harmony—are ratios of numbers, it is clear that the things of which they are ratios are some one [kind of] thing. But if there is this one thing, i.e., the matter, then evidently the numbers themselves will

18. [Eudoxus of Cnidus (c. 408–c. 355 B.C.) was a Greek astronomer, mathematician, and physician.]

also be ratios of one thing to another. If, for instance, Callias is a numerical ratio of fire, earth, water, and air, then his Idea will also be the number of certain other subjects. And Man-itself, even if it is in some way numerical, will nonetheless be a numerical ratio of certain things, not [properly] a number. This argument, then, does not show that any Idea is a number. 20

. . . In general, it is impossible to find the elements of beings without distinguishing the ways they are spoken of, since in fact beings are spoken of in many ways. It is especially impossible to find them if we search in this way for the sorts of elements that compose beings. For what elements compose acting or being affected or the straight? Presumably these cannot be found; at most the elements of substances can be found. Hence it is incorrect either to seek the elements of all beings or to think one has found them. *992b18* 20

And how could one even learn the elements of all things? For clearly one cannot begin with previous cognition. If, for instance, we are learning geometry, we may have previous knowledge of other things [outside geometry], but we have no previous cognition about the subject matter of the science we are to learn about; the same is true in other cases. Hence if there is some science of all things, such as some say there is, we could not have previous cognition of anything before we learn this science. And yet all learning, either through demonstration or through definitions, relies on previous cognition of either all or some things; for one must previously know the elements of the definition, and they must be well known; the same is true for learning through induction. Then is this science actually innate? If so, it is remarkable that we manage not to notice that we possess the supreme science. 25 30 *993a*

Further, how is one to acquire recognition of the elements, and how is this knowledge to be made clear? For there is a puzzle here too, since our answers might be disputed, as in the case of certain syllables; for some say that ZA is from S, D, and A, while others say it is a different sound, and none of the well-known ones. 5

Further, how could one recognize perceptible things without perception? And yet one would have to, if the elements composing all things are indeed the same, as complex sounds are [composed of] their proper elements. 10

BOOK IV

1

There is a science that studies being insofar as it is being, and also the properties of being in its own right. It is not the same as any of the so-called special sciences. For none of them considers being quite generally, insofar as it is being; rather, each of them cuts off some part of being and studies the relevant coincident of that part, as, for instance, the mathematical sciences do. *1003a21* 25

Since we are seeking the principles, i.e., the highest causes, clearly they must be the causes of the nature of some subject as it is in its own right. If, then, those who were seeking the elements of beings were also seeking these highest principles, the elements must also be the elements of being not coincidentally, but insofar as it is being. That is why we also ought to find the first causes of being insofar as it is being. 30

2

Being is spoken of in many ways, but always with reference to one thing—i.e., to some one nature—and not homonymously. Everything healthy, for instance, is spoken of with reference to health—one thing because it preserves health, another because it produces health, another because it indicates health, another because it can receive health. Similarly, the medical is spoken of with reference to medical science; for one thing is called medical because it has the medical science, another because it is naturally suited to medical science, another because it is the function of medical science, and we shall find other things spoken of in ways similar to these. 35 *1003b*

Similarly, then, being is spoken of in many ways, but in all cases it is spoken of with reference to one principle. For some things are called beings because they are substances, others because they are attributes of substance, others because they are a road to substance, or because they are perishings or privations or qualities of substance, or productive or generative of substance or of things spoken of with reference to it, or because they are negations of one of these or of substance. This is why we also say that not being is—i.e., is not being. 5 10

A single science studies all healthy things, and the same applies in the other cases. For it is not only things that are spoken of in accordance with one [common property] that are studied by a single science; the same is true of things that are spoken of with reference to one nature, since these things are 15 also, in a way, spoken of in accordance with one [common property]. Clearly, then, it is also the task of a single science to study beings insofar as they are beings.

In every case the dominant concern of a science is with its primary object, the one on which the others depend and because of which they are spoken of as they are. If, then, this primary object is substance, the philosopher must grasp the principles and causes of substances.

1004a2 There are as many parts of philosophy as there are [types of] substances, and so there must be a first philosophy, and a second philosophy following it; for 5 being is divided immediately into genera, which is why the sciences will also conform to these. For the philosopher is spoken of in the same way as the mathematician is; for mathematical science also has parts, and in mathematics there is a first and a second science and others succeeding in order.

1003b19 For every single genus there is a single [sort of] 20 perception and a single science; there is, for instance, a single grammatical science, and it studies all the [types of] sounds. Hence it is also the task of a science that is one in genus to study all the species of being insofar as it is being; it is the task of the species of that science to study the species [of being].

Being and unity are the same and a single nature, since they imply each other, as principle and cause do, though they are not one and the same in the 25 sense of being revealed by the same account (though indeed it does not matter if we take them to have the same account; that would be even more suitable for our purpose). For one man is the same as a man, and moreover a man who is is the same as a man, and 'he is a man and a man who is' reveals nothing different by the repetition in what is said, since clearly a man and a man who is are separated neither in 30 coming to be nor in perishing. The same also applies to unity. It is evident, then, that in these cases the addition [of 'one'] reveals the same thing [as 'is' reveals], and that unity is nothing different from being. Moreover, the substance of a thing is non-coincidentally one thing; and similarly it is essentially some being.

It follows that there are as many species of being as of unity. Hence it is a task for a science that is the 35 same in genus to study the what-it-is about these species—for instance, about same, similar and other such things. Practically all the contraries are referred 1004a to this principle; our study of these in the Selection of Contraries will suffice.

It is the task of one science to study opposites, and 10 plurality is the opposite of unity. It is also the task of one science to study negation and privation, since in both cases we study the one thing of which it is the negation or the privation. For either we say without qualification that something does not belong to the subject, or we say that it does not belong to some genus of the subject. In the latter case a differentia is added besides what is in the negation—for the 15 negation is the absence of that property, but the privation also involves some nature that is the subject of which the privation is said.

And so it is also the task of the science we have mentioned to know about the contraries of the things we have mentioned—different, unlike, unequal, and everything else that is spoken of either with respect to these or with respect to plurality and unity. Contra- 20 riety is also one of these; for it is a type of difference, and difference is a type of otherness. And so, since unity is spoken of in many ways, these will also be spoken of in many ways; but still it is the task of a single science to know them all. For the mere fact that things are spoken of in many ways does not imply that they cannot be studied by one and the same science; different sciences are required only if it is true both that the things have no one [common property] and that their accounts are not referred to 25 one thing.

Since in each case everything is referred to the primary thing (for instance, everything that is called one is referred to the primary unity), this is also what we ought to say about same, different, and contraries. And so we should first distinguish how many ways each thing is spoken of, and then show how each of the things we have distinguished is spoken of with reference to the primary thing in each predication; for some things will be spoken of as they are because 30 they have that primary thing, others because they produce it, others in other such ways.

Evidently, then, it is the task of a single science to take account both of these things and of substance (this was one of the questions that raised puzzles), 1004b and it is the philosopher's task to be able to study all [these] things. For if this is not his task, who will consider whether Socrates is the same as seated Socrates, or whether one thing has [just] one contrary, or what contrariety is, or how many ways it is spoken of? And the same is true for other questions of that sort.

5 We have found, then, that these are attributes of unity insofar as it is unity, and of being insofar as it is being; each is an attribute of unity and being in their own right, not insofar as they are numbers or lines or fire. Hence it is clearly the task of that science [of being] to know both what being and unity are, and also their coincidents. The mistake of those who currently consider these questions is not that they fail to practise philosophy but that, although substance is prior, they comprehend nothing about it.

There are attributes distinctive of number insofar 10 as it is number (for instance, oddness and evenness, commensurability and inequality, being more and being less), and these belong to numbers both in their own right and in relation to one another. Likewise there are other attributes distinctive of the solid, both moved and unmoved, and [of the moved], both 15 weightless and having weight. In the same way, then, there are also some attributes distinctive of being in so far as it is being, and it is the philosopher's task to investigate the truth about these.

Here is a sign [to show that it is his task]. Dialecticians and Sophists assume the same guise as the philosopher. For sophistic has the appearance of wis- 20 dom, though nothing more, and dialecticians practise dialectic about all things; being is common to all things, and clearly they practice dialectic about all things because all things are proper to philosophy. For sophistic and dialectic treat the same genus as philosophy, but philosophy differs from dialectic in the type of power it has, and it differs from sophistic 25 in its decision about how to live. Dialectic tests in the area where philosophy achieves knowledge, while sophistic has the appearance [of knowledge], but not the reality.

Further, one column of contraries is privation, and all contraries are referred to being and not being, and to unity and plurality—for instance, stability belongs 30 to unity, motion to plurality. And practically everyone agrees that beings and substance are composed of contraries. At any rate, they all say that the principles are contrary; for some say that they are the odd and even, some that they are the hot and cold, some that they are the determinate and indeterminate, others that they are love and strife. All the other contraries are also evidently referred to unity and plurality (let us assume this referral), and the principles recognized 1005a by others fall completely under unity and plurality as their genera.

This also makes it evident, then, that it is the task of a single science to study being insofar as it is being; for all things are either contraries or composed of contraries, and unity and plurality are principles of the contraries. Unity and plurality belong to one science, 5 whether or not they are spoken of as having one [common property] (and presumably in fact they are not). Even if unity is indeed spoken of in many ways, still the nonprimary unities will be spoken of with reference to the primary unity; the same applies to the contraries. This is true even if being or unity is neither universal and the same over them all nor separable; and presumably it is neither of these, but 10 rather some [beings and unities] are spoken of with reference to one thing, and others in succession. That is why it is not the geometer's task to study what a contrary is or what completeness is, or to study unity, or being, or same, or different, but only to study them on the basis of an assumption.

Clearly, then, it is the task of a single science to study both being insofar as it is being and also the things that belong to it insofar as it is being. And clearly the same science studies not only substances 15 but also their attributes—both those we have mentioned and also prior and posterior, genus and species, whole and part, and the other things of this sort.

3

We ought to say whether it is the task of one and the same science or of different sciences to study both the axioms (as they are called in mathematics) and 20 substance. Evidently it is also the task of one and the same science—the philosopher's—to examine these, since these belong to all beings and are not distinctive of one genus in separation from the others.

Every scientist uses the axioms because they belong to being insofar as it is being, and each genus is a being. But each uses them to the extent he needs 25 them, and that is however far the genus about which he presents his demonstrations extends. Clearly, then, the axioms belong to all things insofar as they are beings (for this is what all things have in common); and so it is also the task of the one who knows being insofar as it is being to study the axioms.

This is why none of those who investigate a special area—for instance, a geometer or an arithmetician—30 undertakes to say anything about whether or not the axioms are true. The ones who did so were some of the students of nature; and it is not surprising that they did this, since they were the only ones who thought they were examining the whole of nature and examining being. In fact, however, there is someone still higher than the student of nature, since 35 nature is only one kind of being; and so investigating these axioms will also be a task of this universal scientist, 1005b the one who studies primary substance. The study of nature is also a type of wisdom, but not the primary type.

Now, some of those who argue about when a conclusion should properly be accepted as true object that one should not accept [principles that have not been demonstrated]. They do this because they lack education in analytics; for someone who comes [to 5 the science of being] must already know about analytics and not ask about it when he studies [the science of being].

Clearly, then, study of the principles of deductions is also a task for the philosopher—i.e., for the one who studies the nature of all substance. Whoever has the best claim to knowledge of a given genus ought 10 to be able to state the firmest principles of his subject matter; hence whoever has the best claim to knowledge of beings insofar as they are beings should be able to state the firmest principles of all things—and this person is the philosopher.

The firmest principle of all is one about which it is impossible to be mistaken. For this sort of principle must be known best (for what we make mistakes about is invariably what we do not know), and it cannot be 15 an assumption. For a principle that we must already possess in order to understand anything at all about beings is not an assumption; and what we must know in order to know anything at all is a principle we must already possess. Clearly, then, this sort of principle is the firmest of all.

Let us next say what this principle is: that it is impossible for the same thing both to belong and not to belong at the same time to the same thing and in 20 the same respect (and let us assume we have drawn all the further distinctions that might be drawn to meet logical complaints). This, then, is the firmest principle of all, since it has the distinguishing feature previously mentioned.

For it is impossible for anyone to suppose that the same thing is and is not, though some people take 25 Heraclitus to say this; for what one says need not be what one supposes to be true. For it is impossible for contraries to belong at the same time to the same thing (and let us assume that the customary further distinctions are added to this statement). But what is contrary to a belief is the belief in its contradictory. Hence evidently it is impossible for the same person at the same time to suppose that the same thing is 30 and is not, since someone who makes this mistake would have contrary beliefs at the same time. This is why all those who demonstrate refer back to this belief as ultimate; for this is by nature the principle of all the other axioms as well.

BOOK VII

1

Being is spoken of in many ways, which we dis- 1028a10 tinguished previously in the work on how many ways things are spoken of. For one [type of being] signifies what-it-is and a this; another signifies quality, or quantity, or any of the other things predicated in this way. But while being is spoken of in this many ways, it is evident that among these the primary being is the what-it-is, which signifies substance. For whenever 15 we say what quality this has, we call it good or bad, not six feet long or a man, whereas whenever we say what it is, we call it a man or a god, not pale or hot or six feet long; and the other things are called beings by belonging to this type of being—some as quantities, some as qualities, some as affections, some in some other such way. 20

That is why someone might actually be puzzled about whether walking, flourishing, or sitting signifies a being, for none of these is in its own right nor is any of them capable of being separated from substance, but it is more true that the walking or sitting or flourishing thing is a being (if indeed it is a being). 25 This latter type of thing is apparently more of a being because it has some definite subject—the substance and the particular—which is discerned in such a predication; for this subject is implied in speaking of the good or sitting thing. Clearly, then, it is because 30 of substance that each of those other things is also a being, so that what is in the primary way—what is not something, but is without qualification a being—is substance.

Now the primary is so spoken of in many ways, but still, substance is primary in every way: in nature, in account, and in knowledge. For none of the other things predicated is separable, but only substance. Substance is also primary in account, since its account 35 is necessarily present in the account of each thing. Moreover, we think we know a thing most of all whenever we know what, for instance, man or fire is, 1028b rather than when we know its quality or quantity or place; for indeed we know each of these only when we know *what* the quantity or the quality is.

Indeed, the old question—always pursued from long ago till now, and always raising puzzles—'What 5 is being?' is just the question 'What is substance?'. For it is substance that some say is one and others say is more than one, some saying that it is limited in number, others that it is unlimited. And so we too must make it our main, our primary, indeed (we may say) our only, task to study what it is that is in this way.

2

10 The most evident examples of substances seem to be bodies. That is why we say that animals and plants and their parts are substances, and also natural bodies, such as fire, water, earth, and all such things, and whatever is either a part of these or composed of all or some of them—for instance, the universe and its parts, the stars, moon, and sun. But we ought to 15 consider: Are these the only substances there are, or are there also others? Or are only some of these things substances, or some of these and also some other things? Or are none of these things substances, but only some other things?

Some people think that the limits of a body—for instance, a surface, a line, a point, and a unit—are substances, and are so to a higher degree than a body and a solid. Further, some think there are no substances apart from perceptible things, while to others it seems that there are also everlasting substances, which are more numerous and are beings to a higher degree. Plato, for example, thinks that Forms and mathematicals are two [types of] substances, and 20 that the substance of perceptible bodies is a third [type]. Speusippus posits even more substances, beginning with the one, and posits a principle for each [type of] substance—one for numbers, another for magnitudes, and then another for soul; and in this way he multiplies the [types of] substances. Some say that Forms and numbers have the same nature, and 25 that everything else comes after them—lines, planes, and everything else, extending to the substance of the universe and to perceptible things.

We must consider, then, which of these views are correct or incorrect; what substances there are; whether or not there are any substances apart from perceptible substances, and in what way these perceptible substances are [substances]; and whether or not 30 there is any separable substance apart from perceptible ones, and, if there is, why there is, and in what way it is [substance]. But before doing this, we must first sketch what substance is.

3

Substance is spoken of, if not in several ways, at any rate in four main cases. For the essence, the universal 35 and the genus seem to be the substance of a given thing, and the fourth of these cases is the subject.

Now, the subject is that of which the other things are said, but which is not itself in turn said of any other thing, hence we must first determine what it 1029a is, since the primary subject seems to be substance most of all.

What is spoken of in this way [as the primary subject] is in one way the matter, in another way the form, and in a third way the thing composed of these. (By the matter I mean, for example, the bronze; by the form I mean the figure and character; and by the 5 thing composed of them I mean the statue, i.e., the compound.) And so if the form is prior to the matter, and more of a being, it will also, by the same argument, be prior to the thing composed of both.

We have now said in outline, then, what substance is: it is what is not said of a subject but has the other things said of it.

However, we must not confine ourselves to this answer. For it is inadequate: for, first, it is itself un-

10 clear; and further, the matter turns out to be substance. For if the matter is not substance, it is hard to see what other substance there is; for when all the other things are removed, nothing [but the matter] evidently remains. For the other things are affections, products, and potentialities of bodies; and length, 15 breadth, and depth are kinds of quantities but not substances (for quantity is not substance), but the primary [subject] to which these belong is more of a substance than they are. But when length, breadth, and depth are abstracted, we see that nothing is left, except whatever is determined by these. And so, if we examine it in this way, the matter necessarily appears as the only substance.

20 By matter I mean what is spoken of in its own right neither as being something, nor as having some quantity, nor as having any of the other things by which being is determined. For there is something of which each of these is predicated, something whose being is different from that of each of the things predicated; for the other things are predicated of the substance, and the substance is predicated of the matter. And so the last thing is in its own right neither something nor of some quantity nor any other [of the 25 things mentioned]; nor is it [in its own right] the negations of these, since what we have said implies that the negations as well [as the positive properties] belong to it [only] coincidentally.

And so, if we study it from this point of view, the result is that the matter is substance, but that is impossible. For being separable and being a this seem to belong to substance most of all; that is why the form and the [compound] of both [matter and form] 30 would seem to be substance more than the matter is.

And so the substance composed of both—I mean composed of the matter and the form—should be set aside, since it is posterior to the other two, and clear. The matter is also evident in a way. We must, then, consider the third type of substance, since it is the most puzzling.

1029b Since some of the perceptible substances are agreed to be substances, we should begin our search with these.

4

Since we began by distinguishing the things by which we define substance and since essence seems to be one of these, we ought to study it. For it is useful to advance toward what is better known, since this is how anyone succeeds in learning, by advancing through what is less well known, by nature to what 5 is better known. In questions about action, our task is to advance from what is good to ourselves, and so to make what is good without reservation good to ourselves; in the same way, then, we should advance from what is better known to ourselves, and so make what is well known by nature well known to ourselves. Admittedly, what is well known and known first to any given type of person is only slightly known and 10 has little or no hold on being; still, we must begin from what is poorly known but known by us and try to come to know what is known without reservation, by advancing, as has been said, through the very things that are known to us.

First let us make some logical remarks about it. The essence of a thing is what the thing is said to be in its own right. For being you is not the same as 15 being a musician, since you are not a musician in your own right; hence your essence is what you are in your own right.

Nor indeed is your essence all of what you are in your own right. For a thing's essence is not what belongs to it in its own right in the way that pale belongs in its own right to a surface; for being a surface is not the same as being pale. But neither is a thing's essence the same as the combination of the thing and what belongs in its own right to it—for instance, being a pale surface, since here surface is added. It follows that the account of a thing's essence 20 is the account that describes but does not mention the thing; and so if being a pale surface is the same as being a smooth surface, being pale and being smooth are one and the same.

There are composites [not only among substances but] also in the other predications, since each of these (for instance, quality, quantity, when, where, and motion) has a subject; hence we should ask whether 25 there is an account of the essence of each of these composites, and whether an essence belongs to them—to a pale man, for instance—as well as to substances. Let us, then, call this composite 'cloak.' What is being a cloak?

One might object, however, that a cloak is not spoken of in its own right either. [We reply:] There are two ways in which we speak of what is not in its own right: one way is from addition, the other is not. 30

In the first case, something is said [not to be in its own right] because the thing to be defined is added to something else—if, for instance, one gave the account of pale man as a definition of pale. In the second case, something is said not to be in its own right because something else is added to it—if, for instance, 'cloak' signified a pale man, but one were *1030a* to define cloak as pale. A pale man, then, is pale, but is not what being pale is.

But is being a cloak an essence at all? Perhaps not. For an essence is what something essentially is, but whenever one thing is said of another, the composite *5* of the two is not essentially a this; the pale man, for instance, is not essentially a this, since only a substance is a this. Hence the things that have an essence are those whose account is a definition. But the mere fact that a name and an account signify the same thing does not imply that the account is a definition. If it did, then all accounts would be formulae (since for every account, we can find a name that signifies *10* the same); so that even the *Iliad* would be a definition. Rather, an account is a definition [only] if it is of some primary thing; primary things are those that are spoken of in a way that does not consist in one thing's being said of another. Hence essence will belong only to species of a genus and to nothing else, since [only] these seem to be spoken of in a way that does not consist in one thing's participating in another, or in one thing's being an attribute or coincident of an*15*other. Admittedly, everything else [besides members of a species], if it has a name, will also have an account saying what it signifies (i.e., that this belongs to this) or, instead of an unqualified account, a more exact one; but nothing else will have a definition or essence.

Perhaps, however, definitions, like what-it-is, are spoken of in several ways. For in fact what-it-is in one *20* way signifies substance and a this, and in another way signifies each of the things predicated—quantity, quality, and all the rest. For just as being belongs to them all—not in the same way, but to substance primarily and to the other things derivatively—so also the what-it-is belongs without qualification to substance and derivatively to the other things. For we might ask what a quality is, so that quality is also a *25* what-it-is, though not without qualification; just as some people say, speaking logically, that not-being is (not that it is without qualification, but that it is not-being), so also we say what a quality is.

We must certainly consider what ought to be said about a particular question, but we must consider no less how things really are. That is why, in this case, since what is said is evident [we must consider how things are]. We find that essence, like what-it-is, be- *30* longs primarily and without qualification to substance, and derivatively to the other things, where it will be the essence of quality or quantity, not the essence without qualification. For we must say that these [nonsubstances] are beings either homonymously or by addition and substraction, as we say that what is not known is known [not to be known]. The right answer is that they are beings neither homonymously nor in the same way. What is medical, for *35* instance, is spoken of with reference to one and the same thing, not by being one and the same thing, but not homonymously either—for a body, a proce- *1030b* dure, and an instrument are called medical neither homonymously nor by having one [nature], but with reference to one thing. The same applies to beings.

It does not matter which alternative we accept: in *5* either case substances evidently have a definition and essence of the primary type, i.e., a definition and essence without qualification. Certainly other beings also have definitions and essences, but not primarily. For if we accept this view of definition, not every name that signifies the same as an account will necessarily have a definition corresponding to it; rather, in order to be a definition, the account must be of the right type, namely an account of something that is one—and something that is one not merely by continuity (like the *Iliad*, or like things that are tied together) but that is one in one of the ways in which *10* one is spoken of. Now, one is spoken of in the same ways as being, and one type of being signifies a this, another quantity, another quality. That is why there will also be an account and a definition of the pale man, but not in the way that there is of pale and of the substance.

6

We should investigate whether a thing is the same *1031a15* as or different from its essence. For this is useful for our investigation of substance; for a thing seems to be nothing other than its own substance, and something's substance is said to be its essence.

In the case of things spoken of coincidentally, a *20*

thing might seem to be different from its essence; a pale man, for instance, is different from being a pale man. For if it is the same, then being a man is the same as being a pale man; for, they say, a man is the same as a pale man, so that being a pale man is the same as being a man.

Perhaps, however, it is not necessary for things to be the same if one is a coincident of the other, since the extreme terms are not the same in the same way. But presumably it might seem to follow that the extremes, the coincidental things, turn out to be the same—for instance, being pale and being musical. In fact, however, it seems not to follow.

But is it necessary for things spoken of in their own right to be the same as their essences? For instance, what about substances of the sort some say Ideas are, ones that have no other substances or natures prior to them? If that the good itself [the Idea] is different from the essence of good, and the animal itself from the essence of animal, and the being itself from the essence of being, then there will be further substances, natures, and Ideas apart from those mentioned, and these will be prior substances and substances to a higher degree, if essence is substance.

If, then, [the Ideas and the essences] are severed from each other, it follows that [the Ideas] will not be known and that [the essences] will not be beings. (By 'severed' I mean that the essence of good does not belong to the good itself, and being good does not belong to the essence of good.) For we know a thing whenever we know its essence. Further, what applies to good applies equally to the other essences, so that if the essence of good is not good, then neither will the essence of being be, nor the essence of one be one. But since all essences alike either are or are not, it follows that, if not even the essence of being is a being, none of the other essences is a being either. Moreover, if the essence of good does not belong to a given thing, that thing is not good.

The good, then, is necessarily one with the essence of good, and the fine with the essence of fine. The same applies to all the primary things, those spoken of in their own right, not insofar as they belong to something else. For if this is true [i.e., that something is a primary being], it already implies [that the primary being is identical to its essence], even if it is not a Form—though presumably [the conclusion] is all the more [necessary] if the thing is a Form.

Further, if the Ideas are what some people say they are, then clearly the subject will not be substance. For Ideas must be substances, but not by [being predicated] of a subject, since [if they were predicated of a subject], they would exist [only] by being participated in.

From these arguments, then, we find that a thing itself and its essence are noncoincidentally one and the same, and that knowing a thing is knowing its essence; and so even isolating the Forms shows that a thing and its essence must be some one thing.

But because what is spoken of coincidentally—for instance, the musical or the pale—signifies two things, it is not true to say that it is the same as its essence. For the pale signifies both the subject of which pale is a coincident and the coincident, and so in a way it is the same as its essence, and in a way it is not the same—for [the pale] is not the same as man or as pale man, but it is the same as the attribute.

We can also see that it is absurd [for something not to be the same as its essence], if we give a name to each essence; for apart from that essence there will be another essence as well—for instance, another essence will be the essence of the essence of horse. But why not let some things be essences at once, going no further, since essence is substance? Moreover, not only is [a thing] one [with its essence], but their account is also the same; for one and being one are noncoincidentally one. Moreover, if there is another essence, the essences will go on to infinity; for one thing will be the essence of the one, and another will be the one, so that the same argument will also apply in their case.

Clearly, then, in the case of the primary things, those spoken of in their own right, a thing and its essence are one and the same. And it is evident that the sophistical refutations aimed against this position are all resolved in the same way as is the puzzle of whether Socrates and being Socrates are the same; for there is no difference in the premisses from which one would ask the questions or in the premisses from which one would find a solution.

We have said, then, in what way something's essence is the same as the thing, and in what way it is not.

7

Among things that come to be, some come to be by nature, some by craft, and some by chance, but they all come to be by some agent and from something, and come to be something. (By 'comes to be something' 15 I mean something in any of the predications; for things come to be either this or of some quantity or quality or somewhere.) Things that have natural comings to be are those whose coming to be is from nature. What they come to be from is what we call matter; the agent is something that is by nature; and the something they come to be is a man or a plant or anything 20 of the sort we say are substances most of all.

Everything that comes to be by nature or craft has matter; for these things can both be and not be, and what has this potentiality is a thing's matter.

In general, both what something comes to be from and what it becomes is a nature; for what comes to be has a nature—a plant or an animal, for instance. Moreover, the agent is the nature that is spoken of with reference to form, and this nature is the same in form [as the nature of what comes to be], but it 25 is in another [particular], since a man generates a man. Things that come to be because of nature, then, come to be in this way.

The other comings to be are called productions; these are all from either craft or potentiality or thought. Some productions also come to be from 30 chance or luck, similarly to the way in which things come about from chance or luck among things that come to be from nature; for in the latter case too the same things that [usually] come to be from a seed also [sometimes] come to be without any seed. We must investigate these cases later.

Things that come to be from craft are those whose 1032b form is in the soul. (By 'form' I mean a thing's essence and primary substance.) For even contraries have the same form in a way, since the substance of a privation is the substance opposed to it, so that health, for 5 instance, is the substance of disease because disease results from the absence of health; and health is the account in the soul and the knowledge.

What is healthy comes into being when the producer has had the following sort of thought: since health is this, then if something is to be healthy, it must have this (for instance, a uniform condition of the body), and if it is to have this, it must have heat. This is how he thinks at each stage, until he leads the process back to the last thing, which is what he can produce 10 himself; and then the motion from here on toward health is called a production. And so it turns out that in a way health comes to be from health, and a house from a house—the one that has matter from the one without matter. For the medical or housebuilding [knowledge] is the form of health or house, and substance without matter is what I call the essence.

15 One sort of coming to be and motion is called thinking, another production. Thinking is the motion that proceeds from the principle, i.e., the form; and production is the motion that proceeds from the last stage of thinking. Each of the other things—those in between—comes to be in the same way. I mean, for instance, that if this [body] is to be healthy, its bodily condition must be made uniform. What, then, is it to be made uniform? This. [The body] will have this 20 if it is warmed. What is it to be warmed? This. But this is potentially present. And now he has reached what is up to himself.

If the motion toward health comes from craft, the producer that is its principle is the form in the soul; if it comes from chance, it comes from whatever is the principle of the production if the producer exercises a 25 craft. In medical treatment, for instance, the principle is presumably from warming, which the doctor produces by rubbing; heat in the body, then, either is a part of health or is followed, directly or in several stages, by something that is part of health. This last thing producing the part [of health] is in a way itself also a part of health, just as the last thing (for instance, stones) is a part of the house, and part of the product in other cases. Hence, as is said, nothing can come to 30 be unless something is previously present. Evidently, 1033a then, some part will have to be present; for the matter is a part, since it is present in the product, and it comes to be the product.

But is [the matter] also one of the things in the account? We speak in both ways when we say what bronze circles are. For we speak of the matter when we say that the circle is bronze, and of the form when we say that it is this sort of shape; shape is the genus into which it is primarily placed. The bronze circle, then, has the matter in its account. 5

Some things that come to be from matter, once they have come to be, are called not that, but of-that; the statue, for instance, is called of-stone, not stone, and similarly the healthy man is not called that from which he has come to be. The reason for this is that a thing comes to be from its privation, or from its subject which we call the matter. For instance, the 10 man as well as the sick one comes to be healthy, but he is said to have come to be from the privation rather than the subject, so that he is said to have become healthy from having been sick, rather than from having been a man; that is why the healthy one is said to be a man, not to be sick, and the man is said to be healthy, [not sick]. But in cases where the privation—the privation of some definite shape in bronze, 15 for instance, or of a house in bricks and timbers—is unclear and nameless, the product seems to come to be from this [matter], as in the first case [the man became healthy] from having been sick.

That is why, just as in the first case the product is not called by the name of that [privation] from which it came to be, so also in the second case the statue is not called wood, but rather the name is varied and the statue is called of-wood, not wood, or of-bronze, not bronze, or of-stone, not stone, and the house is 20 of-bricks, not bricks. For if we look at it closely, we would not say without qualification, in this case any more than in the other, that a statue comes to be from wood, or a house from bricks; for that from which something comes to be must change and not remain when the thing comes to be. This, then, is why we speak in this way.

8

What comes to be, then, does so by some agent (i.e., 25 the source of the principle of the coming to be) and from something (not the privation but the matter; we have now determined the sense in which we say this) and becomes something (a sphere or a circle or whatever else it may be). And just as [the producer] 30 does not produce the subject—the bronze—neither does he produce the sphere, unless he does so coincidentally, because he produces the bronze sphere and it is a sphere; for to produce a this is to produce a this from a subject in general.

Let me explain. To make the bronze round is not to produce the round or the sphere, but to produce one thing, this form, in another thing; for if someone 1033b produces the form, he must produce it from another thing, since another thing must have been the subject. For instance, he produces the bronze sphere, and this is so because he produces this, which is a sphere, from this subject, which is bronze; and if he also produces this form itself, i.e., sphere, clearly he will 5 produce it in the same way, and then comings into being will go back to infinity.

Evidently, then, the form (or whatever the shape in the perceptible thing ought to be called) and the essence (i.e., what comes to be in something else by the agency of craft, nature, or potentiality) does not come into being and there is no coming to be of it. But the producer does make a bronze sphere to be; for he produces it from bronze and sphere—he produces this 10 form in this subject, and the product is a bronze sphere.

If the essence of sphere in general is to have a coming to be, this essence will be something from something; for in each case what is coming to be must be divisible into this (i.e., matter) and this (i.e., form). Now, if the sphere is the figure whose circumference is everywhere equidistant from the center, 15 one aspect of it is the matter that the product is in, the other is the form in that matter, and the whole thing—the bronze sphere, for instance—is what has come to be. It is evident, then, that what is called substance as form does not come to be, but the compound substance, which is called substance insofar as it is substance as form, does come to be. It is also evident that matter is present in everything that comes to be, and that one aspect of the product is this matter and the other is this form. 20

Is there, then, some sphere apart from these [perceptible ones], or a house apart from bricks? If there were, then surely there could never have been any coming to be of any this. Rather, [sphere, for instance,] signifies this sort of thing; it is not a this and something definite. On the contrary, one produces or generates this sort of thing from this [matter], and when it has been generated, it is *this* thing of this sort. This whole thing—for instance, Callias or Socrates— 25 corresponds to this bronze sphere, while man and animal correspond to bronze sphere in general.

It is evident, then, that the forms, construed as some people habitually construe them, as things apart from particulars, are useless as causes, at any rate of comings to be and of substances; this role, at any rate, is no reason for these forms to be substances in their own right. 30

In some cases, generator and generated are evidently also of the same sort, but they are not the same thing—they are one in form, not one in number. This is true of natural things (for instance, a man generates a man), except in cases where something contrary to nature comes about, so that a horse, for instance, generates a mule. And even in these cases something similar is true; for the nearest genus, whatever is common to horse and ass, has no name, but is presumably both, as a mule is. 1034a

Evidently, then, there is no need to set up a form as a pattern. For if we sought such forms anywhere, it would be in natural generation, since natural things are substances most of all; but in fact the generator is sufficient to produce the thing and to be the cause of the form in the matter. And the whole—this sort of form in this flesh and bones—is Callias or Socrates; and they differ because of matter, since their matter is different, but they are the same in form, since the form is indivisible. 5

9

A puzzle might arise about why some things—for instance, health—come to be both by craft and also from chance, while others—for instance, houses—do not. The reason is as follows. The matter that is the principle of production and coming to be from craft, and that has some part of the product present in it, in some cases can be moved by its own agency, and in other cases cannot. In some cases of the first sort, the matter can be moved [by its own agency] in a particular way [required for a certain kind of product], and in other such cases it cannot; for many things are capable of being moved by their own agency, but not in a particular way (for instance, dancing). Hence things with matter of this second sort—stones, for instance—cannot be moved in a particular way except by something else, but in another way they can be moved by their own agency. That is why in some cases the result requires a craftsman, but in other cases it does not; in these cases the movers will be agents that have no craft but can themselves be moved, either by other agents that have no craft or from a part [of the eventual product]. 10 15 20

It is also clear from what we have said that in a way every [product of craft] comes to be, just as natural things do, from something with the same name (for instance, a house from a house, insofar as it is produced by mind, since the craft [of building] is the form), or from a part with the same name, or from something that has a part [of the product]. This is true if it does not come to be coincidentally; for the first cause in its own right of the production is a part of the product. Heat in the motion, for example, produces heat in the body, and this heat is either health or a part of it or is followed by a part of health or by health itself; that is why it is also said to produce [health], because it produces that on which health follows and in which it coincides. 25 30

And so, just as in deductions, substance is the principle of everything; for deductions begin from what-it-is, and comings to be are from this too.

Naturally constituted things are similar to the products of craft. For the seed produces in the same way as the efforts of craft do; for it has the form potentially, and in a way the parent providing the seed has the same name as the offspring. For one must not expect all offspring to come to be in the way a man comes to be from a man—even here, indeed, a female comes to be from a male. The offspring has the same name if it is not defective; hence a mule's parent is not a mule [since mules are defective]. 1034b

Things that come to be by chance (just as in the case of crafts) are those whose matter can on some occasions also be moved by its own agency with the motion that the seed [usually] initiates in it; unless this is true of the matter, things cannot come to be except from the parents. 5

Our argument not only shows that form cannot come to be in the case of substance, but it also applies equally to all the primary [genera]—to quantity, quality, and the other predications. For it is the bronze sphere, not sphere or bronze, that comes to be, and the same applies to bronze, if it comes to be; for in every case the matter and the form must previously exist. This is true both for what-it-is and also for quality, quantity, and each of the other predications; for what comes to be is not a quality, but wood of some quality, and not a quantity, but wood or animal of some quantity. 10 15

However, a distinctive feature of substance may be noticed from these cases, that it must be produced by another actual substance preceding it (for instance, by an animal, if an animal comes to be), whereas a quality or quantity needs only a potential quality or quantity to precede it.

10

A definition is an account, and every account has parts; and a part of the account corresponds to a part of the thing defined in the way in the whole account 1034b corresponds to the whole thing. Hence a puzzle arises about whether or not the account of the parts must be present in the account of the whole. For in some cases the accounts of the parts evidently are present and in some cases they evidently are not; 25 the account of a circle, for instance, does not include that of the segments, but the account of a syllable includes that of the letters, even though the circle is divided into its segments just as the syllable is divided into its letters.

Moreover, if a part is prior to a whole, and an acute angle is part of a right angle, and a finger of an animal, 30 then an acute angle would be prior to a right angle, and a finger to a man. In fact, however, the whole seems to be prior, since the account of the part refers to the whole, and the whole is prior by being independent.

Alternatively, perhaps a part is spoken of in many ways, and a quantitative measure is only one type of part; leaving this type aside, we should examine the parts that compose substance.

1035a If, then, there is matter, form, and the compound of these, and matter, form, and the compound of them are all substance, then it follows that in one way matter is also called a part of something, but in another way it is not, and in this second way only the components of the account of the form are parts. For example, flesh is not a part of concavity (since 5 it is the matter in which concavity comes to be), but it is a part of snubness. Again, bronze is a part of the compound statue, but not a part of the statue spoken of as form. For it is the form of the statue—i.e., the statue insofar as it has form—and never the material aspect in its own right, that should be spoken of as the statue.

This is why the account of a circle does not include 10 that of the segments, whereas the account of a syllable does include that of the letters; for the letters are not matter, but parts of the account of the form, while the segments are parts as matter in which the form comes to be. Still, the segments are nearer to the form than bronze is to the circle in the cases where circularity comes to be in bronze.

15 In a way, however, not every sort of letters—for instance, those in wax or those in air—will be included in the account of the syllable; for these also [like the bronze in the circle] are a part of the syllable as its perceptible matter. For if a line is divided and perishes into halves, or a man into bones, sinews, and bits of flesh, it does not follow that these compose the whole as parts of the substance, but 20 only that they compose it as its matter. They are parts of the compound, but when we come to the form, which is what the account is of, they are not parts of it; that is why they are not included in accounts either.

Hence the account of some things will include that of these material parts, but the account of other things, if it is not of something combined with matter, must not include it. For this reason, the principles composing a given thing are, in some but not all cases, the material parts into which it perishes. 25

If, then, something—for instance, the snub or the bronze circle—is form and matter combined, then it perishes into these [material parts], and matter is a part of it. But if something is without matter, not combined with it, so that its account is only of the form, then it does not perish—either not at all, or at least not in this way. Hence these 30 [material parts] are parts and principles of things combined with matter, but neither parts nor principles of the form.

That is why the clay statue perishes into clay, the ball into bronze, and Callias into flesh and bones. Moreover, the circle perishes into its segments, because one type of circle is combined with matter; for *1035b* the circle spoken of without qualification and the particular circle are called circles homonymously, because the particular has no distinctive name.

We have now given the true answer, but let us take up the question again, and state the answer more perspicuously. Parts of the account—i.e., the things 5 into which the account is divided—are, either all or some of them, prior to the whole. The account of the right angle, by contrast, does not include that of the acute angle, but, on the contrary, that of the acute angle includes that of the right angle; for we use the right angle in defining the acute, which is [defined as] less than a right angle. This is also the relation of the circle to a semicircle, since the semicircle is 10 defined by the circle. Similarly, a finger is defined by reference to the whole, since this sort of part of a man is a finger.

And so all the material parts—i.e., those into which the whole is divided as its matter—are posterior to it, but the parts that are parts of the account and of the substance corresponding to the account are, either all or some of them, prior to the whole.

15 Now, an animal's soul—the substance of what is ensouled—is the substance corresponding to the account; it is the form and essence of the right sort of body. At any rate, a proper definition of each part requires reference to its function, and this function requires perception. Hence the parts of the soul, either all or some of them, are prior to the compound animal, and the same is true in the case of the particular.

20 The body and its parts are posterior to this substance [i.e., the soul], and its parts are the matter into which the compound, but not this substance, is divided. In a way they are prior to the compound, but in a way they are not, since they cannot exist when they are separated; for a finger is not an animal's finger in all 25 conditions—on the contrary, a dead finger is only homonymously a finger. Some of them are simultaneous, if they are the controlling parts, those on which the account and the substance primarily depend—the heart or the brain, for instance (for it does not matter which of the two it is).

Now, man or horse or anything else that applies in this way to particulars, but universally, is not a substance, but a sort of compound of this account and 30 this matter as universal. When we come to particulars, Socrates is composed of ultimate matter, and the same is true in the other cases.

A part may be either of the form (by 'form' I mean the essence), or of the compound of the form and the matter, or of the matter itself. But only parts of the form are parts of the account, and the account 1036a is of the universal; for being circle is the same as circle, and being soul is the same as soul. But a compound such as this particular circle, either a perceptible (for instance, bronze or wooden) compound or an intelligible (for instance, mathematical) 5 compound, has no definition, but we know it with the help of thought or perception. When it has departed from actual thought or perception, it is unclear whether or not it exists; but still, we always speak of it and know it by means of the universal account, whereas the matter is unknowable in its own right.

10 One sort of matter is perceptible, another intelligible. Examples of perceptible matter are, for instance, bronze and wood, and all matter that is capable of motion; intelligible matter is the matter present in perceptible things (as, for instance, mathematical objects are present in them), but not insofar as they are perceptible.

We have now stated the facts about whole and part and about prior and posterior. If someone asks whether the right angle, or circle, or animal is prior 15 to the parts composing it, i.e., the parts into which it is divided, or whether, alternatively, the parts are prior to the whole, we must answer that neither is true without qualification.

For suppose first that the soul is the animal, or rather the ensouled thing, or that a thing's soul is the thing itself, that being circle is the circle, and that being right angle, i.e., the essence of the right angle, is the right angle. In that case, we should say that [the particular compound]—both the bronze right angle including [perceptible] matter and the right angle in particular lines—is posterior to the things 20 in the account and to one sort of right angle, and that the right angle without matter is posterior to the things in its account, but prior to the parts in the particular. We should [add these conditions and] not give an unqualified answer. Suppose, alternatively, that the soul is not the animal but different from it. In this case too we should say that some things are 25 [prior] and some are not, as we have said.

11

Not surprisingly, a further puzzle arises: What sorts of parts are parts of the form, and what sorts are parts of the combined thing, not of the form? If this is not clear, we cannot define anything; for definition is of the universal and of the form. If, then, it is not evident which sorts of parts count as matter and which do not, it will not be evident what an account is either. 30

In cases where something evidently occurs in different kinds of things, as a circle, for instance, is found in bronze, stone, and wood, it seems clear that the bronze or stone (for instance) is not part of the substance of a circle, because a circle is [also found] separated from it. Even if it is not seen to be separated, 35 the case may still be similar to those just mentioned. 1036b This would be true if, for example, all the circles that were seen were bronze; for it would still be true that the bronze is not part of the form [of circle], even though it is hard to remove the bronze in thought.

Now the form of man, for instance, always appears in flesh and bones, and in parts of this sort. Does it follow that these are also parts of the form and the account? Perhaps not; perhaps they are only matter, and we are incapable of separating them from the form because it does not also occur in other [sorts of material parts].

Since this sort of thing seems to be possible, but it is unclear when [it is possible], some people are puzzled even when they come to a circle or a triangle. They suppose that it is not suitably defined by lines and by the continuous, and that we speak of these in the same way as we were speaking of the flesh and bones of a man, or the bronze or stone of a statue. Hence they reduce everything to numbers, and say that the account of the line is the account of the two.

Those talk about the Ideas are also affected by this puzzle. Some of them say that the dyad is line-itself; others say that it is the form of line since, they say, in some cases—for instance, dyad and the form of dyad—the form is the same as the thing whose form it is, but in the case of the line it is not. The result is that there is one form for many things whose form appears different (this was also the result of the Pythagorean view); and then it is possible to make this form the one form of all things, and to make nothing else a form. On this argument, however, all things will be one.

We have said, then, that questions about definitions raise a puzzle, and why they raise it. That is why this reduction of everything [to numbers and Forms] and the abstracting of matter goes too far; for presumably some things are [essentially] this form in this matter, or these material parts with this form. And Socrates the Younger was wrong in his habitual comparison of an animal [and its parts with circle and bronze]. For his comparison leads us away from the truth; it makes us suppose that a man can exist without his parts, as a circle can exist without bronze. But in fact the two cases are not similar; for an animal is a perceiver, and cannot be defined without reference to motion, and therefore to parts in the right condition. For a hand is not a part of a man in just any condition, but only when it is capable of fulfilling its function, and hence only when it is ensouled—when it is not ensouled, it is not a part [of a man].

But in the case of mathematical objects, why are accounts [of parts], of semicircles, for instance, not part of accounts [of wholes], of circles, for instance? For these are not perceptible. Perhaps, however, this makes no difference; for some non-perceptible things have matter too, and in fact everything that is not an essence and form itself in its own right, but a this, has some sort of matter. Hence these semicircles will not be parts of the universal circle, but they will be parts of particular circles, as we said before; for one sort of matter is perceptible, one sort intelligible.

It is also clear that the soul is the primary substance, the body is matter, and man or animal is composed of the two as universal. As for Socrates or Coriscus, if [Socrates'] soul is also Socrates, he is spoken of in two ways; for some speak of him as soul, some as the compound. But if he is without qualification this soul and this body, then what was said about the universal also applies to the particular.

We must postpone an investigation of whether there is another sort of matter apart from the matter of these [perceptible] substances, and whether we must search for some other sort of substance—for instance, numbers or something of the sort. For we also have this in view in trying to determine [the answers to questions] about perceptible substances as well [as non-perceptible substances], since in a way the study of nature, i.e., second philosophy, has the task of studying perceptible substances. For the student of nature must know not only about matter but also, and even more, about the substance corresponding to the account.

We must also postpone an investigation of the way in which the things in the account are parts of the definition, and of why the definition is one account. For it is clear that the thing defined is one. But what makes it one, given that it has parts?

We have said generally, then, about all cases, what the essence is; in what way it is itself in its own right; why in some cases the account of the essence includes the parts of the thing defined and in some cases it does not; and that in the account of substance the parts that are matter will not be present, because they are parts of the compound substance, not of the substance corresponding to the account.

The compound substance has an account in one way, but in another way it has none. Taken together with matter, it has no account, since that is indefinable; but it has an account corresponding to the primary substance, so that the account of man, for instance, is the account of soul. For [the primary] 30 substance is the form present in the thing, and the compound substance is spoken of as composed of the form and the matter. Concavity, for instance, [is a form of this sort]; for snub nose and snubness are composed of concavity and nose (for nose will be present twice in these). And the compound substance (for instance snub nose or Callias) will also have matter in it.

1037b We have also said that in some cases, as in the case of primary substances, a thing and its essence are the same; curvature, for instance, is the same as being curvature, if curvature is primary. (By 'primary substance' I mean the substance that is so called not because x is in y and y is the subject of x by being the matter of x.) But if a thing is [a substance] by 5 being matter or by being combined with matter, it is not the same as its essence. Nor, however, are they one [only] coincidentally, as Socrates and the musical are; for these are the same [only] coincidentally.

13

1038b Since we are investigating substance, let us return to it again. Just as the subject and the essence are said to be substance, so too is the universal. We have discussed the first two of these, namely essence and 5 subject; we have seen that something is a subject in one of two ways, either by being a this (as an animal is the subject for its attributes) or as matter is the subject for the actuality. But some also think that the universal is a cause and principle more than anything else is; that is why we should also discuss the universal.

For it would seem impossible for anything spoken of universally to be substance. For, first, the substance 10 of a thing is the substance that is distinctive of it, which does not belong to anything else, whereas the universal is common; for what is called universal is what naturally belongs to more than one thing. Then which thing's substance will the universal be? For it must be the substance either of all or of none of them. It cannot be the substance of all; but if it is the substance of one of them, then the others will be this one too, since things that have one substance 15 also have one essence and are themselves one.

Further, what is called substance is what is not said of a subject, whereas every universal is said of a subject.

Now, suppose someone says: 'Admittedly, a universal cannot belong to something as its essence. Still, it is present in the essence, as animal is present in man and horse.' Surely it is clear that it will be some account of [the essence it is present in]. It does not matter even if it is not an account of everything in the substance; for this [universal] will still be the 20 substance of something, as man is of the man in which it is present. And so the result will be the same once again; for [the universal]—for instance, animal—will be the substance of whatever it is present in by being its distinctive property.

Further, it is both impossible and absurd for a this and substance, if it is composite, to be composed not 25 from substances and not from a this, but from a sort of thing; for it will follow that a nonsubstance, a sort of thing, will be prior to substance, to a this. But that is impossible; for attributes cannot be prior to substance, either in account or in time or in knowledge—for if they were, they would also be separable.

Moreover, a substance will be present in [the substance] Socrates, so that [the universal] will be the 30 substance of two things.

In general, if a man and things spoken of in this way are substances, it follows that nothing in their account is the substance of any of them or exists separately from them or in anything else. I mean, for instance, that there is no animal, or anything else mentioned in the accounts, apart from the particular animals.

If we study them in this way, then, it is evident 35 that nothing that belongs universally is a substance and that what is predicated in common signifies this 1039a sort of thing, not a this. If it is a this, then many [difficulties] result, including the Third Man.

Further, our conclusion can also be made clear from the following points. Substance cannot be composed of substances that are actually present in it; for things that are actually two in this way are never 5 actually one, but if they are potentially two they are [actually] one. A double line, for instance, is composed of halves that are [only] potentially two things; for the actuality separates them. And so if substance is one, it will not be composed of substances that are actually present in it. Democritus is right about actuality, when he says that one cannot come to be 10 from two, or two from one; he says this because he regards the indivisible magnitudes as the substances.

Clearly, then, the same will apply in the case of number if, as some say, number is a combination of units; for either the pair is not one or else a unit is not actually in it.

15 This conclusion, however, raises a puzzle. For if no substance can be composed of universals (because a universal signifies this sort of thing, not a this) and if no substance can be composed of substances actually present in it, then it follows that every substance will be incomposite, so that none will have any account. And yet, it seems to everyone, and we 20 have said much earlier, that substances alone, or most of all, have formulae, whereas now they too turn out not to have them. And so either nothing will have a definition or else in a way things will have definitions, and in a way they will not. What this means will be clearer from what follows.

14

25 It is also evident from this what results for those who both say that the Ideas are separate substances and also, at the same time, take a Form to be composed of genus and differentiae. For if there are Forms, and if animal is in man and horse, then it is either numerically one and the same in both or numerically different in each. (For clearly it is one in account; a 30 statement of the account will state the same thing in each case.) If, then, there is some man himself in his own right that is a this and separated, each of his components—for instance, animal and biped—must also signify a this and be separable and a substance; and so this is also true of animal.

If the animal in horse is one and the same as the animal in man, as you are one and the same as 1039b yourself, then how will this one thing that is in separate things be one, and why will this animal not be separate from itself as well?

Further, if it is to participate in two-footed and many-footed, then something impossible follows; for contraries will belong simultaneously to it, though it is one and a this. But if it is not to participate in 5 them, what is meant by saying that animal is two-footed or footed? Presumably [we might be told] they are combined and in contact or mixed; but all such answers are absurd.

Suppose, alternatively, that animal is different in each [species]; then there will be practically an unlimited number of things whose substance is animal, since man is noncoincidentally composed of animal.

Further, animal itself will be many things. For the 10 animal in each [species] is substance, because [the species] is not called [animal] by reference to anything else—if it were, then that other thing would be a component of man and would be its genus.

Further, all the elements composing man will be Ideas; but nothing will be the Idea of one thing and the substance of another (for that would be impossible). Hence animal itself will be each one of the animals in the different [species of] animals.

Further, what is that [animal in each species] composed of, and how will it be composed of animal 15 itself? Or how can the animal [in each species], whose substance is this animal itself, be something apart from animal itself?

Further, in the case of perceptible things, these and even more absurd results follow. If, then, this cannot be how things are, clearly there are no Forms of perceptible things in the way some say there are.

15

We have found that the compound and the form are 20 different sorts of substance; I mean that the first sort of substance is substance by being the form, combined with matter, and the second sort is the form, without qualification. Now, all the substances spoken of as compounds perish, since all of them also come to be; but the form does not perish in such a way that it is ever [in the process of] perishing, since neither is it ever [in the process of] coming to be. For it is 25 the essence of this house, not the essence of house, that is [in the process of] coming to be, whereas forms are and are not without [any process of] coming to be and perishing, since we have shown that no one generates or produces them.

For this reason there is neither definition nor demonstration about particular perceptible substances, because they have matter whose nature admits of both being and not being; that is why all [perceptible] 30 particulars are perishable.

Now, demonstrations and definitions that express knowledge, are of necessary things. And just as knowledge cannot be knowledge at one time and ignorance at another, but what admits of such variation is belief, so also neither demonstration nor definition admits

1040a of such variation; belief is what is concerned with what admits of being otherwise. It clearly follows that there will be neither definition nor demonstration of these [particular perceptible things]. For whenever perishing things pass from perception, they are unclear to those with knowledge, and though the accounts still remain in the souls of those with knowl- *5* edge, there will be neither definition nor demonstration [about perceptible things]. That is why, whenever anyone who looks for a formula is defining a particular, he ought to realize that the definition can in every case be undermined, since particulars cannot be defined.

Nor, indeed, can Ideas be defined. For Ideas are *10* particulars, they say, and separable. But accounts must be composed of names, and the definer will not make a [new] name (since it would be unknown); yet each of the established names is common to all [the particulars of a given kind], and so they must also belong to something else [as well as to a given particular]. If, for instance, someone defines you, he will say you are a thin or pale animal, or something else that belongs to something else as well as to you.

Someone might say: 'Even though each name [in *15* the definition] belongs separately to many things, still it is possible that all together belong only to this.' We should answer, first, that biped animal, for instance, belongs both to animal and to biped—indeed, this must be so with everlasting things, since they are prior to and parts of the composite thing. Moreover, they are also separable if man is separable; for either none *20* of the three is separable or both animal and biped are. And so if none of them is separable, the genus will not exist apart from the species; but if the genus is separable, so is the differentia. Moreover, [animal and biped] are prior in being [to biped animal], and therefore they are not destroyed when it is.

Further, if Ideas are composed of Ideas (for the things they are composed of are less composite), then the components of the Idea—for instance, animal and biped—will also have to be predicated of many *25* things. If they are not, how will they be known? For there will be an Idea which cannot be predicated of more than one thing. But that does not seem to be so; on the contrary, every Idea can, it seems, be participated in.

As has been said, then, we fail to notice that everlasting things [that are particulars] are indefinable. This is especially true in the case of those that are unique—for instance, the sun and the moon. For sometimes people not only go wrong by adding the sorts of things *30* (for instance, going around the earth, or being hidden at night) that can be removed from the sun without its ceasing to be the sun. (For [this sort of definition implies that] if it stops going around or shows at night, it will no longer be the sun; but that is absurd, since the sun signifies a certain substance.) They also [sometimes go wrong by mentioning only the features] that can be found in something else as well. If, for instance, something else of this sort comes to be, then clearly [according to the alleged definition], it will also have to be the sun, and in that case the *1040b* account will be common [to the two]. But in fact the sun is a particular, as Cleon and Socrates are.

[These objections show why Ideas are indefinable.] For why does none of those [who believe in Ideas] present a formula of any Idea? If they tried to do so, the truth of what we have just said would become clear.

16

5 It is evident that even among the substances that are generally recognized to be such, most are potentialities. These include the parts of animals (for none of them is separated [as long as they remain parts of animals]; whenever they are separated, they all exist as matter), and also earth, fire, and air. For none of these is one, but each is a sort of heap, until they are worked up and some one thing comes to be from them. *10*

One would be most inclined to suppose that the parts of ensouled things that are closely [associated with] the soul are beings both in actuality and in potentiality; for they have principles of motion from some source in their joints, which is why some animals keep on living when they are divided. But nonetheless, all these things exist [only] in potentiality. *15* They exist as long as they are one and continuous by nature, rather than by force or by growing together (that sort of thing is a deformity).

Now, one is spoken of in the same ways as being is; and the substance of one thing is one, and things whose substance is numerically one are numerically one. Evidently, then, neither one nor being can be the substance of things, just as being an element or being a principle cannot [be the substance of things];

20 rather, we ask 'What then is the principle?', so that we may refer [the thing] to something better known. Among these things, then, being and one are substance to a higher degree than principle, element, and cause are; but even being and one are not substance, since nothing else common is substance either. For substance belongs only to itself and to what 25 has it, the thing whose substance it is. Moreover, one thing would not be in many places at once, but what is common exists in many places at once. Hence clearly no universal is found separately apart from particulars.

But those who say there are Forms are right in one way, in separating them, if they are indeed substances; but in another way they are wrong, because they say 30 that the one over many is a Form. The reason is that they cannot describe these imperishable substances apart from particular and perceptible substances, and so they make them the same in kind as perishable things (since these are the substances we know); they speak of man itself and horse itself, adding to perceptibles the word 'itself.'

1041a And yet even if we had not seen the stars, nonetheless, I think, they would have been everlasting substances apart from those we know; and so, as things are, it is equally true that even if we do not know what nonperceptible substances there are, there must presumably be some.

It is clear, then, that nothing said universally is a substance, and that no substance is composed of sub- 5 stances.

17

But let us make a sort of new beginning, and say over again what, and what sort of thing, substance should be said to be; for presumably our answer will also make things clear about the substance that is separated from perceptible substances. Since, then, substance is some sort of principle and cause, we should 10 proceed from here.

In every case, we search for the reason why by asking why one thing belongs to another. For if we ask why a musical man is a musical man, either we are searching for what we have mentioned—for instance, why the man is musical—or else we are searching for something else. Now, to ask why some- 15 thing is itself is to search for nothing. For that [it is so] and its being so—I mean, for instance, that the moon is eclipsed—must be clear already; and the answer 'because it is itself' is one account and one cause applying to every case, to why a man is a man or a musician a musician. Perhaps, however, someone might answer 'because each thing is indivisible from itself, since this is what it is to be one.' But this is a short answer common to all cases. 20

We might, however, ask why a man is this sort of animal. Here, then, we are clearly not asking why something that is a man is a man. We are asking, then, why one thing belongs to another; that it does belong must already be clear, since otherwise we are searching for nothing. For instance, when we ask why it thunders, we are asking why there is a noise in the 25 clouds; here we ask why one thing belongs to another. Similarly, we ask why these things—for instance, bricks and stones—are a house.

Evidently, then, we are searching for the cause; and this is the essence, to speak from a logical point of view. In some cases—for instance, presumably, a house or a bed—the cause is the what something is for; sometimes it is what first initiated the motion, 30 since this is also a cause. We search for the latter type of cause in the case of coming to be and perishing; in the case of being as well [as in the case of coming to be] we search for the former type of cause.

What we are searching for is most easily overlooked when one thing is not said of another (as when we ask, for instance, what a man is), because we speak *1041b* without qualification and do not specify that we are asking why these things are this thing. Instead of speaking without qualification, we must articulate our question before we search, since otherwise we will not have distinguished a genuine search from a search for nothing. Since we must take it as given that the 5 subject exists, clearly we search for why the matter is something. We ask, for instance, 'Why are these things a house?' Because the essence of house belongs to them. Similarly, a man is this, or rather is this body having this. Hence we search for the cause on account of which the matter is something, i.e., for the form; and this cause is the substance.

Evidently, then, there is neither searching nor 10 teaching about incomposite things; the approach to them is different from searching.

Now, a composite is composed of something in such a way that the whole thing is one, not as a heap is, but as a syllable is. A syllable is not the same as its letters—for instance, B and A are not the same thing as BA, nor is flesh fire and earth. For when the 15 components are dispersed, the flesh or syllable no longer exists, though the letters or the fire and earth still do. Hence the syllable is something, and not only the vowel and the consonant but some further thing; and similarly, flesh is not only fire and earth, or the hot and cold, but some further thing.

20 Now suppose that this further thing must be either an element or composed of elements. If it is an element, there will be the same argument over again; for flesh will be composed of this [new element], plus fire and earth, plus some further thing, so that it will go on without limit. If the further thing is composed of an element, it is clearly not composed of just one (otherwise it would itself be this one), but of more 25 than one; and then we will repeat the same argument about it as about flesh or a syllable.

It would seem, however, that this further thing is something, and not an element, and that it is the cause of one thing's being flesh and another thing's being a syllable, and similarly in the other cases.

Now this is the substance of a given thing; for this is the primary cause of the thing's being [what it is]. Some things are not substances, but the things that 30 are substances are naturally constituted; hence this nature—the one that is not an element but a principle—will apparently be substance. An element is what is present in something as the matter into which the thing is divided—for instance, the A and the B in the syllable.

BOOK VIII

1

1042a3 We must, then, draw the conclusions from what has been said, gather together the main points, and so complete the discussion. Here, then, is what we 5 have said:

(1) We are searching for the causes, principles, and elements of substances.

(2) Some substances are agreed by everyone to be substances, while some people have held distinctive views of their own about some other things [that they count as substances]. The agreed substances are the natural ones—for instance, fire, earth, water, air, and the other simple bodies, then plants and their parts, 10 animals and their parts, and, finally, the heaven and its parts. In some people's distinctive views, Forms and mathematical objects are substances.

(3) Some arguments imply that the essence is substance, others that the subject is substance. Other arguments imply that the genus is substance more than the species are, and that the universal is substance more than the particulars are. The Ideas are 15 closely related to the universal and the genus, since the same argument makes all of them seem to be substances.

(4) Since the essence is substance and a definition is an account of the essence, we have discussed definition and what is in its own right.

(5) Since a definition is an account and an account has parts, we also had to consider what a part is, to 20 see what sorts of parts are parts of the substance, and what sorts are not, and whether the same parts [that are parts of the substance] are also parts of the definition.

(6) Further, neither the universal nor the genus is substance.

(7) We should examine Ideas and mathematical objects later, since some say that these are substances apart from perceptible substances.

For now, let us proceed with a discussion of the agreed substances; these are the perceptible ones, and 25 all perceptible substances have matter.

The subject is substance. In one way, matter [is a subject]. (By 'matter' I mean what is potentially but not actually a this.) In another way, the account and the form, which, being a this, is separable in account, [is a subject]. The third [sort of subject] is the composite 30 of these two. Only it comes to be and perishes, and it is separable without qualification; for among substances that correspond to the account some are [separable without qualification] and some are not.

Now, clearly matter as well [as form and compound] is substance; for in all changes between opposites there is some subject for the change. Changes in place, for instance, have a subject that is here at one time, elsewhere at another time; those involving 35 growth have one that is this size at one time, smaller or bigger at another time; changes involving alteration have one that is, [for instance,] healthy at one time, sick at another time. Similarly, changes involving *1042b* substance have a subject that is at one time in [process of] coming to be, at another time in [process of] perishing, and at one time is the sort of subject that is a this and at another time is the sort of subject that corresponds to a privation.

Coming to be and perishing imply all the other sorts of change, but one or two of the other sorts do not imply this sort. For if something has matter for change in place, it need not also have matter for coming to be and perishing. The difference between unqualified and qualified coming to be has been described in the works on nature.

2

The substance that is subject and matter is agreed; this is the substance that is something potentially. It remains, then, to describe the substance of perceptible things that is actuality.

Democritus would seem to think that there are three differentiae; in his view, the body that is the subject—the matter—is one and the same, but [perceptible things] differ either by 'balance', i.e., figure, or by 'turning', i.e., position, or by 'contact', i.e., arrangement. It is evident, however, that there are many differentiae. For things are differentiated by the way their matter is combined (blended together, for instance, as honey-water is); or tied together (for instance, a bundle); or glued (for instance, a book); or nailed (for instance, a box); or by more than one of these; or by having a specific position (a threshold or a lintel, for instance, since their differentia is being in a certain position); or by a specific time (for instance, dinner and breakfast); or by a specific place (for instance, the winds); or by having different perceptible attributes (for instance, hardness or softness, thickness or thinness, dryness or wetness), either some or all of them, and, in general, by excess or deficiency [of them].

Clearly, then, 'is' is also said in just as many ways. Something is a threshold, for instance, because it has this position, and its being a threshold signifies its having this position; and similarly, being ice signifies [water's] having solidified in this way. The being of some things will be defined by all of these things—by some things being mixed, some blended, some bound together, some solidified, and some (a hand or foot, for instance) having the other differentiae.

We must grasp, then, what kinds of differentiae there are, since they will be the principles of [a thing's] being [what it is]. For instance, things differentiated by more and less, or thick and thin, or by other such things, are all differentiated by excess and deficiency; things differentiated by shape, or by roughness and smoothness, are all differentiated by straight and bent; and the being of other things will be being mixed, and their not being will be the opposite.

It is evident from what we have said, then, that if substance is the cause of a thing's being, we should seek the cause of the being of each of these things in these [differentiae]. Although none of them is substance even when combined [with matter], still it is in each case analogous to substance; and just as in substances what is predicated of the matter is the actuality itself, so also in other definitions what is predicated is what is closest to being the actuality. If, for instance, we have to define a threshold, we will say it is wood or stone in this position; we will define a house as bricks and timber in this position (or in some cases we mention the end as well). If we have to define ice, we will say it is water frozen or solidified in this way; we will say harmony is this sort of blending of high and low; and the same is true in the other cases.

It is evident from this that each different sort of matter has a different actuality and account. For in some cases the actuality is the composition, in some it is the mixture, and in others one of the other things we have mentioned.

That is why some people who offer definitions say what a house is by saying it is stones, bricks, and timber; in saying this, they speak of what is potentially a house, since these things are matter. Others say that a house is a container sheltering possessions and [living] bodies (or add something else of that sort); in saying this, they speak of the actuality. Others combine the matter and the actuality; in doing this, they speak of the third sort of substance, which is composed of the first two. For the account giving the differentiae would seem to be the account of the form and the actuality, and the one giving the constituents present in the house would seem to be more an account of the matter. The same is true of the sorts of formulae that Archytas[19] used to accept; for these

19. [Archytas of Tarentum, a friend of Plato, was a mathematician, philosopher, and enlightened political leader.]

are accounts of the composite. What, for instance, is calm weather? Quiet in a large expanse of air; for air is the matter, and quiet is the actuality of the substance. 25 What is calm? Smoothness of sea; the material subject is the sea, and the actuality and form is the smoothness.

It is evident from what we have said, then, both what perceptible substance is and what sort of being it has; for one sort is substance as matter, another is substance as form and actuality, and the third is the substance that is composed of these.

6

1045a7 Let us now return to the puzzle we mentioned about definitions and about numbers, namely about the cause of their being one. If something has several 10 parts, but all together it is not a sort of heap, but, on the contrary, the whole is something apart from the parts, then there is a cause of its being one, since, even among bodies, in some cases the cause of being one is contact, and in others it is viscosity or some other such attribute.

A definition is an account that is one, not by being tied together (like the *Iliad*), but by being of one thing. What, then, is it that makes man one? Why is 15 he one, and not more than one—animal and two-footed, for instance—especially if, as some say, there is some animal itself and two-footed itself? For why is man not these things themselves? If so, men will exist by participating, not in one thing (man), but in 20 two (animal and two-footed); and in general, man would be more than one (animal and two-footed) and not one.

Now, it is evident that it is impossible to explain and solve the puzzle if one continues to define and to speak as they normally do. But if, as we say, one thing is matter and another is form, and the one is [something] potentially, the other actually, then what 25 we are searching for no longer seems to be a puzzle. For this puzzle is the same as the question whether the round bronze is the formula of cloak. [If it is,] then this name ['cloak'] is a sign of the account, and so what we are searching for is what causes the round and the bronze to be one. There no longer appears to be a puzzle, then, because one of them is the matter, and the other is the form.

30 What, then, causes something that is potentially to be actually? That is to say, what is the cause apart from the agent that produced it (in the case of things that come to be)? There is no cause other than [the fact that] the potential sphere is an actual sphere; this is the essence of both [the potential and the actual sphere].

Some matter is intelligible, some perceptible; and in every account one part is the matter, one the actu- 35 ality.

If something has neither intelligible nor perceptible matter, it is thereby essentially one thing, just as *1045b* it is also essentially a being—a this, a quality, a quantity; this is why neither being nor one is present in definitions. Moreover, the essence of these things is thereby one thing, just as it is also a being. Hence none of these things has any other cause than being 5 one or being a being; for each is some being and some one [thing] immediately [by its own nature], not by being in the genus of being or of one, and not in such a way that [being and one] are separable apart from particulars.

This puzzle leads some to speak of participating and to be puzzled about its cause and about what it is. Others speak of communion: Lycophron, for 10 instance, says that knowledge is a communion of knowing and the soul. Others say that life is a compounding or tying together of the soul with the body. But the same thing can be said about all these attempts. For according to them being healthy, for instance, will also be a communion or tying together or compounding of soul and health; and the bronze's being a triangle will be a compounding 15 of bronze and triangle; and something's being pale will be a compounding of surface and paleness. The reason they say these things is that they are searching for an account that makes potentiality and actuality one, and [in doing so] they are searching for the differentia.

In fact, however, as we have said, the ultimate matter and the form are one and the same; the matter [is something] potentially, and the form [is that thing] actually. Hence [to search for what causes them to be one] is like searching for the cause of one and of 20 being one. For each thing [that has matter and form] is some one thing; and what is potentially and what is actually are in a way one. And so nothing else causes [them to be one], unless something has initiated the motion from potentiality to actuality. Anything that lacks matter is without qualification some one thing essentially.

BOOK XII

6

1071b3 Since we have found that there are three types of substance, two of them natural and one unmoved, we must discuss the third kind, to show that there 5 must be an everlasting unmoved substance. For substances are the primary beings, and if all substances are perishable, then everything is perishable. But motion cannot come to be or perish (since it has always been), nor can time (since there cannot be a before and an after if there is no time). Motion is also contin- 10 uous, then, in the same way that time is, since time is either the same as motion or an attribute of it. But the only continuous motion is local motion—specifically, circular motion.

Now if there is something that is capable of initiating motion or of acting, but it does not actually do so, there will be no motion; for what has a potentiality need not actualize it. It will be no use, then, to assume 15 everlasting substances, as believers in Forms do, unless these include some principle capable of initiating change. And even this, or some other type of substance besides the Forms, is not sufficient; for if it does not actualize its potentiality, there will be no motion. Nor yet is it sufficient if it actualizes its potentiality, but its essence is potentiality; for there will be no everlasting motion, since what has a potentiality 20 need not actualize it. There must, then, be a principle of the sort whose essence is actuality. Further, these substances must be without matter; for they must be everlasting if anything else is to be everlasting, and hence they must be actuality.

Now a puzzle arises. For it seems that whatever actualizes a potentiality must have it, but not everything that has a potentiality also actualizes it; and so 25 potentiality is prior. But now, if this is so, nothing that exists will exist, since things can have the potentiality to exist without actualizing it. And yet, if those who have written about the gods are right to generate everything from night, or if the natural philosophers are right to say that 'all things were together', the same impossibility results. For how will things be moved if there is no cause [initiating motion] in actuality? For surely matter will not initiate motion 30 in itself, but carpentry, [for instance, must initiate the motion]; nor will the menstrual fluid or the earth initiate motion in themselves, but the semen and the seeds [must initiate the motion].

Hence some people—Leucippus and Plato, for instance—believe in everlasting actuality; for they say that there is always motion. But they do not say why there is this motion, or what kind of motion it is, and neither do they state the cause of something's being moved in this way or that. For nothing is moved at 35 random, but in every case there must be some [cause]—as in fact things are moved in one way by nature and in another by force or by the agency of mind or something else. Further, what sort of motion is primary? For that makes an enormous difference. Nor can Plato say that the principle is of the sort 1072a that he sometimes thinks it is—what initiates its own motion. For he also says that the soul is later [than motion] and comes into being at the same time as the universe.

The view that potentiality is prior to actuality is in a way correct and in a way incorrect—we have explained how this is so. The priority of actuality is 5 attested by Anaxagoras (since mind is actuality), and by Empedocles (who makes love and strife prior), and by those who say that there is always motion, as Leucippus does. And so chaos or night did not exist for an infinite time, but the same things have always existed (either in a cycle or in some other way), if actuality is prior to potentiality.

If, then, the same things always exist in a cycle, 10 something must always remain actually operating in the same way. And if there is to be coming to be and perishing, then there must be something else that always actually operates, in one way at one time and in another way at another time. This [second mover], then, must actually operate in one way because of itself and in another way because of something else, and hence either because of some third mover or because of the first mover. Hence it must be because of the first mover; for [otherwise] the first mover will 15 cause the motion of both the second and the third. Then surely it is better if the first mover is the cause. For we have seen that it is the cause of what is always the same, and a second mover is the cause of what is different at different times. Clearly both together cause this everlasting succession. Then surely this is also how the motions occur. Why, then, do we need to search for any other principles?

7

Since it is possible for things to be as we have said they 20 are, and since the only alternative is for everything to come to be from night and from all things being together and from what is not, this may be taken as the solution of the puzzles. There is something, then, that is always being moved in a ceaseless motion, and this motion is circular (this is clear not only from argument but also from what actually happens); and so the first heaven is everlasting. Hence there is also something that initiates motion. And since whatever both is moved and initiates motion is an intermediary, 25 there is something that initiates motion without being moved, something that is everlasting and a substance and actuality.

This is how an object of understanding or desire initiates motion; it initiates motion without being moved. The primary objects of desire and of understanding are the same. For what appears fine is the object of appetite, and what is fine is the primary object of wish; and we desire something because it seems [fine], rather than its seeming [fine] because 30 we desire it—for understanding is the principle.

Understanding is moved by its object, and the first column [of opposites] is what is understood in its own right. In this column substance is primary; and the primary substance is the substance that is simple and actually operating. (Being one and being simple are not the same; for being one signifies a measure, while being simple signifies that something is itself in a 35 particular condition.) Further, what is fine and what is choiceworthy for itself are in the same column; 1072b and what is primary is in every case either the best or what is analogous to the best.

Division shows that what something is for is among the things that are unmoved. For it is either the end for some [beneficiary] or the end [aimed at] in some [process]; the first of these is moved, and the second is unmoved. The [end] initiates motion by being an object of love, and it initiates motion in the other things by [something else's] being moved.

5 If, then, something is moved, it can be otherwise. And so, if something's actuality is the primary type of local motion, it follows that insofar as it is in motion, in this respect it admits of being otherwise, in place if not in substance. But since there is something that initiates motion without itself being moved, and this is actually operating, it cannot be otherwise in any respect at all. For local motion is the primary type of motion, and the primary type of local motion is circular motion; and this is the sort of motion that 10 the primary mover initiates. Hence the primary mover exists necessarily; and insofar as it exists necessarily, its being is fine, and insofar as its being is fine, it is a principle. For what is necessary is spoken of in a number of ways—as what is forced because it is contrary to the subject's impulse, as that without which the good cannot be, and as what cannot be otherwise but is necessary without qualification.

This, then, is the sort of principle on which the heaven and nature depend. Its way of life has the 15 same character as our own way of life at its best has for a short time. For the primary mover is always in this state [of complete actuality], whereas we cannot always be in it; for its actuality is also pleasure (that is why being awake, perceiving, and thinking are pleasantest, while expectations and memories are pleasant because of these).

Understanding in its own right is of what is best in its own right, and the highest degree of understanding is of what is best to the highest degree in its own right. And understanding understands itself by sharing 20 the character of the object of understanding; for it becomes an object of understanding by being in contact with and by understanding its object, so that understanding and its object are the same. For understanding is what is capable of receiving the object of understanding and the essence, and it is actually understanding when it possesses its object; and so it is this [actual understanding and possession] rather than [the potentiality to receive the object] that seems to be the divine aspect of understanding, and its actual attention to the object of understanding is pleasantest and best.

If, then, the god is always in the good state that 25 we are in sometimes, that deserves wonder; if he is in a better state, that deserves still more wonder. And that is indeed the state he is in. Further, life belongs to the god. For the actuality of understanding is life, and the god is that actuality; and his actuality in its own right is the best and everlasting life. We say, then, that the god is the best and everlasting living being, so that continuous and everlasting life and duration belong to the god; for that is what the god is.

30 Some, however, suppose, as the Pythagoreans and Speusippus[20] do, that what is finest and best is not present in the principle, claiming that the principles of plants and animals are their causes, whereas what is fine and complete is found in what results from 35 these. Their view is mistaken. For the seed comes from other [principles] that are prior and complete; 1073a and what is primary is not the seed, but the complete [organism]; for instance, one would say that the man is prior to the seed (not the man who comes into being from the seed, but another one, from whom the seed comes).

It is evident from what has been said, then, that there is an everlasting, unmoved substance that is separated from perceptible things. It has also been 5 proved that this substance cannot have any magnitude, but must be without parts and indivisible; for it initiates motion for an infinite time, but nothing finite has infinite potentiality. And since every magnitude is either infinite or finite, [the primary mover] cannot have a finite magnitude, and it cannot have 10 an infinite magnitude, because there is no infinite magnitude at all. Besides, it has also been proved that this substance is not affected or altered, since all other motions depend on local motion. It is clear, then, why these things are so.

20. [Speusippus, disciple and nephew of Plato, was the philosopher who succeeded Plato as head of his Academy.]

Nicomachean Ethics

BOOK I

1

Every craft and every line of inquiry, and likewise every action and decision, seems to seek some good; that is why some people were right to describe the good as what everything seeks. But the ends [that are sought] appear to differ; some are activities, and others are products apart from the activities. Wherever there are ends apart from the actions, the products are by nature better than the activities.

Since there are many actions, crafts, and sciences, the ends turn out to be many as well; for health is the end of medicine, a boat of boat building, victory of generalship, and wealth of household management. But some of these pursuits are subordinate to some one capacity; for instance, bridle making and every other science producing equipment for horses are subordinate to horsemanship, while this and every action in warfare are, in turn, subordinate to generalship, and in the same way other pursuits are subordinate to further ones. In all such cases, then, the ends of the ruling sciences are more choiceworthy than all the ends subordinate to them, since the lower ends are also pursued for the sake of the higher. Here it does not matter whether the ends of the actions are the activities themselves, or something apart from them, as in the sciences we have mentioned.

2

Suppose, then, that the things achievable by action have some end that we wish for because of itself, and because of which we wish for the other things, and that we do not choose everything because of something else—for if we do, it will go on without limit, so that desire will prove to be empty and futile. Clearly, this end will be the good, that is to say, the best good.

Then does knowledge of this good carry great weight for [our] way of life, and would it make us better able, like archers who have a target to aim at, to hit the right mark? If so, we should try to grasp, in outline at any rate, what the good is, and which is its proper science or capacity.

It seems proper to the most controlling science—the highest ruling science. And this appears characteristic of political science. For it is the one that prescribes which of the sciences ought to be studied in cities, and which ones each class in the city should learn, and how far; indeed we see that even the most honored capacities—generalship, household management, and rhetoric, for instance—are subordinate to it. And since it uses the other sciences concerned with action, and moreover legislates what must be done and what avoided, its end will include the ends of the other sciences, and so this will be the human good. For even if the good is the same for a city as for an individual, still the good of the city is apparently a greater and more complete good to acquire and preserve. For while it is satisfactory to acquire and preserve the good even for an individual, it is finer and more divine to acquire and preserve it for a people and for cities. And so, since our line of inquiry seeks these [goods, for an individual and for a community], it is a sort of political science.

3

Our discussion will be adequate if we make things perspicuous enough to accord with the subject matter; for we would not seek the same degree of exactness in all sorts of arguments alike, and more than in the products of different crafts. Now, fine and just things, which political science examines, differ and vary so much as to seem to rest on convention only, not on nature. But [this is not a good reason, since] goods also

Reprinted from Aristotle, *Nicomachean Ethics*, second edition, translated by Terence Irwin (Indianapolis: Hackett Publishing Company, 1999), by permission of the publisher. The use of brackets within the text indicates insertions not found in the manuscript.

vary in the same way, because they result in harm to many people—for some have been destroyed because 20 of their wealth, others because of their bravery. And so, since this is our subject and these are our premises, we shall be satisfied to indicate the truth roughly and in outline; since our subject and our premises are things that hold good usually [but not universally], we shall be satisfied to draw conclusions of the same sort.

Each of our claims, then, ought to be accepted in the same way [as claiming to hold good usually]. For 25 the educated person seeks exactness in each area to the extent that the nature of the subject allows; for apparently it is just as mistaken to demand demonstrations from a rhetorician as to accept [merely] persuasive arguments from a mathematician. Further, each 1095a person judges rightly what he knows, and is a good judge about that; hence the good judge in a given area is the person educated in that area, and the unqualifiedly good judge is the person educated in every area.

This is why a youth is not a suitable student of political science; for he lacks experience of the actions in life, which are the subject and premises of our arguments. Moreover, since he tends to follow his feel- 5 ings, his study will be futile and useless; for the end [of political science] is action, not knowledge. It does not matter whether he is young in years or immature in character, since the deficiency does not depend on age, but results from following his feelings in his life and in a given pursuit; for an immature person, like an incontinent person, gets no benefit from his 10 knowledge. But for those who accord with reason in forming their desires and in their actions, knowledge of political science will be of great benefit.

These are the preliminary points about the student, about the way our claims are to be accepted, and about what we propose to do.

4

Let us, then, begin again. Since every sort of knowl- 15 edge and decision pursues some good, what is the good that we say political science seeks? What, [in other words,] is the highest of all the goods achievable in action?

As far as its name goes, most people virtually agree; for both the many and the cultivated call it happiness, and they suppose that living well and doing well are the same as being happy. But they disagree about 20 what happiness is, and the many do not give the same answer as the wise.

For the many think it is something obvious and evident—for instance, pleasure, wealth, or honor. Some take it to be one thing, others another. Indeed, the same person often changes his mind; for when he has fallen ill, he thinks happiness is health, and when he has fallen into poverty, he thinks it is wealth. And when they are conscious of their own ignorance, they admire anyone who speaks of something grand and 25 above their heads. [Among the wise,] however, some used to think that besides these many goods there is some other good that exists in its own right and that causes all these goods to be goods.

Presumably, then, it is rather futile to examine all these beliefs, and it is enough to examine those that 30 are most current or seem to have some argument for them.

We must notice, however, the difference between arguments from principles and arguments toward principles. For indeed Plato was right to be puzzled about this, when he used to ask if [the argument] set out from the principles or led toward them—just 1095b as on a race course the path may go from the starting line to the far end, or back again. For we should certainly begin from things known, but things are known in two ways; for some are known to us, some known without qualification. Presumably, then, *we* ought to begin from things known to *us*.

That is why we need to have been brought up in 5 fine habits if we are to be adequate students of fine and just things, and of political questions generally. For we begin from the [belief] that [something is true]; if this is apparent enough to us, we can begin without also [knowing] why [it is true]. Someone who is well brought up has the beginnings, or can easily acquire them. Someone who neither has them nor can acquire them should listen to Hesiod:[1] 'He who 10 grasps everything himself is best of all; he is noble also who listens to one who has spoken well; but he who neither grasps it himself nor takes to heart what he hears from another is a useless man.'

1. [Regarding Hesiod, see Aristotle's *Metaphysics*, n.13. —S.M.C.]

5

But let us begin again from the point from which we digressed. For, it would seem, people quite reasonably reach their conception of the good, i.e., of happiness, 15 from the lives [they lead]; for there are roughly three most favored lives: the lives of gratification, of political activity, and third, of study.

The many, the most vulgar, would seem to conceive the good and happiness as pleasure, and hence they also like the life of gratification. In this 20 they appear completely slavish, since the life they decide on is a life for grazing animals. Still, they have some argument in their defense, since many in positions of power feel as Sardanapallus[2] felt, [and also choose this life].

The cultivated people, those active [in politics], conceive the good as honor, since this is more or less the end [normally pursued] in the political life. This, however, appears to be too superficial to be 25 what we are seeking; for it seems to depend more on those who honor than on the one honored, whereas we intuitively believe that the good is something of our own and hard to take from us. Further, it would seem, they pursue honor to convince themselves that they are good; at any rate, they seek to be honored by prudent people, among people who know them, and 30 for virtue. It is clear, then, that—in their view at any rate—virtue is superior [to honor].

Perhaps, indeed, one might conceive virtue more than honor to be the end of the political life. However, this also is apparently too incomplete [to be the good]. For it seems possible for someone to *1096a* possess virtue but be asleep or inactive throughout his life, and, moreover, to suffer the worst evils and misfortunes. If this is the sort of life he leads, no one would count him happy, except to defend a philosopher's paradox. Enough about this, since it has been adequately discussed in the popular works as well.

5 The third life is the life of study, which we shall examine in what follows.

The moneymaker's life is in a way forced on him [not chosen for itself]; and clearly wealth is not the good we are seeking, since it is [merely] useful, [choiceworthy only] for some other end. Hence one would be more inclined to suppose that [any of] the goods mentioned earlier is the end, since they are liked for themselves. But apparently they are not [the end] either; and many arguments have been 10 presented against them. Let us, then, dismiss them.

6

Presumably, though, we had better examine the universal good, and puzzle out what is meant in speaking of it. This sort of inquiry is, to be sure, unwelcome to us, because those who introduced the Forms were friends of ours; still, it presumably seems 15 better, indeed only right, to destroy even what is close to us if that is the way to preserve truth. We must especially do this as philosophers, [lovers of wisdom]; for though we love both the truth and our friends, reverence is due to the truth first.

Those who introduced this view did not mean to produce an Idea for any [series] in which they spoke of prior and posterior [members]; that was why they did not mean to establish an Idea [of number] for [the series of] numbers. But the good is spoken of both in 20 what-it-is [that is, substance], and in quality and relative; and what exists in its own right, that is, substance, is by nature prior to the relative, since a relative would seem to be an appendage and coincident of being. And so there is no common Idea over these.

Further, good is spoken of in as many ways as being [is spoken of]: in what-it-is, as god and mind; in quality, as the virtues; in quantity, as the measured 25 amount; in relative, as the useful; in time, as the opportune moment; in place, as the [right] situation; and so on. Hence it is clear that the good cannot be some common and single universal; for if it were, it would be spoken of in only one [of the types of] predication, not in them all.

Further, if a number of things have a single Idea, 30 there is also a single science of them; hence [if there were an Idea of good] there would also be some single science of all goods. but, in fact, there are many sciences even of the goods under one [type of] predication; for the science of the opportune moment, for instance, in war is generalship, in disease medicine. And similarly the science of the measured amount in food is medicine, in exertion gymnastics. [Hence there is no singles science of the good, and so no Idea.]

One might be puzzled about what [the believers

2. [According to legend, Sardanapallus was an Assyrian ruler who lived in great luxury.]

1096b in Ideas] really mean in speaking of the So-and-So Itself, since Man Itself and man have one and the same account of man; for insofar as each is man, they will not differ at all. If that is so, then [Good Itself and good have the same account of good]; hence they also will not differ at all insofar as each is good, [hence there is no point in appealing to Good Itself].

Moreover, Good Itself will be no more of a good 5 by being eternal; for a white thing is no whiter if it lasts a long time than if it lasts a day.

The Pythagoreans[3] would seem to have a more plausible view about the good, since they place the One in the column of goods. Indeed, Speusippus[4] seems to have followed them. But let us leave this for another discussion.

A dispute emerges, however, about what we have 10 said, because the arguments [in favor of the Idea] are not concerned with every sort of good. Good pursued and liked in their own right are spoken of as one species of goods, whereas those that in some way tend to produce or preserve these goods, or to prevent their contraries, are spoken of as goods because of these and in a different way. Clearly, then, goods are spoken of in two ways, and some are goods in their own right, 15 and others goods because of these. Let us, then, separate the goods in their own right from the [merely] useful goods, and consider whether goods in their own right correspond to a single Idea.

But what sorts of goods may we take to be goods in their own right? Are they the goods that are pursued even on their own—for instance, prudence, seeing, some types of pleasures, and honors? For even if we also pursue these because of something else, we may 20 nonetheless take them to be goods in their own right. Alternatively, is nothing except the Idea good in its own right, so that the Form will be futile? But if these other things are also goods in their own right, then, [if there is an Idea of good,] the same account of good will have to turn up in all of them, just as the same account of whiteness turns up in snow and in chalk. In fact, however, honor, prudence, and pleasure have 25 different and dissimilar accounts, precisely insofar as they are goods. Hence the good is not something common corresponding to a single Idea.

But how, then, is good spoken of? For it is not like homonyms resulting from chance. Is it spoken of from the fact that goods derive from one thing or all contribute to one thing? Or is it spoken of more by analogy? For as sight is to body, so understanding is to soul, and so on for other cases.

Presumably, though, we should leave these ques- 30 tions for now, since their exact treatment is more appropriate for another [branch of] of philosophy. And the same is true about the Idea. For even if there is some one good predicated in common, or some separable good, itself in its own right, clearly that is not the sort of good a human being can achieve in action or possess; but that is the sort we are looking 35 for now.

Perhaps, however, someone might think it is better to get to know the Idea with a view to the goods that 1097a we can possess and achieve in action; for [one might suppose that] if we have this as a sort of pattern, we shall also know better about the goods that are goods for us, and if we know about them, we shall hit on them. This argument certainly has some plausibility, 5 but it would seem to clash with the sciences. For each of these, though it aims at some good and seeks to supply what is lacking, leaves out knowledge of the Idea; but if the Idea were such an important aid, surely it would not be reasonable for all craftsmen to know nothing about it and not even to look for it.

Moreover, it is a puzzle to know what the weaver or carpenter will gain for his own craft from knowing 10 this Good Itself, or how anyone will be better at medicine or generalship from having gazed on the Idea Itself. For what the doctor appears to consider is not even health [universally, let alone good universally], but human health, and presumably the health of this human being even more, since he treats one particular patient at a time.

So much, then, for these questions.

7

But let us return once again to the good we are 15 looking for, and consider just what it could be. For it is apparently one thing in one action or craft, and another thing in another; for it is one thing in medicine, another in generalship, and so on for the rest. What, then, is the good of each action or craft? Surely it is that for the sake of which the other things are done; in medicine this is health, in generalship

3. [Regarding the Pythagoreans, see Aristotle's *Metaphysics*, n.7.]

4. [Regarding Speusippus, see Aristotle's *Metaphysics*, n.20.]

20 victory, in house-building a house, in another case something else, but in every action and decision it is the end, since it is for the sake of the end that everyone does the other actions. And so, if there is some end of everything achievable in action, the good achievable in action will be this end; if there are more ends than one, [the good achievable in action] will be these ends.

Our argument, then, has followed a different route to reach the same conclusion. But we must try 25 to make this still more perspicuous. Since there are apparently many ends, and we choose some of them (for instance, wealth, flutes, and, in general, instruments) because of something else, it is clear that not all ends are complete. But the best good is apparently something complete. And so, if only one end is complete, the good we are looking for will be this 30 end; if more ends than one are complete, it will be the most complete end of these.

We say that an end pursued in its own right is more complete than an end pursued because of something else, and that an end that is never choiceworthy because of something else is more complete than ends that are choiceworthy both in their own right and because of this end. Hence an end that is always choiceworthy in its own right, never because of something else, is complete without qualification.

Now happiness, more than anything else, seems *1097b* complete without qualification. For we always choose it because of itself, never because of something else. Honor, pleasure, understanding, and every virtue we certainly choose because of themselves, since we would choose each of them even if it had no further result; but we also choose them for the sake of happi- 5 ness, supposing that through them we shall be happy. Happiness, by contrast, no one ever chooses for their sake, or for the sake of anything else at all.

The same conclusion [that happiness is complete] also appears to follow from self-sufficiency. For the complete good seems to be self-sufficient. What we count as self-sufficient is not what suffices for a soli- 10 tary person by himself, living an isolated life, but what suffices also for parents, children, wife, and, in general, for friends and fellow citizens, since a human being is a naturally political [animal]. Here, however, we must impost some limit; for if we extend the good to parents' parents and children's children and to friends of friends, we shall go on without limit; but we must examine this another time.

Anyhow, we regard something as self-sufficient when all by itself it makes a life choiceworthy and 15 lacking nothing; and that is what we think happiness does.

Moreover, we think happiness is most choiceworthy of all goods, [since] it is not counted as one good among many. [If it were] counted as one among many, then, clearly, we think it would be more choiceworthy if the smallest of goods were added; for the good that is added becomes an extra quantity of goods, and the larger of two goods is always more choiceworthy.

Happiness, then, is apparently something 20 complete and self-sufficient, since it is the end of the things achievable in action.

But presumably the remark that the best good is happiness is apparently something [generally] agreed, and we still need a clearer statement of what the best good is. Perhaps, then, we shall find this if we first grasp the function of a human being. For just as the good, i.e., [doing] well, for a flautists, a sculptor, and 25 every craftsman, and, in general, for whatever has a function and [characteristic] action, seems to depend on its function, the same seems to be true for a human being, if a human being has some function.

Then do the carpenter and the leather worker 30 have their functions and actions, but has a human being no function? Is he by nature idle, without any function? Or, just as eye, hand, foot, and in general every [bodily] part apparently has its function, may we likewise ascribe to a human being some function apart from all of these?

What, then, could this be? For living is apparently shared with plants, but what we are looking for is the *1098a* special function of a human being; hence we should set aside the life of nutrition and growth. The life next in order is some sort of life of sense perception; but this too is apparently shared with horse, ox, and every animal.

The remaining possibility, then, is some sort of life of action of the [part of the soul] that has reason. One [part] of it has reason as obeying reason; the other has it as itself having reason and thinking. Moreover, 5 life is also spoken of in two ways [as capacity and as activity], and we must take [a human being's special function to be] life as activity, since this seems to be called life more fully. We have found, then, that the human function is activity of the soul in accord with reason or requiring reason.

Now we say that the function of a [kind of thing]—of a harpist, for instance—is the same in kind as the function of an excellent individual of the kind—of an excellent harpist, for instance. And the same is true without qualification in every case, if we add to the function the superior achievement in accord with the virtue; for the function of a harpist is to play the harp, and the function of a good harpist is to play it well. Moreover, we take the human function to be a certain kind of life, and take this life to be activity and actions of the soul that involve reason; hence the function of the excellent man is to do this well and finely.

Now each function is completed well by being completed in accord with the virtue proper [to that kind of thing]. And so the human good proves to be activity of the soul in accord with virtue, and indeed with the best and most complete virtue, if there are more virtues than one. Moreover, in a complete life. For one swallow does not make a spring, nor does one day; nor, similarly, does one day or a short time make us blessed and happy.

This, then, is a sketch of the good; for, presumably, we must draw the outline first, and fill it in later. If the sketch is good, anyone, it seems, can advance and articulate it, and in such cases time discovers more, or is a good partner in discovery. That is also how the crafts have improved, since anyone can add what is lacking [in the outline].

We must also remember our previous remarks, so that we do not look for the same degree of exactness in all areas, but the degree that accords with a given subject matter and is proper to a given line of inquiry. For the carpenter's and the geometer's inquiries about the right angle are different also; the carpenter restricts himself to what helps his work, but the geometer inquires into what, or what sort of thing, the right angle is, since he studies the truth. We must do the same, then, in other areas too, [seeking the proper degree of exactness], so that digressions do not overwhelm our main task.

Nor should we make the same demand for an explanation in all cases. On the contrary, in some cases it is enough to prove rightly that [something is true, without also explaining why it is true]. This is so, for instance, with principles, where the fact that [something is true] is the first thing, that is to say, the principle.

Some principles are studied by means of induction, some by means of perception, some by means of some sort of habituation, and others by other means. In each case we should try to find them out by means suited to their nature, and work hard to define them rightly. For they carry great weight for what follows; for the principle seems to be more than half the whole, and makes evident the answer to many of our questions.

8

We should examine the principle, however, not only from the conclusion and premises [of a deduction], but also from what is said about it; for all the facts harmonize with a true account, whereas the truth soon clashes with a false one.

Goods are divided, then, into three types, some called external, some goods of the soul, others goods of the body. We say that the goods of the soul are goods most fully, and more than the others, and we take actions and activities of the soul to be [goods] of the soul. And so our account [of the good] is right, to judge by this belief anyhow—and it is an ancient belief, and accepted by philosophers.

Our account is also correct in saying that some sort of actions and activities are the end; for in that way the end turns out to be a good of the soul, not an external good.

The belief that the happy person lives well and does well also agrees with our account, since we have virtually said that the end is a sort of living well and doing well.

Further, all the features that people look for in happiness appear to be true of the end described in our account. For to some people happiness seems to be virtue; to others prudence; to others some sort of wisdom; to others again it seems to be these, or one of these, involving pleasure or requiring it to be added; others add in external prosperity as well. Some of these views are traditional, held by many, while others are held by a few men who are widely esteemed. It is reasonable for each group not to be completely wrong, but to be correct on one point at least, or even on most points.

30 First, our account agrees with those who say happiness is virtue [in general] or some [particular] virtue; for activity in accord with virtue is proper to virtue. Presumably, though, it matters quite a bit whether we suppose that the best good consists in possessing or in using—that is to say, in a state or in an activity [that actualizes the state]. For someone may be in a state 1099a that achieves no good—if, for instance, he is asleep or inactive in some other way—but this cannot be true of the activity; for it will necessarily act and act well. And just as Olympic prizes are not for the finest 5 and strongest, but for the contestants—since it is only these who win—the same is true in life; among the fine and good people, only those who act correctly win the prize.

Moreover, the life of these active people is also pleasant in itself. For being pleased is a condition of the soul, [and hence is included in the activity of the soul]. Further, each type of person finds pleasure in whatever he is called a lover of; a horse, for instance, 10 pleases the horse-lover, a spectacle the lover of spectacles. Similarly, what is just pleases the lover of justice, and in general what accords with virtue pleases the lover of virtue.

Now the things that please most people conflict, because they are not pleasant by nature, whereas the things that please lovers of the fine are things pleasant by nature. Actions in accord with virtue are pleasant 15 by nature, so that they both please lovers of the fine and are pleasant in their own right.

Hence these people's life does not need pleasure to be added [to virtuous activity] as some sort of extra decoration; rather it has its pleasure within itself. For besides the reasons already given, someone who does not enjoy fine actions is not good; for no one would call a person just, for instance, if he did not enjoy doing just actions, or generous if he did not enjoy 20 generous actions, and similarly for the other virtues.

If this is so, actions in accord with the virtues are pleasant in their own right. Moreover, these actions are good and fine as well as pleasant; indeed, they are good, fine, and pleasant more than anything else is, since on this question the excellent person judges rightly, and his judgment agrees with what we have said.

Happiness, then, is best, finest, and most pleasant, 25 and the Delian inscription is wrong to distinguish these things: 'What is most just is finest; being healthy is most beneficial; but it is most pleasant to win our heart's desire.' For all three features are found in the best activities, and we say happiness is these activities, or [rather] one of them, the best one.

Nonetheless, happiness evidently also needs external goods to be added, as we said, since we cannot, or cannot easily, do fine actions if we lack the resources. For, first of all, in many actions we use friends, 1099b wealth, and political power just as we use instruments. Further, deprivation of certain [externals]—for instance, good birth, good children, beauty—mars our blessedness. For we do not altogether have the character of happiness if we look utterly repulsive or are ill-born, solitary, or childless; and we have it even less, presumably, if our children or friends are totally 5 bad, or were good but have died.

And so, as we have said, happiness would seem to need this sort of prosperity added also. That is why some people identify happiness with good fortune, and others identify it with virtue.

9

This also leads to a puzzle: Is happiness acquired by learning, or habituation, or by some other form of 10 cultivation? Or is it the result of some divine fate, or even of fortune?

First, then, if the gods give any gift at all to human beings, it is reasonable for them to give us happiness more than any other human good, insofar as it is the best of human goods. Presumably, however, this question is more suitable for a different inquiry.

But even if it is not sent by the gods, but instead 15 results from virtue and some sort of learning or cultivation, happiness appears to be one of the most divine things, since the prize and goal of virtue appears to be the best good, something divine and blessed. Moreover [if happiness comes in this way] it will be widely shared; for anyone who is not deformed [in his capacity] for virtue will be able to achieve happiness through some sort of learning and attention. 20

And since it is better to be happy in this way than because of fortune, it is reasonable for this to be the way [we become] happy. For whatever is natural is naturally in the finest state possible. The same is true of the products of crafts and of every other cause, especially the best cause; and it would be seriously inappropriate to entrust what is greatest and finest to fortune.

The answer to our question is also evident from our account. For we have said that happiness is a certain sort of activity of the soul in accord with virtue, [and hence not a result of fortune]. Of the other goods, some are necessary conditions of happiness, while others are naturally useful and cooperative as instruments [but are not parts of it].

Further, this conclusion agrees with our opening remarks. For we took the goal of political science to be the best good; and most of its attention is devoted to the character of the citizens, to make them good people who do fine actions.

It is not surprising, then, that we regard neither ox, nor horse, nor any other kind of animal as happy; for none of them can share in this sort of activity. For the same reason a child is not happy either, since his age prevents him from doing these sorts of actions. If he is called happy, he is being congratulated [simply] because of anticipated blessedness; for, as we have said, happiness requires both complete virtue and a complete life.

It needs a complete life because life includes many reversals of fortune, good and bad, and the most prosperous person may fall into a terrible disaster in old age, as the Trojan stories tell us about Priam.[5] If someone has suffered those sorts of misfortunes and comes to a miserable end, no one counts him happy.

10

Then should we count no human being happy during his lifetime, but follow Solon's[6] advice to wait to see the end? But if we agree with Solon, can someone really be happy during the time after he has died? Surely that is completely absurd, especially when we say happiness is an activity.

We do not say, then, that someone is happy during the time he is dead, and Solon's point is not this [absurd one], but rather that when a human being has died, we can safely pronounce [that he was] blessed [before he died], on the assumption that he is now finally beyond evils and misfortunes. But this claim is also disputable. For if a living person has good or evil of which he is not aware, a dead person also, it seems, has good or evil, if, for instance, he receives honors or dishonors, and his children, and descendants in general, do well or suffer misfortune.

However, this conclusion also raises a puzzle. For even if someone has lived in blessedness until old age, and has died appropriately, many fluctuations of his descendants' fortunes may still happen to him; for some may be good people and get the life they deserve, while the contrary may be true of others, and clearly they may be as distantly related to their ancestor as you please. Surely, then, it would be an absurd result if the dead person's condition changed along with the fortunes of his descendants, so that at one time he would turn out to have been happy [in his lifetime] and at another time he would turn out to have been miserable. But it would also be absurd if the condition of descendants did not affect their ancestors at all or for any length of time.

But we must return to the previous puzzle, since that will perhaps also show us the answer to our present question. Let us grant that we must wait to see the end, and must then count someone blessed, not as now being blessed [during the time he is dead] but because he previously was blessed. Would it not be absurd, then, if, at the very time when he is happy, we refused to ascribe truly to him the happiness he has? Such refusal results from reluctance to call him happy during his lifetime, because of its ups and downs; for we suppose happiness is enduring and definitely not prone to fluctuate, but the same person's fortunes often turn to and fro. For clearly, if we take our cue from his fortunes, we shall often call him happy and then miserable again, thereby representing the happy person as a kind of chameleon, insecurely based.

But surely it is quite wrong to take our cue from someone's fortunes. For his doing well or badly does not rest on them. A human life, as we said, needs these added, but activities in accord with virtue control happiness, and the contrary activities control its contrary. Indeed, the present puzzle is further evidence for our account [of happiness]. For no human achievement has the stability of activities in accord with virtue, since these seem to be more enduring even than our knowledge of the sciences.

5. [Priam was the legendary king of Troy at the time of its destruction by the Greeks, as related in Homer's *Iliad*.]

6. [Solon (c. 639–c. 559 B.C.) was an Athenian statesman and a wise lawgiver.]

Indeed, the most honorable among the virtues themselves are more enduring than the other virtues, because blessed people devote their lives to them more fully and more continually than to anything else—for this continual activity would seem to be the reason we do not forget them.

It follows, then, that the happy person has the [stability] we are looking for and keeps the character he has throughout his life. For always, or more than anything else, he will do and study the actions in accord with virtue, and will bear fortunes most finely, in every way and in all conditions appropriately, since he is truly 'good, foursquare, and blameless.'

Many events, however, are subject to fortune; some are minor, some major. Hence, minor strokes of good or ill fortune clearly will not carry any weight for his life. But many major strokes of good fortune will make it more blessed; for in themselves they naturally add adornment to it, and his use of them proves to be fine and excellent. Conversely, if he suffers many major misfortunes, they oppress and spoil his blessedness, since they involve pain and impede many activities. And yet, even here what is fine shines through, whenever someone bears many severe misfortunes with good temper, not because he feels no distress, but because he is noble and magnanimous.

And since it is activities that control life, as we said, no blessed person could ever become miserable, since he will never do hateful and base actions. For a truly good and prudent person, we suppose, will bear strokes of fortune suitably, and from his resources at any time will do the finest actions, just as a good general will make the best use of his forces in war, and a good shoemaker will make the finest shoe from the hides given to him, and similarly for all other craftsmen.

If this is so, the happy person could never become miserable, but neither will he be blessed if he falls into misfortunes as bad as Priam's. Nor, however, will he be inconstant and prone to fluctuate, since he will neither be easily shaken from his happiness nor shaken by just any misfortunes. He will be shaken from it, though, by many serious misfortunes, and from these a return to happiness will take no short time. At best, it will take a long and complete length of time that includes great and fine successes.

Then why not say that the happy person is the one whose activities accord with complete virtue, with an adequate supply of external goods, not for just any time but for a complete life? Or should we add that he will also go on living this way and will come to an appropriate end, since the future is not apparent to us, and we take happiness to be the end, and altogether complete in every way? Given these facts [about the future and about happiness], we shall say that a living person who has, and will keep, the goods we mentioned is blessed, but blessed as a human being is. So much for a determination of this question.

13

Since happiness is a certain sort of activity of the soul in accord with complete virtue, we must examine virtue; for that will perhaps also be a way to study happiness better. Moreover, the true politician seems to have put more effort into virtue than into anything else, since he wants to make the citizens good and law-abiding. We find an example of this in the Spartan and Cretan legislators and in any others who share their concerns. Since, then, the examination of virtue is proper for political science, the inquiry clearly suits our decision at the beginning.

It is clear that the virtue we must examine is human virtue, since we are also seeking the human good and human happiness. By human virtue we mean virtue of the soul, not of the body, since we also say that happiness is an activity of the soul. If this is so, it is clear that the politician must in some way know about the soul, just as someone setting out to heal the eyes must know about the whole body as well. This is all the more true to the extent that political science is better and more honorable than medicine; even among doctors, the cultivated ones devote a lot of effort to finding out about the body. Hence the politician as well [as the student of nature] must study the soul. But he must study it for his specific purpose, far enough for his inquiry [into virtue]; for a more exact treatment would presumably take more effort than his purpose requires.

[We] have discussed the soul sufficiently [for our purposes] in [our] popular works as well [as our less popular], and we should use this discussion. We have said, for instance, that on [part] of the soul is nonrational, while one has reason. Are these distinguished as parts of a body and everything divisible into parts are? Or are they two [only] in definition, and inseparable by nature, as the convex and the concave are in a surface? It does not matter for present purposes.

Consider the nonrational [part]. One [part] of it, 1102b i.e., the cause of nutrition and growth, would seem to be plantlike and shared [with all living things]; for we can ascribe this capacity of the soul to everything that is nourished, including embryos, and the same capacity to full-grown living things, since this is more reasonable that to ascribe another capacity to them.

Hence the virtue of this capacity is apparently 5 shared, not [specifically] human. For this part and this capacity more than others seem to be active in sleep, and here the good and the bad person are least distinct; hence happy people are said to be no better off than miserable people for half their lives. This lack of distinction is not surprising, since sleep is inactivity of the soul insofar as it is called excel- 10 lent or base, unless to some small extent some movements penetrate [to our awareness], and in this way the decent person comes to have better images [in dreams] than just any random person has. Enough about this, however, and let us leave aside the nutritive part, since by nature it has no share in human virtue.

Another nature in the soul would also seem to be 15 nonrational, though in a way it shares in reason. For in the continent and the incontinent person we praise their reason, that is to say, the [part] of the soul that has reason, because it exhorts them correctly and toward what is best; but they evidently also have in them some other [part] that is by nature something apart from reason, clashing and struggling with reason. For 20 just as paralyzed parts of a body, when we decide to move them to the right, do the contrary and move off to the left, the same is true of the soul; for incontinent people have impulses in contrary directions. In bodies, admittedly, we see the part go astray, whereas we do not see it in the soul; nonetheless, presumably, we should suppose that the soul also has something 25 apart from reason, countering and opposing reason. The [precise] way it is different does not matter.

However, this [part] as well [as the rational part] appears, as we said, to share in reason. At any rate, in the continent person it obeys reason; and in the temperate and the brave person it presumably listens still better to reason, since there it agrees with reason in everything.

The nonrational [part], then, as well [as the whole soul] apparently has two parts. For while the plantlike 30 [part] shares in reason not at all, the [part] with appetites and in general desires shares in reason in a way, insofar as it both listens to reason and obeys it. This is the way in which we are said to 'listen to reason' from father or friends, as opposed to the way in which [we 'give the reason'] in mathematics. The nonrational part also [obeys and] is persuaded in some way by reason, as is shown by correction, and by every sort of 1103a reproof and exhortation.

If, then, we ought to say that this [part] also has reason, then the [part] that has reason, as well [as the nonrational part], will have two parts. One will have reason fully, by having it within itself; the other will have reason by listening to reason as to a father.

The division between virtues accords with this 5 difference. For some virtues are called virtues of thought, others virtues of character; wisdom, comphrehension, and prudence are called virtues of thought, generosity and temperance virtues of character. For when we speak of someone's character we do not say that he is wise or has good comprehension, but that he is gentle or temperate. And yet, we also praise the wise person for his state, and the states that 10 are praiseworthy are the ones we call virtues.

BOOK II

1

Virtue, then, is of two sorts, virtue of thought and 15 virtue of character. Virtue of thought arises and grows mostly from teaching; that is why it needs experience and time. Virtue of character [i.e., of *ēthos*] results from habit [*ethos*]; hence its name 'ethical,' slightly varied from 'ethos.'

Hence it is also clear that none of the virtues of character arises in us naturally. For if something is 20 by nature in one condition, habituation cannot bring it into another condition. A stone, for instance, by nature moves downwards, and habituation could not make it move upwards, not even if you threw it up ten thousand times to habituate it; nor could habituation make fire move downwards, or bring anything that is by nature in one condition into another condition. And so the virtues arise in us neither by nature 25 nor against nature. Rather, we are by nature able to acquire them, and we are completed through habit.

Further, if something arises in us by nature, we first have the capacity for it, and later perform the activity. This is clear in the case of the senses; for we did not acquire them by frequent seeing or hearing, but we already had them when we exercised them, and did not get them by exercising them. Virtues, by contrast, we acquire, just as we acquire crafts, by having first activated them. For we learn a craft by producing the same product that we must produce when we have learned it; we become builders, for instance, by building, and we become harpists by playing the harp. Similarly, then, we become just by doing just actions, temperate by doing temperate actions, brave by doing brave actions.

What goes on in cities is also evidence for this. For the legislator makes the citizens good by habituating them, and this is the wish of every legislator; if he fails to do it well he misses his goal. Correct habituation distinguishes a good political system from a bad one.

Further, the sources and means that develop each virtue also ruin it, just as they do in a craft. For playing the harp makes both good and bad harpists, and it is analogous in the case of builders and all the rest; for building well makes good builders, and building badly makes bad ones. Otherwise no teacher would be needed, but everyone would be born a good or a bad craftsman.

It is the same, then, with the virtues. For what we do in our dealings with other people makes some of us just, some unjust; what we do in terrifying situations, and the habits of fear or confidence that we acquire, make some of us brave and others cowardly. The same is true of situations involving appetites and anger; for one or another sort of conduct in these situations makes some temperate and mild, others intemperate and irascible. To sum it up in a single account: a state [of character] results from [the repetition of] similar activities.

That is why we must perform the right activities, since differences in these imply corresponding differences in the states. It is not unimportant, then, to acquire one sort of habit or another, right from our youth. On the contrary, it is very important, indeed all-important.

2

Our present discussion does not aim, as our others do, at study; for the purpose of our examination is not to know what virtue is, but to become good, since otherwise the inquiry would be of no benefit to us. And so we must examine the right ways of acting; for, as we have said, the actions also control the sorts of states we acquire.

First, then, actions should accord with the correct reason. That is a common [belief], and let us assume it. We shall discuss it later, and say what the correct reason is and how it is related to the other virtues.

But let us take it as agreed in advance that every account of the actions we must do has to be stated in outline, not exactly. As we also said at the beginning, the type of accounts we demand should accord with the subject matter; and questions about actions and expediency, like questions about health, have no fixed answers.

While this is the character of our general account, the account of particular cases is still more inexact. For these fall under no craft or profession; the agents themselves must consider in each case what the opportune action is, as doctors and navigators do. The account we offer, then, in our present inquiry is of this inexact sort; still, we must try to offer help.

First, then, we should observe that these sorts of states naturally tend to be ruined by excess and deficiency. We see this happen with strength and health—for we must use evident cases [such as these] as witnesses to things that are not evident. For both excessive and deficient exercise ruin bodily strength, and, similarly, too much or too little eating or drinking ruins health, whereas the proportionate amount produces, increases, and preserves it.

The same is true, then, of temperance, bravery, and the other virtues. For if, for instance, someone avoids and is afraid of everything, standing firm against nothing, he becomes cowardly; if he is afraid of nothing at all and goes to face everything, he becomes rash. Similarly, if he gratifies himself with every pleasure and abstains from none, he becomes intemperate; if he avoids them all, as boors do, he becomes some sort of insensible person. Temperance and bravery, then, are ruined by excess and deficiency, but preserved by the mean.

30 But these actions are not only the sources and causes both of the emergence and growth of virtues and of their ruin; the activities of the virtues [once we have acquired them] also consist in these same actions. For this is also true of more evident cases; strength, for instance, arises from eating a lot and from withstanding much hard labor, and it is the strong person who is most capable of these very actions. It is the same with the virtues. For abstaining from plea- 35 sures makes us become temperate, and once we have 1104b become temperate we are most capable of abstaining from pleasures. It is similar with bravery; habituation in disdain for frightening situations and in standing firm against them makes us become brave, and once we have become brave we shall be most capable of standing firm.

3

5 But we must take someone's pleasure or pain following on his actions to be a sign of his state. For if someone who abstains from bodily pleasures enjoys the abstinence itself, he is temperate; if he is grieved by it, he is intemperate. Again, if he stands firm against terrifying situations and enjoys it, or at least does not find it painful, he is brave; if he finds it painful, he is cowardly. For virtue of character is about pleasures and pains.

10 For pleasure causes us to do base actions, and pain causes us to abstain from fine ones. That is why we need to have had the appropriate upbringing—right from early youth, as Plato says—to make us find enjoyment or pain in the right things; for this is the correct education.

Further, virtues are concerned with actions and 15 feelings; but every feeling and every action implies pleasure or pain; hence, for this reason too, virtue is about pleasures and pains. Corrective treatments also indicate this, since they use pleasures and pains; for correction is a form of medical treatment, and medical treatment naturally operates through contraries.

Further, as we said earlier, every state of soul is 20 naturally related to and about whatever naturally makes it better or worse; and pleasures and pains make people base, from pursuing and avoiding the wrong ones, at the wrong time, in the wrong ways, or whatever other distinctions of that sort are needed in an account. These [bad effects of pleasure and pain] are the reason why people actually define the virtues as ways of being unaffected and undisturbed [by pleasures and pains]. They are wrong, however, because 25 they speak of being unaffected without qualification, not of being unaffected in the right or wrong way, at the right or wrong time, and the added qualifications.

We assume, then, that virtue is the sort of state that does the best actions concerning pleasures and pains, and that vice is the contrary state.

The following will also make it evident that virtue 30 and vice are about the same things. For there are three objects of choice—fine, expedient, and pleasant—and three objects of avoidance—their contraries, shameful, harmful, and painful. About all these, then, the good person is correct and the bad person is in error, and especially about pleasure. For pleasure 35 is shared with animals, and implied by every object 1105a of choice, since what is fine and what is expedient appear pleasant as well.

Further, pleasure grows up with all of us from infancy on. That is why it is hard to rub out this feeling that is dyed into our lives. We also estimate actions [as well as feelings]—some of us more, some less—by 5 pleasure and pain. For this reason, our whole discussion must be about these; for good or bad enjoyment or pain is very important for our actions.

Further, it is more difficult to fight pleasure than to fight spirit—and Heraclitus[7] tells us [how difficult it is to fight spirit]. Now both craft and virtue are in 10 every case about what is more difficult, since a good result is even better when it is more difficult. Hence, for this reason also, the whole discussion, for virtue and political science alike, must consider pleasures and pains; for if we use these well, we shall be good, and if badly, bad.

To sum up: Virtue is about pleasures and pains; 15 the actions that are its sources also increase it or, if they are done badly, ruin it; and its activity is about the same actions as those that are its sources.

4

Someone might be puzzled, however, about what we mean by saying that we become just by doing just actions and become temperate by doing temperate actions. For [one might suppose that] if we do grammatical or musical actions, we are grammarians or 20

7. [Regarding Heraclitus, see Aristotle's *Metaphysics*, n.8.]

musicians, and, similarly, if we do just or temperate actions, we are thereby just or temperate.

But surely actions are not enough, even in the case of crafts; for it is possible to produce a grammatical result by chance, or by following someone else's instructions. To be grammarians, then, we must both produce a grammatical result and produce it grammatically—that is to say, produce it in accord with the grammatical knowledge in us.

Moreover, in any case, what is true of crafts is not true of virtues. For the products of a craft determine by their own qualities whether they have been produced well; and so it suffices that they have the right qualities when they have been produced. But for actions in accord with the virtues to be done temperately or justly it does not suffice that they themselves have the right qualities. Rather, the agent must also be in the right state when he does them. First, he must know [that he is doing virtuous actions]; second, he must decide on them, and decide on them for themselves; and, third, he must also do them from a firm and unchanging state.

As conditions for having a craft, these three do not count, except for the bare knowing. As a condition for having a virtue, however, the knowing counts for nothing, or [rather] for only a little, whereas the other two conditions are very important, indeed all-important. And we achieve these other two conditions by the frequent doing of just and temperate actions.

Hence actions are called just or temperate when they are the sort that a just or temperate person would do. But the just and temperate person is not the one who [merely] does these actions, but the one who also does them in the way in which just or temperate people do them.

It is right, then, to say that a person comes to be just from doing just actions and temperate from doing temperate actions; for no one has the least prospect of becoming good from failing to do them.

The many, however, do not do these actions. They take refuge in arguments, thinking that they are doing philosophy, and that this is the way to become excellent people. They are like a sick person who listens attentively to the doctor, but acts on none of his instructions. Such a course of treatment will not improve the state of the sick person's body; nor will the many improve the state of their souls by this attitude to philosophy.

5

Next we must examine what virtue is. Since there are three conditions arising in the soul—feelings, capacities, and states—virtue must be one of these.

By feelings I mean appetite, anger, fear, confidence, envy, joy, love, hate, longing, jealousy, pity, and in general whatever implies pleasure or pain. By capacities I mean what we have when we are said to be capable of these feelings—capable of being angry, for instance, or of being afraid or of feeling pity. By states I mean what we have when we are well or badly off in relation to feelings. If, for instance, our feeling is too intense or slack, we are badly off in relation to anger, but if it is intermediate, we are well off; the same is true in the other cases.

First, then, neither virtues nor vices are feelings. For we are called excellent or base insofar as we have virtues or vices, not insofar as we have feelings. Further, we are neither praised nor blamed insofar as we have feelings; for we do not praise the angry or the frightened person, and do not blame the person who is simply angry, but only the person who is angry in a particular way. We are praised or blamed, however, insofar as we have virtues or vices. Further, we are angry and afraid without decision; but the virtues are decisions of some kind, or [rather] require decision. Besides, insofar as we have feelings, we are said to be moved; but insofar as we have virtues or vices, we are said to be in some condition rather than moved.

For these reasons the virtues are not capacities either; for we are neither called good nor called bad, nor are we praised or blamed, insofar as we are simply capable of feelings. Further, while we have capacities by nature, we do not become good or bad by nature; we have discussed this before.

If, then, the virtues are neither feelings nor capacities, the remaining possibility is that they are states. And so we have said what the genus of virtue is.

6

But we must say not only, as we already have, that it is a state, but also what sort of state it is.

It should be said, then, that every virtue causes its possessors to be in a good state and to perform their functions well. The virtue of eyes, for instance, makes the eyes and their functioning excellent, because it makes us see well; and similarly, the virtue of a horse makes the horse excellent, and thereby good at galloping, at carrying its rider, and at standing steady in the face of the enemy. If this is true in every case, the virtue of a human being will likewise be the state that makes a human being good and makes him perform his function well.

We have already said how this will be true, and it will also be evident from our next remarks, if we consider the sort of nature that virtue has.

In everything continuous and divisible we can take more, less, and equal, and each of them either in the object itself or relative to us; and the equal is some intermediate between excess and deficiency. By the intermediate in the object I mean what is equidistant from each extremity; this is one and the same for all. But relative to us the intermediate is what is neither superfluous nor deficient; this is not one, and is not the same for all.

If, for instance, ten are many and two are few, we take six as intermediate in the object, since it exceeds [two] and is exceeded [by ten] by an equal amount, [four]. This is what is intermediate by numerical proportion. But that is not how we must take the intermediate that is relative to us. For if ten pounds [of food], for instance, are a lot for someone to eat, and two pounds a little, it does not follow that the trainer will prescribe six, since this might also be either a little or a lot for the person who is to take it—for Milo[8] [the athlete] a little, but for the beginner in gymnastics a lot; and the same is true for running and wrestling. In this way every scientific expert avoids excess and deficiency and seeks and chooses what is intermediate—but intermediate relative to us, not in the object.

This, then, is how each science produces its product well, by focusing on what is intermediate and making the product conform to that. This, indeed, is why people regularly comment on well-made products that nothing could be added or subtracted; they assume that excess or deficiency ruins a good [result], whereas the mean preserves it. Good craftsmen also, we say, focus on what is intermediate when they produce their product. And since virtue, like nature, is better and more exact than any craft, it will also aim at what is intermediate.

8. [Milo was a sixth-century-B.C. Greek wrestler of legendary strength.]

By virtue I mean virtue of character; for this is about feelings and actions, and these admit of excess, deficiency, and an intermediate condition. We can be afraid, for instance, or be confident, or have appetites, or get angry, or feel pity, and in general have pleasure or pain, both too much and too little, and in both ways not well. But having these feelings at the right times, about the right things, toward the right people, for the right end, and in the right way, is the intermediate and best condition, and this is proper to virtue. Similarly, actions also admit of excess, deficiency, and an intermediate condition.

Now virtue is about feelings and actions, in which excess and deficiency are in error and incur blame, whereas the intermediate condition is correct and wins praise, which are both proper to virtue. Virtue, then, is a mean, insofar as it aims at what is intermediate.

Moreover, there are many ways to be in error—for badness is proper to the indeterminate, as the Pythagoreans pictured it, and good to the determinate. But there is only one way to be correct. That is why error is easy and correctness is difficult, since it is easy to miss the target and difficult to hit it. And so for this reason also excess and deficiency are proper to vice, the mean to virtue; 'for we are noble in only one way, but bad in all sorts of ways.'

Virtue, then, is a state that decides, consisting in a mean, the mean relative to us, which is defined by reference to reason, that is to say, to the reason by reference to which the prudent person would define it. It is a mean between two vices, one of excess and one of deficiency.

It is a mean for this reason also: Some vices miss what is right because they are deficient, others because they are excessive, in feelings or in actions, whereas virtue finds and chooses what is intermediate.

That is why virtue, as far as its essence and the account stating what it is are concerned, is a mean, but, as far as the best [condition] and the good [result] are concerned, it is an extremity.

Now not every action or feeling admits of the mean. For the names of some automatically include baseness—for instance, spite, shamelessness, envy [among feelings], and adultery, theft, murder, among actions. For all of these and similar things are called by these names because they themselves, not their excesses or deficiencies, are base. Hence in doing these things we can never be correct, but must invariably be in error. We cannot do them well, or not well—by committing adultery, for instance, with the right woman at the right time in the right way. On the contrary, it is true without qualification that to do any of them is to be in error.

[To think these admit of a mean], therefore, is 20 like thinking that unjust or cowardly or intemperate action also admits of a mean, an excess and a deficiency. If it did, there would be a mean of excess, a mean of deficiency, an excess of excess and a deficiency of deficiency. On the contrary, just as there is no excess or deficiency of temperance or of bravery (since the intermediate is a sort of extreme), so also there is no mean of these vicious actions either, but 25 whatever way anyone does them, he is in error. For in general there is no mean of excess or of deficiency, and no excess or deficiency of a mean.

7

However, we must not only state this general account 30 but also apply it to the particular cases. For among accounts concerning actions, though the general ones are common to more cases, the specific ones are truer, since actions are about particular cases, and our account must accord with these.

1107b First, then, in feelings of fear and confidence the mean is bravery. The excessively fearless person is nameless (indeed many cases are nameless), and the one who is excessively confident is rash. The one who is excessive in fear and deficient in confidence is cowardly.

5 In pleasures and pains—though not in all types, and in pains less than in pleasures—the mean is temperance and the excess intemperance. People deficient in pleasure are not often found, which is why they also lack even a name; let us call them insensible.

10 In giving and taking money the mean is generosity, the excess wastefulness and the deficiency ungenerosity. Here the vicious people have contrary excesses and defects; for the wasteful person is excessive in spending and deficient in taking, whereas the ungenerous person is excessive in taking and defi- 15 cient in spending. At the moment we are speaking in outline and summary, and that is enough; later we shall define these things more exactly.

In questions of money there are also other conditions. Another mean is magnificence; for the magnificent person differs from the generous by being concerned with large matters, while the generous person is concerned with small. The excess is osten- 20 tation and vulgarity, and the deficiency is stinginess. These differ from the vices related to generosity in ways we shall describe later.

In honor and dishonor the mean is magnanimity, the excess something called a sort of vanity, 25 and the deficiency pusillanimity. And just as we said that generosity differs from magnificence in its concern with small matters, similarly there is a virtue concerned with small honors, differing in the same way from magnanimity, which is concerned with great honors. For honor can be desired either in the right way or more or less than is right. If someone desires it to excess, he is called an honor-lover, and if his desire 30 is deficient he is called indifferent to honor, but if he is intermediate he has no name. The corresponding conditions have no name either, except the condition of the honor-lover, which is called honor-loving.

This is why people at the extremes lay claim to the intermediate area. Moreover, we also sometimes call the intermediate person an honor-lover, and sometimes call him indifferent to honor; and sometimes we praise the honor-lover, sometimes the person 1108a indifferent to honor. We will mention later the reason we do this; for the moment, let us speak of the other cases in the way we have laid down.

Anger also admits of an excess, deficiency, and 5 mean. These are all practically nameless; but since we call the intermediate person mild, let us call the mean mildness. Among the extreme people, let the excessive person be irascible, and his vice irascibility, and let the deficient person be a sort of inirascible person, and his deficiency inirascibility.

There are also three other means, somewhat simi- 10 lar to one another, but different. For they are all concerned with common dealings in conversations and actions, but differ insofar as one is concerned with truth telling in these areas, the other two with sources of pleasure, some of which are found in amusement, and the others in daily life in general. Hence we should also discuss these states, so that we can better observe that in every case the mean is 15 praiseworthy, whereas the extremes are neither praiseworthy nor correct, but blameworthy. Most of these cases are also nameless, and we must try, as in the other cases also, to supply names ourselves, to make things clear and easy to follow.

20 In truth-telling, then, let us call the intermediate person truthful, and the mean truthfulness; pretense that overstates will be boastfulness, and the person who has it boastful; pretense that understates will be self-deprecation, and the person who has it self-deprecating.

In sources of pleasure in amusements let us call 25 the intermediate person witty, and the condition wit; the excess buffoonery and the person who has it a buffoon; and the deficient person a sort of boor and the state boorishness.

In the other sources of pleasure, those in daily life, let us call the person who is pleasant in the right way friendly, and the mean state friendliness. If someone goes to excess with no [ulterior] aim, he will be ingra- 30 tiating; if he does it for his own advantage, a flatterer. The deficient person, unpleasant in everything, will be a sort of quarrelsome and ill-tempered person.

There are also means in feelings and about feelings. Shame, for instance, is not a virtue, but the person prone to shame as well as [the virtuous people we have described] receives praise. For here also one person is called intermediate, and another—the 35 person excessively prone to shame, who is ashamed about everything—is called excessive; the person who is deficient in shame or never feels shame at all is said 1108b to have no sense of disgrace; and the intermediate one is called prone to shame.

Proper indignation is the mean between envy and spite; these conditions are concerned with pleasure and pain at what happens to our neighbors. For the properly indignant person feels pain when someone 5 does well undeservedly; the envious person exceeds him by feeling pain when anyone does well, while the spiteful person is so deficient in feeling pain that he actually enjoys [other people's misfortunes].

There will also be an opportunity elsewhere to speak of these. We must consider justice after these. Since it is spoken of in more than one way, we shall distinguish its two types and say how each of them is a mean. Similarly, we must also consider the virtues 10 that belong to reason.

BOOK III

1

Virtue, then, is about feelings and actions. These 1109b30 receive praise or blame if they are voluntary, but pardon, sometimes even pity, if they are involuntary. Hence, presumably, in examining virtue we must define the voluntary and the involuntary. This is also useful to legislators, both for honors and for correc- 35 tive treatments.

Now it seems that things coming about by force or 1110a because of ignorance are involuntary.

What is forced has an external principle, the sort of principle in which the agent, or [rather] the victim, contributes nothing—if, for instance, a wind or people who have him in their control were to carry him off.

But what about actions done because of fear of 5 greater evils, or because of something fine? Suppose, for instance, a tyrant tells you to do something shameful, when he has control over your parents and children, and if you do it, they will live, but if not, they will die. These cases raise dispute about whether they are voluntary or involuntary.

However, the same sort [of unwelcome choice] is found in throwing cargo overboard in storms. For no 10 one willingly throws cargo overboard, without qualification, but anyone with any sense throws it overboard to save himself and the others.

These sorts of actions, then, are mixed, but they are more like voluntary actions. For at the time they are done they are choiceworthy, and the goal of an action accords with the specific occasion; hence we should also call the action voluntary or involuntary on the occasion when he does it. Now in fact he 15 does it willingly. For in such actions he has within him the principle of moving the limbs that are the instruments [of the action]; but if the principle of the actions is in him, it is also up to him to do them or not to do them. Hence actions of this sort are voluntary, though presumably the actions without [the appropriate] qualification are involuntary, since no one would choose any such action in its own right.

For such [mixed] actions people are sometimes 20 actually praised, whenever they endure something shameful or painful as the price of great and fine results. If they do the reverse, they are blamed; for it is a base person who endures what is most shameful for nothing fine or for only some moderately fine result. In some cases there is no praise, but there is pardon, 25 whenever someone does a wrong action because of conditions of a sort that overstrain human nature, and that no one would endure.

But presumably there are some things we cannot be compelled to do. Rather than do them we should suffer the most terrible consequences and accept death; for the things that [allegedly] compelled Euripides' Alcmaeon to kill his mother appear ridiculous.[9]

30 It is sometimes difficult, however, to judge what [goods] should be chosen at the price of what [evils], and what [evils] should be endured as the price of what [goods]. It is even more difficult to abide by our judgment, since the results we expect [when we endure] are usually painful, and the actions we are compelled [to endure, when we choose] are 1110b usually shameful. That is why those who have been compelled or not compelled receive praise or blame.

What sorts of things, then, should we say are forced? Perhaps we should say that something is forced without qualification whenever its cause is external and the agent contributes nothing. Other things are involuntary in their own right, but choiceworthy on this 5 occasion and as the price of these [goods], and their principle is in the agent. These are involuntary in their own right, but, on this occasion and as the price of these [goods], voluntary. But they are more like voluntary actions, since the actions are particulars, and [in the case of mixed actions] these particulars are voluntary. But what sort of thing should be chosen as the price of what [good] is not easy to answer, since there are many differences in particular [conditions].

10 But what if someone says that pleasant things and fine things force us, on the ground that they are outside us and compel us? For him, then, everything must be forced, since everyone in every action aims at something fine or pleasant. Moreover, if we are forced and unwilling to act, we find it painful; but if something pleasant or fine is its cause, we do it with pleasure. It is ridiculous, then, for him to ascribe responsi- 15 bility to external causes, not to himself as being easily snared by such things; and ridiculous to hold himself responsible for his fine actions, but pleasant things responsible for his shameful actions.

What is forced, then, would seem to be what has its principle outside the person forced, who contributes nothing.

Everything caused by ignorance is nonvoluntary, but what is involuntary also involves pain and regret. 20 For if someone's action was caused by ignorance, but he now has no objection to the action, he has done it neither willingly, since he did not know what it was, nor unwillingly, since he now feels no pain. Hence, among those who act because of ignorance, the agent who now regrets his action seems to be unwilling, but the agent with no regrets may be called nonwilling, since he is another case—for, since he is different, it is better if he has his own special name.

Further, action caused by ignorance would seem 25 to be different from action done in ignorance. For if the agent is drunk or angry, his action seems to be caused by drunkenness or anger, not by ignorance, though it is done in ignorance, not in knowledge. Certainly every vicious person is ignorant of the actions he must do or avoid, and this sort of error makes people unjust, and in general bad. 30

[This] ignorance of what is beneficial is not taken to make action involuntary. For the cause of involuntary action is not [this] ignorance in the decision, which causes vice; it is not [in other words] ignorance of the universal, since that is a cause for blame. Rather, 1111a the cause is ignorance of the particulars which the action consists in and is concerned with, since these allow both pity and pardon. For an agent acts involuntarily if he is ignorant of one of these particulars.

Presumably, then, it is not a bad idea to define these particulars, and say what they are, and how many. They are: who is doing it; what he is doing; about what or to what he is doing it; sometimes also 5 what he is doing it with—with what instrument, for example; for what result, for example, safety; in what way, for example, gently or hard.

Now certainly someone could not be ignorant of *all* of these unless he were mad. Nor, clearly, could he be ignorant of who is doing it, since he could hardly be ignorant of himself. But he might be ignorant of what he is doing, as when someone says that [the secret] slipped out while he was speaking, or, as Aeschylus said about the mysteries, that he did not

9. [The play by the great fifth-century-B.C. Greek dramatists is not extant. According to Greek mythology, Alcmaeon killed his mother to avenge the death of his father.]

know it was forbidden to reveal it;[10] or, like the person with the catapult, that he let it go when he [only] wanted to demonstrate it. Again, he might think that his son is an enemy, as Merope did;[11] or that the barbed spear has a button on it, or that the stone is pumice stone. By giving someone a drink to save his life we might kill him; and wanting to touch someone, as they do in sparring, we might wound him.

Since an agent may be ignorant of any of these particular constituents of his action, someone who was ignorant of one of these seems to have acted unwillingly, especially if he was ignorant of the most important; these seem to be what he is doing, and the result for which he does it.

Hence the agent who acts involuntarily is the one who acts in accord with this specific sort of ignorance, who must also feel pain and regret for his action.

Since involuntary action is either forced or caused by ignorance, voluntary action seems to be what has its principle in the agent himself, knowing the particulars that constitute the action.

For, presumably, it is not right to say that action caused by spirit or appetite is involuntary. For, first of all, on this view none of the other animals will ever act voluntarily; nor will children. Next, among all the actions caused by appetite or spirit do we do none of them voluntarily? Or do we do the fine actions voluntarily and the shameful involuntarily? Surely [the second answer] is ridiculous, given that one and the same thing [i.e., appetite or spirit] causes [both fine and shameful actions]. And presumably it is also absurd to say [as the first answer implies] that things we ought to desire are involuntary. Indeed, we ought both to be angry at some things and to have appetite for some things—for health and learning, for instance. Again, what is involuntary seems to be painful, whereas what accords with appetite seems to be pleasant.

Moreover, how are errors in accord with spirit any less voluntary than those in accord with rational calculation? For both sorts of errors are to be avoided. Besides, nonrational feelings seem to be no less human than rational calculation; and so actions resulting from spirit or appetite are also proper to a human being. It is absurd, then, to regard them as involuntary.

2

Now that we have defined the voluntary and the involuntary, the next task is to discuss decision; for decision seems to be most proper to virtue, and to distinguish characters from one another better than actions do.

Decision, then, is apparently voluntary, but not the same as the voluntary, which extends more widely. For children and the other animals share in voluntary action, but not in decision; and the actions we do on the spur of the moment are said to be voluntary, but not to accord with decision.

Those who say decision is appetite or spirit or wish or some sort of belief would seem to be wrong. For decision is not shared with nonrational animals, but appetite and spirit are shared with them. Again, the incontinent person acts on appetite, not on decision, but the continent person does the reverse, by acting on decision, not on appetite. Again, appetite is contrary to decision, but not to appetite. Besides, the object of appetite is what is pleasant or painful, whereas neither of these is the object of decision. And still less is spirit decision; for actions caused by spirit seem least of all to accord with decision.

But further, it is not wish either, though it is apparently close to it. For we do not decide on impossible things—anyone claiming to decide on them would seem a fool; but we do wish for impossible things—for immortality, for instance—as well as possible things. Further, we wish [not only for results we can achieve], but also for results that are [possible, but] not achievable through our own agency—victory for some actor or athlete, for instance. But what we decide on is never anything of that sort, but what we think would come about through our own agency. Again, we wish for the end more [than for the things that promote it], but we decide on things that promote the end. We wish, for instance, to be healthy; but we decide to do things that will make us healthy; and we wish to be happy, and say so, but we could not appropriately say we decide to be happy, since in general the things we

10. [The Greek dramatists Aeschylus is said to have been accused but then acquitted of revealing rites of a secret religious cult.]

11. [In a lost play of Euripides, Merope, not recognizing his son, nearly slays him.]

decide on would seem to be things that are up to us.

Nor is it belief. For belief seems to be about everything, no less about things that are eternal and things that are impossible [for us] than about things that are up to us. Moreover, beliefs are divided into true and false, not into good and bad, but decisions are divided into good and bad more than into true and false.

Now presumably no one even claims that decision is the same as belief in general. But it is not the same as any kind of belief either. For our decisions to do good or bad actions, not our beliefs, form the characters we have. Again, we decide to take or avoid something good or bad. We believe what it is, whom it benefits or how; but we do not exactly believe to take or avoid. Further, decision is praised more for deciding on what is right, whereas belief is praised for believing rightly. Moreover, we decide on something [even] when we know most completely that it is good; but [what] we believe [is] what we do not quite know. Again, those who make the best decisions do not seem to be the same as those with the best beliefs; on the contrary, some seem to have better beliefs, but to make the wrong decisions because of vice. We may grant the decision follows or implies belief. But that is irrelevant, since it is not the question we are asking; our question is whether decision is the same as some sort of belief.

Then, what, or what sort of thing, is decision, since it is none of the things mentioned? Well, apparently it is voluntary, but not everything voluntary is decided. Then perhaps what is decided is what has been previously deliberated. For decision involves reason and thought, and even the name itself would seem to indicate that [what is decided, *prohaireton*] is chosen [*haireton*] before [*pro*] other things.

3

Do we deliberate about everything, and is everything open to deliberation? Or is there no deliberation about some things? By 'open to deliberation,' presumably, we should mean that someone with some sense, not some fool or madman, might deliberate about it.

Now no one deliberates about eternal things—about the universe, for instance, or about the incommensurability of the sides and the diagonal; nor about things that are in movement but always come about the same way, either from necessity or by nature or by some other cause—the solstices, for instance, or the rising of the stars; nor about what happens in different ways at different times—droughts and rains, for instance; nor about what results from fortune—the finding of a treasure, for instance. For none of these results could be achieved through our agency.

We deliberate about what is up to us, that is to say, about the actions we can do; and this is what is left [besides the previous cases]. For causes seem to include nature, necessity, and fortune, but besides them mind and everything [operating] through human agency. But we do not deliberate about all human affairs; no Spartan, for instance, deliberates about how the Scythians[12] might have the best political system. Rather, each group of human beings deliberates about the actions that they themselves can do.

There is no deliberation about the sciences that are exact and self-sufficient, as, for instance, about letters, since we are in no doubt about how to write them [in spelling a word]. Rather, we deliberate about what results through our agency, but in different ways on different occasions—about, for instance, medicine and money making. We deliberate about navigation more than about gymnastics, to the extent that it is less exactly worked out, and similarly with other [crafts]. And we deliberate about beliefs more than about sciences, since we are more in doubt about them.

Deliberation concerns what is usually [one way rather than another], where the outcome is unclear and the right way to act is undefined. And we enlist partners in deliberation on large issues and when we distrust our own ability to discern [the right answer].

We deliberate not about ends, but about what promotes ends. A doctor, for instance, does not deliberate about whether he will cure, or an orator about whether he will persuade, or a politician about whether he will produce good order, or any other [expert] about the end [that his science aims at]. Rather, we lay down the end, and then examine the ways and means to achieve it.

If it appears that any of several [possible] means

12. [The Scythians were an association of central Asian tribes, renowned for their horsemanship and decorative horse trappings, who penetrated into eastern Europe in the first millennium B.C.]

will reach it, we examine which of them will reach it most easily and most finely; and if only one [possible] means reaches it, we examine how that means will reach it, and how the means itself is reached, until we 20 come to the first cause, the last thing to be discovered. For a deliberator would seem to inquire and analyze in the way described, as though analyzing a diagram. [The comparison is apt, since], apparently, all deliberation is inquiry, though not all inquiry—in mathematics, for instance—is deliberation. And the last thing [found] in the analysis would seem to be the first that comes into being.

25 If we encounter an impossible step—for instance, we need money but cannot raise it—we desist; but if the action appears possible, we undertake it. What is possible is what we could achieve through our agency [including what our friends could achieve for us]; for what our friends achieve is, in a way, achieved through our agency, since the principle is in us. [In crafts] we sometimes look for instruments, sometimes 30 [for the way] to use them; so also in other cases we sometimes look for the means to the end, sometimes for the proper use of the means, or for the means to that proper use.

As we have said, then, a human being would seem to be a principle of action. Deliberation is about the actions he can do, and actions are for the sake of other things; hence we deliberate about things that 1113a promote an end, not about the end. Nor do we deliberate about particulars, about whether this is a loaf, for instance, or is cooked the right amount; for these are questions for perception, and if we keep on deliberating at each stage we shall go on without end.

What we deliberate about is the same as what we decide to do, except that by the time we decide to 5 do it, it is definite; for what we decide to do is what we have judged [to be right] as a result of deliberation. For each of us stops inquiring how to act as soon as he traces the principle to himself, and within himself to the guiding part; for this is the part that decides. This is also clear from the ancient political systems described by Homer; there the kings would first decide and then announce their decision to the people.

10 We have found, then, that what we decide to do is whatever action, among those up to us, we deliberate about and [consequently] desire to do. Hence also decision will be deliberative desire to do an action that is up to us; for when we have judged [that it is right] as a result of deliberation, we desire to do it in accord with our wish.

We have said in outline, then, what sorts of things decision is about, and [specifically] that we decide on things that promote the end.

4

Wish, we have said, is for the end. But some think 15 that wish is for the good, others that it is for the apparent good.

For those who say the good is wished, it follows that what someone wishes if he chooses incorrectly is not wished at all. For if it is wished, then [on this view] it is good; but what he wishes is in fact bad, if it turns out that way. [Hence what he wishes is not 20 wished, which is self-contradictory.]

But for those who say the apparent good is wished, it follows that nothing is wished by nature. Rather, for each person what is wished is what seems [good to him]; but different things, and indeed contrary things, if it turns out that way, appear good to different people. [Hence contrary things will be wished and nothing will be wished by nature.]

If, then, these views do not satisfy us, should we say that, without qualification and in reality, what is wished is the good, but for each person what is wished is the apparent good? For the excellent person, then, 25 what is wished will be what is [wished] in reality, while for the base person what is wished is whatever it turns out to be [that appears good to him]. Similarly in the case of bodies, really healthy things are healthy to people in good condition, while other things are healthy to sickly people; and the same is true of what 30 is bitter, sweet, hot, heavy, and so on. For the excellent person judges each sort of thing correctly, and in each case what is true appears to him.

For each state [of character] has its own distinctive [view of] what is fine and pleasant. Presumably, then, the excellent person is far superior because he sees what is true in each case, being himself a sort of standard and measure. In the many, however, pleasure would seem to cause deception, since it appears good 1113b when it is not. Certainly, they choose what is pleasant because they assume it is good, and avoid pain because they assume it is evil.

5

We have founds, then, that we wish for the end, and deliberate and decide about things that promote it; hence the actions concerned with things that promote the end are in accord with decision and are voluntary. The activities of the virtues are concerned with these things [that promote the end].

Hence virtue is also up to us, and so also, in the same way, is vice. For when acting is up to us, so is not acting, and when no is up to us, so is yes. And so if acting, when it is fine, is up to us, not acting, when it is shameful, is also up to us; and if not acting, when it is fine, is up to us, then acting, when it is shameful, is also up to us. But if doing, and likewise not doing, fine or shameful actions is up to us, and if, as we saw, [doing or not doing them] is [what it is] to be a good or bad person, being decent or base is up to us.

The claim that 'no one is willingly bad or unwillingly blessed' would seem to be partly true but partly false. For while certainly no one is unwillingly blessed, vice is voluntary.

If this is not so, we must dispute what has been said, and we must deny that a human being is a principle, begetting actions as he begets children. But if what we have said appears true, and we cannot refer back to other principles apart from those that are up to us, those things that have their principle in us are themselves up to us and voluntary.

There would seem to be evidence in favor of our view not only in what each of us does as a private citizen, but also in what legislators themselves do. For they impose corrective treatments and penalties on anyone who does vicious actions, unless his action is forced or is caused by ignorance that he is not responsible for; and they honor anyone who does fine actions. In all this they assume that they will encourage the second sort of person, and restrain the first. But no one encourages us to do anything that is not up to us and voluntary; people assume it is pointless to persuade us not to get hot or distressed or hungry or anything else of that sort, since persuasion will not stop it happening to us.

Indeed, legislators also impose corrective treatments for the ignorance itself, if the agent seems to be responsible for the ignorance. A drunk, for instance, pays a double penalty; for the principle is in him, since he controls whether he gets drunk, and his getting drunk causes his ignorance. They also impose corrective treatment on someone who [does a vicious action] in ignorance of some provision of law that he is required to know and that is not hard [to know]. *1114a* And they impose it in other cases likewise for any other ignorance that seems to be caused by the agent's inattention; they assume it is up to him not to be ignorant, since he controls whether he pays attention.

But presumably he is the sort of person who is inattentive. Still, he is himself responsible for becoming this sort of person, because he has lived carelessly. Similarly, an individual is responsible for being unjust, because he has cheated, and for being intemperate, because he has passed his time in drinking and the like; for each type of activity produces the corresponding sort of person. This is clear from those who train for any contest or action, since they continually practice the appropriate activities. [Only] a totally insensible person would not know that a given type of activity is the source of the corresponding state; [Hence] if someone does what he knows will make him unjust, he is willingly unjust.

Further, it is unreasonable for someone doing injustice not to wish to be unjust, or for someone doing intemperate action not to wish to be intemperate. This does not mean, however, that if he is unjust and wishes to stop, he will thereby stop and be just. For neither does a sick person recover his health [simply by wishing]; nonetheless, he is sick willingly, by living incontinently and disobeying the doctors, if that was how it happened. At that time, then, he was free not to be sick, though no longer free once he has let himself go, just as it was up to someone to throw a stone, since the principle was up to him, though he can no longer take it back once he has thrown it. Similarly, then, the person who is [now] unjust or intemperate was originally free not to acquire this character, so that he has it willingly, though once he has acquired the character, he is no longer free not to have it [now].

It is not only vices of the soul that are voluntary; vices of the body are also voluntary for some people, and we actually censure them. For we never censure someone if nature causes his ugliness; but if his lack of training or attention causes it, we do censure him. The same is true for weakness or maiming; for everyone would pity someone, not reproach him, if he were blind by nature or because of a disease or a wound, but would censure him if his heavy drinking or some other form of intemperance made him blind. Hence bodily vices that are up to us are censured, while those not up to us are not censured. If so, then in the other cases also the vices that are censured will be up to us.

But someone may say that everyone aims at the apparent good, and does not control how it appears, but, on the contrary, his character controls how the end appears to him. [We reply that] if each person is in some way responsible for his own state [of character], he is also himself in some way responsible for how [the end] appears.

Suppose, on the other hand, that no one is responsible for acting badly, but one does so because one is ignorant of the end, and thinks this is the way to gain what is best for oneself. In that case, one's aiming at the end is not one's own choice; one needs a sort of natural, inborn sense of sight, to judge finely and to choose what is really good. Whoever by nature has this sense in a fine condition has a good nature; for [, according to this view,] this sense is the greatest and finest thing, given that one cannot acquire it or learn it from another, but its natural character determines [his] later condition, and when it is naturally good and fine, that is true and complete good nature. If all this is true, then, surely virtue will be no more voluntary than vice.

For how the end appears is laid down, by nature or in whatever way, for the good and the bad person alike; they trace all the other things back to the end in doing whatever actions they do. Let us suppose, then, that nature does not make the end appear however it appears to each person, but something also depends on him. Alternatively, let us suppose that [how] the end [appears] is natural, but virtue is voluntary because the virtuous person does the other things voluntarily. In either case, vice will be no less voluntary than virtue; for the bad person, no less than the good, is responsible for his own actions, even if not for [how] the end [appears].

Now the virtues, as we say, are voluntary. For in fact we are ourselves in a way jointly responsible for our states of character, and the sort of character we have determines the sort of end we lay down. Hence the vices will also be voluntary, since the same is true of them.

We have now discussed the virtues in common. We have described their genus in outline; they are means, and they are states. Certain actions produce them, and they cause us to do these same actions in accord with the virtues themselves, in the way that correct reason prescribes. They are up to us and voluntary.

Actions and states, however, are not voluntary in the same way. For we are in control of actions from the beginning to the end, when we know the particulars. With states, however, we are in control of the beginning, but do not know, any more than with sicknesses, what the cumulative effect of particular actions will be. Nonetheless, since it was up to us to exercise a capacity either this way or another way, states are voluntary.

Let us now take up the virtues again, and discuss them one by one. Let us say what they are, what sorts of thing they are concerned with, and how they are concerned with them. It will also be clear at the same time how many of them there are.

6

First let us discuss bravery. We have already made it apparent that there is a mean about feelings of fear and confidence. What we fear, clearly, is what is frightening, and such things are, speaking without qualification, bad things; hence people define fear as expectation of something bad.

Certainly we fear all bad things—for instance, bad reputation, poverty, sickness, friendlessness, death—but they do not all seem to concern the brave person. For fear of some bad things, such as bad reputation, is actually right and fine, and lack of fear is shameful; for if someone fears bad reputation, he is decent and properly prone to shame, and if he has no fear of it, he has no feeling of disgrace. Some, however, call this fearless person brave, by a transference of the name; for he has some similarity to the brave person, since the brave person is also a type of fearless person.

Presumably it is wrong to fear poverty or sickness or, in general, [bad things] that are not the results of vice or caused by ourselves; still, someone who is fearless about these is not thereby brave. He is also called brave by similarity; for some people who are cowardly in the dangers of war are nonetheless generous, and face with confidence the [danger of] losing money.

Again, if someone is afraid of committing wanton aggression on children or women, or of being envious or anything of that sort, that does not make him cowardly. And if someone is confident when he is going to be whipped for his crimes, that does not make him brave.

Then what sorts of frightening conditions concern the brave person? Surely the most frightening; for no one stands firmer against terrifying conditions. Now death is most frightening of all, since it is a boundary, and when someone is dead nothing beyond it seems either good or bad for him any more. Still, not even death in all conditions—on the sea, for instance, or in sickness—seems to be the brave person's concern.

In what conditions, then, is death his concern? Surely in the finest conditions. Now such deaths are those in war, since they occur in the greatest and finest danger. This judgment is endorsed by the honors given in cities and by monarchs. Hence someone is called fully brave if he is intrepid in facing a fine death and the immediate dangers that bring death. And this is above all true of the dangers of war.

Certainly the brave person is also intrepid on the sea and in sickness, but not in the same way as seafarers are. For he has given up hope of safety, and objects to this sort of death [with nothing fine in it], but seafarers' experience makes them hopeful. Moreover, we act like brave men on occasions when we can use our strength, or when it is fine to be killed; and neither of these is true when we perish from shipwreck or sickness.

7

Now what is frightening is not the same for everyone. We say, however, that some things are too frightening for a human being to resist, these, then, are frightening for everyone, at least for everyone with any sense. What is frightening, but not irresistible for a human being, varies in its seriousness and degree; and the same is true of what inspires confidence.

The brave person is unperturbed, as far as a human being can be. Hence, though he will fear even the sorts of things that are not irresistible, he will stand firm against them, in the right way, as reason prescribes, for the sake of the fine, since this is the end aimed at by virtue.

It is possible to be more or less afraid of these frightening things, and also possible to be afraid of what is not frightening as though it were frightening. The cause of error may be fear of the wrong thing, or in the wrong way, or at the wrong time, or something of that sort; and the same is true for things that inspire confidence.

Hence whoever stands firm against the right things and fears the right things, for the right end, in the right way, at the right time, and is correspondingly confident, is the brave person; for the brave person's actions and feelings accord with what something is worth, and follow what reason prescribes.

Every activity aims at actions in accord with the state of character. Now to the brave person bravery is fine; hence the end it aims at is also fine, since each thing is defined by its end. The braver person, then, aims at the fine when he stands firm and acts in accord with bravery.

Among those who go to excess the excessively fearless person has no name—we said earlier that many causes have no names. He would be some sort of madman, or incapable of feeling distress, if he feared nothing, neither earthquake nor waves, as they say about the Celts.[13]

The person who is excessively confident about frightening things is rash. The rash person also seems to be a boaster, and a pretender to bravery. At any rate, the attitude to frightening things that the brave person really has is the attitude that the rash person wants to appear to have; hence he imitates the brave person where he can. That is why most of them are rash cowards; for, rash though they are on these [occasions for imitation], they do not stand firm against anything frightening. Moreover, rash people are impetuous, wishing for dangers before they arrive, but they shrink from them when they come. Brave people, on the contrary, are eager when in action, but keep quiet until then.

The person who is excessively afraid is the coward, since he fears the wrong things, and in the wrong way, and so on. Certainly, he is also deficient in confidence, but his excessive pain distinguishes him more clearly. Hence, since he is afraid of everything, he is a despairing sort. The brave person, on the contrary,

13. [Members of a group of tribes who, armed with iron weapons and mounted on horses, spread rapidly over Europe and the British Isles in the second millennium B.C.]

is hopeful, since [he is confident and] confidence is proper to a hopeful person.

5 Hence the coward, the rash person, and the brave person are all concerned with the same things, but have different states related to them; the others are 7 excessive or defective, but the brave person has the intermediate and right state.

10 As we have said, then, bravery is a mean about what inspires confidence and about what is frightening in the conditions we have described; it chooses and stands firm because that is fine or because anything else is shameful. Dying to avoid poverty or erotic passion or something painful is proper to a 15 coward, not to a brave person. For shirking burdens is softness, and such a person stands firm [in the face of death] to avoid an evil, not because standing firm is fine.

8

Bravery, then, is something of this sort. But five other sorts of things are also called bravery.

The bravery of citizens comes first, since it looks most like bravery. For citizens seem to stand firm against dangers with the aim of avoiding reproaches 20 and legal penalties and of winning honors; that is why the bravest seem to be those who hold cowards in dishonor and do honor to brave people. That is how Homer also describes them when he speaks of Diomede and Hector: 'Polydamas will be the first 25 to heap disgrace on me', and 'For some time Hector speaking among the Trojans will say, "The son of Tydeus fled from me."'[14] This is the most like the [genuine] bravery described above, because it results 1116a from a virtue; for it is caused by shame and by desire for something fine, namely honor, and by aversion from reproach, which is shameful.

30 In this class we might also place those who are compelled by their superiors. However, they are worse to the extent that they act because of fear, not because of shame, and to avoid pain, not disgrace. For their commanders compel them, as Hector does; 35 'If I notice anyone shrinking back from the battle, nothing will save him from being eaten by the dogs.' Commanders who strike any troops who give ground, 1116b or who post them in front of ditches and suchlike, do the same things, since they all compel them. The brave person, however, must be moved by the fine, not by compulsion.

Experience about a given situation also seems to 5 be bravery; that is why Socrates actually thought that bravery is scientific knowledge. Different people have this sort [of apparent courage] in different conditions. In wartime professional soldiers have it; for there seem to be many groundless alarms in war, and the professionals are the most familiar with these. Hence they appear brave, since others do not know that the alarms are groundless. Moreover, their experience makes them most capable in attack and defense, since they are skilled in the use of their weapons, and have the best weapons for attack and defense. The 10 result is that in fighting nonprofessionals they are like armed troops against unarmed, or trained athletes against ordinary people; for in these contests also the best fighters are the strongest and physically fittest, not the bravest. 15

Professional soldiers, however, turn out to be cowards whenever the danger overstrains them and they are inferior in numbers and equipment. For they are the first to run, whereas the citizen troops stand firm and get killed; this was what happened at the temple of Hermes.[15] For the citizens find it shameful to run, and find death more choiceworthy than safety 20 at this cost. But the professionals from the start were facing the danger on the assumption of their superiority; once they learn their mistake, they run, since they are more afraid of being killed than of doing something shameful. That is not the brave person's character.

Spirit is also counted as bravery; for those who act 25 on spirit also seem to be brave—as beasts seem to be when they attack those who have wounded them—because brave people are also full of spirit. For spirit is most eager to run and face dangers; hence Homer's words, 'put strength in his spirit', 'aroused strength and spirit', and 'his blood boiled'.[16] All these would 30 seem to signify the arousal and the impulse of spirit.

Now brave people act because of the fine, and

14. *Iliad* XXII.100; VIII.148–49.]

15. [The incident occurred in 353 B.C., when mercenaries paid to defend the citizens of Coronea in Boeotia deserted and left the citizen troops to be killed by invaders.]

16. [*Iliad* XI.11; XIV.151; XVI.529; V.470; XV 232, 594; *Odyssey* XXIV.318–19. The last phrase is not Homeric but known to us only in *Idyll* XX.15 by the post-Aristotelian poet Theocritus.]

their spirit cooperates with them. But beasts act because of pain; for they attack only because they have been wounded or frightened (since they keep 35 away from us in a forest). They are not brave, then, since distress and spirit drives them in an impulsive rush to meet danger, foreseeing none of the terrifying prospects. For if they were brave, hungry asses 1117*a* would also be brave, since they keep on feeding even if they are beaten; and adulterers also do many daring actions because of lust.

5 Human beings as well as beasts find it painful to be angered, and pleasant to exact a penalty. But those who fight for these reasons are not brave, though they are good fighters; for they fight because of their feelings, not because of the fine nor as reason prescribes. *4* Still, they have something similar [to bravery]. The *5* [bravery] caused by spirit would seem to be the most natural sort, and to be [genuine] bravery once it has also acquired decision and the goal.

9, 10 Hopeful people are not brave either; for their many victories over many opponents make them confident in dangers. They are somewhat similar to brave people, since both are confident. But whereas brave people are confident for the reason given earlier, the hopeful are confident because they think they are stronger and nothing could happen to them; 15 drunks do the same sort of thing, since they become hopeful. When things turn out differently from how they expected, they run away. The brave person, on the contrary, stands firm against what is and appears frightening to a human being; he does this because it is fine to stand firm and shameful to fail.

Indeed, that is why someone who is unafraid and unperturbed in emergencies seems braver than 20 [someone who is unafraid only] when he is warned in advance; for his action proceeds more from his state of character, because it proceeds less from preparation. For if we are warned in advance, we might decide what to do [not only because of our state of character, but] also by reason and rational calculation; but in emergencies [we must decide] in accord with our state of character.

Those who act in ignorance also appear brave, and indeed they are close to hopeful people, though 25 inferior to them insofar as they lack the self-esteem of hopeful people. That is why the hopeful stand firm for some time, whereas if ignorant people have been deceived and then realize or suspect that things are different, they run. That was what happened to the Argives when they stumbled on the Spartans and took them for Sicyonians.[17]

We have described, then, the character of brave people and of those who seem to be brave.

9

Bravery is about feelings of confidence and fear—not, 30 however, about both in the same way, but more about frightening things. For someone is brave if he is undisturbed and in the right state about these, more than if he is in this state about things inspiring confidence.

As we said, then, standing firm against what is painful makes us call people brave; that is why bravery is both painful and justly praised, since it is harder to stand firm against something painful than 35 to refrain from something pleasant. Nonetheless, the 1117*b* end that bravery aims at seems to be pleasant, though obscured by its surroundings. This is what happens in athletic contests. For boxers find that the end they aim at, the crown and the honors, is pleasant, but, being made of flesh and blood, they find it distressing 5 and painful to take the punches and to bear all the hard work; and because there are so many of these painful things, the end, being small, appears to have nothing pleasant in it.

And so, if the same is true for bravery, the brave person will find death and wounds painful, and suffer them unwillingly, but he will endure them because that is fine or because failure is shameful. Indeed, 10 the truer it is that he has every virtue and the happier he is, the more pain he will feel at the prospect of death. For this sort of person, more than anyone, finds it worthwhile to be alive, and knows he is being deprived of the greatest goods, and this is painful. But he is no less brave for all that; presumably, indeed, he is all the braver, because he chooses what is fine in 15 war at the cost of all these goods. It is not true, then, in the case of every virtue that its active exercise is pleasant; it is pleasant only insofar as we attain the end.

But presumably it is quite possible for brave people, given the character we have described, not

17. [In a battle in 392 B.C. the Spartans were wearing shields taken from their fleeing Sicyonian allies. The Argives, upon discovering the identity of their opponents, fled. The incident is related in *Hellenica* IV.4.10 by the Greek historian Xenophon (c. 430 B.C.–c. 355 B.C.).

to be the best soldiers. Perhaps the best will be those who are less brave, but possess no other good; for they are ready to face dangers, and they sell their lives for 20 small gains.

So much for bravery. It is easy to grasp what it is, in outline at least, from what we have said.

BOOK V

1

1129a The questions we must examine about justice and 5 injustice are these: What sorts of actions are they concerned with? What sort of mean is justice? What are the extremes between which justice is intermediate? Let us investigate them by the same line of inquiry as we used in the topics discussed before.

We see that the state everyone means in speaking of justice is the state that makes us just agents—[that 10 is to say,] the state that makes us do justice and wish what is just. In the same way they mean by injustice the state that makes us do injustice and wish what is unjust. That is why we also should first assume these things as an outline.

For what is true of sciences and capacities is not true of states. For while one and the same capacity or science seems to have contrary activities, a state 15 that is a contrary has no contrary activities. Health, for instance, only makes us do healthy actions, not their contraries; for we say we are walking in the way a healthy person would.

Often one of a pair of contrary states is recognized from the other contrary; and often the states are recognized from their subjects. For if, for instance, the 20 good state is evident, the bad state becomes evident too; and moreover the good state becomes evident from the things that have it, and the things from the state. For if, for instance, the good state is thickness of flesh, the bad state must be thinness of flesh, and the thing that produces the good state must be what produces thickness of flesh.

25 If one of a pair of contraries is spoken of in more ways than one, it follows, usually, that the other is too. If, for instance, the just is spoken of in more ways than one, so is the unjust.

Now it would seem that justice and injustice are both spoken of in more ways than one, but since their homonymy is close, the difference is unnoticed, and is less clear than it is with distant homonyms where 30 the distance in appearance is wide (for instance, the bone below an animal's neck and what we lock doors with are called keys homonymously).

Let us, then, find the number of ways an unjust person is spoken of. Both the lawless person and the overreaching and unfair person seem to be unjust; and so, clearly, both the lawful and the fair person will be just. Hence the just will be both the lawful and 1129b what is fair, and the unjust will be both the lawless and the unfair.

Since the unjust person is an overreacher, he will be concerned with goods—not with all goods, but only with those involved in good and bad fortune, goods which are, [considered] without qualification, always good, but for this or that person not always good. Though human beings pray for these and 5 pursue them, they are wrong; the right thing is to pray that what is good without qualification will also be good for us, but to choose [only] what is good for us.

Now the unjust person [who chooses these goods] does not choose more in every case; in the case of what is bad without qualification he actually chooses less. But since what is less bad also seems to be good 10 in a way, and overreaching aims at more of what is good, he seems to be an overreacher. In fact he is unfair; for unfairness includes [all these actions], and is a common feature [of his choice of the greater good and of the lesser evil].

Since, as we saw, the lawless person is unjust and the lawful person is just, it clearly follows that whatever is lawful is in some way just; for the provisions of legislative science are lawful, and we say that each of them is just. In every matter that they deal with, the 15 laws aim either at the common benefit of all, or at the benefit of those in control, whose control rests on virtue or on some other such basis. And so in one way what we call just is whatever produces and maintains happiness and its parts for a political community.

Now the law instructs us to do the actions of a 20 brave person—for instance, not to leave the battle-line, or to flee, or to throw away our weapons; of a 25 temperate person—not to commit adultery or wanton aggression; of a mild person—not to strike or revile another; and similarly requires actions in accord with the other virtues, and prohibits actions in accord with the vices. The correctly established law does this 25 correctly, and the less carefully framed one does this worse.

This type of justice, then, is complete virtue, not complete virtue without qualification, but complete virtue in relation to another. And that is why justice often seems to be supreme among the virtues, and 'neither the evening star nor the morning star is so marvellous,'[18] and the proverb says, 'And in justice all 30 virtue is summed up.'[19]

Moreover, justice is complete virtue to the highest degree because it is the complete exercise of complete virtue. And it is the complete exercise because the person who has justice is able to exercise virtue in relation to another, not only in what concerns himself; for many are able to exercise virtue in their own concerns, but unable in what relates to another.

1130a That is why Bias[20] seems to have been correct in saying that ruling will reveal the man; for a ruler is automatically related to another, and in a community. That is also why justice is the only virtue that seems 5 to be another person's good, because it is related to another; for it does what benefits another, either the ruler or the fellow member of the community.

The worst person, therefore, is the one who exercises his vice toward himself and his friends as well [as toward others]. And the best person is not the one who exercises virtue [only] toward himself, but the one who [also] exercises it in relation to another, since this is a difficult task.

10 This type of justice, then, is the whole, not a part, of virtue, and the injustice contrary to it is the whole, not a part, of vice.

Our discussion makes clear the difference between virtue and this type of justice. For virtue is the same as justice, but what it is to be virtue is not the same as what it is to be justice. Rather, insofar as virtue is related to another, it is justice, and insofar as it is a certain sort of state without qualification, it is virtue.

2

But we are looking for the type of justice, since we 15 say there is one, that consists in a part of virtue, and correspondingly for the type of injustice that is a part of vice.

A sign that there is this type of justice and injustice is this: If someone's activities accord with the other vices—if, for instance, cowardice made him throw away his shield, or irritability made him revile someone, or ungenerosity made him fail to help someone with money—what he does is unjust, but not over- 20 reaching. But when someone acts from overreaching, in many cases his action accords with none of these vices—certainly not all of them; but it still accords with some type of wickedness, since we blame him, and [in particular] it accords with injustice. Hence there is another type of injustice that is a part of the whole, and a way of being unjust that is a part of the whole that is contrary to law.

Further, if A commits adultery for profit and makes 25 a profit, but B commits adultery because of his appetite, and spends money on it to his own loss, B seems intemperate rather than overreaching, but A seems unjust, not intemperate. Clearly, then, this is because A acts to make a profit.

Further, we can refer every other unjust action to 30 some vice—to intemperance if someone committed adultery, to cowardice if he deserted his comrade in the battle-line, to anger if he struck someone. But if he made an [unjust] profit, we can refer it to no other vice except injustice.

It is evident, then, that there is another type of injustice, special injustice, apart from injustice as a whole, and that it is synonymous with injustice as a whole, since the definition is in the same genus. 1130b For both have their area of competence in relation to another, but special injustice is concerned with honor or wealth or safety (or whatever single name will include all these), and aims at the pleasure that results from making a profit, whereas the concern of 5 injustice as a whole is whatever concerns the excellent person.

Clearly, then, there is more than one type of

18. [The quotation is thought to be from Euripides' lost play *Melanippe*.]

19. [The quotation derives from the work of Theognis, regarding whom see Plato's *Meno*, n.18.]

20. [Bias of Priene was a sixth-century-B.C. Ionian statesman and one of the Seven Wise Men of Greece, who distinguished themselves in public affairs. His most famous saying was "Most men are bad."]

justice, and there is another type besides [the type that is] the whole of virtue; but we must still grasp what it is, and what sort of thing it is.

The unjust is divided into the lawless and the 10 unfair, and the just into the lawful and the fair. The unjustice previously described, then, is concerned with the lawless. But the unfair is not the same as the lawless; it is related to it as part to whole, since whatever is unfair is lawless, but not everything lawless is unfair. Hence also the unfair type of injustice and the unfair way of being unjust are not the same as 15 the lawless type, but differ as parts from wholes. For unfair injustice is a part of the whole of injustice, and, similarly, fair justice is a part of the whole of justice. Hence we must describe special as well as general justice and injustice, and equally this way of being just or unjust.

20 Let us, then, set aside the type of justice and injustice that accords with the whole of virtue, justice being the exercise of the whole of virtue, and injustice of the whole of vice, in relation to another. And it is evident how we must distinguish the way of being just or unjust that accords with this type of justice and injustice. For most lawful actions, we might say, are those produced by virtue as a whole; for the law prescribes living in accord with each virtue, and forbids living in 25 accord with each vice. Moreover, the actions producing the whole of virtue are the lawful actions that the laws prescribe for education promoting the common good. We must wait till later, however, to determine whether the education that makes an individual an unqualifiedly good man is a task for political science or for another science; for, presumably, being a good man is not the same as being every sort of good citizen.

30 Special justice, however, and the corresponding way of being just have one species that is found in the distribution of honors or wealth or anything else that can be divided among members of a community who share in a political system; for here it is possible 1131a for one member to have a share equal or unequal to another's. A second species concerns rectification in transactions.

This second species has two parts, since one sort of transaction is voluntary, and one involuntary. Voluntary transactions (for instance, selling, buying, lending, 5 pledging, renting, depositing, hiring out) are so called because their principle is voluntary. Among involuntary transactions some are secret (for instance, theft, adultery, poisoning, pimping, slave-deception, murder by treachery, false witness), whereas others involve force (for instance, imprisonment, murder, plunder, mutilation, slander, insult).

7

One part of the politically just is natural, and the other 1134b part legal. The natural has the same validity every- 20 where alike, independent of its seeming so or not. The legal originally makes no difference [whether it is done] one way or another, but makes a difference whenever people have laid down the rule—that a mina is the price of a ransom, for instance, or that a goat rather than two sheep should be sacrificed. The legal also includes laws passed for particular cases (for instance, that sacrifices should be offered to Brasidas)[21] and enactments by decree.

Now some people think everything just is merely 25 legal. For the natural is unchangeable and equally valid everywhere—fire, for instance, burns both here and in Persia—whereas they see that the just changes [from city to city].

This is not so, though in a way it is so. With us, though presumably not at all with the gods, there is 30 such a thing as the natural, but still all is changeable; despite the change there is such a thing as what is natural and what is not.

Then what sort of thing, among those that [are changeable and hence] admit of being otherwise, is natural, and what sort is not natural, but legal and conventional, if both natural and legal are changeable? It is clear in other cases also, and the same distinction [between the natural and the unchangeable] will apply; for the right hand, for instance, is naturally superior, even though it is possible for every- 35 one to become ambidextrous.

The sorts of things that are just by convention 1135a and expediency are like measures. For measures for wine and for corn are not of equal size everywhere, but in wholesale markets they are bigger, and in retail smaller. Similarly, the things that are just by human [enactment] and not by nature differ from place to 5 place, since political systems also differ. Still, only one system is by nature the best everywhere. . . .

21. [Regarding Brasidas, see Plato's *Symposium*, n.60.]

10

1137a The next task is to discuss how decency is related to justice and how the decent is related to the just. For on examination they appear as neither the same without qualification nor as states of different kinds. Sometimes we praise what is decent and the decent 35 person, so that even when we praise someone for 1137b other things we transfer the term 'decent' and use it instead of 'good,' making it clear that what is more decent is better. But sometimes, when we reason about the matter, it appears absurd for what is decent to be something apart from what is just, and still praiseworthy. For [apparently] either what is just is not excellent or what is decent is not excellent, if it is 5 something other than what is just; or else, if they are both excellent, they are the same.

These, then, are roughly the claims that raise the puzzle about the decent; but they are all correct in a way, and none is contrary to any other. For the decent 10 is better than one way of being just, but it is still just, and not better than the just by being a different kind of thing. Hence the same thing is just and decent; while both are excellent, what is decent is superior.

The puzzle arises because the decent is just, but is not the legally just, but a rectification of it. This is because all law is universal, but in some areas no 15 universal rule can be correct; and so where a universal rule has to be made, but cannot be correct, the law chooses the [universal rule] that is usually [correct], well aware of the error being made. And the law is no less correct on this account; for the source of the error is not the law or the legislator, but the nature of the object itself, since that is what the subject matter of actions is bound to be like.

20 And so, whenever the law makes a universal rule, but in this particular case what happens violates the [intended scope of] the universal rule, on this point the legislator falls short, and has made an error by making an unqualified rule. Then it is correct to rectify the deficiency; this is what the legislator would have said himself if he had been present there, and what he would have prescribed, had he known, in his legislation.

25 That is why the decent is just, and better than a certain way of being just—not better than the unqualifiedly just, but better than the error that results from the omission of any qualification [in the rule]. And this is the nature of the decent—rectification of law insofar as the universality of law makes it deficient.

This is also the reason why not everything is guided by law. For on some matters legislation is impossible, and so a decree is needed. For the standard applied 30 to the indefinite is itself indefinite, as the lead standard is in Lesbian[22] building, where it is not fixed, but adapts itself to the shape of the stone; similarly, a decree is adapted to fit its objects.

It is clear from this what is decent, and clear that it is just, and better than a certain way of being just. It 35 is also evident from this who the decent person is; for he is the one who decides on and does such actions, 1138a not an exact stickler for justice in the bad way, but taking less than he might even though he has the law on his side. This is the decent person, and his state is decency; it is a sort of justice, and not some state different from it.

BOOK VI

1

Since we have said previously that we must choose 1138b the intermediate condition, not the excess or the deficiency, 20 and that the intermediate condition is as the correct reason says, let us now determine what it says. For in all the states of character we have mentioned, as well as in the others, there is a target that the person who has reason focuses on and so tightens or relaxes; and there is a definition of the means, which we say are between excess and deficiency because 25 they accord with the correct reason.

To say this is admittedly true, but it is not at all clear. For in other pursuits directed by a science, it is equally true that we must labor and be idle neither too much nor too little, but the intermediate amount prescribed by correct reason. But knowing only this, 30 we would be none the wiser about, for instance, the medicines to be applied to the body, if we were told we must apply the ones that medical science 35 prescribes and in the way that the medical scientist applies them.

That is why our account of the states of the soul, in the same way, must not only be true as far as it has

22. [Lesbos, a large, fertile island in the Aegean Sea near Turkey, was a brilliant cultural center.]

gone, but we must also determine what the correct reason is, that is to say, what its definition is.

35 After we divided the virtues of the soul, we said that 1139a some are virtues of character and some of thought. And so, having finished our discussion of the virtues of character, let us now discuss the others as follows, after speaking first about the soul.

5 Previously, then, we said there are two parts of the soul, one that has reason, and one nonrational. Now we should divide in the same way the part that has reason. Let us assume there are two parts that have reason: with one we study beings whose principles do not admit of being otherwise than they are, and with the other we study beings whose principles admit of being otherwise. For when the beings are of different 10 kinds, the parts of the soul naturally suited to each of them are also of different kinds, since the parts possess knowledge by being somehow similar and appropriate [to their objects].

Let us call one of these the scientific part, and the other the rationally calculating part; for deliberating is the same as rationally calculating, and no one deliberates about what cannot be otherwise. Hence 15 the rationally calculating part is one part of the part of the soul that has reason.

Hence we should find the best state of the scientific part and the best state of the rationally calculating part; for this state is the virtue of each of them. Now a thing's virtue is relative to its own proper function, [and so we must consider the function of each part].

2

There are three [capacities] in the soul—sense perception, understanding, desire—that control action and truth. Of these three, sense perception is clearly not the principle of any action, since beasts 20 have perception, but no share in action.

As assertion and denial are to thought, so pursuit and avoidance are to desire. Now virtue of character is a state that decides; and decision is a deliberative desire. If, then, the decision is excellent, the reason must be true and the desire correct, so that 25 what reason asserts is what desire pursues. This, then, is thought and truth concerned with action. The thought concerned with study, not with action or production, has its good or bad state in being true or false; for truth is the function of whatever thinks. But the function of what thinks about action is truth 30 agreeing with correct desire.

The principle of an action—the source of motion, not the goal—is decision; the principle of decision is desire and goal-directed reason. That is why decision requires understanding and thought, and also a state 35 of character; for acting well or badly requires both thought and character.

Thought by itself moves nothing; what moves us is goal-directed thought concerned with action. For this 1139b thought is also the principle of productive thought; for every producer in his production aims at some [further] goal, and the unqualified goal is not the product, which is only the [qualified] goal of some [production], and aims at some [further] goal. [An unqualified goal is] what we achieve in *action*, since acting well is the goal, and desire is for the goal. That is why decision is either understanding combined 5 with desire or desire combined with thought; and this is the sort of principle that a human being is.

We do not decide to do what is already past; no one decides, for instance, to have sacked Troy. For neither do we deliberate about what is past, but only about what will be and admits of being or not being; and what is past does not admit of not having happened. That is why Agathon is correct to say 'Of this alone 10 even a god is deprived—to make what is all done to have never happened.'[23]

The function of each of the understanding parts, then, is truth. And so the virtues of each part will be the states that best direct it toward the truth.

3

Then let us begin again, and discuss these states of 15 the soul. Let us say, then, that there are five states in which the soul grasps the truth in its affirmation or denials. These are craft, scientific knowledge, prudence, wisdom, and understanding; for belief and supposition admit of being false.

What science is, is evident from the following, if we must speak exactly and not be guided by [mere] 20 similarities. For we all suppose that what we know scientifically does not even admit of being otherwise; and whenever that admits of being otherwise escapes

23. [Agathon was a fifth-century B.C. Athenian poet.]

observation, we do not notice whether it is or is not, [and hence we do not know about it]. Hence what is known scientifically is by necessity. Hence it is everlasting; for the things that are by unqualified necessity are all everlasting, and everlasting things are ingenerable and indestructible.

Further, every science seems to be teachable, and what is scientifically knowable is learnable. But all teaching is from what is already known, as we also say in the *Analytics*; for some teaching is through induction, some by deduction, [which both require previous knowledge]. Induction [leads to] the principle, i.e., the universal, whereas deduction proceeds from the universal. Hence deduction has principles from which it proceeds and which are not themselves [reached] by deduction. Hence they are [reached] by induction.

Scientific knowledge, then, is a demonstrative state, and has all the other features that in the *Analytics* we add to the definition. For one has scientific knowledge whenever one has the appropriate sort of confidence, and knows the principles; for if one does not know them better than the conclusion, one will have scientific knowledge [only] coincidentally.

So much for a definition of scientific knowledge.

5

1140a25 To grasp what prudence is, we should first study the sort of people we call prudent. It seems proper to a prudent person to be able to deliberate finely about things that are good and beneficial for himself, not about some restricted area—about what sorts of things promote health or strength, for instance—but about what sorts of things promote living well in general.

A sign of this is the fact that we call people prudent about some [restricted area] whenever they calculate well to promote some excellent end, in an area where there is no craft. Hence where [living well] as a whole is concerned, the deliberative person will also be prudent.

Now no one deliberates about things that cannot be otherwise or about things that cannot be achieved in his action. Hence, if science involves demonstration, but there is no demonstration of anything whose principles admit of being otherwise (since every such *1140b* thing itself admits of being otherwise); and if we cannot deliberate about things that are by necessity; it follows that prudence is not science nor yet craft knowledge. It is not science, because what is achievable in action admits of being otherwise; and it is not craft knowledge, because action and production belong to different kinds.

The remaining possibility, then, is that prudence is a state grasping the truth, involving reason, concerned with action about things that are good or bad for a human being. For production has its end in something other than itself, but action does not, since its end is acting well itself.

That is why Pericles[24] and such people are the ones whom we regard as prudent, because they are able to study what is good for themselves and for human beings; we think that household managers and politicians are such people.

This is also how we come to give temperance (*sōphrosunē*) its name, because we think that it preserves prudence (*sōzousan tēn phronēsin*). It preserves the [right] sort of supposition. For the sort of supposition that is corrupted and perverted by the pleasant or painful is not every sort—not, for instance, the supposition that the triangle does or does not have two right angles—but suppositions about what is achievable in action. For the principles of things achievable in action are their goal, but if someone is corrupted because of pleasure or pain, no [appropriate] principle can appear to him, and it cannot appear that this is the right goal and cause of all his choice and action; for vice corrupts the principle. And so prudence must be a state grasping the truth, involving reason, and concerned with action about human goods.

Moreover, there is virtue [or vice in the use] of craft, but not [in the use] of prudence. Further, in a craft, someone who makes errors voluntarily is more choiceworthy; but with prudence, as with the virtues, the reverse is true. Clearly, then, prudence is a virtue, not craft knowledge.

There are two parts of the soul that have reason. Prudence is a virtue of one of them, of the part that has belief; for belief is concerned, as prudence is, with what admits of being otherwise.

Moreover, it is not only a state involving reason. A

24. [Pericles (c. 495–429 B.C.), the eminent Athenian statesman, was renowned for his incorruptible character and the wisdom of his policies. He was a staunch defender of democracy and a patron of the arts.]

sign of this is the fact that such a state can be forgotten, but prudence cannot.

6

Scientific knowledge is supposition about universals, things that are by necessity. Further, everything demonstrable and every science have principles, since scientific knowledge involves reason. Hence there can be neither scientific knowledge nor craft knowledge nor prudence about the principles of what is scientifically known. For what is scientifically known is demonstrable, [but the principles are not]; and craft and prudence are about what admits of being otherwise. Nor is wisdom [exclusively] about principles; for it is proper to the wise person to have a demonstration of some things.

[The states of the soul] by which we always grasp the truth and never make mistakes, about what can or cannot be otherwise, are scientific knowledge, prudence, wisdom, and understanding. But none of the first three—prudence, scientific knowledge, wisdom—is possible about principles. The remaining possibility, then, is that we have understanding about principles.

7

We ascribe wisdom in crafts to the people who have the most exact expertise in the crafts. For instance, we call Pheidias a wise stoneworker and Polycleitus a wise bronze worker; and by wisdom we signify precisely virtue in a craft. But we also think some people are wise in general, not wise in some [restricted] area, or in some other [specific] way (as Homer says in the *Margites*: 'The gods did not make him a digger or a ploughman or wise in anything else'). Clearly, then, wisdom is the most exact [form] of scientific knowledge.

Hence the wise person must not only know what is derived from the principles of a science, but also grasp the truth about the principles. Therefore wisdom is understanding plus scientific knowledge; it is scientific knowledge of the most honorable things that has received [understanding as] its coping stone.

For it would be absurd for someone to think that political science or prudence is the most excellent science; for the best thing in the universe is not a human being [and the most excellent science must be of the best things].

Moreover, if what is good and healthy for human beings and for fish is not the same, whereas what is white or straight is always the same, everyone would also say that the content of wisdom is the same in every case, but the content of prudence is not. For the agent they would call prudent is the one who studies well each question about his own [good], and he is the one to whom they would entrust such questions. That is why prudence is also ascribed to some of the beasts, the ones that are evidently capable of forethought about their own life.

It is also evident that wisdom is not the same as political science. For if people are to say that science about what is beneficial to themselves [as human beings] counts as wisdom, there will be many types of wisdom [corresponding to the different species of animals]. For if there is no one medical science about all beings, there is no one science about the good of all animals, but a different science about each specific good. [Hence there will be many types of wisdom, contrary to our assumption that it has always been the same content.] It does not matter if human beings are the best among the animals; for there are other beings of a far more divine nature than human beings—most evidently, for instance, the beings composing the universe.

What we have said makes it clear that wisdom is both scientific knowledge and understanding about the things that are by nature most honorable. That is why people say that Anaxagoras[25] or Thales[26] or that sort of person is wise, but not prudent, whenever they see that he is ignorant of what benefits himself. And so they say that what he knows is extraordinary, amazing, difficult, and divine, but useless, because it is not human goods that he looks for.

Prudence, by contrast, is about human concerns, about things open to deliberation. For we say that deliberating well is the function of the prudent person more than anyone else; but no one deliberates about things that cannot be otherwise, or about things lacking any goal that is a good achievable in action. The unqualifiedly good deliberator is the one whose aim accords with rational calculation in pursuit of the best good for a human being that is achievable in action.

Nor is prudence about universals only. It must

25. [Regarding Anaxagoras, see Plato's *Apology*, n.7.]

26. [Regarding Thales, see Aristotle's *Metaphysics*, n.3.]

also acquire knowledge of particulars, since it is concerned with action and action is about particulars. That is why in other areas also some people who lack knowledge but have experience are better in action than others who have knowledge. For someone who 20 knows that light meats are digestible and [hence] healthy, but not which sorts of meats are light, will not produce health; the one who knows that bird meats are light and healthy will be better at producing health. And since prudence is concerned with action, it must possess both [the universal and the particular knowledge] or the [particular] more [than the universal]. Here too, however, [as in medicine] there is a ruling [science].

8

Political science and prudence are the same state, but their being is not the same.

25 One type of prudence about the city is the ruling part; this is legislative science. The type concerned with particulars [often] monopolizes the name 'political science' that [properly] applies to both types in common. This type is concerned with action and deliberation, since [it is concerned with decrees and] the decree is to be acted on as the last thing [reached in deliberation]. Hence these people are the only ones who are said to be politically active; for these are the only ones who put [political science] into practice, as hand-craftsmen put [a craft] into practice.

30 Similarly, prudence concerned with the individual himself seems most of all to be counted as prudence; and this [type of prudence often] monopolizes the name 'prudence' that [properly] applies [to all types] in common. Of the other types, one is household science, another legislative, another political, one type of which is deliberative and another judicial.

In fact knowledge of what is [good] for oneself is 1142a one species [of prudence]. But there is much difference [in opinions] about it. The one who knows about himself, and spends his time on his own concerns, seems to be prudent, while politicians seem to be too active. Hence Euripides says, 'Surely I cannot be prudent, since I could have been inactive, 5 numbered among all the many in the army, and have had an equal share. . . . For those who go too far and are too active. . . .' For people seek what is good for themselves, and suppose that this [inactivity] is the right action [to achieve their good]. Hence this belief has led to the view that these are the prudent people. Presumably, however, one's own welfare requires household management and a political system. Further, [another reason for the difference of opinion 10 is that] it is unclear, and should be examined, how one must manage one's own affairs.

A sign of what has been said [about the unclarity of what prudence requires] is the fact that whereas young people become accomplished in geometry and mathematics, and wise within these limits, prudent young people do not seem to be found. The reason is that prudence is concerned with particulars as well as universals, and particulars become known from expe- 15 rience, but a young person lacks experience, since some length of time is needed to produce it.

Indeed [to understand the difficulty and importance of experience] we might consider why a child can become accomplished in mathematics, but not in wisdom or natural science. Surely it is because mathematical objects are reached through abstraction, whereas in these other cases the principles are reached from experience. Young people, then, [lacking experience], have no real conviction in these 20 other sciences, but only say the words, whereas the nature of mathematical objects is clear to them.

Further, [prudence is difficult because it is deliberative and deliberation may be in error about either the universal or the particular. For [we may wrongly suppose] either that all sorts of heavy water are bad or that this water is heavy.

It is apparent that prudence is not scientific knowl- 25 edge; for, as we said, it concerns the last thing [i.e., the particular], since this is what is achievable in action. Hence it is opposite to understanding. For understanding is about the [first] terms, [those] that have no account of them; but prudence is about the last thing, an object of perception, not of scientific knowledge. This is not the perception of special objects, but the sort by which we perceive that the last among mathematical objects is a triangle; for it will 30 stop there too. This is another species [of perception that perception of special objects]; but it is still perception more than prudence is.

12

One might, however, go through some puzzles about what use they are. For wisdom is not concerned with any sort of coming into being, and hence will not study any source of human happiness. Admittedly, prudence will study this; but what do we need it for? For knowledge of what is healthy or fit (i.e., of what results from the state of health, not of what produces it) makes us no readier to act appropriately if we are already healthy; for having the science of medicine or gymnastics makes us no readier to act appropriately. Similarly, prudence is the science of what is just and what is fine, and what is good for a human being; but this is how the good man acts; and if we are already good, knowledge of them makes us no readier to act appropriately, since virtues are states [activated in actions].

If we concede that prudence is not useful for this, should we say it is useful for becoming good? In that case it will be no use to those who are already excellent. Nor, however, will it be any use to those who are not. For it will not matter to them whether they have it themselves or take the advice of others who have it. The advice of others will be quite adequate for us, just as it is with health: we wish to be healthy, but still do not learn medical science.

Besides, it would seem absurd for prudence, inferior as it is to wisdom, to control it [as a superior. But this will be the result], since the science that produces also rules and prescribes about its product.

We must discuss these questions; for so far we have only raised the puzzles about them.

First of all, let us state that both prudence and wisdom must be choiceworthy in themselves, even if neither produces anything at all; for each is the virtue of one of the two [rational] parts [of the soul].

Secondly, they do produce something. Wisdom produces happiness, not in the way that medical science produces health, but in the way that health produces [health]. For since wisdom is a part of virtue as a whole, it makes us happy because it is a state that we possess and activate.

Further, we fulfill our function insofar as we have prudence and virtue of character; for virtue makes the goal correct, and prudence makes the things promoting the goal [correct]. The fourth part of the soul, the nutritive part, has no such virtue [related to our function], since no action is up to it to do or not to do.

To answer the claim that prudence will make us no better at achieving fine and just actions, we must begin from a little further back [in our discussion]. We begin here: we say that some people who do just actions are not yet thereby just, if, for instance, they do the actions prescribed by the laws of either unwillingly or because of ignorance or because of some other end, not because of the actions themselves, even though they do the right actions, those that the excellent person ought to do. Equally, however, it would seem to be possible for someone to do each type of action in the state that makes him a good person, that is to say, because of decision and for the sake of the actions themselves.

Now virtue makes the decision correct; but the actions that are naturally to be done to fulfill the decision are the concern not of virtue, but of another capacity. We must grasp them more perspicuously before continuing our discussion.

There is a capacity, called cleverness, which is such as to be able to do the actions that tend to promote whatever goal is assumed and to attain them. If, then, the goal is fine, cleverness is praiseworthy, and if the goal is base, cleverness is unscrupulousness. That is why both prudent and unscrupulous people are called clever.

Prudence is not cleverness, though it requires this capacity. [Prudence,] this eye of the soul, requires virtue in order to reach its fully developed state, as we have said and as is clear. For inferences about actions have a principle, 'Since the end and the best good is this sort of thing' (whatever it actually is—let it be any old thing for the sake of argument). And this [best good] is apparent only to the good person; for vice perverts us and produces false views about the principles of actions. Evidently, then, we cannot be prudent without being good.

13

We must, then, also examine virtue over again. For virtue is similar [in this way] to prudence; as prudence is related to cleverness, not the same but similar, so natural virtue is related full virtue. For each of us seems to possess his type of character to some extent by nature; for in fact we are just, brave, prone to temperance, or have another feature, immediately from birth. But still we look for some further condition to be full goodness, and we expect to possess these features in another way. For these natural states belong to children and to beasts as well [as to 10 adults], but without understanding they are evidently harmful. At any rate, this much would seem to be clear: Just as a heavy body moving around unable to see suffers a heavy fall because it has no sight, so it is with virtue. [A naturally well-endowed person without understanding will harm himself.]

But if someone acquires understanding, he improves in his actions; and the state he now has, though still similar [to the natural one], will be fully virtue. And so, just as there are two sorts of conditions, 15 cleverness and prudence, in the part of the soul that has belief, so also there are two in the part that has character, natural virtue and full virtue. And of these full virtue cannot be acquired without prudence.

That is why some say that all the virtues are [instances of] prudence, and why the inquires 20 Socrates used to undertake were in one way correct, and in another way in error. For insofar as he thought all the virtues are [instances of] prudence, he was in error; but insofar as he thought they all require prudence, what he used to say was right.

Here is a sign of this: Whenever people now define virtue, they all say what state it is and what it is related to, and then add that it is the state in accord with the correct reason. Now the correct reason is the reason in accord with prudence; it would seem, then, that 25 they all in a way intuitively believe that the state in accord with prudence is virtue.

But we must make a slight change. For it is not merely the state in accord with the correct reason, but the state involving the correct reason, that is virtue. And it is prudence that is the correct reason in this area. Socrates, then, used to think the virtues are [instances of] reason because he thought they are 30 all [instances of] knowledge, whereas we think they involve reason.

What we have said, then, makes it clear that we cannot be fully good without prudence, or prudent without virtue of character. And in this way we can also solve the dialectical argument that someone might use to show that the virtues are separated from one another. For, [it is argued], since the same person 35 is not naturally best suited for all the virtues, someone will already have one virtue before he gets another. This is indeed possible in the case of the natural virtues. It is not possible, however, in the case of the [full] virtues that someone must have to be called *1145a* good without qualification; for one has all the virtues if and only if one has prudence, which is a single state.

And it is clear that, even if prudence were useless in action, we would need it because it is the virtue of this part of the soul, and because the decision will not be correct without prudence or without virtue— 5 for [virtue] makes us achieve the end, whereas [prudence] makes us achieve the things that promote the end.

Moreover, prudence does not control wisdom or the better part of the soul, just as medical science does not control health. For medical science does not use health, but only aims to bring health into being; hence it prescribes for the sake of health, but does not 10 prescribe to health. Besides, [saying that prudence controls wisdom] would be like saying that political science rules the gods because it prescribes about everything in the city.

BOOK VII

1

Let us now make a new start, and say that there are 15 three conditions of character to be avoided—vice, incontinence, and bestiality. The contraries of two of these are clear; we call one virtue and the other continence.

The contrary to bestiality is most suitably called 20 virtue superior to us, a heroic, indeed divine, sort of virtue. Thus Homer made Priam say that Hector was remarkably good; 'nor did he look as though he were the child of a mortal man, but of a god.'[27] And so, if, as they say, human beings become gods because of exceedingly great virtue, this is clearly the sort of state 25 that would be opposite to the bestial state. For indeed, just as a beast has neither virtue nor vice, so neither does a god, but the god's state is more honorable than virtue, and the beast's belongs to some kind different from vice.

Now it is rare that a divine man exists. (This is what the Spartans habitually call him; whenever they very much admire someone, they say he is a divine 30 man.) Similarly, the bestial person is also rare among

27. [The quotation is from the *Iliad*.]

human beings. He is most often found in foreigners; but some bestial features also result from diseases and deformities. We also use 'bestial' as a term of reproach for people whose vice exceeds the human level.

We must make some remarks about this condition later. We have discussed vice earlier. We must now discuss incontinence, softness, and self-indulgence, and also continence and resistance; for we must not suppose that continence and incontinence are concerned with the same states as virtue and vice, or that they belong to a different kind.

As in the other cases, we must set out the appearances, and first of all go through the puzzles. In this way we must prove the common beliefs about these ways of being affected—ideally, all the common beliefs, but if not all, most of them, and the most important. For if the objections are solved, and the common beliefs are left, it will be an adequate proof.

Continence and resistance seem to be good and praiseworthy conditions, whereas incontinence and softness seem to be base and blameworthy conditions. The continent person seems to be the same as one who abides by his rational calculation; and the incontinent person seems to be the same as one who abandons it. The incontinent person knows that his actions are base, but does them because of his feelings, whereas the continent person knows that his appetites are base, but because of reason does not follow them.

People think the temperate person is continent and resistant. Some think that every continent and resistant person is temperate, while others do not. Some people say the incontinent person is intemperate and the intemperate incontinent, with no distinction; others say they are different.

Sometimes it is said that a prudent person cannot be incontinent; but sometimes it is said that some people are prudent and clever, but still incontinent.

Further, people are called incontinent about spirit, honor, and gain.

These, then, are the things that are said.

2

We might be puzzled about what sort of correct supposition someone has when he acts incontinently.

First of all, some say he cannot have knowledge [at the time he acts]. For it would be terrible, Socrates used to think, for knowledge to be in someone, but mastered by something else, and dragged around like a slave. For Socrates used to oppose the account [of incontinence] in general, in the belief that there is no incontinence; for no one, in Socrates' view, supposes while he acts that his action conflicts with what is best; our action conflicts with what is best only because we are ignorant [of the conflict].

This argument, then, contradicts things that appear manifestly. If ignorance causes the incontinent person to be affected as he is, we must look for the type of ignorance that it turns out to be; for it is evident, at any rate, that before he is affected the person who acts incontinently does not think [he should do the action he eventually does].

Some people concede some of [Socrates' points], but reject some of them. For they agree that nothing is superior to knowledge, but they deny the claim that no one's action conflicts with what has seemed better to him. That is why they say that when the incontinent person is overcome by pleasure he has only belief, not knowledge.

If, however, he has belief, not knowledge, and the supposition that resists is not strong, but only a weak one, such as people have when they are in doubt, we will pardon failure to abide by these beliefs against strong appetites. In fact, however, we do not pardon vice or any other blameworthy condition [and incontinence is one of these].

Then is it prudence that resists, since it is the strongest? This is absurd. For on this view the same person will be both prudent and incontinent; but no one would say that the prudent person is the sort to do the worst actions willingly. Besides, we have shown earlier that the prudent person acts [on his knowledge], since he is concerned with the last things, [i.e., particulars] and that he has the other virtues.

Further, if the continent person must have strong and base appetites, the temperate person will not be continent nor the continent person temperate. For the temperate person is not the sort to have either excessive or base appetites; but [the continent person] must have both. For if his appetites are good, the state that prevents him from following them must be base, so that not all continence is excellent. If, however, the appetites are weak and not base, continence is nothing impressive; and if they are base and weak, it is nothing great.

Further, if continence makes someone prone to abide by every belief, it is bad, if, for instance, it makes him abide by a false as well [as true] belief. And if incontinence makes someone prone to abandon every belief, there will be an excellent type of incontinence. Take, for instance, Neoptolemus in Sophocles' *Philoctetes*. For he is praiseworthy for his failure to abide by [his promise to tell the lies] that Odysseus had persuaded him [to tell]; [he breaks his promise] because he feels pain at lying. 20

Further, the sophistical argument is a puzzle. For [the Sophists] wish to refute an [opponent, by showing] that his views have paradoxical results, so that they will be clever in encounters. Hence the inference that results is a puzzle; for thought is tied up, whenever it does not want to stand still, because the conclusion is displeasing, but it cannot advance, because it cannot solve the argument. A certain argument, then, concludes that foolishness combined with incontinence is virtue. For incontinence makes someone act contrary to what he supposes [is right]; but since he supposes that good things are bad and that it is wrong to do them, he will do the good actions, not the bad. 25 30

Further, someone who acts to pursue what is pleasant because this is what he is persuaded and decides to do seems to be better than someone who acts not because of rational calculation, but because of incontinence. For the first person is the easier to cure, because he might be persuaded to act otherwise; but the incontinent person illustrates the proverb 'If water chokes us, what must we drink to wash it down?' For if he had been persuaded to do the action he does, he would have stopped when he was persuaded to act otherwise; but in fact, though already persuaded to act otherwise, he still acts [wrongly]. 35 *1146b*

Further, is there incontinence and continence about everything? If so, who is simply incontinent? For no one has all the types of incontinence, but we say that some people are simply incontinent. 5

These, then, are the sorts of puzzles that arise. We must undermine some of these claims, and leave others intact; for the solution of the puzzle is the discovery [of what we are seeking].

3

First, then, we must examine whether the incontinent has knowledge or not, and in what way he has it. Second, what should we take to be the range of incontinence and continence—every pleasure and pain, or some definite subclass? Are the continent and the resistant person the same or different? Similarly we must deal with the other questions that are relevant to this study. 10

We begin by examining whether continence and incontinence differ from other things by their range or by their attitudes. In other words, is the incontinent person incontinent because of a specific range of actions, or because of a specific attitude, or because of both? Next, is there incontinence and continence about everything, or not? 15

For the simply incontinent person is not incontinent about everything, but he has the same range as the intemperate person. Nor is he incontinent simply by being inclined toward these things—that would make incontinence the same as intemperance. Rather, he is incontinent by being inclined toward them in this way. For the intemperate person acts on decision when he is led on, since he thinks it is right in every case to pursue the pleasant thing at hand; the incontinent person, however, thinks it is wrong to pursue this pleasant things, yet still pursues it. 20

It is claimed that the incontinent person's action conflicts with the true belief, not with knowledge. But whether it is knowledge or belief that he has does not matter for this argument. For some people with belief are in no doubt, but think they have exact knowledge. 25

If, then, it is the weakness of their conviction that makes people with belief, not people with knowledge, act in conflict with their supposition, it follows that knowledge will [for these purposes] be no different from belief; for, as Heraclitus makes clear, some people's convictions about what they believe are no weaker than other people's convictions about what they know. 30

But we speak of knowing in two ways; we ascribe it both to someone who has it without using it and to someone who is using it. Hence it will matter whether someone has the knowledge that his action is wrong, without attending to his knowledge, or he both has it and attends to it. For this second case seems 35 extraordinary, but wrong action when he does not attend to his knowledge does not seem extraordinary.

Further, since there are two types of premises, someone's action may well conflict with his knowledge if he has both types of premises, but uses only the universal premise and not the particular premise. For it is particulars that are achievable in action. There are also different types of universal, one type referring to the agent himself, and the other referring to the object. Perhaps, for instance, someone knows that dry things benefit every human being, and that he himself is a human being, or that this sort of thing is dry; but he either does not have or does not activate the knowledge that this particular thing is of this sort. These ways [of knowing and not knowing], then, make such a remarkable difference that it seems quite intelligible [for someone acting against his knowledge] to have the one sort of knowledge, but astounding if he has the other sort.

Further, human beings may have knowledge in a way different from those we have described. For we see that having without using includes different types of having; hence some people, such as those asleep or mad or drunk, both have knowledge in a way and do not have it. Moreover, this is the condition of those affected by strong feelings. For spirited reactions, sexual appetites, and some conditions of this sort clearly [both disturb knowledge and] disturb the body as well, and even produce fits of madness in some people. Clearly, then [since incontinents are also affected by strong feelings], we should say that they have knowledge in a way similar to these people.

Saying the words that come from knowledge is no sign [of fully having it]. For people affected in these ways even recite demonstrations and verses of Empedocles. And those who have just learned something do not yet know it, though they string the words together; for it must grow into them, and this takes time. And so we must suppose that those who are acting incontinently also say the words in the way that actors do.

Further, we may also look at the cause in the following way, referring to [human] nature. For one belief is universal; the other is about particulars, and because they are particulars, perception controls them. And in the cases where these two beliefs result in one belief, it is necessary, in one case, for the soul to affirm what has been concluded, but, in the case of beliefs about production, to act at once on what has been concluded. If, for instance, everything sweet must be tasted, and this, some one particular thing, is sweet, it is necessary for someone who is able and unhindered also to act on this at the same time.

Suppose, then, that someone has the universal belief hindering him from tasting; he has the second belief, that everything sweet is pleasant and this is sweet, and this belief is active; but it turns out that appetite is present in him. The belief, then, [that is formed from the previous two beliefs] tells him to avoid this, but appetite leads him on, since it is capable of moving each of the [bodily] parts.

The result, then, is that in a way reason and belief make him act incontinently. The [second] belief is contrary to the correct reason, but only coincidentally, not in its own right. For the appetite, not the belief, is contrary [in its own right to the correct reason]. That is also why beasts are not incontinent, because they have no universal supposition, but [only] appearance and memory of particulars.

How is the ignorance resolved, so that the incontinent person recovers his knowledge? The same account that applies to someone drunk or asleep applies here too, and is not special to this way of being affected. We must hear it from the natural scientists.

Since the last premise is a belief about something perceptible, and controls action, this is what the incontinent person does not have when he is being affected. Or [rather] the way he has it is not knowledge of it, but, as we saw, [merely] saying the words, as the drunk says the words of Empedocles.

And since the last term does not seem to be universal, or expressive of knowledge in the same way as the universal term, even the result Socrates was looking for would seem to come about. For the knowledge that is present when someone is affected by incontinence, and that is dragged about because he is affected, is not the sort that seems to be fully knowledge, but it is only perceptual knowledge.

So much, then, for knowing and not knowing, and for how it is possible to know and still to act incontinently.

BOOK VIII

1

After that, the next topic is friendship; for it is a virtue, or involves virtue.

Further, it is most necessary for our life. For no one would choose to live without friends even if he had all the other goods. Indeed rich people and holders of powerful positions, even more than other people, seem to need friends. For how would one benefit from such prosperity if one had no opportunity for beneficence, which is most often displayed, and most highly praised, in relation to friends? And how would one guard and protect prosperity without friends, when it is all the more precarious the greater it is?

But in poverty also, and in the other misfortunes, people think friends are the only refuge. Moreover, the young need friends to keep them from error. The old need friends to care for them and support the actions that fail because of weakness. And those in their prime need friends to do fine actions; for 'when two go together . . . ,' they are more capable of understanding and acting.

Further, a parent would seem to have a natural friendship for a child, and a child for a parent, not only among human beings but also among birds and most kinds of animals. Members of the same species, and human beings most of all, have a natural friendship for each other; that is why we praise friends of humanity. And in our travels we can see how every human being is akin and beloved to a human being.

Moreover, friendship would seem to hold cities together, and legislators would seem to be more concerned about it than about justice. For concord would seem to be similar to friendship, and they aim at concord among all, while they try above all to expel civil conflict, which is enmity. Further, if people are friends, they have no need of justice, but if they are just they need friendship in addition; and the justice that is most just seems to belong to friendship.

But friendship is not only necessary, but also fine. For we praise lovers of friends, and having many friends seems to be a fine thing. Moreover, people think that the same people are good and also friends.

Still, there are quite a few disputed points about friendship.

For some hold it is a sort of similarity and that similar people are friends. Hence the sayings, 'similar to similar,' and 'birds of a feather,' and so on. On the other side, it is said that similar people are all like the proverbial potters, quarreling with each other.

On these questions some people inquire at a higher level, more proper to natural science. Euripides says that when earth gets dry it longs passionately for rain, and the holy heaven when filled with rain longs passionately to fall into the earth; and Heraclitus says that the opponent cooperates, the finest harmony arises from discordant elements, and all things come to be in struggle. Others, such as Empedocles,[28] oppose this view, and say that similar aims for similar.

Let us, then, leave aside the puzzles proper to natural science, since they are not proper to the present examination, and let us examine the puzzles that concern human [nature], and bear on characters and feelings. For instance, does friendship arise among all sorts of people, or can people not be friends if they are vicious? And is there one species of friendship, or are there more? Some people think there is only one species because friendship allows more and less. But here their confidence rests on an inadequate sign; for things of different species also allow more and less. We have spoken about these earlier.

2

Perhaps these questions will become clear once we find out what it is that is lovable. For, it seems, not everything is loved, but [only] the lovable, and this is either good or pleasant or useful. However, it seems that the useful is the source of some good or some pleasure; hence the good and the pleasant are lovable as ends.

Now do people love the good, or the good for themselves? For sometimes these conflict, and the same is true of the pleasant. Each one, it seems, loves the good for himself; and while the good is lovable without qualification, the lovable for each one is the good for himself. In fact, each one loves not what *is* good for him, but what *appears* good for him; but this will not matter, since [what appears good for him] will be what appears lovable.

There are these three causes, then, of love. Now love for an inanimate things is not called friendship, since there is no mutual loving, and no wishing of good to it. For it would presumably be ridiculous to wish good things to wine; the most you wish is its preservation so that you can have it. To a friend, however, it is said, you must wish goods for his own sake. If you wish good things in this way, but the same wish is

28. [Regarding Empedocles, see Plato's *Meno*, n.6.]

not returned by the other, you would be said to have [only] goodwill for the other. For friendship is said to be *reciprocated* goodwill.

But perhaps we should add that friends are aware of the reciprocated goodwill. For many a one has goodwill to people whom he has not seen but supposes to be decent or useful, and one of these might have the same goodwill toward him. These people, then, apparently have goodwill to each other, but how could we call them friends, given that they are unaware of their attitude to each other? [If they are to be friends], then, they must have goodwill to each other, wish goods and be aware of it, from one of the causes mentioned above.

3

Since these causes differ in species, so do the types of loving and types of friendship. Hence friendship has three species, corresponding to the three objects of love. For each object of love has a corresponding type of mutual loving, combined with awareness of it.

But those who love each other wish goods to each other [only] insofar as they love each other. Those who love each other for utility love the other not in his own right, but insofar as they gain some good for themselves from him. The same is true of those who love for pleasure; for they like a witty person not because of his character, but because he is pleasant to them.

Those who love for utility or pleasure, then, are fond of a friend because of what is good or pleasant for themselves, not insofar as the beloved is who he is, but insofar as he is useful or pleasant. Hence these friendships as well [as the friends] are coincidental, since the beloved is loved not insofar as he is who he is, but insofar as he provides some good or pleasure.

And so these sorts of friendships are easily dissolved, when the friends do not remain similar [to what they were]; for if someone is not longer pleasant or useful, the other stops loving him.

What is useful does not remain the same, but is different at different times. Hence, when the cause of their being friends is removed, the friendship is dissolved too, on the assumption that the friendship aims at these [useful results]. This sort of friendship seems to arise especially among older people, since at that age they pursue the advantageous, not the pleasant, and also among those in their prime or youth who pursue the expedient.

Nor do such people live together very much. For sometimes they do not even find each other pleasant. Hence they have no further need to meet in this way if they are not advantageous [to each other]; for each finds the other pleasant [only] to the extent that he expects some good from him. The friendship of hosts and guests is taken to be of this type too.

The cause of friendship between young people seems to be pleasure. For their lives are guided by their feelings, and they pursue above all what is pleasant for themselves and what is at hand. But as they grow up [what they find] pleasant changes too. Hence they are quick to become friends, and quick to stop; for their friendship shifts with [what they find] pleasant, and the change in such pleasure is quick. Young people are prone to erotic passion, since this mostly accords with feelings, and is caused by pleasure; that is why they love and quickly stop, often changing in a single day.

These people wish to spend their days together and to live together; for this is how they gain [the good things] corresponding to their friendship.

But complete friendship is the friendship of good people similar in virtue; for they wish goods in the same way to each other insofar as they are good, and they are good in their own right. [Hence they wish goods to each other for each other's own sake.] Now those who wish goods to their friend for the friend's own sake are friends most of all; for they have this attitude because of the friend himself, not coincidentally. Hence these people's friendship lasts as long as they are good; and virtue is enduring.

Each of them is both good without qualification and good for his friend, since good people are both good without qualification and advantageous for each other. They are pleasant in the same ways too, since good people are pleasant both without qualification and for each other. [They are pleasant for each other] because each person finds his own actions and actions of that kind pleasant, and the actions of good people are the same or similar.

It is reasonable that this sort of friendship is enduring, since it embraces in itself all the features that friends must have. For the cause of every friendship is good or pleasure, either unqualified or for the lover;

and every friendship accords with some similarity. And all the features we have mentioned are found in this friendship because of [the nature of] the friends themselves. For they are similar in this way [i.e., in being good]. Moreover, their friendship also has the other things—what is good without qualification and what is pleasant without qualification; and these are lovable most of all. Hence loving friendship are found most of all and at their best in these friends.

25 These kinds of friendships are likely to be rare, since such people are few. Further, they need time as well, to grow accustomed to each other; for, as the proverb says, they cannot know each other before they have shared their salt as often as it says, and they cannot accept each other or be friends until each appears lovable to the other and gains the other's 30 confidence. Those who are quick to treat each other in friendly ways wish to be friends, but are not friends, unless they are also lovable, and know this. For though the wish for friendship comes quickly, friendship does not.

9

1159b25 As we said at the beginning, friendship and justice would seem to be about the same things and to be found in the same people. For in every community there seems to be some sort of justice, and some type of friendship also. At any rate, fellow voyages and fellow soldiers are called friends, and so are members of other communities. And the extent of their commu- 30 nity is the extent of their friendship, since it is also the extent of the justice found there. The proverb 'What friends have is common' is correct, since friendship involves community.

But, whereas brothers and companions have everything in common, what people have in common in other types of community is limited, more in some communities and less in others, since some friend- 35 ships are also closer than others, some less close.

1160a What is just is also different, since it is not the same for parents toward children as for one brother toward another, and not the same for companions as for fellow citizens, and similarly with the other types of friendship. Similarly, what is unjust toward each of these is also different, and becomes more unjust as it is practiced on closer friends. It is more shocking, for 5 instance, to rob a companion of money than to rob a fellow citizen, to fail to help a brother than a stranger, and to strike one's father than anyone else. Justice also naturally increases with friendship, since it involves the same people and extends over an equal area.

All the communities [mentioned], however, would seem to be parts of the political community. 10 For people keep company for some advantage and to supply something contributing to their life. And the political community as well [as the others] seems both to have been originally formed and to endure for advantage; for legislators also aim at advantage, and the common advantage is said to be just.

Now the other types of community aim at partial 15 advantage. Sea travellers, for instance, seek the advantage proper to a journey, in making money or something like that, while fellow soldiers seek the advantage proper to war, desiring either money or victory or a city; and the same is true of fellow members of a tribe or deme. Some communities—religious societies and dining clubs—seem to arise for pleasure, 20 since these are, respectively, for religious sacrifices and for companionship.

But all these communities would seem to be subordinate to the political community, since it aims not at some advantage close at hand, but at advantage for the whole of life. . . . [We can see this in the arrangements that cities make for religious festivals. For] in performing sacrifices and arranging gather- 25 ings for these, people both accord honors to the gods and provide themselves with pleasant relaxations. For the long-established sacrifices and gatherings appear to take place after the harvesting of the crops, as a sort of first-fruits, since this was the time when people used to be most at leisure [and the time when relaxation would be most advantageous for the whole of life].

All the types of community, then, appear to be parts 30 of the political community, and these sorts of communities imply the appropriate sorts of friendships.

BOOK IX

4

1166a The defining features of friendship that are found in friendships to one's neighbors would seem to be derived from features of friendship toward oneself.

For a friend is taken to be someone who wishes and does goods or apparent goods to his friend for the 5 friend's own sake; or one who wishes the friend to be and to live for the friend's own sake—this is how mothers feel toward their children, and how friends who have been in conflict feel [toward each other]. Others take a friend to be one who spends his time with his friend, and makes the same choices; or one who shares his friend's distress and enjoyment—and this also is especially true of mothers. And people define friendship by one of these features.

10 Each of these features is found in the decent person's relation to himself, and it is found in other people, insofar as they suppose they are decent. As we have said, virtue and the excellent person would seem to be the standard in each case.

For the excellent person is of one mind with 15 himself, and desires the same things in his whole soul. Hence he wishes goods and apparent goods to himself, and achieves them in his actions, since it is proper to the good person to reach the good by his efforts. He wishes and does them for his own sake, since he does them for the sake of his thinking part, and that is what each person seems to be. Moreover, he wishes himself to live and to be preserved. And he wishes this for his rational part more than for any other part.

20 For being is a good for the good person, and each person wishes for goods for himself. And no one chooses to become another person even if that other will have every good when he has come into being; for, as it is, the god has the good [but no one chooses to be replaced by a god]. Rather [each of us chooses goods] on condition that he remains whatever he is; and each person would seem to be the understanding part, or that most of all. [Hence the good person wishes for goods for the understanding part.]

Further, such a person finds it pleasant to spend 25 time with himself, and so wishes to do it. For his memories of what he has done are agreeable, and his expectations for the future are good, and hence both are pleasant. And besides, his thought is well supplied with topics for study. Moreover, he shares his own distresses and pleasures, more than other people share theirs. For it is always the same thing that is painful or pleasant, not different things at different times. This is because he practically never regrets [what he has done].

The decent person, then, has each of these features 30 in relation to himself, and is related to his friend as he is to himself, since the friend is another himself. Hence friendship seems to be one of these features, and people with these features seem to be friends.

But is there friendship toward oneself, or not? Let us dismiss that question for the present. However, 35 there seems to be friendship insofar as someone is two or more parts. This seems to be true from what we have said, and because an extreme degree of friendship resembles one's friendship to oneself. *1166b*

The many, base though they are, also appear to have these features. But perhaps they share in them only insofar as they approve of themselves and suppose they are decent. For no one who is utterly 5 base and unscrupulous either has these features or appears to have them.

Indeed, even base people hardly have them. For they are at odds with themselves, and have an appetite for one thing and a wish for another, as incontinent people do. For they do not choose things that seem to be good for them, but instead choose pleasant things that are actually harmful; and cowardice or laziness 10 causes others to shrink from doing what they think best for themselves. And those who have done many terrible actions hate and shun life because of their vice, and destroy themselves.

Besides, vicious people seek others to pass their 15 days with, and shun themselves. For when they are by themselves they remember many disagreeable actions, and anticipate others in the future; but they manage to forget these in other people's company. These people have nothing lovable about them, and so have no friendly feelings for themselves.

Hence such a person does not share his own enjoy- 20 ments and distresses. For his soul is in conflict, and because he is vicious one part is distressed at being restrained, and another is pleased [by the intended action]; and so each part pulls in a different direction, as though they were tearing him apart. Even if he cannot be distressed and pleased at the same time, still he is soon distressed because he was pleased, and wishes these things had not become pleasant to him; 25 for base people are full of regret.

Hence the base person appears not to have a friendly attitude even toward himself, because he has nothing lovable about him.

If this state is utterly miserable, everyone should

earnestly shun vice and try to be decent; for that is how someone will have a friendly relation to himself and will become a friend to another.

7

1167b Benefactors seem to love their beneficiaries more than the beneficiaries love them [in return], and this is discussed as though it were an unreasonable thing 20 to happen. In most people's view, this is because the beneficiaries are debtors and the benefactors creditors: The debtor in a loan wishes the creditor did not exist, while the creditor even attends to the safety of the debtor. So also, then, a benefactor wants the 25 beneficiary to exist because he expects gratitude in return, whereas the beneficiary is not attentive about making the return.

Now Epicharmus[29] might say that most people say this because they 'take a bad person's point of view.' Still, it would seem to be a human point of view, since the many are indeed forgetful, and seek to receive benefits more than to give them.

However, it seems that the cause is more proper to 30 [human] nature, and the case of creditors is not even similar. For they do not love their debtors, but in wishing for their safety simply seek repayment. Benefactors, however, love and like their beneficiaries even if they are of no present or future use to them. The same is true of craftsmen; for each likes his own prod- 35 uct more than it would like him if it acquired a soul. 1168a Presumably this is true of poets most of all, since they dearly like their own poems, and are fond of them as though they were their children.

This, then, is what the case of the benefactor resem- 5 bles; here the beneficiary is his product, and hence he likes him more than the product likes its producer. The reason for this is that being is choiceworthy and lovable for all, and we are insofar as we are actualized, since we are insofar as we live and act. Now the product is, in a way, the producer in his actualization; hence the producer is fond of the product, because he loves his own being. This is natural, since what he is potentially is what the product indicates in actualization.

10 At the same time, the benefactor's action is fine for him, so that he finds enjoyment in the person he acts on; but the person acted on finds nothing fine in the agent, but only, at most, some advantage, which is less pleasant and lovable.

What is pleasant is actualization in the present, expectation for the future, and memory of the past; 15 but what is most pleasant is the [action we do] insofar as we are actualized, and this is also most lovable. For the benefactor, then, his product endures, since the fine is long-lasting; but for the person acted on, the useful passes away.

Besides, memory of fine things is pleasant, while memory of [receiving] useful things is not altogether pleasant, or is less pleasant—though the reverse would seem to be true for expectation.

Moreover, loving is like production, while being 20 loved is like being acted on; and [the benefactor's] love and friendliness are the result of his greater activity.

Further, everyone is fond of whatever has taken effort to produce; for instance, people who have made money themselves are fonder of it than people who have inherited it. And while receiving a benefit seems to take no effort, giving one is hard work. This is also 25 why mothers love their children more [than fathers do], since giving birth is more effort for them, and they know better that the children are theirs. And this also would seem to be proper to benefactors.

8

There is also a puzzle about whether one ought to love oneself or someone else most of all; for those who 30 like themselves most are criticized and denounced as self-lovers, as though this were something shameful. Indeed, the base person seems to go to every length for his own sake, and all the more the more vicious he is; hence he is accused, for instance, of doing nothing [for any end apart] from himself. The decent person, on the contrary, acts for what is fine, all the more the 35 better he is, and for his friend's sake, disregarding his own [interest].

The facts, however, conflict with these claims, and 1168b that is not unreasonable. For it is said that we must love most the friend who is most a friend; and one person is a friend to another most of all if he wishes goods to the other for the other's sake, even if no one will know about it. But these are features most of all of one's relation to oneself; and so too are all the other 5

29. [Epicharmus was a fifth-century-B.C. Sicilian comic poet.]

defining features of a friend, since we have said that all the features of friendship extend from oneself to others.

All the proverbs agree with this too, speaking, for instance, of 'one soul,' 'what friends have is common,' 'equality is friendship,' and 'the knee is closer than the shin.' For all these are true most of all in someone's relations with himself, since one is a friend to himself most of all. Hence he should also love himself most of all.

It is not surprising, then, that there is a puzzle about which view we ought to follow, since both inspire some confidence. Presumably, then, we must divide these sorts of arguments, and distinguish how far and in what ways those on each side are true. Perhaps, then, it will become clear, if we grasp how those on each side understand self-love.

Those who make self-love a matter for reproach ascribe it to those who award the biggest share in money, honors, and bodily pleasures to themselves. For these are the goods desired and eagerly pursued by the many on the assumption that they are the best. That is why they are also contested. Those who overreach for these goods gratify their appetites and in general their feelings and the nonrational part of the soul; and this is the character of the many. That is why the application of the term ['self-love'] is derived from the most frequent [kind of self-love], which is base. This type of self-lover, then, is justifiably reproached.

And plainly it is the person who awards himself these goods whom the many habitually call a self-lover. For if someone is always eager above all to do just or temperate actions or any other actions in accord with the virtues, and in general always gains for himself what is fine, no one will call him a self-lover or blame him for it.

This sort of person, however, more than the other sort, seems to be a self-lover. At any rate he awards himself what is finest and best of all, and gratifies the most controlling part of himself, obeying it in everything. And just as a city and every other composite system seems to be above all its most controlling part, the same is true of a human being; hence someone loves himself most if he likes and gratifies this part.

Similarly, someone is called continent or incontinent because his understanding is or is not the master, on the assumption that this is what each person is. Moreover, his own voluntary actions seem above all to be those involving reason. Clearly, then, this, or this above all, is what each person is, and the decent person likes this most of all.

That is why he most of all is a self-lover, but a different kind from the self-lover who is reproached. He differs from him as much as the life guided by reason differs from the life guided by feelings, and as much as the desire for what is fine differs from the desire for what seems advantageous.

Those who are unusually eager to do fine actions are welcomed and praised by everyone. And when everyone strains to achieve what is fine and concentrates on the finest actions, everything that is right will be done for the common good, and each person individually will receive the greatest of goods, since that is the character of virtue. And so the good person must be a self-lover, since he will both help himself and benefit others by doing fine actions. But the vicious person must not love himself, since he will harm both himself and his neighbors by following his base feelings.

For the vicious person, then, the right actions conflict with those he does. The decent person, however, does the right actions, since every understanding chooses what is best for itself and the decent person obeys his understanding.

It is quite true that, as they say, the excellent person labors for his friends and for his native country, and will die for them if he must; he will sacrifice money, honors, and contested goods in general, in achieving the fine for himself. For he will choose intense pleasure for a short time over slight pleasure for a long time; a year of living finely over many years of undistinguished life; and a single fine and great action over many small actions. This is presumably true of one who dies for others; he does indeed choose something great and fine for himself. He is also ready to sacrifice money as long as his friends profit; for the friends gain money, which he gains the fine, and so he awards himself the greater good.

He treats honors and offices in the same way; for he will sacrifice them all for his friends, since this is fine and praiseworthy for himself. It is not surprising, then, that he seems to be excellent, since he chooses the fine at the cost of everything. It is also possible, however, to sacrifice actions to his friend, since it may be finer to be responsible for his friend's doing the action than to do it himself

35 In everything praiseworthy, then, the excellent 1169b person awards more of the fine to himself. In this way, then, we must be self-lovers, as we have said. But in the way the many are, we ought not to be.

9

There is also a dispute about whether the happy person will need friends or not. For it is said that blessedly happy and self-sufficient people have no need 5 of friends. For they already have [all] the goods, and hence, being self-sufficient, need nothing added. But your friend, since he is another yourself, supplies what your own efforts cannot supply. Hence it is said, 'When the god gives well, what need is there of friends?'

It would seem absurd, however, to award the happy 10 person all the goods, without giving him friends; for having friends seems to be the greatest external good. And if it is more proper to a friend to confer benefits than to receive them, and it is proper to the good person and to virtue to do good, and it is finer to benefit friends than to benefit strangers, the excellent person will need people for him to benefit. Indeed, that is why there is a question about whether friends 15 are needed more in good fortune than in ill fortune; for it is assumed that in ill fortune we need people to benefit us, and in good fortune we need others for us to benefit.

Presumably it is also absurd to make the blessed person solitary. For no one would choose to have all [other] goods and yet be alone, since a human being is a political [animal], tending by nature to live together 20 with others. This will also be true, then, of the happy person; for he has the natural goods, and clearly it is better to spend his days with decent friends that with strangers of just any character. Hence the happy person needs friends.

Then what are those on the other side saying, and on what point are they correct? Perhaps they say what 25 they say because the many think that it is the useful people who are friends. Certainly the blessedly happy person will have no need of these, since he has [all] goods. Similarly, he will have no need, or very little, of friends for pleasure; for since his life is pleasant, it has no need of imported pleasures. Since he does not need these sorts of friends, he does not seem to need friends at all.

This conclusion, however, is presumably not true. For we said at the beginning that happiness is a kind 30 of activity; and clearly activity comes into being, and does not belong [to someone all the time], as a possession does. Now if being happy consists in living and being active; the activity of the good person in excellent, and [hence] pleasant in itself, as we said at the beginning; what is our own is pleasant; and we are able to observe our neighbors more than ourselves, 35 and to observe their actions more than our own; it follows that a good person finds pleasure in the actions of excellent people who are his friends, 1170a since these actions have both the naturally pleasant [features—they are good, and they are his own]. The blessed person, therefore, will need virtuous friends, given that he decides to observe virtuous actions that are his own, and the actions of a virtuous friend are of this sort.

Further, it is thought that the happy person must 5 live pleasantly. But the solitary person's life is hard, since it is not easy for him to be continuously active all by himself; but in relation to others and in their company it is easier. Hence his activity will be more continuous. It is also pleasant in itself, as it must be in the blessedly happy person's case. For the excellent person, insofar as he is excellent, enjoys actions in accord with virtue, and objects to actions caused by 10 vice, just as the musician enjoys fine melodies and is pained by bad ones.

Further, good people's life together allows the cultivation of virtue, as Theognis says.

If we examine the question more from the point of view of [human] nature, an excellent friend would seem to be choiceworthy by nature for an excellent person. For, as we have said, what is good by nature is 15 good and pleasant in itself for an excellent person.

For animals, life is defined by the capacity for perception, but for human beings, it is defined by the capacity for perception or understanding; moreover, every capacity refers to an activity, and a thing is present fully in its activity; hence living fully would seem to be perceiving or understanding.

Now life is good and pleasant in itself; for it has 20 definite order, which is proper to the nature of what is good. What is good by nature is also good for the decent person; that is why life would seem to be pleasant for everyone. But we must not consider a 25 life that is vicious and corrupted, or filled with pains; for such a life lacks definite order, just as its proper features do. (The truth about pain will be more evident in what follows.)

Life itself, then, is good and pleasant, as it would seem, at any rate, from the fact that everyone desires it, and decent and blessed people desire it more than others do—for their life is most choiceworthy for them, and their living is most blessed.

30 Now someone who sees perceives that he sees; one who hears perceives that he hears; one who walks perceives that he walks; and similarly in the other cases also there is some [element] that perceives that we are active; so that if we are perceiving, we perceive that we are perceiving, and if we are understanding, we perceive that we are understanding. Now perceiving that we are perceiving or understanding is the same as perceiving that we are, since we agreed that being is perceiving or understanding.

1170b Perceiving that we are alive is pleasant in itself. For life is by nature a good, and it is pleasant to perceive that something good is present in us. Living is also choiceworthy, for a good person most of all, since being good and pleasant for him; for he is pleased to 5 perceive something good in itself together [with his own being].

The excellent person is related to his friend in the same way as he is related to himself, since a friend is another himself. Therefore, just as his own being is choiceworthy for him, his friend's being is choiceworthy for him in the same or a similar way. We agreed that someone's own being is choiceworthy because he perceives that he is good, and this sort of perception is pleasant in itself. He must, then, perceive his friend's 10 being together [with his own], and he will do this when they live together and share conversation and thought. For in the case of human beings what seems to count as living together is this sharing of conversation and thought, not sharing the same pasture, as in the case of grazing animals.

If, then, for the blessedly happy person, being is 15 choiceworthy, since it is naturally good and pleasant, and if the being of his friend is closely similar to his own, his friend will also be choiceworthy. What is choiceworthy for him he must possess, since otherwise he will in this respect lack something. Anyone who is to be happy, then, must have excellent friends.

12

1171b30 What the erotic lover likes most is the sight of his beloved, and this is the sort of perception he chooses over the others, supposing that this above all is what makes him fall in love and remain in love. In the same way, surely, what friends find most choiceworthy is living together. For friendship is community, and we are related to our friend as we are related to ourselves. Hence, since the perception of our own being is choiceworthy, so is the perception of our friend's being. Perception is active when we live with 35 him; hence, not surprisingly, this is what we seek. 1172a

Whatever someone [regards as] his being, or the end for which he chooses to be alive, that is the activity he wishes to pursue in his friend's company. Hence some friends drink together, others play dice, while others do gymnastics and go hunting, or do philos- 5 ophy. They spend their days together on whichever pursuit in life they like most; for since they want to live with their friends, they share the actions in which they find their common life.

Hence the friendship of base people turns out to be vicious. For they are unstable, and share base 10 pursuits; and by becoming similar to each other, they grow vicious. But the friendship of decent people is decent, and increases the more often they meet. And they seem to become still better from their activities and their mutual correction. For each molds the other in what they approve of, so that '[you will learn] what is noble from noble people.'

So much, then, for friendship. The next task will 15 be to discuss pleasure.

BOOK X

4

1174a What, then, or what kind of thing, is pleasure? This will become clearer if we take it up again from the beginning. For seeing seems to be complete at any time, since it has no need for anything else to 15 complete its form by coming to be at a later time. And pleasure is also like this, since it is some sort of whole, and no pleasure is to be found at any time that will have its form completed by coming to be for a longer time.

That is why pleasure is not a process either. For every process, such as constructing a building, takes 20 time, and aims at some end, and is complete when it produces the product it seeks, or, [in other words, is complete] in this whole time [that it takes]. Moreover, each process is incomplete during the processes that are its parts, i.e., during the time it goes on; and it consists of processes that are different in form from the whole process and from one another.

For laying stones together and fluting a column 25 are different processes; and both are different from the [whole] production of the temple. For the production of the temple is a complete production, since it needs nothing further [when it is finished] to achieve the proposed goal; but the production of the foundation or the triglyph is an incomplete production, since [when it is finished] it is [the production] of a part. Hence [processes that are parts of larger processes] differ in form; and we cannot find a process complete in form at any time [while it is going on], but [only], if at all, in the whole time [that it takes].

30 The same is true of walking and the other [processes]. For if locomotion is a process from one place to another, it includes locomotions differing in form—flying, walking, jumping, and so on. And besides these differences, there are differences in walking itself. For the place from which and the place to which are not the same in the whole racecourse as they are in a part of it, or the same in one part as in 1174b another; nor is travelling along one line the same as travelling along another, since what we cover is not just a line, but a line in a [particular] place, and this line and that line are in different places.

Now we have discussed process exactly elsewhere. But, at any rate, a process, it would seem, is not 5 complete at every time; and the many [constituent] processes are incomplete, and differ in form, since the place from which and the place to which make the form of a process [and different processes begin and end in different places].

The form of pleasure, by contrast, is complete at any time. Clearly, then, it is different from a process, and is something whole and complete. This also seems true because a process must take time, but 10 being pleased need not; for what is present in an instant is a whole. This also makes it clear that it is wrong to say that pleasure is a process or a becoming. For this is not said of everything, but only of what is divisible and not a whole; for seeing, or a point, or a unit, has no coming to be, and none of these is either a process or a becoming. But pleasure is a whole; hence it too has no coming to be.

Every perceptual capacity is active in relation to 15 its perceptible object, and completely active when it is in good condition in relation to the finest of its perceptible objects. For this above all seems to be the character of complete activity, whether it is ascribed to the capacity or to the subject that has it. Hence for each capacity the best activity is the activity of the subject in the best condition in relation to the best object of the capacity.

This activity will also be the most complete and 20 the most pleasant. For every perceptual capacity and every sort of thought and study has its pleasure; the most pleasant activity is the most complete; and the most complete is the activity of the subject in good condition in relation to the most excellent object of the capacity. Pleasure completes the activity.

But the way in which pleasure completes the 25 activity is not the way in which the perceptible object and the perceptual capacity complete it when they are both excellent—just as health and the doctor are not the cause of being healthy in the same way.

Clearly a pleasure arises that corresponds to each perceptual capacity, since we say that sights and sounds are pleasant; and clearly it arises most of all whenever the perceptual capacity is best, and is active in relation to the best sort of object. When this is the 30 condition of the perceptible object and of the perceiving subject, there will always be pleasure, when the producer and the subject to be affected are both present.

Pleasure completes the activity—not, however, as the state does, by being present [in the activity], but as a sort of consequent end, like the bloom on youths. Hence as long as the objects of understanding or perception and the subject that judges or attends 1175a are in the right condition, there will be pleasure in the activity. For as long as the subject affected and the productive [cause] remain similar and in the same relation to each other, the same thing naturally arises.

Then how is it that no one is continuously pleased? 5 Is it not because we get tired? For nothing human is capable of continuous activity, and hence no continuous pleasure arises either, since pleasure is a consequence of the activity. Some things delight us when they are new to us, but later delight us less, for the same reason. For at first our thought is stimulated and intensely active toward them, as our sense of sight is when we look closely at something; but later the activity becomes lax and careless, so that the pleasure fades also.

Why does everyone desire pleasure? We might think it is because everyone also aims at being alive. Living is a type of activity, and each of us is active toward the objects he likes most and in the ways he likes most. The musician, for instance, activates his hearing in hearing melodies; the lover of learning activates his thought in thinking about objects of study; and so on for each of the others. Pleasure completes their activities, and hence completes life, which they desire. It is reasonable, then, that they also aim at pleasure, since it completes each person's life for him, and life is choiceworthy.

But do we choose life because of pleasure, or pleasure because of life? Let us set aside this question for now, since the two appear to be combined and to allow no separation; for pleasure never arises without activity, and, equally, it completes every activity.

5

Hence pleasures also seem to differ in species. For we suppose that things of different species are completed by different things. That is how it appears, both with natural things and with artifacts—for instance, with animals, trees, a painting, a statue, a house, or an implement. Similarly, activities that differ in species are also completed by things that differ in species. Now activities of thought differ in species from activities of the capacities for perception, and so do these from each other; so also, then, do the pleasures that complete them.

This is also apparent from the way each pleasure is proper to the activity that it completes. For the proper pleasure increases the activity; for we judge each thing better and more exactly when our activity involves pleasure. If, for instance, we enjoy doing geometry, we become better geometers, and understand each question better; and similarly lovers of music, building, and so on improve at their proper function when they enjoy it. Each pleasure increases the activity; what increases it is proper to it; and since the activities are different in species, what is proper to them is also different in species.

This is even more apparent from the way some activities are impeded by pleasures from others. For lovers of flutes, for instance, cannot pay attention to a conversation if they catch the sound of someone playing the flute, because they enjoy flute playing more than their present activity; and so the pleasure proper to flute playing destroys the activity of conversation.

The same is true in other cases also, whenever we are engaged in two activities at once. For the more pleasant activity pushes out the other one, all the more if it is much more pleasant, so that we no longer even engage in the other activity. Hence if we are enjoying one thing intensely, we do not do another very much. It is when we are only mildly pleased that we do something else; for instance, people who eat nuts in theatres do this most when the actors are bad.

Since, then, the proper pleasure makes an activity more exact, longer, and better, whereas an alien pleasure damages it, clearly the two pleasures differ widely. For an alien pleasure does virtually what a proper pain does. The proper pain destroys activity, so that, if, for instance, writing or rational calculation has no pleasure and is in fact painful for us, we do not write or calculate, since the activity is painful. Hence the proper pleasures and pains have contrary effects on an activity; and the proper ones are those that arise from the activity in itself. And as we have said, the effect of alien pleasures is similar to the effect of pain, since they ruin the activity, though not in the same way as pain.

Since activities differ in degrees of decency and badness, and some are choiceworthy, some to be avoided, some neither, the same is true of pleasures; for each activity has its own proper pleasure. Hence the pleasure proper to an excellent activity is decent, and the one proper to a base activity is vicious; for, similarly, appetites for fine things are praiseworthy, and appetites for shameful things are blameworthy. And in fact the pleasure in an activity is more proper to it than the desire for it. For the desire is distinguished from it in time and in nature; but the pleasure is close to the activity, and so little distinguished from it that disputes arise about whether the activity is the same as the pleasure.

Still, pleasure would seem to be neither thought nor perception, since that would be absurd. Rather, it is because [pleasure and activity] are not separated that to some people they appear the same. Hence, just as activities differ, so do the pleasures. Sight differs from touch in purity, as hearing and smell do from taste; hence the pleasures also differ in the same way. So also do the pleasures of thought differ from these [pleasure of sense]; and both sorts have different kinds within them.

Each kind of animal seems to have its own proper pleasure, just as it has its own proper function; for the proper pleasure will be the one that corresponds to its activity. This is apparent if we also study each kind; for a horse, a dog, and a human being have different pleasures, and, as Heraclitus says, an ass would choose chaff over gold, since asses find food more pleasant than gold. Hence animals that differ in species also have pleasures that differ in species; and it would be reasonable for animals of the same species to have the same pleasures also.

In fact, however, the pleasures differ quite a lot, in human beings at any rate. For the same things delight some people, and cause pain to others; and while some find them painful and hateful, others find them pleasant and lovable. The same is true of sweet things. For the same things do not seem sweet to a feverish and to a healthy person, or hot to an enfeebled and to a vigorous person; and the same is true of other things.

But in all such cases it seems that what is really so is what appears so to the excellent person. If this is right, as it seems to be, and virtue, i.e., the good person insofar as he is good, is the measure of each thing, then what appear pleasures to him will also really be pleasures, and what is pleasant will be what he enjoys.

And if what he finds objectionable appears pleasant to someone, that is not at all surprising; for human beings suffer many sorts of corruption and damage. It is not pleasant, however, except to these people in these conditions. Clearly, then, we should say that the pleasures agreed to be shameful are not pleasures at all, except to corrupted people.

But what about those pleasures that seem to be decent? Of these, which kind, or which particular pleasure, should we take to be the pleasure of a human being? Surely it will be clear from the activities, since the pleasures are consequences of these. Hence the pleasures that complete the activities of the complete and blessedly happy man, whether he has one activity or more than one, will be called the fully human pleasures to the fullest extent. The other pleasures will be human in secondary, or even more remote ways, corresponding to the character of the activities.

6

We have now finished our discussion of the types of virtue; of friendship; and of pleasure. It remains for us to discuss happiness in outline, since we take this to be the end of human [aims]. Our discussion will be shorter if we first take up again what we said before.

We said, then, that happiness is not a state. For if it were, someone might have it and yet be asleep for his whole life, living the life of a plant, or suffer the greatest misfortunes. If we do not approve of this, we count happiness as an activity rather than a state, as we said before.

Some activities are necessary, i.e., choiceworthy for some other end, while others are choiceworthy in their own right. Clearly, then, we should count happiness as one of those activities that are choiceworthy in their own right, not as one of those choiceworthy for some other end. For happiness lacks nothing, but is self-sufficient.

An activity is choiceworthy in its own right if nothing further apart from it is sought from it. This seems to be the character of actions in accord with virtue; for doing fine and excellent actions is choiceworthy for itself. But pleasant amusements also [seem to be choiceworthy in their own right]; for they are not chosen for other ends, since they actually cause more harm than benefit, by causing neglect of our bodies and possessions. Moreover, most of those people congratulated for their happiness resort to these sorts of pastimes. That is why people who are witty participants in them have a good reputation with tyrants, since they offer themselves as pleasant [partners] in the tyrant's aims, and these are the sort of people the tyrant requires. And so these amusements seem to have the character of happiness because people in supreme power spend their leisure in them.

These sorts of people, however, are presumably no evidence. For virtue and understanding, the sources of excellent activities, do not depend on holding supreme power. Further, these powerful people have had no taste of pure and civilized pleasure, and so they resort to bodily pleasures. But that is no reason to think these pleasures are most choiceworthy, since boys also think that the things they honor are best.

Hence, just as different things appear honorable to boys and to men, it is reasonable that in the same way different things appear honorable to base and to decent people.

25 As we have often said, then, what is honorable and pleasant is what is so to the excellent person. To each type of person the activity that accords with his own proper state is most choiceworthy; hence the activity in accord with virtue is most choiceworthy to the excellent person [and hence is most honorable and pleasant].

Happiness, then, is not found in amusement; for 30 it would be absurd if the end were amusement, and our lifelong efforts and sufferings aimed at amusing ourselves. For we choose practically everything for some other end—except for happiness, since it is [the] end; but serious work and toil aimed [only] at amusement appears stupid and excessively childish. Rather, it seems correct to amuse ourselves so that we can do something serious, as Anacharsis says;[30] 35 for amusement would seem to be relaxation, and it is because we cannot toil continuously that we require relaxation. Relaxation, then, is not [the] end; for we 1177a pursue it [to prepare] for activity. But the happy life seems to be a life in accord with virtue, which is a life involving serious actions, and not consisting in amusement.

Besides, we say that things to be taken seriously 5 are better than funny things that provide amusement, and that in each case the activity of the better part and the better person is more serious and excellent; and the activity of what is better is superior, and thereby has more the character of happiness.

Besides, anyone at all, even a slave, no less than the best person, might enjoy bodily pleasures; but no one would allow that a slave shares in happiness, if one does not [also allow that the slave shares in the sort of] life [needed for happiness]. Happiness, then, 10 is found not in these pastimes, but in the activities in accord with virtue, as we also said previously.

7

If happiness is activity in accord with virtue, it is reasonable for it to accord with the supreme virtue, 15 which will be the virtue of the best thing. The best is understanding, or whatever else seems to be the natural ruler and leader, and to understand what is fine and divine, by being itself either divine or the most divine element in us. Hence complete happiness will be its activity in accord with its proper virtue; and we have said that this activity is the activity of study.

This seems to agree with what has been said before, and also with the truth. For this activity is supreme, 20 since understanding is the supreme element in us, and the objects of understanding are the supreme objects of knowledge.

Further, it is the most continuous activity, since we are more capable of continuous study than any continuous action.

Besides, we think pleasure must be mixed into happiness; and it is agreed that the activity in accord 25 with wisdom is the most pleasant of the activities in accord with virtue. Certainly, philosophy seems to have remarkably pure and firm pleasures, and it is reasonable for those who have knowledge to spend their lives more pleasantly than those who seek it.

Moreover, the self-sufficiency we spoke of will be found in study more than in anything else. For admittedly the wise person, the just person, and the other virtuous people all need the good things necessary for life. Still, when these are adequately supplied, the 30 just person needs other people as partners and recipients of his just actions; and the same is true of the temperate person, the brave person, and each of the others. But the wise person is able, and more able the wiser he is, to study even by himself; and though 1177b he presumably does it better with colleagues, even so he is more self-sufficient than any other [virtuous person].

Besides, study seems to be liked because of itself alone, since it has no result beyond having studied. But from the virtues concerned with action we try to a greater or lesser extent to gain something beyond the action itself.

Besides, happiness seems to be found in leisure; 5 for we deny ourselves leisure so that we can be at leisure, and fight wars so that we can be at peace. Now the virtues concerned with action have their activities in politics or war, and actions here seem to require trouble. This seems completely true for actions in war, since no one chooses to fight a war, 10 and no one continues it, for the sake of fighting a war; for someone would have to be a complete murderer

30. [Anacharsis was a sixth-century-B.C. Scythian prince of legendary wisdom.]

if he made his friends his enemies so that there could be battles and killings. But the actions of the politi- 15 cian also deny us leisure; apart from political activities themselves, those actions seek positions of power and honors, or at least they seek happiness for the politician himself and for his fellow citizens, which is something different from political science itself, and clearly is sought on the assumption that it is different.

Hence among actions in accord with the virtues those in politics and war are preeminently fine and great; but they require trouble, aim at some [further] end, and are choiceworthy for something other than 20 themselves. But the activity of understanding, it seems, is superior in excellence because it is the activity of study, aims at no end apart from itself, and has its own proper pleasure, which increases the activity. Further, self-sufficiency, leisure, unwearied activity (as far as is possible for a human being), and any other features ascribed to the blessed person, are evidently 25 features of this activity. Hence a human being's complete happiness will be this activity, if it receives a complete span of life, since nothing incomplete is proper to happiness.

Such a life would be superior to the human level. For someone will live it not insofar as he is a human being, but insofar as he has some divine element in him. And the activity of this divine element is as much superior to the activity in accord with the rest of virtue 30 as this element is superior to the compound. Hence if understanding is something divine in comparison with a human being, so also will the life in accord with understanding be divine in comparison with human life. We ought not to follow the makers of proverbs and 'Think human, since you are human,' or 'Think mortal, since you are mortal.' Rather, as far as we can, we ought to be pro-immortal, and go to all lengths to live a life in accord with our supreme 1178a element; for however much this element may lack in bulk, by much more it surpasses everything in power and value.

Moreover, each person seems to be his understanding, if he is his controlling and better element. It would be absurd, then, if he were to choose not 5 his own life, but something else's. And what we have said previously will also apply now. For what is proper to each thing's nature is supremely best and most pleasant for it; and hence for human being the life in accord with understanding will be supremely best and most pleasant, if understanding, more than anything else, is the human being. This life, then, will also be happiest.

8

The life in accord with the other kind of virtue [i.e., the kind concerned with action] is [happiest] 10 in a secondary way, because the activities in accord with this virtue are human. For we do just and brave actions, and the other actions in accord with the virtues, in relation to other people, by abiding by what fits each person in contracts, services, all types of actions, and also in feelings; and all these appear to be human conditions. Indeed, some feelings actually 15 seem to arise from the body; and in many ways virtue of character seems to be proper to feelings.

Besides, prudence is inseparable from virtue of character, and virtue of character from prudence. For the principles of prudence accord with the virtues of character; and correctness in virtues of character accords with prudence. And since these virtues are 20 also connected to feelings, they are concerned with the compound. Since the virtues of the compound are human virtues, the life and the happiness in accord with these virtues is also human. The virtue of understanding, however, is separated [from the compound]. Let us say no more about it, since an exact account would be too large a task for our present project.

Moreover, it seems to need external supplies 25 very little, or [at any rate] less than virtue of character needs them. For let us grant that they both need necessary goods, and to the same extent; for there will be only a very small difference, even though the politician labors more about the body and suchlike. Still, there will be a large difference in [what is needed] for the [proper] activities [of each type of virtue]. For 30 the generous person will need money for generous actions; and the just person will need it for paying debts, since wishes are not clear, and people who are not just pretend to wish to do justice. Similarly, the brave person will need enough power, and the temperate person will need freedom [to do intemperate actions], if they are to achieve anything that the virtue requires. For how else will they, or any other virtuous people, make their virtue clear?

35 Moreover, it is disputed whether decision or action 1178b is more in control of virtue, on the assumption that virtue depends on both. Well, certainly it is clear that the complete [good] depends on both; but for actions many external goods are needed, and the greater and finer the actions the more numerous are the external good needed.

But someone who is studying needs none of these goods, for that activity at least, indeed, for study at least, we might say they are even hindrances. Insofar 5 as he is a human being, however, and [hence] lives together with a number of other human beings, he chooses to do the actions that accord with virtue. Hence he will need the sorts of external goods [that are needed for the virtues], for living a human life.

In another way also it appears that complete happi- 10 ness is some activity of study. For we traditionally suppose that the gods more than anyone are blessed and happy; but what sorts of actions ought we to ascribe to them? Just actions? Surely they will appear ridiculous making contracts, returning deposits, and so on. Brave actions? Do they endure what [they find] frightening and endure dangers because it is fine? Generous actions? Whom will they give to? And 15 surely it would be absurd for them to have currency or anything like that. What would their temperate actions be? Surely it is vulgar praise to say that they do not have base appetites. When we go through them all, anything that concerns actions appears trivial and unworthy of the gods. Nonetheless, we all tradition- 20 ally suppose that they are alive and active, since surely they are not asleep like Endymion.[31] Then if someone is alive, and action is excluded, and production even more, what is left but study? Hence the gods' activity that is superior in blessedness will be an activity of study. And so the human activity that is most akin to the gods' activity will, more than any others, have the character of happiness.

25 A sign of this is the fact that other animals have no share in happiness, being completely deprived of this activity of study. For the whole life of the gods is blessed, and human life is blessed to the extent that it has something resembling this sort of activity; but none of the other animals is happy, because none of them shares in study at all. Hence happiness extends just as far as study extends, and the more someone 30 studies, the happier he is, not coincidentally but insofar as he studies, since study is valuable in itself. And so [on this argument] happiness will be some kind of study.

But happiness will need external prosperity also, since we are human beings; for our nature is not self- 35 sufficient for study, but we need a healthy body, and need to have food and the other services provided. Still, even though no one can be blessedly happy 1179a without external goods, we must not think that to be happy we will need many large goods. For self-sufficiency and action do not depend on excess.

Moreover, we can do fine actions even if we do not rule earth and sea; for even from moderate resources 5 we can do the actions that accord with virtue. This is evident to see, since many private citizens seem to do decent actions no less than people in power do—even more, in fact. It is enough if moderate resources are provided; for the life of someone whose activity accords with virtue will be happy.

Solon surely described happy people well, when 10 he said they had been moderately supplied with external goods, had done what he regarded as the finest actions, and had lived their lives temperately. For it is possible to have moderate possessions and still to do the right actions. And Anaxagoras would seem to have supposed that the happy person was neither rich 15 nor powerful, since he said he would not be surprised if the happy person appeared an absurd sort of person to the many. For the many judge by externals, since these are all they perceive. Hence the beliefs of the wise would seem to accord with our arguments.

These considerations, then, produce some confidence. But the truth in questions about action is 20 judged from what we do and how we live, since these are what control [the answers to such questions]. Hence we ought to examine what has been said by applying it to what we do and how we live; and if it harmonizes with what we do, we should accept it, but if it conflicts we should count it [mere] words.

The person whose activity accords with understanding and who takes care of understanding would seem to be in the best condition, and most loved by 25 the gods. For if the gods pay some attention to human

31. [According to Greek mythology, Endymion was a remarkably beautiful young man who was placed into everlasting sleep by the Moon so that she might embrace him each night.]

beings, as they seem to, it would be reasonable for them to take pleasure in what is best and most akin to them, namely understanding; and reasonable for them to benefit in return those who most of all like and honor understanding, on the assumption that 30 these people attend to what is beloved by the gods, and act correctly and finely. Clearly, all this is true of the wise person more than anyone else; hence he is most loved by the gods. And it is likely that this same person will be happiest; hence, by this argument also, the wise person, more than anyone else, will be happy.

9

We have now said enough in outlines about happi- 35 ness and the virtues, and about friendship and pleasure also. Should we, then, think that our decision [to *1179b* study these] has achieved its end? On the contrary, the aim of studies about action, as we say, is surely not to study and know about a given thing, but rather to act on our knowledge. Hence knowing about virtue is not enough, but we must also try to possess and exercise virtue, or become good in any other way.

5 Now if arguments were sufficient by themselves to make people decent, the rewards they would command would justifiably have been many and large, as Theognis says, and rightly bestowed. In fact, however, arguments seem to have enough influence to stimulate and encourage the civilized ones among the young people, and perhaps to make virtue take possession of a well-born character that truly loves 10 what is fine; but they seem unable to turn the many toward being fine and good.

For the many naturally obey fear, not shame; they avoid what is base because of the penalties, not because it is disgraceful. For since they live by their feelings, they pursue their proper pleasures and the 15 sources of them, and avoid the opposed pains, and have not even a notion of what is fine and [hence] truly pleasant, since they have had no taste of it.

What argument, then, could reform people like these? For it is impossible, or not easy, to alter by argument what has long been absorbed as a result of one's habits. But, presumably, we should be satisfied to achieve some share in virtue if we already have what we seem to need to become decent.

20 Now some think it is nature that makes people good; some think it is habit; some that it is teaching. The [contribution] of nature clearly is not up to us, but results from some divine cause in those who have it, who are truly the fortunate ones. Arguments and teaching surely do not prevail on everyone, but the 25 soul of the student needs to have been prepared by habits for enjoying and hating finely, like ground that is to nourish seed. For someone who lives in accord with his feelings would not even listen to an argument turning him away, or comprehend it [if he did listen]; and in that state how could he be persuaded to change? And in general feelings seem to yield to 30 force, not to argument. Hence we must already in some way have a character suitable for virtue, fond of what is fine and objecting to what is shameful.

It is difficult, however, for someone to be trained correctly for virtue from his youth if he has not been brought up under correct laws; for the many, especially the young, do not find it pleasant to live in a temperate and resistant way. That is why laws must 15 prescribe their upbringing and practices; for they will not find these things painful when they get used to them.

Presumably, however, it is not enough if they get *1180a* the correct upbringing and attention when they are young; rather, they must continue the same practices and be habituated to them when they become men. Hence we need laws concerned with these things also, and in general with all of life. For the many yield 5 to compulsion more than to argument, and to sanctions more than to the fine.

That is why legislators must, in some people's view, urge people toward virtue and exhort them to aim at the fine—on the assumption that anyone whose good habits have prepared him decently will listen to them—but must impose corrective treatments and penalties on anyone who disobeys or lacks 10 the right nature, and must completely expel an incurable. For the decent person, it is assumed, will attend to reason because his life aims at the fine, whereas the base person, since he desires pleasure, has to receive corrective treatment by pain, like a beast of burden. That is why it is said that the pains imposed must be those most contrary to the pleasures he likes.

As we have said, then, someone who is to be good 15 must be finely brought up and habituated, and then must live in decent practices, doing base actions neither willingly nor unwillingly. And this will be true if his life follows some sort of understanding and correct order that prevails on him.

Now a father's instructions lack this power to prevail and compel; and so in general do the instructions of an individual man, unless he is a king or someone like that. Law, however, has the power that compels; and law is reason that proceeds from a sort of prudence and understanding. Besides, people become hostile to an individual human being who opposes their impulses, even if he is correct in opposing them, whereas a law's prescription of what is decent is not burdensome.

And yet, it is only in Sparta, or in a few other cities as well, that the legislator seems to have attended to upbringing and practices. In most other cities they are neglected, and an individual lives as he wishes, 'laying down the rules for his children and wife,' like a Cyclops.[32]

It is best, then, if the community attends to upbringing, and attends correctly. But if the community neglects it, it seems fitting for each individual to promote the virtue of his children and his friends—to be able to do it, or at least to decide to do it. From what we have said, however, it seems he will be better able to do it if he acquires legislative science. For, clearly, attention by the community works through laws, and decent attention works through excellent laws; and whether the laws are written or unwritten, for the education of one or of many, seems unimportant, as it is in music, gymnastics, and other practices. For just as in a city the provisions of law and the types of character [found in that city] have influence, similarly a father's words and habits have influence, and all the more because of kinship and because of the benefits he does; for his children are already fond of him and naturally ready to obey.

Further, education adapted to an individual is actually better than a common education for everyone, just as individualized medical treatment is better. For though generally a feverish patient benefits from rest and starvation, presumably some patient does not; nor does the boxing instructor impose the same way of fighting on everyone. Hence it seems that treatment in particular cases is more exactly right when each person gets special attention, since he then more often gets the suitable treatment.

Nonetheless a doctor, a gymnastics trainer, and everyone else will give the best individual attention if they also know universally what is good for all, or for these sorts. For sciences are said to be, and are, of what is common [to many particular cases]. Admittedly someone without scientific knowledge may well attend properly to a single person, if his experience has allowed him to take exact note of what happens in a given case, just as some people seem to be their own best doctors, though unable to help anyone else at all. Nonetheless, presumably, it seems that someone who wants to be an expert in a craft and a branch of study should progress to the universal, and come to know that, as far as possible; for that, as we have said, is what the sciences are about.

Then perhaps also someone who wishes to make people better by his attention, many people or few, should try to acquire legislative science, if laws are a means to make us good. For not just anyone can improve the condition of just anyone, or the person presented to him; but if someone can, it is the person with knowledge, just as in medical science and the others that require attention and prudence.

Next, then, should we examine whence and how someone might acquire legislative science? Just as in other cases [we go to the practitioner], should we go to the politicians, since, as we saw, legislative science seems to be a part of political science? Or does the case of political science appear different from the other sciences and capacities? For evidently, in the other cases, the same people, such as doctors or painters, who transmit the capacity to others actively practice it themselves. By contrast, it is the Sophists who advertise that they teach politics but none of them practices it. Instead, those who practice it are the political activists, and they seem to act on some sort of capacity and experience rather than thought.

For evidently they neither write nor speak on such questions, though presumably it would be finer to do this than to compose speeches for the law courts or the Assembly; nor have they made politicians out of their own sons or any other friends of theirs. But it would be reasonable for them to do this if they were able; for there is nothing better than the political capacity that they could leave to their cities, and

32. [The reference is to Homer's *Odyssey*, in which the Cyclopes were portrayed as savage, one-eyed giants living without government or laws.]

nothing better that they could decide to produce in themselves, or, therefore, in their closest friends.

10 Nonetheless, experience would seem to contribute quite a lot; otherwise people would not have become better politicians by familiarity with politics. That is why those who aim to know about political science would seem to need experience as well.

By contrast, those of the Sophists who advertise [that they teach political science] appear to be a long way from teaching; for they are altogether ignorant about the sort of thing political science is, and the 15 sorts of things it is about. For if they had known what it is, they would not have taken it to be the same as rhetoric, or something inferior to it, or thought it an easy task to assemble the laws with good reputations and then legislate. For they think they can select the best laws, as though the selection itself did not require comprehension, and as though correct judgment were not the most important thing, as it is in music. 20 [They are wrong;] for those with experience in each area judge the products correctly and comprehend the ways and means of completing them, and what fits with what; for if we lack experience, we must be satisfied with noticing that the product is well or 1181b badly made, as with painting. Now laws would seem to be the products of political science; how, then, could someone acquire legislative science, or judge which laws are best, from laws alone? For neither do we appear to become experts in medicine by reading textbooks.

And yet doctors not only try to describe the [recognized] treatments, but also distinguish different [bodily] states, and try to say how each type of patient 5 might be cured and must be treated. And what they say seems to be useful to the experienced, though useless to the ignorant. Similarly, then, collections of laws and political systems[33] might also, presumably, be most useful if we are capable of studying them and of judging what is done finely or in the contrary way, and what sorts of [elements] fit with what. Those who lack the [proper] state [of experience] when they go 10 through these collections will not manage to judge finely, unless they can do it all by themselves [without training], though they might come to comprehend them better by going through them.

Since, then, our predecessors have left the area of legislation uncharted, it is presumably better to examine it ourselves instead, and indeed to examine politi- 15 cal systems in general, and so to complete the philosophy of human affairs, as far as we are able.

First, then, let us try to review any sound remarks our predecessors have made on particular topics. Then let us study the collected political systems, to see from them what sorts of things preserve and destroy cities, and political systems of different types; 20 and what causes some cities to conduct politics well, and some badly. For when we have studied these questions, we will perhaps grasp better what sort of political system is best; how each political system should be organized so as to be best; and what habits and laws it should follow.

Let us discuss this, then, starting from the beginning.[34]

33. [Aristotle supervised a collection of the constitutional histories of 158 Greek states, of which only one, the *Constitution of Athens*, is extant.]

34. [Here the *Nicomachean Ethics* ends, reminding us that for Aristotle the study of ethics is inseparable from the study of political philosophy.]

Epicurus

Epicurus (341–271 B.C.) was born on the island of Samos of Athenian parents and was thus counted as an Athenian citizen. In order to fulfill his military obligations, he went to Athens in 323, the year in which Aristotle fled Athens, fearing anti-Macedonian sentiment after the death of Alexander the Great. However, even in Aristotle's absence Athens remained the center for philosophical activity, and Epicurus most certainly became familiar with Platonism and Aristotelianism. The death of Alexander brought about a good deal of political turmoil, some of which affected Epicurus directly. While he was in Athens, his family was evicted from Samos by the Macedonians, as were other Athenian colonists. It may be that Epicurus' evident antipathy to politics began with these events. In any case Epicureanism and the public life do not mix: the latter would upset the tranquillity required by the former.

Epicurus' family migrated to Colophon, in Asia Minor, and Epicurus rejoined them in 321. He spent the next ten years in Colophon, where he came under the tutelage of Nausiphanes, who espoused a version of atomism, a philosophy that had been founded by Leucippus (fifth century B.C.) and Democritus of Abdera (c. 460–c. 370 B.C.). Epicurus himself became a convert to atomism, but his atomism differed from that of his predecessors.

Epicurus' version of atomism contended that the universe is composed of only two kinds of things: bodies and the void. That bodies exist is a matter of observation. The existence of the void or empty space is necessary in order for bodies to move. Bodies of visible size are compounded out of bodies of invisible size, namely, atoms. It is impossible for anything to come into existence out of nothing, and it is impossible for anything to pass into nothingness. Therefore what exists always has existed and always will exist. Now many visible bodies are not everlasting; they can be cut up and disintegrated. But since it is impossible for anything to come out of or pass into nothingness, it must be that at least the ultimate parts or atoms of a visible body are not subject to creation, decomposition, or disintegration; that is, the atoms are everlasting. (Epicurus' arguments explaining why there should be ultimate parts at all and why, if they do exist, they are too small to be seen, are obscure.)

Epicurus' infinitely many atoms possess only three variable qualities. They can differ from each other in size, shape, and weight. Some atoms are larger than others, although none of them is big enough to be seen, and none is infinitely small. Some atoms are heavier than others, but the differences in weight do not result in differences in velocity among various atoms. In fact, all atoms move at exactly the same velocity as they fall directly downward through infinite space and infinite time. If all atoms followed parallel downward paths at the same speed, however, they would never interact with each other, and thus nothing would ever change. In order to avoid that difficulty, Epicurus claimed that the atoms occasionally swerve in a random way from their downward paths. When atoms swerve, they may strike other atoms, thus setting off whole series of collisions. Visible objects are the results of such collisions. These objects are systems of atoms that, for some time, display cohesiveness due to a kind of dynamic equilibrium. But, insisted Epicurus, such systems of atoms, no matter how large and well behaved, are the result of purely mechanical causes. There is no design or providence in the universe. Everything that exists can be explained in principle by the motions of atoms in empty space. Nor is the present world-order in which we find ourselves everlasting. It is, like every visible object in it, a collection of atoms that for the present time exists in a dynamic equilibrium, but that will eventually disperse.

Epicurus regarded his atomic theory as the key to his moral theory. The moral theory was epitomized in antiquity as follows: the gods are not to be feared, death is not to be feared, pleasure is easy to obtain, and it is easy to endure pain. The gods, who are also nothing more than collections of atoms, are not to be feared because they have utterly no concern for the affairs of humans. To have any concern would be to spoil their divine tranquillity. Death is not to be feared because it is simply the dissolution of the atomic structure that makes up the soul, and when that happens, one ceases to exist. Thus one can be confident that no pain will be experienced after death.

The pursuit of pleasure is natural in humans, according to Epicurus, and in fact, a person ought always to seek pleasure. But an Epicurean is not an epicure, one devoted to pleasing the senses. The pursuit of excessive or violent pleasures can only result in pain; thus, such pleasures should be avoided. Rather, the pleasure to be sought is best characterized as the absence of pain of any kind. The most pleasant condition, according to Epicurus, is that in which one is neither hungry, thirsty, nor apprehensive, yet confident that one will remain in that condition. In this condition, one's atomic structure is unperturbed. Thus, true pleasure for Epicurus does not require extravagance.

From the time Epicurus began teaching in Athens in 306 until his death, he and his followers lived an abstemious life together, but one that they regarded as approaching perfect pleasure. Once the Epicureans' concept of pleasure is understood, one can see why they thought that pleasure is easy to obtain.

Epicurus' attitude toward his own painful terminal illness illustrates the thesis that it is easy to endure pain. In a letter written to a disciple shortly before his death, he said that "there is set over against these pains the joy of my heart at the memory of our happy conversations in the past."

• • •

Although Epicurus was a prolific writer, few of his writings survive. His *Letter to Menoeceus* and *Principal Doctrines,* reprinted here, give us the rudiments of his moral theory. An important source of information about Epicureanism is the Roman poet Lucretius (c. 99–c. 55 B.C.), in *On the Nature of Things,* translated by Martin F. Smith (Indianapolis: Hackett Publishing Company, 2001). Important source material, along with ancient commentary (some of it hostile), is contained in Brad Inwood and L. P. Gerson, eds., *Hellenistic Philosophy,* second edition (Indianapolis: Hackett Publishing Company, 1997). Some of this material is topically arranged in A. A. Long and D. N. Sedley, eds., *The Hellenistic Philosophers* (Cambridge: Cambridge University Press, 1987), two volumes (English translations in volume I). J. M. Rist, *Epicurus: An Introduction* (Cambridge: Cambridge University Press, 1972) is a well-balanced account. David J. Furley, *Two Studies in the Greek Atomists* (Princeton, N.J.: Princeton University Press, 1967) is a more specialized but provocative work.

William E. Mann

Letter to Menoeceus

Epicurus to Menoeceus, greetings:

Let no one delay the study of philosophy while young nor weary of it when old. For no one is either too young or too old for the health of the soul. He who says either that the time for philosophy has not yet come or that it has passed is like someone who says that the time for happiness has not yet come or that it has passed. Therefore, both young and old must philosophize, the latter so that although old he may stay young in good things owing to gratitude for what has occurred, the former so that although young he too may be like an old man owing to his lack of fear of what is to come. Therefore, one must practise the things which produce happiness, since if that is present we have everything and if it is absent we do everything in order to have it.

Do and practise what I constantly told you to do, believing these to be the elements of living well. First, believe that god is an indestructible and blessed animal, in accordance with the general conception of god commonly held, and do not ascribe to god anything foreign to his indestructibility or repugnant to his blessedness. Believe of him everything which is able to preserve his blessedness and indestructibility. For gods do exist, since we have clear knowledge of them. But they are not such as the many believe them to be. For they do not adhere to their own views about the gods. The man who denies the gods of the many is not impious, but rather he who ascribes to the gods the opinions of the many. For the pronouncements of the many about the gods are not basic grasps but false suppositions. Hence come the greatest harm from the gods to bad men and the greatest benefits [to the good]. For the gods always welcome men who are like themselves, being congenial to their own virtues and considering that whatever is not such is uncongenial.

Get used to believing that death is nothing to us. For all good and bad consists in sense-experience, and death is the privation of sense-experience. Hence, a correct knowledge of the fact that death is nothing to us makes the mortality of life a matter for contentment, not by adding a limitless time [to life] but by removing the longing for immortality. For there is nothing fearful in life for one who has grasped that there is nothing fearful in the absence of life. Thus, he is a fool who says that he fears death not because it will be painful when present but because it is painful when it is still to come. For that which while present causes no distress causes unnecessary pain when merely anticipated. So death, the most frightening of bad things, is nothing to us; since when we exist, death is not yet present, and when death is present, then we do not exist. Therefore, it is relevant neither to the living nor to the dead, since it does not affect the former, and the latter do not exist. But the many sometimes flee death as the greatest of bad things and sometimes choose it as a relief from the bad things of life. But the wise man neither rejects life nor fears death. For living does not offend him, nor does he believe not living to be something bad. And just as he does not unconditionally choose the largest amount of food but the most pleasant food, so he savours not the longest time but the most pleasant. He who advises the young man to live well and the old man to die well is simple-minded, not just because of the pleasing aspects of life but because the same kind of practice produces a good life and a good death. Much worse is he who says that it is good not to be born, "but when born to pass through the gates of Hades as quickly as possible."[1] For if he really believes what he says, why doesn't he leave life? For it is easy for him to do, if he has firmly decided on it. But if he is joking, he is wasting his time among men who don't welcome it. We must remember that what will happen is neither unconditionally within our power nor unconditionally outside our power, so

Reprinted from *Hellenistic Philosophy*, translated and edited by Brad Inwood and L. P. Gerson (Indianapolis: Hackett Publishing Company, 1988), by permission of the publisher.

1. [Theognis 425, 427.—B.I. and L.P.G.]

that we will not unconditionally expect that it will occur nor despair of it as unconditionally not going to occur.

One must reckon that of desires some are natural, some groundless; and of the natural desires some are necessary and some merely natural; and of the necessary, some are necessary for happiness and some for freeing the body from troubles and some for life itself. The unwavering contemplation of these enables one to refer every choice and avoidance to the health of the body and the freedom of the soul from disturbance, since this is the goal of a blessed life. For we do everything for the sake of being neither in pain nor in terror. As soon as we achieve this state every storm in the soul is dispelled, since the animal is not in a passion to go after some need nor to seek something else to complete the good of the body and the soul. For we are in need of pleasure only when we are in pain because of the absence of pleasure, and when we are not in pain, then we no longer need pleasure.

And this is why we say that pleasure is the starting-point and goal of living blessedly. For we recognized this as our first innate good, and this is our starting point for every choice and avoidance and we come to this by judging every good by the criterion of feeling. And it is just because this is the first innate good, that we do not choose every pleasure; but sometimes we pass up many pleasures when we get a larger amount of what is uncongenial from them. And we believe many pains to be better than pleasures when a greater pleasure follows for a long while if we endure the pains. So every pleasure is a good thing, since it has a nature congenial [to us], but not every one is to be chosen. Just as every pain too is a bad thing, but not every one is such as to be always avoided. It is, however, appropriate to make all these decisions by comparative measurement and an examination of the advantages and disadvantages. For at some times we treat the good things as bad and conversely, the bad things as good.

And we believe that self-sufficiency is a great good, not in order that we might make do with few things under all circumstances, but so that if we do not have a lot we can make do with few, being genuinely convinced that those who least need extravagance enjoy it most; and that everything natural is easy to obtain and whatever is groundless is hard to obtain; and that simple flavours provide a pleasure equal to that of an extravagant life-style when all pain from want is removed, and barley cakes and water provide the highest pleasure when someone in want takes them. Therefore, becoming accustomed to simple, not extravagant, ways of life makes one completely healthy, makes man unhesitant in the face of life's necessary duties, puts us in a better condition for the times of extravagance which occasionally come along, and makes us fearless in the face of chance. So when we say that pleasure is the goal we do not mean the pleasures of the profligate or the pleasures of consumption, as some believe, either from ignorance and disagreement or from deliberate misinterpretation, but rather the lack of pain in the body and disturbance in the soul. For it is not drinking bouts and continuous partying and enjoying boys and women, or consuming fish and the other dainties of an extravagant table, which produce the pleasant life, but sober calculation which searches out the reasons for every choice and avoidance and drives out the opinions which are the source of the greatest turmoil for men's souls.

Prudence is the principle of all these things and is the greatest good. That is why prudence is a more valuable thing than philosophy. For prudence is the source of all the other virtues, teaching that it is impossible to live pleasantly without living prudently, honourably, and justly, and impossible to live prudently, honourably, and justly without living pleasantly. For the virtues are natural adjuncts of the pleasant life and the pleasant life is inseparable from them.

For who do you believe is better than a man who has pious opinions about the gods, is always fearless about death, has reasoned out the natural goal of life and understands that the limit of good things is easy to achieve completely and easy to provide, and that the limit of bad things either has a short duration or causes little trouble?

As to [Fate], introduced by some as the mistress of all, [he is scornful, saying rather that some things happen of necessity,] others by chance and others by our own agency, and that he sees that necessity is not answerable [to anyone], that chance is unstable, while what occurs by our own agency is autonomous, and that it is to this that praise and blame are attached. For it would be better to follow the stories told about the gods than to be a slave to the fate of the natural philosophers. For the former suggests a hope of escaping bad things by honouring the gods, but the latter involves an inescapable and merciless necessity. And he [the wise man] believes that chance is not a god, as the many think, for nothing is done in a disorderly way by god; nor that it is an uncertain cause. For he does not think that anything good or bad with respect to living blessedly is given by chance to men, although it does provide the starting points of great good and bad things. And he thinks it better to be unlucky in a rational way than lucky in a senseless way; for it is better for a good decision not to turn out right in action than for a bad decision to turn out right because of chance.

Practise these and the related precepts day and night, by yourself and with a like-minded friend, and you will never be disturbed either when awake or in sleep, and you will live as a god among men. For a man who lives among immortal goods is in no respect like a mere mortal animal.

The Principal Doctrines

I. What is blessed and indestructible has no troubles itself, nor does it give trouble to anyone else, so that it is not affected by feelings of anger or gratitude. For all such things are a sign of weakness.[1]

II. Death is nothing to us. For what has been dissolved has no sense-experience, and what has no sense-experience is nothing to us.

III. The removal of all feeling of pain is the limit of the magnitude of pleasures. Wherever a pleasurable feeling is present, for as long as it is present, there is neither a feeling of pain nor a feeling of distress, nor both together.

IV. The feeling of pain does not linger continuously in the flesh; rather, the sharpest is present for the shortest time, while what merely exceeds the feeling of pleasure in the flesh lasts only a few days. And diseases which last a long time involve feelings of pleasure which exceed feelings of pain.

V. It is impossible to live pleasantly without living prudently, honourably, and justly and impossible to live prudently, honourably, and justly without living pleasantly. And whoever lacks this cannot live pleasantly.

VI. The natural good of public office and kingship is for the sake of getting confidence from [other] men, [at least] from those from whom one *is* able to provide this.

VII. Some men want to become famous and respected, believing that this is the way to acquire security against [other] men. Thus if the life of such men is secure, they acquire the natural good; but if it is not secure, they do not have that for the sake of which they strove from the beginning according to what is naturally congenial.

VIII. No pleasure is a bad thing in itself. But the things which produce certain pleasures bring troubles many times greater than the pleasures.

IX. If every pleasure were condensed and were present, both in time and in the whole compound [body and soul] or in the most important parts of our nature, then pleasures would never differ from one another.

X. If the things which produce the pleasures of profligate men dissolved the intellect's fears about the phenomena of the heavens and about death and pains and, moreover, if they taught us the limit of our desires, then we would not have reason to criticize them, since they would be filled with pleasures from every source and would contain no feeling of pain or distress from any source—and that is what is bad.

XI. If our suspicions about heavenly phenomena and about death did not trouble us at all and were never anything to us, and, moreover, if not knowing the limits of pains and desires did not trouble us, then we would have no need of natural science.

XII. It was impossible for someone ignorant about the nature of the universe but still suspicious about the subjects of the myths to dissolve his feelings of fear about the most important matters. So it was impossible to receive unmixed pleasures without knowing natural science.

XIII. It was useless to obtain security from men while the things above and below the earth and, generally, the things in the unbounded remained as objects of suspicion.

XIV. The purest security is that which comes from a quiet life and withdrawal from the many, although a certain degree of security from other men does come by means of the power to repel [attacks] and by means of prosperity.

XV. Natural wealth is both limited and easy to acquire. But wealth [as defined by] groundless opinions extends without limit.

XVI. Chance has a small impact on the wise man, while reasoning has arranged for, is arranging for, and will arrange for the greatest and most important matters throughout the whole of his life.

1. [Scholiast: "Elsewhere he says that the gods are contemplated by reason, and that some exist 'numerically' (i.e., are numerically distinct, each being unique in kind) while others are similar in form, because of a continuous flow of similar images to the same place; and that they are anthropomorphic."—B.I. and L.P.G.]

XVII. The just life is most free from disturbance, but the unjust life is full of the greatest disturbance.

XVIII. As soon as the feeling of pain produced by want is removed, pleasure in the flesh will not increase but is only varied. But the limit of mental pleasures is produced by a reasoning out of these very pleasures [of the flesh] and of the things related to these, which used to cause the greatest fears in the intellect.

XIX. Unlimited time and limited time contain equal [amounts of] pleasure, if one measures its limits by reasoning.

XX. The flesh took the limits of pleasure to be unlimited, and [only] an unlimited time would have provided it. But the intellect, reasoning out the goal and limit of the flesh and dissolving the fears of eternity, provided us with the perfect way of life and had no further need of unlimited time. But it [the intellect] did not flee pleasure, and even when circumstances caused an exit from life it did not die as though it were lacking any aspect of the best life.

XXI. He who has learned the limits of life knows that it is easy to provide that which removes the feeling of pain owing to want and makes one's whole life perfect. So there is no need for things which involve struggle.

XXII. One must reason about the real goal and every clear fact, to which we refer mere opinions. If not, everything will be full of indecision and disturbance.

XXIII. If you quarrel with all your sense-perceptions you will have nothing to refer to in judging even those sense-perceptions which you claim are false.

XXIV. If you reject unqualifiedly any sense-perception and do not distinguish the opinion about what awaits confirmation, and what is already present in the sense-perception, and the feelings, and every application of the intellect to presentations, you will also disturb the rest of your sense-perceptions with your pointless opinions; as a result you will reject every criterion. If, on the other hand, in your conceptions formed by opinion, you affirm everything that awaits confirmation as well as what does not, you will not avoid falsehood, so that you will be in the position of maintaining every disputable point in every decision about what is and is not correct.

XXV. If you do not, on every occasion, refer each of your actions to the goal of nature, but instead turn prematurely to some other [criterion] in avoiding or pursuing [things], your actions will not be consistent with your reasoning.

XXVI. The desires which do not bring a feeling of pain when not fulfilled are not necessary, but the desire for them is easy to dispel when they seem to be hard to achieve or to produce harm.

XXVII. Of the things which wisdom provides for the blessedness of one's whole life, by far the greatest is the possession of friendship.

XXVIII. The same understanding produces confidence about there being nothing terrible which is eternal or [even] long-lasting and has also realized that security amid even these limited [bad things] is most easily achieved through friendship.

XXIX. Of desires, some are natural and necessary, some natural and not necessary, and some neither natural nor necessary but occurring as a result of a groundless opinion.[2]

XXX. Among natural desires, those which do not lead to a feeling of pain if not fulfilled and about which there is an intense effort, these are produced by an groundless opinion and they fail to be dissolved not because of their own nature but because of the groundless opinions of mankind.

XXXI. The justice of nature is a pledge of reciprocal usefulness, [i.e.,] neither to harm one another nor be harmed.

XXXII. There was no justice or injustice with respect to all those animals which were unable to make pacts about neither harming one another nor being harmed. Similarly, [there was no justice or injustice] for all those nations which were unable or unwilling to make pacts about neither harming one another nor being harmed.

XXXIII. Justice was not a thing in its own right, but [exists] in mutual dealings in whatever places there [is] a pact about neither harming one another nor being harmed.

XXXIV. Injustice is not a bad thing in its own right, but [only] because of the fear produced by the

2. [Scholiast: "Epicurus thinks that those which liberate us from pains are natural and necessary, for example drinking in the case of thirst; natural and not necessary are those which merely provide variations of pleasure but do not remove the feeling of pain, for example expensive foods; neither natural nor necessary are, for example, crowns and the erection of statues."]

suspicion that one will not escape the notice of those assigned to punish such actions.

XXXV. It is impossible for someone who secretly does something which men agreed [not to do] in order to avoid harming one another or being harmed to be confident that he will escape detection, even if in current circumstances he escapes detection ten thousand times. For until his death it will be uncertain whether he will continue to escape detection.

XXXVI. In general outline justice is the same for everyone; for it was something useful in mutual associations. But with respect to the peculiarities of a region or of other [relevant] causes, it does not follow that the same thing is just for everyone.

XXXVII. Of actions believed to be just, that whose usefulness in circumstances of mutual associations is supported by the testimony [of experience] has the attribute of serving as just whether it is the same for everyone or not. And if someone passes a law and it does not turn out to be in accord with what is useful in mutual associations, this no longer possesses the nature of justice. And if what is useful in the sense of being just changes, but for a while fits our basic grasp [of justice], nevertheless it was just for that length of time, [at least] for those who do not disturb themselves with empty words but simply look to the facts.

XXXVIII. If objective circumstances have not changed and things believed to be just have been shown in actual practice not to be in accord with our basic grasp [of justice], then those things were not just. And if objective circumstances do change and the same things which had been just turn out to be no longer useful, then those things were just as long as they were useful for the mutual associations of fellow citizens; but later, when they were not useful, they were no longer just.

XXXIX. The man who has made the best arrangements for confidence about external threats is he who has made the manageable things akin to himself, and has at least made the unmanageable things not alien to himself. But he avoided all contact with things for which not even this could be managed and he drove out of his life everything which it profited him to drive out.

XL. All those who had the power to acquire the greatest confidence from [the threats posed by] their neighbours also thereby lived together most pleasantly with the surest guarantee; and since they enjoyed the fullest sense of belonging they did not grieve the early death of the departed, as though it called for pity.

Epictetus

Stoicism as an organized philosophical movement flourished for a period of approximately five hundred years, from 300 B.C. to A.D. 180. The dates are, respectively, the approximate year in which the founder of Stoicism, Zeno of Citium (c. 344–c. 262 B.C.), began lecturing from a stoa, or porch, in the marketplace in Athens, and the year in which the last famous Stoic, the Roman emperor Marcus Aurelius, died. Although Stoic doctrine did not remain static in those five hundred years, the doctrinal differences between earlier and later Stoics appear for the most part to be minimal. What *is* remarkable is the difference in emphasis that Stoicism underwent. In the second and first centuries B.C., Stoicism was introduced into Roman intellectual circles. It found an audience so receptive that in the first and second centuries A.D. Stoicism was a powerful influence in the life of the Roman Empire, attracting such figures as Seneca (1–65), Epictetus (c. 50–c. 130), and Marcus Aurelius (121–180).

In the process of change, Stoicism became less of a philosophy and more of a guide to right conduct. The early Stoics had placed equal emphasis on logic, physics, and ethics; but the Roman Stoics were concerned almost exclusively with the ethical and political aspects of Stoicism. It is easy to see why those aspects of Stoicism appealed to a Marcus Aurelius: the Stoic emphasis on duty and the Stoic belief that all people are citizens of one vast city dovetailed nicely with Roman imperialistic policy. But Stoicism also offered consolation to the less fortunate of the time, including Epictetus, a former slave, since it claimed that that which has ultimate value, namely, virtue, is equally open to all; and that such things as wealth, health, and honor are either of no value whatsoever or merely of instrumental value in the attainment of virtue.

The early Stoics saw the three areas of logic, physics, and ethics as intimately related. These early Stoics made significant contributions to logical theory, with much of their work a departure from Aristotelian logic. For their physical theory the early Stoics looked back to what they took to be the teachings of a Pre-Socratic philosopher, Heraclitus of Ephesus, who flourished around 500 B.C. Heraclitus had taught that the universe is a continuously dynamic thing in which nothing remains strictly the same from one moment to the next. Heraclitus had used fire as a symbol for the ceaseless change occurring in the universe; he may also have intended to say that the universe is actually ruled and guided by fire, which would be the noblest kind of matter in nature. The early Stoics interpreted him in this way. Fire was also thought to be the source and seat of human intelligence; thus, if the universe is ruled by fire, the universe is itself intelligent. In fact, the Stoics believed the universe to be a vast rational being that exhibits, through the guidance of fire, order and law-governed behavior. The Stoics thus consciously appealed to a macrocosm-microcosm analogy: the universe is a rational animal writ large, and a person is or should be the universe writ small. This doctrine has four important repercussions for Stoic ethics.

First, since the source of human intelligence is a natural material element, fire, and since intelligence is the hallmark of what it is to be human, it followed for the Stoics that a person is a part of the natural physical universe, and not something over and above it. This belief fit very well with a doctrine that the Stoics adopted from the Cynics, namely, that all persons are "citizens of the world," which implied that all persons are radically equal. Stoic materialism thus provided a metaphysical underpinning for Stoic cosmopolitanism.

Second, if the universe itself is governed by certain laws and if a person is a microcosm of the universe, then it follows that a person is subject to the same laws as those that govern the universe.

The laws in question, moreover, were viewed not merely as *descriptive* but as *prescriptive:* they prescribe how things *ought* to behave. These laws might be at variance with the customs and legal conventions of a particular society, and if so, those customs and conventions are wrong. In other words, a "natural law" supersedes all customary law and is binding on all persons. Natural Law theories in and after the Middle Ages have their roots in Stoicism.

Third, inasmuch as a person is a microcosm of an inherently rational world, a person ought to live a life in perfect conformity with nature, that is, a life in which reason dominates a person's actions and passions. The Stoic "wise man" will live his life so that he does only that which is in accord with nature; moreover, he will do it simply *because* it is in accord with nature. For the Stoic the value of an action resides not in the happiness or pleasure it may happen to bring about, but solely in the virtuous state of mind of the agent. In this respect Stoic ethics foreshadow the ethical theory of Immanuel Kant.

Finally, the Stoics' insistence on the law-governed nature of the universe committed them to determinism, the thesis that everything that happens is the outcome of the operation of unchangeable and all-pervasive laws. As their critics were quick to point out, this seemed to clash with their belief that humans are free, responsible agents. In order to meet this criticism the Stoics stressed that it is important to see what constitutes human freedom. Epictetus' *Encheiridion,* or "Handbook," reprinted here, besides giving a moving account of the Stoic view of life, attempts to resolve the contradiction between human freedom and determinism.

Not much is known of Epictetus' life. He was born in Hieropolis in Asia Minor, was for some time a slave, but was freed by his Roman master. He was educated by a Stoic philosopher and began to teach philosophy himself in Rome until he was banished by the emperor Domitian. Epictetus moved to Nicopolis, in northwestern Greece, where he taught and practiced Stoicism until his death. No written works survive: the *Encheiridion* was dictated to a disciple.

• • •

Important source material on Stoicism is topically arranged in A. A. Long and D. N. Sedley, eds., *The Hellenistic Philosophers* (Cambridge: Cambridge University Press, 1987), two volumes (English translations in volume I). See also Brad Inwood and L. P. Gerson, eds., *Hellenistic Philosophy,* second edition (Indianapolis: Hackett Publishing Company, 1997). F. H. Sandbach's *The Stoics* (New York: W. W. Norton, 1975) gives an elementary account. J. M. Rist, *Stoic Philosophy* (Cambridge: Cambridge University Press, 1969) deals topically with several major issues. Benson Mates, *Stoic Logic* (1953; rpt. Berkeley: University of California Press, 1961); Samuel Sambursky, *Physics of the Stoics* (1959; rpt. London: Hutchinson, 1971); and Brad Inwood, *Ethics and Human Action in Early Stoicism* (Oxford: Clarendon Press, 1985) are excellent in their areas. Important papers are collected in A. A. Long, ed., *Problems in Stoicism* (London: Athlone Press, 1971) and John M. Rist, ed., *The Stoics* (Berkeley: University of California Press, 1978). Two more specialized but rewarding books are Susanne Bobzien, *Determinism and Freedom in Stoic Philosophy* (Oxford: Clarendon Press, 1998) and Richard Sorabji, *Emotion and Peace of Mind: From Stoic Agitation to Christian Temptation* (Oxford: Oxford University Press, 2000).

William E. Mann

Encheiridion

1

Some things are up to us and some are not up to us. Our opinions are up to us, and our impulses, desires, aversions—in short, whatever is our own doing. Our bodies are not up to us, nor are our possessions, our reputations, or our public offices, or, that is, whatever is not our own doing. The things that are up to us are by nature free, unhindered, and unimpeded; the things that are not up to us are weak, enslaved, hindered, not our own. So remember, if you think that things naturally enslaved are free or that things not your own are your own, you will be thwarted, miserable, and upset, and will blame both gods and men. But if you think that only what is yours is yours, and that what is not your own is, just as it is, not your own, then no one will ever coerce you, no one will hinder you, you will blame no one, you will not accuse anyone, you will not do a single thing unwillingly, you will have no enemies, and no one will harm you, because you will not be harmed at all.

As you aim for such great goals, remember that you must not undertake them by acting moderately,[1] but must let some things go completely and postpone others for the time being. But if you want both those great goals and also to hold public office and to be rich then you may perhaps not get even the latter just because you aim at the former too; and you certainly will fail to get the former, which are the only things that yield freedom and happiness.[2]

From the start, then, work on saying to each harsh appearance,[3] "You are an appearance, and not at all the thing that has the appearance." Then examine it and assess it by these yardsticks that you have, and first and foremost by whether it concerns the things that are up to us or the things that are not up to us. And if it is about one of the things that is not up to us, be ready to say, "You are nothing in relation to me."

2

Remember, what a desire proposes is that you gain what you desire, and what an aversion proposes is that you not fall into what you are averse to. Someone who fails to get what he desires is *un*fortunate, while someone who falls into what he is averse to has met *mis*fortune. So if you are averse only to what is against nature among the things that are up to you, then you will never fall into anything that you are averse to; but if you are averse to illness or death or poverty, you will meet misfortune. So detach your aversion from everything not up to us, and transfer it to what is against nature among the things that are up to us. And for the time being eliminate desire completely, since if you desire something that is not up to us, you are bound to be unfortunate, and at the same time none of the things that are up to us, which it would be good to desire, will be available to you. Make use only of impulse and its

Reprinted from *The Handbook of Epictetus*, translated, with introduction and annotations, by Nicholas White (Indianapolis: Hackett Publishing Company, 1983), by permission of the publisher.

1. [This may mean simply that the proposed undertaking is difficult (Oldfather's translation suggests this), or it may mean (as I believe) that the aim cannot be achieved by the Aristotelian policy of pursuing a mean or middle course between extremes.—N.W.]

2. [Epictetus recommends aiming to have one's state of mind in accord with nature, in the sense explained in the previous paragraph and in c. 8. His point here is that if you aim for that and also simultaneously for certain "externals" like wealth, you will probably have neither and clearly will not have the former.]

3. [The word "appearance" translates *phantasia*, which some translators render by "impression" or "presentation." An appearance is roughly the immediate experience of sense or feeling, which may or may not represent an external state of affairs. (The Stoics held, against the Skeptics, that some appearances self-evidently do represent external states of affairs correctly.)]

contrary, rejection,[4] though with reservation, lightly, and without straining.

3

In the case of everything attractive or useful or that you are fond of, remember to say just what sort of thing it is, beginning with the least little things. If you are fond of a jug, say "I am fond of a jug!" For then when it is broken you will not be upset. If you kiss your child or your wife, say that you are kissing a human being; for when it dies you will not be upset.

4

When you are about to undertake some action, remind yourself what sort of action it is. If you are going out for a bath, put before your mind what happens at baths—there are people who splash, people who jostle, people who are insulting, people who steal. And you will undertake the action more securely if from the start you say of it, "I want to take a bath and to keep my choices in accord with nature"; and likewise for each action. For that way if something happens to interfere with your bathing you will be ready to say, "Oh, well, I wanted not only this but also to keep my choices in accord with nature, and I cannot do that if I am annoyed with things that happen."

5

What upsets people is not things themselves but their judgments about the things. For example, death is nothing dreadful (or else it would have appeared dreadful to Socrates), but instead the judgment about death that it is dreadful—*that* is what is dreadful. So when we are thwarted or upset or distressed, let us never blame someone else but rather ourselves, that is, our own judgments. An uneducated person accuses others when he is doing badly; a partly educated person accuses himself, an educated person accuses neither someone else nor himself.

4. [Impulse and rejection (*hormē* and *aphormē*) are, in Stoic terms, natural and non-rational psychological movements, so to speak, that are respectively toward or away from external objects.]

6

Do not be joyful about any superiority that is not your own. If the horse were to say joyfully, "I am beautiful," one could put up with it. But certainly you, when you say joyfully, "I have a beautiful horse," are joyful about the good of the horse. What, then, is your own? Your way of dealing with appearances. So whenever you are in accord with nature in your way of dealing with appearances, then be joyful, since then you are joyful about a good of your own.

7

On a voyage when your boat has anchored, if you want to get fresh water you may pick up a small shellfish and a vegetable by the way, but you must keep your mind fixed on the boat and look around frequently in case the captain calls. If he calls you must let all those other things go so that you will not be tied up and thrown on the ship like livestock. That is how it is in life too: if you are given a wife and a child instead of a vegetable and a small shellfish, that will not hinder you; but if the captain calls, let all those things go and run to the boat without turning back; and if you are old, do not even go very far from the boat, so that when the call comes you are not left behind.

8

Do not seek to have events happen as you want them to, but instead want them to happen as they do happen, and your life will go well.

9

Illness interferes with the body, not with one's faculty of choice,[5] unless that faculty of choice wishes it to. Lameness interferes with the limb, not with one's faculty of choice. Say this at each thing that happens to you, since you will find that it interferes with something else, not with you.

5. ["Faculty of choice" translates *proairesis*, which designates a rational faculty of the soul (cf. n.4).]

10

At each thing that happens to you, remember to turn to yourself and ask what capacity you have for dealing with it. If you see a beautiful boy or woman, you will find the capacity of self-control for that. If hardship comes to you, you will find endurance. If it is abuse, you will find patience. And if you become used to this, you will not be carried away by appearances.

11

Never say about anything, "I have lost it," but instead, "I have given it back." Did your child die? It was given back. Did your wife die? She was given back. "My land was taken." So this too was given back. "But the person who took it was bad!" How does the way the giver[6] asked for it back concern you? As long as he gives it, take care of it as something that is not your own, just as travelers treat an inn.

12

If you want to make progress,[7] give up all considerations like these: "If I neglect my property I will have nothing to live on," "If I do not punish my slave boy he will be bad." It is better to die of hunger with distress and fear gone than to live upset in the midst of plenty. It is better for the slave boy to be bad than for you to be in a bad state. Begin therefore with little things. A little oil is spilled, a little wine is stolen: say, "This is the price of tranquillity; this is the price of not being upset." Nothing comes for free. When you call the slave boy, keep in mind that he is capable of not paying attention, and even if he does pay attention he is capable of not doing any of the things that you want him to. But he is not in such a good position that your being upset or not depends on him.

6. [The "giver" can be taken to be nature, or the natural order of the cosmos, or god, which the Stoics identified with each other.]

7. ["Making progress" (*prokoptein*) is the Stoic expression for movement in the direction of the ideal condition for a human being, embodied by the Stoic "sage" (cf. c. 15, n.8).]

13

If you want to make progress, let people think you are a mindless fool about externals, and do not desire a reputation for knowing about them. If people think you amount to something, distrust yourself. Certainly it is not easy to be on guard both for one's choices to be in accord with nature and also for externals, and a person who concerns himself with the one will be bound to neglect the other.

14

You are foolish if you want your children and your wife and your friends to live forever, since you are wanting things to be up to you that are not up to you, and things to be yours that are not yours. You are stupid in the same way if you want your slave boy to be faultness, since you are wanting badness not to be badness but something else. But wanting not to fail to get what you desire—*this* you are capable of. A person's master is someone who has power over what he wants or does not want, either to obtain it or take it away. Whoever wants to be free, therefore, let him not want or avoid anything that is up to others. Otherwise he will necessarily be a slave.

15

Remember, you must behave as you do at a banquet. Something is passed around and comes to you: reach out your hand politely and take some. It goes by: do not hold it back. It has not arrived yet: do not stretch your desire out toward it, but wait until it comes to you. In the same way toward your children, in the same way toward your wife, in the same way toward public office, in the same way toward wealth, and you will be fit to share a banquet with the gods. But if when things are set in front of you, you do not take them but despise them, then you will not only share a banquet with the gods but also be a ruler along with them. For by acting in this way Diogenes and Heraclitus[8] and people like them were deservedly gods and were deservedly called gods.

8. [Diogenes the Cynic (the one who with his lantern looked for an honest man) and Heraclitus of Ephesus, the Pre-Socratic philosopher, were along with Socrates and Zeno people whom the Stoics said might possibly have reached the perfect condition of being sages, which the

16

When you see someone weeping in grief at the departure of his child or the loss of his property, take care not to be carried away by the appearance that the externals he is involved in are bad, and be ready to say immediately, "What weighs down on this man is not what has happened (since it does not weigh down on someone else), but his judgment about it." Do not hesitate, however, to sympathise with him verbally, and even to moan with him if the occasion arises; but be careful not to moan inwardly.

17

Remember that you are an actor in a play, which is as the playwright wants it to be: short if he wants it short, long if he wants it long. If he wants you to play a beggar, play even this part skillfully, or a cripple, or a public official, or a private citizen. What is yours is to play the assigned part well. But to choose it belongs to someone else.

18

When a raven gives an unfavorable sign by croaking,[9] do not be carried away by the appearance, but immediately draw a distinction to yourself and say, "None of these signs is for me, but only for my petty body or my petty property or my petty judgments or children or wife. For all signs are favorable if I wish, since it is up to me to be benefited by whichever of them turns out correct."

19

You can be invincible if you do not enter any contest in which victory is not up to you. See that you are not carried away by the appearance, in thinking that someone is happy when you see him honored ahead of you or very powerful or otherwise having a good reputation. For if the really good things are up to us, neither envy nor jealousy has a place, and you yourself will want neither to be a general or a magistrate or a consul, but to be free. And there is one road to this: despising what is not up to us.

20

Remember that what is insulting is not the person who abuses you or hits you, but the judgment about them that they *are* insulting. So when someone irritates you be aware that what irritates you is your own belief. Most importantly, therefore, try not to be carried away by appearance, since if you once gain time and delay you will control yourself more easily.

21

Let death and exile and everything that is terrible appear before your eyes every day, especially death; and you will never have anything contemptible in your thoughts or crave anything excessively.

22

If you crave philosophy prepare yourself on the spot to be ridiculed, to be jeered at by many people who will say, "Here he is again, all of a sudden turned philosopher on us!" and "Where did he get that high brow?" But don't *you* put on a high brow, but hold fast to the things that appear best to you, as someone assigned by god to this place. And remember that if you hold to these views, those who previously ridiculed you will later be impressed with you, but if you are defeated by them you will be doubly ridiculed.

23

If it ever happens that you turn outward to want to please another person, certainly you have lost your plan of life. Be content therefore in everything to be a philosopher, and if you want to seem to be one, make yourself appear so to yourself, and you will be capable of it.

Stoics took to be conceptually no different from the perfect condition of a god.]

9. [Most people in antiquity believed in fortune-telling of various kinds, involving bird-calls, the flight of birds, inspection of entrails, stars, and whatnot. Many Stoics, notably Chrysippus, believed in such things, not least because they saw in them manifestations of the order of the cosmos and the tight and intricate interconnections within it, and thus saw them as scientific rather than superstitious.]

24

Do not be weighed down by the consideration, "I shall live without any honor, everywhere a nobody!" For if lack of honors is something bad, I cannot be in a bad state because of another person any more than I can be in a shameful one. It is not your task[10] to gain political office, or be invited to a banquet, is it? Not at all. How then is that a lack of honor? And how will you be a nobody everywhere, if you need to be a somebody only in things that are up to you—in which it is open to you to be of the greatest worth? "But your friends will be without help!" What do you mean, "without help?" Well, they will be without a little cash from you, and you will not make them Roman citizens. Who told you, then, that these things are up to you and not the business of someone else? Who can give to someone else what he does not have himself? "Get money," someone says, "so that we may have some." If I can get it while keeping self-respect and trustworthiness and high-mindedness, show me the way and I will get it. But if you demand that I lose the good things that are mine so that you may acquire things that are not good, see for yourselves how unfair and inconsiderate you are. Which do you want more, money or a self-respecting and trustworthy friend? Then help me more toward this, and do not expect me to do things that will make me lose these qualities. "But my country," he says, "will be without help, in so far as it depends on me!" Again, what sort of "help" is this? So it will not have porticos and baths by your efforts. What does that amount to? For it does not have shoes because of the blacksmith or weapons because of the cobbler, but it is enough if each person fulfills his own task. And if you furnished for it another citizen who was trustworthy and self-respecting, would you in no way be helpful to it? "Yes, I would be." Then neither would you yourself be unhelpful to it. "Then what place," he says "will I have in the city?" The one you can have by preserving your trustworthiness and self-respect. And if while wanting to help it you throw away these things, what use will you be to it if you turn out shameless and untrustworthy?

10. [The word translated "task" here and below is *ergon*, which might also be translated by "function."]

25

Has someone been given greater honor than you at a banquet or in a greeting or by being brought in to give advice? If these things are good, you should be glad that he has got them. If they are bad, do not be angry that you did not get them. And remember, you cannot demand an equal share if you did not do the same things, with a view to getting things that are not up to us. For how can someone who does not hang around a person's door have an equal share with someone who does, or someone who does not escort him with someone who does, or someone who does not praise him with someone who does? You will be unjust and greedy, then, if you want to obtain these things for free when you have not paid the price for which they are bought. Well, what is the price of heads of lettuce? An obol, say. So if someone who has paid an obol takes the heads of lettuce, and you who do not pay do not take them, do not think that you are worse off than the one who did. For just as he has the lettuce, you have the obol that you did not pay. It is the same way in this case. You were not invited to someone's banquet? You did not give the host the price of the meal. He sells it for praise; he sells it for attention. Then give him the balance for which it is sold, if that is to your advantage. But you are greedy and stupid if you want both not to pay and also to take. Have you got nothing, then, in place of the meal? Indeed you do have something; you did not praise someone you did not wish to praise, and you did not have to put up with the people around his door.

26

It is possible to learn the will of nature from the things in which we do not differ from each other. For example, when someone else's little slave boy breaks his cup we are ready to say, "It's one of those things that just happen." Certainly, then, when your own cup is broken you should be just the way you were when the other person's was broken. Transfer the same idea to larger matters. Someone else's child is dead, or his wife. There is no one would not say, "It's the lot of a human being." But when one's own dies, immediately it is, "Alas! Poor me!" But we should have remembered how we feel when we hear of the same thing about others.

27

Just as a target is not set up to be missed, in the same way nothing bad by nature happens in the world.[11]

28

If someone turned your body over to just any person who happened to meet you, you would be angry. But are you not ashamed that you turn over your own faculty of judgment to whoever happens along, so that if he abuses you it is upset and confused?

29

For each action, consider what leads up to it and what follows it, and approach it in the light of that. Otherwise you will come to it enthusiastically at first, since you have not borne in mind any of what will happen next, but later when difficulties turn up you will give up disgracefully. You want to win an Olympic victory? I do too, by the gods, since that is a fine thing. But consider what leads up to it and what follows it, and undertake the action in the light of that. You must be disciplined, keep a strict diet, stay away from cakes, train according to strict routine at a fixed time in heat and in cold, not drink cold water, not drink wine when you feel like it, and in general you must have turned yourself over to your trainer as to a doctor, and then in the contest "dig in,"[12] sometimes dislocate your hand, twist your ankle, swallow a lot of sand, sometimes be whipped, and, after all that, lose. Think about that and then undertake training, if you want to. Otherwise you will be behaving the way children do, who play wrestlers one time, gladiators another time, blow trumpets another time, then act a play. In this way you too are now an athlete, now a gladiator, then an orator, then a philosopher, yet you are nothing wholeheartedly, but like a monkey you mimic each sight that you see, and one thing after another is to your taste, since you do not undertake a thing after considering it from every side, but only randomly and half-heartedly.

In the same way when some people watch a philosopher and hear one speaking like Euphrates[13] (though after all who can speak like him?), they want to be philosophers themselves. Just you consider, as a human being, what sort of thing it is; then inspect your own nature and whether you can bear it. You want to do the pentathlon, or to wrestle? Look at your arms, your thighs, inspect your loins. Different people are naturally suited for different things. Do you think that if you do those things you can eat as you now do, drink as you now do, have the same likes and dislikes? You must go without sleep, put up with hardship, be away from your own people, be looked down on by a little slave boy, be laughed at by people who meet you, get the worse of it in everything, honor, public office, law course, every little thing. Think about whether you want to exchange these things for tranquillity, freedom, calm. If not, do not embrace philosophy, and do not like children be a philosopher at one time, later a tax-collector, then an orator, then a procurator of the emperor. These things do not go together. You must be one person, either good or bad. You must either work on your ruling principle,[14] or work on externals, practise the art either of what is inside or of what is outside, that is, play the role either of a philosopher or of a non-philosopher.

30

Appropriate actions[15] are in general measured by relationships. He is a father: that entails taking care of him, yielding to him in everything, putting up with

11. [According to the Stoic view, the universe as a whole is perfect and everything in it has a place in its overall design, so that nothing can exist or occur that is bad in its relation to that overall design.]

12. [Nobody knows just what this expression means in this context.]

13. [Euphrates was a Stoic lecturer noted for his eloquence.]

14. [The "ruling principle" (or "governing principle"), the *hēgemonikon*, in the rather complicated psychological theory adopted by the Stoics, is that central part of the soul that can understand what is good and decide to act on that understanding.]

15. ["Appropriate actions" are *kathēkonta*, which Cicero called *officia*, and are in English translations often called "duties," though the notion is actually somewhat different from that of duty. They are the actions that are of a type

him when he abuses you or strikes you. "But he is a bad father." Does nature then determine that you have a good father? No, only that you have a father.[16] "My brother has done me wrong." Then keep your place in relation to him; do not consider his action, but instead consider what you can do to bring your own faculty of choice[17] into accord with nature. Another person will not do you harm unless you wish it; you will be harmed at just that time at which you take yourself to be harmed. In this way, then, you will discover the appropriate actions to expect from a neighbor, from a citizen, from a general, if you are in the habit of looking at relationships.

31

The most important aspect of piety toward the gods is certainly both to have correct beliefs about them, as beings that arrange the universe well and justly, and to set yourself to obey them and acquiesce in everything that happens and to follow it willingly, as something brought to completion by the best judgment. For in this way you will never blame the gods or accuse them of neglecting you. And this piety is impossible unless you detach the good and the bad from what is not up to us and attach it exclusively to what is up to us, because if you think that any of what is not up to us is good or bad, then when you fail to get what you want and fall into what you do not want, you will be bound to blame and hate those who cause this. For every animal by nature flees and turns away from things that are harmful and from what causes them, and pursues and admires things that are beneficial and what causes them. There is therefore no way for a person who thinks he is being harmed to enjoy what he thinks is harming him, just as it is impossible to enjoy the harm itself. Hence a son even abuses his father when the father does not give him a share of things that he thinks are good; and thinking that being a tyrant was a good thing is what made enemies of Polyneices and Eteocles.[18] This is why the farmer too abuses the gods, and the sailor, and the merchant, and those who have lost their wives and children. For wherever someone's advantage lies, there he also shows piety. So whoever takes care to have desires and aversions as one should also in the same instance takes care about being pious. And it is always appropriate to make libations and sacrifices and give firstfruits according to the custom of one's forefathers, in a manner that is pure and neither slovenly nor careless, nor indeed cheaply nor beyond one's means.

32

When you make use of fortune-telling, remember that you do not know what will turn out and have gone to the fortune-teller to find out, but that if you really are a philosopher you have gone already knowing what sort of thing it is. For if it is one of the things that is not up to us, it is bound to be neither good nor bad. Therefore do not bring desire or aversion to the fortune-teller and do not approach him trembling but instead realizing that everything that turns out is indifferent[19] and nothing in relation to you, and that whatever sort of thing it may be, you will be able to deal with it well and no one will hinder that. So go confidently to the gods as advisers, and thereafter when some particular advice has been given to you remember who your advisers are and whom you will be disregarding if you disobey. Approach fortune-telling as Socrates thought a person should, in cases where the whole consideration has reference to the outcome, and no resource is available from reason or any other technique to find out about the matter. So, when it is necessary to share a danger with a friend or with your country, do not use fortune-telling about whether you should share the danger. For if the fortune-teller says that the omens are unfavorable, clearly death is signified or the injury of a part of your body or exile. But reason chooses to stand by your friend and to share danger with your country

generally in accord with nature, or with a particular sort of person's place in it.]

16. [The idea here is, roughly, that there are certain relationships of affinity established by the natural order, and that having a father represents one of them, but that having a good father is not entailed by it.]

17. [Cf. c. 9, n.5, and c. 29, n.14.]

18. [The story of the conflict between the brothers Polyneices and Eteocles is best known to modern readers from Sophocles' tragedy *Antigone*.]

19. [Things that are "indifferent" in the Stoic view are all things that are external and not up to oneself (cf. c. 1, e.g.).]

even under these conditions. For this reason pay attention to the greater fortune-teller, Pythian Apollo, who threw out of the temple the man who did not help his brother when he was being murdered.[20]

33

Set up right now a certain character and pattern for yourself which you will preserve when you are by yourself and when you are with people. Be silent for the most part, or say what you have to in a few words. Speak rarely, when the occasion requires speaking, but not about just any topic that comes up, not about gladiators, horse-races, athletes, eating or drinking—the things that always come up; and especially if it is about people, talk without blaming or praising or comparing. Divert by your own talk, if you can, the talk of those with you to something appropriate. If you happen to be stranded among strangers, do not talk. Do not laugh a great deal or at a great many things or unrestrainedly. Refuse to swear oaths, altogether if possible, or otherwise as circumstances allow. Avoid banquets given by those outside philosophy. But if the appropriate occasion arises, take great care not to slide into their ways, since certainly if a person's companion is dirty the person who spends time with him, even if he happens to be clean, is bound to become dirty too. Take what has to do with the body to the point of bare need, such as food, drink, clothing, house, household slaves, and cut out everything that is for reputation or luxury. As for sex stay pure as far as possible before marriage, and if you have it do only what is allowable. But do not be angry or censorious toward those who do engage in it, and do not always be making an exhibition of the fact that you do not.

If someone reports back to you that so-and-so is saying bad things about you, do not reply to them but answer, "Obviously he didn't know my other bad characteristics, since otherwise he wouldn't just have mentioned these."

For the most part there is no need to go to public shows, but if ever the right occasion comes do not show your concern to be for anything but yourself; that is to say, wish to have happen only what does happen, and for the person to win who actually does win, since that way you will not be thwarted. But refrain completely from shouting or laughing at anyone or being very much caught up in it. After you leave, do not talk very much about what has happened, except what contributes to your own improvement, since that would show that the spectacle had impressed you.

Do not go indiscriminately or readily to people's public lectures, but when you do be on guard to be dignified and steady and at the same time try not to be disagreeable.

When you are about to meet someone, especially someone who seems to be distinguished, put to yourself the question, "What would Socrates or Zeno have done in these circumstances?" and you will not be at a loss as to how to deal with the occasion. When you go to see someone who is important, put to yourself the thought that you will not find him at home, that you will be shut out, that the door will be slammed, that he will pay no attention to you. If it is appropriate to go even under these conditions, go and put up with what happens, and never say to yourself, "It wasn't worth all that!" For that is the way of a non-philosopher, someone who is misled by externals.

In your conversations stay away from making frequent and longwinded mention of what you have done and the dangers that you have been in, since it is not as pleasant for others to hear about what has happened to you as it is for you to remember your own dangers.

Stay away from raising a laugh, since this manner slips easily into vulgarity and at the same time is liable to lessen your neighbors' respect for you. It is also risky to fall into foul language. So when anything like that occurs, if a good opportunity arises, go so far as to criticize the person who has done it, and otherwise by staying silent and blushing and frowning you will show that you are displeased by what has been said.

34

Whenever you encounter some kind of apparent pleasure, be on guard, as in the case of other appearances, not to be carried away by it, but let the thing wait for you and allow yourself to delay. Then bring before

20. [The idea is that one does not need a fortune-teller to tell one whether one should defend one's country or one's friends, and that this fact was recognized by the oracle of Apollo at Delphi.]

your mind two times, both the time when you enjoy the pleasure and the time when after enjoying it you later regret it and berate yourself; and set against these the way you will be pleased and will praise yourself if you refrain from it. But if the right occasion appears for you to undertake the action, pay attention so that you will not be overcome by its attractiveness and pleasantness and seductiveness, and set against it how much better it is to be conscious of having won this victory against it.

35

When you do something that you determine is to be done, never try not to be seen doing it, even if most people are likely to think something bad about it. If you are not doing it rightly, avoid the act itself; if you are doing it rightly, why do you fear those who will criticize you wrongly?

36

Just as the propositions "It is day" and "It is night" have their full value when disjoined [*sc.*, in "It is day *or* it is night"] but have negative value when conjoined [*sc.*, in "It is day *and* it is night"], in the same way, granted that taking the larger portion has value for one's body, it has negative value for preserving the fellowship of a banquet in the way one should.[21] So when you eat with another, remember not merely to see the value for your body of what lies in front of you, but also to preserve your respect for your host.

37

If you undertake some role beyond your capacity, you both disgrace yourself by taking it and also thereby neglect the role that you were unable to take.

38

Just as in walking about you pay attention so as not to step on a nail or twist your foot, pay attention in the same way so as not to harm your ruling principle.[22] And if we are on guard about this in every action, we shall set about it more securely.

39

The measure of possessions for each person is the body, as the foot is of the shoe. So if you hold to this principle you will preserve the measure; but if you step beyond it, you will in the end be carried as if over a cliff; just as in the case of the shoe, if you go beyond the foot, you get a gilded shoe, and then a purple embroidered one. For there is no limit to a thing once it is beyond its measure.

40

Women are called ladies by men right after they are fourteen. And so when they see that they have nothing else except to go to bed with men, they begin to make themselves up and place all their hopes in that. It is therefore worthwhile to pay attention so that they are aware that they are honored for nothing other than appearing modest and self-respecting.

41

It shows lack of natural talent to spend time on what concerns the body, as in exercising a great deal, eating a great deal, drinking a great deal, moving one's bowels or copulating a great deal. Instead you must do these things in passing, but turn your whole attention toward your faculty of judgment.[23]

21. [Very roughly, the idea is that the value of an action has to be judged from all features of the context. The parallel is that allegedly the meaningfulness of a sentence depends in a way on its context.]

22. [Cf. c. 29, n.14.]

23. [Cf. c. 29, n.14. The claim is in effect that one should be concerned wholly with the state of the ruling part of one's soul, and not with external states of affairs or with those aspects of the soul, such as one's affective feelings or desires, that are directly dependent on external states of affairs. One can see here the Stoic view, which seems paradoxical to many, that one's feelings and non-rational desires are in a crucial sense external to one's true self (cf. c. 6 and Introduction).]

42

When someone acts badly toward you or speaks badly of you, remember that he does or says it in the belief that it is appropriate for him to do so. Accordingly he cannot follow what appears to you but only what appears to him, so that if things appear badly to him, he is harmed in as much as he has been deceived. For if someone thinks that a true conjunctive proposition[24] is false, the conjunction is not harmed but rather the one who is deceived. Starting from these considerations you will be gentle with the person who abuses you. For you must say on each occasion, "That's how it seemed to him."

43

Everything has two handles, one by which it may be carried and the other not. If your brother acts unjustly toward you, do not take hold of it by this side, that he has acted unjustly (since this is the handle by which it may not be carried), but instead by this side, that he is your brother and was brought up with you, and you will be taking hold of it in the way that it can be carried.

44

These statements are not valid inferences: "I am richer than you; therefore I am superior to you," or "I am more eloquent than you; therefore I am superior to you." But rather these are valid: "I am richer than you; therefore my property is superior to yours," or "I am more eloquent than you; therefore my speaking is superior to yours." But you are identical neither with your property nor with your speaking.

45

Someone takes a bath quickly; do not say that he does it badly but that he does it quickly. Someone drinks a great deal of wine; do not say that he does it badly but that he does a great deal of it. For until you have discerned what his judgment was, how do you know whether he did it badly? In this way it will not turn out that you receive convincing appearances of some things but give assent to quite different ones.[25]

46

Never call yourself a philosopher and do not talk a great deal among non-philosophers about philosophical propositions, but do what follows from them. For example, at a banquet do not say how a person ought to eat, but eat as a person ought to. Remember that Socrates had so completely put aside ostentation that people actually went to him when they wanted to be introduced to philosophers, and he took them.[26] He was that tolerant of being overlooked. And if talk about philosophical propositions arises among non-philosophers, for the most part be silent, since there is a great danger of your spewing out what you have not digested. And when someone says to you that you know nothing and you are not hurt by it, then you know that you are making a start at your task. Sheep do not show how much they have eaten by bringing the feed to the shepherds, but they digest the food inside themselves, and outside themselves they bear wool and milk. So in your case likewise do not display propositions to non-philosophers but instead the actions that come from the propositions when they are digested.

47

When you have become adapted to living cheaply as far as your body is concerned, do not make a show of it, and if you drink water do not say at every opening that you drink water. If you wish to train yourself to hardship, do it for yourself and not for those outside.

24. [Cf. c. 36. A proposition of this sort consists of two component propositions conjoined by "and."]

25. [A "convincing appearance" is a *katalēptikē phantasia*, the sort of appearance that according to the Stoics is a self-evidently correct representation of the way things actually are (cf. n.3). "Assent" is *synkatathesis*. Correct assent would of course be assent to self-evidently correct appearances. The line of thought here is, however, quite compressed, and the student will find it a difficult exercise to explain it.]

26. [The allusion is perhaps to the events in the early part of Plato's *Protagoras*.]

Do not throw your arms around statues.[27] Instead, when you are terribly thirsty, take cold water into your mouth, and spit it out, and do not tell anyone about it.

48

The position and character of a non-philosopher: he never looks for benefit or harm to come from himself but from things outside. The position and character of a philosopher: he looks for all benefit and harm to come from himself.

Signs of someone's making progress: he censures no one; he praises no one; he blames no one; he never talks about himself as a person who amounts to something or knows something. When he is thwarted or prevented in something, he accuses himself. And if someone praises him he laughs to himself at the person who has praised him; and if someone censures him he does not respond. He goes around like an invalid, careful not to move any of his parts that are healing before they have become firm. He has kept off all desire from himself, and he has transferred all aversion onto what is against nature among the things that are up to us. His impulses toward everything are diminished. If he seems foolish or ignorant, he does not care. In a single phrase, he is on guard against himself as an enemy lying in wait.

49

When someone acts grand because he understands and can expound the works of Chrysippus,[28] say to yourself, "If Chrysippus had not written unclearly, this man would have nothing to be proud of."

But what do *I* want? To learn to understand nature and follow it. So I try to find out who explains it. And I hear that Chrysippus does, and I go to him. But I do not understand the things that he has written, so I try to find the person who explains them. Up to this point there is nothing grand. But when I do find someone who explains them, what remains is to carry out what has been conveyed to me. This alone is grand. But if I am impressed by the explaining itself, what have I done but ended up a grammarian instead of a philosopher—except that I am explaining Chrysippus instead of Homer. Instead, when someone says to me, "Read me some Chrysippus," I turn red when I cannot exhibit actions that are similar to his words and in harmony with them.

50

Abide by whatever task is set before you as if it were a law, and as if you would be committing sacrilege if you went against it. But pay no attention to whatever anyone says about you, since that falls outside what is yours.

51

How long do you put off thinking yourself worthy of the best things, and never going against the definitive capacity of reason?[29] You have received the philosophical propositions that you ought to agree to and you have agreed to them. Then what sort of teacher are you still waiting for, that you put off improving yourself until he comes? You are not a boy any more, but already a full-grown man. If you now neglect things and are lazy and are always making delay after delay and set one day after another as the day for paying attention to yourself, then without realizing it you will make no progress but will end up a non-philosopher all through life and death. So decide now that you are worthy of living as a full-grown man who is making progress, and make everything that seems best be a law that you cannot go against. And if you meet with any hardship or anything pleasant or reputable or disreputable, then remember that the contest is *now* and the Olympic games are *now* and you cannot put things off any more and that your progress is made or destroyed by a single day and a single action. Socrates became fully perfect in this way, by not paying attention to anything but his reason in everything that he met with. You, even if you are not

27. [According to a story in Diogenes Laërtius 6.23, Diogenes the Cynic did this nude in cold weather, to toughen himself. But the statues were outdoors, and Diogenes was a bit of a show-off (but cf. n.8!).]

28. [Chrysippus was the third head of the Stoic school at Athens.]

29. [In brief, the capacity of reason here is that of distinguishing different things from each other and defining them.]

yet Socrates, ought to live as someone wanting to be Socrates.

52

The first and most necessary aspect of philosophy is that of dealing with philosophical propositions, such as "not to hold to falsehood." The second is that of demonstrations, for example, "How come one must not hold to falsehood?" The third is that of the confirmation and articulation of these, for example, "How come this is a demonstration? What is demonstration? What is entailment? What is conflict? What is truth? What is falsity?" Therefore the third is necessary because of the second, and the second because of the first; but the most necessary, and the one where one must rest, is the first. We, however, do it backwards, since we spend time in the third and all of our effort goes into it, and we neglect the first completely. Therefore we hold to falsehood, but we are ready to explain how it is demonstrated that one must not hold to falsehood.

53

On every occasion you must have these thoughts ready:

Lead me, Zeus, and you too, Destiny,
Wherever I am assigned by you;
I'll follow and not hesitate,
But even if I do not wish to,
Because I'm bad, I'll follow anyway.

Whoever has complied well with necessity
Is counted wise by us, and understands divine affairs.

Well, Crito, if it is pleasing to the gods this way, then let it happen this way.

Anytus and Meletus can kill me, but they can't harm me.[30]

30. [These four bits of poetry have the following origins. The first is by Cleanthes, who was head of the Stoic school at Athens between Zeno and Chrysippus. The second is a fragment of Euripides (fr. 965 Nauck). The third is Plato, *Crito* 43d, and the fourth is Plato, *Apology* 30c–d (slightly modified as compared with our manuscript texts), both purporting to be quotations from Socrates (cf. n.8).]

Sextus Empiricus

Sextus Empiricus is the only Greek skeptic of whom complete works survive. He stands near the end of the skeptical tradition known as Pyrrhonism, which originated with Pyrrho of Elis, a shadowy figure from the fourth and early third centuries B.C. But the movement to which Sextus belongs began in earnest with Aenesidemus of Cnossos, who in the first century B.C. initiated a method of thinking claiming inspiration from Pyrrho. Scholars have debated whether or how Pyrrhonism changed or developed during its long and discontinuous history.

Virtually nothing is known about the life of Sextus. Most scholars place him in the second century A.D. He makes clear that he was a doctor. The title Empiricus, as well as several ancient sources, suggests that he was a member of the Empiric school of medicine (as were other Pyrrhonists); yet in one puzzling passage, he appears to claim that Pyrrhonism is closer to the rival Methodic school. The indications as to where he may have lived are slender and conflicting.

Three works of Sextus survive whole or in part. *Outlines of Pyrrhonism* consists of three books. The first book (the majority of which is included here) expounds the Pyrrhonist outlook in general terms; the other two dissect the views of nonskeptical philosophers in logic, physics, and ethics, the three standard areas of philosophy. Another work, probably incomplete, covers (at greater length) roughly the same ground as *Outlines of Pyrrhonism* II–III, whereas a third attacks various specific technical fields of study. It is a matter of some dispute whether Sextus' works, taken as a whole, present a single consistent outlook (and this may be related to the issue of developments in the Pyrrhonist tradition). It is generally agreed, however, that *Outlines* I constitutes by far the best introduction both to Sextus and to Pyrrhonism as a whole.

A single sentence of the *Outlines* (at the opening of Chapter IV) gives the essentials of Pyrrhonist skepticism. Sextus says that skepticism is an *ability;* to be a skeptic is to be an expert at a certain type of procedure, not an adherent of any theory or doctrine. The procedure has three stages. First, one assembles a set of opposing arguments or impressions, on any given topic. Second, in virtue of the "equality of force" exhibited by these opposing arguments or impressions—no one of them inclining us to acceptance any more than any other—one suspends judgment; that is, one refrains from adopting any of the alternative positions on offer. (Sextus does not say that one *ought* to suspend judgment—that would itself be taking a position—but that this is what *happens;* suspension of judgment is a psychological reaction, not a rational requirement.) If this process is generalized to all topics, the result is suspension of judgment on a global scale. Third, this suspension of judgment results in "mental tranquillity" (*ataraxia*), assumed to be the common goal of all philosophers.

This bare-bones description invites many questions, some of which Sextus addresses in the ensuing discussion. A few of the most important questions follow.

Why is Sextus so sure that suspension of judgment will be the result of the juxtaposition of opposing arguments? Is one not likely often to find one argument more persuasive than the others—however artfully the skeptic has presented the range of alternatives—rather than seeing them all as equal in force? In practice, Sextus frequently concedes that an opponent will continue to find one alternative more persuasive, and Sextus shifts to deeper questions about the proofs or the criteria on which the opponent relies.

How far does the skeptic's suspension of judgment extend? What kinds of beliefs, if any, is the skeptic permitted to have? Sextus makes clear that skeptics do not hold theoretical doctrines; he also says that they do accept their own plain experience. What is not clear is whether this "acceptance" of one's experience includes commitments concerning objective states of affairs (if so, a great many everyday beliefs might be permitted) or whether one merely registers the fact that one is undergoing certain impressions. Sextus may not tell us enough to settle this issue, or his position may not be fully consistent. A related question is whether he sees himself as arguing on the side of common sense, against the abstractions of philosophers, or whether ordinary beliefs as well as theoretical ones are part of his target; again, there are indications on either side.

How can the skeptic act? Sextus says that the skeptic relies on the appearances. He lists four main species of action-guiding appearances, some natural and some cultural. Given the kind of being that one is, one will naturally experience certain desires and motivations (for example, hunger leads to eating); and given that one has been raised or taught in a certain way, one will be disposed to observe certain customs and exercise certain skills. All of this, it is argued, can occur without any violation of skeptical suspension of judgment; one engages in various forms of behavior, but without the beliefs that, in the case of the nonskeptic, would typically accompany this behavior. Whether the way of life that results is a desirable or an admirable one is another question.

Why is suspension of judgment supposed to result in *tranquillity*—rather than, say, anxiety? Sextus' answer is that the holding of definite beliefs, and especially definite beliefs to the effect that certain things are good (and others bad) by nature, leads to serious mental turmoil, from which the skeptic, through not having these beliefs, is free. The stakes for a skeptic are quite simply much lower than they are for the rest of us.

The Ten Modes, which occupy much of the present selection, are a set of standardized forms of skeptical argumentation. They consist of a multitude of examples of conflicting impressions, arranged into ten categories. The general idea is that, since one is bound to admit that no one of these conflicting impressions is to be preferred over any other, suspension of judgment is the only possible reaction. The Ten Modes, as well as various other groups of Modes not included here, are thus presented as means for the skeptic to induce suspension of judgment—or to maintain it, if it is in danger of lapsing. Sextus takes this to be a project requiring ongoing intellectual activity, rather than a result to be achieved once and for all. Again, skepticism is an ability, not a conclusion.

• • •

A concise and accessible general study of Greek skepticism is Harald Thorsrud, *Ancient Scepticism* (Berkeley: University of California Press, 2009). *The Cambridge Companion to Ancient Scepticism*, ed. Richard Bett (Cambridge: Cambridge University Press, 2010) is a collection of essays by multiple authors. Both volumes devote considerable space to Sextus; both also contain extensive bibliographies organized by topic. The Ten Modes are analyzed in *The Modes of Scepticism* by Julia Annas and Jonathan Barnes (Cambridge: Cambridge University Press, 1985). Myles Burnyeat and Michael Frede, eds., *The Original Sceptics: A Controversy* (Indianapolis: Hackett Publishing Co., 1997) contains five important related essays.

Richard Bett

Outlines of Pyrrhonism

BOOK ONE

Chapter I

The Basic Difference between Philosophies

It is a fair presumption that when people search for a thing the result will be either its discovery, a confession of non-discovery and of its non-apprehensibility, or perseverance in the search. Perhaps this is the reason why in matters of philosophical research some claim to have discovered the truth, while others declare that finding it is an impossibility, and others are still seeking it. There are some who think they have found the truth, such as Aristotle, Epicurus, the Stoics, and certain others. These are, in a special sense of the term, the so-called dogmatists. Clitomachus[1] and Carneades,[2] on the other hand, and other Academics,[3] claim it is a search for inapprehensibles. But the Sceptics go on searching. It is, therefore, a reasonable inference that basically there are three philosophies, the dogmatic, the Academic, and the Sceptic. For the present our task will be to present an outline of the Sceptic discipline, leaving it to such others as it befits to treat of the former two. We declare at the outset that we do not make any positive assertion that anything we shall say is wholly as we affirm it to be. We merely report accurately on each thing as our impressions of it are at the moment.

Reprinted from Sextus Empiricus, *Selections from the Major Writings on Scepticism, Man, and God,* translated by Sanford G. Etheridge (Indianapolis: Hackett Publishing Company, 1985), by permission of the publisher.

1. [Clitomachus, a second-century-B.C. Carthaginian, migrated to Athens in his twenties, became a student of Carneades, and eventually headed the Academy.—S.M.C.]

2. [Carneades, a second-century-B.C. Athenian, led the Academy and was renowned for his defense of withholding judgment. He frequently spoke with equal skill and fervor on one side of a question and then on the other.]

3. [The Academics were philosophers from the Academy, the school founded by Plato, which became during the third and second centuries B.C. the center of skepticism.]

Chapter II

The Arguments of Scepticism

The Sceptic philosophy comprises two types of argument, the general and the special. In the first we undertake an exposition of the character of Scepticism by stating its notion, the principles and methods of reasoning involved, and its criterion and end. We set forth also the various modes of suspension of judgement, the manner in which we use the Sceptic formulae, and the distinction between Scepticism and those philosophies which closely approach it. The special argument is that in which we dispute the validity of so-called philosophy in all its parts. Let us, then, first treat of the general argument and begin our sketch with the various appellations of the Sceptic discipline.

Chapter III

The Names of Scepticism

Now, the Sceptic discipline is called the "zetetic" (searching) from its activity of searching and examining. It is also called the "ephectic" (suspending) from the experience which the inquirer feels after the search. "Aporetic" (doubting) is another name for it, either from the fact that their doubting and searching extends to everything (the opinion of some), or from their inability to give final assent or denial. It is also called "Pyrrhonean," because Pyrrho[4] appears to us to have applied himself to Scepticism more thoroughly and with more distinction than his predecessors.

Chapter IV

The Meaning of Scepticism

Scepticism is an ability to place in antithesis, in any manner whatever, appearances and judgements, and thus—because of the equality of force in the objects

4. [Pyrrho (c. 360–270 B.C.) was the Greek philosopher who founded skepticism.]

and arguments opposed—to come first of all to a suspension of judgement and then to mental tranquillity. Now, we call it an "ability" not in any peculiar sense of the word, but simply as it denotes a "being able." "Appearances" we take as meaning the objects of sense-perception; hence we set over against them the objects of thought. The phrase "in any manner whatever" may attach itself to "ability," so that we may understand that word (as we have said) in its simple sense, or it may be understood as modifying the phrase "to place in antithesis appearances and judgements." For since the antitheses we make take various forms, appearances opposed to appearances, judgements to judgements, or appearances to judgements, we say "in any manner whatever" in order to include all the antitheses. Or, we may understand it as "any manner of appearances and judgements whatever," in order to relieve ourselves of the inquiry into how appearances appear or how judgements are formed, and thus take them at their face value. When we speak of arguments which are "opposed," we do not at all mean denial and affirmation, but use this word in the sense of "conflicting." By "equality of force" we mean equality in respect of credibility and incredibility, since we do not admit that any of the conflicting arguments can take precedence over another on grounds of its being more credible. "Suspension of judgement" is a cessation of the thought processes in consequence of which we neither deny nor affirm anything. "Mental tranquillity" is an undisturbed and calm state of soul. The question how mental tranquillity enters into the soul along with suspension of judgement we shall bring up in the chapter "On the End."

Chapter V

The Sceptic

The definition of the Pyrrhonean philosopher is also virtually included in the concept of the Sceptic discipline. It is, of course, he who shares in the "ability" we have spoken of.

Chapter VI

The Principles of Scepticism

Scepticism has its inception and cause, we say, in the hope of attaining mental tranquillity. Men of noble nature had been disturbed at the irregularity in things, and puzzled as to where they should place their belief. Thus they were led on to investigate both truth and falsehood in things, in order that, when truth and falsehood were determined, they might attain tranquillity of mind. Now, the principle fundamental to the existence of Scepticism is the proposition, "To every argument an equal argument is opposed," for we believe that it is in consequence of this principle that we are brought to a point where we cease to dogmatize.

Chapter VII

Does the Sceptic Dogmatize?

We say that the Sceptic does not dogmatize. But in saying this we do not understand the word "dogma" as some do, in the more general sense of "approval of a thing." The Sceptic, of course, assents to feelings which derive necessarily from sense-impressions; he would not, for example, when feeling warm (or cold), say, "I believe I am not warm (or cold)." But some say that "dogma" is "the assent given to one of the non-evident things which form the object of scientific research." It is this meaning of "dogma" that we have in view when we say that the Sceptic does not dogmatize, for concerning non-evident things the Pyrrhonean philosopher holds no opinion. In fact, he does not even dogmatize when he is uttering the Sceptic formulae in regard to non-evident things (these formulae, the "No more," the "I determine nothing," and the others, we shall speak of later). No—for the dogmatizer affirms the real existence of that thing about which he is said to be dogmatizing, whereas the Sceptic does not take the real existence of these formulae wholly for granted. As he understands them, the formula "All things are false," for example, asserts its own falsity together with that of all other things, and the formula "Nothing is true" likewise. Thus also the formula "No more" asserts not only of other things but of itself also that it is "no more" existent than anything else, and hence cancels itself together with the other things. We say the same about the other Sceptic formulae also. However, if the dogmatizer affirms the real existence of the thing about which he is dogmatizing, while the Sceptic, uttering his own formulae, does so in such a way that they virtually cancel themselves, he can hardly be said to be dogmatizing when he pronounces them. The greatest indication of this is that in the enunciation of these formulae he is saying what appears to him and is reporting his own feeling, without indulging in opinion or making positive statements about the reality of things outside himself.

Chapter VIII

Does the Sceptic Have a System?

Our attitude is the same when we are asked whether the Sceptic has a system. For if one defines "system" as "an adherence to a set of numerous dogmas which are consistent both with one another and with appearances," and if "dogma" is defined as "assent to a non-evident thing," then we shall say that we have no system. But if one means by "system" a "discipline which, in accordance with appearance, follows a certain line of reasoning, that line of reasoning indicating how it is possible to seem to live rightly ('rightly' understood not only with reference to virtue, but more simply), and extending also to the ability to suspend judgement," then we say that we do have a system. For we follow a certain line of reasoning which indicates to us, in a manner consistent with appearances, how to live in accordance with the customs, the laws, and the institutions of our country, and with our own natural feelings.

Chapter IX

Is the Sceptic Concerned with the Study of Physics?

To the inquiry whether the Sceptic should theorize about physics our reply is similar. We do not theorize about physics in order to give firm and confident opinions on any of the things in physical theory about which firm doctrines are held. On the other hand, we do touch on physics in order to have for every argument an equal argument to oppose to it, and for the sake of mental tranquillity. Our approach to the logical and ethical divisions of so-called philosophy is similar.

Chapter X

Do the Sceptics Deny Appearances?

Those who say that the Sceptics deny appearances seem to me to be ignorant of what we say. As we said above, we do not deny those things which, in accordance with the passivity of our sense-impressions, lead us involuntarily to give our assent to them; and these are the appearances. And when we inquire whether an object is such as it appears, we grant the fact of its appearance. Our inquiry is thus not directed at the appearance itself. Rather, it is a question of what is predicated of it, and this is a different thing from investigating the fact of the appearance itself. For example, honey appears to us to have a sweetening quality. This much we concede, because it affects us with a sensation of sweetness. The question, however, is whether it is sweet in an absolute sense. Hence not the appearance is questioned, but that which is predicated of the appearance. Whenever we do expound arguments directly against appearances, we do so not with the intention of denying them, but in order to point out the hasty judgement of the dogmatists. For if reason is such a rogue as to all but snatch even the appearances from under our very eyes, should we not by all means be wary of it, at least not be hasty to follow it, in the case of things non-evident?

Chapter XI

The Criterion of Scepticism

That we pay attention to appearances is clear from what we say about the criterion of the Sceptic discipline. Now, the word "criterion" is used in two senses. First, it is the standard one takes for belief in reality or non-reality. This we shall discuss in our refutation. Second, it is the standard of action the observance of which regulates our actions in life. It is this latter about which we now speak. Now, we say that the criterion of the Sceptic discipline is the appearance, and it is virtually the sense-presentation to which we give this name, for this is dependent on feeling and involuntary affection and hence is not subject to question. Therefore no one, probably, will dispute that an object has this or that appearance; the question is whether it is in reality as it appears to be. Now, we cannot be entirely inactive when it comes to the observances of everyday life. Therefore, while living undogmatically, we pay due regard to appearances. This observance of the requirements of daily life seems to be fourfold, with the following particular heads: the guidance of nature, the compulsion of the feelings, the tradition of laws and customs, and the instruction of the arts. It is by the guidance of nature that we are naturally capable of sensation and thought. It is by the compulsion of the feelings that hunger leads us to food and thirst leads us to drink. It is by virtue of the tradition of laws and customs that in everyday life we accept piety as good and impiety as evil. And it is by virtue of the instruction of the arts that we are not inactive in those arts which we employ. All these statements, however, we make without prejudice.

Chapter XII

The End of Scepticism

The next point to go through would be the end of Scepticism. An end is "that at which all actions or thoughts are directed, and which is itself directed at nothing, in other words, the ultimate of desirable things." Our assertion up to now is that the Sceptic's end, where matters of opinion are concerned, is mental tranquillity; in the realm of things unavoidable, moderation of feeling is the end. His initial purpose in philosophizing was to pronounce judgement on appearances. He wished to find out which are true and which false, so as to attain mental tranquillity. In doing so, he met with contradicting alternatives of equal force. Since he could not decide between them, he withheld judgement. Upon his suspension of judgement there followed, by chance, mental tranquillity in matters of opinion. For the person who entertains the opinion that anything is by nature good or bad is continually disturbed. When he lacks those things which seem to him to be good, he believes he is being pursued, as if by the Furies, by those things which are by nature bad, and pursues what he believes to be the good things. But when he has acquired them, he encounters further perturbations. This is because his elation at the acquisition is unreasonable and immoderate, and also because in his fear of a reversal all his exertions go to prevent the loss of the things which to him seem good. On the other side there is the man who leaves undetermined the question what things are good and bad by nature. He does not exert himself to avoid anything or to seek after anything, and hence he is in a tranquil state.

The Sceptic, in fact, had the same experience as that related in the story about Apelles the artist.[5] They say that when Apelles was painting a horse, he wished to represent the horse's foam in the painting. His attempt was so unsuccessful that he gave it up and at the same time flung at the picture his sponge, with which he had wiped the paints off his brush. As it struck the picture, the sponge produced an image of horse's foam. So it was with the Sceptics. They were in hopes of attaining mental tranquillity, thinking that they could do this by arriving at some rational judgement which would dispel the inconsistencies involved in both appearances and thoughts. When they found this impossible, they withheld judgement. While they were in this state, they made a chance discovery. They found that they were attended by mental tranquillity as surely as a body by its shadow.

Nevertheless, we do not suppose the Sceptic to be altogether free from disturbance; rather, we say that when he is disturbed, it is by things which are unavoidable. Certainly we concede that he is sometimes cold and thirsty, and that he suffers in other such ways. But even here there is a difference. Two circumstances combine to the detriment of the ordinary man: he is hindered both by the feelings themselves and not less by the fact that he believes these conditions to be evil by nature. The Sceptic, on the other hand, rejects this additional notion that each of these things is evil by nature, and thus he gets off more easily. These, then, are our reasons for saying that the Sceptic's end is mental tranquillity where matters of opinion are concerned, and moderate feeling in the realm of things unavoidable. Some notable Sceptics have, however, added to these a third: suspension of judgement in investigations.

Chapter XIII

General Introduction to the Modes of Suspension of Judgement

We were saying that mental tranquillity follows on suspension of judgement in regard to all things. Next, it would be proper for us to state how we attain

5. [Apelles was a leading fourth-century-B.C. painter.]

suspension of judgement. As a general rule, this suspension of judgement is effected by our setting things in opposition. We oppose appearances to appearances, or thoughts to thoughts, or appearances to thoughts. For example, when we say, "The same tower appears round from a distance, but square from close by," we are opposing appearances to appearances. When a person is trying to prove the existence of providence from the order of the celestial bodies, and we counter him with the observation that the good often fare ill while the evil prosper and then conclude from this that there is no providence, we are opposing thoughts to thoughts. And then appearances may be opposed to thoughts. Anaxagoras,[6] for instance, could oppose to the fact that snow is white his reasoning that "Snow is frozen water, and water is black, snow therefore is black also." And sometimes, from the point of view of a different concept, we oppose present things to present things, as in the foregoing, and sometimes present things to past or future things. An example of this is the following. Whenever someone propounds an argument that we are not able to dispose of, we make this reply: "Before the birth of the founder of the school to which you belong, this argument of your school was not yet seen to be a sound argument. From the point of view of nature, however, it existed all the while as such. In like manner it is possible, as far as nature is concerned, that an argument antithetical to the one now set forth by you is in existence, though as yet unknown to us. This being so, the fact that an argument seems valid to us now is not yet a sufficient reason why we must assent to it."

But for a better understanding of these antitheses, I shall now present also the modes by which suspension of judgement is induced. I cannot, however, vouch for their number or validity, since it is possible that they are unsound, and that there are more of them than the ones to be discussed.

Chapter XIV

The Ten Modes

With the older Sceptics the usual teaching is that the modes by which suspension of judgement seems to be brought about are ten in number, which they also term synonymously "arguments" and "forms." These are as follows. First is that in which suspension is caused by the variation in animals. In the second it is caused by the differences in human beings. Third, by the differences in the construction of the organs of sense. Fourth, by the circumstances. Fifth, by the positions, distances, and places involved. Sixth, by the admixtures present. Seventh, by the quantities and compoundings of the underlying objects. Eighth, by the relativity of things. Ninth, by the frequency or rarity of occurrence. Tenth, by the institutions, customs, laws, mythical beliefs, and dogmatic notions. This order, however, is merely arbitrary.

Transcending these are three modes: the argument from the subject judging, the argument from the object judged, and that from both. The first four modes above are subordinate to the argument from the subject judging (for that which judges is either an animal or a human being or a sense, and is in some circumstance or other). The seventh and the tenth are referred to the argument from the object judged. The fifth, sixth, eighth, and ninth are referred to the argument from both combined. These three modes are in turn referred to the mode of relativity, so that the mode of relativity is the *summum genus*, while the three are its species, and the ten are subordinate. This is the most plausible statement we can make concerning their number. In regard to their meaning, we have the following to say.

The First Mode

As we were saying, the first argument is the argument from differences in animals. According to this mode, the same objects do not produce the same impression in different animals. This we conclude both from the fact that they have different origins and from the variety exhibited in the structure of their bodies. Now to consider origin. Some animals are produced without sexual union, others by coition. Of those which are produced without sexual union, some are generated out of fire, such as the little animals that appear in furnaces, others out of stagnant water, such as mosquitoes, and others, from soured wine, such as ants. From the earth come earthworms, from mud come frogs, from dung, maggots. From asses come beetles, and from vegetables caterpillars. Other animals come from fruits, as the gall-insects from wild

6. [Regarding Anaxagoras, see Plato's *Apology*, n.7.]

figs; and still others from rotting animals, as bees from bulls and wasps from horses. Of the animals produced by sexual union, some (most of them, in fact) are the offspring of parents of like kind, some of parents of different kinds, as are mules. Speaking of animals in general again, some are born alive, as are human beings, some are born as eggs, as are birds, and some are born as unformed flesh, as bears. It is reasonable, then, to suppose that the dissimilarities and differences in their respective origins are a cause of greatly contrary affections in animals, and that the discordant, incongruous, and conflicting character of their affections is derived from their different origins.

Moreover, a very great conflict between sense-impressions can be produced even by differences in the most important parts of the body, especially the organs whose natural function is judging and perceiving. For instance, people suffering from jaundice say that what appears to us as white is yellow, and those who had a bloodshot condition of the eyes say it is blood-red. Now, since some animals have yellow eyes, others bloodshot eyes, while others have eyes which are white, and others have eyes of still other colours, it is reasonable to suppose, I think, that their perception of colour is different. Moreover, if we fix our gaze on the sun for a long time and then look down into a book, the letters appear to be gold-coloured and going in circles. Also, some animals have a sort of natural brilliance in their eyes, and send off from them a fine light which travels easily, so that they even see at night. In view of this fact, we might well be right in supposing that the impressions they get of external objects are different from ours. And jugglers, too, by smearing their lamp-wick with copper rust or with the ink of the cuttle-fish, make their onlookers appear to have a copper or black colour, as the case may be. This they effect by the application of only a small quantity of their preparation. It is surely much more reasonable to suppose that if the eyes of animals contain different mixtures of fluids, the impressions they receive of external objects will be different. Also, when we press one side of the eyeball, the objects viewed appear longish and narrow in form, figure, and size. It is probable, therefore, that those animals which have a slanting and elongated pupil, such as goats, cats, and the like, receive impressions of objects which are different from and unlike the impressions had of the same objects by animals with round pupils. And then mirrors: owing to differences in their construction, they sometimes show the external objects as being very small (concave mirror), sometimes as longish and narrow (convex mirror). Some show the mirrored person's head at the bottom and his feet at the top. Now, there are similar differences in the organs of sight of animals. Some of these, owing to their convexity, protrude quite out of the sockets, while others are more concave, and others lie in a flat plane. It is natural to suppose that these conditions also may cause differences in the sense-impressions. If this is so, when dogs and fishes and lions and humans and locusts look at the same objects, they would in such case see objects that are neither equal in size nor similar in shape. Rather, what each perceives would be the impression created by the particular sight that receives the object.

The same argument applies to the other senses. Take the sense of touch. One could hardly postulate a similarity of sensibility between hard-shelled animals, fleshy animals, thorny animals, and feathered or scaly ones. And as for perceptions conveyed through the sense of hearing, one could hardly say that they are the same in those animals which have a very narrow auditory passage as they are in those which have a very wide one, or the same in animals with hairy ears as in those with smooth ears. We can even see the truth of this assertion in ourselves, as far as the sense of hearing is concerned, for when we plug up our ears, our perception through this sense is different from our normal hearing. The sense of smell also would exhibit differences by virtue of the variety in animals. We ourselves, when we have a cold and the phlegm in us is excessive, are affected in one way; but when an excessive amount of blood is collected in the parts about the head, we are affected in another way, and turn away from things which to others seem fragrant, believing ourselves overpowered, as it were, by their smell. Some animals, too, are flaccid by nature and abound in phlegm, while others are very rich in blood; and in others yellow or black bile, present in an excessive amount, is the predominant element. Hence it would be reasonable to assume that this is another reason why objects of smell appear different to each severally. It is the same with objects of taste. In the first place, the tongues of animals are different, some being rough and without moisture, some very moist. In fever our tongues too become very dry, so that we think the food set before us has an earthy, ill-flavoured, and bitter taste; and this experience of ours is caused by the varying predominance of the juices we are said to have in us. Now, since the organs of taste of animals differ from each other, and have different juices in excess, it would follow that they also receive different ideas of the taste of things.

An analogous process is the distribution of food throughout the body. In one place it becomes a vein, in another an artery, a bone, a sinew, and so on. The difference in the power it displays corresponds with the differences between the parts which receive it. Water also, which is one and uniform when it is absorbed by trees, becomes in different places bark, branch, or fruit, and further, fig, pomegranate, or whatever it may be. The breath of the musician, also one and the same when it enters the flute, becomes in turn a high-pitched tone or a low one. Similarly, the same pressure of his hand upon the lyre sometimes produces a low tone, sometimes a high one. In the same manner it is a fair supposition that external objects appear different to the animals receiving the sense-impressions of the objects, and that this is due to differences of constitution in the different animals. But this can be seen more clearly from the preferences and aversions of animals. For example, perfume seems very agreeable to men, but intolerable to beetles and bees. Olive-oil is beneficial to men, but it kills wasps and bees if sprinkled on them. Sea-water is unpleasant for men to drink, even poisonous, but for fish most pleasant—and drinkable. Pigs would much rather wash in the most stinking mire than in clear and pure water. And then some animals subsist on herbs, others on shrubs, and other live in the woods; others live on seeds, flesh, or milk. Some enjoy putrefied food, while others like it prepared by cooking; and in general, what is pleasant to some is unpleasant to others, and may be undesirable, even fatal. Hemlock, for example, fattens quails, and henbane fattens sows. The latter even like to eat salamanders, just as deer eat venomous animals and swallows eat blister-beetles. Ants and wood-lice, if swallowed by humans, produce nausea and colic, while the bear, if he falls sick, licks them up and thus regains his strength. One touch of an oak-twig is sufficient to stun a viper. The leaf of a plane-tree has the same effect on bats. An elephant will run from a ram, a lion from a cock. Sea-monsters will flee from the crackling noise produced by the pounding of beans, and a tiger will run from the mere sound of a drum. We could multiply these examples, but it would mean dwelling unduly long on the subject. In short, if the same things are unpleasant to some animals but pleasant to others, and pleasure and displeasure depend on sense-impression, then the sense-impressions that animals get from the objects are different.

But if the difference in animals is a cause of things appearing different, then we shall, it is true, be able to say what—in our view—a thing is; but on the question what it really is by nature, we shall suspend judgement. And as for acting ourselves as judges between our own sense-impressions and those of the other animals, that is out of the question, because we ourselves are a party to the disagreement. For this reason, in fact, we shall be more in need of a judge than capable ourselves of judging. Moreover, we are unable, either without proof or with proof, to give the preference to our own sense-impressions over those of the irrational animals. For besides the possibility (which we shall mention) that proof is non-existent, the so-called proof itself will be either apparent to us or non-apparent. If it is non-apparent, we cannot even bring it forward with confidence. But suppose it is apparent to us. Then, since what is apparent to animals is the question at issue and we to whom the proof is apparent are animals, we still shall have to investigate whether the proof itself is in the same degree true as it is apparent. It is absurd to attempt to establish the question at issue by means of the question at issue, since that would involve believing and disbelieving the same thing at once—which is impossible. We should have to believe it in so far as it professes to furnish the proof, and disbelieve it in so far as it itself is the thing to be proved. We shall have, then, no proof which will enable us to give the preference to our own sense-impressions over those of the so-called irrational animals. If, therefore, the sense-impressions of animals differ as a consequence of the differences which exist between animals, and we cannot possibly sit in judgement over them, we must of necessity suspend judgement in regard to external objects.

We also allow ourselves the luxury of comparing the so-called irrational animals with man in respect of sense-impressions. For after our practical arguments have done their work, we feel not unqualified to make sport of those demented braggarts the dogmatists. Now, the men of our school are wont to compare the generality of the irrational animals with man. But since the dogmatists sophistically assert that the comparison is unfair, we shall base our argument on one animal only—for instance, the dog, if you please, which seems to be the most worthless—and still continue our jesting at great advantage. Even so, we shall find that as far as the trusthworthiness of appearances goes, the animals we speak of are not inferior to ourselves. Now, the dogmatists concede that this animal excels us in sense-perception. His perception by the sense of smell is superior to ours, and he also has a keen sense of hearing.

Let us now turn to the faculty of reason. One kind of reason is internal reason, and the other kind is uttered reason. Let us look first at internal reason. According to those dogmatists whose doctrines are the most opposed to us, namely, the Stoics, it seems that internal reason is activated in the following cases: in the choice of congenial and the avoidance of alien things; in the knowledge of the arts that contribute to this; in the apprehension and alleviation of one's own sufferings; and in the acquisition of the virtues consistent with one's own nature. Now, the dog—the example we decided to take for the sake of the argument—makes a choice of the congenial when he seeks after food, and he avoids the harmful when he retires before a raised whip. What is more, he possesses an art by which he procures what is congenial to him, the art of hunting. He is not without virtue, either. Certainly, at any rate, if justice means to render each his due, the dog would not be without justice, for he exercises it by guarding and wagging his tail at those who are familiar to him and who treat him well, and by keeping strangers and those who harm him at a distance. But if he possesses this virtue, then, since the virtues are reciprocally implied, he possesses the other virtues also, which according to the claim of the wise men the majority of men do not possess. We see that he is brave from the way he defends us, and intelligent too, as Homer also testified when he represented Odysseus as going unrecognized by all the members of his household and as being recognized only by his dog Argus, who was not deceived by the changes that had come over the body of the man.[7] Neither had his impression of the man lost its immediacy; in fact, it appeared that he had retained this immediacy of impression better than the humans did. But according to Chrysippus,[8] who is hostile, if anybody is, to irrational animals, the dog even shares in the famous science of dialectic. At any rate, the aforesaid man is responsible for the statement that the dog knows intuitively the fifth complex indemonstrable syllogism. He shows this knowledge whenever he is tracking an animal and comes to a meeting of three roads. After he has tried two of the roads and found that the animal has not passed that way, he rushes off immediately on the third without even stopping to pick up the scent. The old philosopher says that the dog virtually reasons this out, as follows: "The animal passed either this way, or this way, or this way; but it did not take this road, nor that; therefore it must have gone by the third road." Moreover, he is capable of apprehending his own sufferings and of relieving them. Thus, if there is a thorn stuck in his foot, he sets about removing it by rubbing his foot against the ground, or by means of his teeth. And if he has a sore anywhere, because dirty sores are slow to heal and clean ones heal easily, he gently wipes off the discharge that gathers. Why, he even observes the teaching of Hippocrates,[9] and very well at that; for if he should receive an injury to his foot, he applies the general rule (that rest will cure it) and elevates the injured foot and keeps it as undisturbed as possible. And when he is troubled by unwholesome humours, he eats grass, which enables him to vomit up the unwholesome matter and get well.

Now, we based our observations on the dog as an example for the sake of the argument. If, then, it appears that he chooses what is good for him and avoids what is troublesome, if he possesses an art which enables him to procure the good things, if he is capable of apprehending and relieving his own sufferings, if he is not without virtue—these being the conditions on which the perfection of internal reason depends—then the dog will be, in this respect,

7. [The story is told in the *Odyssey*.]

8. [Regarding Chrysippus, see Epictetus' *Encheiridion*, n.28.]

9. [Hippocrates (c. 460–c. 370 B.C.) was the Greek physician who is recognized as the father of medicine.]

perfect. This may be the reason why some philosophers have exalted themselves with the name of this animal.[10]

An inquiry concerning uttered reason is for the present unnecessary, since even some of the dogmatists have rejected it on the grounds that it is prejudicial to the acquisition of virtue. For the same reason they also used to practise silence during the time they were learners.[11] And besides, just supposing a man were dumb, no one is going to say that he is irrational. But leaving this consideration aside also, as our subject is animals, we certainly see some animals, jays among others, that can even utter human sounds. But leaving this point aside also, we note simply that even though we do not understand the sounds made by the so-called irrational animals, it is not altogether improbable that they do converse—without our understanding them. But then when we hear the speech of foreigners we do not understand that either; we think it monotonous. Also, the sounds we hear dogs utter are different: when they are keeping people off it is one sound, when they are howling it is another; and when they receive a beating, the sound is different from the sound they utter when they are fawning. And in general, if a person were to look into this matter carefully, he would find that the utterances of both this and the other animals vary greatly under different circumstances. On this account the so-called irrational animals might fairly be said to share in uttered reason also. But if these animals are inferior to humans neither in the accuracy of their perceptions, nor in internal reason, nor—needless to say—in uttered reason, then their sense-impressions will be no more untrustworthy than ours. It is perhaps even possible to prove this by basing our argument on each class of the irrational animals separately. Who, for example, would not admit that birds excel in quickness of wit and that they possess the use of uttered reason? Their understanding is not confined to the present but extends to future things as well, and to those who are able to understand them they show the future beforehand, both by their prophetic cry and by the other signs they give.

The comparison I have here drawn is given into the bargain as a bonus. This I have indicated before. I had previously shown sufficiently, I think, that we cannot give the preference to our own sense-impressions over those of the irrational animals. But then if the irrational animals, as judges of the sense-impressions, are not less reliable than we, and if the discrepancy in sense-impressions is due to the difference between animals, it is true that I shall be able to say what each object appears to me to be, but no more. As to what its real nature is, I shall be forced, for the reasons given above, to suspend judgement.

The Second Mode

Such, then, is the first mode of suspension. The second, as we said, is the argument from the difference between men. Let us make a concession for the sake of the argument and say that human beings are more to be believed than the irrational animals. Even so, inasmuch as we differ from one another, we shall find suspension of judgement being brought in. It is said that man is made up of two elements, soul and body. Well, in both of these we differ from one another.

As for the body, we have different figures and constitutional peculiarities. Now, the Scythian's figure is different from that of an Indian, and the difference is due, it is said, to the varying predominance of the humours. And according as different humours predominate in men, their sense-impressions also are different, as we showed in the first argument. That is why there is also much difference between them in their choice and avoidance of external things. Thus the Indian standard of taste is different from that in our country, and the fact that we enjoy different things is indicative of a difference in the sense-impressions that we get from the external objects. We differ also in our constitutional peculiarities: for some people, beef is easier to digest than rock-fish, and some suffer diarrhoea from inferior Lesbian wine. There used to be an old woman of Attica, they said, who could take thirty drams of hemlock with impunity, and Lysis used to take four drams of opium without harm. And Demophon, Alexander's butler, used to shiver when

10. [The reference is to the Cynics, literally "doggish" followers of Diogenes (404–323 B.C.), the Greek philosopher who urged self-sufficiency and shamelessness. When Alexander the Great offered to fulfill a request from Diogenes, the Cynic replied, "Only step out of my sunlight."]

11. [The reference is to the Pythagoreans, regarding whom see Aristotle's *Metaphysics*, n.7.]

he was in the sun or in a hot bath, but when he was in the shade he felt warm. Athenagoras of Argos was not affected by the sting of scorpions and poisonous spiders; the tribe called the Psyllaeans are not injured by the bite of snakes and asps; and the Tentyritae, an Egyptian people, suffer no harm from the crocodiles. Also, the Ethiopians who live along the Astapous River on the other side of Lake Meroë eat scorpions and snakes and such-like animals without ill effect. Rufinus of Chalcis would drink hellebore without vomiting and without any evacuation at all; he could simply take it and digest it like any of the usual beverages. Chrysermus, of the school of Herophilus, ran the risk of a heart attack whenever he took pepper, and Soterichus the surgeon used to suffer from diarrhoea whenever he caught the odour of fried sheatfish. Andron of Argos was so unaffected by thirst that he even journeyed across the waterless part of Libya without requiring a drink. Tiberius Caesar could see in the dark, and Aristotle tells us of a certain Thracian who had the hallucination that a man was continually leading the way in front of him.

Now, we shall content ourselves with the recitation of these few examples from the many found in the writings of the dogmatists. Even so, it is clear that the bodily differences between men are great, and it is thus natural to assume that these differences extend also to the very soul of man, for the body is in a sense the stamped image of the soul, as the art of physiognomy shows us. But the greatest indication of the wide, indeed infinite, variety to be found in human intelligence is the discrepancy in the statements which the dogmatists make on every subject, particularly on the question what things it is proper to choose or avoid. The poets, too, have expressed themselves on this. Pindar[12] says:

> The honours and wreaths won by wind-swift
>   horses are the delight of one man,
> Others delight in a life in gilded chambers;
> Another man, too, finds joy in traversing
>   the salty main with a fast ship.

And the Poet says:

> Different men take delight in different deeds.[13]

Tragedy also is full of these sentiments. For example:

> If fair and wise meant both the same to all,
> Dispute and strife would be no more.[14]

And again:

> Strange, to say the least, that what gives joy
>   to some,
> Is an object of hate to others.[15]

Now, since choice and avoidance depend on pleasure and displeasure, and pleasure and displeasure in turn depend on sensation and sense-impression, it is logical for us to conclude that whenever the same things are chosen by some and avoided by others they are not even affected in the same manner by the same objects, since otherwise they would agree in their choices and avoidances. But if it is because of the differences between men that the same objects affect us differently, then this would be another good reason for bringing in suspension of judgement. We are, perhaps, able to say what each external object appears to be from our several different points of view, but we are unable to give an account of its true essence. For we shall have to believe either all men or some of them; to believe all would be an impossible undertaking, as we should have to accept contradictory accounts, while if we are to believe some, let them tell us who it is we are supposed to agree with. The Platonist will say Plato, the Epicurean, Epicurus, and so on with the others. They cannot decide as between their own factions, and this only serves to bring us round to suspension again. Furthermore, to say that we should agree with the majority would be puerile, since it is in no one's power to make a survey of all mankind and determine statistically the majority opinion. It is quite possible that there are peoples unknown to us, to whom things rare with us are common occurrences and with whom the conditions

12. [Regarding Pindar, see Plato's *Republic*, Book I, n.7.]

13. [The quotation is from Homer, *Odyssey* 14.228.]

14. [The quotation is from Euripides' play *The Phoenician Women* 499.]

15. [The author of the quotation is unknown.]

obtaining with us are comparatively rare. It might turn out, for example, that those who feel no pain at the bite of spiders are in the majority, and that some feel pain only rarely; and this might be similarly the case with the other constitutional peculiarities mentioned above. The differences in men, therefore, are another compelling reason for invoking suspension of judgement.

The Third Mode

Now, the dogmatists are a rather conceited class of people, and they say that they must give themselves the preference over other men in the matter of judging things; but we know that their claim is absurd because they themselves form a party to the disagreement. Furthermore, if they are thus prejudiced in favour of themselves whenever they judge appearances, then they are begging the question before they even begin their judgement, because they are turning the decision over to themselves. Nevertheless, we can arrive at suspension of judgement even when basing the argument on a single man, for instance on the "wise man" who is the product of their dreams. In order to do this we bring into play the mode which is third in order. This is the one we called the argument from the differences in the senses. And it is clear at the outset that the senses differ from one another. Take paintings, for example. To the eye they seem to have hollows and prominences, but certainly not to the sense of touch. And to some, honey appears to be pleasant to the tongue, but to the eyes it appears unpleasant; thus it is impossible to say whether it is in itself pleasant or unpleasant. With perfume the case is similar; it delights the sense of smell but is disgusting to the taste. Then there is the juice of the spurge. Since it is painful to the eyes but causes pain to no other part of the body, it will not be for us to say whether, as far as its own nature is concerned, it is in itself painful or painless to bodies. And rain-water is beneficial to the eyes, but irritates the windpipe and lungs just as olive-oil does, which to the skin is soothing. The electric ray produces stiffness if applied to the extremities, while application to the rest of the body is without ill effect. Therefore we are not in a position to say what each thing is by nature, although it is possible to say what it appears to be on each occasion.

We could easily cite more examples, but to avoid waste of time, on account of the plan of the treatise, we need say just this. Each appearance that we perceive through the senses seems to present itself under many forms; an apple, for instance, seems smooth, fragrant, sweet, and yellow. It is uncertain, however, whether these are really the only qualities it possesses, or whether it is of one quality only but appears in different forms because the various sense-organs are of different construction. It may also be that it has more qualities than are apparent, and that some of them are not perceived by us. Now, that the apple is of a single quality we can conclude, on the one hand, from our previous statements about the distribution of food throughout the body, of water throughout trees, and about the breathing of wind into flutes, pipes, and similar instruments. For the apple, like these, may well be of a uniform quality, yet still appear to possess several qualities by reason of the differences between the sense-organs through which its perception takes place. On the other hand, we can conclude that the apple possesses more qualities than those which are apparent to us, as follows. Let us imagine a man whose senses of touch, smell, and taste are intact, but who is congenitally deaf and blind. This man will have no idea at all that a thing is visible or audible, but will believe that only those three classes of qualities exist which he is capable of apprehending. With us too it is possible that our apprehension of qualities in the apple is determined by the number of senses we possess—five only. And it is possible that there exist other qualities that fall within the province of other organs of sense. Our not possessing any such other organs of sense would be reason enough why we do not apprehend the type of sense-objects proper to them.

"But," one will say, "nature made the senses commensurate with their objects." In view of the great disagreement amongst the dogmatists on the unsettled question of the existence of nature, we can only reply, "Which nature?" On this question of the existence of nature the layman's judgement will carry no authority with the dogmatists. But a philosopher's judgement is no better, for he is not a judge, but a party to the disagreement, himself subject to judgement. However, given these possible alternatives, that there may subsist in the apple only those qualities which we seem to apprehend, likewise that there may subsist more than just these; or again that even the ones we perceive may not subsist at all; it follows that it will be non-evident to us what kind of thing the apple is. And the same argument holds for the other objects of sense. But then if the senses do not apprehend external objects, the intellect cannot apprehend them either, seeing that it is led astray by its guides, which is all the more reason why suspension of judgement in regard to the external underlying objects will be indicated.

The Fourth Mode

But we can also reach suspension by basing our argument on each sense separately, or even by disregarding the senses. To this end we employ the fourth mode of suspension, which we call the mode based on the circumstances. We understand by "circumstances" the states in which we are. This mode, we say, is seen in cases of natural or unnatural states, in states of waking or sleeping, in cases where age, motion or rest, hating or loving are involved; or where the determining factor is a state of want or satiety, drunkenness or soberness; in cases of predispositions, or when it is a question of confidence or fear, or grief or joy. For example, things appear dissimilar according to whether we are in a natural or unnatural state; delirious people, and those who are possessed by a god, think that they hear divine voices, while we do not. Often they claim that they perceive, among a number of other things, the odour of storax or frankincense, or something of that sort, where we perceive nothing. And the same water that seems hot to a person when poured on inflamed parts seems lukewarm to us. The coat which appears yellowish-orange to men with bloodshot eyes does not appear so to me, yet it is the same coat. And the same honey that appears sweet to me appears bitter to those suffering from jaundice.

Now, one might object that in those whose condition is unnatural it is the intermingling of certain humours that causes them to get unnatural impressions from the external objects. Our reply to this would be that it is possible that the external objects actually are in reality such as they appear to those who are said to be in an unnatural state; and that since persons in a state of good health also have mixed humours, it may be that it is these humours that make the objects appear different to them. For it would be a fabrication to attribute to the humours of sick people a power to change external objects, and to deny this power to the humours of the healthy. After all, it is natural for the healthy to be in a healthy state, and unnatural for them to be in a sick state. By the same token it is unnatural for the sick to be in a healthy state, but natural for them to be in a sick state. Consequently, the sick warrant credence also, since they too are in some respect in a natural state. Whether one is in a sleeping or a waking state also makes a difference in the sense-impressions, since our manner of perception while awake differs from the perception we have in sleep; and our manner of perception in sleep is not like our waking perception. As a result, the existence or non-existence of our sense-impressions is not absolute but relative, since they bear a relation to our sleeping or waking state. It is probable, therefore, that although our dream-images are unreal in our waking state, they are nevertheless not absolutely unreal, for they do exist in our dreams. In the same manner the realities of the waking state, even if they do not exist in dreams, nevertheless exist. Age also makes a difference. Old men, for example, may think the air is cold, but the same air seems mild to those who are in the prime of life. The same colour appears dim to older persons but full to those in their prime. And a sound, likewise the same, seems faint to the former but quite audible to the latter. The matter of choice and avoidance of things also provokes different reactions in people of different ages. Children, perhaps, take their ball-games and their hoops seriously, but grown men have different tastes, and old men prefer still other things. From this it follows that differences of age also can cause the sense-impressions to be different where the external objects are the same. Motion or rest may also be the determining factor when objects appear different. For instance, things which we see to be motionless when we are stationary seem to be moving when we are sailing past them. Loving or hating may also make the difference. For example, there are those to whom pork is extremely repugnant, while others eat it with gusto. Hence also Menander's[16] lines:

16. [Menander was a fourth-century-B.C. Greek author of comic plays].

> And then what does his face look like,
> Since he has come to be like this? Why,
> he's a beast!
> Fair dealing makes us fair as well.

There are also many who have ugly mistresses and yet think them very beautiful. Hunger or satiety may also be the cause, as the same food can seem very tasty to the hungry and yet disagreeable to those who have had their fill. Drunkenness or soberness is another cause, since what we think shameful when sober does not seem shameful to us when we are drunk. Predispositions are another cause, since the same wine seems to be sour if you have eaten dates or dried figs beforehand, and sweet if you have eaten nuts or chick-peas. Also, the vestibule of the bath-house is warming to those who come in from the outside, but chills those who are coming out, if they tarry in it. Fear or confidence is also a cause, as a thing may seem fearful and terrible to the coward, yet not at all so to the man who is more daring. Being in a state of grief or joy would also be a factor, since the same matters are at once burdensome to those who are in grief and pleasant to those who are rejoicing.

Now, considering the fact that so much discrepancy is due to the states we are in, and that men are in different states at different times, it is easy, perhaps, to state the nature of each object as it appears to this or that person, but difficult to say further what its real nature is. This is because the discrepancy does not lend itself to judgement. In fact, whoever attempts to resolve this discrepancy will find himself either in one or the other of the aforesaid states or else in no state at all. But now to say that he is in no state at all, that he is neither healthy nor sick, neither in motion nor at rest, that he is not of any particular age, and that he is free from the other states, is perfectly absurd. On the other hand, the fact of his being in some state or other while attempting to pass judgement will make him a party to the controversy. And moreover, he will be confused by the states in which he finds himself, and this will prevent him from being an absolute judge in the matter. A person, therefore, who is in the waking state cannot compare the impressions of a sleeping person with those of waking persons, and a healthy person cannot compare the impressions of sick people with those of the healthy. We do, after all, tend to give our assent to those things which are present and have a present influence over us rather than to things which are not present.

The discrepancy between such impressions is irresolvable on other grounds also, for if a person prefers one sense-impression to another, and one circumstance to another, he does so either without judging and without proof or by judging and offering proof. But he cannot do so without judgement and proof, for then he will be discredited. Nor can he do so even with judgement and proof, for if he judges the impressions, he must at all events use a criterion in judging them. And this criterion he will declare to be either true or false. If false, he will not be worthy of belief; but if he claims it is true, then his statement that the criterion is true will be offered either without proof or with proof. If without proof, again he will not be worthy of belief; but if he offers proof for his statement, the proof must in any case be a true one, otherwise he will not be worthy of belief. Now, if he says that the proof employed for the confirmation of his criterion is true, will he say this after having passed judgement on the proof, or without having judged it? If he has not judged it, he will not be worthy of belief, but if he has, obviously he will say he has used a criterion in his judgement. We shall ask for a proof for this criterion, and for this proof another criterion. For the proof always needs a criterion to confirm it, and the criterion needs a proof to show that it is true. A proof cannot be sound without the pre-existence of a true criterion, and a criterion cannot be true either without prior confirmation of the proof. And so both the criterion and the proof fall into circular argument, in which both are found to be untrustworthy. The fact that each expects confirmation from the other makes both of them equally untrustworthy. It is impossible, then, for a person to give the preference to one sense-impression over another. This being so, such differences in sense-impressions as arise from a disparity of states will be irresolvable. As a result, this mode also serves to introduce suspension of judgement with regard to the nature of external objects.

The Fifth Mode

The fifth argument is the one based on positions, distances, and places. Each of these can cause the same objects to appear different. Take a portico for example. When seen from either end, it appears tapered, yet the same portico viewed from the middle appears symmetrical on all sides. Also, the same boat appears small and stationary from a distance, and large and moving from close by. And the same tower appears round from afar but square from near by.

These differences are the result of the distances involved. Then there are differences due to the places involved. For example, the light of a lamp appears dim in sunlight but bright in the dark, the same oar appears broken in the water but straight when out of the water, and the egg is soft inside the bird but hard when exposed to the air. Amber is liquid when inside the lynx but hard when exposed to the air, and coral is soft when in the sea but hard in the air. And a sound appears different according to whether it is produced in a pipe, a flute, or simply in the air.

Position also may be the cause of different appearances. The same picture appears smooth when inclined backwards, but seems to have hollows and prominences when inclined forward to a certain angle. Also, the necks of pigeons appear different in colour according to differences in inclination.

Thus all objects appearing to us are seen as being in some place or other, at a certain distance, and in a certain position, and each of these factors makes a great difference in the sense-impressions, as we have mentioned. Hence, by this mode also we shall be compelled to have recourse to suspension of judgement. In point of fact, anyone who wishes to give any of these sense-impressions the preference over the others will be undertaking an impossible task. For if he makes his judgement simply and without proof, he will be discredited; and if he wishes to employ a proof, then says his proof is false, he will be refuting himself; if he says the proof is true, he will be asked for a proof of its truth, and another proof for that one, and so on *ad infinitum*. But it is impossible to present an infinite series of proofs; therefore he will not be able, even by the use of proofs, to prefer one sense-impression to another. And if a person is unable to pass judgement on the above-mentioned impressions either without proof or with proof, then the necessary result is suspension of judgement. Thus, while we are perhaps able to state of what nature each object appears to be in one particular position, at one particular distance, and in one location, it is not in our power, for the reasons just given, to declare what its true nature is.

The Sixth Mode

The sixth mode is the one based on admixtures. By this mode we conclude that, since none of the external objects appears to us singly but always in conjunction with something else, it is perhaps possible to state the nature of the mixture resulting from the conjunction of the external object and that other thing which we perceive together with it, but we are not able to say what the real nature of the external object is in its unmixed state. That no external object is ever perceived singly but in all cases together with something else, and that this causes it to have a different appearance for us, I take as evident fact. Our skin, for instance, shows a different colour according to whether the air is warm or cold; and we cannot say what our true natural colour is, but only what it appears to be in conjunction with each of these conditions. And the same sound appears different according as it occurs in air which is rarefied or dense; and aromatic odours are rather more overpowering in the warm bath and in the sun than in chilled air; and if a body is enclosed by water, it is light, but if enclosed by air, it is heavy.

But to get away from external admixtures, the internal contents of our eyes consist of both membranes and fluid matter. Now, since visible objects, in order to be seen, require both of these, they will not be apprehended with accuracy. What we actually perceive is the mixture, and this is the reason why people sick with jaundice see everything yellow, and those with bloodshot eyes see everything blood-red. And since the same sound appears different according as it occurs in open places or in narrow and winding places, and according as the air is pure or foul, it is probable that our apprehension of the sound is not free from admixture. For the ears have winding, narrow passages and are fouled with vaporous discharges which are said to gather from various parts of the head. And since secreted matter is also present in the nostrils and in the places where the sense of taste is located, our apprehension of the objects of taste and smell is not without admixture but includes the apprehension of that matter as well. Consequently, the admixtures prevent our senses from apprehending with accuracy the true nature of external objects.

But neither can the intellect do this, the chief reason being that the senses, which are its guides, are deceived; though perhaps the intellect, too, produces some peculiar admixture of its own, which then also affects the reports communicated by the senses. For we can perceive the presence of certain humours in each place where the dogmatists think the ruling part of the soul is located, whether one wishes to regard it as located in the brain, in the heart, or in any part of the animal body whatever. We see, therefore, that according to this mode also we are unable to predicate anything about the nature of external objects. As a result, we are compelled to suspend judgement.

The Seventh Mode

The seventh mode, as we said, is based on the quantities and compoundings of the external objects. By their "compounding" we mean in general their composition. And it is evident that this mode too obliges us to suspend judgement as regards the nature of things. For example, the filings from a goat's horn appear white when they are seen by themselves and uncompounded, but when they are compounded so as to constitute a horn they appear black. And filings of silver appear black by themselves, but in conjunction with the whole they are perceived as white. And pieces of the marble of Taenarum look white when they are polished, but when together in the rough stone they appear yellow. Grains of sand appear rough when they are scattered apart, but when combined as a heap they produce the impression of softness. Hellebore causes suffocation if taken as a fine powder, but not if taken coarse. Wine strengthens us if drunk in moderate amounts, but if more than this is taken, it enervates the body. And with food the case is similar, for the efficacy it exhibits varies according to the quantity taken. For instance, taking food in large quantities often causes the body to be purged through attacks of indigestion and diarrhoea. Here also, then, we shall be in a position to state the nature of the small bit of horn and of the whole composed of the many fine parts, and the nature of the chip of Taenarean marble and of the whole composed of the many small pieces. We may also be able to state the nature, in relative terms, of the grains of sand, the hellebore, the wines, and the food. Yet we shall not be able to go further and state the absolute nature of the objects. This we are prevented from doing by the discrepancy in our sense-impressions caused by the varying compositions of things.

In fact, it seems generally true that even things beneficial to us become harmful through their use in immoderate quantities, and that things that seem harmful when taken in excessive quantity are not injurious in very small quantities. The best argument in support of this reasoning is the observation we make regarding the action of medicines. Here we find that an accurate mixing of the component drugs renders the compound beneficial, while sometimes the slightest inclination of the balance, if overlooked, can render the product not only ineffectual but often very harmful, even poisonous. Thus the argument based on the quantities and compoundings makes the question of the real properties of external objects a confused issue. Therefore, since we are unable to state in absolute terms the nature of external objects, this mode also will bring us round naturally to suspension of judgement.

The Eighth Mode

The eighth mode is the argument from relativity. By this mode we conclude that, since all things are relative, we shall suspend judgement as to what they are absolutely and in themselves. But there is one qualification we must realize, both here and elsewhere. This is that we employ the word "are" in place of the word "appear," so that what we are saying amounts virtually to this: "All things appear to be relative." And our statement about relativity has a double sense; in the first place, there is a relationship to the thing judging (for the external object being judged appears to the thing judging it), and there is a relationship—in another way—to the things which are perceived along with it, such as the relationship of right to left. But we have considered the relativity of all things in the foregoing also. With respect to the thing which judges, for instance, we said that each object appears relatively to some particular animal or man or sense, and to such and such a circumstance. With respect to the things perceived along with it, each object appears relatively to some particular admixture or manner or composition or quantity or position.

But it is also possible to prove separately that all things are relative. This is done in the following manner. Do absolutes differ from relatives or not? If they do not differ, then they are themselves relative. But if they do differ, since all things which differ are relative (for it is in relation to that from which it differs that it is said to differ), then absolute things are relative. Also, the dogmatists divide all existent things into three classes, the highest genera, the lowest species, and the things which are both genera and species. But all these are relative; therefore all things are relative. A further statement which they themselves make is that some things are manifest, others non-evident; and they say that apparent things are significative and that it is the non-evident things that are made manifest by the apparent things, for according to them, "Things apparent are an aspect of the things not evident."[17] But that which makes manifest and that which is made manifest are relative; therefore all things are relative. In addition to this, existent things are divided into the similar and the dissimilar, and the equal and the unequal. But now these are relative; therefore all things are relative. But even he who denies that all things are relative confirms, by his opposition to us, the proposition that all things are relative; for he shows that the proposition itself (that all things are relative) is relative to us, and not universal.

The result, however, is clear once we show in this manner that all things are relative. We shall not be able to say what each object is in its own nature and absolutely, but what it appears to be under the aspect of relativity. Hence follows the necessity of our suspending judgement concerning the nature of things.

The Ninth Mode

The mode concerned with frequency or rarity of occurrence, which we said was ninth in order, we expound as follows. The sun is surely a much more amazing thing than a comet. But the sun we see constantly, whereas we rarely see a comet. Hence our astonishment at the sight of a comet is such that we may even believe it to be a divine omen, while we are not at all astonished at the sight of the sun. If, however, we only imagine the sun as appearing rarely and setting rarely, illuminating everything at once and causing everything to be thrown suddenly into shadow, then we shall observe great astonishment at the occurrence. Earthquakes, also, do not cause a like degree of confusion in those who are experiencing one for the first time as they do in those who have become accustomed to them by habit. And how great is the astonishment the sea causes in a man who beholds it for the first time! But also the beauty of the human body, in a subject we see for the first time, and suddenly, excites us more than if the right should become a common one. Rare things seem to be valuable; things familiar to us, and easily obtainable, not at all. For example, if we suppose water to be a rare thing, how much more valuable it will appear to us than all the things which are held to be valuable! Or if we ponder the thought of gold simply lying about in large quantities on the ground like stones, to whom shall we suppose it would be so valuable, or so much worth locking up? Since, therefore, according to the frequency or rarity of their occurrence, the same things seem sometimes to be astonishing or valuable, and sometimes not at all so, we conclude that we shall perhaps be able to say what the nature of each of these things appears to be in the context of its frequent or rare occurrence, but that it is not within our power to state the nature of each external object considered purely and simply in itself. And so this mode too causes us to suspend judgement concerning them.

The Tenth Mode

There is a tenth mode, this one concerned chiefly with ethics. This is the argument from disciplines, customs, laws, mythical beliefs, and dogmatic notions. Now, a "discipline" is a choice of a way of life or of some objective, made by one person or by many. A case in point would be Diogenes,[18] or the Laconians.[19] A law is a written covenant among men who live in organized states, the transgressor of which is punished. A custom or habit (there is no difference) is a common acceptance by many men of a certain thing. Here the transgressor is not punished at all. Examples: It is a law not to commit adultery, but a custom not to have intercourse with a woman publicly. Mythical belief is an acceptance of unhistorical;

17. [A saying of Anaxagoras.]

18. [Regarding Diogenes, see n.10.]

19. [Laconia was the region of Greece whose capital was Sparta, which fought beside Athens in the Persian Wars and then against Athens in the Peloponnesian War.]

and fictitious events, such as—among others—the tales told of Kronos (for there are many who are led to believe these tales). A dogmatic notion is acceptance of a thing in so far as the acceptance seems to be confirmed by a line of reasoning or by some proof, for example, that atoms are the elements of existing things, or homoeomeries, or minimal bodies, or something else.

Each of these we oppose sometimes to itself, sometimes to each of the others. We oppose custom to custom, for instance, in this way. Some of the Ethiopians tattoo their babies, while we do not. And Persians think that the use of bright-coloured, dragging garments is seemly, while we think it is unbecoming. And the Indians have intercourse with their women in public, whereas most other peoples hold this to be shameful. We oppose law to law in the following manner. With the Romans, he who relinquishes claim to the property inherited from his father is not obliged to pay his father's debts, but with the Rhodians one must pay them in any event. And among the Tauri of Scythia there was a law that strangers should be sacrificed to Artemis, while with us the ritual killing of humans is forbidden. We oppose discipline to discipline when we set the discipline of Diogenes in opposition to that of Aristippus, or that of the Laconians to that of the Italians. We oppose mythical belief to mythical belief when we say that in one version Zeus is spoken of as the father of gods and men, while in another version it is Oceanus. To quote:

> Ocean, sire of the gods, and Tethys their mother.[20]

And we set dogmatic notions against one another when we say that some declare that there is only one element, while others assume that they are infinite in number. We do so also when we say that some believe the soul to be mortal, others immortal; and that some declare that human affairs are directed by divine providence, while others claim providence has no hand in them.

We oppose custom to the other things, as for example to a law, when we say that with Persian men it is a custom to indulge in homosexual practices, while with the Romans this practice is prohibited by law. This is also the case when we say that with us adultery is forbidden, while with the Massagetae the custom is traditionally an indifferent matter, as Eudoxus of Cnidos records in the first book of his *Voyage*. And whereas intercourse with our mothers is prohibited by our laws, with the Persians it is a custom to marry thus if one possibly can. Among the Egyptians men marry their sisters, a practice which with us is prohibited by law. The opposition of custom to discipline is seen in the fact that whereas most men have intercourse with their wives in private, Crates did so with Hipparchia in public. And Diogenes went about with only a one-sleeved tunic, while we dress as is customary. Custom is opposed to mythical belief when the stories have it that Kronos devoured his own children, since it is our custom to provide for our children. And while it is habitual practice with us to venerate the gods as being good and unaffected by evils, the poets represent them as getting wounded and being envious of one another. And custom is opposed to dogmatic notion when Epicurus says, in opposition to our custom of begging favours of the gods, that the Divinity does not pay any attention to us; and when Aristippus thinks that dressing in women's clothes is a matter of indifference, whereas we consider this a shameful thing.

We have discipline opposed to law when in the face of a law which forbids the striking of a freeman or a well-born man, pancratiasts strike each other because of the discipline of the life they follow; and when gladiators, for the same reason, kill each other even though homicide is forbidden. We oppose mythical belief to discipline when we say that the myths tell of Heracles that he

> carded wool and endured the lot of a slave,[21]

and that he did things that no one, exercising even a moderate choice, would have done, whereas Heracles' discipline of life was a noble one. Discipline is opposed to dogmatic notion when athletes pursue glory as something good, and for its sake take upon themselves a laborious discipline of life, while many philosophers have the dogmatic notion that glory is a trivial thing. We oppose law to mythical belief when

20. [The quotation is from Homer, *Iliad* 14.201.]

21. [The quotation is from the *Odyssey* 22.423.]

the poets portray the gods as committing adultery and practising paederasty, whereas with us these practices are forbidden by law. And we oppose law to dogmatic notion when Chrysippus says that having intercourse with mothers or sisters is a matter of indifference, while the law forbids this. And we oppose mythical belief to dogmatic notion when the poets tell of Zeus coming down and having intercourse with mortal women, while with the dogmatists it is believed that this is impossible. And the Poet says that Zeus, in his grief over Sarpedon, "poured down showers of blood to the earth,"[22] yet it is a dogma of philosophers that the Deity is impassive; and philosophers confute the story of the horse-centaurs, and offer us the horse-centaur as an example of non-reality.

Now, it would be possible to take up many other examples for each of the antitheses mentioned above, but for a brief account these will be sufficient. However, since this mode too points out how great the discrepancy in things is, we shall not be able to say what quality an object possesses according to nature, but only what quality it appears to possess with reference to a particular discipline, a particular law, a particular custom, and so on with each of the others. This mode also, then, compels us to suspend judgement regarding the nature of external objects. And so in this manner, through the ten modes, we end with suspension of judgement.

22. [The quotation is from the *Iliad* 16.459.]

Augustine

During the second through the fifth centuries or so of the Christian Era, Christian apologists began to graft the shoots of the New Testament onto the roots of Platonism, Aristotelianism, and Stoicism. Such husbandry was the work of the Fathers of the Church; hence, this part of the Christian Era is sometimes called the Patristic Era.

Indisputably the greatest of the Church Fathers was St. Augustine (A.D. 354–430). Born in the North African town of Thagaste (now Souk-Ahras, Algeria), Augustine was sent to Carthage in 370 to receive an education in rhetoric, preparatory to a career in law. Not only was Carthage then renowned for education in rhetoric and law, it was also, by Augustine's account, famous for its iniquity, in which he indulged himself freely. In Carthage Augustine first heard of Manichaeism, a dualistic Oriental religion he followed for some nine years. Augustine was attracted to the Manicheans by their swift solution to the problem of evil; that is, the problem of why an all-good, all-powerful God permits the existence of evil in the world. The Manicheans held that counterpoised to God is an all-powerful malignant force, and the world continually exhibits the endless strife between these two.

Following his education, Augustine taught rhetoric in Thagaste, Carthage, and Rome, and in 384 secured a position as a professor of rhetoric at Milan. His disenchantment with Manichaeism had been growing through the years, and by then it was complete; but still tormented by the problem of evil, he had settled for skepticism. While in Milan he encountered two influences that had a profound effect on his life: St. Ambrose, then bishop of Milan, and the writings of the Neoplatonists. Augustine heard many of the sermons given by Ambrose and was deeply moved by them. He also read, in Latin translation, some of the writings of such Neoplatonist philosophers as Plotinus (205–270), who claimed to be perfecting the philosophy of Plato. These two sources convinced him that his reservations about Christianity were ill founded. In particular, he now thought he saw a way out of the impasse created by the problem of evil: since everything that exists is created by God and everything created by God is good, there could be no all-powerful, perfectly malign being continually thwarting God's efforts. It follows, then, according to Augustine, that evil is nonexistent. As Augustine would have it, evil is not the presence of something that exists, but rather the absence of something, namely, goodness. Augustine finally converted to Christianity in 386 and was baptized in Milan the next year. After his conversion he returned to Africa, where he was ordained as priest in the city of Hippo. He rose rapidly in the ecclesiastical ranks to become the bishop of Hippo, a position he held until his death. He died in 430 as the Vandals were preparing to lay siege to Hippo.

Augustine's prodigious writings cover virtually every aspect of Christian experience, since he spent much of his adult life seeking to define Christianity and defend it not only from the attacks of nonbelievers but also from the challenges of several types of heretical Christians. For example, in addition to combating the Manicheans, Augustine also wrote several treatises against the members of a schismatic North African sect, the Donatists, who maintained that the sacraments, if administered by a sinful priest, had no validity. Augustine also took issue with the Pelagians, who denied the doctrine of original sin, claiming that Adam and Eve's sin was not transmitted to their descendants. The Pelagians believed that God's grace was not necessary for human salvation, a proposition vehemently denied by Augustine. His success against Christian heretics was so complete that subsequent Christian theologians generally consider it sufficient merely to cite his authority on many doctrinal issues. Indeed, his authority was so great that it was appealed to by both sides during the Reformation controversies.

It is commonly said that Augustine Platonized Christianity. This statement must be treated cautiously, for Augustine could not have read many, if any, of Plato's dialogues. In fact, he emphatically rejected many of Plato's most characteristic doctrines, including the doctrines of reincarnation (along with the associated Platonic thesis that the body is the prison of the soul, deserved because of the soul's transgressions in a previous life); recollection (which he replaced with a doctrine of divine illumination); and the denial of moral weakness. Nevertheless, there is a Platonic core to Augustine's thinking. Plato's Forms become for Augustine eternal ideas in God's mind; and, like Plato, Augustine makes a sharp distinction between the things that exist in space or time and that which is outside space and time, the latter being perfect, the former imperfect.

On Free Choice of the Will gives an overview of many of the themes central to Augustine's thought. As the title suggests, the work focuses on the notion of freedom of the will, its importance in dealing with the problem of evil, God's justice in bestowing it upon us, its incompatibility with God's foreknowledge of all our future choices, and its necessity for our happiness.

Augustine's most comprehensive treatment of the problems of time constitutes Book XI of his *Confessions,* which is reprinted here. The *Confessions* is a unique book, a work that is at once autobiographical, didactic, devotional, and philosophical. The first nine books give a detailed account of Augustine's life up to and including his conversion to Christianity. In Book XI, however, the issues are strictly theological and philosophical. Augustine begins with the question, "What was God doing before He created Heaven and Earth?" His treatment of this question leads him to consider the further question, "How is it possible to measure time?" which invokes the more general question, "What is time?" The honesty and evident self-perplexity with which he grapples with these difficult questions have attracted many contemporary philosophers to this book of the *Confessions.*

• • •

A serviceable biography of Augustine's life is Peter Brown, *Augustine of Hippo: A Biography* (Berkeley: University of California Press, 1967), which also contains information about English translations of Augustine's writings. Etienne Gilson, *The Christian Philosophy of Saint Augustine* (New York: Random House, 1960) provides a clear introduction to Augustine's philosophy. R. A. Markus, ed., *Augustine: A Collection of Critical Essays* (Garden City, N.J.: Doubleday, 1972); Gareth B. Matthews, ed., *The Augustinian Tradition* (Berkeley: University of California Press, 1998); and Eleonore Stump and Norman Kretzmann, eds., *The Cambridge Companion to Augustine* (Cambridge: Cambridge University Press, 2001) are valuable collections of papers on Augustine's philosophy. Two useful studies of Augustine as philosopher are Christopher Kirwan, *Augustine* (London: Routledge, 1989) and Gareth B. Matthews, *Augustine* (Malden, Mass.: Blackwell Publishing, 2005). For examinations of several philosophical themes in the *Confessions,* see William E. Mann, ed., *Augustine's Confessions* (Lanham, MD.: Rowman & Littlefield, 2006).

William E. Mann

On Free Choice of the Will

BOOK ONE

1 EVODIUS: Please tell me: isn't God the cause of evil?

AUGUSTINE: I will tell you once you have made clear what kind of evil you are asking about. For we use the word 'evil' in two senses: first, when we say that someone has *done* evil; and second, when we say that someone has *suffered* evil.

EVODIUS: I want to know about both.

AUGUSTINE: But if you know or believe that God is good—and it is not right to believe otherwise—then he does no evil. On the other hand, if we acknowledge that God is just—and it is impious to deny it—then he rewards the good and punishes the wicked. Those punishments are certainly evils for those who suffer them. Therefore, if no one is punished unjustly—and we must believe this, since we believe that this universe is governed by divine providence—it follows that God is a cause of the second kind of evil, but in no way causes the first kind.

EVODIUS: Then is there some other cause of the evil that God does not cause?

AUGUSTINE: There certainly is. Such evil could not occur unless someone caused it. But if you ask who that someone is, it is impossible to say. For there is no single cause of evil; rather, everyone who does evil is the cause of his own evildoing. If you doubt this, recall what I said earlier: Evil deeds are punished by the justice of God. They would not be punished justly if they had not been performed voluntarily.

EVODIUS: It seems that no one could sin unless he had first learned how to sin. And if that is the case, I must ask this: From whom did we learn to sin?

AUGUSTINE: Do you think learning is a good thing?

EVODIUS: Who would dare to say that learning is a bad thing?

AUGUSTINE: What if it is neither good nor bad?

EVODIUS: I think it is good.

AUGUSTINE: Indeed it is, since knowledge is given or awakened through learning and no one comes to know anything except through learning.[1] Don't you agree?

EVODIUS: I think that we come to know only good things through learning.

AUGUSTINE: Then we do not come to know evil things; for the word 'learning' is correctly applied only when we come to know something.[2]

EVODIUS: But if we do not come to know evil things, how is it that human beings perform evil acts?

AUGUSTINE: Perhaps because they turn away from learning and become strangers to it. But whether that is the correct explanation or not, one thing is certainly clear: since learning is good, and the word 'learning' is correctly applied only when we come to know something, we simply cannot come to know evil things. If we could, then they would be part of learning, and so learning would not be a good thing. But it *is* a good thing, as you said yourself. Therefore, we do not come to know evil things, and there is no point in your asking from whom we learn to do evil things. Or else we do come to know them, but only as things to be avoided, not as things to be done. It follows that doing evil is nothing but turning away from learning.

EVODIUS: I rather think that there are two sorts of learning: one by means of which we learn to do

Reprinted from Augustine, *On Free Choice of the Will*, translated by Thomas Williams (Indianapolis: Hackett Publishing Company, 1993), by permission of the publisher.

1. [In the passage that follows, Augustine relies on the similarity between the verb "*discere*" ("to learn") and its noun form "*disciplina*" ("learning"). Unfortunately, the words are so similar in English that a literal translation sounds odd and occasionally nonsensical. I have therefore translated "*discere*" as "come to know" in most cases. The reader should bear in mind that the connection between "come to know" and "learning" is much closer in the Latin than I can safely make it in the English.—T.W.]

2. [Literally, "the word '*disciplina*' is derived from the word '*discere*.'"]

right, and another by means of which we learn to do evil. But when you asked whether learning was good, the love of good itself caught my attention, and I saw only the sort of learning by which we learn to do right. That is why I answered that it is good. But now I remember that there is another sort of learning. I have no doubt that it is evil, and I would like to know its cause.

AUGUSTINE: Do you at least consider understanding good?

EVODIUS: Certainly. I consider it so good that I cannot see how any human trait could be better. And I would in no way say that any understanding can be bad.

AUGUSTINE: When someone is being taught but does not understand, would you think that he has learned?

EVODIUS: Of course not.

AUGUSTINE: Well then, if all understanding is good, and no one who does not understand learns, then everyone who learns is doing good. For everyone who learns, understands; and everyone who understands is doing good. So someone who wants to know the cause of our learning something really wants to know the cause of our doing good. So let's have no more of your wanting to hunt down this mysterious evil teacher. If he is evil, he is no teacher; and if he is a teacher, he is not evil.

2 EVODIUS: Now that you have convinced me that we do not learn to do evil, please explain to me what *is* the source of our evildoing.

AUGUSTINE: You have hit upon the very question that worried me greatly when I was still young, a question that wore me out, drove me into the company of heretics,[3] and knocked me flat on my face. I was so hurt by this fall, buried under a mountain of silly fairy tales, that if my love of finding the truth had not secured divine help, I would not have been able to get out from under them to breathe freely and begin to seek the truth. And since such pains were taken to free me from this difficulty, I will lead you on the same path that I followed in making my escape. God will be with us, and he will make us understand what we have believed. For we are well aware that we are at the stage described by the prophet, who says, "Unless you believe, you will not understand."[4] We believe that everything that exists comes from the one God, and yet we believe that God is not the cause of sins. What is troubling is that if you admit that sins come from the souls that God created, and those souls come from God, pretty soon you'll be tracing those sins back to God.

EVODIUS: You have stated plainly what bothers me in thinking about this question. That is the problem that has compelled me and drawn me into this inquiry.

AUGUSTINE: Be courageous, and go on believing what you believe. There is no better belief, even if you do not yet see the explanation for why it is true. The truest beginning of piety is to think as highly of God as possible; and doing so means that one must believe that he is omnipotent, and not changeable in the smallest respect; that he is the creator of all good things, but is himself more excellent than all of them; that he is the supremely just ruler of everything that he created; and that he was not aided in creating by any other being, as if he were not sufficiently powerful by himself. It follows that he created all things from nothing. He did not create from himself, but generated one who is equal to himself, whom we call the only Son of God. In trying to describe the Son more clearly we call him "the Power of God and the Wisdom of God,"[5] through whom God made all the things that were made from nothing. On that basis let us try, with God's help, to achieve an understanding of the problem you have raised.

3 You want to know the source of our evildoing. So we must first discuss what evildoing *is*. State your view on the matter. If you cannot explain the whole thing at once in a few words, you can at least show me your view by naming particular evil deeds.

EVODIUS: Adultery, murder, and sacrilege, not to mention others that time and memory do not permit me to enumerate. Who could fail to recognize these as evil deeds?

3. [The Manichees, who believed in the existence of an evil "god" equal to and independent of the good "god."]

4. [Isaiah 7:9 (pre-Vulgate text).]

5. [1 Corinthians 1:24.]

AUGUSTINE: Tell me first, why do you think adultery is evil? Because the law forbids it?

EVODIUS: On the contrary. Clearly, it is not evil because the law forbids it; rather, the law forbids it because it is evil.

AUGUSTINE: But suppose someone were to make things difficult for us by extolling the pleasures of adultery and asking why we think adultery evil and deserving of condemnation. Surely you do not think that people who want to understand, and not merely to believe, would have to take refuge in an appeal to the authority of the law? Now like you I do believe, and I believe most firmly, and cry out that all peoples and nations should believe, that adultery is evil. But now we are attempting to know and hold firmly by understanding what we have already accepted by faith. So think this over as carefully as you can, and tell me what reason you have by which you know that adultery is evil.

EVODIUS: I know that it is evil because I would not tolerate it if someone tried to commit adultery with my own wife. Anyone who does to another what he does not want done to himself does evil.

AUGUSTINE: What if someone's lust is so great that he offers his wife to another and willingly allows him to commit adultery with her, and is eager to enjoy the same freedom with the other man's wife? Do you think that this man has done nothing evil?

EVODIUS: Far from it!

AUGUSTINE: But by your rule he does not sin, since he is not doing anything that he is unwilling to have done to himself. You must therefore look for some other argument to show that adultery is evil.

EVODIUS: The reason that I think it is evil is that I have often seen people condemned for this crime.

AUGUSTINE: But haven't people often been condemned for good deeds? Not to refer you to any other books, recall the story that is superior to all others by virtue of its divine authority. There you will find that we must think very poorly of the apostles and martyrs if we intend to make condemnation a sure sign of wrongdoing. All of them were judged worthy of condemnation because of their confession of faith. It follows that if everything that is condemned is evil, it was evil in those days to believe in Christ and to confess that faith. But if not everything that is condemned is evil, find some other way to show why adultery is evil.

EVODIUS: I can't think how to respond.

AUGUSTINE: Then perhaps what makes adultery evil is inordinate desire,[6] whereas so long as you look for the evil in the external, visible act, you are bound to encounter difficulties. In order to understand that inordinate desire is what makes adultery evil, consider this: if a man is unable to sleep with someone else's wife, but it is somehow clear that he would like to, and would do so if he had the chance, he is no less guilty than if he were caught in the act.

EVODIUS: Nothing could be clearer. Now I see that there is no need for a long discussion to persuade me that this is the case with murder and sacrilege and every sin whatsoever. For it is clear now that inordinate desire is what drives every kind of evildoing.

4 AUGUSTINE: Do you know that inordinate desire is also called 'cupidity'?

EVODIUS: Yes.

AUGUSTINE: Do you think there is any difference between cupidity and fear? Or are they quite the same?

EVODIUS: Indeed, I think there is a huge difference between the two.

AUGUSTINE: I suppose you think so because cupidity desires its object, and fear flees from it.

EVODIUS: You're quite right.

AUGUSTINE: Then suppose a man kills someone, not out of cupidity for something that he desires to

6. [The Latin here is "*libido*." There is no single English word that adequately conveys its meaning. Some translators have rendered it "desire," with the result that Augustine often seems to be saying that all desire is sinful, which is not his view at all. The alternative translation of "lust" captures the fact that "*libido*" is one specific kind of desire, but English usage restricts "lust" to blameworthy *sexual desire*; and Augustine certainly does not mean to claim that all murder and sacrilege result from misdirected sexual passion. Therefore, despite the occasional clumsiness of doing so, I have translated "*libido*" as "inordinate desire." The other important term in this passage is "*cupiditas*." Sometimes Augustine treats "*cupiditas*" as synonymous with "*libido*"; in those cases I have translated it as "cupidity."

gain, but because he fears that some harm will come to himself. Would he be a murderer?

EVODIUS: Yes, he would. But even in this deed, cupidity is the driving force: for a man who kills someone out of fear surely desires to live without fear.

AUGUSTINE: Do you think that living without fear is a small good?

EVODIUS: It is a great good, but that murderer cannot achieve it by his action.

AUGUSTINE: I am not asking what he can achieve, but what he desires. Someone who desires a life free from fear certainly desires a good thing, so his desire is not blameworthy; otherwise we will have to blame everyone who loves the good. Consequently, we will have to say that there is an instance of murder in which cupidity is not the driving force; and it will be false that inordinate desire is what drives all sins, to the extent that they are evil. Either that, or there will be an instance of murder that is not sinful.

EVODIUS: If murder is just killing a human being, then there can be murder that is not sinful. When a soldier kills the enemy, when a judge or his representative puts a criminal to death, or when a weapon accidentally slips out of someone's hand without his willing or noticing it: these people do not seem to me to be sinning when they kill someone.

AUGUSTINE: I agree, but such people are not usually called murderers. So consider someone who kills his master because he fears severe torture. Do you think that he should be classed among those who kill a human being but do not deserve to be called murderers?

EVODIUS: I think this case is entirely different. In the earlier examples, those men are acting in accordance with the law, or at least not contrary to the law; but no law approves of the deed in your example.

AUGUSTINE: Again you refer me to authority. You must remember that we took up this discussion in order to understand what we believe. We believe the laws, and so we must try to understand, if we can, whether the law that punishes this deed does so unjustly.

EVODIUS: It is in no way unjust to punish someone who knowingly and willingly kills his master. None of the men in my earlier examples did that.

AUGUSTINE: But do you not remember that a little while ago you said that inordinate desire is what drives every evil deed, and that this is the very reason why the deed is evil?

EVODIUS: Of course I remember.

AUGUSTINE: And did you not also grant that someone who desires to live without fear does not have an evil desire?

EVODIUS: I remember that too.

AUGUSTINE: It follows that, since the master is killed by the slave as a result of this desire, he is not killed as a result of a blameworthy desire. And so we have not yet figured out why this deed is evil. For we are agreed that all wrongdoing is evil only because it results from inordinate desire, that is, from blameworthy cupidity.

EVODIUS: At this point it seems to me that the slave is unjustly condemned, which I would not dream of saying if I could think of some other response.

AUGUSTINE: You have let yourself be persuaded that this great crime should go unpunished, without considering whether the slave wanted to be free of the fear of his master in order to satisfy his own ordinate desires. All wicked people, just like good people, desire to live without fear. The difference is that the good, in desiring this, turn their love away from things that cannot be possessed without the fear of losing them. The wicked, on the other hand, try to get rid of anything that prevents them from enjoying such things securely. Thus they lead a wicked and criminal life, which would better be called death.

EVODIUS: Now I've come to my senses. I am glad that I understand so clearly the nature of that blameworthy cupidity that is called inordinate desire. Obviously it is the love of those things that one can lose against one's will. . . .

BOOK TWO

EVODIUS: Now explain to me, if you can, why God *1* gave human beings free choice of the will, since if we had not received it, we would not have been able to sin.

But sometimes he uses it as a neutral term, and there I have translated it as "desire."]

AUGUSTINE: Do you know for certain that God gave us this thing that you think should not have been given?

EVODIUS: If I understood Book One correctly, we have free choice of the will and we cannot sin without it.

AUGUSTINE: I too remember that that had become quite clear to us. But what I asked just now was whether you knew that it was *God* who gave us this thing, which we clearly have and by which we sin.

EVODIUS: Who else would it be? For we have our existence from God, and it is from him that we deserve punishment for doing wrong and reward for doing good.

AUGUSTINE: Here again I want to know whether you know this for certain, or whether you willingly believe it on the urging of some authority, without actually knowing it.

EVODIUS: I admit that at first I believed this on authority. But what could be truer than that everything good comes from God, that everything just is good, and that it is just for sinners to be punished and the good rewarded? From this I conclude that it is God who afflicts sinners with unhappiness and confers happiness on the good.

AUGUSTINE: I make no objection. But I do have one further question: How do you know that we have our existence from God? You did not explain that; you showed only that it is from him that we deserve punishment or reward.

EVODIUS: That is an obvious consequence of the fact that God, as the source of all justice, punishes sins. It may be that goodness confers benefits on those not committed to its charge, but justice does not punish those not in its jurisdiction. So it is obvious that we belong to God, because he is not only most generous in conferring benefits but also most just in punishing.

Furthermore, I claimed, and you agreed, that everything good is from God. From this we can understand that human beings too are from God. For human beings as such are good things, since they can live rightly if they so will.

AUGUSTINE: If all of this is true, the question you posed has clearly been answered. If human beings are good things, and they cannot do right unless they so will, then they ought to have a free will, without which they cannot do right. True, they can also use free will to sin, but we should not therefore believe that God gave them free will so that they would be able to sin. The fact that human beings could not live rightly without it was sufficient reason for God to give it. The very fact that anyone who uses free will to sin is divinely punished shows that free will was given to enable human beings to live rightly, for such punishment would be unjust if free will had been given both for living rightly and for sinning. After all, how could someone justly be punished for using the will for the very purpose for which it was given? When God punishes a sinner, don't you think he is saying, "Why didn't you use your free will for the purpose for which I gave it to you?"—that is, for living rightly?

And as for the goodness that we so admired in God's justice—his punishing sins and rewarding good deeds—how could it even exist if human beings lacked the free choice of the will? No action would be either a sin or a good deed if it were not performed by the will, and so both punishment and reward would be unjust if human beings had no free will. But it was right for there to be justice in both reward and punishment, since this is one of the goods that come from God. Therefore, it was right for God to give free will to human beings.

2 EVODIUS: I concede that point now. But don't you think that if free will was given to us for living rightly, we ought not to have been able to pervert it and use it for sinning? It should have been like justice, which was also given to human beings to enable them to live well. No one can use justice to live wickedly. In the same way, it ought to be the case that no one could use the will to sin, if indeed the will was given for acting rightly.

AUGUSTINE: God will, I hope, enable me to reply to you—or rather, he will enable you to reply to yourself, as Truth, the greatest teacher of all, teaches you within. But first I want you to tell me this. I asked whether you knew for certain that God gave us free will, and you said that you did. So now that we have agreed that he gave us free will, should we presume to say that it should not have been given? If there is some doubt whether it was God who gave it, it is appropriate for us to ask whether it was a good gift; and if we find that it was, then we have also found that it was given by God, from whom the soul has all good gifts. But if we find that it was not a good gift, we will understand that it was not given by God, whom it is impious to blame. But if it is quite certain that God gave us free will, then we must admit that it ought to have been given, and in exactly the way that it was given; for God gave it, and his deeds are utterly beyond reproach.

EVODIUS: Although I hold these things with unshaken faith, let's investigate them as if they were all uncertain, since I do not yet *know* them. It is uncertain whether free will was given for doing right, since we can also use it to sin; consequently, it is also uncertain whether it ought to have been given. For if it is uncertain whether it was given for doing right, then it is also uncertain whether it ought to have been given. This means in turn that it is doubtful whether it was given by God. For if it is doubtful whether it ought to have been given, then it is also doubtful whether it was given by God, since it is impious to believe that God gave something that should not have been given.

AUGUSTINE: You are at any rate certain that God exists.

EVODIUS: Even that is something I hold by faith, not something I see for myself.

AUGUSTINE: Scripture says, "The fool has said in his heart, 'There is no God.'"[7] Suppose one of those fools were to say that to you. Suppose he did not want to believe what you believe, but to know whether what you believe is true. Would you just give up, or would you think that he could somehow be persuaded of what you firmly believe—especially if he was not merely being contentious, but sincerely wanted to know?

EVODIUS: This last proviso of yours suggests a response. However absurd he might be, he would surely concede that one should not discuss anything, and especially not such an important matter, with a deceitful and obstinate person. Then he would have to get me to believe that he had the proper attitude and was not concealing any deceitfulness or obstinacy regarding this issue. Then I would point out to him that he expects other people to believe things about his own state of mind, things that he knows but other people do not. And I would try to get him to see (as I think anyone easily can) how much more reasonable it is for him to believe that God exists on the authority of the writings of such great men, who left written testimony that they lived with the Son of God, and wrote that they saw things that could not have happened if God did not exist. He would be completely foolish to reproach me for believing them, when he expects me to believe him. And since he could not rightly reproach me, he would have no reason not to join me.

AUGUSTINE: But if you think it is acceptable to believe that God exists because we have found those men to be reliable authorities, why don't you think we should also accept the authority of those same men regarding the other issues that we had found to be uncertain and unknown, rather than toiling on with our inquiry?

EVODIUS: But we want to know and understand what we believe.

AUGUSTINE: Your memory serves you well; we cannot deny what we said at the beginning of our previous discussion. Unless believing and understanding were two different things, and we were first to believe the great and divine things that we desire to understand, there would have been no point in the prophet's saying "Unless you believe, you will not understand."[8] At first our Lord himself by his words and deeds urged those whom he had called to salvation to believe in him. But later, when he spoke of the gift that he was going to give to those who believed, he did not say, "This is eternal life, that they may *believe*," but "This is eternal life, that they may *know* you, the true God, and him whom you have sent, Jesus Christ."[9] And he said to those who already believe, "Seek, and you will find."[10] For something that is believed but not known has not yet been found, and no one becomes ready to find God unless he first believes what he will afterwards know.

Therefore, let us diligently obey the Lord's command as we seek; for he himself will show us what

7. [Psalm 14:1; 53:1.]

8. [Isaiah 7:9 (pre-Vulgate text).]

9. [John 17:3.]

10. [Matthew 7:7.]

we seek at his urging, insofar as it can be found in this life by such people as we are. For we must believe that better people, even in this earthly life, and all good and pious people in the next, see and possess these things more clearly and completely. We must hope one day to be like them, and we must wholeheartedly desire and love these things and place no value on what is earthly and human. . . .

BOOK THREE

1 EVODIUS: It has been demonstrated to my satisfaction that free will is to be numbered among good things, and indeed not among the least of them, and therefore that it was given to us by God, who acted rightly in giving it. So now, if you think that this is a good time, I would like you to explain the source of the movement by which the will turns away from the common and unchangeable good toward its own good, or the good of others, or lower goods, all of which are changeable.

AUGUSTINE: Why do we need to know that?

EVODIUS: Because if the will was given to us in such a way that it had this movement naturally, then it turned to changeable goods by necessity, and there is no blame involved when nature and necessity determine an action.

AUGUSTINE: Does this movement please you or displease you?

EVODIUS: It displeases me.

AUGUSTINE: So you find fault with it.

EVODIUS: Of course.

AUGUSTINE: Then you find fault with a blameless movement of the soul.

EVODIUS: No, it's just that I don't know whether there is any blame involved when the soul deserts the unchangeable good and turns toward changeable goods.

AUGUSTINE: Then you find fault with what you don't know.

EVODIUS: Don't quibble over words. In saying "I don't know whether there is any blame involved," I meant it to be understood that there undoubtedly *is* blame involved. The "I don't know" implied that it was ridiculous to have doubts about such an obvious fact.

AUGUSTINE: Then pay close attention to this most certain truth, which has caused you to forget so quickly what you just said. If that movement existed by nature or necessity, it could in no way be blameworthy. But you are so firmly convinced that this movement is indeed blameworthy that you think it would be ridiculous to entertain doubts about something so certain. Why then did you affirm, or at least tentatively assert, something that now seems to you clearly false? For this is what you said: "If the will was given to us in such a way that it had this movement naturally, then it turned to changeable goods by necessity, and there is no blame involved when nature and necessity determine an action." Since you are sure that this movement was blameworthy, you should have been quite sure that the will was not given to us in such a way.

EVODIUS: I said that this movement was blameworthy and that therefore it displeases me. And I am surely right to find fault with it. But I deny that a soul ought to be blamed when this movement pulls it away from the unchangeable good toward changeable goods, if this movement is so much a part of its nature that it is moved by necessity.

AUGUSTINE: You admit that this movement certainly deserves blame; but *whose* movement is it?

EVODIUS: I see that the movement is in the soul, but I don't know whose it is.

AUGUSTINE: Surely you don't deny that the soul is moved by this movement.

EVODIUS: No.

AUGUSTINE: Do you deny that a movement by which a stone is moved is a movement of the stone? I'm not talking about a movement that is caused by us or some other force, as when it is thrown into the air, but the movement that occurs when it falls to the earth by its own weight.

EVODIUS: I don't deny that this movement, by which the stone seeks the lowest place, is a movement of the stone. But it is a natural movement. If that's the sort of movement the soul has, then the soul's movement is also natural. And if it is moved naturally, it cannot justly be blamed; even if it is moved toward something evil, it is compelled by its own nature. But since we don't doubt that this movement is blameworthy, we must absolutely deny that it is natural, and so it is not similar to the natural movement of a stone.

AUGUSTINE: Did we accomplish anything in our first two discussions?

EVODIUS: Of course we did.

AUGUSTINE: I'm sure you recall that in Book One we agreed that nothing can make the mind a slave to inordinate desire except its own will. For the will cannot be forced into such iniquity by anything superior or equal to it, since that would be unjust; or by anything inferior to it, since that is impossible. Only one possibility remains: the movement by which the will turns from enjoying the Creator to enjoying his creatures belongs to the will itself. So if that movement deserves blame (and you said it was ridiculous to entertain doubts on that score), then it is not natural, but voluntary.

This movement of the will is similar to the downward movement of a stone in that it belongs to the will just as that downward movement belongs to the stone. But the two movements are dissimilar in this respect: the stone has no power to check its downward movement, but the soul is not moved to abandon higher things and love inferior things unless it wills to do so. And so the movement of the stone is natural, but the movement of the soul is voluntary. If someone were to say that a stone is sinning because its weight carries it downward, I would not merely say that he was more senseless than the stone itself; I would consider him completely insane. But we accuse a soul of sin when we are convinced that it has abandoned higher things and chosen to enjoy inferior things. Now we admit that this movement belongs to the will alone, and that it is voluntary and therefore blameworthy; and the only useful teaching on this topic is that which condemns and checks this movement and thus serves to rescue our wills from their fall into temporal goods and turn them toward the enjoyment of the eternal good. Therefore, what need is there to ask about the source of the movement by which the will turns away from the unchangeable good toward changeable good?

EVODIUS: I see that what you are saying is true, and in a way I understand it. There is nothing I feel so firmly and so intimately as that I have a will by which I am moved to enjoy something. If the will by which I choose or refuse things is not mine, then I don't know what I can call mine. So if I use my will to do something evil, whom can I hold responsible but myself? For a good God made me, and I can do nothing good except through my will; therefore, it is quite clear that the will was given to me by a good God so that I might do good. If the movement of the will by which it turns this way or that were not voluntary and under its own control, a person would not deserve praise for turning to higher things or blame for turning to lower things, as if swinging on the hinge of the will. Furthermore, there would be no point in admonishing people to forget about lower things and strive for what is eternal, so that they might refuse to live badly but instead will to live rightly. And anyone who does not think that we ought to admonish people in this way deserves to be banished from the human race.

2 Since these things are true, I very much wonder how God can have foreknowledge of everything in the future, and yet we do not sin by necessity. It would be an irreligious and completely insane attack on God's foreknowledge to say that something could happen otherwise than as God foreknew. So suppose that God foreknew that the first human being was going to sin. Anyone who admits, as I do, that God foreknows everything in the future will have to grant me that. Now I won't say that God would not have made him—for God made him good, and no sin of his can harm God, who not only made him good but showed His own goodness by creating him, as He also shows His justice by punishing him and His mercy by redeeming him—but I will say this: since God foreknew that he was going to sin, his sin necessarily had to happen. How, then, is the will free when such inescapable necessity is found in it?

AUGUSTINE: You have knocked powerfully on the door of God's mercy; may it be present and open the door to those who knock. Nevertheless, I think the only reason that most people are tormented by this question is that they do not ask it piously; they are more eager to excuse than to confess their sins. Some people gladly believe that there is no divine providence in charge of human affairs. They put their bodies and their souls at the mercy of chance and give themselves up to be beaten and mangled by inordinate desires. They disbelieve divine judgments and evade human judgments, thinking that fortune will defend them from those who accuse them. They depict this "fortune" as blind, implying either that they are better than fortune, by which they think they are ruled, or that they themselves suffer from the same blindness. It is perfectly reasonable to admit that such people do everything by chance, since in whatever they do, they fall.[11] But we said enough in Book Two to combat this opinion, which is full of the most foolish and insane error.

Others, however, are not impertinent enough to deny that the providence of God rules over human life; but they prefer the wicked error of believing that it is weak, or unjust, or evil, rather than confessing their sins with humble supplication. If only they would let themselves be convinced that, when they think of what is best and most just and most powerful, the goodness and justice and power of God are far greater and far higher than anything they can conceive; if only they would consider themselves and understand that they would owe thanks to God even if he had willed to make them lower than they are. Then the very bone and marrow of their conscience would cry out, "I said, 'O Lord, have mercy upon me; heal my soul, for I have sinned against you.'"[12] Thus they would be led in the secure paths of divine mercy along the road to wisdom, not becoming conceited when they made new discoveries or disheartened when they failed to do so. Their new knowledge would simply prepare them to see more, and their ignorance would make them more patient in seeking the truth. Of course I'm sure that you already believe this. But you will see how easily I can answer your difficult question once I have answered a few preliminary questions.

3 Surely this is the problem that is disturbing and puzzling you. How is it that these two propositions are not contradictory and inconsistent: (1) God has foreknowledge of everything in the future; and (2) We sin by the will, not by necessity? For, you say, if God foreknows that someone is going to sin, then it is necessary that he sin. But if it is necessary, the will has no choice about whether to sin; there is an inescapable and fixed necessity. And so you fear that this argument forces us into one of two positions: either we draw the heretical conclusion that God does not foreknow everything in the future; or, if we cannot accept this conclusion, we must admit that sin happens by necessity and not by will. Isn't that what is bothering you?

EVODIUS: That's it exactly.

AUGUSTINE: So you think that anything that God foreknows happens by necessity and not by will.

EVODIUS: Precisely.

AUGUSTINE: Now pay close attention. Look inside yourself for a little while, and tell me, if you can, what sort of will you are going to have tomorrow: a will to do right or a will to sin?

EVODIUS: I don't know.

AUGUSTINE: Do you think that God doesn't know either?

EVODIUS: Not at all—God certainly does know.

AUGUSTINE: Well then, if God knows what you are going to will tomorrow, and foresees the future wills of every human being, both those who exist now and those who will exist in the future, he surely foresees how he is going to treat the just and the irreligious.

EVODIUS: Clearly, if I say that God foreknows all of my actions, I can much more confidently say that he foreknows his own actions and foresees with absolute certainty what he is going to do.

AUGUSTINE: Then aren't you worried that someone might object that God himself will act out of necessity rather than by his will in everything that he is going to do? After all, you said that whatever God foreknows happens by necessity, not by will.

EVODIUS: When I said that, I was thinking only of what happens in his creation and not of what happens within himself. For those things do not come into being; they are eternal.

AUGUSTINE: So God does nothing in his creation.

EVODIUS: He has already established, once for all, the ways in which the universe that he created is to be governed; he does not administer anything by a new act of will.

AUGUSTINE: Doesn't he make anyone happy?

EVODIUS: Of course he does.

AUGUSTINE: And he does this when that person is made happy.

11. [The Latin word for "chance" ("*casus*") is derived from the verb "to fall" ("*cado*").]

12. [Psalm 41:4.]

EVODIUS: Right.

AUGUSTINE: Then suppose, for example, that you are going to be happy a year from now. That means that a year from now God is going to make you happy.

EVODIUS: That's right too.

AUGUSTINE: And God knows today what he is going to do a year from now.

EVODIUS: He has always foreknown this, so I admit that he foreknows it now, if indeed it is really going to happen.

AUGUSTINE: Then surely you are not God's creature, or else your happiness does not take place in you.

EVODIUS: But I am God's creature, and my happiness does take place in me.

AUGUSTINE: Then the happiness that God gives you takes place by necessity and not by will.

EVODIUS: His will *is* my necessity.

AUGUSTINE: And so you will be happy against your will.

EVODIUS: If I had the power to be happy I would be happy right now. Even now I will to be happy, but I'm not, since it is God who makes me happy. I cannot do it for myself.

AUGUSTINE: How clearly the truth speaks through you! You could not help thinking that the only thing that is within our power is that which we do when we will it. Therefore, nothing is so much within our power as the will itself, for it is near at hand the very moment that we will. So we can rightly say, "We grow old by necessity, not by will"; or "We become feeble by necessity, not by will"; or "We die by necessity, not by will," and other such things. But who would be crazy enough to say "We do not will by the will"? Therefore, although God foreknows what we are going to will in the future, it does not follow that we do not will by the will.

When you said that you cannot make yourself happy, you said it as if I had denied it. Not at all; I am merely saying that when you do become happy, it will be in accordance with your will, not against your will. Simply because God foreknows your future happiness—and nothing can happen except as God foreknows it, since otherwise it would not be foreknowledge—it does not follow that you will be happy against your will. That would be completely absurd and far from the truth. So God's foreknowledge, which is certain even today of your future happiness, does not take away your will for happiness once you have begun to be happy; and in the same way, your blameworthy will (if indeed you are going to have such a will) does not cease to be a will simply because God foreknows that you are going to have it.

Just notice how imperceptive someone would have to be to argue thus: "If God has foreknown my future will, it is necessary that I will what he has foreknown, since nothing can happen otherwise than as he has foreknown it. But if it is necessary, then one must concede that I will it by necessity and not by will." What extraordinary foolishness! If God foreknew a future will that turned out not to be a will at all, things would indeed happen otherwise than as God foreknew them. And I will overlook this objector's equally monstrous statement that "it is necessary that I will," for by assuming necessity he tries to abolish will. For if his willing is necessary, how does he will, since there is no will?

Suppose he expressed it in another way and said that, since his willing is necessary, his will is not in his own power. This would run up against the same problem that you had when I asked whether you were going to be happy against your will. You replied that you would already be happy if you had the power; you said that you have the will but not the power. I answered that the truth had spoken through you. For we can deny that something is in our power only if it is not present even when we will it; but if we will, and yet the will remains absent, then we are not really willing at all. Now if it is impossible for us not to will when we are willing, then the will is present to those who will; and if something is present when we will it, then it is in our power. So our will would not be a will if it were not in our power. And since it is in our power, we are free with respect to it. But we are not free with respect to anything that we do not have in our power, and anything that we have cannot be nothing.

Thus, we believe both that God has foreknowledge of everything in the future and that nonetheless we will whatever we will. Since God foreknows our will, the very will that he foreknows will be what comes about. Therefore, it will be a will, since it is a will that he foreknows. And it could not be a will unless it were in our power. Therefore, he also foreknows this power. It follows, then, that his foreknowledge does not take away my power; in fact, it is all the more certain that I will have that power, since he whose foreknowledge never errs foreknows that I will have it.

EVODIUS: I agree now that it is necessary that whatever God has foreknown will happen, and that he foreknows our sins in such a way that our wills remain free and are within our power.

4 AUGUSTINE: Then what is troubling you? Have you perhaps forgotten the results of our first discussion? Will you deny that nothing at all, whether superior, equal, or inferior, can coerce the will, and that we sin by our own wills?

EVODIUS: I certainly wouldn't dream of denying any of those things. But still, I must admit that I can't quite see how God's foreknowledge of our sins can be consistent with our free choice in sinning. For we must admit that God is just, and that he has foreknowledge. But I would like to know how it can be just to punish sins that happen necessarily, or how things that God foreknows do not happen necessarily, or how whatever happens necessarily in creation should not be attributed to the Creator.

AUGUSTINE: Why do you think that our free choice is inconsistent with God's foreknowledge? Because it's foreknowledge, or because it's *God's* foreknowledge?

EVODIUS: Because it's God's foreknowledge.

AUGUSTINE: If you knew that someone was going to sin, he wouldn't sin necessarily, would he?

EVODIUS: Indeed he would. Unless I foreknew something with certainty, it wouldn't be foreknowledge at all.

AUGUSTINE: Then it's not *God's* foreknowledge that makes his sin necessary, but any foreknowledge, since if something is not foreknown with certainty, it is not foreknown at all.

EVODIUS: I agree. But where are you headed with this?

AUGUSTINE: Unless I am mistaken, you do not force someone to sin just because you foreknow that he is going to sin. Nor does your foreknowledge force him to sin, even if he is undoubtedly going to sin—since otherwise you would not have genuine foreknowledge. So if your foreknowledge is consistent with his freedom in sinning, so that you foreknow what someone else is going to do by his own will, then God forces no one to sin, even though he foresees those who are going to sin by their own will.

Why then can't our just God punish those things that his foreknowledge does not force to happen? Just as your memory does not force the past to have happened, God's foreknowledge does not force the future to happen. And just as you remember some things that you have done but did not do everything that you remember, God foreknows everything that he causes but does not cause everything that he foreknows. Of such things he is not the evil cause, but the just avenger. Therefore, you must understand that God justly punishes the sins that he foreknows but does not cause. If the fact that God foresees their sins means that he should not punish sinners, then he should also not reward those who act rightly, for he also foresees their righteous actions. Let us rather confess that nothing in the future is hidden from God's foreknowledge, and that no sin is left unpunished by his justice, for sin is committed by the will, not coerced by God's foreknowledge.

5 As for your third question, about how the Creator can escape blame for whatever happens necessarily in his creation, it will not easily overcome that rule of piety that we ought to bear in mind, namely, that we owe thanks to our Creator. His most abundant goodness would be most justly praised even if he had created us at a lower level of creation. For even though our souls are decayed with sin, they are better and more sublime than they would be if they were transformed into visible light. And you see that even souls that are addicted to the bodily senses give God great praise for the grandeur of light. Therefore, don't let the fact that sinful souls are condemned lead you to say in your heart that it would be better if they did not exist. For they are condemned only in comparison with what they would have been if they had refused to sin. Nonetheless, God their Creator deserves the most noble praise that human beings can offer him, not only because he places them in a just order when they sin, but also because he created them in such a way that even the filth of sin could in no way make them inferior to corporeal light, for which he is nonetheless praised.

So you should not say that it would be better if sinful souls had never existed. But I must also warn you not to say that they ought to have been created differently. Whatever might rightly occur to you as being better, you may be sure that God, as the Creator of all good things, has made that too. When you think that something better should have been made, it is not right reason, but grudging weakness, to will that nothing lower had been made, as if you looked upon the heavens and wished that the earth had not been made. Such a wish is utterly unjust.

If you saw that the earth had been made but not the heavens, then you would have a legitimate complaint, for you could say that the earth ought to have been made like the heavens that you can imagine. But since you see that the pattern to which you wanted the earth to conform has indeed been made (but it is called "the heavens" and not "the earth"), I'm sure that you would not begrudge the fact that the inferior thing has also been made, and that the earth exists, since you are not deprived of the better thing. And there is so great a variety of parts in the earth that we cannot conceive of any earthly form that God has not created. By intermediate steps one passes gradually from the most fertile and pleasant land to the briniest and most barren, so that you would not dream of disparaging any of them except in comparison with a better. Thus you ascend through every degree of praise, so that even when you come to the very best land, you would not want it to exist without the others. And how great a distance there is between the whole earth and the heavens! For between the two is interposed the watery and airy nature. From these four elements come a variety of forms and species too numerous for us to count, although God has numbered them all.

Therefore, it is possible for something to exist in the universe that you do not conceive with your reason, but it is not possible for something that you conceive by right reason not to exist. For you cannot conceive anything better in creation that has slipped the mind of the Creator. Indeed, the human soul is naturally connected with the divine reasons on which it depends. When it says "It would be better to make this than that," if what it says is true, and it sees what it is saying, then it sees that truth in the reasons to which it is connected. If, therefore, it knows by right reason that God ought to have made something, let it believe that God has in fact done so, even if it does not see the thing among those that God has made.

For example, suppose we could not see the heavens. Nonetheless, if right reason showed that some such thing ought to have been made, it would be right for us to believe that it was made, even if we did not see it with our own eyes. For if we see by thought that something ought to have been made, we see it only in those reasons by which all things were made. But no truthful thinking can enable someone to see what is not in those reasons, for whatever is not there is not true.

Many people go astray when they have seen better things with their mind because in searching for it with their eyes they look in the wrong places. They are like someone who understands perfect roundness and is angry because he does not find it in a nut, if that is the only round object that he sees. In the same way, some people see by the truest reason that a creature is better if it is so firmly dedicated to God that it will never sin, even though it has free will. Then, when they look upon the sins of human beings, they do not use their sorrow over sin to stop people from sinning; they bemoan the fact that human beings were created in the first place. "He ought to have made us," they say, "so that we would always enjoy his unchangeable truth, so that we would never will to sin." Let them not moan and complain! God, who gave them the power to will, did not force them to sin; and there are angels who never have sinned and never will sin.

Therefore, if you take delight in a creature whose will is so perfectly steadfast that he does not sin, it is by right reason that you prefer this creature to one that sins. And just as you give it a higher rank in your thinking, the Creator gave it a higher rank in his ordering. So be sure that such a creature exists in the higher places and in the splendor of the heavens, since if the Creator manifested his goodness in creating something that he foresaw would sin, he certainly manifested his goodness in creating something that he foreknew would not sin.

That sublime creature has perpetual happiness in the perpetual enjoyment of its Creator, a happiness that it deserves because it perpetually wills to retain justice. Next, there is a proper place even for the sinful nature that by its sins has lost happiness but not thrown away the power to recover happiness. This nature is in turn higher than one that perpetually wills to sin. It occupies a sort of intermediate position between those that persist in willing justice and those that persist in willing to sin. It receives its greatness from the lowliness of repentance.

But God, in the bounty of his goodness, did not

shrink from creating even that creature whom he foreknew would not merely sin, but would persist in willing to sin. For a runaway horse is better than a stone that stays in the right place only because it has no movement or perception of its own; and in the same way, a creature that sins by free will is more excellent than one that does not sin only because it has no free will. I would praise wine as a thing good of its kind, but condemn a person who got drunk on that wine. And yet I would prefer that person, condemned and drunk, to the wine that I praised, on which he got drunk. In the same way, the material creation is rightly praised on its own level, but those who turn away from the perception of the truth by immoderately using the material creation deserve condemnation. And yet even those perverse and drunken people who are ruined by this greed are to be preferred to the material creation, praiseworthy though it is in its own order, not because of the merit of their sins, but because of the dignity of their nature.

Therefore, any soul is better than any material object. Now no sinful soul, however far it may fall, is ever changed into a material object; it never ceases to be a soul. Therefore, no soul ceases to be better than a material object. Consequently, the lowest soul is still better than light, which is the foremost among material objects. It may be that the body in which a certain soul exists is inferior to some other body, but the soul itself can in no way be inferior to a body.

Why, then, should we not praise God with unspeakable praise, simply because when he made those souls who would persevere in the laws of justice, he made others who he foresaw would sin, even some who would persevere in sin? For even such souls are better than souls that cannot sin because they lack reason and the free choice of the will. And these souls are in turn better than the brilliance of any material object, however splendid, which some people mistakenly worship instead of the Most High God. In the order of material creation, from the heavenly choirs to the number of the hairs of our heads, the beauty of good things at every level is so perfectly harmonious that only the most ignorant could say, "What is this? Why is this?"—for all things were created in their proper order. How much more ignorant, then, to say this of a soul whose glory, however dimmed and tarnished it might become, far exceeds the dignity of any material object!

Reason judges in one way, custom in another. Reason judges by the light of truth, so that by right judgment it subjects lesser things to greater. Custom is often swayed by agreeable habits, so that it esteems as greater what truth reveals as lower. Reason accords the heavenly bodies far greater honor than earthly bodies. And yet who among carnal human beings would not much rather have many stars gone from the heavens than one sapling missing from his field or one cow from his pasture? Children would rather see a man die (unless it is someone they love) than their pet bird, especially if the man frightens them and the bird is beautiful and can sing; but adults utterly despise their judgments, or at least wait patiently until they can be corrected. In the same way, there are those who praise God for his lesser creatures, which are better suited to their carnal senses. But when it comes to his superior and better creatures, some of these people praise him less or not at all; some even try to find fault with them or change them; and some do not believe that God created them. But those who have advanced along the road to wisdom regard such people as ignorant judges of things. Until they can correct the ignorant, they learn to bear with them patiently; but if they cannot correct them, they utterly repudiate their judgments.

6 Since this is the case, it is quite wrong to think that the sins of the creature should be attributed to the Creator, even though it is necessary that whatever he foreknows will happen. So much so, that when you said you could find no way to avoid attributing to him everything in his creation that happens necessarily, I on the other hand could find no way—nor can any way be found, for I am convinced that there is no way—to attribute to him anything in his creation that happens necessarily by the will of sinners.

Someone might say, "I would rather not exist at all than be unhappy." I would reply, "You're lying. You're unhappy now, and the only reason you don't want to die is to go on existing. You don't want to be unhappy, but you do want to exist. Give thanks, therefore, for what you are willingly, so that what you are against your will might be taken away; for you willingly exist, but you are unhappy against your will. If you are ungrateful for what you will to be, you are justly compelled to be what you do not will. So I praise the goodness of your Creator, for even though you are ungrateful you have what you will; and I praise the justice of your Lawgiver, for because you are ungrateful you suffer what you do not will."

But then he might say, "It is not because I would rather be unhappy than not exist at all that I am unwilling to die; it's because I'm afraid that I might be even more unhappy after death." I would reply, "If it is unjust for you to be even more unhappy, you won't be so; but if it is just, let us praise him by whose laws you will be so."

Next he might ask, "Why should I assume that if it is unjust I won't be more unhappy?" I would reply, "If at that time you are in your own power, either you will not be unhappy, or you will be governing yourself unjustly, in which case you will deserve your unhappiness. But suppose instead that you wish to govern yourself justly but cannot. That means that you are not in your own power, so either someone else has power over you, or no one has. If no one has power over you, you will act either willingly or unwillingly. It cannot be unwillingly, because nothing happens to you unwillingly unless you are overcome by some force, and you cannot be overcome by any force if no one has power over you. And if it is willingly, you are in fact in your own power, and the earlier argument applies: either you deserve your unhappiness for governing yourself unjustly, or, since you have whatever you will, you have reason to give thanks for the goodness of your Creator.

"Therefore, if you are not in your own power, some other thing must have control over you. This thing is either stronger or weaker than you. If it is weaker than you, your servitude is your own fault and your unhappiness is just; since you could overpower this thing if you willed to do so. And if a stronger thing has control over you, its control is in accordance with proper order, and you cannot rightly think that so right an order is unjust. I was therefore quite correct to say, 'If it is unjust for you to be even more unhappy, you won't be so; but if it is just, let us praise him by whose laws you will be so.'"

7 Then he might say, "The only reason that I will to be unhappy rather than not to exist at all is that I already exist; if somehow I could have been consulted on this matter before I existed, I would have chosen not to exist rather than to be unhappy. The fact that I am now afraid not to exist, even though I am unhappy, is itself part of that very unhappiness because of which I do not will what I ought to will. For I ought to will not to exist rather than to be unhappy. And yet I admit that in fact I would rather be unhappy than be nothing. But the more unhappy I am, the more foolish I am to will this; and the more truly I see that I ought not will this, the more unhappy I am."

I would reply, "Be careful that you are not mistaken when you think you see the truth. For if you were happy, you would certainly prefer existence to nonexistence. Even as it is, although you are unhappy and do not will to be unhappy, you would rather exist and be unhappy than not exist at all. Consider, then, as well as you can, how great is the good of existence, which the happy and the unhappy alike will. If you consider it well, you will realize three things. First, you are unhappy to the extent that you are far from him who exists in the highest degree. Second, the more you think that it is better for someone not to exist than to be unhappy, the less you will see him who exists in the highest degree. Finally, you nonetheless will to exist because you are from him who exists in the highest degree."

So if you will to escape from unhappiness, cherish your will to exist. For if you will more and more to exist, you will approach him who exists in the highest degree. And give thanks that you exist now, for even though you are inferior to those who are happy, you are superior to things that do not have even the will to be happy—and many such things are praised even by those who are unhappy. Nonetheless, all things that exist deserve praise simply in virtue of the fact that they exist, for they are good simply in virtue of the fact that they exist.

The more you love existence, the more you will desire eternal life, and so the more you will long to be refashioned so that your affections are no longer temporal, branded upon you by the love of temporal things that are nothing before they exist, and then, once they do exist, flee from existence until they exist no more. And so when their existence is still to come, they do not yet exist; and when their existence is past, they exist no more. How can you expect such things to endure, when for them to begin to exist is to set out on the road to nonexistence?

Someone who loves existence approves of such things insofar as they exist and loves that which always exists. If once he used to waiver in the love of temporal things, he now grows firm in the love of the eternal. Once he wallowed in the love of fleeting things, but he will stand steadfast in the love of what is permanent. Then he will obtain the very existence that he willed when he was afraid not to exist but could not stand upright because he was entangled in the love of fleeting things.

Therefore, do not grieve that you would rather exist and be unhappy than not exist and be nothing at all. Instead, rejoice greatly, for your will to exist is like a first step. If you go on from there to set your sights more and more on existence, you will rise to him who exists in the highest degree. Thus you will keep yourself from the kind of fall in which that which exists in the lowest degree ceases to exist and thereby devastates the one who loves it. Hence, someone who prefers not to exist rather than to be unhappy has no choice but to be unhappy, since he cannot fail to exist; but someone who loves existence more than he hates being unhappy can banish what he hates by cleaving more and more to what he loves. For someone who has come to enjoy an existence that is perfect for a thing of his kind cannot be unhappy.

8 Notice how absurd and illogical it would be to say "I would prefer not to exist rather than to be unhappy." For someone who says "I would prefer this rather than that" is choosing something. But not to exist is not something, but nothing. Therefore, you can't properly choose it, since what you are choosing does not exist.

Perhaps you will say that you do in fact will to exist, even though you are unhappy, but that you *shouldn't* will to exist. Then what should you will? "Not to exist," you say. Well, if that is what you ought to will, it must be better; but that which does not exist cannot be better. Therefore, you should not will not to exist, and the frame of mind that keeps you from willing it is closer to the truth than your belief that you ought to will it.

Furthermore, if someone is right in choosing to pursue something, it must be the case that he becomes better when he attains it. But whoever does not exist cannot be better; and so no one can be right in choosing not to exist. We should not be swayed by the judgment of those whose unhappiness has driven them to suicide. Either they thought that they would be better off after death, in which case they were doing nothing contrary to our argument (whether they were right in thinking so or not); or else they thought that they would be nothing after death, in which case there is even less reason for us to bother with them, since they falsely chose nothing. For how am I supposed to concur in the choice of someone who, if I asked him what he was choosing, would say "Nothing"? And someone who chooses not to exist is clearly choosing nothing, even if he won't admit it.

To tell you quite frankly what I think about this whole issue, it seems to me that someone who kills himself or in some way wants to die has the feeling that he will not exist after death, whatever his conscious opinion may be. Opinion, whether true or false, has to do with reason or faith; but feeling derives its power from either habit or nature. It can happen that opinion leads in one direction and feeling in another. This is easy to see in cases where we believe that we ought to do one thing but enjoy doing just the opposite. And sometimes feeling is closer to the truth than opinion is, as when the opinion is in error and the feeling is from nature. For example, a sick man will often enjoy drinking cold water, which is good for him, even if he believes that it will kill him. But sometimes opinion is closer to the truth than feeling is, as when someone's knowledge of medicine tells him that cold water would be harmful when in fact it *would* be harmful, even though it would be pleasant to drink. Sometimes both are right, as when one rightly believes that something is beneficial and also finds it pleasing. Sometimes both are wrong, as when one believes that something is beneficial when it is actually harmful and one is also happy not to give it up.

It often happens that right opinion corrects perverted habits and that perverted opinion distorts an upright nature, so great is the power of the dominion and rule of reason. Therefore, someone who believes that after death he will not exist is driven by his unbearable troubles to desire death with all his heart; he chooses death and takes hold of it. His opinion is completely false, but his feeling is simply a natural desire for peace. And something that has peace is not nothing; indeed, it is greater than something that is restless. For restlessness generates one conflicting passion after another, whereas peace has the constancy that is the most conspicuous characteristic of Being.

So the will's desire for death is not a desire for nonexistence but a desire for peace. When someone wrongly believes that he will not exist, he desires by nature to be at peace; that is, he desires to exist in a higher degree. Therefore, just as no one can desire not to exist, no one ought to be ungrateful to the goodness of the Creator for the fact that he exists.

Confessions

Book XI

In the Beginning God Created . . .

I

But, Lord, since You are in eternity, are You unaware of what I am saying to You? Or do you see in time what takes place in time? But if You *do* see, why am I giving You an account of all these things? Not, obviously, that You should learn them from me; but I excite my own love for You and the love of those who read what I write, that we all may say: *The Lord is great, and exceedingly to be praised.* I have said before and I will say again: "It is for love of Your love that I do it." We pray [for what we want], yet Truth Himself has said: *Your Father knows what is needful for you before you ask Him.* Thus we are laying bare our love for You in confessing to You our wretchedness and Your mercies towards us: that You may free us wholly as You have already freed us in part, so that we may cease to be miserable in ourselves and come to happiness in You. For You have called us to be poor in spirit, to be meek, to mourn, to hunger and thirst after justice, to be merciful and clean of heart and peacemakers.

Thus I have told You many things, with such power and will as I had, because You, O Lord my God, had first willed that I should confess to You: *for Thou art good and Thy mercy endureth forever.*

II

But when will the voice of my pen have power to tell all Your exhortations and all Your terrors, Your consolations and the guidance by which You have brought me to be to Your people a preacher of Your word and a dispenser of Your Sacrament? Even had I the power to set down all these things duly, the drops of my time are too precious.

For a long time now I burn with the desire to meditate upon Your law, and to confess to You both my knowledge of it and my ignorance of it—the first beginnings of Your light and what remains of my own darkness—until my weakness shall be swallowed up in Your strength. And I do not want to see scattered and wasted upon other things such time as I find free from necessary care of the body, intellectual labour, and the service which either I owe men or do not owe but render all the same.

O Lord my God, be attentive to my prayer. Let Thy mercy grant my desire, since it does not burn for myself alone, but longs to serve the charity I have for my brethren: and in my heart Thou seest that it is so. Let me offer in sacrifice to Thee the service of my mind and my tongue, and do Thou give me what I may offer Thee. For I am needy and poor, *Thou art rich unto all who call upon Thee.* Thou art free from care for Thyself and full of care for us. Circumcise the lips of my mouth and lips of my mind of all rash speech and lying. May Thy Scriptures be for my chaste delight; let me not deceive others about them nor be myself deceived. O Lord, hearken and have mercy, O Lord my God, Light of the blind and Strength of the weak, but Light too of the clear of sight and Strength of the strong; hearken to my soul, hear it crying from the depths. Unless Thine ears are attentive to us in the abyss, whither shall we go? To whom shall we cry?

Thine is the day, and Thine is the night: at Thy will the moments flow and pass. Grant me, then, space for my meditations upon the hidden things of Thy law, nor close Thy law against me as I knock. Not for nothing hast Thou willed that the deep secrets of all those pages should be written, not for nothing have those woods their *stags*, which retire to them and are restored, walk in them and are fed, lie down in them and ruminate. Complete Thy work in me, O Lord, and open those pages to me. Thy voice is my joy, abounding above all joys. Grant me what I

Reprinted from *Confessions of St. Augustine*, translated by F. J. Sheed (New York: Sheed & Ward, 1943), by permission of the publisher. The words in brackets are amplifications by the translator. The italicized words are biblical quotations.

love, for I do love it. And this too is of Thy gift. Do not abandon what Thou hast given, nor scorn Thy grass that is athirst for Thee. Let me confess to thee whatsoever I shall find in Thy books, and *let me hear the voice of thy praise*, and drink of Thee and *consider the wondrous things of Thy law* from the first beginning, when Thou didst make heaven and earth, until our everlasting reign with Thee in Thy holy city.

O Lord have mercy on me and grant what I desire. For, as I think, my desire is not of earth, not of gold and silver and gems or fine raiment or power and glory or the lusts of the flesh or the necessities of my body and of this our earthly pilgrimage: *all these things shall be added unto us who seek the Kingdom of God and Thy justice.*

See, O my God, whence comes my desire. *The wicked have told me fables but not as Thy law.* That is the source of my desire. See, Father: gaze and see and approve: and may it be pleasing in the sight of Thy mercy that I should find grace before Thee, that the inner secret of Thy words may be laid open at my knock. I beseech it by our Lord Jesus Christ Thy Son, *the Man of Thy right hand, the Son of Man, whom Thou hast confirmed for Thyself* as Mediator between Thyself and us: by whom Thou didst seek us when we sought not Thee, didst seek us indeed that we might seek Thee: Thy Word, by which Thou hast made all things and me among them: The Only One, by whom Thou hast called the people of the faithful, and me among them, unto adoption. I beseech it by Him who sits at Thy right hand and makes intercession for us, *in whom are hidden all the treasures of wisdom and knowledge.* These treasures are what I seek in Thy books. Moses wrote of Him: this He says, who is Truth.

III

Grant me to hear and understand what is meant by *In the beginning You made heaven and earth.* For so Moses wrote, wrote and went his way: passed from this world to You and is no longer here before me. Were he here, I should lay hold of him, and ask him, and in Your name beg him, to explain the sense of those words to me; I should lend my bodily ear to the sounds that should issue from his mouth. If he spoke in Hebrew, his voice would beat upon my ear to no purpose, nothing of what it said would reach my mind: if he spoke in Latin, I should know what he said. But how should I know that what he said was true? And if I did know it, would it be from him that I knew it? No: but within me, in the inner retreat of my mind, the Truth, which is neither Hebrew nor Greek, nor Latin, nor Barbarian, would tell me, without lips or tongue or sounded syllables: "He speaks truth": and I (at once assured) would say to Your servant in all confidence: "You speak truth." Since, then, I cannot question him, I ask Thee, the Truth, filled with whom Moses spoke truth: I ask Thee, my God: pardon my sins, and as Thou didst grant to Thy servant to speak those words, grant me to understand them.

IV

We look upon the heavens and the earth, and they cry aloud that they were made. For they change and vary. (If anything was not made and yet exists, there is nothing in it that was not there before: and it is the essence of change and variation that something should be that was not there before.) They cry aloud, too, that they did not make themselves. "We exist, because we were made; but we did not exist before we existed to be able to give ourselves existence!" And their visible presence is itself the voice with which they speak.

It was You, Lord, who made them: for You are beautiful, and they are beautiful: You are good, and they are good: You are, and they are. But they neither are beautiful nor are good nor simply are as You their Creator: compared with You they are not beautiful and are not good and are not. These truths, thanks to You, we know; and our knowledge compared with Your knowledge is ignorance.

V

But *how* did You make heaven and earth? What instrument did You use for a work so mighty? You are not like an artist; for he forms one body from another as his mind chooses; his mind has the power to give external existence to the form it perceives within itself by its inner eye—and whence should it have that power unless You made it? It impresses that form upon a material already existent and having the capacity to be thus formed, such as clay or stone or wood or gold or such like. And how should these things have come to be unless You had made them to be? It was You who made the workman his body, and the mind that directs his limbs, the matter of which he makes what he makes, the intelligence by which he masters his art and sees inwardly what he is to produce exteriorly, the bodily sense by which he translates what he does from his mind to his material, and then informs the mind of the result of his workmanship, so that the mind may judge by that truth which presides within it whether the work is well done.

All these things praise You, the Creator of them all. But how do You create them? How, O God, did You create heaven and earth? Obviously it was not *in* heaven or on earth that You made heaven and earth; nor in the air nor in the waters, since these belong to heaven and earth; nor did You make the universe in the universe, because there was no place for it to be made in until it was made. Nor had You any material in Your hand when You were making heaven and earth: for where should You have got what You had not yet made to use as material? What exists, save because You exist? You spoke and heaven and earth were created; in Your word You created them.

VI

But *how* did You speak? Was it perhaps as when that voice sounded from the cloud saying: *This is my beloved Son?* That voice sounded and ceased to sound, had a beginning and an end. The syllables sounded and died away, the second after the first, the third after the second, and so in order, until the last after the rest, and silence after the last. From this it is clear beyond question that that voice was sounded by the movement of something created by You, a movement in time but serving Your eternal will.

These words were uttered in time and the bodily ear conveyed them to the understanding mind, whose spiritual ear is attuned to Your eternal Word. And the mind compared these words sounding in time with Your eternal Word and its silence: and it said: "It is other, far other. These words are far less than I, indeed they are not at all, for they pass away and are no more: but the Word of God is above me and endures for ever."

Thus, had it been by words sounding and passing away that You said "Let heaven and earth be made," and so created heaven and earth, there would have had to be some bodily creature before heaven and earth, by the movement of which in time that voice came and went in time.

But there was no bodily thing before heaven and earth: or if there were then certainly You did not use some still earlier utterance in time to produce it, that by it You might utter in time the decree that heaven and earth should be made. Whatever it may have been that produced such a voice, it must have been made by You, otherwise it would not have existed at all. But to produce the bodily thing capable of uttering those words, what word did You utter?

VII

Clearly You are calling us to the realization of that Word—God with You, God as You are God—which is uttered eternally and by which all things are uttered eternally.

For this is not an utterance in which what has been said passes away that the next thing may be said and so finally the whole utterance be complete: but all in one act, yet abiding eternally: otherwise it would be but time and change and no true eternity, no true immortality.

I know it, O my God, and I give You thanks. I know it, Lord, I confess it to You: and every man knows it as I do and praises You as I do who is not ungrateful for Your sure truth. We know, Lord, we know, that in the degree that anything is no longer what it was, and is now what it once was not, it is in the process of dying and beginning anew. But of Your Word nothing passes or comes into being, for it is truly immortal and eternal. Thus it is by a Word coeternal with Yourself that in one eternal act You say all that You say, and all things are made that You say are to be made. You create solely by thus saying. Yet all the things You create by saying are not brought into being in one act and from eternity.

VIII

Tell me, O Lord my God, how this can be? In a kind of way I see, but how to express it I do not know: save that whatever comes into being and ceases to be, begins at the moment and ends at the moment when the eternal reason—which has in itself no beginning or ending—knows that it should begin or end. That eternal reason is Your Word, *the Beginning who also speaks unto us.* This He tells us in the Gospel to our bodily ear, this He uttered exteriorly in the ears of men: that we might believe in Him, and seek Him within us and find Him in the eternal Truth, where the one good Master teaches all His disciples.

There it is that I hear Your voice, Lord, telling me that only one who teaches us is speaking to us, and that whoever does not teach us may be speaking, but not to us. Yet who teaches us save Truth unchanging? When from changing creatures we learn anything, we are led to Truth that does not change: and there we truly learn, as we stand and hear Him and rejoice with you for the voice of the bridegroom, returning to the Source of our being. Thus it is that He is the Beginning: unless He remained when we wandered away, there should be no abiding place for our return. But when we return from error, we return by realizing the Truth; that we may realize it, He instructs us for He is the *Beginning who also speaks unto us.*

IX

This then, O God, was the Beginning in which You created Heaven and Earth: marvellously speaking and marvellously creating in Your Word, Who is Your Son and Your Strength and Your Wisdom and Your Truth. Who shall understand this? Who shall relate it? What is that light which shines upon me but not continuously, and strikes upon my heart with no wounding? I draw back in terror: I am on fire with longing: terror in so far as I am different from it, longing in the degree of my likeness to it. It is Wisdom, Wisdom Itself, which in those moments shines upon me, cleaving through my cloud. And the cloud returns to wrap me round once more as my strength is beaten down under its darkness and the weight of my sins: for *my strength is weakened through poverty,* so that I can no longer support my good, until Thou, Lord who art merciful to my iniquities, shall likewise heal my weakness: redeeming my life from corruption and crowning me with pity and compassion, and filling my desire with good things: *my youth shall be renewed like the eagle's. For we are saved by hope and we wait with patience for Thy promises.*

Let him who can hear Thy voice speaking within him; I, relying upon Thy inspired word, shall cry aloud: *How great are Thy works, O Lord! Thou has made all things in wisdom.* Wisdom is "the Beginning": and it is in that Beginning that You made heaven and earth.

X

Surely those are still in their ancient error who say to us: "What was God doing before He made heaven and earth?" If, they say, He was at rest and doing nothing, why did He not continue to do nothing for ever after as for ever before? If it was a new movement and a new will in God to create something He had never created before, how could that be a true eternity in which a will should arise which did not exist before? For the will of God is not a creature: it is prior to every creature, since nothing would be created unless the will of the Creator first so willed. The will of God belongs to the very substance of God. Now if something arose in the substance of God which was not there before, that substance could not rightly be called eternal; but if God's will that creatures should be is from eternity, why are creatures not from eternity?

XI

Those who speak thus do not yet understand You, O Wisdom of God, Light of minds: they do not yet understand how the things are made that are made by You and in You. They strive for the savour of eternity, but their mind is still tossing about in the past and future movements of things, and is still vain.

Who shall lay hold upon their mind and hold it still, that it may stand a little while, and a little while glimpse the splendour of eternity which stands for ever: and compare it with time whose moments never stand, and see that it is not comparable. Then indeed it would see that a long time is long only from the multitude of movements that pass away in succession, because they cannot co-exist: that in eternity nothing passes but all is present, whereas time cannot be present all at once. It would see that all the past is thrust out by the future, and all the future follows upon the past, and past and future alike are wholly created and upheld in their passage by that which is always present? Who shall lay hold upon the mind of man, that it may stand and see that time with its past and future must be determined by eternity, which stands and does not pass, which has in itself no past or future. Could my hand have the strength [so to lay hold upon the mind of man] or could my mouth by its speaking accomplish so great a thing?

XII

I come now to answer the man who says: "What was God doing before He made Heaven and earth?" I do not give the jesting answer—said to have been given by one who sought to evade the force of the question—"He was getting Hell ready for people who pry too deep." To poke fun at a questioner is not to see the answer. My reply will be different. I would much rather say "I don't know," when I don't, than hold one up to ridicule who had asked a profound question and win applause for a worthless answer.

But, O my God, I say that You are the Creator of all creation, and if by the phrase heaven and earth we mean all creation, then I make bold to reply: Before God made heaven and earth, He did not make anything. For if He had made something, what would it have been but a creature? And I wish I knew all that it would be profitable for me to know, as well as I know that no creature was made before any creature was made.

XIII

But a lighter mind, adrift among images of time and its passing, might wonder that You, O God almighty and all-creating and all-conserving, Maker of heaven and earth, should have abstained from so vast a work for the countless ages that passed before You actually wrought it. Such a mind should awaken and realize how ill-grounded is his wonder.

How could countless ages pass when You, the Author and Creator of all ages, had not yet made them? What time could there be that You had not created? or how could ages pass, if they never were?

Thus, since You are the Maker of all times, if there actually was any time before You made heaven and earth, how can it be said that You were not at work? If there was time, You made it, for time could not pass before You made time. On the other hand, if before heaven and earth were made there was no time, then what is meant by the question "What were You doing *then?*" If there was not any time, there was not any "then."

It is not in time that You are before all time: otherwise You would not be before all time. You are before all the past by the eminence of Your ever-present eternity: and You dominate all the future in as much as it is still to be: and once it has come it will be past: but *Thou art always the self-same and Thy years shall not fail.* Your years neither go nor come: but our years come and go, that all may come. Your years abide all in one act of abiding: for they abide and the years that go are not thrust out by those that come, for none pass: whereas our years shall not be, till all are no more. Your years are as a single day; and Your day comes not daily but is today, a today which does not yield place to any tomorrow or follow upon any yesterday. In You today is eternity: thus it is that You begot one co-eternal with Yourself to whom you said: *Today have I begotten Thee.* You are the Maker of all time, and before all time You are, nor was there ever a time when there was no time!

XIV

At no time then had You not made anything, for time itself You made. And no time is co-eternal with You, for You stand changeless; whereas if time stood changeless, it would not be time. What then is time? Is there any short and easy answer to that? Who can put the answer into words or even see it in his mind? Yet what commoner or more familiar word do we use in speech than time? Obviously when we use it, we know what we mean, just as when we hear another use it, we know what he means.

What then *is* time? If no one asks me, I know; if I want to explain it to a questioner, I do not know. But at any rate this much I dare affirm I know: that if nothing passed there would be no past time; if nothing were approaching, there would be no future time; if nothing were, there would be no present time.

But the two times, past and future, how can they *be,* since the past is no more and the future is not yet? On the other hand, if the present were always present and never flowed away into the past, it would not be time at all, but eternity. But if the present is only time, because it flows away into the past, how can we say that it *is?* For it is, only because it will cease to be. Thus we can affirm that time *is* only in that it tends towards not-being.

XV

Yet we speak of a long time or a short time, applying these phrases only to past or future. Thus for example we call a hundred years ago a long time past, and a hundred years hence a long time ahead, and ten days ago a short time past, ten days hence a short time ahead. But in what sense can that which does not exist be long or short? The past no longer is, the future is not yet. Does this mean that we must not say: "It is long," but of the past "It was long," of the future "It will be long?"

O, my Lord, my Light, here too man is surely mocked by Your truth! If we say the past was long, was it long when it was already past or while it was still present? It could be long only while it was in existence to *be* long. But the past no longer exists; it cannot be long, because it is not at all.

Thus we must not say that the past was long: for we shall find nothing in it capable of being long, since, precisely because it is past, it is not at all. Let us say then that a particular time was long while it was present, because in so far as it was present, it was long. For it had not yet passed away and so become non-existent; therefore it still was something, and therefore capable of being long: though once it passed away, it ceased to be long by ceasing to be.

Let us consider, then, O human soul, whether present time can be long: for it has been given you to feel and measure time's spaces. What will you answer me?

Are the present hundred years a long time? But first see whether a hundred years *can* be present. If it is the first year of the hundred, then that year is present, but the other ninety-nine are still in the future, and so as yet are not: if we are in the second year, then one year is past, one year is present, the rest future. Thus whichever year of our hundred-year period we choose as present, those before it have passed away, those after it are still to come. Thus a hundred years cannot be present.

But now let us see if the chosen year is itself present. If we are in the first month, the others are still to come, if in the second, the first has passed away and the rest are not yet. Thus a year is not wholly present while it runs, and if the whole of it is not present, then the year is not present. For a year is twelve months, and the month that happens to be running its course is the only one present, the others either are no longer or as yet are not. Even the current month is not present, but only one day of it: if that day is the first, the rest are still to come; if the last, the rest are passed away; if somewhere between, it has days past on one side and days still to come on the other.

Thus the present, which we have found to be the only time capable of being long, is cut down to the space of scarcely one day. But if we examine this one day, even it is not wholly present. A day is composed of twenty-four hours—day-hours, night-hours: the first hour finds the rest still to come, the last hour finds the rest passed away, any hour between has hours passed before it, hours to come after it. And that one hour is made of fleeing moments: so much of the hour as has fled away is past, what still remains is future. If we conceive of some point of time which cannot be divided into even the minutest parts of moments, that is the only point that can be called present: and that point flees at such lightning speed from being future to being past, that it has no extent of duration at all. For if it were so extended, it would be divisible into past and future: the present has no length.

Where, then, is there a time that can be called long? Is it the future? But we cannot say of the future "It is long" because as yet it is not at all and therefore is not long. We say "It will be long." By when will it be long? While it is still in the future, it will not be long, because it does not yet exist and so cannot be long. Suppose we say, then, that it is to be long only when, coming out of the future [which is not yet], it begins to be and is now present—and thus something, and thus capable of being long. But the present cries aloud, as we have just heard, that it cannot have length.

XVI

Yet, Lord, we are aware of periods of time; we compare one period with another and say that some are longer, some shorter. We measure how much one is longer than another and say that it is double, or triple, or single, or simply that one is as long as the other. But it is time actually passing that we measure by our awareness; who can measure times past which are now no more or times to come which are not yet, unless you are prepared to say that that which does not exist can be measured? Thus while time is passing, it can be perceived and measured; but when it has passed it cannot, for it *is* not.

XVII

I am seeking, Father, not saying: O, my God, aid me and direct me.

Perhaps it might be said that there are not three times, past, present and future, as we learnt in boyhood and have taught boys: but only present, because the other two do not exist. Or perhaps that these two do exist, but that time comes forth from some secret place when from future it becomes present, and departs into some secret place when from present it becomes past. For where have those who prophesied the future seen the future, if it does not yet exist? What does not exist cannot be seen. And those who describe the past could not describe it truly if they did not mentally see it: and if the past were totally without existence it would be totally impossible to see it. Hence both past and future must exist.

XVIII

Suffer me, Lord, to push my inquiry further; O my Hope, let not my purpose go awry.

If the future and the past exist, I want to know where they are. And if I cannot yet know this, at least I do know that wherever they are, they are there not as future or past, but present. If wherever they are they are future, then in that place they are not yet; if past, then they are there no more. Thus wherever they are and whatever they are, they *are* only as present. When we relate the past truly, it is not the things themselves that are brought forth from our memory—for these have passed away: but words conceived from the images of the things: for the things stamped their prints upon the mind as they passed through it by way of the senses. Thus for example my boyhood, which no longer exists, is in time past, which no longer exists; but the likeness of my boyhood, when I recall it and talk of it, I look upon in time present, because it is still present in my memory.

Whether the case is similar with prophecies of things to come—namely that images of things which are not yet are seen in advance as now existent—I confess, O my God, that I do not know. But this I do know, that we ordinarily consider our future actions in advance, and that this consideration is present, but the action we are thinking of does not yet exist, because it is future; when we have actually set about it and have begun to do what we planned, then that action will exist, because then it will not be future but present.

Whatever may be the mode of this mysterious foreseeing of things to come, unless the thing is it cannot be seen. But what now is, is not future but present. Therefore when we speak of seeing the future, obviously what is seen is not the things which are not yet because they are still to come, but their causes or perhaps the signs that foretell them, for these causes and signs do exist here and now. Thus to those who see them now, they are not future but present, and from them things to come are conceived by the mind and foretold. These concepts already exist, and those who foretell are gazing upon them, present within themselves.

Let me take one example from a vast number of such things.

I am looking at the horizon at dawn: I foretell that the sun is about to rise. What I am looking at is present, what I foretell is future—not the sun, of course, for it now is, but its rising which is not yet. But unless I could imagine the actual rising in my mind, as now when I speak of it, I could not possibly foretell it. But the dawn which I see in the sky is not the sunrise, although it precedes the sunrise; nor is the dawn the image of the sunrise that is in my mind. But both—the dawn and the image of the sunrise—are present and seen by me, so that the sunrise which is future can be told in advance. Thus the future is not yet; and if it is not yet, it is not; and if it is not, then it is totally impossible to see it. But it can be foretold from things present which now exist and are seen.

XIX

But You, O Ruler of Your creation, how is it that you can show souls things that are to come? For such things You have told Your prophets. In what manner do You show the future to man, for whom nothing future yet is? Or do You show only present signs of things to come? For what does not exist obviously cannot be shown. The means You use is altogether beyond my gaze; my eyes have not the strength; of myself I shall never be able to see so deep, but in You I shall be able, when you grant it, O lovely Light of the eyes of my spirit.

XX

At any rate it is now quite clear that neither future nor past actually exists. Nor is it right to say there are three times, past, present and future. Perhaps it would be more correct to say: there are three times, a present of things past, a present of things present, a present of things future. For these three exist in the mind, and I find them nowhere else: the present of things past is memory, the present of things present is sight, the present of things future is expectation. If we are allowed to speak thus, I see and admit that there are three times, that three times truly are.

By all means continue to say that there are three times, past, present and future; for, though it is incorrect, custom allows it. By all means say it. I do not mind, I neither argue nor object: provided that you understand what you are saying and do not think future or past now exists. There are few things that we phrase properly; most things we phrase badly: but what we are trying to say is understood.

XXI

I said a little while ago that we measure time in its passing, so that we are able to say that this period of time is to that as two to one, or that this is of the same duration as that, and can measure and describe any other proportions of time's parts.

Thus, as I said, we measure time *in its passing*. If you ask me how I know this, my answer is that I know it because we measure time, and we cannot measure what does not exist, and past and future do not exist. But how do we measure time present, since it has no extent? It is measured while it is passing; once it has passed, it cannot be measured, for then nothing exists to measure.

But where does time come from, and by what way does it pass, and where does it go, while we are measuring it? Where is it from?—obviously from the future. By what way does it pass?—by the present. Where does it go?—into the past. In other words it passes from that which does not yet exist, by way of that which lacks extension, into that which is no longer.

But how are we measuring time unless in terms of some kind of duration? We cannot say single or double or triple or equal or proportioned in any other way, save of the duration of periods of time. But in what duration do we measure time while it is actually passing? In the future, from which it comes? But what does not yet exist cannot be measured. In the present, then, by which it passes? But that which has no space cannot be measured. In the past, to which it passes? But what no longer exists cannot be measured.

XXII

My mind burns to solve this complicated enigma. O Lord my God, O good Father, for Christ's sake I beseech Thee, do not shut off these obscure familiar problems from my longing, do not shut them off and leave them impenetrable but let them shine clear for me in the light of Thy mercy, O Lord. Yet whom shall I question about them? And to whom more fruitfully than to Thee shall I confess my ignorance: for Thou art not displeased at the zeal with which I am on fire for Thy Scriptures. Grant me what I love: for it is by Your gift that I love. Grant me this gift, Father, *who dost know how to give good gifts to Thy children.* Grant it because I have *studied that I might know and it is a labour in my sight* until Thou shalt open it to me. For Christ's sake I beseech Thee, in the name of Him who is the Holy of Holies, that no one prevent me. *I have believed, therefore have I spoken.* This is my hope; for this do I live, *that I may see the delight of the Lord. Behold Thou hast made my days old,* and they pass away: but how I know not.

We are forever talking of time and of times. "How long did he speak," "How long did it take him to do that," "For how long a time did I fail to see this," "This syllable is double the length of that." So we speak and so we hear others speak, and others understand us, and we them. They are the plainest and commonest of words, yet again they are profoundly obscure and their meaning still to be discovered.

XXIII

I once heard a learned man say that time is simply the movement of the sun and moon and stars. I did not agree. For why should not time rather be the movement of all bodies? Supposing the lights of heaven were to cease and the potter's wheel moved on, would there not be time by which we could measure its rotations and say that these were at equal intervals, or some slower, some quicker, some taking longer, some shorter? And if we spoke thus, should we not ourselves be speaking in time: would there not be in our words some syllables long, some short—because some would sound for a longer time, some for a shorter?

O God, grant unto men to see by some small example the elements in common between small things and great. There are stars and the lights of heaven *to be for signs and for seasons and for days and years.* This is evident; but just as I would not affirm that one turn of that little wooden wheel is a day, neither should my philosopher say that it is no time at all.

What I am trying to come at is the force and nature of time, by which we measure the movement of bodies and say for example that this movement is twice as long as that. A day means not only the length of time that the sun is above the earth—so that we distinguish day from night—but the time of the sun's whole circuit from east to east—as we say that so many days have passed, so many days being used to include their nights, for the nights are not reckoned separately. Thus, since a day is constituted by the movement of the sun and its completed circle from east to east, I wish to know whether a day is that movement itself, or simply the time the movement takes, or both.

If the movement of the sun through one complete circuit were the day, then it would be a day even if the sun sped through its course in a space of time equal to an hour. If the time the sun now takes to complete its circuit is the day, then it would not be a day if between one sunrise and the next there were only the space of an hour: the sun would have to go around twenty-four times to make one day. But if to constitute a day there is needed both the movement of the sun through one circuit and the time the sun now takes, then you would not have a day if the sun completed its whole circuit in an hour, nor again if the sun stood still and as much time passed as the sun normally takes to complete its journey from one morning to the next.

But I shall not at the moment pursue the question of what it is that we call a day. I shall continue to seek what time is, by which we measure the sun's journey: so that we should say that it had gone round in half its accustomed time, if it went round in a space of time equivalent to twelve hours. And comparing its normal time with this twelve-hour time, we should say that the latter was single, the former double; yet the sun would in the one case have made its journey from east to east in the shorter time, in the other in the longer (so that time is something independent of the sun's movement).

Let no one tell me that the movement of the heavenly bodies is time: when at the prayer of a man the sun stood still that he might complete his victory in battle, the sun stood still but time moved on. The battle was continued for the necessary length of time and was finished.

Therefore I see time as in some way extended. But do I see it? Or do I only seem to see it? Thou wilt show me, O Light, O Truth.

XXIV

Would You have me agree with one who said that time is the movement of a body? You would not: for I learn that no body moves save in time: You have said it. But I do not learn that the movement of the body is time: You have not said it. For when a body is in motion, it is by time that I measure how long it is in motion from the beginning of its movement till it ceases to move. And if I did not see when the movement began, and if it moved on without my seeing when it ceased, I should be able to measure only from the movement I began to look until the moment I stopped looking. If I looked for a long time, all I can say is that the time is long, but not how long it is, because when we say how long a time, we say it by comparison: as for example: this is as long as that, or this is twice that, and such like. But if we could note the point of space from which a body in motion comes or the point to which it goes, or could distinguish its parts if it is moving on its axis, we should be able to say how much time has elapsed for the movement of the body, or its part, from one place to another.

Thus since the movement of a body is not the same as our measurement of how long the movement takes, who can fail to see which of these is more deserving of the name of time? A body moves at different speeds, and sometimes stands still; but time enables us to measure not only its motion but its rest as well; and we say "It was at rest for the same length of time as it was in motion," or "It was at rest twice or thrice as long as it was in motion" or any other proportion, whether precisely measured or roughly estimated.

Therefore time is not the movement of a body.

XXV

I confess to You, Lord, that I still do not know what time is. And again I confess to You, Lord, that I know that I am uttering these things in time: I have been talking of time for a long time, and this long time would not be a long time unless time had passed. But how do I know this, since I do not know what time is? Or perhaps I do know, but simply do not know how to express what I know. Alas for me, I do not even know what I do not know! See me, O my God, I stand before You and I do not lie: as my speech is, so is my heart. *For Thou lightest my lamp, O Lord; O my God, enlighten my darkness.*

XXVI

Does not my soul speak truly to You when I say that I can measure time? For so it is, O Lord my God, I measure it and I do not know what it is that I am measuring. I measure the movement of a body, using time to measure it by. Do I not then measure time itself? Could I measure the movement of a body—its duration and how long it takes to move from place to place—if I could not measure the time in which it moves?

But if so, what do I use to measure time with? Do we measure a longer time by a shorter one, as we measure a beam in terms of cubits? Thus we say that the duration of a long syllable is measured by the space of a short syllable and is said to be double. Thus we measure the length of poems by the lengths of the lines, and the lengths of the lines by the lengths of the feet, and the lengths of the feet by the lengths of the syllables, and the lengths of long syllables by the lengths of short. We do not measure poems by pages, for that would be to measure space not time; we measure by the way the voice moves in uttering the poem, and we say: "It is a long poem, for it consists of so many lines; the lines are long for they are composed of so many feet; the feet are long for they include so many syllables; this syllable is long for it is the double of a short syllable."

But not by all this do we arrive at an exact measure of time. It may well happen that a shorter line may take longer if it is recited slowly than a longer line hurried through. And the same is true of a poem or a foot or a syllable.

Thus it seems to me that time is certainly extendedness—but I do not know what it is extendedness of: probably of the mind itself. Tell me, O my God, what am I measuring, when I say either, with no aim at precision, that one period is longer than the other, or precisely, that one is double the other? That I measure time, I know. But I do not measure the future, for it is not yet; nor the present, for it is not extended in space; nor the past, which no longer exists. So what do I measure? Is it time in passage but not past? So I have already said.

XXVII

Persevere, O my soul, fix all the power of your gaze. *God is our helper. He made us, and not we ourselves.* Fix your gaze where truth is whitening toward the dawn.

Consider the example of a bodily voice. It begins to sound, it sounds and goes on sounding, then it ceases: and now there is silence, the sound has passed, the sound no longer is. It was future before it began to sound, and so could not be measured, for as yet it did not exist; and now it cannot be measured because now it exists no longer. Only while sounding could it be measured for then it was, and so was measurable. But even then it was not standing still; it was moving, and moving out of existence. Did this make it more measurable? Only in the sense that by its passing it was spread over a certain space of time which made it measurable: for the present occupies no space.

At any rate, let us grant that it could be measured. And now again imagine a voice. It begins to sound and goes on sounding continuously without anything to break its even flow. Let us measure it, while it is sounding. For when it has ceased to sound, it will be past and will no longer be measurable. Let us measure it then and say how long it is. But it is still sounding and can be measured only from its beginning when it began to sound to its end, when it ceased. For what we measure is the interval between some starting point and some conclusion. This means that a sound which is not yet over cannot be measured so that we may say how long or short it is, nor can it be said either to be equal to some other sound or single or double or any other proportion in relation to it. But when it *is* over, it will no longer be. Then how will it be possible to measure it? Yet we do measure time—not that which is not yet, nor that which is no longer, nor that which has no duration, nor that which lacks beginning and end. Thus it seems that we measure neither time future nor time past nor time present nor time passing: and yet we measure time.

Deus creator omnium:[1] This line is composed of eight syllables, short and long alternately: the four short syllables, the first, third, fifth, seventh are single in relation to the four long syllables, the second, fourth, sixth, eighth. Each long syllable has double the time of each short syllable. I pronounce them and I say that it is so, and so it is, as is quite obvious to the ear. As my ear distinguishes I measure a long syllable by a short and I perceive that it contains it twice. But since I hear a syllable only when the one before it has ceased—the one before being short and the one following long—how am I to keep hold of the short syllable, and how shall I set it against the long one to measure it and find that the long one is twice its length—given that the long syllable does not begin to sound until the short one has ceased? And again can I measure the long one while it is present, since I cannot measure it until it is completed? And its completion is its passing out of existence.

What then is it that I measure? Where is the short syllable by which I measure? Where is the long syllable which I measure? Both have sounded, have fled away, have gone into the past, are now no more: yet I do measure, and I affirm with confidence, in so far as a practised sense can be trusted, that one is single, the other double, in the length of time it occupies. And I could not do this unless they had both passed away and ended. Thus it is not the syllables themselves that I measure, for they are now no more, but something which remains engraved in my memory.

1. [God, the creator of all.—S.M.C.]

It is in you, O my mind, that I measure time. Do not bring against me, do not bring against yourself the disorderly throng of your impressions. In you, I say, I measure time. What I measure is the impress produced in you by things as they pass and abiding in you when they have passed: and it is present. I do not measure the things themselves whose passage produced the impress; it is the impress that I measure when I measure time. Thus either that is what time is, or I am not measuring time at all.

But when we measure silences, and say that some particular silence lasted as long as some particular phrase, do we not stretch our mind to measure the phrase as though it were actually sounded, so as to be able to form a judgment of the relation between the space of the silence and that space of time? For without voice or lips we can go through poems and verses and speeches in our minds, and we can allow for the time it takes for their movement, one part in relation to another, exactly as if we were reciting them aloud. If a man decides to utter a longish sound and settles in his mind how long the sound is to be, he goes through that space of time in silence, entrusts it to his memory, then begins to utter the sound, and it sounds until it reaches the length he had fixed for it. Or rather I should say [not that it sounds but] that it has sounded and will sound: for as much of it as has been uttered at a given moment has obviously sounded, and what remains will sound: and so he completes the sound: at every moment his attention, which is present, causes the future to make its way into the past, the future diminishing and the past growing, until the future is exhausted and everything is past.

XXVIII

But how is the future diminished or exhausted, since the future does not yet exist: or how does the past grow, since it no longer is? Only because, in the mind which does all this, there are three acts. For the mind expects, attends and remembers: what it expects passes, by way of what it attends to, into what it remembers. Would anyone deny that the future is as yet not existent? But in the mind there is already an expectation of the future. Would anyone deny that the past no longer exists? Yet still there is in the mind a memory of the past. Would anyone deny that the present time lacks extension, since it is but a point that passes on? Yet the attention endures, and by it that which is to be passes on its way to being no more. Thus it is not the future that is long, for the future does not exist: a long future is merely a long expectation of the future; nor is the past long since the past does not exist: a long past is merely a long memory of the past.

Suppose that I am about to recite a psalm that I know. Before I begin, my expectation is directed to the whole of it; but when I have begun, so much of it as I pluck off and drop away into the past becomes matter for my memory; and the whole energy of the action is divided between my memory, in regard to what I have said, and my expectation, in regard to what I am still to say. But there is a present act of attention, by which what was future passes on its way to becoming past. The further I go in my recitation, the more my expectation is diminished and my memory lengthened, until the whole of my expectation is used up when the action is completed and has passed wholly into my memory. And what is true of the whole psalm, is true for each part of the whole, and for each syllable: and likewise for any longer action, of which the canticle may be only a part: indeed it is the same for the whole life of man, of which all a man's actions are parts: and likewise for the whole history of the human race, of which all the lives of all men are parts.

XXIX

But *The mercy is better than lives,* and behold my life is but a scattering. *Thy right hand has held me up* in my Lord, the Son of Man who is the Mediator in many things and in divers manners—that *I may apprehend by Him in whom I am apprehended* and may be set free from what I once was, following your Oneness: *forgetting the things that are behind* and not poured out upon things to come and things transient, but *stretching forth to those that are before* (not by dispersal but by concentration of energy) *I press towards the prize of the supernal vocation,* where *I may hear the voice of Thy praise* and contemplate Thy delight which neither comes nor passes away.

But now my years are wasted in sighs, and Thou, O Lord, my eternal Father, art my only solace; but I am divided up in time, whose order I do not know, and my thoughts and the deepest places of my soul are torn with every kind of tumult until the day when I shall be purified and melted in the fire of Thy love and wholly joined to Thee.

XXX

And I shall stand and be established in You, in my own true form, in Your truth. I shall no longer suffer the questions of men who, by a disease they have merited for their punishment, ever thirst for more than they can drink. Thus they ask: "What was God making before He made Heaven and earth?" "Or how did the idea of creating something come into His mind whereas He had never created anything before?"

Grant them, Lord, to think well what they are saying, and to realize that one cannot use the word "never" when there is no time. If you say that he "never" made anything, obviously this means that He did not make anything "at any time." Let them see then that there can be no time apart from creation, and let them cease to talk such nonsense. *Let them stretch forth to the things that are before,* and let them realize that before all times You are the Eternal Creator of all times, and that no times are co-eternal with You, nor is any creature, even if there were a creature above time.

XXXI

O Lord, My God, how deep is the abyss of Thy secret, and how far from it have the consequences of my sins held me? Cleanse my eyes and let me rejoice in Thy Light. Assuredly if there were a mind of such vast knowledge and fore-knowledge that all the past and all the future were as clearly known to it as some familiar canticle is known to me, such a mind would be marvellous beyond measure, would strike us silent with awe. For to such a mind nothing would be hidden of ages past or ages still to come, any more than when I am singing my canticle anything is unknown to me of what I have sung from the beginning, of what remains to me to sing to the end. Yet far from me be it to think that You, O Creator of the Universe, Creator of souls and bodies, had only such knowledge as that of the future and the past. Far more marvellously, far more mysteriously, do You hold Your knowledge. For when a man is singing a song he knows, or hearing a song he knows, his impressions vary and his senses are divided between the expectation of sounds to come and the memory of sounds already uttered. No such thing happens to You, the immutable and eternal, the eternal Creator of minds. In the beginning You knew heaven and earth without any element of change in your knowledge; and similarly in the beginning You created Heaven and earth without any element of change in Your action. Let him who understands praise You, and let him who does not understand praise You likewise. You are the highest, and the humble of heart are Your dwelling place. For You *lift up them that are cast down,* and those do not fall who have You for their high place.

Plotinus

Neoplatonism, the most influential philosophical movement of the Roman Empire, combined metaphysical speculation on the esoteric meanings of Plato's dialogues with a contemplative vision of reality. At once erudite and eclectic, as it drew on the six centuries of philosophical development between Plato's Academy and its own emergence in Alexandria in the third century A.D., Neoplatonism above all used philosophical structures to expound and expand the dimensions of inner experience. Its scholasticism was matched only by its spiritual aspirations, and so its influence continued through its adaptations by the mystical teachers of the Orthodox Church and its prolongation in the Aristotelian Platonism of classical Islam.

It was the brilliantly original work of Plotinus (A.D. 204/5–270) as recorded in the *Enneads,* edited and published by Plotinus' disciple Porphyry, that inspired and provided the foundations for the work of later Neoplatonists such as Iamblichus (active 245) and Proclus (412–485). Virtually all that we know of Plotinus' life comes from Porphyry's essay *The Life of Plotinus,* which Porphyry published alongside his edition of the *Enneads* (the title in Greek means "Nines," as there are six groups of nine essays each, the divisions of which were established by Porphyry). Plotinus was born in Alexandria, studied philosophy for eleven years, joined the emperor Gordian III's campaign against the Persians, and after the failure of that expedition, moved to Rome where he began to teach philosophy. Plotinus committed nothing to writing until almost the age of fifty and instead concerned himself with the difficulties presented by individual students during the course of personal instruction.

Although Plotinus engaged whoever wished to attend the lectures (evidently chaos reigned in Plotinus' classroom, with answers to objections dragging on for days), this public teaching style was modified by two factors. The first qualification for a student of philosophy was basic familiarity with the textual tradition that maintained the philosophical lineage.

The other constraint involved philosophy as a way of life. Senators, doctors, politicians—indeed, the emperor himself—were welcome. But the life of philosophy set one apart, as in the case of Plotinus' student Rogatianus, a senator who renounced his office and became "an example for those who engage in the life of philosophy" (*Life* 7.45–46). Perhaps it was ironically fitting, then, that at the end of his life Plotinus found himself alone, abandoned by all but his attending physician.

Rather than claiming to be innovators or original thinkers, philosophers in the Roman Empire tended to present themselves as exegetes of previous texts or doctrines, and Plotinus was no exception. In *Ennead* V.1, "On the Three Principal Hypostases," reprinted here, Plotinus says concerning his three primary hypostases, the Soul, the Intellect, and the One: "Our present doctrines are an exegesis of those [ancient teachings], and so the writings of Plato himself provide evidence that our doctrines are of ancient origin." (V.1.8.11–15). What exactly does Plotinus mean when he calls his doctrines an exegesis of Plato's text, especially in the context of *Ennead* V.1? To answer this question is to gain a theoretical foothold in the often abstract world of Neoplatonic metaphysics.

Plotinus held that Plato's *Parmenides* was a theological disquisition that charted not only the fundamental principles of reality but also the emergence of any possible form of being from one transcendent source. As we have just seen, in *Ennead* V.1, Plotinus interprets the three initial hypotheses in the second half of the *Parmenides* as adumbrating his own metaphysical doctrine, according to which reality has different levels: the One, Intellect, and Soul. Plotinus' first hypothesis ("if the one is," *Parmenides* 137c4) refers to the One beyond being, the transcendent source of all.

The second hypothesis refers to a subsequent stage of reality that arises when the wisdom inherent within the One turns back on itself, giving rise to Being/Intellect, the intelligible world that consists of intellects each contemplating all the other intellects, rather like a hall of mirrors. This order of reality represents Plotinus' transformation of the Platonic Forms via an Aristotelian conception of divine thought eternally contemplating itself. Transitory being (Greek *genesis,* or "becoming") originates in the third hypostasis, at the level of Soul, which is present both on a cosmic level as caretaker of all that is soulless, and as the embodied individual whose destiny is to return to his origin by recovering his lost unity with the One.

Yet the *Enneads* are certainly not merely scholastic or exegetical. There is also a dynamic aspect of the philosophy that is best understood as a spiritual circuit. In *Ennead* V.1 Plotinus uses the physical similes of perfume, snow, and sunlight to describe the eternal process of emanation, the radiation of all beings from the One. The cosmic respiration or universal pulse that constantly sends forth beings from the One into a state of manifestation derives from the self-giving nature of reality. Plotinus says that all that is perfect produces. Nevertheless, Plotinus also insists that the soul remains very close to the One and prescribes exercises by means of which the soul can begin to recover from its apparent separation. The soul discovers its own native fullness when it undertakes its cosmic mission of returning the multiplicity back to the source. Porphyry ends the *Life of Plotinus* with the dying words of the sage: "Strive to bring the One in yourself back to the One."

Indeed, much of what strikes us as unique in the *Enneads* is Plotinus' attempt to convey this experience of return to the One in the terms of a contemplative vision where ordinary notions of the self, of language, and of reality as a whole are utterly transformed. Plotinus discusses this experience in the first of the treatises reprinted here, *Ennead* IV.8, "On the Descent of the Soul into Bodies." In both *Enneads* V.1 and IV.8, Plotinus dwells at length on the consequences and reasons for the soul's separation from the unity of the One as a desire to be independent, even as "rashness." At the same time, Plotinus is always at pains to make clear, as he does very decisively in IV.8, that the soul is never actually separate from the divine nature of the Intellect and that it does not descend entirely but remains part of the intelligible universe. Much of treatise IV.8 is devoted to teaching the soul how to live in the midst of its guardian duties, caring for the life of the body, but mindful that it nevertheless enjoys a higher calling. Perhaps it is this optimism concerning the possibilities of the human soul, Plotinus' insistence that soul is rooted in and an expression of divine reality, that has made Plotinus and Neoplatonism as a whole such an important vehicle for the shaping of Christian, Islamic, and Jewish mystical traditions.

• • •

The best introduction to Neoplatonism remains R. T. Wallis' *Neoplatonism* (Indianapolis: Hackett Publishing Company, 1995). A. C. Lloyd's *Anatomy of Neoplatonism* (Oxford: Oxford University Press, 1990) and O'Meara's *Plotinus: An Introduction to the Enneads* (Oxford: Oxford University Press, 1993) are also extremely useful. A more analytic approach is taken in Lloyd P. Gerson's *Plotinus* (London: Routledge, 1996).

Sara Ahbel-Rappe

Enneads

IV 8. On the Descent of the Soul into Bodies

§1. I have many times awakened into myself from the body when I exited the things other than myself, and entered into myself, and, seeing a marvelous and great beauty, I was then especially confident that I belonged to the better part and that I was engaging in the best life, and that I had come to that activity having identified myself with the divine and having situated myself in it, that is, having situated myself above all else in the intelligible world. After this repose in the divine, descending from Intellect into discursive reasoning, I am puzzled how I have now descended and how my soul has come to be in the body when it is the way it appeared to itself even while it was in the body.

Heraclitus,[1] who exhorted us to examine this, in supposing "necessary changes from opposites" and saying "the road up and down" and "while changing, it is at rest" and "it is weary to toil at and be ruled by the same things," seemed to leave it to us to imagine what he meant, since he did not care to make clear to us his argument, perhaps on the grounds that it is necessary for one to seek by oneself, just as he found by seeking. And Empedocles,[2] when he said that it was a law that sinful souls enter here and that he himself, "fleeing from the home of the gods," "trusting in mad strife" gave us a peek, I think, as much as did Pythagoras[3] and his followers, who offered riddles about this and about many other things. But it was also possible that Heraclitus did not make himself clear, because he was writing poetry. We are left with the divine Plato, who said many and beautiful things about soul and spoke in many places in his writings about its arrival here [the sensible world], so that we hope to grasp something clear from him. What then does this philosopher say?

He appears not to say the same thing everywhere, so that one could easily know his intention, but everywhere disdaining the whole sensible world and blaming the soul for its association with the body, he says the soul is "in its bonds" and "buried in it" and that great is the saying among the mysteries that claims that the soul is "under detention." And his cave, like the grotto of Empedocles, stands, I think, for this world when he actually says that the "journey" to the intelligible world is a "release from our bonds" and an "ascent from the cave" for the soul. And in *Phaedrus*, "the shedding of wings" is the cause of our arriving here. And according to him, the cycles bring here again the soul that has ascended, and "judgments" send others down here as well as "lots and fortunes," or forces.

In addition, though blaming the soul for its arrival in the body in all these places, in *Timaeus*, when speaking about this universe, he praises it and says that it is a "happy god" and that the soul was given by a good craftsman in order that this universe might be intelligent, since it had to be intelligent, and without soul it was not possible for it to become so. The soul of the universe, then, was sent into it by the god for the sake of this, and the soul of each of us was sent for the universe's perfection. This occurred since it was necessary that there exist in the sensible world the same kinds of living things that there are in the intelligible world.

§2. For us, the result of seeking to learn from Plato about our soul is that we find ourselves also compelled to focus on and to seek out a general account of the soul, investigating how by its nature it can ever be in association with the body, and in regard to the nature of the universe, what sort of thing we should suppose it is in which the soul resides: whether it does so willingly, or under compulsion, or in some other

Reprinted from *Neoplatonic Philosophy: Introductory Readings*, edited and translated by John Dillon and Lloyd P. Gerson (Indianapolis: Hackett Publishing Company, 2004), by permission of the publisher.

1. [Regarding Heraclitus, see Aristotle's *Metaphysics*, n.8.—S.M.C.]

2. [Regarding Empedocles, see Plato's *Meno*, n.6.]

3. [Regarding Pythagoras, see Aristotle's *Metaphysics*, n.7.]

manner; and about its producer: whether it has done its job correctly or, perhaps like our souls, which, since they had to direct inferior bodies, had to sink far below, owing to them, if, that is, they were going to rule over them at all; otherwise, each part of the body would be scattered and borne to its own place—though in the universe everything is in its own place by nature—whereas our bodies are in need of a lot of onerous providential care, since there are many alien things that befall them, and since they are always constrained by want, they need every type of assistance for the great difficulty that they are in.

But since the body of the universe is perfect and sufficient, that is, self-sufficient and having nothing in itself beyond what its nature requires, it is in need of little direction. And as its soul is always as it naturally wanted to be, it has no appetite, nor is it affected. For "there is nothing that goes out of it and nothing that goes into it." For this reason, Plato says that our soul, too, if it should come to be with that perfect soul, is itself perfected and "travels on the heights and directs the universe." When it departs for a state where it neither is within any body nor belongs to any one of them, then it will be like the soul of the universe effortlessly directing the universe with it, since it is not evil in any way for the soul to provide the body with the power of doing well and of existing. This is because not every form of providence for what is inferior removes the superior status for that which is provident.

For there are two types of care for everything: the universal, by the inactive command of the one providing the order with royal oversight, and the particular, which consists in some immediate self-involved doing and, by contact with that which is done, the doer is contaminated with the nature of what is done. Since the divine soul is said always to direct the heavens in the first way, with its higher part transcendent while sending its last [lowest] power into [the body of the universe], God could still not be said to be responsible for having made the soul of the universe be in something worse, and the soul would not be deprived of what belongs to it according to nature, which it has from eternity and will have forever, which cannot possibly be counter to its nature, and which continuously belongs to it forever, without having ever begun.

And when Plato says that the souls of the stars stand to their bodies in the same manner as does the soul of the universe in regard to its body—for he inserts the stars' bodies into the circles of the soul—he preserves the appropriate state of happiness for them, for there are two things, owing to which the association of the soul with the body is made difficult to endure: first, because the association produces an impediment to thought and second, because pleasures and appetites and pains fill it up. Neither of these could happen to a soul that did not descend into the interior of a body that does not belong to anyone nor is the body's possession, but rather the body belongs to it, and it is such as neither to need anything nor to be deficient in some respect, so that the soul is not filled up with appetites or fears, for neither will it expect anything fearful from a body of this kind, nor will any occupation make it incline downward and lead it away from the better and blessed vision, but it is always directed to those [intelligible realities], governing this universe with an effortless power.

§3. Regarding the human soul which, when it is in the body, is said [by Plato] to suffer all forms of evil and to "experience distress," because it comes to be amidst inanities and appetites and fears and other evils—insofar as the body is a chain and a tomb, and the universe is for it a cave or a cavern—let us now express how [Plato] understands its descent; here, he does not contradict what he says about the causes [of the descent of the soul of the universe], which are not, in its case, the same.

Now since universal Intellect is as a whole and universally in the world of thinking, which we suppose to be an intelligible universe, and since there are also intellectual powers and individual intellects contained in this—for the intelligible world is not only one but also one and many—it had to be the case that there be both many souls and one Soul, with the many differing souls coming from the one, just as from one genus come many species, some better and some worse, some more intellectually active, some less actualized; for in the intelligible world, in Intellect, there is Intellect encompassing virtually the others [individual intellects] as a sort of great living being, and there are the individual intellects in actuality, each of which the other encompasses virtually. For example, if a city were ensouled, encompassing other ensouled beings, the [soul of the] city would be more complete and would be more powerful though nothing in its nature prevented other souls from existing. Or arising from a universal fire, there comes a large and a small fire. But it is the universal essence that is the essence of the universal fire, or rather that from which the universal fire also comes.

The function of the more rational Soul is thinking, but it is not just thinking. For if it were, how would it differ from Intellect? For it added to the intellectual something else such that it did not remain Intellect. And it has its own function, if it is the case that every part of intelligible reality has a function. But looking at that which is prior to it, it thinks, while when looking to itself it arranges that which comes after it and manages and rules it, because it was not possible for everything to stay in the intelligible world, when it was possible for something else that is inferior to it to come to be, something that necessarily came to be if that which was prior to it was also necessary.

§4. The individual souls, not only exercise an intellectual desire for their return to that from which they came, but also have a power directed to here below, like a light dependent on the sun above, which does not begrudge its bounty to what comes after it. But they are without pain if they remain with universal Soul in the intelligible world, governing the heaven with that whole Soul, like those living with the king of all, sharing in his rule but not themselves alighting from the royal thrones. For these are all together in the same place.

But they move away from the whole [Soul] into being a part, and being by themselves and, in a way, tiring of being with another, each withdraws into itself. And whenever a soul does this for a time, fleeing the all and standing apart in separateness and not looking in the direction of that which is intelligible, it has become a part isolated and weak and consumed with its own affairs and looks to the part, and by a separation from the whole, it enters some one thing and flees all the rest. And coming to and turning towards that one thing that is beaten up by the totality of things in every way, setting itself apart from the whole, it manages the individual [body] with complications as soon as it has attached itself to it and, caring for externals and being present [to the body], it sinks far into its interior.

It is here that the so-called "molting" occurs, and it comes to be in the "chains" of the body, since it has failed to achieve the immunity that pertains to the more exalted management that belonged to it when it was with universal Soul. It was in every way better for it before, when it was traveling on the upward path. It has, then, been captured and it is falling in the direction of its chains and acting by sense-perception, owing to its being prevented from acting with intellect in its new state. And it is said to be "buried" and "in a cave," but when it is turning in the direction of thinking, it is loosed from its chains and ascends, whenever it might get a start, owing to recollection, to view reality. For it always has, still, something that is transcendent.

Souls, then, in a way become amphibious, necessarily living a part of their life in the intelligible world and a part here, those which are able to consort with Intellect living more of their life there while those who are governed in the opposite way by nature or by chance, live more of their life here. Plato gently shows this when he divides again that which comes from the second mixing, that is, he divides [the mixture] into parts. It is then that he says that they must enter into the world of becoming, since they have become such parts. But if he says that god "sowed" them, this must be taken in the same way as when he says that god is speaking and in a way making a public speech. As for the things that are in nature, these the hypothesis generates and makes as a demonstration, adducing in order things that are always becoming and always being.

§5. There is, then, no discordance between "the sowing in becoming" and "the descent of the all into completion," and the judgment and the cave, and the necessary and the voluntary, since the necessary includes the voluntary and the being in an evil state that is being in a body. There is discordance in neither Empedocles' flight from god and the wandering, nor the error upon which judgment follows, nor the halting of Heraclitus in flight, nor, in general, the voluntariness of the descent and, again, its involuntariness. For while everything that gravitates to the worse does so involuntarily, still, since it does so in fact by its own impetus, when it suffers the worse it is said to receive punishment for the things it did. But it suffers these things and does what it does necessarily by an eternal law of nature, and this occurs when it meets up with the needs of another [the body] in its procession from that which is above it [above the human being]. So if someone were to say that a god had sent it down, he would not be out of tune either with the truth or with himself. For each thing, including the ultimate things, must be referred to the principle from which it comes, even if there are many intermediaries.

But since the error of the soul is twofold, one being the explanation for its descent and one being the evils it does when it has come here, [the punishment] for the first is the fact that it experiences the descent and for the second, that it enters other [inferior] bodies; this occurs quickly, based on the judgment of what it deserves—the word "judgment" shows that it happens by divine decree—whereas the limitless kind of evil deserves a more severe judgment, rendered by the oversight of punishing spirits.

In this way, then, even though the soul is divine and comes to be in a body from divine regions above, since it is a god of a lesser rank, it comes here by a self-determining inclination, and by reason of its power, and to order what comes after it. And if soul flees quickly, there is no harm in its acquiring a knowledge of evil, and knowing the nature of vice, and rendering its own powers manifest, and displaying its works and deeds, which, if they were to have stayed in the bodiless world, would have remained quiet in vain being eternally unactualized. And the soul itself would not have been aware of what it had if these had neither been made manifest nor proceeded forth. This is so, because everywhere it is the case that actuality shows potentiality totally hidden, and in a way nonapparent, and not ever being really real. As it is now, each of its interior properties is an object of wonder, owing to the external variety [of their manifestations] such that it is from this interior that someone achieves these splendid manifestations.

§6. If, then, it had to be the case that there was not one thing only—for if there had been, all things would have been hidden in that one thing, which did not have any shape, and there would not have existed any of the beings had the One remained in itself, neither the multiplicity of these beings generated from the One nor those things which assumed the order of souls, which proceeded after these—in the same way, it had to be that souls not be alone without there being the things that are made apparent through them, if indeed it is the case that each nature makes what comes after it and unfolds itself like a seed from some partless source, proceeding to its perceptible conclusion.

On the one hand, that which is prior remains in its own position; on the other, that which comes after is in a way produced from unspeakably great power, consisting of all that was in those [higher powers]. It had not to remain in itself in a way circumscribed in grudging, but it had to go forward eternally, until all things should arrive at the ultimate limit of power, owing to its enormous power, which, in sending forth itself in every way, does not fail to permit anything to share in its own power. For there was nothing that prevented anything from having a share in the nature of good insofar as it was possible for each thing to share in it.

Either, then, the nature of matter is eternal and it is not possible for it, since it is existing, not to participate in that which provides that which is good to each thing insofar as it is able, or else the generation of it followed from necessity upon the causes that came before it, though even so it was not the case that it had to be separate [from all existing things], owing to the fact that before it came into being, there was an immobilization of activity because of a lack of power in that which gave it existence as a sort of grace.

The most beautiful part of the sensible world, then, is a manifestation of the best among the intelligibles, of their power and of their goodness; and all things, both sensible and intelligible, are eternally connected, the intelligibles existing by themselves, the things that partake always receiving their existence from them, imitating the intelligible nature insofar as they are able.

§7. Even if the nature of the soul is twofold, being both intelligible and sensible and, though it would be better for the soul to be in the intelligible world, still it is necessary for something having such a nature to be able to share in the sensible world, and it should not be irritated with itself, because even if all things are not in the best way, it occupies a middle rank among things. Though it has a "divine portion," it is at the outer limit of intelligibility such that it has a common boundary with the sensible nature, giving something of itself to this while receiving in return something from it, unless it governs the universe in a detached manner rather than, possessed of a greater zeal, entering into the interior, not remaining wholly with the whole Soul. At any rate, it is possible for it to surface again and acquire the narrative of the things it saw and experienced here, and then for it to learn what it is like to be in the intelligible world, and then to learn more clearly which is better by making a comparison of what are, in a way, contrary states.

For the experience of evil is a clearer understanding of the Good for those with a capacity too weak to know evil before experiencing it. And just as the intellectual procession is a descent into the limits of that which is worst—for it is not in it to ascend to that which transcends it, but it necessarily acts from itself and, not being able to remain in its own nature, it must by necessity and law arrive at soul, for this is its goal, and it must hand over that which comes next to soul and return again—so the activity of soul operates in the same way: one part is that which comes after it, namely, the things here, and the other part is the contemplation of the beings that are prior to it.

For some particular souls, such an experience comes with time, when they are in a bad state and they make a return to the better, whereas for the one called the soul of the universe, it has not been involved in inferior work, and, since it is unaffected by evils, it reflects contemplatively on the things below here and remains forever dependent on the things prior to it. In fact, it is able to do both at once; it receives from there, and at the same time provides here, since, being soul, it was unrealistic for it not to be attached to these things.

§8. But if one must, contrary to the opinions of others, dare to say more clearly what appears to be the case, it is not our entire soul that has descended, but rather there is some part of it always in the intelligible world. But if the part that is in the sensible world should rule, rather if it should be ruled and confused, it does not allow us awareness of the things that the upper part of the soul contemplates. In that case, that which is thought comes to us, but only when it comes into our awareness in its descent. For we do not know everything that occurs in every part of our souls before it reaches the whole soul. For example, appetite, while remaining in the appetitive part of the soul, is cognized by us, but only when we grasp it by the internal perceptual power, or by the discursive power, or by both. For every soul has something of that which is below, which is connected to the body, and something of that which is above, which is connected to Intellect.

And universal Soul or the soul of the universe, by means of the part of it that is connected to the body, governs the whole while remaining effortlessly apart, because it does not do this by calculation, as do we, but by intellect, just as "art does not deliberate" that part of the whole governing its [the universe's] inferior part [the body]. But particular souls that occupy part of the universe have a part that stands apart, though they are busy with sense-perception and with the apprehension, apprehending many things that are, contrary to nature, painful and terrifying, since that which gets their attention is a part that is defective, having many alien things around it, many that it desires. And it is pleased, and pleasure deceives it. But there is that part that, being immune to pleasure, the momentary pleasures do not please, and its way of life is like that in the upper region.

V 1. On the Three Principal Hypostases

§1. What can it be, then, that has made the souls forget the god who is their father and be ignorant both of themselves and him even though they are parts of the intelligible world and are completely derived from it?

The starting point for their evil is audacity, that is, generation or primary difference, or wanting to belong to themselves. Since they then appeared to be pleased with their self-determination and to have made much use of their self-motion, running as far away as possible and producing the maximum distance, they were also ignorant that they themselves came from the intelligible world. They were like children who at birth are separated from their fathers and, being raised for a long time far away, are ignorant both of themselves and of their fathers. Since they no longer can see their father or themselves, they dishonor themselves, owing to ignorance of their lineage, honoring instead other things, in fact, everything more than themselves; marveling at and being awestruck and loving and being dependent on these, and they severed themselves as much as possible from those things from which they turned away with their dishonor.

So it follows that it is honor of these things and dishonor of themselves that is the cause of their complete ignorance of god. For one to pursue and marvel at something is at the same time to accept that one is inferior to that which one is pursuing and marveling at. If one supposes oneself inferior to things that come to be and perish and assuming oneself to be the most dishonored and mortal of the things one does honor, neither the nature nor the power of god would ever be impressed in one's heart.

For this reason, the way of arguing with those so disposed should be twofold—that is, if one is going to turn them in the opposite direction and towards the things that are primary and lead them up to that which is highest or first, that is, the One. What, then, are the two ways?

First, one shows how the things now honored by the soul are in fact dishonorable, which we will discuss further elsewhere. Second, one teaches the soul to remember the sort of lineage it has and its worth, a line of reasoning that is, in fact, prior to the other and, once having been set forth, makes that other evident, too. This is the one that needs to be spoken of now. It is close to that which we are seeking and provides the groundwork for that. For that which is doing the seeking is the soul, and it should know that which is doing the seeking so that it can learn, first about itself and next whether it has the ability for seeking such things, whether it has the sort of "eye" that is able to see, and whether it is fitting for it to seek these things, for if the things sought are alien to it, why should it seek them? But if they are of the same lineage, it is fitting for it to seek them, and it is possible to find that which it is seeking.

§2. Let every soul, then, first consider that soul itself made all living things by breathing life into them, those that are nourished by the earth, the sea, and the air, and the divine stars in heaven. Soul itself made the sun and this great heaven, and it ordered it, and it drives it in a regular arrangement, being a nature different from that which it orders, from that which it moves, and from that which it makes to be alive. And it is necessary that it be more honorable than these, since while these are generated and destroyed whenever soul departs from them or supplies them with life, soul itself exists forever by "not departing from itself."

As for the manner in which it supplies life to the whole and to each individual, this is how soul should reason about the matter: let it consider the great soul, being itself another soul of no small stature, worthy of consideration once it has been released from deception and from the things that have enchanted the other souls by being in a state of tranquility. Let not only its encompassing body and its surging waves be tranquil, but all that surrounds it; let the earth be tranquil, the sea and the air be tranquil, and heaven, the better part. Let soul, then, think of itself as, in a way, flowing or pouring everywhere into immobile heaven from "outside," inhabiting and completely illuminating it. Just as rays from the sun light up a dark cloud, make it shine, and give it a golden appearance, so soul entered into the body of heaven and gave it life, gave it immortality, and wakened the sleeping. And heaven, moved with an everlasting motion by the "wise guidance" of soul, became "a happy living being," and acquired its value from soul's dwelling within it, before which it was a dead body, mere earth and water, or rather the darkness of matter and of nonbeing and "what the gods hate," as the poet says.

The power and nature of soul would be more apparent, or clearer, if one would reflect here on how soul encompasses and directs heaven with its own acts of will. For soul has given itself to the entire extent of heaven, such as that is, and every interval both great and small is ensouled, even as one body lies apart from another, one here and one there, some separated by the contraries of which they are composed, and some separated in other ways, though they be mutually interdependent.

The soul is, however, not like that, and it does not make something alive by a part of it being broken up and put in each one, but all things live by the whole of it, and all soul is present everywhere by its being like the father who begat it, according to its unity and its universality. And though heaven is multiple and diverse, it is one by the power of soul, and this universe is a god owing to this. The sun is also a god—because it is ensouled—and the other stars: and we, if we are divine in some way, are so for just this reason, "for corpses are more apt for disposal than dung."

But the explanation for gods being gods must necessarily be a god older than they. Our soul is of the same kind, and when you examine it without the accretions, taking it in its "purified condition," you will find that it is the same honorable thing that soul was found to be, more honorable than everything that is bodily. For all bodily things are earth, but even if they were fire, what would be the cause of its burning? And so, too, for everything composed of these, even if you add water and air. But if the body is worth pursuing just because it is ensouled, why would one ignore oneself to pursue another? If you loved the soul in another, then love yourself.

§3. Since the soul is so honorable and divine a thing—trusting at once that such a thing is able to approach god with [the help of] such a cause—ascend to him. Certainly, you will not have to cast far, "nor are the intermediary steps many." Understand, then, the soul's higher neighboring region, more divine than the divine soul, after which and from which the soul comes. For even though the argument has shown the kind of thing soul is [honorable and divine], it is an image of Intellect. Just as spoken words are an expression of thinking, so, too, Soul is an expression of Intellect, and its whole [external] activity, that which Intellect sends forth as life for the existence of something else. It is just like fire that has both internal heat and radiant heat. But in the intelligible world, one should understand that the internal activity does not flow out of it, but rather one activity remains in it, and the other is the independent reality.

Since, then, Soul is derived from Intellect, it is intellectual, and its own intellect is found in its acts of discursive reasoning, and its perfection comes from Intellect, again like a father raising a child whom he begat as imperfect in relation to himself. Then both its independent reality is from Intellect and the actuality of it as an expression of Intellect occurs when Intellect is seen in it. For whenever it [Soul] looks into Intellect, it has inside of itself objects of thought and activity that belong to it. And these alone should be called activities of Soul, namely, those that are intellectual and belong to it. The inferior activities come from elsewhere, and are states of an inferior soul.

Intellect, then, makes Soul even more divine by being its father and by being present to it. For there is nothing in between them but the fact of their being different, soul as next in order and as receptive, and Intellect as form. Even the matter of Intellect is beautiful, since it is both in the form of Intellect and simple. What Intellect is like, then, is clear from the above, namely, that it is superior to Soul thus described.

§4. One might also see this from the following: if one starts by marveling at this sensible universe, looking at its expanse and its beauty and its everlasting motion and the gods in it, both the visible and the invisible ones, and the spirits, and all the animals and plants, let him then ascend to the archetype of this universe and the truer reality, and there let him see all that is intelligible and eternal in it with its own understanding and life, and "pure Intellect" presiding over these, and indescribable wisdom, and the life that is truly that of Kronos, a god of "fullness" and intellect. For it encompasses every immortal within itself, that is, every intellect, every god, every soul, always at rest. For why should it seek to alter itself from its happy condition? Where should it go to, having all things within itself? It does not even seek to enlarge itself, since it is most perfect.

For this reason, in addition, all the things in it are perfect so as to be perfect in every way, having nothing which is not like this, nothing in it that it does not think, though it thinks not by seeking but by having. Its blessedness is not acquired; rather, everything is in it eternally, and it is true eternity, which time imitates, moving around along with Soul, dropping some things and picking up others. For different things occur at the level of Soul; one time there is a Socrates, one time there is a horse—always some particular reality—whereas Intellect just is everything. So it has all things at rest in it in eternity, and it alone is, and the "is" is always, and the future is nothing to it (for it "is" then, too), nor is there a past for it (for nothing in the intelligible world has passed away), but all things are set in it always, and since they are the same, they are in a way pleased with the condition they are in.

Each of them is Intellect and Being, that is, the totality consists of all Intellect and all Being—Intellect, insofar as it thinks, making Being exist, and Being, by its being thought, giving to Intellect its thinking, which is its Being. But the cause of thinking is something else, something that is also the cause of Being. So the cause of thinking, then, which is also the cause of Being, is something else. Both of these, then, have at the same time a cause other than themselves. For those coexist simultaneously and do not abandon each other, but this one thing is nevertheless two: Intellect and Being, thinking and being thought—Intellect, insofar as it is thinking, Being insofar as it is being thought. For thinking could not occur if there was not Difference as well as Sameness. The first things that occur, then, are Intellect, Being, Difference, and Sameness. And one should include Motion and Rest—Motion if Intellect is thinking, and Rest, so that it thinks the same thing. There must be Difference, so that there can be both thinking and being thought; if you were to remove Difference, it would be made silent, having become one. It also must be that things that are thought are different from each other. There must also be Sameness, since Intellect is one with itself, that is, there is a certain commonality in all its objects, but "differentiation is Difference." And their having become many produces number and quantity, and quality is the unique character of each of these, and from these as principles all the other things arise.

§5. The god, then, who is above the soul is complex, and soul exists within this complex, connected to it, so long as it does not wish to be "separated" from it. Then, when it approaches near to Intellect and in a way becomes one with it, it seeks to know who it is that produced it. It is he who is simple and who is prior to this multiplicity, who is the explanation for the being and the complexity of this god; it is he who is the maker of number.

For number is not primary. Before the Dyad is the One; the Dyad is second and, having come from the One, it has that as limit imposed on it, whereas it is itself unlimited. When it is limited, it is henceforth a number, a number in the sense of a substance. The soul, too, is a number. The first things are neither masses nor magnitudes. The things that have thickness come later, those things that sense-perception takes to be real. Nor is it the moist part in seeds that is valuable, but the part that is not seen. This is number and an expressed principle. So, what are called number and the Dyad in the intelligible world are expressed principles and Intellect. But whereas the Dyad, understood in a way as a substrate, is unlimited, each number that comes from it and the One is a Form, [Intellect] in a way having been shaped by the Forms that come to be in it. In one manner, it is shaped by the One, and in another by itself, as in the way the faculty of sight is actualized. For thinking is [as] sight's seeing, and both are one.

§6. How, then, does it [Intellect] see, and what does it see, and how in general did it get realized and come to be from the One so that it can even see? For the soul now grasps that these things [the Forms] must of necessity be, but in addition it longs to grasp the answer to the question much discussed among the ancient wise men, too, of how from a unity, such as we say the One is, anything acquired existence, whether plurality or duality or number. Why did it not remain by itself, but instead such a plurality flowed from it, which [plurality], though seen among existing things, we think right to lead back to it.

Let us speak of this matter, then, in the following manner, calling to God Himself, not with spoken words, but by extending ourselves with our soul in prayer to Him, in this way being able to pray alone to Him who is alone. Since God is by Himself, as if inside a temple, remaining tranquil while transcending everything, the contemplator should contemplate the fixed statues which are in a way outside the temple already, or rather the first statue which appeared in the following manner.

It must be that for everything in motion there is something towards which it moves. Since the One has nothing towards which it moves, let us not suppose that it is moving, but if something comes to be after it, it has necessarily come to be by being eternally turned towards the One. Let the sort of coming to be that is in time not get in our way, since our discussion is concerned with things that are eternal. When in our discussion we attribute "coming to be" to them, we are doing so in order to give their causal order. We should say, then, that that which comes to be from the intelligible world does so without the One being moved. For if something came to be as a result of its having moved, then that which came to be from it would be third after the motion and not second. It must be, then, that if something came second after it, that came to exist while the One was unmoved, neither inclining, nor having willed anything, nor moving in any way.

How, then, does this happen, and what should we think about what is near to the One while it reposes? A radiation of light comes from it, but from it while it reposes, like the light from the sun, in a way encircling it, eternally coming from it while it reposes. And all things that exist, so long as they continue to exist, necessarily, in virtue of their present power, produce from their own essence a dependent reality around them at their exterior, a sort of image of the archetypes from which it was generated. Fire produces the heat that comes from it. And snow does not only hold its coldness inside itself. Perfumes especially witness to this, for so long as they exist, something flows from them around them, the reality of which a bystander enjoys. Further, all things, as soon as they are perfected, generate. That which is eternally perfect generates eternally an everlasting reality, and it generates something inferior to itself.

What, then, must we say about that which is most perfect? Nothing can come from it except that which is greatest after it. The greatest after it is Intellect, that which is second. For Intellect sees that and is in need of it alone. But the One has no need of Intellect. And that which is generated from something greater than Intellect is Intellect, which is greater than other things, because other things come after it. For example, Soul is an expression of Intellect and a certain activity, just as Intellect is an activity of the One. But Soul's reason is murky, for it is a reflection of Intellect, and, owing to this, it must look to Intellect. Similarly, Intellect has to look to the One, so that it can be Intellect. It sees it not as having been separated from it, but because it is after it and there is nothing in between, as there is nothing in between Soul and Intellect. Everything longs for that which produced it and loves this, especially whenever there is just producer and produced. And "whenever the producer is the best," the produced is necessarily together with it, since they are only separated by difference.

§7. Since we really should speak more clearly, let's say that Intellect is an image of the One. We must say first that that which is produced must somehow be the One and preserve many of its properties, that is, be a likeness in relation to it, just like the light that comes from the sun. But the One is not Intellect. How, then, does it generate Intellect? In fact, by Intellect's reversion to it, Intellect saw the One, and this seeing is Intellect. For that which grasps anything else is either sense-perception or intellect. Sense-perception is a line, etc. But the circle is the sort of thing that can be divided, though intellect is not like that. There is unity here, but the One has the power to produce all things. Thinking observes those things that the One is virtually, in a way cutting itself off from that virtuality. Otherwise, it would not have become Intellect, since it already has by itself a sort of awareness of the One's power to produce essence.

At any rate, Intellect, by means of itself, also defines its own being by the power that comes from the One and, because it is a sort of unitary part of what belongs to the One and is the substance coming from it, it is strengthened by it and brought to perfection as substance by it, and comes from it. It sees what is there by seeing itself, a sort of division of the indivisible, life and thinking and all things, none of which the One is.

For in this way all things come from it, because it is not constrained by some shape, for it is one alone. If it were all things, it would be among the things that are. For this reason, the One is none of the things in Intellect, but from it all things come. For this reason, these are essences, for each has already been defined, and each has a sort of shape. Being should not be suspended, so to speak, in the indefinite, but fixed by definition and stability. Stability in the intelligible world is definition and shape, by means of which it [essence] acquires reality.

"This is the lineage" of this Intellect, worthy of the purest Intellect, born from nowhere else than from the first principle, and, having been generated, at once generating all things together with itself, both all the beauty of the Ideas and all the intelligible gods. And it is full of the beings it has generated and, so to speak, swallowing them again by having them in itself and neither letting them fall into matter nor be reared by Rhea (as the mysteries and myths about the gods enigmatically say that Kronos, the wisest god, before the birth of Zeus, holds back in himself what he generates, so that he is full and is like Intellect in satiety).

After this, so they say, being already sated, he generates Zeus, for Intellect generates Soul, being perfect as Intellect. For since it is perfect, it had to generate and since it was such a great power, it could not be barren. That which was generated by it could, in this case as well, not be superior to it but had to be an inferior reflection of it, first similarly undefined and then defined by that which generated it, in a way made to be a reflection. The offspring of Intellect is an expressed principle and a reality, that which thinks discursively [Soul]. This is what moves around Intellect and is a light and trace of Intellect, dependent on it, on one side attached to Intellect and filled up with it and enjoying it and sharing in it and thinking, and on the other side, attached to the things that came after it, or rather itself generating what is necessarily inferior to Soul. These matters should be discussed later. This is as far as the divine realities go.

§8. And it is for this reason that Plato says that the principles are three: "around the king of all," meaning the primary things, "second around the secondary things," and "third around the tertiary things." And he says "father of the cause" meaning by "cause," Intellect. For the Intellect is his Demiurge. And he says that the Demiurge makes the Soul in that "mixing bowl." And since the Intellect is cause, he means by "father" the Good, or that which is beyond Intellect and "beyond essence." Often he calls Being and the Intellect "Idea," which shows that Plato understood that the Intellect comes from the Good, and the Soul comes from the Intellect. So these statements of ours are not recent or new, but rather were made a long time ago, though not explicitly. The things we are saying now are interpretations of those, relying on the writings of Plato himself as evidence that these are ancient views.

Parmenides[4] previously touched on this doctrine to the extent that he amalgamated Being and Intellect, that is, he did not place Being among sensibles, saying "for thinking and being are the same." And he says that Being is "immobile," though he does attach thinking to it, eliminating all bodily motion from it so that it would remain as it is, likening it to a "spherical mass," because it encompasses all things and because thinking is not external to it, but rather in it itself. Saying that it was "one" in his own writings, he got blamed for saying that this one thing was in fact found to be many.

Plato's Parmenides,[5] speaking more accurately, distinguishes from among other ones the primary One, which is one in a more proper sense, calling the second one "one many" and the third one "one and many." In this way, too, he is in harmony with [the doctrine of] the three natures.

§9. Anaxagoras[6] himself, too, in saying that "intellect is pure and unmixed," is positing the first principle as simple and the One as separate, although he neglects to give an accurate account owing to his antiquity. In addition, Heraclitus knew the One to be everlasting and intelligible, since bodies are always coming into being and are "in flux." And for Empedocles, "Strife" divides and "Love" is the One—this itself is incorporeal—and the elements are posited as matter.

Aristotle later said that the first principle was "separate" and "intelligible," but when he says that "it thinks itself," he no longer makes it the first principle. Further, he makes many other things intelligible (as many as there are spheres in the heavens, so that each intelligible moves each sphere), but by doing so he describes intelligibles in a way different from Plato, supposing an argument from plausibility, since he did not have an argument from necessity. One might pause to consider whether it is even plausible, for it is more plausible that all the spheres, contributing to one system, should look to one thing that is the first principle.

And one might inquire if the many intelligibles are, according to him, derived from one first principle, or whether he holds that there are many principles among the intelligibles. And if they are derived from one, it will be clear that, analogous to the way it is among sensibles, where one sphere encompasses another, until you reach the outermost one that is dominant, so the first there will also encompass everything, that is, there will be an intelligible world. And just as here the spheres are not empty, but the first is full of stars, and the others also have stars, so, too, in the intelligible world the movers will have many things within themselves, and the truer realities will be there. But if each one is a principle, the principles will be an arbitrary collection. And what will be the explanation for their working together and their agreement on a single task, the harmony of the entire universe? How can there be equality [in number] of the sensibles [spheres] in the universe in relation to the intelligibles or movers? How can these incorporeals be thus many, without matter to separate them?

So, among the ancients, those who adhered most closely to the doctrines of Pythagoras and to those who came after him, and to those of Pherecydes,[7]

4. [Regarding Parmenides, see Aristotle's *Metaphysics*, n.11.]

5. [The reference is to the character Parmenides in Plato's *Parmenides* dialogue.]

6. [Regarding Anaxagoras, see Plato's *Apology*, n.7.]

7. [The reference is to Pherecydes of Syros, a sixth-century-B.C. Greek thinker who authored a theory about the origin of the universe.]

held to this account of this nature [the One]. But some among them worked out this view among themselves in their own writings, while some did not do so in writings but demonstrated it in unwritten discussions or, altogether left it alone.

§10. It has already been shown that it is necessary to believe that things are this way: that there is the One beyond Being, that it is such as the argument strove to show to the extent that it is possible to demonstrate anything about these matters; that next, there is Being and Intellect; and third, there is the nature of the Soul.

And just as in nature these aforementioned three are found, so it is necessary to believe as well that these are in us. I do not mean that they are among sensibles—for these three are separate from sensibles—but that they are in things that transcend the sensible order, using the term "transcend" in the same manner in which it is used to refer to those things that transcend the whole universe. In the same way, in saying that they belong to a human being, I mean what Plato means by "the inner human being."

Our soul is, then, something divine and of another nature, like the nature of all soul. But the soul that has intellect is perfect, and one part of intellect is that which reasons and one part is that which makes reasoning possible. The reasoning part of soul is in need of no bodily organ for its reasoning, having its own activity in purity in order that it also be possible for it to reason purely; someone who supposed it to be separate and not mixed with body and in the primary intelligible world would not be mistaken. For we should not search for a place in which to situate it, but we should make it transcend all place. For this is how it is for that which is by itself, transcendent and immaterial, which it is whenever it is alone, retaining nothing from the nature of the body. For this reason, Plato says that the Demiurge "in addition" encircled the soul of the universe from "outside," pointing to the part of the soul that abides in the intelligible world. As for us, hiding his meaning, he said that it is "at the top of our head."

And his exhortation "to be separate" is not meant spatially—for this is by nature separated—but is an exhortation not to incline to the body, even by acts of imagination, and to alienate ourselves from the body, if somehow someone could lead upward the remaining part of the soul and even bear upward that which is situated here below, that part that alone is craftsman of the body and has the job of shaping it and caring for it.

§11. Since, then, there is soul that reasons about just and beautiful things and reasoning that seeks to know if this is just or if this is beautiful, it is necessary that there exist permanently something that is just, from which the reasoning in the soul arises. How else could it reason? And if soul sometimes reasons about these things and sometimes does not, there must be in us Intellect that does not reason but always possesses Justice, and there must be also the principle of Intellect and its cause and god [the One]. And it must be indivisible and remain so, and while not remaining in [any one] place, it is still seen in many things, each one able to receive it [the One] in a way as other than it, just as the center of the circle exists by itself, but each of the points on it has a mark of the center in themselves, that is, the radii bring to the center that which is in each case unique. For it is by something like this in ourselves that we are in contact with God and are with Him and depend on Him. And if we converge on Him, we would be settled in the intelligible world.

§12. How, then, given that we have such great things in us, do we not grasp them, but rather are mostly inactive with respect to these activities; indeed, some are altogether inactive?

Those are always involved with their own activities—I mean, Intellect and that which is prior to Intellect, eternally in itself, and Soul as well, which is thus "always moving." For not everything in soul is immediately perceptible, but it comes to us whenever it comes to our sense-perception. But whenever there is perceptual activity that is not being transmitted to the perceptual faculty, it has not yet come to the entire soul. We do not yet know it, then, since we are the whole soul, including the perceptual faculty, not just a part of it. Further, each of the parts of the soul is always acting always by itself with its own object, but cognizing occurs whenever transmission, that is, apprehension, occurs.

If, then, there is going to be apprehension of things present in this way, then that which is to apprehend must revert inward, and focus attention there. Just as if someone were waiting to hear a voice that he wanted to hear, and, distancing himself from other voices, were to prick up his ears to hear the preferred one, waiting for the time when it would arrive—so, too, in this case one must let go of perceptible sounds, except insofar as they are necessary, and guard the soul's pure power of apprehension and be ready to listen to the sounds from above.

Boethius

Romulus Augustulus, the last Roman emperor, was forcibly sent into retirement in A.D. 476 by Odoacer, a "barbarian" (that is, Germanic) military officer, who thereupon became king of the region now known as Italy. Shortly thereafter, Anicius Manlius Severinus Boethius (A.D. 480–524) was born into a distinguished Roman senatorial family. Two events occurred during Boethius' childhood that were to have an enormous impact on his life. The death of his father resulted in his being adopted into an even more distinguished family, that of Quintus Aurelius Memmius Symmachus. And Odoacer was overthrown and treacherously murdered in 493 by Theodoric the Ostrogoth, who ruled over Italy for thirty-three years.

Boethius flourished in Symmachus' family, both as a precocious learner receiving an excellent education and as a successful suitor marrying Symmachus' daughter. In a normal upper-class family, Boethius' educational achievements might have resulted in a life dedicated solely to scholarship. For someone who died in his mid-forties, Boethius' written accomplishments are impressive. He translated most of Aristotle's logical works into Latin, wrote commentaries on them and on logical treatises written by Porphyry and Cicero, and authored logical treatises of his own. He also wrote works on arithmetic, geometry, and music, along with five essays on theological topics. Many of these writings were highly influential in the development of medieval philosophy and theology for centuries after his death. His philosophical masterpiece, however, is the *Consolation of Philosophy,* the culminating book of which is presented here.

But Symmachus' family was no normal upper-class family. Symmachus was a highly respected and politically influential Roman senator who at one time had held the office of consul, or nominal and by this time mainly ceremonial executive officer of the state. Boethius followed his father-in-law's footsteps, becoming consul in 510. In 522 his two sons became joint consuls, while Boethius himself was appointed Master of the Offices, a position whose closest parallel in contemporary American political organization might be the fusion of White House Chief of Staff and National Security Advisor.

Boethius' and Theodoric's careers were thus intertwined. Theodoric had originally been sent to Italy to depose Odoacer by the Eastern (Byzantine) emperor Zeno. Although Theodoric owed allegiance to Zeno and his successors, he was allowed considerable latitude in his rule over Italy. That rule was marked by political shrewdness in creating and maintaining strategic alliances, respect for Roman legal and religious institutions, and—the universal measure of a successful politician—repair and improvement of public works. At the same time, Theodoric resisted assimilation. He banned Roman citizens from serving in the army and Goths from being educated in Roman schools.

One badge that differentiated Theodoric from his Roman subjects was his Arianism, a doctrine that Roman Christians regarded as heretical. Arianism maintained that, like the material world, Christ had been created by God out of nothing. Although superior to other creatures, Christ was nonetheless inferior to God. Arians claimed that this very inferiority enabled Christ to become flesh and suffer for humans' salvation. Arianism was the target of the Nicene Creed (promulgated in 325), which explicitly declared that Christ was "begotten," not made, "being of one substance with the Father." Theological controversy did not cease, however, for now questions arose about the relation between Christ's divinity and Christ's humanity. The Council of Chalcedon (451) maintained that Christ was one person with two natures, "truly God and truly Man." The expression of these theological doctrines depended heavily on such philosophically significant concepts as substance, relation, person, and nature. Boethius' theological treatises were efforts to clarify the positions enunciated in Nicaea and Chalcedon, using the tools of Aristotelian logic, not so much in an attempt to demonstrate or prove the positions as to show that some views opposed to them rested on confusion.

These seemingly abstruse philosophical exercises were in fact politically dangerous. In the second decade of the sixth century, the soon-to-be Eastern emperor Justinian sought to bring the Roman west into the Byzantine fold. In service of that end, Justinian was willing to accept the Chalcedonian definition of Christ's nature. As an Arian, Theodoric now found himself and his Goths regarded as heretics both by their Roman subjects, with whom they had resisted assimilation, and by their Eastern master. In this political context, it would be easy to read Boethius' treatises as propaganda designed to aid Justinian by stirring up Roman unrest. Theodoric had Boethius arrested and imprisoned in Pavia. A Roman senatorial court 500 miles away found him guilty and imposed a sentence of death without benefit of hearing a defense. He remained in prison for several months, during which time he wrote the Consolation of Philosophy. In it Boethius claims that the charges brought against him include conspiring with the senate against Theodoric, having written documents advocating freedom for Rome (could the evidence have been the theological treatises?), and committing sacrilege by trafficking with evil spirits. The last charge is reminiscent of the charge of impiety brought against Socrates, equally inflammatory and equally groundless. Unlike Socrates, who was put to death in a humane way, Boethius was brutally executed. As if for good measure, Theodoric also had Symmachus killed.

The Consolation of Philosophy is a dialogue between Boethius and Philosophy, personified as a goddess. The earlier books contain discussions of what constitutes the good life, how God is the ultimate good, and how evil can occur in a world governed by God's providence and justice. In Book V, the final book, Boethius raises the question of how it is possible for humans to have freedom of will if God knows in advance what every human choice will be. Philosophy's answer is to claim that the way in which a thing is known depends on the way in which the knower knows it, and that God knows things that are future to us as present to him. In arguing for this thesis, Philosophy offers a definition of eternity that came to exert considerable influence in the subsequent history of philosophy: Eternity is "a possession of life, a possession simultaneously entire and perfect, which has no end."

• • •

Two of Boethius' logical works have been translated, with much helpful commentary, by Eleonore Stump: *Boethius's "De topicis differentiis"* (Ithaca, N.Y.: Cornell University Press, 1978) and *Boethius's "In Ciceronis Topica"* (Ithaca, N.Y.: Cornell University Press, 1988). A magisterial study of Boethius' life and works is Henry Chadwick, *Boethius: The Consolations of Music, Logic, Theology, and Philosophy* (Oxford: Clarendon Press, 1981). A helpful examination of Boethius' philosophy is John Marenbon, *Boethius* (Oxford: Oxford University Press, 2003). A useful collection of recent essays on Boethius is contained in John Marenbon, ed., *The Cambridge Compainion to Boethius* (Cambridge: Cambridge University Press, 2009).

William E. Mann

Consolation of Philosophy

BOOK V

Prose 1

So she concluded, and she was starting to turn the direction of her pleading toward the treatment and explanation of some other things.

But then I said: A proper encouragement to be sure, completely and absolutely worthy of your authority! But as to what you said previously about Providence, that it is a question bound up with many other questions—I know that by personal experience. That is to say, I'm asking you whether you think there is such a thing as chance at all and, tell me, what sort of thing do you think it is?

Then she said: I'm hurrying to make good the debt of my promise, and to open up for you the path by which you may be carried back to your fatherland. But these questions—even though they are quite useful to know, they are all the same a little off to one side of the path of what I had proposed. And it's reasonable for me to be afraid that you'll be exhausted on the sidetracks and won't be able to bear up for traveling the straight path through to its end.

I said: You must have absolutely no fear of that. For it will be like tranquil quiet for me to bring to mind the things in which I take the greatest delight. And at the same time, when every side of your argument stands fixed, its trustworthiness undoubted, I want there to be no doubt at all about what follows.

Then she said: I'll humor you; and as she did so she began as follows.

She said: If someone were to define chance as a result that is a product of random motion, without any interweaving of causes, I would state that chance is nothing at all; my judgment is that it is a word absolutely devoid of meaning, in the absence of any signification of any underlying reality. I mean, what place can be left for randomness, when there is a God who keeps all things in bounds, binding them into order? For that axiom is true, which none of the old philosophers ever spoke against: Nothing comes from nothing. (Granted, they laid this down as a sort of foundation for all of their theories about the natural world only in consideration of the subject material, not the active first principle.) But should something arise from no causes, it will seem to have arisen from nothing; but if this can't happen, then it is impossible that there be chance of the sort that we have just now defined.

Well then! I said. Is there really nothing that can rightly be called chance or accident? Or is there something that these words are appropriate for, even if it is hidden from the common herd?

She said: It is in his *Physics* that my good Aristotle has defined it, in a brief demonstration that is very near to the truth.

I said: Tell me, in what way?

She said: Whenever something is done for some one particular purpose, and something other than what was intended occurs, from whatever causes—this is called chance. For example: if someone plows the earth in order to cultivate a field, and finds a mass of buried gold. And so it is that this is actually believed to have happened accidentally, but it is not from nothing, because it has its own causes, and it is the unforeseen and unexpected confluence of these causes that seems to have engineered a chance occurrence. For if the cultivator of the field were not plowing the earth, and if the one who hid the money had not hidden it in that very place, the gold would not have been found. And so these are the causes of the accidental profit, which arose not from the intention of the doer but from intersecting and confluent causes. For neither the one who buried the gold nor the one who worked the field intended that this money be found but, as I've said, that the one dug where the other had buried—this is a coincidence and a confluence. We may therefore define chance as follows: In the realm of things done for some partic-

Reprinted (without accompanying verses) from Boethius, *Consolation of Philosophy*, translated by Joel C. Relihan (Indianapolis: Hackett Publishing Company, 2001), by permission of the publisher.

ular reason, it is an unexpected outcome, deriving from confluent causes. Further, the order that makes these causes coincident and confluent proceeds in an inescapable interweaving of causes; it descends from the source of Providence and arranges all things in their proper places and in their proper times. . . .

Prose 2

I said: I recognize this, and I concur that things are just as you say they are. But in this sequence of causes, so attached to one another—is there any freedom of our independent judgment? Or does the chain of fate tie together the very motions of human minds as well?

She said: There is; in fact, there can be no rational nature without there being freedom of independent judgment in its possession. For a thing that is able by its own nature to employ reason has the discrimination by which it can tell things apart; consequently, it distinguishes between things that it must avoid and things that it must choose on its own. What it judges must be chosen, it seeks to gain; what it reckons must be avoided, it runs away from. For this reason, within the beings that have reason present within them, a freedom to want and not to want is present as well. However, it is my determination that this freedom is not the same in all of them. For substances that are ethereal and divine have at their disposal a penetrating discrimination, a will that suffers no decomposition, and a true power capable of effecting the things they have chosen.

Now it is necessarily the case that human souls are indeed at their freest when they preserve themselves intact within the contemplation of the divine mind; but they are less free when they fall away toward bodies, and still less free when they are tied to limbs of earthly matter. At their furthest remove there is slavery, when they have fallen away from the possession of the reason that belongs to them because they have surrendered themselves to vices. For once they have cast their eyes down from the light of the highest truth to the lower and shadowy realms, they are soon darkened over by the cloud of unknowing, they are caught in the whirlwind of destructive passions. By yielding to these passions and agreeing with them they help along the slavery that they have brought down upon themselves and, in a certain sense, they are the captives of their own liberty. Nevertheless, the gaze of Providence perceives these things, a gaze that from eternity looks out at all things in advance; it assigns to their merits each and every thing that has been predestined for them.

Prose 3

Then I said: Now look here! Now I am confounded by a still more difficult doubt.

She said: Tell me—what is that? Although I can already guess at the things that are the source of your confusion.

I said: That God has foreknowledge of absolutely everything and that there is any freedom of independent judgment—these things seem to me to be set against each other, and to be at odds with each other, far too much. For if God sees all things in advance and cannot be mistaken in any way, that thing must necessarily happen that Providence foresees will happen. And for this reason, if Providence has foreknowledge from eternity not only of the actions of mortal men but of their deliberations and of their wills as well, then there would be no freedom of independent judgment. For there could exist no action, no will of any sort, other than what divine Providence, which does not know how to be mistaken, perceives beforehand. I mean, if such things could be forcibly turned aside in some other direction than they were foreseen to go, then there would now be no immovable foreknowledge of the future, but only indefinite opinion instead. And this I judge to be a wicked thing to believe about God.

Nor do I approve of the line of argument by which some people believe they can untie the knot of this question. I refer to the people who deny that *this* is the reason that something will happen, that Providence sees in advance that it will be so. Rather to the contrary: Because something is going to be, it cannot escape the notice of divine Providence, and in this way the necessity falls to the other side. For they say that the things that are foreseen are not contingent by necessity; rather, the things that are going to be are necessarily foreseen. Ha! As if the contention were which is the cause of which—whether foreknowledge of future things is the cause of the necessity, or whether the necessity of future things is the cause of the foreseeing. *This* is what we are striving to demonstrate: Exactly how the order of causes is constituted is irrelevant—there is a necessary result of foreknown things, even if the foreknowledge does not seem to impose a necessity of resulting on future events. In fact, if someone is sitting, it is necessarily the case that the opinion that conjectures that he is sitting is true; and then again, from the other side, if it is a true opinion about someone that he is sitting, it is necessarily the case that he is sitting. Consequently, necessity is present in either case: in the latter, the necessity of the sitting; in the other, the necessity of the truth of the opinion. But it is not for *this* reason, that the opinion is true, that someone is sitting; rather, this opinion is true because the fact of a man's sitting preceded it. Thus, even though the cause of truth proceeds from only one side, there is present all the same a common necessity on both sides. A similar line of reasoning is obvious concerning Providence and future events. For even if things are foreseen because they are going to happen, and they do not happen because they are foreseen, it is nevertheless the case that things to come are foreseen by God, or that things foreseen by God happen as they were foreseen to happen. This alone is sufficient to destroy the freedom of independent judgment.

What's more, how utterly backwards it is to say that the outcome of temporal events is the cause of eternal knowledge! To judge that God foresees future things for *this* reason, that they are going to happen—what else is this but to think that things that happened at some point before are the cause of his most high Providence? In addition, just as when I know that something is, it is necessarily the case that that same thing be; similarly, when I know that something will be, it is necessarily the case that that same thing will be. And so it happens that the outcome of a foreseen event cannot be avoided. A last point. If someone were to think that something is otherwise than it is actually constituted—not only is that not knowledge, but it is a deceitful opinion, far removed from the truth of knowledge.

Therefore, if something is going to happen in such a way that its outcome is not a definite and necessary thing, how could it happen that its occurrence be foreknown? For true knowledge admits no admixture of falsity; in just the same way, whatever has been thought by knowledge cannot be in any way other than it was thought to be. Furthermore, the reason why such knowledge has no share of falsehood is that each action is necessarily constituted in just the same way that knowledge grasps that it is constituted. Well then! Tell me, what is the way in which God has foreknowledge that these indefinite things will occur? I mean, if he determines that things will inevitably happen that could possibly not happen, then he is mistaken, and it is wicked not only to hold this opinion but to speak it out loud as well. On the other hand, if it is his judgment that these things will be just as they are, so that he recognizes that they can just as well happen as not happen—what sort of foreknowledge is this, which grasps nothing as definite, nothing as stable? Or in what way is this different from that absurd prophecy of Tiresias in Horace?

Whatever I say either will be or won't be.

And really, how would divine Providence be superior to mere opinion if, just as mortals do, it makes judgments about indefinite things that have indefinite outcomes?

And yet, if within that source of all things, that most definite source, there can be nothing that is indefinite, then there is a definite outcome of those things which he, by his unshakable foreknowledge, knows will be. So for this reason there is no freedom for human resolutions or for human actions: The divine mind that sees all things in advance without the miscalculation of falsity binds them and ties them all together for one and only one result. And as soon as this is accepted, it is clear what a great downfall of human affairs follows as its logical consequence. I mean, rewards and punishments are set before good and evil people in vain—no free and voluntary motion of their minds has deserved them. That the righteous are rewarded and the unrighteous are punished, as is now judged to be perfectly just—this will seem to be the most perfectly unjust thing of all, for it would not be an individual will that directs them, but the definite necessity of the future that forces them, to the one or the other. Consequently, both virtues and vices would be nothing; in their place would be a jumbled and indiscriminate confusion of all merits. Nothing more wicked can be imagined than this: Since that entire order of things is led out from Providence and since there is nothing permitted to mortal resolution, what happens is that our vices too are to be referred to the creator of all good things.

Therefore: There is no reason to hope for something or to pray for deliverance; for what would a person hope for or even pray to be delivered from if an unbendable sequence weaves together all the things that could be chosen? Therefore: That one and only avenue of exchange between human beings and God will be taken away, the avenue of hope and prayer for deliverance; provided, of course, that for the price of our rightful humility we deserve the return of divine grace, which is beyond price. This is the only way by which human beings seem to be able to speak with God—by the act of supplication—and to be joined to that inapproachable light even before they succeed in attaining it. Once the necessity of future events is accepted, if these hopes and prayers are then believed to have no force, what will there be by which we can be woven together with and cling to that most high ruler of all things? And so it is, just as you were singing a little while ago, that it will necessarily be the case that the human race, separated and "cut off from its source, will burst at the seams." . . .

Prose 4

Then she said: This is an old complaint about Providence. It was a topic passionately discussed by Cicero[1] when he broke divination into its constituent parts; you pursued it yourself over quite a long period of time and at great length. However, up until now it has been in no way adequately dealt with by any one of you in a painstaking and rigorous way. Here is the cause of all this darkness: The motion of human rational argument cannot set itself next to the simplicity of divine foreknowledge. If this could in any way be imagined, there would then be absolutely no doubt about it remaining. I shall try at the end to make this clear to you and explain it to you, provided that I can first get the heft of the things that have got you upset. I want to know why you hold that one line of reasoning offered by those who would solve this problem is less than productive—the line of reasoning that holds that freedom of independent judgment is not obstructed by foreknowledge, because it thinks that foreknowledge is not a cause of necessity for future events. You aren't drawing your argument about the necessity of future things from any other source, are you, than that things that are foreseen cannot *not* happen? Therefore: If foreknowledge places no necessity upon future events—a thing that you yourself admitted a little while ago—what reason is there for the voluntary outcomes of events to be forced toward a definite result?

And further, just for the sake of argument, so you can see what the logical consequence is, let us claim that there is no foreknowledge. It isn't the case then, is it, as far as this situation is concerned, that such things as come from independent judgment are forced toward necessity?

Hardly.

Next, let us claim that there is foreknowledge, but that it binds no necessity on events; there will remain unchanged, I think, that same freedom of the will, whole and absolute. But foreknowledge, you will say, even if there is no necessity of their resulting for future things, is nevertheless a sign that such things are necessarily going to occur. And so it is in this way that it would be agreed that the outcomes of future things are necessary, even if there is no cognition beforehand; the point being that every sign merely *shows* what is, but is not *productive* of what it points to. For this reason, what would have to be shown first is that there is no contingency except through necessity, so that it may be manifest that foreknowledge is a sign of this necessity. Otherwise, if there were no such necessity, it could not be a sign of an event that does not exist. However, it is already agreed that a proof that rests upon an unshakable line of argument must be drawn neither from signs nor from arguments that are sought in what is external to it, but rather from causes that are appropriate and necessary. But how can it happen that those things do not come to pass that are foreseen as things that are going to be? As if we were to believe that what Providence foreknows as things that are going to be are not going to happen! As if we were to believe this instead, that, granted that they do happen, they nevertheless had by their own nature no necessity that they happen!

Now this objection you will be able to weigh easily in the balance, from this consideration. There are in fact many things that we gaze upon while they are happening, things subject to our eyes. For example, the things that charioteers are seen to do as they guide

1. [The reference is to Marcus Tullius Cicero (106–43 B.C.), the Roman statesman and philosopher.—S.M.C.]

their teams and give them rein, and all the other things of this sort. Surely it is not the case here, is it, that any necessity compels any of these things to happen as they do?

Hardly; if all these were forced actions that were set into motion, the effect of the driver's skill would be all in vain.

Therefore: The things that lack the necessity of their existence while they are happening are things which, before they happen, are going to exist without necessity. For this reason there are certain things that will happen whose outcome is divorced from all necessity. In fact, I think that no one would say this, that things that are now happening were not about to result before they happened? Consequently, these things, even if there were cognition beforehand, have free outcomes. For knowledge of present events brings in with it no necessity to the things that are happening; and in just the same way foreknowledge of future events brings in no necessity to the things that are going to occur.

But, you say, this is itself a source of doubt: *Can* there be any foreknowledge of those events that do not have necessary outcomes? They do indeed seem to be discordant: you think that if things are foreseen then necessity is the logical consequence; you think that there can in no way be foreknowledge if necessity is absent; you think that nothing can be grasped by knowledge unless it is a definite thing. For if things that are characterized by indefinite outcomes are foreseen as if they were definite, that would be the darkness of opinion and not the truth of knowledge; for you believe that it is opposed to the infallibility of knowledge to think of a thing in some way other than it is constituted. The cause of this miscalculation is that it judges that all the things that a person knows are perceived only in accordance with the force and nature of the things which are known themselves. But it is completely the opposite. Everything that is perceived is grasped not according to its own force but rather according to the capability of those who perceive it.

To make this clear with a brief example: Vision and touch, each in its distinct way, recognize the same three-dimensionality of a body. The former, at a distance, remaining itself unmoved, gazes upon the whole thing all at once by casting its rays; the latter, adhering to its curvature and joined to it, set in motion on all sides of the surface itself, grasps its three-dimensionality part by part. Similarly, sense perception, imagination, reason, and understanding, each in its distinct way, view the same human being. For sense perception judges the shape as it has been constituted in its subject material, while imagination judges the shape alone, without its material; reason transcends this as well and from its universal point of view weighs in the balance that very appearance that is present in all individuals. And the eye of understanding exists as something higher yet; for it has passed beyond what is encompassed by universality and views the one simple form itself in the pure vision of the mind.

In all of this, here is the one point that must be considered in particular: Namely, that the higher power of comprehension embraces the lower, but in no way does the lower rise to the level of the higher. For sense perception has no power beyond what is material; imagination does not view universal appearances; reason does not grasp the simple form. Understanding, however, looking down as it were from on high, grasps the form and then judges separately the things that are beneath it, all of them; but it does so in the way in which it comprehends the form itself, which could not be known to any of the other powers. For it perceives reason's universal and imagination's shape and sense perception's material, but not by using reason or imagination or the senses but by the characteristic single stroke of mind, formally, if I may use the word, seeing all things in advance. And reason similarly: When it views something universal, it comprehends the things that can be perceived by imagination and the senses, but not by using imagination or the senses. This is reason, and it defines the universal of its own conception this way: A human being is a two-legged, rational animal. And although this is a universal knowledge, there is no one who is unaware that its object is a thing of the imagination and a thing of sense perception as well, yet a thing that this knowledge looks at not by imagination and not by sense but in its state of rational conception.

And imagination similarly: Even if it has taken from the senses the starting point of seeing and forming shapes, nevertheless it is in the absence of sense that it casts its gaze over each and every thing of the senses by a rationale of judgment that is not of the senses but of the imagination. So do you see how in perception all things use their own capability rather than the capability of the things that are perceived? And not without cause: For since every judgment exists as an act of the one who judges, it is necessarily the case that all who judge bring their work to completion by their own true powers, and not by a power outside of themselves.

Prose 5

When physical objects are perceived by the senses—even though their qualities, presented from the outside, exert an influence on the instruments of sense perception, even though the strength of the active mind is preceded by the passivity of the body, which calls forth an act of the mind within the body and arouses the forms that have hitherto been dormant within—when, as I was saying, physical objects are perceived by the senses, if it is the case that the mind is not in passivity impressed by a sign, but by its own strength judges the passivity to which the body is subject, well then! To an even greater extent do the things that are divorced from all of the external influences exerted on bodies set the action of their own minds free in their acts of judgment, not pursuing the things presented to them externally. And so it is, according to this line of reasoning, that multiple modes of perception have been allotted to the various substances, different among themselves. For sense and sense alone, deprived of all other modes of perception, has been allotted to animate creatures without self-motion (to the shellfish of the sea, for example, and to other such things as cling to rocks); while imagination is allotted to beasts with self-motion, who seem to have within them already some desire for what must be avoided and what must be chosen. On the other hand, reason is the property of the human race only, just as understanding alone is the property of the divine; and so it is that that particular way of knowing excels all the others which, by its own nature, perceives not only what is properly subject to it, but the subjects of all the other ways of knowing as well.

Well then! What if sense and imagination were to speak against rational argument, and say that the universal which reason thinks it gazes upon is nothing at all? After all, they could say that what can be perceived by sense or imagination cannot be universal; consequently, either reason's judgment is true and nothing that can be perceived by sense truly exists; or, since sense and imagination are well aware that there are many things subject to them, reason's conception is a thing devoid of meaning, since reason contemplates a particular thing, one that can be perceived by sense, as though it were some sort of universal. Now let reason answer these arguments and counter them; let it say that it does indeed look upon what can be perceived by sense and imagination, but in accordance with the reason which is directed toward the universal, while they cannot aim at the mode of perception that is directed toward the universal; let it argue that the knowledge possessed by sense and imagination cannot go beyond the bounds of the shapes of physical bodies, whereas one should rather put one's trust in a stronger and more powerful judgment for the perception of what truly exists. So if there were to be a dispute along these lines, oughtn't we, who have within us the force of reason as well as of imagination and sense perception, give our approval rather to the case presented by reason, you and I?

The situation is similar with human reason: It does not think that divine intelligence gazes upon future things in any other way than it perceives them itself. For your discourse is as follows: If there are some things that are not seen to have definite and necessary outcomes, then there can be no definite foreknowledge of them as outcomes. Consequently, there is *no* foreknowledge of these events; were we to believe that there is foreknowledge in these things as well, there will then be nothing that does not come to pass through necessity. And yet, consequently, were we able to possess the judgment of the divine mind in just the same way as we are partakers of reason, then we would think it most just that human reason surrender to the divine mind in just the same way that we judged that imagination and sense perception ought to yield to reason. And for this reason let us raise ourselves up, if we can, into the head of that highest intelligence, for it is in that place that reason will see what it cannot gaze upon within itself, and that is this: in just what way a fixed and definite foreknowledge can still see even those things that do not have definite outcomes, and how this is not mere conjecture but the simplicity of the highest knowledge instead, knowledge bounded by no limits.

Prose 6

Therefore: Since, as has been shown just a little while ago, everything that is known is perceived not in accordance with its own nature but rather the nature of those who grasp it—let us now look closely, as far as is allowed, at what is the condition of the divine substance, so that we may be able to recognize what its knowledge is as well. Therefore: It is the common judgment of all who live in accordance with reason that God is eternal. Therefore, let us look at what eternity is, for this will make obvious to us the divine nature and the divine knowledge at one and the same time.

Therefore: Eternity is a possession of life, a possession simultaneously entire and perfect, which has no end. This becomes clear in a more transparent way from a comparison with temporal things. For whatever exists in time proceeds as a present thing from the things that have happened into the things that are going to happen, and there is nothing that has been established in time that is able to embrace the entire space of its own life at one and the same time. Instead, it does not yet gain what is tomorrow's, but has already lost what is yesterday's; furthermore, within the life that is today's, none of you lives to any greater extent than in that swift and passing moment. Therefore: That which endures the condition of time—even granted that, as Aristotle has judged to be true about the world, it did not begin to exist at any time, nor would it cease to exist, and its life would be extended to the infinity of time—it is, for all that, not the sort of thing that can rightly be believed to be eternal. For it does not grasp and embrace the entire extent of its life, even though it is infinite, simultaneously; rather, it does not yet have the future things, and the things that have been completed it has no longer. Therefore: That which grasps and possesses the entire fullness of a life that has no end at one and the same time (nothing that is to come being absent to it, nothing of what has passed having flowed away from it) is rightly held to be eternal. Further, it is necessary both that, as master of itself, it always be present to itself as a present thing and that it always have the infinity of swift time as present.

There are certain people who think, when they hear that it was Plato's opinion that the world neither had a beginning in time nor would it ever disappear, that in this way the created world is coeternal with its creator. But from these considerations, they do not think correctly. For it is one thing to be drawn out through a life that has no end (this is what Plato assigned to the world), and quite another to have embraced the entire presentness of a life which has no end at one and the same time (this is what perfectly clearly is appropriate to the divine mind). Further, God ought not to be seen as more ancient and glorious than created things by the measurement of time, but rather by the distinctive character of his own simple nature. For that infinite motion of temporal things imitates this present-moment condition of motionless life. Since the former cannot represent or equal the latter, it falls away from motionlessness into motion and devolves from the simplicity of the present into the infinite quantity of what is to come and what has passed; and since it is not able to possess the entire fullness of its own life at one and the same time, then, for this very reason, because it never ceases to be (in some way or other) that which it cannot satisfy or express, it seems to rival it to some small degree by binding itself to any sort of presentness it can of this minuscule and swiftly-passing moment. Because this presentness carries within itself a sort of image of that other, stable present, it provides *this* to whatever things it happens to come in contact with: that is, that they are seen to be. But, because such a thing could not be stable, it started rapidly down the infinite road of time and it is in this way that it happened that it protracted its life through motion, the life whose fullness it was not able to embrace by remaining unchanged. Consequently, if we want to impose on things names that are worthy of them, let us follow Plato and say that God is eternal, but that the world is perpetual.

Therefore: Since every judgment grasps the things that are subject to it in accordance with its own nature, and since God has an ever-eternal and ever-present-moment condition, his knowledge as well has passed beyond all the motion of time and is stable in the simplicity of its own present; it embraces the infinite reaches of what has passed and what is to come and, in its own simple perception, it looks at all things as if they are being carried out *now*. And so, should you want to ponder the foresight by which God distinguishes all things, you will more accurately determine that it is not a foreknowledge as of something that is to come, but rather a knowledge of a never-failing present. From these considerations, it is not named Previdence (foresight) but Providence (looking out), because, established far from the bottommost things, it looks out at all things as if from some lofty head of things. Well then! Do you demand that the things that the light of the divine eye passes over come about as necessary things, when not even human beings cause the things that they see to be as necessary things? Why would you? Surely your gaze does not add any necessity to those things that you perceive as present? Hardly. And yet, if there is any worthy comparison between the divine present and the human present—just as you humans see certain individual things in this time-bounded present of yours, he perceives all things in his own eternal present. And it is for this reason that this divine foreknowledge does not change the nature and the distinctive character of things; it looks at such things as are present to it just as they will eventually come to pass in time as future things. Nor does it confuse its judgments; rather, with the single gaze of its own mind, it distinguishes both what will happen of necessity as well as what will happen, but not of necessity. Similarly, when you mortals see in the same way both a man walking upon the earth and the sun rising in the heavens, although each of these two has been observed at one and the same time, nevertheless you tell them apart and judge that the former is voluntary and the latter is necessary. Therefore: The divine gaze, by discerning all things in this way, does not at all confuse the quality of the things which are, to be sure, present to it but which, in respect of their condition in time, are going to come to pass. And so it happens that this is not mere opinion but rather perception supported by truth, that the same thing which it knows will arise it does not fail to know lacks the necessity of coming into being.

Now if you should say at this point that what God sees will happen cannot *not* happen, and that what cannot not happen is contingent by necessity, and if you bind me tight to this word "necessity," then I will admit that it is indeed a thing of the most steadfast truth, but one that scarcely anyone but a contemplator of the divine has approached. For I shall answer that the same future event seems to be necessary when it is referred to divine knowledge, but completely and absolutely free when weighed in the balance of its own nature. There are in fact two necessities: One is simple (for example, the fact that all human beings are mortal); the other is conditional (as when it is necessary that a man is walking if you know that he *is* walking). For whatever anyone knows cannot exist in any other way than it is known to exist, but this condition does not at all draw along with it that other, simple necessity. For it is not the thing's own nature that makes this necessity but only the addition of condition; for no necessity compels a man to move forward who is taking a step voluntarily, even though it is a necessary thing that he move forward at the point at which he takes a step. Therefore, it is in just this way that it is necessary that a thing exists if Providence sees it as a present thing, even if it has no necessity in its nature. And yet, God views as present those future things that come to pass from the freedom of independent judgment. Therefore: These things, when referred to the divine gaze, come about as necessary things, because of the condition of divine knowledge; but when looked at in and of themselves they do not cease from the absolute freedom of their natures. Therefore: Beyond any doubt, all the things that God foreknows as future things will come into being, but certain of these things proceed from free and independent judgment; although they do happen, nevertheless they do not lose by their existing their own proper nature, by virtue of which they could have *not* happened before they did come into being.

Well then! Does it make a difference that they are not necessary when, because of the condition of divine knowledge, what is in all respects a facsimile of necessity will happen? Yes it does, and in this way. The examples that I proposed just a little while ago, the rising sun and the man taking a step: while they happen, they cannot *not* happen; nevertheless, it was necessary even before it happened that one of them come into existence, but the other one not at all. So too the things that God possesses as present: They will beyond any doubt exist, but one descends from the necessity of things while another descends from the power of those who do it. Therefore, it is not at all improper that we said that these things are necessary if they are referred to divine knowledge, but divorced from the meshes of necessity if they are looked at in and of themselves. Similarly, everything that is obvious to the senses is universal if you refer it to reason, but particularly if you look to the things themselves.

But, you will say, if it has been placed within my power to change my intention, then I shall gut Providence, since, perhaps, I shall have changed the things that it has foreknowledge of. I shall answer that yes, you can alter the course of your intention; however, since the present truth of Providence observes that you can do so and whether you will do so and to what end you will redirect it, you cannot avoid divine foreknowledge, just as you cannot escape the gaze of its present eye even though you redirect yourself by your free will toward actions of different sorts. Well then! you will say; will divine knowledge be changed by my arrangements, with the result that, when I wish for now this thing, now that, divine knowledge seems to switch back and forth the vicissitudes of its foreknowing? Hardly. For the divine gaze runs on ahead of every thing that will come to pass and twists it back and calls it back to the present of its own proper perception; it does not, as you reckon it, switch back and forth in an alternation of a foreknowledge of now this thing, now another; rather, remaining stable, it anticipates and embraces your changes in its single stroke. It is not from the coming to pass of future events but rather from his own proper simplicity that God has been allotted this present grasping and seeing of all things. And from this also comes an answer to the problem you had posed just a little while ago, that it is an unworthy thing that our future actions be said to provide a cause for the foreknowledge of God. For such is the force of this knowledge, embracing all things by its present-moment knowledge, that it has itself established the status of all things, while it owes nothing to things that are subsequent to it.

And since this is the way things are, this remains unchanged for mortals: an inviolate freedom of independent judgment. Laws are not unjust, and they assign rewards and punishments to wills that are free of every necessity. God also remains unchanged, looking down from on high with foreknowledge of all things; the ever-present eternity of his vision keeps pace with the future qualities of our actions, dispensing rewards to good people and punishments to the bad. Nor are hopes and prayers placed in God in vain; they cannot help but be effective, provided that they are blameless. Therefore, all of you: Avoid vices, cherish virtues; raise up your minds to blameless hopes; extend your humble prayers into the lofty heights. Unless you want to hide the truth, there *is* a great necessity imposed upon you—the necessity of righteousness, since you act before the eyes of a judge who beholds all things.

Anselm

Although he is generally referred to as St. Anselm of Canterbury, Anselm (1033–1109) was not an Englishman by birth or education. He was born in the village of Aosta, in the Piedmont area of what is now Italy. Little is known of his early years, but in 1060 he entered the Benedictine monastery at Bec, in Normandy. Then under the mastership of Lanfranc, Bec had a reputation as an excellent school. When Lanfranc left Bec in 1063, his position fell to the evidently precocious Anselm, who eventually became abbot of the monastery. In the meantime Lanfranc followed William the Conqueror to England in 1066, serving as Archbishop of Canterbury until his death in 1089. William's son, William II, allowed the see of Canterbury to remain vacant for four years, after which time Anselm was made archbishop. He may have been chosen because it was thought that given his relatively advanced age and political inexperience, he would be not a bishop but a pawn in the hands of the king and the other bishops. He turned out to be anything but manipulatable.

Most of the disputes into which Anselm entered revolved around the conflicting claims of secular and spiritual authorities in a highly feudalized society; for example, whether a bishop was a feudal servant of the king, and whether the king had the right to invest bishops with the insignia of their office. Anselm's relations with William II and with William's successor, Henry I, were so fitful that he managed to get himself exiled during the reigns of both kings.

Anselm's philosophical and theological talents are so impressive that he has been called by some the "Father of Scholasticism." His careful, painstaking methods and his insistence on the importance of reason to the life of faith anticipate the works of the great thirteenth-century thinkers' teaching in the cathedral schools. Anselm did not write a magnum opus; his writings consist of several short works, almost all devoted to the philosophical investigation of a particular theological topic. Many of the titles reveal his dominant concerns and his willingness to probe a fairly narrow issue in depth: "On Truth," "On the Fall of the Devil," "Epistle Concerning the Incarnation of the Word," "Why God Became Man," "On the Virgin Conception and on Original Sin," "On the Harmony of Foreknowledge, Predestination, and the Grace of God with Free Will."

Although Anselm's writings may seem piecemeal, the vision that inspired and suffuses them is global. He was above all a believing Christian, but one who believed that mere belief was not enough. The task imposed by belief was to show that one's beliefs were rational. For Anselm there could be no genuine conflict between Christian faith and the findings of reason. Not to support the claims of Christian faith, however, by the use of cogent arguments would be a kind of intellectual laziness. His confidence in the power of reason—not only to show that Christian belief is consistent but to prove that the major tenets of Christianity are *true*—may strike us as absurdly extreme; even by the thirteenth century we find more cautious enunciations of the harmony of faith and reason.

Anselm's *Proslogion*, reprinted in this volume, is his most famous work. In rapid order Anselm argues for the existence of God and His traditionally ascribed divine attributes, such as omnipotence, justice, mercy, simplicity, and timelessness. Anselm concludes by attempting to sketch how great the joy of the blessed will be.

Anselm's attempt to prove the existence of God has attracted the most attention. The argument, now called the ontological argument (a title bestowed on it by Immanuel Kant), is contained in Chapter 2 (some would include Chapter 3) of the *Proslogion*. The ontological argument has been scorned by some philosophers as the most naive of verbal conjuring tricks, and praised by others as sound. Aquinas, Hume, and Kant rejected it, while Descartes, Spinoza, and Leibniz accepted it.

One can find contemporary philosophers on both sides. It is hard to think of any philosophical argument that has excited and agitated philosophers more than this one. For one thing, its sheer audacity is breathtaking. Anselm claims that the existence of God can be demonstrated simply by following out the logical implications of a certain characterization of God. Thus, if Anselm's argument works, atheism does not just happen to be false; it is a logically impossible position. A second source of the argument's philosophical fascination is that in order either to defend or criticize it intelligently, one is forced to probe some controversial philosophical issues. As a contemporary philosopher puts it, "Many of the most knotty and difficult problems in philosophy meet in this argument." For example, how is it possible to deny the existence of something without presupposing the existence of the very thing whose existence is denied? Is existence a property of things? Are there genuinely different modes of existence, and if so, can the same thing exist in several modes?—and so on.

Recorded criticism of the ontological argument began almost before Anselm's quill had dried, with the monk Gaunilo's attack "on behalf of the fool." (Virtually nothing is known of Gaunilo's life.) The most tantalizing point made by Gaunilo is the claim that the same argument Anselm uses to demonstrate the existence of a perfect being would, if sound, also demonstrate the existence of a perfect island. To ask whether Gaunilo's criticism is telling, and whether Anselm's reply to Gaunilo is adequate, is to embark on yet another philosophical inquiry.

• • •

For a brilliant and judicious account of Anselm's life and times, consult R. W. Southern, *Saint Anselm: A Portrait in a Landscape* (Cambridge: Cambridge University Press, 1990). Jasper Hopkins, *A Companion to the Study of St. Anselm* (Minneapolis: University of Minnesota Press, 1972) provides a knowledgeable discussion of virtually all of Anselm's writings, with an informative emphasis on the theological issues with which Anselm was involved. Important essays on all aspects of Anselm's philosophy are contained in Brian Davies and Brian Leftow, eds., *The Cambridge Companion to Anselm* (Cambridge: Cambridge University Press, 2004). For a philosophically sensitive overview of Anselm's writings, see Sandra Visser and Thomas Williams, *Anselm* (Oxford: Oxford University Press, 2009).

The literature on the ontological argument is vast. Two useful anthologies are Alvin Plantinga, ed., *The Ontological Argument* (Garden City, N.J.: Doubleday, 1965) and John H. Hick and Arthur C. McGill, eds., *The Many-Faced Argument* (New York: Macmillan, 1967). The former includes many of the historically important reactions to the argument, along with contemporary assessments. The latter emphasizes the diversity of approaches that have been taken to Anselm's argument.

William E. Mann

Proslogion

Prologue

After I had published, at the urging of some of my brethren, a short work as a pattern for meditation on the rational basis of faith, adopting the role of someone who, by reasoning silently to himself, investigates things he does not know, I began to wonder, when I considered that it is constructed out of a chaining together of many arguments, whether it might be possible to find a single argument that needed nothing but itself alone for proof, that would by itself be enough to show that God really exists; that he is the supreme good, who depends on nothing else, but on whom all things depend for their being and for their well-being; and whatever we believe about the divine nature. And so I often turned my thoughts to this with great diligence. Sometimes I thought I could already grasp what I was looking for, and sometimes it escaped my mind completely. Finally, I gave up hope. I decided to stop looking for something that was impossible to find. But when I tried to stifle that thought altogether, lest by occupying my mind with useless speculation it should keep me from things I could actually accomplish, it began to hound me more and more, although I resisted and fought against it. Then one day, when my violent struggle against its hounding had worn me down, the thing I had despaired of finding presented itself in the very clash of my thoughts, so that I eagerly embraced the thought I had been taking such pains to drive away.

Therefore, thinking that what I had rejoiced to discover would please a reader if it were written down, I wrote about it and about a number of other things in the work that follows, adopting the role of someone trying to raise his mind to the contemplation of God and seeking to understand what he believes. Since I had judged that neither this work nor the one I mentioned earlier deserved to be called a book, or to bear the name of an author, and yet I did not think they ought to be sent out without so much as a title by which they might induce someone who came across them to read them, I gave each a title. The first I called "A pattern for meditation on the rational basis of faith"; the second I called "Faith seeking understanding." But since both works had been transcribed under these titles by several readers, I was encouraged by a number of people (especially by Hugo, the Most Reverend Archbishop of Lyons, Apostolic Legate to France, who commanded me by his apostolic authority) to put my own name on these works. And so, in order to do so more suitably, I named the first *Monologion*, which means a speech made to oneself, and the second *Proslogion*, which means a speech made to another.

Reprinted from Anselm, *Monologion and Proslogion*, translated by Thomas Williams (Indianapolis: Hackett Publishing Company, 1996), by permission of the publisher.

Chapter 1

A rousing of the mind to the contemplation of God

Come now, insignificant mortal. Leave behind your concerns for a little while, and retreat for a short time from your restless thoughts. Cast off your burdens and cares; set aside your labor and toil. Just for a little while make room for God and rest a while in him. "Enter into the chamber" (Matthew 6:6) of your mind, shut out everything but God and whatever helps you to seek him, and seek him "behind closed doors" (Matthew 6:6). Speak now, my whole heart: say to God, "I seek your face; your face, Lord, do I seek" (Psalm 27:8).

Come now, O Lord my God. Teach my heart where and how to seek you, where and how to find you. Lord, if you are not here, where shall I seek you, since you are absent? But if you are everywhere, why do I not see you, since you are present? Truly "you dwell in inaccessible light" (1 Timothy 6:16). And where is this "inaccessible light"? How am I to approach an inaccessible light? Who will lead to it, so that I can see you in it? And by what signs am I to seek you? Under what aspect? I have never seen you,

O Lord my God; I do not know your face. What shall he do, O Lord Most High? What shall he do, this distant exile from you? What shall your servant do, deeply troubled by his love for you and "banished far from your face"? (Psalm 51:11) He longs to see you, but your face is too far away from him. He desires to enter your presence, but your dwelling is inaccessible. He wants to find you, but he does not know where you are. He aspires to seek you, but he does not know your face. Lord, you are my God, and you are my Lord, but I have never seen you. You have made me and remade me, you have given me every good thing that is mine, and still I do not know you. I was created so that I might see you, but I have not yet done what I was created to do.

How wretched human beings are! They have lost the very thing for which they were created. Hard and terrible was their fall! Alas! Think what they have lost and what they have found; think what they left behind and what they kept. They have lost the happiness for which they were created and found an unhappiness for which they were not created. They left behind the only source of happiness and kept what brings nothing but misery. Once "human beings ate the bread of angels" (Psalm 78:25), for which they now hunger; now they "eat the bread of sorrows" (Psalm 127:2), which once they did not know. Alas for the common lamentation of human beings, the universal outcry of the children of Adam! He was satisfied to the full; we sigh with hunger. He had everything he needed; we go begging. He happily possessed those things and abandoned them in misery; we unhappily do without them and miserably desire them, but alas, we remain empty-handed. Why did he not preserve for us, as he could easily have done, what we so woefully lack? Why did he thus shut us out from the light and cover us with darkness? Why did he take away our life and inflict death upon us? What wretches we are! Think whence we have been cast out, whither we have been driven; thrown down from so great a height, and buried so deep. From our homeland into exile; from the vision of God into our blindness; from the joy of immortality into the bitterness and terror of death. What a wretched change! From such great good into such great evil! O woeful loss, woeful sorrow, all is woeful!

Alas, wretched man that I am, one of the wretched children of Eve, far from the presence of God. What have I undertaken, and what have I accomplished? Where was I heading, and where have I come to? What was I reaching toward, and what do I long for? "I have sought the good" (Psalm 122:9), and "behold, confusion!" (Jeremiah 14:19). I was heading for God but stumbled over myself. I sought rest in my solitude but "found trials and sorrows" (Psalm 116:3) deep within. I wanted to laugh as my mind rejoiced, but I am forced to "cry out as my heart weeps" (Psalm 38:8). Joy was hoped for, but look where the sighs are closing in.

"How long, O Lord?" (Psalm 6:3) "How long, O Lord, will you forget us? How long will you turn your face from us?" (Psalm 13:1) When will you look favorably upon us and hear us? When will you "enlighten our eyes" (Psalm 13:3) and "show us your face"? (Psalm 80:3, 7, 19) When will you give yourself to us again? Look favorably upon us, O Lord; hear us, enlighten us, show yourself to us. Give yourself to us again, that it might go well for us; for without you it goes so badly for us. Take pity upon our toils and strivings after you, for without you we can do nothing. You call us; come to our aid. I beseech you, Lord: let me not sigh in despair, but let me breathe hopefully again. I beseech you, Lord: my heart is made bitter with its desolation; sweeten it with your consolation. I beseech you, Lord: in my hunger I began to seek you; let me not depart from you empty. I have come to you starving; let me not leave unsatisfied. I have come as a beggar to one who is rich, as a pitiful wretch to one who has pity; let me not go back penniless and despised. If indeed "I sigh before I eat" (Job 3:24), grant that I might eat after I sigh. Lord, I am bent double; I can only look down. Raise me up so that I can turn my gaze upwards. "My sins are heaped up over my head" and entangle me; "like a heavy burden" they weigh me down (Psalm 38:4). Extricate me; lift my burdens, "lest like a pit they swallow me up" (Psalm 69:15). Let me look up at your light, whether from afar or from the depths. Teach me how to seek you, and show yourself to me when I seek. For I cannot seek you unless you teach me how, and I cannot find you unless you show yourself to me. Let me seek you in desiring you; let me desire you in seeking you. Let me find you in loving you; let me love you in finding you.

I acknowledge, Lord, and I thank you, that you have created in me this image of you so that I may remember you, think of you, and love you. Yet this image is so eroded by my vices, so clouded by the smoke of my sins, that it cannot do what it was created to do unless you renew and refashion it. I am not trying to scale your heights, Lord; my understanding is in no way equal to that. But I do long to understand your truth in some way, your truth which my heart believes and loves. For I do not seek to understand in order to believe; I believe in order to understand. For I also believe that "Unless I believe, I shall not understand."[1]

Chapter 2

That God truly exists

Therefore, Lord, you who grant understanding to faith, grant that, insofar as you know it is useful for me, I may understand that you exist as we believe you exist, and that you are what we believe you to be. Now we believe that you are something than which nothing greater can be thought. So can it be that no such being exists, since "The fool has said in his heart, 'There is no God' "? (Psalm 14:1; 53:1) But when this same fool hears me say "something than which nothing greater can be thought," he surely understands what he hears; and what he understands exists in his understanding,[2] even if he does not understand that it exists [in reality]. For it is one thing for an object to exist in the understanding and quite another to understand that the object exists [in reality]. When a painter, for example, thinks out in advance what he is going to paint, he has it in his understanding, but he does not yet understand that it exists, since he has not yet painted it. But once he has painted it, he both has it in his understanding and understands that it exists because he has now painted it. So even the fool must admit that something than which nothing greater can be thought exists at least in his understanding, since he understands this when he hears it, and whatever is understood exists in the understanding. And surely that than which a greater cannot be thought cannot exist only in the understanding. For if it exists only in the understanding, it can be thought to exist in reality as well, which is greater. So if that than which a greater cannot be thought exists only in the understanding, then that than which a greater *cannot* be thought is that than which a greater *can* be thought. But that is clearly impossible. Therefore, there is no doubt that something than which a greater cannot be thought exists both in the understanding and in reality.

Chapter 3

That he cannot be thought not to exist

This [being] exists so truly that it cannot be thought not to exist. For it is possible to think that something exists that cannot be thought not to exist, and such a being is greater than one that can be thought not to exist. Therefore, if that than which a greater cannot be thought can be thought not to exist, then that than which a greater cannot be thought is *not* that than which a greater cannot be thought; and this is a contradiction. So that than which a greater cannot be thought exists so truly that it cannot be thought not to exist.

And this is you, O Lord our God. You exist so truly, O Lord my God, that you cannot be thought not to exist. And rightly so, for if some mind could think something better than you, a creature would rise above the Creator and sit in judgment upon him, which is completely absurd. Indeed, everything that exists, except for you alone, can be thought not to exist. So you alone among all things have existence most truly, and therefore most greatly. Whatever else exists has existence less truly, and therefore less greatly. So then why did "the fool say in his heart, 'There is no God,' " when it is so evident to the rational mind that you of all beings exist most greatly? Why indeed, except because he is stupid and a fool?

Chapter 4

How the fool said in his heart what cannot be thought

But how has he said in his heart what he could not think? Or how could he not think what he said in his heart, since to say in one's heart is the same as

1. [Anselm is here quoting St. Augustine, who was fond of using this verse (which is an older translation of Isaiah 7:9) in explaining his views on the relationship between faith and reason.—T.W.]

2. [The word here translated "understanding" is "*intellectus*." The text would perhaps read better if I translated it as "intellect," but this would obscure the fact that it is from the same root as the verb "*intelligere*," "to understand." Some of what Anselm says makes a bit more sense if this fact is constantly borne in mind.]

to think? But if he really—or rather, *since* he really—thought this, because he said it in his heart, and did not say it in his heart, because he could not think it, there must be more than one way in which something is 'said in one's heart' or 'thought.' In one sense of the word, to think a thing is to think the word that signifies that thing. But in another sense, it is to understand what exactly the thing is. God can be thought not to exist in the first sense, but not at all in the second sense. No one who understands what God is can think that God does not exist, although he may say these words in his heart with no signification at all, or with some peculiar signification. For God is that than which a greater cannot be thought. Whoever understands this properly, understands that this being exists in such a way that he cannot, even in thought, fail to exist. So whoever understands that God exists in this way cannot think that he does not exist.

Thanks be to you, my good Lord, thanks be to you. For what I once believed through your grace, I now understand through your illumination, so that even if I did not want to *believe* that you exist, I could not fail to *understand* that you exist.

Chapter 5

That God is whatever it is better to be than not to be; and that he alone exists through himself, and makes all other things from nothing

Then what are you, Lord God, than whom nothing greater can be thought? What are you, if not the greatest of all beings, who alone exists through himself and made all other things from nothing? For whatever is not this is less than the greatest that can be thought, but this cannot be thought of you. What good is missing from the highest good, through which every good thing exists? And so you are just, truthful, happy, and whatever it is better to be than not to be. For it is better to be just than unjust, and better to be happy than unhappy.

Chapter 6

How God can perceive even though he is not a body

Now it is better to be percipient, omnipotent, merciful, and impassible than not. But how can you perceive if you are not a body? How can you be omnipotent if you cannot do everything? How can you be both merciful and impassible? If only corporeal things can perceive, because the senses exist in a body and are directed towards bodies, then how can you perceive? For you are not a body but the highest spirit, which is better than any body.

But if to perceive is just to know, or is aimed at knowledge—for whoever perceives knows according to the appropriate sense, as, for example, we know colors through sight and flavors through taste—then it is not inappropriate to say that whatever in some way knows also in some way perceives. Therefore, Lord, although you are not a body, you are indeed supremely percipient in the sense that you supremely know all things, not in the sense that an animal knows things through its bodily senses.

Chapter 7

In what sense God is omnipotent even though there are many things he cannot do

But how are you omnipotent if you cannot do everything?[3] And how can you do everything if you cannot be corrupted, or lie, or cause what is true to be false (as, for example, to cause what has been done not to have been done), or many other such things?

Or is the ability to do these things not power but weakness? For someone who can do these things can do what is not beneficial to himself and what he ought not to do. And the more he can do these things, the more power misfortune and wickedness have over him, and the less he has over them. So whoever can do these things can do them, not in virtue of his power, but in virtue of his weakness. So when we say that he "can" do these things, it is not because he has the power to do them, but because his weakness gives something else power over him. Or else it is some other manner of speaking, such as we often use

3. [This chapter is full of word play in the Latin that does not all come across in English. The words for "power" (*potentia*), "weakness" (*impotentia*), and various forms of the verb "can" (*posse*)—also translated here as "have power"—all share a common stem. And the word for omnipotent (*omnipotens*) means literally "able to do everything" (*omnia potens*).]

in speaking loosely. For example, we sometimes say 'to be' instead of 'not to be,' or 'to do' instead of 'not to do' or 'to do nothing.' For often when someone denies that something exists, we say "It is as you say it is"; but it would seem more correct to say "It is not as you say it is not." Again, we say "This man is sitting just as that man is doing" or "This man is resting just as that man is doing"; but to sit is not to do anything, and to rest is to do nothing. In the same way, then, when someone is said to have the "power" to do or suffer something that is not beneficial to himself or that he ought not to do, by 'power' we really mean 'weakness.' For the more he has this "power," the more power misfortune and wickedness have over him, and the less he has over them. Therefore, Lord God, you are all the more truly omnipotent because you can do nothing through weakness, and nothing has power over you.

Chapter 8

How God is both merciful and impassible

But how are you both merciful and impassible? For if you are impassible, you do not feel compassion, and if you do not feel compassion, your heart is not sorrowful out of compassion for sorrow; and that is what being merciful is. But if you are not merciful, how is it that you are such a comfort to the sorrowful?

So how, Lord, are you both merciful and not merciful? Is it not because you are merciful in relation to us but not in relation to yourself? You are indeed merciful according to what we feel, but not according to what you feel. For when you look with favor upon us in our sorrow, we feel the effect [*effectum*] of mercy, but you do not feel the emotion [*affectum*] of mercy. So you are merciful, because you save the sorrowful and spare those who sin against you; but you are also not merciful, because you are not afflicted with any feeling of compassion for sorrow.

Chapter 9

How the one who is completely and supremely just spares the wicked and justly has mercy on them

But how do you spare the wicked if you are completely and supremely just? For how does the one who is completely and supremely just do something that is not just? And what sort of justice is it to give everlasting life to someone who deserves eternal death? How then, O good God, good to the good and to the wicked, how do you save the wicked if this is not just and you do not do anything that is not just?

Or, since your goodness is incomprehensible, does this lie hidden in the "inaccessible light where you dwell"? (1 Timothy 6:16) It is indeed in the highest and most secret place of your goodness that the spring is hidden whence the river of your mercy flows. For although you are totally and supremely just, you are nonetheless kind even to the wicked, since you are totally and supremely good. You would be less good if you were not kind to any wicked person. For it is better to be good both to the good and to the wicked than to be good only to the good, and it is better to be good to the wicked both in punishing and in sparing them than to be good only in punishing them. So it follows that you are merciful precisely because you are totally and supremely good. And while it may be easy to see why you repay the good with good and the evil with evil, one must certainly wonder why you, who are totally just and lack for nothing, give good things to your evil and guilty creatures. O God, how exalted is your goodness! We can see the source of your mercy, and yet we cannot discern it clearly. We know whence the river flows, but we do not see the spring from which it issues. For it is out of the fullness of goodness that you are kind to sinners, while the reason why you are lies hidden in the heights of goodness. True, out of goodness you repay the good with good and the evil with evil, but the very nature of justice seems to demand this. When you give good things to the wicked, however, one knows that he who is supremely good willed to do this, and yet one wonders why he who is supremely just could have willed such a thing.

O mercy, from what rich sweetness and sweet richness you flow forth for us! O immeasurable goodness of God, how intensely ought sinners to love you! You save the just whom justice commends and set free those whom justice condemns. The just are saved with the help of their merits, sinners despite their merits. The just are saved because you look upon the good things you have given them, sinners because you overlook the evil things you hate. O immeasurable goodness that thus "surpasses all understanding"! (Philippians 4:7) Let the mercy that proceeds from your great riches come upon me. Let that which flows forth from you flow over me. Spare me through your mercy, lest you exact retribution through your justice. For even if it is difficult to understand how your mercy coexists with your justice, one must nonetheless believe that it is in no way opposed to justice, because it flows out of your goodness, and there is no goodness apart from justice—indeed, goodness is actually in harmony with justice. In fact, if you are merciful because you are supremely good, and supremely good only because you are supremely just, then you are indeed merciful precisely because you are supremely just. Help me, O just and merciful God, whose light I seek, help me to understand what I am saying. You are indeed merciful because you are just.

So, then, is your mercy born of[4] your justice? Do you spare the wicked because of your justice? If it is so, Lord, if it is so, teach me how it is so. Is it because it is just for you to be so good that you cannot be understood to be better, and to act so powerfully that you cannot be thought to act more powerfully? For what could be more just than this? And this would certainly not be the case if you were good only in punishing and not in sparing, and if you made only those not yet good to be good and did not do this also for the wicked. And so it is in this sense just that you spare the wicked and make them good. And finally, what is not done justly should not be done, and what should not be donc is done unjustly. So if it were not just for you to be merciful to the wicked, you should not be merciful; and if you should not be merciful, you would act unjustly in being merciful. But if it is wrong to say this, it is right to believe that you act justly in being merciful to the wicked.

Chapter 10

How God justly punishes and justly spares the wicked

But it is also just for you to punish the wicked. For what could be more just than for the good to receive good things and the wicked bad things? So how is it both just that you punish the wicked and just that you spare the wicked?

Or do you justly punish the wicked in one way and justly spare them in another? For when you punish the wicked, this is just because it accords with their merits; but when you spare the wicked, this is just, not because it is in keeping with their merits, but because it is in keeping with your goodness. In sparing the wicked you are just in relation to yourself but not in relation to us, in the same way that you are merciful in relation to us but not in relation to yourself. Thus, in saving us whom you might justly destroy, you are merciful, not because you experience any emotion, but because we experience the effect of your mercy; and in the same way, you are just, not because you give us our due, but because you do what is fitting for you who are supremely good. And so in this way you justly punish and justly pardon without any inconsistency.

Chapter 11

How "all the ways of the Lord are mercy and truth," and yet "the Lord is just in all his ways"

But is it not also just in relation to yourself, O Lord, for you to punish the wicked? It is certainly just for you to be so just that you cannot be thought to be more just. And you would by no means be so just if you only repaid the good with good and did not repay the wicked with evil. For one who treats both the good and the wicked as they deserve is more just than one who does so only for the good. Therefore, O just and benevolent God, it is just in relation to you both when you punish and when you pardon. Thus indeed "all the ways of the Lord are mercy and truth" (Psalm 25:10), and yet "the Lord is just in all his ways" (Psalm 145:17). And there is no inconsistency here, for it is not just for those to be saved whom you will to punish, and it is not just for those to be condemned whom you will to spare. For only what you will is just, and only what you do not will is not just. Thus your mercy is born of your justice, since it is just for you to be so good that you are good even in sparing the wicked. And perhaps this is why the supremely Just One can will good things for the wicked. But even if one can somehow grasp why you can will to save the wicked, certainly no reasoning can comprehend why, from those who are alike in wickedness, you save some

4. [Reading "*nascitur*" for "*noscitur.*"]

rather than others through your supreme goodness and condemn some rather than others through your supreme justice.

Thus you are indeed percipient, omnipotent, merciful, and impassible, just as you are living, wise, good, happy, eternal, and whatever it is better to be than not to be.

Chapter 12

That God is the very life by which he lives, and so on for similar attributes

But clearly, you are whatever you are, not through anything else, but through yourself. Therefore, you are the very life by which you live, the wisdom by which you are wise, and the very goodness by which you are good to the good and to the wicked, and so on for similar attributes.

Chapter 13

How he alone is unbounded and eternal, although other spirits are unbounded and eternal

Everything that is at all enclosed in a place or a time is less than that which is subject to no law of place or time. Therefore, since nothing is greater than you, you are not confined to any place or time; you exist everywhere and always. Since this can be said of you alone, you alone are unbounded and eternal. So how can other spirits also be said to be unbounded and eternal?

And indeed you alone are eternal, because you alone of all beings do not cease to exist, just as you do not begin to exist. But how are you alone unbounded? Is it that a created spirit is bounded compared to you but unbounded compared to a material object? Surely something is completely bounded if, when it is wholly in one place, it cannot at the same time be somewhere else. This is true only of material objects. On the other hand, something is unbounded if it is wholly everywhere at once, and this is true of you alone. But something is both bounded and unbounded if, when it is wholly in one place, it can at the same time be wholly in another place, but not everywhere; and this is true of created spirits. For if the whole soul were not present in each part of its body, it would not as a whole sense each part. Therefore, Lord, you are uniquely unbounded and eternal, and yet other spirits are also unbounded and eternal.

Chapter 14

How and why God is both seen and not seen by those who seek him

Have you found what you were seeking, O my soul? You were seeking God, and you have found that he is the highest of all beings, than which nothing better can be thought; that he is life itself, light, wisdom, goodness, eternal happiness and happy eternity; and that he exists always and everywhere. If you have not found your God, how is he the one whom you have found, whom you have understood with such certain truth and true certainty? But if you have found him, why do you not perceive what you have found? Why does my soul not perceive you, O Lord God, if it has found you?

Or has it not found him whom it found to be light and truth? For how did it understand this, if not by seeing that light and truth? Could it have understood anything at all about you except by "your light and your truth"? (Psalm 43:3) Therefore, if it has seen the light and the truth, it has seen you. If it has not seen you, it has not seen the light or the truth. Or perhaps it was indeed the light and the truth that it saw, but it has not yet seen you, because it saw you only in part and did not "see you as you really are" (1 John 3:2).

O Lord my God, you who have fashioned and refashioned me, tell my longing soul what you are besides what it has seen, that it might see purely what it longs to see. It strives to see more, but beyond what it has already seen it sees nothing but darkness. Or rather, it does not see darkness, for "in you there is no darkness" (1 John 1:5); it sees that it cannot see more because of its own darkness. Why is this, Lord, why is this? Is its eye darkened by its own infirmity, or is it dazzled by your splendor? Surely it is both darkened in itself and dazzled by you. Indeed it is both obscured by its own littleness and overwhelmed by your vastness. Truly it is both pinched by its own narrowness and vanquished by your fullness. How great is that light, for from it flashes every truth that enlightens the rational mind! How full is that truth, for in it is everything that is true, and outside it is only nothingness and falsehood! How vast it is, for in one glance it sees everything that has been created, and it sees by whom and through whom and how it was all created from nothing! What purity, what simplicity, what certainty and splendor are there! Truly it is more than any creature can understand.

Chapter 15

That God is greater than can be thought

Therefore, Lord, you are not merely that than which a greater cannot be thought; you are something greater than can be thought. For since it is possible to think that such a being exists, then if you are not that being, it is possible to think something greater than you. But that is impossible.

Chapter 16

That this is the "inaccessible light where he dwells"

Truly, Lord, this is the "inaccessible light in which you dwell" (1 Timothy 6:16). For surely there is no other being that can penetrate this light so that it might see you there. Indeed, the reason that I do not see it is that it is too much for me. And yet whatever I do see, I see through it, just as a weak eye sees what it sees by the light of the sun, although it cannot look at that light directly in the sun itself. My understanding cannot see that light. It is too dazzling; my understanding does not grasp it, and the eye of my soul cannot bear to look into it for long. It is dazzled by its splendor, vanquished by its fullness, overwhelmed by its vastness, perplexed by its extent. O supreme and inaccessible light, O complete and blessed truth, how far you are from me while I am so close to you! How far you are from my sight while I am so present to yours! You are wholly present everywhere, and yet I do not see you. "In you I move and in you I have my being" (Acts 17:28), and yet I cannot come into your presence. You are within me and all around me, and yet I do not perceive you.

Chapter 17

That in God there is harmony, fragrance, savor, softness, and beauty in his own ineffable way

Still, O Lord, you are hidden from my soul in your light and happiness, and so it still lives in its darkness and misery. It looks around, but it does not see your beauty. It listens, but it does not hear your harmony. It smells, but it does not perceive your fragrance. It tastes, but it does not know your savor. It touches, but it does not sense your softness. For you have these qualities in you, O Lord God, in your own ineffable way; and you have given them in their own perceptible way to the things you created. But the senses of my soul have been stiffened, dulled, and obstructed by the long-standing weakness of sin.

Chapter 18

That there are no parts in God or in his eternity, which he himself is

Once again, "behold, confusion!" (Jeremiah 14:19) Behold, once again mourning and sorrow stand in the way of one seeking joy and happiness. My soul hoped for satisfaction, and once again it is overwhelmed by need. I tried to eat my fill, but I hunger all the more. I strove to rise to the light of God, but I fell back down into my own darkness. Indeed, I did not merely fall into it; I find myself entangled in it. I fell before "my mother conceived me" (Psalm 51:5). I was indeed conceived in darkness; I was born enshrouded in darkness. Truly, we all fell long ago in him "in whom we all sinned" (Romans 5:12). In him, who easily possessed it and wickedly lost it for himself and for us, we all lost what we desire to seek but do not know; what we seek but do not find; what we find but is not what we sought. Help me "because of your goodness, O Lord" (Psalm 25:7). "I have sought your face; your face, Lord, will I seek. Turn not your face from me" (Psalm 27:8–9). Lift me up from myself to you. Cleanse, heal, sharpen, "enlighten the eye" (Psalm 13:3) of my soul so that I may look upon you. Let my soul gather its strength, and let it once more strive with all its understanding to reach you, O Lord.

What are you, Lord, what are you? What shall my

heart understand you to be? Surely you are life, you are wisdom, you are truth, you are goodness, you are happiness, you are eternity, and you are every true good. These are many things; my narrow understanding cannot see so many things in one glance and delight in all of them at once. How then, Lord, are you all these things? Are they parts of you? Or rather, is not each of them all that you are? For whatever is composed of parts is not completely one. It is in some sense a plurality and not identical with itself, and it can be broken up either in fact or at least in the understanding. But such characteristics are foreign to you, than whom nothing better can be thought. Therefore there are no parts in you, Lord, and you are not a plurality. Instead, you are so much a unity, so much identical with yourself, that you are in no respect dissimilar to yourself. You are in fact unity itself; you cannot be divided by any understanding. Therefore, life and wisdom and the rest are not parts of you; they are all one. Each of them is all of what you are, and each is what the rest are. And since you have no parts, and neither does your eternity, which you yourself are, it follows that no part of you or of your eternity exists at a certain place or time. Instead, you exist as a whole in every place, and your eternity exists as a whole always.

Chapter 19

That God is not in a place or a time, but all things are in him

But if by your eternity you have been, and are, and will be, and if to have been is not the same as to be in the future, and to be is not the same as to have been or to be in the future, then how does your eternity exist as a whole always?

Is it that nothing of your eternity is in the past in such a way that it no longer exists, and nothing is in the future as if it did not exist already? So it is not the case that yesterday you were and tomorrow you will be; rather, yesterday, today, and tomorrow you *are*. In fact, it is not even the case that yesterday, today, and tomorrow you *are*; rather, you are simply outside time altogether. Yesterday, today, and tomorrow are merely in time. But you, although nothing exists without you, do not exist in a place or a time; rather, all things exist in you. For nothing contains you, but you contain all things.

Chapter 20

That he is before and beyond even all eternal things

Therefore you fill and embrace all things; you are before and beyond all things. And indeed you are before all things, since "before they came into being, you already are" (cf. Psalm 90:2). But how are you beyond all things? In what way are you beyond those things that will have no end?

Is it because they can in no way exist without you, whereas you do not exist any less even if they return to nothingness? For in this way you are in a certain sense beyond them. And is it also because they can be thought to have an end, whereas you cannot at all? Thus they do in one sense have an end, but you do not in any sense. And certainly what does not in any sense have an end is beyond what does in some sense come to an end. And do you not also surpass even all eternal things in that both your and their eternity is wholly present to you, whereas they do not yet possess the part of their eternity that is yet to come, just as they no longer possess the part that is past? In this way you are indeed always beyond them, because you are always present somewhere they have not yet arrived—or because it is always present to you.

Chapter 21

Whether this is "the age of the age" or "the ages of the ages"

So is this "the age of the age" or "the ages of the ages"?[5] For just as an age of time contains all temporal things, so your eternity contains even the very ages of time. This eternity is indeed "an age" because of its indivisible unity, but it is "ages" because of its boundless greatness. And although you are so great, Lord, that all things are full of you and are in you,

5. [That is, is it more correct to identify God's eternity as "*saeculum saeculi*" or as "*saecula saeculorum*"? Both expressions (usually translated into English as "world without end" or "for ever and ever") were found in Scripture and in the liturgy.]

nonetheless you have no spatial extension, so that there is no middle or half or any other part in you.

Chapter 22

That he alone is what he is and who he is

Therefore, you alone, Lord, are what you are; and you are who you are. For whatever is one thing as a whole and something else in its parts, and whatever has in it something changeable, is not entirely what it is. And whatever began to exist out of nonexistence and can be thought not to exist, and returns to nonexistence unless it subsists through some other being; and whatever has a past that no longer exists and a future that does not yet exist: that thing does not exist in a strict and absolute sense. But you are what you are, since whatever you are in any way or at any time, you are wholly and always that.

And you are the one who exists in a strict and absolute sense, because you have no past and no future but only a present, and you cannot be thought not to exist at any time. And you are life and light and wisdom and happiness and eternity and many such good things; and yet you are nothing other than the one supreme good, utterly self-sufficient, needing nothing, whom all things need for their being and their well-being.

Chapter 23

That this good is equally Father, Son, and Holy Spirit; and that this is the "one necessary thing," which is the complete, total, and only good

This good is you, O God the Father; it is your Word, that is to say, your Son. For there cannot be anything other than what you are, or anything greater or less than you, in the Word by which you utter yourself. For your Word is as true as you are truthful, and therefore he is the same truth that you are and no other. And you are so simple that nothing can be born of you that is other than what you are. And this good is the one love that is shared by you and your Son, that is, the Holy Spirit, who proceeds from you both. For this love is not unequal to you or to your Son, since you love yourself and him, and he loves himself and you, as much as you and he *are*. Moreover, the one who is equal to both you and him is not other than you and he; nothing can proceed from the supreme simplicity that is other than that from which it proceeds. Thus, whatever each of you is individually, that is what the whole Trinity is at once, Father, Son, and Holy Spirit; for each of you individually is nothing other than the supremely simple unity and the supremely united simplicity, which cannot be multiplied or different from itself.

"Moreover, one thing is necessary" (Luke 10:42). And this is that one necessary thing, in which is all good—or rather, which is itself the complete, one, total, and unique good.

Chapter 24

A conjecture as to what sort of good this is, and how great it is

Bestir yourself, O my soul! Lift up your whole understanding, and consider as best you can what sort of good this is, and how great it is. For if particular goods are delightful, consider intently how delightful is that good which contains the joyfulness of all goods—and not such joyfulness as we have experienced in created things, but as different [from that] as the Creator differs from the creature. If created life is good, how good is the life that creates? If the salvation that has been brought about is joyful, how joyful is the salvation that brings about all salvation? If wisdom in the knowledge of created things is desirable, how desirable is the wisdom that created all things from nothing? In short, if there are many and great delights in delightful things, what kind and how great a delight is there in him who made those delightful things?

Chapter 25

What great goods there are for those who enjoy this good

O those who enjoy this good: what will be theirs, and what will not be theirs! Truly they will have everything they want and nothing they do not want. There will be such goods of both body and soul that "neither eye has seen nor ear heard nor the human heart" (1 Corinthians 2:9) conceived. So why are you wandering through many things, you insignificant mortal, seeking the goods of your soul and of your body? Love the one good, in which are all good things, and that is enough. Desire the simple good, which is the complete good, and that is enough. What do you love, O my flesh? What do you long for, O my soul? It is there; whatever you love, whatever you long for, it is there.

If it is beauty that delights you, "the righteous will shine like the sun" (Matthew 13:43). If it is swiftness or strength, or the freedom of a body that nothing can withstand, "they will be like the angels of God" (Matthew 22:30); for "it is sown an animal body, but it will rise a spiritual body" (1 Corinthians 15:44), with a power that is not from nature. If it is a long and healthy life, there is a healthy eternity and eternal health, for "the righteous will live for ever" (Wisdom 5:15) and "the salvation of the righteous is from the Lord" (Psalm 37:39). If it is satisfaction, "they will be satisfied when the glory of God has appeared" (Psalm 17:13). If it is drunkenness, "they will be drunk with the abundance of the house" (Psalm 36:8) of God. If it is music, there the choirs of angels sing unceasingly to God. If it is some pleasure, not impure but pure, God "will give them to drink from the torrent of his pleasure" (Psalm 36:8). If it is wisdom, the very wisdom of God will show itself to them. If it is friendship, they will love God more than themselves and one another as themselves, and God will love them more than they do themselves; for they will love God and themselves and one another through God, and God will love himself and them through himself. If it is concord, everyone will have but one will, for there will be no will among them but the will of God. If it is power, they will be omnipotent through their wills, just as God is through his. For just as God can do what he wills through himself, so they will be able to do what they will through God; for just as they will will only what God wills, so he will will whatever they will—and what he wills cannot fail to be. If it is wealth and honor, God will "set his good and faithful servants over many things" (cf. Matthew 25:21, 23); indeed, they will be called, and will truly be, "sons of God" (Matthew 5:9) and "gods" (Psalm 82:6, John 10:34). Where his Son is, there they too will be, "heirs of God and joint-heirs with Christ" (Romans 8:17). If it is true security, they will be certain that they will never in any way lose this security—or rather, this good; just as certain as they are that they will never give it up voluntarily, and that the loving God will never take it away against their will from those who love him, and that nothing more powerful than God will separate them from God against their will.

What great joy is there where so great a good is present! O human heart, O needy heart, heart that has known troubles, that is indeed overwhelmed by troubles: how greatly would you rejoice if you abounded in all these things! Ask your inmost self whether it can even comprehend its joy at such great happiness. And yet surely if someone else whom you loved in every respect as yourself had that same happiness, your joy would be doubled, for you would rejoice no less for him than for yourself. And if two or three or many more had that same happiness, you would rejoice as much for each of them as you would for yourself, if you loved each one as yourself. Therefore, in that perfect charity of countless happy angels and human beings, where no one will love anyone else less than he loves himself, each one will rejoice for each of the others just as he does for himself. If, then, the human heart will scarcely comprehend its own joy from so great a good, how will it be able to contain so many and such great joys? And indeed, since the more one loves someone, the more one rejoices in his good, it follows that, just as everyone in that perfect happiness will love God incomparably more than himself and all others with him, so everyone will rejoice inconceivably more in God's happiness than in his own, or in that of everyone else with him. But if they love God so much with "their whole heart, mind, and soul" (Matthew 22:37) that their whole heart, mind, and soul are too small for the greatness of their love, they will truly rejoice so much with their whole heart, mind, and soul that their whole heart, mind, and soul will be too small for the fullness of their joy.

Chapter 26

Whether this is the "fullness of joy" that the Lord promises

My God and my Lord, my hope and the joy of my heart, tell my soul whether this is that joy of which you tell us through your Son, "Ask and you shall receive, that your joy may be full" (John 16:24). For I have found a joy that is full and more than full. Indeed, when the heart, the mind, the soul, and the whole human being are filled with that joy, there will still remain joy beyond measure. The whole of that joy will therefore not enter into those who rejoice; instead, those who rejoice will enter wholly into that joy. Speak, Lord, tell your servant inwardly in his heart whether this is the joy into which your servants will enter who "enter into the joy of the Lord" (Matthew 25:21). But surely the joy with which your chosen ones will rejoice is something "no eye has seen, nor ear heard, nor has it entered into the heart of man" (1 Corinthians 2:9). Therefore, Lord, I have not yet expressed or conceived how greatly your blessed ones will rejoice. They will indeed rejoice as much as they love, and they will love as much as they know. How much will they know you then, Lord, and how much will they love you? Truly in this life "eye has not seen, nor has ear heard, nor has it entered into the heart of man" how much they will love and know you in that life.

O God, I pray that I will know and love you that I might rejoice in you. And if I cannot do so fully in this life, I pray that I might grow day by day until my joy comes to fullness. Let the knowledge of you grow in me here, and there let it be full. Let your love grow in me here, and there let it be full, so that my joy here is great in hope, and my joy there is full in reality. O Lord, by your Son you command us—or rather, you counsel us—to ask, and you promise that we will receive, "that our joy may be full." Lord, I ask what you counsel us through our "Wonderful Counselor" (Isaiah 9:6). Let me receive what you promise through your truth, "that my joy may be full." O truthful God, I ask that I may receive, "that my joy may be full." Until then, let my mind ponder on it, my tongue speak of it. Let my heart love it and my mouth proclaim it. Let my soul hunger for it, my flesh thirst for it, my whole being long for it, until I "enter into the joy of my Lord," who is God, Three in One, "blessed for ever. Amen" (Romans 1:25).

Gaunilo's Reply on Behalf of the Fool

Someone who either doubts or denies that there is any such being as that than which nothing greater can be thought is told that its existence is proved in the following way. First, the very person who denies or entertains doubts about this being has it in his understanding, since when he hears it spoken of he understands what is said. Further, what he understands must exist in reality as well, and not only in the understanding. The argument for this claim goes like this: to exist in reality is greater than to exist only in the understanding. Now if that being exists only in the understanding, then whatever also exists in reality is greater than it. Thus, that which is greater than everything else[1] will be less than something, and not greater than everything else, which is of course a contradiction. And so that which is greater than everything else, which has already been proved to exist in the understanding, must exist not only in the understanding but also in reality, since otherwise it could not be greater than everything else.

He can perhaps reply, "The only reason this is said to exist in my understanding is that I understand what is said. But in the same way, could I not also be said to have in my understanding any number of false things that have no real existence at all in themselves, since if someone were to speak of them I would understand whatever he said? Unless perhaps it is established that this being is such that it cannot be had in thought in the same way that any false or doubtful things can, and so I am not said to think of what I have heard or to have it in my thought, but to understand it and have it in my understanding, since I cannot think of it in any other way except by understanding it, that is, by comprehending in genuine knowledge the fact that it actually exists.

"But first of all, if this were the case, there would be no distinction between having a thing in the understanding at one time and then later understanding that the thing exists, as there is in the case of a painting, which exists first in the mind of the painter and then in the finished work.

"Furthermore, it is nearly impossible to believe that this being, once someone had heard it spoken of, cannot be thought not to exist, in just the same way that even God can be thought not to exist. For if that were so, why bother with all this argument against someone who denies or doubts that such a being exists?

"Finally, it must be proved to me by some unassailable argument that this being merely needs to be thought in order for the understanding to perceive with complete certainty that it undoubtedly exists. It is not enough to tell me that it exists in my understanding, since I understand it when I hear about it. I still think I could likewise have any number of other doubtful or even false things in my understanding if I heard them spoken of by someone whose words I understand, and especially if I am so taken in by him that, as often happens, I believe him—as I still do not believe in that being.

"Accordingly, that example of the painter, who already has in his understanding the picture that he is going to paint, is not a close enough analogy to support this argument. For before that picture is painted, it is contained in the craft of the painter, and any such thing in the craft of a craftsman is nothing but a part of his intelligence. For, as Saint Augustine says, 'when a carpenter is about to make a chest in reality, he first has it in his craft. The chest that exists in reality is not a living thing, but the chest that exists in his craft is a living thing, since the soul of the craftsman, in which all those things exist before

1. [Gaunilo regularly says "*maius omnibus*," which literally translated is "greater than everything." English idiom demands "greater than everything *else*," and I have translated it accordingly, but I thought it important to note the discrepancy.]

they are produced, is alive.'[2] Now how can they be living things in the living soul of the craftsman unless they are nothing other than the knowledge or intelligence of his soul itself? By contrast, except for things that are recognized as belonging to the nature of the mind itself, when the intellect upon hearing or thinking of something perceives that it is true, that truth is undoubtedly distinct from the intellect that grasps it. So even if it is true that there is something than which a greater cannot be thought, that thing, when it is heard and understood, is not the same sort of thing as a picture that exists in the understanding of the painter before it is painted.

"There is a further argument, which I mentioned earlier. When I hear someone speak of that which is greater than everything else that can be thought (which, it is alleged, can be nothing other than God himself), I can no more think of it or have it in my understanding in terms of anything whose genus or species I already know, than I can think of God himself—and indeed, for this very reason I can also think of him as not existing. For I do not know the thing itself, and I cannot form an idea of it on the basis of something like it, since you yourself claim that it is so great that nothing else could be like it. Now if I heard something said about a man I do not know at all, whose very existence is unknown to me, I could think of him in accordance with that very thing that a man is, on the basis of that knowledge of genus or species by which I know what a man is or what men are. Nonetheless, it could happen that the one who spoke of this man was lying, and so the man whom I thought of would not exist. But I would still be thinking of him on the basis of a real thing: not what that particular man would be, but what any given man is.

"But when I hear someone speak of 'God' or 'something greater than everything else,' I cannot have it in my thought or understanding in the same way as this false thing. I was able to think of the false thing on the basis of some real thing that I actually knew. But in the case of God, I can think of him only on the basis of the word. And one can seldom or never think of any truth solely on the basis of a word. For in thinking of something solely on the basis of a word, one does not think so much of the word itse[illegible] is at least a real thing: the sound of letters or syllables, as of the meaning of the word that is heard. And in the present case, one does not do this as someone who knows what is customarily meant by the word and thinks of it on the basis of a thing that is real at least in thought. Instead, one thinks of it as someone who does not know the meaning of the word, who thinks only of the impression made on his mind by hearing the word and tries to imagine its meaning. It would be surprising if one ever managed to reach the truth about something in this way. Therefore, when I hear and understand someone saying that there exists something greater than everything else that can be thought, it is in this way, and this way only, that it is present in my understanding. So much, then, for the claim that that supreme nature already exists in my understanding.

"Then I am offered the further argument that this thing necessarily exists in reality, since if it did not, everything that exists in reality would be greater than it. And so this thing, which of course has been proved to exist in the understanding, would not be greater than everything else. To that argument I reply that if we are to say that something exists in the understanding that cannot even be thought on the basis of the true nature of anything whatever, then I shall not deny that even this thing exists in my understanding. But since there is no way to derive from this the conclusion that this thing also exists in reality, there is simply no reason for me to concede to him that this thing exists in reality until it is proved to me by some unassailable argument.

"And when he says that this thing exists because otherwise that which is greater than everything else would not be greater than everything else, he does not fully realize whom he is addressing. For I do not yet admit—indeed, I actually deny, or at least doubt—that this greater being is greater than any real thing. Nor do I concede that it exists at all, except in the sense that something exists (if you want to call it 'existence') when my mind tries to imagine some completely unknown thing solely on the basis of a word that it has heard. How, then, is the fact that this being has been proved to be greater than everything else supposed to show me that it exists in actual fact? For I continue to deny, or at least doubt, that this has been proved, so that I do not admit that this thing

2. [*In Iohannem*, tractate 1, n.17.]

exists in my understanding or thought even in the way that many doubtful and uncertain things exist there. First I must become certain that this thing truly exists somewhere, and only then will the fact that it is greater than everything else show clearly that it also subsists in itself.

"For example, there are those who say that somewhere in the ocean is an island, which, because of the difficulty—or rather, impossibility—of finding what does not exist, some call 'the Lost Island.' This island (so the story goes) is more plentifully endowed than even the Isles of the Blessed with an indescribable abundance of all sorts of riches and delights. And because it has neither owner nor inhabitant, it is everywhere superior in its abundant riches to all the other lands that human beings inhabit. Suppose that someone tells me all this. The story is easily told and involves no difficulty, and so I understand it. But if this person went on to draw a conclusion, and say, 'You cannot any longer doubt that this island, more excellent than all others on earth, truly exists somewhere in reality. For you do not doubt that this island exists in your understanding, and since it is more excellent to exist not merely in the understanding, but also in reality, this island must also exist in reality. For if it did not, any land that exists in reality would be greater than it. And so this more excellent thing that you have understood would not in fact be more excellent.'—If, I say, he should try to convince me by this argument that I should no longer doubt whether the island truly exists, either I would think he was joking, or I would not know whom I ought to think more foolish: myself, if I grant him his conclusion, or him, if he thinks he can establish the existence of that island with any degree of certainty, without first showing that its excellence exists in my understanding as a thing that truly and undoubtedly exists and not in any way like something false or uncertain."

In this way the fool might meet the objections brought against him up to this point. The next assertion is that this greater being is such that even in thought it cannot fail to exist, and that in turn rests entirely on the claim that otherwise this being would not be greater than everything else. To this argument he can make the very same response, and say, "When did I ever say that any such thing as that 'greater than everything else' exists in actual fact, so that on that basis I am supposed to accept the claim that it exists to such a degree that it cannot even be thought not to exist? Therefore you must first prove by some absolutely incontestable argument that there exists some superior being, i.e., one that is greater and better than all others that exist, so that from this we can also prove all of the qualities that that which is greater and better than all other things must necessarily possess." So instead of saying that the highest thing cannot be *thought* not to exist, perhaps it would be better to say that it cannot be *understood* not to exist, or even to be capable of not existing. For in the strict sense of the word, false things cannot be understood, even though they can of course be thought in the same way that the fool thought that God does not exist.

Furthermore, I know with absolute certainty that I myself exist, but nonetheless I also know that I can fail to exist. But I understand beyond all doubt that the highest being that exists, namely God, both exists and cannot fail to exist. Now I do not know whether I can think I do not exist even while I know with absolute certainty that I do exist. But if I can, why can I not do the same for anything else that I know with the same certainty? And if I cannot, it is not God alone who cannot be thought not to exist.

The rest of this book is argued so truly, so lucidly and magnificently, full of so much that is useful, and fragrant with the aroma of devout and holy feelings, that it should by no means be belittled on account of the claims made at the beginning, which are indeed accurately understood, but less compellingly argued. Rather, those claims should be demonstrated more solidly, and then the whole book can be accorded great honor and praise.

Anselm's Reply to Gaunilo

Since the one who takes me to task is not that fool against whom I was speaking in my book, but a Christian who is no fool, arguing on behalf of the fool, it will be enough for me to reply to the Christian.

You say—whoever you are who say that the fool could say these things—that something than which a greater cannot be thought is in the understanding no differently from that which cannot even be thought according to the true nature of anything at all. You also say that it does not follow (as I say it does) that that than which a greater cannot be thought exists in reality as well simply because it exists in the understanding, any more than it follows that the Lost Island most certainly exists simply because someone who hears it described in words has no doubt that it exists in his understanding. I, however, say this: if that than which a greater cannot be thought is neither understood nor thought, and exists neither in the understanding nor in thought, then either God is not that than which a greater cannot be thought, or else he is neither understood nor thought, and exists neither in the understanding nor in thought. I appeal to your own faith and conscience as the most compelling argument that this is false. Therefore, that than which a greater cannot be thought is indeed understood and thought, and exists in the understanding and in thought. So either the premises by which you attempt to prove the contrary are false, or else what you think follows from them does not in fact follow.

You think that from the fact that something than which a greater cannot be thought is understood, it does not follow that it exists in the understanding; nor does it follow that if it exists in the understanding, it therefore exists in reality. But I say with certainty that if it can be so much as thought to exist, it must necessarily exist. For that than which a greater cannot be thought cannot be thought of as beginning to exist. By contrast, whatever can be thought to exist, but does not in fact exist, can be thought of as beginning to exist. Therefore, it is not the case that that than which a greater cannot be thought can be thought to exist, but does not in fact exist. If, therefore, it can be thought to exist, it does necessarily exist.

Furthermore, if it can be thought *at all*, it necessarily exists. For no one who denies or doubts that something than which a greater cannot be thought exists, denies or doubts that if it did exist, it would be unable to fail to exist either in reality or in the understanding, since otherwise it would not be that than which a greater cannot be thought. But whatever can be thought, but does not in fact exist, could (if it did exist) fail to exist either in reality or in the understanding. So if that than which a greater cannot be thought can be thought at all, it cannot fail to exist.

But let us assume instead that it does not exist, although it can be thought. Now something that can be thought but does not exist, would not, if it existed, be that than which a greater cannot be thought. And so, if it existed, that than which a greater cannot be thought would not be that than which a greater cannot be thought, which is utterly absurd. Therefore, if that than which a greater cannot be thought can be thought at all, it is false that it does not exist—and much more so if it can be understood and can exist in the understanding.

I shall say something more. If something does not exist everywhere and always, even if perhaps it does exist somewhere and sometimes, it can undoubtedly be thought not to exist anywhere or at any time, just as it does not exist in this particular place or at this particular time. For something that did not exist yesterday but does exist today can be conceived of as never existing in just the same way that it is understood as not existing yesterday. And something that does not exist here but does exist elsewhere can be thought not to exist anywhere in just the same way that it does not exist here. Similarly, when some parts of a thing do not exist in the same place or at the same time as other parts of that thing, all its parts—and therefore the thing as a whole—can be thought not to exist anywhere or at any time. Even if we say that time always exists and that the universe is everywhere, nevertheless, the whole of time does not always exist, and the whole of the universe is not everywhere. And just as some parts of time do not exist when others do, all of the parts can be thought not to exist at any time. And just as some parts of the universe do not exist where others do, all of the parts can be thought not to exist anywhere. Moreover, whatever is composed of parts can, at least in thought, be divided and fail to exist. Therefore, whatever does not exist as a whole in all places and at all times, even if it does exist, can be thought not to exist. But that than which a greater cannot be thought, if it exists, cannot be thought not to exist. For otherwise, even if it exists, it is not that than which a greater cannot be thought—which is absurd. Therefore, there is no time and no place in which it does not exist as a whole; it exists as a whole always and everywhere.

Do you think the being about whom these things are understood can in any way be thought or understood, or can exist in thought or in the understanding? If it cannot, these claims about it cannot be understood either. Perhaps you will say that it is not understood and does not exist in the understanding because it is not *fully* understood. But then you would have to say that someone who cannot gaze directly upon the purest light of the sun does not see the light of day, which is nothing other than the light of the sun. Surely that than which a greater cannot be thought is understood, and exists in the understanding, at least to the extent that these things about it are understood.

And so I said in the argument that you criticize, that when the fool hears someone utter the words "that than which a greater cannot be thought," he understands what he hears. Someone who does not understand it (if it is spoken in a language he knows) is rather feeble-minded, if indeed he has a mind at all.

Then I said that if it is understood, it exists in the understanding. Or does that which has been shown to exist necessarily in actual fact not exist in any understanding? But you will say that even if it exists in the understanding, it still does not follow that it is understood. Notice, however, that if it is understood, it does follow that it exists in the understanding. For when something is thought, it is thought by means of thinking; and what is thought by means of thinking exists in thinking just as it is thought. And in the same way, when something is understood, it is understood by means of the understanding; and what is understood by means of the understanding exists in the understanding, just as it is understood. What could be clearer than that?

After that I said that if it exists only in the understanding, it can be thought to exist in reality as well, which is greater. Therefore, if it exists only in the understanding, the very same thing is both that than which a greater *cannot* be thought and that than which a greater *can* be thought. Now I ask you, what could be more logical? For if it exists only in the understanding, can it not be thought to exist in reality as well? And if it can, does not the one who thinks it, think something greater than that thing is if it exists only in the understanding? So if that than which a greater *cannot* be thought exists only in the understanding, it is that than which a greater *can* be thought: what more logical conclusion could there be? But of course that than which a greater cannot be thought is not the same in anyone's understanding as that than which a greater can be thought. Does it not follow, therefore, that if that than which a greater cannot be thought exists in any understanding at all, it does not exist only in the understanding? For if it exists only in the understanding, it is that than which a greater can be thought, which is absurd.

But, you say, this is just the same as if someone were to claim that it cannot be doubted that a certain island in the ocean, surpassing all other lands in its fertility (which, from the difficulty—or rather, impossibility—of finding what does not exist, is called "the Lost Island"), exists in reality, because someone can easily understand it when it is described to him in words. I say quite confidently that if anyone can find for me something existing either in reality or only in thought to which he can apply this inference in my argument, besides that than which a greater cannot be thought, I will find and give to him that Lost Island, never to be lost again. In fact, however, it has already become quite clear that that than which a greater cannot be thought cannot be thought not to exist, since its existence is a matter of such certain truth. For otherwise it would not exist at all. Finally, if someone says that he thinks it does not exist, I say that when he thinks this, either he is thinking something than which a greater cannot be thought, or he is not. If he is not, then he is not thinking that it does not exist, since he is not thinking it at all. But if he is, he is surely thinking something that cannot be thought not to exist. For if it could be thought not to exist, it could be thought to have a beginning and an end, which is impossible. Therefore, someone who is thinking it, is thinking something that cannot be thought not to exist. And of course someone who is thinking this, does not think that that very thing does not exist. Otherwise he would be thinking something that cannot be thought. Therefore, that than which a greater cannot be thought cannot be thought not to exist.

When I say that this highest being cannot be *thought* not to exist, you reply that it would perhaps be better to say that it cannot be *understood* not to exist, or even to be capable of not existing. But in fact it was more correct to say that it cannot be *thought* not to exist. For if I had said that this thing cannot be understood not to exist, you (who say that in the strict sense of the word, false things cannot be understood) might well object that nothing that exists can be understood not to exist, since, after all, it is false that something that exists does not exist. Consequently, it is not God alone who cannot be understood not to exist. But if any of those things that most certainly exist can be understood not to exist, then other things that are certain can likewise be understood not to exist. If, however, we say 'thought' [rather than 'understood'] this objection will have no force if it is examined properly. For even if nothing that actually exists can be *understood* not to exist, everything can be *thought* not to exist, except for that which exists in the highest degree. Indeed, all and only those things that have a beginning or end, or are made up of parts, as well as whatever does not exist always and everywhere as a whole (as I discussed earlier), can be thought not to exist. The only thing that cannot be thought not to exist is that which has neither beginning nor end, and is not made up of parts, and which no thought discerns except as wholly present always and everywhere.

So you should realize that you can indeed *think* of yourself as not existing even while you know with absolute certainty that you exist. I am amazed that you said you did not know this. For we think of many things as not existing that we know exist, and we think of many things as existing that we know do not exist—not judging, but imagining, that things are as we are thinking of them. And so we can in fact think of something as not existing even while we know that it exists, since we can think the one thing and know the other at the very same time. And yet we cannot think of something as not existing even while we know that it exists, since we cannot think of it as existing and not existing at the same time. So if someone distinguishes the two senses of this statement in this way, he will understand that in one sense nothing can be thought of as not existing when we know that it exists, and in another sense anything besides that than which a greater cannot be thought can be thought not to exist, even when we know that it exists. Thus God alone cannot be thought not to exist, but nonetheless it is also true that there are many things that cannot be thought not to exist while they actually exist. I think, however, that I adequately explained in my book the sense in which God is thought not to exist.

Now as for the other objections you raise against me on behalf of the fool, anyone with much sense at all can easily see through them, so I had judged it best not to bother proving this. But since I hear that some readers think they have some force against me, I will deal with them briefly. First, you repeatedly say that I argue that that which is greater than everything else exists in the understanding; and that if it exists in the understanding, it also exists in reality, for otherwise that which is greater than everything else would not be greater than everything else. Nowhere in anything I said can such an argument be found. For "that which is greater than everything else" and "that than which nothing greater can be thought" do not have the same force in proving that the thing spoken of exists in reality. For if someone says that that than which a greater cannot be thought is not something existing in reality, or is capable of not existing, or can be thought not to exist, he is easily refuted. For whatever does not exist is capable of not existing, and whatever is capable of not existing can be thought not to exist. Now whatever can be thought not to exist, if it does exist, is not that than which a greater cannot be thought. And if it does not exist, it would not be that than which a greater cannot be thought *even if it were to exist.* But it makes no sense to say that that than which a greater cannot be thought, if it exists, is not that than which a greater cannot be thought, and that if it [does not exist but] were to exist, it would not be that than which a greater cannot be thought. It is therefore evident that it exists, that it is not capable of not existing, and that it cannot be thought not to exist. For otherwise, if it exists, it is not the thing spoken of; and if it [does not exist but] were to exist, it would not be the thing spoken of.

This does not seem to be so easily proved with regard to what is said to be greater than everything else. For it is not as evident that something that can be thought not to exist is not that which is greater than everything else that exists, as it is that such a thing is not that than which a greater cannot be thought. Nor is it indubitable that if there is something greater than everything else, it is the same as that than which a greater cannot be thought, or that if such a thing were to exist, there would not exist another thing just like it. But these things are certainly true of what is called "that than which a greater cannot be thought." For what if someone were to say that something exists that is greater than everything else that exists, and yet that this very thing can be thought not to exist, and that something greater than it can be thought, although that greater thing does not actually exist? Can it be just as easily inferred in this case that it is not greater than everything else that exists, as it was perfectly certain in the previous case that it was not that than which a greater cannot be thought? In the second case we would need another premise, besides the mere fact that this being is said to be "greater than everything else," whereas in the first case there was no need for anything more than the expression "that than which a greater cannot be thought." Therefore, since "that than which a greater cannot be thought" proves things about itself and through itself that cannot be proved in the same way about what is said to be "greater than everything else," you have unjustly criticized me for saying things I did not say, when they differ greatly from what I actually said.

If, however, this can be proved through some further argument, you should not have criticized me for saying what can clearly be proved. And that it can in fact be proved should be easily perceived by anyone who knows that it can be proved for that than which a greater cannot be thought. For that than which a greater cannot be thought cannot be understood as anything other than the one thing that is greater than everything else. Therefore, just as that than which a greater cannot be thought is understood and exists in the understanding, and therefore is affirmed to exist in actual fact, even so that which is said to be greater than everything else is with necessity inferred to be understood, to exist in the understanding, and consequently to exist in reality. So you see how right you were to compare me to that stupid man who was willing to affirm the existence of the Lost Island solely because the island would be understood if someone described it.

But you also raise the objection that all sorts of false or doubtful things can be understood, and exist in the understanding, in the very same way as the being I was talking about. I wonder what force you thought this objection could have against me. I was simply trying to prove something that was still in doubt, and for that it was enough for me to show that this being is understood, and exists in the understanding, in *some way or other*, since on that basis the argument would go on to determine whether it exists only in the understanding, like a false thing, or also in reality, like a real thing. For if false and doubtful things are understood, and exist in the understanding, in the sense that one who hears them spoken of understands what the speaker means, there is no reason that the being I was discussing could not be understood or exist in the understanding. But how can these two claims of yours be consistent: first, that if someone spoke of false things, you would understand whatever he said; and second, that if what you heard is not had in thought in the same way that false things are, you would not say that you think it and have it in your thought, but rather that you understand it and have it in your understanding, since you cannot think this thing without understanding it, that is, comprehending in genuine knowledge that it exists in reality? How, I ask, can these be consistent: that false things are understood in some sense, and that to understand is to comprehend in genuine knowledge that something exists? You should realize that this objection has no force against me. If false things can indeed be understood in some sense, and your definition of understanding applies not to all but only to some cases of understanding, then I should not have been criticized for saying that that than which a greater cannot be thought is understood and exists in the understanding even before it was certain that it exists in reality.

Next, you say that it is nearly impossible to believe that when this thing has been spoken of and heard, it cannot be thought not to exist in the way that even

God can be thought not to exist. Let those who have acquired even a meager knowledge of disputation and argument reply on my behalf. Is it rational for someone to deny [the existence of] what he understands, simply because it is said to be the same as something [whose existence] he denies because he does not understand it? Or if [its existence] is sometimes denied because it is only partly understood, and it is the same as something that is not understood at all, are not things in doubt more easily proved to be true of what exists in some understanding than of what exists in no understanding? Therefore, it is impossible to believe that someone would deny [the existence of] that than which a greater cannot be thought, which he understands to some extent when he hears of it, simply because he denies [the existence of] God, whose meaning he is not thinking of in any way. Or, if he also denies [the existence of] that than which a greater cannot be thought, because he does not fully understand it, is it not easier to prove [the existence of] what is understood to some extent than to prove what is not understood at all? So it was not irrational for me to prove against the fool that God exists by making use of the expression "that than which a greater cannot be thought," since he would understand that expression to some extent, whereas he might not understand "God" at all.

You go to some trouble to show that that than which a greater cannot be thought is not the same sort of thing as a picture, not yet painted, in the understanding of the painter, but your argument is not to the point. I did not bring up the picture that is thought out beforehand in order to claim that it was the same sort of thing as the being I was discussing, but merely so I could show that something exists in the understanding that would not be understood to exist [in reality].

Again, you say that when you hear "that than which a greater cannot be thought," you cannot think it in accordance with some thing that you know by genus or species, or have it in your understanding, since you do not know the thing itself and cannot infer it on the basis of something similar. But that is clearly wrong. For since every lesser good, insofar as it is good, is similar to a greater good, it is clear to every reasonable mind that by raising our thoughts from lesser goods to greater goods, we can infer a great deal about that than which a greater cannot be thought on the basis of those things than which a greater can be thought. Who, for example, is unable to think (even if he does not believe that what he thinks exists in reality) that if something that has a beginning and end is good, then something that has a beginning but never ceases to exist is much better? And that just as the latter is better than the former, so something that has neither beginning nor end is better still, even if it is always moving from the past through the present into the future? And that something that in no way needs or is compelled to change or move is far better even than that, whether any such thing exists in reality or not? Can such a thing not be thought? Can anything greater than this be thought? Or rather, is not this an example of inferring that than which a greater cannot be thought on the basis of those things than which a greater can be thought? So there is in fact a way to infer that than which a greater cannot be thought. And so in this way it is easy to refute a fool who does not accept the sacred authority, if he denies that one can infer that than which a greater cannot be thought on the basis of other things. But if an orthodox Christian were to deny this, he should recall that "since the creation of the world the invisible things of God—his everlasting power and divinity—have been clearly seen through the things that have been made" (Romans 1:20).

But even if it were true that that than which a greater cannot be thought cannot be thought or understood, it would not be false that [the expression] "that than which a greater cannot be thought" can be thought and understood. For just as one can use the word 'ineffable,' even though the thing that is said to be ineffable cannot be spoken of; and just as 'unthinkable' can be thought, even though the thing to which the word 'unthinkable' applies cannot be thought; in the same way, when someone says "that than which a greater cannot be thought," that which is heard can undoubtedly be thought and understood, even though the thing itself than which a greater cannot be thought cannot be thought or understood. For even if someone is foolish enough to say that something than which a greater cannot be thought does not exist, he will surely not be shameless enough to say that he cannot understand or think what he is saying. Or, if such a person does turn up, not only should his words be repudiated, but he himself should be ridiculed. So anyone who denies the existence of something than which a greater cannot be thought surely understands and thinks the denial that he is making. Now he cannot understand or think this denial without its parts. And one part of it is "that than which a greater cannot be thought." Therefore, whoever denies this, understands and thinks that than which a greater cannot be thought. Now it is quite clear that something that cannot fail to exist can be thought and understood in the same way. And one who thinks this is thinking something greater than is one who thinks something that can fail to exist. Therefore, if, while he is thinking that than which a greater cannot be thought, he thinks that it can fail to exist, he is not thinking that than which a greater cannot be thought. But it is not possible for the same thing at the same time both to be thought and not to be thought. Therefore, someone who thinks that than which a greater cannot be thought does not think that it can, but rather that it cannot, fail to exist. For this reason the thing that he is thinking exists necessarily, since whatever can fail to exist is not what he is thinking.

I believe I have now shown that my proof in the foregoing book that that than which a greater cannot be thought exists in reality was no weak argument, but a quite conclusive one, one that is not weakened by the force of any objection. For the meaning of this expression has such great force that, from the mere fact that it is understood or thought, what is said is necessarily proved both to exist in reality and to be whatever we ought to believe about the divine nature. Now we believe about the divine nature everything that can be thought, absolutely speaking, better for something to be than not to be. For example, it is better to be eternal than not eternal, good than not good, and indeed goodness itself, rather than not goodness itself. That than which something greater cannot be thought cannot fail to be anything of this sort. So one must believe that that than which a greater cannot be thought is whatever we ought to believe about the divine nature.

I am grateful for your kindness both in your criticisms and in your praise of my book. For since you lavished such great praise on the things you found worthy of acceptance, it is quite clear that you criticized the things that seemed weak to you, not from ill will but in a friendly spirit.

Moses Maimonides

Rabbi Moses ben Maimon (1138–1204), commonly referred to by his Latinized name Maimonides or the Hebrew acronym RaMBaM, was both a preeminent authority on Halakhah (Jewish law) and the most illustrious Jewish philosopher of all time. A son of a prominent rabbinic scholar and judge, Maimonides was born in Cordova, Spain. At a young age, he was forced to emigrate with his family following the invasion of Spain by the Almohades, a fanatical Muslim group that presented Jews with the choice between conversion and death. Maimonides' wanderings took him through southern Spain, North Africa, the Land of Israel (then dominated by Christian Crusaders), and ultimately Fostat (Old Cairo), Egypt, where he became a court physician as well as the untitled and (on personal principle) unsalaried rabbinic leader of the Jewish community. Overcoming the pressures and distractions of persecution and wandering, prolonged grief over the death of his brother on a business voyage, and, later in Fostat, an exhausting schedule of medical ministration and rabbinic leadership, Maimonides produced a stunning literary output. At twenty-three he began his commentary on the *Mishnah* (a large ancient legal compilation). Later he authored, among other works, a monumental code of Jewish law, *Mishneh Torah* (ca. 1178), that became indispensable for all future codifiers; the landmark philosophical opus *The Guide of the Perplexed* (ca. 1190); and medical treatises. Subsequent thinkers could define themselves as either sympathizers or antagonists, but all had to reckon with the writings of the man often called "the great eagle."

Maimonides' philosophical endeavor, as well as the opposition it aroused, must be understood in terms of the philosophy and theology prevailing in the Muslim societies in which he lived. After their extended conquests beginning in the seventh century, the Muslims translated works of Greek philosophy into Arabic, composed commentaries on those works, and developed their own philosophical-theological systems using categories and principles tracing to the Greeks. Some works of the Neoplatonic mystic Plotinus (d. 270) were mistakenly attributed to Aristotle, leading to a hybrid metaphysical system often called Neoplatonized Aristotelianism. Jews who were familiar with Islamic thought admired and appropriated the philosophical ideas the Muslims had discovered and developed. Maimonides was familiar with works of Arabic philosophers, some of whom sought to understand the Koran's teachings as figurative articulations of philosophical and scientific truth. Maimonides spent considerable effort showing that scriptural and rabbinic texts express philosophical and scientific truths but need to be understood figuratively in order for this meaning to be unveiled. If philosophy demonstrates, for example, that God has no body, but the Bible speaks as if God does, the problematic texts must be reinterpreted. Thus, Maimonides represents the position known as religious rationalism, according to which the exercise of reason serves a positive role in religious life and uncovers the true meaning of religious assertions and practices.

Maimonides recognized, however, that philosophical teachings about creation, divine providence, the afterlife, and the goals of human life were at odds with views held by the masses, who were brought up in ignorance of philosophy and science. How he negotiated those conflicts is a matter of long-standing debate. Some think that on crucial doctrines Maimonides accepted the traditional beliefs and rejected Aristotelianism; others allege that he was a heretic in a pious disguise, which he donned either for the sake of personal protection or the sake of social order; still others maintain he achieved a perfect harmony between philosophical and religious truth. Compounding the interpretive problem, Maimonides wrote his *Guide of the Perplexed* in the "esoteric" style cultivated by Muslim thinkers. This method of writing involved refusing to lay out one's views explicitly, even to the point of deliberately inserting contradictions to veil one's true intent or (as recent scholars suggest about Maimonides' case) to conceal one's own uncertainty about abstruse matters. In the selection that follows, Maimonides, developing a theme of Neoplatonism, maintains that God is beyond all human conceptualization. He possesses no affirmative attributes, for insofar as God is one (simple and without multiplicity), he cannot have any attributes superadded to His essence; nor, of course, can he possess multiple attributes. God's attributes, therefore, must be understood in the *via negativa,* or negative way. When we say "God knows," "God is powerful," and the like, we mean that God is not not-knowing, is not nonpowerful, and so on. Furthermore, these just-mentioned negations are to be understood as is the statement "The wall does not see." Just as sight and blindness cannot apply to a wall, so too, neither knowledge nor ignorance, power nor powerlessness, can apply to God. Maimonides enlists this "negative theology" to explain why God's foreknowledge of how a person will act does not preclude the person's acting freely. The heart of Maimonides' solution is that God's knowledge is unlike human knowledge, and, therefore, to infer a person's lack of freedom from God's foreknowledge is a non sequitur. (For certain attributes, specifically those that appear to describe psychological states—for example, "compassionate" and "long-suffering"—Maimonides provides a different analysis. Such terms are said to refer to God's actions, not inner states.)

Not long after Maimonides' death, medieval Jewry was rocked by a clash between rationalists and antirationalists known as the Maimonidean controversy. A key issue was how much figurative interpretation is admissible when approaching biblical and rabbinic texts. At stake in the answer was how to understand not only language about God but also teachings about prophecy, providence, creation, and the afterlife.

• • •

A fine selection of legal and philosophical material from Maimonides' writing is Isadore Twersky, *A Maimonides Reader* (New York: Behrman House, 1972). Shlomo Pines' outstanding translation of *The Guide of the Perplexed* (Chicago: University of Chicago Press, 1963) includes a very useful analytical survey of Maimonides' philosophical sources. Significant books about Maimonides' philosophy include Joseph Buijs, ed., *Maimonides: A Collection of Critical Essays* (Notre Dame, Ind.: University of Notre Dame Press, 1988); Herbert Davidson, *Maimonides: The Man and His Works* (New York: Oxford University Press, 2005); Marvin Fox, *Interpreting Maimonides* (Chicago: University of Chicago Press, 1989); Menachem Kellner, *Maimonides' Confrontation With Mysticism* (London: Littman Library of Jewish Civilization, 2006); Joel Kraemer, ed., *Perspectives on Maimonides' Political Philosophy: Studies in Ethics, Law, and the Human Ideal* (New York: State University of New York, 1999); Charles Manekin, *On Maimonides* (Belmont, Calif.: Wadsworth, 2005); Shlomo Pines and Yirmiyahu Yovel, eds., *Maimonides and Philosophy* (Dordrecht: Martinus Nijhoff, 1986); Tamar Rudavsky, *Maimonides* (Hoboken, NJ.: Wiley-Blackwell, 2010); Kenneth Seeskin, *Searching for a Distant God* (New York: Oxford University Press, 2000); and Kenneth Seeskin, ed., *The Cambridge Companion to Maimonides* (Cambridge: Cambridge University Press, 2005). A substantial body of work on the *Guide* either accepts or challenges the "esotericist" mode of interpreting Maimonides championed by Leo Strauss in, for example, Strauss' *Persecution and the Art of Writing* (Glencoe, Ill.: Free Press, 1952).

David Shatz

The Guide of the Perplexed

BOOK I

Chapter LVIII

MORE DIFFICULT THAN THE PRECEDING ONES

You must understand that the description of God by means of negative terms is the only sound description which contains no element of loose terminology, and implies altogether in no circumstances a lack of perfection in God. His description by positive terms, on the other hand, comports polytheism and a lack of perfection in God in the way we have demonstrated.

First I must explain how negative terms can in a manner be attributes, and in what way they differ from positive attributes. Then I shall show how it is that we have no way of describing Him except by negative terms and no others. An attribute is not something specifying the thing described in such a way that it cannot share the attribute with anything else. On the contrary, an attribute may describe something even if it shares that attribute with other things and is not peculiar to it. For instance, if you see a man from a distance and ask: what is that which is visible? the reply may be: some living being. This is without a doubt a correct description of the thing seen, though it does not set it aside as a peculiar thing from all others. Some specification does, however, result, namely, that the thing seen is not an object of the vegetable or mineral class. In the same manner also, if there is a man in a certain house, and you know that there is some object in it, but not what it is, you may ask: what is in this house? and may receive the reply: there isn't a vegetable or mineral object in it. Then you obtain some specification and know that a living being is in the house, though you do not know what kind of living being it is. From this point of view the negative attributes have something in common with positive attributes, because they must necessarily produce some specification, even though this specification means merely the removal of the negated items from among those that we had before imagined un-negated. The difference between negative and positive attributes is in this, that positive attributes, even when they do not specify, indicate some part of the totality of the thing which we desire to know. This may be either a part of its substance or one of its accidents. The negative attributes do not in any manner tell us anything about the essence of the thing which we wish to know as it is, except incidentally, as in our example.

After these prefatory remarks I state that it has been proved that God exists by necessity and that He is non-composite, as we shall prove, and we can apprehend only that He is, not what He is. It is therefore meaningless that He should have any positive attribute, since the fact that He is is not something outside of what He is, so that the attribute might indicate one of these two. Much less can what He is be of a composite character, so that the attribute could indicate one of the parts. Even less can He be substrate to accidents, so that the attribute could indicate these. Thus there is no scope for any positive attributes in any way whatsoever.

It is the negative attributes which we must employ to guide our mind to that which we ought to believe concerning God, because from them no plurality can result in any way. They can guide the mind to the utmost limit of what man can apprehend of God. For instance, it has been proved to us that something must exist apart from those objects which our senses apprehend and which our reason can encompass with its knowledge. We say about this thing that it exists, meaning that it is absurd to say that He does not exist. Then we apprehend that its existence is not like the

Reprinted from *The Guide of the Perplexed*, translated by Chaim Rabin (Indianapolis: Hackett Publishing Company, 1995), by permission of the publisher.

existence of, say, the elements, which are lifeless bodies, and consequently say that He lives, meaning that God is not subject to death. Then we apprehend that this being is also not like the existence of heaven, which is a living body, and consequently we say that He is not a body. Then we apprehend that this being is not like the existence of an Intelligence, which is neither a body nor subject to death, but is due to a cause, and consequently say that God is eternal, meaning that there is no cause which called Him into being. Then we apprehend that the existence of this Being, which is its essence, is not only sufficient for that Being itself to exist, but many existences emanate from it. It is, however, not like the emanation of heat from the fire or the automatic connection between light and the sun, but it is an emanation which He perpetually keeps going, giving it a constant flow arranged according to a wise plan, as we shall show. We shall say on account of these arrangements that He is omnipotent, omniscient, and possessed of will. By these attributes we mean to say that He is neither powerless nor ignorant nor distracted or disinterested. When we say He is not powerless, we mean that His existence is sufficient to bring into existence things other than Himself. When we say He is not ignorant, we mean that He apprehends, i.e., lives, for whatever apprehends lives. When we say He is not distracted or disinterested, we mean that all those existing things run along an ordered and planned course, not without supervision and coming into being just by chance, just like anything which a person possessed of will plans with purpose and will. Then we apprehend that there is no other being like this one. When we, therefore, say He is One, we mean thereby to deny any plurality.

Thus it becomes clear that every attribute with which we describe Him is either an attribute of action or has the purport of negating its own absence if our intention thereby is to apprehend His essence rather than His works. These negative terms are also not used absolutely of God, but only in the manner mentioned before, that one denies of a thing something that by the nature of things could not exist in it, as when we say of a wall that it does not see.

You know well, dear reader, that the heaven is a moving body, and that we have measured it in yards and feet and have complete data on the extent of its parts and of most of its movements, and yet our minds are completely unable to apprehend what it is, although we know that it must necessarily possess matter and form, but not matter of the kind that is with us. For this reason we can only describe it by indefinite nouns, not by definite positive terms. We say that the heaven is not light and not heavy, does not suffer action and is therefore not receptive to impressions, it has no taste or smell, and similar negative terms. All this is because we are ignorant of that kind of matter. What will be the position then of our minds when they endeavour to apprehend that which is free from matter, non-composite to the utmost degree, of necessary existence, has no cause and is not attained by anything additional to its perfect essence—the meaning of its perfection being the denial of all shortcomings, as explained before? We can only apprehend that He is; that there exists a Being unlike any other being which He brought into existence, having nothing whatsoever in common with them, who has no plurality in Him, and is not powerless to bring into existence things other than He himself, and that His relation to the world is that of the captain to the ship. This also is not a true relation, and not even remotely resembles the real one, but it serves to guide the mind to the idea that God governs the universe, meaning that He supports it and keeps its order as it should be. This point will be explained in a more concrete manner.

Praise be to Him who is such that when our minds try to visualize His essence, their power of apprehending becomes imbecility; when they study the connection between His works and His will, their knowledge becomes ignorance; and when our tongues desire to declare His greatness by descriptive terms, all eloquence becomes impotence and imbecility.

BOOK III

Chapter XX

It is generally agreed that it would be incorrect to ascribe to God the acquisition of new knowledge, i.e. that He should now know something He did not know before. It would be equally incorrect to ascribe to Him manifold and multiple acts of cognition, even according to the view of those who believe in divine attributes. Assuming this as proven, we, the believers in the Divine Law, say that He knows many and manifold things by the same act of knowledge and that His acts of cognition do not vary according to the variation of things known, as it would be the case with us. We further say that all things that emerge anew were known to Him before they existed, and He knew them continually. For this reason He does not acquire any new knowledge whatsoever. He knows that so-and-so does not exist now, but will exist at such-and-such a time and will remain alive for so-and-so much time and will then be non-existent. When that person comes into being, as God knew he would, no new piece of knowledge has been added. It was not as if something hitherto unknown to Him had occurred, but something occurred which He continually knew would occur just in the way it did.

A consequence of this belief is that knowledge should pertain to non-existent things and should encompass the infinite. That is exactly what we do believe. We say, in effect, that with regard to non-existing things, whose creation pre-exists in God's knowledge—since His is the power to create them—there is no reason why His knowledge should not extend to them. Those things, however, which essentially cannot exist are with regard to His knowledge in a state of absolute non-existence, to which His knowledge cannot extend any more than our knowledge can extend to something that does not exist for us.

The idea of knowledge encompassing the infinite raises a number of difficulties. Some thinkers assume that (divine) knowledge attaches to the species and in some way is extended over all the individuals of the species. This is the belief of everyone who accepts the Divine Law in so far as the requirements of speculative thought demand it.

The philosophers, however, declare without further ado that God's knowledge cannot extend to the non-existent or that any knowledge can encompass the infinite. Therefore, since He does not acquire new knowledge, it is absurd that He should know anything of those things that emerge anew, and thus God does not know anything except permanent things that do not change. Some of them have still another doubt. They say, even if God knows only the permanent things, this would still imply many acts of knowing, since the acts of knowing vary according to the things known, because to every knowable object belongs a particular act of knowing. Therefore, God cannot know anything except His own substance.

My own opinion is that the reason for falling into all these errors is that they treat God's knowledge as something comparable with our own. Each school of thought contemplates things which would be impossible with our own cognitive processes and concludes that the same restrictions should also apply in the case of God, or that he should experience the same difficulties. For their failure in this matter the philosophers deserve more reproach than anyone else, for it is they who proved that His essence does not allow of any plurality and that He possesses no attributes outside His essence and that His knowledge is identical with His essence; it is they who proved that our minds are insufficient to apprehend His true essence as it is, as we have explained before. How then can they assert that they apprehend God's knowledge when it is not something outside His essence? That same insufficiency of our minds to apprehend His essence also prevents us from apprehending His knowledge of how things exist. It is not a knowledge of the same species as our own so that we could treat it analogically, but it is something as different from it as can be. Just as there is a necessarily existing essence from which all existence results, as they say, or which has produced all that is outside it out of non-existence, as we say—in the same way we claim that this essence apprehends everything that is outside it and nothing whatsoever that exists is ever hidden from it. There is nothing in common between our knowledge and his, just as there is nothing in common between our essence and His. What misled them is the homonymous nature of the word knowledge, for there is something common only in nomenclature, but complete difference in nature. This is why absurd conclusions will be reached if we imagine that necessary features of our own cognitive processes are also necessary in His case.

From various phrases in the Scriptures I conclude that God's knowledge with regard to a possibility that it will take place does not deprive that possibility in any way of its nature as a possibility. The nature of a possibility remains attached to it, and God's knowledge of what is going to happen in the case of possible alternatives does not imply the necessity of one or the other of the alternatives happening. This is another principle of the law of Moses concerning which there can be no doubt or scepticism. Had it been otherwise, the Law would not have said: *thou shalt make a battlement for thy roof* (Deuteronomy 22, 8), or *lest he die in the battle and another man take her* (Deuteronomy 20, 7). Similarly the entire law with its commands and prohibitions is based upon this principle, namely that God's knowledge of what is going to happen does not change the contingency from its nature. This is very difficult for our imperfect minds to grasp.

According to our view, who say that God's knowledge is not a thing superadded to His essence, it is really impossible to avoid the conclusion that between His knowledge and ours there exists the same difference of substance as between the substance of heaven and earth. This has been clearly stated by the prophets: *For not my thoughts are your thoughts, and not your ways are my ways, saith the Lord. For as high as the heavens are above the earth, so high are my ways above your ways, and my thoughts above your thoughts* (Isaiah 55, 8–9).

The sum total of the idea I am trying here briefly to explain is the following: we cannot apprehend the true nature of God's essence; yet we know that His existence is the most perfect, without any admixture of imperfection or change or affection in any way. Similarly, though we do not know the true nature of God's knowledge, because it is His substance, yet we know that He does not sometimes apprehend and at other times remain unaware, i.e. that He never acquires any new knowledge; also that His knowledge is not of a multiple nature, nor finite, that nothing of all existing things is hidden from Him and that His knowledge of them does not change their nature, but the possible retains its nature as a possibility. Anything in this enumeration that appears contradictory, is so only owing to the structure of our knowledge, which has nothing in common with His knowledge except the name.

Chapter XXI

Whatever we know, we know from observation of reality. Therefore our knowledge does not extend to what will be or to that which is infinite, and we constantly acquire new and manifold items of knowledge according to the things from which we derive them. It is otherwise with God: He does not derive His knowledge of things from the things, so that His knowledge would be multiple and ever new, but those things themselves are a consequence of His knowledge, which precedes them and establishes them as they are, whether this be as an incorporeal being, as a perpetually existing individual composed of matter, or as a thing possessing matter passing through various individuals according to some consistent law.

This is the reason why in the case of God there is neither a multiplicity of items of knowledge, nor acquisition of any new or different knowledge. Through knowing the true nature of His own unchangeable essence, He knows everything that results from all His works. For us to desire to understand how this takes place, is the same as to desire that we were He and that our perception were the same as His. The proper belief for a person who seeks truth and justice, is to hold that nothing whatsoever is hidden from God, but everything is accessible to His knowledge, which is identical with His substance; further, that it is out of the question for us to know anything of this type of perception. If we knew how it works, then we should ourselves be possessed of that intelligence with which that type of perception is achieved. This, however, is not possessed by anyone in the universe except God alone, whose essence it is.

Take these remarks to heart, for I maintain that it is very wonderful and a sound opinion. When it is followed up, no trace of erroneous or misleading ideas will be found in it, nor will it lead to any absurd conclusions or to the attribution of any shortcomings to God. We must accept it, since in dealing with those momentous and sublime subjects no demonstrative proof of any kind can be brought, be it according to the opinions of ourselves, who believe in revelation, or of the philosophers, whatever their opinions on this subject. In all subjects which do not allow of demonstrative proof, however, the same method must be followed which we have applied in dealing with this subject, God's knowledge of that which is outside Him. It should, therefore, be given full consideration.

Thomas Aquinas

Aquinas (1225–1274) was born at the castle of Roccasecca, near Aquino, which lay between Rome and Naples. His well-to-do parents apparently intended an ecclesiastical career for him. He was sent to the Benedictine abbey at Monte Cassino for his early education; from there he went to the University of Naples in 1239.

While in Naples Aquinas came under the influence of the newly created Order of Preachers founded by St. Dominic (1170–1221). The Dominicans at the time were, like the Franciscans, mendicant, or begging, friars. Espousing absolute poverty, they saw their vocation as the spreading of the Gospel to the people, both by word and by living example. The apostolic zeal of the mendicant friars captured the imagination and admiration of many; both the Franciscans and the Dominicans were to become successful and powerful. To Aquinas' family, however, the Dominicans must have appeared an appalling bunch of rag-tag ne'er-do-wells, especially in comparison with the Benedictines, who had prestige, power, and corporate wealth. When Aquinas joined the Dominican order in 1243, his family reacted strongly, going so far as to lock him up in the castle. He remained unswayed, spending his time studying the Bible. Legend has it that his family even offered him the blandishments of a prostitute in order to change his mind. Legend also has it that he refused. After attaining his freedom, Aquinas went to Paris in about 1244 and to Cologne in 1248 to study philosophy and theology.

The Dominicans placed considerable value on intellectual pursuits, and Aquinas profited from the teaching of Albertus Magnus (Albert the Great), perhaps the first of a long line of outstanding Dominican intellects. In 1252 Aquinas returned to the University of Paris as a lecturer, receiving his doctorate in theology in 1256. The divinity faculty at Paris, however, was reluctant to confer the license to teach upon mendicant friars. Aquinas the Dominican and St. Bonaventure (1217–1274) the Franciscan argued their case before the Pope, and both were licensed in 1257. From 1259 to 1268 Aquinas taught at several Dominican monasteries in Italy. He then returned to Paris, only to go to Naples in 1272. Summoned to participate at the Council of Lyons in 1274, he died on the way at Fossanova, near the place of his birth.

Aquinas did not spend much of his adult life in any one place, but he managed to write a tremendous amount of material. Several of his works are commentaries on the works of Aristotle, a fact that requires some comment. Aristotle's major works had been lost to the non-Arabic West until the beginning of the thirteenth century. Their reappearance caused a good deal of intellectual ferment. To many, the worldview disclosed in Aristotle's writings seemed to be a pagan threat to Christianity. To others, including Aquinas, Aristotle's works provided an exhilarating cosmological, metaphysical, and epistemological framework on which to build a coherent and all-encompassing Christian worldview. However, although Aristotle was "the Philosopher," he was not infallible, and Aquinas felt free to reject those aspects of his philosophy that conflicted with Christian revelation.

Some of the most characteristic features of Aquinas' philosophy derived from Aristotle include the insistence on the primary role of the senses in the acquisition of natural knowledge, and the metaphysical analysis of things in terms of matter and form. On the other hand, while Aristotle had held out little chance for personal survival after death, Aquinas argued for personal immortality. Aristotle's "God," or unmoved mover, would appear not to care one whit about the world, whereas the God of Christianity, insisted Aquinas, must be a personal God.

Another difference between Aristotle and Aquinas served to illustrate Aquinas' views on the relation between reason and faith. Aristotle had asserted that the world was eternal—that is, it had always existed, a doctrine that ran contrary to the Christian doctrine that the world was created by God. Aquinas claimed that nothing in our natural knowledge of the world would force one to conclude either that the world was eternal or that it had been created. Aristotle's position, then, was neither confirmed nor refuted by the evidence of our senses and the operation of human reason. But his position is refuted by revelation, that body of knowledge that transcends our rational faculties and that God has chosen to reveal to us. As a result, the Christian will believe as an item of faith that the world was created by God. For Aquinas, reason is powerless to prove such articles of faith given by revelation. But reason can operate to demonstrate the truth of propositions, which are not themselves articles of faith but are presupposed by the articles of faith. One such proposition is that God exists.

The greatest of Aquinas' philosophical writings is his monumental *Summa Theologiae*. It is divided into three major parts, with each part divided into many questions, and each question into articles. A number of questions and articles from the first part are reprinted here. In the first question, Aquinas asks whether Christian theology is a science—a question that may seem peculiar until one finds out that by "science," Aquinas means nothing more than any body of knowledge that has first principles. In the second question, Aquinas turns to the issue of God's existence. Here he criticizes Anselm's ontological argument but offers five arguments of his own to show that God exists. These "five ways" have attracted lavish philosophical attention through the centuries. The two articles from the thirteenth question address issues concerning the application to God, an infinite being, of terms like "good" and "wise" that have been learned from examples of finite beings. Finally, the excerpts from the nineteenth and the twenty-second questions attempt to resolve problems about the extent of God's providence in the world and whether that providence can allow some events to occur contingently.

• • •

F. C. Copleston's *Aquinas* (Baltimore, MD: Penguin Books, 1955) and Etienne Gilson's *The Christian Philosophy of St. Thomas Aquinas* (New York: Random House, 1956) are two good introductions to Aquinas' philosophy. For more rigorous treatments, see Brian Davies, *The Thought of Thomas Aquinas* (Oxford: Oxford University Press, 1992) and Eleonore Stump, *Aquinas* (New York: Routledge, 2003). Anthony Kenny, ed., *Aquinas: A Collection of Critical Essays* (Garden City, N.J.: Doubleday, 1969); Norman Kretzmann and Eleonore Stump, eds., *The Cambridge Companion to Aquinas* (Cambridge: Cambridge University Press, 1993); and Brian Davies, ed., *Thomas Aquinas: Contemporary Philosophical Perspectives* (Oxford: Oxford University Press, 2002) contain several important essays.

William E. Mann

Summa Theologiae

Part One

GOD

Question I

The Nature and Domain of Sacred Doctrine

(In Ten Articles)

To place our purpose within definite limits, we must first investigate the nature and domain of sacred doctrine. Concerning this there are ten points of inquiry:—

(1) Whether sacred doctrine is necessary? (2) Whether it is a science? (3) Whether it is one or many? (4) Whether it is speculative or practical? (5) How it is compared with other sciences? (6) Whether it is a wisdom? (7) Whether God is its subject-matter? (8) Whether it is argumentative? (9) Whether it rightly employs metaphors and similes? (10) Whether the Sacred Scripture of this doctrine may be expounded in different senses?

First Article

Whether, Besides the Philosophical Sciences, Any Further Doctrine Is Required?

We proceed thus to the First Article:—

Objection 1. It seems that, besides the philosophical sciences, we have no need of any further knowledge. For man should not seek to know what is above reason: *Seek not the things that are too high for thee* (*Ecclus.* iii. 22). But whatever is not above reason is sufficiently considered in the philosophical sciences. Therefore any other knowledge besides the philosophical sciences is superfluous.

Obj. 2. Further, knowledge can be concerned only with being, for nothing can be known, save the true, which is convertible with being. But everything that is, is considered in the philosophical sciences—even God Himself; so that there is a part of philosophy called theology, or the divine science, as is clear from Aristotle. Therefore, besides the philosophical sciences, there is no need of any further knowledge.

On the contrary, It is written (2 *Tim.* iii. 16): *All Scripture inspired of God is profitable to teach, to reprove, to correct, to instruct in justice.* Now Scripture, inspired by God, is not a part of the philosophical sciences discovered by human reason. Therefore it is useful that besides the philosophical sciences there should be another science—*i.e.,* inspired of God.

I answer that, It was necessary for man's salvation that there should be a knowledge revealed by God, besides the philosophical sciences investigated by human reason. First, because man is directed to God as to an end that surpasses the grasp of his reason: *The eye hath not seen, O God, besides Thee, what things Thou hast prepared for them that wait for Thee* (*Isa.* lxiv. 4). But the end must first be known by men who are to direct their thoughts and actions to the end. Hence it was necessary for the salvation of man that certain truths which exceed human reason should be made known to him by divine revelation. Even as regards those truths about God which human reason can investigate, it was necessary that man be taught by a divine revelation. For the truth about God, such as reason can know it, would only be known by a few, and that after a long time, and with the admixture of many errors; whereas man's whole salvation, which is in God, depends upon the knowledge of this truth. Therefore, in order that the salvation of men might be brought about more fitly and more surely, it was necessary that they be taught divine truths by divine revelation. It was therefore necessary that, besides the philosophical sciences investigated by reason, there should be a sacred science by way of revelation.

Reply Obj. 1. Although those things which are beyond man's knowledge may not be sought for by

Reprinted from Aquinas, *Basic Writings of St. Thomas Aquinas*, edited by Anton C. Pegis (Indianapolis: Hackett Publishing Company, reprinted 1997), by permission of the publisher.

man through his reason, nevertheless, what is revealed by God must be accepted through faith. Hence the sacred text continues. *For many things are shown to thee above the understanding of man* (*Ecclus.* iii. 25). And in such things sacred science consists.

Reply Obj. 2. Sciences are diversified according to the diverse nature of their knowable objects. For the astronomer and the physicist both prove the same conclusion—that the earth, for instance is round: the astronomer by means of mathematics (*i.e.*, abstracting from matter), but the physicist by means of matter itself. Hence there is no reason why those things which are treated by the philosophical sciences, so far as they can be known by the light of natural reason, may not also be treated by another science so far as they are known by the light of the divine revelation. Hence the theology included in sacred doctrine differs in genus from that theology which is part of philosophy.

Second Article

Whether Sacred Doctrine Is a Science?

We proceed thus to the Second Article:—

Objection 1. It seems that sacred doctrine is not a science. For every science proceeds from self-evident principles. But sacred doctrine proceeds from articles of faith which are not self-evident, since their truth is not admitted by all: *For all men have not faith* (2 *Thess.* iii. 2). Therefore sacred doctrine is not a science.

Obj. 2. Further, science is not of individuals. But sacred doctrine treats of individual facts, such as the deeds of Abraham, Isaac and Jacob, and the like. Therefore sacred doctrine is not a science.

On the contrary, Augustine says that *to this science alone belongs that whereby saving faith is begotten, nourished, protected and strengthened.* But this can be said of no science except sacred doctrine. Therefore sacred doctrine is a science.

I answer that, Sacred doctrine is a science. We must bear in mind that there are two kinds of sciences. There are some which proceed from principles known by the natural light of the intellect, such as arithmetic and geometry and the like. There are also some which proceed from principles known by the light of a higher science: thus the science of optics proceeds from principles established by geometry, and music from principles established by arithmetic. So it is that sacred doctrine is a science because it proceeds from principles made known by the light of a higher science, namely, the science of God and the blessed. Hence, just as music accepts on authority the principles taught by the arithmetician, so sacred science accepts the principles revealed by God.

Reply Obj. 1. The principles of any science are either in themselves self-evident, or reducible to the knowledge of a higher science; and such, as we have said, are the principles of sacred doctrine.

Reply Obj. 2. Individual facts are not treated in sacred doctrine because it is concerned with them principally; they are rather introduced as examples to be followed in our lives (as in the moral sciences), as well as to establish the authority of those men through whom the divine revelation, on which this sacred scripture or doctrine is based, has come down to us.

Third Article

Whether Sacred Doctrine Is One Science?

We proceed thus to the Third Article:—

Objection 1. It seems that sacred doctrine is not one science, for according to the Philosopher[1] *that science is one which treats only of one class of subjects.* But the creator and the creature, both of whom are treated in sacred doctrine, cannot be grouped together under one class of subjects. Therefore sacred doctrine is not one science.

Obj. 2. Further, in sacred doctrine we treat of angels, corporeal creatures and human morality. But these belong to separate philosophical sciences. Therefore sacred doctrine cannot be one science.

On the contrary, Holy Scripture speaks of it as one science: *Wisdom gave him the knowledge of holy things* (*Wis.* x. 10).

I answer that, Sacred doctrine is one science. The unity of a power or habit is to be gauged by its object, not indeed, in its material aspect, but as regards the formality under which it is an object. For example, man, ass, stone, agree in the one formality of being colored; and color is the formal object of sight. Therefore, because Sacred Scripture (as we have said)

1. [Aquinas often refers to Aristotle as "the Philosopher."—S.M.C.]

considers some things under the formality of being divinely revealed, all things which have been divinely revealed have in common the formality of the object of this science. Hence, they are included under sacred doctrine as under one science.

Reply Obj. 1. Sacred doctrine does not treat of God and creatures equally, but of God primarily, and of creatures only so far as they are referable to God as their beginning or end. Hence the unity of this science is not impaired.

Reply Obj. 2. Nothing prevents inferior powers or habits from being diversified by objects which yet agree with one another in coming together under a higher power or habit; because the higher power or habit regards its own object under a more universal formality. Thus, the object of the *common sense* is the sensible, including, therefore, whatever is visible or audible. Hence the *common sense,* although one power, extends to all the objects of the five senses. Similarly, objects which are the subject-matter of different philosophical sciences can yet be treated by this one single sacred science under one aspect, namely, in so far as they can be included in revelation. So that in this way sacred doctrine bears, as it were, the stamp of the divine science, which is one and simple, yet extends to everything.

Fourth Article

Whether Sacred Doctrine Is a Practical Science?

We proceed thus to the Fourth Article:—

Objection 1. It seems that sacred doctrine is a practical science, for a practical science is that which ends in action, according to the Philosopher. But sacred doctrine is ordained to action: *Be ye doers of the word, and not hearers only* (*Jas.* i. 22). Therefore sacred doctrine is a practical science.

Obj. 2. Further sacred doctrine is divided into the Old and the New Law. But law belongs to moral science, which is a practical science. Therefore sacred doctrine is a practical science.

On the contrary, Every practical science is concerned with the things man can do; as moral science is concerned with human acts, and architecture with buildings. But sacred doctrine is chiefly concerned with God, Who is rather the Maker of man. Therefore it is not a practical but a speculative science.

I answer that, Sacred doctrine, being one, extends to things which belong to the different philosophical sciences, because it considers in each the same formal aspect, namely, so far as they can be known through the divine light. Hence, although among the philosophical sciences some are speculative and others practical, nevertheless, sacred doctrine includes both; as God, by one and the same science, knows both Himself and His works.

Still, it is more speculative than practical, because it is more concerned with divine things than with human acts; though even of these acts it treats inasmuch as man is ordained by them to the perfect knowledge of God, in which consists eternal beatitude.

This is a sufficient answer to the Objections.

Fifth Article

Whether Sacred Doctrine Is Nobler Than Other Sciences?

We proceed thus to the Fifth Article:—

Objection 1. It seems that sacred doctrine is not nobler than other sciences, for the nobility of a science depends on its certitude. But other sciences, the principles of which cannot be doubted, seem to be more certain than sacred doctrine; for its principles—namely, articles of faith—can be doubted. Therefore other sciences seem to be nobler.

Obj. 2. Further, it is the part of a lower science to draw upon a higher; as music draws upon arithmetic. But sacred doctrine does draw upon the philosophical sciences; for Jerome[2] observes, in his Epistle to Magnus, that *the ancient doctors so enriched their books with the doctrines and thoughts of the philosophers, that thou knowest not what more to admire in them, their profane erudition or their scriptural learning.* Therefore sacred doctrine is inferior to other sciences.

On the contrary, Other sciences are called the handmaidens of this one: *Wisdom sent her maids to invite to the tower* (*Prov.* ix. 3).

I answer that, Since this science is partly speculative and partly practical, it transcends all other sciences,

2. [Jerome (c. 347–c. 420), a Father of the Church, was the author of the Vulgate translation of the Bible, the official Latin version of the Roman Catholic Church.]

speculative and practical. Now one speculative science is said to be nobler than another either by reason of its greater certitude, or by reason of the higher dignity of its subject-matter. In both these respects this science surpasses other speculative sciences: in point of greater certitude, because other sciences derive their certitude from the natural light of human reason, which can err, whereas this derives its certitude from the light of the divine knowledge, which cannot err; in point of the higher dignity of its subject-matter, because this science treats chiefly of those things which by their sublimity transcend human reason, while other sciences consider only those things which are within reason's grasp. Of the practical sciences, that one is nobler which is ordained to a more final end, as political science is nobler than military science; for the good of the army is directed to the good of the state. But the purpose of this science, in so far as it is practical, is eternal beatitude, to which as to an ultimate end the ends of all the practical sciences are directed. Hence it is clear that from every standpoint it is nobler than other sciences.

Reply Obj. 1. It may well happen that what is in itself the more certain may seem to us the less certain because of the weakness of our intellect, *which is dazzled by the clearest objects of nature; as the owl is dazzled by the light of the sun.* Hence the fact that some happen to doubt about the articles of faith is not due to the uncertain nature of the truths, but to the weakness of the human intellect; yet the slenderest knowledge that may be obtained of the highest things is more desirable than the most certain knowledge obtained of the lowest things, as is said in *De Animalibus* xi.[3]

Reply Obj. 2. This science can draw upon the philosophical sciences, not as though it stood in need of them, but only in order to make its teaching clearer. For it accepts its principles, not from the other sciences, but immediately from God, by revelation. Therefore it does not draw upon the other sciences as upon its superiors, but uses them as its inferiors and handmaidens: even so the master sciences make use of subordinate sciences, as political science of military science. That it thus uses them is not due to its own defect or insufficiency, but to the defect of our intellect, which is more easily led by what is known through natural reason (from which proceed the other sciences), to that which is above reason, such as are the teachings of this science.

Sixth Article

Whether This Doctrine Is a Wisdom?

We proceed thus to the Sixth Article:—

Objection 1. It seems that this doctrine is not a wisdom. For no doctrine which borrows its principles is worthy of the name of wisdom, seeing that the wise man directs, and is not directed. But this doctrine borrows its principles. Therefore it is not a wisdom.

Obj. 2. Further, it is a part of wisdom to prove the principles of other sciences. Hence it is called the chief of sciences, as is clear in *Ethics* vi.[4] But this doctrine does not prove the principles of other sciences. Therefore it is not a wisdom.

Obj. 3. Further, this doctrine is acquired by study, whereas wisdom is acquired by God's inspiration, and is accordingly numbered among the gifts of the Holy Spirit (*Isa.* xi. 2). Therefore this doctrine is not a wisdom.

On the contrary, It is written (*Deut.* iv. 6): *This is your wisdom and understanding in the sight of nations.*

I answer that, This doctrine is wisdom above all human wisdoms not merely in any one order, but absolutely. For since it is the part of a wise man to order and to judge, and since lesser matters can be judged in the light of some higher cause, he is said to be wise in any genus who considers the highest cause in that genus. Thus in the realm of building, he who plans the form of the house is called wise and architect, in relation to the subordinate laborers who trim the wood and make ready the stones: thus it is said, *As a wise architect I have laid the foundation* (*1 Cor.* ii. 10). Again, in order of all human life, the prudent man is called wise, inasmuch as he directs his acts to a fitting end: thus it is said, *Wisdom is prudence to a man* (*Prov.* x. 23). Therefore, he who considers absolutely the highest cause of the whole universe, namely God, is most of all called wise. Hence wisdom is said to be the knowledge of divine things, as Augustine says. But sacred doctrine essentially treats of God viewed as the highest cause, for

3. [The reference is to a biological work by Aristotle.]

4. [The reference is to Aristotle's *Nicomachean Ethics*.]

it treats of Him not only so far as He can be known through creatures just as philosophers knew Him—*That which is known of God is manifest in them* (*Rom.* i. 19)—but also so far as He is known to Himself alone and revealed to others. Hence sacred doctrine is especially called a wisdom.

Reply Obj. 1. Sacred doctrine derives its principles, not from any human knowledge, but from the divine knowledge, by which, as by the highest wisdom, all our knowledge is ordered.

Reply Obj. 2. The principles of the other sciences either are evident and cannot be proved, or they are proved by natural reason in some other science. But the knowledge proper to this science comes through revelation, and not through natural reason. Therefore it is not its business to prove the principles of the other sciences, but only to judge them. For whatsoever is found in the other sciences contrary to the truth of this science must be condemned as false. Hence, it is said: *Destroying counsels and every height that exalteth itself against the knowledge of God* (2 *Cor.* x. 4, 5).

Reply Obj. 3. Since judgment pertains to wisdom, in accord with a twofold manner of judging there is a twofold wisdom. A man may judge in one way by inclination, as whoever has the habit of a virtue judges rightly of what is virtuous by his very inclination towards it. Hence it is the virtuous man, as we read,[5] who is the measure and rule of human acts. In another way, a man may judge by knowledge, just as a man learned in moral science might be able to judge rightly about virtuous acts, though he had not virtue. The first manner of judging divine things belongs to that wisdom which is numbered as a gift of the Holy Ghost: *The spiritual man judgeth all things* (1 *Cor.* ii. 15). And Dionysius says: *Hierotheus is taught not only as one learning, but also as experiencing divine things.* The second manner of judging belongs to this doctrine, inasmuch as it is acquired by study, though its principles are obtained by revelation.

Seventh Article
Whether God Is the Subject-Matter of This Science?

We proceed thus to the Seventh Article:—

Objection 1. It seems that God is not the subject-matter of this science. For, according to the Philosopher, in every science the essence of its subject is presupposed. But this science cannot presuppose the essence of God, for Damascene says: *It is impossible to express the essence of God.* Therefore God is not the subject-matter of this science.

Obj. 2. Further, whatever conclusions are reached in any science must be comprehended under the subject-matter of that science. But in Holy Scripture we reach conclusions not only concerning God, but concerning many other things, such as creatures and human morality. Therefore God is not the subject-matter of this science.

On the contrary, The subject-matter of a science is that of which it principally treats. But in this science the treatment is mainly about God; for it is called theology, as treating of God. Therefore God is the subject-matter of this science.

I answer that, God is the subject-matter of this science. The relation between a science and its subject-matter is the same as that between a habit or a power and its object. Now properly speaking the object of a power or habit is that under whose formality all things are referred to that power or habit, as man and stone are referred to sight in that they are colored. Hence colored things are the proper object of sight. But in sacred doctrine all things are treated under the aspect of God, either because they are God Himself, or because they refer to God as to their beginning and end. Hence it follows that God is in very truth the subject-matter of this science. This is made clear also from the principles of this science, namely, the articles of faith, for faith is about God. The subject-matter of the principles and of the whole science must be the same, since the whole science is contained virtually in its principles.

Some, however, looking to what is treated in this science, and not to the aspect under which it is treated, have asserted the subject-matter of this science to be something other than God—that is, either things and signs, or the works of salvation, or the whole Christ, that is, the head and members. Of all these things, in truth, we treat in this science, but so far as they are ordered to God.

Reply Obj. 1. Although we cannot know in what consists the essence of God, nevertheless in this doctrine we make use of His effects, either of nature or of grace, in the place of a definition, in regard to whatever is treated in this doctrine concerning God;

5. [The reference is to Aristotle's *Nicomachean Ethics.*]

even as in some philosophical sciences we demonstrate something about a cause from its effect, by taking the effect in the place of a definition of the cause.

Reply Obj. 2. Whatever other conclusions are reached in this sacred science are comprehended under God, not as parts or species or accidents, but as in some way ordained to Him.

Eighth Article

Whether Sacred Doctrine Is Argumentative?

We proceed thus to the Eighth Article:—

Objection 1. It seems this doctrine is not argumentative. For Ambrose[6] says: *Put arguments aside where faith is sought.* But in this doctrine faith especially is sought: *But these things are written that you may believe* (*Jo.* xx. 31). Therefore sacred doctrine is not argumentative.

Obj. 2. Further, if it is argumentative, the argument is either from authority or from reason. If it is from authority, it seems unbefitting its dignity, for the proof from authority is the weakest form of proof according to Boethius.[7] But if from reason, this is unbefitting its end, because, according to Gregory,[8] *faith has no merit in those things of which human reason brings its own experience.* Therefore sacred doctrine is not argumentative.

On the contrary, The Scripture says that a bishop should *embrace that faithful word which is according to doctrine, that he may be able to exhort in sound doctrine and to convince the gainsayers* (*Tit.* i. 9).

I answer that, As the other sciences do not argue in proof of their principles, but argue from their principles to demonstrate other truths in these sciences, so this doctrine does not argue in proof of its principles, which are the articles of faith, but from them it goes on to prove something else; as the Apostle[9] argues from the resurrection of Christ in proof of the general resurrection (*1 Cor.* xv. 12). However, it is to be borne in mind, in regard to the philosophical sciences, that the inferior sciences neither prove their principles nor dispute with those who deny them, but leave this to a higher science; whereas the highest of them, viz., metaphysics, can dispute with one who denies its principles, if only the opponent will make some concession; but if he concedes nothing, it can have no dispute with him, though it can answer his arguments. Hence Sacred Scripture, since it has no science above itself, disputes argumentatively with one who denies its principles only if the opponent admits some at least of the truths obtained through divine revelation. Thus, we can argue with heretics from texts in Holy Scripture, and against those who deny one article of faith we can argue from another. If our opponent believes nothing of divine revelation, there is no longer any means of proving the articles of faith by argument, but only of answering his objections—if he has any—against faith. Since faith rests upon infallible truth, and since the contrary of a truth can never be demonstrated, it is clear that the proofs brought against faith are not demonstrations, but arguments that can be answered.

Reply Obj. 1. Although arguments from human reason cannot avail to prove what belongs to faith, nevertheless, this doctrine argues from articles of faith to other truths.

Reply Obj. 2. It is especially proper to this doctrine to argue from authority, inasmuch as its principles are obtained by revelation; and hence we must believe the authority of those to whom the revelation has been made. Nor does this take away the dignity of this doctrine, for although the argument from authority based on human reason is the weakest, yet the argument from authority based on divine revelation is the strongest. But sacred doctrine also makes use of human reason, not, indeed, to prove faith (for thereby the merit of faith would come to an end), but to make clear other things that are set forth in this doctrine. Since therefore grace does not destroy nature, but perfects it, natural reason should minister to faith as the natural inclination of the will ministers to

6. [Ambrose (c. 340–397) was bishop of Milan and a Father of the Church.]

7. [Boethius (c. 480–524) was a Roman philosopher and statesman whose greatest work, the *Consolation of Philosophy,* was written while he was imprisoned prior to his execution on false charges of treason.)

8. [Gregory I (c. 540–604), a Father of the Church who served as pope, defended the view that the temporal powers of the emperor and the spiritual powers of the pope were each supreme within separate spheres.]

9. [Aquinas often refers to Paul as "the Apostle."]

charity. Hence the Apostle says: *Bringing into captivity every understanding unto the obedience of Christ* (2 *Cor.* x. 5). Hence it is that sacred doctrine makes use also of the authority of philosophers in those questions in which they were able to know the truth by natural reason, as Paul quotes a saying of Aratus:[10] *As some also of your own poets said: For we are also His offspring* (*Acts* xvii. 28). Nevertheless, sacred doctrine makes use of these authorities as extrinsic and probable arguments, but properly uses the authority of the canonical Scriptures as a necessary demonstration, and the authority of the doctors of the Church as one that may properly be used, yet merely as probable. For our faith rests upon the revelation made to the apostles and prophets, who wrote the canonical books, and not on the revelations (if any such there are) made to other doctors. Hence Augustine says: *Only those books of Scripture which are called canonical have I learned to hold in such honor as to believe their authors have not erred in any way in writing them. But other authors I so read as not to deem anything in their works to be true, merely because of their having so thought and written, whatever may have been their holiness and learning.*

Ninth Article

Whether Holy Scripture Should Use Metaphors?

We proceed thus to the Ninth Article:—

Objection 1. It seems that Holy Scripture should not use metaphors. For that which is proper to the lowest science seems not to befit this science, which holds the highest place of all. But to proceed by the aid of various similitudes and figures is proper to poetic, the least of all the sciences. Therefore it is not fitting that this science should make use of such similitudes.

Obj. 2. Further, this doctrine seems to be intended to make truth clear. Hence a reward is held out to those who manifest it: *They that explain me shall have life everlasting* (*Ecclus.* xxiv. 31). But by such similitudes truth is obscured. Therefore to put forward divine truths under the likeness of corporeal things does not befit this doctrine.

Obj. 3. Further, the higher creatures are, the nearer they approach to the divine likeness. If therefore any creature be taken to represent God, this representation ought chiefly to be taken from the higher creatures, and not from the lower; yet this is often found in the Scriptures.

On the contrary, It is written (*Osee* xxii. 10): *I have multiplied visions, and I have used similitudes by the ministry of the prophets.* But to put forward anything by means of similitudes is to use metaphors. Therefore sacred doctrine may use metaphors.

I answer that, It is befitting Holy Scripture to put forward divine and spiritual truths by means of comparisons with material things. For God provides for everything according to the capacity of its nature. Now it is natural to man to attain to intellectual truths through sensible things, because all our knowledge originates from sense. Hence in Holy Scripture spiritual truths are fittingly taught under the likeness of material things. This is what Dionysius[11] says: *We cannot be enlightened by the divine rays except they be hidden within the covering of many sacred veils.* It is also befitting Holy Scripture, which is proposed to all without distinction of persons—*To the wise and to the unwise I am a debtor* (*Rom.* i. 14)—that spiritual truths be expounded by means of figures taken from corporeal things, in order that thereby even the simple who are unable by themselves to grasp intellectual things may be able to understand it.

Reply Obj. 1. Poetry makes use of metaphors to produce a representation, for it is natural to man to be pleased with representations. But sacred doctrine makes use of metaphors as both necessary and useful.

Reply Obj. 2. The ray of divine revelation is not extinguished by the sensible imagery wherewith it is veiled, as Dionysius says; and its truth so far remains that it does not allow the minds of those to whom the revelation has been made, to rest in the likenesses, but raises them to the knowledge of intelligible truths; and through those to whom the revelation has been made others also may receive instruction in these matters. Hence those things that are taught metaphorically in one part of Scripture, in other parts are taught more openly. The very hiding of truth in figures is

10. [Aratus was a third-century-B.C. Greek court poet.]

11. [Dionysius the Areopagite, who lived during the first century, was traditionally considered the first bishop of Athens.]

useful for the exercise of thoughtful minds, and as a defense against the ridicule of the unbelievers, according to the words, *Give not that which is holy to dogs* (*Matt.* vii. 6).

Reply Obj. 3. As Dionysius says, it is more fitting that divine truths should be expounded under the figure of less noble than of nobler bodies; and this for three reasons. First, because thereby men's minds are the better freed from error. For then it is clear that these things are not literal descriptions of divine truths, which might have been open to doubt had they been expressed under the figure of nobler bodies, especially in the case of those who could think of nothing nobler than bodies. Second, because this is more befitting the knowledge of God that we have in this life. For what He is not is clearer to us than what He is. Therefore similitudes drawn from things farthest away from God form within us a truer estimate that God is above whatsoever we may say or think of Him. Third, because thereby divine truths are the better hidden from the unworthy.

Tenth Article

Whether in Holy Scripture a Word May Have Several Senses?

We proceed thus to the Tenth Article:—

Objection 1. It seems that in Holy Scripture a word cannot have several senses, historical or literal, allegorical, tropological or moral, and anagogical. For many different senses in one text produce confusion and deception and destroy all force of argument. Hence no argument, but only fallacies, can be deduced from a multiplicity of propositions. But Holy Scripture ought to be able to state the truth without any fallacy. Therefore in it there cannot be several senses to a word.

Obj. 2. Further, Augustine says that *the Old Testament has a fourfold division: according to history, etiology, analogy, and allegory.* Now these four seem altogether different from the four divisions mentioned in the first objection. Therefore it does not seem fitting to explain the same word of Holy Scripture according to the four different senses mentioned above.

Obj. 3. Further, besides these senses, there is the parabolical, which is not one of these four.

On the contrary, Gregory says: *Holy Scripture by the manner of its speech transcends every science, because in one and the same sentence, while it describes a fact, it reveals a mystery.*

I answer that, The author of Holy Scripture is God, in Whose power it is to signify His meaning, not by words only (as man also can do), but also by things themselves. So, whereas in every other science things are signified by words, this science has the property that the things signified by the words have themselves also a signification. Therefore that first signification whereby words signify things belongs to the first sense, the historical or literal. That signification whereby things signified by words have themselves also a signification is called the spiritual sense, which is based on the literal, and presupposes it. Now this spiritual sense has a threefold division. For as the Apostle says (*Heb.* x. 1) the Old Law is a figure of the New Law, and Dionysius says *the New Law itself is a figure of future glory.* Again, the New Law, whatever our Head has done is a type of what we ought to do. Therefore, so far as the things of the Old Law signify the things of the New Law, there is the allegorical sense; so far as the things done in Christ, or so far as the things which signify Christ, are signs of what we ought to do, there is the moral sense. But so far as they signify what relates to eternal glory, there is the anagogical sense. Since the literal sense is that which the author intends, and since the author of Holy Scripture is God, Who by one act comprehends all things by His intellect, it is not unfitting, as Augustine says, if, even according to the literal sense, one word in Holy Scripture should have several senses.

Reply Obj. 1. The multiplicity of these senses does not produce equivocation or any other kind of multiplicity, seeing that these senses are not multiplied because one word signifies several things, but because the things signified by the words can be themselves signs of other things. Thus in Holy Scripture no confusion results, for all the senses are founded on one—the literal—from which alone can any argument be drawn, and not from those intended allegorically, as Augustine says. Nevertheless, nothing of Holy Scripture perishes because of this, since nothing necessary to faith is contained under the spiritual sense which is not elsewhere put forward clearly by the Scripture in its literal sense.

Reply Obj. 2. These three—history, etiology, analogy—are grouped under the literal sense. For it is called history, as Augustine expounds, whenever anything is simply related; it is called etiology when its cause is assigned, as when Our Lord gave the reason why Moses allowed the putting away of wives—namely, because of the hardness of men's hearts (*Matt.* xix. 8); it is called analogy whenever the truth of one text of Scripture is shown not to contradict the truth of another. Of these four, allegory alone stands for the three spiritual senses. Thus Hugh of St. Victor[12] includes the anagogical under the allegorical sense, laying down three senses only—the historical, the allegorical and the tropological.

Reply Obj. 3. The parabolical sense is contained in the literal, for by words things are signified properly and figuratively. Nor is the figure itself, but that which is figured, the literal sense. When Scripture speaks of God's arm, the literal sense is not that God has such a member, but only what is signified by this member, namely, operative power. Hence it is plain that nothing false can ever underlie the literal sense of Holy Scripture.

Question II
The Existence of God
(In Three Articles)

Because the chief aim of sacred doctrine is to teach the knowledge of God not only as He is in Himself, but also as He is the beginning of things and their last end, and especially of rational creatures, as is clear from what has been already said, therefore, in our endeavor to expound this science, we shall treat: (1) of God; (2) of the rational creature's movement towards God; (3) of Christ Who as man is our way to God.

In treating of God there will be a threefold division:—

For we shall consider (1) whatever concerns the divine essence. (2) Whatever concerns the distinctions of Persons. (3) Whatever concerns the procession of creatures from Him.

Concerning the divine essence, we must consider:—

(1) Whether God exists? (2) The manner of His existence, or, rather, what is *not* the manner of His existence. (3) Whatever concerns His operations—namely, His knowledge, will, power.

Concerning the first, there are three points of inquiry:—

(1) Whether the proposition *God exists* is self-evident? (2) Whether it is demonstrable? (3) Whether God exists?

First Article

Whether the Existence of God Is Self-Evident?

We proceed thus to the First Article:—

Objection 1. It seems that the existence of God is self-evident. For those things are said to be self-evident to us the knowledge of which exists naturally in us, as we can see in regard to first principles. But as Damascene[13] says, *the knowledge of God is naturally implanted in all.* Therefore the existence of God is self-evident.

Obj. 2. Further, those things are said to be self-evident which are known as soon as the terms are known, which the Philosopher says is true of the first principles of demonstration. Thus, when the nature of a whole and of a part is known, it is at once recognized that every whole is greater than its part. But as soon as the signification of the name *God* is understood, it is at once seen that God exists. For by this name is signified that thing than which nothing greater can be conceived. But that which exists actually and mentally is greater than that which exists only mentally. Therefore, since as soon as the name *God* is understood it exists mentally, it also follows that it exists actually. Therefore the proposition *God exists* is self-evident.

Obj. 3. Further, the existence of truth is self-evident. For whoever denies the existence of truth grants that truth does not exist: and, if truth does not exist, then the proposition *Truth does not exist* is true: and if there is anything true there must be truth. But God is truth itself: *I am the way, the truth, and the life* (*Jo.* xiv. 6). Therefore *God exists* is self-evident.

On the contrary, No one can mentally admit the opposite of what is self-evident, as the Philosopher states concerning the first principles of demonstration. But the opposite of the proposition *God is* can

12. [Hugh of St. Victor (1096–1141), born in Saxony, was a noted theologian who also wrote numerous mystical works.]

13. [John Damascene (c. 675–c. 749) was a Syrian theologian and Father of the Church.]

be mentally admitted: *The fool said in his heart, There is no God* (*Ps.* lii. 1). Therefore, that God exists is not self-evident.

I answer that, A thing can be self-evident in either of two ways: on the one hand, self-evident in itself, though not to us; on the other, self-evident in itself, and to us. A proposition is self-evident because the predicate is included in the essence of the subject: *e.g., Man is an animal,* for animal is contained in the essence of man. If, therefore, the essence of the predicate and subject be known to all, the proposition will be self-evident to all; as is clear with regard to the first principles of demonstration, the terms of which are certain common notions that no one is ignorant of, such as being and non-being, whole and part, and the like. If, however, there are some to whom the essence of the predicate and subject is unknown, the proposition will be self-evident in itself, but not to those who do not know the meaning of the predicate and subject of the proposition. Therefore, it happens, as Boethius says, that there are some notions of the mind which are common and self-evident only to the learned, as that incorporeal substances are not in space. Therefore, I say that this proposition, *God exists,* of itself is self-evident, for the predicate is the same as the subject, because God is His own existence as will be hereafter shown. Now because we do not know the essence of God, the proposition is not self-evident to us, but needs to be demonstrated by things that are more known to us, though less known in their nature—namely, by His effects.

Reply Obj. 1. To know that God exists in a general and confused way is implanted in us by nature, inasmuch as God is man's beatitude. For man naturally desires happiness, and what is naturally desired by man is naturally known by him. This, however, is not to know absolutely that God exists; just as to know that someone is approaching is not the same as to know that Peter is approaching, even though it is Peter who is approaching; for there are many who imagine that man's perfect good, which is happiness, consists in riches, and others in pleasures, and others in something else.

Reply Obj. 2. Perhaps not everyone who hears this name *God* understands it to signify something than which nothing greater can be thought, seeing that some have believed God to be a body. Yet, granted that everyone understands that by this name *God* is signified something than which nothing greater can be thought, nevertheless, it does not therefore follow that he understands that what the name signifies exists actually, but only that it exists mentally. Nor can it be argued that it actually exists, unless it be admitted that there actually exists something than which nothing greater can be thought; and this precisely is not admitted by those who hold that God does not exist.

Reply Obj. 3. The existence of truth in general is self-evident, but the existence of a Primal Truth is not self-evident to us.

Second Article

Whether It Can Be Demonstrated That God Exists?

We proceed thus to the Second Article:—

Objection 1. It seems that the existence of God cannot be demonstrated. For it is an article of faith that God exists. But what is of faith cannot be demonstrated, because a demonstration produces scientific knowledge, whereas faith is of the unseen, as is clear from the Apostle (*Heb.* xi. 1). Therefore it cannot be demonstrated that God exists.

Obj. 2. Further, essence is the middle term of demonstration. But we cannot know in what God's essence consists, but solely in what it does not consist, as Damascene says. Therefore we cannot demonstrate that God exists.

Obj. 3. Further, if the existence of God were demonstrated, this could only be from His effects. But His effects are not proportioned to Him, since He is infinite and His effects are finite, and between the finite and infinite there is no proportion. Therefore, since a cause cannot be demonstrated by an effect not proportioned to it, it seems that the existence of God cannot be demonstrated.

On the contrary, the Apostle says: *The invisible things of Him are clearly seen, being understood by the things that are made* (*Rom.* i. 20). But this would not be unless the existence of God could be demonstrated through the things that are made; for the first thing we must know of anything is, whether it exists.

I answer that, Demonstration can be made in two ways: One is through the cause, and is called *propter quid,* and this is to argue from what is prior absolutely. The other is through the effect, and is called a demonstration *quia;* this is to argue from what is prior relatively only to us. When an effect is better known to us than its cause, from the effect we proceed to the knowledge of the cause. And from every effect the existence of its proper cause can be demonstrated, so long as its effects are better known to us; because, since every effect depends upon its cause, if the effect exists, the cause must pre-exist. Hence the existence of God, in so far as it is not self-evident to us, can be demonstrated from those of His effects which are known to us.

Reply Obj. 1. The existence of God and other like truths about God, which can be known by natural reason, are not articles of faith, but are preambles to the articles; for faith presupposes natural knowledge, even as grace presupposes nature and perfection the perfectible. Nevertheless, there is nothing to prevent a man, who cannot grasp a proof, from accepting, as a matter of faith, something which in itself is capable of being scientifically known and demonstrated.

Reply Obj. 2. When the existence of a cause is demonstrated from an effect, this effect takes the place of the definition of the cause in proving the cause's existence. This is especially the case in regard to God, because, in order to prove the existence of anything, it is necessary to accept as a middle term the meaning of the name, and not its essence, for the question of its essence follows on the question of its existence. Now the names given to God are derived from His effects, as will be later shown. Consequently, in demonstrating the existence of God from His effects, we may take for the middle term the meaning of the name *God*.

Reply Obj. 3. From effects not proportioned to the cause no perfect knowledge of that cause can be obtained. Yet from every effect the existence of the cause can be clearly demonstrated, and so we can demonstrate the existence of God from His effects; though from them we cannot know God perfectly as He is in His essence.

Third Article

Whether God Exists?

We proceed thus to the Third Article:—

Objection 1. It seems that God does not exist; because if one of two contraries be infinite, the other would be altogether destroyed. But the name *God* means that He is infinite goodness. If, therefore, God existed, there would be no evil discoverable; but there is evil in the world. Therefore God does not exist.

Obj. 2. Further, it is superfluous to suppose that what can be accounted for by a few principles has been produced by many. But it seems that everything we see in the world can be accounted for by other principles, supposing God did not exist. For all natural things can be reduced to one principle, which is nature; and all voluntary things can be reduced to one principle, which is human reason, or will. Therefore there is no need to suppose God's existence.

On the contrary, It is said in the person of God: *I am Who am* (*Exod.* iii. 14).

I answer that, The existence of God can be proved in five ways.

The first and more manifest way is the argument from motion. It is certain, and evident to our senses, that in the world some things are in motion. Now whatever is moved is moved by another, for nothing can be moved except it is in potentiality to that towards which it is moved; whereas a thing moves inasmuch as it is in act. For motion is nothing else than the reduction of something from potentiality to actuality. But nothing can be reduced from potentiality to actuality, except by something in a state of actuality. Thus that which is actually hot, as fire, makes wood, which is potentially hot, to be actually hot, and thereby moves and changes it. Now it is not possible that the same thing should be at once in actuality and potentiality in the same respect, but only in different respects. For what is actually hot cannot simultaneously be potentially hot; but it is simultaneously potentially cold. It is therefore impossible that in the same respect and in the same way a thing should be both mover and moved, *i.e.*, that it should move itself. Therefore, whatever is moved must be moved by another. If that by which it is moved be itself moved, then this also must needs be moved by another, and that by another again. But this cannot go on to infinity, because then there would be no first mover, and, consequently, no other mover, seeing that subsequent movers move only inasmuch as they are moved by the first mover; as the staff moves only because it is moved by the hand. Therefore it is necessary to arrive at a first mover, moved by no other; and this everyone understands to be God.

The second way is from the nature of efficient cause. In the world of sensible things we find there is an order of efficient causes. There is no case known (neither is it, indeed, possible) in which a thing is found to be the efficient cause of itself; for so it would be prior to itself, which is impossible. Now in efficient causes it is not possible to go on to infinity, because in all efficient causes following in order, the first is the cause of the intermediate cause, and the intermediate is the cause of the ultimate cause, whether the intermediate cause be several, or one only. Now to take away the cause is to take away the effect. Therefore, if there be no first cause among efficient causes, there will be no ultimate, nor any intermediate, cause. But if in efficient causes it is possible to go on to infinity, there will be no first efficient cause, neither will there be an ultimate effect, nor any intermediate efficient causes; all of which is plainly false. Therefore it is necessary to admit a first efficient cause, to which everyone gives the name of God.

The third way is taken from possibility and necessity, and runs thus. We find in nature things that are possible to be and not to be, since they are found to be generated, and to be corrupted, and consequently, it is possible for them to be and not to be. But it is impossible for these always to exist, for that which can not-be at some time is not. Therefore, if everything can not-be, then at one time there was nothing in existence. Now if this were true, even now there would be nothing in existence, because that which does not exist begins to exist only through something already existing. Therefore, if at one time nothing was in existence, it would have been impossible for anything to have begun to exist; and thus even now nothing would be in existence—which is absurd. Therefore, not all beings are merely possible, but there must exist something the existence of which is necessary. But every necessary thing either has its necessity caused by another, or not. Now it is impossible to go on to infinity in necessary things which have their necessity caused by another, as has been already proved in regard to efficient causes. Therefore we cannot but admit the existence of some being having of itself its own necessity, and not receiving it from another, but rather causing in others their necessity. This all men speak of as God.

The fourth way is taken from the gradation to be found in things. Among beings there are some more and some less good, true, noble, and the like. But *more* and *less* are predicated of different things according as they resemble in their different ways something which is the maximum, as a thing is said to be hotter according as it more nearly resembles that which is hottest; so that there is something which is truest, something best, something noblest, and consequently, something which is most being, for those things that are greatest in truth are greatest in being, as it is written in *Metaph* ii.[14] Now the maximum in any genus is the cause of all in that genus, as fire, which is the maximum of heat, is the cause of all hot things, as is said in the same book. Therefore there must also be something which is to all beings the cause of their being, goodness, and every other perfection; and this we call God.

The fifth way is taken from the governance of the world. We see that things which lack knowledge, such as natural bodies, act for an end, and this is evident from their acting always, or nearly always, in the same way, so as to obtain the best result. Hence it is plain that they achieve their end, not fortuitously, but designedly. Now whatever lacks knowledge cannot move towards an end, unless it be directed by some being endowed with knowledge and intelligence; as the arrow is directed by the archer. Therefore some intelligent being exists by whom all natural things are directed to their end; and this being we call God.

Reply Obj. 1. As Augustine says: *Since God is the highest good, He would not allow any evil to exist in His works, unless His omnipotence and goodness were such as to bring good even out of evil.* This is part of the infinite goodness of God, that He should allow evil to exist, and out of it produce good.

Reply Obj. 2. Since nature works for a determinate end under the direction of a higher agent, whatever is done by nature must be traced back to God as to its first cause. So likewise whatever is done voluntarily must be traced back to some higher cause other than human reason and will, since these can change and fail; for all things that are changeable and capable of defect must be traced back to an immovable and self-necessary first principle, as has been shown.

14. [The reference is to Aristotle's *Metaphysics*.]

Question XIII

The Names of God

Second Article

Whether Any Name Can Be Applied to God Substantially?

We proceed thus to the Second Article:—

Objection 1. It seems that no name can be applied to God substantially. For Damascene says: *Everything said of God must not signify His substance, but rather show forth what He is not; or express some relation, or something following from His nature or operation.*

Obj. 2. Further, Dionysius says: *You will find a chorus of holy doctors addressed to the end of distinguishing clearly and praiseworthily the divine processions in the denominations of God.* This means that the names applied by the holy doctors in praising God are distinguished according to the divine processions themselves. But what expresses the procession of anything does not signify anything pertaining to its essence. Therefore the names said of God are not said of Him substantially.

Obj. 3. Further, a thing is named by us according as we understand it. But in this life God is not understood by us in His substance. Therefore, neither is any name we can use applied substantially to God.

On the contrary, Augustine says: *For God to be is to be strong or wise, or whatever else we may say of that simplicity whereby His substance is signified.* Therefore all names of this kind signify the divine substance.

I answer that, Names which are said of God negatively or which signify His relation to creatures manifestly do not at all signify His substance, but rather express the distance of the creature from Him, or His relation to something else, or rather, the relation of creatures to Himself.

But as regards names of God said absolutely and affirmatively, as *good, wise,* and the like, various and many opinions have been held. For some have said that all such names, although they are applied to God affirmatively, nevertheless have been brought into use more to remove something from God than to posit something in Him. Hence they assert that when we say that God lives, we mean that God is not like an inanimate thing; and the same in like manner applies to other names. This was taught by Rabbi Moses.[15] Others say that these names applied to God signify His relationship towards creatures: thus in the words, *God is good,* we mean, God is the cause of goodness in things; and the same interpretation applies to other names.

Both of these opinions, however, seem to be untrue for three reasons. First, because in neither of them could a reason be assigned why some names more than others should be applied to God. For He is assuredly the cause of bodies in the same way as He is the cause of good things; therefore if the words *God is good* signified no more than, *God is the cause of good things,* it might in like manner be said that God is a body, inasmuch as He is the cause of bodies. So also to say that He is a body implies that He is not a mere potentiality, as is primary matter. Secondly, because it would follow that all names applied to God would be said of Him by way of being taken in a secondary sense, as healthy is secondarily said of medicine, because it signifies only the cause of health in the animal which primarily is called healthy. Thirdly, because this is against the intention of those who speak of God. For in saying that God lives, they assuredly mean more than to say that He is the cause of our life, or that He differs from inanimate bodies.

Therefore we must hold a different doctrine—viz., that these names signify the divine substance, and are predicated substantially of God, although they fall short of representing Him. Which is proved thus. For these names express God, so far as our intellects know Him. Now since our intellect knows God from creatures, it knows Him as far as creatures represent Him. But it was shown above that God prepossesses in Himself all the perfections of creatures, being Himself absolutely and universally perfect. Hence every creature represents Him, and is like Him, so far as it possesses some perfection: yet not so far as to represent Him as something of the same species or genus, but as the excelling source of whose form the effects fall short, although they derive some kind of likeness thereto, even as the forms of inferior bodies represent the power of the sun. This was explained above in treating of the divine perfection. Therefore, the afore-

15. [The reference is to Moses Maimonides.]

said names signify the divine substance, but in an imperfect manner, even as creatures represent it imperfectly. So when we say, *God is good,* the meaning is not, *God is the cause of goodness,* or, *God is not Evil;* but the meaning is, *Whatever good we attribute to creatures pre-exists in God,* and in a higher way. Hence it does not follow that God is good because He causes goodness; but rather, on the contrary, He causes goodness in things because He is good. As Augustine says, *Because He is good, we are.*

Reply Obj. 1. Damascene says that these names do not signify what God is because by none of these names is what He is perfectly expressed; but each one signifies Him in an imperfect manner, even as creatures represent Him imperfectly.

Reply Obj. 2. In the signification of names, that from which the name is derived is different sometimes from what it is intended to signify, as for instance this name *stone* [*lapis*] is imposed from the fact that it hurts the foot [*lædit pedem*], yet it is not imposed to signify that which hurts the foot, but rather to signify a certain kind of body; otherwise everything that hurts the foot would be a stone. So we must say that such divine names are imposed from the divine processions; for as according to the diverse processions of their perfections, creatures are the representations of God, although in an imperfect manner, so likewise our intellect knows and names God according to each kind of procession. But nevertheless these names are not imposed to signify the processions themselves, as if when we say *God lives,* the sense were, *life proceeds from Him,* but to signify the principle itself of things, in so far as life pre-exists in Him, although it pre-exists in Him in a more eminent way than is understood or signified.

Reply Obj. 3. In this life, we cannot know the essence of God as it is in itself, but we know it according as it is represented in the perfections of creatures; and it is thus that the names imposed by us signify it.

Fifth Article

Whether What Is Said of God and of Creatures Is Univocally Predicated of Them?

We proceed thus to the Fifth Article:—

Objection 1. It seems that the things attributed to God and creatures are univocal. For every equivocal term is reduced to the univocal, as many are reduced to one: for if the name *dog* be said equivocally of the barking dog and of the dogfish, it must be said of some univocally—viz., of all barking dogs; otherwise we proceed to infinitude. Now there are some univocal agents which agree with their effects in name and definition, as man generates man; and there are some agents which are equivocal, as the sun which causes heat, although the sun is hot only in an equivocal sense. Therefore it seems that the first agent, to which all other agents are reduced, is a univocal agent: and thus what is said of God and creatures is predicated univocally.

Obj. 2. Further, no likeness is understood through equivocal names. Therefore, as creatures have a certain likeness to God, according to the text of *Genesis* (i. 26), *Let us make man to our image and likeness,* it seems that something can be said of God and creatures univocally.

Obj. 3. Further, measure is homogeneous with the thing measured, as is said in *Metaph.* x. But God is the first measure of all beings. Therefore God is homogeneous with creatures; and thus a name may be applied univocally to God and to creatures.

On the contrary, Whatever is predicated of various things under the same name but not in the same sense is predicated equivocally. But no name belongs to God in the same sense that it belongs to creatures; for instance, wisdom in creatures is a quality, but not in God. Now a change in genus changes an essence, since the genus is part of the definition; and the same applies to other things. Therefore whatever is said of God and of creatures is predicated equivocally.

Further, God is more distant from creatures than any creatures are from each other. But the distance of some creatures makes any univocal predication of them impossible, as in the case of those things which are not in the same genus. Therefore much less can anything be predicated univocally of God and creatures; and so only equivocal predication can be applied to them.

I answer that, Univocal predication is impossible between God and creatures. The reason of this is that every effect which is not a proportioned result of the power of the efficient cause receives the similitude of the agent not in its full degree, but in a measure that falls short; so that what is divided and multiplied in the effects resides in the agent simply, and in an unvaried manner. For example, the sun by the exercise of its one power produces manifold and various forms in these sublunary things. In the same way, as was said above, all perfections existing in creatures divided and multiplied pre-exist in God unitedly. Hence, when any name expressing perfection is applied to a creature, it signifies that perfection as distinct from the others according to the nature of its definition; as, for instance, by this term *wise* applied to a man, we signify some perfection distinct from a man's essence, and distinct from his power and his being, and from all similar things. But when we apply *wise* to God, we do not mean to signify anything distinct from His essence or power or being. And thus when this term *wise* is applied to man, in some degree it circumscribes and comprehends the thing signified; whereas this is not the case when it is applied to God, but it leaves the thing signified as uncomprehended and as exceeding the signification of the name. Hence it is evident that this term *wise* is not applied in the same way to God and to man. The same applies to other terms. Hence, no name is predicated univocally of God and of creatures.

Neither, on the other hand, are names applied to God and creatures in a purely equivocal sense, as some have said. Because if that were so, it follows that from creatures nothing at all could be known or demonstrated about God; for the reasoning would always be exposed to the fallacy of equivocation. Such a view is against the Philosopher, who proves many things about God, and also against what the Apostle[16] says: *The invisible things of God are clearly seen being understood by the things that are made* (*Rom.* i. 20). Therefore it must be said that these names are said of God and creatures in an *analogous* sense, that is, according to proportion.

This can happen in two ways: either according as many things are proportioned to one (thus, for example *healthy* is predicated of medicine and urine in relation and in proportion to health of body, of which the latter is the sign and the former the cause), or according as one thing is proportioned to another (thus, *healthy* is said of medicine and an animal, since medicine is the cause of health in the animal body). And in this way some things are said of God and creatures analogically, and not in a purely equivocal nor in a purely univocal sense. For we can name God only from creatures. Hence, whatever is said of God and creatures is said according as there is some relation of the creature to God as to its principle and cause, wherein all the perfections of things pre-exist excellently. Now this mode of community is a mean between pure equivocation and simple univocation. For in analogies the idea is not, as it is in univocals, one and the same; yet it is not totally diverse as in equivocals; but the name which is thus used in a multiple sense signifies various proportions to some one thing; *e.g.*, *healthy*, applied to urine, signifies the sign of animal health; but applied to medicine, it signifies the cause of the same health.

Reply Obj. 1. Although in predications all equivocals must be reduced to univocals, still in actions the non-univocal agent must precede the univocal agent. For the non-univocal agent is the universal cause of the whole species, as the sun is the cause of the generation of all men. But the univocal agent is not the universal efficient cause of the whole species (otherwise it would be the cause of itself, since it is contained in the species), but is a particular cause of this individual which it places under the species by way of participation. Therefore the universal cause of the whole species is not a univocal agent: and the universal cause comes before the particular cause. But this universal agent, while not univocal, nevertheless is not altogether equivocal (otherwise it could not produce its own likeness); but it can be called an analogical agent, just as in predications all univocal names are reduced to one first non-univocal analogical name, which is *being*.

Reply Obj. 2. The likeness of the creature to God is imperfect, for it does not represent the same thing even generically.

Reply Obj. 3. God is not a measure proportioned to the things measured; hence it is not necessary that God and creatures should be in the same genus.

The arguments adduced in the contrary sense prove indeed that these names are not predicated univocally of God and creatures; yet they do not prove that they are predicated equivocally.

16. [The reference is to St. Paul.]

Question XIX
The Will of God

Eighth Article

Whether the Will of God Imposes Necessity on the Things Willed?

We proceed thus to the Eighth Article:—

Objection 1. It seems that the will of God imposes necessity on the things willed. For Augustine says: *No one is saved, except whom God has willed to be saved. He must therefore be asked to will it; for if He wills it, it must necessarily be.*

Obj. 2. Further, every cause that cannot be hindered produces its effect necessarily, because, as the Philosopher says, *nature always works in the same way, if there is nothing to hinder it.* But the will of God cannot be hindered. For the Apostle says (*Rom.* ix. 19): *Who resisteth His will?* Therefore the will of God imposes necessity on the things willed.

Obj. 3. Further, whatever is necessary by its antecedent cause is necessary absolutely; it is thus necessary that animals should die, being compounded of contrary elements. Now things created by God are related to the divine will as to an antecedent cause, whereby they have necessity. For this conditional proposition is true: *if God wills a thing, it comes to pass:* and every true conditional proposition is necessary. It follows therefore that all that God wills is necessary absolutely.

On the contrary, All good things that exist God wills to be. If therefore His will imposes necessity on the things willed, it follows that all good happens of necessity; and thus there is an end of free choice, counsel, and all other such things.

I answer that, The divine will imposes necessity on some things willed, but not on all. The reason of this some have chosen to assign to intermediate causes, holding that what God produces by necessary causes is necessary, and what He produces by contingent causes contingent.

This does not seem to be a sufficient explanation, for two reasons. First, because the effect of a first cause is contingent because of the secondary cause, from the fact that the effect of the first cause is hindered by deficiency in the second cause, as the sun's power is hindered by a defect in the plant. But no defect of a secondary cause can hinder God's will from producing its effect. Secondly, because if the distinction between the contingent and the necessary is to be referred only to secondary causes, this must mean that the distinction itself escapes the divine intention and will; which is inadmissible.

It is better therefore to say that this happens because of the efficacy of the divine will. For when a cause is efficacious to act, the effect follows upon the cause, not only as to the thing done, but also as to its manner of being done or of being. Thus from defect of active power in the seed it may happen that a child is born unlike its father in accidental points, which belong to its manner of being. Since then the divine will is perfectly efficacious, it follows not only that things are done, which God wills to be done, but also that they are done in the way that He wills. Now God wills some things to be done necessarily, some contingently, so that there be a right order in things for the perfection of the universe. Therefore to some effects He has attached unfailing necessary causes, from which the effects follow necessarily; but to others defectible and contingent causes, from which effects arise contingently. Hence it is not because the proximate causes are contingent that the effects willed by God happen contingently; but God has prepared contingent causes for them because He has willed that they should happen contingently.

Reply Obj. 1. By the words of Augustine we must understand a necessity in things willed by God that is not absolute, but conditional. For the conditional proposition that *if God wills a thing, it must necessarily be*, is necessarily true.

Reply Obj. 2. From the very fact that nothing resists the divine will, it follows not only that those things happen that God wills to happen, but that they happen necessarily or contingently according to His will.

Reply Obj. 3. Consequents have necessity from their antecedents according to the mode of the antecedents. Hence things effected by the divine will have that kind of necessity that God wills them to have, either absolute or conditional. Not all things, therefore, are necessary absolutely.

Question XXII
The Providence of God

Second Article

Whether Everything Is Subject to the Providence of God?

We proceed thus to the Second Article:—

Objection 1. It seems that not everything is subject to divine providence. For nothing foreseen can happen by chance. If then everything has been foreseen by God, nothing will happen by chance. And thus chance and fortune disappear; which is against common opinion.

Obj. 2. Further, a wise provider excludes any defect or evil, as far as he can, from those over whom he has a care. But we see many evils existing in things. Either, then, God cannot hinder these, and thus is not omnipotent; or else He does not have care for everything.

Obj. 3. Further, whatever happens of necessity does not require providence or prudence. Hence, according to the Philosopher: *Prudence is the right reason of contingent things concerning which there is counsel and choice.* Since, then, many things happen from necessity, everything cannot be subject to providence.

Obj. 4. Further, whatsoever is left to itself cannot be subject to the providence of a governor. But men are left to themselves by God, in accordance with the words: *God made man from the beginning, and left him in the hand of his own counsel* (*Ecclus.* xv. 14). And particularly in reference to the wicked: *I let them go according to the desires of their heart* (*Ps.* lxxx. 13). Everything, therefore, cannot be subject to divine providence.

Obj. 5. Further, the Apostle says (*1 Cor.* ix. 9): *God doth not care for oxen;* and we may say the same of other irrational creatures. Thus everything cannot be under the care of divine providence.

On the contrary, It is said of divine wisdom: *She reacheth from end to end mightily, and ordereth all things sweetly* (Wis. viii. I).

I answer that, Certain persons totally denied the existence of providence, as Democritus[17] and the Epicureans, maintaining that the world was made by chance. Others taught that incorruptible substances only were subject to providence, while corruptible substances were not in their individual being, but only according to their species; for in this respect they are incorruptible. They are represented as saying (*Job* xxii. 14): *The clouds are His covert; and He doth not consider our things; and He walketh about the poles of heaven.* Rabbi Moses, however, excluded men from the generality of corruptible things, because of the excellence of the intellect which they possess, but in reference to all else that suffers corruption he adhered to the opinion of the others.

We must say, however, that all things are subject to divine providence, not only in general, but even in their own individual being. This is made evident thus. For since every agent acts for an end, the ordering of effects towards that end extends as far as the causality of the first agent extends. Whence it happens that in the effects of an agent something takes place which has no reference towards the end, because the effect comes from some other cause outside the intention of the agent. But the causality of God, Who is the first agent, extends to all beings not only as to the constituent principles of species, but also to the individualizing principles; not only of things incorruptible, but also of things corruptible. Hence all things that exist in whatsoever manner are necessarily directed by God towards the end; as the Apostle says: *Those things that are of God are well ordered* (*Rom.* xiii. I). Since, therefore, the providence of God is nothing other than the notion of the order of things towards an end, as we have said, it necessarily follows that all things, inasmuch as they participate in being, must to that extent be subject to divine providence. It has also been shown that God knows all things, both universal and particular. And since His knowledge may be compared to the things themselves as the knowledge of art to the objects of art, as was said above, all things must of necessity come under His ordering; as all things wrought by an art are subject to the ordering of that art.

Reply Obj. 1. There is a difference between universal and particular causes. A thing can escape the order of a particular cause, but not the order of a universal cause. For nothing escapes the order of a particular cause, except through the intervention and hindrance of some other particular cause; as, for instance, wood may be prevented from burning by the action of water.

17. [Regarding Democritus, see Aristotle's *Physics*, n.3.]

Since, then, all particular causes are included under the universal cause, it is impossible that any effect should escape the range of the universal cause. So far then as an effect escapes the order of a particular cause, it is said to be by chance or fortuitous in respect to that cause; but if we regard the universal cause, outside whose range no effect can happen, it is said to be foreseen. Thus, for instance, the meeting of two servants, although to them it appears a chance circumstance, has been fully foreseen by their master, who has purposely sent them to meet at the one place, in such a way that the one has no knowledge of the other.

Reply Obj. 2. It is otherwise with one who is in charge of a particular thing, and one whose providence is universal, because a particular provider excludes all defects from what is subject to his care as far as he can; whereas one who provides universally allows some little defect to remain, lest the good of the whole should be hindered. Hence, corruption and defects in natural things are said to be contrary to some particular nature, yet they are in keeping with the plan of universal nature, inasmuch as the defect in one thing yields to the good of another, or even to the universal good: for the corruption of one is the generation of another, and through this it is that a species is kept in existence. Since God, then, provides universally for all being, it belongs to His providence to permit certain defects in particular effects, that the perfect good of the universe may not be hindered; for if all evil were prevented, much good would be absent from the universe. A lion would cease to live, if there were no slaying of animals; and there would be no patience of martyrs if there were no tyrannical persecution. Thus Augustine says: *Almighty God would in no wise permit evil to exist in His works, unless He were so almighty and so good as to produce good even from evil.* It would appear that it was because of these two arguments to which we have just replied, that some were persuaded to consider corruptible things—*i.e.*, things in which chance and evil are found—as removed from the care of divine providence.

Reply Obj. 3. Man is not the author of nature; but he uses natural things for his own purposes in his works of art and virtue. Hence human providence does not reach to that which takes place in nature from necessity; but divine providence extends thus far, since God is the author of nature. Apparently it was this argument that moved those who withdrew the course of nature from the care of divine providence, attributing it rather to the necessity of matter as did Democritus, and others of the ancients.

Reply Obj. 4. When it is said that God left man to himself, this does not mean that man is exempt from divine providence, but merely that he has not a prefixed operating power determined to only the one effect; as in the case of natural things, which are only acted upon as though directed by another towards an end: for they do not act of themselves, as if they directed themselves towards an end, like rational creatures, through the possession of free choice, by which these are able to take counsel and make choices. Hence it is significantly said: *In the hand of his own counsel.* But since the very act of free choice is traced to God as to a cause, it necessarily follows that everything happening from the exercise of free choice must be subject to divine providence. For human providence is included under the providence of God as a particular cause under a universal cause. God, however, extends His providence over the just in a certain more excellent way than over the wicked, inasmuch as He prevents anything happening which would impede their final salvation. For *to them that love God, all things work together unto good* (*Rom.* viii. 28). But from the fact that He does not restrain the wicked from the evil of sin, He is said to abandon them. This does not mean that He altogether withdraws His providence from them; otherwise they would return to nothing, if they were not preserved in existence by His providence. This was the reason that had weight with Tully,[18] who withdrew human affairs, concerning which we take counsel, from the care of divine providence.

Reply Obj. 5. Since a rational creature has, through its free choice, control over its actions, as was said above, it is subject to divine providence in an especial manner: something is imputed to it as a fault, or as a merit, and accordingly there is given to it something by way of punishment or reward. In this way the Apostle withdraws oxen from the care of God: not, however, that individual irrational creatures escape

18. [The reference is to Cicero, regarding whom, see Boethius' *Consolation of Philosophy*, n.1.]

the care of divine providence, as was the opinion of the Rabbi Moses.

Third Article

Whether God Has Immediate Providence over Everything?

We proceed thus to the Third Article:—

Objection 1. It seems that God has not immediate providence over all things. For whatever pertains to dignity must be attributed to God. But it belongs to the dignity of a king that he should have ministers, through whose mediation he provides for his subjects. Therefore much less has God Himself immediate providence over all things.

Obj. 2. Further, it belongs to providence to order all things to an end. Now the end of everything is its perfection and its good. But it pertains to every cause to bring its effect to good; and therefore every agent cause is a cause of the effect over which it has providence. If therefore God were to have immediate providence over all things, all secondary causes would be withdrawn.

Obj. 3. Further, Augustine says that, *It is better to be ignorant of some things than to know them, for example, ignoble things*; and the Philosopher says the same. But whatever is better must be attributed to God. Therefore He has not immediate providence over ignoble and wicked things.

On the contrary, It is said (*Job* xxxiv. 13): *What other hath He appointed over the earth? or whom hath He set over the world which He made?* On which passage Gregory says: *Himself He ruleth the world which He Himself hath made.*

I answer that, Two things belong to providence—namely, the exemplar of the order of things foreordained towards an end, and the execution of this order, which is called government. As regards the first of these, God has immediate providence over everything, because he has in His intellect the exemplars of everything, even the smallest; and whatsoever causes He assigns to certain effects, He gives them the power to produce those effects. Whence it must be that He has pre-comprehended the order of those effects in His mind. As to the second, there are certain intermediaries of God's providence, for He governs things inferior by superior, not because of any defect in His power, but by reason of the abundance of His goodness; so that the dignity of causality is imparted even to creatures. Thus Plato's opinion, as narrated by Gregory of Nyssa, is removed. He taught a threefold providence. First, one which belongs to the supreme Deity, Who first and foremost has provision over spiritual things, and thus over the whole world as regards genus, species, and universal causes. The second providence, which is over the individuals of all that can be generated and corrupted, he attributed to the divinities who circulate in the heavens; that is, certain separate substances, which move corporeal things in a circular motion. The third providence, which is over human affairs, he assigned to demons, whom the Platonic philosophers placed between us and the gods, as Augustine tells us.

Reply Obj. 1. It pertains to a king's dignity to have ministers who execute his providence. But the fact that he does not know the plans of what is done by them arises from a deficiency in himself. For every operative science is the more perfect, the more it considers the particular things where action takes place.

Reply Obj. 2. God's immediate provision over everything does not exclude the action of secondary causes, which are the executors of His order, as was said above.

Reply Obj. 3. It is better for us not to know evil and ignoble things, insofar as by them we are impeded in our knowledge of what is better and higher (for we cannot understand many things simultaneously), and insofar as the thought of evil sometimes perverts the will towards evil. This does not hold true of God, Who sees everything simultaneously at one glance, and Whose will cannot turn in the direction of evil.

Fourth Article

Whether Providence Imposes Any Necessity on What Is Foreseen?

We proceed thus to the Fourth Article:—

Objection 1. It seems that divine providence imposes necessity upon what it foresees. For every effect that has an essential cause (present or past) which it necessarily follows, comes to be of necessity; as the Philosopher proves. But the providence of God, since it is eternal, precedes its effect, and the effect flows from it of necessity; for divine providence cannot be frustrated. Therefore divine providence imposes a necessity upon what it foresees.

Obj. 2. Further, every provider makes his work as stable as he can, lest it should fail. But God is most powerful. Therefore He assigns the stability of necessity to things whose providence He is.

Obj. 3. Further, Boethius says: *Fate from the immutable source of providence binds together human acts and fortunes by the indissoluble connexion of causes.* It seems therefore that providence imposes necessity upon what it foresees.

On the contrary, Dionysius says that *to corrupt nature is not the work of providence.* But it is in the nature of some things to be contingent. Divine providence does not therefore impose any necessity upon things so as to destroy their contingency.

I answer that, Divine providence imposes necessity upon some things; not upon all, as some believed. For to providence it belongs to order things towards an end. Now after the divine goodness, which is an extrinsic end to all things, the principal good in things themselves is the perfection of the universe; which would not be, were not all grades of being found in things. Whence it pertains to divine providence to produce every grade of being. And thus for some things it has prepared necessary causes, so that they happen of necessity; for others contingent causes, that they may happen by contingency, according to the disposition of their proximate causes.

Reply Obj. 1. The effect of divine providence is not only that things should happen *somehow;* but that they should happen either by necessity or by contingency. Therefore whatsoever divine providence ordains to happen infallibly and of necessity, happens infallibly and of necessity; and what the divine providence plans to happen contingently, happens contingently.

Reply Obj. 2. The order of divine providence is unchangeable and certain, so far as all things foreseen happen as they have been foreseen, whether from necessity or from contingency.

Reply Obj. 3. The indissolubility and unchangeableness, of which Boethius speaks, pertain to the certainty of providence, which does not fail to produce its effect, and that in the way foreseen; but they do not pertain to the necessity of the effects. We must remember that, properly speaking, *necessary* and *contingent* are consequent upon being as such. Hence the mode both of necessity and of contingency falls under the foresight of God, Who provides universally for all being; not under the foresight of causes that provide only for some particular order of things.

Levi Gersonides

Rabbi Levi ben Gershom, known by his Latinized name Gersonides and his Hebrew acronym RaLBaG, was born in 1288 in the southern French city of Provence, where he lived until his death in 1344. His father was a rabbinic scholar, but little is known about Gersonides' personal life. After the Almohade conquest of Spain in the late 1140s, many Jews migrated to Christian communities in northern Spain and southern France, transporting with them the rich philosophical heritage of Muslim Spain. The resultant philosophical culture of Provençal Jewry met with staunch opposition from the more traditionalist northern French rabbinic authorities, igniting the bans and counterbans of the fierce dispute known as the Maimonidean controversy. Gersonides stands as the preeminent Provençal representative of Jewish rationalism, that is, the view that religious beliefs must be formulated, and the Torah interpreted, in the light of scientific and philosophical knowledge.

Versatility and rigor are Gersonides' hallmarks: He was renowned especially as an astronomer, mathematician, philosopher, and biblical commentator. *The Wars of the Lord* spans the topics of immortality, prophecy, divine knowledge, providence, creation, cosmology, and miracles. His biblical commentaries, which cover almost all the works of the Bible, constitute the most comprehensive and detailed medieval Jewish attempt to interpret Scripture by the light of philosophical reason. In these works and in his supercommentaries on the Muslim philosopherjurist Averroes' commentaries on Aristotle, Gersonides evinces a thorough command of the issues and approaches that earlier had occupied Islamic and Jewish philosophers in Muslim Spain.

Gersonides' ideas long have been the target of suspicion and criticism from Jewish thinkers due to their rigorously Aristotelian and radical strain. Like Maimonides, Gersonides believed that the Torah and reason can never conflict; when they appear to, Scripture must be interpreted to fit reason. However, his conceptions of what reason and Scripture jointly teach sometimes put him sharply at odds with traditional Jewish thinking. For example, although he rejects Aristotle's view that the world is eternal, neither does he accept the traditional Jewish belief in creation *ex nihilo,* creation from nothing, which, according to Maimonides, Scripture teaches. Instead Gersonides submits that both reason and the narrative of Genesis support Plato's position that the world was created by an artisan out of eternal, preexisting matter. By constructing proofs for creation out of eternal matter and against both creation *ex nihilo* and Aristotle's view of an eternal universe, Gersonides was rejecting Maimonides' claims that reason is unable to demonstrate a conclusion about the world's origins and that the choice must be made by appeal to Scripture.

A second controversial view of Gersonides, represented in the selection that follows, is that God does not know which free choices human beings will make in the future. This position emerges as a response to a well-known conundrum: If God knows the future, how can human beings act freely? After all, at the time a person acts, God already has knowledge about what the person will do, and a person clearly lacks the power to make God's knowledge false. Gersonides' bold reply is that God does not know the truth of statements describing "future contingents"—future events whose occurrence or nonoccurrence depends on free human choices. That is because such statements are neither true nor false—no choice has yet been made. But God's lack of *foreknowledge* of free human choices does not spell a lack of *omniscience.* To be omniscient is to know everything that is know*able,* and failing to know propositions that are unknowable (because they are neither true nor false) does not detract from omniscience. Gersonides went further, arguing, with Aristotle and against Maimonides, that God does not know "particulars" (truths about particular beings) but only general laws ("general natures") that order and govern the world, including laws expressing tendencies of human nature that free choices can overcome.

In this context Gersonides expressly dismisses Maimonides' solution that "know" is equivocal; that is, that the word does not mean the same thing when applied to God as when applied to humans. This dismissal is but a special case of Gersonides' larger rejection of Maimonides' "negative theology" and its claims that statements about God are completely equivocal, that affirmative attributes cannot be applied to God, and that God is beyond all conceptualizations in categories that apply to humans. Gersonides argued that among other unpalatable features of Maimonides' view is that it precludes our drawing any inferences about God, for such inferences depend on our knowing the meanings of terms we are using in our premises and conclusions. Furthermore, if Maimonides were right that the true meaning of statements about God is that none of our concepts apply to God, one term would be just as good (or bad) as any other in describing God. Instead of insisting that God is not a body, as Maimonides does, why cannot we just as well say that God is a body and that "body" is completely equivocal in this context? Gersonides' own view is that terms are ascribed to God in the "prior" sense ("primarily") and to created things in the "posterior" sense ("secondarily"). What this means is that, for example, divine knowledge is the cause of wisdom in humans, and that God possesses knowledge to a higher degree than humans do.

• • •

The Wars of the Lord has been translated by Seymour Feldman in a three-volume work (Philadelphia: Jewish Publication Society, 1984–1999) that includes excellent introductions, synopses, notes, and appendices. Two important works that serve both neophytes and scholars are Seymour Feldman, *Gersonides Judaism Within the Limits of Reason* (The Littman Library of Jewish Civilization, 2010) and Menachem Kellner, *Torah in the Observatory: Gersonides, Maimonides, Song of Songs* (Boston: Academic Studies Press, 2010). Robert Eisen's penetrating study, *Gersonides on Providence, Covenant, and the Chosen People* (Albany: State University of New York Press, 1995), illustrates the philosophical richness of Gersonides' biblical commentary. An important counterbalance to the standard portrait of Gersonides as a radical theologian is Charles Manekin's "Conservative Tendencies in Gersonides' Religious Philosophy," in *The Cambridge Companion to Medieval Jewish Philosophy*, eds., Baniel H. Frank and Oliver Leaman (Cambridge: Cambridge University Press, 2003), 304–42. A useful anthology is Gad Freudenthal, ed., *Studies on Gersonides: A Fourteenth-Century Jewish Philosopher-Scientist* (Leiden: E. J. Brill, 1992), which includes a detailed bibliography by Menachem Kellner.

Gersonides' views on free will and divine foreknowledge have attracted considerable attention. On this topic, see Tamar Rudavsky, "Divine Omniscience and Future Contingents in Gersonides," *Journal of the History of Philosophy* 21 (1983): 513–36; Norbert M. Samuelson, "Gersonides' Account of God's Knowledge of Particulars," *Journal of the History of Philosophy* 10 (1972): 399–416; and Charles H. Manekin, "Freedom Within Reason? Gersonides on Human Choice," in C. H. Manekin and Manachem M. Kellner, eds., *Freedom and Moral Responsibility: General and Jewish Perspectives* (Bethesda: University Press of Maryland, 1997). A contemporary defense of Gersonides' solution to the problem of foreknowledge and free will is Steven M. Cahn, "Does God Know the Future?" in Steven M. Cahn and David Shatz, eds., *Questions About God: Today's Philosophers Ponder the Divine,* (New York: Oxford University Press, 2002).

David Shatz

The Wars of the Lord

INTRODUCTORY REMARKS

. . . I have decided to mention all the possible opinions on a given issue of the various problems I shall discuss and the arguments for and against them. For in this way many principles involved in these questions will be established for us, and it will be easier to determine the true from the false so that the truth in these matters will be achieved in an indubitable manner. Doubt arises on a given matter when we have contrary views concerning it; but when the inquiry will be completed and the true will be sifted out from the false, the doubts in this matter will vanish. Since there have been many false opinions among our predecessors on these matters, and we have [therefore, in our] investigation contended with them in order to refute these views in every possible way, and yet everything that we have been able to demonstrate is the view of our Torah,[1] we have accordingly entitled our book "The Wars of the Lord." For we have fought the battles of the Lord in so far as we have refuted the false views of our predecessors.

The reader should not think it is the Torah that has stimulated us to verify what shall be verified in this book, [whereas in reality] the truth itself is something different. It is evident, as Maimonides (may his name be blessed) has said, that we must believe what reason has determined to be true. If the literal sense of the Torah differs from reason, it is necessary to interpret those passages in accordance with the demands of reason. Accordingly, Maimonides (may his name be blessed) explains the words of the Torah that suggest that God (may He be blessed) is corporeal in such a way that reason is not violated. He, therefore, maintains that if the eternity of the universe is demonstrated, it would be necessary to believe in it and to interpret the passages of the Torah that seem to be incompatible with it in such a way that they agree with reason. It is, therefore, evident that if reason causes us to affirm doctrines that are incompatible with the literal sense of Scripture, we are not prohibited by the Torah to pronounce the truth of these matters, for reason is not incompatible with the true understanding of the Torah. The Torah is not a law that forces us to believe false ideas; rather it leads us to the truth to the extent that is possible, as we have explained in the beginning of our commentary on the Torah. Accordingly, it is our practice in these discussions to begin with an exhaustive philosophical inquiry into the question at hand, and then to show that what we have philosophically discovered concerning the question is compatible with the Torah. With respect to some of these problems the Torah itself has, in its marvelous way, directed us toward the truth. Indeed, this should be the case, since the Torah is intended to guide its adherents to human perfection as far as it is attainable. . . .

BOOK THREE

Chapter 1

The Views of Our Predecessors Concerning This Question

It is appropriate to examine whether or not God knows particular, contingent things in the sublunar world, and if He does know them [there is still the question], how He knows them. Since the philosophers and the sages of our Torah have differed with respect to this problem, it is proper that we first examine their views.

Reprinted from *The Wars of the Lord*, vols. 1 and 2, translated by Seymour Feldman (Philadelphia: Jewish Publication Society, 1984 and 1987), by permission of the publisher. The use of brackets within the text indicates insertions by the translator.

1. [The Torah is the first five books of the Bible: Genesis, Exodus, Leviticus, Numbers, and Deuteronomy. — S.M.C.]

Whatever truth we find in them we shall accept, and in whatever falsity we find we shall indicate the truth that is to be found in refuting it.

There are two main views on this topic among the ancients that are worthy of discussion: (1) the views of Aristotle and his followers, and (2) the views of the great sages of the Torah. Aristotle maintained that God (may He be blessed) does not know particular things in the sublunar world. Those who followed him are divided into two camps on this question, the first group maintaining that Aristotle believed that God (may He be blessed) has no knowledge of these things in the sublunar world, either universals or particulars, for if He were to know either universals or particulars, there would be multiplicity in His knowledge and hence in His essence. In short, His essence would be divided into a more perfect part and a less perfect part . . . The second camp holds that Aristotle's view is that God (may He be blessed) knows the things in the sublunar world with respect to their general natures, i.e., their essences, but not insofar as they are particulars, i.e., contingents. Nor is there any multiplicity in His essence on this view, since He knows only Himself and in this knowledge He knows all things with respect to their general natures. For He is the principle of law, order, and regularity in the universe. But God [according to this view] does not know particulars; hence there is no order to them by virtue of [His not knowing them as particulars), although they do exhibit some order and regularity insofar as God knows them [i.e., their general natures]. It shall be demonstrated (with God's help) in Book Five of this treatise that this is the authentic view of Aristotle.

However, the great sages of our Torah, such as the outstanding philosopher Maimonides (may he be blessed) and others of our Torah who have followed him, maintain that God (may He be blessed) does know all particular and contingent things insofar as they are particular. Indeed, they believe that in one piece of knowledge He knows all these things, which in fact are infinite. This is indeed the view of Maimonides (may his memory be blessed), who in Chapter 20 of Part III of his great book *The Guide of the Perplexed* says the following: "Similarly we say that the various things that occur are known to Him before they take place and that He doesn't cease knowing them. Hence, no new knowledge accrues to Him at all. For example, He knows that a particular person is now nonexistent but will exist at some later date, and will continue to exist for some time and then will be nonexistent. Now when this person actually does exist according to [God's prior] knowledge of him, there is no addition to His knowledge and no new piece of information has arisen which was not already known to Him. But something has in fact taken place that previously was known would take place and exactly in the same way [as He knew it would]. This belief implies that [God's] knowledge refers to the nonexistent and encompasses the infinite. We accept this belief. And we say that the nonexistent things, the bringing forth of which pre-exists in His knowledge and falls within His power to bring about, can be objects of God's knowledge." It is clear from this that Maimonides maintains that God (may He be blessed) knows particular, contingent things insofar as they are particular.

Chapter 11

The Arguments in Favor of These Views, As We Have Found Them Explicitly or Implicitly in the Statements of Their Proponents

After having mentioned these opinions on this question, let us now examine them to see which is the true one. It will be necessary to examine the arguments in behalf of these views as well as those that purport to refute them.

Aristotle's thesis that God (may He be blessed) does not know particulars has been thought to be quite plausible. First, a particular is not apprehended except by means of a corporeal faculty, for example, the senses or the imagination. But it is obvious that God (may He be blessed) has no corporeal powers. Hence, God does not know these particulars. The following syllogism can be constructed: God has no corporeal powers; anything that apprehends a particular possesses a corporeal power; hence, God cannot apprehend particulars.

Second, a particular is a temporal phenomenon, i.e., its existence is in some portion of time. But someone who cannot be described as in motion or at rest cannot apprehend temporal phenomena. Now God cannot be described as in motion or at rest;

hence He cannot apprehend particulars. The following syllogism can be constructed: God cannot be described as in motion or at rest; anyone who cannot be described as in motion or at rest cannot apprehend temporal phenomena; hence God cannot apprehend temporal phenomena. To this conclusion we add a self-evident premise, namely, that particulars are temporal phenomena. From this it follows that God cannot apprehend particulars. . . .

Sixth, if it were alleged that God (may He be blessed) knows things that are generated, the following dilemma ensues: either He knows them *before* they occur, or He knows them only *simultaneously* with their occurrence, not beforehand. Now, if we assume that He knows them before their occurrence, His knowledge would refer to nonbeing. But this is absurd, for knowledge is necessarily [the cognition] of an existent, apprehended thing. Moreover, this divine foreknowledge of generated things implies the following dilemma. If He knows generated things as genuine contingents, then His knowledge that one of these contingencies is to occur is compatible with the occurrence of the alternative. If, on the other hand, He knows precisely *which* of the two alternative states of affairs will occur, its alternative will not be genuinely possible. Now, if we assume that God has knowledge of these events as genuine contingencies [the first horn of this dilemma], His foreknowledge of them would change when they actually occurred, for prior to their occurrence they could or could not have happened, but after their occurrence this possibility is removed. And since the intellect is constituted by what it knows, God would be continually changing—but this is utterly absurd. If, on the other hand, God knows *precisely* which of these contingencies will occur [the second horn of this dilemma], it follows that there is no genuine contingency at all; hence everything would be necessary. But this, too, is absurd and repugnant. It is clear, then, that it is false to say that God has knowledge of these generated events before they occur. But if we say that He has knowledge of them simultaneously with their occurrence [the second horn of the original dilemma], new knowledge would continually arise in Him. And since the intellect is constituted by what it knows, the divine essence would be continually changing, which is utterly impossible. . . . [In sum,] these are the arguments that we have been able to extract from the words of the philosophers, explicitly or implicitly, in support of the thesis that God does not know particulars. . . .

Nevertheless, the view of our sages of the Torah (of blessed memory) that God (may He be blessed) does know particulars also has arguments in its favor. First, since it is admitted by all who philosophize that God is the most perfect being, it is improper to attribute to Him the defect of ignorance, i.e., that He does not know *some* thing; for ignorance is one of the greatest defects. Someone who chooses to attribute to Him ignorance of particulars rather than to ascribe to Him the inability to arrange these particulars in an orderly manner escapes from one evil and falls into something worse. For it could be the case that the recipient cannot receive more perfection than it actually does, and this is not a defect with respect to God (may He be blessed).

Second, it is not proper to ascribe to the agent who produces something ignorance of his product. Rather, his knowledge of the product is more perfect than that possessed by someone else. For he knows through one cognition everything that will derive from the produced thing by virtue of the disposition [i.e., structure] according to which he made it. Someone else, however, acquires his knowledge of it from the product, and when he observes that the object exhibits some new property resulting from the nature with which it has been endowed, he acquires new knowledge of that new property. And so new properties of a thing give rise to successive cognitions in the observer, and it is possible that the observer will never obtain complete knowledge of the properties that accrue to this object, [especially] if the properties are quite numerous. Thus, since God (may He be blessed) is the creator of the whole world, He has a complete knowledge of what shall happen to that which He has made, a knowledge that cannot be compared to our knowledge. For He knows in one cognition everything that will happen with respect to the world according to the nature with which He has endowed it, whereas we know these things only as they occur. Hence, it is not proper to compare our knowledge and His knowledge, saying that if God (may He be blessed) were to have this knowledge. He would have many cognitions, and hence His essence would be subject to plurality. What we know by many cognitions is known to God (may He be blessed) in one cognition, as we have seen. Indeed, God knows through one cognition [many things of] these particulars, of which we can have knowledge [only] by means of a plurality of cognitions. For our knowledge does not encompass the many things that are generated in the world according to the nature with which God (may He be blessed) has endowed the world.

These two arguments are given by Maimonides (of blessed memory) in Part III of his celebrated book *The Guide of the Perplexed* in behalf of the claim that God (may He be blessed) knows all these particulars. It is clear that the second argument, in addition to proving that God knows all the things that happen, refutes some of the arguments of the philosophers against the view that God knows particulars. On the other hand, some of the philosophers have countered the first argument in behalf of divine knowledge of all particulars by saying that the denial of this claim does not entail any defect in God. For not every privation is a defect; it is a defect only when the thing is able to have the characteristic in question, not when it cannot. For example, motion is a perfection of animate creatures; when we deny motion of God, however, it is not a defect in Him but a perfection. Similarly, they say that in claiming that God does not know particulars, no imperfection in Him results, only perfection; for His knowledge concerns superior things, not these trivial matters. And so Aristotle says in Book XII of the *Metaphysics* that it is better not to see some things than to see them.

Maimonides (of blessed memory) countered all those difficulties that have been believed to entail the rejection of divine knowledge of particulars by means of his dictum that it is not appropriate to compare divine cognition with human cognition. For to the extent that His being is greater than ours, so, too, is His knowledge greater than ours. And this is a necessary truth, since His knowledge is identical with Himself, as the philosophers have explained. Accordingly, Maimonides frequently rebukes the philosophers for comparing divine knowledge with human knowledge and inferring therefrom that God does not know particulars. They themselves have shown us in some sense that when applied to both God and men, the term "knowledge" is equivocal. And it is obvious that with respect to things having equivocal predicates, inferences from one to the other cannot be made. By means of this argument, Maimonides claimed that it is not impossible, despite the arguments of the philosophers, for God to know all particulars. And when it has been shown that there is no impossibility in this supposition, it is clearly proper then to ascribe this power to Him in order to remove the defect of ignorance from Him. . . .

According to Maimonides, there are five factors by virtue of which God's knowledge differs from our knowledge, i.e., each one of these factors that is present in divine cognition cannot obtain in human cognition. . . .

The fourth differentiating factor is that the divine knowledge of future events does not entail that the predicted event will occur; rather, its opposite is still possible. Maimonides was led to this belief because he could not deny the existence of contingency, for both philosophy and the Torah assert the existence of contingent events. Hence, it would follow that when it is claimed that God has foreknowledge of future events, the opposite of the event predicted by God could occur and the predicted event could [then] not occur. For if [it were maintained] that the predicted event will undoubtedly occur, its opposite could not occur at all, and contingency would thereby be eliminated. And this is what Maimonides wanted to avoid. Now this feature cannot be attributed to human cognition. For if Maimonides meant that God (may He be blessed) knows with respect to two opposite possibilities which one will occur but also that it may not occur (i.e., its opposite is possible)—and this seems to be how his position should be construed—this [kind of cognition] would obviously not be considered by us to be *knowledge* but opinion. For when we say that we *know* that one particular possibility of two contradictory possibilities will occur, we thereby imply that it is impossible that it not occur, whereas if we *think* that it cannot occur, we call this "opinion," not "knowledge." That is, we would then say "we *think* that this possibility will happen" and not "we *know* that it will occur." And if what we thought would occur turns out not to occur, our opinion would be considered by us to have been erroneous; this is obviously not knowledge.

[On the other hand,] if Maimonides meant that God knows determinately which possibility will occur but does not know that it may not occur, and it is the case that the latter is really possible (i.e., the opposite of this event is possible), we would not consider this to be knowledge but error. That is, if the opposite of what we judged would occur happens instead, [we would] obviously [consider our judgment to be mistaken]. Hence, it is evident that according to this principle, what is knowledge with respect to God (may He be blessed) with respect to us is the opposite of knowledge; for error is the contrary of knowledge, and opinion, too, is in some sense the opposite of knowledge. For this reason, then, Maimonides claimed that divine knowledge differs from human knowledge. This difference in these two cognitions is consistent with Maimonides' thesis that the term "knowledge" is absolutely equivocal when applied to God (may He be blessed) and to us. . . .

Chapter III

A Critical Examination of the Adequacy of the Arguments Advanced by the "Master of the *Guide*" [i.e., Maimonides] on This Topic

It is proper that we determine whether Maimonidies' efforts to counter all the possible arguments of the philosophers who differ from him are successful before we examine whether or not these arguments are correct and, if they are correct, whether [or not] they entail what the philosophers concluded from them. For if Maimonides' replies to these arguments are adequate, there will be no need for us to examine them by means of another method.

We claim that the first thing to do is to examine whether the term "knowledge" is equivocal with respect to divine and human knowledge, such that the difference between them is as Maimonides thought—i.e., that divine knowledge is the opposite of our knowledge, so that what we consider to be opinion, error, or confusion is knowledge with respect to God—or whether the equivocation involved here is such that this difference cannot be such [as Maimonides claimed]. It seems to us that Maimonides' position on this question of divine cognition is not implied by any philosophical principles; indeed, reason denies this view, as I will show. It seems rather that theological considerations have forced him to this view. The question of whether the Torah requires this doctrine will be considered after our philosophical analysis of this problem.

That philosophical argument rules out Maimonides' position on this topic will be demonstrated as follows. It would seem that God's knowledge is equivocal with respect to our knowledge in the sense of prior and posterior predication, that is, the term "knowledge" is predicated of God (may He be blessed) *primarily* and of others *secondarily*. For in God knowledge is identical with His essence, whereas in anyone else knowledge is the effect of God's knowledge. In such a case the term is applied to God in a prior sense and to other things in a posterior sense. The same is true with respect to such terms as "exists," "one," "essence," and the like, i.e., they are predicated of God primarily and of other things secondarily. For His existence, unity, and essence belong to Him essentially, whereas the existence, unity, and essence of every [other] existent thing emanate from Him. Now when something is of this kind, the predicate applies to it in a prior sense, whereas the predicate applies in a posterior sense to the other things that are called by it insofar as they are given this property directly by the substance that has the property in the prior sense. . . . Hence, it seems that the difference between divine and human cognition is a difference in terms of greater perfection, for this is what is implied by prior and posterior predication. Now if what we have said is true, and since it is obvious that the most perfect knowledge is more true with respect to specificity and determinateness, it would follow that God's knowledge is more true with respect to specificity and determinateness. Hence, it cannot be that what is considered knowledge with respect to God can be called "belief," "error," or "confusion" with respect to man.

We can show in another way that the difference between divine and human cognition is not as Maimonides thought. It is evident that we proceed to affirm attributes of God from that with which we are familiar. That is, we say that God knows because of the knowledge found in us. For example, since we apprehend that the knowledge belonging to our intellect is a perfection of our intellect—without which it could not be an intellect in act [i.e., perfect]—we predicate of God that He knows by virtue of the fact, which we have demonstrated concerning Him, that God (may He be blessed) is indubitably an intellect in act. It is self-evident that when a predicate is affirmed of some object because it is true of some other thing, it is not predicated of both things in an absolutely equivocal sense, for between things that are absolutely equivocal there is no analogy. . . . Hence, it is clear that the term "knowledge" is not completely equivocal when applied to God (may He be blessed) and man. Since this term cannot be applied univocally with respect to God and man, it must be predicated in the sense of priority and posteriority. The same holds for other attributes that are predicated of both God (may He be blessed) and man. Thus, the difference between divine and human knowledge is one of greater perfection, albeit exceedingly so, and this type of knowledge is more precise and clear. . . .

The inadequacy of Maimonides' contention about the [absolute] difference between our knowledge and God's knowledge can be shown in another way. With respect to those attributes concerning which we want to know whether or not they can be predicated of God, it is evident that such predicates have one meaning regardless whether we affirm or deny them. For example, if we want to know whether God is corporeal or incorporeal, the term "corporeal" has the same meaning in some sense in either case. For if the term "body" has a completely different connotation in the negation from the meaning it has in the affirmation, these statements would not be considered genuine contradictions, as is obvious. . . . Hence, since it is clear when we deny attributes of God that are found in us that such attributes are not completely equivocal with respect to God (may He be blessed) and us, the same is true when we affirm of God predicates that are true of us. For example, we say that God is immovable, since if He were movable He would be a body, for all movable objects [are bodies]. Now it is evident that in this proposition the term "movable" is not completely equivocal with respect to the term "movable" when it is applied to nondivine things. For if it were, there would be no proof that God is not movable, since the movable object that must be a body is that which is movable in the domain of human phenomena, whereas the term "movable" (in the completely equivocal sense) would not imply that it is a body. Hence, since it is evident that the predicates we deny of God are not absolutely equivocal, neither are the terms that we affirm of Him. For at first we were uncertain whether to affirm or deny such predicates of God (may He be blessed). Then when the inquiry was completed, we were able to affirm or deny such predicates of Him. In general, if the terms used in affirming predicates of Him were absolutely equivocal, there would be no term applicable to things in our world that would be more appropriate to deny than to affirm of God or [more appropriate] to affirm than to deny of Him. For example, someone could say "God is a body" but not mean by the term "body," "a magnitude"; rather he would mean something that is completely equivocal with the term "body" as we usually use it. Similarly, someone could say "God does not have knowledge," since the term "knowledge" would not [on this view] have the same meaning for him in this statement as it does for us. It will not do to object that we indeed deny corporeality of God because it is an imperfection for us, whereas we affirm knowledge of Him because it is a perfection for us. For the *term* "corporeality" is not [itself] an imperfection, and it is the term that we deny of Him, but the content of the term is the imperfection. Similarly, the *term* "knowledge" is not [itself] a perfection; its content is. The proof of this is as follows. If by the term "corporeality" we were to connote what the term "knowledge" connotes, and conversely, corporeality would be a perfection for us and knowledge an imperfection. Moreover, we do not affirm or deny anything of God except by determining at the outset whether it is proper or improper for *Him;* we do not ask whether or not it is a perfection for *us.* Thus, it is clear that reason shows that the term "knowledge" is not completely equivocal with respect to God (may He be blessed) and man. . . .

On the basis of this entire discussion, it is now evident that reason shows that the term "knowledge" is predicated of God (may He be blessed) primarily and of creatures secondarily, not absolutely equivocally, and that the principles [of religious language] adopted by Maimonides in order to remove the objections of the philosophers concerning the problem of divine knowledge are not acceptable.

Chapter IV

The Completion of Our Theory of Divine Knowledge, Philosophically Demonstrated; Refutation of the Opposing Arguments

. . . Now, when we consider these arguments that have been brought forth in favor of divine knowledge of particulars and the arguments adduced by the philosophers against this thesis, there is no alternative but to say that God knows particulars in one respect but does not know them in another respect. But what these respects are, would that I knew!

It has been previously shown that these particulars are ordered and determined in one sense, yet contingent in another sense. Accordingly, it is evident that the sense in which God knows these particulars is the sense in which they are ordered and determined. . . . For from this aspect it is possible to have knowledge of them. On the other hand, the sense in which God does not know particulars is the sense in which they are not ordered, i.e., the sense in which they are contingent. For in the latter sense knowledge of them is not possible. However, God does know from this aspect that these events may not occur because of the choice, which He has given man. . . . But He does not know which of the contradictory outcomes will be realized insofar as they are [genuinely] contingent affairs; for if He did, there would not be any contingency at all. [Nevertheless,] the fact that God does not have the knowledge of which possible outcomes will be realized does not imply any defect in God (may He be blessed). For perfect knowledge of something is the knowledge of what that thing is in reality; when the thing is not apprehended as it is, this is error, not knowledge. Hence, God knows these things in the best manner possible, for He knows them insofar as they are ordered in a determinate and certain way, and He knows in addition that these events are contingent, insofar as they fall within the domain of human choice, [and as such knows them] truly as contingent. Thus, God (may He be blessed), by means of the Prophets, commands men who are about to suffer evil fortune that they mend their ways so that they will avert this punishment, as in the case of King Zedekiah who was commanded to make peace with the King of Babylonia.[2] Now this indicates that what God knows of future events is known by Him as not necessarily occurring; however, He knows these events in the sense that they are part of the general order and also as possibly not occurring insofar as they are contingent. . . .

Having established this point, we shall now show that none of the aforementioned arguments of the philosophers against divine knowledge of particulars is valid against our own theory.

The first of these arguments of the philosophers—since God has no corporeal powers, He has no knowledge of particulars—does not prove that God has no knowledge of the intelligible order inherent in them and in terms of which they are ordered and determinate. This argument implies only that He does not know them as particulars in their very individuality. This is evident. Similarly, the second argument—God has no knowledge of particulars because they are temporal phenomena—does not refute our theory. For we have not claimed that His knowledge encompasses their temporal aspects; rather we have claimed that it is concerned with the intelligible order in terms of which these particulars are ordered, and from this aspect they are not temporally specified. . . .

The sixth argument maintains that God cannot know generated events [i.e., particular events], for if He did, He would know them either *before* their occurrence or only simultaneously with their occurrence. If He knows them before their occurrence, His knowledge would refer to nonexistents. Moreover, if this is indeed the case, either He knows them as they really are, i.e., as contingents, and then it is still possible that the opposite of what He predicted will occur; or He knows definitely which alternative of two contradictory states of affairs will occur, such that the other alternative is not possible. If we say that He knows them as genuine contingents, His foreknowledge of these events would be subject to change when the event in question has occurred; for prior to its occurrence the event could or could not have occurred, whereas after its occurrence this possibility has disappeared. And since the intellect is constituted by its knowledge, God's essence would be continually subject to change, which is absurd. On the other hand, if we say that He knows definitely which of two contradictory events will occur, no contingency would exist. Finally, if we say that God knows particulars only as they occur, His knowledge would always be generated and His essence subject to change. Since all of these suppositions are absurd, it follows that God does not know particulars at all.

Nevertheless, this argument does not invalidate our version of the thesis that God knows particulars. In saying that God knows particulars insofar as they are ordered and that He knows them as contingent insofar

2. [Jer. 38:17–18.]

as human choice is involved, we are not subject to any of the above-mentioned absurdities. [In the first place], His knowledge does not refer to nonexistents, since we maintain that His knowledge of particulars is grounded in the intelligible order pertaining to them as it is present in His mind, but not in these particulars themselves. [In the second place], it does not follow that His knowledge is subject to change when any of these events has occurred, for we have not claimed that His knowledge is based upon any of these events; rather, it is grounded in their intelligible order in His mind. And this order is eternally in His mind and never changes. [In the third place], it does not follow from our hypothesis that there is no contingency [merely because] we maintain that God has foreknowledge of which of two contradictory events will occur. According to our theory God knows that a particular event *should* occur given the ordering of phenomena [in the intelligible order of things], but not that it *must absolutely* occur; for God recognizes that by virtue of human choice this event might not occur, and this is the sense in which these things are contingent. . . .

Chapter V

The Advantages of Our Theory

One of the evident advantages of our theory of divine knowledge of particulars is that none of the absurdities that ensue from Maimonides' account of divine knowledge is applicable to it, i.e., the difficulties deriving from the five features that allegedly differentiate divine knowledge from human knowledge. . . .

The fourth feature—God's knowledge of future events does not imply that the event foreknown will necessarily occur; rather its opposite is still possible—is also a characteristic of our knowledge insofar as we have knowledge of these events through dreams, divination, or prophecy. For we do possess such knowledge insofar as such events are ordered. Yet they remain contingent by virtue of the factor of choice. This is the reason why this knowledge has been given to us, that we can recognize the evil that has been prepared for us and take measures to avoid it. . . . This can be understood if we examine the practice of the Prophets (may they rest in peace), who warn us of some [imminent] evil. For it is the case that they give advice on how to prevent this evil from coming. Similarly, Joseph warns Pharaoh, by interpreting his dream, about the famine and suggests a relief measure so that the famine will not be as calamitous as it was originally predicted in the dream.[3] Daniel, for example, tells Nebuchadnezzar, by interpreting his dream, that he will lose his reason and be like an animal for seven years, but he also suggests a way in which this evil can be averted.[4] Since we have claimed that God has knowledge of these events insofar as they are ordered, it is not strange that they are still contingent with respect to human choice. In this way, the difficulty that has continually plagued men—i.e., how can God know future events without these events being necessary—disappears; for these events exhibit two aspects [i.e., an ordered, or regular, pattern and a free, or voluntary, dimension], and not just one aspect.

Chapter VI

The Identity of Our View with the Doctrine of the Torah

It is now incumbent upon us to show that the theory we have established by philosophical argument is identical with the view of our Torah. It is a fundamental and pivotal belief of the Torah that there are contingent events in the world. Accordingly, the Torah commands us to perform certain things and prohibits other things. It is [also] a fundamental principle implicit in all the Prophets (may they rest in peace) that God informs them of these contingent events before they actually occur, as it is said, "God does nothing without having revealed His purpose to His servants the prophets."[5] Yet it is not necessary that any evil predicted by them must occur, as it is said, "God is gracious . . . [abounding in kindness] and renouncing punishment."[6] These principles are reconcilable only on the hypothesis that [first] these contingent events are in some sense ordered, and it is in this respect that knowledge of them is possible, but in another sense not ordered, and it is in the

3. [Gen. 41:25–26.]
4. [Dan. 4:16–24.]
5. [Amos 3:7.]
6. [Joel 2:13.]

latter sense that they are contingent; and [second] that God (may He be blessed) knows all future contingent events insofar as they are ordered and [in addition] knows that they are contingent. It is, therefore, clear that the view of our Torah is identical with the theory that philosophical argument has proved with respect to divine knowledge. Moreover, it can be shown that the view of the Torah is that God knows these things in a general manner, not as particulars, for it is said "He who fashions the hearts of them *all,* who discerns *all* their doings."[7] That is, God created the hearts and thoughts of men *at the same time* insofar as He endowed the heavenly bodies with those patterns from which [these thoughts] are in their entirety derived. In this way God considers *all* their deeds, i.e., simultaneously, not in the sense that His knowledge refers to the particular as particular. This shows that [according to the Torah] God understands all human affairs in a general way.

Moreover, the Torah maintains that the will of God does not change, as it said, "I am the Lord—I have not changed."[8] And Balaam, when he was a prophet, said: "God is not man to be capricious, or mortal to change His mind."[9] [Yet] in some of the Prophets [it is related that] God does repent of His acts, as it is said, "The Lord renounced the punishment He had planned to bring upon His people";[10] "For God is gracious . . . renouncing punishment."[11] Since this difficulty cannot be removed when it is assumed that God (may He be blessed) knows particulars as particulars but can be easily removed when it is assumed that He knows them as we have argued [i.e., generally], it is proper, according to the Torah, that we should interpret the doctrine of divine knowledge according to our philosophical theory.

That our theory of divine cognition can easily solve this problem can be shown as follows. God's knowledge does not imply that a particular event will occur to a particular man, but that it may occur to *any* man who falls under this [general] ordering of events, insofar as these events are ordered; in addition, God knows that this event may *not* occur because of human choice. But if we were to claim that God knows this affair with respect to this particular man as a definite individual, it would follow that His will would be subject to change.

In short, there is nothing in the words of the Prophets (may they rest in peace) that implies anything incompatible with the theory we have developed by means of philosophy. Hence, it is incumbent upon us to follow philosophy in this matter. For, when the Torah, interpreted literally, seems to conflict with doctrines that have been proved by reason, it is proper to interpret these passages according to philosophical understanding, so long as none of the fundamental principles of the Torah are destroyed.

7. [Ps. 33:15 (translator's italics).]

8. [Mal. 3:6.]

9. [Num. 23:19.]

10. [Ex. 32:14.]

11. [Joel 2:13.]

William of Ockham

In 1277, the Bishop of Paris condemned 219 propositions expressing various positions in philosophy and theology. Several of the condemned propositions bore the influence of Aristotle's natural philosophy. It is hard not to see some of the Aristotelian doctrines of Thomas Aquinas, who had died shortly before the promulgation of the condemnation, as its targets. Because of Aquinas' philosophical prominence among the Dominicans, to place elements of his teachings under a cloud of suspicion was to compromise the educational project of the Dominican order. Whether the condemnation was symptom or cause, the first half of the fourteenth century was witness to a different, more critical philosophical atmosphere, created principally by two great Franciscan masters, John Duns Scotus (c. 1266–1308) and William of Ockham (1285–1348). Renaissance humanists, impatient with and perhaps incapable of comprehending the intricate argumentative style of Scotus, derisively referred to him and his followers as "Dunsmen," giving rise to the word "dunce." Until recently, Ockham's reputation has not fared much better. Unlike Scotus, however, whose life was comparatively uneventful, Ockham's disfavor can be attributed both to his maverick philosophical opinions and his controversial political career.

Coming from the village of Ockham, in Surrey, Ockham joined the Franciscans at an early age. He was educated at Oxford and lectured there from about 1315 to 1319. He had hoped to be appointed to a chair at Oxford. The hope never materialized because there were other Franciscans ahead of him and because there was opposition to his appointment, apparently on grounds having to do with Ockham's philosophical writings. Ockham is thus sometimes referred to as "Venerable Inceptor," that is, someone on the verge of incepting or formally assuming a title at a university.

By 1324, Ockham had written several of his major logical and philosophical works. They had attracted the attention of the former chancellor at Oxford, now in residence at the papal court in Avignon, who regarded some of Ockham's philosophical views as heretical. Ockham was summoned to Avignon in 1324 to be examined on these views. He would remain in Avignon for four years. A papal commission charged with the inquiry into Ockham's views took two years in its deliberations, finally declaring several of Ockham's opinions vulnerable to censure. The opinions were never formally condemned. In 1327, Michael of Cesena, minister general of the Franciscan order, who was also in residence at Avignon, set Ockham the task of investigating the issue of apostolic poverty. The Franciscans had contended that Jesus and the apostles had not owned property and thus that the mendicant Franciscans were following in the apostles' footsteps. The contention and the ideal that it fostered provoked Pope John XXII (1316–1334), who believed that the Church could succeed in maintaining its independence from secular rulers only if it were as wealthy as they. Ockham came to believe that John's pronouncements contradicted Scripture and views held by earlier popes. In Ockham's eyes, then, John was a heretic and could not be a true pope. In May 1328, Michael of Cesena and Ockham fled Avignon for Munich, placing themselves under the protection of Louis (or Ludwig) of Bavaria, the Holy Roman Emperor. They were excommunicated by John. Ockham continued to write political treatises aimed at what he took to be the deviations from the Christian mission of John and John's successor, Pope Benedict XII. When Louis died in 1347, Ockham made an attempt to reconcile himself with the Church but died shortly thereafter, probably a victim of the Black Death.

Two salient themes in Ockham's philosophical methodology are his appeals to God's absolute power and his appeals to what is now known as "Ockham's Razor." God's absolute power is God's power to do anything that does not involve a contradiction. Ockham appeals to that power in dealing with issues in metaphysics, ethics, and theology. One might have thought, for example, that spatial extension is an essential property of matter. According to Ockham, however, God can diminish the size of the material universe to an extensionless point without thereby destroying any of the universe's parts. Thus extension cannot be an absolutely essential property of matter. Again, one might have thought that God's commandment to love Him is a necessary consequence of God's perfect goodness. But, Ockham argues, God could have commanded us to hate Him; had He done so, it would have been obligatory for us to hate God. Or one might have thought that faith was necessary for salvation. But God can, if He chooses, save someone who lacks faith. One consequence of the appeal to God's absolute power is Ockham's voluntarism in ethics—his belief that right and wrong are determined entirely by God's will.

Ockham's Razor is commonly expressed as the injunction "Do not multiply entities beyond necessity." Ockham never enunciates the principle in quite these words, but he is clearly committed to its spirit. The reading included here, from Ockham's major work on logic, provides an important example of the Razor's influence. For Ockham, the study of logic begins with the study of terms and their properties. In the sentences "This rose is red" and "That rose is red," it is plausible to say that the subject-terms, "This rose" and "That rose," refer to individual, identifiable roses. But to what does the predicate-term, "red," refer? One view, called realism, maintains that "red" refers to a universal, redness, that is common to both this rose and that rose. Realism thus maintains that in addition to the individual roses, there is another kind of entity, redness, that has the property of being able to exist in more than one place at the same time.

Ockham rejects this kind of realism on grounds that it multiplies entities beyond necessity. The redness of this rose and the redness of that rose are just two individual things, not unlike the roses themselves. More generally, Ockham undertakes the project of arguing for nominalism, the position that the only things that exist are individuals.

• • •

Some of Ockham's individual works have received excellent translations, a few with very helpful introductory essays. Michael J. Loux's *Ockham's Theory of Terms* (South Bend, Ind.: St. Augustine's Press, 1998), from which the following text is taken, is a translation of Part I of Ockham's *Summa Logicae.* Alfred J. Freddoso and Henry Schuurman's *Ockham's Theory of Propositions* (Notre Dame, Ind.: University of Notre Dame Press, 1980) is a translation of Part II. Marilyn McCord Adams and Norman Kretzmann have translated Ockham's *Predestination, God's Foreknowledge, and Future Contingents* (Indianapolis: Hackett Publishing Company, 1983). Alfred J. Freddoso has produced a two-volume translation of Ockham's *Quodlibetal Questions* (New Haven: Yale University Press, 1991). Marilyn McCord Adams' two-volume *William Ockham* (Notre Dame, Ind.: University of Notre Dame Press, 1987) is a magisterial treatment of Ockham's philosophy. For a collection of important essays on various aspects of Ockham's philosophy, see Paul Vincent Spade, ed., *The Cambridge Companion to Ockham* (Cambridge: Cambridge University Press, 1999).

William E. Mann

Summa Logicae

PART I

On Terms

14: On the Universal

It is not enough for the logician to have a merely general knowledge of terms; he needs a deep understanding of the concept of a term. Therefore, after discussing some general divisions among terms we should examine in detail the various headings under these divisions.

First, we should deal with terms of second intention and afterwards with terms of first intention. I have said that 'universal,' 'genus,' and 'species' are examples of terms of second intention. We must discuss those terms of second intention which are called the five universals, but first we should consider the common term 'universal.' It is predicated of every universal and is opposed to the notion of a particular.

First, it should be noted that the term 'particular' has two senses. In the first sense a particular is that which is one and not many. Those who hold that a universal is a certain quality residing in the mind which is predicable of many (not suppositing for itself, of course, but for the many of which it is predicated) must grant that, in this sense of the word, every universal is a particular. Just as a word, even if convention makes it common, is a particular, the intention of the soul signifying many is numerically one thing a particular; for although it signifies many things it is nonetheless one thing and not many.

In another sense of the word we use 'particular' to mean that which is one and not many and which cannot function as a sign of many. Taking 'particular' in this sense no universal is a particular, since every universal is capable of signifying many and of being predicated of many. Thus, if we take the term 'universal' to mean that which is not one in number, as many do, then, I want to say that nothing is a universal. One could, of course, abuse the expression and say that a population constitutes a single universal because it is not one but many. But that would be puerile.

Therefore, it ought to be said that every universal is one particular thing and that it is not a universal except in its signification, in its signifying many things. This is what Avicenna[1] means to say in his commentary on the fifth book of the *Metaphysics*. He says, "One form in the intellect is related to many things, and in this respect it is a universal; for it is an intention of the intellect which has an invariant relationship to anything you choose." He then continues, "Although this form is a universal in its relationship to individuals, it is a particular in its relationship to the particular soul in which it resides; for it is just one form among many in the intellect." He means to say that a universal is an intention of a particular soul. Insofar as it can be predicated of many things not for itself but for these many, it is said to be a universal; but insofar as it is a particular form actually existing in the intellect, it is said to be a particular. Thus 'particular' is predicated of a universal in the first sense but not in the second. In the same way we say that the sun is a universal cause and, nevertheless, that it is really and truly a particular or individual cause. For the sun is said to be a universal cause because it is the cause of many things (i.e., every object that is generable and corruptible), but it is said to be a particular cause because it is one cause and

Reprinted from *Ockham's Theory of Terms: Part I of the Summa Logicae*, translated by Michael J. Loux (South Bend, Ind.: St. Augustine's Press, 1998), by permission of the publisher.

1. [The reference is to the renowned Islamic philosopher and physician Ibn Sina (980–1037), also known as Avicenna.—S.M.C.]

not many. In the same way the intention of the soul is said to be a universal because it is a sign predicable of many things, but it is said to be a particular because it is one thing and not many.

But it should be noted that there are two kinds of universals. Some things are universal by nature; that is, by nature they are signs predicable of many in the same way that the smoke is by nature a sign of fire; weeping, a sign of grief; and laughter, a sign of internal joy. The intention of the soul, of course, is a universal by nature. Thus, no substance outside the soul, nor any accident outside the soul is a universal of this sort. It is of this kind of universal that I shall speak in the following chapters.

Other things are universals by convention. Thus, a spoken word, which is numerically one quality, is a universal; it is a sign conventionally appointed for the signification of many things. Thus, since the word is said to be common, it can be called a universal. But notice it is not by nature, but only by convention, that this label applies.

15: That the Universal Is Not a Thing Outside the Mind

But it is not enough just to state one's position; one must defend it by philosophical arguments. Therefore, I shall set forth some arguments for my view, and then corroborate it by an appeal to the authorities.

That no universal is a substance existing outside the mind can be proved in a number of ways:

No universal is a particular substance, numerically one; for if this were the case, then it would follow that Socrates is a universal; for there is no good reason why one substance should be a universal rather than another. Therefore no particular substance is a universal; every substance is numerically one and a particular. For every substance is either one thing and not many or it is many things. Now, if a substance is one thing and not many, then it is numerically one; for that is what we mean by 'numerically one.' But if, on the other hand, some substance is several things, it is either several particular things or several universal things. If the first alternative is chosen, then it follows that some substance would be several particular substances; and consequently that some substance would be several men. But although the universal would be distinguished from a single particular, it would not be distinguished from several particulars. If, however, some substance were to be several universal entities, I take one of those universal entities and ask, "Is it many things or is it one and not many?" If the second is the case then it follows that the thing is particular. If the first is the case then I ask, "Is it several particular things or several universal things?" Thus, either an infinite regress will follow or it will be granted that no substance is a universal in a way that would be incompatible with its also being a particular. From this it follows that no substance is a universal.

Again, if some universal were to be one substance existing in particular substances, yet distinct from them, it would follow that it could exist without them; for everything that is naturally prior to something else can, by God's power, exist without that thing; but the consequence is absurd.

Again, if the view in question were true, no individual would be able to be created. Something of the individual would pre-exist it, for the whole individual would not take its existence from nothing if the universal which is in it were already in something else. For the same reason it would follow that God could not annihilate an individual substance without destroying the other individuals of the same kind. If He were to annihilate some individual, he would destroy the whole which is essentially that individual and, consequently, He would destroy the universal which is in that thing and in others of the same essence. Consequently, other things of the same essence would not remain, for they could not continue to exist without the universal which constitutes a part of them.

Again, such a universal could not be construed as something completely extrinsic to the essence of an individual; therefore, it would belong to the essence of the individual; and, consequently, an individual would be composed of universals, so that the individual would not be any more a particular than a universal.

Again, it follows that something of the essence of Christ would be miserable and damned, since that common nature really existing in Christ would be damned in the damned individual; for surely that essence is also in Judas. But this is absurd.

Many other arguments could be brought forth, but in the interests of brevity, I shall dispense with them.

Instead, I shall corroborate my account by an appeal to authorities.

First, in the seventh book of the *Metaphysics*, Aristotle is treating the question of whether a universal is a substance. He shows that no universal is a substance. Thus, he says, "it is impossible that substance be something that can be predicated universally."

Again, in the tenth book of the *Metaphysics*, he says, "Thus, if, as we argued in the discussions on substance and being, no universal can be a substance, it is not possible that a universal be a substance in the sense of a one over and against the many."

From these remarks it is clear that, in Aristotle's view, although universals can supposit for substances, no universal is a substance.

Again, the Commentator in his forty-fourth comment on the seventh book of the *Metaphysics* says, "In the individual, the only substance is the particular form and matter out of which the individual is composed."

Again, in the forty-fifth comment, he says, "Let us say, therefore, that it is impossible that one of those things we call universals be the substance of anything, although they do express the substances of things."

And, again, in the forty-seventh comment, "It is impossible that they (universals) be parts of substances existing of and by themselves."

Again, in the second comment on the eighth book of the *Metaphysics*, he says, "No universal is either a substance or a genius."

Again, in the sixth comment on the tenth book, he says, "Since universals are not substances, it is clear that the common notion of being is not a substance existing outside the mind."

Using these and many other authorities, the general point emerges: no universal is a substance regardless of the viewpoint from which we consider the matter. Thus, the viewpoint from which we consider the matter is irrelevant to the question of whether something is a substance. Nevertheless, the meaning of a term is relevant to the question of whether the expression 'substance' can be predicated of the term. Thus, if the term 'dog' in the proposition 'The dog is an animal' is used to stand for the barking animal, the proposition is true; but if it is used for the celestial body which goes by that name, the proposition is false. But it is impossible that one and the same thing should be a substance from one viewpoint and not a substance from another.

Therefore, it ought to be granted that no universal is a substance regardless of how it is considered. On the contrary, every universal is an intention of the mind which, on the most probable account, is identical with the act of understanding. Thus, it is said that the act of understanding by which I grasp men is a natural sign of men in the same way that weeping is a natural sign of grief. It is a natural sign such that it can stand for men in mental propositions in the same way that a spoken word can stand for things in spoken propositions.

That the universal is an intention of the soul is clearly expressed by Avicenna in the fifth book of the *Metaphysics*, in which he comments, "I say, therefore, that there are three senses of 'universal.' For we say that something is a universal if (like 'man') it is actually predicated of many things; and we also call an intention a universal if it could be predicated of many." Then follows the remark, "An intention is also called a universal if there is nothing inconceivable in its being predicated of many."

From these remarks it is clear that the universal is an intention of the soul capable of being predicated of many. The claim can be corroborated by argument. For everyone agrees that a universal is something predicable of many, but only an intention of the soul or a conventional sign is predicated. No substance is ever predicated of anything. Therefore, only an intention of the soul or a conventional sign is a universal; but I am not here using the term 'universal' for conventional signs, but only for signs that are universals by nature. That substance is not capable of functioning as predicate is clear; for if it were, it would follow that a proposition would be composed of particular substances; and, consequently, the subject would be in Rome and the predicate in England which is absurd.

Furthermore, propositions occur only in the mind, in speech, or in writing; therefore, their parts can exist only in the mind, in speech, and in writing. Particular substances, however, cannot themselves exist in the mind, in speech, or in writing. Thus, no proposition can be composed of particular substances. Propositions are, however, composed of universals; therefore, universals cannot conceivably be substances.

16: Against Scotus'[2] Account of the Universal

It may be clear to many that a universal is not a substance outside the mind which exists in, but is distinct from, particulars. Nevertheless, some want to claim that the universal is, in some way, outside the soul and in particulars; and while they do not want to say that a universal is really distinct from particulars, they say that it is formally distinct from particulars. Thus, they say that in Socrates there is human nature which is contracted to Socrates by an individual difference which is not really, but only formally, distinct from that nature. Thus, while there are not two things, one is not formally the other.

I do not find this view tenable:

First, in creatures there can never be any distinction outside the mind unless there are distinct things; if, therefore, there is any distinction between the nature and the difference, it is necessary that they really be distinct things. I prove my premise by the following syllogism: the nature is not formally distinct from itself; this individual difference is formally distinct from this nature; therefore, this individual difference is not this nature.

Again, the same entity is not both common and proper, but in their view the individual difference is proper and the universal is common; therefore, no universal is identical with an individual difference.

Again, opposites cannot be attributed to one and the same created thing, but *common* and *proper* are opposites; therefore, the same thing is not both common and proper. Nevertheless, that conclusion would follow if an individual difference and a common nature were the same thing.

Again, if a common nature were the same thing as an individual difference, there would be as many common natures as there are individual differences; and, consequently, none of those natures would be common, but each would be peculiar to the difference with which it is identical.

Again, whenever one thing is distinct from another it is distinguished from that thing either of and by itself or by something intrinsic to itself. Now, the humanity of Socrates is something different from the humanity of Plato; therefore, they are distinguished of and by themselves and not by differences that are added to them.

Again, according to Aristotle things differing in species also differ in number, but the nature of a man and the nature of a donkey differ in species of and by themselves; therefore, they are numerically distinguished of and by themselves; therefore, each of them is numerically one of and by itself.

Again, that which cannot belong to many cannot be predicated of many; but such a nature, if it really is the same thing as the individual difference, cannot belong to many since it cannot belong to any other particular. Thus, it cannot be predicable of many; but, then, it cannot be a universal.

Again, take an individual difference and the nature which it contracts. Either the difference between these two things is greater or less than the difference between two particulars. It is not greater because they do not differ really; particulars, however, do differ really. But neither is it less because then they would admit of one and the same definition, since two particulars can admit of the same definition. Consequently, if one of them is, by itself, one in number, the other will also be.

Again, either the nature is the individual difference or it is not. If it is the difference I argue as follows: this individual difference is proper and not common; this individual difference is this nature; therefore this nature is proper and not common, but that is what I set out to prove. Likewise, I argue as follows: the individual difference is not formally distinct from the individual difference; the individual difference is the nature; therefore, the nature is not formally distinct from the individual difference. But if it be said that the individual difference is not the nature, my point has been proved; for it follows that if the individual difference is not the nature, the individual difference is not really the nature; for from the opposite of the consequent follows the opposite of the antecedent. Thus, if it is true that the individual difference really is the nature, then the individual difference is the nature. The inference is valid, for from a determinable taken with its determination (where the determination does not detract from or diminish the determinable) one can infer the determinable taken by itself; but 'really' does not express a determination that detracts or diminishes. Therefore, it follows that

2. [The reference is to the influential Scottish philosopher John Duns Scotus (c. 1266–1308).]

if the individual difference is really the nature, the individual difference is the nature.

Therefore, one should grant that in created things there is no such thing as a formal distinction. All things which are distinct in creatures are really distinct and, therefore, different things. In regard to creatures modes of argument like the following ought never be denied: this is *A*; this is *B*; therefore, *B* is *A*; and this is not *A*; this is *B*; therefore, *B* is not *A*. Likewise, one ought never deny that, as regards creatures, there are distinct things where contradictory notions hold. The only exception would be the case where contradictory notions hold true because of some syncategorematic element or similar determination, but in the same present case this is not so.

Therefore, we ought to say with the philosophers that in a particular substance there is nothing substantial except the particular form, the particular matter, or the composite of the two. And, therefore, no one ought to think that in Socrates there is a humanity or a human nature which is distinct from Socrates and to which there is added an individual difference which contracts that nature. The only thing in Socrates which can be construed as substantial is this particular matter, this particular form, or the composite of the two. And, therefore, every essence and quiddity and whatever belongs to substance, if it is really outside the soul, is just matter, form, or the composite of these or, following the doctrine of the Peripatetics, a separated and immaterial substance.

17: Responses to Objections

The ability of a doctrine to handle objections is a sign of its truth. Consequently, I shall outline some objections against the foregoing and show how they can be met. Many men of no small authority hold that the universal is, in some sense, an entity outside the soul and belonging to the essence of particular substances. They bring forth arguments and authorities to show this:

(1) It is claimed that when things both really agree and really differ, there is something by which they agree and something else by which they differ. But Socrates and Plato really agree and really differ; therefore, they must agree and differ with respect to different things. They agree with respect to humanity, matter, and form; therefore, they each include an entity over and above these things, an entity in terms of which they are distinguished. These additional entities are called individual differences.

(2) Again, Socrates and Plato agree more than Socrates and a donkey; therefore, there is something in which Plato and Socrates agree but something in which Socrates and the donkey do not agree. However, Socrates and Plato do not agree in anything that is numerically one. Therefore, that in which they agree is not a particular; it must be something common.

(3) Again, in the tenth book of the *Metaphysics*, Aristotle says that in every genus there is some one thing that is first and the measure of all other things in that genus. But no particular can be the measure of all other particulars in the same genus, for no particular can be the measure of all individuals of the same species; therefore, there is something over and above particulars.

(4) Again, every common notion belongs to the essence of what is subsumed under it; therefore, a universal belongs to the essence of substance. But non-substantiality is not a part of the essence of any substance; therefore, some universal must be a substance.

(5) Again, if no universal were a substance, then all universals would be accidents and, consequently, all the categories would be accidents. Thus, the category of substance would itself be an accident. Consequently, some accident would be more general than substance. Indeed, it would follow that one and the same thing would be more general than itself; for if universals are accidents, they must be placed in the genus of quality; and, consequently, the category of quality would be common to all the universals. Thus, it would be common to the universal which is itself the category of quality.

Other arguments and innumerable authorities are adduced in behalf of this view, but in the interests of brevity I shall not consider them now. I shall, however, refer to them in a number of places later in the book. To the objections raised I respond as follows:

Response to (1) To the first objection I grant that Socrates and Plato both really agree and really differ; they agree specifically and differ numerically. But I want to claim that it is in terms of the same thing that they agree specifically and differ numerically; and here I do not differ from those who distinguish between the common nature and the individual difference, for they are forced to say that it is in terms of the same thing that the individual difference is both really the same as and formally different from the nature. One might object here that the same thing cannot be the cause both of agreement and of the difference which is its opposite. While the claim is true, it is beside the point; for specific identity and numerical difference are not intrinsically opposed. It ought to be granted, therefore, that Socrates agrees specifically with Plato and differs numerically from him by one and the same thing.

Response to (2) In the same way the second argument fails. For it does not follow that if Socrates and Plato agree more than Socrates and the donkey, there is some one thing with respect to which they agree more. But it is sufficient they agree more of and by themselves. Thus, I say that Socrates agrees more with Plato in virtue of his intellective soul; and, similarly, that he agrees with Plato more than with the donkey with respect to his whole being. Thus, if we are to be accurate we should not say that Socrates and Plato agree in some one thing which is their essence; we should say rather that they agree in several things, for they agree in their forms and in themselves taken as wholes.

Of course, if by contradiction there was one nature in both of them, they would agree in that too; but one might as well say that if by contradiction God were frivolous, He would rule the world badly.

Response to (3) With regard to the third point one should say that although an individual may not be the measure of all the individuals of the same genus or the same lowest level species, nonetheless, one and the same individual can be the measure of individuals from another genus or of many individuals from the same species. This is all that is needed to preserve Aristotle's view.

Response to (4) The response to the fourth objection is that, properly speaking, no universal belongs to the essence of any substance, for every universal is an intention of the soul or a conventional sign and nothing of either sort can belong to the essence of substance. Consequently, no genus nor any species nor any other universal belongs to the essence of any substance. But, strictly speaking, it should be said that a universal expresses or indicates the nature of a substance; that is, it expresses the nature which is a substance. The Commentator makes this point in the seventh book of the *Metaphysics*, when he notes that although it is impossible that any universal belong to the essence of anything, universals do express the essence of things. Thus, all authorities who say that universals belong to the essence of substance or are in substance or are parts of substances should be interpreted as saying only that universals indicate, express, designate, and signify the essences of things.

But one might object along the following lines: common names like 'man' and 'animal' signify substantial entities but not particular entities. The items they signify are substantial; but if they were particular substances, the term 'man,' for example, would signify all men and clearly it does not.

In response to this objection I want to claim that common names signify only particulars. Thus, the name 'man' does not signify anything other than the thing which is a particular man. Consequently, the only substantial entity for which it can supposit is a particular man. Indeed, it ought to be granted that the name 'man' signifies indifferently all particular men, but it does not follow that the term 'man' is equivocal. The reason is that although it signifies several individuals equally, it signifies them all by one convention; and in signifying them it is subordinated to only one concept and not several. Thus, it can be predicated of them univocally.

Response to (5) With respect to the last objection it should be noted that those who hold that intentions of the soul are qualities of the mind have to claim that all universals are accidents; nevertheless, not all universals are signs of accidents. On the contrary some are signs of substances only; they constitute the category of substance. Other universals constitute the other categories. Therefore, it should be granted that the category of substance is an accident, although it signifies substances and not accidents; and, consequently, it should be granted that some accident (i.e., the accident which is a sign only of substances) is, of itself, more general than substance. But this is not more perplexing than the claim that some word is a name of many substances.

But does not this imply that one and the same thing is more general than itself?

I think not, for in order that one thing be more general than another a distinction between them is required. Thus, although all universals are qualities, one can deny that all universals are per se less general than the common term 'quality.' The general term 'quality' is a quality; but this is not a case where one term is more or less general than another, for we are dealing here with just one term.

One might also object that since no one term is predicable of different categories, 'quality' cannot be common to different categories. But here we must ask whether the categories are being taken significatively or not. When the categories are not taken significatively, one and the same thing can be predicated of different categories. Thus, the proposition '"Substance" is a quality' is true if the subject supposits materially or simply for an intention. In the same way '"Quantity" is a quality' is true if 'quantity' does not stand significatively. It is in this way that the same thing is predicated of different categories. In the same way the proposition '"Substance" is a word' and '"Quality" is a word' are both true provided the subjects are suppositing materially and not significatively.

Likewise, one might object that the notion of *spiritual quality* is more general than any category, for it is predicated of several different categories and no one category is predicated of all the categories. The correct response here is that the notion *spiritual quality* is not predicated of all the categories when these are taken significatively, but only when they are taken as signs. Thus, it does not follow that the notion of *spiritual quality* is more general than any category; for one term is more general than another if, when both are taken significatively, the first is predicated of more items than the second.

A similar difficulty arises with the name 'expression,' for this name is one subsumed under the notion 'name.' 'Expression' is a name and not every name is the name 'expression.' Nonetheless, the name 'expression' is somehow more general than all names, more general even than the term 'name'; for every name is an expression, but not every expression is a name. Thus, it seems that the same thing is both more general and less general than some other thing. The difficulty is removed when we note that the argument just presented is conclusive only if the relevant common terms are suppositing uniformly in all the propositions in which they appear. Careful consideration shows that they are not.

Nevertheless, one could use the term 'less general' in a different way. He could argue that one term is less general than another if the second is predicated of the first (along with others) when the first is suppositing in some way or other. Thus, it might be that the more general term cannot be predicated of its inferior when the inferior is suppositing in a different way, so that it would not be predicated of that inferior when it supposits in all ways. In this new sense one could hold that the same thing is both more and less general than some other thing, but in the revised usage 'less general' and 'more general' cease to function as opposites. They are simply different notions.

René Descartes

René Descartes lived in an era of geniuses. In the year of his birth, 1596, Shakespeare was writing *Richard II* and *The Merchant of Venice*. When Descartes died in 1650, Newton was seven. Hobbes and Galileo were near-contemporaries.

Descartes was born in La Haye, now La Haye-Descartes, a small town in Touraine, France, and lived much of his life in virtual seclusion in Holland. His interests were extremely wide-ranging. He made major contributions to anatomy and physiology, optics, mathematics, and, of course, philosophy. The *Discourse on the Method of Rightly Conducting Reasoning* gives some sense of his range. Part Five describes his researches into the properties of light, the constitutions of men and animals, including an explanation of why 'lower' animals cannot think, and an account of the circulation of the blood that he takes to be more satisfactory than Harvey's.

At the center of Descartes' thought lies the view that each science is a branch of one unified science of the world, a science based on mathematics. Thus, Descartes was an early champion of Galileo's doctrine that "the book of nature is written in the language of mathematics." In addition to unifying other sciences through mathematics, Descartes effected a major unification within mathematics when he displayed the relation between the geometry of the ancients and the algebra he helped develop through the use of his Cartesian coordinate system.

The value of mathematics in studying natural science seems obvious to us today. How can mathematics advance the study of philosophy? Like Plato before him, Descartes believes that through training in mathematics the mind becomes capable of engaging in philosophical thought. In mathematics, we encounter absolute certainty, according to Descartes. We recognize that our conclusion cannot be mistaken, because our starting assumptions are obviously true and each step in the chain of reasoning is correct. Further, mathematics introduces us to knowledge gained through the understanding, or through reasoning, rather than through the senses. While children may originally come to accept that 1 + 1 = 2 by counting cookies, the mature person's belief that 1 + 1 = 2, always and with no exceptions, seems to have a different basis. Descartes believes that it rests on intellectual understanding: We grasp what a unit is and how the addition operation combines units. It is not mathematical results, but these two striking characteristics of mathematical knowledge, its certainty and its dependence on understanding rather than sensation, that provide illumination for philosophy. Descartes argues that, as with mathematics, certainty must be the touchstone of philosophical truth and the way to that truth must be through the understanding.

The *Meditations on First Philosophy*, reprinted here, is Descartes' most important philosophical treatise. It is an unusual work: Rather than lecturing his readers on the virtues of his conclusions, Descartes invites us to come along with him on the journey of discovering those conclusions. What is required of readers is that we too reflect on the issues that intrigue Descartes, that we ask ourselves such questions as, "If I am thinking, is it possible for me to doubt that I exist?"

Recalling that Descartes wished to bring to philosophy the certainty he discerned in mathematics, it is hardly surprising that the First Meditation begins by attempting to doubt all claims. The doubting has two purposes. Descartes wants to show that beliefs based on sensory data are not certain, thereby establishing the superiority of the understanding in acquiring knowledge. He also wants to discover whether any of our beliefs is in fact immune to doubt. In the Second Meditation, Descartes and his readers come to understand through reasoning that there is a claim that cannot be doubted: When one contemplates one's existence, it is not possible to have the slightest doubt that one does in fact exist. This conclusion is neatly captured in the well-known phrase, *cogito, ergo sum,* or "I think, therefore I am" (although these words do not appear in the *Meditations*). It is crucially important to note that, for Descartes, the "I" in this claim does not refer to a physical person, but to an immaterial mind. "Cartesian dualism" is the view that the world consists of two fundamental types of entities: physical bodies and immaterial minds. Since only minds can think, the *cogito* can only be used to show that a mind exists.

Later in the *Meditations,* Descartes attempts to restore the beliefs that his method of doubt had cast aside, arguing that it is also certain that physical bodies exist. In the Third Meditation, he completes the *cogito* argument and lays the basis for the later arguments concerning the existence of the physical world, contending that any claim that cannot be doubted must actually be true because God exists and would not permit us to be deceived about anything that was completely obvious to us.

• • •

Vere Chappell has collected the best recent work on this topic in Descartes' *Meditations* (Lanham, Md.: Rowman & Littlefield, 1997). Anthony Kenny, *Descartes: A Study of His Philosophy* (New York: Random House, 1968) is designed as an introduction for students but also treats those aspects of Descartes' thought that are the most interesting to contemporary philosophers. Another helpful work on the introductory level is John Cottingham, *Descartes* (Oxford: Basil Blackwell, 1986). John Cottingham, ed., *The Cambridge Companion to Descartes* (Cambridge: Cambridge University Press, 1992) offers introductory essays on a variety of important topics. Harry Frankfurt, *Demons, Dreamers, and Madmen: The Defense of Reason in Descartes' Meditations* (Indianapolis: Bobbs-Merrill, 1970) offers an excellent discussion of the first two meditations as does E. M. Curley, *Descartes Against the Skeptics* (Cambridge, Mass.: Harvard University Press, 1978). Peter J. Markie, *Descartes's Gambit* (Ithaca, N.Y.: Cornell University Press, 1986) presents an incisive study of the strategy of Descartes' argumentation. When Descartes first published the *Meditations,* he included a series of objections by contemporaries and his replies to them, which is still a wonderful companion to the *Meditations.* These are available along with other major works of Descartes, including the *Discourse on Method,* the *Principles of Philosophy,* and *The Passions of the Soul,* in *The Philosophical Writings of Descartes,* 2 vols., translated by J. Cottingham, R. Stoothoff, and D. Murdock (Cambridge: Cambridge University Press, 1985). An influential contemporary critique of Descartes' position is Gilbert Ryle, *The Concept of Mind* (New York: Barnes and Noble, 1949).

Patricia Kitcher

Discourse on the Method for Conducting One's Reason Well and for Seeking Truth in the Sciences

[NOTE ON THE TRANSLATION: The translation is based on the original French version (1637) of the *Discourse on Method* found in volume six of the Adam and Tannery edition of Descartes' works (Paris: Vrin, 1965). The numbers in the margins of this translation refer to the pagination of the Adam and Tannery edition.—D.A.C.]

DISCOURSE ON THE METHOD FOR CONDUCTING ONE'S REASON WELL AND FOR SEEKING THE TRUTH IN THE SCIENCES

1 *If this discourse seems too long to be read at one time, it may be divided into six parts. In the first part, you will find various considerations concerning the sciences; in the second part, the chief rules of the method which the author has sought; in the third part, some of the rules of morality which he has derived from this method; in the fourth part, the arguments by which he proves the existence of God and of the human soul, which are the foundations of his metaphysics; in the fifth part, the order of the questions in physics that he has investigated, and particularly the explanation of the movement of the heart and of other difficulties that pertain to medicine, as well as the difference between our soul and that of beasts; and in the final part, what things the author believes are required in order to advance further in the investigation of nature than the author has done, and what reasons have made him write.*

PART ONE

Good sense is the best distributed thing in the world, for everyone thinks himself to be so well endowed 2 with it that even those who are the most difficult to please in everything else are not at all wont to desire more of it than they have. It is not likely that everyone is mistaken in this. Rather, it provides evidence that the power of judging well and of distinguishing the true from the false (which is, properly speaking, what people call "good sense" or "reason") is naturally equal in all men, and that the diversity of our opinions does not arise from the fact that some people are more reasonable than others, but solely from the fact that we lead our thoughts along different paths and do not take the same things into consideration. For it is not enough to have a good mind; the main thing is to apply it well. The greatest souls are capable of the greatest vices as well as of the greatest virtues. And those who proceed only very slowly can make much greater progress, provided they always follow the right path, than do those who hurry and stray from it.

For myself, I have never presumed that my mind was in any respect more perfect than that of ordinary men. In fact, I have often desired to have as quick a wit, or as keen and distinct an imagination, or as full and responsive a memory as some other people. And other than these I know of no qualities that serve in the perfecting of the mind, for as to reason or sense, inasmuch as it alone makes us men and distinguishes us from the beasts, I prefer to believe that it exists whole and entire in each of us, and in this to follow the opinion commonly held by the philosophers, who 3 say that there are differences of degree only between accidents, but not at all between forms or natures of individuals of the same species.

But I shall have no fear of saying that I think I have been rather fortunate to have, since my youth, found myself on certain paths that have led me to considerations and maxims from which I have formed a method by which, it seems to me, I have the means to increase my knowledge by degrees and to raise it little by little to the highest point which the mediocrity of my mind and the short duration of my life will be able to allow it to attain. For I have already reaped from it such a harvest that, although I try, in judgments I

Reprinted from Descartes, *Discourse on Method* (Third Edition), translated by Donald A. Cress (Indianapolis: Hackett Publishing Co., 1998), by permission of the publisher.

make of myself, always to lean more on the side of diffidence than of presumption, and although, looking with a philosopher's eye at the various actions and enterprises of all men, there is hardly one of them that does not seem to me vain and useless, I cannot but take immense satisfaction in the progress that I think I have already made in the search for truth, and I cannot but envisage such hopes for the future that if, among the occupations of men purely as men, there is one that is solidly good and important, I dare to believe that it is the one I have chosen.

All the same, it could be that I am mistaken, and what I take for gold and diamonds is perhaps nothing but a bit of copper and glass. I know how much we are prone to err in what affects us, and also how much the judgments made by our friends should be [4] distrusted when these judgments are in our favor. But I will be very happy to show in this discourse what paths I have followed and to represent my life in it as if in a picture, so that everyone may judge it for himself; and thus, that, learning from the common response the opinions one will have of it, this may be a new means of teaching myself, which I shall add to those that I am accustomed to using.

Thus my purpose here is not to teach the method that everyone ought to follow in order to conduct his reason well, but merely to show how I have tried to conduct my own. Those who take it upon themselves to give precepts must regard themselves as more competent than those to whom they give them; and if they are found wanting in the least detail, they are to blame. But putting forward this essay merely as a story or, if you prefer, as a fable in which, among some examples one can imitate, one will perhaps also find many others which one will have reason not to follow, I hope that it will be useful to some without being harmful to anyone, and that everyone will be grateful to me for my frankness.

I have been nourished on letters since my childhood, and because I was convinced that by means of them one could acquire a clear and assured knowledge of everything that is useful in life, I had a tremendous desire to master them. But as soon as I had completed this entire course of study, at the end of which one is ordinarily received into the ranks of the learned, I completely changed my mind. For I found myself confounded by so many doubts and errors that it seemed to me that I had not gained any profit from my attempt to teach myself, except that more and more I had discovered my ignorance. And yet I was at one of the most renowned schools of [5] Europe, where I thought there must be learned men, if in fact any such men existed anywhere on earth. There I had learned everything the others were learning; and, not content with the disciplines we were taught there, I had gone through all the books I could lay my hands on that treated those disciplines considered the most curious and most unusual. Moreover, I knew what judgments the others were making about me; and I did not at all see that I was rated inferior to my fellow students, even though there already were some among them who were destined to take the place of our teachers. And finally our age seemed to me to be just as flourishing and as fertile in good minds as any of the preceding ones. This made me feel free to judge all others by myself, and to think that there was no doctrine in the world that was of the sort that I had previously been led to hope for.

I did not, however, cease to hold in high regard the academic exercises with which we occupy ourselves in the schools. I knew that the languages learned there are necessary for the understanding of classical texts; that the charm of fables awakens the mind; that the memorable deeds recounted in histories uplift it, and, if read with discretion, aid in forming one's judgment; that the reading of all good books is like a conversation with the most honorable people of past ages, who were their authors, indeed, even like a set conversation in which they reveal to us only the best of their thoughts; that oratory has incomparable power and beauty; that poetry has quite ravishing delicacy and sweetness; that mathematics has some very [6] subtle stratagems that can serve as much to satisfy the curious as to facilitate all the arts and to lessen men's labor; that writings dealing with morals contain many lessons and many exhortations to virtue that are very useful; that theology teaches one how to reach heaven; that philosophy provides the means of speaking plausibly about all things and of making oneself admired by the less learned; that jurisprudence, medicine, and the other sciences bring honors and riches to those who cultivate them; and, finally, that it is good to have examined all these disciplines, even the most superstition-ridden and the most false of them, in order to know their true worth and to guard against being deceived by them.

But I believed I had already given enough time to languages, and also to the reading of classical texts, both to their histories and to their fables. For conversing with those of other ages is about the same thing as traveling. It is good to know something of the customs of various peoples, so as to judge our own more soundly and so as not to think that everything that is contrary to our ways is ridiculous and against reason, as those who have seen nothing have a habit of doing. But when one takes too much time traveling, one eventually becomes a stranger in one's own country; and when one is too curious about what commonly took place in past ages, one usually remains quite 7 ignorant of what is taking place in one's own country. Moreover, fables make one imagine many events to be possible which are not so at all. And even the most accurate histories, if they neither alter nor exaggerate the significance of things in order to render them more worthy of being read, almost always at least omit the baser and less noteworthy details. Consequently the rest do not appear as they really are, and those who govern their own conduct by means of examples drawn from these texts are liable to fall into the extravagances of the knights of our romances and to conceive plans that are beyond their powers.

I held oratory in high regard and was enamored of poetry, but I thought both were gifts of the mind, rather than fruits of study. Those who possess the strongest reasoning and who best order their thoughts in order to make them clear and intelligible can always best persuade others of what they are proposing, even if they were to speak only Low Breton[1] and had never learned rhetoric. And those who have the most pleasing rhetorical devices and who know how to express themselves with the most embellishment and sweetness would not fail to be the greatest poets, even if the art of poetry were unknown to them.

I delighted most of all in mathematics because of the certainty and the evidence of its reasonings. But I did not yet notice its true use, and, thinking that it was of service merely to the mechanical arts, I was astonished by the fact that no one had built anything more noble upon its foundations, given that they were so solid and firm. On the other hand, I compared the writings of the ancient pagans that deal with morals to very proud and very magnificent palaces that were built on nothing but sand and mud. They place 8 virtues on a high plateau and make them appear to be valued more than anything else in the world, but they do not sufficiently instruct us about how to recognize them; and often what they call by so fine-sounding a name is nothing more than a kind of insensibility, pride, desperation, or parricide.

I revered our theology, and I desired as much as anyone else to reach heaven; but having learned as something very certain that the road to heaven is open no less to the most ignorant than to the most learned, and that the revealed truths guiding us there are beyond our understanding, I would not have dared to submit them to the frailty of my reasonings. And I thought that, in order to undertake an examination of these truths and to succeed in doing so, it would be necessary to have some extraordinary assistance from heaven and to be more than a man.

Concerning philosophy I shall say only that, seeing that it has been cultivated for many centuries by the most excellent minds that have ever lived and that, nevertheless, there still is nothing in it about which there is not some dispute, and consequently nothing that is not doubtful, I was not at all so presumptuous as to hope to fare any better there than the others; and that, considering how many opinions there can be about the very same matter that are held by learned people without there ever being the possibility of more than one opinion being true, I deemed everything that was merely probable to be well-nigh false.

Then, as for the other sciences, I judged that, insofar as they borrow their principles from philosophy, one could not have built anything solid upon such 9 unstable foundations. And neither the honor nor the monetary gain they promised was sufficient to induce me to master them, for I did not perceive myself, thank God, to be in a condition that obliged me to make a career out of science in order to enhance my fortune. And although I did not make a point of rejecting glory after the manner of a Cynic, nevertheless I placed very little value on the glory that I could not hope to acquire except through false pretenses. And finally, as to the false doctrines, I thought I already knew well enough what they were worth, so as not to be liable to be deceived either by the promises of an alchemist, the predictions of an astrologer, the tricks of a magician, or the ruses or boasts of any of those

1. [This dialect was considered rather barbarous and hardly suitable for sophisticated literary endeavors. —D.A.C.]

who profess to know more than they do.

That is why, as soon as age permitted me to emerge from the supervision of my teachers, I completely abandoned the study of letters. And resolving to search for no knowledge other than what could be found within myself, or else in the great book of the world, I spent the rest of my youth traveling, seeing courts and armies, mingling with people of diverse temperaments and circumstances, gathering various experiences, testing myself in the encounters that fortune offered me, and everywhere engaging in such reflection upon the things that presented themselves that I was able to derive some profit from them. For it seemed to me that I could find much more truth in the reasonings that each person makes concerning *10* matters that are important to him, and whose outcome ought to cost him dearly later on if he has judged badly, than in those reasonings engaged in by a man of letters in his study, which touch on speculations that produce no effect and are of no other consequence to him except perhaps that, the more they are removed from common sense, the more pride he will take in them, for he will have to employ that much more wit and ingenuity in attempting to render them plausible. And I have always had an especially great desire to learn to distinguish the true from the false, in order to see my way clearly in my actions, and to go forward with confidence in this life.

It is true that, so long as I merely considered the customs of other men, I found hardly anything there about which to be confident, and that I noticed there was about as much diversity as I had previously found among the opinions of philosophers. Thus the greatest profit I derived from this was that, on seeing many things that, although they seem to us very extravagant and ridiculous, do not cease to be commonly accepted and approved among other great peoples, I learned not to believe anything too firmly of which I had been persuaded only by example and custom; and thus I little by little freed myself from many errors that can darken our natural light and render us less able to listen to reason. But after I had spent some years thus studying in the book of the world and in trying to gain some experience, I resolved one day to study within myself too and to spend all the powers of *11* my mind in choosing the paths that I should follow. In this I had much more success, it seems to me, than had I never left either my country or my books.

PART TWO

I was then in Germany, where the occasion of the wars which are not yet over there[2] had called me; and as I was returning to the army from the coronation of the emperor, the onset of winter detained me in quarters where, finding no conversation to divert me and fortunately having no worries or passions to trouble me, I remained for an entire day shut up by myself in a stove-heated room,[3] where I was completely free to converse with myself about my thoughts. Among them, one of the first was that it occurred to me to consider that there is often not so much perfection in works composed of many pieces and made by the hands of various master craftsmen as there is in those works on which but a single individual has worked. Thus one sees that buildings undertaken and completed by a single architect are usually more attractive and better ordered than those which many architects have tried to patch up by using old walls that had been built for other purposes. Thus those ancient cities that were once mere villages and in the course of time have become large towns are usually so poorly laid out, compared to those well-ordered places that an engineer traces out on a vacant plain as it suits his fancy, that even though, upon considering each building one by one in the former sort, one often finds as much, if not more, art than one finds in those of the latter sort, still, upon seeing how the buildings are arranged—here a large one, there a small one—and how they make the streets crooked and uneven, one would say that it is chance rather *12* than the will of some men using reason that has arranged them thus. And if one considers that there have nevertheless always been officials responsible for seeing that private buildings contribute to the attractiveness of public areas, one will well understand that it is difficult to make things that are very finely crafted by laboring only on the works of others. Thus I imagined that peoples who, having once been half savages and having been civilized only little by little, have made their laws only to the extent that the inconvenience due to crimes and quarrels have forced them

2. [The Thirty Years' War (1618–48).]

3. [There is no need to allege that Descartes sat in or on a stove. A *poêle* is simply a room heated by an earthenware stove. Cf. E. Gilson, *Discours de la méthode: texte et commentaire*, 4th edition (Paris: Vrin, 1967), p. 157.]

to do so, could not be as well ordered as those who, from the very beginning of their coming together, have followed the fundamental precepts of some prudent legislator. Likewise, it is quite certain that the state of the true religion, whose ordinances were made by God alone, must be incomparably better ordered than all the others. And, speaking of things human, I believe that if Sparta was at one time very flourishing, this was not because of the goodness of each one of its laws taken by itself, seeing that many of them were very strange and even contrary to good morals, but because, having been devised by a single individual, they all tended toward the same end. And thus I thought that book learning, at least the kind whose reasonings are merely probable and that do not have any demonstrations, having been composed and enlarged little by little from the opinions of many different persons, does not draw nearly so close to the 13 truth as the simple reasonings that a man of good sense can naturally make about the things he encounters. And thus, too, I thought that, because we were all children before being men and because for a long time it was necessary for us to be governed by our appetites and our teachers (which were frequently in conflict with one another, and of which perhaps neither always gave us the best advice), it is nearly impossible for our judgments to be as pure or as solid as they would have been if we had had the full use of our reason from the moment of our birth and if we had always been guided by it alone.

It is true that we never see anyone pulling down all the houses in a city for the sole purpose of rebuilding them in a different style and of making the streets more attractive; but one does see very well that many people tear down their own houses in order to rebuild them, and that in some cases they are even forced to do so when their houses are in danger of collapsing and when the foundations are not very secure. This example persuaded me that it would not really be at all reasonable for a single individual to plan to reform a state by changing everything in it from the foundations up and by toppling it in order to set it up again, nor even also to reform the body of the sciences or the order established in the schools for teaching them; but that, as regards all the opinions to which I had until now given credence, I could not do better than to try to get rid of them once and for all, in order to replace 14 them later on, either with other ones that are better, or even with the same ones once I had reconciled them to the norms of reason. And I firmly believed that by this means I would succeed in conducting my life much better than if I were to build only upon old foundations and if I were to rely only on the principles of which I had allowed myself to be persuaded in my youth without ever having examined whether they were true. For although I noticed various difficulties in this undertaking, still they were not irremediable, nor were they comparable to those difficulties occurring in the reform of the least things that affect the public. These great bodies are too difficult to raise up once they have been knocked down, or even to hold up once they have been shaken; and their fall can only be very violent. Moreover, as to their imperfections, if they have any (and the mere fact of the diversity that exists among them suffices to assure one that many do have imperfections), custom has doubtless greatly mitigated them and has even prevented or imperceptibly corrected many of them, against which prudence could not provide so well. And finally, these imperfections are almost always more tolerable than changing them would be; similarly, the great roads that wind through mountains little by little become so smooth and so convenient by dint of being frequently used, that it is much better to follow them than to try to take a more direct route by climbing over rocks and descending to the bottom of precipices.

That is why I could in no way approve of those troublemaking and restless personalities who, called neither by their birth nor by their fortune to manage public affairs, are forever coming up with an idea for some new reform in this matter. And if I thought there were in this writing the slightest thing by means 15 of which one might suspect me of such folly, I would be very sorry to permit its publication. My plan has never gone beyond trying to reform my own thoughts and building upon a foundation which is completely my own. And if, my work having pleased me sufficiently, I here show you a model of it, it is not for the reason that I would wish to advise anyone to imitate it. Perhaps those with whom God has better shared his graces will have more lofty plans; but I fear that even this one here may already be too daring for many. The single resolution to rid oneself of all the opinions to which one has heretofore given credence is not an example that everyone ought to follow; and the world consists almost exclusively of two kinds of minds for whom it is not at all suitable. First, there are those who, believing themselves more capable than they are, are unable to avoid being hasty in their judgments or to have enough patience to conduct all their thoughts in an orderly manner; as a result, if they have once taken the liberty of doubting the principles they had accepted and of straying from the common path, they could never keep to the path one must take in order to go in a more straightforward direction, and they would remain lost all their lives. Second, there are those who have enough reason or modesty to judge that they are less capable of distinguishing the true from the false than certain others by whom they can be instructed; they should content themselves more with following the opinions of these others than with looking for better ones themselves.

And as for myself, I would unquestionably have 16 been counted among these latter persons if I had always had only one master or if I had not known at all the differences that have always existed among the opinions of the most learned. But I had learned in my college days that one cannot imagine anything so strange or so little believable that it had not been said by one of the philosophers, and since then, I had recognized in my travels that all those who have sentiments quite contrary to our own are not for that reason barbarians or savages, but that many of them use their reason as much as or more than we do. And I considered how one and the same man with the very same mind, were he brought up from infancy among the French or the Germans, would become different from what he would be had he always lived among the Chinese or the cannibals, and how, even down to the styles of our clothing, the same thing that pleased us ten years ago, and that perhaps will again please us ten years hence, now seems to us extravagant and ridiculous. Thus it is more custom and example that persuades us than any certain knowledge; and yet the majority opinion is worthless as a proof of truths that are at all difficult to discover, since it is much more likely that one man would have found them than a whole multitude of people. Hence I could not choose anyone whose opinions seemed to me should be preferred over those of the others, and I found myself, as it were, constrained to try to guide myself on my own.

But, like a man who walks alone and in the 17 dark, I resolved to go so slowly and to use so much circumspection in all things that, if I advanced only very slightly, at least I would effectively keep myself from falling. Nor did I want to begin to reject totally any of the opinions that had once been able to slip into my head without having been introduced there by reason, until I had first spent sufficient time planning the work I was undertaking and seeking the true method for arriving at the knowledge of everything of which my mind would be capable.

When I was younger, I had studied, among the parts of philosophy, a little logic, and among those of mathematics, a bit of geometrical analysis and algebra—three arts or sciences that, it seemed, ought to contribute something to my plan. But in examining them, I noticed that, in the case of logic, its syllogisms and the greater part of its other lessons served more to explain to someone else the things one knows, or even, like the art of Lully,[4] to speak without judgment concerning matters about which one is ignorant, than to learn them. And although, in effect, it might well contain many very true and very good precepts, nevertheless there are so many others mixed up with them that are either harmful or superfluous, that it is almost as difficult to separate the latter precepts from the former as it is to draw a Diana or a Minerva from a block of marble that has not yet been hewn. Then, as to the analysis of the ancients and the algebra of the moderns, apart from the fact that they apply only to very abstract matters and seem to be of no use, the former is always so closely tied to the consideration of figures that it cannot exercise the understanding without greatly fatiguing the imagination; and in the 18 case of the latter, one is so subjected to certain rules and to certain symbols, that out of it there results a confused and obscure art that encumbers the mind, rather than a science that cultivates it. That is why I thought it necessary to search for some other method embracing the advantages of these three yet free from their defects. And since the multiplicity of

4. [Ramon Llull (ca. 1236–1315), Catalan philosopher and Franciscan who wrote in defense of Christianity against the Moors by attempting to demonstrate the articles of faith by means of logic. Descartes seems to have encountered a Lullist in Dordrecht who could hold forth on any subject whatever for long periods of time. This encounter, more than any direct contact with the writings of Lull, seems to have colored Descartes' understanding of the "art of Lully." Cf. E. Gilson, *Discours de la méthode: texte et commentaire*, pp. 185–86.]

laws often provides excuses for vices, so that a state is much better ruled when it has but very few laws and when these are very strictly observed; likewise, in place of the large number of precepts of which logic is composed, I believed that the following four rules would be sufficient for me, provided I made a firm and constant resolution not even once to fail to observe them:

The first was never to accept anything as true that I did not plainly know to be such; that is to say, carefully to avoid hasty judgment and prejudice; and to include nothing more in my judgments than what presented itself to my mind so clearly and so distinctly that I had no occasion to call it in doubt.

The second, to divide each of the difficulties I would examine into as many parts as possible and as was required in order better to resolve them.

The third, to conduct my thoughts in an orderly fashion, by commencing with those objects that are simplest and easiest to know, in order to ascend little by little, as by degrees, to the knowledge of the most composite things, and by supposing an order even *19* among those things that do not naturally precede one another.

And the last, everywhere to make enumerations so complete and reviews so general that I was assured of having omitted nothing.

Those long chains of utterly simple and easy reasonings that geometers commonly use to arrive at their most difficult demonstrations had given me occasion to imagine that all the things that can fall within human knowledge follow from one another in the same way, and that, provided only that one abstain from accepting any of them as true that is not true, and that one always adheres to the order one must follow in deducing the ones from the others, there cannot be any that are so remote that they are not eventually reached nor so hidden that they are not discovered. And I was not very worried about trying to find out which of them it would be necessary to begin with; for I already knew that it was with the simplest and easiest to know. And considering that, of all those who have hitherto searched for the truth in the sciences, only mathematicians have been able to find any demonstrations, that is to say, certain and evident reasonings, I did not at all doubt that it was with these same things that they had examined [that I should begin]; although I expected from them no other utility but that they would accustom my mind to nourish itself on truths and not to be content with false reasonings. But it was not my plan on that account to try to learn all those particular sciences commonly called "mathematical"; and seeing that, even though their objects differed, these sciences *20* did not cease to be all in accord with one another in considering nothing but the various relations or proportions which are found in their objects, I thought it would be more worthwhile for me to examine only these proportions in general, and to suppose them to be only in subjects that would help me make the knowledge of them easier, and without at the same time in any way restricting them to those subjects, so that later I could apply them all the better to everything else to which they might pertain. Then, having noted that, in order to know these proportions, I would sometimes need to consider each of them individually, and sometimes only to keep them in mind, or to grasp many of them together, I thought that, in order better to consider them in particular, I ought to suppose them to be relations between lines, since I found nothing more simple, or nothing that I could represent more distinctly to my imagination and to my senses; but that, in order to keep them in mind or to grasp many of them together, I would have to explicate them by means of certain symbols, the briefest ones possible; and that by this means I would be borrowing all that is best in geometrical analysis and algebra, and correcting all thc defects of the one by means of the other.

In fact, I dare say the strict adherence to these few precepts I had chosen gave me such facility for disentangling all the questions to which these two sciences extend, that, in the two or three months I spent examining them, having begun with the simplest and most general, and each truth that I found being a rule that *21* later helped me to find others, not only did I arrive at a solution of many problems that I had previously judged very difficult, but also it seemed to me toward the end that, even in those instances where I was ignorant, I could determine by what means and how far it was possible to resolve them. In this perhaps I shall not seem to you to be too vain, if you will consider that, there being but one truth with respect to each thing, whoever finds this truth knows as much about a thing as can be known; and that, for example, if a child who has been instructed in arithmetic has made an addition following its rules, he can be assured of having found everything regarding the sum he was examining that the human mind would know how to find. For ultimately, the method that teaches one to follow the true order and to enumerate exactly all the circumstances of what one is seeking contains everything that gives certainty to the rules of arithmetic.

But what pleased me most about this method was that by means of it I was assured of using my reason in everything, if not perfectly, at least as well as was in my power; and in addition that I felt that in practicing this method my mind was little by little getting into the habit of conceiving its objects more rigorously and more distinctly and that, not having restricted the method to any particular subject matter, I promised myself to apply it as usefully to the problems of the other sciences as I had to those of algebra. Not that, on this account, I would have dared at the outset to undertake an examination of all the problems that presented themselves, for that would itself have been contrary to the order prescribed by the method. But having noted that the principles of these sciences must all be derived from philosophy, in which I did 22 not yet find any that were certain, I thought that it was necessary for me first of all to try to establish some there and that, this being the most important thing in the world, and the thing in which hasty judgment and prejudice were most to feared, I should not try to accomplish that objective until I had reached a much more mature age than that of merely twenty-three, which I was then, and until I had first spent a great deal of time preparing myself for it, as much in rooting out from my mind all the wrong opinions that I had accepted before that time as in accumulating many experiences, in order for them later to be the subject matter of my reasonings, and in always practicing the method I had prescribed for myself so as to strengthen myself more and more in its use.

PART THREE

And finally, just as it is not enough, before beginning to rebuild the house where one is living, simply to pull it down, and to make provision for materials and architects or to train oneself in architecture, and also to have carefully drawn up the building plans for it; but it is also necessary to be provided with someplace else where one can live comfortably while working on it; so, too, in order not to remain irresolute in my actions while reason required me to be so in my judgments, and in order not to cease to live as happily as possible during this time, I formulated a provisional code of morals, which consisted of but three or four maxims, which I very much want to share with you.

The first was to obey the laws and the customs of my country, constantly holding on to the religion in 23 which, by God's grace, I had been instructed from my childhood, and governing myself in everything else according to the most moderate opinions and those furthest from excess—opinions that were commonly accepted in practice by the most judicious of those with whom I would have to live. For, beginning from then on to count my own opinions as nothing because I wished to submit them all to examination, I was assured that I could not do better than to follow those of the most judicious. And although there may perhaps be people among the Persians or the Chinese just as judicious as there are among ourselves, it seemed to me that the most useful thing was to rule myself in accordance with those with whom I had to live, and that, in order to know what their opinions truly were, I ought to pay attention to what they did rather than to what they said, not only because in the corruption of our morals there are few people who are willing to say everything they believe, but also because many do not know what they believe, for, given that the action of thought by which one believes something is different from that by which one knows that one believes it, the one often occurs without the other. And among many opinions that are equally accepted, I would choose only the most moderate, not only because they are always the most suitable for practical affairs and probably the best (every excess usually being bad), but also so as to stray less from the true path, in case I should be mistaken, than if I had chosen one of the two extremes when it was the other one I should have followed. And in 24 particular I counted among the excesses all the promises by which one curtails something of one's freedom. Not that I disapproved of laws that, to remedy the inconstancy of weak minds, permit someone, when he has a good plan or even, for the security of commerce, some plan that is merely indifferent, to make vows or contracts that oblige him to persevere in it, but because I saw nothing in the world that always remained in the same state, and because, for my part, I promised myself to improve my judgments more and more, and never to make them worse, I would have thought I committed a grave indiscretion against good sense if, having once approved of something, I had obliged myself to take it as good again later, when perhaps it might have stopped being so or when I might have stopped considering it as such.

My second maxim was to be as firm and resolute in my actions as I could, and to follow the most doubtful opinions, once I had decided on them, with no less constancy than if they had been very well assured. In this I would be imitating travelers who, finding themselves lost in some forest, should not wander about turning this way and that, nor, worse still, stop in one place, but should always walk in as straight a line as they can in one direction and never change it for feeble reasons, even if at the outset it had perhaps been only chance that made them choose it, for by this means, even if they are not going exactly where they wish, at least they will eventually arrive somewhere where they will probably be better off than in the middle of a forest. And thus the actions of life often tolerating no delay, it is a very certain truth that, 25 when it is not in our power to discern the truest opinions, we must follow the most probable, and even if we notice no more probability in some than in others, nevertheless we must settle on some, and afterwards no longer regard them as doubtful, insofar as they relate to practical matters, but as very true and very certain, because the reason that made us decide on them appears so. And from then on this was able to free me from all the regret and remorse that usually agitate the consciences of those frail and irresolute minds that allow themselves inconstantly to go about treating as if good things they later judge to be bad.

My third maxim was always to try to conquer myself rather than fortune, and to change my desires rather than the order of the world, and generally to accustom myself to believing that there is nothing that is completely within our power except our thoughts, so that, after we have done our best regarding things external to us, everything that is lacking for us to succeed is, from our point of view, absolutely impossible. And this alone seemed to me sufficient to prevent me in the future from desiring anything but what I was to acquire, and thus to make me contented. For, our will tending by nature to desire only what our 26 understanding represents to it as somehow possible, it is certain that, if we consider all the goods that are outside us as equally beyond our power, we will have no more regrets about lacking those that seem owed to us as our birthright when we are deprived of them through no fault of our own, than we have in not possessing the kingdoms of China or Mexico, and that, making a virtue of necessity, as they say, we shall no more desire to be healthy if we are sick, or to be free if we are in prison, than we now do to have a body made of a material as incorruptible as diamonds, or wings to fly like birds. But I admit that long exercise is needed as well as frequently repeated meditation, in order to become accustomed to looking at everything from this point of view; and I believe that it is principally in this that the secret of those philosophers consists, who in earlier times were able to free themselves from fortune's domination and who, despite sorrows and poverty, could rival their gods in happiness. For occupying themselves ceaselessly with considering the limits prescribed to them by nature, they so perfectly persuaded themselves that nothing was in their power but their thoughts, that this alone was sufficient to prevent them from having any affection for other things, and they controlled their thoughts so absolutely that in this they had some reason for reckoning themselves richer, more powerful, freer, and happier than any other men who, not having this philosophy, never thus controlled everything they wished to control, however favored by 27 nature and fortune they might be.

Finally, to conclude this code of morals, I took it upon myself to review the various occupations that men have in this life, in order to try to choose the best one, and, not wanting to say anything about the occupations of others, I thought I could not do better than to continue in that very one in which I found myself, that is to say, spending my whole life cultivating my reason and advancing, as far as I could, in the knowledge of the truth, following the method I had prescribed to myself. I had met with such extreme contentment since the time I had begun to make use of this method, that I did not believe one could obtain any sweeter or more innocent contentment in this life, and, discovering every day by its means some truths that to me seemed quite important and commonly ignored by other men, the satisfaction I had from them so filled my mind that nothing else was of any consequence to me. In addition, the three preceding maxims were founded solely on the plan I had of continuing to instruct myself, for since God has given each of us some light to distinguish the true from the false, I would not have believed I ought to rest content for a single moment with the opinions of others, had I not proposed to use my own judgment to examine them when there would be time; and I would not have been able to free myself of scruples in following these opinions, had I not hoped that I would not, on that account, lose any opportunity of finding better ones, in case there were any. And finally, I could not have limited my desires or have been content, had I not followed a path by which, thinking I was assured of acquiring all the knowledge of which I was capable, I thought I was assured by the same means of the knowledge of all the true goods that would ever be in my power. For, given that our will tends not to pursue or flee anything unless our understanding represents it to the will as either good or bad, it suffices to judge well in order to do well, and to judge as best one can, in order also to do one's very best, that is to say, to acquire all the virtues and in general all the other goods that one could acquire, and, when one is certain that this is the case, one could not fail to be contented.

When I had thus assured myself of these maxims and put them to one side along with the truths of the faith, which have always held first place among my beliefs, I judged that, as for the rest of my opinions, I could freely undertake to rid myself of them. And inasmuch as I hoped to be able to reach my goal better by conversing with men than by staying shut up any longer in the stove-heated room[5] where I had had all these thoughts, the winter was not yet over when I set out again on my travels. And in all the nine years that followed I did nothing but wander here and there in the world, trying to be more a spectator than an actor in all the comedies that are played out there; and reflecting particularly in each matter on what might render it suspect and give us occasion for erring, I meanwhile rooted out from my mind all the errors that had previously been able to slip into it. Not that, in order to do this, I was imitating the skeptics who doubt merely for the sake of doubting and put on the affectation of being perpetually undecided, for, on the contrary, my entire plan tended simply to give me assurance and to cast aside the shifting earth and sand in order to find rock or clay. In this I was quite successful, it seems to me, inasmuch as, trying to discover the falsity or the uncertainty of the propositions I was examining, not by feeble conjectures but by clear and certain reasonings, I never found any that was so doubtful that I could not draw from it some quite certain conclusion, even if it had been merely that it contained nothing certain. And just as in tearing down an old house, one usually saves the wreckage for use in building a new one, similarly, in destroying all those opinions of mine that I judged to be poorly founded, I made various observations and acquired many experiences that have since served me in establishing more certain opinions. Moreover, I continued to practice the method I had prescribed for myself, for, besides taking care generally to conduct all my thoughts according to its rules, from time to time I set aside some hours that I spent particularly in applying it to mathematical problems, or even also to some other problems that I could make as it were similar to those of mathematics, by detaching them from all the principles of the other sciences, which I did not find to be sufficiently firm, as you will see I have done in many problems that are explained in this volume.[6] And thus, without living any differently in outward appearance than do those who, having no task but to live a sweet and innocent life, make a point of separating pleasures from vices, and who, in order to enjoy their leisure without becoming bored, involve themselves in all sorts of honest diversions, I did not cease to carry out my plan and to progress in the knowledge of the truth, perhaps more than if I had done nothing but read books or keep company with men of letters.

Nevertheless, those nine years slipped by before I had as yet taken any stand regarding the difficulties commonly debated among learned men, or had begun to seek the foundations of any philosophy that was more certain than the commonly accepted one. And the example of many excellent minds, who had previously had this plan and had not, it seemed to me, succeeded in it, made me imagine so much difficulty in it that perhaps I would not have dared to undertake it so soon again, if I had not seen that some had

5. [See f.n. 3.]

6. [Descartes also published treatises on optics, geometry, and meteorology in this same volume.]

already spread the rumor that I had achieved my goal. I cannot say on what they based this opinion, and if I have contributed something to it by my conversation, this must have been because I confessed that of which I was ignorant more ingenuously than those who have studied only a little are in the habit of doing, and perhaps also because I showed the reasons I had for doubting many things that other people regard as certain, rather than because I was boasting of any learning. But having a good enough heart not to want someone to take me for something other than I was, I thought it necessary to try by every means to render myself worthy of the reputation that was bestowed on me. And it is exactly eight years ago that this desire made me resolve to take my leave of all those places where I might have acquaintances, and to retire here, to a country where the long duration of the war has led to the establishment of such well-ordered discipline that the armies quartered here seem to serve only to make one enjoy the fruits of peace with even greater security, and where, in the midst of the crowd of a great and very busy people who are more concerned with their own affairs than they are curious about those of others, I have been able, without lacking any of the amenities to be found in the most bustling cities, to live as solitary and as withdrawn a life as I could in the remotest deserts.

PART FOUR

I do not know whether I ought to tell you about the first meditations I engaged in there, for they are so metaphysical and so out of the ordinary that perhaps they will not be to everyone's liking. And yet, in order that it should be possible to judge whether the foundations I have laid are sufficiently firm, I find myself in some sense forced to talk about them. For a long time I had noticed that in matters of morality one must sometimes follow opinions that one knows to be quite uncertain, just as if they were indubitable, as has been said above, but because I then desired to devote myself exclusively to the search for the truth, I thought it necessary that I do exactly the opposite, and that I reject as absolutely false everything in which I could imagine the least doubt, in order to see whether, after this process, something in my beliefs remained that was entirely indubitable. Thus, because our senses sometimes deceive us, I wanted to suppose that nothing was exactly as they led us to imagine. And because there are men who make mistakes in reasoning, even in the simplest matters in geometry, and who commit paralogisms, judging that I was just as prone to err as any other, I rejected as false all the reasonings that I had previously taken for demonstrations. And finally, considering the fact that all the same thoughts we have when we are awake can also come to us when we are asleep, without any of them being true, I resolved to pretend that all the things that had ever entered my mind were no more true than the illusions of my dreams. But immediately afterward I noticed that, while I wanted thus to think that everything was false, it necessarily had to be the case that I, who was thinking this, was something. And noticing that this truth—*I think, therefore I am*—was so firm and so assured that all the most extravagant suppositions of the skeptics were incapable of shaking it, I judged that I could accept it without scruple as the first principle of the philosophy I was seeking.

Then, examining with attention what I was, and seeing that I could pretend that I had no body and that there was no world nor any place where I was, I could not pretend, on that account, that I did not exist at all, and that, on the contrary, from the very fact that I thought of doubting the truth of other things, it followed very evidently and very certainly that I existed; whereas, on the other hand, had I simply stopped thinking, even if all the rest of what I had ever imagined had been true, I would have had no reason to believe that I had existed. From this I knew that I was a substance the whole essence or nature of which is simply to think, and which, in order to exist, has no need of any place nor depends on any material thing. Thus this "I," that is to say, the soul through which I am what I am, is entirely distinct from the body and is even easier to know than the body, and even if there were no body at all, it would not cease to be all that it is.

After this, I considered in general what is needed for a proposition to be true and certain, for since I had just found one of them that I knew to be such, I thought I ought also to know in what this certitude consists. And having noticed that there is nothing at all in this *I think, therefore I am* that assures me that I am speaking the truth, except that I see very clearly that, in order to think, it is necessary to exist, I judged that I could take as a general rule that the things we conceive very clearly and very distinctly are all true, but that there is merely some difficulty in properly discerning which are those that we distinctly conceive.

Following this, reflecting upon the fact that I doubted and that, as a consequence, my being was not utterly perfect (for I saw clearly that it is a greater perfection to know than to doubt), I decided to search for the source from which I had learned to think of something more perfect than I was, and I plainly 34 knew that this had to be from some nature that was in fact more perfect. As to those thoughts I had of many other things outside me, such as the heavens, the earth, light, heat, and a thousand others, I had no trouble at all knowing where they came from, because, noticing nothing in them that seemed to me to make them superior to me, I could believe that, if they were true, they were dependencies of my nature, insofar as it had some perfection, and that, if they were not true, I obtained them from nothing, that is to say, they were in me because I had some defect. But the same could not hold for the idea of a being more perfect than my own, for it is a manifest contradiction to receive this idea from nothing, and because it is no less a contradiction that something more perfect should follow from and depend upon something less perfect than that something should come from nothing, I could not obtain it from myself. It thus remained that this idea had been placed in me by a nature truly more perfect than I was and that it even had within itself all the perfections of which I could have any idea, that is to say, to explain myself in a single word, that it was God. To this I added that, since I knew of some perfections that I did not at all possess, I was not the only being that existed (here, if you please, I shall freely use the terminology of the School), but that of necessity there must be something else more perfect, upon which I depended, and from which I had acquired all that I had. For, had I been alone and independent of 35 everything else, so that I had had from myself all that small amount of perfection in which I participated in the perfect being, I would have been able, for the same reason, to have from myself everything else I knew I lacked, and thus to be myself infinite, eternal, unchanging, all-knowing, all-powerful; in short, to have all the perfections I could observe to be in God. For, following the reasonings I have just gone through, in order to know the nature of God, so far as my own nature was capable of doing so, I had only to consider, regarding all the things of which I found in myself some idea, whether or not it was a perfection to possess them, and I was assured that none of those that indicated any imperfection were in God, but that all others were in him. Thus I saw that doubt, inconstancy, sadness, and the like could not be in God, since I myself would have been happy to be exempt from them. Then, besides this, I had ideas of a number of sensible and corporeal things, for even if I were to suppose that I was dreaming and that everything I saw or imagined was false, I still could not deny that the ideas of these things were truly in my thought. But since I had already recognized very clearly in myself that intelligent nature is distinct from corporeal nature, taking into consideration that all composition attests to dependence and that dependence is manifestly a defect, I judged from this that being composed of these two natures could not be a perfection in God and that, as a consequence, God was not thus composed, but that, if there are bodies in the world, or even intelligences, or other natures 36 that were not at all entirely perfect, their being had to depend on God's power in such wise that they could not subsist without God for a single moment.

After this, I wanted to search for other truths, and, having set before myself the object dealt with by geometers, which I conceived of as a continuous body or a space indefinitely extended in length, breadth, and height or depth, divisible into various parts which could have various shapes and sizes and which may be moved or transposed in all sorts of ways—for the geometers assume all this in their object—I went through some of their simplest demonstrations. And, having noted that the great certitude that everyone attributes to these demonstrations is founded exclusively on the fact that they are plainly conceived, following the rule that I mentioned earlier, I also noted that there was nothing at all in them that assured me of the existence of their object. For I saw very well that if one supposed, for example, a triangle, it was necessary for its three angles to be equal to two right angles, but I did not see anything in all this to assure me that there was any triangle existing in the world. On the other hand, returning to examine the idea I had of a perfect being, I found that existence was contained in it in the same way in which the equality of its three angles to two right angles is contained in the idea of a triangle, or that the equidistance of all its parts from its center is contained in the idea of a sphere, or even more plainly still, and that, consequently, it is, at the very least, just as certain that God, who is this perfect being, is or exists, as any demonstration in geometry could be.

But what brings it about that there are many people 37 who are persuaded that it is difficult to know this and also even to know what their soul is is that they never lift their minds above sensible things and that they are so accustomed to consider nothing except by imagining it (which is a way of thinking appropriate for material things), that everything unimaginable seems to them unintelligible. This is obvious enough from the fact that even philosophers take it as a maxim in the schools that there is nothing in the understanding that has not first been in the senses, where it is nevertheless certain that the ideas of God and the soul have never been. And it seems to me that those who want to use their imagination in order to grasp these ideas are doing the very same thing as if, in order to hear sounds or to smell odors, they wanted to use their eyes. There is just this difference: the sense of sight assures us no less of the truth of its objects than do the senses of smell or hearing, whereas neither our imagination nor our senses could ever assure us of anything if our understanding did not intervene.

Finally, if there still are men who have not been sufficiently persuaded of the existence of God and of their soul by means of the reasons I have brought forward, I very much want them to know that all the other things of which they think themselves perhaps more assured, such as having a body, that there are stars and an earth, and the like, are less certain. For although one might have a moral assurance about these things, which is such that it seems one cannot 38 doubt them without being extravagant, still when it is a question of metaphysical certitude, it seems unreasonable for anyone to deny that there is not a sufficient basis for one's being completely assured about them, when one observes that while asleep one can, in the same fashion, imagine that one has a different body and that one sees different stars and a different earth, without any of these things being the case. For how does one know that the thoughts that come to us in dreams are any more false than the others, given that they are often no less vivid and explicit? And even if the best minds study this as much as they please, I do not believe they can give any reason sufficient to remove this doubt, unless they presuppose the existence of God. For first of all, even what I have already taken for a rule, namely that the things we very clearly and very distinctly conceive are all true, is assured only for the reason that God is or exists, and that he is a perfect being, and that all that is in us comes from him. It follows from this that our ideas or notions, being real things and coming from God, cannot, in all that is clear and distinct in them, be anything but true. Thus, if we quite often have ideas that contain some falsity, this can only be the case with respect to things that have something confused or obscure about them, because in this respect they participate in nothing; that is, they are thus confused in us only because we are not perfect. And it is evident that it is no less a contradiction that falsity or imperfection as 39 such proceeds from God, than that truth or perfection proceeds from nothing. But if we did not know that all that is real and true in us comes from a perfect and infinite being, however clear and distinct our ideas were, we would have no reason that assured us that they had the perfection of being true.

But once the knowledge of God and the soul has thus made us certain of this rule, it is very easy to know that the dreams we imagine while asleep ought in no way to make us doubt the truth of the thoughts we have while awake. For if it did happen, even while asleep, that one had a very distinct idea (as, for example, if a geometer found some new demonstration), one's being asleep would not prevent its being true. And as to the most common error of our dreams, which consists in the fact that they represent to us various objects in the same way as our external senses do, it does not matter that it gives us occasion to question the truth of such ideas, since they can also deceive us quite often without our being asleep, such as when those with jaundice see everything as yellow, or when the stars or other very distant bodies appear to us much smaller than they are. For finally, whether awake or asleep, we should never allow ourselves to be persuaded except by the evidence of our reason. And it is to be observed that I say "of our reason," and not "of our imagination" or "of our senses." Even 40 though we see the sun very clearly, we should not on that account judge that it is only as large as we see it, and we can well imagine distinctly the head of a lion grafted onto the body of a goat, without having to conclude for that reason that there is a chimera in the world, for reason does not at all dictate to us that what we thus see or imagine is true. But it does dictate to us that all our ideas or notions must have some foundation of truth, for it would not be possible that God, who is all-perfect and all-truthful, would have put them in us without that. And because our reasonings are never so evident nor so complete while we are asleep as they are while we are awake, even though our imaginings while we are asleep are sometimes just as vivid and explicit as those we have while we are awake, or even more so, reason also dictates to us that our thoughts cannot all be true, since we are not all-perfect; what truth there is in them must infallibly be encountered in those we have when we are awake rather than in those we have in our dreams.

PART FIVE

I would be quite happy to continue and to show here the whole chain of other truths that I have deduced from these first ones. But because, in order to do this, it would now be necessary for me to speak about many questions that are a matter of controversy among the learned, with whom I have no desire to get into any quarrel, I believe it will be better for me to abstain from this and to state only in a general way what these questions are, in order to let those who are wiser judge whether it would be useful for the public to be more particularly informed about them. I have always remained firm in the resolution I had made not to *41* suppose any principle but the one I have just used to demonstrate the existence of God and of the soul, and not to accept anything as true that did not seem to me clearer and more certain than the demonstrations of the geometers had hitherto seemed. And, nevertheless, I dare say not only that have I found a means of satisfying myself within a short time regarding all the principal difficulties commonly treated in philosophy, but also that I have noted certain laws that God has so established in nature, and of which he has impressed in our souls such notions, that, after having reflected sufficiently on these matters, we cannot doubt that they are strictly adhered to in everything that exists or occurs in the world. Moreover, in considering the consequences of these laws, it seems to me that I have discovered many truths more useful and more important than all that I had previously learned or even hoped to learn.

But because I have tried to explain the principal ones among these truths in a treatise that certain considerations prevented me from publishing,[7] I could not make them better known than by stating here in summary form what the treatise contains. I had intended to include in it everything that I thought I knew, before writing it down, concerning the nature of material things. But just as painters, who are unable to represent equally well on a flat surface all the various sides of a solid body, choose one of the principal sides which they place alone facing the light of day, and, by darkening the rest with shadows, make them appear only as they can be seen by someone *42* who is looking at the principal side, just so, fearing I could not put into my discourse everything I had in mind about it, I undertook in it merely to speak at length about what I conceived with respect to light; then, at the proper time, to add something about the sun and the fixed stars, because light proceeds almost entirely from them; something about the heavens, because they transmit light; about planets, comets, and the earth, because they reflect light; and, in particular, about all terrestrial bodies, because they are either colored, or transparent, or luminous; and finally, about man, because he is the observer of these things. All the same, to cast all these things a little in shadow and to be able to say more freely what I judged about them without being obliged either to follow or to refute the opinions that are accepted among the learned, I resolved to leave this entire world here to their disputes, and to speak only of what would happen in a new world, were God now to create enough matter to compose it, somewhere in imaginary spaces, and were he to agitate in various ways and without order the different parts of this matter, so that he composed from it a chaos as confused as any the poets could concoct and that later he did no more than apply his ordinary concurrence to nature, and let nature act in accordance with the laws he had established. Thus, first, I described this matter and

7. [Descartes' *Le Monde* (*The World*). See René Descartes, *Le Monde ou Traité de la lumière*, translation and introduction by Michael Sean Mahoney (New York: Abaris Books, Inc., 1979). One of the considerations preventing the publication of *Le Monde* was the trial in 1633 of Galileo by the Holy Office in Rome.]

tried to represent it in such a way that there is nothing in the world, it seems to me, clearer and more intel- 43 ligible, with the exception of what has already been said about God and the soul, for I even explicitly supposed that in this matter there were none of those forms or qualities about which disputes occur in the schools, nor generally anything the knowledge of which was not so natural to our souls that one could not even pretend to be ignorant of it. Moreover, I showed what the laws of nature were, and, without supporting my reasons on any other principle but the infinite perfections of God, I tried to demonstrate all those laws about which one might have been able to have any doubt and to show that they are such that, even if God had created many worlds, there could not be any of them in which these laws failed to be observed. After that, I showed how, as a consequence of these laws, the greater part of the matter of this chaos had to be disposed and arranged in a certain way, which made it similar to our heavens; how, at the same time, some of its parts had to compose an earth; others, planets and comets; and still others, a sun and fixed stars. And here, dwelling on the subject of light, I explained at some length what this light was that had to be found in the sun and the stars, and how from thence it travelled in an instant across the immense spaces of the heavens, and how it was reflected from the planets and comets to the earth. To this I added also a number of things touching on the substance, position, motions, and all the various qualities of these heavens and these stars; and as a result, I thought I said enough on these matters to show that there is nothing to be observed in the things of this world which should not, or at least could not, have 44 appeared entirely similar in those of the world I was describing. From there, I went on to speak in particular about the earth: how, although I had expressly supposed that God had not put any weight[8] in the matter out of which the earth was composed, none of its parts ceased to tend precisely toward its center; how, there being water and air on its surface, the disposition of the heavens and of the stars, principally of the moon, had to cause there an ebb and flow similar in all respects to what we observe in our seas, and, in addition, a certain coursing, as much of the water as of the air, from east to west, such as is also observed between the tropics; how mountains, seas, springs, and rivers could naturally be formed there, and how metals could make their way into mines there; how plants could grow naturally in the fields there, and generally how all the bodies called "mixed" or "composed" could be engendered there. And, among other things, because apart from the stars I know of nothing else in the world that would produce light except fire, I tried to make very clearly understood all that belonged to its nature: how it is made, how it is nourished, how sometimes it has only heat but no light, and sometimes only light but no heat; how it can introduce various colors and various other qualities into various bodies; how it melts some bodies and hardens others; how it can consume nearly all of them or turn them into ashes and smoke; and finally, how from these ashes, merely by the force of its action, it produces glass, for since this transmutation of ashes into glass seemed to me to be as awesome as any other that occurs in nature, I took 45 particular pleasure in describing it.

Yet I did not want to infer from all these things that this world has been created in the manner I was proposing, for it is much more likely that, from the beginning, God made it such as it had to be. But it is certain (and this is an opinion commonly accepted among theologians) that the action by which God preserves the world is precisely the same as that by which he created it; so that, even if, in the beginning, he had never given it any other form at all but that of a chaos, provided he established the laws of nature and bestowed his concurrence in order for nature to function just as it does ordinarily, one can believe, without doing injustice to the miracle of creation, that by this means alone all the things that are purely material could over time have been rendered such as we now see them. And their nature is much easier to conceive, when one sees them coming to be little by little in this manner, than when one considers them only in their completed state.

From the description of inanimate bodies and plants I passed to that of animals and in particular to that of human beings. But because I did not yet have sufficient knowledge of them to speak of them in the same manner as I did of the rest, that is to say,

8. [E. Gilson, in his *Discours de la méthode: texte et commentaire*, p. 388, observes that *pesanteur* here means the same thing as *gravitas*, a scholastic term referring to the tendency of terrestrial objects always to tend downwards. Gilson also directs the reader to *The World*, chapter xi: "On Weight."]

by demonstrating effects from causes and by showing from what seeds and in what manner nature must produce them, I contented myself with supposing 46 that God formed the body of a man exactly like one of ours, as much in the outward shape of its members as in the internal arrangement of its organs, without composing it out of any material but the type I had described, and without putting into it, at the start, any rational soul, or anything else to serve there as a vegetative or sensitive soul, but merely kindled in the man's heart one of those fires without light which I had already explained and which I did not at all conceive to be of a nature other than what heats hay when it has been stored before it is dry, or which makes new wines boil when they are left to ferment after crushing. For on examining the functions that could, as a consequence, be in this body, I found there precisely all those things that can be in us without our thinking about them, and hence, without our soul's contributing to them, that is to say, that part distinct from the body of which it has been said previously that its nature is only to think. And these are all the same features in which one can say that animals lacking reason resemble us. But I could not on that account find there any of those functions, which, being dependent on thought, are the only ones that belong to us as men, although I did find them all later on, once I had supposed that God created a rational soul and joined it to this body in a particular manner that I described.

But in order that one might be able to see how I treated this matter there, I want to place here the explanation of the movement of the heart and of the arteries, because, this being the first and most general movement that one observes in animals, on the basis 47 of it one will easily judge what one ought to think about all the others. And, in order that there might be less difficulty in understanding what I shall say on the matter, I would like those who are not at all versed in anatomy to take the trouble, before reading this, to have the heart of some large animal that has lungs dissected in their presence (for such a heart is in all respects sufficiently similar to that of a man), and to be shown the two chambers or cavities that are in it. First, there is the one on the right side of the heart, into which two very large tubes lead, namely the *vena cava*, which is the principal receptacle of the blood, and which is like the trunk of a tree of which the other veins of the body are the branches, and the arterial vein (which has thus been rather ill-named, because it is, in effect, an artery), which, taking its origin from the heart, divides up after leaving the heart into many branches that go on to be spread throughout the lungs. Then there is the chamber or cavity on the left side, into which two tubes lead in the same fashion, which are as large as or larger than the preceding ones: namely, the venous artery (which has also been ill-named, since it is nothing but a vein), which comes from the lungs, where it is divided into many branches interlaced with those of the arterial vein and with those in the passageway called the windpipe, through which the air one breathes enters, and the great artery, which, on leaving the heart, sends its branches throughout the body. I would also like those who are not versed in anatomy to be carefully shown the eleven little membranes that, like so many little doors, open and shut the four openings in the two cavities: namely, three at the entrance to the *vena* 48 *cava*, where they are so disposed that they cannot in any way prevent the blood it contains from flowing into the right cavity of the heart, and yet completely prevent it from being able to leave it: three at the entrance to the arterial vein, which, being arranged totally in the other direction, readily permit the blood in this cavity to pass into the lungs, but do not permit any blood in the lungs to return there; likewise, two others at the entrance to the venous artery, which let blood flow from the lungs into the left cavity of the heart but block its return; and three at the entrance to the great artery, which permit blood to leave the heart but prevent it from returning there. And there is no need at all to search for any other reason for the number of membranes except that the opening of the venous artery, being oval-shaped because of its location, can conveniently be closed with two, while the other openings, being round, can better be closed with three. Further, I would like to make them consider that the great artery and the arterial vein are of a much harder and firmer constitution than the venous artery and the *vena cava*, and that these latter two become enlarged before entering the heart and there form, as it were, sacks, called the "auricles" of the heart, which are made of flesh similar to that of the heart; and that there is always more heat in the heart than anywhere else in the body, and, finally, that this heat is able to bring it about that, if a drop of blood enters its cavities, it promptly expands and is dilated, 49 just as all liquids generally do when one lets them fall drop by drop into some vessel that is very hot.

For, after that, I have no need to say anything else in order to explain the movement of the heart, except that, when its cavities are not full of blood, blood necessarily flows from the *vena cava* into the right cavity and from the venous artery into the left cavity, given that these two vessels are always full of blood, and their openings, which face the heart, cannot then be closed. But as soon as two drops of blood have thus entered the heart, one into each of its cavities, these drops, which can only be very large because the openings through which they enter are very wide and the vessels from whence they come are quite full of blood, are rarified and dilated because of the heat they find there, by means of which, making the whole heart inflate, they push and close the five little doors that are at the entrances to the two vessels from whence they come, thus preventing any more blood from descending into the heart, and, continuing to become more and more rarified, they push and open the six other little doors which are at the entrances to the other two vessels by which they leave. By this means they inflate all the branches of the arterial vein and the great artery, almost at the same instant as the heart; immediately afterward the heart contracts, as do these arteries as well, because the blood that has entered them gets cooled and their six little doors close again, and the five doors of the *vena cava* and 50 the venous artery reopen and grant passage to two other drops of blood, which immediately make the heart and the arteries inflate exactly as before. And, because the blood that thus enters the heart passes through the two sacks called its auricles, it follows from this that their movement is contrary to that of the heart, and that they are deflated while the heart is inflated. As for the rest (in order that those who do not know the force of mathematical demonstrations and are not accustomed to distinguishing true reasons from probable ones should not venture to deny this without examining it), I want to put them on notice that this movement which I have just been explaining follows just as necessarily from the mere disposition of the organs that can be seen in the heart by the naked eye, and from the heat that can be felt with the fingers, and from the nature of blood, which can be known through observation, as does the movement of a clock from the force, placement, and shape of its counterweights and wheels.

But if one asks how it is that the blood in the veins is not at all dissipated in flowing thus continually into the heart, and how the arteries are never overly full of blood, since all the blood that flows through the heart is going to flow into them, to this I need give no other answer than what has already been written by an English physician,[9] to whom homage must be paid for having broken the ice in this area, and for being the first to have taught that there are many small passages at the extremities of the arteries through which the blood they receive enters into the small branches of the veins, from which it flows immediately to the heart, so that its course is merely 51 a perpetual circulation. He proves this very effectively from the common experience of surgeons, who, on binding an arm moderately tightly above the spot where they open the vein, cause the blood to flow out in even greater abundance than if they had not bound the arm at all. And just the opposite would happen if they bound the arm below, between the hand and the opening, or even if they bind it very tightly above the opening, for it is obvious that a moderately tight tourniquet, being able to prevent the blood that is already in the arm from returning to the heart through the veins, does not on that account prevent new blood from coming in through the arteries, because they are located below the veins, and their membranes, being harder, are less easy to press, and also because the blood coming from the heart tends to pass through the arteries toward the hand with greater force than it does in returning from these to the heart through the veins. And since this blood leaves the arm through the opening in one of the veins, there must necessarily be some passages below the tourniquet, that is to say, toward the extremities of the arm, through which it could come from the arteries. He also proves quite effectively what he says regarding the circulation of blood by referring to certain small membranes that are so disposed in various places along the length of the veins that they do not at all permit blood to pass

9. [William Harvey (1578–1657), English physiologist who demonstrated the function of the heart and the complete circulation of blood throughout the body. His most important work is *Anatomical Exercises on the Motion of the Heart and Blood* (1628). Descartes accepted Harvey's account of how blood circulated, but not his account of the heart's motion.]

from the middle of the body toward the extremities, but only to return from the extremities toward the heart; and further, by means of the experiment that shows that all the blood that is in the body can flow out of it in a very short time through just one artery when it is cut open, even if the artery is very tightly bound quite close to the heart, and cut open between the heart and the tourniquet, so that one would have 52 no basis for imagining that the blood that flowed out came from somewhere else.

But there are many other things that attest to the fact that the true cause of this movement of blood is as I have said. First, the difference that one notices between the blood leaving the veins and the blood leaving the arteries can result only from the fact that the blood is rarified and, as it were, distilled, in passing through the heart; it is thinner, livelier, and warmer just after having left the heart, that is to say, while it is in the arteries, than it is shortly before it enters the heart, that is to say, while it is in the veins. And if one takes note of it, one will find that this difference is more readily apparent near the heart and not at all so much in those places furthest removed from the heart. Then the hardness of the membranes of which the arterial vein and the great artery are composed shows well enough that the blood beats against them with more force than it does against the veins. And why would the left cavity of the heart and the great artery be larger and wider than the right cavity and the arterial vein, unless it is because the blood in the venous artery, having been only in the lungs after having passed through the heart, is thinner and is more forcefully and more easily rarified than what comes immediately from the *vena cava*? And what can physicians divine from taking the pulse, if they do not know that, as the blood changes its nature, it can be rarified by the heat of the heart more or less strongly, and more or less quickly than before? And 53 if one examines how this heat is communicated to the other members, must one not admit that it is by means of the blood, which, on passing through the heart, is reheated there and from there is spread throughout the whole body? It follows from this that if one removes the blood from some part of the body, one thereupon also removes the heat; and even if the heart were as hot as a piece of glowing iron, it would not be enough to reheat the feet and hands as much as it does, if it did not continuously send new blood to them. Then, too, it is also evident from this that the true function of respiration is to bring enough fresh air into the lungs to cause the blood which comes there from the right cavity of the heart, where it has been rarified and, as it were, changed into vapors, immediately to be condensed and to be converted once again into blood before returning to the left cavity; without this process the blood could not properly aid in feeding the fire that is in the heart. This is confirmed because one sees that animals without lungs have but one single cavity in their hearts, and that children, who cannot use their lungs while enclosed within their mother's womb, have an opening through which blood flows from the *vena cava* into the left cavity of the heart, as well as a tube through which blood goes from the arterial vein to the great artery without passing through the lungs. Next, how would digestion take place in the stomach if the heart did not send heat there through the arteries, and with it some of the most fluid parts of the blood, which help dissolve the food that has gone there? And is it not easy to understand the action that changes the juice of this food into blood, if one considers that, in passing and repassing through the heart, it is distilled perhaps more than one or two hundred times a day? And is anything else needed to explain nutrition and the 54 production of the various humors that are in the body, except to say that the force with which the blood, in being rarified, passes from the heart toward the extremities of the arteries, makes some of its parts stop in those parts of the members where they are found and there take the place of others that they expel from there; and that, according to the situation or the shape or the smallness of the pores they encounter, some of the parts of the blood tend to go certain places rather than others, in just the same way that anyone can have seen various sieves of different fineness serve to separate out different grains from one another? And finally what is most remarkable in all this is the generation of the animal spirits, which are like a very subtle wind, or rather, like a very pure and lively flame that rises continuously in great abundance from the heart to the brain, and from there goes through the nerves into the muscles, and gives movement to all the members. The parts of the blood that are the most agitated and penetrating, and are thus the best suited to compose these spirits, are going to move toward the brain rather than elsewhere; and there is no need to imagine any reason for this other than that the arteries that carry these parts of the blood there are those that come from the heart in the straightest line of all, and that, according to the laws of mechanics (which are the same as those of nature), when a number of things tend to move together in the same direction, where there is not enough room for all of them, as when the parts of the blood leaving the left cavity of the heart tend toward the brain, the weakest and least 55 agitated must be pushed aside by the strongest which by this means arrive there alone.

I had provided a sufficiently detailed explanation for all these things in the treatise that I had previously intended to publish. And then I had shown what the constitution of the nerves and muscles of the human body must be in order to make the animal spirits within them have the force to move its members, as when one observes that heads, shortly after being severed, still move about and bite the earth, even though they are no longer alive. I had also shown what changes must take place in the brain in order to cause wakefulness, sleep, and dreams; how light, sounds, odors, tastes, heat, and all the other qualities of external objects can imprint various ideas there through the mediation of the senses; how hunger, thirst, and the other internal passions can also send their ideas there; what part of them needs to be taken there for the common sense, where these ideas are received, for the memory, which preserves them, and for the imagination, which can change them in various ways and compose new ones out of them, and, by the same means, distributing the animal spirits into the muscles, make the members of this body move in as many different ways (and in a manner appropriate to the objects that present themselves to the senses and to the internal passions that are in the body), as our own bodies can, without their being guided by the will. This will in no way seem strange to those who are cognizant of how many different automata or moving machines the 56 ingenuity of men can make, without, in doing so, using more than a very small number of parts, in comparison with the great multitude of bones, muscles, nerves, arteries, veins, and all the other parts which are in the body of each animal. For they will regard this body as a machine which, having been made by the hands of God, is incomparably better ordered and has within itself movements far more wondrous than any of those that can be invented by men.

And I paused here in particular in order to show that, if there were such machines having the organs and the shape of a monkey or of some other animal that lacked reason, we would have no way of recognizing that they were not entirely of the same nature as these animals; whereas, if there were any such machines that bore a resemblance to our bodies and imitated our actions as far as this is practically feasible, we would always have two very certain means of recognizing that they were not at all, for that reason, true men. The first is that they could never use words or other signs, or put them together as we do in order to declare our thoughts to others. For one can well conceive of a machine being so made that it utters words, and even that it utters words appropriate to the bodily actions that will cause some change in its organs (such as, if one touches it in a certain place, it asks what one wants to say to it, or, if in another place, it cries out that one is hurting it, and the like). But it could not arrange its words differently so as to respond to the sense of all that will be said in its presence, as 57 even the dullest men can do. The second means is that, although they might perform many tasks very well or perhaps better than any of us, such machines would inevitably fail in other tasks; by this means one would discover that they were acting not through knowledge but only through the disposition of their organs. For while reason is a universal instrument that can be of help in all sorts of circumstances, these organs require some particular disposition for each particular action; consequently, it is for all practical purposes impossible for there to be enough different organs in a machine to make it act in all the contingencies of life in the same way as our reason makes us act.

Now by these two means one can also know the difference between men and beasts. For it is rather remarkable that there are no men so dull and so stupid (excluding not even the insane), that they are incapable of arranging various words together and of composing from them a discourse by means of which they might make their thoughts understood, and that, on the other hand, there is no other animal at all, however perfect and pedigreed it may be, that does the like. This does not happen because they lack the organs, for one sees that magpies and parrots can utter words just as we can, and yet they cannot speak as we do, that is to say, by testifying to the fact that they are thinking about what they are saying; on the other hand, men born deaf and dumb, who are deprived 58 of the organs that aid others in speaking just as much as, or more than beasts, are wont to invent for themselves various signs by means of which they make themselves understood to those who, being with them on a regular basis, have the time to learn their language. And this attests not merely to the fact that beasts have less reason than men but that they have none at all. For it is obvious it does not need much to know how to speak; and since we notice as much inequality among animals of the same species as among men, and that some are easier to train than others, it is unbelievable that a monkey or a parrot that is the most perfect of its species would not equal in this respect one of the most stupid children or at least a child with a disordered brain, if their soul were not of a nature entirely different from our own. And we should not confuse words with the natural movements that attest to the passions and can be imitated by machines as well as by animals. Nor should we think, as did some of the ancients, that beasts speak, although we do not understand their language, for if that were true, since they have many organs corresponding to our own, they could make themselves as well understood by us as they are by their fellow creatures. It is also a very remarkable phenomenon that, although there are many animals that show more skill than we do in some of their actions, we nevertheless see that they show none at all in many other actions. Consequently, the fact that they do something better than we do does not prove that they have any intelligence, for, were that the case, they would have more 59 of it than any of us and would excel us in everything. But rather it proves that they have no intelligence at all, and that it is nature that acts in them, according to the disposition of their organs—just as we see that a clock composed exclusively of wheels and springs can count the hours and measure time more accurately than we can with all our carefulness.

After that, I described the rational soul and showed that it can in no way be derived from the potentiality of matter, as can the other things I have spoken of, but rather that it must be expressly created; and how it is not enough for it to be lodged in the human body like a pilot in his ship, unless perhaps in order to move its members, but rather that it must be more closely joined and united to the body in order to have, in addition to this, feelings and appetites similar to our own, and thus to constitute a true man. As to the rest, I elaborated here a little on the subject of the soul because it is of the greatest importance; for, after the error of those who deny the existence of God (which I think I have sufficiently refuted), there is none at all that puts weak minds at a greater distance from the straight path of virtue than to imagine that the soul of beasts is of the same nature as ours, and that, as a consequence, we have nothing to fear or to hope for after this life any more than do flies and ants. On the other hand, when one knows how different they are, one understands much better the arguments which prove that our soul is of a nature entirely independent of the body, and consequently that it is not subject to die with it. Then, since we do not see any other causes at all for its destruction, we are naturally led to 60 judge from this that it is immortal.

PART SIX

But it is now three years since I arrived at the end of the treatise that contains all these things and began to review it in order to put it into the hands of a printer, when I learned that some people to whom I defer and whose authority over my actions can hardly be less than that of my reason over my thoughts, had disapproved of an opinion in physics, published a short time earlier by someone else,[10] concerning which I do not want to say that I was in agreement, but rather that I had not noticed anything in it, before their censuring of it, that I could imagine to be prejudicial either to religion or to the state, nor, as a consequence, had I found anything that would have prevented me from writing it, had reason persuaded me of it, and this made me fear that there might likewise be found among my opinions one in which I had been mistaken, notwithstanding the great care that I have always taken never to accept into my beliefs any new opinions for which I did not

10. [Galileo Galilei (1564–1642), Italian astronomer, mathematician and physicist. His *Dialogue . . . on the Two Chief Systems of the World* (1632), in which he advanced the theory of the movement of the earth, occasioned the Inquisitors of the Holy Office to conduct a trial in Rome and to extort a retraction of that theory from Galileo. Descartes, who also advocated a theory of terrestrial motion, was not about to let Rome sin twice against philosophy. Cf. E. Gilson, *Discours de la méthode: texte et commentaire*, pp. 439–42.]

have very certain demonstrations and never to write anything that could turn to anyone's disadvantage. This was sufficient to make me change the resolution I had had to publish my opinions. For although the reasons for which I had earlier made the resolution were very strong, my inclination, which has always made me hate the business of writing books, immediately made me find enough other reasons to excuse me from it. And these reasons, both for and *61* against, are such that not only do I have some interest in stating them here, but perhaps also the public has some interest in knowing them.

I had never made much of the things that came from my mind, and so long as I had reaped no other fruits from the method I am using except my own satisfaction regarding certain problems that pertain to the speculative sciences or else my attempt at governing my moral conduct by means of the reasons which the method taught me, I believed I was under no obligation whatever to write anything about it. For as to moral conduct, everyone is so very full of his own viewpoint, that it would be possible to find as many reformers as heads, if anyone other than those God has established as rulers over his peoples or even those to whom he has given sufficient grace and zeal to be prophets were permitted to try to change anything here. And although my speculations pleased me very much, I believed that others also had their own which perhaps pleased them more. But as soon as I had acquired some general notions regarding physics, and, beginning to test them in various particular difficulties, I had noticed where they could lead and how much they differ from the principles that have been in use up to the present, I believed I could not keep them hidden away without sinning grievously against the law that obliges us to procure, as much as is in our power, the common good of all men. For these notions made me see that it is possible to arrive at knowledge that would be very useful in life and that, in place of that speculative philosophy 62 taught in the schools, it is possible to find a practical philosophy, by means of which, knowing the force and the actions of fire, water, air, the stars, the heavens, and all the other bodies that surround us, just as distinctly as we know the various skills of our craftsmen, we might be able, in the same way, to use them for all the purposes for which they are appropriate, and thus render ourselves, as it were, masters and possessors of nature. This is desirable not only for the invention of an infinity of devices that would enable one to enjoy trouble-free the fruits of the earth and all the goods found there, but also principally for the maintenance of health, which unquestionably is the first good and the foundation of all the other goods of this life, for even the mind depends so greatly on the temperament and on the disposition of the organs of the body that, if it is possible to find some means to render men generally more wise and more adroit than they have been up until now, I believe that one should look for it in medicine. It is true that the medicine currently practiced contains few things whose usefulness is so noteworthy, but without intending to ridicule it, I am sure there is no one, not even among those who make a profession of it, who would not admit that everything known in medicine is practically nothing in comparison with what remains to be known, and that one could rid oneself of an infinity of maladies, as much of the body as of the mind, and even perhaps also the frailty of old age, if one had a sufficient knowledge of their causes and of all the remedies that nature has provided us. For, having the intention of spending my entire life in the search for so indispensable a science, and having found a path that 63 seems to me such that, by following it, one ought infallibly to find this science, unless one is prevented from doing so either by the brevity of life or by a lack of experiments,[11] I judged there to be no better remedy against these two obstacles than to communicate faithfully to the public the entirety of what little I had found and to urge good minds to try to advance beyond this by contributing, each according to his inclination and ability, to the experiments that must be performed and also by communicating to the public everything they might learn, in order that, with subsequent inquirers beginning where their predecessors had left off, and thus, joining together the lives and labors of many, we might all advance together much further than a single individual could do on his own.

Moreover, I noticed, in regard to experiments, that they are the more necessary as one is more advanced in knowledge. For in the beginning it is better to make

11. [*Expérience* is used by Descartes to refer to a wide range of activities, from simple observations to sophisticated scientific experiments. *Expérience* will be translated as "observations" or as "experiments," depending on the context.]

use only of those observations which present themselves of their own accord to our senses and which we could not ignore, provided we reflect, however so little, on them, rather than to search for unusual and contrived experiments. The reason for this is that these more unusual experiments often deceive one when one does not know yet the causes of the more common ones, and that the circumstances on which the unusual ones depend are almost always so special and so minute that it is very difficult to notice them. But the order I have held to has been the following. First, I have tried to find in general the principles or first causes of all that is or can be in the world, without considering anything but God alone, who created the world, and without deriving these principles from any other source but from certain seeds of truths that are naturally in our souls. After that I examined what were the first and most ordinary effects that could be deduced from these causes; and it seems to me that by this means I had found the heavens, stars, an earth, and even, on the earth, water, air, fire, minerals, and other such things that are the most common of all and the simplest, and, as a consequence, the easiest to know. Then, when I wanted to descend to those things which were more particular, so many different ones were presented to me that I did not believe it possible for the human mind to distinguish the forms or species of bodies that are on the earth from an infinity of others that could have been there had it been the will of God to have put them there, nor, as a consequence, to make them serviceable to us, unless we advance to the causes through the effects and make use of many particular observations. After this, passing my mind again over all the objects that have ever presented themselves to my senses, I daresay I did not notice anything in them that I could not explain easily enough by means of the principles I had found. But I must also admit that the power of nature is so ample and so vast, and these principles are so simple and so general, that I notice hardly any particular effect without at once knowing that it can be deduced in many different ways from them, and that ordinarily my greatest difficulty is to find in which of these ways it depends on them. For, to this end, I know of no other expedient at all except to search once more for some experiments which are such that their outcomes are not the same, if it is in one of these ways rather than in another that one ought to explain the outcome. As to the rest, I am now at the point where, it seems to me, I see quite well what approach one must take in order to make most of the experiments that can serve this purpose; but I also see that they are of such a kind and of so great a number that neither my adroitness nor my financial resources (even if I had a thousand times more than I have) would suffice for all of them, so that, according as I henceforth have the opportunity to perform more or fewer experiments, I shall also advance more or less in the knowledge of nature. That is what I meant to make known through the treatise I had written, and to show there so clearly the utility that the public could gain from such knowledge that I would oblige all those who desire the general well-being of men (that is to say, all those who really are virtuous, not just appearing to be so through false pretenses or merely by reputation), both to communicate those experiments they have already performed and to assist me in the search for those that remain to be performed.

But since then other reasons have made me change my mind and to think that I really ought to continue to write about all the things I judged to be of some importance, to the extent that I discovered the truth with respect to them, and to take the same care in regard to them as I would take if I wanted to have them published. I did this as much to have all the more of an occasion to examine them well (since without doubt one always looks more carefully at what one believes must be seen by many than at what one does only for oneself, and often the things that have seemed to me to be true when I began to conceive them have appeared false to me when I wanted to put them on paper), as in order not to lose any occasion to benefit the public, if I am able, and in order that, if my writings are worth anything, those who will have them after my death can thus use them as will be most fitting. But I must not in any way consent to their being published during my lifetime, so that neither the hostilities and the controversies to which they might be subject, nor even such reputation as they could gain for me, would give me any occasion for losing the time I have intended to use in instructing myself. For although it may be true that each man is obliged to secure as best he can the good of others, and that to be useful to no one is, strictly speaking, to be worthless, still it is also true that our concerns ought to extend further than to the present time, and that it is well to omit things that perhaps would yield some profit to those who are alive, when it is with the intention of doing other things that would yield even more profit to our posterity. In any event, I very much want people to understand that what little I have learned up until now is almost nothing in comparison to what I do not know and to what I do not despair of being able to learn, for it is almost the same with those who little by little discover the truth in the sciences as it is 67 with those who, upon beginning to acquire wealth, have less trouble making large acquisitions than they had had before, when they were poorer, in making very small ones. Or indeed, one can compare them to army commanders whose forces typically grow in proportion to their victories and who need more skill to maintain themselves after losing a battle than they do to take cities or provinces when they have won one. For it is truly to engage in battle when one tries to overcome all the difficulties and errors that prevent us from arriving at the knowledge of the truth, and it is truly to lose a battle when one accepts a false opinion touching on a matter that is at all general and important. And afterward it requires much more skill to recover one's former position than to make great progress when one already has principles that are assured. For myself, if I have already found some truths in the sciences (and I hope the things contained in this volume will make people judge that I have found some of them), I can say that these are only things that result from and depend on five or six principal difficulties that I have surmounted and that I count as so many battles in which I have had fortune on my side. I will not even fear to say that I think I need to win only two or three more battles like them in order to succeed entirely in my plans, and that my age is not at all so advanced that, in the ordinary 68 course of nature, I might not still have enough time to bring this about. But I believe I am all the more obliged to manage well the time remaining to me, the more hope I have of being able to use it well, and doubtless I would have many opportunities to lose time, had I published the foundations of my physics. For although they are nearly all so evident that it is necessary only to understand them in order to believe them, and although there has not been a single one for which I did not believe I could give demonstrations, nevertheless, because it is impossible for them to be in agreement with all the diverse opinions of other men, I foresee that I would often be distracted by the disputes they would engender.

One could say that these disputes might be useful, as much in order that I be made aware of my faults, as in order that, if I had anything worthwhile to say, others would by this means have greater understanding of it, and that, since many can see more than one man alone, these others, by beginning right now to use it, might also help me with their discoveries. But, although I recognize that I am extremely prone to err and that I almost never rely on the first thoughts that come to me, still the experience I have of the objections that can be made against me prevents me from expecting any profit from them. For I have already often put to the test the judgments of those I took to be my friends, as well as of some others whom I took to be indifferent, and even of those too whose maliciousness and envy I knew would try hard enough to discover what affection would hide from my friends. But it has rarely happened that an objection has been 69 raised against me that I had not at all foreseen, unless it was very far removed from my subject; thus I have almost never found any critic of my opinions who did not seem to me to be either less rigorous or less unbiased than myself. Nor have I ever observed that, through the method of disputations practiced in the schools, any truth has been discovered that had until then been unknown. For, so long as each person in the dispute aims at winning, he is more concerned with making much out of probability than with weighing the arguments on each side; and those who have long been good advocates are not, on that account, afterward better judges.

As to the utility that others might gain from the communication of my thoughts, it could not be so very great, given that I have not yet at all taken them so far that there is no need to add many things to them before applying them to actual practice. And I think I can say without vanity that, if there is anyone who is capable of doing this, it must be myself rather than someone else: not that there could not be in the world many minds incomparably greater than mine, but because one cannot conceive a thing so well and make it one's own when one learns it from someone else as one can when one discovers it for oneself. This is so true in this matter that, although I have often explained some of my opinions to people with good minds, who, while I spoke to them, seemed to understand them quite distinctly, nevertheless, when they repeated them, I noticed that they had almost always changed them in such a way that I could no longer acknowledge them as mine. In this connection, I 70 am very happy here to ask our descendants never to believe the things people tell them came from me, unless I myself have divulged them. And I am in no way surprised by the extravagances attributed to all those ancient philosophers whose writings we do not have, nor do I judge, for that reason, that their thoughts have been so very unreasonable, given that they were the greatest minds of their time, but only that their thoughts have been poorly reported to us. For one also sees that it has almost never happened that any of their followers had ever surpassed them, and I am sure that the most impassioned of those who now follow Aristotle would believe themselves fortunate, if they had as much knowledge of nature as he had, even if it were on the condition that they would never have any more. They are like ivy, which never stretches any higher than the trees supporting it, and which often even descends again after it has reached their tops, for it seems to me that they too are redescending, that is, they are making themselves somehow less knowledgeable than if they abstained from studying; not content with knowing all that is intelligibly explained in their author, they want in addition to find the solutions there to many difficulties about which he says nothing and about which he has perhaps never thought. Still, their manner of philosophizing is very convenient for those who have only very mediocre minds, for the obscurity of the distinctions and the principles they make use of is the reason why they can speak about all things as boldly as if they 71 knew them, and why they can uphold everything they say against the most subtle and the most adroit, without anyone's having the means of convincing them that they are mistaken. In this they seem to me like a blind man who, in order to fight without a disadvantage against someone who is sighted, had made his opponent go into the depths of some very dark cellar. And I may say that these people have an interest in my refraining from publishing the principles of the philosophy I use, for my principles being as very simple and very evident as they are, I would, by publishing them, be doing almost the same as if I were to open some windows and make some daylight enter that cellar they had gone into in order to fight. But even the best minds have no reason for wanting to know these principles, for if they want to know how to speak about all things and to acquire the reputation for being learned, they will achieve their objective more easily by contenting themselves with probability, which can be found without great difficulty in all sorts of matters, than by seeking the truth, which can only be discovered little by little in some and which, when it is a question of speaking about other matters, obliges one to confess frankly that one is ignorant of them. But if they prefer the knowledge of some few truths to the vanity of appearing to be ignorant of nothing, as no doubt it is really preferable to do, and if they want to follow a plan similar to mine, they do not, on that score, need me to say anything more except what I have already said in this discourse. For, if they are capable of advancing further than I have, then *a fortiori* they are also capable of finding for themselves all that I think I have found. Inasmuch as I have never examined anything except in an orderly manner, it is certain that what still remains for me to discover is of itself more difficult and more hidden than what 72 I have heretofore been able to discover, and they would take much less pleasure in learning it from me than from themselves. Moreover, the habit they will acquire of seeking first the easy things and then of passing little by little by degrees to other more difficult ones will serve them better than all my instructions could do. As for myself, I am convinced that, if I had been taught from my youth all the truths for which I have since then sought demonstrations, and if I had not had any difficulty in learning them, I might perhaps have never known any other truths, and at least I would never have acquired the habit and facility I think I have for always finding new truths, to the extent that I apply myself in searching for them. And, in a word, if there is any task in the world that could not be accomplished so well by anyone else but the same person who began it, it is the one on which I am working.

It is true that, with respect to experiments that can help here, one man alone cannot suffice to perform them all, but neither can he usefully employ hands other than his own, except those of craftsmen, or such people as he could pay and whom the hope of gain, which is a very effective means, would cause to do precisely what he ordered them to do. For, as to volunteers, who, out of curiosity or a desire to learn, might offer themselves in order perhaps to help him (aside from the fact that they usually make more promises than they produce achievements, and merely make fine proposals, none of which will come to anything), they would inevitably want to be paid 73 by the explanation of various difficulties, or at least by compliments and useless conversations, which could not cost him so little time that he would not lose by it. And as to the experiments that others have already performed, even if these people did want to communicate them to him (something those who call them "secrets" would never do), they are for the most part composed of so many details and superfluous ingredients that it would be very hard for him to discern the truth in them; besides, he would find almost all of them to be so badly explained or even so false, because those who have done them strove to make them appear to be in conformity with their principles, that, if there were among them some experiments that might serve him, they could not be worth the time he would need to spend in selecting them. In this way, if there were someone in the world whom one assuredly knows to be capable of finding the greatest things and the things as beneficial to the public as possible and whom, for this cause, other men were to exert themselves to help in every way to succeed in his plans, I do not see that they could do a thing for him except to make a donation toward the expenses of the experiments he would need and, for the rest, to prevent his leisure from being wasted by the importunity of anyone. But, although I do not presume so much of myself as to want to promise anything out of the ordinary, or feast on such vain thoughts as to imagine that the public ought to be especially interested in my plans, I do not have so base a soul that I would 74 want to accept from anyone any favor that one might believe I had not deserved.

All these considerations taken together were the reason why, three years ago, I did not at all want to divulge the treatise I had on hand, and why I had even made a resolution not to make public during my lifetime any other treatise which was so general or on the basis of which one could understand the foundations of my physics. But since then there have been yet again two other reasons that have obliged me to place here certain particular essays and to render to the public some account of my actions and my plans. The first is that, if I failed to do so, many who knew of the intention I once had to have certain writings published could imagine that the reasons for which I am abstaining from doing so were more to my disadvantage than they are. For although I do not love glory excessively—indeed, if I dare say so, I hate it, inasmuch as I judge it to be contrary to the tranquility I esteem above all things—still, I have also never tried to hide my actions as if they were crimes, nor have I taken many precautions so as not to be known. This is the case as much because I would have believed I would be doing myself an injustice, as because it would have given me a certain kind of disquiet, which again would have been contrary to the perfect peace of mind I am seeking. And because, having always been thus indifferent about the concern over being known or not known, I could not prevent my acquiring some type of reputation, I thought I ought to do my best at least to spare myself from having a bad one. 75 The other reason that has obliged me to write this is as follows: I saw more and more every day the delay that the plan I have of self-instruction is suffering because of an infinity of experiments of which I have need and which it is impossible for me to perform without the help of others. And although I do not flatter myself so much as to hope that the public will become greatly taken with my interests, still I also do not want to fail myself so much as to give those who will survive me cause to reproach me one day on the grounds that I could have left them many far better things than I had done, if I had not so badly neglected making them understand how they could contribute to my plans.

And I thought that it was easy to choose certain matters that, without being subjected to much controversy or obliging me to declare more of my principles than I desire, would nevertheless allow me to show quite clearly what I can or cannot do in the sciences. I cannot say whether I have been successful in this, and I do not at all want to prejudice the judgments of anyone in speaking for myself about my writings; but I shall be very happy if they are examined, and, in order to have more of an opportunity to do this, I am imploring all who have any objections to make against them to take the trouble to send them to my publisher and, on being advised about them by him, I shall try at the same time to append my reply to the objections, and by this means, seeing both of them together, readers will judge the truth all the more easily. For I promise never to make long replies to them, but only to admit 76 my errors very candidly, if I recognize them, or, even if I cannot perceive any, to say simply what I believe to be required for the defense of what I have written, without adding to it an explanation of any new material, in order not to become endlessly involved in one issue after another.

And, if any of those things about which I have spoken at the beginning of the *Dioptrics* and the *Meteors* are shocking at first glance because I call them suppositions and seem to lack the inclination to prove them, I entreat the reader to have the patience to read the whole thing with attention, and I hope he will find himself satisfied with it. For it seems to me that the reasonings follow each other there in such a way that, just as the last are demonstrated by means of the first, which are their causes, so these first are reciprocally demonstrated by means of the last, which are their effects. And one must not imagine that I am here committing the fallacy that logicians call a circle, for, experience rendering the majority of these effects very certain, the causes from which I deduce these effects serve not so much to prove them as to explain them; on the contrary, it is rather the case that the causes are what are proved by the effects. And I have called them suppositions only to make it understood that I think I can deduce them from these first truths that I have explained above. But I wanted expressly not to do so, in order to prevent certain minds, who imagine that they know in one day all that someone else has thought about for twenty years as soon as he has said but two or three words to them about it, and who are the more subject to error and the less capable of truth, the more penetrating and 77 lively they are, from being able to take this occasion to build some extravagant philosophy on what they believe are my principles, and in order to prevent me from being blamed for it. For as to the opinions that are entirely mine, I do not apologize for their being new, since, if one considers well the arguments for them, I am sure that one will find them so simple and so in conformity with common sense that they will seem less extraordinary and less strange than any others one could have on the same subjects. Nor do I pride myself at all on being the first discoverer of any of them; rather, I pride myself on never having accepted them because they have or have not been said by others, but only because reason has persuaded me of them.

If craftsmen cannot immediately carry out the invention explained in the *Dioptrics*, I do not believe one could say, on that account, that it is bad, for, inasmuch as skill and practice are needed to make and adjust the machines I have described, without any detail being overlooked there, I would be no less astonished if they were to succeed on the first try than if someone were able to learn in one day to play the lute with distinction simply because he had been given a good score. And if I write in French, the language of my country, rather than in Latin, the language of my teachers, it is because I am hoping that those who use only their natural reason in all its purity will judge my opinions better than those who believe only in old books. And as to those who combine good sense with study, whom alone I wish to have as my judges, they will not at all, I am sure, be so 78 partial to Latin that they refuse to listen to my reasons because I explain them in the vernacular.

As to the rest, I do not at all want to speak here in detail about the future progress I hope to make in the sciences, or to involve myself vis-à-vis the public in any promise that I am not assured of keeping; rather I shall say simply that I have resolved to spend the rest of my life on nothing but trying to acquire some knowledge of nature which is such that one could draw from it rules for medicine that are more reliable than those we have had to the present, and that my inclination puts me at such a great distance from all other sorts of plans, and chiefly from those that can be useful to some only by being harmful to others, that if circumstances were to force me to busy myself with them, I do not at all believe I could succeed. About this I am here making a declaration which I know very well cannot serve to make me eminent in the world, but I also have no desire to be so; and I shall always hold myself obliged more to those by whose favor I enjoy my leisure without hindrance than to those who might offer me the most honorable positions on earth.

Meditations on First Philosophy

To those Most Wise and Distinguished Men,
the Dean and Doctors of the Faculty of Sacred Theology of Paris
René Descartes Sends Greetings

So right is the cause that impels me to offer this work to you, that I am confident you too will find it equally right and thus take up its defense, once you have understood the plan of my undertaking; so much is this the case that I have no better means of commending it here than to state briefly what I have sought to achieve in this work.

I have always thought that two issues—namely, God and the soul—are chief among those that ought to be demonstrated with the aid of philosophy rather than theology. For although it suffices for us believers to believe by faith that the human soul does not die with the body, and that God exists, certainly no unbelievers seem capable of being persuaded of any religion or even of almost any moral virtue, until these two are first proven to them by natural reason. And since in this life greater rewards are often granted to vices than to virtues, few would prefer what is right to what is useful, if they neither feared God nor anticipated an afterlife. Granted, it is altogether true that we must believe in God's existence because it is taught in the Holy Scriptures, and, conversely, that we must believe the Holy Scriptures because they have come from God. This is because, of course, since faith is a gift from God, the very same one who gives the grace that is necessary for believing the rest can also give the grace to believe that he exists. Nonetheless, this reasoning cannot be proposed to unbelievers because they would judge it to be circular. In fact, I have observed that not only do you and all other theologians affirm that one can prove the existence of God by natural reason, but also that one may infer from Sacred Scripture that the knowledge of him is easier to achieve than the many things we know about creatures, and is so utterly easy that those without this knowledge are blameworthy. For this is clear from *Wisdom*, Chapter 13, where it is said: "They are not to be excused, for if their capacity for knowing were so great that they could think well of this world, how is it that they did not find the Lord of it even more easily?" And in *Romans*, Chapter 1, it is said that they are "without excuse." And again in the same passage it appears we are being warned with the words: "What is known of God is manifest in them," that everything that can be known about God can be shown by reasons drawn exclusively from our own mind. For this reason, I did not think it unbecoming for me to inquire how this may be the case, and by what path God may be known more easily and with greater certainty than the things of this world.

And as to the soul, there are many who have regarded its nature as something into which one cannot easily inquire, and some have even gone so far as to say that human reasoning convinces them that the soul dies with the body, while it is by faith alone that they hold the contrary position. Nevertheless, because the Lateran Council[1] held under Leo X, in Session 8, condemned such people and expressly enjoined Christian philosophers to refute their arguments and to use all their powers to demonstrate the truth, I have not hesitated to undertake this task as well.

Moreover, I know that there are many irreligious people who refuse to believe that God exists and that the human mind is distinct from the body—for no

Reprinted from Descartes, *Meditations on First Philosophy*, third edition, translated by Donald A. Cress (Indianapolis: Hackett Publishing Company, 1993), by permission of the publisher.

1. [The Council took place between 1512 and 1517. —S.M.C.]

other reason than their claim that up until now no one has been able to demonstrate these two things. By no means am I in agreement with these people; on the contrary, I believe that nearly all the arguments which have been brought to bear on these questions by great men have the force of a demonstration, when they are adequately understood, and I am convinced that hardly any arguments can be given that have not already been discovered by others. Nevertheless, I judge that there is no greater task to perform in philosophy than assiduously to seek out, once and for all, the best of all these arguments and to lay them out so precisely and plainly that henceforth all will take them to be true demonstrations. And finally, I was strongly urged to do this by some people who knew that I had developed a method for solving all sorts of problems in the sciences—not a new one, mind you, since nothing is more ancient than the truth, but one they had seen me use with some success in other areas. Accordingly, I took it to be my task to attempt something on this subject.

This treatise contains all that I have been able to accomplish. Not that I have attempted to gather together in it all the various arguments that could be brought forward as proof of the very same conclusions, for this does not seem worthwhile, except where no one proof is sufficiently certain. Rather, I have sought out the primary and chief arguments, so that I now make bold to propose these as most certain and evident demonstrations. Moreover, I will say in addition that these arguments are such that I believe there is no way open to the human mind whereby better ones could ever be found. For the urgency of the cause, as well as the glory of God, to which this entire enterprise is referred, compels me here to speak somewhat more freely on my own behalf than is my custom. But although I believe these arguments to be certain and evident, still I am not thereby convinced that they are suited to everyone's grasp. In geometry there are many arguments developed by Archimedes,[2] Apollonius,[3] Pappus,[4] and others, which are taken by everyone to be evident and certain because they contain absolutely nothing which, considered by itself, is not quite easily known, and in which what follows does not square exactly with what has come before. Nevertheless they are rather lengthy and require a particularly attentive reader; thus only a small handful of people understand them. Likewise, although the arguments I use here do, in my opinion, equal or even surpass those of geometry in certitude and obviousness, nevertheless I am fearful that many people will not be capable of adequately perceiving them, both because they too are a bit lengthy, with some of them depending on still others, and also because, first and foremost, they demand a mind that is quite free from prejudices and that can easily withdraw itself from association with the senses. Certainly there are not to be found in the world more people with an aptitude for metaphysical studies than those with an aptitude for geometry. Moreover, there is the difference that in geometry everyone is of a mind that usually nothing is put down in writing without there being a sound demonstration for it; thus the inexperienced more frequently err on the side of assenting to what is false, wanting as they do to give the appearance of understanding it, than on the side of denying what is true. But it is the reverse in philosophy: since it is believed that there is no issue that cannot be defended from either side, few look for the truth, and many more prowl about for a reputation for profundity by arrogantly challenging whichever arguments are the best.

And therefore, regardless of the force of my arguments, because they are of a philosophical nature I do not anticipate that what I will have accomplished through them will be very worthwhile unless you assist me with your patronage. Your faculty is held in such high esteem in the minds of all, and the name of the Sorbonne has such authority, that not only in matters of faith has no association, with the exception of the councils of the Church, been held in such high regard as yours, but even in human philosophy nowhere is there thought to be greater insightfulness and solidity, or greater integrity and wisdom in rendering judgments. Should you deign to show any interest in this work, I do not doubt that, first of all, its errors would be corrected by you (for I am mindful not only of my humanity but also, and most especially, of my ignorance, and thus do not

2. [Archimedes (287–212 B.C. was the famed Greek mathematician, physicist, and inventor.]

3. [Apollonius of Perga (c. 262–200 B.C.) was a Greek mathematician best-known for his study of conic sections.]

4. [Pappus of Alexandria was a fourth-century Greek mathematician whose work exerted an influence on the revival of interest in geometry in the seventeenth century.]

claim that there are no errors in it); second, what is lacking would be added, or what is not sufficiently complete would be perfected, or what is in need of further discussion would be expanded upon more fully, either by yourselves or at least by me, after you have given me your guidance; and finally, after the arguments contained in this work proving that God exists and that the mind is distinct from the body have been brought (as I am confident they can be) to such a level of lucidity that these arguments ought to be regarded as the most precise of demonstrations, you may be of a mind to make such a declaration and publicly attest to it. Indeed, should this come to pass, I have no doubt that all the errors that have ever been entertained regarding these issues would shortly be erased from the minds of men. For the truth itself will easily cause other men of intelligence and learning to subscribe to your judgment. Your authority will cause the atheists, who more often than not are dilettantes rather than men of intelligence and learning, to put aside their spirit of contrariness, and perhaps even to defend the arguments which they will come to know are regarded as demonstrations by all who are discerning, lest they appear not to understand them. And finally, everyone else will readily give credence to so many indications of support, and there will no longer be anyone in the world who would dare call into doubt either the existence of God or the real distinction between the soul and the body. Just how great the usefulness of this thing might be, you yourselves, in virtue of your singular wisdom, are in the best position of anyone to judge; nor would it behoove me to commend the cause of God and religion at any greater length to you, who have always been the greatest pillar of the Catholic Church.

Preface to the Reader

I have already touched briefly on the issues of God and the human mind in my *Discourse on the Method of Rightly Conducting One's Reason and Searching for Truth in the Sciences,* published in French in 1637. The intent there was not to provide a precise treatment of them, but only to offer a sample and to learn from the opinions of readers how these issues should be treated in the future. For they seemed to me to be so important that I judged they ought to be dealt with more than once. And the path I follow in order to explain them is so little trodden and so far removed from the one commonly taken that I did not think it useful to hold forth at greater length in a work written in French and designed to be read indiscriminately by everyone, lest weaker minds be in a position to think that they too ought to set out on this path.

In the *Discourse* I asked everyone who might find something in my writings worthy of refutation to do me the favor of making me aware of it. As for what I touched on regarding these issues, only two objections were worth noting, and I will respond briefly to them here before undertaking a more precise explanation of them.

The first is that, from the fact that the human mind, when turned in on itself, does not perceive itself to be anything other than a thinking thing, it does not follow that its nature or *essence* consists only in its being a thinking thing, such that the word *only* excludes everything else that also could perhaps be said to belong to the nature of the soul. To this objection I answer that in that passage I did not intend my exclusion of those things to reflect the order of the truth of the matter (I was not dealing with it then), but merely the order of my perception. Thus what I had in mind was that I was aware of absolutely nothing that I knew belonged to my essence, save that I was a thinking thing, that is, a thing having within itself the faculty of thinking. Later on, however, I will show how it follows, from the fact that I know of nothing else belonging to my essence, that nothing else really does belong to it.

The second objection is that it does not follow from the fact that I have within me an idea of a thing more perfect than me, that this idea is itself more perfect than me, and still less that what is represented by this idea exists. But I answer that there is an equivocation here in the word "idea." For "idea" can be taken either materially, for an operation of the intellect (in which case it cannot be said to be more perfect than me), or objectively, for the thing represented by means of that operation. This thing, even if it is not presumed to exist outside the intellect, can nevertheless be more perfect than me by reason of its essence. I will explain in detail in the ensuing remarks how, from the mere fact that there is within me an idea of something more perfect than me, it follows that this thing really exists.

In addition, I have seen two rather lengthy treatises, but these works, utilizing as they do arguments drawn from atheist commonplaces, focused their attack not so much on my arguments regarding these issues, as on my conclusions. Moreover, arguments of this type exercise no influence over those who understand my arguments, and the judgments of many people are so preposterous and feeble that they are more likely to be persuaded by the first opinions to come along, however false and contrary to reason they may be, than by a true and firm refutation of them which they hear subsequently. Accordingly, I have no desire to respond here to these objections, lest I first have to state what they are. I will only say in general that all the objections typically bandied about by the atheists to assail the existence of God always depend either on ascribing human emotions to God, or on arrogantly claiming for our minds such power and wisdom that we attempt to determine and grasp fully what God can and ought to do. Hence these objections will cause us no difficulty, provided we but remember that our minds are to be regarded as finite, while God is to be regarded as incomprehensible and infinite.

But now, after having, to some degree, conducted an initial review of the judgments of men, here I begin once more to treat the same questions about God and the human mind, together with the starting points of the whole of first philosophy, but not in a way that causes me to have any expectation of widespread approval or a large readership. On the contrary, I do not advise anyone to read these things except those who have both the ability and the desire to meditate seriously with me, and to withdraw their minds from the senses as well as from all prejudices. I know all too well that such people are few and far between. As to those who do not take the time to grasp the order and linkage of my arguments, but will be eager to fuss over statements taken out of context (as is the custom for many), they will derive little benefit from reading this work. Although perhaps they might find an occasion for quibbling in several places, still they will not find it easy to raise an objection that is either compelling or worthy of response.

But because I do not promise to satisfy even the others on all counts the first time around, and because I do not arrogantly claim for myself so much that I believe myself capable of anticipating all the difficulties that will occur to someone, I will first of all narrate in the *Meditations* the very thoughts by means of which I seem to have arrived at a certain and evident knowledge of the truth, so that I may determine whether the same arguments that persuaded me can be useful in persuading others. Next, I will reply to the objections of a number of very gifted and learned gentlemen, to whom these *Meditations* were forwarded for their examination prior to their being sent to press. For their objections were so many and varied that I have dared to hope that nothing will readily occur to anyone, at least nothing of importance, which has not already been touched upon by these gentlemen. And thus I earnestly entreat the readers not to form a judgment regarding the *Meditations* until they have deigned to read all these objections and the replies I have made to them.

Synopsis of the Following Six Meditations

In the First Meditation the reasons are given why we can doubt all things, especially material things, so long, that is, as, of course, we have no other foundations for the sciences than the ones which we have had up until now. Although the utility of so extensive a doubt is not readily apparent, nevertheless its greatest utility lies in freeing us of all prejudices, in preparing the easiest way for us to withdraw the mind from the senses, and finally, in making it impossible for us to doubt any further those things that we later discover to be true.

In the Second Meditation the mind, through the exercise of its own freedom, supposes the nonexistence of all those things about whose existence it can have even the least doubt. In so doing the mind realizes that it is impossible for it not to exist during this time. This too is of the greatest utility, since by means of it the mind easily distinguishes what things belong to it, that is, to an intellectual nature, from what things belong to the body. But because some people will perhaps expect to see proofs for the immortality of the soul in this Meditation, I think they should be put on notice here that I have attempted to write only what I have carefully demonstrated. Therefore the only order I could follow was the one typically used by geometers, which is to lay out everything on which a given proposition depends, before concluding anything about it. But the first and principal prerequisite for knowing that the soul is immortal is that we form a concept of the soul that is as lucid as possible and utterly distinct from every concept of a body. This is what has been done here. Moreover, there is the additional requirement that we know that everything that we clearly and distinctly understand is true, in exactly the manner in which we understand it; however, this could not have been proven prior to the Fourth Meditation. Moreover, we must have a distinct concept of corporeal nature, and this is formulated partly in the Second Meditation itself, and partly in the Fifth and Sixth Meditations. From all this one ought to conclude that all the things we clearly and distinctly conceive as different substances truly are substances that are really distinct from one another. (This, for example, is how mind and body are conceived.) This conclusion is arrived at in the Sixth Meditation. This same conclusion is also confirmed in this Meditation in virtue of the fact that we cannot understand a body to be anything but divisible, whereas we cannot understand the mind to be anything but indivisible. For we cannot conceive of half of a mind, as we can half of any body whatever, no matter how small. From this we are prompted to acknowledge that the natures of mind and body not only are different from one another, but even, in a manner of speaking, are contraries of one another. However, I have not written any further on the matter in this work, both because these considerations suffice for showing that the annihilation of the mind does not follow from the decaying of the body (and thus these considerations suffice for giving mortals hope in an afterlife), and also because the premises from which the immortality of the mind can be inferred depend upon an account of the whole of physics. First, we need to know that absolutely all substances, that is, things that must be created by God in order to exist, are by their very nature incorruptible, and can never cease to exist, unless, by the same God's denying his concurrence to them, they be reduced to nothingness. Second, we need to realize that body, taken in a general sense, is a substance and hence it too can never perish. But the human body, insofar as it differs from other bodies, is composed of merely a certain configuration of members, together with other accidents of the same sort. But the human mind is not likewise composed of any accidents, but is a pure substance. For even if all its accidents were changed, so that it understands different things, wills different things, senses different things, and so on, the mind itself does not on that score become something different. On the other hand, the human body does become something different, merely as a result of the fact that a change in the shape of some of its parts has taken place. It follows from these considerations that a body can very easily perish, whereas the mind by its nature is immortal.

In the Third Meditation I have explained at sufficient length, it seems to me, my principal argument for proving the existence of God. Nevertheless, since my intent was to draw the minds of readers as far as possible from the senses, I had no desire to draw upon comparisons based upon corporeal things. Thus many obscurities may perhaps have remained; but these, I trust, will later be entirely removed in my Replies to the Objections. One such point of contention, among others, is the following: how can the idea that is in us of a supremely perfect being have so much objective reality that it can only come from a supremely perfect cause? This is illustrated in the Replies by a comparison with a very perfect machine, the idea of which is in the mind of some craftsman. For, just as the objective ingeniousness of this idea ought to have some cause (say, the knowledge possessed by the craftsman or by someone else from whom he received this knowledge), so too, the idea of God which is in us must have God himself as its cause.

In the Fourth Meditation it is proved that all that we clearly and distinctly perceive is true, and it is also explained what constitutes the nature of falsity. These things necessarily need to be known both to confirm what has preceded as well as to help readers understand what remains. (But here one should meanwhile bear in mind that in that Meditation there is no discussion whatsoever of sin, that is, the error committed in the pursuit of good and evil, but only the error that occurs in discriminating between what is true and what is false. Nor is there an examination of those matters pertaining to the faith or to the conduct of life, but merely of speculative truths known exclusively by means of the light of nature.)

In the Fifth Meditation, in addition to an explanation of corporeal nature in general, the existence of God is also demonstrated by means of a new proof. But again several difficulties may arise here; however, these are resolved later in my Replies to the Objections. Finally, it is shown how it is true that the certainty of even geometrical demonstrations depends upon the knowledge of God.

Finally, in the Sixth Meditation the understanding is distinguished from the imagination and the marks of this distinction are described. The mind is proved to be really distinct from the body, even though the mind is shown to be so closely joined to the body that it forms a single unit with it. All the errors commonly arising from the senses are reviewed; an account of the ways in which these errors can be avoided is provided. Finally, all the arguments on the basis of which we may infer the existence of material things are presented—not because I believe them to be very useful for proving what they prove, namely, that there really is a world, that men have bodies, and the like (things which no one of sound mind has ever seriously doubted), but rather because, through a consideration of these arguments, one realizes that they are neither so firm nor so evident as the arguments leading us to the knowledge of our mind and of God, so that, of all the things that can be known by the human mind, these latter are the most certain and the most evident. Proving this one thing was for me the goal of these Meditations. For this reason I will not review here the various issues that are also to be treated in these Meditations as the situation arises.

Meditations on First Philosophy in Which the Existence of God and the Distinction between the Soul and the Body Are Demonstrated

Meditation One: Concerning Those Things That Can Be Called into Doubt

Several years have now passed since I first realized how numerous were the false opinions that in my youth I had taken to be true, and thus how doubtful were all those that I had subsequently built upon them. And thus I realized that once in my life I had to raze everything to the ground and begin again from the original foundations, if I wanted to establish anything firm and lasting in the sciences. But the task seemed enormous, and I was waiting until I reached a point in my life that was so timely that no more suitable time for undertaking these plans of action would come to pass. For this reason, I procrastinated for so long that I would henceforth be at fault, were I to waste the time that remains for carrying out the project by brooding over it. Accordingly, I have today suitably freed my mind of all cares, secured for myself a period of leisurely tranquillity, and am withdrawing into solitude. At last I will apply myself earnestly and unreservedly to this general demolition of my opinions.

Yet to bring this about I will not need to show that all my opinions are false, which is perhaps something I could never accomplish. But reason now persuades me that I should withhold my assent no less carefully from opinions that are not completely certain and indubitable than I would from those that are patently false. For this reason, it will suffice for the rejection of all of these opinions, if I find in each of them some reason for doubt. Nor therefore need I survey each opinion individually, a task that would be endless. Rather, because undermining the foundations will cause whatever has been built upon them to crumble of its own accord, I will attack straightaway those principles which supported everything I once believed.

Surely whatever I had admitted until now as most true I received either from the senses or through the senses. However, I have noticed that the senses are sometimes deceptive; and it is a mark of prudence never to place our complete trust in those who have deceived us even once.

But perhaps, even though the senses do sometimes deceive us when it is a question of very small and distant things, still there are many other matters concerning which one simply cannot doubt, even though they are derived from the very same senses: for example, that I am sitting here next to the fire, wearing my winter dressing gown, that I am holding this sheet of paper in my hands, and the like. But on what grounds could one deny that these hands and this entire body are mine? Unless perhaps I were to liken myself to the insane, whose brains are impaired by such an unrelenting vapor of black bile that they steadfastly insist that they are kings when they are utter paupers, or that they are arrayed in purple robes when they are naked, or that they have heads made of clay, or that they are gourds, or that they are made of glass. But such people are mad, and I would appear no less mad, were I to take their behavior as an example for myself.

This would all be well and good, were I not a man who is accustomed to sleeping at night, and to experiencing in my dreams the very same things, or now and then even less plausible ones, as these insane people do when they are awake. How often does my evening slumber persuade me of such ordinary things as these: that I am here, clothed in my dressing gown, seated next to the fireplace—when in fact I am lying undressed in bed! But right now my eyes are certainly wide awake when I gaze upon this sheet of paper. This head which I am shaking is not heavy with sleep. I extend this hand consciously and deliberately, and I feel it. Such things would not be so distinct for someone who is asleep. As if I did not recall having been deceived on other occasions even by similar thoughts in my dreams! As I consider these matters more carefully, I see so plainly that there are no definitive signs by which to distinguish being awake from being asleep. As a result, I am becoming quite dizzy, and this dizziness nearly convinces me that I am asleep.

Let us assume then, for the sake of argument, that we are dreaming and that such particulars as these are not true: that we are opening our eyes, moving our head, and extending our hands. Perhaps we do not even have such hands, or any such body at all. Nevertheless, it surely must be admitted that the things seen during slumber are, as it were, like painted images, which could only have been produced in the likeness of true things, and that therefore at least these general things—eyes, head, hands, and the whole body—are not imaginary things, but are true and exist. For indeed when painters themselves wish to represent sirens and satyrs by means of especially bizarre forms, they surely cannot assign to them utterly new natures. Rather, they simply fuse together the members of various animals. Or if perhaps they concoct something so utterly novel that nothing like it has ever been seen before (and thus is something utterly fictitious and false), yet certainly at the very least the colors from which they fashion it ought to be true. And by the same token, although even these general things—eyes, head, hands and the like—could be imaginary, still one has to admit that at least certain other things that are even more simple and universal are true. It is from these components, as if from true colors, that all those images of things that are in our thought are fashioned, be they true or false.

This class of things appears to include corporeal nature in general, together with its extension; the shape of extended things; their quantity, that is, their size and number; as well as the place where they exist; the time through which they endure, and the like.

Thus it is not improper to conclude from this that physics, astronomy, medicine, and all the other disciplines that are dependent upon the consideration of composite things are doubtful, and that, on the other hand, arithmetic, geometry, and other such disciplines, which treat of nothing but the simplest and most general things and which are indifferent as to whether these things do or do not in fact exist, contain something certain and indubitable. For whether I am awake or asleep, two plus three make five, and a square does not have more than four sides. It does not seem possible that such obvious truths should be subject to the suspicion of being false.

Be that as it may, there is fixed in my mind a certain opinion of long standing, namely that there exists a God who is able to do anything and by whom I, such as I am, have been created. How do I know that he did not bring it about that there is no earth at all, no heavens, no extended thing, no shape, no size, no place, and yet bringing it about that all these things appear to me to exist precisely as they do now? Moreover, since I judge that others sometimes make mistakes in matters that they believe they know most perfectly, may I not, in like fashion, be deceived every time I add two and three or count the sides of a square, or perform an even simpler operation, if that can be imagined? But perhaps God has not willed that I be deceived in this way, for he is said to be supremely good. Nonetheless, if it were repugnant to his goodness to have created me such that I be deceived all the time, it would also seem foreign to that same goodness to permit me to be deceived even occasionally. But we cannot make this last assertion.

Perhaps there are some who would rather deny so powerful a God than believe that everything else is uncertain. Let us not oppose them; rather, let us grant that everything said here about God is fictitious. Now they suppose that I came to be what I am either by fate, or by chance, or by a connected chain of events, or by some other way. But because being deceived and being mistaken appear to be a certain imperfection, the less powerful they take the author of my origin to be, the more probable it will be that I am so imperfect that I am always deceived. I have nothing to say in response to these arguments. But eventually I am forced to admit that there is nothing among the things I once believed to be true which it is not permissible to doubt—and not out of frivolity or lack of forethought, but for valid and considered reasons. Thus I must be no less careful to withhold assent henceforth even from these beliefs than I would from those that are patently false, if I wish to find anything certain.

But it is not enough simply to have realized these things; I must take steps to keep myself mindful of them. For long-standing opinions keep returning, and, almost against my will, they take advantage of my credulity, as if it were bound over to them by long use and the claims of intimacy. Nor will I ever get out of the habit of assenting to them and believing in them, so long as I take them to be exactly what they are, namely, in some respects doubtful, as has just now been shown, but nevertheless highly probable, so that it is much more consonant with reason to believe them than to deny them. Hence, it seems to me I would do well to deceive myself by turning my will in completely the opposite direction and pretend for a time that these opinions are wholly false and imaginary, until finally, as if with prejudices weighing down each side equally, no bad habit should turn my judgment any further from the correct perception of things. For indeed I know that meanwhile there is no danger or error in following this procedure, and that it is impossible for me to indulge in too much distrust, since I am now concentrating only on knowledge, not on action.

Accordingly, I will suppose not a supremely good God, the source of truth, but rather an evil genius, supremely powerful and clever, who has directed his entire effort at deceiving me. I will regard the heavens, the air, the earth, colors, shapes, sounds, and all external things as nothing but the bedeviling hoaxes of my dreams, with which he lays snares for my credulity. I will regard myself as not having hands, or eyes, or flesh, or blood, or any senses, but as nevertheless falsely believing that I possess all these things. I will remain resolute and steadfast in this meditation, and even if it is not within my power to know anything true, it certainly is within my power to take care resolutely to withhold my assent to what is false, lest this deceiver, however powerful, however clever he may be, have any effect on me. But this undertaking is arduous, and a certain laziness brings me back to my customary way of living. I am not unlike a prisoner who enjoyed an imaginary freedom during his sleep, but, when he later begins to suspect that he is dreaming, fears being awakened and nonchalantly conspires with these pleasant illusions. In just the same way, I fall back of my own accord into my old opinions, and dread being awakened, lest the toilsome wakefulness which follows upon a peaceful rest must be spent thenceforward not in the light but among the inextricable shadows of the difficulties now brought forward.

Meditation Two: Concerning the Nature of the Human Mind: That It Is Better Known Than the Body

Yesterday's meditation has thrown me into such doubts that I can no longer ignore them, yet I fail to see how they are to be resolved. It is as if I had suddenly fallen into a deep whirlpool; I am so tossed about that I can neither touch bottom with my foot, nor swim up to the top. Nevertheless I will work my way up and will once again attempt the same path I entered upon yesterday. I will accomplish this by putting aside everything that admits of the least doubt, as if I had discovered it to be completely false. I will stay on this course until I know something certain, or, if nothing else, until I at least know for certain that nothing is certain. Archimedes sought but one firm and immovable point in order to move the entire earth from one place to another. Just so, great things are also to be hoped for if I succeed in finding just one thing, however slight, that is certain and unshaken.

Therefore I suppose that everything I see is false. I believe that none of what my deceitful memory represents ever existed. I have no senses whatever. Body, shape, extension, movement, and place are all chimeras. What then will be true? Perhaps just the single fact that nothing is certain.

But how do I know there is not something else, over and above all those things that I have just reviewed, concerning which there is not even the slightest occasion for doubt? Is there not some God, or by whatever name I might call him, who instills these very thoughts in me? But why would I think that, since I myself could perhaps be the author of these thoughts? Am I not then at least something? But I have already denied that I have any senses and any body. Still I hesitate; for what follows from this? Am I so tied to a body and to the senses that I cannot exist without them? But I have persuaded myself that there is absolutely nothing in the world: no sky, no earth, no minds, no bodies. Is it then the case that I too do not exist? But doubtless I did exist, if I persuaded myself of something. But there is some deceiver or other who is supremely powerful and supremely sly and who is always deliberately deceiving me. Then too there is no doubt that I exist, if he is deceiving me. And let him do his best at deception, he will never bring it about that I am nothing so long as I shall think that I am something. Thus, after everything has been most carefully weighed, it must finally be established that this pronouncement "I am, I exist" is necessarily true every time I utter it or conceive it in my mind.

But I do not yet understand sufficiently what I am—I, who now necessarily exist. And so from this point on, I must be careful lest I unwittingly mistake something else for myself, and thus err in that very item of knowledge that I claim to be the most certain and evident of all. Thus, I will meditate once more on what I once believed myself to be, prior to embarking upon these thoughts. For this reason, then, I will set aside whatever can be weakened even to the slightest degree by the arguments brought forward, so that eventually all that remains is precisely nothing but what is certain and unshaken.

What then did I use to think I was? A man, of course. But what is a man? Might I not say a "rational animal"? No, because then I would have to inquire what "animal" and "rational" mean. And thus from one question I would slide into many more difficult ones. Nor do I now have enough free time that I want to waste it on subtleties of this sort. Instead, permit me to focus here on what came spontaneously and naturally into my thinking whenever I pondered what I was. Now it occurred to me first that I had a face, hands, arms, and this entire mechanism of bodily members: the very same as are discerned in a corpse, and which I referred to by the name "body." It next occurred to me that I took in food, that I walked about, and that I sensed and thought various things; these actions I used to attribute to the soul. But as to what this soul might be, I either did not think about it or else I imagined it a rarified I-know-not-what, like a wind, or a fire, or ether, which had been infused into my coarser parts. But as to the body I was not in any doubt. On the contrary, I was under the impression that I knew its nature distinctly. Were I perhaps tempted to describe this nature such as I conceived it in my mind, I would have described it thus: by "body," I understand all that is capable of being bounded by some shape, of being enclosed in a place, and of filling up a space in such a way as to exclude any other body from it; of being perceived by touch, sight, hearing, taste, or smell; of being moved in several ways, not, of course, by itself, but by whatever else impinges upon it. For it was my view that the power of self-motion, and likewise of sensing or of thinking, in no way belonged to the nature of the body. Indeed I used rather to marvel that such faculties were to be found in certain bodies.

But now what am I, when I suppose that there is some supremely powerful and, if I may be permitted to say so, malicious deceiver who deliberately tries to fool me in any way he can? Can I not affirm that I possess at least a small measure of all those things which I have already said belong to the nature of the body? I focus my attention on them, I think about them, I review them again, but nothing comes to mind. I am tired of repeating this to no purpose. But what about those things I ascribed to the soul? What about being nourished or moving about? Since I now do not have a body, these are surely nothing but fictions. What about sensing? Surely this too does not take place without a body; and I seemed to have sensed in my dreams many things that I later realized I did not sense. What about thinking? Here I make my discovery: thought exists; it alone cannot be separated from me. I am; I exist—this is certain. But for how long? For as long as I am thinking; for perhaps it could also come to pass that if I were to cease all thinking I would then utterly cease to exist. At this time I admit nothing that is not necessarily true. I am therefore precisely nothing but a thinking thing; that is, a mind, or intellect, or understanding, or reason—words of whose meanings I was previously ignorant. Yet I am a true thing and am truly existing; but what kind of thing? I have said it already: a thinking thing.

What else am I? I will set my imagination in motion. I am not that concatenation of members we call the human body. Neither am I even some subtle air infused into these members, nor a wind, nor a fire, nor a vapor, nor a breath, nor anything I devise for myself. For I have supposed these things to be nothing. The assumption still stands; yet nevertheless I am something. But is it perhaps the case that these very things which I take to be nothing, because they are unknown to me, nevertheless are in fact no different from that "me" that I know? This I do not know, and I will not quarrel about it now. I can make a judgment only about things that are known to me. I know that I exist; I ask now who is this "I" whom I know? Most certainly, in the strict sense the knowledge of this "I" does not depend upon things of whose existence I do not yet have knowledge. Therefore it is not dependent upon any of those things that I simulate in my imagination. But this word "simulate"[5] warns me of my error. For I would indeed be simulating were I to "imagine" that I was something, because imagining is merely the contemplating of the shape or image of a corporeal thing. But I now know with certainty that I am and also that all these images—and, generally, everything belonging to the nature of the body—could turn out to be nothing but dreams. Once I have realized this, I would seem to be speaking no less foolishly were I to say: "I will use my imagination in order to recognize more distinctly who I am," than were I to say: "Now I surely am awake, and I see something true; but since I do not yet see it clearly enough, I will deliberately fall asleep so that my dreams might represent it to me more truly and more clearly." Thus I realize that none of what I can grasp by means of the imagination pertains to this knowledge that I have of myself. Moreover, I realize that I must be most diligent about withdrawing my mind from these things so that it can perceive its nature as distinctly as possible.

But what then am I? A thing that thinks. What is that? A thing that doubts, understands, affirms, denies, wills, refuses, and that also imagines and senses.

Indeed it is no small matter if all of these things belong to me. But why should they not belong to me? Is it not the very same "I" who now doubts almost everything, who nevertheless understands something, who affirms that this one thing is true, who denies other things, who desires to know more, who wishes not to be deceived, who imagines many things even against my will, who also notices many things which appear to come from the senses? What is there in all of this that is not every bit as true as the fact that I exist—even if I am always asleep or even if my creator makes every effort to mislead me? Which of these things is distinct from my thought? Which of them can be said to be separate from myself? For it is so obvious that it is I who doubt, I who understand, and I who will, that there is nothing by which it could be explained more clearly. But indeed it is also the same "I" who imagines; for although perhaps, as I supposed before, absolutely nothing that I imagined is true, still the very power of imagining really does exist, and constitutes a part of my thought. Finally, it is this same "I" who senses or who is cognizant of bodily things as if through the senses. For example, I now see a light, I hear a noise, I feel heat. These things are false, since I am asleep. Yet I certainly do seem to see, hear, and feel warmth. This cannot be false. Properly speaking, this is what in me is called "sensing." But this, precisely so taken, is nothing other than thinking.

From these considerations I am beginning to know a little better what I am. But it still seems (and I cannot resist believing) that corporeal things—whose images are formed by thought, and which the senses themselves examine—are much more distinctly known than this mysterious "I" which does not fall within the imagination. And yet it would be strange indeed were I to grasp the very things I consider to be doubtful, unknown, and foreign to me more distinctly than what is true, what is known—than, in short, myself. But I see what is happening: my mind loves to wander and does not yet permit itself to be restricted within the confines of truth. So be it then; let us just this once allow it completely free rein, so that, a little while later, when the time has come to pull in the reins, the mind may more readily permit itself to be controlled.

Let us consider those things which are commonly believed to be the most distinctly grasped of all: namely the bodies we touch and see. Not bodies in general, mind you, for these general perceptions are apt to be somewhat more confused, but one body in particular. Let us take, for instance, this piece of wax. It has been taken quite recently from the honeycomb; it has not yet lost all the honey flavor. It retains some of the scent of the flowers from which it was collected. Its color, shape, and size are manifest. It is hard and cold; it is easy to touch. If you rap on it with your knuckle it will emit a sound. In short, everything is present in it that appears needed to enable a body to be known as distinctly as possible. But notice that, as I am speaking, I am bringing it close to the fire. The remaining traces of the honey flavor are disappearing; the scent is vanishing; the color is changing; the original shape is disappearing. Its size is increasing; it is becoming liquid and hot; you can hardly touch it. And now, when you rap on it, it no longer emits

5. [The Latin word "*effingo*" means "to form an image" or "imagine."]

any sound. Does the same wax still remain? I must confess that it does; no one denies it; no one thinks otherwise. So what was there in the wax that was so distinctly grasped? Certainly none of the aspects that I reached by means of the senses. For whatever came under the senses of taste, smell, sight, touch or hearing has now changed; and yet the wax remains.

Perhaps the wax was what I now think it is: namely that the wax itself never really was the sweetness of the honey, nor the fragrance of the flowers, nor the whiteness, nor the shape, nor the sound, but instead was a body that a short time ago manifested itself to me in these ways, and now does so in other ways. But just what precisely is this thing that I thus imagine? Let us focus our attention on this and see what remains after we have removed everything that does not belong to the wax: only that it is something extended, flexible, and mutable. But what is it to be flexible and mutable? Is it what my imagination shows it to be: namely, that this piece of wax can change from a round to a square shape, or from the latter to a triangular shape? Not at all; for I grasp that the wax is capable of innumerable changes of this sort, even though I am incapable of running through these innumerable changes by using my imagination. Therefore this insight is not achieved by the faculty of imagination. What is it to be extended? Is this thing's extension also unknown? For it becomes greater in wax that is beginning to melt, greater in boiling wax, and greater still as the heat is increased. And I would not judge correctly what the wax is if I did not believe that it takes on an even greater variety of dimensions than I could ever grasp with the imagination. It remains then for me to concede that I do not grasp what this wax is through the imagination; rather, I perceive it through the mind alone. The point I am making refers to this particular piece of wax, for the case of wax in general is clearer still. But what is this piece of wax which is perceived only by the mind? Surely it is the same piece of wax that I see, touch, and imagine; in short it is the same piece of wax I took it to be from the very beginning. But I need to realize that the perception of the wax is neither a seeing, nor a touching, nor an imagining. Nor has it ever been, even though it previously seemed so; rather it is an inspection on the part of the mind alone. This inspection can be imperfect and confused, as it was before, or clear and distinct, as it is now, depending on how closely I pay attention to the things in which the piece of wax consists.

But meanwhile I marvel at how prone my mind is to error. For although I am considering these things within myself silently and without words, nevertheless I seize upon words themselves and I am nearly deceived by the ways in which people commonly speak. For we say that we see the wax itself, if it is present, and not that we judge it to be present from its color or shape. Whence I might conclude straightaway that I know the wax through the vision had by the eye, and not through an inspection on the part of the mind alone. But then were I perchance to look out my window and observe men crossing the square, I would ordinarily say I see the men themselves just as I say I see the wax. But what do I see aside from hats and clothes, which could conceal automata? Yet I judge them to be men. Thus what I thought I had seen with my eyes, I actually grasped solely with the faculty of judgment, which is in my mind.

But a person who seeks to know more than the common crowd ought to be ashamed of himself for looking for doubt in common ways of speaking. Let us then go forward and inquire when it was that I perceived more perfectly and evidently what the piece of wax was. Was it when I first saw it and believed I knew it by the external sense, or at least by the so-called common sense, that is, the power of imagination? Or do I have more perfect knowledge now, when I have diligently examined both what the wax is and how it is known? Surely it is absurd to be in doubt about this matter. For what was there in my initial perception that was distinct? What was there that any animal seemed incapable of possessing? But indeed when I distinguish the wax from its external forms, as if stripping it of its clothing, and look at the wax in its nakedness, then, even though there can be still an error in my judgment, nevertheless I cannot perceive it thus without a human mind.

But what am I to say about this mind, that is, about myself? For as yet I admit nothing else to be in me over and above the mind. What, I ask, am I who seem to perceive this wax so distinctly? Do I not know myself not only much more truly and with greater certainty, but also much more distinctly and evidently? For if I judge that the wax exists from the fact that I see it, certainly from this same fact that I see the wax it follows much more evidently that I myself exist. For it could happen that what I see is not truly wax. It could happen that I have no eyes with which to see anything. But it is utterly impossible that, while I see or think I see (I do not now distinguish these two), I who think am not something. Likewise, if I judge that the wax exists from the fact that I touch it, the same outcome will again obtain, namely that I exist. If I judge that the wax exists from the fact that I imagine it, or for any other reason, plainly the same thing follows. But what I note regarding the wax applies to everything else that is external to me. Furthermore, if my perception of the wax seemed more distinct after it became known to me not only on account of sight or touch, but on account of many reasons, one has to admit how much more distinctly I am now known to myself. For there is not a single consideration that can aid in my perception of the wax or of any other body that fails to make even more manifest the nature of my mind. But there are still so many other things in the mind itself on the basis of which my knowledge of it can be rendered more distinct that it hardly seems worth enumerating those things which emanate to it from the body.

But lo and behold, I have returned on my own to where I wanted to be. For since I now know that even bodies are not, properly speaking, perceived by the senses or by the faculty of imagination, but by the intellect alone, and that they are not perceived through their being touched or seen, but only through their being understood, I manifestly know that nothing can be perceived more easily and more evidently than my own mind. But since the tendency to hang on to long-held beliefs cannot be put aside so quickly, I want to stop here, so that by the length of my meditation this new knowledge may be more deeply impressed upon my memory.

Meditation Three: Concerning God, That He Exists

I will now shut my eyes, stop up my ears, and withdraw all my senses. I will also blot out from my thoughts all images of corporeal things, or rather, since the latter is hardly possible, I will regard these images as empty, false and worthless. And as I converse with myself alone and look more deeply into myself, I will attempt to render myself gradually better known and more familiar to myself. I am a thing that thinks, that is to say, a thing that doubts, affirms, denies, understands a few things, is ignorant of many things, wills, refrains from willing, and also imagines and senses. For as I observed earlier, even though these things that I sense or imagine may perhaps be nothing at all outside me, nevertheless I am certain that these modes of thinking, which are cases of what I call sensing and imagining, insofar as they are merely modes of thinking, do exist within me.

In these few words, I have reviewed everything I truly know, or at least what so far I have noticed that I know. Now I will ponder more carefully to see whether perhaps there may be other things belonging to me that up until now I have failed to notice. I am certain that I am a thinking thing. But do I not therefore also know what is required for me to be certain of anything? Surely in this first instance of knowledge, there is nothing but a certain clear and distinct perception of what I affirm. Yet this would hardly be enough to render me certain of the truth of a thing, if it could ever happen that something that I perceived so clearly and distinctly were false. And thus I now seem able to posit as a general rule that everything I very clearly and distinctly perceive is true.

Be that as it may, I have previously admitted many things as wholly certain and evident that nevertheless I later discovered to be doubtful. What sort of things were these? Why, the earth, the sky, the stars, and all the other things I perceived by means of the senses. But what was it about these things that I clearly perceived? Surely the fact that the ideas or thoughts of these things were hovering before my mind. But even now I do not deny that these ideas are in me. Yet there was something else I used to affirm, which, owing to my habitual tendency to believe it, I used to think was something I clearly perceived, even though I actually did not perceive it at all: namely, that certain things existed outside me, things from which those ideas proceeded and which those ideas completely resembled. But on this point I was mistaken; or rather, if my judgment was a true one, it was not the result of the force of my perception.

But what about when I considered something very simple and easy in the areas of arithmetic or geometry, for example that two plus three make five, and the like? Did I not intuit them at least clearly enough so as to affirm them as true? To be sure, I did decide later on that I must doubt these things, but that was only because it occurred to me that some God could perhaps have given me a nature such that I might be deceived even about matters that seemed most evident. But whenever this preconceived opinion about the supreme power of God occurs to me, I cannot help admitting that, were he to wish it, it would be easy for him to cause me to err even in those matters that I think I intuit as clearly as possible with the eyes of the mind. On the other hand, whenever I turn my attention to those very things that I think I perceive with such great clarity, I am so completely persuaded by them that I spontaneously blurt out these words: "let anyone who can do so deceive me; so long as I think that I am something, he will never bring it about that I am nothing. Nor will he one day make it true that I never existed, for it is true now that I do exist. Nor will he even bring it about that perhaps two plus three might equal more or less than five, or similar items in which I recognize an obvious contradiction." And certainly, because I have no reason for thinking that there is a God who is a deceiver (and of course I do not yet sufficiently know whether there even is a God), the basis for doubting, depending as it does merely on the above hypothesis, is very tenuous and, so to speak, metaphysical. But in order to remove even this basis for doubt, I should at the first opportunity inquire whether there is a God, and, if there is, whether or not he can be a deceiver. For if I am ignorant of this, it appears I am never capable of being completely certain about anything else.

However, at this stage good order seems to demand that I first group all my thoughts into certain classes, and ask in which of them truth or falsity properly resides. Some of these thoughts are like images of things; to these alone does the word "idea" properly apply, as when I think of a man, or a chimera, or the sky, or an angel, or God. Again there are other thoughts that take different forms: for example, when I will, or fear, or affirm, or deny, there is always some thing that I grasp as the subject of my thought, yet I embrace in my thought something more than the likeness of that thing. Some of these thoughts are called volitions or affects, while others are called judgments.

Now as far as ideas are concerned, if they are considered alone and in their own right, without being referred to something else, they cannot, properly speaking, be false. For whether it is a she-goat or a chimera that I am imagining, it is no less true that I imagine the one than the other. Moreover, we need not fear that there is falsity in the will itself or in the affects, for although I can choose evil things or even things that are utterly non-existent, I cannot conclude from this that it is untrue that I do choose these things. Thus there remain only judgments in which I must take care not to be mistaken. Now the principal and most frequent error to be found in judgments consists in the fact that I judge that the ideas which are in me are similar to or in conformity with certain things outside me. Obviously, if I were to consider these ideas merely as certain modes of my thought, and were not to refer them to anything else, they could hardly give me any subject matter for error.

Among these ideas, some appear to me to be innate, some adventitious, and some produced by me. For I understand what a thing is, what truth is, what thought is, and I appear to have derived this exclusively from my very own nature. But say I am now hearing a noise, or looking at the sun, or feeling the fire; up until now I judged that these things proceeded from certain things outside me, and finally, that sirens, hippogriffs, and the like are made by me. Or perhaps I can even think of all these ideas as being adventitious, or as being innate, or as fabrications, for I have not yet clearly ascertained their true origin.

But here I must inquire particularly into those ideas that I believe to be derived from things existing outside me. Just what reason do I have for believing that these ideas resemble those things? Well, I do seem to have been so taught by nature. Moreover, I do know from experience that these ideas do not depend upon my will, nor consequently upon myself, for I often notice them even against my will. Now, for example, whether or not I will it, I feel heat. It is for this reason that I believe this feeling or idea of heat comes to me from something other than myself, namely from the heat of the fire by which I am sitting. Nothing is more obvious than the judgment that this thing is sending its likeness rather than something else into me.

I will now see whether these reasons are powerful enough. When I say here "I have been so taught by nature," all I have in mind is that I am driven by a spontaneous impulse to believe this, and not that some light of nature is showing me that it is true. These are two very different things. For whatever is shown me by this light of nature, for example, that from the fact that I doubt, it follows that I am, and the like, cannot in any way be doubtful. This is owing to the fact that there can be no other faculty that I can trust as much as this light and which could teach that these things are not true. But as far as natural impulses are concerned, in the past I have often judged myself to have been driven by them to make the poorer choice when it was a question of choosing a good; and I fail to see why I should place any greater faith in them than in other matters.

Again, although these ideas do not depend upon my will, it does not follow that they necessarily proceed from things existing outside me. For just as these impulses about which I spoke just now seem to be different from my will, even though they are in me, so too perhaps there is also in me some other faculty, one not yet sufficiently known to me, which produces these ideas, just as it has always seemed up to now that ideas are formed in me without any help from external things when I am asleep.

And finally, even if these ideas did proceed from things other than myself, it does not therefore follow that they must resemble those things. Indeed it seems I have frequently noticed a vast difference in many respects. For example, I find within myself two distinct ideas of the sun. One idea is drawn, as it were, from the senses. Now it is this idea which, of all those that I take to be derived from outside me, is most in need of examination. By means of this idea the sun appears to me to be quite small. But there is another idea, one derived from astronomical reasoning, that is, it is elicited from certain notions that are innate in me, or else is fashioned by me in some other way. Through this idea the sun is shown to be several times larger than the earth. Both ideas surely cannot resemble the same sun existing outside me; and reason convinces me that the idea that seems to have emanated from the sun itself from so close is the very one that least resembles the sun.

All these points demonstrate sufficiently that up to this point it was not a well-founded judgment but only a blind impulse that formed the basis of my belief that things existing outside me send ideas or images of themselves to me through the sense organs or by some other means.

But still another way occurs to me for inquiring whether some of the things of which there are ideas in me do exist outside me: insofar as these ideas are merely modes of thought, I see no inequality among them; they all seem to proceed from me in the same manner. But insofar as one idea represents one thing and another idea another thing, it is obvious that they do differ very greatly from one another. Unquestionably, those ideas that display substances to me are something more and, if I may say so, contain within themselves more objective reality than those which represent only modes or accidents. Again, the idea that enables me to understand a supreme deity, eternal, infinite, omniscient, omnipotent, and creator of all things other than himself, clearly has more objective reality within it than do those ideas through which finite substances are displayed.

Now it is indeed evident by the light of nature that there must be at least as much [reality] in the efficient and total cause as there is in the effect of that same cause. For whence, I ask, could an effect get its reality, if not from its cause? And how could the cause give that reality to the effect, unless it also possessed that reality? Hence it follows that something cannot come into being out of nothing, and also that what is more perfect (that is, what contains in itself more reality) cannot come into being from what is less perfect. But this is manifestly true not merely for those effects whose reality is actual or formal, but also for ideas in which only objective reality is considered. For example, not only can a stone which did not exist previously not now begin to exist unless it is produced by something in which there is, either formally or eminently,[6] everything that is in the stone; nor heat be introduced into a subject which was not already hot unless it is done by something that is of at least as perfect an order as heat—and the same for the rest—but it is also true that there can be in me no idea of heat, or of a stone, unless it is placed in me by some cause that has at least as much reality as I conceive to be in the heat or in the stone. For although this cause conveys none of its actual or formal reality to my idea, it should not be thought for that reason that it must be less real. Rather, the very nature of an idea is such that of itself it needs no formal

6. [By "formal cause" Descartes means one as perfect as its effect; by "eminent cause" he means one more perfect.]

reality other than what it borrows from my thought, of which it is a mode. But that a particular idea contains this as opposed to that objective reality is surely owing to some cause in which there is at least as much formal reality as there is objective reality contained in the idea. For if we assume that something is found in the idea that was not in its cause, then the idea gets that something from nothing. Yet as imperfect a mode of being as this is by which a thing exists in the intellect objectively through an idea, nevertheless it is plainly not nothing; hence it cannot get its being from nothing.

Moreover, even though the reality that I am considering in my ideas is merely objective reality, I ought not on that account to suspect that there is no need for the same reality to be formally in the causes of these ideas, but that it suffices for it to be in them objectively. For just as the objective mode of being belongs to ideas by their very nature, so the formal mode of being belongs to the causes of ideas, at least to the first and preeminent ones, by their very nature. And although one idea can perhaps issue from another, nevertheless no infinite regress is permitted here; eventually some first idea must be reached whose cause is a sort of archetype that contains formally all the reality that is in the idea merely objectively. Thus it is clear to me by the light of nature that the ideas that are in me are like images that can easily fail to match the perfection of the things from which they have been drawn, but which can contain nothing greater or more perfect.

And the longer and more attentively I examine all these points, the more clearly and distinctly I know they are true. But what am I ultimately to conclude? If the objective reality of any of my ideas is found to be so great that I am certain that the same reality was not in me, either formally or eminently, and that therefore I myself cannot be the cause of the idea, then it necessarily follows that I am not alone in the world, but that something else, which is the cause of this idea, also exists. But if no such idea is found in me, I will have no argument whatsoever to make me certain of the existence of anything other than myself, for I have conscientiously reviewed all these arguments, and so far I have been unable to find any other.

Among my ideas, in addition to the one that displays me to myself (about which there can be no difficulty at this point), are others that represent God, corporeal and inanimate things, angels, animals, and finally other men like myself.

As to the ideas that display other men, or animals, or angels, I easily understand that they could be fashioned from the ideas that I have of myself, of corporeal things, and of God—even if no men (except myself), no animals, and no angels existed in the world.

As to the ideas of corporeal things, there is nothing in them that is so great that it seems incapable of having originated from me. For if I investigate them thoroughly and examine each one individually in the way I examined the idea of wax yesterday, I notice that there are only a very few things in them that I perceive clearly and distinctly: namely, size, or extension in length, breadth, and depth; shape, which arises from the limits of this extension; position, which various things possessing shape have in relation to one another; and motion, or alteration in position. To these can be added substance, duration, and number. But as for the remaining items, such as light and colors, sounds, odors, tastes, heat and cold and other tactile qualities, I think of these only in a very confused and obscure manner, to the extent that I do not even know whether they are true or false, that is, whether the ideas I have of them are ideas of things or ideas of non-things. For although a short time ago I noted that falsity properly so called (or "formal" falsity) is to be found only in judgments, nevertheless there is another kind of falsity (called "material" falsity) which is found in ideas whenever they represent a non-thing as if it were a thing. For example, the ideas I have of heat and cold fall so far short of being clear and distinct that I cannot tell from them whether cold is merely the privation of heat or whether heat is the privation of cold, or whether both are real qualities, or whether neither is. And because ideas can only be, as it were, of things, if it is true that cold is merely the absence of heat, then an idea that represents cold to me as something real and positive will not inappropriately be called false. The same holds for other similar ideas.

Assuredly I need not assign to these ideas an author distinct from myself. For if they were false, that is, if they were to represent non-things, I know by the light of nature that they proceed from nothing; that is, they are in me for no other reason than that something is lacking in my nature, and that my nature is not entirely perfect. If, on the other hand, these ideas are true, then because they exhibit so little reality to me that I cannot distinguish it from a non-thing, I see no reason why they cannot get their being from me.

As for what is clear and distinct in the ideas of corporeal things, it appears I could have borrowed some of these from the idea of myself: namely, substance, duration, number, and whatever else there may be of this type. For instance, I think that a stone is a substance, that is to say, a thing that is suitable for existing in itself; and likewise I think that I too am a substance. Despite the fact that I conceive myself to be a thinking thing and not an extended thing, whereas I conceive of a stone as an extended thing and not a thinking thing, and hence there is the greatest diversity between these two concepts, nevertheless they seem to agree with one another when considered under the rubric of substance. Furthermore, I perceive that I now exist and recall that I have previously existed for some time. And I have various thoughts and know how many of them there are. It is in doing these things that I acquire the ideas of duration and number, which I can then apply to other things. However, none of the other components out of which the ideas of corporeal things are fashioned (namely extension, shape, position, and motion) are contained in me formally, since I am merely a thinking thing. But since these are only certain modes of a substance, whereas I am a substance, it seems possible that they are contained in me eminently.

Thus there remains only the idea of God. I must consider whether there is anything in this idea that could not have originated from me. I understand by the name "God" a certain substance that is infinite, independent, supremely intelligent and supremely powerful, and that created me along with everything else that exists—if anything else exists. Indeed all these are such that, the more carefully I focus my attention on them, the less possible it seems they could have arisen from myself alone. Thus, from what has been said, I must conclude that God necessarily exists.

For although the idea of substance is in me by virtue of the fact that I am a substance, that fact is not sufficient to explain my having the idea of an infinite substance, since I am finite, unless this idea proceeded from some substance which really was infinite.

Nor should I think that I do not perceive the infinite by means of a true idea, but only through a negation of the finite, just as I perceive rest and darkness by means of a negation of motion and light. On the contrary, I clearly understand that there is more reality in an infinite substance than there is in a finite one. Thus the perception of the infinite is somehow prior in me to the perception of the finite, that is, my perception of God is prior to my perception of myself. For how would I understand that I doubt and that I desire, that is, that I lack something and that I am not wholly perfect, unless there were some idea in me of a more perfect being, by comparison with which I might recognize my defects?

Nor can it be said that this idea of God is perhaps materially false and thus can originate from nothing, as I remarked just now about the ideas of heat and cold, and the like. On the contrary, because it is the most clear and distinct and because it contains more objective reality than any other idea, no idea is in and of itself truer and has less of a basis for being suspected of falsehood. I maintain that this idea of a being that is supremely perfect and infinite is true in the highest degree. For although I could perhaps pretend that such a being does not exist, nevertheless I could not pretend that the idea of such a being discloses to me nothing real, as was the case with the idea of cold which I referred to earlier. It is indeed an idea that is utterly clear and distinct; for whatever I clearly and distinctly perceive to be real and true and to involve some perfection is wholly contained in that idea. It is no objection that I do not comprehend the infinite or that there are countless other things in God that I can in no way either comprehend or perhaps even touch with my thought. For the nature of the infinite is such that it is not comprehended by a being such as I, who am finite. And it is sufficient that I understand this very point and judge that all those things that I clearly perceive and that I know to contain some perfection—and perhaps even countless other things of which I am ignorant—are in God either formally or eminently. The result is that, of all the ideas that are in me, the idea that I have of God is the most true, the most clear and distinct.

But perhaps I am something greater than I myself understand. Perhaps all these perfections that I am attributing to God are somehow in me potentially, although they do not yet assert themselves and are not yet actualized. For I now observe that my knowledge is gradually being increased, and I see nothing standing in the way of its being increased more and more to infinity. Moreover, I see no reason why, with my knowledge thus increased, I could not acquire all the remaining perfections of God. And, finally, if the potential for these perfections is in me already, I see no reason why this potential would not suffice to produce the idea of these perfections.

Yet none of these things can be the case. First, while it is true that my knowledge is gradually being increased and that there are many things in me potentially that are not yet actual, nevertheless, none of these pertains to the idea of God, in which there is nothing whatever that is potential. Indeed this gradual increase is itself a most certain proof of imperfection. Moreover, although my knowledge may always increase more and more, nevertheless I understand that this knowledge will never by this means be actually infinite, because it will never reach a point where it is incapable of greater increase. On the contrary, I judge God to be actually infinite, so that nothing can be added to his perfection. Finally, I perceive that the objective being of an idea cannot be produced by a merely potential being (which, strictly speaking, is nothing), but only by an actual or formal being.

Indeed there is nothing in all these things that is not manifest by the light of nature to one who is conscientious and attentive. But when I am less attentive, and the images of sensible things blind the mind's eye, I do not so easily recall why the idea of a being more perfect than me necessarily proceeds from a being that really is more perfect. This being the case, it is appropriate to ask further whether I myself who have this idea could exist, if such a being did not exist.

From what source, then, do I derive my existence? Why, from myself, or from my parents, or from whatever other things there are that are less perfect than God. For nothing more perfect than God, or even as perfect as God, can be thought or imagined.

But if I got my being from myself, I would not doubt, nor would I desire, nor would I lack anything at all. For I would have given myself all the perfections of which I have some idea; in so doing, I myself would be God! I must not think that the things I lack could perhaps be more difficult to acquire than the ones I have now. On the contrary, it is obvious that it would have been much more difficult for me (that is, a thing or substance that thinks) to emerge out of nothing than it would be to acquire the knowledge of many things about which I am ignorant (these items of knowledge being merely accidents of that substance). Certainly, if I got this greater thing for myself, I would not have denied myself at least those things that can be had more easily. Nor would I have denied myself any of those other things that I perceive to be contained in the idea of God, for surely none of them seem to me more difficult to bring about. But if any of them were more difficult to bring about, they would certainly also seem more difficult to me, even if the remaining ones that I possess I got from myself, since it would be on account of them that I would experience that my power is limited.

Nor am I avoiding the force of these arguments, if I suppose that perhaps I have always existed as I do now, as if it then followed that no author of my existence need be sought. For because the entire span of one's life can be divided into countless parts, each one wholly independent of the rest, it does not follow from the fact that I existed a short time ago that I must exist now, unless some cause, as it were, creates me all over again at this moment, that is to say, which preserves me. For it is obvious to one who pays close attention to the nature of time that plainly the same force and action are needed to preserve anything at each individual moment that it lasts as would be required to create the same thing anew, were it not yet in existence. Thus conservation differs from creation solely by virtue of a distinction of reason; this too is one of those things that are manifest by the light of nature.

Therefore I must now ask myself whether I possess some power by which I can bring it about that I myself, who now exist, will also exist a little later on. For since I am nothing but a thinking thing—or at least since I am now dealing simply and precisely with that part of me which is a thinking thing—if such a power were in me, then I would certainly be aware of it. But I observe that there is no such power; and from this very fact I know most clearly that I depend upon some being other than myself.

But perhaps this being is not God, and I have been produced either by my parents or by some other causes less perfect than God. On the contrary, as I said before, it is obvious that there must be at least as much in the cause as there is in the effect. Thus, regardless of what it is that eventually is assigned as my cause, because I am a thinking thing and have within me a certain idea of God, it must be granted that what caused me is also a thinking thing and it too has an idea of all the perfections which I attribute to God. And I can again inquire of this cause whether it got its existence from itself or from another cause. For if it got its existence from itself, it is evident from what has been said that it is itself God, because, having the power of existing in and of itself, it unquestionably also has the power of actually possessing all the perfections of which it has in itself an idea—that is, all the perfections that I conceive to be in God. However, if it got its existence from another cause, I will once again inquire in similar fashion about this other cause: whether it got its existence from itself or from another cause, until finally I arrive at the ultimate cause, which will be God. For it is apparent enough that there can be no infinite regress here, especially since I am not dealing here merely with the cause that once produced me, but also and most especially with the cause that preserves me at the present time.

Nor can one fancy that perhaps several partial causes have concurred in bringing me into being, and that I have taken the ideas of the various perfections I attribute to God from a variety of causes, so that all of these perfections are found somewhere in the universe, but not all joined together in a single being—God. On the contrary, the unity, the simplicity, that is, the inseparability of all those features that are in God is one of the chief perfections that I understand to be in him. Certainly the idea of the unity of all his perfections could not have been placed in me by any cause from which I did not also get the ideas of the other perfections; for neither could some cause have made me understand them joined together and inseparable from one another, unless it also caused me to recognize what they were.

Finally, as to my parents, even if everything that I ever believed about them were true, still it is certainly not they who preserve me; nor is it they who in any way brought me into being, insofar as I am a thinking thing. Rather, they merely placed certain dispositions in the matter which I judged to contain me, that is, a mind, which now is the only thing I take myself to be. And thus there can be no difficulty here concerning my parents. Indeed I have no choice but to conclude that the mere fact of my existing and of there being in me an idea of a most perfect being, that is, God, demonstrates most evidently that God too exists.

All that remains for me is to ask how I received this idea of God. For I did not draw it from the senses; it never came upon me unexpectedly, as is usually the case with the ideas of sensible things when these things present themselves (or seem to present themselves) to the external sense organs. Nor was it made by me, for I plainly can neither subtract anything from it nor add anything to it. Thus the only option remaining is that this idea is innate in me, just as the idea of myself is innate in me.

To be sure, it is not astonishing that in creating me, God should have endowed me with this idea, so that it would be like the mark of the craftsman impressed upon his work, although this mark need not be something distinct from the work itself. But the mere fact that God created me makes it highly plausible that I have somehow been made in his image and likeness, and that I perceive this likeness, in which the idea of God is contained, by means of the same faculty by which I perceive myself. That is, when I turn the mind's eye toward myself, I understand not only that I am something incomplete and dependent upon another, something aspiring indefinitely for greater and greater or better things, but also that the being on whom I depend has in himself all those greater things—not merely indefinitely and potentially, but infinitely and actually, and thus that he is God. The whole force of the argument rests on the fact that I recognize that it would be impossible for me to exist, being of such a nature as I am (namely, having in me the idea of God), unless God did in fact exist. God, I say, that same being the idea of whom is in me: a being having all those perfections that I cannot comprehend, but can somehow touch with my thought, and a being subject to no defects whatever. From these considerations it is quite obvious that he cannot be a deceiver, for it is manifest by the light of nature that all fraud and deception depend on some defect.

But before examining this idea more closely and at the same time inquiring into other truths that can be gathered from it, at this point I want to spend some time contemplating this God, to ponder his attributes and, so far as the eye of my darkened mind can take me, to gaze upon, to admire, and to adore the beauty of this immense light. For just as we believe by faith that the greatest felicity of the next life consists solely in this contemplation of the divine majesty, so too we now experience that from the same contemplation, although it is much less perfect, the greatest pleasure of which we are capable in this life can be perceived.

Meditation Four: Concerning the True and the False

Lately I have become accustomed to withdrawing my mind from the senses, and I have carefully taken note of the fact that very few things are truly perceived regarding corporeal things, although a great many more things are known regarding the human mind, and still many more things regarding God. The upshot is that I now have no difficulty directing my thought away from things that can be imagined to things that can be grasped only by the understanding and are wholly separate from matter. In fact the idea I clearly have of the human mind—insofar as it is a thinking thing, not extended in length, breadth or depth, and having nothing else from the body—is far more distinct than the idea of any corporeal thing. And when I take note of the fact that I doubt, or that I am a thing that is incomplete and dependent, there comes to mind a clear and distinct idea of a being that is independent and complete, that is, an idea of God. And from the mere fact that such an idea is in me, or that I who have this idea exist, I draw the obvious conclusion that God also exists, and that my existence depends entirely upon him at each and every moment. This conclusion is so obvious that I am confident that the human mind can know nothing more evident or more certain. And now I seem to see a way by which I might progress from this contemplation of the true God, in whom, namely, are hidden all the treasures of the sciences and wisdom, to the knowledge of other things.

To begin with, I acknowledge that it is impossible for God ever to deceive me, for trickery or deception is always indicative of some imperfection. And although the ability to deceive seems to be an indication of cleverness or power, the will to deceive undoubtedly attests to maliciousness or weakness. Accordingly, deception is incompatible with God.

Next I experience that there is in me a certain faculty of judgment, which, like everything else that is in me, I undoubtedly received from God. And since he does not wish to deceive me, he assuredly has not given me the sort of faculty with which I could ever make a mistake, when I use it properly.

No doubt regarding this matter would remain, but for the fact that it seems to follow from this that I am never capable of making a mistake. For if everything that is in me I got from God, and he gave me no faculty for making mistakes, it seems I am incapable of ever erring. And thus, so long as I think exclusively about God and focus my attention exclusively on him, I discern no cause of error or falsity. But once I turn my attention back on myself, I nevertheless experience that I am subject to countless errors. As I seek a cause of these errors, I notice that passing before me is not only a real and positive idea of God (that is, of a supremely perfect being), but also, as it were, a certain negative idea of nothingness (that is, of what is at the greatest possible distance from any perfection), and that I have been so constituted as a kind of middle ground between God and nothingness, or between the supreme being and non-being. Thus insofar as I have been created by the supreme being, there is nothing in me by means of which I might be deceived or be led into error; but insofar as I participate in nothingness or non-being, that is, insofar as I am not the supreme being and lack a great many things, it is not surprising that I make mistakes. Thus I certainly understand that error as such is not something real that depends upon God, but rather is merely a defect. And thus there is no need to account for my errors by positing a faculty given to me by God for this purpose. Rather, it just so happens that I make mistakes because the faculty of judging the truth, which I got from God, is not, in my case, infinite.

Still this is not yet altogether satisfactory; for error is not a pure negation, but rather a privation or a lack of some knowledge that somehow ought to be in me. And when I attend to the nature of God, it seems impossible that he would have placed in me a faculty that is not perfect in its kind or that is lacking some perfection it ought to have. For if it is true that the more expert the craftsman, the more perfect the works he produces, what can that supreme creator of all things make that is not perfect in all respects? No doubt God could have created me such that I never erred. No doubt, again, God always wills what is best. Is it then better that I should be in error rather than not?

As I mull these things over more carefully, it occurs to me first that there is no reason to marvel at the fact that God should bring about certain things the reasons for which I do not understand. Nor is his existence therefore to be doubted because I happen to experience other things of which I fail to grasp why and how he made them. For since I know now that my nature is very weak and limited, whereas the nature of God is immense, incomprehensible, and infinite, this is sufficient for me also to know that he can make innumerable things whose causes escape me. For this reason alone the entire class of causes which people customarily derive from a thing's "end," I judge to be utterly useless in physics. It is not without rashness that I think myself capable of inquiring into the ends of God.

It also occurs to me that whenever we ask whether the works of God are perfect, we should keep in view not simply some one creature in isolation from the rest, but the universe as a whole. For perhaps something might rightfully appear very imperfect if it were all by itself, and yet be most perfect, to the extent that it has the status of a part in the universe. And although subsequent to having decided to doubt everything, I have come to know with certainty only that I and God exist, nevertheless, after having taken note of the immense power of God, I cannot deny that many other things have been made by him, or at least could have been made by him. Thus I may have the status of a part in the universal scheme of things.

Next, as I focus more closely on myself and inquire into the nature of my errors (the only things that are indicative of some imperfection in me), I note that these errors depend on the simultaneous concurrence of two causes: the faculty of knowing that is in me and the faculty of choosing, that is, the free choice of the will, in other words, simultaneously on the intellect and will. Through the intellect alone I merely perceive ideas, about which I can render a judgment. Strictly speaking, no error is to be found in the intellect when properly viewed in this manner. For although perhaps there may exist countless things about which I have no idea, nevertheless it must not be said that, strictly speaking, I am deprived of these ideas but only that I lack them in a negative sense. This is because I cannot adduce an argument to prove that God ought to have given me a greater faculty of knowing than he did. No matter how expert a craftsman I understand him to be, still I do not for that reason believe he ought to have bestowed on each one of his works all the perfections that he can put into some. Nor, on the other hand, can I complain that the will or free choice I have received from God is insufficiently ample or perfect, since I experience that it is limited by no boundaries whatever. In fact, it seems to be especially worth noting that no other things in me are so perfect or so great but that I understand that they can be still more perfect or greater. If, for example, I consider the faculty of understanding, I immediately recognize that in my case it is very small and quite limited, and at the very same time I form an idea of another much greater faculty of understanding—in fact, an understanding which is consummately great and infinite; and from the fact that I can form an idea of this faculty, I perceive that it pertains to the nature of God. Similarly, were I to examine the faculty of memory or imagination, or any of the other faculties, I would understand that in my case each of these is without exception feeble and limited, whereas in the case of God I understand each faculty to be boundless. It is only the will or free choice that I experience to be so great in me that I cannot grasp the idea of any greater faculty. This is so much the case that the will is the chief basis for my understanding that I bear a certain image and likeness of God. For although the faculty of willing is incomparably greater in God than it is in me, both by virtue of the knowledge and power that are joined to it and that render it more resolute and efficacious and by virtue of its object inasmuch as the divine will stretches over a greater number of things, nevertheless, when viewed in itself formally and precisely, God's faculty of willing does not appear to be any greater. This is owing to the fact that willing is merely a matter of being able to do or not do the same thing, that is, of being able to affirm or deny, to pursue or to shun; or better still, the will consists solely in the fact that when something is proposed to us by our intellect either to affirm or deny, to pursue or to shun, we are moved in such a way that we sense that we are determined to it by no external force. In order to be free I need not be capable of being moved in each direction; on the contrary, the more I am inclined toward one direction—either because I clearly understand that there is in it an aspect of the good and the true, or because God has thus disposed the inner recesses of my thought—the more freely do I choose that direction. Nor indeed does divine grace or natural knowledge ever diminish one's freedom; rather, they increase and strengthen it. However, the indifference that I experience when there is no reason moving me more in one direction than in another is the lowest grade of freedom; it is indicative not of any perfection in freedom, but rather of a defect, that is, a certain negation in knowledge. Were I always to see clearly what is true and good, I would never deliberate about what is to be judged or chosen. In that event, although I would be entirely free, I could never be indifferent.

But from these considerations I perceive that the power of willing, which I got from God, is not, taken by itself, the cause of my errors, for it is most ample as well as perfect in its kind. Nor is my power of understanding the cause of my errors. For since I got my power of understanding from God, whatever I understand I doubtless understand rightly, and it is impossible for me to be deceived in this. What then is the source of my errors? They are owing simply to the fact that, since the will extends further than the intellect, I do not contain the will within the same boundaries; rather, I also extend it to things I do not understand. Because the will is indifferent in regard to such matters, it easily turns away from the true and the good; and in this way I am deceived and I sin.

For example, during these last few days I was examining whether anything in the world exists, and I noticed that, from the very fact that I was making this examination, it obviously followed that I exist. Nevertheless, I could not help judging that what I understood so clearly was true; not that I was coerced into making this judgment because of some external force, but because a great light gave way to a great inclination in my will, and the less indifferent I was, the more spontaneously and freely did I believe it. But now, in addition to my knowing that I exist, insofar as I am a certain thinking thing, I also observe a certain idea of corporeal nature. It happens that I am in doubt as to whether the thinking nature which is in me, or rather which I am, is something different from this corporeal nature, or whether both natures are one and the same thing. And I assume that as yet no consideration has occurred to my intellect to convince me of the one alternative rather than the other. Certainly in virtue of this very fact I am indifferent about whether to affirm or to deny either alternative, or even whether to make no judgment at all in the matter.

Moreover, this indifference extends not merely to things about which the intellect knows absolutely nothing, but extends generally to everything of which the intellect does not have a clear enough knowledge at the very time when the will is deliberating on them. For although probable guesses may pull me in one direction, the mere knowledge that they are only guesses and not certain and indubitable proofs is all it takes to push my assent in the opposite direction. These last few days have provided me with ample experience on this point. For all the beliefs that I had once held to be most true I have supposed to be utterly false, and for the sole reason that I determined that I could somehow raise doubts about them.

But if I hold off from making a judgment when I do not perceive what is true with sufficient clarity and distinctness, it is clear that I am acting properly and am not committing an error. But if instead I were to make an assertion or a denial, then I am not using my freedom properly. Were I to select the alternative that is false, then obviously I will be in error. But were I to embrace the other alternative, it will be by sheer luck that I happen upon the truth; but I will still not be without fault, for it is manifest by the light of nature that a perception on the part of the intellect must always precede a determination on the part of the will. Inherent in this incorrect use of free will is the privation that constitutes the very essence of error: the privation, I say, present in this operation insofar as the operation proceeds for me, but not in the faculty given to me by God, nor even in its operation insofar as it depends upon him.

Indeed I have no cause for complaint on the grounds that God has not given me a greater power of understanding or a greater light of nature than he has, for it is of the essence of a finite intellect not to understand many things, and it is of the essence of a created intellect to be finite. Actually, instead of thinking that he has withheld from me or deprived me of those things that he has not given me, I ought to thank God, who never owed me anything, for what he has bestowed upon me.

Again, I have no cause for complaint on the grounds that God has given me a will that has a wider scope than my intellect. For since the will consists of merely one thing, something indivisible, as it were, it does not seem that its nature could withstand anything being removed from it. Indeed, the more ample the will is, the more I ought to thank the one who gave it to me.

Finally, I should not complain because God concurs with me in eliciting those acts of the will, that is those judgments, in which I am mistaken. For insofar as those acts depend on God, they are absolutely true and good; and in a certain sense, there is greater perfection in me in being able to elicit those acts than in not being able to do so. But privation, in which alone the defining characteristic of falsehood and wrong-doing is to be found, has no need whatever for God's concurrence, since a privation is not a thing, nor, when it is related to God as its cause, is it to be called a privation, but simply a negation. For it is surely no imperfection in God that he has given me the freedom to give or withhold my assent in those instances where he has not placed a clear and distinct perception in my intellect. But surely it is an imperfection in me that I do not use my freedom well and that I make judgments about things I do not properly understand. Nevertheless, I see that God could easily have brought it about that, while still being free and having finite knowledge, I should nonetheless never make a mistake. This result could have been achieved either by his endowing my intellect with a clear and distinct perception of everything about which I would ever deliberate, or by simply impressing the following rule so firmly upon my memory that I could never forget it: I should never judge anything that I do not clearly and distinctly understand. I readily understand that, considered as a totality, I would have been more perfect than I am now, had God made me that way. But I cannot therefore deny that it may somehow be a greater perfection in the universe as a whole that some of its parts are not immune to error, while others are, than if all of them were exactly alike. And I have no right to complain that the part God has wished me to play is not the principal and most perfect one of all.

Furthermore, even if I cannot abstain from errors in the first way mentioned above, which depends upon a clear perception of everything about which I must deliberate, nevertheless I can avoid error in the other way, which depends solely on my remembering to abstain from making judgments whenever the truth of a given matter is not apparent. For although I experience a certain infirmity in myself, namely that I am unable to keep my attention constantly focused on one and the same item of knowledge, nevertheless, by attentive and often repeated meditation, I can bring it about that I call this rule to mind whenever the situation calls for it, and thus I would acquire a certain habit of not erring.

Since herein lies the greatest and chief perfection of man, I think today's meditation, in which I investigated the cause of error and falsity, was quite profitable. Nor can this cause be anything other than the one I have described; for as often as I restrain my will when I make judgments, so that it extends only to those matters that the intellect clearly and distinctly discloses to it, it plainly cannot happen that I err. For every clear and distinct perception is surely something, and hence it cannot come from nothing. On the contrary, it must necessarily have God for its author: God, I say, that supremely perfect being to whom it is repugnant to be a deceiver. Therefore the perception is most assuredly true. Today I have learned not merely what I must avoid so as never to make a mistake, but at the same time what I must do to attain truth. For I will indeed attain it if only I pay enough attention to all the things that I perfectly understand, and separate them off from the rest, which I apprehend more confusedly and more obscurely. I will be conscientious about this in the future.

Meditation Five: Concerning the Essence of Material Things, and Again Concerning God, That He Exists

Several matters remain for me to examine concerning the attributes of God and myself, that is, concerning the nature of my mind. But perhaps I will take these up at some other time. For now, since I have noted what to avoid and what to do in order to attain the truth, nothing seems more pressing than that I try to free myself from the doubts into which I fell a few days ago, and that I see whether anything certain is to be had concerning material things.

Yet, before inquiring whether any such things exist outside me, I surely ought to consider the ideas of these things, insofar as they exist in my thought, and see which ones are distinct and which ones are confused.

I do indeed distinctly imagine the quantity that philosophers commonly call "continuous," that is, the extension of this quantity, or rather of the thing quantified in length, breadth and depth. I enumerate the various parts in it. I ascribe to these parts any sizes, shapes, positions, and local movements whatever; to these movements I ascribe any durations whatever.

Not only are these things manifestly known and transparent to me, viewed thus in a general way, but also, when I focus my attention on them, I perceive countless particulars concerning shapes, number, movement, and the like. Their truth is so open and so much in accord with my nature that, when I first discover them, it seems I am not so much learning something new as recalling something I knew beforehand. In other words, it seems as though I am noticing things for the first time that were in fact in me for a long while, although I had not previously directed a mental gaze upon them.

What I believe must be considered above all here is the fact that I find within me countless ideas of certain things, that, even if perhaps they do not exist anywhere outside me, still cannot be said to be nothing. And although, in a sense, I think them at will, nevertheless they are not something I have fabricated; rather they have their own true and immutable natures. For example, when I imagine a triangle, even if perhaps no such figure exists outside my thought anywhere in the world and never has, the triangle still has a certain determinate nature, essence, or form which is unchangeable and eternal, which I did not fabricate, and which does not depend on my mind. This is evident from the fact that various properties can be demonstrated regarding this triangle: namely, that its three angles are equal to two right angles, that its longest side is opposite its largest angle, and so on. These are properties I now clearly acknowledge, whether I want to or not, even if I previously had given them no thought whatever when I imagined the triangle. For this reason, then, they were not fabricated by me.

It is irrelevant for me to say that perhaps the idea of a triangle came to me from external things through the sense organs because of course I have on occasion seen triangle-shaped bodies. For I can think of countless other figures, concerning which there can be no suspicion of their ever having entered me through the senses, and yet I can demonstrate various properties of these figures, no less than I can those of the triangle. All these properties are patently true because I know them clearly, and thus they are something and not merely nothing. For it is obvious that whatever is true is something, and I have already demonstrated at some length that all that I know clearly is true. And even if I had not demonstrated this, certainly the nature of my mind is such that nevertheless I cannot refrain from assenting to these things, at least while I perceive them clearly. And I recall that even before now, when I used to keep my attention glued to the objects of the senses, I always took the truths I clearly recognized regarding figures, numbers, or other things pertaining to arithmetic, geometry or, in general, to pure and abstract mathematics to be the most certain of all.

But if, from the mere fact that I can bring forth from my thought the idea of something, it follows that all that I clearly and distinctly perceive to belong to that thing really does belong to it, then cannot this too be a basis for an argument proving the existence of God? Clearly the idea of God, that is, the idea of a supremely perfect being, is one I discover to be no less within me than the idea of any figure or number. And that it belongs to God's nature that he always exists is something I understand no less clearly and distinctly than is the case when I demonstrate in regard to some figure or number that something also belongs to the nature of that figure or number. Thus, even if not everything that I have meditated upon during these last few days were true, still the existence of God ought to have for me at least the same degree of certainty that truths of mathematics had until now.

However, this point is not wholly obvious at first glance, but has a certain look of a sophism about it. Since in all other matters I have become accustomed to distinguishing existence from essence, I easily convince myself that it can even be separated from God's essence, and hence that God can be thought of as not existing. But nevertheless, it is obvious to anyone who pays close attention that existence can no more be separated from God's essence than its having three angles equal to two right angles can be separated from the essence of a triangle, or that that the idea of a valley can be separated from the idea of a mountain. Thus it is no less contradictory to think of God (that is, a supremely perfect being) lacking existence (that is, lacking some perfection) than it is to think of a mountain without a valley.

But granted I can no more think of God as not existing than I can think of a mountain without a valley, nevertheless it surely does not follow from the fact that I think of a mountain with a valley that a mountain exists in the world. Likewise, from the fact that I think of God as existing, it does not seem to follow that God exists, for my thought imposes no necessity on things. And just as one may imagine a winged horse, without there being a horse that has wings, in the same way perhaps I can attach existence to God, even though no God exists.

But there is a sophism lurking here. From the fact that I am unable to think of a mountain without a valley, it does not follow that a mountain or a valley exists anywhere, but only that, whether they exist or not, a mountain and a valley are inseparable from one another. But from the fact that I cannot think of God except as existing, it follows that existence is inseparable from God, and that for this reason he really exists. Not that my thought brings this about or imposes any necessity on anything; but rather the necessity of the thing itself, namely of the existence of God, forces me to think this. For I am not free to think of God without existence, that is, a supremely perfect being without a supreme perfection, as I am to imagine a horse with or without wings.

Further, it should not be said here that even though I surely need to assent to the existence of God once I have asserted that God has all perfections and that existence is one of these perfections, nevertheless that earlier assertion need not have been made. Likewise, I need not believe that all four-sided figures can be inscribed in a circle; but given that I posit this, it would then be necessary for me to admit that a rhombus can be inscribed in a circle. Yet this is obviously false. For although it is not necessary that I should ever happen upon any thought of God, nevertheless whenever I am of a mind to think of a being that is first and supreme, and bring forth the idea of God as it were from the storehouse of my mind, I must of necessity ascribe all perfections to him, even if I do not at that time enumerate them all or take notice of each one individually. This necessity plainly suffices so that afterwards, when I realize that existence is a perfection, I rightly conclude that a first and supreme being exists. In the same way, there is no necessity for me ever to imagine a triangle, but whenever I do wish to consider a rectilinear figure having but three angles, I must ascribe to it those properties on the basis of which one rightly infers that the three angles of this figure are no greater than two right angles, even though I do not take note of this at the time. But when I inquire as to the figures that may be inscribed in a circle, there is absolutley no need whatever for my thinking that all four-sided figures are of this sort; for that matter, I cannot even fabricate such a thing, so long as I am of a mind to admit only what I clearly and distinctly understand. Consequently, there is a great difference between false assupmtions of this sort and the true ideas that are inborn in me, the first and chief of which is the idea of God. For there are a great many ways in which I understand that this idea is not an invention that is dependent upon my thought, but is an image of a true and immutable nature. First, I cannot think of anything aside from God alone to whose essence existence belongs. Next, I cannot understand how there could be two or more Gods of this kind. Again, once I have asserted that one God now exists, I plainly see that it is necessary that he has exsted from eternity and will endure for eternity. Finally, I perceive many other features in God, none of which I can remove or change.

But, whatever type of argument I use, it always comes down to the fact that the only things that fully convince me are those that I clearly and distinctly perceive. And although some of these things I thus perceive are obvious to everyone, while others are discovered only by those who look more closely and inquire carefully, nevertheless, once they have been discovered, they are considered no less certain than the others. For example, in the case of a right triangle, although it is not so readily apparent that the square of the hypotenuse is equal to the sum of the squares of the other two sides as it is that the hypotenuse is opposite the largest angle, nevertheless, once the former has been ascertained, it is no less believed. However, as far as God is concerned, if I were not overwhelmed by prejudices and if the images of sensible things were not besieging my thought from all directions, I would certainly acknowledge nothing sooner or more easily than him. For what, in and of itself, is more manifest than that a supreme being exists, that is, that God, to whose essence alone existence belongs, exists?

And although I needed to pay close attention in order to perceive this, nevertheless I now am just as certain about this as I am about everything else that seems most certain. Moreover, I observe also that certitude about other things is so dependent on this, that without it nothing can ever be perfectly known.

For I am indeed of such a nature that, while I perceive something very clearly and distinctly, I cannot help believing it to be true. Nevertheless, my nature is also such that I cannot focus my mental gaze always on the same thing, so as to perceive it clearly. Often the memory of a previously made judgment may return when I am no longer attending to the arguments on account of which I made such a judgment. Thus, other arguments can be brought forward that would easily make me change my opinion, were I ignorant of God. And thus I would never have true and certain knowledge about anything, but merely fickle and changeable opinions. Thus, for example, when I consider the nature of a triangle, it appears most evident to me, steeped as I am in the principles of geometry, that its three angles are equal to two right angles. And so long as I attend to its demonstration I cannot help believing this to be true. But no sooner do I turn the mind's eye away from the demonstration, than, however much I still recall that I had observed it most clearly, nevertheless, it can easily happen that I entertain doubts about whether it is true, were I ignorant of God. For I can convince myself that I have been so constituted by nature that I might occasionally be mistaken about those things I believe I perceive most evidently, especially when I recall that I have often taken many things to be true and certain, which other arguments have subsequently led me to judge to be false.

But once I perceived that there is a God, and also understood at the same time that everything else depends on him, and that he is not a deceiver, I then concluded that everything that I clearly and distinctly perceive is necessarily true. Hence even if I no longer attend to the reasons leading me to judge this to be true, so long as I merely recall that I did clearly and distinctly observe it, no counter-argument can be brought forward that might force me to doubt it. On the contrary, I have a true and certain knowledge of it. And not just of this one fact, but of everything else that I recall once having demonstrated, as in geometry, and so on. For what objections can now be raised against me? That I have been made such that I am often mistaken? But I now know that I cannot be mistaken in matters I plainly understand. That I have taken many things to be true and certain which subsequently I recognized to be false? But none of these were things I clearly and distinctly perceived. But I was ignorant of this rule for determining the truth, and I believed these things perhaps for other reasons which I later discovered were less firm. What then remains to be said? That perhaps I am dreaming, as I recently objected against myself, in other words, that everything I am now thinking of is no truer than what occurs to someone who is asleep? Be that as it may, this changes nothing; for certainly, even if I were dreaming, if anything is evident to my intellect, then it is entirely true.

And thus I see plainly that the certainty and truth of every science depends exclusively upon the knowledge of the true God, to the extent that, prior to my becoming aware of him, I was incapable of achieving perfect knowledge about anything else. But now it is possible for me to achieve full and certain knowledge about countless things, both about God and other intellectual matters, as well as about the entirety of that corporeal nature which is the object of pure mathematics.

Meditation Six: Concerning the Existence of Material Things, and the Real Distinction between Mind and Body

It remains for me to examine whether material things exist. Indeed I now know that they can exist, at least insofar as they are the object of pure mathematics, since I clearly and distinctly perceive them. For no doubt God is capable of bringing about everything that I am capable of perceiving in this way. And I have never judged that God was incapable of something, except when it was incompatible with my perceiving it distinctly. Moreover, from the faculty of imagination, which I notice I use while dealing with material things, it seems to follow that they exist. For to anyone paying very close attention to what imagination is, it appears to be simply a certain application of the knowing faculty to a body intimately present to it, and which therefore exists.

To make this clear, I first examine the difference between imagination and pure intellection. So, for example, when I imagine a triangle, I not only understand that it is a figure bounded by three lines, but at the same time I also envisage with the mind's eye those lines as if they were present; and this is what I call "imagining." On the other hand, if I want to think about a chiliagon, I certainly understand that it is a figure consisting of a thousand sides, just as well as I understand that a triangle is a figure consisting of three sides, yet I do not imagine those thousand sides in the same way, or envisage them as if they were present. And although in that case—because of force of habit I always imagine something whenever I think about a corporeal thing—I may perchance represent to myself some figure in a confused fashion, nevertheless this figure is obviously not a chiliagon. For this figure is really no different from the figure I would represent to myself, were I thinking of a myriagon or any other figure with a large number of sides. Nor is this figure of any help in knowing the properties that differentiate a chiliagon from other polygons. But if the figure in question is a pentagon, I surely can understand its figure, just as was the case with the chiliagon, without the help of my imagination. But I can also imagine a pentagon by turning the mind's eye both to its five sides and at the same time to the area bounded by those sides. At this point I am manifestly aware that I am in need of a peculiar sort of effort on the part of the mind in order to imagine, one that I do not employ in order to understand. This new effort on the part of the mind clearly shows the difference between imagination and pure intellection.

Moreover, I consider that this power of imagining that is in me, insofar as it differs from the power of understanding, is not required for my own essence, that is, the essence of my mind. For were I to be lacking this power, I would nevertheless undoubtedly remain the same entity I am now. Thus it seems to follow that the power of imagining depends upon something distinct from me. And I readily understand that, were a body to exist to which a mind is so joined that it may apply itself in order, as it were, to look at it any time it wishes, it could happen that it is by means of this very body that I imagine corporeal things. As a result, this mode of thinking may differ from pure intellection only in the sense that the mind, when it understands, in a sense turns toward itself and looks at one of the ideas that are in it; whereas when it imagines, it turns toward the body, and intuits in the body something that conforms to an idea either understood by the mind or perceived by sense. To be sure, I easily understand that the imagination can be actualized in this way, provided a body does exist. And since I can think of no other way of explaining imagination that is equally appropriate, I make a probable conjecture from this that a body exists. But this is only a probability. And even though I may examine everything carefully, nevertheless I do not yet see how the distinct idea of corporeal nature that I find in my imagination can enable me to develop an argument which necessarily concludes that some body exists.

But I am in the habit of imagining many other things, over and above that corporeal nature which is the object of pure mathematics, such as colors, sounds, tastes, pain, and the like, though not so distinctly. And I perceive these things better by means of the senses, from which, with the aid of the memory, they seem to have arrived at the imagination. Thus I should pay the same degree of attention to the senses, so that I might deal with them more appropriately. I must see whether I can obtain any reliable argument for the existence of corporeal things from those things that are perceived by the mode of thinking that I call "sense."

First of all, to be sure, I will review here all the things I previously believed to be true because I had perceived them by means of the senses and the causes I had for thinking this. Next I will assess the causes why I later called them into doubt. Finally, I will consider what I must now believe about these things.

So first, I sensed that I had a head, hands, feet, and other members that comprised this body which I viewed as part of me, or perhaps even as the whole of me. I sensed that this body was found among many other bodies, by which my body can be affected in various beneficial or harmful ways. I gauged what was opportune by means of a certain sensation of pleasure, and what was inopportune by a sensation of pain. In addition to pain and pleasure, I also sensed within me hunger, thirst, and other such appetites, as well as certain bodily tendencies toward mirth, sadness, anger, and other such affects. And externally, besides the extension, shapes, and motions of bodies, I also sensed their hardness, heat, and other tactile qualities. I also sensed light, colors, odors, tastes, and sounds, on the basis of whose variety I distinguished the sky, the earth, the seas, and the other bodies, one from the other. Now given the ideas of all these qualities that presented themselves to my thought, and which were all that I properly and immediately sensed, still it was surely not without reason that I thought I sensed things that were manifestly different from my thought, namely, the bodies from which these ideas proceeded. For I knew by experience that these ideas came upon me utterly without my consent, to the extent that, wish as I may, I could not sense any object unless it was present to a sense organ. Nor could I fail to sense it when it was present. And since the ideas perceived by sense were much more vivid and explicit and even, in their own way, more distinct than any of those that I deliberately and knowingly formed through meditation or that I found impressed on my memory, it seemed impossible that they came from myself. Thus the remaining alternative was that they came from other things. Since I had no knowledge of such things except from those same ideas themselves, I could not help entertaining the thought that they were similar to those ideas. Moreover, I also recalled that the use of the senses antedated the use of reason. And since I saw that the ideas that I myself fashioned were not as explicit as those that I perceived through the faculty of sense, and were for the most part composed of parts of the latter, I easily convinced myself that I had absolutely no idea in the intellect that I did not have beforehand in the sense faculty. Not without reason did I judge that this body, which by a certain special right I called "mine," belongs more to me than did any other. For I could never be separated from it in the same way I could be from other bodies. I sensed all appetites and feelings in and on behalf of it. Finally, I noticed pain and pleasurable excitement in its parts, but not in other bodies external to it. But why should a certain sadness of spirit arise from some sensation or other of pain, and why should a certain elation arise from a sensation of excitement, or why should that peculiar twitching in the stomach, which I call hunger, warn me to have something to eat, or why should dryness in the throat warn me to take something to drink, and so on? I plainly had no explanation other than that I had been taught this way by nature. For there is no affinity whatsoever, at least none I am aware of, between this twitching in the stomach and the will to have something to eat, or between the sensation of something causing pain and the thought of sadness arising from this sensation. But nature also seems to have taught me everything else as well that I judged concerning the objects of the senses, for I had already convinced myself that this was how things were, prior to my assessing any of the arguments that might prove it.

Afterwards, however, many experiences gradually weakened any faith that I had in the senses. Towers that had seemed round from afar occasionally appeared square at close quarters. Very large statues mounted on their pedestals did not seem large to someone looking at them from ground level. And in countless other such instances I determined that judgments in matters of the external senses were in error. And not just the external senses, but the internal senses as well. For what can be more intimate than pain? But I had sometimes heard it said by people whose leg or arm had been amputated that it seemed to them that they still occasionally sensed pain in the very limb they had lost. Thus, even in my own case it did not seem to be entirely certain that some bodily member was causing me pain, even though I did sense pain in it. To these causes for doubt I recently added two quite general ones. The first was that everything I ever thought I sensed while awake I could believe I also sometimes sensed while asleep, and since I do not believe that what I seem to sense in my dreams comes to me from things external to me, I saw no reason why I should hold this belief about those things I seem to be sensing while awake. The second was that, since I was still ignorant of the author of my origin (or at least pretended to be ignorant of it), I saw nothing to prevent my having been so constituted by nature that I should be mistaken even about what seemed to me most true. As to the arguments that used to convince me of the truth of sensible things, I found no difficulty responding to them. For since I seemed driven by nature toward many things about which reason tried to dissuade me, I did not think that what I was taught by nature deserved much credence. And even though the perceptions of the senses did not depend on my will, I did not think that we must therefore conclude that they came from things distinct from me, since perhaps there is some faculty in me, as yet unknown to me, that produces these perceptions.

But now, having begun to have a better knowledge of myself and the author of my origin, I am of the opinion that I must not rashly admit everything that I seem to derive from the senses; but neither, for that matter, should I call everything into doubt.

First, I know that all the things that I clearly and distinctly understand can be made by God such as I understand them. For this reason, my ability clearly and distinctly to understand one thing without another suffices to make me certain that the one thing is different from the other, since they can be separated from each other, at least by God. The question as to the sort of power that might effect such a separation is not relevant to their being thought to be different. For this reason, from the fact that I know that I exist, and that at the same time I judge that obviously nothing else belongs to my nature or essence except that I am a thinking thing, I rightly conclude that my essence consists entirely in my being a thinking thing. And although perhaps (or rather, as I shall soon say, assuredly) I have a body that is very closely joined to me, nevertheless, because on the one hand I have a clear and distinct idea of myself, insofar as I am merely a thinking thing and not an extended thing, and because on the other hand I have a distinct idea of a body, insofar as it is merely an extended thing and not a thinking thing, it is certain that I am really distinct from my body, and can exist without it.

Moreover, I find in myself faculties for certain special modes of thinking, namely the faculties of imagining and sensing. I can clearly and distinctly understand myself in my entirety without these faculties, but not vice versa: I cannot understand them clearly and distinctly without me, that is, without a substance endowed with understanding in which they inhere, for they include an act of understanding in their formal concept. Thus I perceive them to be distinguished from me as modes from a thing. I also acknowledge that there are certain other faculties, such as those of moving from one place to another, of taking on various shapes, and so on, that, like sensing or imagining, cannot be understood apart from some substance in which they inhere, and hence without which they cannot exist. But it is clear that these faculties, if in fact they exist, must be in a corporeal or extended substance, not in a substance endowed with understanding. For some extension is contained in a clear and distinct concept of them, though certainly not any understanding. Now there clearly is in me a passive faculty of sensing, that is, a faculty for receiving and knowing the ideas of sensible things; but I could not use it unless there also existed, either in me or in something else, a certain active faculty of producing or bringing about these ideas. But this faculty surely cannot be in me, since it clearly presupposes no act of understanding, and these ideas are produced without my cooperation and often even against my will. Therefore the only alternative is that it is in some substance different from me, containing either formally or eminently all the reality that exists objectively in the ideas produced by that faculty, as I have just noted above. Hence this substance is either a body, that is, a corporeal nature, which contains formally all that is contained objectively in the ideas, or else it is God, or some other creature more noble than a body, which contains eminently all that is contained objectively in the ideas. But since God is not a deceiver, it is patently obvious that he does not send me these ideas either immediately by himself, or even through the mediation of some creature that contains the objective reality of these ideas not formally but only eminently. For since God has given me no faculty whatsoever for making this determination, but instead has given me a great inclination to believe that these ideas issue from corporeal things, I fail to see how God could be understood not to be a deceiver, if these ideas were to issue from a source other than corporeal things. And consequently corporeal things exist. Nevertheless, perhaps not all bodies exist exactly as I grasp them by sense, since this sensory grasp is in many cases very obscure and confused. But at least they do contain everything I clearly and distinctly understand—that is, everything, considered in a general sense, that is encompassed in the object of pure mathematics.

As far as the remaining matters are concerned,

which are either merely particular (for example, that the sun is of such and such a size or shape, and so on) or less clearly understood (for example, light, sound, pain, and the like), even though these matters are very doubtful and uncertain, nevertheless the fact that God is no deceiver (and thus no falsity can be found in my opinions, unless there is also in me a faculty given me by God for the purpose of rectifying this falsity) offers me a definite hope of reaching the truth even in these matters. And surely there is no doubt that all that I am taught by nature has some truth to it; for by "nature," taken generally, I understand nothing other than God himself or the ordered network of created things which was instututed by God. By my own particular nature I understand nothing other than the combination of all the things bestowed upon me by God.

There is nothing that this nature teaches me more explicitly thn that I have a bosy that is ill-disposed when I feel pain, that needs food and drink when I suffer hunger or thirst, and the like. Therefore, I should not doubt that there is some truth in this.

By means of these sensations of pain, hunger, thirst and so on, nature also teaches that I am present not merely to my body in the way a sailor is present in a ship, but that I am most tightly joined and, so to speak, commingled with it, so much so that I and the body constitute one single thing. For if this were not the case, then I, who am only a thinking thing, would not sense pain when the body is injured; rather, I would perceive the wound by means of the pure intellect, just as a sailor perceives by sight whether anything in his ship is broken. And when the body is in need of food or drink, I should understand this explicitly, instead of having confused sensations of hunger and thirst. For clearly these sensations of thirst, hunger, pain, and so on are nothing but certain confused modes of thinking arising from the union and, as it were, the commingling of the mind with the body.

Moreover, I am also taught by nature that various other bodies exist around my body, some of which are to be pursued, while others are to be avoided. And to be sure, from the fact that I sense a wide variety of colors, sounds, odors, tastes, levels of heat, and grades of roughness, and the like, I rightly conclude that in the bodies from which these different perceptions of the senses proceed there are differences corresponding to the different perceptions—though perhaps the latter do not resemble the former. And from the fact that some of these perceptions are pleasant while others are unpleasant, it is plainly certain that my body, or rather my whole self, insofar as I am comprised of a body and a mind, can be affected by various beneficial and harmful bodies in the vicinity.

Granted, there are many other things that I seem to have been taught by nature; nevertheless it was not really nature that taught them to me but a certain habit of making reckless judgments. And thus it could easily happen that these judgments are false: for example, that any space where there is absolutely nothing happening to move my senses is empty; or that there is something in a hot body that bears an exact likeness to the idea of heat that is in me; or that in a white or green body there is the same whiteness or greenness that I sense; or that in a bitter or sweet body there is the same taste, and so on; or that stars and towers and any other distant bodies have the same size and shape that they present to my sense, and other things of this sort. But to ensure that my perceptions in this matter are sufficiently distinct, I ought to define more precisely what exactly I mean when I say that I am "taught something by nature." For I am taking "nature" here more narrowly than the combination of everything betowed on me by God. For this combination embraces many things that belong exclusively to my mind, such as my perceiving that what has been done cannot be undone, and everything else that is known by the light of nature. That is not what I am talking about here. There are also many things that belong excusively to the body, such as that it tends to move downward, and so on. I am not dealing with these either, but only with what God has bestowed on me insofar as I am comprised of mind and body. Accordingly, it is this nature that teaches me to avoid things that produce a sensation of pain and to pursue things that produce a sensation of pleasure, and the like. But it does not appear that nature teaches us to conclude anything, besides these things, from these sense perceptions unless the intellect has first conducated its own inquiry regarding things external to us. For it seems to belong exclusively to the mind, and not to the composite of mind and body, to know the truth in these matters. Thus, although a star affects my eye no more than does the flame from a small torch, still there is no real or positive tendency in my eye toward believing that the star is no larger than the flame. Yet, ever since my youth, I have made this judgment without any reason for doing so. And although I feel heat as I draw closer to the fire, and I also feel pain upon drawing too close to it, there is not a single argument that persuades me that there is something in the fire similar to that heat, any more than to that pain. On the contrary, I am convinced only that there is something in the fire that, regardless of what it finally turns out to be, causes in us those sensations of heat or pain. And although there may be nothing in a given space that moves the senses, it does not therefore follow that there is no body in it. But I see that in these and many other instances I have been in the habit of subverting the order of nature. For admittedly I use the perceptions of the senses (which are properly given by nature only for signifying to the mind what things are useful or harmful to the composite of which it is a part, and to that extent they are clear and distinct enough) as reliable rules for immediately discerning what is the essence of bodies located outside us. Yet they signify nothing about that except quite obscurely and confusedly.

I have already examined in sufficient detail how it could happen that my judgments are false, despite the goodness of God. But a new difficulty now arises regarding those very things that nature shows me are either to be sought out or avoided, as well as the internal sensations where I seem to have detected errors, as for example, when someone is deluded by a food's pleasant taste to eat the poison hidden inside it. In this case, however, he is driven by nature only toward desiring the thing in which the pleasurable taste is found, but not toward the poison, of which he obviously is unaware. I can only conclude that this nature is not omniscient. This is not remarkable, since man is a limited thing, and thus only what is of limited perfection befits him.

But we not infrequently err even in those things to which nature impels us. Take, for example, the case of those who are ill and who desire food or drink that will soon afterwards be injurious to them. Perhaps it could be said here that they erred because their nature was corrupt. However, this does not remove our difficulty, for a sick man is no less a creature of God than a healthy one, and thus it seems no less inconsistent that the sick man got a deception-prone nature from God. And a clock made of wheels and counter-weights follows all the laws of nature no less closely when it has been badly constructed and does not tell time accurately than it does when it completely satisfies the wish of its maker. Likewise, I might regard a man's body as a kind of mechanism that is outfitted with and composed of bones, nerves, muscles, veins, blood and skin in such a way that, even if no mind existed in it, the man's body would still exhibit all the same motions that are in it now except for those motions that proceed either from a command of the will or, consequently, from the mind. I easily recognize that it would be natural for this body, were it, say, suffering from dropsy and experiencing dryness in the throat (which typically produces a thirst sensation in the mind), and also so disposed by its nerves and other parts to take something to drink, the result of which would be to exacerbate the illness. This is as natural as for a body without any such illness to be moved by the same dryness in the throat to take something to drink that is useful to it. And given the intended purpose of the clock, I could say that it deviates from its nature when it fails to tell the right time. And similarly, considering the mechanism of the human body in terms of its being equipped for the motions that typically occur in it, I may think that it too is deviating from its nature, if its throat were dry when having something to drink is not beneficial to its conservation. Nevertheless, I am well aware that this last use of "nature" differs greatly from the other. For this latter "nature" is merely a designation dependent on my thought, since it compares a man in poor health and a poorly constructed clock with the ideas of a healthy man and of a well-made clock, a designation extrinsic to the things to which it is applied. But by "nature" taken in the former sense, I understand something that is really in things, and thus is not without some truth.

When we say, then, in the case of the body suffering from dropsy, that its "nature" is corrupt, given the fact that it has a parched throat and yet does not need something to drink, "nature" obviously is merely an extrinsic designation. Nevertheless, in the case of the composite, that is, of a mind joined to such a body, it is not a pure designation, but a true error of nature that this body should be thirsty when having something to drink would be harmful to it. It therefore remains to inquire here how the goodness of God does not prevent "nature," thus considered, from being deceptive.

Now my first observation here is that there is a great difference between a mind and a body in that a body, by its very nature, is always divisible. On the other hand, the mind is utterly indivisible. For when I consider the mind, that is, myself insofar as I am only a thinking thing, I cannot distinguish any parts within me; rather, I understand myself to be manifestly one complete thing. Although the entire mind seems to be united to the entire body, nevertheless, were a foot or an arm or any other bodily part to be amputated, I know that nothing has been taken away from the mind on that account. Nor can the faculties of willing, sensing, understanding, and so on be called "parts" of the mind, since it is one and the same mind that wills, senses, and understands. On the other hand, there is no corporeal or extended thing I can think of that I may not in my thought easily divide into parts; and in this way I understand that it is divisible. This consideration alone would suffice to teach me that the mind is wholly diverse from the body, had I not yet known it well enough in any other way.

My second observation is that my mind is not immediately affected by all the parts of the body, but only by the brain, or perhaps even by just one small part of the brain, namely, by that part where the "common" sense is said to reside. Whenever this part of the brain is disposed in the same manner, it presents the same thing to the mind, even if the other parts of the body are able meanwhile to be related in diverse ways. Countless experiments show this, none of which need be reviewed here.

My next observation is that the nature of the body is such that whenever any of its parts can be moved by another part some distance away, it can also be moved in the same manner by any of the parts that lie between them, even if this more distant part is doing nothing. For example, in the cord ABCD, if the final part D is pulled, the first part A would be moved in exactly the same manner as it could be, if one of the intermediate parts B or C were pulled, while the end part D remained immobile. Likewise, when I feel a pain in my foot, physics teaches me that this sensation took place by means of nerves distributed throughout the foot, like stretched cords extending from the foot all the way to the brain. When these nerves are pulled in the foot, they also pull on the inner parts of the brain to which they extend, and produce a certain motion in them. This motion has been constituted by nature so as to affect the mind with a sensation of pain, as if it occurred in the foot. But because these nerves need to pass through the skin, thigh, loins, back, and neck to get from the foot to the brain, it can happen that even if it is not the part in the foot but merely one of the intermediate parts that is being struck, the very same movement will occur in the brain that would occur were the foot badly injured. The inevitable result will be that the mind feels the same pain. The same opinion should hold for any other sensation.

My final observation is that, since any given motion occurring in that part of the brain immediately affecting the mind produces but one sensation in it, I can think of no better arrangement than that it produces the one sensation that, of all the ones it is able to produce, is most especially and most often conducive to the maintenance of a healthy man. Moreover, experience shows that all the sensations bestowed on us by nature are like this. Hence there is absolutely nothing to be found in them that does not bear witness to God's power and goodness. Thus, for example, when the nerves in the foot are agitated in a violent and unusual manner, this motion of theirs extends through the marrow of the spine to the inner reaches of the brain, where it gives the mind the sign to sense something, namely, the pain as if it is occurring in the foot. This provokes the mind to do its utmost to move away from the cause of the pain, since it is seen as harmful to the foot. But the nature of man could have been so constituted by God that this same motion in the brain might have indicated something else to the mind: for example, either the motion itself as it occurs in the brain, or in the foot, or in some place in between, or something else entirely different. But nothing else would have served so well the maintenance of the body. Similarly, when we need something to drink, a certain dryness arises in the throat that moves the nerves in the throat, and, by means of them, the inner parts of the brain. And this motion affects the mind with a sensation of thirst, because in this entire affair nothing is more useful for us to know than that we need something to drink in order to maintain our health; the same holds in the other cases.

From these considerations it is utterly apparent that, notwithstanding the immense goodness of God, the nature of man, insofar as it is composed of mind and body, cannot help being sometimes mistaken. For if some cause, not in the foot but in some other part through which the nerves extend from the foot to the brain, or perhaps even in the brain itself, were to produce the same motion that would normally be produced by a badly injured foot, the pain will be felt as if it were in the foot, and the senses will naturally be deceived. For since an identical motion in the brain can only bring about an identical sensation in the mind, and it is more frequently the case that this motion is wont to arise on account of a cause that harms the foot than on account of some other thing existing elsewhere, it is reasonable that the motion should always show pain to the mind as something belonging to the foot rather than to some other part. And if dryness in the throat does not arise, as is normal, because taking something to drink contributes to bodily health, but from a contrary cause, as happens in the case of someone with dropsy, then it is far better that it should deceive on that occasion than that it should always be deceptive when the body is in good health. The same holds for the other cases.

This consideration is most helpful, not only for my noticing all the errors to which my nature is liable, but also for enabling me to correct or avoid them without difficulty. To be sure, I know that all the senses set forth what is true more frequently than what is false regarding what concerns the welfare of the body. Moreover, I can nearly always make use of several of them in order to examine the same thing. Furthermore, I can use my memory, which connects current happenings with past ones, and my intellect, which now has examined all the causes of error. Hence I should no longer fear that those things that are daily shown me by the senses are false. On the contrary, the hyperbolic doubts of the last few days ought to be rejected as ludicrous. This goes especially for the chief reason for doubting, which dealt with my failure to distinguish being asleep from being awake. For I now notice that there is a considerable difference between these two; dreams are never joined by the memory with all the other actions of life, as is the case with those actions that occur when one is awake. For surely, if, while I am awake, someone were suddenly to appear to me and then immediately disappear, as occurs in dreams, so that I see neither where he came from nor where he went, it is not without reason that I would judge him to be a ghost or a phantom conjured up in my brain, rather than a true man. But when these things happen, and I notice distinctly where they come from, where they are now, and when they come to me, and when I connect my perception of them without interruption with the whole rest of my life, I am clearly certain that these perceptions have happened to me not while I was dreaming but while I was awake. Nor ought I have even the least doubt regarding the truth of these things, if, having mustered all the senses, in addition to my memory and my intellect, in order to examine them, nothing is passed on to me by one of these sources that conflicts with the others. For from the fact that God is no deceiver, it follows that I am in no way mistaken in these matters. But because the need to get things done does not always permit us the leisure for such a careful inquiry, we must confess that the life of man is apt to commit errors regarding particular things, and we must acknowledge the infirmity of our nature.

Thomas Hobbes

Thomas Hobbes (1588–1679) was born in Malmesbury, Wiltshire, England. Raised by a well-to-do uncle, he entered Oxford at the age of fourteen and received his bachelor's degree in 1608. His early interests were largely classical. In 1629, however, on a visit to the continent his imagination was captured by the method of geometry, in which he saw a superior way of arriving at certain truths. In his masterpiece, *Leviathan*, Hobbes remarks that geometry is "the only science that it hath pleased God hitherto to bestow upon mankind." On another continental visit, from 1634 through 1637, Hobbes met Galileo in Italy, conversed frequently with eminent thinkers in Paris, and formulated the outlines of his own philosophical position. Returning to England in 1637, he became increasingly concerned about the impending civil war there. His support of monarchy and his fear of the parliamentarians led him to flee to Holland in 1640. Thereafter, Hobbes remained on the continent for eleven productive years, spending a part of this time tutoring the future Charles II. His final years in England, from 1650 on, were marked by continuing controversy over his views and by the banning of his books.

Hobbes' earlier works include the *Little Treatise*, a discussion of sensation (written between 1630 and 1637), and *Elements of Law* (1640), in which he argues for an undivided sovereignty. His masterpiece, *Leviathan* (1651), is a treatise on "the matter, forme, and power of a commonwealth, ecclesiasticall and civil." Among his other works are a trilogy that includes *De Cive* (1642), *De Corpore* (1655), and *De Homine* (1657); *Of Liberty and Necessity* (published without his consent in 1654); and a historical work, *Behemoth* (1668).

Although *Leviathan* is best known as a contribution to political philosophy, it is really a multifaceted work, containing important insights into metaphysics and psychology. Since Hobbes recognized that any adequate theory of government must grow out of a sound conception of the governed, he attempted to develop a comprehensive view of human life from a mechanistic and materialistic base. *Leviathan* thus begins with the claim that sensation is nothing but motion in the appropriate bodily parts, and that the various forms of imagination that we call "memory," "dream," and "apparition" are all echoes of this initial motion. They are, in Hobbes' own vivid phrase, "decaying sense." Associations between thoughts are echoes of connections between past motions; and desire and aversion, the antecedents of action, are the "small beginnings of motion, within the body of man, before they appear in walking, speaking, striking, and other visible actions." Although the details of this materialistic account are crude, the views expressed are recognizable ancestors of views hotly debated today.

Hobbes' political philosophy takes as its starting point an extremely pessimistic view of human nature. According to Hobbes, the basic motivation of humankind is "a perpetual and restless desire of power after power, that ceaseth only in death." Given the universality of this desire for power, life in the state of nature, before the imposition of civil laws backed by sovereign force, must be a perpetual struggle for possessions, supremacy, and glory. In this state, the outcome of one's productive efforts is always uncertain, and life is "solitary, poor, nasty, brutish and short." To avoid this intolerable situation, the law of nature, which dictates self-preservation, commands people to surrender their liberty (although not their ability to defend their lives or persons) to a single sovereign. By covenanting, or contracting, to lend their force to the sovereign's endeavors, they first create the conditions under which the enforcement of laws, and so too the institutions of property and justice, are possible. Thus is born Leviathan, the great artificial being of the commonwealth, whose very soul is sovereignty.

Hobbes' account does not point inevitably to any single form of government. He allows that the sovereignty may reside in a single ruler (monarchy), a group (aristocracy), or the entire population (democracy). He does insist, however, that whatever form the sovereign body takes, its power must be absolute. The reason for this is that the purpose of the original covenant is to create an authority strong enough to protect each member of the populace from the incursions of the others. Given this initial intent, any attempt to separate from the sovereign the abilities to tax, legislate, or deploy the military; to challenge or punish the sovereign's acts; or in any other way to limit his power must violate the original agreement. There may be a risk that the sovereign will abuse his power but for Hobbes this risk is far outweighed by the secure and orderly existence that that power makes possible.

• • •

For a good discussion of Hobbes' life and philosophy, see R. S. Peters, *Hobbes* (Baltimore: Penguin Books, 1956). A number of interesting shorter pieces are collected in Keith Brown, ed., *Hobbes Studies* (Cambridge, Mass.: Harvard University Press, 1965). Two important works are Michael Oakshott, *Hobbes on Civil Association* (Berkeley: University of California Press, 1975) and Leo Strauss, *The Political Philosophy of Hobbes* (1936; rpt. Oxford: Oxford University Press, 1963). An influential study of Hobbes' political and moral philosophy is Howard Warrender, *The Political Philosophy of Thomas Hobbes* (Oxford: Oxford University Press, 1957). Hobbes' work is placed in its historical context in Jean Hampton, *Hobbes and the Social Contract Tradition* (New York: Cambridge University Press, 1986). Also noteworthy is Gregory S. Kavka, *Hobbesian Moral and Political Theory* (Princeton: Princeton University Press, 1986).

George Sher

Leviathan

THE INTRODUCTION

[1] Nature (the art whereby God hath made and governs the world) is by the *art* of man, as in many other things, so in this also imitated, that it can make an artificial animal. For seeing life is but a motion of limbs, the beginning whereof is in some principal part within, why may we not say that all *automata* (engines that move themselves by springs and wheels as doth a watch) have an artificial life? For what is the *heart*, but a *spring*; and the *nerves*, but so many *strings*; and the *joints*, but so many *wheels*, giving motion to the whole body, such as was intended by the artificer? *Art* goes yet further, imitating that rational and most excellent work of nature, *man*. For by art is created that great LEVIATHAN[1] called a COMMONWEALTH, or STATE (in Latin CIVITAS), which is but an artificial man, though of greater stature and strength than the natural, for whose protection and defence it was intended; and in which the *sovereignty* is an artificial soul, as giving life and motion to the whole body; the *magistrates* and other *officers* of judicature and execution, artificial *joints*; *reward* and *punishment* (by which fastened to the seat of the sovereignty every joint and member is moved to perform his duty) are the *nerves*, that do the same in the body natural; the *wealth* and *riches* of all the particular members are the *strength*; *salus populi* (the people's safety) its *business*; *counsellors*, by whom all things needful for it to know are suggested unto it, are the *memory*; *equity* and *laws*, an artificial *reason* and *will*; *concord*, *health*; *sedition*, *sickness*; and *civil war*, *death*. Lastly, the *pacts* and *covenants* by which the parts of this body politic were at first made, set together, and united, resemble that *fiat*, or the *let us make man*, pronounced by God in the creation.

[2] To describe the nature of this artificial man, I will consider

First, the *matter* thereof, and the *artificer*, both which is *man*.

Secondly, *how* and by what *covenants* it is made; what are the *rights* and *just power* or *authority* of a *sovereign*; and what it is that *preserveth* and *dissolveth* it.

Thirdly, what is a *Christian commonwealth*.

Lastly, what is the *kingdom of darkness*.

[3] Concerning the first, there is a saying much usurped of late, that *wisdom* is acquired, not by reading of *books*, but of *men*. Consequently whereunto, those persons that for the most part can give no other proof of being wise take great delight to show what they think they have read in men, by uncharitable censures of one another behind their backs. But there is another saying not of late understood, by which they might learn truly to read one another, if they would take the pains; and that is, *nosce teipsum*, *read thy self*, which was not meant, as it is now used, to countenance either the barbarous state of men in power towards their inferiors, or to encourage men of low degree to a saucy behaviour towards their betters, but to teach us that for the similitude of the thoughts and passions of one man to the thoughts and passions of another, whosoever looketh into himself and considereth what he doth, when he does *think*, *opine*, *reason*, *hope*, *fear*, &c, and upon what grounds, he shall thereby read and know, what are the thoughts and passions of all other men upon the like occasions. I say the similitude of *passions*, which are the same in all men, *desire*, *fear*, *hope*, &c, not the similitude of the *objects* of the passions, which are the things *desired*, *feared*, *hoped*, &c; for these the constitution individual and particular education do so vary, and they are so easy to be kept from our knowledge, that the characters of man's heart, blotted and confounded as they are with dissembling, lying, counterfeiting, and erroneous doctrines, are legible only to him that searcheth hearts. And though by

1. [The leviathan was a biblical sea monster.—S.M.C.]

men's actions we do discover their design sometimes, yet to do it without comparing them with our own, and distinguishing all circumstances by which the case may come to be altered, is to decipher without a key, and be for the most part deceived, by too much trust, or by too much diffidence, as he that reads is himself a good or evil man.

[4] But let one man read another by his actions never so perfectly, it serves him only with his acquaintance, which are but few. He that is to govern a whole nation must read in himself, not this or that particular man, but mankind, which though it be hard to do, harder than to learn any language or science, yet when I shall have set down my own reading orderly and perspicuously, the pains left another will be only to consider if he also find not the same in himself. For this kind of doctrine admitteth no other demonstration.

Part One
OF MAN
CHAPTER 1
Of *Sense*

[1] Concerning the thoughts of man, I will consider them first *singly*, and afterwards in *train*, or dependence upon one another. *Singly*, they are every one a *representation* or *appearance*, of some quality or other accident, of a body without us, which is commonly called an *object*. Which object worketh on the eyes, ears, and other parts of a man's body, and by diversity of working produceth diversity of appearances.

[2] The original of them all is that which we call SENSE. (For there is no conception in a man's mind which hath not at first, totally or by parts, been begotten upon the organs of sense.) The rest are derived from that original.

[3] To know the natural cause of sense is not very necessary to the business now in hand, and I have elsewhere written of the same at large. Nevertheless, to fill each part of my present method, I will briefly deliver the same in this place.

[4] The cause of sense is the external body, or object, which presseth the organ proper to each sense, either immediately, as in the taste and touch, or mediately, as in seeing, hearing, and smelling; which pressure, by the mediation of nerves and other strings and membranes of the body, continued inwards to the brain and heart, causeth there a resistance, or counter-pressure, or endeavour of the heart to deliver itself; which endeavour, because *outward*, seemeth to be some matter without. And this *seeming*, or *fancy*, is that which men call *sense*; and consisteth, as to the eye, in a *light* or *colour figured*; to the ear, in a *sound*; to the nostril, in an *odour*; to the tongue and palate, in a *savour*; and to the rest of the body, in *heat, cold, hardness, softness*, and such other qualities as we discern by *feeling*. All which qualities called *sensible* are in the object that causeth them but so many several motions of the matter, by which it presseth our organs diversely. Neither in us that are pressed are they anything else but divers motions (for motion produceth nothing but motion). But their appearance to us is fancy, the same waking that dreaming. And as pressing, rubbing, or striking the eye, makes us fancy a light, and pressing the ear, produceth a din, so do the bodies also we see, or hear, produce the same by their strong, though unobserved action. For if those colours and sounds were in the bodies, or objects, that cause them, they could not be severed from them, as by glasses, and in echoes by reflection, we see they are, where we know the thing we see is in one place, the appearance in another. And though at some certain distance the real and very object seem invested with the fancy it begets in us, yet still the object is one thing, the image or fancy is another. So that sense in all cases, is nothing else but original fancy, caused (as I have said) by the pressure, that is, by the motion, of external things upon our eyes, ears, and other organs thereunto ordained.

[5] But the philosophy-schools, through all the universities of Christendom, grounded upon certain texts of *Aristotle*, teach another doctrine, and say, for the cause of *vision*, that the thing seen sendeth forth on every side a *visible species* (in English, a *visible show, apparition*, or *aspect*, or a *being seen*), the receiving whereof into the eye is *seeing*. And for the cause of *hearing*, that the thing heard sendeth forth an *audible species*, that is, an *audible aspect*, or *audible being seen*, which entering at the ear maketh *hearing*. Nay for the cause of *understanding* also, they say the thing understood sendeth forth *intelligible species*, that is, an *intelligible being seen*, which coming into

the understanding makes us understand. I say not this as disapproving the use of universities; but because I am to speak hereafter of their office in a commonwealth, I must let you see on all occasions by the way, what things would be amended in them, amongst which the frequency of insignificant speech is one.

CHAPTER II

Of *Imagination*

[1] That when a thing lies still, unless somewhat else stir it, it will lie still for ever, is a truth that no man doubts of. But that when a thing is in motion, it will eternally be in motion, unless somewhat else stay it, though the reason be the same (namely, that nothing can change itself), is not so easily assented to. For men measure, not only other men, but all other things, by themselves; and because they find themselves subject after motion to pain and lassitude, think everything else grows weary of motion and seeks repose of its own accord, little considering whether it be not some other motion wherein that desire of rest they find in themselves consisteth. From hence it is that the schools say heavy bodies fall downwards out of an appetite to rest, and to conserve their nature in that place which is most proper for them, ascribing appetite and knowledge of what is good for their conservation (which is more than man has) to things inanimate, absurdly.

[2] When a body is once in motion, it moveth (unless something else hinder it) eternally; and whatsoever hindreth it, cannot in an instant, but in time and by degrees, quite extinguish it. And as we see in the water, though the wind cease, the waves give not over rolling for a long time after, so also it happeneth in that motion which is made in the internal parts of a man, then when he sees, dreams, &c. For after the object is removed, or the eye shut, we still retain an image of the thing seen, though more obscure than when we see it. And this is it, the Latins call *imagination*, from the image made in seeing, and apply the same, though improperly, to all the other senses. But the Greeks call it *fancy*, which signifies *appearance*, and is as proper to one sense as to another. IMAGINATION therefore is nothing but *decaying sense*, and is found in men and many other living creatures, as well sleeping as waking.

[3] The decay of sense in men waking is not the decay of the motion made in sense, but an obscuring of it, in such manner as the light of the sun obscureth the light of the stars; which stars do no less exercise their virtue, by which they are visible, in the day than in the night. But because amongst many strokes which our eyes, ears, and other organs receive from external bodies, the predominant only is sensible, therefore the light of the sun being predominant, we are not affected with the action of the stars. And any object being removed from our eyes, though the impression it made in us remain, yet other objects more present succeeding and working on us, the imagination of the past is obscured and made weak, as the voice of a man is in the noise of the day.

From whence it followeth that the longer the time is after the sight or sense of any object, the weaker is the imagination. For the continual change of man's body destroys in time the parts which in sense were moved, so that distance of time and of place hath one and the same effect in us. For as, at a great distance of place, that which we look at appears dim and without distinction of the smaller parts, and as voices grow weak and inarticulate, so also, after great distance of time, our imagination of the past is weak, and we lose (for example) of cities we have seen, many particular streets, and of actions, many particular circumstances. This *decaying sense*, when we would express the thing itself (I mean *fancy* itself), we call *imagination*, as I said before; but when we would express the *decay*, and signify that the sense is fading, old, and past, it is called *memory*. So that *imagination* and *memory* are but one thing, which for diverse considerations hath diverse names.

[4] Much memory, or memory of many things, is called *experience*. Again, imagination being only of those things which have been formerly perceived by sense, either all at once or by parts at several times, the former (which is the imagining the whole object, as it was presented to the sense) is *simple imagination*; as when one imagineth a man, or horse, which he hath seen before. The other is *compounded*; as when from the sight of a man at one time, and of a horse at another, we conceive in our mind a Centaur. So when a man compoundeth the image of his own person with the image of the actions of another man, as when a man imagines himself a *Hercules* or an *Alexander* (which happeneth often to them that are

much taken with reading of romances), it is a compound imagination, and properly but a fiction of the mind. There be also other imaginations that rise in men (though waking) from the great impression made in sense, as from gazing upon the sun, the impression leaves an image of the sun before our eyes a long time after; and from being long and vehemently attent upon geometrical figures, a man shall in the dark (though awake) have the images of lines and angles before his eyes, which kind of fancy hath no particular name, as being a thing that doth not commonly fall into men's discourse.

[5] The imaginations of them that sleep are those we call *dreams*. And these also (as all other imaginations) have been before, either totally or by parcels, in the sense. And because the brain and nerves, which are the necessary organs of sense, are so benumbed in sleep as not easily to be moved by the action of external objects, there can happen in sleep no imagination, and therefore no dream, but what proceeds from the agitation of the inward parts of man's body, which inward parts, for the connexion they have with the brain and other organs, when they be distempered, do keep the same in motion; whereby the imaginations there formerly made appear as if a man were waking, saving that the organs of sense being now benumbed, so as there is no new object which can master and obscure them with a more vigorous impression, a dream must needs be more clear, in this silence of sense, than are our waking thoughts. And hence it cometh to pass, that it is a hard matter, and by many thought impossible, to distinguish exactly between sense and dreaming. For my part, when I consider that in dreams I do not often, nor constantly, think of the same persons, places, objects, and actions that I do waking, nor remember so long a train of coherent thoughts dreaming as at other times, and because waking I often observe the absurdity of dreams, but never dream of the absurdities of my waking thoughts, I am well satisfied that being awake I know I dream not, though when I dream, I think myself awake.

[6] And seeing dreams are caused by the distemper of some of the inward parts of the body, diverse distempers must needs cause different dreams. And hence it is that lying cold breedeth dreams of fear and raiseth the thought and image of some fearful object (the motion from the brain to the inner parts, and from the inner parts to the brain, being reciprocal); and that as anger causeth heat in some parts of the body when we are awake, so when we sleep the overheating of the same parts causeth anger and raiseth up in the brain the imagination of an enemy. In the same manner as natural kindness, when we are awake, causeth desire, and desire makes heat in certain other parts of the body, so also too much heat in those parts, while we sleep, raiseth in the brain an imagination of some kindness shown. In sum, our dreams are the reverse of our waking imaginations, the motion when we are awake beginning at one end, and when we dream at another.

[7] The most difficult discerning of a man's dream from his waking thoughts is then, when by some accident we observe not that we have slept, which is easy to happen to a man full of fearful thoughts, and whose conscience is much troubled, and that sleepeth without the circumstances of going to bed, or putting off his clothes, as one that noddeth in a chair. For he that taketh pains, and industriously lays himself to sleep, in case any uncouth and exorbitant fancy come unto him, cannot easily think it other than a dream. We read of *Marcus Brutus* (one that had his life given him by *Julius Caesar*, and was also his favourite, and notwithstanding murdered him), how at *Philippi*, the night before he gave battle to *Augustus Caesar*, he saw a fearful apparition, which is commonly related by historians as a vision, but considering the circumstances, one may easily judge to have been but a short dream. For sitting in his tent, pensive and troubled with the horror of his rash act, it was not hard for him, slumbering in the cold, to dream of that which most affrighted him, which fear, as by degrees it made him wake, so also it must needs make the apparition by degrees to vanish; and having no assurance that he slept, he could have no cause to think it a dream, or anything but a vision. And this is no very rare accident; for even they that be perfectly awake, if they be timorous and superstitious, possessed with fearful tales and alone in the dark, are subject to the like fancies, and believe they see spirits and dead men's ghosts walking in churchyards; whereas it is either their fancy only, or else the knavery of such persons as make use of such superstitious fear to pass disguised in the night to places they would not be known to haunt.

[8] From this ignorance of how to distinguish

dreams and other strong fancies from vision and sense did arise the greatest part of the religion of the gentiles in times past, that worshipped satyrs, fawns, nymphs, and the like; and now-a-days the opinion that rude people have of fairies, ghosts, and goblins, and of the power of witches. For as for witches, I think not that their witchcraft is any real power, but yet that they are justly punished, for the false belief they have that they can do such mischief, joined with their purpose to do it if they can, their trade being nearer to a new religion than to a craft or science. And for fairies and walking ghosts, the opinion of them has I think been on purpose, either taught or not confuted, to keep in credit the use of exorcism, of crosses, of holy water, and other such inventions of ghostly men.

Nevertheless, there is no doubt but God can make unnatural apparitions. But that he does it so often as men need to fear such things more than they fear the stay or change of the course of nature, which he also can stay and change, is no point of Christian faith. But evil men, under pretext that God can do anything, are so bold as to say anything when it serves their turn, though they think it untrue; it is the part of a wise man to believe them no further than right reason makes that which they say appear credible. If this superstitious fear of spirits were taken away, and with it prognostics from dreams, false prophecies, and many other things depending thereon, by which crafty ambitious persons abuse the simple people, men would be much more fitted than they are for civil obedience.

[9] And this ought to be the work of the schools; but they rather nourish such doctrine. For (not knowing what imagination or the senses are) what they receive, they teach, some saying that imaginations rise of themselves and have no cause, others that they rise most commonly from the will, and that good thoughts are blown (inspired) into a man by God, and evil thoughts by the Devil, or that good thoughts are poured (infused) into a man by God, and evil ones by the Devil. Some say the senses receive the species of things and deliver them to the common sense, and the common sense delivers them over to the fancy, and the fancy to the memory, and the memory to the judgment, like handing of things from one to another, with many words making nothing understood.

[10] The imagination that is raised in man (or any other creature endued with the faculty of imagining) by words or other voluntary signs is that we generally call *understanding*, and is common to man and beast. For a dog by custom will understand the call or the rating of his master; and so will many other beasts. That understanding which is peculiar to man is the understanding not only his will, but his conceptions and thoughts, by the sequel and contexture of the names of things into affirmations, negations, and other forms of speech; and of this kind of understanding I shall speak hereafter [cf. v, 6].

CHAPTER III

Of the Consequence or *Train* of Imaginations

[1] By *Consequence*, or TRAIN of thoughts, I understand that succession of one thought to another which is called (to distinguish it from discourse in words) *mental discourse*.

[2] When a man thinketh on anything whatsoever, his next thought after, is not altogether so casual as it seems to be. Not every thought to every thought succeeds indifferently. But as we have no imagination whereof we have not formerly had sense, in whole or in parts, so we have no transition from one imagination to another whereof we never had the like before in our senses. The reason whereof is this. All fancies are motions within us, relics of those made in the sense; and those motions that immediately succeed one another in the sense continue also together after sense, insomuch as the former coming again to take place and be predominant, the latter followeth by coherence of the matter moved, in such manner as water upon a plain table is drawn which way any one part of it is guided by the finger. But because in sense, to one and the same thing perceived, sometimes one thing, sometimes another succeedeth, it comes to pass in time that in the imagining of anything there is no certainty what we shall imagine next; only this is certain, it shall be something that succeeded the same before, at one time or another.

[3] This train of thoughts, or mental discourse, is of two sorts. The first is *unguided, without design*, and inconstant, wherein there is no passionate thought to govern and direct those that follow to itself, as the end and scope of some desire or other passion; in which case the thoughts are said to wander, and seem

impertinent one to another, as in a dream. Such are commonly the thoughts of men that are not only without company, but also without care of anything, though even then their thoughts are as busy as at other times, but without harmony, as the sound which a lute out of tune would yield to any man, or in tune, to one that could not play. And yet in this wild ranging of the mind, a man may oft-times perceive the way of it, and the dependence of one thought upon another. For in a discourse of our present civil war, what could seem more impertinent than to ask (as one did) what was the value of a Roman penny? Yet the coherence to me was manifest enough. For the thought of the war introduced the thought of the delivering up the king to his enemies; the thought of that brought in the thought of the delivering up of Christ; and that again the thought of the 30 pence which was the price of that treason; and thence easily followed that malicious question; and all this in a moment of time, for thought is quick.

[4] The second is more constant, as being *regulated* by some desire, and design. For the impression made by such things as we desire or fear is strong and permanent, or (if it cease for a time) of quick return; so strong it is sometimes as to hinder and break our sleep. From desire ariseth the thought of some means we have seen produce the like of that which we aim at; and from the thought of that, the thought of means to that mean; and so continually, till we come to some beginning within our own power. And because the end, by the greatness of the impression, comes often to mind, in case our thoughts begin to wander, they are quickly again reduced into the way; which, observed by one of the seven wise men, made him give men this precept, which is now worn out, *Respice finem*, that is to say, in all your actions, look often upon what you would have, as the thing that directs all your thoughts in the way to attain it.

[5] The train of regulated thoughts is of two kinds: one, when of an effect imagined, we seek the causes, or means that produce it; and this is common to man and beast. The other is when, imagining anything whatsoever, we seek all the possible effects that can by it be produced; that is to say, we imagine what we can do with it, when we have it. Of which I have not at any time seen any sign, but in man only; for this is a curiosity hardly incident to the nature of any living creature that has no other passion but sensual, such as are hunger, thirst, lust, and anger. In sum, the discourse of the mind, when it is governed by design, is nothing but *seeking*, or the faculty of invention, which the Latins called *sagacitas*, and *solertia*; a hunting out of the causes of some effect, present or past, or of the effects of some present or past cause. Sometimes a man seeks what he hath lost, and from that place and time wherein he misses it, his mind runs back, from place to place, and time to time, to find where and when he had it; that is to say, to find some certain and limited time and place in which to begin a method of seeking. Again, from thence his thoughts run over the same places and times, to find what action or other occasion might make him lose it. This we call *remembrance*, or calling to mind; the Latins call it *reminiscentia*, as it were a *re-conning* of our former actions.

[6] Sometimes a man knows a place determinate, within the compass whereof he is to seek; and then his thoughts run over all the parts thereof, in the same manner as one would sweep a room to find a jewel, or as a spaniel ranges the field till he find a scent, or as a man should run over the alphabet to start a rhyme.

[7] Sometimes a man desires to know the event of an action; and then he thinketh of some like action past, and the events thereof one after another, supposing like events will follow like actions. As he that foresees what will become of a criminal re-cons what he has seen follow on the like crime before, having this order of thoughts: the crime, the officer, the prison, the judge, and the gallows. Which kind of thoughts is called *foresight*, and *prudence*, or *providence*, and sometimes *wisdom*, though such conjecture, through the difficulty of observing all circumstances, be very fallacious. But this is certain: by how much one man has more experience of things past than another, by so much also he is more prudent, and his expectations the seldomer fail him. The *present* only has a being in nature; things *past* have a being in the memory only; but things *to come* have no being at all, the *future* being but a fiction of the mind, applying the sequels of actions past to the actions that are present; which with most certainty is done by him that has most experience, but not with certainty enough. And though it be called prudence when the event answereth our expectation, yet in its own nature it is but presumption. For the foresight

of things to come, which is providence, belongs only to him by whose will they are to come. From him only, and supernaturally, proceeds prophecy. The best prophet naturally is the best guesser; and the best guesser, he that is most versed and studied in the matters he guesses at, for he hath most *signs* to guess by.

[8] A *sign* is the event antecedent of the consequent, and contrarily, the consequent of the antecedent, when the like consequences have been observed before; and the oftener they have been observed, the less uncertain is the sign. And therefore he that has most experience in any kind of business has most signs whereby to guess at the future time, and consequently is the most prudent; and so much more prudent than he that is new in that kind of business, as not to be equalled by any advantage of natural and extemporary wit, though perhaps many young men think the contrary.

[9] Nevertheless it is not prudence that distinguisheth man from beast. There be beasts that at a year old observe more, and pursue that which is for their good more prudently, than a child can do at ten.

[10] As prudence is a *presumption* of the *future*, contracted from the *experience* of time *past*, so there is a presumption of things past taken from other things (not future but) past also. For he that hath seen by what courses and degrees a flourishing state hath first come into civil war and then to ruin, upon the sight of the ruins of any other state will guess the like war and the like courses have been there also. But this conjecture has the same uncertainty almost with the conjecture of the future, both being grounded only upon experience.

[11] There is no other act of man's mind that I can remember, naturally planted in him so as to need no other thing to the exercise of it but to be born a man, and live with the use of his five senses. Those other faculties of which I shall speak by and by, and which seem proper to man only, are acquired and increased by study and industry, and of most men learned by instruction and discipline, and proceed all from the invention of words and speech. For besides sense, and thoughts, and the train of thoughts, the mind of man has no other motion, though by the help of speech and method the same faculties may be improved to such a height as to distinguish men from all other living creatures.

[12] Whatsoever we imagine is *finite*. Therefore there is no idea or conception of anything we call *infinite*. No man can have in his mind an image of infinite magnitude, nor conceive infinite swiftness, infinite time, or infinite force, or infinite power. When we say anything is infinite, we signify only that we are not able to conceive the ends and bounds of the thing named, having no conception of the thing, but of our own inability. And therefore the name of *God* is used, not to make us conceive him (for he is *incomprehensible*, and his greatness and power are unconceivable), but that we may honour him. Also because whatsoever (as I said before) we conceive has been perceived first by sense, either all at once or by parts, a man can have no thought representing anything not subject to sense. No man therefore can conceive anything, but he must conceive it in some place, and endued with some determinate magnitude, and which may be divided into parts; nor that anything is all in this place, and all in another place at the same time; nor that two or more things can be in one and the same place at once; for none of these things ever have, or can be, incident to sense, but are absurd speeches, taken upon credit (without any signification at all) from deceived philosophers, and deceived or deceiving schoolmen.[2]

CHAPTER V

Of Reason, and Science

[1] When a man *reasoneth*, he does nothing else but conceive a sum total from *addition* of parcels, or conceive a remainder from *subtraction* of one sum from another; which (if it be done by words) is conceiving of the consequence of the names of all the parts to the name of the whole, or from the names of the whole and one part to the name of the other part. And though in some things (as in numbers) besides *adding* and *subtracting* men name other operations, as *multiplying* and *dividing*, yet they are the same; for multiplication is but adding together of things equal, and division, but subtracting of one thing as often as we can. These operations are not

2. [The term "schoolmen" was applied to medieval theologians and philosophers, often with a connotation of pedantry.]

incident to numbers only, but to all manner of things that can be added together and taken one out of another. For as arithmeticians teach to add and subtract in *numbers*, so the geometricians teach the same in *lines*, *figures* (solid and superficial), *angles*, *proportions*, *times*, degrees of *swiftness*, *force*, *power*, and the like; the logicians teach the same in *consequences of words*, adding together *two names* to make an *affirmation*, and *two affirmations* to make a *syllogism*; and *many syllogisms* to make a *demonstration*; and from the *sum*, or *conclusion*, of a *syllogism* they subtract one *proposition* to find the other. Writers of politics add together *pactions* to find men's *duties*; and lawyers, *laws* and *facts*, to find what is *right* and *wrong* in the actions of private men. In sum, in what matter soever there is place for *addition* and *subtraction*, there also is place for *reason*; and where these have no place, there *reason* has nothing at all to do.

[2] Out of all which we may define (that is to say determine) what that is which is meant by this word *reason*, when we reckon it amongst the faculties of the mind. For REASON, in this sense, is nothing but *reckoning* (that is, adding and subtracting) of the consequences of general names agreed upon for the *marking* and *signifying* of our thoughts; I say *marking* them when we reckon by ourselves, and *signifying*, when we demonstrate or approve our reckonings to other men.

[3] And as in arithmetic, unpractised men must, and professors themselves may, often err and cast up false, so also in any other subject of reasoning, the ablest, most attentive, and most practised men may deceive themselves and infer false conclusions; not but that reason itself is always right reason, as well as arithmetic is a certain and infallible art, but no one man's reason, nor the reason of any one number of men, makes the certainty, no more than an account is therefore well cast up, because a great many men have unanimously approved it. And therefore, as when there is a controversy in an account, the parties must by their own accord set up for right reason the reason of some arbitrator or judge to whose sentence they will both stand, or their controversy must either come to blows or be undecided, for want of a right reason constituted by nature, so is it also in all debates of what kind soever. And when men that think themselves wiser than all others clamour and demand right reason for judge, yet seek no more but that things should be determined by no other men's reason but their own, it is as intolerable in the society of men as it is in play, after trump is turned, to use for trump on every occasion that suit whereof they have most in their hand. For they do nothing else, that will have every of their passions, as it comes to bear sway in them, to be taken for right reason, and that in their own controversies, bewraying their want of right reason by the claim they lay to it.

[4] The use and end of reason is not the finding of the sum and truth of one or a few consequences, remote from the first definitions and settled significations of names, but to begin at these, and proceed from one consequence to another. For there can be no certainty of the last conclusion without a certainty of all those affirmations and negations on which it was grounded and inferred. As when a master of a family, in taking an account, casteth up the sums of all the bills of expense into one sum, and not regarding how each bill is summed up by those that give them in account, nor what it is he pays for, he advantages himself no more than if he allowed the account in gross, trusting to every of the accountants' skill and honesty, so also in reasoning of all other things, he that takes up conclusions on the trust of authors, and doth not fetch them from the first items in every reckoning (which are the significations of names settled by definitions), loses his labour, and does not know anything, but only believeth.

[5] When a man reckons without the use of words, which may be done in particular things (as when upon the sight of any one thing, we conjecture what was likely to have preceded, or is likely to follow upon it), if that which he thought likely to follow, follows not, or that which he thought likely to have preceded it, hath not preceded it, this is called ERROR, to which even the most prudent men are subject. But when we reason in words of general signification, and fall upon a general inference which is false, though it be commonly called *error*, it is indeed an ABSURDITY, or senseless speech. For error is but a deception, in presuming that somewhat is past, or to come, of which, though it were not past, or not to come, yet there was no impossibility discoverable. But when we make a general assertion, unless it be a true one, the possibility of it is inconceivable. And words whereby we conceive nothing but the sound are those we call *absurd*, *insignificant*, and *nonsense*. And therefore if

a man should talk to me of a *round quadrangle*, or *accidents of bread in cheese*, or *immaterial substances*, or of *a free subject*, *a free will*, or any *free*, but free from being hindered by opposition, I should not say he were in an error, but that his words were without meaning, that is to say, absurd.

[6] I have said before (in the second chapter [¶10]) that a man did excel all other animals in this faculty: that when he conceived anything whatsoever, he was apt to inquire the consequences of it, and what effects he could do with it. And now I add this other degree of the same excellence: that he can by words reduce the consequences he finds to general rules, called *theorems*, or *aphorisms*; that is, he can reason, or reckon, not only in number, but in all other things whereof one may be added unto or subtracted from another.

[7] But this privilege is allayed by another, and that is by the privilege of absurdity, to which no living creature is subject but man only. And of men, those are of all most subject to it that profess philosophy. For it is most true that *Cicero*[3] saith of them somewhere: that there can be nothing so absurd, but may be found in the books of philosophers. And the reason is manifest. For there is not one of them that begins his ratiocination from the definitions, or explications of the names they are to use; which is a method that hath been used only in geometry, whose conclusions have thereby been made indisputable.

[8] The first cause of absurd conclusions I ascribe to the want of method, in that they begin not their ratiocination from definitions, that is, from settled significations of their words, as if they could cast account without knowing the value of the numeral words, *one*, *two*, and *three*.

[9] And whereas all bodies enter into account upon diverse considerations [. . .] these considerations being diversely named, diverse absurdities proceed from the confusion and unfit connexion of their names into assertions. And therefore,

[10] The second cause of absurd assertions I ascribe to the giving of names of *bodies* to *accidents*, or of *accidents* to *bodies*, as they do that say *faith is infused* or *inspired*, when nothing can be *poured* or *breathed* into anything but body, and that *extension* is *body*, that *phantasms* are *spirits*, &c.

3. [Marcus Tullius Cicero (106–43 B.C.) was a Roman philosopher.]

[11] The third I ascribe to the giving of the names of the *accidents of bodies without us* to the *accidents* of our *own bodies*, as they do that say the *colour is in the body*, *the sound is in the air*, &c.

[12] The fourth, to the giving of the names of *bodies* to *names* or *speeches*, as they do that say that *there be things universal*, that *a living creature is genus*, or *a general thing*, &c.

[13] The fifth, to the giving of the names of *accidents* to *names* and *speeches*, as they do that say *the nature of a thing is its definition*, *a man's command is his will*, and the like.

[14] The sixth, to the use of metaphors, tropes, and other rhetorical figures, instead of words proper. For though it be lawful to say (for example) in common speech *the way goeth, or leadeth hither, or thither, the proverb says this or that* (whereas ways cannot go, nor proverbs speak), yet in reckoning and seeking of truth such speeches are not to be admitted.

[15] The seventh, to names that signify nothing, but are taken up and learned by rote from the schools, as *hypostatical*, *transubstantiate*, *consubstantiate*, *eternal-now*, and the like canting of schoolmen.

[16] To him that can avoid these things it is not easy to fall into any absurdity, unless it be by the length of an account, wherein he may perhaps forget what went before. For all men by nature reason alike, and well, when they have good principles. For who is so stupid as both to mistake in geometry, and also to persist in it when another detects his error to him?

[17] By this it appears that reason is not, as sense and memory, born with us, nor gotten by experience only, as prudence is, but attained by industry, first in apt imposing of names, and secondly by getting a good and orderly method in proceeding from the elements, which are names, to assertions made by connexion of one of them to another, and so to syllogisms, which are the connexions of one assertion to another, till we come to a knowledge of all the consequences of names appertaining to the subject in hand; and that is it men call SCIENCE. And whereas sense and memory are but knowledge of fact, which is a thing past and irrevocable, *Science* is the knowledge of consequences, and dependence of one fact upon another, by which, out of that we can presently do, we know how to do something else when we will, or the like, another time; because when we see how anything comes about, upon what causes, and by

what manner, when the like causes come into our power, we see how to make it produce the like effects.

[18] Children therefore are not endued with reason at all till they have attained the use of speech, but are called reasonable creatures for the possibility apparent of having the use of reason in time to come. And the most part of men, though they have the use of reasoning a little way, as in numbering to some degree, yet it serves them to little use in common life, in which they govern themselves, some better, some worse, according to their differences of experience, quickness of memory, and inclinations to several ends, but specially according to good or evil fortune, and the errors of one another. For as for *science*, or certain rules of their actions, they are so far from it that they know not what it is. Geometry they have thought conjuring; but for other sciences, they who have not been taught the beginnings and some progress in them, that they may see how they be acquired and generated, are in this point like children, that having no thought of generation are made believe by the women that their brothers and sisters are not born, but found in the garden.

[19] But yet they that have no *science* are in better and nobler condition with their natural prudence than men that by mis-reasoning, or by trusting them that reason wrong, fall upon false and absurd general rules. For ignorance of causes and of rules does not set men so far out of their way as relying on false rules, and taking for causes of what they aspire to, those that are not so, but rather causes of the contrary.

[20] To conclude, the light of human minds is perspicuous words, but by exact definitions first snuffed and purged from ambiguity; *reason* is the *pace*; increase of *science*, the *way*; and the benefit of mankind, the *end*. And on the contrary, metaphors, and senseless and ambiguous words, are like *ignes fatui* [a fool's fire], and reasoning upon them is wandering amongst innumerable absurdities; and their end, contention and sedition, or contempt.

[21] As much experience is *prudence*, so is much science *sapience*. For though we usually have one name of wisdom for them both, yet the Latins did always distinguish between *prudentia* and *sapientia*, ascribing the former to experience, the latter to science. But to make their difference appear more clearly, let us suppose one man endued with an excellent natural use and dexterity in handling his arms, and another to have added to that dexterity an acquired science of where he can offend or be offended by his adversary in every possible posture or guard; the ability of the former would be to the ability of the latter as prudence to sapience; both useful, but the latter infallible. But they that trusting only to the authority of books follow the blind blindly are like him that, trusting to the false rules of a master of fence, ventures presumptuously upon an adversary that either kills or disgraces him.

[22] The signs of science are some, certain and infallible, some, uncertain. Certain, when he that pretendeth the science of anything can teach the same, that is to say, demonstrate the truth thereof perspicuously to another; uncertain, when only some particular events answer to his pretence, and upon many occasions prove so as he says they must. Signs of prudence are all uncertain, because to observe by experience and remember all circumstances that may alter the success is impossible. But in any business whereof a man has not infallible science to proceed by, to forsake his own natural judgment and be guided by general sentences read in authors (and subject to many exceptions) is a sign of folly, and generally scorned by the name of pedantry. And even of those men themselves that in councils of the commonwealth love to show their reading of politics and history, very few do it in their domestic affairs, where their particular interest is concerned, having prudence enough for their private affairs; but in public they study more the reputation of their own wit than the success of another's business.

CHAPTER VI

Of the Interiour Beginnings of Voluntary Motions Commonly Called the *Passions*, and the Speeches by Which They Are Expressed

[1] There be in animals two sorts of *motions* peculiar to them: one called *vital*, begun in generation and continued without interruption through their whole life, such as are the *course* of the *blood*, the *pulse*, the *breathing*, the *concoction*, *nutrition*, *excretion*, &c, to which motions there needs no help of imagination; the other is *animal motion*, otherwise

called *voluntary motion* as to *go*, to *speak*, to *move* any of our limbs, in such manner as is first fancied in our minds. That sense is motion in the organs and interior parts of man's body, caused by the action of the things we see, hear, &c, and that fancy is but the relics of the same motion, remaining after sense, has been already said in the first and second chapters. And because *going, speaking*, and the like voluntary motions depend always upon a precedent thought of *whither, which way*, and *what*, it is evident that the imagination is the first internal beginning of all voluntary motion. And although unstudied men do not conceive any motion at all to be there, where the thing moved is invisible, or the space it is moved in is (for the shortness of it) insensible, yet that doth not hinder, but that such motions are. For let a space be never so little, that which is moved over a greater space whereof that little one is part must first be moved over that. These small beginnings of motion within the body of man, before they appear in walking, speaking, striking, and other visible actions, are commonly called ENDEAVOUR.

[2] This endeavour, when it is toward something which causes it, is called APPETITE or DESIRE, the latter being the general name, and the other oftentimes restrained to signify the desire of food, namely *hunger* and *thirst*. And when the endeavour is fromward something, it is generally called AVERSION. These words, *appetite* and *aversion*, we have from the *Latins*, and they both of them signify the motions, one of approaching, the other of retiring. So also do the Greek words for the same, which are *horme* and *aphorme*. For nature itself does often press upon men those truths which afterwards, when they look for somewhat beyond nature, they stumble at. For the Schools find in mere appetite to go, or move, no actual motion at all; but because some motion they must acknowledge, they call it metaphorical motion, which is but an absurd speech; for though words may be called metaphorical, bodies and motions cannot.

[3] That which men desire they are also said to LOVE, and to HATE those things for which they have aversions. So that desire and love are the same thing, save that by desire we always signify the absence of the object; by love, most commonly the presence of the same. So also by aversion we signify the absence, and by hate, the presence of the object.

[4] Of appetites and aversions some are born with men, as appetite of food, appetite of excretion and exoneration (which may also and more properly be called aversions from somewhat they feel in their bodies) and some other appetites, not many. The rest, which are appetites of particular things, proceed from experience and trial of their effects upon themselves or other men. For of things we know not at all, or believe not to be, we can have no further desire than to taste and try. But aversion we have for things, not only which we know have hurt us, but also that we do not know whether they will hurt us or not.

[5] Those things which we neither desire nor hate we are said to *contemn*, CONTEMPT being nothing else but an immobility or contumacy of the heart in resisting the action of certain things, and proceeding from that the heart is already moved otherwise, by other more potent objects, or from want of experience of them.

[6] And because the constitution of a man's body is in continual mutation, it is impossible that all the same things should always cause in him the same appetites and aversions; much less can all men consent in the desire of almost any one and the same object.

[7] But whatsoever is the object of any man's appetite or desire that is it which he for his part calleth *good*; and the object of his hate and aversion, *evil*; and of his contempt, *vile* and *inconsiderable*. For these words of good, evil, and contemptible are ever used with relation to the person that useth them, there being nothing simply and absolutely so, nor any common rule of good and evil to be taken from the nature of the objects themselves, but from the person of the man (where there is no commonwealth), or (in a commonwealth) from the person that representeth it, or from an arbitrator or judge whom men disagreeing shall by consent set up, and make his sentence the rule thereof.

[8] The Latin tongue has two words whose significations approach to those of good and evil, but are not precisely the same; and those are *pulchrum* and *turpe*. Whereof the former signifies that which by some apparent signs promiseth good; and the latter, that which promiseth evil. But in our tongue we have not so general names to express them by. But for *pulchrum* we say, in some things, *fair*; in others, *beau-*

tiful, or *handsome*, or *gallant*, or *honourable*, or *comely*, or *amiable*, and for *turpe, foul, deformed, ugly, base, nauseous*, and the like, as the subject shall require; all which words, in their proper places, signify nothing else but the *mien*, or countenance, that promiseth good and evil. So that of good there be three kinds: good in the promise, that is *pulchrum*; good in effect, as the end desired, which is called *jucundum, delightful*; and good as the means, which is called *utile, profitable*; and as many of evil; for *evil* in promise is that they call *turpe*; evil in effect and end is *molestum, unpleasant, troublesome*; and evil in the means *inutile, unprofitable, hurtful*.

[9] As in sense that which is really within us is (as I have said before) only motion caused by the action of external objects (but in appearance, to the sight, light and colour, to the ear, sound, to the nostril, odour, &c.), so when the action of the same object is continued from the eyes, ears, and other organs to the heart, the real effect there is nothing but motion or endeavour, which consisteth in appetite or aversion, to or from the object moving. But the appearance, or sense of that motion, is that we either call DELIGHT, or TROUBLE OF MIND.

[10] This motion which is called appetite, and for the appearance of it *delight* and *pleasure*, seemeth to be a corroboration of vital motion, and a help thereunto; and therefore such things as caused delight were not improperly called *jucunda* (*a juvando*, from helping or fortifying); and the contrary, *molesta, offensive*, from hindering and troubling the motion vital.

[11] *Pleasure*, therefore, or *delight*, is the appearance, or sense, of good; and *molestation* or *displeasure*, the appearance, or sense, of evil. And consequently all appetite, desire, and love is accompanied with some delight more or less; and all hatred and aversion, with more or less displeasure and offence.

[12] Of pleasures or delights, some arise from the sense of an object present, and those may be called *pleasures of sense* (the word *sensual*, as it is used by those only that condemn them, having no place till there be laws). Of this kind are all onerations and exonerations of the body, as also all that is pleasant in the *sight, hearing, smell, taste*, or *touch*. Others arise from the expectation that proceeds from foresight of the end or consequence of things, whether those things in the sense please or displease. And these are *pleasures of the mind* of him that draweth those consequences, and are generally called JOY. In the like manner displeasures are some in the sense, and called PAIN; others in the expectation of consequences, and are called GRIEF.

[13] These simple passions, called *appetite, desire, love, aversion, hate, joy*, and *grief*, have their names for diverse considerations diversified. As first, when they one succeed another, they are diversely called from the opinion men have of the likelihood of attaining what they desire. Secondly, from the object loved or hated. Thirdly, from the consideration of many of them together. Fourthly, from the alteration or succession itself.

[14] For *appetite* with an opinion of attaining is called HOPE.

[15] The same without such opinion, DESPAIR.

[16] *Aversion* with opinion of *hurt* from the object, FEAR.

[17] The same with hope of avoiding that hurt by resistance, COURAGE.

[18] Sudden *courage*, ANGER.

[19] Constant *hope*, CONFIDENCE of ourselves.

[20] Constant *despair*, DIFFIDENCE of ourselves.

[21] *Anger* for great hurt done to another, when we conceive the same to be done by injury, INDIGNATION.

[22] *Desire* of good to another, BENEVOLENCE, GOOD WILL, CHARITY. If to man generally, GOOD NATURE.

[23] *Desire* of riches, COVETOUSNESS, a name used always in signification of blame, because men contending for them are displeased with one another's attaining them, though the desire in itself be to be blamed or allowed, according to the means by which those riches are sought.

[24] *Desire* of office or precedence, AMBITION, a name used also in the worse sense, for the reason before mentioned.

[25] *Desire* of things that conduce but a little to our ends, and fear of things that are but of little hindrance, PUSILLANIMITY.

[26] *Contempt* of little helps and hindrances, MAGNANIMITY.

[27] *Magnanimity* in danger of death or wounds, VALOUR, FORTITUDE.

[28] *Magnanimity* in the use of riches, LIBERALITY.

[29] *Pusillanimity*, in the same, WRETCHEDNESS, MISERABLENESS, or PARSIMONY; as it is liked or disliked.

[30] *Love* of persons for society, KINDNESS.

[31] *Love* of persons for pleasing the sense only, NATURAL LUST.

[32] *Love* of the same, acquired from rumination, that is, imagination of pleasure past, LUXURY.

[33] *Love* of one singularly, with desire to be singularly beloved, THE PASSION OF LOVE. The same, with fear that the love is not mutual, JEALOUSY.

[34] *Desire*, by doing hurt to another, to make him condemn some fact of his own, REVENGEFULNESS.

[35] *Desire* to know why, and how, CURIOSITY, such as is in no living creature but *man*, so that man is distinguished, not only by his reason, but also by this singular passion from other *animals*, in whom the appetite of food and other pleasures of sense by predominance take away the care of knowing causes, which is a lust of the mind that by a perseverance of delight in the continual and indefatigable generation of knowledge exceedeth the short vehemence of any carnal pleasure.

[36] *Fear* of power invisible, feigned by the mind, or imagined from tales publicly allowed, RELIGION; not allowed, SUPERSTITION. And when the power imagined is truly such as we imagine, TRUE RELIGION.

[37] *Fear* without the apprehension of why or what, PANIC TERROR, called so from the fables, that make *Pan* the author of them; whereas in truth there is always in him that so feareth first, some apprehension of the cause, though the rest run away by example, every one supposing his fellow to know why. And therefore this passion happens to none but in a throng, or multitude of people.

[38] *Joy* from apprehension of novelty, ADMIRATION; proper to man, because it excites the appetite of knowing the cause.

[39] *Joy* arising from imagination of a man's own power and ability is that exultation of the mind which is called GLORYING; which, if grounded upon the experience of his own former actions, is the same with *confidence*; but if grounded on the flattery of others, or only supposed by himself, for delight in the consequences of it, is called VAINGLORY; which name is properly given, because a well grounded *confidence* begetteth attempt, whereas the supposing of power does not, and is therefore rightly called *vain*.

[40] *Grief* from opinion of want of power is called DEJECTION of mind.

[41] The *vain-glory* which consisteth in the feigning or supposing of abilities in ourselves (which we know are not) is most incident to young men, and nourished by the histories or fictions of gallant persons; and is corrected oftentimes by age and employment.

[42] *Sudden glory* is the passion which maketh those *grimaces* called LAUGHTER, and is caused either by some sudden act of their own that pleaseth them, or by the apprehension of some deformed thing in another, by comparison whereof they suddenly applaud themselves. And it is incident most to them that are conscious of the fewest abilities in themselves, who are forced to keep themselves in their own favour by observing the imperfections of other men. And therefore much laughter at the defects of others is a sign of pusillanimity. For of great minds one of the proper works is to help and free others from scorn, and compare themselves only with the most able.

[43] On the contrary, *sudden dejection* is the passion that causeth WEEPING, and is caused by such accidents as suddenly take away some vehement hope, or some prop of their power; and they are most subject to it that rely principally on helps external, such as are women and children. Therefore some weep for the loss of friends; others for their unkindness; others for the sudden stop made to their thoughts of revenge, by reconciliation. But in all cases, both laughter and weeping are sudden motions, custom taking them both away. For no man laughs at old jests, or weeps for an old calamity.

[44] *Grief* for the discovery of some defect of ability is SHAME, or the passion that discovereth itself in BLUSHING, and consisteth in the apprehension of some thing dishonourable; and in young men is a sign of the love of good reputation and commendable; in old men it is a sign of the same, but because it comes too late, not commendable.

[45] The *contempt* of good reputation is called IMPUDENCE.

[46] *Grief* for the calamity of another is PITY, and ariseth from the imagination that the like calamity may befall himself; and therefore is called also COMPASSION, and in the phrase of this present time a FELLOW-FEELING; and therefore for calamity arriving from great wickedness, the best men have the least pity; and for the same calamity, those have least pity that think themselves least obnoxious to the same.

[47] *Contempt*, or little sense, of the calamity of others is that which men called CRUELTY, proceeding from security of their own fortune. For, that any man should take pleasure in other men's great harms without other end of his own I do not conceive it possible.

[48] *Grief* for the success of a competitor in wealth, honour, or other good, if it be joined with endeavour to enforce our own abilities to equal or exceed him, is called EMULATION; but joined with endeavour to supplant or hinder a competitor, ENVY.

[49] When in the mind of man appetites and aversions, hopes and fears, concerning one and the same thing arise alternately, and diverse good and evil consequences of the doing or omitting the thing propounded come successively into our thoughts, so that sometimes we have an appetite to it, sometimes an aversion from it, sometimes hope to be able to do it, sometimes despair or fear to attempt it, the whole sum of desires, aversions, hopes and fears, continued till the thing be either done or thought impossible, is what we call DELIBERATION.

[50] Therefore of things past, there is no *deliberation*, because manifestly impossible to be changed; nor of things known to be impossible, or thought so, because men know or think such deliberation vain. But of things impossible which we think possible, we may deliberate, not knowing it is in vain. And it is called *deliberation*, because it is a putting an end to the *liberty* we had of doing or omitting, according to our own appetite or aversion.

[51] This alternate succession of appetites, aversions, hopes and fears is no less in other living creatures than in man; and therefore beasts also deliberate.

[52] Every *deliberation* is then said to *end*, when that whereof they deliberate is either done or thought impossible, because till then we retain the liberty of doing or omitting, according to our appetite or aversion.

[53] In deliberation, the last appetite or aversion immediately adhering to the action, or to the omission thereof, is that we call the WILL, the act (not the faculty) of *willing*. And beasts that have *deliberation* must necessarily also have *will*. The definition of the *will* given commonly by the Schools, that it is a *rational appetite*, is not good. For if it were, then could there be no voluntary act against reason. For a *voluntary act* is that which proceedeth from the *will*, and no other. But if instead of a rational appetite, we shall say an appetite resulting from a precedent deliberation, then the definition is the same that I have given here. *Will* therefore *is the last appetite in deliberating*. And though we say in common discourse, a man had a will once to do a thing, that nevertheless he forbore to do, yet that is properly but an inclination, which makes no action voluntary; because the action depends not of it, but of the last inclination or appetite. For if the intervenient appetites make any action voluntary, then by the same reason all intervenient aversions should make the same action involuntary; and so one and the same action should be both voluntary and involuntary.

[54] By this it is manifest that not only actions that have their beginning from covetousness, ambition, lust, or other appetites to the thing propounded, but also those that have their beginning from aversion or fear of those consequences that follow the omission are *voluntary actions*.

[55] The forms of speech by which the passions are expressed are partly the same and partly different from those by which we express our thoughts. And first, generally all passions may be expressed *indicatively*, as *I love, I fear, I joy, I deliberate, I will, I command*; but some of them have particular expressions by themselves, which nevertheless are not affirmations (unless it be when they serve to make other inferences besides that of the passion they proceed from). Deliberation is expressed *subjunctively*, which is a speech proper to signify suppositions, with their consequences, as *if this be done, then this will follow*, and differs not from the language of reasoning, save that reasoning is in general words, but deliberation for the most part is of particulars. The language of desire and aversion is *imperative*, as *do this, forbear that*, which, when the party is obliged to do or forbear, is *command*; otherwise *prayer*, or else *counsel*. The language of vain-glory, of indignation, pity and revengefulness, *optative*; but of the desire to know there is a peculiar expression, called *interrogative*, as *what is it, when shall it, how is it done*, and *why so?* other language of the passions I find none; for cursing, swearing, reviling, and the like, do not signify as speech, but as the actions of a tongue accustomed.

[56] These forms of speech, I say, are expressions, or voluntary significations, of our passions; but certain signs they be not, because they may be used arbitrarily, whether they that use them have such passions

or not. The best signs of passions present are in the countenance, motions of the body, actions, and ends or aims which we otherwise know the man to have.

[57] And because in deliberation the appetites and aversions are raised by foresight of the good and evil consequences and sequels of the action whereof we deliberate, the good or evil effect thereof dependeth on the foresight of a long chain of consequences, of which very seldom any man is able to see to the end. But for so far as a man seeth, if the good in those consequences be greater than the evil, the whole chain is that which writers call *apparent* or *seeming good*. And contrarily, when the evil exceedeth the good, the whole is *apparent* or *seeming evil*; so that he who hath by experience or reason the greatest and surest prospect of consequences deliberates best himself, and is able, when he will, to give the best counsel unto others.

[58] *Continual success* in obtaining those things which a man from time to time desireth, that is to say, continual prospering, is that men call FELICITY; I mean the felicity of this life. For there is no such thing as perpetual tranquillity of mind, while we live here; because life itself is but motion, and can never be without desire, nor without fear, no more than without sense. What kind of felicity God hath ordained to them that devoutly honour Him, a man shall no sooner know than enjoy, being joys that now are as incomprehensible as the word of school-men *beatifical vision* is unintelligible.

[59] The form of speech whereby men signify their opinion of the goodness of anything is PRAISE. That whereby they signify the power and greatness of anything is MAGNIFYING. And that whereby they signify the opinion they have of a man's felicity is by the Greeks called *makarismos*, for which we have no name in our tongue. And thus much is sufficient for the present purpose, to have been said of the PASSIONS.

CHAPTER XI

Of the Difference of *Manners*

[1] By *manners* I mean not here decency of behaviour, as how one man should salute another, or how a man should wash his mouth or pick his teeth before company, and such other points of the *small morals*, but those qualities of mankind that concern their living together in peace and unity. To which end we are to consider that the felicity of this life consisteth not in the repose of a mind satisfied. For there is no such *Finis ultimus* (utmost aim) nor *Summum Bonum* (greatest good) as is spoken of in the books of the old moral philosophers. Nor can a man any more live, whose desires are at an end, than he whose senses and imaginations are at a stand. Felicity is a continual progress of the desire, from one object to another, the attaining of the former being still but the way to the latter. The cause whereof is that the object of man's desire is not to enjoy once only, and for one instant of time, but to assure forever the way of his future desire. And therefore the voluntary actions and inclinations of all men tend, not only to the procuring, but also to the assuring of a contented life, and differ only in the way; which ariseth partly from the diversity of passions in divers men, and partly from the difference of the knowledge or opinion each one has of the causes which produce the effect desired.

[2] So that in the first place, I put for a general inclination of all mankind, a perpetual and restless desire of power after power, that ceaseth only in death. And the cause of this is not always that a man hopes for a more intensive delight than he has already attained to, or that he cannot be content with a moderate power, but because he cannot assure the power and means to live well which he hath present, without the acquisition of more. And from hence it is that kings, whose power is greatest, turn their endeavours to the assuring it at home by laws or abroad by wars; and when that is done, there succeedeth a new desire, in some of fame from new conquest, in others of ease and sensual pleasure, in others of admiration or being flattered for excellence in some art or other ability of the mind.

[3] Competition of riches, honour, command, or other power, inclineth to contention, enmity, and war; because the way of one competitor to the attaining of his desire is to kill, subdue, supplant, or repel the other. Particularly, competition of praise inclineth to a reverence of antiquity. For men contend with the living, not with the dead, to these ascribing more than due, that they may obscure the glory of the other.

[4] Desire of ease and sensual delight disposeth men to obey a common power, because by such desires a man doth abandon the protection might be

hoped for from his own industry and labour. Fear of death and wounds disposeth to the same, and for the same reason. On the contrary, needy men, and hardy, not contented with their present condition, as also all men that are ambitious of military command, are inclined to continue the causes of war, and to stir up trouble and sedition; for there is no honour military but by war, nor any such hope to mend an ill game as by causing a new shuffle.

[5] Desire of knowledge, and arts of peace, inclineth men to obey a common power. For such desire containeth a desire of leisure, and consequently protection from some other power than their own.

[6] Desire of praise disposeth to laudable actions, such as please them whose judgment they value; for of those men whom we contemn, we contemn also the praises. Desire of fame after death does the same. And though after death there be no sense of the praise given us on earth, as being joys that are either swallowed up in the unspeakable joys of Heaven, or extinguished in the extreme torments of hell, yet is not such fame vain, because men have a present delight therein, from the foresight of it and of the benefit that may redound thereby to their posterity, which though they now see not, yet they imagine; and anything that is pleasure in the sense, the same also is pleasure in the imagination.

CHAPTER XIII

Of the *Natural Condition* of *Mankind*, as Concerning Their Felicity, and Misery

[1] Nature hath made men so equal in the faculties of body and mind as that, though there be found one man sometimes manifestly stronger in body or of quicker mind than another, yet when all is reckoned together the difference between man and man is not so considerable as that one man can thereupon claim to himself any benefit to which another may not pretend as well as he. For as to the strength of body, the weakest has strength enough to kill the strongest, either by secret machination, or by confederacy with others that are in the same danger with himself.

[2] And as to the faculties of the mind—setting aside the arts grounded upon words, and especially that skill of proceeding upon general and infallible rules called science (which very few have, and but in few things), as being not a native faculty (born with us), nor attained (as prudence) while we look after somewhat else—I find yet a greater equality amongst men than that of strength. For prudence is but experience, which equal time equally bestows on all men in those things they equally apply themselves unto. That which may perhaps make such equality incredible is but a vain conceit of one's own wisdom, which almost all men think they have in a greater degree than the vulgar, that is, than all men but themselves and a few others whom, by fame or for concurring with themselves, they approve. For such is the nature of men that howsoever they may acknowledge many others to be more witty, or more eloquent, or more learned, yet they will hardly believe there be many so wise as themselves. For they see their own wit at hand, and other men's at a distance. But this proveth rather that men are in that point equal, than unequal. For there is not ordinarily a greater sign of the equal distribution of anything than that every man is contented with his share.

[3] From this equality of ability ariseth equality of hope in the attaining of our ends. And therefore, if any two men desire the same thing, which nevertheless they cannot both enjoy, they become enemies; and in the way to their end, which is principally their own conservation, and sometimes their delectation only, endeavour to destroy or subdue one another. And from hence it comes to pass that, where an invader hath no more to fear than another man's single power, if one plant, sow, build, or possess a convenient seat, others may probably be expected to come prepared with forces united, to dispossess and deprive him, not only of the fruit of his labour, but also of his life or liberty. And the invader again is in the like danger of another.

[4] And from this diffidence of one another, there is no way for any man to secure himself so reasonable as anticipation, that is, by force or wiles to master the persons of all men he can, so long till he see no other power great enough to endanger him. And this is no more than his own conservation requireth, and is generally allowed. Also, because there be some that taking pleasure in contemplating their own power in the acts of conquest, which they pursue farther than their security requires, if others (that otherwise would be glad to be at ease within modest bounds) should not by invasion increase their power, they would not

be able, long time, by standing only on their defence, to subsist. And by consequence, such augmentation of dominion over men being necessary to a man's conservation, it ought to be allowed him.

[5] Again, men have no pleasure, but on the contrary a great deal of grief, in keeping company where there is no power able to over-awe them all. For every man looketh that his companion should value him at the same rate he sets upon himself, and upon all signs of contempt, or undervaluing, naturally endeavours, as far as he dares (which amongst them that have no common power to keep them in quiet, is far enough to make them destroy each other), to extort a greater value from his contemners, by damage, and from others, by the example.

[6] So that in the nature of man we find three principal causes of quarrel: first, competition; secondly, diffidence; thirdly, glory.

[7] The first maketh men invade for gain; the second, for safety; and the third, for reputation. The first use violence to make themselves masters of other men's persons, wives, children, and cattle; the second, to defend them; the third, for trifles, as a word, a smile, a different opinion, and any other sign of undervalue, either direct in their persons, or by reflection in their kindred, their friends, their nation, their profession, or their name.

[8] Hereby it is manifest that during the time men live without a common power to keep them all in awe, they are in that condition which is called war, and such a war as is of every man against every man. For WAR consisteth not in battle only, or the act of fighting, but in a tract of time wherein the will to contend by battle is sufficiently known. And therefore, the notion of *time* is to be considered in the nature of war, as it is in the nature of weather. For as the nature of foul weather lieth not in a shower or two of rain, but in an inclination thereto of many days together, so the nature of war consisteth not in actual fighting, but in the known disposition thereto during all the time there is no assurance to the contrary. All other time is PEACE.

[9] Whatsoever therefore is consequent to a time of war, where every man is enemy to every man, the same is consequent to the time wherein men live without other security than what their own strength and their own invention shall furnish them withal. In such condition there is no place for industry, because the fruit thereof is uncertain, and consequently, no culture of the earth, no navigation, nor use of the commodities that may be imported by sea, no commodious building, no instruments of moving and removing such things as require much force, no knowledge of the face of the earth, no account of time, no arts, no letters, no society, and which is worst of all, continual fear and danger of violent death, and the life of man, solitary, poor, nasty, brutish, and short.

[10] It may seem strange, to some man that has not well weighed these things, that nature should thus dissociate, and render men apt to invade and destroy one another. And he may, therefore, not trusting to this inference made from the passions, desire perhaps to have the same confirmed by experience. Let him therefore consider with himself—when taking a journey, he arms himself, and seeks to go well accompanied; when going to sleep, he locks his doors; when even in his house, he locks his chests; and this when he knows there be laws, and public officers, armed, to revenge all injuries shall be done him—what opinion he has of his fellow subjects, when he rides armed; of his fellow citizens, when he locks his doors; and of his children and servants, when he locks his chests. Does he not there as much accuse mankind by his actions, as I do by my words? But neither of us accuse man's nature in it. The desires and other passions of man are in themselves no sin. No more are the actions that proceed from those passions, till they know a law that forbids them—which till laws be made they cannot know. Nor can any law be made, till they have agreed upon the person that shall make it.

[11] It may peradventure be thought, there was never such a time nor condition of war as this; and I believe it was never generally so, over all the world. But there are many places where they live so now. For the savage people in many places of *America* (except the government of small families, the concord whereof dependeth on natural lust) have no government at all, and live at this day in that brutish manner as I said before. Howsoever, it may be perceived what manner of life there would be where there were no common power to fear, by the manner of life which men that have formerly lived under a peaceful government use to degenerate into, in a civil war.

[12] But though there had never been any time wherein particular men were in a condition of war

one against another, yet in all times kings and persons of sovereign authority, because of their independency, are in continual jealousies and in the state and posture of gladiators, having their weapons pointing and their eyes fixed on one another, that is, their forts, garrisons, and guns upon the frontiers of their kingdoms, and continual spies upon their neighbours, which is a posture of war. But because they uphold thereby the industry of their subjects, there does not follow from it that misery which accompanies the liberty of particular men.

[13] To this war of every man against every man, this also is consequent: that nothing can be unjust. The notions of right and wrong, justice and injustice, have there no place. Where there is no common power, there is no law; where no law, no injustice. Force and fraud are in war the two cardinal virtues. Justice and injustice are none of the faculties neither of the body, nor mind. If they were, they might be in a man that were alone in the world, as well as his senses and passions. They are qualities that relate to men in society, not in solitude. It is consequent also to the same condition that there be no propriety, no dominion, no *mine* and *thine* distinct, but only that to be every man's that he can get, and for so long as he can keep it. And thus much for the ill condition which man by mere nature is actually placed in, though with a possibility to come out of it, consisting partly in the passions, partly in his reason.

[14] The passions that incline men to peace are fear of death, desire of such things as are necessary to commodious living, and a hope by their industry to obtain them. And reason suggesteth convenient articles of peace, upon which men may be drawn to agreement. These articles are they which otherwise are called the Laws of Nature, whereof I shall speak more particularly in the two following chapters.

CHAPTER XIV

Of the First and Second *Natural Laws* and of *Contracts*

[1] The Right of Nature, which writers commonly call *jus naturale*, is the liberty each man hath to use his own power, as he will himself, for the preservation of his own nature, that is to say, of his own life, and consequently of doing anything which, in his own judgment and reason, he shall conceive to be the aptest means thereunto.

[2] By Liberty is understood, according to the proper signification of the word, the absence of external impediments, which impediments may oft take away part of a man's power to do what he would, but cannot hinder him from using the power left him, according as his judgment and reason shall dictate to him.

[3] A Law of Nature (*lex naturalis*) is a precept or general rule, found out by reason, by which a man is forbidden to do that which is destructive of his life or taketh away the means of preserving the same, and to omit that by which he thinketh it may be best preserved. For though they that speak of this subject use to confound *jus* and *lex* (*right* and *law*), yet they ought to be distinguished, because Right consisteth in liberty to do or to forbear, whereas Law determineth and bindeth to one of them; so that law and right differ as much as obligation and liberty, which in one and the same matter are inconsistent.

[4] And because the condition of man (as hath been declared in the precedent chapter) is a condition of war of everyone against everyone (in which case everyone is governed by his own reason and there is nothing he can make use of that may not be a help unto him in preserving his life against his enemies), it followeth that in such a condition every man has a right to everything, even to one another's body. And therefore, as long as this natural right of every man to everything endureth, there can be no security to any man (how strong or wise soever he be) of living out the time which nature ordinarily alloweth men to live. And consequently it is a precept, or general rule of reason *that every man ought to endeavour peace, as far as he has hope of obtaining it, and when he cannot obtain it, that he may seek and use all helps and advantages of war*. The first branch of which rule containeth the first and fundamental law of nature, which is *to seek peace, and follow it*. The second, the sum of the right of nature, which is *by all means we can, to defend ourselves*.

[5] From this fundamental law of nature, by which men are commanded to endeavour peace, is derived this second law: *that a man be willing, when others are so too, as far-forth as for peace and defence of himself he shall think it necessary, to lay down this right to all things, and be contented with so much*

liberty against other men, as he would allow other men against himself. For as long as every man holdeth this right of doing anything he liketh, so long are all men in the condition of war. But if other men will not lay down their right as well as he, then there is no reason for anyone to divest himself of his; for that were to expose himself to prey (which no man is bound to), rather than to dispose himself to peace. This is that law of the Gospel: "whatsoever you require that others should do to you, that do ye to them." And that law of all men: *quod tibi fieri non vis, alteri ne feceris.*

[6] To *lay down* a man's *right* to anything is to *divest* himself of the *liberty* of hindering another of the benefit of his own right to the same. For he that renounceth or passeth away his right giveth not to any other man a right which he had not before (because there is nothing to which every man had not right by nature), but only standeth out of his way, that he may enjoy his own original right without hindrance from him, not without hindrance from another. So that the effect which redoundeth to one man by another man's defect of right is but so much diminution of impediments to the use of his own right original.

[7] Right is laid aside either by simply renouncing it or by transferring it to another. By *simply* RENOUNCING, when he cares not to whom the benefit thereof redoundeth. By TRANSFERRING, when he intendeth the benefit thereof to some certain person or persons. And when a man hath in either manner abandoned or granted away his right, then is he said to be OBLIGED or BOUND not to hinder those to whom such right is granted or abandoned from the benefit of it; and [it is said] that he *ought*, and it is his DUTY, not to make void that voluntary act of his own, and that such hindrance is INJUSTICE, and INJURY, as being *sine jure* [without right], the right being before renounced or transferred. So that *injury* or *injustice*, in the controversies of the world, is somewhat like to that which in the disputations of scholars is called absurdity. For as it is there called an *absurdity* to contradict what one maintained in the beginning, so in the world it is called injustice and injury voluntarily to undo that which from the beginning he had voluntarily done.

The way by which a man either simply renounceth or transferreth his right is a declaration, or signification by some voluntary and sufficient sign or signs, that he doth so renounce or transfer, or hath so renounced or transferred the same, to him that accepteth it. And these signs are either words only, or actions only, or (as it happeneth most often) both words and actions. And the same are the BONDS by which men are bound and obliged, bonds that have their strength, not from their own nature (for nothing is more easily broken than a man's word) but from fear of some evil consequence upon the rupture.

[8] Whensoever a man transferreth his right or renounceth it, it is either in consideration of some right reciprocally transferred to himself or for some other good he hopeth for thereby. For it is a voluntary act, and of the voluntary acts of every man the object is some *good to himself.* And therefore there be some rights which no man can be understood by any words or other signs to have abandoned or transferred. As, first, a man cannot lay down the right of resisting them that assault him by force, to take away his life, because he cannot be understood to aim thereby at any good to himself. [Second], the same may be said of wounds, and chains, and imprisonment, both because there is no benefit consequent to such patience (as there is to the patience of suffering another to be wounded or imprisoned), as also because a man cannot tell, when he seeth men proceed against him by violence, whether they intend his death or not. [Third], and lastly, the motive and end for which this renouncing and transferring of right is introduced, is nothing else but the security of a man's person, in his life and in the means of so preserving life as not to be weary of it. And therefore if a man by words or other signs seem to despoil himself of the end for which those signs were intended, he is not to be understood as if he meant it, or that it was his will, but that he was ignorant of how such words and actions were to be interpreted.

[9] The mutual transferring of right is that which men call CONTRACT.

[10] There is difference between transferring of right to the thing and transferring (or tradition, that is, delivery) of the thing itself. For the thing may be delivered together with the translation of the right (as in buying and selling with ready money, or exchange of goods or lands); and it may be delivered some time after.

[11] Again, one of the contractors may deliver the

thing contacted for on his part, and leave the other to perform his part at some determinate time after (and in the meantime be trusted); and then the contract on his part is called PACT, or COVENANT; or both parts may contract now, to perform hereafter, in which cases he that is to perform in time to come, being trusted, his performance is called *keeping of promise*, or *faith*, and the failing of performance (if it be voluntary) *violation of faith*.

[12] When the transferring of right is not mutual, but one of the parties transferreth in hope to gain thereby friendship or service from another (or from his friends), or in hope to gain the reputation of charity or magnanimity, or to deliver his mind from the pain of compassion, or in hope of reward in heaven, this is not contract, but GIFT, FREE-GIFT, GRACE, which words signify one and the same thing.

[13] Signs of contract are either *express* or *by inference*. Express are words spoken with understanding of what they signify; and such words are either of the time *present* or *past* (as, *I give, I grant, I have given, I have granted, I will that this be yours*), or of the future (as, *I will give, I will grant*), which words of the future are called PROMISE.

[14] Signs by inference are: sometimes the consequence of words, sometimes the consequence of silence; sometimes the consequence of actions, sometimes the consequence of forbearing an action; and generally a sign by inference of any contract is whatsoever sufficiently argues the will of the contractor.

[15] Words alone, if they be of the time to come, and contain a bare promise, are an insufficient sign of a free-gift, and therefore not obligatory. For if they be of the time to come (as, *tomorrow I will give*), they are a sign I have not given yet, and consequently that my right is not transferred, but remaineth till I transfer it by some other act. But if the words be of the time present or past (as, *I have given, or do give to be delivered tomorrow*), then is my tomorrow's right given away today; and that by the virtue of the words, though there were no other argument of my will. And there is a great difference in the signification of these words: *volo hoc tuum esse cras* and *cras dabo* (that is, between *I will that this be thine tomorrow* and *I will give it thee tomorrow*); for the word *I will* in the former manner of speech signifies an act of the will present, but in the latter it signifies a promise of an act of the will to come; and therefore the former words, being of the present, transfer a future right; the latter, that be of the future, transfer nothing.

But if there be other signs of the will to transfer a right besides words, then though the gift be free, yet may the right be understood to pass by words of the future (as, if a man propound a prize to him that comes first to the end of a race, the gift is free, and though the words be of the future, yet the right passeth; for if he would not have his words so be understood, he should not have let them run).

[16] In contracts the right passeth, not only where the words are of the time present or past, but also where they are of the future, because all contract is mutual translation, or change of right; and therefore he that promiseth only (because he hath already received the benefit for which he promiseth) is to be understood as if he intended the right should pass; for unless he had been content to have his words so understood, the other would not have performed his part first. And for that cause, in buying and selling, and other acts of contract, a promise is equivalent to a covenant, and therefore obligatory.

[17] He that performeth first in the case of a contract is said to MERIT that which he is to receive by the performance of the other, and he hath it as *due*. Also when a prize is propounded to many, which is to be given to him only that winneth (or money is thrown amongst many, to be enjoyed by them that catch it), though this be a free gift, yet so to win (or so to catch) is to *merit*, and to have it as DUE. For the right is transferred in the propounding of the prize (and in throwing down the money), though it be not determined to whom but by the event of the contention.

But there is between these two sorts of merit, this difference: that in contract I merit by virtue of my own power, and the contractor's need; but in this case of free gift, I am enabled to merit only by the benignity of the giver; in contract I merit at the contractor's hand that he should depart with his right; in this case of gift, I merit not that the giver should part with his right, but that when he has parted with it, it should be mine rather than another's.

And this I think to be the meaning of that distinction of the Schools between *meritum congrui* and *meritum condigni*.[4] For God Almighty having prom-

4. [Merit by coincidence and merit deserved.]

ised Paradise to those men (hoodwinked with carnal desires) that can walk through this world according to the precepts and limits prescribed by him, they say: he that shall so walk shall merit Paradise *ex congruo*. But because no man can demand a right to it, by his own righteousness or any other power in himself, but by the free grace of God only, they say: no man can merit Paradise *ex condigno*. This, I say, I think is the meaning of that distinction; but because disputers do not agree upon the signification of their own terms of art longer than it serves their turn, I will not affirm anything of their meaning. Only this I say: when a gift is given indefinitely, as a prize to be contended for, he that winneth meriteth, and may claim the prize as due.

[18] If a covenant be made wherein neither of the parties perform presently, but trust one another, in the condition of mere nature (which is a condition of war of every man against every man) upon any reasonable suspicion it is void; but if there be a common power set over them both, with right and force sufficient to compel performance, it is not void. For he that performeth first has no assurance the other will perform after, because the bonds of words are too weak to bridle men's ambition, avarice, anger, and other passions, without the fear of some coercive power; which in the condition of mere nature, where all men are equal and judges of the justness of their own fears, cannot possibly be supposed. And therefore, he which performeth first does but betray himself to his enemy, contrary to the right (he can never abandon) of defending his life and means of living.

[19] But in a civil estate, where there is a power set up to constrain those that would otherwise violate their faith, that fear is no more reasonable; and for that cause, he which by the covenant is to perform first is obliged so to do.

[20] The cause of fear which maketh such a covenant invalid must be always something arising after the covenant made (as some new fact or other sign of the will not to perform), else it cannot make the covenant void. For that which could not hinder a man from promising, ought not to be admitted as a hindrance of performing.

[21] He that transferreth any right transferreth the means of enjoying it, as far as lieth in his power. As he that selleth land is understood to transfer the herbage and whatsoever grows upon it; nor can he that sells a mill turn away the stream that drives it. And they that give to a man the right of government in sovereignty are understood to give him the right of levying money to maintain soldiers, and of appointing magistrates for the administration of justice.

[22] To make covenants with brute beasts is impossible because, not understanding our speech, they understand not, nor accept of, any translation of right, nor can translate any right to another; and without mutual acceptation, there is no covenant.

[23] To make covenant with God is impossible, but by mediation of such as God speaketh to (either by revelation supernatural or by his lieutenants that govern under him, and in his name); for otherwise we know not whether our covenants be accepted or not. And therefore, they that vow anything [OL: to God] contrary to any law of nature vow in vain, as being a thing unjust to pay such vow. And if it be a thing commanded by the law of nature, [OL: they vow in vain;] it is not the vow, but the law that binds them.

[24] The matter or subject of a covenant is always something that falleth under deliberation (for to covenant is an act of the will; that is to say an act, and the last act, of deliberation) and is therefore always understood to be something to come, and which is judged possible for him that covenanteth to perform.

[25] And therefore, to promise that which is known to be impossible is no covenant. But if that prove impossible afterwards which before was thought possible, the covenant is valid and bindeth, though not to the thing itself, yet to the value; or, if that also be impossible, to the unfeigned endeavour of performing as much as is possible (for to more no man can be obliged).

[26] Men are freed of their covenants two ways: by performing or by being forgiven. For performance is the natural end of obligation; and forgiveness, the restitution of liberty (as being a retransferring of that right in which the obligation consisted).

[27] Covenants entered into by fear, in the condition of mere nature, are obligatory. For example, if I covenant to pay a ransom, or service, for my life, to an enemy, I am bound by it. For it is a contract wherein one receiveth the benefit of life; the other is to receive money, or service, for it; and consequently, where no other law (as in the condition of mere nature) forbiddeth the performance, the covenant is valid. Therefore prisoners of war, if trusted with the

payment of their ransom, are obliged to pay it; and if a weaker prince make a disadvantageous peace with a stronger, for fear, he is bound to keep it, unless (as hath been said before [¶20]) there ariseth some new and just cause of fear, to renew the war. And even in commonwealths, if I be forced to redeem myself from a thief by promising him money, I am bound to pay it, till the civil law discharge me. For whatsoever I may lawfully do without obligation, the same I may lawfully covenant to do through fear; and what I lawfully covenant, I cannot lawfully break.

[28] A former covenant makes void a later. For a man that hath passed away his right to one man today, hath it not to pass tomorrow to another; and therefore the later promise passeth no right, but is null.

[29] A covenant not to defend myself from force by force is always void. For (as I have showed before) no man can transfer or lay down his right to save himself from death, wounds, and imprisonment (the avoiding whereof is the only end of laying down any right), and therefore the promise of not resisting force in no covenant transferreth any right, nor is obliging. For though a man may covenant thus *unless I do so, or so, kill me*, he cannot covenant thus *unless I do so, or so, I will not resist you, when you come to kill me*. For man by nature chooseth the lesser evil, which is danger of death in resisting, rather than the greater, which is certain and present death in not resisting. And this is granted to be true by all men, in that they lead criminals to execution and prison with armed men, notwithstanding that such criminals have consented to the law by which they are condemned.

[30] A covenant to accuse oneself, without assurance of pardon, is likewise invalid. For in the condition of nature, where every man is judge, there is no place for accusation; and in the civil state the accusation is followed with punishment, which being force, a man is not obliged not to resist. The same is also true of the accusation of those by whose condemnation a man falls into misery (as, of a father, wife, or benefactor). For the testimony of such an accuser, if it be not willingly given, is presumed to be corrupted by nature, and therefore not to be received; and where a man's testimony is not to be credited, he is not bound to give it. Also accusations upon torture are not to be reputed as testimonies. For torture is to be used but as means of conjecture and light in the further examination and search of truth; and what is in that case confessed tendeth to the ease of him that is tortured, not to the informing of the torturers, and therefore ought not to have the credit of a sufficient testimony; for whether he deliver himself by true or false accusation, he does it by the right of preserving his own life.

[31] The force of words being (as I have formerly noted) too weak to hold men to the performance of their covenants, there are in man's nature but two imaginable helps to strengthen it. And those are either a fear of the consequence of breaking their word, or a glory or pride in appearing not to need to break it. This latter is a generosity too rarely found to be presumed on, especially in the pursuers of wealth, command, or sensual pleasure (which are the greatest part of mankind).

The passion to be reckoned upon is fear, whereof there be two very general objects: one, the power of spirits invisible; the other, the power of those men they shall therein offend. Of these two, though the former be the greater power, yet the fear of the latter is commonly the greater fear. The fear of the former is in every man his own religion, which hath place in the nature of man before civil society. The latter hath not so, at least not place enough to keep men to their promises, because in the condition of mere nature the inequality of power is not discerned but by the event of battle.

So that before the time of civil society, or in the interruption thereof by war, there is nothing can strengthen a covenant of peace agreed on, against the temptations of avarice, ambition, lust, or other strong desire, but the fear of that invisible power which they every one worship as God and fear as a revenger of their perfidy. All therefore that can be done between two men not subject to civil power is to put one another to swear by the God he feareth; which *swearing*, or OATH, is a *form of speech, added to a promise, by which he that promiseth signifieth that unless he perform, he renounceth the mercy of his God, or calleth to him for vengeance on himself*. Such was the heathen form *Let* Jupiter *kill me else, as I kill this beast*. So is our form *I shall do thus, and thus, so help me God*. And this, with the rites and ceremonies which everyone useth in his own religion, that the fear of breaking faith might be the greater.

[32] By this it appears that an oath taken according to any other form or rite than his that sweareth is in vain,

and no oath, and that there is no swearing by anything which the swearer thinks not God. For though men have sometimes used to swear by their kings, for fear or flattery, yet they would have it thereby understood they attributed to them divine honour. And that swearing unnecessarily by God is but prophaning of his name, and swearing by other things, as men do in common discourse, is not swearing, but an impious custom, gotten by too much vehemence of talking.

[33] It appears also that the oath adds nothing to the obligation. For a covenant, if lawful, binds in the sight of God without the oath as much as with it; if unlawful, bindeth not at all, though it be confirmed with an oath.

CHAPTER XV

Of Other Laws of Nature

[1] From that law of nature by which we are obliged to transfer to another such rights as, being retained, hinder the peace of mankind, there followeth a third, which is this *that men perform their covenants made*, without which covenants are in vain, and but empty words, and the right of all men to all things remaining, we are still in the condition of war.

[2] And in this law of nature consisteth the fountain and original of JUSTICE. For where no covenant hath preceded, there hath no right been transferred, and every man has right to everything; and consequently, no action can be unjust. But when a covenant is made, then to break it is *unjust*; and the definition of INJUSTICE is no other than *the not performance of covenant*. And whatsoever is not unjust, is *just*.

[3] But because covenants of mutual trust where there is a fear of not performance on either part (as hath been said in the former chapter [xiv, 18–20]) are invalid, though the original of justice be the making of covenants, yet injustice actually there can be none till the cause of such fear be taken away, which, while men are in the natural condition of war, cannot be done. Therefore, before the names of just and unjust can have place, there must be some coercive power to compel men equally to the performance of their covenants, by the terror of some punishment greater than the benefit they expect by the breach of their covenant, and to make good that propriety which by mutual contract men acquire, in recompense of the universal right they abandon; and such power there is none before the erection of a commonwealth. And this is also to be gathered out of the ordinary definition of justice in the Schools; for they say that *justice is the constant will of giving to every man his own*. And therefore where there is no *own*, that is, no propriety, there in no injustice; and where there is no coercive power erected, that is, where there is no commonwealth, there is no propriety, all men having right to all things; therefore where there is no commonwealth, there nothing is unjust. So that the nature of justice consisteth in keeping of valid covenants; but the validity of covenants begins not but with the constitution of a civil power sufficient to compel men to keep them; and then it is also that propriety begins.

[4] The fool hath said in his heart: "there is no such thing as justice"; and sometimes also with his tongue, seriously alleging that: "every man's conservation and contentment being committed to his own care, there could be no reason why every man might not do what he thought conduced thereunto, and therefore also to make or not make, keep or not keep, covenants was not against reason, when it conduced to one's benefit." He does not therein deny that there be covenants, and that they are sometimes broken, sometimes kept, and that such breach of them may be called injustice, and the observance of them justice; but he questioneth whether injustice, taking away the fear of God (for the same fool hath said in his heart there is no God), may not sometimes stand with that reason which dictateth to every man his own good; and particularly then, when it conduceth to such a benefit as shall put a man in a condition to neglect, not only the dispraise and revilings, but also the power of other men.

"The kingdom of God is gotten by violence; but what if it could be gotten by unjust violence? were it against [OL: right] reason so to get it, when it is impossible to receive hurt by it [OL: but only the supreme good]? and if it be not against reason, it is not against justice; or else justice is not to be approved for good."

From such reasoning as this, successful wickedness hath obtained the name of virtue, and some that in all other things have disallowed the violation of faith, yet have allowed it when it is for the getting of a kingdom. And the heathen that believed that *Saturn* was deposed by his son *Jupiter* believed nevertheless the same *Jupiter* to be the avenger of injustice, somewhat like to a piece of law in *Coke's* Commentaries on *Littleton*,[5] where he says: if the right heir of the crown be attainted of treason, yet the crown shall descend to him, and *eo instante* [immediately] the attainder be void; from which instances a man will be very prone to infer that "when the heir apparent of a kingdom shall kill him that is in possession, though his father, you may call it injustice, or by what other name you will, yet it can never be against reason, seeing all the voluntary actions of men tend to the benefit of themselves, and those actions are most reasonable that conduce most to their ends." This specious reasoning is nevertheless false.

[5] For the question is not of promises mutual where there is no security of performance on either side (as when there is no civil power erected over the parties promising), for such promises are no covenants, but either where one of the parties has performed already, or where there is a power to make him perform, there is the question whether it be against reason, that is, against the benefit of the other to perform or not. And I say it is not against reason. For the manifestation whereof we are to consider: first, that when a man doth a thing which, notwithstanding anything can be foreseen and reckoned on, tendeth to his own destruction (howsoever some accident which he could not expect, arriving, may turn it to his benefit), yet such events do not make it reasonably or wisely done. Secondly, that in a condition of war wherein every man to every man (for want of a common power to keep them all in awe) is an enemy, there is no man can hope by his own strength or wit to defend himself from destruction without the help of confederates (where everyone expects the same defence by the confederation that anyone else does); and therefore, he which declares he thinks it reason to deceive those that help him can in reason expect no other means of safety than what can be had from his own single power. He, therefore, that breaketh his covenant, and consequently declareth that he thinks he may with reason do so, cannot be received into any society that unite themselves for peace and defence but by the error of them that receive him; nor when he is received, be retained in it without seeing the danger of their error; which errors a man cannot reasonably reckon upon as the means of his security; and therefore, if he be left or cast out of society, he perisheth; and if he live in society, it is by the errors of other men, which he could not foresee nor reckon upon; and consequently [he has acted] against the reason of his preservation, and so as all men that contribute not to his destruction forbear him only out of ignorance of what is good for themselves.

[6] As for the instance of gaining the secure and perpetual felicity of heaven by any way, it is frivolous, there being but one way imaginable, and that is not breaking, but keeping of covenant.

[7] And for the other instance of attaining sovereignty by rebellion, it is manifest that, though the event follow, yet because it cannot reasonably be expected (but rather the contrary), and because (by gaining it so) others are taught to gain the same in like manner, the attempt thereof is against reason. Justice, therefore, that is to say, keeping of covenant, is a rule of reason by which we are forbidden to do anything destructive to our life, and consequently a law of nature.

[8] There be some that proceed further, and will not have the law of nature to be those rules which conduce to the preservation of man's life on earth, but to the attaining of an eternal felicity after death, to which they think the breach of covenant may conduce, and consequently be just and reasonable (such are they that think it a work of merit to kill, or depose, or rebel against the sovereign power constituted over them by their own consent). But because there is no natural knowledge of man's estate after death, much less of the reward that is then to be given to breach of faith, but only a belief grounded upon other men's saying that they know it supernaturally, or that they know those that knew them that knew others that knew it supernaturally, breach of faith cannot be called a precept of reason or nature.

[9] Others, that allow for a law of nature the keeping of faith, do nevertheless make exception of certain persons (as heretics and such as use not to perform their covenant to others); and this also is against reason.

5. [Edward Coke (1552–1634) was an eminent English jurist who defended common law against encroachments by the crown. Thomas Littleton (c. 1442–1481), an English barrister and judge, wrote a work on property law that, in an edition expanded by Coke, was the standard text on the subject until the nineteenth century.]

For if any fault of a man be sufficient to discharge our covenant made, the same ought in reason to have been sufficient to have hindered the making of it.

[10] The names of just and unjust, when they are attributed to men, signify one thing; and when they are attributed to actions, another. When they are attributed to men, they signify conformity or inconformity of manners to reason. But when they are attributed to actions, they signify the conformity or inconformity to reason, not of manners or manner of life, but of particular actions. A just man, therefore, is he that taketh all the care he can that his actions may be all just; and an unjust man is he that neglecteth it. And such men are more often in our language styled by the names of righteous and unrighteous, than just and unjust, though the meaning be the same. Therefore a righteous man does not lose that title by one or a few unjust actions that proceed from sudden passion or mistake of things or persons; nor does an unrighteous man lose his character for such actions as he does or forbears to do for fear, because his will is not framed by the justice, but by the apparent benefit of what he is to do. That which gives to human actions the relish of justice is a certain nobleness or gallantness of courage (rarely found) by which a man scorns to be beholden for the contentment of his life to fraud or breach of promise. This justice of the manners is that which is meant where justice is called a virtue, and injustice a vice.

[11] But the justice of actions denominates men, not just, but *guiltless*; and the injustice of the same (which is also called injury) gives them but the name of *guilty*.

[12] Again, the injustice of manners is the disposition or aptitude to do injury, and is injustice before it proceed to act and without supposing any individual person injured. But the injustice of an action (that is to say injury) supposeth an individual person injured, namely, him to whom the covenant was made; and therefore, many times the injury is received by one man, when the damage redoundeth to another. As when the master commandeth his servant to give money to a stranger; if it be not done, the injury is done to the master, whom he had before covenanted to obey, but the damage redoundeth to the stranger, to whom he had no obligation, and therefore could not injure him. And so also in commonwealths, private men may remit to one another their debts, but not robberies or other violences whereby they are endamaged; because the detaining of debt is an injury to themselves, but robbery and violence are injuries to the person of the commonwealth.

[13] Whatsoever is done to a man conformable to his own will, signified to the doer, is no injury to him. For if he that doeth it hath not passed away his original right to do what he please by some antecedent covenant, there is no breach of covenant, and therefore no injury done him. And if he have, then his will [i.e., that of the person acted on] to have it done being signified, is a release of that covenant; and so again there is no injury done him.

[14] Justice of actions is by writers divided into *commutative* and *distributive*; and the former they say consisteth in proportion arithmetical; the latter, in proportion geometrical. Commutative, therefore, they place in the equality of value of the things contracted for; and distributive, in the distribution of equal benefit to men of equal merit (as if it were injustice to sell dearer than we buy, or to give more to a man than he merits). The value of all things contracted for is measured by the appetite of the contractors; and therefore the just value is that which they be contented to give. And merit (besides that which is by covenant, where the performance on one part meriteth the performance of the other part, and falls under justice commutative, not distributive) is not due by justice, but is rewarded of grace only.

And therefore, this distinction, in the sense wherein it useth to be expounded, is not right. To speak properly, commutative justice is the justice of a contractor, that is, a performance of covenant (in buying and selling, hiring and letting to hire, lending and borrowing, exchanging, bartering, and other acts of contract).

[15] And distributive justice [is] the justice of an arbitrator, that is to say, the act of defining what is just. Wherein (being trusted by them that make him arbitrator) if he perform his trust, he is said to distribute to every man his own; and this is indeed just distribution, and may be called (though improperly) distributive justice (but more properly, equity, which also is a law of nature). . . .

[16] As justice dependeth on antecedent covenant, so does GRATITUDE depend on antecedent grace, that is to say, antecedent free-gift; and is the fourth law of nature, which may be conceived in this form *that*

a man which receiveth benefit from another of mere grace endeavour that he which giveth it have no reasonable cause to repent him of his good will. For no man giveth but with intention of good to himself, because gift is voluntary, and of all voluntary acts the object is to every man his own good; of which, if men see they shall be frustrated, there will be no beginning of benevolence or trust; nor, consequently, of mutual help, nor of reconciliation of one man to another; and therefore they are to remain still in the condition of war, which is contrary to the first and fundamental law of nature, which commandeth men to *seek peace*. The breach of this law is called *ingratitude*, and hath the same relation to grace that injustice hath to obligation by covenant.

[17] A fifth law of nature is COMPLAISANCE, that is to say, *that every man strive to accommodate himself to the rest.* For the understanding whereof we may consider that there is, in men's aptness to society, a diversity of nature rising from their diversity of affections, not unlike to that we see in stones brought together for building of an edifice. For as that stone which (by the asperity and irregularity of figure) takes more room from others than itself fills, and (for the hardness) cannot be easily made plain, and thereby hindereth the building, is by the builders cast away as unprofitable and troublesome, so also a man that (by asperity of nature) will strive to retain those things which to himself are superfluous and to others necessary, and (for the stubbornness of his passions) cannot be corrected, is to be left or cast out of society as cumbersome thereunto. For seeing every man, not only by right, but also by necessity of nature, is supposed to endeavour all he can to obtain that which is necessary for his conservation, he that shall oppose himself against it for things superfluous is guilty of the war that thereupon is to follow; and, therefore, doth that which is contrary to the fundamental law of nature, which commandeth *to seek peace*. The observers of this law may be called SOCIABLE (the Latins call them *commodi*); the contrary, *stubborn, insociable, froward, intractable*.

[18] A sixth law of nature is this *that upon caution of the future time, a man ought to pardon the offences past of them that, repenting, desire it.* For PARDON is nothing but granting of peace, which (though granted to them that persevere in their hostility be not peace but fear, yet) not granted to them that give caution of the future time is sign of an aversion to peace; and therefore contrary to the law of nature.

[19] A seventh is *that in revenges* (that is, retribution of evil for evil) *men look not at the greatness of the evil past, but the greatness of the good to follow.* Whereby we are forbidden to inflict punishment with any other design than for correction of the offender, or direction of others. For this law is consequent to the next before it, that commandeth pardon upon security of the future time. Besides, revenge without respect to the example and profit to come is a triumph, or glorying, in the hurt of another, tending to no end (for the end is always somewhat to come); and glorying to no end is vainglory, and contrary to reason; and to hurt without reason tendeth to the introduction of war, which is against the law of nature, and is commonly styled by the name of *cruelty*.

[20] And because all signs of hatred or contempt provoke to fight, insomuch as most men choose rather to hazard their life than not to be revenged, we may in the eighth place, for a law of nature, set down this precept *that no man by deed, word, countenance, or gesture, declare hatred or contempt of another.* The breach of which law is commonly called *contumely*.

[21] The question 'who is the better man?' has no place in the condition of mere nature, where (as has been shewn before) all men are equal. The inequality that now is, has been introduced by the laws civil. I know that *Aristotle* (in the first book of his Politics [ch. iii–vii], for a foundation of his doctrine) maketh men by nature, some more worthy to command (meaning the wiser sort, such as he thought himself to be for his philosophy), others to serve (meaning those that had strong bodies, but were not philosophers as he), as if master and servant were not introduced by consent of men, but by difference of wit; which is not only against reason, but also against experience. For there are very few so foolish that had not rather govern themselves than be governed by others; nor when the wise in their own conceit contend by force with them who distrust their own wisdom, do they always, or often, or almost at any time, get the victory. If nature therefore have made men equal, that equality is to be acknowledged; or if nature have made men unequal, yet because men that think themselves equal will not enter into conditions of peace but upon equal terms, such equality must be admitted. And therefore for the ninth law of nature,

I put this *that every man acknowledge other for his equal by nature*. The breach of this precept is *pride*.

[22] On this law dependeth another: *that at the entrance into conditions of peace, no man require to reserve to himself any right which he is not content should be reserved to every one of the rest*. As it is necessary, for all men that seek peace, to lay down certain rights of nature (that is to say, not to have liberty to do all they list), so is it necessary, for man's life, to retain some (as, right to govern their own bodies, [right to] enjoy air, water, motion, ways to go from place to place, and all things else without which a man cannot live, or not live well). If in this case, at the making of peace, men require for themselves that which they would not have to be granted to others, they do contrary to the precedent law, that commandeth the acknowledgment of natural equality, and therefore also against the law of nature. The observers of this law are those we call *modest*, and the breakers *arrogant* men. The Greeks call the violation of this law *pleonexia*, that is, a desire of more than their share.

[23] Also *if a man be trusted to judge between man and man*, it is a precept of the law of nature that *he deal equally between them*. For without that, the controversies of men cannot be determined but by war. He, therefore, that is partial in judgment doth what in him lies to deter men from the use of judges and arbitrators; and consequently (against the fundamental law of nature), is the cause of war.

[24] The observance of this law (from the equal distribution to each man of that which in reason belongeth to him) is called EQUITY, and (as I have said before) distributive justice; the violation [is called] *acception of persons (prosopolepsia)*.

[25] And from this followeth another law: *that such things as cannot be divided be enjoyed in common, if it can be; and if the quantity of the thing permit, without stint; otherwise proportionably to the number of them that have right*. For otherwise the distribution is unequal, and contrary to equity.

[26] But some things there be that can neither be divided nor enjoyed in common. Then the law of nature which prescribeth equity requireth *that the entire right (or else, making the use alternate, the first possession) be determined by lot*. For equal distribution is of the law of nature, and other means of equal distribution cannot be imagined.

[27] Of *lots* there be two sorts: *arbitrary* and *natural*. Arbitrary is that which is agreed on by the competitors; natural is either *primogeniture* (which the Greek calls *kleronomia*, which signifies, *given by lot*) or *first seizure*.

[28] And therefore those things which cannot be enjoyed in common, nor divided, ought to be adjudged to the first possessor; and in some cases to the firstborn, as acquired by lot.

[29] It is also a law of nature *that all men that mediate peace be allowed safe conduct*. For the law that commandeth peace, as the *end*, commandeth intercession, as the *means*; and to intercession the means is safe conduct.

[30] And because (though men be never so willing to observe these laws) there may nevertheless arise questions concerning a man's action (first, whether it were done or not done; secondly, if done, whether against the law or not against the law; the former whereof is called a question *of fact*; the latter a question *of right*), therefore unless the parties to the question covenant mutually to stand to the sentence of another, they are as far from peace as ever. This other to whose sentence they submit is called an ARBITRATOR. And therefore it is of the law of nature *that they that are at controversy, submit their right to the judgment of an arbitrator*.

[31] And seeing every man is presumed to do all things in order to his own benefit, *no man is a fit arbitrator in his own cause*; and if he were never so fit, yet (equity allowing to each party equal benefit) if one be admitted to judge, the other is to be admitted also; and so the controversy, that is, the cause of war, remains, against the law of nature.

[32] For the same reason no man in any cause ought to be received for arbitrator, to whom greater profit, or honour, or pleasure apparently ariseth out of the victory of one party, than of the other; for he hath taken (though an unavoidable bribe, yet) a bribe; and no man can be obliged to trust him. And thus also the controversy, and the condition of war remaineth, contrary to the law of nature.

[33] And in a controversy of *fact* the judge (being to give no more credit to one [litigant] than to the other, if there be no other arguments) must give credit to a third [a non-litigant witness], or to a third and fourth; or more; for else the question is undecided, and left to force, contrary to the law of nature.

[34] These are the laws of nature dictating peace for a means of the conservation of men in multitudes; and which only concern the doctrine of civil society. There be other things tending to the destruction of particular men (as drunkenness and all other parts of intemperance), which may therefore also be reckoned amongst those things which the law of nature hath forbidden; but are not necessary to be mentioned, nor are pertinent enough to this place.

[35] And though this may seem too subtle a deduction of the laws of nature to be taken notice of by all men (whereof the most part are too busy in getting food, and the rest too negligent, to understand), yet to leave all men inexcusable they have been contracted into one easy sum, intelligible even to the meanest capacity, and that is *Do not that to another, which thou wouldst not have done to thyself*; which sheweth him that he has no more to do in learning the laws of nature but (when, weighing the actions of other men with his own, they seem too heavy) to put them into the other part of the balance, and his own into their place, that his own passions and self-love may add nothing to the weight; and then there is none of these laws of nature that will not appear unto him very reasonable.

[36] The laws of nature oblige *in foro interno*, that is to say, they bind to a desire they should take place; but *in foro externo*, that is, to the putting them in act, not always. For he that should be modest and tractable, and perform all he promises, in such time and place where no man else should do so, should but make himself a prey to others, and produce his own certain ruin, contrary to the ground of all laws of nature, which tend to nature's preservation. And again, he that having sufficient security that others shall observe the same laws towards him, observes them not himself, seeketh not peace, but war, and consequently the destruction of his nature by violence.

[37] And whatsoever laws bind *in foro interno* may be broken, not only by a fact contrary to the law, but also by a fact according to it, in case a man think it contrary. For though his action in this case be according to the law, yet his purpose was against the law, which, where the obligation is *in foro interno*, is a breach.

[38] The laws of nature are immutable and eternal; for injustice, ingratitude, arrogance, pride, iniquity, acception of persons, and the rest, can never be made lawful. For it can never be that war shall preserve life, and peace destroy it.

[39] The same laws, because they oblige only to a desire and endeavour (I mean an unfeigned and constant endeavour) are easy to be observed. For in that they require nothing but endeavour, he that endeavoureth their performance fulfilleth them; and he that fulfilleth the law is just.

[40] And the science of them [the laws of nature] is the true and only moral philosophy. For moral philosophy is nothing else but the science of what is *good* and *evil* in the conversation and society of mankind. *Good* and *evil* are names that signify our appetites and aversions, which in different tempers, customs, and doctrines of men are different; and divers men differ not only in their judgment on the senses (of what is pleasant and unpleasant to the taste, smell, hearing, touch, and sight), but also of what is conformable or disagreeable to reason in the actions of common life. Nay, the same man in divers times differs from himself, and one time praiseth (that is, calleth good) what another time he dispraiseth (and calleth evil); from whence arise disputes, controversies, and at last war. And therefore so long a man is in the condition of mere nature (which is a condition of war) as private appetite is the measure of good and evil; and consequently, all men agree on this, that peace is good; and therefore also the way or means of peace (which, as I have shewed before, are *justice, gratitude, modesty, equity, mercy,* and the rest of the laws of nature) are good (that is to say, *moral virtues*), and their contrary vices, evil.

Now the science of virtue and vice is moral philosophy; and therefore the true doctrine of the laws of nature is the true moral philosophy. But the writers of moral philosophy, though they acknowledge the same virtues and vices, yet not seeing wherein consisted their goodness, nor that they come to be praised as the means of peaceable, sociable, and comfortable living, place them in a mediocrity of passions (as if not the cause, but the degree of daring, made fortitude; or not the cause, but the quantity of a gift, made liberality).

[41] These dictates of reason men use to call by the name of laws, but improperly; for they are but conclusions or theorems concerning what conduceth to the conservation and defence of themselves, whereas law, properly, is the word of him that by right hath command over others. But yet if we consider the

same theorems, as delivered in the word of God, that by right commandeth all things; then are they properly called laws.

Part Two
OF COMMONWEALTH
CHAPTER XVII
Of the Causes, Generation, and Definition of a *Commonwealth*

[1] The final cause, end, or design of men (who naturally love liberty and dominion over others) in the introduction of that restraint upon themselves in which we see them live in commonwealths is the foresight of their own preservation, and of a more contented life thereby; that is to say, of getting themselves out from that miserable condition of war, which is necessarily consequent (as hath been shown [ch. xiii]) to the natural passions of men, when there is no visible power to keep them in awe, and tie them by fear of punishment to the performance of their covenants and observation of those laws of nature set down in the fourteenth and fifteenth chapters.

[2] For the laws of nature (as *justice, equity, modesty, mercy,* and (in sum) *doing to others as we would be done to*) of themselves, without the terror of some power to cause them to be observed, are contrary to our natural passions, that carry us to partiality, pride, revenge, and the like. And covenants without the sword are but words, and of no strength to secure a man at all. Therefore notwithstanding the laws of nature (which every one hath then kept, when he has the will to keep them, when he can do it safely), if there be no power erected, or not great enough for our security, every man will, and may lawfully rely on his own strength and art, for caution against all other men. And in all places where men have lived by small families, to rob and spoil one another has been a trade, and so far from being reputed against the law of nature that the greater spoils they gained, the greater was their honour; and men observed no other laws therein but the laws of honour, that is, to abstain from cruelty, leaving to men their lives and instruments of husbandry. And as small families did then, so now do cities and kingdoms (which are but greater families) for their own security enlarge their dominions upon all pretences of danger and fear of invasion or assistance that may be given to invaders, [and] endeavour as much as they can to subdue or weaken their neighbours, by open force and secret arts for want of other caution, justly (and are remembered for it in after ages with honour).

[3] Nor is it the joining together of a small number of men that gives them this security; because in small numbers, small additions on the one side or the other make the advantage of strength so great as is sufficient to carry the victory; and therefore gives encouragement to an invasion. The multitude sufficient to confide in for our security is not determined by any certain number, but by comparison with the enemy we fear, and is then sufficient, when the odds of the enemy is not of so visible and conspicuous moment, to determine the event of war, as to move him to attempt.

[4] And be there never so great a multitude, yet if their actions be directed according to their particular judgments and particular appetites, they can expect thereby no defence, nor protection, neither against a common enemy, nor against the injuries of one another. For being distracted in opinions concerning the best use and application of their strength, they do not help, but hinder one another, and reduce their strength by mutual opposition to nothing; whereby they are easily, not only subdued by a very few that agree together, but also when there is no common enemy, they make war upon each other, for their particular interests. For if we could suppose a great multitude of men to consent in the observation of justice and other laws of nature without a common power to keep them all in awe, we might as well suppose all mankind to do the same; and then there neither would be, nor need to be, any civil government or commonwealth at all, because there would be peace without subjection.

[5] Nor is it enough for the security, which men desire should last all the time of their life, that they be governed and directed by one judgment for a limited time, as in one battle or one war. For though they obtain a victory by their unanimous endeavour against a foreign enemy, yet afterwards, when either they have no common enemy, or he that by one part is held for an enemy is by another part held for a friend, they must needs by the difference of their interests dissolve, and fall again into a war amongst themselves.

[6] It is true that certain living creatures (as bees and ants) live sociably one with another (which are therefore by *Aristotle* numbered amongst political creatures), and yet have no other direction than their particular judgments and appetites, nor speech whereby one of them can signify to another what he thinks expedient for the common benefit; and therefore some man may perhaps desire to know why mankind cannot do the same. To which I answer,

[7] First, that men are continually in competition for honour and dignity, which these creatures are not; and consequently, amongst men there ariseth, on that ground, envy and hatred, and finally war; but amongst these not so.

[8] Secondly, that amongst these creatures the common good differeth not from the private; and being by nature inclined to their private, they procure thereby the common benefit. But man, whose joy consisteth in comparing himself with other men, can relish nothing but what is eminent.

[9] Thirdly, that these creatures (having not, as man, the use of reason) do not see, nor think they see, any fault in the administration of their common business; whereas amongst men there are very many that think themselves wiser, and abler to govern the public, better than the rest; and these strive to reform and innovate, one this way, another that way; and thereby bring it into distraction and civil war.

[10] Fourthly, that these creatures, though they have some use of voice (in making known to one another their desires and other affections), yet they want that art of words by which some men can represent to others that which is good in the likeness of evil, and evil in the likeness of good, and augment or diminish the apparent greatness of good and evil, discontenting men, and troubling their peace at their pleasure.

[11] Fifthly, irrational creatures cannot distinguish between *injury* and *damage*; and therefore, as long as they be at ease, they are not offended with their fellows, whereas man is then most troublesome, when he is most at ease; for then it is that he loves to shew his wisdom, and control the actions of them that govern the commonwealth.

[12] Lastly, the agreement of these creatures is natural; that of men is by covenant only, which is artificial; and therefore, it is no wonder if there be somewhat else required (besides covenant) to make their agreement constant and lasting, which is a common power to keep them in awe, and to direct their actions to the common benefit.

[13] The only way to erect such a common power as may be able to defend them from the invasion of foreigners and the injuries of one another, and thereby to secure them in such sort as that by their own industry, and by the fruits of the earth, they may nourish themselves and live contentedly, is to confer all their power and strength upon one man, or upon one assembly of men, that may reduce all their wills, by plurality of voices, unto one will, which is as much as to say, to appoint one man or assembly of men to bear their person, and every one to own and acknowledge himself to be author of whatsoever he that so beareth their person shall act, or cause to be acted, in those things which concern the common peace and safety, and therein to submit their wills, every one to his will, and their judgments, to his judgment. This is more than consent, or concord; it is a real unity of them all, in one and the same person, made by covenant of every man with every man, in such manner as if every man should say to every man *I authorize and give up my right of governing myself to this man, or to this assembly of men, on this condition, that thou give up thy right to him, and authorize all his actions in like manner*. This done, the multitude so united in one person is called a COMMONWEALTH, in Latin CIVITAS. This is the generation of that great LEVIATHAN, or rather (to speak more reverently) of that *Mortal God* to which we owe, under the *Immortal God*, our peace and defence. For by this authority, given him by every particular man in the commonwealth, he hath the use of so much power and strength conferred on him that by terror thereof he is enabled to conform the wills of them all to peace at home and mutual aid against their enemies abroad. And in him consisteth the essence of the commonwealth, which (to define it) is *one person, of whose acts a great multitude, by mutual covenants one with another, have made themselves every one the author, to the end he may use the strength and means of them all, as he shall think expedient, for their peace and common defence*.

[14] And he that carrieth this person is called SOVEREIGN, and said to have *Sovereign Power*; and every one besides, his SUBJECT.

Baruch Spinoza

Baruch Spinoza (1632–1677) was born in Amsterdam, his parents Jewish refugees from the Spanish Inquisition. Educated in the traditional religious studies of his people, he absorbed a profound knowledge of the Bible and Hebrew, later mastering Latin, the language in which he wrote.

Spinoza not only kept abreast of the scientific and philosophical developments of his own time but, as a result of his dissatisfaction with anthropomorphism and mysticism, also studied the works of the important Jewish medieval philosophers who had grappled with these issues—men such as Maimonides (1138–1204), Gersonides (1288–1344), and Crescas (1340–1410). When questioned by a tribunal of his congregation, Spinoza was unwilling to disavow his heterodox theological opinions. Subsequently, the Jewish community of Holland, not at that time entitled to citizenship and fearful of reprisals for permitting such heresies, excommunicated him at the age of twenty-four. For the next four years he stayed in Amsterdam, pursuing his studies while earning a living grinding and polishing lenses. He then moved to the small village of Rijnsburg, near Leyden, and later to Voorburg, outside The Hague, continuing his lonely life as a scholar and lens-grinder. He was offered a chair of philosophy at the University of Heidelberg but refused it, fearful of losing his freedom of expression. He died at forty-four, the victim of tuberculosis, his frail constitution weakened by arduous labor as well as by the glass dust he had inhaled while practicing his vocation. He was regarded as a person of great courtesy, unusual modesty, and equanimity.

Only two books by Spinoza appeared during his lifetime: *Principles of Cartesian Philosophy*, an expository volume in geometrical form and the anonymously published *Theological-Political Treatise*. The latter is perhaps the earliest example of what two centuries later became known as "higher criticism," the study of the Bible as a historical document open to rational interpretation. His posthumous works included an unfinished Hebrew grammar, intended to support his scientific approach to scriptural exegesis; the *Short Treatise on God, Man, and His Well-Being*, an early, partial draft of his philosophical system; the fragmentary *Treatise on the Emendation of the Intellect*, an introduction to his methodology; the incomplete *Political Treatise*, which stresses the value of individual liberty and religious toleration, as well as supporting democracy against the claims of monarchy and aristocracy; and his masterpiece, the *Ethics, Demonstrated in Geometrical Order*, one of the most majestic of all philosophical works.

Spinoza viewed the world as possessing an intelligible structure according to which every event was in principle comprehensible as a necessary part of the whole. The logical order of that whole was to be understood only "through itself" and was variously termed "substance," "Nature," or "God." The geometric format of the *Ethics* illustrates this central thesis, since the propositions, corollaries, and notes are all intended as deductions from the initial definitions and axioms, which are presented as self-explanatory.

Part I contains Spinoza's detailed demonstration of the essence of God. In Part II he offers his solution to the traditional philosophical problem of the relation between mind and body, regarding these not, as Descartes had, as two separate substances, but rather as two aspects of the one Substance. The remainder of the *Ethics* (not reprinted here) contains Spinoza's moral theory and his view of the ideal life. The terms "good" and "bad" are, according to Spinoza, merely words we use to express our own desires. In order to achieve salvation, we need to free ourselves from the bondage of these emotions and strive through reason to achieve knowledge of and identification with the order of the universe, thus coming to possess "the intellectual love of God" that is "blessedness." By thus reinterpreting the concept of God and imparting spirituality to the study of nature, Spinoza fused his commitment to the scientific model of knowledge with the monotheistic vision of his religious heritage.

• • •

An illuminating biography is Steven Nadler, *Spinoza: A Life* (Cambridge: Cambridge University Press, 1999). Helpful overviews of Spinoza's thought are Stuart Hampshire, *Spinoza* (Middlesex: Penguin Books, 1951) and Henry E. Allison, *Benedict de Spinoza: An Introduction*, Revised Edition (New Haven: Yale University Press, 1987). An incisive presentation of Spinoza's philosophical perspective is Chapter 5 of John Herman Randall, Jr., *The Career of Philosophy: From the Middle Ages to the Enlightenment* (1962; rpt. New York: Columbia University Press, 1970). Also useful as a concise presentation of the major themes in Spinoza's system is the essay by P. H. Nidditch in D. J. O'Connor, ed., *A Critical History of Western Philosophy* (Glencoe, Ill.: Free Press, 1964). Two detailed examinations of the *Ethics* are Jonathan Bennett, *A Study of Spinoza's "Ethics"* (Indianapolis: Hackett Publishing Company, 1984) and Edwin Curley, *Behind the Geometrical Method: A Reading of Spinoza's "Ethics"* (Princeton: Princeton University Press, 1988). A detailed study of Spinoza's view of God is Richard Mason, *The God of Spinoza: A Philosophical Study* (Cambridge: Cambridge University Press, 1997). A useful collection of essays is Derk Pereboom, ed., *The Rationalists: Descartes, Spinoza, Leibniz* (Lanham, Md.: Rowman & Littlefield, 1999). An especially fine essay that penetrates to the heart of Spinoza's thought is the text of a lecture by Frederick J. F. Woodbridge, delivered at Columbia University in 1933 and reprinted in the edition of the *Ethics* edited by James Gutmann (New York: Hafner, 1957). The classic study of the *Ethics* from a historical point of view, exhibiting in immense detail its connections to the work of Aristotle, Descartes, and others, is Harry Austryn Wolfson, *The Philosophy of Spinoza* (1934; rpt. Cleveland: Meridian Books, 1958). A comprehensive guide to Spinoza's thought is Don Garrett, ed., *The Cambridge Companion to Spinoza* (Cambridge: Cambridge University Press, 1996).

Steven M. Cahn

Ethics

Part I
CONCERNING GOD

DEFINITIONS

1. By that which is self-caused I mean that whose essence involves existence; or that whose nature can be conceived only as existing.

2. A thing is said to be finite in its own kind [*in suo genere finita*] when it can be limited by another thing of the same nature. For example, a body is said to be finite because we can always conceive of another body greater than it. So, too, a thought is limited by another thought. But body is not limited by thought, nor thought by body.

3. By substance I mean that which is in itself and is conceived through itself; that is, that the conception of which does not require the conception of another thing from which it has to be formed.

4. By attribute I mean that which the intellect perceives of substance as constituting its essence.

5. By mode I mean the affections of substance, that is, that which is in something else and is conceived through something else.

6. By God I mean an absolutely infinite being, that is, substance consisting of infinite attributes, each of which expresses eternal and infinite essence.

Explication

I say 'absolutely infinite,' not 'infinite in its kind.' For if a thing is only infinite in its kind, one may deny that it has infinite attributes. But if a thing is absolutely infinite, whatever expresses essence and does not involve any negation belongs to its essence.

Reprinted from Spinoza, *The Ethics, TIE, and Selected Letters*, translated by Samuel Shirley (Indianapolis: Hackett Publishing Company, 1992), by permission of the publisher.

7. That thing is said to be free [*liber*] which exists solely from the necessity of its own nature, and is determined to action by itself alone. A thing is said to be necessary [*necessarius*] or rather, constrained [*coactus*], if it is determined by another thing to exist and to act in a definite and determinate way.

8. By eternity I mean existence itself insofar as it is conceived as necessarily following solely from the definition of an eternal thing.

Explication

For such existence is conceived as an eternal truth, just as is the essence of the thing, and therefore cannot be explicated through duration or time, even if duration be conceived as without beginning and end.

AXIOMS

1. All things that are, are either in themselves or in something else.

2. That which cannot be conceived through another thing must be conceived through itself.

3. From a given determinate cause there necessarily follows an effect; on the other hand, if there be no determinate cause, it is impossible that an effect should follow.

4. The knowledge of an effect depends on, and involves, the knowledge of the cause.

5. Things which have nothing in common with each other cannot be understood through each other; that is, the conception of the one does not involve the conception of the other.

6. A true idea must agree with that of which it is the idea [*ideatum*].

7. If a thing can be conceived as not existing, its essence does not involve existence.

PROPOSITION 1

Substance is by nature prior to its affections.

Proof

This is evident from Defs. 3 and 5.

PROPOSITION 2

Two substances having different attributes have nothing in common.

Proof

This too is evident from Def. 3; for each substance must be in itself and be conceived through itself; that is, the conception of the one does not involve the conception of the other.

PROPOSITION 3

When things have nothing in common, one cannot be the cause of the other.

Proof

If things have nothing in common, then (Ax. 5) they cannot be understood through one another, and so (Ax. 4) one cannot be the cause of the other.

PROPOSITION 4

Two or more distinct things are distinguished from one another either by the difference of the attributes of the substances or by the difference of the affections of the substances.

Proof

All things that are, are either in themselves or in something else (Ax. 1); that is (Defs. 3 and 5), nothing exists external to the intellect except substances and their affections. Therefore, there can be nothing external to the intellect through which several things can be distinguished from one another except substances or (which is the same thing) (Def. 4) the attributes and the affections of substances.

PROPOSITION 5

In the universe there cannot be two or more substances of the same nature or attribute.

Proof

If there were several such distinct substances, they would have to be distinguished from one another either by a difference of attributes or by a difference of affections (Pr. 4). If they are distinguished only by a difference of attributes, then it will be granted that there cannot be more than one substance of the same attribute. But if they are distinguished by a difference of affections, then, since substance is by nature prior to its affections (Pr. 1), disregarding therefore its affections and considering substance in itself, that is (Def. 3 and Ax. 6) considering it truly, it cannot be conceived as distinguishable from another substance. That is (Pr. 4), there cannot be several such substances but only one.

PROPOSITION 6

One substance cannot be produced by another substance.

Proof

In the universe there cannot be two substances of the same attribute (Pr. 5), that is (Pr. 2), two substances having something in common. And so (Pr. 3) one cannot be the cause of the other; that is, one cannot be produced by the other.

Corollary

Hence it follows that substance cannot be produced by anything else. For in the universe there exists nothing but substances and their affections, as is evident from Ax. 1 and Defs. 3 and 5. But, by Pr. 6, it cannot be produced by another substance. Therefore, substance cannot be produced by anything else whatsoever.

Another Proof

This can be proved even more readily by the absurdity of the contradictory. For if substance could be produced by something else, the knowledge of substance would have to depend on the knowledge of its cause (Ax. 4), and so (Def. 3) it would not be substance.

PROPOSITION 7

Existence belongs to the nature of substance.

Proof

Substance cannot be produced by anything else (Cor. Pr. 6) and is therefore self-caused [*causa sui*]; that is (Def. 1), its essence necessarily involves existence; that is, existence belongs to its nature.

PROPOSITION 8

Every substance is necessarily infinite.

Proof

There cannot be more than one substance having the same attribute (Pr. 5), and existence belongs to the nature of substance (Pr. 7). It must therefore exist either as finite or as infinite. But it cannot exist as finite, for (Def. 2) it would have to be limited by another substance of the same nature, and that substance also would have to exist (Pr. 7). And so there would exist two substances of the same attribute, which is absurd (Pr. 5). Therefore, it exists as infinite.

Scholium 1

Since in fact to be finite is in part a negation and to be infinite is the unqualified affirmation of the existence of some nature, it follows from Proposition 7 alone that every substance must be infinite.

Scholium 2

I do not doubt that for those who judge things confusedly and are not accustomed to know things through their primary causes it is difficult to grasp the proof of Proposition 7. Surely, this is because they neither distinguish between the modification of substances and substances themselves, nor do they know how things are produced. And so it comes about that they ascribe to substances a beginning which they see natural things as having; for those who do not know the true causes of things confuse everything. Without any hesitation they imagine trees as well as men talking and stones as well as men being formed from seeds; indeed, any forms whatsoever are imagined to change into any other forms. So too, those who confuse the divine nature with human nature easily ascribe to God human emotions, especially so long as they are ignorant of how the latter are produced in the mind. But if men were to attend to the nature of substance, they would not doubt at all the truth of Proposition 7; indeed, this Proposition would be an axiom to all and would be ranked among universally accepted truisms. For by substance they would understand that which is in itself and is conceived through itself; that is, that the knowledge of which does not require the knowledge of any other thing. By modifications they would understand that which is in another thing, and whose conception is formed from the thing in which they are. Therefore, in the case of nonexistent modifications we can have true ideas of them since their essence is included in something else, with the result that they can be conceived through that something else, although they do not exist in actuality externally to the intellect. However, in the case of substances, because they are conceived only through themselves, their truth external to the intellect is only in themselves. So if someone were to say that he has a clear and distinct—that is, a true—idea of substance and that he nevertheless doubts whether such a substance exists, this would surely be just the same as if he were to declare that he has a true idea but nevertheless suspects that it may be false (as is obvious to anyone who gives his mind to it). Or if anyone asserts that substance is created, he at the same time asserts that a false idea has become true, than which nothing more absurd can be conceived. So it must necessarily be admitted that the existence of substance is as much an eternal truth as is its essence.

From here we can derive in another way that there cannot be but one [substance] of the same nature, and I think it worthwhile to set out the proof here. Now to do this in an orderly fashion I ask you to note:

1. The true definition of each thing involves and expresses nothing beyond the nature of the thing defined. Hence it follows that—

2. No definition involves or expresses a fixed number of individuals, since it expresses nothing but the nature of the thing defined. For example, the

definition of a triangle expresses nothing other than simply the nature of a triangle, and not a fixed number of triangles.

3. For each individual existent thing there must necessarily be a definite cause for its existence.

4. The cause for the existence of a thing must either be contained in the very nature and definition of the existent thing (in effect, existence belongs to its nature) or must have its being independently of the thing itself.

From these premises it follows that if a fixed number of individuals exist in Nature, there must necessarily be a cause why those individuals and not more or fewer exist. If, for example, in Nature twenty men were to exist (for the sake of greater clarity I suppose that they exist simultaneously and that no others existed in Nature before them), in order to account for the existence of these twenty men, it will not be enough for us to demonstrate the cause of human nature in general; it will furthermore be necessary to demonstrate the cause why not more or fewer than twenty men exist, since (Note 3) there must necessarily be a cause for the existence of each one. But this cause (Notes 2 and 3) cannot be contained in the nature of man, since the true definition of man does not involve the number twenty. So (Note 4) the cause of the existence of these twenty men, and consequently of each one, must necessarily be external to each one, and therefore we can reach the unqualified conclusion that whenever several individuals of a kind exist, there must necessarily be an external cause for their existence. Now since existence belongs to the nature of substance (as has already been shown in this Scholium) the definition of substance must involve necessary existence, and consequently the existence of substance must be concluded solely from its definition. But the existence of several substances cannot follow from the definition of substance (as I have already shown in Notes 2 and 3). Therefore, from the definition of substance it follows necessarily that there exists only one substance of the same nature, as was proposed.

PROPOSITION 9

The more reality or being a thing has, the more attributes it has.

Proof

This is evident from Definition 4.

PROPOSITION 10

Each attribute of one substance must be conceived through itself.

Proof

For an attribute is that which intellect perceives of substance as constituting its essence (Def. 4), and so (Def. 3) it must be conceived through itself.

Scholium

From this it is clear that although two attributes be conceived as really distinct, that is, one without the help of the other, still we cannot deduce therefrom that they constitute two entities, or two different substances. For it is in the nature of substance that each of its attributes be conceived through itself, since all the attributes it possesses have always been in it simultaneously, and one could not have been produced by another; but each expresses the reality or being of substance. So it is by no means absurd to ascribe more than one attribute to one substance. Indeed, nothing in Nature is clearer than that each entity must be conceived under some attribute, and the more reality or being it has, the more are its attributes which express necessity, or eternity, and infinity. Consequently, nothing can be clearer than this, too, that an absolutely infinite entity must necessarily be defined (Def. 6) as an entity consisting of infinite attributes, each of which expresses a definite essence, eternal and infinite. Now if anyone asks by what mark can we distinguish between different substances, let him read the following Propositions, which show that in Nature there exists only one substance, absolutely infinite. So this distinguishing mark would be sought in vain.

PROPOSITION 11

God, or substance consisting of infinite attributes, each of which expresses eternal and infinite essence, necessarily exists.

Proof

If you deny this, conceive, if you can, that God does not exist. Therefore (Ax. 7), his essence does not involve existence. But this is absurd (Pr. 7). Therefore, God necessarily exists.

Second Proof

For every thing a cause or reason must be assigned either for its existence or for its nonexistence. For example, if a triangle exists, there must be a reason, or cause, for its existence. If it does not exist, there must be a reason or cause which prevents it from existing, or which annuls its existence. Now this reason or cause must either be contained in the nature of the thing or be external to it. For example, the reason why a square circle does not exist is indicated by its very nature, in that it involves a contradiction. On the other hand, the reason for the existence of substance also follows from its nature alone, in that it involves existence (Pr. 7). But the reason for the existence or nonexistence of a circle or a triangle does not follow from their nature, but from the order of universal corporeal Nature. For it is from this latter that it necessarily follows that either the triangle necessarily exists at this moment or that its present existence is impossible. This is self-evident, and therefrom it follows that a thing necessarily exists if there is no reason or cause which prevents its existence. Therefore if there can be no reason or cause which prevents God from existing or which annuls his existence, we are bound to conclude that he necessarily exists. But if there were such a reason or cause, it would have to be either within God's nature or external to it; that is, it would have to be in another substance of another nature. For if it were of the same nature, by that very fact it would be granted that God exists. But a substance of another nature would have nothing in common with God (Pr. 2), and so could neither posit nor annul his existence. Since therefore there cannot be external to God's nature a reason or cause that would annul God's existence, then if indeed he does not exist, the reason or cause must necessarily be in God's nature, which would therefore involve a contradiction. But to affirm this of a Being absolutely infinite and in the highest degree perfect is absurd. Therefore neither in God nor external to God is there any cause or reason which would annul his existence. Therefore, God necessarily exists.

A Third Proof

To be able to not exist is weakness; on the other hand, to be able to exist is power, as is self-evident. So if what now necessarily exists is nothing but finite entities, then finite entities are more potent than an absolutely infinite Entity—which is absurd. Therefore either nothing exists, or an absolutely infinite Entity necessarily exists, too. But we do exist, either in ourselves or in something else which necessarily exists (Ax. 1 and Pr. 7). Therefore, an absolutely infinite Entity—that is (Def. 6), God—necessarily exists.

Scholium

In this last proof I decided to prove God's existence *a posteriori* so that the proof may be more easily perceived, and not because God's existence does not follow *a priori* from this same basis. For since the ability to exist is power, it follows that the greater the degree of reality that belongs to the nature of a thing, the greater amount of energy it has for existence. So an absolutely infinite Entity or God will have from himself absolutely infinite power to exist, and therefore, exists absolutely.

But perhaps many will not readily find this proof convincing because they are used to considering only such things as derive from external causes. Of these things they observe that those which come quickly into being—that is, which readily exist—likewise readily perish, while things which they conceive as more complex they regard as more difficult to bring into being—that is, not so ready to exist. However, to free them from these misconceptions I do not need at this point to show what measure of truth there is in the saying, "Quickly come, quickly go," neither need I raise the question whether or not everything is equally easy in respect of Nature as a whole. It is enough to note simply this, that I am not here speaking of things that come into being through external causes, but only of substances, which (Pr. 6) cannot be produced by any external cause. For whether they consist of many parts or few, things that are brought about by external causes owe whatever degree of perfection or reality they possess entirely to the power of the external cause, and so their existence has its origin solely in the perfection of the external cause, and not in their own perfection. On the other hand, whatever perfection substance possesses is due to no external cause; therefore its existence, too, must follow solely from its own nature, and is therefore nothing else but its essence. So perfection does not annul a thing's existence: on the contrary, it posits it; whereas imperfection annuls a thing's existence. So there is nothing of which we can be more certain than the existence of an absolutely infinite or perfect Entity; that is, God. For since his essence excludes all imperfection and involves absolute perfection, it thereby removes all reason for doubting his existence and affords the utmost certainty of it. This, I think, must be quite clear to all who give a modicum of attention to the matter.

PROPOSITION 12

No attribute of substance can be truly conceived from which it would follow that substance can be divided.

Proof

The parts into which substance thus conceived would be divided will either retain the nature of substance or they will not. In the first case each part will have to be infinite (Pr. 8) and self-caused (Pr. 6) and consist of a different attribute (Pr. 5); and so several substances could be formed from one substance, which is absurd (Pr. 6). Furthermore, the parts would have nothing in common with the whole (Pr. 2), and the whole could exist and be conceived without its parts (Def. 4 and Pr. 10), the absurdity of which none can doubt. But in the latter case in which the parts will not retain the nature of substance—then when the whole substance would have been divided into equal parts it would lose the nature of substance and would cease to be. This is absurd (Pr. 7).

PROPOSITION 13

Absolutely infinite substance is indivisible.

Proof

If it were divisible, the parts into which it would be divided will either retain the nature of absolutely infinite substance, or not. In the first case, there would therefore be several substances of the same nature, which is absurd (Pr. 5). In the second case, absolutely infinite substance can cease to be, which is also absurd (Pr. 11).

Corollary

From this it follows that no substance, and consequently no corporeal substance, insofar as it is substance, is divisible.

Scholium

The indivisibility of substance can be more easily understood merely from the fact that the nature of substance can be conceived only as infinite, and that a part of substance can mean only finite substance, which involves an obvious contradiction (Pr. 8).

PROPOSITION 14

There can be, or be conceived, no other substance but God.

Proof

Since God is an absolutely infinite being of whom no attribute expressing the essence of substance can be denied (Def. 6) and since he necessarily exists (Pr. 11), if there were any other substance but God, it would have to be explicated through some attribute of God, and so there would exist two substances with the same attribute, which is absurd (Pr. 5). So there can be no substance external to God, and consequently no such substance can be conceived. For if it could be conceived, it would have to be conceived necessarily as existing; but this is absurd (by the first part of this proof). Therefore, no substance can be or be conceived external to God.

Corollary 1

Hence it follows quite clearly that God is one: that is (Def. 6), in the universe there is only one substance, and this is absolutely infinite, as I have already indicated in Scholium Pr. 10.

Corollary 2

It follows that the thing extended and the thing thinking are either attributes of God or (Ax. 1) affections of the attributes of God.

PROPOSITION 15

Whatever is, is in God, and nothing can be or be conceived without God.

Proof

Apart from God no substance can be or be conceived (Pr. 14), that is (Def. 3), something which is in itself and is conceived through itself. Now modes (Def. 5) cannot be or be conceived without substance; therefore, they can be only in the divine nature and can be conceived only through the divine nature. But nothing exists except substance and modes (Ax. 1). Therefore, nothing can be or be conceived without God.

Scholium

Some imagine God in the likeness of man, consisting of mind and body, and subject to passions. But it is clear from what has already been proved how far they stray from the true knowledge of God. These I dismiss, for all who have given any consideration to the divine nature deny that God is corporeal. They find convincing proof of this in the fact that by body we understand some quantity having length, breadth, and depth, bounded by a definite shape; and nothing more absurd than this can be attributed to God, a being absolutely infinite.

At the same time, however, by other arguments which they try to prove their point, they show clearly that in their thinking corporeal or extended substance is set completely apart from the divine nature, and they assert that it is created by God. But they have no idea from what divine power it could have been created, which clearly shows that they don't know what they are saying. Now I have clearly proved—at any rate, in my judgment (Cor. Pr. 6 and Sch. 2 Pr. 8)—that no substance can be produced or created by anything else. Furthermore, in Proposition 14 we showed that apart from God no substance can be or be conceived, and hence we deduced that extended substance is one of God's infinite attributes.

However, for a fuller explanation I will refute my opponents' arguments, which all seem to come down to this. Firstly, they think that corporeal substance, insofar as it is substance, is made up of parts, and so they deny that it can be infinite, and consequently that it can pertain to God. This they illustrate with many examples, of which I will take one or two. They say that if corporeal substance is infinite, suppose it to be divided into two parts. Each of these parts will be either finite or infinite. If the former, then the infinite is made up of two finite parts, which is absurd. If the latter, then there is an infinite which is twice as great as another infinite, which is also absurd.

Again, if an infinite length is measured in feet, it will have to consist of an infinite number of feet; and if it is measured in inches, it will consist of an infinite number of inches. So one infinite number will be twelve times greater than another infinite number.

Lastly, if from one point in an infinite quantity two lines, AB and AC, be drawn of fixed and determinate length, and thereafter be produced to infinity, it is clear that the distance between B and C continues to increase and finally changes from a determinate distance to an indeterminate distance.

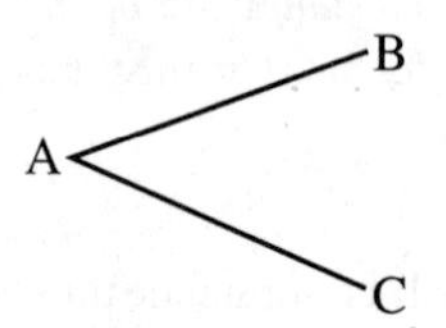

As these absurdities follow, they think, from supposing quantity to be infinite, they conclude that corporeal substance must be finite and consequently cannot pertain to God's essence.

The second argument is also drawn from God's consummate perfection. Since God, they say, is a supremely perfect being, he cannot be that which is acted upon. But corporeal substance, being divisible, can be acted upon. It therefore follows that corporeal substance does not pertain to God's essence.

These are the arguments I find put forward by writers who thereby seek to prove that corporeal substance is unworthy of the divine essence and cannot pertain to it. However, the student who looks carefully into these arguments will find that I have already replied to them, since they are all founded on the same supposition that material substance is composed of parts, and this I have already shown to be absurd (Pr. 12 and Cor. Pr. 13). Again, careful reflection will show that all those alleged absurdities (if indeed they are absurdities, which is not now under discussion) from which they seek to prove that extended substance is finite do not at all follow from the supposition that quantity is infinite, but that infinite quantity is measurable and is made up of finite parts. Therefore, from the resultant absurdities no other conclusion can be reached but that infinite quantity is not measurable and cannot be made up of finite parts. And this is exactly what we have already proved (Pr. 12). So the weapon they aimed at us is in fact turned against themselves. If therefore from this 'reductio ad absurdum' argument of theirs they still seek to deduce that extended substance must be finite, they are surely just like one who, having made the supposition that a circle has the properties of a square, deduces therefrom that a circle does not have a center from which all lines drawn to the circumference are equal. For corporeal substance, which can be conceived only as infinite, one, and indivisible (Prs. 8, 5, and 12), they conceive as made up of finite parts, multiplex, and divisible, so as to deduce that it is finite. In the same way others, too, having supposed that a line is composed of points, can find many arguments to prove that a line cannot be infinitely divided. Indeed, it is just as absurd to assert that corporeal substance is composed of bodies or parts as that a body is composed of surfaces, surfaces of lines, and lines of points. This must be admitted by all who know clear reason to be infallible, and particularly those who say that a vacuum cannot exist. For if corporeal substance could be so divided that its parts were distinct in reality, why could one part not be annihilated while the others remain joined together as before? And why should all the parts be so fitted together as to leave no vacuum? Surely, in the case of things which are in reality distinct from one another, one can exist without the other and remain in its original state. Since therefore there is no vacuum in Nature (of which [more] elsewhere) and all its parts must so harmonize that there is no vacuum, it also follows that the parts cannot be distinct in reality; that is, corporeal substance, insofar as it is substance, cannot be divided.

If I am now asked why we have this natural inclination to divide quantity, I reply that we conceive quantity in two ways, to wit, abstractly, or superficially—in other words, as represented in the imagination—or as substance, which we do only through the intellect. If therefore we consider quantity insofar as we represent it in the imagination—and this is what we more frequently and readily do—we find it to be finite, divisible, and made up of parts. But if we consider it intellectually and conceive it insofar as it is substance—and this is very difficult—then it will be found to be infinite, one, and indivisible, as we have already sufficiently proved. This will be quite clear to those who can distinguish between the imagination and the intellect, especially if this point also is stressed, that matter is everywhere the same, and there are no distinct parts in it except insofar as we conceive matter as modified in various ways. Then its parts are distinct, not really but only modally. For example, we conceive water to be divisible and to have separate parts insofar as it is water, but not insofar as it is material substance. In this latter respect it is not capable of separation or division. Furthermore, water, qua water, comes into existence and goes out of existence; but qua substance it does not come into existence nor go out of existence [*corrumpitur*].

I consider that in the above I have also replied to the second argument, since this too is based on the supposition that matter, insofar as it is substance, is divisible and made up of parts. And even though this were not so, I do not know why matter should be unworthy of the divine nature, since (Pr. 14) there can be no substance external to God by which it can be acted upon. All things, I repeat, are in God, and all things that come to pass do so only through the laws of God's infinite nature and follow through the necessity of his essence (as I shall later show). Therefore, by no manner of reasoning can it be said that God is acted upon by anything else or that extended substance is unworthy of the divine nature, even though it be supposed divisible, as long as it is granted to be eternal and infinite.

But enough of this subject for the present.

PROPOSITION 16

From the necessity of the divine nature there must follow infinite things in infinite ways [modis], *(that is, everything that can come within the scope of infinite intellect).*

Proof

This proposition should be obvious to everyone who will but consider this point, that from the given definition of any one thing the intellect infers a number of properties which necessarily follow in fact from the definition (that is, from the very essence of the thing), and the more reality the definition of the thing expresses (that is, the more reality the essence of the thing defined involves), the greater the number of its properties. Now since divine nature possesses absolutely infinite attributes (Def. 6), of which each one also expresses infinite essence in its own kind, then there must necessarily follow from the necessity of the divine nature an infinity of things in infinite ways (that is, everything that can come within the scope of the infinite intellect).

Corollary 1: Hence it follows that God is the efficient cause of all things that can come within the scope of the infinite intellect.

Corollary 2: Secondly, it follows that God is the cause through himself, not however *per accidens.*

Corollary 3: Thirdly, it follows that God is absolutely the first cause.

PROPOSITION 17

God acts solely from the laws of his own nature, constrained by none.

Proof

We have just shown that an infinity of things follow, absolutely, solely from the necessity of divine nature, or—which is the same thing—solely from the laws of that same nature (Pr. 16); and we have proved (Pr. 15) that nothing can be or be conceived without God, but that everything is in God. Therefore, there can be nothing external to God by which he can be determined or constrained to act. Thus God acts solely from the laws of his own nature and is constrained by none.

Corollary 1

Hence it follows, firstly, that there is no cause, except the perfection of his nature, which either extrinsically or intrinsically moves God to act.

Corollary 2

It follows, secondly, that God alone is a free cause. For God alone exists solely from the necessity of his own nature (Pr. 11 and Cor. 1 Pr. 14) and acts solely from the necessity of his own nature (Pr. 17). So he alone is a free cause (Def. 7).

Scholium

Others take the view that God is a free cause because—so they think—he can bring it about that those things which we have said follow from his nature—that is, which are within his power—should not come about; that is, they should not be produced by him. But this is as much as to say that God can bring it about that it should not follow from the nature of a triangle that its three angles are equal to two right angles, or that from a given cause the effect should not follow, which is absurd.

Furthermore, I shall show later on without the help of this proposition that neither intellect nor will pertain to the nature of God. I know indeed that there are many who think they can prove that intellect in the highest degree and free will belong to the nature of God; for they say they know of nothing more perfect which they may attribute to God than that which is the highest perfection in us. Again, although they conceive of God as having in actuality intellect in the highest degree, they yet do not believe he can bring about the existence of everything which in actuality he understands, for they think they would thereby be nullifying God's power. If, they say, he had created everything that is within his intellect, then he would not have been able to create anything more; and this they regard as inconsistent with God's omnipotence. So they have preferred to regard God as indifferent to everything and as creating nothing but what he has decided, by some absolute exercise of will, to create. However, I think I have shown quite clearly (Pr. 16) that from God's supreme power or infinite nature an infinity of things in infinite ways—that is, everything—has necessarily flowed or is always following from that same necessity, just as from the nature of a triangle it follows from eternity to eternity that its three angles are equal to two right angles. Therefore, God's omnipotence has from eternity been actual and will remain for eternity in the same actuality. In this way, I submit, God's omnipotence is established as being far more perfect. Indeed my opponents—let us speak frankly—seem to be denying God's omnipotence. For they are obliged to admit that God understands an infinite number of creatable things which nevertheless he can never create. If this were not so, that is, if he were to create all the things that he understands, he would exhaust his omnipotence, according to them, and render himself imperfect. Thus, to affirm God as perfect they are reduced to having to affirm at the same time that he cannot bring about everything that is within the bounds of his power. I cannot imagine anything more absurd than this, or more inconsistent with God's omnipotence.

Furthermore, I have something here to say about the intellect and will that is usually attributed to God. If intellect and will do indeed pertain to the eternal essence of God, one must understand in the case of both these attributes something very different from the meaning widely entertained. For the intellect and will that would constitute the essence of God would have to be vastly different from human intellect and will, and would have no point of agreement except the name. They could be no more alike than the celestial constellation of the Dog and the dog that barks. This I will prove as follows. If intellect does pertain to the divine nature, it cannot, like man's intellect, be posterior to (as most thinkers hold) or simultaneous with the objects of understanding, since God is prior in causality to all things (Cor. 1 Pr. 16). On the contrary, the truth and formal essence of things is what it is because it exists as such in the intellect of God as an object of thought. Therefore, God's intellect, insofar as it is conceived as constituting God's essence, is in actual fact the cause of things, in respect both of their essence and their existence. This seems to have been recognized also by those who have asserted that God's intellect, will, and power are one and the same. Since therefore God's intellect is the one and only cause of things, both of their essence and their existence, as we have shown, it must necessarily be different from them both in respect of essence and existence. For that which is caused differs from its cause precisely in what it has from its cause. For example, a man is the cause of the existence of another man, but not of the other's essence; for the essence is an eternal truth. So with regard to their essence the two men can be in full agreement, but they must differ with regard to existence; and for that reason if the existence of the one should cease, the existence of the other would not thereby cease. But if the essence of the one could be destroyed and rendered false, so too would the essence of the other. Therefore, a thing which is the cause of the essence and existence of some effect must differ from that effect both in respect of essence and existence. But God's intellect is the cause of the essence and existence of man's intellect. Therefore, God's intellect, insofar as it is conceived as constituting the divine essence, differs from man's intellect both in respect of essence and existence, and cannot agree with it in any respect other than name—which is what I sought to prove. In the matter of will, the proof is the same, as anyone can readily see.

PROPOSITION 18

God is the immanent, not the transitive, cause of all things.

Proof

All things that are, are in God, and must be conceived through God (Pr. 15), and so (Cor. 1 Pr. 16) God is the cause of the things that are in him, which is the first point. Further, there can be no substance external to God (Pr. 14); that is (Def. 3), a thing which is in itself external to God—which is the second point. Therefore, God is the immanent, not the transitive, cause of all things.

PROPOSITION 19

God [is eternal], that is, all the attributes of God are eternal.

Proof

God is substance (Def. 6) which necessarily exists (Pr. 11); that is (Pr. 7), a thing to whose nature it pertains to exist, or—and this is the same thing—a thing from whose definition existence follows; and so (Def. 8) God is eternal. Further, by the attributes of God must be understood that which expresses the essence of the Divine substance (Def. 4), that is, that which pertains to substance. It is this, I say, which the attributes themselves must involve. But eternity pertains to the nature of substance (as I have shown in Pr. 7). Therefore, each of the attributes must involve eternity, and so they are all eternal.

Scholium

This proposition is also perfectly clear from the manner in which I proved the existence of God (Pr. 11). From this proof, I repeat, it is obvious that God's existence is, like his essence, an eternal truth. Again, I have also proved God's eternity in another way in

Proposition 19 of my *Descartes's Principles of Philosophy*, and there is no need here to go over that ground again.

PROPOSITION 20

God's existence and his essence are one and the same.

Proof

God and all his attributes are eternal (Pr. 19); that is, each one of his attributes expresses existence (Def. 8). Therefore, the same attributes of God that explicate his eternal essence (Def. 4) at the same time explicate his eternal existence; that is, that which constitutes the essence of God at the same time constitutes his existence, and so his existence and his essence are one and the same.

Corollary 1

From this it follows, firstly, that God's existence, like his essence, is an eternal truth.

Corollary 2

It follows, secondly, that God is immutable; that is, all the attributes of God are immutable. For if they were to change in respect of existence, they would also have to change in respect of essence (Pr. 10); that is—and this is self-evident—they would have to become false instead of true, which is absurd.

PROPOSITION 21

All things that follow from the absolute nature of any attribute of God must have existed always, and as infinite; that is, through the said attribute they are eternal and infinite.

Proof

Suppose this proposition be denied and conceive, if you can, that something in some attribute of God, following from its absolute nature, is finite and has a determinate existence or duration; for example, the idea of God in Thought. Now Thought, being assumed to be an attribute of God, is necessarily infinite by its own nature (Pr. 11). However, insofar as it has the idea of God, it is being supposed as finite. Now (Def. 2) it cannot be conceived as finite unless it is determined through Thought itself. But it cannot be determined through Thought itself insofar as Thought constitutes the idea of God, for it is in that respect that Thought is supposed to be finite. Therefore, it is determined through Thought insofar as Thought does not constitute the idea of God, which Thought must nevertheless necessarily exist (Pr. 11). Therefore, there must be Thought which does not constitute the idea of God, and so the idea of God does not follow necessarily from its nature insofar as it is absolute Thought. (For it is conceived as constituting and as not constituting the idea of God.) This is contrary to our hypothesis. Therefore, if the idea of God in Thought, or anything in some attribute of God (it does not matter what is selected, since the proof is universal), follows from the necessity of the absolute nature of the attribute, it must necessarily be infinite. That was our first point.

Furthermore, that which thus follows from the necessity of the nature of some attribute cannot have a determinate existence, or duration. If this be denied, suppose that there is in some attribute of God a thing following from the necessity of the nature of the attribute, for example, the idea of God in Thought, and suppose that this thing either did not exist at some time, or will cease to exist in the future. Now since Thought is assumed as an attribute of God, it must necessarily exist, and as immutable (Pr. 11 and Cor. 2 Pr. 20). Therefore, outside the bounds of the duration of the idea of God (for this idea is supposed at some time not to have existed, or will at some point cease to exist) Thought will have to exist without the idea of God. But this is contrary to the hypothesis, for it is supposed that when Thought is granted the idea of God necessarily follows. Therefore, the idea of God in Thought, or anything that necessarily follows from the absolute nature of some attribute of God, cannot have a determinate existence, but is eternal through that same attribute. That was our second point. Note that the same holds for anything in an attribute of God which necessarily follows from the absolute nature of God.

PROPOSITION 22

Whatever follows from some attribute of God, insofar as the attribute is modified by a modification that exists necessarily and as infinite through that same attribute, must also exist both necessarily and as infinite.

Proof

This proposition is proved in the same way as the preceding one.

PROPOSITION 23

Every mode which exists necessarily and as infinite must have necessarily followed either from the absolute nature of some attribute of God or from some attribute modified by a modification which exists necessarily and as infinite.

Proof

A mode is in something else through which it must be conceived (Def. 5); that is (Pr. 15), it is in God alone and can be conceived only through God. Therefore, if a mode is conceived to exist necessarily and to be infinite, both these characteristics must necessarily be inferred or perceived through some attribute of God insofar as that attribute is conceived to express infinity and necessity of existence, or (and by Def. 8 this is the same) eternity; that is (Def. 6 and Pr. 19), insofar as it is considered absolutely. Therefore, a mode which exists necessarily and as infinite must have followed from the absolute nature of some attribute of God, either directly (Pr. 21) or through the mediation of some modification which follows from the absolute nature of the attribute; that is (Pr. 22), which exists necessarily and as infinite.

PROPOSITION 24

The essence of things produced by God does not involve existence.

Proof

This is evident from Def. 1. For only that whose nature (considered in itself) involves existence is self-caused and exists solely from the necessity of its own nature.

Corollary

Hence it follows that God is the cause not only of the coming into existence of things but also of their continuing in existence, or, to use a scholastic term, God is the cause of the being of things [*essendi rerum*]. For whether things exist or do not exist, in reflecting on their essence we realize that this essence involves neither existence nor duration. So it is not their essence which can be the cause of either their existence or their duration, but only God, to whose nature alone existence pertains (Cor. 1 Pr. 14).

PROPOSITION 25

God is the efficient cause not only of the existence of things but also of their essence.

Proof

If this is denied, then God is not the cause of the essence of things, and so (Ax. 4) the essence of things can be conceived without God. But this is absurd (Pr. 15). Therefore, God is also the cause of the essence of things.

Scholium

This proposition follows more clearly from Pr. 16; for from that proposition it follows that from the given divine nature both the essence and the existence of things must be inferred. In a word, in the same sense that God is said to be self-caused he must also be said to be the cause of all things. This will be even clearer from the following Corollary.

Corollary

Particular things are nothing but affections of the attributes of God, that is, modes wherein the attributes of God find expression in a definite and determinate way. The proof is obvious from Pr. 15 and Def. 5.

PROPOSITION 26

A thing which has been determined to act in a particular way has necessarily been so determined by God; and a thing which has not been determined by God cannot determine itself to act.

Proof

That by which things are said to be determined to act in a particular way must necessarily be something positive (as is obvious). So God, from the necessity of his nature, is the efficient cause both of its essence and its existence (Prs. 25 and 16)—which was the first point. From this the second point quite clearly follows as well. For if a thing which has not been determined by God could determine itself, the first part of this proposition would be false, which, as I have shown, is absurd.

PROPOSITION 27

A thing which has been determined by God to act in a particular way cannot render itself undetermined.

Proof

This proposition is evident from Axiom 3.

PROPOSITION 28

Every individual thing, i.e., anything whatever which is finite and has a determinate existence, cannot exist or be determined to act unless it be determined to exist and to act by another cause which is also finite and has a determinate existence, and this cause again cannot exist or be determined to act unless it be determined to exist and to act by another cause which is also finite and has a determinate existence, and so ad infinitum.

Proof

Whatever is determined to exist and to act has been so determined by God (Pr. 26 and Cor. Pr. 24). But that which is finite and has a determinate existence cannot have been produced by the absolute nature of one of God's attributes, for whatever follows from the absolute nature of one of God's attributes is infinite and eternal (Pr. 21). It must therefore have followed from God or one of his attributes insofar as that is considered as affected by some mode; for nothing exists but substance and its modes (Ax. 1 and Defs. 3 and 5), and modes (Cor. Pr. 25) are nothing but affections of God's attributes. But neither could a finite and determined thing have followed from God or one of his attributes insofar as that is affected by a modification which is eternal and infinite (Pr. 22). Therefore, it must have followed, or been determined to exist and to act, by God or one of his attributes insofar as it was modified by a modification which is finite and has a determinate existence. That was the first point. Then again this cause or this mode (the reasoning is the same as in the first part of this proof) must also have been determined by another cause, which is also finite and has a determinate existence, and again this last (the reasoning is the same) by another, and so *ad infinitum*.

Scholium

Since some things must have been produced directly by God (those things, in fact, which necessarily follow from his absolute nature) and others through the medium of these primary things (which other things nevertheless cannot be or be conceived without God), it follows, firstly, that God is absolutely the proximate cause of things directly produced by him. I say 'absolutely' [*absolute*], and not 'in its own kind' [*suo genere*], as some say. For the effects of God can neither be nor be conceived without their cause (Pr. 15 and Cor. Pr. 24). It follows, secondly, that God cannot properly be said to be the remote cause of individual things, unless perchance for the purpose of distinguishing these things from things which he has produced directly, or rather, things which follow from his absolute nature. For by 'remote cause' we understand a cause which is in no way conjoined with its effect. But all things that are, are in God, and depend on God in such a way that they can neither be nor be conceived without him.

PROPOSITION 29

Nothing in nature is contingent, but all things are from the necessity of the divine nature determined to exist and to act in a definite way.

Proof

Whatever is, is in God (Pr. 15). But God cannot be termed a contingent thing, for (Pr. 11) he exists necessarily, not contingently. Again, the modes of the divine nature have also followed from it necessarily, not contingently (Pr. 16), and that, too, whether insofar as the divine nature is considered absolutely (Pr. 21) or insofar as it is considered as determined to act in a definite way (Pr. 27). Furthermore, God is the cause of these modes not only insofar as they simply exist (Cor. Pr. 24), but also insofar as they are considered as determined to a particular action (Pr. 26). Now if they are not determined by God (Pr. 26), it is an impossibility, not a contingency, that they should determine themselves. On the other hand (Pr. 27), if they are determined by God, it is an impossibility, not a contingency, that they should render themselves undetermined. Therefore, all things are determined from the necessity of the divine nature not only to exist but also to exist and to act in a definite way. Thus, there is no contingency.

Scholium

Before I go any further, I wish to explain at this point what we must understand by 'Natura naturans' and 'Natura naturata.' I should perhaps say not 'explain,' but 'remind the reader,' for I consider that it is already clear from what has gone before that by 'Natura naturans' we must understand that which is in itself and is conceived through itself; that is, the attributes of substance that express eternal and infinite essence; or (Cor. 1 Pr. 14 and Cor. 2 Pr. 17), God insofar as he is considered a free cause. By 'Natura naturata' I understand all that follows from the necessity of God's nature, that is, from the necessity of each one of God's attributes; or all the modes of God's attributes insofar as they are considered as things which are in God and can neither be nor be conceived without God.

PROPOSITION 30

The finite intellect in act or the infinite intellect in act must comprehend the attributes of God and the affections of God, and nothing else.

Proof

A true idea must agree with its object [*ideatum*] (Ax. 6); that is (as is self-evident), that which is contained in the intellect as an object of thought must necessarily exist in Nature. But in Nature (Cor. 1 Pr. 14) there is but one substance—God—and no other affections (Pr. 15) than those which are in God and that can neither be nor be conceived (Pr. 15) without God. Therefore, the finite intellect in act or the infinite intellect in act must comprehend the attributes of God and the affections of God, and nothing else.

PROPOSITION 31

The intellect in act, whether it be finite or infinite, as also will, desire, love etc., must be related to Natura naturata, not to Natura naturans.

Proof

By intellect (as is self-evident) we do not understand absolute thought, but only a definite mode of thinking which differs from other modes such as desire, love, etc., and so (Def. 5) must be conceived through absolute thought—that is (Pr. 15 and Def. 6), an attribute of God which expresses the eternal and infinite essence of thought—in such a way that without this attribute it can neither be nor be conceived; and therefore (Sch. Pr. 29) it must be related to Natura naturata, not to Natura naturans, just like the other modes of thinking.

Scholium

The reason for my here speaking of the intellect in act is not that I grant there can be any intellect in potentiality, but that, wishing to avoid any confusion, I want to confine myself to what we perceive with the utmost clarity, to wit, the very act of understanding, than which nothing is more clearly apprehended by us. For we can understand nothing that does not lead to a more perfect cognition of the understanding.

PROPOSITION 32

Will cannot be called a free cause, but only a necessary cause.

Proof

Will, like intellect, is only a definite mode of thinking, and so (Pr. 28) no single volition can exist or be determined to act unless it is determined by another cause, and this cause again by another, and so *ad infinitum*. Now if will be supposed infinite, it must also be determined to exist and to act by God, not insofar as he is absolutely infinite substance, but insofar as he possesses an attribute which expresses the infinite and eternal essence of Thought (Pr. 23). Therefore, in whatever way will is conceived, whether finite or infinite, it requires a cause by which it is determined to exist and to act; and so (Def. 7) it cannot be said to be a free cause, but only a necessary or constrained cause.

Corollary 1

Hence it follows, firstly, that God does not act from freedom of will.

Corollary 2

It follows, secondly, that will and intellect bear the same relationship to God's nature as motion-and-rest and, absolutely, as all natural phenomena that must be determined by God (Pr. 29) to exist and to act in a definite way. For will, like all the rest, stands in need of a cause by which it may be determined to exist and to act in a definite manner. And although from a given will or intellect infinite things may follow, God cannot on that account be said to act from freedom of will any more than he can be said to act from freedom of motion-and-rest because of what follows from motion-and-rest (for from this, too, infinite things follow). Therefore, will pertains to God's nature no more than do other natural phenomena. It bears the same relationship to God's nature as does motion-and-rest and everything else that we have shown to follow from the necessity of the divine nature and to be determined by that divine nature to exist and to act in a definite way.

PROPOSITION 33

Things could not have been produced by God in any other way or in any other order than is the case.

Proof

All things have necessarily followed from the nature of God (Pr. 16) and have been determined to exist and to act in a definite way from the necessity of God's nature (Pr. 29). Therefore, if things could have been of a different nature or been determined to act in a different way so that the order of Nature would have been different, then God's nature, too, could have been other than it now is, and therefore (Pr. 11) this different nature, too, would have had to exist, and consequently there would have been two or more Gods, which (Cor. 1 Pr. 14) is absurd. Therefore, things could not have been produced by God in any other way or in any other order than is the case.

Scholium 1

Since I have here shown more clearly than the midday sun that in things there is absolutely nothing by virtue of which they can be said to be 'contingent,' I now wish to explain briefly what we should understand by 'contingent'; but I must first deal with 'necessary' and 'impossible.' A thing is termed 'necessary' either by reason of its essence or by reason of its cause. For a thing's existence necessarily follows either from its essence and definition or from a given efficient cause. Again, it is for these same reasons that a thing is termed 'impossible'—that is, either because its essence or definition involves a contradiction or because there is no external cause determined to bring it into existence. But a thing is termed 'contingent' for no other reason than the deficiency of our knowledge. For if we do not know whether the essence of a thing involves a contradiction, or if, knowing full well that its essence does not involve a contradiction, we still cannot make any certain judgment as to its existence because the chain of causes is hidden from us, then that thing cannot appear to us either as necessary or as impossible. So we term it either 'contingent' or 'possible.'

Scholium 2

It clearly follows from the above that things have been brought into being by God with supreme perfection, since they have necessarily followed from a most perfect nature. Nor does this imply any imperfection in God, for it is his perfection that has constrained us to make this affirmation. Indeed, from its contrary it would clearly follow (as I have just shown) that God is not supremely perfect, because if things had been brought into being in a different way by God, we should have to attribute to God another nature different from that which consideration of a most perfect Being has made us attribute to him.

However, I doubt not that many will ridicule this view as absurd and will not give their minds to its examination, and for this reason alone, that they are in the habit of attributing to God another kind of freedom very different from that which we (Def. 7) have assigned to him, that is, an absolute will. Yet I do not doubt that if they were willing to think the matter over and carefully reflect on our chain of proofs they would in the end reject the kind of freedom which they now attribute to God not only as nonsensical but as a serious obstacle to science. It is needless for me here to repeat what was said in the Scholium to Proposition 17. Yet for their sake I shall proceed to show that, even if it were to be granted that will pertains to the essence of God, it would nevertheless follow from his perfection that things could not have been created by God in any other way or in any other order. This will readily be shown if we first consider—as they themselves grant—that on God's decree and will alone does it depend that each thing is what it is. For otherwise God would not be the cause of all things. Further, there is the fact that all God's decrees have been sanctioned by God from eternity, for otherwise he could be accused of imperfection and inconstancy. But since the eternal does not admit of 'when' or 'before' or 'after,' it follows merely from God's perfection that God can never decree otherwise nor ever could have decreed otherwise; in other words, God could not have been prior to his decrees nor can he be without them. "But," they will say, "granted the supposition that God had made a different universe, or that from eternity he had made a different decree concerning Nature and her order, no imperfection in God would follow therefrom." But if they say this, they will be granting at the same time that God can change his decrees. For if God's decrees had been different from what in fact he has decreed regarding Nature and her order—that is, if he had willed and conceived differently concerning Nature—he would necessarily have had a different intellect and a different will from that which he now has. And if it is permissible to attribute to God a different intellect and a different will without any change in his essence and perfection, why should he not now be able to change his decrees concerning created things, and nevertheless remain equally perfect? For his intellect and will regarding created things and their order have the same relation to his essence and perfection, in whatever manner it be conceived.

Then again, all philosophers whom I have read grant that in God there is no intellect in potentiality but only intellect in act. Now since all of them also grant that his intellect and will are not distinct from his essence, it therefore follows from this, too, that if God had had a different intellect in act and a different will, his essence too would necessarily have been different. Therefore—as I deduced from the beginning—if things had been brought into being by God so as to be different from what they now are, God's intellect and will—that is (as is granted), God's essence—must have been different, which is absurd. Therefore, since things could not have been brought into being by God in any other way or order—and it follows from God's supreme perfection that this is true—surely we can have no sound reason for believing that God did not wish to create all the things that are in his intellect through that very same perfection whereby he understands them.

"But," they will say, "there is in things no perfection or imperfection; that which is in them whereby they are perfect or imperfect, and are called good or bad, depends only on the will of God. Accordingly, if God had so willed it he could have brought it about that that which is now perfection should be utmost imperfection, and vice versa." But what else is this but an open assertion that God, who necessarily understands that which he wills, can by his will bring it about that he should understand things in a way different from the way he understands them—and this, as I have just shown, is utterly absurd. So I can turn their own argument against them, as follows. All things depend on the power of God. For things to be able to be otherwise than as they are, God's will, too, would necessarily have to be different. But God's will cannot be different (as we have just shown most clearly from the consideration of God's perfection). Therefore, neither can things be different.

I admit that this view which subjects everything to some kind of indifferent will of God and asserts that everything depends on his pleasure diverges less from the truth than the view of those who hold that God does everything with the good in mind. For these people seem to posit something external to God that does not depend upon him, to which in acting God looks as if it were a model, or to which he aims, as if it were a fixed target. This is surely to subject God to fate; and no more absurd assertion can be made about God, whom we have shown to be the first and the only free cause of both the essence and the existence of things. So I need not spend any more time in refuting this absurdity.

PROPOSITION 34

God's power is his very essence.

Proof

From the sole necessity of God's essence it follows that God is self-caused (Pr. 11) and the cause of all things (Pr. 16 and Cor.). Therefore, God's power, whereby he and all things are and act, is his very essence.

PROPOSITION 35

Whatever we conceive to be within God's power necessarily exists.

Proof

Whatever is within God's power must be so comprehended in his essence (Pr. 34) that it follows necessarily from it, and thus necessarily exists.

PROPOSITION 36

Nothing exists from whose nature an effect does not follow.

Proof

Whatever exists expresses God's nature or essence in a definite and determinate way (Cor. Pr. 25); that is (Pr. 34), whatever exists expresses God's power, which is the cause of all things, in a definite and determinate way, and so (Pr. 16) some effect must follow from it.

APPENDIX

I have now explained the nature and properties of God: that he necessarily exists, that he is one alone, that he is and acts solely from the necessity of his own nature, that he is the free cause of all things and how so, that all things are in God and are so dependent on him that they can neither be nor be conceived without him, and lastly, that all things have been predetermined by God, not from his free will or absolute pleasure, but from the absolute nature of God, his infinite power. Furthermore, whenever the opportunity arose I have striven to remove prejudices that might hinder the apprehension of my proofs. But since there still remain a considerable number of prejudices, which have been, and still are, an obstacle—indeed, a very great obstacle—to the acceptance of the concatenation of things in the manner which I have expounded, I have thought it proper at this point to bring these prejudices before the bar of reason.

Now all the prejudices which I intend to mention here turn on this one point, the widespread belief among men that all things in Nature are like themselves in acting with an end in view. Indeed, they hold it as certain that God himself directs everything to a fixed end; for they say that God has made everything for man's sake and has made man so that he should worship God. So this is the first point I shall consider, seeking the reason why most people are victims of this prejudice and why all are so naturally disposed to accept it. Secondly, I shall demonstrate its falsity; and lastly I shall show how it has been the source of misconceptions about good and bad, right and wrong, praise and blame, order and confusion, beauty and ugliness, and the like.

However, it is not appropriate here to demonstrate the origin of these misconceptions from the nature of the human mind. It will suffice at this point if I take as my basis what must be universally admitted, that all men are born ignorant of the causes of things, that they all have a desire to seek their own advantage, a desire of which they are conscious. From this it follows, firstly, that men believe that they are free, precisely because they are conscious of their volitions and desires; yet concerning the causes that have determined them to desire and will they do not think, not even dream about, because they are ignorant of them. Secondly, men act always with an end in view, to wit, the advantage that they seek. Hence it happens that they are always looking only for the final causes of things done, and are satisfied when they find them, having, of course, no reason for further doubt. But if they fail to discover them from some external source, they have no recourse but to turn to themselves, and to reflect on what ends would normally determine them to similar actions, and so they necessarily judge other minds by their own. Further, since they find within themselves and outside themselves a considerable number of means very convenient for the pursuit of their own advantage—as, for instance, eyes for seeing, teeth for chewing, cereals and living creatures for food, the sun for giving light, the sea for breeding fish—the result is that they look on all the things of Nature as means to their own advantage. And realizing that these were found, not produced by them, they come to believe that there is someone else who produced these means for their use. For looking on things as means, they could not believe them to be self-created, but on the analogy of the means which they are accustomed to produce for themselves, they were bound to conclude that there was some governor or governors of Nature, endowed with human freedom, who have attended to all their needs and made everything for their use. And having no information on the subject, they also had to estimate the character of these rulers by their own, and so they asserted that the gods direct everything for man's use so that they may bind men to them and be held in the highest honor by them. So it came about that every individual devised different methods of worshipping God as he thought fit in order that God should love him beyond others and direct the whole of Nature so as to serve his blind cupidity and insatiable greed. Thus it was that this misconception developed into superstition and became deep-rooted in the minds of men, and it was for this reason that every man strove most earnestly to understand and to explain the final causes of all things. But in seeking to show that Nature does nothing in vain—that is, nothing that is not to man's advantage—they seem to have shown only this, that Nature and the gods are as crazy as mankind.

Consider, I pray, what has been the upshot. Among so many of Nature's blessings they were bound to discover quite a number of disasters, such as storms, earthquakes, diseases, and so forth, and they maintained that these occurred because the gods were angry at the wrongs done to them by men, or the faults committed in the course of their worship. And although daily experience cried out against this and showed by any number of examples that blessings and disasters befall the godly and the ungodly alike without discrimination, they did not on that account abandon their ingrained prejudice. For they found it easier to regard this fact as one among other mysteries they could not understand and thus maintain their innate condition of ignorance rather than to demolish in its entirety the theory they had constructed and devise a new one. Hence they made it axiomatic that the judgment of the gods is far beyond man's understanding. Indeed, it is for this reason, and this reason only, that truth might have evaded mankind forever had not Mathematics, which is concerned not with ends but only with the essences and properties of figures, revealed to men a different standard of truth. And there are other causes too—there is no need to mention them here—which could have made men aware of these widespread misconceptions and brought them to a true knowledge of things.

I have thus sufficiently dealt with my first point. There is no need to spend time in going on to show that Nature has no fixed goal and that all final causes are but figments of the human imagination. For I think that this is now quite evident, both from the basic causes from which I have traced the origin of this misconception and from Proposition 16 and the Corollaries to Proposition 32, and in addition from the whole set or proofs I have adduced to show that all things in Nature proceed from all eternal necessity and with supreme perfection. But I will make this additional point, that this doctrine of Final Causes turns Nature completely upside down, for it regards as an effect that which is in fact a cause, and vice versa. Again, it makes that which is by nature first to be last; and finally, that which is highest and most perfect is held to be the most imperfect. Omitting the first two points as self-evident, Propositions 21, 22, and 23 make it clear that that effect is most perfect which is directly produced by God, and an effect is the less perfect in proportion to the number of intermediary causes required for its production. But if the things produced directly by God were brought about to enable him to attain an end, then of necessity the last things for the sake of which the earlier things were brought about would excel all others. Again, this doctrine negates God's perfection; for if God acts with an end in view, he must necessarily be seeking something that he lacks. And although theologians and metaphysicians may draw a distinction between a purpose arising from want and an assimilative purpose, they still admit that God has acted in all things for the sake of himself, and not for the sake of the things to be created. For prior to creation they are not able to point to anything but God as a purpose for God's action. Thus they have to admit that God lacked and desired those things for the procurement of which he willed to create the means—as is self-evident.

I must not fail to mention here that the advocates of this doctrine, eager to display their talent in assigning purpose to things, have introduced a new style of argument to prove their doctrine, i.e., a reduction, not to the impossible, but to ignorance, thus revealing the lack of any other argument in its favor. For example, if a stone falls from the roof on somebody's head and kills him, by this method of arguing they will prove that the stone fell in order to kill the man; for if it had not fallen for this purpose by the will of God, how could so many circumstances (and there are often many coinciding circumstances) have chanced to concur? Perhaps you will reply that the event occurred because the wind was blowing and the man was walking that way. But they will persist in asking why the wind blew at that time and why the man was walking that way at that very time. If you again reply that the wind sprang up at that time because on the previous day the sea had begun to toss after a period of calm and that the man had been invited by a friend, they will again persist—for there is no end to questions—"But why did the sea toss, and why was the man invited for that time?" And so they will go on and on asking the causes of causes, until you take refuge in the will of God—that is, the sanctuary of ignorance. Similarly, when they consider the structure of the human body, they are astonished, and being ignorant of the causes of such skillful work they conclude that it is fashioned not by mechanical art but by divine or supernatural art, and is so arranged that no one part shall injure another.

As a result, he who seeks the true causes of miracles and is eager to understand the works of Nature as a scholar, and not just to gape at them like a fool, is universally considered an impious heretic and denounced by those to whom the common people bow down as interpreters of Nature and the gods. For these people know that the dispelling of ignorance would entail the disappearance of that astonishment, which is the one and only support for their argument and for safeguarding their authority. But I will leave this subject and proceed to the third point that I proposed to deal with.

When men become convinced that everything that is created is created on their behalf, they were bound to consider as the most important quality in every individual thing that which was most useful to them, and to regard as of the highest excellence all those things by which they were most benefited. Hence they came to form these abstract notions to explain the natures of things: Good, Bad, Order, Confusion, Hot, Cold, Beauty, Ugliness; and since they believe that they are free, the following abstract notions came into being: Praise, Blame, Right, Wrong. The latter I shall deal with later on after I have treated of human nature; at this point I shall briefly explain the former.

All that conduces to well being and to the worship of God they call Good, and the contrary, Bad. And since those who do not understand the nature of things, but only imagine things, make no affirmative judgments about things themselves and mistake their imagination for intellect, they are firmly convinced that there is order in things, ignorant as they are of things and of their own nature. For when things are in such arrangement that, being presented to us through our senses, we can readily picture them and thus readily remember them, we say that they are well arranged; if the contrary, we say that they are ill arranged, or confused. And since those things we can readily picture we find pleasing compared with other things, men prefer order to confusion, as though order were something in Nature other than what is relative to our imagination. And they say that God has created all things in an orderly way, without realizing that they are thus attributing human imagination to God—unless perchance they mean that God, out of consideration for the human imagination, arranged all things in the way that men could most easily imagine. And perhaps they will find no obstacle in the fact that there are any number of things that far surpass our imagination, and a considerable number that confuse the imagination because of its weakness.

But I have devoted enough time to this. Other notions, too, are nothing but modes of imagining whereby the imagination is affected in various ways, and yet the ignorant consider them as important attributes of things because they believe—as I have said—that all things were made on their behalf, and they call a thing's nature good or bad, healthy or rotten and corrupt, according to its effect on them. For instance, if the motion communicated to our nervous system by objects presented through our eyes is conducive to our feeling of well being, the objects which are its cause are said to be beautiful, while the objects which provoke a contrary motion are called ugly. Those things that we sense through the nose are called fragrant or fetid; through the tongue, sweet or bitter, tasty or tasteless; those that we sense by touch are called hard or soft, rough or smooth, and so on. Finally, those that we sense through our ears are said to give forth noise, sound, or harmony, the last of which has driven men to such madness that they used to believe that even God delights in harmony. There are philosophers who have convinced themselves that the motions of the heavens give rise to harmony. All this goes to show that everyone's judgment is a function of the disposition of his brain, or rather, that he mistakes for reality the way his imagination is affected. Hence it is no wonder—as we should note in passing—that we find so many controversies arising among men, resulting finally in skepticism. For although human bodies agree in many respects, there are very many differences, and so one man thinks good what another thinks bad; what to one man is well ordered, to another is confused; what to one is pleasing, to another is displeasing, and so forth. I say no more here because this is not the place to treat at length of this subject, and also because all are well acquainted with it from experience. Everybody knows those sayings: "So many heads, so many opinions," "everyone is wise in his own sight," "brains differ as much as palates," all of which show clearly that men's judgment is a function of the disposition of the brain, and they are guided by imagination rather than intellect. For if men understood things, all that I have put forward would be found, if not attractive, at any rate convincing, as Mathematics attests.

We see therefore that all the notions whereby the common people are wont to explain Nature are merely modes of imagining, and denote not the nature of any thing but only the constitution of the imagination. And because these notions have names as if they were the names of entities existing independently of the imagination I call them 'entities of imagination' [*entia imaginationis*] rather than 'entities of reason' [*entia rationis*]. So all arguments drawn from such notions against me can be easily refuted. For many are wont to argue on the following lines: If everything has followed from the necessity of God's most perfect nature, why does Nature display so many imperfections, such as rottenness to the point of putridity, nauseating ugliness, confusion, evil, sin, and so on? But, as I have just pointed out, they are easily refuted. For the perfection of things should be measured solely from their own nature and power; nor are things more or less perfect to the extent that they please or offend human senses, serve or oppose human interests. As to those who ask why God did not create men in such a way that they should be governed solely by reason, I make only this reply, that he lacked not material for creating all things from the highest to the lowest degree of perfection; or, to speak more accurately, the laws of his nature were so comprehensive as to suffice for the production of everything that can be conceived by an infinite intellect, as I proved in Proposition 16.

These are the misconceptions which I undertook to deal with at this point. Any other misconception of this kind can be corrected by everyone with a little reflection.

Part II

OF THE NATURE AND ORIGIN OF THE MIND

I now pass on to the explication of those things that must necessarily have followed from the essence of God, the eternal and infinite Being; not indeed all of them—for we proved in Proposition 16 Part I that from his essence there must follow infinite things in infinite ways—but only those things that can lead us as it were by the hand to the knowledge of the human mind and its utmost blessedness.

DEFINITIONS

1. By 'body' I understand a mode that expresses in a definite and determinate way God's essence insofar as he is considered as an extended thing. (See Cor. Pr. 25, I.)

2. I say that there pertains to the essence of a thing that which, when granted, the thing is necessarily posited, and by the annulling of which the thing is necessarily annulled; or that without which the thing can neither be nor be conceived, and, vice versa, that which cannot be or be conceived without the thing.

3. By idea I understand a conception of the Mind which the Mind forms because it is a thinking thing.

Explication

I say 'conception' rather than 'perception' because the term perception seems to indicate that the Mind is passive to its object, whereas conception seems to express an activity of the Mind.

4. By an adequate idea I mean an idea which, insofar as it is considered in itself without relation to its

object, has all the properties—that is, intrinsic characteristics—of a true idea [*ideatum*].

Explication

I say 'intrinsic' so as to exclude the extrinsic characteristic—to wit, the agreement of the idea with that of which it is an idea.

5. Duration is the indefinite continuance of existing.

Explication

I say 'indefinite' because it can in no wise be determined through the nature of the existing thing, nor again by the thing's efficient cause which necessarily posits, but does not annul, the existence of the thing.

6. By reality and perfection I mean the same thing.
7. By individual things [*res singulares*] I mean things that are finite and have a determinate existence. If several individual things concur in one act in such a way as to be all together the simultaneous cause of one effect, I consider them all, in that respect, as one individual.

AXIOMS

1. The essence of man does not involve necessary existence; that is, from the order of Nature it is equally possible that a certain man exists or does not exist.
2. Man thinks.
3. Modes of thinking such as love, desire, or whatever emotions are designated by name, do not occur unless there is in the same individual the idea of the thing loved, desired, etc. But the idea can be without any other mode of thinking.
4. We feel a certain body to be affected in many ways.
5. We do not feel or perceive any individual things except bodies and modes of thinking. [N.B.: For Postulates, see after Proposition 13.]

PROPOSITION 1

Thought is an attribute of God; i.e., God is a thinking thing.

Proof

Individual thoughts, or this and that thought, are modes expressing the nature of God in a definite and determinate way (Cor. Pr. 25, I). Therefore there belongs to God (Def. 5, I) an attribute the conception of which is involved in all individual thoughts, and through which they are conceived. Thought, therefore, is one of God's infinite attributes, expressing the eternal and infinite essence of God (Def. 6, I); that is, God is a thinking thing.

Scholium

This Proposition is also evident from the fact that we can conceive of an infinite thinking being. For the more things a thinking being can think, the more reality or perfection we conceive it to have. Therefore a being that can think infinite things in infinite ways is by virtue of its thinking necessarily infinite. Since therefore by merely considering Thought we conceive an infinite being, Thought is necessarily one of the infinite attributes of God (Defs. 4 and 6, I), as we set out to prove.

PROPOSITION 2

Extension is an attribute of God; i.e., God is an extended thing.

Proof

This Proposition is proved in the same way as the preceding proposition.

PROPOSITION 3

In God there is necessarily the idea both of his essence and of everything that necessarily follows from his essence.

Proof

For God can (Pr. 1, II) think infinite things in infinite ways, or (what is the same thing, by Pr. 16, I) can form the idea of his own essence and of everything that necessarily follows from it. But all that is in God's power necessarily exists (Pr. 35, I). Therefore such an idea necessarily exists, and only in God (Pr. 15, I).

Scholium

By God's power the common people understand free will and God's right over all things that are, which things are therefore commonly considered as contingent. They say that God has power to destroy everything and bring it to nothing. Furthermore, they frequently compare God's power with that of kings. But this doctrine we have refuted in Cors. 1 and 2, Pr. 32, I; and in Pr. 16, I, we proved that God acts by the same necessity whereby he understands himself; that is, just as it follows from the necessity of the divine nature (as is universally agreed) that God understands himself, by that same necessity it also follows that God acts infinitely in infinite ways. Again, we showed in Pr. 34, I that God's power is nothing but God's essence in action, and so it is as impossible for us to conceive that God does not act as that God does not exist. Furthermore, if one wished to pursue the matter, I could easily show here that the power that common people assign to God is not only a human power (which shows that they conceive God as a man or like a man) but also involves negation of power. But I am reluctant to hold forth so often on the same subject. I merely request the reader most earnestly to reflect again and again on what we said on this subject in Part I from Proposition 16 to the end. For nobody will rightly apprehend what I am trying to say unless he takes great care not to confuse God's power with a king's human power or right.

PROPOSITION 4

The idea of God, from which infinite things follow in infinite ways, must be one, and one only.

Proof

Infinite intellect comprehends nothing but the attributes of God and his affections (Pr. 30, I). But God is one, and one only (Cor. 1 Pr. 14, I). Therefore the idea of God, from which infinite things follow in infinite ways, must be one, and one only.

PROPOSITION 5

The formal being of ideas recognizes God as its cause only insofar as he is considered as a thinking thing, and not insofar as he is explicated by any other attribute; that is, the ideas both of God's attributes and of individual things recognize as their efficient cause not the things of which they are ideas,—that is, the things perceived,—but God himself insofar as he is a thinking thing.

Proof

This is evident from Pr. 3, II. For there our conclusion that God can form the idea of his own essence and of everything that necessarily follows therefrom was inferred solely from God's being a thinking thing, and not from his being the object of his own idea. Therefore the formal being of ideas recognizes God as its cause insofar as he is a thinking thing. But there is another proof, as follows. The formal being of ideas is a mode of thinking (as is self-evident); that is (Cor. Pr. 25, I), a mode which expresses in a definite manner the nature of God insofar as he is a thinking thing, and so does not involve (Pr. 10, I) the conception of any other attribute of God. Consequently (Ax. 4, I), it is the effect of no other attribute but Thought; and so the formal being of ideas recognizes God as its cause only insofar as he is considered as a thinking thing.

PROPOSITION 6

The modes of any attribute have God for their cause only insofar as he is considered under that attribute, and not insofar as he is considered under any other attribute.

Proof

Each attribute is conceived through itself independently of any other (Pr. 10, I). Therefore the modes of any attribute involve the conception of their own attribute, and not that of any other. Therefore they have God for their cause only insofar as he is considered under the attribute of which they are modes, and not insofar as he is considered under any other attribute (Ax. 4, I).

Corollary

Hence it follows that the formal being of things that are not modes of thinking does not follow from the nature of God by reason of his first having known them; rather, the objects of ideas follow and are inferred from their own attributes in the same way and by the same necessity as we have shown ideas to follow from the attribute of Thought.

PROPOSITION 7

The order and connection of ideas is the same as the order and connection of things.

Proof

This is evident from Ax. 4, I; for the idea of what is caused depends on the knowledge of the cause of which it is the effect.

Corollary

Hence it follows that God's power of thinking is coextensive with his actualized power of acting. That is, whatever follows formally from the infinite nature of God, all this follows from the idea of God as an object of thought in God according to the same order and connection.

Scholium

At this point, before proceeding further, we should recall to mind what I have demonstrated above—that whatever can be perceived by infinite intellect as constituting the essence of substance pertains entirely to the one sole substance. Consequently, thinking substance and extended substance are one and the same substance, comprehended now under this attribute, now under that. So, too, a mode of Extension and the idea of that mode are one and the same thing, expressed in two ways. This truth seems to have been glimpsed by some of the Hebrews,[1] who hold that God, God's intellect, and the things understood by God are one and the same. For example, a circle existing in Nature and the idea of the existing circle—which is also in God—are one and the same thing, explicated through different attributes. And so, whether we conceive Nature under the attribute of Extension or under the attribute of Thought or under any other attribute, we find one and the same order, or one and the same connection of causes—that is, the same things following one another. When I said that God is the cause, e.g., of the idea of a circle only insofar as he is a thinking thing, and of a circle only insofar as he is an extended thing, my reason was simply this, that the formal being of the idea of a circle can be perceived only through another mode of thinking as its proximate cause, and that mode through another, and so *ad infinitum*, with the result that as long as things are considered as modes of thought, we must explicate the order of the whole of Nature, or the connection of causes, through the attribute of Thought alone; and insofar as things are considered as modes of Extension, again the order of the whole of Nature must be explicated through the attribute of Extension only. The same applies to other attributes. Therefore God, insofar as he consists of infinite attributes, is in fact the cause of things as they are in themselves. For the present, I cannot give a clearer explanation.

PROPOSITION 8

The ideas of nonexisting individual things or modes must be comprehended in the infinite idea of God in the same way as the formal essences of individual things or modes are contained in the attributes of God.

Proof

This proposition is obvious from the preceding one, but may be understood more clearly from the preceding Scholium.

Corollary

Hence it follows that as long as individual things do not exist except insofar as they are comprehended in the attributes of God, their being as objects of thought—that is, their ideas—do not exist except insofar as the infinite idea of God exists; and when individual things are said to exist not only insofar as they are comprehended in the attributes of God but also insofar as they are said to have duration, their

1. [The reference is most likely to Moses Maimonides, *The Guide of the Perplexed*, Part 1, Chapter 68.—S.S.]

ideas also will involve the existence through which they are said to have duration.

Scholium

Should anyone want an example for a clearer understanding of this matter, I can think of none at all that would adequately explicate the point with which I am here dealing, for it has no parallel. Still, I shall try to illustrate it as best I can. The nature of a circle is such that the rectangles formed from the segments

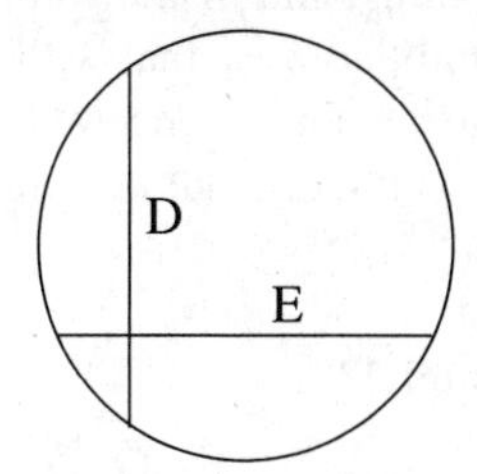

of its intersecting chords are equal. Hence an infinite number of equal rectangles are contained in a circle, but none of them can be said to exist except insofar as the circle exists, nor again can the idea of any one of these rectangles be said to exist except insofar as it is comprehended in the idea of the circle. Now of this infinite number of intersecting chords let two, E and D, exist. Now indeed their ideas also exist not only insofar as they are merely comprehended in the idea of the circle but also insofar as they involve the existence of those rectangles, with the result that they are distinguished from the other ideas of the other rectangles.

PROPOSITION 9

The idea of an individual thing existing in actuality has God for its cause not insofar as he is infinite but insofar as he is considered as affected by another idea of a thing existing in actuality, of which God is the cause insofar as he is affected by a third idea, and so ad infinitum.

Proof

The idea of an individual actually existing thing is an individual mode of thinking distinct from other modes (Cor. and Sch. Pr. 8, II), and so (Pr. 6, II) it has God as its cause only insofar as he is a thinking thing. But not (Pr. 28, I) insofar as he is a thinking thing absolutely, but insofar as he is considered as affected by another definite mode of thinking. And of this latter God is also the cause insofar as he is affected by another definite mode of thinking, and so *ad infinitum*. But the order and connection of ideas is the same as the order and connection of causes (Pr. 7, II). Therefore an individual idea is caused by another idea; i.e., God insofar as he is considered as affected by another idea. And this last idea is caused by God, insofar as he is affected by yet another idea, and so *ad infinitum*.

Corollary

Whatsoever happens in the individual object of any idea, knowledge of it is in God only insofar as he has the idea of that object.

Proof

Whatsoever happens in the object of any idea, the idea of it is in God (Pr. 3, II) not insofar as he is infinite, but insofar as he is considered as affected by another idea of an individual thing (preceding Pr.). But the order and connection of ideas is the same as the order and connection of things (Pr. 7, II). Therefore the knowledge of what happens in an individual object is in God only insofar as he has the idea of that object.

PROPOSITION 10

The being of substance does not pertain to the essence of man; i.e., substance does not constitute the form [forma] *of man.*

Proof

The being of substance involves necessary existence (Pr. 7, I). So if the being of substance pertained to the essence of man, man would necessarily be granted together with the granting of substance (Def. 2, II), and consequently man would necessarily exist, which is absurd (Ax. 1, II). Therefore . . . etc.

Scholium

This Proposition is also proved from Pr. 5, I, which states that there cannot be two substances of the same nature. Now since many men can exist, that which constitutes the form of man is not the being of substance. This Proposition is furthermore evident from the other properties of substance—that substance is by its own nature infinite, immutable, indivisible, etc., as everyone can easily see.

Corollary

Hence it follows that the essence of man is constituted by definite modifications of the attributes of God.

Proof

For the being of substance does not pertain to the essence of man (preceding Pr.), which must therefore (Pr. 15, I) be something that is in God, and which can neither be nor be conceived without God; i.e., an affection or mode (Cor. Pr. 25, I) which expresses the nature of God in a definite and determinate way.

Scholium

All must surely admit that nothing can be or be conceived without God. For all are agreed that God is the sole cause of all things, both of their essence and their existence; that is, God is the cause of things not only in respect of their coming into being [*secundum fieri*], as they say, but also in respect of their being. But at the same time many assert that that without which a thing can neither be nor be conceived pertains to the essence of the thing, and so they believe that either the nature of God pertains to the essence of created things or that created things can either be or be conceived without God; or else, more probably, they hold no consistent opinion. I think that the reason for this is their failure to observe the proper order of philosophical enquiry. For the divine nature, which they should have considered before all else—it being prior both in cognition and in Nature—they have taken to be last in the order of cognition, and the things that are called objects of sense they have taken as prior to everything. Hence it has come about that in considering natural phenomena, they have completely disregarded the divine nature. And when thereafter they turned to the contemplation of the divine nature, they could find no place in their thinking for those fictions on which they had built their natural science, since these fictions were of no avail in attaining knowledge of the divine nature. So it is little wonder that they have contradicted themselves on all sides.

But I pass over these points, for my present purpose is restricted to explaining why I have not said that that without which a thing can neither be nor be perceived pertains to the essence of the thing. My reason is that individual things can neither be nor be conceived without God, and yet God does not pertain to their essence. But I did say that that necessarily constitutes the essence of a thing which, when posited, posits the thing, and by the annulling of which the thing is annulled; i.e., that without which the thing can neither be nor be conceived, and vice versa, that which can neither be nor be conceived without the thing.

PROPOSITION 11

That which constitutes the actual being of the human mind is basically nothing else but the idea of an individual actually existing thing.

Proof

The essence of man (Cor. Pr. 10, II) is constituted by definite modes of the attributes of God, to wit (Ax. 2, II), modes of thinking. Of all these modes the idea is prior in nature (Ax. 3, II), and when the idea is granted, the other modes—modes to which the idea is prior by nature—must be in the same individual (Ax. 3, II). And so the idea is that which basically constitutes the being of the human mind. But not the idea of a nonexisting thing; for then (Cor. Pr. 8, II) the idea itself could not be said to exist. Therefore, it is the idea of an actually existing thing. But not the idea of an infinite thing, for an infinite thing (Prs. 21 and 22, I) must always necessarily exist, and this is absurd (Ax. 1, II). Therefore that which first constitutes the actual being of the human mind is the idea of an individual actually existing thing.

Corollary

Hence it follows that the human mind is part of the infinite intellect of God; and therefore when we say that the human mind perceives this or that, we are saying nothing else but this: that God—not insofar as he is infinite but insofar as he is explicated through the nature of the human mind, that is, insofar as he constitutes the essence of the human mind—has this or that idea. And when we say that God has this or that idea not only insofar as he constitutes the essence of the human mind but also insofar as he has the idea of another thing simultaneously with the human mind, then we are saying that the human mind perceives a thing partially or inadequately.

Scholium

At this point our readers will no doubt find themselves in some difficulty and will think of many things that will give them pause. So I ask them to proceed slowly step by step with me, and to postpone judgment until they have read to the end.

PROPOSITION 12

Whatever happens in the object of the idea constituting the human mind is bound to be perceived by the human mind; i.e., the idea of that thing will necessarily be in the human mind. That is to say, if the object of the idea constituting the human mind is a body, nothing can happen in that body without its being perceived by the mind.

Proof

Whatever happens in the object of any idea, knowledge thereof is necessarily in God (Cor. Pr. 9, II) insofar as he is considered as affected by the idea of that object; that is, (Pr. 11, II) insofar as he constitutes the mind of some thing. So whatever happens in the object of the idea constituting the human mind, knowledge thereof is necessarily in God insofar as he constitutes the nature of the human mind; that is (Cor. Pr. 11, II), knowledge of that thing is necessarily in the mind; i.e., the mind perceives it.

Scholium

This Proposition is also obvious, and is more clearly understood from Sch. Pr. 7, II, q.v.

PROPOSITION 13

The object of the idea constituting the human mind is the body—i.e., a definite mode of extension actually existing, and nothing else.

Proof

If the body were not the object of the human mind, the ideas of the affections of the body would not be in God (Cor. Pr. 9, II) insofar as he constitutes our mind, but insofar as he constitutes the mind of another thing; that is, (Cor. Pr. 11, II) the ideas of the affections of the body would not be in our mind. But (Ax. 4, II) we do have ideas of the affections of a body. Therefore the object of the idea constituting the human mind is a body, a body actually existing (Pr. 11, II). Again, if there were another object of the mind apart from the body, since nothing exists from which some effect does not follow (Pr. 36, I), there would necessarily have to be in our mind the idea of some effect of it (Pr. 12, II). But (Ax. 5, II) there is no such idea. Therefore the object of our mind is an existing body, and nothing else.

Corollary

Hence it follows that man consists of mind and body, and the human body exists according as we sense it.

Scholium

From the above we understand not only that the human Mind is united to the Body but also what is to be understood by the union of Mind and Body. But nobody can understand this union adequately or distinctly unless he first gains adequate knowledge of the nature of our body. For what we have so far demonstrated is of quite general application, and applies to men no more than to other individuals, which are all animate, albeit in different degrees. For there is necessarily in God an idea of each thing whatever, of which idea God is the cause in the same way as he is the cause of the idea of the human body. And so whatever we have asserted of the idea of the human body must necessarily be asserted of the idea of each thing. Yet we cannot deny, too, that ideas differ among themselves as do their objects, and that one is more excellent and contains more reality than another, just as the object of one idea is more excellent than that of another and contains more reality. Therefore, in order to determine the difference between the human mind and others and in what way it surpasses them, we have to know the nature of its object, (as we have said); that is, the nature of the human body. Now I cannot here explain this nature, nor is it essential for the points that I intend to demonstrate. But I will make this general assertion, that in proportion as a body is more apt than other bodies to act or be acted upon simultaneously in many ways, so is its mind more apt than other minds to perceive many things simultaneously; and in proportion as the actions of one body depend on itself alone and the less that other bodies concur with it in its actions, the more apt is its mind to understand distinctly. From this we can realise the superiority of one mind over others, and we can furthermore see why we have only a very confused knowledge of our body, and many other facts which I shall deduce from this basis in what follows. Therefore I have thought it worthwhile to explicate and demonstrate these things more carefully. To this end there must be a brief preface concerning the nature of bodies.

Axiom 1

All bodies are either in motion or at rest.

Axiom 2

Each single body can move at varying speeds.

Lemma 1

Bodies are distinguished from one another in respect of motion and rest, quickness and slowness, and not in respect of substance.

Proof

The first part of this Lemma I take to be self-evident. As to bodies not being distinguished in respect of substance, this is evident from both Pr. 5 and Pr. 8, Part I, and still more clearly from Sch. Pr. 15, Part I.

Lemma 2

All bodies agree in certain respects.

Proof

All bodies agree in this, that they involve the conception of one and the same attribute (Def. 1, II), and also in that they may move at varying speeds, and may be absolutely in motion or absolutely at rest.

Lemma 3

A body in motion or at rest must have been determined to motion or rest by another body, which likewise has been determined to motion or rest by another body, and that body by another, and so *ad infinitum*.

Proof

Bodies are individual things (Def. 1, II) which are distinguished from one another in respect of motion and rest (Lemma 1), and so (Pr. 28, I) each body must have been determined to motion or rest by another individual thing, namely, another body (Pr. 6, II), which is also in motion or at rest (Ax. 1). But this body again—by the same reasoning—could not have been in motion or at rest unless it had been determined to motion or rest by another body, and this body again—by the same reasoning—by another body, and so on, *ad infinitum*.

Corollary

Hence it follows that a body in motion will continue to move until it is determined to rest by another body, and a body at rest continues to be at rest until it is determined to move by another body. This, too, is self-evident; for when I suppose, for example, that a body A is at rest and I give no consideration to other moving bodies, I can assert nothing about body A but that it is at rest. Now if it should thereafter happen that body A is in motion, this surely could not have resulted from the fact that it was at rest; for from that fact nothing else could have followed than that body A should be at rest. If on the other hand A were supposed to be in motion, as long as we consider only A, we can affirm nothing of it but that it is in motion. If it should thereafter happen that A should be at rest, this surely could not have resulted from its previous motion; for from its motion nothing else could have followed but that A was in motion. So this comes about from a thing that was not in A, namely, an external cause by which the moving body A was determined to rest.

Axiom 1

All the ways in which a body is affected by another body follow from the nature of the affected body together with the nature of the body affecting it, so that one and the same body may move in various ways in accordance with the various natures of the bodies causing its motion; and, on the other hand, different bodies may be caused to move in different ways by one and the same body.

Axiom 2

When a moving body collides with a body at rest and is unable to cause it to move, it is reflected so as to continue its motion, and the angle between the line of motion of the reflection and the plane of the body at rest with which it has collided is equal to the angle between the line of incidence of motion and the said plane.

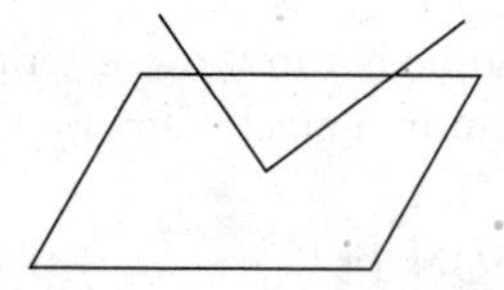

So far we have been discussing the simplest bodies, those which are distinguished from one another solely by motion and rest, quickness and slowness. Now let us advance to composite bodies.

Definition

When a number of bodies of the same or different magnitude form close contact with one another through the pressure of other bodies upon them, or if they are moving at the same or different rates of speed so as to preserve an unvarying relation of movement among themselves, these bodies are said to be united with one another and all together to form one body or individual thing, which is distinguished from other things through this union of bodies.

Axiom 3

The degree of difficulty with which the parts of an individual thing or composite body can be made to change their position and consequently the degree of difficulty with which the individual takes on different shapes, is proportional to the extent of the surface areas along which they are in close contact. Hence bodies whose parts maintain close contact along large areas of their surfaces I term hard; those whose parts maintain contact along small surface areas I term soft; while those whose parts are in a state of motion among themselves I term liquid.

Lemma 4

If from a body, or an individual thing composed of a number of bodies, certain bodies are separated, and at the same time a like number of other bodies of the same nature take their place, the individual thing will retain its nature as before, without any change in its form [*forma*].

Proof

Bodies are not distinguished in respect of substance (Lemma 1). That which constitutes the form of the individual thing consists in a union of bodies (preceding definition). But this union, by hypothesis, is retained in spite of the continuous change of component bodies. Therefore the individual thing will retain its own nature as before, both in respect of substance and of mode.

Lemma 5

If the parts of an individual thing become greater or smaller, but so proportionately that they all preserve the same mutual relation of motion-and-rest as before, the individual thing will likewise retain its own nature as before without any change in its form.

Proof

The reasoning is the same as in the preceding Lemma.

Lemma 6

If certain bodies composing an individual thing are made to change the existing direction of their motion, but in such a way that they can continue their motion and keep the same mutual relation as before, the individual thing will likewise preserve its own nature without any change of form.

Proof

This is self-evident; for, by hypothesis, the individual thing retains all that we, in defining it, asserted as constituting its form.

Lemma 7

Furthermore, the individual thing so composed retains its own nature, whether as a whole it is moving or at rest, and in whatever direction it moves, provided that each constituent part retains its own motion and continues to communicate this motion to the other parts.

Proof

This is evident from its definition, which you will find preceding Lemma 4.

Scholium

We thus see how a composite individual can be affected in many ways and yet preserve its nature. Now hitherto we have conceived an individual thing composed solely of bodies distinguished from one another only by motion-and-rest and speed of movement; that is, an individual thing composed of the simplest bodies. If we now conceive another individual thing composed of several individual things of different natures, we shall find that this can be affected in many other ways while still preserving its nature. For since each one of its parts is composed of several bodies, each single part can therefore (preceding Lemma), without any change in its nature, move with varying degrees of speed and consequently communicate its own motion to other parts with varying degrees of speed. Now if we go on to conceive a third kind of individual things composed of this second kind, we shall find that it can be affected in many other ways without any change in its form. If we thus continue to infinity, we shall readily conceive the whole of Nature as one individual whose parts—that is, all the constituent bodies—vary in infinite ways without any change in the individual as a whole.

If my intention had been to write a full treatise on body, I should have had to expand my explications and demonstrations. But I have already declared a different intention, and the only reason for my dealing with this subject is that I may readily deduce therefrom what I have set out to prove.

POSTULATES

1. The human body is composed of very many individual parts of different natures, each of which is extremely complex.
2. Of the individual components of the human body, some are liquid, some are soft, and some are hard.
3. The individual components of the human body, and consequently the human body itself, are affected by external bodies in a great many ways.
4. The human body needs for its preservation a great many other bodies, by which, as it were [*quasi*], it is continually regenerated.
5. When a liquid part of the human body is determined by an external body to impinge frequently on another part which is soft, it changes the surface of that part and impresses on it certain traces of the external body acting upon it.
6. The human body can move external bodies and dispose them in a great many ways.

PROPOSITION 14

The human mind is capable of perceiving a great many things, and this capacity will vary in proportion to the variety of states which its body can assume.

Proof

The human body (Posts. 3 and 6) is affected by external bodies in a great many ways and is so structured that it can affect external bodies in a great many ways. But the human mind must perceive all that happens in the human body (Pr. 12, II). Therefore the human mind is capable of perceiving very many things, and . . . etc.

PROPOSITION 15

The idea which constitutes the formal being of the human mind is not simple, but composed of very many ideas.

Proof

The idea which constitutes the formal being of the human mind is the idea of the body (Pr. 13, II), which is composed of a great number of very composite individual parts (Postulate 1). But in God there is necessarily the idea of every individual component part (Cor. Pr. 8, II). Therefore (Pr. 7, II) the idea of the human body is composed of these many ideas of the component parts.

PROPOSITION 16

The idea of any mode wherein the human body is affected by external bodies must involve the nature of the human body together with the nature of the external body.

Proof

All the modes wherein a body is affected follow from the nature of the body affected together with the nature of the affecting body (Ax. 1 after Cor. Lemma 3). Therefore the idea of these modes will necessarily involve the nature of both bodies (Ax. 4, I). So the idea of any mode wherein the human body is affected by an external body involves the nature of the human body and the external body.

Corollary 1

Hence it follows that the human mind perceives the nature of very many bodies along with the nature of its own body.

Corollary 2

Secondly, the ideas that we have of external bodies indicate the constitution of our own body more than the nature of external bodies. This I have explained with many examples in Appendix, Part I.

PROPOSITION 17

If the human body is affected in a way [modo] *that involves the nature of some external body, the human mind will regard that same external body as actually existing, or as present to itself, until the human body undergoes a further modification which excludes the existence or presence of the said body.*

Proof

This is evident; for as long as the human body is thus affected, so long will the human mind (Pr. 12, II) regard this affection of the body; that is (by the preceding Proposition), so long will it have the idea of a mode existing in actuality, an idea involving the nature of an external body; that is, an idea which does not exclude but posits the existence or presence of the nature of the external body. So the mind (Cor.1 of the preceding Proposition) will regard the external body as actually existing, or as present, until . . . etc.

Corollary

The mind is able to regard as present external bodies by which the human body has been once affected, even if they do not exist and are not present.

Proof

When external bodies so determine the fluid parts of the human body that these frequently impinge on the softer parts, they change the surfaces of these softer parts (Post. 5). Hence it comes about (Ax. 2 after Cor. Lemma 3) that the fluid parts are reflected therefrom in a manner different from what was previously the case; and thereafter, again coming into contact with the said changed surfaces in the course of their own spontaneous motion, they are reflected in the same way as when they were impelled towards those surfaces by external bodies. Consequently, in continuing this reflected motion they affect the human body in the same manner, which manner will again be the object of thought in the mind (Pr. 12, II); that is (Pr. 17, II), the mind will again regard the external body as present. This will be repeated whenever the fluid parts of the human body come into contact with those same surfaces in the course of their own spontaneous motion. Therefore, although the external bodies by which the human body has once been affected may no longer exist, the mind will regard them as present whenever this activity of the body is repeated.

Scholium

So we see how it can come about that we regard as present things which are not so, as often happens. Now it is possible that there are other causes for this fact, but it is enough for me at this point to have indicated one cause through which I can explicate the matter just as if I had demonstrated it through its true cause. Yet I do not think that I am far from the truth, since all the postulates that I have assumed contain scarcely anything inconsistent with experience; and after demonstrating that the human body exists just as we sense it (Cor. Pr. 13, II), we may not doubt experience.

In addition (preceding Cor. and Cor. 2 Pr. 16, II), this gives a clear understanding of the difference between the idea, e.g., of Peter which constitutes the essence of Peter's mind, and on the other hand the idea of Peter which is in another man, say Paul. The former directly explicates the essence of Peter's body, and does not involve existence except as long as Peter exists. The latter indicates the constitution of Paul's body rather than the nature of Peter; and so, while that constitution of Paul's body continues to be, Paul's mind will regard Peter as present to him although Peter may not be in existence. Further, to retain the usual terminology, we will assign the word 'images' [*imagines*] to those affections of the human body the ideas of which set forth external bodies as if they were present to us, although they do not represent shapes. And when the mind regards bodies in this way, we shall say that it 'imagines' [*imaginari*].

At this point, to begin my analysis of error, I should like you to note that the imaginations of the mind, looked at in themselves, contain no error; i.e., the mind does not err from the fact that it imagines, but only insofar as it is considered to lack the idea which excludes the existence of those things which it imagines to be present to itself. For if the mind, in imagining nonexisting things to be present to it, knew at the same time that those things did not exist in fact, it would surely impute this power of imagining not to the defect but to the strength of its own nature, especially if this faculty of imagining were to depend solely on its own nature; that is (Def. 7, I), if this faculty of imagining were free.

PROPOSITION 18

If the human body has once been affected by two or more bodies at the same time, when the mind afterwards imagines one of them, it will straightway remember the others too.

Proof

The mind imagines (preceding Cor.) any given body for the following reason, that the human body is affected and conditioned by the impressions of an external body in the same way as it was affected when certain of its parts were acted upon by the external body. But, by hypothesis, the human mind was at that time conditioned in such a way that the mind imagined two bodies at the same time. Therefore it will now also imagine two bodies at the same time, and the mind, in imagining one of them, will straightway remember the other as well.

Scholium

Hence we clearly understand what memory is. It is simply a linking of ideas involving the nature of things outside the human body, a linking which occurs in the mind parallel to the order and linking of the affections of the human body. I say, firstly, that it is only the linking of those ideas that involve the nature of things outside the human body, not of those ideas that explicate the nature of the said things. For they are in fact (Pr. 16, II) ideas of the affections of the human body which involve the nature both of the human body and of external bodies. Secondly, my purpose in saying that this linking occurs in accordance with the order and linking of the affections of the human body is to distinguish it from the linking of ideas in accordance with the order of the intellect whereby the mind perceives things through their first causes, and which is the same in all men.

Furthermore, from this we clearly understand why the mind, from thinking of one thing, should straightway pass on to thinking of another thing which has no likeness to the first. For example, from thinking of the word 'pomum' [apple] a Roman will straightway fall to thinking of the fruit, which has no likeness to that articulated sound nor anything in common with it other than that the man's body has often been affected by them both; that is, the man has often heard the word 'pomum' while seeing the fruit. So everyone will pass on from one thought to another according as habit in each case has arranged the images in his body. A soldier, for example, seeing the tracks of a horse in the sand will straightway pass on from thinking of the horse to thinking of the rider, and then thinking of war, and so on. But a peasant, from thinking of a horse, will pass on to thinking of a plough, and of a field, and so on. So every person will pass on from thinking of one thing to thinking of another according as he is in the habit of joining together and linking the images of things in various ways.

PROPOSITION 19

The human mind has no knowledge of the body, nor does it know it to exist, except through ideas of the affections by which the body is affected.

Proof

The human mind is the very idea or knowledge of the human body (Pr. 13, II), and this idea is in God (Pr. 9, II) insofar as he is considered as affected by another idea of a particular thing; or, since (Post. 4) the human body needs very many other bodies by which it is continually regenerated, and the order and connection of ideas is the same (Pr. 7, II) as the order and connection of causes, this idea is in God insofar as he is considered as affected by the ideas of numerous particular things. Therefore God has the idea of the human body, or knows the human body, insofar as he is affected by numerous other ideas, and not insofar as he constitutes the nature of the human mind; that is, (Cor. Pr. 11, II), the human mind does not know the human body. But the ideas of the affections of the body are in God insofar as he does constitute the nature of human mind; i.e., the human mind perceives these affections (Pr. 12, II) and consequently perceives the human body (Pr. 16, II), and perceives it as actually existing (Pr. 17, II). Therefore, it is only to that extent that the human mind perceives the human body.

PROPOSITION 20

There is also in God the idea or knowledge of the human mind, and this follows in God and is related to God in the same way as the idea or knowledge of the human body.

Proof

Thought is an attribute of God (Pr. 1, II), and so (Pr. 3, II) the idea of both Thought and its affections—and consequently of the human mind as well—must necessarily be in God. Now this idea or knowledge of the mind does not follow in God insofar as he is infinite, but insofar as he is affected by another idea of a particular thing (Pr. 9, II). But the order and connection of ideas is the same as the order and connection of causes (Pr. 7, II). Therefore, the idea or knowledge of the mind follows in God and is related to God in the same way as the idea or knowledge of the body.

PROPOSITION 21

This idea of the mind is united to the mind in the same way as the mind is united to the body.

Proof

That the mind is united to the body we have shown from the fact that the body is the object of the mind (Prs. 12 and 13, II), and so by the same reasoning the idea of the mind must be united to its object—that is, to the mind itself—in the same way as the mind is united to the body.

Scholium

This proposition is understood far more clearly from Sch. Pr. 7, II. There we showed that the idea of the body and the body itself—that is, (Pr. 13, II) mind and body—are one and the same individual thing, conceived now under the attribute of Thought and now under the attribute of Extension. Therefore, the idea of the mind and the mind itself are one and the same thing, conceived under one and the same attribute, namely, Thought. The idea of the mind, I repeat, and the mind itself follow in God by the same necessity and from the same power of thought. For in fact the idea of the mind—that is, the idea of an idea—is nothing other than the form [*forma*] of the idea insofar as the idea is considered as a mode of thinking without relation to its object. For as soon as anyone knows something, by that very fact he knows that he knows, and at the same time he knows that he knows that he knows, and so on *ad infinitum*. But I will deal with this subject later.

PROPOSITION 22

The human mind perceives not only the affections of the body but also the ideas of these affections.

Proof

The ideas of ideas of affections follow in God and are related to God in the same way as ideas of affections, which can be proved in the same manner as Pr. 20, II. But the ideas of affections of the body are in the human mind (Pr. 12, II); that is (Cor. Pr. 11, II), in God insofar as he constitutes the essence of the human mind. Therefore the ideas of these ideas will be in God insofar as he has knowledge or the idea of the human mind; that is (Pr. 21, II), they will be in the human mind itself, which therefore perceives not only the affections of the body but also the ideas of these affections.

PROPOSITION 23

The mind does not know itself except insofar as it perceives ideas of affections of the body.

Proof

The idea or knowledge of the mind (Pr. 20, II) follows in God and is related to God in the same way as the idea or knowledge of the body. But since (Pr. 19, II) the human mind does not know the human body—that is, (Cor. Pr. 11, II) since the knowledge of the human body is not related to God insofar as he constitutes the nature of the human mind—therefore neither is knowledge of the mind related to God insofar as he constitutes the essence of the human mind. And so (Cor. Pr. 11, II) the human mind to that extent does not know itself. Again, the ideas of the affections by which the body is affected involve the nature of the human body (Pr. 16, II); that is, (Pr. 13, II) they are in agreement [*conveniunt*] with the nature of the mind. Therefore, the knowledge of these ideas will necessarily involve knowledge of the mind. But (preceding Pr.) the knowledge of these ideas is in the human mind. Therefore, the human mind knows itself only to that extent.

PROPOSITION 24

The human mind does not involve an adequate knowledge of the component parts of the human body.

Proof

The component parts of the human body do not pertain to the essence of the body itself save insofar as they preserve an unvarying relation of motion with one another (Def. after Cor. Lemma 3), and not insofar as they can be considered as individual things apart from their relation to the human body. For the parts of the human body (Post. 1) are very composite individual things, whose parts can be separated from the human body (Lemma 4) without impairing in any way its nature and specific reality [*forma*], and can establish a quite different relation of motion with other bodies (Ax. 1 after Lemma 3). Therefore (Pr. 3, II), the idea or knowledge of any component part will be in God, and will be so (Pr. 9, II) insofar as he is considered as affected by another idea of a particular thing, a particular thing which is prior in Nature's order to the part itself (Pr. 7, II). Further, the same holds good of any part of an individual component part of the human body, and so of any component part of the human body there is knowledge in God insofar as he is affected by very many ideas of things, and not insofar as he has the idea only of the human body, that is (Pr. 13, II), the idea that constitutes the nature of the human mind. So (Cor. Pr. 11, II) the human mind does not involve adequate knowledge of the component parts of the human body.

PROPOSITION 25

The idea of any affection of the human body does not involve an adequate knowledge of an external body.

Proof

We have shown that the idea of an affection of the human body involves the nature of an external body insofar as the external body determines the human body in some definite way (Pr. 16, II). But insofar as the external body is an individual thing that is not related to the human body, the idea or knowledge of it is in God (Pr. 9, II) insofar as God is considered as affected by the idea of another thing which is (Pr. 7, II) prior in nature to the said external body. Therefore, an adequate knowledge of the external body is not in God insofar as he has the idea of an affection of the human body; i.e., the idea of an affection of the human body does not involve an adequate knowledge of an external body.

PROPOSITION 26

The human mind does not perceive any external body as actually existing except through the ideas of affections of its own body.

Proof

If the human body is not affected in any way by an external body, then (Pr. 7, II) neither is the idea of the human body—that is (Pr. 13, II), the human mind—affected in any way by the idea of the existence of that body; i.e., it does not in any way perceive the existence of that external body. But insofar as the human body is affected in some way by an external body, to that extent it perceives the external body (Pr. 16, II, with Cor.1).

Corollary

Insofar as the human mind imagines [*imaginatur*] an external body, to that extent it does not have an adequate knowledge of it.

Proof

When the human mind regards external bodies through the ideas of affections of its own body, we say that it imagines [*imaginatur*] (see Sch. Pr. 17, II), and in no other way can the mind imagine external bodies as actually existing (preceding Pr.). Therefore, insofar as the mind imagines external bodies (Pr. 25, II), it does not have adequate knowledge of them.

PROPOSITION 27

The idea of any affection of the human body does not involve adequate knowledge of the human body.

Proof

Any idea whatsoever of any affection of the human body involves the nature of the human body only to the extent that the human body is considered to be affected in some definite way (Pr. 16, II). But insofar as the human body is an individual thing that can be affected in many other ways, the idea . . . etc. (See Proof Pr. 25, II.)

PROPOSITION 28

The ideas of the affections of the human body, insofar as they are related only to the human mind, are not clear and distinct, but confused.

Proof

The ideas of the affections of the human body involve the nature both of external bodies and of the human body itself (Pr. 16, II), and must involve the nature not only of the human body but also of its parts. For affections are modes in which parts of the human body (Post. 3), and consequently the body as a whole, is affected. But (Prs. 24 and 25, II) an adequate knowledge of external bodies, as also of the component parts of the human body, is not in God insofar as he is considered as affected by the human mind, but insofar as he is considered as affected by other ideas. Therefore, these ideas of affections, insofar as they are related only to the human mind, are like conclusions without premises; that is, as is self-evident, confused ideas.

Scholium

The idea that constitutes the nature of the human mind is likewise shown, when considered solely in itself, not to be clear and distinct, as is also the idea of the human mind and the ideas of affections of the human body insofar as they are related only to the human mind, as everyone can easily see.

PROPOSITION 29

The idea of the idea of any affection of the human body does not involve adequate knowledge of the human mind.

Proof

The idea of an affection of the human body (Pr. 27, II) does not involve adequate knowledge of the body itself; in other words, it does not adequately express the nature of the body; that is (Pr. 13, II), it does not adequately agree [*convenit*] with the nature of the mind. So (Ax. 6, I) the idea of this idea does not adequately express the nature of the human mind; i.e., it does not involve an adequate knowledge of it.

Corollary

Hence it follows that whenever the human mind perceives things after the common order of nature, it does not have an adequate knowledge of itself, nor of its body, nor of external bodies, but only a confused and fragmentary knowledge. For the mind does not know itself save insofar as it perceives ideas of the affections of the body (Pr. 23, II). Now it does not perceive its own body (Pr. 19, II) except through ideas of affections of the body, and also it is only through these affections that it perceives external bodies (Pr. 26, II). So insofar as it has these ideas, it has adequate knowledge neither of itself (Pr. 29, II) nor of its own body (Pr. 27, II) nor of external bodies (Pr. 25, II), but only a fragmentary [*multilatam*] and confused knowledge (Pr. 28, II and Sch.).

Scholium

I say expressly that the mind does not have an adequate knowledge, but only a confused and fragmentary knowledge, of itself, its own body, and external bodies whenever it perceives things from the common order of nature, that is, whenever it is determined externally—namely, by the fortuitous run of circumstance—to regard this or that, and not when it is determined internally, through its regarding several things at the same time, to understand their agreement, their differences, and their opposition. For whenever it is conditioned internally in this or in another way, then it sees things clearly and distinctly, as I shall later show.

PROPOSITION 30

We can have only a very inadequate knowledge of the duration of our body.

Proof

The duration of our body does not depend on its essence (Ax. 1, II), nor again on the absolute nature of God (Pr. 21, I), but (Pr. 28, I) it is determined to exist and to act by causes which are also determined by other causes to exist and to act in a definite and determinate way, and these again by other causes, and so *ad infinitum*. Therefore, the duration of our body depends on the common order of nature and the structure of the universe. Now there is in God adequate knowledge of the structure of the universe insofar as he has ideas of all the things in the universe, and not insofar as he has only the idea of the human body (Cor. Pr. 9, II). Therefore, knowledge of the duration of our body is very inadequate in God insofar as he is considered only to constitute the nature of the human mind. That is (Cor. Pr. 11, II), this knowledge is very inadequate in the human mind.

PROPOSITION 31

We can have only a very inadequate knowledge of the duration of particular things external to us.

Proof

Each particular thing, just like the human body, must be determined by another particular thing to exist and to act in a definite and determinate way, and this latter thing again by another, and so on *ad infinitum* (Pr. 28, I). Now since we have shown in the preceding Proposition that from this common property of particular things we can have only a very inadequate knowledge of the duration of the human body, in the case of the duration of particular things we have to come to the same conclusion: that we can have only a very inadequate knowledge thereof.

Corollary

Hence it follows that all particular things are contingent and perishable. For we can have no adequate knowledge of their duration (preceding Pr.), and that is what is to be understood by contingency and perishability (Sch. I, Pr. 33, I). For apart from this there is no other kind of contingency (Pr. 29, I).

PROPOSITION 32

All ideas are true insofar as they are related to God.

Proof

All ideas, which are in God, agree completely with the objects of which they are ideas (Cor. Pr. 7, II), and so they are all true (Ax. 6, I).

PROPOSITION 33

There is nothing positive in ideas whereby they can be said to be false.

Proof

If this be denied, conceive, if possible, a positive mode of thinking which constitutes the form [*forma*] of error or falsity. This mode of thinking cannot be in God (preceding Pr.), but neither can it be or be conceived externally to God (Pr. 15, I). Thus there can be nothing positive in ideas whereby they can be called false.

PROPOSITION 34

Every idea which in us is absolute, that is, adequate and perfect, is true.

Proof

When we say that there is in us an adequate and perfect idea, we are saying only this (Cor. Pr. 11, II), that there is an adequate and perfect idea in God insofar as he constitutes the essence of our mind. Consequently we are saying only this, that such an idea is true (Pr. 32, II).

PROPOSITION 35

Falsity consists in the privation of knowledge which inadequate ideas, that is, fragmentary and confused ideas, involve.

Proof

There is nothing positive in ideas which constitutes the form [*forma*] of falsity (Pr. 33, II). But falsity cannot consist in absolute privation (for minds, not bodies, are said to err and be deceived), nor again in absolute ignorance, for to be ignorant and to err are different. Therefore it consists in that privation of knowledge which inadequate knowledge, that is, inadequate and confused ideas, involves.

Scholium

In Sch. Pr. 17, II I explained how error consists in the privation of knowledge, but I will give an example to enlarge on this explanation. Men are deceived in thinking themselves free, a belief that consists only in this, that they are conscious of their actions and ignorant of the causes by which they are determined. Therefore, the idea of their freedom is simply the ignorance of the cause of their actions. As to their saying that human actions depend on the will, these are mere words without any corresponding idea. For none of them knows what the will is and how it moves the body, and those who boast otherwise and make up stories of dwelling places and habitations of the soul provoke either ridicule or disgust.

As another example, when we gaze at the sun, we see it as some two hundred feet distant from us. The error does not consist in simply seeing the sun in this way but in the fact that while we do so we are not aware of the true distance and the cause of our seeing it so. For although we may later become aware that the sun is more than six hundred times the diameter of the earth distant from us, we shall nevertheless continue to see it as close at hand. For it is not our ignorance of its true distance that causes us to see the sun to be so near; it is that the affection of our body involves the essence of the sun only to the extent that the body is affected by it.

PROPOSITION 36

Inadequate and confused ideas follow by the same necessity as adequate, or clear and distinct, ideas.

Proof

All ideas are in God (Pr. 15, I), and insofar as they are related to God, they are true (Pr. 32, II) and adequate (Cor. Pr. 7, II). So there are no inadequate or confused ideas except insofar as they are related to the particular mind of someone (see Prs. 24 and 28, II). So all ideas, both adequate and inadequate, follow by the same necessity (Cor. Pr. 6, II).

PROPOSITION 37

That which is common to all things (see Lemma 2 above) and is equally in the part as in the whole, does not constitute the essence of any one particular thing.

Proof

If this be denied, conceive, if possible, that it does constitute the essence of one particular thing, B. Therefore it can neither be nor be conceived without B (Def. 2, II). But this is contrary to our hypothesis. Therefore, it does not pertain to B's essence, nor does it constitute the essence of any other particular thing.

PROPOSITION 38

Those things that are common to all things and are equally in the part as in the whole, can be conceived only adequately.

Proof

Let A be something common to all bodies, and equally in the part of any body as in the whole. I say that A can be conceived only adequately. For its idea (Cor. Pr. 7, II) will necessarily be in God both insofar as he has the idea of the human body and insofar as he has the ideas of affections of the human body, affections which partly involve the natures of both the human body and external bodies (Prs. 16, 25 and 27, II). That is (Prs. 12 and 13, II), this idea will necessarily be adequate in God insofar as he constitutes the human mind; that is, insofar as he has the ideas which are in the human mind. Therefore, the mind (Cor. Pr. 11, II) necessarily perceives A adequately, and does so both insofar as it perceives itself and insofar as it perceives its own body or any external body; nor can A be perceived in any other way.

Corollary

Hence it follows that there are certain ideas or notions common to all men. For (by Lemma 2) all bodies agree in certain respects, which must be (preceding Pr.) conceived by all adequately, or clearly and distinctly.

PROPOSITION 39

Of that which is common and proper to the human body and to some external bodies by which the human body is customarily affected, and which is equally in the part as well as in the whole of any of these bodies, the idea also in the mind will be adequate.

Proof

Let A be that which is common and proper to the human body and to some external bodies and which is equally in the human body as in those same external bodies, and which is finally equally in the part of any external body as in the whole. There will be in God an adequate idea of A (Cor. Pr. 7, II) both insofar as he has the idea of the human body and insofar as he has ideas of those posited external bodies. Let it now be supposed that the human body is affected by an external body through that which is common to them both, that is, A. The idea of this affection will involve the property A (Pr. 16, II), and so (Cor. Pr. 7, II) the idea of this affection, insofar as it involves the property A, will be adequate in God insofar as he is affected by the idea of the human body; that is (Pr. 13, II), insofar as he constitutes the nature of the human mind. So this idea will also be adequate in the human mind (Cor. Pr. 11, II).

Corollary

Hence it follows that the mind is more capable of perceiving more things adequately in proportion as its body has more things in common with other bodies.

PROPOSITION 40

Whatever ideas follow in the mind from ideas that are adequate in it are also adequate.

Proof

This is evident. For when we say that an idea follows in the human mind from ideas that are adequate in it, we are saying no more than that there is in the divine intellect an idea of which God is the cause, not insofar as he is infinite nor insofar as he is affected by ideas of numerous particular things, but only insofar as he constitutes the essence of the human mind.

Scholium 1

I have here set forth the cause of those notions that are called 'common,' and which are the basis of our reasoning processes. Now certain axioms or notions have other causes which it would be relevant to set forth by this method of ours; for thus we could establish which notions are more useful compared with others, and which are of scarcely any value. And again, we could establish which notions are common to all, which ones are clear and distinct only to those not laboring under prejudices [*praejudiciis*] and which ones are ill-founded. Furthermore, this would clarify the origin of those notions called 'secondary'—and consequently the axioms which are based on them—as well as other related questions to which I have for some time given thought. But I have decided not to embark on these questions at this point because I have set them aside for another treatise,[2] and also to avoid wearying the reader with too lengthy a discussion of this subject. Nevertheless, to omit nothing that it is essential to know, I shall briefly deal with the question of the origin of the so-called 'transcendental terms,' such as 'entity,' 'thing,' 'something' [*ens, res, aliquid*].

These terms originate in the following way. The human body, being limited, is capable of forming simultaneously in itself only a certain number of distinct images. (I have explained in Sch. Pr. 17, II what an image is.) If this number be exceeded, these images begin to be confused, and if the number of distinct images which the body is capable of forming simultaneously in itself be far exceeded, all the images will be utterly confused with one another. This being so, it is evident from Cor. Pr. 17 and Pr. 18, II that the human mind is able to imagine simultaneously and distinctly as many bodies as there are images that can be formed simultaneously in its body. But when the images in the body are utterly confused, the mind will also imagine all the bodies confusedly without any distinction, and will comprehend them, as it were, under one attribute, namely, that of entity, thing, etc. This conclusion can also be reached from the fact that images are not always equally vivid, and also from other causes analogous to these, which I need not here explicate. For it all comes down to this, that these terms signify ideas confused in the highest degree.

Again, from similar causes have arisen those notions called 'universal,' such as 'man,' 'horse,' 'dog,' etc; that is to say, so many images are formed in the human body simultaneously (e.g., of man) that our capacity to imagine them is surpassed, not indeed completely, but to the extent that the mind is unable to imagine the unimportant differences of individuals (such as the complexion and stature of each, and their exact number) and imagines distinctly only their common characteristic insofar as the body is affected by them. For it was by this that the body was affected most repeatedly, by each single individual. The mind expresses this by the word 'man,' and predicates this word of an infinite number of individuals. For, as we said, it is unable to imagine the determinate number of individuals.

But it should be noted that not all men form these notions in the same way; in the case of each person the notions vary according as that thing varies whereby the body has more frequently been affected, and which the mind more readily imagines or calls to mind. For example, those who have more often regarded with admiration the stature of men will understand by the word 'man' an animal of upright stature, while those who are wont to regard a different aspect will form a different common image of man, such as that man is a laughing animal, a featherless biped, or a rational animal. Similarly, with regard to other aspects, each will form universal images according to the conditioning of his body. Therefore, it is not surprising that so many controversies have arisen among philosophers who have sought to explain natural phenomena through merely the images of these phenomena.

Scholium 2

From all that has already been said it is quite clear that we perceive many things and form universal notions:

1. From individual objects presented to us through the senses in a fragmentary [*mutilate*] and confused manner without any intellectual order (see Cor. Pr. 29, II); and therefore I call such perceptions 'knowledge from casual experience.'

2. From symbols. For example, from having heard or read certain words we call things to mind and we form certain ideas of them similar to those through which we imagine things (Sch. Pr. 18, II). Both these ways of regarding things I shall in future refer to as 'knowledge of the first kind,' 'opinion' or 'imagination.'

3. From the fact that we have common notions and adequate ideas of the properties of things (see Cor. Pr. 38 and 39 with its Cor., and Pr. 40, II). I shall refer to this as 'reason' and 'knowledge of the second kind.'

Apart from these two kinds of knowledge there is, as I shall later show, a third kind of knowledge, which

2. [This is Spinoza's incomplete essay, *On the Improvement of the Understanding.*]

I shall refer to as 'intuition.' This kind of knowledge proceeds from an adequate idea of the formal essence of certain attributes of God to an adequate knowledge of the essence of things. I shall illustrate all these kinds of knowledge by one single example. Three numbers are given; it is required to find a fourth which is related to the third as the second to the first. Tradesmen have no hesitation in multiplying the second by the third and dividing the product by the first, either because they have not yet forgotten the rule they learnt without proof from their teachers, or because they have in fact found this correct in the case of very simple numbers, or else from the force of the proof of Proposition 19 of the Seventh Book of Euclid, to wit, the common property of proportionals. But in the case of very simple numbers, none of this is necessary. For example, in the case of the given numbers 1, 2, 3, everybody can see that the fourth proportional is 6, and all the more clearly because we infer in one single intuition the fourth number from the ratio we see the first number bears to the second.

PROPOSITION 41

Knowledge of the first kind is the only cause of falsity; knowledge of the second and third kind is necessarily true.

Proof

In the preceding Scholium we asserted that all those ideas which are inadequate and confused belong to the first kind of knowledge; and thus (Pr. 35, II), this knowledge is the only cause of falsity. Further, we asserted that to knowledge of the second and third kind there belong those ideas which are adequate. Therefore (Pr. 34, II), this knowledge is necessarily true.

PROPOSITION 42

Knowledge of the second and third kind, and not knowledge of the first kind, teaches us to distinguish true from false.

Proof

This Proposition is self-evident. For he who can distinguish the true from the false must have an adequate idea of the true and the false; that is (Sch. 2 Pr. 40, II), he must know the true and the false by the second or third kind of knowledge.

PROPOSITION 43

He who has a true idea knows at the same time that he has a true idea, and cannot doubt its truth.

Proof

A true idea in us is one which is adequate in God insofar as he is explicated through the nature of the human mind (Cor. Pr. 11, II). Let us suppose, then, that there is in God, insofar as he is explicated through the nature of the human mind, an adequate idea, A. The idea of this idea must also necessarily be in God, and is related to God in the same way as the idea A (Pr. 20, II, the proof being of general application). But by our supposition the idea A is related to God insofar as he is explicated through the nature of the human mind. Therefore, the idea of the idea A must be related to God in the same way; that is (Cor. Pr. 11, II), this adequate idea of the idea A will be in the mind which has the adequate idea A. So he who has an adequate idea, that is, he who knows a thing truly (Pr. 34, II), must at the same time have an adequate idea, that is, a true knowledge of his knowledge; that is, (as is self-evident) he is bound at the same time to be certain.

Scholium

I have explained in the Scholium to Pr. 21, II what is an idea of an idea; but it should be noted that the preceding proposition is sufficiently self-evident. For nobody who has a true idea is unaware that a true idea involves absolute certainty. To have a true idea means only to know a thing perfectly, that is, to the utmost degree. Indeed, nobody can doubt this, unless he thinks that an idea is some dumb thing like a picture on a tablet, and not a mode of thinking, to wit, the very act of understanding. And who, pray, can know that he understands some thing unless he first understands it? That is, who can know that he is certain of something unless he is first certain of it? Again, what standard of truth can there be that is clearer and more certain than a true idea? Indeed, just as light makes manifest both itself and darkness, so truth is the standard both of itself and falsity.

I think I have thus given an answer to those questions which can be stated as follows: If a true idea is distinguished from a false one only inasmuch as it is said to correspond with that of which it is an idea, then a true idea has no more reality or perfection than a false one (since they are distinguished only by an extrinsic characteristic) and consequently neither is a man who has true ideas superior to one who has only false ideas. Secondly, how do we come to have false ideas? And finally, how can one know for certain that one has ideas which correspond with that of which they are ideas? I have now given an answer, I repeat, to these problems. As regards the difference between a true and a false idea, it is clear from Pr. 35, II that the former is to the latter as being to non-being. The causes of falsity I have quite clearly shown from Propositions 19 to 35 with the latter's Scholium, from which it is likewise obvious what is the difference between a man who has true ideas and one who has only false ideas. As to the last question, how can a man know that he has an idea which corresponds to that of which it is an idea, I have just shown, with abundant clarity, that this arises from the fact that he does have an idea that corresponds to that of which it is an idea; that is, truth is its own standard. Furthermore, the human mind, insofar as it perceives things truly, is part of the infinite intellect of God (Cor. Pr. 11, II), and thus it is as inevitable that the clear and distinct ideas of the mind are true as that God's ideas are true.

PROPOSITION 44

It is not in the nature of reason to regard things as contingent, but as necessary.

Proof

It is in the nature of reason to perceive things truly (Pr. 41, II), to wit, (Ax. 6, I) as they are in themselves; that is (Pr. 29, I), not as contingent, but as necessary.

Corollary 1

Hence it follows that it solely results from imagination [*imaginatio*] that we regard things, both in respect of the past and of the future, as contingent.

Scholium

I shall explain briefly how this comes about. We have shown above (Pr. 17, II and Cor.) that although things may not exist, the mind nevertheless always imagines them as present unless causes arise which exclude their present existence. Further, we have shown (Pr. 18, II) that if the human body has once been affected by two external bodies at the same time, when the mind later imagines one of them, it will straightway call the other to mind as well; that is, it will regard both as present to it unless other causes arise which exclude their present existence. Furthermore, nobody doubts that time, too, is a product of the imagination, and arises from the fact that we see some bodies move more slowly than others, or more quickly, or with equal speed. Let us therefore suppose that yesterday a boy saw Peter first of all in the morning, Paul at noon, and Simon in the evening, and that today he again sees Peter in the morning. From Pr. 18, II it is clear that as soon as he sees the morning light, forthwith he will imagine the sun as traversing the same tract of sky as on the previous day, that is, he will imagine a whole day, and he will imagine Peter together with morning, Paul with midday, and Simon with evening; that is, he will imagine the existence of Paul and Simon with reference to future time. On the other hand, on seeing Simon in the evening he will refer Paul and Peter to time past by imagining them along with time past. This train of events will be the more consistent the more frequently he sees them in that order. If it should at some time befall that on another evening he sees James instead of Simon, then the following morning he will imagine along with evening now Simon, now James, but not both together. For we are supposing that he has seen only one of them in the evening, not both at the same time. Therefore, his imagination will waver, and he will imagine, along with a future evening, now one, now the other; that is, he will regard neither of them as going to be there for certain, but both of them contingently. This wavering of the imagination occurs in the same way if the imagination be of things which we regard with relation to past or present time, and consequently we shall imagine things, as related both to present and past or future time, as contingent.

Corollary 2

It is in the nature of reason to perceive things in the light of eternity [*sub quadam specie aeternitatis*].

Proof

It is in the nature of reason to regard things as necessary, not as contingent (previous Pr.). Now it perceives this necessity truly (Pr. 41, II); that is, as it is in itself (Ax. 6, I). But (Pr. 16, I) this necessity is the very necessity of God's eternal nature. Therefore, it is in the nature of reason to regard things in this light of eternity. Furthermore, the basic principles of reason are those notions (Pr. 38, II) which explicate what is common to all things, and do not explicate (Pr. 37, II) the essence of any particular thing, and therefore must be conceived without any relation to time, but in the light of eternity.

PROPOSITION 45

Every idea of any body or particular thing existing in actuality necessarily involves the eternal and infinite essence of God.

Proof

The idea of a particular thing actually existing necessarily involves both the essence and the existence of the thing (Cor. Pr. 8, II). But particular things cannot be conceived without God (Pr. 15, I). Now since they have God for their cause (Pr. 6, II) insofar as he is considered under that attribute of which the things themselves are modes, their ideas (Ax. 4, I) must necessarily involve the conception of their attribute; that is (Def. 6, I), the eternal and infinite essence of God.

Scholium

Here by existence I do not mean duration, that is, existence insofar as it is considered in the abstract as a kind of quantity. I am speaking of the very nature of existence, which is attributed to particular things because they follow in infinite numbers in infinite ways from the eternal necessity of God's nature (Pr. 16, I). I am speaking, I repeat, of the very existence of particular things insofar as they are in God. For although each particular thing is determined by another particular thing to exist in a certain manner, the force by which each perseveres in existing follows from the eternal necessity of God's nature. See Cor. Pr. 24, I.

PROPOSITION 46

The knowledge of the eternal and infinite essence of God which each idea involves is adequate and perfect.

Proof

The proof of the preceding proposition is universally valid, and whether a thing be considered as a part or a whole, its idea, whether of whole or part, involves the eternal and infinite essence of God (preceding Pr.). Therefore, that which gives knowledge of the eternal and infinite essence of God is common to all things, and equally in the part as in the whole. And so this knowledge will be adequate (Pr. 38, II).

PROPOSITION 47

The human mind has an adequate knowledge of the eternal and infinite essence of God.

Proof

The human mind has ideas (Pr. 22, II) from which (Pr. 23, II) it perceives itself, its own body (Pr. 19, II) and external bodies (Cor. 1, Pr. 16 and Pr. 17, II) as actually existing, and so it has an adequate knowledge of the eternal and infinite essence of God (Prs. 45 and 46, II).

Scholium

Hence we see that God's infinite essence and his eternity are known to all. Now since all things are in God and are conceived through God, it follows that from this knowledge we can deduce a great many things so as to know them adequately and thus to form that third kind of knowledge I mentioned in Sch. 2 Pr. 40, II, of the superiority and usefulness of which we shall have occasion to speak in Part V. That men do not have as clear a knowledge of God as they do of common notions arises from the fact that they are unable to imagine God as they do bodies, and that they have connected the word 'God' with the images of things which they commonly see; and this they can scarcely avoid, being affected continually by external bodies. Indeed, most errors result solely from the incorrect application of words to things. When somebody says that the lines joining the center of a circle to its circumference are unequal, he surely understands by circle, at least at that time, something different from what mathematicians understand. Likewise, when men make mistakes in arithmetic, they have different figures in mind from those on paper. So if you look only to their minds, they indeed are not mistaken; but they seem to be wrong because we think that they have in mind the figures on the page. If this were not the case, we would not think them to be wrong, just as I did not think that person to be wrong whom I recently heard shouting that his hall had flown into his neighbour's hen, for I could see clearly what he had in mind. Most controversies arise from this, that men do not correctly express what is in their mind, or they misunderstand another's mind. For, in reality, while they are hotly contradicting one another, they are either in agreement or have different things in mind, so that the apparent errors and absurdities of their opponents are not really so.

PROPOSITION 48

In the mind there is no absolute, or free, will. The mind is determined to this or that volition by a cause, which is likewise determined by another cause, and this again by another, and so ad infinitum.

Proof

The mind is a definite and determinate mode of thinking (Pr. 11, II), and thus (Cor. 2, Pr. 17, I) it cannot be the free cause of its actions: that is, it cannot possess an absolute faculty of willing and non-willing. It must be determined to will this or that (Pr. 28, I) by a cause, which likewise is determined by another cause, and this again by another, etc.

Scholium

In the same way it is proved that in the mind there is no absolute faculty of understanding, desiring, loving, etc. Hence it follows that these and similar faculties are either entirely fictitious or nothing more than metaphysical entities or universals which we are wont to form from particulars. So intellect and will bear the same relation to this or that idea, this or that volition, as stoniness to this or that stone, or man to Peter and Paul. As to the reason why men think they are free, we explained that in the Appendix to Part I.

But before proceeding further, it should here be noted that by the will I mean the faculty of affirming and denying, and not desire. I mean, I repeat, the faculty whereby the mind affirms or denies what is true or what is false, not the desire whereby the mind seeks things or shuns them. But now that we have proved that these faculties are universal notions which are not distinct from the particulars from which we form them, we must inquire whether volitions themselves are anything more than ideas of things. We must inquire, I say, whether there is in the mind any other affirmation and denial apart from that which the idea, insofar as it is an idea, involves. On this subject see the following proposition and also Def. 3, II, lest thought becomes confused with pictures. For by ideas I do not mean images such as are formed at the back of the eye—or, if you like, in the middle of the brain—but conceptions of thought.

PROPOSITION 49

There is in the mind no volition, that is, affirmation and negation, except that which an idea, insofar as it is an idea, involves.

Proof

There is in the mind (preceding Pr.) no absolute faculty of willing and non-willing, but only particular volitions, namely, this or that affirmation, and this or that negation. Let us therefore conceive a particular volition, namely, a mode of thinking whereby the mind affirms that the three angles of a triangle are equal to two right angles. This affirmation involves the conception, or idea, of a triangle; that is, it cannot be conceived without the idea of a triangle. For to say that A must involve the conception of B is the same as to say that A cannot be conceived without B. Again, this affirmation (Ax. 3, II) cannot even be without the idea of a triangle. Therefore, this idea can neither be nor be conceived without the idea of a triangle. Furthermore, this idea of a triangle must involve this same affirmation, namely, that its three angles are equal to two right angles. Therefore, vice versa, this idea of a triangle can neither be nor be conceived without this affirmation, and so (Def. 2, II) this affirmation belongs to the essence of the idea of a triangle, and is nothing more than the essence itself. And what I have said of this volition (for it was arbitrarily selected) must also be said of every volition, namely, that it is nothing but an idea.

Corollary

Will and intellect are one and the same thing.

Proof

Will and intellect are nothing but the particular volitions and ideas (Pr. 48, II and Sch.). But a particular volition and idea are one and the same thing (preceding Pr.). Therefore will and intellect are one and the same thing.

Scholium

By this means we have removed the cause to which error is commonly attributed. We have previously shown that falsity consists only in the privation that fragmentary and confused ideas involve. Therefore, a false idea, insofar as it is false, does not involve certainty. So when we say that a man acquiesces in what is false and has no doubt thereof, we are not thereby saying that he is certain, but only that he does not doubt, or that he acquiesces in what is false because there is nothing to cause his imagination to waver. On this point see Sch. Pr. 44, II. So however much we suppose a man to adhere to what is false, we shall never say that he is certain. For by certainty we mean something positive (Pr. 43, II and Sch.), not privation of doubt. But by privation of certainty we mean falsity.

But for a fuller explanation of the preceding proposition some things remain to be said. Then, again, there is the further task of replying to objections that may be raised against this doctrine of ours. Finally, to remove every shred of doubt, I have thought it worthwhile to point out certain advantages of this doctrine. I say certain advantages, for the most important of them will be better understood from what we have to say in Part V.

I begin, then, with the first point, and I urge my readers to make a careful distinction between an idea—i.e., a conception of the mind—and the images of things that we imagine. Again, it is essential to distinguish between ideas and the words we use to signify things. For since these three—images, words, and ideas—have been utterly confused by many, or else they fail to distinguish between them through lack of accuracy, or, finally, through lack of caution, our doctrine of the will, which it is essential to know both for theory and for the wise ordering of life, has never entered their minds. For those who think that ideas consist in images formed in us from the contact of external bodies are convinced that those ideas of things whereof we can form no like image are not ideas, but mere fictions fashioned arbitrarily at will. So they look on ideas as dumb pictures on a tablet, and misled by this preconception they fail to see that an idea, insofar as it is an idea, involves affirmation or negation. Again, those who confuse words with idea, or with the affirmation which an idea involves, think that when they affirm or deny something merely by words contrary to what they feel, they are able to will contrary to what they feel. Now one can easily dispel these misconceptions if one attends to the nature of thought, which is quite removed from the concept of extension. Then one will clearly understand that an idea, being a mode of thinking, consists neither in the image of a thing nor in words. For the essence of words and images is constituted solely by corporeal motions, far removed from the concept of thought. With these few words of warning, I turn to the aforementioned objections.

The first of these rests on the confident claim that the will extends more widely than the intellect, and therefore is different from it. The reason for their belief that the will extends more widely than the intellect is that they find—so they say—that they do not need a greater faculty of assent, that is, of affirming and denying, than they already possess, in order to assent to an infinite number of other things that we do not perceive, but that we do need an increased faculty of understanding. Therefore will is distinct from intellect, the latter being finite and the former infinite.

Second, it may be objected against us that experience appears to tell us most indisputably that we are able to suspend judgment so as not to assent to things that we perceive, and this is also confirmed by the fact that nobody is said to be deceived insofar as he perceives something, but only insofar as he assents or dissents. For instance, he who imagines a winged horse does not thereby grant that there is a winged horse; that is, he is not thereby deceived unless at the same time he grants that there is a winged horse. So experience appears to tell us most indisputably that the will, that is, the faculty of assenting, is free, and different from the faculty of understanding.

Third, it may be objected that one affirmation does not seem to contain more reality than another; that is, we do not seem to need greater power in order to affirm that what is true is true than to affirm that what is false is true. On the other hand, we do perceive that one idea has more reality or perfection than another. For some ideas are more perfect than others in proportion as some objects are superior to others. This, again, is a clear indication that there is a difference between will and intellect.

Fourthly, it may be objected that if man does not act from freedom of will, what would happen if he should be in a state of equilibrium like Buridan's ass? Will he perish of hunger and thirst? If I were to grant this, I would appear to be thinking of an ass or a statue, not of a man. If I deny it, then the man will be determining himself, and consequently will possess the faculty of going and doing whatever he wants.

Besides these objections there may possibly be others. But since I am not obliged to stress every objection that can be dreamed up, I shall make it my task to reply to these objections only, and as briefly as possible.

To the first objection I reply that, if by the intellect is meant clear and distinct ideas only, I grant that the will extends more widely than the intellect, but I deny that the will extends more widely than perceptions, that is, the faculty of conceiving. Nor indeed do I see why the faculty of willing should be termed infinite any more than the faculty of sensing. For just as by the same faculty of willing we can affirm an infinite number of things (but in succession, for we cannot affirm an infinite number of things simultaneously), so also we can sense or perceive an infinite number of bodies (in succession) by the same faculty of sensing. If my objectors should say that there are an infinite number of things that we cannot sense, I retort that we cannot grasp them by any amount of thought, and consequently by any amount of willing. But, they say, if God wanted to bring it about that we should perceive these too, he would have had to give us a greater faculty of perceiving, but not a greater faculty of willing than he has already given us. This is the same as saying that if God wishes to bring it about that we should understand an infinite number of other entities, he would have to give us a greater intellect than he already has, so as to encompass these same infinite entities, but not a more universal idea of entity. For we have shown that the will is a universal entity, or the idea whereby we explicate all particular volitions; that is, that which is common to all particular volitions. So if they believe that this common or universal idea of volitions is a faculty, it is not at all surprising that they declare this faculty to extend beyond the limits of the intellect to infinity. For the term 'universal' is applied equally to one, to many, and to an infinite number of individuals.

To the second objection I reply by denying that we have free power to suspend judgment. For when we say that someone suspends judgment, we are saying only that he sees that he is not adequately perceiving the thing. So suspension of judgment is really a perception, not free will. To understand this more clearly, let us conceive a boy imagining a winged horse and having no other perception. Since this imagining involves the existence of a horse (Cor. Pr. 17, II), and the boy perceives nothing to annul the existence of the horse, he will regard the horse as present and he will not be able to doubt its existence, although he is not certain of it. We experience this quite commonly in dreams, nor do I believe there is anyone who thinks that while dreaming he has free power to suspend judgment regarding the contents of his dream, and of bringing it about that he should not dream what he dreams that he sees. Nevertheless, it does happen that even in dreams we suspend judgment, to wit, when we dream that we are dreaming. Furthermore, I grant that nobody is deceived insofar as he has a perception; that is, I grant that the imaginings of the mind, considered in themselves, involve no error (see Sch. Pr. 17, II). But I deny that a man makes no affirmation insofar as he has a perception. For what else is perceiving a winged horse than affirming wings of a horse? For if the mind were to perceive nothing apart from the winged horse, it would regard the horse as present to it, and would have no cause to doubt the existence of the horse, nor would it have any faculty of dissenting, unless the imagining of the winged horse were joined to an idea which annuls the existence of the said horse, or unless the mind perceives that the idea which it has of the winged horse is inadequate. Then it will either necessarily deny the existence of the said horse or it will necessarily doubt it.

In the above I think I have also answered the third objection by my assertion that the will is a universal term predicated of all ideas and signifying only what is common to all ideas, namely, affirmation, the adequate essence of which, insofar as it is thus conceived as an abstract term, must be in every single idea, and the same in all in this respect only. But not insofar as it is considered as constituting the essence of the idea, for in that respect particular affirmations differ among themselves as much as do ideas. For example, the affirmation which the idea of a circle involves differs from the affirmation which the idea of a triangle involves as much as the idea of a circle differs from the idea of a triangle. Again, I absolutely deny that we need an equal power of thinking to affirm that what is true is true as to affirm that what is false is true. For these two affirmations, if you look to their meaning and not to the words alone, are related to one another as being to non-being. For there is nothing in ideas that constitutes the form of falsity (see Pr. 35, II with Sch. and Sch. Pr. 47, II). Therefore, it is important to note here how easily we are deceived when we confuse universals with particulars, and mental constructs [*entia rationis*] and abstract terms with the real.

As to the fourth objection, I readily grant that a man placed in such a state of equilibrium (namely, where he feels nothing else but hunger and thirst and perceives nothing but such-and-such food and drink at equal distances from him) will die of hunger and thirst. If they ask me whether such a man is not to be reckoned an ass rather than a man, I reply that I do not know, just as I do not know how one should reckon a man who hangs himself, or how one should reckon babies, fools, and madmen.

My final task is to show what practical advantages accrue from knowledge of this doctrine, and this we shall readily gather from the following points:

1. It teaches that we act only by God's will, and that we share in the divine nature, and all the more as our actions become more perfect and as we understand God more and more. Therefore this doctrine, apart from giving us complete tranquillity of mind, has the further advantage of teaching us wherein lies our greatest happiness or blessedness, namely, in the knowledge of God alone, as a result of which we are induced only to such actions as are urged on us by love and piety. Hence we clearly understand how far astray from the true estimation of virtue are those who, failing to understand that virtue itself and the service of God is happiness itself and utmost freedom, expect God to bestow on them the highest rewards in return for their virtue and meritorious actions as if in return for the basest slavery.

2. It teaches us what attitude we should adopt regarding fortune, or the things that are not in our power, that is, the things that do not follow from our nature; namely, to expect and to endure with patience both faces of fortune. For all things follow from God's eternal decree by the same necessity as it follows from the essence of a triangle that its three angles are equal to two right angles.

3. This doctrine assists us in our social relations, in that it teaches us to hate no one, despise no one, ridicule no one, be angry with no one, envy no one. Then again, it teaches us that each should be content with what he has and should help his neighbor, not from womanish pity, or favour, or superstition, but solely from the guidance of reason as occasion and circumstance require. This I shall demonstrate in Part IV.

4. Finally, this doctrine is also of no small advantage to the commonwealth, in that it teaches the manner in which citizens should be governed and led; namely, not so as to be slaves, but so as to do freely what is best.

And thus I have completed the task I undertook in this Scholium, and thereby I bring to an end Part II, in which I think I have explained the nature of the human mind and its properties at sufficient length and as clearly as the difficult subject matter permits, and that from my account can be drawn many excellent lessons, most useful and necessary to know, as will partly be disclosed in what is to follow.

Gottfried Leibniz

Leibniz was born in 1646 in Leipzig, in what is now Germany, the son of a professor of moral philosophy. He studied at the University of Leipzig from 1661 until 1666 and then at the University of Altdorf from 1666 to 1667, earning degrees in law and philosophy. After graduating, he rejected an academic offer from the University of Leipzig and instead entered the service of the Elector of Mainz. In 1672 he traveled to Paris as a diplomat, where he stayed until 1676. There, benefiting from the guidance of Christian Huygens, one of the most important physicists of the time, he became thoroughly acquainted with modern science and philosophy. In Paris he also developed calculus, independently of Newton, who developed it around the same time. After his years in Paris, Leibniz traveled to England and then to the Netherlands, where he met Spinoza. When he returned to Germany he became a counselor at the court in Hanover, which was to be his principal residence until his death in 1716.

In Hanover, Leibniz wrote numerous philosophical works, many of which were not published until after his death. In several of these works—the *Discourse on Metaphysics* (1686), the *New System of Nature* (1695), and the *Monadology* (1714)—he displays his metaphysical system in outline form. Leibniz's philosophical views on physics are set out in the *Specimen of Dynamics* (1698), *On Nature Itself* (1697), and in his correspondence with De Volder (1699–1706) and with Samuel Clarke, Newton's friend (1715–1716). Theology is treated at length in the *Theodicy,* published in 1710, and in his correspondence with Antoine Arnauld (1686–1690). In 1704 Leibniz finished a substantial commentary of Locke's *Essay,* entitled *New Essays on Human Understanding.*

At the center of Leibniz's system is the notion of a *monad,* which is an immaterial, simple, mind-like entity, modeled on the Cartesian soul. In Leibniz's view, monads are the only substances that exist. Matter, therefore, is not among the fundamental constituents of reality, but is rather an appearance of systems of monads: Matter is *phenomenal.* Hence physics is a study of appearances, and not of ultimately real things. Metaphysics, by contrast, since it has monads in its purview, is about ultimately real things.

In Leibniz's conception, monads are *windowless,* that is, they do not have any real causal relations with other monads. All causal relations among different created things are merely phenomenal. God gives each monad its own internal program that consists of various perceptions, none of which involve real interactions with other monads. However, God does set up all of the monads in preestablished harmony, so that, for example, when the monad that is you has a perception of speaking to me, God has set up my monad so that at the same time I will have a perception of you speaking to me, despite the fact that you are not *really* interacting with me at all. Leibniz's idea comes partly from his view that all relations, like *speaking to* and *being next to* must, in the end, be reducible to *intrinsic* properties, properties that are not relational at all, and thus make no reference to any entity other than the thing that possesses it. In his analysis of Leibniz, Kant points out that the Cartesian soul provides a model of a substance all of whose properties—thoughts or perceptions—are intrinsic to it, and that this is why Leibniz believes that all substances are like Cartesian souls.

In Leibniz's view, all of the monads *express* the entire universe: Each of them has perceptions of everything that has occurred, is occurring, and will occur in the universe. In this respect, all monads are the very same. But each of them differs from every other in the *point of view* from which it expresses the universe. This is partly a matter of which perceptions are clear and distinct, and which are more confused and obscure. Certain perceptions may be conscious and clear in you but merely unconscious and confused in me, for example, perceptions of what you did in the last hour. Some monads, such as those that provide the metaphysical foundations of rocks and buildings, lack any conscious perceptions at all.

Leibniz was a determinist in that he held that, in virtue of choosing the best of all possible worlds, God determines every event that occurs, including each of our actions. One of Leibniz's great philosophical struggles involved attempting to show that human moral responsibility is compatible with this divine determinism. He devised several solutions to this problem, one of which involves the renowned formulation that in our choices, God inclines our souls without necessitating them.

• • •

For a classic account of Leibniz's philosophical system, see Bertrand Russell, *A Critical Exposition of the Philosophy of Leibniz* (London, 1900). Nicholas Rescher's *The Philosophy of Leibniz* (Englewood Cliffs, N.J.: Prentice-Hall, 1967) provides a good introduction to Leibniz's views. Important critical studies include Robert M. Adams, *Leibniz: Determinist, Theist, Idealist* (Oxford: Oxford University Press, 1994); Nicholas Jolley, *Leibniz and Locke* (Oxford: Oxford University Press, 1984); Robert McRae, *Leibniz: Perception, Apperception, and Thought* (Toronto: University of Toronto Press, 1976); Robert Sleigh, *Leibniz and Arnauld* (New Haven: Yale University Press, 1990); and Catherine Wilson, *Leibniz's Metaphysics: A Comparative and Historical Study* (Princeton: Princeton University Press, 1989). Some collections of essays on Leibniz are Harry Frankfurt, ed., *Leibniz: A Collection of Critical Essays* (Garden City, N.J.: Doubleday, 1972); Michael Hooker, ed., *Leibniz: Critical and Interpretive Essays* (Minneapolis: University of Minnesota Press, 1982); R. S. Woolhouse, ed., *Leibniz: Metaphysics and Philosophy of Science* (Oxford: Oxford University Press, 1981); and Derk Pereboom, ed., *The Rationalists: Descartes, Spinoza, Leibniz* (Lanham, Md.: Rowman & Littlefield, 1999).

Derk Pereboom

Discourse on Metaphysics

1. *On divine perfection, and that God does everything in the most desirable way.* The most widely accepted and meaningful notion we have of God is expressed well enough in these words, that God is an absolutely perfect being; yet the consequences of these words are not sufficiently considered. And, to penetrate more deeply into this matter, it is appropriate to remark that there are several entirely different perfections in nature, that God possesses all of them together, and that each of them belongs to him in the highest degree.

We must also know what a perfection is. A fairly sure test for being a perfection is that forms or natures that are not capable of a highest degree are not perfections, as for example, the nature of number or figure. For the greatest of all numbers (or even the number of all numbers), as well as the greatest of all figures, imply a contradiction, but the greatest knowledge and omnipotence do not involve any impossibility. Consequently, power and knowledge are perfections, and, insofar as they belong to God, they do not have limits.

Whence it follows that God, possessing supreme and infinite wisdom, acts in the most perfect manner, not only metaphysically, but also morally speaking, and that, with respect to ourselves, we can say that the more enlightened and informed we are about God's works, the more we will be disposed to find them excellent and in complete conformity with what we might have desired.

2. *Against those who claim that there is no goodness in God's works, or that the rules of goodness and beauty are arbitrary.* Thus I am far removed from the opinion of those who maintain that there are no rules of goodness and perfection in the nature of things or in the ideas God has of them and who say that the works of God are good solely for the formal reason that God has made them.[1] For, if this were so, God, knowing that he is their author, would not have had to consider them afterwards and find them good, as is testified by the Sacred Scriptures—which seem to have used such anthropomorphic expressions only to make us understand that the excellence of God's works can be recognized by considering them in themselves, even when we do not reflect on this empty external denomination which relates them to their cause. This is all the more true, since it is by considering his works that we can discover the creator. His works must therefore carry his mark in themselves. I confess that the contrary opinion seems to me extremely dangerous and very near to the opinion of the recent innovators[2] who hold that the beauty of the universe and the goodness we attribute to the works of God are but the chimeras of those who conceive of God in terms of themselves. Thus, in saying that things are not good by virtue of any rule of goodness but solely by virtue of the will of God, it seems to me that we unknowingly destroy all of God's love and all of his glory. For why praise him for what he has done if he would be equally praiseworthy in doing the exact contrary? Where will his justice and wisdom reside if there remains only a certain despotic power, if will holds the place of reason, and if, according to the definition of tyrants, justice consists in whatever pleases the most powerful? Besides, it seems that all acts of will presuppose a reason for willing and that this reason is naturally prior to the act of will. That is why I also find completely strange the expression of some other philosophers who say that the eternal truths of metaphysics and geometry and consequently also the rules of goodness, justice, and perfection are merely the effects of the will of God; instead, it seems to me, they are only the consequences of his understanding, which, assuredly, does not depend on his will, any more than does his essence.

3. *Against those who believe that God might have made things better.* Nor can I approve of the opin-

Reprinted from Leibniz, *Philosophical Essays*, edited and translated by Roger Ariew and Daniel Garber (Indianapolis: Hackett Publishing Company, 1989), by permission of the publisher.

1. [This is Descartes' view.—R.A. and D.G.]

2. [Spinoza and, by extension, Descartes.]

ion of some moderns who maintain boldly that what God has made is not of the highest perfection and that he could have done much better.[3] For it seems to me that the consequences of this opinion are wholly contrary to the glory of God: as a lesser evil is relatively good, so a lesser good is relatively evil. And to act with less perfection than one could have is to act imperfectly. To show that an architect could have done better is to find fault with his work. This opinion is also contrary to the Sacred Scripture, which assure us of the goodness of God's works. For, if their view were sufficient, then since the series of imperfections descends to infinity, God's works would always have been good in comparison with those less perfect, no matter how he created them but something is hardly praiseworthy if it can be praised only in this way. I also believe that a great many passages from Sacred Scripture and the holy fathers will be found favoring my opinion, but scarcely any will be found favoring the opinion of these moderns, an opinion which is, in my judgment, unknown to all antiquity and which is based only on the inadequate knowledge we have of the general harmony of the universe and of the hidden reasons for God's conduct. This enables us to judge audaciously that many things could have been rendered better. Besides, these moderns insist on certain dubious subtleties, for they imagine that nothing is so perfect that there is not something more perfect—this is an error.

They also believe that in this way they are able to safeguard God's freedom, as though it were not freedom of the highest sort to act in perfection following sovereign reason. For to believe that God does something without having any reason for his will—overlooking the fact that this seems impossible—is an opinion that conforms little to his glory. Let us assume, for example, that God chooses between A and B and that he takes A without having any reason to prefer it to B. I say that this action of God is at the very least not praiseworthy; for all praise must be based on some reason, and by hypothesis there is none here. Instead I hold that God does nothing for which he does not deserve to be glorified.

4. *That the love of God requires our complete satisfaction and acquiescence with respect to what he has done without our being quietists as a result.* The general knowledge of this great truth, that God acts always in the most perfect and desirable way possible, is, in my judgment, the foundation of the love that we owe God in all things, since he who loves seeks his satisfaction in the happiness or perfection of the object loved and in his actions. To will the same and dislike the same is true friendship. And I believe that it is difficult to love God well when we are not disposed to will what God wills, when we might have the power to change it. In fact, those who are not satisfied with what God does seem to me like dissatisfied subjects whose attitudes are not much different from those of rebels.

I hold, therefore, that, according to these principles, in order to act in accordance with the love of God, it is not sufficient to force ourselves to be patient; rather, we must truly be satisfied with everything that has come to us according to his will. I mean this acquiescence with respect to the past. As for the future, we must not be quietists[4] and stand ridiculously with arms folded, awaiting that which God will do, according to the sophism that the ancients called *logon aergon*, the lazy reason. But we must act in accordance with what we presume to be the *will of God*, insofar as we can judge it, trying with all our might to contribute to the general good and especially to the embellishment and perfection of that which affects us or that which is near us, that which is, so to speak, in our grasp. For, although the outcome might perhaps demonstrate that God did not wish our good will to have effect at present, it does not follow that he did not wish us to act as we have. On the contrary, since he is the best of all masters, he never demands more than the right intention, and it is for him to know the proper hour and place for letting the good designs succeed.

5. *What the rules of the perfection of divine conduct consist in, and that the simplicity of the ways is in balance with the richness of the effects.* Therefore it is sufficient to have the confidence that God does everything for the best and that nothing can harm

3. [Malebranche's *Traité* seems to be one of the main targets of this essay.]

4. [The quietists were followers of Miguel de Molinos (c. 1640–97), author of the *Guida spirituale* (1675), and others, who stressed passive contemplation and complete resignation to the will of God.]

those who love him. But to know in detail the reasons that could have moved him to choose this order of the universe—to allow sins, to dispense his saving grace in a certain way—surpasses the power of a finite mind, especially when it has not yet attained the enjoyment of the vision of God.

However, we can make some general remarks concerning the course of providence in the governance of things. We can therefore say that one who acts perfectly is similar to an excellent geometer who can find the best constructions for a problem; or to a good architect who makes use of his location and the funds set aside for a building in the most advantageous manner, allowing nothing improper or lacking in the beauty of which it is capable; or to a good householder, who makes use of his holdings in such a way that there remains nothing uncultivated and sterile; or to a skilled machinist who produces his work in the least difficult way possible; or to a learned author who includes the greatest number of truths [*realités*] in the smallest possible volume. Now, the most perfect of all beings, those that occupy the least volume, that is, those that least interfere with one another, are minds, whose perfections consist in their virtues. That is why we mustn't doubt that the happiness of minds is the principal aim of God and that he puts this into practice to the extent that general harmony permits it. We shall say more about this below.

As for the simplicity of the ways of God, this holds properly with respect to his means, as opposed to the variety, richness, and abundance, which holds with respect to his ends or effects. And the one must be in balance with the others, as are the costs of a building and the size and beauty one demands of it. It is true that nothing costs God anything—even less than it costs a philosopher to build the fabric of his imaginary world out of hypotheses—since God has only to make decrees in order that a real world come into being. But in matters of wisdom, decrees or hypotheses take the place of expenditures to the extent that they are more independent of one another, because reason requires that we avoid multiplying hypotheses or principles, in somewhat the same way that the simplest system is always preferred in astronomy.

6. *God does nothing which is not orderly and it is not even possible to imagine events that are not regular.* The volitions or acts of God are commonly divided into ordinary or extraordinary. But it is good to consider that God does nothing which is not orderly. Thus, what passes for extraordinary is extraordinary only with some particular order established among creatures; for everything is in conformity with respect to the universal order. This is true to such an extent that not only does nothing completely irregular occur in the world, but we would not even be able to imagine such a thing. Thus, let us assume, for example, that someone jots down a number of points at random on a piece of paper, as do those who practice the ridiculous art of geomancy.[5] I maintain that it is possible to find a geometric line whose notion is constant and uniform, following a certain rule, such that this line passes through all the points in the same order in which the hand jotted them down.

And if someone traced a continuous line which is sometimes straight, sometimes circular, and sometimes of another nature, it is possible to find a notion, or rule, or equation common to all the points of this line, in virtue of which these very changes must occur. For example, there is no face whose contours are not part of a geometric line and cannot be traced in one stroke by a certain regular movement. But, when a rule is extremely complex, what is in conformity with it passes for irregular.

Thus, one can say, in whatever manner God might have created the world, it would always have been regular and in accordance with a certain general order. But God has chosen the most perfect world, that is, the one which is at the same time the simplest in hypotheses and the richest in phenomena, as might be a line in geometry whose construction is easy and whose properties and effects are extremely remarkable and widespread. I use these comparisons to sketch an imperfect likeness of divine wisdom and to point out something that can at least elevate our minds to conceive in some way what cannot be sufficiently expressed. But I do not claim to explain in this way the great mystery upon which the entire universe depends.

7. *That miracles conform to the general order, even though they may be contrary to the subordinate maxims; and about what God wills or permits by a*

5. [Geomancy is the art of divination by means of lines or figures.]

general or particular volition. Now, since nothing can happen which is not in the order, one can say that miracles are as much within the order as are natural operations, operations which are called natural because they are in conformity with certain subordinate maxims that we call the nature of things. For one can say that this nature is only God's custom, with which he can dispense for any stronger reason than the one which moved him to make use of these maxims.

As for the general or particular volitions, depending upon how the matter is understood, we can say that God does everything following his most general will, which is in conformity with the most perfect order he has chosen, but we can also say that he has particular volitions which are exceptions to these aforementioned subordinate maxims. For the most general of God's laws, the one that rules the whole course of the universe, is without exception.

We can say also that God wills everything that is an object of his particular volition. But we must make a distinction with respect to the objects of his general volition, such as the actions of other creatures, particularly the actions of those that are reasonable, actions with which God wishes to concur. For, if the action is good in itself, we can say that God wills it and sometimes commands it, even when it does not take place. But if the action is evil in itself and becomes good only by accident, because the course of things (particularly punishment and atonement) corrects its evilness and repays the evil with interest in such a way that in the end there is more perfection in the whole sequence than if the evil had not occurred, then we must say that God permits this but does not will it, even though he concurs with it because of the laws of nature he has established and because he knows how to draw a greater good from it.

8. *To distinguish the actions of God from those of creatures we explain the notion of an individual substance.* It is rather difficult to distinguish the actions of God from those of creatures; for some believe that God does everything, while others imagine that he merely conserves the force he has given to creatures. What follows will let us see the extent to which we can say the one or the other. And since actions and passions properly belong to individual substances [*actiones sunt suppositorum*],[6] it will be necessary to explain what such an individual substance is.

It is indeed true that when several predicates are attributed to a single subject and this subject is attributed to no other, it is called an individual substance; but this is not sufficient, and such an explanation is merely nominal. We must therefore consider what it is to be attributed truly to a certain subject.

Now it is evident that all true predication has some basis in the nature of things and that, when a proposition is not an identity, that is, when the predicate is not explicitly contained in the subject, it must be contained in it virtually. That is what the philosophers call *in-esse*, when they say that the predicate is in the subject. Thus the subject term must always contain the predicate term, so that one who understands perfectly the notion of the subject would also know that the predicate belongs to it.

Since this is so, we can say that the nature of an individual substance or of a complete being is to have a notion so complete that it is sufficient to contain and to allow us to deduce from it all the predicates of the subject to which this notion is attributed. An accident, on the other hand, is a being whose notion does not include everything that can be attributed to the subject to which the notion is attributed. Thus, taken in abstraction from the subject, the quality of being a king which belongs to Alexander the Great is not determinate enough to constitute an individual and does not include the other qualities of the same subject, nor does it include everything that the notion of this prince includes. On the other hand, God, seeing Alexander's individual notion or haecceity,[7] sees in it at the same time the basis and reason for all the predicates which can be said truly of him, for example, that he vanquished Darius and Porus; he even knows *a priori* (and not by experience) whether he died a natural death or whether he was poisoned,

6. [Leibniz is making use of Scholastic logical terminology: a *suppositum* is an individual subsistent substance; *actiones sunt suppositorum* therefore means that actions are of individual subsistent substances.]

7. [The word *haecceitas* (or *hecceïté*, what we are translating as "haecceity") was coined by John Duns Scotus (c. 1266–1308) to refer to an individual essence or "thisness"—what *haecceitas* means literally.]

something we can know only through history. Thus when we consider carefully the connection of things, we can say that from all time in Alexander's soul there are vestiges of everything that has happened to him and marks of everything that will happen to him and even traces of everything that happens in the universe, even though God alone could recognize them all.

9. *That each singular substance expresses the whole universe in its own way, and that all its events, together with all their circumstances and the whole sequence of external things, are included in its notion.* Several notable paradoxes follow from this; among others, it follows that it is not true that two substances can resemble each other completely and differ only in number [*solo numero*], and that what Saint Thomas asserts on this point about angels or intelligences (that here every individual is a lowest species)[8] is true of all substances, provided that one takes the specific difference as the geometers do with respect to their figures. It also follows that a substance can begin only by creation and end only by annihilation; that a substance is not divisible into two; that one substance cannot be constructed from two; and that thus the number of substances does not naturally increase and decrease, though they are often transformed.

Moreover, every substance is like a complete world and like a mirror of God or of the whole universe, which each one expresses in its own way, somewhat as the same city is variously represented depending upon the different positions from which it is viewed. Thus the universe is in some way multiplied as many times as there are substances, and the glory of God is likewise multiplied by as many entirely different representations of his work. It can even be said that every substance bears in some way the character of God's infinite wisdom and omnipotence and imitates him as much as it is capable. For it expresses, however confusedly, everything that happens in the universe, whether past, present, or future—this has some resemblance to an infinite perception or knowledge. And since all other substances in turn express this substance and accommodate themselves to it, one can say that it extends its power over all the others, in imitation of the creator's omnipotence.

10. *That the belief in substantial forms has some basis, but that these forms do not change anything in the phenomena and must not be used to explain particular effects.* It seems that the ancients, as well as many able men accustomed to deep meditation who have taught theology and philosophy some centuries ago (some of whom are respected for their saintliness) have had some knowledge of what we have just said; this is why they introduced and maintained the substantial forms which are so decried today. But they are not so distant from the truth nor so ridiculous as the common lot of our new philosophers imagines.

I agree that the consideration of these forms serves no purpose in the details of physics and must not be used to explain particular phenomena. That is where the Scholastics failed, as did the physicians of the past who followed their example, believing that they could account for the properties of bodies by talking about forms and qualities without taking the trouble to examine their manner of operation. It is as if we were content to say that a clock has a quality of clockness derived from its form without considering in what all of this consists; that would be sufficient for the person who buys the clock, provided that he turns over its care to another.

But this misunderstanding and misuse of forms must not cause us to reject something whose knowledge is so necessary in metaphysics that, I hold, without it one cannot properly know the first principles or elevate our minds sufficiently well to the knowledge of incorporeal natures and the wonders of God.

However, just as a geometer does not need to burden his mind with the famous labyrinth of the composition of the continuum, there is no need for any moral philosopher and even less need for a jurist or statesman to trouble himself with the great difficulties involved in reconciling free will and God's providence, since the geometer can achieve all his demonstrations and the statesman can complete all his deliberations without entering into these discussions, discussions that remain necessary and important in philosophy and theology. In the same way, a physicist can explain some experiments, at times using previous simpler experiments and at times using geometric and me-

8. [See St. Thomas Aquinas, *Summa Theologiae* I, q. 50, art. 4.]

chanical demonstrations, without needing general considerations from another sphere. And if he uses God's concourse, or else a soul, animating force [*archée*], or something else of this nature, he is raving just as much as the person who, in the course of an important practical deliberation, enters into a lofty discussion concerning the nature of destiny and the nature of our freedom. In fact, people often commit this fault without thinking when they encumber their minds with the consideration of fatalism and sometimes are even diverted from a good resolution or a necessary duty in this way.

11. *That the thoughts of the theologians and philosophers who are called Scholastics are not entirely to be disdained.* I know that I am advancing a great paradox by attempting to rehabilitate the old philosophy in some fashion and to restore the almost banished substantial forms to their former place. But perhaps I will not be condemned so easily when it is known that I have long meditated upon the modern philosophy, that I have given much time to experiments in physics and demonstrations in geometry, and that I had long been persuaded about the futility of these beings, which I finally was required to embrace in spite of myself and, as it were, by force, after having myself carried out certain studies. These studies made me recognize that our moderns do not give enough credit to Saint Thomas and to the other great men of his time and that there is much more solidity than one imagines in the opinions of the Scholastic philosophers and theologians, provided that they are used appropriately and in their proper place. I am even convinced that, if some exact and thoughtful mind took the trouble to clarify and summarize their thoughts after the manner of the analytic geometers, he would find there a great treasure of extremely important and wholly demonstrative truths.

12. *That the notions involved in extension contain something imaginary and cannot constitute the substance of body.* But, to resume the thread of our discussion, I believe that anyone who will meditate about the nature of substance, as I have explained it above, will find that the nature of body does not consist merely in extension, that is, in size, shape, and motion, but that we must necessarily recognize in body something related to souls, something we commonly call substantial form, even though it makes no change in the phenomena, any more than do the souls of animals, if they have any. It is even possible to demonstrate that the notions of size, shape, and motion are not as distinct as is imagined and that they contain something imaginary and relative to our perception, as do (though to a greater extent) color, heat, and other similar qualities, qualities about which one can doubt whether they are truly found in the nature of things outside ourselves. That is why qualities of this kind cannot constitute any substance. And if there were no other principle of identity in body other than the one just mentioned, a body could not subsist for more than a moment.

Yet the souls and substantial forms of other bodies are entirely different from intelligent souls, which alone know their actions. Not only don't intelligent souls perish naturally, but they also always preserve the basis for the knowledge of what they are; this is what renders them alone susceptible to punishment and reward and makes them citizens of the republic of the universe, whose monarch is God. It also follows that all other creatures must serve them—something which we will later discuss more fully.

13. *Since the individual notion of each person includes once and for all everything that will ever happen to him, one sees in it the* a priori *proofs of the truth of each event, or, why one happened rather than another. But these truths, however certain, are nevertheless contingent, being based on the free will of God or of his creatures, whose choice always has its reasons, which incline without necessitating.* But before going further, we must attempt to resolve a great difficulty that can arise from the foundations we have set forth above. We have said that the notion of an individual substance includes once and for all everything that can ever happen to it and that, by considering this notion, one can see there everything that can truly be said of it, just as we can see in the nature of a circle all the properties that can be deduced from it. But it seems that this would eliminate the difference between contingent and necessary truths, that there would be no place for human freedom, and that an absolute fatalism would rule all our actions as well as all the other events of the world. To this I reply that we must distinguish between what is certain and what is necessary. Everyone grants that

future contingents are certain, since God foresees them, but we do not concede that they are necessary on that account. But (someone will say) if a conclusion can be deduced infallibly from a definition or notion, it is necessary. And it is true that we are maintaining that everything that must happen to a person is already contained virtually in his nature or notion, just as the properties of a circle are contained in its definition; thus the difficulty still remains. To address it firmly, I assert that connection or following [*consécution*] is of two kinds. The one whose contrary implies a contradiction is absolutely necessary; this deduction occurs in the eternal truths, for example, the truths of geometry. The other is necessary only *ex hypothesi* and, so to speak, accidentally, but it is contingent in itself, since its contrary does not imply a contradiction. And this connection is based not purely on ideas and God's simple understanding, but on his free decrees and on the sequence of the universe.

Let us take an example. Since Julius Caesar will become perpetual dictator and master of the republic and will overthrow the freedom of the Romans, this action is contained in his notion, for we assume that it is the nature of such a perfect notion of a subject to contain everything, so that the predicate is included in the subject, *ut possit inesse subjecto.*[9] It could be said that it is not in virtue of this notion or idea that he must perform this action, since it pertains to him only because God knows everything. But someone might insist that his nature or form corresponds to this notion, and, since God has imposed this personality on him, it is henceforth necessary for him to satisfy it. I could reply by citing future contingents, since they have no reality as yet, save in God's understanding and will, and, because God gave them this form in advance, they must in the same way correspond to it.

But I much prefer to overcome difficulties rather than to excuse them by giving some other similar difficulties, and what I am about to say will illuminate the one as well as the other. It is here, then, that we must apply the distinction concerning connections, and I say that whatever happens in conformity with these predeterminations [*avances*] is certain but not necessary, and if one were to do the contrary, he would not be doing something impossible in itself, even though it would be impossible [*ex hypothesi*] for this to happen. For if someone were able to carry out the whole demonstration by virtue of which he could prove this connection between the subject, Caesar, and the predicate, his successful undertaking, he would in fact be showing that Caesar's future dictatorship is grounded in his notion or nature, that there is a reason why he crossed the Rubicon rather than stopped at it and why he won rather than lost at Pharsalus and that it was reasonable, and consequently certain, that this should happen. But this would not show that it was necessary in itself nor that the contrary implies a contradiction. It is reasonable and certain in almost the same way that God will always do the best, even though what is less perfect does not imply a contradiction.

For it will be found that the demonstration of this predicate of Caesar is not as absolute as those of numbers or of geometry, but that it supposes the sequence of things that God has freely chosen, a sequence based on God's first free decree always to do what is most perfect and on God's decree with respect to human nature, following out of the first decree, that man will always do (although freely) that which appears to be best. But every truth based on these kinds of decrees is contingent, even though it is certain; for these decrees do not change the possibility of things, and, as I have already said, even though it is certain that God always chooses the best, this does not prevent something less perfect from being and remaining possible in itself, even though it will not happen, since it is not its impossibility but its imperfection which causes it to be rejected. And nothing is necessary whose contrary is possible.

We will therefore be in a position to satisfy these sorts of difficulties, however great they may appear (and in fact they are not made any the less pressing by considering the other thinkers who have ever treated this matter), as long as we recognize that all contingent propositions have reasons to be one way rather than another or else (what comes to the same thing) that they have *a priori* proofs of their truth which render them certain and which show that the connection between subject and predicate of these propositions has its basis in the natures of both. But they do not have necessary demonstrations, since

9. [The Latin is an approximate paraphrase of the preceding clause.]

these reasons are based only on the principle of contingency or the principle of the existence of things, that is, based on what is or appears to be best from among several equally possible things. On the other hand, necessary truths are based on the principle of contradiction and on the possibility or impossibility of essences themselves, without regard to the free will of God or his creatures.

14. *God produces various substances according to the different views he has of the universe, and through God's intervention the proper nature of each substance brings it about that what happens to one corresponds with what happens to all the others, without their acting upon one another directly.* After having seen, in some way, what the nature of substances consists in, we must try to explain the dependence they have upon one another and their actions and passions. Now, first of all, it is very evident that created substances depend upon God, who preserves them and who even produces them continually by a kind of emanation, just as we produce our thoughts. For God, so to speak, turns on all sides and in all ways the general system of phenomena which he finds it good to produce in order to manifest his glory, and he views all the faces of the world in all ways possible, since there is no relation that escapes his omniscience. The result of each view of the universe, as seen from a certain position, is a substance which expresses the universe in conformity with this view, should God see fit to render his thought actual and to produce this substance. And since God's view is always true, our perceptions are always true; it is our judgments, which come from ourselves, that deceive us.

Now we said above, and it follows from what we have just said, that each substance is like a world apart, independent of all other things, except for God; thus all our phenomena, that is, all the things that can ever happen to us, are only consequences of our being. And since these phenomena maintain a certain order in conformity with our nature or, so to speak, in conformity with the world which is in us, an order which enables us to make useful observations to regulate our conduct, observations justified by the success of future phenomena, an order which thus allows us often to judge the future from the past without error, this would be sufficient to enable us to say that these phenomena are true without bothering with whether they are outside us and whether others also perceive them. Nevertheless, it is very true that the perceptions or expressions of all substances mutually correspond in such a way that each one, carefully following certain reasons or laws it has observed, coincides with others doing the same—in the same way that several people who have agreed to meet in some place at some specified time can really do this if they so desire. But although they all express the same phenomena, it does not follow that their expressions are perfectly similar; it is sufficient that they are proportional. In just the same way, several spectators believe that they are seeing the same thing and agree among themselves about it, even though each sees and speaks in accordance with his view.

And God alone (from whom all individuals emanate continually and who sees the universe not only as they see it but also entirely differently from all of them) is the cause of this correspondence of their phenomena and makes that which is particular to one of them public to all of them; otherwise, there would be no interconnection. We could therefore say in some way and properly speaking, though not in accordance with common usage, that one particular substance never acts upon another particular substance nor is acted upon by it, if we consider that what happens to each is solely a consequence of its complete idea or notion alone, since this idea already contains all its predicates or events and expresses the whole universe. In fact, nothing can happen to us except thoughts and perceptions, and all our future thoughts and perceptions are merely consequences, though contingent, of our preceding thoughts and perceptions, in such a way that, if I were capable of considering distinctly everything that happens or appears to me at this time, I could see in it everything that will ever happen or appear to me. This would never fail, and it would happen to me regardless, even if everything outside of me were destroyed, provided there remained only God and me. But since we attribute what we perceive in a certain way to other things as causes acting on us, we must consider the basis for this judgment and the element of truth there is in it.

15. *The action of one finite substance on another consists only in the increase of degree of its expression*

together with the diminution of the expression of the other, insofar as God requires them to accommodate themselves to one another. But, without entering into a long discussion, in order to reconcile the language of metaphysics with practice, it is sufficient for now to remark that we ascribe to ourselves—and with reason—the phenomena that we express most perfectly and that we attribute to other substances the phenomena that each expresses best. Thus a substance, which is of infinite extension insofar as it expresses everything, becomes limited in proportion to its more or less perfect manner of expression. This, then, is how one can conceive that substances impede or limit each other, and consequently one can say that, in this sense, they act upon one another and are required, so to speak, to accommodate themselves to one another. For it can happen that a change that increases the expression of one diminishes that of another. Now, the efficacy [*vertu*] a particular substance has is to express well the glory of God, and it is by doing this that it is less limited. And whenever something exercises its efficacy or power, that is, when it acts, it improves and extends itself insofar as it acts. Therefore, when a change takes place by which several substances are affected (in fact every change affects all of them), I believe one may say that the substance which immediately passes to a greater degree of perfection or to a more perfect expression exercises its power and *acts*, and the substance which passes to a lesser degree shows its weakness and is *acted upon* [*pâtit*]. I also hold that every action of a substance which has perfection involves some *pleasure*, and every passion some *pain* and vice versa. However, it can happen that a present advantage is destroyed by a greater evil in what follows, whence one can sin in acting, that is, in exercising one's power and finding pleasure.

16. *God's extraordinary concourse is included in that which our essence expresses, for this expression extends to everything. But this concourse surpasses the powers of our nature or of our distinct expression, which is finite and follows certain subordinate maxims.* It now only remains to explain how God can sometimes influence men and other substances by an extraordinary and miraculous concourse, since it seems that nothing extraordinary and supernatural can happen to them, given that all their events are only consequences of their nature. But we must remember what we have said above concerning miracles in the universe—that they are always in conformity with the universal law of the general order, even though they may be above the subordinate maxims. And to the extent that every person or substance is like a small world expressing the large world, we can say equally that the extraordinary action of God on this substance does not fail to be miraculous, despite the fact that it is included in the general order of the universe insofar as it is expressed by the essence or individual notion of this substance. That is why, if we include in our nature everything that it expresses, nothing is supernatural to it, for our nature extends everywhere, since an effect always expresses its cause and God is the true cause of substances. But what our nature expresses more perfectly belongs to it in a particular way, since it is in this that its power consists. But since it is limited, as I have just explained, there are many things that surpass the powers of our nature and even surpass the powers of all limited natures. Thus, to speak more clearly, I say that God's miracles and extraordinary concourse have the peculiarity that they cannot be foreseen by the reasoning of any created mind, no matter how enlightened, because the distinct comprehension of the general order surpasses all of them. On the other hand, everything that we call natural depends on the less general maxims that creatures can understand. Thus, in order that my words may be as irreproachable as my meaning, it would be good to connect certain ways of speaking with certain thoughts. We could call that which includes everything we express our essence or idea; since this expresses our union with God himself, it has no limits and nothing surpasses it. But that which is limited in us could be called our nature or our power; and in that sense, that which surpasses the natures of all created substances is supernatural.

17. *An example of a subordinate maxim or law of nature; in which it is shown, against the Cartesians and many others, that God always conserves the same force but not the same quantity of motion.* I have already mentioned the subordinate maxims or laws of nature often enough, and it seems appropriate to give an example of one. Our new philosophers commonly make use of the famous rule that God always conserves the same quantity of motion in the

world. In fact, this rule is extremely plausible, and, in the past, I held it as indubitable. But I have since recognized what is wrong with it. It is that Descartes and many other able mathematicians have believed that the quantity of motion, that is, the speed multiplied by the size of the moving body, coincides exactly with the moving force, or, to speak geometrically, that the forces are proportional to the product of the speeds and [sizes of] bodies. Now, it is extremely reasonable that the same force is always conserved in the universe. Also, when we attend to the phenomena, we see that there is no perpetual mechanical motion, because then the force of a machine, which is always diminished somewhat by friction and which must sooner or later come to an end, would restore itself, and consequently would increase by itself without any new external impulsion. We observe also that the force of a body is diminished only in proportion to the force it imparts to some bodies contiguous to it or to its own parts, insofar as they have separate motion.

Thus they believed that what can be said about force can also be said about the quantity of motion. But to show the difference between them, I assume that a body falling from a certain height acquires the force to rise up that height, if its direction carries it that way, at least, if there are no impediments. For example, a pendulum would rise again exactly to the height from which it descended if the resistance of the air and some other small obstacles did not diminish its acquired force a little.

I *assume* also that as much force is required to elevate A, a body of one pound, to CD, a height of four fathoms, as to elevate B, a body of four pounds, to EF, a height of one fathom. All this is admitted by our new philosophers.

It is therefore evident that, having fallen from height CD, body A acquired exactly as much force as did body B, which fell from height EF; for since body (B) reached F and acquired the force to rise to E (by the first assumption), it has the force to carry a body of four pounds, that is, itself, to EF, the height of one fathom; similarly, since body (A) reached D and acquired the force to rise to C, it has the force to carry a body of one pound, that is, itself, to CD, a height of four fathoms. Therefore (by the second assumption), the force of these two bodies is equal.

Let us now see whether the quantity of motion is also the same in each. But here we will be surprised to

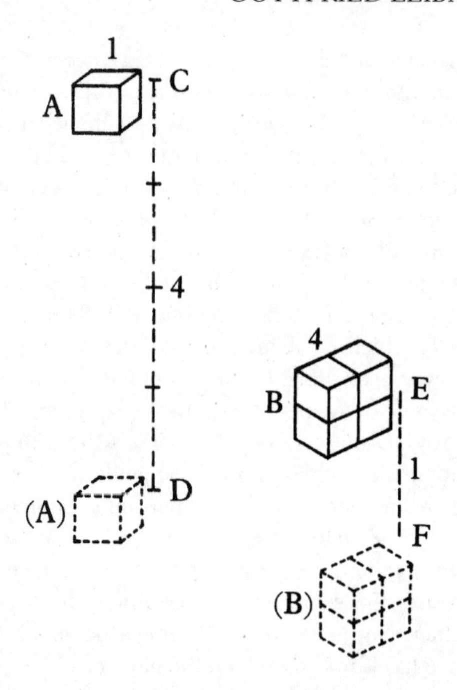

find a very great difference. For Galileo demonstrated that the speed acquired by the fall CD is twice the speed acquired by the fall EF, even though the one height is four times the other. Let us therefore multiply body A, proportional to 1, with its speed, proportional to 2; the product or quantity of motion will be proportional to 2. On the other hand, let us multiply body B, proportional to 4, by its speed, proportional to 1; the product or quantity of motion will be proportional to 4. Therefore the quantity of motion of body (A) at point D is half of the quantity of motion of body (B) at point F; yet their forces are equal. Hence, there is a great difference between quantity of motion and force—which is what needed to be proved.

Thus we see that force must be calculated from the quantity of the effect it can produce, for example, by the height to which a heavy body of a certain size and kind can be raised; this is quite different from the speed that can be imparted to it. And to give it double the speed, it must be given more than double the force.

Nothing is simpler that this proof. Descartes fell into error here only because he had too much confidence in his own thoughts, even when they were not sufficiently ripe. But I am surprised that his followers have not since then discovered this mistake; and I fear that they are beginning, little by little, to imitate some of the Peripatetics, whom they ridicule, like them gradually acquiring the habit of consulting their master's writings rather than reason and nature.

18. *The distinction between force and quantity of motion is important, among other reasons, for judging that one must have recourse to metaphysical considerations distinct from extension in order to explain the phenomena of bodies.* This consideration, the distinction between force and quantity of motion, is rather important, not only in physics and mechanics, in order to find the true laws of nature and rules of motion and even to correct the several errors of practice which have slipped into the writings of some able mathematicians, but also in metaphysics, in order to understand the principles better. For if we consider only what motion contains precisely and formally, that is, change of place, motion is not something entirely real, and when several bodies change position among themselves, it is not possible to determine, merely from a consideration of these changes, to which body we should attribute motion or rest, as I could show geometrically, if I wished to stop and do this now.

But the force or proximate cause of these changes is something more real, and there is sufficient basis to attribute it to one body more than to another. Also, it is only in this way that we can know to which body the motion belongs. Now, this force is something different from size, shape, and motion, and one can therefore judge that not everything conceived in body consists solely in extension and in its modifications, as our moderns have persuaded themselves. Thus we are once again obliged to reestablish some beings or forms they have banished. And it becomes more and more apparent that, although all the particular phenomena of nature can be explained mathematically or mechanically by those who understand them, nevertheless the general principles of corporeal nature and of mechanics itself are more metaphysical than geometrical, and belong to some indivisible forms or natures as the causes of appearances, rather than to corporeal mass or extension. This is a reflection capable of reconciling the mechanical philosophy of the moderns with the caution of some intelligent and well-intentioned persons who fear, with some reason, that we are withdrawing too far from immaterial beings, to the disadvantage of piety.

19. *The utility of final causes in physics.* Since I do not like to judge people wrongly, I do not accuse our new philosophers, who claim to banish final causes from physics.[10] But I am nevertheless obliged to confess that the consequences of this opinion appear dangerous to me, especially if I combine it with the one I refuted at the beginning of this discourse, which seems to go so far as to eliminate final causes altogether, as if God proposed no end or good in acting or as if the good were not the object of his will. As for myself, I hold, on the contrary, that it is here we must seek the principle of all existences and laws of nature, because God always intends the best and most perfect.

I am quite willing to admit that we are subject to deception when we wish to determine God's ends or counsels. But this is only when we try to limit them to some particular design, believing that he had only one thing in view, when instead he regards everything at the same time. For instance, it is a great mistake to believe that God made the world only for us, although it is quite true that he made it in its entirety for us and that there is nothing in the universe which does not affect us and does not also accommodate itself in accordance with his regard for us, following the principles set forth above. Thus when we see some good effect or perfection occurring or ensuing from God's works, we can say with certainty that God had proposed it. For he does nothing by chance and is not like us, who sometimes fail to do the good. That is why, far from being able to fall into error in this, as do extreme politicians who imagine too much subtlety in the designs of princes or as do commentators who look for too much erudition in their author, we cannot attribute too much reflection to this infinite wisdom, and there is no subject in which error is to be feared less, provided we limit ourselves to affirmations and avoid negative propositions that limit God's designs.

Anyone who sees the admirable structure of animals will find himself forced to recognize the wisdom of the author of things. And I advise those who have any feelings of piety and even feelings of true philosophy to keep away from the phrases of certain would-

10. [The "new philosophers" Leibniz has in mind include Descartes and Spinoza, who explain everything mechanically and reject final causes.]

be free thinkers who say that we see because it happens that we have eyes and not that eyes were made for seeing. When one seriously holds these opinions ascribing everything to the necessity of matter or to some chance (even though both must appear ridiculous to those who understand what we have explained above), it is difficult to recognize an intelligent author of nature. For the effect must correspond to its cause; indeed, the effect is best recognized through a knowledge of the cause. Moreover, it is unreasonable to introduce a supreme intelligence as orderer of things and then, instead of using his wisdom, use only the properties of matter to explain the phenomena. This is as if, in order to account for the conquest of an important place by a great prince, a historian were to claim that it occurred because the small particles of gunpowder, set off by the contact of a spark, escaped with sufficient speed to push a hard and heavy body against the walls of the place, while the little particles that make up the brass of the cannon were so firmly interlaced that this speed did not separate them, instead of showing how the foresight of the conqueror enabled him to choose the suitable means and times and how his power overcame all obstacles.

20. A *noteworthy passage by Socrates in Plato against the philosophers who are overly materialistic.* This reminds me of a beautiful passage by Socrates in Plato's *Phaedo*. This passage agrees marvelously with my opinions on this point and seems to be directed expressly against our overly materialistic philosophers. Thus I have been tempted to translate this account, even though it is a little long; perhaps this sample will give an incentive to some of us to share in many of the other beautiful and solid thoughts which can be found in the writings of this famous author.[11]

21. *If mechanical rules depended only on geometry without metaphysics, the phenomena would be entirely different.* Now, since we have always recognized God's wisdom in the detail of the mechanical structure of some particular bodies, it must also be displayed in the general economy of the world and in the constitution of the laws of nature. This is true to such an extent that one can observe the counsels of this wisdom in the laws of motion in general. For if there were nothing in bodies but extended mass and nothing in motion but change of place and if everything should and could be deduced solely from these definitions by geometrical necessity, it would follow, as I have shown elsewhere, that, upon contact, the smallest body would impart its own speed to the largest body without losing any of this speed; and we would have to accept a number of such rules which are completely contrary to the formation of a system. But the decree of divine wisdom always to conserve the same total force and the same total direction has provided for this.

I even find that several effects of nature can be demonstrated doubly, that is, by considering first the efficient cause and then by considering the final cause, making use, for example, of God's decree always to produce his effect by the easiest and most determinate ways, as I have shown elsewhere in accounting for the rules of catoptrics and dioptrics;[12] I shall say more about this soon.

22. *Reconciliation of two ways of explaining things, by final causes and by efficient causes, in order to satisfy both those who explain nature mechanically and those who have recourse to incorporeal natures.* It is appropriate to make this remark in order to reconcile those who hope to explain mechanically the formation of the first tissue of an animal and the whole machinery of its parts, with those who account for this same structure using final causes. Both ways are good and both can be useful, not only for admiring the skill of the Great Worker, but also for discovering something useful in physics and in medicine. And the authors who follow these different routes should not malign each other.

For I see that those who apply themselves to explaining the beauty of the divine anatomy laugh at others who imagine that a movement of certain fluids that seems fortuitous could have produced such a beautiful variety of limbs, and call these people rash and profane. And the latter, on the other hand, call

11. Leibniz's marginal note: "The passage from Plato's *Phaedo* where Socrates ridicules Anaxagoras, who introduces mind but does not make use of it, is to be inserted."

12. [The reference is to the "Unicum Opticae, Catoptricae et Dioptricae Principium, Autore G. G. L.," from the *Acta Eridutorum* (June 1682).]

the former simple and superstitious, comparing them to the ancients who regarded physicists as impious when they maintained that it is not Jupiter that thunders, but some matter present in the clouds. It would be best to join together both considerations, for if it is permitted to use a humble comparison I recognize and praise the skill of a worker not only by showing his designs in making the parts of his machine, but also by explaining the instruments he used in making each part, especially when these instruments are simple and cleverly contrived. *And God is a skillful enough artisan* to produce a machine which is a thousand times more ingenious than that of our body, while using only some very simple fluids explicitly concocted in such a way that only the ordinary laws of nature are required to arrange them in the right way to produce so admirable an effect; but it is also true that this would not happen at all unless God were the author of nature.

However, I find that the way of efficient causes, which is in fact deeper and in some sense more immediate and *a priori*, is, on the other hand, quite difficult when one comes to details, and I believe that, for the most part, our philosophers are still far from it. But the way of final causes is easier, and is not infrequently of use in divining important and useful truths which one would be a long time in seeking by the other, more physical way; anatomy can provide significant examples of this. I also believe that Snell, who first discovered the rules of refraction, would have waited a long time before discovering them if he first had to find out how light is formed. But he apparently followed the method which the ancients used for catoptrics, which is in fact that of final causes. For, by seeking the easiest way to lead a ray from a given point to another point given by reflection on a given plane (assuming that this is nature's design), they discovered the equality of angles of incidence and angles of reflection, as can be seen in a little treatise by Heliodorus of Larissa, and elsewhere.[13] That is what, I believe, Snell and Fermat after him (though without knowing anything about Snell) have most ingeniously applied to refraction. For when, in the same media, rays observe the same proportion between sines (which is proportional to the resistances of the media), this happens to be the easiest or, at least, the most determinate way to pass from a given point in a medium to a given point in another. And the demonstration Descartes attempted to give of this same theorem by way of efficient causes is not nearly as good. At least there is room for suspicion that he would never have found the law in this way, if he had learned nothing in Holland of Snell's discovery.[14]

23. *To return to immaterial substances, we explain how God acts on the understanding of minds and whether we always have the idea of that about which we think.* I found it appropriate to insist a bit on these considerations of final causes, incorporeal natures, and an intelligent cause with respect to bodies, in order to show their use even in physics and mathematics: on the one hand, to purge the mechanical philosophy of the impiety with which it is charged and, on the other hand, to elevate the minds of our philosophers from material considerations alone to nobler meditations. It is now appropriate to return from bodies to immaterial natures, in particular to minds, and to say something of the means God uses to enlighten them and act on them. In this matter, too, we must not doubt that there are certain laws of nature, of which I could speak more fully elsewhere. But for now it will be sufficient to touch somewhat on ideas, whether we see all things in God and how God is our light.

It may be appropriate to observe that the improper use of ideas gives rise to several errors. For when we reason about something, we imagine ourselves to have the idea of that thing; and that is the foundation upon which certain ancient and new philosophers have built a certain extremely imperfect demonstration of God. For, they say, I must have an idea of God or of a perfect being since I think of him, and one cannot think without an idea. Now, the idea of this being

13. [Heliodorus of Larissa, or Damianos, was a Greek mathematician who flourished after Ptolemy.]

14. [The law of refraction was first published in the second discourse of Descartes' *Dioptrics*. Descartes does indeed attempt to derive the law from hypotheses about the nature of light. Snell discovered the same laws at roughly the same time as Descartes, and there was (and continues to be) a lively dispute about who discovered the law first, and whether Descartes actually discovered the law or learned it from Snell. Leibniz seems to favor Snell.]

contains all perfections, and existence is a perfection, so consequently he exists. But since we often think of impossible chimeras—for example, of the highest degree of speed, of the greatest number, of the intersection of the conchoid with its base or rule—this reasoning is insufficient. It is therefore in this sense that we can say that there are true and false ideas, depending upon whether the thing in question is possible or not. And it is only when we are certain of its possibility that we can boast of having an idea of the thing. Thus the argument above proves, at least, that God exists necessarily, if he is possible. It is indeed a prerogative of divine nature, one that surpasses all others, that divine nature needs only its possibility or essence in order actually to exist, and it is precisely this that is called *ens a se*.

24. *What is clear or obscure, distinct or confused, adequate and intuitive or suppositive knowledge; nominal, real, causal, and essential definition.* In order to understand better the nature of ideas, we must to some extent touch on the varieties of knowledge. When I can recognize a thing from among others without being able to say what its differences or properties consist in, the knowledge is *confused*. It is in this way that we sometimes know something *clearly*, without being in any doubt whether a poem or a picture is done well or badly, simply because it has a certain something, I know not what, that satisfies or offends us. But when I can explain the marks which I have, the knowledge is called *distinct*. And such is the knowledge of an assayer, who discerns the true from the false by means of certain tests or marks which make up the definition of gold.

But distinct knowledge has degrees, for ordinarily the notions that enter into the definition would themselves need definition and are known only confusedly. But when everything that enters into a distinct definition or distinct knowledge is known distinctly, down to the primitive notions, I call this knowledge *adequate*. And when my mind understands all the primitive ingredients of a notion at once and distinctly, it has *intuitive* knowledge of it; this is extremely rare, since the greater part of human knowledge is only confused or *suppositive*.

It is also good to distinguish nominal and real definitions. I call a definition *nominal* when one can still doubt whether the notion defined is possible, as, for example, if I say that an endless helix is a solid line whose parts are congruent or can be superimposed on one another; anyone who does not know from elsewhere what an endless helix is could doubt whether such a line is possible, even though having such congruent parts is in fact one of the reciprocal properties of the endless helix, for other lines whose parts are congruent (which are only the circumference of a circle and the straight line) are planar, that is, they can be inscribed on a plane. This shows that any reciprocal property can serve as a nominal definition; but when the property makes known the possibility of the thing, it constitutes a real definition. As long as we have only a nominal definition, we cannot be certain of the consequences we derive, for if it concealed some contradiction or impossibility, the opposite conclusions could be derived from it. That is why truths do not depend upon names and are not arbitrary, as some new philosophers have believed.[15]

Furthermore, there are still great differences between the kinds of real definitions. For when possibility is proved only by experience, as in the definition of quicksilver, whose possibility we know because we know that there actually is such a body which is an extremely heavy but rather volatile fluid, the definition is merely real and nothing more; but when the proof of the possibility is *a priori*, the definition is both real and *causal*, as when it contains the possible generation of the thing. And when a definition pushes the analysis back to the primitive notions without assuming anything requiring an *a priori* proof of its possibility, it is perfect or *essential*.

25. *In what case our knowledge is joined to the contemplation of the idea.* Now, it is evident that we have no idea of a notion when it is impossible. And in the case where knowledge is only *suppositive*, even when we have the idea, we do not contemplate it, for such a notion is only known in the way in which we know notions involving a hidden impossibility [*occultement impossibles*]; and if a notion is possible, we do not learn its possibility in this way. For example, when I think of a thousand or of a chiliagon, I often do this without contemplating the idea—as when I

15. [Leibniz probably has Hobbes in mind here.]

say that a thousand is ten times a hundred without bothering to think of what 10 and 100 are because I *suppose* I know it and do not believe I need to stop now and conceive it. Thus, it could happen, as in fact it often happens, that I am mistaken with respect to a notion I suppose or believe that I understand, although in fact the notion is impossible, or at least incompatible with those to which I join it. And whether I am mistaken or not, this suppositive way of conceiving remains the same. Therefore, only in confused notions when our knowledge is *clear* or in distinct notions when it is *intuitive* do we see the entire idea in them.

26. *That we have all ideas in us; and of Plato's doctrine of reminiscence.* In order properly to conceive what an idea is, we must prevent an equivocation. For some take the idea to be the form or difference of our thoughts, and thus we have an idea in the mind only insofar as we think of it; every time we think of it again, we have other ideas of the same thing, though similar to the preceding ideas. But it seems that others take the idea as an immediate object of thought or as some permanent form that remains when we are not contemplating it. And, in fact, our soul always has in it the quality of representing to itself any nature or form whatsoever, when the occasion to think of it presents itself. And I believe that this quality of our soul, insofar as it expresses some nature, form, or essence, is properly the idea of the thing, which is in us and which is always in us, whether we think of it or not. For our soul expresses God, the universe, and all essences, as well as all existences.

This agrees with my principles, for nothing ever enters into our mind naturally from the outside; and we have a bad habit of thinking of our soul as if it received certain species as messengers and as if it has doors and windows. We have all these forms in our mind; we even have forms from all time, for the mind always expresses all its future thoughts and already thinks confusedly about everything it will ever think about distinctly. And nothing can be taught to us whose idea we do not already have in our mind, an idea which is like the matter of which that thought is formed.

This is what Plato so excellently recognized when he proposed his doctrine of reminiscence, a very solid doctrine, provided that it is taken rightly and purged of the error of preexistence and provided that we do not imagine that at some earlier time the soul must already have known and thought distinctly what it learns and thinks now. Plato also strengthened his view by way of a fine experiment, introducing a little boy, whom he leads insensibly to extremely difficult truths of geometry concerning incommensurables without teaching him anything, merely by asking appropriate questions in proper order.[16] This demonstrates that our soul knows all these things virtually and requires only *attention* to recognize truths, and that, consequently, it has, at very least, the ideas upon which these truths depend. One can even say that it already possesses these truths, if they are taken as relations of ideas.

27. *How our soul can be compared to empty tablets and how our notions come from the senses.* Aristotle preferred to compare our soul to tablets that are still blank, where there is room for writing,[17] and he maintained that nothing is in our understanding that does not come from the senses. That agrees better with the popular notions, as is Aristotle's way, but Plato goes deeper. However, these kinds of doxologies or practicologies may be acceptable in ordinary usage, much as we see that those who follow Copernicus do not stop saying that the sun rises and sets. I even find that they can be given a good sense, a sense according to which they have nothing false in them, just as I have already noted how one can truly say that particular substances act on one another. In this same way, one can also say that we receive knowledge from the outside by way of the senses, because some external things contain or express more particularly the reasons that determine our soul to certain thoughts. But when we are concerned with the exactness of metaphysical truths, it is important to recognize the extent and independence of our soul, which

16. [This is a reference to Plato's *Meno*, 82b *et seq.*, where, in a familiar passage, Socrates leads a young slave boy through some geometrical arguments.]

17. [Aristotle, *De Anima*, Book II, chap. 4. The doctrine that nothing is in the intellect that was not first in the senses, attributed to Aristotle by the Scholastics, does not actually occur in Aristotle; perhaps it is a rendering of *Posterior Analytics*, Book II, chap. 19, or *Nicomachean Ethics*, Book VI, chap. 3, sec. 3.]

goes infinitely further than is commonly thought, though in ordinary usage in life we attribute to it only what we perceive most manifestly and what belongs to us most particularly, for it serves no purpose to go any further.

However, it would be good to choose terms proper to each conception [*sens*] in order to avoid equivocation. Thus, the expressions in our soul, whether we conceive them or not, can be called *ideas*, but those we conceive or form can be called *notions, concepts* [*conceptus*]. But however we take these expressions, it is always false to say that all our notions come from the external senses, for the notions I have of myself and of my thoughts, and consequently of being, substance, action, identity, and of many others, arise from an internal experience.

28. *God alone is the immediate object of our perceptions, which exist outside of us, and he alone is our light.* Now, in rigorous metaphysical truth, there is no external cause acting on us except God alone, and he alone communicates himself to us immediately in virtue of our continual dependence. From this it follows that there is no other external object that touches our soul and immediately excites our perception. Thus we have ideas of everything in our soul only by virtue of God's continual action on us, that is to say, because every effect expresses its cause, and thus the essence of our soul is a certain expression, imitation or image of the divine essence, thought, and will, and of all the ideas comprised in it. It can then be said that God is our immediate external object and that we see all things by him. For example, when we see the sun and the stars, it is God who has given them to us and who conserves the ideas of them in us, and it is God who determines us really to think of them by his ordinary concourse while our senses are disposed in a certain manner, according to the laws he has established. God is the sun and the light of souls, the light that lights every man that comes into this world,[18] and this is not an opinion new to our times. After Holy Scripture and the Church Fathers, who have always preferred Plato to Aristotle, I remember having previously noted that from the time of the Scholastics, several believed that God is the light of the soul and, in their way of speaking, the active intellect of the rational soul. The Averroists gave the sense of this a bad turn,[19] but others, among whom was, I believe, William of St. Amour, and several mystical theologians, have taken it in a manner worthy of God and capable of elevating the soul to the knowledge of its good.

29. *Yet we think immediately through our own ideas and not through those of God.* However, I am not of the opinion of certain able philosophers who seem to maintain that our very ideas are in God and not at all in us.[20] In my opinion, this arises from the fact that they have not yet considered sufficiently either what we have just explained about substances or the full extent and independence of our soul, which makes it contain everything that happens to us and makes it express God and, with him, all possible and actual beings, just as an effect expresses its cause. Also, it is inconceivable that I think through the ideas of others. The soul must actually be affected in a certain way when it thinks of something, and it must already have in itself not only the passive power of being able to be affected in this way (which is already wholly determined) but also an active power, a power by virtue of which there have always been in its nature marks of the future production of this thought and dispositions to produce it in its proper time. And all this already involves the idea included in this thought.

30. *How God inclines our soul without necessitating it; that we do not have the right to complain and that we must not ask why Judas sins but only why Judas the sinner is admitted to existence in preference to some other possible persons. On original imperfection before sin and on the degrees of grace.* There are a number of considerations with respect to the action of God on human will which are so difficult that it would be inordinately lengthy to pursue them here. Roughly speaking, however,

18. [John 1:9.]

19. [Averroists were Christian followers of Averroes (or Ibn Rushd—1126–98), the great Arabic commentator on Aristotle, who held that the active intellect in each man is part of a single active intellect. The doctrine of a single world-soul was condemned as heresy.]

20. [Malebranche, again, is Leibniz's primary target, as above in sec. 23.]

here is what can be said. In concurring with our actions, God ordinarily does no more than follow the laws he has established, that is, he continually conserves and produces our being in such a way that thoughts come to us spontaneously or freely in the order that the notion pertaining to our individual substance contains them, a notion in which they could be foreseen from all eternity. Moreover, in virtue of his decree that the will always tend toward the apparent good, expressing or imitating his will in certain particular respects (so that this apparent good always has some truth in it), God determines our will to choose what seems better, without, however, necessitating it. For, absolutely speaking, the will is in a state of indifference, as opposed to one of necessity, and it has the power to do otherwise or even to suspend its action completely; these two alternatives are possible and remain so.

Therefore the soul must guard itself against deceptive appearances [*les surprises des apparences*] through a firm will to reflect and neither to act nor to judge in certain circumstances except after having deliberated fully. But it is true, and it is even assured from all eternity, that a certain soul will not make use of this power in such a situation. But who is to blame? Can the soul complain about anything other than itself? All these complaints after the fact are unjust, if they would have been unjust before the fact. Now, could this soul, a little before sinning, complain about God in good faith, as if God determined it to sin? Since God's determinations in these matters cannot be foreseen, how does the soul know that it is determined to sin, unless it is actually sinning already? It is only a matter of not willing, and God could not put forth an easier and more just condition; thus judges do not seek the reasons which have disposed a man to have a bad will, but only stop to consider the extent to which this particular will is bad. But perhaps it is certain from all eternity that I shall sin? Answer this question for yourself: perhaps not; and without considering what you cannot know and what can give you no light, act according to your duty, which you do know.

But someone else will say, why is it that this man will assuredly commit this sin? The reply is easy: otherwise he would not be this man. For God sees from all time that there will be a certain Judas whose notion or idea (which God has) contains this free and future action. Therefore only this question remains, why does such a Judas, the traitor, who is merely possible in God's idea, actually exist? But no reply to this question is to be expected on earth, except that, in general, one must say that, since God found it good that he should exist, despite the sin that God foresaw, it must be that this sin is paid back with interest in the universe, that God will derive a greater good from it, and that it will be found that, in sum, the sequence of things in which the existence of that sinner is included is the most perfect among all the possible sequences. But we cannot always explain the admirable economy of this choice while we are travellers in this world; it is enough to know it without understanding it. And here is the occasion to recognize the *altitudinem divitarum*, the depth and abyss of divine wisdom, without seeking a detail that involves infinite considerations.[21]

Yet one sees clearly that God is not the cause of evil. For not only did original sin take possession of the soul after the innocence of men had been lost, but even before this, there was an original imperfection or limitation connatural to all creatures, which makes them liable to sin or capable of error. Thus, the supralapsarians[22] raise no more problems than the others do. And it is to this, in my view, that we must reduce the opinion of Saint Augustine and other authors, the opinion that the root of evil is in nothingness, that is to say, in the privation or limitation of creatures, which God graciously remedies by the degree of perfection it pleases him to give. This grace of God, whether ordinary or extraordinary, has its degrees and its measures; in itself, it is always efficacious in producing a certain proportionate effect, and, further, it is always sufficient, not only to secure us from sin, but even to produce salvation, assuming that man unites himself to it by what derives from him. But it is not always sufficient to overcome man's inclinations, for otherwise he would have nothing more to strive for; this is reserved solely for the absolutely efficacious grace which is always victorious, whether it is so by itself or by way of appropriate circumstances.

21. [The Latin translates: "depth of riches," a reference to Romans 11:33.]

22. [Calvinists who held that God's decrees of election and reprobation preceded the fall.]

31. *On the motives of election, on faith foreseen, on middle knowledge, on the absolute decree and that it all reduces to the reason why God has chosen for existence such a possible person whose notion includes just such a sequence of graces and free acts; this puts an end to all difficulties at once.* Finally, God's graces are wholly pure graces, upon which creatures have no claim. However, just as it is not sufficient to appeal to God's absolute or conditional foresight into the future actions of men in order to account for his choice in the dispensation of these graces, we also must not imagine absolute decrees that have no reasonable motive. As for God's foreknowledge of faith or good works, it is very true that he has elected only those whose faith and charity he foresaw, whom he foreknew he would endow with faith. But the same question returns, why will God give the grace of faith or of good works to some rather than to others? And as for this knowledge God has, which is the foresight not of faith and good works, but of their grounds [*matière*] and predisposition, that is, foresight of what a man would contribute to them on his side (for it is true that there are differences among men whenever there are differences in grace and that, in fact, although a man needs to be stimulated to the good and be converted, he must also act in that direction afterward), it seems to several people that one could say that God, seeing what a man would do without grace or extraordinary assistance, or at least seeing the sort of person he is, leaving grace aside, might resolve to give grace to those whose natural dispositions were better or, at least, less imperfect or less bad. But even if that were the case, one can say that these natural dispositions, insofar as they are good, are still the effect of grace, although ordinary grace, since God has favored some more than others. And since he knows that these natural advantages he gives will serve as motives for grace or extraordinary assistance, is it not true, according to this doctrine, that in the end everything is completely reduced to his mercy?

Since we do not know how much and in what way God takes account of natural dispositions in the dispensation of grace, I believe, then, that the most exact and surest thing to say, according to our principles, as I have already noted, is that among the possible beings there must be the person of Peter or John, whose notion or idea contains this entire sequence of ordinary and extraordinary graces and all the rest of these events with their circumstances, and that it pleased God to choose him for actual existence from among an infinity of equally possible persons. After this it seems that there is nothing more to ask and that all difficulties vanish.

For, with respect to this single great question, why it pleased God to choose him from among so many other possible persons, one would have to be very unreasonable not to be content with the general reasons we have given, reasons whose details lie beyond us. Thus, instead of having recourse to an absolute decree which is unreasonable, since it is without reason, or to reasons which do not solve the difficulty completely and are in need of further reasons, it would be best to say with Saint Paul, that God here followed certain great reasons of wisdom or appropriateness, unknown to mortals and based on the general order, whose aim is the greatest perfection of the universe. It is to this that the motives of the glory of God and the manifestation of his justice are reduced, as well as of his mercy and generally of his perfections and finally the immense depth of his riches, with which the soul of Saint Paul was enraptured.

32. *The utility of these principles in matters of piety and religion.* For the rest, it seems that the thoughts we have just explained, particularly the great principle of the perfection of the operations of God and the principle that the notion of a substance contains all its events with all their circumstances, far from harming, serve to confirm religion, to dispel enormous difficulties, to enflame souls with a divine love, and to elevate minds to the knowledge of incorporeal substances, much more than hypotheses we have seen until now. For one sees clearly that all other substances depend on God, in the same way as thoughts emanate from our substance, that God is all in all, and that he is intimately united with all creatures, in proportion to their perfection, that it is he alone who determines them from the outside by his influence, and, if to act is to determine immediately, it can be said in this sense, in the language of metaphysics, that God alone operates on me, and God alone can do good or evil to me; the other substances contribute only by reason of these determinations, because God, having regard for all, shares his blessings and requires them to accommodate themselves to one another. Hence God alone brings about the connection and communication among substances, and it is through

him that the phenomena of any substance meet and agree with those of others and consequently, that there is reality in our perceptions. But, in practice, one ascribes an action to particular reasons in the sense that I have explained above, because it is not necessary always to mention the universal cause in particular cases.

We also see that every substance has a perfect spontaneity (which becomes freedom in intelligent substances), that everything that happens to it is a consequence of its idea or of its being, and that nothing determines it, except God alone. And that is why a person of very exalted mind, revered for her saintliness, was in the habit of saying that the soul must often think as if there were nothing but God and itself in the world.[23]

Now, nothing gives us a stronger understanding of immortality than the independence and extent of the soul in question here, which shelters it absolutely from all external things, since the soul alone makes up its whole world and is sufficient to itself with God. And it is as impossible that it should perish without annihilation, as it is that the world (of which it is a perpetual living expression) should destroy itself; hence, it is impossible that the changes in this extended mass called our body should do anything to the soul or that the dissolution of this body should destroy what is indivisible.

33. *Explanation of the union of soul and body, a matter which has been considered as inexplicable or miraculous, and on the origin of confused perceptions.* We also see the unexpected illumination of this great mystery of the union of the soul and the body, that is, how it happens that the passions and actions of the one are accompanied by the actions and passions, or by the corresponding phenomena, of the other. For there is no way to conceive that the one has any influence on the other, and it is unreasonable simply to appeal to the extraordinary operation of the universal cause in an ordinary and particular thing. But here is the true reason: we have said that everything that happens to the soul and to each substance follows from its notion, and therefore the very idea or essence of the soul carries with it the fact that all its appearances or perceptions must arise spontaneously from its own nature and precisely in such a way that they correspond by themselves to what happens in the whole universe. But they correspond more particularly and more perfectly to what happens in the body assigned to it, because the soul expresses the state of the universe in some way and for some time, according to the relation other bodies have to its own body. This also allows us to know how our body belongs to us, without, however, being attached to our essence. And I believe that persons who can meditate will judge our principles favorably, because they will be able to see easily what the connection between the soul and the body consists in, a connection which seems inexplicable in any other way.

We also see that the perceptions of our senses, even when they are clear, must necessarily contain some confused feelings [*sentiment*], for our body receives the impression of all other bodies, since all the bodies of the universe are in sympathy, and, even though our senses are related to everything, it is impossible for our soul to attend to everything in particular; that is why our confused sensations are the result of a truly infinite variety of perceptions. This is almost like the confused murmur coming from the innumerable set of breaking waves heard by those who approach the seashore. Now, if from several perceptions (which do not come together to make one), there is none which stands out before the others and if they make impressions that are almost equally strong or equally capable of gaining the attention of the soul, the soul can only perceive them confusedly.

34. *On the difference between minds and other substances, souls or substantial forms, and that the immortality required includes memory.* Assuming that the bodies that make up an *unum per se*, as does man, are substances, that they have substantial forms, and that animals have souls, we must admit that these souls and these substantial forms cannot entirely perish, no more than atoms or the ultimate parts of matter can, on the view of other philosophers. For no substance perishes, although it can become completely different. They also express the whole universe, although more imperfectly than minds do. But the principal difference is that they do not know what they are nor what they do, and consequently, since they do not reflect on themselves, they cannot dis-

23. [Leibniz probably had St. Theresa in mind here.]

cover necessary and universal truths. It is also because they lack reflection about themselves that they have no moral qualities. As a result, though they may pass through a thousand transformations, like those we see when a caterpillar changes into a butterfly, yet from the moral or practical point of view, the result is as if they had perished; indeed, we may even say that they have perished physically, in the sense in which we say that bodies perish through their corruption. But the intelligent soul, knowing what it is—having the ability to utter the word "I," a word so full of meaning—does not merely remain and subsist metaphysically, which it does to a greater degree than the others, but also remains the same morally and constitutes the same person. For it is memory or the knowledge of this self that renders it capable of punishment or reward. Thus the immortality required in morality and religion does not consist merely in this perpetual subsistence common to all substances, for without the memory of what one has been, there would be nothing desirable about it. Suppose that some person all of a sudden becomes the king of China, but only on the condition that he forgets what he has been, as if he were born anew; practically, or as far as the effects could be perceived, wouldn't that be the same as if he were annihilated and a king of China created at the same instant in his place? That is something this individual would have no reason to desire.

35. *The excellence of minds and that God considers them preferable to other creatures. That minds express God rather than the world, but that the other substances express the world rather than God.* But so that we may judge by natural reasons that God will always preserve not only our substance, but also our person, that is, the memory and knowledge of what we are (though distinct knowledge is sometimes suspended during sleep and fainting spells), we must join morals to metaphysics, that is, we must not only consider God as the principle and cause of all substances and all beings, but also as the leader of all persons or intelligent substances and as the absolute monarch of the most perfect city or republic, which is what the universe composed of all minds together is, God himself being the most perfect of all minds and the greatest of all beings. For certainly minds are the most perfect beings and best express divinity. And since the whole nature, end, virtue, and function of substance is merely to express God and the universe, as has been sufficiently explained, there is no reason to doubt that the substances which express the universe with the knowledge of what they are doing and which are capable of knowing great truths about God and the universe, express it incomparably better than do those natures, which are either brutish and incapable of knowing truths or completely destitute of sensation and knowledge. And the difference between intelligent substances and substances that have no intelligence at all is just as great as the difference between a mirror and someone who sees.

Since God himself is the greatest and wisest of all minds, it is easy to judge that the beings with whom he can, so to speak, enter into conversation, and even into a society—by communicating to them his views and will in a particular manner and in such a way that they can know and love their benefactor—must be infinitely nearer to him than all other things, which can only pass for the instruments of minds. So we see that all wise persons value a man infinitely more than any other thing, no matter how precious it is, and it seems that the greatest satisfaction that a soul, content in other ways, can have is to see itself loved by others. With respect to God, though, there is the difference that his glory and our worship cannot add anything to his satisfaction, since knowledge of creatures is only a consequence of his supreme and perfect happiness—far from contributing to it or being its partial cause. However, what is good and reasonable in finite minds is found preeminently in him, and, just as we would praise a king who would prefer to preserve the life of a man rather than the most precious and rarest of his animals, we should not doubt that the most enlightened and most just of all monarchs is of the same opinion.

36. *God is the monarch of the most perfect republic, composed of all minds, and the happiness of this city of God is his principal purpose.* Indeed, minds are the most perfectible substances, and their perfections are peculiar in that they interfere with each other the least, or rather they aid one another the most, for only the most virtuous can be the most perfect friends. Whence it obviously follows that God, who always aims for the greatest perfection in general, will pay the greatest attention to minds and will give

them the greatest perfection that universal harmony can allow, not only in general, but to each of them in particular.

One can even say that God, insofar as he is a mind, is the originator of existences; otherwise, if he lacked the will to choose the best, there would be no reason for a possible thing to exist in preference to others. Thus the quality that God has of being a mind himself takes precedence over all the other considerations he can have toward creatures; only minds are made in his image and are, as it were, of his race or like children of his household, since they alone can serve him freely and act with knowledge in imitation of the divine nature; a single mind is worth a whole world, since it does not merely express the world but it also knows it and it governs itself after the fashion of God. In this way we may say that, although all substances express the whole universe, nevertheless the other substances express the world rather than God, while minds express God rather than the world. And this nature of minds, so noble that it brings them as near to divinity as it is possible for simple creatures, has the result that God draws infinitely more glory from them than from all other beings, or rather the other beings only furnish minds the matter for glorifying him.

That is why this moral quality God has, which makes him the lord or monarch of minds, relates to him, so to speak, personally and in a quite singular manner. It is because of this that he humanizes himself, that he is willing to allow anthropomorphism, and that he enters into society with us, as a prince with his subjects; and this consideration is so dear to him that the happy and flourishing state of his empire, which consists in the greatest possible happiness of its inhabitants, becomes the highest of his laws. For happiness is to people what perfection is to beings. And if the first principle of the existence of the physical world is the decree to give it the greatest perfection possible, the first intent of the moral world or the City of God, which is the noblest part of the universe, must be to diffuse in it the greatest possible happiness.

Therefore we must not doubt that God has ordered everything in such a way that minds not only may live always, which is certain, but also that they may always preserve their moral quality, so that the city does not lose a single person, just as the world does not lose any substance. And consequently they will always know what they are, otherwise they would not be susceptible to reward or punishment, something, however, essential to a republic, but above all essential to the most perfect republic, in which nothing can be neglected.

Finally, since God is at the same time the most just and most good-natured of monarchs and since he demands only a good will, as long as it is sincere and serious, his subjects cannot wish for a better condition, and, to make them perfectly happy, he wants only for them to love him.

37. *Jesus Christ has revealed to men the mystery and admirable laws of the kingdom of heaven and the greatness of the supreme happiness that God prepares for those who love him.* The ancient philosophers knew very little of these important truths; Jesus Christ alone has expressed them divinely well and in a manner so clear and familiar that the coarsest of minds have grasped them. Thus his gospel has entirely changed the course of human affairs; he has brought us to know the kingdom of heaven, or that perfect republic of minds which deserves the title of City of God, whose admirable laws he has disclosed to us. He alone has made us see how much God loves us and with what exactitude he has provided for everything that concerns us; that, caring for sparrows, he will not neglect the rational beings which are infinitely more dear to him; that all the hairs on our head are numbered; that heaven and earth will perish rather than the word of God and what pertains to the economy of our salvation; that God has more regard for the least of the intelligent souls than for the whole machinery of the world; that we must not fear those who can destroy bodies but cannot harm souls, because God alone can make souls happy or unhappy; and that the souls of the just, in his hands, are safe from all the upheavals of the universe, God alone being able to act upon them; that none of our actions are forgotten; that everything is taken account of, even idle words or a spoonful of water well used; finally, that everything must result in the greatest welfare of those who are good; that the just will be like suns; and that neither our senses nor our mind has ever tasted anything approaching the happiness that God prepares for those who love him.

Monadology

1. The monad, which we shall discuss here, is nothing but a simple substance that enters into composites—simple, that is, without parts.

2. And there must be simple substances, since there are composites; for the composite is nothing more than a collection, or *aggregate*, of simples.

3. But where there are no parts, neither extension, nor shape, nor divisibility is possible. These monads are the true atoms of nature and, in brief, the elements of things.

4. There is also no dissolution to fear, and there is no conceivable way in which a simple substance can perish naturally.

5. For the same reason, there is no conceivable way a simple substance can begin naturally, since it cannot be formed by composition.

6. Thus, one can say that monads can only begin or end all at once, that is, they can only begin by creation and end by annihilation, whereas composites begin or end through their parts.

7. There is also no way of explaining how a monad can be altered or changed internally by some other creature, since one cannot transpose anything in it, nor can one conceive of any internal motion that can be excited, directed, augmented, or diminished within it, as can be done in composites, where there can be change among the parts. The monads have no windows through which something can enter or leave. Accidents cannot be detached, nor can they go about outside of substances, as the sensible species of the Scholastics once did. Thus, neither substance nor accident can enter a monad from without.

8. However, monads must have some qualities, otherwise they would not even be beings. And if simple substances did not differ at all in their qualities, there would be no way of perceiving any change in things, since what there is in a composite can only come from its simple ingredients; and if the monads had no qualities, they would be indiscernible from one another, since they also do not differ in quantity. As a result, assuming a plenum, in motion, each place would always receive only the equivalent of what it already had, and one state of things would be indistinguishable from another.

9. It is also necessary that each monad be different from each other. For there are never two beings in nature that are perfectly alike, two beings in which it is not possible to discover an internal difference, that is, one founded on an intrinsic denomination.

10. I also take for granted that every created being, and consequently the created monad as well, is subject to change, and even that this change is continual in each thing.

11. It follows from what we have just said that the monad's natural changes come from an *internal principle*, since no external cause can influence it internally.

12. But, besides the principle of change, there must be *diversity* [*un détail*] *in that which changes*, which produces, so to speak, the specification and variety of simple substances.

13. This diversity must involve a multitude in the unity or in the simple. For, since all natural change is produced by degrees, something changes and something remains. As a result, there must be a plurality of properties [*affections*] and relations in the simple substance, although it has no parts.

14. The passing state which involves and represents a multitude in the unity or in the simple substance is nothing other than what one calls *perception*, which should be distinguished from apperception, or consciousness, as will be evident in what follows. This is where the Cartesians have failed badly, since they took no account of the perceptions that we do not apperceive. This is also what made them believe that minds alone are monads and that there are no animal souls or other entelechies. With the common people, they have confused a long stupor with death, properly speaking, which made them fall again into the Scholastic prejudice of completely separated souls, and

Reprinted from Leibniz, *Philosophical Essays*, edited and translated by Roger Ariew and Daniel Garber (Indianapolis: Hackett Publishing Company, 1989), by permission of the publisher.

they have even confirmed unsound minds in the belief in the mortality of souls.

15. The action of the internal principle which brings about the change or passage from one perception to another can be called *appetition*; it is true that the appetite cannot always completely reach the whole perception toward which it tends, but it always obtains something of it, and reaches new perceptions.

16. We ourselves experience a multitude in a simple substance when we find that the least thought we ourselves apperceive involves variety in its object. Thus, all those who recognize that the soul is a simple substance should recognize this multitude in the monad; and Mr. Bayle should not find any difficulty in this as he has done in his *Dictionary* article, "Rorarius."[1]

17. Moreover, we must confess that the *perception*, and what depends on it, is *inexplicable in terms of mechanical reasons*, that is, through shapes and motions. If we imagine that there is a machine whose structure makes it think, sense, and have perceptions, we could conceive it enlarged, keeping the same proportions, so that we could enter into it, as one enters into a mill. Assuming that, when inspecting its interior, we will only find parts that push one another, and we will never find anything to explain a perception. And so, we should seek perception in the simple substance and not in the composite or in the machine. Furthermore, this is all one can find in the simple substance—that is, perception and their changes. It is also in this alone that all the *internal actions* of simple substances can consist.

18. One can call all simple substances or created monads entelechies, for they have in themselves a certain perfection (*echousi to enteles*); they have a sufficiency (*autarkeia*) that makes them the sources of their internal actions, and, so to speak, incorporeal automata.

19. If we wish to call *soul* anything that has *perceptions* and *appetites* in the general sense I have just explained, then all simple substances or created monads can be called souls. But, since sensation is something more than a simple perception, I think that the general name of monad and entelechy is sufficient for simple substances which only have perceptions, and that we should only call those substances *souls* where perception is more distinct and accompanied by memory.

20. For we experience within ourselves a state in which we remember nothing and have no distinct perception; this is similar to when we faint or when we are overwhelmed by a deep, dreamless sleep. In this state the soul does not differ sensibly from a simple monad; but since this state does not last, and since the soul emerges from it, our soul is something more.

21. And it does not at all follow that in such a state the simple substance is without any perception. This is not possible for the previous reasons; for it cannot perish, and it also cannot subsist without some property [*affection*], which is nothing other than its perception. But when there is a great multitude of small perceptions in which nothing is distinct, we are stupefied. This is similar to when we continually spin in the same direction several times in succession, from which arises a dizziness that can make us faint and does not allow us to distinguish anything. Death can impart this state to animals for a time.

22. And since every present state of a simple substance is a natural consequence of its preceding state, the present is pregnant with the future.

23. Therefore, since on being awakened from a stupor we apperceive our perceptions, it must be the case that we had some perceptions immediately before, even though we did not apperceive them; for a perception can only come naturally from another perception, as a motion can only come naturally from a motion.

24. From this we see that if, in our perceptions, we had nothing distinct or, so to speak, in relief and stronger in flavor, we would always be in a stupor. And this is the state of bare monads.

25. We also see that nature has given heightened perceptions to animals from the care she has taken to furnish them organs that collect several rays of light or several waves of air, in order to make them

1. [Leibniz's *Theodicy* was, to a large extent, an attempt to answer the skeptical arguments, from Bayle's *Historical and Critical Dictionary*, regarding the impossibility of reconciling faith with reason. "Rorarius," an article of the *Dictionary*, was Bayle's occasion for a discussion of the problem of the souls of animals: Jerome Rorarius (1485–1566) wrote a treatise maintaining that men are less rational than the lower animals. In "Rorarius" Bayle criticizes Leibniz's views.—R.A. and D.G.]

more effectual by bringing them together. There is something similar to this in odor, taste, and touch, and perhaps in many other senses which are unknown to us. I will soon explain how what occurs in the soul represents what occurs in the organs.

26. Memory provides a kind of sequence in souls, which imitates reason, but which must be distinguished from it. We observe that when animals have the perception of something which strikes them, and when they previously had a similar perception of that thing, then, through a representation in their memory, they expect that which was attached to the thing in the preceding perception, and are led to have sensations similar to those they had before. For example, if we show dogs a stick, they remember the pain that it caused them and they flee.

27. And the strong imagination that strikes and moves them comes from the magnitude or the multitude of the preceding perceptions. For often a strong impression produces, all at once, the effect produced by a long *habit* or by many lesser, reiterated perceptions.

28. Men act like beasts insofar as the sequence of their perceptions results from the principle of memory alone; they resemble the empirical physicians who practice without theory. We are all mere Empirics in three fourths of our actions. For example, when we expect that the day will dawn tomorrow, we act like an Empiric,[2] because until now it has always been thus. Only the astronomer judges this by reason.

29. But the knowledge of eternal and necessary truths is what distinguishes us from simple animals and furnishes us with *reason* and the sciences, by raising us to a knowledge of ourselves and of God. And that is what we call the rational soul, or *mind*, in ourselves.

30. It is also through the knowledge of necessary truths and through their abstractions that we rise to *reflective acts*, which enable us to think of that which is called "I" and enable us to consider that this or that is in us. And thus, in thinking of ourselves, we think of being, or substance, of the simple and of the composite, of the immaterial and of God himself, by conceiving that that which is limited in us is limitless in him. And these reflective acts furnish the principal objects of our reasonings.

31. Our reasonings are based on *two great principles, that of contradiction*, in virtue of which we judge that which involves a contradiction to be false, and that which is opposed or contradictory to the false to be true.

32. And *that of sufficient reason*, by virtue of which we consider that we can find no true or existent fact, no true assertion, without there being a sufficient reason why it is thus and not otherwise, although most of the time these reasons cannot be known to us.

33. There are also two kinds of *truths*, those of *reasoning* and those of *fact*. The truths of reasoning are necessary and their opposite is impossible; the truths of fact are contingent, and their opposite is possible. When a truth is necessary, its reason can be found by analysis, resolving it into simpler ideas and simpler truths until we reach the primitives.

34. This is how the speculative *theorems* and practical *canons* of mathematicians are reduced by analysis to *definitions, axioms,* and *postulates*.

35. And there are, finally, *simple ideas,* whose definition cannot be given. There are also axioms and postulates, in brief, *primitive principles,* which cannot be proved and which need no proof. And these are *identical propositions,* whose opposite contains an explicit contradiction.

36. But there must also be a *sufficient reason* in *contingent truths*, or *truths of fact*, that is, in the series of things distributed throughout the universe of creatures, where the resolution into particular reasons could proceed into unlimited detail because of the immense variety of things in nature and because of the division of bodies to infinity. There is an infinity of past and present shapes and motions that enter into the efficient cause of my present writing, and there is an infinity of small inclinations and dispositions of my soul, present and past, that enter into its final cause.

37. And since all this *detail* involves nothing but other prior or more detailed contingents, each of which needs a similar analysis in order to give its reason, we do not make progress in this way. It must be the case that the sufficient or ultimate reason is outside the sequence or *series* of this multiplicity of contingencies, however infinite it may be.

2. [The Empirics were a sect of physicians before Galen (c. A.D. 150). In later times, the epithet "Empiric" was given to physicians who despised theoretical study and trusted tradition and their own experience.]

38. And that is why the ultimate reason of things must be in a necessary substance in which the diversity of changes is only eminent, as in its source. This is what we call *God.*

39. Since this substance is a sufficient reason for all this diversity, which is utterly interconnected, *there is only one God, and this God is sufficient.*

40. We can also judge that this supreme substance which is unique, universal, and necessary must be incapable of limits and must contain as much reality as is possible, insofar as there is nothing outside it which is independent of it, and insofar as it is a simple consequence of its possible existence.

41. From this it follows that God is absolutely perfect—*perfection* being nothing but the magnitude of positive reality considered as such, setting aside the limits or bounds in the things which have it. And here, where there are no limits, that is, in God, perfection is absolutely infinite.

42. It also follows that creatures derive their perfections from God's influence, but that they derive their imperfections from their own nature, which is incapable of being without limits. For it is in this that they are distinguished from God.

43. It is also true that God is not only the source of existences, but also that of essences insofar as they are real, that is, or the source of that which is real in possibility. This is because God's understanding is the realm of eternal truths or that of the ideas on which they depend; without him there would be nothing real in possibles, and not only would nothing exist, but also nothing would be possible.

44. For if there is reality in essences or possibles, or indeed, in eternal truths, this reality must be grounded in something existent and actual, and consequently, it must be grounded in the existence of the necessary being, in whom essence involves existence, that is, in whom possible being is sufficient for actual being.

45. Thus God alone (or the necessary being) has this privilege, that he must exist if he is possible. And since nothing can prevent the possibility of what is without limits, without negation, and consequently without contradiction, this by itself is sufficient for us to know the existence of God *a priori.* We have also proved this by the reality of the eternal truths. But we have also just proved it *a posteriori* since there are contingent beings, which can only have their final or sufficient reason in the necessary being, a being that has the reason of its existence in itself.

46. However, we should not imagine, as some do, that since the eternal truths depend on God, they are arbitrary and depend on his will, as Descartes appears to have held, and after him Mr. Poiret.[3] This is true only of contingent truths, whose principle is *fitness* [*convenance*] or the choice of the *best.* But necessary truths depend solely on his understanding, and are its internal object.

47. Thus God alone is the primitive unity or the first [*originaire*] simple substance; all created or derivative monads are products, and are generated, so to speak, by continual fulgurations of the divinity from moment to moment, limited by the receptivity of the creature, to which it is essential to be limited.

48. God has *power,* which is the source of everything, *knowledge,* which contains the diversity of ideas, and finally *will,* which brings about changes or products in accordance with the principle of the best. And these correspond to what, in created monads, is the subject or the basis, the perceptive faculty and the appetitive faculty. But in God these attributes are absolutely infinite or perfect, while in the created monads or in entelechies (or *perfectihabies,* as Hermolaus Barbarus translated that word)[4] they are only imitations of it, in proportion to the perfection that they have.

49. The creature is said to *act* externally insofar as it is perfect, and *to be acted upon* [*patir*] by another, insofar as it is imperfect. Thus we attribute *action* to a monad insofar as it has distinct perceptions, and *passion,* insofar as it has confused perceptions.

50. And one creature is more perfect than another insofar as one finds in it that which provides an *a priori* reason for what happens in the other; and this is why we say that it acts on the other.

3. [Pierre Poiret (1646–1719) was initially one of Descartes' followers; he published a book of reflections on God, soul, and evil, *Cogitationum rationalium de Deo, anima, et malo libri quattuor* (1677), which was attacked by Bayle.]

4. [Hermolaus Barbarus (1454–93) was an Italian scholar who attempted, through retranslations of Aristotle, to recover Aristotle's original doctrine from under the layers of Scholastic interpretations. His works include popular compendia of ethics and natural philosophy, drawn from the writings of Aristotle.]

51. But in simple substances the influence of one monad over another can only be ideal, and can only produce its effect through God's intervention, when in the ideas of God a monad reasonably asks that God take it into account in regulating the others from the beginning of things. For, since a created monad cannot have an internal physical influence upon another, this is the only way in which one can depend on another.

52. It is in this way that actions and passions among creatures are mutual. For God, comparing two simple substances, finds in each reasons that require him to adjust the other to it; and consequently, what is active in some respects is passive from another point of view: *active* insofar as what is known distinctly in one serves to explain what happens in another; and *passive* insofar as the reason for what happens in one is found in what is known distinctly in another.

53. Now, since there is an infinity of possible universes in God's ideas, and since only one of them can exist, there must be a sufficient reason for God's choice, a reason which determines him towards one thing rather than another.

54. And this reason can only be found in *fitness*, or in the degree of perfection that these worlds contain, each possible world having the right to claim existence in proportion to the perfection it contains.

55. And this is the cause of the existence of the best, which wisdom makes known to God, which his goodness makes him choose, and which his power makes him produce.

56. This interconnection or accommodation of all created things to each other, and each to all the others, brings it about that each simple substance has relations that express all the others, and consequently, that each simple substance is a perpetual, living mirror of the universe.

57. Just as the same city viewed from different directions appears entirely different and, as it were, multiplied perspectively, in just the same way it happens that, because of the infinite multitude of simple substances, there are, as it were, just as many different universes, which are, nevertheless, only perspectives on a single one, corresponding to the different points of view of each monad.

58. And this is the way of obtaining as much variety as possible, but with the greatest order possible, that is, it is the way of obtaining as much perfection as possible.

59. Moreover, this is the only hypothesis (which I dare say is demonstrated) that properly enhances God's greatness. Mr. Bayle recognized this when, in his *Dictionary* (article "Rorarius"), he set out objections to it; indeed, he was tempted to believe that I ascribed too much to God, more than is possible. But he was unable to present any reason why this universal harmony, which results in every substance expressing exactly all the others through the relations it has to them, is impossible.

60. Furthermore, in what I have just discussed, we can see the *a priori* reasons why things could not be otherwise. Because God, in regulating the whole, had regard for each part, and particularly for each monad, and since the nature of the monad is representative, nothing can limit it to represent only a part of things. However, it is true that this representation is only confused as to the detail of the whole universe, and can only be distinct for a small portion of things, that is, either for those that are closest, or for those that are greatest with respect to each monad, otherwise each monad would be a divinity. Monads are limited, not as to their objects, but with respect to the modifications of their knowledge of them. Monads all go confusedly to infinity, to the whole; but they are limited and differentiated by the degrees of their distinct perceptions.

61. In this respect, composites are analogous to simples. For everything is a plenum, which makes all matter interconnected. In a plenum, every motion has some effect on distant bodies, in proportion to their distance. For each body is affected, not only by those in contact with it, and in some way feels the effects of everything that happens to them, but also, through them, it feels the effects of those in contact with the bodies with which it is itself immediately in contact. From this it follows that this communication extends to any distance whatsoever. As a result, every body is affected by everything that happens in the universe, to such an extent that he who sees all can read in each thing what happens everywhere, and even what has happened or what will happen, by observing in the present what is remote in time as well as in space. "All things conspire [*sympnoia panta*]," said Hippocrates. But a soul can read in itself only what is distinctly represented there; it cannot unfold all its folds at once, because they go to infinity.

62. Thus, although each created monad represents the whole universe, it more distinctly represents the body which is particularly affected by it, and whose entelechy it constitutes. And just as this body expresses the whole universe through the interconnection of all matter in the plenum, the soul also represents the whole universe by representing this body, which belongs to it in a particular way.

63. The body belonging to a monad (which is the entelechy or soul of that body) together with an entelechy constitutes what may be called a *living being*, and together with a soul constitutes what is called an *animal*. Now, the body of a living being or an animal is always organized; for, since every monad is a mirror of the universe in its way, and since the universe is regulated in a perfect order, there must also be an order in the representing being, that is, in the perceptions of the soul, and consequently, in the body in accordance with which the universe is represented therein.

64. Thus each organized body of a living being is a kind of divine machine or natural automaton, which infinitely surpasses all artificial automata. For a machine constructed by man's art is not a machine in each of its parts. For example, the tooth of a brass wheel has parts or fragments which, for us, are no longer artificial things, and no longer have any marks to indicate the machine for whose use the wheel was intended. But natural machines, that is, living bodies, are still machines in their least parts, to infinity. That is the difference between nature and art, that is, between divine art and our art.

65. And the author of nature has been able to practice this divine and infinitely marvelous art, because each portion of matter is not only divisible to infinity, as the ancients have recognized, but is also actually subdivided without end, each part divided into parts having some motion of their own; otherwise, it would be impossible for each portion of matter to express the whole universe.

66. From this we see that there is a world of creatures, of living beings, of animals, of entelechies, of souls in the least part of matter.

67. Each portion of matter can be conceived as a garden full of plants, and as a pond full of fish. But each branch of a plant, each limb of an animal, each drop of its humors, is still another such garden or pond.

68. And although the earth and air lying between the garden plants, or the water lying between the fish of the pond, are neither plant nor fish, they contain yet more of them, though of a subtleness imperceptible to us, most often.

69. Thus there is nothing fallow, sterile, or dead in the universe, no chaos and no confusion except in appearance, almost as it looks in a pond at a distance, where we might see the confused and, so to speak, teeming motion of the fish in the pond, without discerning the fish themselves.

70. Thus we see that each living body has a dominant entelechy, which in the animal is the soul; but the limbs of this living body are full of other living beings, plants, animals, each of which also has its entelechy, or its dominant soul.

71. But we must not imagine, as some who have misunderstood my thought do, that each soul has a mass or portion of matter of its own, always proper to or allotted by it, and that it consequently possesses other lower living beings, forever destined to serve it. For all bodies are in a perpetual flux, like rivers, and parts enter into them and depart from them continually.

72. Thus the soul changes body only little by little and by degrees, so that it is never stripped at once of all its organs. There is often metamorphosis in animals, but there is never metempsychosis nor transmigration of souls; there are also no completely *separated souls*, nor spirits [*Génies*] without bodies. God alone is completely detached from bodies.

73. That is why there is never total generation nor, strictly speaking, perfect death, death consisting in the separation of the soul. And what we call *generations* are developments and growths, as what we call deaths are enfoldings and diminutions.

74. Philosophers have been greatly perplexed about the origin of forms, entelechies, or souls. But today, when exact inquiries on plants, insects, and animals have shown us that organic bodies in nature are never produced from chaos or putrefaction, but always through seeds in which there is, no doubt, some *preformation*, it has been judged that, not only the organic body was already there before conception, but there was also a soul in this body; in brief, the animal itself was there, and through conception this animal was merely prepared for a great transformation, in order to become an animal of another kind.

Something similar is seen outside generation, as when worms become flies, and caterpillars become butterflies.

75. Those *animals*, some of which are raised by conception to the level of the larger animals, can be called *spermatic*. But those of them that remain among those of their kind, that is, the majority, are born, multiply, and are destroyed, just like the larger animals. There are but a small number of Elect that pass onto a larger stage [*théatre*].

76. But this was only half the truth. I have, therefore, held that if the animal never begins naturally, it does not end naturally, either; and not only will there be no generation, but also no complete destruction, nor any death, strictly speaking. These *a posteriori* reasonings, derived from experience, agree perfectly with my principles deduced *a priori*, as above.

77. Thus one can state that not only is the soul (mirror of an indestructible universe) indestructible, but so is the animal itself, even though its mechanism often perishes in part, and casts off or puts on its organic coverings.

78. These principles have given me a way of naturally explaining the union, or rather the conformity of the soul and the organic body. The soul follows its own laws and the body also follows its own; and they agree in virtue of the harmony pre-established between all substances, since they are all representations of a single universe.

79. Souls act according to the laws of final causes, through appetitions, ends, and means. Bodies act according to the laws of efficient causes or of motions. And these two kingdoms, that of efficient causes and that of final causes, are in harmony with each other.

80. Descartes recognized that souls cannot impart a force to bodies because there is always the same quantity of force in matter. However, he thought that the soul could change the direction of bodies. But that is because the law of nature, which also affirms the conservation of the same total direction in matter, was not known at that time. If he had known it, he would have hit upon my system of pre-established harmony.

81. According to this system, bodies act as if there were no souls (though this is impossible); and souls act as if there were no bodies; and both act as if each influenced the other.

82. As for *minds* or rational souls, I find that, at bottom, what we just said holds for all living beings and animals, namely that animals and souls begin only with the world and do not end any more than the world does. However, rational animals have this peculiarity, that their little spermatic animals, as long as they only remain in this state, have only ordinary or sensitive souls. But that as soon as the Elect among them, so to speak, attain human nature by actual conception, their sensitive souls are elevated to the rank of reason and to the prerogative of minds.

83. Among other differences which exist between ordinary souls and minds, some of which I have already noted, there are also the following: that souls, in general, are living mirrors or images of the universe of creatures, but that minds are also images of the divinity itself, or of the author of nature, capable of knowing the system of the universe, and imitating something of it through their schematic representations [*échantillons architectoniques*] of it, each mind being like a little divinity in its own realm.

84. That is what makes minds capable of entering into a kind of society with God, and allows him to be, in relation to them, not only what an inventor is to his machine (as God is in relation to the other creatures) but also what a prince is to his subjects, and even what a father is to his children.

85. From this it is easy to conclude that the collection of all minds must make up the city of God, that is, the most perfect possible state under the most perfect of monarchs.

86. This city of God, this truly universal monarchy, is a moral world within the natural world, and the highest and most divine of God's works. The glory of God truly consists in this city, for he would have none if his greatness and goodness were not known and admired by minds. It is also in relation to this divine city that God has goodness, properly speaking, whereas his wisdom and power are evident everywhere.

87. Since earlier we established a perfect harmony between two natural kingdoms, the one of efficient causes, the other the final causes, we ought to note here yet another harmony between the physical kingdom of nature and the moral kingdom of grace, that is, between God considered as the architect of the mechanism of the universe, and God considered as the monarch of the divine city of minds.

88. This harmony leads things to grace through

the very path of nature. For example, this globe must be destroyed and restored by natural means at such times as the governing of minds requires it, for the punishment of some and the reward of others.

89. It can also be said that God the architect pleases in every respect God the legislator, and, as a result, sins must carry their penalty with them by the order of nature, and even in virtue of the mechanical structure of things. Similarly, noble actions will receive their rewards through mechanical means with regard to bodies, even though this cannot, and must not, always happen immediately.

90. Finally, under this perfect government, there will be no good action that is unrewarded, no bad action that goes unpublished, and everything must result in the well-being of the good, that is, of those who are not dissatisfied in this great state, those who trust in providence, after having done their duty, and who love and imitate the author of all good, as they should, finding pleasure in the consideration of his perfections according to the nature of genuinely *pure love*, which takes pleasure in the happiness of the beloved. This is what causes wise and virtuous persons to work for all that appears to be in conformity with the presumptive or antecedent divine will, and nevertheless, to content themselves with what God brings about by his secret, consequent, or decisive will, since they recognize that if we could understand the order of the universe well enough, we would find that it surpasses all the wishes of the wisest, and that it is impossible to make it better than it is.[5] This is true not only for the whole in general, but also for ourselves in particular, if we are attached, as we should be, to the author of the whole, not only as the architect and efficient cause of our being, but also as to our master and final cause; he ought to be the whole aim of our will, and he alone can make us happy.

5. [The distinction between God's antecedent and consequent will can be found in Thomas Aquinas, *Summa Theologiae* I, q. 23, art. 2, ad 1.]

John Locke

John Locke was born in Wrington, England, a town near Bristol, in 1632. He was raised in a Puritan household and there received an elementary education, as well as instruction in theology and politics. He entered Westminster School in 1647 and then was elected to a scholarship at Christ Church, Oxford. Locke was to make Oxford his home for about thirty years. For his bachelor's and master's degrees he studied metaphysics, logic, rhetoric, and classical languages. The philosophy taught at Oxford at the time was Aristotelian, and his lack of enthusiasm for that system was to be reflected in his mature views. During this period he developed an interest in medicine, which he pursued with an eye toward understanding the methodology of experimental science. Consideration of this methodology, as well as his friendships with the chemist Robert Boyle and the physicist Isaac Newton, was to influence his philosophical views profoundly. From 1675 to 1679, he went to France due to his poor health, where he devoted his time to his studies. For many years Locke served as physician and later also as secretary and advisor to Lord Ashley, later Earl of Shaftesbury. In 1683, because of his connections with Shaftesbury's anti-Stuart politics, he felt compelled to flee to the Netherlands. Here he was able to finish his two greatest works, *Two Treatises of Government* (1690) and *An Essay Concerning Human Understanding* (1690). Another work he completed during this time is *A Letter Concerning Toleration* (1689). Locke returned to England in 1689 with William of Orange, who, together with his wife Mary, assumed the British throne in the Glorious Revolution. He then retired to Oates in Essex, the home of his friend Lady Masham and her husband, where he spent the remainder of his life. Works published in this final period include *Some Thoughts Concerning Education* (1693) and *The Reasonableness of Christianity* (1695). Locke died in 1704.

In *An Essay Concerning Human Understanding* Locke develops an empiricist account of science and of knowledge. In his view, all of our ideas and all of our knowledge have their origin in sensory experience. Locke contrasts this position with the rationalist claim that some of our ideas and consequently some of our knowledge are *innate,* that is, part of the structure of the mind from birth. By contrast, Locke argues that all human ideas and knowledge derive either from sensation of the external world or from reflection, a kind of sensation of the elements of one's mind: "All those sublime thoughts, which tower above the clouds, and reach as high as heaven itself, take their rise and footing here: In all that great extent wherein the mind wanders, in those remote speculations, it may seem to be elevated with, it stirs not one jot beyond those ideas, which sense or reflection have offered for its contemplation" (*Essay* 2.1.24).

Locke associates his empiricist view with a degree of pessimism about the extent of our ability to acquire knowledge. Human beings have only a limited range of sensory capacities, and our understanding is limited in its operations to the ideas it can acquire by means of these capacities. And further, our understanding is limited in its power, so that, for example, it cannot apprehend the relations among all of its ideas at once.

In the *Essay,* Locke also develops views about the central issues that faced the emerging modern scientific conception of the physical world. He criticizes Descartes' claim that the essence of matter consists solely in extension—spatial three-dimensionality—on the grounds that this claim leads to unacceptable results, such as the indistinguishability of matter and space and the inconceivability of a vacuum. In Locke's view, the essence of matter does not consist simply in extension, but also in solidity or impenetrability—the physical force that hinders the approach of two bodies when they are moving toward each other. His view is akin to the *dynamical* views of matter of Leibniz and Kant, according to which its essence consists primarily in force.

Siding with Galileo and Descartes, Locke also argues that the real characteristics of matter are the primary qualities, such as extension and motion, and that by contrast with the Aristotelian view, matter has no qualities that resemble secondary-quality ideas, such as the ideas of color, shape, sound, taste, odor, and temperature. Locke presents a much-discussed *perceptual relativity* argument for claims of this sort: If one hand is initially warm, and the other cold, and both are placed in the same bowl of water, it will feel cooler to one hand than the other. Since the water couldn't have a quality that resembles the temperature sensations of each of the hands, one should conclude that the water really has no such quality at all. Nevertheless Locke does want to maintain the commonsensical view that physical objects really have secondary qualities, and accordingly he characterizes a secondary quality as a power that an object has in virtue of its primary qualities to produce a secondary-quality idea in a perceiver. Redness, therefore, is not a quality in a physical object that resembles one's sensation of red, but rather a power that an object has in virtue of its primary qualities—perhaps in virtue of its surface texture—to produce sensations of red in perceivers.

A further feature of the *Essay* is Locke's attack on Aristotelian science, which he thought to be on the wrong track, since its primary concerns seemed to him to involve characterizing natural kinds by merely superficial definitions of their essences. According to his own account, inspired by the revival of the ancient Greek atomism, natural kinds have "corpuscular" real essences, consisting of arrangements of unobservable particles, from which their observable primary qualities result. Yet Locke does not think that we can gain any genuine knowledge of real essences of material substances. He also denies that we can come to know the nature of the connections between the real essences of material substances and the secondary-quality ideas they produce in us. The only hypothesis we can grasp on this issue, he claims, is that this connection is established by God. Locke does, however, argue that we can acquire knowledge of real essences in geometry and in morality.

Locke believes in dualism of body and mind—that the body is material while the mind is immaterial—but he does not think that this view can be firmly established, since the hypothesis that God annexes thought to a purely material system cannot be ruled out. What makes us the same persons over time, he argues, is continuity of consciousness or memory. Locke also claims that the existence of God can be established with "mathematical certainty." His religion is in a sense rationalist, since he maintains that beliefs based solely on revelation are inferior to beliefs supported by reasoned argument. In this respect, Locke's religion is a forerunner of the deism that was to become so influential in the eighteenth century.

• • •

Important scholarly books on Locke include Peter Alexander, *Ideas, Qualities, and Corpuscles: Locke and Boyle on the External World* (Cambridge: Cambridge University Press, 1985); Michael R. Ayers, *Locke* (London: Routledge and Kegan Paul, 1991); Jonathan Bennett, *Locke, Berkeley, Hume: Central Themes* (Oxford: Oxford University Press, 1971); Nicholas Jolley, *Leibniz and Locke* (Oxford: Oxford University Press, 1984); J. L. Mackie, *Problems from Locke* (Oxford: Oxford University Press, 1971); and R. S. Woolhouse, *Locke* (Brighton: Harvester Press, 1983). Good collections of essays are C. B. Martin and D. M. Armstrong, eds., *Locke and Berkeley: A Collection of Critical Essays* (Garden City, N.J.: Doubleday, 1968) and Margaret Atherton, ed., *The Empiricists: Locke, Berkeley, Hume* (Lanham, Md.: Rowman & Littlefield, 1998).

Derk Pereboom

An Essay Concerning Human Understanding

INTRODUCTION

1. *An Inquiry into the Understanding pleasant and useful.* Since it is the *understanding* that sets man above the rest of sensible beings, and gives him all the advantage and dominion which he has over them; it is certainly a subject, even for its nobleness, worth our labour to inquire into. The understanding, like the eye, whilst it makes us see and perceive all other things, takes no notice of itself; and it requires art and pains to set it at a distance and make it its own object. But whatever be the difficulties that lie in the way of this inquiry; whatever it be that keeps us so much in the dark to ourselves; sure I am that all the light we can let in upon our minds, all the acquaintance we can make with our own understandings, will not only be very pleasant, but bring us great advantage, in directing our thoughts in the search of other things.

2. *Design.* This, therefore, being my purpose—to inquire into the original, certainty, and extent of *human knowledge*, together with the grounds and degrees of *belief, opinion,* and *assent*;—I shall not at present meddle with the physical consideration of the mind; or trouble myself to examine wherein its essence consists; or by what motions of our spirits or alterations of our bodies we come to have any *sensation* by our organs, or any *ideas* in our understandings; and whether those ideas do in their formation, any or all of them, depend on matter or not. These are speculations which, however curious and entertaining, I shall decline, as lying out of my way in the design I am now upon. It shall suffice to my present purpose, to consider the discerning faculties of a man, as they are employed about the objects which they have to do with. And I shall imagine I have not wholly misemployed myself in the thoughts I shall have on this occasion, if, in this historical, plain method, I can give any account of the ways whereby our understandings come to attain those notions of things we have; and can set down any measures of the certainty of our knowledge; or the grounds of those persuasions which are to be found amongst men, so various, different, and wholly contradictory; and yet asserted somewhere or other with such assurance and confidence, that he that shall take a view of the opinions of mankind, observe their opposition, and at the same time consider the fondness and devotion wherewith they are embraced, the resolution and eagerness wherewith they are maintained, may perhaps have reason to suspect, that either there is no such thing as truth at all, or that mankind hath no sufficient means to attain a certain knowledge of it.

3. *Method.* It is therefore worth while to search out the bounds between opinion and knowledge; and examine by what measures, in things whereof we have no certain knowledge, we ought to regulate our assent and moderate our persuasion. In order whereunto I shall pursue this following method:—

First, I shall inquire into the original of those *ideas*, notions, or whatever else you please to call them, which a man observes, and is conscious to himself he has in his mind; and the ways whereby the understanding comes to be furnished with them.

Secondly, I shall endeavour to show what *knowledge* the understanding hath by those ideas; and the certainty, evidence, and extent of it.

Thirdly, I shall make some inquiry into the nature and grounds of *faith* or *opinion*: whereby I mean that assent which we give to any proposition as true, of whose truth yet we have no certain knowledge. And here we shall have occasion to examine the reasons and degrees of *assent*.

8. *What Idea stands for.* Before I proceed on to what I have thought on this subject, I must here in the entrance beg pardon of my reader for the frequent use of the word *idea*, which he will find in the following treatise. It being that term which, I think, serves best to stand for whatsoever is the *object* of the understanding when a man thinks, I have used it to express whatever is meant by *phantasm, notion, species,* or

whatever it is which the mind can be employed about in thinking; and I could not avoid frequently using it.

I presume it will be easily granted me, that there are such *ideas* in men's minds: every one is conscious of them in himself; and men's words and actions will satisfy him that they are in others.

BOOK I

NEITHER PRINCIPLES NOR IDEAS ARE INNATE

Chapter I

NO INNATE SPECULATIVE PRINCIPLES

1. *The way shown how we come by any knowledge, sufficient to prove it not innate.* It is an established opinion amongst some men, that there are in the understanding certain *innate principles*; some primary notions, κοιναὶ ἔννοιαι, characters, as it were, stamped upon the mind of man; which the soul receives in its very first being, and brings into the world with it. It would be sufficient to convince unprejudiced readers of the falseness of this supposition, if I should only show (as I hope I shall in the following parts of this Discourse) how men, barely by the use of their natural faculties, may attain to all the knowledge they have, without the help of any innate impressions; and may arrive at certainty, without any such original notions or principles. For I imagine any one will easily grant that it would be impertinent to suppose the ideas of colours innate in a creature to whom God hath given sight, and a power to receive them by the eyes from external objects; and no less unreasonable would it be to attribute several truths to the impressions of nature, and innate characters, when we may observe in ourselves faculties fit to attain as easy and certain knowledge of them as if they were originally imprinted on the mind.

But because a man is not permitted without censure to follow his own thoughts in the search of truth, when they lead him ever so little out of the common road, I shall set down the reasons that made me doubt of the truth of that opinion, as an excuse for my mistake, if I be in one; which I leave to be considered by those who, with me, dispose themselves to embrace truth wherever they find it.

2. *General Assent the great Argument.* There is nothing more commonly taken for granted than that there are certain *principles*, both *speculative* and *practical*, (for they speak of both), universally agreed upon by all mankind: which therefore, they argue, must needs be the constant impressions which the souls of men receive in their first beings, and which they bring into the world with them, as necessarily and really as they do any of their inherent faculties.

3. *Universal Consent proves nothing innate.* This argument, drawn from universal consent, has this misfortune in it, that if it were true in matter of fact, that there were certain truths wherein all mankind agreed, it would not prove them innate, if there can be any other way shown how men may come to that universal agreement, in the things they do consent in, which I presume may be done.

4. *'What is, is,' and 'It is impossible for the same Thing to be and not to be,' not universally assented to.* But, which is worse, this argument of universal consent which is made use of to prove innate principles, seems to me a demonstration that there are none such: because there are none to which all mankind give an universal assent. I shall begin with the speculative, and instance in those magnified principles of demonstration, 'Whatsoever is, is,' and 'It is impossible for the same thing to be and not to be'; which, of all others, I think have the most allowed title to innate. These have so settled a reputation of maxims universally received, that it will no doubt be thought strange if any one should seem to question it. But yet I take liberty to say, that these propositions are so far from having an universal assent, that there are a great part of mankind to whom they are not so much as known.

5. *Not on the Mind naturally imprinted, because not known to Children, Idiots, &c.* For, first, it is evident, that all children and idiots have not the least apprehension or thought of them. And the want of that is enough to destroy that universal assent which must needs be the necessary concomitant of all innate truths: it seeming to me near a contradiction to say, that there are truths imprinted on the soul, which it perceives or understands not: imprinting, if it signify anything, being nothing else but the making certain

truths to be perceived. For to imprint anything on the mind without the mind's perceiving it, seems to me hardly intelligible. If therefore children and idiots have souls, have minds, with those impressions upon them, *they* must unavoidably perceive them, and necessarily know and assent to these truths; which since they do not, it is evident that there are no such impressions. For if they are not notions naturally imprinted, how can they be innate? and if they are notions imprinted, how can they be unknown? To say a notion is imprinted on the mind, and yet at the same time to say, that the mind is ignorant of it, and never yet took notice of it, is to make this impression nothing. No proposition can be said to be in the mind which it never yet knew, which it was never yet conscious of. For if any one may, then, by the same reason, all propositions that are true, and the mind is capable ever of assenting to, may be said to be in the mind, and to be imprinted: since, if any one can be said to be in the mind, which it never yet knew, it must be only because it is capable of knowing it; and so the mind is of all truths it ever shall know. Nay, thus truths may be imprinted on the mind which it never did, nor ever shall know; for a man may live long, and die at last in ignorance of many truths which his mind was capable of knowing, and that with certainty. So that if the capacity of knowing be the natural impression contended for, all the truths a man ever comes to know will, by this account, be every one of them innate; and this great point will amount to no more, but only to a very improper way of speaking; which, whilst it pretends to assert the contrary, says nothing different from those who deny innate principles. For nobody, I think, ever denied that the mind was capable of knowing several truths. The capacity, they say, is innate; the knowledge acquired. But then to what end such contest for certain innate maxims? If truths can be imprinted on the understanding without being perceived, I can see no difference there can be between any truths the mind is *capable* of knowing in respect of their original: they must all be innate or all adventitious: in vain shall a man go about to distinguish them. He therefore that talks of innate notions in the understanding, cannot (if he intend thereby any distinct sort of truths) mean such truths to be in the understanding as it never perceived, and is yet wholly ignorant of. For if these words 'to be in the understanding' have any propriety, they signify to be understood. So that to be in the understanding, and not to be understood; to be in the mind and never to be perceived, is all one as to say anything is and is not in the mind or understanding. If therefore these two propositions, 'Whatsoever is, is,' and 'It is impossible for the same thing to be and not to be,' are by nature imprinted, children cannot be ignorant of them: infants, and all that have souls, must necessarily have them in their understandings, know the truth of them, and assent to it.

BOOK II

OF IDEAS

Chapter I

OF IDEAS IN GENERAL, AND THEIR ORIGINAL

1. *Idea is the Object of Thinking.* Every man being conscious to himself that he thinks; and that which his mind is applied about whilst thinking being the *ideas* that are there, it is past doubt that men have in their minds several ideas,—such as are those expressed by the words *whiteness, hardness, sweetness, thinking, motion, man, elephant, army, drunkenness,* and others: it is in the first place then to be inquired, *How he comes by them?*

I know it is a received doctrine, that men have native ideas, and original characters, stamped upon their minds in their very first being. This opinion I have at large examined already; and, I suppose what I have said in the foregoing Book will be much more easily admitted, when I have shown whence the understanding may get all the ideas it has; and by what ways and degrees they may come into the mind;—for which I shall appeal to every one's own observation and experience.

2. *All Ideas come from Sensation or Reflection.* Let us then suppose the mind to be, as we say, white paper, void of all characters, without any ideas:—How comes it to be furnished? Whence comes it by that vast store which the busy and boundless fancy of man has painted on it with an almost endless variety? Whence has it all the *materials* of reason and knowledge? To this I answer, in one word, from EXPERIENCE. In that all our knowledge is founded;

and from that it ultimately derives itself. Our observation employed either, about external sensible objects, or about the internal operations of our minds perceived and reflected on by ourselves, is that which supplies our understandings with all the *materials* of thinking. These two are the fountains of knowledge, from whence all the ideas we have, or can naturally have, do spring.

3. *The Objects of Sensation and Source of Ideas.* First, our Senses, conversant about particular sensible objects, do convey into the mind several distinct perceptions of things, according to those various ways wherein those objects do affect them. And thus we come by those *ideas* we have of *yellow, white, heat, cold, soft, hard, bitter, sweet,* and all those which we call sensible qualities; which when I say the senses convey into the mind, I mean, they from external objects convey into the mind what produces there those perceptions. This great source of most of the ideas we have, I call our senses, and derived by them to the understanding, I call SENSATION.

4. *The Operations of our Minds, the other Source of them.* Secondly, the other fountain from which experience furnisheth the understanding with ideas is,—the perception of the operations of our own mind within us, as it is employed about the ideas it has got;—which operations, when the soul comes to reflect on and consider, do furnish the understanding with another set of ideas, which could not be had from things without. And such are *perception, thinking, doubting, believing, reasoning, knowing, willing,* and all the different actings of our own minds;—which we being conscious of, and observing in ourselves, do from these receive into our understandings as distinct ideas as we do from bodies affecting our senses. This source of ideas every man has wholly in himself; and though it be not sense, as having nothing to do with external objects, yet it is very like it, and might properly enough be called *internal sense.* But as I call the other *sensation,* so I call this REFLECTION, the ideas it affords being such only as the mind gets by reflecting on its own operations within itself. By reflection then, in the following part of this discourse, I would be understood to mean, that notice which the mind takes of its own operations, and the manner of them, by reason whereof there come to be ideas of these operations in the understanding. These two, I say, viz. external material things, as the objects of SENSATION, and the operations of our own minds within, as the objects of REFLECTION, are to me the only originals from whence all our ideas take their beginnings. The term *operations* here I use in a large sense, as comprehending not barely the actions of the mind about its ideas, but some sort of passions arising sometimes from them, such as is the satisfaction or uneasiness arising from any thought.

5. *All our Ideas are of the one or the other of these.* The understanding seems to me not to have the least glimmering of any ideas which it doth not receive from one of these two. *External objects* furnish the mind with the ideas of sensible qualities, which are all those different perceptions they produce in us; and *the mind* furnishes the understanding with ideas of its own operations.

These, when we have taken a full survey of them, and their several modes, combinations, and relations, we shall find to contain all our whole stock of ideas; and that we have nothing in our minds which did not come in one of these two ways. Let any one examine his own thoughts, and thoroughly search into his understanding; and then let him tell me, whether all the original ideas he has there, are any other than of the objects of his senses, or of the operations of his mind, considered as objects of his reflection. And how great a mass of knowledge soever he imagines to be lodged there, he will, upon taking a strict view, see that he has not any idea in his mind but what one of these two have imprinted;—though perhaps, with infinite variety compounded and enlarged by the understanding, as we shall see hereafter.

10. *The Soul thinks not always; for this wants Proofs.* But whether the soul be supposed to exist antecedent to, or coeval with, or some time after the first rudiments of organization, or the beginnings of life in the body, I leave to be disputed by those who have better thought of that matter. I confess myself to have one of those dull souls, that doth not perceive itself always to contemplate ideas; nor can conceive it any more necessary for the soul always to think, than for the body always to move: the perception of ideas

being (as I conceive) to the soul, what motion is to the body; not its essence, but one of its operations. And therefore, though thinking be supposed never so much the proper action of the soul, yet it is not necessary to suppose that it should be always thinking, always in action. That, perhaps, is the privilege of the infinite Author and Preserver of all things, who 'never slumbers nor sleeps'; but is not competent to any finite being, at least not to the soul of man. We know certainly, by experience, that we *sometimes* think; and thence draw this infallible consequence,—that there is something in us that has a power to think. But whether that substance *perpetually* thinks or no, we can be no further assured than experience informs us. For, to say that actual thinking is essential to the soul, and inseparable from it, is to beg what is in question, and not to prove it by reason;—which is necessary to be done, if it be not a self-evident proposition. But whether this, 'That the soul always thinks,' be a self-evident proposition, that everybody assents to at first hearing, I appeal to mankind. It is doubted whether I thought at all last night or no. The question being about a matter of fact, it is begging it to bring, as a proof for it, an hypothesis, which is the very thing in dispute: by which way one may prove anything, and it is but supposing that all watches, whilst the balance beats, think, and it is sufficiently proved, and past doubt, that my watch thought all last night. But he that would not deceive himself, ought to build his hypothesis on matter of fact, and make it out by sensible experience, and not presume on matter of fact, because of his hypothesis, that is, because he supposes it to be so; which way of proving amounts to this, that I must necessarily think all last night, because another supposes I always think, though I myself cannot perceive that I always do so.

But men in love with their opinions may not only suppose what is in question, but allege wrong matter of fact. How else could any one make it an inference of mine, that a thing is not, because we are not sensible of it in our sleep? I do not say there is no *soul* in a man, because he is not sensible of it in his sleep; but I do say, he cannot *think* at any time, waking or sleeping, without being sensible of it. Our being sensible of it is not necessary to anything but to our thoughts; and to them it is; and to them it always will be necessary, till we can think without being conscious of it.

Chapter II

OF SIMPLE IDEAS

1. *Uncompounded Appearances.* The better to understand the nature, manner, and extent of our knowledge, one thing is carefully to be observed concerning the ideas we have; and that is, that some of them are *simple* and some *complex*.

Though the qualities that affect our senses are, in the things themselves, so united and blended, that there is no separation, no distance between them; yet it is plain, the ideas they produce in the mind enter by the senses simple and unmixed. For, though the sight and touch often take in from the same object, at the same time, different ideas;—as a man sees at once motion and colour; the hand feels softness and warmth in the same piece of wax: yet the simple ideas thus united in the same subject, are as perfectly distinct as those that come in by different senses. The coldness and hardness which a man feels in a piece of ice being as distinct ideas in the mind as the smell and whiteness of a lily; or as the taste of sugar, and smell of a rose. And there is nothing can be plainer to a man than the clear and distinct perception he has of those simple ideas; which, being each in itself uncompounded, contains in it nothing but *one uniform appearance, or conception in the mind*, and is not distinguishable into different ideas.

2. *The Mind can neither make nor destroy them.* These simple ideas, the materials of all our knowledge, are suggested and furnished to the mind only by those two ways above mentioned, viz. sensation and reflection. When the understanding is once stored with these simple ideas, it has the power to repeat, compare, and unite them, even to an almost infinite variety, and so can make at pleasure new complex ideas. But it is not in the power of the most exalted wit, or enlarged understanding, by any quickness or variety of thought, to *invent* or *frame* one new simple idea in the mind, not taken in by the ways before mentioned: nor can any force of the understanding *destroy* those that are there. The dominion of man, in this little world of his own understanding being much what the same as it is in the great world of visible things; wherein his power, however managed by art and skill, reaches no farther than to compound and divide the materials that are made to his

hand; but can do nothing towards the making the least particle of new matter, or destroying one atom of what is already in being. The same inability will every one find in himself, who shall go about to fashion in his understanding one simple idea, not received in by his senses from external objects, or by reflection from the operations of his own mind about them. I would have any one try to fancy any taste which had never affected his palate; or frame the idea of a scent he had never smelt: and when he can do this, I will also conclude that a blind man hath ideas of colours, and a deaf man true distinct notions of sounds.

Chapter III

OF SIMPLE IDEAS OF SENSE

1. *Division of simple Ideas.* The better to conceive the ideas we receive from sensation, it may not be amiss for us to consider them, in reference to the different ways whereby they make their approaches to our minds, and make themselves perceivable by us.

First, then, There are some which come into our minds *by one sense only*.

Secondly, There are others that convey themselves into the mind *by more senses than one*.

Thirdly, Others that are had from *reflection only*.

Fourthly, There are some that make themselves way, and are suggested to the mind *by all the ways of sensation and reflection*.

We shall consider them apart under these several heads.

Ideas of one Sense.—There are some ideas which have admittance only through one sense, which is peculiarly adapted to receive them. Thus light and colours, as white, red, yellow, blue, with their several degrees or shades and mixtures, as green, scarlet, purple, sea-green, and the rest, come in only by the eyes. All kinds of noises, sounds, and tones, only by the ears. The several tastes and smells, by the nose and palate. And if these organs, or the nerves which are the conduits to convey them from without to their audience in the brain,—the mind's presence-room (as I may so call it)—are any of them so disordered as not to perform their functions, they have no postern to be admitted by; no other way to bring themselves into view, and be perceived by the understanding.

The most considerable of those belonging to the touch, are heat and cold, and solidity: all the rest, consisting almost wholly in the sensible configuration, as smooth and rough; or else, more or less firm adhesion of the parts, as hard and soft, tough and brittle, are obvious enough.

2. *Few simple Ideas have Names.* I think it will be needless to enumerate all the particular simple ideas belonging to each sense. Nor indeed is it possible if we would; there being a great many more of them belonging to most of the senses than we have names for. The variety of smells, which are as many almost, if not more, than species of bodies in the world, do most of them want names. Sweet and stinking commonly serve our turn for these ideas, which in effect is little more than to call them pleasing or displeasing; though the smell of a rose and violet, both sweet, are certainly very distinct ideas. Nor are the different tastes, that by our palates we receive ideas of, much better provided with names. Sweet, bitter, sour, harsh, and salt are almost all the epithets we have to denominate that numberless variety of relishes, which are to be found distinct, not only in almost every sort of creatures, but in the different parts of the same plant, fruit, or animal. The same may be said of colours and sounds. I shall, therefore, in the account of simple ideas I am here giving, content myself to set down only such as are most material to our present purpose, or are in themselves less apt to be taken notice of though they are very frequently the ingredients of our complex ideas; amongst which, I think, I may well account solidity, which therefore I shall treat of in the next chapter.

Chapter IV

IDEA OF SOLIDITY

1. *We receive this Idea from Touch.* The idea of *solidity* we receive by our touch: and it arises from the resistance which we find in body to the entrance of any other body into the place it possesses, till it has left it. There is no idea which we receive more constantly from sensation than solidity. Whether we move or rest, in what posture soever we are, we always

feel something under us that supports us, and hinders our further sinking downwards; and the bodies which we daily handle make us perceive that, whilst they remain between them, they do, by an insurmountable force, hinder the approach of the parts of our hands that press them. *That which thus hinders the approach of two bodies, when they are moved one towards another, I call solidity.* I will not dispute whether this acceptation of the word solid be nearer to its original signification than that which mathematicians use it in. It suffices that I think the common notion of solidity will allow, if not justify, this use of it; but if any one think it better to call it *impenetrability*, he has my consent. Only I have thought the term solidity the more proper to express this idea, not only because of its vulgar use in that sense, but also because it carries something more of positive in it than impenetrability; which is negative, and is perhaps more a consequence of solidity, than solidity itself. This, of all other, seems the idea most intimately connected with, and essential to body; so as nowhere else to be found or imagined, but only in matter. And though our senses take no notice of it, but in masses of matter, of a bulk sufficient to cause a sensation in us: yet the mind, having once got this idea from such grosser sensible bodies, traces it further, and considers it, as well as figure, in the minutest particle of matter that can exist; and finds it inseparably inherent in body, wherever or however modified.

2. *Solidity fills Space.* This is the idea which belongs to body, whereby we conceive it to fill space. The idea of which filling of space is,—that where we imagine any space taken up by a solid substance, we conceive it so to possess it, that it excludes all other solid substances; and will for ever hinder any other two bodies, that move towards one another in a straight line, from coming to touch one another, unless it removes from between them in a line not parallel to that which they move in. This idea of it, the bodies which we ordinarily handle sufficiently furnish us with.

6. *What Solidity is.* If any one asks me, *What this solidity is*, I send him to his senses to inform him. Let him put a flint or a football between his hands, and then endeavour to join them, and he will know. If he thinks this not a sufficient explication of solidity, what it is, and wherein it consists; I promise to tell him what it is, and wherein it consists, when he tells me what thinking is, or wherein it consists; or explains to me what extension or motion is, which perhaps seems much easier. The simple ideas we have, are such as experience teaches them us; but if, beyond that, we endeavour by words to make them clearer in the mind, we shall succeed no better than if we went about to clear up the darkness of a blind man's mind by talking; and to discourse into him the ideas of light and colours. The reason of this I shall show in another place.

Chapter V

OF SIMPLE IDEAS OF DIVERS SENSES

Ideas received both by seeing and touching. The ideas we get by more than one sense are, of *space* or *extension*, *figure*, *rest*, and *motion*. For these make perceivable impressions, both on the eyes and touch; and we can receive and convey into our minds the ideas of the extension, figure, motion, and rest of bodies, both by seeing and feeling. But having occasion to speak more at large of these in another place, I here only enumerate them.

Chapter VI

OF SIMPLE IDEAS OF REFLECTION

1. *Simple Ideas are the Operations of Mind about its other Ideas.* The mind receiving the ideas mentioned in the foregoing chapters from without, when it turns its view inward upon itself, and observes its own actions about those ideas it has, takes from thence other ideas, which are as capable to be the objects of its contemplation as any of those it received from foreign things.

2. *The Idea of Perception, and Idea of Willing, we have from Reflection.* The two great and principal actions of the mind, which are most frequently considered, and which are so frequent that every one that pleases may take notice of them in himself, are these two:—

Perception, or *Thinking*; and
Volition, or *Willing*.

The power of thinking is called the *Understanding*, and the power of volition is called the *Will*; and these two powers or abilities in the mind are denominated faculties.

Of some of the *modes* of these simple ideas of reflection, such as are *remembrance, discerning, reasoning, judging, knowledge, faith*, &c., I shall have occasion to speak hereafter.

Chapter VII

OF SIMPLE IDEAS OF BOTH SENSATION AND REFLECTION

1. *Ideas of Pleasure and Pain.* There be other simple ideas which convey themselves into the mind by all the ways of sensation and reflection, viz, *pleasure* or *delight*, and its opposite, *pain*, or *uneasiness; power, existence; unity.*

2. *Mix with almost all our other Ideas.* Delight or uneasiness, one or other of them, join themselves to almost all our ideas both of sensation and reflection: and there is scarce any affection of our senses from without, any retired thought of our mind within, which is not able to produce in us pleasure or pain. By pleasure and pain, I would be understood to signify, whatsoever delights or molests us; whether it arises from the thoughts of our minds, or anything operating on our bodies. For, whether we call it satisfaction, delight, pleasure, happiness, &c., on the one side, or uneasiness, trouble, pain, torment, anguish, misery, &c., on the other, they are still but different degrees of the same thing, and belong to the ideas of pleasure and pain, delight or uneasiness; which are the names I shall most commonly use for those two sorts of ideas.

7. *Ideas of Existence and Unity.* *Existence* and *Unity* are two other ideas that are suggested to the understanding by every object without, and every idea within. When ideas are in our minds, we consider them as being actually there, as well as we consider things to be actually without us;—which is, that they exist, or have existence. And whatever we can consider as one thing, whether a real being or idea, suggests to the understanding the idea of unity.

8. *Idea of Power.* *Power* also is another of those simple ideas which we receive from sensation and reflection. For, observing in ourselves that we do and can think, and that we can at pleasure move several parts of our bodies which were at rest; the effects, also, that natural bodies are able to produce in one another, occurring every moment to our senses,—we both these ways get the idea of power.

9. *Idea of Succession.* Besides these there is another idea, which, though suggested by our senses, yet is more constantly offered to us by what passes in our minds; and that is the idea of *succession*. For if we look immediately into ourselves, and reflect on what is observable there, we shall find our ideas always, whilst we are awake, or have any thought, passing in train, one going and another coming, without intermission.

10. *Simple Ideas the materials of all our Knowledge.* These, if they are not all, are at least (as I think) the most considerable of those simple ideas which the mind has, and out of which is made all its other knowledge; all which it receives only by the two forementioned ways of sensation and reflection.

Nor let any one think these too narrow bounds for the capacious mind of man to expatiate in, which takes its flight further than the stars, and cannot be confined by the limits of the world; that extends its thoughts often even beyond the utmost expansion of Matter, and makes excursions into that incomprehensible Inane. I grant all this, but desire any one to assign any *simple idea* which is not received from one of those inlets before mentioned, or any *complex idea* not made out of those simple ones. Nor will it be so strange to think these few simple ideas sufficient to employ the quickest thought, or largest capacity; and to furnish the materials of all that various knowledge, and more various fancies and opinions of all mankind, if we consider how many words may be made out of the various composition of twenty-four letters; or if, going one step further, we will but reflect on the variety of combinations that may be made with barely one of the above-mentioned ideas, viz. number, whose stock is inexhaustible and truly infinite: and what a large and immense field doth extension alone afford the mathematicians?

Chapter VIII

SOME FURTHER CONSIDERATIONS CONCERNING OUR SIMPLE IDEAS OF SENSATION

7. *Ideas in the Mind, Qualities in Bodies.* To discover the nature of our *ideas* the better, and to discourse of them intelligibly, it will be convenient to distinguish them *as they are ideas or perceptions in our minds*; and *as they are modifications of matter in the bodies that cause such perceptions in us*: that so we may not think (as perhaps usually is done) that they are exactly the images and resemblances of something inherent in the subject; most of those of sensation being in the mind no more the likeness of something existing without us, than the names that stand for them are the likeness of our ideas, which yet upon hearing they are apt to excite in us.

8. *Our Ideas and the Qualities of Bodies.* Whatsoever the mind perceives *in itself*, or is the immediate object of perception, thought, or understanding, that I call *idea*; and the power to produce any idea in our mind, I call *quality* of the subject wherein that power is. Thus a snowball having the power to produce in us the ideas of white, cold, and round,—the power to produce those ideas in us, as they are in the snowball, I call qualities; and as they are sensations or perceptions in our understandings, I call them ideas; which *ideas*, if I speak of sometimes as in the things themselves, I would be understood to mean those qualities in the objects which produce them in us.

9. *Primary Qualities of Bodies.* Qualities thus considered in bodies are,

First, such as are utterly inseparable from the body, in what state soever it be; and such as in all the alterations and changes it suffers, all the force can be used upon it, it constantly keeps; and such as sense constantly finds in every particle of matter which has bulk enough to be perceived; and the mind finds inseparable from every particle of matter, though less than to make itself singly be perceived by our senses: v.g. Take a grain of wheat, divide it into two parts; each part has still solidity, extension, figure, and mobility: divide it again, and it retains still the same qualities; and so divide it on, till the parts become insensible; they must retain still each of them all those qualities. For division (which is all that a mill, or pestle, or any other body, does upon another, in reducing it to insensible parts) can never take away either solidity, extension, figure or mobility from any body, but only makes two or more distinct separate masses of matter, of that which was but one before; all which distinct masses, reckoned as so many distinct bodies, after division, make a certain number. These I call *original* or *primary qualities* of body, which I think we may observe to produce simple ideas in us, viz. solidity, extension, figure, motion or rest, and number.

10. *Secondary Qualities of Bodies.* *Secondly*, such qualities which in truth are nothing in the objects themselves but powers to produce various sensations in us by their primary qualities, i.e. by the bulk, figure, texture, and motion of their insensible parts, as colours, sounds, tastes, &c. These I call *secondary qualities*. To these might be added a *third* sort, which are allowed to be barely powers; though they are as much real qualities in the subject as those which I, to comply with the common way of speaking, call qualities, but for distinction, secondary qualities. For the power in fire to produce a new colour, or consistency, in *wax* or *clay*,—by its primary qualities, is as much a quality in fire, as the power it has to produce in *me* a new idea or sensation of warmth or burning, which I felt not before,—by the same primary qualities, viz. the bulk, texture, and motion of its insensible parts.

11. *How Bodies produce Ideas in us.* The next thing to be considered is, how bodies produce ideas in us; and that is manifestly by impulse, the only way which we can conceive bodies to operate in.

12. *By motions, external, and in our organism.* If then external objects be not united to our minds when they produce ideas therein; and yet we perceive these *original* qualities in such of them as singly fall under our senses, it is evident that some motion must be thence continued by our nerves, or animal spirits, by some parts of our bodies, to the brains or the seat of sensation, there to produce in our minds the particular ideas we have of them. And since the extension, figure, number, and motion of bodies of an observable bigness, may be perceived at a distance by the sight, it is evident some singly imperceptible

bodies must come from them to the eyes, and thereby convey to the brain some motion; which produces these ideas which we have of them in us.

13. *How secondary Qualities produce their ideas.* After the same manner that the ideas of these original qualities are produced in us, we may conceive that the ideas of *secondary* qualities are also produced, viz. by the operation of insensible particles on our senses. For, it being manifest that there are bodies and good store of bodies, each whereof are so small, that we cannot by any of our senses discover either their bulk, figure, or motion,—as is evident in the particles of the air and water, and others extremely smaller than those; perhaps as much smaller than the particles of air and water, as the particles of air and water are smaller than peas or hail-stones;—let us suppose at present that the different motions and figures, bulk and number, of such particles, affecting the several organs of our senses, produce in us those different sensations which we have from the colours and smells of bodies; v.g. that a violet, by the impulse of such insensible particles of matter, of peculiar figures and bulks, and in different degrees and modifications of their motions, causes the ideas of the blue colour, and sweet scent of that flower to be produced in our minds. It being no more impossible to conceive that God should annex such ideas to such motions, with which they have no similitude, than that he should annex the idea of pain to the motion of a piece of steel dividing our flesh, with which that idea hath no resemblance.

14. *They depend on the primary Qualities.* What I have said concerning colours and smells may be understood also of tastes and sounds, and other the like sensible qualities; which, whatever reality we by mistake attribute to them, are in truth nothing in the objects themselves, but powers to produce various sensations in us; and depend on those primary qualities, viz. bulk, figure, texture, and motion of parts as I have said.

15. *Ideas of primary Qualities are Resemblances; of secondary, not.* From whence I think it easy to draw this observation,—that the ideas of primary qualities of bodies are resemblances of them, and their patterns do really exist in the bodies themselves, but the ideas produced in us by these secondary qualities have no resemblance of them at all. There is nothing like our ideas, existing in the bodies themselves. They are, in the bodies we denominate from them, only a power to produce those sensations in us; and what is sweet, blue, or warm in idea, is but the certain bulk, figure, and motion of the insensible parts, in the bodies themselves, which we call so.

16. *Examples.* Flame is denominated hot and light; snow, white and cold; and manna, white and sweet, from the ideas they produce in us. Which qualities are commonly thought to be the same in those bodies that those ideas are in us, the one the perfect resemblance of the other, as they are in a mirror, and it would by most men be judged very extravagant if one should say otherwise. And yet he that will consider that the same fire that, at one distance produces in us the sensation of warmth, does, at a nearer approach, produce in us the far different sensation of pain, ought to bethink himself what reason he has to say—that this idea of warmth, which was produced in him by the fire, is *actually in the fire*; and his idea of pain, which the same fire produced in him the same way, is *not* in the fire. Why are whiteness and coldness in snow, and pain not, when it produces the one and the other idea in us; and can do neither, but by the bulk, figure, number, and motion of its solid parts?

17. *The ideas of the Primary alone really exist.* The particular bulk, number, figure, and motion of the parts of fire or snow are really in them,—whether any one's senses perceive them or no: and therefore they may be called *real* qualities, because they really exist in those bodies. But light, heat, whiteness, or coldness, are no more really in them than sickness or pain is in manna. Take away the sensation of them; let not the eyes see light or colours, nor the ears hear sounds; let the palate not taste, nor the nose smell, and all colours, tastes, odours, and sounds, *as they are such particular ideas*, vanish and cease, and are reduced to their causes, i.e. bulk, figure, and motion of parts.

18. *The secondary exist in things only as modes of the primary.* A piece of manna of a sensible bulk is able to produce in us the idea of a round or square

figure; and by being removed from one place to another, the idea of motion. This idea of motion represents it as it really is in manna moving: a circle or square are the same, whether in idea or existence, in the mind or in the manna. And this, both motion and figure, are really in the manna, whether we take notice of them or no: this everybody is ready to agree to. Besides, manna, by the bulk, figure, texture, and motion of its parts, has a power to produce the sensations of sickness, and sometimes of acute pains or gripings in us. That these ideas of sickness and pain are *not* in the manna, but effects of its operations on us, and are nowhere when we feel them not; this also every one readily agrees to. And yet men are hardly to be brought to think that sweetness and whiteness are not really in manna; which are but the effects of the operations of manna, by the motion, size, and figure of its particles, on the eyes and palate: as the pain and sickness caused by manna are confessedly nothing but the effects of its operations on the stomach and guts, by the size, motion, and figure of its insensible parts, (for by nothing else can a body operate, as has been proved): as if it could not operate on the eyes and palate, and thereby produce in the mind particular distinct ideas, which in itself it has not, as well as we allow it can operate on the guts and stomach, and thereby produce distinct ideas, which in itself it has not. These ideas, being all effects of the operations of manna on several parts of our bodies, by the size, figure, number, and motion of its parts;—why those produced by the eyes and palate should rather be thought to be really in the manna, than those produced by the stomach and guts; or why the pain and sickness, ideas that are the effect of manna, should be thought to be nowhere when they are not felt; and yet the sweetness and whiteness, effects of the same manna on other parts of the body, by ways equally as unknown, should be thought to exist in the manna, when they are not seen or tasted, would need some reason to explain.

19. *Examples.* Let us consider the red and white colours in porphyry. Hinder light from striking on it, and its colours vanish; it no longer produces any such ideas in us: upon the return of light it produces these appearances on us again. Can any one think any real alterations are made in the porphyry by the presence or absence of light; and that those ideas of whiteness and redness are really in porphyry in the light, when it is plain *it has no colour in the dark*? It has, indeed, such a configuration of particles, both night and day, as are apt, by the rays of light rebounding from some parts of that hard stone, to produce in us the idea of redness, and from others the idea of whiteness; but whiteness or redness are not in it at any time, but such a texture that hath the power to produce such a sensation in us.

20. Pound an almond, and the clear white colour will be altered into a dirty one, and the sweet taste into an oily one. What real alteration can the beating of the pestle make in any body, but an alteration of the texture of it?

21. *Explains how water felt as cold by one hand may be warm to the other.* Ideas being thus distinguished and understood, we may be able to give an account how the same water, at the same time, may produce the idea of cold by one hand and of heat by the other: whereas it is impossible that the same water, if those ideas were really in it, should at the same time be both hot and cold. For, if we imagine *warmth*, as it is in our hands, to be nothing but a certain sort and degree of motion in the minute particles of our nerves or animal spirits, we may understand how it is possible that the same water may, at the same time, produce the sensations of heat in one hand and cold in the other; which yet *figure* never does, that never producing the idea of a square by one hand which has produced the idea of a globe by another. But if the sensation of heat and cold be nothing but the increase or diminution of the motion of the minute parts of our bodies, caused by the corpuscles of any other body, it is easy to be understood, that if that motion be greater in one hand than in the other; if a body be applied to the two hands, which has in its minute particles a greater motion than in those of one of the hands, and a less than in those of the other, it will increase the motion of the one hand and lessen it in the other; and so cause the different sensations of heat and cold that depend thereon.

23. *Three Sorts of Qualities in Bodies.* The qualities, then, that are in bodies, rightly considered, are of three sorts:—

First, The bulk, figure, number, situation, and motion or rest of their solid parts. Those are in them, whether we perceive them or not; and when they are of that size that we can discover them, we have by these an idea of the thing as it is in itself; as is plain in artificial things. These I call *primary qualities.*

Secondly, The power that is in any body, by reason of its insensible primary qualities, to operate after a peculiar manner on any of our senses, and thereby produce in *us* the different ideas of several colours, sounds, smells, tastes, &c. These are usually called *sensible qualities.*

Thirdly, The power that is in any body, by reason of the particular constitution of its primary qualities, to make such a change in the bulk, figure, texture, and motion of *another body*, as to make it operate on our senses differently from what it did before. Thus the sun has a power to make wax white, and fire to make lead fluid. These are usually called *powers*.

The first of these, as has been said, I think may be properly called real, original, or primary qualities; because they are in the things themselves, whether they are perceived or not: and upon their different modifications it is that the secondary qualities depend.

The other two are only powers to act differently upon other things: which powers result from the different modifications of those primary qualities.

24. *The first are Resemblances; the second thought to be Resemblances, but are not; the third neither are, nor are thought so.*' But, though the two latter sorts of qualities are powers barely, and nothing but powers, relating to several other bodies, and resulting from the different modifications of the original qualities, yet they are generally otherwise thought of. For the *second* sort, viz. the powers to produce several ideas in us, by our senses, are looked upon as real qualities in the things thus affecting us: but the *third* sort are called and esteemed barely powers. v.g. The idea of heat or light, which we receive by our eyes, or touch, from the sun, are commonly thought real qualities existing in the sun, and something more than mere powers in it. But when we consider the sun in reference to wax, which it melts or blanches, we look on the whiteness and softness produced in the wax, not as qualities in the sun, but effects produced by powers in it. Whereas, if rightly considered, these qualities of light and warmth, which are perceptions in me when I am warmed or enlightened by the sun, are no otherwise in the sun, than the changes made in the wax, when it is blanched or melted, are in the sun. They are all of them equally *powers in the sun, depending on its primary qualities*; whereby it is able, in the one case, so to alter the bulk, figure, texture, or motion of some of the insensible parts of my eyes or hands, as thereby to produce in me the idea of light or heat; and in the other, it is able so to alter the bulk, figure, texture, or motion of the insensible parts of the wax, as to make them fit to produce in me the distinct ideas of white and fluid.

Chapter IX

OF PERCEPTION

1. *Perception the first simple Idea of Reflection.* Perception, as it is the first faculty of the mind exercised about our ideas; so it is the first and simplest idea we have from reflection, and is by some called thinking in general. Though thinking, in the propriety of the English tongue, signifies that sort of operation in the mind about its ideas, wherein the mind is active; where it, with some degree of voluntary attention, considers anything. For in bare naked perception, the mind is, for the most part, only passive; and what it perceives, it cannot avoid perceiving.

2. *Reflection alone can give us the idea of what perception is.* What perception is, every one will know better by reflecting on what he does himself, when he sees, hears, feels, &c., or thinks, than by any discourse of mine. Whoever reflects on what passes in his own mind cannot miss it. And if he does not reflect, all the words in the world cannot make him have any notion of it.

3. *Arises in sensation only when the mind notices the organic impression.* This is certain, that whatever alterations are made in the body, if they reach not the mind; whatever impressions are made on the outward parts, if they are not taken notice of within, there is no perception. Fire may burn our bodies with no other effect than it does a billet, unless the motion

be continued to the brain, and there the sense of heat, or idea of pain, be produced in the mind; wherein consists actual perception.

4. *Impulse on the organ insufficient.* How often may a man observe in himself, that whilst his mind is intently employed in the contemplation of some objects, and curiously surveying some ideas that are there, it takes no notice of impressions of sounding bodies made upon the organ of hearing, with the same alteration that uses to be for the producing the idea of sound? A sufficient impulse there may be on the organ; but it not reaching the observation of the mind, there follows no perception: and though the motion that uses to produce the idea of sound be made in the ear, yet no sound is heard. Want of sensation, in this case, is not through any defect in the organ, or that the man's ears are less affected than at other times when he does hear: but that which uses to produce the idea, though conveyed in by the usual organ, not being taken notice of in the understanding, and so imprinting no idea in the mind, there follows no sensation. So that wherever there is sense or perception, there some idea is actually produced, and present in the understanding.

8. *Sensations often changed by the Judgment.* We are further to consider concerning perception, that the ideas we receive by sensation are often, in grown people, altered by the judgment, without our taking notice of it. When we set before our eyes a round globe of any uniform colour, v.g. gold, alabaster, or jet, it is certain that the idea thereby imprinted on our minds is of a flat circle, variously shadowed, with several degrees of light and brightness coming to our eyes. But we having, by use, been accustomed to perceive what kind of appearance convex bodies are wont to make in us; what alterations are made in the reflections of light by the difference of the sensible figures of bodies;—the judgment presently, by an habitual custom, alters the appearances into their causes. So that from that which is truly variety of shadow or colour, collecting the figure, it makes it pass for a mark of figure, and frames to itself the perception of a convex figure and an uniform colour; when the idea we receive from thence is only a plane variously coloured, as is evident in painting. To which purpose I shall here insert a problem of that very ingenious and studious promoter of real knowledge, the learned and worthy Mr. Molineux,[1] which he was pleased to send me in a letter some months since; and it is this:—'Suppose a man *born* blind, and now adult, and taught by his *touch* to distinguish between a cube and a sphere of the same metal, and nighly of the same bigness, so as to tell, when he felt one and the other, which is the cube, which the sphere. Suppose then the cube and sphere placed on a table, and the blind man be made to see: *quaere*, whether *by his sight, before he touched them*, he could now distinguish and tell which is the globe, which the cube?' To which the acute and judicious proposer answers, 'Not. For, though he has obtained the experience of how a globe, how a cube affects his touch, yet he has not yet obtained the experience, that what affects his touch so or so, must affect his sight so or so; or that a protuberant angle in the cube, that pressed his hand unequally, shall appear to his eye as it does in the cube.'—I agree with this thinking gentleman, whom I am proud to call my friend, in his answer to this problem; and am of opinion that the blind man, at first sight, would not be able with certainty to say which was the globe, which the cube, whilst he only saw them; though he could unerringly name them by his touch, and certainly distinguish them by the difference of their figures felt. This I have set down, and leave with my reader, as an occasion for him to consider how much he may be beholden to experience, improvement, and acquired notions, where he thinks he had not the least use of, or help from them. And the rather, because this observing gentleman further adds, that 'having, upon the occasion of my book, proposed this to divers very ingenious men, he hardly ever met with one that at first gave the answer to it which he thinks true, till by hearing his reasons they were convinced.'

Chapter X

OF RETENTION

1. *Contemplation.* The next faculty of the mind, whereby it makes a further progress towards knowledge, is that which I call *retention*; or the keeping of

1. [William Molineux (1656–1698), a Dubliner who was a Member of Parliament and who published a work on optics, entered into correspondence with Locke, and the two became close friends. The letter Locke refers to was

those simple ideas which from sensation or reflection it hath received. This is done two ways.

First, by keeping the idea which is brought into it, for some time actually in view, which is called *contemplation.*

2. *Memory.* The other way of retention is, the power to revive again in our minds those ideas which, after imprinting, have disappeared, or have been as it were laid aside out of sight. And thus we do, when we conceive heat or light, yellow or sweet,—the object being removed. This is *memory*, which is as it were the storehouse of our ideas. For, the narrow mind of man not being capable of having many ideas under view and consideration at once, it was necessary to have a repository, to lay up those ideas which, at another time, it might have use of. But, our *ideas* being nothing but actual perceptions in the mind, which cease to be anything when there is no perception of them; this laying up of our ideas in the repository of the memory signifies no more but this,—that the mind has a power in many cases to revive perceptions which it has once had, with this additional perception annexed to them, that *it has had them before*. And in this sense it is that our ideas are said to be in our memories, when indeed they are actually nowhere;—but only there is an ability in the mind when it will to revive them again, and as it were paint them anew on itself, though some with more, some with less difficulty; some more lively, and other more obscurely. And thus it is, by the assistance of this faculty, that we are said to have all those ideas in our understandings which, though we do not actually contemplate, yet we *can* bring in sight, and make appear again, and be the objects of our thoughts, without the help of those sensible qualities which first imprinted them there.

7. *In Remembering, the Mind is often active.* In this secondary perception, as I may so call it, or viewing again the ideas that are lodged in the memory, the mind is oftentimes more than barely passive; the appearance of those dormant pictures depending sometimes on the *will*. The mind very often sets itself on work in search of some hidden idea, and turns as it were the eye of the soul upon it; though sometimes too they start up in our minds of their own accord, and offer themselves to the understanding; and very often are roused and tumbled out of their dark cells into open daylight, by turbulent and tempestuous passions; our affections bringing ideas to our memory, which had otherwise lain quiet and unregarded. This further is to be observed, concerning ideas lodged in the memory, and upon occasion revived by the mind, that they are not only (as the word *revive* imports) none of them new ones, but also that the mind takes notice of them as of a former impression, and renews its acquaintance with them, as with ideas it had known before. So that though ideas formerly imprinted are not all constantly in view, yet in remembrance they are constantly known to be such as have been formerly imprinted; i.e. in view, and taken notice of before, by the understanding.

sent in 1693, and the discussion of Molineux's problem was added to the *Essay* in its second edition (1694).—S.M.C.]

Chapter XI

OF DISCERNING, AND OTHER OPERATIONS OF THE MIND

1. *No Knowledge without Discernment.* Another faculty we may take notice of in our minds is that of *discerning* and *distinguishing* between the several ideas it has. It is not enough to have a confused perception of something in general. Unless the mind had a distinct perception of different objects and their qualities, it would be capable of very little knowledge, though the bodies that affect us were as busy about us as they are now, and the mind were continually employed in thinking. On this faculty of distinguishing one thing from another depends the evidence and certainty of several, even very general, propositions, which have passed for innate truths;—because men, overlooking the true cause why those propositions find universal assent, impute it wholly to native uniform impressions; whereas it in truth depends upon this clear discerning faculty of the mind, whereby it *perceives* two ideas to be the same, or different. But of this more hereafter.

4. *Comparing.* The COMPARING them one with another, in respect of extent, degrees, time, place, or any other circumstances, is another operation of the mind about its ideas, and is that upon which depends all that large tribe of ideas comprehended under *rela-*

tion; which, of how vast an extent it is, I shall have occasion to consider hereafter.

6. *Compounding.* The next operation we may observe in the mind about its ideas is COMPOSITION; whereby it puts together several of those simple ones it has received from sensation and reflection, and combines them into complex ones. Under this of composition may be reckoned also that of *enlarging*, wherein, though the composition does not so much appear as in more complex ones, yet it is nevertheless a putting several ideas together, though of the same kind. Thus, by adding several units together, we make the idea of a dozen; and putting together the repeated ideas of several perches, we frame that of a furlong.

8. *Naming.* When children have, by repeated sensations, got ideas fixed in their memories, they begin by degrees to learn the use of signs. And when they have got the skill to apply the organs of speech to the framing of articulate sounds, they begin to make use of words, to signify their ideas to others. These verbal signs they sometimes borrow from others, and sometimes make themselves, as one may observe among the new and unusual names children often give to things in the first use of language.

9. *Abstraction.* The use of words then being to stand as outward marks of our internal ideas, and those ideas being taken from particular things, if every particular idea that we take in should have a distinct name, names must be endless. To prevent this, the mind makes the particular ideas received from particular objects to become general; which is done by considering them as they are in the mind such appearances,—separate from all other existences, and the circumstances of real existence, as time, place, or any other concomitant ideas. This is called ABSTRACTION, whereby ideas taken from particular beings become general representatives of all of the same kind; and their names general names, applicable to whatever exists conformable to such abstract ideas. Such precise, naked appearances in the mind, without considering how, whence, or with what others they came there, the understanding lays up (with names commonly annexed to them) as the standards to rank real existences into sorts, as they agree with these patterns, and to denominate them accordingly. Thus the same colour being observed to-day in chalk or snow, which the mind yesterday received from milk, it considers that appearance alone, makes it a representative of all of that kind; and having given it the name *whiteness*, it by that sound signifies the same quality wheresoever to be imagined or met with; and thus universals, whether ideas or terms, are made.

10. *Brutes abstract not.* If it may be doubted whether beasts compound and enlarge their ideas that way to any degree; this, I think, I may be positive in,—that the power of abstracting is not at all in them; and that the having of general ideas is that which puts a perfect distinction betwixt man and brutes, and is an excellency which the faculties of brutes do by no means attain to. For it is evident we observe no footsteps in them of making use of general signs for universal ideas; from which we have reason to imagine that they have not the faculty of abstracting, or making general ideas, since they have no use of words, or any other general signs.

11. *Brutes abstract not, yet are not bare machines.* Nor can it be imputed to their want of fit organs to frame articulate sounds, that they have no use or knowledge of general words; since many of them, we find, can fashion such sounds, and pronounce words distinctly enough, but never with any such application. And, on the other side, men who, through some defect in the organs, want words, yet fail not to express their universal ideas by signs, which serve them instead of general words, a faculty which we see beasts come short in. And, therefore, I think, we may suppose, that it is in this that the species of brutes are discriminated from man: and it is that proper difference wherein they are wholly separated, and which at last widens to so vast a distance. For if they have any ideas at all, and are not bare machines, (as some would have them,)[2] we cannot deny them to have some reason. It seems as evident to me, that they do reason, as that they have sense; but it is only in particular ideas, just as they received them from their senses. They are the best of them tied up within those narrow bounds, and have not (as I think) the faculty to enlarge them by any kind of abstraction.

2. [Descartes, for example.]

15. *The true Beginning of Human Knowledge.* And thus I have given a short, and, I think, true *history of the first beginnings of human knowledge*;—whence the mind has its first objects; and by what steps it makes it progress to the laying in and storing up those ideas, out of which is to be framed all the knowledge it is capable of: wherein I must appeal to experience and observation whether I am in the right: the best way to come to truth being to examine things as really they are, and not to conclude they are, as we fancy of ourselves, or have been taught by others to imagine.

17. *Dark Room.* I pretend not to teach, but to inquire; and therefore cannot but confess here again,—that external and internal sensation are the only passages I can find of knowledge to the understanding. These alone, as far as I can discover, are the windows by which light is let into this *dark room*. For, methinks, the understanding is not much unlike a closet wholly shut from light, with only some little openings left, to let in external visible resemblances, or ideas of things without: would the pictures coming into such a dark room but stay there, and lie so orderly as to be found upon occasion, it would very much resemble the understanding of a man, in reference to all objects of sight, and the ideas of them.

These are my guesses concerning the means whereby the understanding comes to have and retain simple ideas, and the modes of them, with some other operations about them.

I proceed now to examine some of these simple ideas and their modes a little more particularly.

Chapter XII

OF COMPLEX IDEAS

1. *Made by the Mind out of simple Ones.* We have hitherto considered those ideas, in the reception whereof the mind is only passive, which are those simple ones received from sensation and reflection before mentioned, whereof the mind cannot make one to itself, nor have any idea which does not wholly consist of them. But as the mind is wholly passive in the reception of all its simple ideas, so it exerts several acts of its own, whereby out of its simple ideas, as the materials and foundations of the rest, the others are framed. The acts of the mind, wherein it exerts its power over its simple ideas, are chiefly these three: (1) Combining several simple ideas into one compound one; and thus all *complex ideas* are made. (2) The second is bringing two ideas, whether simple or complex, together, and setting them by one another, so as to take a view of them at once, without uniting them into one; by which way it gets all its *ideas of relations*. (3) The third is separating them from all other ideas that accompany them in their real existence: this is called abstraction: and thus all its *general ideas* are made. This shows man's power, and its ways of operation, to be much the same in the material and intellectual world. For the materials in both being such as he has no power over, either to make or destroy, all that man can do is either to unite them together, or to set them by one another, or wholly separate them. I shall here begin with the first of these in the consideration of complex ideas, and come to the other two in their due places. As simple ideas are observed to exist in several combinations united together, so the mind has a power to consider several of them united together as one idea; and that not only as they are united in external objects, but as itself has joined them together. Ideas thus made up of several simple ones put together, I call *complex*;—such as are beauty, gratitude, a man, an army, the universe; which, though complicated of various simple ideas, or complex ideas made up of simple ones, yet are, when the mind pleases, considered each by itself, as one entire thing, and signified by one name.

2. *Made voluntarily.* In this faculty of repeating and joining together its ideas, the mind has great power in varying and multiplying the objects of its thoughts, infinitely beyond what sensation or reflection furnished it with: but all this still confined to those simple ideas which it received from those two sources, and which are the ultimate materials of all its compositions. For simple ideas are all from things themselves, and of these the mind *can* have no more, nor other than what are suggested to it. It can have no other ideas of sensible qualities than what come from without by the senses; nor any ideas of other kind of operations of a thinking substance, than what it finds in itself. But when it has once got these simple ideas, it is not confined barely to observation, and what offers itself from without; it can, by its own power, put together those ideas it has, and make new complex ones, which it never received so united.

3. *Complex ideas are either of Modes, Substances, or Relations.* Complex ideas, however compounded and decompounded, though their number be infinite, and the variety endless, wherewith they fill and entertain the thoughts of men; yet I think they may be all reduced under these three heads:—

1. *Modes.*
2. *Substances.*
3. *Relations.*

4. *Ideas of Modes.* First, *Modes* I call such complex ideas which, however compounded, contain not in them the supposition of subsisting by themselves, but are considered as dependences on, or affections of substances;—such as are the ideas signified by the words triangle, gratitude, murder, &c. And if in this I use the word mode in somewhat a different sense from its ordinary signification, I beg pardon; it being unavoidable in discourses, differing from the ordinary received notions, either to make new words, or to use old words in somewhat a new signification; the later whereof, in our present case, is perhaps the more tolerable of the two.

5. *Simple and mixed Modes of simple ideas.* Of these *modes*, there are two sorts which deserve distinct consideration:—

First, there are some which are only variations, or different combinations of the same simple idea, without the mixture of any other;—as a dozen, or score; which are nothing but the ideas of so many distinct units added together, and these I call *simple modes* as being contained within the bounds of one simple idea.

Secondly, there are others compounded of simple ideas of several kinds, but together to make one complex one;—v.g. beauty, consisting of a certain composition of colour and figure, causing delight to the beholder; theft, which being the concealed change of the possession of anything, without the consent of the proprietor, contains, as is visible, a combination of several ideas of several kinds: and these I call *mixed modes.*

6. *Ideas of Substances, single or collective.* Secondly, the ideas of *substances* are such combinations of simple ideas as are taken to represent distinct *particular* things subsisting by themselves; in which the supposed or confused idea of substance, such as it is, is always the first and chief. Thus if to substance be joined the simple idea of a certain dull whitish colour, with certain degrees of weight, hardness, ductility, and fusibility, we have the idea of lead; and a combination of the ideas of a certain sort of figure, with the powers of motion, thought and reasoning, joined to substance, make the ordinary idea of a man. Now of substances also, there are two sorts of ideas:—one of *single* substances, as they exist separately, as of a man or a sheep; the other of several of those put together, as an army of men, or flock of sheep—which *collective* ideas of several substances thus put together are as much each of them one single idea as that of a man or an unit.

7. *Ideas of Relation.* Thirdly, the last sort of complex ideas is that we call *relation*, which consists in the consideration and comparing one idea with another.

Of these several kinds we shall treat in their order.

Chapter XXI

OF POWER

1. *This Idea, how got.* The mind being every day informed, by the senses, of the alteration of those simple ideas it observes in things without; and taking notice how one comes to an end, and ceases to be, and another begins to exist which was not before; reflecting also on what passes within itself, and observing a constant change of its ideas, sometimes by the impression of outward objects on the senses, and sometimes by the determination of its own choice; and concluding from what it has so constantly observed to have been, that the like changes will for the future be made in the same things, by like agents, and by the like ways,—considers in one thing the possibility of having any of its simple ideas changed, and in another the possibility of making that change; and so comes by the idea which we call *power.* Thus we say, Fire has a power to melt gold, i.e. to destroy the consistency of its insensible parts, and consequently its hardness, and make it fluid; and gold has a power to be melted; that the sun has a power to

blanch wax, and wax a power to be blanched by the sun, whereby the yellowness is destroyed, and whiteness made to exist in its room. In which, and the like cases, the power we consider is in reference to the change of perceivable ideas. For we cannot observe any alteration to be made in, or operation upon anything, but by the observable change of its sensible ideas; nor conceive any alteration to be made, but by conceiving a change of some of its ideas.

2. *Power, active and passive.* Power thus considered is two-fold, viz. as able to make, or able to receive any change. The one may be called *active*, and the other *passive* power. Whether matter be not wholly destitute of active power, as its author, God, is truly above all passive power; and whether the intermediate state of created spirits be not that alone which is capable of both active and passive power, may be worth consideration. I shall not now enter into that inquiry, my present business being not to search into the original of power, but how we come by the *idea* of it. But since active powers make so great a part of our complex ideas of natural substances, (as we shall see hereafter,) and I mention them as such, according to common apprehension; yet they being not, perhaps, so truly *active* powers as our hasty thoughts are apt to represent them, I judge it not amiss, by this intimation, to direct our minds to the consideration of God and spirits, for the clearest idea of *active* power.

4. *The clearest Idea of active Power had from Spirit.* We are abundantly furnished with the idea of *passive* power by almost all sorts of sensible things. In most of them we cannot avoid observing their sensible qualities, nay, their very substances, to be in a continual flux. And therefore with reason we look on them as liable still to the same change. Nor have we of *active* power (which is the more proper signification of the word power) fewer instances. Since whatever change is observed, the mind must collect a power somewhere able to make that change, as well as a possibility in the thing itself to receive it. But yet, if we will consider it attentively, bodies, by our senses, do not afford us so clear and distinct an idea of active power, as we have from reflection on the operations of our minds. For all power relating to action, and there being but two sorts of action whereof we have an idea, viz. thinking and motion, let us consider whence we have the clearest ideas of the powers which produce these actions. (1) Of thinking, body affords us no idea at all; it is only from reflection that we have that. (2) Neither have we from body any idea of the beginning of motion. A body at rest affords us no idea of any active power to move; and when it is set in motion itself, that motion is rather a passion than an action in it. For, when the ball obeys the motion of a billiard-stick, it is not any action of the ball, but bare passion. Also when by impulse it sets another ball in motion that lay in its way, it only communicates the motion it had received from another, and loses in itself so much as the other received: which gives us but a very obscure idea of an *active* power of moving in body, whilst we observe it only to *transfer*, but not *produce* any motion. For it is but a very obscure idea of power which reaches not the production of the action, but the continuation of the passion. For so is motion in a body impelled by another; the continuation of the alteration made in it from rest to motion being little more an action, than the continuation of the alteration of its figure by the same blow is an action. The idea of the *beginning* of motion we have only from reflection on what passes in ourselves; where we find by experience, that, barely by willing it, barely by a thought of the mind, we can move the parts of our bodies, which were before at rest. So that it seems to me, we have, from the observation of the operation of bodies by our senses, but a very imperfect obscure idea of *active* power; since they afford us not any idea in themselves of the power to begin any action, either motion or thought.

5. *Will and Understanding two Powers in Mind or Spirit.* This, at least, I think evident,—That we find in ourselves a power to begin or forbear, continue or end several actions of our minds, and motions of our bodies, barely by a thought or preference of the mind ordering, or as it were commanding, the doing or not doing such or such a particular action. This power which the mind has thus to order the consideration of any idea, or the forebearing to consider it; or to prefer the motion of any part of the body to its rest, and *vice versa*, in any particular instance, is that which we call the *Will*. The actual exercise of that power, by directing any particular action, or its forbearance, is that which we call *volition* or *willing*. The forbear-

ance of that action, consequent to such order or command of the mind, is called *voluntary*. And whatsoever action is performed without such a thought of the mind, is called *involuntary*. The power of perception is that which we call the *Understanding*. Perception, which we make the act of the understanding, is of three sorts:—1. The perception of ideas in our minds. 2. The perception of the signification of signs. 3. The perception of the connexion or repugnancy, agreement or disagreement, that there is between any of our ideas. All these are attributed to the understanding, or perceptive power, though it be the two latter only that use allows us to say we understand.

7. *Whence the idea of liberty and necessity.* Everyone, I think, finds in himself a power to begin or forbear, continue or put an end to several actions in himself. From the consideration of the extent of this power of the mind over the actions of the man, which everyone finds in himself, arise the ideas of liberty and necessity.

8. *Liberty, what.* All the actions that we have any idea of reducing themselves, as has been said, to these two, viz. thinking and motion; so far as a man has power to think or not to think, to move or not to move, according to the preference or direction of his own mind, so far is a man *free*. Whenever any performance or forbearance are not equally in a man's power; wherever doing or not doing will not equally *follow* upon the preference of his mind directing it, there he is not free, though perhaps the action may be voluntary. So, that the idea of *liberty* is, the idea of a power in any agent to do or forbear any particular action, according to the determination or thought of the mind, whereby either of them is preferred to the other: where either of them is not in the power of the agent to be produced by him according to his volition, there he is not at liberty; that agent is under *necessity*. So that liberty cannot be where there is no thought, no volition, no will; but there may be thought, there may be will, there may be volition, where there is no liberty. A little consideration of an obvious instance or two may make this clear.

9. *Supposes Understanding and Will.* A tennis-ball, whether in motion by the stroke of a racket, or lying still at rest, is not by any one taken to be a free agent. If we inquire into the reason, we shall find it is because we conceive not a tennis-ball to think, and consequently not to have any volition, or *preference* of motion to rest, or *vice versâ*; and therefore has not liberty, is not a free agent; but all its both motion and rest come under our idea of necessary, and are so called. Likewise a man falling into the water, (a bridge breaking under him,) has not herein liberty, is not a free agent. For though he has volition, though he prefers his not falling to falling; yet the forbearance of that motion not being in his power, the stop or cessation of that motion follows not upon his volition; and therefore herein he is not free. So a man striking himself, or his friend, by a convulsive motion of his arm, which it is not in his power, by volition or the direction of his mind, to stop or forbear, nobody thinks he has in this liberty; every one pities him, as acting by necessity and constraint.

10. *Belongs not to Volition.* Again: suppose a man be carried, whilst fast asleep, into a room where is a person he longs to see and speak with; and be there locked fast in, beyond his power to get out: he awakes, and is glad to find himself in so desirable company, which he stays willingly in, i.e. prefers his stay to going away. I ask, is not this stay voluntary? I think nobody will doubt it: and yet, being locked fast in, it is evident he is not at liberty not to stay, he has not freedom to be gone. So that liberty is not an idea belonging to volition, or preferring; but to the person having the power of doing, or forbearing to do, according as the mind shall choose or direct. Our idea of liberty reaches as far as that power, and no farther. For wherever restraint comes to check that power, or compulsion takes away that indifferency of ability to act, or to forbear acting, there liberty, and our notion of it, presently ceases.

11. *Voluntary opposed to involuntary, not to necessary.* We have instances enough, and often more than enough, in our own bodies. A man's heart beats, and the blood circulates, which it is not in his power by any thought or volition to stop; and therefore in respect of these motions, where rest depends not on his choice, nor would follow the determination of his mind, if it should prefer it, he is not a free agent. Convulsive motions agitate his legs, so that though he wills it ever so much, he cannot by any power of

his mind stop their motion, (as in that odd disease called *chorea sancti viti*), but he is perpetually dancing; he is not at liberty in this action, but under as much necessity of moving, as a stone that falls, or a tennis-ball struck with a racket. On the other side, a palsy or the stocks hinder his legs from obeying the determination of his mind, if it would thereby transfer his body to another place. In all these there is want of freedom; though the sitting still, even of a paralytic, whilst he prefers it to a removal, is truly voluntary. Voluntary, then, is not opposed to necessary, but to involuntary. For a man may prefer what he can do, to what he cannot do; the state he is in, to its absence or change; though necessity has made it in itself unalterable.

12. *Liberty, what.* As it is in the motions of the body, so it is in the thoughts of our minds: where any one is such, that we have power to take it up, or lay it by, according to the preference of the mind, there we are at liberty. A waking man, being under the necessity of having some ideas constantly in his mind, is not at liberty to think or not to think; no more than he is at liberty, whether his body shall touch any other or no: but whether he will remove his contemplation from one idea to another is many times in his choice; and then he is, in respect of his ideas, as much at liberty as he is in respect of bodies he rests on; he can at pleasure remove himself from one to another. But yet some ideas to the mind, like some motions to the body, are such as in certain circumstances it cannot avoid, nor obtain their absence by the utmost effort it can use. A man on the rack is not at liberty to lay by the idea of pain, and divert himself with other contemplations: and sometimes a boisterous passion hurries our thoughts, as a hurricane does our bodies, without leaving us the liberty of thinking on other things, which we would rather choose. But as soon as the mind regains the power to stop or continue, begin or forbear, any of these motions of the body without, or thoughts within, according as it thinks fit to prefer either to the other, we then consider the man as a *free agent* again.

13. *Necessity, what.* Wherever thought is wholly wanting, or the power to act or forbear according to the direction of thought, there necessity takes place. This, in an agent capable of volition, when the beginning or continuation of any action is contrary to that preference of his mind, is called compulsion; when the hindering or stopping any action is contrary to his volition, it is called restraint. Agents that have no thought, no volition at all, are in everything *necessary agents*.

14. *Liberty belongs not to the Will.* If this be so, (as I imagine it is,) I leave it to be considered, whether it may not help to put an end to that long agitated, and, I think, unreasonable, because unintelligible question, viz. *Whether man's will be free or no?* For if I mistake not, it follows from what I have said, that the question itself is altogether improper; and it is as insignificant to ask whether man's *will* be free, as to ask whether his sleep be swift, or his virtue square: liberty being as little applicable to the will, as swiftness of motion is to sleep, or squareness to virtue. Every one would laugh at the absurdity of such a question as either of these: because it is obvious that the modifications of motion belong not to sleep, nor the difference of figure to virtue; and when any one well considers it, I think he will as plainly perceive that liberty, which is but a power, belongs only to *agents*, and cannot be an attribute or modification of the will, which is also but a power.

15. *Volition.* Such is the difficulty of explaining and giving clear notions of internal actions by sounds, that I must here warn my reader, that *ordering, directing, choosing, preferring*, &c., which I have made use of, will not distinctly enough express volition, unless he will reflect on what he himself does when he wills. For example, preferring, which seems perhaps best to express the act of volition, does it not precisely. For though a man would prefer flying to walking, yet who can say he ever wills it? Volition, it is plain, is an act of the mind knowingly exerting that dominion it takes itself to have over any part of the man, by employing it in, or withholding it from, any particular action. And what is the will, but the faculty to do this? And is that faculty anything more in effect than a power; the power of the mind to determine its thought, to the producing, continuing, or stopping any action, as far as it depends on us? For can it be denied that whatever agent has a power to think on its own actions, and to prefer their doing or omission either to other, has that faculty called will? *Will*, then,

is nothing but such a power. *Liberty*, on the other side, is the power a *man* has to do or forbear doing any particular action according as its doing or forbearance has the actual preference in the mind; which is the same thing as to say, according as he himself wills it.

16. *Powers belonging to Agents.* It is plain then that the will is nothing but one power or ability, and *freedom* another power or ability so that, to ask, whether the will has freedom, is to ask whether one power has another power, one ability another ability; a question at first sight too grossly absurd to make a dispute, or need an answer. For, who is it that sees not that powers belong only to agents, and are attributes only of substances, and not of powers themselves? So that this way of putting the question (viz. whether the will be free) is in effect to ask, whether the will be a substance, an agent, or at least to suppose it, since freedom can properly be attributed to nothing else. If freedom can with any propriety of speech be applied to power, it may be attributed to the power that is in a man to produce, or forbear producing, motion in parts of his body, by choice or preference; which is that which denominates him free, and is freedom itself. But if any one should ask, whether freedom were free, he would be suspected not to understand well what he said; and he would be thought to deserve Midas's ears,[3] who, knowing that rich was a denomination for the possession of riches, should demand whether riches themselves were rich.

21. *But to the Agent or Man.* To return, then, to the inquiry about liberty, I think the question is not proper, *whether the will be free*, but *whether a man be free*. Thus, I think.

First, That so far as any one can, by the direction or choice of his mind, preferring the existence of any action to the non-existence of that action, and *vice versa*, make *it* to exist or not exist, so far *he* is free. For if I can, by a thought directing the motion of my finger, make it move when it was at rest, or *vice versa*, it is evident, that in respect of that I am free: and if I can, by a like thought of my mind, preferring one to the other, produce either words or silence, I am at liberty to speak or hold my peace: and as far as this power reaches, of acting or not acting, by the determination of his own thought preferring either, so far is a man free. For how can we think any one freer, than to have the power to do what he will? And so far as any one can, by preferring any action to its not being, or rest to any action, produce that action or rest, so far can he do what he will. For such a preferring of action to its absence, is the willing of it: and we can scarce tell how to imagine any being freer, than *to be able to do what he wills*. So that in respect of actions within the reach of such a power in him, a man seems as free as it is possible for freedom to make him.

22. *In respect of willing, a Man is not free.* But the inquisitive mind of man, willing to shift off from himself, as far as he can, all thoughts of guilt, though it be by putting himself into a worse state than that of fatal necessity, is not content with this: freedom, unless it reaches further than this, will not serve the turn: and it passes for a good plea, that a man is not free at all, if he be not as *free to will* as he is to *act what he wills*. Concerning a man's liberty, there yet, therefore, is raised this further question, *Whether a man be free to will?* which I think is what is meant, when it is disputed whether the will be free. And as to that I imagine.

23. *How a man cannot be free to will.* Secondly, That willing, or volition, being an action, and freedom consisting in a power of acting or not acting, a man in respect of willing or the act of volition, when any action in his power is once proposed to his thoughts, as presently to be done, cannot be free. The reason whereof is very manifest. For, it being unavoidable that the action depending on his will should exist or not exist, and its existence or not existence following perfectly the determination and preference of his will, he cannot avoid willing the existence or non-existence of that action; it is absolutely necessary that he will the one or the other; i.e., prefer the one to the other: since one of them must necessarily follow; and that which does follow follows by the choice and determination of his mind; that is, by his willing it: for if he did not will it, it would not be. So that, in respect of

3. [According to Greek mythology, King Midas argued that Apollo, the god of music, had lost a musical contest, and Apollo then punished Midas by turning his ears into those of an ass.]

the act of willing, a man in such a case is not free: liberty consisting in a power to act or not to act; which, in regard of volition, a man, upon such a proposal, has not. For it is unavoidably necessary to prefer the doing or forbearance of an action in a man's power, which is once so proposed to his thoughts; a man must necessarily will the one or the other of them; upon which preference or volition, the action or its forbearance certainly follows, and is truly voluntary. But the act of volition, or preferring one of the two, being that which he cannot avoid, a man, in respect of that act of willing, is under a necessity, and so cannot be free; unless necessity and freedom can consist together, and a man can be free and bound at once. Besides to make a man free after this manner, by making the action of willing to depend on his will, there must be another antecedent will, to determine the acts of this will, and another to determine that, and so *in infinitum*: for wherever one stops, the actions of the last will cannot be free. Nor is any being, as far I can comprehend beings above, capable of such a freedom of will, that it can forbear to will, i.e. to prefer the being or not being of anything in its power, which it has once considered as such.

24. *Liberty is freedom to execute what is willed.* This, then, is evident. That *a man is not at liberty to will, or not to will, anything in his power that he once considers of*: liberty consisting in a power to act or to forbear acting, and in that only. For a man that sits still is said yet to be at liberty; because he can walk if he wills it. A man that walks is at liberty also, not because he walks or moves; but because he can stand still if he wills it. *But if a man sitting still has not a power to remove himself, he is not at liberty;* so likewise a man falling down a precipice, though in motion, is not at liberty, because he cannot stop that motion if he would. This being so, it is plain that a man that is walking, to whom it is proposed to give off walking, is not at liberty, whether he will determine himself to walk, or give off walking or not: he must necessarily prefer one or the other of them; walking or not walking. And so it is in regard of all other actions in our power so proposed, which are the far greater number. For, considering the vast number of voluntary actions that succeed one another every moment that we are awake in the course of our lives, there are but few of them that are thought on or proposed to the will, till the time they are to be done; and in all such actions, as I have shown, the mind, in respect of willing, has not a power to act or not to act, wherein consists liberty. The mind, in that case, has not a power to forbear *willing*; it cannot avoid some determination concerning them, let the consideration be as short, the thought as quick as it will, it either leaves the man in the state he was before thinking, or changes it; continues the action, or puts an end to it. Whereby it is manifest, that *it* orders and directs one, in preference to, or with neglect of the other, and thereby either the continuation or change becomes *unavoidably* voluntary.

25. *The Will determined by something without it.* Since then it is plain that, in most cases, a man is not at liberty, whether he will nor no, (for, when an action in his power is proposed to his thoughts, he *cannot* forbear volition; he *must* determine one way or the other;) the next thing demanded is,—*Whether a man be at liberty to will which of the two he pleases, motion or rest?* This question carries the absurdity of it so manifestly in itself, that one might thereby sufficiently be convinced that liberty concerns not the will. For, to ask whether a man be at liberty to will either motion or rest, speaking or silence, which he pleases, is to ask whether a man can will what he wills, or be pleased with what he is pleased with? A question which, I think, needs no answer: and they who can make a question of it must suppose one will to determine the acts of another, and another to determine that, and so on *in infinitum*.

26. *The ideas of* liberty *and* volition *must be defined.* To avoid these and the like absurdities, nothing can be of greater use than to establish in our minds determined ideas of the things under consideration. If the ideas of liberty and volition were well fixed in our understandings, and carried along with us in our minds, as they ought, through all the questions that are raised about them, I suppose a great part of the difficulties that perplex men's thoughts, and entangle their understandings, would be much easier resolved; and we should perceive where the confused signification of terms, or where the nature of the thing caused the obscurity.

27. *Freedom.* First, then, it is carefully to be remembered, That freedom consists in the dependence

of the existence, or not existence of any *action*, upon our *volition* of it; and not in the dependence of any action, or its contrary, on our *preference*. A man standing on a cliff, is at liberty to leap twenty yards downwards into the sea, not because he has a power to do the contrary action, which is to leap twenty yards upwards, for that he cannot do; but he is therefore free, because he has a power to leap or not to leap. But if a greater force than his, either holds him fast, or tumbles him down, he is no longer free in that case; because the doing or forbearance of that particular action is no longer in his power. He that is a close prisoner in a room twenty feet square, being at the north side of his chamber, is at liberty to walk twenty feet southward, because he can walk or not walk it; but is not, at the same time, at liberty to do the contrary, i.e. to walk twenty feet northward.

In this, then, consists freedom, viz. in our being able to act or not to act, according as we shall choose or will.

28. *What Volition and action mean.* Secondly, we must remember, that *volition* or *willing* is an act of the mind directing its thought to the production of any action, and thereby exerting its power to produce it. To avoid multiplying of words, I would crave leave here, under the word *action*, to comprehend the forbearance too of any action proposed: sitting still, or holding one's peace, when walking or speaking are proposed, though mere forbearances, requiring as much the determination of the will, and being as often weighty in their consequences, as the contrary actions, may, on that consideration, well enough pass for actions too: but this I say, that I may not be mistaken, if (for brevity's sake) I speak thus.

29. *What determines the Will.* Thirdly, the will being nothing but a power in the mind to direct the operative faculties of a man to motion or rest, as far as they depend on such direction; to the question, What is it determines the will? the true and proper answer is, The mind. For that which determines the general power of directing, to this or that particular direction, is nothing but the agent itself exercising the power it has that particular way. If this answer satisfies not, it is plain the meaning of the question, What determines the will? is this,—What moves the mind, in every particular instance, to determine its general power of directing, to this or that particular motion or rest? And to this I answer,—*The motive for continuing in the same state or action, is only the present satisfaction in it; the motive to change is always some uneasiness*: nothing setting us upon the change of state, or upon any new action, but some uneasiness. This is the great motive that works on the mind to put it upon action, which for shortness' sake we will call determining of the will, which I shall more at large explain.

48. *The Power to suspend the Prosecution of any Desire makes way for Consideration.* There being in us a great many uneasinesses, always soliciting and ready to determine the will, it is natural, as I have said, that the greatest and most pressing should determine the will to the next action; and so it does for the most part, but not always. For, the mind having in most cases, as is evident in experience, a power to *suspend* the execution and satisfaction of any of its desires; and so all, one after another; is at liberty to consider the objects of them, examine them on all sides, and weigh them with others. In this lies the liberty man has; and from the not using of it right comes all that variety of mistakes, errors, and faults which we run into in the conduct of our lives, and our endeavours after happiness; whilst we precipitate the determination of our wills, and engage too soon, before due examination. To prevent this, we have a power to suspend the prosecution of this or that desire; as every one daily may experiment in himself. This seems to me the source of all liberty; in this seems to consist that which is (as I think improperly) called *free-will*. For, during this suspension of any desire, before the will be determined to action, and the action (which follows that determination) done, we have opportunity to examine, view, and judge of the good or evil of what we are going to do; and when, upon due examination, we have judged, we have done our duty, all that we can, or ought to do, in pursuit of our happiness; and it is not a fault, but a perfection of our nature, to desire, will, and act according to the last result of a fair examination.

73. *Recapitulation—Liberty of indifferency.* To conclude this inquiry into *human liberty*, which, as it stood before, I myself from the beginning fearing, and a very judicious friend of mine, since the publication, suspecting to have some mistake in it, though he could not particularly show it me, I was put upon a stricter review of this chapter. Wherein lighting upon a very easy and scarce observable slip I had

made, in putting one seemingly indifferent word for another that discovery opened to me this present view, which here, in this second edition, I submit to the learned world, and which, in short, is this: *Liberty* is a power to act or not to act, according as the mind directs. A power to direct the operative faculties to motion or rest in particular instances is that which we call the *will*. That which in the train of our voluntary actions determines the will to any change of operation is *some present uneasiness*, which is, or at least is always accompanied with that of *desire*. Desire is always moved by evil, to fly it: because a total freedom from pain always makes a necessary part of our happiness: but every good, nay, every greater good, does not constantly move desire, because it may not make, or may not be taken to make, any necessary part of our happiness. For all that we desire, is only to be happy. But, though this general desire of happiness operates constantly and invariably, yet the satisfaction of any particular desire *can be suspended* from determining the will to any subservient action, till we have maturely examined whether the particular apparent good which we then desire makes a part of our real happiness, or be consistent or inconsistent with it. The result of our judgment upon that examination is what ultimately determines the man; who could not be *free* if his will were determined by anything but his own desire, guided by his own judgment. I know that liberty, by some, is placed in an indifferency of the man; antecedent to the determination of his will. I wish they who lay so much stress on such an antecedent indifferency, as they call it, had told us plainly, whether this supposed indifferency be antecedent to the thought and judgment of the understanding, as well as to the decree of the will. For it is pretty hard to state it between them, i.e. immediately *after* the judgment of the understanding, and *before* the determination of the will: because the determination of the will immediately follows the judgment of the understanding: and to place liberty in an indifferency, antecedent to the thought and judgment of the understanding, seems to me to place liberty in a state of darkness, wherein we can neither see nor say anything of it; at least it places it in a subject incapable of it, no agent being allowed capable of liberty, but in consequence of thought and judgment. I am not nice about phrases, and therefore consent to say with those that love to speak so, that liberty is placed in indifferency; but it is an indifferency which remains after the judgment of the understanding, yea, even after the determination of the will: and that is an indifferency not of the *man*, (for after he has once judged which is best, viz. to do or forbear, he is no longer indifferent,) but an indifferency of *the operative powers of the man*, which remaining equally able to operate or to forbear operating after as before the decree of the will, are in a state, which, if one pleases, may be called indifferency; and as far as this indifferency reaches, a man is free, and no further: v.g. I have the ability to move my hand, or to let it rest; that operative power is indifferent to move or not to move my hand. I am then, in that respect perfectly free; my will determines that operative power to rest: I am yet free, because the indifferency of that my operative power to act, or not to act, still remains; the power of moving my hand is not at all impaired by the determination of my will, which at present orders rest; the indifferency of that power to act, or not to act, is just as it was before, as will appear, if the will puts it to the trial, by ordering the contrary. But if, during the rest of my hand, it be seized with a sudden palsy, the indifferency of that operative power is gone, and with it my liberty; I have no longer freedom in that respect, but am under a necessity of letting my hand rest. On the other side, if my hand be put into motion by a convulsion, the indifferency of that operative faculty is taken away by that motion; and my liberty in that case is lost, for I am under a necessity of having my hand move. I have added this, to show in what sort of indifferency liberty seems to me to consist, and not in any other, real or imaginary.

74. *Active and passive power, in motions and in thinking.* Before I close this chapter, it may perhaps be to our purpose, and help to give us clearer conceptions about *power*, if we make our thoughts take a little more exact survey of *action*. I have said above, that we have ideas but of two sorts of action, viz. motion and thinking. These, in truth, though called and counted actions, yet, if nearly considered, will not be found to be always perfectly so. For, if I mistake not, there are instances of both kinds, which, upon due consideration, will be found rather passions than actions; and consequently so far the effects barely of *passive powers* in those subjects, which yet on their

accounts are thought agents. For, in these instances, the substance that hath motion or thought receives the impression, whereby it is put into that action, purely from without, and so acts merely by the capacity it has to receive such an impression from some external agent; and such a power is not properly an active power, but a mere passive capacity in the subject. Sometimes the substance or agent puts itself into action by its own power, and this is properly *active power*. Whatsoever modification a substance has, whereby it produces any effect, that is called action: v.g. a solid substance, by motion, operates on or alters the sensible ideas of another substance, and therefore this modification of motion we call action. But yet this motion in that solid substance is, when rightly considered, but a passion, if it received it only from some external agent. So that the active power of motion is in no substance which cannot begin motion in itself or in another substance when at rest. So likewise in thinking, a power to receive ideas or thoughts from the operation of any external substance is called a power of thinking: but this is but a passive power, or capacity. But to be able to bring into view ideas out of sight at one's own choice, and to compare which of them one thinks fit, this is an active power. This reflection may be of some use to preserve us from mistakes about powers and actions, which grammar, and the common frame of languages, may be apt to lead us into. Since what is signified by verbs that grammarians call active, does not always signify action: v.g. this proposition: I *see* the moon, or a star, or I *feel* the heat of the sun, though expressed by a verb active, does not signify any action in me, whereby I operate on those substances, but only the reception of the ideas of light, roundness, and heat; wherein I am not active, but barely passive, and cannot, in that position of my eyes or body, avoid receiving them. But when I turn my eyes another way, or remove my body out of the sunbeams, I am properly active; because of my own choice, by a power within myself, I put myself into that motion. Such an action is the product of active power.

Chapter XXIII
OF OUR COMPLEX IDEAS OF SUBSTANCES

1. *Ideas of particular Substances, how made.* The mind being, as I have declared, furnished with a great number of the simple ideas, conveyed in by the senses as they are found in exterior things, or by reflection on its own operations, takes notice also that a certain number of these simple ideas go constantly together; which being presumed to belong to one thing, and words being suited to common apprehensions, and made use of for quick dispatch, are called, so united in one subject, by one name; which, by inadvertency, we are apt afterward to talk of and consider as one simple idea, which indeed is a complication of many ideas together: because, as I have said, not imaging how these simple ideas *can* subsist by themselves, we accustom ourselves to suppose some *substratum* wherein they do subsist, and from which they do result, which therefore we call *substance*.

2. *Our obscure Idea of Substance is general.* So that if any one will examine himself concerning his notion of pure substance in general, he will find he has no other idea of it at all, but only a supposition of he knows not what *support* of such qualities which are capable of producing simple ideas in us; which qualities are commonly called accidents. If any one should be asked, what is the subject wherein colour or weight inheres, he would have nothing to say, but the solid extended parts; and if he were demanded, what is it that solidity and extension adhere in, he would not be in a much better case than the Indian before mentioned who, saying that the world was supported by a great elephant, was asked what the elephant rested on; to which his answer was—a great tortoise: but being again pressed to know what gave support to the broad-backed tortoise, replied—*something, he knew not what*. And thus here, as in all other cases where we use words without having clear and distinct ideas, we talk like children: who, being questioned what such a thing is, which they know not, readily give this satisfactory answer, that it is *something*: which in truth signifies no more, when so used, either by children or men, but that they know not what; and that the thing they pretend to know, and talk of, is what they have no distinct idea of at all, and so are perfectly ignorant of it, and in the dark. The idea then we have, to which we give the *general* name substance, being nothing but the supposed, but unknown, support of those qualities we find existing, which we imagine cannot subsist *sine re substante*, without something to support them, we call that sup-

port *substantia*; which, according to the true import of the word, is, in plain English, standing under or upholding.

3. *Of the Sorts of Substances.* An obscure and relative idea of *substance in general* being thus made we come to have the ideas of *particular sorts of substances*, by collecting *such* combinations of simple ideas as are, by experience and observation of men's senses, taken notice of to exist together; and are therefore supposed to flow from the particular internal constitution, or unknown essence of that substance. Thus we come to have the ideas of a man, horse, gold, water, &c.; of which substances, whether any one has any other *clear* idea, further than of certain simple ideas coexistent together, I appeal to every one's own experience. It is the ordinary qualities observable in iron, or a diamond, put together, that make the true complex idea of those substances, which a smith or a jeweller commonly knows better than a philosopher; who, whatever *substantial forms* he may talk of, has no other idea of those substances, than what is framed by a collection of those simple ideas which are to be found in them: only we must take notice, that our complex ideas of substances, besides all those simple ideas they are made up of, have always the confused idea of something to which they belong, and in which they subsist: and therefore when we speak of any sort of substance, we say it is a thing having such or such qualities; as body is a thing that is extended, figured, and capable of motion; spirit, a thing capable of thinking; and so hardness, friability, and power to draw iron, we say, are qualities to be found in a loadstone. These, and the like fashions of speaking, intimate that the substance is supposed always *something besides* the extension, figure, solidity, motion, thinking, or other observable ideas, though we know not what it is.

4. *No clear or distinct idea of Substance in general.* Hence, when we talk or think of any particular sort of corporeal substances, as horse, stone, &c., though the idea we have of either of them be but the complication or collection of those several simple ideas of sensible qualities, which we used to find united in the thing called horse or stone; yet, *because we cannot conceive how they should subsist alone, nor one in another,* we suppose them existing in and supported by some common subject; which support we denote by the name substance, though it be certain we have no clear or distinct idea of that thing we suppose a support.

5. *As clear an Idea of spiritual substance as of corporeal substance.* The same thing happens concerning the operations of the mind, viz. thinking, reasoning, fearing, &c., which we concluding not to subsist of themselves, nor apprehending how they can belong to body, or be produced by it, we are apt to think these the actions of some other *substance*, which we call *spirit*; whereby yet it is evident that, having no other idea or notion of matter, but something wherein those many sensible qualities which affect our senses do subsist; by supposing a substance wherein thinking, knowing, doubting, and a power of moving, &c., do subsist, we have as clear a notion of the substance of spirit, as we have of body; the one being supposed to be (without knowing what it is) the *substratum* to those simple ideas we have from without; and the other supposed (with a like ignorance of what it is) to be the *substratum* to those operations we experiment in ourselves within. It is plain then, that the idea of *corporeal substance* in matter is as remote from our conceptions and apprehensions, as that of *spiritual substance*, or spirit: and therefore, from our not having any notion of the substance of spirit, we can no more conclude its non-existence, than we can, for the same reason, deny the existence of body; it being as rational to affirm there is no body, because we have no clear and distinct idea of the substance of matter, as to say there is no spirit, because we have no clear and distinct idea of the substance of a spirit.

6. *Our ideas of particular Sorts of Substances.* Whatever therefore be the secret abstract nature of substance in general, all the ideas we have of particular distinct sorts of substances are nothing but several combinations of simple ideas, co-existing in such, though unknown, cause of their union, as makes the whole subsist of itself. It is by such combinations of simple ideas, and nothing else, that we represent particular sorts of substances to ourselves; such are the ideas we have of their several species in our minds; and such only do we, by their specific names, signify to others, v.g. man, horse, sun, water, iron: upon

hearing which words, every one who understands the language, frames in his mind a combination of those several simple ideas which he has usually observed, or fancied to exist together under that denomination; all which he supposes to rest in and be, as it were, adherent to that unknown common subject, which inheres not in anything else. Though, in the meantime, it be manifest, and every one, upon inquiry into his own thoughts, will find, that he has no other idea of any substance, v.g. let it be gold, horse, iron, man, vitriol, bread, but what he has barely of those sensible qualities, which he supposes to inhere; with a supposition of such a *substratum* as gives, as it were, a support to those qualities or simple ideas, which he has observed to exist united together. Thus, the idea of the sun,—what is it but an aggregate of those several simple ideas, bright, hot, roundish, having a constant regular motion, at a certain distance from us, and perhaps some other: as he who thinks and discourses of the sun has been more or less accurate in observing those sensible qualities, ideas, or properties, which are in that thing which he calls the sun.

9. *Three sorts of Ideas make our complex ones of Corporeal Substances.* The ideas that make our complex ones of corporeal substances, are of these three sorts. First, the ideas of the primary qualities of things, which are discovered by our senses, and are in them even when we perceive them not; such are the bulk, figure, number, situation, and motion of the parts of bodies; which are really in them, whether we take notice of them or not. Secondly, the sensible secondary qualities, which, depending on these, are nothing but the powers those substances have to produce several ideas in us by our senses; which ideas are not in the things themselves, otherwise than as anything in its cause. Thirdly, the aptness we consider in any substance, to give or receive such alterations of primary qualities, as that the substance so altered should produce in us different ideas from what it did before; these are called active and passive powers: all which powers, as far as we have any notice or notion of them, terminate only in sensible simple ideas. For whatever alteration a loadstone has the power to make in the minute particles of iron, we should have no notion of any power it had at all to operate on iron, did not its sensible motion discover it: and I doubt not, but there are a thousand changes, that bodies we daily handle have a power to cause in one another, which we never suspect, because they never appear in sensible effects.

10. *Powers thus make a great Part of our complex Ideas of particular Substances.* *Powers* therefore justly make a great part of our complex ideas of substances. He that will examine his complex idea of gold, will find several of its ideas that make it up to be only powers; as the power of being melted, but of not spending itself in the fire; of being dissolved in *aqua regia*, are ideas as necessary to make up our complex idea of gold, as its colour and weight: which, if duly considered, are also nothing but different powers. For, to speak truly, yellowness is not actually in gold, but is a power in gold to produce that idea in us by our eyes, when placed in a due light: and the heat, which we cannot leave out of our ideas of the sun, is no more really in the sun, than the white colour it introduced into wax. These are both equally powers in the sun, operating, by the motion and figure of its sensible parts, so on a man, as to make him have the idea of heat; and so on wax, as to make it capable to produce in a man the idea of white.

11. *The now secondary Qualities of Bodies would disappear, if we could discover the primary ones of their minute Parts.* Had we senses acute enough to discern the minute particles of bodies, and the real constitution on which their sensible qualities depend, I doubt not but they would produce quite different ideas in us: and that which is now the yellow colour of gold, would then disappear, and instead of it we should see an admirable texture of parts, of a certain size and figure. This microscopes plainly discover to us; for what to our naked eyes produces a certain colour, is, by thus augmenting the acuteness of our senses, discovered to be quite a different thing; and the thus altering, as it were, the proportion of the bulk of the minute parts of a coloured object to our usual sight, produces different ideas from what it did before. Thus, sand or pounded glass, which is opaque, and white to the naked eye, is pellucid in a microscope; and a hair seen in this way, loses its former colour, and is, in a great measure, pellucid, with a mixture of some bright sparkling colours, such as appear from the refraction of diamonds, and other pellucid bodies. Blood, to the naked eye, appears all

red; but by a good microscope, wherein its lesser parts appear, shows only some few globules of red, swimming in a pellucid liquor, and how these red globules would appear, if glasses could be found that could yet magnify them a thousand or ten thousand times more, is uncertain.

14. *Our specific Ideas of Substances.* But to return to the matter in hand,—the ideas we have of substances, and the ways we come by them. I say, our *specific* ideas of substances are nothing else but *a collection of a certain number of simple ideas, considered as united in one thing.* These ideas of substances, though they are commonly simple apprehensions, and the names of them simple terms, yet in effect are complex and compounded. Thus the idea which an Englishman signifies by the name swan, is white colour, long neck, red beak, black legs, and whole feet, and all these of a certain size, with a power of swimming in the water, and making a certain kind of noise, and perhaps, to a man who has long observed this kind of birds, some other properties: which all terminate in sensible simple ideas, all united in one common subject.

15. *Our Ideas of spiritual Substances, as clear as of bodily Substances.* Besides the complex ideas we have of material sensible substances, of which I have last spoken,—by the simple ideas we have taken from those operations of our own minds, which we experiment daily in ourselves, as thinking, understanding, willing, knowing, and power of beginning motion, &c., co-existing in some substance, we are able to frame the *complex idea of an immaterial spirit.* And thus, by putting together the ideas of thinking, perceiving, liberty, and power of moving themselves and other things, we have as clear a perception and notion of immaterial substances as we have of material. For putting together the ideas of thinking and willing, or the power of moving or quieting corporeal motion, joined to substance, of which we have no distinct idea, we have the idea of an immaterial spirit; and by putting together the ideas of coherent solid parts, and a power of being moved, joined with substance, of which likewise we have no positive idea, we have the idea of matter. The one is as clear and distinct an idea as the other: the idea of thinking, and moving a body, being as clear and distinct ideas as the ideas of extension, solidity, and being moved. For our idea of substance is equally obscure, or none at all, in both: it is but a supposed I know not what, to support those ideas we call accidents. It is for want of reflection that we are apt to think that our senses show us nothing but material things. Every act of sensation, when duly considered, gives us an equal view of both parts of nature, the corporeal and spiritual. For whilst I know, by seeing or hearing, &c., that there is some corporeal being without me, the object of that sensation, I do more certainly know, that there is some spiritual being within me that sees and hears. This, I must be convinced, cannot be the action of bare insensible matter; nor ever could be, without an immaterial thinking being.

16. *No Idea of abstract Substance either in Body or Spirit.* By the complex idea of extended, figured, coloured, and all other sensible qualities, which is all that we know of it, we are as far from the idea of the substance of body, as if we knew nothing at all: nor after all the acquaintance and familiarity which we imagine we have with matter, and the many qualities men assure themselves they perceive and know in bodies, will it perhaps upon examination be found, that they have any more or clearer primary ideas belonging to body, than they have belonging to immaterial spirit.

17. *Cohesion of solid parts and Impulse, the primary ideas peculiar to Body.* The primary ideas we have *peculiar to body,* as contradistinguished to spirit, are the *cohesion of solid, and consequently separable, parts,* and a *power of communicating motion by impulse.* These, I think, are the original ideas proper and peculiar to body; for figure is but the consequence of finite extension.

18. *Thinking and Motivity.* The ideas we have belonging and *peculiar to spirit,* are *thinking,* and *will,* or *a power of putting body into motion by thought, and, which is consequent to it, liberty.* For, as body cannot but communicate its motion by impulse to another body, which it meets with at rest, so the mind can put bodies into motion, or forbear to do so, as it pleases. The ideas of *existence, duration,* and *mobility,* are common to them both.

37. *Recapitulation.* And thus we have seen what kind of ideas we have of *substances of all kinds*, wherein they consist, and how we came by them. From whence, I think, it is very evident,

First, That all our ideas of the several *sorts* of substances are nothing but collections of simple ideas: with a supposition of *something* to which they belong, and in which they subsist: though of this supposed something we have no clear distinct idea at all.

Secondly, That all the simple ideas, that thus united in one common *substratum*, make up our complex ideas of several *sorts* of substances, are no other but such as we have received from sensation or reflection. So that even in those which we think we are most intimately acquainted with, and that come nearest the comprehension of our most enlarged conceptions, we cannot go beyond those simple ideas. And even in those which seem most remote from all we have to do with, and do infinitely surpass anything we can perceive in ourselves by reflection; or discover by sensation in other things, we can attain to nothing but those simple ideas, which we originally received from sensation or reflection; as is evident in the complex ideas we have of angels, and particularly of God himself.

Thirdly, That most of the simple ideas that make up our complex ideas of substances, when truly considered, are only *powers*, however we are apt to take them for positive qualities; v.g. the greatest part of the ideas that make our complex idea of *gold* are yellowness, great weight, ductility, fusibility, and solubility in *aqua regia*, &c., all united together in an unknown *substratum*: all which ideas are nothing else but so many relations to other substances; and are not really in the gold, considered barely in itself, though they depend on those real and primary qualities of its internal constitution, whereby it has a fitness differently to operate, and be operated on by several other substances.

Chapter XXVII

OF IDENTITY AND DIVERSITY

1. *Wherein Identity consists.* Another occasion the mind often takes of comparing, is the very being of things, when, considering *anything as existing at any determined time and place*, we compare it with *itself existing at another time*, and thereon form the ideas of *identity* and *diversity*. When we see anything to be in any place in any instant of time, we are sure (be it what it will) that it is that very thing, and not another which at that same time exists in another place, how like and undistinguishable soever it may be in all other respects: and in this consists *identity*, when the ideas it is attributed to vary not at all from what they were that moment wherein we consider their former existence, and to which we compare the present. For never finding, nor conceiving it possible, that two things of the same kind should exist in the same place at the same time, we rightly conclude, that, whatever exists anywhere at any time, excludes all of the same kind, and is there itself alone. When therefore we demand whether anything be the *same* or no, it refers always to something that existed such a time in such a place, which it was certain, at that instant, was the same with itself, and no other. From whence it follows, that one thing cannot have two beginnings of existence, nor two things one beginning; it being impossible for two things of the same kind to be or exist in the same instant, in the very same place; or one and the same thing in different places. That, therefore, that had one beginning, is the same thing; and that which had a different beginning in time and place from that, is not the same, but divers. That which has made the difficulty about this relation has been the little care and attention used in having precise notions of the things to which it is attributed.

2. *Identity of Substances and of Modes.* We have the ideas but of three sorts of substances: 1. *God*. 2. *Finite intelligences*. 3. *Bodies*.

First, *God* is without beginning, eternal, unalterable, and everywhere, and therefore concerning his identity there can be no doubt.

Secondly, *Finite spirits* having had each its determinate time and place of beginning to exist, the relation to that time and place will always determine to each of them its identity, as long as it exists.

Thirdly, The same will hold of every *particle of matter*, to which no addition or subtraction of matter being made, it is the same. For, though these three sorts of substances, as we term them, do not exclude one another out of the same place, yet we cannot conceive but that they must necessarily each of them exclude any of the same kind out of the same place: or else the notions and names of identity and diversity would be in vain, and there could be no such distinctions of substances, or anything else one from another. For example: could two bodies be in the same place at the same time; then those two parcels of matter must be one and the same, take them great or little; nay, all bodies must be one and the same. For, by the same reason that two particles of matter may be in one place, all bodies may be in one place: which, when it can be supposed, takes away the distinction of identity and diversity of one and more, and renders it ridiculous. But it being a contradiction that two or more should be one, identity and diversity are relations and ways of comparing well founded, and of use to the understanding. All other things being but modes or relations ultimately terminated in substances, the identity and diversity of each particular existence of them too will be by the same way determined: only as to things whose existence is in succession, such as are the actions of finite beings, v.g. *motion* and *thought*, both which consist in a continued train of succession, concerning *their* diversity there can be no question: because each perishing the moment it begins, they cannot exist in different times, or in different places, as permanent beings can at different times exist in distant places; and therefore no motion or thought, considered as at different times, can be the same, each part thereof having a different beginning of existence.

3. *Principium Individuationis.* From what has been said, it is easy to discover what is so much inquired after, the *principium individuationis*; and that, it is plain, is existence itself; which determines a being of any sort to a particular time and place, incommunicable to two beings of the same kind. Thus, though it seems easier to conceive in simple substances or modes; yet, when reflected on, is not more difficult in compound ones, if care be taken to what it is applied: v.g. let us suppose an atom, i.e. a continued body under one immutable superficies, existing in a determined time and place; it is evident, that, considered in any instant of its existence, it is in that instant the same with itself. For, being at that instant what it is, and nothing else, it is the same, and so must continue as long as its existence is continued; for so long it will be the same, and no other. In like manner, if two or more atoms be joined together into the same mass, every one of those atoms will be the same, by the foregoing rule: and whilst they exist united together, the mass, consisting of the same atoms, must be the same mass, or the same body, let the parts be ever so differently jumbled. But if one of these atoms be taken away, or one new one added, it is no longer the same mass or the same body. In the state of living creatures, their identity depends not on a mass of the same particles, but on something else. For in them the variation of great parcels of matter alters not the identity: an oak growing from a plant to a great tree, and then lopped, is still the same oak; and a colt grown up to a horse, sometimes fat, sometimes lean, is all the while the same horse: though, in both these cases, there may be a manifest change of the parts; so that truly they are not either of them the same masses of matter, though they be truly one of them the same oak, and the other the same horse. The reason whereof is, that, in these two cases—a *mass of matter* and a *living body*—identity is not applied to the same thing.

4. *Identity of Vegetables.* We must therefore consider wherein an oak differs from a mass of matter, and that seems to me to be in this, that the one is only the cohesion of particles of matter any how united, the other such a disposition of them as constitutes the parts of an oak; and such an organization of those parts as is fit to receive and distribute nourishment, so as to continue and frame the wood, bark, and leaves, &c., of an oak, in which consists the vegetable life. That being then one plant which has such an organization of parts in one coherent body, partaking of one common life, it continues to be the same plant as long as it partakes of the same life, though that life be communicated to new particles of matter vitally united to the living plant, in a like continued organization conformable to that sort of plants. For this organization, being at any one instant in any one collection of matter, is in that particular concrete distinguished from all other, and *is* that individual life, which existing constantly from that moment both forwards and backwards, in the same continuity of insensibly succeeding parts united to the living body of the plant, it has that identity which makes the same plant, and all the parts of it, parts of the same plant, during all the time that they exist united in that

continued organization, which is fit to convey that common life to all the parts so united.

5. *Identity of Animals.* The case is not so much different in *brutes* but that any one may hence see what makes an animal and continues it the same. Something we have like this in machines, and may serve to illustrate it. For example, what is a watch? It is plain it is nothing but a fit organization or construction of parts to a certain end, which, when a sufficient force is added to it, it is capable to attain. If we would suppose this machine one continued body, all whose organized parts were repaired, increased, or diminished by a constant addition or separation of insensible parts, with one common life, we should have something very much like the body of an animal; with this difference, that, in an animal the fitness of the organization, and the motion wherein life consists, begin together, the motion coming from within; but in machines the force coming sensibly from without, is often away when the organ is in order, and well fitted to receive it.

6. *The Identity of Man.* This also shows wherein the identity of the same *man* consists; viz. in nothing but a participation of the same continued life, by constantly fleeting particles of matter, in succession vitally united to the same organized body. He that shall place the identity of man in anything else, but, like that of other animals, in one fitly organized body, taken in any one instant, and from thence continued, under one organization of life, in several successively fleeting particles of matter united to it, will find it hard to make an embryo, one of years, mad and sober, the *same* man, by any supposition, that will not make it possible for Seth, Ismael, Socrates, Pilate, St. Austin, and Caesar Borgia, to be the same man. For if the identity of *soul alone* makes the same *man*; and there be nothing in the nature of matter why the same individual spirit may not be united to different bodies, it will be possible that those men, living in distant ages, and of different tempers, may have been the same man: which way of speaking must be from a very strange use of the word man, applied to an idea out of which body and shape are excluded. And that way of speaking would agree yet worse with the notions of those philosophers who allow of transmigration, and are of opinion that the souls of men may, for their miscarriages, be detruded into the bodies of beasts, as fit habitations, with organs suited to the satisfaction of their brutal inclinations. But yet I think nobody, could he be sure that the *soul* of Heliogabalus were in one of his hogs, would yet say that hog were a *man* or *Heliogabalus*.

9. *Personal Identity.* This being premised, to find wherein personal identity consists, we must consider what *person* stands for;—which, I think, is a thinking intelligent being, that has reason and reflection, and can consider itself as itself, the same thinking thing, in different times and places; which it does only by that consciousness which is inseparable from thinking, and, as it seems to me, essential to it: it being impossible for any one to perceive without *perceiving* that he does perceive. When we see, hear, smell, taste, feel, meditate, or will anything, we know that we do so. Thus it is always as to our present sensations and perceptions: and by this every one is to himself that which he calls *self*:—it not being considered, in this case, whether the same self be continued in the same or divers substances. For, since consciousness always accompanies thinking, and it is that which makes everyone to be what he calls self, and thereby distinguishes himself from all other thinking things, in this alone consists personal identity, i.e. the sameness of a rational being: and as far as this consciousness can be extended backwards to any past action or thought, so far reaches the identity of that person; it is the same self now it was then; and it is by the same self with this present one that now reflects on it, that that action was done.

10. *Consciousness makes personal Identity.* But it is further inquired, whether it be the same identical substance. This few would think they had reason to doubt of, if these perceptions, with their consciousness, always remained present in the mind, whereby the same thinking thing would be always consciously present, and, as would be thought, evidently the same to itself. But that which seems to make the difficulty is this, that this consciousness being interrupted always by forgetfulness, there being no moment of our lives wherein we have the whole train of all our past actions before our eyes in one view, but even the best memories losing the sight of one part whilst they are viewing another; and we sometimes, and that the

greatest part of our lives, not reflecting on our past selves, being intent on our present thoughts, and in sound sleep having no thoughts at all, or at least none with that consciousness which remarks our waking thoughts,—I say, in all these cases, our consciousness being interrupted, and we losing the sight of our past selves, doubts are raised whether we are the same thinking thing, i.e., the same *substance* or no. Which, however reasonable or unreasonable, concerns not *personal* identity at all. The question being what makes the same person, and not whether it be the same identical substance, which always thinks in the same person, which, in this case, matters not at all: different substances, by the same consciousness (where they do partake in it) being united into one person, as well as different bodies by the same life are united into one animal, whose identity is preserved in that change of substances by the unity of one continued life. For, it being the same consciousness that makes a man be himself to himself, personal identity depends on that only, whether it be annexed solely to one individual substance, or can be continued in a succession of several substances. For as far as any intelligent being *can* repeat the idea of any past action with the same consciousness it had of it at first, and with the same consciousness it has of any present action; so far it is the same personal self. For it is by the consciousness it has of its present thoughts and actions, that it is *self to itself* now, and so will be the same self, as far as the same consciousness can extend to actions past or to come; and would be by distance of time, or change of substance, no more two persons, than a man be two men by wearing other clothes today than he did yesterday, with a long or a short sleep between: the same consciousness uniting those distant actions into the same person, whatever substances contributed to their production.

16. *Consciousness alone unites actions into the same Person.* But though the same immaterial substance or soul does not alone, wherever it be, and in whatsoever state, make the same *man*; yet it is plain, consciousness, as far as ever it can be extended—should it be to ages past—unites existences and actions very remote in time into the same *person*, as well as it does the existences and actions of the immediately preceding moment: so that whatever has the consciousness of present and past actions, is the same person to whom they both belong. Had I the same consciousness that I saw the ark and Noah's flood, as that I saw an overflowing of the Thames last winter, or as that I write now, I could no more doubt that I who write this now, that saw the Thames overflowed last winter, and that viewed the flood at the general deluge, was the same *self*,—place that self in what *substance* you please—than that I who write this am the same *myself* now while I write (whether I consist of all the same substance, material or immaterial, or no) that I was yesterday. For as to this point of being the same self, it matters not whether this present self be made up of the same or other substances—I being as much concerned, and as justly accountable for any action that was done a thousand years since, appropriated to me now by this self-consciousness, as I am for what I did the last moment.

17. *Self depends on Consciousness, not on Substance.* *Self* is that conscious thinking thing,—whatever substance made up of, (whether spiritual or material, simple or compounded, it matters not)—which is sensible or conscious of pleasure and pain, capable of happiness or misery, and so is concerned for itself, as far as that consciousness extends. Thus every one finds that, whilst comprehended under that consciousness, the little finger is as much a part of himself as what is most so. Upon separation of this little finger, should this consciousness go along with the little finger, and leave the rest of the body, it is evident the little finger would be the person, the same person; and self then would have nothing to do with the rest of the body. As in this case it is the consciousness that goes along with the substance, when one part is separate from another, which makes the same person, and constitutes this inseparable self: so it is in reference to substances remote in time. That with which the consciousness of this present thinking thing *can* join itself, makes the same person, and is one self with it, and with nothing else; and so attributes to itself, and owns all the actions of that thing, as its own, as far as that consciousness reaches, and no further; as every one who reflects will perceive.

18. *Persons, not Substances, the Objects of Reward and Punishment.* In this personal identity is

founded all the right and justice of reward and punishment; happiness and misery being that for which every one is concerned for *himself*, and not mattering what becomes of any *substance*, not joined to, or affected with that consciousness. For, as it is evident in the instance I gave but now, if the consciousness went along with the little finger when it was cut off, that would be the same self which was concerned for the whole body yesterday, as making part of itself, whose actions then it cannot but admit as its own now. Though, if the same body should still live, and immediately from the separation of the little finger have its own peculiar consciousness, whereof the little finger knew nothing, it would not at all be concerned for it, as a part of itself, or could own any of its actions, or have any of them imputed to him.

20. *Absolute oblivion separates what is thus forgotten from the person, but not from the man.* But yet possibly it will still be objected,—Suppose I wholly lose the memory of some parts of my life, beyond a possibility of retrieving them, so that perhaps I shall never be conscious of them again; yet am I not the same person that did those actions, had those thoughts that I once was conscious of, though I have now forgot them? To which I answer, that we must here take notice what the word *I* is applied to; which, in this case, is the *man* only. And the same man being presumed to be the same person, I is easily here supposed to stand also for the same person. But if it be possible for the same man to have distinct incommunicable consciousness at different times, it is past doubt the same man would at different times make different persons; which, we see, is the sense of mankind in the solemnest declaration of their opinions, human laws not punishing the mad man for the sober man's actions, nor the sober man for what the mad man did,—thereby making them two persons: which is somewhat explained by our way of speaking in English when we say such an one is 'not himself,' or is 'beside himself'; in which phrases it is insinuated, as if those who now, or at least first used them, thought that self was changed; the self-same person was no longer in that man.

22. But is not a man drunk and sober the same person? Why else is he punished for the fact he commits when drunk, though he be never afterwards conscious of it? Just as much the same person as a man that walks, and does other things in his sleep, is the same person, and is answerable for any mischief he shall do in it. Human laws punish both, with a justice suitable to *their* way of knowledge;—because, in these cases, they cannot distinguish certainly what is real, what counterfeit: and so the ignorance in drunkenness or sleep is not admitted as a plea. For, though punishment be annexed to personality, and personality to consciousness, and the drunkard perhaps be not conscious of what he did, yet human judicatures justly punish him; because the fact is proved against him, but want of consciousness cannot be proved for him. But in the Great Day, wherein the secrets of all hearts shall be laid open, it may be reasonable to think, no one shall be made to answer for what he knows nothing of; but shall receive his doom, his conscience accusing or excusing him.

25. *Consciousness unites substances, material or spiritual, with the same personality.* I agree, the more probable opinion is, that this consciousness is annexed to, and the affection of, one individual immaterial substance.

But let men, according to their diverse hypotheses, resolve of that as they please. This every intelligent being, sensible of happiness or misery, must grant—that there is something that is *himself*, that he is concerned for, and would have happy; that this self has existed in a continued duration more than one instant, and therefore it is possible may exist, as it has done, months and years to come, without any certain bounds to be set to its duration; and may be the same self, by the same consciousness continued on for the future. And thus, by this consciousness he finds himself to be the same self which did such and such an action some years since, by which he comes to be happy or miserable now. In all which account of self, the same numerical *substance* is not considered as making the same self; but the same continued *consciousness*, in which several substances may have been united, and again separated from it, which, whilst they continued in a vital union with that wherein this consciousness then resided, made a part of that same self. Thus any part of our bodies, vitally united to that which is conscious in us, makes a part of ourselves: but upon separation from the vital union by which that consciousness is communicated, that which a moment since was part of ourselves, is now no more so than a part of another man's self is a part of me: and it is not impossible but in a little time may become a real part of another person. And so we have the same numerical substance become a part of two different persons; and the same person preserved under the change of various substances. Could we suppose any spirit wholly stripped of all its memory or consciousness of past actions, as we find our minds always are of a great part of ours, and sometimes of them all; the union or separation of such a spiritual substance would make no variation of personal identity, any more than that of any particle of matter does. Any substance vitally united to the present thinking being is a part of that very same self which now is; anything united to it by a consciousness of former actions, makes also a part of the same self, which is the same both then and now.

BOOK III

OF WORDS

Chapter II

OF THE SIGNIFICATION OF WORDS

1. *Words are sensible Signs, necessary for Communication of Ideas.* Man, though he have great variety of thoughts, and such from which others as well as himself might receive profit and delight; yet they are all within his own breast, invisible and hidden from others, nor can of themselves be made to appear. The comfort and advantage of society not being to be had without communication of thoughts, it was necessary that man should find out some external sensible signs, whereof those invisible ideas, which his thoughts are made up of, might be made known to others. For this purpose nothing was so fit, either for plenty or quickness, as those articulate sounds, which with so much ease and variety he found himself able to make. Thus we may conceive how *words*, which were by nature so well adapted to that purpose, came to be made use of by men as the signs of their ideas; not by any natural connexion that there is between particular articulate sounds and certain ideas, for then there would be but one language amongst all men; but by a voluntary imposition, whereby such a word is made arbitrarily the mark of such an idea. The use, then, of words, is to be sensible marks of ideas; and the ideas they stand for are their proper and immediate signification.

3. *Examples of this.* This is so necessary in the use of language, that in this respect the knowing and the ignorant, the learned and the unlearned, use the words they speak (with any meaning) all alike. They, in every man's mouth, stand for the ideas he has, and which he would express by them. A child having taken notice of nothing in the metal he hears called *gold*, but the bright shining yellow colour, he applies the word gold only to his own idea of that colour, and nothing else; and therefore calls the same colour in a peacock's tail gold. Another that hath better observed, adds to shining yellow great weight: and then the sound gold, when he uses it, stands for a complex idea of a shining yellow and a very weighty substance. Another adds to those qualities fusibility: and then the word gold signifies to him a body, bright, yellow, fusible, and very heavy. Another adds malleability. Each of these uses equally the word gold, when they have occasion to express the idea which they have applied it to: but it is evident that each can apply it only to his own idea; nor can be make it stand as a sign of such a complex idea as he has not.

Chapter III

OF GENERAL TERMS

1. *The greatest Part of Words are general terms.* All things that exist being particulars, it may perhaps be thought reasonable that words, which ought to be conformed to things, should be so too,—I mean in their signification: but yet we find quite the contrary. The far greatest part of the words that make all languages are general terms: which has not been the effect of neglect or chance, but of reason and necessity.

2. *That every particular Thing should have a Name for itself is impossible.* First, It is impossible that every particular thing should have a distinct peculiar name. For, the signification and use of words depending on that connexion which the mind makes between its ideas and the sounds it uses as signs of them, it is necessary, in the application of names to things,

that the mind should have distinct ideas of the things, and retain also the particular name that belongs to every one, with its peculiar appropriation to that idea. But it is beyond the power of human capacity to frame and retain distinct ideas of all the particular things we meet with: every bird and beast men saw; every tree and plant that affected the senses, could not find a place in the most capacious understanding. If it be looked on as an instance of a prodigious memory, that some generals have been able to call every soldier in their army by his proper name, we may easily find a reason why men have never attempted to give names to each sheep in their flock, or crow that flies over their heads; much less to call every leaf of plants, or grain of sand that came in their way, by a peculiar name.

3. *And would be useless, if it were possible.* Secondly, If it were possible, it would yet be useless; because it would not serve to the chief end of language. Men would in vain heap up names of particular things, that would not serve them to communicate their thoughts. Men learn names, and use them in talk with others, only that they may be understood: which is then only done when, by use or consent, the sound I make by the organs of speech, excites in another man's mind who hears it, the idea I apply it to in mine, when I speak it. This cannot be done by names applied to particular things; whereof I alone having the ideas in my mind, the names of them could not be significant or intelligible to another, who was not acquainted with all those very particular things which had fallen under my notice.

4. *A distinct name for every particular thing, not fitted for enlargement of knowledge.* Thirdly, But yet, granting this also feasible, (which I think is not,) yet a distinct name for every particular thing would not be of any great use for the improvement of knowledge: which, though founded in particular things, enlarges itself by general views; to which things reduced into sorts, under general names, are properly subservient. These, with the names belonging to them, come within some compass, and do not multiply every moment, beyond what either the mind can contain, or use requires. And therefore, in these, men have for the most part stopped: but yet not so as to hinder themselves from distinguishing particular things by appropriated names, where convenience demands it. And therefore in their own species, which they have most to do with, and wherein they have often occasion to mention particular persons, they make use of proper names; and there distinct individuals have distinct denominations.

5. *What things have proper Names and why.* Besides persons, countries also, cities, rivers, mountains, and other the like distinctions of place have usually found peculiar names, and that for the same reason; they being such as men have often an occasion to mark particularly, and, as it were, set before others in their discourses with them. And I doubt not but, if we had reason to mention particular horses as often as we have to mention particular men, we should have proper names for the one, as familiar as for the other, and Bucephalus would be a word as much in use as Alexander. And therefore we see that, amongst jockeys, horses have their proper names to be known and distinguished by, as commonly as their servants: because, amongst them, there is often occasion to mention this or that particular horse when he is out of sight.

6. *How general words are made.* The next thing to be considered is,—How general words come to be made. For, since all things that exist are only particulars, how come we by general terms; or where find we those general natures they are supposed to stand for? Words become general by being made the signs of general ideas: and ideas become general, by separating from them the circumstances of time and place, and any other ideas that may determine them to this or that particular existence. By this way of abstraction they are made capable of representing more individuals than one; each of which having in it a conformity to that abstract idea, is (as we call it) of that sort.

7. *Shown by the way we enlarge our complex ideas from infancy.* But, to deduce this a little more distinctly, it will not perhaps be amiss to trace our notions and names from their beginning, and observe by what degrees we proceed, and by what steps we enlarge our ideas from our first infancy. There is nothing more evident, than that the ideas of the persons children converse with (to instance in them alone) are like

the persons themselves, only particular. The ideas of the nurse and the mother are well framed in their minds; and, like pictures of them there, represent only those individuals. The names they first gave to them are confined to these individuals; and the names of *nurse* and *mamma*, the child uses, determine themselves to those persons. Afterwards, when time and a larger acquaintance have made them observe that there are a great many other things in the world, that in some common agreements of shape, and several other qualities, resemble their father and mother, and those persons they have been used to, they frame an idea, which they find those many particulars do partake in; and to that they give, with others, the name *man*, for example. And thus they come to have a general name, and a general idea. Wherein they make nothing new; but only leave out of the complex idea they had of Peter and James, Mary and Jane, that which is peculiar to each, and retain only what is common to them all.

8. *And further enlarge our complex ideas, by still leaving out properties contained in them.* By the same way that they come by the general name and idea of *man*, they easily advance to more general names and notions. For, observing that several things that differ from their idea of man, and cannot therefore be comprehended under that name, have yet certain qualities wherein they agree with man, by retaining only those qualities, and uniting them into one idea, they have again another and more general idea; to which having given a name they make a term of a more comprehensive extension: which new idea is made, not by any new addition, but only as before, by leaving out the shape, and some other properties signified by the name man, and retaining only a body, with life, sense, and spontaneous motion, comprehended under the name *animal*.

9. *General natures are nothing but abstract and partial ideas of more complex ones.* That this is the way whereby men first formed general ideas, and general names to them, I think is so evident, that there needs no other proof of it but the considering of a man's self, or others, and the ordinary proceedings of their minds in knowledge. And he that thinks *general natures* or *notions* are anything else but such abstract and partial ideas of more complex ones, taken at first from particular existences, will, I fear, be at a loss where to find them. For let any one effect, and then tell me, wherein does his idea of *man* differ from that of *Peter* and *Paul*, or his idea of *horse* from that of *Bucephalus*, but in the leaving out something that is peculiar to each individual, and retaining so much of those particular complex ideas of several particular existences as they are found to agree in? Of the complex ideas signified by the names *man* and *horse*, leaving out but those particulars wherein they differ, and retaining only those wherein they agree, and of those making a new distinct complex idea, and giving the name *animal* to it, one has a more general term, that comprehends with man several other creatures. Leave out of the idea of *animal*, sense and spontaneous motion, and the remaining complex idea, made up of the remaining simple ones of body, life, and nourishment, becomes a more general one, under the more comprehensive term, *vivens*. And, not to dwell longer upon this particular, so evident in itself; by the same way the mind proceeds to *body, substance*, and at last to *being, thing*, and such universal terms, which stand for any of our ideas whatsoever. To conclude: this whole mystery of genera and species, which make such a noise in the schools, and are with justice so little regarded out of them, is nothing else but *abstract ideas*, more or less comprehensive, with names annexed to them. In all which this is constant and unvariable, that every more general term stands for such an idea, and is but a part of any of those contained under it.

10. *Why the Genus is ordinarily made Use of in Definitions.* This may show us the reason why, in the defining of words, which is nothing but declaring their signification, we make use of the *genus*, or next general word that comprehends it. Which is not out of necessity, but only to save the labour of enumerating the several simple ideas which the next general word or *genus* stands for; or, perhaps, sometimes the shame of not being able to do it. But though defining by *genus* and *differentia* (I crave leave to use these terms of art, though originally Latin, since they most properly suit those notions they are applied to), I say, though defining by the *genus* be the shortest way, yet I think it may be doubted whether it be the best. This I am sure, it is not the only, and so not absolutely necessary. For, definition being nothing but making

another understand by words what idea the term defined stands for, a definition is best made by enumerating those simple ideas that are combined in the signification of the term defined: and, if, instead of such an enumeration, men have accustomed themselves to use the next general term, it has not been out of necessity, or for greater clearness, but for quickness and dispatch sake. For I think that, to one who desired to know what idea the word *man* stood for; if it should be said, that man was a solid extended substance, having life, sense, spontaneous motion, and the faculty of reasoning, I doubt not but the meaning of the term man would be as well understood, and the idea it stands for be at least as clearly made known, as when it is defined to be a rational animal: which, by the several definitions of *animal*, *vivens*, and *corpus*, resolves itself into those enumerated ideas. I have, in explaining the term *man*, followed here the ordinary definition of the schools; which, though perhaps not the most exact, yet serves well enough to my present purpose. And one may, in this instance, see what gave occasion to the rule, that a definition must consist of *genus* and *differentia*; and it suffices to show us the little necessity there is of such a rule, or advantage in the strict observing of it. For, definitions, as has been said, being only the explaining of one word by several others, so that the meaning or idea it stands for may be certainly known; languages are not always so made according to the rules of logic, that every term can have its signification exactly and clearly expressed by two others. Experience sufficiently satisfies us to the contrary; or else those who have made this rule have done ill, that they have given us so few definitions conformable to it. But of definitions more in the next chapter.

11. *General and Universal are Creatures of the Understanding, and belong not to the Real Existence of things.* To return to general words: it is plain, by what has been said, that *general* and *universal* belong not to the real existence of things; but are the inventions and creatures of the understanding, made by it for its own use, and concern only signs, whether words or ideas. Words are general, as has been said, when used for signs of general ideas, and so are applicable indifferently to many particular things; and ideas are general when they are set up as the representatives of many particular things: but universality belongs not to things themselves, which are all of them particular in their existence, even those words and ideas which in their signification are general. When therefore we quit particulars, the generals that rest are only creatures of our own making; their general nature being nothing but the capacity they are put into, by the understanding, of signifying or representing many particulars. For the signification they have is nothing but a relation that, by the mind of man, is added to them.

12. *Abstract Ideas are the Essences of Genera and Species.* The next thing therefore to be considered is, What kind of signification it is that general words have. For, as it is evident that they do not signify barely one particular thing; for then they would not be general terms, but proper names, so, on the other side, it is as evident they do not signify a plurality; for *man* and *men* would then signify the same; and the distinction of numbers (as the grammarians call them) would be superfluous and useless. That then which general words signify is a *sort* of things; and each of them does that, by being a sign of an abstract idea in the mind; to which idea, as things existing are found to agree, so they come to be ranked under that name, or, which is all one, be of that sort. Whereby it is evident that the *essences* of the sorts, or, if the Latin word pleases better, *species* of things, are nothing else but these abstract ideas. For the having the essence of any species, being that which makes anything to be of that species; and the conformity to the idea to which the name is annexed being that which gives a right to that name; the having the essence, and the having that conformity, must needs be the same thing: since to be of any species, and to have a right to the name of that species, is all one. As, for example, to be a *man*, or of the *species* man, and to have right to the *name* man, is the same thing, Again, to be a man, or of the species man, and have the *essence* of a man, is the same thing, Now, since nothing can be a man, or have a right to the name man, but what has a conformity to the abstract idea the name man stands for, nor anything be a man, or have a right to the species man, but what has the essence of that species; it follows, that the abstract idea for which the name stands, and the essence of the species, is one and the same. From whence it is easy to observe, that the essences of the sorts of things,

and, consequently, the sorting of things, is the workmanship of the understanding that abstracts and makes those general ideas.

13. *They are the Workmanship of the Understanding, but have their Foundation in the Similitude of Things.* I would not here be thought to forget, much less to deny, that Nature, in the production of things, makes several of them alike: there is nothing more obvious, especially in the races of animals, and all things propagated by seed. But yet I think we may say, *the sorting of them under names is the workmanship of the understanding, taking occasion, from the similitude it observes amongst them, to make abstract general ideas*, and set them up in the mind, with names annexed to them, as patterns or forms, (for, in that sense, the word *form* has a very proper signification,) to which as particular things existing are found to agree, so they come to be of that species, have that denomination, or are put into that *classis*. For when we say this is a man, that a horse; this justice, that cruelty; this a watch, that a jack; what do we else but rank things under different specific names, as agreeing to those abstract ideas, of which we have made those names the signs? And what are the essences of those species set out and marked by names, but those abstract ideas in the mind; which are, as it were, the bonds between particular things that exist, and the names they are to be ranked under? And when general names have any connexion with particular beings, these abstract ideas are the medium that unites them: so that the essences of species, as distinguished and denominated by us, neither are nor can be anything but those precise abstract ideas we have in our minds. And therefore the supposed real essences of substances, if different from our abstract ideas, cannot be the essences of the species *we* rank things into. For two species may be one, as rationally as two different essences be the essence of one species: and I demand what are the alterations [which] may, or may not be made in a *horse* or *lead*, without making either of them to be of another species? In determining the species of things by *our* abstract ideas, this is easy to resolve, but if any one will regulate himself herein by supposed *real* essences, he will, I suppose, be at a loss: and he will never be able to know when anything precisely cease to be of the species of a *horse* or *lead*.

14. *Each distinct abstract Idea is a distinct Essence.* Nor will any one wonder that I say these essences, or abstract ideas (which are the measures of name, and the boundaries of species) are the workmanship of the understanding, who considers that at least the complex ones are often, in several men, different collections of simple ideas; and therefore that is *covetousness* to one man, which is not so to another. Nay, even in substances, where their abstract ideas seem to be taken from the things themselves, they are not constantly the same; no, not in that species which is most familiar to us, and with which we have the most intimate acquaintance: it having been more than once doubted, whether the *foetus* born of a woman were a *man*, even so far as that it hath been debated, whether it were or were not to be nourished and baptized: which could not be, if the abstract idea or essence to which the name man belonged were of nature's making; and were not the uncertain and various collection of simple ideas, which the understanding put together, and then, abstracting it, affixed a name to it. So that, in truth, every distinct abstract idea is a distinct essence; and the names that stand for such distinct ideas are the names of things essentially different. Thus a circle is as essentially different from an oval as a sheep from a goat; and rain is as essentially different from snow as water from earth: that abstract idea which is the essence of one being impossible to be communicated to the other. And thus any two abstract ideas, that in any part vary one from another, with two distinct names annexed to them, constitute two distinct sorts, or, if you please, *species*, as essentially different as any two of the most remote or opposite in the world.

15. *Several significations of the word Essence.* But since the essences of things are thought by some (and not without reason) to be wholly unknown, it may not be amiss to consider the several significations of the word *essence*.

First, Essence may be taken for the very being of anything, whereby it is what it is. And thus the real internal, but generally (in substances) unknown constitution of things, whereon their discoverable qualities depend, may be called their essence. This is the proper original signification of the word, as is evident from the formation of it; *essentia*, in its primary notation, signifying properly, being. And in this sense it is still used, when we speak of the essence of *particular* things, without giving them any name.

Secondly, The learning and disputes of the schools having been much busied about *genus* and *species*, the word *essence* has almost lost its primary signification: and, instead of the real constitution of things, has been almost wholly applied to the artificial constitution of *genus* and *species*. It is true, there is ordinarily supposed a real constitution of the sorts of things; and it is past doubt there must be some real constitution, on which any collection of simple ideas co-existing must depend. But, it being evident that things are ranked under names into sorts or species, only as they agree to certain abstract ideas, to which we have annexed those names, the essence of each *genus*, or sort, comes to be nothing but that abstract idea which the general, or sortal (if I may have leave so to call it from sort, as I do general from genus,) name stands for. And this we shall find to be that which the word essence imports in its most familiar use.

These two sorts of essences, I suppose, may not unfitly be termed, the one the *real*, the other *nominal essence*.

16. *Constant Connexion between the Name and nominal Essence.* Between the *nominal essence* and the *name* there is so near a connexion, that the name of any sort of things cannot be attributed to any particular being but what has this essence, whereby it answers that abstract idea whereof that name is the sign.

17. *Supposition, that Species are distinguished by their real Essences useless.* Concerning the *real essences* of corporeal substances (to mention these only) there are, if I mistake not, two opinions. The one is of those who, using the word essence for they know not what, suppose a certain number of those essences, according to which all natural things are made, and wherein they do exactly every one of them partake, and so become of this or that species. The other and more rational opinion is of those who look on all natural things to have a real, but unknown, constitution of their insensible parts; from which flow those sensible qualities which serve us to distinguish them one from another, according as we have occasion to rank them into sorts, under common denominations. The former of these opinions, which supposes these essences as a certain number of forms or moulds, wherein all natural things that exist are cast, and do equally partake, has, I imagine, very much perplexed the knowledge of natural things. The frequent productions of monsters, in all the species of animals, and of changelings, and other strange issues of human birth, carry with them difficulties, not possible to consist with this hypothesis; since it is as impossible that two things partaking exactly of the same real essence should have different properties, as that two figures partaking of the same real essence of a circle should have different properties. But were there no other reason against it, yet the supposition of essences that cannot be known; and the making of them, nevertheless, to be that which distinguishes the species of things, is so wholly useless and unserviceable to any part of our knowledge, that that alone were sufficient to make us lay it by, and content ourselves with such essences of the sorts or species of things as come within the reach of our knowledge: which, when seriously considered, will be found, as I have said, to be nothing else but, those *abstract* complex ideas to which we have annexed distinct general names.

18. *Real and nominal Essence, the same in simple Ideas and Modes, different in Substances.* Essences being thus distinguished into nominal and real, we may further observe, that, in the species of simple ideas and modes, they are always the same; but in substances always quite different. Thus, a figure including a space between three lines, is the real as well as nominal essence of a triangle; it being not only the abstract idea to which the general name is annexed, but the very *essentia* or being of the thing itself; that foundation from which all its properties flow, and to which they are all inseparably annexed. But it is far otherwise concerning that parcel of matter which makes the ring on my finger; wherein these two essences are apparently different. For, it is the real constitution of its insensible parts, on which depend all those properties of colour, weight, fusibility, fixedness, &c., which are to be found in it; which constitution we know not, and so, having no particular idea of, having no name that is the sign of it. But yet it is its colour, weight, fusibility, fixedness, &c., which makes it to be gold, or gives it a right to that name, which is therefore its nominal essence. Since nothing can be called gold but what has a conformity of qualities to that abstract complex idea to which that

name is annexed. But this distinction of essences, belonging particularly to substances, we shall, when we come to consider their names, have an occasion to treat of more fully.

19. *Essences ingenerable and incorruptible.* That such abstract ideas, with names to them, as we have been speaking of are essences, may further appear by what we are told concerning essences, viz. that they are all ingenerable and incorruptible. Which cannot be true of the real constitutions of things, which begin and perish with them. All things that exist, besides their Author, are all liable to change; especially those things we are acquainted with, and have ranked into bands under distinct names or ensigns. Thus, that which was grass to-day is to-morrow the flesh of a sheep; and, within a few days after, becomes part of a man: in all which and the like changes, it is evident their real essence—i.e. that constitution whereon the properties of these several things depended—is destroyed, and perishes with them. But essences being taken for ideas established in the mind, with names annexed to them, they are supposed to remain steadily the same, whatever mutations the particular substances are liable to. For, whatever becomes of *Alexander* and *Bucephalus*, the ideas to which *man* and *horse* are annexed, are supposed nevertheless to remain the same; and so the essences of those species are preserved whole and undestroyed, whatever changes happen to any or all of the individuals of those species. By this means the essence of a species rests safe and entire, without the existence of so much as one individual of that kind. For, were there now no circle existing anywhere in the world, (as perhaps that figure exists not anywhere exactly marked out,) yet the idea annexed to that name would not cease to be what it is; nor cease to be as a pattern to determine which of the particular figures we meet with have or have not a right to the *name* circle, and so to show which of them, by having that essence, was of that species. And though there neither were nor had been in nature such a beast as *unicorn*, or such a fish as a *mermaid*; yet, supposing those names to stand for complex abstract ideas that contained no inconsistency in them, the essence of a mermaid is as intelligible as that of a man; and the idea of an unicorn as certain, steady, and permanent as that of a horse. From what has been said, it is evident, that the doctrine of the immutability of essences proves them to be only abstract ideas; and is founded on the relation established between them and certain sounds as signs of them; and will always be true, as long as the same name can have the same signification.

20. *Recapitulation.* To conclude. This is that which in short I would say, viz. that all the great business of *genera* and *species*, and their *essences*, amounts to no more but this:—That men making abstract ideas, and settling them in their minds with names annexed to them, do thereby enable themselves to consider things, and discourse of them, as it were in bundles, for the easier and readier improvement and communication of their knowledge, which would advance but slowly were their words and thoughts confined only to particulars.

Chapter IV

OF SIMPLE IDEAS

5. *If all names were definable, it would be a Process* in infinitum. I will not here trouble myself to prove that all terms are not definable, from that progress *in infinitum*, which it will visibly lead us into, if we should allow that all names could be defined. For, if the terms of one definition were still to be defined by another, where at last should we stop? But I shall, from the nature of our ideas, and the signification of our words, show *why some names can, and others cannot be defined*; and *which they are.*

6. *What a Definition is.* I think it is agreed, that a *definition* is nothing else but *the showing the meaning of one word by several other not synonymous terms.* The meaning of words being only the ideas they are made to stand for by him that uses them, the meaning of any term is then showed, or the word is defined, when, by other words, the idea it is made the sign of, and annexed to, in the mind of the speaker, is as it were represented, or set before the view of another; and thus its signification ascertained. This is the only use and end of definitions; and therefore the only measure of what is, or is not a good definition.

7. *Simple Ideas, why undefinable.* This being premised, I say that the *names of simple ideas, and*

those only, are incapable of being defined. The reason whereof is this, That the several terms of a definition, signifying several ideas, they can all together by no means represent an idea which has no composition at all: and therefore a definition, which is properly nothing but the showing the meaning of one word by several others not signifying each the same thing, can in the names of simple ideas have no place.

Chapter VI

OF THE NAMES OF SUBSTANCES

1. *The common Names of Substances stand for Sorts.* The common names of substances, as well as other general terms, stand for *sorts*: which is nothing else but the being made signs of such complex ideas wherein several particular substances do or might agree, by virtue of which they are capable of being comprehended in one common conception, and signified by one name. I say do or might agree: for though there be but one sun existing in the world, yet the idea of it being abstracted, so that more substances (if there were several) might each agree in it, it is as much a sort as if there were as many suns as there are stars. They want not their reasons who think there are, and that each fixed star would answer the idea the name sun stands for, to one who was placed in a due distance: which, by the way, may show us how much the sorts, or, if you please, *genera* and *species* of things (for those Latin terms signify to me no more than the English word sort) depend on such collections of ideas as men have made, and not on the real nature of things; since it is not impossible but that, in propriety of speech, that might be a sun to one which is a star to another.

2. *The Essence of each Sort of substance is our abstract Idea to which the name is annexed.* The measure and boundary of each sort or species, whereby it is constituted that particular sort, and distinguished from others, is that we call its *essence*, which is nothing but that abstract idea to which the name is annexed; so that everything contained in that idea is essential to that sort. This, though it be all the essence of natural substances that *we* know, or by which we distinguish them into sorts, yet I call it by a peculiar name, the *nominal essence*, to distinguish it from the real constitution of substances, upon which depends this nominal essence, and all the properties of that sort; which, therefore, as has been said, may be called the *real essence*: v.g. the nominal essence of gold is that complex idea the word gold stands for, let it be, for instance, a body yellow, of a certain weight, malleable, fusible, and fixed. But the real essence is the constitution of the insensible parts of that body, on which those qualities and all the other properties of gold depend. How far these two are different, though they are both called essence, is obvious at first sight to discover.

3. *The nominal and real Essence different.* For, though perhaps voluntary motion, with sense and reason, joined to a body of a certain shape, be the complex idea to which I and others annex the name *man*, and so be the nominal essence of the species so called: yet nobody will say that complex idea is the real essence and source of all those operations which are to be found in any individual of that sort. The foundation of all those qualities which are the ingredients of our complex idea, is something quite different: and had we such a knowledge of that constitution of man, from which his faculties of moving, sensation, and reasoning, and other powers flow, and on which his so regular shape depends, as it is possible angels have, and it is certain his Maker has, we should have a quite other idea of his essence than what now is contained in our definition of that species, be it what it will: and our idea of any individual man would be as far different from what it is now, as is his who knows all the springs and wheels and other contrivances within of the famous clock at Strasburg, from that which a gazing countryman has of it, who barely sees the motion of the hand, and hears the clock strike, and observes only some of the outward appearances.

4. *Nothing essential to Individuals.* That *essence*, in the ordinary use of the word, relates to sorts, and that it is considered in particular beings no further than as they are ranked into sorts, appears from hence: that, take but away the abstract ideas by which we sort individuals, and rank them under common names, and then the thought of anything essential to any of them instantly vanishes: we have no notion of the one without the other, which plainly shows their relation. It is necessary for me to be as I am; God and nature has made me so: but there is nothing I

have is essential to me. An accident or disease may very much alter my colour or shape; a fever or fall may take away my reason or memory, or both; and an apoplexy leave neither sense, nor understanding, no, nor life. Other creatures of my shape may be made with more and better, or fewer and worse faculties than I have; and others may have reason and sense in a shape and body very different from mine. None of these are essential to the one or the other, or to any individual whatever, till the mind refers it to some sort of species of things; and then presently, according to the abstract idea of that sort, something is found essential. Let any one examine his own thoughts, and he will find that as soon as he supposes or speaks of essential, the consideration of some species, or the complex idea signified by some general name, comes into his mind; and it is in reference to that that this or that quality is said to be essential. So that if it be asked, whether it be essential to me or any other particular corporeal being, to have reason? I say, no; no more than it is essential to this white thing I write on to have words in it. But if that particular being be to be counted of the sort *man*, and to have the name *man* given it, then reason is essential to it; supposing reason to be a part of the complex idea the name man stands for: as it is essential to this thing I write on to contain words, if I will give it the name *treatise*, and rank it under that species. So that essential and not essential relate only to our abstract ideas, and the names annexed to them; which amounts to no more than this, that whatever particular thing has not in it those qualities which are contained in the abstract idea which any general term stands for, cannot be ranked under that species, nor be called by that name; since that abstract idea is the very essence of that species.

5. *The only essences perceived by us in individual substances are those qualities which entitle them to receive their names.* Thus, if the idea of *body* with some people be bare extension or space, then solidity is not essential to body: if others make the idea to which they give the name *body* to be solidity and extension, then solidity is essential to body. That therefore, and that alone, is considered as essential, which makes a part of the complex idea the name of a sort stands for; without which no particular thing can be reckoned of that sort, nor be entitled to that name. Should there be found a parcel of matter that had all the other qualities that are in iron, but wanted obedience to the loadstone, and would neither be drawn by it nor receive direction from it, would any one question whether it wanted anything essential? It would be absurd to ask, Whether a thing really existing wanted anything essential to it. Or could it be demanded, Whether this made an essential or specific difference or no, since *we* have no other measure of essential or specific but our abstract ideas? And to talk of specific differences in *nature*, without reference to general ideas in names, is to talk unintelligibly. For I would ask for any one, What is sufficient to make an essential difference in nature between any two particular beings, without any regard had to some abstract idea, which is looked upon as the essence and standard of a species? All such patterns and standards being quite laid aside, particular beings, considered barely in themselves, will be found to have all their qualities equally essential; and everything in each individual will be essential to it; or, which is more, nothing at all. For, though it may be reasonable to ask, Whether obeying the magnet be essential to iron? yet I think it is very improper and insignificant to ask, whether it be essential to the particular parcel of matter I cut my pen with; without considering it under the name *iron*, or as being of a certain species. And if, as has been said, our abstract ideas, which have names annexed to them, are the boundaries of species, nothing can be essential but what is contained in those ideas.

6. *Even the real essences of individual substances imply potential sorts.* It is true, I have often mentioned a *real essence*, distinct in substances from those abstract ideas of them, which I call their nominal essence. By this real essence I mean, that real constitution of anything, which is the foundation of all those properties that are combined in, and are constantly found to co-exist with the nominal essence; that particular constitution which everything has within itself, without any relation to anything without it. But essence, even in this sense, *relates to a sort, and supposes a species.* For, being that real constitution on which the properties depend, it necessarily supposes a sort of things, properties belonging only to species, and not to individuals: v.g. supposing the nominal essence of gold to be a body of such a peculiar colour and

weight, with malleability and fusibility, the real essence is that constitution of the parts of matter on which these qualities and their union depend; and is also the foundation of its solubility in *aqua regia* and other properties, accompanying that complex idea. Here are essences and properties, but all upon supposition of a sort or general abstract idea, which is considered as immutable; but there is no individual parcel of matter to which any of these qualities are so annexed as to be essential to it or inseparable from it. That which is essential belongs to it as a condition whereby it is of this or that sort: but take away the consideration of its being ranked under the name of some abstract idea, and then there is nothing necessary to it, nothing inseparable from it. Indeed, as to the real essences of substances, we only suppose their being, without precisely knowing what they are; but that which annexes them still to the species is the nominal essence, of which they are the supposed foundation and cause.

7. *The nominal Essence bounds the Species for us.* The next thing to be considered is, by which of those essences it is that substances are determined into sorts or species; and that, it is evident, is by the nominal essence. For it is that alone that the name, which is the mark of the sort, signifies. It is impossible, therefore, that anything should determine the sorts of things, which *we* rank under general names, but that idea which that name is designed as a mark for; which is that, as has been shown, which we call nominal essence. Why do we say this is a horse, and that a mule; this is an animal, that an herb? How comes any particular thing to be of this or that sort, but because it has that nominal essence; or, which is all one, agrees to that abstract idea, that name is annexed to? And I desire any one but to reflect on his own thoughts, when he fears or speaks any of those or other names of substances, to know what sort of essences they stand for.

8. *The nature of Species, as formed by us.* And that the species of things to us are nothing but the ranking them under distinct names, according to the complex ideas in *us*, and not according to precise, distinct, real essences in *them*, is plain from hence:—That we find many of the individuals that are ranked into one sort, called by one common name, and so received as being of one species, have yet qualities, depending on their real constitutions, as far different one from another as from others from which they are accounted to differ specifically. This, as it is easy to be observed by all who have to do with natural bodies, so chemists especially are often, by sad experience, convinced of it, when they, sometimes in vain, seek for the same qualities in one parcel of sulphur, antimony, or vitriol, which they have found in others. For, though they are bodies of the same species, having the same nominal essence, under the same name, yet do they often, upon severe ways of examination, betray qualities so different one from another, as to frustrate the expectation and labour of very wary chemists. But if things were distinguished into species, according to their real essences, it would be as impossible to find different properties in any two individual substances of the same species, as it is to find different properties in two circles, or two equilateral triangles. That is properly the essence to *us*, which determines every particular to this or that *classis*; or, which is the same thing, to this or that general name: and what can that be else, but that abstract idea to which that name is annexed; and so has, in truth, a reference, not so much to the being of particular things, as to their general denominations?

9. *Not the real Essence, or texture of parts, which we know not.* Nor indeed can we rank and sort things, and consequently (which is the end of sorting) denominate them, by their real essences; because we know them not. Our faculties carry us no further towards the knowledge and distinction of substances, than a collection of *those sensible ideas which we observe in them*; which, however made with the greatest diligence and exactness we are capable of, yet is more remote from the true internal constitution from which those qualities flow, than, as I said, a countryman's idea is from the inward contrivance of that famous clock at Strasburg, whereof he only sees the outward figure and motions. There is not so contemptible a plant or animal, that does not confound the most enlarged understanding. Though the familiar use of things about us take off our wonder, yet it cures not our ignorance. When we come to examine the stones we tread on, or the iron we daily handle, we presently find we know not their make; and can give no reason of the different qualities we find in them.

It is evident the internal constitution, whereon their properties depend, is unknown to us: for to go no further than the grossest and most obvious we can imagine amongst them, What is that texture of parts, that real essence, that makes lead and antimony fusible, wood and stones not? What makes lead and iron malleable, antimony and stones not? And yet how infinitely these come short of the fine contrivances and inconceivable real essences of plants or animals, every one knows. The workmanship of the all-wise and powerful God in the great fabric of the universe, and every part thereof, further exceeds the capacity and comprehension of the most inquisitive and intelligent man, than the best contrivance of the most ingenious man doth the conceptions of the most ignorant of rational creatures. Therefore we in vain pretend to range things into sorts, and dispose them into certain classes under names, by their real essences, that are so far from our discovery or comprehension. A blind man may as soon sort things by their colours, and he that has lost his smell as well distinguish a lily and a rose by their odours, as by those internal constitutions which he knows not. He that thinks he can distinguish sheep and goats by their real essences, that are unknown to him, may be pleased to try his skill in those species called *cassiowary* and *querechinchio*; and by their internal real essences determine the boundaries of those species, without knowing the complex idea of sensible qualities that each of those names stand for, in the countries where those animals are to be found.

13. *The Nominal Essence that of the Species, as conceived by us, proved from Water and Ice.* But to return to the species of corporeal substances. If I should ask any one whether ice and water were two distinct species of things, I doubt not but I should be answered in the affirmative: and it cannot be denied but he that says they are two distinct species is in the right. But if an Englishman bred in Jamaica, who perhaps had never seen nor heard of ice, coming into England in the winter, find the water he put in his basin at night in a great part frozen in the morning, and, not knowing any peculiar name it had, should call it hardened water; I ask whether this would be a new species to him, different from water? And I think it would be answered here, It would not be to him a new species, no more than congealed jelly, with it is cold, is a distinct species from the same jelly fluid and warm; or than liquid gold in the furnace is a distinct species from hard gold in the hands of a workman. And if this be so, it is plain that *our distinct species* are *nothing but distinct complex ideas, with distinct names annexed to them.* It is true every substance that exists has its peculiar constitution, whereon depend those sensible qualities and powers we observe in it; but the ranking of things into species (which is nothing but sorting them under several titles) is done by us according to the ideas that *we* have of them: which, though sufficient to distinguish them by names, so that we may be able to discourse of them when we have them not present before us; yet if we suppose it to be done by their real internal constitutions, and that things existing are distinguished by nature into species, by real essences, according as we distinguish them into species by names, we shall be liable to great mistakes.

14. *Difficulties in the supposition of a certain number of real Essences.* To distinguish substantial being into species, according to the usual supposition, that there are certain precise essences of forms of things, whereby all the individuals existing are, by nature distinguished into species, these things are necessary:—

15. *A crude supposition.* First, To be assured that nature, in the production of things, always designs them to partake of certain regulated established essences, which are to be the models of all things to be produced. This, in that crude sense it is usually proposed, would need some better explication, before it can fully be assented to.

16. *Monstrous births.* Secondly, It would be necessary to know whether nature always attains that essence it designs in the production of things. The irregular and monstrous births, that in divers sorts of animals have been observed, will always give us reason to doubt of one or both of these.

17. *Are monsters really a distinct species?*
Thirdly, It ought to be determined whether those we call monsters be really a distinct species, according to the scholastic notion of the word species; since it is certain that everything that exists has its particular

constitution. And yet we find that some of these monstrous productions have few or none of those qualities which are supposed to result from, and accompany, the essence of that species from whence they derive their originals, and to which, by their descent, they seem to belong.

18. *Men can have no ideas of Real Essences.* Fourthly, The real essences of those things which we distinguish into species, and as so distinguished we name, ought to be known; i.e. we ought to have ideas of them. But since we are ignorant in these four points, the supposed real essences of things stand *us* not in stead for the distinguishing substances into species.

19. *Our Nominal Essences of Substances not perfect collections of the properties that flow from their Real Essences.* Fifthly, The only imaginable help in this case would be, that, having framed perfect complex ideas of the properties of things flowing from their different real essences, we should thereby distinguish them into species. But neither can this be done. For, being ignorant of the real essence itself, it is impossible to know all those properties that flow from it, and are so annexed to it, that any one of them being away, we may certainly conclude that that essence is not there, and so the thing is not of that species. We can never know what is the precise number of properties depending on the real essence of gold, any one of which failing, the real essence of gold, and consequently gold, would not be there, unless we knew the real essence of gold itself, and by that determined that species. By the word *gold* here, I must be understood to design a particular piece of matter; v.g. the last guinea that was coined. For, if it should stand here, in its ordinary signification, for that complex idea which I or any one else calls gold, i.e. for the nominal essence of gold, it would be jargon. So hard is it to show the various meaning and imperfection of words, when we have nothing else but words to do it by.

20. *Hence names independent of Real Essences.* By all which it is clear, that our distinguishing substances into species by names, is not at all founded on their real essences; nor can we pretend to range and determine them exactly into species, according to internal essential differences.

21. *But stand for such a collection of simple ideas as we have made the Name stand for.* But since, as has been remarked, we have need of *general* words, though we know not the real essences of things; all we can do is, to collect such a number of simple ideas as, by examination, we find to be united together in things existing, and thereof to make one complex idea. Which, though it be not the real essence of any substance that exists, is yet the specific essence to which our name belongs, and is convertible with it; by which we may at least try the truth of these nominal essences. For example: there be that say that the essence of body is *extension*; if it be so, we can never mistake in putting the essence of anything for the thing itself. Let us then in discourse put extension for body, and when we would say that body moves, let us say that extension moves, and see how ill it will look. He that should say that one extension by impulse moves another extension, would, by the bare expression, sufficiently show the absurdity of such a notion. The essence of anything in respect of us, is the whole complex idea comprehended and marked by that name; and in substances, besides the several distinct simple ideas that make them up, the confused one of substance, or of an unknown support and cause of their union, is always a part: and therefore the essence of body is not bare extension, but an extended solid thing; and so to say, an extended solid thing moves, or impels another, is all one, and as intelligible, as to say, *body* moves or impels. Likewise, to say that a rational animal is capable of conversation, is all one as to say a man; but no one will say that rationality is capable of conversation, because it makes not the whole essence to which we give the name man.

22. *Our Abstract Ideas are to us the Measures of the Species we make: instance in that of Man.* There are creatures in the world that have shapes like ours, but are hairy, and want language and reason. There are naturals amongst us that have perfectly our shape, but want reason, and some of them language too. There are creatures, as it is said, (*sit fides penes authorem*, but there appears no contradiction that there should be such,) that, with language and reason and a shape in other things agreeing with ours, have

hairy tails; others where the males have no beards, and others where the females have. If it be asked whether these be all *men* or no, all of human species? it is plain, the question refers only to the nominal essence: for those of them to whom the definition of the word man, or the complex idea signified by that name, agrees, are men, and the other not. But if the inquiry be made concerning the supposed real essence; and whether the internal constitution and frame of these several creatures be specifically different, it is wholly impossible for us to answer, no part of that going into our specific idea: only we have reason to think, that where the faculties or outward frame so much differs, the internal constitution is not exactly the same. But what difference in the real internal constitution makes a specific difference it is in vain to inquire; whilst our measures of species be, as they are, only our abstract ideas, which we know; and not that internal constitution, which makes no part of them. Shall the difference of hair only on the skin be a mark of a different internal specific constitution between a changeling and a drill, when they agree in shape, and want of reason and speech? And shall not the want of reason and speech be a sign to us of different real constitutions and species between a changeling and a reasonable man? And so of the rest, if we pretend that distinction of species or sorts is fixedly established by the real frame and secret constitutions of things.

25. *The specific Essences that are commonly made by Men.* But supposing that the *real* essences of substances were discoverable by those that would severely apply themselves to that inquiry, yet we could not reasonably think that the ranking of things under general names was regulated by those internal real constitutions, or anything else but their *obvious* appearances; since languages, in all countries, have been established long before sciences. So that they have not been philosophers or logicians, or such who have troubled themselves about forms and essences, that have made the general names that are in use amongst the several nations of men: but those more or less comprehensive terms have, for the most part, in all languages, received their birth and signification from ignorant and illiterate people, who sorted and denominated things by those sensible qualities they found in them; thereby to signify them, when absent, to others, whether they had an occasion to mention a sort or a particular thing.

26. *Therefore very various and uncertain in the ideas of different men.* Since then it is evident that we sort and name substances by their nominal and not by their real essences, the next thing to be considered is how, and by whom these essences come to be made. As to the latter, it is evident they are made by the mind, and not by nature: for were they Nature's workmanship, they could not be so various and different in several men as experience tells us they are. For if we will examine it, we shall not find the nominal essence of any one species of substances in all men the same: no, not of that which of all others we are the most intimately acquainted with. It could not possibly be that the abstract idea to which the name *man* is given should be different in several men, if it were of Nature's making; and that to one it should be *animal rationale*, and to another, *animal implume bipes latis unguibus*. He that annexes the name man to a complex idea, made up of sense and spontaneous motion, joined to a body of such a shape, has thereby one essence of the species man; and he that, upon further examination, adds rationality, has another essence of the species he calls man: by which means the same individual will be a true man to the one which is not so to the other. I think there is scarce any one will allow this upright figure, so well known, to be the essential difference of the species man; and yet how far men determine of the sorts of animals rather by their shape than descent, is very visible; since it has been more than once debated, whether several human foetuses should be preserved or received to baptism or no, only because of the difference of their outward configuration from the ordinary make of children, without knowing whether they were not as capable of reason as infants cast in another mould: some whereof, though of an approved shape, are never capable of as much appearance of reason all their lives as is to be found in an ape, or an elephant, and never give any signs of being acted by a rational soul. Whereby it is evident, that the outward figure, which only was found wanting, and not the faculty of reason, which nobody could know would be wanting in its due season, was made essential to the human species. The learned divine and lawyer must, on such occasions, renounce his sacred definition of *animal ratio-*

nale, and substitute some other essence of the human species. Monsieur Menage[4] furnishes us with an example worth the taking notice of on this occasion: 'When the abbot of Saint Martin,' says he, 'was born, he had so little of the figure of a man, that it bespake him rather a monster. It was for some time under deliberation, whether he should be baptized or no. However, he was baptized, and declared a man provisionally till time should show what he would prove. Nature had moulded him so untowardly, that he was called all his life the Abbot Malotru; i.e. ill-shaped. He was of Caen.' (*Menagiana*, 278, 430.) This child, we see, was very near being excluded out of the species of man, barely by his shape. He escaped very narrowly as he was; and it is certain, a figure a little more oddly turned had cast him, and he had been executed, as a thing not to be allowed to pass for man. And yet there can be no reason given why, if the lineaments of his face had been a little altered, a rational soul could not have been lodged in him; why a visage somewhat longer, or a nose flatter, or a wider mouth, could not have consisted, as well as the rest of his ill figure, with such a soul, such parts, as made him, disfigured as he was, capable to be a dignitary in the church.

27. *Nominal Essences of particular substances are undetermined by nature, and therefore various as men vary.* Wherein, then, would I gladly know, consist the precise and unmovable boundaries of that species? It is plain, if we examine, there is no such thing made by Nature, and established by her amongst men. The real essence of that or any other sort of substances, it is evident, we know not; and therefore are so undetermined in our nominal essences, which we make ourselves, that, if several men were to be asked concerning some oddly-shaped *foetus*, as soon as born, whether it were a *man* or no, it is past doubt one should meet with different answers. Which could not happen, if the nominal essences whereby we limit and distinguish the species of substances, were not made by man with some liberty; but were exactly copied from precise boundaries set by nature, whereby it distinguished all substances into certain species. Who would undertake to resolve what species that monster was of which is mentioned by Licetus (lib. i. c. 3),[5] with a man's head and hog's body? Or those other which to the bodies of men had the heads of beasts, as dogs, horses, &c. If any of these creatures had lived, and could have spoke, it would have increased the difficulty. Had the upper part to the middle been of human shape, and all below swine, had it been murder to destroy it? Or must the bishop have been consulted, whether it were man enough to be admitted to the font or no? As I have been told it happened in France some years since, in somewhat a like case. So uncertain are the boundaries of species of animals to us, who have no other measures than the complex ideas of our own collecting: and so far are we from certainly knowing what a *man* is; though perhaps it will be judged great ignorance to make any doubt about it. And yet I think I may say, that the certain boundaries of that species are so far from being determined, and the precise number of simple ideas which make the nominal essence so far from being settled and perfectly known, that very material doubts may still arise about it. And I imagine none of the definitions of the word *man* which we yet have, nor descriptions of that sort of animal, are so perfect and exact as to satisfy a considerate inquisitive person; much less to obtain a general consent, and to be that which men would everywhere stick by, in the decision of cases, and determining of life and death, baptism or no baptism, in productions that might happen.

28. *But not so arbitrary as Mixed Modes.* But though these nominal essences of substances are made by the mind, they are not yet made so arbitrarily as those of mixed modes. To the making of any nominal essence, it is necessary, First, that the ideas whereof it consists have such a union as to make but one idea, how compounded soever. Secondly, that the particular ideas so united be exactly the same, neither more nor less. For if two abstract complex ideas differ either in number or sorts of their component parts, they make two different, and not one and the same essence. In the first of these, the mind, in making its complex ideas of substances, only follows nature; and puts none together which are not sup-

4. [Giles Menage (1613–1690) was a French philologist and critic.]

5. [Fortunato Liceto (1577–1657) was an Italian physician. The reference is to his *De Monstrorum Causis* (Of the Causes of Monsters).]

posed to have a union in nature. Nobody joins the voice of a sheep with the shape of a horse; nor the colour of lead with the weight and fixedness of gold, to be the complex ideas of any real substances; unless he has a mind to fill his head with chimeras, and his discourse with unintelligible words. Men observing certain qualities always joined and existing together, therein copied nature; and of ideas so united made their complex ones of substances. For, though men may make what complex ideas they please, and give what names to them they will; yet, if they will be understood *when they speak of things really existing*, they must in some degree conform their ideas to the things they would speak of; or else men's language will be like that of Babel,[6] and every man's words, being intelligible only to himself, would no longer serve to conversation and the ordinary affairs of life, if the ideas they stand for be not some way answering the common appearances and agreement of substances as they really exist.

29. *Our Nominal Essences of substances usually consist of a few obvious qualities observed in things.* Secondly, Though the mind of man, in making its complex ideas of substances, never puts any together that do not really, or are not supposed to, co-exist; and so it truly borrows that union from nature: yet the number it combines depends upon the various care, industry, or fancy of him that makes it. Men generally content themselves with some few sensible obvious qualities; and often, if not always, leave out others as material and as firmly united as those that they take. Of sensible substances there are two sorts: one of organized bodies, which are propagated by seed; and in these the *shape* is that which to us is the leading quality, and most characteristical part, that determines the species. And therefore in vegetables and animals, an extended solid substance of such a certain figure usually serves the turn. For however some men seem to prize their definition of *animal rationale*, yet should there a creature be found that had language and reason, but partaked not of the usual shape of a man, I believe it would hardly pass for a man, how much soever it were *animal rationale*. And if Balaam's ass[7] had all his life discoursed as rationally as he did once with his master, I doubt yet whether any one would have thought him worthy the name man, or allowed him to be of the same species with himself. As in vegetables and animals it is the shape, so in most other bodies, not propagated by seed, it is the *colour* we most fix on, and are most led by. Thus where we find the colour of gold, we are apt to imagine all the other qualities comprehended in our complex idea to be there also: and we commonly take these two obvious qualities, viz. shape and colour, for so presumptive ideas of several species, that in a good picture, we readily say, this is a lion, and that a rose; this is a gold, and that a silver goblet, only by the different figures and colours represented to the eye by the pencil.

30. *Yet, imperfect as they thus are, they serve for common converse.* But though this serves well enough for gross and confused conceptions, and inaccurate ways of talking and thinking; yet *men are far enough from having agreed on the precise number of simple ideas or qualities belonging to any sort of things, signified by its name.* Nor is it a wonder; since it requires much time, pains, and skill, strict inquiry, and long examination to find out what, and how many, those simple ideas are, which are constantly and inseparably united in nature, and are always to be found together in the same subject. Most men, wanting either time, inclination, or industry enough for this, even to some tolerable degree, content themselves with some few obvious and outward appearances of things, thereby readily to distinguish and sort them for the common affairs of life: and so, without further examination, give them names, or take up the names already in use. Which, though in common conversation they pass well enough for the signs of some few obvious qualities co-existing, are yet far enough from comprehending, in a settled signification, a precise number of simple ideas, much less all those which are united in nature. He that shall

6. [The reference is to a biblical story related in the Book of Genesis, according to which, at a time when all people spoke the same language, they attempted to build a tower that reached to heaven, but they were prevented from doing so by God, who confounded their language so they could not understand one another.]

7. [The reference is to a biblical story related in the Book of Numbers, according to which God gave the power of speech to the prophet Balaam's ass.]

consider, after so much stir about genus and species, and such a deal of talk of specific differences, how few words we have yet settled definitions of, may with reason imagine, that those *forms* which there hath been so much noise made about are only chimeras, which give us no light into the specific natures of things. And he that shall consider how far the names of substances are from having significations wherein all who use them do agree, will have reason to conclude that, though the nominal essences of substances are all supposed to be copied from nature, yet they are all, or most of them, very imperfect. Since the composition of those complex ideas are, in several men, very different: and therefore that these boundaries of species are as men, and not as Nature, makes them, if at least there are in nature any such prefixed bounds. It is true that many particular substances are so made by Nature, that they have agreement and likeness one with another, and so afford a foundation of being ranked into sorts. But the sorting of things by us, or the making of determinate species, being in order to naming and comprehending them under general terms, I cannot see how it can be properly said, that Nature sets the boundaries of the species of things: or, if it be so, our boundaries of species are not exactly conformable to those in nature. For we, having need of general names for present use, stay not for a perfect discovery of all those qualities which would *best* show us their most material differences and agreements; but we ourselves divide them, by certain obvious appearances, into species, that we may the easier under general names communicate our thoughts about them. For, having no other knowledge of any substance but of the simple ideas that are united in it; and observing several particular things to agree with others in several of those simple ideas; we make that collection our specific idea, and give it a general name; that in recording our thoughts, and in our discourse with others, we may in one short word designate all the individuals that agree in that complex idea, without enumerating the simple ideas that make it up; and so not waste our time and breath in tedious descriptions: which we see they are fain to do who would discourse of any new sort of things they have not yet a name for.

31. *Essences of Species under the same Name very different in different minds.* But however these species of substances pass well enough in ordinary conversation, it is plain that this complex idea, wherein they observe several individuals to agree, is by different men made very differently; by some more, and others less accurately. In some, this complex idea contains a greater, and in others a smaller number of qualities; and so is apparently such as the mind makes it. The yellow shining colour makes gold to children; others add weight, malleableness, and fusibility; and others yet other qualities, which they find joined with that yellow colour, as constantly as its weight and fusibility. For in all these and the like qualities, one has as good a right to be put into the complex idea of that substance wherein they are all joined as another. And therefore different men, leaving out or putting in several simple ideas which others do not, according to their various examination, skill, or observation of that subject, have different essences of gold, which must make therefore be of their own and not of nature's making.

32. *The more general our Ideas of Substances are, the more incomplete and partial they are.* If the number of simple ideas that make the nominal essence of the lowest species, or first sorting, of individuals, depends on the mind of man, variously collecting them, it is much more evident that they do so in the more comprehensive classes, which, by the masters of logic, are called *genera*. These are complex ideas designedly imperfect: and it is visible at first sight, that several of those qualities that are to be found in the things themselves are purposely left out of generical ideas. For, as the mind, to make general ideas comprehending several particulars, leaves out those of time and place, and such other, that make them incommunicable to more than one individual; so to make other yet more general ideas, that may comprehend different sorts, it leaves out those qualities that distinguish them, and puts into its new collection only such ideas as are common to several sorts. The same convenience that made men express several parcels of yellow matter coming from Guinea and Péru under one name, sets them also upon making of one name that may comprehend both gold and silver, and some other bodies of different sorts. This is done by leaving out those qualities, which are peculiar to each sort, and retaining a complex idea made up of those that are common to them all. To which

the name *metal* being annexed, there is a genus constituted; the essence whereof being that abstract idea, containing only malleableness and fusibility, with certain degrees of weight and fixedness, wherein some bodies of several kinds agree, leaves out the colour and other qualities peculiar to gold and silver, and the other sorts comprehended under the name metal. Whereby it is plain that men follow not exactly the patterns set them by nature, when they make their general ideas of substances; since there is no body to be found which has barely malleableness and fusibility in it, without other qualities as inseparable as those. But men, in making their general ideas, seeking more the convenience of language, and quick dispatch by short and comprehensive signs, that the true and precise nature of things as they exist, have, in the framing their abstract ideas, chiefly pursued that end; which was to be furnished with store of general and variously comprehensive names. So that in this whole business of genera and species, the genus, or more comprehensive, is but a partial conception of what is in the species; and the species but a partial idea of what is to be found in each individual. If therefore any one will think that a man, and a horse, and an animal, and a plant, &c., are distinguished by real essences made by nature, he must think nature to be very liberal of these real essences, making one for body, another for an animal, and another for a horse; and all these essences liberally bestowed upon Bucephalus. But if we would rightly consider what is done in all these genera and species, or sorts, we should find that there is no new thing made, but only more or less comprehensive signs, whereby we may be enabled to express in a few syllables great numbers of particular things, as they agree in more or less general conceptions, which we have framed to that purpose. In all which we may observe, that the more general term is always the name of a less complex idea; and that each genus is but a partial conception of the species comprehended under it. So that if these abstract general ideas be thought to be complete, it can only be in respect of a certain established relation between them and certain names which are made use of to signify them; and not in respect of anything existing, as made by nature.

33. *This all accommodated to the end of Speech.* This is adjusted to the true end of speech, which is to be the easiest and shortest way of communicating our notions. For thus he that would discourse of things, as they agreed in the complex idea of extension and solidity, needed but use the word *body* to denote all such. He that to these would join others, signified by the words life, sense, and spontaneous motion, needed but use the word *animal* to signify all which partaked of those ideas, and he that had made a complex idea of a body, with life, sense, and motion, with the faculty of reasoning, and a certain shape joined to it, needed but use the short monosyllable *man*, to express all particulars that correspond to that complex idea. This is the proper business of genus and species: and this men do without any consideration of real essences, or substantial forms; which come not within the reach of our knowledge when we think of those things, nor within the signification of our words when we discourse with others.

34. *Instance in Cassowaries.* Were I to talk with any one of a sort of birds I lately saw in St. James's Park, about three or four feet high, with a covering of something between feathers and hair, of a dark brown colour, without wings, but in the place thereof two or three little branches coming down like sprigs of Spanish broom, long great legs, with feet only of three claws, and without a tail; I must make this description of it, and so may make others understand me. But when I am told that the name of it is *cassuaris*, I may then use that word to stand in discourse for all my complex idea mentioned in that description; though by that word, which is now become a specific name, I know no more of the real essence or constitution of that sort of animals than I did before; and knew probably as much of the nature of that species of birds before I learned the name, as many Englishmen do of swans or herons, which are specific names, very well known, of sorts of birds common in England.

35. *Men determine the Sorts of Substances, which may be sorted variously.* From what has been said, it is evident that *men* make sorts of things. For, it being different essences alone that make different species, it is plain that they who make those abstract ideas which are the nominal essences do thereby make the species, or sort. Should there be a body found, having all the other qualities of gold except malleableness, it would no doubt be made a question

whether it were gold or not, i.e. whether it were of that species. This could be determined only by that abstract idea to which every one annexed the name gold: so that it would be true gold to him, and belong to that species, who included not malleableness in his nominal essence, signified by the sound gold; and on the other side it would not be true gold, or of that species, to him who included malleableness in his specific idea. And how, I pray, is it that makes these diverse species, even under one and the same name, but men that make two different abstract ideas, consisting not exactly of the same collection of qualities? Nor is it a mere supposition to imagine that a body may exist wherein the other obvious qualities of gold may be without malleableness; since it is certain that gold itself will be sometimes so eager, (as artists call it,) that it will as little endure the hammer as glass itself. What we have said of the putting in, or leaving out of malleableness, in the complex idea the name gold is by any one annexed to, may be said of its peculiar weight, fixedness, and several other the like qualities: for whatever is left out, or put in, it is still the complex idea to which that name is annexed that makes the species: and as any particular parcel of matter answers that idea, so the name of the sort belongs truly to it; and it is of that species. And thus anything is true gold, perfect metal. All which determination of the species, it is plain, depends on the understanding of man, making this or that complex idea.

36. *Nature makes the Similitudes of Substances.* This, then, in short, is the case: Nature makes many *particular things*, which do agree one with another in many sensible qualities, and probably too in their internal frame and constitution: but it is not this real essence that distinguishes them into species; it is men who, taking occasion from the qualities they find united in them, and wherein they observe often several individuals to agree, range them into sorts, in order to their naming, for the convenience of comprehensive signs; under which individuals, according to their conformity to this or that abstract idea, come to be ranked as under ensigns: so that this is of the blue, that the red regiment; this is a man, that a drill: and in this, I think, consists the whole business of genus and species.

BOOK IV

OF KNOWLEDGE AND PROBABILITY

Chapter I

OF KNOWLEDGE IN GENERAL

1. *Our Knowledge conversant about our Ideas only.* Since the mind, in all its thoughts and reasonings, hath no other immediate object but its own ideas, which it alone does or can contemplate, it is evident that our knowledge is only conversant about them.

2. *Knowledge is the Perception of the Agreement or Disagreement of two Ideas.* *Knowledge* then seems to me to be nothing but *the perception of the connexion of and agreement, or disagreement and repugnancy of any of our ideas.* In this alone it consists. Where this perception is, there is knowledge, and where it is not, there, though we may fancy, guess, or believe, yet we always come short of knowledge. For when we know that white is not black, what do we else but perceive, that these two ideas do not agree? When we possess ourselves with the utmost security of the demonstration, that the three angles of a triangle are equal to two right ones, what do we more but perceive, that equality to two right ones does necessarily agree to, and is inseparable from, the three angles of a triangle.

3. *This Agreement or Disagreement may be any of four sorts.* But to understand a little more distinctly wherein this agreement or disagreement consists, I think we may reduce it all to these four sorts:

I. *Identity*, or *diversity*.

II. *Relation*.

III. *Co-existence*, or *necessary connexion*.

IV. *Real existence*.

4. *First, Of Identity, or Diversity in ideas.* As to the first sort of agreement or disagreement, viz. *identity* or *diversity*. It is the first act of the mind, when it has any sentiments or ideas at all, to perceive its ideas; and so far as it perceives them, to know each what

it is, and thereby also to perceive their difference, and that one is not another. This is so absolutely necessary, that without it there could be no knowledge, no reasoning, no imagination, no distinct thoughts at all. By this the mind clearly and infallibly perceives each idea to agree with itself, and to be what it is; and all distinct ideas to disagree, i.e. the one not to be the other: and this it does without pains, labour, or deduction; but at first view, by its natural power of perception and distinction. And though men of art have reduced this into those general rules, *What is, is,* and *It is impossible for the same thing to be and not to be*, for ready application in all cases, wherein there may be occasion to reflect on it: yet it is certain that the first exercise of this faculty is about particular ideas. A man infallibly knows, as soon as ever he has them in his mind, that the ideas he calls *white* and *round* are the very ideas they are; and that they are not other ideas which he calls *red* or *square*. Nor can any maxim or proposition in the world make him know it clearer or surer than he did before, and without any such general rule. This then is the first agreement or disagreement which the mind perceives in its ideas; which it always perceives at first sight: and if there ever happen any doubt about it, it will always be found to be about the names, and not the ideas themselves, whose identity and diversity will always be perceived, as soon and clearly as the ideas themselves are; nor can it possibly be otherwise.

5. *Secondly, Of abstract Relations between ideas.* The next sort of agreement or disagreement the mind perceives in any of its ideas may, I think, be called *relative*, and is nothing but the perception of the *relation* between any two ideas, of what kind soever, whether substances, modes, or any other. For, since all distinct ideas must eternally be known not to be the same, and so be universally and constantly denied one of another, there could be no room for any positive knowledge at all, if we could not perceive any relation between our ideas, and find out the agreement or disagreement they have one with another, in several ways the mind takes of comparing them.

6. *Thirdly, Of their necessary Co-existence in Substances.* The third sort of agreement or disagreement to be found in our ideas, which the perception of the mind is employed about, is *co-existence* or *non-co-existence* in the *same subject*; and this belongs particularly to substances. Thus when we pronounce concerning gold, that it is fixed, our knowledge of this truth amounts to no more but this, that fixedness, or a power to remain in the fire unconsumed, is an idea that always accompanies and is joined with that particular sort of yellowness, weight, fusibility, malleableness, and solubility in *aqua regia*, which make our complex idea signified by the word gold.

7. *Fourthly, Of real Existence agreeing to any idea.* The fourth and last sort is that of *actual real existence* agreeing to any idea.

Within these four sorts of agreement or disagreement is, I suppose, contained all the knowledge we have, or are capable of. For all the inquiries we can make concerning any of our ideas, all that we know or can affirm concerning any of them, is, That it is, or is not, the same with some other; that it does or does not always co-exist with some other idea in the same subject; that it has this or that relation with some other idea; or that it has a real existence without the mind. Thus, 'blue is not yellow,' is of identity. 'Two triangles upon equal bases between two parallels are equal,' is of relation. 'Iron is susceptible of magnetical impressions,' is of co-existence. 'God is,' is of real existence. Though identity and co-existence are truly nothing but relations, yet they are such peculiar ways of agreement or disagreement of our ideas, that they deserve well to be considered as distinct heads, and not under relation in general; since they are so different grounds of affirmation and negation, as will easily appear to any one, who will but reflect on what is said in several places of this *Essay*.

Chapter II

OF THE DEGREES OF OUR KNOWLEDGE

1. *Of the degrees, or differences in clearness, of our Knowledge: I. Intuitive.* All our knowledge consisting, as I have said, in the view the mind has of its own ideas, which is the utmost light and greatest certainty we, with our faculties, and in our way of knowledge, are capable of, it may not be amiss to consider a little the degrees of its evidence. The different clearness of our knowledge seems to me to lie in the different way of perception the mind has of the

agreement or disagreement of any of its ideas. For if we will reflect on our own ways of thinking, we will find, that sometimes the mind perceives the agreement or disagreement of two ideas *immediately by themselves*, without the intervention of any other: and this I think we may call *intuitive knowledge*. For in this the mind is at no pains of proving or examining, but perceives the truth as the eye doth light, only by being directed towards it. Thus the mind perceives that *white* is not *black*, that a *circle* is not a *triangle*, that *three* are more than *two* and equal to *one and two*. Such kinds of truths the mind perceives at the first sight of the ideas together, by bare intuition; without the intervention of any other idea: and this kind of knowledge is the clearest and most certain that human frailty is capable of. This part of knowledge is irresistible, and, like bright sunshine, forces itself immediately to be perceived, as soon as ever the mind turns its view that way; and leaves no room for hesitation, doubt, or examination, but the mind is presently filled with the clear light of it. *It is on this intuition that depends all the certainty and evidence of all our knowledge*; which certainty every one finds to be so great, that he cannot imagine, and therefore not require a greater: for a man cannot conceive himself capable of a greater certainty than to know that any idea in his mind is such as he perceives it to be; and that two ideas, wherein he perceives a difference, are different and not precisely the same. He that demands a greater certainty than this, demands he knows not what, and shows only that he has a mind to be a sceptic, without being able to be so. Certainty depends so wholly on this intuition, that, in the next degree of knowledge which I call demonstrative, this intuition is necessary in all the connexions of the intermediate ideas, without which we cannot attain knowledge and certainty.

2. *II. Demonstrative.* The next degree of knowledge is, where the mind perceives the agreement or disagreement of any ideas, but not immediately. Though wherever the mind perceives the agreement or disagreement of any of its ideas, there be certain knowledge; yet it does not always happen, that the mind sees that agreement or disagreement, which there is between them, even where it is discoverable; and in that case remains in ignorance, and at most gets no further than a probable conjecture. The reason why the mind cannot always perceive presently the agreement or disagreement of two ideas, is, because those ideas, concerning whose agreement or disagreement the inquiry is made, cannot by the mind be so put together as to show it. In this case then, when the mind cannot so bring its ideas together as by their immediate comparison, and as it were juxtaposition or application one to another, to perceive their agreement or disagreement, it is fain, *by the intervention of other ideas* (one or more, as it happens) to discover the agreement or disagreement which it searches; and this is that which we call *reasoning*. Thus, the mind being willing to know the agreement or disagreement in bigness between the three angles of a triangle and two right ones, cannot by an immediate view and comparing them do it: because the three angles of a triangle cannot be brought at once, and be compared with any other one, or two, angles; and so of this the mind has no immediate, no intuitive knowledge. In this case the mind is fain to find out some other angles, to which the three angles of a triangle have an equality; and, finding those equal to two right ones, comes to know their equality to two right ones.

7. *Each Step in Demonstrated knowledge must have Intuitive Evidence.* Now, in every step reason makes in demonstrative knowledge, there is an intuitive knowledge of that agreement or disagreement it seeks with the next intermediate idea which it uses as a proof: for if it were not so, that yet would need a proof; since without the perception of such agreement or disagreement, there is no knowledge produced: if it be perceived by itself, it is intuitive knowledge: if it cannot be perceived by itself, there is need of some intervening idea, as a common measure, to show their agreement or disagreement. By which it is plain, that every step in reasoning that produces knowledge, has intuitive certainty; which when the mind perceives, there is no more required but to remember it, to make the agreement or disagreement of the ideas concerning which we inquire visible and certain. So that to make anything a demonstration, it is necessary to perceive the immediate agreement of the intervening ideas, whereby the agreement or disagreement of the two ideas under examination (whereof the one is always the first, and the other the last in the account) is found. This intu-

itive perception of the agreement or disagreement of the intermediate ideas, in each step and progression of the demonstration, must also be carried exactly in the mind, and a man must be sure that no part is left out: which, because in long deductions, and the use of many proofs, the memory does not always so readily and exactly retain; therefore it comes to pass, that this is more imperfect than intuitive knowledge, and men embrace often falsehood for demonstrations.

14. *III. Sensitive Knowledge of the particular Existence of finite beings without us.* These two, viz. intuition and demonstration, are the degrees of our *knowledge*; whatever comes short of one of these, with what assurance soever embraced, is but *faith*, or *opinion*, but not knowledge, at least in all general truths. There is, indeed, another perception of the mind, employed about *the particular existence of finite beings without us*, which, going beyond bare probability, and yet not reaching perfectly to either of the foregoing degrees of certainty, passes under the name of *knowledge*. There can be nothing more certain than that the idea we receive from an external object is in our minds: this is intuitive knowledge. But whether there be anything more than barely that idea in our minds; whether we can thence certainly infer the existence of anything without us, which corresponds to that idea, is that whereof some men think there may be a question made; because men may have such ideas in their minds, when no such thing exists, no such object affects their senses. But yet here I think we are provided with an evidence that puts us past doubting. For I ask any one, Whether he be not invincibly conscious to himself of a different perception, when he looks on the sun by day, and thinks on it by night; when he actually tastes wormwood, or smells a rose, or only thinks on that savour or odour? We as plainly find the difference there is between any idea revived in our minds by our own memory, and actually coming into our minds by our senses, as we do between any two distinct ideas. If any one say, a dream may do the same thing, and all these ideas may be produced in us without any external objects; he may please to dream that I make him this answer:—1. That it is no great matter, whether I remove his scruple or no: where all is but dream, reasoning and arguments are of no use, truth and knowledge nothing. 2. That I believe he will allow a very manifest difference between dreaming of being in the fire, and being actually in it. But yet if he be resolved to appear so sceptical as to maintain, that what I call being actually in the fire is nothing but a dream; and that we cannot thereby certainly know, that any such thing as fire actually exists without us: I answer, That we certainly finding that pleasure or pain follows upon the application of certain objects to us, whose existence we perceive, or dream that we perceive, by our senses; this certainty is as great as our happiness or misery, beyond which we have no concernment to know or to be. So that, I think, we may add to the two former sorts of knowledge this also, of the existence of particular external objects, by that perception and consciousness we have of the actual entrance of ideas from them, and allow these three degrees of knowledge, viz. *intuitive, demonstrative,* and *sensitive*: in each of which there are different degrees and ways of evidence and certainty.

Chapter III

OF THE EXTENT OF HUMAN KNOWLEDGE

1. *First, it extends no further than we have Ideas.* Knowledge, as has been said, lying in the perception of the agreement or disagreement of any of our ideas, it follows from hence, That,

First, we can have knowledge no further than we have *ideas*.

2. *It extends no further than we can perceive their Agreement or Disagreement.* Secondly, That we can have no knowledge further than we can have *perception* of that agreement or disagreement. Which perception being: 1. Either by *intuition*, or the immediate comparing any two ideas; or, 2. By *reason*, examining the agreement or disagreement of two ideas, by the intervention of some others; or, 3. By *sensation*, perceiving the existence of particular things: hence it also follows:

3. *Intuitive Knowledge extends itself not to all the relations of all our Ideas.* Thirdly, That we cannot have an *intuitive knowledge* that shall extend itself to all our ideas, and all that we would know about them; because we cannot examine and perceive all the relations they have one to another, by juxta-position, or

an immediate comparison one with another. Thus, having the ideas of an obtuse and an acute angled triangle, both drawn from equal bases, and between parallels, I can, by intuitive knowledge, perceive the one not to be the other, but cannot that way know whether they be equal or no; because their agreement or disagreement in equality can never be perceived by an immediate comparing them: the difference of figure makes their parts incapable of an exact immediate application; and therefore there is need of some intervening qualities to measure them by, which is demonstration, or rational knowledge.

4. *Nor does Demonstrative Knowledge.* Fourthly, It follows, also, from what is above observed, that our *rational knowledge* cannot reach to the whole extent of our ideas: because between two different ideas we would examine, we cannot always find such mediums as we can connect one to another with an intuitive knowledge in all the parts of the deduction; and wherever that fails, we come short of knowledge and demonstration.

5. *Sensitive Knowledge narrower than either.* Fifthly, *Sensitive knowledge* reaching no further than the existence of things actually present to our senses, is yet much narrower than either of the former.

6. *Our Knowledge, therefore, narrower than our Ideas.* Sixthly, From all which it is evident, that the *extent of our knowledge* comes not only short of the reality of things, but even of the extent of our own ideas. Though our knowledge be limited to our ideas, and cannot exceed them either in extent or perfection; and though these be very narrow bounds, in respect of the extent of All-being, and far short of what we may justly imagine to be in some even created understandings, not tied down to the dull and narrow information that is to be received from some few, and not very acute, ways of perception, such as are our senses; yet it would be well with us if our knowledge were but as large as our ideas, and there were not many doubts and inquiries *concerning the ideas we have,* whereof we are not, nor I believe ever shall be in this world resolved. Nevertheless, I do not question but that human knowledge, under the present circumstances of our beings and constitutions, may be carried much further than it has hitherto been, if men would sincerely, and with freedom of mind, employ all that industry and labour of thought, in improving the means of discovering truth, which they do for the colouring or support of falsehood, to maintain a system, interest, or party they are once engaged in. But yet after all, I think I may, without injury to human perfection, be confident, that our knowledge would never reach to all we might desire to know concerning those ideas we have; nor be able to surmount all the difficulties, and resolve all the questions that might arise concerning any of them. We have the ideas of a *square*, a *circle*, and *equality*; and yet, perhaps, shall never be able to find a circle equal to a square, and certainly know that it is so. We have the ideas of *matter* and *thinking*, but possibly shall never be able to know whether any mere material being thinks or no; it being impossible for us, by the contemplation of our own ideas, without revelation, to discover whether Omnipotency has not given to some systems of matter, fitly disposed, a power to perceive and think, or else joined and fixed to matter, so disposed, a thinking immaterial substance: it being, in respect of our notions, not much more remote from our comprehension to conceive that God can, if he pleases, superadd to matter a *faculty of thinking*, than that he should superadd to it *another substance with a faculty of thinking*; since we know not wherein thinking consists, nor to what sort of substances the Almighty has been pleased to give that power, which cannot be in any created being, but merely by the good pleasure and bounty of the Creator. For I see no contradiction in it, that the first Eternal thinking Being, or Omnipotent Spirit, should, if he pleased, give to certain systems of created senseless matter, put together as he thinks fit, some degrees of sense, perception, and thought: though, as I think I have proved, lib iv. ch. 10, § 14, &c., it is no less than a contradiction to suppose matter (which is evidently in its own nature void of sense and thought) should be that Eternal first-thinking Being. What certainty of knowledge can any one have, that some perceptions, such as, v.g., pleasure and pain, should not be in some bodies themselves, after a certain manner modified and moved, as well as that they should be in an immaterial substance, upon the motion of the parts of the body: Body, as far as we can conceive, being able only to strike and affect body, and motion, according to the utmost reach of our ideas, being able to produce

nothing but motion; so that when we allow it to produce pleasure or pain, or the idea of a colour or sound, we are fain to quit our reason, go beyond our ideas, and attribute it wholly to the good pleasure of our Maker. For, since we must allow He has annexed effects to motion which we can no way conceive motion able to produce, what reason have we to conclude that He could not order them as well to be produced in a subject we cannot conceive capable of them, as well as in a subject we cannot conceive the motion of matter can any way operate upon?

But to return to the argument in hand: our knowledge, I say, is not only limited to the paucity and imperfections of the ideas we have, and which we employ it about, but even comes short of that too: but how far it reaches, let us now inquire.

7. *How far our Knowledge reaches.* The affirmations or negations we make concerning the ideas we have, may, as I have before intimated in general, be reduced to these four sorts, viz. identity, co-existence, relation, and real existence. I shall examine how far our knowledge extends in each of these:

8. *Firstly, Our Knowledge of Identity and Diversity in ideas extends as far as our Ideas themselves.* First, as to *identity* and *diversity*. In this way of agreement or disagreement of our ideas, our intuitive knowledge is as far extended as our ideas themselves: and there can be no idea in the mind, which it does not, presently, by an intuitive knowledge, perceive to be what it is, and to be different from any other.

9. *Secondly, Of their Co-existence, extends only a very little way.* As to the second sort, which is the agreement or disagreement of our ideas in *co-existence*, in this our knowledge is very short; though in this consists the greatest and most material part of our knowledge concerning substances. For our ideas of the species of substances being, as I have showed, nothing but certain collections of simple ideas united in one subject, and so co-existing together; v.g. our idea of flame is a body hot, luminous, and moving upward; of gold, a body heavy to a certain degree, yellow, malleable, and fusible: for these, or some such complex ideas as these, in men's minds, do these two names of the different substances, flame and gold, stand for. When we would know anything further concerning these, or any other sort of substances, what do we inquire, but what *other* qualities or powers these substances have or have not? Which is nothing else but to know what *other* simple ideas do, or do not co-exist with those that make up that complex idea?

10. *Because the Connexion between simple Ideas in substances is for the most part unknown.* This, how weighty and considerable a part soever of human science, is yet very narrow, and scarce any at all. The reason whereof is, that the simple ideas whereof our complex ideas of substances are made up are, for the most part, such as carry with them, in their own nature, no *visible necessary* connexion or inconsistency with any other simple ideas, whose co-existence with them we would inform ourselves about.

11. *Especially of the secondary Qualities of Bodies.* The ideas that our complex ones of substances are made up of, and about which our knowledge concerning substances is most employed, are those of their secondary qualities; which depending all (as has been shown) upon the primary qualities of their minute and insensible parts; or, if not upon them, upon something yet more remote from our comprehension; it is impossible we should know which have a *necessary* union or inconsistency one with another. For, not knowing the root they spring from, not knowing what size, figure, and texture of parts they are, on which depend, and from which result those qualities which make our complex idea of gold, it is impossible we should know what *other* qualities result from, or are incompatible with, the same constitution of the insensible parts of gold; and so consequently must always co-exist with that complex idea we have of it, or else are inconsistent with it.

12. *Because necessary Connexion between any secondary and the primary Qualities is undiscoverable by us.* Besides this ignorance of the primary qualities of the insensible parts of bodies, on which depend all their secondary qualities, there is yet another and more incurable part of ignorance, which sets us more remote from a certain knowledge of the co-existence or *inco-existence* (if I may so say) of different ideas in the same subject; and that is, that there is no discoverable connexion between any secondary quality and those primary qualities which it depends on.

13. *We have no perfect knowledge of their Primary Qualities.* That the size, figure, and motion of one body should cause a change in the size, figure, and motion of another body, is not beyond our conception; the separation of the parts of one body upon the intrusion of another; and the change from rest to motion upon impulse; these and the like seem to have *some connexion* one with another. And if we knew these primary qualities of bodies, we might have reason to hope we might be able to know a great deal more of these operations of them one upon another: but our minds not being able to discover any connexion betwixt these primary qualities of bodies and the sensations that are produced in us by them, we can never be able to establish certain and undoubted rules of the *consequence* or *co-existence* of any secondary qualities, though we could discover the size, figure, or motion of those invisible parts which immediately produce them. We are so far from knowing *what* figure, size, or motion of parts produce a yellow colour, a sweet taste, or a sharp sound, that we can by no means conceive how *any* size, figure, or motion of any particles, can possibly produce in us the idea of any colour, taste, or sound whatsoever: there is no conceivable connexion between the one and the other.

14. *And seek in vain for certain and universal knowledge of unperceived qualities in substances.* In vain, therefore, shall we endeavour to discover by our ideas (the only true way of certain and universal knowledge) what other ideas are to be found constantly joined with that of *our* complex idea of any substance: since we neither know the real constitution of the minute parts on which their qualities do depend; nor, did we know them, could we discover any necessary connexion between them and any of the secondary qualities: which is necessary to be done before we can certainly know their necessary co-existence. So, that, let our complex idea of any species of substances be what it will, we can hardly, from the simple ideas contained in it, certainly determine the necessary co-existence of any other quality whatsoever. Our knowledge in all these inquiries reaches very little further than our experience. Indeed some few of the primary qualities have a necessary dependence and visible connexion one with another, as figure necessarily supposes extension; receiving or communicating motion by impulse, supposes solidity. But, though these, and perhaps some others of our ideas have: yet there are so few of them that have a visible connexion one with another, that we can by intuition or demonstration discover the co-existence of very few of the qualities that are to be found united in substances: and we are left only to the assistance of our senses to make known to us what qualities they contain. For of all the qualities that are co-existent in any subject, without this dependence and evident connexion of their ideas one with another, we cannot know certainly any two to co-exist, any further than experience, by our senses, informs us. Thus, though we see the yellow colour, and, upon trial, find the weight, malleableness, fusibility, and fixedness that are united in a piece of gold; yet, because no one of these ideas has any evident dependence or necessary connexion with the other, we cannot certainly know that where any four of these are, the fifth will be there also, how highly probable soever it may be; because the highest probability amounts not to certainty, without which there can be no true knowledge. For this co-existence can be no further known than it is perceived; and it cannot be perceived but either in particular subjects, by the observation of our senses, or, in general, by the necessary connexion of the ideas themselves.

18. *Thirdly, Of Relations between abstracted ideas it is not easy to say how far our knowledge extends.* As to the third sort of our knowledge, viz. the agreement or disagreement of any of our ideas in any other relation: this, as it is the largest field of our knowledge, so it is hard to determine how far it may extend: because the advances that are made in this part of knowledge, depending on our sagacity in finding intermediate ideas, that may show the relations and habitudes of ideas whose coexistence is not considered, it is a hard matter to tell when we are at an end of such discoveries; and when reason has all the helps it is capable of, for the finding of proofs, or examining the agreement or disagreement of remote ideas. They that are ignorant of Algebra cannot imagine the wonders in this kind are to be done by it: and what further improvements and helps advantageous to other parts of knowledge the sagacious mind of man may yet find out, it is not easy to determine. This at least I believe, that the *ideas of quantity* are not those alone

that are capable of demonstration and knowledge; and that other, and perhaps more useful, parts of contemplation, would afford us certainty, if vices, passions, and domineering interest did not oppose or menace such endeavours.

21. *Fourthly, Of the three real Existences of which we have certain knowledge.* As to the fourth sort of our knowledge, viz. of the *real actual existence of things*, we have an intuitive knowledge of *our own existence*, and a demonstrative knowledge of the existence of a *God*: of the existence of *anything else*, we have no other but a sensitive knowledge; which extends not beyond the objects present to our senses.

Chapter IV

OF THE REALITY OF KNOWLEDGE

1. *Objection. 'Knowledge placed in our Ideas may be all unreal or chimerical.'* I doubt not but my reader, by this time, may be apt to think that I have been all this while only building a castle in the air; and be ready to say to me:—

'To what purpose all this stir? Knowledge, say you, is only the perception of the agreement or disagreement of our own ideas: but who knows what those ideas may be? Is there anything so extravagant as the imaginations of men's brains? Where is the head that has no chimeras in it? Or if there be a sober and a wise man, what difference will there be, by your rules, between his knowledge and that of the most extravagant fancy in the world? They both have their ideas, and perceive their agreement and disagreement one with another. If there be any difference between them, the advantage will be on the warm-headed man's side, as having the more ideas, and the more lively. And so, by your rules, he will be the more knowing. If it be true, that all knowledge lies only in the perception of the agreement or disagreement of our own ideas, the visions of an enthusiast and the reasonings of a sober man will be equally certain. It is no matter how things are: so a man observe but the agreement of his own imaginations, and talk conformably, it is all truth, all certainty. Such castles in the air will be as strongholds of truth, as the demonstrations of Euclid. That an harpy is not a centaur is by this way as certain knowledge, and as much a truth, as that a square is not a circle.

'But of what use is all this fine knowledge of *men's own imaginations*, to a man that inquires after the reality of things? It matters not what men's fancies are, it is the knowledge of things that is only to be prized: it is this alone gives a value to our reasonings, and preference to one man's knowledge over another's, that it is of things as they really are, and not of dreams and fancies.'

2. *Answer. Not so, where Ideas agree with Things.* To which I answer, That if our knowledge of our ideas terminate in them, and reach no further, where there is something further intended, our most serious thoughts will be of little more use than the reveries of a crazy brain; and the truths built thereon of no more weight than the discourses of a man who sees things clearly in a dream, and with great assurance utters them. But I hope, before I have done, to make it evident, that this way of certainty, by the knowledge of our own ideas, goes a little further than bare imagination: and I believe it will appear that all the certainty of general truths a man has lies in nothing else.

3. *But what shall be the criterion of this agreement?* It is evident the mind knows not things immediately, but only by the intervention of the ideas it has of them. Our knowledge, therefore, is real only so far as there is a *conformity* between our ideas and the reality of things. But what shall be here the criterion? How shall the mind, when it perceives nothing but its own ideas, know that they agree with things themselves? This, though it seems not to want difficulty, yet, I think, there be two sorts of ideas that we may be assured agree with things.

4. *As, First, All Simple Ideas are really conformed to Things.* The first are simple ideas, which since the mind, as has been showed, can by no means make to itself, must necessarily be the product of things operating on the mind, in a natural way, and producing therein those perceptions which by the Wisdom and Will of our Maker they are ordained and adapted to. From whence it follows, that simple ideas are not fictions of our fancies, but the natural and regular productions of things without us, really operating upon us; and so carry with them all the conformity which is intended; or which our state requires: for they represent to us things under those appearances

which they are fitted to produce in us: whereby we are enabled to distinguish the sorts of particular substances, to discern the states they are in, and so to take them for our necessities, and apply them to our uses. Thus, the idea of whiteness, or bitterness, as it is in the mind, exactly answering that power which is in any body to produce it there, has all the real conformity it can or ought to have, with things without us. And this conformity between our simple ideas and the existence of things, is sufficient for real knowledge.

5. *Secondly, All Complex Ideas, except ideas of Substances, are their own archetypes.* Secondly, All our complex ideas, *except those of substances*, being archetypes of the mind's own making, not intended to be the copies of anything, nor referred to the existence of anything, as to their originals, cannot want any conformity necessary to real knowledge. For that which is not designed to represent anything but itself, can never be capable of a wrong representation, nor mislead us from the true apprehension of anything, by its dislikeness to it: and such, excepting those of substances, are all our complex ideas. Which, as I have showed in another place, are combinations of ideas, which the mind, by its free choice, puts together, without considering any connexion they have in nature. And hence it is, that in all these sorts the ideas themselves are considered as the archetypes, and things no otherwise regarded, but as they are conformable to them. So that we cannot but be infallibly certain, that all the knowledge we attain concerning these ideas is real, and reaches things themselves. Because in all our thoughts, reasonings, and discourses of this kind, we intend things no further than as they are conformable to our ideas. So that in these we cannot miss of a certain and undoubted reality.

6. *Hence the reality of Mathematical Knowledge.* I doubt not but it will be easily granted, that the knowledge we have of mathematical truths is not only certain, but real knowledge; and not the bare empty vision of vain, insignificant chimeras of the brain: and yet, if we will consider, we shall find that it is only of our own ideas. The mathematician considers the truth and properties belonging to a rectangle or circle only as they are an idea in his own mind. For it is possible he never found either of them existing mathematically, i.e. precisely true, in his life. But yet the knowledge he has of any truths or properties belonging to a circle, or any other mathematical figure, are nevertheless true and certain, even of real things existing: because real things are no further concerned, nor intended to be meant by any such propositions, than as things really agree to those archetypes in his mind. Is it true of the *idea* of a triangle, that its three angles are equal to two right ones? It is true also of a triangle, wherever it *really exists*. Whatever other figure exists, that it is not exactly answerable to that idea of a triangle in his mind, is not at all concerned in that proposition. And therefore he is certain all his knowledge concerning such ideas is real knowledge: because, intending things no further than they agree with those his ideas, he is sure what he knows concerning those figures, when they have *barely an ideal existence* in his mind, will hold true of them also when they have *a real existence* in matter: his consideration being barely of those figures, which are the same wherever or however they exist.

7. *And of Moral.* And hence it follows that moral knowledge is as capable of real certainty as mathematics. For certainty being but the perception of the agreement or disagreement of our ideas, and demonstration nothing but the perception of such agreement, by the intervention of other ideas or mediums; our moral ideas, as well as mathematical, being archetypes themselves, and so adequate and complete ideas; all the agreement or disagreement which we shall find in them will produce real knowledge, as well as in mathematical figures.

11. *Thirdly, Our complex Ideas of Substances have their Archetypes without us; and here knowledge comes short.* Thirdly, There is another sort of complex ideas, which, being referred to archetypes without us, may differ from them, and so our knowledge about them may come short of being real. Such are our ideas of substances, which, consisting of a collection of simple ideas, supposed taken from the works of nature, may yet vary from them; by having more or different ideas united in them than are to be found united in the things themselves. From whence it

comes to pass, that they may, and often do, fail of being exactly conformable to things themselves.

18. *Recapitulation.* Wherever we perceive the agreement or disagreement of any of our ideas, there is certain knowledge: and wherever we are sure those ideas agree with the reality of things, there is certain real knowledge. Of which agreement of our ideas with the reality of things, having here given the marks, I think, I have shown *wherein it is that certainty, real certainty, consists*. Which, whatever it was to others, was, I confess, to me heretofore, one of those desiderata which I found great want of.

Chapter VI
OF UNIVERSAL PROPOSITIONS: THEIR TRUTH AND CERTAINTY

1. *Treating of Words necessary to Knowledge.* Though the examining and judging of ideas by themselves, their names being quite laid aside, be the best and surest way to clear and distinct knowledge: yet, through the prevailing custom of using sounds for ideas, I think it is very seldom practised. Every one may observe how common it is for names to be made use of, instead of the ideas themselves, even when men think and reason within their own breasts; especially if the ideas be very complex, and made up of a great collection of simple ones. This makes the consideration of *words* and *propositions* so necessary a part of the Treatise of Knowledge, that it is very hard to speak intelligibly of the one, without explaining the other.

2. *General Truths hardly to be understood, but in verbal Propositions.* All the knowledge we have, being only of particular or general truths, it is evident that whatever may be done in the former of these, the latter, which is that which with reason is most sought after, can never be well made known, and is very seldom apprehended, but as conceived and expressed in words. It is not, therefore, out of our way, in the examination of our knowledge, to inquire into the truth and certainty of universal propositions.

3. *Certainty twofold—of Truth and of Knowledge.* But that we may not be misled in this case by that which is the danger everywhere, I mean by the doubtfulness of terms, it is fit to observe that certainty is twofold; *certainty of truth* and *certainty of knowledge*. Certainty of truth is, when words are so put together in propositions as exactly to express the agreement or disagreement of the ideas they stand for, as really it is. Certainty of knowledge is to perceive the agreement or disagreement of ideas, as expressed in any proposition. This we usually call knowing, or being certain of the truth of any proposition.

4. *No Proposition can be certainly known to be true, where the real Essence of each Species mentioned is not known.* Now, because we cannot be certain of the truth of any general proposition, unless we know the precise bounds and extent of the species its terms stand for, it is necessary we should know the essence of each species, which is that which constitutes and bounds it.

This, in all simple ideas and modes, is not hard to do. For in these the real and nominal essence being the same, or, which is all one, the abstract idea which the general term stands for being the sole essence and boundary that is or can be supposed of the species, there can be no doubt how far the species extends, or what things are comprehended under each term; which, it is evident, are all that have an exact conformity with the idea it stands for, and no other.

But in substances, wherein a real essence, distinct from the nominal, is supposed to constitute, determine, and bound the species, the extent of the general word is very uncertain; because, not knowing this real essence, we cannot know what is, or what is not of that species; and, consequently, what may or may not with certainty be affirmed of it. And thus, speaking of a *man*, or *gold*, or any other species of natural substances, as supposed constituted by a precise and real essence which nature regularly imparts to every individual of that kind, whereby it is made to be of that species, we cannot be certain of the truth of any affirmation or negation made of it. For man or gold, taken in this sense, and used for species of things constituted by real essences, different from the complex idea in the mind of the speaker, stand for we know not what; and the extent of these species, with such boundaries, are so unknown and undetermined, that it is impossible with any certainty to affirm, that all men are rational, or that all gold is yellow. But where the nominal essence is kept to, as the boundary of each species, and men extend the application of any general term no further than to the particular things in which the complex idea it stands for is to be found, there they are in no danger to mistake the bounds of each species, nor can be in doubt, on this account, whether any proposition be true or not. I have chosen to explain this uncertainty of propositions in this scholastic way, and have made use of the terms of *essences*, and *species*, on purpose to show the absurdity and inconvenience there is to think of them as of any other sort of realities, than barely abstract ideas with names to them. To suppose that the species of things are anything but the sorting of them under general names, according as they agree to several abstract ideas of which we make those names the signs, is to confound truth, and introduce uncertainty into all general propositions that can be made about them. Though therefore these things might, to people not possessed with scholastic learning, be treated of in a better and clearer way; yet those wrong notions of essences or species having got root in most people's minds who have received any tincture from the learning which has prevailed in this part of the world, are to be discovered and removed, to make way for that use of words which should convey certainty with it.

5. *This more particularly concerns Substances.* The names of substances, then, whenever made to stand for species which are supposed to be constituted by real essences which we know not, are not capable to convey certainty to the understanding. Of the truth of general propositions made up of such terms we cannot be sure. The reason whereof is plain: for how can we be sure that this or that quality is in gold, when we know not what is or is not gold? Since in this way of speaking, nothing is gold but what partakes of an essence, which we, not knowing, cannot know where it is or is not, and so cannot be sure that any parcel of matter in the world is or is not in this sense gold; being incurably ignorant whether *it* has or has not that which makes anything to be called gold; i.e. that real essence of gold whereof we have no idea at all. This being as impossible for us to know as it is for a blind man to tell in what flower the colour of a pansy is or is not to be found, whilst he has no idea of the colour of a pansy at all. Or if we could (which is impossible) certainly know where a real essence, which we know not, is, v.g. in what parcels of matter the real essence of gold is, yet could we not be sure that this or that quality could with truth be affirmed of gold; since it is impossible for us to know that this or that quality or idea has a necessary connexion with a real essence of which we have no idea at all, whatever species that supposed real essence may be imagined to constitute.

6. *The Truth of few universal Propositions concerning Substances is to be known.* On the other side, the names of substances, when made use of as they should be, for the ideas men have in their minds, though they carry a clear and determinate signification with them, will not yet serve us to make many universal propositions of whose truth we can be certain. Not because in this use of them we are uncertain what things are signified by them, but because the complex ideas they stand for are such combinations of simple ones as carry not with them any discoverable connexion or repugnancy, but with a very few other ideas.

7. *Because necessary Co-existence of simple Ideas in Substances can in few Cases be known.* The complex ideas that our names of the species of substances properly stand for, are collections of such qualities as have been observed to co-exist in an unknown substratum, which we call substance; but what other qualities necessarily co-exist with such combinations, we cannot certainly know, unless we can discover their natural dependence; which, in their primary qualities, we can go but a very little way in; and in all their secondary qualities we can discover no connexion at all: for the reasons mentioned, chap. iii. Viz. I. Because we know not the real constitutions of substances, on which each secondary quality particularly depends. 2. Did we know that, it would serve us only for experimental (not universal) knowledge; and reach with certainty no further than that bare instance: because our understandings can discover no conceivable connexion between any secondary quality and any modification whatsoever of any of the primary ones. And therefore there are very few general propositions to be made concerning substances, which can carry with them undoubted certainty.

8. *Instances in Gold.* 'All gold is fixed,' is a proposition whose truth we cannot be certain of, how univer-

sally soever it be believed. For if, according to the useless imagination of the Schools, any one supposes the term gold to stand for a species of things set out by nature, by a real essence belonging to it, it is evident he knows not what particular substances are of that species; and so cannot with certainty affirm anything universally of gold. But if he makes gold stand for a species determined by its nominal essence, let the nominal essence, for example, be the complex idea of a body of a certain yellow colour, malleable, fusible, and heavier than any other known;—in this proper use of the word gold, there is no difficulty to know what is or is not gold. But yet no other quality can with certainty be universally affirmed or denied of gold, but what hath a *discoverable* connexion or inconsistency with that nominal essence. Fixedness, for example, having no necessary connexion that we can discover, with the colour, weight, or any other simple idea of our complex one, or with the whole combination together; it is impossible that we should certainly know the truth of this proposition, that all gold is fixed.

9. *No discoverable necessary connexion between nominal essence of gold and other simple ideas.* As there is no discoverable connexion between fixedness and the colour, weight, and other simple ideas of that nominal essence of gold; so, if we make our complex idea of gold, a body yellow, fusible, ductile, weighty, and fixed, we shall be at the same uncertainty concerning solubility in *aqua regia*, and for the same reason. Since we can never, from consideration of the ideas themselves, with certainty affirm or deny of a body whose complex idea is made up of yellow, very weighty, ductile, fusible, and fixed, that it is soluble in *aqua regia*: and so on of the rest of its qualities. I would gladly meet with one general affirmation concerning any quality of gold, that any one can certainly know is true. It will, no doubt, be presently objected, Is not this an universal proposition, *All gold is malleable?* To which I answer, It is a very certain proposition, if malleableness be a part of the complex idea the word gold stands for. But then here is nothing affirmed of gold, but that that sound stands for an idea in which malleableness is contained: and such a sort of truth and certainty as this it is, to say a centaur is four-footed. But if malleableness make not a part of the specific essence the name of gold stands for, it is plain, *all gold is malleable*, is not a certain proposition. Because, let the complex idea of gold be made up of whichsoever of its other qualities you please, malleableness will not appear to depend on that complex idea, nor follow from any simple one contained in it: the connexion that malleableness has (if it has any) with those other qualities being only by the intervention of the real constitution of its insensible parts; which, since we know not, it is impossible we should perceive that connexion, unless we could discover that which ties them together.

10. *As far as any such Co-existence can be known, so far Universal Propositions may be certain. But this will go but a little way.* The more, indeed, of these coexisting qualities we unite into one complex idea, under one name, the more precise and determinate we make the signification of that word; but never yet make it thereby more capable of universal certainty, *in respect of other qualities not contained in our complex idea*: since we perceive not their connexion or dependence on one another; being ignorant both of that real constitution in which they are all founded, and also how they flow from it. For the chief part of our knowledge concerning substances is not, as in other things, barely of the relation of two ideas that may exist separately; but is of the necessary connexion and co-existence of several distinct ideas in the same subject, or of their repugnancy so to coexist. Could we begin at the other end, and discover what it was wherein that colour consisted, what made a body lighter or heavier, what texture of parts made it malleable, fusible, and fixed, and fit to be dissolved in this sort of liquor, and not in another;—if, I say, we had such an idea as this of bodies, and could perceive therein all sensible qualities originally consist, and how they are produced; we might frame such abstract ideas of them as would furnish us with matter of more general knowledge, and enable us to make universal propositions, that should carry general truth and certainty with them. But whilst our complex ideas of the sorts of substances are so remote from that internal real constitution on which their sensible qualities depend, and are made up of nothing but an imperfect collection of those apparent qualities our senses can discover, there can be few general propositions concerning substances of whose real truth we can be certainly assured; since there are but few sim-

ple ideas of whose real truth we can be certainly assured; since there are but few simple ideas of whose connexion and necessary co-existence we can have certain and undoubted knowledge. I imagine, amongst all the secondary qualities of substances, and the powers relating to them, there cannot any two be named, whose necessary co-existence, or repugnance to co-exist, can certainly be known; unless in those of the same sense, which necessarily exclude one another, as I have elsewhere showed. No one, I think, by the colour that is in any body, can certainly know what smell, taste, sound, or tangible qualities it has, nor what alterations it is capable to make or receive on or from other bodies. The same may be said of the sound or taste, &c. Our specific names of substances standing for any collections of such ideas, it is not to be wondered that we can with them make very few general propositions of undoubted real certainty. But yet so far as any complex idea of any sort of substances contains in it any simple idea, whose *necessary* co-existence with any other *may* be discovered, so far universal propositions may with certainty be made concerning it: v.g. could any one discover a necessary connexion between malleableness and the colour or weight of gold, or any other part of the complex idea signified by that name, he might make a certain universal proposition concerning gold in this respect; and the real truth of this proposition, that *all gold is malleable*, would be as certain as of this, *the three angles of all right-lined triangles are all equal to two right ones*.

Chapter IX

OF OUR THREEFOLD KNOWLEDGE OF EXISTENCE

1. *General Propositions that are certain concern not Existence.* Hitherto we have only considered the essences of things; which being only abstract ideas, and thereby removed in our thoughts from particular existence, (that being the proper operation of the mind, in abstraction, to consider an idea under no other existence but what it has in the understanding,) gives us no knowledge of real existence at all. Where, by the way, we may take notice, that universal propositions of whose truth or falsehood we can have certain knowledge concern not existence: and further, that all particular affirmations or negations that would not be certain if they were made general, are only concerning existence; they declaring only the accidental union or separation of ideas in things existing, which, in their abstract natures, have no known necessary union or repugnancy.

2. *A threefold Knowledge of Existence.* But, leaving the nature of propositions, and different ways of predication to be considered more at large in another place, let us proceed now to inquire concerning our knowledge of the *existence of things*, and how we come by it. I say, then, that we have the knowledge of *our own* existence by intuition; of the existence of *God* by demonstration; and of *other things* by sensation.

3. *Our Knowledge of our own Existence is Intuitive.* As for *our own existence*, we perceive it so plainly and so certainly, that it neither needs nor is capable of any proof. For nothing can be more evident to us than our own existence. I think, I reason, I feel pleasure and pain: can any of these be more evident to me than my own existence? If I doubt of all other things, that very doubt makes me perceive my own existence, and will not suffer me to doubt of that. For if I know I feel pain, it is evident I have as certain perception of my own existence, as of the existence of the pain I feel: or if I know I doubt, I have as certain perception of the existence of the thing doubting, as of that thought which I *call doubt*. Experience then convinces us, that we have an *intuitive knowledge* of our own existence, and an internal infallible perception that we are. In every act of sensation, reasoning, or thinking, we are conscious to ourselves of our own being; and, in this matter, come not short of the highest degree of certainty.

Chapter X

OF OUR KNOWLEDGE OF THE EXISTENCE OF A GOD

1. *We are capable of knowing certainly that there is a God.* Though God has given us no innate ideas of himself; though he has stamped no original characters on our minds, wherein we may read his being; yet having furnished us with those faculties our minds are endowed with, he hath not left himself without witness: since we have sense, perception, and

reason, and cannot want a clear proof of him, as long as we carry *ourselves* about us. Nor can we justly complain of our ignorance in this great point; since he has so plentifully provided us with the means to discover and know him; so far as is necessary to the end of our being, and the great concernment of our happiness. But, though this be the most obvious truth that reason discovers, and though its evidence be (if I mistake not) equal to mathematical certainty; yet it requires thought and attention; and the mind must apply itself to a regular deduction of it from some part of our intuitive knowledge, or else we shall be as uncertain and ignorant of this as of other propositions, which are in themselves capable of clear demonstration. To show, therefore, that we are capable of *knowing*, i.e. *being certain* that there is a God, and *how we may come by* this certainty, I think we need go no further than *ourselves*, and that undoubted knowledge we have of our own existence.

2. *For Man knows that he himself exists.* I think it is beyond question, that man has a clear idea of his own being; he knows certainly he exists, and that he is something. He that can doubt whether he be anything or no, I speak not to; no more than I would argue with pure nothing, or endeavour to convince nonentity that it were something. If any one pretends to be so sceptical as to deny his own existence, (for really to doubt of it is manifestly impossible,) let him for me enjoy his beloved happiness of being nothing, until hunger or some other pain convince him of the contrary. This, then, I think I may take for a truth, which every one's certain knowledge assures him of, beyond the liberty of doubting, viz. that he is *something that actually exists*.

3. *He knows also that Nothing cannot produce a Being; therefore Something must have existed from Eternity.* In the next place, man knows, by an intuitive certainty, that bare *nothing can no more produce any real being, than it can be equal to two right angles*. If a man knows not that nonentity, or the absence of all being, cannot be equal to two right angles, it is impossible he should know any demonstration in Euclid. If, therefore, we know there is some real being, and that nonentity cannot produce any real being, it is an evident demonstration, that *from eternity there has been something*; since what was not from eternity had a beginning; and what had a beginning must be produced by something else.

4. *And that eternal Being must be most powerful.* Next, it is evident, that what had its being and beginning from another, must also have all that which is in and belongs to its being from another too. All the powers it has must be owing to and received from the same source. This eternal source, then, of all being must also be the source and original of all power; and so *this eternal Being must be also the most powerful*.

5. *And most knowing.* Again, a man finds in *himself* perception and knowledge. We have then got one step further; and we are certain now that there is not only some being, but some knowing, intelligent being in the world. There was a time, then, when there was no knowing being, and when knowledge began to be; or else there had been also *a knowing being from eternity*. If it be said, there was a time when no being had any knowledge, when that eternal being was void of all understanding; I reply, that then it was impossible there should ever have been any knowledge: it being as impossible that things wholly void of knowledge, and operating blindly, and without any perception, should produce a knowing being, as it is impossible that a triangle should make itself three angles bigger than two right ones. For it is as repugnant to the idea of senseless matter, that it should put into itself sense, perception, and knowledge, as it is repugnant to the idea of a triangle, that it should put into itself greater angles than two right ones.

6. *And therefore God.* Thus, from the consideration of ourselves, and what we infallibly find in our own constitutions, our reason leads us to the knowledge of this certain and evident truth,—*That there is an eternal, most powerful, and most knowing Being*; which whether any one will please to call God, it matters not. The thing is evident; and from this idea duly considered, will easily be deduced all those other attributes, which we ought to ascribe to this eternal Being. If, nevertheless, any one should be found to senselessly arrogant, as to suppose man alone knowing and wise, but yet the product of mere ignorance and chance; and that all the rest of the universe acted only by that blind haphazard; I shall leave with him

that very rational and emphatical rebuke of Tully[8] (1. ii. De Leg.), to be considered at his leisure: 'What can be more sillily arrogant and misbecoming, than for a man to think that he has a mind and understanding in him, but yet in all the universe beside there is no such thing? Or that those things, which with the utmost stretch of his reason he can scarce comprehend, should be moved and managed without any reason at all?' *Quid est enim verius, quam neminem esse oportere tam stulte arrogantem, ut in se mentem et rationem putet inesse, in caelo mundoque non putet? Aut ea quae vix summa ingenii ratione comprehendat, nulla ratione moveri putet?*

From what has been said, it is plain to me we have a more certain knowledge of the existence of a God, than of anything our senses have not immediately discovered to us. Nay, I presume I may say, that we more certainly know that there is a God, than that there is anything else without us. When I say we *know*, I mean there is such a knowledge within our reach which we cannot miss, if we will but apply our minds to that, as we do to several other inquiries.

Chapter XI

OF OUR KNOWLEDGE OF THE EXISTENCE OF OTHER THINGS

1. *Knowledge of the existence of other Finite Beings is to be had only by actual Sensation.* The knowledge of our own being we have by intuition. The existence of a God, reason clearly makes known to us, as has been shown.

The knowledge of the existence of *any other thing* we can have only by *sensation*: for there being no necessary connexion of real existence with any *idea* a man hath in his memory; nor of any other existence but that of God with the existence of any particular man: no particular man can know the existence of any other being, but only when, by actual operating upon him, it makes itself perceived by him. For, the having the idea of anything in our mind, no more proves the existence of that thing, than the picture of a man evidences his being in the world, or the visions of a dream make thereby a true history.

2. *Instance: Whiteness of this Paper.* It is therefore the *actual receiving* of ideas from without that gives us notice of the existence of other things, and makes us know, that something doth exist at that time without us, which causes that idea in us; though perhaps we neither know nor consider how it does it. For it takes not from the certainty of our sense, and the ideas we receive by them, that we know not the manner wherein they are produced: v.g. whilst I write this, I have, by the paper affecting my eyes, that idea produced in my mind, which, whatever object causes, I call *white*; by which I know that that quality or accident (i.e. whose appearance before my eyes always causes that idea) doth really exist, and hath a being without me. And of this, the greatest assurance I can possibly have, and to which my faculties can attain, is the testimony of my eyes, which are the proper and sole judges of this thing; whose testimony I have reason to rely on as so certain, that I can no more doubt, whilst I write this, that I see white and black, and that something really exists that causes that sensation in me, than that I write or move my hand; which is a certainty as great as human nature is capable of, concerning the existence of anything, but a man's self alone, and of God.

3. *This notice by our Senses, though not so certain as Demonstration, yet may be called Knowledge, and proves the Existence of Things without us.* The notice we have by our senses of the existing of things without us, though it be not altogether so certain as our intuitive knowledge, or the deductions of our reason employed about the clear abstract ideas of our own minds; yet it is an assurance that deserves the name of *knowledge*. If we persuade ourselves that our faculties act and inform us right concerning the existence of those objects that affect them, it cannot pass for an ill-grounded confidence: for I think nobody can, in earnest, be so sceptical as to be uncertain of the existence of those things which he sees and feels. At least, he that can doubt so far, (whatever he may have with his own thoughts,) will never have any controversy with me; since he can never be sure I say anything contrary to his own opinion. As to myself, I think God has given me assurance enough of the existence of things without me: since, by their different application, I can produce in myself both pleasure and pain, which is one great concernment of my

8. [Marcus Tullius Cicero (106–43 B.C.), the statesman and philosopher, was considered the greatest Roman orator. Locke's reference is to *De Legibus*, a political dialogue.]

present state. This is certain: the confidence that our faculties do not herein deceive us, is the greatest assurance we are capable of concerning the existence of material beings. For we cannot act anything but by our faculties; nor talk of knowledge itself, but by the help of those faculties which are fitted to apprehend even what knowledge is.

But besides the assurance we have from our senses themselves, that they do not err in the information they give us of the existence of things without us, when they are affected by them, we are further confirmed in this assurance by other concurrent reasons:—

4. *Confirmed by concurrent reasons:—First, Because we cannot have ideas of Sensation but by the Inlet of the Senses.* I. It is plain those perceptions are produced in us by exterior causes affecting our senses: because those that want the *organs* of any sense, never can have the ideas belonging to that sense produced in their minds. This is too evident to be doubted: and therefore we cannot but be assured that they come in by the organs of that sense, and no other way. The organs themselves, it is plain, do not produce them: for then the eyes of a man in the dark would produce colours, and his nose smell roses in the winter: but we see nobody gets the relish of a pineapple, till he goes to the Indies, where it is, and tastes it.

5. *Secondly, Because we find that an Idea from actual Sensation, and another from Memory, are very distinct Perceptions.* II. Because sometimes I find that *I cannot avoid the having those ideas produced in my mind.* For though, when my eyes are shut, or windows fast, I can at pleasure recall to my mind the ideas of light, or the sun, which former sensations had lodged in my memory; so I can at pleasure lay by *that* idea, and take into my view that of the smell of a rose, or taste sugar. But, if I turn my eyes at noon towards the sun, I cannot avoid the ideas which the light or sun then produces in me. So that there is a manifest difference between the ideas laid up in my memory, (over which, if they were there only, I should have constantly the same power to dispose of them, and lay them by at pleasure,) and those which force themselves upon me, and I cannot avoid having. And therefore it must needs be some exterior cause, and the brisk acting of some objects without me, whose efficacy I cannot resist, that produces those ideas in my mind, whether I will or no. Besides, there is nobody who doth not perceive the difference in himself between contemplating the sun, as he hath the idea of it in his memory, and actually looking upon it: of which two, his perception is so distinct, that few of his ideas are more distinguishable one from another. And therefore he hath certain knowledge that they are not *both* memory, or the actions of his mind, and fancies only within him; but that actual seeing hath a cause without.

6. *Thirdly, Because Pleasure or Pain, which accompanies actual Sensation, accompanies not the returning of those Ideas without the external Objects.* III. Add to this, that many of those ideas are *produced in us with pain*, which afterwards we remember without the least offence. Thus, the pain of heat or cold, when the idea of it is revived in our minds, gives us no disturbance; which, when felt, was very troublesome; and is again, when actually repeated: which is occasioned by the disorder the external object causes in our bodies when applied to them: and we remember the pains of hunger, thirst, or the headache, without any pain at all; which would either never disturb us, or else constantly do it, as often as we thought of it, were there nothing more but ideas floating in our minds, and appearances entertaining our fancies, without the real existence of things affecting us from abroad. The same may be said of *pleasure*, accompanying several actual sensations. And though mathematical demonstration depends not upon sense, yet the examining them by diagrams gives great credit to the evidence of our sight, and seems to give it a certainty approaching to that of demonstration itself. For, it would be very strange, that a man should allow it for an undeniable truth, that two angles of a figure, which he measures by lines and angles of a diagram, should be bigger one than the other, and yet doubt of the existence of those lines and angles, which by looking on he makes use of to measure that by.

7. *Fourthly, Because our Senses assist one another's Testimony of the Existence of outward Things, and enable us to predict.* IV. Our *senses* in many cases *bear witness to the truth of each other's report*, concerning the existence of sensible things without us. He that *sees* a fire, may, if he doubt whether it be anything

more than a bare fancy, *feel* it too; and be convinced, by putting his hand in it. Which certainly could never be put into such exquisite pain by a bare idea or phantom, unless that the pain be a fancy too: which yet he cannot, when the burn is well, by raising the idea of it, bring upon himself again.

Thus I see, whilst I write this, I can change the appearance of the paper; and by designing the letters, tell *beforehand* what new idea it shall exhibit the very next moment, by barely drawing my pen over it: which will neither appear (let me fancy as much as I will) if my hands stand still; or though I move my pen, if my eyes be shut: nor, when those characters are once made on the paper, can I choose afterwards but see them as they are; that is, have the ideas of such letters as I have made. Whence it is manifest, that they are not barely the sport and play of my own imagination, when I find that the characters that were made at the pleasure of my own thoughts, do not obey them; nor yet cease to be, whenever I shall fancy it, but continue to affect my senses constantly and regularly, according to the figures I made them. To which if we will add, that the sight of those shall, from another man, draw such sounds as I beforehand design they shall stand for, there will be little reason left to doubt that those words I write do really exist without me, when they cause a long series of regular sounds to affect my ears, which could not be the effect of my imagination, nor could my memory retain them in that order.

8. *This Certainty is as great as our Condition needs.* But yet, if after all this any one will be so sceptical as to distrust his senses, and to affirm that all we see and hear, feel and taste, think and do, during our whole being, is but the series and deluding appearances of a long dream, whereof there is no reality; and therefore will question the existence of all things, or our knowledge of anything: I must desire him to consider, that, if all be a dream, then he doth but dream that he makes the question, and so it is not much matter that a waking man should answer him. But yet, if he pleases, he may dream that I make him this answer, That the certainty of things existing in *rerum natura* when we have the testimony of our senses for it is not only as great as our frame can attain to, but as our condition needs. For, our faculties being suited not to the full extent of being, nor to a perfect, clear, comprehensive knowledge of things free from all doubt and scruple; but to the preservation of us, in whom they are; and accommodated to the use of life: they serve to our purpose well enough, if they will but give us certain notice of those things, which are convenient or inconvenient to us. For he that sees a candle burning, and hath experimented the force of its flame by putting his finger in it, will little doubt that this is something existing without him, which does him harm, and puts him to great pain: which is assurance enough, when no man requires greater certainty to govern his actions by than what is as certain as his actions themselves. And if our dreamer pleases to try whether the glowing heat of a glass furnace be barely a wandering imagination in a drowsy man's fancy, by putting his hand into it, he may perhaps be wakened into a certainty greater than he could wish, that it is something more than bare imagination. So that this evidence is as great as we can desire, being as certain to us as our pleasure or pain, i.e. happiness or misery; beyond which we have no concernment, either of knowing or being. Such an assurance of the existence of things without us is sufficient to direct us in the attaining the good and avoiding the evil which is caused by them, which is the important concernment we have of being made acquainted with them.

9. *But reaches no further than actual Sensation.* In fine, then, when our senses do actually convey into our understandings any idea, we cannot but be satisfied that there doth something *at that time* really exist without us, which doth affect our senses, and by them give notice of itself to our apprehensive faculties, and actually produce that idea which we then perceive: and we cannot so far distrust their testimony, as to doubt that such *collections* of simple ideas as we have observed by our senses to be united together, do really exist together. But this knowledge extends as far as the present testimony of our senses, employed about particular objects that do then affect them, and no further. For if I saw such a collection of simple ideas as is wont to be called *man*, existing together one minute since, and am now alone, I cannot be certain that the same man exists now, since there is no *necessary connexion* of his existence a minute since with his existence now: by a thousand ways he may cease to be, since I had the testimony of my senses for his existence. And if I cannot be

certain that the man I saw last to-day is now in being, I can less be certain that he is so who hath been longer removed from my senses, and I have not seen since yesterday, or since the last year: and much less can I be certain of the existence of men that I never saw. And, therefore, though it be highly probable that millions of men do now exist, yet, whilst I am alone, writing this, I have not that certainty of it which we strictly call knowledge; though the great likelihood of it puts me past doubt, and it be reasonable for me to do several things upon the confidence that there are men (and men also of my acquaintance, with whom I have to do) now in the world: but this is but probability, not knowledge.

12. *The Existence of other finite Spirits not knowable, and rests on Faith.* What ideas we have of spirits, and how we come by them, I have already shown. But though we have those ideas in our minds, and know we have them there, the having the ideas of spirits does not make us know that any such things do exist without us, or that there are any finite spirits, or any other spiritual beings, but the Eternal God. We have ground from revelation, and several other reasons, to believe with assurance that there are such creatures: but our senses not being able to discover them, we want the means of knowing their particular existences. For we can no more know that there are finite spirits really existing, by the idea we have of such beings in our minds, than by the ideas any one has of fairies or centaurs, he can come to know that things answering those ideas do really exist.

And therefore concerning the existence of finite spirits, as well as several other things, we must content ourselves with the evidence of faith; but universal, certain propositions concerning this matter are beyond our reach. For however true it may be, v.g., that all the intelligent spirits that God ever created do still exist, yet it can never make a part of our certain knowledge. These and the like propositions we may assent to, as highly probable, but are not, I fear, in this state capable of knowing. We are not, then, to put others upon demonstrating, nor ourselves upon search of universal certainty in all those matters; wherein we are not capable of any other knowledge, but what our senses give us in this or that particular.

13. *Only particular Propositions concerning concrete Existences are knowable.* By which it appears that there are two sorts of propositions:—(1) There is one sort of propositions concerning the *existence* of anything answerable to such an idea: as having the idea of an elephant, phoenix, motion, or an angel, in my mind, the first and natural inquiry is, Whether such a thing does anywhere exist? And this knowledge is only of particulars. No existence of anything without us, but only of God, can certainly be known further than our senses inform us. (2) There is another sort of propositions, wherein is expressed the agreement or disagreement of *our abstract ideas*, and their dependence on one another. Such propositions may be universal and certain. So, having the idea of God and myself, of fear and obedience, I cannot but be sure that God is to be feared and obeyed by me: and this proposition will be certain, concerning man in general, if I have made an abstract idea of such a species, whereof I am one particular. But yet this proposition, how certain soever, that 'men ought to fear and obey God' proves not to me the *existence of men* in the world; but will be true of all such creatures, whenever they do exist: which certainty of such general propositions depends on the agreement or disagreement to be discovered in those abstract ideas.

14. *And all general Propositions that are known to be true concern abstract Ideas.* In the former case, our knowledge is the consequence of the existence of things, producing ideas in our minds by our senses: in the latter, knowledge is the consequence of the ideas (be they what they will) that are in our minds, producing there general certain propositions. Many of these are called *aeternae veritates*, and all of them indeed are so; not from being written, all or any of them, in the minds of all men; or that they were any of them propositions in any one's mind, till he, having got the abstract ideas, joined or separated them by affirmation or negation. But wheresoever we can suppose such a creature as man is, endowed with such faculties, and thereby furnished with such ideas as we have, we must conclude, he must needs, when he applies his thoughts to the consideration of his ideas, know the truth of certain propositions that will arise from the agreement or disagreement which he will perceive in his own ideas. Such propositions are therefore called *eternal truths*, not because they are eternal propositions actually formed, and antecedent to the understanding that at any time makes them;

nor because they are imprinted on the mind from any patterns that are anywhere out of the mind, and existed before: but because, being once made about abstract ideas, so as to be true, they will, whenever they can be supposed to be made again at any time, past or to come, by a mind having those ideas, always actually be true. For names being supposed to stand perpetually for the same ideas, and the same ideas having immutably the same habitudes one to another, propositions concerning any abstract ideas that are once true must needs be *eternal verities*.

George Berkeley

George Berkeley was born in Kilkenny, Ireland, in 1685. He studied at Trinity College, Dublin, where he received his B.A. in 1704 and his M.A. in 1707. Subsequently, he joined the faculty at Trinity, where he stayed until 1712. During this time at Trinity, Berkeley wrote his most important philosophical works, *An Essay Towards a New Theory of Vision* (1709), *A Treatise Concerning the Principles of Human Knowledge* (the *Principles*) (1710), and *Three Dialogues between Hylas and Philonous* (the *Dialogues*) (1713). In this period he also became an Anglican clergyman. For several years beginning in 1713, he lived in London, where he associated with the literati of the time. In 1721, the year he published *De Motu*, a book on the philosophy of physics, he returned to Trinity, where he remained until 1724. From 1724 until 1728 he promoted a plan to establish a college in Bermuda for sons of settlers and Native Americans. In 1728 he married Anne Forster and then sailed to Newport, Rhode Island, where he waited in vain until 1731 for the promised government subsidy for the college. The college was never established, and in 1731 he returned to London. During his stay in America, he wrote *Alciphron: or, the Minute Philosopher* (1734), a defense of Christianity. Around this time he also wrote *The Theory of Vision* (1733) and two books on the philosophy of mathematics, *The Analyst* (1734) and a *Defense of Free Thinking in Mathematics* (1735), and he published the third edition of the *Principles* (1734), which incorporates certain significant revisions. While in London, Berkeley was made bishop of Cloyne, a diocese in Ireland, where he lived from 1734 until 1752. In this period he produced an unusual work, *Siris: A Chain of Philosophical Reflections and Inquiries Concerning the Virtues of Tar-water, and Divers Other Subjects* (1744). In 1752 he moved his family to Oxford because his son George, one of his five children, was to study there, and in the next year, 1753, he died.

Berkeley is best known for his immaterialism, his view that there is no matter in the universe, and all that exists are minds (*spirits*) and their states. Matter, in his view, is by definition stuff external to any mind. Berkeley did not deny that there are objects such as books and trees, but he held that such physical objects exist only in minds, wholly constituted of ideas. A tree, for example, consists entirely of certain ideas in the mind of a perceiver—ideas of, for example, size, shape, weight, resistance, and color.

In both the *Principles* and the *Dialogues* the most prominent place is given to a series of arguments against the existence of matter. Berkeley's most basic antimaterialistic intuition is that, when we consider carefully what it means for a physical object to exist, we will see that it is just that its various qualities are perceived—its color is seen, its texture felt, its odor smelled, and its flavor tasted. For physical things, as Berkeley puts it, their *esse* is *percipi;* that is, for them *to be* is *to be perceived.* Beyond this basic consideration, Berkeley advances two types of argument against the existence of matter. In one sort, Berkeley contends that we would never come to know the existence of material objects. All we directly perceive are sensations, and indirectly, by means of inference from the sensations we directly perceive, we could never conclude that material objects exist, because we have no explanation of how material objects can cause sensations in immaterial minds.

The second sort of argument is devoted to the claim that matter cannot even be conceived by us. We cannot conceive of matter by forming an idea that resembles a material object, because ideas cannot resemble material objects—they can resemble only other ideas. But further, when I attempt to conceive of a material object by forming an idea of a physical object that is external to any mind, I do not succeed, because the physical object is nevertheless in *my* mind, the mind of the conceiver.

Perhaps Berkeley's most important consideration against the existence of matter involves his attack on the supposed mind-independence of primary qualities. In the tradition of Galileo, Descartes, and Locke, we can form a conception of mind-independent physical things by forming an idea of entities possessing only primary qualities—for example, extension, size, shape, motion, location, and duration. By contrast, secondary qualities—such as color, taste, odor, and temperature—do not provide us with a conception of mind-independent physical things. This is partly because perception of secondary qualities varies with the state or nature of the perceptual organs. For example, a bowl of water can feel warmer or cooler depending on the initial temperature of the hand one is feeling the water with, and thus, temperature is perception- or mind-dependent. Berkeley argues that perception of primary qualities varies in the very same way and that consequently primary qualities are as mind-dependent as secondary qualities.

Berkeley's universe is a community of immaterial spirits. God is the greatest of the spirits, and he sends the other spirits sensations in an orderly way, giving rise to a physical world consisting wholly of sensations and governed by laws of nature. Despite the incredulity with which Berkeley's claims are often received, he nevertheless argued that his views are commonsensical, and that those of the materialists are mere philosophers' inventions. Berkeley's legacy is a creative alternative to commonly held metaphysical views, offering resourceful and important challenges to the modern understanding of matter.

• • •

Important studies of Berkeley's views include Margaret Atherton, *Berkeley's Revolution in Vision* (Ithaca, N.Y.: Cornell University Press, 1990); A. A. Luce, *The Dialectic of Immaterialism: An Account of the Making of Berkeley's Principles* (London: Hodder and Stoughton, 1963); Keota Fields, *Berkeley: Ideas, Immaterialism, and Objective Presence* (Lanham, Md.: Lexington Books, 2011); Robert Muehlmann, *Berkeley's Ontology* (Indianapolis: Hackett Publishing Company, 1992); George Pitcher, *Berkeley* (London: Routledge & Kegan Paul, 1977); I. C. Tipton, *Berkeley: The Philosophy of Immaterialism* (London: Methuen, 1974); and Kenneth P. Winkler, *Berkeley: An Interpretation* (Oxford: Oxford University Press, 1989). Some of the best collections of critical essays are C. B. Martin and D. M. Armstrong, eds., *Locke and Berkeley: A Collection of Critical Essays* (Garden City, N.J.: Doubleday, 1968); Ernest Sosa, ed., *Essays on the Philosophy of George Berkeley* (Dordrecht: D. Reidel, 1987); Colin Turbayne, ed., *Berkeley: Critical and Interpretive Essays* (Minneapolis: University of Minnesota Press, 1987); and Margaret Atherton, ed., *The Empiricists: Locke, Berkeley, Hume* (Lanham, Md.: Rowman & Littlefield, 1998).

Derk Pereboom

A Treatise Concerning the Principles of Human Knowledge

The Preface

What *I here make public has, after a long and scrupulous inquiry, seemed to me evidently true, and not unuseful to be known, particularly to those who are tainted with skepticism, or want a demonstration of the existence and immateriality of God, or the natural immortality of the soul. Whether it be so or no, I am content the reader should impartially examine. Since I do not think myself any farther concerned for the success of what I have written, than as it is agreeable to* truth. *But to the end this may not suffer, I make it my request that the reader suspend his judgment, till he has once,* at least, *read the whole through with that degree of attention and thought which the subject matter shall seem to deserve. For as there are some passages that, taken by themselves, are very liable (nor could it be remedied) to gross misinterpretation, and to be charged with most absurd consequences, which, nevertheless, upon an entire perusal will appear not to follow from them: so likewise, though the whole should be read over, yet, if this be done transiently, 'tis very probable my sense may be mistaken; but to a thinking reader, I flatter myself, it will be throughout clear and obvious. As for the characters of novelty and singularity, which some of the following notions may seem to bear, 'tis, I hope, needless to make any apology on that account. He must surely be either very weak, or very little acquainted with the sciences, who shall reject a truth, that is capable of demonstration, for no other reason but because it's newly known and contrary to the prejudices of mankind. Thus much I thought fit to premise, in order to prevent, if possible, the hasty censures of a sort of men, who are too apt to condemn an opinion before they rightly comprehend it.*

Reprinted from Berkeley, *A Treatise Concerning the Principles of Human Knowledge,* edited by Kenneth Winkler (Indianapolis: Hackett Publishing Co., 1982), by permission of the publisher.

Introduction

1. Philosophy being nothing else but the study of wisdom and truth, it may with reason be expected, that those who have spent most time and pains in it should enjoy a greater calm and serenity of mind, a greater clearness and evidence of knowledge, and be less disturbed with doubts and difficulties than other men. Yet so it is we see the illiterate bulk of mankind that walk the high-road of plain, common sense, and are governed by the dictates of nature, for the most part easy and undisturbed. To them nothing that's familiar appears unaccountable or difficult to comprehend. They complain not of any want of evidence in their senses, and are out of all danger of becoming *skeptics.* But no sooner do we depart from sense and instinct to follow the light of a superior principle, to reason, meditate, and reflect on the nature of things, but a thousand scruples spring up in our minds, concerning those things which before we seemed fully to comprehend. Prejudices and errors of sense do from all parts discover themselves to our view; and endeavoring to correct these by reason we are insensibly drawn into uncouth paradoxes, difficulties, and inconsistencies, which multiply and grow upon us as we advance in speculation; till at length, having wandered through many intricate mazes, we find ourselves just where we were, or, which is worse, sit down in a forlorn skepticism.

2. The cause of this is thought to be the obscurity of things, or the natural weakness and imperfection of our understandings. It is said the faculties we have are few, and those designed by nature for the support and comfort of life, and not to penetrate into the inward essence and constitution of things. Besides, the mind of man being finite, when it treats of things which partake of infinity, it is not to be wondered at, if it runs into absurdities and contradictions; out of which it is impossible it should ever extricate itself, it being of the nature of infinite not to be comprehended by that which is finite.

3. But perhaps we may be too partial to ourselves in placing the fault originally in our faculties, and not rather in the wrong use we make of them. It is a hard thing to suppose, that right deductions from true principles should ever end in consequences which cannot be maintained or made consistent. We should believe that God has dealt more bountifully with the sons of men, than to give them a strong desire for that knowledge, which he had placed quite out of their reach. This were not agreeable to the wonted, indulgent methods of providence, which, whatever appetites it may have implanted in the creatures, does usually furnish them with such means as, if rightly made use of, will not fail to satisfy them. Upon the whole, I am inclined to think that the far greater part, if not all, of those difficulties which have hitherto amused philosophers, and blocked up the way to knowledge, are entirely owing to ourselves. That we have first raised a dust, and then complain, we cannot see.

4. My purpose therefore is, to try if I can discover what those principles are, which have introduced all that doubtfulness and uncertainty, those absurdities and contradictions into the several sects of philosophy; insomuch that the wisest men have thought our ignorance incurable, conceiving it to arise from the natural dullness and limitation of our faculties. And surely it is a work well deserving our pains, to make a strict inquiry concerning the first principles of *human knowledge*, to sift and examine them on all sides: especially since there may be some grounds to suspect that those lets and difficulties, which stay and embarrass the mind in its search after truth, do not spring from any darkness and intricacy in the objects, or natural defect in the understanding, so much as from false principles which have been insisted on, and might have been avoided.

5. How difficult and discouraging soever this attempt may seem, when I consider how many great and extraordinary men have gone before me in the same designs: yet I am not without some hopes, upon the consideration that the largest views are not always the clearest, and that he who is short-sighted will be obliged to draw the object nearer, and may, perhaps, by a close and narrow survey discern that which had escaped far better eyes.

6. In order to prepare the mind of the reader for the easier conceiving what follows, it is proper to premise somewhat, by way of introduction, concerning the nature and abuse of language. But the unraveling this matter leads me in some measure to anticipate my design, by taking notice of what seems to have had a chief part in rendering speculation intricate and perplexed, and to have occasioned innumerable errors and difficulties in almost all parts of knowledge. And that is the opinion that the mind has a power of framing *abstract ideas* or notions of things. He who is not a perfect stranger to the writings and disputes of philosophers, must needs acknowledge that no small part of them are spent about abstract ideas. These are in a more especial manner, thought to be the object of those sciences which go by the name of *logic* and *metaphysics*, and of all that which passes under the notion of the most abstracted and sublime learning, in all which one shall scarce find any question handled in such a manner, as does not suppose their existence in the mind, and that it is well acquainted with them.

7. It is agreed on all hands, that the qualities or modes of things do never really exist each of them apart by itself, and separated from all others, but are mixed, as it were, and blended together, several in the same object. But we are told, the mind being able to consider each quality singly, or abstracted from those other qualities with which it is united, does by that means frame to itself abstract ideas. For example, there is perceived by sight an object extended, colored, and moved: this mixed or compound idea the mind resolving into its simple, constituent parts, and viewing each by itself, exclusive of the rest, does frame the abstract ideas of extension, color, and motion. Not that it is possible for color or motion to exist without extension: but only that the mind can frame to itself by *abstraction* the idea of color exclusive of extension, and of motion exclusive of both color and extension.

8. Again, the mind having observed that in the particular extensions perceived by sense, there is something common and alike in all, and some other things peculiar, as this or that figure or magnitude, which distinguish them one from another; it considers apart or singles out by itself that which is common, making thereof a most abstract idea of extension, which is neither line, surface, nor solid, nor has any figure or magnitude but is an idea entirely prescinded from all these. So likewise the mind by leaving out of the particular colors perceived by sense, that which

distinguishes them one from another, and retaining that only which is common to all, makes an idea of color in abstract which is neither red, nor blue, nor white, nor any other determinate color. And in like manner by considering motion abstractedly not only from the body moved, but likewise from the figure it describes, and all particular directions and velocities, the abstract idea of motion is framed; which equally corresponds to all particular motions whatsoever that may be perceived by sense.

9. And as the mind frames to itself abstract ideas of qualities or modes, so does it, by the same precision or mental separation, attain abstract ideas of the more compounded beings, which include several coexistent qualities. For example, the mind having observed that *Peter, James*, and *John*, resemble each other, in certain common agreements of shape and other qualities, leaves out of the complex or compounded idea it has of *Peter, James*, and any other particular man, that which is peculiar to each, retaining only what is common to all; and so makes an abstract idea wherein all the particulars equally partake, abstracting entirely from and cutting off all those circumstances and differences, which might determine it to any particular existence. And after this manner it is said we come by the abstract idea of *man* or, if you please, humanity or human nature; wherein it is true there is included color, because there is no man but has some color, but then it can be neither white, nor black, nor any particular color; because there is no one particular color wherein all men partake. So likewise there is included stature, but then it is neither tall stature nor low stature, nor yet middle stature, but something abstracted from all these. And so of the rest. Moreover, there being a great variety of other creatures that partake in some parts, but not all, of the complex idea of *man*, the mind leaving out those parts which are peculiar to men, and retaining those only which are common to all the living creatures, frames the idea of *animal*, which abstracts not only from all particular men, but also all birds, beasts, fishes, and insects. The constituent parts of the abstract idea of animal are body, life, sense, and spontaneous motion. By *body* is meant, body without any particular shape or figure, there being no one shape or figure common to all animals, without covering, either of hair or feathers, or scales, etc. nor yet naked: hair, feathers, scales, and nakedness being the distinguishing properties of particular animals, and for that reason left out of the *abstract idea*. Upon the same account the spontaneous motion must be neither walking, nor flying, nor creeping, it is nevertheless a motion, but what that motion is, it is not easy to conceive.

10. Whether others have this wonderful faculty of *abstracting their ideas*, they best can tell: for myself I find indeed I have a faculty of imagining, or representing to myself the ideas of those particular things I have perceived and of variously compounding and dividing them. I can imagine a man with two heads or the upper parts of a man joined to the body of a horse. I can consider the hand, the eye, the nose, each by itself abstracted or separated from the rest of the body. But then whatever hand or eye I imagine, it must have some particular shape and color. Likewise the idea of man that I frame to myself, must be either of a white, or a black, or a tawny, a straight, or a crooked, a tall, or a low, or a middle-sized man. I cannot by any effort of thought conceive the abstract idea above described. And it is equally impossible for me to form the abstract idea of motion distinct from the body moving, and which is neither swift nor slow, curvilinear nor rectilinear; and the like may be said of all other abstract general ideas whatsoever. To be plain, I own myself able to abstract in one sense, as when I consider some particular parts or qualities separated from others, with which though they are united in some object, yet, it is possible they may really exist without them. But I deny that I can abstract one from another, or conceive separately, those qualities which it is impossible should exist so separated; or that I can frame a general notion by abstracting from particulars in the manner aforesaid. Which two last are the proper acceptations of *abstraction*. And there are grounds to think most men will acknowledge themselves to be in my case. The generality of men which are simple and illiterate never pretend to *abstract notions*. It is said they are difficult and not to be attained without pains and study. We may therefore reasonably conclude that, if such there be, they are confined only to the learned.

11. I proceed to examine what can be alleged in defense of the doctrine of abstraction, and try if I can discover what it is that inclines the men of speculation to embrace an opinion, so remote from common sense as that seems to be. There has been a late deservedly esteemed philosopher, who, no doubt, has given

it very much countenance by seeming to think the having abstract general ideas is what puts the widest difference in point of understanding betwixt man and beast.[1] "The having of general ideas (*says he*) is that which puts a perfect distinction betwixt man and brutes, and is an excellency which the faculties of brutes do by no means attain unto. For it is evident we observe no footsteps in them of making use of general signs for universal ideas; from which we have reason to imagine that they have not the faculty of *abstracting* or making general ideas, since they have no use of words or any other general signs. *And a little after.* Therefore, I think, we may suppose that it is in this that the species of brutes are discriminated from men, and 'tis that proper difference wherein they are wholly separated, and which at last widens to so wide a distance. For if they have any ideas at all, and are not bare machines (as some would have them) we cannot deny them to have some reason. It seems as evident to me that they do some of them in certain instances reason as that they have sense, but it is only in particular ideas, just as they receive them from their senses. They are the best of them tied up within those narrow bounds, and have not (as I think) the faculty to enlarge them by any kind of *abstraction.*" *Essay on Hum. Underst.* B. 2. C. 11. Sect. 10 and 11. I readily agree with this learned author, that the faculties of brutes can by no means attain to *abstraction.* But then if this be made the distinguishing property of that sort of animals, I fear a great many of those that pass for men must be reckoned into their number. The reason that is here assigned why we have no grounds to think brutes have abstract general ideas, is that we observe in them no use of words or any other general signs; which is built on this supposition, to wit, that the making of use of words, implies the having general ideas. From which it follows, that men who use language are able to abstract or generalize their ideas. That this is the sense and arguing of the author will further appear by his answering the question he in another place puts. "Since all things that exist are only particulars, how come we by general terms? *His answer is,* Words become general by being made the signs of general ideas." *Essay on Hum. Underst.* B. 3. C. 3. Sect. 6. But it seems that a word becomes general by being made the sign, not of an abstract general idea but, of several particular ideas, any one of which it indifferently suggests to the mind. For example, when it is said *the change of motion is proportional to the impressed force,* or that *whatever has extension is divisible;* these propositions are to be understood of motion and extension in general, and nevertheless it will not follow that they suggest to my thoughts an idea of motion without a body moved, or any determinate direction and velocity, or that I must conceive an abstract general idea of extension, which is neither line, surface nor solid, neither great nor small, black, white, nor red, nor of any other determinate color. It is only implied that whatever motion I consider, whether it be swift or slow, perpendicular, horizontal or oblique, or in whatever object, the axiom concerning it holds equally true. As does the other of every particular extension, it matters not whether line, surface or solid, whether of this or that magnitude or figure.

12. By observing how ideas become general, we may the better judge how words are made so. And here it is to be noted that I do not deny absolutely there are general ideas, but only that there are any *abstract general ideas:* for in the passages above quoted, wherein there is mention of general ideas, it is always supposed that they are formed by *abstraction,* after the manner set forth in Sect. 8 and 9. Now if we will annex a meaning to our words, and speak only of what we can conceive, I believe we shall acknowledge, that an idea, which considered in itself is particular, becomes general, by being made to represent or stand for all other particular ideas of the same sort. To make this plain by an example, suppose a geometrician is demonstrating the method, of cutting a line in two equal parts. He draws, for instance, a black line of an inch in length, this which in itself is a particular line is nevertheless with regard to its signification general, since as it is there used, it represents all particular lines whatsoever; so that what is demonstrated of it, is demonstrated of all lines, or, in other words, of a line in general. And as that particular line becomes general, by being made a sign, so the name *line* which is taken absolutely is particular, by being a sign is made general. And as the former owes its generality, not to its being the sign of an abstract or general line, but of all particular right lines that may possibly exist, so the latter must be thought to derive

1. [The philosopher is John Locke (1632–1704), whose *An Essay concerning Human Understanding* was first published in 1690. —K.W.]

its generality from the same cause, namely, the various particular lines which it indifferently denotes.

13. To give the reader a yet clearer view of the nature of abstract ideas, and the uses they are thought necessary to, I shall add one more passage out of the *Essay on Human Understanding*, which is as follows. "*Abstract ideas* are not so obvious or easy to children or the yet unexercised mind as particular ones. If they seem so to grown men, it is only because by constant and familiar use they are made so. For when we nicely reflect upon them, we shall find that general ideas are fictions and contrivances of the mind, that carry difficulty with them, and do not so easily offer themselves, as we are apt to imagine. For example, does it not require some pains and skill to form the general idea of a triangle (which is yet none of the most abstract comprehensive and difficult) for it must be neither oblique nor rectangle, neither equilateral, equicrural, nor scalenon, but *all and none* of these at once. In effect, it is something imperfect that cannot exist, an idea wherein some parts of several different and *inconsistent* ideas are put together. It is true the mind in this imperfect state has need of such ideas, and makes all the haste to them it can, for the conveniency of communication and enlargement of knowledge, to both which it is naturally very much inclined. But yet one has reason to suspect such ideas are marks of our imperfection. At least this is enough to show that the most abstract and general ideas are not those that the mind is first and most easily acquainted with, nor such as its earliest knowledge is conversant about. B. 4. C. 7. Sect. 9."[2] If any man has the faculty of framing in his mind such an idea of a triangle as is here described, it is in vain to pretend to dispute him out of it, nor would I go about it. All I desire is, that the reader would fully and certainly inform himself whether he has such an idea or no. And this, methinks, can be no hard task for anyone to perform. What more easy than for anyone to look a little into his own thoughts, and there try whether he has, or can attain to have, an idea that shall correspond with the description that is here given of the general idea of a triangle, which is, *neither oblique, nor rectangle, equilateral, equicrural, nor scalenon, but all and none of these at once?*

2. [The emphasis on "all and none" and "inconsistent" is Berkeley's.]

14. Much is here said of the difficulty that abstract ideas carry with them, and the pains and skill requisite to the forming them. And it is on all hands agreed that there is need of great toil and labor of the mind, to emancipate our thoughts from particular objects, and raise them to those sublime speculations that are conversant about abstract ideas. From all which the natural consequence should seem to be, that so difficult a thing as the forming abstract ideas was not necessary for *communication*, which is so easy and familiar to all sorts of men. But we are told, if they seem obvious and easy to grown men, *it is only because by constant and familiar use they are made so.* Now I would fain know at what time it is, men are employed in surmounting that difficulty, and furnishing themselves with those necessary helps for discourse. It cannot be when they are grown up, for then it seems they are not conscious of any such pains-taking; it remains therefore to be the business of their childhood. And surely, the great and multiplied labor of framing abstract notions, will be found a hard task for that tender age. It is not a hard thing to imagine, that a couple of children cannot prate together, of their sugar-plums and rattles and the rest of their little trinkets, till they have first tacked together numberless inconsistencies, and so framed in their minds *abstract general ideas*, and annexed them to every common name they make use of?

15. Nor do I think them a whit more needful for the *enlargement of knowledge* than for *communication.* It is I know a point much insisted on, that all knowledge and demonstration are about universal notions, to which I fully agree: but then it does not appear to me that those notions are formed by *abstraction* in the manner premised; *universality*, so far as I can comprehend, not consisting in the absolute, positive nature or conception of anything, but in the relation it bears to the particulars signified or represented by it: by virtue whereof it is that things, names, or notions, being in their own nature *particular,* are rendered *universal.* Thus when I demonstrate any proposition concerning triangles, it is to be supposed that I have in view the universal idea of a triangle; which ought not to be understood as if I could frame an idea of a triangle which was neither equilateral nor scalenon nor equicrural. But only that the particular triangle I consider, whether of this or that sort it matters not, does equally stand for and

represent all rectilinear triangles whatsoever, and is in that sense *universal*. All which seems very plain and not to include any difficulty in it.

16. But here it will be demanded, how we can know any proposition to be true of all particular triangles, except we have first seen it demonstrated of the abstract idea of a triangle which equally agrees to all? For because a property may be demonstrated to agree to some one particular triangle, it will not thence follow that it equally belongs to any other triangle, which in all respects is not the same with it. For example, having demonstrated that the three angles of an isosceles rectangular triangle are equal to two right ones, I cannot therefore conclude this affection agrees to all other triangles, which have neither a right angle, nor two equal sides. It seems therefore that, to be certain this proposition is universally true, we must either make a particular demonstration for every particular triangle, which is impossible, or once for all demonstrate it of the *abstract idea of a triangle*, in which all the particulars do indifferently partake, and by which they are all equally represented. To which I answer, that though the idea I have in view whilst I make the demonstration, be, for instance, that of an isosceles rectangular triangle, whose sides are of a determinate length, I may nevertheless be certain it extends to all other rectilinear triangles, of what sort or bigness soever. And that, because neither the right angle, nor the equality, nor determinate length of the sides, are at all concerned in the demonstration. It is true, the diagram I have in view includes all these particulars, but then there is not the least mention made of them in the proof of the proposition. It is not said, the three angles are equal to two right ones, because one of them is a right angle, or because the sides comprehending it are of the same length. Which sufficiently shows that the right angle might have been oblique, and the sides unequal, and for all that the demonstration have held good. And for this reason it is, that I conclude that to be true of any obliquangular or scalenon, which I had demonstrated of a particular right-angled, equicrural triangle; and not because I demonstrated the proposition of the abstract idea of a triangle. And here it must be acknowledged that a man may consider a figure merely as triangular, without attending to the particular qualities of the angles, or relations of the sides. So far he may abstract: but this will never prove, that he can frame an abstract general inconsistent idea of a triangle. In like manner we may consider *Peter* so far forth as man, or so far forth as animal, without framing the forementioned abstract idea, either of man or of animal, inasmuch as all that is perceived is not considered.

17. It were an endless, as well as a useless thing, to trace the *Schoolmen*, those great masters of abstraction, through all the manifold inextricable labyrinths of error and dispute, which their doctrine of abstract natures and notions seems to have led them into.[3] What bickerings and controversies, and what a learned dust have been raised about those matters, and what mighty advantage has been from thence derived to mankind, are things at this day too clearly known to need being insisted on. And it had been well if the ill effects of that doctrine were confined to those only who make the most avowed profession of it. When men consider the great pains, industry and parts, that have for so many ages been laid out on the cultivation and advancement of the sciences, and that notwithstanding all this, the far greater part of them remain full of darkness and uncertainty, and disputes that are like never to have an end, and even those that are thought to be supported by the most clear and cogent demonstrations, contain in them paradoxes which are perfectly irreconcilable to the understandings of men, and that taking all together, a small portion of them does supply any real benefit to mankind, otherwise than by being an innocent diversion and amusement: I say, the consideration of all this is apt to throw them into a despondency, and perfect contempt of all study. But this may perhaps cease, upon a view of the false principles that have obtained in the worlds, amongst all which there is none, methinks, has a more wide influence over the thoughts of speculative men, than this of abstract general ideas.

3. ["Schoolmen" refers to the philosophers and theologians who taught in the medieval universities (the "Schools") and to later figures who philosophized in their style. They were also known as "Scholastics." Berkeley does not refer to any of the Schoolmen by name in the *Principles*, but in *Alciphron* IV he briefly discusses St. Thomas Aquinas (c. 1224–1274) and Francisco Suarez (1548–1617). Berkeley's opinion of the Schoolmen is typical of its time: he thinks their "bickerings and controversies" are over-subtle and useless (a view expressed in the present section), and that they too often defer to the authority of Aristotle.]

18. I come now to consider the source of this prevailing notion, and that seems to me to be language. And surely nothing of less extent than reason itself could have been the source of an opinion so universally received. The truth of this appears as from other reasons, so also from the plain confession of the ablest patrons of abstract ideas, who acknowledge that they are made in order to naming; from which it is a clear consequence, that if there had been no such things as speech or universal signs, there never had been any thought of abstraction. *See* B. 3. C. 6. Sect. 39. *and elsewhere of the Essay on Human Understanding.* Let us therefore examine the manner wherein words have contributed to the origin of that mistake. First then, 'tis thought that every name has, or ought to have, one only precise and settled signification, which inclines men to think there are certain *abstract, determinate ideas,* which constitute the true and only immediate signification of each general name. And that it is by the mediation of these abstract ideas, that a general name comes to signify any particular thing. Whereas, in truth, there is no such thing as one precise and definite signification annexed to any general name, they all signifying indifferently a great number of particular ideas. All which does evidently follow from what has been already said, and will clearly appear to anyone by a little reflection. To this it will be objected, that every name that has a definition, is thereby restrained to one certain signification. For example, a *triangle* is defined to be a *plain surface comprehended by three right lines;* by which that name is limited to denote one certain idea and no other. To which I answer, that in the definition it is not said whether the surface be great or small, black or white, nor whether the sides are long or short, equal or unequal, nor with what angles they are inclined to each other; in all which there may be great variety, and consequently there is no one settled idea which limits the signification of the word *triangle.* 'Tis one thing for to keep a name constantly to the same definition, and another to make it stand everywhere for the same idea: the one is necessary, the other useless and impracticable.

19. But to give a farther account how words came to produce the doctrine of abstract ideas, it must be observed that it is a received opinion, that language has no other end but the communicating our ideas, and that every significant name stands for an idea. This being so, and it being withal certain, that names, which yet are not thought altogether insignificant, do not always mark out particular conceivable ideas, it is straightway concluded that they stand for abstract notions. That there are many names in use amongst speculative men, which do not always suggest to others determinate particular ideas, is what nobody will deny. And a little attention will discover, that it is not necessary (even in the strictest reasonings) significant names which stand for ideas should, every time they are used, excite in the understanding the ideas they are made to stand for: in reading and discoursing, names being for the most part used as letters are in *algebra,* in which though a particular quantity be marked by each letter, yet to proceed right it is not requisite that in every step each letter suggest to your thoughts, that particular quantity it was appointed to stand for.

20. Besides, the communicating of ideas marked by words is not the chief and only end of language, as is commonly supposed. There are other ends, as the raising of some passion, the exciting to, or deterring from an action, the putting the mind in some particular disposition; to which the former is in many cases barely subservient, and sometimes entirely omitted, when these can be obtained without it, as I think does not infrequently happen in the familiar use of language. I entreat the reader to reflect with himself, and see if it does not often happen either in hearing or reading a discourse, that the passions of fear, love, hatred, admiration, disdain, and the like, arise immediately in his mind upon the perception of certain words, without any ideas coming between. At first, indeed, the words might have occasioned ideas that were fit to produce those emotions; but, if I mistake not, it will be found that when language is once grown familiar, the hearing of the sounds or sight of the characters is oft immediately attended with those passions, which at first were wont to be produced by the intervention of ideas, that are now quite omitted. May we not, for example, be affected with the promise of a *good thing,* though we have not an idea of what it is? Or is not the being threatened with danger sufficient to excite a dread, though we think not of any particular evil likely to befall us, nor yet frame to ourselves an idea of danger in abstract? If anyone shall join ever so little reflection of his own to what has been said, I believe it will evidently appear to him, that general names are often used in the propriety of

language without the speaker's designing them for marks of ideas in his own, which he would have them raise in the mind of the hearer. Even proper names themselves do not seem always spoken, with a design to bring into our view the ideas of those individuals that are supposed to be marked by them. For example, when a Schoolman tells me *Aristotle has said it,* all I conceive he means by it, is to dispose me to embrace his opinion with the deference and submission which custom has annexed to that name. And this effect may be so instantly produced in the minds of those who are accustomed to resign their judgment to the authority of that philosopher, as it is impossible any idea either of his person, writings, or reputation should go before. Innumerable examples of this kind may be given, but why should I insist on those things, which everyone's experience will, I doubt not, plentifully suggest unto him?

21. We have, I think, shown the impossibility of *abstract ideas.* We have considered what has been said for them by their ablest patrons; and endeavored to show they are of no use for those ends, to which they are thought necessary. And lastly, we have traced them to the source from whence the flow, which appears to be language. It cannot be denied that words are of excellent use, in that by their means all that stock of knowledge which has been purchased by the joint labors of inquisitive men in all ages and nations, may be drawn into the view and made the possession of one single person. But at the same time it must be owned that most parts of knowledge have been strangely perplexed and darkened by the abuse of words, and general ways of speech wherein they are delivered. Since therefore words are so apt to impose on the understanding, whatever ideas I consider, I shall endeavor to take them bare and naked into my view, keeping out of my thoughts, so far as I am able, those names which long and constant use has so strictly united with them; from which I may expect to derive the following advantages.

22. First, I shall be sure to get clear of all controversies purely verbal; the springing up of which weeds in almost all the sciences has been a main hindrance to the growth of true and sound knowledge. Secondly, this seems to be a sure way to extricate myself out of that fine and subtle net of *abstract ideas*, which has so miserably perplexed and entangled the minds of men, and that with this peculiar circumstance, that by how much the finer and more curious was the wit of any man, by so much the deeper was he like to be ensnared, and faster held therein. Thirdly, so long as I confine my thoughts to my own ideas divested of words, I do not see how I can easily be mistaken. The objects I consider, I clearly and adequately know. I cannot be deceived in thinking I have an idea which I have not. It is not possible for me to imagine, that any of my own ideas are alike or unlike, that are not truly so. To discern the agreements or disagreements there are between my ideas, to see what ideas are included in any compound idea, and what not, there is nothing more requisite, than an attentive perception of what passes in my own understanding.

23. But the attainment of all these advantages does presuppose an entire deliverance from the deception of words, which I dare hardly promise myself; so difficult a thing it is to dissolve a union so early begun, and confirmed by so long a habit as that betwixt words and ideas. Which difficulty seems to have been very much increased by the doctrine of *abstraction.* For so long as men thought abstract ideas were annexed to their words, it does not seem strange that they should use words for ideas: it being found an impracticable thing to lay aside the word, and retain the abstract idea in the mind, which in itself was perfectly inconceivable. This seems to me the principal cause, why those men who have so emphatically recommended to others, the laying aside all use of words in their meditations, and contemplating their bare ideas, have yet failed to perform it themselves.[4] Of late many have been very sensible of the absurd opinions and insignificant disputes, which grow out of the abuse of words. And in order to remedy these evils they advise well, that we attend to the ideas signified, and draw off our attention from the words which signify them. But how good soever this advice may be, they have given others, it is plain they could not have a due regard to it themselves, so long as they thought the only immediate use of words was to signify ideas, and that the immediate signification of every general name was a *determinate, abstract idea*.

24. But these being known to be mistakes, a man may with greater ease prevent his being imposed on

4. [No doubt Berkeley is thinking of Locke, who often advises his readers to lay aside words and attend to ideas. See for example *Essay* IV iv 17 and IV iii 30.]

by words. He that knows he has no other than particular ideas, will not puzzle himself in vain to find out and conceive the abstract idea, annexed to any name. And he that knows names do not always stand for ideas, will spare himself the labor of looking for ideas, where there are none to be had. It were therefore to be wished that everyone would use his utmost endeavors, to obtain a clear view of the ideas he would consider, separating from them all that dress and encumbrance of words which so much contribute to blind the judgment and divide the attention. In vain do we extend our view into the heavens, and pry into the entrails of the earth, in vain do we consult the writings of learned men, and trace the dark footsteps of antiquity; we need only draw the curtain of words, to behold the fairest tree of knowledge, whose fruit is excellent, and within the reach of our hand.

25. Unless we take care to clear the first principles of knowledge, from the embarras and delusion of words, we may make infinite reasonings upon them to no purpose; we may draw consequences from consequences, and be never the wiser. The farther we go, we shall only lose ourselves the more irrecoverably, and be the deeper entangled in difficulties and mistakes. Whoever therefore designs to read the following sheets, I entreat him to make my words the occasion of his own thinking, and endeavor to attain the same train of thoughts in reading, that I had in writing them. By this means it will be easy for him to discover the truth or falsity of what I say. He will be out of all danger of being deceived by my words, and I do not see how he can be led into an error by considering his own naked, undisguised ideas.

Of the Principles of Human Knowledge

1. It is evident to anyone who takes a survey of the objects of human knowledge, that they are either ideas actually imprinted on the senses, or else such as are perceived by attending to the passions and operations of the mind, or lastly ideas formed by help of memory and imagination, either compounding, dividing, or barely representing those originally perceived in the aforesaid ways. By sight I have the ideas of light and colors with their several degrees and variations. By touch I perceive, for example, hard and soft, heat and cold, motion and resistance, and of all these more and less either as to quantity or degree. Smelling furnishes me with odors; the palate with tastes, and hearing conveys sounds to the mind in all their variety of tone and composition. And as several of these are observed to accompany each other, they come to be marked by one name, and so to be reputed as one thing. Thus, for example, a certain color, taste, smell, figure and consistence having been observed to go together, are accounted one distinct thing, signified by the name *apple*. Other collections of ideas constitute a stone, a tree, a book, and the like sensible things; which, as they are pleasing or disagreeable, excite the passions of love, hatred, joy, grief, and so forth.

2. But besides all that endless variety of ideas or objects of knowledge, there is likewise something which knows or perceives them, and exercises divers operations, as willing, imagining, remembering about them. This perceiving, active being is what I call *mind, spirit, soul* or *myself*. By which words I do not denote any one of my ideas, but a thing entirely distinct from them, wherein they exist, or, which is the same thing, whereby they are perceived; for the existence of an idea consists in being perceived.

3. That neither our thoughts, nor passions, nor ideas formed by the imagination, exist without the mind, is what everybody will allow. And it seems no less evident that the various sensations or ideas imprinted on the sense, however blended or combined together (that is, whatever objects they compose) cannot exist otherwise than in a mind perceiving them. I think an intuitive knowledge may be obtained of this, by anyone that shall attend to what is meant by the term *exist* when applied to sensible things. The table I write on, I say, exists, that is, I see and feel it; and if I were out of my study I should say it existed, meaning thereby that if I was in my study I might perceive it, or that some other spirit actually does perceive it. There was an odor, that is, it was smelled; there was a sound, that is to say, it was heard; a color or figure, and it was perceived by sight or touch. This is all that I can understand by these and the like expressions. For as to what is said of the absolute existence of unthinking things without any relation to their being perceived, that seems perfectly unintelligible. Their *esse* is *percipi*, nor is it possible they should have any

existence, out of the minds or thinking things which perceive them.[5]

4. It is indeed an opinion strangely prevailing amongst men, that houses, mountains, rivers, and in a word all sensible objects have an existence natural or real, distinct from their being perceived by the understanding. But with how great an assurance and acquiescence soever this principle may be entertained in the world; yet whoever shall find in his heart to call it in question, may, if I mistake not, perceive it to involve a manifest contradiction. For what are the forementioned objects but the things we perceive by sense, and what do we perceive besides our own ideas or sensations; and is it not plainly repugnant that any one of these or any combination of them should exist unperceived?

5. If we thoroughly examine this tenet, it will, perhaps, be found at bottom to depend on the doctrine of *abstract ideas.* For can there be a nicer strain of abstraction than to distinguish the existence of sensible objects from their being perceived, so as to conceive them existing unperceived? Light and colors, heat and cold, extension and figures, in a word the things we see and feel, what are they but so many sensations, notions, ideas or impressions on the sense; and is it possible to separate, even in thought, any of these from perception? For my part I might as easily divide a thing from itself. I may indeed divide in my thoughts or conceive apart from each other those things which, perhaps, I never perceived by sense so divided. Thus I imagine the trunk of a human body without the limbs, or conceive the smell of a rose without thinking on the rose itself. So far I will not deny I can abstract, if that may properly be called *abstraction,* which extends only to the conceiving separately such objects, as it is possible may really exist or be actually perceived asunder. But my conceiving or imagining power does not extend beyond the possibility of real existence or perception. Hence as it is impossible for me to see or feel anything without an actual sensation of that thing, so is it impossible for me to conceive in my thoughts any sensible thing or object distinct from the sensation or perception of it.

6. Some truths there are so near and obvious to the mind, that a man need only open his eyes to see them. Such I take this important one to be, to wit, that all the choir of heaven and furniture of the earth, in a word all those bodies which compose the mighty frame of the world, have not any subsistence without a mind, that their being is to be perceived or known; that consequently so long as they are not actually perceived by me, or do not exist in my mind or that of any other created spirit, they must either have no existence at all, or else subsist in the mind of some eternal spirit: it being perfectly unintelligible and involving all the absurdity of abstraction, to attribute to any single part of them an existence independent of a spirit. To be convinced of which, the reader need only reflect and try to separate in his own thoughts the being of a sensible thing from its being perceived.

7. From what has been said, it follows, there is not any other substance than *spirit,* or that which perceives. But for the fuller proof of this point, let it be considered, the sensible qualities are color, figure, motion, smell, taste, and such like, that is, the ideas perceived by sense. Now for an idea to exist in an unperceiving thing, is a manifest contradiction; for to have an idea is all one as to perceive: that therefore wherein color, figure, and the like qualities exist, must perceive them; hence it is clear there can be no unthinking substance or *substratum* of those ideas.

8. But say you, though the ideas themselves do not exist without the mind, yet there may be things like them whereof they are copies or resemblances, which things exist without the mind, in an unthinking substance. I answer, an idea can be like nothing but an idea; a color or figure can be like nothing but another color or figure. If we look but ever so little into our thoughts, we shall find it impossible for us to conceive a likeness except only between our ideas. Again, I ask whether those supposed originals or external things, of which our ideas are the pictures or representations, be themselves perceivable or no? If they are, then they are ideas, and we have gained our point; but if you say they are not, I appeal to anyone whether it be sense, to assert a color is like something which is invisible; hard or soft, like something which is intangible; and so of the rest.

9. Some there are who make a distinction betwixt *primary* and *secondary* qualities: by the former, they mean extension, figure, motion, rest, solidity or impenetrability and number: by the latter they denote all other sensible qualities, as colors, sounds,

5. [*esse*, to be; *percipi*, to be perceived.]

tastes, and so forth.[6] The ideas we have of these they acknowledge not to be the resemblances of anything existing without the mind or unperceived; but they will have our ideas of the primary qualities to be patterns or images of things which exist without the mind, in an unthinking substance which they call *matter.* By matter therefore we are to understand an inert, senseless substance, in which extension, figure, and motion, do actually subsist. But it is evident from what we have already shown, that extension, figure and motion are only ideas existing in the mind, and that an idea can be like nothing but another idea, and that consequently neither they nor their archetypes can exist in an unperceiving substance. Hence it is plain, that the very notion of what is called *matter* or *corporeal substance,* involves a contradiction in it.

10. They who assert that figure, motion, and the rest of the primary or original qualities do exist without the mind, in unthinking substances, do at the same time acknowledge that colors, sounds, heat, cold, and such like secondary qualities, do not, which they tell us are sensations existing in the mind alone, that depend on and are occasioned by the different size, texture and motion of the minute particles of matter. This they take for an undoubted truth, which they can demonstrate beyond all exception. Now if it be certain, that those original qualities are inseparably united with the other sensible qualities, and not, even in thought, capable of being abstracted from them, it plainly follows that they exist only in the mind. But I desire anyone to reflect and try, whether he can by any abstraction of thought, conceive the extension and motion of a body, without all other sensible qualities. For my own part, I see evidently that it is not in my power to frame an idea of a body extended and moved, but I must withal give it some color or other sensible quality which is acknowledged to exist only in the mind. In short, extension, figure, and motion, abstracted from all other qualities, are inconceivable. Where therefore the other sensible qualities are, there must these be also, to wit, in the mind and nowhere else.

11. Again, *great* and *small, swift* and *slow,* are allowed to exist nowhere without the mind, being entirely relative, and changing as the frame or position of the organs of sense varies. The extension therefore which exists without the mind, is neither great nor small, the motion neither swift nor slow, that is, they are nothing at all. But say you, they are extension in general, and motion in general: thus we see how much the tenet of extended, moveable substances existing without the mind, depends on that strange doctrine of *abstract ideas.* And here I cannot but remark, how nearly the vague and indeterminate description of matter or corporeal substance, which the modern philosophers are run into by their own principles, resembles that antiquated and so much ridiculed notion of *materia prima,* to be met with in *Aristotle* and his followers.[7] Without extension solidity cannot be conceived; since therefore it has been shown that extension exists not in an unthinking substance, the same must also be true of solidity.

12. That number is entirely the creature of the mind, even though the other qualities be allowed to exist without, will be evident to whoever considers, that the same thing bears a different denomination of numbers, as the mind views it with different respects. Thus, the same extension is one or three or thirty six, according as the mind considers it with reference to a yard, a foot, or an inch. Number is so visibly relative, and dependent on men's understanding, that it is strange to think how anyone should give it an absolute existence without the mind. We say one book, one page, one line; all these are equally units, though some contain several of the others. And in each instance it is plain, the unit relates to some particular combination of ideas arbitrarily put together by the mind.

13. Unity I know some will have to be a simple or uncompounded idea, accompanying all other ideas into the mind.[8] That I have any such idea answering the word *unity,* I do not find; and if I had, methinks I could not miss finding it; on the contrary it should be the most familiar to my understanding, since it is

6. [Locke makes the distinction at *Essay* II viii 9–26.]

7. [Aristotle calls the wood of a casket its *matter.* He thinks the various kinds of matter can be arranged in a hierarchy: wood, for example, is matter for a casket, while earth (one of the four basic elements) is matter for wood. *Materia prima,* or prime matter, is a totally indeterminate substratum, the most basic item in the hierarchy. Berkeley follows a long tradition when he attributes belief in prime matter to Aristotle, but it is a tradition many scholars now dispute.]

8. [Locke makes these observations about unity at *Essay* II xvi 1.]

said to accompany all other ideas, and to be perceived by all the ways of sensation and reflection. To say no more, it is an *abstract idea*.

14. I shall farther add, that after the same manner, as modern philosophers prove certain sensible qualities to have no existence in matter, or without the mind, the same thing may be likewise proved of all other sensible qualities whatsoever. Thus, for instance, it is said that heat and cold are affections only of the mind, and not at all patterns of real beings, existing in the corporeal substances which excite them, for that the same body which appears cold to one hand, seems warm to another. Now why may we not as well argue that figure and extension are not patterns or resemblances of qualities existing in matter, because to the same eye at different stations, or eyes of a different texture at the same station, they appear various, and cannot therefore be the images of anything settled and determinate without the mind? Again, it is proved that sweetness is not really in the sapid thing, because the thing remaining unaltered the sweetness is changed into bitter, as in case of a fever or otherwise vitiated palate. It is not as reasonable to say, that motion is not without the mind, since if the succession of ideas in the mind become swifter, the motion, it is acknowledged, shall appear slower without any alteration in any external object.

15. In short, let anyone consider those arguments, which are thought manifestly to prove that colors and tastes exist only in the mind, and he shall find they may with equal force, be brought to prove the same thing of extension, figure, and motion. Though it must be confessed this method of arguing does not so much prove that there is no extension or color in an outward object, as that we do not know by sense which is the true extension or color of the object. But the arguments foregoing plainly show it to be impossible that any color or extension at all, or other sensible quality whatsoever, should exist in an unthinking subject without the mind, or in truth, that there should be any such thing as an outward object.

16. But let us examine a little the received opinion. It is said extension is a mode or accident of matter, and that matter is the *substratum* that supports it. Now I desire that you would explain what is meant by matter's *supporting* extension: say you, I have no idea of matter, and therefore cannot explain it. I answer, though you have no positive, yet if you have any meaning at all, you must at least have a relative idea of matter; though you know not what it is, yet you must be supposed to know what relation it bears to accidents, and what is meant by its supporting them. It is evident *support* cannot here be taken in its usual or literal sense, as when we say that pillars support a building: in what sense therefore must it be taken?

17. If we inquire into what the most accurate philosophers declare themselves to mean by *material substance*; we shall find them acknowledge, they have no other meaning annexed to those sounds, but the idea of being in general, together with the relative notion of its supporting accidents.[9] The general idea of being appears to me the most abstract and incomprehensible of all other; and as for its supporting accidents, this, as we have just now observed, cannot be understood in the common sense of those words; it must therefore be taken in some other sense, but what that is they do not explain. So that when I consider the two parts or branches which make the signification of the words *material substance*, I am convinced there is no distinct meaning annexed to them. But why should we trouble ourselves any farther, in discussing this material *substratum* or support of figure and motion, and other sensible qualities? Does it not suppose they have an existence without the mind? And is not this a direct repugnancy, and altogether inconceivable?

18. But though it were possible that solid, figured, moveable substances may exist without the mind, corresponding to the ideas we have of bodies, yet how is it possible for us to know this? Either we must know it by sense, or by reason. As for our senses, by them we have the knowledge only of our sensations, ideas, or those things that are immediately perceived by sense, call them what you will: but they do not inform us that things exist without the mind, or unperceived, like to those which are perceived. This the materialists themselves acknowledge. It remains therefore that if we have any knowledge at all of external things, it must be by reason, inferring their existence from what is immediately perceived by sense. But what reason can induce us to believe the existence of bodies without the mind, from what we perceive, since the very patrons of matter themselves do not pretend, there is any necessary connection betwixt them and our ideas?

9. [Berkeley is probably referring to Locke's remarks on "pure substance in general" at *Essay* II xxiii 2.]

I say it is granted on all hands (and what happens in dreams, frenzies, and the like, puts it beyond dispute) that it is possible we might be affected with all the ideas we have now, though no bodies existed without, resembling them. Hence it is evident the supposition of external bodies is not necessary for the producing our ideas: since it is granted they are produced sometimes, and might possibly be produced always in the same order we see them in at present, without their concurrence.

19. But though we might possibly have all our sensations without them, yet perhaps it may be thought easier to conceive and explain the manner of their production, by supposing external bodies in their likeness rather than otherwise; and so it might be at least probable there are such things as bodies that excite their ideas in our minds. But neither can this be said; for though we give the materialists their external bodies, they by their own confession are never the nearer knowing how our ideas are produced: since they own themselves unable to comprehend in what manner body can act upon spirit, or how it is possible it should imprint any idea in the mind. Hence it is evident the production of ideas or sensations in our minds, can be no reason why we should suppose matter or corporeal substances, since that is acknowledged to remain equally inexplicable with, or without this supposition. If therefore it were possible for bodies to exist without the mind, yet to hold they do so, must needs be a very precarious opinion; since it is to suppose, without any reason at all, that God has created innumerable beings that are entirely useless, and serve to no manner of purpose.

20. In short, if there were external bodies, it is impossible we should ever come to know it; and if there were not, we might have the very same reasons to think there were that we have now. Suppose, what no one can deny possible, an intelligence, without the help of external bodies, to be affected with the same train of sensations or ideas that you are, imprinted in the same order and with like vividness in his mind. I ask whether that intelligence has not all the reason to believe the existence of corporeal substances, represented by his ideas, and exciting them in his mind, that you can possibly have for believing the same thing? Of this there can be no question; which one consideration is enough to make any reasonable person suspect the strength of whatever arguments he may think himself to have, for the existence of bodies without the mind.

21. Were it necessary to add any farther proof against the existence of matter, after what has been said, I could instance several of those errors and difficulties (not to mention impieties) which have sprung from that tenet. It has occasioned numberless controversies and disputes in philosophy, and not a few of far greater moment in religion. But I shall not enter into the detail of them in this place, as well because I think, arguments *a posteriori* are unnecessary for confirming what has been, if I mistake not, sufficiently demonstrated *a priori*, as because I shall hereafter find occasion to say somewhat of them.[10]

22. I am afraid I have given cause to think me needlessly prolix in handling this subject. For to what purpose is it to dilate on that which may be demonstrated with the utmost evidence in a line or two, to anyone that is capable of the least reflection? It is but looking into your own thoughts, and so trying whether you can conceive it possible for a sound, or figure, or motion, or color, to exist without the mind, or unperceived. This easy trial may make you see, that what you contend for, is a downright contradiction. Insomuch that I am content to put the whole upon this issue; if you can but conceive it possible for one extended moveable substance, or in general, for any one idea or anything like an idea, to exist otherwise than in a mind perceiving it, I shall readily give up the cause: and as for all that *compages* of external bodies which you contend for, I shall grant you its existence, though you cannot either give me any reason why you believe it exists, or assign any use to it when it is supposed to exist. I say, the bare possibility of your opinion's being true, shall pass for an argument that it is so.

23. But say you, surely there is nothing easier than

10. [*a posteriori*, from what comes after; *a priori*, from what comes before. These are among the first appearances of these expressions in English. Berkeley does not use the expressions as philosophers do today. According to Berkeley, an *a posteriori* argument against a belief attacks the belief through its effects or consequences, which in the case of matter include skepticism, atheism, and various difficulties in physics and mathematics. An *a priori* argument attacks the belief directly. Berkeley's promise to present the *a posteriori* case against matter is fulfilled in sections 85–96 and 101–34.]

to imagine trees, for instance, in a park, or books existing in a closet, and nobody by to perceive them. I answer, you may so, there is no difficulty in it: but what is all this, I beseech you, more than framing in your mind certain ideas which you call *books* and *trees*, and at the same time omitting to frame the idea of anyone that may perceive them? But do not you yourself perceive or think of them all the while? This therefore is nothing to the purpose: it only shows you have the power of imagining or forming ideas in your mind; but it does not show that you can conceive it possible, the objects of your thought may exist without the mind: to make out this, it is necessary that you conceive them existing unconceived or unthought of, which is a manifest repugnancy. When we do our utmost to conceive the existence of external bodies, we are all the while only contemplating our own ideas. But the mind taking no notice of itself, is deluded to think it can and does conceive bodies existing unthought of or without the mind; though at the same time they are apprehended by or exist in itself. A little attention will discover to anyone the truth and evidence of what is here said, and make it unnecessary to insist on any other proofs against the existence of material substance.

24. It is very obvious, upon the least inquiry into our own thoughts, to know whether it be possible for us to understand what is meant, by the *absolute existence of sensible objects in themselves, or without the mind.* To me it is evident those words mark out either a direct contradiction, or else nothing at all. And to convince others of this, I know no readier or fairer way, than to entreat they would calmly attend to their own thoughts: and if by this attention, the emptiness or repugnancy of those expressions does appear, surely nothing more is requisite for their conviction. It is on this therefore that I insist, to wit, that the absolute existence of unthinking things are words without a meaning, or which include a contradiction. This is what I repeat and inculcate, and earnestly recommend to the attentive thoughts of the reader.

25. All our ideas, sensations, or the things which we perceive, by whatsoever names they may be distinguished, are visibly inactive, there is nothing of power or agency included in them. So that one idea or object of thought cannot produce, or make any alteration in another. To be satisfied of the truth of this, there is nothing else requisite but a bare observation of our ideas. For since they and every part of them exist only in the mind, it follows that there is nothing in them but what is perceived. But whoever shall attend to his ideas, whether of sense or reflection, will not perceive in them any power or activity; there is therefore no such thing contained in them. A little attention will discover to us that the very being of an idea implies passiveness and inertness in it, insomuch that it is impossible for an idea to do anything, or, strictly speaking, to be the cause of anything: neither can it be the resemblance or pattern of any active being, as is evident from Sect. 8. Whence it plainly follows that extension, figure and motion, cannot be the cause of our sensations. To say therefore, that these are the effects of powers resulting from the configuration, number, motion, and size of corpuscles, must certainly be false.

26. We perceive a continual succession of ideas, some are anew excited, others are changed or totally disappear. There is therefore some cause of these ideas whereon they depend, and which produces and changes them. That this cause cannot be any quality or idea or combination of ideas, is clear from the preceding section. It must therefore be a substance; but it has been shown that there is no corporeal or material substance: it remains therefore that the cause of ideas is an incorporeal active substance or spirit.

27. A spirit is one simple, undivided, active being: as it perceives ideas, it is called the *understanding*, and as it produces or otherwise operates about them, it is called the *will*. Hence there can be no idea formed of a soul or spirit: for all ideas whatever, being passive and inert, *vide* Sect. 25, they cannot represent unto us, by way of image or likeness, that which acts. A little attention will make it plain to anyone, that to have an idea which shall be like that active principle of motion and change of ideas, is absolutely impossible. Such is the nature of *spirit* or that which acts, that it cannot be of itself perceived, but only by the effects which it produces. If any man shall doubt of the truth of what is here delivered, let him but reflect and try if he can frame the idea of any power or active being; and whether he has ideas of two principal powers, marked by the names *will* and *understanding*, distinct from each other as well as from a third idea of substance or being in general, with a relative notion of its supporting or being the subject of the

aforesaid powers, which is signified by the name *soul* or *spirit*. This is what some hold; but so far as I can see, the words *will, soul, spirit,* do not stand for different ideas, or in truth, for any idea at all, but for something which is very different from ideas, and which being an agent cannot be like unto, or represented by, any idea whatsoever. Though it must be owned at the same time, that we have some notion of soul, spirit, and the operations of the mind, such as willing, loving, hating, inasmuch as we know or understand the meaning of those words.

28. I find I can excite ideas in my mind at pleasure, and vary and shift the scene as oft as I think fit. It is no more than willing, and straightaway this or that idea arises in my fancy: and by the same power it is obliterated, and makes way for another. This making and unmaking of ideas does very properly denominate the mind active. Thus much is certain, and grounded on experience: but when we talk of unthinking agents, or of exciting ideas exclusive of volition, we only amuse ourselves with words.

29. But whatever power I may have over my own thoughts, I find the ideas actually perceived by sense have not a like dependence on my will. When in broad daylight I open my eyes, it is not in my power to choose whether I shall see or no, or to determine what particular objects shall present themselves to my view; and so likewise as to the hearing and other senses, the ideas imprinted on them are not creatures of my will. There is therefore some other will or spirit that produces them.

30. The ideas of sense are more strong, lively, and distinct than those of the imagination; they have likewise a steadiness, order, and coherence, and are not excited at random, as those which are the effects of human will often are, but in a regular train or series, the admirable connection whereof sufficiently testifies the wisdom and benevolence of its author. Now the set rules or established methods, wherein the mind we depend on excites in us the ideas of sense, are called the *laws of nature*: and these we learn by experience, which teaches us that such and such ideas are attended with such and such other ideas, in the ordinary course of things.

31. This gives us a sort of foresight, which enables us to regulate our actions for the benefit of life. And without this we should be eternally at a loss: we could not know how to act anything that might procure us the least pleasure, or remove the least pain of sense. That food nourishes, sleep refreshes, and fire warms us; that to sow in the seed-time is the way to reap in the harvest, and, in general, that to obtain such or such ends, such or such means are conducive, all this we know, not by discovering any necessary connection between our ideas, but only by the observations of the settled laws of nature, without which we should be all in uncertainty and confusion, and a grown man no more know how to manage himself in the affairs of life, than an infant just born.

32. And yet this consistent uniform working, which so evidently displays the goodness and wisdom of that governing spirit whose will constitutes the laws of nature, is so far from leading our thoughts to him, that it rather sends them awandering after second causes. For when we perceive certain ideas of sense constantly followed by other ideas, and we know this is not of our own doing, we forthwith attribute power and agency to the ideas themselves, and make one the cause of another, than which nothing can be more absurd and unintelligible. Thus, for example, having observed that when we perceive by sight a certain round luminous figure, we at the same time perceive by touch the idea or sensation called *heat*, we do from thence conclude the sun to be the cause of heat. And in like manner perceiving the motion and collision of bodies to be attended with sound, we are inclined to think the latter an effect of the former.

33. The ideas imprinted on the senses by the Author of Nature are called *real things*: and those excited in the imagination being less regular, vivid and constant, are more properly termed *ideas*, or *images of things*, which they copy and represent. But then our sensations, be they never so vivid and distinct, are nevertheless *ideas*, that is, they exist in the mind, or are perceived by it, as truly as the ideas of its own framing. The ideas of sense are allowed to have more reality in them, that is, to be more strong, orderly, and coherent than the creatures of the mind; but this is no argument that they exist without the mind. They are also less dependent on the spirit, or thinking substance which perceives them, in that they are excited by the will of another and more powerful spirit: yet still they are *ideas*, and certainly no *idea*, whether faint or strong, can exist otherwise than in a mind perceiving it.

34. Before we proceed any farther, it is necessary to

spend some time in answering objections which may probably be made against the principles hitherto laid down. In doing of which, if I seem too prolix to those of quick apprehensions, I hope it may be pardoned, since all men do not equally apprehend things of this nature; and I am willing to be understood by everyone. First then, it will be objected that by the foregoing principles, all that is real and substantial in nature is banished out of the world: and instead thereof a chimerical scheme of ideas takes place. All things that exist, exist only in the mind, that is, they are purely notional. What therefore becomes of the sun, moon, and stars? What must we think of houses, rivers, mountains, trees, stones; nay, even of our own bodies? Are all these but so many chimeras and illusions on the fancy? To all which, and whatever else of the same sort may be objected, I answer, that by the principles premised, we are not deprived of any one thing in nature. Whatever we see, feel, hear, or any wise conceive or understand, remains as secure as ever, and is as real as ever. There is a *rerum natura*, and the distinction between realities and chimeras retains its full force. This is evident from Sect. 29, 30, and 33, where we have shown what is meant by *real things* in opposition to *chimeras*, or ideas of our own framing; but then they both equally exist in the mind, and in that sense are alike *ideas*.

35. I do not argue against the existence of any one thing that we can apprehend, either by sense or reflection. That the things I see with mine eyes and touch with my hands do exist, really exist, I make not the least question. The only thing whose existence we deny, is that which philosophers call matter or corporeal substance. And in doing of this, there is no damage done to the rest of mankind, who, I dare say, will never miss it. The atheist indeed will want the color of an empty name to support his impiety; and the philosophers may possibly find, they have lost a great handle for trifling and disputation.

36. If any man thinks this detracts from the existence or reality of things, he is very far from understanding what has been premised in the plainest terms I could think of. Take here an abstract of what has been said. There are spiritual substances, minds, or human souls, which will or excite ideas in themselves at pleasure: but these are faint, weak, and unsteady in respect of others they perceive by sense, which being impressed upon them according to certain rules or laws of nature, speak themselves the effects of a mind more powerful and wise than human spirits. These latter are said to have more *reality* in them than the former: by which is meant that they are more affecting, orderly, and distinct, and that they are not fictions of the mind perceiving them. And in this sense, the sun that I see by day is the real sun, and that which I imagine by night is the idea of the former. In the sense here given of *reality*, it is evident that every vegetable, star, mineral, and in general each part of the mundane system, is as much a *real being* by our principles as by any other. Whether others mean anything by the term *reality* different from what I do, I entreat them to look into their own thoughts and see.

37. It will be urged that thus much at least is true, to wit, that we take away all corporeal substances. To this my answer is, that if the word *substance* be taken in the vulgar sense, for a combination of sensible qualities, such as extension, solidity, weight, and the like; this we cannot be accused of taking away. But if it be taken in a philosophic sense, for the support of accidents or qualities without the mind: then indeed I acknowledge that we take it away, if one may be said to take away that which never had any existence, not even in the imagination.

38. But, say you, it sounds very harsh to say we eat and drink ideas, and are clothed with ideas. I acknowledge it does so, the word *idea* not being used in common discourse to signify the several combinations of sensible qualities, which are called *things*: and it is certain that any expression which varies from the familiar use of language, will seem harsh and ridiculous. But this does not concern the truth of the proposition, which in other words is no more than to say, we are fed and clothed with those things which we perceive immediately by our senses. The hardness or softness, the color, taste, warmth, figure, and such like qualities, which combined together constitute the several sorts of victuals and apparel, have been shown to exist only in the mind that perceives them; and this is all that is meant by calling them *ideas*; which word, if it was as ordinarily used as *thing*, would sound no harsher nor more ridiculous than it. I am not for disputing about the propriety, but the truth of the expression. If therefore you agree with me that we eat and drink, and are clad with the immediate objects of sense which cannot exist unperceived or without the mind: I shall readily grant it is more

proper or conformable to custom, that they should be called things rather than ideas.

39. If it be demanded why I make use of the word *idea*, and do not rather in compliance with custom call them things. I answer, I do it for two reasons: first, because the term *thing*, in contradistinction to *idea*, is generally supposed to denote somewhat existing without the mind: secondly, because *thing* has a more comprehensive signification than *idea*, including spirits or thinking things as well as ideas. Since therefore the objects of sense exist only in the mind, and are withal thoughtless and inactive, I chose to mark them by the word *idea*, which implies those properties.

40. But say what we can, someone perhaps may be apt to reply, he will still believe his senses, and never suffer any arguments, how plausible soever, to prevail over the certainty of them. Be it so, assert the evidence of sense as high as you please, we are willing to do the same. That what I see, hear and feel does exist, that is to say, is perceived by me, I no more doubt than I do of my own being. But I do not see how the testimony of sense can be alleged, as a proof for the existence of anything, which is not perceived by sense. We are not for having any man turn *skeptic*, and disbelieve his senses; on the contrary we give them all the stress and assurance imaginable; nor are there any principles more opposite to skepticism, than those we have laid down, as shall be hereafter clearly shown.

41. Secondly, it will be objected that there is a great difference betwixt real fire, for instance, and the idea of fire, betwixt dreaming or imagining oneself burnt, and actually being so: this and the like may be urged in opposition to our tenets. To all which the answer is evident from what has been already said, and I shall only add in this place, that if real fire be very different from the idea of fire, so also is the real pain that it occasions, very different from the idea of the same pain: and yet nobody will pretend that real pain either is, or can possibly be, in an unperceiving thing or without the mind, any more than its idea.

42. Thirdly, it will be objected that we see things actually without or at a distance from us, and which consequently do not exist in the mind, it being absurd that those things which are seen at the distance of several miles, should be as near to us as our own thoughts. In answer to this, I desire it may be considered, that in a dream we do oft perceive things as existing at a great distance off, and yet for all that, those things are acknowledged to have their existence only in the mind.

43. But for the fuller clearing of this point, it may be worthwhile to consider, how it is that we perceive distance and things placed at a distance by sight. For that we should in truth see external space, and bodies actually existing in it, some nearer, others farther off, seems to carry with it some opposition to what has been said, of their existing nowhere without the mind. The consideration of this difficulty it was, that gave birth to my *Essay towards a New Theory of Vision*, which was published not long since. Wherein it is shown that *distance* or outness is neither immediately of itself perceived by sight, nor yet apprehended or judged of by lines and angles, or anything that has a necessary connection with it: but that it is only suggested to our thoughts, by certain visible ideas and sensations attending vision, which in their own nature have no manner of similitude or relation, either with distance, or things placed at a distance. But by a connection taught us by experience, they come to signify and suggest them to us, after the same manner that words of any language suggest the ideas they are made to stand for. Insomuch that a man born blind, and afterwards made to see, would not, at first sight, think the things he saw, to be without his mind, or at any distance from him. See Sect. 41 of the forementioned treatise.

44. The ideas of sight and touch make two species, entirely distinct and heterogeneous. The former are marks and prognostics of the latter. That the proper objects of sight neither exist without the mind, nor are the images of external things, was shown even in that treatise. Though throughout the same, the contrary be supposed true of tangible objects: not that to suppose that vulgar error, was necessary for establishing the notion therein laid down; but because it was beside my purpose to examine and refute it in a discourse concerning *vision*. So that in strict truth the ideas of sight, when we apprehend by them distance and things placed at a distance, do not suggest or mark out to us things actually existing at a distance, but only admonish us what ideas of touch will be imprinted in our minds at such and such distances of time, and in consequence of such or such actions. It is, I say, evident from what has been said in the foregoing parts of this treatise, and in Sect. 147, and

elsewhere of the essay concerning vision, that visible ideas are the language whereby the governing spirit, on whom we depend, informs us what tangible ideas he is about to imprint upon us, in case we excite this or that motion in our own bodies. But for a fuller information in this point, I refer to the essay itself.

45. Fourthly, it will be objected that from the foregoing principles it follows, things are every moment annihilated and created anew. The objects of sense exist only when they are perceived: the trees therefore are in the garden, or the chairs in the parlor, no longer than while there is somebody by to perceive them. Upon shutting my eyes all the furniture in the room is reduced to nothing, and barely upon opening them it is again created. In answer to all which, I refer the reader to what has been said in Sect. 3, 4, etc. and desire he will consider whether he means anything by the actual existence of an idea, distinct from its being perceived. For my part, after the nicest inquiry I could make, I am not able to discover that anything else is meant by those words. And I once more entreat the reader to sound his own thoughts, and not suffer himself to be imposed on by words. If he can conceive it possible either for his ideas or their archetypes to exist without being perceived, then I give up the cause: but if he cannot, he will acknowledge it is unreasonable for him to stand up in defense of he knows not what, and pretend to charge on me as an absurdity, the not assenting to those propositions which at bottom have no meaning in them.

46. It will not be amiss to observe, how far the received principles of philosophy are themselves chargeable with those pretended absurdities. It is thought strangely absurd that upon closing my eyelids, all the visible objects round me should be reduced to nothing; and yet is not this what philosophers commonly acknowledge, when they agree on all hands, that light and colors, which alone are the proper and immediate objects of sight, are mere sensations that exist no longer than they are perceived? Again, it may to some perhaps seem very incredible, that things should be every moment creating, yet this very notion is commonly taught in the Schools. For the *Schoolmen*, though they acknowledge the existence of matter, and that the whole mundane fabric is framed out of it, are nevertheless of opinion that it cannot subsist without the divine conservation, which by them is expounded to be a continual creation.

47. Farther, a little thought will discover to us, that though we allow the existence of matter or corporeal substance, yet it will unavoidably follow from the principles which are now generally admitted, that the particular bodies of what kind soever, do none of them exist whilst they are not perceived. For it is evident from Sect. 11 and the following sections, that the matter philosophers contend for, is an incomprehensible somewhat which has none of those particular qualities, whereby the bodies falling under our senses are distinguished one from another. But to make this more plain, it must be remarked, that the infinite divisibility of matter is now universally allowed, at least by the most approved and considerable philosophers, who on the received principles demonstrate it beyond all exception. Hence it follows, that there is an infinite number of parts in each particle of matter, which are not perceived by sense. The reason therefore, that any particular body seems to be of a finite magnitude, or exhibits only a finite number of parts to sense, is, not because it contains no more, since in itself it contains an infinite number of parts, but because the sense is not acute enough to discern them. In proportion therefore as the sense is rendered more acute, it perceives a greater number of parts in the object, that is, the object appears greater, and its figure varies, those parts in its extremities which were before unperceivable, appearing now to bound it in very different lines and angles from those perceived by an obtuser sense. And at length, after various changes of size and shape, when the sense becomes infinitely acute, the body shall seem infinite. During all which there is no alteration in the body, but only in the sense. Each body therefore considered in itself, is infinitely extended, and consequently void of all shape or figure. From which it follows, that though we should grant the existence of matter to be ever so certain, yet it is withal as certain, the materialists themselves are by their own principles forced to acknowledge, that neither the particular bodies perceived by sense, nor anything like them exists without the mind. Matter, I say, and each particle thereof is according to them infinite and shapeless, and it is the mind that frames all that variety of bodies which compose the visible world, any one whereof does not exist longer than it is perceived.

48. If we consider it, the objection proposed in Sect. 45 will not be found reasonably charged on the

principles we have premised, so as in truth to make any objection at all against our notions. For though we hold indeed the objects of sense to be nothing else but ideas which cannot exist unperceived; yet we may not hence conclude they have no existence except only while they are perceived by us, since there may be some other spirit that perceives them, though we do not. Wherever bodies are said to have no existence without the mind, I would not be understood to mean this or that particular mind, but all minds whatsoever. It does not therefore follow from the foregoing principles, that bodies are annihilated and created every moment, or exist not at all during the intervals between our perception of them.

49. Fifthly, it may perhaps be objected, that if extension and figure exist only in the mind, it follows that the mind is extended and figured; since extension is a mode or attribute, which (to speak with the Schools) is predicated of the subject in which it exists. I answer, those qualities are in the mind only as they are perceived by it, that is, not by way of *mode* or *attribute*, but only by way of *idea*; and it no more follows, that the soul or mind is extended because extension exists in it alone, than it does that it is red or blue, because those colors are on all hands acknowledged to exist in it, and nowhere else. As to what philosophers say of subject and mode, that seems very groundless and unintelligible. For instance, in this proposition, a die is hard, extended and square, they will have it that the word *die* denotes a subject or substance, distinct from the hardness, extension and figure, which are predicated of it, and in which they exist. This I cannot comprehend: to me a die seems to be nothing distinct from those things which are termed its modes or accidents. And to say a die is hard, extended and square, is not to attribute those qualities to a subject distinct from and supporting them, but only an explication of the meaning of the word *die*.

50. Sixthly, you will say there have been a great many things explained by matter and motion: take away these, and you destroy the whole corpuscular philosophy, and undermine those mechanical principles which have been applied with so much success to account for the *phenomena*. In short, whatever advances have been made, either by ancient or modern philosophers, in the study of nature, do all proceed on the supposition, that corporeal substance or matter does really exist. To this I answer, that there is not any one *phenomenon* explained on that supposition, which may not as well be explained without it, as might easily be made appear by an induction of particulars. To explain the *phenomena*, is all one as to show, why upon such and such occasions we are affected with such and such ideas. But how matter should operate on a spirit, or produce any idea in it, is what no philosopher will pretend to explain. It is therefore evident, there can be no use of matter in natural philosophy. Besides, they who attempt to account for things, do it not by corporeal substance, but by figure, motion, and other qualities, which are in truth no more than mere ideas, and therefore cannot be the cause of anything, as has been already shown. See Sect. 25.

51. Seventhly, it will upon this be demanded whether it does not seem absurd to take away natural causes, and ascribe everything to the immediate operation of spirits? We must no longer say upon these principles that fire heats, or water cools, but that a spirit heats, and so forth. Would not a man be deservedly laughed at, who should talk after this manner? I answer, he would so; in such things we ought to *think with the learned, and speak with the vulgar.* They who to demonstration are convinced of the truth of the *Copernican* system, do nevertheless say the sun rises, the sun sets, or comes to the meridian: and if they affected a contrary style in common talk, it would without doubt appear very ridiculous. A little reflection on what is here said will make it manifest, that the common use of language would receive no manner of alteration or disturbance from the admission of our tenets.

52. In the ordinary affairs of life, any phrases may be retained, so long as they excite in us proper sentiments, or dispositions to act in such a manner as is necessary for our well-being, how false soever they may be, if taken in a strict and speculative sense. Nay this is unavoidable, since propriety being regulated by custom, language is suited to the received opinions, which are not always the truest. Hence it is impossible, even in the most rigid philosophic reasonings, so far to alter the bent and genius of the tongue we speak, as never to give a handle for cavillers to pretend difficulties and inconsistencies. But a fair and ingenuous reader will collect the sense, from the scope and

tenor and connection of a discourse, making allowances for those inaccurate modes of speech, which use has made inevitable.

53. As to the opinion that there are no corporeal causes, this has been heretofore maintained by some of the Schoolmen, as it is of late by others among the modern philosophers, who though they allow matter to exist, yet will have God alone to be the immediate efficient cause of all things.[11] These men saw, that amongst all the objects of sense, there was none which had any power or activity included in it, and that by consequence this was likewise true of whatever bodies they supposed to exist without the mind, like unto the immediate objects of sense. But then, that they should suppose an innumerable multitude of created beings, which they acknowledge are not capable of producing any one effect in nature, and which therefore are made to no manner of purpose, since God might have done everything as well without them; this I say, though we should allow it possible, must yet be a very unaccountable and extravagant supposition.

54. In the eighth place, the universal concurrent assent of mankind may be thought by some, an invincible argument in behalf of matter, or the existence of external things. Must we suppose the whole world to be mistaken? And if so, what cause can be assigned of so widespread and predominant an error? I answer, first, that upon a narrow inquiry, it will not perhaps be found, so many as is imagined do really believe the existence of matter or things without the mind. Strictly speaking, to believe that which involves a contradiction, or has no meaning in it, is impossible: and whether the foregoing expressions are not of that sort, I refer it to the impartial examination of the reader. In one sense indeed, men may be said to believe that matter exists, that is, they act as if the immediate cause of their sensations, which affects them every moment and is so nearly present to them, were some senseless unthinking being. But that they should clearly apprehend any meaning marked by those words, and form thereof a settled speculative opinion, is what I am not able to conceive. This is not the only instance wherein men impose upon themselves, by imagining they believe those propositions they have often heard, though at bottom they have no meaning in them.

55. But secondly, though we should grant a notion to be ever so universally and steadfastly adhered to, yet this is but a weak argument of its truth, to whoever considers what a vast number of prejudices and false opinions are everywhere embraced with the utmost tenaciousness, by the unreflecting (which are the far greater) part of mankind. There was a time when the *antipodes* and motion of the earth were looked upon as monstrous absurdities, even by men of learning: and if it be considered what a small proportion they bear to the rest of mankind, we shall find that at this day, those notions have gained but a very inconsiderable footing in the world.

56. But it is demanded, that we assign a cause of this prejudice, and account for its obtaining in the world. To this I answer, that men knowing they perceived several ideas, whereof they themselves were not the authors, as not being excited from within, nor depending on the operation of their wills, this made them maintain, those ideas or objects of perception had an existence independent of, and without the mind, without ever dreaming that a contradiction was involved in those words. But philosophers having plainly seen, that the immediate objects of perception do not exist without the mind, they in some degree corrected the mistake of the vulgar, but at the same time run into another which seems no less absurd, to wit, that there are certain objects really existing without the mind, or having a subsistence distinct from being perceived, of which our ideas are only images or resemblances, imprinted by those objects on the mind. And this notion of the philosophers owes its origin to the same cause with the former, namely, their being conscious that they were not the authors of their own sensations, which they evidently knew were imprinted from without, and which therefore must have some cause, distinct from the minds on which they are imprinted.

57. But why they should suppose the ideas of sense to be excited in us by things in their likeness, and not rather have recourse to *spirit* which alone can act, may be accounted for, first, because they were not aware of the repugnancy there is, as well in supposing things like unto our ideas existing without, as in attributing to them power or activity. Secondly, because

11. [One of the "modern philosophers" is Nicolas Malebranche (1638–1715). See his *The Search after Truth*, Book 6, Part 2, chapter 3.]

the supreme spirit which excites those ideas in our minds, is not marked out and limited to our view by any particular finite collection of sensible ideas, as human agents are by their size, complexion, limbs, and motions. And thirdly, because his operations are regular and uniform. Whenever the course of nature is interrupted by a miracle, men are ready to own the presence of a superior agent. But when we see things go on in the ordinary course, they do not excite in us any reflection; their order and concatenation, though it be an argument of the greatest wisdom, power, and goodness in their creator, is yet so constant and familiar to us, that we do not think them the immediate effects of a *free spirit*: especially since inconstancy and mutability in acting, though it be an imperfection, is looked on as a mark of *freedom*.

58. Tenthly, it will be objected, that the notions we advance, are inconsistent with several sound truths in philosophy and mathematics. For example, the motion of the earth is now universally admitted by astronomers, as a truth grounded on the clearest and most convincing reasons; but on the foregoing principles, there can be no such thing. For motion being only an idea, it follows that if it be not perceived, it exits not; but the motion of the earth is not perceived by sense. I answer, that tenet, if rightly understood, will be found to agree with the principles we have premised: for the question, whether the earth moves or no, amounts in reality to no more than this, to wit, whether we have reason to conclude from what has been observed by astronomers, that if we were placed in such and such circumstances, and such or such a position and distance, both from the earth and sun, we should perceive the former to move among the choir of the planets, and appearing in all respects like one of them: and this, by the established rules of nature, which we have no reason to mistrust, is reasonably collected from the phenomena.

59. We may, from the experience we have had of the train and succession of ideas in our minds, often make, I will not say uncertain conjectures, but sure and well-grounded predictions, concerning the ideas we shall be affected with, pursuant to a great train of actions, and be enabled to pass a right judgment of what would have appeared to us, in case we were placed in circumstances very different from those we are in at present. Herein consists the knowledge of nature, which may preserve its use and certainty very consistently with what has been said. It will be easy to apply this to whatever objections of the like sort may be drawn from the magnitude of the stars, or any other discoveries in astronomy or nature.

60. In the eleventh place, it will be demanded to what purpose serves that curious organization of plants, and the admirable mechanism in the parts of animals; might not vegetables grow, and shoot forth leaves and blossoms, and animals perform all their motions, as well without as with all that variety of internal parts so elegantly contrived and put together, which being ideas have nothing powerful or operative in them, nor have any necessary connection with the effects ascribed to them? If it be a spirit that immediately produces every effect by a *fiat*, or act of his will, we must think all that is fine and artificial in the works, whether of man or nature, to be made in vain. By this doctrine, though an artist has made the spring and wheels, and every movement of a watch, and adjusted them in such a manner as he knew would produce the motions he designed; yet he must think all this done to no purpose, and that it is an intelligence which directs the index, and points to the hour of the day. If so, why may not the intelligence do it, without his being at the pains of making the movements, and putting them together? Why does not an empty case serve as well as another? And how comes it to pass, that whenever there is any fault in the going of a watch, there is some corresponding disorder to be found in the movements, which being mended by a skillful hand, all is right again? The like may be said of all the clockwork of nature, great part whereof is so wonderfully fine and subtle, as scarce to be discerned by the best microscope. In short, it will be asked, how upon our principles any tolerable account can be given, or any final cause assigned of an innumerable multitude of bodies and machines framed with the most exquisite art, which in the common philosophy have very apposite uses assigned them, and serve to explain abundance of phenomena.

61. To all which I answer, first, that though there were some difficulties relating to the administration of providence, and the uses by it assigned to the several parts of nature, which I could not solve by the foregoing principles, yet this objection could be of small weight against the truth and certainty of those things which may be proved *a priori*, with the utmost evidence. Secondly, but neither are the

received principles free from the like difficulties; for it may still be demanded, to what end God should take those roundabout methods of effecting things by instruments and machines, which no one can deny might have been effected by the mere command of his will, without all that *apparatus*: nay, if we narrowly consider it, we shall find the objection may be retorted with greater force on those who hold the existence of those machines without the mind; for it has been made evident, that solidity, bulk, figure, motion and the like, have no *activity* or *efficacy* in them, so as to be capable of producing any one effect in nature. See Sect. 25. Whoever therefore supposes them to exist (allowing the supposition possible) when they are not perceived, does it manifestly to no purpose; since the only use that is assigned to them, as they exist unperceived, is that they produce those perceivable effects, which in truth cannot be ascribed to anything but spirit.

62. But to come nearer the difficulty, it must be observed, that though the fabrication of all those parts and organs be not absolutely necessary to the producing any effect, yet it is necessary to the producing of things in a constant, regular way, according to the laws of nature. There are certain general laws that run through the whole chain of natural effects: these are learned by the observation and study of nature, and are by men applied as well to the framing artificial things for the use and ornament of life, as to the explaining the various *phenomena*: which explication consists only in showing the conformity any particular phenomenon has to the general laws of nature, or, which is the same thing, in discovering the *uniformity* there is in the production of natural effects; as will be evident to whoever shall attend to the several instances, wherein philosophers pretend to account for appearances. That there is a great and conspicuous use in these regular constant methods of working observed by the Supreme Agent, has been shown in Sect. 31. And it is no less visible, that a particular size, figure, motion and disposition of parts are necessary, though not absolutely to the producing any effect, yet to the producing it according to the standing mechanical laws of nature. Thus, for instance, it cannot be denied that God, or the intelligence which sustains and rules the ordinary course of things might, if he were minded to produce a miracle, cause all the motions on the dial-plate of a watch, though nobody had ever made the movements, and put them in it: but yet if he will act agreeably to the rules of mechanism, by him for wise ends established and maintained in the creation, it is necessary that those actions of the watchmaker, whereby he makes the movements and rightly adjusts them, precede the production of the aforesaid motions; as also that any disorder in them be attended with the perception of some corresponding disorder in the movements, which being once corrected all is right again.

63. It may indeed on some occasions be necessary, that the Author of Nature display his overruling power in producing some appearance out of the ordinary series of things. Such exceptions from the general rules of nature are proper to surprise and awe men into an acknowledgment of the Divine Being: but then they are to be used but seldom, otherwise there is a plain reason why they should fail of that effect. Besides, God seems to choose the convincing our reason of his attributes by the works of nature, which discover so much harmony and contrivance in their make, and are such plain indications of wisdom and beneficence in their author, rather than to astonish us into a belief of his being by anomalous and surprising events.

64. To set this matter in a yet clearer light, I shall observe that what has been objected in Sect. 60 amounts in reality to no more than this: ideas are not anyhow and at random produced, there being a certain order and connection between them, like to that of cause and effect: there are also several combinations of them, made in a very regular and artificial manner, which seem like so many instruments in the hand of nature, that being hid as it were behind the scenes, have a secret operation in producing those appearances which are seen on the theater of the world, being themselves discernible only to the curious eye of the philosopher. But since one idea cannot be the cause of another, to what purpose is that connection? And since those instruments, being barely *inefficacious perceptions* in the mind, are not subservient to the production of natural effects; it is demanded why they are made, or, in other words, what reason can be assigned why God should make us, upon a close inspection into his works, behold so great variety of ideas, so artfully laid together, and so much according to rule; it not being credible, that he would be at the expense (if one may so speak) of all

that art and regularity to no purpose?

65. To all which my answer is, first, that the connection of ideas does not imply the relation of *cause* and *effect*, but only a mark or *sign* with the things *signified*. The fire which I see is not the cause of the pain I suffer upon my approaching it, but the mark that forewarns me of it. In like manner, the noise that I hear is not the effect of this or that motion or collision of the ambient bodies, but the sign thereof. Secondly, the reason why ideas are formed into machines, that is, artificial and regular combinations, is the same with that for combining letters into words. That a few original ideas may be made to signify a great number of effects and actions, it is necessary they be variously combined together: and to the end their use be permanent and universal, these combinations must be made by *rule*, and with *wise contrivance*. By this means abundance of information is conveyed unto us, concerning what we are to expect from such and such actions, and what methods are proper to be taken, for the exciting such and such ideas: which in effect is all that I conceive to be distinctly meant, when it is said that by discerning the figure, texture, and mechanism of the inward parts of bodies, whether natural or artificial, we may attain to know the several uses and properties depending thereon, or the nature of the thing.

66. Hence it is evident, that those things which under the notion of a cause cooperating or concurring to the production of effects, are altogether inexplicable, and run us into great absurdities, may be very naturally explained, and have a proper and obvious use assigned them, when they are considered only as marks or signs for our information. And it is the searching after, and endeavoring to understand those signs instituted by the Author of Nature, that ought to be the employment of the natural philosopher, and not the pretending to explain things by corporeal causes; which doctrine seems to have too much estranged the minds of men from that active principle, that supreme and wise spirit, *in whom we live, move, and have our being*.[12]

67. In the twelfth place, it may perhaps be objected, that though it be clear from what has been said, that there can be no such thing as an inert, senseless, extended, solid, figured, moveable substance, existing without the mind, such as philosophers describe matter: yet if any man shall leave out of his idea of *matter*, the positive ideas of extension, figure, solidity and motion, and say that he means only by that word, an inert senseless substance, that exists without the mind, or unperceived, which is the occasion of our ideas, or at the presence whereof God is pleased to excite ideas in us: it does not appear, but that matter taken in this sense may possibly exist. In answer to which I say, first, that it seems no less absurd to suppose a substance without accidents, than it is to suppose accidents without a substance. But secondly, though we should grant this unknown substance may possibly exist, yet where can it be supposed to be? That it exists not in the mind is agreed, and that it exists not in place is no less certain; since all extension exists only in the mind, as has been already proved. It remains therefore that it exists nowhere at all.

68. Let us examine a little the description that is here given us of *matter*. It neither acts, nor perceives, nor is perceived: for this is all that is meant by saying it is an inert, senseless, unknown substance; which is a definition entirely made up of negatives, excepting only the relative notion of its standing under or supporting: but then it must be observed, that it *supports* nothing at all; and how nearly this comes to the description of a *non-entity*, I desire may be considered. But, say you, it is the *unknown occasion*, at the presence of which, ideas are excited in us by the will of God. Now I would fain know how anything can be present to us, which is neither perceivable by sense nor reflection, nor capable of producing any idea in our minds, not is it at all extended, nor has any form, nor exists in any place. The words *to be present*, when thus applied, must needs be taken in some abstract and strange meaning, and which I am not able to comprehend.

69. Again, let us examine what is meant by *occasion*: so far as I can gather from the common use of language, that word signifies, either the agent which produces any effect, or else something that is observed to accompany, or go before it, in the ordinary course of things. But when it is applied to matter as above described, it can be taken in neither of those senses. For matter is said to be passive and inert, and so cannot be an agent or efficient cause. It is also unperceivable, as being devoid of all sensible qualities, and so cannot be the occasion of our perceptions in the

12. [Acts 17:28.]

latter sense: as when the burning my finger is said to be the occasion of the pain that attends it. What therefore can be meant by calling matter an *occasion*? This term is either used in no sense at all, or else in some sense very distant from its received signification.

70. You will perhaps say that matter, though it be not perceived by us, is nevertheless perceived by God, to whom it is the occasion of exciting ideas in our minds. For, say you, since we observe our sensations to be imprinted in an orderly and constant manner, it is but reasonable to suppose there are certain constant and regular occasions of their being produced. That is to say, that there are certain permanent and distinct parcels of matter, corresponding to our ideas, which, though they do not excite them in our minds, or any ways immediately affect us, as being altogether passive and unperceivable to us, they are nevertheless to God, by whom they are perceived, as it were so many occasions to remind him when and what ideas to imprint on our minds: that so things may go on in a constant uniform manner.

71. In answer to this I observe, that as the notion of matter is here stated, the question is no longer concerning the existence of a thing distinct from *spirit* and *idea*, from perceiving and being perceived: but whether there are not certain ideas, of I know not what sort, in the mind of God, which are so many marks or notes that direct him how to produce sensations in our minds, in a constant and regular method: much after the same manner as a musician is directed by the notes of music to produce that harmonious train and composition of sound, which is called a *tune*; though they who hear the music do not perceive the notes, and may be entirely ignorant of them. But this notion of matter seems too extravagant to deserve a confutation. Besides, it is in effect no objection against what we have advanced, to wit, that there is no senseless, unperceived *substance*.

72. If we follow the light of reason, we shall, from the constant uniform method of our sensations, collect the goodness and wisdom of the *spirit* who excites them in our minds. But this is all that I can see reasonably concluded from thence. To me, I say, it is evident that the being of a *spirit infinitely wise, good, and powerful* is abundantly sufficient to explain all the appearances of nature. But as for *inert senseless matter*, nothing that I perceive has any the least connection with it, or leads to the thoughts of it. And I would fain see anyone explain any the meanest *phenomenon* in nature by it, or show any manner of reason, though in the lowest rank of probability, that he can have for its existence; or even make any tolerable sense or meaning of that supposition. For as to its being an occasion, we have, I think, evidently shown that with regard to us it is no occasion: it remains therefore that it must be, if at all, the occasion to God of exciting ideas in us; and what this amounts to, we have just now seen.

73. It is worthwhile to reflect a little on the motives which induced men to suppose the existence of material substance; that so having observed the gradual ceasing, and expiration of those motives or reasons, we may proportionably withdraw the assent that was grounded on them. First therefore, it was thought that color, figure, motion, and the rest of the sensible qualities or accidents, did really exist without the mind; and for this reason, it seemed needful to suppose some unthinking *substratum* or *substance* wherein they did exist, since they could not be conceived to exist by themselves. Afterwards, in process of time, men being convinced that colors, sounds, and the rest of the sensible secondary qualities had no existence without the mind, they stripped this *substratum* or material substance of those qualities, leaving only the primary ones, figure, motion, and such like, which they still conceived to exist without the mind, and consequently to stand in need of a material support. But it having been shown, that none, even of these, can possibly exist otherwise than in a spirit or mind which perceives them, it follows that we have no longer any reason to suppose the being of *matter*. Nay, that it is utterly impossible there should be any such thing, so long as that word is taken to denote an *unthinking substratum* of qualities or accidents, wherein they exist without the mind.

74. But though it be allowed by the *materialists* themselves, that matter was thought of only for the sake of supporting accidents; and the reason entirely ceasing, one might expect the mind should naturally, and without any reluctance at all, quit the belief of what was solely grounded thereon. Yet the prejudice is riveted so deeply in our thoughts, that we can scarce tell how to part with it, and are therefore inclined, since the *thing* itself is indefensible, at least to retain the *name*; which we apply to I know not what abstracted and indefinite notions of *being*, or

occasion, though without any show of reason, at least so far as I can see. For what is there on our part, or what do we perceive amongst all the ideas, sensations, notions, which are imprinted on our minds, either by sense or reflection, from whence may be inferred the existence of an inert, thoughtless, unperceived occasion? And on the other hand, on the part of an *all-sufficient spirit*, what can there be that should make us believe, or even suspect, he is *directed* by an inert occasion to excite ideas in our minds?

75. It is a very extraordinary instance of the force of prejudice, and much to be lamented, that the mind of man retains so great a fondness against all the evidence of reason, for a stupid thoughtless *somewhat*, by the interposition whereof it would, as it were, screen itself from the providence of God, and remove him farther off from the affairs of the world. But though we do the utmost we can, to secure the belief of *matter*, though when reason forsakes us, we endeavor to support our opinion on the bare possibility of the thing, and though we indulge ourselves in the full scope of an imagination not regulated by reason, to make out that poor *possibility*, yet the upshot of all is, that there are certain *unknown ideas* in the mind of God; for this, if anything, is all that I conceive to be meant by *occasion* with regard to God. And this, at the bottom, is no longer contending for the *thing*, but for the *name*.

76. Whether therefore there are such ideas in the mind of God, and whether they may be called by the name *matter*, I shall not dispute. But if you stick to the notion of an unthinking substance, or support of extension, motion, and other sensible qualities, then to me it is most evidently impossible there should be any such thing. Since it is a plain repugnancy, that those qualities should exist in or be supported by an unperceiving substance.

77. But say you, though it be granted that there is no thoughtless support of extension, and the other qualities or accidents which we perceive; yet there may, perhaps, be some inert unperceiving substance, or *substratum* of some other qualities, as incomprehensible to us as colors are to a man born blind, because we have not a sense adapted to them. But if we had a new sense, we should possibly no more doubt of their existence, than a blind man made to see does of the existence of light and colors. I answer, first, if what you mean by the word *matter* be only the unknown support of unknown qualities, it is no matter whether there is such a thing or no, since it no way concerns us: and I do not see the advantage there is in disputing about we know not *what*, and we know not *why*.

78. But secondly, if we had a new sense, it could only furnish us with new ideas or sensations: and then we should have the same reason against their existing in an unperceiving substance, that has been already offered with relation to figure, motion, color, and the like. Qualities, as has been shown, are nothing else but *sensations* or *ideas*, which exist only in a *mind* perceiving them; and this is true not only of the ideas we are acquainted with at present, but likewise of all possible ideas whatsoever.

79. But you will insist, what if I have no reason to believe the existence of matter, what if I cannot assign any use to it, or explain anything by it, or even conceive what is meant by that word? Yet still it is no contradiction to say that matter exists, and that this matter is *in general* a *substance*, or *occasion of ideas*; though, indeed, to go about to unfold the meaning, or adhere to any particular explication of those words, may be attended with great difficulties. I answer, when words are used without a meaning, you may put them together as you please, without danger of running into a contradiction. You may say, for example, that *twice two* is equal to *seven*, so long as you declare you do not take the words of that proposition in their usual acceptation, but for marks of you know not what. And by the same reason you may say, there is an inert thoughtless substance without accidents, which is the occasion of our ideas. And we shall understand just as much by one proposition, as the other.

80. In the last place, you will say, what if we give up the cause of material substance, and assert, that matter is an unknown *somewhat*, neither substance nor accident, spirit nor idea, inert, thoughtless, indivisible, immoveable, unextended, existing in no place? For, say you, whatever may be urged against *substance* or *occasion*, or any other positive or relative notion of matter, has no place at all, so long as the *negative* definition of matter is adhered to. I answer, you may, if so it shall seem good, use the word *matter* in the same sense, that other men use *nothing*, and so make those terms convertible in your style. For after all, this is what appears to me to be the result of that

definition, the parts whereof when I consider with attention, either collectively, or separate from each other, I do not find that there is any kind of effect or impression made on my mind, different from what is excited by the term *nothing*.

81. You will reply perhaps, that in the foresaid definition is included, what does sufficiently distinguish it from nothing, the positive abstract idea of *quiddity*, *entity*, or *existence*. I own indeed, that those who pretend to the faculty of framing abstract general ideas, so talk as if they had such an idea, which is, say they, the most abstract and general notion of all, that is to me the most incomprehensible of all others. That there are a great variety of spirits of different orders and capacities, whose faculties, both in number and extent, are far exceeding those the author of my being has bestowed on me, I see no reason to deny. And for me to pretend to determine by my own few, stinted, narrow inlets of perception, what ideas the inexhaustible power of the Supreme Spirit may imprint upon them, were certainly the utmost folly and presumption. Since there may be, for ought that I know, innumerable sorts of ideas or sensations, as different from one another, and from all that I have perceived, as colors are from sounds. But how ready soever I may be, to acknowledge the scantiness of my comprehension, with regard to the endless variety of spirits and ideas, that might possibly exist, yet for anyone to pretend to a notion of entity or existence, *abstracted* from *spirit* and *idea*, from perceiving and being perceived, is, I suspect, a downright repugnancy and trifling with words. It remains that we consider the objections, which may possibly be made on the part of religion.

82. Some there are who think, that though the arguments for the real existence of bodies, which are drawn from reason, be allowed not to amount to demonstration, yet the Holy Scriptures are so clear in the point, as will sufficiently convince every good Christian, that bodies do really exist, and are something more than mere ideas; there being in Holy Write innumerable facts related, which evidently suppose the reality of timber, and stone, mountains, and rivers, and cities, and human bodies. To which I answer, that no sort of writings whatever, sacred or profane, which use those and the like words in the vulgar acceptation, or so as to have a meaning in them, are in danger of having their truth called in question by our doctrine. That all those things do really exist, that there are bodies, even corporeal substances, when taken in the vulgar sense, has been shown to be agreeable to our principles: and the difference betwixt *things* and *ideas*, *realities* and *chimeras*, has been distinctly explained.[13] And I do not think, that either what philosophers call *matter*, or the existence of objects without the mind, is anywhere mentioned in Scripture.

83. Again, whether there be, or be not external things, it is agreed on all hands, that the proper use of words, is the marking our conceptions, or things only as they are known and perceived by us; whence it plainly follows, that in the tenets we have laid down, there is nothing inconsistent with the right use and significancy of *language*, and that discourse of what kind soever, so far as it is intelligible, remains undisturbed. But all this seems so manifest, from what has been set forth in the premises, that it is needless to insist any farther on it.

84. But it will be urged, that miracles do, at least, lose much of their stress and import by our principles. What must we think of *Moses's* rod, was it not *really* turned into a serpent, or was there only a change of *ideas* in the minds of the spectators? And can it be supposed, that our Savior did no more at the marriage-feast in *Cana*, than impose on the sight, and smell, and taste of the guests, so as to create in them the appearance or idea only of wine? The same may be said of all other miracles: which, in consequence of the foregoing principles, must be looked upon only as so many cheats, or illusions of fancy. To this I reply, that the rod was changed into a real serpent, and the water into real wine. That this does not, in the least, contradict what I have elsewhere said, will be evident from Sect. 34, and 35. But this business of *real* and *imaginary* has been already so plainly and fully explained, and so often referred to, and the difficulties about it are so easily answered from what has gone before, that it were an affront to the reader's understanding, to resume the explication of it in this place. I shall only observe, that if at table all who were present should see, and smell, and taste, and drink wine, and find the effects of it, with me there could be no doubt of its reality. So that, at bottom, the scruple concerning real miracles has no place at all on ours,

13. Sect. 29, 30, 33, 36, etc.

but only on the received principles, and consequently makes rather *for*, than *against* what has been said.

85. Having done with the objections, which I endeavored to propose in the clearest light, and gave them all the force and weight I could, we proceed in the next place to take a view of our tenets in their consequences. Some of these appear at first sight, as that several difficult and obscure questions, on which abundance of speculation has been thrown away, are entirely banished from philosophy. Whether corporeal substance can think? Whether matter be infinitely divisible? And how it operates on spirit? These and the like inquiries have given infinite amusement to philosophers in all ages. But depending on the existence of *matter*, they have no longer any place on our principles. Many other advantages there are, as well with regard to *religion* as the *sciences*, which it is easy for anyone to deduce from what has been premised. But this will appear more plainly in the sequel.

86. From the principles we have laid down, it follows, human knowledge may naturally be reduced to two heads, that of *ideas*, and that of *spirits*. Of each of these I shall treat in order. And first as to ideas or unthinking things, our knowledge of these has been very much obscured and confounded, and we have been led into very dangerous errors, by supposing a twofold existence of the objects of sense, the one *intelligible*, or in the mind, the other *real* and without the mind: whereby unthinking things are thought to have a natural subsistence of their own, distinct from being perceived by spirits. This which, if I mistake not, has been shown to be a most groundless and absurd notion, is the very root of *skepticism*; for so long as men thought that real things subsisted without the mind, and that their knowledge was only so far forth *real* as it was conformable to *real things*, it follows, that they could not be certain that they had any real knowledge at all. For how can it be known, that the things which are perceived, are conformable to those which are not perceived, or exist without the mind?

87. Color, figure, motion, extension and the like, considered only as so many *sensations* in the mind, are perfectly known, there being nothing in them which is not perceived. But if they are looked on as notes or images, referred to *things* or *archetypes* existing without the mind, then are we involved all in *skepticism*. We see only the appearances, and not the real qualities of things. What may be the extension, figure, or motion of anything really and absolutely, or in itself, it is impossible for us to know, but only the proportion or the relation they bear to our senses. Things remaining the same, our ideas vary, and which of them, or even whether any of them at all represent the true quality really existing in the thing, it is out of our reach to determine. So that, for ought we know, all we see, hear, and feel, may be only phantom and vain chimera, and not at all agree with the real things, existing in *rerum natura*. All this skepticism follows, from our supposing a difference between *things* and *ideas*, and that the former have a subsistence without the mind, or unperceived. It were easy to dilate on this subject, and show how the arguments urged by *skeptics* in all ages, depend on the supposition of external objects.

88. So long as we attribute a real existence to unthinking things, distinct from their being perceived, it is not only impossible for us to know with evidence the nature of any real unthinking being, but even that it exists. Hence it is, that we see philosophers distrust their senses, and doubt of the existence of heaven and earth, of everything they see or feel, even of their own bodies. And after all their labor and struggle of thought, they are forced to own, we cannot attain to any self-evident or demonstrative knowledge of the existence of sensible things. But all this doubtfulness, which so bewilders and confounds the mind, and makes *philosophy* ridiculous in the eyes of the world, vanishes, if we annex a meaning to our words, and do not amuse ourselves with the terms *absolute*, *external*, *exist*, and such like, signifying we know not what. I can as well doubt of my own being, as of the being of those things which I actually perceive by sense: it being a manifest contradiction, that any sensible object should be immediately perceived by sight or touch, and at the same time have no existence in nature, since the very existence of an unthinking being consists in *being perceived*.

89. Nothing seems of more importance, towards erecting a firm system of sound and real knowledge, which may be proof against the assaults of *skepticism*, than to lay the beginning in a distinct explication of what is meant by *thing*, *reality*, *existence*: for in vain shall we dispute concerning the real existence of things, or pretend to any knowledge thereof, so long as we have not fixed the meaning of those words.

Thing or *being* is the most general name of all, it comprehends under it two kinds entirely distinct and heterogeneous, and which have nothing common but the name, to wit, *spirits* and *ideas*. The former are *active, indivisible substances*: the latter are *inert, fleeting, dependent beings*, which subsist not by themselves, but are supported by, or exist in minds or spiritual substances. We comprehend our own existence by inward feeling or reflection, and that of other spirits by reason. We may be said to have some knowledge or notion of our own minds, of spirits and active beings, whereof in a strict sense we have not ideas. In like manner we know and have a notion of relations between things or ideas, which relations are distinct from the ideas or things related, inasmuch as the latter may be perceived by us without our perceiving the former. To me it seems that ideas, spirits and relations are all in their respective kinds, the object of human knowledge and subject of discourse: and that the term *idea* would be improperly extended to signify everything we know or have any notion of.

90. Ideas imprinted on the senses are real things, or do really exist; this we do not deny, but we deny they can subsist without the minds which perceive them, or that they are resemblances of any archetypes existing without the mind: since the very being of a sensation or idea consists in being perceived, and an idea can be like nothing but an idea. Again, the things perceived by sense may be termed *external*, with regard to their origin, in that they are not generated from within, by the mind itself, but imprinted by a spirit distinct from that which perceives them. Sensible objects may likewise be said to be without the mind, in another sense, namely when they exist in some other mind. Thus when I shut my eyes, the things I saw may still exist, but it must be in another mind.

91. It were a mistake to think, that what is here said derogates in the least from the reality of things. It is acknowledged on the received principles, that extension, motion, and in a word all sensible qualities, have need of a support, as not being able to subsist by themselves. But the objects perceived by sense, are allowed to be nothing but combinations of those qualities, and consequently cannot subsist by themselves. Thus far it is agreed on all hands. So that in denying the things perceived by sense, an existence independent of a substance, or support wherein they may exist, we detract nothing from the received opinion of their *reality*, and are guilty of no innovation in that respect. All the difference is, that according to us the unthinking beings perceived by sense, have no existence distinct from being perceived, and cannot therefore exist in any other substance, than those unextended, indivisible substances, or *spirits*, which act, and think, and perceive them: whereas philosophers vulgarly hold, that the sensible qualities exist in an inert, extended, unperceiving substance, which they call *matter*, to which they attribute a natural subsistence, exterior to all thinking beings, or distinct from being perceived by any mind whatsoever, even the eternal mind of the Creator, wherein they suppose only ideas of the corporeal substances created by him: if indeed they allow them to be at all created.

92. For as we have shown the doctrine of matter or corporeal substance, to have been the main pillar and support of *skepticism*, so likewise upon the same foundation have been raised all the impious schemes of *atheism* and irreligion. Nay so great a difficulty has it been thought, to conceive matter produced out of nothing, that the most celebrated among the ancient philosophers, even of these who maintained the being of a God, have thought matter to be uncreated and coeternal with him. How great a friend material substance has been to *atheists* in all ages, were needless to relate. All their monstrous systems have so visible and necessary a dependence on it, that when this cornerstone is once removed, the whole fabric cannot choose but fall to the ground; insomuch that it is no longer worthwhile, to bestow a particular consideration on the absurdities of every wretched sect of *atheists*.

93. That impious and profane persons should readily fall in with those systems which favor their inclinations, by deriding immaterial substance, and supposing the soul to be divisible and subject to corruption as the body; which exclude all freedom, intelligence, and design from the formation of things, and instead thereof make a self-existent, stupid, unthinking substance the root and origin of all beings. That they should hearken to those who deny a providence, or inspection of a superior mind over the affairs of the world, attributing the whole series of events either to blind chance or fatal necessity, arising from the impulse of one body on another. All this is very natural. And on the other hand, when men

of better principles observe the enemies of religion lay so great a stress on *unthinking matter*, and all of them use so much industry and artifice to reduce everything to it; methinks they should rejoice to see them deprived of their grand support, and driven from that only fortress, without which your *Epicureans*, *Hobbists*, and the like, have not even the shadow of a pretense, but become the most cheap and easy triumph in the world.[14]

94. The existence of matter, or bodies unperceived, has not only been the main support of *atheists* and *fatalists*, but on the same principle does *idolatry* likewise in all its various forms depend. Did men but consider that the sun, moon, and stars, and every other object of the senses, are only so many sensations in their minds, which have no other existence but barely being perceived, doubtless they would never fall down, and worship their own *ideas*; but rather address their homage to that Eternal Invisible Mind which produces and sustains all things.

95. The same absurd principle, by mingling itself with the articles of our faith, has occasioned no small difficulties to Christians. For example, about the *resurrection*, how many scruples and objections have been raised by *Socinians* and others?[15] But do not the most plausible of them depend on the supposition, that a body is denominated the *same*, with regard not to the form or that which is perceived by sense, but the material substance which remains the same under several forms? Take away this *material substance*, about the identity whereof all the dispute is, and mean by *body* what every plain ordinary person means by that word, to wit, that which is immediately seen and felt, which is only a combination of sensible qualities, or ideas: and then their most unanswerable objections come to nothing.

96. Matter being once expelled out of nature, drags with it so many skeptical and impious notions, such an incredible number of disputes and puzzling questions, which have been thorns in the sides of divines, as well as philosophers, and made so much fruitless work for mankind; that if the arguments we have produced against it, are not found equal to demonstration (as to me they evidently seem) yet I am sure all friends to knowledge, peace, and religion, have reason to wish they were.

97. Beside the external existence of the objects of perception, another great source of errors and difficulties, with regard to ideal knowledge, is the doctrine of *abstract ideas*, such as it has been set forth in the Introduction. The plainest things in the world, those we are most intimately acquainted with, and perfectly know, when they are considered in an abstract way, appear strangely difficult and incomprehensible. Time, place, and motion, taken in particular or concrete, are what everybody knows; but having passed through the hands of a metaphysician, they become too abstract and fine, to be apprehended by men of ordinary sense. Bid your servant meet you at such a *time*, in such a *place*, and he shall never stay to deliberate on the meaning of those words: in conceiving that particular time and place, or the motion by which he is to get thither, he finds not the least difficulty. But if *time* be taken, exclusive of all those particular actions and ideas that diversify the day, merely for the continuation of existence, or duration in abstract, then it will perhaps gravel even a philosopher to comprehend it.

98. Whenever I attempt to frame a simple idea of *time*, abstracted from the succession of ideas in my mind, which flows uniformly, and is participated by all beings, I am lost and embrangled in inextricable difficulties. I have no notion of it at all, only I hear others say, it is infinitely divisible, and speak of it in such a manner as leads me to entertain odd thoughts of my existence: since that doctrine lays one under an absolute necessity of thinking, either that he passes away innumerable ages without a thought, or else that he is annihilated every moment of his life: both which seem equally absurd. Time therefore being nothing, abstracted from the succession of ideas in our minds,

14. [Epicurus and Thomas Hobbes both maintain that the universe is nothing but matter in motion. Epicurus acknowledges the existence of gods, but he believes they have no interest in the world. Hobbes writes as if he believes in God, and even offers a proof of God's existence, but he has always been suspected of atheism, in part because his metaphysics commits him to the view that God, if he exists, is a material thing.]

15. [The Socinians were followers of Fausto Sozzini (Latinized "Socinus," 1539–1604), and forerunners of the Unitarians. Though they denied the divinity of Christ, their leading catechism affirms the resurrection. In Berkeley's day the word "Socinian" was often applied to anyone who challenged Christian orthodoxy, and this probably explains Berkeley's use of it here.]

it follows that the duration of any finite spirit must be estimated by the number of ideas or actions succeeding each other in that same spirit or mind. Hence it is a plain consequence that the soul always thinks: and in truth whoever shall go about to divide in his thoughts, or abstract the *existence* of a spirit from its *cogitation*, will, I believe, find it no easy task.

99. So likewise, when we attempt to abstract extension and motion from all other qualities, and consider them by themselves, we presently lose sight of them, and run into great extravagancies. All which depend on a twofold abstraction: first, it is supposed that extension, for example, may be abstracted from all other sensible qualities; and secondly, that the entity of extension may be abstracted from its being perceived. But whoever shall reflect, and take care to understand what he says, will, if I mistake not, acknowledge that all sensible qualities are alike *sensations*, and alike *real*; that where the extension is, there is the color too, to wit, in his mind, and that their archetypes can exist only in some other *mind*: and that the objects of sense are nothing but those sensations combined, blended, or (if one may so speak) concreted together: none of all which can be supposed to exist unperceived.

100. What it is for a man to be happy, or an object good, everyone may think he knows. But to frame an abstract idea of *happiness*, prescinded from all particular pleasure, or of *goodness*, from everything that is good, this is what few can pretend to. So likewise, a man may be just and virtuous, without having precise ideas of *justice* and *virtue*. The opinion that those and the like words stand for general notions abstracted from all particular persons and actions, seems to have rendered morality difficult, and the study thereof of less use to mankind. And in effect, the doctrine of *abstraction* has not a little contributed towards spoiling the most useful parts of knowledge.

101. The two great provinces of speculative science, conversant about ideas received from sense and their relations, are *natural philosophy* and *mathematics*; with regard to each of these I shall make some observations. And first, I shall say somewhat of natural philosophy. On this subject it is, that the *skeptics* triumph: all that stock of arguments they produce to depreciate our faculties, and make mankind appear ignorant and low, are drawn principally from this head, to wit, that we are under an invincible blindness as to the *true* and *real* nature of things. This they exaggerate, and love to enlarge on. We are miserably bantered, say they, by our senses, and amused only with the outside and show of things. The real essence, the internal qualities, and constitution of every the meanest object, is hid from our view; something there is in every drop of water, every grain of sand, which it is beyond the power of human understanding to fathom or comprehend. But it is evident from what has been shown, that all this complaint is groundless, and that we are influenced by false principles to that degree as to mistrust our senses, and think we know nothing of those things which we perfectly comprehend.

102. One great inducement to our pronouncing ourselves ignorant of the nature of things, is the current opinion that everything includes within itself the cause of its properties: or that there is in each object an inward essence, which is the source whence its discernible qualities flow, and whereon they depend. Some have pretended to account for appearances by occult qualities, but of late they are mostly resolved into mechanical causes, to wit, the figure, motion, weight, and such like qualities of insensible particles: whereas in truth, there is no other agent or efficient cause than *spirit*, it being evident that motion, as well as all other *ideas*, is perfectly inert. See Sect. 25. Hence, to endeavor to explain the production of colors or sounds, by figure, motion, magnitude and the like, must needs be labor in vain. And accordingly, we see the attempts of that kind are not at all satisfactory. Which may be said, in general, of those instances, wherein one idea or quality is assigned for the cause of another. I need not say, how many *hypotheses* and speculations are left out, and how much the study of nature is abridged by this doctrine.

103. The great mechanical principle now in vogue is *attraction*. That a stone falls to the earth, or the sea swells towards the moon, may to some appear sufficiently explained thereby. But how are we enlightened by being told this is done by attraction? Is it that that word signifies the manner of the tendency, and that it is by the mutual drawing of bodies, instead of their being impelled or protruded towards each other? But nothing is determined of the manner of action, and it may as truly (for ought we know) be termed *impulse* or *protrusion* as *attraction*. Again, the parts of steel we see cohere firmly together, and this

also is accounted for by attraction; but in this, as in the other instances, I do not perceive that anything is signified besides the effect itself; for as to the manner of the action whereby it is produced, or the cause which produces it, these are not so much as aimed at.

104. Indeed, if we take a view of the several *phenomena*, and compare them together, we may observe some likeness and conformity between them. For example, in the falling of a stone to the ground, in the rising of the sea towards the moon, in cohesion and crystallization, there is something alike, namely a union or mutual approach of bodies. So that any one of these or the like *phenomena*, may not seem strange or surprising to a man who has nicely observed and compared the effects of nature. For that only is thought so which is uncommon, or a thing by itself, and out of the ordinary course of our observation. That bodies should tend towards the center of the earth, is not thought strange, because it is what we perceive every moment of our lives. But that they should have a like gravitation towards the center of the moon, may seem odd and unaccountable to most men, because it is discerned only in the tides. But a philosopher, whose thoughts take in a larger compass of nature, having observed a certain similitude of appearances, as well in the heavens as the earth, that argue innumerable bodies to have a mutual tendency towards each other, which he denotes by the general name *attraction*, whatever can be reduced to that, he thinks justly accounted for. Thus he explains the tides by the attraction of the terraqueous globe towards the moon, which to him does not appear odd or anomalous, but only a particular example of a general rule or law of nature.

105. If therefore we consider the difference there is betwixt natural philosophers and other men, with regard to their knowledge of the *phenomena*, we shall find it consists, not in an exacter knowledge of the efficient cause that produces them, for that can be no other than the *will of a spirit*, but only in a greater largeness of comprehension, whereby analogies, harmonies, and agreements are discovered in the works of nature, and the particular effects explained, that is, reduced to general rules, see Sect. 62, which rules grounded on the analogy, and uniformness observed in the production of natural effects, are most agreeable, and sought after by the mind; for that they extend our prospect beyond what is present, and near to us, and enable us to make very probable conjectures, touching things that may have happened at very great distances of time and place, as well as to predict things to come; which sort of endeavor towards omniscience, is much affected by the mind.

106. But we should proceed warily in such things: for we are apt to lay too great a stress on analogies, and to the prejudice of truth, humor that eagerness of the mind, whereby it is carried to extend its knowledge into general theorems. For example, gravitation, or mutual attraction, because it appears in many instances, some are straightaway for pronouncing *universal*; and that to *attract, and be attracted by every other body, is an essential quality inherent in all bodies whatsoever*. Whereas it appears the fixed stars have no such tendency towards each other: and so far is that gravitation, from being *essential* to bodies, that, in some instances a quite contrary principle seems to show itself: as in the perpendicular growth of plants, and the elasticity of the air. There is nothing necessary or essential in the case, but it depends entirely on the will of the *governing spirit*, who causes certain bodies to cleave together, or tend towards each other, according to various laws, whilst he keeps others at a fixed distance; and to some he gives a quite contrary tendency to fly asunder, just as he sees convenient.

107. After what has been premised, I think we may lay down the following conclusions. First, it is plain philosophers amuse themselves in vain, when they inquire for any natural efficient cause, distinct from a *mind* or *spirit*. Secondly, considering the whole creation is the workmanship of a *wise and good agent*, it should seem to become philosophers, to employ their thoughts (contrary to what some hold) about the final causes of things: and I must confess, I see no reason, why pointing out the various ends, to which natural things are adapted, and for which they were originally with unspeakable wisdom contrived, should not be thought one good way of accounting for them, and altogether worthy a philosopher.[16] Thirdly, from what has been premised no reason can be drawn, why the history of nature should not still be studied, and observations and experiments made,

16. [Among the philosophers who deny either the existence of final causes or the propriety of inquiry into them are René Descartes in *The Principles of Philosophy*, Part I, xxviii, and Baruch Spinoza in the Appendix to Part I of his *Ethics*.]

which, that they are of use to mankind, and enable us to draw any general conclusions, is not the result of any immutable habitudes, or relations between things themselves, but only of God's goodness and kindness to men in the administration of the world. See Sect. 30 and 31. Fourthly, by a diligent observation of the *phenomena* within our view, we may discover the general laws of nature, and from them deduce the other *phenomena*, I do not say *demonstrate*; for all deductions of that kind depend on a supposition that the Author of Nature always operates uniformly, and in a constant observance of those rules we take for principles: which we cannot evidently know.

108. Those men who frame general rules from the *phenomena*, and afterwards derive the *phenomena* from those rules, seem to consider signs rather than causes. A man may well understand natural signs without knowing their analogy, or being able to say by what rule a thing is so or so. And as it is very possible to write improperly, through too strict an observance of general grammar-rules: so in arguing from general rules of nature, it is not impossible we may extend the analogy too far, and by that means run into mistakes.

109. As in reading other books, a wise man will choose to fix his thoughts on the sense and apply it to use, rather than lay them out in grammatical remarks on the language; so in perusing the volume of nature, it seems beneath the dignity of the mind to affect an exactness in reducing each particular *phenomenon* to general rules, or showing how it follows from them. We should propose to ourselves nobler views, such as to recreate and exalt the mind, with a prospect of the beauty, order, extent, and variety of natural things: hence, by proper inferences, to enlarge our notions of the grandeur, wisdom, and beneficence of the Creator: and lastly, to make the several parts of the creation so far as in us lies, subservient to the ends they were designed for, God's glory, and the sustentation and comfort of our selves and fellow-creatures.

110. The best key for the aforesaid analogy, or natural science, will be easily acknowledged to be a certain celebrated treatise of *mechanics*: in the entrance of which justly admired treatise, time, space and motion, are distinguished into *absolute* and *relative*, *true* and *apparent*, *mathematical* and *vulgar*: which distinction, as it is at large explained by the author, does suppose those quantities to have an existence without the mind: and that they are ordinarily conceived with relation to sensible things, to which nevertheless in their own nature, they bear no relation at all.[17]

111. As for *time*, as it is there taken in an absolute or abstracted sense, for the duration or perseverance of the existence of things, I have nothing more to add concerning it, after what has been already said on that subject, Sect. 97 and 98. For the rest, this celebrated author holds there is an *absolute space*, which, being unperceivable to sense, remains in itself similar and immoveable: and relative space to be the measure thereof, which being moveable, and defined by its situation in respect of sensible bodies, is vulgarly taken for immoveable space. *Place* he defines to be that part of space which is occupied by any body. And according as the space is absolute or relative, so also is the place. *Absolute motion* is said to be the translation of a body from absolute place to absolute place, as relative motion is from one relative place to another. And because the parts of absolute space, do not fall under our senses, instead of them we are obliged to use their sensible measures: and so define both place and motion with respect to bodies, which we regard as immoveable. But it is said, in philosophical matters we must abstract from our senses, since it may be, that none of those bodies which seem to be quiescent, are truly so: and the same thing which is moved relatively, may be really at rest. As likewise one and the same body may be in relative rest and motion, or even moved with contrary relative motions at the same time, according as its place is variously defined. All which ambiguity is to be found in the apparent motions, but not at all in the true or absolute, which should therefore be alone regarded in philosophy. And the true, we are told, are distinguished from the apparent or relative motions by the following properties. First, in true or absolute motion, all parts which preserve the same position with respect to the whole, partake of the motions of the whole. Secondly, the place being moved, that which is placed therein is also moved: so that a body moving in a place which is in motion, does participate the motion of its place. Thirdly, true motion is never generated or changed,

17. [The treatise is *Mathematical Principles of Natural Philosophy*, published by Isaac Newton (1642–1727) in 1687. Berkeley refers to it under its Latin title in section 114.]

otherwise than by force impressed on the body itself. Fourthly, true motion is always changed by force impressed on the body moved. Fifthly, in circular motion barely relative, there is no centrifugal force, which nevertheless in that which is true or absolute, is proportional to the quantity of motion.

112. But notwithstanding what has been said, it does not appear to me, that there can be any motion other than *relative*: so that to conceive motion, there must be at least conceived two bodies, whereof the distance or position in regard to each other is varied. Hence if there was one only body in being, it could not possibly be moved. This seems evident, in that the idea I have of motion does necessarily include relation.

113. But though in every motion it be necessary to conceive more bodies than one, yet it may be that one only is moved, namely that on which the force causing the change of distance is impressed, or in other words, that to which the action is applied. For however some may define relative motion, so as to term that body *moved*, which changes its distance from some other body, whether the force or action causing that change were applied to it, or no: yet as relative motion is that which is perceived by sense, and regarded in the ordinary affairs of life, it should seem that every man of common sense knows what it is, as well as the best philosopher: now I ask anyone, whether in his sense of motion as he walks along the streets, the stones he passes over may be said to *move*, because they change distance with his feet? To me it seems, that though motion includes a relation of one thing to another, yet it is not necessary that each term of relation be denominated from it. As a man may think of somewhat which does not think, so a body may be moved to or from another body, which is not therefore itself in motion.

114. As the place happens to be variously defined, the motion which is related to it varies. A man in a ship may be said to be quiescent, with relation to the sides of the vessel, and yet move with relation to the land. Or he may move eastward in respect of the one, and westward in respect of the other. In the common affairs of life, men never go beyond the earth to define the place of any body: and what is quiescent in respect of that, is accounted *absolutely* to be so. But philosophers who have a greater extent of thought, and juster notions of the system of things, discover even the earth itself to be moved. In order therefore to fix their notions, they seem to conceive the corporeal world as finite, and the utmost unmoved walls or shell thereof to be the place, whereby they estimate true motions. If we sound our own conceptions, I believe we may find all the absolute motion we can frame an idea of, to be at bottom no other than relative motion thus defined. For as has been already observed, absolute motion exclusive of all external relation is incomprehensible: and to this kind of relative motion, all the abovementioned properties, causes, and effects ascribed to absolute motion, will, if I mistake not, be found to agree. As to what is said of the centrifugal force, that it does not at all belong to circular relative motion: I do not see how this follows from the experiment which is brought to prove it. See *Philosophiae Naturalis Principia Mathematica, in Schol. Def.* VIII. For the water in the vessel, at that time wherein it is said to have the greatest relative circular motion, has, I think, no motion at all: as is plain from the foregoing section.

115. For to denominate a body *moved*, it is requisite, first, that it change its distance or situation with regard to some other body: and secondly, that the force or action occasioning that change be applied to it. If either of these be wanting, I do not think that agreeably to the sense of mankind, or the propriety of language, a body can be said to be in motion. I grant indeed, that it is possible for us to think a body, which we see change its distance from some other, to be moved, though it have no force applied to it (in which sense there may be apparent motion), but then it is, because the force causing the change of distance, is imagined by us to be applied or impressed on that body thought to move. Which indeed shows we are capable of mistaking a thing to be in motion which is not, and that is all.

116. From what has been said, it follows that the philosophic consideration of motion does not imply the being of an *absolute space*, distinct from that which is perceived by sense, and related to bodies: which that it cannot exist without the mind, is clear upon the same principles, that demonstrate the like of all other objects of sense. And perhaps, if we inquire narrowly, we shall find we cannot even frame an idea of *pure space*, exclusive of all body. This I must confess seems impossible, as being a most abstract idea. When I excite a motion in some part of my

body, if it be free or without resistance, I say there is *space*: but if I find a resistance, then I say there is *body*: and in proportion as the resistance to motion is lesser or greater, I say the *space* is more or less *pure*. So that when I speak of pure or empty space, it is not to be supposed, that the word *space* stands for an idea distinct from, or conceivable without body and motion. Though indeed we are apt to think every noun substantive stands for a distinct idea, that may be separated from all others: which has occasioned infinite mistakes. When therefore supposing all the world to be annihilated besides my own body, I say there still remains *pure space*: thereby nothing else is meant, but only that I conceive it possible, for the limbs of my body to be moved on all sides without the least resistance: but if that too were annihilated, then there could be no motion, and consequently no space. Some perhaps may think the sense of seeing does furnish them with the idea of pure space; but it is plain from what we have elsewhere shown, that the ideas of space and distance are not obtained by that sense. See the *Essay concerning Vision*.

117. What is here laid down, seems to put an end to all those disputes and difficulties, which have sprung up amongst the learned concerning the nature of *pure space*. But the chief advantage arising from it, is, that we are freed from that dangerous *dilemma*, to which several who have employed their thoughts on this subject, imagine themselves reduced, to wit, of thinking either that real space is God, or else that there is something besides God which is eternal, uncreated, infinite, indivisible, immutable. Both which may justly be thought pernicious and absurd notions. It is certain that not a few divines, as well as philosophers of great note, have, from the difficulty they found in conceiving either limits or annihilation of space, concluded it must be *divine*. And some of late have set themselves particularly to show, that the incommunicable attributes of God agree to it. Which doctrine, how unworthy soever it may seem of the divine nature, yet I do not see how we can get clear of it, so long as we adhere to the received opinions.

118. Hitherto of natural philosophy: we come now to make some inquiry concerning that other great branch of speculative knowledge, to wit, *mathematics*. These, how celebrated soever they may be, for their clearness and certainty of demonstration, which is hardly anywhere else to be found, cannot nevertheless be supposed altogether free from mistakes; if in their principles there lurks some secret error, which is common to the professors of those sciences with the rest of mankind. Mathematicians, though they deduce their theorems from a great height of evidence, yet their first principles are limited by the consideration of quantity: and they do not ascend into any inquiry concerning those transcendental maxims, which influence all the particular sciences, each part whereof, mathematics not excepted, does consequently participate of the errors involved in them. That the principles laid down by mathematicians are true, and their way of deduction from those principles clear and incontestable, we do not deny. But we hold, there may be certain erroneous maxims of greater extent than the object of mathematics, and for that reason not expressly mentioned, though tacitly supposed throughout the whole progress of that science; and that the ill effects of those secret unexamined errors are diffused through all the branches thereof. To be plain, we suspect the mathematicians are, as well as other men, concerned in the errors arising from the doctrine of abstract general ideas, and the existence of objects without the mind.

119. *Arithmetic* has been thought to have for its object abstract ideas of *number*. Of which to understand the properties and mutual habitudes is supposed no mean part of speculative knowledge. The opinion of the pure and intellectual nature of numbers in abstract, has made them in esteem with those philosophers, who seem to have affected an uncommon fineness and elevation of thought. It has set a price on the most trifling numerical speculations which in practice are of no use, but serve only for amusement: and has therefore so far infected the minds of some, that they have dreamt of mighty *mysteries* involved in numbers, and attempted the explication of natural things by them. But if we inquire into our own thoughts, and consider what has been premised, we may perhaps entertain a low opinion of those high flights and abstractions, and look on all inquiries about numbers, only as so many *difficiles nugae*, so far as they are not subservient to practice, and promote the benefit of life.

120. Unity in abstract we have before considered in Sect. 13, from which and what has been said in the Introduction, it plainly follows there is not any such idea. But number being defined a *collection*

of units, we may conclude that, if there be no such thing as unity or unit in abstract, there are no ideas of number in abstract denoted by the numeral names and figures. The theories therefore in arithmetic, if they are abstracted from the names and figures, as likewise from all use and practice, as well as from the particular things numbered, can be supposed to have nothing at all for their object. Hence we may see, how entirely the science of numbers is subordinate to practice, and how jejune and trifling it becomes, when considered as a matter of mere speculation.

121. However since there may be some, who, deluded by the specious show of discovering abstracted verities, waste their time in arithmetical theorems and problems, which have not any use: it will not be amiss, if we more fully consider, and expose the vanity of that pretense; and this will plainly appear, by taking a view of arithmetic in its infancy, and observing what it was that originally put men on the study of that science, and to what scope they directed it. It is natural to think that at first, men, for ease of memory and help of computation, made use of counters, or in writing of single strokes, points or the like, each whereof was made to signify a unit, that is, some one thing of whatever kind they had occasion to reckon. Afterwards they found out the more compendious ways, of making one character stand in place of several strokes, or points. And lastly, the notation of the *Arabians* or *Indians* came into use, wherein by the repetition of a few characters or figures, and varying the signification of each figure according to the place it obtains, all numbers may be most aptly expressed: which seems to have been done in imitation of language, so that an exact analogy is observed betwixt the notation by figures, and names, the nine simple figures answering the nine first numeral names, and place in the former corresponding to denominations in the latter. And agreeably to those conditions of the simple and local value of figures, were contrived methods of finding from the given figures or marks of the parts, what figures and how placed, are proper to denote the whole or *vice versa*. And having found the sought figures, the same rule or analogy being observed throughout, it is easy to read them into words; and so the number becomes perfectly known. For then the number of any particular things is said to be known, when we know the name or figures (with their due arrangement) that according to the standing analogy belong to them. For these signs being known, we can by the operations of arithmetic, know the signs of any part of the particular sums signified by them; and thus computing in signs (because of the connection established betwixt them and the distinct multitudes of things, whereof one is taken for a unit), we may be able rightly to sum up, divide, and proportion the things themselves that we intend to number.

122. In *arithmetic* therefore we regard not the *things* but the *signs*, which nevertheless are not regarded for their own sake, but because they direct us how to act with relation to things, and dispose rightly of them. Now agreeably to what we have before observed, of words in general (Sect. 19, *Introd.*) it happens here likewise, that abstract ideas are thought to be signified by numeral names or characters, while they do not suggest ideas of particular things to our minds. I shall not at present enter into a more particular dissertation on this subject; but only observe that it is evident from what has been said, those things which pass for abstract truths and theorems concerning numbers, are, in reality, conversant about no object distinct from particular numerable things, except only names and characters; which originally came to be considered, on no other account but their being *signs*, or capable to represent aptly, whatever particular things men had need to compute. Whence it follows, that to study them for their own sake would be just as wise, and to as good purpose, as if a man, neglecting the true use or original intention and subserviency of language, should spend his time in impertinent criticisms upon words, or reasonings and controversies purely verbal.

123. From numbers we proceed to speak of *extension*, which considered as relative, is the object of geometry. The *infinite* divisibility of *finite* extension, though it is not expressly laid down, either as an axiom or theorem in the elements of that science, yet is throughout the same everywhere supposed, and thought to have so inseparable and essential a connection with the principles and demonstrations in geometry, that mathematics never admit it into doubt, or make the least question of it. And as this notion is the source from whence do spring all those amusing geometrical paradoxes, which have such a direct repugnancy to the plain common sense of mankind, and are admitted with so much reluctance

into a mind not yet debauched by learning: so is it the principal occasion of all that nice and extreme subtlety, which renders the study of *mathematics* so difficult and tedious. Hence if we can make it appear, that no finite extension contains innumerable parts, or is infinitely divisible, it follows that we shall at once clear the science of geometry from a great number of difficulties and contradictions, which have ever been esteemed a reproach to human reason, and withal make the attainment thereof a business of much less time and pains, than it hitherto has been.

124. Every particular finite extension, which may possibly be the object of our thought, is an *idea* existing only in the mind, and consequently each part thereof must be perceived. If therefore I cannot perceive innumerable parts in any finite extension that I consider, it is certain they are not contained in it: but it is evident, that I cannot distinguish innumerable parts in any particular line, surface, or solid, which I either perceive by sense, or figure to myself in my mind: wherefore I conclude they are not contained in it. Nothing can be plainer to me, than that the extensions I have in view are no other than my own ideas, and it is no less plain, that I cannot resolved any one of my ideas into an infinite number of other ideas, that is, that they are not infinitely divisible. If by *finite extension* be meant something distinct from a finite idea, I declare I do not know what that is, and so cannot affirm or deny anything of it. But if the terms *extension*, *parts*, and the like, are taken in any sense conceivable, that is, for ideas; then to say a finite quantity or extension consists of parts infinite in number, is so manifest a contradiction, that everyone at first sight acknowledges it to be so. And it is impossible it should ever gain the assent of any reasonable creature, who is not brought to it by gentle and slow degrees, as a converted gentile to the belief of *transubstantiation*.[18] Ancient and rooted prejudices do often pass into principles: and those propositions which once obtain the force and credit of a *principle*, are not only themselves, but likewise whatever is deducible from them, thought privileged from all examination. And there is no absurdity so gross, which by this means the mind of man may not be prepared to swallow.

18. [Transubstantiation is the conversion of the substance of the bread and wine of the Eucharist into the substance of the body and blood of Christ.]

125. He whose understanding is prepossessed with the doctrine of abstract general ideas, may be persuaded, that (whatever be thought of the ideas of sense), extension in *abstract* is infinitely divisible. And one who thinks the objects of sense exist without the mind, will perhaps in virtue thereof be brought to admit, that a line but an inch long may contain innumerable parts really existing, though too small to be discerned. These errors are grafted as well in the minds of *geometricians*, as of other men, and have a like influence on their reasonings; and it were no difficult thing, to show how the arguments from geometry made use of to support the infinite divisibility of extension, are bottomed on them. At present we shall only observe in general, whence it is that the mathematicians are all so fond and tenacious of this doctrine.

126. It has been observed in another place, that the theorems and demonstrations in geometry are conversant about universal ideas. Sect 15, *Introd*. Where it is explained in what sense this ought to be understood, to wit, that the particular lines and figures included in the diagram, are supposed to stand for innumerable others of different sizes: or in other words, the geometer considers them abstracting from their magnitude: which does not imply that he forms an abstract idea, but only that he cares not what the particular magnitude is, whether great or small, but looks on that as a thing indifferent to the demonstration: hence it follows, that a line in the scheme, but an inch long, must be spoken of, as though it contained ten thousand parts, since it is regarded not in itself, but as it is universal; and it is universal only in its signification, whereby it represents innumerable lines greater than itself, in which may be distinguished ten thousand parts or more, though there may not be above an inch in it. After this manner the properties of the lines signified are (by a very usual figure) transferred to the sign, and thence through mistake thought to appertain to it considered in its own nature.

127. Because there is no number of parts so great, but it is possible there may be a line containing more, the inch-line is said to contain parts more than any assignable number; which is true, not of the inch taken absolutely, but only for the things signified by it. But men not retaining that distinction in their thoughts, slide into a belief that the small particular line described on paper contains in itself

parts innumerable. There is no such thing as the ten-thousandth part of an *inch*; but there is of a *mile* or *diameter of the earth*, which may be signified by that inch. When therefore I delineate a triangle on paper, and take one side not above an inch, for example, in length to be the *radius*: this I consider as divided into ten thousand or a hundred thousand parts, or more. For though the ten-thousandth part of that line considered in itself, is nothing at all, and consequently may be neglected without any error or inconveniency; yet these described lines being only marks standing for greater quantities, whereof it may be the ten-thousandth part is very considerable, it follows, that to prevent notable errors in practice, the *radius* must be taken of ten thousand parts, or more.

128. From what has been said the reason is plain why, to the end any theorem may become universal in its use, it is necessary we speak of the lines described on paper, as though they contained parts which really they do not. In doing of which, if we examine the matter thoroughly, we shall perhaps discover that we cannot conceive an inch itself as consisting of, or being divisible into a thousand parts, but only some other line which is far greater than an inch, and represented by it. And that when we say a line is *infinitely divisible*, we must mean a line which is *infinitely great*. What we have here observed seems to be the chief cause, why to suppose the infinite divisibility of finite extension has been thought necessary in geometry.

129. The several absurdities and contradictions which flowed from this false principle might, one would think, have been esteemed so many demonstrations against it. But by I know not what *logic*, it is held that proofs *a posteriori* are not to be admitted against propositions relating to infinity. As though it were not impossible even for an infinite mind to reconcile contradictions. Or as if anything absurd and repugnant could have a necessary connection with truth, or flow from it. But whoever considers the weakness of this pretense, will think it was contrived on purpose to humor the laziness of the mind, which had rather acquiesce in an indolent skepticism, than be at the pains to go through with a severe examination of those principles it has ever embraced for true.

130. Of late the speculations about infinites have run so high, and grown to such strange notions, as have occasioned no small scruples and disputes among the geometers of the present age. Some there are of great note, who not content with holding that finite lines may be divided into an infinite number of parts, do yet farther maintain, that each of those infinitesimals is itself subdivisible into an infinity of other parts, or infinitesimals of a second order, and so on *ad infinitum*. These, I say, assert there are infinitesimals of infinitesimals of infinitesimals, without ever coming to an end. So that according to them an inch does not barely contain an infinite number of parts, but an infinity of an infinity of an infinity *ad infinitum* of parts. Others there be who hold all orders of infinitesimals below the first to be nothing at all, thinking it with good reason absurd, to imagine there is any positive quantity or part of extension, which though multiplied infinitely, can ever equal the smallest given extension. And yet on the other hand it seems no less absurd, to think the square, cube, or other power of a positive real root, should itself be nothing at all; which they who hold infinitesimals of the first order, denying all of the subsequent orders, are obliged to maintain.

131. Have we not therefore reason to conclude, that they are *both* in the wrong, and that there is in effect no such thing as parts infinitely small, or an infinite number of parts contained in any finite quantity? But you will say, that if this doctrine obtains, it will follow the very foundations of geometry are destroyed: and those great men who have raised that science to so astonishing a height, have been all the while building a castle in the air. To this it may be replied, that whatever is useful in geometry and promotes the benefit of human life, does still remain firm and unshaken on our principles. That science considered as practical, will rather receive advantage than any prejudice from what has been said. But to set this in a due light, may be the subject of a distinct inquiry. For the rest, though it should follow that some of the more intricate and subtle parts of *speculative mathematics* may be pared off without any prejudice to truth; yet I do not see what damage will be thence derived to mankind. On the contrary, it were highly to be wished, that men of great abilities and obstinate application would draw off their thoughts from those amusements, and employ them in the study of such things as lie nearer the concerns of life, or have a more direct influence on the manners.

132. If it be said that several theorems undoubtedly true, are discovered by methods in which infinitesimals are made use of, which could never have been, if their existence included a contradiction in it. I answer, that upon a thorough examination it will not be found, that in any instance it is necessary to make use of or conceive infinitesimal parts of finite lines, or even quantities less than the *minimum sensibile*: nay, it will be evident this is never done, it being impossible.[19]

133. By what we have premised, it is plain that very numerous and important errors have taken their rise from those false principles, which were impugned in the foregoing parts of this treatise. And the opposites of those erroneous tenets at the same time appear to be most fruitful principles, from whence do flow innumerable consequences highly advantageous to true philosophy as well as to religion. Particularly, *matter* or *the absolute existence of corporeal objects*, has been shown to be that wherein the most avowed and pernicious enemies of all knowledge, whether human or divine, have ever placed their chief strength and confidence. And surely, if by distinguishing the real existence of unthinking things from their being perceived, and allowing them a subsistence of their own out of the minds of spirits, no one thing is explained in nature; but on the contrary a great many inexplicable difficulties arise: if the supposition of matter is barely precarious, as not being grounded on so much as one single reason: if its consequences cannot endure the light of examination and free inquiry, but screen themselves under the dark and general pretense of *infinites being incomprehensible*: if withal the removal of this *matter* be not attended with the least evil consequence, if it be not even missed in the world, but everything as well, nay much easier conceived without it: if lastly, both *skeptics* and *atheists* are forever silenced upon supposing only spirits and ideas, and this scheme of things is perfectly agreeable both to *reason* and *religion*: methinks we may expect it should be admitted and firmly embraced, though it were proposed only as a *hypothesis*, and the existence of matter had been allowed possible, which yet I think we have evidently demonstrated that it is not.

19. [The *minimum sensible* is the smallest quantity capable of being sensed, a "sensible point."]

134. True it is, that in consequence of the foregoing principles, several disputes and speculations, which are esteemed no mean parts of learning, are rejected as useless. But how great a prejudice soever against our notions, this may give to those who have already been deeply engaged, and made large advances in studies of that nature: yet by others, we hope it will not be thought any just ground of dislike to the principles and tenets herein laid down, that they abridge the labor of study, and make human sciences more clear, compendious, and attainable, than they were before.

135. Having dispatched what we intended to say concerning the knowledge of *ideas*, the method we proposed leads us, in the next place, to treat of *spirits*: with regard to which, perhaps human knowledge is not so deficient as is vulgarly imagined. The great reason that is assigned for our being thought ignorant of the nature of spirits, is, our not having an idea of it. But surely it ought not to be looked on as a defect in a human understanding, that it does not perceive the idea of *spirit*, if it is manifestly impossible there should be any such *idea*. And this, if I mistake not, has been demonstrated in Sect. 27: to which I shall here add that a spirit has been shown to be the only substance or support, wherein the unthinking beings or ideas can exist: but that this *substance* which supports or perceives ideas should itself be an *idea* or like an *idea*, is evidently absurd.

136. It will perhaps be said, that we want a sense (as some have imagined) proper to know substances withal, which if we had, we might know our own soul, as we do a triangle. To this I answer, that in case we had a new sense bestowed upon us, we could only receive thereby some new sensations or ideas of sense. But I believe nobody will say, that what he means by the terms *soul* and *substance*, is only some particular sort of idea or sensation. We may therefore infer, that all things duly considered, it is not more reasonable to think our faculties defective, in that they do not furnish us with an idea of spirit or active thinking substance, than it would be if we should blame them for not being able to comprehend a *round square*.

137. From the opinion that spirits are to be known after the manner of an idea or sensation, have risen many absurd and heterodox tenets, and much skepticism about the nature of the soul. It is even probable, that this opinion may have produced a doubt in some,

whether they had any soul at all distinct from their body, since upon inquiry they could not find they had an idea of it. That an *idea* which is inactive, and the existence whereof consists in being perceived, should be the image or likeness of an agent subsisting by itself, seems to need no other refutation, than barely attending to what is meant by those words. But perhaps you will say, that though an *idea* cannot resemble a *spirit*, in its thinking, acting, or subsisting by itself, yet it may in some other respects: and it is not necessary that an idea or image be in all respects like the original.

138. I answer, if it does not in those mentioned, it is impossible it should represent it in any other thing. Do but leave out the power of willing, thinking, and perceiving ideas, and there remains nothing else wherein the idea can be like a spirit. For by the word *spirit* we mean only that which thinks, wills, and perceives; this, and this alone, constitutes the signification of that term. If therefore it is impossible that any degree of those powers should be represented in an idea, it is evident there can be no idea of a spirit.

139. But it will be objected, that if there is no idea signified by the terms *soul*, *spirit*, and *substance*, they are wholly insignificant, or have no meaning in them. I answer, those words do mean or signify a real thing, which is neither an idea nor like an idea, but that which perceives ideas, and wills, and reasons about them. What I am myself, that which I denote by the term I, is the same with what is meant by *soul* or *spiritual substance*. If it be said that this is only quarrelling at a word, and that since the immediate significations of other names are by common consent called *ideas*, no reason can be assigned, why that which is signified by the name *spirit* or *soul* may not partake in the same appellation. I answer, all the unthinking objects of the mind agree, in that they are entirely passive, and their existence consists only in being perceived: whereas a soul or spirit is an active being, whose existence consists not in being perceived, but in perceiving ideas and thinking. It is therefore necessary, in order to prevent equivocation and confounding natures perfectly disagreeing and unlike, that we distinguish between *spirit* and *idea*. See Sect. 27.

140. In a large sense indeed, we may be said to have an idea, or rather a notion of *spirit*, that is, we understand the meaning of the word, otherwise we could not affirm or deny anything of it. Moreover, as we conceive the ideas that are in the minds of other spirits by means of our own, which we suppose to be resemblances of them: so we know other spirits by means of our own soul, which in that sense is the image or idea of them, it having a like respect to other spirits, that blueness or heat by me perceived has to those ideas perceived by another.

141. It must not be supposed, that they who assert the natural immortality of the soul are of opinion, that it is absolutely incapable of annihilation even by the infinite power of the Creator who first gave it being: but only that it is not liable to be broken or dissolved by the ordinary laws of nature or motion. They indeed, who hold the soul of man to be only a thin vital flame, or system of animal spirits, make it perishing and corruptible as the body, since there is nothing more easily dissipated than such a being, which it is naturally impossible should survive the ruin of the tabernacle, wherein it is enclosed. And this notion has been greedily embraced and cherished by the worst part of mankind, as the most effectual antidote against all impressions of virtue and religion. But it has been made evident, that bodies of what frame or texture soever, are barely passive ideas in the mind, which is more distant and heterogeneous from them, than light is from darkness. We have shown that the soul is indivisible, incorporeal, unextended, and it is consequently incorruptible. Nothing can be plainer, than that the motions, changes, decays, and dissolutions which we hourly see befall natural bodies (and which is what we mean by the *course of nature*) cannot possibly affect an active, simple, uncompounded substance: such a being therefore is indissoluble by the force of nature, that is to say, *the soul of man is naturally immortal*.

142. After what has been said, it is I suppose plain, that our souls are not to be known in the same manner as senseless inactive objects, or by way of *idea*. *Spirits* and *ideas* are things so wholly different, that when we say, *they exist*, *they are known*, or the like, these words must not be thought to signify anything common to both natures. There is nothing alike or common in them: and to expect that by any multiplication or enlargement of our faculties, we may be enabled to know a spirit as we do a triangle, seems as absurd as if we should hope to *see a sound*. This is inculcated because I imagine it may be of moment towards clearing several important questions, and preventing some

very dangerous errors concerning the nature of the soul. (We may not I think strictly be said to have an idea of an active being, or of an action, although we may be said to have a notion of them. I have some knowledge or notion of my mind, and its acts about ideas, inasmuch as I know or understand what is meant by those words. What I know, that I have some notion of, I will not say, that the terms *idea* and *notion* may not be used convertibly, if the world will have it so. But yet it conduces to clearness and propriety, that we distinguish things very different by different names. It is also to be remarked, that all relations including an act of the mind, we cannot so properly be said to have an idea, but rather a notion of the relations or habitudes between things. But if in the modern way the word *idea* is extended to spirits, and relations and acts; this is after all an affair of verbal concern.)

143. It will not be amiss to add, that the doctrine of *abstract ideas* has had no small share in rendering those sciences intricate and obscure, which are particularly conversant about spiritual things. Men have imagined they could frame abstract notions of the powers and acts of the mind, and consider them prescinded, as well from the mind or spirit itself, as from their respective objects and effects. Hence a great number of dark and ambiguous terms presumed to stand for abstract notions, have been introduced into metaphysics and morality, and from these have grown infinite distractions and disputes amongst the learned.

144. But nothing seems more to have contributed towards engaging men in controversies and mistakes, with regard to the nature and operations of the mind, than the being used to speak of those things, in terms borrowed from sensible ideas. For example, the will is termed the *motion* of the soul: this infuses a belief, that the mind of man is as a ball in motion, impelled and determined by the objects of sense, as necessarily as that is by the stroke of a racket.[20] Hence arise endless scruples and errors of dangerous consequence in morality. All which I doubt not may be cleared, and truth appear plain, uniform, and consistent, could but philosophers be prevailed on to retire into themselves, and attentively consider their own meaning.

20. [Berkeley is apparently thinking of Hobbes.]

145. From what has been said, it is plain that we cannot know the existence of other spirits, otherwise than by their operations, or the ideas by them excited in us. I perceive several motions, changes, and combinations of ideas, that inform me there are certain particular agents like myself, which accompany them, and concur in their production. Hence the knowledge I have of other spirits is not immediate, as is the knowledge of my ideas: but depending on the intervention of ideas, by me referred to agents or spirits distinct from myself, as effects or concomitant signs.

146. But though there be some things which convince us, human agents are concerned in producing them; yet it is evident to everyone, that those things which are called the works of nature, that is, the far greater part of the ideas or sensations perceived by us, are not produced by, or dependent on the wills of men. There is therefore some other spirit that causes them, since it is repugnant that they should subsist by themselves. See Sect. 29. But if we attentively consider the constant regularity, order, and concatenation of natural things, the surprising magnificence, beauty, and perfection of the larger, and the exquisite contrivance of the smaller parts of the creation, together with the exact harmony and correspondence of the whole, but above all, the never enough admired laws of pain and pleasure, and the instincts or natural inclinations, appetites, and passions of animals; I say if we consider all these things, and at the same time attend to the meaning and import of the attributes, one, eternal, infinitely wise, good, and perfect, we shall clearly perceive that they belong to the aforesaid spirit, *who works all in all*, and *by whom all things consist*.[21]

147. Hence it is evident, that God is known as certainly and immediately as any other mind or spirit whatsoever, distinct from ourselves. We may even assert, that the existence of God is far more evidently perceived than the existence of men; because the effects of nature are infinitely more numerous and considerable, than those ascribed to human agents. There is not any one mark that denotes a man, or effect produced by him, which does not more strongly evince the being of that spirit who is the

21. [*who works all in all*, 1 Corinthians 12:6; *by whom all things consist*, Colossians 1:17.]

Author of Nature. For it is evident that in affecting other persons, the will of man has no other object, than barely the motion of the limbs of his body; but that such a motion should be attended by, or excite any idea in the mind of another, depends wholly on the will of the Creator. He alone it is who *upholding all things by the word of his power,* maintains that intercourse between spirits, whereby they are able to perceive the existence of each other.[22] And yet this pure and clear light which enlightens everyone, is itself invisible.

148. It seems to be a general pretense of the unthinking herd, that they cannot see God. Could we but see him, say they, as we see a man, we should believe that he is, and believing obey his commands. But alas we need only open our eyes to see the sovereign lord of all things with a more full and clear view, than we do any one of our fellow-creatures. Not that I imagine we see God (as some will have it) by a direct and immediate view, or see corporeal things, not by themselves, but by seeing that which represents them in the essence of God, which doctrine is I must confess to me incomprehensible.[23] But I shall explain my meaning. A human spirit or person is not perceived by sense, as not being an idea; when therefore we see the color, size, figure, and motions of a man, we perceive only certain sensations or ideas excited in our own minds: and these being exhibited to our view in sundry distinct collections, serve to mark out unto us the existence of finite and created spirits like ourselves. Hence it is plain, we do not see a man, if by *man* is meant that which lives, moves, perceives, and thinks as we do: but only such a certain collection of ideas, as directs us to think there is a distinct principle of thought and motion like to ourselves, accompanying and represented by it. And after the same manner we see God; all the difference is, that whereas some one finite and narrow assemblage of ideas denotes a particular human mind, whithersoever we direct our view, we do at all times and in all places perceive manifest tokens of the Divinity: everything we see, hear, feel, or any wise perceive by sense, being a sign or effect of the power of God; as is our perception of those very motions, which are produced by men.

149. It is therefore plain, that nothing can be more evident to anyone that is capable of the least reflection, than the existence of God, or a spirit who is intimately present to our minds, producing in them all that variety of ideas or sensations, which continually affect us, on whom we have an absolute and entire dependence, in short, *in whom we live, and move, and have our being.*[24] That the discovery of this great truth which lies so near and obvious to the mind, should be attained to by the reason of so very few, is a sad instance of the stupidity and inattention of men, who, though they are surrounded with such clear manifestations of the Deity, are yet so little affected by them, that they seem as it were blinded with excess of light.

150. But you will say, has nature no share in the production of natural things, and must they be all ascribed to the immediate and sole operation of God? I answer, if by *nature* is meant only the visible *series* of effects, or sensations imprinted on our minds according to certain fixed and general laws: then it is plain, that nature taken in this sense cannot produce anything at all. But if by *nature* is meant some being distinct from God, as well as from the laws of nature, and things perceived by sense, I must confess that word is to me an empty sound, without any intelligible meaning annexed to it. Nature in this acceptation is a vain *chimera* introduced by those heathens, who had not just notions of the omnipresence and infinite perfection of God. But it is more unaccountable, that it should be received among *Christians* professing belief in the Holy Scriptures, which constantly ascribe those effects to the immediate hand of God, that heathen philosophers are wont to impute to *nature. The Lord, he causeth the vapors to ascend; he maketh lightnings with rain; he bringeth forth the wind out of his treasures,* Jerem. Chap. 10 ver. 13. *He turneth the shadow of death into the morning, and maketh the day dark with night,* Amos Chap. 5. ver. 8. *He visiteth the earth, and maketh it soft with showers: he blesseth the springing thereof, and crowneth the year with his goodness; so that the pastures are clothed with flocks, and the valleys are covered over with corn.* See *Psalm* 65. But notwithstanding that this is the constant language of Scripture; yet we have I know not what aversion

22. [*upholding all things by . . . his power,* Hebrews 1:3.]

23. [Malebranche believes that "we see all things in God." See *The Search after Truth,* Book 3, Part 2, chapter 6. Berkeley explains how he differs from Malebranche in *Three Dialogues* 2.]

24. [Acts 17:28.]

from believing, that God concerns himself so nearly in our affairs. Fain would we suppose him at a great distance off, and substitute some blind unthinking deputy in his stead, though (if we may believe Saint Paul) *he be not far from every one of us*.[25]

151. It will I doubt not be objected, that the slow and gradual methods observed in the production of natural things, do not seem to have for their cause the immediate hand of an *almighty agent*. Besides, monsters, untimely births, fruits blasted in the blossom, rains falling in desert places, miseries incident to human life, are so many arguments that the whole frame of nature is not immediately actuated and superintended by a spirit of infinite wisdom and goodness. But the answer to this objection is in a good measure plain from Sect. 62, it being visible, that the aforesaid methods of nature are absolutely necessary, in order to working by the most simple and general rules, and after a steady and consistent manner; which argues both the *wisdom* and *goodness* of God. Such is the artificial contrivance of this mighty machine of nature, that whilst its motions and various phenomena strike on our senses, the hand which actuates the whole is itself unperceivable to men of flesh and blood. *Verily* (says the prophet) *thou art a God that hidest thyself*, Isaiah Chap. 45 ver. 15. But though God conceal himself from the eyes of the *sensual* and *lazy*, who will not be at the least expense of thought; yet to an unbiased and attentive mind, nothing can be more plainly legible, than the intimate presence of an *all-wise spirit*, who fashions, regulates, and sustains the whole system of being. It is clear from what we have elsewhere observed, that the operating according to general and stated laws, is so necessary for our guidance in the affairs of life, and letting us into the secret of nature, that without it, all reach and compass of thought, all human sagacity and design could serve to no manner of purpose: it were even impossible there should be any such faculties or powers in the mind. See Sect. 31. Which one consideration abundantly out-balances whatever particular inconveniences may thence arise.

152. We should further consider, that the very blemishes and defects of nature are not without their use, in that they make an agreeable sort of variety, and augment the beauty of the rest of the creation, as shades in a picture serve to set off the brighter and more enlightened parts. We would likewise do well to examine, whether our taxing the waste of seeds and embryos, and accidental destruction of plants and animals, before they come to full maturity, as an imprudence in the Author of Nature, be not the effect of prejudice contracted by our familiarity with impotent and saving mortals. In *man* indeed a thrifty management of those things, which he cannot procure without much pains and industry, may be esteemed *wisdom*. But we must not imagine, that the inexplicably fine machines of an animal or vegetable, costs the great Creator any more pains or trouble in its production than a pebble does: nothing being more evident, than that an omnipotent spirit can indifferently produce everything by a mere *fiat* or act of his will. Hence it is plain, that the splendid profusion of natural things should not be interpreted, weakness or prodigality in the agent who produces them, but rather be looked on as an argument of the riches of his power.

153. As for the mixture of pain or uneasiness which is in the world, pursuant to the general laws of nature, and the actions of finite imperfect spirits: this, in the state we are in at present, is indispensably necessary to our well-being. But our prospects are too narrow: we take, for instance, the idea of some one particular pain into our thoughts, and account it *evil*; whereas if we enlarge our view, so as to comprehend the various ends, connections, and dependencies of things, on what occasions and in what proportions we are affected with pain and pleasure, the nature of human freedom, and the design with which we are put into the world; we shall be forced to acknowledge that those particular things, which considered in themselves appear to be *evil*, have the nature of *good*, when considered as linked with the whole system of beings.

154. From what has been said it will be manifest to any considering person, that it is merely for want of attention and comprehensiveness of mind, that there are any favorers of *atheism* or the *Manichean heresy* to be found.[26] Little and unreflecting souls may indeed burlesque the works of providence, the beauty

25. [Acts 17:27.]

26. [The Manicheans (followers of Mani, c. 216–276) believed that the world is governed by two competing principles, one good, the other evil.]

and order whereof they have not capacity, or will not be at the pains to comprehend. But those who are masters of any justness and extent of thought, and are withal used to reflect, can never sufficiently admire the divine traces of wisdom and goodness that shine throughout the economy of nature. But what truth is there which shines so strongly on the mind, that by an aversion of thought, a willful shutting of the eyes, we may not escape seeing it? Is it therefore to be wondered at, if the generality of men, who are ever intent on business or pleasure, and little used to fix or open the eye of their mind, should not have all that conviction and evidence of the being of God, which might be expected in reasonable creatures?

155. We should rather wonder, that men can be found so stupid as to neglect, than that neglecting they should be unconvinced of such an evident and momentous truth. And yet it is to be feared that too many of parts and leisure, who live in Christian countries, are merely through a supine and dreadful negligence sunk into a sort of *atheism*. Since it is downright impossible, that a soul pierced and enlightened with a thorough sense of the omnipresence, holiness, and justice of that *Almighty Spirit*, should persist in a remorseless violation of his laws. We ought therefore earnestly to meditate and dwell on those important points; that so we may attain conviction without all scruple, *that the eyes of the Lord are in every place beholding the evil and the good; that he is with us and keepeth us in all places whither we go, and giveth us bread to eat, and raiment to put on*; that he is present and conscious to our innermost thoughts; and that we have a most absolute and immediate dependence on him.[27] A clear view of which great truths cannot choose but fill our hearts with an awful circumspection and holy fear, which is the strongest incentive to *virtue*, and the best guard against *vice*.

156. For after all, what deserves the first place in our studies, is the consideration of *God*, and our *duty*; which to promote, as it was the main drift and design of my labors, so shall I esteem them altogether useless and ineffectual, if by what I have said I cannot inspire my readers with a pious sense of the presence of God: and having shown the falseness or vanity of those barren speculations, which make the chief employment of learned men, the better dispose them to reverence and embrace the salutary truths of the Gospel, which to know and to practice is the highest perfection of human nature.

27. [*that the eyes are . . . beholding the evil and the good*, Proverbs 15:3; *that he is with us . . . and giveth us . . . raiment to put on*, Genesis 28:20.]

Three Dialogues between Hylas and Philonous, in Opposition to Skeptics and Atheists

THE FIRST DIALOGUE

PHILONOUS: Good morning, Hylas; I did not expect to find you up so early.

HYLAS: It is indeed something unusual, but my thoughts were so taken up with a subject I was discoursing of last night that, finding I could not sleep, I resolved to rise and take a turn in the garden.

P: It happened well to let you see what innocent and agreeable pleasures you lose every morning. Can there be a pleasanter time of the day, or a more delightful season of the year? That purple sky, those wild but sweet notes of birds, the fragrant bloom upon the trees and flowers, the gentle influence of the rising sun, these and a thousand nameless beauties of nature inspire the soul with secret transports; its faculties too being at this time fresh and lively are fit for these meditations, which the solitude of a garden and tranquillity of the morning naturally dispose us to. But I am afraid I interrupt your thoughts, for you seemed very intent on something.

H: It is true, I was, and shall be obliged to you if you will permit me to go on in the same vein; not that I would by any means deprive myself of your company, for my thoughts always flow more easily in conversation with a friend than when I am alone, but my request is that you would allow me to impart my reflections to you.

P: With all my heart, it is what I should have requested myself, if you had not prevented me.

H: I was considering the odd fate of those men who have in all ages, through an affectation of being distinguished from the vulgar—or some unaccountable turn of thought—pretended either to believe nothing at all or to believe the most extravagant things in the world. This, however, might be borne, if their paradoxes and skepticism did not draw after them some consequences of general disadvantage to mankind. But the mischief lies here, that when men of less leisure see them who are supposed to have spent their whole time in the pursuits of knowledge, professing an entire ignorance of all things or advancing such notions as are repugnant to plain and commonly received principles, they will be tempted to entertain suspicions concerning the most important truths, which they had up to now held sacred and unquestionable.

P: I entirely agree with you as to the ill tendency of the affected doubts of some philosophers and fantastic conceits of others. I am even so far gone of late in this way of thinking that I have discarded several of the sublime notions I had got in their schools for vulgar opinions. And I give it you on my word, since this revolt from metaphysical notions to the plain dictates of nature and common sense, I find my understanding strangely enlightened so that I can now easily comprehend a great many things which before were all mystery and riddle.

H: I am glad to find there was nothing in the accounts I heard of you.

P: Pray, what were those?

H: You were represented in last night's conversation as one who maintained the most extravagant opinion that ever entered into the mind of man, namely, that there is no such thing as *material substance* in the world.

P: That there is no such thing as what philosophers call *material substance*, I am seriously per-

From *The Works of George Berkeley*, edited by G. N. Wright (London, 1843), 2 vols., English, modified by Roger Ariew. Reprinted from *Modern Philosophy*, edited by Roger Ariew and Eric Watkins (Indianapolis: Hackett Publishing Company, 1998), by permission of the publisher.

suaded, but if I were made to see anything absurd or skeptical in this, I should then have the same reason to renounce this, that I imagine I have now to reject the contrary opinion.

H: What! Can anything be more fantastic, more repugnant to common sense, or a more manifest piece of skepticism, than to believe there is no such thing as *matter*?

P: Softly, good Hylas. What if it should prove that you, who hold there is, are by virtue of that opinion a greater skeptic and maintain more paradoxes and repugnancies to common sense than I who believe no such thing?

H: You may as soon persuade me the part is greater than the whole, as that, in order to avoid absurdity and skepticism, I should ever be obliged to give up my opinion in this point.

P: Well then, are you content to admit that opinion for true which upon examination shall appear most agreeable to common sense and remote from skepticism?

H: With all my heart. Since you are for raising disputes about the plainest things in nature, I am content for once to hear what you have to say.

P: Pray, Hylas, what do you mean by a *skeptic*?

H: I mean what all men mean, one that doubts of everything.

P: He then who entertains no doubt concerning some particular point, with regard to that point, cannot be thought a *skeptic*.

H: I agree with you.

P: Whether doubting consists in embracing the affirmative or negative side of a question?

H: In neither; for whoever understands English cannot but know that *doubting* signifies a suspense between both.

P: He then who denies any point can no more be said to doubt of it than he who affirms it with the same degree of assurance.

H: True.

P: And, consequently, in this case his denial is no more to be esteemed *skeptical* than the other.

H: I acknowledge it.

P: How does it come to pass then, Hylas, that you pronounce me a *skeptic*, because I deny what you affirm, namely, the existence of matter? Since, for all you can tell, I am as peremptory in my denial as you in your affirmation.

H: Hold on, Philonous, I have been a little out in my definition, but every false step a man makes in discourse is not to be insisted on. I said, indeed, that a *skeptic* was one who doubted of everything, but I should have added: or who denies the reality and truth of things.

P: What things? Do you mean the principles and theorems of sciences? But these you know are universal intellectual notions and consequently independent of matter; the denial of this therefore does not imply denying them.

H: I grant it. But are there no other things? What do you think of distrusting the senses, of denying the real existence of sensible things, or pretending to know nothing of them? Is not this sufficient to call a man a *skeptic*?

P: Shall we therefore examine which of us it is that denies the reality of sensible things or professes the greatest ignorance of them, since, if I take you rightly, he is to be esteemed the greatest *skeptic*?

H: That is what I desire.

P: What do you mean by sensible things?

H: Those things which are perceived by the senses. Can you imagine that I mean anything else?

P: Pardon me, Hylas, if I am desirous clearly to apprehend your notions, since this may much shorten our inquiry. Allow me then to ask you this further question. Are those things only perceived by the senses which are perceived immediately? Or may those things properly be said to be *sensible* which are perceived mediately or not without the intervention of others?

H: I do not sufficiently understand you.

P: In reading a book, what I immediately perceive are the letters, but mediately, or by means of these, are suggested to my mind the notions of God, virtue, truth, etc. Now that the letters are truly sensible things, or perceived by sense, there is no doubt; but I would like to know whether you take the things suggested by them to be so too.

H: No, certainly, it would be absurd to think *God* or *virtue* sensible things, though they may be signified and suggested to the mind by sensible marks with which they have an arbitrary connection.

P: It seems then, that by *sensible things* you mean those only which can be perceived immediately by sense.

H: Right.

P: Does it not follow from this that though I see one part of the sky red, and another blue, and that my reason does then evidently conclude there must be some cause of that diversity of colors, yet that cause cannot be said to be a sensible thing or perceived by the sense of seeing?

H: It does.

P: In like manner, though I hear a variety of sounds, yet I cannot be said to hear the causes of those sounds.

H: You cannot.

P: And when by my touch I perceive a thing to be hot and heavy, I cannot say with any truth or propriety that I feel the cause of its heat or weight.

H: To prevent any more questions of this kind, I tell you once and for all that by *sensible things* I mean those only which are perceived by sense and that in truth the senses perceive nothing which they do not perceive immediately, for they make no inferences. The deducing therefore of causes or occasions from effects and appearances, which alone are perceived by sense, entirely relates to reason.

P: This point then is agreed between us—that *sensible things are those only which are immediately perceived by sense*. You will further inform me whether we immediately perceive by sight anything besides light, and colors, and figures; or by hearing anything but sounds; by the palate, anything besides tastes; by the smell, besides odors; or by the touch, more than tangible qualities.

H: We do not.

P: It seems, therefore, that if you take away all sensible qualities, there remains nothing sensible.

H: I grant it.

P: Sensible things therefore are nothing else but so many sensible qualities or combinations of sensible qualities.

H: Nothing else.

P: Heat then is a sensible thing.

H: Certainly.

P: Does the reality of sensible things consist in being perceived? Or, is it something distinct from their being perceived and that bears no relation to the mind?

H: To *exist* is one thing and to be *perceived* is another.

P: I speak with regard to sensible things only; and of these I ask whether by their real existence you mean a subsistence exterior to the mind and distinct from their being perceived?

H: I mean a real absolute being, distinct from and without any relation to their being perceived.

P: Heat, therefore, if it is allowed a real being, must exist without the mind.

H: It must.

P: Tell me, Hylas, is this real existence equally compatible to all degrees of heat which we perceive, or is there any reason why we should attribute it to some and deny it others? And if there is, pray let me know that reason.

H: Whatever degree of heat we perceive by sense, we may be sure the same exists in the object that occasions it.

P: What! The greatest as well as the least?

H: I tell you, the reason is plainly the same in respect of both: They are both perceived by sense; no, the greater degree of heat is more sensibly perceived and, consequently, if there is any difference, we are more certain of its real existence than we can be of the reality of a lesser degree.

P: But is not the most vehement and intense degree of heat a very great pain?

H: No one can deny it.

P: And is any unperceiving thing capable of pain or pleasure?

H: No certainly.

P: Is your material substance a senseless being or a being endowed with sense and perception?

H: It is senseless without doubt.

P: It cannot therefore be the subject of pain.

H: By no means.

P: Nor consequently of the greatest heat perceived by sense, since you acknowledge this to be no small pain.

H: I grant it.

P: What shall we say then of your external object; is it a material substance or not?

H: It is a material substance with the sensible qualities inhering in it.

P: How then can a great heat exist in it, since you admit it cannot in a material substance? I desire you would clear this point.

H: Hold on, Philonous, I fear I was wrong in yielding intense heat to be a pain. It should seem rather that pain is something distinct from heat and the consequence or effect of it.

P: Upon putting your hand near the fire, do you perceive one simple uniform sensation or two distinct sensations?

H: But one simple sensation.

P: Is not the heat immediately perceived?

H: It is.

P: And the pain?

H: True.

P: Seeing therefore they are both immediately perceived at the same time and the fire affects you only with one simple or uncompounded idea, it follows that this same simple idea is both the intense heat immediately perceived and the pain, and, consequently, that the intense heat immediately perceived is nothing distinct from a particular sort of pain.

H: It seems so.

P: Again, try in your thoughts, Hylas, if you can conceive a vehement sensation to be without pain or pleasure.

H: I cannot.

P: Or can you frame to yourself an idea of sensible pain or pleasure in general, abstracted from every particular idea of heat, cold, tastes, smells, etc.?

H: I do not find that I can.

P: Does it not therefore follow that sensible pain is nothing distinct from those sensations or ideas in an intense degree?

H: It is undeniable, and, to speak the truth, I begin to suspect a very great heat cannot exist but in a mind perceiving it.

P: What! Are you then in that *skeptical* state of suspense between affirming and denying?

H: I think I may be positive in the point. A very violent and painful heat cannot exist without the mind.

P: It does not, therefore, according to you, have any real being.

H: I admit it.

P: Is it therefore certain that there is no body in nature really hot?

H: I have not denied there is any real heat in bodies. I only say there is no such thing as an intense real heat.

P: But did you not say before that all degrees of heat were equally real or, if there was any difference, that the greater would be more undoubtedly real than the lesser?

H: True, but it was because I did not then consider the ground there is for distinguishing between them which I now plainly see. And it is this: Because intense heat is nothing else but a particular kind of painful sensation and pain cannot exist but in a perceiving being, it follows that no intense heat can really exist in an unperceiving corporeal substance. But this is no reason why we should deny heat in an inferior degree to exist in such a substance.

P: But how shall we be able to discern those degrees of heat which exist only in the mind, from those which exist without it?

H: That is no difficult matter. You know the least pain cannot exist unperceived; therefore, whatever degree of heat is a pain exists only in the mind. But as for all other degrees of heat nothing obliges us to think the same of them.

P: I think you granted before that no unperceiving being was capable of pleasure any more than of pain.

H: I did.

P: And is not warmth, or a more gentle degree of heat than what causes uneasiness, a pleasure?

H: What then?

P: Consequently, it cannot exist without the mind in any unperceiving substance or body.

H: So it seems.

P: Since, therefore, those degrees of heat that are not painful as well as those that are can exist only in a thinking substance, may we not conclude that external bodies are absolutely incapable of any degree of heat whatsoever?

H: On second thought, I do not think it so evident that warmth is a pleasure as that a great degree of heat is a pain.

P: I do not pretend that warmth is as great a pleasure as heat is a pain. But if you grant it to be even a small pleasure, it serves to make good my conclusion.

H: I could rather call it an *indolence*. It seems to be nothing more than a privation of both pain and pleasure. And that such a quality or state as this may agree to an unthinking substance, I hope you will not deny.

P: If you are resolved to maintain that warmth, or a gentle degree of heat, is no pleasure, I do not know how to convince you otherwise than by appealing to your own sense. But what do you think of cold?

H: The same that I do of heat. An intense degree

of cold is a pain, for to feel a very great cold is to perceive a great uneasiness; it cannot, therefore, exist without the mind, but a lesser degree of cold may as well as a lesser degree of heat.

P: Those bodies, therefore, upon whose application to our own we perceive a moderate degree of heat, must be concluded to have a moderate degree of heat or warmth in them; and those, upon whose application we feel a like degree of cold, must be thought to have cold in them.

H: They must.

P: Can any doctrine be true that necessarily leads a man into an absurdity?

H: Without doubt it cannot.

P: Is it not an absurdity to think that the same thing should be at the same time both cold and warm?

H: It is.

P: Suppose now one of your hands hot, and the other cold, and that they are both at once put into the same vessel of water in an intermediate state; will not the water seem cold to one hand and warm to the other?

H: It will.

P: Ought we not therefore by your principles conclude: It is really both cold and warm at the same time, that is, according to your own concession, believe an absurdity?

H: I confess it seems so.

P: Consequently, the principles themselves are false, since you have granted that no true principle leads to an absurdity.

H: But, after all, can anything be more absurd than to say *there is no heat in the fire*?

P: To make the point still clearer, tell me whether in two cases exactly alike we ought not make the same judgment?

H: We ought.

P: When a pin pricks your finger, does it not rend and divide the fibers of your flesh?

H: It does.

P: And when a coal burns your finger, does it do so any more?

H: It does not.

P: Since, therefore, you neither judge the sensation itself occasioned by the pin, nor anything like it to be in the pin, you should not, conformably to what you have now granted, judge the sensation occasioned by the fire, or anything like it, to be in the fire.

H: Well, since it must be so, I am content to yield this point and acknowledge that heat and cold are only sensations existing in our minds, but there still remain qualities enough to secure the reality of external things.

P: But what will you say, Hylas, if it shall appear that the case is the same with regard to all other sensible qualities and that they can no more be supposed to exist without the mind than heat and cold?

H: Then indeed you will have done something to the purpose, but that is what I despair of seeing proved.

P: Let us examine them in order. What think you of tastes—do they exist without the mind or not?

H: Can any man in his senses doubt whether sugar is sweet or wormwood bitter?

P: Inform me, Hylas. Is a sweet taste a particular kind of pleasure or pleasant sensation, or is it not?

H: It is.

P: And is not bitterness some kind of uneasiness or pain?

H: I grant it.

P: If therefore sugar and wormwood are unthinking corporeal substances existing without the mind, how can sweetness and bitterness, that is, pleasure and pain, agree to them?

H: Hold on, Philonous, I now see what deluded me all this time. You asked whether heat and cold, sweetness and bitterness, were not particular sorts of pleasure and pain—to which I answered simply that they were. Whereas I should have distinguished thus: Those qualities, as perceived by us, are pleasures or pains, but not as existing in the external objects. We must not, therefore, conclude absolutely that there is no heat in the fire or sweetness in the sugar, but only that heat or sweetness, as perceived by us, is not in the fire or sugar. What do you say to this?

P: I say it is nothing to the purpose. Our discourse proceeded altogether concerning sensible things, which you defined to be the things we *immediately perceive by our senses*. Therefore, whatever other qualities you speak of as distinct from these, I know nothing of them, nor do they at all belong to the point in dispute. You may indeed pretend to have discovered certain qualities which you do not perceive and assert those insensible qualities exist in fire and sugar. But what use can be made of this to your present purpose, I am at a loss to conceive. Tell me then once more—

do you acknowledge that heat and cold, sweetness and bitterness (meaning those qualities which are perceived by the senses), do not exist without the mind?

H: I see it is to no purpose to hold out, so I give up the cause as to those mentioned qualities. Though I profess it sounds odd to say that sugar is not sweet.

P: But for your further satisfaction, take this along with you: That which at other times seems sweet shall to a distempered palate appear bitter. And nothing can be plainer than that various persons perceive different tastes in the same food, since that which one man delights in, another abhors. And how could this be, if the taste was something really inherent in the food?

H: I acknowledge I do not know how.

P: In the next place, odors are to be considered. And with regard to these, I would gladly know whether what has been said of tastes does not exactly agree to them? Are they not so many pleasing or displeasing sensations?

H: They are.

P: Can you then conceive it possible that they should exist in an unperceiving thing?

H: I cannot.

P: Or can you imagine that filth and garbage affect those brute animals that feed on them out of choice with the same smells which we perceive in them?

H: By no means.

P: May we not therefore conclude of smells, as of the other aforementioned qualities, that they cannot exist in any but a perceiving substance or mind?

H: I think so.

P: Then as to sounds, what must we think of them—are they accidents really inherent in external bodies or not?

H: That they do not inhere in the sonorous bodies is plain from this: because a bell struck in the exhausted receiver of an air pump sends forth no sound. The air, therefore, must be thought the subject of sound.

P: What reason is there for that, Hylas?

H: Because, when any motion is raised in the air, we perceive a greater or lesser sound in proportion to the air's motion, but without some motion in the air we never hear any sound at all.

P: And granting that we never hear a sound but when some motion is produced in the air, yet I do not see how you can infer from this that the sound itself is in the air.

H: It is this very motion in the external air that produces in the mind the sensation of *sound*. For striking on the drum of the ear, it causes a vibration, which, being communicated to the brain by the auditory nerves, then affects the soul with the sensation called sound.

P: What! Is sound then a sensation?

H: I tell you, as perceived by us, it is a particular sensation in the mind.

P: And can any sensation exist without the mind?

H: No, certainly.

P: How then can sound, being a sensation, exist in the air if by the air you mean a senseless substance existing without the mind.

H: You must distinguish, Philonous, between sound as it is perceived by us and as it is in itself, or (which is the same thing) between the sound we immediately perceive and that which exists without us. The former indeed is a particular kind of sensation, but the latter is merely a vibrational or undulatory motion in the air.

P: I thought I had already obviated that distinction by the answer I gave when you were applying it in a like case before. But, to say no more of that, are you sure then that sound is really nothing but motion?

H: I am.

P: Whatever therefore agrees to real sound may with truth be attributed to motion.

H: It may.

P: It is then good sense to speak of *motion*, as of a thing that is *loud*, *sweet*, *acute*, or *grave*.

H: I see you are resolved not to understand me. Is it not evident those accidents or modes belong only to sensible sound, or *sound* in the common meaning of the word, but not to *sound* in the real and philosophic sense, which, as I just now told you, is nothing but a certain motion of the air?

P: It seems then there are two sorts of sound, the one vulgar, or that which is heard, the other philosophical and real.

H: Even so.

P: And the latter consists in motion.

H: I told you so before.

P: Tell me, Hylas, to which of the senses, do you think, the idea of motion belongs—to the hearing?

H: No, certainly, but to the sight and touch.

P: It should follow then, that according to you, real sounds may possibly be *seen* or *felt*, but never *heard*.

H: Look, Philonous, you may if you please make a jest of my opinion, but that will not alter the truth of things. I admit, indeed, the inferences you draw me into sound something odd, but common language, you know, is framed by and for the use of the vulgar. We must not therefore wonder if expressions adapted to exact philosophic notions seem uncouth and out of the way.

P: Is it come to that? I assure you, I imagine myself to have gained no small point, since you make so light of departing from common phrases and opinions, it being a main part of our inquiry to examine whose notions are widest of the common road and most repugnant to the general sense of the world. But can you think it no more than a philosophical paradox to say that *real sounds are never heard* and that the idea of them is obtained by some other sense. And is there nothing in this contrary to nature and the truth of things?

H: To deal ingenuously, I do not like it. And after the concessions already made, I granted as well that sounds too have no real being without the mind.

P: And I hope you will make no difficulty to acknowledge the same of colors.

H: Pardon me, the case of colors is very different. Can anything be plainer than that we see them on the objects?

P: The objects you speak of are, I suppose, corporeal substances existing without the mind.

H: They are.

P: And have true and real colors inhering in them?

H: Each visible object has that color which we see in it.

P: How! Is there anything visible but what we perceive by sight?

H: There is not.

P: And do we perceive anything by sense which we do not perceive immediately?

H: How often must I be obliged to repeat the same thing? I tell you, we do not.

P: Have patience, good Hylas, and tell me once more whether there is anything immediately perceived by the senses except sensible qualities. I know you asserted there was not, but I would now be informed whether you still persist in the same opinion.

H: I do.

P: Pray, is your corporeal substance either a sensible quality or made up of sensible qualities?

H: What a question that is! Who ever thought it was?

P: My reason for asking was because in saying *each visible object has that color which we see in it*, you make visible objects be corporeal substances, which implies either that corporeal substances are sensible qualities or else that there is something besides sensible qualities perceived by sight; but as this point was formerly agreed between us and is still maintained by you, it is a clear consequence that your corporeal substance is nothing distinct from sensible qualities.

H: You may draw as many absurd consequences as you please and endeavor to perplex the plainest things, but you shall never persuade me out of my senses. I clearly understand my own meaning.

P: I wish you would make me understand it too. But since you are unwilling to have your notion of corporeal substance examined, I shall urge that point no further. Only be pleased to let me know whether the same colors which we see exist in external bodies or some other.

H: The very same.

P: What! Are then the beautiful red and purple we see on yonder clouds really in them? Or do you imagine they have in themselves any other form than that of a dark mist or vapor?

H: I must admit, Philonous, those colors are not really in the clouds as they seem to be at this distance. They are only apparent colors.

P: *Apparent* call you them? How shall we distinguish these apparent colors from real?

H: Very easily. Those are to be thought apparent which, appearing only at a distance, vanish upon a nearer approach.

P: And those, I suppose, are to be thought real which are discovered by the most near and exact survey.

H: Right.

P: Is the nearest and most exact survey made by the help of a microscope or by the naked eye?

H: By a microscope, doubtless.

P: But a microscope often discovers colors in an

object different from those perceived by the unassisted sight. And in case we had microscopes magnifying to any assigned degree, it is certain that no object whatsoever viewed through them would appear in the same color which it exhibits to the naked eye.

H: And what will you conclude from all this? You cannot argue that there are really and naturally no colors on objects because they may be altered or made to vanish by artificial managements.

P: I think it may evidently be concluded from your own concessions that all the colors we see with our naked eyes are only apparent as those on the clouds, since they vanish upon a more close and accurate inspection, which is afforded us by a microscope. Then as to what you say by way of prevention, I ask you whether the real and natural state of an object is better discovered by a very sharp and piercing sight or by one which is less sharp.

H: By the former without doubt.

P: Is it not plain from *Dioptrics* that microscopes make the sight more penetrating and represent objects as they would appear to the eye, in case it were naturally endowed with a most exquisite sharpness?

H: It is.

P: Consequently, the microscopic representation is to be thought that which best sets forth the real nature of the thing or what it is in itself. The colors therefore perceived by it are more genuine and real than those perceived otherwise.

H: I confess there is something in what you say.

P: Besides, it is not only possible but manifest that there actually are animals whose eyes are by nature framed to perceive those things which by reason of their minuteness escape our sight. What do you think of those inconceivably small animals perceived by glasses? Must we suppose they are all stark blind? Or, in case they see, can it be imagined their sight does not have the same use in preserving their bodies from injuries which appears in that of all other animals? And if it does, is it not evident they must see particles less than their own bodies, which will present them with a far different view in each object from that which strikes our senses? Even our own eyes do not always represent objects to us after the same manner. With *jaundice*, everyone knows that all things seem yellow. Is it not therefore highly probable that those animals in whose eyes we discern a very different texture from that of ours and whose bodies abound with different humors, do not see the same colors in every object that we do? From all of which, should it not seem to follow that all colors are equally apparent and that none of those which we perceive are really inherent in any outward object?

H: It should.

P: The point will be past all doubt if you consider that in case colors were real properties or affections inherent in external bodies, they could admit of no alteration without some change made in the very bodies themselves. But is it not evident from what has been said that upon the use of microscopes, upon a change happening in the humors of the eye, or a variation of distance, without any manner of real alteration in the thing itself, the colors of any object are either changed or totally disappear? No, all other circumstances remaining the same, change but the situation of some objects and they shall present different colors to the eye. The same thing happens upon viewing an object in various degrees of light. And what is more known than that the same bodies appear differently colored by candlelight from what they do in the open day? Add to these the experiment of a prism which, separating the heterogeneous rays of light, alters the color of any object and will cause the whitest to appear of a deep blue or red to the naked eye. And now tell me whether you are still of the opinion that every body has its true, real color inhering in it; and if you think it has, I would gladly know further from you what certain distance and position of the object, what peculiar texture and formation of the eye, what degree or kind of light is necessary for ascertaining that true color and distinguishing it from apparent ones.

H: I admit myself entirely satisfied that they are all equally apparent and that there is no such thing as color really inhering in external bodies, but that it is altogether in the light. And what confirms me in this opinion is that, in proportion to the light, colors are still more or less vivid, and if there is no light, then there are no colors perceived. Besides, allowing there are colors on external objects, yet how is it possible for us to perceive them? For no external body affects the mind unless it acts first on our organs of sense. But the only action of bodies is motion, and motion cannot be communicated otherwise than by impulse. A distant object, therefore, cannot act on the eye, nor consequently make itself or its properties perceivable to the soul. From this it plainly follows that it is immediately some contiguous substance which, operating on the eye, occasions a perception of colors—and such is light.

P: How! Is light then a substance?

H: I tell you, Philonous, external light is nothing but a thin fluid substance whose minute particles, being agitated with a brisk motion and in various manners reflected from the different surfaces of outward objects to the eyes, communicate different motions to the optic nerves, which being propagated to the brain, cause various impressions in it; and these are attended with the sensations of red, blue, yellow, etc.

P: It seems, then, the light does no more than shake the optic nerves.

H: Nothing else.

P: And, consequent to each particular motion of the nerves, the mind is affected with a sensation, which is some particular color.

H: Right.

P: And these sensations have no existence without the mind.

H: They do not.

P: How then do you affirm that colors are in the light, since by light you understand a corporeal substance external to the mind?

H: Light and colors, as immediately perceived by us, I grant cannot exist without the mind. But in themselves they are only the motions and configurations of certain insensible particles of matter.

P: Colors then, in the vulgar sense, or taken for the immediate objects of sight, cannot agree to any but a perceiving substance.

H: That is what I say.

P: Well then, since you give up the point as to those sensible qualities which are alone thought colors by all mankind besides, you may hold what you please with regard to those invisible ones of the philosophers. It is not my business to dispute about them; only I would advise you to envision yourself, whether, considering the inquiry we are upon, it would be prudent for you to affirm: *The red and blue which we see are not real colors, but certain unknown motions and figures which no man ever did or can see are truly so.* Are not these shocking notions, and are not they subject to as many ridiculous inferences as those you were obliged to renounce before in the case of sounds?

H: I frankly admit, Philonous, that it is in vain to stand out any longer. Colors, sounds, tastes, in a word, all those termed *secondary qualities*, have certainly no existence without the mind. But by this acknowledgment I must not be supposed to derogate anything from the reality of matter or external objects, seeing it is no more than several philosophers maintain who nevertheless are the furthest imaginable from denying matter. For the clearer understanding of this you must know sensible qualities are by philosophers divided into *primary* and *secondary*.[1] The former are extension, figure, solidity, gravity, motion, and rest. And these they hold exist really in bodies. The latter are those above enumerated or, briefly, all sensible qualities besides the primary, which they assert are only so many sensations or ideas existing nowhere but in the mind. But all this, I do not doubt, you are already apprised of. For my part, I have been a long time sensible there was such an opinion current among philosophers, but was never thoroughly convinced of its truth until now.

P: You are still then of the opinion that extension and figures are inherent in external unthinking substances.

H: I am.

P: But what if the same arguments which are brought against secondary qualities will hold proof against these also?

H: Why then I shall be obliged to think they too exist only in the mind.

P: Is it your opinion that the very figure and extension which you perceive by sense exist in the outward object or material substance?

H: It is.

P: Have all other animals as good grounds to think the same of the figure and extension which they see and feel?

H: Without doubt, if they have any thought at all.

P: Answer me, Hylas. Do you think the senses were bestowed upon all animals for their preservation and well being in life? Or were they given to men alone for this end?

H: I make no question but they have the same use in all other animals.

P: If so, is it not necessary they should be enabled

1. [See Locke's *Essay*, Bk. II, ch. VIII.—S.M.C.]

by them to perceive their own limbs and those bodies which are capable of harming them?

H: Certainly.

P: A mite therefore must be supposed to see his own foot, and things equal or even less than it, as bodies of some considerable dimension, though at the same time they appear to you scarce discernible or at best as so many visible points.

H: I cannot deny it.

P: And to creatures less than the mite they will seem yet larger.

H: They will.

P: To the extent that what you can hardly discern will to another extremely minute animal appear as some huge mountain.

H: All this I grant.

P: Can one and the same thing be at the same time in itself of different dimensions?

H: That would be absurd to imagine.

P: But from what you have laid down it follows that both the extension perceived by you and that perceived by the mite itself, as likewise all those perceived by lesser animals, are each of them the true extension of the mite's foot—that is to say, by your own principles you are led into an absurdity.

H: There seems to be some difficulty in the point.

P: Again, have you not acknowledged that no real inherent property of any object can be changed without some change in the thing itself?

H: I have.

P: But as we approach to or recede from an object, the visible extension varies, being at one distance ten or a hundred times greater than at another. Does it not therefore follow from this, likewise, that it is not really inherent in the object?

H: I admit I am at a loss what to think.

P: Your judgment will soon be determined if you will venture to think as freely concerning this quality as you have done concerning the rest. Was it not admitted as a good argument that neither heat nor cold was in the water because it seemed warm to one hand and cold to the other?

H: It was.

P: Is it not the very same reasoning to conclude there is no extension or figure in an object because to one eye it shall seem little, smooth, and round, when at the same time it appears to the other, great, uneven, and angular?

H: The very same. But does this latter fact ever happen?

P: You may at any time make the experiment by looking with one eye bare and with the other through a microscope.

H: I do not know how to maintain it, and yet I am loath to give up *extension*; I see so many odd consequences following upon such a concession.

P: Odd, you say? After the concessions already made, I hope you will stick at nothing for its oddness. But on the other hand should it not seem very odd if the general reasoning which includes all other sensible qualities did not also include extension? If it is allowed that no idea nor anything like an idea can exist in an unperceiving substance, then surely it follows that no figure or mode of extension, which we can either perceive or imagine or have any idea of, can be really inherent in matter—not to mention the peculiar difficulty there must be in conceiving a material substance, prior to and distinct from extension, to be the *substratum* of extension. Whatever the sensible quality is, figure, or sound, or color, it seems equally impossible it should subsist in that which does not perceive it.

H: I give up the point for the present, reserving still a right to retract my opinion, in case I shall hereafter discover any false step in my progress to it.

P: That is a right you cannot be denied. Figures and extension being dispatched, we proceed next to *motion*. Can a real motion in any external body be at the same time both very swift and very slow?

H: It cannot.

P: Is not the motion of a body swift in a reciprocal proportion to the time it takes up in describing any given space? Thus a body that describes a mile in an hour moves three times faster than it would in case it described only a mile in three hours.

H: I agree with you.

P: And is not time measured by the succession of ideas in our minds?

H: It is.

P: And is it not possible ideas should succeed one another twice as fast in your mind as they do in mine or in that of some spirit of another kind?

H: I admit it.

P: Consequently, the same body may to another seem to perform its motion over any space in half the time that it does to you. And the same reasoning will hold as to any other proportion—that is to say, according to your principles (since the motions perceived are both really in the object) it is possible one and the same body shall be really moved the same way at once, both very swift and very slow. How is this consistent either with common sense or with what you just now granted?

H: I have nothing to say to it.

P: Then as for *solidity*, either you do not mean any sensible quality by that word, and so it is beside our inquiry, or if you do, it must be either hardness or resistance. But both the one and the other are plainly relative to our senses, it being evident that what seems hard to one animal may appear soft to another who has greater force and firmness of limbs. Nor is it less plain that the resistance I feel is not in the body.

H: I admit the very sensation of resistance, which is all you immediately perceive, is not in the *body*, but the cause of that sensation is.

P: But the causes of our sensations are not things immediately perceived, and, therefore, not sensible. This point I thought had been already determined.

H: I admit it was, but you will pardon me if I seem a little embarrassed; I do not know how to quit my old notions.

P: To help you out, do but consider that if extension is once acknowledged to have no existence without the mind, the same must necessarily be granted of motion, solidity, and gravity, since they all evidently suppose extension. It is therefore superfluous to inquire particularly concerning each of them. In denying extension, you have denied them all to have any real existence.

H: I wonder, Philonous, if what you say is true, why those philosophers who deny the secondary qualities any real existence should yet attribute it to the primary. If there is no difference between them, how can this be accounted for?

P: It is not my business to account for every opinion of the philosophers. But among other reasons which may be assigned for this, it seems probable that pleasure and pain being annexed to the former rather than the latter may be one. Heat and cold, tastes and smells, have something more vividly pleasing or disagreeable than the ideas of extension, figure, and motion affect us with. And it being too visibly absurd to hold that pain or pleasure can be in an unperceiving substance, men are more easily weaned from believing the external existence of the secondary than the primary qualities. You will be satisfied there is something in this if you recollect the difference you made between an intense and more moderate degree of heat, allowing the one a real existence, while you denied it to the other. But after all, there is no rational ground for that distinction, for surely an indifferent sensation is as truly *a sensation* as one more pleasing or painful, and consequently should not any more than they be supposed to exist in an unthinking subject.

H: It has just come into my head, Philonous, that I have somewhere heard of a distinction between absolute and sensible extension. Now though it is acknowledged that great and small, consisting merely in the relation which other extended beings have to the parts of our own bodies, do not really inhere in the substances themselves, yet nothing obliges us to hold the same with regard to *absolute extension*, which is something abstracted from *great* and *small*, from this or that particular magnitude or figure. So likewise as to motion, *swift* and *slow* are altogether relative to the succession of ideas in our own minds. But it does not follow, because those modifications of motion do not exist without the mind, that absolute motion abstracted from them therefore does not.

P: Pray what is it that distinguishes one motion or one part of extension from another? Is it not something sensible, as some degree of swiftness or slowness, some certain magnitude or figure peculiar to each?

H: I think so.

P: These qualities, therefore, stripped of all sensible properties, are without all specific and numerical differences, as the schools call them.

H: They are.

P: That is to say, they are extension in general and motion in general.

H: Let it be so.

P: But it is a universally received maxim that *everything which exists is particular*. How then can motion in general or extension in general exist in any corporeal substance?

H: I will take time to solve your difficulty.

P: But I think the point may be speedily decided. Without doubt you can tell whether you are able to frame this or that idea. Now I am content to put our dispute on this issue. If you can frame in your thoughts a distinct abstract idea of motion or extension, divested of all those sensible modes as swift and slow, great and small, round and square, and the like, which are acknowledged to exist only in the mind, I will then yield the point you contend for. But if you cannot, it will be unreasonable on your side to insist any longer upon what you have no notion of.

H: To confess ingenuously, I cannot.

P: Can you even separate the ideas of extension and motion from the ideas of all those qualities which they who make the distinction term *secondary*?

H: What! Is it not an easy matter to consider extension and motion by themselves, abstracted from all other sensible qualities? Pray how do the mathematicians treat of them?

P: I acknowledge, Hylas, it is not difficult to form general propositions and reasonings about those qualities without mentioning any other and in this sense to consider or treat of them abstractly. But how does it follow that because I can pronounce the word *motion* by itself, I can form the idea of it in my mind exclusive of body? Or because theorems may be made of extension and figures without any mention of *great* or *small*, or any other sensible mode or quality, that therefore it is possible such an abstract idea of extension without any particular size or figure, or sensible quality, should be distinctly formed and apprehended by the mind? Mathematicians treat of quantity without regarding what other sensible qualities it is attended with, as being altogether indifferent to their demonstrations. But when, laying aside the words, they contemplate the bare ideas, I believe you will find they are not the pure abstracted ideas of extension.

H: But what do you say to *pure intellect*? May not abstracted ideas be framed by that faculty?

P: Since I cannot frame abstract ideas at all, it is plain I cannot frame them by the help of *pure intellect*, whatever faculty you understand by those words. Besides, not to inquire into the nature of pure intellect and its spiritual objects, as *virtue*, *reason*, *God*, or the like—this much seems manifest—that sensible things are only to be perceived by sense or represented by the imagination. Figures, therefore, and extension, being originally perceived by sense, do not belong to pure intellect. But for your further satisfaction, try if you can frame the idea of any figure abstracted from all particularities of size or even from other sensible qualities.

H: Let me think a little—I do not find that I can.

P: And can you think it possible that what implies a repugnance in its conception should really exist in nature?

H: By no means.

P: Since, therefore, it is impossible even for the mind to disunite the ideas of extension and motion from all other sensible qualities, does it not follow that where the one exists, there necessarily the other exists likewise?

H: It should seem so.

P: Consequently, the very same arguments which you admitted as conclusive against the secondary qualities are without any further application of force against the primary too. Besides, if you will trust your senses, is it not plain all sensible qualities coexist or appear to them as being in the same place? Do they ever represent a motion, or figure, as being divested of all other visible and tangible qualities?

H: You need say no more on this head. I am free to admit, if there is no secret error or oversight in our proceedings up to now, that all sensible qualities are alike to be denied existence without the mind. But my fear is that I have been too liberal in my former concessions or overlooked some fallacy or other. In short, I did not take time to think.

P: For that matter, Hylas, you may take what time you please in reviewing the progress of our inquiry. You are at liberty to recover any slips you might have made or offer whatever you have omitted, which makes for your first opinion.

H: One great oversight I take to be this: that I did not sufficiently distinguish the *object* from the *sensation*. Now though this latter may not exist without the mind, yet it will not follow from this that the former cannot.

P: What object do you mean? The object of the senses?

H: The same.

P: It is then immediately perceived?

H: Right.

P: Make me understand the difference between what is immediately perceived and a sensation.

H: The sensation I take to be an act of the mind perceiving, besides which there is something perceived, and this I call the *object*. For example, there is red and yellow on that tulip. But then the act of perceiving those colors is in me only, and not in the tulip.

P: What tulip do you speak of? Is it that which you see?

H: The same.

P: And what do you see besides color, figure, and extension?

H: Nothing.

P: What you would say then is that the red and yellow are coexistent with the extension; is it not?

H: That is not all. I would say they have a real existence without the mind in some unthinking substance.

P: That the colors are really in the tulip, which I see, is manifest. Neither can it be denied that this tulip may exist independent of your mind or mine; but that any immediate object of the senses, that is, any idea or combination of ideas, should exist in an unthinking substance or exterior to all minds, is in itself an evident contradiction. Nor can I imagine how this follows from what you said just now, namely, that the red and yellow were on the tulip *you saw*, since you do not pretend to see that unthinking substance.

H: You have an artful way, Philonous, of diverting our inquiry from the subject.

P: I see you have no mind to be pressed that way. To return then to your distinction between *sensation* and *object*; if I take you right, you distinguish in every perception two things, the one an action of the mind, the other not.

H: True.

P: And this action cannot exist in or belong to any unthinking thing, but whatever besides is implied in a perception, may.

H: That is my meaning.

P: So that if there was a perception without any act of the mind, it was possible such a perception should exist in an unthinking substance.

H: I grant it. But it is impossible there should be such a perception.

P: When is the mind said to be active?

H: When it produces, puts an end to, or changes anything.

P: Can the mind produce, discontinue, or change anything but by an act of the will?

H: It cannot.

P: The mind therefore is to be accounted active in its perceptions, insofar as volition is included in them.

H: It is.

P: In plucking this flower I am active, because I do it by the motion of my hand, which was consequent upon my volition—so likewise in applying it to my nose. But is either of these smelling?

H: No.

P: I act too in drawing the air through my nose, because my breathing so rather than otherwise is the effect of my volition. But neither can this be called *smelling*, for if it were, I should smell every time I breathed in that manner.

H: True.

P: Smelling then is somewhat consequent to all this.

H: It is.

P: But I do not find my will concerned any further. Whatever more there is, as that I perceive such a particular smell or any smell at all, this is independent of my will and I am altogether passive in this. Do you find it otherwise with you, Hylas?

H: No, the very same.

P: Then as to seeing, is it not in your power to open your eyes or keep them shut, to turn them this or that way?

H: Without doubt.

P: But does it in like manner depend on your will that, in looking on this flower, you perceive *white* rather than any other color? Or directing your open eyes towards that part of the heaven beyond, can you avoid seeing the sun? Or is light or darkness the effect of your volition?

H: No, certainly.

P: You are then in these respects altogether passive.

H: I am.

P: Tell me now, whether *seeing* consists in perceiving light and colors or in opening and turning the eyes?

H: Without doubt, in the former.

P: Since, therefore, you are in the very perception of light and colors altogether passive, what has become of that action you were speaking of as an ingredient in every sensation? And does it not follow from your own concessions that the perception of light and colors, including no action in it, may exist in an unperceiving substance? And is this not a plain contradiction?

H: I do not know what to think of it.

P: Besides, since you distinguish the *active* and *passive* in every perception, you must do it in that of pain. But how is it possible that pain—let it be as little active as you please—should exist in an unperceiving substance? In short, do but consider the point and then confess ingenuously whether light and colors, tastes, sounds, etc., are not all equally passions or sensations in the soul. You may indeed call them *external objects* and give them in words what subsistence you please. But examine your own thoughts and then tell me whether it is not as I say?

H: I acknowledge, Philonous, that upon a fair observation of what passes in my mind, I can discover nothing else but that I am a thinking being, affected with variety of sensations; neither is it possible to conceive how a sensation should exist in an unperceiving substance. But then, on the other hand, when I look on sensible things in a different view, considering them as so many modes and qualities, I find it necessary to suppose a material *substratum*, without which they cannot be conceived to exist.

P: *Material substratum* call you it? Pray, by which of your senses did you become acquainted with that being?

H: It is not itself sensible, its modes and qualities only being perceived by the senses.

P: I presume, then, it was by reflection and reason you obtained the idea of it.

H: I do not pretend to any proper positive idea of it. However, I conclude it exists, because qualities cannot be conceived to exist without a support.

P: It seems then you have only a relative notion of it, or that you conceive it not otherwise than by conceiving the relation it bears to sensible qualities.

H: Right.

P: Be pleased, therefore, to let me know in what that relation consists.

H: Is it not sufficiently expressed in the term *substratum* or *substance*?

P: If so, the word *substratum* should import that it is spread under the sensible qualities or accidents.

H: True.

P: And consequently under extension.

H: I admit it.

P: It is therefore somewhat in its own nature entirely distinct from extension.

H: I tell you extension is only a mode, and matter is something that supports modes. And is it not evident the thing supported is different from the thing supporting?

P: So that something distinct from and exclusive of extension is supposed to be the *substratum* of extension.

H: Just so.

P: Answer me, Hylas. Can a thing be spread without extension? Or is not the idea of extension necessarily included in *spreading*?

H: It is.

P: Whatever, therefore, you suppose spread under anything must have in itself an extension distinct from the extension of that thing under which it is spread.

H: It must.

P: Consequently, every corporeal substance being the *substratum* of extension must have in itself another extension by which it is qualified to be a *substratum*, and so on to infinity. And I ask whether this is not absurd in itself and repugnant to what you granted just now, namely, that the *substratum* was something distinct from and exclusive of extension.

H: Yes, but, Philonous, you take me wrong. I do not mean that matter is *spread* in a gross literal sense under extension. The word *substratum* is used only to express in general the same thing with *substance*.

P: Well then, let us examine the relation implied in the term *substance*. Is it not that it stands under accidents?

H: The very same.

P: But that one thing may stand under or support another, must it not be extended?

H: It must.

P: Is not therefore this supposition liable to the same absurdity with the former?

H: You still take things in a strict literal sense; that is not fair, Philonous.

P: I am not for imposing any sense on your words; you are at liberty to explain them as you please. Only I beseech you, make me understand something by them. You tell me matter supports or stands under accidents. How? Is it as your legs support your body?

H: No; that is the literal sense.

P: Pray let me know any sense, literal or not

literal, that you understand it in. How long must I wait for an answer, Hylas?

H: I declare I do not know what to say. I once thought I understood well enough what was meant by matter's supporting accidents. But now the more I think on it, the less can I comprehend it; in short, I find that I know nothing of it.

P: It seems then you have no idea at all, neither relative nor positive, of matter; you know neither what it is in itself nor what relation it bears to accidents.

H: I acknowledge it.

P: And yet you asserted that you could not conceive how qualities or accidents should really exist without conceiving at the same time a material support of them.

H: I did.

P: That is to say, when you conceive the real existence of qualities, you do in addition conceive something which you cannot conceive.

H: It was wrong, I admit. But still I fear there is some fallacy or other. Pray what do you think of this? It has just come into my head that the ground of all our mistake lies in your treating of each quality by itself. Now, I grant that each quality cannot singly subsist without the mind. Color cannot exist without extension, neither can figure without some other sensible quality. But as the several qualities united or blended together form entire sensible things, nothing hinders why such things may not be supposed to exist without the mind.

P: Either, Hylas, you are jesting or have a very bad memory. Though indeed we went through all the qualities by name one after another, yet my arguments, or rather your concessions, nowhere tended to prove that the secondary qualities did not subsist each alone by itself, but that they were not *at all* without the mind. Indeed in treating of figure and motion, we concluded they could not exist without the mind because it was impossible even in thought to separate them from all secondary qualities so as to conceive them existing by themselves. But then this was not the only argument made use of upon that occasion. But (to pass by all that has been said up to now, and reckon it for nothing, if you will have it so) I am content to put the whole upon this issue. If you can conceive it possible for any mixture or combination of qualities or any sensible object whatever to exist without the mind, then I will grant it actually to be so.

H: If it comes to that, the point will soon be decided. What is more easy than to conceive a tree or house existing by itself, independent of, and unperceived by any mind whatsoever? I do at this present time conceive them existing after that manner.

P: What are you saying, Hylas—can you see a thing which is at the same time unseen?

H: No, that would be a contradiction.

P: Is it not as great a contradiction to talk of *conceiving* a thing which is *unconceived*?

H: It is.

P: The tree or house, therefore, which you think of is conceived by you.

H: How should it be otherwise?

P: And what is conceived is surely in the mind.

H: Without question, that which is conceived is in the mind.

P: How then did you come to say you conceived a house or tree existing independent and out of all minds whatsoever?

H: That was, I admit, an oversight; but stay, let me consider what led me into it. It is a pleasant mistake enough. As I was thinking of a tree in a solitary place where no one was present to see it, I thought that was to conceive a tree as existing unperceived or unthought of, not considering that I myself conceived it all the while. But now I plainly see that all I can do is to frame ideas in my own mind. I may indeed conceive in my own thoughts the idea of a tree, or a house, or a mountain, but that is all. And this is far from proving that I can conceive them *existing out of the minds of all spirits*.

P: You acknowledge then that you cannot possibly conceive how any one corporeal sensible thing should exist otherwise than in a mind.

H: I do.

P: And yet you will earnestly contend for the truth of that which you cannot so much as conceive.

H: I profess I do not know what to think, but still some scruples remain with me. Is it not certain I see things at a distance? Do we not perceive the stars and moon, for example, to be a great way off? Is this not, I say, manifest to the senses?

P: Do you not in a dream too perceive those or the like objects?

H: I do.

P: And do they not then have the same appearance of being distant?

H: They have.

P: But you do not then conclude the apparitions in a dream to be without the mind?

H: By no means.

P: You ought not therefore conclude that sensible objects are without the mind from their appearance or manner in which they are perceived.

H: I acknowledge it. But does not my sense deceive me in those cases?

P: By no means. Of the idea or thing which you immediately perceive, neither sense nor reason informs you that it actually exists without the mind. By sense you only know that you are affected with such certain sensations of light and colors, etc. And these you will not say are without the mind.

H: True, but besides all that, do you not think the sight suggests something of *outness* or *distance*?

P: Upon approaching a distant object, do the visible size and figure change perpetually or do they appear the same at all distances?

H: They are in a continual change.

P: Sight, therefore, does not suggest or in any way inform you that the visible object you immediately perceive exists at a distance or will be perceived when you advance further onward, there being a continued series of visible objects succeeding each other during the whole time of your approach.

H: It does not; but still I know, upon seeing an object, what object I shall perceive after having passed over a certain distance—no matter whether it be exactly the same or no—there is still something of distance suggested in the case.

P: Good Hylas, do but reflect a little on the point and then tell me whether there is any more in it than this: From the ideas you actually perceive by sight, you have by experience learned to collect what other ideas you will (according to the standing order of nature) be affected with, after such a certain succession of time and motion.

H: Upon the whole, I take it to be nothing else.

P: Now is it not plain that if we suppose a man born blind was suddenly made to see, he could at first have no experience of what may be suggested by sight.

H: It is.

P: He would not then, according to you, have any notion of distance annexed to the things he saw; but would take them for a new set of sensations existing only in his mind.

H: It is undeniable.

P: But to make it still more plain: is not *distance* a line turned endwise to the eye?

H: It is.

P: And can a line so situated be perceived by sight?

H: It cannot.

P: Does it not therefore follow that distance is not properly and immediately perceived by sight?

H: It should seem so.

P: Again, is it your opinion that colors are at a distance?

H: It must be acknowledged they are only in the mind.

P: But do not colors appear to the eye as coexisting in the same place with extension and figures?

H: They do.

P: How can you then conclude from sight that figures exist without, when you acknowledge colors do not, the sensible appearance being the very same with regard to both?

H: I do not know what to answer.

P: But allowing that distance was truly and immediately perceived by the mind, yet it would not then follow it existed out of the mind. For whatever is immediately perceived is an idea; and can any idea exist out of the mind?

H: To suppose that would be absurd, but inform me, Philonous, can we perceive or know nothing besides our ideas?

P: As for the rational deducing of causes from effects, that is besides our inquiry. And by the senses you can best tell whether you perceive anything which is not immediately perceived. And I ask you whether the things immediately perceived are other than your own sensations or ideas? You have indeed more than once, in the course of this conversation, declared yourself on those points; but you seem, by this last question, to have departed from what you then thought.

H: To speak the truth, Philonous, I think there are two kinds of objects, the one perceived immediately, which are likewise called ideas, the other are real things or external objects perceived by the mediation of ideas, which are their images and representations. Now I admit ideas do not exist without the mind, but the latter sort of object does. I am sorry I did not think of this distinction sooner; it would probably have cut short your discourse.

P: Are those external objects perceived by sense or by some other faculty?

H: They are perceived by sense.

P: How! Is there anything perceived by sense which is not immediately perceived?

H: Yes, Philonous, in some sort there is. For example, when I look on a picture or statue of Julius Caesar, I may be said, after a manner, to perceive him (though not immediately) by my senses.

P: It seems then you will have our ideas, which alone are immediately perceived, to be pictures of external things, and that these also are perceived by sense inasmuch as they have a conformity or resemblance to our ideas.

H: That is my meaning.

P: And in the same way that Julius Caesar, in himself invisible, is nevertheless perceived by sight; real things, in themselves imperceptible, are perceived by sense.

H: In the very same.

P: Tell me, Hylas, when you behold the picture of Julius Caesar, do you see with your eyes any more than some colors and figures, with a certain symmetry and composition of the whole?

H: Nothing else.

P: And would not a man who had never known anything of Julius Caesar see as much?

H: He would.

P: Consequently, he has his sight and the use of it in as perfect a degree as you.

H: I agree with you.

P: From where does it come then that your thoughts are directed to the Roman emperor and his are not? This cannot proceed from the sensations or ideas of sense by you then perceived, since you acknowledge you have no advantage over him in that respect. It should seem therefore to proceed from reason and memory, should it not?

H: It should.

P: Consequently, it will not follow from that instance that anything is perceived by sense which is not immediately perceived. Though I grant we may in one meaning be said to perceive sensible things mediately by sense, that is, when, from a frequently perceived connection, the immediate perception of ideas by one sense suggests to the mind others perhaps belonging to another sense which are accustomed to be connected with them. For instance, when I hear a coach drive along the streets, immediately I perceive only the sound; but, from the experience I have had that such a sound is connected with a coach, I am said to hear the coach. It is nevertheless evident that, in truth and strictness, nothing can be *heard* but *sound*, and the coach is not then properly perceived by sense, but suggested from experience. So likewise when we are said to see a red-hot bar of iron, the solidity and heat of the iron are not the objects of sight, but suggested to the imagination by the color and figure, which are properly perceived by that sense. In short, those things alone are actually and strictly perceived by any sense which would have been perceived in case that same sense had then been first conferred on us. As for other things, it is plain they are only suggested to the mind by experience grounded on former perceptions. But to return to your comparison of Caesar's picture, it is plain, if you keep to that, you must hold that the real things or archetypes of our ideas are not perceived by sense, but by some internal faculty of the soul as reason or memory. I would therefore gladly know what arguments you can draw from reason for the existence of what you call *real things* or *material objects*, or whether you remember to have seen them formerly as they are in themselves, or if you have heard or read of anyone who did.

H: I see, Philonous, you are disposed to raillery, but that will never convince me.

P: My aim is only to learn from you the way to come at the knowledge of *material beings*. Whatever we perceive is perceived either immediately or mediately, by sense, or by reason and reflection. But as you have excluded sense, pray show me what reason you have to believe their existence, or what *medium* you can possibly make use of to prove it, either to mine or your own understanding.

H: To deal ingenuously, Philonous, now that I consider the point, I do not find I can give you any good reason for it. But this much seems pretty plain—that it is at least possible such things may really exist, and as long as there is no absurdity in supposing them, I am resolved to believe as I did, until you bring good reasons to the contrary.

P: What! Has it come to this that you only believe the existence of material objects and that your belief is founded barely on the possibility of its being true? Then you will have me bring reasons against it, though another would think it reasonable the proof should lie on him who holds the affirmative. And after all, this very point which you are now resolved to maintain without any reason is, in effect, what you have more than once during this discourse seen good reason to give up. But to pass over all this—if I understand you rightly, you say our ideas do not exist without the mind, but that they are copies, images, or representations of certain originals that do.

H: You take me right.

P: They are then like external things.

H: They are.

P: Have those things a stable and permanent nature independent of our senses, or are they in a perpetual change upon our producing any motions in our bodies, suspending, exerting, or altering our faculties or organs of sense?

H: Real things, it is plain, have a fixed and real nature, which remains the same, notwithstanding any change in our senses or in the posture and motion of our bodies, which indeed may affect the ideas in our minds, but it would be absurd to think they had the same effect on things existing without the mind.

P: How then is it possible that things perpetually fleeting and variable as our ideas should be copies or images of anything fixed and constant? Or, in other words, since all sensible qualities, as size, figure, color, etc., that is, our ideas, are continually changing upon every alteration in the distance, medium, or instruments of sensation, how can any determinate material objects be properly represented or painted forth by several distinct things, each of which is so different from and unlike the rest? Or if you say it resembles some one only of our ideas, how shall we be able to distinguish the true copy from all the false ones?

H: I profess, Philonous, I am at a loss. I do not know what to say to this.

P: But neither is this all. Which are material objects in themselves—perceptible or imperceptible?

H: Properly and immediately nothing can be perceived but ideas. All material things, therefore, are in themselves insensible and to be perceived only by their ideas.

P: Ideas then are sensible, and their archetypes or originals insensible.

H: Right.

P: But how can that which is sensible be like that which is insensible? Can a real thing in itself *invisible* be like a *color*; or a real thing which is not *audible* be like a *sound*? In a word, can anything be like a sensation or idea but another sensation or idea?

H: I must admit, I think not.

P: Is it possible there should be any doubt in the point? Do you not perfectly know your own ideas?

H: I know them perfectly, since what I do not perceive or know can be no part of my idea.

P: Consider, therefore, and examine them, and then tell me if there is anything in them which can exist without the mind or if you can conceive anything like them existing without the mind.

H: Upon inquiry, I find it is impossible for me to conceive or understand how anything but an idea can be like an idea. And it is most evident that *no idea can exist without the mind*.

P: You are, therefore, by your principles forced to deny the reality of sensible things, since you made it to consist in an absolute existence exterior to the mind. That is to say, you are a downright *skeptic*. So I have gained my point, which was to show your principles led to skepticism.

H: For the present I am, if not entirely convinced, at least silenced.

P: I would gladly know what more you would require in order to have a perfect conviction. Have you not had the liberty of explaining yourself all manner of ways? Were any little slips in discourse laid hold and insisted on? Or were you not allowed to retract or reinforce anything you had offered, as best served your purpose? Has not everything you could say been heard and examined with all the fairness imaginable? In a word, have you not in every point been convinced out of your own mouth? And if you can at present discover any flaw in any of your former concessions, or think of any remaining subterfuge, any new distinction, color, or comment whatsoever, why do you not produce it?

H: A little patience, Philonous. I am at present so amazed to see myself ensnared, and as it were imprisoned in the labyrinths you have drawn me into, that on the sudden it cannot be expected I should find my way out. You must give me time to look about me and recollect myself.

P: Listen, is not this the college bell?

H: It rings for prayers.

P: We will go in then if you please, and meet here again tomorrow morning. In the meantime you may employ your thoughts on this morning's discourse, and try if you can find any fallacy in it, or invent any new means to extricate yourself.

H: Agreed.

THE SECOND DIALOGUE

HYLAS: I beg your pardon, Philonous, for not meeting you sooner. All this morning my head was so filled with our late conversation that I had not leisure to think of the time of the day, or indeed of anything else.

PHILONOUS: I am glad you were so intent upon it, in hopes if there were any mistakes in your concessions or fallacies in my reasonings from them, you will now discover them to me.

H: I assure you, I have done nothing ever since I saw you but search after mistakes and fallacies—and, with that view, have minutely examined the whole series of yesterday's discourse—but all in vain, for the notions it led me into, upon review, appear still more clear and evident, and the more I consider them, the more irresistibly do they force my assent.

P: And is this not, you think, a sign that they are genuine, that they proceed from nature and are conformable to right reason? Truth and beauty are in this alike, that the strictest survey sets them both off to advantage. While the false luster of error and disguise cannot endure being reviewed or too nearly inspected.

H: I admit there is a great deal in what you say. Nor can anyone be more entirely satisfied of the truth of those odd consequences so long as I have in view the reasonings that lead to them. But when these are out of my thoughts, there seems, on the other hand, something so satisfactory, so natural and intelligible in the modern way of explaining things that I profess I do not know how to reject it.

P: I do not know what way you mean.

H: I mean the way of accounting for our sensations or ideas.

P: How is that?

H: It is supposed the soul makes her residence in some part of the brain from which the nerves take their rise and are thus extended to all parts of the body, and that outward objects, by the different impressions they make on the organs of sense, communicate certain vibrational motions to the nerves, and these being filled with spirits, propagate them to the brain or seat of the soul, which, according to the various impressions or traces thereby made in the brain, is variously affected with ideas.

P: And do you call this an explication of the manner whereby we are affected with ideas?

H: Why not, Philonous? Have you anything to object against it?

P: I would first know whether I rightly understand your hypothesis. You make certain traces in the brain to be the causes or occasions of our ideas. Pray tell me whether by the *brain* you mean any sensible thing?

H: What else do you think I could mean?

P: Sensible things are all immediately perceivable; and those things which are immediately perceivable are ideas; and these exist only in the mind. This much you have, if I am not mistaken, long since agreed to.

H: I do not deny it.

P: The brain therefore you speak of, being a sensible thing, exists only in the mind. Now, I would gladly know whether you think it reasonable to suppose that one idea or thing existing in the mind occasions all other ideas. And if you think so, pray how do you account for the origin of that primary idea or brain itself?

H: I do not explain the origin of our ideas by that brain which is perceivable to sense, this being itself only a combination of sensible ideas, but by another which I imagine.

P: But are not things imagined as truly *in the mind* as things perceived?

H: I must confess they are.

P: It comes, therefore, to the same thing, and you have been all this while accounting for ideas by certain motions or impressions in the brain, that is, by some alterations in an idea—whether sensible or imaginable, it does not matter.

H: I begin to suspect my hypothesis.

P: Beside spirits, all that we know or conceive are our own ideas. When, therefore, you say all ideas are occasioned by impressions in the brain, do you conceive this brain or not? If you do, then you talk of ideas imprinted in an idea causing that same idea, which is absurd. If you do not conceive it, you talk unintelligibly instead of forming a reasonable hypothesis.

H: I now clearly see it was a mere dream. There is nothing in it.

P: You need not be much concerned at it; for, after all, this way of explaining things, as you called it, could never have satisfied any reasonable man. What connection is there between a motion in the nerves and the sensations of sound or color in the mind? Or how is it possible these should be the effect of that?

H: But I could never think it had so little in it as now it seems to have.

P: Well then, are you at length satisfied that no sensible things have a real existence, and that you are in truth a thoroughgoing *skeptic*?

H: It is too plain to be denied.

P: Look! Are not the fields covered with a delightful greenery? Is there not something in the woods and groves, in the rivers and clear springs, that soothes, that delights, that transports the soul? At the prospect of the wide and deep ocean, or some huge mountain whose top is lost in the clouds, or of an old gloomy forest, are not our minds filled with a pleasing horror? Even in rocks and deserts, is there not an agreeable wildness? How sincere a pleasure is it to behold the natural beauties of the earth! To preserve and renew our relish for them, is not the veil of night alternately drawn over her face, and does she not change her dress with the seasons? How aptly are the elements disposed! What variety and use in the meanest production of nature! What delicacy, what beauty, what contrivance in animal and vegetable bodies! How exquisitely are all things suited as well to their particular ends as to constitute opposite parts of the whole! And while they mutually aid and support, do they not also set off and illustrate each other! Raise now your thoughts from this ball of earth to all those glorious luminaries that adorn the high arch of heaven. The motion and situation of the planets, are they not admirable for use and order? Were those (miscalled *erratic*) globes ever known to stray in their repeated journeys through the pathless void? Do they not measure areas round the sun ever proportioned to the times? So fixed, so immutable, are the laws by which the unseen Author of nature actuates the universe. How vivid and radiant is the luster of the fixed stars! How magnificent and rich that negligent profusion with which they appear to be scattered throughout the whole azure vault! Yet if you take the telescope, it brings into your sight a new host of stars that escape the naked eye. Here they seem contiguous and minute, but to a nearer view immense orbs of light at various distances, far sunk in the abyss of space. Now you must call imagination to your aid. The feeble narrow sense cannot ascertain innumerable worlds revolving round the central fires, and in those worlds the energy of an all-perfect mind displayed in endless forms. But neither sense nor imagination is big enough to comprehend the boundless extent with all its glittering furniture. Though the laboring mind exerts and strains each power to its utmost reach, there still stands out ungrasped an immeasurable surplus. Yet all the vast bodies that compose this mighty frame, however distant and remote, are by some secret mechanism, some divine art and force, linked in a mutual dependence and intercourse with each other, even with this earth, which was almost slipped from my thoughts and lost in the crowd of worlds. Is not the whole system immense, beautiful, glorious beyond expression and beyond thought? What treatment then do those philosophers deserve who would deprive these noble and delightful scenes of all reality? How should those principles be entertained that lead us to think all the visible beauty of the creation a false imaginary glare? To be plain, can you expect this skepticism of yours will not be thought extravagantly absurd by all men of sense?

H: Other men may think as they please, but for your part you have nothing to reproach me with. My comfort is you are as much a skeptic as I am.

P: There, Hylas, I must beg leave to differ from you.

H: What! Have you all along agreed to the premises, and do you now deny the conclusion and leave me to maintain these paradoxes which you led me into by myself? This surely is not fair.

P: I deny that I agreed with you in those notions that led to skepticism. You indeed said the reality of sensible things consisted in an *absolute existence* out of the minds of spirits or distinct from their being perceived. And, pursuant to this notion of reality, you are obliged to deny sensible things any real existence, that is, according to your own definition, you profess yourself a *skeptic*. But I neither said nor thought the reality of sensible things was to be defined after that manner. To me it is evident, for the reasons you allow of, that sensible things cannot exist otherwise than in a mind or spirit. From this I conclude, not that they have no real existence, but that, seeing they do not depend on my thought, and have an existence distinct from being perceived by me, *there must be some other mind in which they exist.* As sure, therefore, as the sensible world really exists, so sure is there an infinite, omnipresent Spirit who contains and supports it.

H: What! This is no more than I and all Christians hold—no, and all others too who believe there is a God and that he knows and comprehends all things.

P: Yes, but here lies the difference. Men commonly believe that all things are known or perceived by God because they believe the being of a God, whereas I, on the other side, immediately and necessarily conclude the being of a God because all sensible things must be perceived by him.

H: But so long as we all believe the same thing, what matter is it how we come by that belief?

P: But neither do we agree in the same opinion. For philosophers, though they acknowledge all corporeal beings to be perceived by God, yet they attribute to them an absolute subsistence distinct from their being perceived by any mind whatever, which I do not. Besides, is there no difference between saying *there is a God, therefore he perceives all things*, and saying *sensible things do really exist—and if they really exist, they are necessarily perceived by an infinite mind—therefore there is an infinite mind, or God*? This furnishes you with a direct and immediate demonstration, from a most evident principle, of the *being of a God*. Theologians and philosophers had proved beyond all controversy, from the beauty and usefulness of the several parts of the creation, that it was the workmanship of God. But that—setting aside all help of astronomy and natural philosophy, all contemplation of the contrivance, order, and adjustment of things—an infinite mind should be necessarily inferred from the bare existence of the sensible world is an advantage peculiar to them only who have made this easy reflection: that the sensible world is that which we perceive by our several senses; and that nothing is perceived by the senses besides ideas; and that no idea or archetype of an idea can exist otherwise than in a mind. You may now, without any laborious search into the sciences, without any subtlety of reason or tedious length of discourse, oppose and baffle the most strenuous advocate for atheism. Those miserable refuges, whether in an eternal succession of unthinking causes and effects or in a fortuitous concourse of atoms—those wild imaginations of Vanini,[2] Hobbes, and Spinoza, in a word, the whole system of atheism—is it not entirely overthrown by this single reflection on the repugnance included in supposing the whole or any part, even the most rude and shapeless, of the visible world to exist without a mind? Let anyone of those abettors of impiety but look into his own thoughts and there try if he can conceive how so much as a rock, a desert, a chaos, or confused jumble of atoms, how anything at all, either sensible or imaginable, can exist independent of a mind, and he need go no further to be convinced of his folly. Can anything be fairer than to put a dispute on such an issue and leave it to a man himself to see if he can conceive, even in thought, what he holds to be true in fact, and to allow it a real existence from a notion?

H: It cannot be denied, there is something highly serviceable to religion in what you advance. But do you not think it looks very like a notion entertained by some eminent moderns,[3] of *seeing all things in God*?

P: I would gladly know that opinion; pray explain it to me.

H: They conceive that the soul, being immaterial, is incapable of being united with material things so as to perceive them in themselves, but that she perceives them by her union with the substance of God, which, being spiritual, is therefore purely intelligible or capable of being the immediate object of a spirit's thought. Besides, the divine essence contains in it perfections correspondent to each created being, and which are, for that reason, proper to exhibit or represent them to the mind.

P: I do not understand how our ideas, which are things altogether passive and inert, can be the essence or any part (or like any part) of the essence or substance of God, who is an impassive, indivisible, purely

2. [Giulio Cesare Lucilio Vanini (1585–1619) was an Italian philosopher burned at the stake at Toulouse, France on charges of atheism and witchcraft.]

3. [The reference is to Nicolas Malebranche (1638–1715), one of the occasionalists, who maintained that no interaction occurs between mental and physical events nor among events in either realm. The appearance of interaction was ascribed to the intervention of God, whose actions were said to produce regularities.]

active being. Many more difficulties and objections occur at first view against this hypothesis, but I shall only add that it is liable to all the absurdities of the common hypotheses in making a created world exist otherwise than in the mind of a spirit. Besides all which, it has this peculiar to itself that it makes that material world serve to no purpose. And if it passes for a good argument against other hypotheses in the sciences that they suppose nature or the Divine Wisdom to make something in vain or do by tedious round-about methods what might have been performed in a much more easy and compendious way, what shall we think of that hypothesis which supposes the whole world made in vain?

H: But what do you say, are not you too of the opinion that we see all things in God? If I am not mistaken, what you advance comes near it.

P: Few men think, yet all will have opinions. Hence men's opinions are superficial and confused. It is nothing strange that tenets which in themselves are ever so different should nevertheless be confounded with each other by those who do not consider them attentively. I shall not therefore be surprised if some men imagine that I run into the enthusiasm of Malebranche, though in truth I am very remote from it. He builds on the most abstract general ideas, which I entirely disclaim. He asserts an absolute external world, which I deny. He maintains that we are deceived by our senses and do not know the real natures or the true forms and figures of extended beings—to all of which I hold the direct contrary. So that, upon the whole, there are no principles more fundamentally opposite than his and mine. It must be admitted I entirely agree with what the Holy Scripture says that "in God we live, and move, and have our being."[4] But that we see things in his essence, after the manner above set forth, I am far from believing. Take here in brief my meaning. It is evident that the things I perceive are my own ideas and that no idea can exist unless it be in a mind. Nor is it less plain that these ideas, or things perceived by me, either themselves or their archetypes, exist independently of my mind, since I do not know myself to be their author, it being out of my power to determine at pleasure what particular ideas I shall be affected with upon opening my eyes or ears. They must therefore exist in some other mind, whose will it is they should be exhibited to me. The things, I say, immediately perceived, are ideas or sensations, call them which you will. But how can any idea or sensation exist in, or be produced by, anything but a mind or spirit? This indeed is inconceivable, and to assert that which is inconceivable is to talk nonsense, is it not?

H: Without doubt.

P: But, on the other hand, it is very conceivable that they should exist in and be produced by a spirit, since this is no more than I daily experience in myself—inasmuch as I perceive numberless ideas and, by an act of my will, can form a great variety of them and raise them up in my imagination, though it must be confessed, these creatures of the fancy are not altogether so distinct, so strong, vivid, and permanent, as those perceived by my senses, which latter are called *real things*. From all which I conclude *there is a mind which affects me every moment with all the sensible impressions I perceive*. And from the variety, order, and manner of these, I conclude the author of them to be *wise, powerful, and good beyond comprehension*. Mark it well: I do not say I see things by perceiving that which represents them in the intelligible substance of God. This I do not understand; but I say the things perceived by me are known by the understanding and produced by the will of an infinite Spirit. And is not all this most plain and evident? Is there any more in it than what a little observation of our own minds, and that which passes in them, not only enables us to conceive but also obliges us to acknowledge?

H: I think I understand you very clearly and admit the proof you give of a Deity seems no less evident than it is surprising. But allowing that God is the supreme and universal cause of all things, yet may not there be still a third nature besides spirits and ideas? May we not admit a subordinate and limited cause of our ideas? In a word, may there not for all that be *matter*?

P: How often must I inculcate the same thing? You allow the things immediately perceived by sense to exist nowhere without the mind, but there is nothing perceived by sense which is not perceived immediately. Therefore, there is nothing sensible that exists without the mind. The matter, therefore, which you still insist on is something intelligible, I suppose,

4. [The quotation is from Acts 17:28.]

something that may be discovered by reason and not by sense.

H: You are in the right.

P: Pray let me know what reasoning your belief of matter is grounded on, and what this matter is in your present sense of it.

H: I find myself affected with various ideas of which I know I am not the cause; neither are they the cause of themselves or of one another, or capable of subsisting by themselves, as being altogether inactive, fleeting, dependent beings. They have therefore some cause distinct from me and them, of which I pretend to know no more than that it is *the cause of my ideas*. And this thing, whatever it is, I call matter.

P: Tell me, Hylas, has everyone a liberty to change the current proper signification annexed to a common name in any language? For example, suppose a traveler should tell you that in a certain country men might pass unhurt through the fire, and, upon explaining himself, you found he meant by the word *fire* that which others call *water*, or if he should assert there are trees which walk upon two legs, meaning men by the term *trees*. Would you think this reasonable?

H: No, I should think it very absurd. Common custom is the standard of propriety in language. And for any man to affect speaking improperly is to pervert the use of speech and can never serve to a better purpose than to protract and multiply disputes where there is no difference in opinion.

P: And does not *matter*, in the common current meaning of the word, signify an extended, solid, moveable, unthinking, inactive substance?

H: It does.

P: And has it not been made evident that no such substance can possibly exist? And though it should be allowed to exist, yet how can that which is *inactive* be a *cause* or that which is *unthinking* be a *cause of thought*? You may, indeed, if you please, annex to the word *matter* a contrary meaning to what is vulgarly received, and tell me you understand by it an unextended, thinking, active being, which is the cause of our ideas. But what else is this than to play with words and run into that very fault you just now condemned with so much reason? I do by no means find fault with your reasoning, in that you collect a cause from the *phenomena*, but I deny that the cause deducible by reason can properly be termed matter.

H: There is indeed something in what you say. But I am afraid you do not thoroughly comprehend my meaning. I would by no means be thought to deny that God, or an infinite spirit, is the supreme cause of all things. All I contend for is that subordinate to the supreme agent there is a cause of a limited and inferior nature, which concurs in the production of our ideas, not by any act of will or spiritual efficiency, but by that kind of action which belongs to matter, namely *motion*.

P: I find you are at every turn relapsing into your old exploded conceit of a moveable and consequently an extended substance existing without the mind. What! Have you already forgot you were convinced, or are you willing I should repeat what has been said on that head? In truth this is not fair dealing in you still to suppose the being of that which you have so often acknowledged to have no being. But not to insist further on what has been so largely handled, I ask whether all your ideas are not perfectly passive and inert, including nothing of action in them?

H: They are.

P: And are sensible qualities anything else but ideas?

H: How often have I acknowledged that they are not?

P: But is not motion a sensible quality?

H: It is.

P: Consequently, it is no action.

H: I agree with you. And indeed it is very plain that when I stir my finger, it remains passive, but my will which produced the motion is active.

P: Now I desire to know, in the first place, whether motion being allowed to be no action, you can conceive any action besides volition; and, in the second place, whether to say something and conceive nothing is not to talk nonsense; and, lastly, whether having considered the premises, you do not perceive that to suppose any efficient or active cause of our ideas other than *spirit* is highly absurd and unreasonable?

H: I give up the point entirely. But though matter may not be a cause, yet what hinders its being an *instrument* subservient to the supreme agent in the production of our ideas?

P: An instrument, you say; pray what may be the figure, springs, wheels, and motions of that instrument?

H: Those I pretend to determine nothing of, both the substance and its qualities being entirely unknown to me.

P: What? You are then of the opinion, it is made up of unknown parts, that it has unknown motions, and an unknown shape.

H: I do not believe it has any figure or motion at all, being already convinced that no sensible qualities can exist in an unperceiving substance.

P: But what notion is it possible to frame of an instrument void of all sensible qualities, even extension itself?

H: I do not pretend to have any notion of it.

P: And what reason do you have to think this unknown, this inconceivable somewhat does exist? Is it that you imagine God cannot act as well without it or that you find by experience the use of some such thing when you form ideas in your own mind?

H: You are always teasing me for reasons of my belief. Pray what reasons do you have not to believe it?

P: It is to me a sufficient reason not to believe the existence of anything if I see no reason for believing it. But, not to insist on reasons for believing, you will not so much as let me know what it is you would have me believe, since you say you have no manner of notion of it. After all, let me entreat you to consider whether it is like a philosopher, or even like a man of common sense, to pretend to believe you do not know what and you do not know why.

H: Hold on, Philonous. When I tell you matter is an *instrument*, I do not mean altogether nothing. It is true, I do not know the particular kind of instrument, but, however, I have some notion of *instrument in general*, which I apply to it.

P: But what if it should prove that there is something, even in the most general notion of *instrument*, as taken in a distinct sense from *cause*, which makes the use of it inconsistent with the divine attributes?

H: Make that appear and I shall give up the point.

P: What do you mean by the general nature or notion of *instrument*?

H: That which is common to all particular instruments composes the general notion.

P: Is it not common to all instruments that they are applied to the doing those things only which cannot be performed by the mere act of our wills? Thus, for instance, I never use an instrument to move my finger because it is done by a volition. But I should use one if I were to remove part of a rock or tear up a tree by the roots. Are you of the same mind? Or can you show any example where an instrument is made use of in producing an effect immediately depending on the will of the agent?

H: I admit I cannot.

P: How, therefore, can you suppose that an all-perfect Spirit, on whose will all things have an absolute and immediate dependence, should need an instrument in his operations or, not needing it, make use of it? Thus it seems to me that you are obliged to admit the use of a lifeless inactive instrument to be incompatible with the infinite perfection of God—that is, by your own confession to give up the point.

H: It does not readily occur what I can answer you.

P: But I think you should be ready to admit the truth when it has been fairly proved to you. We, indeed, who are beings of finite powers, are forced to make use of instruments. And the use of an instrument shows the agent to be limited by rules of another's prescription and that he cannot obtain his end, but in such a way and by such conditions. From this it seems a clear consequence that the supreme unlimited agent uses no tool or instrument at all. The will of an omnipotent Spirit is no sooner exerted than executed, without the application of means, which, if they are employed by inferior agents, it is not upon account of any real efficacy that is in them or necessary aptitude to produce any effect, but merely in compliance with the laws of nature or those conditions prescribed to them by the first cause, who is himself above all limitation or prescription whatsoever.

H: I will no longer maintain that matter is an instrument. However, I would not be understood to give up its existence either, since, notwithstanding what has been said, it may still be an *occasion*.

P: How many shapes is your matter to take? Or how often must it be proved not to exist before you are content to part with it? But to say no more of this (though by all the laws of disputation I may justly blame you for so frequently changing the signification of the principal term) I would gladly know what you mean by affirming that matter is an occasion, having already denied it to be a cause. And when you have shown in what sense you understand *occasion*, pray, in the next place, be pleased to show me what reason induces you to believe there is such an occasion of our ideas.

H: As to the first point: By *occasion* I mean an inactive, unthinking being, at the presence of which God excites ideas in our minds.

P: And what may be the nature of that inactive, unthinking being?

H: I know nothing of its nature.

P: Proceed then to the second point and assign some reason why we should allow an existence to this inactive, unthinking, unknown thing.

H: When we see ideas produced in our minds after an orderly and constant manner, it is natural to think they have some fixed and regular occasions at the presence of which they are excited.

P: You acknowledge then God alone to be the cause of our ideas and that he causes them at the presence of those occasions.

H: That is my opinion.

P: Those things which you say are present to God, without doubt he perceives.

H: Certainly. Otherwise they could not be to him an occasion of acting.

P: Not to insist now on your making sense of this hypothesis or answering all the puzzling questions and difficulties it is liable to: I only ask whether the order and regularity observable in the series of our ideas, or the course of nature, are not sufficiently accounted for by the wisdom and power of God, and whether it does not derogate from those attributes to suppose he is influenced, directed, or put in mind, when and how he is to act, by any unthinking substance. And, lastly, whether in case I granted all you contend for, it would make anything to your purpose, it not being easy to conceive how the external or absolute existence of an unthinking substance, distinct from its being perceived, can be inferred from my allowing that there are certain things perceived by the mind of God which are to him the occasion of producing ideas in us.

H: I am perfectly at a loss what to think, this notion of *occasion* seeming now altogether as groundless as the rest.

P: Do you not at length perceive that in all these different meanings of *matter*, you have been only supposing you do not know what, for no manner of reason, and to no kind of use?

H: I freely admit myself less fond of my notions since they have been so accurately examined. But still, I think I have some confused perception that there is such a thing as *matter*.

P: Either you perceive the being of matter immediately or mediately. If immediately, pray inform me by which of the senses you perceive it. If mediately, let me know by what reasoning it is inferred from those things which you perceive immediately. So much for the perception. Then for the matter itself, I ask whether it is object, *substratum*, cause, instrument, or occasion? You have already pleaded for each of these, shifting your notions and making matter to appear sometimes in one shape, then in another. And what you have offered has been disapproved and rejected by yourself. If you have anything new to advance, I would gladly hear it.

H: I think I have already offered all I had to say on those heads. I am at a loss what more to urge.

P: And yet you are loath to part with your old prejudice. But to make you quit it more easily, I desire that, besides what has been suggested up to now, you will further consider whether, upon the supposition that matter exists, you can possibly conceive how you should be affected by it? Or, supposing it did not exist, whether it is not evident you might for all that be affected with the same ideas you now are, and consequently have the very same reasons to believe its existence that you now can have?

H: I acknowledge it is possible we might perceive all things just as we do now, though there was no matter in the world; neither can I conceive, if there is matter, how it should produce any idea in our minds. And I do further grant you have entirely satisfied me that it is impossible there should be such a thing as matter in any of the foregoing senses. But still I cannot help supposing that there is *matter* in some sense or other. What that is I do not indeed pretend to determine.

P: I do not expect you should define exactly the nature of that unknown being. Only be pleased to tell me whether it is a substance, and if so, whether you can suppose a substance without accidents, or in case you suppose it to have accidents or qualities, I desire you will let me know what those qualities are, at least what is meant by matter's supporting them.

H: We have already argued on those points. I have no more to say to them. But to prevent any further questions, let me tell you, I at present understand by *matter* neither substance nor accident, thinking nor extended being, neither cause, instrument, nor occasion, but something entirely unknown, distinct from all these.

P: It seems then you include in your present notion of matter nothing but the general abstract of idea of *entity*.

H: Nothing else, save only that I superadd to this general idea the negation of all those particular things, qualities, or ideas that I perceive, imagine, or in any way apprehend.

P: Pray where do you suppose this unknown matter to exist?

H: Oh Philonous! Now you think you have entangled me; for if I say it exists in place, then you will infer that it exists in the mind, since it is agreed that place or extension exists only in the mind, but I am not ashamed to admit my ignorance. I do not know where it exists; only I am sure it does not exist in place. There is a negative answer for you and you must expect no other to all the questions you put for the future about matter.

P: Since you will not tell me where it exists, be pleased to inform me after what manner you suppose it to exist or what you mean by its existence.

H: It neither thinks nor acts, neither perceives, nor is perceived.

P: But what is there positive in your abstracted notion of its existence?

H: Upon a nice observation, I do not find I have any positive notion or meaning at all. I tell you again I am not ashamed to admit my ignorance. I do not know what is meant by its *existence* or how it exists.

P: Continue, good Hylas, to act the same ingenuous part and tell me sincerely whether you can frame a distinct idea of entity in general, prescinded from and exclusive of all thinking and corporeal beings, all particular things whatsoever.

H: Hold on, let me think a little—I profess, Philonous, I do not find that I can. At first glance I thought I had some dilute and airy notion of pure entity in abstract, but upon closer attention it has quite vanished out of sight. The more I think on it, the more am I confirmed in my prudent resolution of giving none but negative answers and not pretending to the least degree of any positive knowledge or conception of matter, its *where*, its *how*, its *entity*, or anything belonging to it.

P: When, therefore, you speak of the existence of matter, you do not have any notion in your mind.

H: None at all.

P: Pray tell me if the case does not stand thus: At first, from a belief in material substance, you would have it that the immediate objects existed without the mind; then, that they are archetypes; then causes; next instruments; then occasions; lastly, *something in general*, which being interpreted proves *nothing*. So matter comes to nothing. What do you think, Hylas? Is not this a fair summary of your whole proceeding?

H: Be that as it will, yet I still insist upon it that our not being able to conceive a thing is no argument against its existence.

P: That from a cause, effect, operation, sign, or other circumstance, there may reasonably be inferred the existence of a thing not immediately perceived, and that it would be absurd for any man to argue against the existence of that thing from his having no direct and positive notion of it, I freely admit. But where there is nothing of all this; where neither reason nor revelation induces us to believe the existence of a thing; where we have not even a relative notion of it; where an abstraction is made from perceiving and being perceived, from spirit and idea; lastly, where there is not so much as the most inadequate or faint idea pretended to, I will not, indeed, then conclude against the reality of any notion or existence of anything, but my inference shall be that you mean nothing at all, that you imply words to no manner of purpose, without any design or signification whatsoever. And I leave it to you to consider how mere jargon should be treated.

H: To deal frankly with you, Philonous, your arguments seem in themselves unanswerable, but they do not have so great an effect on me as to produce that entire conviction, that hearty acquiescence which attends demonstration. I find myself still relapsing into an obscure surmise of I do not know what—*matter*.

P: But are you not sensible, Hylas, that two things must concur to take away all scruple and work a plenary assent in the mind? Let a visible object be set in never so clear a light, yet, if there is any imperfection in the sight, or if the eye is not directed towards it, it will not be distinctly seen. And though a demonstration be never so well grounded and fairly proposed, yet, if there is in addition a stain of prejudice or a wrong bias on the understanding, can it be expected on a sudden to perceive clearly and adhere firmly to the truth? No, there is need of time and pains; the attention must be awakened and detained by a frequent repetition of the same thing placed often in the same, often in different lights. I have said it already, and find I must still repeat and inculcate, that it is an unaccountable license you take in pretending to maintain you do not know what, you do not know for what reason, you do not know to what purpose. Can this be paralleled in any art or science, any sect or profession of men? Or is there anything so barefacedly groundless and unreasonable to be met with even in the lowest of common conversation? But perhaps you will still say, matter may exist, though at the same time you neither know what is meant by *matter*, nor by its *existence*. This indeed is surprising, and the more so because it is altogether voluntary, you not being led to it by any one reason; for I challenge you to show me that thing in nature which needs matter to explain or account for it.

H: The reality of things cannot be maintained without supposing the existence of matter. And is not this, you think, a good reason why I should be earnest in its defense?

P: The reality of things! What things, sensible or intelligible?

H: Sensible things.

P: My glove, for example?

H: That or any other thing perceived by the senses.

P: But to fix on some particular thing, is it not a sufficient evidence to me of the existence of this *glove* that I see it, and feel it, and wear it? Or if this will not do, how is it possible I should be assured of the reality of this thing, which I actually see in this place, by supposing that some unknown thing, which I never did or can see, exists after an unknown manner, in an unknown place, or in no place at all? How can the supposed reality of that which is intangible be a proof that anything tangible really exists? Or of that which is invisible, that any visible thing, or in general of anything which is imperceptible, that a perceptible exists? Do but explain this and I shall think nothing too hard for you.

H: Upon the whole, I am content to admit the existence of matter is highly improbable; but the direct and absolute impossibility of it does not appear to me.

P: But granting matter to be possible, yet, upon that account merely, it can have no more claim to existence than a golden mountain or a centaur.

H: I acknowledge it, but still you do not deny it is possible; and that which is possible, for all you know, may actually exist.

P: I deny it to be possible, and have, if I am not mistaken, evidently proved from your own concessions that it is not. In the common meaning of the word *matter*, is there any more implied than an extended, solid, figured, moveable substance, existing without the mind? And have not you acknowledged over and over that you have seen evident reason for denying the possibility of such a substance?

H: True, but that is only one sense of the term *matter*.

P: But is it not the only proper genuine received sense? And if matter in such a sense is proved impossible, may it not be thought with good grounds absolutely impossible? How else could anything be proved impossible? Or indeed how could there be any proof at all one way or the other to a man who takes the liberty to unsettle and change the common signification of words?

H: I thought philosophers might be allowed to speak more accurately than the vulgar and were not always confined to the common meaning of a term.

P: But this now mentioned is the common received sense among philosophers themselves. But not to insist on that, have you not been allowed to take matter in what sense you pleased? And have you not used this privilege in the utmost extent, sometimes entirely changing, at others leaving out or putting into the definition of it whatever for the present best served your design, contrary to all the known rules of reason and logic? And has not this shifting, unfair method of yours spun out our dispute to an unnecessary length, matter having been particularly examined and by your own confession refuted in each of those senses? And can any more be required to prove the absolute impossibility of a thing than the proving it impossible in every particular sense that either you or anyone else understands it in?

H: But I am not so thoroughly satisfied that you have proved the impossibility of matter in the last most obscure, abstracted, and indefinite sense.

P: When is a thing shown to be impossible?

H: When a repugnance is demonstrated between the ideas comprehended in its definition.

P: But where there are no ideas, there no repugnance can be demonstrated between ideas.

H: I agree with you.

P: Now, in that which you call the obscure, indefinite sense of the word matter, it is plain, by your own confession, there was included no idea at all, no sense except an unknown sense, which is the same thing as none. You are not, therefore, to expect I should prove a repugnance between ideas where there are no ideas, or the impossibility of matter taken in an *unknown* sense—that is, no sense at all. My business was only to show you meant *nothing*, and this you were brought to admit. So that in all your various senses, you have been shown either to mean nothing at all or, if anything, an absurdity. And if this is not sufficient to prove the impossibility of a thing, I desire you will let me know what is.

H: I acknowledge you have proved that matter is impossible; nor do I see what more can be said in defense of it. But, at the same time that I give up this, I suspect all my other notions. For surely none could be more seemingly evident than this once was, and yet it now seems as false and absurd as ever it did true before. But I think we have discussed the point sufficiently for the present. The remaining part of the day I would willingly spend in running over in my thoughts the several heads of this morning's conversation, and tomorrow shall be glad to meet you here again about the same time.

P: I will not fail to attend you.

THE THIRD DIALOGUE

Philonous: Tell me, Hylas, what are the fruits of yesterday's meditation? Has it confirmed you in the same mind you were in at parting? Or have you since seen cause to change your opinion?

Hylas: Truly my opinion is that all our opinions are alike vain and uncertain. What we approve today, we condemn tomorrow. We keep a stir about knowledge and spend our lives in the pursuit of it, when, alas, we know nothing all the while; nor do I think it possible for us ever to know anything in this life. Our faculties are too narrow and too few. Nature certainly never intended us for speculation.

P: What! You say we can know nothing, Hylas?

H: There is not that single thing in the world of which we can know the real nature, or what it is in itself.

P: Will you tell me I do not really know what fire or water is?

H: You may indeed know that fire appears hot and water fluid, but this is no more than knowing what sensations are produced in your own mind, upon the application of fire and water to your organs of sense. Their internal constitution, their true and real nature, you are utterly in the dark as to *that*.

P: Do I not know this to be a real stone that I stand on and that which I see before my eyes to be a real tree?

H: *Know*? No, it is impossible you or any man alive should know it. All you know is that you have such a certain idea or appearance in your own mind. But what is this to the real tree or stone? I tell you that color, figure, and hardness, which you perceive, are not the real natures of those things or in the least like them. The same may be said of all other real things or corporeal substances which compose the world. They have, none of them, anything in themselves like those sensible qualities perceived by us. We should not, therefore, pretend to affirm or know anything of them as they are in their own nature.

P: But surely, Hylas, I can distinguish gold, for example, from iron, and how could this be, if I knew not what either truly was?

H: Believe me, Philonous, you can only distinguish between your own ideas. That yellowness, that weight, and other sensible qualities, do you think they are really in the gold? They are only relative to the senses and have no absolute existence in nature. And in pretending to distinguish the species of real things by the appearances in your mind, you may perhaps act as wisely as he who should conclude two men were of a different species because their clothes were not of the same color.

P: It seems, then, we are altogether put off with the appearances of things, and those false ones too. The very meat I eat and the cloth I wear have nothing in them like what I see and feel.

H: Even so.

P: But is it not strange the whole world should be thus imposed on and so foolish as to believe their senses? And yet I do not know how it is, but men eat, and drink, and sleep, and perform all the offices of life as comfortably and conveniently as if they really knew the things they are conversant about.

H: They do so, but you know ordinary practice does not require a nicety of speculative knowledge. Hence the vulgar retain their mistakes, and for all that make a shift to bustle through the affairs of life. But philosophers know better things.

P: You mean, they know that they *know nothing*.

H: That is the very top and perfection of human knowledge.

P: But are you all this while in earnest, Hylas; and are you seriously persuaded that you know nothing real in the world? Suppose you are going to write, would you not call for pen, ink, and paper, like another man; and do you not know what it is you call for?

H: How often must I tell you that I do not know the real nature of any one thing in the universe? I may, indeed, upon occasion, make use of pen, ink, and paper. But what any one of them is in its own true nature, I declare positively I do not know. And the same is true with regard to every other corporeal thing. And, what is more, we are not only ignorant of the true and real nature of things, but even of their existence. It cannot be denied that we perceive such certain appearances or ideas; but it cannot be concluded from this that bodies really exist. No, now I think on it, I must, agreeably to my former concessions, further declare that it is impossible any real corporeal thing should exist in nature.

P: You amaze me. Was anything ever more wild and extravagant than the notions you now maintain, and is it not evident you are led into all these extravagances by the belief of *material substance*? This makes you dream of those unknown natures in everything. It is this which occasions your distinguishing between the reality and sensible appearances of things. It is to this you are indebted for being ignorant of what everybody else knows perfectly well. Nor is this all: you are not only ignorant of the true nature of everything, but you do not know whether anything really exists or whether there are any true natures at all. For as much as you attribute to your material beings an absolute or external existence, in which you suppose their reality consists, and as you are forced, in the end, to acknowledge such an existence means either a direct repugnance or nothing at all, it follows that you are obliged to pull down your own hypothesis of material substance and positively to deny the real existence of any part of the universe. And so you are plunged into the deepest and most deplorable *skepticism* that ever man was. Tell me, Hylas, is it not as I say?

H: I agree with you. *Material substance* was no more than an hypothesis, and a false and groundless one too. I will no longer spend my breath in defense of it. But whatever hypothesis you advance, or whatever scheme of things you introduce in its stead, I do not doubt it will appear every whit as false; let me but be allowed to question you upon it. That is, allow me to serve you in your own kind and I warrant it shall conduct you through as many perplexities and contradictions to the very same state of skepticism that I myself am in at present.

P: I assure you, Hylas, I do not pretend to frame any hypothesis at all. I am of a vulgar cast, simple enough to believe my senses and leave things as I find them. To be plain, it is my opinion that the real things are those very things I see and feel and perceive by my senses. These I know, and, finding they answer all the necessities and purposes of life, have no reason to be solicitous about any other unknown beings. A piece of sensible bread, for instance, would stay my stomach better than ten thousand times as much of that insensible, unintelligible, real bread you speak of. It is likewise my opinion that colors and other sensible qualities are in the objects. I cannot for my life help thinking that snow is white and fire hot. You indeed, who by *snow* and *fire* mean certain external, unperceived, unperceiving substances, are in the right to deny whiteness or heat to be affections inherent in them. But I, who understand by those words the things I see and feel, am obliged to think like other folks. And as I am no skeptic with regard to the nature of things, so neither am I as to their existence. That a thing should be really perceived by my senses and at the same time not really exist is to me a plain contradiction, since I cannot prescind or abstract, even in thought, the existence of a sensible thing from its being perceived. Wood, stones, fire, water, flesh, iron, and the like things, which I name and discourse of, are things that I know. And I should not have known them but that I perceived them by my senses; and things perceived by the senses are immediately perceived; and things immediately perceived are ideas; and ideas cannot exist without the mind; their existence, therefore, consists in being perceived;

when, therefore, they are actually perceived, there can be no doubt of their existence. Away then with all that skepticism, all those ridiculous philosophical doubts. What a jest is it for a philosopher to question the existence of sensible things until he has it proved to him from the veracity of God or to pretend our knowledge in this point falls short of intuition or demonstration! I might as well doubt of my own being as of the being of those things I actually see and feel.

H: Not so fast, Philonous; you say you cannot conceive how sensible things should exist without the mind. Do you not?

P: I do.

H: Supposing you were annihilated, cannot you conceive it possible that things perceivable by sense may still exist?

P: I can; but then it must be in another mind. When I deny sensible things an existence out of the mind, I do not mean my mind in particular, but all minds. Now it is plain they have an existence exterior to my mind, since I find them by experience to be independent of it. There is, therefore, some other mind in which they exist during the intervals between the times of my perceiving them, as likewise they did before my birth and would do after my supposed annihilation. And as the same is true with regard to all other finite created spirits, it necessarily follows there is an *omnipresent, eternal Mind* which knows and comprehends all things, and exhibits them to our view in such a manner and according to such rules as he himself has ordained and are by us termed the *laws of nature*.

H: Answer me, Philonous. Are all our ideas perfectly inert beings? Or do they have any agency included in them?

P: They are altogether passive and inert.

H: And is not God an agent, a being purely active?

P: I acknowledge it.

H: No idea, therefore, can be like or represent the nature of God.

P: It cannot.

H: Since, therefore, you have no idea of the mind of God, how can you conceive it possible that things should exist in his mind? Or, if you can conceive the mind of God without having an idea of it, why may I not be allowed to conceive the existence of matter, notwithstanding that I have no idea of it?

P: As to your first question, I admit I have properly no idea, either of God or any other spirit; for these, being active, cannot be represented by things perfectly inert as our ideas are. I do nevertheless know that I, who am a spirit or thinking substance, exist as certainly as I know my ideas exist. Further, I know what I mean by the terms *I* and *myself*; and I know this immediately, or intuitively, though I do not perceive it as I perceive a triangle, a color, or a sound. The mind, spirit, or soul, is that indivisible, unextended thing, which thinks, acts, and perceives. I say *indivisible*, because unextended, and *unextended*, because extended, figured, moveable things are ideas; and that which perceives ideas, which thinks and wills, is plainly itself no idea, nor like an idea. Ideas are things inactive and perceived, and spirits a sort of beings altogether different from them. I do not therefore say my soul is an idea or like an idea. However, taking the word *idea* in a large sense, my soul may be said to furnish me with an idea, that is, an image or likeness of God, though indeed extremely inadequate. For all the notion I have of God is obtained by reflecting on my own soul, heightening its powers and removing its imperfections. I have, therefore, though not an inactive idea, yet in myself some sort of an active thinking image of the Deity. And though I do not perceive him by sense, yet I have a notion of him or know him by reflection and reasoning. My own mind and my own ideas I have an immediate knowledge of, and, by the help of these, do mediately apprehend the possibility of the existence of other spirits and ideas. Further, from my own being and from the dependency I find in myself and my ideas, I do by an act of reason necessarily infer the existence of a God and of all created things in the mind of God. So much for your first question. For the second, I suppose by this time you can answer it yourself. For you neither perceive matter objectively, as you do an inactive being or idea, nor know it, as you do yourself, by a reflective act—neither do you mediately apprehend it by similitude of the one or the other, nor yet collect it by reasoning from that which you know immediately—all of which makes the case of *matter* widely different from that of the *Deity*.

H: You say your own soul supplies you with some sort of an idea or image of God. But at the same time you acknowledge you have, properly speaking, no idea of your own soul. You even affirm that spirits are a sort of beings altogether different from ideas, consequently, that no idea can be like a spirit. We have, therefore, no idea of any spirit. You admit nevertheless that there is spiritual substance, although you have no idea of it, while you deny there can be such a thing as material substance, because you have no notion or idea of it. Is this fair dealing? To act consistently, you must either admit matter or reject spirit. What do you say to this?

P: I say, in the first place, that I do not deny the existence of material substance merely because I have no notion of it, but because the notion of it is inconsistent or, in other words, because it is repugnant that there should be a notion of it. Many things, for all I know, may exist, of which neither I nor any other man has or can have any idea or notion whatsoever. But then those things must be possible; that is, nothing inconsistent must be included in their definition. I say, secondly, that, although we believe things to exist which we do not perceive, yet we may not believe that any particular thing exists without some reason for such belief, but I have no reason for believing the existence of matter. I have no immediate intuition of this; neither can I mediately from my sensations, ideas, notions, actions, or passions infer an unthinking, unperceiving, inactive substance, either by probable deduction or necessary consequence, whereas the being of myself, that is, my own soul, mind, or thinking principle, I evidently know by reflection. You will forgive me if I repeat the same things in answer to the same objections. In the very notion or definition of material substance, there is included a manifest repugnance and inconsistency. But this cannot be said of the notion of spirit. That ideas should exist in what does not perceive, or be produced by what does not act, is repugnant. But it is no repugnance to say that a perceiving thing should be the subject of ideas or an active thing the cause of them. It is granted we have neither an immediate evidence nor a demonstrative knowledge of the existence of other finite spirits, but it will not then follow that such spirits are on a foot with material substances, if to suppose the one is inconsistent and it is not inconsistent to suppose the other; if the one can be inferred by no argument, and there is a probability for the other; if we see signs and effects indicating distinct finite agents like ourselves, and see no sign or symptom whatever that leads to a rational belief of matter. I say, lastly, that I have a notion of spirit, though I do not have, strictly speaking, an idea of it. I do not perceive it as an idea or by means of an idea, but know it by reflection.

H: Notwithstanding all you have said, it seems to me that, according to your own way of thinking, and in consequence of your own principles, it should follow that you are only a system of floating ideas without any substance to support them. Words are not to be used without a meaning. And as there is no more meaning in spiritual substance than in material substance, the one is to be exploded as well as the other.

P: How often must I repeat that I know or am conscious of my own being and that I myself am not my ideas, but something else, a thinking, active principle that perceives, knows, wills, and operates about ideas? I know that I, one and the same self, perceive both colors and sounds; that a color cannot perceive a sound nor a sound a color; that I am therefore one individual principle, distinct from color and sound, and, for the same reason, from all other sensible things and inert ideas. But I am not in like manner conscious of either the existence or the essence of matter. On the contrary, I know that nothing inconsistent can exist and that the existence of matter implies an inconsistency. Further, I know what I mean when I affirm that there is a spiritual substance or support of ideas, that is, that a spirit knows and perceives ideas. But I do not know what is meant when it is said that an unperceiving substance has inherent in it and supports either ideas or the archetypes of ideas. There is, therefore, upon the whole no parity of case between spirit and matter.

H: I admit myself satisfied in this point. But do you in earnest think the real existence of sensible things consists in their being actually perceived? If so, how does it come that all mankind distinguishes between them? Ask the first man you meet, and he shall tell you, *to be perceived* is one thing and *to exist* is another.

P: I am content, Hylas, to appeal to the common sense of the world for the truth of my notion. Ask the gardener why he thinks the cherry tree over there exists in the garden, and he shall tell you because he sees and feels it—in a word, because he perceives it by his senses. Ask him why he thinks an orange tree is not there, and he shall tell you because he does not perceive it. What he perceives by sense, that he terms a real being and says it *is*, or *exists*; but that which is not perceivable, the same, he says, has no being.

H: Yes, Philonous, I grant the existence of a sensible thing consists in being perceivable, but not in being actually perceived.

P: And what is perceivable but an idea? And can an idea exist without being actually perceived? These are points long since agreed between us.

H: But be your opinion never so true, yet surely you will not deny it is shocking and contrary to the common sense of men. Ask the fellow, whether tree over there has an existence out of his mind, what answer, do you think, he would make?

P: The same that I should myself, namely, that it does exist out of his mind. But then to a Christian it cannot surely be shocking to say the real tree existing without his mind is truly known and comprehended by (that is, *exists in*) the infinite mind of God. Probably he may not at first glance be aware of the direct and immediate proof there is of this, inasmuch as the very being of a tree or any other sensible thing implies a mind in which it is. But the point itself he cannot deny. The question between the materialists and me is not whether things have a real existence out of the mind of this or that person, but whether they have an absolute existence, distinct from being perceived by God and exterior to all minds. This, indeed, some heathens and philosophers have affirmed, but whoever entertains notions of the Deity suitable to the Holy Scriptures will be of another opinion.

H: But, according to your notions, what difference is there between real things and chimeras formed by the imagination or the visions of a dream, since they are all equally in the mind?

P: The ideas formed by the imagination are faint and indistinct; they have, besides, an entire dependence on the will. But the ideas perceived by sense, that is, real things, are more vivid and clear, and, being imprinted on the mind by a spirit distinct from us, have not a like dependence on our will. There is, therefore, no danger of confounding these with the foregoing, and there is as little of confounding them with the visions of a dream, which are dim, irregular, and confused. And though they should happen to be never so lively and natural, yet, by their not being connected and of a piece with the preceding and subsequent transactions of our lives, they might easily be distinguished from realities. In short, by whatever method you distinguish *things* from *chimeras* on your own scheme, the same, it is evident, will hold also upon mine. For it must be, I presume, by some perceived difference, and I am not for depriving you of any one thing that you perceive.

H: But still, Philonous, you hold there is nothing in the world but spirits and ideas. And this, you must necessarily acknowledge, sounds very odd.

P: I admit the word *idea*, not being commonly used for *thing*, sounds something out of the way. My reason for using it was because a necessary relation to the mind is understood to be implied by that term and it is now commonly used by philosophers to denote the immediate objects of the understanding. But however odd the proposition may sound in words, yet it includes nothing so very strange or shocking in its sense, which in effect amounts to no more than this, namely, that there are only things perceiving and things perceived; or that every unthinking being is necessarily and from the very nature of its existence perceived by some mind, if not by any finite created mind, yet certainly by the infinite mind of God, in whom "we live, and move, and have our being" (Acts 17:28). Is this as strange as to say the sensible qualities are not in the objects or that we cannot be sure of the existence of things, or know anything of their real natures, though we both see and feel them and perceive them by all our senses?

H: And, in consequence of this, must we not think there are no such things as physical or corporeal causes, but that a spirit is the immediate cause of all the *phenomena* in nature? Can there be anything more extravagant than this?

P: Yes, it is infinitely more extravagant to say a thing which is inert operates on the mind and a thing which is unperceiving is the cause of our perceptions. Besides, that which to you, I do not know for what reason, seems so extravagant is no more than the Holy Scriptures assert in a hundred places. In them God is represented as the sole and immediate author of all those effects which some heathens and philosophers are accustomed to ascribe to nature, matter, fate, or the like unthinking principle. This is so much the constant language of Scripture that it would be needless to confirm it by citations.

H: You are not aware, Philonous, that in making

God the immediate author of all the motions in nature, you make him the author of murder, sacrilege, adultery, and the like heinous sins.

P: In answer to that I observe, first, that the imputation of guilt is the same whether a person commits an action with or without an instrument. In case, therefore, you suppose God to act by the mediation of an instrument or occasion called *matter*, you as truly make him the author of sin as I, who think him the immediate agent in all those operations vulgarly ascribed to nature. I further observe that sin or moral turpitude does not consist in the outward physical action or motion, but in the internal deviation of the will from the laws of reason and religion. This is plain, in that the killing an enemy in a battle, or putting a criminal legally to death, is not thought sinful, though the outward acts are the very same with that in the case of murder. Since, therefore, sin does not consist in the physical action, making God an immediate cause of all such actions is not making him the author of sin. Lastly, I have nowhere said that God is the only agent who produces all the motions in bodies. It is true I have denied there are any other agents besides spirits, but this is very consistent with allowing to thinking, rational beings, in the production of motions, the use of limited powers ultimately indeed derived from God, but immediately under the direction of their own wills, which is sufficient to entitle them to all the guilt of their actions.

H: But denying matter, Philonous, or corporeal substance—there is the point. You can never persuade me that this is not repugnant to the universal sense of mankind. Were our dispute to be determined by most voices, I am confident you would give up the point without gathering the votes.

P: I wish both our opinions were fairly stated and submitted to the judgment of men who had plain common sense without the prejudices of a learned education. Let me be represented as one who trusts his senses, who thinks he knows the things he sees and feels and entertains no doubts of their existence, and you fairly set forth with all your doubts, your paradoxes, and your skepticism about you, and I shall willingly acquiesce in the determination of any indifferent person. That there is no substance in which ideas can exist besides spirit is evident to me. And that the objects immediately perceived are ideas is agreed on all hands. And that sensible qualities are objects immediately perceived no one can deny. It is therefore evident there can be no *substratum* of those qualities but spirit, in which they exist, not by way of mode or property, but as a thing perceived in that which perceives it. I deny, therefore, that there is any unthinking *substratum* of the objects of sense and, in that meaning, that there is any material substance. But if by *material substance* is meant only sensible body, that which is seen and felt (and the unphilosophical part of the world, I dare say, mean no more), then I am more certain of matter's existence than you or any other philosopher pretend to be. If there is anything which makes the generality of mankind averse from the notions I espouse, it is a misapprehension that I deny the reality of sensible things, but as it is you who are guilty of that and not I, it follows that in truth their aversion is against your notions and not mine. I do therefore assert that I am as certain of my own being as that there are bodies or corporeal substances (meaning the things I perceive by my senses), and that, granting this, the bulk of mankind will take no thought about, nor think themselves at all concerned in the fate of those unknown natures and philosophical quiddities, which some men are so fond of.

H: What do you say to this? Since, according to you, men judge of the reality of things by their senses, how can a man be mistaken in thinking the moon a plain lucid surface about a foot in diameter; or a square tower, seen at a distance, round; or an oar, with one end in the water, crooked?

P: He is not mistaken with regard to the ideas he actually perceives, but in the inferences he makes from his present perceptions. Thus, in the case of the oar, what he immediately perceives by sight is certainly crooked, and so far he is in the right. But if he then concludes that upon taking the oar out of the water he shall perceive the same crookedness, or that it would affect his touch as crooked things are accustomed to do, in that he is mistaken. In like manner, if he should conclude from what he perceives in one station, that, in case he advances toward the moon or tower, he should still be affected with the like ideas, he is mistaken. But his mistake does not lie in what he perceives immediately and at present (it being a manifest contradiction to suppose he should err in respect of that), but in the wrong judgment he makes concerning the ideas he apprehends to be connected with those immediately perceived, or concerning the ideas that, from what he perceives at present, he imagines would be perceived in other circumstances. The case is the same with regard to the Copernican system. We do not here perceive any motion of the earth, but it would be erroneous to conclude from this that, in case we were placed at as great a distance from that as we are now from the other planets, we should not then perceive its motion.

H: I understand you and must necessarily admit you say things plausible enough, but give me leave to put you in mind of one thing. Pray, Philonous, were you not formerly as positive that matter existed as you are now that it does not?

P: I was. But here lies the difference. Before, my positiveness was founded without examination, upon prejudice; but now, after inquiry, upon evidence.

H: After all, it seems our dispute is rather about words than things. We agree in the thing, but differ in the name. That we are affected with ideas from without is evident; and it is no less evident that there must be (I will not say archetypes, but) powers outside the mind corresponding to those ideas. And as these powers cannot subsist by themselves, there is some subject of them necessarily to be admitted, which I call *matter* and you call *spirit*. This is all the difference.

P: Pray, Hylas, is that powerful being, or subject of powers, extended?

H: It has not extension; but it has the power to raise in you the idea of extension.

P: It is therefore itself unextended.

H: I grant it.

P: Is it not also active?

H: Without doubt; otherwise, how could we attribute powers to it?

P: Now let me ask you two questions: *First*, whether it is agreeable to the usage either of philosophers or others to give the name *matter* to an unextended active being? And *secondly*, whether it is not ridiculously absurd to misapply names contrary to the common use of language?

H: Well then, let it not be called matter, since you will have it so, but some *third nature* distinct from matter and spirit. For what reason is there why you should call it spirit? Does not the notion of spirit imply that it is thinking as well as active and unextended?

P: My reason is this: Because I have a mind to have some notion or meaning in what I say, but I have no notion of any action distinct from volition, neither can I conceive volition to be anywhere but in a spirit; therefore, when I speak of an active being, I am obliged to mean a spirit. Besides, what can be plainer than that a thing which has no ideas in itself cannot impart them to me; and if it has ideas, surely it must be a spirit. To make you comprehend the point still more clearly, if it is possible, I assert as well as you that since we are affected from without, we must allow powers to be without in a being distinct from ourselves. So far we are agreed. But then we differ as to the kind of this powerful being. I will have it to be spirit, you matter or I do not know what (I may add too, you do not know what) third nature. Thus I prove it to be spirit. From the effects I see produced, I conclude there are actions; and because actions, volitions; and because there are volitions, there must be a will. Again, the things I perceive must have an existence, they or their archetypes, out of my mind, but, being ideas, neither they nor their archetypes can exist otherwise than in an understanding; there is therefore an understanding. But will and understanding constitute in the strictest sense a mind or spirit. The powerful cause, therefore, of my ideas is in strict propriety of speech a *spirit*.

H: And now I warrant you think you have made the point very clear, little suspecting that what you advance leads directly to a contradiction. Is it not an absurdity to imagine any imperfection in God?

P: Without doubt.

H: To suffer pain is an imperfection.

P: It is.

H: Are we not sometimes affected with pain and uneasiness by some other being?

P: We are.

H: And have you not said that being is a spirit, and is not that spirit God?

P: I grant it.

H: But you have asserted that whatever ideas we perceive from without are in the mind which affects us. The ideas, therefore, of pain and uneasiness are in God; or in other words, God suffers pain—that is to say, there is an imperfection in the divine nature, which you acknowledged was absurd. So you are caught in a plain contradiction.

P: That God knows or understands all things and

that he knows among other things what pain is, even every sort of painful sensation, and what it is for his creatures to suffer pain, I make no question. But that God, though he knows and sometimes causes painful sensations in us, can himself suffer pain, I positively deny. We, who are limited and dependent spirits, are liable to impressions of sense, the effects of an external agent, which, being produced against our wills, are sometimes painful and uneasy. But God, whom no external being can affect, who perceives nothing by sense as we do, whose will is absolute and independent, causing all things and liable to be thwarted or resisted by nothing, it is evident such a being as this can suffer nothing, nor be affected with any painful sensation, or indeed any sensation at all. We are chained to a body, that is to say, our perceptions are connected with corporeal motions. By the law of our nature we are affected upon every alteration in the nervous parts of our sensible body—which sensible body rightly considered is nothing but a complexion of such qualities or ideas as have no existence distinct from being perceived by a mind—so that this connection of sensations with corporeal motions means no more than a correspondence in the order of nature between two sets of ideas or things immediately perceivable. But God is a pure spirit, disengaged from all such sympathy or natural ties. No corporeal motions are attended with the sensations of pain or pleasure in his mind. To know everything knowable is certainly a perfection; but to endure, or suffer, or feel anything by sense, is an imperfection. The former, I say, agrees to God, but not the latter. God knows or has ideas, but his ideas are not conveyed to him by sense as ours are. Your not distinguishing where there is so manifest a difference makes you fancy you see an absurdity where there is none.

H: But all this while you have not considered that the quantity of matter has been demonstrated to be proportioned to the gravity of bodies. And what can withstand demonstration?

P: Let me see how you demonstrate that point.

H: I lay it down for a principle that the moments or quantities of motion in bodies are in a direct compounded reason of the velocities and quantities of matter contained in them. Hence, where the velocities are equal, it follows the moments are directly as the quantity of matter in each. But it is found by experience that all bodies (bating the small inequalities arising from the resistance of the air) descend with an equal velocity; the motion therefore of descending bodies, and consequently their gravity, which is the cause or principle of that motion, is proportional to the quantity of matter—which was to be demonstrated.

P: You lay it down as a self-evident principle that the quantity of motion in any body is proportional to the velocity and *matter* taken together; and this is made use of to prove a proposition from which the existence of *matter* is inferred. Pray is not this arguing in a circle?

H: In the premise I only mean that the motion is proportional to the velocity, jointly with the extension and solidity.

P: But allowing this to be true, yet it will not then follow that gravity is proportional to *matter* in your philosophic sense of the word, except you take it for granted that unknown *substratum*, or whatever else you call it, is proportional to those sensible qualities—which to suppose is plainly begging the question. That there is magnitude and solidity, or resistance, perceived by sense, I readily grant, as likewise that gravity may be proportional to those qualities, I will not dispute. But that either these qualities as perceived by us or the powers producing them do exist in a *material substratum*; this is what I deny and you indeed affirm, but notwithstanding your demonstration have not yet proved.

H: I shall insist no longer on that point. Do you think, however, you shall persuade me that natural philosophers have been dreaming all this while? Pray what becomes of all their hypotheses and explications of the *phenomena* which suppose the existence of matter?

P: What do you mean, Hylas, by the *phenomena*?

H: I mean the appearances which I perceive by my senses.

P: And the appearances perceived by sense, are they not ideas?

H: I have told you so a hundred times.

P: Therefore, to explain the *phenomena* is to show how we come to be affected with ideas, in that manner and order in which they are imprinted on our senses. Is it not?

H: It is.

P: Now if you can prove that any philosopher has explained the production of any one idea in our minds by the help of *matter*, I shall forever acquiesce and look on all that has been said against it as nothing, but if you cannot, it is in vain to urge the explication of *phenomena*. That a being endowed with knowledge and will should produce or exhibit ideas is easily understood. But that a being which is utterly destitute of these faculties should be able to produce ideas, or in any sort to affect an intelligence, this I can never understand. This I say, though we had some positive conception of matter, though we knew its qualities and could comprehend its existence, would yet be so far from explaining things that it is itself the most inexplicable thing in the world. And yet for all this, it will not follow that philosophers have been doing nothing; for by observing and reasoning upon the connection of ideas, they discover the laws and methods of nature, which is a part of knowledge both useful and entertaining.

H: After all, can it be supposed God would deceive all mankind? Do you imagine he would have induced the whole world to believe the being of matter if there was no such thing?

P: That every epidemic opinion arising from prejudice, or passion, or thoughtlessness, may be imputed to God, as the author of it, I believe you will not affirm. Whatever opinion we father on him, it must be either because he has discovered it to us by supernatural revelation or because it is so evident to our natural faculties, which were framed and given us by God, that it is impossible we should withhold our assent from it. But where is the revelation or where is the evidence that extorts the belief of matter? No, how does it appear that matter, taken for something distinct from what we perceive by our senses, is thought to exist by all mankind, or indeed by any except a few philosophers who do not know what they would be at? Your question supposes these points are clear; and when you have cleared them, I shall think myself obliged to give you another answer. In the meantime let it suffice that I tell you I do not suppose God has deceived mankind at all.

H: But the novelty, Philonous, the novelty! There lies the danger. New notions should always be discountenanced; they unsettle men's minds and nobody knows where they will end.

P: Why rejecting a notion that has no foundation either in sense or in reason or in divine authority should be thought to unsettle the belief of such opinions as are grounded on all or any of these, I cannot imagine. That innovations in government and religion are dangerous and ought to be discountenanced, I freely admit. But is there the like reason why they should be discouraged in philosophy? Making anything known which was unknown before is an innovation in knowledge, and if all such innovations had been forbidden, men would [not] have made a notable progress in the arts and sciences. But it is none of my business to plead for novelties and paradoxes. That the qualities we perceive are not in the objects; that we must not believe our senses; that we know nothing of the real nature of things and can never be assured even of their existence; that real colors and sounds are nothing but certain unknown figures and motions; that motions are in themselves neither swift nor slow; that there are in bodies absolute extensions, without any particular magnitude or figure; that a thing stupid, thoughtless, and inactive operates on a spirit; that the least particle of a body contains innumerable extended parts. These are the novelties, these are the strange notions which shock the genuine uncorrupted judgment of all mankind, and, being once admitted, embarrass the mind with endless doubts and difficulties. And it is against these and the like innovations I endeavor to vindicate common sense. It is true, in doing this, I may perhaps be obliged to use some *ambages* and ways of speech not common. But if my notions are once thoroughly understood, that which is most singular in them will in effect be found to amount to no more than this: that it is absolutely impossible and a plain contradiction to suppose that any unthinking being should exist without being perceived by a mind. And if this notion is singular, it is a shame it should be so at this time of day and in a Christian country.

H: As for the difficulties other opinions may be liable to, those are out of the question. It is your business to defend your own opinion. Can anything be plainer than that you are for changing all things into ideas? You, I say, who are not ashamed to charge me with *skepticism*. This is so plain there is no denying it.

P: You mistake me. I am not for changing things into ideas, but rather ideas into things, since those immediate objects of perception, which, according to you, are only appearances of things, I take to be the real things themselves.

H: Things! You may pretend what you please, but it is certain you leave us nothing but the empty forms of things, the outside only which strikes the senses.

P: What you call the empty forms and outside of things seems to me the very things themselves. Nor are they empty or incomplete otherwise than upon your supposition that matter is an essential part of all corporeal things. We both, therefore, agree in this: that we perceive only sensible forms, but we differ in this: You will have them to be empty appearances; I, real beings. In short, you do not trust your senses; I do.

H: You say you believe your senses and seem to applaud yourself that in this you agree with the vulgar. According to you, therefore, the true nature of a thing is discovered by the senses. If so, where does that disagreement come from? Why is not the same figure and other sensible qualities perceived all manner of ways? And why should we use a microscope, the better to discover the true nature of a body, if it were discoverable to the naked eye?

P: Strictly speaking, Hylas, we do not see the same object that we feel; neither is the same object perceived by the microscope which was by the naked eye. But in case every variation was thought sufficient to constitute a new kind or individual, the endless number or confusion of names would render language impracticable. Therefore, to avoid this as well as other inconveniences which are obvious upon a little thought, men combine together several ideas, apprehended by various senses, or by the same sense at different times, or in different circumstances, but observed, however, to have some connection in nature, either with respect to coexistence or succession; all which they refer to one name and consider as one thing. Hence it follows that when I examine by my other senses a thing I have seen, it is not in order to understand better the same object which I had perceived by sight, the object of one sense not being perceived by the other senses. And when I look through a microscope, it is not that I may perceive more clearly what I perceived already with my bare eyes, the object perceived by the glass being quite different from the former. But in both cases my aim is only to know what ideas are connected together; and the more a man knows of the connection of ideas, the more he is said to know of the nature of things. What, therefore, if our ideas are variable? What if our senses are not in all circumstances affected with the same appearances? It will not then follow they are not to be trusted, or that they are inconsistent either with themselves or anything else, except with your preconceived notion of (I do not know what) one single, unchanged, unperceivable, real nature, marked by each name, which prejudice seems to have taken its rise from not rightly understanding the common language of men speaking of several distinct ideas as united into one thing by the mind. And, indeed, there is cause to suspect several erroneous conceits of the philosophers are owing to the same original: while they began to build their schemes, not so much on notions as words which were framed by the vulgar merely for convenience and dispatch in the common actions of life, without any regard to speculation.

H: I think I apprehend your meaning.

P: It is your opinion the ideas we perceive by our senses are not real things, but images or copies of them. Our knowledge, therefore, is no further real than as our ideas are the true representations of those originals. But as these supposed originals are in themselves unknown, it is impossible to know how far our ideas resemble them or whether they resemble them at all. We cannot, therefore, be sure we have any real knowledge. Further, as our ideas are perpetually varied, without any change in the supposed real things, it necessarily follows they cannot all be true copies of them, or, if some are and others are not, it is impossible to distinguish the former from the latter. And this plunges us yet deeper in uncertainty. Again, when we consider the point, we cannot conceive how any idea, or anything like an idea, should have an absolute existence out of a mind, nor consequently, according to you, how there should be any real thing in nature. The result of all this is that we are thrown into the most hopeless and abandoned *skepticism*. Now give me leave to ask you, *first*, whether your referring ideas to certain absolutely existing unperceived substances, as their originals, is not the source of all this *skepticism*? *Secondly*, whether you are informed, either by sense or reason, of the existence of those unknown originals? And in case you are not, whether it is not absurd to suppose them? *Thirdly*, whether upon inquiry, you find there is anything distinctly conceived or meant by the *absolute or external existence of unperceiving substances*? *Lastly*, whether, the premises considered, it is not the wisest way to follow nature, trust your senses, and laying aside all anxious thought about unknown natures or substances, admit with the vulgar those for real things which are perceived by the senses?

H: For the present, I have no inclination to the answering part. I would much rather see how you can get over what follows. Pray, are not the objects perceived by the senses of one likewise perceivable to others present? If there were a hundred more here, they would all see the garden, the trees, and flowers as I see them. But they are not in the same manner affected with the ideas I frame in my imagination. Does not this make a difference between the former sort of objects and the latter?

P: I grant it does. Nor have I ever denied a difference between the objects of sense and those of imagination. But what would you infer from this? You cannot say that sensible objects exist unperceived because they are perceived by many.

H: I admit I can make nothing of that objection, but it has led me into another. Is it not your opinion that by our senses we perceive only the ideas existing in our minds?

P: It is.

H: But the same idea which is in my mind cannot be in yours or in any other mind. Does it not, therefore, follow from your principles that no two can see the same thing? And is not this highly absurd?

P: If the term *same* be taken in the vulgar meaning, it is certain (and not at all repugnant to the principles I maintain) that different persons may perceive the same thing, or the same thing or idea exist in different minds. Words are of arbitrary imposition; and since men are accustomed to apply the word *same* where no distinction or variety is perceived, and I do not pretend to alter their perceptions, it follows that, as men have said before, *several saw the same thing*, so they may upon like occasions, still continue to use the same phrase without any deviation either from propriety of language or the truth of things. But if the term *same* is used in the meaning of philosophers who pretend to an abstracted notion of identity, then, according to their sundry definitions of this notion (for it is not yet agreed in what that philosophic identity consists), it may or may not be possible for various persons to perceive the same thing. But whether philosophers shall think fit to call a thing the *same* or not, is, I conceive, of small importance. Let us suppose several men together, all endowed with the same faculties, and consequently affected in like sort by their senses, and who had yet never known the use of language; they would without question agree in their perceptions. Though perhaps, when they came to the use of speech, some regarding the uniformity of what was perceived might call it the *same* thing; others, especially regarding the diversity of persons who perceived, might choose the denomination of different things. But who does not see that all the dispute is about a word—namely, whether what is perceived by different persons may yet have the term *same* applied to it? Or suppose a house whose walls or outward shell remaining unaltered, the chambers are all pulled down, and new ones built in their place, and that you should call this the *same*, and I should say it was not the *same* house—would we not for all this perfectly agree in our thoughts of the house considered in itself? And would not all the difference consist in a sound? If you should say we differ in our notions, for that you superadded to your idea of the house the simple abstracted idea of identity, whereas I did not; I would tell you I do not know what you mean by that *abstracted idea of identity*; and I should desire you to look into your own thoughts and be sure you understood yourself.—Why so silent, Hylas? Are you not yet satisfied that men may dispute about identity and diversity without any real difference in their thoughts and opinions abstracted from names? Take this further reflection with you, that whether matter be allowed to exist or not, the case is exactly the same as to the point in hand. For the materialists themselves acknowledge what we immediately perceive by our senses to be our own ideas. Your difficulty, therefore, that no two see the same thing makes equally against the materialists and me.

H: But they suppose an external archetype to which, referring their several ideas, they may truly be said to perceive the same thing.

P: And (not to mention your having discovered those archetypes) so may you suppose an external archetype on my principles—*external*, I mean, to your own mind, though indeed it must be supposed to exist in that mind which comprehends all things; but then this serves all the ends of identity as well as if it existed out of a mind. And I am sure you yourself will not say it is less intelligible.

H: You have indeed clearly satisfied me, either that there is no difficulty at bottom in this point or if there is, it counts equally against both opinions.

P: But that which counts equally against two contradictory opinions can be a proof against neither.

H: I acknowledge it. But, after all, Philonous, when I consider the substance of what you advance against *skepticism*, it amounts to no more than this: We are sure that we really see, hear, feel—in a word, that we are affected with sensible impressions.

P: And how are we concerned any further? I see this *cherry*, I feel it, I taste it—and I am sure *nothing* cannot be seen or felt or tasted—it is therefore *real*. Take away the sensations of softness, moisture, redness, tartness, and you take away the *cherry*. Since it is not a being distinct from sensations, a *cherry*, I say, is nothing but a congeries of sensible impressions or ideas perceived by various senses, which ideas are united into one thing (or have one name given them) by the mind because they are observed to attend each other. Thus, when the palate is affected with such a particular taste, the sight is affected with a red color, the touch with roundness, softness, etc. Hence, when I see and feel and taste in sundry certain manners, I am sure the *cherry* exists or is real, its reality being in my opinion nothing abstracted from those sensations. But if by the word *cherry* you mean an unknown nature distinct from all those sensible qualities, and by its existence something distinct from its being perceived, then indeed I admit neither you nor I nor anyone else can be sure it exists.

H: But what would you say, Philonous, if I should bring the very same reasons against the existence of sensible things in a mind which you have offered against their existing in a material *substratum*?

P: When I see your reasons, you shall hear what I have to say to them.

H: Is the mind extended or unextended?

P: Unextended, without doubt.

H: Do you say the things you perceive are in your mind?

P: They are.

H: Again, have I not heard you speak of sensible impressions?

P: I believe you may.

H: Explain to me now, O Philonous, how it is possible there should be room for all those trees and houses to exist in your mind. Can extended things be contained in that which is unextended? Or are we to imagine impressions made on a thing void of all solidity? You cannot say objects are in your mind as books in your study or that things are imprinted on it as the figure of a seal upon wax. In what sense, therefore, are we to understand those expressions? Explain this to me, if you can, and I shall then be able to answer all those queries you formerly put to me about my *substratum*.

P: Look you, Hylas, when I speak of objects as existing in the mind or imprinted on the senses, I would not be understood in the gross literal sense, as when bodies are said to exist in a place or a seal to make an impression upon wax. My meaning is only that the mind comprehends or perceives them and that it is affected from without or by some being distinct from itself. This is my explication of your difficulty, and how it can serve to make your tenet of an unperceiving material *substratum* intelligible, I would gladly know.

H: No, if that be all, I confess I do not see what use can be made of it. But are you not guilty of some abuse of language in this?

P: None at all, it is no more than common custom, which you know is the rule of language, has authorized, nothing being more usual than for philosophers to speak of the immediate objects of the understanding as things existing in the mind. Nor is there anything in this, but what is conformable to the general analogy of language, most part of the mental operations being signified by words borrowed from sensible things—as is plain in the terms *comprehend, reflect, discourse*, etc., which being applied to the mind, must not be taken in their gross original sense.

H: You have, I admit, satisfied me in this point. But there still remains one great difficulty, which I do not know how you will get over. And, indeed, it is of such importance that if you could solve all others, without being able to find a solution for this, you must never expect to make me a proselyte to your principles.

P: Let me know this mighty difficulty.

H: The Scripture account of the creation is what appears to me utterly irreconcilable with your notions. Moses tells us of a creation,[5] a creation of what? of

5. [This and subsequent references are to the first chapter of the Book of Genesis.]

ideas? No, certainly, but of things, of real things, solid corporeal substances. Bring your principles to agree with this and I shall perhaps agree with you.

P: Moses mentions the sun, moon, and stars, earth and sea, plants and animals—that all these do really exist and were in the beginning created by God, I make no question. If by *ideas* you mean fictions and fancies of the mind, then these are no ideas. If by *ideas* you mean immediate objects of the understanding, or sensible things which cannot exist unperceived, or out of a mind, then these things are ideas. But whether you do or do not call them *ideas*, it matters little. The difference is only about a name. And whether that name is retained or rejected, the sense, the truth, and reality of things continues the same. In common talk, the objects of our senses are not termed *ideas*, but *things*. Call them so still, provided you do not attribute to them any absolute external existence, and I shall never quarrel with you for a word. The creation, therefore, I allow to have been a creation of things, of *real* things. Neither is this in the least inconsistent with my principles, as is evident from what I have now said, and would have been evident to you without this, if you had not forgotten what had been so often said before. But as for solid corporeal substances, I desire you to show where Moses makes any mention of them, and if they should be mentioned by him or any other inspired writer, it would still be incumbent on you to show those words were not taken in the vulgar meaning, for things falling under our senses, but in the philosophic meaning, for matter, or an unknown quiddity, with an absolute existence. When you have proved these points, then (and not until then) may you bring the authority of Moses into our dispute.

H: It is in vain to dispute about a point so clear. I am content to refer it to your own conscience. Are you not satisfied there is some peculiar repugnance between the Mosaic account of the creation and your notions?

P: If all possible sense which can be put on the first chapter of Genesis may be conceived as consistently with my principles as any other, then it has no peculiar repugnance with them. But there is no sense you may not as well conceive, believing as I do. Since, besides spirits, all you conceive are ideas, and the existence of these I do not deny. Neither do you pretend they exist without the mind.

H: Pray let me see any sense you can understand it in.

P: Why I imagine that if I had been present at the creation, I should have seen things produced into being, that is, become perceptible, in the order described by the sacred historian. I ever before believed the Mosaic account of the creation and now find no alteration in my manner of believing it. When things are said to begin or end their existence, we do not mean this with regard to God, but his creatures. All objects are eternally known by God, or, which is the same thing, have an eternal existence in his mind, but when things, before imperceptible to creatures, are by a decree of God made perceptible to them, then are they said to begin a relative existence with respect to created minds. Upon reading therefore the Mosaic account of the creation, I understand that the several parts of the world became gradually perceivable to finite spirits, endowed with proper faculties, so that, whoever such were present, they were in truth perceived by them. This is the literal, obvious sense suggested to me by the words of the Holy Scripture, in which is included no mention or no thought, either of *substratum*, instrument, occasion, or absolute existence. And upon inquiry, I do not doubt it will be found that most plain, honest men, who believe the creation, never think of those things any more than I. What metaphysical sense you may understand it in, you only can tell.

H: But, Philonous, you do not seem to be aware that you allow created things in the beginning only a relative, and, consequently, hypothetical being—that is to say, upon supposition there were men to perceive them, without which they have no actuality of absolute existence in which creation might terminate. Is it not, therefore, according to you, plainly impossible that the creation of any inanimate creatures should precede that of man? And is not this directly contrary to the Mosaic account?

P: In answer to that, I say, *first*, created beings might begin to exist in the mind of other created intelligences besides men. You will not, therefore, be able to prove any contradiction between Moses and my notions unless you first show there was no other order of finite created spirits in being before man. I say further—in case we conceive the creation as we should at this time a parcel of plants or vegetables of all sorts produced by an invisible power in a desert where nobody was present—that this way of explaining or conceiving it is consistent with my principles, since they deprive you of nothing, either sensible or imaginable; that it exactly suits with the common, natural, undebauched notions of mankind; that it manifests the dependence of all things on God, and consequently has all the good effect or influence which it is possible that important article of our faith should have in making men humble, thankful, and resigned to their Creator. I say, moreover, that in this naked conception of things, divested of words, there will not be found any notion of what you call the *actuality of absolute existence*. You may indeed raise a dust with those terms and so lengthen our dispute to no purpose. But I entreat you calmly to look into your own thoughts and then tell me if they are not a useless and unintelligible jargon.

H: I admit I have no very clear notion annexed to them. But what do you say to this? Do you not make the existence of sensible things consist in their being in a mind? And were not all things eternally in the mind of God? Did they not therefore exist from all eternity, according to you? And how could that which was eternal be created in time? Can anything be clearer or better connected than this?

P: And are not you too of the opinion that God knew all things from eternity?

H: I am.

P: Consequently, they always had a being in the divine intellect.

H: This I acknowledge.

P: By your own confession, therefore, nothing is new, or begins to be, in respect of the mind of God. So we are agreed in that point.

H: What shall we make then of the creation?

P: May we not understand it to have been entirely in respect of finite spirits, so that things with regard to us may properly be said to begin their existence, or be created, when God decreed they should become perceptible to intelligent creatures in that order and manner which he then established and we now call the laws of nature? You may call this a *relative*, or *hypothetical existence* if you please. But so long as it supplies us with the most natural, obvious, and literal sense of the Mosaic history of the creation—so long as it answers all the religious ends of that great article—in a word, so long as you can assign no other sense or meaning in its stead, why should we reject this? Is it to comply with a ridiculous skeptical humor of making everything nonsense and unintelligible? I am sure you cannot say it is for the glory of God. For allowing it to be a thing possible and conceivable that the corporeal world should have an absolute subsistence extrinsic to the mind of God, as well as to the minds of all created spirits, yet how could this set forth either the immensity or omniscience of the Deity or the necessary and immediate dependence of all things on him? No, would it not rather seem to derogate from those attributes?

H: Well, but as to this decree of God's for making things perceptible, what do you say, Philonous, is it not plain God did either execute that decree from all eternity or at some certain time began to will what he had not actually willed before, but only designed to will? If the former, then there could be no creation or beginning of existence in finite things. If the latter, then we must acknowledge something new to befall the Deity, which implies a sort of change; and all change argues imperfection.

P: Pray consider what you are doing. Is it not evident this objection concludes equally against a creation in any sense, no, against every other act of the Deity discoverable by the light of nature? None of which can we conceive otherwise than as performed in time and having a beginning. God is a being of transcendent and unlimited perfections; his nature, therefore, is incomprehensible to finite spirits. It is not, therefore, to be expected that any man, whether *materialist* or *immaterialist*, should have exactly just notions of the Deity, his attributes, and ways of operation. If then you would infer anything against me, your difficulty must not be drawn from the inadequateness of our conceptions of the divine nature, which is unavoidable on any scheme, but from the denial of matter, of which there is not one word directly or indirectly in what you have now objected.

H: I must acknowledge the difficulties you are concerned to clear are such only as arise from the nonexistence of matter and are peculiar to that notion. So far you are in the right. But I cannot by any means bring myself to think there is no such peculiar repugnance between the creation and your opinion, though indeed where to fix it I do not distinctly know.

P: What would you have? Do I not acknowledge a twofold state of things, the one ectypal or natural, the other archetypal and eternal? The former was created in time, the latter existed from everlasting in the mind of God. Is not this agreeable to the common notions of theologians? Or is any more than this necessary in order to conceive the creation? But you suspect some peculiar repugnance, though you do not know where it lies. To take away all possibility of scruple in the case, do but consider this one point. Either you are not able to conceive the creation on any hypothesis whatsoever, and if so, there is no ground for dislike or complaint against my particular opinion on that score, or you are able to conceive it, and if so, why not on my principles, since nothing conceivable is taken away by that means? You have all along been allowed the full scope of sense, imagination, and reason. Whatever, therefore, you could before apprehend, either immediately or mediately by your senses, or by ratiocination from your senses, whatever you could perceive, imagine, or understand remains still with you. If, therefore, the notion you have of the creation by other principles is intelligible, you have it still upon mine; if it is not intelligible, I conceive it to be no notion at all, and so there is no loss of it. And, indeed, it seems to me very plain that the supposition of matter, that is, a thing perfectly unknown and inconceivable, cannot serve to make us conceive anything. And I hope it does not need to be proved to you that if the existence of matter does not make the creation conceivable, the creation's being without it inconceivable can be no objection against its nonexistence.

H: I confess, Philonous, you have almost satisfied me in this point of the creation.

P: I would gladly know why you are not quite satisfied. You tell me indeed of a repugnance between the Mosaic history and immaterialism, but you do not know where it lies. Is this reasonable, Hylas? Can you expect I should solve a difficulty without knowing what it is? But to pass by all that, would not a man think you were assured there is no repugnance between the received notions of materialists and the inspired writings?

H: And so I am.

P: Ought the historical part of Scripture to be understood in a plain, obvious sense, or in a sense which is metaphysical and out of the way?

H: In the plain sense, doubtless.

P: When Moses speaks of herbs, earth, water, etc., as having been created by God, do you not think the sensible things, commonly signified by those words, are suggested to every unphilosophical reader?

H: I cannot help thinking so.

P: And are not all ideas, or things perceived by sense, to be denied a real existence by the doctrine of the materialists?

H: This I have already acknowledged.

P: The creation, therefore, according to them, was not the creation of sensible things, which have only a relative being, but of certain unknown natures, which have an absolute being in which creation might terminate.

H: True.

P: Is it not, therefore, evident the asserters of matter destroy the plain obvious sense of Moses, with which their notions are utterly inconsistent, and instead of it obtrude on us I do not know what, something equally unintelligible to themselves and me.

H: I cannot contradict you.

P: Moses tells us of a creation. A creation of what? Of unknown quiddities, of occasions, or *substratums*? No, certainly; but of things obvious to the senses. You must first reconcile this with your notions if you expect I should be reconciled to them.

H: I see you can assault me with my own weapons.

P: Then as to *absolute existence*, was there ever known a more jejune notion than that? Something it is, so abstracted and unintelligible, that you have frankly owned you could not conceive it, much less explain anything by it. But allowing matter to exist and the notion of absolute existence to be as clear as light, yet was this ever known to make the creation more credible? No, has it not furnished the *atheists* and *infidels* of all ages with the most plausible argument against a creation? That a corporeal substance, which has an absolute existence without the minds of spirits, should be produced out of nothing by the mere will of a spirit has been looked upon as a thing so contrary to all reason, so impossible and absurd that not only the most celebrated among the ancients, but even various modern and Christian philosophers have thought matter coeternal with the Deity. Lay these things together and then judge whether materialism disposes men to believe the creation of things.

H: I admit, Philonous, I think it does not. This of the *creation* is the last objection I can think of, and I must necessarily admit it has been sufficiently answered as well as the rest. Nothing now remains to be overcome but a sort of unaccountable backwardness that I find in myself toward your notions.

P: When a man is swayed to one side of a question, he does not know why; can this, do you think, be anything else but the effect of prejudice, which never fails to attend old and rooted notions? And indeed in this respect I cannot deny the belief of matter to have very much the advantage over the contrary opinion with men of a learned education.

H: I confess it seems to be as you say.

P: As a balance, therefore, to this weight of prejudice, let us throw into the scale the great advantages that arise from the belief of immaterialism, both in regard to religion and human learning. The being of a God and incorruptibility of the soul, those great articles of religion, are they not proved with the clearest and most immediate evidence? When I say the being of a *God*, I do not mean an obscure, general cause of things, of which we have no conception, but *God* in the strict and proper sense of the word. A being whose spirituality, omnipresence, providence, omniscience, infinite power, and goodness are as conspicuous as the existence of sensible things, of which (notwithstanding the fallacious pretenses and affected scruples of *skeptics*) there is no more reason to doubt than of our own being. Then with relation to human sciences: In natural philosophy, what intricacies, what obscurities, what contradictions, has the belief of matter led men into! To say nothing of the numberless disputes about its extent, continuity, homogeneity, gravity, divisibility, etc., do they not pretend to explain all things by bodies operating on bodies, according to the laws of motion? And yet, are they able to comprehend how any one body should move another? No, admitting there was no difficulty in reconciling the notion of an inert being with a cause or in conceiving how an accident might pass from one body to another, yet by all their strained thoughts and extravagant suppositions, have they been able to reach the mechanical production of any one animal or vegetable body? Can they account, by the laws of motion, for sounds, tastes, smells, or colors, or for the regular course of things? Have they accounted, by physical principles, for the aptitude and contrivance even of the most inconsiderable parts of the universe? But laying aside matter and corporeal causes and admitting only the efficiency of an all-perfect mind, are not all the effects of nature easy and intelligible? If the *phenomena* are nothing else but *ideas*, God is a *spirit*, but matter an unintelligent, unperceiving being. If they demonstrate an unlimited power in their cause, God is active and omnipotent, but matter an inert mass. If the order, regularity, and usefulness of them can never be sufficiently admired, God is infinitely wise and provident, but matter destitute of all contrivance and design. These surely are great advantages in *physics*. Not to mention that the apprehension of a distant Deity naturally disposes men to a negligence in their *moral* actions, which they would be more cautious of in case they thought him immediately present and acting on their minds without the interposition of matter or unthinking second causes. Then in *metaphysics*; what difficulties concerning entity in abstract, substantial forms, hylarchic principles, plastic natures, substance and accident, principle of individuation, possibility of matter's thinking, origin of ideas, the manner how two independent substances, so widely different as *spirit* and *matter*, should mutually operate on each other! What difficulties, I say, and endless disquisitions concerning these and innumerable other like points, do we escape by supposing only spirits and ideas? Even *mathematics* itself, if we take away the absolute existence of extended things, becomes much more clear and easy, the most shocking paradoxes and intricate speculations in those sciences depending on the infinite divisibility of finite extension, which depends on that supposition. But what need is there to insist on the particular sciences? Is not that opposition to all science whatsoever, that frenzy of the ancient and modern *skeptics*, built on the same foundation? Or can you produce so much as one argument against the reality of corporeal things, or in behalf of that avowed utter ignorance of their natures which does not suppose their reality to consist in an external absolute existence? Upon this supposition indeed the objections from the change of colors in a pigeon's neck or the appearances of a broken oar in the water must be allowed to have weight. But those and the like objections vanish if we do not maintain the being of absolute external originals, but place the reality of things in ideas, fleeting indeed, and changeable, however, not changed at random, but according to the fixed order of nature. For in this consists that constancy and truth of things which secures all the concerns of life and distinguishes that which is *real* from the irregular visions of the fancy.

H: I agree to all you have now said and must admit that nothing can incline me to embrace your opinion more than the advantages I see it is attended with. I am by nature lazy and this would be a mighty abridgment in knowledge. What doubts, what hypotheses, what labyrinths of amusement, what fields of disputation, what an ocean of false learning may be avoided by that single notion of *immaterialism*?

P: After all, is there anything further remaining to be done? You may remember you promised to embrace that opinion which upon examination should appear most agreeable to common sense and remote from *skepticism*. This, by your own confession, is that which denies matter or the absolute existence of corporeal things. Nor is this all; the same notion has been proved several ways, viewed in different lights, pursued in its consequences, and all objections against it cleared. Can there be a greater evidence of its truth? Or is it possible it should have all the marks of a true opinion and yet be false?

H: I admit myself entirely satisfied for the present in all respects. But what security can I have that I shall still continue the same full assent to your opinion and that no unthought-of objection or difficulty will occur hereafter?

P: Pray, Hylas, do you in other cases, when a point is once evidently proved, withhold your assent on account of objections or difficulties it may be liable to? Are the difficulties that attend the doctrine of incommensurable quantities, of the angle of contact, of the asymptotes to curves, or the like, sufficient to make you hold out against mathematical demonstration? Or will you disbelieve the providence of God because there may be some particular things which you do not know how to reconcile with it? If there are difficulties attending immaterialism, there are at the same time direct and evident proofs for it. But for the existence of matter there is not one proof and far more numerous and insurmountable objections lie against it. But where are those mighty difficulties you insist on? Alas, you do not know where or what they are—something which may possibly occur later. If this is a sufficient pretense for withholding your full assent, you should never yield it to any proposition, however free from exceptions, however clearly and solidly demonstrated.

H: You have satisfied me, Philonous.

P: But to arm you against all future objections, do but consider that what bears equally hard on two contradictory opinions can be a proof against neither. Whenever, therefore, any difficulty occurs, try if you can find a solution for it on the hypothesis of the *materialists*. Be not deceived by words, but sound your own thoughts. And in case you cannot conceive it easier by the help of *materialism*, it is plain it can be no objection against *immaterialism*. Had you proceeded all along by this rule, you would probably have spared yourself abundance of trouble in objecting, since of all your difficulties I challenge you to show one that is explained by matter, no, which is not more unintelligible with than without that supposition, and consequently makes rather *against* than *for* it. You should consider, in each particular, whether the difficulty arises from the *nonexistence of matter*. If it does not, you might as well argue from the infinite divisibility of extension against divine foreknowledge as from such a difficulty against *immaterialism*. And yet, upon recollection, I believe you will find this to have been often if not always the case. You should likewise take heed not to argue on a *petitio principii*. One is apt to say the unknown substances ought to be esteemed real things rather than the ideas in our minds; and who can tell but the unthinking external substance may concur as a cause or instrument in the production of our ideas? But is not this proceeding on a supposition that there are such external substances? And to suppose this, is it not begging the question? But, above all things, you should beware of imposing on yourself by that vulgar sophism, which is called *ignoratio elenchi*. You talked often as if you thought I maintained the nonexistence of sensible things, whereas in truth no one can be more thoroughly assured of their existence than I am, and it is you who doubt—I should have said, positively deny it. Everything that is seen, felt, heard, or any way perceived by the senses is, on the principles I embrace, a real being, but not on yours. Remember, the matter you contend for is an unknown somewhat (if indeed it may be termed *somewhat*), which is quite stripped of all sensible qualities, and can be neither perceived by sense, nor apprehended by the mind. Remember, I say that it is not any object which is hard or soft, hot or cold, blue or white, round or square, etc. For all these things I affirm do exist.

Though, indeed, I deny they have existence distinct from being perceived or that they exist out of all minds whatsoever. Think on these points; let them be attentively considered and still kept in view. Otherwise you will not comprehend the state of the question—without which your objections will always be wide of the mark and, instead of mine, may possibly be directed (as more than once they have been) against your own notions.

H: I must necessarily admit, Philonous, nothing seems to have kept me from agreeing with you more than this same *mistaking the question*. In denying matter, at first glimpse I am tempted to imagine you deny the things we see and feel, but, upon reflection, find there is no ground for it. What do you think, therefore, of retaining the name *matter* and applying it to sensible things? This may be done without any change in your sentiments, and, believe me, it would be a means of reconciling them to some persons who may be more shocked at an innovation in words than in opinion.

P: With all my heart, retain the word *matter* and apply it to the objects of sense, if you please, provided you do not attribute to them any subsistence distinct from their being perceived. I shall never quarrel with you for an expression. *Matter* or *material substance* are terms introduced by philosophers, and, as used by them, imply a sort of independence or a subsistence distinct from being perceived by a mind, but are never used by common people, or if ever, it is to signify the immediate objects of sense. One would think, therefore, so long as the names of all particular things, with the terms *sensible, substance, body, stuff*, and the like, are retained, the word *matter* should be never missed in common talk. And in philosophical discourses it seems the best way to leave it quite out, since there is not perhaps any one thing that has more favored and strengthened the depraved bent of the mind toward atheism than the use of that general confused term.

H: Well, but, Philonous, since I am content to give up the notion of an unthinking substance exterior to the mind, I think you ought not deny me the privilege of using the word *matter* as I please and annexing it to a collection of sensible qualities subsisting only in the mind. I freely admit there is no other substance in a strict sense than *spirit*. But I have been so long accustomed to the term *matter* that I do not know how to part with it. To say there is no *matter* in the world is still shocking to me. Whereas to say there is no *matter*, if by that term is meant an unthinking substance existing without the mind, but if by *matter* is meant some sensible thing whose existence consists in being perceived, then there is *matter*—this distinction gives it quite another turn—and men will come into your notions with small difficulty when they are proposed in that manner. For, after all, the controversy about *matter* in the strict meaning of it lies altogether between you and the philosophers, whose principles, I acknowledge, are not near so natural or so agreeable to the common sense of mankind and Holy Scripture as yours. There is nothing we either desire or shun but as it makes or is apprehended to make some part of our happiness or misery. But what has happiness or misery, joy or grief, pleasure or pain, to do with absolute existence or with unknown entities, abstracted from all relation to us? It is evident, things regard us only as they are pleasing or displeasing, and they can please or displease only insofar as they are perceived. Further, therefore, we are not concerned; and thus far you leave things as you found them. Yet still there is something new in this doctrine. It is plain, I do not now think with the philosophers, nor yet altogether with the vulgar. I would like to know how the case stands in that respect, precisely what you have added to or altered in my former notions.

P: I do not pretend to be a setter-up of *new notions*. My endeavors tend only to unite and place in a clearer light that truth which was before shared between the vulgar and the philosophers—the former being of opinion that *those things they immediately perceive are the real things* and the latter that *the things immediately perceived are ideas which exist only in the mind*—which two notions put together do in effect constitute the substance of what I advance.

H: I have been a long time distrusting my senses; I thought I saw things by a dim light and through false glasses. Now the glasses are removed and a new light breaks in upon my understanding. I am clearly convinced that I see things in their native forms and am no longer in pain about their unknown natures or absolute existence. This is the state I find myself in at present, though, indeed, the course that brought me to it I do not yet thoroughly comprehend. You set out upon the same principles that Academics,

Cartesians, and the like sects usually do; and for a long time it looked as if you were advancing their philosophical *skepticism*; but, in the end, your conclusions are directly opposite to theirs.

P: You see, Hylas, the water of the fountain over there, how it is forced upwards in a round column to a certain height, at which it breaks and falls back into the basin from which it rose, its ascent as well as descent proceeding from the same uniform law or principle of *gravitation*. Just so, the same principles which, at first view, lead to *skepticism*, pursued to a certain point, bring men back to common sense.

David Hume

David Hume was born in 1711 in Edinburgh. At the age of fifteen he had completed his education at Edinburgh University, and he began to study law. Three years later, convinced that he had made a major philosophical discovery, he abandoned his legal studies to devote his entire attention to philosophy. In 1739, Hume published his *Treatise of Human Nature*, which, in his own words, "fell deadborn from the press." Disappointed by his failure to obtain an audience for his ideas, Hume decided that the style of the *Treatise* was at fault, and in 1748 he published an abbreviated version of Book I of the *Treatise*. This later work, *An Enquiry Concerning Human Understanding*, is reprinted here, along with three excerpts from the *Treatise*. The first excerpt presents Hume's famous dismissal of personal identity and his reflections on what he has accomplished. The second contains his important contributions to the free will debate, and the last his seminal discussion of the foundations of ethics.

Hume continued to write on philosophical topics, publishing his *Enquiry Concerning the Principles of Morals* in 1751. He also wrote works on political theory, as well as a history of England; in his lifetime, his fame rested chiefly on these nonphilosophical writings. A sociable and witty man, he had numerous friends and, at his death in 1776, was widely mourned. The *Dialogues Concerning Natural Religion* was published posthumously.

Hume's official aim in the *Enquiry* is to investigate the powers of human reason. Yet from its first page, the work has a very definite thrust. A vigorous opponent of superstition, Hume is interested in disclosing the pretensions of traditional metaphysics, which he regards as providing cover for dogmatism and prejudice.

An important weapon in Hume's attack is his distinction between "relations of ideas" and "matter of fact." In some areas of inquiry, says Hume, we establish our conclusions by reasoning deductively from first principles, but these merely record the meanings we have given to our terms. Arithmetic and geometry are prime examples of sciences in which, according to Hume's theory, we work out the logical consequences of our definitions. However, not all our knowledge is founded on definition and deduction. The laws of nature cannot be deduced from definitions but are established by experiment and observation. Hume points out that we are not able to deduce these laws from statements that record our observations. Rather, our acceptance of them is based on a kind of inference that is more risky than deduction. In a deductive argument the truth of the premises guarantees the truth of the conclusion. But, as Hume notes, our belief that the sun will rise every morning is founded on our past experience; and even though it may be true that the sun has risen every morning of our lives that evidence does not guarantee the truth of the thesis that the sun will always rise.

Hume poses for us the problem of how we can reasonably accept statements about the entire course of nature. What justifies us in generalizing, from our own limited experience, about principles that allegedly hold true throughout the universe? Hume offers a simple and devastating argument in response: we cannot find any a priori guarantee for the orderliness of the universe, and we can appeal to past experience to support the idea that nature is regular only by arguing in a circle, since past experience is a good indicator of the future only if we assume the orderliness of nature.

Hume's own solution to this problem is to claim that no rational justifications can be given for our ordinary nondeductive inferences. We make these inferences through the operation of habit, or, as Hume calls it, custom. A similar operation is at work when we make causal judgments. Hume argues that such judgments have a complex logical structure. Custom determines us to expect a regular succession in which an earlier event, which we call the cause, is followed by events of the type of the effect. Hume then applies this analysis of causation to the issue of human freedom. He argues that once we have a clear understanding of what is involved in causation, and once we know what is meant by human freedom, we will recognize that there is no inconsistency between the thesis that all human actions are caused and the claim that humans sometimes act freely.

The second passage from the *Treatise* adds two crucial points to the argument about free will. Hume distinguishes the "liberty of spontaneity" that is essential to freedom from the "liberty of indifference" that no one has any reason to want. He also observes that the practice of praise and blame itself required an ability to impute an action to an agent, which in turn requires that we understand the action as caused by the agent's character. So, far from being inimical to moral responsibility, causation is crucial in assigning responsibility. The last section of this excerpt maintains that what determines the will is not reason, but passion. This section lays the groundwork for the discussion of the third excerpt, where Hume considers the basis of ethical judgments: as reason is impotent to move the will, so it is impotent to judge actions. Despite the sloppy formulations of moralists, there is no way to reason from facts about what is, to moral judgments about what ought to be. Morality does not rest on the calculations of reason but on the warmth of feeling.

In the excerpt from Book I of the *Treatise*, Hume turns his formidable critical powers on the problem of understanding persons themselves. What justifies us in believing that we preserve our identity as persons through time? When he looks inward, he can find no simple and continuing self. The weakness of previous philosophical arguments for a self leads him to the startling claim that the identity of persons is a fiction.

In the *Dialogues Concerning Natural Religion*, Hume's principal aim is to show that religious debates are futile. Since we cannot reason deductively to conclusions about the nature and existence of God, our reasoning in this area must be nondeductive. That is, we must examine the evidence of the creation to look for clues about the Creator. As Hume notes, however, the evidence is morally ambiguous. Since both good and bad things happen, how is an inference to an all-good Creator to be justified?

• • •

David Fate Norton, ed., *The Cambridge Companion to Hume* (Cambridge: Cambridge University Press, 1993) offers accessible essays on important topics. Don J. Garrett's *Cognition of Commitment* (Oxford: Oxford University Press, 1997) is a clear account of central themes in Hume's philosophy. Annette C. Baier, *The Progress of Sentiments* (Cambridge, Mass.: Harvard University Press, 1991) links Hume's epistemological researches to his positive contributions to ethics. An older, but widely influential, survey of Hume's entire philosophy is Norman Kemp Smith, *The Philosophy of David Hume* (1941; rpt. London: Macmillan, 1964). Helpful anthologies are V. C. Chappell, ed., *Hume: A Collection of Essays* (Garden City, N.J.: Doubleday, 1966) and Margaret Atherton, ed., *The Empiricists: Locke, Berkeley, Hume* (Lanham, Md.: Rowman & Littlefield, 1998). Barry Stroud's *Hume* (London: Routledge, 1978) provides a systematic and illuminating discussion of Hume's epistemology.

Patricia Kitcher
Philip Kitcher

An Enquiry Concerning Human Understanding

SECTION I
Of the Different Species of Philosophy.

Moral philosophy, or the science of human nature, may be treated after two different manners, each of which has its peculiar merit and may contribute to the entertainment, instruction, and reformation of mankind. The one considers man chiefly as born for action and as influenced in his measures by taste and sentiment, pursuing one object and avoiding another according to the value which these objects seem to possess and according to the light in which they present themselves. As virtue, of all objects, is allowed to be the most valuable, this species of philosophers paint her in the most amiable colors, borrowing all help from poetry and eloquence and treating their subject in an easy and obvious manner, and such as is best fitted to please the imagination and engage the affections. They select the most striking observations and instances from common life, place opposite characters in a proper contrast, and, alluring us into the paths of virtue by the views of glory and happiness, direct our steps in these paths by the soundest precepts and most illustrious examples. They make us *feel* the difference between vice and virtue; they excite and regulate our sentiments; and so they can but bend our hearts to the love of probity and true honor, they think, that they have fully attained the end of all their labors.

The other species of philosophers consider man in the light of a reasonable rather than an active being and endeavor to form his understanding more than cultivate his manners. They regard human nature as a subject of speculation and, with a narrow scrutiny, examine it in order to find those principles which regulate our understanding, excite our sentiments, and make us approve or blame any particular object, action, or behavior. They think it a reproach to all literature that philosophy should not yet have fixed, beyond controversy, the foundation of morals, reasoning, and criticism, and should forever talk of truth and falsehood, vice and virtue, beauty and deformity, without being able to determine the source of these distinctions. While they attempt this arduous task, they are deterred by no difficulties; but proceeding from particular instances to general principles, they still push on their inquiries to principles more general and rest not satisfied until they arrive at those original principles by which, in every science, all human curiosity must be bounded. Though their speculations seem abstract and even unintelligible to common readers, they aim at the approbation of the learned and the wise and think themselves sufficiently compensated for the labor of their whole lives, if they can discover some hidden truths which may contribute to the instruction of posterity.

It is certain that the easy and obvious philosophy will always, with the generality of mankind, have the preference above the accurate and abstruse, and by many will be recommended not only as more agreeable, but more useful than the other. It enters more into common life, molds the heart and affections, and, by touching those principles which actuate men, reforms their conduct and brings them nearer to that model of perfection which it describes. On the contrary, the abstruse philosophy, being founded on a turn of mind which cannot enter into business and action, vanishes when the philosopher leaves the shade and comes into open day, nor can its principles easily retain any influence over our conduct and behavior. The feelings of our heart, the agitation of our passions, the vehemence of our affections, dissipate all its conclusions and reduce the profound philosopher to a mere plebeian.

This also must be confessed that the most durable as well as most just fame has been acquired by the easy philosophy and that abstract reasoners seem up to now to have enjoyed only a momentary reputation

Reprinted from Hume's *An Enquiry Concerning Human Understanding,* edited by Eric Steinberg (Indianapolis: Hackett Publishing Company, 1977), by permission of the publisher.

from the caprice or ignorance of their own age, but have not been able to support their renown with more equitable posterity. It is easy for a profound philosopher to commit a mistake in his subtle reasonings; and one mistake is the necessary parent of another, while he pushes on his consequences and is not deterred from embracing any conclusion by its unusual appearance or its contradiction to popular opinion. But a philosopher whose only purpose is to represent the common sense of mankind in more beautiful and more engaging colors, if by accident he falls into error, goes no further, but, renewing his appeal to common sense and the natural sentiments of the mind, returns into the right path and secures himself from any dangerous illusions. The fame of Cicero[1] flourishes at present, but that of Aristotle is utterly decayed. La Bruyère[2] passes the seas and still maintains his reputation. But the glory of Malebranche[3] is confined to his own nation and to his own age. And Addison,[4] perhaps, will be read with pleasure when Locke shall be entirely forgotten.

The mere philosopher is a character which is commonly but little acceptable in the world, as being supposed to contribute nothing either to the advantage or pleasure of society, while he lives remote from communication with mankind and is wrapped up in principles and notions equally remote from their comprehension. On the other hand, the mere ignorant is still more despised, nor is anything deemed a surer sign of an illiberal genius in an age and nation where the sciences flourish than to be entirely destitute of all relish for those noble entertainments. The most perfect character is supposed to lie between those extremes: retaining an equal ability and taste for books, company, and business; preserving in conversation that discernment and delicacy which arise from polite letters, and in business that probity and accuracy which are the natural result of a just philosophy. In order to diffuse and cultivate so accomplished a character, nothing can be more useful than compositions of the easy style and manner which do not draw too much from life, require no deep application or retreat to be comprehended, and send back the student among mankind full of noble sentiments and wise precepts applicable to every exigency of human life. By means of such compositions virtue becomes amiable, science agreeable, company instructive, and retirement entertaining.

Man is a reasonable being and, as such, receives from science his proper food and nourishment. But so narrow are the bounds of human understanding that little satisfaction can be hoped for in this particular, either from the extent or security of his acquisitions. Man is a sociable no less than a reasonable being. But neither can he always enjoy company agreeable and amusing or preserve the proper relish for them. Man is also an active being and, from that disposition, as well as from the various necessities of human life, must submit to business and occupation. But the mind requires some relaxation and cannot always support its bent to care and industry. It seems, then, that nature has pointed out a mixed kind of life as most suitable to human race and secretly admonished them to allow none of these biases to *draw* too much, so as to incapacitate them for other occupations and entertainments. Indulge your passion for science, she says, but let your science be human and such as may have a direct reference to action and society. Abstruse thought and profound researches I prohibit and will severely punish by the pensive melancholy which they introduce, by the endless uncertainty in which they involve you and by the cold reception which your pretended discoveries shall meet with, when communicated. Be a philosopher, but, amid all your philosophy, be still a man.

Were the generality of mankind contented to prefer the easy philosophy to the abstract and profound, without throwing any blame or contempt on the latter, it might not be improper, perhaps, to comply with this general opinion and allow every man to enjoy, without opposition, his own taste and sentiment. But as the matter is often carried further, even to the absolute rejecting of all profound reasonings, or what is commonly called *metaphysics*, we shall now proceed to consider what can reasonably be pleaded in their behalf.

We may begin with observing that one considerable advantage which results from the accurate and ab-

1. [See Locke's *Essay*, n.8.—S.M.C.]

2. [A French author of character sketches and maxims, Jean de La Bruyère (1645–1696) was also a literary critic.]

3. [See Berkeley's *Three Dialogues*, n.3.]

4. [Joseph Addison (1672–1719) was an English poet, essayist, and critic.]

stract philosophy is its subservience to the easy and humane, which, without the former, can never attain a sufficient degree of exactness in its sentiments, precepts, or reasonings. All polite letters are nothing but pictures of human life in various attitudes and situations, and inspire us with different sentiments of praise or blame, admiration or ridicule, according to the qualities of the object which they set before us. An artist must be better qualified to succeed in this undertaking who, besides a delicate taste and a quick apprehension, possesses an accurate knowledge of the internal fabric, the operations of the understanding, the workings of the passions, and the various species of sentiment which discriminate vice and virtue. However painful this inward search or inquiry may appear, it becomes in some measure requisite to those who would describe with success the obvious and outward appearances of life and manners. The anatomist presents to the eye the most hideous and disagreeable objects, but his science is useful to the painter in delineating even a Venus[5] or a Helen.[6] While the latter employs all the richest colors of his art and gives his figures the most graceful and engaging airs, he must still carry his attention to the inward structure of the human body, the position of the muscles, the fabric of the bones, and the use and figure of every part or organ. Accuracy is, in every case, advantageous to beauty, and just reasoning to delicate sentiment. In vain would we exalt the one by depreciating the other.

Besides, we may observe, in every art or profession, even those which most concern life or action, that a spirit of accuracy, however acquired, carries all of them nearer their perfection and renders them more subservient to the interests of society. And though a philosopher may live remote from business, the genius of philosophy, if carefully cultivated by several, must gradually diffuse itself throughout the whole society and bestow a similar correctness on every art and calling. The politician will acquire greater foresight and subtlety in the subdividing and balancing of power, the lawyer more method and finer principles in his reasonings, and the general more regularity in his discipline and more caution in his plans and operations. The stability of modern governments above the ancient and the accuracy of modern philosophy have improved, and probably will still improve, by similar gradations.

Were there no advantage to be reaped from these studies beyond the gratification of an innocent curiosity, yet ought not even this be despised as being one accession to those few safe and harmless pleasures which are bestowed on human race. The sweetest and most inoffensive path of life leads through the avenues of science and learning; and whoever can either remove any obstructions in this way or open up any new prospect ought so far to be esteemed a benefactor to mankind. And though these researches may appear painful and fatiguing, it is with some minds as with some bodies, which, being endowed with vigorous and florid health, require severe exercise, and reap a pleasure from what, to the generality of mankind, may seem burdensome and laborious. Obscurity, indeed, is painful to the mind as well as to the eye, but to bring light from obscurity, by whatever labor, must necessarily be delightful and rejoicing.

But this obscurity in the profound and abstract philosophy is objected to, not only as painful and fatiguing, but as the inevitable source of uncertainty and error. Here indeed lies the most just and most plausible objection against a considerable part of metaphysics that they are not properly a science, but arise either from the fruitless efforts of human vanity, which would penetrate into subjects utterly inaccessible to the understanding, or from the craft of popular superstitions, which, being unable to defend themselves on fair ground, raise these entangling brambles to cover and protect their weakness. Chased from the open country, these robbers fly into the forest and lie in wait to break in upon every unguarded avenue of the mind and overwhelm it with religious fears and prejudices. The stoutest antagonist, if he remits his watch a moment, is oppressed. And many, through cowardice and folly, open the gates to the enemies and willingly receive them with reverence and submission as their legal sovereigns.

But is this a sufficient reason why philosophers should desist from such researches and leave superstition still in possession of her retreat? Is it not proper to draw an opposite conclusion and perceive the necessity of carrying the war into the most secret recesses of the enemy? In vain do we hope that men, from frequent disappointment, will at last abandon such

5. [The Roman goddess of love and beauty.]
6. [In Greek mythology the most beautiful of women.]

airy sciences and discover the proper province of human reason. For, besides the fact that many persons find too sensible an interest in perpetually recalling such topics—besides this, I say, the motive of blind despair can never reasonably have place in the sciences, since, however unsuccessful former attempts may have proved, there is still room to hope that the industry, good fortune, or improved sagacity of succeeding generations may reach discoveries unknown to former ages. Each adventurous genius will still leap at the arduous prize and find himself stimulated, rather than discouraged by the failures of his predecessors, while he hopes that the glory of achieving so hard an adventure is reserved for him alone. The only method of freeing learning at once from these abstruse questions is to inquire seriously into the nature of human understanding and show, from an exact analysis of its powers and capacity, that it is by no means fitted for such remote and abstruse subjects. We must submit to this fatigue in order to live at ease ever after and must cultivate true metaphysics with some care in order to destroy the false and adulterate. Indolence, which to some persons affords a safeguard against this deceitful philosophy, is, with others, overbalanced by curiosity; and despair, which at some moments prevails, may give place afterwards to sanguine hopes and expectations. Accurate and just reasoning is the only catholic remedy fitted for all persons and all dispositions and is alone able to subvert that abstruse philosophy and metaphysical jargon which, being mixed up with popular superstition, renders it in a manner impenetrable to careless reasoners and gives it the air of science and wisdom.

Besides this advantage of rejecting, after deliberate inquiry, the most uncertain and disagreeable part of learning, there are many positive advantages which result from an accurate scrutiny into the powers and faculties of human nature. It is remarkable concerning the operations of the mind that, though most intimately present to us, yet, whenever they become the object of reflection, they seem involved in obscurity, nor can the eye readily find those lines and boundaries which discriminate and distinguish them. The objects are too fine to remain long in the same aspect or situation and must be apprehended in an instant by a superior penetration derived from nature and improved by habit and reflection. It becomes, therefore, no inconsiderable part of science barely to know the different operations of the mind, to separate them from each other, to class them under their proper heads, and to correct all that seeming disorder in which they lie involved when made the object of reflection and inquiry. This task of ordering and distinguishing, which has no merit when performed with regard to external bodies, the objects of our senses, rises in its value when directed towards the operations of the mind in proportion to the difficulty and labor which we meet with in performing it. And if we can go no further than this mental geography or delineation of the distinct parts and powers of the mind, it is at least a satisfaction to go so far; and the more obvious this science may appear (and it is by no means obvious), the more contemptible still must the ignorance of it be esteemed in all pretenders to learning and philosophy.

Nor can there remain any suspicion that this science is uncertain and chimerical, unless we should entertain such a skepticism as is entirely subversive of all speculation and even action. It cannot be doubted that the mind is endowed with several powers and faculties, that these powers are distinct from each other, that what is really distinct to immediate perception may be distinguished by reflection, and consequently that there is a truth and falsehood in all propositions on this subject, and a truth and falsehood which does not lie beyond the compass of human understanding. There are many obvious distinctions of this kind, such as those between the will and understanding, the imagination and passions, which fall within the comprehension of every human creature; and the finer and more philosophical distinctions are no less real and certain, though more difficult to be comprehended. Some instances, especially late ones, of success in these inquiries may give us a more just notion of the certainty and solidity of this branch of learning. And shall we esteem it worthy the labor of a philosopher to give us a true system of the planets and adjust the position and order of those remote bodies, while we affect to overlook those who, with so much success, delineate the parts of the mind in which we are so intimately concerned?

But may we not hope that philosophy, if cultivated with care and encouraged by the attention of the public, may carry its researches still further and discover, at least in some degree, the secret springs and principles by which the human mind is actuated in its operations? Astronomers had long contented themselves with proving, from the phenomena, the true motions, order, and magnitude of the heavenly bodies, until a philosopher at last arose[7] who seems, from the happiest reasoning, to have also determined the laws and forces by which the revolutions of the planets are governed and directed. The like has been performed with regard to other parts of nature. And there is no reason to despair of equal success in our inquiries concerning the mental powers and economy, if prosecuted with equal capacity and caution. It is probable that one operation and principle of the mind depends on another, which again may be resolved into one more general and universal. And how far these researches may possibly be carried, it will be difficult for us, before or even after a careful trial, exactly to determine. This much is certain—that attempts of this kind are made every day even by those who philosophize the most negligently. And nothing can be more requisite than to enter upon the enterprise with thorough care and attention that, if it lies within the compass of human understanding, it may at last be happily achieved; if not, it may, however, be rejected with some confidence and security. This last conclusion, surely, is not desirable nor ought it be embraced too rashly. For how much must we diminish from the beauty and value of this species of philosophy upon such a supposition? Moralists have been accustomed up to now, when they considered the vast multitude and diversity of those actions that excite our approbation or dislike, to search for some common principle on which this variety of sentiments might depend. And though they have sometimes carried the matter too far, by their passion for some one general principle, it must, however, be confessed that they are excusable in expecting to find some general principles into which all the vices and virtues were justly to be resolved. The like has been the endeavor of critics, logicians, and even politicians; nor have their attempts been wholly unsuccessful, though perhaps longer time, greater accuracy, and more ardent application may bring these sciences still nearer their perfection. To throw up at once all pretensions of this kind may justly be deemed more rash, precipitate, and dogmatic than even the boldest and most affirmative philosophy that has ever attempted to impose its crude dictates and principles on mankind.

7. [The reference is to the famed English scientist Sir Isaac Newton (1642–1721).]

What? Though these reasonings concerning human nature seem abstract and of difficult comprehension, this affords no presumption of their falsehood. On the contrary, it seems impossible that what has escaped so many wise and profound philosophers up to now can be very obvious and easy. And whatever pains these researches may cost us, we may think ourselves sufficiently rewarded, not only in point of profit but of pleasure, if, by that means, we can make any addition to our stock of knowledge in subjects of such unspeakable importance.

But as, after all, the abstractedness of these speculations is no recommendation, but rather a disadvantage to them, and as this difficulty may perhaps be surmounted by care and art and the avoiding of all unnecessary detail, we have, in the following inquiry, attempted to throw some light upon subjects from which uncertainty has deterred the wise up to now, and obscurity the ignorant. Happy if we can unite the boundaries of the different species of philosophy by reconciling profound inquiry with clearness and truth with novelty! And still more happy if, reasoning in this easy manner, we can undermine the foundations of an abstruse philosophy which seems to have up to now served only as a shelter to superstition and a cover to absurdity and error!

Section II
Of the Origin of Ideas.

Everyone will readily allow that there is a considerable difference between the perceptions of the mind when a man feels the pain of excessive heat or the pleasure of moderate warmth and when he afterwards recalls to his memory this sensation or anticipates it by his imagination. These faculties may mimic or copy the perceptions of the senses, but they never can entirely reach the force and vivacity of the original sentiment. The utmost we say of them, even when they operate with greatest vigor, is that they represent their object in so lively a manner that we could *almost* say we feel or see it: But, unless the mind is disordered by disease or madness, they never can arrive at such a pitch of vivacity as to render these perceptions altogether indistinguishable. All the colors of poetry, however splendid, can never paint natural objects in such a manner as to make the description be taken for a real landscape. The most lively thought is still inferior to the dullest sensation.

We may observe a like distinction to run through all the other perceptions of the mind. A man in a fit of anger is actuated in a very different manner from one who only thinks of that emotion. If you tell me that any person is in love, I easily understand your meaning and form a just conception of his situation, but never can mistake that conception for the real disorders and agitations of the passion. When we reflect on our past sentiments and affections, our thought is a faithful mirror and copies its objects truly, but the colors which it employs are faint and dull in comparison of those in which our original perceptions were clothed. It requires no nice discernment or metaphysical head to mark the distinction between them.

Here, therefore, we may divide all the perceptions of the mind into two classes or species which are distinguished by their different degrees of force and vivacity. The less forcible and lively are commonly denominated thoughts or ideas. The other species want a name in our language and in most others, I suppose, because it was not requisite for any but philosophical purposes to rank them under a general term or appellation. Let us, therefore, use a little freedom and call them impressions, employing that word in a sense somewhat different from the usual. By the term *impression*, then, I mean all our more lively perceptions, when we hear, or see, or feel, or love, or hate, or desire, or will. And impressions are distinguished from ideas, which are the less lively perceptions of which we are conscious when we reflect on any of those sensations or movements above mentioned.

Nothing, at first view, may seem more unbounded than the thought of man, which not only escapes all human power and authority, but is not even restrained within the limits of nature and reality. To form monsters and join incongruous shapes and appearances costs the imagination no more trouble than to conceive the most natural and familiar objects. And while the body is confined to one planet, along which it creeps with pain and difficulty, the thought can in an instant transport us into the most distant regions of the universe or even beyond the universe into the unbounded chaos where nature is supposed to lie in total confusion. What never was seen or heard of, may yet be conceived, nor is anything beyond the power of thought except what implies an absolute contradiction.

But though our thought seems to possess this unbounded liberty, we shall find upon a nearer examination that it is really confined within very narrow limits and that all this creative power of the mind amounts to no more than the faculty of compounding, transposing, augmenting, or diminishing the materials afforded us by the senses and experience. When we think of a golden mountain, we only join two consistent ideas, *gold* and *mountain*, with which we were formerly acquainted. A virtuous horse we can conceive, because, from our own feeling, we can conceive virtue; and this we may unite to the figure and shape of a horse, which is an animal familiar to us. In short, all the materials of thinking are derived either from our outward or inward sentiment. The mixture and composition of these belongs alone to the mind and will. Or, to express myself in philosophical language, all our ideas or more feeble perceptions are copies of our impressions or more lively ones.

To prove this, the two following arguments will, I hope, be sufficient. *First*, when we analyze our thoughts or ideas, however compounded or sublime, we always find that they resolve themselves into such simple ideas as were copied from a precedent feeling or sentiment. Even those ideas which at first view seem the most wide of this origin are found, upon a nearer scrutiny, to be derived from it. The idea of God, as meaning an infinitely intelligent, wise, and good being, arises from reflecting on the operations of our own mind and augmenting, without limit, those qualities of goodness and wisdom. We may prosecute this inquiry to what length we please; where we shall always find that every idea which we examine is copied from a similar impression. Those who would assert that this position is not universally true, nor without exception, have only one method, and an easy one at that, of refuting it by producing that idea which, in their opinion, is not derived from this source. It will then be incumbent on us, if we would maintain our doctrine, to produce the impression or lively perception which corresponds to it.

Secondly, if it happens, from a defect of the organ,

that a man is not susceptible of any species of sensation, we always find that he is as little susceptible of the correspondent ideas. A blind man can form no notion of colors, a deaf man of sounds. Restore either of them that sense in which he is deficient by opening this new inlet for his sensations, you also open an inlet for the ideas and he finds no difficulty in conceiving these objects. The case is the same if the object proper for exciting any sensation has never been applied to the organ. A Laplander[8] or Negro has no notion of the relish of wine. And though there are few or no instances of a like deficiency in the mind where a person has never felt or is wholly incapable of a sentiment or passion that belongs to his species, yet we find the same observation to take place in a less degree. A man of mild manners can form no idea of inveterate revenge or cruelty, nor can a selfish heart easily conceive the heights of friendship and generosity. It is readily allowed that other beings may possess many senses of which we can have no conception, because the ideas of them have never been introduced to us in the only manner by which an idea can have access to the mind, namely, by the actual feeling and sensation.

There is, however, one contradictory phenomenon which may prove that it is not absolutely impossible for ideas to arise independent of their correspondent impressions. I believe it will readily be allowed that the several distinct ideas of color which enter by the eye or those of sound which are conveyed by the ear are really different from each other, though at the same time resembling. Now if this is true of different colors, it must be no less so of the different shades of the same color; and each shade produces a distinct idea, independent of the rest. For if this should be denied, it is possible, by the continual gradation of shades, to run a color insensibly into what is most remote from it; and if you will not allow any of the means to be different, you cannot without absurdity deny the extremes to be the same. Suppose, therefore, a person to have enjoyed his sight for thirty years and to have become perfectly acquainted with colors of all kinds, except one particular shade of blue, for instance, which it never has been his fortune to meet with. Let all the different shades of that color, except that single one, be placed before him, descending gradually from the deepest to the lightest, it is plain that he will perceive a blank where that shade is wanting, and will be sensible that there is a greater distance in that place between the contiguous colors than in any other. Now I ask whether it is possible for him, from his own imagination, to supply this deficiency and raise up to himself the idea of that particular shade, though it had never been conveyed to him by his senses? I believe there are few but will be of the opinion that he can. And this may serve as a proof that the simple ideas are not always, in every instance, derived from the correspondent impressions, though this instance is so singular that it is scarcely worth our observing and does not merit that for it alone we should alter our general maxim.

Here, therefore, is a proposition which not only seems in itself simple and intelligible, but, if a proper use were made of it, might render every dispute equally intelligible and banish all that jargon, which has so long taken possession of metaphysical reasonings and drawn disgrace upon them. All ideas, especially abstract ones, are naturally faint and obscure. The mind has but a slender hold of them. They are apt to be confounded with other resembling ideas; and when we have often employed any term, though without a distinct meaning, we are apt to imagine that it has a determinate idea annexed to it. On the contrary, all impressions, that is, all sensations either outward or inward, are strong and vivid. The limits between them are more exactly determined; nor is it easy to fall into any error or mistake with regard to them. When we entertain, therefore, any suspicion that a philosophical term is employed without any meaning or idea (as is but too frequent), we need but inquire *from what impression is that supposed idea derived*? And if it is impossible to assign any, this will serve to confirm our suspicion. By bringing ideas into so clear a light, we may reasonably hope to remove all dispute which may arise concerning their nature and reality.[9]

8. [Lapland is an area of Scandinavia above the Arctic Circle.]

9. It is probable that no more was meant by those, who denied innate ideas, than that all ideas were copies of our impressions; though it must be confessed, that the terms, which they employed, were not chosen with such caution, nor so exactly defined, as to prevent all mistakes about their doctrine. For what is meant by *innate*? If innate be

Section III
Of the Association of Ideas.

It is evident that there is a principle of connection between the different thoughts or ideas of the mind and that, in their appearance to the memory or imagination, they introduce each other with a certain degree of method and regularity. In our more serious thinking or discourse this is so observable that any particular thought which breaks in upon the regular tract or chain of ideas is immediately remarked and rejected. And even in our wildest and most wandering reveries, no, in our very dreams, we shall find, if we reflect, that the imagination did not run altogether at adventures, but that there was still a connection upheld among the different ideas which succeeded each other. Were the loosest and freest conversation to be transcribed, there would immediately be observed something which connected it in all its transitions. Or where this is wanting, the person who broke the thread of discourse might still inform you that there had secretly revolved in his mind a succession of thought which had gradually led him from the subject of conversation. Among different languages, even where we cannot suspect the least connection or communication, it is found that the words expressive of ideas the most compounded do yet nearly correspond to each other—certain proof that the simple ideas comprehended in the compound ones were bound together by some universal principle which had an equal influence on all mankind.

Though it is too obvious to escape observation that different ideas are connected together, I do not find that any philosopher has attempted to enumerate or class all the principles of association—a subject, however, that seems worthy of curiosity. To me there appear to be only three principles of connection among ideas, namely, *resemblance, contiguity* in time or place, and *cause* or *effect.*

That these principles serve to connect ideas will not, I believe, be much doubted. A picture naturally leads our thoughts to the original.[10] The mention of one apartment in a building naturally introduces an inquiry or discourse concerning the others;[11] and if we think of a wound, we can scarcely forbear reflecting on the pain which follows it.[12] But that this enumeration is complete, and that there are no other principles of association except these, may be difficult to prove to the satisfaction of the reader or even to a man's own satisfaction. All we can do, in such cases, is to run over several instances and examine carefully the principle which binds the different thoughts to each other, never stopping until we render the principle as general as possible.[13] The more instances we examine and the more care we employ, the more assurance shall we acquire that the enumeration, which we form from the whole, is complete and entire.

---

equivalent to natural, then all the perceptions and ideas of the mind must be allowed to be innate or natural, in whatever sense we take the latter word, whether in opposition to what is uncommon, artificial, or miraculous. If by innate be meant, contemporary to our birth, the dispute seems to be frivolous; nor is it worth while to enquire at what time thinking begins, whether before, at, or after our birth. Again, the word *idea,* seems to be commonly taken in a very loose sense, by *Locke* and others: As standing for any of our perceptions, our sensations and passions, as well as thoughts. Now in this sense, I should desire to know, what can be meant by asserting, that self-love, or resentment of injuries, or the passion between the sexes is not innate?

But admitting these terms, *impressions* and *ideas,* in the sense above explained, and understanding by *innate,* what is original or copied from no precedent perception, then may we assert, that all our impressions are innate, and our ideas not innate.

To be ingenuous, I must own it to be my opinion, that Locke was betrayed into this question by the schoolmen, who, making use of undefined terms, draw out their disputes to a tedious length, without ever touching the point in question. A like ambiguity and circumlocution seem to run through that great philosopher's reasonings on this as well as most other subjects.

10. Resemblance.

11. Contiguity.

12. Cause and Effect.

13. For instance, *Contrast* or *Contrariety* is also a connexion among ideas: But it may, perhaps, be considered as a mixture of *Causation* and *Resemblance.* Where two objects are contrary, the one destroys the other; that is, the cause of its annihilation, and the idea of the annihilation of an object, implies the idea of its former existence.

Section IV
Skeptical Doubts Concerning the Operations of the Understanding.

Part I.

All the objects of human reason or inquiry may naturally be divided into two kinds, namely, *relations of ideas* and *matters of fact*. Of the first kind are the sciences of geometry, algebra, and arithmetic, and, in short, every affirmation which is either intuitively or demonstratively certain. *That the square of the hypotenuse is equal to the squares of the two sides* is a proposition which expresses a relation between these figures. *That three times five is equal to the half of thirty* expresses a relation between these numbers. Propositions of this kind are discoverable by the mere operation of thought, without dependence on what is anywhere existent in the universe. Though there never were a circle or triangle in nature, the truths demonstrated by Euclid would forever retain their certainty and evidence.

Matters of fact, which are the second objects of human reason, are not ascertained in the same manner; nor is our evidence of their truth, however great, of a like nature with the foregoing. The contrary of every matter of fact is still possible, because it can never imply a contradiction and is conceived by the mind with the same facility and distinctness, as if ever so conformable to reality. *That the sun will not rise tomorrow* is no less intelligible a proposition and implies no more contradiction than the affirmation that *it will rise*. We should in vain, therefore, attempt to demonstrate its falsehood. Were it demonstratively false, it would imply a contradiction and could never be distinctly conceived by the mind.

It may, therefore, be a subject worthy of curiosity to inquire what is the nature of that evidence which assures us of any real existence and matter of fact beyond the present testimony of our senses or the records of our memory. This part of philosophy, it is observable, has been little cultivated either by the ancients or moderns, and, therefore, our doubts and errors in the prosecution of so important an inquiry may be the more excusable, while we march through such difficult paths without any guide or direction. They may even prove useful by exciting curiosity and destroying that implicit faith and security which is the bane of all reasoning and free inquiry. The discovery of defects in the common philosophy, if there are any, will not, I presume, be a discouragement, but rather an incitement, as is usual, to attempt something more full and satisfactory than has yet been proposed to the public.

All reasonings concerning matter of fact seem to be founded on the relation of *cause and effect*. By means of that relation alone we can go beyond the evidence of our memory and senses. If you were to ask a man why he believes any matter of fact which is absent—for instance, that his friend is in the country or in France—he would give you a reason, and this reason would be some other fact: as a letter received from him or the knowledge of his former resolutions and promises. A man finding a watch or any other machine on a desert island would conclude that there had once been men on that island. All our reasonings concerning fact are of the same nature. And here it is constantly supposed that there is a connection between the present fact and that which is inferred from it. Were there nothing to bind them together, the inference would be entirely precarious. The hearing of an articulate voice and rational discourse in the dark assures us of the presence of some person. Why? Because these are the effects of the human make and fabric, and closely connected with it. If we anatomize all the other reasonings of this nature, we shall find that they are founded on the relation of cause and effect and that this relation is either near or remote, direct or collateral. Heat and light are collateral effects of fire and the one effect may justly be inferred from the other.

If we would satisfy ourselves, therefore, concerning the nature of that evidence which assures us of matters of fact, we must inquire how we arrive at the knowledge of cause and effect.

I shall venture to affirm, as a general proposition which admits of no exception, that the knowledge of this relation is not, in any instance, attained by reasonings *a priori*, but arises entirely from experience when we find that any particular objects are constantly conjoined with each other. Let an object be presented to a man of ever so strong natural reason and abilities; if that object is entirely new to him, he will not be able, by the most accurate examination of its sensible qualities, to discover any of its causes or effects. Adam, though his rational faculties are supposed entirely perfect at the very first, could not have inferred from the fluidity and transparency of water that it would suffocate him, or from the light and warmth of fire that it would consume him. No object ever discovers, by the qualities which appear to the senses, either the causes which produced it or the effects which will arise from it; nor can our reason, unassisted by experience, ever draw any inference concerning real existence and matter of fact.

This proposition, *that causes and effects are discoverable, not by reason but by experience*, will readily be admitted with regard to such objects as we remember to have once been altogether unknown to us, since we must be conscious of the utter inability which we then lay under of foretelling what would arise from them. Present two smooth pieces of marble to a man who has no tincture of natural philosophy; he will never discover that they will adhere together in such a manner as to require great force to separate them in a direct line, while they make so small a resistance to a lateral pressure. Such events as bear little analogy to the common course of nature are also readily confessed to be known only by experience, nor does any man imagine that the explosion of gunpowder or the attraction of a lodestone could ever be discovered by *a priori* arguments. In like manner, when an effect is supposed to depend upon an intricate machinery or secret structure of parts, we make no difficulty in attributing all our knowledge of it to experience. Who will assert that he can give the ultimate reason why milk or bread is proper nourishment for a man, not for a lion or a tiger?

But the same truth may not appear at first sight to have the same evidence with regard to events which have become familiar to us from our first appearance in the world, which bear a close analogy to the whole course of nature, and which are supposed to depend on the simple qualities of objects without any secret structure of parts. We are apt to imagine that we could discover these effects by the mere operation of our reason without experience. We fancy that were we brought, all of the sudden, into this world, we could at first have inferred that one billiard ball would communicate motion to another upon impulse and that we did not need to have waited for the event in order to pronounce with certainty concerning it. Such is the influence of custom that where it is strongest it not only covers our natural ignorance, but even conceals itself and seems not to take place, merely because it is found in the highest degree.

But to convince us that all the laws of nature and all the operations of bodies without exception are known only by experience, the following reflections may perhaps suffice. Were any object presented to us and were we required to pronounce concerning the effect which will result from it without consulting past observation, after what manner, I beseech you, must the mind proceed in this operation? It must invent or imagine some event which it ascribes to the object as its effect and it is plain that this invention must be entirely arbitrary. The mind can never possibly find the effect in the supposed cause by the most accurate scrutiny and examination. For the effect is totally different from the cause and consequently can never be discovered in it. Motion in the second billiard ball is a quite distinct event from motion in the first, nor is there anything in the one to suggest the smallest hint of the other. A stone or piece of metal raised into the air and left without any support immediately falls. But to consider the matter *a priori*, is there anything we discover in this situation which can beget the idea of a downward rather than an upward or any other motion in the stone or metal?

And as the first imagination or invention of a particular effect in all natural operations is arbitrary where we do not consult experience, so must we also esteem the supposed tie or connection between the cause and effect which binds them together and renders it impossible that any other effect could result from the operation of that cause. When I see, for instance, a billiard ball moving in a straight line towards another, even suppose motion in the second ball should by accident be suggested to me as the result of their contact or impulse, may I not conceive that a hundred different events might as well follow from that cause? May not both these balls remain at absolute rest? May not the first ball return in a straight line or leap off from the second in any line or direction? All these suppositions are consistent and conceivable. Why then should we give the preference to one which is no more consistent or conceivable than the rest? All our reasonings *a priori* will never be able to show us any foundation for this preference.

In a word, then, every effect is a distinct event from

its cause. It could not, therefore, be discovered in the cause and the first invention or conception of it, *a priori*, must be entirely arbitrary. And even after it is suggested, the conjunction of it with the cause must appear equally arbitrary, since there are always many other effects which, to reason, must seem fully as consistent and natural. In vain, therefore, should we pretend to determine any single event or infer any cause or effect without the assistance of observation and experience.

Hence we may discover the reason why no philosopher who is rational and modest has ever pretended to assign the ultimate cause of any natural operation or to show distinctly the action of that power which produces any single effect in the universe. It is confessed that the utmost effort of human reason is to reduce the principles productive of natural phenomena to a greater simplicity and to resolve the many particular effects into a few general causes by means of reasonings from analogy, experience, and observation. But as to the causes of these general causes, we should in vain attempt their discovery, nor shall we ever be able to satisfy ourselves by any particular explication of them. These ultimate springs and principles are totally shut up from human curiosity and inquiry. Elasticity, gravity, cohesion of parts, communication of motion by impulse—these are probably the ultimate causes and principles which we shall ever discover in nature; and we may esteem ourselves sufficiently happy if, by accurate inquiry and reasoning, we can trace up the particular phenomena to, or near to, these general principles. The most perfect philosophy of the natural kind only staves off our ignorance a little longer, as perhaps the most perfect philosophy of the moral or metaphysical kind serves only to discover larger portions of it. Thus the observation of human blindness and weakness is the result of all philosophy and meets us at every turn in spite of our endeavors to elude or avoid it.

Nor is geometry, when taken into the assistance of natural philosophy, ever able to remedy this defect or lead us into the knowledge of ultimate causes by all that accuracy of reasoning for which it is so justly celebrated. Every part of mixed mathematics proceeds upon the supposition that certain laws are established by nature in her operations and abstract reasonings are employed either to assist experience in the discovery of these laws or to determine their influence in particular instances where it depends upon any precise degree of distance and quantity. Thus, it is a law of motion, discovered by experience, that the moment or force of any body in motion is in the compound ratio or proportion of its solid contents and its velocity, and consequently that a small force may remove the greatest obstacle or raise the greatest weight if, by any contrivance or machinery, we can increase the velocity of that force so as to make it an overmatch for its antagonist. Geometry assists us in the application of this law by giving us the just dimensions of all the parts and figures which can enter into any species of machine, but still the discovery of the law itself is owing merely to experience and all the abstract reasonings in the world could never lead us one step towards the knowledge of it. When we reason *a priori* and consider merely any object or cause as it appears to the mind, independent of all observation, it never could suggest to us the notion of any distinct object, such as its effect, much less show us the inseparable and inviolable connection between them. A man must be very sagacious who could discover by reasoning that crystal is the effect of heat, and ice of cold, without being previously acquainted with the operation of these qualities.

Part II.

But we have not yet attained any tolerable satisfaction with regard to the question first proposed. Each solution still gives rise to a new question as difficult as the foregoing and leads us on to further inquiries. When it is asked, *What is the nature of all our reasonings concerning matter of fact?* the proper answer seems to be that they are founded on the relation of cause and effect. When again it is asked, *What is the foundation of all our reasonings and conclusions concerning that relation?* it may be replied in one word, experience. But if we still carry on our sifting humor and ask, *What is the foundation of all conclusions from experience?* this implies a new question which may be of more difficult solution and explication. Philosophers who give themselves airs of superior wisdom and sufficiency have a hard task when they encounter persons of inquisitive dispositions, who push them from every corner to which they retreat, and who are sure at last to bring them to some dangerous dilemma. The best expedient to prevent this confusion is to be modest in our pretensions and even to discover the difficulty ourselves before it is objected to us. By this means we may make a kind of merit of our very ignorance.

I shall content myself in this section with an easy task and shall pretend only to give a negative answer to the question here proposed. I say, then, that even after we have experience of the operations of cause and effect, our conclusions from that experience are not founded on reasoning or any process of the understanding. This answer we must endeavor both to explain and to defend.

It must certainly be allowed that nature has kept us at a great distance from all her secrets and has afforded us only the knowledge of a few superficial qualities of objects, while she conceals from us those powers and principles on which the influence of these objects entirely depends. Our senses inform us of the color, weight, and consistency of bread, but neither sense nor reason can ever inform us of those qualities which fit it for the nourishment and support of a human body. Sight or feeling conveys an idea of the actual motion of bodies, but as to that wonderful force or power which would carry on a moving body forever in a continued change of place and which bodies never lose but by communicating it to others, of this we cannot form the most distant conception. But notwithstanding this ignorance of natural powers[14] and principles, we always presume when we see like sensible qualities that they have like secret powers and expect that effects similar to those which we have experienced will follow from them. If a body of like color and consistency with that bread which we have formerly eaten is presented to us, we make no scruple of repeating the experiment and foresee with certainty like nourishment and support. Now this is a process of the mind or thought of which I would willingly know the foundation. It is allowed on all hands that there is no known connection between the sensible qualities and the secret powers, and consequently that the mind is not led to form such a conclusion concerning their constant and regular conjunction by anything which it knows of their nature. As to past *experience*, it can be allowed to give *direct* and *certain* information of those precise objects only and that precise period of time which fell under its cognizance. But why this experience should be extended to future times and to other objects which, for all we know, may be only similar in appearance; this is the main question on which I would insist. The bread which I formerly ate nourished me—that is, a body of such sensible qualities was, at that time, endowed with such secret powers. But does it follow that other bread must also nourish me at another time and that like sensible qualities must always be attended with like secret powers? The consequence seems in no way necessary. At least, it must be acknowledged that there is here a consequence drawn by the mind that there is a certain step taken, a process of thought, and an inference which wants to be explained. These two propositions are far from being the same: *I have found that such an object has always been attended with such an effect*, and *I foresee that other objects which are similar in appearance will be attended with similar effects*. I shall allow, if you please, that the one proposition may justly be inferred from the other; I know in fact that it always is inferred. But if you insist that the inference is made by a chain of reasoning, I desire you to produce that reasoning. The connection between these propositions is not intuitive. There is required a medium which may enable the mind to draw such an inference, if indeed it is drawn by reasoning and argument. What that medium is, I must confess, passes my comprehension; and it is incumbent on those to produce it who assert that it really exists and is the origin of all our conclusions concerning matter of fact.

This negative argument must certainly, in process of time, become altogether convincing if many penetrating and able philosophers shall turn their inquiries this way and no one is ever able to discover any connecting proposition or intermediate step which supports the understanding in this conclusion. But as the question is yet new, every reader may not trust so far to his own penetration as to conclude that, because an argument escapes his inquiry, therefore it does not really exist. For this reason it may be requisite to venture upon a more difficult task, and, enumerating all the branches of human knowledge, endeavor to show that none of them can afford such an argument.

All reasonings may be divided into two kinds, namely, demonstrative reasoning, or that concerning relations of ideas, and moral reasoning, or that con-

14. "Power" is used loosely, in a popular sense. A more detailed explanation of the word would lend strength to the argument. See Section VII.

cerning matter of fact and existence. That there are no demonstrative arguments in the case seems evident, since it implies no contradiction that the course of nature may change and that an object, seemingly like those which we have experienced, may be attended with different or contrary effects. May I not clearly and distinctly conceive that a body, falling from the clouds and which in all other respects resembles snow, has yet the taste of salt or feeling of fire? Is there any more intelligible proposition than to affirm that all the trees will flourish in December and January and decay in May and June? Now, whatever is intelligible and can be distinctly conceived implies no contradiction and can never be proved false by any demonstrative argument or abstract reasoning *a priori*.

If we are, therefore, engaged by arguments to put trust in past experience and make it the standard of our future judgment, these arguments must be probable only, or such as regard matter of fact and real existence according to the division above mentioned. But that there is no argument of this kind must appear if our explication of that species of reasoning is admitted as solid and satisfactory. We have said that all arguments concerning existence are founded on the relation of cause and effect, that our knowledge of that relation is derived entirely from experience, and that all our experimental conclusions proceed upon the supposition that the future will be conformable to the past. To endeavor, therefore, the proof of this last supposition by probable arguments, or arguments regarding existence, must be evidently going in a circle and taking that which is the very point in question for granted.

In reality, all arguments from experience are founded on the similarity which we discover among natural objects and by which we are induced to expect effects similar to those which we have found to follow from such objects. And though none but a fool or madman will ever pretend to dispute the authority of experience or to reject that great guide of human life, it may surely be allowed a philosopher to have so much curiosity at least as to examine the principle of human nature which gives this mighty authority to experience and makes us draw advantage from that similarity which nature has placed among different objects. From causes which appear *similar*, we expect similar effects. This is the sum of all our experimental conclusions. Now it seems evident that, if this conclusion were formed by reason, it would be as perfect at first, and upon one instance, as after ever so long a course of experience. But the case is far otherwise. Nothing so like as eggs, yet no one, on account of this appearing similarity, expects the same taste and relish in all of them. It is only after a long course of uniform experiments in any kind that we attain a firm reliance and security with regard to a particular event. Now where is that process of reasoning which, from one instance, draws a conclusion so different from that which it infers from a hundred instances that are in no way different from that single one? This question I propose as much for the sake of information as with an intention of raising difficulties. I cannot find, I cannot imagine any such reasoning. But I keep my mind still open to instruction, if anyone will vouchsafe to bestow it on me.

Should it be said that, from a number of uniform experiments, we *infer* a connection between the sensible qualities and the secret powers? This, I must confess, seems the same difficulty couched in different terms. The question still recurs: on what process of argument this *inference* is founded? Where is the medium, the interposing ideas which join propositions so very wide of each other? It is confessed that the color, consistency, and other sensible qualities of bread do not appear of themselves to have any connection with the secret powers of nourishment and support. For otherwise we could infer these secret powers from the first appearance of these sensible qualities without the aid of experience, contrary to the sentiment of all philosophers and contrary to plain matter of fact. Here, then, is our natural state of ignorance with regard to the powers and influence of all objects. How is this remedied by experience? It only shows us a number of uniform effects resulting from certain objects and teaches us that those particular objects, at that particular time, were endowed with such powers and forces. When a new object endowed with similar sensible qualities is produced, we expect similar powers and forces and look for a like effect. From a body of like color and consistency with bread, we expect like nourishment and support. But this surely is a step or progress of the mind which wants to be explained. When a man says, *I have found, in all past instances, such sensible qualities conjoined with such secret powers*: And when he says, *Similar sensible qualities will always be conjoined with similar secret powers*; he is not guilty of a tautology, nor are these propositions in any respect the same. You say that the one proposition is an inference from the other. But you must confess that the inference is not intuitive, neither is it demonstrative. Of what nature is it then? To say it is experimental is begging the question. For all inferences from experience suppose as their foundation that the future will resemble the past and that similar powers will be conjoined with similar sensible qualities. If there is any suspicion that the course of nature may change, and that the past may be no rule for the future, all experience becomes useless and can give rise to no inference or conclusion. It is impossible, therefore, that any arguments from experience can prove this resemblance of the past to the future, since all these arguments are founded on the supposition of that resemblance. Let the course of things be allowed up to now ever so regular, that alone, without some new argument or inference, does not prove that for the future it will continue so. In vain do you pretend to have learned the nature of bodies from your past experience. Their secret nature and, consequently, all their effects and influence may change without any change in their sensible qualities. This happens sometimes and with regard to some objects. Why may it not happen always and with regard to all objects? What logic, what process of argument secures you against this supposition? My practice, you say, refutes my doubts. But you mistake the purport of my question. As an agent, I am quite satisfied in the point; but as a philosopher who has some share of curiosity—I will not say skepticism—I want to learn the foundation of this inference. No reading, no inquiry has yet been able to remove my difficulty or give me satisfaction in a matter of such importance. Can I do better than propose the difficulty to the public, even though, perhaps, I have small hopes of obtaining a solution? We shall at least, by this means, be sensible of our ignorance, if we do not augment our knowledge.

I must confess that a man is guilty of unpardonable arrogance who concludes, because an argument has escaped his own investigation, that therefore it does not really exist. I must also confess that, though all the learned for several ages should have employed themselves in fruitless search upon any subject, it may still, perhaps, be rash to conclude positively that the subject must therefore pass all human comprehension. Even though we examine all the sources of our knowledge and conclude them unfit for such a subject, there may still remain a suspicion that the enumeration is not complete or the examination not accurate. But with regard to the present subject, there are some considerations which seem to remove all this accusation of arrogance or suspicion of mistake.

It is certain that the most ignorant and stupid peasants, no infants, no even brute beasts, improve by experience and learn the qualities of natural objects by observing the effects which result from them. When a child has felt the sensation of pain from touching the flame of a candle, he will be careful not to put his hand near any candle, but will expect a similar effect from a cause which is similar in its sensible qualities and appearance. If you assert, therefore, that the understanding of the child is led into this conclusion by any process of argument or ratiocination, I may justly require you to produce that argument, nor have you any pretense to refuse so equitable a demand. You cannot say that the argument is abstruse and may possibly escape your inquiry, since you confess that it is obvious to the capacity of a mere infant. If you hesitate therefore a moment or if, after reflection, you produce any intricate or profound argument, you, in a manner, give up the question and confess that it is not reasoning which engages us to suppose the past resembling the future and to expect similar effects from causes which are similar to appearance. This is the proposition which I intended to enforce in the present section. If I am right, I pretend not to have made any mighty discovery. And if I am wrong, I must acknowledge myself to be indeed a very backward scholar, since I cannot now discover an argument which, it seems, was perfectly familiar to me long before I was out of my cradle.

Section V
Skeptical Solution of These Doubts.

Part I.

The passion for philosophy, like that for religion, seems liable to this inconvenience that, though it aims at the correction of our manners and extirpation of our vices, it may only serve, by imprudent management, to foster a predominant inclination and push the mind, with more determined resolution, towards that side which already *draws* too much by the bias and propensity of the natural temper. It is certain that, while we aspire to the magnanimous firmness of the philosophic sage and endeavor to confine our pleasures altogether within our own minds, we may, at last, render our philosophy like that of Epictetus and other *Stoics*, only a more refined system of selfishness, and reason ourselves out of all virtue as well as social enjoyment. While we study with attention the vanity of human life and turn all our thoughts towards the empty and transitory nature of riches and honors, we are, perhaps, all the while flattering our natural indolence which, hating the bustle of the world and drudgery of business, seeks a pretense of reason to give itself a full and uncontrolled indulgence. There is, however, one species of philosophy which seems little liable to this inconvenience, and that because it strikes in with no disorderly passion of the human mind, nor can mingle itself with any natural affection or propensity; and that is the Academic or skeptical philosophy. The academics always talk of doubt and suspense of judgment, of danger in hasty determinations, of confining to very narrow bounds the inquiries of the understanding, and of renouncing all speculations which do not lie within the limits of common life and practice. Nothing, therefore, can be more contrary than such a philosophy to the supine indolence of the mind, its rash arrogance, its lofty pretensions, and its superstitious credulity. Every passion is mortified by it except the love of truth; and that passion never is nor can be carried to too high a degree. It is surprising, therefore, that this philosophy, which in almost every instance must be harmless and innocent, should be the subject of so much groundless reproach and blame. But, perhaps, the very circumstance which renders it so innocent is what chiefly exposes it to the public hatred and resentment. By flattering no irregular passion, it gains few partisans. By opposing so many vices and follies, it raises to itself abundance of enemies who stigmatize it as libertine, profane, and irreligious.

Nor need we fear that this philosophy, while it endeavors to limit our inquiries to common life, should ever undermine the reasonings of common life and carry its doubts so far as to destroy all action as well as speculation. Nature will always maintain her rights and prevail in the end over any abstract reasoning whatsoever. Though we should conclude, for instance, as in the foregoing section that, in all reasonings from experience, there is a step taken by the mind which is not supported by any argument or process of the understanding, there is no danger that these reasonings, on which almost all knowledge depends, will ever be affected by such a discovery. If the mind is not engaged by argument to make this step, it must be induced by some other principle of equal weight and authority and that principle will preserve its influence as long as human nature remains the same. What that principle is may well be worth the pains of inquiry.

Suppose a person, though endowed with the strongest faculties of reason and reflection, to be brought on a sudden into this world; he would, indeed, immediately observe a continual succession of objects and one event following another, but he would not be able to discover anything further. He would not at first, by any reasoning, be able to reach the idea of cause and effect, since the particular powers by which all natural operations are performed never appear to the senses; nor is it reasonable to conclude, merely because one event in one instance precedes another, that therefore the one is the cause, the other the effect. Their conjunction may be arbitrary and casual. There may be no reason to infer the existence of one from the appearance of the other. And in a word, such a person without more experience could never employ his conjecture or reasoning concerning any matter of fact or be assured of anything beyond what was immediately present to his memory and senses.

Suppose again that he has acquired more experience and has lived so long in the world as to have observed similar objects or events to be constantly conjoined together—what is the consequence of this experience? He immediately infers the existence of one object from the appearance of the other. Yet he has not, by all his experience, acquired any idea or knowledge of the secret power by which the one object produces the other, nor is it by any process of reasoning he is engaged to draw this inference. But still he finds himself determined to draw it. And though he should be convinced that his understanding has no part in the operation, he would nevertheless continue in the same course of thinking. There is some other principle which determines him to form such a conclusion.

This principle is *custom* or *habit*. For wherever the repetition of any particular act or operation produces a propensity to renew the same act or operation without being impelled by any reasoning or process of the understanding, we always say that this propensity is the effect of *custom*. By employing that word we pretend not to have given the ultimate reason of such a propensity. We only point out a principle of human nature which is universally acknowledged and which is well known by its effects. Perhaps we can push our inquiries no further or pretend to give the cause of this cause, but must rest contented with it as the ultimate principle which we can assign of all our conclusions from experience. It is sufficient satisfaction that we can go so far without repining at the narrowness of our faculties because they will carry us no further. And it is certain we here advance a very intelligible proposition at least, if not a true one, when we assert that after the constant conjunction of two objects, heat and flame, for instance, or weight and solidity, we are determined by custom alone to expect the one from the appearance of the other. This hypothesis seems even the only one which explains the difficulty why we draw, from a thousand instances, an inference which we are not able to draw from one instance that is in no respect different from them. Reason is incapable of any such variation. The conclusions which it draws from considering one circle are the same which it would form upon surveying all the circles in the universe. But no man, having seen only one body move after being impelled by another, could infer that every other body will move after a like impulse. All inferences from experience, therefore, are effects of custom, not of reasoning.[15]

Custom, then, is the great guide of human life. It is that principle alone which renders our experience useful to us and makes us expect, for the future, a similar train of events with those which have appeared in the past. Without the influence of custom we

15. Nothing is more usual than for writers, even on *moral*, *political*, or *physical* subjects, to distinguish between *reason* and *experience*, and to suppose, that these species of argumentation are entirely different from each other. The former are taken for the mere result of our intellectual faculties, which, by considering *a priori* the nature of things, and examining the effects, that must follow from their operation, establish particular principles of science and philosophy. The latter are supposed to be derived entirely from sense and observation, by which we learn what has actually resulted from the operation of particular objects, and are thence able to infer, what will, for the future, result from them. Thus, for instance, the limitations and restraints of civil government, and a legal constitution, may be defended, either from *reason*, which reflecting on the great frailty and corruption of human nature, teaches, that no man can safely be trusted with unlimited authority; or from *experience* and history, which inform us of the enormous abuses, that ambition, in every age and country, has been found to make of so imprudent a confidence.

The same distinction between reason and experience is maintained in all our deliberations concerning the conduct of life; while the experienced statesman, general, physician, or merchant is trusted and followed; and the unpractised novice, with whatever natural talents endowed, neglected and despised. Though it be allowed, that reason may form very plausible conjectures with regard to the consequences of such a particular conduct in such particular circumstances; it is still supposed imperfect, without the assistance of experience, which is alone able to give stability and certainty to the maxims, derived from study and reflection.

But notwithstanding that this distinction be thus universally received, both in the active and speculative scenes of life, I shall not scruple to pronounce, that it is, at bottom, erroneous, at least, superficial.

If we examine those arguments which, in any of the sciences above-mentioned, are supposed to be the mere effects of reasoning and reflection, they will be found to terminate, at last, in some general principle or conclusion, for which we can assign no reason but observation and experience. The only difference between them and those maxims, which are vulgarly esteemed the result of pure experience, is, that the former cannot be established without some process of thought, and some reflection on what we have observed, in order to distinguish its circumstances, and trace its consequences: Whereas in the latter, the experienced event is exactly and fully similar to that which we infer as the result of any particular situation. The history of a Tiberius [Roman emperor (14–37)] or a Nero [Roman emperor (54–69)] makes us dread a tyranny, were our monarchs freed from the restraints of laws and senates: But the observation of any fraud or cruelty in private life is sufficient, with the aid of a little thought, to give us the same apprehension; while it serves as an instance of the general curruption of human nature, and shows us the danger which we must incur by reposing an entire confidence in mankind. In both

should be entirely ignorant of every matter of fact beyond what is immediately present to the memory and senses. We should never know how to adjust means to ends or to employ our natural powers in the production of any effect. There would be an end at once of all action as well as of the chief part of speculation.

But here it may be proper to remark that though our conclusions from experience carry us beyond our memory and senses and assure us of matters of fact, which happened in the most distant places and most remote ages, yet some fact must always be present to the senses or memory from which we may first proceed in drawing these conclusions. A man who should find in a desert country the remains of pompous buildings would conclude that the country had, in ancient times, been cultivated by civilized inhabitants, but did nothing of this nature occur to him, he could never form such an inference. We learn the events of former ages from history, but then we must peruse the volumes in which this instruction is contained and from this carry up our inferences from one testimony to another, until we arrive at the eyewitnesses and spectators of these distant events. In a word, if we proceed not upon some fact present to the memory or senses, our reasonings would be merely hypothetical; and however the particular links might be connected with each other, the whole chain of inferences would have nothing to support it, nor could we ever, by its means, arrive at the knowledge of any real existence. If I ask, why you believe any particular matter of fact which you relate, you must tell me some reason; and this reason will be some other fact connected with it. But as you cannot proceed after this manner *in infinitum*, you must at last terminate in some fact which is present to your memory or senses or must allow that your belief is entirely without foundation.

What then is the conclusion of the whole matter? A simple one, though it must be confessed, pretty remote from the common theories of philosophy. All belief of matter of fact or real existence is derived merely from some object present to the memory or senses and a customary conjunction between that and some other object. Or, in other words, having found in many instances that any two kinds of objects, flame and heat, snow and cold, have always been conjoined together, if flame or snow is presented anew to the senses, the mind is carried by custom to expect heat or cold and to *believe* that such a quality does exist and will discover itself upon a nearer approach. This belief is the necessary result of placing the mind in such circumstances. It is an operation of the soul when we are so situated, as unavoidable as feeling the passion of love, when we receive benefits—or hatred, when we meet with injuries. All these operations are a species of natural instincts which no reasoning or process of the thought and understanding is able either to produce or to prevent.

At this point, it would be very allowable for us to stop our philosophical researches. In most questions we can never make a single step further; and in all questions, we must terminate here at last, after our most restless and curious inquiries. But still our curiosity will be pardonable, perhaps commendable, if it carry us on to still further researches and make us examine more accurately the nature of this *belief* and of the *customary conjunction* from which it is derived. By this means we may meet with some explications and analogies that will give satisfaction, at least to such as love the abstract sciences and can be entertained with speculations which, however accurate,

---

cases, it is experience which is ultimately the foundation or our inference and conclusion.

There is no man so young and unexperienced, as not to have formed, from observation, many general and just maxims concerning human affairs and the conduct of life; but it must be confessed, that when a man comes to put these in practice, he will be extremely liable to error, till time and farther experience both enlarge these maxims, and teach him their proper use and application. In every situation or incident, there are many particular and seemingly minute circumstances, which the man of greatest talents is, at first, apt to overlook, though on them the justness of his conclusions, and consequently the prudence of his conduct, entirely depend. Not to mention, that, to a young beginner, the general observations and maxims occur not always on the proper occasions, nor can be immediately applied with due calmness and distinction. The truth is, an unexperienced reasoner could be no reasoner at all, were he absolutely unexperienced; and when we assign that character to any one, we mean it only in a comparative sense, and suppose him possessed of experience, in a smaller and more imperfect degree.

may still retain a degree of doubt and uncertainty. As to readers of a different taste, the remaining part of this section is not calculated for them and the following inquiries may well be understood, though it is neglected.

Part II.

Nothing is more free than the imagination of man, and though it cannot exceed that original stock of ideas furnished by the internal and external senses, it has unlimited power of mixing, compounding, separating, and dividing these ideas, in all the varieties of fiction and vision. It can feign a train of events with all the appearance of reality, ascribe to them a particular time and place, conceive them as existent, and paint them out to itself with every circumstance that belongs to any historical fact which it believes with the greatest certainty. In what, therefore, consists the difference between such a fiction and belief? It lies not merely in any peculiar idea which is annexed to such a conception as commands our assent and which is wanting to every known fiction. For as the mind has authority over all its ideas, it could voluntarily annex this particular idea to any fiction and consequently be able to believe whatever it pleases; contrary to what we find by daily experience. We can, in our conception, join the head of a man to the body of a horse, but it is not in our power to believe that such an animal has ever really existed.

It follows, therefore, that the difference between *fiction* and *belief* lies in some sentiment or feeling which is annexed to the latter, not to the former, and which depends not on the will, nor can be commanded at pleasure. It must be excited by nature like all other sentiments and must arise from the particular situation in which the mind is placed at any particular juncture. Whenever any object is presented to the memory or senses, it immediately, by the force of custom, carries the imagination to conceive that object which is usually conjoined to it; and this conception is attended with a feeling or sentiment different from the loose reveries of the fancy. In this consists the whole nature of belief. For as there is no matter of fact which we believe so firmly that we cannot conceive the contrary, there would be no difference between the conception assented to and that which is rejected were it not for some sentiment which distinguishes the one from the other. If I see a billiard ball moving towards another on a smooth table, I can easily conceive it to stop upon contact. This conception implies no contradiction, but still it feels very differently from that conception by which I represent to myself the impulse and the communication of motion from one ball to another.

Were we to attempt a *definition* of this sentiment, we should, perhaps, find it a very difficult, if not an impossible task; in the same manner as if we should endeavor to define the feeling of cold, or passion of anger, to a creature who never had any experience of these sentiments. Belief is the true and proper name of this feeling, and no one is ever at a loss to know the meaning of that term, because every man is every moment conscious of the sentiment represented by it. It may not, however, be improper to attempt a *description* of this sentiment, in hopes we may by that means arrive at some analogies which may afford a more perfect explication of it. I say then that belief is nothing but a more vivid, lively, forcible, firm, steady conception of an object than what the imagination alone is ever able to attain. This variety of terms, which may seem so unphilosophical, is intended only to express that act of the mind which renders realities, or what is taken for such, more present to us than fictions, causes them to weigh more in the thought, and gives them a superior influence on the passions and imagination. Provided we agree about the thing, it is needless to dispute about the terms. The imagination has the command over all its ideas and can join and mix and vary them in all the ways possible. It may conceive fictitious objects with all the circumstances of place and time. It may set them in a manner before our eyes, in their true colors, just as they might have existed. But as it is impossible that this faculty of imagination can ever, of itself, reach belief, it is evident that belief consists not in the peculiar nature or order of ideas, but in the *manner* of their conception and in their *feeling* to the mind. I confess that it is impossible perfectly to explain this feeling or manner of conception. We may make use of words which express something near it. But its true and proper name, as we observed before, is *belief*, which is a term that everyone sufficiently understands in common life. And in philosophy we can go no further than assert that *belief* is something felt by the mind which distinguishes the ideas of the judgment from the fictions of the imagination. It gives them more weight and influence, makes them appear of greater importance, enforces them in the mind, and renders them the governing principle of our actions. I hear at present, for instance, a person's voice with whom I am acquainted and the sound comes as from the next room. This impression of my senses immediately conveys my thought to the person, together with all the surrounding objects. I paint them out to myself as existing at present with the same qualities and relations of which I formerly knew them possessed. These ideas take faster hold of my mind than ideas of an enchanted castle. They are very different to the feeling and have a much greater influence of every kind, either to give pleasure or pain, joy or sorrow.

Let us, then, take in the whole compass of this doctrine and allow that the sentiment of belief is nothing but a conception more intense and steady than what attends the mere fictions of the imagination and that this *manner* of conception arises from a customary conjunction of the object with something present to the memory or senses. I believe that it will not be difficult, upon these suppositions, to find other operations of the mind analogous to it and to trace up these phenomena to principles still more general.

We have already observed that nature has established connections among particular ideas and that no sooner one idea occurs to our thoughts than it introduces its correlative and carries our attention towards it by a gentle and insensible movement. These principles of connection or association we have reduced to three, namely, *resemblance*, *contiguity*, and *causation*; these are the only bonds that unite our thoughts together and beget that regular train of reflection or discourse which, in a greater or less degree, takes place among all mankind. Now here arises a question on which the solution of the present difficulty will depend. Does it happen in all these relations that when one of the objects is presented to the senses or memory the mind is not only carried to the conception of the correlative, but reaches a steadier and stronger conception of it than what otherwise it would have been able to attain? This seems to be the case with that belief which arises from the relation of cause and effect. And if the case is the same with the other relations or principles of association, this may be established as a general law which takes place in all the operations of the mind.

We may, therefore, observe, as the first experiment to our present purpose, that upon the appearance of the picture of an absent friend, our idea of him is evidently enlivened by the *resemblance*, and that every passion which that idea occasions, whether of joy or sorrow, acquires new force and vigor. In producing this effect there concur both a relation and a present impression. Where the picture bears him no resemblance, at least was not intended for him, it never so much as conveys our thought to him. And where it is absent, as well as the person, though the mind may pass from the thought of the one to that of the other, it feels its idea to be rather weakened than enlivened by that transition. We take a pleasure in viewing the picture of a friend when it is set before us; but when it is removed, rather choose to consider him directly than by reflection in an image which is equally distant and obscure.

The ceremonies of the Roman Catholic religion may be considered as instances of the same nature. The devotees of that superstition usually plead in excuse for the mummeries with which they are upbraided that they feel the good effect of those external motions, and postures, and actions in enlivening their devotion and quickening their fervor, which otherwise would decay, if directed entirely to distant and immaterial objects. We shadow out the objects of our faith, they say, in sensible types and images, and render them more present to us by the immediate presence of these types than it is possible for us to do merely by an intellectual view and contemplation. Sensible objects have always a greater influence on the fancy than any other, and this influence they readily convey to those ideas to which they are related and which they resemble. I shall only infer from these practices and this reasoning that the effect of resemblance in enlivening the ideas is very common; and as in every case a resemblance and a present impression must concur, we are abundantly supplied with experiments to prove the reality of the foregoing principle.

We may add force to these experiments by others of a different kind, in considering the effects of *contiguity* as well as of *resemblance*. It is certain that distance diminishes the force of every idea and that, upon our approach to any object, though it does not discover itself to our senses, it operates upon the mind with an influence which imitates an immediate impression. The thinking on any object readily transports the mind to what is contiguous; but it is only the actual presence of an object that transports it with a superior vivacity. When I am a few miles from home, whatever relates to it touches me more nearly than when I am two hundred leagues distant, though even at that distance the reflecting on anything in the neighborhood of my friends or family naturally produces an idea of them. But, as in this latter case, both the objects of the mind are ideas, notwithstanding there is an easy transition between them; that transition alone is not able to give a superior vivacity to any of the ideas, for want of some immediate impression.

No one can doubt but causation has the same influence as the other two relations of resemblance and contiguity. Superstitious people are fond of the relics of saints and holy men, for the same reason that they seek after types or images in order to enliven their devotion and give them a more intimate and strong conception of those exemplary lives which they desire to imitate. Now it is evident that one of the best relics which a devotee could procure would be the handiwork of a saint; and if his clothes and furniture are ever to be considered in this light, it is because they were once at his disposal and were moved and affected by him; in this respect they are to be considered as imperfect effects and as connected with him by a shorter chain of consequences than any of those by which we learn the reality of his existence.

Suppose that the son of a friend who had been long dead or absent were presented to us; it is evident that this object would instantly revive its correlative idea and recall to our thoughts all past intimacies and familiarities in more lively colors than they would otherwise have appeared to us. This is another phenomenon which seems to prove the principle above mentioned.

We may observe that in these phenomena the belief of the correlative object is always presupposed, without which the relation could have no effect. The influence of the picture supposes that we *believe* our friend to have once existed. Contiguity to home can never excite our ideas of home unless we *believe* that it really exists. Now I assert that this belief, where it reaches beyond the memory or senses, is of a similar nature and arises from similar causes with the transition of thought and vivacity of conception here explained. When I throw a piece of dry wood into a fire, my mind is immediately carried to conceive that it augments, not extinguishes, the flame. This transition of thought from the cause to the effect does not proceed from reason. It derives its origin altogether from custom and experience. And as it first begins from an object present to the senses, it renders the idea or conception of flame more strong and lively than any loose, floating reverie of the imagination. That idea arises immediately. The thought moves instantly towards it and conveys to it all that force of conception which is derived from the impression present to the senses. When a sword is leveled at my breast, does not the idea of wound and pain strike me more strongly than when a glass of wine is presented to me, even though by accident this idea should occur after the appearance of the latter object? But what is there in this whole matter to cause such a strong conception except only a present object and a customary transition to the idea of another object which we have been accustomed to conjoin with the former? This is the whole operation of the mind in all our conclusions concerning matter of fact and existence; and it is a satisfaction to find some analogies by which it may be explained. The transition from a present object does in all cases give strength and solidity to the related idea.

Here, then, is a kind of preestablished harmony between the course of nature and the succession of our ideas; and though the powers and forces by which the former is governed are wholly unknown to us, yet our thoughts and conceptions have still, we find, gone on in the same train with the other works of nature. Custom is that principle by which this correspondence has been effected, so necessary to the subsistence of our species and the regulation of our conduct in every circumstance and occurrence of human life. Had not the presence of an object instantly excited the idea of those objects commonly conjoined with it, all our knowledge must have been limited to the narrow sphere of our memory and senses and we should never have been able to adjust means to ends or employ our natural powers either to the producing of good or avoiding of evil. Those who delight in the discovery and contemplation of *final causes* have here ample subject to employ their wonder and admiration.

I shall add, for a further confirmation of the foregoing theory, that as this operation of the mind by which we infer like effects from like causes, and *vice versa*, is so essential to the subsistence of all human creatures, it is not probable that it could be trusted to the fallacious deductions of our reason, which is slow in its operations, does not appear, in any degree, during the first years of infancy, and at best is in every age and period of human life extremely liable to error and mistake. It is more conformable to the ordinary wisdom of nature to secure so necessary an act of the mind by some instinct or mechanical tendency which may be infallible in its operations, may discover itself at the first appearance of life and thought, and may be independent of all the labored deductions of the understanding. As nature has taught us the use of our limbs without giving us the knowledge of the muscles and nerves by which they are actuated, so has she implanted in us an instinct which carries forward the thought in a correspondent course to that which she has established among external objects, though we are ignorant of those powers and forces on which this regular course and succession of objects totally depends.

Section VI
Of Probability.[16]

Though there is no such thing as *chance* in the world, our ignorance of the real cause of any event has the same influence on the understanding and begets a like species of belief or opinion.

There is certainly a probability which arises from a superiority of chances on any side and, according as this superiority increases and surpasses the opposite chances, the probability receives a proportional increase and begets still a higher degree of belief or assent to that side in which we discover the superiority. If a die were marked with one figure or number of spots on four sides, and with another figure or number of spots on the two remaining sides, it would be more probable that the former would turn up than the latter, though, if it had a thousand sides marked in the same manner and only one side different, the probability would be much higher and our belief or expectation of the event more steady and secure. This process of the thought or reasoning may seem trivial and obvious, but to those who consider it more narrowly, it may, perhaps, afford matter for curious speculation.

It seems evident that when the mind looks forward to discover the event which may result from the throw of such a die, it considers the turning up of each particular side as alike probable and it is the very nature of chance to render all the particular events comprehended in it entirely equal. But finding a greater number of sides concur in the one event than in the other, the mind is carried more frequently to that event and meets it more often in revolving the various possibilities or chances on which the ultimate result depends. This concurrence of several views in one particular event begets immediately, by an inexplicable contrivance of nature, the sentiment of belief and gives that event the advantage over its antagonist which is supported by a smaller number of views and recurs less frequently to the mind. If we allow that belief is nothing but a firmer and stronger conception of an object than what attends the mere fictions of the imagination, this operation may, perhaps, in some measure be accounted for. The concurrence of these several views or glimpses imprints the idea more strongly on the imagination, gives it superior force and vigor, renders its influence on the passions and affections more sensible, and, in a word, begets that reliance or security which constitutes the nature of belief and opinion.

The case is the same with the probability of causes as with that of chance. There are some causes which are entirely uniform and constant in producing a particular effect and no instance has ever yet been found of any failure or irregularity in their operation. Fire has always burned, and water suffocated, every human creature. The production of motion by impulse and gravity is a universal law which has up to now admitted of no exception. But there are other causes which have been found more irregular and

16. Mr. Locke divides all arguments into demonstrative and probable. In this view, we must say, that it is only probable all men must die, or that the sun will rise tomorrow. But to conform our language more to common use, we ought to divide arguments into *demonstrations*, *proofs*, and *probabilities*. By proofs meaning such arguments from experience as leave no room for doubt or opposition.

uncertain; nor has rhubarb always proved a purge, or opium a soporific, to everyone who has taken these medicines. It is true, when any cause fails of producing its usual effect, philosophers do not ascribe this to any irregularity in nature, but suppose that some secret causes in the particular structure of parts have prevented the operation. Our reasonings, however, and conclusions concerning the event are the same as if this principle had no place. Being determined by custom to transfer the past to the future in all our inferences, where the past has been entirely regular and uniform, we expect the event with the greatest assurance and leave no room for any contrary supposition. But where different effects have been found to follow from causes which are to *appearance* exactly similar, all these various effects must occur to the mind in transferring the past to the future and enter into our consideration when we determine the probability of the event. Though we give the preference to that which has been found most usual and believe that this effect will exist, we must not overlook the other effects, but must assign to each of them a particular weight and authority in proportion as we have found it to be more or less frequent. It is more probable, in almost every country of Europe, that there will be frost sometime in January than that the weather will continue open throughout that whole month, though this probability varies according to the different climates and approaches to a certainty in the more northern kingdoms. Here, then, it seems evident that when we transfer the past to the future in order to determine the effect which will result from any cause, we transfer all the different events in the same proportion as they have appeared in the past and conceive one to have existed a hundred times, for instance, another ten times, and another once. As a great number of views do here concur in one event, they fortify and confirm it to the imagination, beget that sentiment which we call *belief*, and give its object the preference above the contrary event which is not supported by an equal number of experiments and does not recur so frequently to the thought in transferring the past to the future. Let anyone try to account for this operation of the mind upon any of the received systems of philosophy and he will be sensible of the difficulty. For my part, I shall think it sufficient if the present hints excite the curiosity of philosophers and make them sensible how defective all common theories are in treating of such curious and such sublime subjects.

Section VII
Of the Idea of Necessary Connection.

Part I.

The great advantage of the mathematical sciences above the moral consists in this, that the ideas of the former, being sensible, are always clear and determinate, the smallest distinction between them is immediately perceptible, and the same terms are still expressive of the same ideas without ambiguity or variation. An oval is never mistaken for a circle, nor an hyperbola for an ellipsis. The isosceles and scalene are distinguished by boundaries more exact than vice and virtue, right and wrong. If any term is defined in geometry, the mind readily, of itself, substitutes on all occasions the definition for the term defined. Or even when no definition is employed, the object itself may be presented to the senses and by that means be steadily and clearly apprehended. But the finer sentiments of the mind, the operations of the understanding, the various agitations of the passions, though really in themselves distinct, easily escape us when surveyed by reflection; nor is it in our power to recall the original object as often as we have occasion to contemplate it. Ambiguity, by this means, is gradually introduced into our reasonings. Similar objects are readily taken to be the same and the conclusion becomes at last very wide of the premises.

One may safely, however, affirm that if we consider these sciences in a proper light, their advantages and disadvantages nearly compensate each other and reduce both of them to a state of equality. If the mind, with greater facility, retains the ideas of geometry clear and determinate, it must carry on a much longer and more intricate chain of reasoning and compare ideas much wider of each other in order to reach the more abstruse truths of that science. And if moral ideas are apt, without extreme care, to fall into obscurity and confusion, the inferences are always much shorter in these disquisitions and the intermediate steps which lead to the conclusion much fewer than in the sciences which treat of quantity and number. In reality, there is scarcely a proposition in Euclid so simple as not to consist of more parts than are to be found in any moral reasoning which runs not into chimera and conceit. Where we trace the principles of the human mind through a few steps, we may be very well satisfied with our progress, considering how soon nature throws a bar to all our inquiries concerning causes and reduces us to an acknowledgment of our ignorance. The chief obstacle, therefore, to our improvement in the moral or metaphysical sciences is the obscurity of the ideas and ambiguity of the terms. The principal difficulty in mathematics is the length of inferences and compass of thought requisite to the forming of any conclusion. And, perhaps, our progress in natural philosophy is chiefly retarded by the want of proper experiments and phenomena which are often discovered by chance and cannot always be found when requisite, even by the most diligent and prudent inquiry. As moral philosophy seems up to now to have received less improvement than either geometry or physics, we may conclude that if there is any difference in this respect among these sciences, the difficulties which obstruct the progress of the former require superior care and capacity to be surmounted.

There are no ideas which occur in metaphysics more obscure and uncertain than those of *power*, *force*, *energy*, or *necessary connection*, of which it is every moment necessary for us to treat in all our disquisitions. We shall, therefore, endeavor in this section to fix, if possible, the precise meaning of these terms and thereby remove some part of that obscurity which is so much complained of in this species of philosophy.

It seems a proposition which will not admit of much dispute that all our ideas are nothing but copies of our impressions, or, in other words, that it is impossible for us to *think* of anything which we have not antecedently *felt* either by our external or internal senses. I have endeavored[17] to explain and prove this proposition, and have expressed my hopes that by a proper application of it men may reach a greater clearness and precision in philosophical reasonings than what they have up to now been able to attain. Complex ideas may, perhaps, be well known by definition, which is nothing but an enumeration of those parts or simple ideas that compose them. But when we have pushed up definitions to the most simple ideas and find still some ambiguity and obscurity, what resource are we then possessed of? By what invention can we throw light upon these ideas and render them altogether precise and determinate to our intellectual view? Produce the impressions or original sentiments from which the ideas are copied. These impressions are all strong and sensible. They do not admit of ambiguity. They are not only placed in a full light themselves, but may throw light on their correspondent ideas, which lie in obscurity. And by this means we may, perhaps, attain a new microscope or species of optics by which, in the moral sciences, the most minute and most simple ideas may be so enlarged as to fall readily under our apprehension and be equally known with the grossest and most sensible ideas that can be the object of our inquiry.

To be fully acquainted, therefore, with the idea of power or necessary connection, let us examine its impression and, in order to find the impression with greater certainty, let us search for it in all the sources from which it may possibly be derived.

When we look about us towards external objects and consider the operation of causes, we are never able, in a single instance, to discover any power or necessary connection, any quality which binds the effect to the cause and renders the one an infallible consequence of the other. We only find that the one does actually in fact follow the other. The impulse of one billiard ball is attended with motion in the second. This is the whole that appears to the *outward* senses. The mind feels no sentiment or *inward* impression from this succession of objects. Consequently, there is not, in any single particular instance of cause and effect, anything which can suggest the idea of power or necessary connection.

From the first appearance of an object we never can conjecture what effect will result from it. But were the power or energy of any cause discoverable by the mind, we could foresee the effect, even without experience, and might, at first, pronounce with certainty concerning it by the mere dint of thought and reasoning.

In reality, there is no part of matter that ever does, by its sensible qualities, discover any power or energy or give us ground to imagine that it could produce

17. Section II. Of the Origin of Ideas.

anything or be followed by any other object which we could denominate its effect. Solidity, extension, motion—these qualities are all complete in themselves and never point out any other event which may result from them. The scenes of the universe are continually shifting and one object follows another in an uninterrupted succession; but the power or force which actuates the whole machine is entirely concealed from us and never discovers itself in any of the sensible qualities of body. We know that, in fact, heat is a constant attendant of flame, but what is the connection between them we have no room so much as to conjecture or imagine. It is impossible, therefore, that the idea of power can be derived from the contemplation of bodies in single instances of their operation, because no bodies ever discover any power which can be the original of this idea.[18]

Since, therefore, external objects as they appear to the senses give us no idea of power or necessary connection by their operation in particular instances, let us see whether this idea is derived from reflection on the operations of our own minds and is copied from any internal impression. It may be said that we are every moment conscious of internal power, while we feel that, by the simple command of our will, we can move the organs of our body or direct the faculties of our mind. An act of volition produces motion in our limbs or raises a new idea in our imagination. This influence of the will we know by consciousness. Hence we acquire the idea of power or energy and are certain that we ourselves and all other intelligent beings are possessed of power. This idea, then, is an idea of reflection, since it arises from reflecting on the operations of our own mind and on the command which is exercised by will, both over the organs of the body and faculties of the mind.

We shall proceed to examine this pretension and, first, with regard to the influence of volition over the organs of the body. This influence, we may observe, is a fact which, like all other natural events, can be known only by experience and can never be foreseen from any apparent energy or power in the cause which connects it with the effect and renders the one an infallible consequence of the other. The motion of our body follows upon the command of our will. Of this we are every moment conscious. But the means by which this is effected, the energy by which the will performs so extraordinary an operation, of this we are so far from being immediately conscious that it must forever escape our most diligent inquiry.

For *first*, is there any principle in all nature more mysterious than the union of soul with body, by which a supposed spiritual substance acquires such an influence over a material one that the most refined thought is able to actuate the grossest matter? Were we empowered by a secret wish to remove mountains or control the planets in their orbit, this extensive authority would not be more extraordinary, nor more beyond our comprehension. But if by consciousness we perceived any power or energy in the will, we must know this power; we must know its connection with the effect; we must know the secret union of soul and body, and the nature of both these substances by which the one is able to operate in so many instances upon the other.

Secondly, we are not able to move all the organs of the body with a like authority, though we cannot assign any reason besides experience for so remarkable a difference between one and the other. Why has the will an influence over the tongue and fingers, not over the heart or liver? This question would never embarrass us were we conscious of a power in the former case, not in the latter. We should then perceive, independent of experience, why the authority of will over the organs of the body is circumscribed within such particular limits. Being in that case fully acquainted with the power or force by which it operates, we should also know why its influence reaches precisely to such boundaries, and no further.

A man suddenly struck with a palsy in the leg or arm or who had newly lost those members frequently endeavors, at first, to move them and employ them in their usual offices. Here he is as much conscious of power to command such limbs as a man in perfect health is conscious of power to actuate any member which remains in its natural state and condition. But consciousness never deceives. Consequently, neither

18. Mr. Locke, in his chapter of power, says, that, finding from experience, that there are several new productions in matter, and concluding that there must somewhere be a power capable of producing them, we arrive at last by this reasoning at the idea of power. But no reasoning can ever give us a new, original, simple idea; as this philosopher himself confesses. This, therefore, can never be the origin of that idea. [The reference is to Locke's *Essay*, Bk. II, ch. XXI.]

in the one case nor in the other are we ever conscious of any power. We learn the influence of our will from experience alone. And experience only teaches us how one event constantly follows another, without instructing us in the secret connection which binds them together and renders them inseparable.

Thirdly, we learn from anatomy that the immediate object of power in voluntary motion is not the member itself which is moved, but certain muscles and nerves and animal spirits and, perhaps, something still more minute and more unknown through which the motion is successively propagated before it reaches the member itself whose motion is the immediate object of volition. Can there be a more certain proof that the power by which this whole operation is performed, so far from being directly and fully known by an inward sentiment or consciousness, is to the last degree mysterious and unintelligible? Here the mind wills a certain event. Immediately another event, unknown to ourselves and totally different from the one intended, is produced. This event produces another, equally unknown, until at last, through a long succession the desired event is produced. But if the original power was felt, it must be known. If it was known, its effect must also be known, since all power is relative to its effect. And *vice versa*, if the effect is not known, the power cannot be known nor felt. How indeed can we be conscious of a power to move our limbs when we have no such power, but only that to move certain animal spirits which, though they produce at last the motion of our limbs, yet operate in such a manner as is wholly beyond our comprehension?

We may, therefore, conclude from the whole, I hope, without any temerity, though with assurance, that our idea of power is not copied from any sentiment or consciousness of power within ourselves when we give rise to animal motion or apply our limbs to their proper use and office. That their motion follows the command of the will is a matter of common experience, like other natural events. But the power or energy by which this is effected, like that in other natural events, is unknown and inconceivable.[19]

Shall we then assert that we are conscious of a power or energy in our own minds when, by an act or command of our will, we raise up a new idea, fix the mind to the contemplation of it, turn it on all sides, and at last dismiss it for some other idea when we think that we have surveyed it with sufficient accuracy? I believe the same arguments will prove that even this command of the will gives us no real idea of force or energy.

First, it must be allowed that when we know a power, we know that very circumstance in the cause by which it is enabled to produce the effect, for these are supposed to be synonymous. We must, therefore, know both the cause and effect and the relation between them. But do we pretend to be acquainted with the nature of the human soul and the nature of an idea or the aptitude of the one to produce the other? This is a real creation, a production of something out of nothing, which implies a power so great that it may seem, at first sight, beyond the reach of any being less than infinite. At least it must be admitted that such a power is not felt, nor known, nor even conceivable by the mind. We only feel the event, namely, the existence of an idea consequent to a command of the will. But the manner in which this operation is performed, the power by which it is produced, is entirely beyond our comprehension.

Secondly, the command of the mind over itself is limited, as well as its command over the body; and these limits are not known by reason or any acquaintance with the nature of cause and effect, but only by experience and observation, as in all other natural events and in the operation of external objects. Our

19. It may be pretended, that the resistance which we meet with in bodies, obliging us frequently to exert our force, and call up all our power, this gives us the idea of force and power. It is this *nisus* or strong endeavour, of which we are conscious, that is the original impression from which this idea is copied. But, first, we attribute power to a vast number of objects, where we never can suppose this resistance or exertion of force to take place; to the Supreme Being, who never meets with any resistance; to the mind in its command over its ideas and limbs, in common thinking and motion, where the effect follows immediately upon the will, without any exertion or summoning up of force; to inanimate matter, which is not capable of this sentiment. *Secondly*, This sentiment of an endeavour to overcome resistance has no known connexion with any event: What follows it, we know by experience; but could not know it *a priori*. It must, however, be confessed, that the animal *nisus*, which we experience, though it can afford no accurate precise idea of power, enters very much into that vulgar, inaccurate idea, which is formed of it.

authority over our sentiments and passions is much weaker than that over our ideas; and even the latter authority is circumscribed within very narrow boundaries. Will anyone pretend to assign the ultimate reason of these boundaries or show why the power is deficient in one case, not in another?

Thirdly, this self-command is very different at different times. A man in health possesses more of it than one languishing with sickness. We are more master of our thoughts in the morning than in the evening—fasting, than after a full meal. Can we give any reason for these variations except experience? Where, then, is the power of which we pretend to be conscious? Is there not here, either in a spiritual or material substance or both, some secret mechanism or structure of parts upon which the effect depends and which, being entirely unknown to us, renders the power or energy of the will equally unknown and incomprehensible?

Volition is surely an act of the mind with which we are sufficiently acquainted. Reflect upon it. Consider it on all sides. Do you find anything in it like this creative power by which it raises from nothing a new idea and, with a kind of fiat, imitates the omnipotence of its Maker—if I may be allowed so to speak—who called forth into existence all the various scenes of nature? So far from being conscious of this energy in the will, it requires as certain experience as that of which we are possessed to convince us that such extraordinary effects do ever result from a simple act of volition.

The generality of mankind never find any difficulty in accounting for the more common and familiar operations of nature, such as the descent of heavy bodies, the growth of plants, the generation of animals, or the nourishment of bodies by food. But suppose that in all these cases they perceive the very force or energy of the cause by which it is connected with its effect and is forever infallible in its operation. They acquire, by long habit, such a turn of mind that upon the appearance of the cause they immediately expect with assurance its usual attendant and hardly conceive it possible that any other event could result from it. It is only on the discovery of extraordinary phenomena, such as earthquakes, pestilence, and prodigies of any kind, that they find themselves at a loss to assign a proper cause and to explain the manner in which the effect is produced by it. It is usual for men, in such difficulties, to have recourse to some invisible intelligent principle as the immediate cause of that event which surprises them and which they think cannot be accounted for from the common powers of nature. But philosophers, who carry their scrutiny a little further, immediately perceive that, even in the most familiar events, the energy of the cause is as unintelligible as in the most unusual and that we only learn by experience the frequent conjunction of objects, without being ever able to comprehend anything like connection between them. Here, then, many philosophers[20] think themselves obliged by reason to have recourse, on all occasions, to the same principle which the vulgar never appeal to but in cases that appear miraculous and supernatural. They acknowledge mind and intelligence to be not only the ultimate and original cause of all things, but the immediate and sole cause of every event which appears in nature. They pretend that those objects which are commonly denominated *causes* are in reality nothing but *occasions*; and that the true and direct principle of every effect is not any power or force in nature, but a volition of the Supreme Being, who wills that such particular objects should forever be conjoined with each other. Instead of saying that one billiard ball moves another by a force which it has derived from the author of nature, it is the Deity himself, they say, who, by a particular volition, moves the second ball, being determined to this operation by the impulse of the first ball, in consequence of those general laws which he has laid down to himself in the government of the universe. But philosophers advancing still in their inquiries, discover that as we are totally ignorant of the power on which depends the mutual operation of bodies, we are no less ignorant of that power on which depends the operation of mind on body or of body on mind; nor are we able, either from our senses or consciousness, to assign the ultimate principle in one case more than in the other. The same ignorance, therefore, reduces them to the same conclusion. They assert that the Deity is the immediate cause of the union between soul and body and that they are not the organs of sense which, being agitated by external objects, produce sensations in the mind, but that it is a particular volition of our

20. [The reference is to the "occasionalists," regarding whom see Berkeley's *Three Dialogues*, n.3.]

omnipotent Maker which excites such a sensation in consequence of such a motion in the organ. In like manner, it is not any energy in the will that produces local motion in our members. It is God himself, who is pleased to second our will, in itself impotent, and to command that motion which we erroneously attribute to our own power and efficacy. Nor do philosophers stop at this conclusion. They sometimes extend the same inference to the mind itself in its internal operations. Our mental vision or conception of ideas is nothing but a revelation made to us by our Maker. When we voluntarily turn our thoughts to any object and raise up its image in the fancy, it is not the will which creates that idea, it is the universal Creator who discovers it to the mind and renders it present to us.

Thus, according to these philosophers, every thing is full of God. Not content with the principle that nothing exists but by his will, that nothing possesses any power but by his concession, they rob nature and all created beings of every power in order to render their dependence on the Deity still more sensible and immediate. They do not consider that by this theory they diminish, instead of magnifying, the grandeur of those attributes which they affect so much to celebrate. It argues surely more power in the Deity to delegate a certain degree of power to inferior creatures than to produce everything by his own immediate volition. It argues more wisdom to contrive at first the fabric of the world with such perfect foresight that, of itself and by its proper operation, it may serve all the purposes of providence than if the great Creator were obliged every moment to adjust its parts and animate by his breath all the wheels of that stupendous machine.

But if we would have a more philosophical confutation of this theory, perhaps the two following reflections may suffice.

First, it seems to me that this theory of the universal energy and operation of the Supreme Being is too bold ever to carry conviction with it to a man sufficiently apprised of the weakness of human reason and the narrow limits to which it is confined in all its operations. Though the chain of arguments which conduct to it were ever so logical, there must arise a strong suspicion, if not an absolute assurance, that it has carried us quite beyond the reach of our faculties when it leads to conclusions so extraordinary and so remote from common life and experience. We arrived in fairyland long before we have reached the last steps of our theory; and *there* we have no reason to trust our common methods of argument or to think that our usual analogies and probabilities have any authority. Our line is too short to fathom such immense abysses. And however we may flatter ourselves that we are guided, in every step which we take, by a kind of verisimilitude and experience, we may be assured that this fancied experience has no authority when we thus apply it to subjects that lie entirely out of the sphere of experience. But on this we shall have occasion to touch afterwards.[21]

Secondly, I cannot perceive any force in the arguments on which this theory is founded. We are ignorant, it is true, of the manner in which bodies operate on each other. Their force or energy is entirely incomprehensible. But are we not equally ignorant of the manner or force by which a mind, even the supreme mind, operates either on itself or on body? From where, I beseech you, do we acquire any idea of it? We have no sentiment or consciousness of this power in ourselves. We have no idea of the Supreme Being but what we learn from reflection on our own faculties. Were our ignorance, therefore, a good reason for rejecting anything, we should be led into that principle of denying all energy in the Supreme Being as much as in the grossest matter. We surely comprehend as little the operations of one as of the other. Is it more difficult to conceive that motion may arise from impulse than that it may arise from volition? All we know is our profound ignorance in both cases.[22]

21. Section XII.

22. I need not examine at length the *vis inertiae* which is so much talked of in the new philosophy, and which is ascribed to matter. We find by experience, that a body at rest or in motion continues for ever in its present state, till put from it by some new cause: And that a body impelled takes as much motion from the impelling body as it acquires itself. These are facts. When we call this a *vis inertiae*, we only mark these facts, without pretending to have any idea of the inert power; in the same manner as, when we talk of gravity, we mean certain effects without comprehending that active power. It was never the meaning of Sir Isaac Newton to rob second causes of all force or energy; though some of his followers have endeavoured to establish that theory upon his authority. On the contrary, that great philosopher had recourse to an ethereal active fluid to explain his universal attraction; though he was so cautious and

Part II.

But to hasten to a conclusion of this argument, which is already drawn out to too great a length. We have sought in vain for an idea of power or necessary connection in all the sources from which we could suppose it to be derived. It appears that in single instances of the operation of bodies we never can, by our utmost scrutiny, discover anything but one event following another, without being able to comprehend any force or power by which the cause operates or any connection between it and its supposed effect. The same difficulty occurs in contemplating the operations of mind on body, where we observe the motion of the latter to follow upon the volition of the former, but are not able to observe or conceive the tie which binds together the motion and volition, or the energy by which the mind produces this effect. The authority of the will over its own faculties and ideas is not a whit more comprehensible, so that, upon the whole, there does not appear, throughout all nature, any one instance of connection which is conceivable by us. All events seem entirely loose and separate. One event follows another, but we never can observe any tie between them. They seem *conjoined*, but never *connected*. And as we can have no idea of anything which never appeared to our outward sense or inward sentiment, the necessary conclusion *seems* to be that we have no idea of connection or power at all and that these words are absolutely without any meaning when employed either in philosophical reasonings or common life.

But there still remains one method of avoiding this conclusion and one source which we have not yet examined. When any natural object or event is presented, it is impossible for us, by any sagacity or penetration to discover, or even conjecture, without experience, what event will result from it, or to carry our foresight beyond that object which is immediately present to the memory and senses. Even after one instance or experiment where we have observed a particular event to follow upon another, we are not entitled to form a general rule or foretell what will happen in like cases, it being justly esteemed an unpardonable temerity to judge of the whole course of nature from one single experiment, however accurate or certain. But when one particular species of event has always, in all instances, been conjoined with another, we make no longer any scruple of foretelling one upon the appearance of the other and of employing that reasoning which can alone assure us of any matter of fact or existence. We then call the one object *cause*, the other *effect*. We suppose that there is some connection between them, some power in the one by which it infallibly produces the other and operates with the greatest certainty and strongest necessity.

It appears, then, that this idea of a necessary connection among events arises from a number of similar instances which occur, of the constant conjunction of these events, nor can that idea ever be suggested by any one of these instances surveyed in all possible lights and positions. But there is nothing in a number of instances, different from every single instance, which is supposed to be exactly similar, except only that after a repetition of similar instances the mind is carried by habit, upon the appearance of one event, to expect its usual attendant and to believe that it will exist. This connection, therefore, which we *feel* in the mind, this customary transition of the imagination from one object to its usual attendant, is the sentiment or impression from which we form the idea of power or necessary connection. Nothing further is in the case. Contemplate the subject on all sides, you will never find any other origin of that idea. This is the sole difference between one instance, from which we can never receive the idea of connection, and a number of similar instances by which it is suggested. The first time a man saw the communication of motion by impulse, as by the shock of two billiard balls,

---

modest as to allow, that it was a mere hypothesis, not to be insisted on, without more experiments. I must confess, that there is something in the fate of opinions a little extraordinary. Descartes insinuated that doctrine of the universal and sole efficacy of the Deity, without insisting on it. Malebranche and other Cartesians made it the foundation of all their philosophy. It had, however, no authority in England. Locke, Clarke [the Cambridge philosopher Samuel Clarke (1675–1729)], and Cudworth [the English philosopher and theologian Ralph Cudworth (1617–1688)] never so much as take notice of it, but supposed all along that matter has a real, though subordinate and derived power. By what means has it become so prevalent among our modern metaphysicians?

he could not pronounce that the one event was *connected*, but only that it was *conjoined* with the other. After he has observed several instances of this nature, he then pronounces them to be *connected*. What alteration has happened to give rise to this new idea of *connection*? Nothing but that he now *feels* these events to be *connected* in his imagination and can readily foretell the existence of one from the appearance of the other. When we say, therefore, that one object is connected with another, we mean only that they have acquired a connection in our thought and give rise to this inference by which they become proofs of each other's existence—a conclusion, which is somewhat extraordinary, but which seems founded on sufficient evidence. Nor will its evidence be weakened by any general diffidence of the understanding or skeptical suspicion concerning every conclusion which is new and extraordinary. No conclusions can be more agreeable to skepticism than such as make discoveries concerning the weakness and narrow limits of human reason and capacity.

And what stronger instance can be produced of the surprising ignorance and weakness of the understanding than the present? For surely, if there is any relation among objects which it imports to us to know perfectly, it is that of cause and effect. On this are founded all our reasonings concerning matter of fact or existence. By means of it alone we attain any assurance concerning objects which are removed from the present testimony of our memory and senses. The only immediate utility of all sciences is to teach us how to control and regulate future events by their causes. Our thoughts and inquiries are, therefore, every moment employed about this relation; yet so imperfect are the ideas which we form concerning it that it is impossible to give any just definition of cause, except what is drawn from something extraneous and foreign to it. Similar objects are always conjoined with similar. Of this we have experience. Suitably to this experience, therefore, we may define a cause to be *an object followed by another and where all the objects similar to the first are followed by objects similar to the second*. Or, in other words, *where, if the first object had not been, the second never had existed*. The appearance of a cause always conveys the mind, by a customary transition, to the idea of the effect. Of this also we have experience. We may, therefore, suitably to this experience, form another definition of cause, and call it *an object followed by another and whose appearance always conveys the thought to that other*. But though both these definitions are drawn from circumstances foreign to the cause, we cannot remedy this inconvenience or attain any more perfect definition which may point out that circumstance in the cause which gives it a connection with its effect. We have no idea of this connection, nor even any distinct notion what it is we desire to know when we endeavor at a conception of it. We say, for instance, that the vibration of this string is the cause of this particular sound. But what do we mean by that affirmation? We either mean that *this vibration is followed by this sound, and that all similar vibrations have been followed by similar sounds*: Or that *this vibration is followed by this sound and that upon the appearance of one, the mind anticipates the senses and forms immediately an idea of the other*. We may consider the relation of cause and effect in either of these two lights; but beyond these, we have no idea of it.[23]

23. According to these explications and definitions, the idea of *power* is relative as much as that of *cause*; and both have a reference to an effect, or some other event constantly conjoined with the former. When we consider the *unknown* circumstance of an object, by which the degree or quantity of its effect is fixed and determined, we call that its power: And accordingly, it is allowed by all philosophers, that the effect is the measure of the power. But if they had any idea of power, as it is in itself, why could not they measure it in itself? The dispute whether the force of a body in motion be as its velocity, or the square of its velocity; this dispute, I say, needed not be decided by comparing its effects in equal or unequal times; but by a direct mensuration and comparison.

As to the frequent use of the words, Force, Power, Energy, etc. which every where occur in common conversation, as well as in philosophy; that is no proof, that we are acquainted, in any instance, with the connecting principle between cause and effect, or can account ultimately for the production of one thing by another. These words, as commonly used, have very loose meanings annexed to them; and their ideas are very uncertain and confused. No animal can put external bodies in motion without the sentiment of a *nisus* or endeavour; and every animal has a sentiment or feeling from the stroke or blow of an external object, that is in motion. These sensations, which are merely animal, and from which we can *a priori* draw no inference,

To recapitulate, therefore, the reasonings of this section: Every idea is copied from some preceding impression or sentiment; and where we cannot find any impression, we may be certain that there is no idea. In all single instances of the operation of bodies or minds, there is nothing that produces any impression, nor consequently can suggest any idea of power or necessary connection. But when many uniform instances appear and the same object is always followed by the same event, we then begin to entertain the notion of cause and connection. We then *feel* a new sentiment or impression, namely, a customary connection in the thought or imagination between one object and its usual attendant and this sentiment is the original of that idea which we seek for. For as this idea arises from a number of similar instances and not from any single instance, it must arise from that circumstance in which the number of instances differ from every individual instance. But this customary connection or transition of the imagination is the only circumstance in which they differ. In every other particular they are alike. The first instance which we saw of motion communicated by the shock of two billiard balls (to return to this obvious illustration) is exactly similar to any instance that may, at present, occur to us, except only that we could not at first *infer* one event from the other, which we are enabled to do at present, after so long a course of uniform experience. I do not know whether the reader will readily apprehend this reasoning. I am afraid that, should I multiply words about it or throw it into a greater variety of lights, it would only become more obscure and intricate. In all abstract reasonings, there is one point of view which, if we can happily hit, we shall go further towards illustrating the subject than by all the eloquence and copious expression in the world. This point of view we should endeavor to reach, and reserve the flowers of rhetoric for subjects which are more adapted to them.

---

we are apt to transfer to inanimate objects, and to suppose, that they have some such feelings, whenever they transfer or receive motion. With regard to energies, which are exerted, without our annexing to them any idea of communicated motion, we consider only the constant experienced conjunction of the events; and as we *feel* a customary connexion between the ideas, we transfer that feeling to the objects; as nothing is more usual than to apply to external bodies every internal sensation, which they occasion.

Section VIII
Of Liberty and Necessity.

Part I.

It might reasonably be expected in questions which have been canvassed and disputed with great eagerness since the first origin of science and philosophy that the meaning of all the terms, at least, should have been agreed upon among the disputants, and our inquiries, in the course of two thousand years, been able to pass from words to the true and real subject of the controversy. For how easy may it seem to give exact definitions of the terms employed in reasoning and make these definitions, not the mere sound of words, the object of future scrutiny and examination? But if we consider the matter more narrowly, we shall be apt to draw a quite opposite conclusion. From this circumstance alone that a controversy has been long kept on foot and remains still undecided, we may presume that there is some ambiguity in the expression and that the disputants affix different ideas to the terms employed in the controversy. For as the faculties of the mind are supposed to be naturally alike in every individual—otherwise nothing could be more fruitless than to reason or dispute together—it would be impossible, if men affix the same ideas to their terms, that they could so long form different opinions of the same subject, especially when they communicate their views and each party turn themselves on all sides in search of arguments which may give them the victory over their antagonists. It is true that if men attempt the discussion of questions which lie entirely beyond the reach of human capacity, such as those concerning the origin of worlds or the economy of the intellectual system or region of spirits, they may long beat the air in their fruitless contests and never arrive at any determinate conclusion. But if the question regards any subject of common life and experience, nothing, one would think, could preserve the dispute so long undecided, but some ambiguous expressions which keep the antagonists still at a distance and hinder them from grappling with each other.

This has been the case in the long disputed question concerning liberty and necessity and to so remarkable a degree that, if I am not much mistaken, we shall find that all mankind, both learned and ignorant, have always been of the same opinion with regard to this subject and that a few intelligible definitions would immediately have put an end to the whole controversy. I admit that this dispute has been so much canvassed on all hands and has led philosophers into such a labyrinth of obscure sophistry that it is no wonder if a sensible reader indulge his ease so far as to turn a deaf ear to the proposal of such a question from which he can expect neither instruction nor entertainment. But the state of the argument here proposed may, perhaps, serve to renew his attention, as it has more novelty, promises at least some decision of the controversy, and will not much disturb his ease by any intricate or obscure reasoning.

I hope, therefore, to make it appear that all men have ever agreed in the doctrine both of necessity and of liberty, according to any reasonable sense which can be put on these terms, and that the whole controversy has up to now turned merely upon words. We shall begin with examining the doctrine of necessity.

It is universally allowed that matter, in all its operations, is actuated by a necessary force and that every natural effect is so precisely determined by the energy of its cause that no other effect, in such particular circumstances, could possibly have resulted from it. The degree and direction of every motion are, by the laws of nature, prescribed with such exactness that a living creature may as soon arise from the shock of two bodies as motion in any other degree or direction than what is actually produced by it. Would we, therefore, form a just and precise idea of *necessity*, we must consider from where that idea arises when we apply it to the operation of bodies.

It seems evident that, if all the scenes of nature were continually shifted in such a manner that no two events bore any resemblance to each other, but every object was entirely new, without any similitude to whatever had been seen before, we should never, in that case, have attained the least idea of necessity or of a connection among these objects. We might say, upon such a supposition, that one object or event has followed another, not that one was produced by the other. The relation of cause and effect must be utterly unknown to mankind. Inference and reasoning concerning the operations of nature would, from that moment, be at an end; and the memory and senses remain the only canals by which the knowledge of any real existence could possibly have access to the mind. Our idea, therefore, of necessity and causation arises entirely from the uniformity observable in the operations of nature, where similar objects are constantly conjoined together and the mind is determined by custom to infer the one from the appearance of the other. These two circumstances form the whole of that necessity which we ascribe to matter. Beyond the constant *conjunction* of similar objects and the consequent *inference* from one to the other, we have no notion of any necessity or connection.

If it appears, therefore, that all mankind have ever allowed, without any doubt or hesitation, that these two circumstances take place in the voluntary actions of men and in the operations of mind, it must follow that all mankind have ever agreed in the doctrine of necessity and that they have up to now disputed merely for not understanding each other.

As to the first circumstance, the constant and regular conjunction of similar events, we may possibly satisfy ourselves by the following considerations. It is universally acknowledged that there is a great uniformity among the actions of men in all nations and ages and that human nature remains still the same in its principles and operations. The same motives always produce the same actions. The same events follow from the same causes. Ambition, avarice, self-love, vanity, friendship, generosity, public spirit—these passions, mixed in various degrees and distributed through society, have been, from the beginning of the world, and still are the source of all the actions and enterprises which have ever been observed among mankind. Would you know the sentiments, inclinations, and course of life of the Greeks and Romans? Study well the temper and actions of the French and English. You cannot be much mistaken in transferring to the former *most* of the observations which you have made with regard to the latter. Mankind are so much the same, in all times and places, that history informs us of nothing new or strange in this particular. Its chief use is only to discover the constant and universal principles of human nature by showing men in all varieties of circumstances and situations and furnishing us with materials from which we may form our observations and become acquainted with the regular springs of human action and behavior. These records of wars, intrigues, factions, and revolutions are so many collections of experiments by which the politician or moral philosopher fixes the principles of his science, in the same manner as the physician or natural philosopher becomes acquainted with the nature of plants, minerals, and other external objects by the experiments which he forms concerning them. Nor are the earth, water, and other elements examined by Aristotle and Hippocrates[24] more like to those which at present lie under our observation than the men described by Polybius[25] and Tacitus[26] are to those who now govern the world.

Should a traveler, returning from a far country, bring us an account of men, wholly different from any with whom we were ever acquainted, men, who were entirely divested of avarice, ambition, or revenge, who knew no pleasure but friendship, generosity, and public spirit, we should immediately, from these circumstances, detect the falsehood and prove him a liar with the same certainty as if he had stuffed his narration with stories of centaurs and dragons, miracles and prodigies. And if we would explode any forgery in history, we cannot make use of a more convincing argument than to prove that the actions ascribed to any person are directly contrary to the course of nature and that no human motives, in such circumstances, could ever induce him to such a conduct. The veracity of Quintus Curtius[27] is as much to be suspected when he describes the supernatural courage of Alexander[28] by which he was hurried on singly to attack multitudes, as when he describes his supernatural force and activity by which he was able to resist them. So readily and universally do we acknowledge a uniformity in human motives and actions as well as in the operations of body.

Hence, likewise, the benefit of that experience acquired by long life and a variety of business and company, in order to instruct us in the principles of human nature and regulate our future conduct as well as speculation. By means of this guide we mount up to the knowledge of men's inclinations and motives from their actions, expressions, and even gestures, and again descend to the interpretation of their actions from our knowledge of their motives and inclinations. The general observations, treasured up by a course of experience, give us the clue of human nature and teach us to unravel all its intricacies. Pretexts and appearances no longer deceive us. Public declarations pass for the specious coloring of a cause. And though virtue and honor are allowed their proper weight and authority, that perfect disinterestedness, so often pretended to, is never expected in multitudes and parties, seldom in their leaders, and scarcely even in individuals of any rank or station. But were there no uniformity in human actions and were every experiment which we could form of this kind irregular and anomalous, it would be impossible to collect any general observations concerning mankind and no experience, however accurately digested by reflection, would ever serve to any purpose. Why is the aged husband more skillful in his calling than the young beginner, but because there is a certain uniformity in the operation of the sun, rain, and earth towards the production of vegetables, and experience teaches the old practitioner the rules by which this operation is governed and directed?

We must not, however, expect that this uniformity of human actions should be carried to such a length as that all men, in the same circumstances, will always act precisely in the same manner, without making any allowance for the diversity of characters, prejudices, and opinions. Such a uniformity in every particular is found in no part of nature. On the contrary, from observing the variety of conduct in different men, we are enabled to form a greater variety of maxims which still suppose a degree of uniformity and regularity.

Are the manners of men different in different ages and countries? We learn from this the great force of custom and education which mold the human mind from its infancy and form it into a fixed and established character. Is the behavior and conduct of the one sex very unlike that of the other? It is from this we become acquainted with the different characters which nature has impressed upon the sexes and which

24. [Hippocrates (c. 460–c. 370 B.C.), a Greek physician, became known as "The Father of Medicine."]

25. [Polybius (c. 201–120 B.C.), a Greek historian, wrote of the rise of Rome.]

26. [Tacitus (55–c. 117), a Roman historian, wrote about the Germanic tribes and about the luxurious habits of Romans, which he criticized sharply.]

27. [Quintus Curtius Rufus, a first-century Roman author, wrote a history of Alexander the Great.]

28. [Alexander the Great (356–323 B.C.) was king of Macedon and conqueror of much of Asia.]

she preserves with constancy and regularity. Are the actions of the same person much diversified in the different periods of his life from infancy to old age? This affords room for many general observations concerning the gradual change of our sentiments and inclinations and the different maxims which prevail in the different ages of human creatures. Even the characters which are peculiar to each individual have a uniformity in their influence; otherwise our acquaintance with the persons and our observation of their conduct could never teach us their dispositions or serve to direct our behavior with regard to them.

I grant it possible to find some actions which seem to have no regular connection with any known motives and are exceptions to all the measures of conduct which have ever been established for the government of men. But if we would willingly know what judgment should be formed of such irregular and extraordinary actions, we may consider the sentiments commonly entertained with regard to those irregular events which appear in the course of nature and the operations of external objects. All causes are not conjoined to their usual effects with like uniformity. An artificer who handles only dead matter may be disappointed of his aim as well as the politician who directs the conduct of sensible and intelligent agents.

The vulgar, who take things according to their first appearance, attribute the uncertainty of events to such an uncertainty in the causes as makes the latter often fail of their usual influence, though they meet with no impediment in their operation. But philosophers, observing that almost in every part of nature there is contained a vast variety of springs and principles which are hid by reason of their minuteness or remoteness, find that it is at least possible the contrariety of events may not proceed from any contingency in the cause but from the secret operation of contrary causes. This possibility is converted into certainty by further observation, when they remark that, upon an exact scrutiny, a contrariety of effects always betrays a contrariety of causes and proceeds from their mutual opposition. A peasant can give no better reason for the stopping of any clock or watch than to say that it does not commonly go right. But an artist easily perceives that the same force in the spring or pendulum always has the same influence on the wheels, but fails of its usual effect, perhaps by reason of a grain of dust which puts a stop to the whole movement. From the observation of several parallel instances, philosophers form a maxim that the connection between all causes and effects is equally necessary and that its seeming uncertainty in some instances proceeds from the secret opposition of contrary causes.

Thus, for instance, in the human body, when the usual symptoms of health or sickness disappoint our expectation, when medicines do not operate with their wonted powers, when irregular events follow from any particular cause, the philosopher and physician are not surprised at the matter, nor are ever tempted to deny, in general, the necessity and uniformity of those principles by which the animal economy is conducted. They know that a human body is a mighty complicated machine, that many secret powers lurk in it which are altogether beyond our comprehension, that to us it must often appear very uncertain in its operations, and that therefore the irregular events which outwardly discover themselves can be no proof that the laws of nature are not observed with the greatest regularity in its internal operations and government.

The philosopher, if he is consistent, must apply the same reasoning to the actions and volitions of intelligent agents. The most irregular and unexpected resolutions of men may frequently be accounted for by those who know every particular circumstance of their character and situation. A person of an obliging disposition gives a peevish answer; but he has a toothache or has not dined. A stupid fellow discovers an uncommon alacrity in his carriage; but he has met with a sudden piece of good fortune. Or even when an action, as sometimes happens, cannot be particularly accounted for either by the person himself or by others, we know, in general, that the characters of men are to a certain degree inconstant and irregular. This is, in a manner, the constant character of human nature, though it is applicable in a more particular manner to some persons who have no fixed rule for their conduct, but proceed in a continued course of caprice and inconstancy. The internal principles and motives may operate in a uniform manner, notwithstanding these seeming irregularities—in the same manner as the winds, rain, clouds, and other variations of the weather are supposed to be governed by steady principles, though not easily discoverable by human sagacity and inquiry.

Thus, it appears not only that the conjunction between motives and voluntary actions is as regular and uniform as that between the cause and effect in any part of nature, but also that this regular conjunction has been universally acknowledged among mankind and has never been the subject of dispute either in philosophy or common life. Now, as it is from past experience that we draw all inferences concerning the future and as we conclude that objects will always be conjoined together which we find to have always been conjoined, it may seem superfluous to prove that this experienced uniformity in human actions is a source from which we draw *inferences* concerning them. But in order to throw the argument into a greater variety of lights, we shall also insist, though briefly, on this latter topic.

The mutual dependence of men is so great in all societies that scarcely any human action is entirely complete in itself or is performed without some reference to the actions of others, which are requisite to make it answer fully the intention of the agent. The poorest artificer who labors alone expects at least the protection of the magistrate to ensure him the enjoyment of the fruits of his labor. He also expects that, when he carries his goods to market and offers them at a reasonable price, he shall find purchasers and shall be able, by the money he acquires, to engage others to supply him with those commodities which are requisite for his subsistence. In proportion as men extend their dealings and render their intercourse with others more complicated, they always comprehend in their schemes of life a greater variety of voluntary actions which they expect, from the proper motives, to cooperate with their own. In all these conclusions they take their measures from past experience in the same manner as in their reasonings concerning external objects, and firmly believe that men as well as all the elements are to continue in their operations the same that they have ever found them. A manufacturer reckons upon the labor of his servants for the execution of any work as much as upon the tools which he employs and would be equally surprised were his expectations disappointed. In short, this experimental inference and reasoning concerning the actions of others enters so much into human life that no man, while awake, is ever a moment without employing it. Have we not reason, therefore, to affirm that all mankind have always agreed in the doctrine of necessity, according to the foregoing definition and explication of it?

Nor have philosophers ever entertained a different opinion from the people in this particular. For not to mention that almost every action of their life supposes that opinion, there are even few of the speculative parts of learning to which it is not essential. What would become of *history* had we not a dependence on the veracity of the historian, according to the experience which we have had of mankind? How could *politics* be a science, if laws and forms of government had not a uniform influence upon society? Where would be the foundation of *morals*, if particular characters had no certain or determinate power to produce particular sentiments and if these sentiments had no constant operation on actions? And with what pretense could we employ our *criticism* upon any poet or polite author, if we could not pronounce the conduct and sentiments of his actors either natural or unnatural to such characters and in such circumstances? It seems almost impossible, therefore, to engage either in science or action of any kind without acknowledging the doctrine of necessity and this *inference* from motives to voluntary actions, from characters to conduct.

And indeed, when we consider how aptly *natural* and *moral* evidence link together and form only one chain of argument, we shall make no scruple to allow that they are of the same nature and derived from the same principles. A prisoner who has neither money nor interest discovers the impossibility of his escape as well when he considers the obstinacy of the jailer as the walls and bars with which he is surrounded and in all attempts for his freedom chooses to work upon the stone and iron of the one rather than upon the inflexible nature of the other. The same prisoner, when conducted to the scaffold, foresees his death as certainly from the constancy and fidelity of his guards as from the operation of the ax or wheel. His mind runs along a certain train of ideas: the refusal of the soldiers to consent to his escape; the action of the executioner; the separation of the head and body; bleeding, convulsive motions, and death. Here is a connected chain of natural causes and voluntary actions, but the mind feels no difference between them in passing from one link to another, nor is less certain of the future event than if it were connected with the objects present to the memory or senses by a train of causes cemented together by what we are pleased to call a *physical* necessity. The same experienced union has the same effect on the mind, whether the united objects are motives, volition, and actions, or figure and motion. We may change the names of things, but their nature and their operation on the understanding never change.

Were a man whom I know to be honest and opulent and with whom I live in intimate friendship to come into my house where I am surrounded with my servants, I rest assured that he is not to stab me before he leaves it in order to rob me of my silver standish; and I no more suspect this event than the falling of the house itself which is new and solidly built and founded.—*But he may have been seized with a sudden and unknown frenzy.*—So may a sudden earthquake arise, and shake and tumble my house about my ears. I shall therefore change the suppositions. I shall say that I know with certainty that he is not to put his hand into the fire and hold it there until it is consumed. And this event I think I can foretell with the same assurance as that, if he threw himself out at the window and met with no obstruction, he will not remain a moment suspended in the air. No suspicion of an unknown frenzy can give the least possibility to the former event which is so contrary to all the known principles of human nature. A man who at noon leaves his purse full of gold on the pavement at Charing Cross[29] may as well expect that it will fly away like a feather as that he will find it untouched an hour after. Over one half of human reasonings contain inferences of a similar nature, attended with more or less degrees of certainty, proportioned to our experience of the usual conduct of mankind in such particular situations.

I have frequently considered what could possibly be the reason why all mankind, though they have ever, without hesitation, acknowledged the doctrine of necessity in their whole practice and reasoning, have yet discovered such a reluctance to acknowledge it in words and have rather shown a propensity, in all ages, to profess the contrary opinion. The matter, I think, may be accounted for after the following manner. If we examine the operations of body and the production of effects from their causes, we shall find that all our faculties can never carry us further in our knowledge of this relation than barely to observe that particular objects are *constantly conjoined* together and that the mind is carried, by a *customary transition*, from the appearance of one to the belief of the other. But though this conclusion concerning human ignorance is the result of the strictest scrutiny of this subject, men still entertain a strong propensity to believe that they penetrate further into the powers of nature and perceive something like a necessary connection between the cause and the effect. When again they turn their reflections towards the operations of their own minds and *feel* no such connection of the motive and the action, they are apt to suppose from this that there is a difference between the effects which result from material force and those which arise from thought and intelligence. But being once convinced that we know nothing further of causation of any kind than merely the *constant conjunction* of objects and the consequent *inference* of the mind from one to another and finding that these two circumstances are universally allowed to have place in voluntary actions, we may be more easily led to admit the same necessity common to all causes. And though this reasoning may contradict the systems of many philosophers in ascribing necessity to the determinations of the will, we shall find, upon reflection, that they dissent from it in words only, not in their real sentiment. Necessity, according to the sense in which it is here taken, has never yet been rejected, nor can ever, I think, be rejected by any philosopher. It may only, perhaps, be pretended that the mind can perceive in the operations of matter some further connection between the cause and effect and a connection that has no place in the voluntary actions of intelligent beings. Now whether it is so or not can only appear upon examination, and it is incumbent on these philosophers to make good their assertion by defining or describing that necessity and pointing it out to us in the operations of material causes.

It would seem, indeed, that men begin at the wrong end of this question concerning liberty and necessity when they enter upon it by examining the faculties of the soul, the influence of the understanding, and the operations of the will. Let them first discuss a more simple question, namely, the operations of body and of brute unintelligent matter, and try whether they can there form any idea of causation and neces-

29. [An area in central London.]

sity, except that of a constant conjunction of objects and subsequent inference of the mind from one to another. If these circumstances form, in reality, the whole of that necessity which we conceive in matter and if these circumstances are also universally acknowledged to take place in the operations of the mind, the dispute is at an end—at least must be admitted to be merely verbal thereafter. But as long as we will rashly suppose that we have some further idea of necessity and causation in the operations of external objects, at the same time that we can find nothing further in the voluntary actions of the mind, there is no possibility of bringing the question to any determinate issue while we proceed upon so erroneous a supposition. The only method of undeceiving us is to mount up higher, to examine the narrow extent of science when applied to material causes, and to convince ourselves that all we know of them is the constant conjunction and inference above mentioned. We may, perhaps, find that it is with difficulty we are induced to fix such narrow limits to human understanding. But we can afterwards find no difficulty when we come to apply this doctrine to the actions of the will. For as it is evident that these have a regular conjunction with motives and circumstances and characters and as we always draw inferences from one to the other, we must be obliged to acknowledge in words that necessity which we have already avowed in every deliberation of our lives and in every step of our conduct and behavior.[30]

But to proceed in this reconciling project with regard to the question of liberty and necessity—the most contentious question of metaphysics, the most contentious science—it will not require many words to prove that all mankind have ever agreed in the doctrine of liberty as well as in that of necessity, and that the whole dispute, in this respect also, has been up to now merely verbal. For what is meant by liberty when applied to voluntary actions? We cannot surely mean that actions have so little connection with motives, inclinations, and circumstances that one does not follow with a certain degree of uniformity from the other and that one affords no inference by which we can conclude the existence of the other. For these are plain and acknowledged matters of fact. By liberty, then, we can only mean *a power of acting or not acting according to the determinations of the will*—that is, if we choose to remain at rest, we may; if we choose to move, we also may. Now this hypothetical liberty is universally allowed to belong to everyone who is not a prisoner and in chains. Here then is no subject of dispute.

Whatever definition we may give of liberty, we should be careful to observe two requisite circumstances: *first*, that it is consistent with plain matter of

30. The prevalence of the doctrine of liberty may be accounted for, from another cause, *viz.* a false sensation or seeming experience which we have, or may have, of liberty or indifference, in many of our actions. The necessity of any action, whether of matter or of mind, is not, properly speaking, a quality in the agent, but in any thinking or intelligent being, who may consider the action; and it consists chiefly in the determination of his thoughts to infer the existence of that action from some preceding objects; as liberty, when opposed to necessity, is nothing but the want of that determination, and a certain looseness or indifference, which we feel, in passing, or not passing, from the idea of one object to that of any succeeding one. Now we may observe, that, though, in *reflecting* on human actions, we seldom feel such a looseness or indifference, but are commonly able to infer them with considerable certainty from their motives, and from the dispositions of the agent; yet is frequently happens, that, in *performing* the actions themselves, we are sensible of something like it: And as all resembling objects are readily taken for each other, this has been employed as a demonstrative and even intuitive proof of human liberty. We feel, that our actions are subject to our will, on most occasions; and imagine we feel, that the will itself is subject to nothing, because, when by a denial of it we are provoked to try, we feel, that it moves easily every way, and produces an image of itself, (or a *Velleïty*, as it is called in the schools) even on that side, on which it did not settle. This image, or faint motion, we persuade ourselves, could, at that time, have been completed into the thing itself; because, should that be denied, we find, upon a second trial, that, at present, it can. We consider not, that the fantastical desire of showing liberty, is here the motive of our actions. And it seems certain, that, however we may imagine we feel a liberty within ourselves, a spectator can commonly infer our actions from our motives and character; and even where he cannot, he concludes in general, that he might, were he perfectly acquainted with every circumstance of our situation and temper, and the most secret springs of our complexion and disposition. Now this is the very essence of necessity, according to the foregoing doctrine.

fact; *secondly*, that it is consistent with itself. If we observe these circumstances and render our definition intelligible, I am persuaded that all mankind will be found of one opinion with regard to it.

It is universally allowed that nothing exists without a cause of its existence, and that chance, when strictly examined, is a mere negative word and does not mean any real power which has anywhere a being in nature. But it is pretended that some causes are necessary, some not necessary. Here then is the advantage of definitions. Let anyone *define* a cause without comprehending, as a part of the definition, a *necessary connection* with its effect, and let him show distinctly the origin of the idea expressed by the definition, and I shall readily give up the whole controversy. But if the foregoing explication of the matter is received, this must be absolutely impracticable. Had not objects a regular conjunction with each other, we should never have entertained any notion of cause and effect and this regular conjunction produces that inference of the understanding which is the only connection that we can have any comprehension of. Whoever attempts a definition of cause exclusive of these circumstances will be obliged either to employ unintelligible terms or such as are synonymous to the term which he endeavors to define.[31] And if the definition above mentioned is admitted, liberty, when opposed to necessity, not to constraint, is the same thing with chance, which is universally allowed to have no existence.

Part II.

There is no method of reasoning more common and yet none more blamable than in philosophical disputes to endeavor the refutation of any hypothesis by a pretense of its dangerous consequences to religion and morality. When any opinion leads to absurdities, it is certainly false; but it is not certain that an opinion is false because it is of dangerous consequence. Such topics, therefore, ought entirely to be forborne, as serving nothing to the discovery of truth, but only to make the person of an antagonist odious. This I observe in general, without pretending to draw any advantage from it. I frankly submit to an examination of this kind and shall venture to affirm that the doctrines both of necessity and of liberty, as above explained, are not only consistent with morality, but are absolutely essential to its support.

Necessity may be defined two ways, conformably to the two definitions of cause of which it makes an essential part. It consists either in the constant conjunction of like objects or in the inference of the understanding from one object to another. Now necessity, in both these senses, (which, indeed, are at bottom the same) has universally, though tacitly, in the schools, in the pulpit, and in common life been allowed to belong to the will of man and no one has ever pretended to deny that we can draw inferences concerning human actions and that those inferences are founded on the experienced union of like actions with like motives, inclinations, and circumstances. The only particular in which anyone can differ is that either, perhaps, he will refuse to give the name of necessity to this property of human actions—but as long as the meaning is understood I hope the word can do no harm—or that he will maintain it possible to discover something further in the operations of matter. But this, it must be acknowledged, can be of no consequence to morality or religion, whatever it may be to natural philosophy or metaphysics. We may here be mistaken in asserting that there is no idea of any other necessity or connection in the actions of body. But surely we ascribe nothing to the actions of the mind but what everyone does and must readily allow of. We change no circumstance in the received orthodox system with regard to the will, but only in that with regard to material objects and causes. Nothing, therefore, can be more innocent at least than this doctrine.

All laws being founded on rewards and punishments, it is supposed as a fundamental principle that these motives have a regular and uniform influence on the mind and both produce the good and prevent the evil actions. We may give to this influence what name we please; but, as it is usually conjoined with

31. Thus, if a cause be defined, *that which produces any thing*; it is easy to observe, that *producing* is synonymous to *causing*. In like manner, if a cause be defined, *that by which anything exists*; this is liable to the same objection. For what is meant by these words, *by which?* Had it been said, that a cause is *that* after which *anything constantly exists*; we should have understood the terms. For this is, indeed, all we know of the matter. And this constancy forms the very essence of necessity, nor have we any other idea of it.

the action, it must be esteemed a *cause* and be looked upon as an instance of that necessity which we would here establish.

The only proper object of hatred or vengeance is a person or creature endowed with thought and consciousness, and when any criminal or injurious actions excite that passion, it is only by their relation to the person or connection with him. Actions are, by their very nature, temporary and perishing, and where they do not proceed from some cause in the character and disposition of the person who performed them, they can neither redound to his honor if good, nor infamy if evil. The actions themselves may be blamable; they may be contrary to all the rules of morality and religion. But the person is not answerable for them and, as they proceeded from nothing in him that is durable and constant and leave nothing of that nature behind them, it is impossible he can, upon their account, become the object of punishment or vengeance. According to the principle, therefore, which denies necessity and consequently causes that a man is as pure and untainted after having committed the most horrid crime as at the first moment of his birth, nor is his character any way concerned in his actions, since they are not derived from it, and the wickedness of the one can never be used as a proof of the depravity of the other.

Men are not blamed for such actions as they perform ignorantly and casually, whatever may be the consequences. Why? But because the principles of these actions are only momentary and terminate in them alone. Men are less blamed for such actions as they perform hastily and unpremeditatedly than for such as proceed from deliberation. For what reason? But because a hasty temper, though a constant cause or principle in the mind, operates only by intervals and does not infect the whole character. Again, repentance wipes off every crime, if attended with a reformation of life and manners. How is this to be accounted for? But by asserting that actions render a person criminal merely as they are proofs of criminal principles in the mind; and when, by an alteration of these principles, they cease to be just proofs, they likewise cease to be criminal. But, except upon the doctrine of necessity, they never were just proofs and consequently never were criminal.

It will be equally easy to prove, and from the same arguments, that *liberty*, according to that definition above mentioned, in which all men agree, is also essential to morality and that no human actions, where it is wanting, are susceptible of any moral qualities or can be the objects either of approbation or dislike. For as actions are objects of our moral sentiment only so far as they are indications of the internal character, passions, and affections, it is impossible that they can give rise either to praise or blame where they do not proceed from these principles, but are derived altogether from external violence.

I do not pretend to have obviated or removed all objections to this theory with regard to necessity and liberty. I can foresee other objections derived from topics which have not here been treated of. It may be said, for instance, that if voluntary actions are subjected to the same laws of necessity with the operations of matter, there is a continued chain of necessary causes, preordained and predetermined, reaching from the original cause of all to every single volition of every human creature. No contingency anywhere in the universe, no indifference, no liberty. While we act, we are at the same time acted upon. The ultimate Author of all our volitions is the Creator of the world, who first bestowed motion on this immense machine and placed all beings in that particular position from which every subsequent event, by an inevitable necessity, must result. Human actions, therefore, either can have no moral turpitude at all, as proceeding from so good a cause, or if they have any turpitude, they must involve our Creator in the same guilt, while he is acknowledged to be their ultimate cause and author. For as a man who fired a mine is answerable for all the consequences, whether the train he employed is long or short, so wherever a continued chain of necessary causes is fixed, that Being, either finite or infinite, who produces the first is likewise the author of all the rest and must both bear the blame and acquire the praise which belong to them. Our clear and unalterable ideas of morality establish this rule upon unquestionable reasons when we examine the consequences of any human action and these reasons must still have greater force when applied to the volitions and intentions of a Being infinitely wise and powerful. Ignorance or impotence may be pleaded for so limited a creature as man, but those imperfections have no place in our Creator. He foresaw, he ordained, he intended all those actions of men which we so rashly pronounce criminal. And we must therefore conclude either that they are not criminal or that the Deity, not man, is accountable for them. But as either of these positions is absurd and impious, it follows that the doctrine from which they are deduced cannot possibly be true, as being liable to all the same objections. An absurd consequence, if necessary, proves the original doctrine to be absurd in the same manner as criminal actions render criminal the original cause, if the connection between them is necessary and inevitable.

This objection consists of two parts, which we shall examine separately: *First*, that if human actions can be traced up, by a necessary chain, to the Deity, they can never be criminal, on account of the infinite perfection of that Being from whom they are derived and who can intend nothing but what is altogether good and laudable. Or, *secondly*, if they are criminal, we must retract the attribute of perfection which we ascribe to the Deity and must acknowledge him to be the ultimate author of guilt and moral turpitude in all his creatures.

The answer to the first objection seems obvious and convincing. There are many philosophers who, after an exact scrutiny of all the phenomena of nature, conclude that the whole, considered as one system, is, in every period of its existence, ordered with perfect benevolence, and that the utmost possible happiness will, in the end, result to all created beings without any mixture of positive or absolute ill and misery. Every physical ill, they say, makes an essential part of this benevolent system and could not possibly be removed, even by the Deity himself, considered as a wise agent, without giving entrance to greater ill or excluding greater good which will result from it. From this theory some philosophers, and the ancient *Stoics* among the rest, derived a topic of consolation under all afflictions, while they taught their pupils that those ills under which they labored were in reality goods to the universe and that to an enlarged view which could comprehend the whole system of nature every event became an object of joy and exultation. But though this topic is specious and sublime, it was soon found in practice weak and ineffectual. You would surely more irritate than appease a man lying under the racking pains of gout by preaching up to him the rectitude of those general laws which produced the malignant humors in his body and led them through the proper canals to the sinews and nerves, where they now excite such acute torments. These enlarged views may, for a moment, please the imagination of a speculative man who is placed in ease and security, but neither can they dwell with constancy on his mind, even though undisturbed by the emotions of pain or passion, much less can they maintain their ground when attacked by such powerful antagonists. The affections take a narrower and more natural survey of their object, and, by an economy more suitable to the infirmity of human minds, regard alone the beings around us, and are actuated by such events as appear good or ill to the private system.

The case is the same with *moral* as with *physical* ill. It cannot reasonably be supposed that those remote considerations which are found of so little efficacy with regard to one will have a more powerful influence with regard to the other. The mind of man is so formed by nature that, upon the appearance of certain characters, dispositions, and actions, it immediately feels the sentiment of approbation or blame; nor are there any emotions more essential to its frame and constitution. The characters which engage our approbation are chiefly such as contribute to the peace and security of human society, as the characters which excite blame are chiefly such as tend to public detriment and disturbance. From this it may reasonably be presumed that the moral sentiments arise, either mediately or immediately, from a reflection of these opposite interests. What though philosophical meditations establish a different opinion or conjecture that everything is right with regard to the whole, and that the qualities which disturb society are, in the main, as beneficial and are as suitable to the primary intention of nature as those which more directly promote its happiness and welfare? Are such remote and uncertain speculations able to counterbalance the sentiments which arise from the natural and immediate view of the objects? A man who is robbed of a considerable sum, does he find his vexation for the loss any way diminished by these sublime reflections? Why then should his moral resentment against the crime be supposed incompatible with them? Or why should not the acknowledgment of a real distinction between vice and virtue be reconcilable to all speculative systems of philosophy, as well as that of a real distinction between personal beauty and deformity? Both these distinctions are founded in the natural sentiments of the human mind. And these sentiments are not to be controlled or altered by any philosophical theory or speculation whatsoever.

The *second* objection does not admit of so easy and satisfactory an answer, nor is it possible to explain distinctly how the Deity can be the mediate cause of all the actions of men without being the author of sin and moral turpitude. These are mysteries which mere natural and unassisted reason is very unfit to handle; and whatever system she embraces, she must find herself involved in inextricable difficulties, and even contradictions, at every step which she takes with regard to such subjects. To reconcile the indifference and contingency of human actions with prescience or to defend absolute decrees and yet free the Deity from being the author of sin has been found up to now to exceed all the power of philosophy. Happy, if she is sensible of her temerity from there, when she pries into these sublime mysteries, and, leaving a scene so full of obscurities and perplexities, returns with suitable modesty to her true and proper province, the examination of common life, where she will find difficulties enough to employ her inquiries without launching into so boundless an ocean of doubt, uncertainty, and contradiction!

Section IX
Of the Reason of Animals.

All our reasonings concerning matter of fact are founded on a species of analogy which leads us to expect from any cause the same events which we have observed to result from similar causes. Where the causes are entirely similar, the analogy is perfect and the inference drawn from it is regarded as certain and conclusive. Nor does any man ever entertain a doubt where he sees a piece of iron that it will have weight and cohesion of parts, as in all other instances which have ever fallen under his observation. But where the objects do not have so exact a similarity, the analogy is less perfect and the inference is less conclusive, though still it has some force in proportion to the degree of similarity and resemblance. The anatomical observations formed upon one animal are, by this species of reasoning, extended to all animals; and it is certain that, when the circulation of the blood, for instance, is clearly proved to have place in one creature, as a frog, or fish, it forms a strong presumption that the same principle has place in all. These analogical observations may be carried further, even to this science of which we are now treating, and any theory by which we explain the operations of the understanding or the origin and connection of the passions in man will acquire additional authority, if we find that the same theory is requisite to explain the same phenomena in all other animals. We shall make trial of this with regard to the hypothesis by which we have, in the foregoing discourse, endeavored to account for all experimental reasoning and it is hoped that this new point of view will serve to confirm all our former observations.

First, it seems evident that animals, as well as men, learn many things from experience and infer that the same events will always follow from the same causes. By this principle they become acquainted with the more obvious properties of external objects and gradually, from their birth, treasure up a knowledge of the nature of fire, water, earth, stones, heights, depths, etc., and of the effects which result from their operation. The ignorance and inexperience of the young are here plainly distinguishable from the cunning and sagacity of the old, who have learned, by long observation, to avoid what hurt them and to pursue what gave ease or pleasure. A horse that has been accustomed to the field becomes acquainted with the proper height which he can leap, and will never attempt what exceeds his force and ability. An old greyhound will trust the more fatiguing part of the chase to the younger and will place himself so as to meet the hare in her doubles; nor are the conjectures which he forms on this occasion founded in anything but his observation and experience.

This is still more evident from the effects of discipline and education on animals who, by the proper application of rewards and punishments, may be taught any course of action the most contrary to their natural instincts and propensities. Is it not experience which renders a dog apprehensive of pain when you menace him or lift up the whip to beat him? Is it not even experience which makes him answer to his name and infer, from such an arbitrary sound, that you mean him rather than any of his fellows and intend to call him when you pronounce it in a certain manner and with a certain tone and accent?

In all these cases we may observe that the animal infers some fact beyond what immediately strikes his senses and that this inference is altogether founded on past experience, while the creature expects from the present object the same consequences which it has always found in its observation to result from similar objects.

Secondly, it is impossible that this inference of the animal can be founded on any process of argument or reasoning by which he concludes that like events must follow like objects and that the course of nature will always be regular in its operations. For if there are in reality any arguments of this nature, they surely lie too abstruse for the observation of such imperfect understandings, since it may well employ the utmost care and attention of a philosophic genius to discover and observe them. Animals, therefore, are not guided in these inferences by reasoning. Neither are children. Neither are the generality of mankind in their ordinary actions and conclusions. Neither are philosophers themselves, who, in all the active parts of life, are in the main the same with the vulgar and are governed by the same maxims. Nature must have provided some other principle, of more ready and more general use and application; nor can an operation of such immense consequence in life as that of inferring effects from causes be trusted to the uncertain process of reasoning and argumentation. Were this doubtful with regard to men, it seems to admit of no question with regard to the brute creation; and the conclusion being once firmly established in the one, we have a strong presumption, from all the rules of analogy, that it ought to be universally admitted without any exception or reserve. It is custom alone which engages animals from every object that strikes their senses to infer its usual attendant and carries their imagination from the appearance of the one to conceive the other in that particular manner which we denominate *belief*. No other explication can be given of this operation, in all the higher as well as lower classes of sensitive beings which fall under our notice and observation.[32]

But though animals learn many parts of their knowledge from observation, there are also many parts of it which they derive from the original hand of nature, which much exceed the share of capacity they possess on ordinary occasions and in which they improve little or nothing by the longest practice and experience. These we denominate instincts and are

32. Since all reasonings concerning facts or causes is derived merely from custom, it may be asked how it happens, that men so much surpass animals in reasoning, and one man so much surpasses another? Has not the same custom the same influence on all?

We shall here endeavour briefly to explain the great difference in human understandings: After which the reason of the difference between men and animals will easily be comprehended.

1. When we have lived any time, and have been accustomed to the uniformity of nature, we acquire a general habit, by which we always transfer the known to the unknown, and conceive the latter to resemble the former. By means of this general habitual principle, we regard even one experiment as the foundation of reasoning, and expect a similar even with some degree of certainty, where the experiment has been made accurately, and free from all foreign circumstances. It is therefore considered as a matter of great importance to observe the consequences of things; and as one man may very much surpass another in attention and memory and observation, this will make a very great difference in their reasoning.

2. Where there is a complication of causes to produce any effect, one mind may be much larger than another, and better able to comprehend the whole system of objects, and to infer justly their consequences.

3. One man is able to carry on a chain of consequences to a greater length than another.

4. Few men can think long without running into a confusion of ideas, and mistaking one for another; and there are various degrees of this infirmity.

5. The circumstance, on which the effect depends, is frequently involved in other circumstances, which are foreign and extrinsic. The separation of it often requires great attention, accuracy, and subtilty.

6. The forming of general maxims from particular observation is a very nice operation; and nothing is more usual, from haste or a narrowness of mind, which sees not on all sides, than to commit mistakes in this particular.

7. When we reason from analogies, the man, who has the greater experience or the greater promptitude of suggesting analogies, will be the better reasoner.

8. Biases from prejudice, education, passion, party, etc. hang more upon one mind than another.

9. After we have acquired a confidence in human testimony, books and conversation enlarge much more the sphere of one man's experience and thought than those of another.

It would be easy to discover many other circumstances that make a difference in the understandings of men.

so apt to admire as something very extraordinary and inexplicable by all the disquisitions of human understanding. But our wonder will perhaps cease or diminish when we consider that the experimental reasoning itself which we possess in common with beasts and on which the whole conduct of life depends is nothing but a species of instinct or mechanical power that acts in us unknown to ourselves and in its chief operations is not directed by any such relations or comparisons of ideas as are the proper objects of our intellectual faculties. Though the instinct is different, yet still it is an instinct which teaches a man to avoid the fire, as much as that which teaches a bird, with such exactness, the art of incubation and the whole economy and order of its nursery.

SECTION X
Of Miracles.

Part I.

There is, in Dr. Tillotson's writings,[33] an argument against the *real presence*[34] which is as concise and elegant and strong as any argument can possibly be supposed against a doctrine so little worthy of a serious refutation. It is acknowledged on all hands, says that learned prelate, that the authority either of the Scripture or of tradition is founded merely in the testimony of the Apostles who were eyewitnesses to those miracles of our Savior by which he proved his divine mission. Our evidence, then, for the truth of the *Christian* religion is less than the evidence for the truth of our senses, because even in the first authors of our religion it was no greater; and it is evident it must diminish in passing from them to their disciples, nor can anyone rest such confidence in their testimony as in the immediate object of his senses. But a weaker evidence can never destroy a stronger; and, therefore, were the doctrine of the real presence ever so clearly revealed in scripture, it would be directly contrary to the rules of just reasoning to give our assent to it. It contradicts sense, though both the Scripture and tradition, on which it is supposed to be built, do not carry such evidence with them as sense, when they are considered merely as external evidences and are not brought home to everyone's breast by the immediate operation of the Holy Spirit.

Nothing is so convenient as a decisive argument of this kind, which must at least *silence* the most arrogant bigotry and superstition and free us from their impertinent solicitations. I flatter myself that I have discovered an argument of a like nature which, if just, will, with the wise and learned, be an everlasting check to all kinds of superstitious delusion and consequently will be useful as long as the world endures. For so long, I presume, will the accounts of miracles and prodigies be found in all history, sacred and profane.

Though experience is our only guide in reasoning concerning matters of fact, it must be acknowledged that this guide is not altogether infallible, but in some cases is apt to lead us into errors. One who in our climate should expect better weather in any week of June than in one of December would reason justly and conformably to experience, but it is certain that he may happen, in the event, to find himself mistaken. However, we may observe that in such a case he would have no cause to complain of experience, because it commonly informs us beforehand of the uncertainty by that contrariety of events which we may learn from a diligent observation. All effects do not follow with like certainty from their supposed causes. Some events are found, in all countries and all ages, to have been constantly conjoined together. Others are found to have been more variable and sometimes to disappoint our expectations, so that in our reasonings concerning matter of fact there are all imaginable degrees of assurance from the highest certainty to the lowest species of moral evidence.

A wise man, therefore, proportions his belief to the evidence. In such conclusions as are founded on an infallible experience, he expects the event with the last degree of assurance and regards his past experience as a full *proof* of the future existence of that event. In other cases he proceeds with more caution. He weighs the opposite experiments. He considers which side is supported by the greater number of experiments—to that side he inclines with doubt and hesitation; and when at last he fixes his judgment, the evidence does not exceed what we properly call

33. [John Tilloston (1630–1694), a Presbyterian theologian who became archbishop of Canterbury in 1691.]

34. [The reference is to the presence of the body and blood of Jesus in the bread and wine of the Christian sacrament of Holy Communion.]

probability. All probability, then, supposes an opposition of experiments and observations where the one side is found to overbalance the other and to produce a degree of evidence proportioned to the superiority. A hundred instances or experiments on one side and fifty on another afford a doubtful expectation of any event, though a hundred uniform experiments with only one that is contradictory reasonably beget a pretty strong degree of assurance. In all cases we must balance the opposite experiments where they are opposite and deduct the smaller number from the greater in order to know the exact force of the superior evidence.

To apply these principles to a particular instance, we may observe that there is no species of reasoning more common, more useful, and even necessary to human life than that which is derived from the testimony of men and the reports of eyewitnesses and spectators. This species of reasoning, perhaps, one may deny to be founded on the relation of cause and effect. I shall not dispute about a word. It will be sufficient to observe that our assurance in any argument of this kind is derived from no other principle than our observation of the veracity of human testimony and of the usual conformity of facts to the reports of witnesses. It being a general maxim that no objects have any discoverable connection together and that all the inferences which we can draw from one to another are founded merely on our experience of their constant and regular conjunction, it is evident that we ought not make an exception to this maxim in favor of human testimony whose connection with any event seems in itself as little necessary as any other. Were not the memory tenacious to a certain degree, had not men commonly an inclination to truth and a principle of probity, were they not sensible to shame when detected in a falsehood, were not these, I say, discovered by *experience* to be qualities inherent in human nature, we should never repose the least confidence in human testimony. A man delirious or noted for falsehood and villainy has no manner of authority with us.

And as the evidence derived from witnesses and human testimony is founded on past experience, so it varies with the experience and is regarded either as a *proof* or a *probability*, according as the conjunction between any particular kind of report and any kind of object has been found to be constant or variable. There are a number of circumstances to be taken into consideration in all judgments of this kind; and the ultimate standard by which we determine all disputes that may arise concerning them is always derived from experience and observation. Where this experience is not entirely uniform on any side, it is attended with an unavoidable contrariety in our judgments and with the same opposition and mutual destruction of argument as in every other kind of evidence. We frequently hesitate concerning the reports of others. We balance the opposite circumstances which cause any doubt or uncertainty; and when we discover a superiority on any side, we incline to it, but still with a diminution of assurance in proportion to the force of its antagonist.

This contrariety of evidence, in the present case, may be derived from several different causes: from the opposition of contrary testimony, from the character or number of the witnesses, from the manner of their delivering their testimony, or from the union of all these circumstances. We entertain a suspicion concerning any matter of fact when the witnesses contradict each other, when they are but few or of a doubtful character, when they have an interest in what they affirm, when they deliver their testimony with hesitation or, on the contrary, with too violent affirmations. There are many other particulars of the same kind which may diminish or destroy the force of any argument derived from human testimony.

Suppose, for instance, that the fact which the testimony endeavors to establish partakes of the extraordinary and the marvelous—in that case, the evidence resulting from the testimony admits of a diminution, greater or less in proportion as the fact is more or less unusual. The reason why we place any credit in witnesses and historians is not derived from any *connection* which we perceive *a priori* between testimony and reality, but because we are accustomed to find a conformity between them. But when the fact attested is such a one as has seldom fallen under our observation, here is a contest of two opposite experiences, of which the one destroys the other as far as its force goes and the superior can only operate on the mind by the force which remains. The very same principle of experience which gives us a certain degree of assurance in the testimony of witnesses gives us also, in this case, another degree of assurance against the fact which they endeavor to establish—

from which contradiction there necessarily arises a counterpoise and mutual destruction of belief and authority.

I should not believe such a story were it told me by Cato[35] was a proverbial saying in Rome, even during the lifetime of that philosophical patriot.[36] The incredibility of a fact, it was allowed, might invalidate so great an authority.

The Indian prince[37] who refused to believe the first relations concerning the effects of frost reasoned justly, and it naturally required very strong testimony to engage his assent to facts that arose from a state of nature with which he was unacquainted and which bore so little analogy to those events of which he had had constant and uniform experience. Though they were not contrary to his experience, they were not conformable to it.[38]

35. [The reference is to Marcus Porcius Cato (Cato the Younger) (95–46 B.C.), a Roman statesman and philosopher.]

36. Plutarch in *Vita Catonis*.

37. [An apparent reference to a story about the King of Siam.]

38. No Indian, it is evident, could have experience that water did not freeze in cold climates. This is placing nature in a situation quite unknown to him; and it is impossible for him to tell *a priori* what will result from it. It is making a new experiment, the consequence of which is always uncertain. One may sometimes conjecture from analogy what will follow; but still this is but conjecture. And it must be confessed, that, in the present case of freezing, the event follows contrary to the rules of analogy, and is such as a rational Indian would not look for. The operations of cold upon water are not gradual, according to the degrees of cold; but whenever it comes to the freezing point, the water passes in a moment, from the utmost liquidity to perfect hardness. Such an event, therefore, may be denominated *extraordinary*, and requires a pretty strong testimony, to render it credible to people in a warm climate. But still it is not *miraculous*, nor contrary to uniform experience of the course of nature in cases where all the circumstances are the same. The inhabitants of Sumatra have always seen water fluid in their own climate, and the freezing of their rivers ought to be deemed a prodigy: But they never saw water in Muscovy during the winter; and therefore they cannot reasonably be positive what would there be the consequence.

But in order to increase the probability against the testimony of witnesses, let us suppose that the fact which they affirm, instead of being only marvelous, is really miraculous, and suppose also that the testimony, considered apart and in itself, amounts to an entire proof—in that case, there is proof against proof, of which the strongest must prevail, but still with a diminution of its force in proportion to that of its antagonist.

A miracle is a violation of the laws of nature; and as a firm and unalterable experience has established these laws, the proof against a miracle, from the very nature of the fact, is as entire as any argument from experience can possibly be imagined. Why is it more than probable that all men must die, that lead cannot of itself remain suspended in the air, that fire consumes wood and is extinguished by water, unless it is that these events are found agreeable to the laws of nature and there is required a violation of these laws or, in other words, a miracle to prevent them? Nothing is esteemed a miracle if it ever happen in the common course of nature. It is no miracle that a man, seemingly in good health, should die all of a sudden, because such a kind of death, though more unusual than any other, has yet been frequently observed to happen. But it is a miracle that a dead man should come to life, because that has never been observed in any age or country. There must, therefore, be a uniform experience against every miraculous event; otherwise the event would not merit that appellation. And as a uniform experience amounts to a proof, there is here a direct and full *proof*, from the nature of the fact, against the existence of any miracle, nor can such a proof be destroyed or the miracle rendered credible but by an opposite proof which is superior.[39]

39. Sometimes an event may not, *in itself*, *seem* to be contrary to the laws of nature, and yet, if it were real, it might, by reason of some circumstances, be denominated a miracle; because, in *fact*, it is contrary to these laws. Thus if a person, claiming a divine authority, should command a sick person to be well, a healthful man to fall down dead, the clouds to pour rain, the winds to blow, in short, should order many natural events, which immediately follow upon his command; these might justly be esteemed miracles, because they are really, in this case, contrary to the laws of nature. For if any suspicion remain, that the event and command

The plain consequence is (and it is a general maxim worthy of our attention): that no testimony is sufficient to establish a miracle, unless the testimony is of such a kind that its falsehood would be more miraculous than the fact which it endeavors to establish; and even in that case there is a mutual destruction of arguments and the superior only gives us an assurance suitable to that degree of force which remains after deducting the inferior. When anyone tells me that he saw a dead man restored to life, I immediately consider with myself whether it is more probable that this person should either deceive or be deceived or that the fact which he relates should really have happened. I weigh the one miracle against the other and, according to the superiority which I discover, I pronounce my decision and always reject the greater miracle. If the falsehood of his testimony would be more miraculous than the event which he relates, then, and not until then, can he pretend to command my belief or opinion.

Part II.

In the foregoing reasoning we have supposed that the testimony upon which a miracle is founded may possibly amount to an entire proof and that the falsehood of that testimony would be a real prodigy. But it is easy to show that we have been a great deal too liberal in our concession and that there never was a miraculous event established on so full an evidence.

For *first*, there is not to be found, in all history, any miracle attested by a sufficient number of men of such unquestioned good sense, education, and learning, as to secure us against all delusion in themselves; of such undoubted integrity as to place them beyond all suspicion of any design to deceive others; of such credit and reputation in the eyes of mankind as to have a great deal to lose in case of their being detected in any falsehood, and at the same time attesting facts performed in such a public manner and in so celebrated a part of the world as to render the detection unavoidable—all which circumstances are requisite to give us a full assurance in the testimony of men.

Secondly, we may observe in human nature a principle which, if strictly examined, will be found to diminish extremely the assurance which we might, from human testimony, have in any kind of prodigy. The maxim by which we commonly conduct ourselves in our reasonings is that the objects of which we have no experience resemble those of which we have; that what we have found to be most usual is always most probable; and that where there is an opposition of arguments, we ought to give the preference to such as are founded on the greatest number of past observations. But though, in proceeding by this rule, we readily reject any fact which is unusual and incredible in an ordinary degree, yet in advancing further, the mind does not observe always the same rule; but when anything is affirmed utterly absurd and miraculous, it rather the more readily admits of such a fact upon account of that very circumstance which ought to destroy all its authority. The passion of *surprise* and *wonder*, arising from miracles, being an agreeable emotion, gives a sensible tendency towards the belief of those events from which it is derived. And this goes so far that even those who cannot enjoy this pleasure immediately, nor can believe those miraculous events of which they are informed, yet love to partake of the satisfaction at secondhand or by rebound, and place a pride and delight in exciting the admiration of others.

With what greediness are the miraculous accounts of travelers received, their descriptions of sea and land monsters, their relations of wonderful adventures, strange men, and uncouth manners? But if the spirit of religion joins itself to the love of wonder, there is an end of common sense and human testimony in these circumstances loses all pretensions to authority. A religionist may be an enthusiast and imagine he sees what has no reality. He may know his narrative to be false and yet persevere in it with the best

concurred by accident, there is no miracle, and a transgression of these laws; because nothing can be more contrary to nature than that the voice or command of a man should have such an influence. A miracle may be accurately defined, *a transgression of a law of nature by a particular volition of the Deity, or by the interposition of some invisible agent.* A miracle may either be discoverable by men or not. This alters not its nature and essence. The raising of a house or ship into the air is a visible miracle. The raising of a feather, when the wind wants ever so little of a force requisite for that purpose, is as real a miracle, though not so sensible with regard to us.

intentions in the world, for the sake of promoting so holy a cause. Or even where this delusion does not have place, vanity, excited by so strong a temptation, operates on him more powerfully than on the rest of mankind in any other circumstances, and self-interest with equal force. His auditors may not have and commonly do not have sufficient judgment to canvass his evidence. What judgment they have, they renounce by principle in these sublime and mysterious subjects. Or if they were ever so willing to employ it, passion and a heated imagination disturb the regularity of its operations. Their credulity increases his impudence and his impudence overpowers their credulity.

Eloquence, when at its highest pitch, leaves little room for reason or reflection, but, addressing itself entirely to the fancy or the affections, captivates the willing hearers and subdues their understanding. Happily, this pitch it seldom attains. But what a Tully[40] or a Demosthenes[41] could scarcely effect over a Roman or Athenian audience, every Capuchin,[42] every itinerant or stationary teacher can perform over the generality of mankind, and in a higher degree by touching such gross and vulgar passions.

The many instances of forged miracles and prophecies and supernatural events, which, in all ages, have either been detected by contrary evidence or which detect themselves by their absurdity, prove sufficiently the strong propensity of mankind to the extraordinary and the marvelous and ought reasonably to beget a suspicion against all relations of this kind. This is our natural way of thinking, even with regard to the most common and most credible events. For instance, there is no kind of report which rises so easily and spreads so quickly, especially in country places and provincial towns, as those concerning marriages, insomuch that two young persons of equal condition never see each other twice, but the whole neighborhood immediately join them together. The pleasure of telling a piece of news so interesting, of propagating it, and of being the first reporters of it spreads the intelligence. And this is so well known that no man of sense gives attention to these reports until he finds them confirmed by some greater evidence. Do not the same passions, and others still stronger, incline the generality of mankind to believe and report with the greatest vehemence and assurance all religious miracles?

Thirdly, it forms a strong presumption against all supernatural and miraculous relations that they are observed chiefly to abound among ignorant and barbarous nations; or if a civilized people has ever given admission to any of them that people will be found to have received them from ignorant and barbarous ancestors, who transmitted them with that inviolable sanction and authority which always attend received opinions. When we peruse the first histories of all nations, we are apt to imagine ourselves transported into some new world where the whole frame of nature is disjointed and every element performs its operations in a different manner from what it does at present. Battles, revolutions, pestilence, famine, and death are never the effect of those natural causes which we experience. Prodigies, omens, oracles, judgments quite obscure the few natural events that are intermingled with them. But as the former grow thinner every page, in proportion as we advance nearer the enlightened ages, we soon learn that there is nothing mysterious or supernatural in the case, but that all proceeds from the usual propensity of mankind towards the marvelous, and that, though this inclination may at intervals receive a check from sense and learning, it can never be thoroughly extirpated from human nature.

It is strange, a judicious reader is apt to say, upon the perusal of these wonderful historians, that *such prodigious events never happen in our days*. But it is nothing strange, I hope, that men should lie in all ages. You must surely have seen instances enough of that frailty. You have yourself heard many such marvelous relations started which, being treated with scorn by all the wise and judicious, have at last been abandoned even by the vulgar. Be assured that those renowned lies which have spread and flourished to such a monstrous height arose from like beginnings, but being sown in a more proper soil, shot up at last into prodigies almost equal to those which they relate.

It was a wise policy in that false prophet Alexander, who, though now forgotten, was once so famous, to

40. [Marcus Tullius Cicero (106–43 B.C.), the statesman and philosopher, was considered the greatest Roman orator.]

41. [Demosthenes (c. 384–322 B.C.), was a famous Greek orator.]

42. [The Capuchins, founded in the sixteenth century, were Franciscan friars who did extensive preaching and missionary work.]

lay the first scene of his impostures in Paphlagonia, where, as Lucian tells us,[43] the people were extremely ignorant and stupid and ready to swallow even the grossest delusion. People at a distance, who are weak enough to think the matter at all worth inquiry, have no opportunity of receiving better information. The stories come magnified to them by a hundred circumstances. Fools are industrious in propagating the imposture, while the wise and learned are contented, in general, to deride its absurdity, without informing themselves of the particular facts by which it may be distinctly refuted. And thus the impostor above mentioned was enabled to proceed from his ignorant Paphlagonians to the enlisting of votaries, even among the Greek philosophers and men of the most eminent rank and distinction in Rome—No, could engage the attention of that sage emperor Marcus Aurelius[44] so far as to make him trust the success of a military expedition to his delusive prophecies.

The advantages are so great of starting an imposture among an ignorant people that, even though the delusion should be too gross to impose on the generality of them (*which, though seldom, is sometimes the case*), it has a much better chance for succeeding in remote countries than if the first scene had been laid in a city renowned for arts and knowledge. The most ignorant and barbarous of these barbarians carry the report abroad. None of their countrymen have a large correspondence or sufficient credit and authority to contradict and beat down the delusion. Men's inclination to the marvelous has full opportunity to display itself. And thus a story which is universally exploded in the place where it was first started shall pass for certain at a thousand miles distance. But had Alexander fixed his residence at Athens, the philosophers of that renowned mart of learning had immediately spread throughout the whole Roman empire their sense of the matter, which, being supported by so great authority and displayed by all the force of reason and eloquence, had entirely opened the eyes of mankind. It is true, Lucian, passing by chance through, had an opportunity of performing this good office. But, though much to be wished, it does not always happen that every Alexander meets with a Lucian, ready to expose and detect his impostures.

I may add, as a *fourth* reason which diminishes the authority of prodigies, that there is no testimony for any, even those which have not been expressly detected, that is not opposed by an infinite number of witnesses, so that not only the miracle destroys the credit of testimony, but the testimony destroys itself. To make this the better understood, let us consider, that in matters of religion whatever is different is contrary and that it is impossible the religions of ancient Rome, of Turkey, of Siam, and of China should all of them be established on any solid foundation. Every miracle, therefore, pretended to have been wrought in any of these religions (and all of them abound in miracles), as its direct scope is to establish the particular system to which it is attributed, so it has the same force, though more indirectly, to overthrow every other system. In destroying a rival system, it likewise destroys the credit of those miracles on which that system was established, so that all the prodigies of different religions are to be regarded as contrary facts and the evidences of these prodigies, whether weak or strong, as opposite to each other. According to this method of reasoning, when we believe any miracle of Mahomet or his successors, we have for our warrant the testimony of a few barbarous Arabians. And, on the other hand, we are to regard the authority of Titus Livius,[45] Plutarch, Tacitus, and, in short, of all the authors and witnesses, Greek, Chinese, and Roman Catholic, who have related any miracle in their particular religion—I say, we are to regard their testimony in the same light as if they had mentioned that Mahometan miracle and had in express terms contradicted it with the same certainty as they have for the miracle they relate. This argument may appear over subtle and refined, but is not in reality different from the reasoning of a judge who supposes that the credit of two witnesses maintaining a crime against anyone is destroyed by the testimony of two others

43. [In *Alexander, the False Prophet*, the Greek writer Lucian (c. 120–c. 180) relates how Alexander of Abonoteichos was hailed as an oracle because of a hoax perpetrated on the people of Paphlagonia, an ancient country in Asia Minor located in what is now Turkey.]

44. [Marcus Aurelius (121–180) was a Roman emperor and a major Stoic philosopher.]

45. [Titus Livius (59 B.C.–17 A.D.), commonly known as Livy, was a Roman historian; his major work, the 142-book *History of Rome*, covered Rome's beginnings until his own time.]

who affirm him to have been two hundred leagues distant at the same instant when the crime is said to have been committed.

One of the best attested miracles in all profane history is that which Tacitus[46] reports of Vespasian,[47] who cured a blind man in Alexandria by means of his spittle and a lame man by the mere touch of his foot, in obedience to a vision of the god Serapis, who had enjoined them to have recourse to the Emperor for these miraculous cures. The story may be seen in that fine historian,[48] where every circumstance seems to add weight to the testimony, and might be displayed at large with all the force of argument and eloquence, if anyone were now concerned to enforce the evidence of that exploded and idolatrous superstition: the gravity, solidity, age, and probity of so great an emperor, who, through the whole course of his life, conversed in a familiar manner with his friends and courtiers and never affected those extraordinary airs of divinity assumed by Alexander and Demetrius;[49] the historian, a contemporary writer noted for candor and veracity, and in addition the greatest and most penetrating genius perhaps of all antiquity, and so free from any tendency to credulity that he even lies under the contrary imputation of atheism and profaneness; the persons from whose authority he related the miracle of established character for judgment and veracity, as we may well presume; eyewitnesses of the fact, and confirming their testimony after the Flavian family was despoiled of the empire and could no longer give any reward as the price of a lie. *Utrumque, qui interfuere, nunc quoque memorant, postquam nullum mendacio pretium.*[50] To which, if we add the public nature of the facts, as related, it will appear that no evidence can well be supposed stronger for so gross and so palpable a falsehood.

There is also a memorable story related by Cardinal de Retz,[51] which may well deserve our consideration. When that intriguing politician fled into Spain to avoid the persecution of his enemies, he passed through Saragossa, the capital of Arragon, where he was shown, in the cathedral, a man who had served seven years as a doorkeeper and was well known to everybody in town who had ever paid his devotions at that church. He had been seen for so long a time wanting a leg, but recovered that limb by the rubbing of holy oil upon the stump; and when the Cardinal examined it, he found it to be a true natural leg like the other. This miracle was vouched by all the canons of the church; and the whole company in town were appealed to for a confirmation of the fact, whom the cardinal found, by their zealous devotion, to be thorough believers of the miracle. Here the relater was also contemporary to the supposed prodigy, of an incredulous and libertine character, as well as of great genius; the miracle of so *singular* a nature as could scarcely admit of a counterfeit, and the witnesses very numerous, and all of them, in a manner, spectators of the fact to which they gave their testimony. And what adds mightily to the force of the evidence and may double our surprise on this occasion is that the Cardinal himself, who relates the story, does not seem to give any credit to it and, consequently, cannot be suspected of any concurrence in the holy fraud. He considered justly that it was not requisite, in order to reject a fact of this nature, to be able accurately to disprove the testimony and to trace its falsehood through all the circumstances of knavery and credulity which produced it. He knew that, as this was commonly altogether impossible at any small distance of time and place, so was it extremely difficult, even where one was immediately present, by reason of the bigotry, ignorance, cunning, and roguery of a great part of mankind. He therefore

46. [Vespasian (9–79) was emperor of Rome and founder of the Flavian dynasty, which ruled from 69 to 96.]

47. Hist. Bk. IV, Chap. 81. Suetonius gives nearly the same account in VESP.7. [Suetonius (69–140) was a Roman biographer.]

48. [Demetrius I (c. 336–283 B.C.) was a ruler of Macedon.]

49. Those who were present recount both events even now, when nothing is to be gained from deceit.

50. [Cardinal de Retz (1613–1679) was a French political leader.]

51. [Miraculous cures were said to occur at the tomb of François de Paris (1690–1727), a follower of the doctrine of Bishop Cornelius Jansen (1585–1638), founder of Jansenism, a Roman Catholic movement that stressed moral austerity and predestination. Notable French Jansenists included the scientist and philosopher Blaise Pascal (1623–1662), the dramatist Jean Racine (1639–1699), the priest and philosopher Antoine Arnauld (1612–1694), and the writer Pierre Nicole (1625–1695).]

concluded, like a just reasoner, that such an evidence carried falsehood upon the very face of it and that a miracle supported by any human testimony was more properly a subject of derision than of argument.

There surely never was a greater number of miracles ascribed to one person than those which were lately said to have been wrought in France upon the tomb of Abbé Paris, the famous Jansenist,[52] with whose sanctity the people were so long deluded. The curing of the sick, giving hearing to the deaf and sight to the blind, were everywhere talked of as the usual effects of that holy sepulcher. But what is more extraordinary, many of the miracles were immediately proved upon the spot, before judges of unquestioned integrity, attested by witnesses of credit and distinc-

52. This book was writ by Mons. Montgerron, counsellor or judge of the parliament of Paris, a man of figure and character, who was also a martyr to the cause, and is now said to be somewhere in a dungeon on account of his book.

There is another book in three volumes (called *Recuiel des Miracles de l'Abbé Paris*) giving an account of many of these miracles, and accompanied with prefatory discourses, which are very well written. There runs, however, through the whole of these a ridiculous comparison between the miracles of our Saviour and those of the Abbé; wherein it is asserted, that the evidence for the latter is equal to that for the former: As if the testimony of men could ever be put in the balance with that of God himself, who conducted the pen of the inspired writers. If these writers, indeed, were to be considered merely as human testimony, the French author is very moderate in his comparison: Since he might, with some appearance of reason, pretend, that the Jansenist miracles much surpass the other in evidence and authority. The following circumstances are drawn from authentic papers, inserted in the above-mentioned book.

Many of the miracles of Abbé Paris were proved immediately by witnesses before the officiality or bishop's court at Paris, under the eye of cardinal Noailles, whose character for integrity and capacity was never contested even by his enemies.

His successor in the archbishopric was an enemy to the Jansenists, and for that reason promoted to the see by the court. Yet 22 rectors or *curés* of Paris, with infinite earnestness, press him to examine those miracles, which they assert to be known to the whole world, and undisputably certain: But he wisely forbore.

The Molinist party had tried to discredit these miracles in one instance, that of Madamoiselle le Franc. [The Molinists were Jesuits who followed the teachings of the Spanish theologian Luis de Molina (1535–1600).] But, besides that their proceedings were in many respects the most irregular in the world, particularly in citing only a few of the Jansenist witnesses, whom they tampered with: Besides this, I say, they soon found themselves overwhelmed by a cloud of new witnesses, one hundred and twenty in number, most of them persons of credit and substance in Paris, who gave oath for the miracle. This was accompanied with a solemn and earnest appeal to the parliament. But the parliament were forbidden by authority to meddle in the affair. It was at last observed, that where men are heated by zeal and enthusiasm, there is no degree of human testimony so strong as may not be procured for the greatest absurdity: And those who will be so silly as to examine the affair by that medium, and seek particular flaws in the testimony, are almost sure to be confounded. It must be a miserable imposture, indeed, that does not prevail in that contest.

All who have been in France about that time have heard of the reputation of Mons. Heraut, the *lieutenant de Police*, whose vigilance, penetration, activity, and extensive intelligence have been much talked of. This magistrate, who by the nature of his office is almost absolute, was invested with full powers, on purpose to suppress or discredit these miracles; and he frequently seized immediately, and examined the witnesses and subjects of them: But never could reach any thing satisfactory against them.

In the case of Madamoiselle Thibaut he sent the famous De Sylva to examine her; whose evidence is very curious. The physician declares, that it was impossible she could have been so ill as was proved by witnesses; because it was impossible she could, in so short a time, have recovered so perfectly as he found her. He reasoned, like a man of sense, from natural causes; but the opposite party told him, that the whole was a miracle, and that his evidence was the best proof of it.

The Molinists were in a sad dilemma. They durst not assert the absolute insufficiency of human evidence, to prove a miracle. They were obliged to say, that these miracles were wrought by witchcraft and the devil. But they were told, that this was the resource of the Jews of old.

No Jansenist was ever embarrassed to account for the cessation of the miracles, when the church-yard was shut up by the king's edict. It was the touch of the tomb, which produced these extraordinary effects; and when no one could approach the tomb, no effects could be expected. God, indeed, could have thrown down the walls in a moment; but he is master of his own graces and works, and it belongs not to us to account for them. He did not throw down the walls of every city like those of Jericho, on the sounding of the rams' horns, nor break up the prison of every apostle, like that of St. Paul.

tion, in a learned age, and on the most eminent theater that is now in the world. Nor is this all: A relation of them was published and dispersed everywhere, nor were the *Jesuits*, though a learned body supported by the civil magistrate and determined enemies to those opinions in whose favor the miracles were said to have been wrought, ever able distinctly to refute or detect them. Where shall we find such a number of circumstances agreeing to the corroboration of one fact? And what have we to oppose to such a cloud of witnesses but the absolute impossibility or miraculous nature of the events which they relate? And this, surely, in the eyes of all reasonable people, will alone be regarded as a sufficient refutation.

Is the consequence just, because some human testimony has the utmost force and authority in some cases, when it relates the battle of Philippi[53] or Pharsalia,[54] for instance, that therefore all kinds of testimony must in all cases have equal force and authority? Suppose that the Caesarean and Pompeian factions had, each of them, claimed the victory in these battles, and that the historians of each party had uniformly ascribed the advantage to their own side, how could mankind, at this distance, have been able to determine between them? The contrariety is equally strong between the miracles related by Herodotus[55] or Plutarch and those delivered by Mariana,[56] Bede,[57] or any monkish historian.

The wise lend a very academic faith to every report which favors the passion of the reporter, whether it magnifies his country, his family, or himself, or in any other way strikes in with his natural inclinations and propensities. But what greater temptation than to appear a missionary, a prophet, an ambassador from heaven? Who would not encounter many dangers and difficulties in order to attain so sublime a character? Or if, by the help of vanity and a heated imagination, a man has first made a convert of himself and entered seriously into the delusion, who ever scruples to make use of pious frauds in support of so holy and meritorious a cause?

The smallest spark may here kindle into the greatest

No less a man, than the Duc de Chatillon, a duke and peer of France, of the highest rank and family, gives evidence of a miraculous cure, performed upon a servant of his, who had lived several years in his house with a visible and palpable infirmity.

I shall conclude with observing, that no clergy are more celebrated for strictness of life and manners than the secular clergy of France, particularly the rectors of curés of Paris, who bear testimony to these impostures.

The learning, genius, and probity of the gentlemen, and the austerity of the nuns of Port-Royal, have been much celebrated all over Europe. Yet they all give evidence for a miracle, wrought on the niece of the famous Pascal, whose sanctity of life, as well as extraordinary capacity, is well known. The famous Racine gives an account of this miracle in his famous history of Port-Royal, and fortifies it with all the proofs, which a multitude of nuns, priests, physicians, and men of the world, all of them of undoubted credit, could bestow upon it. Several men of letters, particularly the bishop of Tournay, thought this miracle so certain, as to employ it in the refutation of atheists and free-thinkers. The queen-regent of France, who was extremely prejudiced against the Port-Royal, sent her own physician to examine the miracle, who returned an absolute convert. In short, the supernatural cure was so uncontestable, that it saved, for a time, that famous monastery from the ruin with which it was threatened by the Jesuits. Had it been a cheat, it had certainly been detected by such sagacious and powerful antagonists, and must have hastened the ruin of the contrivers. Our divines, who can build up a formidable castle from such despicable materials; what a prodigious fabric could they have reared from these and many other circumstances, which I have not mentioned! How often would the great names of Pascal, Racine, Arnauld, Nicole, have resounded in our ears? But if they be wise, they had better adopt the miracle, as being more worth, a thousand times, than all the rest of their collection. Besides, it may serve very much to their purpose. For that miracle was really performed by the touch of an authentic holy prickle of the holy thorn, which composed the holy crown, which, &c.

53. [Philippi, a city in Eastern Macedonia, was in 42 B.C. the scene of two decisive battles in Roman history, at which Octavian (Augustus) and Marc Antony defeated Brutus and Cassius.]

54. [The battle of Pharsalia was fought in 48 B.C. in Pharsalus, a city in Thessaly, Greece, where, at a vital juncture in Roman history, Julius Caesar triumphed over Pompey.]

55. [Herodotus (c. 484–c. 425 B.C.) was the Greek historian, often referred to as "the Father of History," who wrote *The Persian Wars*.]

56. [The reference is to Juan de Mariana (c. 1536–c. 1623), a Spanish Jesuit and historian, who wrote a history of Spain.]

57. [Bede (673–735), an English historian and Benedictine monk, wrote an ecclesiastical history of England.]

flame, because the materials are always prepared for it. The *avidum genus auricularum*,[58] the gazing populace, receive greedily, without examination, whatever soothes superstition and promotes wonder.

How many stories of this nature have, in all ages, been detected and exploded in their infancy? How many more have been celebrated for a time and have afterwards sunk into neglect and oblivion? Where such reports, therefore, fly about, the solution of the phenomenon is obvious and we judge in conformity to regular experience and observation when we account for it by the known and natural principles of credulity and delusion. And shall we, rather than have a recourse to so natural a solution, allow of a miraculous violation of the most established laws of nature?

I need not mention the difficulty of detecting a falsehood in any private or even public history at the place where it is said to happen, much more when the scene is removed to ever so small a distance. Even a court of judicature, with all the authority, accuracy, and judgment, which they can employ, find themselves often at a loss to distinguish between truth and falsehood in the most recent actions. But the matter never comes to any issue, if trusted to the common method of altercation and debate and flying rumors, especially when men's passions have taken part on either side.

In the infancy of new religions, the wise and learned commonly esteem the matter too inconsiderable to deserve their attention or regard. And when afterwards they would willingly detect the cheat in order to undeceive the deluded multitude, the season is now past and the records and witnesses which might clear up the matter have perished beyond recovery.

No means of detection remain but those which must be drawn from the very testimony itself of the reporters. And these, though always sufficient with the judicious and knowing, are commonly too fine to fall under the comprehension of the vulgar.

Upon the whole, then, it appears that no testimony for any kind of miracle has ever amounted to a probability, much less to a proof; and that, even supposing it amounted to a proof, it would be opposed by another proof derived from the very nature of the fact which it would endeavor to establish. It is experience only which gives authority to human testimony and it is the same experience which assures us of the laws of nature. When, therefore, these two kinds of experience are contrary, we have nothing to do but subtract the one from the other and embrace an opinion either on one side or the other with that assurance which arises from the remainder. But according to the principle here explained, this subtraction with regard to all popular religions amounts to an entire annihilation and, therefore, we may establish it as a maxim that no human testimony can have such force as to prove a miracle and make it a just foundation for any such system of religion.

I beg the limitations here made may be remarked, when I say that a miracle can never be proved so as to be the foundation of a system of religion. For I admit that otherwise there may possibly be miracles or violations of the usual course of nature of such a kind as to admit of proof from human testimony; though perhaps it will be impossible to find any such in all the records of history. Thus, suppose all authors, in all languages, agree that from the first of January 1600 there was a total darkness over the whole earth for eight days; suppose that the tradition of this extraordinary event is still strong and lively among the people—that all travelers who return from foreign countries bring us accounts of the same tradition without the least variation or contradiction—it is evident that our present philosophers, instead of doubting the fact, ought to receive it as certain and ought to search for the causes from which it might be derived. The decay, corruption, and dissolution of nature is an event rendered probable by so many analogies that any phenomenon which seems to have a tendency towards that catastrophe comes within the reach of human testimony, if that testimony is very extensive and uniform.

But suppose that all the historians who treat of England should agree that on the first of January 1600, Queen Elizabeth died; that both before and after her death she was seen by her physicians and the whole court, as is usual with persons of her rank; that her successor was acknowledged and proclaimed by the parliament; and that, after being interred a month, she again appeared, resumed the throne, and governed England for three years—I must confess that I should be surprised at the concurrence of so

58. [Gossipy race.]

many odd circumstances, but should not have the least inclination to believe so miraculous an event. I should not doubt of her pretended death and of those other public circumstances that followed it; I should only assert it to have been pretended, and that it neither was nor possibly could be real. You would in vain object to me the difficulty and almost impossibility of deceiving the world in an affair of such consequence; the wisdom and solid judgment of that renowned queen, with the little or no advantage which she could reap from so poor an artifice—all this might astonish me, but I would still reply that the knavery and folly of men are such common phenomena that I should rather believe the most extraordinary events to arise from their concurrence than admit of so signal a violation of the laws of nature.

But should this miracle be ascribed to any new system of religion, men in all ages have been so much imposed on by ridiculous stories of that kind that this very circumstance would be a full proof of a cheat and sufficient, with all men of sense, not only to make them reject the fact, but even reject it without further examination. Though the Being to whom the miracle is ascribed is in this case Almighty, it does not, upon that account, become a whit more probable, since it is impossible for us to know the attributes or actions of such a Being otherwise than from the experience which we have of his productions in the usual course of nature. This still reduces us to past observation and obliges us to compare the instances of the violation of truth in the testimony of men with those of the violation of the laws of nature by miracles, in order to judge which of them is most likely and probable. As the violations of truth are more common in the testimony concerning religious miracles than in that concerning any other matter of fact, this must diminish very much the authority of the former testimony and make us form a general resolution, never to lend any attention to it, with whatever specious pretense it may be covered.

Lord Bacon seems to have embraced the same principles of reasoning. "We ought," says he, "make a collection or particular history of all monsters and prodigious births or productions and, in a word, of everything new, rare, and extraordinary in nature. But this must be done with the most severe scrutiny, lest we depart from truth. Above all, every relation must be considered as suspicious which depends in any degree upon religion, as the prodigies of Livy. And no less so, everything that is to be found in the writers of natural magic or alchemy or such authors who seem, all of them, to have an unconquerable appetite for falsehood and fable."[59]

I am the better pleased with the method of reasoning here delivered, as I think it may serve to confound those dangerous friends or disguised enemies to the *Christian Religion* who have undertaken to defend it by the principles of human reason. Our most holy religion is founded on Faith, not on reason; and it is a sure method of exposing it to put it to such a trial as it is by no means fitted to endure. To make this more evident, let us examine those miracles related in Scripture and, not to lose ourselves in too wide a field, let us confine ourselves to such as we find in the *Pentateuch*,[60] which we shall examine according to the principles of these pretended Christians, not as the word or testimony of God himself, but as the production of a mere human writer and historian. Here then we are first to consider a book presented to us by a barbarous and ignorant people, written in an age when they were still more barbarous, and in all probability long after the facts which it relates, corroborated by no concurring testimony, and resembling those fabulous accounts which every nation gives of its origin. Upon reading this book we find it full of prodigies and miracles. It gives an account of a state of the world and of human nature entirely different from the present: of our fall from that state; of the age of man extended to near a thousand years; of the destruction of the world by a deluge; of the arbitrary choice of one people as the favorites of heaven, and that people the countrymen of the author; of their deliverance from bondage by prodigies the most astonishing imaginable: I desire anyone to lay his hand upon his heart and, after a serious consideration, declare whether he thinks that the falsehood of such a book, supported by such a testimony, would be more extraordinary and miraculous than all the

59. *Novum Organum* lib.11.aph.29. [The reference is to Francis Bacon (1561–1626), an English philosopher and statesman, who stressed the importance of scientific methodology in the acquisition of knowledge.]

60. [The Pentateuch, the Five Books of Moses, is the first five books of the Bible: Genesis, Exodus, Leviticus, Numbers, and Deuteronomy.]

miracles it relates—which is, however, necessary to make it be received according to the measures of probability above established.

What we have said of miracles may be applied without any variation to prophecies; and, indeed, all prophecies are real miracles and as such only can be admitted as proofs of any revelation. If it did not exceed the capacity of human nature to foretell future events, it would be absurd to employ any prophecy as an argument for a divine mission or authority from heaven. So that, upon the whole, we may conclude that the Christian religion not only was at first attended with miracles, but even at this day cannot be believed by any reasonable person without one. Mere reason is insufficient to convince us of its veracity. And whoever is moved by faith to assent to it is conscious of a continued miracle in his own person which subverts all the principles of his understanding and gives him a determination to believe what is most contrary to custom and experience.

Section XI
Of a Particular Providence and of a Future State.

I was lately engaged in conversation with a friend who loves skeptical paradoxes, where, though he advanced many principles of which I can by no means approve, yet as they seem to be curious and to bear some relation to the chain of reasoning carried on throughout this inquiry, I shall here copy them from my memory as accurately as I can in order to submit them to the judgment of the reader.

Our conversation began with my admiring the singular good fortune of philosophy, which, as it requires entire liberty above all other privileges and chiefly flourishes from the free opposition of sentiments and argumentation, received its first birth in an age and country of freedom and toleration, and was never cramped, even in its most extravagant principles, by any creeds, confessions, or penal statutes. For, except the banishment of Protagoras[61] and the death of Socrates, which last event proceeded partly from other motives, there are scarcely any instances to be met with, in ancient history, of this bigoted jealousy with which the present age is so much infested. Epicurus lived at Athens to an advanced age in peace and tranquillity. Epicureans[62] were even admitted to receive the sacerdotal character and to officiate at the altar in the most sacred rites of the established religion. And the public encouragement[63] of pensions and salaries was afforded equally by the wisest of all the Roman emperors[64] to the professors of every sect of philosophy. How requisite such kind of treatment was to philosophy, in her early youth, will easily be conceived, if we reflect that even at present, when she may be supposed more hardy and robust, she bears with much difficulty the inclemency of the seasons and those harsh winds of calumny and persecution which blow upon her.

You admire, says my friend, as the singular good fortune of philosophy what seems to result from the natural course of things and to be unavoidable in every age and nation. This pertinacious bigotry, of which you complain as so fatal to philosophy, is really her offspring who, after allying with superstition, separates himself entirely from the interest of his parent and becomes her most inveterate enemy and persecutor. Speculative dogmas of religion, the present occasions of such furious dispute, could not possibly be conceived or admitted in the early ages of the world, when mankind, being wholly illiterate, formed an idea of religion more suitable to their weak apprehension and composed their sacred tenets of such tales chiefly as were the objects of traditional belief more than of argument or disputation. After the first alarm, therefore, was over, which arose from the new paradoxes and principles of the philosophers, these teachers seem ever after, during the ages of antiquity, to have lived in great harmony with the established superstition and to have made a fair partition of mankind between them—the former claiming all the learned and wise, the latter possessing all the vulgar and illiterate.

It seems then, I say, that you leave politics entirely

61. [Protagoras of Abdera (c. 490–c. 421 B.C.) was an outstanding Sophist who was exiled from Athens because of his religious views, which were said to be impious.]

62. Luciani συμπ. ἢ λαπίθαι. 9. [*The Drinking Party* or *Lapiths* (a mythological people).]

63. Luciani εὐνοῦχος 3. [*The Eunuch.*]

64. Id. & Dio. [*The Eunuch* and Dio Cassius (c. 150–c. 235), *History of Rome,* Bk. LXXII.]

out of the question and never suppose that a wise magistrate can justly be jealous of certain tenets of philosophy, such as those of Epicurus, which, denying a divine existence and consequently a providence and a future state, seem to loosen in a great measure the ties of morality and may be supposed, for that reason, pernicious to the peace of civil society.

I know, he replied, that in fact these persecutions never, in any age, proceeded from calm reason or from experience of the pernicious consequences of philosophy, but arose entirely from passion and prejudice. But what if I should advance further and assert that, if Epicurus had been accused before the people by any of the *sycophants* or informers of those days, he could easily have defended his cause and proved his principles of philosophy to be as salutary as those of his adversaries who endeavored with such zeal to expose him to the public hatred and jealousy?

I wish, I said, you would try your eloquence upon so extraordinary a topic and make a speech for Epicurus which might satisfy, not the mob of Athens, if you will allow that ancient and polite city to have contained any mob, but the more philosophical part of his audience, such as might be supposed capable of comprehending his arguments.

The matter would not be difficult upon such conditions, he replied; and if you please, I shall suppose myself Epicurus for a moment and make you stand for the Athenian people, and shall deliver you such an harangue as will fill all the urn with white beans and leave not a black one to gratify the malice of my adversaries.[65]

Very well. Pray proceed upon these suppositions.

I come here, O you Athenians, to justify in your assembly what I maintained in my school and I find myself impeached by furious antagonists, instead of reasoning with calm and dispassionate inquirers. Your deliberations, which of right should be directed to questions of public good and the interest of the commonwealth, are diverted to the disquisitions of speculative philosophy, and these magnificent, but perhaps fruitless inquiries take place of your more familiar, but more useful occupations. But so far as in me lies I will prevent this abuse. We shall not here dispute concerning the origin and government of worlds. We shall only inquire how far such questions concern the public interest. And if I can persuade you that they are entirely indifferent to the peace of society and security of government, I hope that you will presently send us back to our schools, there to examine at leisure the question, the most sublime, but, at the same time, the most speculative of all philosophy.

The religious philosophers, not satisfied with the tradition of your forefathers and doctrine of your priests (in which I willingly acquiesce), indulge a rash curiosity in trying how far they can establish religion upon the principles of reason; and they thereby excite, instead of satisfying, the doubts which naturally arise from a diligent and scrutinous inquiry. They paint in the most magnificent colors the order, beauty, and wise arrangement of the universe and then ask if such a glorious display of intelligence could proceed from the fortuitous concourse of atoms or if chance could produce what the greatest genius can never sufficiently admire. I shall not examine the justness of this argument. I shall allow it to be as solid as my antagonists and accusers can desire. It is sufficient if I can prove, from this very reasoning, that the question is entirely speculative, and that, when, in my philosophical disquisitions, I deny a providence and a future state, I do not undermine the foundations of society, but advance principles which they themselves, upon their own topics, if they argue consistently, must allow to be solid and satisfactory.

You then, who are my accusers, have acknowledged that the chief or sole argument for a divine existence (which I never questioned) is derived from the order of nature, where there appear such marks of intelligence and design that you think it extravagant to assign for its cause either chance or the blind and unguided force of matter. You allow that this is an argument drawn from effects to causes. From the order of the work you infer that there must have been project and forethought in the workman. If you cannot make out this point, you allow that your conclusion fails and you do not pretend to establish the conclusion in a greater latitude than the phenomena of nature will justify. These are your concessions. I desire you to mark the consequences.

When we infer any particular cause from an effect, we must proportion the one to the other and can never be allowed to ascribe to the cause any qualities but what are exactly sufficient to produce the effect.

65. [In Athenian balloting white beans signified agreement, black ones disagreement.]

A body of ten ounces raised in any scale may serve as a proof that the counterbalancing weight exceeds ten ounces, but can never afford a reason that it exceeds a hundred. If the cause assigned for any effect is not sufficient to produce it, we must either reject that cause or add to it such qualities as will give it a just proportion to the effect. But if we ascribe to it further qualities or affirm it capable of producing other effects, we can only indulge the license of conjecture and arbitrarily suppose the existence of qualities and energies without reason or authority.

The same rule holds whether the cause assigned is brute unconscious matter or a rational intelligent being. If the cause is known only by the effect, we never ought to ascribe to it any qualities beyond what are precisely requisite to produce the effect; nor can we, by any rules of just reasoning, return back from the cause and infer other effects from it, beyond those by which alone it is known to us. No one, merely from the sight of one of Zeuxis's[66] pictures, could know that he was also a statuary or architect and was an artist no less skillful in stone and marble than in colors. The talents and taste displayed in the particular work before us—these we may safely conclude the workman to be possessed of. The cause must be proportioned to the effect; and if we exactly and precisely proportion it, we shall never find in it any qualities that point further or afford an inference concerning any other design or performance. Such qualities must be somewhat beyond what is merely requisite for producing the effect which we examine.

Allowing, therefore, the gods to be the authors of the existence or order of the universe, it follows that they possess that precise degree of power, intelligence, and benevolence which appears in their workmanship, but nothing further can ever be proved, except we call in the assistance of exaggeration and flattery to supply the defects of argument and reasoning. So far as the traces of any attributes at present appear, so far may we conclude these attributes to exist. The supposition of further attributes is mere hypothesis, much more the supposition that in distant regions of space or periods of time there has been or will be a more magnificent display of these attributes and a scheme of administration more suitable to such imaginary virtues. We can never be allowed to mount up from the universe, the effect, to Jupiter,[67] the cause, and then descend downwards to infer any new effect from that cause, as if the present effects alone were not entirely worthy of the glorious attributes which we ascribe to that deity. The knowledge of the cause being derived solely from the effect, they must be exactly adjusted to each other and the one can never refer to anything further or be the foundation of any new inference and conclusion.

You find certain phenomena in nature. You seek a cause or author. You imagine that you have found him. You afterwards become so enamored of this offspring of your brain that you imagine it impossible but he must produce something greater and more perfect than the present scene of things, which is so full of ill and disorder. You forget that this superlative intelligence and benevolence are entirely imaginary or, at least, without any foundation in reason and that you have no ground to ascribe to him any qualities but what you see he has actually exerted and displayed in his productions. Let your gods, therefore, O philosophers, be suited to the present appearances of nature and do not presume to alter these appearances by arbitrary suppositions in order to suit them to the attributes which you so fondly ascribe to your deities.

When priests and poets, supported by your authority, O Athenians, talk of a golden or silver age which preceded the present state of vice and misery, I hear them with attention and with reverence. But when philosophers who pretend to neglect authority and to cultivate reason hold the same discourse, I do not pay them, I admit, the same obsequious submission and pious deference. I ask: Who carried them into the celestial regions, who admitted them into the councils of the gods, who opened to them the book of fate that they thus rashly affirm that their deities have executed or will execute any purpose beyond what has actually appeared? If they tell me that they have mounted on the steps or by the gradual ascent of reason and by drawing inferences from effects to causes, I still insist that they have aided the ascent of reason by the wings of imagination; otherwise they could not thus change their manner of inference and argue from causes to effects, presuming that a more

66. [Zeuxis was a fifth-century-B.C. Greek painter.]

67. [According to Roman mythology, Jupiter was the supreme deity.]

perfect production than the present world would be more suitable to such perfect beings as the gods and forgetting that they have no reason to ascribe to these celestial beings any perfection or any attribute but what can be found in the present world.

Hence all the fruitless industry to account for the ill appearances of nature and save the honor of the gods, while we must acknowledge the reality of that evil and disorder with which the world so much abounds. The obstinate and intractable qualities of matter, we are told, or the observance of general laws, or some such reason, is the sole cause which controlled the power and benevolence of Jupiter and obliged him to create mankind and every sensible creature so imperfect and so unhappy. These attributes, then, are, it seems, beforehand taken for granted in their greatest latitude. And upon that supposition, I admit that such conjectures may, perhaps, be admitted as plausible solutions of the ill phenomena. But still I ask: Why take these attributes for granted or why ascribe to the cause any qualities but what actually appear in the effect? Why torture your brain to justify the course of nature upon suppositions which, for all you know, may be entirely imaginary and of which there are to be found no traces in the course of nature?

The religious hypothesis, therefore, must be considered only as a particular method of accounting for the visible phenomena of the universe. But no just reasoner will ever presume to infer from it any single fact and alter or add to the phenomena in any single particular. If you think that the appearances of things prove such causes, it is allowable for you to draw an inference concerning the existence of these causes. In such complicated and sublime subjects, everyone should be indulged in the liberty of conjecture and argument. But here you ought to rest. If you come backward and, arguing from your inferred causes, conclude that any other fact has existed or will exist in the course of nature which may serve as a fuller display of particular attributes I must admonish you that you have departed from the method of reasoning attached to the present subject and have certainly added something to the attributes of the cause beyond what appears in the effect; otherwise you could never, with tolerable sense or propriety, add anything to the effect in order to render it more worthy of the cause.

Where, then, is the odiousness of that doctrine which I teach in my school, or rather, which I examine in my gardens? Or what do you find in this whole question in which the security of good morals or the peace and order of society are in the least concerned?

I deny a providence, you say, and supreme governor of the world who guides the course of events and punishes the vicious with infamy and disappointment, and rewards the virtuous with honor and success in all their undertakings. But surely I do not deny the course itself of events, which lies open to everyone's inquiry and examination. I acknowledge that, in the present order of things, virtue is attended with more peace of mind than vice and meets with a more favorable reception from the world. I am sensible that, according to the past experience of mankind, friendship is the chief joy of human life and moderation the only source of tranquillity and happiness. I never balance between the virtuous and the vicious course of life, but am sensible that, to a well-disposed mind, every advantage is on the side of the former. And what can you say more, allowing all your suppositions and reasonings? You tell me, indeed, that this disposition of things proceeds from intelligence and design. But whatever it proceeds from, the disposition itself, on which depends our happiness or misery and consequently our conduct and deportment in life, is still the same. It is still open for me, as well as you, to regulate my behavior by my experience of past events. And if you affirm that, while a divine providence is allowed, and a supreme distributive justice in the universe, I ought to expect some more particular reward of the good and punishment of the bad beyond the ordinary course of events, I here find the same fallacy which I have before endeavored to detect. You persist in imagining that, if we grant that divine existence for which you so earnestly contend, you may safely infer consequences from it and add something to the experienced order of nature by arguing from the attributes which you ascribe to your gods. You do not seem to remember that all your reasonings on this subject can only be drawn from effects to causes and that every argument deduced from causes to effects must of necessity be a gross sophism, since it is impossible for you to know anything of the cause but what you have antecedently not inferred, but discovered to the full in the effect.

But what must a philosopher think of those vain reasoners who, instead of regarding the present scene of things as the sole object of their contemplation, so far reverse the whole course of nature as to render this life merely a passage to something further—a porch which leads to a greater and vastly different building, a prologue which serves only to introduce the piece and give it more grace and propriety? From where, do you think, can such philosophers derive their idea of the gods? From their own conceit and imagination surely. For if they derived it from the present phenomena, it would never point to anything further, but must be exactly adjusted to them. That the divinity may *possibly* be endowed with attributes which we have never seen exerted, may be governed by principles of action which we cannot discover to be satisfied. All this will freely be allowed. But still this is mere *possibility* and hypothesis. We never can have reason to *infer* any attributes or any principles of action in him, but so far as we know them to have been exerted and satisfied.

Are there any marks of a distributive justice in the world? If you answer in the affirmative, I conclude that, since justice here exerts itself, it is satisfied. If you reply in the negative, I conclude that you have then no reason to ascribe justice, in our sense of it, to the gods. If you hold a medium between affirmation and negation, by saying that the justice of the gods at present exerts itself in part, but not in its full extent, I answer that you have no reason to give it any particular extent, but only so far as you see it, *at present*, exert itself.

Thus I bring the dispute, O Athenians, to a short issue with my antagonists. The course of nature lies open to my contemplation as well as to theirs. The experienced train of events is the great standard by which we all regulate our conduct. Nothing else can be appealed to in the field or in the senate. Nothing else ought ever to be heard of in the school or in the closet. In vain would our limited understanding break through those boundaries which are too narrow for our fond imagination. While we argue from the course of nature and infer a particular intelligent cause which first bestowed and still preserves order in the universe, we embrace a principle which is both uncertain and useless. It is uncertain because the subject lies entirely beyond the reach of human experience. It is useless because our knowledge of this cause being derived entirely from the course of nature, we can never, according to the rules of just reasoning, return back from the cause with any new inference or, making additions to the common and experienced course of nature, establish any new principles of conduct and behavior.

I observe (I said, finding he had finished his harangue) that you do not neglect the artifice of the demagogues of old and as you were pleased to make me stand for the people, you insinuate yourself into my favor by embracing those principles to which, you know, I have always expressed a particular attachment. But allowing you to make experience (as indeed I think you ought) the only standard of our judgment concerning this and all other questions of fact, I do not doubt but, from the very same experience to which you appeal, it may be possible to refute this reasoning which you have put into the mouth of Epicurus. If you saw, for instance, a half-finished building surrounded with heaps of brick and stone and mortar and all the instruments of masonry, could you not *infer* from the effect that it was a work of design and contrivance? And could you not return again, from this inferred cause, to infer new additions to the effect and conclude that the building would soon be finished and receive all the further improvements which art could bestow upon it? If you saw upon the seashore the print of one human foot, you would conclude that a man had passed that way and that he had also left the traces of the other foot, though effaced by the rolling of the sands or inundation of the waters. Why then do you refuse to admit the same method of reasoning with regard to the order of nature? Consider the world and the present life only as an imperfect building from which you can infer a superior intelligence and, arguing from that superior intelligence which can leave nothing imperfect, why may you not infer a more finished scheme or plan which will receive its completion in some distant point of space or time? Are not these methods of reasoning exactly similar? And under what pretense can you embrace the one while you reject the other?

The infinite difference of the subjects, he replied, is a sufficient foundation for this difference in my conclusions. In works of human art and contrivance, it is allowable to advance from the effect to the cause, and, returning back from the cause, to form new inferences concerning the effect and examine the alterations which it has probably undergone or may still undergo. But what is the foundation of this method of reasoning? Plainly this: that man is a being whom we know by experience, whose motives and designs we are acquainted with, and whose projects and inclinations have a certain connection and coherence according to the laws which nature has established for the government of such a creature. When, therefore, we find that any work has proceeded from the skill and industry of man, as we are otherwise acquainted with the nature of the animal, we can draw a hundred inferences concerning what may be expected from him; and these inferences will all be founded in experience and observation. But did we know man only from the single work or production which we examine, it would be impossible for us to argue in this manner, because our knowledge of all the qualities which we ascribe to him, being in that case derived from the production, it is impossible they could point to anything further or be the foundation of any new inference. The print of a foot in the sand can only prove, when considered alone, that there was some figure adapted to it by which it was produced. But the print of a human foot proves likewise, from our other experience, that there was probably another foot which also left its impression, though effaced by time or other accidents. Here we mount from the effect to the cause, and, descending again from the cause, infer alterations in the effect; but this is not a continuation of the same simple chain of reasoning. We comprehend in this case a hundred other experiences and observations concerning the *usual* figure and members of that species of animal without which this method of argument must be considered as fallacious and sophistical.

The case is not the same with our reasonings from the works of nature. The Deity is known to us only by his productions and is a single being in the universe, not comprehended under any species or genus, from whose experienced attributes or qualities we can, by analogy, infer any attribute or quality in him. As the universe shows wisdom and goodness, we infer wisdom and goodness. As it shows a particular degree of these perfections, we infer a particular degree of them precisely adapted to the effect which we examine. But further attributes or further degrees of the same attributes we can never be authorized to infer or suppose by any rules of just reasoning. Now, without some such license of supposition, it is impossible for us to argue from the cause or infer any alteration in the effect beyond what has immediately fallen under our observation. Greater good produced by this Being must still prove a greater degree of goodness. A more impartial distribution of rewards and punishments must proceed from a greater regard to justice and equity. Every supposed addition to the works of nature makes an addition to the attributes of the Author of nature, and, consequently, being entirely unsupported by any reason or argument, can never be admitted but as mere conjecture and hypothesis.[68]

The great source of our mistake in this subject and of the unbounded license of conjecture which we indulge is that we tacitly consider ourselves as in the place of the Supreme Being and conclude that he will, on every occasion, observe the same conduct which we ourselves, in his situation, would have embraced as reasonable and eligible. But, besides that the ordinary course of nature may convince us that almost everything is regulated by principles and maxims very different from ours—besides this, I say, it must evidently appear contrary to all rules of analogy to reason from the intentions and projects of men to those of a Being so different and so much superior.

68. In general, it may, I think, be established as a maxim, that where any cause is known only by its particular effects, it must be impossible to infer any new effects from that cause; since the qualities, which are requisite to produce these new effects along with the former, must either be different, or superior, or of more extensive operation, than those which simply produced the effect, whence alone the cause is supposed to be known to us. We can never, therefore, have any reason to suppose the existence of these qualities. To say, that the new effects proceed only from a continuation of the same energy, which is already known from the first effects, will not remove the difficulty. For even granting this to be the case (which can seldom be supposed), the very continuation and exertion of a like energy (for it is impossible it can be absolutely the same), I say, this exertion of a like energy, in a different period of space and time, is a very arbitrary supposition, and what there cannot possibly be any traces of in the effects, from which all our knowledge of the cause is originally derived. Let the *inferred* cause be exactly proportioned (as it should be) to the known effect; and it is impossible that it can possess any qualities, from which new or different effects can be *inferred*.

In human nature there is a certain experienced coherence of designs and inclinations, so that when, from any fact, we have discovered one intention of any man, it may often be reasonable, from experience, to infer another and draw a long chain of conclusions concerning his past or future conduct. But this method of reasoning can never have place with regard to a Being so remote and incomprehensible, who bears much less analogy to any other being in the universe than the sun to a waxen taper, and who discovers himself only by some faint traces or outlines beyond which we have no authority to ascribe to him any attribute or perfection. What we imagine to be a superior perfection may really be a defect. Or were it ever so much a perfection, the ascribing of it to the Supreme Being, where it does not appear to have been really exerted to the full in his works, savors more of flattery and panegyric than of just reasoning and sound philosophy. All the philosophy, therefore, in the world and all the religion, which is nothing but a species of philosophy, will never be able to carry us beyond the usual course of experience or give us measures of conduct and behavior different from those which are furnished by reflections on common life. No new fact can ever be inferred from the religious hypothesis, no event foreseen or foretold, no reward or punishment expected or dreaded beyond what is already known by practice and observation. So that my apology for Epicurus will still appear solid and satisfactory, nor have the political interests of society any connection with the philosophical disputes concerning metaphysics and religion.

There is still one circumstance, I replied, which you seem to have overlooked. Though I should allow your premises, I must deny your conclusion. You conclude that religious doctrines and reasonings *can* have no influence on life because they *ought* to have no influence, never considering that men reason not in the same manner you do, but draw many consequences from the belief of a divine Existence and suppose that the Deity will inflict punishments on vice and bestow rewards on virtue beyond what appear in the ordinary course of nature. Whether this reasoning of theirs is just or not is no matter. Its influence on their life and conduct must still be the same. And those who attempt to disabuse them of such prejudices may, for all I know, be good reasoners, but I cannot allow them to be good citizens and politicians, since they free men from one restraint upon their passions and make the infringement of the laws of society in one respect more easy and secure.

After all, I may perhaps agree to your general conclusion in favor of liberty, though upon different premises from those on which you endeavor to found it. I think that the state ought to tolerate every principle of philosophy, nor is there an instance that any government has suffered in its political interests by such indulgence. There is no enthusiasm among philosophers; their doctrines are not very alluring to the people and no restraint can be put upon their reasonings but what must be of dangerous consequence to the sciences and even to the state, by paving the way for persecution and oppression in points where the generality of mankind are more deeply interested and concerned.

But there occurs to me (I continued) with regard to your main topic a difficulty which I shall just propose to you, without insisting on it, lest it lead into reasonings of too nice and delicate a nature. In a word, I much doubt whether it is possible for a cause to be known only by its effect (as you have all along supposed) or to be of so singular and particular a nature as to have no parallel and no similarity with any other cause or object that has ever fallen under our observation. It is only when two species of objects are found to be constantly conjoined that we can infer the one from the other; and were an effect presented which was entirely singular and could not be comprehended under any known species, I do not see that we could form any conjecture or inference at all concerning its cause. If experience and observation and analogy are, indeed, the only guides which we can reasonably follow in inferences of this nature, both the effect and cause must bear a similarity and resemblance to other effects and causes which we know, and which we have found in many instances to be conjoined with each other. I leave it to your own reflection to pursue the consequences of this principle. I shall just observe that, as the antagonists of Epicurus always suppose the universe, an effect quite singular and unparalleled, to be the proof of a Deity, a cause no less singular and unparalleled, your reasonings upon that supposition seem, at least, to merit our attention. There is, I admit, some difficulty how we can ever return from the cause to the effect and, reasoning from our ideas of the former, infer any alteration on the latter or any addition to it.

Section XII
Of the Academic or Skeptical Philosophy.

Part I.

There is not a greater number of philosophical reasonings displayed upon any subject than those which prove the existence of a Deity and refute the fallacies of *atheists*; and yet the most religious philosophers still dispute whether any man can be so blinded as to be a speculative atheist. How shall we reconcile these contradictions? The knights-errant who wandered about to clear the world of dragons and giants never entertained the least doubt with regard to the existence of these monsters.

The *skeptic* is another enemy of religion, who naturally provokes the indignation of all divines and graver philosophers, though it is certain that no man ever met with any such absurd creature or conversed with a man who had no opinion or principle concerning any subject, either of action or speculation. This begets a very natural question: What is meant by a skeptic? And how far it is possible to push these philosophical principles of doubt and uncertainty?

There is a species of skepticism, *antecedent* to all study and philosophy, which is much inculcated by Descartes and others as a sovereign preservative against error and precipitate judgment. It recommends a universal doubt not only of all our former opinions and principles, but also of our very faculties, of whose veracity, they say, we must assure ourselves by a chain of reasoning deduced from some original principle which cannot possibly be fallacious or deceitful. But neither is there any such original principle which has a prerogative above others that are self-evident and convincing. Or if there were, could we advance a step beyond it but by the use of those very faculties of which we are supposed to be already diffident. The Cartesian doubt, therefore, were it ever possible to be attained by any human creature (as it plainly is not) would be entirely incurable and no reasoning could ever bring us to a state of assurance and conviction upon any subject.

It must, however, be confessed that this species of skepticism, when more moderate, may be understood in a very reasonable sense and is a necessary preparative to the study of philosophy by preserving a proper impartiality in our judgments and weaning our mind from all those prejudices which we may have imbibed from education or rash opinion. To begin with clear and self-evident principles, to advance by timorous and sure steps, to review frequently our conclusions and examine accurately all their consequences—though by these means we shall make both a slow and a short progress in our systems—are the only methods by which we can ever hope to reach truth and attain a proper stability and certainty in our determinations.

There is another species of skepticism, *consequent* to science and inquiry, when men are supposed to have discovered either the absolute fallaciousness of their mental faculties or their unfitness to reach any fixed determination in all those curious subjects of speculation about which they are commonly employed. Even our very senses are brought into dispute by a certain species of philosophers and the maxims of common life are subjected to the same doubt as the most profound principles or conclusions of metaphysics and theology. As these paradoxical tenets (if they may be called tenets) are to be met with in some philosophers, and the refutation of them in several, they naturally excite our curiosity and make us inquire into the arguments on which they may be founded.

I need not insist upon the more trite topics employed by the skeptics in all ages against the evidence of *sense* such as those which are derived from the imperfection and fallaciousness of our organs on numberless occasions: the crooked appearance of an oar in water, the various aspects of objects according to their different distances, the double images which arise from the pressing one eye, with many other appearances of a like nature. These skeptical topics, indeed, are only sufficient to prove that the senses alone are not implicitly to be depended on, but that we must correct their evidence by reason and by considerations derived from the nature of the medium, the distance of the object, and the disposition of the organ, in order to render them, within their sphere, the proper *criteria* of truth and falsehood. There are other more profound arguments against the senses which do not admit of so easy a solution.

It seems evident that men are carried by a natural instinct or prepossession to repose faith in their senses, and that without any reasoning, or even almost before the use of reason, we always suppose an external universe which does not depend on our perception, but would exist though we and every sensible creature were absent or annihilated. Even the animal creation are governed by a like opinion and preserve this belief of external objects, in all their thoughts, designs, and actions.

It seems also evident that when men follow this blind and powerful instinct of nature they always suppose the very images presented by the senses to be the external objects and never entertain any suspicion that the one are nothing but representations of the other. This very table which we see white and which we feel hard is believed to exist independent of our perception and to be something external to our mind which perceives it. Our presence does not bestow being on it. Our absence does not annihilate it. It preserves its existence uniform and entire, independent of the situation of intelligent beings who perceive or contemplate it.

But this universal and primary opinion of all men is soon destroyed by the slightest philosophy which teaches us that nothing can ever be present to the mind but an image or perception, and that the senses are only the inlets through which these images are conveyed, without being able to produce any immediate intercourse between the mind and the object. The table which we see seems to diminish as we remove further from it. But the real table which exists independent of us suffers no alteration. It was, therefore, nothing but its image which was present to the mind. These are the obvious dictates of reason and no man who reflects ever doubted that the existences which we consider when we say *this house* and *that tree* are nothing but perceptions in the mind and fleeting copies or representations of other existences which remain uniform and independent.

So far, then, are we necessitated by reasoning to contradict or depart from the primary instincts of nature and to embrace a new system with regard to the evidence of our senses. But here philosophy finds herself extremely embarrassed when she would justify this new system and obviate the cavils and objections of the skeptics. She can no longer plead the infallible and irresistible instinct of nature, for that led us to a quite different system which is acknowledged fallible and even erroneous. And to justify this pretended philosophical system by a chain of clear and convincing argument, or even any appearance of argument, exceeds the power of all human capacity.

By what argument can it be proved that the perceptions of the mind must be caused by external objects entirely different from them, though resembling them (if that is possible), and could not arise either from the energy of the mind itself, or from the suggestion of some invisible and unknown spirit, or from some other cause still more unknown to us? It is acknowledged that in fact many of these perceptions arise not from anything external, as in dreams, madness, and other diseases. And nothing can be more inexplicable than the manner in which body should so operate upon mind as ever to convey an image of itself to a substance supposed of so different and even contrary a nature.

It is a question of fact whether the perceptions of the senses are produced by external objects resembling them; how shall this question be determined? By experience surely as all other questions of a like nature. But here experience is and must be entirely silent. The mind never has anything present to it but the perceptions and cannot possibly reach any experience of their connection with objects. The supposition of such a connection is, therefore, without any foundation in reasoning.

To have recourse to the veracity of the supreme Being in order to prove the veracity of our senses is surely making a very unexpected circuit. If his veracity were at all concerned in this matter, our senses would be entirely infallible, because it is not possible that he can ever deceive. Not to mention that, if the external world is once called in question, we shall be at a loss to find arguments by which we may prove the existence of that Being or any of his attributes.

This is a topic, therefore, in which the profounder and more philosophical skeptics will always triumph when they endeavor to introduce a universal doubt into all subjects of human knowledge and inquiry. Do you follow the instincts and propensities of nature, may they say, in assenting to the veracity of sense? But these lead you to believe that the very perception or sensible image is the external object. Do you disclaim this principle in order to embrace a more rational opinion that the perceptions are only representations of something external? You here depart from your natural propensities and more obvious sentiments and yet are not able to satisfy your reason, which can never find any convincing argument from experience to prove that the perceptions are connected with any external objects.

There is another skeptical topic of a like nature, derived from the most profound philosophy, which might merit our attention were it requisite to dive so deep in order to discover arguments and reasonings which can so little serve to any serious purpose. It is universally allowed by modern inquirers that all the sensible qualities of objects, such as hard, soft, hot, cold, white, black, etc., are merely secondary and do not exist in the objects themselves, but are perceptions of the mind, without any external archetype or model which they represent. If this is allowed with regard to secondary qualities, it must also follow with regard to the supposed primary qualities of extension and solidity, nor can the latter be any more entitled to that denomination than the former. The idea of extension is entirely acquired from the senses of sight and feeling and if all the qualities perceived by the senses are in the mind, not in the object, the same conclusion must reach the idea of extension which is wholly dependent on the sensible ideas or the ideas of secondary qualities. Nothing can save us from this conclusion but the asserting that the ideas of those primary qualities are attained by *abstraction*; an opinion which, if we examine it accurately, we shall find to be unintelligible and even absurd. An extension that is neither tangible nor visible cannot possibly be conceived; and a tangible or visible extension which is neither hard nor soft, black nor white, is equally beyond the reach of human conception. Let any man try to conceive a triangle in general which is neither *isosceles* nor *scalene*, nor has any particular length or proportion of sides, and he will soon perceive the absurdity of all the scholastic notions with regard to abstraction and general ideas.[69]

Thus the first philosophical objection to the evidence of sense or to the opinion of external existence consists in this, that such an opinion, if rested on natural instinct, is contrary to reason and, if referred to reason, is contrary to natural instinct and at the same time carries no rational evidence with it to convince an impartial inquirer. The second objection goes further and represents this opinion as contrary to reason, at least, if it is a principle of reason that all sensible qualities are in the mind, not in the object. Deprive matter of all its intelligible qualities, both primary and secondary, you in a manner annihilate it and leave only a certain unknown, inexplicable *something* as the cause of our perceptions—a notion so imperfect that no skeptic will think it worthwhile to contend against it.

Part II.

It may seem a very extravagant attempt of the skeptics to destroy *reason* by argument and ratiocination, yet is this the grand scope of all their inquiries and disputes. They endeavor to find objections both to our abstract reasonings and to those which regard matter of fact and existence.

The chief objection against all *abstract* reasonings is derived from the ideas of space and time—ideas which, in common life and to a careless view, are very clear and intelligible, but when they pass through the scrutiny of the profound sciences (and they are the chief object of these sciences) afford principles which seem full of absurdity and contradiction. No priestly *dogmas* invented on purpose to tame and subdue the rebellious reason of mankind ever shocked common sense more than the doctrine of the infinite divisibility of extension, with its consequences, as they are pompously displayed by all geometers and metaphysicians with a kind of triumph and exultation. A real quantity, infinitely less than any finite quantity, containing quantities infinitely less than itself, and so on *in infinitum*; this is an edifice so bold and prodigious that it is too weighty for any pretended

69. This argument is drawn from Dr. Berkeley; and indeed most of the writings of that very ingenious author form the best lessons of skepticism, which are to be found either among the ancient or modern philosophers, Bayle [Pierre Bayle (1647–1706), a French skeptical philosopher] not excepted. He professes, however, in his title-page (and undoubtedly with great truth) to have composed his book against the skeptics as well as against the atheists and freethinkers. But that all his arguments, though otherwise intended, are, in reality, merely skeptical, appears from this, *that they admit of no answer and produce no conviction.* Their only effect is to cause that momentary amazement and irresolution and confusion, which is the result of skepticism.

demonstration to support because it shocks the clearest and most natural principles of human reason.[70] But what renders the matter more extraordinary is that these seemingly absurd opinions are supported by a chain of reasoning, the clearest and most natural, nor is it possible for us to allow the premises without admitting the consequences. Nothing can be more convincing and satisfactory than all the conclusions concerning the properties of circles and triangles, and yet, when these are once received, how can we deny that the angle of contact between a circle and its tangent is infinitely less than any rectilinear angle—that as you may increase the diameter of the circle *in infinitum*, this angle of contact becomes still less, even *in infinitum*, and that the angle of contact between other curves and their tangents may be infinitely less than those between any circle and its tangent, and so on, *in infinitum*? The demonstration of these principles seems as unexceptionable as that which proves the three angles of a triangle to be equal to two right ones, though the latter opinion is natural and easy and the former big with contradiction and absurdity. Reason here seems to be thrown into a kind of amazement and suspense which, without the suggestions of any skeptic, gives her a diffidence of herself and of the ground on which she treads. She sees a full light which illuminates certain places, but that light borders upon the most profound darkness. And between these she is so dazzled and confounded that she scarcely can pronounce with certainty and assurance concerning any one object.

The absurdity of these bold determinations of the abstract sciences seems to become, if possible, still more palpable with regard to time than extension. An infinite number of real parts of time, passing in succession and exhausted one after another, appears so evident a contradiction that no man, one should think, whose judgment is not corrupted, instead of being improved by the sciences, would ever be able to admit of it.

Yet still reason must remain restless and unquiet, even with regard to that skepticism to which she is driven by these seeming absurdities and contradictions. How any clear, distinct idea can contain circumstances contradictory to itself, or to any other clear, distinct idea, is absolutely incomprehensible and is, perhaps, as absurd as any proposition which can be formed—so that nothing can be more skeptical or more full of doubt and hesitation than this skepticism itself which arises from some of the paradoxical conclusions of geometry or the science of quantity.[71]

The skeptical objections to *moral* evidence or to the reasonings concerning matter of fact are either *popular* or *philosophical*. The popular objections are derived from the natural weakness of human understanding: the contradictory opinions which have been entertained in different ages and nations; the variations of our judgment in sickness and health, youth and old age, prosperity and adversity; the perpetual contradiction of each particular man's

70. Whatever disputes there may be about mathematical points, we must allow that there are physical points; that is, parts of extension, which cannot be divided or lessened, either by the eye or imagination. These images, then, which are present to the fancy or senses, are absolutely indivisible, and consequently must be allowed by mathematicians to be infinitely less than any real part of extension; and yet nothing appears more certain to reason, than that an infinite number of them composes an infinite extension. How much more an infinite number of those infinitely small parts of extension, which are still supposed infinitely divisible?

71. It seems to me not impossible to avoid these absurdities and contradictions, if it be admitted, that there is no such thing as abstract or general ideas, properly speaking; but that all general ideas are, in reality, particular ones, attached to a general term, which recalls, upon occasion, other particular ones, that resemble, in certain circumstances, the idea, present to the mind. Thus when the term *horse* is pronounced, we immediately figure to ourselves the idea of a black or a white animal, of a particular size or figure: But as that term is also usually applied to animals of other colors, figures, and sizes, these ideas, though not actually present to the imagination, are easily recalled; and our reasoning and conclusion proceed in the same way, as if they were actually present. If this is admitted (as seems reasonable), it follows that all the ideas of quantity upon which mathematicians reason are nothing but particular, and such as are suggested by the senses and imagination and, consequently, cannot be infinitely divisible. It is sufficient to have dropped this hint at present without prosecuting it any farther. It certainly concerns all lovers of science not to expose themselves to the ridicule and contempt of the ignorant by their conclusions; and this seems the readiest solution of these difficulties.

opinions and sentiments with many other topics of that kind. It is needless to insist further on this head. These objections are but weak. For, as in common life, we reason every moment concerning fact and existence and cannot possibly subsist without continually employing this species of argument, any popular objections derived from this must be insufficient to destroy that evidence. The great subverter of *Pyrrhonism*, or the excessive principles of skepticism, is action, and employment, and the occupations of common life. These principles may flourish and triumph in the schools, where it is indeed difficult, if not impossible, to refute them. But as soon as they leave the shade and by the presence of the real objects which actuate our passions and sentiments are put in opposition to the more powerful principles of our nature, they vanish like smoke and leave the most determined skeptic in the same condition as other mortals.

The skeptic, therefore, had better keep within his proper sphere and display those *philosophical* objections which arise from more profound researches. Here he seems to have ample matter of triumph, while he justly insists that all our evidence for any matter of fact which lies beyond the testimony of sense or memory is derived entirely from the relation of cause and effect; that we have no other idea of this relation than that of two objects which have been frequently *conjoined* together; that we have no argument to convince us that objects which have, in our experience, been frequently conjoined, will likewise, in other instances, be conjoined in the same manner; and that nothing leads us to this inference but custom or a certain instinct of our nature which it is indeed difficult to resist, but which, like other instincts, may be fallacious and deceitful. While the skeptic insists upon these topics, he shows his force, or rather, indeed, his own and our weakness, and seems, for the time at least, to destroy all assurance and conviction. These arguments might be displayed at greater length, if any durable good or benefit to society could ever be expected to result from them.

For here is the chief and most confounding objection to *excessive* skepticism, that no durable good can ever result from it while it remains in its full force and vigor. We need only ask such a skeptic *What his meaning is? And what he proposes by all these curious researches?* He is immediately at a loss and does not know what to answer. A Copernican[72] or Ptolemaist[73] who each supports his different system of astronomy may hope to produce a conviction which will remain constant and durable with his audience. A Stoic or Epicurean displays principles which may not only be durable, but which have an effect on conduct and behavior. But a Pyrrhonian cannot expect that his philosophy will have any constant influence on the mind or, if it had, that its influence would be beneficial to society. On the contrary, he must acknowledge, if he will acknowledge anything, that all human life must perish, were his principles universally and steadily to prevail. All discourse, all action would immediately cease and men would remain in a total lethargy until the necessities of nature, unsatisfied, put an end to their miserable existence. It is true—so fatal an event is very little to be dreaded. Nature is always too strong for principle. And though a Pyrrhonian may throw himself or others into a momentary amazement and confusion by his profound reasonings, the first and most trivial event in life will put to flight all his doubts and scruples and leave him the same, in every point of action and speculation, with the philosophers of every other sect or with those who never concerned themselves in any philosophical researches. When he awakes from his dream, he will be the first to join in the laugh against himself and to confess that all his objections are mere amusement and can have no other tendency than to show the whimsical condition of mankind, who must act and reason and believe, though they are not able, by their most diligent inquiry, to satisfy themselves concerning the foundation of these operations or to remove the objections which may be raised against them.

Part III.

There is, indeed, a more *mitigated* skepticism or *academic* philosophy which may be both durable and useful and which may, in part, be the result of this Pyrrhonism or *excessive* skepticism when its undistinguished doubts are in some measure corrected by common sense and reflection. The greater part of

72. [Nicolas Copernicus (1473–1543), the Polish astronomer, maintained that the earth revolved around the sun.]

73. [The second-century Greco-Egyptian astronomer Ptolemy maintained that the sun revolved around the earth.]

mankind are naturally apt to be affirmative and dogmatic in their opinions and while they see objects only on one side and have no idea of any counterpoising argument, they throw themselves precipitately into the principles to which they are inclined, nor have they any indulgence for those who entertain opposite sentiments. To hesitate or balance perplexes their understanding, checks their passion, and suspends their action. They are, therefore, impatient until they escape from a state which to them is so uneasy and they think that they can never remove themselves far enough from it by the violence of their affirmations and obstinacy of their belief. But could such dogmatic reasoners become sensible of the strange infirmities of human understanding, even in its most perfect state and when most accurate and cautious in its determinations, such a reflection would naturally inspire them with more modesty and reserve, and diminish their fond opinion of themselves and their prejudice against antagonists. The illiterate may reflect on the disposition of the learned who, amid all the advantages of study and reflection, are commonly still diffident in their determinations. And if any of the learned are inclined, from their natural temper, to haughtiness and obstinacy, a small tincture of Pyrrhonism might abate their pride by showing them that the few advantages which they may have attained over their fellows are but inconsiderable, if compared with the universal perplexity and confusion which is inherent in human nature. In general, there is a degree of doubt and caution and modesty which, in all kinds of scrutiny and decision, ought forever accompany a just reasoner.

Another species of *mitigated* skepticism which may be of advantage to mankind and which may be the natural result of the Pyrrhonian doubts and scruples is the limitation of our inquiries to such subjects as are best adapted to the narrow capacity of human understanding. The *imagination* of man is naturally sublime, delighted with whatever is remote and extraordinary, and running without control into the most distant parts of space and time in order to avoid the objects which custom has rendered too familiar to it. A correct *judgment* observes a contrary method and, avoiding all distant and high inquiries, confines itself to common life and to such subjects as fall under daily practice and experience, leaving the more sublime topics to the embellishment of poets and orators or to the arts of priests and politicians. To bring us to so salutary a determination, nothing can be more serviceable than to be once thoroughly convinced of the force of the Pyrrhonian doubt and of the impossibility that anything but the strong power of natural instinct could free us from it. Those who have a propensity to philosophy will still continue their researches, because they reflect that, besides the immediate pleasure attending such an occupation, philosophical decisions are nothing but the reflections of common life, methodized and corrected. But they will never be tempted to go beyond common life so long as they consider the imperfection of those faculties which they employ, their narrow reach, and their inaccurate operations. While we cannot give a satisfactory reason why we believe, after a thousand experiments, that a stone will fall or fire burn, can we ever satisfy ourselves concerning any determination which we may form with regard to the origin of worlds and the situation of nature from and to eternity?

This narrow limitation, indeed, of our inquiries is in every respect so reasonable that it suffices to make the slightest examination into the natural powers of the human mind and to compare them with their objects, in order to recommend it to us. We shall then find what are the proper subjects of science and inquiry.

It seems to me that the only objects of the abstract sciences or of demonstration are quantity and number and that all attempts to extend this more perfect species of knowledge beyond these bounds are mere sophistry and illusion. As the component parts of quantity and number are entirely similar, their relations become intricate and involved and nothing can be more curious, as well as useful, than to trace, by a variety of mediums, their equality or inequality through their different appearances. But as all other ideas are clearly distinct and different from each other, we can never advance further, by our utmost scrutiny, than to observe this diversity and, by an obvious reflection, pronounce one thing not to be another. Or if there is any difficulty in these decisions, it proceeds entirely from the indeterminate meaning of words, which is corrected by more just definitions. That *the square of the hypotenuse is equal to the squares of the other two sides* cannot be known, let the terms be ever so exactly defined, without a train of reasoning and inquiry. But to convince us of this proposition, *that where there is no property there can be no injustice*, it is only necessary to define the terms and explain injustice to be a violation of property. This proposition is, indeed, nothing but a more imperfect definition. It is the same case with all those pretended syllogistic reasonings which may be found in every other branch of learning except the sciences of quantity and number; and these may safely, I think, be pronounced the only proper objects of knowledge and demonstration.

All other inquiries of men regard only matter of fact and existence and these are evidently incapable of demonstration. Whatever *is* may *not be*. No negation of a fact can involve a contradiction. The nonexistence of any being, without exception, is as clear and distinct an idea as its existence. The proposition which affirms it not to be, however false, is no less conceivable and intelligible than that which affirms it to be. The case is different with the sciences, properly so called. Every proposition which is not true is there confused and unintelligible. That the cube root of 64 is equal to the half of 10 is a false proposition and can never be distinctly conceived. But that Caesar, or the angel Gabriel, or any being never existed may be a false proposition, but still is perfectly conceivable, and implies no contradiction.

The existence, therefore, of any being can only be proved by arguments from its cause or its effect and these arguments are founded entirely on experience. If we reason *a priori*, anything may appear able to produce anything. The falling of a pebble may, for all we know, extinguish the sun or the wish of a man control the planets in their orbits. It is only experience which teaches us the nature and bounds of cause and effect and enables us to infer the existence of one object from that of another.[74] Such is the foundation of moral reasoning, which forms the greater part of human knowledge and is the source of all human action and behavior.

Moral reasonings are either concerning particular or general facts. All deliberations in life regard the former, as also all disquisitions in history, chronology, geography, and astronomy.

The sciences which treat of general facts are politics, natural philosophy, physics, chemistry, etc., where the qualities, causes, and effects of a whole species of objects are inquired into.

Divinity or theology, as it proves the existence of a Deity and the immortality of souls, is composed partly of reasonings concerning particular, partly concerning general facts. It has a foundation in *reason* so far as it is supported by experience. But its best and most solid foundation is *faith* and divine revelation.

Morals and criticism are not so properly objects of the understanding as of taste and sentiment. Beauty, whether moral or natural, is felt more properly than perceived. Or if we reason concerning it and endeavor to fix its standard, we regard a new fact, namely, the general taste of mankind or some such fact which may be the object of reasoning and inquiry.

When we run over libraries, persuaded of these principles, what havoc must we make? If we take in our hand any volume—of divinity or school metaphysics, for instance—let us ask: *Does it contain any abstract reasoning concerning quantity or number?* No. *Does it contain any experimental reasoning concerning matter of fact and existence?* No. Commit it then to the flames, for it can contain nothing but sophistry and illusion.

74. That impious maxim of the ancient philosophy, *Ex nihilo, nihil fit* [From nothing, nothing comes], by which the creation of matter was excluded, ceases to be a maxim, according to this philosophy. Not only the will of the supreme Being may create matter; but, for aught we know *a priori*, the will of any other being might create it, or any other cause, that the most whimsical imagination can assign.

A Treatise of Human Nature

BOOK I

Of the Understanding

Of Personal Identity

There are some philosophers who imagine we are every moment intimately conscious of what we call our self, that we feel its existence and its continuance in existence, and are certain beyond the evidence of a demonstration both of its perfect identity and simplicity. The strongest sensation, the most violent passion, they say, instead of distracting us from this view, only fix it the more intensely and make us consider their influence on *self* either by their pain or pleasure. To attempt a further proof of this would be to weaken its evidence, since no proof can be derived from any fact of which we are so intimately conscious, nor is there anything of which we can be certain if we doubt of this.

Unluckily all these positive assertions are contrary to that very experience which is pleaded for them, nor have we any idea of *self* after the manner it is here explained. For from what impression could this idea be derived? This question it is impossible to answer without a manifest contradiction and absurdity, and yet it is a question which must necessarily be answered, if we would have the idea of self pass for clear and intelligible. It must be some one impression that gives rise to every real idea. But self or person is not any one impression, but that to which our several impressions and ideas are supposed to have a reference. If any impression gives rise to the idea of self, that impression must continue invariably the same through the whole course of our lives, since self is supposed to exist after that manner. But there is no impression constant and invariable. Pain and pleasure, grief and joy, passions and sensations succeed each other and never all exist at the same time.

From *The Philosophical Works of David Hume*, edited by T. H. Green and T. H. Grose (London: Longman's, Green, and Co., 1898), 4 vols., English, modified.

It cannot, therefore, be from any of these impressions or from any other that the idea of self is derived, and, consequently, there is no such idea.

But further, what must become of all our particular perceptions upon this hypothesis? All these are different, and distinguishable, and separable from each other, and may be separately considered, and may exist separately, and have no need of anything to support their existence. After what manner therefore do they belong to self and how are they connected with it? For my part, when I enter most intimately into what I call *myself,* I always stumble on some particular perception or other, of heat or cold, light or shade, love or hatred, pain or pleasure. I never can catch *myself* at any time without a perception and never can observe anything but the perception. When my perceptions are removed for any time, as by sound sleep, so long am I insensible of myself and may truly be said not to exist. And were all my perceptions removed by death and could I neither think, nor feel, nor see, nor love, nor hate after the dissolution of my body, I should be entirely annihilated, nor do I conceive what is further requisite to make me a perfect nonentity. If anyone, upon serious and unprejudiced reflection, thinks he has a different notion of *himself,* I must confess I can reason no longer with him. All I can allow him is that he may be in the right as well as I and that we are essentially different in this particular. He may, perhaps, perceive something simple and continued which he calls *himself,* though I am certain there is no such principle in me.

But setting aside some metaphysicians of this kind, I may venture to affirm of the rest of mankind that they are nothing but a bundle or collection of different perceptions which succeed each other with an inconceivable rapidity and are in a perpetual flux and movement. Our eyes cannot turn in their sockets without varying our perceptions. Our thought is still more variable than our sight and all our other senses and faculties contribute to this change; nor is there any single power of the soul which remains unalterably the same perhaps for one moment. The mind is a kind of theater where several perceptions successively make their appearance, pass, repass, glide away, and mingle in an infinite variety of postures and situations. There is properly no *simplicity* in it at one time nor *identity* in different, whatever natural propensity we may have to imagine that simplicity and identity. The comparison of the theater must not mislead us. They are the successive perceptions only that constitute the mind, nor have we the most distant notion of the place where these scenes are represented or of the materials of which it is composed.

What, then, gives us so great a propensity to ascribe an identity to these successive perceptions and to suppose ourselves possessed of an invariable and uninterrupted existence through the whole course of our lives? In order to answer this question we must distinguish between personal identity as it regards our thought or imagination and as it regards our passions or the concern we take in ourselves. The first is our present subject and to explain it perfectly we must take the matter pretty deep and account for that identity which we attribute to plants and animals, there being a great analogy between it and the identity of a self or person.

We have a distinct idea of an object that remains invariable and uninterrupted through a supposed variation of time and this idea we call that of *identity* or *sameness*. We have also a distinct idea of several different objects existing in succession and connected together by a close relation, and this, to an accurate view, affords as perfect a notion of *diversity* as if there was no manner of relation among the objects. But though these two ideas of identity and a succession of related objects be in themselves perfectly distinct and even contrary, yet it is certain that, in our common way of thinking, they are generally confounded with each other. That action of the imagination by which we consider the uninterrupted and invariable object and that by which we reflect on the succession of related objects are almost the same to the feeling, nor is there much more effort of thought required in the latter case than in the former. The relation facilitates the transition of the mind from one object to another and renders its passage as smooth as if it contemplated one continued object. This resemblance is the cause of the confusion and mistake and makes us substitute the notion of identity instead of that of related objects. However at one instant we may consider the related succession as variable or interrupted, we are sure the next to ascribe to it a perfect identity and regard it as invariable and uninterrupted. Our propensity to this mistake is so great from the resemblance above mentioned that we fall into it before we are aware, and though we incessantly correct ourselves by reflection and return to a more accurate method of thinking, yet we cannot long sustain our philosophy or take off this bias from the imagination. Our last resource is to yield to it and boldly assert that these different related objects are in effect the same, however interrupted and variable. In order to justify to ourselves this absurdity, we often feign some new and unintelligible principle that connects the objects together and prevents their interruption or variation. Thus we feign the continued existence of the perceptions of our senses to remove the interruption and run into the notion of a *soul*, and *self*, and *substance* to disguise the variation. But, we may further observe that where we do not give rise to such a fiction, our propensity to confound identity with relation is so great that we are apt to imagine something unknown and mysterious, connecting the parts, besides their relation, and this I take to be the case with regard to the identity we ascribe to plants and vegetables. And even when this does not take place, we still feel a propensity to confound these ideas, though we are not able fully to satisfy ourselves in that particular nor find anything invariable and uninterrupted to justify our notion of identity.

Thus the controversy concerning identity is not merely a dispute of words. For when we attribute identity, in an improper sense, to variable or interrupted objects, our mistake is not confined to the expression, but is commonly attended with a fiction, either of something invariable and uninterrupted, or of something mysterious and inexplicable, or at least with a propensity to such fictions. What will suffice to prove this hypothesis to the satisfaction of every fair inquirer is to show from daily experience and observation that the objects which are variable or interrupted, and yet are supposed to continue the same, are such only as consist of a succession of parts, connected together by resemblance, contiguity, or causation. For as such a succession answers evidently to our notion of diversity, it can only be by mistake we ascribe to it an identity, and as the relation of parts, which leads us into this mistake, is really nothing but a quality which produces an association of ideas and an easy transition of the imagination from one to another, it can only be from the resemblance which this act of the mind bears to that by which we contemplate one continued object that the error arises. Our chief business, then, must be to prove that all objects to which we ascribe identity without observing their invariableness and uninterruptedness are such as consist of a succession of related objects.

In order to [see] this, suppose any mass of matter of which the parts are contiguous and connected to be placed before us. It is plain we must attribute a perfect identity to this mass, provided all the parts continue uninterruptedly and invariably the same, whatever motion or change of place we may observe either in the whole or in any of the parts. But supposing some very *small* or *inconsiderable* part to be added to the mass or subtracted from it, though this absolutely destroys the identity of the whole, strictly speaking, yet as we seldom think so accurately, we scruple not to pronounce a mass of matter the same where we find so trivial an alteration. The passage of the thought from the object before the change to the object after it is so smooth and easy that we scarce perceive the transition and are apt to imagine that it is nothing but a continued survey of the same object.

There is a very remarkable circumstance that attends this experiment, which is that though the change of any considerable part in a mass of matter destroys the identity of the whole, yet we must measure the greatness of the part, not absolutely, but by its *proportion* to the whole. The addition or diminution of a mountain would not be sufficient to produce a diversity in a planet, though the change of a very few inches would be able to destroy the identity of some bodies. It will be impossible to account for this but by reflecting that objects operate upon the mind and break or interrupt the continuity of its actions not according to their real greatness, but according to their proportion to each other, and therefore, since this interruption makes an object cease to appear the same, it must be the uninterrupted progress of the thought which constitutes the imperfect identity.

This may be confirmed by another phenomenon. A change in any considerable part of a body destroys its identity, but it is remarkable that where the change is produced *gradually* and *insensibly* we are less apt to ascribe to it the same effect. The reason can plainly be no other than that the mind, in following the successive changes of the body, feels an easy passage from surveying its condition in one moment to viewing of it in another and at no particular time perceives any interruption in its actions—from which continued perception it ascribes a continued existence and identity to the object.

But whatever precaution we may use in introducing the changes gradually and making them proportional to the whole, it is certain that where the changes are at last observed to become considerable, we make a scruple of ascribing identity to such different objects. There is, however, another artifice by which we may induce the imagination to advance a step further, and that is by producing a reference of the parts to each other and a combination to some *common end* or purpose. A ship of which a considerable part has been changed by frequent repairs is still considered as the same, nor does the difference of the materials hinder us from ascribing an identity to it. The common end, in which the parts conspire, is the same under all their variations and affords an easy transition of the imagination from one situation of the body to another.

But this is still more remarkable when we add a *sympathy* of parts to their *common end* and suppose that they bear to each other the reciprocal relation of cause and effect in all their actions and operations. This is the case with all animals and vegetables, where not only the several parts have a reference to some general purpose, but also a mutual dependence on and connection with each other. The effect of so strong a relation is that though everyone must allow that in a very few years both vegetables and animals endure a *total* change, yet we still attribute identity to them, while their form, size, and substance are entirely altered. An oak that grows from a small plant to a large tree is still the same oak, though there is not one particle of matter or figure of its parts the same. An infant becomes a man and is sometimes fat, sometimes lean without any change in his identity.

We may also consider the two following phenomena, which are remarkable in their kind. The first is that though we are commonly able to distinguish pretty exactly between numerical and specific identity, yet it sometimes happens that we confound them and in our thinking and reasoning employ the one for the other. Thus, a man who hears a noise that is frequently interrupted and renewed says it is still the same noise, though it is evident the sounds have only a specific identity or resemblance and there is nothing numerically the same but the cause which produced them. In like manner it may be said without breach of the propriety of language that such a church, which was formerly of brick, fell to ruin and that the parish rebuilt the same church of freestone and according to modern architecture. Here neither the form nor materials are the same, nor is there anything common to the two objects but their relation to the inhabitants of the parish. Yet this alone is sufficient to make us denominate them the same. But we must observe that in these cases the first object is in a manner annihilated before the second comes into existence, by which means we are never presented in any one point of time with the idea of difference and multiplicity and, for that reason, are less scrupulous in calling them the same.

Secondly, we may remark that though in a succession of related objects it is in a manner requisite that the change of parts are not sudden nor entire in order to preserve the identity, yet where the objects are in their nature changeable and inconstant, we admit of a more sudden transition than would otherwise be consistent with that relation. Thus, as the nature of a river consists in the motion and change of parts, though in less than twenty-four hours these are totally altered, this does not hinder the river from continuing the same during several ages. What is natural and essential to anything is, in a manner, expected, and what is expected makes less impression and appears of less moment than what is unusual and extraordinary. A considerable change of the former kind seems really less to the imagination than the most trivial alteration of the latter and, by breaking less the continuity of the thought, has less influence in destroying the identity.

We now proceed to explain the nature of *personal identity*, which has become so great a question in philosophy, especially of late years, in *England*, where all the more abstruse sciences are studied with a peculiar ardor and application. And here it is evident the same method of reasoning must be continued which has so successfully explained the identity of plants and animals, and ships and houses, and of all the compounded and changeable productions either of art or nature. The identity which we ascribe to the mind of man is only a fictitious one and of a like kind with that which we ascribe to vegetables and animal bodies. It cannot, therefore, have a different origin, but must proceed from a like operation of the imagination upon like objects.

But lest this argument should not convince the reader, though in my opinion perfectly decisive, let him weigh the following reasoning, which is still closer and more immediate. It is evident that the identity which we attribute to the human mind, however perfect we may imagine it to be, is not able to run the several different perceptions into one and make them lose their characters of distinction and difference which are essential to them. It is still true that every distinct perception which enters into the composition of the mind is a distinct existence, and is different, and distinguishable, and separable from every other perception, either contemporary or successive. But as, notwithstanding this distinction and separability, we suppose the whole train of perceptions to be united by identity, a question naturally arises concerning this relation of identity, whether it is something that really binds our several perceptions together or only associates their ideas in the imagination, that is, in other words, whether, in pronouncing concerning the identity of a person, we observe some real bond among his perceptions or only feel one among the ideas we form of them. This question we might easily decide if we would recollect what has been already proved at large, namely, that the understanding never observes any real connection among objects and that even the union of cause and effect, when strictly examined, resolves itself into a customary association of ideas. For from this it evidently follows that identity is nothing really belonging to these different perceptions and uniting them together but rather is merely a quality which we attribute to them because of the union of their ideas in the imagination when we reflect upon them. Now, the only qualities which can give ideas a union in the imagination are these three relations above mentioned. These are the uniting principles in the ideal world, and without them every distinct object is separable by the mind, and may be separately considered, and appears not to have any more connection with any other object than if disjoined by the greatest difference and remoteness. It is, therefore, on some of these three relations of resemblance, contiguity, and causation that identity depends, and as the very essence of these relations consists in their producing an easy transition of ideas, it follows that our notions of personal identity proceed entirely from the smooth and uninterrupted progress of the thought along a train of connected ideas, according to the principles above explained.

The only question, therefore, which remains is by what relations this uninterrupted progress of our thought is produced when we consider the successive existence of a mind or thinking person. And here it is evident we must confine ourselves to resemblance and causation and must drop contiguity, which has little or no influence in the present case.

To begin with *resemblance*: Suppose we could see clearly into the breast of another and observe that succession of perceptions which constitutes his mind or thinking principle, and suppose that he always preserves the memory of a considerable part of past perceptions, it is evident that nothing could more contribute to bestowing a relation on this succession amid all its variations. For what is the memory but a faculty by which we raise up the images of past perceptions? And as an image necessarily resembles its object, must not the frequent placing of these resembling perceptions in the chain of thought convey the imagination more easily from one link to another and make the whole seem like the continuance of one object? In this particular, then, the memory not only discovers the identity, but also contributes to its production by producing the relation of resemblance among the perceptions. The case is the same whether we consider ourselves or others.

As to *causation*, we may observe that the true idea of the human mind is to consider it as a system of different perceptions or different existences which are linked together by the relation of cause and effect, and mutually produce, destroy, influence, and modify each other. Our impressions give rise to their correspondent ideas, and these ideas, in their turn, produce other impressions. One thought chases another and draws after it a third by which it is expelled in its turn. In this respect, I cannot compare the soul more properly to anything than to a republic or commonwealth in which the several members are united by the reciprocal ties of government and subordination and give rise to other persons who propagate the same republic in the incessant changes of its parts. And as the same individual republic may not only change its members, but also its laws and constitutions, in like manner the same person may vary his character and disposition as well as his impressions and ideas without losing his identity. Whatever changes he endures, his several parts are still connected by the relation of causation. And in this view our identity with regard to the passions serves to corroborate that with regard to the imagination by making our distant perceptions influence each other and by giving us a present concern for our past or future pains or pleasures.

As memory alone acquaints us with the continuance and extent of this succession of perceptions, it is to be considered upon that account chiefly as the source of personal identity. Had we no memory, we never should have any notion of causation nor consequently of that chain of causes and effects which constitute our self or person. But having once acquired this notion of causation from the memory, we can extend the same chain of causes and consequently the identity of our persons beyond our memory and can comprehend times, circumstances, and actions which we have entirely forgotten, but suppose in general to have existed. For how few of our past actions are there of which we have any memory? Who can tell me, for instance, what were his thoughts and actions on the 1st of January 1715, the 11th of March 1719, and the 3rd of August 1733? Or will he affirm, because he has entirely forgotten the incidents of these days, that the present self is not the same person with the self of that time, and by that means overturn all the most established notions of personal identity? In this view, therefore, memory does not so much *produce* as *discover* personal identity by showing us the relation of cause and effect among our different perceptions. It will be incumbent on those who affirm that memory produces entirely our personal identity to give a reason why we can thus extend our identity beyond our memory.

The whole of this doctrine leads us to a conclusion which is of great importance in the present affair, namely that all the nice and subtle questions concerning personal identity can never possibly be decided and are to be regarded rather as grammatical than as philosophical difficulties. Identity depends on the relations of ideas, and these relations produce identity by means of that easy transition they occasion. But as the relations and the easiness of the transition may diminish by insensible degrees, we have no just standard by which we can decide any dispute concerning the time when they acquire or lose a title to the name of identity. All the disputes concerning the identity of connected objects are merely verbal, except so far as the relation of parts gives rise to some fiction or imaginary principle of union as we have already observed.

What I have said concerning the first origin and uncertainty of our notion of identity, as applied to the human mind, may be extended with little or no variation to that of *simplicity*. An object whose different coexistent parts are bound together by a close relation operates upon the imagination after much the same manner as one perfectly simple and indivisible and does not require a much greater stretch of thought in order to [form] its conception. From this similarity of operation we attribute a simplicity to it and feign a principle of union as the support of this simplicity and the center of all the different parts and qualities of the object.

Thus we have finished our examination of the several systems of philosophy, both of the intellectual and moral world; and, in our miscellaneous way of reasoning, have been led into several topics, which will either illustrate and confirm some preceding part of this discourse, or prepare the way for our following opinions. It is now time to return to a more close examination of our subject, and to proceed in the accurate anatomy of human nature, having fully explained the nature of our judgment and understanding.

Conclusion of This Book

But before I launch out into those immense depths of philosophy which lie before me, I find myself inclined to stop a moment in my present station, and to ponder that voyage which I have undertaken, and which undoubtedly requires the utmost art and industry to be brought to a happy conclusion. Methinks I am like a man, who, having struck on many shoals, and having narrowly escaped shipwreck in passing a small frith, has yet the temerity to put out to sea in the same leaky weather-beaten vessel, and even carries his ambition so far as to think of compassing the globe under these disadvantageous circumstances. My memory of past errors and perplexities makes me diffident for the future. The wretched condition, weakness, and disorder of the faculties, I must employ in my inquiries, increase my apprehensions. And the impossibility of amending or correcting these faculties, reduces me almost to despair, and makes me resolve to perish on the barren rock, on which I am at present, rather than venture myself upon that boundless ocean which runs out into immensity. This sudden view of my danger strikes me with melancholy; and, as it is usual for that passion, above all others, to indulge itself, I cannot forbear feeding my despair with all those desponding reflections which the present subject furnishes me with in such abundance.

I am first affrighted and confounded with that forlorn solitude in which I am placed in my philosophy, and fancy myself some strange uncouth monster, who, not being able to mingle and unite in society, has been expelled all human commerce, and left utterly abandoned and disconsolate. Fain would I run into the crowd for shelter and warmth, but cannot prevail with myself to mix with such deformity. I call upon others to join me, in order to make a company apart, but no one will hearken to me. Every one keeps at a distance, and dreads that storm which beats upon me from every side. I have exposed myself to the enmity of all metaphysicians, logicians, mathematicians, and even theologians; and can I wonder at the insults I must suffer? I have declared my disapprobation of their systems; and can I be surprised if they should express a hatred of mine and of my person? When I look abroad, I foresee on every side dispute, contradiction, anger, calumny, and detraction. When I turn my eye inward, I find nothing but doubt and ignorance. All the world conspires to oppose and contradict me; though such is my weakness, that I feel all my opinions loosen and fall of themselves, when unsupported by the approbation of others. Every step I take is with hesitation, and every new reflection makes me dread an error and absurdity in my reasoning.

For with what confidence can I venture upon such bold enterprises, when, beside those numberless infirmities peculiar to myself, I find so many which are common to human nature? Can I be sure that, in leaving all established opinions, I am following truth? and by what criterion shall I distinguish her, even if fortune should at last guide me on her footsteps? After the most accurate and exact of my reasonings, I can give no reason why I should assent to it, and feel nothing but a *strong* propensity to consider objects *strongly* in that view under which they appear to me. Experience is a principle which instructs me in the several conjunctions of objects for the past. Habit is another principle which determines me to expect the same for the future; and both of them conspiring to operate upon the imagination, make me form certain ideas in a more intense and lively manner than others which are not attended with the same advantages. Without this quality, by which the mind enlivens some ideas beyond others (which seemingly is so trivial, and so little founded on reason), we could never assent to any argument, nor carry our view beyond those few objects which are present to our senses. Nay, even to these objects we could never attribute any existence but what was dependent on the senses, and must comprehend them entirely in that succession of perceptions which constitutes our self or person. Nay, further, even with relation to that succession, we could only admit of those perceptions which are immediately present to our consciousness; nor could those lively images, with which the memory presents us, be ever received as true pictures of past perceptions. The memory, senses, and understanding are therefore all of them founded on the imagination, or the vivacity of our ideas.

No wonder a principle so inconstant and fallacious should lead us into errors when implicitly followed (as it must be) in all its variations. It is this principle which makes us reason from cause and effect; and it is the same principle which convinces us of the continued existence of external objects when absent from the senses. But though these two operations be equally natural and necessary in the human mind, yet in some circumstances they are directly contrary; nor is it possible for us to reason justly and regularly from causes and effects, and at the same time believe the continued existence of matter? How shall we adjust those principles together? Which of them shall we prefer? Or in case we prefer neither of them, but successively assent to both, as is usual among philosophers, with what confidence can we afterwards usurp that glorious title, when we thus knowingly embrace a manifest contradiction?

This contradiction would be more excusable were it compensated by any degree of solidity and satisfaction in the other parts of our reasoning. But the case is quite contrary. When we trace up the human understanding to its first principles, we find it to lead us into such sentiments as seem to turn into ridicule all our past pains and industry, and to discourage us from future inquiries. Nothing is more curiously inquired after by the mind of man than the causes of every phenomenon; nor are we content with knowing the immediate causes, but push on our inquiries till we arrive at the original and ultimate principle. We would not willingly stop before we are acquainted with that energy in the cause by which it operates on its effect; that tie, which connects them together; and that efficacious quality on which the tie depends. This is our aim in all our studies and reflections. and how must we be disappointed when we learn that this connection, tie, or energy lies merely in ourselves, and is nothing but that determination of the mind which is acquired by custom, and causes us to make a transition from an object to its usual attendant, and from the impression of one to the lively idea of the other? Such a discovery not only cuts off all hope of ever attaining satisfaction, but even prevents our very wishes; since it appears, that when we say we desire to know the ultimate and operating principle as something which resides in the external object, we either contradict ourselves, or talk without a meaning.

This deficiency in our ideas is not indeed perceived in common life, nor are we sensible that, in the most usual conjunctions of cause and effect, we are as ignorant of the ultimate principle which binds them together, as in the most unusual and extraordinary. But this proceeds merely from an illusion of the imagination; and the question is, how far we ought to yield to these illusions. This question is very difficult, and reduces us to a very dangerous dilemma, whichever way we answer it. For if we assent to every trivial suggestion of the fancy, beside that these suggestions are often contrary to each other, they lead us into such errors, absurdities, and obscurities, that we must at last become ashamed of our credulity. Nothing is more dangerous to reason than the flights of the imagination, and nothing has been the occasion of more mistakes among philosophers. Men of bright fancies may in this respect be compared to those angels, whom the Scripture represents as covering their eyes with their wings. This has already appeared in so many instances, that we may spare ourselves the trouble of enlarging upon it any further.

But, on the other hand, if the consideration of these instances makes us take a resolution to reject all the trivial suggestions of the fancy, and adhere to the understanding, that is, to the general and more established properties of the imagination; even this resolution, if steadily executed, would be dangerous, and attended with the most fatal consequences. For I have already shown that the understanding, when it acts alone, and according to its most general principles, entirely subverts itself, and leaves not the lowest degree of evidence in any proposition, either in philosophy or common life. We save ourselves from this total scepticism only by means of that singular and seemingly trivial property of the fancy, by which we enter with difficulty into remote views of things, and are not able to accompany them with so sensible an impression, as we do those which are more easy and natural. Shall we, then, establish it for a general maxim, that no refined or elaborate reasoning is ever to be received? Consider well the consequences of such a principle. By this means you cut off entirely all science and philosophy: you proceed upon one singular quality of the imagination, and by a parity of reason must embrace all of them; and you expressly contradict yourself; since this maxim must be built on the preceding reasoning, which will be allowed to be sufficiently refined and metaphysical. What party, then, shall we choose among these difficulties? If we embrace this principle, and condemn all refined reasoning, we run into the most manifest absurdities. If we reject it in favour of these reasonings, we subvert entirely the human understanding. We have therefore no choice left, but betwixt a false reason and none at all. For my part, I know not what ought to be done in the present case. I can only observe what is commonly done; which is, that this difficulty is seldom or never thought of; and even where it has once been present to the mind, is quickly forgot, and leaves but a small impression behind it. Very refined reflections have little or no influence upon us; and yet we do not, and cannot establish it for a rule, that they ought not to have any influence; which implies a manifest contradiction.

But what have I here said, that reflections very refined and metaphysical have little or no influence upon us? This opinion I can scarce forbear retracting, and condemning from my present feeling and experience. The *intense* view of these manifold contradictions and imperfections in human reason has so wrought upon me, and heated my brain, that I am ready to reject all belief and reasoning, and can look upon no opinion even as more probable or likely than another. Where am I, or what? From what causes do I derive my existence, and to what condition shall I return? Whose favour shall I court, and whose anger must I dread? What beings surround me? and on whom have I any influence, or who have any influence on me? I am confounded with all these questions, and begin to fancy myself in the most deplorable condition imaginable, environed with the deepest darkness, and utterly deprived of the use of every member and faculty.

Most fortunately it happens, that since reason is incapable of dispelling these clouds, Nature herself suffices to that purpose, and cures me of this philosophical melancholy and delirium, either by relaxing this bent of mind, or by some avocation, and lively impression of my senses, which obliterate all these chimeras. I dine, I play a game of backgammon, I converse, and am merry with my friends; and when, after three or four hours' amusement, I would return to these speculations, they appear so cold, and strained, and ridiculous, that I cannot find in my heart to enter into them any further.

Here, then, I find myself absolutely and necessarily determined to live, and talk, and act like other people in the common affairs of life. But notwithstanding that my natural propensity, and the course of my animal spirits and passions reduce me to this indolent belief in the general maxims of the world, I still feel such remains of my former disposition, that I am ready to throw all my books and papers into the fire, and resolve never more to renounce the pleasures of life for the sake of reasoning and philosophy. For those are my sentiments in that splenetic humour which governs me at present. I may, nay I must yield to the current of nature, in submitting to my senses and understanding; and in this blind submission I show most perfectly my sceptical disposition and principles. But does it follow that I must strive against the current of nature, which leads me to indolence and pleasure; that I must seclude myself, in some measure, from the commerce and society of men, which is so agreeable; and that I must torture my brain with subtilties and sophistries, at the very time that I cannot satisfy myself concerning the reasonableness of so painful an application, nor have any tolerable prospect of arriving by its means at truth and certainty? Under what obligation do I lie of making such an abuse of time? And to what end can it serve, either for the service of mankind, or for my own private interest? No: if I must be a fool, as all those who reason or believe anything *certainly* are, my follies shall at least be natural and agreeable. Where I strive against my inclination, I shall have a good reason for my resistance; and will no more be led a wandering into such dreary solitudes, and rough passages, as I have hitherto met with.

These are the sentiments of my spleen and indolence; and indeed I must confess, that philosophy has nothing to oppose to them, and expects a victory more from the returns of a serious good-humoured disposition, than from the force of reason and conviction. In all the incidents of life, we ought still to preserve our scepticism. If we believe that fire warms, or water refreshes, it is only because it costs us too much pains to think otherwise. Nay, if we are philosophers, it ought only to be upon sceptical principles, and from an inclination which we feel to the employing ourselves after that manner. Where reason is lively, and mixes itself with some propensity, it ought to be assented to. Where it does not, it never can have any title to operate upon us.

At the time, therefore, that I am tired with amusement and company, and have indulged a *reverie* in my chamber, or in a solitary walk by a river side, I feel my mind all collected within itself, and am naturally *inclined* to carry my view into all those subjects, about which I have met with so many disputes in the course of my reading and conversation. I cannot forbear having a curiosity to be acquainted with the principles of moral good and evil, the nature and foundation of government, and the cause of those several passions and inclinations which actuate and govern me. I am uneasy to think I approve of one object, and disapprove of another; call one thing beautiful, and another deformed; decide concerning truth and falsehood, reason and folly, without knowing upon what principles I proceed. I am concerned for the condition of the learned world, which lies under such a deplorable ignorance in all these particulars. I feel an ambition to arise in me of contributing to the instruction of mankind, and of acquiring a name by my inventions and discoveries. These sentiments spring up naturally in my present disposition; and should I endeavour to banish them, by attaching myself to any other business or diversion, I *feel* I should be a loser in point of pleasure; and this is the origin of my philosophy.

But even to suppose this curiosity and ambition should not transport me into speculations without the sphere of common life, it would necessarily happen that from my very weakness I must be led into such inquiries. It is certain that superstition is much more bold in its systems and hypotheses than philosophy; and while the latter contents itself with assigning new causes and principles to the phenomena which appear in the visible world, the former opens a world of its own, and presents us with scenes, and beings, and objects, which are altogether new. Since, therefore, it is almost impossible for the mind of man to rest, like those of beasts, in that narrow circle of objects, which are the subject of daily conversation and action, we ought only to deliberate concerning the choice of our guide, and ought to prefer that which is safest and most agreeable. And in this respect I make bold to recommend philosophy, and shall not scruple to give it the preference to superstition of every kind or denomination. For as superstition arises naturally and easily from the popular opinions of mankind, it seizes more strongly on the mind, and is often able to disturb us in the conduct of our lives and actions. Philosophy, on the contrary, if just, can present us only with mild and moderate sentiments; and if false and extravagant, its opinions are merely the objects of a cold and general speculation, and seldom go so far as to interrupt the course of our natural propensities. The *Cynics*[1] are an extraordinary instance of philosophers, who, from reasonings purely philosophical, ran into as great extravagancies of conduct as any *monk* or *dervish* that ever was in the world. Generally speaking, the errors in religion are dangerous; those in philosophy only ridiculous.

I am sensible that these two cases of the strength and weakness of the mind will not comprehend all

1. [The Cynics were members of an Athenian philosophical school who, considering themselves followers of Socrates, maintained that virtue is self-sufficiency and the suppression of desires.]

mankind, and that there are in England, in particular, many honest gentlemen, who, being always employed in their domestic affairs, or amusing themselves in common recreations, have carried their thoughts very little beyond those objects, which are every day exposed to their senses. And indeed, of such as these I pretend not to make philosophers, nor do I expect them either to be associates in these researches, or auditors of these discoveries. They do well to keep themselves in their present situation; and, instead of refining them into philosophers, I wish we could communicate to our founders of systems, a share of this gross earthy mixture, as an ingredient, which they commonly stand much in need of, and which would serve to temper those fiery particles, of which they are composed. While a warm imagination is allowed to enter into philosophy, and hypotheses embraced merely for being spacious and agreeable, we can never have any steady principles, nor any sentiments, which will suit with common practice and experience. But were these hypotheses once removed, we might hope to establish a system or set of opinions, which if not true (for that, perhaps, is too much to be hoped for), might at least be satisfactory to the human mind, and might stand the test of the most critical examination. Nor should we despair of attaining this end, because of the many chimerical systems, which have successively arisen and decayed away among men, would we consider the shortness of that period, wherein these questions have been the subjects of inquiry and reasoning. Two thousand years with such long interruptions, and under such mighty discouragements, are a small space of time to give any tolerable perfection to the sciences; and perhaps we are still in too early an age of the world to discover any principles which will bear the examination of the latest posterity. For my part, my only hope is, that I may contribute a little to the advancement of knowledge, by giving in some particulars a different turn to the speculations of philosophers, and pointing out to them more distinctly those subjects where alone they can expect assurance and conviction. Human Nature is the only science of man; and yet has been hitherto the most neglected. It will be sufficient for me, if I can bring it a little more into fashion; and the hope of this serves to compose my temper from that spleen, and invigorate it from that indolence, which sometimes prevail upon me. If the reader finds himself in the same easy disposition, let him follow me in my future speculations. If not, let him follow his inclination, and wait the returns of application and good humour. The conduct of a man who studies philosophy in this careless manner, is more truly sceptical than that of one who, feeling in himself an inclination to it, is yet so overwhelmed with doubts and scruples, as totally to reject it. A true sceptic will be diffident of his philosophical doubts, as well as of his philosophical convictions; and will never refuse any innocent satisfaction which offers itself, upon account of either of them.

Nor is it only proper we should in general indulge our inclination in the most elaborate philosophical researches, notwithstanding our sceptical principles, but also that we should yield to that propensity, which inclines us to be positive and certain in *particular points*, according to the light in which we survey them in any *particular instant*. It is easier to forbear all examination and inquiry, than to check ourselves in so natural a propensity, and guard against that assurance, which always arises from an exact and full survey of an object. On such an occasion we are apt not only to forget our scepticism, but even our modesty too; and make use of such terms as these, *it is evident, it is certain, it is undeniable*; which a due deference to the public ought, perhaps, to prevent. I may have fallen into this fault after the example of others; but I here enter a *caveat* against any objections which may be offered on that head; and declare that such expressions were extorted from me by the present view of the object, and imply no dogmatical spirit, nor conceited idea of my own judgment, which are sentiments that I am sensible can become nobody, and a sceptic still less than any other.

Every one has observed how much more dogs are animated when they hunt in a pack, than when they pursue their game apart; and it is evident this can proceed from nothing but from sympathy. It is also well known to hunters, that this effect follows in a greater degree, and even in too great a degree, where two packs that are strangers to each other are joined together. We might, perhaps, be at a loss to explain this phenomenon, if we had not experience of a similar in ourselves.

Envy and malice are passions very remarkable in animals. They are perhaps more common than pity; as requiring less effort of thought and imagination.

BOOK II
Of the Passions

Of Liberty and Necessity

We come now to explain the *direct* passions, or the impressions which arise immediately from good or evil, from pain or pleasure. Of this kind are, *desire and aversion, grief and joy, hope and fear.*

Of all the immediate effects of pain and pleasure, there is none more remarkable than the *will*; and though, properly speaking, it be not comprehended among the passions, yet, as the full understanding of its nature and properties is necessary to the explanation of them, we shall here make it the subject of our inquiry. I desire it may be observed, that, by the *will*, I mean nothing but *the internal impression we feel, and are conscious of, when we knowingly give rise to any new motion of our body, or new perception of our mind.* This impression, like the preceding ones of pride and humility, love and hatred, it is impossible to define, and needless to describe any further; for which reason we shall cut off all those definitions and distinctions with which philosophers are wont to perplex rather than clear up this question; and entering at first upon the subject, shall examine that long-disputed question concerning *liberty and necessity*, which occurs so naturally in treating of the will.

It is universally acknowledged that the operations of external bodies are necessary; and that, in the communication of their motion, in their attraction, and mutual cohesion, there are not the least traces of indifference or liberty. Every object is determined by an absolute fate to a certain degree and direction of its motion, and can no more depart from that precise line in which it moves, than it can convert itself into an angel, or spirit, or any superior substance. The actions, therefore, of matter, are to be regarded as instances of necessary actions; and whatever is, in this respect, on the same footing with matter, must be acknowledged to be necessary. That we may know whether this be the case with the actions of the mind, we shall begin with examining matter, and considering on what the idea of a necessity in its operations are founded, and why we conclude one body or action to be the infallible cause of another.

It has been observed already, that in no single instance the ultimate connection of any objects is discoverable either by our senses or reason, and that we can never penetrate so far into the essence and construction of bodies, as to perceive the principle on which their mutual influence depends. It is their constant union alone with which we are acquainted; and it is from the constant union the necessity arises. If objects had not an uniform and regular conjunction with each other, we should never arrive at any idea of cause and effect; and even after all, the necessity which enters into that idea, is nothing but a determination of the mind to pass from one object to its usual attendant, and infer the existence of one from that of the other. Here then are two particulars which we are to consider as essential to necessity, viz. the constant *union* and the *inference* of the mind; and whenever we discover these, we must acknowledge a necessity. As the actions of matter have no necessity but what is derived from these circumstances, and it is not by any insight into the essence of bodies we discover their connection, the absence of this insight, while the union and inference remain, will never, in any case, remove the necessity. It is the observation of the union which produces the inference; for which reason it might be thought sufficient, if we prove a constant union in the actions of the mind, in order to establish the inference along with the necessity of these actions. But that I may bestow a greater force on my reasoning, I shall examine these particulars apart, and shall first prove from experience that our actions have a constant union with our motives, tempers, and circumstances, before I consider the inferences we draw from it.

To this end a very slight and general view of the common course of human affairs will be sufficient. There is no light in which we can take them that does not confirm this principle. Whether we consider mankind according to the difference of sexes, ages, governments, conditions, or methods of education; the same uniformity and regular operation of natural principles are discernible. Like causes still produce like effects; in the same manner as in the mutual action of the elements and powers of nature.

There are different trees which regularly produce fruit, whose relish is different from each other; and this regularity will be admitted as an instance of necessity and causes in external bodies. But are the products of Guienne and of Champagne more regularly different than the sentiments, actions, and passions of the two sexes, of which the one are distinguished by their force and maturity, the other by their delicacy and softness?

Are the changes of our body from infancy to old age more regular and certain than those of our mind and conduct? And would a man be more ridiculous, who would expect that an infant of four years old will raise a weight of three hundred pounds, than one who, from a person of the same age, would look for a philosophical reasoning, or a prudent and well concerted action?

We must certainly allow, that the cohesion of the parts of matter arises form natural and necessary principles, whatever difficulty we may find in explaining them: and for a like reason we must allow, that human society is founded on like principles; and our reason in the latter case is better than even that in the former; because we not only observe that men *always* seek society, but can also explain the principles on which this universal propensity is founded. For is it more certain that two flat pieces of marble will unite together, than two young savages of different sexes will copulate? Do the children arise from this copulation more uniformly, than does the parents' care for their safety and preservation? And after they have arrived at years of discretion by the care of their parents, are the inconveniences attending their separation more certain than their foresight of these inconveniences, and their care of avoiding them by a close union and confederacy?

The skin, pores, muscles, and nerves of a day-labourer, are different from those of a man of quality: so are his sentiments, actions, and manners. The different stations of life influence the whole fabric, external and internal; and these different stations arise necessarily, because uniformly, from the necessary and uniform principles of human nature. Men cannot live without society, and cannot be associated without government. Government makes a distinction of property, and establishes the different ranks of men. This produces industry, traffic, manufactures, law-suits, war, leagues, alliances, voyages, travels, cities, fleets, ports, and all those other actions and objects which cause such a diversity, and at the same time maintain such an uniformity in human life.

Should a traveler, returning from a far country, tell us, that he had seen a climate in the fiftieth degree of northern latitude, where all the fruits ripen and come to perfection in the winter, and decay in the summer, after the same manner as in England they are produced and decay in the contrary seasons, he would find few so credulous as to believe him. I am apt to think a traveler would meet with as little credit, who should inform us of people exactly of the same character with those in Plato's republic on the one hand, or those in Hobbes's *Leviathan* on the other. There is a general course of nature in human actions, as well as in the operations of the sun and the climate. There are also characters peculiar to different nations and particular persons, as well as common to mankind. The knowledge of these characters is founded on the observation of an uniformity in the actions that flow from them; and this uniformity forms the very essence of necessity.

I can imagine only one way of eluding this argument, which is by denying that uniformity of human actions, on which it is founded. As long as actions have a constant union and connection with the situation and temper of the agent, however we may in words refuse to acknowledge the necessity, we really allow the thing. Now, some may perhaps find a pretext to deny this regular union and connection. For what is more capricious than human actions? What more inconstant than the desires of man? And what creature departs more widely, not only from right reason, but from his own character and disposition? An hour, a moment is sufficient to make him change from one extreme to another, and overturn what cost the greatest pain and labour to establish. Necessity is regular and certain. Human conduct is irregular and uncertain. The one therefore proceeds not from the other.

To this I reply, that in judging of the actions of men we must proceed upon the same maxims, as when we reason concerning external objects. When any phenomena are constantly and invariably conjoined together, they acquire such a connection in the imagination, that it passes from one to the other without any doubt or hesitation. But below this there are many inferior degrees of evidence and probability, nor does one single contrariety of experiment entirely destroy all our reasoning. The mind balances the contrary experiments, and, deducting the inferior from the superior, proceeds with that degree of assurance or evidence, which remains. Even when these contrary experiments are entirely equal, we remove not the notion of causes and necessity; but, supposing that the usual contrariety proceeds from the operation of contrary and concealed causes, we conclude, that the chance or indifference lies only in our judgment on account of our imperfect knowledge, not in the things themselves, which are in every case equally necessary, though, to appearance, not equally constant or certain. No union can be more constant and certain than that of some actions with some motives and characters; and it, in other cases, the union is uncertain, it is no more than what happens in the operations of body; nor can we conclude anything from the one irregularity which will not follow equally from the other.

It is commonly allowed that madmen have no liberty. But, were we to judge by their actions, these have less regularity and constancy than the actions of wise men, and consequently are further removed from necessity. Our way of thinking in this particular is, therefore, absolutely inconsistent; but is a natural consequence of these confused ideas and undefined terms, which we so commonly make use of in our reasonings, especially on the present subject.

We must now show, that, as the *union* betwixt motives and actions has the same constancy as that in any natural operations, so its influence on the understanding is also the same in *determining* us to infer the existence of one from that of another. If this shall appear, there is no known circumstance that enters into the connection and production of the actions of matter that is not to be found in all the operations of the mind; and consequently we cannot, without a manifest absurdity, attribute necessity to the one, and refuse it to the other.

There is no philosopher, whose judgment is so riveted to this fantastical system of liberty, as not to acknowledge the force of *moral evidence*, and both in speculation and practice proceed upon it as upon a reasonable foundation. Now, moral evidence is nothing but a conclusion concerning the actions of men, derived from the consideration of their motives, temper, and situation. Thus, when we see certain characters or figures described upon paper, we infer that the person who produced them would affirm such facts, the death of Caesar, the success of Augustus, the cruelty of Nero; and, remembering many other concurrent testimonies, we conclude that those facts were once really existent, and that so many men, without any interest, would never conspire to deceive us; especially since they must, in the attempt, expose themselves to the derision of all their contemporaries, when these facts were asserted to be recently and universally known. The same kind of reasoning runs through politics, war, commerce, economy, and indeed mixes itself so entirely in human life, that it is impossible to act or subsist a moment without having recourse to it. A prince who imposes a tax upon his subjects, expects their compliance. A general who conducts an army, makes account of a certain degree of courage. A merchant looks for fidelity and skill in his factor or supercargo. A man who gives orders for his dinner, doubts not of the obedience of his servants. In short, as nothing more nearly interests us than our own actions and those of others, the greatest part of our reasonings is employed in judgments concerning them. Now I assert, that whoever reasons after this manner, does *ipso facto* believe the actions of the will to arise from necessity, and that he knows not what he means when he denies it.

All those objects, of which we call the one *cause* and the other *effect*, considered in themselves, are as distinct and separate from each other as any two things in nature; nor can we ever, by the most accurate survey of them, infer the existence of the one from that of the other. It is only from experience and the observation of their constant union, that we are able to form this inference; and even after all, the inference is nothing but the effects of custom on the imagination. We must not here be content with saying, that the idea of cause and effect arises from objects constantly united; but must affirm, that it is the very same with the idea of these objects, and that the *necessary connection* is not discovered by a conclusion of the understanding, but is merely a perception of the mind. Wherever, therefore, we observe the same union, and wherever the union operates in the same manner upon the belief and opinion, we have the idea of cause and necessity, though perhaps we may avoid those expressions. Motion in one body, in all past instances that have fallen under our observation, is followed upon impulse by motion in another. It is impossible for the mind to penetrate further. From this constant union it *forms* the idea of cause and effect, and by its influence *feels* the necessity. As there is the same constancy, and the same influence, in what we call moral evidence, I ask no more. What remains can only be a dispute of words.

And indeed, when we consider how aptly *natural* and *moral* evidence cement together, and form only one chain of argument betwixt them, we shall make no scruple to allow, that they are of the same nature, and derived from the same principles. A prisoner, who has neither money nor interest discovers the impossibility of his escape, as well from the obstinacy of the gaoler, as from the walls and bars with which he is surrounded; and in all attempts for his freedom, chooses rather to work upon the stone and iron of the one, than upon the inflexible nature of the other. The same prisoner, when conducted to the scaffold, foresees his death as certainly from the constancy and fidelity of his guards, as from the operation of the axe or wheel. His mind runs along a certain train of ideas: the refusal of the soldiers to consent to his escape; the action of the executioner; the separation of the head and body, bleeding, convulsive motions, and death. Here is a connected chain of natural causes and voluntary actions; but the mind feels no difference betwixt them in passing from one link to another; nor is less certain of the future event that if it were connected with the present impressions of the memory and senses by a train of causes cemented together by what we are pleased to call a *physical necessity*. The same experienced union has the same effect on the mind, whether the united objects be motives, volitions, and actions, or figure and motion. We may change the names of things, but their nature and their operation on the understanding never change.

I dare be positive no one will ever endeavour to refute these reasonings otherwise than by altering my definitions, and assigning a different meaning to the terms of *cause, and effect, and necessity, and liberty, and chance*. According to my definitions, necessity makes an essential part of causation; and consequently liberty, by removing necessity, removes all causes, and is the very same thing with chance. As chance is commonly thought to imply a contradiction, and is at least directly contrary to experience, there are always the same arguments against liberty or free-will. If any one alters the definitions, I cannot pretend to argue with him till I know the meaning he assigns to these terms.

The Same Subject Continued

I believe we may assign the three following reasons for the prevalence of the doctrine of liberty, however absurd it may be in one sense, and unintelligible in any other. First, after we have performed any action, though we confess we were influenced by particular views and motives, it is difficult for us to persuade ourselves we were governed by necessity, and that it was utterly impossible for us to have acted otherwise, the idea of necessity seeming to imply something of force, and violence, and constraint, of which we are not sensible. Few are capable of distinguishing betwixt the liberty of *spontaneity*, as it is called in the schools, and the liberty of *indifference*; betwixt that which is opposed to violence, and that which means a negation of necessity and causes. The first is even the most common sense of the word; and as it is only that species of liberty which it concerns us to preserve, our thoughts have been principally turned towards it, and have almost universally confounded it with the other.

Secondly, there is a *false sensation* or *experience* even of the liberty of indifference, which is regarded as an argument for its real existence. The necessity of any action, whether of matter or of mind, is not properly a quality in the agent, but in any thinking or intelligent being who may consider the action, and consists in the determination of his thought to infer its existence from some preceding objects: as liberty or chance, on the other hand, is nothing but the want of that determination, and a certain looseness, which we feel in passing or not passing from the idea of one to that of the other. Now, we may observe, that though in reflecting on human actions, we seldom feel such a looseness or indifference, yet it very commonly happens, that, in performing the actions themselves, we are sensible of something like it: and as all related or resembling objects are readily taken for each other, this has been employed as a demonstrative, or even an intuitive proof of human liberty. We feel that our actions are subject to our will on most occasions, and imagine we feel that the will itself is subject to nothing; because when, by a denial of it, we are provoked to try, we feel that it moves easily every way, and produces an image of itself even on that side on which it did not settle. This image or faint motion, we persuade ourselves, could have been completed into the thing itself; because, should that be denied, we find, upon a second trial, that it can. But these efforts are all in vain; and whatever capricious and irregular actions we may perform, as the desire of showing our liberty is the sole motive of our actions, we can never free ourselves from the bonds of necessity. We may imagine we feel a liberty within ourselves, but a spectator can commonly infer our actions from our motives and character; and even where he cannot, he concludes in general that he might, were he perfectly acquainted with every circumstance of our situation and temper, and the most secret springs of our complexion and disposition. Now, this is the very essence of necessity, according to the foregoing doctrine.

A third reason why the doctrine of liberty has generally been better received in the world than its antagonist, proceeds from *religion*, which has been very unnecessarily interested in this question. There is no method of reasoning more common, and yet none more blamable, than in philosophical debates to endeavour to refute any hypothesis by a pretext of its dangerous consequences to religion and morality. When any opinion leads us into absurdities, it is certainly false; but it is not certain an opinion is false because it is of dangerous consequence. Such topics, therefore, ought entirely to be forborne, as serving nothing to the discovery of truth, but only to make the person of an antagonist odious. This I observe in general, without pretending to draw any advantage from it. I submit myself frankly to an examination of this kind, and dare venture to affirm, that the doctrine of necessity, according to my explication of it, is not only innocent, but even advantageous to religion and morality.

I define necessity two ways, conformable to the two definitions of *cause*, of which it makes an essential part. I place it either in the constant union and conjunction of like objects, or in the inference of the mind from the one to the other. Now, necessity, in both these senses, has universally, though tacitly, in the schools, in the pulpit, and in common life, been allowed to belong to the will of man; and no one has ever pretended to deny, that we can draw inferences concerning human actions, and that those inferences are founded on the experienced union of like actions with like motives and circumstances. The only particular in which any one can differ from me is, either that perhaps he will refuse to call this necessity; but as long as the meaning is understood, I hope the word can do no harm; or, that he will maintain there is something else in the operations of matter. Now, whether it be so or not, is of no consequence to religion, whatever it may be to natural philosophy. I may be mistaken in asserting, that we have no idea of any other connection in the actions of body, and shall be glad to be further instructed on that head: but sure I am, I ascribe nothing to the actions of the mind, but what must readily be allowed of. Let no one, therefore, put an invidious construction on my words, by saying simply, that I assert the necessity of human actions, and place them on the same footing with the operations of senseless matter. I do not ascribe to the will that unintelligible necessity, which is supposed to lie in matter. But I ascribe to matter that intelligible quality, call it necessity or not, which the most rigorous orthodoxy does or must allow to belong to the will. I change, therefore, nothing in the received systems, with regard to the will, but only with regard to material objects.

Nay, I shall go further, and assert, that this kind of necessity is so essential to religion and morality, that without it there must ensue an absolute subversion of both, and that every other supposition is entirely destructive to all laws, both *divine* and *human*. It is indeed certain, that as all human laws are founded on rewards and punishments, it is supposed as a fundamental principle, that these motives have an influence on the mind, and both produce the good and prevent the evil actions. We may give to this influence what name we please; but as it is usually conjoined with the action, common sense requires it should be esteemed a cause, and be looked upon as an instance of that necessity, which I would establish.

This reasoning is equally solid, when applied to *divine* laws, so far as the Deity is considered as a legislator, and is supposed to inflict punishment and bestow rewards with a design to produce obedience. But I also maintain, that even where he acts not in his magisterial capacity, but is regarded as the avenger of crimes merely on account of their odiousness and deformity, not only it is impossible, without the necessary connection of cause and effect in human actions, that punishments could be inflicted compatible with justice and moral equity; but also that it could ever enter into the thoughts of any reasonable being to inflict them. The constant and universal object of hatred or anger is a person or creature endowed with thought and consciousness; and when any criminal or injurious actions excite that passion, it is only by their relation to the person or connection with him. But according to the doctrine of liberty or chance, this connection is reduced to nothing, nor are men more accountable for those actions, which are designed and premeditated, than for such as are the most casual and accidental. Actions are, by their very nature, temporary and perishing; and where they proceed not from some cause in the characters and dispositions of the person who performed them, they infix not themselves upon him, and can neither redound to his honour, if good, nor infamy, if evil. The action itself may be blamable; it may be contrary to all the rules of morality and religion: but the person is not responsible for it; and as it proceeded from nothing in him that is durable or constant, and leaves nothing of that nature behind it, it is impossible he can, upon its account, become the object of punishment or vengeance. According to the hypothesis of liberty, therefore, a man is as pure and untainted, after having committed the most horrid crimes, as at the first moment of his birth, nor is his character any way concerned in his actions, since they are derived from it, and the wickedness of the one can never be used as a proof of the depravity of the other. It is only upon the principles of necessity, that a person acquires any merit or demerit from his actions, however the common opinion may incline to the contrary.

But so inconsistent are men with themselves, that though they often assert that necessity utterly destroys all merit and demerit either towards mankind or superior powers, yet they continue still to reason upon these very principles of necessity in all their judgments concerning this matter. Men are not blamed for such evil actions as they perform ignorantly and casually, whatever may be their consequences. Why? but because the causes of these actions are only momentary, and terminate in them alone. Men are less blamed for such evil actions as they perform hastily and unpremeditatedly, than for such as proceed from thought and deliberation. For what reason? but because a hasty temper, though a constant cause in the mind, operates only by intervals, and infects not the whole character. Again, repentence wipes off every crime, especially if attended with an evident reformation of life and manners. How is this to be accounted for? but by asserting that actions render a person criminal, merely as they are proofs of criminal passions or principles in the mind; and when, by any alteration of these principles, they cease to be just proofs, they likewise cease to be criminal. But according to the doctrine of *liberty* or *chance*, they never were just proofs, and consequently never were criminal.

Here then I turn to my adversary, and desire him to free his own system from these odious consequences before he charges them upon others. Or, if he rather chooses that this question should be decided by fair arguments before philosophers, than by declamations before the people, let him return to what I have advanced to prove that liberty and chance are synonymous; and concerning the nature of moral evidence and the regularity of human actions. Upon a review of these reasonings, I cannot doubt of an entire victory; and therefore, having proved that all actions of the will have particular causes, I proceed to explain what these causes are, and how they operate.

Of the Influencing Motives of the Will

Nothing is more usual in philosophy, and even in common life, than to talk of the combat of passion and reason, to give the preference to reason, and assert that men are only so far virtuous as they conform themselves to its dictates. Every rational creature, it is said, is obliged to regulate his actions by reason; and if any other motive or principle challenge the direction of his conduct, he ought to oppose it, till it be entirely subdued, or at least brought to a conformity with that superior principle. On this method of thinking the greatest part of moral philosophy, ancient and modern, seems to be founded; nor is there an ampler field, as well for metaphysical arguments, as popular declamations, than this supposed preëminence of reason above passion. The eternity, invariableness, and divine origin of the former, have been displayed to the best advantage: the blindness, inconstancy, and deceitfulness of the latter, have been as strongly insisted on. In order to show the fallacy of all this philosophy, I shall endeavour to prove *first*, that reason alone can never be a motive to any action of the will; and *secondly*, that it can never oppose passion in the direction of the will.

The understanding exerts itself after two different ways, as it judges from demonstration or probability; as it regards the abstract relations of our ideas, or those relations of objects of which experience only gives us information. I believe it scarce will be asserted, that the first species of reasoning alone is ever the cause of any action. As its proper province is the world of ideas, and as the will always places us in that of realities, demonstration and volition seem upon that account to be totally removed from each other. Mathematics, indeed, are useful in all mechanical operations, and arithmetic in almost every art and profession: but it is not of themselves they have any influence. Mechanics are the art of regulating the motions of bodies *to some designed end or purpose*; and the reason why we employ arithmetic in fixing the proportions of numbers, is only that we may discover the proportions of their influence and operation. A merchant is desirous of knowing the sum total of his accounts with any person: why? but that he may learn what sum will have the same *effects* in paying his debt, and going to market, as all the particular articles taken together. Abstract or demonstrative reasoning, therefore, never influences any of our actions, but only as it directs our judgment concerning causes and effects; which leads us to the second operation of the understanding.

It is obvious, that when we have the prospect of pain or pleasure from any object, we feel a consequent emotion of aversion or propensity, and are carried to avoid or embrace what will give us this uneasiness or satisfaction. It is also obvious, that this emotion rests not here, but, making us cast our view on every side, comprehends whatever objects are connected with its original one by the relation of cause and effect. Here then reasoning takes place to discover this relation; and according as our reasoning varies, our actions receive a subsequent variation. But it is evident, in this case, that the impulse arises not from reason, but is only directed by it. It is from the prospect of pain or pleasure that the aversion or propensity arises towards any object: and these emotions extend themselves to the causes and effects of that object, as they are pointed out to us by reason and experience. It can never in the least concern us to know, that such objects are causes, and such others effects, if both the causes and effects be indifferent to us. Where the objects themselves do not affect us, their connection can never give them any influence; and it is plain that, as reason is nothing but the discovery of this connection, it cannot be by its means that the objects are able to affect us.

Since reason alone can never produce any action, or give rise to volition, I infer, that the same faculty is as incapable of preventing volition, or of disputing the preference with any passion or emotion. This consequence is necessary. It is impossible reason could have the latter effect of preventing volition, but by giving an impulse in a contrary direction to our passions; and that impulse, had it operated alone, would have been ample to produce volition. Nothing can oppose or retard the impulse of passion, but a contrary impulse; and if this contrary impulse ever arises from reason, that latter faculty must have an original influence on the will, and must be able to cause, as well as hinder, any act of volition. But if reason has no original influence, it is impossible it can withstand any principle which has such an efficacy, or ever keep the mind in suspense a moment. Thus, it appears, that the principle which opposes our passion cannot be the same with reason, and is only called so in an improper sense. We speak not strictly and philosophically, when we talk of the combat of passion and of reason. Reason is, and ought only to be, the slave of the passions, and can never pretend to any other office than to serve and obey them. As this opinion may appear somewhat extraordinary, it may not be improper to confirm it by some other considerations.

A passion is an original existence, or, if you will, modification of existence, and contains not any representative quality, which renders it a copy of any other existence or modification. When I am angry, I am actually possessed with the passion, and in that emotion have no more a reference to any other object, than when I am thirsty, or sick, or more than five feet high. It is impossible, therefore, that this passion can be opposed by, or be contradictory to truth and reason; since this contradiction consists in the disagreement of ideas, considered as copies, with those objects which they represent.

What may at first occur on this head is, that as nothing can be contrary to truth or reason, except what has a reference to it, and as the judgments of our understanding only have this reference, it must follow that passions can be contrary to reason only, so far as they are *accompanied* with some judgment or opinion. According to this principle, which is so obvious and natural, it is only in two senses that any affection can be called unreasonable. First, When a passion, such as hope or fear, grief or joy, despair or security, is founded on the supposition of the existence of objects, which really do not exist. Secondly, When in exerting any passion in action, we choose means sufficient for the designed end, and deceive ourselves in our judgment of causes and effects. Where a passion is neither founded on false suppositions, nor chooses means insufficient for the end, the understanding can neither justify nor condemn it. It is not contrary to reason to prefer the destruction of the whole world to the scratching of my finger. It is not contrary to reason for me to choose my total ruin, to prevent the least uneasiness of an Indian, or person wholly unknown to me. It is as little contrary to reason to prefer even my own acknowledged lesser good to my greater, and have a more ardent affection for the former than the latter. A trivial good may, from certain circumstances, produce a desire superior to what arises from the greatest and most valuable enjoyment; nor is there anything more extraordinary in this, than in mechanics to see one pound weight raise up a hundred by the advantage of its situation. In short, a passion must be accompanied with some false judgment, in order to its being unreasonable; and even then it is not the passion, properly speaking, which is unreasonable, but the judgment.

The consequences are evident. Since a passion can never, in any sense, be called unreasonable, but when founded on a false supposition, or when it chooses means insufficient for the designed end, it is impossible that reason and passion can ever oppose each other, or dispute for the government of the will and actions. The moment we perceive the falsehood of any supposition, or the insufficiency of any means, our passions yield to our reason without any opposition. I may desire any fruit as of an excellent relish; but whenever you convince me of my mistake, my longing ceases. I may will the performance of certain actions as means of obtaining any desired good; but as my willing of these actions is only secondary, and founded on the supposition that they are causes of the proposed effect; as soon as I discover the falsehood of that supposition, they must become indifferent to me.

It is natural for one, that does not examine objects with a strict philosophic eye, to imagine, that those actions of the mind are entirely the same, which produce not a different sensation, and are not immediately distinguishable to the feeling and perception. Reason, for instance, exerts itself without producing any sensible emotions; and except in the more sublime disquisitions of philosophy, or in the frivolous subtilties of the schools, scarce ever conveys any pleasure or uneasiness. Hence it proceeds, that every action of the mind which operates with the same calmness and tranquillity, is confounded with reason by all those who judge of things from the first view and appearance. Now it is certain there are certain calm desires and tendencies, which, though they be real passions, produce little emotion in the mind, and are more known by their effects than by the immediate feeling or sensation. These desires are of two kinds; either certain instincts originally implanted in our natures, such as benevolence and resentment, the love of life, and kindness to children; or the general appetite to good, and aversion to evil, considered merely as such. When any of these passions are calm, and cause no disorder in the soul, they are very readily taken for the determinations of reason, and are supposed to proceed from the same faculty with that which judges of truth and falsehood. Their nature and principles have been supposed the same, because their sensations are not evidently different.

Besides these calm passions, which often determine the will, there are certain violent emotions of the same kind, which have likewise a great influence on that faculty. When I receive any injury from another, I often feel a violent passion of resentment, which makes me desire his evil and punishment, independent of all considerations of pleasure and advantage to myself. When I am immediately threatened with any grievous ill, my fears, apprehensions, and aversions rise to a great height, and produce a sensible emotion.

The common error of metaphysicians has lain in ascribing the direction of the will entirely to one of these principles, and supposing the other to have no influence. Men often act knowingly against their interest; for which reason, the view of the greatest possible good does not always influence them. Men often counteract a violent passion in prosecution of their interests and designs; it is not, therefore, the present uneasiness alone which determines them. In general we may observe that both these principles operate on the will; and where they are contrary, that either of them prevails, according to the *general* character or *present* disposition of the person. What we call strength of mind, implies the prevalence of the calm passions above the violent; though we may easily observe, there is no man so constantly possessed of this virtue as never on any occasion to yield to the solicitations of passion and desire. From these variations of temper proceeds the great difficulty of deciding concerning the actions and resolutions of men, where there is any contrariety of motives and passions.

BOOK III

Of Morals

Moral Distinctions Not Derived from Reason

There is an inconvenience which attends all abstruse reasoning, that it may silence, without convincing an antagonist, and requires the same intense study to make us sensible of its force, that was at first requisite for its invention. When we leave our closet, and engage in the common affairs of life, its conclusions seem to vanish like the phantoms of the night on the appearance of the morning; and it is difficult for us to retain even that conviction which we had attained with difficulty. This is still more conspicuous in a long chain of reasoning, where we must preserve to the end the evidence of the first propositions, and where we often lose sight of all the most received maxims, either of philosophy or common life. I am not, however, without hopes, that the present system of philosophy will acquire new force as it advances; and that our reasonings concerning *morals* will corroborate whatever has been said concerning the *understanding* and the *passions*. Morality is a subject that interests us above all others; we fancy the peace of society to be at stake in every decision concerning it; and it is evident that this concern must make our speculations appear more real and solid, than where the subject is in a great measure indifferent to us. What affects us, we conclude, can never be a chimera; and, as our passion is engaged on the one side or the other, we naturally think that the question lies within human comprehension; which, in other cases of this nature, we are apt to entertain some doubt of. Without this advantage, I never should have ventured upon a third volume of such abstruse philosophy, in an age wherein the greatest part of men seem agreed to convert reading into an amusement, and to reject everything that requires any considerable degree of attention to be comprehended.

It has been observed, that nothing is ever present to the mind but its perceptions; and that all the actions of seeing, hearing, judging, loving, hating, and thinking, fall under this denomination. The mind can never exert itself in any action which we may not comprehend under the term of *perception*; and consequently that term is no less applicable to those judgments by which we distinguish moral good and evil, than to every other operation of the mind. To approve of one character, to condemn another, are only so many different perceptions.

Now, as perceptions resolve themselves into two kinds, viz. *impressions* and *ideas*, this distinction gives rise to a question, with which we shall open up our present inquiry concerning morals, *whether it is by means of our ideas or impressions we distinguish betwixt vice and virtue, and pronounce an action blamable or praiseworthy*? This will immediately cut off all loose discourses and declamations, and reduce us to something precise and exact on the present subject.

Those who affirm that virtue is nothing but a conformity to reason; that there are eternal fitnesses and unfitnesses of things, which are the same to every rational being that considers them; that the immutable measure of right and wrong impose an obligation, not only on human creatures, but also on the Deity himself: all these systems concur in the opinion, that morality, like truth, is discerned merely by ideas, and by their juxtaposition and comparison. In order, therefore, to judge of these systems, we need only consider whether it be possible from reason alone, to distinguish betwixt moral good and evil, or whether there must concur some other principles to enable us to make that distinction.

If morality had naturally no influence on human passions and actions, it were in vain to take such pains to inculcate it; and nothing would be more fruitless than that multitude of rules and precepts with which all moralists abound. Philosophy is commonly divided into *speculative* and *practical*; and as morality is always comprehended under the latter division, it is supposed to influence our passions and actions, and to go beyond the calm and indolent judgments of the understanding. And this is confirmed by common experience, which informs us that men are often governed by their duties, and are deterred from some actions by the opinion of injustice, and impelled to others by that of obligation.

Since morals, therefore, have an influence on the actions and affections, it follows that they cannot be derived from reason; and that because reason alone, as we have already proved, can never have any such influence. Morals excite passions, and produce or prevent actions. Reason of itself is utterly impotent in this particular. The rules of morality, therefore, are not conclusions of our reason.

No one, I believe, will deny the justness of this inference; nor is there any other means of evading it, than by denying that principle on which it is founded. As long as it is allowed, that reason has no influence on our passions and actions, it is in vain to pretend that morality is discovered only by a deduction of reason. An active principle can never be founded on an inactive; and if reason be inactive in itself, it must remain so in all its shapes and appearances, whether it exerts itself in natural or moral subjects, whether it considers the powers of external bodies, or the actions of rational beings.

It would be tedious to repeat all the arguments by which I have proved that reason is perfectly inert, and can never either prevent or produce any action or affection. It will be easy to recollect what has been said upon that subject. I shall only recall on this occasion one of these arguments, which I shall endeavour to render still more conclusive, and more applicable to the present subject.

Reason is the discovery of truth or falsehood. Truth or falsehood consists in an agreement or disagreement either to the *real* relations of ideas, or to *real* existence and matter of fact. Whatever therefore is not susceptible of this agreement or disagreement, is incapable of being true or false, and can never be an object of our reason. Now, it is evident our passions, volitions, and actions, are not susceptible of any such agreement or disagreement; being original facts and realities, complete in themselves, and implying no reference to other passions, volitions, and actions. It is impossible, therefore, they can be pronounced either true or false, and be either contrary or conformable to reason.

This argument is of double advantage to our present purpose. For it proves *directly*, that actions do not derive their merit from a conformity to reason, nor their blame from a contrariety to it; and it proves the same truth more *indirectly*, by showing us, that as reason can never immediately prevent or produce any action by contradicting or approving of it, it cannot be the source of moral good and evil, which are found to have that influence. Actions may be laudable or blamable; but they cannot be reasonable or unreasonable: laudable or blamable, therefore, are not the same with reasonable or unreasonable. The merit and demerit of actions frequently contradict, and sometimes control our natural propensities. But reason has no such influence. Moral distinctions, therefore, are not the offspring of reason. Reason is wholly inactive, and can never be the source of so active a principle as conscience, or a sense of morals.

But perhaps it may be said, that though no will or action can be immediately contradictory to reason, yet we may find such a contradiction in some of the attendants of the actions, that is, in its causes or effects. The action may cause a judgment, or may be *obliquely* caused by one, when the judgment concurs with a passion; and by an abusive way of speaking, which philosophy will scarce allow of, the same contrariety may, upon that account, be ascribed to the action. How far this truth or falsehood may be the source of morals, it will now be proper to consider.

It has been observed that reason, in a strict and philosophical sense, can have an influence on our conduct only after two ways: either when it excites a passion, by informing us of the existence of something which is a proper object of it; or when it discovers the connection of causes and effects, so as to afford us means of exerting any passion. These are the only kinds of judgment which can accompany our actions, or can be said to produce them in any manner; and it must be allowed, that these judgments may often be false and erroneous. A person may be affected with passion, by supposing a pain or pleasure to lie in an object which has no tendency to produce either of these sensations, or which produces the contrary to what is imagined. A person may also take false measures for the attaining of his end, and may retard, by his foolish conduct, instead of forwarding the execution of any object. These false judgments may be thought to affect the passions and actions, which are connected with them, and may be said to render them unreasonable, in a figurative and improper way of speaking. But though this be acknowledged, it is easy to observe, that these errors are so far from being the source of all immorality, that they are commonly very innocent, and draw no manner of guilt upon the person who is so unfortunate as to fall into them. They extend not beyond a mistake of *fact*, which moralists have not generally supposed criminal, as being perfectly involuntary. I am more to be lamented than blamed, if I am mistaken with regard to the influence of objects in producing pain or pleasure, or if I know not the proper means of satisfying my desires. No one can ever regard such errors as a defect in my moral character. A fruit, for instance, that is really disagreeable, appears to me at a distance, and, through mistake, I fancy it to be pleasant and delicious. Here is one error. I choose certain means of reaching this fruit, which are not proper for my end. Here is a second error; nor is there any third one, which can ever possibly enter into our reasonings concerning actions. I ask, therefore, if a man in this situation, and guilty of these two errors, is to be regarded as vicious and criminal, however unavoidable they might have been? Or if it be possible to imagine that such errors are the sources of all immorality?

And here it may be proper to observe, that if moral distinctions be derived from the truth or falsehood of those judgments, they must take place wherever we form the judgments; nor will there be any difference, whether the question be concerning an apple or a kingdom, or whether the error be avoidable or unavoidable.

For as the very essence of morality is supposed to consist in an agreement or disagreement to reason, the other circumstances are entirely arbitrary, and can never either bestow on any action the character of virtuous or vicious, or deprive it of that character. To which we may add, that this agreement or disagreement, not admitting of degrees, all virtues and vices would of course be equal.

Should it be pretended, that though a mistake of *fact* be not criminal, yet a mistake of *right* often is; and that this may be the source of immorality: I would answer, that it is impossible such a mistake can ever be the original source of immorality, since it supposes a real right and wrong; that is, a real distinction in morals, independent of these judgments. A mistake, therefore, of right, may become a species of immorality; but it is only a secondary one, and is founded on some other antecedent to it.

As to those judgments which are the *effects* of our actions, and which, when false, give occasion to pronounce the actions contrary to truth and reason; we may observe, that our actions never cause any judgment, either true or false, in ourselves, and that it is only on others they have such an influence. It is certain that an action, on many occasions, may give rise to false conclusions in others; and that a person, who, through a window, sees any lewd behaviour of mine with my neighbour's wife, may be so simple as to imagine she is certainly my own. In this respect my action resembles somewhat a lie or falsehood; only with this difference, which is material, that I perform not the action with any intention of giving rise to a false judgment in another, but merely to satisfy my lust and passion. It causes, however, a mistake and false judgment by accident; and the falsehood of its effects may be ascribed, by some odd figurative way of speaking, to the action itself. But still I can see no pretext of reason for asserting, that the tendency to cause such an error is the first spring or original source of all immorality.

Thus, upon the whole, it is impossible that the distinction betwixt moral good and evil can be made by reason; since that distinction has an influence upon our actions, of which reason alone is incapable. Reason and judgment may, indeed, be the mediate cause of an action, by prompting or by directing a passion; but it is not pretended that a judgment of this kind, either in its truth or falsehood, is attended with virtue or vice. And as to the judgments, which are caused by our judgments, they can still less bestow those moral qualities on the actions which are their causes.

But, to be more particular, and to show that those eternal immutable fitnesses and unfitnesses of things cannot be defended by sound philosophy, we may weigh the following considerations.

If the thought and understanding were alone capable of fixing the boundaries of right and wrong, the character of virtuous and vicious either must lie in some relations of objects, or must be a matter of fact which is discovered by our reasoning. This consequence is evident. As the operations of human understanding divide themselves into two kinds, the comparing of ideas, and the inferring of matter of fact, were virtue discovered by the understanding, it must be an object of one of these operations; nor is there any third operation of the understanding which can discover it. There has been an opinion very industriously propagated by certain philosophers, that morality is susceptible of demonstration; and though no one has ever been able to advance a single step in those demonstrations, yet it is taken for granted that this science may be brought to an equal certainty with geometry or algebra. Upon this supposition, vice and virtue must consist in some relations; since it is allowed on all hands, that no matter of fact is capable of being demonstrated. Let us therefore begin with examining this hypothesis, and endeavour, if possible, to fix those moral qualities which have been so long the objects of our fruitless researches; point out distinctly the relations which constitute morality or obligation, that we may know wherein they consist, and after what manner we must judge of them.

If you assert that vice and virtue consist in relations susceptible of certainty and demonstration, you must confine yourself to those *four* relations which alone admit of that degree of evidence; and in that case you run into absurdities from which you will never be able to extricate yourself. For as you make the very essence of morality to lie in the relations, and as there is no one of these relations but what is applicable, not only to an irrational but also to an inanimate object, it follows that even such objects must be susceptible of merit or demerit. *Resemblance, contrariety, degrees in quality*, and *proportions in quantity and number*; all these relations belong as properly to matter as to our actions, passions, and volitions. It is unquestionable, therefore, that morality lies not in any of these relations, nor the sense of it in their discovery.

Should it be asserted, that the sense of morality consists in the discovery of some relation distinct from these, and that our enumeration was not complete when we comprehended all demonstrable relations under four general heads; to this I know not what to reply, till some one be so good as to point out to me this new relation. It is impossible to refute a system which has never yet been explained. In such a manner of fighting in the dark, a man loses his blows in the air, and often places them where the enemy is not present.

I must therefore, on this occasion, rest contented with requiring the two following conditions of any one that would undertake to clear up this system. *First*, as moral good and evil belong only to the actions of the mind, and are derived from our situation with regard to external objects, the relations from which these moral distinctions arise must lie only betwixt internal actions and external objects, and must not be applicable either to internal actions, compared among themselves, or to external objects, when placed in opposition to other external objects. For as morality is supposed to attend certain relations, if these relations could belong to internal actions considered singly, it would follow, that we might be guilty of crimes in ourselves, and independent of our situation with respect to the universe; and in like manner, if these moral relations could be applied to external objects, it would follow that even inanimate beings would be susceptible of moral beauty and deformity. Now, it seems difficult to imagine that any relation can be discovered betwixt our passions, volitions, and actions, compared to external objects, which relation might not belong either to these passions and volitions, or to these external objects, compared among *themselves*.

But it will be still more difficult to fulfill the *second* condition, requisite to justify this system. According to the principles of those who maintain an abstract rational difference betwixt moral good and evil, and a natural fitness and unfitness of things, it is not only supposed, that these relations, being eternal and immutable, are the same, when considered by every rational creature, but their *effects* are also supposed to be necessarily the same; and it is concluded they have no less, or rather a greater, influence in directing the will of the Deity, than in governing the rational and virtuous of our own species. These two particulars are evidently distinct. It is one thing to know virtue, and another to conform the will to it. In order, therefore, to prove that the measures of right and wrong are eternal laws, *obligatory* on every rational mind, it is not sufficient to show the relations upon which they are founded: we must also point out the connection betwixt the relation and the will; and must prove that this connection is so necessary, that in every well-disposed mind, it must take place and have its influence; though the difference betwixt these minds be in other respects immense and infinite. Now, besides what I have already proved, that even in human nature no relation can ever alone produce any action; besides this, I say, it has been shown, in treating of the understanding, that there is no connection of cause and effect, such as this is supposed to be, which is discoverable otherwise than by experience, and of which we can pretend to have any security by the simple consideration of the objects. All beings in the universe, considered in themselves, appear entirely loose and independent of each other. It is only by experience we learn their influence and connection; and this influence we ought never to extend beyond experience.

Thus it will be impossible to fulfill the *first* condition required to the system of eternal rational measures of right and wrong; because it is impossible to show those relations, upon which such a distinction may be founded: and it is as impossible to fulfill the *second* condition; because we cannot prove *a priori*, that these relations, if they really existed and were perceived, would be universally forcible and obligatory.

But to make these general reflections more clear and convincing, we may illustrate them by some particular instances, wherein this character of moral good or evil is the most universally acknowledged. Of all crimes that human creatures are capable of committing, the most horrid and unnatural is ingratitude, especially when it is committed against parents, and appears in the more flagrant instances of wounds and death. This is acknowledged by all mankind, philosophers as well as the people: the question only arises among philosophers, whether the guilt or moral deformity of this action be discovered by demonstrative reasoning, or be felt by an internal sense, and by means of some sentiment, which the reflecting on such an action naturally occasions. This question will soon be decided against the former opinion, if we can show the same relations in other objects, without the notion of any guilt or iniquity attending them. Reason or science is nothing but the comparing of ideas, and the discovery of their relations; and if the same relations have different characters, it must evidently follow, that those characters are not discovered merely by reason. To put the affair, therefore, to this trial, let us choose any inanimate object, such as an oak or elm; and let us suppose, that, by the dropping of its seed, it produces a sapling below it, which, springing up by degrees, at last overtops and destroys the parent tree: I ask, if, in this instance, there be wanting any relation which is discoverable in parricide or ingratitude? Is not the one tree the cause of the other's existence; and the latter the cause of the destruction of the former, in the same manner as when a child murders his parent? It is not sufficient to reply, that a choice or will is wanting. For in the case of parricide, a will does not give rise to any *different* relations, but is only the cause from which the action is derived; and consequently produces the *same* relations, that in the oak or elm arise from some other principles. It is a will or choice that determines a man to kill his parent: and they are the laws of matter and motion that determine a sapling to destroy the oak from which it sprung. Here then the same relations have different causes; but still the relations are the same: and as their discovery is not in both cases attended with a notion of immorality, it follows, that that notion does not arise from such a discovery.

But to choose an instance still more resembling; I would fain ask any one, why incest in the human species is criminal, and why the very same action, and the same relations in animals, have not the smallest moral turpitude and deformity? If it be answered, that this action is innocent in animals, because they have not reason sufficient to discover its turpitude; but that man, being endowed with that faculty, which *ought* to restrain him to his duty, the same action instantly becomes criminal to him. Should this be said, I would reply, that this is evidently arguing in a circle. For, before reason can perceive this turpitude, the turpitude must exist; and consequently is independent of the decisions of our reason, and is their object more properly than their effect. According to this system, then, every animal that has sense and appetite and will, that is, every animal must be susceptible of all the same virtues and vices, for which we ascribe praise and blame to human creatures. All the difference is, that our superior reason may serve to discover the vice or virtue, and by that means may augment the blame or praise: but still this discovery supposes a separate being in these moral distinctions, and a being which depends only on the will and appetite, and which, both in thought and reality, may be distinguished from reason. Animals are susceptible of the same relations with respect to each other as the human species, and therefore would also be susceptible of the same morality, if the essence of morality consisted in these relations. Their want of a sufficient degree of reason may hinder them from perceiving the duties and obligations of morality, but can never hinder these duties from existing; since they must antecedently exist, in order to their being perceived. Reason must find them, and can never produce them. This argument deserves to be weighed, as being, in my opinion, entirely decisive.

Nor does this reasoning only prove, that morality consists not in any relations that are the objects of science; but if examined, will prove with equal certainty, that it consists not in any *matter of fact*, which can be discovered by the understanding. This is the *second* part of our argument; and if it can be made evident, we may conclude that morality is not an object of reason. But can there be any difficulty in proving that vice and virtue are not matters of fact, whose existence we can infer by reason? Take any action allowed to be vicious; wilful murder, for instance. Examine it in all lights, and see if you can find that matter of fact, or real existence, which you call *vice*. In whichever way you take it, you find only certain passions, motives, volitions, and thoughts. There is no other matter of fact in the case. The vice entirely escapes you, as long as you consider the object. You never can find it, till you turn your reflection into your own breast, and find a sentiment of disapprobation, which arises in you, towards this action. Here is a matter of fact; but it is the object of feeling, not of reason. It lies in yourself, not in the object. So that when you pronounce any action or character to be vicious, you mean nothing, but that from the constitution of your nature you have a feeling or sentiment of blame from the contemplation of it. Vice and virtue, therefore, may be compared to sounds, colours, heat, and cold, which, according to modern philosophy, are not qualities in objects, but perceptions in the mind: and this discovery in morals, like that other in physics, is to be regarded as a considerable advancement of the speculative sciences; though, like that too, it has little or no influence on practice. Nothing can be more real, or concern us more, than our own sentiments of pleasure and uneasiness; and if these be favourable to virtue, and unfavourable to vice, no more can be requisite to the regulation of our conduct and behaviour.

I cannot forbear adding to these reasonings an observation, which may, perhaps, be found of some importance. In every system of morality which I have hitherto met with, I have always remarked, that the author proceeds for some time in the ordinary way of reasoning, and establishes the being of a God, or makes observations concerning human affairs; when of a sudden I am surprised to find, that instead of the usual copulations of propositions, *is*, and *is not*, I meet with no proposition that is not connected with an *ought*, or an *ought not*. This change is imperceptible; but is, however, of the last consequence. For as this *ought*, or *ought not*, expresses some new relation or affirmation, it is necessary that it should be observed and explained; and at the same time that a reason should be given, for what seems altogether inconceivable, how this new relation can be a deduction from others, which are entirely different from it. But as authors do not commonly use this precaution, I shall presume to recommend it to the readers; and am persuaded, that this small attention would subvert all the vulgar systems of morality, and let us see that the distinction of vice and virtue is not founded merely on the relations of objects, nor is perceived by reason.

Moral Distinctions Derived from a Moral Sense

Thus the course of the argument leads us to conclude, that since vice and virtue are not discoverable merely by reason, or the comparison of ideas, it must be by means of some impression or sentiment they occasion, that we are able to mark the difference betwixt them. Our decisions concerning moral rectitude and depravity are evidently perceptions; and as all perceptions are either impressions or ideas, the exclusion of the one is a convincing argument for the other. Morality, therefore, is more properly felt than judged of; though this feeling or sentiment is commonly so soft and gentle that we are apt to confound it with an idea, according to our common custom of taking all things for the same which have any near resemblance to each other.

The next question is, of what nature are these impressions, and after what manner do they operate upon us? Here we cannot remain long in suspense, but must pronounce the impression arising from virtue to be agreeable, and that proceeding from vice to be uneasy. Every moment's experience must convince us of this. There is no spectacle so fair and beautiful as a noble and generous action; nor any which gives us more abhorrence than one that is cruel and treacherous. No enjoyment equals the satisfaction we receive from the company of those we love and esteem; as the greatest of all punishments is to be obliged to pass our lives with those we hate or contemn. A very play or romance may afford us instances of this pleasure which virtue conveys to us; and pain, which arises from vice.

Now, since the distinguishing impressions by which moral good or evil is known, are nothing but *particular* pains or pleasures, it follows, that in all inquiries concerning these moral distinctions, it will be sufficient to show the principles which make us feel a satisfaction or uneasiness from the survey of any character, in order to satisfy us why the character is laudable or blamable. An action, or sentiment, or character, is virtuous or vicious; why? because its view causes a pleasure or uneasiness of a particular kind. In giving a reason, therefore, for the pleasure or uneasiness, we sufficiently explain the vice or virtue. To have the sense of virtue, is nothing but to *feel* a satisfaction of a particular kind from the contemplation of a character. The very *feeling* constitutes our praise or admiration. We go no further; nor do we inquire into the cause of the satisfaction. We do not infer a character to be virtuous, because it pleases; but in feeling that it pleases after such a particular manner, we in effect feel that it is virtuous. The case is the same as in our judgments concerning all kinds of beauty, and tastes, and sensations. Our approbation is implied in the immediate pleasure they convey to us.

I have objected to the system which establishes eternal rational measures of right and wrong, that it is impossible to show, in the actions of reasonable creatures, any relations which are not found in external objects; and therefore, if morality always attended these relations, it were possible for inanimate matter to become virtuous or vicious. Now it may, in like manner, be objected to the present system, that if virtue and vice be determined by pleasure and pain, these qualities must, in every case, arise from the sensations; and consequently any object, whether animate or inanimate, rational or irrational, might become morally good or evil, provided it can excite a satisfaction or uneasiness. But though this objection seems to be the very same, it has by no means the same force in the one case as in the other. For, *first*, it is evident that, under the term *pleasure*, we comprehend sensations, which are very different from each other, and which have only such a distant resemblance as is requisite to make them be expressed by the same abstract term. A good composition of music and a bottle of good wine equally produce pleasure; and, what is more, their goodness is determined merely by the pleasure. But shall we say, upon that account, that the wine is harmonious, or the music of a good flavour? In like manner, an inanimate object, and the character or sentiments of any person, may, both of them, give satisfaction; but, as the satisfaction is different, this keeps our sentiments concerning them from being confounded, and makes us ascribe virtue to the one and not to the other. Nor is every sentiment of pleasure or pain, which arises from characters and actions, of that *peculiar* kind which makes us praise or condemn. The good qualities of an enemy are hurtful to us, but may still command our esteem and respect. It is only when a character is considered in general, without reference to our particular interest, that it causes such a feeling or sentiment as denominates it morally good or evil. It is true, those sentiments from interest and morals are apt to be confounded, and naturally run into one another. It seldom happens that we do not think an enemy vicious, and can distinguish betwixt his opposition to our interest and real villainy or baseness. But this hinders not but that the sentiments are in themselves distinct; and a man of temper and judgment may preserve himself from these illusions. In like manner, though it is certain a musical voice is nothing but one that naturally gives a *particular* kind of pleasure; yet it is difficult for a man to be sensible that the voice of an enemy is agreeable, or to allow it to be musical. But a person of a fine ear, who has the command of himself, can separate these feelings, and give praise to what deserves it.

Secondly, we may call to remembrance the preceding system of the passions, in order to remark a still more considerable difference among our pains and pleasures. Pride and humility, love and hatred, are excited, when there is anything presented to us that both bears a relation to the object of the passion, and produces a separate sensation, related to the sensation of the passion. Now, virtue and vice are attended with these circumstances. They must necessarily be placed either in ourselves or others, and excite either pleasure or uneasiness; and therefore must give rise to one of these four passions, which clearly distinguishes them from the pleasure and pain arising from inanimate objects, that often bear no relation to us; and this is, perhaps, the most considerable effect that virtue and vice have upon the human mind.

It may now be asked, *in general*, concerning this pain or pleasure that distinguishes moral good and evil, *From what principle is it derived, and whence does it arise in the human mind*? To this I reply, *first*, that it is absurd to imagine that, in every particular instance, these sentiments are produced by an *original* quality and *primary* constitution. For as the number of our duties is in a manner infinite, it is impossible that our original instincts should extend to each of them, and from our very first infancy impress on the human mind all that multitude of precepts which are contained in the completest system of ethics. Such a method of proceeding is not conformable to the usual maxims by which nature is conducted, where a few principles produce all that variety we observe in the universe, and everything is carried on in the easiest and most simple manner. It is necessary, therefore, to abridge these primary impulses, and find some more general principles upon which all our notions of morals are founded.

But, in the *second* place, should it be asked, whether we ought to search for these principles in *nature*, or whether we must look for them in some other origin? I would reply, that our answer to this question depends upon the definition of the word Nature, than which there is none more ambiguous and equivocal. If *nature* be opposed to miracles, not only the distinction betwixt vice and virtue is natural, but also every event which has ever happened in the world, *excepting those miracles on which our religion is founded*. In saying, then, that the sentiments of vice and virtue are natural in this sense, we make no very extraordinary discovery.

But *nature* may also be opposed to rare and unusual; and in this sense of the word, which is the common one, there may often arise disputes concerning what is natural or unnatural; and one may in general affirm, that we are not possessed of any very precise standard by which these disputes can be decided. Frequent and rare depend upon the number of examples we have observed; and as this number may gradually increase or diminish, it will be impossible to fix any exact boundaries betwixt them. We may only affirm on this head, that if ever there was anything which could be called natural in this sense, the sentiments of morality certainly may; since there never was any nation of the world, nor any single person in any nation, who was utterly deprived of them, and who never, in any instance, showed the least approbation or dislike of manners. These sentiments are so rooted in our constitution and temper, that, without entirely confounding the human mind by disease or madness, it is impossible to extirpate and destroy them.

But *nature* may also be opposed to artifice, as well as to what is rare and unusual; and in this sense it may be disputed, whether the notions of virtue be natural or not. We readily forget that the designs, and projects, and views of men are principles as necessary in their operation as heat and cold, moist and dry; but, taking them to be free and entirely our own, it is usual for us to set them in opposition to the other principles of nature. Should it therefore be demanded, whether the sense of virtue be natural or artificial, I am of opinion that it is impossible for me at present to give any precise answer to this question. Perhaps it will appear afterwards that our sense of some virtues is artificial, and that of others natural. The discussion of this question will be more proper, when we enter upon an exact detail of each particular vice and virtue.

Meanwhile, it may not be amiss to observe, from these definitions of *natural* and *unnatural*, that nothing can be more unphilosophical than those systems which assert that virtue is the same with what is natural, and vice with what is unnatural. For, in the first sense of the word, nature, as opposed to miracles, both vice and virtue are equally natural; and, in the second sense, as opposed to what is unusual, perhaps virtue will be found to be the most unnatural. At least it must be owned, that heroic virtue, being as unusual, is as little natural as the most brutal barbarity. As to the third sense of the word, it is certain that both vice and virtue are equally artificial and out of nature. For, however it may be disputed, whether the notion of a merit or demerit in certain actions, be natural or artificial, it is evident that the actions themselves are artificial, and performed with a certain design and intention; otherwise they could never be ranked under any of these denominations. It is impossible, therefore, that the character of natural and unnatural can ever, in any sense, mark the boundaries of vice and virtue.

Thus we are still brought back to our first position, that virtue is distinguished by the pleasure, and vice by the pain, that any action, sentiment, or character, gives us by the mere view and contemplation. This decision is very commodious; because it reduces us to this simple question, *Why any action or sentiment, upon the general view or survey, gives a certain satisfaction or uneasiness*, in order to show the origin of its moral rectitude or depravity, without looking for any incomprehensible relations and qualities, which never did exist in nature, nor even in our imagination, by any clear and distinct conception? I flatter myself I have executed a great part of my present design by a state of the question, which appears to me so free from ambiguity and obscurity.

Dialogues Concerning Natural Religion

Pamphilus to Hermippus

It has been remarked, my Hermippus, that, though the ancient philosophers conveyed most of their instruction in the form of dialogue, this method of composition has been little practiced in later ages, and has seldom succeeded in the hands of those who have attempted it. Accurate and regular argument, indeed, such as is now expected of philosophical inquirers, naturally throws a man into the methodical and didactic manner; where he can immediately, without preparation, explain the point at which he aims; and thence proceed, without interruption, to deduce the proofs on which it is established. To deliver a *system* in conversation scarcely appears natural; and while the dialogue writer desires, by departing from the direct style of composition, to give a freer air to his performance, and avoid the appearance of *author* and *reader*, he is apt to run into a worse inconvenience and convey the image of *pedagogue* and *pupil*. Or if he carries on the dispute in the natural spirit of good company, by throwing in a variety of topics and preserving a proper balance among the speakers, he often loses so much time in preparations and transitions that the reader will scarcely think himself compensated, by all the graces of dialogue, for the order, brevity, and precision, which are sacrificed to them.

There are some subjects, however, to which dialogue-writing is peculiarly adapted, and where it is still preferable to the direct and simple method of composition.

Any point of doctrine which is so *obvious* that it scarcely admits of dispute, but at the same time so *important* that it cannot be too often inculcated, seems to require some such method of handling it; where the novelty of the manner may compensate the triteness of the subject, where the vivacity of conversation may enforce the precept, and where the variety of lights, presented by various personages and characters, may appear neither tedious nor redundant.

Any question of philosophy, on the other hand, which is so *obscure* and *uncertain* that human reason can reach no fixed determination with regard to it—if it should be treated at all—seems to lead us naturally into the style of dialogue and conversation. Reasonable men may be allowed to differ where no one can reasonably be positive: Opposite sentiments, even without any decision, afford an agreeable amusement; and if the subject be curious and interesting, the book carries us, in a manner, into company, and unites the two greatest and purest pleasures of human life—study and society.

Happily, these circumstances are all to be found in the subject of *natural religion*. What truth so obvious, so certain, as the *being* of a God, which the most ignorant ages have acknowledged, for which the most refined geniuses have ambitiously striven to produce new proofs and arguments? What truth so important as this, which is the ground of all our hopes, the surest foundation of morality, the firmest support of society, and the only principle which ought never to be a moment absent from our thoughts and meditations? But, in treating of this obvious and important truth, what obscure questions occur concerning the *nature* of that Divine Being; his attributes, his decrees, his plan of providence? These have been always subjected to the disputations of men: Concerning these, human reason has not reached any certain determination. But these are topics so interesting that we cannot restrain our restless inquiry with regard to them; though nothing but doubt, uncertainty, and contradiction have as yet been the result of our most accurate researches.

This I had lately occasion to observe, while I passed, as usual, part of the summer season with Cleanthes, and was present at those conversations of his with Philo and Demea, of which I gave you lately some imperfect account. Your curiosity, you then told me, was so excited that I must, of necessity, enter into a more exact detail of their reasonings, and display those various systems which they advanced with regard to so delicate a subject as that of natural religion. The remarkable contrast in their characters still further raised your expectations; while you opposed the accurate philosophical turn of Cleanthes to the careless scepticism of Philo, or compared either of their dispositions with the rigid inflexible orthodoxy of Demea. My youth rendered me a mere auditor of their disputes; and that curiosity, natural to the early season of life, has so deeply imprinted in my memory the whole chain and connection of their arguments, that, I hope, I shall not omit or confound any considerable part of them in the recital.

Part I

After I joined the company, whom I found sitting in Cleanthes' library, Demea paid Cleanthes some compliments on the great care which he took of my education, and on his unwearied perseverance and constancy in all his friendships. The father of Pamphilus, said he, was your intimate friend; the son is your pupil, and may indeed be regarded as your adopted son, were we to judge by the pains which you bestow in conveying to him every useful branch of literature and science. You are no more wanting, I am persuaded, in prudence than in industry. I shall, therefore, communicate to you a maxim which I have observed with regard to my own children, that I may learn how far it agrees with your practice. The method I follow in their education is founded on the saying of an ancient, "*That students of philosophy ought first to learn logics, then ethics, next physics, last of all the nature of the gods.*"[1] This science of natural theology, according to him, being the most profound and abstruse of any, required the maturest judgment in its students; and none but a mind enriched with all the other sciences can safely be entrusted with it.

Are you so late, says Philo, in teaching your children the principles of religion? Is there no danger of their neglecting or rejecting altogether those opinions of which they have heard so little during the whole course of their education? It is only as a science, replied Demea, subjected to human reasoning and disputation, that I postpone the study of natural theology. To season their minds with early piety is my chief care; and by continual precept and instruction and I hope too, by example, I imprint deeply on their tender minds an habitual reverence for all the principles of religion. While they pass through every other science, I still remark the uncertainty of each part; the eternal disputations of men; the obscurity of all philosophy; and the strange, ridiculous conclusions which some of the greatest geniuses have derived from the principles of mere human reason. Having thus tamed their minds to a proper submission and self-diffidence, I have no longer any scruple of opening to them the greatest mysteries of religion, nor apprehend any danger from that assuming arrogance of philosophy, which may lead them to reject the most established doctrines and opinions.

Your precaution, says Philo, of seasoning your children's minds early with piety is certainly very reasonable, and no more than is requisite in this profane and irreligious age. But what I chiefly admire in your plan of education is your method of drawing advantage from the very principles of philosophy and learning which, by inspiring pride and self-sufficiency, have commonly, in all ages, been found so destructive to the principles of religion. The vulgar, indeed, we may remark, who are unacquainted with science and profound inquiry, observing the endless disputes of the learned, have commonly a thorough contempt for philosophy; and rivet themselves the faster, by that means, in the great points of theology which have been taught them. Those who enter a little into study and inquiry, finding many appearances of evidence in doctrines the newest and most extraordinary, think nothing too difficult for human reason; and, presumptuously breaking through all fences, profane the inmost sanctuaries of the temple. But Cleanthes will, I hope, agree with me that, after we have abandoned ignorance, the surest remedy, there is still one expedient left to prevent this profane liberty. Let Demea's principles be improved and cultivated: Let us become thoroughly sensible of the weakness, blindness, and narrow limits of human reason: Let us duly consider its uncertainty and endless contrarieties, even in subjects of common life and practice: Let the errors and deceits of our very senses be set before us; the insuperable difficulties which attend first principles in all systems; the contradictions which adhere to the very ideas of matter, cause and effect, extension,

1. Chrysippus *apud Plut., De repug. Stoicorum.* [Chrysippus (c. 279–206 B.C.), a Greek philosopher, is said to have been one of the greatest logicians of ancient times.—S.M.C.]

space, time, motion; and, in a word, quantity of all kinds, the object of the only science that can fairly pretend to any certainty or evidence. When these topics are displayed in their full light, as they are by some philosophers and almost all divines, who can retain such confidence in this frail faculty of reason as to pay any regard to its determinations in points so sublime, so abstruse, so remote from common life and experience? When the coherence of the parts of a stone, or even that composition of parts which renders it extended; when these familiar objects, I say, are so inexplicable, and contain circumstances so repugnant and contradictory; with what assurance can we decide concerning the origin of worlds or trace their history from eternity to eternity?

While Philo pronounced these words, I could observe a smile in the countenance both of Demea and Cleanthes. That of Demea seemed to imply an unreserved satisfaction in the doctrines delivered; but in Cleanthes' features I could distinguish an air of finesse, as if he perceived some raillery or artificial malice in the reasonings of Philo.

You propose then, Philo, said Cleanthes, to erect religious faith on philosophical scepticism; and you think that, if certainty or evidence be expelled from every other subject of inquiry, it will all retire to these theological doctrines, and there acquire a superior force and authority. Whether your scepticism be as absolute and sincere as you pretend, we shall learn by and by, when the company breaks up; we shall then see whether you go out at the door or the window, and whether you really doubt if your body has gravity or can be injured by its fall, according to popular opinion derived from our fallacious senses and more fallacious experience. And this consideration, Demea, may, I think, fairly serve to abate our ill-will to this humorous sect of the sceptics. If they be thoroughly in earnest, they will not long trouble the world with their doubts, cavils, and disputes; if they be only in jest, they are, perhaps, bad railers, but can never be very dangerous, either to the state, to philosophy, or to religion.

In reality, Philo, continued he, it seems certain that, though a man in a flush of humor, after intense reflection on the many contradictions and imperfections of human reason, may entirely renounce all belief and opinion, it is impossible for him to persevere in this total scepticism or make it appear in his conduct for a few hours. External objects press in upon him: Passions solicit him: His philosophical melancholy dissipates; and even the utmost violence upon his own temper will not be able, during any time, to preserve the poor appearance of scepticism. And for what reason impose on himself such a violence? This is a point in which it will be impossible for him ever to satisfy himself, consistently with his sceptical principles. So that, upon the whole, nothing could be more ridiculous than the principles of the ancient Pyrrhonians;[2] if, in reality, they endeavored, as is pretended, to extend throughout the same scepticism which they had learned from the declamations of their schools, and which they ought to have confined to them.

In this view, there appears a great resemblance between the sects of the Stoics and Pyrrhonians, though perpetual antagonists; and both of them seem founded on this erroneous maxim: that what a man can perform sometimes, and in some dispositions, he can perform always and in every disposition. When the mind, by Stoical reflections, is elevated into a sublime enthusiasm of virtue and strongly smit with any *species* of honor or public good, the utmost bodily pain and sufferings will not prevail over such a high sense of duty; and it is possible, perhaps, by its means, even to smile and exult in the midst of tortures. If this sometimes may be the case in fact and reality, much more may a philosopher, in his school or even in his closet, work himself up to such an enthusiasm, and support, in imagination, the acutest pain or most calamitous event which he can possibly conceive. But how shall he support this enthusiasm itself? The bent of his mind relaxes and cannot be recalled at pleasure; avocations lead him astray; misfortunes attack him unawares; and the *philosopher* sinks, by degrees, into the *plebeian*.

I allow of your comparison between the Stoics and Sceptics, replied Philo. But you may observe, at the same time, that though the mind cannot, in Stoicism, support the highest flights of philosophy, yet, even when it sinks lower, it still retains somewhat of its former disposition; and the effects of the Stoic's reasoning will appear in his conduct in common life, and through the whole tenor of his actions. The ancient

2. [The reference is to followers of Pyrrho of Ellis (c. 360–270 B.C.), regarding whom see Sextus Empiricus, n.4.]

schools, particularly that of Zeno,[3] produced examples of virtue and constancy which seem astonishing to present times.

> Vain Wisdom all and false Philosophy.
> Yet with a pleasing sorcery could charm
> Pain, for a while, or anguish; and excite
> Fallacious Hope, or arm the obdurate breast
> With stubborn Patience, as with triple steel.[4]

In like manner, if a man has accustomed himself to sceptical considerations on the uncertainty and narrow limits of reason, he will not entirely forget them when he turns his reflection on other subjects; but in all his philosophical principles and reasoning, I dare not say, in his common conduct, he will be found different from those who either never formed any opinions in the case or have entertained sentiments more favorable to human reason.

To whatever length anyone may push his speculative principles of scepticism, he must act, I own, and live, and converse like other men; and for this conduct he is not obliged to give any other reason than the absolute necessity he lies under of so doing. If he ever carries his speculations farther than this necessity constrains him, and philosophizes either on natural or moral subjects, he is allured by a certain pleasure and satisfaction which he finds in employing himself after that manner. He considers, besides, that everyone, even in common life, is constrained to have more or less of this philosophy; that from our earliest infancy we make continual advances in forming more general principles of conduct and reasoning; that the larger experience we acquire, and the stronger reason we are endued with, we always render our principles the more general and comprehensive; and that what we call *philosophy* is nothing but a more regular and methodical operation of the same kind. To philosophize on such subjects is nothing essentially different from reasoning on common life, and we may only expect greater stability, if not greater truth, from our philosophy on account of its exacter and more scrupulous method of proceeding.

But when we look beyond human affairs and the properties of the surrounding bodies—when we carry our speculations into the two eternities, before and after the present state of things; into the creation and formation of the universe; the existence and properties of spirits; the powers and operations of one universal Spirit existing without beginning and without end, omnipotent, omniscient, immutable, infinite, and incomprehensible—we must be far removed from the smallest tendency to scepticism not to be apprehensive that we have here got quite beyond the reach of our faculties. So long as we confine our speculations to trade, or morals, or politics, or criticism, we make appeals, every moment, to common sense and experience, which strengthen our philosophical conclusions and remove (at least in part) the suspicion, which we so justly entertain with regard to every reasoning, that is very subtile and refined. But in theological reasonings, we have not this advantage; while at the same time we are employed upon objects which, we must be sensible, are too large for our grasp, and of all others, require most to be familiarized to our apprehension. We are like foreigners in a strange country to whom everything must seem suspicious, and who are in danger every moment of transgressing against the laws and customs of the people with whom they live and converse. We know not how far we ought to trust our vulgar methods of reasoning in such a subject, since, even in common life, and in that province which is peculiarly appropriated to them, we cannot account for them and are entirely guided by a kind of instinct or necessity in employing them.

All sceptics pretend that, if reason be considered in an abstract view, it furnishes invincible arguments against itself, and that we could never retain any conviction or assurance, on any subject, were not the sceptical reasonings so refined and subtile that they are not able to counterpoise the more solid and more natural arguments derived from the senses and experience. But it is evident, whenever our arguments lose this advantage and run wide of common life, that the most refined scepticism comes to be upon a footing with them, and is able to oppose and counterbalance

3. [Zeno of Citium (c. 334–c. 262 B.C.) was the Greek philosopher who founded Stoicism, a philosophical system offering a unified logical, epistemological, metaphysical, ethical, and political outlook. He is not to be confused with Zeno of Elea (c. 490–430 B.C.), creator of the immortal paradoxes.]

4. [The quotation is from *Paradise Lost*, the epic poem by the eminent English poet John Milton (1608–1674).]

them. The one has no more weight than the other. The mind must remain in suspense between them; and it is that very suspense or balance which is the triumph of scepticism.

But I observe, says Cleanthes, with regard to you, Philo, and all speculative sceptics that your doctrine and practice are as much at variance in the most abstruse points of theory as in the conduct of common life. Wherever evidence discovers itself, you adhere to it, notwithstanding your pretended scepticism; and I can observe, too, some of your sect to be as decisive as those who make greater professions of certainty and assurance. In reality, would not a man be ridiculous who pretended to reject Newton's[5] explication of the wonderful phenomenon of the rainbow because that explication gives a minute anatomy of the rays of light—a subject, forsooth, too refined for human comprehension? And what would you say to one who, having nothing particular to object to the arguments of Copernicus[6] and Galileo[7] for the motion of the earth, should withhold his assent on that general principle that these subjects were too magnificent and remote to be explained by the narrow and fallacious reason of mankind?

There is indeed a kind of brutish and ignorant scepticism, as you well observed, which gives the vulgar a general prejudice against what they do not easily understand, and makes them reject every principle which requires elaborate reasoning to prove and establish it. This species of scepticism is fatal to knowledge, not to religion; since we find that those who make greatest profession of it give often their assent, not only to the great truths of theism and natural theology, but even to the most absurd tenets which a traditional superstition has recommended to them. They firmly believe in witches, though they will not believe nor attend to the most simple proposition of Euclid.[8] But the refined and philosophical sceptics fall into an inconsistence of an opposite nature. They push their researches into the most abstruse corners of science, and their assent attends them in every step, proportioned to the evidence which they meet with. They are even obliged to acknowledge that the most abstruse and remote objects are those which are best explained by philosophy. Light is in reality anatomized; the true system of the heavenly bodies is discovered and ascertained. But the nourishment of bodies by food is still an inexplicable mystery; the cohesion of the parts of matter is still incomprehensible. These sceptics, therefore, are obliged, in every question, to consider each particular evidence apart, and proportion their assent to the precise degree of evidence which occurs. This is their practice in all natural, mathematical, moral, and political science. And why not the same, I ask, in the theological and religious? Why must conclusions of this nature be alone rejected on the general presumption of the insufficiency of human reason, without any particular discussion of the evidence? Is not such an unequal conduct a plain proof of prejudice and passion?

Our senses, you say, are fallacious; our understanding erroneous; our ideas, even of the most familiar objects—extension, duration, motion—full of absurdities and contradictions. You defy me to solve the difficulties or reconcile the repugnancies which you discover in them. I have not capacity for so great an undertaking: I have not leisure for it: I perceive it to be superfluous. Your own conduct, in every circumstance, refutes your principles, and shows the firmest reliance on all the received maxims of science, morals, prudence, and behavior.

I shall never assent to so harsh an opinion as that of a celebrated writer,[9] who says that the Sceptics are not a sect of philosophers: they are only a sect of liars. I may, however, affirm (I hope without offence) that they are a sect of jesters or railers. But for my part, whenever I find myself disposed to mirth and amusement, I shall certainly choose my entertainment of a less perplexing and abstruse nature. A comedy, a novel, or, at most, a history seems a more natural

5. [The reference is to Isaac Newton (1642–1727), the towering British mathematician and physicist.]

6. [Regarding Copernicus, see Hume's *Enquiry*, n.72.]

7. [The reference is to Galileo Galilei (1564–1642), the renowned Italian astronomer, mathematician, and physicist.]

8. [Euclid was a fourth-century-B.C. Greek thinker, whose *Elements*, formalizing geometry, is one of the greatest works in the history of mathematics.]

9. *L'art de penser.* [This work, the influential *Port-Royal Logic*, was coauthored by French theologians Pierre Nicole (1625–1695) and Antoine Arnauld (1612–1694).]

recreation than such metaphysical subtilties and abstractions.

In vain would the sceptic make a distinction between science and common life, or between one science and another. The arguments employed in all, if just, are of a similar nature and contain the same force and evidence. Or if there be any difference among them, the advantage lies entirely on the side of theology and natural religion. Many principles of mechanics are founded on very abstruse reasoning; yet no man who has any pretensions to science, even no speculative sceptic, pretends to entertain the least doubt with regard to them. The Copernican system contains the most surprising paradox, and the most contrary to our natural conceptions, to appearances, and to our very senses; yet even monks and inquisitors are now constrained to withdraw their opposition to it. And shall Philo, a man of so liberal a genius and extensive knowledge, entertain any general undistinguished scruples with regard to the religious hypothesis, which is founded on the simplest and most obvious arguments and, unless it meets with artificial obstacles, has such easy access and admission into the mind of man?

And here we may observe, continued he, turning himself towards Demea, a pretty curious circumstance in the history of the sciences. After the union of philosophy with the popular religion, upon the first establishment of Christianity, nothing was more usual, among all religious teachers, than declamations against reason, against the senses, against every principle derived merely from human research and inquiry. All the topics of the ancient Academics[10] were adopted by the Fathers,[11] and thence propagated for several ages in every school and pulpit throughout Christendom. The Reformers embraced the same principles of reasoning or rather declamation; and all panegyrics on the excellence of faith were sure to be interlarded with some severe strokes of satire against natural reason. A celebrated prelate, too,[12] of the Romish communion, a man of the most extensive learning, who wrote a demonstration of Christianity, has also composed a treatise which contains all the cavils of the boldest and most determined Pyrrhonism. Locke seems to have been the first Christian who ventured openly to assert that *faith* was nothing but a species of *reason;* that religion was only a branch of philosophy; and that a chain of arguments, similar to that which established any truth in morals, politics, or physics, was always employed in discovering all the principles of theology, natural and revealed. The ill use which Bayle[13] and other libertines made of the philosophical scepticism of the Fathers and first Reformers still further propagated the judicious sentiment of Mr. Locke. And it is now in a manner avowed, by all pretenders to reasoning and philosophy, that atheist and sceptic are almost synonymous. And as it is certain that no man is in earnest when he professes the latter principle, I would fain hope that there are as few who seriously maintain the former.

Don't you remember, said Philo, the excellent saying of Lord Bacon[14] on this head? That a little philosophy, replied Cleanthes, makes a man an atheist; a great deal converts him to religion. That is a very judicious remark, too, said Philo. But what I have in my eye is another passage, where, having mentioned David's fool, who said in his heart there is no God, this great philosopher observes that the atheists nowadays have a double share of folly; for they are not contented to say in their hearts there is no God, but they also utter that impiety with their lips, and are thereby guilty of multiplied indiscretion and imprudence. Some people, though they were ever so much in earnest, cannot, methinks, be very formidable.

But though you should rank me in this class of fools, I cannot forbear communicating a remark that occurs to me from the history of the religious and irreligious scepticism with which you have enter-

10. [The reference is to the philosophers of the Greek Academy founded by Plato, more specifically, to the philosophers of the Academy in the second and third centuries B.C., in which a form of moderate skepticism reputedly was espoused.]

11. [The reference is to orthodox Christian writers of early times.]

12. Mons. Huet. [The reference is to Peter Daniel Huet (1630–1721), a renowned French scholar who was bishop of Avranches.]

13. [The reference is to Pierre Bayle (1647–1706), a French skeptical philosopher.]

14. [Francis Bacon (1561–1626) was an English philosopher and statesman who stressed the importance of scientific methodology in the acquisition of knowledge.]

tained us. It appears to me that there are strong symptoms of priestcraft in the whole progress of this affair. During ignorant ages, such as those which followed the dissolution of the ancient schools, the priests perceived that atheism, deism, or heresy of any kind, could only proceed from the presumptuous questioning of received opinions, and from a belief that human reason was equal to everything. Education had then a mighty influence over the minds of men, and was almost equal in force to those suggestions of the senses and common understanding by which the most determined sceptic must allow himself to be governed. But at present, when the influence of education is much diminished and men, from a more open commerce of the world, have learned to compare the popular principles of different nations and ages, our sagacious divines have changed their whole system of philosophy and talk the language of Stoics, Platonists, and Peripatetics,[15] not that of Pyrrhonians and Academics. If we distrust human reason we have now no other principle to lead us into religion. Thus sceptics in one age, dogmatists in another—whichever system best suits the purpose of these reverend gentlemen in giving them an ascendant over mankind—they are sure to make it their favorite principle and established tenet.

It is very natural, said Cleanthes, for men to embrace those principles by which they find they can best defend their doctrines, nor need we have any recourse to priestcraft to account for so reasonable an expedient. And surely, nothing can afford a stronger presumption that any set of principles are true and ought to be embraced than to observe that they tend to the confirmation of true religion, and serve to confound the cavils of atheists, libertines, and freethinkers of all denominations.

Part II

I must own, Cleanthes, said Demea, that nothing can more surprise me than the light in which you have all along put this argument. By the whole tenor of your discourse, one would imagine that you were maintaining the Being of a God against the cavils of atheists and infidels, and were necessitated to become a champion for that fundamental principle of all religion. But this, I hope, is not by any means a question among us. No man; no man, at least of common sense, I am persuaded, ever entertained a serious doubt with regard to a truth so certain and self-evident. The question is not concerning the *being* but the *nature of God*. This I affirm, from the infirmities of human understanding, to be altogether incomprehensible and unknown to us. The essence of that supreme mind, his attributes, the manner of his existence, the very nature of his duration—these and every particular which regards so divine a being are mysterious to men. Finite, weak, and blind creatures, we ought to humble ourselves in his august presence, and, conscious of our frailties, adore in silence his infinite perfections which eye hath not seen, ear hath not heard, neither hath it entered into the heart of man to conceive. They are covered in a deep cloud from human curiosity; it is profaneness to attempt penetrating through these sacred obscurities; and, next to the impiety of denying his existence, is the temerity of prying into his nature and essence, decrees and attributes.

But lest you should think that my *piety* has here got the better of my *philosophy*, I shall support my opinion, if it needs any support, by a very great authority. I might cite all the divines, almost from the foundation of Christianity, who have ever treated of this or any other theological subject; but I shall confine myself, at present, to one equally celebrated for piety and philosophy. It is Father Malebranche who, I remember, thus expresses himself.[16] "One ought not so much (says he) to call God a spirit in order to express positively what he is, as in order to signify that he is not matter. He is a Being infinitely perfect—of this we cannot doubt. But in the same manner as we ought not to imagine, even supposing him corporeal, that he is clothed with a human body, as the anthropomorphites asserted, under color that that figure was the most perfect of any, so neither ought we to imagine that the spirit of God has human ideas or bears

15. [The term "Peripatetics," derived from a Greek word meaning "walking about," is applied to the followers of Aristotle since he is said to have taught in this manner.]

16. *Recherche de la Verite*, liv. 3, cap. 9. [Nicolas Malebranche (1638–1715) was a French philosopher who maintained that no interaction occurs between mental and physical events nor among events in either realm, but that the appearance of interaction is due to the intervention of God, whose actions produce regularities.]

any resemblance to our spirit, under color that we know nothing more perfect than a human mind. We ought rather to believe that as he comprehends the perfections of matter without being material . . . he comprehends also the perfections of created spirits without being spirit, in the manner we conceive spirit: That his true name is *He that is*, or, in other words, Being without restriction, All Being, the Being infinite and universal."

After so great an authority, Demea, replied Philo, as that which you have produced, and a thousand more which you might produce, it would appear ridiculous in me to add my sentiment or express my approbation of your doctrine. But surely, where reasonable men treat these subjects, the question can never be concerning the *being* but only the *nature* of the Deity. The former truth, as you well observe, is unquestionable and self-evident. Nothing exists without a cause; and the original cause of this universe (whatever it be) we call *God*, and piously ascribe to him every species of perfection. Whoever scruples this fundamental truth deserves every punishment which can be inflicted among philosophers, to wit, the greatest ridicule, contempt, and disapprobation. But as all perfection is entirely relative, we ought never to imagine that we comprehend the attributes of this divine Being, or to suppose that his perfections have any analogy or likeness to the perfections of a human creature. Wisdom, thought, design, knowledge—these we justly ascribe to him because these words are honorable among men, and we have no other language or other conceptions by which we can express our adoration of him. But let us beware lest we think that our ideas anywise correspond to his perfections, or that his attributes have any resemblance to these qualities among men. He is infinitely superior to our limited view and comprehension; and is more the object of worship in the temple than of disputation in the schools.

In reality, Cleanthes, continued he, there is no need of having recourse to that affected scepticism so displeasing to you in order to come at this determination. Our ideas reach no farther than our experience: We have no experience of divine attributes and operations. I need not conclude my syllogism: You can draw the inference yourself. And it is a pleasure to me (and I hope to you, too) that just reasoning and sound piety here concur in the same conclusion, and both of them establish the adorably mysterious and incomprehensible nature of the Supreme Being.

Not to lose any time in circumlocutions, said Cleanthes, addressing himself to Demea, much less in replying to the pious declamations of Philo, I shall briefly explain how I conceive this matter. Look round the world: Contemplate the whole and every part of it: You will find it to be nothing but one great machine, subdivided into an infinite number of lesser machines, which again admit of subdivisions to a degree beyond what human senses and faculties can trace and explain. All these various machines, and even their most minute parts, are adjusted to each other with an accuracy which ravishes into admiration all men who have ever contemplated them. The curious adapting of means to ends, throughout all nature, resembles exactly, though it much exceeds, the productions of human contrivance—of human design, thought, wisdom, and intelligence. Since therefore the effects resemble each other, we are led to infer, by all the rules of analogy, that the causes also resemble, and that the Author of Nature is somewhat similar to the mind of man, though possessed of much larger faculties, proportioned to the grandeur of the work which he has executed. By this argument *a posteriori*, and by this argument alone, do we prove at once the existence of a Deity and his similarity to human mind and intelligence.

I shall be so free, Cleanthes, said Demea, as to tell you that from the beginning I could not approve of your conclusion concerning the similarity of the Deity to men, still less can I approve of the mediums by which you endeavor to establish it. What! No demonstration of the Being of God! No abstract arguments! No proofs *a priori!* Are these which have hitherto been so much insisted on by philosophers all fallacy, all sophism? Can we reach no farther in this subject than experience and probability? I will say not that this is betraying the cause of a Deity; but surely, by this affected candor, you give advantages to atheists which they never could obtain by the mere dint of argument and reasoning.

What I chiefly scruple in this subject, said Philo, is not so much that all religious arguments are by Cleanthes reduced to experience, as that they appear not to be even the most certain and irrefragable of that inferior kind. That a stone will fall, that fire will burn, that the earth has solidity, we have observed a thousand and a thousand times; and when any new instance of this nature is presented, we draw without hesitation the accustomed inference. The exact similarity of the cases gives us a perfect assurance of a similar event, and a stronger evidence is never desired nor sought after. But wherever you depart, in the least, from the similarity of the cases, you diminish proportionably the evidence; and may at last bring it to a very weak *analogy*, which is confessedly liable to error and uncertainty. After having experienced the circulation of the blood in human creatures, we make no doubt that it takes place in Titius and Maevius;[17] but from its circulation in frogs and fishes it is only a presumption, though a strong one, from analogy that it takes place in men and other animals. The analogical reasoning is much weaker when we infer the circulation of the sap in vegetables from our experience that the blood circulates in animals; and those who hastily followed that imperfect analogy are found, by more accurate experiments, to have been mistaken.

If we see a house, Cleanthes, we conclude, with the greatest certainty, that it had an architect or builder because this is precisely that species of effect which we have experienced to proceed from that species of cause. But surely you will not affirm that the universe bears such a resemblance to a house that we can with the same certainty infer a similar cause, or that the analogy is here entire and perfect. The dissimilitude is so striking that the utmost you can here pretend to is a guess, a conjecture, a presumption concerning a similar cause; and how that pretension will be received in the world, I leave you to consider.

It would surely be very ill received, replied Cleanthes; and I should be deservedly blamed and detested did I allow that the proofs of a Deity amounted to no more than a guess or conjecture. But is the whole adjustment of means to ends in a house and in the universe so slight a resemblance? the economy of final causes? the order, proportion, and arrangement of every part? Steps of a stair are plainly contrived that human legs may use them in mounting; and this inference is certain and infallible. Human legs are also contrived for walking and mounting; and this inference, I allow, is not altogether so certain because of the dissimilarity which you remark; but does it, therefore, deserve the name only of presumption or conjecture?

Good God! cried Demea, interrupting him, where are we? Zealous defenders of religion allow that the proofs of a Deity fall short of perfect evidence! And you, Philo, on whose assistance I depended in proving the adorable mysteriousness of the Divine Nature, do you assent to all these extravagant opinions of Cleanthes? For what other name can I give them? or, why spare my censure when such principles are advanced, supported by such an authority, before so young a man as Pamphilus?

You seem not to apprehend, replied Philo, that I argue with Cleanthes in his own way, and, by showing him the dangerous consequences of his tenets, hope at last to reduce him to our opinion. But what sticks most with you, I observe, is the representation which Cleanthes has made of the argument *a posteriori;* and, finding that that argument is likely to escape your hold and vanish into air, you think it so disguised that you can scarcely believe it to be set in its true light. Now, however much I may dissent, in other respects, from the dangerous principle of Cleanthes, I must allow that he has fairly represented that argument, and I shall endeavor so to state the matter to you that you will entertain no further scruples with regard to it.

Were a man to abstract from everything which he knows or has seen, he would be altogether incapable, merely from his own ideas, to determine what kind of scene the universe must be, or to give the preference to one state or situation of things above another. For as nothing which he clearly conceives could be esteemed impossible or implying a contradiction, every chimera of his fancy would be upon an equal footing; nor could he assign just reason why he adheres to one idea or system, and rejects the others which are equally possible.

Again, after he opens his eyes and contemplates the world as it really is, it would be impossible for him at first to assign the cause of any one event, much less the whole of things, or of the universe. He might set his fancy a rambling, and she might bring him in an infinite variety of reports and representations. These would all be possible; but, being all equally possible, he would never of himself give a satisfactory account for his preferring one of them to the rest.

17. [Conventional names of ordinary persons, such as Smith and Jones.]

Experience alone can point out to him the true cause of any phenomenon.

Now, according to this method of reasoning, Demea, it follows (and is, indeed, tacitly allowed by Cleanthes himself) that order, arrangement, or the adjustment of final causes, is not of itself any proof of design, but only so far as it has been experienced to proceed from that principle. For aught we can know *a priori*, matter may contain the source or spring of order originally within itself, as well as mind does; and there is no more difficulty in conceiving that the several elements, from an internal unknown cause, may fall into the most exquisite arrangement, than to conceive that their ideas, in the great universal mind, from a like internal unknown cause, fall into that arrangement. The equal possibility of both these suppositions is allowed. But, by experience, we find (according to Cleanthes) that there is a difference between them. Throw several pieces of steel together, without shape or form, they will never arrange themselves so as to compose a watch. Stone and mortar and wood, without an architect, never erect a house. But the ideas in a human mind, we see, by an unknown, inexplicable economy, arrange themselves so as to form the plan of a watch or house. Experience, therefore, proves that there is an original principle of order in mind, not in matter. From similar effects we infer similar causes. The adjustment of means to ends is alike in the universe, as in a machine of human contrivance. The causes, therefore, must be resembling.

I was from the beginning scandalized, I must own, with this resemblance which is asserted between the Deity and human creatures, and must conceive it to imply such a degradation of the Supreme Being as no sound theist could endure. With your assistance, therefore, Demea, I shall endeavor to defend what you justly call the adorable mysteriousness of the Divine Nature, and shall refute this reasoning of Cleanthes, provided he allows that I have made a fair representation of it.

When Cleanthes had assented, Philo, after a short pause, proceeded in the following manner.

That all inferences, Cleanthes, concerning fact are founded on experience, and that all experimental reasonings are founded on the supposition that similar causes prove similar effects, and similar effects similar causes, I shall not at present much dispute with you. But observe, I entreat you, with what extreme caution all just reasoners proceed in the transferring of experiments to similar cases. Unless the cases be exactly similar, they repose no perfect confidence in applying their past observation to any particular phenomenon. Every alteration of circumstances occasions a doubt concerning the event; and it requires new experiments to prove certainly that the new circumstances are of no moment or importance. A change in bulk, situation, arrangement, age, disposition of the air, or surrounding bodies—any of these particulars may be attended with the most unexpected consequences. And unless the objects be quite familiar to us, it is the highest temerity to expect with assurance, after any of these changes, an event similar to that which before fell under our observation. The slow and deliberate steps of philosophers here, if anywhere, are distinguished from the precipitate march of the vulgar, who, hurried on by the smallest similitude, are incapable of all discernment or consideration.

But can you think, Cleanthes, that your usual phlegm and philosophy have been preserved in so wide a step as you have taken when you compared to the universe houses, ships, furniture, machines; and, from their similarity in some circumstances, inferred a similarity in their causes? Thought, design, intelligence, such as we discover in men and other animals, is no more than one of the springs and principles of the universe, as well as heat or cold, attraction or repulsion, and a hundred others which fall under daily observation. It is an active cause by which some particular parts of nature, we find, produce alterations on other parts. But can a conclusion, with any propriety, be transferred from parts to the whole? Does not the great disproportion bar all comparison and inference? From observing the growth of a hair, can we learn anything concerning the generation of a man? Would the manner of a leaf's blowing, even though perfectly known, afford us any instruction concerning the vegetation of a tree?

But allowing that we were to take the *operations* of one part of nature upon another for the foundation of our judgment concerning the *origin* of the whole (which never can be admitted), yet why select so minute, so weak, so bounded a principle as the reason and design of animals is found to be upon this planet? What peculiar privilege has this little agitation of the brain which we call *thought*, that we must thus make it the model of the whole universe? Our partiality in our own favor does indeed present it on all occasions, but sound philosophy ought carefully to guard against so natural an illusion.

So far from admitting, continued Philo, that the operations of a part can afford us any just conclusion concerning the origin of the whole, I will not allow any one part to form a rule for another part if the latter be very remote from the former. Is there any reasonable ground to conclude that the inhabitants of other planets possess thought, intelligence, reason, or anything similar to these faculties in men? When nature has so extremely diversified her manner of operation in this small globe, can we imagine that she incessantly copies herself throughout so immense a universe? And if thought, as we may well suppose, be confined merely to this narrower corner and has even there so limited a sphere of action, with what propriety can we assign it for the original cause of all things? The narrow views of a peasant who makes his domestic economy the rule for the government of kingdoms is in comparison a pardonable sophism.

But were we ever so much assured that a thought and reason resembling the human were to be found throughout the whole universe, and were its activity elsewhere vastly greater and more commanding than it appears in this globe; yet I cannot see why the operations of a world constituted, arranged, adjusted, can with any propriety be extended to a world which is in its embryo-state, and is advancing towards that constitution and arrangement. By observation we know somewhat of the economy, action, and nourishment of a finished animal; but we must transfer with great caution that observation to the growth of a foetus in the womb, and still more to the formation of an animalcule in the loins of its male parent. Nature, we find, even from our limited experience, possesses an infinite number of springs and principles which incessantly discover themselves on every change of her position and situation. And what new and unknown principles would actuate her in so new and unknown a situation as that of the formation of a universe, we cannot, without the utmost temerity, pretend to determine.

A very small part of this great system, during a very short time, is very imperfectly discovered to us; and do we thence pronounce decisively concerning the origin of the whole?

Admirable conclusion! Stone, wood, brick, iron, brass, have not, at this time, in this minute globe of earth, an order or arrangement without human art and contrivance; therefore, the universe could not originally attain its order and arrangement without something similar to human art. But is a part of nature a rule for another part very wide of the former? Is it a rule for the whole? Is a very small part a rule for the universe? Is nature in one situation a certain rule for nature in another situation vastly different from the former?

And can you blame me, Cleanthes, if I here imitate the prudent reserve of Simonides,[18] who, according to the noted story, being asked by Hiero,[19] *What God was?* desired a day to think of it, and then two days more; and after that manner continually prolonged the term, without ever bringing in his definition or description? Could you even blame me if I had answered, at first, *that I did not know,* and was sensible that this subject lay vastly beyond the reach of my faculties? You might cry out sceptic and railer, as much as you pleased; but, having found in so many other subjects much more familiar the imperfections and even contradictions of human reason, I never should expect any success from its feeble conjectures in a subject so sublime and so remote from the sphere of our observation. When two *species* of objects have always been observed to be conjoined together, I can *infer,* by custom, the existence of one wherever I *see* the existence of the other; and this I call an argument from experience. But how this argument can have place where the objects, as in the present case, are single, individual, without parallel or specific resemblance, may be difficult to explain. And will any man tell me with a serious countenance that an orderly universe must arise from some thought and art like the human because we have experience of it? To ascertain this reasoning it were requisite that we had experience of the origin of the worlds; and it is not sufficient, surely, that we have seen ships and cities arise from human art and contrivance. . . .

Philo was proceeding in this vehement manner, somewhat between jest and earnest, as it appeared to

18. [Simonides of Ceos (c. 548–468 B.C.) was a Greek poet.]

19. [The reference is to Hiero I, a fifth-century-B.C. ruler of Syracuse, noted as a patron of literature.]

me, when he observed some signs of impatience in Cleanthes, and then immediately stopped short. What I had to suggest, said Cleanthes, is only that you would not abuse terms, or make use of popular expressions to subvert philosophical reasonings. You know that the vulgar often distinguish reason from experience, even where the question relates only to matter of fact and existence, though it is found, where that *reason* is properly analyzed, that it is nothing but a species of experience. To prove by experience the origin of the universe from mind is not more contrary to common speech than to prove the motion of the earth from the same principle. And a caviller might raise all the same objections to the Copernican system which you have urged against my reasonings. Have you other earths, might he say, which you have seen to move? Have. . . .

Yes! cried Philo, interrupting him, we have other earths. Is not the moon another earth, which we see to turn round its center? Is not Venus another earth, where we observe the same phenomenon? Are not the revolutions of the sun also a confirmation, from analogy, of the same theory? All the planets, are they not earths which revolve about the sun? Are not the satellites moons which move round Jupiter and Saturn, and along with these primary planets round the sun? These analogies and resemblances, with others which I have not mentioned, are the sole proofs of the Copernican system; and to you it belongs to consider whether you have any analogies of the same kind to support your theory.

In reality, Cleanthes, continued he, the modern system of astronomy is now so much received by all inquirers, and has become so essential a part even of our earliest education, that we are not commonly very scrupulous in examining the reasons upon which it is founded. It is now become a matter of mere curiosity to study the first writers on that subject who had the full force of prejudice to encounter, and were obliged to turn their arguments on every side in order to render them popular and convincing. But if we peruse Galileo's famous *Dialogues*[20] concerning the system of the world, we shall find that that great genius, one of the sublimest that ever existed, first bent all his endeavors to prove that there was no foundation for the distinction commonly made between elementary and celestial substances. The schools, proceeding from the illusions of sense, had carried this distinction very far; and had established the latter substances to be ingenerable, incorruptible, unalterable, impassible; and had assigned all the opposite qualities to the former. But Galileo, beginning with the moon, proved its similarity in every particular to the earth: its convex figure, its natural darkness when not illuminated, its density, its distinction into solid and liquid, the variations of its phases, the mutual illuminations of the earth and moon, their mutual eclipses, the inequalities of the lunar surface, etc. After many instances of this kind, with regard to all the planets, men plainly saw that these bodies became proper objects of experience, and that the similarity of their nature enabled us to extend the same arguments and phenomena from one to the other.

In this cautious proceeding of the astronomers you may read your own condemnation, Cleanthes; or rather may see that the subject in which you are engaged exceeds all human reason and inquiry. Can you pretend to show any such similarity between the fabric of a house and the generation of a universe? Have you ever seen nature in any such situation as resembles the first arrangement of the elements? Have worlds ever been formed under your eye, and have you had leisure to observe the whole progress of the phenomenon, from the first appearance of order to its final consummation? If you have, then cite your experience and deliver your theory.

Part III

How the most absurd argument, replied Cleanthes, in the hands of a man of ingenuity and invention, may acquire an air of probability! Are you not aware, Philo, that it became necessary for Copernicus and his first disciples to prove the similarity of the terrestrial and celestial matter because several philosophers, blinded by old systems and supported by some sensible appearances, had denied this similarity; but that it is by no means necessary that theists should prove the similarity of the works of nature to those of art, because this similarity is self-evident and undeniable? The same matter, a like form; what more is requisite to show an analogy between their causes, and to

20. [The reference is to Galileo's *Dialogue Concerning the Two Chief World Systems* (1632).]

ascertain the origin of all things from a divine purpose and intention? Your objections, I must freely tell you, are no better than the abstruse cavils of those philosophers who denied motion, and ought to be refuted in the same manner—by illustrations, examples, and instances rather than by serious argument and philosophy.

Suppose, therefore, that an articulate voice were heard in the clouds, much louder and more melodious than any which human art could ever reach; suppose that this voice were extended in the same instant over all nations and spoke to each nation in its own language and dialect; suppose that the words delivered not only contain a just sense and meaning, but convey some instruction altogether worthy of a benevolent Being superior to mankind—could you possibly hesitate a moment concerning the cause of this voice, and must you not instantly ascribe it to some design or purpose? Yet I cannot see but all the same objections (if they merit that appellation) which lie against the system of theism may also be produced against this inference.

Might you not say that all conclusions concerning fact were founded on experience; that, when we hear an articulate voice in the dark and thence infer a man, it is only the resemblance of the effects which leads us to conclude that there is a like resemblance in the cause; but that this extraordinary voice, by its loudness, extent, and flexibility to all languages, bears so little analogy to any human voice that we have no reason to suppose any analogy in their causes; and, consequently, that a rational, wise, coherent speech proceeded, you know not whence, from some accidental whistling of the winds, not from any divine reason or intelligence? You see clearly your own objections in these cavils; and I hope too, you see clearly that they cannot possibly have more force in the one case than in the other.

But to bring the case still nearer the present one of the universe, I shall make two suppositions which imply not any absurdity or impossibility. Suppose that there is a natural, universal, invariable language, common to every individual of human race, and that books are natural productions which perpetuate themselves in the same manner with animals and vegetables, by descent and propagation. Several expressions of our passions contain a universal language: All brute animals have a natural speech, which, however limited, is very intelligible to their own species. And as there are infinitely fewer parts and less contrivance in the finest composition of eloquence than in the coarsest organized body, the propagation of an *Iliad*[21] or *Aeneid*[22] is an easier supposition than that of any plant or animal.

Suppose, therefore, that you enter into your library thus peopled by natural volumes containing the most refined reason and most exquisite beauty; could you possibly open one of them and doubt that its original cause bore the strongest analogy to mind and intelligence? When it reasons and discourses; when it expostulates, argues, and enforces its views and topics; when it applies sometimes to the pure intellect, sometimes to the affections; when it collects, disposes, and adorns every consideration suited to the subject; could you persist in asserting that all this, at the bottom, had really no meaning, and that the first formation of this volume in the loins of its original parent proceeded not from thought and design? Your obstinacy, I know, reaches not that degree of firmness; even your sceptical play and wantonness would be abashed at so glaring an absurdity.

But if there be any difference, Philo, between this supposed case and the real one of the universe, it is all to the advantage of the latter. The anatomy of an animal affords many stronger instances of design than the perusal of Livy[23] or Tacitus;[24] and any objection which you start in the former case, by carrying me back to so unusual and extraordinary a scene as the first formation of worlds, the same objection has place on the supposition of our vegetating library. Choose, then, your party, Philo, without ambiguity or evasion; assert either that a rational volume is no proof of a rational cause or admit of a similar cause to all the works of nature.

Let me here observe, too, continued Cleanthes, that this religious argument, instead of being weakened by that scepticism so much affected by you, rather acquires force from it and becomes more firm

21. [The reference is to the epic poem by Homer, the Greek writer who probably lived in the eighth century B.C.]

22. [The reference is to the epic poem by the Roman author Virgil (70–19 B.C.).]

23. [Regarding Livy, see Hume's *Enquiry*, n.45.]

24. [Regarding Tacitus, see Hume's *Enquiry*, n.26.]

and undisputed. To exclude all argument or reasoning of every kind is either affectation or madness. The declared profession of every reasonable sceptic is only to reject abstruse, remote, and refined arguments; to adhere to common sense and the plain instincts of nature; and to assent, wherever any reasons strike him with so full a force that he cannot, without the greatest violence, prevent it. Now the arguments for natural religion are plainly of this kind; and nothing but the most perverse, obstinate metaphysics can reject them. Consider, anatomize the eye; survey its structure and contrivance, and tell me, from your own feeling, if the idea of a contriver does not immediately flow in upon you with a force like that of sensation. The most obvious conclusion, surely, is in favor of design; and it requires time, reflection, and study, to summon up those frivolous though abstruse objections which can support infidelity. Who can behold the male and female of each species, the correspondence of their parts and instincts, their passions and whole course of life before and after generation, but must be sensible that the propagation of the species is intended by nature? Millions and millions of such instances present themselves through every part of the universe, and no language can convey a more intelligible, irresistible meaning than the curious adjustment of final causes. To what degree, therefore, of blind dogmatism must one have attained to reject such natural and such convincing arguments?

Some beauties in writing we may meet with which seem contrary to rules, and which gain the affections and animate the imagination in opposition to all the precepts of criticism and to the authority of the established masters of art. And if the argument for theism be, as you pretend, contradictory to the principles of logic, its universal, its irresistible influence proves clearly that there may be arguments of a like irregular nature. Whatever cavils may be urged, an orderly world, as well as a coherent, articulate speech, will still be received as an incontestable proof of design and intention.

It sometimes happens, I own, that the religious arguments have not their due influence on an ignorant savage and barbarian; not because they are obscure and difficult, but because he never asks himself any question with regard to them. Whence arises the curious structure of an animal? From the copulation of its parents. And these whence? From *their* parents? A few removes set the objects at such a distance that to him they are lost in darkness and confusion; nor is he actuated by any curiosity to trace them farther. But this is neither dogmatism nor scepticism, but stupidity: a state of mind very different from your sifting, inquisitive disposition, my ingenious friend. You can trace causes from effects; you can compare the most distant and remote objects; and your greatest errors proceed not from barrenness of thought and invention, but from too luxuriant a fertility which suppresses your natural good sense by a profusion of unnecessary scruples and objections.

Here I could observe, Hermippus, that Philo was a little embarrassed and confounded; but, while he hesitated in delivering an answer, luckily for him, Demea broke in upon the discourse and saved his countenance.

Your instance, Cleanthes, said he, drawn from books and language, being familiar, has, I confess, so much more force on that account; but is there not some danger, too, in this very circumstance, and may it not render us presumptuous, by making us imagine we comprehend the Deity and have some adequate idea of his nature and attributes? When I read a volume, I enter into the mind and intention of the author; I become him, in a manner, for the instant, and have an immediate feeling and conception of those ideas which revolved in his imagination while employed in that composition. But so near an approach we never surely can make to the Deity. His ways are not our ways. His attributes are perfect but incomprehensible. And this volume of nature contains a great and inexplicable riddle, more than any intelligible discourse or reasoning.

The ancient Platonists, you know, were the most religious and devout of all the pagan philosophers; yet many of them, particularly Plotinus, expressly declare that intellect or understanding is not to be ascribed to the Deity, and that our most perfect worship of him consists, not in acts of veneration, reverence, gratitude, or love, but in a certain mysterious self-annihilation or total extinction of all our faculties. These ideas are, perhaps, too far stretched; but still it must be acknowledged that, by representing the Deity as so intelligible and comprehensible, and so similar to a human mind, we are guilty of the grossest and most narrow partiality, and make ourselves the model of the whole universe.

All the *sentiments* of the human mind, gratitude, resentment, love, friendship, approbation, blame, pity, emulation, envy, have a plain reference to the state and situation of man, and are calculated for preserving the existence and promoting the activity of such a being in such circumstances. It seems, therefore, unreasonable to transfer such sentiments to a supreme existence or to suppose him actuated by them; and the phenomena, besides, of the universe will not support us in such a theory. All our *ideas* derived from the senses are confessedly false and illusive, and cannot therefore be supposed to have place in a supreme intelligence. And as the ideas of internal sentiment, added to those of the external senses, compose the whole furniture of human understanding, we may conclude that none of the *materials* of thought are in any respect similar in the human and in the divine intelligence. Now, as to the *manner* of thinking, how can we make any comparison between them or suppose them anywise resembling? Our thought is fluctuating, uncertain, fleeting, successive, and compounded; and were we to remove these circumstances, we absolutely annihilate its essence, and it would in such a case be an abuse of terms to apply to it the name of thought or reason. At least, if it appear more pious and respectful (as it really is) still to retain these terms when we mention the Supreme Being, we ought to acknowledge that their meaning, in that case, is totally incomprehensible; and that the infirmities of our nature do not permit us to reach any ideas which in the least correspond to the ineffable sublimity of the Divine attributes.

Part IV

It seems strange to me, said Cleanthes, that you, Demea, who are so sincere in the cause of religion, should still maintain the mysterious, incomprehensible nature of the Deity, and should insist so strenuously that he has no manner of likeness or resemblance to human creatures. The Deity, I can readily allow, possesses many powers and attributes of which we can have no comprehension; but, if our ideas, so far as they go, be not just and adequate and correspondent to his real nature, I know not what there is in this subject worth insisting on. Is the name, without any meaning, of such mighty importance? Or how do you *mystics*, who maintain the absolute incomprehensibility of the Deity, differ from sceptics or atheists, who assert that the first cause of all is unknown and unintelligible? Their temerity must be very great if, after rejecting the production by a mind—I mean a mind resembling the human (for I know of no other)—they pretend to assign, with certainty, any other specific intelligible cause; and their conscience must be very scrupulous, indeed, if they refuse to call the universal unknown cause a God or Deity, and to bestow on him as many sublime eulogies and unmeaning epithets as you shall please to require of them.

Who could imagine, replied Demea, that Cleanthes, the calm philosophical Cleanthes, would attempt to refute his antagonists by affixing a nickname to them; and, like the common bigots and inquisitors of the age, have recourse to invective and declamation instead of reasoning? Or does he not perceive that these topics are easily retorted, and that *anthropomorphite* is an appellation as invidious, and implies as dangerous consequences, as the epithet of *mystic* with which he has honored us? In reality, Cleanthes, consider what it is you assert when you represent the Deity as similar to a human mind and understanding. What is the soul of man? A composition of various faculties, passions, sentiments, ideas—united, indeed, into one self or person, but still distinct from each other. When it reasons, the ideas which are the parts of its discourse arrange themselves in a certain form or order which is not preserved entire for a moment, but immediately gives place to another arrangement. New opinions, new passions, new affections, new feelings arise which continually diversify the mental scene and produce in it the greatest variety and most rapid succession imaginable. How is this compatible with that perfect immutability and simplicity which all true theists ascribe to the Deity? By the same act, say they, he sees past, present, and future; his love and hatred, his mercy and justice, are one individual operation; he is entire in every point of space, and complete in every instant of duration. No succession, no change, no acquisition, no diminution. What he is implies not in it any shadow of distinction or diversity. And what he is this moment he ever has been and ever will be, without any new judgment, sentiment, or operation. He stands fixed in one simple, perfect state; nor can you ever say, with any propriety, that this act of his is different from that other, or that this judgment or idea has been lately formed and will give place, by succession, to any different judgment or idea.

I can readily allow, said Cleanthes, that those who maintain the perfect simplicity of the Supreme Being, to the extent in which you have explained it, are complete *mystics*, and chargeable with all the consequences which I have drawn from their opinion. They are, in a word, *atheists*, without knowing it. For though it be allowed that the Deity possesses attributes of which we have no comprehension, yet ought we never to ascribe to him any attributes which are absolutely incompatible with that intelligent nature essential to him. A mind whose acts and sentiments and ideas are not distinct and successive, one that is wholly simple and totally immutable, is a mind which has no thought, no reason, no will, no sentiment, no love, no hatred; or, in a word, is no mind at all. It is an abuse of terms to give it that appellation, and we may as well speak of limited extension without figure, or of number without composition.

Pray consider, said Philo, whom you are at present inveighing against. You are honoring with the appellation of *atheist* all the sound, orthodox divines, almost, who have treated of this subject; and you will at last be, yourself, found, according to your reckoning, the only sound theist in the world. But if idolaters be atheists, as, I think, may justly be asserted, and Christian theologians the same, what becomes of the argument, so much celebrated, derived from the universal consent of mankind?

But, because I know you are not much swayed by names and authorities, I shall endeavor to show you, a little more distinctly, the inconveniences of that anthropomorphism which you have embraced, and shall prove that there is no ground to suppose a plan of the world to be formed in the Divine mind, consisting of distinct ideas, differently arranged, in the same manner as an architect forms in his head the plan of a house which he intends to execute.

It is not easy, I own, to see what is gained by this supposition, whether we judge of the matter by *reason* or by *experience*. We are still obliged to mount higher in order to find the cause of this cause which you had assigned as satisfactory and conclusive.

If *reason* (I mean abstract reason derived from inquiries *a priori*) be not alike mute with regard to all questions concerning cause and effect, this sentence at least it will venture to pronounce: that a mental world or universe of ideas requires a cause as much as does a material world or universe of objects; and, if similar in its arrangement, must require a similar cause. For what is there in this subject which should occasion a different conclusion or inference? In an abstract view, they are entirely alike; and no difficulty attends the one supposition which is not common to both of them.

Again, when we will needs force *experience* to pronounce some sentence, even on these subjects which lie beyond her sphere, neither can she perceive any material difference in this particular between these two kinds of worlds, but finds them to be governed by similar principles, and to depend upon an equal variety of causes in their operations. We have specimens in miniature of both of them. Our own mind resembles the one; a vegetable or animal body the other. Let experience, therefore, judge from these samples. Nothing seems more delicate, with regard to its causes, than thought; and as these causes never operate in two persons after the same manner, so we never find two persons who think exactly alike. Nor indeed does the same person think exactly alike at any two different periods of time. A difference of age, of the disposition of his body, of weather, of food, of company, of books, of passions—any of these particulars, or others more minute, are sufficient to alter the curious machinery of thought and communicate to it very different movements and operations. As far as we can judge, vegetables and animal bodies are not more delicate in their motions, nor depend upon a greater variety or more curious adjustment of springs and principles.

How, therefore, shall we satisfy ourselves concerning the cause of that Being whom you suppose the Author of Nature, or, according to your system of anthropomorphism, the ideal world into which you trace the material? Have we not the same reason to trace that ideal world into another ideal world or new intelligent principle? But if we stop and go no farther, why go so far—why not stop at the material world? How can we satisfy ourselves without going on *in infinitum*? And, after all, what satisfaction is there in that infinite progression? Let us remember the story of the Indian philosopher and his elephant. It was never more applicable than to the present subject. If the material world rests upon a similar ideal world, this ideal world must rest upon some other, and so

recur upon me. Naturalists, indeed, very justly explain particular effects by more general causes, though these general causes themselves should remain in the end totally inexplicable; but they never surely thought it satisfactory to explain a particular effect by a particular cause which was no more to be accounted for than the effect itself. An ideal system, arranged of itself, without a precedent design, is not a whit more explicable than a material one which attains its order in a like manner; nor is there any more difficulty in the latter supposition than in the former.

Part V

But to show you still more inconveniences, continued Philo, in your anthropomorphism, please to take a new survey of your principles. *Like effects prove like causes.* This is the experimental argument; and this, you say too, is the sole theological argument. Now it is certain that the liker the effects are which are seen and the liker the causes which are inferred, the stronger is the argument. Every departure on either side diminishes the probability and renders the experiment less conclusive. You cannot doubt of the principle; neither ought you to reject its consequences.

All the new discoveries in astronomy which prove the immense grandeur and magnificence of the works of nature are so many additional arguments for a Deity, according to the true system of theism; but, according to your hypothesis of experimental theism, they become so many objections, by removing the effect still farther from all resemblance to the effects of human art and contrivance. For if Lucretius,[25] even following the old system of the world, could exclaim:

> Quis regere immensi summam, quis habere profundi
> Indu manu validas potis est moderanter habenas?
> Quis pariter coelos omnes convertere? et omnes
> Ignibus aetheriis terras suffire feraces?
> Omnibus inque locis esse omni tempore praesto?[26]

If Tully[27] esteemed this reasoning so natural as to put it into the mouth of his Epicurean:

> Quibus enim oculis animi intueri potuit vester Plato fabricam illam tanti operis, qua construi a Deo atque aedificari mundum facit? quae molitio? quae ferramenta? qui vectes? quae machinae? qui ministri tanti muneris fuerunt? quemadmodum autem obedire et parere voluntati architecti aer, ignis, aqua, terra potuerunt?[28]

If this argument, I say, had any force in former ages, how much greater must it have at present when the bounds of nature are so infinitely enlarged and such a magnificent scene is opened to us? It is still more unreasonable to form our idea of so unlimited a cause from our experience of the narrow productions of human design and invention.

The discoveries by microscopes, as they open a new universe in miniature, are still objections, according to you; arguments, according to me. The further we push our researches of this kind, we are still led to infer the universal cause of all to be vastly different from mankind, or from any object of human experience and observation.

And what say you to the discoveries in anatomy,

25. [Lucretius (c. 99–c. 55 B.C.) was a Roman poet and philosopher who espoused the view of Epicurus that the universe is composed of everlasting atoms that move in a void, the whole exhibiting beauty and majesty but without purpose or divine providence.]

26. Lib. Xi. 1094. [The quotation is from *On the Nature of the Universe.* "Who is able to rule the whole of the immeasurable; who is able, with control, to hold in hand the strong reins of the boundless? Who equally is able to turn all the heavens? And who is able to warm all fertile grounds with ethereal fire? Who is able to be present in all places at every time?"]

27. [Regarding Tully (Cicero), see Locke's *Essay*, n.8.]

28. *De. Nat. Deor.*, lib. i. [The quotation is from *On the Nature of the Gods.* "For with which of the soul's eyes has your [master] Plato been able to contemplate that fabrication of such great labor, by which he establishes that the universe is furnished and even constructed by God? What preparation [was involved]? What tools? What levers? What machines? What agents were there for such a great enterprise? Moreover, how were air, fire, water, and earth able to obey and to come forth at the will of the architect?"]

chemistry, botany? . . . These surely are no objections, replied Cleanthes; they only discover new instances of art and contrivance. It is still the image of mind reflected on us from innumerable objects. Add a mind *like the human*, said Philo. I know of no other, replied Cleanthes. And the liker, the better, insisted Philo. To be sure, said Cleanthes.

Now, Cleanthes, said Philo, with an air of alacrity and triumph, mark the consequences. *First*, by this method of reasoning you renounce all claim to infinity in any of the attributes of the Deity. For, as the cause ought only to be proportioned to the effect, and the effect, so far as it falls under our cognizance, is not infinite, what pretensions have we, upon your suppositions, to ascribe that attribute to the divine Being? You will still insist that, by removing him so much from all similarity to human creatures, we give in to the most arbitrary hypothesis, and at the same time weaken all proofs of his existence.

Secondly, you have no reason, on your theory, for ascribing perfection to the Deity, even in his finite capacity; or for supposing him free from every error, mistake, or incoherence, in his undertakings. There are many inexplicable difficulties in the works of nature which, if we allow a perfect author to be proved *a priori*, are easily solved, and become only seeming difficulties from the narrow capacity of man, who cannot trace infinite relations. But according to your method of reasoning, these difficulties become all real; and, perhaps, will be insisted on as new instances of likeness to human art and contrivance. At least, you must acknowledge that it is impossible for us to tell, from our limited views, whether this system contains any great faults or deserves any considerable praise if compared to other possible and even real systems. Could a peasant, if the *Aeneid* were read to him, pronounce that poem to be absolutely faultless, or even assign to it its proper rank among the productions of human wit, he who had never seen any other production?

But were this world ever so perfect a production, it must still remain uncertain whether all the excellences of the work can justly be ascribed to the workman. If we survey a ship, what an exalted idea must we form of the ingenuity of the carpenter who framed so complicated, useful, and beautiful a machine? And what surprise must we feel when we find him a stupid mechanic who imitated others, and copied an art which, through a long succession of ages, after multiplied trials, mistakes, corrections, deliberations, and controversies, had been gradually improving? Many worlds might have been botched and bungled, throughout an eternity, ere this system was struck out; much labor lost; many fruitless trials made; and a slow but continued improvement carried on during infinite ages in the art of world-making. In such subjects, who can determine where the truth, nay, who can conjecture where the probability lies, amidst a great number of hypotheses which may be proposed, and a still greater which may be imagined?

And what shadow of an argument, continued Philo, can you produce from your hypothesis to prove the unity of the Deity? A great number of men join in building a house or ship, in rearing a city, in framing a commonwealth; why may not several deities combine in contriving and framing a world? This is only so much greater similarity to human affairs. By sharing the work among several, we may so much further limit the attributes of each, and get rid of that extensive power and knowledge which must be supposed in one deity, and which, according to you, can only serve to weaken the proof of his existence. And if such foolish, such vicious creatures as man can yet often unite in framing and executing one plan, how much more those deities or demons, whom we may suppose several degrees more perfect?

To multiply causes without necessity is indeed contrary to true philosophy, but this principle applies not to the present case. Were one deity antecedently proved by your theory who were possessed of every attribute requisite to the production of the universe, it would be needless, I own (though not absurd), to suppose any other deity existent. But while it is still a question whether all these attributes are united in one subject or dispersed among several independent beings; by what phenomena in nature can we pretend to decide the controversy? Where we see a body raised in a scale, we are sure that there is in the opposite scale, however concealed from sight, some counterpoising weight equal to it; but it is still allowed to doubt whether that weight be an aggregate of several distinct bodies or one uniform united mass. And if the weight requisite very much exceeds anything which we have ever seen conjoined in any single body, the former supposition becomes still more probable and natural. An intelligent being of such vast power and capacity as is necessary to produce the universe—or, to speak in the language of ancient philosophy, so prodigious an animal—exceeds all analogy and even comprehension.

But further, Cleanthes, men are mortal, and renew their species by generation; and this is common to all living creatures. The two great sexes of male and female, says Milton, animate the world. Why must this circumstance, so universal, so essential, be excluded from those numerous and limited deities? Behold, then, the theogeny of ancient times brought back upon us.

And why not become a perfect anthropomorphite? Why not assert the deity or deities to be corporeal, and to have eyes, a nose, mouth, ears, etc? Epicurus maintained that no man had ever seen reason but in a human figure; therefore, the gods must have a human figure. And this argument, which is deservedly so much ridiculed by Cicero, becomes, according to you, solid and philosophical.

In a word, Cleanthes, a man who follows your hypothesis is able, perhaps, to assert or conjecture that the universe sometime arose from something like design; but beyond that position he cannot ascertain one single circumstance, and is left afterwards to fix every point of his theology by the utmost license of fancy and hypothesis. This world, for aught he knows, is very faulty and imperfect, compared to a superior standard; and was only the first rude essay of some infant deity who afterwards abandoned it, ashamed of his lame performance; it is the work only of some dependent, inferior deity, and is the object of derision to his superiors; it is the production of old age and dotage in some superannuated deity; and ever since his death has run on at adventures, from the first impulse and active force which it received from him. You justly give signs of horror, Demea, at these strange suppositions; but these, and a thousand more of the same kind, are Cleanthes' suppositions, not mine. From the moment the attributes of the Deity are supposed finite, all these have place. And I cannot, for my part, think that so wild and unsettled a system of theology is, in any respect, preferable to none at all.

These suppositions I absolutely disown, cried Cleanthes; they strike me, however, with no horror, especially when proposed in that rambling way in which they drop from you. On the contrary, they give me pleasure when I see that, by the utmost indulgence of your imagination, you never get rid of the hypothesis of design in the universe, but are obliged at every turn to have recourse to it. To this concession I adhere steadily; and this I regard as a sufficient foundation for religion.

Part VI

It must be a slight fabric, indeed, said Demea, which can be erected on so tottering a foundation. While we are uncertain whether there is one deity or many, whether the deity or deities, to whom we owe our existence, be perfect or imperfect, subordinate or supreme, dead or alive, what trust or confidence can we repose in them? What devotion or worship address to them? What veneration or obedience pay them? To all the purposes of life the theory of religion becomes altogether useless; and even with regard to speculative consequences its uncertainty, according to you, must render it totally precarious and unsatisfactory.

To render it still more unsatisfactory, said Philo, there occurs to me another hypothesis which must acquire an air of probability from the method of reasoning so much insisted on by Cleanthes. That like effects arise from like causes—this principle he supposes the foundation of all religion. But there is another principle of the same kind, no less certain and derived from the same source of experience, that, where several known circumstances are observed to be similar, the unknown will also be found similar. Thus, if we see the limbs of a human body, we conclude that it is also attended with a human head, though hid from us. Thus, if we see, through a chink in a wall, a small part of the sun, we conclude that were the wall removed we should see the whole body. In short, this method of reasoning is so obvious and familiar that no scruple can ever be made with regard to its solidity.

Now, if we survey the universe, so far as it falls under our knowledge, it bears a great resemblance to an animal or organized body, and seems actuated with a like principle of life and motion. A continual circulation of matter in it produces no disorder; a continual waste in every part is incessantly repaired; the closest sympathy is perceived throughout the entire system; and each part or member, in performing its proper offices, operates both to its own preservation and to that of the whole. The world, therefore, I infer, is an animal; and the Deity is the *soul* of the world, actuating it, and actuated by it.

You have too much learning, Cleanthes, to be at all surprised at this opinion which, you know, was maintained by almost all the theists of antiquity, and chiefly prevails in their discourses and reasonings. For though sometimes the ancient philosophers reason from final causes, as if they thought the world the workmanship of God, yet it appears rather their favorite notion to consider it as his body whose organization renders it subservient to him. And it must be confessed that, as the universe resembles more a human body than it does the works of human art and contrivance, if our limited analogy could ever, with any propriety, be extended to the whole of nature, the inference seems juster in favor of the ancient than the modern theory.

There are many other advantages, too, in the former theory which recommended it to the ancient theologians. Nothing more repugnant to all their notions—because nothing more repugnant to common experience—than mind without body; a mere spiritual substance which fell not under their senses nor comprehension, and of which they had not observed one single instance throughout all nature. Mind and body they knew because they felt both; an order, arrangement, organization, or internal machinery, in both they likewise knew, after the same manner; and it could not but seem reasonable to transfer this experience to the universe, and to suppose the divine mind and body to be also coeval and to have, both of them, order and arrangement naturally inherent in them and inseparable from them.

Here, therefore, is a new species of *anthropomorphism*, Cleanthes, on which you may deliberate; and a theory which seems not liable to any considerable difficulties. You are too much superior, surely, to *systematical prejudices* to find any more difficulty in supposing an animal body to be, originally, of itself or from unknown causes, possessed of order and organization, than in supposing a similar order to belong to mind. But the *vulgar prejudice* that body and mind ought always to accompany each other ought not, one should think, to be entirely neglected; since it is founded on *vulgar experience*, the only guide which you profess to follow in all these theological inquiries. And if you assert that our limited experience is an unequal standard by which to judge of the unlimited extent of nature, you entirely abandon your own hypothesis, and must thenceforward adopt our mysticism, as you call it, and admit of the absolute incomprehensibility of the Divine Nature.

This theory, I own, replied Cleanthes, has never before occurred to me, though a pretty natural one; and I cannot readily, upon so short an examination and reflection, deliver any opinion with regard to it. You are very scrupulous, indeed, said Philo; were I to examine any system of yours, I should not have acted with half that caution and reserve, in starting objections and difficulties to it. However, if anything occur to you, you will oblige us by proposing it.

Why then, replied Cleanthes, it seems to me that, though the world does, in many circumstances, resemble an animal body, yet is the analogy also defective in many circumstances the most material: no organ of sense, no seat of thought or reason; no one precise origin of motion and action. In short, it seems to bear a stronger resemblance to a vegetable than to an animal, and your inference would be so far inconclusive in favor of the soul of the world.

But, in the next place, your theory seems to imply the eternity of the world; and that is a principle which, I think, can be refuted by the strongest reasons and probabilities. I shall suggest an argument to this purpose which, I believe, has not been insisted on by any writer. Those who reason from the late origin of arts and sciences, though their inference wants not force, may perhaps be refuted by considerations derived from the nature of human society, which is in continual revolution between ignorance and knowledge, liberty and slavery, riches and poverty; so that it is impossible for us, from our limited experience, to foretell with assurance what events may or may not be expected. Ancient learning and history seem to have been in great danger of entirely perishing after the inundation of the barbarous nations; and had these convulsions continued a little longer, or been a little more violent, we should not probably have now known what passed in the world a few centuries before us. Nay, were it not for the superstition of the popes, who preserved a little jargon of Latin in order to support the appearance of an ancient and universal church, that tongue must have been utterly lost; in which case the Western world, being totally barbarous, would not have been in a fit disposition for receiving the Greek language and learning, which was conveyed to them after the sacking of Constantinople. When learning and books had been extinguished, even the mechanical arts would have fallen considerably to decay; and it is easily imagined that fable or tradition might ascribe to them a much later origin than the true one. This vulgar argument, therefore, against the eternity of the world seems a little precarious.

But here appears to be the foundation of a better argument. Lucullus[29] was the first that brought cherry-trees from Asia to Europe; though that tree thrives so well in many European climates that it grows in the woods without any culture. Is it possible that, throughout a whole eternity, no European had ever passed into Asia and thought of transplanting so delicious a fruit into his own country? Or if the tree was once transplanted and propagated, how could it ever afterwards perish? Empires may rise and fall; liberty and slavery succeed alternately; ignorance and knowledge give place to each other; but the cherry-tree will still remain in the woods of Greece, Spain, and Italy, and will never be affected by the revolutions of human society.

It is not two thousand years since vines were transplanted into France, though there is no climate in the world more favorable to them. It is not three centuries since horses, cows, sheep, swine, dogs, corn, were known in America. Is it possible that during the revolutions of a whole eternity there never arose a Columbus who might open the communication between Europe and that continent? We may as well imagine that all men would wear stockings for ten thousand years, and never have the sense to think of garters to tie them. All these seem convincing proofs of the youth or rather infancy of the world, as being founded on the operation of principles more constant and steady than those by which human society is governed and directed. Nothing less than a total convulsion of the elements will ever destroy all the European animals and vegetables which are now to be found in the Western world.

And what argument have you against such convulsions? replied Philo. Strong and almost incontestable proofs may be traced over the whole earth that every part of this globe has continued for many ages entirely covered with water. And though order were supposed inseparable from matter, and inherent in it; yet may matter be susceptible of many and great revolutions, through the endless periods of eternal duration. The incessant changes to which every part of it is subject seem to intimate some such general transformations; though, at the same time, it is observable that all the changes and corruptions of which we have ever had experience are but passages from one state of order to another; nor can matter ever rest in total deformity and confusion. What we see in the parts, we may infer in the whole; at least, that is the method of reasoning on which you rest your whole theory. And were I obliged to defend any particular system of this nature, which I never willingly should do, I esteem none more plausible than that which ascribes an eternal, inherent principle of order to the world, though attended with great and continual revolutions and alterations. This at once solves all difficulties; and if the solution, by being so general, is not entirely complete and satisfactory, it is at least a theory that we must sooner or later have recourse to, whatever system we embrace. How could things have been as they are, were there not an original inherent principle of order somewhere, in thought or in matter? And it is very indifferent to which of these we give the preference. Chance has no place, on any hypothesis, sceptical or religious. Everything is surely governed by steady, inviolable laws. And were the inmost essence of things laid open to us, we should then discover a scene of which, at present, we can have no idea. Instead of admiring the order of natural beings, we should clearly see that it was absolutely impossible for them, in the smallest article, ever to admit of any other disposition.

Were anyone inclined to revive the ancient pagan theology which maintained, as we learn from Hesiod,[30] that this globe was governed by 30,000 deities, who arose from the unknown powers of nature, you would naturally object, Cleanthes, that nothing is gained by this hypothesis; and that it is as easy to suppose all men and animals, beings more numerous but less perfect, to have sprung immediately from a like origin. Push the same inference a step further, and you will find a numerous society of deities as

29. [Lucullus (c. 110–56 B.C.) was a Roman general who fought in Asia and eventually returned to life on a luxurious estate in Rome.]

30. [Regarding Hesiod, see Aristotle's *Metaphysics*, n.13.]

explicable as one universal deity who possesses within himself the powers and perfections of the whole society. All these systems, then, of scepticism, polytheism, and theism, you must allow, on your principles, to be on a like footing, and that no one of them has any advantage over the others. You may thence learn the fallacy of your principles.

Part VII

But here, continued Philo, in examining the ancient system of the soul of the world there strikes me, all of a sudden, a new idea which, if just, must go near to subvert all your reasoning, and destroy even your first inferences on which you repose such confidence. If the universe bears a greater likeness to animal bodies and to vegetables than to the works of human art, it is more probable that its cause resembles the cause of the former than that of the latter, and its origin ought rather to be abscribed to generation or vegetation than to reason or design. Your conclusion, even according to your own principles, is therefore lame and defective.

Pray open up this argument a little further, said Demea, for I do not rightly apprehend it in that concise manner in which you have expressed it.

Our friend Cleanthes, replied Philo, as you have heard, asserts that since no question of fact can be proved otherwise than by experience, the existence of a Deity admits not of proof from any other medium. The world, says he, resembles the works of human contrivance; therefore its cause must also resemble that of the other. Here we may remark that the operation of one very small part of nature, to wit, man, upon another very small part, to wit, that inanimate matter lying within his reach, is the rule by which Cleanthes judges of the origin of the whole; and he measures objects, so widely disproportioned, by the same individual standard. But to waive all objections drawn from this topic, I affirm that there are other parts of the universe (besides the machines of human invention) which bear still a greater resemblance to the fabric of the world, and which, therefore, afford a better conjecture concerning the universal origin of this system. These parts are animals and vegetables. The world plainly resembles more an animal or a vegetable than it does a watch or a knitting-loom. Its cause, therefore, it is more probable, resembles the cause of the former. The cause of the former is generation or vegetation. The cause, therefore, of the world we may infer to be something similar or analogous to generation or vegetation.

But how is it conceivable, said Demea, that the world can arise from anything similar to vegetation or generation?

Very easily, replied Philo. In like manner as a tree sheds its seed into the neighboring fields and produces other trees; so the great vegetable, the world, or this planetary system, produces within itself certain seeds which, being scattered into the surrounding chaos, vegetate into new worlds. A comet, for instance, is the seed of a world; and after it has been fully ripened, by passing from sun to sun, and star to star, it is at last tossed into the unformed elements which everywhere surround this universe, and immediately sprouts up into a new system.

Or if, for the sake of variety (for I see no other advantage) we should suppose this world to be an animal; a comet is the egg of this animal; and in like manner as an ostrich lays its egg in the sand, which, without any further care, hatches the egg and produces a new animal, so . . . I understand you, says Demea: But what wild, arbitrary suppositions are these? What *data* have you for such extraordinary conclusions? And is the slight, imaginary resemblance of the world to a vegetable or an animal sufficient to establish the same inference with regard to both? Objects which are in general so widely different; ought they to be a standard for each other?

Right, cries Philo: This is the topic on which I have all along insisted. I have still asserted that we have no *data* to establish any system of cosmogony. Our experience, so imperfect in itself and so limited both in extent and duration, can afford us no probable conjecture concerning the whole of things. But if we must needs fix on some hypothesis, by what rule, pray, ought we to determine our choice? Is there any other rule than the great similarity of the objects compared? And does not a plant or an animal, which springs from vegetation or generation, bear a stronger resemblance to the world than does any artificial machine, which arises from reason and design?

But what is this vegetation and generation of which you talk? said Demea. Can you explain their operations, and anatomize that fine internal structure on which they depend?

As much, at least, replied Philo, as Cleanthes can explain the operations of reason, or anatomize that internal structure on which *it* depends. But without any such elaborate disquisitions, when I see an animal, I infer that it sprang from generation; and that with as great certainty as you conclude a house to have been reared by design. These words *generation, reason* mark only certain powers and energies in nature whose effects are known, but whose essence is incomprehensible; and one of these principles, more than the other, has no privilege for being made a standard to the whole of nature.

In reality, Demea, it may reasonably be expected that the larger the views are which we take of things, the better will they conduct us in our conclusions concerning such extraordinary and such magnificent subjects. In this little corner of the world alone, there are four principles, *reason, instinct, generation, vegetation,* which are similar to each other, and are the causes of similar effects. What a number of other principles may we naturally suppose in the immense extent and variety of the universe could we travel from planet to planet, and from system to system, in order to examine each part of this mighty fabric? Any one of these four principles above mentioned (and a hundred others which lie open to our conjecture) may afford us a theory by which to judge of the origin of the world; and it is a palpable and egregious partiality to confine our view entirely to that principle by which our own minds operate. Were this principle more intelligible on that account, such a partiality might be somewhat excusable; but reason, in its internal fabric and structure, is really as little known to us as instinct or vegetation; and, perhaps, even that vague, undeterminate word *nature* to which the vulgar refer everything is not at the bottom more inexplicable. The effects of these principles are all known to us from experience; but the principles themselves and their manner of operation are totally unknown; nor is it less intelligible or less conformable to experience to say that the world arose by vegetation, from a seed shed by another world, than to say that it arose from a divine reason or contrivance, according to the sense in which Cleanthes understands it.

But methinks, said Demea, if the world had a vegetative quality and could sow the seeds of new worlds into the infinite chaos, this power would be still an additional argument for design in its author. For whence could arise so wonderful a faculty but from design? Or how can order spring from anything which perceives not that order which it bestows?

You need only look around you, replied Philo, to satisfy yourself with regard to this question. A tree bestows order and organization on that tree which springs from it, without knowing the order; an animal in the same manner on its offspring; a bird on its nest; and instances of this kind are even more frequent in the world than those of order which arise from reason and contrivance. To say that all this order in animals and vegetables proceeds ultimately from design is begging the question; nor can that great point be ascertained otherwise than by proving, *a priori,* both that order is, from its nature, inseparably attached to thought, and that it can never of itself or from original unknown principles belong to matter.

But further, Demea, this objection which you urge can never be made use of by Cleanthes, without renouncing a defence which he has already made against one of my objections. When I inquired concerning the cause of that supreme reason and intelligence into which he resolves everything, he told me that the impossibility of satisfying such inquiries could never be admitted as an objection in any species of philosophy. *We must stop somewhere,* says he; *nor is it ever within the reach of human capacity to explain ultimate causes or show the last connections of any objects. It is sufficient if any steps, so far as we go, are supported by experience and observation.* Now, that vegetation and generation, as well as reason, are experienced to be principles of order in nature is undeniable. If I rest my system of cosmogony on the former, preferably to the latter, it is at my choice. The matter seems entirely arbitrary. And when Cleanthes asks me what is the cause of my great vegetative or generative faculty, I am equally entitled to ask him the cause of his great reasoning principle. These questions we have agreed to forbear on both sides; and it is chiefly his interest on the present occasion to stick to this agreement. Judging by our limited and imperfect experience, generation has some privileges above reason; for we see every day the latter arise from the former, never the former from the latter.

Compare, I beseech you, the consequences on both sides. The world, say I, resembles an animal; therefore it is an animal, therefore it arose from generation. The steps, I confess, are wide; yet there is some small appearance of analogy in each step. The world, says Cleanthes, resembles a machine; therefore it is a machine, therefore it arose from design. The steps are here equally wide, and the analogy less striking. And if he pretends to carry on *my* hypothesis a step further, and to infer design or reason from the great principle of generation on which I insist, I may, with better authority, use the same freedom to push further *his* hypothesis, and infer a divine generation or theogony from his principle of reason. I have at least some faint shadow of experience, which is the utmost that can ever be attained in the present subject. Reason, in innumerable instances, is observed to arise from the principle of generation, and never to arise from any other principle.

Hesiod and all the ancient mythologists were so struck with this analogy that they universally explained the origin of nature from an animal birth, and copulation. Plato, too, so far as he is intelligible, seems to have adopted some such notion in his *Timaeus*.

The Brahmins[31] assert that the world arose from an infinite spider, who spun this whole complicated mass from his bowels, and annihilates afterwards the whole or any part of it, by absorbing it again and resolving it into his own essence. Here is a species of cosmogony which appears to us ridiculous because a spider is a little contemptible animal whose operations we are never likely to take for a model of the whole universe. But still here is a new species of analogy, even in our globe. And were there a planet wholly inhabited by spiders (which is very possible), this inference would there appear as natural and irrefragable as that which in our planet ascribes the origin of all things to design and intelligence, as explained by Cleanthes. Why an orderly system may not be spun from the belly as well as from the brain, it will be difficult for him to give a satisfactory reason.

I must confess, Philo, replied Cleanthes, that, of all men living, the task which you have undertaken, of raising doubts and objections, suits you best and seems, in a manner, natural and unavoidable to you. So great is your fertility of invention that I am not ashamed to acknowledge myself unable, on a sudden, to solve regularly such out-of-the-way difficulties as you incessantly start upon me; though I clearly see, in general, their fallacy and error. And I question not, but you are yourself, at present, in the same case, and have not the solution so ready as the objection; while you must be sensible that common sense and reason are entirely against you, and that such whimsies as you have delivered may puzzle but never can convince us.

31. [Brahmins are members of the highest Hindu caste.]

Part VIII

What you ascribe to the fertility of my invention, replied Philo, is entirely owing to the nature of the subject. In subjects adapted to the narrow compass of human reason there is commonly but one determination which carries probability or conviction with it; and to a man of sound judgment all other suppositions but that one appear entirely absurd and chimerical. But in such questions as the present, a hundred contradictory views may preserve a kind of imperfect analogy, and invention has here full scope to exert itself. Without any great effort of thought, I believe that I could, in an instant, propose other systems of cosmogony which would have some faint appearance of truth; though it is a thousand, a million to one if either yours or any one of mine be the true system.

For instance, what if I should revive the old Epicurean hypothesis? This is commonly, and I believe justly, esteemed the most absurd system that has yet been proposed; yet I know not whether, with a few alterations, it might not be brought to bear a faint appearance of probability. Instead of supposing matter infinite, as Epicurus did, let us suppose it finite. A finite number of particles is only susceptible of finite transpositions, and it must happen, in an eternal duration, that every possible order or position must be tried an infinite number of times. This world, therefore, with all its events, even the most minute, has before been produced and destroyed, and will again be produced and destroyed, without any bounds and limitations. No one who has a conception of the powers of infinite, in comparison of finite, will ever scruple this determination.

But this supposes, said Demea, that matter can acquire motion without any voluntary agent or first mover.

And where is the difficulty, replied Philo, of that supposition? Every event, before experience, is equally difficult and incomprehensible; and every event, after experience, is equally easy and intelligible. Motion, in many instances, from gravity, from elasticity, from electricity, begins in matter, without any known voluntary agent; and to suppose always, in these cases, an unknown voluntary agent is mere hypothesis—and hypothesis attended with no advantages. The beginning of motion in matter itself is as conceivable *a priori* as its communication from mind and intelligence.

Besides, why may not motion have been propagated by impulse through all eternity, and the same stock of it, or nearly the same, be still upheld in the universe? As much as is lost by the composition of motion, as much is gained by its resolution. And whatever the causes are, the fact is certain that matter is and always has been in continual agitation, as far as human experience or tradition reaches. There is not probably, at present, in the whole universe, one particle of matter at absolute rest.

And this very consideration, too, continued Philo, which we have stumbled on in the course of the argument suggests a new hypothesis of cosmogony that is not absolutely absurd and improbable. Is there a system, an order, an economy of things, by which matter can preserve that perpetual agitation which seems essential to it, and yet maintain a constancy in the forms which it produces? There certainly is such an economy, for this is actually the case with the present world. The continual motion of matter, therefore, in less than infinite transpositions, must produce this economy or order; and, by its very nature, that order, when once established, supports itself for many ages if not to eternity. But wherever matter is so poised, arranged, and adjusted, as to continue in perpetual motion, and yet preserve a constancy in the forms, its situation must, of necessity, have all the same appearance of art and contrivance which we observe at present. All the parts of each form must have a relation to each other and to the whole; and the whole itself must have a relation to the other parts of the universe, to the element in which the form subsists, to the materials with which it repairs its waste and decay, and to every other form which is hostile or friendly. A defect in any of these particulars destroys the form; and the matter of which it is composed is again set loose, and is thrown into irregular motions and fermentations till it unite itself to some other regular form. If no such form be prepared to receive it, and if there be a great quantity of this corrupted matter in the universe, the universe itself is entirely disordered, whether it be the feeble embryo of a world in its first beginnings that is thus destroyed or the rotten carcass of one languishing in old age and infirmity. In either case, a chaos ensues till finite though innumerable revolutions produce, at last, some forms whose parts and organs are so adjusted as to support the forms amidst a continued succession of matter.

Suppose (for we shall endeavor to vary the expression) that matter were thrown into any position by a blind, unguided force; it is evident that this first position must, in all probability, be the most confused and most disorderly imaginable, without any resemblance to those works of human contrivance which, along with a symmetry of parts, discover an adjustment of means to ends and a tendency to self-preservation. If the actuating force cease after this operation, matter must remain forever in disorder, and continue an immense chaos, without any proportion or activity. But suppose that the actuating force, whatever it be, still continues in matter, this first position will immediately give place to a second which will likewise, in all probability, be as disorderly as the first, and so on through many successions of changes and revolutions. No particular order or position ever continues a moment unaltered. The original force, still remaining in activity, gives a perpetual restlessness to matter. Every possible situation is produced, and instantly destroyed. If a glimpse or dawn of order appears for a moment, it is instantly hurried away and confounded by that never-ceasing force which actuates every part of matter.

Thus the universe goes on for many ages in a continued succession of chaos and disorder. But is it not possible that it may settle at last, so as not to lose its motion and active force (for that we have supposed inherent in it), yet so as to preserve a uniformity of appearance, amidst the continual motion and fluctuation of its parts? This we find to be the case with the universe at present. Every individual is perpetually changing, and every part of every individual; and yet the whole remains, in appearance, the same. May we not hope for such a position or rather be assured of it from the eternal revolutions of unguided matter; and may not this account for all the appearing wisdom and contrivance which is in the universe? Let us contemplate the subject a little, and we shall find this adjustment if attained by matter of a seeming stability in the forms, with a real and perpetual revolution or motion of parts, affords a plausible, if not a true, solution of the difficulty.

It is in vain, therefore, to insist upon the uses of the parts in animals or vegetables, and their curious adjustment to each other. I would fain know how an animal could subsist unless its parts were so adjusted? Do we not find that it immediately perishes whenever this adjustment ceases, and that its matter, corrupting, tries some new form? It happens indeed that the parts of the world are so well adjusted that some regular form immediately lays claim to this corrupted matter; and if it were not so, could the world subsist? Must it not dissolve, as well as the animal, and pass through new positions and situations till in great but finite succession it fall, at last, into the present or some such order?

It is well, replied Cleanthes, you told us that this hypothesis was suggested on a sudden, in the course of the argument. Had you had leisure to examine it, you would soon have perceived the insuperable objections to which it is exposed. No form, you say, can subsist unless it possess those powers and organs requisite for its subsistence; some new order or economy must be tried, and so on, without intermission, till at last some order which can support and maintain itself is fallen upon. But according to this hypothesis, whence arise the many conveniences and advantages which men and all animals possess? Two eyes, two ears are not absolutely necessary for the subsistence of the species. Human race might have been propagated and preserved without horses, dogs, cows, sheep, and those innumerable fruits and products which serve to our satisfaction and enjoyment. If no camels had been created for the use of man in the sandy deserts of Africa and Arabia, would the world have been dissolved? If no loadstone had been framed to give that wonderful and useful direction to the needle, would human society and the human kind have been immediately extinguished? Though the maxims of nature be in general very frugal, yet instances of this kind are far from being rare; and any one of them is sufficient proof of design—and of a benevolent design—which gave rise to the order and arrangement of the universe.

At least, you may safely infer, said Philo, that the foregoing hypothesis is so far incomplete and imperfect, which I shall not scruple to allow. But can we ever reasonably expect greater success in any attempts of this nature? Or can we ever hope to erect a system of cosmogony that will be liable to no exceptions, and will contain no circumstance repugnant to our limited and imperfect experience of the analogy of nature? Your theory itself cannot surely pretend to any such advantage; even though you have run into *anthropomorphism*, the better to preserve a conformity to common experience. Let us once more put it to trial. In all instances which we have ever seen, ideas are copied from real objects, and are ectypal, not archetypal, to express myself in learned terms. You reserve this order and give thought the precedence. In all instances which we have ever seen, thought has no influence upon matter except where that matter is so conjoined with it as to have an equal reciprocal influence upon it. No animal can move immediately anything but the members of its own body; and, indeed, the equality of action and reaction seems to be an universal law of nature; but your theory implies a contradiction to this experience. These instances, with many more which it were easy to collect (particularly the supposition of a mind or system of thought that is eternal or, in other words, an animal ingenerable and immortal)—these instances, I say, may teach all of us sobriety in condemning each other, and let us see that no system of this kind ought ever to be received from a slight analogy, so neither ought any to be rejected on account of a small incongruity. For that is an inconvenience from which we can justly pronounce no one to be exempted.

All religious systems, it is confessed, are subject to great and insuperable difficulties. Each disputant triumphs in his turn, while he carries on an offensive war, and exposes the absurdities, barbarities, and pernicious tenets of his antagonist. But all of them, on the whole, prepare a complete triumph for the *sceptic*, who tells them that no system ought ever to be embraced with regard to such subjects; for this plain reason, that no absurdity ought ever to be assented to with regard to any subject. A total suspense of judgment is here our only reasonable resource. And if every attack, as is commonly observed, and no defence among theologians is successful, how complete must be *his* victory who remains always, with all mankind, on the offensive, and has himself no fixed station or abiding city which he is ever, on any occasion, obliged to defend?

Part IX

But if so many difficulties attend the argument *a posteriori*, said Demea, had we not better adhere to that simple and sublime argument *a priori* which, by offering to us infallible demonstration, cuts off at once all doubt and difficulty? By this argument, too, we may prove the *infinity* of the Divine attributes, which, I am afraid, can never be ascertained with certainty from any other topic. For how can an effect which either is finite or, for aught we know, may be so—how can such an effect, I say, prove an infinite cause? The unity, too, of the Divine Nature it is very difficult, if not absolutely impossible, to deduce merely from contemplating the works of nature; nor will the uniformity alone of the plan, even were it allowed, give us any assurance of that attribute. Whereas the argument *a priori* . . .

You seem to reason, Demea, interposed Cleanthes, as if those advantages and conveniences in the abstract argument were full proofs of its solidity. But it is first proper, in my opinion, to determine what argument of this nature you choose to insist on; and we shall afterwards, from itself, better than from its *useful* consequences, endeavor to determine what value we ought to put upon it.

The argument, replied Demea, which I would insist on is the common one. Whatever exists must have a cause or reason of its existence, it being absolutely impossible for anything to produce itself or be the cause of its own existence. In mounting up, therefore, from effects to causes, we must either go on in tracing an infinite succession, without any ultimate cause at all, or must at last have recourse to some ultimate cause that is *necessarily* existent. Now, that the first supposition is absurd may be thus proved. In the infinite chain or succession of causes and effects, each single effect is determined to exist by the power and efficacy of that cause which immediately preceded; but the whole eternal chain or succession, taken together, is not determined or caused by anything; and yet it is evident that it requires a cause or reason, as much as any particular object which begins to exist in time. The question is still reasonable why this particular succession of causes existed from eternity, and not any other succession or no succession at all. If there be no necessarily existent being, any supposition which can be formed is equally possible; nor is there any more absurdity in nothing's having existed from eternity than there is in that succession of causes which constitutes the universe. What was it, then, which determined something to exist rather than nothing, and bestowed being on a particular possibility, exclusive of the rest? *External causes*, there are supposed to be none. *Chance* is a word without meaning. Was it *nothing?* But that can never produce anything. We must, therefore, have recourse to a necessarily existent Being who carries the *reason* of his existence in himself; and who cannot be supposed not to exist, without an express contradiction. There is, consequently, such a Being—that is, there is a Deity.

I shall not leave it to Philo, said Cleanthes (though I know that the starting objections is his chief delight), to point out the weakness of this metaphysical reasoning. It seems to me so obviously ill-grounded, and at the same time of so little consequence to the cause of true piety and religion, that I shall myself venture to show the fallacy of it.

I shall begin with observing that there is an evident absurdity in pretending to demonstrate a matter of fact, or to prove it by any arguments *a priori*. Nothing is demonstrable unless the contrary implies a contradiction. Nothing that is distinctly conceivable implies a contradiction. Whatever we conceive as existent, we can also conceive as non-existent. There is no being, therefore, whose non-existence implies a contradiction. Consequently there is no being whose existence is demonstrable. I propose this argument as entirely decisive, and am willing to rest the whole controversy upon it.

It is pretended that the Deity is a necessarily existent being; and this necessity of his existence is attempted to be explained by asserting that, if we knew his whole essence or nature, we should perceive it to be as impossible for him not to exist, as for twice two not to be four. But it is evident that this can never happen, while our faculties remain the same as at present. It will still be possible for us, at any time, to conceive the non-existence of what we formerly conceived to exist; nor can the mind ever lie under a necessity of supposing any object to remain always in being; in the same manner as we lie under a necessity of always conceiving twice two to be four. The words, therefore, *necessary existence* have no meaning; or, which is the same thing, none that is consistent.

But further, why may not the material universe be the necessarily existent Being, according to this pretended explication of necessity? We dare not affirm that we know all the qualities of matter; and, for aught we can determine, it may contain some qualities which, were they known, would make its non-existence appear as great a contradiction as that twice two is five. I find only one argument employed to prove that the material world is not the necessarily existent Being; and this argument is derived from the contingency both of the matter and the form of the world. "Any particle of matter," it is said, "may be *conceived* to be annihilated, and any form may be *conceived* to be altered. Such an annihilation or alteration, therefore, is not impossible."[32] But it seems a great partiality not to perceive that the same argument extends equally to the Deity, so far as we have any conception of him; and that the mind can at least imagine him to be non-existent, or his attributes to be altered. It must be some unknown, inconceivable qualities which can make his non-existence appear impossible or his attributes unalterable: And no reason can be assigned why these qualities may not belong to matter. As they are altogether unknown and inconceivable, they can never be proved incompatible with it.

Add to this that in tracing an eternal succession of objects it seems absurd to inquire for a general cause or first author. How can anything that exists from eternity have a cause, since that relation implies a priority in time and in a beginning of existence?

In such a chain, too, or succession of objects, each part is caused by that which preceded it, and causes that which succeeds it. Where then is the difficulty? But the *whole*, you say, wants a cause. I answer that the uniting of these parts into a whole, like the uniting of several distinct countries into one kingdom, or several distinct members into one body, is performed merely by an arbitrary act of the mind, and has no influence on the nature of things. Did I show you the particular causes of each individual in a collection of twenty particles of matter, I should think it very unreasonable should you afterwards ask me what was the cause of the whole twenty. This is sufficiently explained in explaining the cause of the parts.

Though the reasonings which you have urged, Cleanthes, may well excuse me, said Philo, from starting any further difficulties; yet I cannot forbear insisting still upon another topic. It is observed by arithmeticians that the products of 9 compose always either 9 or some lesser product of 9 if you add together all the characters of which any of the former products is composed. Thus, of 18, 27, 36, which are products of 9, you make 9 by adding 1 to 8, 2 to 7, 3 to 6. Thus 369 is a product also of 9; and if you add 3, 6, and 9, you make 18, a lesser product of 9.[33] To a superficial observer so wonderful a regularity may be admired as the effect either of chance or design; but a skilful algebraist immediately concludes it to be the work of necessity, and demonstrates that it must forever result from the nature of these numbers. Is it not probable, I ask, that the whole economy of the universe is conducted by a like necessity, though no human algebra can furnish a key which solves the difficulty? And instead of admiring the order of natural beings, may it not happen that, could we penetrate into the intimate nature of bodies, we should clearly see why it was absolutely impossible they could ever admit of any other disposition? So dangerous is it to introduce this idea of necessity into the present question! and so naturally does it afford an inference directly opposite to the religious hypothesis!

But dropping all these abstractions, continued Philo, and confining ourselves to more familiar topics, I shall venture to add an observation that the argument *a priori* has seldom been found very convincing, except to people of a metaphysical head who have accustomed themselves to abstract reasoning, and who, finding from mathematics that the understanding frequently leads to truth through obscurity, and contrary to first appearances, have transferred the

32. Dr. Clark. [The quotation is from A *Demonstration of the Being and Attributes of God* by Samuel Clarke, regarding whom see Hume's *Enquiry*, n.22.]

33. *République des Lettres*, Août 1685. [The reference is to the *Nouvelles de la république des lettres*, a journal edited in Holland by Pierre Bayle, regarding whom see Hume's *Enquiry*, n.69. The article cited by Hume appeared not in the August issue, as he stated, but in the September issue and was written by Bernard le Bovier de Fontenelle (1657–1757), a French scientist and man of letters.]

same habit of thinking to subjects where it ought not to have place. Other people, even of good sense and the best inclined to religion, feel always some deficiency in such arguments, though they are not perhaps able to explain distinctly where it lies—a certain proof that men ever did and ever will derive their religion from other sources than from this species of reasoning.

Part X

It is my opinion, I own, replied Demea, that each man feels, in a manner, the truth of religion within his own breast; and, from a consciousness of his imbecility and misery rather than from any reasoning, is led to seek protection from that Being on whom he and all nature are dependent. So anxious or so tedious are even the best scenes of life that futurity is still the object of all our hopes and fears. We incessantly look forward and endeavor, by prayers, adoration, and sacrifice, to appease those unknown powers whom we find, by experience, so able to afflict and oppress us. Wretched creatures that we are! What resource for us amidst the innumerable ills of life did not religion suggest some methods of atonement, and appease those terrors with which we are incessantly agitated and tormented?

I am indeed persuaded, said Philo, that the best and indeed the only method of bringing everyone to a due sense of religion is by just representations of the misery and wickedness of men. And for that purpose a talent of eloquence and strong imagery is more requisite than that of reasoning and argument. For is it necessary to prove what everyone feels within himself? It is only necessary to make us feel it, if possible, more intimately and sensibly.

The people, indeed, replied Demea, are sufficiently convinced of this great and melancholy truth. The miseries of life, the unhappiness of man, the general corruptions of our nature, the unsatisfactory enjoyment of pleasures, riches, honors—these phrases have become almost proverbial in all languages. And who can doubt of what all men declare from their own immediate feeling and experience?

In this point, said Philo, the learned are perfectly agreed with the vulgar; and in all letters, *sacred* and *profane*, the topic of human misery has been insisted on with the most pathetic eloquence that sorrow and melancholy could inspire. The poets, who speak from sentiment, without a system, and whose testimony has therefore the more authority, abound in images of this nature. From Homer down to Dr. Young,[34] the whole inspired tribe have ever been sensible that no other representation of things would suit the feeling and observation of each individual.

As to authorities, replied Demea, you need not seek them. Look round this library of Cleanthes. I shall venture to affirm that, except authors of particular sciences, such as chemistry or botany, who have no occasion to treat of human life, there is scarce one of those innumerable writers from whom the sense of human misery has not, in some passage or other, extorted a complaint and confession of it. At least, the chance is entirely on that side; and no one author has ever, so far as I can recollect, been so extravagant as to deny it.

There you must excuse me, said Philo: Leibniz has denied it, and is perhaps the first[35] who ventured upon so bold and paradoxical an opinion; at least, the first who made it essential to his philosophical system.

And by being the first, replied Demea, might he not have been sensible of his error? For is this a subject in which philosophers can propose to make discoveries especially in so late an age? And can any man hope by a simple denial (for the subject scarcely admits of reasoning) to bear down the united testimony of mankind, founded on sense and consciousness?

And why should man, added he, pretend to an exemption from the lot of all other animals? The whole earth, believe me, Philo, is cursed and polluted. A perpetual war is kindled amongst all living creatures. Necessity, hunger, want stimulate the strong and courageous; fear, anxiety, terror agitate the weak and infirm. The first entrance into life gives anguish to the new-born infant and to its wretched parent; weakness, impotence, distress attend each stage of that life, and it is, at last, finished in agony and horror.

Observe, too, says Philo, the curious artifices of

34. [The reference is to Edward Young (1683–1765), an English poet.]

35. That sentiment has been maintained by Dr. King [William King (1650–1729), an Irish clergyman] and some few others before Leibniz, though by none of so great fame as that German philosopher.

nature in order to embitter the life of every living being. The stronger prey upon the weaker and keep them in perpetual terror and anxiety. The weaker, too, in their turn, often prey upon the stronger, and vex and molest them without relaxation. Consider that innumerable race of insects, which either are bred on the body of each animal or, flying about, infix their stings in him. These insects have others still less than themselves which torment them. And thus on each hand, before and behind, above and below, every animal is surrounded with enemies which incessantly seek his misery and destruction.

Man alone, said Demea, seems to be, in part, an exception to this rule. For by combination in society he can easily master lions, tigers, and bears, whose greater strength and agility naturally enable them to prey upon him.

On the contrary, it is here chiefly, cried Philo, that the uniform and equal maxims of nature are most apparent. Man, it is true, can, by combination, surmount all his *real* enemies and become master of the whole animal creation; but does he not immediately raise up to himself *imaginary* enemies, the demons of his fancy, who haunt him with superstitious terrors and blast every enjoyment of life? His pleasure, as he imagines, becomes in their eyes a crime; his food and repose give them umbrage and offence; his very sleep and dreams furnish new materials to anxious fear; and even death, his refuge from every other ill, presents only the dread of endless and innumerable woes. Nor does the wolf molest more the timid flock than superstition does the anxious breast of wretched mortals.

Besides, consider, Demea: This very society by which we surmount those wild beasts, our natural enemies, what new enemies does it not raise to us? What woe and misery does it not occasion? Man is the greatest enemy of man. Oppression, injustice, contempt, contumely, violence, sedition, war, calumny, treachery, fraud—by these they mutually torment each other, and they would soon dissolve that society which they had formed were it not for the dread of still greater ills which must attend their separation.

But though these external insults, said Demea, from animals, from men, from all the elements, which assault us form a frightful catalogue of woes, they are nothing in comparison of those which arise within ourselves, from the distempered condition of our mind and body. How many lie under the lingering torment of diseases? Hear the pathetic enumeration of the great poet.

> Intestine stone and ulcer, colic-pangs,
> Demoniac frenzy, moping melancholy,
> And moon-struck madness, pining atrophy,
> Marasmus, and wide-wasting pestilence.
> Dire was the tossing, deep the groans: *Despair*
> Tended the sick, busiest from couch to couch.
> And over them triumphant *Death* his dart
> Shook: but delay'd to strike, though oft invok'd
> With vows, as their chief good and final hope.[36]

The disorders of the mind, continued Demea, though more secret, are not perhaps less dismal and vexatious. Remorse, shame, anguish, rage, disappointment, anxiety, fear, dejection, despair—who has ever passed through life without cruel inroads from these tormentors? How many have scarcely ever felt any better sensations? Labor and poverty, so abhorred by everyone, are the certain lot of the far greater number; and those few privileged persons who enjoy ease and opulence never reach contentment or true felicity. All the goods of life united would not make a very happy man, but all the ills united would make a wretch indeed; and any one of them almost (and who can be free from every one), nay, often the absence of one good (and who can possess all) is sufficient to render life ineligible.

Were a stranger to drop on a sudden into this world, I would show him, as a specimen of its ills, a hospital full of diseases, a prison crowded with malefactors and debtors, a field of battle strewed with carcasses, a fleet foundering in the ocean, a nation languishing under tyranny, famine, or pestilence. To turn the gay side of life to him and give him a notion of its pleasures—whither should I conduct him? To a ball, to an opera, to court? He might justly think that I was only showing him a diversity of distress and sorrow.

There is no evading such striking instances, said Philo, but by apologies which still further aggravate the charge. Why have all men, I ask, in all ages, complained incessantly of the miseries of life? . . .

36. [The quotation is from *Paradise Lost*.]

They have no just reason, says one: These complaints proceed only from their discontented, repining, anxious disposition. . . . And can there possibly, I reply, be a more certain foundation of misery than such a wretched temper?

But if they were really as unhappy as they pretend, says my antagonist, why do they remain in life? . . .

> Not satisfied with life, afraid of death.

This is the secret chain, say I, that holds us. We are terrified, not bribed to the continuance of our existence.

It is only a false delicacy, he may insist, which a few refined spirits indulge, and which has spread these complaints among the whole race of mankind. . . . And what is this delicacy, I ask, which you blame? Is it anything but a greater sensibility to all the pleasures and pains of life? And if the man of a delicate, refined temper, by being so much more alive than the rest of the world, is only so much more unhappy, what judgment must we form in general of human life?

Let men remain at rest, says our adversary, and they will be easy. They are willing artificers of their own misery. . . . No! reply I: An anxious languor follows their repose; disappointment, vexation, trouble, their activity and ambition.

I can observe something like what you mention in some others, replied Cleanthes; but I confess I feel little or nothing of it in myself, and hope that it is not so common as you represent it.

If you feel not human misery yourself, cried Demea, I congratulate you on so happy a singularity. Others, seemingly the most prosperous, have not been ashamed to vent their complaints in the most melancholy strains. Let us attend to the great, the fortunate emperor, Charles V,[37] when, tired with human grandeur, he resigned all his extensive dominions into the hands of his son. In the last harangue which he made on that memorable occasion, he publicly avowed *that the greatest prosperities which he had ever enjoyed had been mixed with so many adversities that he might truly say he had never enjoyed any satisfaction or contentment.* But did the retired life in which he sought for shelter afford him any greater happiness? If we may credit his son's account, his repentance commenced the very day of his resignation.

Cicero's fortune, from small beginnings, rose to the greatest luster and renown; yet what pathetic complaints of all ills of life do his familiar letters, as well as philosophical discourses, contain? And suitably to his own experience, he introduces Cato,[38] the great, the fortunate Cato protesting in his old age that had he a new life in his offer he would reject the present.

As yourself, ask any of your acquaintance, whether they would live over again the last ten or twenty years of their life. No! but the next twenty, they say, will be better:

> And from the dregs of life, hope to receive
> What the first sprightly running could not give.[39]

Thus, at last, they find (such is the greatness of human misery, it reconciles even contradictions) that they complain at once of the shortness of life and of its vanity and sorrow.

And is it possible, Cleanthes, said Philo, that after all these reflections, and infinitely more which might be suggested, you can still persevere in your anthropomorphism, and assert the moral attributes of the Deity, his justice, benevolence, mercy, and rectitude, to be of the same nature with these virtues in human creatures? His power, we allow, is infinite; whatever he wills is executed; but neither man nor any other animal is happy; therefore, he does not will their happiness. His wisdom is infinite; he is never mistaken in choosing the means to any end; but the course of nature tends not to human or animal felicity; therefore, it is not established for that purpose. Through the whole compass of human knowledge there are no inferences more certain and infallible than these. In what respect, then, do his benevolence and mercy resemble the benevolence and mercy of men?

Epicurus' old questions are yet unanswered.

Is he willing to prevent evil, but not able? then is

37. [Charles V (1500–1588) was for forty years king of Spain.]

38. [The reference is to Marcus Porcius Cato the Elder (234–149 B.C.), a Roman statesman.]

39. [The quotation is from the heroic drama *Aureng-Zebe* by the English poet and dramatist John Dryden (1631–1700).]

he impotent. Is he able, but not willing? then is he malevolent. Is he both able and willing? whence then is evil?

You ascribe, Cleanthes (and I believe justly), a purpose and intention to nature. But what, I beseech you, is the object of that curious artifice and machinery which she has displayed in all animals—the preservation alone of individuals, and propagation of the species? It seems enough for her purpose, if such a rank be barely upheld in the universe, without any care or concern for the happiness of the members that compose it. No resource for this purpose: no machinery in order merely to give pleasure or ease: no fund of pure joy and contentment: no indulgence without some want or necessity accompanying it. At least, the few phenomena of this nature are overbalanced by opposite phenomena of still greater importance.

Our sense of music, harmony, and indeed beauty of all kinds, gives satisfaction, without being absolutely necessary to the preservation and propagation of the species. But what racking pains, on the other hand, arise from gouts, gravels, megrims, toothaches, rheumatisms, where the injury to the animal machinery is either small or incurable? Mirth, laughter, play, frolic seem gratuitous satisfactions which have no further tendency; spleen, melancholy, discontent, superstition are pains of the same nature. How then does the divine benevolence display itself, in the sense of you anthropomorphites? None but we mystics, as you were pleased to call us, can account for this strange mixture of phenomena, by deriving it from attributes infinitely perfect but incomprehensible.

And have you, at last, said Cleanthes smiling, betrayed your intentions, Philo? Your long agreement with Demea did indeed a little surprise me, but I find you were all the while erecting a concealed battery against me. And I must confess that you have now fallen upon a subject worthy of your noble spirit of opposition and controversy. If you can make out the present point, and prove mankind to be unhappy or corrupted, there is an end at once of all religion. For to what purpose establish the natural attributes of the Deity, while the moral are still doubtful and uncertain?

You take umbrage very easily, replied Demea, at opinions the most innocent and the most generally received, even amongst the religious and devout themselves; and nothing can be more surprising than to find a topic like this—concerning the wickedness and misery of man—charged with no less than atheism and profaneness. Have not all pious divines and preachers who have indulged their rhetoric on so fertile a subject; have they not easily, I say, given a solution of any difficulties which may attend it? This world is but a point in comparison of the universe; this life but a moment in comparison of eternity. The present evil phenomena, therefore, are rectified in other regions, and in some future period of existence. And the eyes of men, being then opened to larger views of things, see the whole connection of general laws, and trace, with adoration, the benevolence and rectitude of the Deity through all the mazes and intricacies of his providence.

No! replied Cleanthes, no! These arbitrary suppositions can never be admitted, contrary to matter of fact, visible and uncontroverted. Whence can any cause be known but from its known effects? Whence can any hypothesis be proved but from the apparent phenomena? To establish one hypothesis upon another is building entirely in the air; and the utmost we ever attain by these conjectures and fictions is to ascertain the bare possibility of our opinion, but never can we, upon such terms, establish its reality.

The only method of supporting divine benevolence—and it is what I willingly embrace—is to deny absolutely the misery and wickedness of man. Your representations are exaggerated; your melancholy views mostly fictitious; your inferences contrary to fact and experience. Health is more common than sickness; pleasure than pain; happiness than misery. And for one vexation which we meet with, we attain, upon computation, a hundred enjoyments.

Admitting your position, replied Philo, which yet is extremely doubtful, you must at the same time allow that, if pain be less frequent than pleasure, it is infinitely more violent and durable. One hour of it is often able to outweigh a day, a week, a month of our common insipid enjoyments; and how many days, weeks, and months are passed by several in the most acute torments? Pleasure, scarcely in one instance, is ever able to reach ecstasy and rapture; and in no one instance can it continue for any time at its highest pitch and altitude. The spirits evaporate, the nerves relax, the fabric is disordered, and the enjoyment quickly degenerates into fatigue and uneasiness. But pain often, good God, how often! rises to torture and agony; and the longer it continues, it becomes still more genuine agony and torture. Patience is exhausted, courage languishes, melancholy seizes us, and nothing terminates our misery but the removal of its cause or another event which is the sole cure of all evil, but which, from our natural folly, we regard with still greater horror and consternation.

But not to insist upon these topics, continued Philo, though most obvious, certain, and important, I must use the freedom to admonish you, Cleanthes, that you have put the controversy upon a most dangerous issue, and are unawares introducing a total scepticism into the most essential articles of natural and revealed theology. What! no method of fixing a just foundation for religion unless we allow the happiness of human life, and maintain a continued existence even in this world, with all our present pains, infirmities, vexations, and follies, to be eligible and desirable! But this is contrary to everyone's feeling and experience; it is contrary to an authority so established as nothing can subvert. No decisive proofs can ever be produced against this authority; nor is it possible for you to compute, estimate, and compare all the pains and all the pleasures in the lives of all men and of all animals; and thus, by your resting the whole system of religion on a point which, from its very nature, must forever be uncertain, you tacitly confess that that system is equally uncertain.

But allowing you what never will be believed, at least, what you never possibly can prove, that animal or, at least, human happiness in this life exceeds its misery, you have yet done nothing; for this is not, by any means, what we expect from infinite power, infinite wisdom, and infinite goodness. Why is there any misery at all in the world? Not by chance, surely. From some cause then. Is it from the intention of the Deity? But he is perfectly benevolent. Is it contrary to his intention? But he is almighty. Nothing can shake the solidity of this reasoning, so short, so clear, so decisive, except we assert that these subjects exceed all human capacity, and that our common measures of truth and falsehood are not applicable to them—a topic which I have all along insisted on, but which you have, from the beginning, rejected with scorn and indignation.

But I will be contented to retire still from this intrenchment, for I deny that you can ever force me in it. I will allow that pain or misery in man is *compatible* with infinite power and goodness in the Deity, even in your sense of these attributes: what are you advanced by all these concessions? A mere possible compatibility is not sufficient. You must *prove* these pure, unmixed and uncontrollable attributes from the present mixed and confused phenomena, and from these alone. A hopeful undertaking! Were the phenomena ever so pure and unmixed, yet, being finite, they would be insufficient for that purpose. How much more, where they are also so jarring and discordant!

Here, Cleanthes, I find myself at ease in my argument. Here I triumph. Formerly, when we argued concerning the natural attributes of intelligence and design, I needed all my sceptical and metaphysical subtilty to elude your grasp. In many views of the universe and of its parts, particularly the latter, the beauty and fitness of final causes strike us with such irresistible force that all objections appear (what I believe they really are) mere cavils and sophisms; nor can we then imagine how it was ever possible for us to repose any weight on them. But there is no view of human life or of the condition of mankind from which, without the greatest violence, we can infer the moral attributes or learn that infinite benevolence, conjoined with infinite power and infinite wisdom, which we must discover by the eyes of faith alone. It is your turn now to tug the laboring oar, and to support your philosophical subtilties against the dictates of plain reason and experience.

Part XI

I scruple not to allow, said Cleanthes, that I have been apt to suspect the frequent repetition of the word *infinite*, which we meet with in all theological writers, to savor more of panegyric than of philosophy, and that any purposes of reasoning, and even of religion, would be better served were we to rest contented with more accurate and more moderate expressions. The terms *admirable, excellent, superlatively great, wise*, and *holy*—these sufficiently fill the imaginations of men, and anything beyond, besides that it leads into absurdities, has no influence on the affections or sentiments. Thus, in the present subject, if we abandon all human analogy, as seems your intention, Demea, I am afraid we abandon all religion and retain on without end. It were better, therefore, never to look beyond the present material world. By supposing it to contain the principle of its order within itself, we really assert it to be God; and the sooner we arrive at that Divine Being, so much the better. When you go one step beyond the mundane system, you only excite an inquisitive humor which it is impossible ever to satisfy.

To say that the different ideas which compose the reason of the Supreme Being fall into order of themselves and by their own nature is really to talk without any precise meaning. If it has a meaning, I would fain know why it is not as good sense to say that the parts of the material world fall into order of themselves and by their own nature. Can the one opinion be intelligible, while the other is not so?

We have, indeed, experience of ideas which fall into order of themselves and without any *known* cause. But, I am sure, we have a much larger experience of matter which does the same, as in all instances of generation and vegetation where the accurate analysis of the cause exceeds all human comprehension. We have also experience of particular systems of thought and of matter which have no order; of the first in madness, of the second in corruption. Why, then, should we think that order is more essential to one than the other? And if it requires a cause in both, what do we gain by your system, in tracing the universe of objects into a similar universe of ideas? The first step which we make leads us on forever. It were, therefore, wise in us to limit all our inquiries to the present world, without looking farther. No satisfaction can ever be attained by these speculations which so far exceed the narrow bounds of human understanding.

It was usual with the Peripatetics, you know, Cleanthes, when the cause of any phenomenon was demanded, to have recourse to their *faculties* or *occult qualities*, and to say, for instance, that bread nourished by its nutritive faculty, and senna purged by its purgative. But it has been discovered that this subterfuge was nothing but the disguise of ignorance, and that these philosophers, though less ingenuous, really said the same thing with the sceptics or the vulgar who fairly confessed that they knew not the cause of these phenomena. In like manner, when it is asked, what cause produces order in the ideas of the Supreme Being, can any other reason be assigned by you, anthropomorphites, than that it is a *rational* faculty, and that such is the nature of the Deity? But why a similar answer will not be equally satisfactory in accounting for the order of the world, without having recourse to any such intelligent creator as you insist on, may be difficult to determine. It is only to say that *such* is the nature of material objects, and that they are all originally possessed of a *faculty* of order and proportion. These are only more learned and elaborate ways of confessing our ignorance; nor has the one hypothesis any real advantage above the other, except in its greater conformity to vulgar prejudices.

You have displayed this argument with great emphasis, replied Cleanthes: You seem not sensible how easy it is to answer it. Even in common life, if I assign a cause for any event, is it any objection, Philo, that I cannot assign the cause of that cause, and answer every new question which may incessantly be started? And what philosophers could possibly submit to so rigid a rule?—philosophers who confess ultimate causes to be totally unknown, and are sensible that the most refined principles into which they trace the phenomena are still to them as inexplicable as these phenomena themselves are to the vulgar. The order and arrangement of nature, the curious adjustment of final causes, the plain use and intention of every part and organ—all of these bespeak in the clearest language an intelligent cause or author. The heavens and the earth join in the same testimony: The whole chorus of nature raises one hymn to the praises of its Creator. You alone, or almost alone, disturb this general harmony. You start abstruse doubts, cavils, and objections; you ask me what is the cause of this cause? I know not; I care not; that concerns not me. I have found a Deity; and here I stop my inquiry. Let those go farther who are wiser or more enterprising.

I pretend to be neither, replied Philo; and for that very reason I should never, perhaps, have attempted to go so far, especially when I am sensible that I must at least be contented to sit down with the same answer which, without further trouble, might have satisfied me from the beginning. If I am still to remain in utter ignorance of causes and can absolutely give an explication of nothing, I shall never esteem it any advantage to shove off for a moment a difficulty which you acknowledge must immediately, in its full force, no conception of the great object of our adoration. If we preserve human analogy, we must forever find it impossible to reconcile any mixture of evil in the universe with infinite attributes; much less can we ever prove the latter from the former. But supposing the Author of Nature to be finitely perfect, though far exceeding mankind, a satisfactory account may then be given of natural and moral evil, and every untoward phenomenon be explained and adjusted. A less evil may then be chosen in order to avoid a greater; inconveniences be submitted to in order to reach a desirable end; and, in a word, benevolence, regulated by wisdom and limited by necessity, may produce just such a world as the present. You, Philo, who are so prompt at starting views and reflections and analogies, I would gladly hear, at length, without interruption, your opinion of this new theory; and if it deserves our attention, we may afterwards, at more leisure, reduce it into form.

My sentiments, replied Philo, are not worth being made a mystery of; and, therefore, without any ceremony, I shall deliver what occurs to me with regard to the present subject. It must, I think, be allowed that, if a very limited intelligence whom we shall suppose utterly unacquainted with the universe were assured that it were the production of a very good, wise, and powerful being, however finite, he would, from his conjectures, form *beforehand* a different notion of it from what we find it to be by experience; nor would he ever imagine, merely from these attributes of the cause of which he is informed, that the effect could be so full of vice and misery and disorder, as it appears in this life. Supposing now that this person were brought into the world, still assured that it was the workmanship of such a sublime and benevolent being, he might, perhaps, be surprised at the disappointment, but would never retract his former belief if founded on any very solid argument, since such a limited intelligence must be sensible of his own blindness and ignorance, and must allow that there may be many solutions of those phenomena which will forever escape his comprehension. But supposing, which is the real case with regard to man, that this creature is not antecedently convinced of a supreme intelligence, benevolent, and powerful, but is left to gather such a belief from the appearances of things—this entirely alters the case, nor will he ever find any reason for such a conclusion. He may be fully convinced of the narrow limits of his understanding, but this will not help him in forming an inference concerning the goodness of superior powers, since he must form that inference from what he knows, not from what he is ignorant of. The more you exaggerate his weakness and ignorance, the more diffident you render him, and give him the greater suspicion that such subjects are beyond the reach of his faculties. You are obliged, therefore, to reason with him merely from the known phenomena, and to drop every arbitrary supposition or conjecture.

Did I show you a house or palace where there was not one apartment convenient or agreeable; where the windows, doors, fires, passages, stairs, and the whole economy of the building were the source of noise, confusion, fatigue, darkness, and the extremes of heat and cold, you would certainly blame the contrivance, without any further examination. The architect would in vain display his subtilty, and prove to you that, if this door or that window were altered, greater ills would ensue. What he says may be strictly true: The alteration of one particular, while the other parts of the building remain, may only augment the inconveniences. But still you would assert in general that, if the architect had had skill and good intentions, he might have formed such a plan of the whole, and might have adjusted the parts in such a manner as would have remedied all or most of these inconveniences. His ignorance, or even your own ignorance of such a plan, will never convince you of the impossibility of it. If you find any inconveniences and deformities in the building, you will always, without entering into any detail, condemn the architect.

In short, I repeat the question: Is the world, considered in general and as it appears to us in this life, different from what a man or such a limited being would, *beforehand*, expect from a very powerful, wise, and benevolent Deity? It must be strange prejudice to assert the contrary. And from thence I conclude that, however consistent the world may be, allowing certain suppositions and conjectures with the idea of such a Deity, it can never afford us an inference concerning his existence. The consistency is not absolutely denied, only the inference. Conjectures, especially where infinity is excluded from the divine attributes, may perhaps be sufficient to prove a consistency, but can never be foundations for any inference.

There seem to be *four* circumstances on which depend all or the greatest part of the ills that molest sensible creatures; and it is not impossible but all these circumstances may be necessary and unavoidable. We know so little beyond common life, or even of common life, that, with regard to the economy of a universe, there is no conjecture, however wild, which may not be just; nor any one, however plausible, which may not be erroneous. All that belongs to human understanding, in this deep ignorance and obscurity, is to be sceptical or at least cautious, and not to admit of any hypothesis whatever, much less of any which is supported by no appearance of probability. Now this I assert to be the case with regard to all the causes of evil and the circumstances on which it depends. None of them appear to human reason in the least degree necessary or unavoidable, nor can we suppose them such, without the utmost license of imagination.

The *first* circumstance which introduces evil is that contrivance or economy of the animal creation by which pains, as well as pleasures, are employed to excite all creatures to action, and make them vigilant in the great work of self-preservation. Now pleasure alone, in its various degrees, seems to human understanding sufficient for this purpose. All animals might be constantly in a state of enjoyment; but when urged by any of the necessities of nature, such as thirst, hunger, weariness; instead of pain, they might feel a diminution of pleasure by which they might be prompted to seek that object which is necessary to their subsistence. Men pursue pleasure as eagerly as they avoid pain; at least, they might have been so constituted. It seems, therefore, plainly possible to carry on the business of life without any pain. Why then is any animal ever rendered susceptible of such a sensation? If animals can be free from it an hour, they might enjoy a perpetual exemption from it, and it required as particular a contrivance of their organs to produce that feeling as to endow them with sight, hearing, or any of the senses. Shall we conjecture that such a contrivance was necessary, without any appearance of reason; and shall we build on that conjecture as on the most certain truth?

But a capacity of pain would not alone produce pain were it not for the *second* circumstance, viz., the conducting of the world by general laws; and this seems nowise necessary to a very perfect being. It is true, if everything were conducted by particular volitions, the course of nature would be perpetually broken, and no man could employ his reason in the conduct of life. But might not other particular volitions remedy this inconvenience? In short, might not the Deity exterminate all ill, wherever it were to be found, and produce all good, without any preparation or long progress of causes and effects?

Besides, we must consider that, according to the present economy of the world, the course of nature, though supposed exactly regular, yet to us appears not so, and many events are uncertain, and many disappoint our expectations. Health and sickness, calm and tempest, with an infinite number of other accidents whose causes are unknown and variable, have a great influence both on the fortunes of particular persons and on the prosperity of public societies; and indeed all human life, in a manner, depends on such accidents. A being, therefore, who knows the secret springs of the universe might easily, by particular volitions, turn all these accidents to the good of mankind and render the whole world happy, without discovering himself in any operation. A fleet whose purposes were salutary to society might always meet with a fair wind; good princes enjoy sound health and long life; persons born to power and authority be framed with good tempers and virtuous dispositions. A few such events as these, regularly and wisely conducted, would change the face of the world; and yet would no more seem to disturb the course of nature or confound human conduct than the present economy of things where the causes are secret and variable and compounded. Some small torches given to Caligula's[40] brain in his infancy might have converted him into a Trajan.[41] One wave, a little higher than the rest, by burying Caesar and his fortune in the bottom of the ocean, might have restored liberty to a considerable part of mankind. There may, for aught we know, be good reasons why Providence interposes not in this manner, but they are unknown to us; and, though the mere supposition that such reasons exist may be sufficient to *save* the conclusion concerning the

40. [Caligula (12–41) was a Roman emperor, conspicuous for his cruelty.]

41. [Trajan (c. 53–117) was a Roman emperor who pursued benevolent social policies.]

divine attributes, yet surely it can never be sufficient to *establish* that conclusion.

If everything in the universe be conducted by general laws, and if animals be rendered susceptible of pain, it scarcely seems possible but some ill must arise in the various shocks of matter and the various concurrence and opposition of general laws; but this ill would be very rare were it not for the *third* circumstance which I proposed to mention, viz., the great frugality with which all powers and faculties are distributed to every particular being. So well adjusted are the organs and capacities of all animals, and so well fitted to their preservation, that, as far as history or tradition reaches, there appears not to be any single species which has yet been extinguished in the universe. Every animal has the requisite endowments, but these endowments are bestowed with so scrupulous an economy that any considerable diminution must entirely destroy the creature. Wherever one power is increased, there is a proportional abatement in the other. Animals which excel in swiftness are commonly defective in force. Those which possess both are either imperfect in some of their senses or are oppressed with the most craving wants. The human species, whose chief excellence is reason and sagacity, is of all others the most necessitous, and the most deficient in bodily advantages, without clothes, without arms, without food, without lodging, without any convenience of life, except what they owe to their own skill and industry. In short, nature seems to have formed an exact calculation of the necessities of her creatures; and, like a *rigid master*, has afforded them little more powers or endowments than what are strictly sufficient to supply those necessities. An *indulgent parent* would have bestowed a large stock in order to guard against accidents, and secure the happiness and welfare of the creature in the most unfortunate concurrence of circumstances. Every course of life would not have been so surrounded with precipices that the least departure from the true path, by mistake or necessity, must involve us in misery and ruin. Some reserve, some fund, would have been provided to ensure happiness, nor would the powers and the necessities have been adjusted with so rigid an economy. The Author of Nature is inconceivably powerful; his force is supposed great, if not altogether inexhaustible; nor is there any reason, as far as we can judge, to make him observe this strict frugality in his dealings with his creatures. It would have been better, were his power extremely limited, to have created fewer animals, and to have endowed these with more faculties for their happiness and preservation. A builder is never esteemed prudent who undertakes a plan beyond what his stock will enable him to finish.

In order to cure most of the ills of human life, I require not that man should have the wings of the eagle, the swiftness of the stag, the force of the ox, the arms of the lion, the scales of the crocodile or rhinoceros; much less do I demand the sagacity of an angel or cherubim. I am contented to take an increase in one single power or faculty of his soul. Let him be endowed with a greater propensity to industry and labor, a more vigorous spring and activity of mind, a more constant bent to business and application. Let the whole species possess naturally an equal diligence with that which many individuals are able to attain by habit and reflection, and the most beneficial consequences, without any allay of ill, is the immediate and necessary result of this endowment. Almost all the moral as well as natural evils of human life arise from idleness; and were our species, by the original constitution of their frame, exempt from this vice or infirmity, the perfect cultivation of land, the improvement of arts and manufactures, the exact execution of every office and duty, immediately follow; and men at once may fully reach that state of society which is so imperfectly attained by the best regulated government. But as industry is a power, and the most valuable of any, nature seems determined, suitably to her usual maxims, to bestow it on men with a very sparing hand; and rather to punish him severely for his deficiency in it than to reward him for his attainments. She has so contrived his frame that nothing but the most violent necessity can oblige him to labor; and she employs all his other wants to overcome, at least in part, the want of diligence, and to endow him with some share of a faculty of which she has thought fit naturally to bereave him. Here our demands may be allowed very humble, and therefore the more reasonable. If we required the endowments of superior penetration and judgment, of a more delicate taste of beauty, of a nicer sensibility to benevolence and friendship, we might be told that we impiously pretend to break the order of nature, that we want to exalt ourselves into a higher rank of being, that the presents which we require, not being suitable to our state and condition, would only be pernicious to us. But it is hard, I dare to repeat it, it is hard that, being placed in a world so full of wants and necessities, where almost every being and element is either our foe or refuses its assistance . . . we should also have our own temper to struggle with, and should be deprived of that faculty which can alone fence against these multiplied evils.

The *fourth* circumstance whence arises the misery and ill of the universe is the inaccurate workmanship of all the springs and principles of the great machine of nature. It must be acknowledged that there are few parts of the universe which seem not to serve some purpose, and whose removal would not produce a visible defect and disorder in the whole. The parts hang all together, nor can one be touched without affecting the rest, in a greater or less degree. But at the same time, it must be observed that none of these parts or principles, however useful, are so accurately adjusted as to keep precisely within those bounds in which their utility consists; but they are, all of them, apt, on every occasion, to run into the one extreme or the other. One would imagine that this grand production had not received the last hand of the maker—so little finished is every part, and so coarse are the strokes with which it is executed. Thus the winds are requisite to convey the vapors along the surface of the globe, and to assist men in navigation; but how often, rising up to tempests and hurricanes, do they become pernicious? Rains are necessary to nourish all the plants and animals of the earth; but how often are they defective? how often excessive? Heat is requisite to all life and vegetation, but is not always found in the due proportion. On the mixture and secretion of the humors and juices of the body depend the health and prosperity of the animal; but the parts perform not regularly their proper function. What more useful than all the passions of the mind, ambition, vanity, love, anger? But how often do they break their bounds and cause the greatest convulsions in society? There is nothing so advantageous in the universe but what frequently becomes pernicious, by its excess or defect; nor has nature guarded, with the requisite accuracy, against all disorder or confusion. The irregularity is never perhaps so great as to destroy any species, but is often sufficient to involve the individuals in ruin and misery.

On the concurrence, then, of these *four* circumstances does all or the greatest part of natural evil depend. Were all living creatures incapable of pain, or were the world administered by particular volitions, evil never could have found access into the universe; and were animals endowed with a large stock of powers and faculties, beyond what strict necessity requires, or were the several springs and principles of the universe so accurately framed as to preserve always the just temperament and medium, there must have been very little ill in comparison of what we feel at present. What then shall we pronounce on this occasion? Shall we say that these circumstances are not necessary, and that they might easily have been altered in the contrivance of the universe? This decision seems too presumptuous for creatures so blind and ignorant. Let us be more modest in our conclusions. Let us allow that, if the goodness of the Deity (I mean a goodness like the human) could be established on any tolerable reasons *a priori*, these phenomena, however untoward, would not be sufficient to subvert that principle, but might easily, in some unknown manner, be reconcilable to it. But let us still assert that, as this goodness is not antecedently established but must be inferred from the phenomena, there can be no grounds for such an inference while there are so many ills in the universe, and while these ills might so easily have been remedied, as far as human understanding can be allowed to judge on such a subject. I am sceptic enough to allow that the bad appearances, notwithstanding all my reasonings, may be compatible with such attributes as you suppose, but surely they can never prove these attributes. Such a conclusion cannot result from scepticism, but must arise from the phenomena, and from our confidence in the reasonings which we deduce from these phenomena.

Look round this universe. What an immense profusion of beings, animated and organized, sensible and active! You admire this prodigious variety and fecundity. But inspect a little more narrowly these living existences, the only beings worth regarding. How hostile and destructive to each other! How insufficient all of them for their own happiness! How contemptible or odious to the spectator! The whole presents nothing but the idea of a blind nature, impregnated by a great vivifying principle, and pouring forth from her lap, without discernment or parental care, her maimed and abortive children!

Here the Manichaean[42] system occurs as a proper hypothesis to solve the difficulty; and, no doubt, in some respects it is very specious and has more probability than the common hypothesis, by giving a plausible account of the strange mixture of good and ill which appears in life. But if we consider, on the other hand, the perfect uniformity and agreement of the parts of the universe, we shall not discover in it any marks of the combat of a malevolent with a benevolent being. There is indeed an opposition of pains and pleasures in the feelings of sensible creatures; but are not all the operations of nature carried on by an opposition of principles, of hot and cold, moist and dry, light and heavy? The true conclusion is that the original source of all things is entirely indifferent to all these principles, and has no more regard to good above ill than to heat above cold, or to drought above moisture, or to light above heavy.

There may *four* hypotheses be framed concerning the first causes of the universe: that they are endowed with perfect goodness; that they have perfect malice; that they are opposite and have both goodness and malice; that they have neither goodness nor malice. Mixed phenomena can never prove the two former unmixed principles; and the uniformity and steadiness of general laws seem to oppose the third. The fourth, therefore, seems by far the most probable.

What I have said concerning natural evil will apply to moral with little or no variation; and we have no more reason to infer that the rectitude of the Supreme Being resembles human rectitude than that his benevolence resembles the human. Nay, it will be thought that we have still greater cause to exclude from him moral sentiments, such as we feel them, since moral evil, in the opinion of many, is much more predominant above moral good than natural evil above natural good.

But even though this should not be allowed, and though the virtue which is in mankind should be acknowledged much superior to the vice; yet, so long as there is any vice at all in the universe, it will very much puzzle you anthropomorphites how to account for it. You must assign a cause for it, without having recourse to the first cause. But as every effect must have a cause, and that cause another, you must either carry on the progression *in infinitum* or rest on that original principle, who is the ultimate cause of all things. . . .

Hold! hold! cried Demea: Whither does your imagination hurry you? I joined in alliance with you in order to prove the incomprehensible nature of the Divine Being, and refute the principles of Cleanthes, who would measure everything by human rule and standard. But I now find you running into all the topics of the greatest libertines and infidels, and betraying that holy cause which you seemingly espoused. Are you secretly, then, a more dangerous enemy than Cleanthes himself?

And are you so late in perceiving it? replied Cleanthes. Believe me, Demea, your friend Philo, from the beginning, has been amusing himself at both our expense; and it must be confessed that the injudicious reasoning of our vulgar theology has given him but too just a handle of ridicule. The total infirmity of human reason, the absolute incomprehensibility of the Divine Nature, the great and universal misery, and still greater wickedness of men—these are strange topics, surely, to be so fondly cherished by orthodox divines and doctors. In ages of stupidity and ignorance, indeed, these principles may safely be espoused; and perhaps no views of things are more proper to promote superstition than such as encourage the blind amazement, the diffidence, and melancholy of mankind. But at present. . . .

Blame not so much, interposed Philo, the ignorance of these reverend gentlemen. They know how to change their style with the times. Formerly, it was a most popular theological topic to maintain that human life was vanity and misery, and to exaggerate all the ills and pains which are incident to men. But of late years, divines, we find, begin to retract this position and maintain, though still with some hesitation, that there are more goods than evils, more pleasures than pains, even in this life. When religion stood entirely upon temper and education, it was thought proper to encourage melancholy; as indeed, mankind never have recourse to superior powers so readily as in that disposition. But as men have now

42. [Manichaeism, a religion founded by the Persian Mani (c. 216–c. 276), strongly influenced the development of Christianity. Basic to the Manichaean outlook is the doctrine that the universe is the scene of an eternal struggle between two antagonistic powers, Light and Darkness (or Good and Evil).]

learned to form principles and to draw consequences, it is necessary to change the batteries, and to make use of such arguments as will endure at least some scrutiny and examination. This variation is the same (and from the same causes) with that which I formerly remarked with regard to scepticism.

Thus Philo continued to the last his spirit of opposition, and his censure of established opinions. But I could observe that Demea did not at all relish the latter part of the discourse; and he took occasion soon after, on some pretence or other, to leave the company.

Part XII

After Demea's departure, Cleanthes and Philo continued the conversation in the following manner. Our friend, I am afraid, said Cleanthes, will have little inclination to revive this topic of discourse while you are in company; and to tell the truth, Philo, I should rather wish to reason with either of you apart on a subject so sublime and interesting. Your spirit of controversy, joined to your abhorrence of vulgar superstition, carries you strange lengths when engaged in an argument; and there is nothing so sacred and venerable, even in your own eyes, which you spare on that occasion.

I must confess, replied Philo, that I am less cautious on the subject of Natural Religion than on any other; both because I know that I can never, on that head, corrupt the principles of any man of common sense and because no one, I am confident, in whose eyes I appear a man of common sense will ever mistake my intentions. You, in particular, Cleanthes, with whom I live in unreserved intimacy; you are sensible that, notwithstanding the freedom of my conversation and my love of singular arguments, no one has a deeper sense of religion impressed on his mind, or pays more profound adoration to the Divine Being, as he discovers himself to reason in the inexplicable contrivance and artifice of nature. A purpose, an intention, a design strikes everywhere the most careless, the most stupid thinker; and no man can be so hardened in absurd systems as at all times to reject it. *That nature does nothing in vain* is a maxim established in all the schools, merely from the contemplation of the works of nature, without any religious purpose; and, from a firm conviction of its truth, an anatomist who had observed a new organ or canal would never be satisfied till he had also discovered its use and intention. One great foundation of the Copernican system is the maxim *that nature acts by the simplest methods, and chooses the most proper means to any end*; and astronomers often, without thinking of it, lay this strong foundation of piety and religion. The same thing is observable in other parts of philosophy; and thus all the sciences almost lead us insensibly to acknowledge a first intelligent Author; and their authority is often so much the greater as they do not directly profess that intention.

It is with pleasure I hear Galen[43] reason concerning the structure of the human body. The anatomy of a man, says he, discovers above 600 different muscles; and whoever duly considers these will find that, in each of them, nature must have adjusted at least ten different circumstances in order to attain the end which she proposed: proper figure, just magnitude, right disposition of the several ends, upper and lower position of the whole, the due insertion of the several nerves, veins, and arteries; so that, in the muscles alone, above 6000 several views and intentions must have been formed and executed. The bones he calculates to be 284; the distinct purposes aimed at in the structure of each, above forty. What a prodigious display of artifice, even in these simple and homogeneous parts! But if we consider the skin, ligaments, vessels, glandules, humors, the several limbs and members of the body, how must our astonishment rise upon us, in proportion to the number and intricacy of the parts so artificially adjusted! The further we advance in these researches, we discover new scenes of art and wisdom; but descry still, at a distance, further scenes beyond our reach; in the fine internal structure of the parts, in the economy of the brain, in the fabric of the seminal vessels. All these artifices are repeated in every different species of animal, with wonderful variety, and with exact propriety, suited to the different intentions of nature in framing each species. And

43. *De Formatione Foetus.* [Galen (c. 130–c. 200) was a Greek physicist and devotee of philosophy who wrote prolifically, most notably in the fields of anatomy and physiology, and served at the court of Marcus Aurelius, regarding whom see Hume's *Enquiry*, n.44.]

if the infidelity of Galen, even when these natural sciences were still imperfect, could not withstand such striking appearances, to what pitch of pertinacious obstinacy must a philosopher in this age have attained who can now doubt of a Supreme Intelligence!

Could I meet with one of this species (who, I thank God, are very rare), I would ask him: Supposing there were a God who did not discover himself immediately to our senses, were it possible for him to give stronger proofs of his existence than what appear on the whole face of nature? What indeed could such a Divine Being do but copy the present economy of things, render many of his artifices so plain that no stupidity could mistake them, afford glimpses of still greater artifices which demonstrate his prodigious superiority above our narrow apprehensions, and conceal altogether a great many from such imperfect creatures? Now, according to all rules of just reasoning, every fact must pass for undisputed when it is supported by all the arguments which its nature admits of, even though these arguments be not, in themselves, very numerous or forcible: How much more in the present case where no human imagination can compute their number, and no understanding estimate their cogency.

I shall further add, said Cleanthes, to what you have so well urged, that one great advantage of the principle of theism is that it is the only system of cosmogony which can be rendered intelligible and complete, and yet can throughout preserve a strong analogy to what we every day see and experience in the world. The comparison of the universe to a machine of human contrivance is so obvious and natural, and is justified by so many instances of order and design in nature, that it must immediately strike all unprejudiced apprehensions and procure universal approbation. Whoever attempts to weaken this theory cannot pretend to succeed by establishing in its place any other that is precise and determinate: It is sufficient for him if he start doubts and difficulties; and, by remote and abstract views of things reach that suspense of judgment which is here the utmost boundary of his wishes. But, besides that this state of mind is in itself unsatisfactory, it can never be steadily maintained against such striking appearances as continually engage us into the religious hypothesis. A false, absurd system, human nature, from the force of prejudice, is capable of adhering to with obstinacy and perseverance; but no system at all, in opposition to a theory supported by strong and obvious reason, by natural propensity, and by early education, I think it absolutely impossible to maintain or defend.

So little, replied Philo, do I esteem this suspense of judgment in the present case to be possible that I am apt to suspect there enters somewhat of a dispute of words into this controversy, more than is usually imagined. That the works of nature bear a great analogy to the productions of art is evident; and, according to all the rules of good reasoning, we ought to infer, if we argue at all concerning them, that their causes have a proportional analogy. But as there are also considerable differences, we have reason to suppose a proportional difference in the causes, and, in particular, ought to attribute a much higher degree of power and energy to the supreme cause than any we have ever observed in mankind. Here, then, the existence of a *Deity* is plainly ascertained by reason; and if we make it a question whether, on account of these analogies, we can properly call him a *mind* or *intelligence*, notwithstanding the vast difference which may reasonably be supposed between him and human minds; what is this but a mere verbal controversy? No man can deny the analogies between the effects: to restrain ourselves from inquiring concerning the causes is scarcely possible. From this inquiry the legitimate conclusion is that the causes have also an analogy; and if we are not contented with calling the first and supreme cause a *God* or *Deity*, but desire to vary the expression, what can we call him but *Mind* or *Thought*, to which he is justly supposed to bear a considerable resemblance?

All men of sound reason are disgusted with verbal disputes, which abound so much in philosophical and theological inquiries; and it is found that the only remedy for this abuse must arise from clear definitions, from the precision of those ideas which enter into any argument, and from the strict and uniform use of those terms which are employed. But there is a species of controversy which, from the very nature of language and of human ideas, is involved in perpetual ambiguity, and can never, by any precaution or any definitions, be able to reach a reasonable certainty or precision. These are the controversies concerning the degrees of any quality or circumstance. Men may argue to all eternity whether Hannibal[44] be a great, or a very great, or a superlatively great man, what degree of beauty Cleopatra[45] possessed, what epithet of praise Livy or Thucydides[46] is entitled to, without bringing the controversy to any determination. The disputants may here agree in their sense and differ in the terms, or *vice versa*, yet never be able to define their terms so as to enter into each other's meaning; because the degrees of these qualities are not, like quantity or number, susceptible of any exact mensuration, which may be the standard in the controversy. That the dispute concerning theism is of this nature, and consequently is merely verbal, or, perhaps, if possible, still more incurably ambiguous, will appear upon the slightest inquiry. I ask the theist if he does not allow that there is a great and immeasurable, because incomprehensible, difference between the *human* and the *divine* mind: The more pious he is, the more readily will he assent to the affirmative, and the more will he be disposed to magnify the difference; he will even assert that the difference is of a nature which cannot be too much magnified. I next turn to the atheist, who, I assert, is only nominally so and can never possibly be in earnest, and I ask him whether, from the coherence and apparent sympathy in all the parts of this world, there be not a certain degree of analogy among all the operations of nature, in every situation and in every age; whether the rotting of a turnip, the generation of an animal, and the structure of human thought, be not energies that probably bear some remote analogy to each other. It is impossible he can deny it: He will readily acknowledge it. Having obtained this concession, I push him still further in his retreat, and I ask him if it be not probable that the principle which first arranged and still maintains order in this universe bears not also some remote inconceivable analogy to the other operations of nature and, among the rest, to the economy of human mind and thought. However reluctant, he must give his assent. Where then, cry I to both these antagonists, is the subject of your dispute? The theist allows that the original intelligence is very different from human reason; the atheist allows that the original principle of order bears some remote analogy to it. Will you quarrel, Gentlemen, about the degrees, and enter into a controversy which admits not of any precise meaning, nor consequently of any determination? If you should be so obstinate, I should not be surprised to find you insensibly change sides; while the theist, on the one hand, exaggerates the dissimilarity between the Supreme Being and frail, imperfect, variable, fleeting, and mortal creatures; and the atheist, on the other, magnifies the analogy among all the operations of nature, in every period, every situation, and every position. Consider then where the real point of controversy lies; and if you cannot lay aside your disputes, endeavor, at least, to cure yourselves of your animosity.

And here I must also acknowledge, Cleanthes, that, as the works of nature have a much greater analogy to the effects of *our* art and contrivance than to those of *our* benevolence and justice, we have reason to infer that the natural attributes of the Deity have a greater resemblance to those of men than his moral have to human virtues. But what is the consequence? Nothing but this, that the moral qualities of man are more defective in their kind than his natural abilities. For, as the Supreme Being is allowed to be absolutely and entirely perfect, whatever differs most from him departs the farthest from the supreme standard of rectitude and perfection.[47]

These, Cleanthes, are my unfeigned sentiments on

44. [Hannibal (247–c. 183 B.C.) was the general of Carthage, who invaded Rome during the Second Punic War.]

45. [Cleopatra (69–30 B.C.) was the queen of Egypt renowned for her charm.]

46. [Thucydides (c. 460–400 B.C.) was the noted Greek historian who authored the *History of the Peloponnesian War.*]

47. It seems evident that the dispute between the sceptics and dogmatists is entirely verbal, or, at least, regards only the degrees of doubt and assurance which we ought to indulge with regard to all reasoning; and such disputes are commonly, at the bottom, verbal and admit not of any precise determination. No philosophical dogmatist denies that there are difficulties both with regard to the senses and to all science, and that these difficulties are, in a regular, logical method, absolutely insolvable. No sceptic denies that we lie under an absolute necessity, notwithstanding these difficulties, of thinking, and believing, and reasoning, with regard to all kinds of subjects, and even of frequently assenting with confidence and security. The only difference, then, between these sects, if they merit that name, is that the sceptic, from habit, caprice, or inclination, insists most on the difficulties, the dogmatist, for like reasons, on the necessity.

this subject; and these sentiments, you know, I have ever cherished and maintained. But in proportion to my veneration for true religion is my abhorrence of vulgar superstitions; and I indulge a peculiar pleasure, I confess, in pushing such principles sometimes into absurdity, sometimes into impiety. And you are sensible that all bigots, notwithstanding their great aversion to the latter above the former, are commonly equally guilty of both.

My inclination, replied Cleanthes, lies, I own, a contrary way. Religion, however corrupted, is still better than no religion at all. The doctrine of a future state is so strong and necessary a security to morals that we never ought to abandon or neglect it. For if finite and temporary rewards and punishments have so great an effect, as we daily find, how much greater must be expected from such as are infinite and eternal?

How happens it then, said Philo, if vulgar superstition be so salutary to society, that all history abounds so much with accounts of its pernicious consequences on public affairs? Factions, civil wars, persecutions, subversions of government, oppression, slavery—these are the dismal consequences which always attend its prevalence over the minds of men. If the religious spirit be ever mentioned in any historical narration, we are sure to meet afterwards with a detail of the miseries which attend it. And no period of time can be happier or more prosperous than those in which it is never regarded or heard of.

The reason of this observation, replied Cleanthes, is obvious. The proper office of religion is to regulate the hearts of men, humanize their conduct, infuse the spirit of temperance, order, and obedience; and, as its operation is silent and only enforces the motives of morality and justice, it is in danger of being overlooked and confounded with these other motives. When it distinguishes itself, and acts as a separate principle over men, it has departed from its proper sphere and has become only a cover to faction and ambition.

And so will all religion, said Philo, except the philosophical and rational kind. Your reasonings are more easily eluded than my facts. The inference is not just—because finite and temporary rewards and punishments have so great influence that therefore such as are infinite and eternal must have so much greater. Consider, I beseech you, the attachment which we have to present things, and the little concern which we discover for objects so remote and uncertain. When divines are declaiming against the common behavior and conduct of the world, they always represent this principle as the strongest imaginable (which indeed it is), and describe almost all human kind as lying under the influence of it, and sunk into the deepest lethargy and unconcern about their religious interests. Yet these same divines, when they refute their speculative antagonists, suppose the motives of religion to be so powerful that, without them, it were impossible for civil society to subsist; nor are they ashamed of so palpable a contradiction. It is certain, from experience, that the smallest grain of natural honesty and benevolence has more effect on men's conduct than the most pompous views suggested by theological theories and systems. A man's natural inclination works incessantly upon him; it is forever present to the mind, and mingles itself with every view and consideration; whereas religious motives, where they act at all, operate only by starts and bounds; and it is scarcely possible for them to become altogether habitual to the mind. The force of the greatest gravity, say the philosophers, is infinitely small, in comparison of that of the least impulse, yet it is certain that the smallest gravity will, in the end, prevail above a great impulse because no strokes or blows can be repeated with such constancy as attraction and gravitation.

Another advantage of inclination: It engages on its side all the wit and ingenuity of the mind, and, when set in opposition to religious principles, seeks every method and art of eluding them; in which it is almost always successful. Who can explain the heart of man, or account for those strange salvos and excuses with which people satisfy themselves when they follow their inclinations in opposition to their religious duty? This is well understood in the world; and none but fools ever repose less trust in a man because they hear that, from study and philosophy, he has entertained some speculative doubts with regard to theological subjects. And when we have to do with a man who makes a great profession of religion and devotion, has this any other effect upon several who pass for prudent than to put them on their guard, lest they be cheated and deceived by him?

We must further consider that philosophers, who

cultivate reason and reflection, stand less in need of such motives to keep them under the restraint of morals; and that the vulgar, who alone may need them, are utterly incapable of so pure a religion as represents the Deity to be pleased with nothing but virtue in human behavior. The recommendations to the Divinity are generally supposed to be either frivolous observances or rapturous ecstasies or a bigoted credulity. We need not run back into antiquity or wander into remote regions to find instances of this degeneracy. Amongst ourselves, some have been guilty of that atrociousness, unknown to the Egyptian and Grecian superstitions, of declaiming, in express terms, against morality, and representing it as a sure forfeiture of the divine favor if the least trust or reliance be laid upon it.

But even though superstition or enthusiasm should not put itself in direct opposition to morality, the very diverting of the attention, the raising up a new and frivolous species of merit, the preposterous distribution which it makes of praise and blame, must have the most pernicious consequences, and weaken extremely men's attachment to the natural motives of justice and humanity.

Such a principle of action likewise, not being any of the familiar motives of human conduct, acts only by intervals on the temper, and must be roused by continual efforts in order to render the pious zealot satisfied with his own conduct and make him fulfil his devotional task. Many religious exercises are entered into with seeming fervor where the heart, at the time, feels cold and languid. A habit of dissimulation is by degrees contracted, and fraud and falsehood become the predominant principle. Hence the reason of that vulgar observation that the highest zeal in religion and the deepest hypocrisy, so far from being inconsistent, are often or commonly united in the same individual character.

The bad effects of such habits, even in common life, are easily imagined; but, where the interests of religion are concerned, no morality can be forcible enough to bind the enthusiastic zealot. The sacredness of the cause sanctifies every measure which can be made use of to promote it.

The steady attention alone to so important an interest as that of eternal salvation is apt to extinguish the benevolent affections, and beget a narrow, contracted selfishness. And when such a temper is encouraged, it easily eludes all the general precepts of charity and benevolence.

Thus the motives of vulgar superstition have no great influence on general conduct, nor is their operation favorable to morality, in the instances where they predominate.

Is there any maxim in politics more certain and infallible than that both the number and authority of priests should be confined within very narrow limits, and that the civil magistrate ought, for ever, to keep his *fasces* and *axes*[48] from such dangerous hands? But if the spirit of popular religion were so salutary to society, a contrary maxim ought to prevail. The greater number of priests and their greater authority and riches will always augment the religious spirit. And though the priests have the guidance of this spirit, why may we not expect a superior sanctity of life and greater benevolence and moderation from persons who are set apart for religion, who are continually inculcating it upon others, and who must themselves imbibe a greater share of it? Whence comes it then that, in fact, the utmost a wise magistrate can propose with regard to popular religions is, as far as possible, to make a saving game of it, and to prevent their pernicious consequences with regard to society? Every expedient which he tries for so humble a purpose is surrounded with inconveniences. If he admits only one religion among his subjects, he must sacrifice, to an uncertain prospect of tranquillity, every consideration of public liberty, science, reason, industry, and even his own independence. If he gives indulgence to several sects, which is the wiser maxim, he must preserve a very philosophical indifference to all of them and carefully restrain the pretensions of the prevailing sect; otherwise he can expect nothing but endless disputes, quarrels, factions, persecutions, and civil commotions.

True religion, I allow, has no such pernicious consequences; but we must treat of religion as it has commonly been found in the world, nor have I anything to do with that speculative tenet of theism which, as it is a species of philosophy, must partake of the beneficial influence of that principle, and, at the same time, must lie under a like inconvenience of being always confined to very few persons.

48. [Rods and axes, a Roman symbol of authority.]

Oaths are requisite in all courts of judicature, but it is a question whether their authority arises from any popular religion. It is the solemnity and importance of the occasion, the regard to reputation, and the reflecting on the general interests of society, which are the chief restraints upon mankind. Customhouse oaths and political oaths are but little regarded even by some who pretend to principles of honesty and religion; and a Quaker's asseveration is with us justly put upon the same footing with the oath of any other person. I know that Polybius[49] ascribes the infamy of Greek faith to the prevalence of the Epicurean philosophy; but I know also that Punic faith had as bad a reputation in ancient times as Irish evidence has in modern, though we cannot account for these vulgar observations by the same reason. Not to mention that Greek faith was infamous before the rise of the Epicurean philosophy; and Euripides,[50] in a passage which I shall point out to you, has glanced a remarkable stroke of satire against his nation, with regard to this circumstance.

Take care, Philo, replied Cleanthes, take care; push not matters too far, allow not your zeal against false religion to undermine your veneration for the true. Forfeit not this principle—the chief, the only great comfort in life and our principal support amidst all the attacks of adverse fortune. The most agreeable reflection which it is possible for human imagination to suggest is that of genuine theism, which represents us as the workmanship of a Being perfectly good, wise, and powerful; who created us for happiness; and who, having implanted in us immeasurable desires of good, will prolong our existence to all eternity, and will transfer us into an infinite variety of scenes, in order to satisfy those desires and render our felicity complete and durable. Next to such a Being himself (if comparison be allowed), the happiest lot which we can imagine is that of being under his guardianship and protection.

These appearances, said Philo, are most engaging and alluring; and, with regard to the true philosopher, they are more than appearances. But it happens here, as in the former case, that, with regard to the greater part of mankind, the appearances are deceitful, and that the terrors of religion commonly prevail above its comforts.

It is allowed that men never have recourse to devotion so readily as when dejected with grief or depressed with sickness. Is not this a proof that the religious spirit is not so nearly allied to joy as to sorrow?

But men, when afflicted, find consolation in religion, replied Cleanthes. Sometimes, said Philo; but it is natural to imagine that they will form a notion of those unknown beings, suitable to the present gloom and melancholy of their temper, when they betake themselves to the contemplation of them. Accordingly, we find the tremendous images to predominate in all religions, and we ourselves, after having employed the most exalted expression in our descriptions of the Deity, fall into the flattest contradiction in affirming that the damned are infinitely superior in number to the elect.

I shall venture to affirm that there never was a popular religion which represented the state of departed souls in such a light as would render it eligible for human kind that there should be such a state. These fine models of religion are the mere product of philosophy. For as death lies between the eye and the prospect of futurity, that event is so shocking to nature that it must throw a gloom on all the regions which lie beyond it; and suggest to the generality of mankind the idea of Cerberus[51] and Furies, devils, and torrents of fire and brimstone.

It is true, both fear and hope enter into religion because both these passions, at different times, agitate the human mind, and each of them forms a species of divinity suitable to itself. But when a man is in a cheerful disposition, he is fit for business, or company, or entertainment of any kind; and he naturally applies himself to these and thinks not of religion. When melancholy and dejected, he has nothing to do but brood upon the terrors of the invisible world, and to plunge himself still deeper in affliction. It may indeed happen that, after he has, in this manner, engraved the religious opinions deep into his thought and imagination, there may arrive a change of health or circumstances which may restore his good humor and,

49. Lib. vi, cap. 54. [The reference is to the *Histories* of Polybius, regarding whom see Hume's *Enquiry*, n.25.]

50. *Iphigenia in Tauride*. [Euripides (c. 480–406 B.C.), the Greek tragic poet, lived most of his life in Athens.]

51. [According to Greek mythology, Cerberus was the monstrous dog that guarded the entrance to the underworld.]

raising cheerful prospects of futurity, make him run into the other extreme of joy and triumph. But still it must be acknowledged that, as terror is the primary principle of religion, it is the passion which always predominates in it, and admits but of short intervals of pleasure.

Not to mention that these fits of excessive, enthusiastic joy, by exhausting the spirits, always prepare the way for equal fits of superstitious terror and dejection, nor is there any state of mind so happy as the calm and equable. But this state it is impossible to support where a man thinks that he lies in such profound darkness and uncertainty, between an eternity of happiness and an eternity of misery. No wonder that such an opinion disjoints the ordinary frame of mind and throws it into the utmost confusion. And though that opinion is seldom so steady in its operation as to influence all the actions; yet it is apt to make a considerable breach in the temper, and to produce that gloom and melancholy so remarkable in all devout people.

It is contrary to common sense to entertain apprehensions or terrors upon account of any opinion whatsoever, or to imagine that we run any risk hereafter, by the freest use of our reason. Such a sentiment implies both an *absurdity* and an *inconsistency*. It is an absurdity to believe that the Deity has human passions, and one of the lowest human passions, a restless appetite for applause. It is an inconsistency to believe that, since the Deity has this human passion, he has not others also; and, in particular, a disregard to the opinions of creatures so much inferior.

To know God, says Seneca,[52] *is to worship him*. All other worship is indeed absurd, superstitious, and even impious. It degrades him to the low condition of mankind, who are delighted with entreaty, solicitation, presents, and flattery. Yet is this impiety the smallest of which superstition is guilty. Commonly, it depresses the Deity far below the condition of mankind, and represents him as a capricious demon who exercises his power without reason and without humanity! And were that Divine Being disposed to be offended at the vices and follies of silly mortals, who are his own workmanship, ill would it surely fare with the votaries of most popular superstitions. Nor would any of human race merit his *favor* but a very few, the philosophical theists, who entertain or rather indeed endeavor to entertain suitable notions of his divine perfections. As the only persons entitled to his *compassion* and *indulgence* would be the philosophical sceptics, a sect almost equally rare, who, from a natural diffidence of their own capacity, suspend or endeavor to suspend all judgment with regard to such sublime and such extraordinary subjects.

If the whole of natural theology, as some people seem to maintain, resolves itself into one simple, though somewhat ambiguous, at least undefined, proposition, *That the cause or causes of order in the universe probably bear some remote analogy to human intelligence*—if this proposition be not capable of extension, variation, or more particular explication; if it affords no inference that affects human life, or can be the source of any action or forbearance; and if the analogy, imperfect as it is, can be carried no further than to the human intelligence, and cannot be transferred, with any appearance of probability, to the other qualities of the mind; if this really be the case, what can the most inquisitive, contemplative, and religious man do more than give a plain, philosophical assent to the proposition, as often as it occurs, and believe that the arguments on which it is established exceed the objections which lie against it? Some astonishment, indeed, will naturally arise from the greatness of the object: Some melancholy from its obscurity: Some contempt of human reason that it can give no solution more satisfactory with regard to so extraordinary and magnificent a question. But believe me, Cleanthes, the most natural sentiment which a well-disposed mind will feel on this occasion is a longing desire and expectation that heaven would be pleased to dissipate, at least alleviate, this profound ignorance by affording some more particular revelation to mankind, and making discoveries of the nature, attributes, and operations of the divine object of our faith. A person, seasoned with a just sense of the imperfections of natural reason, will fly to revealed truth with the greatest avidity; while the haughty dogmatist, persuaded that he can erect a complete system

52. [Lucius Annaeus Seneca (c. 4/1 B.C.–A.D. 65), born in Córdoba, Spain, was a Stoic philosopher who tutored the young future Roman emperor Nero (37–68) and became his political advisor, although later, having left the court, Seneca was accused of conspiracy against the emperor and forced to commit suicide.]

of theology by the mere help of philosophy, disdains any further aid and rejects this adventitious instructor. To be a philosophical sceptic is, in a man of letters, the first and most essential step towards being a sound, believing Christian—a proposition which I would willingly recommend to the attention of Pamphilus; and I hope Cleanthes will forgive me for interposing so far in the education and instruction of his pupil.

Cleanthes and Philo pursued not this conversation much further; and as nothing ever made greater impression on me than all the reasonings of that day, so I confess that, upon a serious review of the whole, I cannot but think that Philo's principles are more probable than Demea's, but that those of Cleanthes approach still nearer to the truth.

Immanuel Kant

Born in Königsburg, East Prussia, Immanuel Kant (1724–1804) is widely regarded as the most important figure in philosophy after Aristotle. His novel approaches to questions of knowledge, metaphysics, morality, art, politics, science, and mathematics have dominated the discussions of many subsequent generations. This influence has sometimes produced intellectual rebellion, only to be followed a generation or two later by another "back to Kant" movement.

Although the *Critique of Pure Reason* (reprinted here in part) is famous for being difficult to read, its central topics can be captured in two questions: What can we know and how can we know it? What can't we know and why can't we know these things? Kant's highly original answer to the first question is best understood in the context of his empiricist predecessors. The empiricists claimed that all knowledge came from the senses: Nothing is in the mind that was not first in the senses. Kant's rationalist predecessor Leibniz had offered an important modification of this position: Nothing is in the mind that was not first in the senses, except the mind itself. In a sense, Kant's view is a detailed extension of this cryptic claim from Leibniz. Kant regarded knowledge as the joint product of sensory evidence and the mind's ways of combining those data into usable form.

To illustrate Kant's view, consider three highly general claims: "All external objects are in space," "All mental states must belong to some subject," and "All events have causes." He agrees with the empiricists that all knowledge has to originate in the evidence of the senses. If all knowledge has to come from the senses, however, then how can anyone ever amass enough evidence to show that all objects are in [one] space? Kant's novel theory is that the claim is true because it reflects the mind's ways of handling sensory data. When given sensory data, the mind produces representations of objects arrayed in an all-comprehending Euclidean space. With this theory, he is in a position to explain the unusual status of mathematical truths. Like Descartes, he believes that mathematical claims such as "the shortest distance between two points is a straight line" are necessarily true. In contrast to Descartes, he does not believe that this status is due to their being known by some mysterious process of intellectual insight. Rather, mathematical claims are necessarily true of the objects that we perceive, because of the way in which we represent them in perception. He also argues that unless objects were represented in this way it would be impossible to keep track of them, and so to have any knowledge of them.

Kant offers a similar explanation for the other two examples. Although none of his predecessors or contemporaries (except Hume) doubted that different mental states were properties of a single mental subject, they were hard-pressed to explain why this is so. Locke created a problem in separating the identity of the human being from that of the moral person. The identity of a human being through time would be carried by his body. If, as Locke argued, a moral person could survive a change of bodies, then her identity as a person cannot be a matter of bodily continuity. What then makes you the same mind through time? This problem was pressing, because most agreed with Descartes' view that each person is certain of her existence as a thinker.

Kant's answer is that your different thoughts are necessarily connected with one another. For example, if you can recognize chartreuse objects, then at some time you must have perceived similar objects and been told the name of the color. If you know that Washington was the first U.S. president, then you must have learned it—even if you cannot remember when. Kant's argument is that insofar as we think of ourselves as having any knowledge, then we must understand our different mental states as necessarily connected to each other and so as belonging to a single cognitive (if not moral) subject. Again, we do not arrive at the view that all mental states belong to some subject by carrying out the impossible task of checking every case. Rather, our minds are so constituted that they expect to find such connections across mental states and, when they do, they declare the states to be states of a single mind.

Let's consider, finally, the case of causation. Hume argued that there was no way to show that every event must have a cause. Kant accepts Hume's point that this claim cannot be established empirically. Again, however, he believes that he can demonstrate that the claim is necessarily true, by showing that the mind cannot make any sense of the data it receives unless it interprets those data as representing causally interacting objects. In sum, Kant argues that the mind must understand its own states as necessarily connected and external objects as causally interacting in a single space if it is to have any knowledge of such objects.

Kant's answer to the second, negative, question is that we cannot know the traditional claims of metaphysics except in the manner just illustrated—by showing that they express conditions that are necessary for cognition from sensory data. He argues in particular that we cannot answer three central metaphysical questions either through the methods of metaphysics or through his own new approach: Are humans free? Does God exist? Is the soul immortal? Given this result, he maintains that these questions do not belong in metaphysics, but should be relocated in a different area—ethics. Because his contemporaries had difficulty following the twists and turns of the *Critique*'s arguments, he offered a more reader-friendly version, the *Prolegomena*, presented here in its entirety.

Both the *Critique of Practical Reason* and the more widely read *Grounding for the Metaphysics of Morals* (reprinted here) try to establish the practical or moral need for assuming freedom of the will, immortality and the existence of God. They also offer a moral theory that is a major player in contemporary debates. Through Socratic questioning, the *Grounding* tries to get readers to see that their own moral views are that an action is permissible/obligatory/forbidden for one if and only if it is permissible/obligatory/forbidden for all. It also argues that the most basic value for any rational moral agent is the value of a person. In the end, all moral action is a matter of respecting the humanity in yourself and in others.

Religion within the Bounds of Mere Reason traces some of the implications of basing belief in God on moral rather than metaphysical considerations. *Perpetual Peace* argues that a lasting peace requires the formation defensive league of nations that could rebuff attacks by aggressors.

• • •

Paul Guyer, ed., *The Cambridge Companion to Kant* (Cambridge: Cambridge University Press, 1992) contains broad and clear essays on many of Kant's central themes. Patricia Kitcher, ed., Kant's *Critique of Pure Reason* (Lanham, Md.: Rowman & Littlefield, 1998) is a collection of recent essays on that book; Paul Guyer, ed., *Kant's Groundwork of the Metaphysics of Morals* (Lanham, Md.: Rowman & Littlefield, 1998) is a collection of recent essays on the *Grounding*. Allen W. Wood, *Kant* (Hoboken, N.J.: Wiley-Blackwell, 2005) provides a brief but comprehensive account of Kant's major theories. Onora [O'Neill] Nell, *Acting on Principle* (Columbia University Press, 1975), Onora O'Neill, *Constructions of Reason* (New York: Cambridge University Press, 1990), Christine Korsgaard, *Creating the Kingdom of Ends* (Cambridge: Cambridge University Press, 1996), and Barbara Herman, *The Practice of Moral Judgment* (Cambridge, Mass.: Harvard University Press, 1993) are useful book-length treatments of Kant's ethics.

Patricia Kitcher

Prolegomena to Any Future Metaphysics

PREFACE

These *Prolegomena* are not for the use of pupils but of [255] future teachers, and even the latter should not expect that they will be serviceable for the systematic exposition of a ready-made science, but merely for the discovery of the science itself.

There are scholars for whom the history of philosophy (both ancient and modern) is philosophy itself; for these the present *Prolegomena* are not written. They must wait until those who endeavor to draw from the fountain of reason itself have completed their work; it will then be the turn of such scholars to inform the world of what has been done. Unfortunately, nothing can be said which, in their opinion, has not been said before, and truly the same prophecy applies to all future time; for since the human reason has for many centuries speculated upon innumerable objects in various ways, it is hardly to be expected that we should not be able to discover analogies for every new idea among the old sayings of past ages.

My object is to persuade all those who think metaphysics worth studying that it is absolutely necessary to pause a moment and, disregarding all that has been done, to propose first the preliminary question, "Whether such a thing as metaphysics be at all possible?"

If it is a science, how does it happen that it cannot, like other sciences, obtain universal and permanent [256] recognition? If not, how can it maintain its pretensions and keep the human understanding in suspense with hopes never ceasing, yet never fulfilled? Whether then we demonstrate our knowledge or our ignorance in this field, we must come once and for all to a definite conclusion respecting the nature of this so-called science, which cannot possibly remain on its present footing. It seems almost ridiculous, while every other science is continually advancing, that in this, which pretends to be wisdom incarnate, for whose oracle every one inquires, we should constantly move around the same spot, without gaining a single step. And so its supporters having melted away, we do not find that men who are confident of their ability to shine in other sciences venture their reputation here, where everybody, however ignorant in other matters, presumes to deliver a final verdict, inasmuch as in this domain there is as yet no standard weight and measure to distinguish soundness from shallow talk.

After all, it is nothing extraordinary in the elaboration of a science, when men begin to wonder how far it has advanced, that the question should at last occur as to whether and how in general such a science is possible? Human reason so delights in constructions that it has several times built up a tower and then razed it to examine the nature of the foundation. It is never too late to become reasonable and wise; but if the insight comes late, there is always more difficulty in starting the change.

The question whether a science be possible presupposes a doubt as to its actuality. But such a doubt offends the man whose entire goods may perhaps consist in this supposed jewel; hence he who raises the doubt must expect opposition from all sides. Some, in the proud consciousness of their possessions, which are ancient and therefore considered legitimate, will take their metaphysical compendia in their hands and look down on him with contempt; others who never see anything except it be identical with what they have somewhere else seen before will not understand him, and everything will remain for a time as if nothing had happened to excite the concern or the hope for an impending change.

Nevertheless, I venture to predict that the independent reader of these Prolegomena will not only doubt his previous science, but ultimately be fully persuaded [257] that it cannot exist unless the demands here stated on which its possibility depends be satisfied; and, as this

Reprinted from Kant, *Prolegomena to Any Future Metaphysics* (Second Edition), translated by James W. Ellington (Indianapolis: Hackett Publishing Co., 2002), by permission of the publisher.

has never been done, that there is, as yet, no such thing as metaphysics. But as it can never cease to be in demand[1]—since the interests of human reason in general are intimately interwoven with it—he must confess that a radical reform, or rather a rebirth of the science according to a new plan, is unavoidable, however much men may struggle against it for a while.

Since the *Essays* of Locke and Leibniz, or rather since the origin of metaphysics so far as we know its history, nothing has ever happened which could have been more decisive to its fate than the attack made upon it by David Hume. He threw no light on this kind of knowledge; but he certainly struck a spark from which light might have been obtained, had it caught some inflammable substance and had its smouldering fire been carefully nursed and developed.

Hume started mainly from a single but important concept in metaphysics, namely, that of the connection of cause and effect (including its derivative concepts of force and action, etc.). He challenged reason, which pretends to have given birth to this concept of herself, to answer him by what right she thinks anything could be so constituted that if that thing be posited, something else also must necessarily be posited; for this is the meaning of the concept of cause. He demonstrated irrefutably that it was entirely impossible for reason to think *a priori* and by means of concepts such a combination as involves necessity. We cannot at all see why, in consequence of the existence of one thing, another must necessarily exist, or how the concept of such a combination can arise *a priori*. Hence he inferred that reason was altogether deluded with reference to this concept, which she erroneously considered as one of her children, whereas in reality it was nothing but a bastard of imagination, impregnated by experience, which subsumed certain representations under the law of association, and mistook a subjective necessity (custom) for an objective necessity arising from insight. Hence he inferred that reason had no power to think such connections, even in general, because her concepts would then be purely fictitious and all her pretended *a priori* cognitions nothing but common experiences marked with a false stamp. This is as much as to say that there is not, and cannot be, any such thing as metaphysics at all.[2]

However hasty and mistaken Hume's conclusion may appear, it was at least founded upon investigation, and this investigation deserved the concentrated attention of the brighter spirits of his day as well as determined efforts on their part to discover, if possible, a happier solution of the problem in the sense proposed by him, all of which would have speedily resulted in a complete reform of the science.

But Hume suffered the usual misfortune of metaphysicians, of not being understood. It is positively painful to see how utterly his opponents, Reid, Oswald, Beattie, and lastly Priestley, missed the point of the problem; for while they were ever taking for granted that which he doubted, and demonstrating with zeal and often with impudence that which he never thought of doubting, they so misconstrued his valuable suggestion that everything remained in its old condition, as if nothing had happened. The question was not whether the concept of cause was right, useful, and even indispensable for our knowledge of nature, for this Hume had never doubted; but whether that concept could be thought by reason *a priori*, and consequently whether it possessed an inner truth, independent of all experience, implying a more widely extended usefulness, not limited merely to objects of experience. This was Hume's problem. It was a question concerning the *origin* of the concept, not concerning its indispensability in use. Were the former decided, the conditions of its use and the sphere of its valid application would have been determined as a matter of course.

But to satisfy the conditions of the problem, the

1. Says Horace: *Rusticus expectat, dum defluat amnis, at ille labitur et labetur in omne volubilis aevum.* ["A peasant waits for the river to flow away, but it flows on and will so flow forever." —J.W.E.] Epistle I, 2, 42f.

2. Nevertheless Hume called such destructive philosophy metaphysics and attached to it great value. "Metaphysics and morals," he says, "are the most important branches of science; mathematics and natural philosophy are not half so important." [*Essays Moral, Political, and Literary* (edited by Green and Grose) vol. I, p. 187. Essay XIV: Of the Rise and Progress of the Arts and Sciences] But the acute man merely regarded the negative use arising from the moderation of extravagant claims of speculative reason, and the complete settlement of the many endless and troublesome controversies that mislead mankind. He overlooked the positive injury which results if reason be deprived of its most important prospects, which can alone supply to the will the highest aim for all its endeavors.

opponents of the great thinker should have penetrated very deeply into the nature of reason, so far as it is concerned with pure thought—a task which did not suit them. They found a more convenient method of being defiant without any insight, viz., the appeal to *common sense*. It is indeed a great gift of heaven to possess right or (as they now call it) plain common sense. But this common sense must be shown in deeds by well-considered and reasonable thoughts and words, not by appealing to it as an oracle when no rational justification of oneself can be advanced. To appeal to common sense when insight and science fail, and no sooner—this is one of the subtle discoveries of modern times, by means of which the most superficial ranter can safely enter the lists with the most thorough thinker and hold his own. But as long as a particle of insight remains, no one would think of having recourse to this subterfuge. Seen in a clear light, it is but an appeal to the opinion of the multitude, of whose applause the philosopher is ashamed, while the popular charlatan glories and confides in it. I should think that Hume might fairly have laid as much claim to common sense as Beattie and, in addition, to a critical reason (such as the latter did not possess), which keeps common sense in check and prevents it from speculating, or, if speculations are under discussion, restrains the desire to decide because it cannot satisfy itself concerning its own principles. By this means alone can common sense remain sound. Chisels and hammers may suffice to work a piece of wood, but for etching we require an etcher's needle. Thus common sense and speculative understanding are both useful, but each in *260* its own way: the former in judgments which apply immediately to experience; the latter when we judge universally from mere concepts, as in metaphysics, where sound common sense, so called in spite of the inappropriateness of the word, has no right to judge at all.

I openly confess that my remembering David Hume was the very thing which many years ago first interrupted my dogmatic slumber and gave my investigations in the field of speculative philosophy a quite new direction. I was far from following him in the conclusions to which he arrived by considering, not the whole of his problem, but a part, which by itself can give us no information. If we start from a well-founded, but undeveloped, thought which another has bequeathed to us, we may well hope by continued reflection to advance further than the acute man to whom we owe the first spark of light.

So I tried first whether Hume's objection could not be put into a general form, and soon found that the concept of the connection of cause and effect was by no means the only concept by which the understanding thinks the connection of things *a priori*, but rather that metaphysics consists altogether of such concepts. I sought to ascertain their number; and when I had satisfactorily succeeded in this by starting from a single principle, I proceeded to the deduction of these concepts, which I was now certain were not derived from experience, as Hume had tried, but sprang from the pure understanding. This deduction (which seemed impossible to my acute predecessor and had never even occurred to anyone else, though no one had hesitated to use the concepts without investigating the basis of their objective validity) was the most difficult task ever undertaken in the service of metaphysics; and the worst was that metaphysics, such as it then existed, could not assist me in the least because this deduction alone can render metaphysics possible. But as soon as I had succeeded in solving Hume's problem, not merely in a particular case, but with respect to the whole faculty of pure reason, I could *261* proceed safely, though slowly, to determine the whole sphere of pure reason completely and from universal principles, in its boundaries as well as in its contents. This was required for metaphysics in order to construct its system according to a sure plan.

But I fear that the working out of Hume's problem in its widest extent (namely, my *Critique of Pure Reason*) will fare as the problem itself fared when first proposed. It will be misjudged because it is misunderstood, and misunderstood because men choose to skim through the book and not to think through it—a disagreeable task, because the work is dry, obscure, opposed to all ordinary notions, and moreover long-winded. Now I confess that I did not expect to hear from philosophers complaints of want of popularity, entertainment, and facility when the existence of a highly prized and indispensable cognition is at stake, which cannot be established otherwise than by the strictest rules of scholarly precision. Popularity may follow, but is inadmissible at the beginning. Yet as regards a certain obscurity, arising particularly from the diffuseness of the plan, owing to which the principal points of the investigation are easily lost sight of, the complaint is just, and I intend to remove it by the present *Prolegomena.*

The first-mentioned work, which discusses the pure faculty of reason in its whole extent and bounds, will remain the foundation, to which the *Prolegamena,* as a preliminary exercise, refer; for that critique must exist as a science, systematic and complete as to its smallest parts, before we can think of letting metaphysics appear on the scene, or even have the most distant hope of so doing.

We have been long accustomed to seeing antiquated knowledge produced as new by taking it out of its former context, and fitting it into a systematic dress 262 of any fancy pattern under new titles. Most readers will set out by expecting nothing else from the *Critique*; but these *Prolegomena* may persuade him that it is a perfectly new science, of which no one has ever even thought, the very idea of which was unknown, and for which nothing hitherto accomplished can be of the smallest use, except it be the suggestion of Hume's doubts. Yet even he did not suspect such a formal science, but ran his ship ashore, for safety's sake, landing on skepticism, there to let it lie and rot; whereas my object is rather to give it a pilot who, by means of safe navigational principles drawn from a knowledge of the globe and provided with a complete chart and compass, may steer the ship safely whither he listeth.

If in a new science that is wholly isolated and unique in its kind we started with the prejudice that we can judge of things by means of would-be knowledge previously acquired, even though this is precisely what has first to be called in question; then we should only fancy we saw everywhere what we had already known, because the expressions have a similar sound. Yet everything would appear utterly metamorphosed, senseless, and unintelligible, because we should have as a foundation our own thoughts, made by long habit a second nature, instead of the author's. However, the longwindedness of the work, so far as it depends on the science itself and not on the exposition, its consequent unavoidable dryness, and its scholastic precision are qualities which can only benefit the science, though they may discredit the book.

Few writers are gifted with the subtlety and, at the same time, with the grace of David Hume, or with the depth, as well as the elegance of, Moses Mendelssohn. Yet I flatter myself that I might have made my own exposition popular, if my object had been merely to sketch out a plan and leave its completion to others, instead of having my heart in the welfare of the science to which I had devoted myself so long; in truth, it required no little constancy, and even self-denial, to postpone the sweets of an immediate success to the prospect of a slower, but more lasting, reputation.

Making plans is often the occupation of an opulent and boastful mind, which thus obtains the reputation of a creative genius by demanding what it cannot itself supply, by censuring what it cannot 263 improve, and by proposing what it knows not where to find. And yet something more should belong to a sound plan of a general critique of pure reason than mere conjectures, if this plan is to be other than the usual declamations of pious aspirations. But pure reason is a sphere so separate and self-contained that we cannot touch a part without affecting all the rest. We can therefore do nothing without first determining the position of each part and its relation to the rest. For inasmuch as our judgment cannot be corrected by anything outside of pure reason, so the validity and use of every part depends upon the relation in which it stands to all the rest within the domain of reason, just as in the structure of an organized body the end of each member can only be deduced from the full conception of the whole. It may, then, be said of such a critique that it is never trustworthy except it be perfectly complete, down to the smallest elements of pure reason. In the sphere of this faculty you can determine either everything or nothing.

But although a mere sketch preceding the *Critique of Pure Reason* would be unintelligible, unreliable, and useless, it is all the more useful as a sequel which enables us to grasp the whole, to examine in detail the chief points of importance in the science, and to improve in many respects our exposition, as compared with the first execution of the work.

That work being completed, I offer here such a plan which is sketched out after an analytical method, while the *Critique* itself had to be executed in the synthetical style, in order that the science may present all its articulations, as the structure of a peculiar cognitive faculty, in their natural combination. But should any reader find this plan, which I publish as the *Prolegomena to Any Future Metaphysics,* still obscure, let him consider that not everyone is bound to study metaphysics, that many minds will succeed very well in the exact and even in deep sciences more closely allied to intuition while they cannot succeed in investigations dealing exclusively with abstract concepts. In such cases men should apply their talents to other subjects. But he who undertakes to judge or, still more, to construct a system of metaphysics must satisfy the demands here made, either by adopting my solution or by thoroughly refuting it and substituting another. To evade it is impossible. In conclusion, let it be remembered that this much-abused obscurity (frequently serving as a mere pretext under which people hide their own indolence or dullness) has its uses, since all who in other sciences observe a judicious silence speak authoritatively in metaphysics and make bold decisions, because their ignorance is not here contrasted with the knowledge of others. Yet it does contrast with sound critical principles, which we may therefore commend in the words of Virgil:

Ignavum, fucos, pecus a praesepibus arcent.[3]

PROLEGOMENA

Preamble on the Peculiarities of All Metaphysical Cognition

§1. Of the Sources of Metaphysics

If it becomes desirable to present any cognition as science, it will be necessary first to determine exactly its differentia, which no other science has in common with it and which constitutes its peculiarity; otherwise the boundaries of all sciences become confused, and none of them can be treated thoroughly according to its nature.

The peculiar features of a science may consist of a simple difference of object, or of the sources of cognition, or of the kind of cognition, or perhaps of all three conjointly. On these features, therefore, depends the idea of a possible science and its territory.

First, as concerns the sources of metaphysical cognition, its very concept implies that they cannot be empirical. Its principles (including not only its basic propositions but also its basic concepts) must never be derived from experience. It must not be physical but metaphysical knowledge, i.e., knowledge lying beyond experience. It can therefore have for its basis neither external experience, which is the source of physics proper, nor internal, which is the basis of empirical psychology. It is therefore *a priori* cognition, coming from pure understanding and pure reason.

But so far metaphysics would not be distinguishable from pure mathematics; it must therefore be called pure philosophical cognition; and for the meaning of this term I refer to the *Critique of Pure Reason* ("Methodology," Chap. I, Sec. 1), where the distinction between these two employments of reason is sufficiently explained. So much for the sources of metaphysical cognition.

§2. Concerning the Kind of Cognition Which Can Alone Be Called Metaphysical

a. Of the Distinction between Analytic and Synthetic Judgments in General—The peculiarity of its sources demands that metaphysical cognition must consist of nothing but *a priori* judgments. But whatever be their origin or their logical form, there is a distinction in judgments, as to their content, according to which they are either merely *explicative*, adding nothing to the content of the cognition, or *ampliative*, increasing the given cognition: the former may be called *analytic*, the latter *synthetic*, judgments.

Analytic judgments express nothing in the predicate but what has been already actually thought in the concept of the subject, though not so clearly and with the same consciousness. If I say: "All bodies are extended," I have not amplified in the least my concept of body, but have only analyzed it, as extension was really thought to belong to that concept before the judgment was made, though it was not expressed; this judgment is therefore analytic. On the other hand, this judgment, "All bodies have weight," contains in its predicate something not actually thought in the universal concept of body; it amplifies my knowledge by adding something to my concept, and must therefore be called synthetic.

b. The Common Principle of All Analytic Judgments Is That of Contradiction.—All analytic judgments depend wholly on the principle of contradiction, and are in their nature *a priori* cognitions, whether the concepts that supply them with matter be empirical or not. For the predicate of an affirmative analytic judgment is already thought in the concept

3. ["They keep out of the hives the drones, an indolent bunch."] *Georgics*, IV, 168.

of the subject, of which it cannot be denied without contradiction. In the same way its opposite is necessarily denied of the subject in an analytic, but negative, judgment, by the same principle of contradiction. Such is the case of the judgments: "All bodies are extended," and "No bodies are unextended (i.e., simple)."

For this very reason all analytic judgments are *a priori* even when the concepts are empirical, as, for example, "Gold is a yellow metal"; for to know this I require no experience beyond my concept of gold, which contained the thought that this body is yellow and metal. It is, in fact, this thought that constituted my concept; and I need only analyze it, without looking beyond it elsewhere.

c. Synthetic Judgments Require a Different Principle from That of Contradiction.—There are synthetic *a posteriori* judgments of empirical origin; but there are also others which are certain *a priori*, and which spring from pure understanding and reason. Yet they both agree in this, that they cannot possibly spring from the principle of analysis, namely, the principle of contradiction, alone, but require another quite different principle. But whatever principle they may be deduced from, they must be subject to the principle of contradiction, which must never be violated, even though everything cannot be deduced from it. I shall first classify synthetic judgments.

1. *Judgments of Experience* are always synthetic. For it would be absurd to base an analytic judgment on 268 experience, as our concept suffices for the purpose without requiring any testimony from experience. That a body is extended is a judgment which holds *a priori*, and is not a judgment of experience. For before appealing to experience, we already have all the conditions for the judgment in the concept, from which we have then but to elicit the predicate according to the principle of contradiction, and thereby to become conscious of the necessity of the judgment, which experience could not at all teach us.

2. *Mathematical Judgments* are all synthetic. This fact seems hitherto to have altogether escaped the observation of those who have analyzed human reason; it even seems directly opposed to all their conjectures, though it is incontestably certain and most important in its consequences. For as it was found that the conclusions of mathematicians all proceed according to the principle of contradiction (as is demanded by all apodeictic certainty), men persuaded themselves that the fundamental propositions were known from the principle of contradiction. This was a great mistake, for a synthetic proposition can indeed be comprehended according to the principle of contradiction, but only by presupposing another synthetic proposition from which it follows, but never in and by itself.

First of all, we must observe that properly mathematical propositions are always judgments *a priori*, and not empirical, because they carry with them necessity, which cannot be obtained from experience. But if this be not conceded to me, very well; I shall confine my assertion to *pure mathematics*, the very concept of which implies that it contains pure *a priori* and not empirical cognition.

It might at first be thought that the proposition $7 + 5 = 12$ is a mere analytic judgment, following from the concept of the sum of seven and five, according to the principle of contradiction. But on closer examination it appears that the concept of the sum of $7 + 5$ contains merely their union in a single number, without its being at all thought what the particular number is that unites them. The concept of twelve is by no means thought by merely thinking of the combination of seven and five; and, analyze this possible sum 269 as we may, we shall not discover twelve in the concept. We must go beyond these concepts by calling to our aid some intuition corresponding to one of them, i.e., either our five fingers or five points (as Segner[4] has it in his *Arithmetic*); and we must add successively the units of the five given in the intuition to the concept of seven. Hence our concept is really amplified by the proposition $7 + 5 = 12$, and we add to the first concept a second one not thought in it. Arithmetical judgments are therefore synthetic, and the more plainly according as we take larger numbers; for in such cases it is clear that, however closely we analyze our concepts without calling intuition to our aid, we can never find the sum by such mere analysis.

All principles of geometry are no less synthetic. That a straight line is the shortest path between two points is a synthetic proposition. For my concept of straight contains nothing of quantity, but only a quality. The concept of the shortest is therefore altogether

4. [J. A. Segner: *Elementa Arithmeticae et Geometriae*, Göttingen, 1739.]

additional and cannot be obtained by any analysis of the concept of the straight line. Here, too, intuition must come to aid us. It alone makes the synthesis possible.

(Some other principles, assumed by geometers, are indeed actually analytic and depend on the principle of contradiction; but they only serve, as identical propositions, as a method of concatenation, and not as principles, e.g., $a = a$, the whole is equal to itself, or $a + b > a$, the whole is greater than its part. And yet even these, though they are recognized as valid from mere concepts, are only admitted in mathematics because they can be presented in some intuition.)

What actually makes us believe that the predicate of such apodeictic judgments is already contained in our concept, and that the judgment is therefore analytic, is the duplicity of the expression. We must think a certain predicate as joined to a given concept, and this necessity inheres in the concepts themselves. But the question is not what we must join in thought *to* the given concept, but what we actually think together with and in it, though obscurely; and so it is manifest that the predicate belongs to this concept necessarily indeed, yet not directly but indirectly by means of a necessarily present intuition.[5]

The essential and distinguishing feature of pure mathematical cognition among all other *a priori* cognitions is that it cannot at all proceed from concepts, but only by means of the construction of concepts (see *Critique of Pure Reason*, "Methodology," Chap. I, Sect. 1). As therefore in its judgments it must proceed beyond the concept to that which its corresponding intuition contains, these judgments neither can, nor ought to arise analytically, by dissecting the concept, but are all synthetic.

I cannot refrain from pointing out the disadvantage resulting to philosophy from the neglect of this easy and apparently insignificant observation. Hume, feeling the call (which is worthy of a philosopher) to cast his eye over the whole field of *a priori* cognitions in which human understanding claims such mighty possessions, heedlessly severed from it a whole, and indeed its most valuable, province, viz., pure mathematics. For he imagined that its nature, or, so to speak, the constitution of this province, depended on totally different principles, namely, on the principle of contradiction alone, and although he did not divide judgments in this manner formally and universally and did not use the same terminology as I have done here, what he said was equivalent to this: that pure mathematics contains only analytic, but metaphysics synthetic, *a priori* judgments. In this, however, he was greatly mistaken, and the mistake had a decidedly injurious effect upon his whole conception. But for this, he would have extended his question concerning the origin of our synthetic judgments far beyond the metaphysical concept of causality and included in it the possibility of mathematics *a priori* also; for this latter he must have assumed to be equally synthetic. And then he could not have based his metaphysical judgments on mere experience without subjecting the axioms of mathematics equally to experience, a thing which he was far too acute to do. The good company into which metaphysics would thus have been brought would have saved it from the danger of a contemptuous ill-treatment; for the thrust intended for it must have reached mathematics, which was not and could not have been Hume's intention. Thus that acute man would have been led into considerations which must needs be similar to those that now occupy us, but which would have gained inestimably from his intimitably elegant style.

[3.] *Metaphysical Judgments*, properly so-called, are all synthetic. We must distinguish judgments belonging to metaphysics from metaphysical judgments properly so-called. Many of the former are analytic, but they only afford the means to metaphysical judgments, which are the whole aim of the science and which are always synthetic. For if there be concepts belonging to metaphysics (as, for example, that of substance), the judgments springing from simple analysis of them also belong to metaphysics, as, for example, substance is that which only exists as subject, etc. By means of several such analytic judgments we seek to arrive at the definition of a concept. But as the analysis of a pure concept of the understanding (such as metaphysics contains) does not proceed in any different manner from the dissection of any other, even empirical, concepts, not belonging to metaphysics (such as, air is an elastic fluid, the elasticity of which is not destroyed by any known degree of cold), it follows that the concept indeed, but not the analytic

5. [In the next several pages the order of the German text as it appears in the *Philosophische Bibliothek* Edition of Kant's *Works* is followed rather than the *Akademie* Edition.]

judgment, is properly metaphysical. This science has something special and peculiar to itself in the production of its *a priori* cognitions, which must therefore be distinguished from the features it has in common with other rational knowledge. Thus the judgment that all the substance in things is permanent is a synthetic and properly metaphysical judgment.

If the *a priori* concepts which constitute the materials and building blocks of metaphysics have first been collected according to fixed principles, then their analysis will be of great value. It might be taught as a particular part (as a *philosophia definitiva*), containing nothing but analytic judgments pertaining to 274 metaphysics, and could be treated separately from the synthetic which constitute metaphysics proper. For indeed these analyzes are not elsewhere of much value except in metaphysics, i.e., as regards the synthetic judgments which are to be generated out of these previously analyzed concepts.

The conclusion drawn in this section then is that metaphysics is properly concerned with synthetic propositions *a priori,* and these alone constitute its end, for which it indeed requires various dissections of its concepts, viz., analytic judgments, but wherein the procedure is not different from that in every other kind of cognition, in which we merely seek to render our concepts distinct by analysis. But the generation of *a priori* cognition by intuition as well as by concepts, in fine, of synthetic propositions *a priori* in philosophical cognition, constitutes the essential content of metaphysics.

§3. A Remark on the General Division of Judgments into Analytic and Synthetic

270

This division is indispensable as concerns the critique of human understanding and therefore deserves to be classical in it, though otherwise it is of little use. But this is the reason why dogmatic philosophers, who always seek the sources of metaphysical judgments in metaphysics itself and not outside of it in the pure laws of reason generally, altogether neglected this apparently obvious distinction. Thus the celebrated Wolff and his acute follower Baumgarten came to seek the proof of the principle of sufficient reason, which is clearly synthetic, in the principle of contradiction. In Locke's *Essay,* however, I find an indication of my division. For in the fourth book (chap. iii, § 9, seq.), having discussed the various connections of representations in judgments, and their sources, one of which he makes "identity or contradiction" (analytic judgments) and another the coexistence of representations in a subject (synthetic judgments), he confesses (§ 10) that our (*a priori*) knowledge of the latter is very narrow and almost nothing. But in his remarks on this species of cognition, there is so little of what is definite and reduced to rules that we cannot wonder if no one, not even Hume, was led to make investigations concerning judgments of this kind. For such universal and yet determinate principles are not easily learned from other men who have only had them obscurely in their minds. One must hit on them first by one's own reflection; then one finds them elsewhere, where one could not possibly have found them at first because the authors themselves did not know that such an idea lay at the basis of their observations. Men who never think independently have nevertheless the acuteness to discover everything, after it has been once shown them, in what was said long since, though no one could ever see it there before.

§ 4. The General Question of the Prolegomena: Is Metaphysics at All Possible?

271

Were a metaphysics that could maintain its place as a science really in existence, were we able to say: here is metaphysics, learn it, and it will convince you irresistibly and irrevocably of its truth, then the above question would be pointless, and there would only remain that other question (which would rather be a test of our acuteness than a proof of the existence of the thing itself): how is the science possible, and how does reason come to attain it? But human reason has not been so fortunate in this case. There is no single book to which you can point, as you do to Euclid, and say: this is metaphysics; here you may find the noblest aim of this science, namely, the knowledge of a highest being, and of a future existence, proved from principles of pure reason. We can be shown indeed many judgments, apodeictically certain, and never questioned; but these are all analytic, and rather concern the materials and the scaffolding for metaphysics than the extension of knowledge, which is our proper object in studying it (§ 2). Even supposing you point to synthetic judgments (such as the principles of sufficient reason, which you have never proved, as you ought to, from pure reason *a priori,* though we gladly concede its truth), you lapse, when you try to use them for your principal purpose, into such inadmissible and uncertain assertions that in all ages one metaphysics has contradicted another, either in its assertions or their proofs, and thus has itself destroyed its own claim to lasting assent. Nay, the very attempts to set up such a science are the main cause of the early appearance of skepticism, a way of thinking in which reason treats itself with such violence that it could never have arisen save from complete despair of ever satisfying our most important aspirations. For long before men began to inquire into nature methodically, they consulted abstract reason, which had to some extent been exercised by means of ordinary experience; for reason is ever present, while laws of nature must usually be discovered with labor. So metaphysics floated to the surface, like foam, which dissolved the moment it was scooped off. But immediately there appeared a new supply on the surface, to be ever eagerly gathered up by some; while others, instead of seeking in the depths the cause of the phenomenon, thought they showed their wisdom by ridiculing the idle labor of their neighbors.

274 Weary therefore of dogmatism, which teaches us nothing, and of skepticism, which does not even promise us anything, not even to rest in permitted ignorance; disquieted by the importance of knowledge so much needed; and, lastly, rendered suspicious by long experience of all knowledge which we believe we possess or which offers itself under the title of pure reason—we have left but one critical question upon whose answer depends our future conduct, viz., *is metaphysics at all possible?* But this question must be answered not by skeptical objections to the asseverations of some actual system of metaphysics (for we do not as yet admit such a thing to exist), but from the conception, as yet only problematic, of a science of this sort.

In the *Critique of Pure Reason* I have treated this question synthetically, by making inquiries into pure reason itself and endeavoring in this source to determine the elements as well as the laws of its pure use according to principles. The task is difficult and requires a resolute reader to penetrate by degrees into a system based on no data except reason itself, and which therefore seeks, without resting upon any fact, to unfold knowledge from its original germs. These *Prolegomena,* however, are designed for preparatory exercises; they are intended to point out what must be done in order to make a science actual if it is possible, rather than to expound it. They must therefore 275 rest upon something already known as trustworthy, from which we can set out with confidence and ascend to sources as yet unknown, the discovery of which will not only explain to us what we knew but exhibit a sphere of many cognitions which all spring from the same sources. The method of such *Prolegomena,* especially of those designed as a preparation for future metaphysics, is consequently analytical.

But it happens, fortunately, that though we cannot assume metaphysics to be an actual science, we can say with confidence that certain pure *a priori* synthetic cognitions are actual and given, namely, pure mathematics and pure physics; for both contain propositions which are everywhere recognized as apodeictically certain, partly by mere reason, partly by universal agreement from experience, and yet as independent of experience. We have therefore some, at least uncontested, synthetic knowledge *a priori,* and need not ask *whether* it be possible (for it is actual) but *how* it is possible, in order that we may deduce from the principle which makes the given knowledge possible the possibility of all the rest.

§ 5. The General Problem: How Is Cognition from Pure Reason Possible?

We have above learned the significant distinction between analytic and synthetic judgments. The possibility of analytic propositions was easily comprehended, being entirely founded on the principle of contradiction. The possibility of synthetic *a posteriori* judgments, of those which are gathered from experience, also requires no special explanation; for experience is nothing but a continual joining together (synthesis) of perceptions. There remain therefore only synthetic propositions *a priori,* of which the possibility must be sought or investigated, because they must depend upon other principles than that of contradiction.

But here we need not first establish the possibility of 276 such propositions so as to ask whether they are possible. For there are enough of them which indeed are of undoubted certainty, and as our present method is analytical, we shall start from the fact that such synthetic but purely rational cognition actually exists; but we must now inquire into the ground of this possibility and ask *how* such cognition is possible, in order that we may, from the principles of its possibility, be enabled to determine the conditions of its use, its sphere, and its limits. The proper problem upon which all depends, when expressed with scholastic precision, is therefore:

How are synthetic propositions *a priori* possible?

For the sake of popularity I have above expressed this problem somewhat differently, as an inquiry into purely rational cognition, which I could do for once without detriment to the desired insight, because, as we have only to do here with metaphysics and its sources, the reader will, I hope, after the foregoing remarks, keep in mind that when we speak of purely rational cognition we do not mean analytic but synthetic cognition.[6]

Metaphysics stands or falls with the solution of this 277 problem; its very existence depends upon it. Let anyone make metaphysical assertions with ever so much plausibility, let him overwhelm us with conclusions; but if he has not first been able to answer this question satisfactorily, I have the right to say: this is all vain, baseless philosophy and false wisdom. You speak through pure reason and claim, as it were, to create cognitions *a priori* not only by dissecting given concepts, but also by asserting connections which do not rest upon the principle of contradiction, and which you believe you conceive quite independently of all experience; how do you arrive at this, and how will you justify such pretensions? An appeal to the consent of the common sense of mankind cannot be allowed, for that is a witness whose authority depends merely upon rumor. Says Horace:

Quodcunque ostendis mihi sic, incredulus odi.[7]

The answer to this question is as indispensable as it is difficult; and though the principal reason that it was not attempted long ago is that the possibility of the question never occurred to anybody, there is yet another reason, viz., that a satisfactory answer to this one question requires a much more persistent, profound, and painstaking reflection than the most diffuse work on metaphysics, which on its first appearance promised immortality to its author. And every intelligent reader, when he carefully reflects what this problem requires, must at first be struck with its difficulty, and would regard it as insoluble and even impossible did there not actually exist pure synthetic cognitions *a priori*. This actually happened to David Hume, though he did not conceive the question in its entire universality as is done here and as must be done, if the answer is to be decisive for all metaphysics. For how is it possible, says that acute man, that when a concept is given me I can go beyond it and connect with it another which is not contained in it, in such a manner as if the latter *necessarily* belonged to the former? Nothing but experience can furnish us with such connections (thus he concluded from the difficulty which he took to be an impossibility), and all that vaunted necessity or, what is the same thing, all cognition assumed to be *a priori* is nothing but a long habit of accepting something as true, and hence of mistaking subjective necessity for objective.

Should my reader complain of the difficulty and the trouble which I occasion him in the solution of 278 this problem, he is at liberty to solve it himself in an easier way. Perhaps he will then feel under obligation to the person who has undertaken for him a labor of so profound research and will rather be surprised at the facility with which, considering the nature of the subject, the solution has been attained. Yet it has cost years of work to solve the problem in its whole universality (using the term in the mathematical sense, viz.,

6. It is unavoidable that as knowledge advances certain expressions which have become classical after having been used since the infancy of science will be found inadequate and unsuitable, and a newer and more appropriate application of the terms will give rise to confusion. [This is the case with the term "analytic."] The analytical method, insofar as it is opposed to the synthetical, is very different from an aggregate of analytic propositions. It signifies only that we start from what is sought, as if it were given, and ascend to the only conditions under which it is possible. In this method we often use nothing but synthetic propositions, as in mathematical analysis, and it were better to term it the regressive method, in contradistinction to the synthetic or progressive. A principal part of logic too is distinguished by the name of analytic, which here signifies the logic of truth in contrast to dialectic, without considering whether the cognitions belonging to it are analytic or synthetic.

7. ["Whatever is shown me thus, I do not believe and do hate."] *Epistle* II, 3, 188.

for that which is sufficient for all cases), and finally to exhibit it in the analytical form, as the reader will find it here.

All metaphysicians are therefore solemnly and legally suspended from their occupations until they shall have satisfactorily answered the question: *How are synthetic cognitions a priori possible?* For the answer contains the only credentials which they must show when they have anything to offer us in the name of pure reason. But if they do not possess these credentials, they can expect nothing else of reasonable people, who have been deceived so often, than to be dismissed without further ado.

If they, on the other hand, desire to carry on their business, not as a science, but as an art of wholesome persuasion suitable for the common sense of man, they cannot in fairness be prevented from pursuing this trade. They will then speak the modest language of a rational belief; they will grant that they are not allowed even to conjecture, far less to know, anything which lies beyond the bounds of all possible experience, but only to assume (not for speculative use, which they must abandon, but for practical use only) the existence of something that is possible and even indispensable for the guidance of the understanding and of the will in life. In this manner alone can they be called useful and wise men, and the more so as they renounce the title of metaphysicians. For the latter profess to be speculative philosophers; and since, when judgments *a priori* are under discussion, poor proba- 279 bilities cannot be admitted (for what is declared to be known *a priori* is thereby announced as necessary), such men cannot be permitted to play with conjectures, but their assertions must be either science or else nothing at all.

It may be said that the entire transcendental philosophy, which necessarily precedes all metaphysics, is nothing but the complete solution of the problem here propounded, in systematic order and completeness, and that we have hitherto never had any transcendental philosophy. For what goes by its name is properly a part of metaphysics, whereas the former science has first to settle the possibility of the latter and must therefore precede all metaphysics. And it is not surprising that when a whole science, deprived of all help from other sciences and consequently in itself quite new, is required to answer a single question satisfactorily, we should find the answer troublesome and difficult, nay, even shrouded in obscurity.

As we now proceed to this solution according to the analytical method, in which we assume that such cognitions from pure reason usually exist, we can only appeal to two sciences of theoretical cognition (which alone is under consideration here), namely, pure mathematics and pure natural science. For these alone can exhibit to us objects in intuition and consequently (if there should occur in them a cognition *a priori*) can show the truth or conformity of the cognition to the object *in concreto,* that is, its actuality, from which we could proceed to the ground of its possibility by the analytical method. This facilitates our work greatly, for here universal considerations are not only applied to facts, but even start from them, while in a synthetic procedure they must strictly be derived *in abstracto* from concepts.

But in order to ascend from these actual and, at the same time, well-grounded pure cognitions *a priori* to a possible cognition of the kind that we are seeking, viz., to metaphysics as a science, we must comprehend that which occasions it, namely, the mere natural (though not above suspicion as to its truth) cognition *a priori* which lies at the foundation of that science, the elaboration of which without any critical investigation of its possibility is commonly called metaphysics. In a word, we must comprehend the natural conditions of such a science as a part of our inquiry, 280 and thus the transcendental problem will be gradually answered by a division into four questions:

1. *How is pure mathematics possible?*
2. *How is pure natural science possible?*
3. *How is metaphysics in general possible?*
4. *How is metaphysics as a science possible?*

It may be seen that the solution of these problems, though chiefly designed to exhibit the essential content of the *Critique,* has yet something peculiar, which for itself alone deserves attention. This is the search for the sources of given sciences in reason itself, so that its faculty of knowing something *a priori* may by its own deeds be investigated and measured. By this procedure these sciences gain, if not with regard to their contents, yet as to their proper use; and while they throw light on the higher question concerning their common origin, they give, at the same time, an occasion for better explaining their own nature.

FIRST PART OF THE MAIN TRANSCENDENTAL QUESTION

How Is Pure Mathematics Possible?

§ 6. Here is a great and established branch of knowledge, encompassing even now a wonderfully large domain and promising an unlimited extension in the future, and carrying with it thoroughly apodeictical certainty, i.e., absolute necessity, which therefore rests upon no empirical grounds. Consequently, it is a pure product of reason, and moreover is thoroughly synthetic. [Here the question arises:] "How then is it possible for human reason to produce such cognition entirely *a priori?*" Does not this faculty [which produces mathematics], as it neither is nor can be based upon experience, presuppose some ground of cognition *a priori*, which lies deeply hidden but which might reveal itself by these its effects, if their first beginnings were but diligently ferreted out?

§ 7. But we find that all mathematical cognition 281 has this peculiarity: it must first exhibit its concept in intuition, and do so *a priori*, in an intuition that is not empirical but pure. Without this mathematics cannot take a single step, hence its judgments are always *intuitive*; whereas philosophy must be satisfied with *discursive* judgments from mere concepts, and though it may illustrate its apodeictic doctrines through intuition, can never derive them from it. This observation on the nature of mathematics gives us a clue to the first and highest condition of its possibility, which is that some pure intuition must form its basis, in which all its concepts can be exhibited or constructed, *in concreto* and yet *a priori*.[8] If we can discover this pure intuition and its possibility, we may thence easily explain how synthetic propositions *a priori* are possible in pure mathematics, and consequently how this science itself is possible. For just as empirical intuition [viz., sense-perception] enables us without difficulty to enlarge the concept which we frame of an object of intuition by new predicates which intuition itself presents synthetically in experience, so pure intuition also does likewise, only with this difference: that in the latter case the synthetic judgment is *a priori* certain and apodeictic, in the former only *a posteriori* and empirically certain, because the *a posteriori* case contains only that which occurs in contingent empirical intuition, but the *a priori* case contains that which must necessarily be discovered in pure intuition. Here intuition, being an intuition *a priori*, is inseparably joined with the concept before all experience or particular perception.

§8. But with this step our perplexity seems rather to increase than to lessen. For the question now is, "How is it possible to intuit anything *a priori?*" An intu- 282 ition is such a representation as would immediately depend upon the presence of the object. Hence it seems impossible to intuit anything *a priori* originally, because intuition would in that event have to take place without either a former or a present object to refer to, and hence could not be intuition. Concepts indeed are such that we can easily form some of them *a priori*, viz., such as contain nothing but the thought of an object in general; and we need not find ourselves in an immediate relation to the object. Take, for instance, the concepts of quantity, of cause, etc. But even these require, in order to be meaningful and significant, certain concrete use—that is, an application to some intuition by which an object of them is given us. But how can the intuition of the object precede the object itself?

§ 9. If our intuition had to be of such a nature as to represent things as they are in themselves, there would not be any intuition *a priori*, but intuition would be always empirical. For I can only know what is contained in the object in itself if it is present and given to me. It is indeed even then inconceivable how the intuition of a present thing should make me know this thing as it is in itself, as its properties cannot migrate into my faculty of representation. But even if this possibility be granted, an intuition of that sort would not take place *a priori*, that is, before the object were presented to me; for without this latter fact no ground of a relation between my representation and the object can be conceived, unless it rested on inspiration. Therefore in one way only can my intuition anticipate the actuality of the object, and be a cognition *a priori*, viz., *if my intuition contains nothing but the form of sensibility, which in me as subject precedes all the actual impressions through which I am affected by objects.* For that objects of sense can only be intuited according to this form of sensibility I can know *a priori*. Hence it follows that propositions which concern this form of sensuous intuition only are possible and valid for objects of the senses; as also, conversely,

8. [See *Critique of Pure Reason*, B 741.]

that intuitions which are possible *a priori* can never concern any other things than objects of our senses.

§ 10. Accordingly, it is only the form of sensuous 283 intuition by which we can intuit things *a priori*, but by which we can know objects only as they *appear* to us (to our senses), not as they are in themselves; and this assumption is absolutely necessary if synthetic propositions *a priori* be granted as possible or if, in case they actually occur, their possibility is to be conceived and determined beforehand.

Now, the intuitions which pure mathematics lay at the foundation of all its cognitions and judgments which appear at once apodeictic and necessary are space and time. For mathematics must first present all its concepts in intuition, and pure mathematics in pure intuition, i.e., it must construct them. If it proceeded in any other way, it would be impossible to make a single step; for mathematics proceeds, not analytically by dissection of concepts, but synthetically, and if pure intuition be wanting there is nothing in which the matter for synthetic judgments *a priori* can be given. Geometry is based upon the pure intuition of space. Arithmetic attains its concepts of numbers by the successive addition of units in time, and pure mechanics especially can attain its concepts of motion only by employing the representation of time. Both representations, however, are merely intuitions; for if we omit from the empirical intuitions of bodies and their alterations (motion) everything empirical, i.e., belonging to sensation, space and time still remain, and are therefore pure intuitions that lie *a priori* at the basis of the empirical. Hence they can never be omitted, but at the same time, by their being pure intuitions *a priori*, they prove that they are mere forms of our sensibility, which must precede all empirical intuition, i.e., perception of actual objects, and in conformity with which objects can be known *a priori* but only as they appear to us.

§ 11. The problem of the present section is therefore solved. Pure mathematics, as synthetic cognition *a priori*, is possible only by referring to no other 284 objects than those of the senses. At the basis of their empirical intuition lies a pure intuition (of space and time), which is *a priori*. This is possible because the latter intuition is nothing but the mere form of sensibility, which precedes the actual appearance of the objects, since in fact it makes them possible. Yet this faculty of intuiting *a priori* concerns not the matter of the appearance (that is, the sensation in it, for this constitutes what is empirical), but its form, viz., space and time. Should any man venture to doubt that both are not determinations of things in themselves but are merely determinations of their relation to sensibility, I should be glad to know how it can be possible to know *a priori* how their intuition will be characterized before we have any acquaintance with them and before they are presented to us. Such, however, is the case with space and time. But this is quite conceivable as soon as both count for nothing more than formal conditions of our sensibility, while the objects count merely as appearance; for then the form of the appearance, i.e., pure intuition, can by all means be represented as proceeding from ourselves, that is, *a priori*.

§ 12. In order to add something by way of illustration and confirmation, we need only watch the ordinary and unavoidably necessary procedure of geometers. All proofs of the complete congruence of two given figures (where the one can in every respect be substituted for the other) ultimately come down to the fact that they may be made to coincide. This is evidently nothing but a synthetic proposition resting upon immediate intuition; and this intuition must be pure and given *a priori*, else the proposition could not hold as apodeictically certain but would have empirical certainty only. In that case it could only be said that it is always found to be so and holds good only as far as our perception reaches. That complete space (which is not itself the boundary of another space) has three dimensions and that space in general cannot have more is based on the proposition that not more 285 than three lines can intersect at right angles in one point. This proposition cannot at all be shown from concepts, but rests immediately on intuition, and indeed on pure intuition *a priori* because it is apodeictically certain. That we can require a line to be drawn to infinity (*in indefinitum*) or that a series of changes (for example, spaces traversed by motion) shall be infinitely continued presupposes a representation of space and time, which can only attach to intuition, namely, so far as it in itself is bounded by nothing, for from concepts it could never be inferred. Consequently, the basis of mathematics actually is pure intuitions, which make its synthetic and apodeictically valid propositions possible. Hence our transcendental deduction of the concepts of space and of time explains at the same time the possibility of pure mathematics. Without some such deduction its truth may be granted, but its existence could by no means be understood, and we must assume "that everything which can be given to our senses (to the external senses in space and to the internal sense in time) is intuited by us as it appears to us, not as it is in itself."

§ 13. Those who cannot yet rid themselves of the notion that space and time are actual qualities inherent in things in themselves may exercise their acumen on the following paradox. When they have in vain attempted its solution and are free from prejudices at least for a few moments, they will suspect that the reduction of space and time to mere forms of our sensuous intuition may perhaps be well founded.

If two things are quite equal in all respects as much as can be ascertained by all means possible, quantitatively and qualitatively, it must follow that the one can in all cases and under all circumstances replace the other, and this substitution would not occasion the least recognizable difference. This in fact is true of plane figures in geometry; but some spherical figures exhibit, notwithstanding a complete internal agreement, such a difference in their external relation that the one figure cannot possibly be put in the place of the other. For instance, two spherical triangles on opposite hemispheres which have an arc of the equator 286 as their common base may be quite equal, both as regards sides and angles, so that nothing is to be found in either, if it be described for itself alone and completed, that would not equally be applicable to both; and yet the one cannot be put in the place of the other (on the opposite hemisphere). Here, then, is an internal difference between the two triangles; this difference our understanding cannot show to be internal but only manifests itself by external relations in space. But I shall adduce examples, taken from common life, that are more obvious still.

What can be more similar in every respect and in every part more alike to my hand and to my ear than their images in a mirror? And yet I cannot put such a hand as is seen in the mirror in the place of its original, for if this is a right hand, that in the mirror is a left one, and the image or reflection of the right ear is a left one, which never can serve as a substitute for the other. There are in this case no internal differences which our understanding could determine by thinking alone. Yet the differences are internal as the senses teach, for, notwithstanding their complete equality and similarity, the left hand cannot be enclosed in the same bounds as the right one (they are not congruent); the glove of one hand cannot be used for the other. What is the solution? These objects are not representations of things as they are in themselves, and as some pure understanding would cognize them, but sensuous intuitions, that is, appearances, whose possibility rests upon the relation of certain things unknown in themselves to something else, viz., to our sensibility. Space is the form of the external intuition of this sensibility, and the internal determination of any space is possible only by the determination of its external relation to the whole of space, of which it is a part (in other words, by its relation to external sense). That is to say, the part is possible only through the whole, which is never the case with things in themselves as objects of the mere understanding, but can well be the case with mere appearances. Hence the difference between similar and equal things which are not congruent (for instance, helices winding in opposite ways), cannot be made intelligible by any concept, but only by the relation to the right and the left hands, which immediately refers to intuition.

Remark I

Pure mathematics, and especially pure geometry, can 287 only have objective reality on condition that it refers merely to objects of sense. But in regard to the latter the principle holds good that our sense representation is not a representation of things in themselves, but of the way in which they appear to us. Hence it follows that the propositions of geometry are not determinations of a mere creation of our poetic imagination, which could therefore not be referred with assurance to actual objects; but rather that they are necessarily valid of space, and consequently of all that may be found in space, because space is nothing but the form of all external appearances, and it is this form alone in which objects of sense can be given to us. Sensibility, the form of which is the basis of geometry, is that upon which the possibility of external appearance depends. Therefore these appearances can never contain anything but what geometry prescribes to them. It would be quite otherwise if the senses were so constituted as to represent objects as they are in themselves. For then it would not by any means follow from the representation of space, which with all its properties serves the geometer as an *a priori* foundation, that this foundation together with what is inferred from it must be so in nature. The space of the geometer would be considered a mere fiction, and it would not be credited with objective validity because we cannot see how things must of necessity agree with an image of them which we make spontaneously and previous to our acquaintance with them. But if this image, or rather this formal intuition, is the essential property of our sensibility by means of which alone objects are given to us, and if this sensibility represents not things in themselves but their appearances, then we shall easily comprehend, and at the same time indisputably prove, that all external objects of our world of sense must necessarily coincide in the most rigorous way with the propositions of geometry. This is so because sensibility by means of its form of external intuition (space), with which the geometer is concerned, makes those objects possible as mere appearances. It will always remain a remarkable phenomenon in the history of philosophy that there was a time when even mathematicians who at the same time were philosophers began to doubt, not 288 of the correctness of their geometrical propositions so far as they merely concerned space, but of their objective validity and the applicability to nature of this concept itself and all its geometrical determinations. They showed much concern whether a line in nature might not consist of physical points, and consequently that true space in the object might consist of simple parts, while the space which the geometer has in his mind cannot be such. They did not recognize that this thought space renders possible the physical space, i.e., the extension of matter itself, and that this pure space is not at all a quality of things in themselves but a form of our sensuous faculty of representation, and that furthermore all objects in space are mere appearances, i.e., not things in themselves but representations of our sensuous intuition. But such is the case, for the space of the geometer is exactly the form of sensuous intuition which we find *a priori* in us, and contains the ground of the possibility of all external appearances (according to their form); and the latter must necessarily and most precisely agree with the propositions of the geometer, which he draws not from any fictitious concept but from the subjective basis of all external appearances, viz., sensibility itself. In this and no other way can geometry be made secure as to the undoubted objective reality of its propositions against all the chicaneries of a shallow metaphysics, however strange this may seem to a metaphysics that does not go back to the sources of its concepts.

Remark II

Whatever is given us as object must be given us in intuition. All our intuition, however, takes place only by means of the senses, the understanding intuits nothing but only reflects. And as we have just shown that the senses never and in no manner enable us to know things in themselves, but only their appearances, which are mere representations of the sensibility, we conclude that "all bodies, together with the space in which they are, must be considered nothing but mere representations in us, and exist nowhere but in our thoughts." Now is not this manifest idealism?

Idealism consists in the assertion that there are none but thinking beings; all other things which we believe are perceived in intuitions are nothing but 289 representations in the thinking beings, to which no object external to them in fact corresponds. On the contrary, I say that things as objects of our senses existing outside us are given, but we know nothing of what they may be in themselves, knowing only their appearances, i.e., the representations which they cause in us by affecting our senses. Consequently, I grant by all means that there are bodies without us, that is, things which, though quite unknown to us as to what they are in themselves, we yet know by the representations which their influence on our sensibility procures us, and which we call bodies. This word merely means the appearance of the thing, which is unknown to us but is not therefore less real. Can this be termed idealism? It is the very contrary.

Long before Locke's time, but assuredly since him, it has been generally assumed and granted without detriment to the actual existence of external things that many of their predicates may be said to belong, not to the things in themselves, but to their appearances, and to have no proper existence outside our representation. Heat, color, and taste, for instance, are of this kind. Now, if I go further and, for weighty reasons, rank as mere appearances also the remaining qualities of bodies, which are called primary—such as extension, place, and, in general, space, with all that which belongs to it (impenetrability or materiality, shape, etc.)—no one in the least can adduce the reason of its being inadmissible. As little as the man who admits colors not to be properties of the object in itself but only to be modifications of the sense of sight should on that account be called an idealist, so little can my doctrine be named idealistic merely because I find that more, nay, *all the properties which constitute the intuition of a body belong merely to its appearance*. The existence of the thing that appears is thereby not destroyed, as in genuine idealism, but it is only shown that we cannot possibly know it by the senses as it is in itself.

I should be glad to know what my assertions must be in order to avoid all idealism. Undoubtedly, I should say that the representation of space is not only perfectly conformable to the relation which our sensibility has to objects—that I have said—but 290 that it is completely like the object—an assertion in which I can find as little meaning as if I said that the sensation of red has a similarity to the property of cinnabar which excites this sensation in me.

Remark III

Hence we may at once dismiss as easily foreseen but futile objection, "that by our admitting the ideality of space and of time the whole sensible world would be turned into mere illusion." After all philosophical insight into the nature of sensuous cognition was spoiled by making the sensibility merely a confused mode of representation, according to which we still know things as they are, but without being able to reduce everything in this our representation to a clear consciousness; whereas on the contrary proof is offered by us that sensibility consists, not in this logical distinction of clearness and obscurity, but in the genetic one of the origin of cognition itself. For sensuous perception represents things not at all as they are, but only the mode in which they affect our senses; and consequently by sensuous perception appearances only, and not things themselves, are given to the understanding for reflection. After this necessary correction, an objection rises from an unpardonable and almost intentional misconception, as if my doctrine turned all the things of the world of sense into mere illusion.

When an appearance is given us, we are still quite free as to how we should judge the matter. The appearance depends upon the senses, but the judgment upon the understanding; and the only question is whether in the determination of the object there is truth or not. But the difference between truth and dreaming is not ascertained by the nature of the representations which are referred to objects (for they are the same in both cases), but by their connection according to those rules which determine the coherence of the representations in the concept of an object, and by ascertaining whether they can subsist together in experience or not. And it is not the fault of the appearances if our cognition takes illusion for truth, i.e., if 291 the intuition, by which an object is given us, is taken for the concept of the thing or even of its existence, which the understanding only can think. The senses represent to us the paths of the planets as now progressive, now retrogressive; and herein is neither falsehood nor truth, because as long as we hold this to be nothing but appearance we do not judge of the objective nature of their motion. But as a false judgment may easily arise when the understanding is not on its guard against this subjective mode of representation being considered objective, we say they appear to move backward; it is not the senses however which must be charged with the illusion, but the understanding, whose province alone it is to make an objective judgment on appearances.

Thus, even if we did not at all reflect on the origin of our representations, whenever we connect our intuitions of sense (whatever they may contain) in space and in time, according to the rules of the coherence of all cognition in experience, illusion or truth will arise according as we are negligent or careful. It is merely a question of the use of sensuous representations in the understanding, and not of their origin. In the same way, if I consider all the representations of the senses, together with their form, space and time, to be nothing but appearances, and space and time to be a mere form of the sensibility, which is not to be met with in objects out of it, and if I make use of these representations in reference to possible experience only, there is nothing in my regarding them as appearances that can lead astray or cause illusion. For all that, they can correctly cohere according to rules of truth in experience. Thus all the propositions of geometry hold good of space as well as of all the objects of the senses, consequently, of all possible experience, whether I consider space as a mere form of the sensibility or as something adhering to the things themselves. In the former case, however, I comprehend how I can know *a priori* these propositions concerning all the objects of external intuition. Otherwise, everything else as regards all possible experience remains just as if I had not departed from the ordinary view.

But if I venture to go beyond all possible experience with my concepts of space and time, which I cannot refrain from doing if I proclaim them qualities 292 inherent in things in themselves (for what should prevent me from letting them hold good of the same things, even though my senses might be different, and unsuited to them?), then a grave error may arise due to illusion, in which I proclaim to be universally valid what is merely a subjective condition of the intuition of things and certain only for all objects of sense, viz., for all possible experience; I would refer this condition to things in themselves, and not limit it to the conditions of experience.

My doctrine of the ideality of space and of time, therefore, far from reducing the whole sensible world to mere illusion, is the only means of securing the application of one of the most important cognitions (that which mathematics propounds *a priori*) to actual objects and of preventing its being regarded as mere illusion. For without this observation it would be quite impossible to make out whether the intuitions of space and time, which we borrow from no experience and which yet lie in our representation *a priori*, are not mere phantasms of our brain to which no objects correspond, at least not adequately; and, consequently, whether we have been able to show geometry's unquestionable validity with regard to all the objects of the sensible world just because they are mere appearances.

Secondly, though these my principles make appearances of the representations of the senses, they are so far from turning the truth of experience into mere illusion that they are rather the only means of preventing the transcendental illusion, by which metaphysics has been deceived hitherto and misled into childish efforts of catching at bubbles, because appearances, which are mere representations, were taken for things in themselves. Here originated the remarkable event of the antinomy of reason, which I shall mention later on and which is cancelled by the single observation that appearance, as long as it is employed in experience, produces truth, but the moment it transgresses the bounds of experience, and consequently becomes transcendent, produces nothing but illusion [see §§ 50–54 below].

Inasmuch, therefore, as I leave to things as we obtain them by the senses their actuality and only limit our sensuous intuition of these things to this—that it 293 represents in no respect, not even in the pure intuitions of space and of time, anything more than mere appearance of those things, but never their constitution in themselves—so is this position of mine not a sweeping illusion invented by me for nature. My protestation, too, against all charges of idealism is so valid and clear as even to seem superfluous, were there not incompetent judges who, while they would have an old name for every deviation from their perverse though common opinion and never judge of the spirit of philosophic nomenclature, but cling to the letter only, are ready to put their own conceits in the place of well-defined concepts, and thereby deform and distort them. I have myself given this my theory the name of transcendental idealism, but that cannot authorize anyone to confound it either with the empirical idealism of Descartes (indeed, his was only an insoluble problem, owing to which he thought every one at liberty to deny the existence of the corporeal world because it could never be proved satisfactorily), or with the mystical and visionary idealism of Berkeley (against which and other similar phantasms, our *Critique* contains the proper antidote). My idealism concerns not the existence of things (the doubting of which, however, constitutes idealism in the ordinary sense), since it never came into my head to doubt it; but it concerns the sensuous representation of things, to which space and time especially belong. Regarding space and time and, consequently, regarding all appearances in general, I have only shown that they are neither things (but are mere modes of representation) nor are they determinations belonging to things in themselves. But the word "transcendental," which for me never means a reference of our cognition to things, but only to our faculty of cognition, was meant to obviate this misconception. Yet rather than give further occasion to it by this word, I now retract it and desire this idealism of mine to be called "critical." But if it be really an objectionable idealism to convert actual things (not appearances) into mere representations, by what name shall we call that which, con-

294 versely, changes mere representations into things? It may, I think, be called *dreaming* idealism, in contradistinction to the former, which may be called *visionary* idealism, both of which are to be refuted by my transcendental, or better, *critical* idealism.

SECOND PART OF THE MAIN TRANSCENDENTAL QUESTION

How Is Pure Natural Science Possible?

§ 14. *Nature* is the *existence* of things, so far as it is determined according to universal laws. Should nature signify the existence of things in themselves, we could never cognize it either *a priori* or *a posteriori*. Not *a priori*, for how can we know what belongs to things in themselves, since this never can be done by the dissection of our concepts (in analytic judgments)? For I do not want to know what is contained in my concept of a thing (for that belongs to its logical being), but what in the actuality of the thing is superadded to my concept and by what the thing itself is determined in its existence outside the concept. My understanding and the conditions on which alone it can connect the determinations of things in their existence do not prescribe any rule to things in themselves; these do not conform to my understanding, but it would have to conform to them; they would therefore have to be first given to me in order to gather these determinations from them, wherefore they would not be cognized *a priori*.

A cognition of the nature of things in themselves *a posteriori* would be equally impossible. For if experience is to teach us laws to which the existence of things is subject, these laws, if they refer to things in themselves, would have to refer to them of necessity even outside our experience. But experience teaches us what exists and how it exists, but never that it must necessarily exist so and not otherwise. Experience therefore can never teach us the nature of things in themselves.

§ 15. We nevertheless actually possess a pure natural science in which are propounded, *a priori* and 295 with all the necessity requisite to apodeictic propositions, laws to which nature is subject. I need only call to witness that propaedeutic to natural knowledge which, under the title of universal natural science,[9] precedes all physics (which is founded upon empirical principles). In it we have mathematics applied to appearances, and also merely discursive principles (from concepts),[10] which constitute the philosophical part of the pure cognition of nature. But there is much in it which is not quite pure and independent of empirical sources, such as the concept of *motion*, that of *impenetrability* (upon which the empirical concept of matter rests), that of *inertia*, and many others, which prevent its being called a quite pure [transcendental] natural science. Besides, it only refers to objects of the external senses, and therefore does not give an example of a universal natural science in the strict sense; for such a science must bring nature in general, whether it regards the object of the external senses or that of the internal sense (the object of physics as well as psychology), under universal laws. But among the principles of this universal physics there are a few which actually have the required universality; for instance, the propositions that "substance is permanent," and that "every event is determined by a cause according to constant laws," etc. These are actually universal laws of nature, which subsist completely *a priori*. There is then in fact a pure [transcendental] natural science, and the question arises: how is it possible?

§ 16. The word *nature* assumes yet another meaning, which determines the object, whereas in the former sense it only denotes the conformity to law of the determinations of the existence of things generally. Nature considered *materialiter* is the *totality of all objects of experience*. And with this only are we now concerned; for, besides, things which can never be objects of experience, if they were to be cognized as to their nature, would oblige us to have recourse to concepts whose meaning could never be given *in concreto* (by any example of possible experience). Consequently, we would have to form for ourselves a list of concepts of their nature, the reality whereof [i.e., whether they actually referred to objects or were mere creations of 296 thought] could never be determined. The cognition of what cannot be an object of experience would be hyperphysical, and with things hyperphysical we are here not concerned, but only with the cognition of nature, the actuality of which can be confirmed by experience, though this cognition is possible *a priori* and precedes all experience.

9. [Contained in Kant's *Metaphysical Foundations of Natural Science* (1786).]

10. [Rather than intuitive principles, like mathematics.]

§17. The formal aspect of nature in this narrower sense is therefore the conformity to law of all the objects of experience and, so far as it is cognized *a priori*, their necessary conformity. But it has just been shown that the laws of nature can never be cognized *a priori* in objects so far as they are considered, not in reference to possible experience, but as things in themselves. And our inquiry here extends, not to things in themselves (the properties of which we pass by), but to things as objects of possible experience, and the totality of these is properly what we here call nature. And now I ask, when the possibility of cognition of nature *a priori* is in question, whether it is better to arrange the problem thus: how can we cognize *a priori* that things as objects of experience necessarily conform to law? or thus: how is it possible to cognize *a priori* the necessary conformity to law of experience itself as regards all its objects generally?

Closely considered, the solution of the question represented in either way amounts, with regard to the pure cognition of nature (which is the point of the question at issue), entirely to the same thing. For the subjective laws, under which alone an empirical cognition of things is possible, hold good of these things as objects of possible experience (not as things in themselves, which are not considered here). Either of the following statements means quite the same: a judgment of perception can never rank as experience without the law that, whenever an event is observed, it is always referred to some antecedent, which it follows according to a universal rule; or else, everything of which experience teaches that it happens must have a cause.

It is, however, more convenient to choose the first 297 formula. For we can *a priori* and before all given objects have a cognition of those conditions on which alone experience of them is possible, but never of the laws to which things may in themselves be subject, without reference to possible experience. We cannot, therefore, study the nature of things *a priori* otherwise than by investigating the conditions and the universal (though subjective) laws, under which alone such a cognition as experience (as to mere form) is possible, and we determine accordingly the possibility of things as objects of experience. For if I should choose the second formula and seek the *a priori* conditions under which nature as an object of experience is possible, I might easily fall into error and fancy that I was speaking of nature as a thing in itself, and then move around in endless circles, in a vain search for laws concerning things of which nothing is given me.

Accordingly, we shall here be concerned merely with experience and the universal conditions of its possibility, which are given *a priori*. Thence we shall determine nature as the whole object of all possible experience. I think it will be understood that I here do not mean the rules of the observation of a nature that is already given, for these already presuppose experience. I do not mean how (through experience) we can study the laws of nature; for these would not then be laws *a priori* and would yield us no pure natural science; but [I mean to ask] how the conditions *a priori* of the possibility of experience are at the same time the sources from which all the universal laws of nature must be derived.

§ 18. In the first place we must state that while all judgments of experience are empirical (i.e., have their ground in immediate sense-perception), yet conversely, all empirical judgments are not therefore judgments of experience; but, besides the empirical, and in general besides what is given to sensuous intuition, special concepts must yet be superadded—concepts which have their origin quite *a priori* in the pure understanding, and under which every perception must be first of all subsumed and then by their means changed into experience.

Empirical judgments, so far as they have objective 298 validity, are *judgments of experience*; but those which are only subjectively valid I name mere *judgments of perception*. The latter require no pure concept of the understanding, but only the logical connection of perception in a thinking subject. But the former always require, besides the representation of the sensuous intuition, special *concepts originally generated in the understanding*, which make the judgment of experience objectively valid.

All our judgments are at first merely judgments of perception; they hold good only for us (i.e., for our subject), and we do not until afterward give them a new reference (to an object) and want that they shall always hold good for us and in the same way for everybody else; for if a judgment agrees with an object, all judgments concerning the same object must likewise agree with one another, and thus the objective validity of the judgment of experience signifies nothing else than its necessary universal validity. And, conversely, if we have reason to hold a judgment to be necessarily universally valid (which never rests on perception, but on the pure concept of the understanding under which the perception is subsumed), we must consider it to be objective also, that is, that it expresses not merely a reference of our perception to a subject, but a quality of the object. For there would be no reason for the judgments of other men necessarily to agree with mine, if it were not the unity of the object to which they all refer and with which they accord; hence they must all agree with one another.

§ 19. Therefore objective validity and necessary universal validity (for everybody) are equivalent concepts, and though we do not know the object in itself, yet when we consider a judgment as universally valid, and hence necessary, we understand it thereby to have objective validity. By this judgment we cognize the object (though it remains unknown as it is in itself) by the universally valid and necessary connection of the given perceptions. As this is the case with all objects of sense, judgments of experience take their 299 objective validity, not from the immediate cognition of the object (which is impossible), but merely from the condition of universal validity of empirical judgments, which, as already said, never rests upon empirical or, in short, sensuous conditions, but upon a pure concept of the understanding. The object in itself always remains unknown; but when by the concept of the understanding the connection of the representations of the object, which are given by the object to our sensibility, is determined as universally valid, the object is determined by this relation, and the judgment is objective.

To illustrate the matter: when we say, "The room is warm, sugar sweet, and wormwood nasty,"[11] we have only subjectively valid judgments. I do not at all expect that I or any other person shall always find it as I now do; each of these sentences only expresses a reference of two sensations to the same subject, i.e., myself, and that only in my present state of perception; consequently, they are not intended to be valid of the object. Such are judgments of perception. Judgments of experience are of quite a different nature. What experience teaches me under certain circumstances, it must always teach me and everybody; and its validity is not limited to the subject nor to its state at a particular time. Hence I pronounce all such judgments as being objectively valid. For instance, when I say the air is elastic, this judgment is as yet a judgment of perception only—I do nothing but refer two sensations in my senses to one another. But if I would have it called a judgment of experience, I require this connection to stand under a condition which makes it universally valid. I desire therefore that I and everybody else should always necessarily connect the same perceptions under the same circumstances.

§ 20. We must therefore analyze experience in gen- 300 eral in order to see what is contained in this product of the senses and of the understanding, and how the judgment of experience itself is possible. The foundation is the intuition of which I become conscious, i.e., perception (*perceptio*), which pertains merely to the senses. But in the next place, there is judging (which belongs only to the understanding). But this judging may be twofold: first, I may merely compare perceptions and connect them in a consciousness of my state; or, secondly, I may connect them in consciousness in general. The former judgment is merely a judgment of perception and is of subjective validity only; it is merely a connection of perceptions in my mental state, without reference to the object. Hence it is not, as is commonly imagined, enough for experience to compare perceptions and connect them in consciousness through judgment; there arises no universal validity and necessity, by virtue of which alone consciousness can become objectively valid and be called experience.

Quite another judgment therefore is required before perception can become experience. The given intuition must be subsumed under a concept which determines the form of judging in general with regard to the intuition, connects the empirical consciousness of the intuition in consciousness in general, and

11. I freely grant that these examples do not represent such judgments of perception as ever could become judgments of experience, even though a concept of the understanding were superadded, because they refer merely to feeling, which everybody knows to be merely subjective and which, of course, can never be attributed to the object and, consequently, never can become objective. I only wished to give here an example of a judgment that is merely subjectively valid, containing no ground for necessary universal validity and thereby for a relation to the object. An example of the judgments of perception which become judgments of experience by superadded concepts of the understanding will be given in the next note.

thereby procures universal validity for empirical judgments. A concept of this nature is a pure *a priori* concept of the understanding, which does nothing but determine for an intuition the general way in which it can be used for judging. Let the concept be that of cause; then it determines the intuition which is subsumed under it, e.g., that of air, with regard to judging in general, viz., the concept of air as regards its expansion serves in the relation of antecedent to consequent in a hypothetical judgment. The concept of cause accordingly is a pure concept of the understanding, which is totally disparate from all possible perception and only serves to determine the representation contained under it with regard to judging in general, and so to make a universally valid judgment possible.

Before, therefore, a judgment of perception can 301 become a judgment of experience, it is requisite that the perception should be subsumed under some such concept of the understanding; for instance, air belongs under the concept of cause, which determines our judgment about it with regard to its expansion as hypothetical.[12] Thereby the expansion of the air is represented, not as merely belonging to the perception of the air in my present state or in several states of mine, or in the state of perception of others, but as belonging to it necessarily. The judgment that air is elastic becomes universally valid and a judgment of experience only because certain judgments precede it which subsume the intuition of air under the concepts of cause and effect; and they thereby determine the perceptions, not merely as regards one another in me, but as regards the form of judging in general (which is here hypothetical), and in this way they render the empirical judgment universally valid.

If all our synthetic judgments are analyzed so far as they are objectively valid, it will be found that they never consist of mere intuitions connected only (as is commonly supposed) by comparison into a judgment; but that they would be impossible were not a pure concept of the understanding superadded to the concepts abstracted from intuition, under which pure concept these latter concepts are subsumed and in this manner only combined into an objectively valid judgment. Even the judgments of pure mathematics in their simplest axioms are not exempt from this condition. The principle that a straight line is the shortest distance between two points presupposes that the line is subsumed under the concept of quantity, which certainly is no mere intuition but has its seat in the understanding alone and serves to determine the intuition (of the line) with regard to the judgments which may be made about it in respect to the quantity, 302 that is, to plurality (as *judica plurativa*).[13] For under them it is understood that in a given intuition there is contained a plurality of homogeneous parts.

§ 21. To prove, then, the possibility of experience so far as it rests upon pure *a priori* concepts of the understanding, we must first represent what belongs to judgments in general and the various moments (functions) of the understanding in them, in a complete table. For the pure concepts of the understanding must run parallel to these moments, inasmuch as such concepts are nothing more than concepts of intuitions in general, so far as these are determined by one or other of these moments of judging, in themselves, i.e., necessarily and universally. Hereby also the *a priori* principles of the possibility of all experience, as objectively valid empirical cognition, will be precisely determined. For they are nothing but propositions which subsume all perception (conformably to certain universal conditions of intuition) under those pure concepts of the understanding.

12. As an easier example, we may take the following: when the sun shines on the stone, it grows warm. This judgment, however often I and others may have perceived it, is a mere judgment of perception and contains no necessity; perceptions are only usually conjoined in this manner. But if I say: the sun warms the stone, I add to the perception a concept of the understanding, viz., that of cause, which necessarily connects with the concept of sunshine that of heat, and the synthetic judgment becomes of necessity universally valid, viz., objective, and is converted from a perception into experience.

13. This name seems preferable to the term *particularia*, which is used for these judgments in logic. For the latter already contains the thought that they are not universal. But when I start from unity (in singular judgments) and proceed to totality, I must not [even indirectly and negatively] include any reference to totality. I think plurality merely without totality, and not the exclusion of totality. This is necessary, if the logical moments are to underlie the pure concepts of the understanding. In logical usage one may leave things as they were.

Logical Table of Judgments

1	2
As to Quantity	*As to Quality*
Universal	Affirmative
Particular	Negative
Singular	Infinite

3	4
As to Relation	*As to Modality*
Categorical	Problematic
Hypothetical	Assertoric
Disjunctive	Apodeictic

303

Transcendental Table of the Concepts of the Understanding

1	2
As to Quantity	*As to Quality*
Unity (Measure)	Reality
Plurality (Quantity)	Negation
Totality (Whole)	Limitation

3	4
As to Relation	*As to Modality*
Substance	Possibility
Cause	Existence
Community	Necessity

Pure Physiological[14] Table of the Universal Principles of Natural Science

1	2
Axioms of Intuition	Anticipations of Perception

3	4
Analogies of Experience	Postulates of Empirical Thought in General

§ 21a. In order to comprise the whole matter in 304 one idea, it is first necessary to remind the reader that we are discussing, not the origin of experience, but what lies in experience. The former pertains to empirical psychology and would even then never be adequately developed without the latter, which belongs to the critique of cognition, and particularly of the understanding.

Experience consists of intuitions, which belong to the sensibility, and of judgments, which are entirely a work of the understanding. But the judgments which the understanding makes entirely out of sensuous intuitions are far from being judgments of experience. For in the one case the judgment connects only the perceptions as they are given in sensuous intuition, while in the other the judgments must express what experience in general and not what the mere perception (which possesses only subjective validity) contains. The judgment of experience must therefore add to the sensuous intuition and its logical connection in a judgment (after it has been rendered universal by comparison) something that determines the synthetic judgment as necessary and therefore as universally valid. This can be nothing but that concept which represents the intuition as determined in itself with regard to one form of judgment rather than another, viz., a concept of that synthetic unity of intuitions which can only be represented by a given logical function of judgments.

§ 22. The sum of the matter is this: the business of the senses is to intuit, that of the understanding is to think. But thinking is uniting representations in a consciousness. This unification originates either merely relative to the subject and is contingent and subjective, or it happens absolutely and is necessary or objective. The uniting of representations in a consciousness is judgment. Thinking therefore is the same as judging, or referring representations to judgments in general. Hence judgments are either merely subjective when representations are referred to a conscious- 305 ness in one subject only and are united in it, or they are objective when they are united in a consciousness in general, that is, necessarily. The logical moments of all judgments are so many possible ways of uniting representations in consciousness. But if they serve as concepts, they are concepts of the necessary unification of representations in a consciousness and so are principles of objectively valid judgments. This uniting in a consciousness is either analytic by identity, or synthetic by the combination and addition of various representations one to another. Experience consists in the synthetic connection of appearances (perceptions) in consciousness, so far as this connection is necessary. Hence the pure concepts of the understanding are those under which all perceptions must first be subsumed before they can serve for judgments

14. [See last sentence of § 23.]

of experience, in which the synthetic unity of the perceptions is represented as necessary and universally valid.[15]

§ 23. Judgments, when considered merely as the condition of the unification of given representations in a consciousness, are rules. These rules, so far as they represent the unification as necessary, are rules *a priori*, and so far as they cannot be deduced from higher rules, are principles. But in regard to the possibility of all experience, merely in relation to the form of thinking in it, no conditions of judgments of experience are higher than those which bring the 306 phenomena, according to the different form of their intuition, under pure concepts of the understanding, and render the empirical judgments objectively valid. These are therefore the *a priori* principles of possible experience.

The principles of possible experience are then at the same time universal laws of nature, which can be cognized *a priori*. And thus the problem in our second question: How is pure natural science possible? is solved. For the systematization which is required for the form of a science is to be met with in perfection here, because, beyond the above-mentioned formal conditions of all judgments in general and of all rules in general, that are offered in logic, no others are possible, and these constitute a logical system. The concepts grounded thereupon, which contain the *a priori* conditions of all synthetic and necessary judgments, accordingly constitute a transcendental system. Finally, the principles by means of which all appearances are subsumed under these concepts constitute a physiological system, that is, a system of nature, which precedes all empirical cognition of nature, first makes it possible, and hence may in strictness be called the universal and pure natural science.

§ 24. The first[16] of the physiological principles[17] subsumes all appearances, as intuitions in space and time, under the concept of *quantity*, and is so far a principle of the application of mathematics to experience. The second[18] subsumes the strictly empirical element, viz., sensation, which denotes the real in intuitions, not indeed directly under the concept of *quantity*, because sensation is not an intuition that *contains* either space or time, though it puts the object corresponding to sensation in both space and time. But still there is between reality (sense-representation) and zero, or total lack of intuition in time, a difference which has a quantity. For between any given degree of light and darkness, between any degree of heat and complete cold, between any degree of weight and absolute lightness, between any 307 degree of occupied space and of totally empty space, ever smaller degrees can be thought, just as even between consciousness and total unconsciousness (psychological darkness) ever smaller degrees obtain. Hence there is no perception that can show an absolute absence; for instance, no psychological darkness that cannot be regarded as a consciousness only surpassed by a stronger consciousness. This occurs in all cases of sensation; and so the understanding can anticipate sensations, which constitute the peculiar quality of empirical representations (appearances), by means of the principle that they all have a degree, consequently, that what is real in all appearance has a degree. Here is the second application of mathematics (*mathesis intensorum*) to natural science.

§ 25. As regards the relation of appearances merely with a view to their existence, the determination is not mathematical but dynamical, and can never be

15. But how does the proposition that judgments of experience contain necessity in the synthesis of perceptions agree with my statement so often before inculcated that experience, as cognition *a posteriori*, can afford contingent judgments only? When I say that experience teaches me something, I mean only the perception that lies in experience—for example, that heat always follows the shining of the sun on a stone; consequently, the proposition of experience is always so far contingent. That this heat necessarily follows the shining of the sun is contained indeed in the judgment of experience (by means of the concept of cause), yet is a fact not learned by experience; for, conversely, experience is first of all generated by this addition of the concept of the understanding (of cause) to perception. How perception attains this addition may be seen by referring in the *Critique* itself to the section on the transcendental faculty of judgment, B 176 *et seq.*

16. The three following paragraphs will hardly be understood unless reference be made to what the *Critique* itself says on the subject of the principles; they will, however, be of service in giving a general view of the principles, and in fixing the attention on the main moments. [See *Critique*, B 187–294.]

17. [The Axioms of Intuition. See *Critique*, B 202–207.]

18. [The Anticipations of Perception. See *ibid.*, B 207–218.]

objectively valid and fit for experience, if it does not come under *a priori* principles[19] by which the cognition of experience relative to appearances first becomes possible. Hence appearances must be subsumed under the concept of substance, which as a concept of the thing itself is the foundation of all determination of existence; or, secondly—so far as a succession is found among appearances, that is, an event—under the concept of an effect with reference to cause; or, lastly—so far as coexistence is to be known objectively, that is, by a judgment of experience—under the concept of community (action and reaction). Thus *a priori* principles form the basis of objectively valid, though empirical, judgments—that is, of the possibility of experience so far as it must connect objects as existing in nature. These principles are properly the laws of nature, which may be called dynamical.

Finally[20] the cognition of the agreement and connection, not only of appearances among themselves in experience, but of their relation to experience in general, belongs to judgments of experience. This relation contains either their agreement with the formal conditions which the understanding cognizes, or their coherence with the material of the senses and of perception, or combines both into one concept and consequently contains possibility, actuality, and necessity according to universal laws of nature. This would constitute the physiological doctrine of method (distinction between truth and hypotheses, and the bounds of the reliability of the latter).

§ 26. The third table of principles drawn from the nature of the understanding itself according to the critical method shows an inherent perfection, which raises it far above every other table which has hitherto, though in vain, been tried or may yet be tried by analyzing the objects themselves dogmatically. It exhibits all synthetic *a priori* principles completely and according to one principle, viz., the faculty of judging in general, which constitutes the essence of experience as regards the understanding, so that we can be certain that there are no more such principles. This affords a satisfaction such as can never be attained by the dogmatic method. Yet this is not all; there is a still greater merit in it.

We must carefully bear in mind the ground of proof which shows the possibility of this cognition *a priori* and, at the same time, limits all such principles to a condition which must never be lost sight of, if they are not to be misunderstood and extended in use beyond what is allowed by the original sense which the understanding places in them. This limit is that they contain nothing but the conditions of possible experience in general so far as it is subjected to laws *a priori*. Consequently, I do not say that things *in themselves* possess a quantity, that their reality possesses a degree, their existence a connection of accidents in a substance, etc. This nobody can prove, because such a synthetic connection from mere concepts, without any reference to sensuous intuition on the one side or connection of such intuition in a possible experience on the other, is absolutely impossible. The essential limitation of the concepts in these principles, then, is that all things stand necessarily *a priori* under the aforementioned conditions only *as objects of experience*.

Hence there follows, secondly, a specifically peculiar mode of proof of these principles; they are not directly referred to appearances and to their relation, but to the possibility of experience, of which appearances constitute the matter only, not the form. Thus they are referred to objectively and universally valid synthetic propositions, in which we distinguish judgments of experience from those of perception. This takes place because appearances, as mere intuitions *occupying a part of space and time,* come under the concept of quantity, which synthetically unites their multiplicity *a priori* according to rules. Again, insofar as the perception contains, besides intuition, sensation, and between the latter and nothing (i.e., the total disappearance of sensation), there is an ever-decreasing transition, it is apparent that the real in appearances must have a degree, so far as it (viz., the sensation) *does not itself occupy any part of space or of time.*[21] Still the transition to sensation from empty

19. [The Analogies of Experience. See *ibid.*, B 218–265.]

20. [The Postulates of Empirical Thought. See *ibid.*, B 265–294.]

21. Heat and light are in a small space just as large, as to degree, as in a large one; in like manner the internal representations, pain, consciousness in general, whether they last a short or a long time, need not vary as to the degree. Hence the quantity is here in a point and in a moment just as great as in any space or time, however great. Degrees are thus quantities not in intuition but in mere sensation (or the quantity of the content of an intuition). Hence they can only

time or empty space is only possible in time. Consequently, although sensation, as the quality of empirical intuition in respect of its specific difference from other sensations, can never be cognized *a priori*, yet it can, in a possible experience in general, as a quantity of perception be intensively distinguished from every other similar perception. Hence the application of mathematics to nature, as regards the sensuous intuition by which nature is given to us, is first made possible and determined.

Above all, the reader must pay attention to the mode of proof of the principles which occur under the title of Analogies of Experience. For these do not refer to the generation of intuitions, as do the principles of applying mathematics to natural science in 310 general, but to the connection of their existence in experience; and this can be nothing but the determination of their existence in time according to necessary laws, under which alone the connection is objectively valid and thus becomes experience. The proof, therefore, does not turn on the synthetic unity in the connection of things in themselves, but merely of perceptions, and of these, not in regard to their content, but to the determination of time and of the relation of their existence in it according to universal laws. If the empirical determination in relative time is indeed to be objectively valid (i.e., experience), these universal laws thus contain the necessity of the determination of existence in time generally (viz., according to a rule of the understanding *a priori*). Since these are prolegomena I cannot further descant on the subject, but my reader (who has probably long been accustomed to consider experience as a mere empirical synthesis of perceptions, and hence has not considered that it goes much beyond them since it imparts to empirical judgments universal validity, and for that purpose requires a pure and *a priori* unity of the understanding) is recommended to pay special attention to this distinction of experience from a mere aggregate of perceptions and to judge the mode of proof from this point of view.

§ 27. Now we are prepared to remove Hume's doubt. He justly maintains that we cannot comprehend by reason the possibility of causality, that is, of the reference of the existence of one thing to the existence of another which is necessitated by the former. I add that we comprehend just as little the concept of subsistence, that is, the necessity that at the foundation of the existence of things there lies a subject which cannot itself be a predicate of any other thing; nay, we cannot even form a concept of the possibility of such a thing (though we can point out examples of its use in experience). The very same incomprehensibility affects the community of things, as we cannot comprehend how from the state of one thing an inference to the state of quite another thing beyond it, and *vice versa*, can be drawn, and how substances which have each their own separate existence should depend upon one another necessarily. But I am very 311 far from holding these concepts to be derived merely from experience, and the necessity represented in them to be fictitious and a mere illusion produced in us by long habit. On the contrary, I have amply shown that they and the principles derived from them are firmly established *a priori* before all experience and have their undoubted objective rightness, though only with regard to experience.

§ 28. Though I have no conception of such a connection of things in themselves, how they can either exist as substances, or act as causes, or stand in community with others (as parts of a real whole) and I can just as little think such properties in appearances as such (because those concepts contain nothing that lies in the appearances, but only what the understanding alone must think), we have yet a concept of such a connection of representations in our understanding and in judgments generally. This is the concept that representations belong in one sort of judgments as subject in relation to predicates; in another as ground in relation to consequent; and, in a third, as parts which constitute together a total possible cognition. Further we know *a priori* that without considering the representation of an object as determined with regard to one or the other of these moments, we can have no valid cognition of the object; and, if we should occupy ourselves with the object in itself, there is not a single possible attribute by which I could know that it is determined with regard to one or the other of these moments, that is, belonged under the concept of substance, or of cause, or (in relation to other

---

be estimated quantitatively by the relation of 1 to 0, viz., by their capability of decreasing by infinite intermediate degrees to disappearance, or of increasing from naught through infinite gradations to a determinate sensation in a certain time. *Quantitas qualitatis est gradus* [the quantity of quality is degree].

substances) of community, for I have no conception of the possibility of such a connection of existence. But the question is not how things in themselves but how the empirical cognition of things is determined, as regards the above moments of judgments in general, that is, how things, as objects of experience, can and must be subsumed under these concepts of the understanding. And then it is clear that I completely comprehend, not only the possibility, but also the necessity, of subsuming all appearances under these concepts, that is, of using them as principles of the possibility of experience.

312 § 29. In order to put to a test Hume's problematic concept (his *crux metaphysicorum*), the concept of cause, we have, in the first place, given *a priori* by means of logic the form of a conditional judgment in general, i.e., we have one given cognition as antecedent and another as consequent. But it is possible that in perception we may meet with a rule of relation which runs thus: that a certain appearance is constantly followed by another (though not conversely); and this is a case for me to use the hypothetical judgment and, for instance, to say that if the sun shines long enough upon a body it grows warm. Here there is indeed as yet no necessity of connection, or concept of cause. But I proceed and say that if this proposition, which is merely a subjective connection of perceptions, is to be a judgment of experience, it must be regarded as necessary and universally valid. Such a proposition would be that the sun is by its light the cause of heat. The empirical rule is now considered as a law, and as valid not merely of appearances but valid of them for the purposes of a possible experience which requires universal and therefore necessarily valid rules. I therefore easily comprehend the concept of cause as a concept necessarily belonging to the mere form of experience, and its possibility as a synthetic unification of perceptions in a consciousness in general; but I do not at all comprehend the possibility of a thing in general as a cause, inasmuch as the concept of cause denotes a condition not at all belonging to things, but to experience. For experience can only be an objectively valid cognition of appearances and of their succession, only so far as the antecedent appearances can be conjoined with the consequent ones according to the rule of hypothetical judgments.

§ 30. Hence if the pure concepts of the understanding try to go beyond objects of experience and be referred to things in themselves (*noumena*), they have no meaning whatever. They serve, as it were, only to spell out appearances, so that we may be able to read them as experience. The principles which arise from their reference to the sensible world only serve 313 our understanding for use in experience. Beyond this they are arbitrary combinations without objective reality; and we can neither cognize their possibility *a priori*, nor verify their reference to objects, let alone make such reference understandable, by any example, because examples can only be borrowed from some possible experience, and consequently the objects of these concepts can be found nowhere but in a possible experience.

This complete (though to its originator unexpected) solution of Hume's problem rescues for the pure concepts of the understanding their *a priori* origin and for the universal laws of nature their validity as laws of the understanding, yet in such a way as to limit their use to experience, because their possibility depends solely on the reference of the understanding to experience, but with a completely reversed mode of connection which never occurred to Hume: they are not derived from experience, but experience is derived from them.

This is, therefore, the result of all our foregoing inquiries: "All synthetic principles *a priori* are nothing more than principles of possible experience" and can never be referred to things in themselves, but only to appearances as objects of experience. And hence pure mathematics as well as pure natural science can never be referred to anything more than mere appearances, and can only represent either that which makes experience in general possible, or else that which, as it is derived from these principles, must always be capable of being represented in some possible experience.

§ 31. And thus we have at last something determinate upon which to depend in all metaphysical enterprises, which have hitherto, boldly enough but always at random, attempted everything without discrimination. That the goal of their exertions should be set up so close struck neither the dogmatic thinkers nor those who, confident in their supposed sound common sense, started with concepts and principles of pure reason (which were legitimate and natural, but des- 314 tined for mere empirical use) in search of insights for which they neither knew nor could know any determinate bounds, because they had never reflected nor were able to reflect on the nature or even on the possibility of such a pure understanding.

Many a naturalist of pure reason (by which I mean the man who believes he can decide in matters of metaphysics without any science) may pretend that he, long ago, by the prophetic spirit of his sound sense, not only suspected but knew and comprehended what is here propounded with so much ado, or, if he likes, with prolix and pedantic pomp: "that with all our reason we can never reach beyond the field of experience." But when he is questioned about his rational principles individually, he must grant that there are many of them which he has not taken from experience and which are therefore independent of it and valid *a priori.* How then and on what grounds will he restrain both himself and the dogmatist, who makes use of these concepts and principles beyond all possible experience because they are recognized to be independent of it? And even he, this adept in sound sense, in spite of all his assumed and cheaply acquired wisdom, is not exempt from wandering inadvertently beyond objects of experience into the field of chimeras. He is often deeply enough involved in them, though in announcing everything as mere probability, rational conjecture, or analogy, he gives by his popular language a color to his groundless pretensions.

§ 32. Since the oldest days of philosophy, inquirers into pure reason have thought that, besides the things of sense, or appearances (*phenomena*), which make up the sensible world, there were certain beings of the understanding (*noumena*), which should constitute an intelligible world. And as appearance and illusion were by those men identified (a thing which we may well excuse in an undeveloped epoch) actuality was only conceded to the beings of the understanding.

And we indeed, rightly considering objects of sense as mere appearances, confess thereby that they

315 are based upon a thing in itself, though we know not this thing as it is in itself but only know its appearances, viz., the way in which our senses are affected by this unknown something. The understanding therefore, by assuming appearances, grants also the existence of things in themselves, and thus far we may say that the representation of such things as are the basis of appearances, consequently of mere beings of the understanding, is not only admissible but unavoidable.

Our critical deduction by no means excludes things of that sort (*noumena*), but rather limits the principles of the Aesthetic[22] in such a way that they shall not extend to all things (as everything would then be turned into mere appearance) but that they shall hold good only of objects of possible experience. Hereby, then, beings of the understanding are admitted, but with the inculcation of this rule which admits of no exception: that we neither know nor can know anything determinate whatever about these pure beings of the understanding, because our pure concepts of the understanding as well as our pure intuitions extend to nothing but objects of possible experience, consequently to mere things of sense; and as soon as we leave this sphere, these concepts retain no meaning whatever.

§ 33. There is indeed something seductive in our pure concepts of the understanding which tempts us to a transcendent use—a use which transcends all possible experience. Not only are our concepts of substance, of power, of action, of reality, and others, quite independent of experience, containing nothing of sense appearance, and so apparently applicable to things in themselves (*noumena*), but, what strengthens this conjecture, they contain a necessity of determination in themselves, which experience never attains. The concept of cause contains a rule according to which one state follows another necessarily; but experience can only show us that one state of things often or, at most, commonly follows another, and therefore affords neither strict universality nor necessity.

Hence concepts of the understanding seem to have a deeper meaning and content than can be exhausted by their merely empirical use, and so the understand- 316 ing inadvertently adds for itself to the house of experience a much more extensive wing which it fills with nothing but beings of thought, without ever observing that it has transgressed with its otherwise legitimate concepts the bounds of their use.

§ 34. Two important and even indispensable, though very dry, investigations therefore became indispensable in the *Critique of Pure Reason* [viz.,

22. [The principles of sensibility (space and time). See *Critique of Pure Reason*, B33–B 73.]

the two chapters "The Schematism of the Pure Concepts of the Understanding" and "The Ground of the Distinction of All Objects in General into Phenomena and Noumena"]. In the former there is shown that the senses furnish, not the pure concepts of the understanding *in concreto*, but only the schema for their use, and that the object conformable to it occurs only in experience (as the product of the understanding from materials of sensibility). In the latter there is shown that, although our pure concepts of the understanding and our principles are independent of experience, and despite the apparently greater sphere of their use, still nothing whatever can be thought by them beyond the field of experience, because they can do nothing but merely determine the logical form of the judgment with regard to given intuitions. But as there is no intuition at all beyond the field of sensibility, these pure concepts, since they cannot possibly be exhibited *in concreto*, are void of all meaning; consequently all these *noumena*, together with their sum total, the intelligible world,[23] are nothing but representations of a problem, the object of which in itself is quite possible but the solution, from the nature of our understanding, totally impossible. For our understanding is not a faculty of intuition but of the connection of given intuitions in an experience. Experience must therefore contain all the objects for our 317 concepts; but beyond it no concepts have any meaning, since no intuition can be subsumed under them.

§ 35. The imagination may perhaps be forgiven for occasional vagaries and for not keeping carefully within the limits of experience, since it gains life and vigor by such flights and since it is always easier to moderate its boldness than to stimulate its languor. But the understanding which ought to *think* can never be forgiven for indulging in vagaries; for we depend upon it alone for assistance to set bounds, when necessary, to the vagaries of the imagination.

But the understanding begins its aberrations very innocently and modestly. It first discerns the elementary cognitions which inhere in it prior to all experience, but yet must always have their application in experience. It gradually drops these limits; and what is there to prevent it, inasmuch as it has quite freely derived its principles from itself? And then it proceeds first to newly thought out forces in nature, then to beings outside nature—in short, to a world for whose construction the materials cannot be wanting, because fertile fiction furnishes them abundantly, and though not confirmed is yet never refuted by experience. This is the reason why young thinkers are so partial to metaphysics in the truly dogmatical manner, and often sacrifice to it their time and their talents, which might be otherwise better employed.

But there is no use in trying to moderate these fruitless endeavors of pure reason by all manner of cautions as to the difficulties of solving questions so occult, by complaints of the limits of our reason, and by degrading our assertions into mere conjectures. For if their impossibility is not distinctly shown, and reason's knowledge of itself does not become a true science, in which the field of its right use is distinguished, so to say, with geometrical certainty from that of its worthless and idle use, these fruitless efforts will never be entirely abandoned.

§ 36. *How is nature itself possible?* This question— 318 the highest point that transcendental philosophy can ever reach, and to which, as its boundary and completion, it must proceed—properly contains two questions.

First: How is nature possible in general in the *material* sense, i.e., according to intuition, as the totality of appearances; how are space, time, and that which fills both—the object of sensation—possible in general? The answer is: by means of the constitution of our sensibility, according to which it is in its special way affected by objects which are in themselves unknown to it and totally distinct from those appearances. This answer is given in the *Critique* itself in the Transcendental Aesthetic, and in these *Prolegomena* by the solution of the first main question.

Secondly: How is nature possible in the *formal* sense, as the totality of the rules under which all appearances must come in order to be thought as connected in an experience? The answer must be

23. We speak of the "intelligible world," not (as the usual expression is) "intellectual world." For cognitions are intellectual through the understanding and refer to our world of sense also, but objects, insofar as they can be represented merely by the understanding, and to which none of our sensible intuitions can refer, are termed "intelligible." But as some possible intuition must correspond to every object, we would have to think an understanding that intuits things immediately; but of such we have not the least concept, nor of beings of the understanding to which it should be applied.

this: it is only possible by means of the constitution of our understanding, according to which all those representations of sensibility are necessarily referred to a consciousness, and by which the peculiar way in which we think (viz., by rules) and hence experience also are possible, but must be clearly distinguished from an insight into the objects in themselves. This answer is given in the *Critique* itself in the Transcendental Logic, and in these *Prolegomena* in the course of the solution of the second main question.

But how this peculiar property of our sensibility itself is possible, or that of our understanding and of the apperception which is necessarily its basis and also that of all thinking, cannot be further analyzed or answered, because it is of them that we are in need for all our answers and for all our thinking about objects.

There are many laws of nature which we can only know by means of experience; but conformity to law 319 in the connection of appearances, i.e., nature in general, we cannot discover by any experience, because experience itself requires laws which are *a priori* at the basis of its possibility.

The possibility of experience in general is therefore at the same time the universal law of nature, and the principles of experience are the very laws of nature. For we know nature as nothing but the totality of appearances, i.e., of representations in us; and hence we can only derive the law of their connection from the principles of their connection in us, that is, from the conditions of their necessary unification in a consciousness, which constitutes the possibility of experience.

Even the main proposition expounded throughout this section—that universal laws of nature can be cognized *a priori*—leads of itself to the proposition that the highest legislation of nature must lie in ourselves, i.e., in our understanding; and that we must not seek the universal laws of nature in nature by means of experience, but conversely must seek nature, as to its universal conformity to law, in the conditions of the possibility of experience, which lie in our sensibility and in our understanding. For how would it otherwise be possible to know *a priori* these laws, as they are not rules of analytic cognition but truly synthetic extensions of it? Such a necessary agreement of the principles of possible experience with the laws of the possibility of nature can only proceed from one of two reasons: either these laws are drawn from nature by means of experience, or conversely nature is derived from the laws of the possibility of experience in general and is quite the same as the mere universal conformity to law of the latter. The former is self-contradictory, for the universal laws of nature can and must be cognized *a priori* (that is, independent of all experience) and be the foundation of all empirical use of the understanding; the latter alternative therefore alone remains.[24]

But we must distinguish the empirical laws of nature, which always presuppose particular percep- 320 tions, from the pure or universal laws of nature, which, without being based on particular perceptions, contain merely the conditions of their necessary unification in experience. With regard to the latter, nature and possible experience are quite the same, and as the conformity to law in the latter depends upon the necessary connection of appearances in experience (without which we cannot cognize any object whatever in the sensible world), consequently upon the original laws of the under-standing, it seems at first strange, but is not the less certain, to say: *the understanding does not derive its laws (a priori) from, but prescribes them to, nature.*

§ 37. We shall illustrate this seemingly bold proposition by an example, which will show that laws which we discover in objects of sensuous intuition (especially when these laws are cognized as necessary) are already held by us to be such as have been placed there by the understanding, in spite of their being similar in all points to the laws of nature which we ascribe to experience.

§ 38. If we consider the properties of the circle, by which this figure at once combines into a universal rule so many arbitrary determinations of the space in it, we cannot avoid attributing a nature to this geometrical thing. Two lines, for example, which intersect each other and the circle, however they may be drawn, are always divided so that the rectangle con-

24. Crusius alone thought of a compromise: that a spirit who can neither err nor deceive implanted these laws in us originally. But since false principles often intrude themselves, as indeed the very system of this man shows in not a few examples, we are involved in difficulties as to the use of such a principle in the absence of sure criteria to distinguish the genuine origin from the spurious, for we never can know certainly what the spirit of truth or the father of lies may have instilled into us.

structed with the segments of the one is equal to that constructed with the segments of the other. The question now is: Does this law lie in the circle or in the understanding? That is, does this figure, independently of the understanding, contain in itself the ground of the law; or does the understanding, having 321 constructed according to its concepts (of the equality of the radii) the figure itself, introduce into it this law of the chords intersecting in geometrical proportion? When we follow the proofs of this law, we soon perceive that it can only be derived from the condition on which the understanding founds the construction of this figure, viz., the equality of the radii. But if we enlarge this concept to pursue further the unity of manifold properties of geometrical figures under common laws and consider the circle as a conic section, which of course is subject to the same fundamental conditions of construction as other conic sections, we shall find that all the chords which intersect within the circle, ellipse, parabola, and hyperbola always intersect so that the rectangles of their segments are not indeed equal but always bear a constant ratio to one another. If we proceed still further to the fundamental doctrines of physical astronomy, we find a physical law of reciprocal attraction extending over the whole material nature, the rule of which is that it decreases inversely as the square of the distance from each attracting point, just as the spherical surfaces through which this force diffuses itself increase; and this law seems to be necessarily inherent in the very nature of things, so that it is usually propounded as cognizable *a priori*. Simple as the sources of this law are, merely resting upon the relation of spherical surfaces of different radii, its consequence is so excellent with regard to the variety and regularity of its agreement that not only are all possible orbits of the celestial bodies conic sections, but such a relation of these orbits to each other results that no other law of attraction than that of the inverse square of the distance can be thought as fit for a cosmical system.

Here, accordingly, is nature resting on laws which the understanding cognizes *a priori*, and chiefly from universal principles of the determination of space. Now I ask: do the laws of nature lie in space, and does the understanding learn them by merely endeavoring to find out the enormous wealth of meaning that lies in space; or do they inhere in the understanding and in the way in which it determines space according to the conditions of the synthetic unity in which its concepts are all centered? Space is something so uniform and as to all particular properties so indeterminate that we should certainly not seek a store of laws of nature in it. Whereas that which determines space 322 to assume the form of a circle, or the figures of a cone and a sphere is the understanding, so far as it contains the ground of the unity of their constructions. The mere universal form of intuition, called space, must therefore be the substratum of all intuitions determinable to particular objects; and in it, of course, the condition of the possibility and of the variety of these intuitions lies. But the unity of the objects is entirely determined by the understanding, and according to conditions which lie in its own nature; and thus the understanding is the origin of the universal order of nature, in that it comprehends all appearances under its own laws and thereby brings about, in an *a priori* way, experience (as to its form), by means of which whatever is to be cognized only by experience is necessarily subjected to its laws. For we are not concerned with the nature of things in themselves, which is independent of the conditions both of our sensibility and our understanding, but with nature as an object of possible experience; and in this case the understanding, because it makes experience possible, thereby insists that the sensuous world is either not an object of experience at all, or else is nature.

Appendix to Pure Natural Science

§ 39. *Of the system of the categories.* There can be nothing more desirable to a philosopher than to be able to derive the scattered multiplicity of the concepts or the principles which had occurred to him in concrete use from a principle *a priori*, and to unite everything in this way in one cognition. He formerly only believed that those things which remained after a certain abstraction, and seemed by comparison among one another to constitute a particular kind of cognitions, were completely collected; but this was only an *aggregate*. Now he knows that just so many, neither more nor less, can constitute this kind of cognition, and perceives the necessity of his division; this constitutes comprehension. And only now has he attained a *system*.

To search in our ordinary knowledge for the concepts which do not rest upon particular experience and yet occur in all knowledge from experience, 323 of which they constitute as it were the mere form of connection, presupposes neither greater reflection nor deeper insight than to detect in a language the rules of the actual use of words generally and thus to collect elements for a grammar (in fact both inquiries are very closely related), even though we are not able to give a reason why each language has just this and no other formal constitution, and still less why exactly so many, neither more nor less, of such formal determinations in general can be found in it.

Aristotle collected ten pure elementary concepts under the name of categories.[25] To these, which were also called predicaments, he found himself obliged afterward to add five post predicaments,[26] some of which however (*prius*, *simul*, and *motus*) are contained in the former; but this rhapsody must be considered (and commended) as a mere hint for future inquiries, not as a regularly worked out idea, and hence it has, in the present more advanced state of philosophy, been rejected as quite useless.

After long reflection on the pure elements of human knowledge (those which contain nothing empirical), I at last succeeded in distinguishing with certainty and in separating the pure elementary concepts of sensibility (space and time) from those of the understanding. Thus the 7th, 8th, and 9th categories had to be excluded from the old list. And the others were of no service to me because there was no principle on which the understanding could be fully mapped out and all the functions, whence its pure concepts arise, determined exhaustively and with precision.

But in order to discover such a principle, I looked about for an act of the understanding which comprises all the rest and is differentiated only by various modifications or moments, in bringing the manifold of representation under the unity of thinking in general. I found this act of the understanding to consist in judging. Here, then, the labors of the logicians were ready at hand, though not yet quite free from defects; and with this help I was enabled to exhibit a complete table of the pure functions of the understanding, 324 which were however undetermined in regard to any object. I finally referred these functions of judging to objects in general, or rather to the condition of determining judgments as objectively valid; and so there arose the pure concepts of the understanding, concerning which I could make certain that these, and this exact number only, constitute our whole cognition of things from pure understanding. I was justified in calling them by their old name of *categories*, while I reserved for myself the liberty of adding, under the title of *predicables*, a complete list of all the concepts deducible from them by combinations, whether among themselves, or with the pure form of the appearance, i.e., space or time, or with its matter, so far as it is not yet empirically determined (viz., the object of sensation in general), as soon as a system of transcendental philosophy should be completed, with the construction of which I was engaged in the *Critique of Pure Reason* itself.

Now the essential point in this system of categories, which distinguishes it from the old rhapsody (which proceeded without any principle) and for which point alone this system deserves to be considered as philosophy, consists in this: that, by means of it, the true meaning of the pure concepts of the understanding and the condition of their use could be exactly determined. For here it became obvious that they are themselves nothing but logical functions, and as such do not constitute the least concept of an object in itself, but require some sensuous intuitions as a basis. These concepts, therefore, only serve to determine empirical judgments (which are otherwise undetermined and indifferent with respect to all functions of judging) as regards these functions, thereby procuring them universal validity, and by means of them, making judgments of experience in general possible.

Such an insight into the nature of the categories, which limits them at the same time to use merely in experience, never occurred either to their first author, or to any of his successors; but without this insight (which exactly depends upon their derivation or deduction), they are quite useless and only a miserable list of names, without explanation or rule for their use. Had the ancients ever conceived such a notion, doubtless the whole study of pure rational knowledge, 325 which under the name of metaphysics has for centuries spoiled many a sound mind, would have reached us in quite another shape and would have enlightened the human understanding instead of actually exhausting it in obscure and vain subtleties and rendering it useless for true science.

25. 1. *Substantia*. 2. *Qualitas*. 3. *Quantitas*. 4. *Relatio*. 5. *Actio*. 6. *Passio*. 7. *Quando*. 8. *Ubi*. 9. *Situs*. 10. *Habitus*.

26. *Oppositum, Prius, Simul, Motus, Habere*.

This system of categories makes all treatment of every object of pure reason itself systematic, and affords a direction or clue how and through what points of inquiry any metaphysical consideration must proceed in order to be complete; for it exhausts all the moments of the understanding, under which every other concept must be brought. In like manner the table of principles has been formulated, the completeness of which we can only vouch for by the system of the categories. Even in the division of the concepts which are to go beyond the physiological application of the understanding,[27] it is still the same clue, which, as it must always be determined *a priori* by the same fixed points of the human understanding, always forms a closed circle. There is no doubt that the object of a pure concept, either of the understanding or of reason, so far as it is to be estimated philosophically and on *a priori* principles, can in this way be completely cognized. I could not therefore omit to make use of this clue with regard to one of the most abstract ontological divisions, viz., the various distinctions of the concepts of something and of nothing, and to construct accordingly[28] a regular and necessary table of their divisions.[29]

27. [Cf. *Critique of Pure Reason*, B 402 and B 442–443.]
28. [Cf. *ibid.* B 348.]
29. On the table of the categories many neat observations may be made, for instance: (1) that the third arises from the first and the second, joined in one concept; (2) that in those of quantity and of quality there is merely a progress from unity to totality or from something to nothing (for this purpose the categories of quality must stand thus: reality, limitation, total negation), without *correlata* or *opposita*, whereas those of relation and of modality have them; (3) that, as in logic categorical judgments are the basis of all others, so the category of substance is the basis of all concepts of actual things; (4) that, as modality in a judgment is not a distinct predicate, so by the modal concepts a determination is not superadded to things, etc. Such observations are of great use. If we, besides, enumerate all the predicables, which we can find pretty completely in any good ontology (for example, Baumgarten's), and arrange them in classes under the categories, in which operation we must not neglect to add as complete a dissection of all these concepts as possible, there will then arise a merely analytic part of metaphysics, which does not contain a single synthetic proposition and might precede the second (the synthetic), and would, by its precision and completeness, be not only useful, but, in virtue of its system, be even to some extent elegant.

And this system, like every other true one founded on a universal principle, shows its inestimable use- 326 fulness in that it excludes all foreign concepts which might otherwise intrude among the pure concepts of the understanding, and determines the place of every cognition. Those concepts, which under the name of *concepts of reflection* have been likewise arranged in a table according to the clue of the categories, intrude into ontology without having any privilege or legitimate claim to be among the pure concepts of the understanding. The latter are concepts of connection, and thereby of the objects themselves, whereas the former are only concepts of a mere comparison of concepts already given, and therefore are of quite another nature and use. By my systematic division[30] they are saved from this confusion. But the utility of this separate table of the categories will be still more obvious when, as will soon happen, we separate the table of the transcendental concepts of reason from the concepts of the understanding. The concepts of reason being of quite another nature and origin, their table must have quite another form from that of the concepts of understanding. This so necessary separation has never yet been made in any system of metaphysics, where as a rule, these ideas of reason are all mixed up with the concepts of the understanding, like children belonging to one family—a confusion that was unavoidable in the absence of a definite system of categories.

THIRD PART OF THE MAIN TRANSCENDENTAL QUESTION

327

How Is Metaphysics in General Possible?

§ 40. Pure mathematics and pure natural science had no need for such a deduction (as has been made for both) for the sake of their own safety and certainty. For the former rests upon its own evidence, and the latter (though sprung from pure sources of the understanding) upon experience and its thorough confirmation. Pure natural science cannot altogether refuse and dispense with the testimony of experience; hence with all its certainty it can never, as philosophy, rival mathematics. Both sciences therefore stood in need of this inquiry, not for themselves, but for the sake of another science, namely, metaphysics.

Metaphysics has to do not only with concepts of nature, which always find their application in expe-

30. [See *Critique of Pure Reason*, B 316.]

rience, but also with pure rational concepts, which never can be given in any possible experience whatsoever. Consequently, the objective reality of these concepts (viz., that they are not mere chimeras) and also the truth or falsity of metaphysical assertions cannot be discovered or confirmed by any experience. This part of metaphysics, however, is precisely what constitutes its essential end, to which the rest is only a means, and thus this science is in need of such a deduction for its own sake. The third question now proposed relates therefore, as it were, to the root and peculiarity of metaphysics, i.e., the occupation of reason merely with itself and the supposed knowledge of objects arising immediately from this brooding over its own concepts, without requiring experience or indeed being able to reach that knowledge through experience.[31]

Without solving this question, reason will never be satisfied. The empirical use to which reason limits the pure understanding does not fully satisfy reason's own 328 proper destination. Every single experience is only a part of the whole sphere of its domain, but the absolute totality of all possible experience is itself not experience. Yet it is a necessary problem for reason, the mere representation of which requires concepts quite different from other pure concepts of the understanding, whose use is only immanent, i.e., refers to experience so far as it can be given. Whereas the concepts of reason aim at the completeness, i.e., the collective unity of all possible experience, and thereby go beyond every given experience. Thus they become *transcendent*.

As the understanding stands in need of categories for experience, reason contains in itself the ground of ideas, by which I mean necessary concepts whose object *cannot* be given in any experience. The latter are inherent in the nature of reason, as the former are in that of the understanding. While the ideas carry with them an illusion likely to mislead, this illusion is unavoidable though it certainly can be kept from misleading us.

31. If we can say that a science is actual, at least in the idea of all men, as soon as it appears that the problems which lead to it are proposed to everybody by the nature of human reason, and hence that at all times many (though faulty) endeavors are unavoidably made in its behalf; then we are bound to say that metaphysics is subjectively (and indeed necessarily) actual, and then we justly ask how is it (objectively) possible.

Since all illusion consists in holding the subjective ground of our judgments to be objective, a self-knowledge of pure reason in its transcendent (hyperbolical) use is the only safeguard against the aberrations into which reason falls when it mistakes its destination, and transcendently refers to the object in itself that which only concerns reason's own subject and its guidance in all immanent use.

§ 41. The distinction of *ideas*, i.e., of pure concepts of reason, from the categories, or pure concepts of the understanding, as cognitions of a quite different species, origin, and use is so important a point in founding a science which is to contain the system of 329 all these *a priori* cognitions that, without this distinction, metaphysics is absolutely impossible or is at best a random, bungling attempt to build a castle in the air without a knowledge of the materials or of their fitness for one purpose or another. Had the *Critique of Pure Reason* done nothing but first point out this distinction, it would thereby have contributed more to clear up our conception of, and to guide our inquiry in, the field of metaphysics than all the vain efforts which have hitherto been made to satisfy the transcendent problems of pure reason; for one never even suspected that he was in quite another field from that of the understanding, and hence that he was classing concepts of the understanding and those of reason together, as if they were of the same kind.

§ 42. All pure cognitions of the understanding have the feature that the concepts can be given in experience, and the principles can be confirmed by it; whereas the transcendent cognitions of reason cannot either, as ideas, be given in experience or, as propositions, ever be confirmed or refuted by it. Hence whatever errors may slip in unawares can only be discovered by pure reason itself—a discovery of much difficulty, because this very reason naturally becomes dialectical by means of its ideas; and this unavoidable illusion cannot be limited by any objective and dogmatic inquiries into things, but only by a subjective investigation of reason itself as a source of ideas.

§ 43. In the *Critique of Pure Reason* it was always my greatest care to endeavor, not only carefully to distinguish the several kinds of cognition, but to derive concepts belonging to each one of them from their common source. I did this in order that by knowing whence they originated, I might determine their use with safety and also have the invaluable, but never previously anticipated, advantage of knowing the 330 completeness of my enumeration, classification, and specification of concepts *a priori*, and of knowing it according to principles. Without this, metaphysics is mere rhapsody, in which no one knows whether he has enough or whether and where something is still wanting. We can indeed have this advantage only in pure philosophy, but of this philosophy it constitutes the very essence.

As I had found the origin of the categories in the four logical functions of all judgments of the understanding, it was quite natural to seek the origin of the ideas in the three functions of syllogisms. For as soon as these pure concepts of reason (the transcendental ideas) are given, they could hardly, except they be held innate, be found anywhere else than in the same activity of reason, which, so far as it regards mere form, constitutes the logical element of syllogisms; but, so far as it represents judgments of the understanding as determined with respect to one or anther form *a priori*, constitutes transcendental concepts of pure reason.

The formal difference of syllogisms makes their division into categorical, hypothetical, and disjunctive necessary. The concepts of reason founded on them contain therefore, first, the idea of the complete subject (the substantial); secondly, the idea of the complete series of conditions; thirdly, the determination of all concepts in the idea of a complete complex of that which is possible.[32] The first idea is psychological, the second cosmological, the third theological; and, as all three give occasion to dialectic, yet each in its own way, the division of the whole dialectic of pure reason into its paralogism, its antimony, and its ideal was arranged accordingly. Through this derivation we may feel assured that all the claims of pure reason are completely represented and that none can be wanting, because the faculty of reason itself, whence they all take their origin, is thereby completely surveyed.

§ 44. In these general considerations it is also remarkable that the ideas of reason, unlike the cate- 331 gories, are of no service to the use of our understanding in experience, but quite dispensable, and become even an impediment to the maxims of a rational cognition of nature. Yet in another aspect still to be determined they are necessary. Whether the soul is or is not a simple substance is of no consequence to us in the explanation of its phenomena. For we cannot render the concept of a simple being understandable sensuously and concretely by any possible experience. The concept is therefore quite void as regards all hoped-for insight into the cause of appearances and cannot at all serve as a principle of the explanation of that which internal or external experience supplies. Likewise the cosmological ideas of the beginning of the world or of its eternity (*a parte ante*) cannot be of any service to us for the explanation of any event in the world itself. And finally we must, according to a right maxim of the philosophy of nature, refrain from all explanation of the design of nature as being drawn from the will of a Supreme Being, because this would not be natural philosophy but an admission that we have come to the end of it. The use of these ideas, therefore, is quite different from that of those categories by which (and by the principles built upon which) experience itself first becomes possible. But our laborious analytic of the understanding would be superfluous if we had nothing else in view than the mere cognition of nature as it can be given in experience; for reason does its work, both in mathematics and in natural science, quite safely and well without any of this subtle deduction. Therefore our critique of the understanding combines with the ideas of pure reason for a purpose which lies beyond the empirical use of the understanding; but we have above declared the use of the understanding in this respect to be totally inadmissible and without any object or meaning. Yet there must be a harmony between the nature of reason and that of the understanding, and the former must contribute to the perfection of the latter and cannot possibly upset it.

The solution of this question is as follows. Pure rea- 332 son does not in its ideas point to particular objects

32. In disjunctive judgments we consider all possibility as divided in respect to a particular concept. By the ontological principle of the thoroughgoing determination of a thing in general, I understand the principle that either the one or the other of all possible contradictory predicates must be assigned to any object. This is at the same time the principle of all disjunctive judgments, constituting the foundation of the totality of all possibility, and in it the possibility of every object in general is considered as determined. This may serve as a brief explanation of the above proposition: that the activity of reason in disjunctive syllogisms is formally the same as that by which it fashions the idea of a totality of all reality, containing in itself the positive member of all contradictory predicates.

which lie beyond the field of experience, but only requires completeness of the use of the understanding in the complex of experience. But this completeness can be a completeness of principles only, not of intuitions and of objects. In order, however, to represent the ideas definitely, reason conceives them after the fashion of the cognition of an object. This cognition is, as far as these rules are concerned, completely determined; but the object is only an idea invented for the purpose of bringing the cognition of the understanding as near as possible to the completeness indicated by that idea.

Prefatory Remark to the Dialectic of Pure Reason

§ 45. We have above shown in §§ 33 and 34 that the purity of the categories from all admixture of sensuous determinations may mislead reason into extending their use beyond all experience to things in themselves; for though these categories themselves find no intuition which can give them meaning or sense *in concreto*, they, as mere logical functions, can represent a thing in general, but not give by themselves alone a determinate concept of anything. Such hyperbolical objects are distinguished by the appellation of *noumena*, or pure beings of the understanding (or better, beings of thought)—such as, for example, "substance," but conceived without permanence in time; or "cause," but not acting in time, etc. Here predicates that only serve to make the conformity-to-law of experience possible are applied to these concepts, and yet they are deprived of all the conditions of intuition on which alone experience is possible, and so these concepts lose all significance.

There is no danger, however, of the understanding spontaneously making an excursion so very wantonly beyond its own bounds into the field of the mere beings of thought, unless being impelled by alien laws. But when reason, which cannot be fully satisfied with any empirical use of the rules of the understanding, as being always conditioned, requires a completion of this chain of conditions, then the understanding is forced out of its sphere. And then reason partly represents objects of experience in a series so extended that 333 no experience can grasp it, partly even (with a view to complete the series) it seeks entirely beyond experience *noumena*, to which it can attach that chain; and so, having at last escaped from the conditions of experience, reason makes its hold complete. These are then the transcendental ideas, which, (though in accord with the true but hidden ends of the natural determination of our reason) may aim, not at extravagant concepts, but at an unbounded extension of their empirical use, yet seduce the understanding by an unavoidable illusion to a transcendent use, which, though deceitful, cannot be restrained within the bounds of experience by any resolution, but only by scientific instruction and with much difficulty.

I. The Psychological Ideas[33]

§ 46. People have long since observed that in all substances the subject proper, that which remains after all the accidents (as predicates) are abstracted, hence the substantial itself, remains unknown, and various complaints have been made concerning these limits to our insight. But it will be well to consider that the human understanding is not to be blamed for its inability to know the substance of things, i.e., to determine it by itself, but rather for demanding to cognize it determinately as though it were a given object, it being a mere idea. Pure reason requires us to seek for every predicate of a thing its own subject, and for this subject, which is itself necessarily nothing but a predicate, its subject, and so on indefinitely (or as far as we can reach). But hence it follows that we must not hold anything at which we can arrive to be an ultimate subject, and that substance itself never can be thought by our understanding, however deep we may penetrate, even if all nature were unveiled to us. For the specific nature of our understanding consists in thinking everything discursively, i.e., by concepts, and so by mere predicates, to which, therefore, the absolute subject must always be wanting. Hence all the real properties by which we cognize bodies are mere accidents, not even excepting impenetrability, which we can only represent to ourselves as the effect 334 of a force for which the subject is unknown to us.

Now we appear to have this substance in the consciousness of ourselves (in the thinking subject), and indeed in an immediate intuition; for all the predicates of an internal sense refer to the *ego*, as a subject, and I cannot conceive myself as the predicate of any

33. [See *Critique of Pure Reason*, "The Paralogisms of Pure Reason," A 341/B 399–A 405/B 432.]

other subject. Hence completeness in the reference of the given concepts as predicates to a subject—not merely an idea, but an object—that is, the *absolute subject* itself, seems to be given in experience. But this expectation is disappointed. For the ego is not a concept,[34] but only the indication of the object of the internal sense, so far as we cognize it by no further predicate. Consequently, it cannot be itself a predicate of any other thing; but just as little can it be a determinate concept of an absolute subject, but is, as in all other cases, only the reference of the internal phenomena to their unknown subject. Yet this idea (which serves very well as a regulative principle totally to destroy all materialistic explanations of the internal phenomena of the soul) occasions by a very natural misunderstanding a very specious argument, which infers the nature of the soul from this supposed cognition of the substance of our thinking being. This argument is specious insofar as the knowledge of this substance falls quite without the complex of experience.

§ 47. But though we may call this thinking self (the soul) substance, as being the ultimate subject of thinking which cannot be further represented as the predicate of another thing, it remains quite empty and inconsequential if permanence—the quality which renders the concept of substances in experience fruitful—cannot be proved of it.

But permanence can never be proved of the concept 335 of a substance as a thing in itself, but only for the purposes of experience. This is sufficiently shown by the first Analogy of Experience,[35] and whoever will not yield to this proof may try for himself whether he can succeed in proving, from the concept of a subject which does not exist itself as the predicate of another thing, that its existence is thoroughly permanent and that it cannot either in itself or by any natural cause come into being or pass out of it. These synthetic *a priori* propositions can never be proved in themselves, but only in reference to things as objects of possible experience.

§ 48. If, therefore, from the concept of the soul as a substance we would infer its permanence, this can hold good as regards possible experience only, not of the soul as a thing in itself and beyond all possible experience. Now life is the subjective condition of all our possible experience; consequently we can only infer the permanence of the soul in life, for the death of man is the end of all the experience that concerns the soul as an object of experience, except the contrary be proved—which is the very question in hand. The permanence of the soul can therefore only be proved (and no one cares for that) during the life of man, but not, as we desire to do, after death. This is so because the concept of substance, insofar as it is to be considered as necessarily combined with the concept of permanence, can be so combined only according to the principles of possible experience, and therefore for the purposes of experience only.[36]

§ 49. That there is something real outside us which 336 not only corresponds but must correspond to our

34. Were the representation of the apperception (the ego) a concept by which anything could be thought, it could be used as a predicate of other things or contain predicates in itself. But it is nothing more than the feeling of an existence without the slightest concept and is only the representation of that to which all thinking stands in relation (*relatione accidentis*).

35. [Cf. *Critique*, B 224–232.]

36. It is indeed very remarkable how carelessly metaphysicians have always passed over the principle of the permanence of substances without ever attempting a proof of it; doubtless because they found themselves abandoned by all proofs as soon as they began to deal with the concept of substance. Common sense, which felt distinctly that without this presupposition no union of perceptions in experience is possible, supplied the want by a postulate. From experience itself it never could derive such a principle, partly because material objects (substances) cannot be so traced in all their alterations and dissolutions that the matter can always be found undiminished, partly because the principle contains *necessity*, which is always the sign of an *a priori* principle. People then boldly applied this postulate to the concept of soul as a *substance*, and concluded a necessary continuance of the soul after the death of man (especially as the simplicity of this substance, which is inferred from the indivisibility of consciousness, secured it from destruction by dissolution). Had they found the genuine source of this principle—a discovery which requires deeper researches than they were ever inclined to make—they would have seen that the law of the permanence of substances finds a place for the purposes of experience only, and hence can hold good of things so far as they are to be cognized and conjoined with others in experience, but never independently of all possible experience, and consequently cannot hold good of the soul after death.

external perceptions can likewise be proved to be, not a connection of things in themselves, but for the sake of experience. This means that there is something empirical, i.e., some appearance in space outside us, that admits of a satisfactory proof; for we have nothing to do with other objects than those which belong to possible experience, because objects which cannot be given us in any experience are nothing for us. Empirically outside me is that which is intuited in space; and space, together with all the appearances which it contains, belongs to the representations whose connection, according to laws of experience, proves their objective truth, just as the connection of the appearances of the internal sense proves the actuality of my soul (as an object of the internal sense). By means of external experience I am conscious of the actuality of bodies as external appearances in space, in the same manner as by means of internal experience I am conscious of the existence of my soul in time; but this soul is cognized only as an object of the internal sense by appearances that constitute an internal state and of which the being in itself, which forms the basis of these appearances, is unknown. Cartesian idealism therefore does nothing but distinguish external experience from dreaming and the conformity to law (as a criterion of its truth) of the former from the irregularity and the false illusion of the latter. In both it presupposes space and time as conditions of the existence of objects, and it only inquires whether the objects of the external senses which we, when awake, put in space, are as actually to be found in it as the object of the internal sense, the soul, is in time; that is, whether experience carries with it sure criteria to distinguish it from imagination. This doubt, however, may easily be disposed of, and we always do so in common life by investigating the connection of appearances in both space and time according to universal laws of experience; and we cannot doubt, when the representation of external things throughout agrees therewith, that they constitute truthful experience. Material idealism, in which appearances are considered as such only according to their connection in experience may accordingly be very easily refuted; and it is just as sure an experience that bodies exist outside us (in space) as that I myself exist according to the representation of the internal sense (in time), for the concept "outside us" only signifies existence in space. However, as the ego in the proposition "I am" means not only the object of internal intuition (in time) but the subject of consciousness, just as body means not only external intuition (in space) but the thing in itself which is the basis of this appearance, then the question whether bodies (as appearances of the external sense) exist as bodies in nature apart from my thoughts may without any hesitation be denied. But the question whether I myself as an appearance of the internal sense (the soul according to empirical psychology) exist apart from my faculty of representation in time is an exactly similar question and must likewise be answered in the negative. And in this manner everything, when it is reduced to its true meaning, is decided and certain. The formal (which I have also called transcendental) actually abolishes the material, or Cartesian, idealism. For if space be nothing but a form of my sensibility, it is as a representation in me just as actual as I myself am, and nothing but the empirical truth of the appearances in it remains for consideration. But if this is not the case, if space and the appearances in it are something existing outside us, then all the criteria of experience outside our perception can never prove the actuality of these objects outside us.

II. The Cosmological Ideas[37]

§ 50. This product of pure reason in its transcendent use is its most remarkable phenomenon. It serves as a very powerful agent to rouse philosophy from its dogmatic slumber and to stimulate it to the arduous task of undertaking a criticism of reason itself.

I term this idea cosmological because it always takes its object only from the sensible world and does not need any other world than that whose object is given to sense; consequently, it remains in this respect in its native home, does not become transcendent, and is therefore so far not an idea; whereas to conceive the soul as a simple substance, on the contrary, means to conceive such an object (the simple) as cannot be presented to the senses. Notwithstanding, the cosmological idea extends the connection of the conditioned with its condition (whether mathematical or dynamical) so far that experience never can keep up with it. It is therefore with regard to this point always an idea, whose object never can be adequately given in any experience.

37. [Cf. *Critique*, "The Antinomy of Pure Reason," B 432–595.]

§ 51. In the first place, the use of a system of categories becomes here so obvious and unmistakable that, even if there were not several other proofs of it, this alone would sufficiently prove it indispensable in the system of pure reason. There are only four such transcendent ideas, as many as there are classes of categories; in each of which, however, they refer only to the absolute completeness of the series of the conditions for a given condition. In conformity with these cosmological ideas, there are only four kinds of dialectical assertions of pure reason, which, being dialectical, prove that to each of them, on equally specious principles of pure reason, a contradictory assertion stands 339 opposed. As all the metaphysical art of the most subtle distinction cannot prevent this opposition, it compels the philosopher to recur to the first sources of pure reason itself. This antinomy, not arbitrarily invented but founded in the nature of human reason, and hence unavoidable and never ceasing, contains the following four theses together with their antitheses:

1

Thesis

The world has, as to time and space,
a beginning (limit).

Antithesis

The world is, as to time and space, infinite.

2

Thesis

Everything in the world is constituted
out of the simple.

Antithesis

There is nothing simple,
but everything is composite.

3

Thesis

There are in the world causes through freedom.

Antithesis

There is no freedom, but all is nature.

4

Thesis

In the series of world-causes there is
some necessary being.

Antithesis

There is nothing necessary in the world,
but in this series all is contingent.

§ 52a. Here is the most singular phenomenon of human reason, no other instance of which can be shown in its any other use. If we, as is commonly done, represent to ourselves the appearance of the sensible world as things in themselves, if we assume the principles of their combination as principles universally valid of things in themselves and not merely of experience, as is usually, nay, without our *Critique*, unavoidably done, there arises an unexpected conflict which never can be removed in the common dogmatic way; because the thesis, as well as the antithesis, can be shown by equally clear, evident, and irresistible proofs—for I pledge myself as to the correctness of all these proofs—and reason therefore perceives that it is divided against itself, a state at which the skeptic rejoices, but which must make the critical philosopher pause and feel ill at ease.

§ 52b. We may blunder in various ways in metaphysics without any fear of being detected in false- 340 hood. For we never can be refuted by experience if we but avoid self-contradiction, which in synthetic though purely fictitious propositions may be done whenever the concepts which we connect are mere ideas that cannot be given (as regards their whole content) in experience. For how can we make out by experience whether the world is from eternity or had a beginning, whether matter is infinitely divisible or consists of simple parts? Such concepts cannot be given in any experience, however extensive, and consequently the falsehood either of the affirmative or the negative proposition cannot be discovered by this touchstone.

The only possible way in which reason could have revealed unintentionally its secret dialectic, falsely announced as dogmatics, would be when it were made to ground an assertion upon a universally admitted principle and to deduce the exact contrary with the greatest accuracy of inference from another which is equally granted. This is actually here the case with regard to four natural ideas of reason, whence four assertions on the one side and as many counter-assertions on the other arise, each consistently following from universally acknowledged principles. Thus they reveal, by the use of these principles, the dialectical illusion of pure reason, which would otherwise forever remain concealed.

This is therefore a decisive experiment, which must necessarily expose any error lying hidden in the 341 assumptions of reason.[38] Contradictory propositions cannot both be false, unless the concept lying at the ground of both of them is self-contradictory; for example, the propositions, "A square circle is round," and "A square circle is not round," are both false. For, as to the former, it is false that the circle is round because it is quadrangular; and it is likewise false that it is not round, i.e., angular, because it is a circle. For the logical criterion of the impossibility of a concept consists in this, that if we presuppose it, two contradictory propositions both become false; consequently, as no middle between them is conceivable, nothing at all is thought by that concept.

§ 52c. The first two antinomies, which I call mathematical because they are concerned with the addition or division of the homogeneous, are founded on such a contradictory concept; and hence I explain how it happens that both the thesis and antithesis of the two are false.

When I speak of objects in time and in space, it is not of things in themselves, of which I know nothing, but of things in appearance, i.e., of experience, as a particular way of cognizing objects which is only afforded to man. I must not say of that which I think in time or in space, that in itself, and independent of these my thoughts, it exists in space and in time, for in that case I would contradict myself, because space and time, together with the appearances in them, are nothing existing in themselves and outside of my rep- 342 resentations, but are themselves only modes of representation, and it is palpably contradictory to say that a mere mode of representation exists outside our representation. Objects of the senses therefore exist only in experience, whereas to give them a self-subsisting existence apart from experience or prior to it is merely to represent to ourselves that experience actually exists apart from experience or prior to it.

Now if I ask about the magnitude of the world, as to space and time, it is equally impossible, with regard to all my concepts, to declare it infinite or to declare it finite. For neither assertion can be contained in experience, because experience either of an infinite space or of an infinite time elapsed, or again, of the boundary of the world by an empty space or by an antecedent empty time, is impossible; these are mere ideas. This magnitude of the world, be it determined in either way, would therefore have to exist in the world itself apart from all experience. But this contradicts the concept of a world of sense, which is merely a complex of the appearances whose existence and connection occur only in our representations, i.e., in experience; since this latter is not an object in itself but a mere mode of representation. Hence it follows that, as the concept of an absolutely existing world of sense is self-contradictory, the solution of the problem concerning its magnitude, whether attempted affirmatively or negatively, is always false.

The same holds of the second antinomy, which relates to the division of appearances. For these are mere representations; and the parts exist merely in their representation, consequently in the division (i.e., in a possible experience where they are given) and the division reaches only as far as such experience reaches. To assume that an appearance, e.g., that of a body, contains in itself before all experience all the parts which any possible experience can ever reach is to impute to a mere appearance, which can exist only in experience, an existence previous to experience. In other words, it would mean that mere representations exist before they can be found in our faculty of representation. Such an assertion is self-contradictory, as also every solution of our misunderstood problem, whether we maintain that bodies in themselves consist of an infinite number of parts or of a finite number of simple parts.

§ 53. In the first (the mathematical) class of antin- 343 omies the falsehood of the presupposition consists in representing in one concept something self-contradictory as if it were compatible (i.e., an appearance as an object in itself). But as to the second (the dynamical) class of antinomies, the falsehood of the presupposition consists in representing as contradictory what is compatible. Consequently, whereas in the first case the opposed assertions were both false, in this case, on

38. I therefore would be pleased to have the critical reader to devote to this antinomy of pure reason his chief attention, because nature itself seems to have established it with a view to stagger reason in its daring pretentions and to force it to self-examination. For every proof which I have given both of the thesis and the antithesis, I pledge myself to be responsible, and thereby to show the certainty of the inevitable antinomy of reason. When the reader is brought by this curious phenomenon to fall back upon the proof of the presumption upon which it rests, he will feel himself obliged to investigate the ultimate foundation of all the cognition of pure reason with me more thoroughly.

the other hand, where they are opposed to one another by mere misunderstanding, they may both be true.

Any mathematical connection necessarily presupposes homogeneity of what is connected (in the concept of magnitude), while the dynamical one by no means requires this. When we have to deal with extended magnitudes, all the parts must be homogeneous with one another and with the whole. But in the connection of cause and effect homogeneity may indeed likewise be found but is not necessary, for the concept of causality (by means of which something is posited through something else quite different from it) does not in the least require it.

If the objects of the world of sense are taken for things in themselves and the above-mentioned laws of nature for the laws of things in themselves, the contradiction would be unavoidable. So also, if the subject of freedom were, like other objects, represented as mere appearance, the contradiction would be just as unavoidable; for the same predicate would at once be affirmed and denied of the same kind of object in the same sense. But if natural necessity is referred merely to appearances and freedom merely to things in themselves, no contradiction arises if we at the same time assume or admit both kinds of causality, however difficult or impossible it may be to make the latter kind conceivable.

In appearance every effect is an event, or something that happens in time; the effect must, according to the universal law of nature, be preceded by a determination of the causality of its cause (a state of the cause) on which the effect follows according to a constant law. But this determination of the cause to causal action must likewise be something that takes place or happens; the cause must have begun to act, otherwise no succession between it and the effect 344 could be thought. Otherwise the effect, as well as the causality of the cause, would have always existed. Therefore the determination of the cause to act must also have originated among appearances and must consequently, just like its effect, be an event, which must again have its cause, and so on; hence natural necessity must be the condition according to which efficient causes are determined. Whereas if freedom is to be a property of certain causes of appearances, it must, as regards the latter as events, be a faculty of starting them spontaneously, i.e., without the causality of the cause itself needing to begin and hence needing no other ground to determine its beginning. But then the cause, as to its causality, must not stand under time-determinations of its state, i.e., it cannot be an appearance, and must be considered a thing in itself, while only its effects would be appearances.[39] If without contradiction we can think of the beings of understanding as exercising such an influence on appearances, then natural necessity will attach to all connections of cause and effect in the sensuous world, though, on the other hand, freedom can be granted to the cause which is itself not an appearance (but the foundation of appearance). Nature and freedom therefore can without contradiction be attributed to the very same thing, but in different relations—on one side as an appearance, on the other as a thing in itself.

We have in us a faculty which not only stands in connection with its subjective determining grounds that are the natural causes of its actions and is so far 345 the faculty of a being that itself belongs to appearances, but is also related to objective grounds that are only ideas so far as they can determine this faculty; this connection is expressed by *ought*. This faculty is called *reason*, and, so far as we consider a being (man) entirely according to this objectively determinable reason, he cannot be considered as a being of sense; but, rather, this property is that of a thing in itself, and we cannot comprehend the possibility of this property—I mean how the *ought* (which might never yet

39. The idea of freedom occurs only in the relation of the intellectual, as cause, to the appearance, as effect. Hence we cannot attribute freedom to matter in regard to the incessant action by which it fills its space, though this action takes place from an internal principle. We can likewise find no concept of freedom suitable to purely rational beings, for instance, to God, so far as his action is immanent. For his action, though independent of external determining causes, is determined in his eternal reason, that is, in the divine *nature*. It is only, if *something is to start* by an action, and so the effect occurs in the sequence of time, or in the world of sense (e.g., the beginning of the world), that we can put the question whether the causality of the cause must in its turn have been started or whether the cause can originate an effect without its causality itself beginning. In the former case the concept of this causality is a concept of natural necessity; in the latter, that of freedom. From this the reader will see that as I explained freedom to be the faculty of starting an event spontaneously, I have exactly hit the concept which is the problem of metaphysics.

have taken place) should determine its activity and could become the cause of actions whose effect is an appearance in the sensible world. Yet the causality of reason would be freedom with regard to the effects in the sensuous world, so far as we can consider *objective grounds*, which are themselves ideas, as their determinants. For its action in that case would not depend upon subjective conditions, consequently not upon those of time, and of course not upon the law of nature which serves to determine them, because grounds of reason give the rule universally to actions, according to principles, without influence of the circumstances of either time or place.

What I adduce here is merely meant as an example to make the thing intelligible, and does not necessarily belong to our problem, which must be decided from mere concepts independently of the properties which we meet in the actual world.

Now I may say without contradiction that all the actions of rational beings, so far as they are appearances (encountered in some experience), are subject to the necessity of nature; but the same actions, as regards merely the rational subject and its faculty of acting according to mere reason, are free. For what is required for the necessity of nature? Nothing more than the determinability of every event in the world of sense according to constant laws, i.e., a reference to cause in the appearance; in this process the thing in itself as its foundation and its causality remain unknown. But, I say, the law of nature remains, whether the rational being is the cause of the effects in the sensuous world from reason, i.e., through freedom, or whether it does not determine 346 them on grounds of reason. For if the former is the case, the action is performed according to maxims, the effect of which as appearance is always conformable to constant laws; if the latter is the case, and the action not performed on principles of reason, it is subject to the empirical laws of sensibility, and in both cases the effects are connected according to constant laws; more than this we do not require or know concerning natural necessity. But in the former case reason is the cause of these laws of nature, and therefore free; in the latter, the effects follow according to mere natural laws of sensibility, because reason does not influence it; but reason itself is not determined on that account by the sensibility (which is impossible) and is therefore free in this case too. Freedom is therefore no hindrance to natural law in appearances; neither does this law abrogate the freedom of the practical use of reason, which is connected with things in themselves as determining grounds.

Thus practical freedom, viz., the freedom in which reason possesses causality according to objectively determining grounds, is rescued; and yet natural necessity is not in the least curtailed with regard to the very same effects, as appearances. The same remarks will serve to explain what we had to say concerning transcendental freedom and its compatibility with natural necessity (in the same subject, but not taken in one and the same reference). For, as to this, every beginning of the action of a being from objective causes regarded as determining grounds is always a first beginning, though the same action is in the series of appearances only a subordinate beginning, which must be preceded by a state of the cause which determines it and is itself determined in the same manner by another immediately preceding. Thus we are able, in rational beings, or in beings generally so far as their causality is determined in them as things in themselves, to think of a faculty of beginning of themselves a series of states without falling into contradiction with the laws of nature. For the relation of the action to objective grounds of reason is not a time-relation; in this case that which determines the causality does not precede in time the action, because such determining grounds represent, not a reference to objects of sense, e.g., to causes in the appearances, but to determining causes as things in themselves, which do not stand under conditions of time. And in this way the action, with regard to the causality of reason, can be considered as a first beginning, while in respect to the series of appearances as a merely 347 subordinate beginning. We may therefore without contradiction consider it in the former aspect as free, but in the latter (insofar as it is merely appearance) as subject to natural necessity.

As to the fourth antinomy, it is solved in the same way as the conflict of reason with itself in the third. For, provided the cause *in* the appearance is distinguished from the cause *of* the appearances (so far as it can be thought as a thing in itself), both propositions are perfectly reconcilable: the one, that there is nowhere in the sensuous world a cause (according to similar laws of causality) whose existence is absolutely necessary; the other, that this world is nevertheless connected with a necessary being as its cause (but of another kind and according to another law). The incompatibility of these two propositions rests entirely upon the misunderstanding of extending what is valid merely of appearances to things in themselves and in general of mixing both in one concept.

§ 54. This, then, is the exposition, and this is the solution of the whole antinomy in which reason finds itself involved in the application of its principles to the sensible world. The former alone (the mere exposition) would be a considerable service in the cause of our knowledge of human reason, even though the solution might fail to fully satisfy the reader, who has here to combat a natural illusion which has been but recently exposed to him and which he had hitherto always regarded as true. For one result at least is unavoidable. As it is quite impossible to prevent this conflict of reason with itself—so long as the objects of the sensible world are taken for things in themselves and not for mere appearances, which they are in fact—the reader is thereby compelled to examine over again the deduction of all our *a priori* cognition and the proof which I have given of my deduction in order to come to a decision on the question. This is all I require at present; for when in this occupation he shall have thought himself deep enough into the nature of pure reason, those concepts by which 348 alone the solution of the conflict of reason is possible will become sufficiently familiar to him. Without this preparation I cannot expect an unreserved assent even from the most attentive reader.

III. The Theological Idea[40]

§ 55. The third transcendental idea, which affords material for the most important but, if pursued only speculatively, transcendent and thereby dialectical use of reason, is the ideal of pure reason. Reason in this case does not, as with the psychological and the cosmological ideas, start from experience and err by exaggerating its grounds in striving to attain, if possible, the absolute completeness of their series. Rather, it totally breaks with experience and from mere concepts of what constitutes the absolute completeness of a thing in general (hence by means of the idea of a most perfect primal being) proceeds to determine the possibility and therefore the actuality of all other things. And so the mere presupposition of a being which, although not in the series of experiences is thought for the purposes of experience and for the sake of conceiving its connection, order, and unity, i.e., the idea, is more easily distinguished from the concept of the understanding here than in the former cases. Hence we can easily expose the dialectical illusion which arises from our making the subjective conditions of our thinking objective conditions of objects themselves, and from making an hypothesis necessary for the satisfaction of our reason into a dogma. As the observations of the *Critique* on the pretensions of transcendental theology are intelligible, clear, and decisive, I have nothing more to add on the subject.

40. [Cf. *Critique*, "The Ideal of Pure Reason," B 595–670.]

General Remark on the Transcendental Ideas

§ 56. The objects which are given us by experience are in many respects inconceivable, and many questions to which the law of nature leads us when carried 349 beyond a certain point (though still quite conformably to the laws of nature) admit of no answer, as, for example, the question as to why material objects attract one another? But if we entirely quit nature or, in pursuing its combinations, exceed all possible experience, and so enter the realm of mere ideas, we cannot then say that the object is inconceivable and that the nature of things proposes to us insoluble problems. For we are not then concerned with nature or with given objects at all, but with mere concepts which have their origin solely in our reason, and with mere beings of thought; and all the problems that arise from our concepts of them must be solved, because of course reason can and must give a full account of its own procedure.[41]

41. Herr Platner, in his *Aphorisms*, acutely says (§§ 728, 729), "If reason be a criterion, no concept which is incomprehensible to human reason can be possible. Incomprehensibility has place in what is actual only. Here incomprehensibility arises from the insufficiency of the acquired ideas." It sounds paradoxical, but is otherwise not strange to say that in nature there is much that is incomprehensible (e.g., the faculty of generation); but if we mount still higher and go even beyond nature, everything again becomes conceivable. For we then quit entirely the objects which can be given us and occupy ourselves merely about ideas, in which occupation we can easily conceive the law that reason prescribes by them to the understanding for its use in experience, because the law is reason's own product.

As the psychological, cosmological, and theological ideas are nothing but pure concepts of reason, which cannot be given in any experience, the questions which reason asks us about them are put to us, not by the objects, but by mere maxims of our reason for the sake of its own satisfaction. They must all be capable of satisfactory answers, which are provided by showing that they are principles which bring our use of the understanding into thorough agreement, completeness, and synthetical unity, and that they thus hold good of experience only, but of experience as a whole. Although an absolute whole of experience is impossible, the idea of a whole of cognition according to principles in general must impart to our knowledge a peculiar kind of unity, that of a system, without which 350 it is nothing but piece work and cannot be used for the highest purpose (which is always only the system of all purposes); I do not here refer only to the practical, but also to the highest purpose of the speculative use of reason.

The transcendental ideas therefore express the peculiar application of reason as a principle of systematic unity in the use of the understanding. Yet if we assume this unity of the mode of cognition to pertain to the object of cognition, if we regard that which is merely *regulative* to be *constitutive*, and if we persuade ourselves that we can by means of these ideas enlarge our cognition transcendently or far beyond all possible experience, while it only serves to render experience within itself as nearly complete as possible, i.e., to limit its progress by nothing that cannot belong to experience—if we do all this, then we suffer from a mere misunderstanding in our estimate of the proper application of our reason and of its principles and suffer from a dialectic which confuses the empirical use of reason and also sets reason at variance with itself.

CONCLUSION

On the Determination of the Bounds of Pure Reason

§ 57. The clearest arguments having been adduced, it would be absurd for us to hope that we can know more of any object than belongs to the possible experience of it or lay claim to the least knowledge of how anything not assumed to be an object of possible experience is determined according to the constitution that it has in itself. For how could we determine anything in this way, since time, space, and all the concepts of the understanding, and still more all the concepts formed by empirical intuition (or perception) in the sensible world have and can have no other use than to make experience possible? And if this condition is omitted from the pure concepts of the understanding, they do not determine any object and have no meaning whatever.

But it would be, on the other hand, a still greater absurdity if we conceded no things in themselves or declared our experience to be the only possible mode 351 of knowing things, our intuition of them in space and in time to be the only possible intuition, our discursive understanding to be the archetype of every possible understanding, and to have the principles of the possibility of experience taken for universal conditions of things in themselves.

Our principles, which limit the use of reason to possible experience, might in this way become transcendent and the limits of our reason be set up as limits of the possibility of things in themselves (as Hume's *Dialogues*[42] may illustrate) if a careful critique did not guard the bounds of our reason with respect to its empirical use and set a limit to its pretensions. Skepticism originally arose from metaphysics and its lawless dialectic. At first it might, merely to favor the empirical use of reason, announce everything that transcends this use as worthless and deceitful; but by and by, when it was perceived that the very same principles that are used in experience insensibly and apparently with the same right led still further than experience extends, then men began to doubt even the propositions of experience. But here there is no danger, for common sense will doubtless always assert its rights. A certain confusion, however, arose in science, which cannot determine how far reason is to be trusted, and why only so far and no further; and this confusion can only be cleared up and all future relapses obviated by a formal determination, on principle, of the boundary of the use of our reason.

We cannot indeed, beyond all possible experience, form a definite notion of what things in themselves may be. Yet we are not at liberty to abstain entirely from inquiring into them; for experience never satisfies reason fully but, in answering questions, refers

42. [David Hume, *Dialogues Concerning Natural Religion* (1779).]

us further and further back and leaves us dissatisfied with regard to their complete solution. This anyone may gather from the dialectic of pure reason, which therefore has its good subjective grounds. Having acquired, as regards the nature of our soul, a clear 352 conception of the subject, and having come to the conviction that its appearances cannot be explained materialistically, who can refrain from asking what the soul really is and, if no concept of experience suffices for the purpose, from accounting for it by a concept of reason (that of a simple immaterial being), though we cannot by any means prove its objective reality? Who can satisfy himself with mere empirical knowledge in all the cosmological questions of the duration and of the magnitude of the world, of freedom or of natural necessity, since every answer given on principles of experience begets a fresh question, which likewise requires its answer and thereby clearly shows the insufficiency of all physical modes of explanation to satisfy reason? Finally, who does not see in the thoroughgoing contingency and dependence of all his thoughts and assumptions on mere principles of experience the impossibility of stopping there? And who does not feel himself compelled, notwithstanding all interdictions against losing himself in transcendent ideas, to seek rest and contentment, beyond all the concepts which he can vindicate by experience, in the concept of a being, the possibility of which cannot be conceived but at the same time cannot be refuted, because it relates to a mere being of the understanding and without it reason must needs remain forever dissatisfied?

Bounds (in extended beings) always presuppose a space existing outside a certain definite place and inclosing it; limits do not require this, but are mere negations which affect a quantity so far as it is not absolutely complete. But our reason, as it were, sees in its surroundings a space for the cognition of things in themselves though we can never have determinate concepts of them and are limited to appearances only.

As long as the cognition of reason is homogeneous, determinate bounds to it cannot be thought. In mathematics and natural science human reason admits of limits but not of bounds, viz., that something indeed lies outside it, at which it can never arrive, but not that it will at any point find completion in its internal progress. The enlarging of insights in mathematics and the possibility of new discoveries are infinite; and the same is the case with the discovery of new properties of nature, of new forces and laws, by continued experience and its rational unification. But limits 353 cannot fail to be seen here; for mathematics refers to appearances only, and what cannot be an object of sensuous intuition (such as the concepts of metaphysics and of morals) lies entirely without its sphere. It can never lead to them, but neither does it require them. There is therefore a continuous progress and approach to these sciences; and there is, as it were, a point or line of contact. Natural science will never reveal to us the internal constitution of things, which, though not appearance, yet can serve as the ultimate ground for explaining appearances. Nor does that science need this for its physical explanations. Nay, even if such grounds should be offered from other sources (for instance, the influence of immaterial beings), they must be rejected and not used in the progress of its explanations. For these explanations must only be grounded upon that which as an object of sense can belong to experience and be brought into connection with our actual perceptions according to empirical laws.

But metaphysics leads us toward bounds in the dialectical attempts of pure reason (not undertaken arbitrarily or wantonly, but stimulated thereto by the nature of reason itself). And the transcendental ideas, as they do not admit of evasion and yet are never capable of realization, serve to point out to us actually not only the bounds of the use of pure reason, but also the way to determine them. Such is the end and the use of this natural predisposition of our reason, which has brought forth metaphysics as its favorite child, whose generation, like every other in the world, is not to be ascribed to blind chance but to an original germ, wisely organized for great ends. For metaphysics, in its fundamental features, perhaps more than any other science, is placed in us by nature itself and cannot be considered the production of an arbitrary choice or casual enlargement in the progress of experience from which it is quite disparate.

Reason with all its concepts and laws of the understanding, which are adequate to it for empirical use, i.e., within the sensible world, finds for itself no satisfaction because ever-recurring questions deprive us of all hope of their complete solution. The transcendental ideas, which have that completion in view, are such problems of reason. But it sees clearly that the 354 sensible world cannot contain this completion; neither, consequently, can all the concepts which serve merely for understanding the world of sense, e.g., space and time, and whatever we have adduced under the name of pure concepts of the understanding. The sensible world is nothing but a chain of appearances connected according to universal laws; it has therefore no subsistence by itself; it is not the thing in itself, and consequently must point to that which contains the basis of this appearance, to beings which cannot be cognized merely as appearances, but as things in themselves. In the cognition of them alone can reason hope to satisfy its desire for completeness in proceeding from the conditioned to its conditions.

We have above (§§ 33, 34) indicated the limits of reason with regard to all cognition of mere beings of thought. Now, since the transcendental ideas have urged us to approach them and thus have led us, as it were, to the spot where the occupied space (viz., experience) touches the void (that of which we can know nothing, viz., *noumena*), we can determine the bounds of pure reason. For in all bounds there is something positive (e.g., a surface is the boundary of corporeal space, and is therefore itself a space; a line is a space, which is the boundary of the surface, a point the boundary of the line, but yet always a place in space), whereas limits contain mere negations. The limits pointed out in those paragraphs are not enough after we have discovered that beyond them there still lies something (though we can never cognize what it is in itself). For the question now is, What is the attitude of our reason in this connection of what we know with what we do not, and never shall, know? This is an actual connection of a known thing with one quite unknown (and which will always remain so), and though what is unknown should not become the least more known—which we cannot even hope—yet the notion of this connection must be definite, and capable of being rendered distinct.

We must therefore think an immaterial being, a world of understanding, and a Supreme Being (all mere *noumena*), because in them only, as things in themselves, reason finds that completion and satisfaction, which it can never hope for in the derivation of 355 appearances from their homogeneous grounds, and because these actually have reference to something distinct from them (and totally heterogeneous), as appearances always presuppose an object in itself and therefore suggest its existence whether we can know more of it or not.

But as we can never cognize these beings of understanding as they are in themselves, that is, determinately, yet must assume them as regards the sensible world and connect them with it by reason, we are at least able to think this connection by means of such concepts as express their relation to the world of sense. Yet if we represent to ourselves a being of the understanding by nothing but pure concepts of the understanding, we then indeed represent nothing determinate to ourselves, and consequently our concept has no significance; but if we think of it by properties borrowed from the sensible world, then it is no longer a being of understanding but is conceived as a phenomenon and belongs to the sensible world. Let us take an instance from the concept of the Supreme Being.

The deistic concept is quite a pure concept of reason, but represents only a thing containing all realities, without being able to determine any one of them; because for that purpose an example must be taken from the world of sense, in which case I should have an object of sense only, not something quite heterogeneous which can never be an object of sense. Suppose I attribute to the Supreme Being understanding, for instance; I have no concept of an understanding other than my own, one that must receive its intuitions by the senses and which is occupied in bringing them under rules of the unity of consciousness. Then the elements of my concept would always lie in the appearance; I should, however, by the insufficiency of the appearances be required to go beyond them to the concept of a being which neither depends upon appearances nor is bound up with them as conditions of its determination. But if I separate understanding from sensibility to obtain a pure understanding, then nothing remains but the mere form of thinking without intuition, by which form alone I can cognize nothing determinate and consequently no object. For that purpose I should have to think another understanding, such as would intuit its objects but of which I have not the least concept, because the human understanding is discursive, and can cognize only by means of general concepts. And the very same dif- 356 ficulties arise if we attribute a will to the Supreme Being; for I have this concept only by drawing it from my inner experience, and therefore from my dependence for satisfaction upon objects whose existence

I require; and so the concept rests upon sensibility, which is wholly incompatible with the pure concept of the Supreme Being.

Hume's objections to deism are weak, and affect only the proofs, and not the deistic assertion itself. But as regards theism, which depends on a stricter determination of the concept of the Supreme Being, which in deism is merely transcendent, they are very strong and, as this concept is formed, in certain (in fact in all common) cases irrefutable. Hume always insists that by the mere concept of an original being to which we apply only ontological predicates (eternity, omnipresence, omnipotence) we think nothing determinate, and that properties which can yield a concept *in concreto* must be superadded. He insists also that it is not enough to say that it is cause, but we must explain the nature of it causality, e.g., that of an understanding and of a will. He then begins his attacks on the essential point itself, i.e., theism, as he had previously directed his battery only against the proofs of deism, an attack which is not very dangerous to it in its consequences. All his dangerous arguments refer to anthropomorphism, which he holds to be inseparable from theism and to make it contradictory in itself; but if the former can be abandoned, the latter must vanish with it and nothing remain but deism, of which nothing can come, which is of no value and which cannot serve as any foundation to religion or morals. If this anthropomorphism were really unavoidable, no proofs whatever of the existence of a Supreme Being, even were they all granted, could determine for us the concept of this Being without involving us in contradictions.

If we connect with the command to avoid all transcendent judgments of pure reason the command (which apparently conflicts with it) to proceed to concepts that lie beyond the field of its immanent (empirical) use, we discover that both can subsist together, but only at the boundary of all permitted use of reason. 357 For this boundary belongs to the field of experience as well as to that of the beings of thought, and we are thereby taught how these remarkable ideas serve merely for marking the bounds of human reason. On the one hand, they give warning not boundlessly to extend cognition by experience, as if nothing but world remained for us to cognize, and yet, on the other hand, not to transgress the bounds of experience and to think of judging about things beyond them as things in themselves.

But we stop at this boundary if we limit our judgment merely to the relation which the world may have to a being whose very concept lies beyond all the cognition which we can attain within the world. For we then do not attribute to the Supreme Being any of the properties in themselves by which we represent objects of experience, and thereby avoid *dogmatic* anthropomorphism; but we attribute them to his relation to the world and allow ourselves a *symbolic* anthropomorphism, which in fact concerns language only and not the object itself.

If I say that we are compelled to consider the world *as if* it were the work of a Supreme Understanding and Will, I really say nothing more than that a watch, a ship, a regiment bears the same relation to the watchmaker, the shipbuilder, the commanding officer as the world of sense (or whatever constitutes the substratum of this complex of appearances) does to the unknown, which I do not hereby cognize as it is in itself but as it is for me, i.e., in relation to the world of which I am a part.

§ 58. Such a cognition is one of analogy and does not signify (as is commonly understood) an imperfect similarity of two things, but a perfect similarity of relations between two quite dissimilar things.[43] By means 358 of this analogy, however, there remains a concept of the Supreme Being sufficiently determined *for us*,

43. Thus there is an analogy between the juridical relation of human actions and the mechanical relation of moving forces. I never can do anything to another man without giving him a right to do the same to me on the same conditions; just as no body can act with its moving force on another body without thereby causing the other to react equally against it. Here right and moving force are quite dissimilar things, but in their relations there is complete similarity. By means of such an analogy, I can obtain a relational concept of things which are absolutely unknown to me. For instance, as the promotion of the welfare of children (= a) is to the love of parents (= b), so the welfare of the human species (= c) is to that unknown in God (= x), which we call love; not as if it had the least similarity to any human inclination, but because we can posit its relation to the world to be similar to that which things of the world bear one another. But the relational concept in this case is a mere category, viz., the concept of cause, which has nothing to do with sensibility.

though we have left out everything that could determine it absolutely and *in itself*; for we determine it as regards the world and therefore as regards ourselves, and more do we not require. The attacks which Hume makes upon those who would determine this concept absolutely, by taking the materials for so doing from themselves and the world, do not affect us; and he cannot object to us that we have nothing left if we take away the objective anthropomorphism from our concept of the Supreme Being.

For let us assume at the outset (as Hume in his *Dialogues* makes Philo grant Cleanthes), as a necessary hypothesis, the deistic concept of the First Being, in which this Being is thought by the mere ontological predicates of substance, of cause, etc. This must be done because reason, actuated in the sensible world by mere conditions which are themselves in turn always conditioned, cannot otherwise have any satisfaction; and it therefore can be done without falling into anthropomorphism (which transfers predicates from the world of sense to a being quite distinct from the world) because those predicates are mere categories which, though they do not give a determinate concept of this being, yet give a concept not limited to any conditions of sensibility. Thus nothing can prevent our predicating of this being a causality through reason with regard to the world, and thus passing to 359 theism, without being obliged to attribute to this being itself this kind of reason, as a property inhering in it. For as to the former, the only possible way of pushing the use of reason (as regards all possible experience in complete harmony with itself) in the world of sense to the highest point is to assume a supreme reason as a cause of all the connections in the world. Such a principle must be quite advantageous to reason and can hurt it nowhere in its application to nature. As to the latter, reason is thereby not transferred as a property to the First Being in itself, but only to its relation to the world of sense, and so anthropomorphism is entirely avoided. For nothing is considered here but the cause of the rational form which is found everywhere in the world, and reason is attributed to the Supreme Being so far as it contains the ground of this rational form in the world, but according to analogy only, i.e., so far as this expression shows merely the relation which the Supreme Cause, unknown to us, has to the world in order to determine everything in it conformably to reason in the highest degree. We are thereby kept from using reason as an attribute in order to think God, but not kept from thinking the world in such a manner as is necessary to have the greatest possible use of reason within it according to principle. We thereby acknowledge that the Supreme Being is quite inscrutable and even unthinkable in any determinate way as to what it is in itself. We are thereby kept, on the one hand, from making a transcendent use of the concepts which we have of reason as an efficient cause (by means of the will), in order to determine the Divine Nature by properties which are only borrowed from human nature, and from losing ourselves in gross and extravagant concepts; and, on the other hand, from deluging the contemplation of the world with hyperphysical modes of explanation according to our concepts of human reason which we transfer to God, and so from losing for this contemplation its proper role, according to which it should be a rational study of mere nature and not a presumptuous derivation of its appearances from a Supreme Reason. The expression suited to our feeble concepts is that we conceive the world *as if* it came, regarding its existence and its inner determination, from a Supreme Reason. By this conception we both cognize the constitution which belongs to the world itself without pretending to determine the nature of its cause in itself, and we transfer the ground of this constitution (of the rational form of the world) to the *relation* of the Supreme Cause to the world, without 360 finding the world sufficient by itself for that purpose.[44]

Thus the difficulties which seem to oppose theism disappear by combining with Hume's principle, "not to carry the use of reason dogmatically beyond the field of all possible experience," this other principle, which he quite overlooked, "not to consider the field of experience as one which bounds itself in the eyes of our reason." The *Critique of Pure Reason* here points out the true mean between dogma-

44. I may say that the causality of the Supreme Cause holds the same place with regard to the world that human reason does with regard to its works of art. Here the nature of the Supreme Cause itself remains unknown to me; I only compare its effects (the order of the world), which I know, and their conformity to reason to the effects of human reason, which I also know; and hence I term the former reason, without attributing to it on that account what I understand in man by this term, or attaching to it anything else known to me as its property.

tism, which Hume combats, and skepticism, which he would substitute for it—a mean which is not like other means that we find advisable to determine for ourselves as it were mechanically (by adopting something from one side and something from the other), and by which nobody is taught a better way, but such a one as can be exactly determined on principles.

§ 59. At the beginning of this note I made use of the metaphor of a boundary in order to establish the limits of reason in regard to its suitable use. The world of sense contains merely appearances, which are not things in themselves; but the understanding must assume these latter ones, viz., *noumena*, because it knows the objects of experience to be mere appearances. In our reason both are comprised together, and the question is, How does reason proceed to set boundaries to the understanding as regards both these fields? Experience, which contains all that belongs to the sensible world, does not bound itself; it only proceeds in every case from the conditioned to some other equally conditioned thing. Its boundary must 361 lie quite without it, and this is the field of the pure beings of the understanding. But this field, so far as the determination of the nature of these beings is concerned, is an empty space for us; and if dogmatically determined concepts are being considered, we cannot pass beyond the field of possible experience. But as a boundary is itself something positive, which belongs to what lies within as well as to the space that lies without the given complex, it is still an actual positive cognition which reason only acquires by enlarging itself to this boundary, yet without attempting to pass it because it there finds itself in the presence of an empty space in which it can think forms of things but not things themselves. But the setting of a boundary to the field of experience by something which is otherwise unknown to reason, is still a cognition which belongs to it even at this point, and by which it is neither confined within the sensible nor strays beyond the sensible, but only limits itself, as befits the knowledge of a boundary, to the relation between what lies beyond it and what is contained within it.

Natural theology is such a concept at the boundary of human reason, being constrained to look beyond this boundary to the idea of a Supreme Being (and, for practical purposes, to that of an intelligible world also), not in order to determine anything relatively to this mere being of the understanding, which lies beyond the world of sense, but in order to guide the use of reason within the world of sense according to principles of the greatest possible (theoretical as well as practical) unity. For this purpose reason makes use of the reference of the world of sense to an independent reason as the cause of all that world's connections. Thereby reason does not merely invent a being, but, as beyond the sensible world there must be something that can be thought only by the pure understanding, reason determines that something in this particular way, though only of course according to analogy.

And thus there remains our original proposition, which is the result of the whole *Critique*: "that reason by all its *a priori* principles never teaches us anything more than objects of possible experience, and even of these nothing more than can be cognized in experience." But this limitation does not prevent reason from leading us to the objective boundary of experience, viz., to the reference to something which is not itself an object of experience but must be the highest ground of all experience. Reason does not, however, teach us anything concerning the thing in itself; 362 it only instructs us as regards its own complete and highest use in the field of possible experience. But this is all that can be reasonably desired in the present case, and with it we have cause to be satisfied.

§ 60. Thus we have fully exhibited metaphysics according to its subjective possibility, as it is actually given in the natural predisposition of human reason and in that which constitutes the essential end of its pursuit. We have found that this merely natural use of such a predisposition of our reason, if no discipline arising only from a scientific critique bridles and sets limits to it, involves us in transcendent dialectical inferences, that are in part merely illusory and in part even self-contradictory, and that this fallacious metaphysics is not only unnecessary as regards the promotion of our knowledge of nature but even disadvantageous to it. There yet remains a problem worthy of inquiry, which is to find out the natural ends intended by this disposition to transcendent concepts in our reason, because everything that lies in nature must be originally intended for some useful purpose.

Such an inquiry is of a doubtful nature, and I acknowledge that what I can say about it is conjecture only, like every speculation about the first ends of nature. This conjecture may be allowed to me in this case alone, because the question does not concern the objective validity of metaphysical judgments but our natural predisposition to them, and therefore does not belong to the system of metaphysics but to anthropology.

When I compare all the transcendental ideas, the totality of which constitutes the particular problem of natural pure reason, compelling it to quit the mere contemplation of nature, to transcend all possible experience, and in this endeavor to produce the thing (be it knowledge or fiction) called metaphysics; I think I perceive that the aim of this natural tendency is to free our concepts from the fetters of experience and from the limits of the mere contemplation of nature so far as at least to open to us a field containing mere objects for the pure understanding which 363 no sensibility can reach, not indeed for the purpose of speculatively occupying ourselves with them (for there we can find no ground to stand on), but in order that practical principles might find some such scope for their necessary expectation and hope and might expand to the universality which reason unavoidably requires from a moral point of view.

So I find that the psychological idea (however little it may reveal to me the nature of the human soul, which is elevated above all concepts of experience) shows the insufficiency of these concepts plainly enough and thereby deters me from materialism, a psychological concept which is unfit for any explanation of nature and which in addition confines reason in practical respects. The cosmological ideas, by the obvious insufficiency of all possible cognition of nature to satisfy reason in its legitimate inquiry, serve in the same manner to keep us from naturalism, which asserts nature to be sufficient for itself. Finally, all natural necessity in the sensible world is conditional, as it always presupposes the dependence of things upon others, and unconditional necessity must be sought only in the unity of a cause different from the world of sense. But as the causality of this cause, in its turn, were it merely nature, could never render the existence of the contingent (as is consequent) comprehensible, reason frees itself by means of the theological idea from fatalism (both as a blind natural necessity in the coherence of nature itself, without a first principle, and as a blind causality of this principle itself) and leads to the concept of a cause possessing freedom and hence of a Supreme Intelligence. Thus the transcendental ideas serve, if not to instruct us positively, at least to destroy the impudent and restrictive assertions of materialism, of naturalism, and of fatalism, and thus to afford scope for the moral ideas beyond the field of speculation. These considerations, I should think, explain in some measure the natural predisposition of which I spoke.

The practical value which a merely speculative science may have lies outside the bounds of this science, and can therefore be considered as a scholium merely, and like all scholia does not form part of the science itself. This application, however, surely lies within the bounds of philosophy, especially of philosophy drawn from the pure sources of reason, where its speculative use in metaphysics must necessarily be at one with its practical use in morals. Hence the unavoidable dialectic of pure reason, considered in metaphysics as a natural tendency, deserves to 364 be explained not as a mere illusion, which is to be removed, but also, if possible, as a natural provision as regards its end, though this task, a work of supererogation, cannot justly be assigned to metaphysics proper.

The solutions of these questions which are treated in the *Critique*[45] should be considered a second scholium, which, however, has a greater affinity with the subject of metaphysics. For there certain rational principles are expounded which determine *a priori* the order of nature or rather of the understanding, which seeks nature's laws through experience. They seem to be constitutive and legislative with regard to experience, though they spring from mere reason, which cannot be considered, like the understanding, as a principle of possible experience. Now whether or not this harmony rests upon the fact that, just as nature does not inhere in appearances or in their source (the sensibility) itself, but only in the relation of the latter to the understanding, so also a thoroughgoing unity in the use of the understanding to bring about an entirety of all possible experience (in a system) can only belong to the understanding when in relation to reason, with the result that experience is in this way mediately subordinate to the legislation of reason: this question may be discussed by those who desire to trace the nature of reason even

45. [*Critique of Pure Reason*, "The Regulative Employment of the Ideas of Pure Reason," B 670–696.]

beyond its use in metaphysics into the general principles for making systematic a history of nature in general. I have presented this task as important, but not attempted its solution in the book itself.[46]

365 And thus I conclude the analytical solution of the main question which I had proposed: "How is metaphysics in general possible?" by ascending from the data of its actual use, at least in its consequences, to the grounds of its possibility.

SOLUTION OF THE GENERAL QUESTION OF THE *PROLEGOMENA*

"How Is Metaphysics Possible as Science?"

Metaphysics, as a natural disposition of reason, is actual; but if considered by itself alone (as the analytical solution of the third principal question showed), it is dialectical and illusory. If we think of taking principles from it, and in using them follow the natural, but on that account not less false, illusion, we can never produce science, but only a vain dialectical art, in which one school may outdo another but none can ever acquire a just and lasting approbation.

In order that as a science metaphysics may be entitled to claim, not mere fallacious plausibility, but insight and conviction, a critique of reason must itself exhibit the whole stock of *a priori* concepts, their division according to their various sources (sensibility, understanding, and reason), together with a complete table of them, the analysis of all these concepts, with all their consequences and especially the possibility of synthetic cognition *a priori* by means of the deduction of these concepts, the principles and bounds of their use, all in a complete system. Critique, therefore, and critique alone contains in itself the whole well-proved and well-tested plan, and even all the means required to establish metaphysics as a science; by other ways and means it is impossible. The question here, therefore, is not so much how this performance is possible as how to set it going and induce men of clear heads to quit their hitherto perverted and fruitless cultivation for one that will not deceive, and how such a union for the common end may best be directed.

This much is certain: whoever has once tasted critique will be ever after disgusted with all dogmatical 366 twaddle which he formerly put up with because his reason had to have something and could find nothing better for its support. Critique stands in the same relation to the common metaphysics of the schools as chemistry does to alchemy, or as astronomy to the astrology of the fortune teller. I pledge myself that nobody who has thought through and grasped the principles of critique, even only in these *Prolegomena*, will ever return to that old and sophistical pseudoscience; but he will, rather, with a certain delight look forward to a metaphysics which is now indeed in his power, requiring no more preparatory discoveries, and now at last affording permanent satisfaction to reason. For here is an advantage upon which, of all possible sciences, metaphysics alone can with certainty reckon: that it can be brought to such completion and fixity as to require no further change or be capable of any augmentation by new discoveries, because here reason has the sources of its knowledge in itself, not in objects and their observation, by which its stock of knowledge could be further increased. When, therefore, it has exhibited the fundamental laws of its faculty completely and so determinately as to avoid all misunderstanding, there remains nothing more for pure reason to cognize *a priori*; nay, there is even no ground to raise further questions. The sure prospect of knowledge so determinate and so compact has a peculiar charm, even though we should set aside all its advantages, of which I shall hereafter speak.

All false art, all vain wisdom, lasts its time but finally destroys itself, and its highest culture is also the epoch of its decay. That this time is come for metaphysics appears from the state into which it has fallen among all learned nations, despite all the zeal with which other sciences of every kind are prosecuted. The old arrangement of our university studies still preserves its shadow; now and then an academy of science tempts men by offering prizes to write essays on it, but it is no longer numbered among sound sciences; and let

46. Throughout in the *Critique* I never lost sight of the plan not to neglect anything, were it ever so recondite, that could render the inquiry into the nature of pure reason complete. Everybody may afterward carry his researches as far as he pleases, when he has been merely shown what yet remains to be done. This can reasonably be expected of him who has made it his business to survey the whole field, in order to consign it to others for future cultivation and allotment. And to this branch both the scholia belong, which will hardly recommend themselves by their dryness to amateurs, and hence are added here for connoisseurs only.

anyone judge for himself how a sophisticated man, if he were called a great metaphysician, would receive the compliment, which may be well meant but is scarcely envied by anybody.

367 Yet, though the period of the downfall of all dogmatic metaphysics has undoubtedly arrived, we are yet far from being able to say that the period of its regeneration is come by means of a thorough and complete critique of reason. All transitions from an inclination to its contrary pass through the stage of indifference, and this moment is the most dangerous for an author but, in my opinion, the most favorable for the science. For when party spirit has died out by a total dissolution of former connections, minds are in the best state to listen to several proposals for an organization according to a new plan.

When I say that I hope these *Prolegomena* will excite investigation in the field of critique and afford a new and promising object to sustain the general spirit of philosophy, which seems on its speculative side to want sustenance, I can imagine beforehand that everyone whom the thorny paths of my *Critique* have tried and put out of humor will ask me upon what I found this hope. My answer is: upon the irresistible law of necessity.

That the human spirit will ever give up metaphysical researches is as little to be expected as that we should prefer to give up breathing altogether, in order to avoid inhaling impure air. There will, therefore, always be metaphysics in the world; nay, everyone, especially every reflective man, will have it and, for want of a recognized standard, will shape it for himself after his own pattern. What has hitherto been called metaphysics cannot satisfy any critical mind, but to forego it entirely is impossible; therefore a critique of pure reason itself must now be attempted or, if one exists, investigated and brought to the full test, because there is no other means of supplying this pressing want which is something more than mere thirst for knowledge.

Ever since I have come to know critique, whenever I finish reading a book of metaphysical contents which, by the determination of its concepts, by variety, 368 order, and an easy style, was not only entertaining but also helpful, I cannot help asking "Has this author indeed advanced metaphysics a single step?" The learned men whose works have been useful to me in other respects and always contributed to the culture of my mental powers will, I hope, forgive me for saying that I have never been able to find either their essays or my own less important ones (though self-love may recommend them to me) to have advanced the science of metaphysics in the least, and why? Here is the very obvious reason: metaphysics did not then exist as a science, nor can it be gathered piecemeal; but its germ must be fully preformed in critique. But in order to prevent all misconception, we must remember what has already been said—that by the analytic treatment of our concepts the understanding gains indeed a great deal, but the science (of metaphysics) is thereby not in the least advanced because these analyzes of concepts are nothing but the materials from which the intention is to carpenter our science. Let the concepts of substance and of accident be ever so well analyzed and determined; all this is very well as a preparation for some future use. But if we cannot prove that in all which exists the substance endures and only the accidents vary, our science is not the least advanced by all our analyzes. Metaphysics has hitherto never been able to prove *a priori* either this proposition or that of sufficient reason, still less any more complex theorem such as belongs to psychology or cosmology, or indeed any synthetic proposition. By all its analyzing, therefore, nothing is affected, nothing obtained or forwarded; and the science, after all this bustle and noise, still remains as it was in the days of Aristotle, though far better preparations were made for it than of old if only the clue to synthetic cognitions had been discovered.

If anyone thinks himself offended, he is at liberty to refute my charge by producing a single synthetic proposition belonging to metaphysics which he would prove dogmatically *a priori*; for until he has actually performed this feat, I shall not grant that he has truly advanced the science, even though this proposition should be sufficiently confirmed by common experience. No demand can be more moderate 369 or more equitable and, in the (inevitably certain) event of its nonperformance, no assertion more just than that hitherto metaphysics has never existed as a science.

But there are two things which, in case the challenge be accepted, I must deprecate: first, trifling about probability and conjecture, which are suited as little to metaphysics as to geometry; and secondly, a decision by means of the magic wand of so-called sound common sense, which does not convince everyone but accommodates itself to personal peculiarities.

For as to the former, nothing can be more absurd than in metaphysics, a philosophy from pure reason, to try to ground our judgments upon probability and conjecture. Everything that is to be cognized *a priori* is thereby announced as apodeictically certain and must therefore be proved in this way. We might as well try to ground geometry or arithmetic upon conjectures. As to the calculus of probabilities in the latter, it does not contain probable but perfectly certain judgments concerning the degree of the possibility of certain cases under given uniform conditions, which, in the sum of all possible cases, must infallibly happen according to the rule, though it is not sufficiently determined as regards every single instance. Conjectures (by means of induction and analogy) can be suffered in an empirical natural science only, yet even there at least the possibility of what we assume must be quite certain.

The appeal to common sense is even more absurd, when concepts and principles are said to be valid, not insofar as they hold with regard to experience, but outside the conditions of experience. For what is common sense? It is normal good sense, so far as it judges right. What is normal good sense? It is the faculty of the knowledge and use of rules *in concreto*, as distinguished from the speculative understanding, which is a faculty of knowing rules *in abstracto*. Common sense can hardly understand the rule that every event is determined by means of its cause and can never comprehend it thus generally. It therefore demands an example from experience; and when it hears that this rule means nothing but what it always thought 370 when a pane was broken or a kitchen-utensil missing, it then understands the principle and grants it. Common sense, therefore, is only of use so far as it can see its rules (though they actually are *a priori*) confirmed by experience; consequently, to comprehend them *a priori*, or independently of experience, belongs to the speculative understanding and lies quite beyond the horizon of common sense. But the province of metaphysics is entirely confined to the latter kind of knowledge, and it is certainly a bad sign of common sense to appeal to it as a witness, for it cannot here form any opinion whatever, and men look down upon it with contempt until they are in trouble and can find in their speculation neither advice nor help.

It is a common subterfuge of those false friends of common sense (who occasionally prize it highly, but usually despise it) to say that there must surely be at all events some propositions which are immediately certain and of which there is no occasion to give any proof, or even any account at all, because we otherwise could never stop inquiring into the grounds of our judgments. But if we accept the principle of contradiction, which is not sufficient to show the truth of synthetic judgments, they can never adduce, in proof of this privilege, anything else indubitable which they can immediately ascribe to common sense, except mathematical propositions, such as twice two make four, between two points there is but one straight line, etc. But these judgments are radically different from those of metaphysics. For in mathematics I can by thinking construct whatever I represent to myself as possible by a concept: I add to the first two the other two, one by one, and myself make the number four, or I draw in thought from one point to another all manner of lines, equal as well as unequal; yet I can draw one only which is like itself in all its parts. But I cannot, by all my power of thinking, extract from the concept of a thing the concept of something else whose existence is necessarily connected with the former, but I must call upon experience. And though my understanding furnishes me *a priori* (yet only in reference to possible experience) with the concept of such a connection (i.e., causation), I cannot exhibit it *a priori* in intuition, like the concepts of mathe- 371 matics, and so show its possibility *a priori*. This concept, together with the principles of its application, always requires, if it is to hold *a priori*—as is requisite in metaphysics—a justification and deduction of its possibility, because we cannot otherwise know how far it holds good and whether it can be used in experience only or beyond it also. Therefore in metaphysics, as a speculative science of pure reason, we can never appeal to common sense, but may do so only when (in certain matters) we are forced to surrender it and renounce all pure speculative cognition, which must always be theoretic knowledge, and therefore are forced to forego metaphysics itself and its instruction for the sake of adopting a rational faith which alone may be possible for us, sufficient to our wants, and perhaps even more salutary than knowledge itself. For then the shape of the thing is quite altered. Metaphysics must be science, not only as a whole but in all its parts; otherwise it is nothing at all, because as speculation of pure reason it finds a hold only on universal insights. Beyond its field, however, probability and common sense may be used advantageously and justly, but on quite special principles, the importance of which always depends on their reference to the practical.

This is what I hold myself justified in requiring for the possibility of metaphysics as a science.

APPENDIX

On What Can Be Done to Make Metaphysics as a Science Actual

Since all the ways heretofore taken have failed to attain the goal, and since without a preceding critique of pure reason it is not likely ever to be attained, the 372 attempt before us has a right to an accurate and careful examination, unless it be thought more advisable to give up all pretensions to metaphysics, to which, if men would but consistently adhere to their purpose, no objection can be made. If we take the course of things as it is, not as it ought to be, there are two sorts of judgments: (1) one a judgment which precedes investigation (in our case one in which the reader from his own metaphysics pronounces judgment on the *Critique of Pure Reason*, which was intended to discuss the very possibility of metaphysics); (2) the other a judgment subsequent to investigation. In the latter, the reader is enabled to ignore for a while the consequences of the critical researches that may be repugnant to his formerly adopted metaphysics, and first examines the grounds whence those consequences are derived. If what common metaphysics propounds were demonstrably certain (like geometry) the former way of judging would hold good. For if the consequences of certain principles are repugnant to established truths, these principles are false and without further inquiry to be repudiated. But if metaphysics does not possess a stock of indisputably certain (synthetic) propositions, and should it even be the case that there are a number of them, which, though among the most plausible, are by their consequences in mutual conflict, and if no sure criterion of the truth of peculiarly metaphysical (synthetic) propositions is to be met with in it, then the former way of judging is not admissible, but the investigation of the principles of the *Critique* must precede all judgments as to its value.

A Specimen of a Judgment about the Critique *Prior to Its Examination*

Such a judgment is to be found in the *Göttingische gelehrte Anzeigen*, in the supplement to the third part, of January 19, 1782, pages 40 *et seq.*[47]

When an author who is familiar with the subject of his work and endeavors to present his independent reflections in its elaboration falls into the hands of a reviewer who, in his turn, is keen enough to discern the points on which the worth or worthlessness of the books rests, who does not cling to words but goes to the heart of the subject, sifting and testing the principles which the author takes as his point of departure, the severity of the judgment may indeed displease 373 the author, but the public does not care, as it gains thereby. And the author himself may be satisfied at having an opportunity of correcting or explaining his positions at an early date by the examination of a competent judge, in such a manner that if he believes himself fundamentally right, he can remove in time any stumbling-block that might hurt the success of his work.

I find myself, with my reviewer, in quite another position. He seems not to see at all the real matter of the investigation, with which (successfully or unsuccessfully) I have been occupied. It is either impatience at thinking out a lengthy work, or vexation at a threatened reform of a science in which he believed he had brought everything to perfection long ago, or, what I am reluctant to suppose, real narrow-mindedness that prevents him from ever carrying his thoughts beyond his school metaphysics. In short, he passes impatiently in review a long series of propositions, of which, without knowing their premises, one can comprehend nothing, intersperses here and there his censure, the reason of which the reader understands just as little as the propositions against which it is directed; and hence [his report] can neither serve the public nor damage me in the judgment of experts. I should, for these reasons, have passed over this judgment altogether, were it not that it may afford me occasion for some explanations which may in some cases save the readers of these *Prolegomena* from a misconception.

In order to take a position from which my reviewer

47. [This review was given by Christian Garve.]

could most easily set the whole work in a most unfavorable light, without venturing to trouble himself with any special investigation, he begins and ends by saying: "This work is a system of transcendental (or, as he translates it, of higher)[48] idealism."

A glance at this line soon showed me the sort of 374 criticism that I had to expect, much as though the reviewer were one who had never seen or heard of geometry, having found a Euclid and coming upon various figures in turning over its leaves, were to say, on being asked his opinion of it: "The work is a textbook of drawing; the author introduces a peculiar terminology in order to give dark, incomprehensible directions, which in the end teach nothing more than what everyone can effect by a fair natural accuracy of eye, etc."

Let us see, in the meantime, what sort of an idealism it is that goes through my whole work, although it does not by a long way constitute the soul of the system.

The dictum of all genuine idealists, from the Eleatic school to Bishop Berkeley, is contained in this formula: "All cognition through the senses and experience is nothing but sheer illusion, and only in the ideas of the pure understanding and reason is there truth."

The principle that throughout dominates and determines my idealism is, on the contrary: "All cognition of things merely from pure understanding or pure reason is nothing but sheer illusion, and only in experience is there truth."

But this is directly contrary to idealism proper. How came I then to use this expression for quite an opposite purpose, and how came my reviewer to see it everywhere?

The solution of this difficulty rests on something that could have been very easily understood from the context of the work, if the reader had only desired to do so. Space and time, together with all that they contain, are not things in themselves or their qualities but belong merely to the appearances of the things in themselves; up to this point I am one in confession with the above idealists. But these, and among them more particularly Berkeley, regarded space as a mere empirical representation that, like the appearances it contains, is, together with its determinations, 375 known to us only by means of experience or perception. I, on the contrary, prove in the first place that space (and also time, which Berkeley did not consider) and all its determinations can be cognized *a priori* by us, because, no less than time, it inheres in us as a pure form of our sensibility before all perception of experience and makes possible all intuition of sensibility, and therefore all appearances. It follows from this that, as truth rests on universal and necessary laws as its criteria, experience, according to Berkeley, can have no criteria of truth because its appearances (according to him) have nothing *a priori* at their foundation, whence it follows that experience is nothing but sheer illusion; whereas with us, space and time (in conjunction with the pure concepts of the understanding) prescribe their law *a priori* to all possible experience and, at the same time, afford the certain criterion for distinguishing truth from illusion therein.[49]

My so-called (properly critical) idealism is of quite a special kind, in that it reverses the usual idealism and through my kind all *a priori* cognition, even that of geometry, first receives objective reality, which, without my demonstrated ideality of space and time, could not be maintained by the most zealous real-

48. By no means "higher." High towers and metaphysically great men resembling them, around both of which there is commonly much wind, are not for me. My place is the fruitful bathos of experience; and the word "transcendental," the meaning of which is so often indicated by me but not once grasped by my reviewer (so carelessly has he regarded everything), does not signify something passing beyond all experience but something that indeed precedes it *a priori*, but that is intended simply to make cognition of experience possible. If these concepts overstep experience, their use is termed "transcendent," which must be distinguished from the immanent use, i.e., use restricted to experience. All misunderstandings of this kind have been sufficiently guarded against in the work itself, but my reviewer found his advantage in misunderstanding me.

49. Idealism proper always has a mystical tendency, and can have no other; but mine is solely designed for the purpose of comprehending the possibility of our *a priori* cognition of objects of experience, which is a problem never hitherto solved or even suggested. In this way all mystical idealism falls to the ground, for (as may be seen in Plato) it inferred from our cognitions *a priori* (even from those of geometry) another intuition different from that of the senses (namely, an intellectual intuition), because it never occurred to anyone that the senses themselves might intuit *a priori*.

ists. This being the state of the case, I could wish, in order to avoid all misunderstanding, to have named this concept of mine otherwise, but to alter it altogether is probably impossible. It may therefore be permitted me in future, as has been above intimated, to term it "formal" or, better still, "critical" idealism, to distinguish it from the dogmatic idealism of Berkeley and from the skeptical idealism of Descartes.

Beyond this, I find nothing remarkable in the judgment of my book. The reviewer makes sweeping criticisms, a mode prudently chosen, since it does not betray one's own knowledge or ignorance; a single thorough criticism in detail, had it touched the main question, as is only fair, would have exposed either my error or my reviewer's measure of insight into this kind of inquiry. It was, moreover, not a badly conceived plan, in order at once to take from readers (who are accustomed to form their conceptions of books from newspaper reports) the desire to read the book itself, to pour out one after the other in one breath a number of propositions which, torn from their connection with their premises and explanations, must necessarily sound senseless, especially considering how antipathetic they are to all school metaphysics; to exhaust the reader's patience *ad nauseam*, and then, having made me acquainted with the lucid proposition that persistent illusion is truth, to conclude with the crude paternal moralization: to what end, then, the quarrel with accepted language; to what end, and whence, the idealistic distinction? A judgment which seeks all that is characteristic of my book, first supposed to be metaphysically heterodox, in a mere innovation of the nomenclature proves clearly that my would-be judge has understood nothing of the subject and, in addition, has not understood himself.[50]

50. The reviewer often fights with his own shadow. When I oppose the truth of experience to dream, he never thinks that I am here speaking simply of the well-known *somnio objective sumto* ["dreams taken objectively"—Christian Wolff's *German Metaphysics*, § 142] of the Wolffian philosophy, which is merely formal, and with which the distinction between sleeping and waking is in no way concerned—a distinction which can indeed have no place in a transcendental philosophy. For the rest, he calls my deduction of the categories and table of the principles of the understanding "common well-known axioms of logic and ontology, expressed in an idealistic manner." The reader need only consult these *Prolegomena* upon this point to convince himself that a more miserable and historically incorrect judgment could hardly be made.

My reviewer speaks like a man who is conscious of important and superior insight which he keeps hidden, for I am aware of nothing recent with respect to metaphysics that could justify his tone. But he is quite wrong to withhold his discoveries from the world, for there are doubtless many who, like myself, have not been able to find in all the fine things that have for long past been written in this department anything that has advanced the science by so much as a finger's breadth. We find indeed the giving a new point to definitions, the supplying of lame proofs with new crutches, the adding to the crazy-quilt of metaphysics fresh patches or changing its pattern; but all this is not what the world requires. The world is tired of metaphysical assertions; what is wanted is the possibility of this science, the sources from which certainty therein can be derived, and certain criteria by which it may distinguish the dialectical illusion of pure reason from truth. To this the critic seems to possess a key, otherwise he would never have spoken out in such a high tone.

But I am inclined to suspect that no such requirement of the science has ever entered his thoughts, or in that case he would have directed his judgment to this point, and even a mistaken attempt in such an important matter would have won his respect. If that be the case, we are once more good friends. He may penetrate as deeply as he likes into his metaphysics, without anyone hindering him; only as concerns that which lies outside metaphysics, its sources, which are to be found in reason, he cannot form a judgment. That my suspicion is not without foundation is proved by the fact that he does not mention a word about the possibility of synthetic knowledge *a priori*, the special problem upon the solution of which the fate of metaphysics wholly rests and upon which my *Critique* (as well as the present *Prolegomena*) entirely hinges. The idealism he encountered and which he hung upon was only taken up in the doctrine as the sole means of solving the above problem (although it received its confirmation on other grounds), and hence he must have shown either that the above problem does not possess the importance I attribute to it (even in these *Prolegomena*) or that, by my concept of appearances, it is either not solved at all or can be better solved in another way; but I do not find a word of this in the criticism. The reviewer, then, understands nothing of my work and possibly also nothing of the spirit and essential nature of metaphysics itself; and it is not, what I would rather assume, the haste of a reviewer to finish his review, incensed at the labor of plodding through so many obstacles, that threw an unfavorable shadow over the work lying before him and made its fundamental features unrecognizable.

378 There is a great deal to be done before a learned journal, it matters not with what care its writers may be selected, can maintain its otherwise well-merited reputation in the field of metaphysics as elsewhere. Other sciences and branches of knowledge have their standard. Mathematics has it in itself, history and theology in secular or sacred books, natural science and the art of medicine in mathematics and experience, jurisprudence in law books, and even matters of taste in the examples of the ancients. But for the judgment of the thing called metaphysics, the standard has yet to be found. I have made an attempt to determine it, as well as its use. What is to be done, then, until it be found, when works of this kind have to be judged? If they are of a dogmatic character, one may do what one likes; no one will play the master over others here for long before someone else appears to deal with him in the same manner. If, however, they are critical in character, not indeed with reference to other works but to reason itself, so that the standard of judgment cannot be assumed but has first of all to be sought for, then, though objection and blame may indeed be permitted, yet a certain degree of leniency is indispensable, since the need is common to us all and the lack of the necessary insight makes the high-handed attitude of judge unwarranted.

In order, however, to connect my defense with the interest of the philosophical commonwealth, I propose a test, which must be decisive as to the mode whereby all metaphysical investigations may be directed to their common purpose. This is nothing more than what mathematicians have done in establishing the advantage of their methods by competition. I challenge my critic to demonstrate, as is only just, on *a priori* grounds, in his own way, any single really metaphysical principle asserted by him. Being metaphysical, it must be synthetic and cognized *a priori* from concepts, but it may also be any one of the most indispensable propositions, as, for instance, the principle of the permanence of substance or of the necessary determination of events in the world by their causes. If he cannot do this (silence however is confession), he must admit that, since metaphysics without apodeictic certainty of propositions of this kind is nothing at all, its possibility or impossibility must before all things be established in a critique of 379 pure reason. Thus he is bound either to confess that my principles in the *Critique* are correct, or he must prove their invalidity. But as I can already foresee that, confidently as he has hitherto relied on the certainty of his principles, when it comes to a strict test he will not find a single one in the whole range of metaphysics he can boldly bring forward, I will concede to him an advantageous condition, which can only be expected in such a competition, and will relieve him of the *onus probandi* by laying it on myself.

He finds in these *Prolegomena* and in my *Critique*[51] eight propositions, of which one in each pair contradicts the other, but each of which necessarily belongs to metaphysics, by which it must either be accepted or rejected (although there is not one that has not in its time been accepted by some philosopher). Now he has the liberty of selecting any one of these eight propositions at his pleasure and accepting it without any proof, of which I shall make him a present, but only one (for waste of time will be just as little serviceable to him as to me), and then of attacking my proof of the opposite proposition. If I can save this one and at the same time show that, according to principles which every dogmatic metaphysics must necessarily recognize, the contrary of the proposition adopted by him can be just as clearly proved, it is thereby established that metaphysics has an hereditary failing not to be explained, much less set aside, until we ascend to its birthplace, pure reason itself. And thus my *Critique* must either be accepted or a better one take its place; at least it must be studied, which is the only thing I now require. If, on the other hand, I cannot save my demonstration, then a synthetic proposition *a priori* from dogmatic principles is to be reckoned to the score of my opponent, and I shall deem my impeachment of ordinary metaphysics unjust and pledge myself to recognize his censure of my *Critique* as justified (although this would not be the consequence by a long way). To this end it would be necessary, it seems to me, that he should step out of his incognito. Otherwise I do not see how it could be avoided that, instead of dealing with one, I should be honored or besieged by several challenges coming 380 from anonymous and unqualified opponents.

51. [The theses and antitheses of "The Antinomy of Pure Reason" in the *Critique*, B 454–489.]

Proposals as to an Investigation of the Critique upon Which a Judgment May Follow

I feel obliged to the learned public even for the silence with which it for a long time honored my *Critique*, for this proves at least a postponement of judgment and some supposition that, in a work leaving all beaten tracks and striking out on a new path, in which one cannot at once perhaps so easily find one's way, something may perchance lie from which an important but at present dead branch of human knowledge may derive new life and productiveness. Hence may have originated a solicitude for the as yet tender shoot, lest it be destroyed by a hasty judgment. A specimen of a judgment, delayed for the above reasons, is now before my eye in the *Gothaische gelehrte Zeitung*,[52] the thoroughness of which (leaving out of account my praise, which might be suspicious) every reader will himself perceive from the clear and unperverted presentation of a fragment of one of the first principles of my work.

Since an extensive structure cannot be judged at once as a whole from a hurried glance, I propose that it be tested piece by piece from its foundation up, and in this, the present *Prolegomena* may be used as a general outline with which the work itself may conveniently be compared. This suggestion, if it were founded on nothing more than my conceit of importance, such as vanity ordinarily attributes to all of one's own productions, would be immodest and would deserve to be rejected with indignation. But now the interests of all speculative philosophy have arrived at the point of total extinction, while human reason hangs upon them with inextinguishable affection; and only after having been endlessly disappointed, does it vainly attempt to change this into indifference.

In our thinking age, it is not to be supposed but that many deserving men would use any good opportunity of working for the common interest of an ever more 381 enlightened reason, if there were only some hope of attaining the goal. Mathematics, natural science, laws, arts, even morality, etc. do not completely fill the soul; there is always a space left over reserved for pure and speculative reason, the emptiness of which prompts us to seek in vagaries, buffooneries, and mysticism for what seems to be employment and entertainment, but what actually is mere pastime undertaken in order to deaden the troublesome voice of reason, which, in accordance with its nature, requires something that can satisfy it and does not merely subserve other ends or the interests of our inclinations. A consideration, therefore, which is concerned only with this extent of reason as it subsists for itself has, as I may reasonably suppose, a great fascination for everyone who has attempted thus to extend his concept, and I may even say a greater fascination than any other theoretical branch of knowledge, for which he would not willingly exchange it because here all other branches of knowledge and even purposes must meet and unite themselves in a whole.

I offer, therefore, these *Prolegomena* as a plan and guide for this investigation, and not the work itself. Although I am even now perfectly satisfied with the latter as far as contents, order, and mode of presentation, and the care that I have expended in weighing and testing every sentence before writing it down are concerned (for it has taken me years to satisfy myself fully, not only as regards the whole, but in some cases even as to the sources of one particular proposition); yet I am not quite satisfied with my exposition in some sections of the Doctrine of Elements,[53] as for instance in the deduction of the concepts of the understanding or in the chapter on the paralogisms of pure reason,[54] because a certain diffuseness takes away from their clearness, and in place of them what is here said in the *Prolegomena* respecting these sections may be made the basis of the test.

It is the boast of the Germans that, where steady and continuous industry are requisite, they can carry things further than other nations. If this opinion be well founded, an opportunity, a task, presents itself; the successful issue of this task can scarcely be doubted and all thinking men can equally take part in it, though they have hitherto been unsuccessful in accomplishing it and in thus confirming the above good opinion. This is chiefly because the science in question is of such a special kind that it can all at 382 once be brought to completion and to that permanent state beyond which it can never be developed,

52. [The issue of August 24, 1782.]

53. [The first part of the *Critique of Pure Reason*, the second part being the Methodology.]

54. [These sections were almost entirely rewritten in the second edition of the *Critique* (1787).]

in the least degree enlarged by later discoveries, or changed if we leave out of account adornment by greater clearness in some places or additional utility for all sorts of purposes. This is an advantage no other science has or can have, because there is none so completely isolated and independent of others and so exclusively concerned with the faculty of cognition pure and simple. And the present moment seems not to be unfavorable to my expectation; for in Germany no one seems now to know how to occupy himself, apart from the so-called useful sciences, so as to pursue not mere play but a business possessing an enduring purpose.

To discover how the endeavors of the learned may be united in such a purpose I must leave to others. In the meantime, it is not my intention to persuade anyone merely to follow my theses or even to flatter me with the hope that he will do so; but attacks, repetitions, limitations, or confirmation, completion, and extension, as the case may be, should be appended. If the matter be but investigated from its foundation, it cannot fail that a system, albeit not my own, shall be erected that shall be a possession for future generations for which they may have reason to be grateful.

It would lead us too far here to show what kind of metaphysics may be expected when the principles of criticism have been perfected and how, though the old false feathers have been pulled out, it need by no means appear poor and reduced to an insignificant figure but may be in other respects richly and respectably adorned. But other and great uses which would result from such a reform strike one immediately. The ordinary metaphysics had its uses, in that it sought out the elementary concepts of the pure understanding in order to make them clear through analysis and determinate through explications. In this way it was a training for reason, in whatever direction it might be turned. But this was all the good it did. This merit was subsequently destroyed when it favored conceit by venturesome assertions, sophistry by subtle dodges and prettifying, and shallowness by the ease with which it decided the most difficult problems by means of a little school wisdom, which is only the more seductive the more it has the choice, 383 on the one hand, of taking on something of the language of science and, on the other, from that of popular discourse—thus being everything to everybody but in reality being nothing at all. By criticism, however, a standard is given to our judgment whereby knowledge may be with certainty distinguished from pseudo-knowledge and firmly founded, being brought into full operation in metaphysics—a mode of thought extending by degrees its beneficial influence over every other use of reason, at once infusing into it the true philosophical spirit. But the service that metaphysics performs also for theology, by making it independent of the judgment of dogmatic speculation and thereby securing it completely against the attacks of all such opponents, is certainly not to be valued lightly. For ordinary metaphysics, although it promised theology much advantage, could not keep this promise, and by summoning speculative dogmatics to its assistance did nothing but arm enemies against itself. Mysticism, which can prosper in a rationalistic age only when it hides itself behind a system of school metaphysics, under the protection of which it may venture to rave with a semblance of rationality, is driven from theology, its last hiding place, by critical philosophy. Last, but not least, it cannot be otherwise than important to a teacher of metaphysics to be able to say with universal assent that what he expounds is *science*, and that by it actual service will be rendered to the commonweal.

Critique of Pure Reason

Preface [Second Edition]

Whether someone's treatment of the cognitions pertaining to reason's business does or does not follow the secure path of a science—this we can soon judge from the result. If, after many preparations and arrangements have been made, the treatment falters as soon as it turns to its purpose; or if, in order to reach that purpose, it repeatedly has to retrace its steps and enter upon a different path; or, again, if the various collaborators cannot be brought to agree on the manner in which their common aim is to be achieved—then we may rest assured that such an endeavor is still far from having entered upon the secure path of a science, but is a mere groping about. We shall indeed be rendering a service to reason if we can possibly discover that path, even if we should have to give up as futile much that was included in the purpose which we had previously adopted without deliberation.

Bviii *Logic* has been following that secure path from the earliest times. This is evident from the fact that since *Aristotle* it has not needed to retrace a single step, unless perhaps removing some of its dispensable subtleties, or setting it forth in a more distinct and determinate way, were to be counted as improvements of logic, even though they pertain more to the elegance of that science than to its being secure. Another remarkable fact about logic is that thus far it also has not been able to advance a single step, and hence is to all appearances closed and completed. It is true that some of the more recent [philosophers] have meant to expand logic. Some of them have inserted into it *psychological* chapters on the different cognitive powers (e.g., on our power of imagination, or on ingenuity). Others have inserted *metaphysical* chapters on the origin of cognition, or the origin of the different kinds of certainty according to the difference in the objects (i.e., chapters on idealism, skepticism, etc.). Still others have inserted into logic *anthropological* chapters on prejudices (as well as their causes and remedies). But all these attempts to expand logic are the result of ignorance concerning the peculiar nature of this science. We do not augment sciences, but corrupt them, if we allow their boundaries to overlap. But the boundary of logic is determined quite precisely by the fact that logic is a science that provides nothing but a comprehensive exposition and Bix strict proof of the formal rules of all thought. (Such thought may be a priori or empirical, may have any origin or object whatsoever, and may encounter in our minds obstacles that are accidental or natural.)

That logic has been so successful in following the secure path of a science is an advantage that it owes entirely to its limitations. They entitle it, even obligate it, to abstract from all objects of cognition and their differences; hence in logic the understanding deals with nothing more than itself and its form. Reason naturally had to find it far more difficult to enter upon the secure path of science when dealing not just with itself, but also with objects. By the same token, logic is a propaedeutic and forms, as it were, only the vestibule of the sciences; and when knowledge is at issue, while for the judging of such knowledge we do indeed presuppose a logic, yet for its acquisition we must look to what are called sciences properly and objectively.

Now insofar as there is to be reason in these sciences, something in them must be cognized a priori. Moreover, reason's cognition can be referred to the object of that cognition in two ways: either in order merely to *determine* the object and its concept (which Bx must be supplied from elsewhere), or in order to *make*

Reprinted from Immanuel Kant, *Critique of Pure Reason*, translated by Werner S. Pluhar (Indianapolis: Hackett Publishing Company, 1996), by permission of the publisher.

it actual as well. The first is reason's *theoretical*, the second its *practical cognition*. In both the pure part, i.e., the part in which reason determines its object entirely a priori, must be set forth all by itself beforehand, no matter how much or how little it may contain. We must not mix with this part what comes from other sources. For we follow bad economic procedures if we blindly spend what comes in and are afterwards unable, when the procedure falters, to distinguish which part of the income can support the expenditure and which must be cut from it.

Two [sciences involving] theoretical cognitions by reason are to determine their *objects* a priori: they are *mathematics* and *physics*. In mathematics this determination is to be entirely pure; in physics it is to be at least partly pure, but to some extent also in accordance with sources of cognition other than reason.

Mathematics has been following the secure path of a science since the earliest times to which the history of human reason extends; it did so already among that admirable people, the Greeks. But we must not think that it was as easy for mathematics to Bxi hit upon that royal road—or, rather, to build it on its own—as it was for logic, where reason deals only with itself. Rather, I believe that for a long time (above all, it was still so among the Egyptians) mathematics did no more than grope about, and that its transformation into a science was due to a *revolution* brought about by the fortunate idea that occurred to one man during an experiment. From that time onward, the route that mathematics had to take could no longer be missed, and the secure path of a science had been entered upon and traced out for all time and to an infinite distance. This revolution in the way of thinking was much more important than the discovery of the passage around the celebrated Cape.[1] Its history, and that of the fortunate man who brought this revolution about, is lost to us. But *Diogenes Laërtius*[2] always names the reputed authors of even the minutest elements of geometrical demonstration, elements that in ordinary people's judgment do not even stand in need of proof; and Diogenes hands down to us a story concerning the change that was brought about by the first indication of this new path's discovery. This story shows that the memory of this change must have seemed exceedingly important to mathematicians, and thus became indelible. When the *isosceles triangle* was first demonstrated, something dawned on the man who did so. (He may have been called *Thales*,[3] or by some other name.) He found that what he Bxii needed to do was not to investigate what he saw in the figure, nor—for that matter—to investigate the mere concept of that figure, and to let that inform him, as it were, of the figure's properties. He found, rather, that he must bring out (by constructing the figure) the properties that the figure had by virtue of what he himself was, according to concepts, thinking into it a priori and exhibiting. And he found that in order for him to know anything a priori and with certainty about the figure, he must attribute to this thing nothing but what follows necessarily from what he has himself put into it in accordance with his concept.

Natural science took much longer to hit upon the high road of science. For only about a century and a half have passed since the ingenious *Bacon*, Baron Verulam,[4] made the proposal that partly prompted this road's discovery, and partly—insofar as some were already on the trail of this discovery—invigorated it further. This discovery, too, can be explained only by a sudden revolution in people's way of thinking. I shall here take account of natural science only insofar as it is founded on *empirical* principles.

Something dawned on all investigators of nature when *Galileo* let balls, of a weight chosen by himself, roll down his inclined plane; or when *Torricelli*[5] made

1. [The Cape of Good Hope.—W.S.P.]

2. [Author of the only extant continuous account of the lives and doctrines of the main Greek philosophers. He is thought to have flourished (where is not clear) in the early part of the third century A.D. His work is known under various titles, such as *The Lives of Philosophers*, *Lives and Opinions of Famous Philosophers*, and several others.]

3. [Thales of Miletus (in Asia Minor), who was considered one of the Seven Wise Men of ancient Greece, flourished around 585 B.C. He has been regarded, since early antiquity, as the founder of the Ionian school of natural philosophy, and is generally credited with having introduced geometry to Greece.]

4. [Francis Bacon (1561–1626), Baron Verulam, Viscount St. Albans, lord chancellor of England, philosopher, and man of letters.]

5. [Evangelista Torricelli (1608–1647), Italian physicist and mathematician. He was first to create a sustained vacuum, and he invented the barometer.]

the air carry a weight that he had judged beforehand to be equal to the weight of a water column known to Bxiii him; or when, in more recent times, *Stahl*[6] converted metals into calx and that in turn into metal, by withdrawing something[7] from the metals and then restoring it to them.[8] What all these investigators of nature comprehended[9] was that reason has insight only into what it itself produces according to its own plan; and that reason must not allow nature by itself to keep it in leading strings, as it were, but reason must—using principles that underlie its judgments—proceed according to constant laws and compel nature to answer reason's own questions. For otherwise our observations, made without following any plan outlined in advance, are contingent, i.e., they have no coherence at all in terms of a necessary law—even though such a law is what reason seeks and requires. When approaching nature, reason must hold in one hand its principles, in terms of which alone concordant appearances can count as laws, and in the other hand the experiment that it has devised in terms of those principles. Thus reason must indeed approach nature in order to be instructed by it; yet it must do so not in the capacity of a pupil who lets the teacher tell him whatever the teacher wants, but in the capacity of an appointed judge who compels the witnesses to answer the question that he puts to them. Thus even Bxiv physics owes that very advantageous revolution in its way of thinking to this idea: the idea that we must, in accordance with what reason itself puts into nature, seek in nature (not attribute to it fictitiously) whatever reason must learn from nature and would know nothing of on its own. This is what put natural science, for the very first time, on the secure path of a science, after it had for so many centuries been nothing more than a mere groping about.

Metaphysics is a speculative cognition by reason that is wholly isolated and rises entirely above being instructed by experience. It is cognition through mere concepts (not, like mathematics, cognition through the application of concepts to intuition), so that here reason is to be its own pupil. But although metaphysics is older than all the other sciences, and would endure even if all the others were to be engulfed utterly in the abyss of an all-annihilating barbarism, fate thus far has not favored it to the point of enabling it to enter upon the secure path of a science. For in metaphysics reason continually falters, even when the laws into which it seeks to gain (as it pretends) a priori insight are those that are confirmed by the commonest experience. Countless times, in metaphysics, we have to retrace our steps, because we find that our path does not lead us where we want to go. As regards agreement in the assertions made by its Bxv devotees, metaphysics is very far indeed from such agreement. It is, rather, a combat arena which seems to be destined quite specifically for practicing one's powers in mock combat, and in which not one fighter has ever been able to gain even the smallest territory and to base upon his victory a lasting possession. There can be no doubt, therefore, that the procedure of metaphysics has thus far been a mere groping about, and—worst of all—a groping about among mere concepts.

Why is it, then, that in metaphysics we have thus far been unable to find the secure path of science? Might this path be impossible here? Why, then, has nature inflicted on reason, as one of reason's most important concerns, the restless endeavor to discover that path? What is more: how little cause have we to place confidence in our reason, when in one of the most important matters where we desire knowledge reason not merely forsakes us, but puts us off with mere pretenses and in the end betrays us! Or if we have only missed the path thus far, what indication do we have that if we renew our search, we may hope

6. [Georg Ernst Stahl (1660–1734), German physician and chemist. He developed the phlogiston theory of combustion, which offered the first comprehensive explanation of combustion and of such related biological processes as respiration, fermentation, and decay. The theory dominated chemical thought for almost a century, until its replacement by Lavoisier's oxidation theory of combustion.]

7. [The "something" was thought to be phlogiston. On the phlogiston theory of combustion (cf. previous note), the processes involved are these: Metals, when heated, lose phlogiston and become calces (or calx, in the singular), kinds of ashy powder now known to be oxides. Calces, when heated with charcoal, reabsorb phlogiston and become metals again. (The original phlogiston having been scattered and lost, the new phlogiston absorbed by the calx comes from the charcoal, which is especially rich in phlogiston.)]

8. I am not here following with precision the course of the history of the experimental method; indeed, the first beginnings of that history are not well known.

9. [As a result of the mentioned experiments.]

to be more fortunate than others before us have been?

I would think that the examples of mathematics and natural science, which have become what they Bxvi now are by a revolution accomplished all at once, are sufficiently remarkable to [suggest that we should] reflect on the essential component in that revolution, viz., the transformation of the way of thinking that became so advantageous for them; and as far as is permitted by the fact that they, as rational cognitions, are analogous to metaphysics, we should [there] imitate them with regard to that transformation, at least by way of an experiment. Thus far it has been assumed that all our cognition must conform to objects. On that presupposition, however, all our attempts to establish something about them a priori, by means of concepts through which our cognition would be expanded, have come to nothing. Let us, therefore, try to find out by experiment whether we shall not make better progress in the problems of metaphysics if we assume that objects must conform to our cognition.—This assumption already agrees better with the demanded possibility of an a priori cognition of objects—i.e., a cognition that is to ascertain something about them before they are given to us. The situation here is the same as was that of *Copernicus* when he first thought of explaining the motions of celestial bodies.[10] Having found it difficult to make progress there when he assumed that the entire host of stars revolved around the spectator, he tried to find out by experiment whether he might not be more successful if he had the spectator revolve and the stars remain at rest. Now, we can try a similar experiment in meta- Bxvii physics, with regard to our *intuition* of objects. If our intuition had to conform to the character of its objects, then I do not see how we could know anything a priori about that character. But I can quite readily conceive of this possibility if the object (as object of the senses) conforms to the character of our power of intuition. However, if these intuitions are to become cognitions, I cannot remain with them but must refer them, as presentations, to something or other as their object, and must determine this object by means of them. [Since for this determination I require concepts, I must make one of two assumptions.] I can assume that the *concepts* by means of which I bring about this determination likewise conform to the object;[11] and in that case I am again in the same perplexity as to how I can know anything a priori about that object. Or else I assume that the objects, or—what amounts to the same[12]—the *experience* in which alone they (as objects that are given to us) can be cognized, conform to those concepts. On this latter assumption, I immediately see an easier way out. For experience is itself a way of cognizing for which I need understanding. But understanding has its rule, a rule that I must presuppose within me even before objects are given to me, and hence must presuppose a priori; and that rule is expressed in a priori concepts. Hence all objects of experience must necessarily conform Bxviii to these concepts and agree with them. Afterwards, however, we must also consider objects insofar as they can merely be thought, though thought necessarily, but cannot at all be given in experience (at least not in the way in which reason thinks them). Our attempts to think these objects (for they must surely be thinkable) will afterwards provide us with a splendid touchstone of what we are adopting as the changed method in our way of thinking, viz., that all we cognize a priori about things is what we ourselves put into them.[13]

10. [Nicolaus Copernicus (1473–1543), the Polish astronomer, reinvented the heliocentric hypothesis. The hypothesis had been advanced previously by Aristarchus, a Greek astronomer of the third century B.C. But his work was lost a few decades after he wrote it, and we know about it only through other writers' testimony that itself was not recovered until long after the time of Copernicus.]

11. [As do the intuitions.]

12. [Because the objects under discussion are objects of our experience, i.e., objects as experienced (objects given to us in experience).]

13. This method, then, which imitates that of the investigator of nature, consists in searching for the elements of pure reason in what can be *confirmed or refuted by an experiment.* Now the propositions of pure reason, especially if they venture beyond all bounds of possible experience, cannot be tested by doing (as we do in natural science) an experiment with their *objects.* Hence testing such propositions will be feasible only by doing an experiment with *concepts* and *principles* that we assume a priori. In that experiment we must arrange [to use] these concepts and principles in such a way that the same objects can be contemplated from two different standpoints: *on the one hand,* for the sake of experience, as objects of the senses and of the understanding; yet *on the other hand,* for the sake of isolated reason

This experiment is as successful as was desired. It promises that metaphysics will be on the secure path of a science in its first part, viz., the part where it deals with those a priori concepts for which corresponding *Bxix* objects adequate to these concepts can be given in experience. For on the changed way of thinking we can quite readily explain how a priori cognition is possible; what is more, we can provide satisfactory proofs for the laws that lie a priori at the basis of nature considered as the sum of objects of experience. Neither of these accomplishments was possible on the kind of procedure used thus far. On the other hand, this deduction—provided in the first part of metaphysics—of our power to cognize a priori[14] produces a disturbing result that seems highly detrimental to the whole purpose of metaphysics as dealt with in the second part: viz., that with this power to cognize a priori we shall never be able to go beyond the boundary of possible experience, *Bxx* even though doing so is precisely the most essential concern of this science. Yet this very [situation permits] the experiment that will countercheck the truth of the result that we obtained from the first assessment of our a priori rational cognition: viz., that our rational cognition applies only to appearances, and leaves the thing in itself uncognized by us, even though inherently actual. For what necessarily impels us to go beyond the boundary of experience and of all appearances is the *unconditioned* that reason demands in things in themselves; reason—necessarily and quite rightfully—demands this unconditioned for everything conditioned, thus demanding that the series of conditions be completed by means of that unconditioned. Suppose, now, we find that the unconditioned *cannot be thought at all without contradiction* if we assume that our experiential cognition conforms to objects as things in themselves, yet that *the contradiction vanishes* if we assume that our presentation of things, as these are given to us, does not conform to them as things in themselves, but that these objects are, rather, appearances that conform to our way of presenting. Suppose that we find, consequently, that the unconditioned is not to be met with in things insofar as we are acquainted with them (i.e., insofar as they are given to us), but is to be met with in them [only] insofar as we are not acquainted with them, viz., insofar as they are things in themselves. If this is what we find, it will show that what we assumed initially only by way of an experiment[15] does in fact *Bxxi* have a foundation.[16] Now, once we have denied that speculative reason can make any progress in that realm of the suprasensible,[17] we still have an option available to us. We can try to discover whether perhaps in reason's practical cognition data can be found that would allow us to determine reason's transcendent concept of the unconditioned.[18] Perhaps in this way our a priori cognition, though one that is possible only from a practical point of view, would still allow us to get beyond the boundary of all possible experience, as is the wish of metaphysics. Moreover, when we follow this kind of procedure,[19] still speculative reason has at least provided us with room for such an expansion [of our cognition], even if it had to leave that room empty. And hence there is as yet nothing to keep us from filling in that room, if we can, with practical *data* of reason; indeed, reason summons us to do so.[20] *Bxxii*

that strives to transcend all bounds of experience, as objects that we merely think. Now if it turns out that contemplating things from that twofold point of view results in harmony with the principle of reason, but that doing so from one and the same point of view puts reason into an unavoidable conflict with itself, then the experiment decides in favor of the correctness of distinguishing the two points of view.

14. [I.e., legitimation of the claim that we have such a power.]

15. [Viz., that our power of a priori cognition can inform us only about appearances, but can never take us beyond the boundary of possible experience and allow us to cognize the thing in itself.]

16. This experiment of pure reason is very similar to that done in *chemistry*, which is called sometimes the experiment of *reduction*, but generally the *synthetic procedure*. The *analysis* of the *metaphysician* has divided pure a priori cognition into two very heterogeneous elements, viz., such cognition of things as appearances, and of things in themselves. The [metaphysician's] *dialectic* recombines the two so as to yield *agreement* with reason's necessary idea of the *unconditioned*, and finds that this agreement can never be obtained except through that distinction, which is therefore [a] true one.

17. [I.e., the realm of objects considered as things in themselves rather than as objects of sense.]

18. [I.e., make the concept determinate, give it content by means of attributes or "determinations."]

19. [I.e., the use of practical reason.]

20. In the same way [as Kant has just described in the case of metaphysics] the central laws governing the motions of the celestial bodies provided with established certainty what

The task, then, of this critique of pure speculative reason consists in the described attempt to transform the procedure previously followed in metaphysics, by subjecting metaphysics to a complete revolution, thus following the example set by the geometricians and investigators of nature. The critique is a treatise on the method [of the science of metaphysics], not a system of the science itself. Yet it does set down the *Bxxiii* entire outline of metaphysics, including the bounds of this science as well as its entire internal structure. For pure speculative reason has a twofold peculiarity. First, it both can and ought to measure what its own ability is according to the different ways in which it selects objects for its thought. For in a priori cognition nothing can be attributed to objects except what the thinking subject takes from itself. Second, pure speculative reason also can and ought to enumerate completely and on its own the various ways it has of posing problems to itself, and thus to set down in advance the entire outline for a system of metaphysics. For, as regards its cognitive principles, it is an entirely separate, self-subsistent unity in which, as in an organized body, each member exists for the sake of all the others, and all exist for the sake of each one. In this unity no principle can safely be taken in *one* reference unless we have also investigated it in [its] *thoroughgoing* reference to our entire pure use of reason. But [as a consequence of this unity of pure speculative reason] metaphysics is also exceptionally fortunate in a way that is denied to all other rational sciences dealing with objects (as distinguished from *logic*, which deals only with the form of thought as such): Once metaphysics has been brought by this critique onto the secure path of a science, it is able to encompass completely the entire realm of the cognitions pertaining to it. Hence it can complete its work *Bxxiv* and put it aside for the use of posterity, as capital that can never be increased. What enables metaphysics to complete its work is that it deals merely with principles, and with the restrictions on their use as determined by these principles themselves. Moreover, being a basic science, it is also obligated to achieve this completeness; regarding metaphysics we must be able to say: *nil actum reputans, si quid superesset agendum.*[21]

But, it will be asked, what sort of treasure is this that we mean to bequeath to posterity, in leaving them a metaphysics that has been purified by critique, though thereby also made durable? A cursory survey of this work will leave one with the impression that such a metaphysics benefits us only *negatively*, viz., by instructing us that in [using] speculative reason we must never venture beyond the boundary of experience; and this instruction is indeed its primary benefit. But this benefit becomes *positive* as soon as we become aware that the principles with which speculative reason ventures beyond its boundary do not in fact *expand* our use of reason; they unfailingly *narrow* it, as we find when we examine them more closely. For these principles, which properly pertain to sensibility, do actually threaten[22] to expand the bounds of sensibility until they include everything, thus threatening *Bxxv* even to displace the pure (practical) use of reason. Hence a critique that restricts speculative reason is, to that extent, indeed *negative*. But because, by doing so, the critique also removes an obstacle that restricts—or even threatens to annihilate—the practical

Copernicus had initially assumed only as a hypothesis, and at the same time provided proof of the invisible force (*Newtonian* attraction) that links together the world edifice. That force would have remained forever undiscovered if Copernicus had not dared, in a manner that conflicted with the senses but yet was true, to seek the observed motions not in the celestrial objects but in the spectator. The transformation in the way of thinking [in metaphysics] which I set forth in the *Critique* is analogous to the Copernician hypothesis. Here in the preface I likewise put it forth only as a hypothesis, even though in the treatise itself it will be proved, not hypothetically but apodeictically, from the character of our presentations of space and time and from the elementary concepts [i.e., the categories] of the understanding. Here I put it forth as a hypothesis in order merely to draw attention to the first attempts at such a transformation; and such attempts are always hypothetical.

21. ["Thinking that nothing was done as long as anything remained to be done." The quote is from the (unfinished) *De bello civili* (*On the Civil War*) by the Roman poet Lucan (Marcus Annaeus Lucanus, A.D. 39–65), ii, 657. The poem, which is also called *Pharsalia* (after the battle of Pharsalos described in Book vii), deals with the contest between Julius Caesar and the Senate, and the person referred to in the quote is Caesar. Actually, instead of *reputans* (thinking) the original has *credens* (believing), and instead of *si* it has *dum* or possibly *cum* (a switch that does not affect the meaning here).]

22. [If used in the way described.]

use of reason, its benefit is in fact *positive* and very important. We see this as soon as we become convinced that there is a use of pure reason which is practical and absolutely necessary (viz., its moral use). When used practically, pure reason inevitably expands and reaches beyond the bounds of sensibility; and although it does not require for this any help from speculative pure reason, it must still be assured against interference from it in order not to fall into contradiction with itself. To deny that this service rendered by the critique has a *positive* benefit would be like saying that the police provides no positive benefit; after all, one might say, the main task of the police is only to put a stop to the violence on whose account citizens must fear each other, in order that everyone may carry on his business calmly and safely. Now in the analytic part of the critique I shall prove that space and time are only forms of our sensible intuition and hence are only conditions of the existence of things as appearances, and that, furthermore, we have no concepts of understanding, and hence *Bxxvi* also no elements whatever for the cognition of things, except insofar as intuition can be given corresponding to these concepts. That will prove, consequently, that we cannot have [speculative] cognition of any object as thing in itself, but can have such cognition only insofar as the object is one of sensible intuition, i.e., an appearance. And from this it does indeed follow that any possible speculative cognition of reason is restricted to mere objects of *experience.* On the other hand, it must be noted carefully that this [conclusion] is always subject to this reservation: that we must be able at least to *think*, even if not [speculatively] *cognize*, the same objects also as things in themselves.[23] For otherwise an absurd proposition would follow, *Bxxvii* viz., that there is appearance without anything that appears. Now let us suppose that the distinction, necessitated by our critique, between objects of experience and these same objects as things in themselves, had not been made at all. In that case the principle of causality, and hence nature's mechanism as governing the determination of [the exercise of] that causality, would definitely have to hold for all things as such[24] [construed] as efficient causes. Hence I could not, without manifest contradiction, say of the same being, for example the human soul, that its will is free and yet is subject to natural necessity, i.e., not free. For I would be taking the soul *in the same sense* in the two propositions, viz., as a thing as such (thing in itself); nor, without prior critique, could I help taking it so. Suppose, on the other hand, that the *Critique* is not in error when it teaches us to take the object in *two different senses,* viz., as appearance and as thing in itself: and that the deduction of the *Critique's* concepts of understanding is correct, so that the principle of causality applies to things only in the first sense, viz., insofar as they are objects of experience, but that these same objects are not subject to that principle when taken in the second sense.[25] On these suppositions, no contradiction arises when we *Bxxviii* think the same will in both these ways: in its appearance (i.e., in its visible acts), as conforming necessarily to natural law and as to that extent *not free;* yet on the other hand, *qua* belonging to a thing in itself,[26] as not subject to that law, and hence as *free.* Now as regards my soul when considered from this second standpoint, I cannot *cognize* it through any [use of] speculative reason (let alone through empirical observation); nor, therefore, can I in this way cognize freedom as the property of a being to which I attribute effects in the world of sense. For otherwise I would have to cognize such a being as a being determined with regard to its existence and yet as not determined in time (which is impossible, because I cannot base such a concept on any intuition). Nevertheless, [although I cannot in this way cognize my freedom,] I can still *think* freedom. I.e., at least my presentation

23. In order for me to *cognize* an object I must be able to prove its [real] possibility (either from its actuality as attested by experience, or a priori by means of reason). But I can *think* whatever I want to, even if I am unable to commit myself to there being, in the sum of all [logical] possibilities, an object corresponding to the concept. All that is required in order for me to think something is that I do not contradict myself, i.e., that my concept be a [logically] possible thought. But I require something further in order to attribute objective reality to a concept (i.e., real possibility, as distinguished from the merely logical possibility just mentioned). However—and this is my point—this something further need not be sought in theoretical sources of cognition, but may also lie in practical ones.

24. [I.e., including things in themselves.]

25. [I.e., as things in themselves.]

26. [A soul.]

of freedom contains no contradiction, if we make our critical distinction between the two ways of presenting (sensible and intellectual), and restrict accordingly the pure concepts of understanding and hence also the principles that flow from them. Now let us suppose that morality necessarily presupposes freedom (in the strictest sense) as a property of our will; for morality adduces a priori, as *data* of reason, original practical principles residing in reason, and these principles *Bxxix* would be absolutely impossible without the presupposition of freedom. But then suppose that speculative reason had proved that freedom cannot be thought at all.[27] In that case the moral presupposition[28] would have to yield to the other [supposition].[29] For this other [supposition]'s opposite involves a manifest contradiction[30] (whereas the opposite of freedom and morality involves no contradiction, unless freedom has already been presupposed).[31] Hence *freedom*, and with it morality, would have to give way to the *mechanism of nature*. But in fact the situation is different. All I need for morality is that freedom does not contradict itself and hence can at least be thought; I do not need to have any further insight into it. In other words, all I need is that freedom [in my act] puts no obstacle whatever in the way of the natural mechanism [that governs] the same act (when the act is taken in a different reference). Thus the doctrine of morality maintains its own place, and so does natural science. But this would not have happened if the critique had not instructed us beforehand about our unavoidable ignorance regarding things in themselves, restricting to mere appearances what we can *cognize* theoretically. This same exposition of the positive benefit found in critical principles of pure reason can be produced again in regard to the concept of *God* and of the *simple nature* of our *soul*; but for the sake of brevity I shall omit it. Thus[32] I cannot even *assume God, freedom*, and *immortality*, [as I must] for *Bxxx* the sake of the necessary practical use of my reason, if I do not at the same time *deprive* speculative reason of its pretensions to transcendent insight. For in order to reach God, freedom, and immortality, speculative reason must use principles that in fact extend merely to objects of possible experience; and when these principles are nonetheless applied to something that cannot be an object of experience, they actually do always transform it into an appearance, and thus they declare all *practical expansion* of reason to be impossible. I therefore had to annul *knowledge* in order to make room for *faith*. And the true source of all the lack of faith which conflicts with morality—and is always highly dogmatic—is dogmatism in metaphysics, i.e., the prejudice according to which we can make progress in metaphysics without a [prior] critique of pure reason.

Although, therefore, it cannot be difficult to leave to posterity the bequest of a metaphysics drawn up systematically in accordance with a critique of pure reason, yet such a metaphysics is a gift that is not to be despised. For consider merely how reason is cultivated generally by pursuing the secure path of a science, as compared to its baseless groping and careless roaming-about when there is no critique. Con- *Bxxxi* sider also our youth with their desire for knowledge, who can then make better use of their time than they can under the usual dogmatism. That dogmatism encourages them quite early and strongly to reason with ease about things of which they understand nothing and into which, moreover, neither they nor anyone else in the world will ever have any insight. It may even encourage them to seek to invent new ideas and opinions and thus to neglect the study of well-founded sciences. Above all, however, [we see the value of] such a metaphysics if we take into ac-

27. [Viz., as ruled out by the necessary mechanism of nature.]

28. [Of freedom, as presupposed by morality.]

29. [That freedom cannot be thought.]

30. [Which would thus prove the original supposition, viz., that freedom cannot be thought. The opposite (or denial) of this supposition is that freedom *can* be thought, which would contradict a necessary mechanism that (as would have been proved by speculative reason) rules out freedom.]

31. [Here the opposite (or denial) is that there is no freedom and hence no (possibility of) morality, which would not contradict a necessary mechanism, obviously not even one that ruled out freedom. Hence here the opposite or denial cannot prove the original supposition, viz., of freedom as presupposed by morality. A contradiction would arise only if we had already presupposed freedom: freedom would contradict both its own denial and that of (the possibility of) morality.]

32. [By the same reasoning that has just been used.]

count the inestimable advantage of putting an end, for all future time, to all objections against morality and religion, and of doing so in the *Socratic* manner, viz., by the clearest proof of the opponents' ignorance. For there has always been some metaphysics in the world; and some metaphysics will presumably continue to be found in it, but with it also a dialectic of pure reason, because a dialectic is natural to pure reason. Hence the primary and most important concern of philosophy is to deprive metaphysics, once and for all, of its detrimental influence, by obstructing the source of its errors.

Despite this important change in the realm of the sciences and the *loss* that speculative reason must suffer in what it has thus far imagined to be its possession, the situation remains entirely as favorable as ever with regard to the universal human concern, and with regard to the benefit that the world has thus far obtained from the teachings of pure reason. The loss affects only the *monopoly of the schools*; in no way does it affect the *interests of the people*. Let me ask the most adamant dogmatist whether any of the following proofs have ever been able, after emerging from the schools, to reach the public and exert the slightest influence on its conviction: the one that proves our soul's continuance after death from the simplicity of substance; or the one that proves the freedom of the will as opposed to universal mechanism by means of subtle but ineffectual distinctions between subjective and objective practical necessity; or the one that proves the existence of God from the concept of a maximally real being ([or] from the contingency of what is changeable and the necessity of a prime mover). I take it that these proofs have never reached the public and influenced it in that way; nor can they ever be expected to do so, because the common human understanding is unfit for such subtle speculation. Rather, the conviction spreading to the public, insofar as it rests on rational grounds, has had to arise from quite different causes. As regards the soul's continuance after death, the hope for a *future life* arose solely from a predisposition discernible to every human being in his [own] nature, viz., the inability ever to be satisfied by what is temporal (and thus is inadequate for the predispositions of his whole vocation). As regards the freedom of the will, the consciousness of *freedom* arose from nothing but the clear exhibition of duties in their opposition to all claims of the inclinations. Finally, as regards the existence of God, the faith in [the existence of] a wise and great *author of the world* arose solely from the splendid order, beauty, and provisions manifested everywhere in nature. Indeed, not only does this possession [of convictions held by the public] remain undisturbed, but it even gains further authority through what the schools are [here] being told: viz., that on a point dealing with the universal human concern they should not claim to have a higher and more extensive insight than that which can be attained just as readily by the great multitude (most worthy of our respect); and that they should therefore confine themselves solely to the cultivation of these universally comprehensible and for moral aims sufficient bases of proof. Hence the change[33] affects merely the arrogant claims of the schools, who would like to be considered in these matters (as they are rightly considered in many other matters) as the sole experts and guardians for truths whose key they keep to themselves, telling the public only how to use them (*quod mecum nescit, solus vult scire videri*).[34] On the other hand, a more legitimate claim of the speculative philosopher is nonetheless being taken care of here. He remains always the exclusive trustee of a science that is useful to the public without its knowing this: viz., the critique of reason. For that critique can never become popular; nor does it need to be. For just as finely spun arguments for useful truths never make it into the heads of the people, so do the equally subtle objections against those arguments never occur to them. The school, on the other hand, inevitably gets involved in both the arguments and the objections, as does anyone who advances to [the point where he can] speculate. Hence the school is obligated to investigate thoroughly the rights of speculative reason, in order to forestall once and for all the scandal that sooner or later must become apparent, even to the people, from [all] the controversies—the controversies in which, when there is no critique,

Bxxxii Bxxxiii Bxxxiv

33. [In the realm of the sciences.]

34. ["What he is as ignorant of as I am he wants to appear to be the only one to understand." I am grateful to Francis E. Sparshott for identifying this quote (and to Geoffrey Payzant for knowing whom to ask). It is from Horace's *Epistles*, II, i, 87. The original text actually has *ignorat* instead of (the synonymous) *nescit*.]

metaphysicians (and, as such, finally also the clergy) inevitably become entangled, and which thereafter even corrupt their teachings. Solely by means of critique can we cut off, at the very root, *materialism*, *fatalism*, *atheism*, freethinking *lack of faith*, *fanaticism*, and *superstition*, which can become harmful universally; and, finally, also *idealism* and *skepticism*, which are dangerous mainly to the schools and cannot *Bxxxv* easily cross over to the public. If governments do indeed think it proper to occupy themselves with the concerns of scholars, they should promote the freedom for such critique, by which alone the works of reason can be put on a firm footing. Promoting such freedom would conform much better to their wise care for both sciences and people than does supporting the ridiculous despotism of the schools. The schools raise a loud cry about danger to the public if one tears up the webs they have spun, even though in fact the public has never taken notice of these webs and hence can never feel the loss of them.

Critique does not stand in contrast to the *dogmatic procedure* that reason follows in its pure cognitions; for that procedure is science (and science must always be dogmatic, i.e., it must always do strict proofs from secure a priori principles). Rather, critique stands in contrast to *dogmatism*. Dogmatism is the pretension that we can make progress[35] by means of no more than a pure cognition from concepts (i.e., philosophical cognition) in accordance with principles—such concepts and principles as reason has been using for a long time—without inquiring into the manner and the right by which reason has arrived at them. Hence dogmatism is the dogmatic procedure followed by reason *without prior critique of its own ability*. The contrast, therefore, is not one that is meant to support *Bxxxvi* a garrulous shallowness with claims to the name of popularity; let alone one to support skepticism, which makes short work of all metaphysics. Rather, critique is the preliminary operation necessary for promoting a metaphysics that is well-founded and [thus] a science. Such a metaphysics must necessarily be carried out dogmatically, and systematically according to the strictest demand, and hence carried out in a way that complies with school standards (rather than in a popular way). For this demand cannot be remitted because metaphysics promises to carry out its task entirely a priori, and therefore to the complete satisfaction of speculative reason. Hence in carrying out some day the plan prescribed by the critique, i.e., in [composing] the future system of metaphysics, we shall have to follow the strict method of the illustrious *Wolff*, the greatest among all the dogmatic philosophers.[36] He was first to provide the example (through which he became the originator of the—not yet extinct—spirit of thoroughness in Germany) as to how one is to take the secure path of a science: viz., by establishing principles in a law-governed way, determining concepts distinctly, trying for strictness in proofs, and avoiding bold leaps in inferences. He was, by the same token, superbly suited to transfer into that secure state such a science as metaphysics is—provided it had occurred to him to prepare the ground in advance by a critique of the organ,[37] viz., pure *Bxxxvii* reason itself. His failure to do so must be imputed not so much to him as rather to the dogmatic way of thinking [characteristic] of his age; and for this failure neither the philosophers of his own period, nor those of all the previous ones, have any [grounds] to reproach one another. Those who reject Wolff's method and yet simultaneously also the procedure of the critique of pure reason can have in mind nothing but [the aim of] shaking off the fetters of *Science* altogether, thus converting work into play, certainty into opinion, and philosophy into philodoxy.[38]

As regards this second edition, I wanted, as is proper, to seize this opportunity in order to remedy as much as possible any difficulties and obscurity, from which many of the misinterpretations may have arisen that acute men—perhaps not without my fault—have hit upon in judging this book. I have not found anything to change in the propositions themselves and in the bases used for proving them, nor in the form and completeness of the plan. This is due partly to the long examination to which I had subjected them

35. [In metaphysics.]

36. [Baron Christian von Wolff (1679–1754), German mathematician, natural scientist, and, above all, rationalist philosopher of the Enlightenment. He is the author of numerous writings. Although his work follows the tradition of Descartes and Leibniz, he developed his own philosophical system within that tradition.]

37. [I.e., instrument. See B 86.]

38. [Pursuit of a creed.]

before submitting the book to the public, and partly to the character of the matter itself, i.e., the nature of a pure speculative reason. For pure speculative reason has a true structure. In such a structure everything is an organ, i.e., everything is there for the sake of each member, and each individual member is *Bxxxviii* there for the sake of all, and hence even the slightest defect,[39] whether it be a mistake (error) or an omission, must inevitably betray itself when we use that plan or system. I hope, moreover, that this system will continue to maintain itself in this unchangeable state. What entitles me to this confidence is not self-conceit, but merely the fact that this [unchangeable state of the system] is evident from the following experiment: We obtain the same result whether we proceed from the minutest elements all the way to the whole of pure reason, or proceed backward to each part when starting from the whole (for this whole also is given by itself, through reason's final aim in the practical sphere); and the result is the same because any attempt to alter even the smallest part immediately gives rise to contradictions, not merely in the system, but in human reason in general. On the other hand, much remains to be done as regards the [manner of] *exposition,* and in this regard I have tried to make improvements by providing this new edition. Some of these improvements are meant to remedy the misunderstanding concerning the Aesthetic, especially the concept of time; others, the obscurity in the deduction of the concepts of understanding. Yet other improvements are meant to remedy the supposed lack of sufficient evidence in the proofs of the principles of pure understanding; and others still, finally, to remedy the misinterpretation of the paralogisms advanced against rational psychology. That is how far the alterations extend that I have made in the manner of exposition. (I.e., they extend only to *Bxxxix* the end of the first chapter of the Transcendental *Bxl* Dialectic.)[40] I did not extend them further because there was not enough time, and also because with regard to the remainder I had not come upon any misunderstanding by competent and impartial critics. *Bxli* Although I cannot name these critics and praise them *Bxlii* as they deserve, they will doubtless find on their own the places where I have taken their suggestions into

39. [In the plan displaying that systematic structure.]

40. Only one of my alterations could I call, properly speaking, an addition, and even it concerns only the kind of proof I offer. It consists—see p. [B] 275—in a new refutation of psychological *idealism,* and a strict proof (also, I believe, the only possible proof) of the objective reality of outer intuition. However innocuous idealism may be considered to be (without in fact being so) as regards the essential purposes of metaphysics, there always remains this scandal for philosophy and human reason in general [if we accept idealism]: that we have to accept merely on faith the existence of things outside us (even though they provide us with all the material we have for cognitions, even for those of our inner sense); and that, if it occurs to someone to doubt their existence, we have no satisfactory proof with which to oppose him. Since there is some obscurity in the expressions I used in that proof, from the third to the sixth line, I request that the passage be changed to the following: "*But this permanent something cannot be an intuition within me. For all bases determining my existence that can be encountered within me are presentations; and, being presentations, they themselves require something permanent distinct from them, by reference to which their variation, and hence my existence in the time in which they vary, can be determined.*" I suppose some will object to this proof by saying: But all I am conscious of directly is what is within me, i.e., my *presentation* of external things, and hence we still have not established whether or not there is anything corresponding to it outside me. However, through inner *experience* I am *Bxl* conscious of *my existence in time* (and hence also of its determinability in time), and that is more than to be conscious merely of my presentation. But this consciousness of my existence (and of its determinability) in time is the same thing as *empirical consciousness of my existence,* and that can be determined only by reference to something linked with my existence that is *outside me.* Therefore this consciousness of my existence in time is linked, by way of identity, with the consciousness of a relation to something outside me; and hence what inseparably connects what is outside me with my inner sense is experience rather than invention, [outer] sense rather than my power of imagination. For outer sense is in itself already the referring of intuition to something actual outside me; and the reality of outer sense, as distinguished from imagination, rests only on our linking outer sense inseparably, as we are doing here, with inner experience itself, viz., as the condition of the possibility of inner experience. [This empirical consciousness of my existence contrasts with] the *intellectual consciousness* of my existence that I have in the conception I am, which accompanies all my judgments and acts of understanding; if with that intellectual consciousness of my existence I could at the same time link a determination of my existence through intellectual intuition, then this

account.[41] The improvements do, however, involve a small loss for the reader, a loss that I could not prevent without making the book rather too voluminous: I had to omit or abbreviate various materials that, while not required essentially for the completeness of the whole, will yet be missed by many readers as possibly useful for some other aim. I had to do this in order to make room for my new exposition, which, as I hope, is more comprehensible now. Basically, my exposition changes absolutely nothing in the propositions or even in the bases used for proving them. But now and then the way in which it departs from my previous method of setting forth the material is such that I could not have accomplished this exposition by means of mere interpolations. I hope that this small loss, which anyone who so wishes can make up anyway by comparing this edition with the first one, is more than made up by the fact that the new version is more comprehensible. I have been pleased and gratified by what I have seen in various published writings (including reviews of some books, as well as separate treatises). I saw there that the spirit of thoroughness in Germany has not faded away, but has only been drowned out for a short time by the tone in vogue, whereby people employ in their thinking a Bxliii freedom that befits [only] a genius. And I saw that courageous and bright minds have gained mastery of my *Critique* despite its thorny paths—paths that lead to a science of pure reason which complies with school standards, but which as such is the only science that lasts, and hence is exceedingly necessary. These worthy men have that happy combination of thorough insight with a talent for lucid exposition (the very talent that I am not aware of in myself), and I leave it to them to perfect my treatment of the material, which here and there may still be deficient as regards lucidity of exposition. For although there is in this case no danger of my being refuted, there certainly is a danger of my not being understood. As for myself, although I shall from now on be unable to enter into controversy, I shall pay careful attention to all suggestions, whether from friends or opponents, in order to use them in the future when I carry out the system of metaphysics in accordance with this propaedeutic. In the course of these labors, I have advanced considerably in age (this month I reach my sixty-fourth year). I must therefore spend my time frugally, if I want to carry out my plan of providing the metaphysics both of nature and of morals, and thus confirm the correctness of my critique of both speculative and practical reason. Hence I must rely on the help of those worthy men who have made this work their own, expecting them to clear up the Bxliv obscurities in it that could hardly have been avoided initially, as well as to defend it as a whole. Any philo-

determination would not include necessarily the consciousness of a relation to something outside me. But in fact I am unable to do so. That intellectual consciousness of my existence does indeed lead the way; but the inner intuition in which alone my existence can be determined is sensible intuition, and is tied to the condition of time. But this [kind of] determination [of my existence], and hence inner experience itself, depends on something permanent to which I must regard myself as related by way of contrast; and anything permanent is not within me and hence is to Bxli be found only in something outside me. Hence the reality of outer sense is linked necessarily with the reality of inner sense, and this [link] makes experience as such possible. In other words, I am conscious with just as much certainty that there are things outside me that have reference to my sense, as I am conscious that I myself exist as determined in time. On the other hand, for which of my given intuitions there actually are objects outside me that correspond to them, objects that must hence be attributed not to the power of imagination but to outer *sense*, as belonging to it, must be established in each particular case. It must be established—and here the proposition that there actually is outer experience must always lie at the basis—in accordance with the rules by which experience as such (even inner experience) is distinguished from imagination. We may add to this a comment: The presentation of something *permanent* in one's existence is not the same thing as a *permanent presentation*. For although—like all our presentations, even those of matter—the presentation of something permanent may be quite mutable and may vary greatly, it yet refers to something permanent. Hence this permanent something must be a thing that is distinct from all my presentations and is external. The existence of this thing is included necessarily in the *determination* of my own existence, and [together] with it amounts to only a single experience; and this experience would not take place even inwardly if it were not (in part) outer at the same time. As to how this occurs, we cannot explain that any further, just as in general we cannot explain further how what is constant is thought by us [as constant] in time, with the concept of change arising from the simultaneity of what is constant with what varies.

41. In making the alterations I mentioned above.

sophical treatise can be tweaked in individual places (for it cannot come forward in all the armor worn by mathematical treatises), while yet the structure of the system, considered as a unity, is not in the slightest danger. Few people have the intellectual agility to survey such a system when it is new, but fewer still have the inclination to do so, because they find all innovation inconvenient. Again, in any work that for the most part uses language freely, we can easily dig up seeming contradictions if we tear individual passages from their contexts and compare them with one another. In the eyes of those who rely on the judgment of others, such seeming contradictions cast an unfavorable light on the work; but they are quite easily resolved by someone who has gained command of the idea as a whole. Moreover, if a theory is internally stable, then any action and reaction that initially portend great danger will in time serve only to smooth away the theory's unevenness; and in a short time they will even provide the theory with the requisite elegance, if those who deal with it are men of impartiality, insight, and true popularity.

Königsberg, in the month of April, 1787.

B1

Introduction [Second Edition]

I. On the Distinction between Pure and Empirical Cognition

There can be no doubt that all our cognition begins with experience. For what else might rouse our cognitive power to its operation if objects stirring our senses did not do so? In part these objects by themselves bring about presentations. In part they set in motion our understanding's activity, by which it compares these presentations, connects or separates them, and thus processes the raw material of sense impressions into a cognition of objects that is called experience. *In terms of time*, therefore, no cognition in us precedes experience, and all our cognition begins with experience.

But even though all our cognition starts **with** experience, that does not mean that all of it arises **from** experience. For it might well be that even our experiential cognition is composite, consisting of what we receive through impressions and what our own cognitive power supplies from itself (sense impressions merely prompting it to do so). If our cognitive power does make such an addition, we may not be able to distinguish it from that basic material until long B2 practice has made us attentive to it and skilled in separating it from the basic material.

This question, then, whether there is such a cognition that is independent of experience and even of all impressions of the senses, is one that cannot be disposed of as soon as it comes to light, but that at least still needs closer investigation. Such cognitions are called *a priori cognitions*; they are distinguished from empirical cognitions, whose sources are a posteriori, namely, in experience.

But that expression, [viz., *a priori*,] is not yet determinate enough to indicate adequately the full meaning of the question just posed. For it is customary, I suppose, to say of much cognition derived from experiential sources that we can or do partake of it a priori. We say this because we derive the cognition not directly from experience but from a universal rule, even though that rule itself was indeed borrowed by us from experience. Thus if someone has undermined the foundation of his house, we say that he could have known a priori that the house would cave in, i.e., he did not have to wait for the experience of its actually caving in. And yet he could not have known this completely a priori. For he did first have to find out through experience that bodies have weight and hence fall when their support is withdrawn.

In what follows, therefore, we shall mean by a priori cognitions not those that occur independently of this B3 or that experience, but those that occur *absolutely* independently of all experience. They contrast with empirical cognitions, which are those that are possible only a posteriori, i.e., through experience. But we call a priori cognitions *pure* if nothing empirical whatsoever is mixed in with them. Thus, e.g., the proposition, Every change has its cause, is an a priori proposition; yet it is not pure, because change is a concept that can be obtained only from experience.

II. We Are in Possession of Certain A Priori Cognitions, and Even Common Understanding Is Never without Them

What matters here is that we find a characteristic by which we can safely distinguish a pure cognition from empirical ones. Now, experience does indeed teach us that something is thus or thus, but not that it cannot be otherwise. **First**, then, if we find a proposition such that in thinking it we think at the same time its *necessity*, then it is an a priori judgment; and if, in addition, it is not derived from any proposition except one that itself has the validity of a necessary proposition, then it is absolutely a priori. **Second**, experience never provides its judgments with true or strict *universality*, but only (through induction) with assumed and comparative universality; hence [there] we should, properly speaking, say [merely] that as far as we have B4 observed until now, no exception is to be found to this or that rule. If, therefore, a judgment is thought with strict universality, i.e., thought in such a way that no exception whatever is allowed as possible, then the judgment is not derived from experience, but is valid absolutely a priori. Hence empirical universality is only [the result of] our choosing to upgrade validity from one that holds in most cases to one that holds in all, as, e.g., in the proposition, all bodies have weight. But when universality is strict and belongs to a judgment essentially, then it points to a special cognitive source for the judgment, viz., a power of a priori cognition. Hence necessity and strict universality are safe indicators of a priori cognition, and they do moreover belong together inseparably. It is nevertheless advisable to make separate use of the two criteria, even though each is infallible by itself. For, in using them, there are times when showing the empirical limitedness of a cognition is easier than showing the contingency of the judgments based on it; and there are times when showing the unlimited universality that we attribute to a judgment is more convincing than is showing the judgment's necessity.

Now, it is easy to show that in human cognition there actually are such judgments [as we are looking for, viz.], judgments that are necessary and in the strictest sense universal, and hence are pure a priori judgments. If we want an example from the sciences, we need only B5 look to all the propositions of mathematics; if we want one from the most ordinary use of understanding, then we can use the proposition that all change must have a cause. Indeed, in this latter proposition the very concept of a cause so manifestly contains the concept of a necessity in [the cause's] connection with an effect, and of a strict universality of the rule [governing that connection], that the concept of a cause would get lost entirely if we derived it as *Hume* did: viz., from a repeated association of what happens with what precedes, and from our resulting habit[42] of connecting presentations (hence from a merely subjective necessity). But we do not need such examples[43] in order to prove that pure a priori principles actual[ly exist] in our cognition. We could, alternatively, establish that these principles are indispensable for the possibility of experience as such, and hence establish [their existence] a priori. For where might even experience get its certainty if all the rules by which it proceeds were always in turn[44] empirical and hence contingent, so that they could hardly be considered first principles? But here we may settle for having established as a matter of fact [that there is a] pure use of our cognitive power, and to have established what its indicators are. However, we can see such an a priori origin not merely in judgments, but even in some concepts. If from your experiential concept of a *body* you gradually omit everything that is empirical in a body—the color, the hardness or softness, the weight, even the impenetrability—there yet remains the *space* that was occupied by the body (which has now entirely vanished), and this space you cannot omit [from the B6 concept]. Similarly, if from your empirical concept of any object whatever, corporeal or incorporeal, you omit all properties that experience has taught you, you still cannot take away from the concept the property through which you think the object either as a *substance* or as *attaching* to a substance (even though this concept of substance is more determinate than that of an object as such).[45] Hence you must, won over by the necessity with which this concept of substance forces itself upon you, admit that this concept resides a priori in your cognitive power.

III. Philosophy Needs a Science That Will Determine the Possibility, the Principles, and the Range of All A Priori Cognitions

Much more significant yet than all the preceding[46] is the fact that there are certain cognitions that [not only extend to but] even leave the realm of all possible experiences. These cognitions, by means of concepts

42. [Or "custom": *Enquiry Concerning Human Understanding*, V, Pt. I, and cf. VII, Pt. II. Cf. also below, B 19–20, 127. Kant knew Hume's *Treatise of Human Nature* only indirectly, through citations (translated into German) from James Beattie's *Essay on the Nature and Immutability of Truth*, of 1770.]

43. [Examples from the sciences or from ordinary understanding.]

44. [I.e., even the higher-order rules.]

45. [The concept of an object as such does not include even (the property or "determination" of) permanence.]

46. [I.e., than the fact that we have a priori cognitions as described.]

to which no corresponding object can be given in experience at all, appear to expand the range of our judgments beyond all bounds of experience.

And precisely in these latter cognitions, which go beyond the world of sense, where experience cannot provide us with any guide or correction, reside our B7 reason's inquiries. We regard these inquiries as far superior in importance, and their final aim as much more sublime, than anything that our understanding can learn in the realm of appearances. Indeed, we would sooner dare anything, even at the risk of error, than give up such treasured inquiries [into the unavoidable problems of reason], whether on the ground that they are precarious somehow, or from disdain and indifference. These unavoidable problems of reason themselves are *God, freedom, and immortality*. But the science whose final aim, involving the science's entire apparatus, is in fact directed solely at solving these problems is called *metaphysics*. Initially, the procedure of metaphysics is *dogmatic*: i.e., [metaphysics], without first examining whether reason is capable or incapable of so great an enterprise, confidently undertakes to carry it out.

Now, suppose that we had just left the terrain of experience. Would we immediately erect an edifice by means of what cognitions we have, though we do not know from where? Would we erect it on credit, i.e., on principles whose origin is unfamiliar to us? It does seem natural that we would not, but that we would first seek assurance through careful inquiries that the foundation had been laid. In other words, it does seem natural that we would, rather, long since have raised the question as to just how our understanding could arrive at all these a priori cognitions, and what might be their range, validity, and value. And in fact nothing would be more natural, if by the term *natural* we mean what properly and reasonably B8 ought to happen. If, on the other hand, we mean by this term what usually happens, then nothing is more natural and comprehensible than the fact that for a long time this inquiry had to remain unperformed. For, one part of these [a priori] cognitions, viz., the mathematical ones, possess long-standing reliability, and thereby raise favorable expectations concerning other [a priori] cognitions as well, even though these may be of a quite different nature. Moreover, once we are beyond the sphere of experience, we are assured of not being refuted by experience. The appeal of expanding our cognitions is so great that nothing but hitting upon a clear contradiction can stop our progress. On the other hand, we can avoid such contradiction by merely being cautious in our inventions—even though they remain nonetheless inventions. Mathematics provides us with a splendid example of how much we can achieve, independently of experience, in a priori cognition. Now, it is true that mathematics deals with objects and cognitions only to the extent that they can be exhibited in intuition. But this detail is easily overlooked because that intuition can itself be given a priori and hence is rarely distinguished from a mere pure concept. Captivated by such a proof of reason's might, our urge to expand [our cognitions] sees no boundaries. When the light dove parts the air in free flight and feels the air's resistance, it might come to think that it would do much better still in space devoid of air. In the B9 same way *Plato* left the world of sense because it sets such narrow limits to our understanding; on the wings of the ideas, he ventured beyond that world and into the empty space of pure understanding. He did not notice that with all his efforts he made no headway. He failed to make headway because he had no resting point against which—as a foothold, as it were—he might brace himself and apply his forces in order to set the understanding in motion. But [Plato is no exception]: it is human reason's usual fate, in speculation, to finish its edifice as soon as possible, and not to inquire until afterwards whether a good foundation has in fact been laid for it. Then all sorts of rationalizations are hunted up in order to reassure us that the edifice is sturdy, or, preferably, even to reject altogether so late and risky an examination of it. But what keeps us, while we are building, free from all anxiety and suspicion, and flatters us with a seeming thoroughness, is the following. A large part—perhaps the largest—of our reason's business consists in dissecting what concepts of objects we already have. This [procedure] supplies us with a multitude of cognitions. And although these cognitions are nothing more than clarifications or elucidations of what has already been thought in our concepts (although thought as yet in a confused way), they are yet rated equal to new insights at least in form, even though in matter or content they do not expand the concepts we have B10 but only spell them out. Now since this procedure yields actual a priori cognition that progresses in a safe and useful way, reason uses this pretense, though without itself noticing this, to lay claim surreptitiously to assertions of a quite different kind. In these assertions, reason adds to given concepts others quite foreign to them, doing so moreover a priori. Yet how reason arrived at these concepts is not known; indeed, such a question is not even thought of. Hence I shall deal at the very outset with the distinction between these two kinds of cognition.

IV. On the Distinction between Analytic and Synthetic Judgments

In all judgments in which we think the relation of a subject to the predicate (I here consider affirmative judgments only, because the application to negative judgments is easy afterwards), this relation is possible in two ways. Either the predicate B belongs to the subject A as something that is (covertly) contained in this concept A; or B, though connected with concept A, lies quite outside it. In the first case I call the judgment *analytic*; in the second, *synthetic*. Hence (affirmative) analytic judgments are those in which the predicate's connection with the subject is thought by [thinking] identity, whereas those judgments in which this connection is thought without [thinking] B11 identity are to be called synthetic. Analytic judgments could also be called *elucidatory*. For they do not through the predicate add anything to the concept of the subject; rather, they only dissect the concept, breaking it up into its component concepts which had already been thought in it (although thought confusedly). Synthetic judgments, on the other hand, could also be called *expansive*. For they do add to the concept of the subject a predicate that had not been thought in that concept at all and could not have been extracted from it by any dissection. For example, if I say: All bodies are extended—then this is an analytic judgment. For I do not need to go beyond the concept that I link with the word body in order to find that extension is connected with it. All I need to do in order to find this predicate in the concept is to dissect the concept, i.e., become conscious of the manifold that I always think in it. Hence the judgment is analytic. By contrast, if I say: All bodies are heavy—then the predicate is something quite different from what I think in the mere concept of a body as such. Hence adding such a predicate yields a synthetic judgment.

Experiential judgments, as such, are one and all synthetic. For to base an analytic judgment on experience would be absurd, because in its case I can formulate my judgment without going outside my concept, and hence do not need for it any testimony of experience. Thus the [analytic] proposition that bodies are extended is one that holds a priori and is not an experiential judgment. For before I turn to experi- B12 ence, I already have in the concept [of body] all the conditions required for my judgment. I have only to extract from it, in accordance with the principle of contradiction, the predicate [of extension]; in doing so, I can at the same time become conscious of the judgment's necessity, of which experience would not even inform me. On the other hand, though in the concept of a body as such I do not at all include the predicate of heaviness, yet the concept designates an object of experience by means of part of this experience; hence I can [synthetically] add to this part further parts, of the same experience, in addition to those that belonged to the concept of a body as such. I can begin by cognizing the concept of a body *analytically* through the characteristics of extension, impenetrability, shape, etc., all of which are thought in this concept. But then I expand my cognition: by looking back to the experience from which I have abstracted this concept of body, I also find heaviness to be always connected with the above characteristics; and so I add it, as a predicate, to that concept *synthetically*. Hence experience is what makes possible the synthesis of the predicate of heaviness with the concept of body. For although neither of the two concepts is contained in the other, yet they belong to each other, though only contingently, as parts of a whole; that whole is experience, which is itself a synthetic combination of intuitions.

In synthetic judgments that are a priori, however, this remedy[47] is entirely lacking. If I am to go beyond B13 the concept A in order to cognize another concept B as combined with it, I rely on something that makes the synthesis possible: what is that something, considering that here I do not have the advantage of looking around for it in the realm of experience? Take the

47. [I.e., experience.]

proposition: Everything that happens has its cause.—In the concept of something that happens I do indeed think an existence preceded by a time, etc., and from this one can obtain analytic judgments. But the concept of a cause lies quite outside that earlier concept and indicates something different from what happens; hence it is not part of what is contained in this latter presentation. In speaking generally of what happens, how can I say about it something quite different from it, and cognize as belonging to it—indeed, belonging to it necessarily—the concept of cause, even though this concept is not contained in the concept of what happens? What is here the unknown = X on which the understanding relies when it believes that it discovers, outside the concept A, a predicate B that is foreign to concept A but that the understanding considers nonetheless to be connected with that concept? This unknown cannot be experience. For in adding the presentation of cause to the presentation of what happens, the above principle does so not only with greater universality than experience can provide, but also with the necessity's being expressed; hence it does so entirely a priori and on the basis of mere concepts. Now, on such synthetic, i.e., expansive, principles depends the whole final aim of our speculative a priori cognition. For, analytic principles are indeed B14 exceedingly important and needed, but only for attaining that distinctness in concepts which is required for a secure and extensive synthesis that, as such, will actually be a new acquisition [of cognition].

V. All Theoretical Sciences of Reason Contain Synthetic A Priori Judgments as Principles

1. Mathematical judgments are one and all synthetic. Although this proposition is incontestably certain and has very important consequences, it seems thus far to have escaped the notice of those who have analyzed human reason; indeed, it seems to be directly opposed to all their conjectures. For they found that all the inferences made by mathematicians proceed (as the nature of all apodeictic certainty requires) according to the principle of contradiction; and thus they came to be persuaded that the principle of contradiction is also the basis on which we recognize the principles [of mathematics]. In this they were mistaken. For though we can indeed gain insight into a synthetic proposition according to the principle of contradiction, we can never do so [by considering] that proposition by itself, but can do so only by presupposing another synthetic proposition from which it can be deduced.

We must note, first of all, that mathematical propositions, properly so called, are always a priori judgments rather than empirical ones; for they carry with them necessity, which we could never glean from experience. But if anyone refuses to grant that all B15 such propositions are a priori—all right: then I restrict my assertion to *pure mathematics*, in the very concept of which is implied that it contains not empirical but only pure a priori cognition.

It is true that one might at first think that the proposition 7 + 5 = 12 is a merely analytic one that follows, by the principle of contradiction, from the concept of a sum of seven and five. Yet if we look more closely, we find that the concept of the sum of 7 and 5 contains nothing more than the union of the two numbers into one; but in [thinking] that union we are not thinking in any way at all what that single number is that unites the two. In thinking merely that union of seven and five, I have by no means already thought the concept of twelve; and no matter how long I dissect my concept of such a possible sum, still I shall never find in it that twelve. We must go beyond these concepts and avail ourselves of the intuition corresponding to one of the two: e.g., our five fingers, or (as *Segner* docs in his *Arithmetic*)[48] five dots. In this way we must gradually add, to the concept of seven, the units of the five given in intuition. For I start by taking the number 7. Then, for the concept of the 5, I avail myself of the fingers of my hand as intuition. Thus, in that image of mine, I gradually add to the number 7 the units that I B16 previously gathered together in order to make up the number 5. In this way I see the number 12 arise. That 5 *were to be added* to 7, this I had indeed already thought in the concept of a sum = 7 + 5, but not

48. [Johann Andreas von Segner (1704–1777), German physicist and mathematician at Jena, Gottingen, and Halle. He is the author of several significant works, and introduced the concept of the surface tension of liquids. The work mentioned here, as translated from the Latin, is his *Anfangsgründe der Arithmetik* (*Elements of Arithmetic*). See the second edition (Halle/Saale: Renger, 1773), pp. 27, 79.]

that this sum is equal to the number 12. Arithmetic propositions are therefore always synthetic. We become aware of this all the more distinctly if we take larger numbers. For then it is very evident that, no matter how much we twist and turn our concepts, we can never find the [number of the] sum by merely dissecting our concepts, i.e., without availing ourselves of intuition.

Just as little are any principles of pure geometry analytic. That the straight line between two points is the shortest is a synthetic proposition. For my concept of *straight* contains nothing about magnitude, but contains only a quality. Therefore the concept of shortest is entirely added to the concept of a straight line and cannot be extracted from it by any dissection. Hence we must here avail ourselves of intuition; only by means of it is the synthesis possible.

It is true that a few propositions presupposed by geometricians are actually analytic and based on the principle of contradiction. But, like identical proposi- B17 tions, they serve not as principles but only [as links in] the chain of method. Examples are a = a; the whole is equal to itself; or (a + b) > a, i.e., the whole is greater than its part. And yet even these principles, although they hold according to mere concepts, are admitted in mathematics only because they can be exhibited in intuition. [As for mathematics generally,] what commonly leads us to believe that the predicate of its apodeitic judgments is contained in our very concept, and that the judgment is therefore analytic, is merely the ambiguity with which we express ourselves. For we say that we *are to* add in thought a certain predicate to a given concept, and this necessity adheres indeed to the very concepts. But here the question is not what we *are to* add in thought to the given concept, but what we *actually* think in the concept, even if only obscurely; and there we find that, although the predicate does indeed adhere necessarily to such concepts, yet it does so not as something thought in the concept itself, but by means of an intuition that must be added to the concept.

2. *Natural science (physica) contains synthetic a priori judgments as principles.* Let me cite as examples just a few propositions: e.g., the proposition that in all changes in the corporeal world the quantity of matter remains unchanged; or the proposition that in all communication of motion, action and reaction must always be equal to each other. Both propositions are clearly not only necessary, and hence of a priori B18 origin, but also synthetic. For in the concept of matter I do not think permanence, but think merely the matter's being present in space insofar as it occupies space. Hence I do actually go beyond the concept of matter, in order to add to it a priori in thought something that I have not thought *in it.* Hence the proposition is thought not analytically but synthetically and yet a priori, and the same occurs in the remaining propositions of the pure part of natural science.

3. *Metaphysics* is to *contain synthetic a priori cognitions.* This holds even if metaphysics is viewed as a science that thus far has merely been attempted, but that because of the nature of human reason is nonetheless indispensable. Metaphysics is not at all concerned merely to dissect concepts of things that we frame a priori, and thereby to elucidate them analytically. Rather, in metaphysics we want to expand our a priori cognition. In order to do this, we must use principles which go beyond the given concept and which add to it something that was not contained in it; and, by means of such synthetic a priori judgments, we must presumably go so far beyond such concepts that even experience[49] can no longer follow us; as in the proposition: The world must have a first beginning—and others like that. And hence metaphysics consists, at least *in terms of its purpose,* of nothing but synthetic a priori propositions.

VI. The General Problem of Pure Reason B19

Much is gained already when we can bring a multitude of inquiries under the formula of a single problem. For we thereby facilitate not only our own business by defining it precisely, but also—for anyone else who wants to examine it—the judgment as to whether or not we have carried out our project adequately. Now the proper problem of pure reason is contained in this question:

How are synthetic judgments possible a priori?

That metaphysics has thus far remained in such a shaky state of uncertainty and contradictions is attributable to a sole cause: the fact that this problem, and

49. [Actual *or possible* experience.]

perhaps even the distinction between *analytic* and *synthetic* judgments, has not previously occurred to anyone.[50] Whether metaphysics stands or falls depends on the solution of this problem, or on an adequate proof that the possibility which metaphysics demands to see explained[51] does not exist at all. *David Hume* at least came closer to this problem than any other philosopher. Yet he did not think of it nearly determinately enough and in its universality, but merely remained with the synthetic proposition about the connection of an effect with its causes (*principium* B20 *causalitatis*).[52] He believed he had discovered that such a proposition is quite impossible a priori. Thus, according to his conclusions, everything that we call metaphysics would amount to no more than the delusion of a supposed rational insight into what in fact is merely borrowed from experience and has, through habit, acquired a seeming necessity. This assertion, which destroys all pure philosophy, would never have entered Hume's mind if he had envisaged our problem in its universality. For he would then have seen that by his argument there could be no pure mathematics either, since it certainly does contain synthetic a priori propositions: and from such an assertion his good sense would surely have saved him.

In solving the above problem we solve at the same time another one, concerning the possibility of the pure use of reason in establishing and carrying out all sciences that contain theoretical a priori cognition of objects; i.e., we also answer these questions:

How is pure mathematics possible?
How is pure natural science possible?

Since these sciences are actually given [as existent], it is surely proper for us to ask **how** they are possible; for that they must be possible is proved by their being actual.[53] As regards *metaphysics*, however, there are B21 grounds on which everyone must doubt its possibility: its progress thus far has been poor; and thus far not a single metaphysics has been put forth of which we can say, as far as the essential purpose of metaphysics is concerned, that it is actually at hand.

Yet in a certain sense this *kind of cognition* must likewise be regarded as given; and although metaphysics is not actual as a science, yet it is actual as a natural predisposition (i.e., as a *metaphysica naturalis*[54]). For human reason, impelled by its own need rather than moved by the mere vanity of gaining a lot of knowledge, proceeds irresistibly to such questions as cannot be answered by any experiential use of reason and any principles taken from such use. And thus all human beings, once their reason has expanded to [the point where it can] speculate, actually have always had in them, and always will have in them,

50. [The problem, roughly, is this: In the case of *analytic* judgments (judgments whose truth depends solely on the meanings of their terms, i.e., on the content of the concepts involved) it is easy to see how such judgments can (by which Kant means "can legitimately") be made a priori (independently of experience). But the truth of *synthetic* (nonanalytic) judgments depends on *more* than their meaning (conceptual content). An example is the judgment (see B 17) that in all changes in the corporeal world the quantity of matter remains unchanged. This judgment is clearly not analytic, but asserts something (not merely conceptual) about the world (and hence about any possible experience that we may have of it). How then can we make such judgments a priori? Kant's answer lies in his "Copernican revolution" (B xvi–xviii). We can make synthetic judgments a priori insofar as objects of experience (which are the same thing as object-experiences) must conform a priori to what we contribute to experience (and hence to them), instead of experience's conforming a priori to totally independent objects (things in themselves) by means of some preestablished harmony. By the same token, as Kant will show in the Transcendental Dialectic, synthetic a priori judgments that go *beyond* all possible experience (make assertions about things in themselves) cannot be justified (legitimated) theoretically at all (though they may still be justifiable *morally-practically*).]

51. [I.e., how synthetic judgments are possible a priori.]

52. [Principle of causality.]

53. This actuality may still be doubted by some in the case of pure natural science. Yet we need only examine the propositions that are to be found at the beginning of physics proper (empirical physics), such as those about the permanence of the quantity of matter, about inertia, about the equality of action and reaction, etc., in order to soon be convinced that these propositions themselves amount to a *physica pura* (or *physica rationalis*). Such a physics, as a science in its own right, surely deserves to be put forth separately and in its whole range, whether this range be narrow or broad.

54. [Natural metaphysics.]

some metaphysics. Now concerning it, too, there is this question:

How is metaphysics as a natural B22 predisposition possible?

i.e., how, from the nature of universal human reason, do the questions arise that pure reason poses to itself and is impelled, by its own need, to answer as best it can?

Thus far, however, all attempts to answer these natural questions—e.g., whether the world has a beginning or has been there from eternity, etc.—have met with unavoidable contradictions. Hence we cannot settle for our mere natural predisposition for metaphysics, i.e., our pure power of reason itself, even though some metaphysics or other (whichever it might be) always arises from it. Rather, it must be possible, by means of this predisposition[55] to attain certainty either concerning our knowledge or lack of knowledge of the objects [of metaphysics], i.e., either concerning a decision about the objects that its questions deal with, or certainty concerning the ability or inability of reason to make judgments about these objects. In other words, it must be possible to expand our pure reason in a reliable way, or to set for it limits that are determinate and safe. This last question, which flows from the general problem above,[56] may rightly be stated thus:

How is metaphysics as science possible?

Ultimately, therefore, critique of pure reason leads necessarily to science; the dogmatic use of pure reason without critique, on the other hand, to baseless assertions B23 that can always be opposed by others that seem equally plausible, and hence to *skepticism*.

This science, moreover, cannot be overly, forbiddingly voluminous. For it deals not with objects of reason, which are infinitely diverse, but merely with [reason] itself. [Here reason] deals with problems that issue entirely from its own womb; they are posed to it not by the nature of things distinct from it, but by its own nature. And thus, once it has become completely acquainted with its own ability regarding the objects that it may encounter in experience, reason must find it easy to determine, completely and safely, the range and the bounds of its use [when] attempted beyond all bounds of experience.

Hence all attempts that have been made thus far to bring a metaphysics about *dogmatically* can and must be regarded as if they had never occurred. For whatever is analytic in one metaphysics or another, i.e., is mere dissection of the concepts residing a priori in our reason, is only a prearrangement for metaphysics proper, and is not yet its purpose at all. That purpose is to expand our a priori cognition synthetically, and for this purpose the dissection of reason's a priori concepts is useless. For it shows merely what is contained in these concepts; it does not show how we arrive at such concepts a priori, so that we could then also determine the valid use of such concepts in regard to the objects of all cognition B24 generally. Nor do we need much self-denial to give up all these claims;[57] for every metaphysics put forth thus far has long since been deprived of its reputation by the fact that it gave rise to undeniable, and in the dogmatic procedure indeed unavoidable, contradictions of reason with itself. A different treatment, completely opposite to the one used thus far, must be given to metaphysics—a science, indispensable to human reason, whose every new shoot can indeed be lopped off but whose root cannot be eradicated. We shall need more perseverance in order to keep from being deterred—either from within by the difficulty of this science or from without by people's resistance to it—from thus finally bringing it to a prosperous and fruitful growth.

VII. Idea and Division of a Special Science under the Name of Critique of Pure Reason

From all of the above we arrive at the idea of a special science that may be called the *critique of pure reason*. For reason is the power that provides us with the *principles* of a priori cognition. Hence pure reason is that reason which contains the principles for cognizing something absolutely a priori. An *organon* of pure reason would be the sum of those principles by which B25

55. [I.e., our power of reason.]

56. [The problem as to how (in general) synthetic judgments are possible a priori: B 19.]

57. [Of dogmatic metaphysics.]

all pure a priori cognitions can be acquired and actually brought about. Comprehensive application of such an organon would furnish us with a system of pure reason. Such a system, however, is a tall order; and it remains to be seen whether indeed an expansion of our cognition is possible here at all, and in what cases it is possible. Hence a science that merely judges pure reason, its sources, and its bounds may be regarded as the *propaedeutic* to the system of pure reason. Such a propaedeutic would have to be called not a *doctrine* but only a *critique* of pure reason. Its benefit, in regard to speculation, would actually only be negative. For such a critique would serve only to purify our reason, not to expand it, and would keep our reason free from errors, which is a very great gain already. I call *transcendental* all cognition that deals not so much with objects as rather with our way of cognizing objects in general insofar as that way of cognizing is to be possible a priori. A *system* of such concepts[58] would be called *transcendental philosophy*. But, once again, this [system of] transcendental philosophy is too much for us as yet, here at the beginning. For since such a science would have to contain both analytic cognition and synthetic a priori cognition, in their completeness, it has too broad a range as far as our aim is concerned. For we need to carry the analysis only as far as it is indispensably necessary for gaining insight, in their entire range, into the principles of a priori synthesis, which is all that we B26 are concerned with. What we are now dealing with is [not such a science, but only] this inquiry, which properly speaking can be called only a transcendental critique, not a doctrine. For its aim is not to expand the cognitions themselves, but only to correct them; and it is to serve as the touchstone of the value, or lack of value, of all a priori cognitions. Accordingly, such a critique is a preparation; if possible, for an organon of those [cognitions]; or, should the [attempt to produce an] organon be unsuccessful, at least for a canon of them. Such a canon would, at any rate, some day allow us to exhibit, analytically as well as synthetically, the complete system of the philosophy of pure reason, whether that system were to consist in expanding the cognition of pure reason or merely in setting boundaries for it. That such a system is possible—and, indeed, that it cannot be overly wide-ranging, so that we may hope to complete it entirely—can be gathered even in advance from the following: What here constitutes the object[59] is not the nature of things, which is inexhaustible, but the understanding that makes judgments about the nature of things, and even this understanding, again, only in regard to its a priori cognition. Moreover, the understanding's supply of a priori cognition cannot be hidden from us, because, after all, we need not search for it outside the understanding; and we may indeed suppose that supply to be small enough in order for us to record it completely, judge it for its value or lack of value, and make a correct assessment of it. B27 [But my readers must not expect to find in this critique more than the mentioned preparation.] Still less must they expect here a critique of books and systems of pure reason, but should expect the critique of our power of pure reason itself. Only if we use that critique as our basis do we have a reliable touchstone for assessing the philosophical content of old and new works in this field. Without such critique, unqualified historians and judges pass judgment on other people's baseless assertions by means of their own, which are just as baseless.

Transcendental philosophy is the idea of a science for which the critique of pure reason is to outline the entire plan *architectonically*, i.e., from principles, with full guarantee of the completeness and reliability of all the components that make up this edifice. Transcendental philosophy is the system of all principles of pure reason. That this critique is not itself already called transcendental philosophy is due solely to this: in order for this critique to be a complete system, it would have to include a comprehensive analysis of the whole of human a priori cognition. Now, it is indeed true that our critique must also put before us a complete enumeration of all the root concepts that make up that pure cognition. Yet the critique refrains, and properly so, from providing either the comprehensive analysis of these concepts themselves, or the complete review of the concepts derived from them. [There are two reasons for this.] First, this dissection of concepts would not serve our purpose; for it lacks B28 that precariousness which we find in synthesis, [the

58. [I.e., a system of a priori concepts of objects in general.]

59. [Of our inquiry.]

precariousness] on account of which the whole critique is in fact there. Second, taking on the responsibility for the completeness of such an analysis and derivation (a responsibility from which we could, after all, have been exempted in view of our aim) would go against the unity of our plan. On the other hand, this completeness in the dissection of the a priori concepts yet to be supplied, as well as in the derivation [of other concepts] from them, can easily be added later: provided that first of all these [concepts] are there, as comprehensive principles of synthesis, and nothing is lacking as regards this essential aim.[60]

Accordingly, the critique of pure reason [in a way] includes everything that makes up transcendental philosophy; it is the complete idea of transcendental philosophy. But the critique is not yet that science itself, because it carries the analysis [of a priori concepts] only as far as is required for making a complete judgment about synthetic a priori cognition.

The foremost goal in dividing such a science is this: no concepts whatever containing anything empirical must enter into this science; or, differently put, the goal is that the a priori cognition in it be completely pure.[61] Hence, although the supreme principles and basic concepts of morality are a priori cognitions, they still do not belong in transcendental philosophy. For B29 they do of necessity also bring [empirical concepts] into the formulation of the system of pure morality:[62] viz., the concepts of pleasure and displeasure, of desires and inclinations, etc., all of which are of empirical origin. Although the supreme principles and basic concepts of morality do not lay these empirical concepts themselves at the basis of their precepts, they must still bring in such pleasure and displeasure, desires and inclinations, etc. in [formulating] the concept of duty: viz., as an obstacle to be overcome, or as a stimulus that is not to be turned into a motive. Hence transcendental philosophy is a philosophy of merely speculative pure reason. For everything practical, insofar as it contains incentives, refers to feelings, and these belong to the empirical sources of cognition.

If, then, the division of the science being set forth here is to be performed in terms of the general viewpoint of a system as such, then this science must contain in the first place a *doctrine of elements,* and in the second a *doctrine of method,* of pure reason. Each of these two main parts would be subdivided; but the bases on which that subdivision would be made cannot yet be set forth here. Only this much seems to be needed here by way of introduction or advance notice: Human cognition has two stems, viz., *sensibility* and *understanding,* which perhaps spring from a common root, though one unknown to us. Through sensibility objects are *given* to us; through understanding they are *thought.* Now if sensibility were to contain a priori presentations constituting the B30 condition under which objects are given to us, it would to that extent belong to transcendental philosophy. And since the conditions under which alone the objects of human cognition are given to us precede the conditions under which these objects are thought, the transcendental doctrine of sense[63] would have to belong to the *first* part of the science of elements.

60. [Of supplying these concepts, as such principles.]

61. [For the distinction between "a priori" and "pure," see B 3.]

62. Whereupon the system is *no longer* pure, though it is still a priori.

63. [I.e., in effect, of sensibility.]

PART I
TRANSCENDENTAL AESTHETIC
§1

In whatever way and by whatever means a cognition may refer to objects, still *intuition* is that by which a cognition refers to objects directly, and at which all thought aims as a means.[64] Intuition, however, takes place only insodar as the object is given to us; but that, in turn, is possible only—for us human beings, at any rate—by the mind's being affected by the object in a certain manner. The capacity (a receptivity) to acquire presentations as a result of the way in which we are affected by objects is called **sensibility.** Hence by means of sensibility objects are *given* to us, and it alone supplies us with *intutions*. Through understanding, on the other hand, objects are thought, and from it arise concepts. But all thought must, by means of certain characteristics, refer ultimately to intu—itions, whether it does so straightforwardly (directe) or circuitously (indirecte); and hence it must, in us [human beings], refer ultimately to sensibility, because no object can be given to us in any other manner than through sensibility.

The efffect of an object on our capacity for presentation, insofar as we are affected by the object, is *sensation*. Intuition that refers to the object through sensation is called *empirical* intuition. The undetermined object of an empirical intuation is called *appearance*.

Whatever in an appearance corresponds to sensation I call its *matter;* but whatever in an appearance brings about the fact that the manifold of the appearance can be ordered in certain relations I call the *form* of appearance. Now, that in which alone sensations can be ordered and put into a certain form cannot itself be sensation again. Therefore, although the matter of all appearance is given to us only a posteriori, the form of all appearance must altogether lie ready for the sensations a priori in the mind; and hence that form must be capable of being examined apart from all sensation.

All presentations in which nothing is found that belongs to sensation I call *pure* (in the transcendental sense of the term). Accordingly, the pure form of sensible intuitions generally, in which everything manifold in experience is intuited in certain relations, will be found in the mind a priori. This pure form of sensibility will also itself be called *pure intuition*. Thus, if from the presentation of a body I separate what the understanding thinks in it, such as substance, force, divisibility, etc., and if I similarly separate from it what belongs to sensation in it, such as impenetrability, hardness, color, etc., I am still left with something from this empirical intutition, namely, extension and shape. These belong to pure intuition, which, even if there is no actual object of the senses or of sensation, has its place in the mind a priori, as a mere form of sensibility.

There must, therefore, be a science of all principles of a priori sensibility. I call such a science *transcendental aesthetic*. It constitutes the first part of the transcendental doctrine of elements, and stands in contrast to that [part of the] transcendental doctrine of elements which contains the principles of pure thought and is called transcendental logic.

Hence in the transcendental aesthetic we shall, first of all, *isolate* sensibility, by separating from it everything that the understanding through its concepts thinks [in connection] with it, so that nothing other than empirical intuition will remain.[65] Second,

64. [I.e., as a means to such cognition.]

65. The Germans are the only people who have come to use the word *aesthetic*[s] to designate what others call the critique of taste. They are doing so on the basis of a false hope conceived by that superb analyst, *Baumgarten* [Alexander Gottlieb Baumgarten (1714–1762), philosopher in the Leibnizian tradition and disciple of Wolff. He introduced the term "aesthetics" in a sense close to the modern one. Kant himself later found a way to base the critique of taste on a priori principles; his aesthetic theory forms the first part of

we shall also segregate from sensibility everything that belongs to sensation, so that nothing will remain but pure intuition and the mere form of appearances, which is all that sensibility can supply a priori. In the course of that inquiry it will be found that there are two pure forms of sensible intuition, which are principles for a priori cognition: viz., space and time. We now proceed to the task of examining these.

B37 TRANSCENDENTAL AESTHETIC

Section I Space

§2

Metaphysical Exposition[66] of This Concept

By means of outer sense (a property of our mind) we present objects as outside us, and present them one and all in space. In space their shape, magnitude, and relation to one another are determined or determinable. By means of inner sense the mind intuits itself, or its inner state. Although inner sense provides no intuition of the soul itself as an object, yet there is a determinate form under which alone [as condition] we can intuit the soul's inner state. [That form is time.] Thus everything belonging to our inner determinations is presented in relations of time. Time cannot be intuited outwardly, any more than space can be intuited as something within us. What, then, are space and time? Are they actual beings? Are they only determinations of things, or, for that matter, relations among them? If so, are they at least determinations or relations that would belong to things intrinsically also, i.e., even if these things were not intuited? Or are they determinations and relations that adhere only to the form of the intuition and hence to the subjective character of our mind, so that apart from B38 that character these predicates cannot be ascribed to any thing at all? In order to inform ourselves on these points, let us first of all give an exposition of the concept of space. Now, by *exposition* (*expositio*) I mean clear (even if not comprehensive) presentation of what belongs to a concept; and such exposition is *metaphysical* if it contains what exhibits the concept as *given a priori.*

1. Space is not an empirical concept that has been abstracted from outer experiences. For the presentation of space must already lie at the basis in order for certain sensations to be referred to something outside me (i.e., referred to something in a location of space other than the location in which I am). And it must similarly already lie at the basis in order for me to be able to present [the objects of] these sensations as outside and *alongside* one another, and hence to present them not only as different but as being in different locations. Accordingly, the presentation of space cannot be one that we take from the relations of outer appearance by means of experience; rather, only through the presentation of space is that outer experience possible in the first place.

2. Space is a necessary a priori presentation that underlies all outer intuitions. We can never have a presentation of there being no space, even though we are quite able to think of there being no objects B39 encountered in it. Hence space must be regarded as the condition for the possibility of appearances, and not as a determination dependent on them. Space

---

the third *Critique,* published in 1790. Kant there reacts to the aesthetic theories prevalent at the time, including that of Baumgarten.], who hoped to bring one critical judging of the beautiful under rational principles, and to raise the rules for such judging to the level of a science. Yet that endeavor is futile. For, as regards their principal sources, those rules or criteria are merely empirical. Hence they can never serve as determinate a priori laws to which our judgment of taste would have to conform; it is, rather, our judgment of taste which constitutes the proper touchstone for the correctness of those rules or criteria. Because of this it is advisable to follow either of two alternatives. One of these is to let this new name *aesthetic*[s] become extinct again, and to reserve the name *aesthetic* for the doctrine that is true science. (In doing so we would also come closer to the language of the ancients and its meaning: among the ancients the division of cognition into αἰσθητά καὶ νοητά [the sensible and the intelligible] was quite famous. The other alternative would be for the new aesthetic[s] to share the name with speculative philosophy; we would then take the name partly in its transcendental sense, and partly in the psychological meaning.

66. [The metaphysical exposition investigates the nature of the presentation of space and shows that this presentation is given a priori. The transcendental exposition of space (in § 3) shows that and how from the a priori presentation of space something else that is a priori follows—viz., synthetic a priori cognitions (propositions of geometry). Cf. B 133–34.]

is an a priori presentation that necessarily underlies outer appearances.

3. Space is not a discursive or, as we say, universal concept of things as such; rather, it is a pure intuition. For, first, we can present only one space; and when we speak of many spaces, we mean by that only parts of one and the same unique space. Nor, second, can these parts precede the one all-encompassing space, as its constituents, as it were (from which it can be assembled); rather, they can be thought only as *in it*. Space is essentially one; the manifold in it, and hence also the universal concept of spaces as such, rests solely on [our bringing in] limitations. It follows from this that, as far as space is concerned, an a priori intuition of it (i.e., one that is not empirical) underlies all concepts of space. By the same token, no geometric principles—e.g., the principle that in a triangle two sides together are greater than the third—are ever derived from universal concepts of *line* and *triangle*; rather, they are all derived from intuition, and are derived from it moreover a priori, with apodeictic certainty.

4. We present space as an infinite *given* magnitude. Now it is true that every concept must be thought as B40 a presentation that is contained in an infinite multitude of different possible presentations (as their common characteristic) and hence the concept contains these presentations *under itself*. But no concept, as such, can be thought as containing an infinite multitude of presentations *within itself*. Yet that is how we think space (for all parts of space, *ad infinitum*, are simultaneous). Therefore the original presentation of space is an a priori *intuition*, not a *concept*.[67]

§3

Transcendental Exposition of the Concept of Space

By a *transcendental exposition* I mean the explication of a concept as a principle that permits insight into the possibility of other synthetic a priori cognitions. Such explication requires (1) that cognitions of that sort do actually flow from the given concept, and (2) that these cognitions are possible only on the presupposition of a given way of explicating that concept.

Geometry is a science that determines the properties of space synthetically and yet a priori. What, then, must the presentation of space be in order for such cognition of space to be possible? Space must originally be intuition. For from a mere concept one B41 cannot obtain propositions that go beyond the concept; but we do obtain such propositions in geometry (Introduction, V). This intuition must, however, be encountered in us a priori, i.e., prior to any perception of an object; hence this intuition must be pure rather than empirical. For geometric propositions are one and all apodeictic, i.e., linked with the consciousness of their necessity—e.g., the proposition that space has only three dimensions. But propositions of that sort cannot be empirical judgments or judgments of experience; nor can they be inferred from such judgments (Introduction, II).

How, then, can the mind have an outer intuition which precedes the objects themselves, and in which the concept of these objects can be determined a priori? Obviously, this can be so only insofar as this intuition resides merely in the subject, as the subject's formal character of being affected by objects and of thereby acquiring from them *direct presentation*, i.e., *intuition*, and hence only as form of outer *sense* in general.

Our explication of the concept of space is, therefore, the only one that makes comprehensible the *possibility of geometry* as a [kind of] synthetic a priori cognition. Any way of explicating the concept that fails to make this possibility comprehensible, even if it should otherwise seem to have some similarity to ours, can be distinguished from it most safely by these criteria.[68]

Conclusions from the Above Concepts B42

(a) Space represents no property whatever of any things in themselves, nor does it represent things in themselves in their relation to one another.[69] That is,

67. [But, as Kant has indicated, from this original intuition of space concepts can be formed, including such concepts as those of empirical space, relative space, Euclidean space, mathematical space.]

68. [The criteria numbered (1) and (2) at the beginning of this subsection.]

69. [As Leibniz claimed when he said that space involves nothing but the relations among the monads (things in themselves).]

space represents no determination of such things, no determination that adheres to objects themselves and that would remain even if we abstracted from all subjective conditions of intuition. For determinations, whether absolute or relative, cannot be intuited prior to the existence of the things to which they belong, and hence cannot be intuited a priori.

(b) Space is nothing but the mere form of all appearances of outer senses; i.e., it is the subjective condition of sensibility under which alone outer intuition is possible for us. Now, the subject's receptivity for being affected by objects precedes necessarily all intuitions of these objects. Thus we can understand how the form of all appearances can be given in the mind prior to all actual perceptions, and hence given a priori; and we can understand how this form, as a pure intuition in which all objects must be determined, can contain, prior to all experience, principles for the relations among these objects.

Only from the human standpoint, therefore, can we speak of space, of extended beings, etc. If we depart from the subjective condition under which alone we can—viz., as far as we may be affected by objects—acquire outer intuition, then the presentation of space means nothing whatsoever. *B43* This predicate is ascribed to things only insofar as they appear to us, i.e., only insofar as they are objects of sensibility. The constant form of this receptivity which we call sensibility is a necessary condition of all relations in which objects are intuited as outside us; and if we abstract from these objects, then the form of that receptivity is a pure intuition that bears the name of space. We cannot make the special conditions of sensibility to be conditions of the possibility of things, but only of the possibility of their appearances. Hence we can indeed say that space encompasses all things that appear to us externally, but not that it encompasses all things in themselves, intuited or not, or intuited by whatever subject. For we can make no judgment at all about the intuitions of other thinking beings, as to whether they are tied to the same conditions that limit our intuition and that are valid for us universally. If the limitation on a judgment is added to the concept of the subject [term], then the judgment holds unconditionally. The proposition, All things are side by side in space, holds under the limitation: if these things are taken as objects of our sensible intuition. If I here add the condition to the concept and say, All things considered as outer appearances are side by side in space, then this rule holds universally and without limitation. Accordingly, our exposition *B44* teaches that space is *real* (i.e., objectively valid) in regard to everything that we can encounter externally as object, but teaches at the same time that space is *ideal* in regard to things when reason considers them in themselves, i.e., without taking into account the character of our sensibility. Hence we assert that space is *empirically real* (as regards all possible outer experience), despite asserting that space is *transcendentally ideal,* i.e., that it is nothing as soon as we omit [that space is] the condition of the possibility of all experience and suppose space to be something underlying things in themselves.

Besides space, on the other hand, no other subjective presentation that is referred to something external could be called an a priori objective presentation. For from none of them can we derive synthetic a priori propositions, as we can from intuition in space (§3). Hence, strictly speaking, ideality does not apply to them, even though they agree with the presentation of space inasmuch as they belong merely to the subjective character of the kind of sense involved. They may belong, e.g., to the sense of sight, of hearing, or of touch, by [being] sensations of colors, sounds, or heat. Yet because they are mere sensations rather than intuitions, they do not allow us to cognize any object at all, let alone a priori.

The only aim of this comment is to forestall an error: it might occur to someone to illustrate the *B45* ideality of space asserted above by means of examples such as colors or taste, etc. These are thoroughly insufficient for this, because they are rightly regarded not as properties of things, but merely as changes in ourselves as subjects, changes that may even be different in different people. For in this case, something that originally is itself only appearance—e.g., a rose—counts as a thing in itself in the empirical meaning of this expression, a thing in itself that in regard to color can nonetheless appear differently to every eye. The transcendental concept of appearances in space, on the other hand, is a critical reminder. It reminds us that nothing whatever that is intuited in space is a thing in itself, and that space is not a form of things, one that might belong to them as they are in themselves. Rather, what we call external objects are nothing but mere presentations of our sensibility. The form of this sensibility is space; but its true correlate, i.e., the thing in itself, is not cognized at all through these presentations, and cannot be. Nor, on the other hand, is the thing in itself ever at issue in experience.

B46 **TRANSCENDENTAL AESTHETIC**

Section II
Time

§4

Metaphysical Exposition of the Concept of Time

1. Time is not an empirical concept that has been abstracted from any experience. For simultaneity or succession would not even enter our perception if the presentation of time did not underlie them a priori. Only on the presupposition of this presentation can we present this and that as being at one and the same time (simultaneously) or at different times (sequentially).

2. Time is a necessary presentation that underlies all intuitions. As regards appearances in general, we cannot annul time itself, though we can quite readily remove appearances from time. Hence time is given a priori. All actuality of appearances is possible only in time. Appearances, one and all, may go away; but time itself (as the universal condition of their possibility) cannot be annulled.

B47 3. This a priori necessity, moreover, is the basis for the possibility of apodeictic principles about relations of time, or for the possibility of axioms about time in general. Time has only one dimension; different times are not simultaneous but sequential (just as different spaces are not sequential but simultaneous). These principles cannot be obtained from experience. For experience would provide neither strict universality nor apodeictic certainty; we could say only that common perception teaches us that it is so, but not that it must be so. These principles hold as rules under which alone experiences are possible at all; and they instruct us prior to experience, not through it.

4. Time is not a discursive or, as it is called, universal concept; rather it is a pure form of sensible intuition. Different times are only parts of one and the same time; and the kind of presentation that can be given only through a single object is intuition. Moreover, the proposition that different times cannot be simultaneous could not be derived from a universal concept. The proposition is synthetic, and [therefore] cannot arise from concepts alone. Hence it is contained directly in the intuition and presentation of time.

5. To say that time is infinite means nothing more than that any determinate magnitude of time is possible only through limitations [put] on a single underlying time. B48 Hence the original presentation *time* must be given as unlimited. But if something is such that its parts themselves and any magnitude of an object in it can be presented determinately only through limitation, then the whole presentation of it cannot be given through concepts (for they contain only partial presentations), but any such presentation must be based on direct intuition.

§5

Transcendental Exposition of the Concept of Time

I may refer for this exposition to No. 3, where, for the sake of brevity, I put among the items of the metaphysical exposition what in fact is transcendental. Let me add here that the concept of change, and with it the concept of motion (as change of place), is possible only through and in the presentation of time; and that if this presentation were not (inner) a priori intuition, no concept whatsoever could make comprehensible the possibility of a change, i.e., of a combination, in one and the same object, of contradictory opposed predicates (e.g., one and the same thing's being in a place and not being in that same place). Only in time can both of two contradictorily opposed determinations be met with in one thing: B49 viz., *sequentially*. Hence our concept of time explains the possibility of all that synthetic a priori cognition which is set forth by the—quite fertile—general theory of motion.

§6

Conclusions from These Concepts

(a) Time is not something that is self-subsistent or that attaches to things as an objective determination, and that hence would remain if one abstracted from all subjective conditions of our intuition of it. For if time were self-sufficient, then it would be something that without there being an actual object would yet be actual.[70] But if, on the second alternative, time were a determination or order attaching to things themselves,[71] then it could not precede the objects as their condition, and could not a priori be cognized through synthetic propositions and intuited. But this a priori cognition and intuition can take place quite readily if time is nothing but the subjective condition under which alone any intuition can take place in us. For in that case this form of inner intuition can be presented prior to the objects, and hence presented a priori.

(b) Time is nothing but the form of inner sense, i.e., of the intuiting we do of ourselves and of our inner state. For time cannot be a determination of B50 outer appearances, [because] it does not belong to any shape or position, etc., but rather determines the relation of presentations in our inner state. And precisely because this inner intuition gives us no shape, do we try to make up for this deficiency by means of analogies. We present time sequence by a line progressing *ad infinitum*, a line in which the manifold constitutes a series of only one dimension. And from the properties of that line we infer all the properties of time, except for the one difference that the parts of the line are simultaneous whereas the parts of time are always sequential. This fact, moreover, that all relations of time can be expressed by means of outer intuition, shows that the presentation of time is itself intuition.

(c) Time is the formal a priori condition of all appearances generally. Space is the pure form of all outer appearances; as such it is limited, as an a priori condition, to just outer appearances. But all presentations, whether or not they have outer things as their objects, do yet in themselves, as determinations of the mind, belong to our inner state; and this inner state is subject to the formal condition of inner intuition, and hence to the condition of time. Therefore time is an a priori condition of all appearance generally: it is the direct condition of inner appearances (of our souls), and precisely thereby also, indirectly, B51 a condition of outer appearances. If I can say a priori that all outer appearances are in space and are determined a priori according to spatial relations, then the principle of inner sense allows me to say, quite universally, that all appearances generally, i.e., all objects of the senses, are in time and stand necessarily in relations of time.

If we take objects as they may be in themselves—i.e., if we abstract from the way in which we intuit ourselves inwardly, and in which by means of this intuition we also take into our power of presentation all outer intuitions—then time is nothing. Time has objective validity only with regard to appearances, because these are already things considered as *objects of our senses*. But time is no longer objective if we abstract from the sensibility of our intuition, and hence from the way of presenting peculiar to us, and speak of *things as such*. Hence time is merely a subjective condition of our (human) intuition (an intuition that is always sensible—i.e., inasmuch as we are affected by objects); in itself, i.e., apart from the subject, time is nothing. Nevertheless, time is necessarily objective in regard to all appearances, and hence also in regard to all things that we can encounter in experience. We cannot say that all things [as such] are in time; for in the concept of things as such B52 we abstract from all ways of intuiting them, while yet this intuition is the very condition under which[72] time belongs in the presentation of objects. If now we add the condition to the concept, and say that all things as appearances (objects of sensible intuition) are in time, then this principle has all its objective correctness and a priori universality.

Hence the doctrine we are asserting is that time is *empirically real*, i.e., objectively valid in regard to all objects that might ever be given to our senses. And since our intuition is always sensible, no object that is not subject to the condition of time can ever be given to us in experience. On the other hand, we dispute that time has any claim to absolute reality; i.e., we dispute any claim whereby time would, quite without taking into account the form of our sensible intuition, attach to things absolutely, as a condition or property. Nor indeed can such properties, properties

70. [As in the case of Newton's absolute space.]

71. [As in the case of Leibniz, who held that time involves nothing but relations among the monads (things in themselves).]

72. [As added to the concept of a thing as such.]

belonging to things in themselves, ever be given to us through the senses. In this, then, consists the *transcendental ideality* of time. According to this view,[73] if we abstract from the subjective conditions of sensible intuition, then time is nothing, and cannot be included among objects in themselves (apart from their relation to our intuition) either as subsisting [as such B53 an object] or as inhering [in one]. But this ideality of time is not to be compared, any more than is the ideality of space, with the subreptions of sensations.[74] For in their case we presuppose that the appearance itself in which these predicates[75] [allegedly] inhere has objective reality.[76] In the case of time, such objective reality is entirely absent,[77] except insofar as this reality is merely empirical, i.e., except insofar as we regard the object itself as merely appearance. See, on this, the above comment, in SECTION 1.[78]

§7

Elucidation

Against this theory, which grants that time is empirically real but disputes that it is real absolutely and transcendentally, I have heard men of insight raise quite unanimously an objection. I gather from this great unanimity that the objection must occur naturally to every reader who is not accustomed to contemplations such as these. The objection is the following. Changes are actual. (This is proved by the variation on the part of our own presentations—even if one were to deny all outer appearances, along with their changes.) Now changes are possible only in time. Therefore time is something actual. There is no difficulty in replying to the objection. I concede the whole argument. Time is indeed something actual, viz., the actual form of inner intuition. It therefore has subjective reality in regard to inner experience; i.e., I B54 actually have the presentation of time and of my determinations in time. Hence time is to be regarded as actual, though not as an object but as the way of presenting that I myself have as an object. Suppose, on the other hand, that I could intuit myself without being subject to this condition of sensibility, or that another being could so intuit me; in that case the very same determinations that we now present as changes would provide a cognition in which the presentation of time, and hence also that of change, would not occur at all. Hence time retains its empirical reality as condition of all our experiences. Only absolute reality must, by the reasons adduced above, be denied to time. Time is nothing but the form of our inner intuition.[79] If we take away from time [the qualification that it is] the special condition of our sensibility, then the concept of time vanishes as well; time attaches not to objects themselves, but merely to the subject intuiting them.

But what causes this objection to be raised so unanimously, and raised, moreover, by those who nonetheless cannot think of any plausible objection against B55 the doctrine that space is ideal, is the following. They had no hope of establishing apodeictically that space is real absolutely; for they are confronted by idealism, according to which the actuality of external objects is incapable of strict proof. By contrast, the actuality of the object of our inner sense (the actuality of myself and of my state) is directly evident through consciousness. External objects might be a mere illusion; but the object of inner sense is, in their opinion, undeniably something actual. They failed to bear in mind, however, that both of them, though their actuality as presentations is indisputable, still belong only to appearance. Appearance always has two sides. One is the side where the object is regarded in itself (without regard to the way in which it is intuited, which is

73. [The transcendental idealism of time, properly speaking.]

74. [I.e., (instances of) their surreptitious substitution for, and thus confusion with, something in the object, as discussed: B 44–45.]

75. [I.e., the colors, sounds, etc., surreptitiously treated as properties of the object.]

76. [Whereas the colors, sounds, etc., do not.]

77. [And is here treated as such, subreption thus being precluded.]

78. [See the end of the section on space: B 44–45.]

79. I can indeed say: My presentations follow one another. But that means only that we are conscious of them as being in a time sequence—in accordance, i.e., with the form of inner sense. Time is not, on that account, something in itself, nor is it a determination attaching to things objectively.

precisely why its character always remains problematic).[80] The other is the side where we take account of the form of the intuition of this object. This form must be sought not in the object in itself, but in the subject to whom the object appears. Yet this form belongs to the appearance of this object actually and necessarily.

Time and space are, accordingly, two sources of cognition. From these sources we can draw a priori different synthetic cognitions—as is shown above all by the splendid example that pure mathematics provides in regard to our cognitions of space and its *B56* relations. For time and space, taken together, are pure forms of all sensible intuition, and thereby make synthetic propositions possible a priori. But precisely thereby (i.e., by being merely conditions of sensibility), these a priori sources of cognition determine their own bounds; viz., they determine that they apply to objects merely insofar as these are regarded as appearances, but do not exhibit things in themselves. Appearances are the sole realm where these a priori sources of cognition are valid; if we go outside that realm, there is no further objective use that can be made of them. This [limited] reality of space and time leaves the reliability of experiential cognition otherwise untouched; for we have equal certainty in that cognition, whether these forms necessarily attach to things in themselves or only to our intuition of these things. Those, on the other hand, who assert that space and time—whether they assume these as subsistent or as only inherent—are real absolutely must be at variance with the principles of experience itself.[81] For suppose they decide to assume space and time as subsistent (thus taking what is usually the side of the mathematical investigators of nature): then they must assume two eternal and infinite self-subsistent nonentities (space and time), which exist (yet without there being anything actual) only in order to encompass everything actual. Or suppose they assume space and time as only inherent (thus taking the side to which some metaphysical natural scientists belong). Here space and time count for them as relations of appearances (occurring concurrently or sequentially)—relations abstracted from experience but, as thus separated, presented confusedly. If they take this *B57* second side, then they must dispute that the mathematical a priori doctrines are valid for actual things (e.g., things in space), or at least that they are apodeictically certain. For a posteriori there is no such certainty at all. According to this second opinion, the a priori concepts of space and time are only creatures of the imagination, and their source must actually be sought in experience: the relations[82] are abstracted from experience; and the imagination has made from them something that, while containing what is universal in these relations, yet cannot occur without the restrictions that nature has connected with them. Those who assume space and time as [real absolutely and] subsistent do gain this much: they make the realm of appearances free[83] for mathematical assertions. On the other hand, these very conditions[84] create great confusion for them when the understanding wants to go beyond the realm of appearances. Those, on the other hand, who assume space and time as [real absolutely but as] only inherent gain on this latter point. I.e., they do not find the presentations of space and time getting in their way when they want to judge objects not as appearances but merely as they relate to the understanding. But they can neither indicate a basis for the possibility of mathematical a priori cognitions (since they lack a true and objectively valid a priori intuition),[85] nor bring the propositions of experience into necessary agreement with those a priori mathematical assertions. Our theory of the true character of these two original *B58* forms of sensibility provides the remedy for both [sets of] difficulties.

Finally, transcendental aesethetic cannot contain more than these two elements, i.e., space and time. This is evident from the fact that all other concepts

80. [For Kant's view that things in themselves are (thought of as) what appears, see B xxvii.]

81. [For Kant's discussion of these two alternatives, representing (respectively) the Newtonian and the Leibnizian views, cf. the beginning of the preceding subsection, B 49.]

82. [Of space and time.]

83. [Which on the opposing view just mentioned it was not.]

84. [The self-subsistent space and time as being eternal and infinite.]

85. [To which to appeal.]

belonging to sensibility presuppose something empirical. This holds even for the concept of motion, which unites the two components.[86] For [the concept of] motion presupposes the perception of something movable.[87] But in space, considered in itself, there is nothing movable; therefore the movable must be something that we find *in space only through experience,* and hence must be an empirical datum. Similarly, transcendental aesthetic cannot include among its a priori data the concept of change. For time itself does not change; rather, what changes is something that is in time. Therefore the concept of change requires the perception of some existent and of the succession of its determinations; hence it requires experience.

B59

§8

General Comments on Transcendental Aesthetic

I. In order to forestall any misinterpretation of our opinion regarding the basic character of sensible cognition as such, we must first explain as distinctly as possible what that opinion is.

What we have tried to say, then, is the following. All our intuition is nothing but the presentation of appearance. The things that we intuit are not in themselves what we intuit them as being. Nor do their relations in themselves have the character that they appear to us as having. And if we annul ourselves as subject, or even annul only the subjective character of the senses generally, then this entire character of objects and all their relations in space and time—indeed, even space and time themselves—would vanish; being appearances, they cannot exist in themselves, but can exist only in us. What may be the case regarding objects in themselves and apart from all this receptivity of our sensibility remains to us entirely unknown. All we know is the way in which we perceive them. That way is peculiar to us and does not necessarily have to apply to all beings, even though it applies necessarily to all human beings. Solely with B60 that way of perceiving are we dealing here. Space and time are its pure forms; sensation as such as its matter. Only that way of perceiving can we cognize a priori, i.e., prior to all actual perception, and that is why it is called pure intuition. Sensation, on the other hand, is that component in our cognition on whose account it is called a posteriori cognition, i.e., empirical intuition. The forms [of intuition] attach to our sensibility with absolute necessity, no matter of what kind our sensations may be; the sensations can differ very much. Even if we could bring this institution of ours to the highest degree of distinctness, that would still not get us closer to the character of objects in themselves. For what we would cognize, and cognize completely, would still be only our way of intuiting, i.e., our sensibility; and we would always cognize it only under the conditions attaching to the subject originally: space and time. What objects may be in themselves would still never become known to us, not even through the most enlightened cognition of what alone is given to us, viz., their appearance.

Hence we must reject the view[88] that our entire sensibility is nothing but our confused presentation of things, a presentation that contains solely what belongs to them in themselves, but contains it only by way of an accumulation of characteristics and partial presentations that we do not consciously discriminate. For this view falsifies the concept of sensibility and of appearance, thus rendering the entire doctrine of sensibility useless and empty. The distinction between an indistinct and a distinct presentation B61 is merely logical and does not concern the content. No doubt the concept of *rightness* as employed by common sense contains just the same as can be extricated from it by the most subtle speculation, except that in its common and practical use one is not conscious of the diverse presentations contained in that thought. But that does not entitle us to say that the common concept is sensible and contains a mere appearance. For rightness cannot be an appearance at all; rather, its concept lies in the understanding,[89] and we present by it a character of acts (their moral character) which belongs to them in themselves. On the other hand, when a *body* is presented in intuition,

86. [Space and time.]

87. [Namely, matter.]

88. [Held by Leibniz.]

89. [And not in intuition.]

this presentation contains nothing whatever that could belong to an object in itself. It contains, rather, merely the appearance of something, and the way we are affected by that something. This receptivity of our cognitive capacity is called sensibility; and even if we were to see through that appearance and to its very bottom, yet this receptivity remains as different as day and night from cognition of the object in itself.

Hence the philosophy of Leibniz and Wolff, by considering the distinction between what is sensible and what is intellectual as a merely logical one, has imposed an entirely wrong point of view on all investigations about the nature and origin of our cognitions. For plainly the distinction is transcendental, and does not concern merely the forms of these cognitions, B62 i.e., their distinctness or indistinctness, but concerns their origin and content. Hence sensibility does not merely fail to provide us with a distinct cognition of the character of things in themselves; it provides us with none whatsoever. And once we remove our subjective character, then the presented object, along with the properties contributed to it by sensible intuition, is not to be found anywhere at all; nor can it possibly be found, because this subjective character is precisely what determines the form of that object as appearance.[90]

It is true that we commonly make this distinction about appearances: we distinguish what attaches to their intuition essentially and holds for the sense of every human being in general, from what belongs to that intuition only contingently by being valid only for a special position of this or that sense, or for the special organization of that sense, but not valid for the relation of [the intuition to] sensibility in general. We then speak of the first kind of cognition as presenting the object in itself, and of the second as presenting only its appearance. This distinction, however, is only empirical. If (as is commonly done) we fail to go beyond it and do not (as we ought to do) regard that empirical intuition in turn as mere appearance, in which nothing whatever belonging to some thing in itself is to be found, then our transcendental distinction is lost. We then believe after all that we cognize B63 things in themselves, even though in the world of sense, however deeply we explore its objects, we deal with nothing whatever but appearances. Thus it is true, e.g., that when during a rain accompanied by sunshine we see a rainbow, we will call it a mere appearance, while calling the rain the thing in itself. And this is indeed correct, provided that we here take the concept of a thing in itself as meaning only something physical. We then mean by it something that in general experience, and in all its different positions in relation to the senses, is yet determined thus, and not otherwise, in intuition. But suppose that we take this empirical something as such, and that—without being concerned about its being the same for the sense of every human being—we ask whether it presents also an object in itself (not whether it presents the rain drops, for these, as appearances, will already be empirical objects). In that case our question about the presentation's relation to the object is transcendental, and the answer is: Not only are these drops mere appearances; rather, even their round shape, and indeed even the space in which they fall, are nothing in themselves. They are, rather, mere modifications, or foundations, of our sensible intuition. The transcendental object, however, remains unknown to us.

Our second important concern in this transcendental aesthetic is that it should not merely gain some favor as a plausible hypothesis, but should be as certain and indubitable as can possibly be demanded of a theory that is to serve as an organon. In order to make this certainty fully evident, let us select some case that can render the validity of this organon obvi- B64 ous and can serve to clarify further what has been set forth in §3.

Suppose, then, that space and time are in themselves objective, and are conditions of the possibility of things in themselves. We then find, in the first place, that we encounter a large number of synthetic a priori propositions about both space and time—above all about space, which we shall therefore investigate here as our prime example. The propositions of geometry are cognized synthetically a priori and with apodeictic certainty. And so I ask: From where do you obtain such propositions, and on what does the understanding rely in order to arrive at such absolutely necessary and universally valid truths? There is no other way [to arrive at truths] than through concepts

90. [This is exactly what is involved in Kant's Copernican revolution. See B xvi–xvii.]

or through intuition. But these concepts and intuitions are both given either a priori or a posteriori. The a posteriori ones, i.e., empirical concepts as well as the empirical intuition on which they are based, can yield only such synthetic propositions as are likewise merely empirical, i.e., propositions of experience. As such, these propositions can never contain necessity and absolute universality; yet these are what characterize all geometric propositions. The first and sole means of arriving at such cognitions is a priori, through mere concepts or through intuitions. From mere concepts, however, we clearly can obtain no *B65* synthetic cognition at all, but only analytic cognition. Just take the proposition that two straight lines cannot enclose any space and hence do not permit [construction of] any figure, and try to derive it from the concept of straight lines and of the number two. Or take the proposition that three straight lines permit [construction of] a figure, and try similarly to derive it from these mere concepts. All your endeavor is futile, and you find yourselves compelled to have recourse to intuition, as indeed geometry always does. Hence you give yourselves an object in intuition. But of which kind is this intuition? Is it a pure a priori intuition or an empirical one? If it were an empirical intuition, then it could never turn into a universally valid proposition, let alone an apodeictic one; for experience can never supply anything like that. Hence you must give your object to yourselves a priori in intuition, and base your synthetic proposition on this object. Now suppose that there did not lie within you a power to intuit a priori; that this subjective condition were not, as regards its form, at the same time the universal a priori condition under which alone the object of this (outer) intuition is itself possible; and that the object (the triangle) were something in itself, even apart from any relation to yourselves as subject. If that were so, how could you say that what necessarily lies in [or belongs to] your subjective conditions for constructing a triangle must also belong necessarily to the triangle itself? For, after all, you could not add to your concepts (of three lines) anything new (the *B66* figure) that would therefore have to be met with necessarily in the object, since this object would be given prior to your cognition rather than through it. Hence you could not synthetically a priori establish anything whatsoever about external objects if space (and similarly time) were not a mere form of your intuition, an intuition that a priori contains conditions under which alone things can be external objects for you—these objects being nothing in themselves, apart from these subjective conditions. Therefore the following is not merely possible—or probable, for that matter—but indubitably certain: Space and time, as the necessary conditions of all (outer and inner) experience, are merely subjective conditions of all our intuition. Hence in relation to these conditions all objects are mere appearances, and are not given to us in this way on their own. And that is why much can be said a priori about these objects as regards their form, but not the least can ever be said about the thing in itself that may underlie these appearances.

II. This theory, according to which both outer and inner sense are ideal and hence all objects of the senses are mere appearances, can be confirmed superbly by the following observation. Whatever in our cognition belongs to intuition (excluding, therefore, what are not cognitions at all, i.e., both the feeling of pleasure and displeasure and the will) contains nothing but mere relations; of places in an intuition *B67* (extension), of change of places (motion), and of laws according to which this change is determined (motive forces). But what is present in that place, or what effect—besides the change of place—it produces in the things themselves, is not given to us by [what belongs to intuition]. Now through mere relations we do not, of course, cognize a thing in itself. Hence our judgment must surely be this: since through outer sense we are given nothing but mere relational presentations, outer sense can, by the same token, contain in its presentation only the relation of an object to the subject, but not the intrinsic character belonging to the object in itself. The same applies to inner intuition. For not only does the proper material in it, with which we occupy our mind, consist in presentations of *outer senses;* but the time in which we place these presentations, and which itself precedes the consciousness of them in experience and underlies, as formal condition, the way in which we place them within the mind, already contains relations: of succession, of simultaneity, and of what is simultaneous with succession (the permanent). Now, presentation that can precede all acts of thinking anything is intuition; and if this intuition contains nothing but relations then it is the form of intuition. But this form does not present anything except insofar as something is being placed within the mind. Therefore this form B68 can be nothing but the way in which the mind is affected by its own activity—viz., this placing of its presentation—and hence affected by itself; i.e., it is an inner sense insofar as that sense's form is concerned. Whatever is presented through a sense is, to that extent, always appearance. Hence either we must not grant that there is an inner sense at all; or we must grant that the subject who is the object of this sense can be presented through it only as appearance, and not as he would judge himself if his intuition were self-activity only, i.e., if it were intellectual intuition. What underlies this whole difficulty is this: how can a subject inwardly intuit himself? But this difficulty is shared by every theory. The consciousness of oneself (apperception) is the simple presentation of the *I*; and if through this consciousness by itself all the manifold in the subject were given *self-actively*, then the inner intuition would be intellectual. But in man this consciousness requires also inner perception of the manifold given in the subject beforehand; and the way in which this manifold is given in the mind—viz., without spontaneity—must, for the sake of marking this distinction, be called sensibility. If the power to become conscious of oneself is to locate (apprehend) what lies in the mind, then it must affect the mind; and only in that way can it produce an intuition of itself. But the form of this intuition lies at the basis B69 beforehand in the mind; and this form determines, in the presentation of time, the way in which the manifold is [placed] together in the mind. And thus this power does not intuit itself as it would if it presented itself directly and self-actively; rather, it intuits itself according to the way in which it is affected from within, and hence intuits itself as it appears to itself, not as it is.

III. I am saying, then, that the intuition of external objects and the self-intuition of the mind both present these objects and the mind, in space and in time, as they affect our senses, i.e., as they appear. But I do not mean by this that these objects are a mere *illusion*. For when we deal with appearance, the objects, and indeed even the properties that we ascribe to them, are always regarded as something actually given—except that insofar as the object's character depends only on the subject's way of intuiting this given object in its relation to him, we do also distinguish this object as *appearance* from the same object as object *in itself*.[91] Thus when I posit both bodies and my soul as being in accordance with the quality of space and time, as condition of their existence, I do indeed assert that this quality lies in my way of intuiting and not in those objects in themselves. But in asserting this I am not saying that the bodies merely *seem* to be outside me, or that my soul only *seems* to be given in my self-consciousness. It would be my own fault if I turned into mere illusion what I ought to class with appearance.[92] This is not, however, what happens B70 if we follow our principle that all our sensible intuitions are ideal. On the contrary: it is when we attribute *objective reality* to those forms of presentation that we cannot prevent everything from being thereby transformed into mere *illusion*. For suppose that we regard space and time as properties that, as far as their very possibility is concerned, must be found in things in themselves. And now reflect on the absurdities in which we then become entangled, inasmuch as [we then have] two infinite things that must not be substances nor anything actually inhering in substances, but that yet must be something existent—indeed, B71 must be the necessary condition for the existence of all things—and must moreover remain even if all existing things are annulled. If we thus reflect on this supposition, then we can hardly blame the good *Berkeley* for downgrading bodies to mere illusion.

91. [In Kant's usual (transcendental) sense of this expression, rather than in its empirical sense (found, e.g., at B 45 and B 62).]

92. The predicates of the appearance can be ascribed to the object itself in relation to our sense: e.g., to the rose, the red color or the scent. But what is mere illusion can never be ascribed as predicate to an object, precisely because illusion ascribes to the object taken *by itself* what belongs to it only in relation to the senses or in general to the subject—an example being the two handles initially ascribed to Saturn. If something is not to be met with at all in the object in itself, but is always to be met with in the object's relation to the subject and is inseparable from the presentation of the object, then it is appearance. And thus the predicates of space and time are rightly ascribed to objects of the senses, as such; and in this there is no illusion. Illusion first arises if, by contrast, I ascribe the redness to the rose *in itself*, or the handles to Saturn, or extension to all external objects *in themselves*, without taking account of—and limiting my judgment to—a determinate relation of these objects to the subject.

Indeed, even our own existence, which would in this way be made dependent on the self-subsistent reality of a nonentity such as time would be, would be transformed along with this time into nothing but illusion—an absurdity of which no one thus far has made himself guilty.

IV. In natural theology we think an object [viz., God] that not only cannot possibly be an object of intuition for us, but that cannot in any way be an object of sensible intuition even to itself. [When we think of God in this way,] we take great care to remove the conditions of time and space from all his intuition. (All his cognition must be intuition rather than *thought*, which always manifests limits.) But what right do we have to do this if we have beforehand turned space and time into forms of things in themselves—such forms, moreover, as are a priori conditions of the existence of things and hence would remain even if we had annulled the things themselves? For as conditions of all existence in general, they would have to be conditions also of the existence of God. If we are not to make space and time objective B72 forms of all things, then we are left with only one alternative: we must make them subjective forms of our kind of intuition, inner and outer. Our kind of intuition is called sensible[93] because it is *not original.* I.e., it is not such that through this intuition itself the existence of its object is given (the latter being a kind of intuition that, as far as we can see, can belong only to the original being). Rather, our kind of intuition is dependent on the existence of the object, and hence is possible only by the object's affecting the subject's capacity to present.

There is, moreover, no need for us to limit this kind of intuition—intuition in space and time—to the sensibility of man. It may be (though we cannot decide this) that any finite thinking being must necessarily agree with man in this regard. Yet even if this kind of intuition were thus universally valid, it would not therefore cease to be sensibility. It would remain sensibility precisely because it is derivative (*intuitus derivativus*) rather than original (*intuitus originarius*), and hence is not intellectual intuition. For the reason just set forth, intellectual intuition seems to belong solely to the original being, and never to a being that is dependent as regards both its existence and its intuition (an intuition that determines that being's existence by reference to given objects). This last remark, however, must be considered as included in our aesthetic theory only as an illustration, not as a basis of proof.

Concluding the Transcendental Aesthetic B73

Thus in our pure a priori intuitions, space and time, we now have one of the components required for solving the general problem of transcendental philosophy: *How are synthetic propositions possible a priori?* When in an a priori judgment about space and time we want to go beyond the given concept, we encounter[94] what cannot be discovered a priori in the given concept, but can indeed be so discovered in the intuition corresponding to that concept and can be combined with it synthetically. Because of this,[95] however, such judgments can never reach beyond objects of the senses, and can hold only for objects of possible experience.

93. [Rather than intellectual.]

94. [In the a priori intuition.]

95. [The judgment's dependence on intuition and the merely synthetic connection to the concept.]

PART II

TRANSCENDENTAL LOGIC

Introduction
Idea of a Transcendental Logic

I

On Logic As Such

Our cognition arises from two basic sources of the mind. The first is [our ability] to receive presentations (and is our receptivity for impressions); the second is our ability to cognize an object through these presentations (and is the spontaneity of concepts).[96] Through receptivity an object is *given* to us; through spontaneity an object is *thought* in relation to that [given] presentation (which [otherwise][97] is a mere determination of the mind). Intuition and concepts, therefore, constitute the elements of all our cognition. Hence neither concepts without an intuition corresponding to them in some way or other, nor intuition without concepts can yield cognition. Both intuition and concepts are either pure or empirical. They are *empirical* if they contain sensation (sensation presupposes the actual presence of the object); they are *pure* if no sensation is mixed in with the presentation.[98] Sensation may be called the matter of sensible cognition. B75 Hence pure intuition contains only the form under which something is intuited, and a pure concept contains solely the form of the thought of an object as such. Only pure intuitions or concepts are possible a priori; empirical ones are possible only a posteriori.

Let us give the name *sensibility* to our mind's *receptivity*, [i.e., to its ability] to receive presentations insofar as it is affected in some manner. *Understanding*, on the other hand, is our ability to produce presentations ourselves, i.e., our *spontaneity* of cognition. Our *intuition*, by our very nature, can never be other than *sensible* intuition;[99] i.e., it contains only the way in which we are affected by objects. *Understanding*, on the other hand, is our ability to *think* the object of sensible intuition. Neither of these properties is to be preferred to the other. Without sensibility no object would be given to us; and without understanding no object would be thought. Thoughts without content are empty; intuitions without concepts are blind. Hence it is just as necessary that we make our concepts sensible (i.e., that we add the object to them in intuition) as it is necessary that we make our intuitions understandable (i.e., that we bring them under concepts). Moreover, this capacity and this ability[100] cannot exchange their functions. The understanding cannot intuit anything,[101] and the senses cannot think anything. Only from their union can cognition arise. B76 This fact, however, must not lead us to confuse their respective contributions;[102] it provides us, rather, with a strong reason for carefully separating and distinguishing sensibility and understanding from each other. Hence we distinguish the science of the rules of sensibility as such, i.e., aesthetic, from the science of the rules of the understanding as such, i.e., logic.

Now logic, in turn, can be done from two points of view, either as logic of the understanding's general use or as logic of its special use. The logic of the understanding's general use contains the absolutely necessary rules of thought without which the understanding cannot be used at all. Hence it deals with the understanding without regard to the difference among the objects to which the understanding may

96. [I.e., the self-activity (cf. B 68) of using concepts in thought and cognition and of expanding them to frame new ones.]

97. [I.e., apart from that thought, whereby this determination enters into our cognition of the object.]

98. [I.e., the intuition or concept.]

99. [Only an intuitive understanding (ours is discursive, i.e., conceptual) can have *intellectual* intuition. See B 72.]

100. [I.e., sensibility and understanding.]

101. [See n.99, just above.]

102. [To cognition.]

be directed. This logic may be called elementary logic. The logic of the understanding's special use, which may be called the organon of this or that science, contains the rules for thinking correctly about a certain kind of objects. The schools usually make this logic a preface to the sciences, using it as a propaedeutic, even though in terms of the progression of human reason it comes last: reason does not arrive at this logic until long after the science is done and needs only finishing touches that will correct and B77 perfect it. For if we are to state the rule as to how a [particular] science can be brought about, then the objects of that science must already be familiar to us to a fairly high degree.

Now general logic is either pure or applied logic. In general logic we abstract from all empirical conditions under which we exercise our understanding. We abstract, e.g., from the influence of the senses, from the play of imagination, from the laws of memory, from the force of habit, from inclination, etc.; hence we abstract also from the sources of prejudices, and indeed from all causes generally that give rise, or may be alleged to give rise, to such and such cognitions. For these empirical conditions concern the understanding only as applied under certain circumstances, and becoming acquainted with these circumstances requires experience. Hence a logic that is *general* but also *pure* deals with nothing but a priori principles. Such a logic is a *canon of understanding* and of reason, but only as regards what is formal in our use of them—i.e., we disregard what the content may be (whether it is empirical or transcendental). A *general logic* is called *applied*, on the other hand, if it is concerned with the rules of the understanding as used under the subjective empirical conditions taught us by psychology. Hence such a logic has empirical principles, although it is general insofar as it deals with our use of the understanding without distinguishing the understanding's objects. That is also the reason why applied general logic is neither a canon of the understanding as such nor an organon B78 of special sciences, but solely a cathartic for the common understanding.[103] In general logic, therefore, the part that is to constitute the pure doctrine of reason must be separated entirely from the part that is to constitute applied (though still general) logic. Only the first of these parts[104] is, properly speaking, a science, although it is brief and dry and thus is such as the exposition of a doctrine of the understanding's elements is required to be in order to comply with school standards. In such pure general logic, therefore, the logicians must always have in mind two rules:

1. As general logic, it abstracts from all content of the cognition of understanding and from the difference among the objects of that cognition, and deals with nothing but the mere form of thought.
2. As pure logic, it has no empirical principles. Hence it does not (as people have sometimes come to be persuaded) take anything from psychology; and therefore psychology has no influence whatever on the canon of the understanding. Pure general logic is demonstrated doctrine, and everything in it must be certain completely a priori.

What I call applied logic is a presentation of the understanding and of the rules governing its necessary use *in concreto*, viz., its use under the contingent conditions attaching to the subject, conditions that B79 can impede or promote this use and that are, one and all, given only empirically. (This definition of applied logic is contrary to the ordinary meaning of the expression, according to which applied logic should contain certain exercises for which pure logic gives the rule.) On my definition, applied logic deals with attention; attention's being impeded and the consequences thereof; the origin of error; the states of doubt, of having scruples, of conviction, etc. Pure general logic relates to applied general logic as pure morality relates to the doctrine proper of virtue. Pure morality contains merely the moral laws of a free will as such; the doctrine of virtue examines these laws as impeded by the feelings, inclinations, and passions to which human beings are more or less subject. The doctrine of virtue can never serve as true and demonstrated science; for, just like applied logic, it requires empirical and psychological principles.

II

On Transcendental Logic

General logic, as we have shown, abstracts from all content of cognition, i.e., from all reference of cogni-

103. [I.e., common sense.]

104. [Pure general logic.]

tion to its object. It examines only the logical form in the relation that cognitions have to one another, i.e., only the form of thought as such. But (as the Transcendental Aesthetic establishes) there are both pure and empirical intuitions; and hence we might B80 well find it appropriate to distinguish also between pure and empirical thought of objects. In that case there would be a logic in which we would not abstract from all content of cognition. For a logic containing merely the rules governing the pure thought of an object would only exclude all those cognitions that have empirical content. Such a logic, moreover, would also deal with the origin of our cognitions of objects insofar as that origin cannot be attributed to the objects, whereas general logic has nothing to do with the origin of cognition. Rather, general logic examines presentations, whether these have their basic origin a priori in ourselves, or are given only empirically; and it examines these presentations merely in terms of the laws according to which the understanding, when it thinks, uses them in their relation to one another. Hence general logic deals only with that form of the understanding which can be imparted to the presentations, whatever their origin may be irrespective of that form.

And here I shall make a comment; it extends its influence to all subsequent contemplations, and hence must be remembered carefully. We must not call just any a priori cognition transcendental, but must call transcendental (i.e., concerning the a priori possibility or the a priori use of cognition) only that a priori cognition whereby we cognize that—and how—certain presentations (intuitions or concepts) B81 are applied, or are possible, simply a priori. Hence neither space nor any a priori geometric determination of it is a transcendental presentation. Rather, we may call transcendental only the cognition that these presentations are not at all of empirical origin, and the possibility whereby they can nonetheless refer a priori to objects of experience. Similarly, the use of space regarding objects in general[105] would also be transcendental. But if the use of space is limited to objects of the senses only, then it is called empirical. The distinction between the transcendental and the empirical belongs, therefore, only to the critique of cognitions, and does not concern the reference of these cognitions to their object.

We shall expect, then, that there may perhaps be concepts referring a priori to objects. Not being pure or sensible intuitions, but being merely acts of pure thought, they would be concepts, but such concepts as originate neither empirically nor aesthetically.[106] In this expectation, then, we frame in advance the idea of a science of pure understanding and of rational cognition, whereby we think objects completely a priori. Such a science would determine the origin, the range, and the objective validity of such rational cognitions. It would have to be called *transcendental logic*. For it deals merely with the laws of understanding and of reason; yet it does so only insofar as this B82 logic is referred a priori to objects—unlike general logic, which is referred indiscriminately to empirical as well as pure rational cognitions.

III

On the Division of General Logic into Analytic and Dialectic

What is truth? is the ancient and famous question with which people meant to drive logicians into a corner, trying to get them to the point where either they must let themselves be caught in a pitiful circle, or they must confess their ignorance and hence admit the futility of their whole art. In asking logicians this question, these people took for granted, and they presupposed, the explication of the name *truth*,[107] viz., that truth is the agreement of cognition with its object. They demanded to know, instead, what is the universal and safe criterion of the truth of any cognition. [They failed to see, however, the absurdity of their own question.]

To know what question one should, reasonably, ask is already a great and necessary proof of one's sagacity and insight. For if the question is in itself absurd and demands answers that are unnecessary, then it not only embarrasses the person raising it, but sometimes has the further disadvantage of misleading the incautious listener: it may prompt him to give

105. [Objects of experience (which includes sensation) and objects of pure geometry.]

106. [I.e., concepts originating neither from empirical intuition nor from intuition generally.]

107. [I.e., in effect, the definition.]

B83 absurd answers and to provide us with the ridiculous spectacle where (as the ancients said) one person milks the ram[108] while the other holds a sieve underneath.

Thus if truth consists in the agreement of a cognition with its object, then this object must here be distinguished from others. For if a cognition does not agree with the object to which it is referred then it is false, even if it contains something that might well hold for other objects. Now a universal criterion of truth would be one that is valid for all cognitions, without distinction of their objects. But while in such a universal criterion of truth we thus abstract from all content of cognition (i.e., from its reference to its object), yet truth concerns this very content. Clearly, therefore, asking questions about a mark for the truth of this content of cognitions is quite impossible and absurd; and hence one cannot possibly give an indicator of truth that is sufficient and yet universal at the same time. Now we have already earlier called the content of a cognition its matter. Hence we shall have to say that no universal indicator can be demanded for the truth of cognition in terms of its matter, because such an indicator would be intrinsically contradictory.

As regards cognition in terms of its mere form (setting aside all content), on the other hand, and thus as regards a logic insofar as it puts forth the universal and B84 necessary rules of the understanding, it is equally clear that such a logic must in these very rules set down criteria of truth. For whatever contradicts these rules is false, because the understanding is then in conflict with its own universal rules of thought, and hence with itself. These criteria, however, concern only the form of truth, i.e., the truth of thought as such, and are to that extent quite correct. But they are not sufficient. For even if a cognition accorded completely with logical form, i.e., even if it did not contradict itself, it could still contradict its object. Therefore the merely logical criterion of truth, viz., a cognition's agreement with the universal and formal laws of understanding and reason, is indeed the *conditio sine qua non*,[109] and hence the negative condition, of all truth. But logic cannot go any farther than this; it has no touchstone by which it can discover an error that concerns content rather than form.

Now general logic analyzes the whole formal business of understanding and reason into its elements, and exhibits these elements as principles governing all logical judging of our cognition. Hence this part of logic may be called an analytic. This analytic is at least the negative touchstone of truth, precisely because all cognition must first of all be tested and assessed, in terms of its form, by these rules;[110] this must be done before we examine these rules themselves in terms of their content in order to establish whether they contain positive truth as regards their B85 object. On the other hand, the mere form of cognition, however much it may agree with logical laws, is far from being sufficient to establish that a cognition is true objectively (materially). Hence with mere logic no one can venture to make judgments about objects and assert anything about them. Rather, we must first go outside logic to obtain well-based information about objects, in order then to attempt merely employing this information and connecting it in a coherent whole in accordance with logical laws, or—better yet—in order only to test the information by these laws. Yet there is something very tempting about possessing so plausible an art, whereby we give to all our cognitions the form of our understanding—even though we may still be very empty-handed and poor as regards the cognition's content. So great is this temptation that this general logic, which is merely a *canon* for judging, has been used—like an *organon*, as it were—for the actual production of at least deceptive objective assertions, and thus has in fact been misused. Now general logic, when used as supposed organon, is called *dialectic*.

Although the ancients used this name *dialectic*, as standing for a science or art, in quite different senses, still from their actual use of the name we can safely glean that dialectic was for them nothing other than B86 the *logic of illusion*. I.e., it was the sophistical art of giving an air of truth to one's ignorance, and indeed even to one's deliberate deceptions; this was done by imitating the method of thoroughness prescribed by logic as such, and by employing the topic of

108. [Reference works characterize this saying as a Greco-Roman proverb quoted (e.g.) in Samuel Hieron, *Works* (1616), i, 586; and in John Hales, *Several Tracts* (1656), 40. Milking of rams is mentioned also in Vergil's *Eclogues*, iii, 91.]

109. [Indispensable (or necessary) condition.]

110. [I.e., the principles just mentioned.]

logic[111] to paint over any empty pretense. Now we may note (as a sure and useful warning) that general logic, when *regarded as an organon*, is always a logic of illusion, i.e., it is always dialectical. For general logic teaches us nothing whatever about the content of cognition; it teaches us merely the formal conditions for the agreement [of cognition] with the understanding, and these conditions are wholly inconsequential otherwise, i.e., as regards the [cognition's] objects. Hence the impudent use of general logic as an instrument (organon), in order (at least allegedly) to broaden and expand one's knowledge, comes down to nothing but idle chatter, where anything one wishes is—with some semblance of plausibility—asserted or, for that matter, challenged at will.

Such instruction is in no way compatible with the dignity of philosophy. For this reason the name *dialectic* has been [redefined so that a dialectic is] included with logic as a *critique* of *dialectical illusion*; and this is how we want it to be understood here as well.

B87

IV

On the Division of Transcendental Logic into Transcendental Analytic and Dialectic

In a transcendental logic we isolate the understanding (just as in the transcendental aesthetic above we isolated sensibility), and we select from our cognition merely that part of thought which has its origin solely in the understanding. The use of this pure cognition rests on the condition, however, that objects to which it can be applied are given to us in intuition. For without intuition, all our cognition lacks objects, and thus remains completely empty. That part, then, of transcendental logic which sets forth the elements of understanding's pure cognition, as well as the principles without which no object can be thought at all, is transcendental analytic. It is at the same time a logic of truth. For no cognition can contradict it without at the same time losing all content, i.e., all reference to any object, and hence without losing all truth. On the other hand, there is great enticement and temptation to employ these pure cognitions of understanding and these principles by themselves, and to do so even beyond the bounds of experience, even though only experience can provide us with B88 the matter (objects) to which those pure concepts of understanding can be applied. As a consequence, the understanding runs the risk that, by idly engaging in subtle reasoning, it will put the merely formal principles of pure understanding to a material use, and will make judgments indiscriminately even about objects that are not given, or indeed about objects that perhaps cannot be given in any way at all. Properly, then, transcendental analytic should be only a canon for judging the empirical use.[112] Hence we misuse transcendental analytic if we accept it as the organon of a universal and unlimited use, and if with pure understanding alone we venture to judge, assert, and decide anything synthetically about objects as such. Hence[113] the use of pure understanding would then be dialectical. Therefore the second part of transcendental logic must be a critique of this dialectical illusion, and is called transcendental dialectic. It is to be regarded not as an art of dogmatically creating such illusion (an art that is unfortunately quite prevalent in diverse cases of metaphysical jugglery), but as a critique of understanding and reason as regards their hyperphysical use. We need such a critique in order to uncover the deceptive illusion in the baseless pretensions of understanding and reason; and we need it in order to downgrade reason's claim that it discovers and expands [cognition]—which it supposedly accomplishes by merely using transcendental principles—[to the claim that it] merely judges pure understanding and guards it against sophistical deceptions.

TRANSCENDENTAL LOGIC B89

Division I

Transcendental Analytic

Transcendental analytic consists in the dissection of our entire a priori cognition into the elements of

111. [The topic (or topics) of (general) logic is the art, developed above all by Aristotle in his *Topics*, of discovering plausible (though not demonstrative) arguments to establish or refute a given position. This discovery is accomplished by means of general argument forms that, being prepared in advance, serve as the "places" (Greek τόποι [*tópoi*], Latin *topica*) or headings to which the more specific arguments are referred.]

112. [Of the understanding; similarly for "universal and unlimited use" just below.]

113. [I.e., as such a misuse.]

understanding's pure cognition. The following points are what matters in this dissection: (1) The concepts must be pure rather than empirical. (2) They must belong not to intuition and sensibility, but to thought and understanding. (3) They must be elementary concepts, and must be distinguished carefully from concepts that are either derivative or composed of such elementary concepts. (4) Our table of these concepts must be complete, and the concepts must occupy fully the whole realm of pure understanding. Now, this completeness [characteristic] of a science cannot be assumed reliably by gauging an aggregate of concepts that was brought about merely through trials. Hence this completeness is possible only by means of an *idea of the whole* of understanding's a priori cognition, and through the division, determined by that idea, of the concepts amounting to that cognition; and hence this completeness is possible only through the *coherence* of these concepts *in a system.* Pure understanding differentiates itself fully not only from everything empirical, but even from all sensibility [generally].[114] Therefore it is a unity that is self-sub- *B90* sistent, sufficient to itself, and that cannot be augmented by supplementing it with any extrinsic additions. Hence the sum of pure understanding's cognition will constitute a system that can be encompassed and determined by an idea. The system's completeness and structure can at the same time serve as a touchstone of the correctness and genuineness of whatever components of cognition fit into the system. This entire part of the Transcendental Logic[115] consists, however, of two *books;* one of these contains the *concepts*, the other the *principles*, of pure understanding.

Transcendental Analytic

Book I
Analytic of Concepts

By *analytic of concepts* I do not mean the analysis of concepts, i.e., the usual procedure in philosophical inquiries of dissecting already available concepts in terms of their content and bringing them to distinctness; rather, I mean the hitherto rarely attempted *dissection*[116] *of the power of understanding itself.* The purpose of this dissection is to explore the possibility of a priori concepts, by locating them solely in the understanding, as their birthplace, and by analyzing the understanding's pure use as such. For this exploration is the proper task of a transcendental philosophy; *B91* the rest[117] is the logical treatment of concepts in philosophy generally. Hence we shall trace the pure concepts all the way to their first seeds and predispositions in the human understanding, where these concepts lie prepared until finally, on the occasion of experience, they are developed and are exhibited by that same understanding in their purity, freed from the empirical conditions attaching to them.

Analytic of Concepts

Chapter I
On the Guide for the Discovery of All Pure Concepts of Understanding

When we bring into play a cognitive power, then, depending on the various ways in which we may be prompted to do so, different concepts come to the fore that allow us to recognize this power. These concepts can be collected[118] in an essay that will be more or less comprehensive, once the concepts have been observed fairly long or with significant mental acuity. But by this—as it were, mechanical—procedure we can never reliably determine at what point that inquiry will be completed. Moreover, if concepts are discovered only on given occasions, then they reveal themselves in no order or systematic unity; *B92* instead they are ultimately only paired according to similarities, and arranged in series according to the quantity of their content, from the simple concepts on to the more composite. The way in which these series are brought about, despite being methodical in a certain manner, is anything but systematic.

Transcendental philosophy has the advantage, but also the obligation, of locating its concepts according to a principle. For these concepts arise, pure and unmixed, from the understanding, which is an abso-

114. [I.e., even from a priori intuition.]

115. [Viz., the Transcendental Analytic.]

116. [I.e., analysis.]

117. [The analysis of concepts mentioned above.]

118. [And set forth.]

lute unity; and hence these concepts themselves must cohere with each other according to one concept or idea. Such coherence, however, provides us with a rule by which we can determine a priori the proper place for each pure concept of understanding, and the completeness of all of them taken together—whereas otherwise all of this would be subject to one's own discretion or to chance.

Transcendental Guide for the Discovery of All Pure Concepts of Understanding

Section I
On the Understanding's Logical Use As Such

The understanding was explicated merely negatively above, viz., as a non-sensible cognitive power. And since independently of sensibility we cannot partake of any intuition, it follows that the understanding is not a power of intuition. Apart from intuition, however, B93 there is only one way of cognizing, viz., through concepts. Hence the cognition of any understanding, or at least of the human understanding, is a cognition through concepts; it is not intuitive, but discursive. All our intuitions, as sensible, rest on our being affected; concepts, on the other hand, rest on functions. By *function* I mean the unity of the act of arranging various presentations under one common presentation. Hence concepts[119] are based on the spontaneity of thought, whereas sensible intuitions are based on the receptivity for impressions. Now the only use that the understanding can make of these concepts is to judge by means of them. But in such judging, a concept is never referred directly to an object, because the only kind of presentation that deals with its object directly is intuition. Instead the concept is referred directly to some other presentation of the object (whether that presentation be an intuition or itself already a concept). Judgment, therefore, is the indirect cognition of an object, viz., the presentation of a presentation of it. In every judgment there is a concept that [comprises and thus] holds for many [presentations], and, among them, comprises also a given presentation that is referred directly to the object. E.g., in the judgment, *All bodies are divisible,* the concept of the divisible refers to various other concepts; but, among these, it is here referred specifically to the concept of body, and the concept of body is referred in turn to certain appearances that we B94 encounter. Hence these objects are presented indirectly through the concept of divisibility. Accordingly, all judgments are functions of unity among our presentations. For instead of cognizing the object by means of a direct presentation, we do so by means of a higher presentation comprising both this direct presentation and several other presentations; and we thereby draw many possible cognitions together into one. Now since all acts of the understanding can be reduced to judgments, the *understanding* as such can be presented as a *power of judgment.* For, according to what we said above, the understanding is a power of thought. But thought is cognition through concepts; and concepts, as predicates of possible judgments, refer to some presentation of an as yet undetermined object. Thus the concept of body signifies something—e.g., metal—that can be cognized through that concept. Hence it is a concept only because there are contained under it other presentations by means of which it can refer to objects. Therefore the concept of body is the predicate for a possible judgment, e.g., the judgment that every metal is a body. Therefore we can find all of the functions of the understanding if we can exhibit completely the functions of unity in judgments. This, however, can be accomplished quite readily, as the following section will show.

[Transcendental] Guide for the Discovery of All Pure Concepts of Understanding B95

Section II

§9

ON THE UNDERSTANDING'S LOGICAL FUNCTION IN JUDGMENTS

If we abstract from all content of a judgment as such and pay attention only to the mere form of understanding in it, then we find that the function of

119. [Inasmuch as they involve such an act.]

thought in judgment can be brought under four headings, each containing under it three moments. They can conveniently be presented in the following table.

1
Quantity of Judgments
Universal
Particular
Singular

2
Quality
Affirmative
Negative
Infinite

3
Relation
Categorical
Hypothetical
Disjunctive

4
Modality
Problematic
Assertoric
Apodeictic

B96 Since this division departs in some respects, even though not in essential ones, from the customary technical apparatus used by logicians, there will be some point in my offering the following safeguards against the worrisome possibility of its being misunderstood.

1. Logicians are right in saying that, when judgments are used in syllogisms, singular judgments can be treated like universal ones. For precisely because singular judgments have no range at all, any predicate of them cannot be referred to some part of what is contained under the concept of the subject and be excluded from some other part of it. Hence the predicate of a singular judgment holds for the subject concept without exception, just as if this concept were a generally valid[120] one and the predicate held for the whole denotation within the concept's range. On the other hand, if[121] a singular judgment is compared in terms of quantity with a generally valid one merely as [two kinds of] cognition,[122] then the singular judgment relates to the generally valid one as unity relates to infinity, and hence is in itself essentially distinct from it. Suppose, therefore, that I assess a singular judgment (*iudicium singulare*) not merely in terms of its intrinsic validity but also as cognition as such, and assess it in terms of the quantity that it has by comparison with other cognitions. In that case the singular judgment is indeed distinct from generally valid judgments (*iudicia communia*); and hence it then deserves a separate place in a complete table of the moments of thought as such (although it does indeed not deserve a separate place in the logic that B97 is limited to the use of judgments merely in relation to one another).

2. Similarly, in a transcendental logic we must distinguish from *affirmative* judgments [not only negative ones but] also *infinite judgments*, even though in general logic they are rightly included with affirmative ones and do not constitute a separate member in the division of judgments. For general logic abstracts from all content of the predicate (even if the predicate is negative), and has regard only for whether the predicate is being ascribed to the subject or is being opposed to it. But transcendental logic considers the judgment also in terms of what value or content there is in this logical affirmation made by means of a merely negative predicate, and in terms of what gain for cognition as a whole is provided by this affirmation. If in speaking of the soul I had said, It is not mortal, then by this negative judgment I would at least have avoided an error. Now if I say instead, The soul is nonmortal, then I have indeed, in terms of logical form, actually affirmed something; for I have posited the soul in the unlimited range of nonmortal beings. Now what is mortal comprises one part of the whole range of possible beings, and what is nonmortal comprises the other. Hence my proposition[123] says nothing more than that the soul is one of the infinite multitude of things that remain if I take away whatever is mortal. But to say that is only to limit the infinite sphere of all that is possible, viz., to limit it to the extent that what is mortal is separated from it and the B98 soul is posited in the remaining space of the sphere's range.[124] But despite this exclusion [of what is mortal

120. [I.e., in effect, universal.]

121. [As is done in transcendental logic (as distinguished from general logic).]

122. [I.e., as two kinds of judgments (propositions), rather than as parts of a syllogism.]

123. [That the soul is nonmortal.]

124. [I.e., the space (of the sphere's range) that includes whatever is nonmortal.]

from it], this space still remains infinite; and even if we take away from it still more parts, this does not in the least increase the concept of the soul and determine it affirmatively. Hence although such judgments[125] are infinite as regards logical range, they are actually merely limitive as regards the content of cognition as such. In view of this, they must not be omitted from the transcendental table of all moments of the thought occurring in judgments, because the function that the understanding performs in these infinite judgments may perhaps be important in the realm of the understanding's pure a priori cognition.

3. The following are all the relations of thought in judgments: (a) the relation of the predicate to the subject; (b) the relation of the ground to its consequence; (c) the relation, in a divided cognition, of all of the division's members to one another. In these three kinds of judgments we consider, in relation to one another: in the first kind of judgments, two concepts only; in the second, two judgments; in the third, several judgments. To illustrate the second kind, take a hypothetical proposition: If there is a perfect justice, then the persistently evil person is punished. This proposition in fact contains the relation of two propositions: There is a perfect justice; and, The persistently evil person is punished. Whether these two propositions are in themselves true remains undecided here; only the implication is thought through this hypothetical judgment. Finally, to illustrate the third kind: a B99 disjunctive judgment contains a relation of two, or of several, propositions to one another. But this relation is not one of sequence. Rather, it is a relation of logical opposition, insofar as the sphere of the one proposition excludes the sphere of the other; yet it is at the same time a relation of community, insofar as the two propositions together occupy the sphere of the proper cognition involved. Hence the relation of the propositions in a disjunctive judgment is a relation of the parts of a cognition's sphere. For the sphere of each part complements the sphere of the other part, to yield the whole sum of the divided cognition. Take this judgment, e.g.: The world exists either through blind chance, or through internal necessity, or through an external cause. Each of these propositions occupies a part of the sphere of possible cognition concerning the existence of a world as such; all of them together occupy the whole sphere. To remove the cognition from one of these spheres means placing it into one of the other spheres; and, on the other hand, to place it into one sphere means to remove it from the others. Hence in a disjunctive judgment there is a certain community of cognitions. This community consists in the fact that the cognitions reciprocally exclude one another, and yet as a *whole* determine thereby the true cognition; for, taken together, they constitute the whole content of a single given cognition. And this, moreover, is all that I here need to point out in view of what follows.

4. The modality of judgments is a very special function of them. What distinguishes this function is the fact that it contributes nothing to the judgment's B100 content (for besides quantity, quality, and relation there is nothing else to constitute a judgment's content). Rather, modality concerns only the value that the copula has in reference to thought as such. *Problematic* judgments are those where the affirmation or negation is taken as merely *possible* (optional); *assertoric* ones are those where the affirmation or negation is considered as *actual* (true); *apodeictic* ones are those in which it is regarded as *necessary*.[126] Thus the two judgments (*antecedens* and *consequens*) whose relation constitutes the hypothetical judgment, and similarly the judgments (members of the division) in whose interaction the disjunctive judgment consists, are one and all problematic only. In the above example, the proposition, There is a perfect justice, is not uttered assertorically, but is thought only as an optional judgment, i.e., one that it is possible for someone to assume; only the implication is assertoric. This is also the reason why such optional judgments, even if manifestly false, can still, when taken problematically, be conditions for the cognition of truth. Thus in the disjunctive judgment used above, the judgment *The world exists through blind chance* has only problematic meaning; viz., to the effect that someone might perhaps assume this proposition for an instant. B101 And yet it serves us in finding the true proposition

125. [As the judgment that the soul is nonmortal.]

126. Just as if thought were a function of the *understanding* in the case of problematic judgments, of our *power of judgment* in the case of assertoric ones, and of *reason* in the case of apodeictic judgments. This remark must wait for its clarification until later.

(just as indicating the wrong road serves us in finding the right one among the number of all the roads that one can take). Hence a problematic proposition is one that expresses only logical possibility (which is not objective possibility). I.e., it expresses a free choosing to let such a proposition stand—a mere electing to admit it into the understanding. An assertoric proposition speaks of logical actuality or truth; thus in a hypothetical syllogism, e.g., the antecedent occurs problematically in the major premise but assertorically in the minor premise. And the assertoric proposition indicates that it is already linked with the understanding in accordance with the understanding's law. An apodeictic proposition thinks the assertoric one as determined by these laws of the understanding themselves, and hence thinks it as maintaining [this or that] a priori; and in this way it expresses logical necessity. Thus everything is incorporated in the understanding by degrees: at first we judge something problematically; then perhaps we also accept it assertorically as true; and finally we maintain it as linked inseparably with the understanding, i.e., as necessary and apodeictic. And hence these three functions of modality may also be called so many moments of thought as such.

[Transcendental] Guide for the Discovery of All Pure Concepts of Understanding

B102

Section III

§10

On the Pure Concepts of Understanding, or Categories

General logic, as we have said several times already, abstracts from all content of cognition. It expects presentations to be given to it from somewhere else—no matter where—in order then to transform these presentations into concepts in the first place. This it does analytically. Transcendental logic, on the other hand, has lying before it a manifold of a priori sensibility, offered to it by transcendental aesthetic. Transcendental aesthetic offers it this manifold in order to provide it with a material for the pure concepts of understanding. Without this material, transcendental logic would have no content, and hence would be completely empty. Now space and time contain a manifold of pure a priori intuition. But they belong nonetheless to the conditions of our mind's receptivity under which alone the mind can receive presentations of objects, and which, by the same token, must always affect the concept of these objects. Yet the spontaneity of our thought requires that this manifold, in order to be turned into a cognition, must first be gone through, taken up, and combined in a certain manner. This act I call synthesis.

By *synthesis*, in the most general sense of the term, I mean the act of putting various presentations with one another and of comprising their manifoldness in one cognition. Such synthesis is *pure* if the manifold is given not empirically but a priori (as is the manifold in space and time). Before any analysis of our presentations can take place, these presentations must first be given, and hence in terms of *content* no concepts can originate analytically. Rather, synthesis of a manifold (whether this manifold is given empirically or a priori) is what first gives rise to a cognition. Although this cognition may still be crude and confused at first and hence may require analysis, yet synthesis is what in fact gathers the elements for cognition and unites them to [form] a certain content. Hence if we want to make a judgment about the first origin of our cognition, then we must first direct our attention to synthesis. B103

Synthesis as such, as we shall see hereafter, is the mere effect produced by the imagination, which is a blind but indispensable function of the soul without which we would have no cognition whatsoever, but of which we are conscious only very rarely. Bringing this synthesis to *concepts*, on the other hand, is a function belonging to the understanding; and it is through this function that the understanding first provides us with cognition in the proper meaning of the term.

Now *pure synthesis, conceived of generally*, yields the pure concept of understanding. By pure synthesis I mean the synthesis that rests on a basis of synthetic a priori unity. E.g., our act of counting (as is more noticeable primarily with larger numbers) is a *synthesis according to concepts*, because it is performed according to a common basis of unity (such as the B104 decimal system). Hence under this concept the unity of the manifold's synthesis becomes necessary.

Bringing various presentations *under* a concept (a task dealt with by general logic) is done analytically. But bringing, not presentations but the *pure synthesis* of presentations, *to* concepts is what transcendental logic teaches. The first [thing] that we must be given a priori in order to cognize any object is the *manifold* of pure intuition. The second [thing] is the *synthesis* of this manifold by the imagination. But this synthesis does not yet yield cognition. The third [thing we need] in order to cognize an object that we encounter is the concepts which give *unity* to this pure synthesis and which consist solely in the presentation of this necessary synthetic unity. And these concepts rest on the understanding.

The same function that gives unity to the various presentations *in a judgment* also gives unity to the B105 mere synthesis of various presentations *in an intuition*. This unity—speaking generally—is called pure concept of understanding. Hence the same understanding—and indeed through the same acts whereby it brought about, in concepts, the logical form of a judgment by means of analytic unity—also brings into its presentations a transcendental content, by means of the synthetic unity of the manifold in intuition as such; and because of this, these presentations are called pure concepts of understanding applying a priori to objects. Bringing such a transcendental content into these presentations is something that general logic cannot accomplish.

Thus there arise precisely as many pure concepts of understanding applying a priori to objects of intuition as such, as in the preceding table there were logical functions involved in all possible judgments. For these functions of the understanding are completely exhaustive and survey its power entirely. Following Aristotle, we shall call these functions *categories*. For our aim is fundamentally the same as his, even though it greatly deviates from his in its execution.

This, then, is the list of all the original pure concepts of synthesis that the understanding contains a priori. Indeed, it is a pure understanding only because of these concepts; for through them alone can it understand something in the manifold of intuition, i.e., think an object of intuition. This division of the categories has been generated systematically from a common principle, viz., our ability to judge (which is equivalent to our

TABLE OF CATEGORIES B106

1
Of Quantity
Unity
Plurality
Allness

2
Of Quality
Reality
Negation
Limitation

3
Of Relation
of *Inherence* and Subsistence (*substantia et accidens*)
of *Causality* and Dependence (Cause and Effect)
of *Community* (Interaction between Agent and Patient)

4
Of Modality
Possibility—Impossibility
Existence—Nonexistence
Necessity—Contingency

ability to think). It has not been generated rhapsodically, by locating pure concepts haphazardly, where B107 we can never be certain that the enumeration of the concepts is complete. For we then infer the division only by induction, forgetting that in this way we never gain insight into why precisely these concepts, rather than others, reside in the pure understanding. Locating these basic concepts was a project worthy of an acute man like Aristotle. But having no principle,[127] he snatched them up as he came upon them. He hunted up ten of them at first, and called them *categories* (predicaments).[128] He later believed that he had discovered five more categories, and added them under the name of postpredicaments.[129] But his table remained deficient even then. Moreover, we also find in it some modes of pure sensibility (*quando*, *ubi*, *situs*, and *prius*,

127. [For locating these concepts.]

128. [Substance, quantity, quality, relation, place, time, posture, state, action, undergoing.]

129. [The five relational categories, of doubtful authenticity, found in chs. 10–15 of the *Categories*: opposition, priority, simultaneity, motion, having.]

simul),[130] as well as an empirical mode (*motus*),[131] none of which belong at all in this register of the root [concepts] of the understanding. Again, derivative concepts (*actio, passio*)[132] are also included among the original concepts,[133] while some of the original concepts[134] are missing entirely.

Hence for the sake of [distinguishing] the original concepts, we must note also that the categories, as the true *root concepts* of pure understanding, have also their equally pure *derivative concepts*. In a complete system of transcendental philosophy these derivative concepts can by no means be omitted. In a merely critical essay, on the other hand, I can settle for merely mentioning them.

B108 Let me call these pure but derivative concepts of understanding the *predicables* of pure understanding (in contrast to the predicaments).[135] Once we have the original and primitive concepts, we can easily add the derivative and subsidiary ones and thus depict completely the genealogical tree of pure understanding. Since I am here concerned with the completeness not of the system but only of the principles for a system, I am reserving that complementary work for another enterprise.[136] We can, however, come close to achieving that aim of completing the tree if we pick up a textbook on ontology and subordinate the predicables to the categories: e.g., to the category of causality, the predicables of force, action, undergoing; to the category of community, the predicables of presence, resistance; to the predicaments of modality, the predicables of arising, passing away, change; and so on. When the categories are combined either with the modes of pure sensibility or with one another, they yield a great multitude of derivative a priori concepts. Mentioning these concepts and, if possible, listing them completely would be a useful and not disagreeable endeavor, but one that we can here dispense with.

130. [Respectively, when (time), where (place), posture, prior (priority), simultaneous (simultaneity).]

131. [Motion.]

132. [Action, passion (undergoing).]

133. [On Aristotle's list.]

134. [I.e., as contained in Kant's own table of categories.]

135. [I.e., categories.]

136. [Presumably the activity of producing a metaphysics of nature. Cf. B xliii.]

In this treatise I deliberately refrain from offering definitions of these categories, even though I may possess them. I shall hereafter dissect the concepts only to a degree adequate for the doctrine of method that I here produce. Whereas definitions of the catego- B109 ries could rightly be demanded of me in a system of pure reason, here they would only make us lose sight of the main point of the inquiry. For they would give rise to doubts and charges that we may readily relegate to another activity without in any way detracting from our essential aim. Still, from what little I have mentioned about this, we can see distinctly that a complete lexicon with all the requisite explications not only is possible but could easily be brought about. The compartments are now at hand. They only need to be filled in; and a systematic [transcendental] topic, such as the present one, will make it difficult to miss the place where each concept properly belongs, and at the same time will make it easy to notice any place that is still empty.

§11

Concerning this table of categories one can make nice observations that might perhaps have important consequences regarding the scientific form of all rational cognitions. For in the theoretical part of philosophy this table is exceedingly useful—indeed, indispensable—for drawing up completely *the plan for a science as a whole* insofar as this science rests on a priori concepts, and for *dividing* it systematically *according to determinate principles*. This is self-evident already from these facts: The table lists completely all the elementary concepts of understanding; indeed, it contains even the form of a system of them residing in the human understanding. Conse- B110 quently the table directs us to all the *moments* of a projected speculative science—indeed, even to their *order*. In fact, a sample of their so directing us has already been provided by me elsewhere. Here now are some of those comments that can be made about the table of categories.

The *first comment* is that this table containing four classes of concepts of understanding can be broken up, initially, into two divisions. The concepts in the first division are directed to objects of intuition (both pure and empirical), while those in the second are directed to the existence of these objects (these objects being referred either to each other or to the understanding).

The first division I would call that of the *mathematical* categories, the second, that of the *dynamical* categories. The first division of categories, as we can see by inspecting the table, has no correlates; only in the second division do we find correlates. This distinction must surely have a basis in the nature of the understanding.

The *second comment* to be made about the table is that the number of categories in each class is equal everywhere, viz., three; this, too, calls for meditation, because normally all a priori division by concepts must be dichotomous. Add to this, moreover, the fact that in each case the third category of the class arises from the combination of the second category with the first of the same class.

B111 Thus *allness* (totality) is nothing but plurality considered as unity; *limitation* is nothing but reality combined with negation; *community* is the causality of a substance reciprocally determining [and being determined by] another substance; *necessity*, finally, is nothing but the existence that is given through possibility itself. This fact, however, must by no means lead us to think that the third category is a mere derivative concept, rather than a root concept, of pure understanding. For combining the first and second categories, in order to produce the third concept, requires that the understanding perform a special act that is not the same as the act it performs in the case of the first and second concepts. Thus the concept of a *number* (which belongs to the category of allness) is not possible in every case where we have the concepts of multitude and unity (e.g., it is not possible in the presentation of infinity). Again, combining the two concepts of a *cause* and of a *substance* does not yet provide me with an immediate understanding of *influence*, i.e., understanding of how a substance can become the cause of something in another substance. This shows that a special act of the understanding is required;[137] and thus it is with the remaining classes of categories.

The *third comment* to be made about the table of categories concerns the category of *community*, which is to be found under the third heading. This is the one category whose agreement with the form corres- B112 ponding to it in the table of logical functions—viz., the form of a disjunctive judgment—is not so obvious as in the case of the others.

In order to assure ourselves of this agreement, we must note the following: In all disjunctive judgments the sphere (the multitude of everything contained under the judgment) is presented as a whole divided into parts (the subordinate concepts). And because the parts cannot be contained one under another, they are thought as *coordinated* with rather than as *subordinated* to one another, so that they determine one another not *unilaterally* as in a *series*, but *reciprocally* as in an *aggregate* (wherein, when one member of the division is posited, all the rest are excluded, and conversely).

Now a similar connection is thought in [thinking] a *whole* of *things*. In such a whole, one thing is not *subordinated*, as effect, to another as cause of its existence; rather, it is simultaneously and reciprocally *coordinated* with others, as cause regarding their determination (as, e.g., in a body whose parts reciprocally attract—or, for that matter, repel—one another). This kind of connection is entirely different from the one found in the mere relation of cause to effect (ground to consequence), where the consequence does not in turn reciprocally determine the ground and hence does not together with it constitute a whole (e.g., the world together with its creator does not constitute a whole). When the understanding presents the sphere of a divided concept, it follows a certain procedure; B113 it observes that same procedure when it thinks a thing as divisible. And in the divided concept the members of the division exclude one another and yet are combined in one sphere; in the same way, the understanding[138] presents the thing's parts as being such that while the existence of each part also belongs to it alone (as a substance) to the exclusion of the others, yet the parts are combined in one whole.

§12

In the transcendental philosophy of the ancients, however, we find an additional chapter containing pure concepts of understanding. Although these concepts are not there included among the categories, yet according to the ancients they were to count as a priori concepts of objects. In that case, however, these concepts would in fact increase the number

137. [To produce the category of community.]

138. [In thinking a thing as divisible.]

of categories—which cannot be. These additional concepts are set forth in this proposition, so famous among the scholastics: *quodlibet ens est unum verum, bonum.*[139] Now it is true that the use of this principle turned out to permit only very meager inferences (yielding nothing but tautological propositions); by the same token, in more recent times the principle has come to receive little more than honorable mention in metaphysics. Yet whenever a thought—no matter how empty it seems to be—has maintained itself for such a long time, then it deserves an inquiry into its origin, and entitles us to conjecture that it has its basis in some rule of the understanding that, as often happens, has only been wrongly interpreted. *B114* But in fact these supposedly transcendental predicates of *things* are nothing but logical requirements and criteria for all *cognition* of *things* in general; and they lay at the basis of such cognition the categories of quantity, viz., those of *unity*, *plurality*, and *allness*. These categories, however, should properly be taken materially, as belonging to the possibility of things themselves. Those [philosophers], on the other hand, used them in fact only in their formal meaning, as belonging to the logical demands concerning any cognition; yet, through carelessness, they still turned these criteria of thought into properties of things in themselves. Let me explain. In every cognition there are three components. First, there is *unity* of the concept; we may call it *qualitative unity*, provided that in [thinking] it we think only the unity in the collating of the manifold of cognitions: e.g., the unity of the topic in a play, a speech, or a story. Second, in every cognition there is *truth* as regards the consequences. The more true consequences arise from a given concept, the more indicators there are of its objective reality. We might call this the *qualitative plurality* of the characteristics that belong to a concept as their common ground (rather than are thought, in the concept, as a quantity). Finally, third, in every cognition there is *perfection;* it consists in the fact that the plurality together leads back again to the unity of the concept, and that it agrees fully with this and with no other concept. This perfection may be *B115* called *qualitative completeness* (totality). This shows that these logical criteria for the possibility of cognition as such only transform the three categories of quantity. In these categories, the unity in the production of the quantum must be assumed as homogeneous throughout. Here, however, they are only transformed, in order to connect components of cognition—even *heterogeneous* ones—in one consciousness, using as principle for this connection the quality of a cognition. Thus the criterion for the possibility of a concept (rather than for the possibility of the concept's object) is the concept's definition; in it the *unity* of the concept, the *truth* of everything that may be derived from it initially, and finally the *completeness* of what has been extracted from it constitute what the whole concept requires for its construction. Or, again, the *criterion of a hypothesis* is the understandability of the assumed *basis of explanation,* or, i.e.: its *unity* (without an auxiliary hypothesis); the *truth* of the consequences derivable from it (their agreement with one another and with experience); and, finally, the *completeness* of the basis for the explanation of these consequences—which means that these consequences point back to no more and no less than was assumed in the hypothesis, and that they analytically a posteriori bring back and agree with what was thought synthetically a priori in the hypothesis. Therefore by adding the concepts of unity, truth, and perfection to the transcendental table of categories we do not at all complement that table—as if perhaps it were deficient. Rather, while setting aside entirely the relation of these concepts to objects[140] *B116* we bring the procedure used with these concepts under general logical rules governing the agreement of cognition with itself.

Analytic of Concepts

Chapter II
On the Deduction of the Pure Concept of Understanding

Section I

§13

On the Principles of a Transcendental Deduction as Such

When teachers of law talk about rights and claims, they distinguish in a legal action the question regard-

139. [Any being is one, true, good.]

140. [I.e., the relation implied in the categories.]

ing what is legal (*quid iuris*) from the question concerning fact (*quid facti*), and they demand proof of both.[141] The first proof, which is to establish the right, or for that matter the legal entitlement, they call the *deduction*. [This term also applies to philosophy.] We employ a multitude of empirical concepts without being challenged by anyone. And we consider ourselves justified, even without having offered a deduction, to assign to these empirical concepts a meaning B117 and imagined signification, because we always have experience available to us to prove their objective reality. But there are also concepts that we usurp, as, e.g., *fortune, fate*. And although these concepts run loose, with our almost universal forbearance, yet they are sometimes confronted by the question [of their legality], *quid iuris*. This question then leaves us in considerable perplexity regarding the deduction[142] of these concepts; for neither from experience nor from reason can we adduce any distinct legal basis from which the right to use them emerges distinctly.

But there are, among the various concepts making up the highly mixed fabric of human cognition, some that are determined for pure a priori use as well (i.e., for a use that is completely independent of all experience); and their right to be so used always requires a deduction. For proofs based on experience are insufficient to establish the legitimacy of using them in that way; yet we do need to know how these concepts can refer to objects even though they do not take these objects from any experience. Hence when I explain in what way concepts can refer to objects a priori, I call that explanation the *transcendental deduction* of these concepts. And I distinguish transcendental deduction from *empirical* deduction, which indicates in what way a concept has been acquired through experience and through reflection upon experience, and which therefore concerns not the concept's legitimacy but only the fact whereby we came to possess it.

B118 We already have, at this point, two types of concepts that, while being wholly different in kind, do yet agree inasmuch as both of them refer to objects completely a priori: viz., on the one hand, the concepts of space and time as forms of sensibility; and, on the other hand, the categories as concepts of understanding. To attempt an empirical deduction of these two types of concepts would be a futile job. For what is distinctive in their nature is precisely the fact that they refer to their objects without having borrowed anything from experience in order to present these objects. Hence if a deduction of these concepts is needed, then it must always be transcendental.

But even for these concepts, as for all cognition, we can locate in experience, if not the principle of their possibility, then at least the occasioning causes of their production. Thus the impressions of the senses first prompt [us] to open up the whole cognitive power in regard to them, and to bring about experience. Experience contains two quite heterogeneous elements: viz., a *matter* for cognition, taken from the senses; and a certain *form* for ordering this matter, taken from the inner source of pure intuition and thought. It is on the occasion of the impressions of the senses that pure intuition and thought are first brought into operation and produce concepts. Such exploration of our cognitive power's first endeavors to ascend from singular perceptions to universal concepts is doubtless highly beneficial, and we are indebted to the illustrious *Locke* for first opening up the path to it.[143] Yet such exploration can never yield a *deduction*[144] of the pure a priori concepts, which does not lie on that path at all. For in view of these concepts' later use, which is to be wholly independent of experience, they must be able to display a birth certificate quite different from that of descent from experiences. The attempted[145] physiological derivation concerns a *quaestio facti*,[146] and therefore cannot properly be called a deduction at all. Hence I shall name it the explanation of our *possession* of a pure cognition. Clearly, then, the only possible deduction of this pure cognition is a transcendental and by no means an empirical one, and empirical deductions regarding the pure a priori concepts are nothing but futile attempts—attempts that only those can engage B119

141. [Legality and factuality.]

142. [I.e., legitimation.]

143. [See *An Essay Concerning Human Understanding*, Bk. II.]

144. [I.e., legitimation.]

145. [By philosophers such as Locke.]

146. [Question of fact (rather than of legality or legitimation).]

in who have not comprehended the quite peculiar nature of these cognitions.

Yet even if it be granted that the only possible kind of deduction of pure a priori cognition is one along the transcendental path, that still does not show that this deduction is inescapably necessary. We did earlier trace the concepts of space and time to their sources by means of a transcendental deduction, and B120 we explained and determined their a priori objective validity. Yet geometry, using nothing but a priori cognitions, follows its course securely without needing to ask philosophy for a certificate of the pure and legitimate descent of geometry's basic concept of space. On the other hand, the use of the concept of space in this science does apply only to the external world of sense. Space is the pure form of the intuition of that world. In that world, therefore, all geometric cognition is directly evident, because it is based on a priori intuition; and, through cognition itself, objects are (as regards their form) given a priori in intuition. With the *pure concepts of understanding*, on the other hand, begins the inescapable requirement to seek a transcendental deduction—not only of these concepts themselves, but also of space. For these concepts speak of objects through predicates of pure a priori thought, not through predicates of intuition and sensibility; hence they refer to objects universally, i.e., apart from all conditions of sensibility. They are, then, concepts that are not based on experience; and in a priori intuition, too, they cannot display any object on which they might, prior to all experience, base their synthesis. Hence these concepts not only arouse suspicion concerning the objective validity and limits of their use, but they also make ambiguous B121 the *concept of space*; for they tend to use it even beyond the conditions of sensible intuition—and this indeed is the reason why a transcendental deduction of this concept was needed above. I must therefore convince the reader, before he has taken a single step in the realm of pure reason, that such a deduction is inescapably necessary. For otherwise he proceeds blindly, and after manifold wanderings must yet return to the ignorance from which he started. But the reader must also distinctly see in advance the inevitable difficulty of providing such a deduction. For otherwise he might complain of obscurity when in fact the matter itself is deeply shrouded, or might be too quickly discouraged during the removal of obstacles. For we either must entirely abandon all claims to pure rational insights into the realm that we care about most, viz., the realm beyond the bounds of all possible experience, or else must bring this critical inquiry to completion.

We had little trouble above in making comprehensible how the concepts of space and time, despite being a priori cognitions, must yet refer necessarily to objects, and how they make possible, independently of any experience, a synthetic cognition of objects. For only by means of such pure forms of sensibility can an object appear to us, i.e., can it be an object of empirical intuition. Hence space and B122 time are pure intuitions containing a priori the condition for the possibility of objects as appearances, and the synthesis in space and time has objective validity.

The categories of understanding, on the other hand, do not at all present to us the conditions under which objects are given in intuition. Therefore objects can indeed appear to us without having to refer necessarily to functions of understanding, and hence without the understanding's containing a priori the conditions of these objects. Thus we find here a difficulty that we did not encounter in the realm of sensibility: viz., how *subjective conditions of thought* could have *objective validity*, i.e., how they could yield conditions for the possibility of all cognition of objects. For appearances can indeed be given in intuition without functions of understanding. Let me take, e.g., the concept of cause. This concept signifies a special kind of synthesis where upon [the occurrence of] something, A, something quite different, B, is posited according to a rule. Why appearances should contain anything like that is not evident a priori. (I say *a priori* because experience cannot be adduced as proof, since we must be able to establish this concept's objective validity a priori.) Hence there is doubt a priori whether perhaps such a concept might not even be empty and encounter no object at all among appearances. For while it is evident that objects of sensible intuition must conform to the formal conditions of B123 sensibility lying a priori in the mind, since otherwise they would not be objects for us, it is not so easy to see the inference whereby they must in addition conform to the conditions that the understanding requires for the synthetic unity of thought. For, I suppose, appearances might possibly be of such a character that the understanding would not find them to conform at all to the conditions of its unity. Everything might then be so confused that, e.g., the sequence of appearances would offer us nothing providing us with a rule of synthesis and thus corresponding to the concept of cause and effect, so that this concept would then be quite empty, null, and without signification. But appearances would nonetheless offer objects to our intuition; for intuition in no way requires the functions of thought.

Suppose that we planned to extricate ourselves from these troublesome inquiries by saying that examples of such regularity among appearances are offered to us incessantly by experience, and that these examples give us sufficient prompting to isolate from them the concept of cause and thus to verify at the same time the objective validity of such a concept. In that case we would be overlooking the fact that the concept of cause cannot arise in that way at all; rather, it either must have its basis completely a priori in the *B124* understanding, or must be given up entirely as a mere chimera. For this concept definitely requires that something, A, be of such a kind that something else, B, follows from it *necessarily* and according to an *absolutely universal rule.* Although appearances do provide us with cases from which we can obtain a rule whereby something usually happens, they can never provide us with a rule whereby the result is *necessary.* This is, moreover, the reason why the synthesis of cause and effect is imbued with a dignity that cannot at all be expressed empirically: viz., that the effect is not merely added to the cause, but is posited *through* the cause and results *from* it. And the strict universality of the rule is indeed no property whatever of empirical rules; empirical rules can, through induction, acquire none but comparative universality, i.e., extensive usability. But if we treated the pure concepts of understanding as merely empirical products, then our use of them would change entirely.

§14

Transition to the Transcendental Deduction of the Categories

Only two cases are possible where synthetic presentation and its objects can concur, can necessarily refer to each other, and can—as it were—meet each other: viz., either if the object makes the presentation possible, or if the presentation alone makes the object possible. If the object makes the presentation possible, *B125* then the reference is only empirical and the presentation is never possible a priori. This is what happens in the case of appearances, as regards what pertains to sensation in them. But suppose that the presentation alone makes the object possible. In that case, while presentation in itself does not produce its object *as regards existence* (for the causality that presentation has by means of the will is not at issue here at all), yet presentation is a priori determinative in regard to the object if *cognizing* something *as an object* is possible only through it. Now there are two conditions under which alone there can be cognition of an object. The first condition is *intuition;* through it the object is given, though only as appearance. The second condition is the *concept;* through it an object is thought that corresponds to this intuition. Now it is evident from the above that the first condition, viz., the condition under which alone objects can be intuited, does indeed, as far as their form is concerned, underlie objects a priori in the mind. Hence all appearances necessarily agree with this formal condition of sensibility, because only through it can they appear, i.e., be empirically intuited and given. Now the question arises whether concepts do not also a priori precede [objects], as conditions under which alone something can be, if not intuited, yet thought as object as such. For in that case all empirical cognition of *B126* objects necessarily conforms to such concepts, because nothing is possible as *object of experience* unless these concepts are presupposed. But all experience, besides containing the senses' intuition through which something is given, does also contain a *concept* of an object that is given in intuition, or that appears. Accordingly, concepts of objects as such presumably underlie all experiential cognition as its a priori conditions. Hence presumably the objective validity of the categories, as a priori concepts, rests on the fact that through them alone is experience possible (as far as the form of thought in it is concerned). For in that case the categories refer to objects of experience necessarily and a priori, because only by means of them can any experiential object whatsoever be thought at all.

Hence the transcendental deduction of all a priori concepts has a principle to which the entire investigation must be directed: viz., the principle that these concepts must be cognized as a priori conditions for the possibility of experience (whether the possibility of the intuition found in experience, or the possibility of the thought). If concepts serve as the objective basis for the possibility of experience, then—precisely because of this—they are necessary. But to unfold the experience in which these concepts are found is not to deduce them (but is only to illustrate them); for otherwise they would, after all, be only contingent. *B127* Without that original reference of these concepts to possible experience wherein all objects of cognition occur, their reference to any object whatever would be quite incomprehensible.

The illustrious **Locke,** not having engaged in this contemplation, and encountering pure concepts of understanding in experience, also derived them from experience. Yet he proceeded so *inconsistently* that he dared to try using these concepts for cognitions that go far beyond any boundary of experience. **David Hume** recognized that in order for us to be able to do this, the origin of these concepts must be a priori. But he was quite unable to explain how it is possible that concepts not in themselves combined in the understanding should nonetheless have to be thought by it as necessarily combined in the object. Nor did it occur to him that perhaps the understanding itself might, through these concepts, be the author of the experience wherein we encounter the understanding's objects. Thus, in his plight, he derived these concepts from experience (viz., from *habit,* a subjective necessity that arises in experience through repeated association and that ultimately is falsely regarded as objective). But he proceeded quite consistently after that, for he declared that we cannot use these concepts and the principles that they occasion in order to go beyond the boundary of experience. *B128* Yet the *empirical* derivation of these concepts which occurred to both[147] cannot be reconciled with the scientific a priori cognitions that we actually have, viz., our a priori cognitions of *pure mathematics* and *universal natural science,* and hence this empirical derivation is refuted by that fact.

Of these two illustrious men, Locke left the door wide open for *fanaticism;* for once reason has gained possession of such rights, it can no longer be kept within limits by indefinite exhortations to moderation. Hume, believing that he had uncovered so universal a delusion—regarded as reason—of our cognitive power, surrendered entirely to *skepticism.* We are now about to try to find out whether we cannot provide for human reason safe passage between these two cliffs, assign to it determinate bounds, and yet keep open for it the entire realm of its appropriate activity.

The only thing that I still want to do before we start is to *explicate the categories:* they are concepts of an object as such whereby the object's intuition is regarded as *determined* in terms of one of the logical functions in judging. Thus the function of the *categorical* judgment—i.e., All bodies are divisible—is that of the relation of subject to predicate. But the understanding's merely logical use left undetermined to which of the two concepts we want to give the function of the subject, and to which the function of the predicate. *B129* For we can also say, Something divisible is a body. If, on the other hand, I bring the concept of a body under the category of substance, then through this category is determined the fact that the body's empirical intuition in experience must be considered always as subject only, never as mere predicate. And similarly in all the remaining categories.

Deduction of the Pure Concepts of Understanding

Section II
[Second Edition]
Transcendental Deduction of the Pure Concepts of Understanding

§15

On the Possibility of a Combination as Such

The [uncombined] manifold of presentations can be given in an intuition that is merely sensible, i.e., nothing but receptivity,[148] and the form of this intuition can lie a priori in our power of presentation without being anything but the way in which the subject is affected. But a manifold's *combination (coniunctio)* as such can never come to us through the senses; nor, therefore, can it already be part of what

147. [Locke and Hume.]

148. [In contrast to an intellectual intuition. See B 72.]

B130 is contained in the pure form of sensible intuition. For this combination is an act of spontaneity by the power of presentation; and this power must be called understanding, in order to be distinguished from sensibility. Hence all combination is an act of understanding—whether or not we become conscious of such combination; whether it is a combination of the manifold of intuition or of the manifold of various concepts; and whether, in the case of intuition, it is a combination of sensible or of nonsensible intuition. I would assign to this act of understanding the general name *synthesis,* in order to point out at the same time: that we cannot present anything as combined in the object without ourselves' having combined it beforehand; and that, among all presentations, *combination* is the only one that cannot be given through objects, but—being an act of the subject's self-activity—can be performed only by the subject himself. We readily become aware here that this act of synthesis must originally be a single act and must hold equally for all combination; and that resolution or *analysis,* which seems to be its opposite yet always presupposes it. For where the understanding has not beforehand combined anything, there it also cannot resolve anything, because only *through the understanding* could the power of presentation have been given something as combined.

But the concept of combination carries with it, besides the concept of the manifold and of its synthesis, also the concept of the manifold's unity. Combi- B131 nation is presentation of the *synthetic* unity of the manifold.[149] Hence the presentation of this unity cannot arise from the combination; rather, by being added to the presentation of the manifold, it makes possible the concept of combination in the first place. This unity, which thus precedes a priori all concepts of combination, is by no means the category of unity mentioned earlier (in § 10[150]). For all categories are based on logical functions occurring in judgments; but in these functions combination, and hence unity of given concepts, is already thought. Hence a category already presupposes combination. We must therefore search for this unity (which is qualitative unity; see § 12[151]) still higher up, viz., in what itself contains the basis for the unity of different concepts in judgments, and hence contains the basis for the possibility of understanding, even as used logically.

§16

On the Original Synthetic Unity of Apperception

The *I think* must be *capable* of accompanying all my presentations. For otherwise something would be presented to me that could not be thought at all—which B132 is equivalent to saying that the presentation either would be impossible, or at least would be nothing to me. Presentation that can be given prior to all thought is called *intuition.* Hence everything manifold in intuition has a necessary reference to the *I think* in the same subject in whom this manifold is found. But this presentation [i.e., the *I think*] is an act of spontaneity; i.e., it cannot be regarded as belonging to sensibility. I call it *pure apperception,* in order to distinguish it from *empirical* apperception. Or, again, I call it *original apperception;* for it is the self-consciousness which, because it produces the presentation *I think* that must be capable of accompanying all other presentations[,] and [because it] is one and the same in all consciousness, cannot be accompanied by any further presentation. I also call the *unity* of this apperception the *transcendental* unity of self-consciousness, in order to indicate that a priori cognition can be obtained from it. For the manifold presentations given in a certain intuition would not one and all be *my* presentations, if they did not one and all belong to one self-consciousness. I.e., as my presentations (even if I am not conscious of them as being mine), they surely must conform necessarily to the condition under which alone they *can* stand together in one universal self-consciousness, since otherwise they would not thoroughly belong to me. And B133 from this original combination much can be inferred.

This same thoroughgoing identity of the appercep-

149. We need not here consider whether the [manifold] presentations themselves are identical, so that one can be thought analytically through the other: the *consciousness* of the one presentation can nonetheless, insofar as we are talking about the manifold, always be distinguished from the consciousness of the other presentation; and what matters here is solely the synthesis of this (possible) consciousness.

150. [Specifically, B 106.]

151. [Specifically, B 114.]

tion of a manifold given in intuition contains a synthesis of presentations, and is possible only through the consciousness of this synthesis. For the empirical consciousness that accompanies different presentations is intrinsically sporadic and without any reference to the subject's identity. Hence this reference comes about not through my merely accompanying each presentation with consciousness, but through my *adding* one presentation to another and being conscious of their synthesis. Hence only because I can combine a manifold of given presentations *in one consciousness*, is it possible for me to present the *identity itself of the consciousness in these presentations.*[152] I.e., the *analytic* unity of apperception is possible only under B134 the presupposition of some *synthetic* unity of apperception.[153] The thought that these presentations given in intuition belong one and all to me is, accordingly, tantamount to the thought that I unite them, or at least can unite them, in one self-consciousness. And although that thought itself is not yet the consciousness of the *synthesis* of the presentations, it still presupposes the possibility of that synthesis. I.e., only because I can comprise the manifold of the presentations in one consciousness, do I call them one and all *my* presentations. For otherwise I would have a self as many-colored and varied as I have presentations that I am conscious of. Hence synthetic unity of the manifold of intuitions, as given a priori, is the basis of the identity itself of apperception, which precedes a priori all *my* determinate thought. But combination does not lie in objects, and can by no means be borrowed from them by perception and thus be taken up only then into the understanding. It is, rather, solely something performed by the understanding; B135 and understanding itself is nothing more than the power to combine a priori and to bring the manifold of given intuitions under the unity of apperception—the principle of this unity being the supreme principle in all of human cognition.

Now, it is true that this principle of the necessary unity of apperception is itself merely an identical[154] and hence an analytic proposition. Yet it does declare as necessary a synthesis of the manifold given in an intuition, a synthesis without which that thoroughgoing identity of self-consciousness cannot be thought. For through the *I*, as simple presentation, nothing manifold is given; only in intuition, which is distinct from this presentation, can a manifold be given, and only through *combination* can it be thought in one consciousness. An understanding wherein through self-consciousness alone everything manifold would at the same time be given would be an understanding that *intuits.*[155] Our understanding can only *think*, and must seek intuition in the senses. I am, then, conscious of the self as identical, as regards the manifold of the presentations given to me in an intuition, because I call them one and all *my* presentations that make up one presentation. That, however, is tantamount to saying that I am conscious of a necessary a priori synthesis of them. This synthesis is called the original synthetic unity of apperception. All presentations given to me are subject to this unity; but they B136 must also be brought under it through a synthesis.

§17

The Principle of the Synthetic Unity of Apperception Is the Supreme Principle for All Use of the Understanding

The supreme principle for the possibility of all intuition in reference to sensibility was, according to the

152. [I.e., across these presentations.]

153. The analytic unity of consciousness attaches to all concepts that are, and inasmuch as they are, common [to several presentations]. E.g., in thinking *red* as such, I present a property that can be found (as a characteristic) in something or other or can be combined with other presentations; hence only by virtue of a possible synthetic unity that I think beforehand can I present the analytic unity. A presentation that is to be thought as common to different presenta- B134 tions is regarded as belonging to presentations that, besides having it, also have something *different* about them. Consequently it must beforehand be thought in synthetic unity with other presentations (even if only possible ones). Only then can I think in it the analytic unity of consciousness that makes the presentation a *conceptus communis.* And thus the synthetic unity of apperception is the highest point, to which we must attach all use of the understanding, even the whole of logic, and in accordance with it transcendental philosophy; indeed, this power is the understanding itself.

154. [I.e., based, for its truth, on identity.]

155. [On intuitive understanding and its (intellectual) intuition, see above, B 72.]

Transcendental Aesthetic, that everything manifold in intuition is subject to the formal conditions of space and time. The supreme principle for the possibility of all intuition in reference to understanding is that everything manifold in intuition is subject to conditions of the original synthetic unity of apperception.[156] All manifold presentations of intuition are subject to the first principle insofar as they are *given* to us. They are subject to the second principle insofar as they B137 must be capable of being *combined* in one consciousness. For without that combination, nothing can be thought or cognized through such presentations, because the given presentations do then not have in common the act of apperception, *I think*, and thus would not be collated[157] in one self-consciousness.

Understanding—speaking generally—is the power of *cognitions*. Cognitions consist in determinate reference of given presentations to an object. And an *object* is that in whose concept the manifold of a given intuition is *united*. But all unification of presentations requires that there be unity of consciousness in the synthesis of them. Consequently the reference of presentations to an object consists solely in this unity of consciousness, and hence so does their objective validity and consequently their becoming cognitions. On this unity, consequently, rests the very possibility of the understanding.

Hence the principle of the original *synthetic* unity of apperception is the primary pure cognition of understanding, on which the entire remaining use of the understanding is based; and this cognition is at the same time entirely independent of all conditions of sensible intuition. Thus the mere form of outer sensible intuition, i.e., space, is as yet no cognition at all; it provides only the manifold of a priori intuition for a possible cognition. Rather, in order to cognize something or other—e.g., a line—in space, I must *draw* it; and hence I must bring about synthetically B138 a determinate combination of the given manifold, so that the unity of this act[158] is at the same time the unity of consciousness (in the concept of a line), and so that an object (a determinate space) is thereby first cognized. The synthetic unity of consciousness is, therefore, an objective condition of all cognition. Not only do I myself need this condition in order to cognize an object, but every intuition must be subject to it *in order to become an object for me*. For otherwise, and without that synthesis, the manifold would *not* unite in one consciousness.

Although this last proposition makes the synthetic unity [of consciousness] a condition of all thought, it is—as I have said—itself analytic. For it says no more than that all *my* presentations in some given intuition must be subject to the condition under which alone I can ascribe them—as *my* presentations—to the identical self, and hence under which alone I can collate them, as combined synthetically in one apperception, through the universal expression *I think*.

On the other hand, this principle is not one for every possible understanding as such, but is a principle only for that [kind of] understanding through whose pure apperception, in the presentation *I think*, nothing manifold whatever is yet given. An alternative [kind of] understanding would be that understanding through whose self-consciousness the manifold of intuition would at the same time be given—i.e., an B139 understanding through whose presentation the objects of this presentation would at the same time exist.[159] Such an understanding would not require, for the unity of consciousness, a special act of synthesis of the manifold. The human understanding, which merely thinks but does not intuit, does need that

156. Space and time, and all their parts, are *intuitions*; hence they, with the manifold that they contain, are singular presentations. (See the Transcendental Aesthetic.[a]) Hence space and time are not mere concepts, through which the very same consciousness is encountered as contained in many presentations. They are, rather, [presentations through which] many presentations are encountered as contained in one presentation and in the consciousness thereof, and hence [they are presentations] encountered as composite; and consequently the unity of this consciousness is encountered as *synthetic*, but yet as original. This *singularity* of [intuition] is important when applied [to specific contexts]. (See §25.[b])

[a][Although Kant did not there use the term 'singular,' the reference seems to be to ¶ numbers 3 and 4 (A 24–25/B 39), and § 4, numbers 4 and 5 (A 31–2/B 47).]

[b][B 157–59.]

157. [I.e., arranged and held together.]

158. [Of synthesis.]

159. [This would be an intuitive understanding, and its intuition would be intellectual. See B 72.]

synthesis. But still, for the human understanding the principle[160] is unavoidably the first principle. And thus our understanding cannot even frame the slightest concept of a different possible understanding—whether of an understanding that itself would intuit; or of an understanding that would indeed have lying at its basis a sensible intuition, yet one of a different kind from that in space and time.

§18

What Objective Unity of Self-Consciousness Is

The *transcendental unity* of apperception is the unity whereby everything manifold given in an intuition is united in a concept of the object. Hence this unity is called *objective,* and must be distinguished from *subjective* unity of consciousness, which is a *determination of inner sense* whereby that manifold of intuition for such [objective] combination is given empirically. Whether I can be conscious *empirically* of the manifold as simultaneous or as sequential depends on circumstances or empirical conditions. B140 Hence empirical unity of consciousness, through association of presentations, itself concerns an appearance and is entirely contingent. On the other hand, the pure form of intuition in time, merely as intuition as such containing a given manifold, is subject to the original unity of consciousness. It is subject to that unity solely through the necessary reference of the manifold of intuition to the one [self], i.e., to the *I think,* and hence through the understanding's pure synthesis that lies a priori at the basis of the empirical synthesis. Only the original unity of consciousness is valid objectively. The empirical unity of apperception, which we are not examining here and which moreover is only derived from the original unity under given conditions *in concreto,* has only subjective validity. One person will link the presentation of a certain word with one thing, another with some other thing; and the unity of consciousness in what is empirical is not, as regards what is given, necessary and universally valid.

§19

The Logical Form of All Judgments Consists in the Objective Unity of Apperception of the Concepts Contained in Them

I have never been able to settle for the explication that logicians give of a judgment as such. A judgment, they say, is the presentation of a relation between two concepts. Now, I shall not here quarrel with them B141 about one respect in which this explication is defective (although this oversight has given rise to many irksome consequences for logic): viz., that it fits at most *categorical* judgments only, but not hypothetical and disjunctive ones (since these contain a relation not of concepts but of further judgments).[161] I shall point out only that this explication of a judgment leaves undetermined wherein this *relation*[162] consists.

But suppose that I inquire more precisely into the [relation or] reference of given cognitions in every judgment, and that I distinguish it, as belonging to the understanding, from the relation in terms of laws of the reproductive imagination (a relation that has only subjective validity). I then find that a judgment is nothing but a way of bringing given cognitions to the objective unity of apperception. This is what the little relational word *is* in judgments intends [to indi- B142 cate], in order to distinguish the objective unity of given presentations from the subjective one. For this word indicates the reference of the presentations to original apperception and its *necessary unity.* The reference to this necessary unity is there even if the judgment itself is empirical and hence contingent—e.g., Bodies are heavy. By this I do not mean that

160. [Of the synthetic unity of apperception.]

161. The voluminous doctrine of the four syllogistic figures concerns only categorical syllogisms. Now, this doctrine is nothing more than the art of surreptitiously creating, by concealing immediate inferences (*consequentiae immediatae*) among the premises of a pure syllogism, the illusion that there are more kinds of inference than that of the first figure. Still, the doctrine would not on account of that illusion alone have met with special fortune, had it not also succeeded in procuring for categorical judgments an exclusive reputation, viz. as judgments to which all others must be capable of being referred [as their basis]—which, however, is false by § 9.

162. [Between the concepts.]

these presentations belong *necessarily to one another* in the empirical intuition. Rather, I mean that they belong to one another *by virtue of the necessary unity* of apperception in the synthesis of intuitions; i.e., they belong to one another according to principles of the objective determination of all presentations insofar as these presentations can become cognition—all of these principles being derived from the principle of the transcendental unity of apperception. Only through this [reference to original apperception and its necessary unity] does this relation [among presentations] become a *judgment*, i.e., a relation that is *valid objectively* and can be distinguished adequately from a relation of the same presentations that would have only subjective validity—e.g., a relation according to laws of association. According to these laws, all I could say is: When I support a body, then I feel a pressure of heaviness. I could not say: It, the body, is heavy—which amounts to saying that these two presentations are not merely together in perception (no matter how often repeated), but are combined in the object, i.e., combined independently of what the subject's state is.

B143

§20

All Sensible Intuitions Are Subject to the Categories, Which Are Conditions under Which Alone Their Manifold Can Come Together in One Consciousness

The manifold given [which is found] in a sensible intuition is subject necessarily to the original synthetic unity of apperception; for solely through this unity is the *unity* of intuition possible. (§ 17.) But the act of understanding whereby the manifold of given presentations (whether intuitions or concepts) are brought under one apperception as such is the logical function of judgments. (§ 19.) Therefore everything manifold, insofar as it is given in one empirical intuition, is *determined* in regard to one of the logical functions of judging, inasmuch as through this function it is brought to one consciousness as such. The *categories*, however, are indeed nothing but precisely these functions of judging insofar as the manifold of a given intuition is determined in regard to them. (§ 13.) Hence, by the same token, the manifold in a given intuition is subject necessarily to the categories.

§21

B144

Comment

Through the synthesis of understanding, a manifold contained in an intuition that I call mine is presented as belonging to the *necessary* unity of self-consciousness, and this presenting is done by means of the category.[163] Hence the category indicates that the empirical consciousness of a given manifold of one intuition is just as subject to a pure a priori self-consciousness, as empirical intuition is subject to a pure sensible intuition that likewise takes place a priori. Hence in the above proposition[164] I have made the beginning of a *deduction* of the pure concepts of understanding. Since the categories are *independent of sensibility* and arise in the understanding alone, I must still abstract, in this deduction, from the way in which the manifold for an empirical intuition is given, in order to take account solely of the unity that the understanding contributes to the intuition by means of the category. Afterwards (§ 26) I shall show, from the way in which the empirical intuition B145 is given in sensibility, that the intuition's unity is none other than the unity that (by § 20, above) the category prescribes to the manifold of a given intuition as such; and that hence by my explaining the category's a priori validity regarding all objects of our senses, the deduction's aim will first be fully attained.

From one point, however, I could not abstract in the above proof: viz., from the fact that the manifold for the intuition must be given still prior to the understanding's synthesis, and independently of it; but how it is given remains undetermined here. For if I were to think of an understanding[165] that itself intuited[166]

163. The basis of proof for this rests on the presented *unity of intuition*, through which an *object*[a] is given. That unity always implies[b] a synthesis of the manifold given[c] for an intuition, and already contains this manifold given's reference to unity of apperception.

[a][Emphasis added.]

[b][Or 'includes': *in sich schließ.*]

[c][Here again 'manifold' is an adjective, and 'given' is a participle that is about to be construed as a noun. Cf. B 143.]

164. [The proposition at the beginning of § 21.]

165. [Other than our own.]

166. [See, B 72.]

(as, e.g., a divine understanding that did not present given objects[167] but through whose presentation the objects would at the same time be given or produced), then in regard to such cognition the categories would have no signification whatever. The categories are only rules for an understanding whose entire power consists in thought, i.e., in the act of bringing to the unity of apperception the synthesis of the manifold that has, in intuition, been given to it from elsewhere. Hence such an understanding by itself cognizes nothing whatever, but only combines and orders the material for cognition, i.e., the intuition, which must be given to it by the object. But why our understanding has this peculiarity, that it a priori brings about unity *B146* of apperception only by means of the categories, and only by just this kind and number of them—for this no further reason can be given, just as no reason can be given as to why we have just these and no other functions in judging, or why time and space are the only forms of our possible intuition.

§22

A Category Cannot Be Used for Cognizing Things Except When It Is Applied to Objects of Experience

Thinking an object and *cognizing* an object are, then, not the same. For cognition involves two components: first, the concept (the category), through which an object as such is thought; and second, the intuition, through which the object is given. For if no intuition corresponding to the concept could be given at all, then in terms of its form the concept would indeed be a thought; but it would be a thought without any object, and no cognition at all of any thing whatsoever would be possible by means of it. For as far as I would know, there would be nothing, and could be nothing, to which my thought could be applied. Now, all intuition that is possible for us is sensible (see the Transcendental Aesthetic). Hence in us, thinking an object as such by means of a pure concept of understanding can become cognition only insofar as this concept is referred to objects of the senses. Sensible *B147* intuition is either pure intuition (space and time) or empirical intuition of what, through sensation, is presented directly as actual in space and time. By determining pure intuition we can (in mathematics) acquire a priori cognition of objects as appearances, but only in terms of their form; that, however, still leaves unestablished whether there can be things that must be intuited in this form. Consequently all mathematical concepts are, by themselves, no cognitions—except insofar as one presupposes that there are things that can be exhibited to us only in accordance with the form of that pure sensible intuition. But *things in space and time* are given only insofar as they are perceptions (i.e., presentations accompanied by sensation), and hence are given only through empirical presentation. Consequently the pure concepts of understanding, even when they are (as in mathematics) applied to a priori intuitions, provide cognition only insofar as these intuitions—and hence, by means of them, also the concepts of understanding—can be applied to empirical intuitions. Consequently the categories also do not supply us, by means of intuition, with any cognition of things, except through their possible application to *empirical* intuition. I.e., the categories serve only for the possibility of *empirical cognition*. Such cognition, however, is called *experience*. Consequently the categories cannot be used for *B148* cognizing things except insofar as these things are taken as objects of possible experience.

§23

The last proposition above is of the greatest importance. For it determines the bounds for the use of the pure concepts of understanding in regard to objects just as much as the Transcendental Aesthetic determined the bounds for the use of the pure form of our sensible intuition. Space and time, as conditions for the possibility as to how objects can be given to us, hold no further than for objects of the senses, and hence hold for objects of experience only. Beyond these bounds, space and time present nothing whatsoever; for they are only in the senses and have no actuality apart from them. The pure concepts of understanding are free from this limitation and extend to objects of intuition as such, whether this intuition is similar to ours or not, as long as it is sensible rather than intellectual. But this further extension of the concepts beyond *our* sensible intuition is of no benefit

167. [As does our understanding, which presents objects given outside of itself, viz., in sensible intuition.]

to us whatsoever. For they are then empty concepts of objects, i.e., concepts through which we cannot judge at all whether or not these objects are so much as possible. I.e., the pure concepts of understanding are then mere forms of thought, without objective reality; for we then have available no intuition to which the synthetic unity of apperception—which is all that those concepts contain—could be applied so B149 that the concepts could determine an object. Solely *our* sensible and empirical intuition can provide them with meaning and significance.

Hence if we suppose an object of a *nonsensible* intuition[168] as given, then we can indeed present it through all the predicates that are already contained in the presupposition *that the object has as a property nothing belonging to sensible intuition:* hence we can present that it is not extended or in space, that its duration is not a time, that no change (i.e., succession of determinations in time) is to be found in it, etc. But yet I have no proper cognition if I merely indicate how the intuition of the object is *not,* without being able to say what the intuition does contain. For I have not then presented the possibility of there being an object for my pure concept of understanding, since I was unable to give an intuition corresponding to the concept, but was able only to say that our intuition does not hold for it. However, the foremost point here is that to such a something not even one single category could be applied. E.g., one could not apply to it the concept of a substance, i.e., the concept of something that can exist as subject but never as mere predicate. For I do not know at all, concerning this concept, whether there can be anything whatever corresponding to this conceptual determination [of substance], unless empirical intuition gives me the instance for applying it. But more about this later.

B150

§24

On Applying the Categories to Objects of the Senses as Such

The pure concepts of understanding refer, through mere understanding, to objects of intuition as such—i.e., we leave undetermined whether this intuition is ours or some other, although it must be sensible intuition. But the concepts are, precisely because of this, mere *forms of thought,* through which as yet no determinate object is cognized. We saw that the synthesis or combination of the manifold in them referred merely to the unity of apperception, and was thereby the basis for the possibility of a priori cognition insofar as such cognition rests on the understanding; and hence this synthesis was not just transcendental but was also purely intellectual only. But there lies at the basis in us a priori a certain form of sensible intuition, a form that is based on the receptivity of our capacity to present (i.e., based on our sensibility). Hence the understanding (as spontaneity) can, by means of the manifold of given presentations, determine inner sense in accordance with the synthetic unity of apperception; and thus it can think synthetic unity of the apperception of the manifold of a priori *sensible intuition*—this unity being the condition to which all objects of our (i.e., human) intuition must necessarily be subject. And thereby the categories, as themselves mere forms of thought, acquire objective reality. I.e., they acquire application B151 to objects that can be given to us in intuition. But they apply to these objects only as appearances; for only of appearances are we capable of having a priori intuition.

This *synthesis* of the manifold of sensible intuition, which is a priori possible and necessary, may be called *figurative* synthesis (*synthesis speciosa*). This serves to distinguish it from the synthesis that would be thought in the mere category, in regard to the manifold of an intuition as such;[169] this latter synthesis is called combination of understanding (*synthesis intellectualis*). Both these syntheses are *transcendental,* not just because they themselves proceed a priori, but because they also are the basis for the possibility of other a priori cognition.

However, when the figurative synthesis concerns merely the original synthetic unity of apperception, i.e., merely this transcendental unity thought in the categories, then it must be called the *transcendental synthesis of imagination,* to distinguish it from the merely intellectual combination.[170] **Imagination** is the power of presenting an object in intuition even *without the object's being present.* Now, all our intu-

168. [I.e., intellectual intuition. See, B 72.]

169. [I.e., sensible or intellectual.]

170. [Of understanding.]

ition is sensible; and hence the imagination, because of the subjective condition under which alone it can give to the concepts of understanding a corresponding intuition, belongs to *sensibility*. Yet the synthesis of imagination is an exercise of spontaneity, which is B152 determinative, rather than merely determinable, as is sense; hence this synthesis can a priori determine sense in terms of its form in accordance with the unity of apperception. To this extent, therefore, the imagination is a power of determining sensibility a priori; and its synthesis of intuitions *in accordance with the categories* must be the transcendental synthesis of *imagination*. This synthesis is an action of the understanding upon sensibility, and is the understanding's first application (and at the same time the basis of all its other applications) to objects of the intuition that is possible for us. As figurative, this synthesis is distinct from the intellectual synthesis, which proceeds without any imagination but merely through understanding. Now insofar as the imagination is spontaneity, I sometimes also call it the *productive* imagination, thereby distinguishing it from the *reproductive* imagination. The synthesis of the reproductive imagination is subject solely to empirical laws, viz., to the laws of association. Therefore this synthesis contributes nothing to the explanation of the possibility of a priori cognition, and hence belongs not in transcendental philosophy but in psychology.

Now, this is the place to clarify something paradoxical that must have struck everyone in reading the exposition of the form of inner sense (§ 6): viz., how this sense exhibits to consciousness even ourselves B153 only as we appear to ourselves, not as we are in ourselves. For we intuit ourselves only as we are inwardly *affected*; and this seems contradictory, because we [despite being active] would then have to relate to ourselves as passive.[171] And this is the reason why people in their systems of psychology usually prefer to pass *inner sense* off as being the same as the power of *apperception* (which we carefully distinguish from inner sense).

However, what determines inner sense is the understanding and its original power of combining the manifold of intuition, i.e., the power of bringing that manifold under one apperception (on which apperception the understanding's possibility itself rests). Now in us human beings the understanding is not itself a power of intuitions; and even if an intuition were already given in sensibility, the understanding cannot take it up *into itself*, in order—as it were—to combine the manifold of [what would then be] *its own* intuition. Hence when the understanding is considered by itself alone, then its synthesis is nothing but the unity of the understanding's act: the act of which the understanding is conscious as an act even apart from sensibility, but through which the understanding itself is able to determine sensibility inwardly as regards the manifold that may, in accordance with the form of sensibility's intuition, be given to the understanding. Hence it is understanding which performs, on the *passive* subject whose *power* it is, that act—under the name of a *transcendental synthesis of imagination*—of which we rightly say that inner sense B154 is affected by it. Apperception and its synthetic unity is so far from being the same as inner sense that, as the source of all combination, it applies rather to the manifold of *intuitions as such*,[172] and—under the name of the categories—applies, prior to all sensible intuition, to objects as such. Inner sense, on the other hand, contains the mere *form* of intuition, but without combination of the manifold in this form, and hence contains as yet no *determinate* intuition at all. Determinate intuition is possible only through the consciousness of the manifold's determination by the transcendental act of imagination (i.e., by the synthetic influence of understanding on inner sense)—the act that I have called figurative synthesis.

This [need for figurative synthesis], moreover, we always perceive in ourselves. We cannot think a line without *drawing* it in thought. We cannot think a circle without *describing* it.[173] We cannot at all present the three dimensions of space without *placing* three lines perpendicularly to one another from the same point. And even time we cannot present except inasmuch as, in *drawing* a straight line (meant to be the externally figurative presentation[174] of time), we

171. [I.e., even though as intuiting we would be active, as *being intuited* we (the same subject) would simultaneously be passive.]

172. [Sensible or intellectual.]

173. [I.e., without tracing it in thought.]

174. [I.e., the presentation that is figurative in the external way.]

attend merely to the act of the manifold's synthesis whereby we successively determine inner sense, and thereby attend to the succession of this determination in inner sense. Indeed, what first produces the con- B155 cept of succession is motion, taken as act of the subject (rather than as a determination of an object)[175] and consequently as the synthesis of the manifold in space, if we abstract from this manifold and attend merely to the act whereby we determine *inner sense* according to its form. Hence by no means does the understanding already find in inner sense such a combination of the manifold; rather, the understanding *produces it,* inasmuch as the understanding *affects* that sense. But how (inasmuch as in addition to sensible intuition I can present, at least as possible, a different kind of intuition) can the *I* who thinks be distinct from the *I* that intuits itself,[176] and yet be the same as it by being the same subject? And hence how can I say: I, as intelligence and *thinking* subject, cognize *my*self as an object that is *thought,* viz., I so cognize myself insofar as in addition[177] I am also given to myself in intuition—except that I cognize myself, as I do other phenomena, not as I am to the understanding, but as I appear to myself? This question involves neither more nor less difficulty than does the question as to how I can be an object to myself at all, viz., an object B156 of intuition and of inner perceptions. Yet so it must actually be, as we can easily establish if space is already accepted as being merely a pure form of the appearances of outer senses. For as regards time, which after all is not an object of outer intuition at all, we cannot present it to ourselves except under the image of a line insofar as we draw that line; without exhibiting time in this way, we could not cognize the singleness of its dimension. Likewise, in seeking for all inner perceptions the determination of length of time, or again of time positions, we must always get this determination from what changeable features are exhibited to us by outer things. Consequently the determinations of inner sense must be arranged by us as appearances in time in precisely the same way as the determinations of the outer senses are arranged by us in space. Hence if concerning the determinations of the outer senses we grant that we cognize objects through them only insofar as we are outwardly affected, then we must also concede concerning inner sense that we intuit ourselves through it only as we are inwardly affected *by ourselves;* i.e., we must concede that, as far as inner intuition is concerned, our own [self as] subject is cognized by us only as appearance, but not in terms of what it is in itself.[178]

§25

B157

By contrast, in the transcendental synthesis of the manifold of presentations as such, and hence in the synthetic original unity of apperception, I am not conscious of myself as I appear to myself, nor as I am in myself, but am conscious only that I am. This *presentation* is a *thought,* not an *intuition.* Now *cognition* of ourselves requires not only the act of thought that brings the manifold of every possible intuition to the unity of apperception, but requires in addition a definite kind of intuition whereby this manifold is given. Hence although my own existence is not appearance (still less mere illusion), determination B158

175. Motion of an *object* in space does not belong in a pure science, and consequently not in geometry. For the fact that something is movable cannot be cognized a priori, but can be cognized only through experience. But motion taken as the *describing* [i.e., outlining] of a space is a pure act of the successive synthesis, by productive imagination, of the manifold in outer intuition as such, and belongs not only to geometry but even to transcendental philosophy.

176. [The point of the parenthetical remark may be that this distinctness combined with sameness seems even *more* problematic if we consider intuition *as such*—including, i.e., the intellectual intuition of an intuitive understanding—than if we consider sensible intuition, which at least is not the intuition of an understanding. Or perhaps Kant is saying merely that this issue of distinctness arises because in our case intuition and understanding are *not* united.]

177. [To being thought.]

178. I fail to see how one can find so many difficulties in the view that inner sense is affected by ourselves—of which every act of *attention* can provide us with an example. In such acts the understanding always determines inner sense, in accordance with the combination that the understanding thinks, turning it into the inner intuition that corresponds to the manifold in the understanding's synthesis. Everyone will be able to perceive in himself how much the mind is commonly affected by this.

of my existence[179] can occur only in conformity with the form of inner sense and according to the particular way in which the manifold that I combine is given in inner intuition. Accordingly I have no *cognition* of myself as I am but merely cognition of how I appear to myself. Hence consciousness of oneself is far from being a cognition of oneself, regardless of all the categories, which make up the thought of an *object as such* through the combination of the manifold in one apperception. We saw that in order for me to cognize an object different from myself, I not only require the thinking (which I have in the category) of an object as such, but do also require an intuition whereby I determine that universal concept. In the same way, in order to cognize myself, too, I not only require the consciousness of myself or the fact that I think myself, but require also an intuition of the manifold in me whereby I determine this thought. And I exist as an intelligence. This intelligence is B159 conscious solely in its power of combination. But as regards the manifold that it is to combine, this intelligence is subjected to a limiting condition (which it calls inner sense). As subjected to this condition, it can make that combination intuitable only in terms of time relations, which lie wholly outside the concepts of understanding, properly so called.[180] And hence this intelligence can still cognize itself only as, in regard to an intuition (one that cannot be intellectual and given by the understanding itself), it merely appears to itself; it cannot cognize itself as it would if its *intuition* were intellectual.

179. The *I think* expresses the act of determining my existence. Hence the existence [of myself] is already given through this *I think*; but there is not yet given through it the way in which I am to determine that existence, i.e., posit the manifold belonging to it. In order for that manifold to be given, self-intuition is required; and at the basis of this self-intuition lies a form given a priori, viz., time, which is sensible and belongs to the ability to receive the deter- B158 minable. Now unless I have in addition a different [viz., intellectual] self-intuition that gives, prior to the act of *determination*, the *determinative* in me (only of its spontaneity am I in fact conscious) just as time so gives the determinable, then I cannot determine my existence as that of a self-active being; instead I present only the spontaneity of my thought, i.e., of the [act of] determination, and my existence remains determinable always only sensibly, i.e., as the existence of an appearance. But it is on account of this spontaneity that I call myself an *intelligence*.

180. [I.e., unschematized.]

§26

Transcendental Deduction of the Universally Possible Use in Experience of the Pure Concepts of Understanding

In the *metaphysical deduction*[181] we established the a priori origin of the categories as such through their complete concurrence with the universal logical functions of thought. But in the *transcendental deduction* we exhibited the possibility of them[182] as a priori cognitions of objects of an intuition as such (§§ 20, 21). We must now explain how it is possible, through *categories*, to cognize a priori whatever objects *our senses may encounter*—to so cognize them as regards not the form of their intuition, but the laws of their combination—and hence, as it were, to prescribe laws to nature, and even to make nature possible. For B160 without this suitability of the categories,[183] one would fail to see how everything that our senses may encounter would have to be subject to the laws that arise a priori from the understanding alone.

First of all, let me point out that by *synthesis of apprehension* I mean that combination of the manifold in an empirical intuition whereby perception, i.e., empirical consciousness of the intuition (as appearance), becomes possible.

We have a priori, in the presentations of space and time, *forms* of both outer and inner sensible intuition; and to these forms the synthesis of apprehension of the manifold of appearance must always conform, because that synthesis itself can take place only according to this form. But space and time are presented a priori not merely as *forms* of sensible intuition, but as themselves *intuitions* (containing a manifold), and hence are presented with the determination[184] of the *unity* of this manifold in them (see the Transcenden- B161

181. [B 90–116. Kant did not there use this name.]

182. [The categories as such.]

183. [For such cognition and prescription.]

184. [I.e., here, property.]

tal Aesthetic).[185] Therefore even *unity of synthesis* of the manifold outside or within us, and hence also a *combination* to which everything that is to be presented determinately in space or time must conform, is already given a priori as condition of the synthesis of all *apprehension*—given along with (not in) these intuitions. This synthetic unity, however, can be none other than the unity of the combination, conforming to the categories but applied to our *sensible intuition*, of the manifold of a given *intuition as such* in an original consciousness. Consequently all synthesis, the synthesis through which even perception becomes possible, is subject to the categories; and since experience is cognition through connected perceptions, the categories are conditions of the possibility of experience and hence hold a priori also for all objects of experience.

B162 Hence, e.g., when I turn the empirical intuition of a house into a perception by apprehending the intuition's manifold, then in this apprehension I use as a basis the *necessary unity* of space and of outer sensible intuition as such; and I draw, as it were, the house's shape in conformity with this synthetic unity of the manifold in space. But this same unity, if I abstract from the form of space, resides in the understanding, and is the category of the synthesis of the homogeneous in an intuition as such, i.e., the category of *magnitude*.[186] Hence the synthesis of apprehension, i.e., perception,[187] must conform throughout to that category.[188]

When (to take a different example) I perceive the freezing of water, then I apprehend two states (fluidity and solidity) as states that stand to each other in a relation of time. Since the appearance is inner *intuition*, I lay time at its basis. But in time I necessarily present B163 synthetic *unity* of the manifold; without this unity, that relation[189] could not be given *determinately* (as regards time sequence) in an intuition. However, this synthetic unity, as a priori condition under which I combine the manifold of an *intuition as such*, is—if I abstract from the constant form of *my* inner intuition, i.e., from time—the category of *cause*; through this category, when I apply it to my sensibility, *everything that happens is, in terms of its relation, determined* by me *in time as such*. Therefore apprehension in such an event, and hence the event itself, is subject—as regards possible perception—to the concept of the *relation of effects and causes*; and thus it is in all other cases.

Categories are concepts that prescribe laws a priori to appearances, and hence to nature regarded as the sum of all appearances (*natura materialiter spectata*).[190] And now this question arises: Since the categories are not derived from nature and do not conform to it as their model (for then they would be merely empirical), how are we to comprehend the fact that nature must conform to the categories, i.e., how can the categories determine a priori the combination of nature's manifold without gleaning that combination from nature? Here now is the solution of this puzzle.

185. Space, presented as *object* (as we are actually required to present it in geometry), contains more than mere form of intuition; viz., it contains also *combination*, of the manifold given[a] according to the form of sensibility, into an *intuitive*[b] presentation—so that the *form of intuition* gives us merely a manifold, but *formal intuition* gives us unity of presentation. In the Transcendental Aesthetic I had merely included B161 this unity with sensibility, wanting only to point out that it precedes any concept. But in fact this unity presupposes a synthesis; this synthesis does not belong to the senses, but through it do all concepts of space and time first become possible. For through this unity (inasmuch as understanding determines sensibility) space or time are first *given* as intuitions, and hence the unity of this a priori intuition belongs to space and time, and not to the concept of understanding (see § 24).

[a][*Des mannigfaltigen . . . Gegebenen*. I.e., 'manifold' is an adjective, and 'given' is a participle functioning as a noun.]

[b][*anschaulich*.]

186. [I.e., quantity.]

187. [Not apprehension but the synthesis of apprehension is being equated with perception.]

188. In this way we prove that the synthesis of apprehension, which is empirical, must conform necessarily to the synthesis of apperception, which is intellectual and is contained wholly a priori in the category. The spontaneity that brings combination into the manifold of intuition is one and the same in the two cases: in apprehension it does so under the name of power of imagination; in apperception it does so under the name of understanding.

189. [Of time.]

190. [Nature considered materially.]

B164 How it is that the laws of appearances in nature must agree with the understanding and its a priori form, i.e., with the understanding's power to combine the manifold as such, is not any stranger than how it is that appearances themselves must agree with the form of a priori sensible intuition. For just as appearances exist not in themselves but only relatively to the subject in whom the appearances inhere insofar as the subject has senses, so the laws exist not in the appearances but only relatively to that same being insofar as that being has understanding. Things in themselves would have their law-governedness necessarily, even apart from an understanding that cognizes them. But appearances are only presentations of things that exist uncognized as regards what they may be in themselves. As mere appearances, however, they are subject to no law of connection whatever except the one prescribed by the connecting power. Now what connects the manifold of sensible intuition is imagination; and imagination depends on understanding as regards the unity of its intellectual synthesis, and on sensibility as regards the manifoldness of apprehension. Now all possible perception depends on this synthesis of apprehension; but it itself, this empirical synthesis, depends on transcendental synthesis and hence on the categories. Therefore all possible perceptions, and hence also everything whatever B165 that can reach empirical consciousness, i.e., all appearances of nature, must in regard to their combination be subject to the categories. Nature (regarded merely as nature as such) depends (as *natura formaliter spectata*)[191] on the categories as the original basis of its necessary law-governedness. But even the pure power of understanding does not suffice for prescribing a priori to appearances, through mere categories, more laws than those underlying a *nature as such* considered as law-governedness of appearances in space and time. Particular laws, because they concern appearances that are determined empirically, are not *derivable completely* from those laws,[192] although the particular laws are one and all subject to the categories. Experience must be added in order for us to become acquainted with particular laws *at all*; but the a priori laws alone give us information about experience as such and about what can be cognized as an object of that experience.

§27

Result of This Deduction of the Concepts of Understanding

We cannot *think* an object except through categories; we cannot cognize an object thought by us except through intuitions corresponding to those concepts. Now all our intuitions are sensible, and this [sensible] cognition is empirical insofar as its object is given. B166 Empirical cognition, however, is experience. *Consequently no cognition is possible for us a priori except solely of objects of possible experience.*[193]

But this cognition, which is limited to just objects of experience, is not therefore all taken from experience. Rather, as far as pure intuitions as well as pure concepts of understanding are concerned, they are elements of cognition that are found in us a priori. Now, there are only two ways in which one can conceive of a *necessary* agreement of experience with the concepts of its objects: either experience makes these concepts possible, or these concepts make experience possible. The first alternative is not what happens as B167 regards the categories (nor as regards pure sensible intuition). For they are a priori concepts and hence are independent of experience. (To assert that their origin is empirical would be to assert a kind of *generatio aequivoca*).[194] There remains, consequently, only

191. [Nature considered formally.]

192. [The a priori laws underlying a nature as such.]

193. In order to keep my readers from being troubled prematurely by the worrisome detrimental consequences of this proposition, let me just remind them that in our *thinking* the categories are not limited by the conditions of our sensible intuition, but have an unbounded realm. Intuition is required only for *cognizing* what we think, i.e., only for determining the object. Thus if intuition is lacking, the thought of the object can otherwise still have its true and useful consequences for the subject's *use of reason*. But because the use of reason is not always directed to the determination of the object and hence to cognition, but is sometimes directed also to the determination of the subject and his volition, it cannot yet be set forth here. [Kant is here referring to the practical use of pure reason in the realm of morality.]

194. [A generation of something by something so different from it that such generation would be an absurdity.]

the second alternative (a system[195] of *epigenesis*, as it were, of pure reason):[196] viz., that the categories contain the bases, on the part of the understanding, of the possibility of all experience as such. But as to how the categories make experience possible, and as to what principles of the possibility of experience they provide us with when applied to appearances, more information will be given in the following chapter on the transcendental use of our power of judgment.

Someone might want to propose, in addition to the two sole ways mentioned above, a middle course between them: viz., that the categories are neither *self-thought* a priori first principles of our cognition, nor again are drawn from experience, but are subjective predispositions for thinking that are implanted in us [and given to us] simultaneously with our existence; and that they were so arranged by our originator that their use harmonizes exactly with the laws of nature governing the course of experience (this theory would be a kind of *preformation system* of pure reason).[197] If such a middle course were proposed, the following would decide against it (apart from the fact that with such a hypothesis one can see no end to B168 how far the presupposition of predetermined predispositions to future judgments might be carried): viz., that the categories would in that case lack the *necessity* which belongs essentially to the concept of them. For, the concept of cause, e.g., which asserts the necessity of a result under a presupposed condition, would be false if it rested only on an arbitrary subjective necessity, implanted in us, to link certain empirical presentations according to such a rule of relation. I could then not say that the effect is connected with the cause in the object (i.e., connected with it necessarily), but could say only that I am so equipped that I cannot think this presentation otherwise than as thus connected. And this is just what the skeptic most longs [to hear]. For then all our insight, achieved through the supposed objective validity of our judgments, is nothing but sheer illusion; and there would also be no lack of people who would not concede this subjective necessity (which must be felt) in themselves. At the very least one could not quarrel with anyone about something that rests merely on the way in which his [self as] subject is organized.

BRIEF SKETCH OF THIS DEDUCTION

This deduction is the exhibition of the pure concepts of understanding (and, with them, of all theoretical a priori cognition) as principles of the possibility of experience; the exhibition of these principles, however, as the *determination* of appearances in space B169 and time *as such*; and the exhibition, finally, of this determination as arising from the *original* synthetic unity of apperception, this unity being the form of understanding as referred to space and time, the original forms of sensibility.

Only up to this point do I consider the division into subsections to be necessary, because we have been dealing with the elementary concepts. Now that we want to present to ourselves the use of these concepts, the treatise may go on without such division, cohering in terms of continuity.

B
SECOND ANALOGY

PRINCIPLE OF TEMPORAL SUCCESSION
ACCORDING TO THE LAW OF CAUSALITY

All changes occur according to the law of the connection of cause and effect.

Proof

(The previous principle has established that all appearances [forming part] of the temporal succession[198] are one and all only *changes*;[199] i.e., they are a successive being and not-being of the determinations of substance, which itself is permanent. The principle has established, therefore, that there is no such thing as the being of substance itself as succeeding its not-being, or its not-being as succeeding its existence; B233 in other words, there is no such thing as the arising

195. [Or, i.e., theory.]

196. [I.e., a system of pure reason whereby experience comes about by epigenesis.]

197. [I.e., a system of pure reason whereby experience is formed in advance.]

198. [And hence all variation (cf. the restatement of the principle, just below).]

199. [Of substance.]

or passing away of substance itself. The principle could also have been expressed thus: *All variation (succession) on the part of appearances is only change*; for an arising or passing away of substance would not be changes of it, because the concept of change presupposes the same subject as existing, and hence as being permanent, with two opposite determinations. After this preliminary reminder, there now follows the proof.)

I perceive that appearances succeed one another, i.e., that at one time there is a state of things whose opposite was there in the things' previous state. Hence I am in fact connecting two perceptions in time. Now connection is not the work of mere sense and intuition, but is here the product of a synthetic ability of our imagination which determines inner sense in regard to time relation. But imagination can link those two states in two ways, so that either the one or the other state precedes in time. For time cannot in itself be perceived, and what precedes or follows cannot be determined by reference to it in the object—empirically, as it were. I am, therefore, conscious only that my imagination places one state before and the other after, but not that the one state *B234* precedes the other in the object. In other words, mere perception leaves indeterminate the *objective relation* of the appearances following one another. Now in order for this objective relation to be cognized as determinate, the relation between the two states must be thought as being such that it determines as necessary which of the states must be placed before and which after, rather than vice versa. But a concept carrying with it a necessity of synthetic unity can only be a pure concept of understanding, which therefore does not reside in perception. Here this concept is that of the *relation of cause and effect*; of these two, the cause is what determines the effect in time, and determines it as the consequence, rather than as something that [as occurring] merely in imagination might [instead] precede (or might not even be perceived at all). Therefore experience itself—i.e., empirical cognition of appearances—is possible only inasmuch as we subject the succession of appearances, and hence all change, to the law of causality. Hence appearances themselves, taken as objects of experience, are possible only in accordance with this law.

Apprehension of the manifold of appearances is always successive. The presentations of the parts succeed one another. Whether they also follow one another in the object is a second point for reflection which is not already contained in the first point.[200] Now it is true that anything, even every presentation insofar as one is conscious of it, can be called an object. Yet what this word might signify in the case *B235* of appearances, not insofar as they (as presentations) are objects but insofar as they only designate an object, calls for deeper investigation. Insofar as appearances, taken only as presentations, are simultaneously objects of consciousness, they are not at all distinct from apprehension, i.e., from the taking up into the synthesis of imagination; and we must say, therefore, that the manifold of appearances is always produced in the mind successively. If appearances were things in themselves, then no human being could gather[201] from the succession of presentations how their manifold is combined in the object. For we deal, after all, only with our presentations; how things may be in themselves (i.e., apart from taking account of presentations whereby they affect us), is entirely outside our sphere of cognition. Appearances, then, are indeed not things in themselves; but they are all that can be given to us for cognition. And now, whereas the presentation [as such] of the manifold in apprehension is always successive, I am to indicate what sort of combination in time belongs to the manifold in appearances themselves. Thus, e.g., the apprehension of the manifold in the appearance of a house standing before me is successive. Now the question is whether the manifold of this house itself is successive intrinsically as well; and this, to be sure, no one will grant. *B236* But once I raise my concepts of an object to the level of transcendental signification, the house is not at all a thing in itself, but is only an appearance, i.e., a presentation, whose transcendental object is unknown. What, then, do I mean by the question as to how the manifold may be combined in appearance itself (which, after all, is nothing in itself)? Here what lies in the successive apprehension is regarded as presentation; but the appearance that is given to me, despite being nothing more than a sum of these pre-

200. [The first point being that the presentations of the parts succeed one another.]

201. [Human beings lack the intellectual intuition (viz., of things in themselves) that an intuitive understanding would have. See B 72.]

sentations, is regarded as their object, with which the concept that I obtain from the presentations of apprehension is to agree. We soon see that, since agreement of cognition with the object is truth, the question can only be inquiring after the formal conditions of empirical truth; and we see that appearance, as contrasted with the presentations of apprehension, can be presented as an object distinct from them only if it is subject to a rule that distinguishes it from any other apprehension and that makes necessary one kind of combination of the manifold. That [element] in the appearance which contains the condition of this necessary rule of apprehension is the object.

Let us now proceed to our problem. That something occurs, i.e., that something, or a state that was not there before, comes to be cannot be perceived *B237* empirically[202] unless it is preceded by an appearance that does not contain this state. For an actuality succeeding an empty time, i.e., an arising not preceded by any state of things, cannot be apprehended any more than empty time itself. Hence any apprehension of an event is a perception succeeding another perception. But because, as I showed above by reference to the appearance of a house, this is so in all synthesis of apprehension, the apprehension of an event is not yet distinguished thereby from other apprehensions. Yet I also observe that if, in an appearance containing an occurrence, I call A the preceding state of the perception and B the succeeding state, then B can in apprehension only succeed A, and similarly perception A cannot succeed B but can only precede it. For example, I see a ship floating down the river. My perception of its position lower down in the course of the river succeeds the perception of its position higher up, and there is no possibility that in the apprehension of this appearance the ship should be perceived first lower down and afterwards higher up in the river. Hence the order in the perceptions' succession in apprehension is here determinate, and apprehension is tied to this order. In the previous example of a house my perceptions could, in appre- *B238* hension, start from the house's top and end at the bottom, but they could also start from below and end above; and they could likewise apprehend the manifold of the empirical intuition by proceeding either to the right or to the left. Hence in the series of these perceptions there was no determinate order making necessary the point in apprehension where I must begin in order to combine the manifold empirically. In the perception of what occurs,[203] however, this rule[204] is always to be found, and through it the order of the perceptions succeeding one another (in the apprehension of this appearance) is made *necessary*.

In our case,[205] therefore, I shall have to derive the *subjective succession* of apprehension from the *objective succession* of appearances; for otherwise the subjective succession is entirely indeterminate and fails to distinguish any one appearance from some other appearance. The subjective succession by itself, being entirely arbitrary, proves nothing about the connection of the manifold in the object. Hence the objective succession will consist in the order of the manifold of appearance whereby the apprehension of the one item (viz., what occurs) succeeds the apprehension of the other (viz., what precedes) *according to a rule*. This alone can entitle me to say of the appearance itself, and not merely of my apprehension, that a succession is to be found in it—which means the same as that I cannot perform the apprehension except in precisely this succession.[206]

In accordance with such a rule, therefore, what precedes an event as such must contain the condition *B239* for a rule whereby this event always and necessarily follows. But I cannot go, conversely, from the event backward and determine (through apprehension) what precedes. For no appearance goes back from the succeeding point of time to the previous one, although it does refer *to some previous one*. The progression from a given time to the determinate following time, on the other hand, is necessary. Hence because it[207] is, after all, something that follows, I must necessarily refer it to something else as such that precedes it and that it succeeds according to a rule, i.e., necessarily. Thus the event, as the conditioned, directs us reliably to some condition, while this condition determines the event.

202. [As Kant uses the term 'perceive,' 'empirically' is actually redundant.]

203. [As in the case of the ship floating down the river.]

204. [As to where I must begin.]

205. [I.e., the case of an event.]

206. [Or "sequence."]

207. [I.e., the event.]

Suppose that an event is not preceded by anything that it must succeed according to a rule. Then all succession of perception would be determined solely in apprehension, i.e., merely subjectively; but this would not at all determine objectively which item in fact precedes in perception and which follows. We would in that way have only a play of presentations that would not refer to any object whatever; i.e., our perception would not at all distinguish one appearance from all others in terms of time relation. For the succession in apprehending is in that case everywhere the same, and hence there is in appearance *B240* nothing determining this succession so that a certain[208] succession is, as objective, made necessary by it. Hence I shall in that case not say that two states succeed each other in appearance. Rather, I shall say only that one apprehension succeeds the other; and this is merely something *subjective* and determines no object, and hence cannot count as cognition of any object (not even of an object in [the realm of] appearance).

Hence when we experience that something occurs, then in doing so we always presuppose that it is preceded by something or other that it succeeds according to a rule. Otherwise I would not say of the object that it succeeds; for the mere succession in my apprehension, if it is not determined by a rule by reference to something preceding it, justifies no [assumption of a] succession in the object. Hence it is always on account of a rule that I make my subjective synthesis (of apprehension) objective, viz., a rule according to which appearances in their succession, i.e., as they occur, are determined by the previous state. And the experience itself of something that occurs is possible solely and exclusively under this presupposition.

It is true that this seems to contradict all the remarks that people have always made about the course taken by our understanding. According to those remarks, it is only by perceiving and comparing the agreeing successions of events that follow upon preceding appearances that we are first led to discover a rule *B241* whereby certain events always succeed certain appearances, and only thereby we are first prompted to frame the concept of cause. This concept would, on such a basis, be merely empirical. And the rule whereby everything that occurs has a cause, as this concept provides it, would be just as contingent as the experience itself.[209] The rule's universality and necessity would then be attributed to it only fictitiously and would have no true universal validity, because they would be based not on anything a priori, but only on induction. But the case with this rule is the same as that with other pure a priori presentations (e.g., space and time): we can extract them as clear concepts from experience solely because we have put them into experience and hence have brought experience about through them in the first place. To be sure, this presentation of a rule determining the series of events, as a concept of cause, can have logical clarity only once we have made use of it in experience. Yet [our] taking account of this presentation, [viz.,] as a condition of the synthetic unity in time of appearances, was nonetheless the basis of the experience itself, and hence the experience was preceded a priori by this condition.

Hence we must show, in the example [of an event], that even in experience we never attribute succession (in the case of an event—where something occurs that was not there before) to the object and we never distinguish this succession from the subjective one *B242* in our apprehension, except when there lies at the basis a rule that compels us to observe this order of perceptions rather than some other order; indeed, we must show that this compulsion is what in fact makes the presentation of a succession in the object possible in the first place.

We have within us presentations of which we can also become conscious. But no matter how far this consciousness[210] may extend and how accurate and punctilious it may be, they still remain forever only presentations, i.e., inner determinations of our mind in this or that time relation. How is it, then, that we posit an object for these presentations; or how is it that in addition to the subjective reality that they have as modifications [of the mind], we also attribute to them who knows what sort of objective reality? Their objective signification cannot consist in the reference

208. [I.e., specific or particular.]

209. [On which it is based.]

210. [Of our presentations.]

to another presentation (of what one would want to call object). For otherwise the question returns: how does this other presentation, in turn, go beyond itself and acquire objective signification in addition to the subjective one that it possesses by being a determination of the mental state? Suppose that we inquire what new character is given to our presentations by the *reference to an object,* and what is the dignity that they thereby obtain. We then find that this reference does nothing beyond making necessary the presentations' being combined[211] in a certain way and being B243 subjected to a rule; and we find, conversely, that only through the necessity of a certain order in the time relation of our presentations is objective signification conferred on them.

In the synthesis of appearances the manifold of presentations is always successive. Now, through this succession no object whatever is presented; for through this succession, which is common to all apprehensions, nothing is distinguished from anything else. But once I perceive, or assume in advance, that there is in this succession a reference to the preceding state, upon which the presentation follows according to a rule, then something presents itself as an event, or as something that occurs. I.e., I then cognize an object that I must posit in a certain determinate position in time—a position that in view of the preceding state cannot be assigned to it differently. Hence when I perceive that something occurs, then this presentation contains, first, [the presupposition] that something precedes; for precisely by reference to this preceding something does the appearance acquire its time relation, viz., its existing after a preceding time in which it was not. But, second, it can obtain its determinate time position in this relation only inasmuch as in the preceding state something is presupposed that it succeeds always, i.e., succeeds according to a rule. And from this results, first, that I cannot reverse the series, taking what occurs and putting it ahead of what it succeeds; and, second, that if the state that precedes is posited, then this specific event B244 succeeds unfailingly and necessarily. Thus it is that among our presentations there comes to be an order in which what is present directs us (insofar as it has come to be) to some preceding state as a correlate of the happening that is given. And although this correlate is still indeterminate, it does refer determinatively to this happening as its consequence and in the time series connects it with itself necessarily.

Suppose, then, that it is a necessary law of our sensibility, and hence a *formal condition* of all perceptions, that the previous time necessarily determines the following one (inasmuch as I cannot arrive at the following time except through the preceding one). If this is so, then it is also an indispensable *law of empirical presentation* of the time series that the appearances of past time determine every existent in the following time; and that these existents, as events, do not take place except insofar as their existence is determined in time—i.e., fixed in time according to a rule—by those appearances of past time. For *only in appearances can we cognize empirically this continuity in the coherence of times.*

Understanding is required for all experience and for its possibility. And the first thing that understanding does for these is not that of making the presentation of objects distinct, but that of making the presentation of an object possible at all. Now, this is B245 done through the understanding's transferring the time order to the appearances and to their existence, by allotting to each appearance, as consequence, a position in time determined a priori with regard to the preceding appearances; without this position in time the appearance would not agree with time itself, which a priori determines for all its parts their position. Now this determination of an appearance's position cannot be taken from the relation of appearances toward absolute time (for absolute time is not an object of perception). Rather, conversely, the appearances must themselves determine for one another their positions in time, and must make these positions necessary in the time order; i.e., what follows or occurs must succeed what was contained in the previous state and must do so according to a universal rule. This results in a series of appearances that, by means of the understanding, produces and makes necessary in the series of possible perceptions the same order and steady coherence that is found a priori in the form of inner intuition (i.e., in time), in which all [such] perceptions would have to have their position.

211. [Or "linked": *Verbindang.*]

Hence that something occurs is a perception belonging to a possible experience. This experience becomes actual when I view the appearance as determined as regards its position in time, and hence view it as an object that in the coherence of perceptions can always be found according to a rule. This rule, B246 however, for determining something in regard to temporal succession, is that the condition under which an event always (i.e., necessarily) follows is to be found in what precedes the event. Hence the principle of sufficient basis[212] is the basis of possible experience, i.e., of objective cognition of appearances with regard to their relation in time sequence.

The basis for proving this proposition, however, rests solely on the following moments. All empirical cognition involves the synthesis of the manifold by the imagination. This synthesis is always successive, i.e., in it the presentations always succeed one another. In the imagination itself, however, the sequence is not at all determined as regards order (i.e., as to what must precede and what must follow), and the series of the presentations following one another can be taken as proceeding backward just as well as forward. But if this synthesis is a synthesis of apprehension (of the manifold of a given appearance), then the order is determined in the object, or—to speak more accurately—there is in this apprehension an order of successive synthesis that determines an object; and according to this order something must necessarily precede, and when this something is posited then the other event must necessarily follow. Hence if my perception is to contain the cognition of an event, i.e., of something's actually occurring, then it must be an empirical judgment in which we think of the consequence as B247 determined, i.e., as presupposing in terms of time another appearance that it succeeds necessarily, or according to a rule. Otherwise, if I posited what precedes and the event did not succeed it necessarily, then I would have to regard this event as only a subjective play of my imaginings; and if I still presented by it something objective, then I would have to call it a mere dream. Therefore the relation of appearances (as possible perceptions) whereby what follows (occurs) is with regard to its existence determined in time, necessarily and according to a rule, by something preceding it—in other words, the relation of cause to effect—is the condition of the objective validity of our empirical judgments as regards the series of perceptions, and hence is the condition of these judgments' empirical truth and therefore of experience. The principle of the causal relation in the succession of appearances holds, therefore, also for all objects of experience ([insofar as they are] under the conditions of succession), because it is itself the basis of the possibility of such experience.

Here, however, emerges a perplexity that must still be removed. The principle of the causal connection among appearances is, in our formulation, limited to their [occurring in] sequence. Yet in using the principle we find that it fits also the case of their concomitance, and that cause and effect can be simultaneous. E.g., there is heat in the room which is not found in the open air. I look around for the B248 cause, and discover a heated stove. Now this stove, as cause, is simultaneous with its effect, the room's heat. Hence here there is between cause and effect no sequence in terms of time. They are, rather, simultaneous; and yet the law of cause and effect does hold. The majority of efficient causes in nature are simultaneous with their effects, and the temporal succession of the effects is due only to the fact that the cause cannot accomplish its entire effect in one instant. But at the instant when the effect first arises, it is always simultaneous with the causality of its cause. For if the cause had ceased to be an instant before, then the effect would not have arisen at all. It must be noted carefully, here, that what we are considering is the *order* of time, not the *lapse* of time; the relation remains even if no time has elapsed. The time between the causality of the cause and the cause's direct effect may be *vanishingly brief*, but yet the relation of the cause to the effect always remains determinable in terms of time. If I consider as cause a [lead] ball that lies on a stuffed cushion and makes an indentation in it, then this cause is simultaneous with the effect. But I nonetheless distinguish the two by the time relation of their dynamical connection. For if I lay the ball on the cushion, then the previous smooth shape of the

212. [Kant is reinterpreting, in accordance with the second analogy, the principle of sufficient reason used by Leibniz and later broadened by Wolff (to include not only the contingent).]

cushion is succeeded by the indentation; but if the B249 cushion has an indentation (no matter from where), then this is not succeeded by a lead ball.[213]

Hence temporal succession is indeed an effect's sole empirical criterion in reference to the causality of the cause preceding it. The [totally filled] tumbler is the cause of the water's rising above the horizontal plane [at the top] of the tumbler, although the two appearances are simultaneous. For as soon as water is scooped from a larger vessel with [an empty] tumbler, there ensues this: the horizontal level that the water had in the larger vessel changes to a concave level in the [partially filled] tumbler.

This causality leads to the concept of action; action leads to the concept of force and thereby to the concept of substance. Since my critical project deals solely with the sources of synthetic a priori cognition and I do not want to mingle with it dissections [of concepts], which concern merely the elucidation (rather than the expansion) of concepts, I leave the detailed exposition of these concepts to a future system of pure reason—although such an analysis can also be found in abundance in the textbooks of this kind that are already familiar. What I must, however, touch upon is the empirical criterion of a substance insofar as it seems to manifest itself not through the permanence of appearance but better and more easily through action.

B250 Where there is action and hence activity and force, there is also substance, and in substance alone must be sought the seat of that fertile source of appearances. That is nicely said; but if we are to explain what we mean by substance and want to avoid the fallacy of circular reasoning, then the answer is not so easy. How, from action on something, are we to infer at once *the agent's permanence*—this permanence being, after all, so essential and peculiar a characteristic of substance ([as] *phaenomenon*[214]). Yet according to our previous remarks, solving the question is not so difficult after all, even though the question would be quite insoluble according to the usual way (of proceeding with one's concepts, viz., merely analytically). Action already means the relation of the causality's subject to the effect. Now any effect consists in what occurs, and hence in the mutable that designates time in terms of succession. Therefore the ultimate subject of the mutable is the *permanent* as the substratum of everything that varies, i.e., substance. For according to the principle of causality actions are always the first basis of all variation by appearances; hence actions cannot reside in a subject that itself varies, since otherwise other actions and another subject determining that variation would be required. By virtue of this does action prove, as a sufficient empirical criterion, the substantiality of a subject, without my B251 needing first of all to search for the subject's permanence by perceptions that I have compared. Nor could proving this substantiality along this path of comparison be accomplished as comprehensively as is required by the magnitude and strict universality of the concept of substance. For, that the first subject of the causality of all arising and passing away cannot itself arise and pass away (in the realm of appearances) is a safe inference that issues in empirical necessity and permanence in existence, and hence in the concept of a substance as appearance.

When something occurs then the mere arising, even if we take no account of what arises, is in itself already an object of inquiry. The transition itself from a state's not-being to this state, even supposing that this state contained no quality in [the realm] of appearance, already calls for inquiry. This arising, as was shown in the First Analogy, concerns not substance (for substance does not arise) but its state. Hence arising is only change, and not origination from nothing. For if this origination from nothing is regarded as effect of an extraneous cause, then it is called creation; and creation cannot be admitted as an event among appearances, because its very possibility would already annul the unity of experience. If, on the other hand, I regard all things not as phenomena but as things in themselves and as objects merely of understanding, then despite their being substances B252 they can still be regarded as being dependent, in terms of their existence, on an extraneous cause. That alternative, however, would then entail quite different significations of the words, and would not fit appearances, as possible objects of experience.

Now, we do not a priori have the least concept as to how anything can be changed at all, i.e., how it

213. [Kant's point is that temporal succession decides empirically what is the cause and what is the effect. The indentation did not cause the lead ball, because it is not succeeded by the lead ball.]

214. [I.e., substance ([taken as] phenomenal).]

is possible that one state occurring at one point of time can be succeeded by an opposite state occurring at another point of time. This [concept of how change is possible] requires knowledge of actual forces—e.g., knowledge of the motive forces, or, which is the same, of certain successive appearances (as motions) indicating such forces—and such knowledge can be given only empirically. But we can nonetheless examine a priori, according to the law of causality and the conditions of time, the form of every change, i.e., the condition under which alone, as an arising of a different state, change can take place (no matter what may be its content, i.e., the state being changed); and hence we can so examine the succession itself of the states (i.e., the occurrence).[215]

B253 When a substance passes from one state, a, to another, b, then the point of time of the second state is different from the point of time of the first, and follows it. In the same way, too, the second state as reality (in [the realm of] appearance) differs from the first, in which this reality was not, as b differs from zero; i.e., even if state b were to differ from state *a* only in magnitude, the change is [still] an arising of b – a;[216] which in the previous state was not and in regard to which that state = 0.

The question, therefore, is how a thing passes from one state, = a, to another, = b. Between two instants there is always a time, and between two states at those instants there is always a difference that has a magnitude (for all parts of appearances are always magnitudes in turn). Hence any transition from one state to another occurs in a time that is contained between two instants, the first instant determining the state that the thing leaves and the second instant determining the state that it enters. Both instants, therefore, are bounds of the time of a change and hence bounds of the intermediate state between the two states, and as such belong also to the entire change. Now every change has a cause that manifests its causality in the entire time wherein the change takes place. Hence this cause produces its B254 change not suddenly (i.e., all at once, or in one instant), but in a time; so that, as the time increases from its initial instant (a) up to its completion (in b), the reality's magnitude (b – a) is also produced through all the smaller degrees contained between the first degree and the last. Hence all change is possible only through a continuous action of the causality; this action, insofar as it is uniform, is called a moment. Change does not consist of these moments, but is produced by them as their effect.

This, then, is the law of the continuity of all change. The basis of this law is this fact: that neither time nor, for that matter, appearance in time consists of parts that are the smallest; and that nonetheless, as a thing changes, its state passes through all these parts, as elements, to the thing's second state. *No difference* of the real in [the realm of] appearance is *the smallest*, just as no difference in the magnitude of times is the smallest. And thus the reality's new state grows, starting from the first state, in which it was not, through all the infinite degrees of this reality; and the differences of the degrees from one another are all smaller than the difference between 0 and a.

What benefit this principle may have for the investigation of nature is of no concern to us here. But how is such a principle, which thus seems to expand our cognition of nature, possible completely a priori? This question very much requires our examination, even though what the principle says is [so] obviously actual and correct that we might believe ourselves to be B255 exempted from the question as to how the principle was possible. For there is such a variety of unfounded claims about our cognition's expansion by pure reason, that we must adopt as a universal principle [the resolve] to be throughout distrustful on that account, and not to believe or assume anything of the sort, even upon the clearest dogmatic proof, without documentation that can provide a well-founded deduction.

All increase of empirical cognition and any progress of perception—no matter what the objects may be, whether appearances or pure intuitions—is nothing but an expansion of the determination of inner sense, i.e., a progression in time. This progression in time determines everything and is in itself determined through nothing further. I.e., the progression's parts are given only in time and through the synthesis of time; they are not given prior to the synthesis. Because of this, every transition in perception to something that follows in time is a determination of time through

215. It should be noted carefully that I am talking not about the change of certain relations as such, but about change of a state. Thus if a body moves uniformly then it does not change its state (of motion) at all; but it does change its state if its motion increases or decreases.

216. [I.e., *b* minus *a*.]

the production of this perception; and since time is always and in all its parts a magnitude, every such transition is the production of a perception as a magnitude that goes through all degrees, none of which is the smallest, from zero onward up to the perception's determinate degree. From this, then, is evident the possibility of cognizing a priori a law governing B256 changes as regards their form. For we only anticipate our own apprehension, whose formal condition, since it resides in ourselves prior to all given appearance, must indeed be capable of being cognized a priori.

We have seen that time contains the sensible a priori condition for the possibility of a continuous progression of what exists to what follows. In the same way the understanding, by means of the unity of apperception, is the a priori condition for the possibility of a continuous determination, through the series of causes and effects, of all positions for appearances in this time—the causes entailing unfailingly the existence of the effects, and thereby making the empirical cognition of time relations valid for every time (i.e., universally) and hence valid objectively.

Refutation of Idealism

Idealism (I mean *material* idealism) is the theory that declares the existence of objects in space outside us either to be merely doubtful and *unprovable*, or to be *false* and *impossible*. The *first* is the *problematic* idealism of *Descartes*; it declares only one empirical assertion (*assertio*) to be indubitable, viz.: *I am*. The *second* is the *dogmatic* idealism of Berkeley; it declares space, with all the things to which space attaches as inseparable condition, to be something that is in itself impossible, and hence also declares the things in space to be mere imaginings. Dogmatic idealism is unavoidable if one regards space as a property that is to belong to things in themselves; for then space, with everything that space serves as condition, is a nonentity. However, the basis for this idealism has already been removed by us in the Transcendental Aesthetic. Problematic idealism, which asserts noth- B275 ing about this but only alleges that we are unable to prove by direct experience an existence apart from our own, is reasonable and is in accordance with a thorough philosophical way of thinking—viz., in permitting no decisive judgment before a sufficient proof has been found. The proof it demands must, therefore, establish that regarding external things we have not merely *imagination* but also *experience*. And establishing this surely cannot be done unless one can prove that even our *inner* experience, indubitable for Descartes, is possible only on the presupposition of *outer* experience.

Theorem

The mere, but empirically determined, consciousness of my own existence proves the existence of objects in space outside me.

Proof

I am conscious of my existence as determined in time. All time determination presupposes something *permanent* in perception. But this permanent something cannot be something within me, precisely because my existence can be determined in time only by this permanent something. Therefore perception of this permanent something is possible only through a *thing* outside me and not through mere *presentation* of a thing outside me. Hence determination of my existence in time is possible only through the existence of actual things that I perceive outside me. Now B276 consciousness of my existence in time is necessarily linked with consciousness of the possibility of this time determination; therefore it is necessarily linked also with the existence of things outside me, as condition of the time determination. I.e., the consciousness of my own existence is simultaneously a direct consciousness of the existence of other things outside me.

Comment 1. In the preceding proof one becomes aware that the game that idealism played is being turned around and against it—and more rightly so. Idealism assumed that the only direct experience is inner experience and that from it we only *infer* external things; but[217] we infer them only unreliably, as happens whenever we infer *determinate* causes from given effects, because the cause of the presentations that we ascribe—perhaps falsely—to external things may also reside in ourselves. Yet here we have proved

217. [Or "*definite* (or *specific*) causes," as distinguished from inferring *some* cause or other.]

that outer experience is in fact direct,[218] and that only by means of it can there be inner experience—i.e., B277 not indeed consciousness of our own existence, but yet determination of that existence in time. To be sure, the presentation *I am*, which expresses the consciousness that can accompany all thinking, is what directly includes the existence of a subject; but it is not yet a *cognition* of that subject, and hence is also no empirical cognition—i.e., experience—of it. For such experience involves, besides the thought of something existent, also intuition, and here specifically inner intuition, in regard to which—viz., time—the subject must be determined; and this determination definitely requires external objects. Thus, consequently, inner experience is itself only indirect and is possible only through outer experience.

Comment 2. Now, all experiential use that we make of our cognitive power in determining time agrees completely with this view. Not only can we perceive any time determination solely through the variation in external relations (i.e., through motion) by reference to the permanent in space (e.g., the sun's motion with respect to the earth's objects); but except merely B278 for *matter* we do not even have anything permanent on which, as intuition, we could base the concept of a substance. And even this permanence is not drawn from outer experience, but is presupposed a priori as necessary condition of all time determination, and hence presupposed also as determination of inner sense, with regard to our own existence, through the existence of external things. The consciousness that I have of myself in the presentation *I* is not an intuition at all, but is a merely *intellectual* presentation of a thinking subject's self-activity. Hence this *I* also does not have the least predicate of intuition that, as *permanent*, could serve as correlate for the time determination in inner sense—as, say, *impenetrability* is such a predicate of *empirical* intuition in matter.

Comment 3. It does not follow, from the fact that the existence of external objects is required for the possibility of a determinate consciousness of ourselves, that every intuitive presentation of external things implies also these things' existence; for the presentation may very well be (as it is in dreams as well as in madness) the mere effect of the imagination. Yet it is this effect merely through the reproduction of former outer perceptions; and these, as has been shown, are possible only through the actuality of external objects. What was here to be proved is only that inner experience as such is possible only through B279 outer experience as such. Whether this or that supposed experience is not perhaps a mere imagining must be ascertained by reference to its particular determinations and by holding it up to the criteria of all actual experience.

218. In the preceding theorem, the *direct* consciousness of the existence of external things is not presupposed but proved, whether or not we have insight into the possibility of this consciousness. The question concerning that possibility would be whether we have only an inner sense, and no outer sense but merely outer imagination. Clearly, however, in order for us even to imagine something—i.e., exhibit it to sense in intuition—as external, we must already have an outer sense, and must thereby distinguish directly the mere receptivity of an outer intuition from the spontaneity that characterizes all imagining. For if even outer sense were merely imagined, this would annul our very power of intuition which is to be determined by the imagination.

Grounding for the Metaphysics of Morals

PREFACE

387 Ancient Greek philosophy was divided into three sciences: physics, ethics, and logic. This division is perfectly suitable to the nature of the subject, and the only improvement that can be made in it is perhaps only to supply its principle so that there will be a possibility on the one hand of insuring its completeness and on the other of correctly determining its necessary subdivisions.

All rational knowledge is either material and concerned with some object, or formal and concerned only with the form of understanding and of reason themselves and with the universal rules of thought in general without regard to differences of its objects. Formal philosophy is called logic. Material philosophy, however, has to do with determinate objects and with the laws to which these objects are subject; and such philosophy is divided into two parts, because these laws are either laws of nature or laws of freedom. The science of the former is called physics, while that of the latter is called ethics; they are also called doctrine of nature and doctrine of morals respectively.

Logic cannot have any empirical part, i.e., a part in which the universal and necessary laws of thought would be based on grounds taken from experience; for in that case it would not be logic, i.e., a canon for understanding and reason, which is valid for all thinking and which has to be demonstrated.[1] Natural and moral philosophy, on the contrary, can each have an empirical part. The former has to because it must determine the laws of nature as an object of experience, and the latter because it must determine the will of man insofar as 388 the will is affected by nature. The laws of the former are those according to which everything does happen, while the laws of the latter are those according to which everything ought to happen, although these moral laws also consider the conditions under which what ought to happen frequently does not.

All philosophy insofar as it is founded on experience may be called empirical, while that which sets forth its doctrines as founded entirely on a priori principles may be called pure. The latter, when merely formal, is called logic; but when limited to determinate objects of the understanding, it is called metaphysics.

In this way there arises the idea of a twofold metaphysics: a metaphysics of nature and a metaphysics of morals.[2] Physics will thus have its empirical part, but also a rational one. Ethics will too, though here the empirical part might more specifically be called practical anthropology,[3] while the rational part might properly be called morals.

All industries, crafts, and arts have gained by the division of labor, viz., one man does not do everything, but each confines himself to a certain kind of work that is distinguished from all other kinds by the treatment it requires, so that the work may be done with the highest perfection and with greater ease. Where work is not so distinguished and divided, where everyone is a jack of all trades, there industry remains sunk in the greatest barbarism. Whether or not pure philosophy in all its parts requires its own special man might well be in itself a subject worthy of consideration. Would not the whole of this learned industry be better off if those who are accustomed, as the public taste demands, to purvey a mixture of the empirical with the rational in all sorts of proportions unknown even to themselves and who style themselves independent thinkers, while giving the name of hair-splitters to those who apply themselves to the purely rational part, were to be given warning about

Reprinted from Kant, *Grounding for the Metaphysics of Morals,* translated by James W. Ellington (Indianapolis: Hackett Publishing Company, 1981), by permission of the publisher.

1. [Kant's *Logic* was first published in 1800 in a version edited by Gottlob Benjamin Jäsche, who was one of Kant's students.—J.W.E.]

2. [*The Metaphysical Foundations of Natural Science* was published in 1786. *The Metaphysics of Morals* appeared in 1797.]

3. [*Anthropology from a Pragmatic Point of View* first appeared in 1798.]

pursuing simultaneously two jobs which are quite different in their technique, and each of which perhaps requires a special talent that when combined with the other talent produces nothing but bungling? But I only ask here whether the nature of science does not require that the empirical part always be carefully separated from the rational part. Should not physics proper (i.e., empirical physics) be preceded by a metaphysics of nature, and practical anthropology by a metaphysics of morals? Both of these 389 metaphysics must be carefully purified of everything empirical in order to know how much pure reason can accomplish in each case and from what sources it draws its a priori teaching, whether such teaching be conducted by all moralists (whose name is legion) or only by some who feel a calling thereto.

Since I am here primarily concerned with moral philosophy, the foregoing question will be limited to a consideration of whether or not there is the utmost necessity for working out for once a pure moral philosophy that is wholly cleared of everything which can only be empirical and can only belong to anthropology. That there must be such a philosophy is evident from the common idea of duty and of moral laws. Everyone must admit that if a law is to be morally valid, i.e., is to be valid as a ground of obligation, then it must carry with it absolute necessity. He must admit that the command, "Thou shalt not lie," does not hold only for men, as if other rational beings had no need to abide by it, and so with all the other moral laws properly so called; and he must concede that the ground of obligation here must therefore be sought not in the nature of man nor in the circumstances of the world in which man is placed, but must be sought a priori solely in the concepts of pure reason; he must grant that every other precept which is founded on principles of mere experience—even a precept that may in certain respects be universal—insofar as it rests in the least on empirical grounds—perhaps only in its motive—can indeed be called a practical rule, but never a moral law.

Thus not only are moral laws together with their principles essentially different from every kind of practical cognition in which there is anything empirical, but all moral philosophy rests entirely on its pure part. When applied to man, it does not in the least borrow from acquaintance with him (anthropology) but gives a priori laws to him as a rational being. To be sure, these laws require, furthermore, a power of judgment sharpened by experience, partly in order to distinguish in what cases they are applicable, and partly to gain for them access to the human will as well as influence for putting them into practice. For man is affected by so many inclinations that, even though he is indeed capable of the idea of a pure practical reason, he is not so easily able to make that idea effective *in concreto* in the conduct of his life.

A metaphysics of morals is thus indispensably nec- 390 essary, not merely because of motives of speculation regarding the source of practical principles which are present a priori in our reason, but because morals themselves are liable to all kinds of corruption as long as the guide and supreme norm for correctly estimating them are missing. For in the case of what is to be morally good, that it conforms to the moral law is not enough; it must also be done for the sake of the moral law. Otherwise that conformity is only very contingent and uncertain, since the non-moral ground may now and then produce actions that conform with the law but quite often produces actions that are contrary to the law. Now the moral law in its purity and genuineness (which is of the utmost concern in the practical realm) can be sought nowhere but in a pure philosophy. Therefore, pure philosophy (metaphysics) must precede; without it there can be no moral philosophy at all. That philosophy which mixes pure principles with empirical ones does not deserve the name of philosophy (for philosophy is distinguished from ordinary rational knowledge by its treatments in a separate science of what the latter comprehends only confusedly). Still less does it deserve the name of moral philosophy, since by this very confusion it spoils even the purity of morals and counteracts its own ends.

There must be no thought that what is required here is already contained in the propaedeutic that precedes the celebrated Wolff's moral philosophy, i.e., in what he calls *Universal Practical Philosophy*,[4] and that hence there is no need to break entirely new ground. Just because his work was to be a universal practical philosophy, it has not taken into consider-

4. [This work of Christian Wolff was published in 1738–1739; this and other of his works served for many years as the standard philosophy textbooks in German universities. Wolff's philosophy was founded on that of Leibniz.]

ation any special kind of will, such as one determined solely by a priori principles without any empirical motives and which could be called a pure will, but has considered volition in general, together with all the actions and conditions belonging to it under this general signification. And thereby does his propaedeutic differ from a metaphysics of morals in the same way that general logic, which expounds the acts and rules of thinking in general, differs from transcendental philosophy, which treats merely of the particular acts and rules of pure thinking, i.e., of that thinking whereby objects are cognized completely a priori. For the metaphysics of morals has to investigate the idea and principles of a possible pure will and not the 391 actions and conditions of human volition as such, which are for the most part drawn from psychology. Moral laws and duty are discussed in this universal practical philosophy (though quite improperly), but this is no objection to what has been said about such philosophy. For the authors of this science remain true to their idea of it on the following point also: they do not distinguish the motives which, as such, are presented completely a priori by reason alone and are properly moral, from the empirical motives which the understanding raises to general concepts merely by the comparison of experiences. Rather, they consider motives irrespective of any difference in their source; and inasmuch as they regard all motives as being homogeneous, they consider nothing but their relative strength or weakness. In this way they frame their concept of obligation, which is certainly not moral, but is all that can be expected from a philosophy which never decides regarding the origin of all possible practical concepts whether they are a priori or merely a posteriori.

I intend some day to publish a metaphysics of morals,[5] but as a preliminary to that I now issue this *Grounding* [1785]. Indeed there is properly no other foundation for such a metaphysics than a critical examination of pure practical reason, just as there is properly no other foundation for a metaphysics [of nature] than the critical examination of pure speculative reason, which has already been published.[6] But, in the first place, the former critique is not so absolutely necessary as the latter one, because human reason can, even in the most ordinary mind, be easily brought in moral matters to a high degree of correctness and precision, while on the other hand in its theoretical but pure use it is wholly dialectical. In the second place, if a critical examination of pure practical reason is to be complete, then there must, in my view, be the possibility at the same time of showing the unity of practical and speculative reason in a common principle; for in the final analysis there can be only one and the same reason, which is to be differentiated solely in its application. But there is no possibility here of bringing my work to such completeness, without introducing considerations of an entirely different kind and without thereby confusing the reader. Instead of calling the present work a *Critique of Pure Practical Reason*, I have, therefore, adopted the title *Grounding for the Metaphysics of Morals* [*Grundlegung zur Metaphysik der Sitten*].[7]

But, in the third place, since a metaphysics of morals, despite the forbidding title, is nevertheless capable of a high degree of popularity and adaptation to the ordinary understanding, I find it useful to separate from the aforementioned metaphysics this preliminary work on its foundation [*Grundlage*] in order later to have no need to introduce unavoidable subtleties into doctrines that are easier to grasp. 392

The present *Grounding* [*Grundlegung*] is, however, intended for nothing more than seeking out and establishing the supreme principle of morality. This constitutes by itself a task which is complete in its purpose and should be kept separate from every other moral inquiry. The application of this supreme principle to the whole ethical system would, to be sure, shed much light on my conclusions regarding this central question, which is important but has not heretofore been at all satisfactorily discussed; and the adequacy manifested by the principle throughout such application would provide strong confirmation for the principle. Nevertheless, I must forego this advantage, which after all would be more gratifying for myself than helpful for others, since ease of use and apparent adequacy of a principle do not provide any certain

5. [This appeared in 1797.]

6. [The first edition of the *Critique of Pure Reason* appeared in 1781, while the second edition appeared in 1787. The *Critique of Practical Reason* was published in 1788.]

7. [This might be translated as *Laying the Foundation for the Metaphysics of Morals*. But for the sake of brevity *Grounding for the Metaphysics of Morals* has been chosen.]

proof of its soundness, but do awaken, rather, a certain bias which prevents any rigorous examination and estimation of it for itself, without any regard to its consequences.

The method adopted in this work is, I believe, one that is most suitable if we proceed analytically from ordinary knowledge to a determination of the supreme principle and then back again synthetically from an examination of this principle and its sources to ordinary knowledge where its application is found. Therefore, the division turns out to be the following:

1. *First Section.* Transition from the Ordinary Rational Knowledge of Morality to the Philosophical.
2. *Second Section.* Transition from Popular Moral Philosophy to a Metaphysics of Morals.
3. *Third Section.* Final Step from a Metaphysics of Morals to a Critique of Pure Practical Reason.

393

FIRST SECTION

Transition from the Ordinary Rational Knowledge of Morality to the Philosophical

There is no possibility of thinking of anything at all in the world, or even out of it, which can be regarded as good without qualification, except, a *good will.* Intelligence, wit, judgment, and whatever talents of the mind one might want to name are doubtless in many respects good and desirable, as are such qualities of temperament as courage, resolution, perseverance. But they can also become extremely bad and harmful if the will, which is to make use of these gifts of nature and which in its special constitution is called character, is not good. The same holds with gifts of fortune; power, riches, honor, even health, and that complete well-being and contentment with one's condition which is called happiness make for pride and often hereby even arrogance, unless there is a good will to correct their influence on the mind and herewith also to rectify the whole principle of action and make it universally conformable to its end. The sight of a being who is not graced by any touch of a pure and good will but who yet enjoys an uninterrupted prosperity can never delight a rational and impartial spectator. Thus a good will seems to constitute the indispensable condition of being even worthy of happiness.

394 Some qualities are even conducive to this good will itself and can facilitate is work. Nevertheless, they have no intrinsic unconditional worth; but they always presuppose, rather, a good will, which restricts the high esteem in which they are otherwise rightly held, and does not permit them to be regarded as absolutely good. Moderation in emotions and passions, self-control, and calm deliberation are not only good in many respects but even seem to constitute part of the intrinsic worth of a person. But they are far from being rightly called good without qualification (however unconditionally they were commended by the ancients). For without the principles of a good will, they can become extremely bad; the coolness of a villain makes him not only much more dangerous but also immediately more abominable in our eyes than he would have been regarded by us without it.

A good will is good not because of what it effects or accomplishes, nor because of its fitness to attain some proposed end; it is good only through its willing, i.e., it is good in itself. When it is considered in itself, then it is to be esteemed very much higher than anything which it might ever bring about merely in order to favor some inclination, or even the sum total of all inclinations. Even if, by some especially unfortunate fate or by the niggardly provision of stepmotherly nature, this will should be wholly lacking in the power to accomplish its purpose; if with the greatest effort it should yet achieve nothing, and only the good will should remain (not, to be sure, as a mere wish but as the summoning of all the means in our power), yet would it, like a jewel, still shine by its own light as something which has its full value in itself. Its usefulness or fruitlessness can neither augment nor diminish this value. Its usefulness would be, as it were, only the setting to enable us to handle it in ordinary dealings or to attract to it the attention of those who are not yet experts, but not to recommend it to real experts or to determine its value.

But there is something so strange in this idea of the absolute value of a mere will, in which no account is taken of any useful results, that in spite of all the agreement received even from ordinary reason, yet there must arise the suspicion that such an idea may perhaps have as its hidden basis merely some high-flown fancy, and that we may have misunderstood the purpose of nature in assigning to reason the gov- 395 erning of our will. Therefore, this idea will be examined from this point of view.

In the natural constitution of an organized being, i.e., one suitably adapted to the purpose of life, let there be taken as a principle that in such a being no organ is to be found for any end unless it be the most fit and the best adapted for that end. Now if that being's preservation, welfare, or in a word its happiness, were the real end of nature in the case of a being having reason and will, then nature would have hit upon a very poor arrangement in having the reason of the creature carry out this purpose. For all the actions which such a creature has to perform with this purpose in view, and the whole rule of his conduct would have been prescribed much more exactly by instinct; and the purpose in question could have been attained much more certainly by instinct than it ever can be by reason. And if in addition reason had been imparted to this favored creature, then it would have had to serve him only to contemplate the happy constitution of his nature, to admire that nature, to rejoice in it, and to feel grateful to the cause that bestowed it; but reason would not have served him to subject his faculty of desire to its weak and delusive guidance nor would it have served him to meddle incompetently with the purpose of nature. In a word, nature would have taken care that reason did not strike out into a practical use nor presume, with its weak insight, to think out for itself a plan for happiness and the means for attaining it. Nature would have taken upon herself not only the choice of ends but also that of the means, and would with wise foresight have entrusted both to instinct alone.

And, in fact, we find that the more a cultivated reason devotes itself to the aim of enjoying life and happiness, the further does man get away from true contentment. Because of this there arises in many persons, if only they are candid enough to admit it, a certain degree of misology, i.e., hatred of reason. This is especially so in the case of those who are the most experienced in the use of reason, because after calculating all the advantages they derive, I say not from the invention of all the arts of common luxury, but even from the sciences (which in the end seem to them to be also a luxury of the understanding), they yet find that they have in fact only brought 396 more trouble on their heads than they have gained in happiness. Therefore, they come to envy, rather than despise, the more common run of men who are closer to the guidance of mere natural instinct and who do not allow their reason much influence on their conduct. And we must admit that the judgment of those who would temper, or even reduce below zero, the boastful eulogies on behalf of the advantages which reason is supposed to provide as regards the happiness and contentment of life is by no means morose or ungrateful to the goodness with which the world is governed. There lies at the root of such judgments, rather, the idea that existence has another and much more worthy purpose, for which, and not for happiness, reason is quite properly intended, and which must, therefore, be regarded as the supreme condition to which the private purpose of men must, for the most part, defer.

Reason, however, is not competent enough to guide the will safely as regards its objects and the satisfaction of all our needs (which it in part even multiplies); to this end would an implanted natural instinct have led much more certainly. But inasmuch as reason has been imparted to us as a practical faculty, i.e., as one which is to have influence on the will, its true function must be to produce a will which is not merely good as a means to some further end, but is good in itself. To produce a will good in itself reason was absolutely necessary, inasmuch as nature in distributing her capacities has everywhere gone to work in a purposive manner. While such a will may not indeed be the sole and complete good, it must, nevertheless, be the highest good and the condition of all the rest, even of the desire for happiness. In this case there is nothing inconsistent with the wisdom of nature that the cultivation of reason, which is requisite for the first and unconditioned purpose, may in many ways restrict, at least in this life, the attainment of the second purpose, viz., happiness, which is always conditioned. Indeed happiness can even be reduced to less than nothing, without nature's failing thereby in her purpose; for reason recognizes as its highest practical function the establishment of a good will, whereby in the attainment of this end reason is capable only of its own kind of satisfaction, viz., that of fulfilling a purpose which is in turn determined only by reason, even though such fulfillment should often interfere with the purposes of inclination.

The concept of a will estimable in itself and good 397

without regard to any further end must now be developed. This concept already dwells in the natural sound understanding and needs not so much to be taught as merely to be elucidated. It always holds first place in estimating the total worth of our actions and constitutes the condition of all the rest. Therefore, we shall take up the concept of *duty*, which includes that of a good will, though with certain subjective restrictions and hindrances, which far from hiding a good will or rendering it unrecognizable, rather bring it out by contrast and make it shine forth more brightly.

I here omit all actions already recognized as contrary to duty, even though they may be useful for this or that end; for in the case of these the question does not arise at all as to whether they might be done from duty, since they even conflict with duty. I also set aside those actions which are really in accordance with duty, yet to which men have no immediate inclination, but perform them because they are impelled thereto by some other inclination. For in this [second] case to decide whether the action which is in accord with duty has been done from duty or from some selfish purpose is easy. This difference is far more difficult to note in the [third] case where the action accords with duty and the subject has in addition an immediate inclination to do the action. For example,[8] that a dealer should not overcharge an inexperienced purchaser certainly accords with duty; and where there is much commerce, the prudent merchant does not overcharge but keeps to a fixed price for everyone in general, so that a child may buy from him just as well as everyone else may. Thus customers are honestly served, but this is not nearly enough for making us believe that the merchant has acted this way from duty and from principles of honesty; his own advantage required him to do it. He cannot, however, be assumed to have in addition [as in the third case] an immediate inclination toward his buyers, causing him, as it were, out of love to give no one as far as price is concerned any advantage over another. Hence the action was done neither from duty nor from immediate inclination, but merely for a selfish purpose.

On the other hand,[9] to preserve one's life is a duty; and, furthermore, everyone has also an immediate inclination to do so. But on this account the often anxious care taken by most men for it has no intrinsic worth, 398 and the maxim of their action has no moral content. They preserve their lives, to be sure, in accordance with duty, but not from duty. On the other hand,[10] if adversity and hopeless sorrow have completely taken away the taste for life, if an unfortunate man, strong in soul and more indignant at his fate than despondent or dejected, wishes for death and yet preserves his life without loving it—not from inclination or fear, but from duty—then his maxim indeed has a moral content.[11]

To be beneficent where one can is a duty; and

8. [The ensuing example provides an illustration of the second case.]

9. [This next example illustrates the third case.]

10. [The ensuing example illustrates the fourth case.]

11. [Four different cases have been distinguished in the two foregoing paragraphs. Case 1 involves those actions which are contrary to duty (lying, cheating, stealing, etc.). Case 2 involves those which accord with duty but for which a person perhaps has no immediate inclination, though he does have a mediate inclination thereto (one pays his taxes not because he likes to but in order to avoid the penalties set for delinquents, one treats his fellows well not because he really likes them but because he wants their votes when at some future time he runs for public office, etc.). A vast number of so-called "morally good" actions actually belong to this case 2—they accord with duty because of self-seeking inclinations. Case 3 involves those which accord with duty and for which a person does have an immediate inclination (one does not commit suicide because all is going well with him, one does not commit adultery because he considers his wife to be the most desirable creature in the whole world, etc.). Case 4 involves those actions which accord with duty but are contrary to some immediate inclination (one does not commit suicide even when he is in dire distress, one does not commit adultery even though his wife has turned out to be an impossible shrew, etc.). Now case 4 is the crucial test case of the will's possible goodness—but Kant does not claim that one should lead his life in such a way as to encounter as many such cases as possible in order constantly to test his virtue (deliberately marry a shrew so as to be able to resist the temptation to commit adultery). Life itself forces enough such cases upon a person without his seeking them out. But when there is a conflict between duty and inclination, duty should always be followed. Case 3 makes for the easiest living and the greatest contentment, and anyone would wish that life might present him with far more of these cases than with cases 2 or 4.

besides this, there are many persons who are so sympathetically constituted that, without any further motive of vanity or self-interest, they find an inner pleasure in spreading joy around them and can rejoice in the satisfaction of others as their own work. But I maintain that in such a case an action of this kind, however dutiful and amiable it may be, has nevertheless no true moral worth.[12] It is on a level with such actions as arise from other inclinations, e.g., the inclination for honor, which if fortunately directed to what is in fact beneficial and accords with duty and is thus honorable, deserves praise and encouragement, but not esteem; for its maxim lacks the moral content of an action done not from inclination but from duty. Suppose then the mind of this friend of mankind to be clouded over with his own sorrow so that all sympathy with the lot of others is extinguished, and suppose him still to have the power to benefit others in distress, even though he is not touched by their trouble because he is sufficiently absorbed with his own; and now suppose that, even though no inclination moves him any longer, he nevertheless tears himself from this deadly insensibility and performs the action without any inclination at all, but solely from duty—then for the first time his action has genuine moral worth.[13] Further still, if nature has put little sympathy in this or that man's heart, if (while being an honest man in other respects) he is by temperament cold and indifferent to the sufferings of others, perhaps because as regards his own sufferings he is endowed with the special gift of patience and fortitude and expects or even requires that others should have the same; if such a man (who would truly not be nature's worst product) had not been exactly fashioned by her to be a philanthropist, would he not yet find in himself a source from which he might give himself a worth far higher than any that a good-natured temperament might have? By all means, because just here does the 399 worth of the character come out; this worth is moral and incomparably the highest of all, viz., that he is beneficent, not from inclination, but from duty.[14]

To secure one's own happiness is a duty (at least indirectly); for discontent with one's condition under many pressing cares and amid unsatisfied wants might easily become a great temptation to transgress one's duties. But here also do men of themselves already have, irrespective of duty, the strongest and deepest inclination toward happiness, because just in this idea are all inclinations combined into a sum total.[15] But the precept of happiness is often so constituted as greatly to interfere with some inclinations, and yet men cannot form any definite and certain concept of the sum of satisfaction of all inclinations that is called happiness. Hence there is no wonder that a single inclination which is determinate both as to what it promises and as to the time within which it can be satisfied may outweigh a fluctuating idea; and there is no wonder that a man, e.g., a gouty patient, can choose to enjoy what he likes and to suffer what he may, since by his calculation he has here at least not sacrificed the enjoyment of the present moment to some possibly groundless expectations of the good fortune that is supposed to be found in health. But even in this case, if the universal inclination to happiness did not determine his will and if health, at least for him, did not figure as so necessary an element in his calculations; there still remains here, as in all other cases, a law, viz., that he should promote his happiness not from inclination but from duty, and thereby for the first time does his conduct have real moral worth.[16]

Undoubtedly in this way also are to be understood those passages of Scripture which command us to love our neighbor and even our enemy. For love as an inclination cannot be commanded; but beneficence from duty, when no inclination impels us[17] and even

But yet one should not arrange his life in such a way as to avoid case 4 at all costs and to seek out case 3 as much as possible (become a recluse so as to avoid the possible rough and tumble involved with frequent association with one's fellows, avoid places where one might encounter the sick and the poor so as to spare oneself the pangs of sympathy and the need to exercise the virtue of benefiting those in distress, etc.). For the purpose of philosophical analysis Kant emphasizes case 4 as being the test case of the will's possible goodness, but he is not thereby advocating puritanism.]

12. [This is an example of case 3.]

13. [This is an example of case 4.]

14. [This is an even more extreme example of case 4.]

15. [This is an example of case 3.]

16. [This example is a weak form of case 4; the action accords with duty but is not contrary to some immediate inclination.]

17. [This is case 4 in its weak form.]

when a natural and unconquerable aversion opposes such beneficence,[18] is practical, and not pathological, love. Such love resides in the will and not in the propensities of feeling, in principles of action and not in tender sympathy; and only this practical love can be commanded.

The second proposition[19] is this: An action done from duty has its moral worth, not in the purpose that is to be attained by it, but in the maxim according to which the action is determined. The moral worth depends, therefore, not on the realization of the object *400* of the action, but merely on the principle of volition according to which, without regard to any objects of the faculty of desire, the action has been done. From what has gone before it is clear that the purposes which we may have in our actions, as well as their effects regarded as ends and incentives of the will, cannot give to actions any unconditioned and moral worth. Where, then, can this worth lie if it is not to be found in the will's relation to the expected effect? Nowhere but in the principle of the will, with no regard to the ends that can be brought about through such action. For the will stands, as it were, at a crossroads between its a priori principle, which is formal, and its a posteriori incentive, which is material; and since it must be determined by something, it must be determined by the formal principle of volition, if the action is done from duty—and in that case every material principle is taken away from it.

The third proposition, which follows from the other two, can be expressed thus: Duty is the necessity of an action done out of respect for the law. I can indeed have an inclination for an object as the effect of my proposed action; but I can never have respect for such an object, just because it is merely an effect and is not an activity of the will. Similarly, I can have no respect for inclination as such, whether my own or that of another. I can at most, if my own inclination, approve it; and, if that of another, even love it, i.e., consider it to be favorable to my own advantage. An object of respect can only be what is connected with my will solely as ground and never as effect—something that does not serve my inclination but, rather, outweighs it, or at least excludes it from consideration when some choice is made—in other words, only the law itself can be an object of respect and hence can be a command. Now an action done from duty must altogether exclude the influence of inclination and therewith every object of the will. Hence there is nothing left which can determine the will except objectively the law and subjectively pure respect for this practical law, i.e., the will can be subjectively determined by the maxim[20] that I should follow such a law even if all my inclinations are thereby thwarted. *401*

Thus the moral worth of an action does not lie in the effect expected from it nor in any principle of action that needs to borrow its motive from this expected effect. For all these effects (agreeableness of one's condition and even the furtherance of other people's happiness) could have been brought about also through other causes and would not have required the will of a rational being, in which the highest and unconditioned good can alone be found. Therefore, the pre-eminent good which is called moral can consist in nothing but the representation of the law in itself, and such a representation can admittedly be found only in a rational being insofar as this representation, and not some expected effect, is the determining ground of the will. This good is already present in the person who acts according to this representation, and such good need not be awaited merely from the effect.[21]

18. [This is case 4 in its strong form.]

19. [The first proposition of morality says that an action must be done from duty in order to have any moral worth. It is implicit in the preceding examples but was never explicitly stated.]

20. A maxim is the subjective principle of volition. The objective principle (i.e., one which would serve all rational beings also subjectively as a practical principle if reason had full control over the faculty of desire) is the practical law. [See Kant's footnote at Ak. 420–21.]

21. There might be brought against me here an objection that I take refuge behind the word "respect" in an obscure feeling, instead of giving a clear answer to the question by means of a concept of reason. But even though respect is a feeling, it is not one received through any outside influence but is, rather, one that is self-produced by means of a rational concept; hence it is specifically different from all feelings of the first kind, which can all be reduced to inclination or fear. What I recognize immediately as a law for me, I recognize with respect; this means merely the consciousness of the subordination of my will to a law without the mediation of other influences upon my sense. The immediate determination of the will by the law, and

402 But what sort of law can that be the thought of which must determine the will without reference to any expected effect, so that the will can be called absolutely good without qualification? Since I have deprived the will of every impulse that might arise for it from obeying any particular law, there is nothing left to serve the will as principle except the universal conformity of its actions to law as such, i.e., I should never act except in such a way that I can also will that my maxim should become a universal law.[22] Here mere conformity to law as such (without having as its basis any law determining particular actions) serves the will as principle and must so serve it if duty is not to be a vain delusion and a chimerical concept. The ordinary reason of mankind in its practical judgments agrees completely with this, and always has in view the aforementioned principle.

For example, take this question. When I am in distress, may I make a promise with the intention of not keeping it? I readily distinguish here the two meanings which the question may have; whether making a false promise conforms with prudence or with duty. Doubtless the former can often be the case. Indeed I clearly see that escape from some present difficulty by means of such a promise is not enough. In addition I must carefully consider whether from this lie there may later arise far greater inconvenience for me than from what I now try to escape. Furthermore, the consequences of my false promise are not easy to forsee, even with all my supposed cunning; loss of confidence in me might prove to be far more disadvantageous than the misfortune which I now try to avoid. The more prudent way might be to act according to a universal maxim and to make it a habit not to promise anything without intending to keep it. But that such a maxim is, nevertheless, always based on nothing but a fear of consequences becomes clear to me at once. To be truthful from duty is, however, quite different from being truthful from fear of disadvantageous consequences; in the first case the concept of the action itself contains a law for me, while in the second I must first look around elsewhere to see what are the results for me that might be connected with the action. For to deviate from the principle of duty is quite certainly bad; but to abandon my 403 maxim of prudence can often be very advantageous for me, though to abide by it is certainly safer. The most direct and infallible way, however, to answer the question as to whether a lying promise accords with duty is to ask myself whether I would really be content if my maxim (of extricating myself from difficulty by means of a false promise) were to hold as a universal law for myself as well as for others, and could I really say to myself that everyone may promise falsely when he finds himself in a difficulty from which he can find no other way to extricate himself. Then I immediately become aware that I can indeed will the lie but can not at all will a universal law to lie. For by such a law there would really be no promises at all, since in vain would my willing future actions be professed to other people who would not believe what I professed, or if they over-hastily did believe, then they would pay me back in like coin. Therefore, my maxim would necessarily destroy itself just as soon as it was made a universal law.[23]

Therefore, I need no far-reaching acuteness to discern what I have to do in order that my will may be morally good. Inexperienced in the course of the world and incapable of being prepared for all its

the consciousness thereof, is called respect, which is hence regarded as the effect of the law upon the subject and not as the cause of the law. Respect is properly the representation of a worth that thwarts my self-love. Hence respect is something that is regarded as an object of neither inclination nor fear, although it has at the same time something analogous to both. The object of respect is, therefore, nothing but the law—indeed that very law which we impose on ourselves and yet recognize as necessary in itself. As law, we are subject to it without consulting self-love; as imposed on us by ourselves, it is a consequence of our will. In the former aspect, it is analogous to fear; in the latter, to inclination. All respect for a person is properly only respect for the law (of honesty, etc.) of which the person provides an example. Since we regard the development of our talents as a duty, we think of a man of talent as being also a kind of example of the law (the law of becoming like him by practice), and that is what constitutes our respect for him. All so-called moral interest consists solely in respect for the law.

22. [This is the first time in the *Grounding* that the categorical imperative is stated.]

23. [This means that when you tell a lie, you merely take exception to the general rule that says everyone should always tell the truth and believe that what you are saying is true. When you lie, you do not thereby will that everyone else lie and not believe that what you are saying is true, because in such a case your lie would never work to get you what you want.]

contingencies, I only ask myself whether I can also will that my maxim should become a universal law. If not, then the maxim must be rejected, not because of any disadvantage accruing to me or even to others, but because it cannot be fitting as a principle in a possible legislation of universal law, and reason exacts from me immediate respect for such legislation. Indeed I have as yet no insight into the grounds of such respect (which the philosopher may investigate). But I at least understand that respect is an estimation of a worth that far outweighs any worth of what is recommended by inclination, and that the necessity of acting from pure respect for the practical law is what constitutes duty, to which every other motive must give way because duty is the condition of a will good in itself, whose worth is above all else.

Thus within the moral cognition of ordinary human reason we have arrived at its principle. To be sure, such reason does not think of this principle abstractly in its universal form, but does always have it actually in view and does use it as the standard of 404 judgment. It would here be easy to show how ordinary reason, with this compass in hand, is well able to distinguish, in every case that occurs, what is good or evil, in accord with duty or contrary to duty, if we do not in the least try to teach reason anything new but only make it attend, as Socrates did, to its own principle—and thereby do we show that neither science nor philosophy is needed in order to know what one must do to be honest and good, and even wise and virtuous. Indeed we might even have conjectured beforehand that cognizance of what every man is obligated to do, and hence also to know, would be available to every man, even the most ordinary. Yet we cannot but observe with admiration how great an advantage the power of practical judgment has over the theoretical in ordinary human understanding. In the theoretical, when ordinary reason ventures to depart from the laws of experience and the perceptions of sense, it falls into sheer inconceivabilities and self-contradictions, or at least into a chaos of uncertainty, obscurity, and instability. In the practical, however, the power of judgment first begins to show itself to advantage when ordinary understanding excludes all sensuous incentives from practical laws. Such understanding then becomes even subtle, whether in quibbling with its own conscience or with other claims regarding what is to be called right, or whether in wanting to determine correctly for its own instruction the worth of various actions. And the most extraordinary thing is that ordinary understanding in this practical case may have just as good a hope of hitting the mark as that which any philosopher may promise himself. Indeed it is almost more certain in this than even a philosopher is, because he can have no principle other than what ordinary understanding has, but he may easily confuse his judgment by a multitude of foreign and irrelevant considerations and thereby cause it to swerve from the right way. Would it not, therefore, be wiser in moral matters to abide by the ordinary rational judgment or at most to bring in philosophy merely for the purpose of rendering the system of morals more complete and intelligible and of presenting its rules in a way that is more convenient for use (especially in disputation), but not for the purpose of leading ordinary human understanding away from its happy simplicity in practical matters and of bringing it by means of philosophy into a new path of inquiry and instruction?

Innocence is indeed a glorious thing; but, unfortu- 405 nately, it does not keep very well and is easily led astray. Consequently, even wisdom—which consists more in doing and not doing than in knowing—needs science, not in order to learn from it, but in order that wisdom's precepts may gain acceptance and permanence. Man feels within himself a powerful counterweight to all the commands of duty, which are presented to him by reason as being so pre-eminently worthy of respect; this counterweight consists of his needs and inclinations, whose total satisfaction is summed up under the name of happiness. Now reason irremissibly commands its precepts, without thereby promising the inclinations anything; hence it disregards and neglects these impetuous and at the same time so seemingly plausible claims (which do not allow themselves to be suppressed by any command). Hereby arises a natural dialectic, i.e., a propensity to quibble with these strict laws of duty, to cast doubt upon their validity, or at least upon their purity and strictness, and to make them, where possible, more compatible with our wishes and inclinations. Thereby are such laws corrupted in their very foundations and their whole dignity is destroyed—something which even ordinary practical reason cannot in the end call good.

Thus is ordinary human reason forced to go outside

its sphere and take a step into the field of practical philosophy, not by any need for speculation (which never befalls such reason so long as it is content to be mere sound reason) but on practical grounds themselves. There it tries to obtain information and clear instruction regarding the source of its own principle and the correct determination of this principle in its opposition to maxims based on need and inclination, so that reason may escape from the perplexity of opposite claims and may avoid the risk of losing all genuine moral principles through the ambiguity into which it easily falls. Thus when ordinary practical reason cultivates itself, there imperceptibly arises in it a dialectic which compels it to seek help in philosophy. The same thing happens in reason's theoretical use; in this case, just as in the other, peace will be found only in a thorough critical examination of our reason.

406

SECOND SECTION

Transition from Popular Moral Philosophy to a Metaphysics of Morals

If we have so far drawn our concept of duty from the ordinary use of our practical reason, one is by no means to infer that we have treated it as a concept of experience. On the contrary, when we pay attention to our experience of the way human beings act, we meet frequent and—as we ourselves admit—justified complaints that there cannot be cited a single certain example of the disposition to act from pure duty; and we meet complaints that although much may be done that is in accordance with what duty commands, yet there are always doubts as to whether what occurs has really been done from duty and so has moral worth. Hence there have always been philosophers who have absolutely denied the reality of this disposition in human actions and have ascribed everything to a more or less refined self-love. Yet in so doing they have not cast doubt upon the rightness of the concept of morality. Rather, they have spoken with sincere regret as to the frailty and impurity of human nature, which they think is noble enough to take as its precept an idea so worthy of respect but yet is too weak to follow this idea: reason, which should legislate for human nature, is used only to look after the interest of inclinations, whether singly or, at best, in their greatest possible harmony with one another.

In fact there is absolutely no possibility by means *407* of experience to make out with complete certainty a single case in which the maxim of an action that may in other respects conform to duty has rested solely on moral grounds and on the representation of one's duty. It is indeed sometimes the case that after the keenest self-examination we can find nothing except the moral ground of duty that could have been strong enough to move us to this or that good action and to such great sacrifice. But there cannot with certainty be at all inferred from this that some secret impulse of self-love, merely appearing as the idea of duty, was not the actual determining cause of the will. We like to flatter ourselves with the false claim to a more noble motive; but in fact we can never, even by the strictest examination, completely plumb the depths of the secret incentives of our actions. For when moral value is being considered, the concern is not with the actions, which are seen, but rather with their inner principles, which are not seen.

Moreover, one cannot better serve the wishes of those who ridicule all morality as being a mere phantom of human imagination getting above itself because of self-conceit than by conceding to them that the concepts of duty must be drawn solely from experience (just as from indolence one willingly persuades himself that such is the case as regards all other concepts as well). For by so conceding, one prepares for them a sure triumph. I am willing to admit out of love for humanity that most of our actions are in accordance with duty; but if we look more closely at our planning and striving, we everywhere come upon the dear self, which is always turning up, and upon which the intent of our actions is based rather than upon the strict command of duty (which would often require self-denial). One need not be exactly an enemy of virtue, but only a cool observer who does not take the liveliest wish for the good to be straight off its realization, in order to become doubtful at times whether any true virtue is actually to be found in the world. Such is especially the case when years increase and one's power of judgment is made shrewder by experience and keener in observation. Because of these things nothing can protect us from a complete falling away from our ideas of duty and preserve in the soul a well-grounded respect for duty's law except

408 the clear conviction that, even if there never have been actions springing from such pure sources, the question at issue here is not whether this or that has happened but that reason of itself and independently of all experience commands what ought to happen. Consequently, reason unrelentingly commands actions of which the world has perhaps hitherto never provided an example and whose feasibility might well be doubted by one who bases everything upon experience; for instance, even though there might never yet have been a sincere friend, still pure sincerity in friendship is nonetheless required of every man, because this duty, prior to all experience, is contained as duty in general in the idea of a reason that determines the will by means of a priori grounds.

There may be noted further that unless we want to deny to the concept of morality all truth and all reference to a possible object, we cannot but admit that the moral law is of such widespread significance that it must hold not merely for men but for all rational beings generally, and that it must be valid not merely under contingent conditions and with exceptions but must be absolutely necessary. Clearly, therefore, no experience can give occasion for inferring even the possibility of such apodeictic laws. For with what right could we bring into unlimited respect as a universal precept for every rational nature what is perhaps valid only under the contingent conditions of humanity? And how could laws for the determination of our will be regarded as laws for the determination of a rational being in general and of ourselves only insofar as we are rational beings, if these laws were merely empirical and did not have their source completely a priori in pure, but practical, reason?

Moreover, worse service cannot be rendered morality than that an attempt be made to derive it from examples. For every example of morality presented to me must itself first be judged according to principles of morality in order to see whether it is fit to serve as an original example, i.e., as a model. But in no way can it authoritatively furnish the concept of morality. Even the Holy One of the gospel must first be compared with our ideal of moral perfection before he is recognized as such. Even he says of himself, 409 "Why do you call me (whom you see) good? None is good (the archetype of the good) except God only (whom you do not see)." But whence have we the concept of God as the highest good? Solely from the idea of moral perfection, which reason frames a priori and connects inseparably with the concept of a free will. Imitation has no place at all in moral matters. And examples serve only for encouragement, i.e., they put beyond doubt the feasibility of what the law commands and they make visible what the practical rule expresses more generally. But examples can never justify us in setting aside their true original, which lies in reason, and letting ourselves be guided by them.

If there is then no genuine supreme principle of morality that must rest merely on pure reason, independently of all experience, I think it is unnecessary even to ask whether it is a good thing to exhibit these concepts generally (*in abstracto*), which, along with the principles that belong to them, hold a priori, so far as the knowledge involved is to be distinguished from ordinary knowledge and is to be called philosophical. But in our times it may well be necessary to do so. For if one were to take a vote as to whether pure rational knowledge separated from everything empirical, i.e., metaphysics of morals, or whether popular practical philosophy is to be preferred, one can easily guess which side would be preponderant.

This descent to popular thought is certainly very commendable once the ascent to the principles of pure reason has occurred and has been satisfactorily accomplished. That would mean that the doctrine of morals has first been grounded on metaphysics and that subsequently acceptance for morals has been won by giving it a popular character after it has been firmly established. But it is quite absurd to try for popularity in the first inquiry, upon which depends the total correctness of the principles. Not only can such a procedure never lay claim to the very rare merit of a true philosophical popularity, inasmuch as there is really no art involved at all in being generally intelligible if one thereby renounces all basic insight, but such a procedure turns out a disgusting mishmash of patchwork observations and half-reasoned principles in which shallowpates revel because all this is something quite useful for the chitchat of everyday life. Persons of insight, on the other hand, feel confused by all this and turn their eyes away with a dissatisfaction which they nevertheless cannot cure. Yet philosophers, who quite see through the delusion, 410 get little hearing when they summon people for a time from this pretended popularity in order that they may be rightfully popular only after they have attained definite insight.

One need only look at the attempts to deal with morality in the way favored by popular taste. What he will find in an amazing mixture is at one time the particular constitution of human nature (but along with this also the idea of a rational nature in general), at another time perfection, at another happiness; here moral feeling, and there the fear of God; something of this, and also something of that. But the thought never occurs to ask whether the principles of morality are to be sought at all in the knowledge of human nature (which can be had only from experience). Nor does the thought occur that if these principles are not to be sought here but to be found, rather, completely a priori and free from everything empirical in pure rational concepts only, and are to be found nowhere else even to the slightest extent—then there had better be adopted the plan of undertaking this investigation as a separate inquiry, i.e., as pure practical philosophy or (if one may use a name so much decried) as a metaphysics[24] of morals. It is better to bring this investigation to full completeness entirely by itself and to bid the public, which demands popularity, to await the outcome of this undertaking.

But such a completely isolated metaphysics of morals, not mixed with any anthropology, theology, physics, or hyperphysics, and still less with occult qualities (which might be called hypophysical), is not only an indispensable substratum of all theoretical and precisely defined knowledge of duties, but is at the same time a desideratum of the highest importance for the actual fulfillment of their precepts. For the pure thought of duty and of the moral law generally, unmixed with any extraneous addition of empirical inducements, has by the way of reason alone (which first becomes aware hereby that it can of itself be practical) an influence on the human heart so much more powerful than all other incentives[25] which may *411* be derived from the empirical field that reason in the consciousness of its dignity despises such incentives and is able gradually to become their master. On the other hand, a mixed moral philosophy, compounded both of incentives drawn from feelings and inclinations and at the same time of rational concepts, must make the mind waver between motives that cannot be brought under any principle and that can only by accident lead to the good but often can also lead to the bad.

It is clear from the foregoing that all moral concepts have their seat and origin completely a priori in reason, and indeed in the most ordinary human reason just as much as in the most highly speculative. They cannot be abstracted from any empirical, and hence merely contingent, cognition. In this purity of their origin lies their very worthiness to serve us as supreme practical principles; and to the extent that something empirical is added to them, just so much is taken away from their genuine influence and from the absolute worth of the corresponding actions. Moreover, it is not only a requirement of the greatest necessity from a theoretical point of view, when it is a question of speculation, but also of the greatest practical importance, to draw these concepts and laws from pure reason, to present them pure and unmixed, and indeed to determine the extent of this entire practical

24. Pure philosophy of morals (metaphysics) may be distinguished from the applied (viz., applied to human nature) just as pure mathematics is distinguished from applied mathematics and pure logic from applied logic. By this designation one is also immediately reminded that moral principles are not grounded on the peculiarities of human nature but must subsist a priori of themselves, and that from such principles practical rules must be derivable for every rational nature, and accordingly for human nature.

25. I have a letter from the late excellent Sulzer [Johann Georg Sulzer (1720–1779), an important Berlin savant, who translated Hume's *Enquiry Concerning the Principles of Morals* into German in 1755] in which he asks me why it is that moral instruction accomplishes so little, even though it contains so much that is convincing to reason. My answer was delayed so that I might make it complete. But it is just that the teachers themselves have not purified their concepts: since they try to do too well by looking everywhere for motives for being morally good, they spoil the medicine by trying to make it really strong. For the most ordinary observation shows that when a righteous act is represented as being done with a steadfast soul and sundered from all view to any advantage in this or another world, and even under the greatest temptations of need or allurement, it far surpasses and eclipses any similar action that was in the least affected by any extraneous incentive; it elevates the soul and inspires the wish to be able to act in this way. Even moderately young children feel this impression, and duties should never be represented to them in any other way.

and pure rational cognition, i.e., to determine the 412 whole faculty of pure practical reason. The principles should not be made to depend on the particular nature of human reason, as speculative philosophy may permit and even sometimes finds necessary; but, rather, the principles should be derived from the universal concept of a rational being in general, since moral laws should hold for every rational being as such. In this way all morals, which require anthropology in order to be applied to humans, must be entirely expounded at first independently of anthropology as pure philosophy, i.e., as metaphysics (which can easily be done in such distinct kinds of knowledge). One knows quite well that unless one is in possession of such a metaphysics, then the attempt is futile. I shall not say to determine exactly for speculative judgment the moral element of duty in all that accords with duty, but that the attempt is impossible, even in ordinary and practical usage, especially in that of moral instruction, to ground morals on their genuine principles and thereby to produce pure moral dispositions and engraft them on men's minds for the promotion of the highest good in the world.

In this study we must advance by natural stages not merely from ordinary moral judgment (which is here ever so worthy of respect) to philosophical judgment, as has already been done, but also from popular philosophy, which goes no further than it can get by groping about with the help of examples, to metaphysics (which does not permit itself to be held back any longer by what is empirical, and which, inasmuch as it must survey the whole extent of rational knowledge of this kind, goes right up to ideas, where examples themselves fail us). In order to make such an advance, we must follow and clearly present the practical faculty of reason from its universal rules of determination to the point where the concept of duty springs from it.

Everything in nature works according to laws. Only a rational being has the power to act according to his conception of laws, i.e., according to principles, and thereby has he a will. Since the derivation of actions from laws requires reason, the will is nothing but practical reason. If reason infallibly determines the will, then in the case of such a being actions which are recognized to be objectively necessary are also subjectively necessary, i.e., the will is a faculty of choosing only that which reason, independently of inclination, recognizes as being practically necessary, i.e., as good. But if reason of itself does not sufficiently determine the will, and if the will submits also to subjective conditions (certain incentives) which do 413 not always agree with objective conditions; in a word, if the will does not in itself completely accord with reason (as is actually the case with men), the actions which are recognized as objectively necessary are subjectively contingent, and the determination of such a will according to objective laws is necessitation. That is to say that the relation of objective laws to a will not thoroughly good is represented as the determination of the will of a rational being by principles of reason which the will does not necessarily follow because of its own nature.

The representation of an objective principle insofar as it necessitates the will is called a command (of reason), and the formula of the command is called an imperative.

All imperatives are expressed by an *ought* and thereby indicate the relation of an objective law of reason to a will that is not necessarily determined by this law because of its subjective constitution (the relation of necessitation). Imperatives say that something would be good to do or to refrain from doing, but they say it to a will that does not always therefore do something simply because it has been represented to the will as something good to do. That is practically good which determines the will by means of representations of reason and hence not by subjective causes, but objectively, i.e., on grounds valid for every rational being as such. It is distinguished from the pleasant as that which influences the will only by means of sensation from merely subjective causes, which hold only for this or that person's senses but do not hold as a principle of reason valid for everyone.[26]

26. The dependence of the faculty of desire on sensations is called inclination, which accordingly always indicates a need. The dependence of a contingently determinable will on principles of reason, however, is called interest. Therefore an interest is found only in a dependent will which is not of itself always in accord with reason; in the divine will no interest can be thought. But even the human will can take an interest in something without thereby acting from interest. The former signifies practical interest in the action, while the latter signifies pathological interest in the object of the action. The former indicates only dependence of the will on principles of reason by itself, while the latter indicates

A perfectly good will would thus be quite as much 414 subject to objective laws (of the good), but could not be conceived as thereby necessitated to act in conformity with law, inasmuch as it can of itself, according to its subjective constitution, be determined only by the representation of the good. Therefore no imperatives hold for the divine will, and in general for a holy will; the *ought* is here out of place, because the *would* is already of itself necessarily in agreement with the law. Consequently, imperatives are only formulas for expressing the relation of objective laws of willing in general to the subjective imperfection of the will of this or that rational being, e.g., the human will.

Now all imperatives command either hypothetically or categorically. The former represent the practical necessity of a possible action as a means for attaining something else that one wants (or may possibly want). The categorical imperative would be one which represented an action as objectively necessary in itself, without reference to another end.

Every practical law represents a possible action as good and hence as necessary for a subject who is practically determinable by reason; therefore all imperatives are formulas for determining an action which is necessary according to the principle of a will that is good in some way. Now if the action would be good merely as a means to something else, so is the imperative hypothetical. But if the action is represented as good in itself, and hence as necessary in a will which of itself conforms to reason as the principle of the will, then the imperative is categorical.

An imperative thus says what action possible by me would be good, and it presents the practical rule in relation to a will which does not forthwith perform an action simply because it is good, partly because the subject does not always know that the action is good and partly because (even if he does know it is good) his maxims might yet be opposed to the objective principles of practical reason.

A hypothetical imperative thus says only that an 415 action is good for some purpose, either possible or actual. In the first case it is a problematic practical principle; in the second case an assertoric one. A categorical imperative, which declares an action to be of itself objectively necessary without reference to any purpose, i.e., without any other end, holds as an apodeictic practical principle.

Whatever is possible only through the powers of some rational being can be thought of as a possible purpose of some will. Consequently, there are in fact infinitely many principles of action insofar as they are represented as necessary for attaining a possible purpose achievable by them. All sciences have a practical part consisting of problems saying that some end is possible for us and of imperatives telling us how it can be attained. These can, therefore, be called in general imperatives of skill. Here there is no question at all whether the end is reasonable and good, but there is only a question as to what must be done to attain it. The prescriptions needed by a doctor in order to make his patient thoroughly healthy and by a poisoner in order to make sure of killing his victim are of equal value so far as each serves to bring about its purpose perfectly. Since there cannot be known in early youth what ends may be presented to us in the course of life, parents especially seek to have their children learn many different kinds of things, and they provide for skill in the use of means to all sorts of arbitrary ends, among which they cannot determine whether any one of them could in the future become an actual purpose for their ward, though there is always the possibility that he might adopt it. Their concern is so great that they commonly neglect to form and correct their children's judgment regarding the worth of things which might be chosen as ends.

There is, however, one end that can be presupposed as actual for all rational beings (so far as they are dependent beings to whom imperatives apply); and thus there is one purpose which they not merely can have but which can certainly be assumed to be such that they all do have by a natural necessity, and this is happiness. A hypothetical imperative which represents the practical necessity of an action as means for the promotion of happiness is assertoric. It may be

---

the will's dependence on principles of reason for the sake of inclination, i.e., reason merely gives the practical rule for meeting the need of inclination. In the former case the action interests me, while in the latter case what interests me is the object of the action (so far as this object is pleasant for me). In the First Section we have seen that in the case of an action done from duty regard must be given not to the interest in the object, but only to interest in the action itself and in its rational principle (viz., the law).

416 expounded not simply as necessary to an uncertain, merely possible purpose, but as necessary to a purpose which can be presupposed a priori and with certainty as being present in everyone because it belongs to his essence. Now skill in the choice of means to one's own greatest well-being can be called prudence[27] in the narrowest sense. And thus the imperative that refers to the choice of means to one's own happiness, i.e., the precept of prudence, still remains hypothetical; the action is commanded not absolutely but only as a means to a further purpose.

Finally, there is one imperative which immediately commands a certain conduct without having as its condition any other purpose to be attained by it. This imperative is categorical. It is not concerned with the matter of the action and its intended result, but rather with the form of the action and the principle from which it follows; what is essentially good in the action consists in the mental disposition, let the consequences be what they may. This imperative may be called that of morality.

Willing according to these three kinds of principles is also clearly distinguished by dissimilarity in the necessitation of the will. To make this dissimilarity clear I think that they are most suitably named in their order when they are said to be either *rules of skill*, *counsels of prudence*, or *commands (laws) of morality*. For law alone involves the concept of a necessity that is unconditioned and indeed objective and hence universally valid, and commands are laws which must be obeyed, i.e., must be followed even in opposition to inclination. Counsel does indeed involve necessity, but involves such necessity as is valid only under a subjectively contingent condition, viz., whether this or that man counts this or that as belonging to his happiness. On the other hand, the categorical imperative is limited by no condition, and can quite properly be called a command since it is absolutely, though practically, necessary. The first kind of imperatives might also be called technical (belonging to art), the second kind pragmatic[28] (belonging to welfare), the third kind moral (belonging 417 to free conduct as such, i.e., to morals).

The question now arises: how are all of these imperatives possible?[29] This question does not seek to know how the fulfillment of the action commanded by the imperative can be conceived, but merely how the necessitation of the will expressed by the imperative in setting a task can be conceived. How an imperative of skill is possible requires no special discussion. Whoever wills the end, wills (so far as reason has decisive influence on his actions) also the means that are indispensably necessary to his actions and that lie in his power. This proposition, as far as willing is concerned, is analytic. For in willing an object as my effect there is already thought the causality of myself as an acting cause, i.e., the use of means. The imperative derives the concept of actions necessary to this end from the concept of willing this end. (Synthetic propositions are indeed required for determining the means to a proposed end; but such propositions are concerned not with the ground, i.e., the act of the will, but only with the way to realize the object of the will.) Mathematics teaches by nothing but synthetic propositions that in order to bisect a line according to a sure principle I must from each of its extremities draw arcs such that they intersect. But when I know that the proposed result can come about only by means of such an action, then the proposition (if I fully will the effect, then I also will the action required for it) is analytic. For it is one and the same thing to conceive of something as an effect that is possible in a certain way through me and to conceive of myself as acting in the same way with regard to the aforesaid effect.

27. The word "prudence" is used in a double sense: firstly, it can mean worldly wisdom, and, secondly, private wisdom. The former is the skill of someone in influencing others so as to use them for his own purposes. The latter is the sagacity to combine all these purposes for his own lasting advantage. The value of the former is properly reduced to the latter, and it might better be said of one who is prudent in the former sense but not in the latter that he is clever and cunning, but on the whole imprudent.

28. It seems to me that the proper meaning of the word "pragmatic" could be defined most accurately in this way. For those sanctions are called pragmatic which properly flow not from the law of states as necessary enactments but from provision for the general welfare. A history is pragmatically written when it teaches prudence, i.e., instructs the world how it can provide for its interests better than, or at least as well as, has been done in former times.

29. [That is, why should one let his actions be determined at various times by one or the other of these three kinds of imperatives?]

If it were only as easy to give a determinate concept 418 of happiness, then the imperatives of prudence would exactly correspond to those of skill and would be likewise analytic. For there could be said in this case just as in the former that whoever wills the end also wills (necessarily according to reason) the sole means thereto which are in his power. But, unfortunately, the concept of happiness is such an indeterminate one that even though everyone wishes to attain happiness, yet he can never say definitely and consistently what it is that he really wishes and wills. The reason for this is that all the elements belonging to the concept of happiness are unexceptionally empirical, i.e., they must be borrowed from experience, while for the idea of happiness there is required an absolute whole, a maximum of well-being in my present and in every future condition. Now it is impossible for the most insightful and at the same time most powerful, but nonetheless finite, being to frame here a determinate concept of what it is that he really wills. Does he want riches? How much anxiety, envy, and intrigue might he not thereby bring down upon his own head! Or knowledge and insight? Perhaps these might only give him an eye that much sharper for revealing that much more dreadfully evils which are at present hidden but are yet unavoidable, or such an eye might burden him with still further needs for the desires which already concern him enough. Or long life? Who guarantees that it would not be a long misery? Or health at least? How often has infirmity of the body kept one from excesses into which perfect health would have allowed him to fall, and so on? In brief, he is not able on any principle to determine with complete certainty what will make him truly happy, because to do so would require omniscience. Therefore, one cannot act according to determinate principles in order to be happy, but only according to empirical counsels, e.g., of diet, frugality, politeness, reserve, etc., which are shown by experience to contribute on the average the most to well-being. There follows from this that imperatives of prudence, strictly speaking, cannot command at all, i.e., present actions objectively as practically necessary. They are to be taken as counsels (*consilia*) rather than as commands (*praecepta*) of reason. The problem of determining certainly and universally what action will promote the happiness of a rational being is completely insoluble. Therefore, regarding such action no imperative that in the strictest sense could command what is to be done to make one happy is possible, inasmuch as happiness is not an ideal of reason but of imagination. 419 Such an ideal rests merely on empirical grounds; in vain can there be expected that such grounds should determine an action whereby the totality of an infinite series of consequences could be attained. This imperative of prudence would, nevertheless, be an analytic practical proposition if one assumes that the means of happiness could with certainty be assigned; for it differs from the imperative of skill only in that for it the end is given while for the latter the end is merely possible. Since both, however, command only the means to what is assumed to be willed as an end, the imperative commanding him who wills the end to will likewise the means thereto is in both cases analytic. Hence there is also no difficulty regarding the possibility of an imperative of prudence.

On the other hand, the question as to how the imperative of morality is possible is undoubtedly the only one requiring a solution. For it is not at all hypothetical; and hence the objective necessity which it presents cannot be based on any presupposition, as was the case with the hypothetical imperatives. Only there must never here be forgotten that no example can show, i.e., empirically, whether there is any such imperative at all. Rather, care must be taken lest all imperatives which are seemingly categorical may nevertheless be covertly hypothetical. For instance, when it is said that you should not make a false promise, the assumption is that the necessity of this avoidance is no mere advice for escaping some other evil, so that it might be said that you should not make a false promise lest you ruin your credit when the falsity comes to light. But when it is asserted that an action of this kind must be regarded as bad in itself, then the imperative of prohibition is therefore categorical. Nevertheless, it cannot with certainty be shown by means of an example that the will is here determined solely by the law without any other incentive, even though such may seem to be the case. For it is always possible that secretly there is fear of disgrace and perhaps also obscure dread of other dangers; such fear and dread may have influenced the will. Who can prove by experience that a cause is not present? Experience only shows that a cause is not perceived. But in such a case the so-called moral imperative, which as such appears to be categorical and unconditioned, would actually be only a pragmatic precept which makes us pay attention to our own advantage and merely teaches us to take such advantage into consideration.

We shall, therefore, have to investigate the possibility of a categorical imperative entirely a priori, inasmuch as we do not here have the advantage of *420* having its reality given in experience and consequently of thus being obligated merely to explain its possibility rather than to establish it. In the meantime so much can be seen for now: the categorical imperative alone purports to be a practical law, while all the others may be called principles of the will but not laws. The reason for this is that whatever is necessary merely in order to attain some arbitrary purpose can be regarded as in itself contingent, and the precept can always be ignored once the purpose is abandoned. Contrariwise, an unconditioned command does not leave the will free to choose the opposite at its own liking. Consequently, only such a command carries with it that necessity which is demanded from a law.

Secondly, in the case of this categorical imperative, or law of morality, the reason for the difficulty (of discerning its possibility) is quite serious.The categorical imperative is an a priori synthetic practical proposition;[30] and since discerning the possibility of propositions of this sort involves so much difficulty in theoretic knowledge, there may readily be gathered that there will be no less difficulty in practical knowledge.

In solving this problem, we want first to inquire whether perhaps the mere concept of a categorical imperative may not also supply us with the formula containing the proposition that can alone be a categorical imperative. For even when we know the purport of such an absolute command, the question as to how it is possible will still require a special and difficult effort, which we postpone to the last section.[31]

If I think of a hypothetical imperative in general, I do not know beforehand what it will contain until its condition is given. But if I think of a categorical imperative, I know immediately what it contains. For since, besides the law, the imperative contains only the necessity that the maxim[32] should accord with *421* this law, while the law contains no condition to restrict it, there remains nothing but the universality of a law as such with which the maxim of the action should conform. This conformity alone is properly what is represented as necessary by the imperative.

Hence there is only one categorical imperative and it is this: Act only according to that maxim whereby you can at the same time will that it should become a universal law.[33]

Now if all imperatives of duty can be derived from this one imperative as their principle, then there can at least be shown what is understood by the concept of duty and what it means, even though there is left undecided whether what is called duty may not be an empty concept.

The universality of law according to which effects are produced constitutes what is properly called nature in the most general sense (as to form), i.e., the existence of things as far as determined by universal laws. Accordingly, the universal imperative of duty may be expressed thus: Act as if the maxim of your action were to become through your will a universal law of nature.[34]

We shall now enumerate some duties, following the usual division of them into duties to ourselves

30. I connect a priori, and therefore necessarily, the act with the will without presupposing any condition taken from some inclination (though I make such a connection only objectively, i.e., under the idea of a reason having full power over all subjective motives). Hence this is a practical proposition which does not analytically derive the willing of an action from some other willing already presupposed (for we possess no such perfect will) but which connects the willing of an action immediately with the concept of the will of a rational being as something which is not contained in this concept.

31. [See Ak. 446–63.]

32. A maxim is the subjective principle of acting and must be distinguished from the objective principle, viz., the practical law. A maxim contains the practical rule which reason determines in accordance with the conditions of the subject (often his ignorance or his inclinations) and is thus the principle according to which the subject does act. But the law is the objective principle valid for every rational being, and it is the principle according to which he ought to act, i.e., an imperative.

33. [This formulation of the categorical imperative is often referred to as the formula of universal law.]

34. [This is often called the formula of the law of nature.]

and to others and into perfect and imperfect duties.[35]

422 1. A man reduced to despair by a series of misfortunes feels sick of life but is still so far in possession of his reason that he can ask himself whether taking his own life would not be contrary to his duty to himself.[36] Now he asks whether the maxim of his action could become a universal law of nature. But his maxim is this: from self-love I make as my principle to shorten my life when its continued duration threatens more evil than it promises satisfaction. There only remains the question as to whether this principle of self-love can become a universal law of nature. One sees at once a contradiction in a system of nature whose law would destroy life by means of the very same feeling that acts so as to stimulate the furtherance of life, and hence there could be no existence as a system of nature. Therefore, such a maxim cannot possibly hold as a universal law of nature and is, consequently, wholly opposed to the supreme principle of all duty.

2. Another man in need finds himself forced to borrow money. He knows well that he won't be able to repay it, but he sees also that he will not get any loan unless he firmly promises to repay it within a fixed time. He wants to make such a promise, but he still has conscience enough to ask himself whether it is not permissible and is contrary to duty to get out of difficulty in this way. Suppose, however, that he decides to do so. The maxim of his action would then be expressed as follows: when I believe myself to be in need of money, I will borrow money and promise to pay it back, although I know that I can never do so. Now this principle of self-love or personal advantage may perhaps be quite compatible with one's entire future welfare, but the question is now whether it is right.[37] I then transform the requirement of self-love into a universal law and put the question thus: how would things stand if my maxim were to become a universal law? He then sees at once that such a maxim could never hold as a universal law of nature and be consistent with itself, but must necessarily be self-contradictory. For the universality of a law which says that anyone believing himself to be in difficulty could promise whatever he pleases with the intention of not keeping it would make promising itself and the end to be attained thereby quite impossible, inasmuch as no one would believe what was promised him but would merely laugh at all such utterances as being vain pretenses.

3. A third finds in himself a talent whose cultivation could make him a man useful in many respects. But he finds himself in comfortable circumstances and 423 prefers to indulge in pleasure rather than to bother himself about broadening and improving his fortunate natural aptitudes. But he asks himself further whether his maxim of neglecting his natural gifts, besides agreeing of itself with his propensity to indulgence, might agree also with what is called duty.[38] He then sees that a system of nature could indeed always subsist according to such a universal law, even though every man (like South Sea Islanders) should let his talents rust and resolve to devote his life entirely to idleness, indulgence, propagation, and, in a word, to enjoyment. But he cannot possibly will that this should become a universal law of nature or be implanted in us as such a law by a natural instinct. For as a rational being he necessarily wills that all his faculties should be developed, inasmuch as they are given him for all sorts of possible purposes.

4. A fourth man finds things going well for himself but sees others (whom he could help) struggling with great hardships; and he thinks: what does it matter to me? Let everybody be as happy as Heaven wills or as he can make himself; I shall take nothing from

35. There should be noted here that I reserve the division of duties for a future *Metaphysics of Morals* [in Part II of the *Metaphysics of Morals*, entitled *The Metaphysical Principles of Virtue*, Ak. 417–474]. The division presented here stands as merely an arbitrary one (in order to arrange my examples). For the rest, I understand here by a perfect duty one which permits no exception in the interest of inclination. Accordingly, I have perfect duties which are external [to others], while other ones are internal [to oneself]. This classification runs contrary to the accepted usage of the schools, but I do not intend to justify it here, since there is no difference for my purpose whether this classification is accepted or not.

36. [Not committing suicide is an example of a perfect duty to oneself. See *Metaphysical Principles of Virtue*, Ak. 422–24.]

37. [Keeping promises is an example of a perfect duty to others. See *ibid.*, Ak. 423–31.]

38. [Cultivating one's talents is an example of an imperfect duty to oneself. See *ibid.*, Ak. 444–46.]

him nor even envy him; but I have no desire to contribute anything to his well-being or to his assistance when in need. If such a way of thinking were to become a universal law of nature, the human race admittedly could very well subsist and doubtless could subsist even better than when everyone prates about sympathy and benevolence and even on occasions exerts himself to practice them but, on the other hand, also cheats when he can, betrays the rights of man, or otherwise violates them. But even though it is possible that a universal law of nature could subsist in accordance with that maxim, still it is impossible to will that such a principle should hold everywhere as a law of nature.[39] For a will which resolved in this way would contradict itself, inasmuch as cases might often arise in which one would have need of the love and sympathy of others and in which he would deprive himself, by such a law of nature springing from his own will, of all hope of the aid he wants for himself.

424 These are some of the many actual duties, or at least what are taken to be such, whose derivation from the single principle cited above is clear. We must be able to will that a maxim of our action become a universal law; this is the canon for morally estimating any of our actions. Some actions are so constituted that their maxims cannot without contradiction even be thought as a universal law of nature, much less be willed as what should become one. In the case of others this internal impossibility is indeed not found, but there is still no possibility of wiling that their maxim should be raised to the universality of a law of nature, because such a will would contradict itself. There is no difficulty in seeing that the former kind of action conflicts with strict or narrow [perfect] (irremissible) duty, while the second kind conflicts only with broad [imperfect] (meritorious) duty.[40] By means of these examples there has thus been fully set forth how all duties depend as regards the kind of obligation (not the object of their action) upon the one principle.

If we now attend to ourselves in any transgression of a duty, we find that we actually do not will that our maxim should become a universal law—because this is impossible for us—but rather that the opposite of this maxim should remain a law universally.[41] We only take the liberty of making an exception to the law for ourselves (or just for this one time) to the advantage of our inclination. Consequently, if we weighed up everything from one and the same standpoint, namely, that of reason, we would find a contradiction in our own will, viz., that a certain principle be objectively necessary as a universal law and yet subjectively not hold universally but should admit of exceptions. But since we at one moment regard our action from the standpoint of a will wholly in accord with reason and then at another moment regard the very same action from the standpoint of a will affected by inclination, there is really no contradiction here. Rather, there is an opposition (*antagonismus*) of inclination to the precept of reason, whereby the universality (*universalitas*) of the principle is changed into a mere generality (*generalitas*) so that the practical principle of reason may meet the maxim halfway. Although this procedure cannot be justified in our own impartial judgment, yet it does show that we actually acknowledge the validity of the categorical imperative and (with all respect for it) merely allow ourselves a few exceptions which, as they seem to us, are unimportant and forced upon us.

We have thus at least shown that if duty is a concept *425* which is to have significance and real legislative authority for our actions, then such duty can be expressed only in categorical imperatives but not at all in hypothetical ones. We have also—and this is already a great deal—exhibited clearly and definitely for every application what is the content of the categorical imperative, which must contain the principle of all duty (if there is such a thing at all). But we have not yet advanced far enough to prove a priori that there actually is an imperative of this kind, that there is a practical law which of itself commands absolutely and without any incentives, and that following this law is duty.

In order to attain this proof there is the utmost

39. [Benefiting others is an example of an imperfect duty to others. See *ibid.*, Ak. 452–54.]

40. [Compare *ibid.*, Ak. 390–94, 410–11, 421–51.]

41. [This is to say, for example, that when you tell a lie, you do so on the condition that others are truthful and believe that what you are saying is true, because otherwise your lie will never work to get you what you want. When you tell a lie, you simply take exception to the general rule that says everyone should always tell the truth.]

importance in being warned that we must not take it into our mind to derive the reality of this principle from the special characteristics of human nature. For duty has to be a practical, unconditioned necessity of action; hence it must hold for all rational beings (to whom alone an imperative is at all applicable) and for this reason only can it also be a law for all human wills. On the other hand, whatever is derived from the special natural condition of humanity, from certain feelings and propensities, or even, if such were possible, from some special tendency peculiar to human reason and not holding necessarily for the will of every rational being—all of this can indeed yield a maxim valid for us, but not a law. This is to say that such can yield a subjective principle according to which we might act if we happen to have the propensity and inclination, but cannot yield an objective principle according to which we would be directed to act even though our every propensity, inclination, and natural tendency were opposed to it. In fact, the sublimity and inner worth of the command are so much the more evident in a duty, the fewer subjective causes there are for it and the more they oppose it; such causes do not in the least weaken the necessitation exerted by the law or take away anything from its validity.

Here philosophy is seen in fact to be put in a precarious position, which should be firm even though there is neither in heaven nor on earth anything upon which it depends or is based. Here philosophy must show its purity as author of its laws, and not as the herald of such laws as are whispered to it by an implanted sense or by who knows what tutelary nature. Such laws may be better than nothing at all, but they can never give us principles dictated by 426 reason. These principles must have an origin that is completely a priori and must at the same time derive from such origin their authority to command. They expect nothing from the inclination of men but, rather, expect everything from the supremacy of the law and from the respect owed to the law. Without the latter expectation, these principles condemn man to self-contempt and inward abhorrence.

Hence everything empirical is not only quite unsuitable as a contribution to the principle of morality, but is even highly detrimental to the purity of morals. For the proper and inestimable worth of an absolutely good will consists precisely in the fact that the principle of action is free of all influences from contingent grounds, which only experience can furnish. This lax or even mean way of thinking which seeks its principle among empirical motives and laws cannot too much or too often be warned against, for human reason in its weariness is glad to rest upon this pillow. In a dream of sweet illusions (in which not Juno but a cloud is embraced) there is substituted for morality some bastard patched up from limbs of quite varied ancestry and looking like anything one wants to see in it but not looking like virtue to him who has once beheld her in her true form.[42]

Therefore, the question is this: is it a necessary law for all rational beings always to judge their actions according to such maxims as they can themselves will that such should serve as universal laws? If there is such a law, then it must already be connected (completely a priori) with the concept of the will of a rational being in general. But in order to discover this connection we must, however reluctantly, take a step into metaphysics, although into a region of it different from speculative philosophy, i.e., we must enter the metaphysics of morals. In practical philosophy the concern is not with accepting grounds for 427 what happens but with accepting laws of what ought to happen, even though it never does happen—that is, the concern is with objectively practical laws. Here there is no need to inquire into the reasons as to why something pleases or displeases, how the pleasure of mere sensation differs from taste, and whether taste differs from a general satisfaction of reason, upon what does the feeling of pleasure and displeasure rest, and how from this feeling desires and inclinations arise, and how, finally, from these there arise maxims through the cooperation of reason. All of this belongs to an empirical psychology, which would constitute the second part of the doctrine of nature, if this doctrine is regarded as the philosophy of nature insofar as this philosophy is grounded on empirical laws. But here the concern is with objectively practical laws,

42. To behold virtue in her proper form is nothing other than to present morality stripped of all admixture of what is sensuous and of every spurious adornment of reward or self-love. How much she then eclipses all else that appears attractive to the inclinations can be easily seen by everyone with the least effort of his reason, if it be not entirely ruined for all abstraction.

and hence with the relation of a will to itself insofar as it is determined solely by reason. In this case everything related to what is empirical falls away of itself, because if reason entirely by itself determines conduct (and the possibility of such determination we now wish to investigate), then reason must necessarily do so a priori.

The will is thought of as a faculty of determining itself to action in accordance with the representation of certain laws, and such a faculty can be found only in rational beings. Now what serves the will as the objective ground of its self-determination is an end; and if this end is given by reason alone, then it must be equally valid for all rational beings. On the other hand, what contains merely the ground of the possibility of the action, whose effect is an end, is called the means. The subjective ground of desire is the incentive; the objective ground of volition is the motive. Hence there arises the distinction between subjective ends, which rest on incentives, and objective ends, which depend on motives valid for every rational being. Practical principles are formal when they abstract from all subjective ends; they are material, however, when they are founded upon subjective ends, and hence upon certain incentives. The ends which a rational being arbitrarily proposes to himself as effects of this action (material ends) are all merely relative, for only their relation to a specially constituted faculty of desire in the subject gives them their worth. Consequently, such worth cannot provide any universal principles, which are valid and necessary 428 for all rational beings and, furthermore, are valid for every volition, i.e., cannot provide any practical laws. Therefore, all such relative ends can be grounds only for hypothetical imperatives.

But let us suppose that there were something whose existence has in itself an absolute worth, something which as an end in itself could be a ground of determinate laws. In it, and in it alone, would there be the ground of a possible categorical imperative, i.e., of a practical law.

Now I say that man, and in general every rational being, exists as an end in himself and not merely as a means to be arbitrarily used by this or that will. He must in all his actions, whether directed to himself or to other rational beings, always be regarded at the same time as an end. All the objects of inclinations have only a conditioned value; for if there were not these inclinations and the needs founded on them, then their object would be without value. But the inclinations themselves, being sources of needs, are so far from having an absolute value such as to render them desirable for their own sake that the universal wish of every rational being must be, rather, to be wholly free from them. Accordingly, the value of any object obtainable by our action is always conditioned. Beings whose existence depends not on our will but on nature have, nevertheless, if they are not rational beings, only a relative value as means and are therefore called things. On the other hand, rational beings are called persons inasmuch as their nature already marks them out as ends in themselves, i.e., as something which is not to be used merely as means and hence there is imposed thereby a limit on all arbitrary use of such beings, which are thus objects of respect. Persons are, therefore, not merely subjective ends, whose existence as an effect of our actions has a value for us; but such beings are objective ends, i.e., exist as ends in themselves. Such an end is one for which there can be substituted no other end to which such beings should serve merely as means, for otherwise nothing at all of absolute value would be found anywhere. But if all value were conditioned and hence contingent, then no supreme practical principle could be found for reason at all.

If then there is to be a supreme practical principle and, as far as the human will is concerned, a categorical imperative, then it must be such that from the conception of what is necessarily an end for everyone because this end is an end in itself it constitutes an objective principle of the will and can hence serve as a practical law. The ground of such a principle is this: rational nature exists as an end in itself. In this 429 way man necessarily thinks of his own existence; thus far is it a subjective principle of human actions. But in this way also does every other rational being think of his existence on the same rational ground that holds also for me;[43] hence it is at the same time an objective principle, from which, as a supreme practical ground, all laws of the will must be able to be derived. The practical imperative will therefore be the following: Act in such a way that you treat

43. This proposition I here put forward as a postulate. The grounds for it will be found in the last section. [See Ak. 446–63.]

humanity, whether in your own person or in the person of another, always at the same time as an end and never simply as a means.[44] We now want to see whether this can be carried out in practice.

Let us keep to our previous examples.[45]

First, as regards the concept of necessary duty to oneself, the man who contemplates suicide will ask himself whether his action can be consistent with the idea of humanity as an end in itself. If he destroys himself in order to escape from a difficult situation, then he is making use of his person merely as a means so as to maintain a tolerable condition till the end of his life. Man, however, is not a thing and hence is not something to be used merely as a means; he must in all his actions always be regarded as an end in himself. Therefore, I cannot dispose of man in my own person by mutilating, damaging, or killing him. (A more exact determination of this principle so as to avoid all misunderstanding, e.g., regarding the amputation of limbs in order to save oneself, or the exposure of one's life to danger in order to save it, and so on, must here be omitted; such questions belong to morals proper.)

Second, as concerns necessary or strict duty to others, the man who intends to make a false promise will immediately see that he intends to make use of another man merely as a means to an end which the latter does not likewise hold. For the man whom I 430 want to use for my own purposes by such a promise cannot possibly concur with my way of acting toward him and hence cannot himself hold the end of this action. This conflict with the principle of duty to others becomes even clearer when instances of attacks on the freedom and property of others are considered. For then it becomes clear that a transgressor of the rights of men intends to make use of the persons of others merely as a means, without taking into consideration that, as rational beings, they should always be esteemed at the same time as ends, i.e., be esteemed only as beings who must themselves be able to hold the very same action as an end.[46]

Third, with regard to contingent (meritorious) duty to oneself, it is not enough that the action does not conflict with humanity in our own person as an end in itself; the action must also harmonize with this end. Now there are in humanity capacities for greater perfection which belong to the end that nature has in view as regards humanity in our own person. To neglect these capacities might perhaps be consistent with the maintenance of humanity as an end in itself, but would not be consistent with the advancement of this end.

Fourth, concerning meritorious duty to others, the natural end that all men have is their own happiness. Now humanity might indeed subsist if nobody contributed anything to the happiness of others, provided he did not intentionally impair their happiness. But this, after all, would harmonize only negatively and not positively with humanity as an end in itself, if everyone does not also strive, as much as he can, to further the ends of others. For the ends of any subject who is an end in himself must as far as possible be my ends also, if that conception of an end in itself is to have its full effect in me.

This principle of humanity and of every rational 431 nature generally as an end in itself is the supreme limiting condition of every man's freedom of action. This principle is not borrowed from experience, first, because of its universality, inasmuch as it applies to all rational beings generally, and no experience is capable of determining anything about them; and, secondly, because in experience (subjectively) humanity is not thought of as the end of men, i.e., as an object that we of ourselves actually make our end which as a law ought to constitute the supreme limiting condition of all subjective ends (whatever they may be); and hence this principle must arise from pure reason [and not from experience]. That is to say that the ground of all practical legislation lies

44. [This oft-quoted version of the categorical imperative is usually referred to as the formula of the end in itself.]

45. [See Ak. 422–23.]

46. Let it not be thought that the trivial *quod tibi non vis fieri, etc.* [do not do to others what you do not want done to yourself] can here serve as a standard or principle. For it is merely derived from our principle, although with several limitations. It cannot be a universal law, for it contains the ground neither of duties to oneself nor of duties of love toward others (for many a man would gladly consent that others should not benefit him, if only he might be excused from benefiting them). Nor, finally, does it contain the ground of strict duties toward others, for the criminal would on this ground be able to dispute with the judges who punish him; and so on.

objectively in the rule and in the form of universality, which (according to the first principle) makes the rule capable of being a law (say, for example, a law of nature). Subjectively, however, the ground of all practical legislation lies in the end; but (according to the second principle) the subject of all ends is every rational being as an end in himself. From this there now follows the third practical principle of the will as the supreme condition of the will's conformity with universal practical reason, viz., the idea of the will of every rational being as a will that legislates universal law.[47]

According to this principle all maxims are rejected which are not consistent with the will's own legislation of universal law. The will is thus not merely subject to the law but is subject to the law in such a way that it must be regarded also as legislating for itself and only on this account as being subject to the law (of which it can regard itself as the author).

In the previous formulations of imperatives, viz., that based on the conception of the conformity of actions to universal law in a way similar to a natural order and that based on the universal prerogative of rational beings as ends in themselves, these imperatives just because they were thought of as categorical excluded from their legislative authority all admixture of any interest as an incentive. They were, however, only assumed to be categorical because such an assumption had to be made if the concept of duty was to be explained. But that there were practical propositions which commanded categorically could not itself be proved, nor can it be proved anywhere in this section. But one thing could have been done, viz., to indicate that in willing from duty the renunciation of all interest is the specific mark distinguishing a categorical imperative from a hypothetical one and that such renunciation was expressed in the imperative itself by means of some determination contained 432 in it. This is done in the present (third) formulation of the principle, namely, in the idea of the will of every rational being as a will that legislates universal law.

When such a will is thought of, then even though a will which is subject to law may be bound to this law by means of some interest, nevertheless a will that is itself a supreme lawgiver is not able as such to depend on any interest. For a will which is so dependent would itself require yet another law restricting the interest of its self-love to the condition that such interest should itself be valid as a universal law.

Thus the principle that every human will as a will that legislates universal law in all its maxims,[48] provided it is otherwise correct, would be well suited to being a categorical imperative in the following respect: just because of the idea of legislating universal law such an imperative is not based on any interest, and therefore it alone of all possible imperatives can be unconditional. Or still better, the proposition being converted, if there is a categorical imperative (i.e., a law for the will of every rational being), then it can only command that everything be done from the maxim of such a will as could at the same time have as its object only itself regarded as legislating universal law. For only then are the practical principle and the imperative which the will obeys unconditional, inasmuch as the will can be based on no interest at all.

When we look back upon all previous attempts that have been made to discover the principle of morality, there is no reason now to wonder why they one and all had to fail. Man was viewed as bound to laws by his duty; but it was not seen that man is subject only to his own, yet universal, legislation and that he is bound only to act in accordance with his own will, which is, however, a will purposed by nature to legislate universal laws. For when man is thought as being merely subject to a law (whatever it might be), then the law had to carry with it some interest 433 functioning as an attracting stimulus or as a constraining force for obedience, inasmuch as the law did not arise as a law from his own will. Rather, in order that his will conform with law, it had to be necessitated by something else to act in a certain way. By this absolutely necessary conclusion, however, all the labor spent in finding a supreme ground for duty was irretrievably lost; duty was never discovered, but only

47. [This is usually called the formula of autonomy.]

48. I may here be excused from citing instances to elucidate this principle inasmuch as those which were first used to elucidate the categorical imperative and its formula can all serve the same purpose here. [See Ak. 421–23, 429–30.]

the necessity of acting from a certain interest. This might be either one's own interest or another's, but either way the imperative had to be always conditional and could never possibly serve as a moral command. I want, therefore, to call my principle the principle of the autonomy of the will, in contrast with every other principle, which I accordingly count under heteronomy.

The concept of every rational being as one who must regard himself as legislating universal law by all his will's maxims, so that he may judge himself and his actions from this point of view, leads to another very fruitful concept, which depends on the aforementioned one, viz., that of a kingdom of ends.

By "kingdom" I understand a systematic union of different rational beings through common laws. Now laws determine ends as regards their universal validity; therefore, if one abstracts from the personal differences of rational beings and also from all content of their private ends, then it will be possible to think of a whole of all ends in systematic connection (a whole both of rational being as ends in themselves and also of the particular ends which each may set for himself); that is, one can think of a kingdom of ends that is possible on the aforesaid principles.

For all rational beings stand under the law that each of them should treat himself and all others never merely as means but always at the same time as an end in himself. Hereby arises a systematic union of rational beings through common objective laws, i.e., a kingdom that may be called a kingdom of ends (certainly only an ideal), inasmuch as these laws have in view the very relation of such beings to one another as ends and means.[49]

A rational being belongs to the kingdom of ends as a member when he legislates in it universal laws while also being himself subject to these laws. He belongs to it as sovereign, when as legislator he is himself subject to the will of no other.

434 A rational being must always regard himself as legislator in a kingdom of ends rendered possible by freedom of the will, whether as member or as sovereign. The position of the latter can be maintained not merely through the maxims of his will but only if he is a completely independent being without needs and with unlimited power adequate to his will.

Hence morality consists in the relation of all action to that legislation whereby alone a kingdom of ends is possible. This legislation must be found in every rational being and must be able to arise from his will, whose principle then is never to act on any maxim except such as can also be a universal law and hence such as the will can thereby regard itself as at the same time the legislator of universal law. If now the maxims do not by their very nature already necessarily conform with this objective principle of rational beings as legislating universal laws, then the necessity of acting on that principle is called practical necessitation, i.e., duty. Duty does not apply to the sovereign in the kingdom of ends, but it does apply to every member and to each in the same degree.

The practical necessity of acting according to this principle, i.e., duty, does not rest at all on feelings, impulses, and inclinations, but only on the relation of rational beings to one another, a relation in which the will of a rational being must always be regarded at the same time as legislative, because otherwise he could not be thought of as an end in himself. Reason, therefore, relates every maxim of the will as legislating universal laws to every other will and also to every action toward oneself; it does so not on account of any other practical motive or future advantage but rather from the idea of the dignity of a rational being who obeys no law except what he at the same time enacts himself.

In the kingdom of ends everything has either a price or a dignity. Whatever has a price can be replaced by something else as its equivalent; on the other hand, whatever is above all price, and therefore admits of no equivalent, has a dignity.

Whatever has reference to general human inclinations and needs has a market price; whatever, without presupposing any need, accords with a certain taste, i.e., a delight in the mere unpurposive play of our mental powers,[50] has an affective price; but that which constitutes the condition under which alone something can be an end in itself has not merely a relative worth, i.e., a price, but has an intrinsic worth, i.e., dignity. 435

49. [This is usually called the formula of the kingdom of ends.]

50. [See Kant, *Critique of Aesthetic Judgment*, §'s 1–5.]

Now morality is the condition under which alone a rational being can be an end in himself, for only thereby can he be a legislating member in the kingdom of ends. Hence morality and humanity, insofar as it is capable of morality, alone have dignity. Skill and diligence in work have market price; wit, lively imagination, and humor have an affective price; but fidelity to promises and benevolence based on principles (not on instinct) have intrinsic worth. Neither nature nor art contain anything which in default of these could be put in their place; for their worth consists, not in the effects which arise from them, nor in the advantage and profit which they provide, but in mental dispositions, i.e., in the maxims of the will which are ready in this way to manifest themselves in action, even if they are not favored with success. Such actions also need no recommendation from any subjective disposition or taste so as to meet with immediate favor and delight; there is no need of any immediate propensity or feeling toward them. They exhibit the will performing them as an object of immediate respect; and nothing but reason is required to impose them upon the will, which is not to be cajoled into them, since in the case of duties such cajoling would be a contradiction. This estimation, therefore, lets the worth of such a disposition be recognized as dignity and puts it infinitely beyond all price, with which it cannot in the least be brought into competition or comparison without, as it were, violating its sanctity,

What then is it that entitles the morally good disposition, or virtue, to make such lofty claims? It is nothing less than the share which such a disposition affords the rational being of legislating universal laws, so that he is fit to be a member in a possible kingdom of ends, for which his own nature has already determined him as an end in himself and therefore as a legislator in the kingdom of ends.Thereby is he free as regards all laws of nature, and he obeys only those laws which he gives to himself. Accordingly, his maxims can belong to a universal legislation to which he at the 436 same time subjects himself. For nothing can have any worth other than what the law determines. But the legislation itself which determines all worth must for that very reason have dignity, i.e., unconditional and incomparable worth; and the word "respect" alone provides a suitable expression for the esteem which a rational being must have for it. Hence autonomy is the ground of the dignity of human nature and of every rational nature.

The aforementioned three ways of representing the principle of morality are at bottom only so many formulas of the very same law: one of them by itself contains a combination of the other two. Nevertheless, there is a difference in them, which is subjectively rather than objectively practical, viz., it is intended to bring an idea of reason closer to intuition (in accordance with a certain analogy) and thereby closer to feeling. All maxims have, namely,

1. A form, which consists in universality; and in this respect the formula of the moral imperative is expressed thus: maxims must be so chosen as if they were to hold as universal laws of nature.

2. A matter, viz., an end; and here the formula says that a rational being, inasmuch as he is by his very nature an end and hence an end in himself, must serve in every maxim as a condition limiting all merely relative and arbitrary ends.

3. A complete determination of all maxims by the formula that all maxims proceeding from his own legislation ought to harmonize with a possible kingdom of ends as a kingdom of nature.[51] There is a progression here through the categories of the *unity* of the form of the will (its universality), the *plurality* of its matter (its objects, i.e., its ends), and the *totality* of completeness of its system of ends. But one does better if in moral judgment he follows the rigorous method and takes as his basis the universal formula of the categorical imperative: Act according to that 437 maxim which can at the same time make itself a universal law. But if one wants also to secure acceptance for the moral law, it is very useful to bring one and the same action under the three aforementioned concepts and thus, as far as possible, to bring the moral law nearer to intuition.

We can now end where we started in the beginning, viz., the concept of an unconditionally good will.

51. Teleology considers nature as a kingdom of ends; morals regards a possible kingdom of ends as a kingdom of nature. In the former the kingdom of ends is a theoretical idea for explaining what exists. In the latter it is a practical idea for bringing about what does not exist but can be

That will is absolutely good which cannot be evil, i.e., whose maxim, when made into a universal law, can never conflict with itself. This principle is therefore also its supreme law: Act always according to that maxim whose universality as a law you can at the same time will. This is the only condition under which a will can never be in conflict with itself, and such an imperative is categorical. Inasmuch as the validity of the will as a universal law for possible actions is analogous to the universal connection of the existence of things in accordance with universal laws, which is the formal aspect of nature in general, the categorical imperative can also be expressed thus: Act according to maxims which can at the same time have for their object themselves as universal laws of nature. In this way there is provided the formula for an absolutely good will.

Rational nature is distinguished from the rest of nature by the fact that it sets itself an end. This end would be the matter of every good will. But in the idea of an absolutely good will—good without any qualifying condition (of attaining this or that end)—complete abstraction must be made from every end that has to come about as an effect (since such would make every will only relatively good). And so the end must here be conceived, not as an end to be effected, but as an independently existing end. Hence it must be conceived only negatively, i.e., as an end which should never be acted against and therefore as one which in all willing must never be regarded merely as means but must always be esteemed at the same time as an end. Now this end can be nothing but the subject of all possible ends themselves, because this subject is at the same time the subject of a possible absolutely good will; for such a will cannot without contradiction be subordinated to any other object. 438 The principle: So act in regard to every rational being (yourself and others) that he may at the same time count in your maxim as an end in himself, is thus basically the same as the principle: Act on a maxim which at the same time contains in itself its own universal validity for every rational being. That in the use of means for every end my maxim should be restricted to the condition of its universal validity as a law for every subject says just the same as that a subject of ends, i.e., a rational being himself, must be made the ground for all maxims of actions and must thus be used never merely as means but as the supreme limiting condition in the use of all means, i.e., always at the same time as an end.

Now there follows incontestably from this that every rational being as an end in himself must be able to regard himself with reference to all laws to which he may be subject as being at the same time the legislator of universal law, for just this very fitness of his maxims for the legislation of universal law distinguishes him as an end in himself. There follows also that his dignity (prerogative) of being above all the mere things of nature implies that his maxims must be taken from the viewpoint that regards himself, as well as every other rational being, as being legislative beings (and hence are they called persons). In this way there is possible a world of rational beings (*mundus intelligibilis*) as a kingdom of ends, because of the legislation belonging to all persons as members. Therefore, every rational being must so act as if he were through his maxim always a legislating member in the universal kingdom of ends. The formal principle of these maxims is this: So act as if your maxims were to serve at the same time as a universal law (for all rational beings). Thus a kingdom of ends is possible only on the analogy of a kingdom of nature; yet the former is possible only through maxims, i.e., self-imposed rules, while the latter is possible only through laws of efficient causes necessitated from without. Regardless of this difference and even though nature as a whole is viewed as a machine, yet insofar as nature stands in a relation to rational beings as its ends, it is on this account given the name of a kingdom of nature. Such a kingdom of ends would actually be realized through maxims whose rule is prescribed to all rational beings by the categorical imperative, if these maxims were universally obeyed. But even if a rational being himself strictly obeys such a maxim, he cannot for that reason count on everyone else's being true to it, nor can he expect the kingdom of nature and its purposive order to be in harmony with him as a fitting member of a kingdom of ends made possible by himself, i.e., he cannot expect the kingdom of nature to favor his expectation of happi- 439 ness. Nevertheless, the law: Act in accordance with the maxims of a member legislating universal laws for a merely possible kingdom of ends, remains in

made actual by our conduct, i.e., what can be actualized in accordance with this very idea.

full force, since it commands categorically. And just in this lies the paradox that merely the dignity of humanity as rational nature without any further end or advantage to be thereby gained—and hence respect for a mere idea—should yet serve as an inflexible precept for the will; and that just this very independence of the maxims from all such incentives should constitute the sublimity of maxims and the worthiness of every rational subject to be a legislative member in the kingdom of ends, for otherwise he would have to be regarded as subject only to the natural law of his own needs. And even if the kingdom of nature as well as the kingdom of ends were thought of as both united under one sovereign so that the latter kingdom would thereby no longer remain a mere idea but would acquire true reality, then indeed the kingdom of ends would gain the addition of a strong incentive, but never any increase in its intrinsic worth. For this sole absolute legislator must, in spite of all this, always be thought of as judging the worth of rational beings solely by the disinterested conduct prescribed to themselves by means of this idea alone. The essence of things is not altered by their external relations; and whatever without reference to such relations alone constitutes the absolute worth of man is also what he must be judged by, whoever the judge may be, even the Supreme Being. Hence morality is the relation of actions to the autonomy of the will, i.e., to the possible legislation of universal law by means of the maxims of the will. That action which is compatible with the autonomy of the will is permitted; that which is not compatible is forbidden. That will whose maxims are necessarily in accord with the laws of autonomy is a holy, or absolutely good, will. The dependence of a will which is not absolutely good upon the principle of autonomy (i.e., moral necessitation) is obligation, which cannot therefore be applied to a holy will. The objective necessity of an action from obligations is called duty.

From what has just been said, there can now easily be explained how it happens that, although in the concept of duty we think of subjection to the law, 440 yet at the same time we thereby ascribe a certain dignity and sublimity to the person who fulfills all his duties. For not insofar as he is subject to the moral law does he have sublimity, but rather has it only insofar as with regard to this very same law he is at the same time legislative, and only thereby is he subject to the law. We have also shown above[52] how neither fear nor inclination, but solely respect for the law, is the incentive which can give an action moral worth. Our own will, insofar as it were to act only under the condition of its being able to legislate universal law by means of its maxims—this will, ideally possible for us, is the proper object of respect. And the dignity of humanity consists just in its capacity to legislate universal law, though with the condition of humanity's being at the same time itself subject to this very same legislation.

Autonomy of the Will as the Supreme Principle of Morality

Autonomy of the will is the property that the will has of being a law to itself (independently of any property of the objects of volition). The principle of autonomy is this: Always choose in such a way that in the same volition the maxims of the choice are at the same time present as universal law. That this practical rule is an imperative, i.e., that the will of every rational being is necessarily bound to the rule as a condition, cannot be proved by merely analyzing the concepts contained in it, since it is a synthetic proposition. For proof one would have to go beyond cognition of objects to a critical examination of the subject, i.e. go to a critique of pure practical reason, since this synthetic proposition which commands apodeictically must be capable of being cognized completely a priori. This task, however, does not belong to the present section. But that the above principle of autonomy is the sole principle of morals can quite well be shown by mere analysis of the concepts of morality; for thereby the principle of morals is found to be necessarily a categorical imperative, which commands nothing more nor less than this very autonomy.

Heteronomy of the Will as the Source of All Spurious Principles of Morality 441

If the will seeks the law that is to determine it anywhere but in the fitness of its maxims for its own legislation of universal laws, and if it thus goes outside

52. [Ak. 400–402.]

of itself and seeks this law in the character of any of its objects, then heteronomy always results. The will in that case does not give itself the law, but the object does so because of its relation to the will. This relation, whether it rests on inclination or on representations of reason, admits only of hypothetical imperatives: I ought to do something because I will something else. On the other hand, the moral, and hence categorical, imperative says that I ought to act in this way or that way, even though I did not will something else. For example, the former says that I ought not to lie if I would maintain my reputation; the latter says that I ought not to lie even though lying were to bring me not the slightest discredit. The moral imperative must therefore abstract from every object to such an extent that no object has any influence at all on the will, so that practical reason (the will) may not merely minister to an interest not belonging to it but may merely show its own commanding authority as the supreme legislation. Thus, for example, I ought to endeavor to promote the happiness of others, not as though its realization were any concern of mine (whether by immediate inclination or by any satisfaction indirectly gained through reason), but merely because a maxim which excludes it cannot be comprehended as a universal law in one and the same volition.

Classification of All Possible Principles of Morality Founded upon the Assumed Fundamental Concept of Heteronomy

Here as elsewhere human reason in its pure use, so long as it lacks a critical examination, first tried every possible wrong way before it succeeded in finding the only right way.

All principles that can be taken from this point of 442 view are either empirical or rational. The first kind, drawn from the principle of happiness, are based upon either physical or moral feeling. The second kind, drawn from the principle of perfection, are based upon either the rational concept of perfection as a possible effect of our will or else upon the concept of an independent perfection (the will of God) as a determining cause of our will.

Empirical principles are wholly unsuited to serve as the foundation for moral laws. For the universality with which such laws ought to hold for all rational beings without exception (the unconditioned practical necessity imposed by moral laws upon such beings) is lost if the basis of these laws is taken from the particular constitution of human nature or from the accidental circumstances in which such nature is placed. But the principle of one's own happiness is the most objectionable. Such is the case not merely because this principle is false and because experience contradicts the supposition that well-being is always proportional to well-doing, nor yet merely because this principle contributes nothing to the establishment of morality, inasmuch as making a man happy is quite different from making him good and making him prudent and sharp-sighted for his own advantage quite different from making him virtuous. Rather, such is the case because this principle of one's own happiness bases morality upon incentives that undermine it rather than establish it and that totally destroy its sublimity, inasmuch as motives to virtue are put in the same class as motives to vice and inasmuch as such incentives merely teach one to become better at calculation, while the specific difference between virtue and vice is entirely obliterated. On the other hand, moral feeling, this alleged special sense,[53] remains closer to morality than does the aforementioned principle of one's own happiness. Yet the appeal to the principle of moral feeling is superficial, since men who cannot think believe that they will be helped out by feeling, even when the question is solely one of universal laws. They do so even though feelings naturally differ from one another by an infinity of degrees, so that feelings are not capable of providing a uniform measure of good and evil; furthermore, they do so even though one man cannot by his feeling judge validly at all for other men. Nevertheless, the principle of moral feeling is closer to morality

53. I count the principle of moral feeling under that of happiness, because every empirical interest promises to contribute to our well-being through the amenity afforded by something, whether immediately and without any reference to advantage or with reference to advantage. Similarly, the principle of sympathy for the happiness of others must with Hutcheson be counted along with the principle of moral sense as adopted by him. [Francis Hutcheson (1694–1746) was Professor of Moral Philosophy in the University of Glasgow, Scotland. He was the main proponent of the doctrine of moral sense.]

and its dignity than is the principle of one's own happiness inasmuch as the former principle pays vir- 443 tue the honor of ascribing to her directly the satisfaction and esteem that is held for her, and does not, as it were, tell her to her face that our attachment to her rests not on her beauty but only on our advantage.

Among the rational principles of morality (or those arising from reason rather than from feeling) there is the ontological concept of perfection. It is empty, indeterminate, and hence is no use for finding in the immeasurable field of possible reality the maximum sum suitable for us. Furthermore, in attempting to distinguish specifically between the reality just mentioned and every other, it exhibits an inevitable tendency for turning about in a circle and cannot avoid tacitly presupposing the morality that it has to explain. Nevertheless, it is better than the theological concept, whereby morality is derived from a divine and most perfect will. It is better not merely because we cannot intuit divine perfection but can only derive it from our own concepts, among which morality is foremost; but also because if it is not so derived (and being thus derived would involve a crudely circular explanation), then the only remaining concept of God's will is drawn from such characteristics as desire for glory and dominion combined with such frightful representations as those of might and vengeance. Any system of morals based on such notions would be directly opposed to morality.

But if I had to choose between the concept of moral sense and that of perfection in general (both of which at least do not weaken morality, even though they are not at all capable of serving as its foundation), I would decide for the latter because it at least withdraws the decision of the question from sensibility and brings it to the court of pure reason, though it does not even here get any decision. Furthermore, I would choose the concept of perfection in general because it preserves the indeterminate idea (of a will good in itself) free from falsity until it can be more precisely determined.

For the rest, I believe that I may be excused from a lengthy refutation of all these doctrines. Such a refutation would be merely superfluous labor, since it is so easy and is presumably so well understood even by those whose office requires them to declare themselves for one of these theories (since their hearers would not tolerate suspension of judgment). But what interests us more here is to know that these principles never lay down anything but heteronomy of the will as the first ground of morality and that they must, consequently, necessarily fail in their purpose.

In every case where an object of the will must be 444 laid down as the foundation for prescribing a rule to determine the will, there the rule is nothing but heteronomy. The imperative is then conditioned, viz., if or because one wills this object, one should act thus or so. Hence the imperative can never command morally, i.e., categorically. Now the object may determine the will by means of inclination, as in the case of the principle of one's own happiness, or by means of reason directed to objects of our volition in general, as in the case of the principle of perfection. Yet in both cases the will never determines itself immediately by the thought of an action, but only by the incentive that the anticipated effect of the action has upon the will: I ought to do something because I will something else. And here must yet another law be assumed in me the subject, whereby I necessarily will this something else; this other law in turn requires an imperative to restrict this maxim. For the impulse which the representation of an object that is possible by means of our powers is to exert upon the will of a subject in accordance with his natural constitution belongs to the nature of the subject, whether to his sensibility (his inclination and taste) or to his understanding and reason, whose employment on an object is by the particular arrangement of their nature attended with satisfaction; consequently, the law would, properly speaking, be given by nature. This law, insofar as it is a law of nature, must be known and proved through experience and is therefore in itself contingent and hence is not fit to be an apodeictic practical rule, such as a moral rule must be. The law of nature under discussion is always merely heteronomy of the will; the will does not give itself the law, but a foreign impulse gives the law to the will by means of the subject's nature, which is adapted to receive such an impulse.

An absolutely good will, whose principle must be a categorical imperative, will therefore be indeterminate as regards all objects and will contain merely the form of willing; and indeed that form is autonomy. This is to say that the fitness of the maxims of every good will to make themselves universal laws is itself the only law that the will of every rational being imposes on itself, without needing to assume any incentive or interest as a basis.

How such a synthetic practical a priori proposition is possible and why it is necessary are problems whose solution does not lie any longer within the bounds of a metaphysics of morals. Furthermore, we have not here asserted the truth of this proposition, much 445 less professed to have within our power a proof of it. We simply showed by developing the universally accepted concept of morality that autonomy of the will is unavoidably bound up with it, or rather is its very foundation. Whoever, then, holds morality to be something real, and not a chimerical idea without any truth, must also admit the principle here put forward. Hence this section, like the first, was merely analytic. To show that morality is not a mere phantom of the brain, which morality cannot be if the categorical imperative, and with it the autonomy of the will, is true and absolutely necessary as an a priori principle, we require a possible synthetic use of pure practical reason. But we must not venture on this use without prefacing it with a critical examination of this very faculty of reason. In the last section we shall give the main outlines of this critical examination as far as sufficient for our purpose.[54]

446

THIRD SECTION

Transition from a Metaphysics of Morals to a Critique of Pure Practical Reason

The Concept of Freedom Is the Key for an Explanation of the Autonomy of the Will

The will is a kind of causality belonging to living beings insofar as they are rational; freedom would be the property of this causality that makes it effective independent of any determination by alien causes. Similarly, natural necessity is the property of the causality of all non-rational beings by which they are determined to activity through the influence of alien causes.

The foregoing explanation of freedom is negative and is therefore unfruitful for attaining an insight regarding its essence; but there arises from it a positive concept, which as such is richer and more fruitful. The concept of causality involves that of laws according to which something that we call cause must entail something else—namely, the effect. Therefore freedom is certainly not lawless, even though it is not a property of will in accordance with laws of nature. It must, rather, be a causality in accordance with immutable laws, which, to be sure, is of a special kind; otherwise a free will would be something absurd. As we have already seen [in the preceding paragraph], natural necessity is a heteronomy of efficient causes, 447 inasmuch as every effect is possible only in accordance with the law that something else determines the efficient cause to exercise its causality. What else, then, can freedom of the will be but autonomy, i.e., the property that the will has of being a law to itself? The proposition that the will is in every action a law to itself expresses, however, nothing but the principle of acting according to no other maxim than that which can at the same time have itself as a universal law for its object. Now this is precisely the formula of the categorical imperative and is the principle of morality. Thus a free will and a will subject to moral laws are one and the same.

Therefore if freedom of the will is presupposed, morality (together with its principle) follows by merely analyzing the concept of freedom. However, the principle of morality is, nevertheless, a synthetic proposition: viz., an absolutely good will is one whose maxim can always have itself as content when such maxim is regarded as a universal law; it is synthetic because this property of the will's maxim can never be found by analyzing the concept of an absolutely good will. Now such synthetic propositions are possible only as follows—two cognitions are bound together through their connection with a third in which both of them are to be found. The positive concept of freedom furnishes this third cognition, which cannot, as is the case with physical causes, be the nature of the world of sense (in whose concept is combined the concept of something as cause in relation to something else as effect). We cannot here yet show straight away what this third cognition is which freedom indicates to us and of which we have an a priori idea, nor can we as yet conceive of the deduction of the concept of freedom from pure practical reason and

54. [The ensuing Third Section is difficult to grasp. Kant expressed himself more clearly regarding the topics discussed there in the *Critique of Practical Reason*, Part I, Book I ("Analytic of Pure Practical Reason").]

therewith also the possibility of a categorical imperative. Rather, we require some further preparation.

Freedom Must Be Presupposed as a Property of the Will of All Rational Beings

It is not enough to ascribe freedom to our will, on whatever ground, if we have not also sufficient reason for attributing it to all rational beings. For inasmuch as morality serves as a law for us only insofar as we are rational beings, it must also be valid for all rational beings. And since morality must be derived solely from the property of freedom, one must show that freedom is also the property of the will of all rational 448 beings. It is not enough to prove freedom from certain alleged experiences of human nature (such a proof is indeed absolutely impossible, and so freedom can be proved only a priori). Rather, one must show that freedom belongs universally to the activity of rational beings endowed with a will. Now I say that every being who cannot act in any way other than under the idea of freedom is for this very reason free from a practical point of view. This is to say that for such a being all the laws that are inseparably bound up with freedom are valid just as much as if the will of such a being could be declared to be free in itself for reasons that are valid for theoretical philosophy.[55] Now I claim that we must necessarily attribute to every rational being which has a will also the idea of freedom, under which only can such a being act. For in such a being we think of a reason that is practical, i.e., that has causality in reference to its objects. Now we cannot possibly think of a reason that consciously lets itself be directed from outside as regards its judgments; for in that case the subject would ascribe the determination of his faculty of judgment not to his reason, but to an impulse. Reason must regard itself as the author of its principles independent of foreign influences. Therefore as practical reason or as the will of a rational being must reason regard itself as free. This is to say that the will of a rational being can be a will of its own only under the idea of freedom, and that such a will must therefore, from a practical point of view, be attributed to all rational beings.

Concerning the Interest Attached to the Ideas of Morality

We have finally traced the determinate concept of morality back to the idea of freedom, but we could not prove freedom to be something actual in ourselves and in human nature. We saw merely that we must 449 presuppose it if we want to think of a being as rational and as endowed with consciousness of its causality as regards actions, i.e., as endowed with a will. And so we find that on the very same ground we must attribute to every being endowed with reason and a will this property of determining itself to action under the idea of its own freedom.

Now there resulted from the presupposition of this idea of freedom also the consciousness of a law of action: that the subjective principles of actions, i.e., maxims, must always be so adopted that they can also be valid objectively, i.e., universally, as principles, and can therefore serve as universal laws of our own legislation. But why, then, should I subject myself to this principle simply as a rational being and by so doing also subject to this principle all other beings endowed with reason? I am willing to grant that no interest impels me to do so, because this would not give a categorical imperative. But nonetheless I must necessarily take an interest in it and discern how this comes about, for this *ought* is properly a *would* which is valid for every rational being, provided that reason is practical for such a being without hindrances. In the case of beings who, like ourselves, are also affected by sensibility, i.e., by incentives of a kind other than the purely rational, and who do not always act as reason by itself would act, this necessity of action is expressed only as an *ought*, and the subjective necessity is to be distinguished from the objective.

It therefore seems as if we have in the idea of freedom actually only presupposed the moral law, namely, the principle of the autonomy of the will, and as if we could not prove its reality and objective necessity independently. In that case we should in-

55. I adopt this method of assuming as sufficient for our purpose that freedom is presupposed merely as an idea by rational beings in their actions in order that I may avoid the necessity of having to prove freedom from a theoretical point of view as well. For even if this latter problem is left unresolved, the same laws that would bind a being who was really free are valid equally for a being who cannot act otherwise than under the idea of its own freedom. Thus we can relieve ourselves of the burden which presses on the theory.

deed still have gained something quite considerable by at least determining the genuine principle more exactly than had previously been done. But as regards its validity and the practical necessity of subjecting oneself to it, we would have made no progress. We could give no satisfactory answer if asked the following questions: why must the universal validity of our maxim taken as a law be a condition restricting our actions; upon what do we base the worth that we assign to this way of acting—a worth that is supposed to be so great that there can be no higher interest; 450 how does it happen that by this alone does man believe that he feels his own personal worth, in comparison with which that of an agreeable or disagreeable condition is to be regarded as nothing.

Indeed we do sometimes find that we can take an interest in a personal characteristic which involves no interest in any [external] condition but only makes us capable of participating in the condition in case reason were to effect the allotment. This is to say that the mere worthiness of being happy can of itself be of interest even without the motive of participating in this happiness. This judgment, however, is in fact only the result of the importance that we have already presupposed as belonging to moral laws (when by the idea of freedom we divorce ourselves from all empirical interest). However, in this way we are not as yet able to have any insight into why it is that we should divorce ourselves from such interest, i.e., that we should consider ourselves as free in action and yet hold ourselves as subject to certain laws so as to find solely in our own person a worth that can compensate us for the loss of everything that gives worth to our condition. We do not see how this is possible and hence how the moral law can obligate us.

One must frankly admit that there is here a sort of circle from which, so it seems, there is no way to escape. In the order of efficient causes we assume that we are free so that we may think of ourselves as subject to moral laws in the order of ends. And we then think of ourselves as subject to these laws because we have attributed to ourselves freedom of the will. Freedom and self-legislation of the will are both autonomy and are hence reciprocal concepts. Since they are reciprocal, one of them cannot be used to explain the other or to supply its ground, but can at most be used only for logical purposes to bring seemingly different conceptions of the same object under a single concept (just as different fractions of the same value are reduced to lowest terms).

However, one recourse still remains open to us, namely, to inquire whether we do not take one point of view when by means of freedom we think of ourselves as a priori efficient causes, and another point of view when we represent ourselves with reference to our actions as effects which we see before our eyes.

No subtle reflection is required for the following observation, which even the commonest understanding may be supposed to make, though it does so in its own fashion through some obscure discrimination of the faculty of judgment which it calls feeling: all representations that come to us without our choice 451 (such as those of the senses) enable us to know objects only as they affect us; what they may be in themselves remains unknown to us. Therefore, even with the closest attention and the greatest clarity that the understanding can bring to such representations, we can attain to a mere knowledge of appearances but never to knowledge of things in themselves. Once this distinction is made (perhaps merely as a result of observing the difference between representations which are given to us from without and in which we are passive from those which we produce entirely from ourselves and in which we show our own activity); then there follows of itself that we must admit and assume that behind the appearances there is something else which is not appearance, namely, things in themselves. Inasmuch as we can never cognize them except as they affect us [through our senses], we must admit that we can never come any nearer to them nor ever know what they are in themselves. This must provide a distinction, however crude, between a world of sense and a world of understanding; the former can vary considerably according to the difference of sensibility [and sense impressions] in various observers, while the latter, which is the basis of the former, remains always the same. Even with regard to himself, a man cannot presume to know what he is in himself by means of the acquaintance which he has through internal sensation. For since he does not, as it were, create himself and since he acquires the concept of himself not a priori but empirically, it is natural that he can attain knowledge even about himself only through inner sense and therefore only through the appearance of his nature and the way in which his consciousness is affected. But yet he must necessarily assume that beyond his own subject's constitution as composed of nothing but appearances there must be something else as basis, namely, his ego as constituted in itself. Therefore with regard to mere perception and the receptivity of sensations, he must count himself as belonging to the world of sense; but with regard to whatever there may be in him of pure activity (whatever reaches consciousness immediately and not through affecting the senses) he must count himself as belonging to the intellectual world, of which he has, however, no further knowledge.

Such a conclusion must be reached by a reflective man regarding all the things that may be presented 452 to him. It is presumably to be found even in the most ordinary understanding, which, as is well known, is quite prone to expect that behind objects of the senses there is something else invisible and acting of itself. But such understanding spoils all this by making the invisible again sensible, i.e., it wants to make the invisible an object of intuition; and thereby does it become not a bit wiser.

Now man really finds in himself a faculty which distinguishes him from all other things and even from himself insofar as he is affected by objects. That faculty is reason, which as pure spontaneity is elevated even above understanding. For although the latter is also spontaneous and does not, like sense, merely contain representations that arise only when one is affected by things (and is therefore passive), yet understanding can produce by its activity no other concepts than those which merely serve to bring sensuous representations [intuitions] under rules and thereby to unite them in one consciousness. Without this use of sensibility, understanding would think nothing at all. Reason, on the other hand, shows such a pure spontaneity in the case of what are called ideas that it goes far beyond anything that sensibility can offer and shows its highest occupation in distinguishing the world of sense from the world of understanding, thereby prescribing limits to the understanding itself.

Therefore a rational being must regard himself qua intelligence (and hence not from the side of his lower powers) as belonging not to the world of sense but to the world of understanding. Therefore he has two standpoints from which he can regard himself and know laws of the use of his powers and hence of all his actions; first, insofar as he belongs to the world of sense subject to laws of nature (heteronomy); secondly, insofar as he belongs to the intelligible world subject to laws which, independent of nature, are not empirical but are founded only on reason.

As a rational being and hence as belonging to the intelligible world, can man never think of the causality of his own will except under the idea of freedom; for independence from the determining causes of the world of sense (an independence which reason must always attribute to itself) is freedom. Now the idea of freedom is inseparably connected with the concept of autonomy, and this in turn with the universal principle of morality, which ideally is the ground of all 453 actions of rational beings, just as natural law is the ground of all appearances.

The suspicion that we raised earlier is now removed, viz., that there might be a hidden circle involved in our inference from freedom to autonomy, and from this to the moral law—this is to say that we had perhaps laid down the idea of freedom only for the sake of the moral law in order subsequently to infer this law in its turn from freedom, and that we had therefore not been able to assign any ground at all for this law but had only assumed it by begging a principle which well-disposed souls would gladly concede us but which we could never put forward as a demonstrable proposition. But now we see that when we think of ourselves as free, we transfer ourselves into the intelligible world as members and know the autonomy of the will together with its consequence, morality; whereas when we think of ourselves as obligated, we consider ourselves as belonging to the world of sense and yet at the same time to the intelligible world.

How Is a Categorical Imperative Possible?

The rational being counts himself, qua intelligence, as belonging to the intelligible world, and only insofar as he is an efficient cause belonging to the intelligible world does he call his causality a will. But on the other side, he is conscious of himself as being also a part of the world of sense, where his actions are found as mere appearances of that causality. The possibility of these actions cannot, however, be discerned through such causality, which we do not know; rather, these actions as belonging to the world of sense must be viewed as determined by other appearances, namely, desires and inclinations. Therefore, if I were solely a member of the intelligible world, then all my actions would perfectly conform to the principle of the autonomy of a pure will; if I were solely a part of the world of sense, my actions would have to be taken as in complete conformity with the natural law of desires and inclinations, i.e., with the heteronomy of nature. (My actions would in the first case rest on the supreme principle of morality, in the second case on that of happiness.) But the intelligible world contains the ground of the world of sense and therefore also the ground of its laws; consequently, the intelligible world is (and must be thought of as) directly legislative for my will (which belongs wholly to the intelligible world). Therefore, even though on the one hand I must regard myself as a being belonging to the world of sense, yet on the other hand shall I have to know myself as an intelligence and as subject 454 to the law of the intelligible world, i.e., to reason, which contains this law in the idea of freedom, and hence to know myself as subject to the autonomy of the will. Consequently, I must regard the laws of the intelligible world as imperatives for me, and the actions conforming to this principle as duties.

And thus are categorical imperatives possible because the idea of freedom makes me a member of an intelligible world. Now if I were a member of only that world, all my actions *would* always accord with autonomy of the will. But since I intuit myself at the same time as a member of the world of sense, my actions *ought* so to accord. This categorical *ought* presents a synthetic a priori proposition, whereby in addition to my will as affected by sensuous desires there is added further the idea of the same will, but as belonging to the intelligible world, pure and practical of itself, and as containing the supreme condition of the former will insofar as reason is concerned. All this is similar to the way in which concepts [categories] of the understanding, which of themselves signify nothing but the form of law in general, are added to intuitions of the world of sense and thus make possible synthetic a priori propositions, upon which all knowledge of nature rests.

The practical use of ordinary human reason bears out the correctness of this deduction. There is no one, not even the meanest villain, provided only that he is otherwise accustomed to the use of reason, who, when presented with examples of honesty of purpose, of steadfastness in following good maxims, and of sympathy and general benevolence (even when involved with great sacrifices of advantages and comfort) does not wish that he might also possess these qualities. Yet he cannot attain these in himself only because of his inclinations and impulses; but at the same time he wishes to be free from such inclinations which are a burden to him. He thereby proves that by having a will free of sensuous impulses he transfers himself in thought into an order of things entirely different from that of his desires in the field of sensibility. Since he cannot expect to obtain by the aforementioned wish any gratification of his desires or any condition that would satisfy any of his actual or even conceivable inclinations (inasmuch as through such an expectation the very idea that elicited the wish would be deprived of its preeminence) he can only expect a greater intrinsic worth of his own person. This better person he believes himself to be when he transfers himself to the standpoint of a member of the intelligi- 455 ble world, to which he is involuntarily forced by the idea of freedom, i.e., of being independent of determination by causes of the world of sense. From this standpoint he is conscious of having a good will, which by his own admission constitutes the law for the bad will belonging to him as a member of the world of sense—a law whose authority he acknowledges even while he transgresses it. The moral *ought* is, therefore, a necessary *would* insofar as he is a member of the intelligible world, and is thought by him as an *ought* only insofar as he regards himself as being at the same time a member of the world of sense.

Concerning the Extreme Limit of All Practical Philosophy

All men think of themselves as free as far as their will is concerned. Hence arise all judgments upon actions as being such as ought to have been done, even though they were not done. But this freedom is not a concept of experience, nor can it be such, since it always holds, even though experience shows the opposite of those requirements represented as necessary under the presupposition of freedom. On the other hand, it is just as necessary that whatever happens should be determined without any exception according to laws of nature; and this necessity of nature is likewise no concept of experience, just because it involves the concept of necessity and thus of a priori knowledge. But this concept of nature is confirmed by experience and must inevitably be presupposed if there is to be possible experience, which is coherent knowledge of the objects of sense in accordance with universal laws. Freedom is, therefore, only an idea of reason whose objective reality is in itself questionable; but nature is a concept of the understanding, which proves, and necessarily must prove, its reality by examples from experience.

There arises from this a dialectic of reason, since the freedom attributed to the will seems to contradict the necessity of nature. And even though at this parting of the ways reason for speculative purposes finds the road of natural necessity much better worn and more serviceable than that of freedom, yet for practi- 456 cal purposes the footpath of freedom is the only one upon which it is possible to make use of reason in our conduct. Therefore, it is just as impossible for the most subtle philosophy as for the most ordinary human reason to argue away freedom. Hence philosophy must assume that no real contradiction will be found between freedom and natural necessity in the same human actions, for it cannot give up the concept of nature any more than that of freedom.

Nevertheless, even though one might never be able to comprehend how freedom is possible, yet this apparent contradiction must at least be removed in a convincing manner. For if the thought of freedom contradicts itself or nature, which is equally necessary, then freedom would have to be completely given up in favor of natural necessity.

It would, however, be impossible to escape this contradiction if the subject, deeming himself free, were to think of himself in the same sense or in the very same relationship when he calls himself free as when he assumes himself subject to the law of nature regarding the same action. Therefore, an unavoidable problem of speculative philosophy is at least to show that its illusion regarding the contradiction rests on our thinking of man in a different sense and relation when we call him free from when we regard him as being a part of nature and hence as subject to the laws of nature. Hence it must show not only that both can coexist very well, but that both must be thought of as necessarily united in the same subject; for otherwise no explanation could be given as to why reason should be burdened with an idea which involves us in a perplexity that is solely embarrassing to reason in its theoretic use, even though it may without contradiction be united with another idea that is sufficiently established. This duty, however, is incumbent solely on speculative philosophy in order that it may clear the way for practical philosophy. Thus the philosopher has no option as to whether he will remove the apparent contradiction or leave it untouched; for in the latter case the theory regarding this could be *bonum vacans*,[56] into the possession of which the fatalist can justifiably enter and chase all morality out of its supposed property as occupying it without title.

Nevertheless, one cannot here say as yet that the boundary of practical philosophy begins. For the settlement of the controversy does not belong to practical philosophy; the latter only requires speculative reason 457 to put an end to the dissension in which it is entangled as regards theoretical questions in order that practical reason may have rest and security from external attacks that might make disputable the ground upon which it wants to build.

The just claim to freedom of the will made even by ordinary human reason is founded on the consciousness and the admitted presupposition that reason is independent of mere subjective determination by causes which together make up what belongs only to sensation and comes under the general designation of sensibility. Regarding himself in this way as intelligence, man thereby puts himself into another order of things. And when he thinks of himself as intelligence endowed with a will and consequently with causality, he puts himself into relation with determining grounds of a kind altogether different from the kind when he perceives himself as a phenomenon in the world of sense (as he really is also) and subjects his causality to external determination according to laws of nature. Now he soon realizes that both can—and indeed must—hold good at the same time. For there is not the slightest contradiction involved in saying that a thing as appearance (belonging to the world of sense) is subject to certain laws, while it is independent of those laws when regarded as a thing or being in itself. That man must represent and think of himself in this twofold way rests, on the one hand, upon the consciousness of himself as an object affected through

56. [Vacant property.]

the senses and, on the other hand, upon the consciousness of himself as intelligence, i.e., as independent of sensuous impulses in his use of reason (and hence as belonging to the intelligible world).

And hence man claims that he has a will which reckons to his account nothing that belongs merely to his desires and inclinations, and which, on the contrary, thinks of actions that can be performed only by disregarding all desires and sensuous incitements as being possible and as indeed being necessary for him. The causality of such actions lies in man as intelligence and lies in the laws of such effects and actions as are in accordance with principles of an intelligible world, of which he knows nothing more than that in such a world reason alone, and indeed pure reason independent of sensibility, gives the law. Furthermore, since he is in such a world his proper self only as intelligence (whereas regarded as a human being he is merely an appearance of himself), those laws apply to him immediately and categorically. Consequently, incitements from inclinations and impulses (and hence from the whole nature of the world of senses) cannot impair the laws of his willing insofar 458 as he is intelligence. Indeed he does not even hold himself responsible for such inclinations and impulses or ascribe them to his proper self, i.e., his will, although he does ascribe to his will any indulgence which he might extend to them if he allowed them any influence on his maxims to the detriment of the rational laws of his will.

When practical reason thinks itself into an intelligible world, it does not in the least thereby transcend its limits, as it would if it tried to enter it by intuition or sensation. The thought of an intelligible world is merely negative as regards the world of sense. The latter world does not give reason any laws for determining the will and is positive only in this single point, viz., it simultaneously combines freedom as negative determination with a positive faculty and even a causality of reason. This causality is designated as a will to act in such a way that the principle of actions may accord with the essential character of a rational cause, i.e., with the condition that the maxim of these actions have universal validity as a law. But if practical reason were to bring in an object of the will, i.e., a motive of action, from the intelligible world, then it would overstep its boundaries and pretend to be acquainted with something of which it knows nothing. The concept of an intelligible world is thus only a point of view which reason sees itself compelled to take outside of appearances in order to think of itself as practical. If the influences of sensibility were determining for man, reason would not be able to take this point of view, which is nonetheless necessary if he is not to be denied the consciousness of himself as intelligence and hence as a rational cause that is active through reason, i.e., free in its operation. This thought certainly involves the idea of an order and a legislation different from that of the mechanism of nature which applies to the world of sense; and it makes necessary the concept of an intelligible world (i.e., the whole of rational beings as things in themselves). But it makes not the slightest claim to anything more than to think of such a world as regards merely its formal condition—i.e., the universality of the will's maxims as laws and thus the will's autonomy, which alone is consistent with freedom. On the contrary, all laws determined by reference to an object yield heteronomy, which can be found only in laws of nature and can apply only to the world of sense.

But reason would overstep all its bounds if it under- 459 took to explain how pure reason can be practical. This is exactly the same problem as explaining how freedom is possible.

For we can explain nothing but what we can reduce to laws whose object can be given in some possible experience. But freedom is a mere idea, whose objective reality can in no way be shown in accordance with laws of nature and consequently not in any possible experience. Therefore, the idea of freedom can never admit of comprehension or even of insight, because it cannot by any analogy have an example falling under it. It holds only as a necessary presupposition of reason in a being who believes himself conscious of a will, i.e., of a faculty distinct from mere desire (namely, a faculty of determining himself to action as intelligence and hence in accordance with laws of reason independently of natural instincts). But where determination according to laws of nature ceases, there likewise ceases all explanation and nothing remains but defense, i.e., refutation of the objections of those who profess to have seen deeper into the essence of things and thereupon boldly declare freedom to be impossible. One can only show them that their supposed discovery of a contradiction lies nowhere but here: in order to make the law of nature applicable to human actions, they have necessarily had to regard man as an appearance; and now when they are required to think of man qua intelligence as thing in himself as well, they still persist in regarding him as appearance. In that case, to be sure, the exemption of man's causality (i.e., his will) from all the natural laws of the world of sense would, as regards one and the same subject, give rise to a contradiction. But this disappears if they would but bethink themselves and admit, as is reasonable, that behind appearances there must lie as their ground also things in themselves (though hidden) and that the laws of their operations cannot be expected to be the same as those that govern their appearances.

460 The subjective impossibility of explaining freedom of the will is the same as the impossibility of discovering and explaining an interest[57] which man can take in moral laws. Nevertheless, he does indeed take such an interest, the basis of which in us is called moral feeling. Some people have falsely construed this feeling to be the standard of our moral judgment, whereas it must rather be regarded as the subjective effect that the law exercises upon the will, while reason alone furnishes the objective grounds of such moral feeling.

In order to will what reason alone prescribes as an *ought* for sensuously affected rational beings, there certainly must be a power of reason to infuse a feeling of pleasure or satisfaction in the fulfillment of duty, and hence there has to be a causality of reason to determine sensibility in accordance with rational principles. But it is quite impossible to discern, i.e., to make a priori conceivable, how a mere thought which itself contains nothing sensuous can produce a sensation of pleasure or displeasure. For here is a special kind of causality regarding which, as with all causality, we can determine nothing a priori but must consult experience alone. However, experience can provide us with no relation of cause and effect except between two objects of experience. But in this case pure reason by means of mere ideas (which furnish no object at all for experience) is to be the cause of an effect that admittedly lies in experience. Consequently, there is for us men no possibility at all for an explanation as to how and why the universality of a maxim as a law, and hence morality, interests us. This much only is certain: the moral law is valid for us not because it interests us (for this is heteronomy and the dependence of practical reason on sensibility, viz., on an underlying feeling whereby reason could *461* never be morally legislative); but, rather, the moral law interests us because it is valid for us as men, since it has sprung from our will as intelligence and hence from our proper self. But what belongs to mere appearance is necessarily subordinated by reason to the nature of the thing in itself.

Thus the question as to how a categorical imperative is possible can be answered to the extent that there can be supplied the sole presupposition under which such an imperative is alone possible—namely, the idea of freedom. The necessity of this presupposition is discernible, and this much is sufficient for the practical use of reason, i.e., for being convinced as to the validity of this imperative, and hence also of the moral law; but how this presupposition itself is possible can never be discerned by any human reason. However, on the presupposition of freedom of the will of an intelligence, there necessarily follows the will's autonomy as the formal condition under which alone the will can be determined. To presuppose this freedom of the will (without involving any contradiction with the principle of natural necessity in the connection of appearances in the world of sense) is not only quite possible (as speculative philosophy can show), but is without any further condition also necessary for a rational being conscious of his causality through reason and hence conscious of a will (which is different from desires) as he makes such freedom in practice, i.e., in idea, the underlying con-

57. Interest is that by which reason becomes practical, i.e., a cause determining the will. Therefore one says of rational beings only that they take an interest in something; nonrational creatures feel only sensuous impulses. Reason takes an immediate interest in the action only when the universal validity of the maxim of the action is a sufficient determining ground of the will. Such an interest alone is pure. But when reason is able to determine the will only by means of another object of desire or under the presupposition of some special feeling in the subject, then reason takes only a mediate interest in the action. And since reason of itself alone without the help of experience can discover neither objects of the will nor a special feeling underlying the will, the latter interest would be only empirical and not a pure rational interest. The logical interest of reason (viz., to extend its insights) is never immediate, but presupposes purposes for which reason might be used.

dition of all his voluntary actions. But how pure reason can be practical by itself without other incentives taken from whatever source—i.e., how the mere principle of the universal validity of all reason's maxims as laws (which would certainly be the form of a pure practical reason) can by itself, without any matter (object) of the will in which some antecedent interest might be taken, furnish an incentive and produce an interest which could be called purely moral; or, in other words, how pure reason could be practical: to explain all this is quite beyond the power of human reason, and all the effort and work of seeking such an explanation is wasted.

It is just the same as if I tried to find out how freedom itself is possible as causality of a will. For I 462 thereby leave the philosophical basis of explanation, and I have no other basis. Now I could indeed flutter about in the world of intelligences, i.e., in the intelligible world still remaining to me. But even though I have an idea of such a world—an idea which has its own good grounds—yet I have not the slightest acquaintance with such a world and can never attain such acquaintance by all the efforts of my natural faculty of reason. This intelligible world signifies only a something that remains over when I have excluded from the determining grounds of my will everything that belongs to the world of sense, so as to restrict the principle of having all motives come from the field of sensibility. By so doing I set bounds to this field and show that it does not contain absolutely everything within itself but that beyond it there is still something more, regarding which, however, I have no further acquaintance. After the exclusion of all matter, i.e., cognition of objects, from pure reason which thinks this ideal, nothing remains over for me except such reason's form, viz., the practical law of the universal validity of maxims; and in conformity with this law I think of reason in its relation to a pure intelligible world as a possible efficient cause, i.e., as a cause determining the will. An incentive must in this case be wholly absent; this idea of an intelligible world would here have to be itself the incentive or have to be that in which reason originally took an interest. But to make this conceivable is precisely the problem that we cannot solve.

Here then is the extreme limit of all moral inquiry. To determine this limit is of great importance for the following considerations. On the one hand, reason should not, to the detriment of morals, search around in the world of sense for the supreme motive and for some interest that is conceivable but is nonetheless empirical. On the other hand, reason should not flap its wings impotently, without leaving the spot, in a space that for it is empty, namely, the space of transcendent concepts that is called the intelligible world, and thereby lose itself among mere phantoms of the brain. Furthermore, the idea of a pure intelligible world regarded as a whole of all intelligences to which we ourselves belong as rational beings (even though we are from another standpoint also members of the world of sense) remains always a useful and permissible idea for the purpose of a rational belief, although all knowledge ends at its boundary. This idea produces in us a lively interest in the moral law by means of the splendid ideal of a universal kingdom of ends in themselves (rational beings), to which we can be- 463 long as members only if we carefully conduct ourselves according to maxims of freedom as if they were laws of nature.

Concluding Remark

The speculative use of reason with regard to nature leads to the absolute necessity of some supreme cause of the world. The practical use of reason with reference to freedom leads also to absolute necessity, but only to the necessity of the laws of the actions of a rational being as such. Now it is an essential principle of all use of our reason to push its knowledge to a consciousness of its necessity (for without necessity there would be no rational knowledge). But there is an equally essential restriction of the same reason that it cannot have insight into the necessity either of what is or what does happen or of what should happen, unless there is presupposed a condition under which it is or does happen or should happen. In this way, however, the satisfaction of reason is only further and further postponed by the continual inquiry after the condition. Reason, therefore, restlessly seeks the unconditionally necessary and sees itself compelled to assume this without having any means of making such necessity conceivable; reason is happy enough if only it can find a concept which is compatible with this assumption. Hence there is no fault in our deduction of the supreme principle of morality, but rather a reproach which must be made against human reason generally, involved in the fact that reason cannot render conceivable the absolute necessity of an unconditioned practical law (such as the categorical imperative must be). Reason cannot be blamed for not being willing to explain this necessity by means of a condition, namely, by basing it on some underlying interest, because in that case the law would no longer be moral, i.e., a supreme law of freedom. And so even though we do not indeed grasp the practical unconditioned necessity of the moral imperative, we do nevertheless grasp its inconceivability. This is all that can be fairly asked of a philosophy which strives in its principles to reach the very limit of human reason.

G.W.F. Hegel

G. W.F. Hegel was born in Stuttgart, Germany, in 1770. He taught at the University of Jena, served eight years as rector at a Gymnasium in Nuremberg and two years at the University of Heidelberg, and taught at the University of Berlin until his death in 1831.

Hegel's philosophy is called "Absolute Idealism," the view that all reality is shaped and constituted by the mind. But it is important to see that this kind of idealism is quite different from the subjective idealism of someone like Berkeley. First, the German word for "mind," *Geist*, refers not just to individual minds, but to something that is essentially shared and is realized in what people *do*. It is closer to what we mean by "spirit" when we speak of the "spirit on campus" or a team's "fighting spirit." And, second, instead of denying the existence of matter, Hegel's idealism holds that mind needs a material world in order to be able to express and fulfill itself in a concrete form. In this respect, the "ideas" in this idealism are more like the ordering Ideas in Plato's philosophy than like Berkeley's mental ideas. To say that mind constitutes reality, then, is to say that there is a rational order underlying all reality. Or, as Hegel puts it, "the real is rational and the rational is real."

Hegel's philosophy grows out of Kant's theory in *Critique of Pure Reason*. Kant argued that reality is not something that is simply "out there" waiting for us to try to grasp it, but is instead something that is constituted through our cognitive activity as knowers. The point is that "transcendental apperception," the pure subject, confers form on reality through pure intuition and, most important for Hegel, through the synthesizing power of its concepts. Since our conceptualizing makes possible the objective world we encounter in our experience, we can have knowledge only of "phenomena," that is, things as they appear to us through our concepts.

Hegel draws from Kant the idea that the pure conceptualizing subject (or, as he calls it, the "concept") is the source of the necessary and universal structure permeating all reality. But he rejects Kant's claim that we can never know reality as it is in itself. If we can talk about a reality that is supposedly beyond our comprehension, Hegel says, then we have already comprehended it, and so it *is* known. Thus, there is no room for the notion of a reality that is alien to or totally distinct from the mind. Moreover, Hegel rejects Kant's uncritical assumption that the Newtonian science of his own day was the highest truth to which science could aspire. In Hegel's view, any science that regards the world as consisting of natural kinds simply "out there" in the world is only a temporary stage on the way to true science. Such a view, which Hegel calls "Understanding," will have to give way to "Reason," a more holistic science that grasps the fact that the nature of anything is defined by its relation to what it is not—its "other" or "negation"—within the systematic whole constituted by *Geist*. At the level of Reason, all dualistic oppositions—including those of subject and object, mind and matter, self and others—will be seen for what they are: only partial and distorted manifestations of *Geist*.

The *Phenomenology of Spirit* is supposed to lead us to true science and its recognition of the identity of thinking and being. The book's Introduction begins with a critique of the assumption, fundamental to traditional epistemology, that we are at the most basic levels *minds* attempting to correctly represent an ultimate *reality* (the "Truth," the "Absolute," or the "in itself") presumed to exist totally independent of our minds. Given this subject/object model of our situation, Hegel believes, skepticism is inevitable, for once subject and object are separated, there is no way to find out whether our knowing (regarded as an active tool or a passive medium) is giving us an accurate picture of reality. Despite this problem, however, scientific inquiry keeps making important advances in knowledge, and this seems to suggest that what is problematic is not science, but the uncritical presuppositions built into epistemology's subject/object model.

In order to overcome the subject/object model, it is necessary to work within the confines of science as it is today, within what Hegel calls "apparent science," and to get that science to recognize that it is inadequate by its own criteria. Hegel's conception of knowledge as an appearing, a phenomenon, displays his profound insight into the *historical* nature of knowledge. In his view, history has been characterized by a series of different "shapes" (*Gestalten*) of consciousness, what we today might call "world-views" or "paradigms," which have evolved from the most elementary models to the most sophisticated ones in our contemporary world. What leads consciousness to move from more primitive models to more sophisticated ones is the discovery of internal inconsistencies within the earlier outlooks. This "dialectical" movement will continue, Hegel thinks, until consciousness goes through all possible models of knowledge and arrives at absolute truth (the unity of all reality under the Concept, which he calls the "Idea").

The two excerpted sections of the *Phenomenology* following the Introduction show Hegel's method of immanent critique and determinate negation at work. The section called "Sense Certainty" is especially interesting because it tries to show that the idea of "knowledge by acquaintance"—a knowledge of particulars that is directly "given" in sensory experience—is incoherent. This attack on "the myth of the given" (as it is now called) builds on the assumption that any form of knowledge must be able to formulate its knowledge-claim in such a way that it gives determinate information valid for different times and contexts. The argument then points out that the purely ostensive specification of the known presupposed by sense certainty must take the form of a bare "this—here—now." Such a knowledge-claim will be inadequate by the criteria of genuine knowledge, however, because the indexicals "this," "here," and "now" change their referents depending on context and so cannot provide fixed and determinate information. In order to tie down the meanings of such terms, we would need to say something like *this* red pen is *here*, on so-and-so's desk, *now*, on such-and-such a day and time. But these specifications require the use of concepts or universals, showing that the attempt to understand knowledge must move from immediate sensation to what Hegel calls "perception."

"Mastery and Slavery" appears later in the *Phenomenology* and marks a transition from considering knowledge as the personal undertaking of an individual (as in Descartes) to a social conception of knowledge in which a universal "Reason" is grounded in mutual recognition among subjects. The upshot of the master/slave dialectic is to show that relations based on subordination preclude the possibility of recognition and so must be superseded if the "pure universality of thought" is to be achieved.

• • •

Among the many fine overviews of Hegel's thought are Robert C. Solomon's *In the Spirit of Hegel* (Oxford: Oxford University Press, 1983), Charles Taylor's *Hegel* (Cambridge: Cambridge University Press, 1975), and Robert B. Pippin's *Hegel's Idealism: The Satisfaction of Self-Consciousness* (Cambridge: Cambridge University Press, 1989). Kenneth R. Westphal, *Hegel's Epistemology: A Philosophical Introduction to the "Phenomenology of Spirit"* (Indianapolis: Hackett Publishing Company, 2003) provides insight into Hegel's method. Frederick Beiser's *Cambridge Companion to Hegel* (Cambridge: Cambridge University Press, 1993) is a good collection.

Charles Guignon

Phenomenology of Spirit

INTRODUCTION

It is a natural supposition that in philosophy, prior to entering into the matter itself—namely, the actual knowledge of that which truly is—it is first necessary to examine that knowledge either regarded as the tool through which we master the Absolute, or else regarded as the means by which we get a glimpse of it. The concern seems justified, partly because there are different types of knowledge and, among these, one might be more expeditious than the other for reaching this final goal, and thus there could be a wrong choice among them. And this is also partly because—inasmuch as knowledge is a faculty of a specific type and compass—without more precise specifications of its nature and limits, clouds of error could be grasped rather than the heaven of truth. This concern must in fact transform itself into the conviction that the entire starting-point is contradictory in its concept, i.e., that what is in itself can be acquired for consciousness by means of knowledge, and also that there is an absolute divide and boundary between knowledge and the Absolute. For if knowledge is the tool for mastering the Absolute, then it is immediately striking that the application of a tool to any material does not leave it as it was for itself, but rather undertakes a formation and alteration of it. But if knowledge is not a tool of our own making, but to a certain extent a passive medium instead, through which the light of truth reaches us, then too we do not attain to it as it is in itself, but rather the way it is through and in this medium. In both cases we make use of a means, which immediately produces the opposite of its purpose; or rather the contradiction is the fact that we make use of any means at all. It seems indeed that this sorry state of affairs could be remedied through an acquaintance with the ways *the tool* works, for that is what makes it possible in the representation of the Absolute we gain through the tool, to subtract from the result gained with the tool that part which belongs to the tool, and thereby attain the truth in a pure way. However, this improvement would in fact only bring us back where we were before. If we remove from a crafted thing the ways in which a tool has affected it, then the thing—in this case, the Absolute—is for us precisely whatever it was before such a superfluous effort. If through the tool the Absolute is only brought nearer to us generally, without changing anything about it, somewhat like the lime-twig[1] used for catching birds, then it would likely mock this cunning, if it were not in and for itself already with us and did not want to be so. Knowledge would in such a case be cunning, since through its manifold efforts it puts on airs of doing something entirely different than bringing out the immediate and thus effortless relation. Or, if the test of the knowledge that we represent to ourselves as a *medium* teaches us to know the law of its refraction, then it is likewise of no use to subtract it from the result; for it is not the refraction of the beam, but the beam itself through which the truth moves us and that is knowledge, and abstracted from this only the mere direction or the empty locus would be indicated for us.

Meanwhile, if the concern about falling into error brings with it a distrust of science, which, without any such reservations, goes on with the work itself and actually knows things, then it cannot be said ahead of time why the opposite would not apply, that we should mistrust this mistrust, that this fear of error is not itself the error. In point of fact this concern presupposes that something is true, indeed that many things are true, and props its reservations and consequences on these grounds, which have to be tested first as to whether they are the truth. To wit, it presupposes *representations* of *knowledge* as a *tool* and *medium,* and also a *differentiation of ourselves from that knowledge;* but primarily this, that the Absolute stands *on one side* and *knowledge on the other side* for itself

1. [Spreading lime on twigs was a common way of luring birds.—A.T. and J.H.S.]

and separate from the Absolute, but nevertheless knowledge is something real or true, even though it is outside the Absolute and in fact outside of truth—an assumption by virtue of which that which is called a fear of error can be recognized instead as a fear of the truth.

This consequence derives from the fact that the Absolute alone is true, or that the true alone is absolute. It can be refuted by differentiating a kind of knowledge which is not recognized as Absolute, as science desires it, but is yet true; and knowledge in general, even if it is incapable of grasping the Absolute, is still capable of grasping other truths. But we see right away that such talking back and forth results in a nebulous distinction between something absolutely true and something otherwise true, and then "Absolute," "Knowledge," etc., are words which presuppose a meaning, and establishing that is our first concern.

Instead of concerning ourselves with such useless representations and ways of speaking about knowledge as a tool for grasping the Absolute or as a medium through which we can glimpse the truth, etc., relationships which come at the end of all these representations of knowledge separated from the Absolute, and an Absolute separated from knowledge;—instead of making up excuses which the very incapacity of science itself creates out of the assumptions about such relations, we could be freed from the strains of science and simultaneously give the appearance of a serious and zealous effort, if the use of related terms like "Absolute," "Knowledge," "Objective," and "Subjective" (and countless others whose meaning is assumed to be generally known) could be seen as a deception. And then, instead of plaguing ourselves with answers to all these things, they could be rejected right off as accidental and arbitrary representations. The pretense, partly that the significance of these terms is generally known, and partly that anybody even has the concept of them, seems rather to spare us from the main issue, which is to present this concept. On the contrary, with more justification one could spare the effort of taking any notice of such representations and ways of speaking by means of which we would be protected from science itself; for they only constitute a mere appearance of knowledge, which immediately disappears once science emerges. But science itself, inasmuch as it takes the stage, makes an appearance; its taking the stage is not yet science amplified and extended in its truth. To that extent it is a matter of indifference *that* it presents itself as an appearing, because it takes the stage *alongside another* knowledge, or calls that other untrue knowledge the appearance. Science must liberate itself from this seeming, and it can only do this by turning against it. For science can neither simply discard untrue knowledge as an ordinary view of things, and insure that it is an entirely different [kind of] knowledge and that such knowing is nothing at all as far as science is concerned, nor can it appeal to the intimation of something better in itself. Through such an *assurance* science clarified its Being as power; but the untrue knowing also makes the same appeal, that *it is*, and *assures* that science is nothing as far as it is concerned. *One* bland assurance counts exactly as much as the other. Even less can science invoke the better intuition which is present in the untrue knowledge, and which is therein the pointer toward science, for on the one hand that would once again be invoking a Being; but on the other hand science would be appealing to itself as the manner in which the untrue knowing exists, i.e., a bad manner of its being, and rather appealing to its appearing than the way it is in and for itself. For this reason the presentation of knowing as it appears should be undertaken next.

But since this presentation has as its object only knowing as it appears, this presentation itself does not appear to be free science in its characteristically self-moving form, but from this standpoint it can be taken as the way of natural consciousness, which presses toward true knowledge; or the way of the soul, which traverses the series of its forms as though stations marked out for it ahead of time by its own nature,[2] so that it might purify itself into spirit, to the extent that it arrives at a recognition of what it is in itself by means of the complete experience of itself.

Natural consciousness will prove to be merely the concept of knowledge, not real knowledge. But to the extent that it considers itself to be unmediated real knowledge, this path has a negative significance for it, and that which is rather a loss of itself counts

2. [A possible reference to the Stations of the Cross, a series of representations of the sufferings of Jesus, set up in a church and visited for prayer.]

instead as a realization of the concept; for along this path natural consciousness loses its own truth. For that reason it can be seen as the way of *doubt,* or more properly the way of despair. For along that path what happens is not what is usually understood as doubt—a jogging of this or that presumed truth, whereupon there is an appropriate re-disappearance of the doubt and a return to the truth, so that in the end the matter is understood as it was before. Rather this way is the conscious insight into the untruth of apparent knowledge, for which the unrealized concept is instead what is truly most real. Thus this self-fulfilling skepticism also is not that for which a serious zeal for truth and science had imagined it had prepared and armed itself to gain mastery, namely with the *intention* of proving everything oneself through science and only following one's own convictions, not giving oneself over to the thoughts of others, on their authority—or better yet, to produce everything oneself and to consider only one's own activity as true. The series of these forms, which consciousness itself traverses along this path, is really the thoroughgoing history of the *education* of consciousness itself in the direction of science. That intention presents education in a simplistic manner as though the intention immediately made the matter over and done with, whereas this path is really a pursuit against untruth. To follow one's own conviction is, to be sure, something more than submitting to authority; but the content itself does not necessarily change on account of the reversal—maintaining something on the basis of authority and maintaining it because of one's own conviction—nor has truth necessarily replaced error. To be stuck in a system of opining or pre-judgments on the basis of the authority of others or out of one's own conviction is differentiated only by the vanity which dwells in the latter mode. The skepticism which extends to the entire compass of appearing consciousness, in contrast, first renders spirit fit to test what truth is, by bringing to bear a despair of the so-called natural representations, thoughts, and opinions. It is a matter of indifference whether they are called one's own or come from elsewhere, and with which consciousness, proceeding *straightaway* to proofs, is still filled and burdened, but for that reason it is in fact incapable of that which it wants to undertake.

The *completeness* of the forms of the not-real consciousness will manifest itself through the necessity of their progression and connection. To make this understandable, it can be remarked in general at the outset that the presentation of the not-true consciousness in its untruth is not merely a *negative* movement. Natural consciousness generally has such a one-sided view of not-real consciousness. And any knowledge which makes this one-sidedness into its essence is one of the shapes of such an incomplete consciousness as will occur along the pathway itself and which will eventually show up there. It is skepticism, to be precise, which always sees only *pure Nothing* in the result, and abstracts therefrom, that this Nothing is certainly the Nothing *of that from which it results.* The Nothing, however, taken as the Nothing of that from which it derives, is in fact only the true result. It is therewith itself something *determinate* and it has a *content.* Skepticism, which concludes with the abstraction of the Nothing or with emptiness, can go no further with this, but must await whether and what new thing presents itself, in order to cast it into the same empty abyss. Contrariwise, inasmuch as the result is grasped as *determinate* negation, as it is in truth, a new form has immediately sprung up, and in the negation the transition is made through which the progress over the complete series of forms results of itself.

The *goal,* however, is as necessarily marked out for knowledge as is the series of progressive steps. The goal is the point where knowledge no longer has to surpass itself, where it discovers itself, and where the concept corresponds to the object and the object corresponds to the concept. Progress toward this goal is therefore also unstoppable, and cannot find satisfaction at any earlier station. Whatever is limited to a natural life is incapable of going on its own beyond its immediate existence; but it is driven beyond that through something else, and this "being torn from itself" is its death. But consciousness for itself *is* its *concept,* and therewith immediately a going beyond the limited, and, since that limited belongs to it, going beyond itself. Thus even with the particular the Beyond is also posited, even if it is only *next to* the limited, as in the case of spatial perception. Consciousness therefore suffers this violence coming from within itself, spoiling its limited satisfaction. In the presence of the feeling of this force its anxiety in the face of the truth may recede, and strive to uphold that whose loss is threatened. But it can find no rest: Even if it gets stuck in thoughtless inertia, thought encroaches on thoughtlessness, and its restlessness disturbs inertia. Or if it fortifies itself as sensitivity, which insures that it will find everything *good after its own kind,* this insurance suffers a parallel violence from reason, which, on just those grounds, finds something that is not good, namely the fact that it is only a "kind." Or else fear of the truth may lead this fear to hide from itself and others behind seeming, as though precisely the heated fervor for truth makes it so difficult, in fact impossible, to find any other truth than that of vanity, and these thoughts are at least more clever than those which somebody has from himself or from somebody else. This vanity, which knows how to make every truth vain and thus returns back to itself on the basis of that, and ruminates on this its own understanding, which always knows how to dissolve all thoughts and to find the dry Ego instead of any content—this vanity is a satisfaction for which it must be left to itself, for it flees the universal and seeks only that which is for itself.

Since this has been said in a preliminary and general way about the manner and necessity of the progression, it could be helpful to remind ourselves of the *method of explication.* This presentation as the *posture* of *science* toward *apparent knowledge,* represented as the *investigation* and *testing of the reality of recognition,* apparently cannot take place without some presupposition underlying it as its *measure.* The test consists in laying down the accepted measure and in the resulting equality or inequality of that which is being tested, and therewith the decision whether it is correct or incorrect; and the measure in general, and likewise science, if it were the measure, is thereby taken to be the *essence* or *the in-itself.* But here, where science first comes upon the stage, it has justified neither itself as the essence or the in-itself, nor anything else; and without some such thing no proof can apparently take place.

This contradiction and its disposal will become more determinate when we first remember the abstract determinations of knowledge and of truth, as they come before consciousness. Consciousness, namely, *distinguishes* something from itself, to which it is simultaneously *related;* or as this takes on expression, it is something *for consciousness,* and the determinate side of this *relation,* or of the *Being* of something *for a consciousness* is *knowledge.* From this Being for an other, however, we distinguish the *Being-in-itself;* and that which is related to knowledge is likewise distinguished therefrom and posited as *being* even outside this relationship; this side of the in-itself is called *truth.* What may actually be in these determinations does not concern us any further here; inasmuch as appearing knowledge is our present object, its determinations are at first taken up as they immediately present themselves; and in that way they likely do present themselves just about as they are grasped.

If we now investigate the truth of knowledge, it seems that we investigate what it is *in itself.* But in this investigation it is *our* object, it is *for us;* and its *in-itself,* which manifests itself, would instead be its Being *for us.* What we would maintain to be its essence is instead not its truth, but only our knowledge of the object. The essence, or the measure, would fall within us, and that which is supposedly contrasted with it and which should be decided by means of that contrast, does not have to recognize that.

But the nature of the object we investigate spares us this separation—or this seeming separation—and presupposition. Consciousness finds its measure within itself, and the investigation thereby becomes a comparison of itself with itself; for the investigation just undertaken falls within itself. There is in it something which is *for an other;* in other words, it has in general the determination of the moment of knowledge in itself; at the same time for consciousness this other is not only *for it,* but also outside this relation or *in itself:* the moment of truth. We do have the measure for what consciousness clarifies within itself as the *in-itself* or the *true,* which it itself establishes as something to measure its knowledge against. If we call *knowledge* the *concept,* but refer to the essence or the *true* as the Being or the *object,* then the test consists in making sure that the concept corresponds to the object. But if we call *the essence* or the in-itself *of the object* the concept, and instead understand by *object,* i.e., as it is *for another,* then the test consists in making sure that the object corresponds to its concept. One can probably see that both are the same; but it is essential to hold fast to this for the entire investigation, so that both these moments, *concept* and *object, being-for-another* and *being-in-itself* themselves fall within the knowledge that we are investigating. For this reason it is not necessary for us to bring along measures and apply *our* brainstorms and thoughts in the investigation; and by virtue of the fact that we leave these aside, we arrive at the point that we observe the thing as it is *in and for itself*.

But it is not only from this angle that any additional contribution from us is superfluous—that concept and object, measure and the thing to be tested, are both present in consciousness itself. But we are also spared the effort of comparing the two and of the actual *testing*, so that, to the extent that consciousness tests itself, from this angle also the only thing remaining is merely to watch what happens. For consciousness is on the one hand consciousness of the object and on the other hand consciousness of itself; consciousness of that which is true for it and consciousness of its knowledge thereof. Inasmuch as both are *for the same*, namely consciousness, it itself is their comparison; it comes to be *for the same*, whether its knowledge of the object corresponds to that or not. For consciousness the object seems in fact to be only as it knows it; and it seems as though it cannot get behind the way the object is *not for consciousness*, but the way it is *in itself*; and therefore it also cannot test its knowledge therewith. But precisely because it is aware of an object at all, the distinction is already at hand, so that for it the *in itself* is a different moment, whereas knowledge or the Being of the object is *for* consciousness. Testing rests on this differentiation, which is at hand. If neither of these corresponds to the other, then it seems that consciousness must change its knowledge, in order to make it fit the object; but in the changing of the knowledge, the object itself in actuality changes for consciousness; because the knowledge at hand was essentially a knowledge of the object; and with this knowledge the object too becomes something different, because it belonged essentially to this knowledge. It thus develops for consciousness that what for it was previously *in itself* is not in-itself, or that it was only an *in-itself* for it. Since it thus finds that its knowledge does not correspond to the object, the object does not persist either. In other words the measure of the test is changed, when that whose measure it was supposed to be does not survive the test. And the test is not only a test of knowledge, but also of the measure.

This *dialectical* movement, which consciousness exercises on itself—on its knowledge as well as on its object—*to the extent that the new true object arises* from it, this is actually that which is called *experience*. It is in this connection that a moment is to be highlighted in the above-mentioned course of things, through which a new light will spread on the scientific side of the following presentation. Consciousness knows *something*, and this object is the essence or the *in-itself*; but it is also the *in-itself* for consciousness, and therewith enters the ambiguity of this truth. We see that consciousness now has two objects, the one is the first *in-itself*, the second is the *being this in-itself for consciousness*. The latter seems at first to be only the reflection of consciousness into its own self, a representation, not of an object, but only of its knowledge of the object. However, as was previously shown, the first object changes itself thereby for consciousness; it stops being the in-itself and becomes for it something which is an *in-itself* only *for it*; but then it results that *the being-in-itself of this for-it* is the true, but that means this is the *essence*, or its *object*. This new object contains the nullity of the first, the object is now the experience attained on the basis of the former.

In this representation of the course of experience there is a moment which makes it seem that it does not conform to what is usually understood by experience: The transition, namely, from the first object and the knowledge of it, to the other object, *in reference to which* one says that experience has been established, was presented as though the knowledge of the first object—i.e., the *for*-consciousness of the first in-itself—should become the second object itself. Contrariwise it would seem that we establish the experience of the untruth of our first concept *on the basis of another* object, which we somehow find by chance and on the outside, so that the only thing that falls within us is the pure *grasping* of that which is in and for itself. In that regard, however, the new object is manifested as having come into being through a *reversal of consciousness* itself. This view of the matter is our contribution, whereby the series of experiences of consciousness elevates itself into a scientific progression, but that does not exist for the consciousness which we observe. In actuality this is the same circumstance which was earlier discussed with regard to the relation of this presentation to skepticism, namely, that the regular result that eventuates in the case of any untrue knowledge can never flow together into an empty nothing, but rather must be understood as the nothing of *that thing,* whose *result* it is; a result, which retains the truth which the prior knowledge had within it. This presents itself here in such a way that, whatever at first it seemed to be, for consciousness the object sinks to the level of our knowledge of it, and the *in-itself* becomes a *being-for-consciousness* of the *in-itself.* And this is the new object whereby a new form of consciousness takes the stage, for which something other than the previous object is the essence. It is this circumstance which guides the entire sequence of the forms of consciousness in its necessity. It is only this necessity itself, or the *genesis* of this new object, which presents itself to consciousness, without its knowing how that happens to it, which occurs for us as though it were behind our back. There comes thus into its movement a moment of the *being-in-itself* or of *being-for-us* which does not present itself for consciousness, which is grasped in experience itself. But the *content* of that which comes to be for us is *for it,* and we only grasp the formal aspect of it, or its pure genesis; *for it* this thing that has come to pass is only an object, but *for us* it is simultaneously motion and becoming.

Through this necessity, this way to science is itself already *science,* and according to its content it is thus the science of the *experience of consciousness.*

That experience which consciousness gains concerning itself can, by virtue of its concept, grasp and conceive nothing less than its entire system, i.e., the entire realm of the truth of Spirit, so that the moments of that truth present themselves in this peculiar determinateness, not as abstract, pure moments, but as they are for consciousness; or as consciousness itself takes the stage in its relation to them, whereby the moments of the whole are *forms of consciousness.* To the extent that consciousness presses on to its true existence—it will reach the point at which it lays aside its seeming, burdened with something strange that is only for it and only as something other than it—where the appearing is the same as the essence, and where its presentation thus corresponds with exactly this point of the actual science of Spirit. And finally, inasmuch as consciousness itself grasps this Being, it will itself characterize the nature of absolute knowledge.

Sense Certainty, or the "This" and "Opining"[3]

That knowledge which is our first and unmediated object can be nothing other than that which is itself unmediated knowledge, *knowledge* of the *immediate* or *the existent.* We must likewise conduct ourselves in an unmediated and receptive manner, thus changing nothing in the way that the object presents itself, keeping a distance between the apprehending and the conceiving of it.

The concrete content of sense certainty makes sense certainty appear unmediated as the richest cognition, indeed as a cognition of infinite richness, for which we can find no limit, whether we go outward into the space and time where this content extends or whether we go inward into it by taking a piece of its fullness and dividing it off. Sense certainty, moreover, appears as the most truthful cognition, for it has not yet neglected any part of the object, but has it in its complete totality in front of itself. This certainty, however, in fact presents itself as the most abstract and poorest *truth.* Of the object which sense certainty knows, it only declares the following: It *is;* and its truth contains only the *being* of the thing; consciousness, on its side, is present in this certainty only as pure *ego [I],*[4] or *I* am therein only as a pure *this* and the object likewise is present only as *this.* I, *this one,* am therefore certain of *this thing,* not because *I* as consciousness developed myself along with it and affected the thought in many ways. Also not because the thing of which I am certain would be a rich relation to itself by virtue of a host of varied characteristics, or a multiple relation to other things. Neither of these concern the truth of sense certainty: Neither I nor the thing has therein the meaning of a manifold mediation. The *I* does not have the meaning of a manifold representation or thought, nor has the thing the meaning of manifold characteristics; but rather the thing *is;* and it *is* only because it *is;* it *is* and that is what is essential for sense knowledge,

3. [*Meinung,* which we here translate as "Opining," connotes subjectivity and contrasts with knowledge, certainty, and proof. The first syllable of *Meinung* means "mine," and Hegel takes advantage of this feature of the word.]

4. [*Das Ich* can be translated either as "ego" or as "I." We use either, depending on the context.]

and this pure *Being* or this simple immediacy constitutes its *truth*. Likewise certainty as relation is *immediate relation*; consciousness is *I*, nothing more, a pure *This*; the *individual* knows a pure this, or *the individual*.

With regard to *pure Being*, however, which constitutes the essence of this certainty, and which it declares as its truth, many other things also play a role, if we pay attention to them. An actual sense certainty is not only this pure immediacy, but an example of the immediacy. Among the countless differences that arise, we encounter on all sides the main differentiation, namely that the two aforementioned "this'es" right away stand out from pure being: a *this* as *I* and a *this* as *object*. But if *we* reflect on this difference, it turns out that neither the one nor the other is merely *immediate* in sense certainty, but is simultaneously *mediated*: I have this certainty *through* something else, namely through the thing; and this thing is likewise a certainty *through* something else, namely through the *I*.

It is not only we who make this distinction between essence and example, between immediacy and mediation, but we find it in sense certainty itself; and it is to be taken up in the form in which the distinction exists in sense certainty, not the way we just determined it. One thing is posited in sense certainty as the simple immediate being, as the essence, the *object*; whereas the other is posited as the inessential and mediated, which thus is not *in itself*, but through something else—I, *a knowledge*, that knows the object only because it is, but which could either be or not be. The object, however, *is*, it is the true and the essence: It *is*, regardless whether it is known or not known, it remains, even if it is not known; but there is no knowledge unless the object exists.

The object therefore is to be considered as to whether in sense certainty itself it is in fact the sort of essence as which sense certainty presents it; whether this its concept of being an essence corresponds to the way that concept is present to sense certainty. To that end we do not have to reflect about it and ponder what it might be in truth, but only consider the way that sense certainty has it in itself.

Sense certainty itself must be asked: *What is the "this"*? If we take it in the doubled form of its Being, as the "Now" and the "Here," then the dialectic which develops out of this Being will take a form which is just as understandable as that Being itself is. To the question *"What is the 'Now'?"* we might answer, for example, *The "Now" is the night*. To test the truth of this sense certainty a simple experiment is sufficient. We make a note of this truth—a truth can lose nothing by being written down, just as it loses nothing by being preserved. And if now at this noontime we look again at this truth we wrote down, then we have to say that the truth we wrote down, the night, has become stale.

The Now which is night is preserved—i.e., it is treated as that as which it was presented, as a *Being*, but it shows itself rather as a not-being thing. The "Now" itself maintains itself indeed, but as something which is not Night; likewise that "Now" maintains itself as over against the day, which it is now, as something which is also not day: or as a *negative* in general. This self-maintaining "Now" is therefore not something immediate, but something mediated; for as something persisting and self-maintaining it is determined through the fact that something else, the day and the night, are not. Nevertheless it is just as simply as it was before *Now*; and in this simplicity it is a matter of indifference what is at play, just as little as the night and the day are its Being, it is also the case that it is night and day; it is not at all affected by this its otherness. Such a simple thing, which *is* through negation neither this nor that—a *Not-this*, and just as indifferent whether it is this or that—we can call a *universal*, and the universal is therefore in fact the truth of sense certainty.

We also *express* the sensible as a universal: What we say is: *This*, i.e., the *universal This*; or: *it is*, i.e., *Being in general*. By this, to be sure, we do not *represent* to ourselves the universal "This" or Being in general, but we express the universal. In other words, we do not say exactly what we *opine* in this sense certainty. Language, however, is, as we see, more truthful: In language we ourselves immediately contradict our *opinion*, and since the universal is the truth of sense certainty, and language is only expressing this truth, it is entirely impossible that we can ever express the sensuous being that we *opine*.

The same will be the case with the other form of the "This," with *the "Here."* The "Here," for example, is a *tree*. I turn around and this truth has disappeared and has changed into its opposite. *The "Here" is not a tree*, but rather *a house*. *The "Here"* itself does not disappear; but *it is* permanently in the disappearing of the house, the tree, and so on, and it is indifferent to its being whether it is a house or tree. The "This" therefore again shows itself as *mediated simplicity*, or as *universality*.

For this sense certainty—showing in itself that the universal is the truth of its object—*pure Being* remains its essence, not as immediate, however, but rather as the sort for which negation and mediation is essential. And thus sense certainty does not show itself as that which we *opine* as *Being*, but rather *Being* together with the *determination* that it is the abstraction or the purely universal. And *our opinion*, for which the truth of sense certainty is not the universal, is the only thing left over against this empty or indifferent "Here" and "Now."

If we compare the relation in which *knowledge* and the object first showed itself with the same relation as it stands in this result, it has reversed itself. The object, which was supposed to be the essential, is now the inessential of sense certainty. The Universal, which the object has become, is no longer the sort of thing which is essential for sense certainty. Rather it is now present in the opposed, in that which was previously the inessential, namely the knowledge. Sense certainty's truth is in the object as *my* object, or in the *mine*, the *opined*. It is because *I* know about it. Sense certainty is therefore actually driven out of the object, but not eliminated thereby, but only driven back into the I. It remains to be seen what experience will show us about this reality.

Thus the force of the truth of sense certainty is now located in the *I*, in the immediacy of my *seeing*, *hearing*, and so on. The disappearance of the individual "Here" and "Now," which we opine, is held off by virtue of the fact that *I* hold it fast. *The "Now" is day*, because I see it; *the "Here" is a tree* for the same reason. Sense certainty experiences in this relation, however, the same dialectic as in the previous case. *I, this I*, see the tree and *insist that the tree is the "Here"*; but *another I* sees the house and asserts that the "here" is not a tree but rather a house. Both truths have the same confirmation, namely the immediacy of seeing, and the certainty and assurance of both about their knowledge; but the one disappears in the other.

What does not disappear in all of this, is *I* as a *universal*, whose seeing is neither a seeing of the tree nor of this house, but simple seeing, that mediates through the negation of this house and so on, which is just as simple and indifferent in relation to that which plays out here, as it was in relation to the house and the tree. *I* am only a universal, just like *"Now," "Here,"* or *"This"* in general; I opine, to be sure, an *individual I*, but as little as I can express what I opine by "here" and "now," no more can I express of "I." To the extent that I say *"this Here, Now"* or an *individual*, I am saying ***all** this'es, all here's, now's, individuals*. Likewise by saying, *I, this individual I*, I say in general: ***all** I's*. Everybody is that which I say: *I, this individual I*. If this demand is presented to science as its touchstone—something which science absolutely could not endure—to deduce, to construct, to discover a priori a so-called *this thing* or *this human being* or whatever one wants to call it, then it is fair that the demand would *specify*, which *this* thing or which *this* I is meant; but it is impossible to express this.

Sense certainty thus experiences that its essence is neither in the object nor in the I, and that the immediacy is neither an immediacy of the one nor the other, for in both cases that which I opine is rather something inessential, and the object and the I are universals, in which the particular Here and Now and I which I opine, does not remain constant, or *they are not*. And so we come to the point of positing the *entirety* of sense certainty itself as its *essence*, no longer only one of its moments, as happened in both cases, wherein at first the object set in opposition to the I should be its reality, and then the I. It is thus only the *entire* sense certainty itself which is steadfast as *immediacy*, and thus excludes all the opposition which occurred in the foregoing.

This pure immediacy therefore does not concern the otherness of the "here" as tree, which changes into a "here" that is non-tree, the otherness of the "now" as day, which becomes the "now" which is night, or an other I for which something else is the object. The truth of sense certainty maintains itself as a relation which remains the same for itself, which doesn't differentiate between essentiality and inessentiality, between the I and the object, and in which therefore no difference whatsoever can intrude. I, this [I], therefore assert the here as a tree, and do not turn around, so that the here would become a non-tree. And I take no notice of the fact that another I sees the "here" as non-tree, or that I myself, at another time, take the "here" to be non-tree, and the "now" as non-day, but I am pure intuition. I, for my part, remain steadfast whether the "now" is the day or the "here" is a tree, and I for my part do not compare the here and now one with the other. But I hold steadfast to the immediate relation: The now is day.

Since this certainty does not want to step forward when we want to call its attention to a "now" which is night or an "I" for which it is night, then we step up to it and let ourselves be shown the "Now" that is asserted. We must let ourselves be shown because the truth of this immediate relation is the truth of *this* I, which confines itself to one *"Here"* and one *"Now."* If we wanted to take up this truth *later*, or stand *at a distance* from it, then it would have no meaning, since we would have eliminated the immediacy which is essential to it. We must therefore enter into the same point of space and time, show it to ourselves, and let ourselves be transformed into the same "this I" which is the one knowing with certainty. We thus see how the immediate which is shown to us is constituted.

The *"now"* is indicated: *This now. Now!* it has already ceased to be. Inasmuch as it is pointed to, the *now* that *is* is another one from the one that was indicated, and we see that the "now" is precisely this one, to the extent that it already is no more. The "now" as it is indicated to us is something which *has been*; and this is its truth. It does not have the truth of Being. But what is still true, is that it has been. But what *has been* is in fact no *essence*; *it is not*, and the issue was Being.

In this exhibition we thus see only a movement and the following unfolding: (1) I point to the "now" and it is asserted as the truth; but I exhibit it as something which has been, or something lifted and I thus lifted the first truth;[5] (2) I now assert the I as the second truth, that it *has been* lifted; (3) But that which has been is not; I lift the having been or having been lifted, the second truth, and negate therewith the negation of the "now," and thus return to the first assertion: that *"now"* is. The "now" and the exhibition of the "now," therefore, is so constituted that neither the "now" nor the exhibition of the "now" is an unmediated simple, but a movement which has different moments in it: *This* is posited, but more than that *an other* is posited, i.e., the *This* is lifted. And this *being-other* or lifting of the first is itself *in turn lifted* and thus returns to the first. But this first thing reflected into itself is not exactly the same as it was at first, namely something *immediate*; but it is something *reflected into itself* or *simple*, which remains what it is in its otherness; a "now," which is absolutely many "now's," an hour is also many minutes, and this "now" is likewise many "now's" and so forth. —The exhibition is therefore itself the movement which it expresses, which is the "now" in truth; namely a result or a multiplicity of "now's" grasped together; and the exhibition is the experiencing that "now" is *universal*.

The *here pointed to,* which I hold steady, is likewise a *this* here, which in fact is *not this* here, but a before and behind, above and below, right and left. The above is likewise this manifold otherness by virtue of being above, below, and so forth. The here which was supposed to be exhibited disappears in another here. But the exhibited disappears as well, that which is held fast and remains, is a *negative this,* which *is* only to the extent that the here's are taken as they should be, but to that extent they are themselves lifted. It is a simple complex of many here's. The "here" that is opined would be the point; however, it *is* not, but to the extent that it is exhibited as being, the exhibiting exhibits itself, not immediate knowledge, but a movement beginning with the opined "here" and going through the many here's into the universal "here," which, just as the day is a simple multiplicity of "now's," so this is a simple multiplicity of "here's."

It becomes clear that the dialectic of sense certainty is nothing other than the simple history of its movement or its experience, and sense certainty itself is nothing other than this history alone. Natural consciousness therefore also comes to this result, that what is true about it is always absent itself and just that constitutes the experience about it; but then it always forgets it again, and begins the movement once again from the beginning. It is therefore remarkable whenever, over against this experience, it is proposed as universal experience—even as a philosophical assertion, and indeed as the result of skepticism—that

5. [Hegel uses the word *aufheben* as a triple pun: its meaning is "to lift up," but colloquially it means both "to cancel" and "to preserve." In the dialectical process any given state of affairs will be preserved as it is cancelled or overcome and lifted up.]

the reality or being of external things as *this* or as sensuous holds absolute truth for consciousness. Such an assertion at the same time doesn't realize what it is saying, doesn't realize that it is saying the opposite of what it is trying to say. The truth of the sensuous *this* for consciousness is supposed to be universal experience. But actually universal experience is the opposite: All consciousness itself lifts such a truth as, for example, *the "here" is a tree*, or *the "now" is midday*, and expresses the opposite: The "here" is *not* a tree, *but rather* a house. And what in this first lifting assertion is once again an assertion of a sensuous this, that too is lifted right away. And in all sense certainty only that is experienced which we have seen, namely that *this* is assured as a *universal*, the opposite of that which such a claim insures as universal experience.—

With this appeal to universal experience it may be permitted to anticipate the consideration of the practical. In this respect it can be said to those who assert that truth and certainty of the reality of sensuous objects, that they are to be referred back to the lowest school of wisdom, namely the Eleusinian mysteries of Ceres and Bacchus, and that they first have to learn the secret of eating bread and drinking wine: for he who is initiated into these mysteries not only comes to doubt the being of sensuous things, but at a despair of them; and accomplishes in them partly their very nullity, and partly he sees them completed. Even the animals are not excluded from this wisdom, but prove themselves rather to be initiated in them in the deepest degree, for they do not stick with the sensuous things as existing themselves, but, despairing of this reality and in complete certainty of their nullity, they reach out for them and devour them; and all of Nature celebrates these revealed mysteries which teach this, which is the truth of sensible things.

But even those who put forward such an assertion, in accordance with the previous remarks, also immediately say the opposite of that which they opine; a phenomenon perhaps the most capable of getting us to ponder the nature of sense certainty. They speak of the existence of *external* objects, which can be more precisely determined as *actual*, absolutely *particular*, *entirely personal, individual* things, of which each no longer has its absolute equal; as if this existence has absolute certainty and truth. They opine *this* piece of paper on which I am writing *this*, or rather I have written it; but what it is that they opine, that they do not say. If they really wanted to *say* this piece of paper which they opine, and they wanted to *say* that, this would be impossible, because the sensuous This that is opined is inaccessible to language, which belongs to consciousness, which is in itself universal. In the actual attempt to say it, it would thus decay: Those who have undertaken its description could never complete it, but would have to leave it to others, who would in the end have to admit that they are speaking of a single thing that *is* not. They may very well opine *this* piece of paper, which is here entirely different from the previous one; but they express actual *things*, *external* or *sensuous objects*, *absolutely individual essences*, and so forth, that is, they say of them only the *universal*; and therefore that which is called the unspeakable is nothing other than the untrue, the irrational, the merely opined.

If nothing further is said about something than that it is an *actual thing*, an *external object*, then it is only expressed as the entirely universal, and thus what is expressed is its sameness with everything else rather than its differentiation, for every thing is a single thing; and likewise *this* thing is anything that anyone wants it to be. More precisely characterized, as *this piece of paper*, *every* and *each* piece of paper is a *this* piece of paper, and I have in each case only said the universal. But if I want to come to the aid of speaking—speech which has the divine nature of immediately inverting opinion and making it into something else—and thus not have speech even *get a word in*, so that I *point to* this piece of paper, then I have the experience of what the truth of sense certainty in fact is: I point to it as a *here*, which is a here of other here's, or in itself a simple togetherness of many here's, i.e., a universal. I take it up as it is in truth, and instead of knowing it as something immediate, I perceive it.[6]

Sense certainty was undermined because the "here and now" constantly change, and what remained certain was we, the observers, not the external world. The next move of consciousness is to stipulate something that remains constant despite all these fluctuations, a thing-in-itself. Sense certainty is replaced by self-certainty. In becoming self-conscious, consciousness recognizes the importance of Desire in two regards. Desire is

6. [The German word for "perception" is *Wahrnehmung*, which literally means "truth-taking" or "taking to be true."]

reflective, making me aware of myself as desiring, but it is always of something or someone, making me aware of the Other. Desire is a desire for mastery of Nature. Because of impediments, however, Desire is deflected into a master of other human beings. Thus the master/slave relation is an aberration, a temporary state over which freedom will ultimately triumph. —A.T. and J.H.S.

Mastery and Slavery

A. Independence and Non-independence of Self-Consciousness: Mastery and Slavery

Self-consciousness is, *in-and-for-itself*, thereby and to the extent that it is *in-and-for-itself for an Other*, that is, it exists only as something recognized.[7] The concept of this its unity in its duplication, of the infinity which realizes itself in self-consciousness, has many sides and many meanings, so that its moments must be kept precisely separate on the one hand, but must in this differentiation simultaneously be kept as undifferentiated on the other hand—or they must always be understood and recognized in their opposed meanings. The double meaning of the differentiated lies in the essence of self-consciousness as being infinite, or as immediately the opposite of the determinateness in which it is posited. The exposition of the concept by taking apart the spiritual unity in its duplication presents us with the motion of recognition.

There is another self-consciousness *for* self-consciousness; it has come out of itself. This has a double meaning: First of all, it has lost itself, since it discovers itself to be *another* essence; second, it has thereby lifted the other, for it does not see the other as an essence, but it sees itself in the other.

It must therefore lift this its otherness: This is the lifting of the first double meaning, and therefore it is itself a second double meaning. First, it must be concerned with lifting the other independent essence, in order thereby to be certain of its own independent essence; secondly, this is a matter of lifting its [own] self, because this other is its self.

This double-sensed lifting of its double-sensed otherness is likewise a double-sensed return into itself; for, first, it gets itself back through this lifting, since it again becomes equal to itself by lifting this otherness. Secondly, however, the other self-consciousness gives back equally in turn, for it was for itself in the other, it lifts this *its* being in the other, and thus also lets the other [go] free.

This movement of self-consciousness in relation to an other self-consciousness is represented, however, as the activity of the one; but this activity of the one has itself the double meaning of being *his* activity just as much as the activity of the other; for the other is equally independent and self-contained, and there is nothing in it which has not come about through it itself. The first does not have the object before it merely as it was for Desire, but as an [object] which exists for itself independently, concerning which it is therefore unable to do anything unless it does the same in itself which the other does to it. The movement, therefore, is simply the double movement of both self-consciousnesses. Each sees *the other* do what *he* does; and each does himself what the other demands; and he therefore does that which he does only to the extent that the other does the same: [for] one-sided activity would be pointless, since that which is supposed to happen can only come about through both of them.

This activity therefore is not only double-sensed to the degree that it is activity equally *toward itself* and *toward the other*, but also to the degree that it is inseparably as much *the activity of the one* as of *the other*.

In this movement we see the process repeating itself which was earlier exhibited as the "play of forces," but now in consciousness. That which was *for us* in the former is here true for the extremes themselves. The middle term[8] is self-consciousness, which diffuses itself into the extremes, and each extreme is this exchange of its own determinateness and an absolute transition into its opposite. As consciousness, however, it surely comes *outside itself*, and nevertheless is simultaneously held back *for itself*, in its *being-*

7. [Hegel here emphasizes the social and political sense of "recognition" as in "recognizing the authority of government."]

8. [The terms "middle" and "extreme" are taken from Aristotelian logic. In the syllogism "All humans are rational; all slaves are human; therefore, all slaves are rational," "human" is the middle term, the extreme term "rational."]

outside-itself, and its *outside-itself* is *for it.* It is for it that it *is* and *is not* immediately another consciousness; and likewise this other is only for itself, inasmuch as it lifts itself as *being-for-itself,* and is *for itself* only in the *being-for-itself* of the other. Each is the middle for the other, through which each mediates itself with itself and merges with itself, and each is to itself and to the other an immediate Essence *being-for-itself,* which simultaneously is only *for itself* by virtue of this mediation. They recognize one another as mutually recognizing one another.

This pure concept of recognition, of the duplication of self-consciousness in its unity, is now to be observed in the way its process appears for self-consciousness. It will first exhibit the side of the inequality of both, the emergence of the middle into the extremes, which, as extremes, are opposed to one another, so that the one is only the recognized and the other only the recognizing.

Self-consciousness is, first of all, simple *being-for-itself,* self-identical through the exclusion *from itself* of everything *other;* its essence and absolute object is, for it, *the I;* and it is an individual in this immediacy, that is in this *being* of its *being-for-itself.* What[ever] is *Other* for it is an object characterized as unessential, with the character of the negative. But *the Other* is also self-consciousness; it emerges as an individual over against an individual. Emerging in such immediacy, they *are* for one another in the manner of ordinary objects, independent shapes, individual consciousnesses immersed in the *Being* of *Life*—for the being Object determines itself as life. They have not yet completed *for-[one]-another* the movement of absolute abstraction, destroying all immediate Being, being only the pure negative Being of self-identical consciousness—that is, they have not yet represented themselves to one another as pure *being-for-itself,* i.e., as *self*-consciousness. Each is no doubt sure of itself, but not of the other, and therefore its own self-certainty does not yet have any truth; for its truth would only consist in its having its own *being-for-itself* as an independent object, or—what amounts to the same thing—as if the object had presented itself as this pure certainty of its own self. But this, according to the concept of Recognition, is not possible unless each is for the other what the other is for him, and each is itself as such through its own activity, and through the activity of the other, in turn, it accomplishes this pure abstraction of *being-for-itself.*

The presentation of itself as the pure abstraction of self-consciousness, however, consists in showing itself as the pure negation of its objective mode—or in showing that it is not tied to any determinate *existence,* nor to the universal particularity of existence in general, i.e., that it is not tied to Life. This presentation is a double activity—activity of the other and activity through itself. To the extent that it is activity of the other, each aims at the death of the other. But therein the second activity is also present, activity on its own: for the former includes risking its own life. The relationship of both self-consciousnesses, therefore, is determined in such a way that they test themselves and each other through a life-and-death struggle. —They must enter into this struggle because they must elevate their certainty of themselves, of *being-for-themselves,* into a truth with regard to the other and with regard to themselves. And it is only through the risking of life that there is freedom, and it is thus proved that, for self-consciousness, it is not *Being,* not the immediate mode in which it appears, not its submergence in the expanse of Life—the Essence—but rather there is nothing present in it which would not be for it a vanishing moment, that it is only pure *being-for-itself.* Any individual that has not yet risked its life can be recognized as a *person* to be sure; but it has not attained to the truth of this being recognized as an independent self-consciousness. Likewise, each must aim at the other's death, inasmuch as it risks its life; for the other no longer counts for him as itself; its essence presents itself to him as an other, it is outside itself; it must lift its *being-outside-itself;* the other is multiply ensnared, and *being consciousness;* it must view its *being other* as pure *being-for-itself* or absolute negation.

This trial by death, however, also lifts the truth which was supposed to proceed from it, and so too is lifted the certainty of itself in general; for just as life is the *natural* position of consciousness, independence without absolute negativity, just so [death] is its *natural* negation, negation without independence, which therefore remains even without the required significance of recognition. It is through death in fact that the certainty has come about that both risked their lives, and each disdained life, both his own and that of the other; but not for those who survived this struggle. They lift their consciousness, posited in this alien essentiality which is natural existence; or they lift themselves and are lifted as extremes wanting to be *for themselves*. But therewith disappears from the play of change the essential moment, that of diffusing into the extremes of opposed determinations. And the middle collapses into a dead unity, which is broken up into dead, merely existing, non-contrary extremes; and neither of them gives or receives the other reciprocally through consciousness, but rather they leave each other free, but indifferently so, like things. Their activity is abstract negation, not the negation of consciousness, which lifts in such a way that it preserves and upholds the lifted, and in this way survives its becoming lifted.

In this experience it becomes clear to self-consciousness that life is as essential to it as pure self-consciousness. In immediate self-consciousness the simple *I* is the absolute object, which, however, *for us* or *in itself*, is absolute mediation, and has enduring independence as its essential moment. The dissolution of that simple unity is the result of the first experience: There is posited through it a pure self-consciousness, and also a consciousness which is not purely *for itself*, but *for another*—that is, as *existing* consciousness or consciousness in the form of *thinghood*. Both moments are essential: Since they are, to begin with, unequal and opposite, and their reflection into unity has not yet been achieved, they exist as two opposed shapes of consciousness—the one independent, for which the essence is *being-for-itself*, the other non-independent, for which the essence is *life* or *being-for-another*. The former is the master, the latter the slave.

The master is consciousness as being *for itself*, but no longer only as the concept thereof; but rather consciousness as *being* for-itself, is mediated with itself through an *other* consciousness, namely through one whose essence entails that it is synthesized with independent Being or with thinghood in general. The master is related to both these moments: to a thing, as such, the object of desire; and to consciousness, for which thinghood is the essence. And to the extent that he, the master, (a) is immediate relation of *being-for-itself* as the concept of self-consciousness, but (b) now he is at the same time mediation, or *being-for-itself*, which is for itself only by virtue of an other; therefore he is related (a) immediately to both, and (b) mediately to each by virtue of the other. The master is related mediately to the slave through [an] *independent being;* for precisely therein the slave is bound: It is his chain, from which he could not "abstract" himself in the struggle, and therefore showed himself to be non-independent, to have his independence in thinghood. The master, however, is the power over this Being, because he proved in the struggle, that, for him, that only counts as something negative. Inasmuch as he, the master, has the power over this, but this being has the power over the Other, in this conclusion he holds the other subject to him. In precisely this way the master is related mediately to the thing through the slave; whereas the slave is also related to the thing as self-consciousness generally, and lifts it; but it is simultaneously independent for him, the slave, and he can therefore not negate it to the point of annihilating and being rid of it: In other words he only works on it. For the master, in contrast, this *immediate* relation becomes, through such mediation, the pure negation of the thing, or enjoyment: What did not succeed for Desire, he thus succeeds in being rid of, and contents himself with enjoyment. Desire failed to accomplish this because of the independence of the thing; but the master, who has now interposed the slave between himself and the thing, is only connected to the non-independence of the thing and enjoys it purely. The aspect of its independence he leaves to the slave, who works on it.

In both of these moments, for the master recognition comes about through another consciousness; for in [the masters] this consciousness is posited as something unessential—in the first instance because of its working on the thing, and in the second instance because of its dependence on a determinate existence. In neither case can it be master over its being and achieve its absolute negation. Thus is at hand this moment of recognition, namely that the other consciousness lifts its *being-for-itself*, and therewith itself does that which the first does to it. Likewise, here is the other moment, that this action of the second is the first one's own action as well: for what the slave does is really the action of the master. For the latter there is only *being-for-himself*, essence: He is the pure negative power, for which the thing is nothing, and therefore the pure essential action in this relationship is his: whereas the slave's is not pure, but rather a non-essential action. But the moment is lacking for the actual recognition that what the master does against the other, he also does against himself, and what the slave does against himself he also does against the other. There has therefore emerged a recognition which is one-sided and unequal.

In this [recognition], the unessential consciousness is the object for the master, which amounts to the *truth* of his certainty. It becomes clear, however, that this object does not correspond to its own concept, but that which the master has achieved has become for him something entirely other than an independent consciousness. It is not such for him at all, but rather something non-independent; and he is therefore not certain of the *being-for-itself* as his own truth, but rather his truth is instead an unessential consciousness and the unessential activity of the same.

The *truth* of the independent consciousness is therefore slavish consciousness. This appears indeed, at first, *outside* itself, not as the truth of self-consciousness. But just as mastery showed that its essence was the inverse of what it wanted to be, so too slavery will become in its completion the opposite of what it is immediately: It will return into itself as consciousness forced back into itself, and will be turned around into true independence.

We have only seen what slavery is in comparison with mastery. But it too is a self-consciousness and we must now observe what it accordingly is *in-and-for-itself*. At first, for slavery, the master is the essence; and thus the independent consciousness *being-for-itself* is the truth for it, which nonetheless is *for it* but not yet *in it*. Still, it has in fact in itself this truth of pure negativity and of *being-for-itself*; for it has experienced this essence therein. To be precise, this consciousness did not have fear of this or that [thing], nor of this or that moment, but of its entire essence, for it has experienced the fear of death, of the absolute master. In that it has been inwardly dissolved, and has thoroughly trembled inside itself, and everything fixed in it has quaked. This pure universal motion, the absolute fluidity of all endurance, is, however, the simple essence of self-consciousness—absolute negativity, pure *being-for-itself*, that is herewith present in this consciousness. This moment of pure *being-for-itself* is also *for it*, for the slave, since it exists for him in the master *as his object*. Furthermore, this is not only this universal dissolution *in general*, but in serving it actually accomplishes it. In all the *individual* moments [of his service] he lifts his dependence on natural existence and works it away.

The feeling of absolute power, however, in general and in the particulars of service, is only the dissolution *in itself*; and although indeed "the fear of the Lord is the beginning of wisdom,"[9] consciousness is therein *for its own self*, not *being-for-itself*. Through work, however, the slave "comes to" himself. In the moment which corresponds to desire in the consciousness of the master, it appeared indeed that the aspect of the unessential relation to the thing fell to the slave consciousness, since in that relation the thing maintained its independence. Desire kept to itself the pure negation of the object and thereby its unmixed self-feeling. This satisfaction, however, is for that reason itself only something vanishing, for it is lacking the objective side, permanence. Work, in contrast, is Desire *held in check*, the vanishing halted: Work is formative. The negative relation to the object becomes its *Form* and becomes something permanent; and it is precisely for the worker that the Object has independence. This negative middle [term], or the formative activity, is simultaneously the particularity or the pure *being-for-itself* of consciousness, which now, in the work outside it, comes upon the element of permanence: The working consciousness thus comes through this to the intuition of independent being as its own independence.

The formative activity, however, does not only have this positive meaning that the slave consciousness, as pure *being-for-itself*, thereby becomes *the being thing*; but also the negative meaning, counter to its first moment, fear. For in the making of the thing its own negativity, its *being-for-itself*, becomes an Object by virtue of the fact that it lifts the existing form opposed to it. But this opposed and objective negative is precisely the alien essence before which it had trembled. Now, however, it destroys this alien, sets itself up as such, [the negative,] in the element of permanence; and thereby becomes for itself a *being-for-itself*. For

9. [Psalm 111:10 and Proverbs 9:10. Throughout *Herr/Herrschaft* can be translated either as "lord/lordship" or "master/mastery." In passages such as this one the religious connotations of the former version are clear—and ironic. Similarly, *Knecht/Knechtschaft* can be translated as "slave/slavery," "servant/servitude," or "bondsman/bondage."]

the slave the *being-for-itself* in the master is an other, but only *for it;* in fear, *being-for-itself* is present for the slave himself; in formative activity *being-for-itself* becomes its very own for it, and it "comes to" consciousness that it itself is *in-and-for-itself.* The form does not become something other than itself by the fact that it is posited outside itself; for that very form is its pure *being-for-itself,* which thereby becomes its truth. And therefore through this rediscovery of himself through himself comes about his own sense, precisely in work, which had only seemed to have an alien meaning.—Both moments, fear and servitude in general, are necessary for this reflexion, as is formative activity, and simultaneously both of them in a universal manner. Without the discipline of service and obedience, fear remains stuck at something formal and does not spread out to the conscious actuality of existence. Without formative activity fear remains inward and mute, and consciousness does not become *for itself.* If consciousness forms the thing without absolute, it is only a vain stubbornness, having only its own sense, for its form or negativity is not negative *in itself;* and its formative activity therefore cannot give it the consciousness of itself as its essence. If he has not endured absolute fear, but only some anxiety, then the negative essence would have remained something external for him, its substance has not been thoroughly infected by it. To the extent that not all fulfillments of its natural consciousness have remained shaky, it belongs *in itself* to determinate being; its own sense is just self-will, a freedom which remains within the bonds of slavery. Just as little as pure form can become essence for him, just so little is that form, considered as extended over the particular, a universal formation or an absolute concept; rather it is a skill which is only powerful over some things, but not the universal power and the whole objective essence.

Arthur Schopenhauer

Arthur Schopenhauer was born in 1788 in Danzig and died in 1860. He is notorious for his pessimism and hostility toward women. His obstinacy is revealed in his volunteering to teach a course at the University of Berlin at the same time the popular Hegel was lecturing. Schopenhauer did not attract students, and his course was cancelled.

Schopenhauer's dissertation, *The Fourfold Root of the Principle of Sufficient Reason* (1813), draws on the Kantian distinction between the noumenal and phenomenal worlds and elaborates on the causal conditions for every type of phenomenon (empirical representations, concepts, time and space, and individual selves). The principle of sufficient reason asserts that every phenomenon depends on the presence of sufficient causal conditions. The definitive statement of Schopenhauer's system is *The World as Will and Representation,* first published in 1819 (revised second edition, 1844; third edition, 1859). He later added a second volume.

Schopenhauer sought to integrate central ideas from the systems of his three heroes—Plato, Kant, and Buddha. *The World as Will and Representation* begins with an announcement of its thoroughly idealistic metaphysical view: "The world is my representation." The world as representation is governed by the principle of sufficient reason. By contrast, the inner reality of the world is Will, an irrational striving. We experience this inner reality through our personal emotions and striving, and in this sense we have a direct awareness of noumenal reality. Every other entity and force within the phenomenal world, the world that we experience, also has a comparable inner side. In light of the fact that we experience the inner reality as will, Schopenhauer uses the term "Will" for the inner reality of everything. In contract with the Will, which is ultimately the only reality, the phenomenal world, as Kant tells us, is a construction of our own powers of representation.

To account for natural kinds as they are observed in the phenomenal world and the orderly relations between them, Schopenhauer conjoins the Kantian distinction between the noumenal and phenomenal with Plato's Theory of Forms or Ideas. Things within the phenomenal world are classifiable into natural kinds, because each participates in a Platonic Idea for the kind of thing that it is. Schopenhauer characterizes the Platonic Ideas as modes or "grades" through which the Will manifests itself. He describes each Platonic Idea as a perfectly adequate manifestation of the Will at a given grade. In other words, a perfect prototype for a particular type of thing manifests the Will. Phenomenal entities, by contrast, imperfectly embody the Platonic Ideas in which they participate.

Although the Will is the same inner reality in all things, we are captivated and deluded by the Will's phenomenal manifestations. Schopenhauer analyzes our belief in the reality of the individuated entities of the phenomenal world as a natural illusion. This illusion gives rise to our practical motivations toward the entities we perceive, including other sentient beings. Because our own inner nature is Will, we are filled with desires. We want some things, and we want to avoid others; we desire some individuals, and we view others as obstacles. All of these consequences of our belief in the reality of individuation motivate our various ambitions, which we typically pursue without regard to any harm we do to others or ourselves in the process. Schopenhauer concludes that Buddha was right to claim that the suffering of life stems from our selfish cravings, and that elimination of these cravings is necessary to eliminate suffering.

Most of us, however, will not achieve the radical resignation required for spiritual liberation. Aside from the saints of various traditions, most human beings escape what Schopenhauer calls "the penal servitude of willing" only occasionally through aesthetic experience, which involves a shift in perspective from seeing an object as a particular, individuated thing to seeing the Platonic Idea in which it participates. This shift dislocates the object from its location in the time-space continuum in which we relate to objects in accordance with egotistical agendas. The object becomes for the perceiver a timeless manifestation of Will, and the observer is transformed into the "pure, will-less subject of knowledge." In other words, during aesthetic experience the observer stops conceiving of him- or herself as an individuated being with desires and comes to an awareness of the self as a manifestation of universal consciousness. At such moments, one no longer identifies oneself with the hankerings of one's personal will. These desires are momentarily silenced, and one experiences peace. In this way aesthetic experience liberates us, but only temporarily.

Ultimately, the only method for lasting liberation is to overcome the illusion of individuation and renounce one's own willfulness. Schopenhauer contends that this ethical aim is the core of ethics and religion. If one fully absorbs the insight that individuation is merely illusory and that the inner reality of other sentient beings is actually the same as one's own, motivation to struggle against others and against one's circumstances would be destroyed. In practice, however, the destruction of one's willful tendencies is achieved only through ascetic practice, which in exceptional cases like those of the saints weakens and eventually undercuts willfulness and even the desire to continue to live. Schopenhauer is not optimistic that many people will actually achieve this state, so aesthetic experience is the closest that most people come to the condition of sanctity. Because the liberated state of pure will-lessness is achieved through the cessation of the desires that structure our personal existence, its positive content is unknown, although saints describe this condition as blissful.

• • •

Rudiger Safranski's *Schopenhauer and the Wild Years of Philosophy,* trans. Ewald Osers (Cambridge, Mass.: Harvard University Press, 1989), is a colorful and detailed biography of Schopenhauer. A critical survey of Schopenhauer's philosophy is provided in Patrick L. Gardiner, *Schopenhauer* (Baltimore: Penguin Books, 1963), which also relates features of Schopenhauer's thought to more recent phenomena in the arts and the history of ideas. Bryan Magee's *The Philosophy of Schopenhauer,* rev. ed. (Oxford: Oxford University Press, 1997) thoroughly considers the internal details of Schopenhauer's thought, including a number of chapters focusing on his influence on other thinkers and artists.

Because *The World as Will and Representation* is the summary statement of Schopenhauer's thought, many of the secondary works on Schopenhauer focus on it specifically. Julian Young offers a lucid and nicely organized reading of the work in *Willing and Unwilling: A Study in the Philosophy of Arthur Schopenhauer* (Norwell, Mass.: Martinus Nijhoff, 1987). D. W. Hamlyn provides a good analysis of both *The World as Will and Representation* and *The Fourfold Root of the Principle of Sufficient Reason* in his *Schopenhauer* (London: Routledge, 1999). Both of these books also stress Schopenhauer's Kantian roots, as does Christopher Janaway, *Self and World in Schopenhauer's Philosophy* (Oxford: Oxford University Press, 1999), although Janaway emphasizes Schopenhauer's ambivalence toward Kant. John E. Atwell argues that Schopenhauer's central thought is that the world is the self-knowledge of the Will in *Schopenhauer on the Character of the World: The Metaphysics of Will* (Berkeley: University of California Press, 1995). Christopher Janaway, ed., *The Cambridge Companion to Schopenhauer* (New York: Cambridge University Press, 1999) is a scholarly but accessible selection of essays.

Kathleen Higgins

The World as Will and Representation

BOOK II

§17.

. . . [D]irecting our attention entirely to the representation of perception, we shall endeavour to arrive at a knowledge of its content, its more precise determinations, and the forms it presents to us. It will be of special interest for us to obtain information about its real significance, that significance, otherwise merely felt, by virtue of which these pictures or images do not march past us strange and meaningless, as they would otherwise inevitably do, but speak to us directly, are understood, and acquire an interest that engrosses our whole nature.

We direct our attention to mathematics, natural science, and philosophy, each of which holds out the hope that it will furnish a part of the information desired. In the first place, we find philosophy to be a monster with many heads, each of which speaks a different language. Of course, they are not all at variance with one another on the point here mentioned, the significance of the representation of perception. For, with the exception of the Sceptics and Idealists, the others in the main speak fairly consistently of an *object* forming the *basis* of the representation. This object indeed is different in its whole being and nature from the representation, but yet is in all respects as like it as one egg is like another. But this does not help us, for we do not at all know how to distinguish that object from the representation. We find that the two are one and the same, for every object always and eternally presupposes a subject, and thus remains representation. We then recognize also that being-object belongs to the most universal form of the representation, which is precisely the division into object and subject. Further, the principle of sufficient reason, to which we here refer, is also for us only the form of the representation, namely the regular and orderly combination of one representation with another, and not the combination of the whole finite or infinite series of representations with something which is not representation at all, and is therefore not capable of being in any way represented. We spoke above of the Sceptics and Idealists, when discussing the controversy about the reality of the external world.

Now if we look to mathematics for the desired more detailed knowledge of the representation of perception, which we have come to know only quite generally according to the mere form, then this science will tell us about these representations only in so far as they occupy time and space, in other words, only in so far as they are quantities. It will state with extreme accuracy the How-many and the How-large; but as this is always only relative, that is to say, a comparison of one representation with another and even that only from the one-sided aspect of quantity, this too will not be the information for which principally we are looking.

Finally, if we look at the wide province of natural science, which is divided into many fields, we can first of all distinguish two main divisions. It is either a description of forms and shapes, which I call *Morphology;* or an explanation of changes, which I call *Etiology*. The former considers the permanent forms, the latter the changing matter, according to the laws of its transition from one form into another. Morphology is what we call natural history in its whole range, though not in the literal sense of the word. As botany and zoology especially, it teaches us about the various, permanent, organic, and thus definitely determined forms in spite of the incessant change of individuals; and these forms constitute a great part of the content of the perceptive representation. In natural history they are classified, separated, united, and arranged according to natural and artificial systems, and brought under concepts that render possible a survey and knowledge of them all. There is further demonstrated an infinitely fine and shaded analogy in the whole and in the parts of these forms which runs through them all (*unité de plan*),[1] by virtue of which they are like the many different variations on an unspecified theme. The passage of matter into those forms, in other words the origin of individuals, is not a main part of the consideration, for every individual springs from its like through generation, which everywhere is equally mysterious, and has so far baffled clear knowledge. But the little that is known of this finds its place in physiology, which belongs to etiological natural science. Mineralogy, especially where it becomes geology, though it belongs mainly to morphology, also inclines to this etiological science. Etiology proper includes all the branches of natural science in which the main concern everywhere is knowledge of cause and effect. These sciences teach how, according to an invariable rule, one state of matter is necessarily followed by another definite state; how one definite change necessarily conditions and brings about another definite change; this demonstration is called *explanation.* Here we find principally mechanics, physics, chemistry, and physiology.

But if we devote ourselves to its teaching, we soon become aware that the information we are chiefly looking for no more comes to us from etiology than it does from morphology. The latter presents us with innumerable and infinitely varied forms that are nevertheless related by an unmistakable family likeness. For us they are representations that in this way remain eternally strange to us, and, when considered merely in this way, they stand before us like hieroglyphics that are not understood. On the other hand, etiology teaches us that, according to the law of cause and effect, this definite condition of matter produces that other condition, and with this it has explained it, and has done its part. At bottom, however, it does nothing more than show the orderly arrangement according to which the states or conditions appear in space and time, and teach for all cases what phenomenon must necessarily appear at this time and in this place. It therefore determines for them their position in time and space according to a law whose definite content has been taught by experience, yet whose universal form and necessity are known to us independently of experience. But in this way we do not obtain the slightest information about the inner nature of any one of these phenomena. This is called a *natural force,* and lies outside the province of etiological explanation, which calls the unalterable constancy with which the manifestation of such a force appears whenever its known conditions are present, *a law of nature.* But this law of nature, these conditions, this appearance in a definite place at a definite time, are all that it knows, or ever can know. The force itself that is manifested, the inner nature of the phenomena that appear in accordance with those laws, remain for it an eternal secret, something entirely strange and unknown, in the case of the simplest as well as of the most complicated phenomenon. For although etiology has so far achieved its aim most completely in mechanics, and least so in physiology, the force by virtue of which a stone falls to the ground, or one body repels another, is, in its inner nature, just as strange and mysterious as that which produces the movements and growth of an animal. Mechanics presupposes matter, weight, impenetrability, communicability of motion through impact, rigidity, and so on as unfathomable; it calls them forces of nature, and their necessary and regular appearance under certain conditions a law of nature. Only then does its explanation begin, and that consists in stating truly and with mathematical precision how, where, and when each force manifests itself, and referring to one of those forces every phenomenon that comes before it. Physics, chemistry, and physiology do the same in their province, only they presuppose much more and achieve less. Consequently, even the most perfect etiological explanation of the whole of nature would never be more in reality than a record of inexplicable forces, and a reliable statement of the rule by which their phenomena appear, succeed, and make way for one another in time and space. But the inner nature of the forces that thus appear was always bound to be left unexplained by etiology, which had to stop at the phenomenon and its arrangement, since the law followed by etiology does not go beyond this. In this respect it could be compared to a section of a piece of marble showing different veins side by side, but not letting us know the course of these veins from the interior of the marble to the surface. Or, if I may be permitted a facetious comparison, because it is more striking, the philosophical investigator must always feel in regard to the complete etiology of the

1. [Unity of plan—S.M.C.]

whole of nature like a man who, without knowing how, is brought into a company quite unknown to him, each member of which in turn presents to him another as his friend and cousin, and thus makes them sufficiently acquainted. The man himself, however, while assuring each person introduced of his pleasure at meeting him, always has on his lips the question: "But how the deuce do I stand to the whole company?"

Hence, about those phenomena by us only as our representations, etiology can never give us the desired information that leads us beyond them. For after all its explanations, they still stand quite strange before us, as mere representations whose significance we do not understand. The causal connexion merely gives the rule and relative order of their appearance in space and time, but affords us no further knowledge of that which so appears. Moreover, the law of causality itself has validity only for representations, for objects of a definite class, and has meaning only when they are assumed. Hence, like these objects themselves, it always exists only in relation to the subject, and so conditionally. Thus it is just as well known when we start from the subject, i.e., *a priori*, as when we start from the object, i.e., *a posteriori*, as Kant has taught us.

But what now prompts us to make enquiries is that we are not satisfied with knowing that we have representations, that they are such and such, and that they are connected according to this or that law, general expression is always the principle of sufficient reason. We want to know the significance of those representations; we ask whether this world is nothing more than representation. In that case, it would inevitably pass by us like an empty dream, or a ghostly vision not worth our consideration. Or we ask whether it is something else, something in addition, and if so what that something is. This much is certain, namely that this something about which we are enquiring must be by its whole nature completely and fundamentally different from the representation; and so the forms and laws of the representation must be wholly foreign to it. We cannot, then, reach it from the representation under the guidance of those laws that merely combine objects, representations, with one another; these are the forms of the principle of sufficient reason.

Here we already see that we can never get at the inner nature of things *from without*. However much we may investigate, we obtain nothing but images and names. We are like a man who goes round a castle, looking in vain for an entrance, and sometimes sketching the façades. Yet this is the path that all philosophers before me have followed.

§ 18.

In fact, the meaning that I am looking for of the world that stands before me simply as my representation, or the transition from it as mere representation of the knowing subject to whatever it may be besides this, could never be found if the investigator himself were nothing more than the purely knowing subject (a winged cherub without a body). But he himself is rooted in that world; and thus he finds himself in it as an *individual*, in other words, his knowledge, which is the conditional supporter of the whole world as representation, is nevertheless given entirely through the medium of a body, and the affections of this body are, as we have shown, the starting-point for the understanding in its perception of this world. For the purely knowing subject as such, this body is a representation like any other, an object among objects. Its movements and actions are so far known to him in just the same way as the changes of all other objects of perception; and they would be equally strange and incomprehensible to him, if their meaning were not unravelled for him in an entirely different way. Otherwise, he would see his conduct follow on presented motives with the constancy of a law of nature, just as the changes of other objects follow upon causes, stimuli, and motives. But he would be no nearer to understanding the influence of the motives than he is to understanding the connexion with its cause of any other effect that appears before him. He would then also call the inner, to him incomprehensible, nature of those manifestations and actions of his body a force, a quality, or a character, just as he pleased, but he would have no further insight into it. All this, however, is not the case; on the contrary, the answer to the riddle is given to the subject of knowledge appearing as individual, and this answer is given in the word *Will*. This and this alone gives him the key to his own phenomenon, reveals to him the significance and shows him the inner mechanism of his being, his actions, his movements. To the subject of knowing, who appears as an individual only through his identity with the body, this body is given in two entirely different ways. It is given in intelligent perception as representation, as an object among objects, liable to the laws of these objects, But it is also given in quite a different way, namely as what is known immediately to everyone, and is denoted by the word *will*. Every true act of his will is also at once and inevitably a movement of his body; he cannot actually will the act without at the same time being aware that it appears as a movement of the body. The act of will and the action of the body are not two different states objectively known, connected by the bond of causality; they do not stand in the relation of cause and effect, but are one and the same thing, though given in two entirely different ways, first quite directly, and then in perception for the understanding. The action of the body is nothing but the act of will objectified, i.e., translated into perception. Later on we shall see that this applies to every movement of the body, not merely to movement following on motives, but also to involuntary movement following on mere stimuli; indeed, that the whole body is nothing but the objectified will, i.e., will that has become representation. All this will follow and become clear in the course of our discussion. Therefore the body . . . will . . . be called the *objectivity of the will*. Therefore, in a certain sense, it can also be said that the will is knowledge *a priori* of the body, and that the body is knowledge *a posteriori* of the will. Resolutions of the will relating to the future are mere deliberations of reason about what will be willed at some time, not real acts of will. Only the carrying out stamps the resolve; till then, it is always a mere intention that can be altered; it exists only in reason, in the abstract. Only in reflection are willing and acting different; in reality they are one. Every true, genuine, immediate act of the will is also at once and directly a manifest act of the body; and correspondingly, on the other hand, every impression on the body is also at once and directly an impression on the will. As such, it is called pain when it is contrary to the will, and gratification or pleasure when in accordance with the will. The gradations of the two are very different. However, we are quite wrong in calling pain and pleasure representations, for they are not these at all, but immediate affections of the will in its phenomenon, the body; an enforced, instantaneous willing or not-willing of the impression undergone by the body. There are only a certain few impressions on the body which do not rouse the will, and through these alone is the body an immediate object of knowledge; for, as perception in the understanding, the body is an indirect object like all other objects. These impressions are therefore to be regarded directly as mere representations, and hence to be excepted from what has just been said. Here are meant the affections of the purely objective senses of sight, hearing, and touch, although only in so far as their organs are affected in the specific natural way that is specially characteristic of them. This is such an exceedingly feeble stimulation of the enhanced and specifically modified sensibility of these parts that it does not affect the will, but, undisturbed by any excitement of the will, only furnishes for the understanding data from which perception arises. But every stronger or heterogeneous affection of these sense-organs is painful, in other words, is against the will; hence they too belong to its objectivity. Weakness of the nerves shows itself in the fact that the impressions which should have merely that degree of intensity that is sufficient to make them data for the understanding, reach the higher degree at which they stir the will, that is to say, excite pain or pleasure, though more often pain. This pain, however, is in part dull and inarticulate; thus it not merely causes us to feel painfully particular tones and intense light, but also gives rise generally to a morbid and hypochondriacal disposition without being distinctly recognized. The identity of the body and the will further shows itself, among other things, in the fact that every vehement and excessive movement of the will, in other words, every emotion, agitates the body and its inner workings directly and immediately, and disturbs the course of its vital functions." . . .

Finally, the knowledge I have of my will, although an immediate knowledge, cannot be separated from that of my body. I know my will not as a whole, not as a unity, not completely according to its nature, but only in its individual acts, and hence in time, which is the form of my body's appearing, as it is of every body. Therefore, the body is the condition of knowledge of my will. Accordingly, I cannot really imagine this will without my body. . . .

The identity of the will and of the body . . . can never be demonstrated, that is to say, deduced as indirect knowledge from some other more direct knowledge, for the very reason that it is itself the most direct knowledge. If we do not apprehend it and stick to it as such, in vain shall we expect to obtain it again in some indirect way as derived knowledge. . . . For it is not . . . the reference of an abstract representation to another representation, or to the necessary form of intuitive or of abstract representing, but it is the reference of a judgement to the relation that a representation of perception, namely the body, has to that which is not a representation at all, but is *toto genere*[2] different therefrom, namely will. I should therefore like to distinguish this truth from every other, and call it *philosophical truth*. . . . We can turn the expression of this truth in different ways and say: My body and my will are one; or, What as representation of perception I call my body, I call my will in so far as I am conscious of it in an entirely different way comparable with no other; or, My body is the *objectivity* of my will; or, Apart from the fact that my body is my representation, it is still my will, so on.

§ 19.

. . . [I]t has now become clear to us that something in the consciousness of everyone distinguishes the representation of his own body from all others that are in other respects quite like it. This is that the body occurs in consciousness in quite another way, *toto genere* different, that is denoted by the word *will*. It is just this double knowledge of our own body which gives us information about that body itself, about its action and movement following on motives, as well as about its suffering through outside impressions, in a word, about what it is, not as representation, but as something over and above this, and hence what it is *in itself*. We do not have such immediate information about the nature, action, and suffering of any other real objects.

The knowing subject is an individual precisely by reason of this special relation to the one body which, considered apart from this, is for him only a representation like all other representations. But the relation by virtue of which the knowing subject is an *individual*, subsists for that very reason only between him and one particular representation among all his representations. He is therefore conscious of this particular representation not merely as such, but at the same time in a quite different way, namely as a will. But if he abstracts from that special relation, from that twofold and completely heterogeneous knowledge of one and the same thing, then that one thing, the body, is a representation like all others. Therefore, in order to understand where he is in this matter, the knowing individual must either assume that the distinctive feature of that one representation is to be found merely in the fact that his knowledge stands in this double reference only to that one representation; that only into this one object of perception is an insight in two ways at the same time open to him; and that this is to be explained not by a difference of this object from all others, but only by a difference between the relation of his knowledge to this one object and its relation to all others. Or he must assume that this one object is essentially different from all others; that it alone among all objects is at the same time will and representation, the rest, on the other hand, being mere representation, i.e., mere phantoms. Thus, he must assume that his body is the only real individual in the world, i.e., the only phenomenon of will, and the only immediate object of the subject. That the other objects, considered as mere *representations*, are like his body, in other words, like this body fill space (itself perhaps existing only as representation), and also, like this body, operate in space—this, I say, is demonstrably certain from the law of causality, which is *a priori* certain for representations, and admits of no effect without a cause. But apart from the fact that we can infer from the effect only a cause in general, not a similar cause, we are still always in the realm of the mere representation, for which alone the law of causality is valid, and beyond which it can never lead us. But whether the objects known to the individual only as representations are yet, like his own body, phenomena of a will, is . . . the proper meaning of the question as to the reality of the external world. To deny this is the meaning of *theoretical egoism*, which in this way regards as phantoms all phenomena outside its own will, just as practical egoism does in a practical respect; thus in it a man regards and treats only his own person as a real person, and all others as mere phantoms, Theoretical egoism, of course, can never be refuted by proofs, yet in philosophy it has never been posi-

2. [In every way.]

tively used otherwise than as a sceptical sophism, i.e., for the sake of appearance. As a serious conviction, on the other hand, it could be found only in a madhouse; as such it would then need not so much a refutation as a cure. Therefore we do not go into it any further, but regard it as the last stronghold of scepticism, which is always polemical. Thus our knowledge, bound always to individuality and having its limitation in this very fact, necessarily means that everyone can *be* only one thing, whereas he can *know* everything else, and it is this very limitation that really creates the need for philosophy. Therefore we, who for this very reason are endeavouring to extend the limits of our knowledge through philosophy, shall regard this sceptical argument of theoretical egoism, which here confronts us, as a small frontier fortress. Admittedly the fortress is impregnable, but the garrison can never sally forth from it, and therefore we can pass it by and leave it in our rear without danger.

The double knowledge which we have of the nature and action of our own body, and which is given in two completely different ways, has now been clearly brought out. Accordingly, we shall use it further as a key to the inner being of every phenomenon in nature. We shall judge all objects which are not our own body, and therefore are given to our consciousness not in the double way, but only as representations, according to the analogy of this body. We shall therefore assume that as, on the one hand, they are representation, just like our body, and are in this respect homogeneous with it, so on the other hand, if we set aside their existence as the subject's representation, what still remains over must be, according to its inner nature, the same as what in ourselves we call *will*. For what other kind of existence or reality could we attribute to the rest of the material world? From what source could we take the elements out of which we construct such a world? Besides the will and the representation, there is absolutely nothing known or conceivable for us. If we wish to attribute the greatest known reality to the material world, which immediately exists only in our representation, then we give it that reality which our own body has for each of us, for to each of us this is the most real of things. But if now we analyse the reality of this body and its actions, then, beyond the fact that it is our representation, we find nothing in it but the will; with this even its reality is exhausted. Therefore we can nowhere find another kind of reality to attribute to the material world. If, therefore, the material world is to be something more than our mere representation, we must say that, besides being the representation, and hence in itself and of its inmost nature, it is what we find immediately in ourselves as will. I say 'of its inmost nature,' but we have first of all to get to know more intimately this inner nature of the will, so that we may know how to distinguish from it what belongs not to it itself, but to its phenomenon, which has many grades. Such, for example, is the circumstance of its being accompanied by knowledge, and the determination by motives which is conditioned by this knowledge. As we proceed, we shall see that this belongs not to the inner nature of the will, but merely to its most distinct phenomenon as animal and human being. Therefore, if I say that the force which attracts a stone to the earth is of its nature, in itself, and apart from all representation, will, then no one will attach to this proposition the absurd meaning that the stone moves itself according to a known motive, because it is thus that the will appears in man. But we will now prove, establish, and develop to its full extent, clearly and in more detail, what has hitherto been explained provisionally and generally.

§ 20.

As the being-in-itself of our own body, as that which this body is besides being object of perception, namely representation, the *will*, as we have said, proclaims itself first of all in the voluntary movements of this body, in so far as these movements are nothing but the visibility of the individual acts of the will. These movements appear directly and simultaneously with those acts of will; they are one and the same thing with them, and are distinguished from them only by the form of perceptibility into which they have passed, that is to say, in which they have become representation.

But these acts of the will always have a ground or reason outside themselves in motives. Yet these motives never determine more than what I will at *this* time, in *this* place, in *these* circumstances, not *that* I will in general, or *what* I will in general, in other words, the maxim characterizing the whole of my willing. Therefore, the whole inner nature of my willing cannot be explained from the motives, but they determine merely its manifestation at a given point of time; they are merely the occasion on which my will shows itself. This will itself, on the other hand, lies outside the province of the law of motivation; only the phenomenon of the will at each point of time is determined by this law. Only on the presupposition of my empirical character is the motive a sufficient ground of explanation of my conduct. But if I abstract from my character, and then ask why in general I will this and not that, no answer is possible, because only the *appearance* or *phenomenon* of the will is subject to the principle of sufficient reason, not the will itself, which in this respect may be called *groundless*. . . .

Now if every action of my body is an appearance or phenomenon of an act of will in which my will itself in general and as a whole, and hence my character, again expresses itself under given motives, then phenomenon or appearance of the will must also be the indispensable condition and presupposition of every action. For the will's appearance cannot depend on something which does not exist directly and only through it, and would therefore be merely accidental for it, whereby the will's appearance itself would be only accidental. But that condition is the whole body itself. Therefore this body itself must be phenomenon of the will, and must be related to my will as a whole, that is to say, to my intelligible character, the phenomenon of which in time is my empirical character, in the same way as the particular action of the body is to the particular act of the will. Therefore the whole body must be nothing but my will become visible, must be my will itself, in so far as this is object of perception, representation of the first class. It has already been advanced in confirmation of this that every impression on my body also affects my will at once and immediately, and in this respect is called pain or pleasure, or in a lower degree, pleasant or unpleasant sensation. Conversely, it has also been advanced that every violent movement of the will, and hence every emotion and passion, convulses the body, and disturbs the course of its functions. Indeed, an etiological, though very incomplete, account can be given of the origin of my body, and a somewhat better account of its development and preservation. Indeed this is physiology; but this explains its theme only in exactly the same way as motives explain action. Therefore the establishment of the individual action through the motive, and the necessary sequence of the action from the motive, do not conflict with the fact that action, in general and by its nature, is only phenomenon or appearance of a will that is in itself groundless. . . . [N]o etiological explanation can ever state more than the necessarily determined position in time and space of a particular phenomenon and its necessary appearance there according to a fixed rule. On the other hand, the inner nature of everything that appears in this way remains for ever unfathomable, and is presupposed by every etiological explanation; it is merely expressed by the name force, or law of nature, or, when we speak of actions, the name character or will. Thus, although every particular action, under the presupposition of the definite character, necessarily ensues with the presented motive, and although growth, the process of nourishment, and all the changes in the animal body take place according to necessarily acting causes (stimuli), the whole series of actions, and consequently every individual act and likewise its condition, namely the whole body itself which performs it, and therefore also the process through which and in which the body exists, are nothing but the phenomenal appearance of the will, its becoming visible, the *objectivity of the will*. On this rests the perfect suitability of the human and animal body to the human and animal will in general, resembling, but far surpassing, the suitability of a purposely made instrument to the will of its maker, and on this account appearing as fitness or appropriateness, i.e., the teleological accountability of the body. Therefore the parts of the body must correspond completely to the chief demands and desires by which the will manifests itself; they must be the visible expression of these desires. Teeth, gullet, and intestinal canal are objectified hunger; the genitals are objectified sexual impulse; grasping hands and nimble feet correspond to the more indirect strivings of the will which they represent. Just as the general human form corresponds to the general human will, so to the individually modified will, namely the character of the individual, there corresponds the individual bodily structure, which is therefore as a whole and in all its parts characteristic and full of expression. . . .

§ 21.

From all these considerations the reader has now gained in the abstract, and hence in clear and certain terms, a knowledge which everyone possesses directly in the concrete, namely as feeling. This is the knowledge that the inner nature of his own phenomenon, which manifests itself to him as representation both through his actions and through the permanent substratum of these his body, is his *will*. This will constitutes what is most immediate in his consciousness, but as such it has not wholly entered into the form of the representation, in which object and subject stand over against each other; on the contrary, it makes itself known in an immediate way in which subject and object are not quite clearly distinguished, yet it becomes known to the individual himself not as a whole, but only in its particular acts. The reader who with me has gained this conviction, will find that of itself it will become the key to the knowledge of the innermost being of the whole of nature, since he now transfers it to all those phenomena that are given to him, not like his own phenomenon both in direct and in indirect knowledge, but in the latter solely, and hence merely in a one-sided way, as *representation* alone. He will recognize that same will not only in those phenomena that are quite similar to his own, in men and animals, as their innermost nature, but continued reflection will lead him to recognize the force that shoots and vegetates in the plant, indeed the force by which the crystal is formed, the force that turns the magnet to the North Pole, the force whose shock he encounters from the contact of metals of different kinds, the force that appears in the elective affinities of matter as repulsion and attraction, separation and union, and finally even gravitation, which acts so powerfully in all matter, pulling the stone to the earth and the earth to the sun; all these he will recognize as different only in the phenomenon, but the same according to their inner nature. He will recognize them all as that which is immediately known to him so intimately and better than everything else, and where it appears most distinctly is called *will*. It is only this application of reflection which no longer lets us stop at the phenomenon, but leads us on to the *thing-in-itself*. Phenomenon means representation and nothing more. All representation, be it of whatever kind it may, all *object*, is *phenomenon*. But only the *will* is *thing-in-itself*; as such it is not representation at all, but *toto genere* different therefrom. It is that of which all representation, all object, is the phenomenon, the visibility, the *objectivity*. It is the innermost essence, the kernel, of every particular thing and also of the whole. It appears in every blindly acting force of nature, and also in the deliberate conduct of man, and the great difference between the two concerns only the degree of the manifestation, not the inner nature of what is manifested.

Søren Kierkegaard

Søren Kierkegaard was born in Copenhagen, Denmark, in 1813, the youngest child of a large family. He was raised in a wealthy middle-class home, with the strictest devotion to church and religion. His father was a successful merchant and an avid reader of theology, and his mother had been his father's servant before she became his second wife. Kierkegaard had a hunchback, and this, according to some, is the "thorn in his flesh" he often mentions in his writings. He viewed his life as governed by a deep melancholy, which he self-consciously attempted to hide with wit and gaiety. An event of crucial importance for Kierkegaard was his breaking of his engagement to Regine Olsen in 1841. His reason for this action is an important but unsolved mystery. First educated at home, he began university as a student of theology but soon turned to literature and philosophy. Kierkegaard was especially steeped in the philosophy of Hegel, which he studied in Berlin. A dominant theme in his life was his opposition to official state Christianity, seen by him as encumbered by a passionless conformity to bourgeois respectability and stability. Instead, Kierkegaard advocated a life of intense religious commitment, free from superficiality and empty formalism. His works include *Either/Or* (1843), *Fear and Trembling* (1843), *Philosophical Fragments* (1844), *Concluding Unscientific Postscript* (1846), *The Sickness unto Death* (1849), *Training in Christianity* (1851), and *The Attack upon "Christendom"* (1854–1855). His writings were largely ignored outside of Denmark until the twentieth century, when they became very influential. Kierkegaard died in 1855, at the age of 42, after collapsing while carrying the last of his inheritance from the bank.

The overriding concern in Kierkegaard's religious and philosophical writings is to provide insight into meaning and fulfillment in human life. Achieving meaning in life, in his view, is not something simply given to us, but it is accomplished through our decisions. But Kierkegaard does not believe that we are ultimately on our own in making the best possible choice for our lives. His final recommendations are religious, and he argues that the best decision we can make is one in which we are dependent on God.

Kierkegaard claims that human existence involves a profound tension or conflict between two dimensions. A self is a tension between the finite and the infinite, between the temporal and the eternal. The notion of the temporal signifies the events of our lives considered as separate and particular moments, immediate and distinct from one another. As temporal beings, we are no different from the other animals, which also have sensations and try to satisfy desires. The notion of the eternal, by contrast, signifies the overarching unity that these events can have just for humans. Though we are beings governed by basic passions and desires, aiming at momentary satisfactions, we are also beings who can make life something more coherent and unified, something more than just a series of fragmented projects aimed at transitory enjoyments.

One can come to understand Kierkegaard's views by considering his threefold classification of the ways we humans can attempt to achieve fulfillment. For him there are three main "spheres of existence" or modes of life: the aesthetic, the ethical, and the religious. The most fundamental characteristic of the person living the aesthetic life is that his purposes are exhausted by the satisfaction of desires for momentary or short-term fulfillments. Kierkegaard believes that the aesthetic option will always fail as a route to meaning in life. Both the attraction and the failure of the aesthetic life can be explained by the fact that it expresses only one side of the self, the temporal aspect.

Kierkegaard believes that the expression of the eternal side can be achieved only by means of a decisive, continuously renewed choice that produces an overarching unity among the disparate moments in one's experience. This choice calls for a commitment, a "leap," that will unify one's life. Such a commitment might be ethical, for example, a commitment to another person in marriage; or religious, a commitment to God. The mark of the ethical life is a constantly renewed decision, made by one's own will alone, to live in accord with ethical duty. By continuously renewing this commitment, one can attempt to provide a unity to the various moments in one's life that expresses one's eternal nature. But Kierkegaard describes striving to express the eternal through one's own will alone as the most agonizing, albeit the highest, form of despair.

Kierkegaard maintains that there is a better solution to be found in the religious life, in part because in making a religious commitment one need not rely on oneself. His most thorough work on religion, the *Concluding Unscientific Postscript*, poses the claim that *truth is subjectivity*. Yet Kierkegaard does not mean to deny that there are objective facts. Rather, "truth is subjectivity" means that, when meaning in one's life is at stake, one's attitude toward the object of one's concerns takes precedence over the issue of whether one is actually right about some fact. In Kierkegaard's view, what is especially important for meaning in life is one's attitude in a relationship with a person or thing, by contrast with merely having true beliefs about that person or thing.

For example, someone might master all of the true sentences about something that is genuinely important, while maintaining a detached, theoretical stance. Imagine, for example, a psychologist who develops a theory about human relationships so accurate and insightful that it has changed the lives of many people. But suppose further that as a scientist she has developed so detached an attitude that she is unable to live in accordance with her theory in her own relationships, with the result that her life is empty and unfulfilled. Such a person possesses the truth objectively, but not subjectively. By contrast, another person might deeply and passionately live her relationships in accord with her insights. She would be in the truth subjectively.

In Kierkegaard's view, what is most important in the search for meaning and fulfillment for one's life is the nature of one's relationship. If one is attempting to relate oneself to God, the infinite being, the appropriate kind of relationship is one of infinite intensity. To illustrate these claims about truth, Kierkegaard argues that a pagan praying with infinite passion, "although his eyes rest on the image of an idol," has a more appropriate relationship to the truth, or is more "in the truth," than someone who has fewer false beliefs and more true beliefs about religion but holds them without deep feeling.

• • •

Significant studies of Kierkegaard's philosophy include C. Stephen Evans, *Kierkegaard's Fragments and Postscript: The Religious Philosophy of Johannes Climacus* (Atlantic Highlands, N.J.: Humanities Press, 1983) and Louis Mackey, *Kierkegaard: A Kind of Poet* (Philadelphia: University of Pennsylvania Press, 1971). Two important essays on Kierkegaard, both by Robert Adams, are "Truth and Subjectivity," in Eleonore Stump, ed., *Reasoned Faith: Essays in Philosophical Theology in Honor of Norman Kretzmann* (Ithaca: Cornell University Press, 1993) and "The Knight of Truth," *Faith and Philosophy* 7 (October 1990). An important collection of essays is Alastair Hannay and Gordon Marino, eds., *The Cambridge Companion to Kierkegaard* (Cambridge: Cambridge University Press, 1997).

Derk Pereboom

Concluding Unscientific Postscript

The Subjective Truth, Inwardness, Truth Is Subjectivity

. . . The way of objective reflection makes the subject accidental, and thereby transforms existence into something indifferent, something vanishing. Away from the subject the objective way of reflection leads to the objective truth, and while the subject and his subjectivity become indifferent, the truth also becomes indifferent, and this indifference is precisely its objective validity; for all interest, like all decisiveness, is rooted in subjectivity. The way of objective reflection leads to abstract thought, to mathematics, to historical knowledge of different kinds; and always it leads away from the subject, whose existence or non-existence, and from the objective point of view quite rightly, becomes infinitely indifferent. Quite rightly, since as Hamlet says,[1] existence and non-existence have only subjective significance. At its maximum this way will arrive at a contradiction, and in so far as the subject does not become wholly indifferent to himself, this merely constitutes a sign that his objective striving is not objective enough. At its maximum this way will lead to the contradiction that only the objective has come into being, while the subjective has gone out; that is to say, the existing subjectivity has vanished, in that it has made an attempt to become what in the abstract sense is called subjectivity, the mere abstract form of an abstract objectivity. And yet, the objectivity which has thus come into being is, from the subjective point of view at the most, either an hypothesis or an approximation, because all eternal decisiveness is rooted in subjectivity.

However, the objective way deems itself to have a security which the subjective way does not have (and, of course, existence and existing cannot be thought in combination with objective security); it thinks to escape a danger which threatens the subjective way, and this danger is at its maximum: madness. In a merely subjective determination of the truth, madness and truth become in the last analysis indistinguishable, since they may both have inwardness.[2] Nevertheless, perhaps I may here venture to offer a little remark, one which would seem to be not wholly superfluous in an objective age. The absence of inwardness is also madness. The objective truth as such, is by no means adequate to determine that whoever utters it is sane; on the contrary, it may even betray the fact that he is mad, although what he says may be entirely true, and especially objectively true. I shall here permit myself to tell a story, which without any sort of adaptation on my part comes direct from an asylum. A patient in such an institution seeks to escape, and actually succeeds in effecting his purpose by leaping out of a window, and prepares to start on the road to freedom, when the thought strikes him (shall I say sanely enough or madly enough?): "When you come to town you will be recognized, and you will at once be brought back here again; hence you need to prepare yourself fully to convince everyone by the objective truth of what you say, that all is in order as far as your sanity is concerned." As he walks

1. [Act III, Scene 1.—S.M.C.]

2. Even this is not really true, however for madness never has the specific inwardness of the infinite. Its fixed idea is precisely some sort of objectivity, and the contradiction of madness consists in embracing this with passion. The critical point in such madness is this again not the subjective, but the little finitude which has become a fixed idea, which is something that can never happen to the infinite.

along and thinks about this, he sees a ball lying on the ground, picks it up, and puts it into the tail pocket of his coat. Every step he takes the ball strikes him, politely speaking, on his hinder parts, and every time it thus strikes him he says: "Bang, the earth is round." He comes to the city, and at once calls on one of his friends; he wants to convince him that he is not crazy, and therefore walks back and forth, saying continually: "Bang, the earth is round!" But is not the earth round? Does the asylum still crave yet another sacrifice for this opinion, as in the time when all men believed it to be flat as a pancake? Or is a man who hopes to prove that he is sane, by uttering a generally accepted and generally respected objective truth, insane? And yet it was clear to the physician that the patient was not yet cured; though it is not to be thought that the cure would consist in getting him to accept the opinion that the earth is flat. But all men are not physicians, and what the age demands seems to have a considerable influence upon the question of what madness is. Aye, one could almost be tempted sometimes to believe that the modern age, which has modernized Christianity, has also modernized the question of Pontius Pilate,[3] and that its urge to find something in which it can rest proclaims itself in the question: What is madness? When a *Privatdocent*,[4] every time his scholastic gown reminds him that he ought to say something, says *de omnibus dubitandum est*,[5] and at the same time writes away at a system which offers abundant internal evidence in every other sentence that the man has never doubted anything at all: he is not regarded as mad.

Don Quixote[6] is the prototype for a subjective madness, in which the passion of inwardness embraces a particular finite fixed idea. But the absence of inwardness gives us on the other hand the prating madness, which is quite as comical; and it might be a very desirable thing if an experimental psychologist would delineate it by taking a handful of such philosophers and bringing them together. In the type of madness which manifests itself as an aberrant inwardness, the tragic and the comic is that the something which is of such infinite concern to the unfortunate individual is a particular fixation which does not really concern anybody. In the type of madness which consists in the absence of inwardness, the comic is that though the something which the happy individual knows really is the truth, the truth which concerns all men, it does not in the slightest degree concern the much respected prater. This type of madness is more inhuman than the other. One shrinks from looking into the eyes of a madman of the former type lest one be compelled to plumb there the depths of his delirium; but one dares not look at a madman of the latter type at all, from fear of discovering that he has eyes of glass and hair made from carpet-rags; that he is, in short, an artificial product. If you meet someone who suffers from such a derangement of feeling, the derangement consisting in his not having any, you listen to what he says in a cold and awful dread, scarcely knowing whether it is a human being who speaks, or a cunningly contrived walking stick in which a talking machine has been concealed. It is always unpleasant for a proud man to find himself unwittingly drinking a toast of brotherhood with the public hangman;[7] but to find oneself engaged in rational and philosophical conversation with a walking stick is almost enough to make a man lose his mind.

The subjective reflection turns its attention inwardly to the subject, and desires in this intensification of inwardness to realize the truth. And it proceeds in such fashion that, just as in the preceding objective reflection, when the objectivity had come into being, the subjectivity had vanished, so here the subjectivity of the subject becomes the final stage, and objectivity a vanishing factor. Not for a single moment is it forgotten that the subject is an existing individual, and that existence is a process of becoming, and that therefore the notion of the truth as identity of thought and being is a chimera of abstraction, in its truth only an expectation of the creature; not because the truth

3. [The reference is to the first-century Roman governor of Judea who, according to the New Testament, officiated at the trial of Jesus.]

4. [An unsalaried university teacher in German-speaking countries paid directly by students' fees.]

5. [Everything is to be doubted.]

6. [In the remarkable novel of that name by the Spanish writer Miguel de Cervantes Saavedra (1547–1616), Don Quixote is a country gentleman who sets forth on a series of adventures in which he has difficulty distinguishing illusion from reality.]

7. [An incident in the play *Geert Westphaler* by the Danish writer Baron Ludwig Holberg (1684–1754).]

is not such an identity, but because the knower is an existing individual for whom the truth cannot be such an identity as long as he lives in time. Unless we hold fast to this, speculative philosophy will immediately transport us into the fantastic realism of the I-am-I,[8] which modern speculative thought has not hesitated to use without explaining how a particular individual is related to it; and God knows, no human being is more than such a particular individual.

If an existing individual were really able to transcend himself, the truth would be for him something final and complete; but where is the point at which he is outside himself? The I-am-I is a mathematical point which does not exist, and in so far there is nothing to prevent everyone from occupying this standpoint; the one will not be in the way of the other. It is only momentarily that the particular individual is able to realize existentially a unity of the infinite and the finite which transcends existence. This unity is realized in the moment of passion. Modern philosophy has tried anything and everything in the effort to help the individual to transcend himself objectively, which is a wholly impossible feat; existence exercises its restraining influence, and if philosophers nowadays had not become mere scribblers in the service of a fantastic thinking and its preoccupation, they would long ago have perceived that suicide was the only tolerable practical interpretation of its striving. But the scribbling modern philosophy holds passion in contempt; and yet passion is the culmination of existence for an existing individual—and we are all of us existing individuals. In passion the existing subject is rendered infinite in the eternity of the imaginative representation, and yet he is at the same time most definitely himself. The fantastic I-am-I is not an identity of the infinite and the finite, since neither the one nor the other is real; it is a fantastic rendezvous in the clouds,[9] an unfruitful embrace, and the relationship of the individual self to this mirage is never indicated.

All essential knowledge relates to existence, or only such knowledge as has an essential relationship to existence is essential knowledge. All knowledge which does not inwardly relate itself to existence, in the reflection of inwardness, is, essentially viewed, accidental knowledge; its degree and scope is essentially indifferent. That essential knowledge is essentially related to existence does not mean the above-mentioned identity which abstract thought postulates between thought and being; nor does it signify, objectively, that knowledge corresponds to something existent as its object. But it means that knowledge has a relationship to the knower, who is essentially an existing individual, and that for this reason all essential knowledge is essentially related to existence. Only ethical and ethico-religious knowledge has an essential relationship to the existence of the knower.

Mediation is a mirage, like the I-am-I. From the abstract point of view everything is and nothing comes into being. Mediation can therefore have no place in abstract thought, because it presupposes *movement*. Objective knowledge may indeed have the existent for its object; but since the knowing subject is an existing individual, and through the fact of his existence in process of becoming, philosophy must first explain how a particular existing subject is related to a knowledge of mediation. It must explain what he is in such a moment, if not pretty nearly *distrait*; where he is, if not in the moon? There is constant talk of mediation and mediation; is mediation then a man, as Peter Deacon[10] believes that *Imprimatur* is a man? How does a human being manage to become something of this kind? Is this dignity, this great *philosophicum*, the fruit of study, or does the magistrate give it away, like the office of deacon or grave-digger? Try merely to enter into these and other such plain questions of a plain man, who would gladly become mediation if it could be done in some lawful and honest manner, and not either by saying abracadabra, or by forgetting that he is himself an existing human being, for whom existence is therefore something essential, and an ethico-religious existence a suitable *quantum satis*.[11] A speculative philosopher may perhaps find it in bad taste to ask such questions. But it is important not to direct the polemic to the wrong point, and hence not to begin in a fantastic objective

8. [The reference is to the thought of Johann Gottlieb Fichte (1762–1814), the German philosopher who maintained that the essence of the I lies in self-awareness.]

9. [Distracted.]

10. [A reference to an incident in Holberg's comedy *Erasmus Montanus*.]

11. [Sufficiency.]

manner to discuss *pro* and *contra*[12] whether there is a mediation or not, but to hold fast what it means to be a human being.

In an attempt to make clear the difference of way that exists between an objective and a subjective reflection, I shall now proceed to show how a subjective reflection makes its way inwardly in inwardness. Inwardness in an existing subject culminates in passion; corresponding to passion in the subject the truth becomes a paradox; and the fact that the truth becomes a paradox is rooted precisely in its having a relationship to an existing subject. Thus the one corresponds to the other. By forgetting that one is an existing subject, passion goes by the board and the truth is no longer a paradox; the knowing subject becomes a fantastic entity rather than a human being, and the truth becomes a fantastic object for the knowledge of this fantastic entity.

When the question of truth is raised in an objective manner, reflection is directed objectively to the truth, as an object to which the knower is related. Reflection is not focussed upon the relationship, however, but upon the question of whether it is the truth to which the knower is related. If only the object to which he is related is the truth, the subject is accounted to be in the truth. When the question of the truth is raised subjectively, reflection is directed subjectively to the nature of the individual's relationship; if only the mode of this relationship is in the truth, the individual is in the truth even if he should happen to be thus related to what is not true.[13] Let us take as an example the knowledge of God. Objectively, reflection is directed to the problem of whether this object is the true God; subjectively, reflection is directed to the question whether the individual is related to a something *in such a manner* that his relationship is in truth a God-relationship. On which side is the truth now to be found? Ah, may we not here resort to a mediation, and say: It is on neither side, but in the mediation of both? Excellently well said, provided we might have it explained how an existing individual manages to be in a state of mediation. For to be in a state of mediation is to be finished, while to exist is to become. Nor can an existing individual be in two places at the same time—he cannot be an identity of subject and object. When he is nearest to being in two places at the same time he is in passion; but passion is momentary, and passion is also the highest expression of subjectivity.

The existing individual who chooses to pursue the objective way enters upon the entire approximation-process by which it is proposed to bring God to light objectively. But this is in all eternity impossible, because God is a subject, and therefore exists only for subjectivity in inwardness. The existing individual who chooses the subjective way apprehends instantly the entire dialectical difficulty involved in having to use some time, perhaps a long time, in finding God objectively; and he feels this dialectical difficulty in all its painfulness, because every moment is wasted in which he does not have God.[14] That very instant he has God, not by virtue of any objective deliberation, but by virtue of the infinite passion of inwardness. The objective inquirer, on the other hand, is not embarrassed by such dialectical difficulties as are involved in devoting an entire period of investigation to finding God—since it is possible that the inquirer may die tomorrow; and if he lives he can scarcely regard God as something to be taken along if convenient, since God is precisely that which one takes *a tout prix*,[15] which in the understanding of passion constitutes the true inward relationship to God.

It is at this point, so difficult dialectically, that the way swings off for everyone who knows what it means to think, and to think existentially; which is something very different from sitting at a desk and writing about what one has never done, something very different

12. [For and against.]

13. The reader will observe that the question here is about essential truth, or about the truth that is essentially related to existence, and that it is precisely for the sake of clarifying it as inwardness or as subjectivity that this contrast is drawn.

14. In this manner, God certainly becomes a postulate, but not in the otiose manner in which this word is commonly understood. It becomes clear rather that the only way in which an existing individual comes into relation with God is when the dialectical contradictions brings his passion to the point of despair and helps him to embrace God with the "category of despair" (faith). Then the postulate is so far from being arbitrary that it is precisely a life-necessity. It is then not so much that God is a postulate as that the existing individual's postulation of God is a necessity.

15. [At any cost.]

from writing *de omnibus dubitandum*[16] and at the same time being as credulous existentially as the most sensuous of men. Here is where the way swings off, and the change is marked by the fact that while objective knowledge rambles comfortably on by way of the long road of approximation without being impelled by the urge of passion, subjective knowledge counts every delay a deadly peril, and the decision so infinitely important and so instantly pressing that it is as if the opportunity had already passed.

Now when the problem is to reckon up on which side there is most truth, whether on the side of one who seeks the true God objectively, and pursues the approximate truth of the God-idea; or on the side of one who, driven by the infinite passion of his need of God, feels an infinite concern for his own relationship to God in truth (and to be at one and the same time on both sides equally, is as we have noted not possible for an existing individual, but is merely the happy delusion of an imaginary I-am-I): the answer cannot be in doubt for anyone who has not been demoralized with the aid of science. If one who lives in the midst of Christendom goes up to the house of God, the house of the true God, with the true conception of God in his knowledge, and prays, but prays in a false spirit; and one who lives in an idolatrous community prays with the entire passion of the infinite, although his eyes rest upon the image of an idol: where is there most truth? The one prays in truth to God though he worships an idol; the other prays falsely to the true God, and hence worships in fact an idol.

When one man investigates objectively the problem of immortality, and another embraces an uncertainty with the passion of the infinite: where is there most truth, and who has the greater certainty? The one has entered upon a never-ending approximation, for the certainty of immortality lies precisely in the subjectivity of the individual; the other is immortal, and fights for his immortality by struggling with the uncertainty. Let us consider Socrates. Nowadays everyone dabbles in a few proofs; some have several such proofs, others fewer. But Socrates! He puts the question objectively in a problematic manner: *if* there is an immortality. He must therefore be accounted a doubter in comparison with one of our modern thinkers with the three proofs? By no means. On this "if" he risks his entire life, he has the courage to meet death, and he has with the passion of the infinite so determined the pattern of his life that it must be found acceptable—*if* there is an immortality. Is any better proof capable of being given for the immortality of the soul? But those who have the three proofs do not at all determine their lives in conformity therewith; if there is an immortality it must feel disgust over their manner of life: can any better refutation be given of the three proofs? The bit of uncertainty that Socrates had, helped him because he himself contributed the passion of the infinite; the three proofs that the others have do not profit them at all, because they are dead to spirit and enthusiasm, and their three proofs, in lieu of proving anything else, prove just this. A young girl may enjoy all the sweetness of love on the basis of what is merely a weak hope that she is beloved, because she rests everything on this weak hope; but many a wedded matron more than once subjected to the strongest expressions of love, has in so far indeed had proofs, but strangely enough has not enjoyed *quod erat demonstrandum*.[17] The Socratic ignorance, which Socrates held fast with the entire passion of his inwardness, was thus an expression for the principle that the eternal truth is related to an existing individual, and that this truth must therefore be a paradox for him as long as he exists; and yet it is possible that there was more truth in the Socratic ignorance as it was in him, than in the entire objective truth of the System, which flirts with what the times demand and accommodates itself to *Privatdocents*.

The objective accent falls on WHAT is said, the subjective accent on HOW it is said. This distinction holds even in the aesthetic realm, and receives definite expression in the principle that what is in itself true may in the mouth of such and such a person become untrue. In these times this distinction is particularly worthy of notice, for if we wish to express in a single sentence the difference between ancient times and our own, we should doubtless have to say: "In ancient times only an individual here and there knew the truth; now all know it, except that the inwardness of its appropriation stands in an inverse

16. [About everything that can be doubted.]

17. [What was to be demonstrated.]

relationship to the extent of its dissemination."[18] Aesthetically the contradiction that truth becomes untruth in this or that person's mouth, is best construed comically: In the ethico-religious sphere, accent is again on the "how." But this is not to be understood as referring to demeanor, expression, or the like; rather it refers to the relationship sustained by the existing individual, in his own existence, to the content of his utterance. Objectively the interest is focussed merely on the thought-content, subjectively on the inwardness. At its maximum this inward "how" is the passion of the infinite, and the passion of the infinite is the truth. But the passion of the infinite is precisely subjectivity, and thus subjectivity becomes the truth. Objectively there is no infinite decisiveness, and hence it is objectively in order to annul the difference between good and evil, together with the principle of contradiction, and therewith also the infinite difference between the true and the false. Only in subjectivity is there decisiveness, to seek objectivity is to be in error. It is the passion of the infinite that is the decisive factor and not its content, for its content is precisely itself. In this manner subjectivity and the subjective "how" constitute the truth.

But the "how" which is thus subjectively accentuated precisely because the subject is an existing individual, is also subject to a dialectic with respect to time. In the passionate moment of decision, where the road swings away from objective knowledge, it seems as if the infinite decision were thereby realized. But in the same moment that existing individual finds himself in the temporal order, and the subjective "how" is transformed into a striving, a striving which receives indeed its impulse and a repeated renewal from the decisive passion of the infinite, but is nevertheless a striving.

When subjectivity is the truth, the conceptual determination of the truth must include an expression for the antithesis to objectivity, a memento of the fork in the road where the way swings off; this expression will at the same time serve as an indication of the tension of the subjective inwardness. Here is such a definition of truth: *An objective uncertainty held fast in an appropriation-process of the most passionate inwardness is the truth*, the highest truth attainable for an *existing* individual. At the point where the way swings off (and where this is cannot be specified objectively, since it is a matter of subjectivity), there objective knowledge is placed in abeyance. Thus the subject merely has, objectively, the uncertainty; but it is this which precisely increases the tension of that infinite passion which constitutes his inwardness. The truth is precisely the venture which chooses an objective uncertainty with the passion of the infinite. I contemplate the order of nature in the hope of finding God, and I see omnipotence and wisdom; but I also see much else that disturbs my mind and excites anxiety. The sum of all this is an objective uncertainty. But it is for this very reason that the inwardness becomes as intense as it is, for it embraces this objective uncertainty with the entire passion of the infinite. In the case of a mathematical proposition the objectivity is given, but for this reason the truth of such a proposition is also an indifferent truth.

But the above definition of truth is an equivalent expression for faith. Without risk there is no faith. Faith is precisely the contradiction between the infinite passion of the individual's inwardness and the objective uncertainty. If I am capable of grasping God objectively, I do not believe, but precisely because I cannot do this I must believe. If I wish to preserve myself in faith I must constantly be intent upon holding fast the objective uncertainty, so as to remain out upon the deep, over seventy thousand fathoms of water, still preserving my faith.

18. *Stages on Life's Way*, Note on p. 426. Though ordinarily not wishing an expression of opinion on the part of reviewers, I might at this point almost desire it, provided such opinions, so far from flattering me, amounted to an assertion of the daring truth that what I say is something that everybody knows, even every child, and that the cultured know infinitely much better. If it only stands fast that everyone knows it, my standpoint is in order, and I shall doubtless make shift to manage with the unity of the comic and the tragic. If there were anyone who did not know it I might perhaps be in danger of being dislodged from my position of equilibrium by the thought that I might be in a position to communicate to someone the needful preliminary knowledge. It is just this which engages my interest so much, this that the cultured are accustomed to say: that everyone knows what the highest is. This was not the case in paganism, nor in Judaism, not in the seventeen centuries of Christianity. Hail to the nineteenth century! Everyone knows it. What progress has been made since the time when only a few knew it. To make up for this, perhaps, we must assume that no one nowadays does it.

John Stuart Mill

John Stuart Mill (1806–1873) was born in London, the son of a well-known philosopher, James Mill. He was extremely well educated by his father, beginning his studies of Greek and Latin at the ages of three and eight, and subsequently reading widely in the classics, history, philosophy, logic, and mathematics. In 1826, at the age of twenty, he underwent a period of acute depression: his ability to feel emotion, he believed, had been weakened by his intensive analytic training. He responded to this crisis by turning to the arts, taking special solace in the poetry of Wordsworth. Eventually he recovered fully. Hired as a clerk by the East India Company in 1823, he supported himself by working for this concern in various capacities until his retirement in 1858. In 1831 he met Harriet Taylor, a merchant's wife with whom he fell in love. Mill and Harriet Taylor were close and constant friends for many years, collaborating on many literary enterprises and finally marrying in 1851 after her husband's death. In his later years, Mill served a term in Parliament (1865–1868).

Mill's contributions to philosophy and social thought are varied. *A System of Logic* (1843) and *An Examination of Sir William Hamilton's Philosophy* (1865) deal with questions of logic and epistemology. *On Liberty* (1859) is a well-known discussion of the extent to which society may interfere with individuals' liberties. In *Utilitarianism* (first published in *Fraser's Magazine*, 1861), Mill expounds his own version of utilitarian ethics. Other topics of social importance are discussed in *Principles of Political Economy* (1848), *Considerations on Representative Government* (1861), *August Comte and Positivism* (1865), and *The Subjection of Women* (1869). His *Autobiography* (1873) presents a fascinating picture of his life.

Like the earlier empiricists, Mill believed that sensation and the mind's awareness of its own activity are the sole sources of all knowledge. However, his empiricism differs from earlier versions on a number of important issues, among them the nature of ordinary objects and the role of induction. Mill accepted Berkeley's contention that ordinary objects are collections of sense-impressions but rejected his contention that the continuous existence of these objects is due mainly to God's continuing perception of them. Rather, Mill argued, the continuous existence of tables, chairs, and other objects resides entirely in the fact that we *could* perceive them at any moment. Ordinary objects are just "permanent possibilities of sensation." Concerning induction, or reasoning that extrapolates from known regularities to conclusions about what is likely to happen in unknown instances, Mill did not share Hume's skepticism. Inductive reasoning, he argued, is licensed by a general axiom of nature's uniformity (itself arrived at inductively) and is the fundamental element in all forms of inference, including deductive inference. Even the truths of mathematics and geometry, generally held to be known a priori, are actually determined by generalizing from past experience.

Mill's moral philosophy is known as utilitarianism. Its fundamental principle is that we should always perform those acts that will bring the most happiness or, failing that, the least unhappiness. This "greatest happiness principle" did not originate with Mill but was pioneered by Jeremy Bentham (1748–1832), the English philosopher and social reformer. However, Mill's essay *Utilitarianism* is the principle's best-known formulation. In support of the greatest happiness principle, Mill argued that "the sole evidence it is possible to produce that anything is desirable is that people do actually desire it"; and that, as a matter of fact, happiness is the one and only thing that people desire. When they seem to desire other things, such as wealth or virtue, it is always because these things are either means to their happiness or "part of their happiness." Given this reasoning, Mill naturally differed with Bentham over the values of different types of pleasure. Bentham had held that the intensity of a pleasure is the only criterion of its worth. For him, sublime moments of intellect or sentiment were worth no more than equally intense moments of animal gratification. For Mill, however, pleasures of equal intensity could differ in worth. Anyone who has experienced both the pleasures of the brute and the pleasures of the civilized person will prefer the latter to the former; and so, according to Mill, the civilized pleasures must be preferable.

At first glance, Mill's greatest-happiness principle may seem to imply that society should interfere with people's liberties whenever such interference will maximize overall happiness. However, Mill did not take any such position. Rather, he argued in *On Liberty* that "the only purpose for which power can be rightfully exercised over any member of a civilised community, against his will, is to prevent harm to others. His own good, either physical or moral, is not a sufficient warrant." In support of this principle, Mill cited the varied benefits of liberty in self-regarding actions. Such liberty, he argued, leads to the discovery of useful new truths and modes of life; confirms and strengthens the insights we already possess; and promotes the happiness of each individual more surely than any enforced and uniform standard can. In this and other ways, Mill attempted to reconcile his utilitarianism with the plurality of values that we possess.

• • •

For general discussions of Mill's work, see R. P. Anschutz, *The Philosophy of John Stuart Mill* (Oxford: Oxford University Press, 1953); Alan Ryan, *J. S. Mill* (London: Routledge & Kegan Paul, 1974); John Skorupski, *John Stuart Mill* (London and New York: Routledge, 1989); and David Lyons, *Rights, Welfare, and Mill's Moral Theory* (Oxford: Clarendon, 1994). For shorter essays, see J. P. Schneewind, ed., *Mill: A Collection of Critical Essays* (Garden City, N.J.: Doubleday, 1968); Samuel Gorovitz, ed., *Utilitarianism with Critical Essays* (Indianapolis: Bobbs-Merrill, 1971); David Lyons, ed., *Mill's Utilitarianism* (Lanham, Md.: Rowman & Littlefield, 1997); and John Skorupski, ed., *The Cambridge Companion to Mill* (Cambridge: Cambridge University Press, 1998). A clear general discussion of utilitarianism can be found in J. J. C. Smart and Bernard Williams, *Utilitarianism: For and Against* (Cambridge: Cambridge University Press, 1973).

George Sher

Utilitarianism

CHAPTER I

General Remarks

There are few circumstances among those which make up the present condition of human knowledge more unlike what might have been expected, or more significant of the backward state in which speculation on the most important subjects still lingers, than the little progress which has been made in the decision of the controversy respecting the criterion of right and wrong. From the dawn of philosophy, the question concerning the *summum bonum*, or, what is the same thing, concerning the foundation of morality, has been accounted the main problem in speculative thought, has occupied the most gifted intellects and divided them into sects and schools carrying on a vigorous warfare against one another. And after more than two thousand years the same discussions continue, philosophers are still ranged under the same contending banners, and neither thinkers nor mankind at a large seem nearer to being unanimous on the subject than when the youth Socrates listened to the old Protagoras[1] and asserted (if Plato's dialogue be grounded on a real conversation) the theory of utilitarianism against the popular morality of the so-called sophist.

It is true that similar confusion and uncertainty and, in some cases, similar discordance exist respecting the first principles of all the sciences, not excepting that which is deemed the most certain of them—mathematics, without much impairing, generally indeed without impairing at all, the trustworthiness of the conclusions of those sciences. An apparent anomaly, the explanation of which is that the detailed doctrines of a science are not usually deduced from, nor depend for their evidence upon, what are called its first principles. Were it not so, there would be no science more precarious, or whose conclusions were more insufficiently made out, than algebra, which derives none of its certainty from what are commonly taught to learners as its elements, since these, as laid down by some of its most eminent teachers, are as full of fictions as English law, and of mysteries as theology. The truths which are ultimately accepted as the first principles of a science are really the last results of metaphysical analysis practiced on the elementary notions with which the science is conversant; and their relation to the science is not that of foundations to an edifice, but of roots to a tree, which may perform their office equally well though they be never dug down to and exposed to light. But though in science the particular truths precede the general theory, the contrary might be expected to be the case with a practical art, such as morals or legislation. All action is for the sake of some end, and rules of action, it seems natural to suppose, must take their whole character and color from the end to which they are subservient. When we engage in pursuit, a clear and precise conception of what we are pursuing would seem to be the first thing we need, instead of the last we are to look forward to. A test of right and wrong must be the means, one would think, of ascertaining what is right or wrong, and not a consequence of having already ascertained it.

The difficulty is not avoided by having recourse to the popular theory of a natural faculty, a sense of instinct, informing us of right and wrong. For—besides that the existence of such a moral instinct is itself one of the matters in dispute—those believers in it who have any pretensions to philosophy have been obliged to abandon the idea that it discerns what is right or wrong in the particular case in hand, as our other senses discern the sight or sound actually present. Our moral faculty, according to all those of its interpreters who are entitled to the name of thinkers, supplies us only with the general principles of moral judgments; it is a branch of our reason, not of our sensitive faculty, and must be looked to for the abstract doctrines of morality, not for perception of it in the concrete. The intuitive, no less than what may be termed the inductive, school of ethics insists on the necessity of general laws. They both agree that the

1. [Regarding Protagoras, see Hume's *Enquiry*, n.60. —S.M.C.]

morality of an individual action is not a question of direct perception, but of the application of a law to an individual case. They recognize also, to a great extent, the same moral laws, but differ as to their evidence and the source from which they derive their authority. According to the one opinion, the principles of morals are evident *a priori*, requiring nothing to command assent except that the meaning of the terms be understood. According to the other doctrine, right and wrong, as well as truth and falsehood, are questions of observation and experience. But both hold equally that morality must be deduced from principles; and the intuitive school affirm as strongly as the inductive that there is a science of morals. Yet they seldom attempt to make out a list of the *a priori* principles which are to serve as the premises of the science; still more rarely do they make any effort to reduce those various principles to one first principle or common ground of obligation. They either assume the ordinary precepts of morals as of *a priori* authority, or they lay down as the common groundwork of those maxims some generality much less obviously authoritative than the maxims themselves, and which has never succeeded in gaining popular acceptance. Yet to support their pretensions there ought either to be some one fundamental principle or law at the root of all morality, or, if there be several, there should be a determinate order of precedence among them; and the one principle, or the rule for deciding between the various principles when they conflict, ought to be self-evident.

To inquire how far the bad effects of this deficiency have been mitigated in practice, or to what extent the moral beliefs of mankind have been vitiated or made uncertain by the absence of any distinct recognition of an ultimate standard, would imply a complete survey and criticism of past and present ethical doctrine. It would, however, be easy to show that whatever steadiness or consistency these moral beliefs have attained has been mainly due to the tacit influence of a standard not recognized. Although the nonexistence of an acknowledged first principle has made ethics not so much a guide as a consecration of men's actual sentiments, still, as men's sentiments, both of favor and of aversion, are greatly influenced by what they suppose to be the effects of things upon their happiness, the principle of utility, or, as Bentham latterly called it, the greatest happiness principle, has had a large share in forming the moral doctrines even of those who most scornfully reject its authority. Nor is there any school of thought which refuses to admit that the influence of actions on happiness is a most material and even predominant consideration in many of the details of morals, however unwilling to acknowledge it as the fundamental principle of morality and the source of moral obligation. I might go much further and say that to all those *a priori* moralists who deem it necessary to argue at all, utilitarian arguments are indispensable. It is not my present purpose to criticize these thinkers; but I cannot help referring, for illustration, to a systematic treatise by one of the most illustrious of them, the *Metaphysics of Ethics* by Kant. This remarkable man, whose system of thought will long remain one of the landmarks in the history of philosophical speculation, does, in the treatise in question, lay down a universal first principle as the origin and ground of moral obligation; it is this: "So act that the rule on which thou actest would admit of being adopted as a law by all rational beings." But when he begins to deduce from this precept any of the actual duties of morality, he fails, almost grotesquely, to show that there would be any contradiction, any logical (not to say physical) impossibility, in the adoption by all rational beings of the most outrageously immoral rules of conduct. All he shows is that the *consequences* of their universal adoption would be such as no one would choose to incur.

On the present occasion, I shall, without further discussion of the other theories, attempt to contribute something toward the understanding and appreciation of the "utilitarian" or "happiness" theory, and toward such proof as it is susceptible of. It is evident that this cannot be proof in the ordinary and popular meaning of the term. Questions of ultimate ends are not amenable to direct proof. Whatever can be proved to be good must be so by being shown to be a means to something admitted to be good without proof. The medical art is proved to be good by its conducing to health; but how is it possible to prove that health is good? The art of music is good, for the reason, among others, that it produces pleasure; but what proof is it possible to give that pleasure is good? If, then, it is asserted that there is a comprehensive formula, including all things which are in themselves good, and that whatever else is good is not so as an end but as a means, the formula may be accepted or rejected, but is not a subject of what is commonly understood by proof. We are not, however, to infer that its acceptance or rejection must depend on blind impulse or arbitrary choice. There is a larger meaning of the word "proof," in which this question is as amenable to it as any other of the disputed questions of philosophy. The subject is within the cognizance of the rational faculty; and neither does that faculty deal with it solely in the way of intuition. Considerations may be presented capable of determining the intellect either to give or withhold its assent to the doctrine; and this is equivalent to proof.

We shall examine presently of what nature are these considerations; in what manner they apply to the case, and what rational grounds, therefore, can be given for accepting or rejecting the utilitarian formula. But it is a preliminary condition of rational acceptance or rejection that the formula should be correctly understood. I believe that the very imperfect notion ordinarily formed of its meaning is the chief obstacle which impedes its reception, and that, could it be cleared even from only the grosser misconceptions, the question would be greatly simplified and a large proportion of its difficulties removed. Before, therefore, I attempt to enter into the philosophical grounds which can be given for assenting to the utilitarian standard, I shall offer some illustrations of the doctrine itself, with the view of showing more clearly what it is, distinguishing it from what it is not, and disposing of such of the practical objections to it as either originate in, or are closely connected with, mistaken interpretations of its meaning. Having thus prepared the ground, I shall afterwards endeavor to throw such light as I can call upon the question considered as one of philosophical theory.

CHAPTER II

What Utilitarianism Is

A passing remark is all that needs be given to the ignorant blunder of supposing that those who stand up for utility as the test of right and wrong use the term in that restricted and merely colloquial sense in which utility is opposed to pleasure. An apology is due to the philosophical opponents of utilitarianism for even the momentary appearance of confounding them with anyone capable of so absurd a misconception; which is the more extraordinary, inasmuch as the contrary accusation, of referring everything to pleasure, and that, too, in its grossest form, is another of the common charges against utilitarianism: and, as has been pointedly remarked by an able writer, the same sort of persons, and often the very same persons, denounce the theory "as impracticably dry when the word 'utility' precedes the word 'pleasure,' and as too practicably voluptuous when the word 'pleasure' precedes the word 'utility.'" Those who know anything about the matter are aware that every writer, from Epicurus to Bentham, who maintained the theory of utility meant by it, not something to be contradistinguished from pleasure, but pleasure itself, together with exemption from pain; and instead of opposing the useful to the agreeable or the ornamental, have always declared that the useful means these, among other things. Yet the common herd, including the herd of writers, not only in newspapers and periodicals, but in books of weight and pretension, are perpetually falling into this shallow mistake. Having caught up the word "utilitarian," while knowing nothing whatever about it but its sound, they habitually express by it the rejection or the neglect of pleasure in some of its forms: of beauty, of ornament, or of amusement. Nor is the term thus ignorantly misapplied solely in disparagement, but occasionally in compliment, as though it implied superiority to frivolity and the mere pleasures of the moment. And this perverted use is the only one in which the word is popularly known, and the one from which the new generation are acquiring their sole notion of its meaning. Those who introduced the word, but who had for many years discontinued it as a distinctive appellation, may well feel themselves called upon to resume it if by doing so they can hope to contribute anything toward rescuing it from this utter degradation.[2]

2. The author of this essay has reason for believing himself to be the first person who brought the word "utilitarian" into use. He did not invent it, but adopted it from a passing expression in Mr. Galt's *Annals of the Parish*. [John Galt (1779–1839) was a Scottish novelist.] After using it as a designation for several years, he and others abandoned it from a growing dislike to anything resembling a badge or watchword of sectarian distinction. But as a name for one single opinion, not a set of opinions—to denote the recognition of utility as a standard, not any particular way of applying it—the term supplies a want in the language, and offers,

The creed which accepts as the foundation of morals "utility" or the "greatest happiness principle" holds that actions are right in proportion as they tend to promote happiness; wrong as they tend to produce the reverse of happiness. By happiness is intended pleasure and the absence of pain; by unhappiness, pain and the privation of pleasure. To give a clear view of the moral standard set up by the theory, much more requires to be said; in particular, what things it includes in the ideas of pain and pleasure, and to what extent this is left an open question. But these supplementary explanations do not affect the theory of life on which this theory of morality is grounded—namely, that pleasure and freedom from pain are the only things desirable as ends; and that all desirable things (which are as numerous in the utilitarian as in any other scheme) are desirable either for pleasure inherent in themselves or as means to the promotion of pleasure and the prevention of pain.

Now such a theory of life excites in many minds, and among them in some of the most estimable in feeling and purpose, inveterate dislike. To suppose that life has (as they express it) no higher end than pleasure—no better and nobler object of desire and pursuit—they designate as utterly mean and groveling, as a doctrine worthy only of swine, to whom the followers of Epicurus were, at a very early period, contemptuously likened; and modern holders of the doctrine are occasionally made the subject of equally polite comparisons by its German, French, and English assailants.

When thus attacked, the Epicureans have always answered that it is not they, but their accusers, who represent human nature in a degrading light, since the accusation supposes human beings to be capable of no pleasures except those of which swine are capable. If this supposition were true, the charge could not be gainsaid, but would then be no longer an imputation; for if the sources of pleasure were precisely the same to human beings and to swine, the rule of life which is good enough for the one would be good enough for the other. The comparison of the Epicurean life to that of beasts is felt as degrading, precisely because a beast's pleasures do not satisfy a human being's conceptions of happiness. Human beings have faculties more elevated than the animal appetites and, when once made conscious of them, do not regard anything as happiness which does not include their gratification. I do not indeed, consider the Epicureans to have been by any means faultless in drawing out their scheme of consequences from the utilitarian principle. To do this in any sufficient manner, many Stoic, as well as Christian, elements require to be included. But there is no known Epicurean theory of life which does not assign to the pleasures of the intellect, of the feelings and imagination, and of the moral sentiments a much higher value as pleasures than to those of mere sensation. It must be admitted, however, that utilitarian writers in general have placed the superiority of mental over bodily pleasures chiefly in the greater permanency, safety, uncostliness, etc., of the former—that is, in their circumstantial advantages rather than in their intrinsic nature. And on all these points utilitarians have fully proved their case; but they might have taken the other and, as it may be called, higher ground with entire consistency. It is quite compatible with the principle of utility to recognize the fact that some kinds of pleasure are more desirable and more valuable than others. It would be absurd that, while in estimating all other things quality is considered as well as quantity, the estimation of pleasure should be supposed to depend on quantity alone.

If I am asked what I mean by difference of quality in pleasures, or what makes one pleasure more valuable than another, merely as a pleasure, except its being greater in amount, there is but one possible answer. Of two pleasures, if there be one to which all or almost all who have experience of both give a decided preference, irrespective of any feeling of moral obligation to prefer it, that is the more desirable pleasure. If one of the two is, by those who are competently acquainted with both, placed so far above the other that they prefer it, even though knowing it to be attended with a greater amount of discontent, and would not resign it for any quantity of the other pleasure which their nature is capable of, we are justified in ascribing to the preferred enjoyment a superiority in quality so far outweighing quantity as to render it, in comparison, of small account.

Now it is an unquestionable fact that those who are equally acquainted with and equally capable of appreciating and enjoying both do give a most marked

in many cases, a convenient mode of avoiding tiresome circumlocutions.

preference to the manner of existence which employs their higher faculties. Few human creatures would consent to be changed into any of the lower animals for a promise of the fullest allowance of a beast's pleasures; no intelligent human being would consent to be a fool, no instructed person would be an ignoramus, no person of feeling and conscience would be selfish and base, even though they should be persuaded that the fool, the dunce, or the rascal is better satisfied with his lot than they are with theirs. They would not resign what they possess more than he for the most complete satisfaction of all the desires which they have in common with him. If they ever fancy they would, it is only in cases of unhappiness so extreme that to escape from it they would exchange their lot for almost any other, however undesirable in their own eyes. A being of higher faculties requires more to make him happy, is capable probably of more acute suffering, and certainly accessible to it at more points, than one of an inferior type; but in spite of these liabilities, he can never really wish to sink into what he feels to be a lower grade of existence. We may give what explanation we please of this unwillingness; we may attribute it to pride, a name which is given indiscriminately to some of the most and to some of the least estimable feelings of which mankind are capable; we may refer it to the love of liberty and personal independence, an appeal to which was with the Stoics one of the most effective means for the inculcation of it; to the love of power or to the love of excitement, both of which do really enter into and contribute to it; but its most appropriate appellation is a sense of dignity, which all human beings possess in one form or other, and in some, though by no means in exact, proportion to their higher faculties, and which is so essential a part of the happiness of those in whom it is strong that nothing which conflicts with it could be otherwise than momentarily an object of desire to them. Whoever supposes that this preference takes place at a sacrifice of happiness—that the superior being, in anything like equal circumstances, is not happier than the inferior—confounds the two very different ideas of happiness and content. It is indisputable that the being whose capacities of enjoyment are low has the greatest chance of having them fully satisfied; and a highly endowed being will always feel that any happiness which he can look for, as the world is constituted, is imperfect. But he can learn to bear its imperfections, if they are at all bearable; and they will not make him envy the being who is indeed unconscious of the imperfections, but only because he feels not at all the good which those imperfections qualify. It is better to be a human being dissatisfied than a pig satisfied; better to be Socrates dissatisfied than a fool satisfied. And if the fool, or the pig, are of a different opinion, it is because they only know their own side of the question. The other party to the comparison knows both sides.

It may be objected that many who are capable of the higher pleasures occasionally, under the influence of temptation, postpone them to the lower. But this is quite compatible with a full appreciation of the intrinsic superiority of the higher. Men often, from infirmity of character, make their election for the nearer good, though they know it to be the less valuable; and this no less when the choice is between two bodily pleasures than when it is between bodily and mental. They pursue sensual indulgences to the injury of health, though perfectly aware that health is the greater good. It may be further objected that many who begin with youthful enthusiasm for everything noble, as they advance in years, sink into indolence and selfishness. But I do not believe that those who undergo this very common change voluntarily choose the lower description of pleasures in preference to the higher. I believe that, before they devote themselves exclusively to the one, they have already become incapable of the other. Capacity for other nobler feelings is in most natures a very tender plant, easily killed, not only by hostile influences, but by mere want of sustenance; and in the majority of young persons it speedily dies away if the occupations to which their position in life has devoted them, and the society into which it has thrown them, are not favorable to keeping that higher capacity in exercise. Men lose their high aspirations as they lose their intellectual tastes, because they have not time or opportunity for indulging them; and they addict themselves to inferior pleasures, not because they deliberately prefer them, but because they are either the only ones to which they have access or the only ones which they are any longer capable of enjoying. It may be questioned whether anyone who has remained equally susceptible to both classes of pleasures ever knowingly and calmly preferred the lower, though many, in all ages, have broken down in an ineffectual attempt to combine both.

From this verdict of the only competent judges, I apprehend there can be no appeal. On a question which is the best worth having of two pleasures, or which of two modes of existence is the most grateful to the feelings, apart from its moral attributes and from its consequences, the judgment of those who are qualified by knowledge of both, or, if they differ, that of the majority among them, must be admitted as final. And there needs be the less hesitation to accept this judgment respecting the quality of pleasures, since there is no other tribunal to be referred to even on the question of quantity. What means are there of determining which is the acutest of two pains, or the intensest of two pleasurable sensations, except the general suffrage of those who are familiar with both? Neither pains nor pleasures are homogeneous, and pain is always heterogeneous with pleasure. What is there to decide whether a particular pleasure is worth purchasing at the cost of a particular pain, except the feelings and judgment of the experienced? When, therefore, those feelings and judgment declare the pleasures derived from the higher faculties to be preferable *in kind*, apart from the question of intensity, to those of which the animal nature, disjoined from the higher faculties, is susceptible, they are entitled on this subject to the same regard.

I have dwelt on this point as being a necessary part of a perfectly just conception of utility or happiness considered as the directive rule of human conduct. But it is by no means an indispensable condition to the acceptance of the utilitarian standard; for that standard is not the agent's own greatest happiness, but the greatest amount of happiness altogether; and if it may possibly be doubted whether a noble character is always the happier for its nobleness, there can be no doubt that it makes other people happier, and that the world in general is immensely a gainer by it. Utilitarianism, therefore, could only attain its end by the general cultivation of nobleness of character, even if each individual were only benefited by the nobleness of others, and his own, so far as happiness is concerned, were a sheer deduction from the benefit. But the bare enunciation of such an absurdity as this last renders refutation superfluous.

According to the greatest happiness principle, as above explained, the ultimate end, with reference to and for the sake of which all other things are desirable—whether we are considering our own good or that of other people—is an existence exempt as far as possible from pain, and as rich as possible in enjoyments, both in point of quantity and quality; the test of quality and the rule of measuring it against quantity being the preference felt by those who, in their opportunities of experience, to which must be added their habits of self-consciousness and self-observation, are best furnished with the means of comparison. This, being according to the utilitarian opinion the end of human action, is necessarily also the standard of morality, which may accordingly be defined "the rules and precepts for human conduct," by the observance of which an existence such as has been described might be, to the greatest extent possible, secured to all mankind; and not to them only, but, so far as the nature of things admits, to the whole sentient creation.

Against this doctrine, however, arises another class of objectors who say that happiness, in any form, cannot be the rational purpose of human life and action; because, in the first place, it is unattainable; and they contemptuously ask, What right hast thou to be happy?—a question which Mr. Carlyle[3] clinches by the addition, What right, a short time ago, hadst thou even *to be*? Next they say that men can do *without* happiness; that all noble human beings have felt this, and could not have become noble but by learning the lesson of *Entsagen*, or renunciation; which lesson, thoroughly learned and submitted to, they affirm to be the beginning and necessary condition of all virtue.

The first of these objections would go to the root of the matter were it well founded; for if no happiness is to be had at all by human beings, the attainment of it cannot be the end of morality or of any rational conduct. Though, even in that case, something might still be said for the utilitarian theory, since utility includes not solely the pursuit of happiness, but the prevention or mitigation of unhappiness; and if the

3. [Thomas Carlyle (1795–1881) was a Scottish author and social critic who wrote a multivolume history of the French Revolution. His theistic view stressed the essential spirituality of the world and its leaders.]

former aim be chimerical, there will be all the greater scope and more imperative need for the latter, so long at least as mankind think fit to live and do not take refuge in the simultaneous act of suicide recommended under certain conditions by Novalis.[4] When, however, it is thus positively asserted to be impossible that human life should be happy, the assertion, if not something like a verbal quibble, is at least an exaggeration. If by happiness be meant a continuity of highly pleasurable excitement, it is evident enough that this is impossible. A state of exalted pleasure lasts only moments or in some cases, and with some intermissions, hours or days, and is the occasional brilliant flash of enjoyment, not its permanent and steady flame. Of this the philosophers who have taught that happiness is the end of life were as fully aware as those who taunt them. The happiness which they meant was not a life of rapture, but moments of such, in an existence made up of few and transitory pains, many and various pleasures, with a decided predominance of the active over the passive, and having as the foundation of the whole not to expect more from life than it is capable of bestowing. A life thus composed, to those who have been fortunate enough to obtain it, has always appeared worthy of the name of happiness. And such an existence is even now the lot of many during some considerable portion of their lives. The present wretched education and wretched social arrangements are the only real hindrance to its being attainable by almost all.

The objectors perhaps may doubt whether human beings, if taught to consider happiness as the end of life,would be satisfied with such a moderate share of it. But great numbers of mankind have been satisfied with much less. The main constituents of a satisfied life appear to be two, either of which by itself is often found sufficient for the purpose: tranquillity and excitement. With much tranquillity, many find that they can be content with very little pleasure; with much excitement, many can reconcile themselves to a considerable quantity of pain. There is assuredly no inherent impossibility of enabling even the mass of mankind to unite both, since the two are so far from being incompatible that they are in natural alliance, the prolongation of either being a preparation for, and exciting a wish for, the other. It is only those in whom indolence amounts to a vice that do not desire excitement after an interval of repose; it is only those in whom the need of excitement is a disease that feel the tranquillity which follows excitement dull and insipid, instead of pleasurable in direct proportion to the excitement which preceded it. When people who are tolerably fortunate in their outward lot do not find in life sufficient enjoyment to make it valuable to them, the cause generally is caring for nobody but themselves. To those who have neither public nor private affections, the excitements of life are much curtailed, and in any case dwindle in value as the time approaches when all selfish interests must be terminated by death; while those who leave after them objects of personal affection, and especially those who have also cultivated a fellow-feeling with the collective interests of mankind, retain as lively an interest in life on the eve of death as in the vigor of youth and health. Next to selfishness, the principal cause which makes life unsatisfactory is want of mental cultivation. A cultivated mind—I do not mean that of a philosopher, but any mind to which the fountains of knowledge have been opened, and which has been taught, in any tolerable degree, to exercise its faculties—finds sources of inexhaustible interest in all that surrounds it: in the objects of nature, the achievements of art, the imaginations of poetry, the incidents of history, the ways of mankind, past and present, and their prospects in the future. It is possible, indeed, to become indifferent to all this, and that too without having exhausted a thousandth part of it, but only when one has had from the beginning no moral or human interest in these things and has sought in them only the gratification of curiosity.

Now there is absolutely no reason in the nature of things why an amount of mental culture sufficient to give an intelligent interest in these objects of contemplation should not be the inheritance of everyone born in a civilized country. As little is there an inherent necessity that any human being should be a selfish egotist, devoid of every feeling or care but those which center in his own miserable individuality. Something far superior to this is sufficiently common even now, to give ample earnest of what the human species may be made. Genuine private affections and a sincere interest in the public good are possible, though in unequal degrees, to every rightly brought up human

4. [Pseudonym of Friedrich Leopold Freiherr von Hardenberg (1771–1801), a German romantic poet.]

being. In a world in which there is so much to interest, so much to enjoy, and so much also to correct and improve, everyone who has this moderate amount of moral and intellectual requisites is capable of an existence which may be called enviable; and unless such a person, through bad laws or subjection to the will of others, is denied the liberty to use the sources of happiness within his reach, he will not fail to find this enviable existence, if he escapes the positive evils of life, the great sources of physical and mental suffering—such as indigence, disease, and the unkindness, worthlessness, or premature loss of objects of affection. The main stress of the problem lies, therefore, in the contest with these calamities from which it is a rare good fortune entirely to escape; which, as things now are, cannot be obviated, and often cannot be in any material degree mitigated. Yet no one whose opinion deserves a moment's consideration can doubt that most of the great positive evils of the world are in themselves removable, and will, if human affairs continue to improve, be in the end reduced within narrow limits. Poverty, in any sense implying suffering, may be completely extinguished by the wisdom of society combined with the good sense and providence of individuals. Even that most intractable of enemies, disease, may be indefinitely reduced in dimensions by good physical and moral education and proper control of noxious influences, while the progress of science holds out a promise for the future of still more direct conquests over this detestable foe. And every advance in that direction relieves us from some, not only of the chances which cut short our own lives, but, what concerns us still more, which deprive us of those in whom our happiness is wrapt up. As for vicissitudes of fortune and other disappointments connected with worldly circumstances, these are principally the effect either of gross imprudence, of ill-regulated desires, or of bad or imperfect social institutions. All the grand sources, in short, of human suffering are in a great degree, many of them almost entirely, conquerable by human care and effort; and though their removal is grievously slow—though a long succession of generations will perish in the breach before the conquest is completed, and this world becomes all that, if will and knowledge were not wanting, it might easily be made—yet every mind sufficiently intelligent and generous to bear a part, however small and inconspicuous, in the endeavor will draw a noble enjoyment from the contest itself, which he would not for any bribe in the form of selfish indulgence consent to be without.

And this leads to the true estimation of what is said by the objectors concerning the possibility and the obligation of learning to do without happiness. Unquestionably it is possible to do without happiness; it is done involuntarily by nineteen-twentieths of mankind, even in those parts of our present world which are least deep in barbarism; and it often has to be done voluntarily by the hero or the martyr, for the sake of something which he prizes more than his individual happiness. But this something, what is it, unless the happiness of others or some of the requisites of happiness? It is noble to be capable of resigning entirely one's own portion of happiness, or chances of it; but, after all, this self-sacrifice must be for some end; it is not its own end; and if we are told that its end is not happiness but virtue, which is better than happiness, I ask, would the sacrifice be made if the hero or martyr did not believe that it would earn for others immunity from similar sacrifices? Would it be made if he thought that his renunciation of happiness for himself would produce no fruit for any of his fellow creatures, but to make their lot like his and place them also in the condition of persons who have renounced happiness? All honor to those who can abnegate for themselves the personal enjoyment of life when by such renunciation they contribute worthily to increase the amount of happiness in the world; but he who does it or professes to do it for any other purpose is no more deserving of admiration than the ascetic mounted on his pillar. He may be an inspiring proof of what men *can* do, but assuredly not an example of what they *should*.

Though it is only in a very imperfect state of the world's arrangements that anyone can best serve the happiness of others by the absolute sacrifice of his own, yet, so long as the world is in that imperfect state, I fully acknowledge that the readiness to make such a sacrifice is the highest virtue which can be found in man. I will add that in this condition of the world, paradoxical as the assertion may be, the conscious ability to do without happiness gives the best prospect of realizing such happiness as is attainable. For nothing except that consciousness can raise a person above the chances of life by making him feel that, let fate and fortune do their worst, they have not power to subdue him; which, once felt, frees him from excess of anxiety concerning the evils of life and enables him, like many a Stoic in the worst times of the Roman Empire, to cultivate in tranquillity the sources of satisfaction accessible to him, without concerning himself about the uncertainty of their duration any more than about their inevitable end.

Meanwhile, let utilitarians never cease to claim the morality of self-devotion as a possession which belongs by as good a right to them as either to the Stoic or to the Transcendentalist.[5] The utilitarian morality does recognize in human beings the power of sacrificing their own greatest good for the good of others. It only refuses to admit that the sacrifice is itself a good. A sacrifice which does not increase or tend to increase the sum total of happiness, it considers as wasted. The only self-renunciation which it applauds is devotion to the happiness, or to some of the means of happiness, of others, either of mankind collectively or of individuals within the limits imposed by the collective interests of mankind.

I must again repeat what the assailants of utilitarianism seldom have the justice to acknowledge, that the happiness which forms the utilitarian standard of what is right in conduct is not the agent's own happiness but that of all concerned. As between his own happiness and that of others, utilitarianism requires him to be as strictly impartial as a disinterested and benevolent spectator. In the golden rule of Jesus of Nazareth, we read the complete spirit of the ethics of utility. "To do as you would be done by," and "to love your neighbor as yourself," constitute the ideal perfection of utilitarian morality. As the means of making the nearest approach to this ideal, utility would enjoin, first, that laws and social arrangements should place the happiness or (as, speaking practically, it may be called) the interest of every individual as nearly as possible in harmony with the interest of the whole; and, secondly, that education and opinion, which have so vast a power over human character, should so use that power as to establish in the mind of every individual an indissoluble association between his own happiness and the good of the whole, especially between his own happiness and the practice of such modes of conduct, negative and positive, as regard for the universal happiness prescribes; so that not only he may be unable to conceive the possibility of happiness to himself, consistently with conduct opposed to the general good, but also that a direct impulse to promote the general good may be in every individual one of the habitual motives of action, and the sentiments connected therewith may fill a large and prominent place in every human being's sentient existence. If the impugners of the utilitarian morality represented it to their own minds in this its true character, I know not what recommendation possessed by any other morality they could possibly affirm to be wanting to it; what more beautiful or more exalted developments of human nature any other ethical system can be supposed to foster, or what springs of action, not accessible to the utilitarian, such systems rely on for giving effect to their mandates.

The objectors to utilitarianism cannot always be charged with representing it in a discreditable light. On the contrary, those among them who entertain anything like a just idea of its disinterested character sometimes find fault with its standard as being too high for humanity. They say it is exacting too much to require that people shall always act from the inducement of promoting the general interests of society. But this is to mistake the very meaning of a standard of morals and confound the rule of action with the motive of it. It is the business of ethics to tell us what are our duties, or by what test we may know them; but no system of ethics requires that the sole motive of all we do shall be a feeling of duty; on the contrary, ninety-nine hundredths of all our actions are done from other motives, and rightly so done if the rule of duty does not condemn them. It is the more unjust to utilitarianism that this particular misapprehension should be made a ground of objection to it, inasmuch as utilitarian moralists have gone beyond almost all others in affirming that the motive has nothing to do with the morality of the action, though much with the worth of the agent. He who saves a fellow creature from drowning does what is morally right, whether his motive be duty or the hope of being paid for his trouble; he who betrays the friend that trusts him is guilty of a crime, even if his object

5. [Transcendentalism was a literary and philosophical movement that flourished in New England from about 1835 to 1860. It emphasized intuition as the source of knowledge and enlightened individualism as the basis of ethics. Its leading spokesmen were Ralph Waldo Emerson (1803–1882) and Henry David Thoreau (1817–1862).]

be to serve another friend to whom he is under greater obligations.[6] But to speak only of actions done from the motive of duty, and in direct obedience to principle: it is a misapprehension of the utilitarian mode of thought to conceive it as implying that people should fix their minds upon so wide a generality as the world, or society at large. The great majority of good actions are intended not for the benefit of the world, but for that of individuals, of which the good of the world is made up; and the thoughts of the most virtuous man need not on these occasions travel beyond the particular persons concerned, except so far as is necessary to assure himself that in benefiting them he is not violating the rights, that is, the legitimate and authorized expectations, of anyone else. The multiplication of happiness is, according to the utilitarian ethics, the object of virtue: the occasions on which any person (except one in a thousand) has it in his power to do this on an extended scale—in other words, to be a public benefactor—are but exceptional; and on these occasions alone is he called on to consider public utility; in every other case, private utility, the interest or happiness of some few persons, is all he has to attend to. Those alone the influence of whose actions extends to society in general need concern themselves habitually about so large an object. In the case of abstinences indeed—of things which people forbear to do from moral considerations, though the consequences in the particular case might be beneficial—it would be unworthy of an intelligent agent not to be consciously aware that the action is of a class which, if practiced generally, would be generally injurious, and that this is the ground of the obligation to abstain from it. The amount of regard for the public interest implied in this recognition is no greater than is demanded by every system of morals, for they all enjoin to abstain from whatever is manifestly pernicious to society.

The same considerations dispose of another reproach against the doctrine of utility, founded on a still grosser misconception of the purpose of a standard of morality and of the very meaning of the words "right" and "wrong." It is often affirmed that utilitarianism renders men cold and unsympathizing; that it chills their moral feelings toward individuals; that it makes them regard only the dry and hard consideration of the consequences of actions, not taking into their moral estimate the qualities from which those actions emanate. If the assertion means that they do not allow their judgment respecting the rightness or wrongness of an action to be influenced by their opinion of the qualities of the person who does it, this is a complaint not against utilitarianism, but against any standard or morality at all; for certainly no known ethical standard decides an action to be good or bad because it is done by a good or bad man, still less because done by an amiable, a brave, or a

6. An opponent, whose intellectual and moral fairness it is a pleasure to acknowledge (the Rev. J. Llewellyn Davies), has objected to this passage, saying, "Surely the rightness or wrongness of saving a man from drowning does depend very much upon the motive with which it is done. Suppose that a tyrant, when his enemy jumped into the sea to escape from him, saved him from drowning simply in order that he might inflict upon him more exquisite tortures, would it tend to clearness to speak of that rescue as 'a morally right action'? Or suppose again, according to one of the stock illustrations of ethical inquiries, that a man betrayed a trust received from a friend, because the discharge of it would fatally injure that friend himself or someone belonging to him, would utilitarianism compel one to call the betrayal 'a crime' as much as if it had been done from the meanest motive?"

I submit that he who saves another from drowning in order to kill him by torture afterwards does not differ only in motive from him who does the same thing from duty or benevolence; the act itself is different. The rescue of the man is, in the case supposed, only the necessary first step of an act far more atrocious than leaving him to drown would have been. Had Mr. Davies said, "The rightness or wrongness of saving a man from drowning does depend very much"—not upon the motive, but—"upon the *intention*," no utilitarian would have differed from him. Mr. Davies, by an oversight too common not to be quite venial, has in this case confounded the very different ideas of Motive and Intention. There is no point which utilitarian thinkers (and Bentham pre-eminently) have taken more pains to illustrate than this. The morality of the action depends entirely upon the intention—that is, upon what the agent *wills to do*. But the motive, that is, the feeling which makes him will so to do, if it makes no difference in the act, makes none in the morality: though it makes a great difference in our moral estimation of the agent, especially if it indicates a good or a bad habitual *disposition*—a bent of character from which useful, or from which hurtful actions are likely to arise.

[This note appeared in the second edition of *Utilitarianism* but not in subsequent ones.]

benevolent man, or the contrary. These considerations are relevant, not to the estimation of actions, but of persons; and there is nothing in the utilitarian theory inconsistent with the fact that there are other things which interest us in persons besides the rightness and wrongness of their actions. The Stoics, indeed, with the paradoxical misuse of language which was part of their system, and by which they strove to raise themselves above all concern about anything but virtue, were fond of saying that he who has that has everything; that he, and only he, is rich, is beautiful, is a king. But no claim of this description is made for the virtuous man by the utilitarian doctrine. Utilitarians are quite aware that there are other desirable possessions and qualities besides virtue, and are perfectly willing to allow to all of them their full worth. They are also aware that a right action does not necessarily indicate a virtuous character, and that actions which are blamable often proceed from qualities entitled to praise. When this is apparent in any particular case, it modifies their estimation, not certainly of the act, but of the agent. I grant that they are, notwithstanding, of opinion that in the long run the best proof of a good character is good actions; and resolutely refuse to consider any mental disposition as good of which the predominant tendency is to produce bad conduct.This makes them unpopular with many people, but it is an unpopularity which they must share with everyone who regards the distinction between right and wrong in a serious light; and the reproach is not one which a conscientious utilitarian need be anxious to repel.

If no more be meant by the objection than that many utilitarians look on the morality of actions, as measured by the utilitarian standards, with too exclusive a regard, and do not lay sufficient stress upon the other beauties of character which go toward making a human being lovable or admirable, this may be admitted. Utilitarians who have cultivated their moral feelings, but not their sympathies, nor their artistic perceptions, do fall into this mistake; and so do all other moralists under the same conditions. What can be said in excuse for other moralists is equally available for them, namely, that, if there is to be any error, it is better that it should be on that side. As a matter of fact, we may affirm that among utilitarians, as among adherents of other systems, there is every imaginable degree of rigidity and of laxity in the application of their standard; some are even puritanically rigorous, while others are as indulgent as can possibly be desired by sinner or by sentimentalist. But on the whole, a doctrine which brings prominently forward the interest that mankind have in the repression and prevention of conduct which violates the moral law is likely to be inferior to no other in turning the sanctions of opinion against such violations. It is true, the question "What does violate the moral law?" is one on which those who recognize different standards of morality are likely now and then to differ. But difference of opinion on moral questions was not first introduced into the world by utilitarianism, while that doctrine does supply, if not always an easy, at all events a tangible and intelligible, mode of deciding such differences.

It may not be superfluous to notice a few more of the common misapprehensions of utilitarian ethics, even those which are so obvious and gross that it might appear impossible for any person of candor and intelligence to fall into them; since persons, even of considerable mental endowment, often give themselves so little trouble to understand the bearings of any opinion against which they entertain a prejudice, and men are in general so little conscious of this voluntary ignorance as a defect that the vulgarest misunderstandings of ethical doctrines are continually met with in the deliberate writings of persons of the greatest pretensions both to high principle and to philosophy. We not uncommonly hear the doctrine of utility inveighed against a *godless* doctrine. If it be necessary to say anything at all against so mere an assumption, we may say that the question depends upon what idea we have formed of the moral character of the Deity. If it be a true belief that God desires, above all things, the happiness of his creatures, and that this was his purpose in their creation, utility is not only not a godless doctrine, but more profoundly religious than any other. If it be meant that utilitarianism does not recognize the revealed will of God as the supreme law of morals, I answer that a utilitarian who believes in the perfect goodness and wisdom of *God* necessarily believes that whatever God has thought fit to reveal on the subject of morals must fulfill the requirements of utility in a supreme degree. But others besides utilitarians have been of opinion that the Christian revelation was intended, and is fitted, to inform the hearts and minds of mankind with a spirit which should enable them to find for themselves what is right, and incline them to do it when found, rather than to tell them, except in a very general way, what it is; and that we need a doctrine of ethics, carefully followed out, to *interpret* to us the will of God. Whether this opinion is correct or not, it is superfluous here to discuss; since whatever aid religion, either natural or revealed, can afford to ethical investigation is as open to the utilitarian moralist as to any other. He can use it as the testimony of God to the usefulness or hurtfulness of any given course of action by as good a right as others can use it for the indication of a transcendental law having no connection with usefulness or with happiness.

Again, utility is often summarily stigmatized as an immoral doctrine by giving it the name of "expediency," and taking advantage of the popular use of that term to contrast it with principle. But the expedient, in the sense in which it is opposed to the right, generally means that which is expedient for the particular interest of the agent himself; as when a minister sacrifices the interests of his country to keep himself in place. When it means anything better than this, it means that which is expedient for some immediate object, some temporary purpose, but which violates a rule whose observance is expedient in a much higher degree. The expedient, in this sense, instead of being the same thing with the useful, is a branch of the hurtful. Thus it would often be expedient, for the purpose of getting over some momentary embarrassment, or attaining some object immediately useful to ourselves or others, to tell a lie. But inasmuch as the cultivation in ourselves of a sensitive feeling on the subject of veracity is one of the most useful, and the enfeeblement of that feeling one of the most hurtful, things to which our conduct can be instrumental; and inasmuch as any, even unintentional, deviation from truth does that much toward weakening the trustworthiness of human assertion, which is not only the principal support of all present social well-being, but the insufficiency of which does more than any one thing that can be named to keep back civilization, virtue, everything on which human happiness on the largest scale depends—we feel that the violation, for a present advantage, of a rule of such transcendent expediency is not expedient, and that he who, for the sake of convenience to himself or to some other individual, does what depends on him to deprive mankind of the good, and inflict upon them the evil, involved in the greater or less reliance which they can place in each other's word, acts the part of one of their worst enemies. Yet that even this rule, sacred as it is, admits of possible exceptions is acknowledged by all moralists; the chief of which is when the withholding of some fact (as of information from a malefactor, or of bad news from a person dangerously ill) would save an individual (especially an individual other than oneself) from great and unmerited evil, and when the withholding can only be effected by denial. But in order that the exception may not extend itself beyond the need, and may have the least possible effect in weakening reliance on veracity, it ought to be recognized and, if possible, its limits defined; and, if the principle of utility is good for anything, it must be good for weighing these conflicting utilities against one another and marking out the region within which one or the other preponderates.

Again, defenders of utility often find themselves called upon to reply to such objections as this—that there is not time, previous to action, for calculating and weighing the effects of any line of conduct on the general happiness. This is exactly as if anyone were to say that it is impossible to guide our conduct by Christianity because there is not time, on every occasion on which anything has to be done, to read through the Old and New Testaments. The answer to the objection is that there has been ample time, namely, the whole past duration of the human species. During all that time mankind have been learning by experience the tendencies of actions; on which experience all the prudence as well as all the morality of life are dependent. People talk as if the commencement of this course of experience had hitherto been put off, and as if, at the moment when some man feels tempted to meddle with the property or life of another, he had to begin considering for the first time whether murder and theft are injurious to human happiness. Even then I do not think that he would find the question very puzzling; but, at all events, the matter is now done to his hand. It is truly a whimsical supposition that, if mankind were agreed in considering utility to be the test of morality, they would remain without any agreement as to what *is* useful, and would take no measures for having their notions on the subject taught to the young and enforced by law and opinion. There is no difficulty in proving any ethical standard whatever to work ill if we suppose universal idiocy to be conjoined with it; but on any hypothesis short of that, mankind must by this time have acquired positive beliefs as to the effects of some actions on their happiness; and the beliefs which have thus come down are the rules of morality for the multitude, and for the philosopher until he has succeeded in finding better. That philosophers might easily do this, even now, on many subjects; that the received code of ethics is by no means of divine right; and that mankind have still much to learn as to the effects of actions on the general happiness, I admit or rather earnestly maintain. The corollaries from the principle of utility, like the precepts of every practical art, admit of indefinite improvement, and, in a progressive state of the human mind, their improvement is perpetually going on. But to consider the rules of morality as improvable is one thing; to pass over the intermediate generalization entirely and endeavor to test each individual action directly by the first principle is another. It is a strange notion that the acknowledgment of a first principle is inconsistent with the admission of secondary ones. To inform a traveler respecting the place of his ultimate destination is not to forbid the use of landmarks and direction-posts on the way. The proposition that happiness is the end and aim of morality does not mean that no road ought to be laid down to that goal, or that persons going thither should not be advised to take one direction rather than another. Men really ought to leave off talking a kind of nonsense on this subject, which they would neither talk nor listen to on other matters of practical concernment. Nobody argues that the art of navigation is not founded on astronomy because sailors cannot wait to calculate the Nautical Almanac. Being rational creatures, they go to sea with it ready calculated; and all rational creatures go out upon the sea of life with their minds made up on the common questions of right and wrong, as well as on many of the far more difficult questions of wise and foolish. And this, as long as foresight is a human quality, it is to be presumed they will continue to do. Whatever we adopt as the fundamental principle of morality, we require subordinate principles to apply it by; the impossibility of doing without them, being common to all systems, can afford no argument against any one in particular; but gravely to argue as if no such secondary principles could be had, and as if mankind had remained till now, and always must remain, without drawing any general conclusions from the experience of human life is as high a pitch, I think, as absurdity has ever reached in philosophical controversy.

The remainder of the stock arguments against utilitarianism mostly consist in laying to its charge the common infirmities of human nature, and the general difficulties which embarrass conscientious persons in shaping their course through life. We are told that a utilitarian will be apt to make his own particular case an exception to moral rules, and, when under temptation, will see a utility in the breach of a rule, greater than he will see in its observance. But is utility the only creed which is able to furnish us with excuses for evil-doing and means of cheating our own conscience? They are afforded in abundance by all doctrines which recognize as a fact in morals the existence of conflicting considerations, which all doctrines do that have been believed by sane persons. It is not the fault of any creed, but of the complicated nature of human affairs, that rules of conduct cannot be so framed as to require no exceptions, and that hardly any kind of action can safely be laid down as either always obligatory or always condemnable. There is no ethical creed which does not temper the rigidity of its laws by giving a certain latitude, under the moral responsibility of the agent, for accommodation to peculiarities of circumstances; and under every creed, at the opening thus made, self-deception and dishonest casuistry get in. There exists no moral system under which there do not arise unequivocal cases of conflicting obligation. These are the real difficulties, the knotty points both in the theory of ethics and in the conscientious guidance of personal conduct. They are overcome practically, with greater or with less success, according to the intellect and virtue of the individual; but it can hardly be pretended that anyone will be the less qualified for dealing with them, from possessing an ultimate standard to which conflicting rights and duties can be referred. If utility is the ultimate source of moral obligations, utility may be invoked to decide between them when their demands are incompatible. Though the application of the standard may be difficult, it is better than none at all; while in other systems, the moral laws all claiming independent authority, there is no common umpire entitled to interfere between them; their claims to precedence one over another rest on little better than sophistry, and, unless determined, as they generally are, by the unacknowledged influence of consideration of utility, afford a free scope for the action of personal desires and partialities. We must remember that only in these cases of conflict between secondary principles is it requisite that first principles should be appealed to. There is no case of moral obligation in which some secondary principle is not involved; and if only one, there can seldom be any real doubt which one it is, in the mind of any person by whom the principle itself is recognized.

CHAPTER III

Of the Ultimate Sanction of the Principle of Utility

The question is often asked, and properly so, in regard to any supposed moral standard—What is its sanction? what are the motives to obey? or, more specifically, what is the source of its obligation? whence does it derive its binding force? It is a necessary part of moral philosophy to provide the answer to this question, which, though frequently assuming the shape of an objection to the utilitarian morality, as if it had some special applicability to that above others, really arises in regard to all standards. It arises, in fact, whenever a person is called on to *adopt* a standard, or refer morality to any basis on which he has not been accustomed to rest it. For the customary morality, that which education and opinion have consecrated, is the only one which presents itself to the mind with the feeling of being *in itself* obligatory; and when a person is asked to believe that this morality *derives* its obligation from some general principle round which custom has not thrown the same halo, the assertion is to him a paradox; the supposed corollaries seem to have a more binding force than the original theorem; the superstructure seems to stand better without than with what is represented as its foundation. He says to himself, I feel that I am bound not to rob or murder, betray or deceive; but why am I bound to promote the general happiness? If my own happiness lies in something else, why may I not give that the preference?

If the view adopted by the utilitarian philosophy of the nature of the moral sense be correct, this difficulty will always present itself until the influences which form moral character have taken the same hold of the principle which they have taken of some of the consequences—until, by the improvement of education, the feeling of unity with our fellow creatures shall be (what it cannot be denied that Christ intended it to be) as deeply rooted in our character, and to our own consciousness as completely a part of our nature, as the horror of crime is in an ordinarily well-brought up young person. In the meantime, however, the difficulty has no peculiar application to the doctrine of utility, but is inherent in every attempt to analyze morality and reduce it to principles; which, unless the principle is already in men's minds invested with as much sacredness as any of its applications, always seems to divest them of a part of their sanctity.

The principle of utility either has, or there is no reason why it might not have, all the sanctions which belong to any other system of morals. Those sanctions are either external or internal. Of the external sanctions it is not necessary to speak at any length. They are the hope of favor and the fear of displeasure from our fellow creatures or from the Ruler of the universe, along with whatever we may have of sympathy or affection for them, or of love and awe of Him, inclining us to do His will independently of selfish consequences. There is evidently no reason why all these motives for observance should not attach themselves to the utilitarian morality as completely and as powerfully as to any other. Indeed, those of them which refer to our fellow creatures are sure to do so, in proportion to the amount of general intelligence; for whether there be any other ground of moral obligation than the general happiness or not, men do desire happiness; and however imperfect may be their own practice, they desire and commend all conduct in others toward themselves by which they think their happiness is promoted. With regard to the religious motive, if men believe, as most profess to do, in the goodness of God, those who think that conduciveness to the general happiness is the essence or even only the criterion of good must necessarily believe that it is also that which God approves. The whole force therefore of external reward and punishment, whether physical or moral, and whether proceeding from God or from our fellow men, together with all that the capacities of human nature admit of disinterested devotion to either, become available to enforce the utilitarian morality, in proportion as that morality is recognized; and the more powerfully, the more the appliances of education and general cultivation are bent to the purpose.

So far as to external sanctions. The internal sanction of duty, whatever our standard of duty may be, is one and the same—a feeling in our own mind; a pain, more or less intense, attendant on violation of duty, which in properly cultivated moral natures rises, in the more serious cases, into shrinking from it as an impossibility. This feeling, when disinterested and connecting itself with the pure idea of duty, and not with some particular form of it, or with any of the merely accessory circumstances, is the essence of conscience; though in that complex phenomenon as it actually exists, the simple fact is in general all encrusted over with collateral associations derived from sympathy, from love, and still more from fear; from all the forms of religious feeling; from the recollections of childhood and of all our past life; from self-esteem, desire of the esteem of others, and occasionally even self-abasement. This extreme complication is, I apprehend, the origin of the sort of mystical character which, by a tendency of the human mind of which there are many other examples, is apt to be attributed to the idea of moral obligation, and which leads people to believe that the idea cannot possibly attach itself to any other objects than those which, by a supposed mysterious law, are found in our present experience to excite it. Its binding force, however, consists in the existence of a mass of feeling which must be broken through in order to do what violates our standard of right, and which, if we do nevertheless violate that standard, will probably have to be encountered afterwards in the form of remorse. Whatever theory we have of the nature or origin of conscience, this is what essentially constitutes it.

The ultimate sanction, therefore, of all morality (external motives apart) being a subjective feeling in our own minds, I see nothing embarrassing to those whose standard is utility in the question, What is the sanction of that particular standard? We may answer, the same as of all other moral standards—the conscientious feelings of mankind. Undoubtedly this sanction has no binding efficacy on those who do not possess the feelings it appeals to; but neither will these persons be more obedient to any other moral principle than to the utilitarian one. On them morality of any kind has no hold but through the external sanctions. Meanwhile the feelings exist, a fact in human nature, the reality of which, and the great power with which they are capable of acting on those in whom they have been duly cultivated, are proved by experience. No reason has ever been shown why they may not be cultivated to as great intensity in connection with the utilitarian as with any other rule of morals.

There is, I am aware, a disposition to believe that a person who sees in moral obligation a transcendental fact, an objective reality belonging to the province of "things in themselves," is likely to be more obedient to it than one who believes it to be entirely subjective, having its seat in human consciousness only. But whatever a person's opinion may be on this point of ontology, the force he is really urged by is his own subjective feeling, and is exactly measured by its strength. No one's belief that duty is an objective reality is stronger than the belief that God is so; yet the belief in God, apart from the expectation of actual reward and punishment, only operates on conduct through and in proportion to, the subjective religious feeling. The sanction, so far as it is disinterested, is always in the mind itself; and the notion, therefore, of the transcendental moralists must be that this sanction will not exist *in* the mind unless it is believed to have its root out of the mind; and that if a person is able to say to himself, "That which is restraining me and which is called my conscience is only a feeling in my own mind," he may possibly draw the conclusion that when the feeling ceases the obligation ceases, and that if he find the feeling inconvenient, he may disregard it and endeavor to get rid of it. But is this danger confined to the utilitarian morality? Does the belief that moral obligation has its seat outside the mind make the feeling of it too strong to get rid of it? The fact is so far otherwise that all moralists admit and lament the ease with which, in the generality of minds, conscience can be silenced or stifled. The question, "Need I obey my conscience?" is quite as often put to themselves by persons who never heard of the principle of utility as by its adherents. Those whose conscientious feelings are so weak as to allow of their asking this question, if they answer it affirmatively, will not do so because they believe in the transcendental theory, but because of the external sanctions.

It is not necessary, for the present purpose, to decide

whether the feeling of duty is innate or implanted. Assuming it to be innate, it is an open question to what objects it naturally attaches itself; for the philosophic supporters of that theory are now agreed that the intuitive perception is of principles of morality and not of the details. If there be anything innate in the matter, I see no reason why the feeling which is innate should not be that of regard to the pleasures and pains of others. If there is any principle of morals which is intuitively obligatory, I should say it must be that. If so, the intuitive ethics would coincide with the utilitarian, and there would be no further quarrel between them. Even as it is, the intuitive moralists, though they believe that there are other intuitive moral obligations, do already believe this to be one; for they unanimously hold that a large *portion* of morality turns upon the consideration due to the interests of our fellow creatures. Therefore, if the belief in the transcendental origin of moral obligation gives any additional efficacy to the internal sanction, it appears to me that the utilitarian principle has already the benefit of it.

On the other hand, if, as is my own belief, the moral feelings are not innate but acquired, they are not for that reason the less natural. It is natural to man to speak, to reason, to build cities, to cultivate the ground, though these are acquired faculties. The moral feelings are not indeed a part of our nature in the sense of being in any perceptible degree present in all of us; but this, unhappily, is a fact admitted by those who believe the most strenuously in their transcendental origin. Like the other acquired capacities above referred to, the moral faculty, if not a part of our nature, is a natural outgrowth from it; capable, like them, in a certain small degree, of springing up spontaneously; and susceptible of being brought by cultivation to a high degree of development. Unhappily it is also susceptible, by a sufficient use of the external sanctions and of the force of early impressions, of being cultivated in almost any direction, so that there is hardly anything so absurd or so mischievous that it may not, by means of these influences, be made to act on the human mind with all the authority of conscience. To doubt that the same potency might be given by the same means to the principle of utility, even if it had no foundation in human nature, would be flying in the face of all experience.

But moral associations which are wholly of artificial creation, when the intellectual culture goes on, yield by degrees to the dissolving force of analysis; and if the feeling of duty, when associated with utility, would appear equally arbitrary; if there were no leading department of our nature, no powerful class of sentiments, with which that association would harmonize, which would make us feel congenial and incline us not only to foster it in others (for which we have abundant interested motives), but also to cherish it in ourselves—if there were not, in short, a natural basis of sentiment for utilitarian morality, it might well happen that this association also, even after it had been implanted by education, might be analyzed away.

But there *is* this basis of powerful natural sentiment; and that it is which, when once the general happiness is recognized as the ethical standard, will constitute the strength of the utilitarian morality. This firm foundation is that of the social feelings of mankind—the desire to be in unity with our fellow creatures, which is already a powerful principle in human nature, and happily one of those which tend to become stronger, even without express inculcation, from the influences of advancing civilization. The social state is at once so natural, so necessary, and so habitual to man, that, except in some unusual circumstances or by an effort of voluntary abstraction, he never conceives himself otherwise than as a member of a body; and this association is riveted more and more, as mankind are further removed from the state of savage independence. Any condition, therefore, which is essential to a state of society becomes more and more an inseparable part of every person's conception of the state of things which he is born into, and which is the destiny of a human being. Now society between human beings, except in the relation of master and slave, is manifestly impossible on any other footing than that the interests of all are to be consulted. Society between equals can only exist on the understanding that the interests of all are to be regarded equally. And since in all states of civilization, every person, except an absolute monarch, has equals, everyone is obliged to live on these terms with somebody; and in every age some advance is made toward a state in which it will be impossible to live permanently on other terms with anybody. In this way people grow up unable to conceive as possible to them a state of total disregard of other people's interests. They are under a necessity of conceiving themselves as at least abstaining from all the grosser injuries, and (if only for their own protection) living in a state of constant protest against them. They are also familiar with the fact of co-operating with others and proposing to themselves a collective, not an individual, interest as the aim (at least for the time being) of their actions. So long as they are co-operating, their ends are identified with those of others; there is at least a temporary feeling that the interests of others are their own interests. Not only does all strengthening of social ties, and all healthy growth of society, give to each individual a stronger personal interest in practically consulting the welfare of others, it also leads him to identify his *feelings* more and more with their good, or at least with an even greater degree of practical consideration for it. He comes, as though instinctively, to be conscious of himself as a being who *of course* pays regard to others. The good of others becomes to him a thing naturally and necessarily to be attended to, like any of the physical conditions of our existence. Now, whatever amount of this feeling a person has, he is urged by the strongest motives both of interest and of sympathy to demonstrate it, and to the utmost of his power encourage it in others; and even if he has none of it himself, he is as greatly interested as anyone else that others should have it. Consequently, the smallest germs of the feeling are laid hold of and nourished by the contagion of sympathy and the influences of education; and a complete web of corroborative association is woven round it by the powerful agency of the external sanctions. This mode of conceiving ourselves and human life, as civilization goes on, is felt to be more and more natural. Every step in political improvement renders it more so, by removing the sources of opposition of interest and leveling those inequalities of legal privilege between individuals or classes, owing to which there are large portions of mankind whose happiness it is still practicable to disregard. In an improving state of the human mind, the influences are constantly on the increase which tend to generate in each individual a feeling of unity with all the rest; which, if perfect, would make him never think of, or desire, any beneficial condition for himself in the benefits of which they are not included. If we now suppose this feeling of unity to be taught as a religion, and the whole force of eduction, of institutions, and of opinion directed, as it once was in the case of religion, to make every person grow up from infancy surrounded on all sides both by the profession and the practice of it, I think that no one who can realize this conception will feel any misgiving about the sufficiency of the ultimate sanction for the happiness morality. To any ethical student who finds the realization difficult, I recommend, as a means of facilitating it, the second of M. Comte's two principal works, the *Traité de politique positive.*[7] I entertain the strongest objections to the system of politics and morals set forth in that treatise, but I think it has superabundantly shown the possibility of giving to the service of humanity, even without the aid of belief in a Providence, both the psychological power and the social efficacy of a religion, making it take hold of human life, and color all thought, feeling, and action in a manner of which the greatest ascendancy ever exercised by any religion may be but a type and foretaste; and of which the danger is, not that it should be insufficient, but that it should be so excessive as to interfere unduly with human freedom and individuality.

Neither is it necessary to the feeling which constitutes the binding force of the utilitarian morality on those who recognize it to wait for those social influences which would make its obligation felt by mankind at large. In the comparatively early state of human advancement in which we now live, a person cannot, indeed, feel that entireness of sympathy with all others which would make any real discordance in the general direction of their conduct in life impossible, but already a person in whom the social feeling is at all developed cannot bring himself to think of the rest of his fellow creatures as struggling rivals with him for the means of happiness, whom he must desire to see defeated in their object in order that he may succeed in his. The deeply rooted conception which every individual even now has of himself as a social being tends to make him feel it one of his natural wants that there should be harmony between his feel-

7. [Auguste Comte (1798–1857) was the French philosopher who founded positivism, a view that denies the sense of speculative metaphysics and stresses the role of scientific observation in achieving understanding. As a social reformer he called for a moral order in which all people and nations could live in harmony. The work referred to is his *Treatise of Positive Polity*.]

ings and aims and those of his fellow creatures. If differences of opinion and of mental culture make it impossible for him to share many of their actual feelings—perhaps make him denounce and defy those feelings—he still needs to be conscious that his real aim and theirs do not conflict; that he is not opposing himself to what they really wish for, namely, their own good, but is, on the contrary, promoting it. This feeling in most individuals is much inferior in strength to their selfish feelings, and is often wanting altogether. But to those who have it, it possesses all the characters of a natural feeling. It does not present itself to their minds as a superstition of education or a law despotically imposed by the power of society, but as an attribute which it would not be well for them to be without. This conviction is the ultimate sanction of the greatest happiness morality. This it is which makes any mind of well-developed feelings work with, and not against, the outward motives to care for others, afforded by what I have called the external sanctions; and, when those sanctions are wanting or act in an opposite direction, constitutes in itself a powerful internal binding force, in proportion to the sensitiveness and thoughtfulness of the character, since few but those whose mind is a moral blank could bear to lay out their course of life on the plan of paying no regard to others except so far as their own private interest compels.

CHAPTER IV

Of What Sort of Proof the Principle of Utility Is Susceptible

It has already been remarked that questions of ultimate ends do not admit of proof, in the ordinary acceptation of the term. To be incapable of proof by reasoning is common to all first principles, to the first premises of our knowledge, as well as to those of our conduct. But the former, being matters of fact, may be the subject of a direct appeal to the faculties which judge of fact—namely, our senses and our internal consciousness. Can an appeal be made to the same faculties on questions of practical ends? Or by what other faculty is cognizance taken of them?

Questions about ends are, in other words, questions what things are desirable. The utilitarian doctrine is that happiness is desirable, and the only thing desirable, as an end; all other things being only desirable as means to that end. What ought to be required of this doctrine, what conditions is it requisite that the doctrine should fulfill—to make good its claim to be believed?

The only proof capable of being given that an object is visible is that people actually see it. The only proof that a sound is audible is that people hear it; and so of the other sources of our experience. In like manner, I apprehend, the sole evidence it is possible to produce that anything is desirable is that people do actually desire it. If the end which the utilitarian doctrine proposes to itself were not, in theory and in practice, acknowledged to be an end, nothing could ever convince any person that it was so. No reason can be given why the general happiness is desirable, except that each person, so far as he believes it to be attainable, desires his own happiness. This, however, being a fact, we have not only all the proof which the case admits of, but all which it is possible to require, that happiness is a good: that each person's happiness is a good to that person, and the general happiness, therefore, a good to the aggregate of all persons. Happiness has made out its title as *one* of the ends of conduct and, consequently, one of the criteria of morality.

But it has not, by this alone, proved itself to be the sole criterion. To do that, it would seem, by the same rule, necessary to show, not only that people desire happiness, but that they never desire anything else. Now it is palpable that they do desire things which, in common language, are decidedly distinguished from happiness. They desire, for example, virtue and the absence of vice no less really than pleasure and the absence of pain. The desire of virtue is not as universal, but it is as authentic a fact as the desire of happiness. And hence the opponents of the utilitarian standard deem that they have a right to infer that there are other ends of human action besides happiness, and that happiness is not the standard of approbation and disapprobation.

But does the utilitarian doctrine deny that people desire virtue, or maintain that virtue is not a thing to be desired? The very reverse. It maintains not only that virtue is to be desired, but that it is to be desired disinterestedly, for itself. Whatever may be the opinion of utilitarian moralists as to the original conditions by which virtue is made virtue, however they may believe (as they do) that actions and dispositions are only virtuous because they promote another end than virtue, yet this being granted, and it having been decided, from considerations of this description, what *is* virtuous, they not only place virtue at the very head of the things which are good as means to the ultimate end, but they also recognize as a psychological fact the possibility of its being, to the individual, a good in itself, without looking to any end beyond it; and hold that the mind is not in a right state, not in a state conformable to utility, not in the state most conducive to the general happiness, unless it does love virtue in this manner—as a thing desirable in itself, even although, in the individual instance, it should not produce those other desirable consequences which it tends to produce, and on account of which it is held to be virtue. This opinion is not, in the smallest degree, a departure from the happiness principle. The ingredients of happiness are very various, and each of them is desirable in itself, and not merely when considered as swelling an aggregate. The principle of utility does not mean that any given pleasure, as music, for instance, or any given exemption from pain, as for example health, is to be looked upon as means to a collective something termed happiness, and to be desired on that account. They are desired and desirable in and for themselves; besides being means, they are a part of the end. Virtue, according to the utilitarian doctrine, is not naturally and originally part of the end, but it is capable of becoming so; and in those who live it disinterestedly it has become so, and is desired and cherished, not as a means to happiness, but as a part of their happiness.

To illustrate this further, we may remember that virtue is not the only thing originally a means, and which if it were not a means to anything else would be and remain indifferent, but which by association with what it is a means to comes to be desired for itself, and that too with the utmost intensity. What, for example, shall we say of the love of money? There is nothing originally more desirable about money than about any heap of glittering pebbles. Its worth is solely that of the things which it will buy; the desires for other things than itself, which it is a means of gratifying. Yet the love of money is not only one of the strongest moving forces of human life, but money is, in many cases, desired in and for itself; the desire to possess it is often stronger than the desire to use it, and goes on increasing when all the desires which point to ends beyond it, to be compassed by it, are falling off. It may, then, be said truly that money is desired not for the sake of an end, but as part of the end. From being a means to happiness, it has come to be itself a principal ingredient of the individual's conception of happiness. The same may be said of the majority of the great objects of human life: power, for example, or fame, except that to each of these there is a certain amount of immediate pleasure annexed, which has at least the semblance of being naturally inherent in them—a thing which cannot be said of money. Still, however, the strongest natural attraction, both of power and of fame, is the immense aid they give to the attainment of our other wishes; and it is the strong association thus generated between them and all our objects of desire which gives to the direct desire of them the intensity it often assumes, so as in some characters to surpass in strength all other desires. In these cases the means have become a part of the end, and a more important part of it than any of the things which they are means to. What was once desired as an instrument for the attainment of happiness has come to be desired for its own sake. In being desired for its own sake it is, however, desired as *part* of happiness. The person is made, or thinks he would be made, happy by its mere possession; and is made unhappy by failure to obtain it. The desire of it is not a different thing from the desire of happiness any more than the love of music or the desire of health. They are included in happiness.They are some of the elements of which the desire of happiness is made up. Happiness is not an abstract idea but a concrete whole; and these are some of its parts. And the utilitarian standard sanctions and approves their being so. Life would be a poor thing, very ill provided with sources of happiness, if there were not this provision of nature by which things originally indifferent, but conducive to, or otherwise associated with, the satisfaction of our primitive desires, become in themselves sources of pleasure more valuable than the primitive pleasures, both in permanency, in the space of human existence that they are capable of covering, and even in intensity.

Virtue, according to the utilitarian conception, is a good of this description. There was no original desire of it, or motive to it, save its conduciveness to pleasure, and especially to protection from pain. But through the association thus formed it may be felt a good in itself, and desired as such with as great intensity as any other good; and with this difference between it and the love of money, of power, or of fame—that all of these may, and often do, render the individual noxious to the other members of the society to which he belongs, whereas there is nothing which makes him so much a blessing to them as the cultivation of the disinterested love of virtue. And consequently, the utilitarian standard, while it tolerates and approves those other acquired desires, up to the point beyond which they would be more injurious to the general happiness than promotive of it, enjoins and requires the cultivation of the love of virtue up to the greatest strength possible, as being above all things important to the general happiness.

It results from the preceding considerations that there is in reality nothing desired except happiness. Whatever is desired otherwise than as a means to some end beyond itself, and ultimately to happiness, is desired as itself a part of happiness, and is not desired for itself until it has become so. Those who desire virtue for its own sake desire it either because the consciousness of it is a pleasure, or because the consciousness of being without it is a pain, or for both reasons united; as in truth the pleasure and pain seldom exist separately, but almost always together—the same person feeling pleasure in the degree of virtue attained, and pain in not having attained more. If one of these gave him no pleasure, and the other no pain, he would not love or desire virtue, or would desire it only for the other benefits which it might produce to himself or to persons whom he cared for.

We have now, then, an answer to the question, of what sort of proof the principle of utility is susceptible. If the opinion which I have now stated is psychologically true—if human nature is so constituted as to desire nothing which is not either a part of happiness or a means of happiness—we can have no other proof, and we require no other, that these are the only things desirable. If so, happiness is the sole end of human action, and the promotion of it the test by which to judge of all human conduct; from whence it necessarily follows that it must be the criterion of morality, since a part is included in the whole.

And now to decide whether this is really so, whether mankind do desire nothing for itself but that which is a pleasure to them, or of which the absence is a pain, we have evidently arrived at a question of fact and experience, dependent, like all similar questions, upon evidence. It can only be determined by practiced self-consciousness and self-observation, assisted by observation of others. I believe that these sources of evidence, impartially consulted, will declare that desiring a thing and finding it pleasant, aversion to it and thinking of it as painful, are phenomena entirely inseparable or, rather, two parts of the same phenomenon—in strictness of language, two different modes of naming the same psychological fact; that to think of an object as desirable (unless for the sake of its consequences) and to think of it as pleasant are one and the same thing; and that to desire anything except in proportion as the idea of it is pleasant is a physical and metaphysical impossibility.

So obvious does this appear to me that I expect it will hardly be disputed; and the objection made will be, not that desire can possibly be directed to anything ultimately except pleasure and exemption from pain, but that the will is a different thing from desire; that a person of confirmed virtue or any other person whose purposes are fixed carries out his purposes without any thought of the pleasure he has in contemplating them or expects to derive from their fulfillment, and persists in acting on them, even though these pleasures are much diminished by changes in his character or decay of his passive sensibilities, or are outweighed by the pains which the pursuit of the purposes may bring upon him. All this I fully admit and have stated it elsewhere as positively and emphatically as anyone. Will, the active phenomenon, is a different thing from desire, the state of passive sensibility, and, though originally an offshoot from it, may in time take root and detach itself from the parent stock, so much so that in the case of a habitual purpose, instead of willing the thing because we desire it, we often desire it only because we will it. This, however, is but an instance of that familiar fact, the power of habit, and is nowise confined to the case of virtuous actions. Many indifferent things which men originally did from a motive of some sort they continue to do from habit. Sometimes this is done unconsciously, the consciousness coming only after the action; at other times with conscious volition, but volition which has become habitual and is put in operation by the force of habit, in opposition perhaps to the deliberate preference, as often happens with those who have contracted habits of vicious or hurtful indulgence. Third and last comes the case in which the habitual act of will in the individual instance is not in contradiction to the general intention prevailing at other times, but in fulfillment of it, as in the case of the person of confirmed virtue and of all who pursue deliberately and consistently any determinate end. The distinction between will and desire thus understood is an authentic and highly important psychological fact; but the fact consists solely in this—that will, like all other parts of our constitution, is amenable to habit, and that we may will from habit what we no longer desire for itself, or desire only because we will it. It is not the less true that will, in the beginning, is entirely produced by desire, including in that term the repelling influence of pain as well as the attractive one of pleasure. Let us take into consideration no longer the person who has a confirmed will to do right, but him in whom that virtuous will is still feeble, conquerable by temptation, and not to be fully relied on; by what means can it be strengthened? How can the will to be virtuous, where it does not exist in sufficient force, be implanted or awakened? Only by making the person *desire* virtue—by making him think of it in a pleasurable light, or of its absence in a painful one. It is by associating the doing right with pleasure, or the wrong with pain, or by eliciting and impressing and bringing home to the person's experience the pleasure naturally involved in the one or the pain in the other, that it is possible to call forth that will to be virtuous which, when confirmed, acts without any thought of either pleasure or pain. Will is the child of desire, and passes out of the dominion of its parent only to come under that of habit. That which is the result of habit affords no presumption of being intrinsically good; and there would be no reason for wishing that the purpose of virtue should become independent of pleasure and pain were it not that the influence of the pleasurable and painful associations which prompt to virtue is not sufficiently to be depended on for unerring constancy of action until it has acquired the support of habit. Both in feeling and in conduct, habit is the only thing which imparts certainty; and it is because of the importance to others of being able to rely absolutely on one's feelings and conduct, and to oneself of being able to rely on one's own, that the will to do right ought to be cultivated into this habitual independence. In other words, this state of the will is a means to good, not intrinsically a good; and does not contradict the doctrine that nothing is a good to human beings but in so far as it is either itself pleasurable or a means of attaining pleasure or averting pain.

But if this doctrine be true, the principle of utility is proved. Whether it is so or not must now be left to the consideration of the thoughtful reader.

CHAPTER V

On the Connection between Justice and Utility

In all ages of speculation one of the strongest obstacles to the reception of the doctrine that utility or happiness is the criterion of right and wrong has been drawn from the idea of justice. The powerful sentiment and apparently clear perception which that word recalls with a rapidity and certainty resembling an instinct have seemed to the majority of thinkers to point to an inherent quality in things; to show that the just must have an existence in nature as something absolute, generically distinct from every variety of the expedient and, in idea, opposed to it, though (as is commonly acknowledged) never, in the long run, disjoined from it in fact.

In the case of this, as of our other moral sentiments, there is no necessary connection between the question of its origin and that of its binding force. That a feeling is bestowed on us by nature does not necessarily legitimate all its promptings. The feeling of justice might be a peculiar instinct, and might yet require, like our other instincts, to be controlled and enlightened by a higher reason. If we have intellectual instincts leading us to judge in a particular way, as well as animal instincts that prompt us to act in a particular way, there is no necessity that the former should be more infallible in their sphere than the latter in theirs; it may as well happen that wrong judgments are occasionally suggested by those, as wrong actions by these. But though it is one thing to believe that we have natural feelings of justice, and another to acknowledge them as an ultimate criterion of conduct, these two opinions are very closely connected in point of fact. Mankind are always predisposed to believe that any subjective feeling, not otherwise accounted for, is a revelation of some objective reality. Our present object is to determine whether the reality to which the feeling of justice corresponds is one which needs any such special revelation, whether the justice or injustice of an action is a thing intrinsically peculiar and distinct from all its other qualities or only a combination of certain of those qualities presented under a peculiar aspect. For the purpose of this inquiry it is practically important to consider whether the feeling itself, of justice and injustice, is *sui generis* like our sensations of color and taste or a derivative feeling formed by a combination of others. And this it is the more essential to examine, as people are in general willing enough to allow that objectively the dictates of justice coincide with a part of the field of general expediency; but inasmuch as the subjective mental feeling of justice is different from that which commonly attaches to simple expediency, and, except in the extreme cases of the latter, is far more imperative in its demands, people find it difficult to see in justice only a particular kind or branch of general utility, and think that its superior binding force requires a totally different origin.

To throw light upon this question, it is necessary to attempt to ascertain what is the distinguishing character of justice, or of injustice; what is the quality, or whether there is any quality, attributed in common to all modes of conduct designated as unjust (for justice, like many other moral attributes, is best defined by its opposite), and distinguishing them from such modes of conduct as are disapproved, but without having that particular epithet of disapprobation applied to them. If in everything which men are accustomed to characterize as just or unjust some one common attribute or collection of attributes is always present, we may judge whether this particular attribute or combination of attributes would be capable of gathering round it a sentiment of that peculiar character and intensity by virtue of the general laws of our emotional constitution, or whether the sentiment is inexplicable and requires to be regarded as a special provision of nature. If we find the former to be the case, we shall, in resolving this question, have resolved also the main problem; if the latter, we shall have to seek for some other mode of investigating it.

To find the common attributes of a variety of objects, it is necessary to begin by surveying the objects themselves in the concrete. Let us therefore advert successively to the various modes of action and arrangements of human affairs which are classed, by universal or widely spread opinion, as just or as unjust. The things well known to excite the sentiments associated with those names are of a very multifarious character. I shall pass them rapidly in review, without studying any particular arrangement.

In the first place, it is mostly considered unjust to deprive anyone of his personal liberty, his property, or any other thing which belongs to him by law. Here, therefore, is one instance of the application of the terms "just" and "unjust" in a perfectly definite sense, namely, that it is just to respect, unjust to violate, the *legal rights* of anyone. But this judgment admits of several exceptions, arising from the other forms in which the notions of justice and injustice present themselves. For example, the person who suffers the deprivation may (as the phrase is) have *forfeited* the rights which he is so deprived of—a case to which we shall return presently. But also—

Secondly, the legal rights of which he is deprived may be rights which *ought* not to have belonged to him; in other words, the law which confers on him these rights may be a bad law. When it is so or when (which is the same thing for our purpose) it is supposed to be so, opinions will differ as to the justice or injustice of infringing it. Some maintain that no law, however bad, ought to be disobeyed by an individual citizen; that his opposition to it, if shown at all, should only be shown in endeavoring to get it altered by competent authority. This opinion (which condemns many of the most illustrious benefactors of mankind, and would often protect pernicious institutions against the only weapons which, in the state of things existing at the time, have any chance of succeeding against them) is defended by those who hold it on grounds of expediency, principally on that of the importance to the common interest of mankind, of maintaining inviolate the sentiment of submission to law. Other persons, again, hold the directly contrary opinion that any law, judged to be bad, may blamelessly be disobeyed, even though it be not judged to be unjust but only inexpedient, while others would confine the license of disobedience to the case of unjust laws; but, again, some say that all laws which are inexpedient are unjust, since every law imposes some restriction on the natural liberty of mankind, which restriction is an injustice unless legitimated by tending to their good. Among these diversities of opinion it seems to be universally admitted that there may be unjust laws, and that law, consequently, is not the ultimate criterion of justice, but may give to one person a benefit, or impose on another an evil, which justice condemns. When, however, a law is thought to be unjust, it seems always to be regarded as being so in the same way in which a breach of law is unjust, namely, by infringing somebody's right, which, as it cannot in this case be a legal right, receives a different appellation and is called a moral right. We may say, therefore, that a second case of injustice consists in taking or withholding from any person that to which he has a *moral right*.

Thirdly, it is universally considered just that each person should obtain that (whether good or evil) which he *deserves*, and unjust that he should obtain a good or be made to undergo an evil which he does not deserve. This is, perhaps, the clearest and most emphatic form in which the idea of justice is conceived by the general mind. As it involves the notion of desert, the question arises what constitutes desert? Speaking in a general way, a person is understood to deserve good if he does right, evil if he does wrong; and in a more particular sense, to deserve good from those to whom he does or has done good, and evil from those to whom he does or has done evil. The precept of returning good for evil has never been regarded as a case of the fulfillment of justice, but as one in which the claims of justice are waived, in obedience to other considerations.

Fourthly, it is confessedly unjust to *break faith* with anyone: to violate an engagement, either express or implied, or disappoint expectations raised by our own conduct, at least if we have raised those expectations knowingly and voluntarily. Like the other obligations of justice already spoken of, this one is not regarded as absolute, but as capable of being overruled by a stronger obligation of justice on the other side, or by such conduct on the part of the person concerned as is deemed to absolve us from our obligation to him and to constitute a *forfeiture* of the benefit which he has been led to expect.

Fifthly, it is, by universal admission, inconsistent with justice to be *partial*—to show favor or preference to one person over another in matters to which favor and preference do not properly apply. Impartiality, however, does not seem to be regarded as a duty in itself, but rather as instrumental to some other duty; for it is admitted that favor and preference are not always censurable, and, indeed, the cases in which they are condemned are rather the exception than the rule. A person would be more likely to be blamed than applauded for giving his family or friends no superiority in good offices over strangers when he could do so without violating any other duty; and no one thinks it unjust to seek one person in preference to another as a friend, connection, or companion. Impartiality where rights are concerned is of course obligatory, but this is involved in the more general obligation of giving to everyone his right. A tribunal, for example, must be impartial because it is bound to award, without regard to any other consideration, a disputed object to the one of two parties who has the right to it. There are other cases in which impartiality means being solely influenced by desert, as with those who, in the capacity of judges, preceptors, or parents, administer reward and punishment as such. There are cases, again, in which it means being solely influenced by consideration for the public interest, as in making a selection among candidates for a government employment. Impartiality, in short, as an obligation of justice, may be said to mean being exclusively influenced by the considerations which it is supposed ought to influence the particular case in hand, and resisting solicitation of any motives which prompt to conduct different from what those considerations would dictate.

Nearly allied to the idea of impartiality is that of *equality*, which often enters as a component part both into the conception of justice and into the practice of it, and, in the eyes of many persons, constitutes its essence. But in this, still more than in any other case, the notion of justice varies in different persons, and always conforms in its variations to their notion of utility. Each person maintains that equality is the dictate of justice, except where he thinks that expediency requires inequality. The justice of giving equal protection to the rights of all is maintained by those who support the most outrageous inequality in the rights themselves. Even in slave countries it is theoretically admitted that the rights of the slave, such as they are, ought to be as sacred as those of the master, and that a tribunal which fails to enforce them with equal strictness is wanting in justice; while, at the same time, institutions which leave to the slave scarcely any rights to enforce are not deemed unjust because they are not deemed inexpedient. Those who think that utility requires distinctions of rank do not consider it unjust that riches and social privileges should be unequally dispensed; but those who think this inequality inexpedient think it unjust also. Whoever thinks that government is necessary sees no injustice in as much inequality as is constituted by giving to the magistrate powers not granted to other people. Even among those who hold leveling doctrines, there are differences of opinion about expediency. Some communists consider it unjust that the produce of the labor of the community should be shared on any other principle than that of exact equality; others think it just that those should receive most whose wants are greatest; while others hold that those who work harder, or who produce more, or whose services are more valuable to the community, may justly claim a larger quota in the division of the produce. And the sense of natural justice may be plausibly appealed to in behalf of every one of these opinions.

Among so many diverse applications of the term "justice," which yet is not regarded as ambiguous, it is a matter of some difficulty to seize the mental link which holds them together, and on which the moral sentiment adhering to the term essentially depends. Perhaps, in this embarrassment, some help may be derived from the history of the word, as indicated by its etymology.

In most if not in all languages, the etymology of the word which corresponds to "just" points distinctly to an origin connected with the ordinances of law. *Justum* is a form of *jussum*, that which has been ordered. *Dikaion* comes directly from *dike*, a suit at law. *Recht*, from which came *right* and *righteous*, is synonymous with law. The courts of justice, the administration of justice, are the courts and the administration of law. *La justice*, in French, is the established term for judicature. I am not committing the fallacy, imputed with some show of truth to Horne Tooke,[8] of assuming that a word must still continue to mean what it originally meant. Etymology is slight evidence of what the idea now signified is, but the very best evidence of how it sprang up. There can, I think, be no doubt that the *idée mère*, the primitive element, in the formation of the notion of justice was conformity to law. It constituted the entire idea among the Hebrews, up to the birth of Christianity; as might be expected in the case of a people whose laws attempted to embrace all subjects on which precepts were required, and who believed those laws to be a direct emanation from the Supreme Being. But other nations, and in particular the Greeks and Romans, who knew that their laws had been made originally, and still continued to be made, by men, were not afraid to admit that those men might make bad laws; might do, by law, the same things, and from the same motives, which if done by individuals without the sanction of law would be called unjust. And hence the sentiment of injustice came to be attached, not to all violations of law, but only to violations of such laws as *ought* to exist, including such as ought to exist but do not, and to laws themselves if supposed to be contrary to what ought to be law. In this manner the idea of law and of its injunctions was still predominant in the notion of justice, even when the laws actually in force ceased to be accepted as the standard of it.

It is true that mankind consider the idea of justice and its obligations as applicable to many things which neither are, nor is it desired that they should be, regulated by law. Nobody desires that laws should interfere with the whole detail of private life; yet everyone allows that in all daily conduct a person may and does show himself to be either just or unjust. But even here, the idea of the breach of what ought to be law still lingers in a modified shape. It would always give us pleasure, and chime in with our feelings of fitness, that acts which we deem unjust should be punished, though we do not always think it expedient that this should be done by the tribunals. We forego that gratification on account of incidental inconveniences. We should be glad to see just conduct enforced and injustice repressed, even in the minutest details, if we were not, with reason, afraid of trusting the magistrate with so unlimited an amount of power over individuals. When we think that a person is bound in justice to do a thing, it is an ordinary form of language to say that he ought to be compelled to do it. We should be gratified to see the obligation

8. [John Horne Tooke (1736–1812) was an English politician and philologist who supported both the American and French revolutions.]

enforced by anybody who had the power. If we see that its enforcement by law would be inexpedient, we lament the impossibility, we consider the impunity given to injustice as an evil, and strive to make amends for it by bringing a strong expression of our own and the public disapprobation to bear upon the offender. Thus the idea of legal constraint is still the generating idea of the notion of justice, though undergoing several transformations before that notion as it exists in an advanced state of society becomes complete.

The above is, I think, a true account, as far as it goes, of the origin and progressive growth of the idea of justice. But we must observe that it contains as yet nothing to distinguish that obligation from moral obligation in general. For the truth is that the idea of penal sanction, which is the essence of law, enters not only into the conception of injustice, but into that of any kind of wrong. We do not call anything wrong unless we mean to imply that a person ought to be punished in some way or other for doing it—if not by law, by the opinion of his fellow creatures; if not by opinion, by the reproaches of his own conscience. This seems the real turning point of the distinction between morality and simple expediency. It is a part of the notion of duty in every one of its forms that a person may rightfully be compelled to fulfill it. Duty is a thing which may be *exacted* from a person, as one exacts a debt. Unless we think that it may be exacted from him, we do not call it his duty. Reasons of prudence, or the interest of other people, may militate against actually exacting it, but the person himself, it is clearly understood, would not be entitled to complain. There are other things, on the contrary, which we wish that people should do, which we like or admire them for doing, perhaps dislike or despise them for not doing, but yet admit that they are not bound to do; it is not a case of moral obligation; we do not blame them, that is, we do not think that they are proper objects of punishment. How we come by these ideas of deserving and not deserving punishment will appear, perhaps, in the sequel; but I think there is no doubt that this distinction lies at the bottom of the notions of right and wrong; that we call any conduct wrong, or employ, instead, some other term of dislike or disparagement, according as we think that the person ought, or ought not, to be punished for it; and we say it would be right to do so and so, or merely that it would be desirable or laudable, according as we would wish to see the person whom it concerns compelled, or only persuaded and exhorted, to act in that manner.[9]

This, therefore, being the characteristic difference which marks off, not justice, but morality in general from the remaining provinces of expediency and worthiness, the character is still to be sought which distinguishes justice from other branches of morality. Now it is known that ethical writers divide moral duties into two classes, denoted by the ill-chosen expressions, duties of perfect and of imperfect obligation; the latter being those in which, though the act is obligatory, the particular occasions of performing it are left to our choice, as in the case of charity or beneficence, which we are indeed bound to practice but not toward any definite person, nor at any prescribed time. In the more precise language of philosophic jurists, duties of perfect obligation are those duties in virtue of which a correlative *right* resides in some person or persons; duties of imperfect obligation are those moral obligations which do not give birth to any right. I think it will be found that this distinction exactly coincides with that which exists between justice and the other obligations of morality. In our survey of the various popular acceptations of justice, the term appeared generally to involve the idea of a personal right—a claim on the part of one or more individuals, like that which the law gives when it confers a proprietary or other legal right. Whether the injustice consists in depriving a person of a possession, or in breaking faith with him, or in treating him worse than he deserves, or worse than other people who have no greater claims—in each case the supposition implies two things: a wrong done, and some assignable person who is wronged. Injustice may also be done by treating a person better than others; but the wrong in this case is to his competitors, who are also assignable persons. It seems to me that this feature in the case—a right in some person, correlative to the moral obligation—constitutes the specific difference between justice and

9. See this point enforced and illustrated by Professor Bain, in an admirable chapter (entitled "The Ethical Emotions, or the Moral Sense"), of the second of the two treatises composing his elaborate and profound work on the Mind. [Alexander Bain (1818–1903) was a Scottish philosopher and psychologist. The work referred to is his *The Emotions and the Will*.]

generosity of beneficence. Justice implies something which it is not only right to do, and wrong not to do, but which some individual person can claim from us as his moral right. No one has a moral right to our generosity or beneficence because we are not morally bound to practice those virtues toward any given individual. And it will be found with respect to this as to every correct definition that the instances which seem to conflict with it are those which most confirm it. For if a moralist attempts, as some have done, to make out that mankind generally, though not any given individual, have a right to all the good we can do them, he at once, by that thesis, includes generosity and beneficence within the category of justice. He is obliged to say that our utmost exertions are *due* to our fellow creatures, thus assimilating them to a debt; or that nothing less can be a sufficient *return* for what society does for us, thus classing the case as one of gratitude; both of which are acknowledged cases of justice, and not of the virtue of beneficence; and whoever does not place the distinction between justice and morality in general, where we have now placed it, will be found to make no distinction between them at all, but to merge all morality in justice.

Having thus endeavored to determine the distinctive elements which enter into the composition of the idea of justice, we are ready to enter on the inquiry whether the feeling which accompanies the idea is attached to it by a special dispensation of nature, or whether it could have grown up, by any known laws, out of the idea itself; and, in particular, whether it can have originated in considerations of general expediency.

I conceive that the sentiment itself does not arise from anything which would commonly or correctly be termed an idea of expediency, but that, though the sentiment does not, whatever is moral in it does.

We have seen that the two essential ingredients in the sentiment of justice are the desire to punish a person who has done harm and the knowledge or belief that there is some definite individual or individuals to whom harm has been done.

Now it appears to me that the desire to punish a person who has done harm to some individual is a spontaneous outgrowth from two sentiments, both in the highest degree natural and which either are or resemble instincts: the impulse of self-defense and the feeling of sympathy.

It is natural to resent and to repel or retaliate any harm done or attempted against ourselves or against those with whom we sympathize. The origin of this sentiment it is not necessary here to discuss. Whether it be an instinct or a result of intelligence, it is, we know, common to all animal nature; for every animal tries to hurt those who have hurt, or who it thinks are about to hurt, itself or its young. Human beings, on this point, only differ from other animals in two particulars. First, in being capable of sympathizing, not solely with their offspring, or, like some of the more noble animals, with some superior animal who is kind to them, but with all human, and even with all sentient, beings; secondly, in having a more developed intelligence, which gives a wider range to the whole of their sentiments, whether self-regarding or sympathetic. By virtue of his superior intelligence, even apart from his superior range of sympathy, a human being is capable of apprehending a community of interest between himself and the human society of which he forms a part, such that any conduct which threatens the security of the society generally is threatening to his own, and calls forth his instinct (if instinct it be) of self-defense. The same superiority of intelligence, joined to the power of sympathizing with human beings generally, enables him to attach himself to the collective idea of his tribe, his country, or mankind in such a manner that any act hurtful to them raises his instinct of sympathy and urges him to resistance.

The sentiment of justice, in that one of its elements which consists of the desire to punish, is thus, I conceive, the natural feeling of retaliation or vengeance, rendered by intellect and sympathy applicable to those injuries, that is, to those hurts, which wound us through, or in common with, society at large. This sentiment, in itself, has nothing moral in it; what is moral is the exclusive subordination of it to the social sympathies, so as to wait on and obey their call. For the natural feeling would make us resent indiscriminately whatever anyone does that is disagreeable to us; but, when moralized by the social feeling, it only acts in the directions conformable to the general good: just persons resenting a hurt to society, though not otherwise a hurt to themselves, and not resenting a hurt to themselves, however painful, unless it be of the kind which society has a common interest with them in the repression of.

It is no objection against this doctrine to say that, when we feel our sentiment of justice outraged, we are not thinking of society at large or of any collective interest, but only of the individual case. It is common enough, certainly, though the reverse of commendable, to feel resentment merely because we have suffered pain; but a person whose resentment is really a moral feeling, that is, who considers whether an act is blamable before he allows himself to resent it—such a person, though he may not say expressly to himself that he is standing up for the interest of society, certainly does feel that he is asserting a rule which is for the benefit of others as well as for his own. If he is not feeling this, if he is regarding the act solely as it affects him individually, he is not consciously just; he is not concerning himself about the justice of his actions. This is admitted even by anti-utilitarian moralists. When Kant (as before remarked) propounds as the fundamental principle of morals, "So act that thy rule of conduct might be adopted as a law by all rational beings," he virtually acknowledges that the interest of mankind collectively, or at least of mankind indiscriminately, must be in the mind of the agent when conscientiously deciding on the morality of the act. Otherwise he uses words without a meaning; for that a rule even of utter selfishness could not *possibly* be adopted by all rational beings—that there is any insuperable obstacle in the nature of things to its adoption—cannot be even plausibly maintained. To give any meaning to Kant's principle, the sense put upon it must be that we ought to shape our conduct by a rule which all rational beings might adopt *with benefit to their collective interest*.

To recapitulate: the idea of justice supposes two things—a rule of conduct and a sentiment which sanctions the rule. The first must be supposed common to all mankind and intended for their good. The other (the sentiment) is a desire that punishment may be suffered by those who infringe the rule. There is involved, in addition, the conception of some definite person who suffers by the infringement, whose rights (to use the expression appropriated to the case) are violated by it. And the sentiment of justice appears to me to be the animal desire to repel or retaliate a hurt or damage to oneself or to those with whom one sympathizes, widened so as to include all persons, by the human capacity of enlarged sympathy and the human conception of intelligent self-interest. From the latter elements the feeling derives its morality; from the former, its peculiar impressiveness and energy of self-assertion.

I have, throughout, treated the idea of a *right* residing in the injured person and violated by the injury, not as a separate element in the composition of the idea and sentiment, but as one of the forms in which the other two elements clothe themselves. These elements are a hurt to some assignable person or persons, on the one hand, and a demand for punishment, on the other. An examination of our own minds, I think, will show that these two things include all that we mean when we speak of violation of a right. When we call anything a person's right, we mean that he has a valid claim on society to protect him in the possession of it, either by the force of law or by that of education and opinion. If he has what we consider a sufficient claim, on whatever account, to have something guaranteed to him by society, we say that he has a right to it. If we desire to prove that anything does not belong to him by right, we think this done as soon as it is admitted that society ought not to take measure for securing it to him, but should leave him to chance or to his own exertions. Thus a person is said to have a right to what he can earn in fair professional competition, because society ought not to allow any other person to hinder him from endeavoring to earn in that manner as much as he can. But he has not a right to three hundred a year, though he may happen to be earning it; because society is not called on to provide that he shall earn that sum. On the contrary, if he owns ten thousand pounds three-per-cent stock, he *has* a right to three hundred a year because society has come under an obligation to provide him with an income of that amount.

To have a right, then, is, I conceive, to have something which society ought to defend me in the possession of. If the objector goes on to ask why it ought, I can give him no other reason than general utility. If that expression does not seem to convey a sufficient feeling of the strength of the obligation, nor to account for the peculiar energy of the feeling, it is because there goes to the composition of the sentiment, not a rational only but also an animal element—the thirst for retaliation; and this thirst derives its intensity, as well as its moral justification, from the extraordinarily important and impressive kind of utility which is concerned. The interest involved is that of security, to everyone's feelings the most vital of all interests. All other earthly benefits are needed by one person, not needed by another; and many of them can, if necessary, be cheerfully foregone or replaced by something else; but security no human being can possibly do without; on it we depend for all our immunity from evil and for the whole value of all and every good, beyond the passing moment, since nothing but the gratification of the instant could be of any worth to us if we could be deprived of everything the next instant by whoever was momentarily stronger than ourselves. Now this most indispensable of all necessaries, after physical nutriment, cannot be had, unless the machinery for providing it is kept unintermittedly in active play. Our notion, therefore, of the claim we have on our fellow creatures to join in making safe for us the very groundwork of our existence gathers feelings around it so much more intense than those concerned in any of the more common cases of utility that the difference in degree (as is often the case in psychology) becomes a real difference in kind. The claim assumes that character of absoluteness, that apparent infinity and incommensurability with all other considerations which constitute the distinction between the feeling of right and wrong and that of ordinary expediency and inexpediency. The feelings concerned are so powerful, and we count so positively on finding a responsive feeling in others (all being alike interested) that *ought* and *should* grow into *must*, and recognized indispensability becomes a moral necessity, analogous to physical, and often not inferior to it in binding force.

If the preceding analysis, or something resembling it, be not the correct account of the notion of justice—if justice be totally independent of utility, and be a standard *per se*, which the mind can recognize by simple introspection of itself—it is hard to understand why that internal oracle is so ambiguous, and why so many things appear either just or unjust, according to the light in which they are regarded.

We are continually informed that utility is an uncertain standard, which every different person interprets differently, and that there is no safety but in the immutable, ineffaceable, and unmistakable dictates of justice, which carry their evidence in themselves and are independent of the fluctuations of opinion. One would suppose from this that on questions of justice there could be no controversy; that, if we take that for our rule, its application to any given case could leave us in as little doubt as a mathematical demonstration. So far is this from being the fact that there is as much difference of opinion, and as much discussion, about what is just as about what is useful to society. Not only have different nations and individuals different notions of justice, but in the mind of one and the same individual, justice is not some one rule, principle, or maxim, but many which do not always coincide in their dictates, and, in choosing between which, he is guided either by some extraneous standard or by his own personal predilections.

For instance, there are some who say that it is unjust to punish anyone for the sake of example to others, that punishment is just only when intended for the good of the sufferer himself. Others maintain the extreme reverse, contending that to punish persons who have attained years of discretion, for their own benefit, is despotism and injustice, since, if the matter at issue is solely their own good, no one has a right to control their own judgment of it; but that they may justly be punished to prevent evil to others, this being the exercise of the legitimate right of self-defense. Mr. Owen,[10] again, affirms that it is unjust to punish at all, for the criminal did not make his own character; his education and the circumstances which surrounded him have made him a criminal, and for these he is not responsible. All these opinions are extremely plausible; and so long as the question is argued as one of justice simply, without going down to the principles which lie under justice and are the source of its authority, I am unable to see how any of these reasoners cam be refuted. For in truth every one of the three builds upon rules of justice confessedly true. The first appeals to the acknowledged injustice of singling out an individual and making him a sacrifice, without his consent, for other people's benefit. The second relies on the acknowledged justice of self-defense and the admitted injustice of forcing one person to conform to another's notions of what constitutes his good. The Owenite invokes the

10. [Robert Owen (1771–1858) was a British social reformer who believed that individual character is determined by environment. He proposed the formation of self-sufficient cooperative communities, one of which was established in 1825 in New Harmony, Indiana, but lasted only a few years.]

admitted principle that it is unjust to punish anyone for what he cannot help. Each is triumphant so long as he is not compelled to take into consideration any other maxims of justice than the one he has selected; but as soon as their several maxims are brought face to face, each disputant seems to have exactly as much to say for himself as the others. No one of them can carry out his own notion of justice without trampling upon another equally binding. These are difficulties; they have always been felt to be such; and many devices have been invented to turn rather than to overcome them. As a refuge from the last of the three, men imagined what they called the freedom of the will—fancying that they could not justify punishing a man whose will is in a thoroughly hateful state unless it be supposed to have come into that state through no influence of anterior circumstances. To escape from the other difficulties, a favorite contrivance has been the fiction of a contract whereby at some unknown period all the members of society engaged to obey the laws and consented to be punished for any disobedience to them, thereby giving to their legislators the right, which it is assumed they would not otherwise have had, of punishing them, either for their own good or for that of society. This happy thought was considered to get rid of the whole difficulty and to legitimate the infliction of punishment, in virtue of another received maxim of justice, *volenti non fit injuria*—that is not unjust which is done with the consent of the person who is supposed to be hurt by it. I need hardly remark that, even if the consent were not mere fiction, this maxim is not superior in authority to the others which it is brought in to supersede. It is, on the contrary, an instructive specimen of the loose and irregular manner in which supposed principles of justice grow up. This particular one evidently came into use as a help to the coarse exigencies of courts of law, which are sometimes obliged to be content with very uncertain presumptions, on account of the greater evils which would often arise from any attempt on their part to cut finer. But even courts of law are not able to adhere consistently to the maxim, for they allow voluntary engagements to be set aside on the ground of fraud, and sometimes on that of mere mistake or misinformation.

Again, when the legitimacy of inflicting punishment is admitted, how many conflicting conceptions of justice come to light in discussing the proper apportionment of punishments to offenses. No rule on the subject recommends itself so strongly to the primitive and spontaneous sentiment of justice as the *lex talionis*, an eye for an eye and a tooth for a tooth. Though this principle of the Jewish and of the Mohammedan law has been generally abandoned in Europe as a practical maxim, there is, I suspect, in most minds, a secret hankering after it; and when retribution accidentally falls on an offender in that precise shape, the general feeling of satisfaction evinced bears witness how natural is the sentiment to which this repayment in kind is acceptable. With many, the test of justice in penal infliction is that the punishment should be proportioned to the offense, meaning that it should be exactly measured by the moral guilt of the culprit (whatever be their standard for measuring moral guilt), the consideration what amount of punishment is necessary to deter from the offense having nothing to do with the question of justice, in their estimation; while there are others to whom that consideration is all in all, who maintain that it is not just, at least for man, to inflict on a fellow creature, whatever may be his offenses, any amount of suffering beyond the least that will suffice to prevent him from repeating, and others from imitating, his misconduct.

To take another example from a subject already once referred to. In co-operative industrial associations, is it just or not that talent or skill should give a title to superior remuneration? On the negative side of the question it is argued that whoever does the best he can deserves equally well, and ought not in justice to be put in a position of inferiority for no fault of his own; that superior abilities have already advantages more than enough, in the admiration they excite, the personal influence they command, and the internal sources of satisfaction attending them, without adding to these a superior share of the world's goods; and that society is bound in justice rather to make compensation to the less favored for this unmerited inequality of advantages than to aggravate it. On the contrary side it is contended that society receives more from the efficient laborer; that, his services being more useful, society owes him a larger return for them; that a greater share of the joint result is actually his work, and not to allow his claim to it is a kind of robbery; that, if he is only to receive as much as others, he can only be justly required to produce as much, and to give a smaller amount of time and exertion, proportioned to his superior efficiency. Who shall decide between these appeals to conflicting principles of justice? Justice has in this case two sides to it, which it is impossible to bring into harmony, and the two disputants have chosen opposite sides; the one looks to what it is just that the individual should receive, the other to what it is just that the community should give. Each, from his own point of view, is unanswerable; and any choice between them, on grounds of justice, must be perfectly arbitrary. Social utility alone can decide the preference.

How many, again, and how irreconcilable are the standards of justice to which reference is made in discussing the repartition of taxation. One opinion is that payment to the state should be in numerical proportion to pecuniary means. Others think that justice dictates what they term graduated taxation—taking a higher percentage from those who have more to spare. In point of natural justice a strong case might be made for disregarding means altogether, and taking the same absolute sum (whenever it could be got) from everyone; as the subscribers to a mess or to a club all pay the same sum for the same privileges, whether they can all equally afford it or not. Since the protection (it might be said) of law and government is afforded to and is equally required by all, there is no injustice in making all buy it at the same price. It is reckoned justice, not injustice, that a dealer should charge to all customers the same price for the same article, not a price varying according to their means of payment. This doctrine, as applied to taxation, finds no advocates because it conflicts so strongly with man's feelings of humanity and of social expediency; but the principle of justice which it invokes is as true and as binding as those which can be appealed to against it. Accordingly it exerts a tacit influence on the line of defense employed for other modes of assessing taxation. People feel obliged to argue that the state does more for the rich man than for the poor, as a justification for its taking more from them, though this is in reality not true, for the rich would be far better able to protect themselves, in the absence of law or government, than the poor, and indeed would probably be successful in converting the poor into their slaves. Others, again, so far defer to the same conception of justice as to maintain that all should pay an equal capitation tax for the protection of their persons (these being of equal value to all), and an unequal tax for the protection of their property, which is unequal. To this others reply that the all of one man is as valuable to him as the all of another. From these confusions there is no other mode of extrication than the utilitarian.

Is, then, the difference between the just and the expedient a merely imaginary distinction? Have mankind been under a delusion in thinking that justice is a more sacred thing than policy, and that the latter ought only to be listened to after the former has been satisfied? By no means. The exposition we have given of the nature and origin of the sentiment recognizes a real distinction; and no one of those who profess the most sublime contempt for the consequences of actions as an element in their morality attaches more importance to the distinction than I do. While I dispute the pretensions of any theory which sets up an imaginary standard of justice not grounded on utility, I account the justice which is grounded on utility to be the chief part, and incomparably the most sacred and binding part, of all morality. Justice is a name for certain classes of moral rules which concern the essentials of human well-being more nearly, and are therefore of more absolute obligation, than any other rules for the guidance of life; and the notion which we have found to be of the essence of the idea of justice—that of a right residing in an individual—implies and testifies to this more binding obligation.

The moral rules which forbid mankind to hurt one another (in which we must never forget to include a wrongful interference with each other's freedom) are more vital to human well-being than any maxims, however important, which only point out the best mode of managing some department of human affairs. They have also the peculiarity that they are the main element in determining the whole of the social feelings of mankind. It is their observance which alone preserves peace among human beings; if obedience to them were not the rule, and disobedience the exception, everyone would see in everyone else an enemy against whom he must be perpetually guarding himself. What is hardly less important, these are the precepts which mankind have the strongest and the most direct inducements for impressing upon one another. By merely giving to each other prudential instruction or exhortation, they may gain, or think they gain, nothing; in inculcating on each other the duty of positive beneficence, they have an unmistakable interest, but far less in degree; a person may possibly not need the benefits of others, but he always needs that they should not do him hurt. Thus the moralities which protect every individual from being harmed by others, either directly or by being hindered in his freedom of pursuing his own good, are at once those which he himself has most at heart and those which he has the strongest interest in publishing and enforcing by word and deed. It is by a person's observance of these that his fitness to exist as one of the fellowship of human beings is tested and decided; for on that depends his being a nuisance or not to those with whom he is in contact. Now it is these moralities primarily which compose the obligation of justice. The most marked cases of injustice, and those which give the tone to the feeling of repugnance which characterizes the sentiment, are acts of wrongful aggression or wrongful exercise of power over someone; the next are those which consist in wrongfully withholding from him something which is his due—in both cases inflicting on him a positive hurt, either in the form of direct suffering or of the privation of some good which he had reasonable ground, either of a physical or of a social kind, for counting upon.

The same powerful motives which command the observance of these primary moralities enjoin the punishment of those who violate them; and as the impulses of self-defense, of defense of others, and of vengeance are all called forth against such persons, retribution, or evil for evil, becomes closely connected with the sentiment of justice, and is universally included in the idea. Good for good is also one of the dictates of justice; and this, though its social utility is evident, and though it carries with it a natural human feeling, has not at first sight that obvious connection with hurt or injury which, existing in the most elementary cases of just and unjust, is the source of the characteristic intensity of the sentiment. But the connection, though less obvious, is not less real. He who accepts benefits and denies a return of them when needed inflicts a real hurt by disappointing one of the most natural and reasonable of expectations, and one which he must at least tacitly have encouraged, otherwise the benefits would seldom have been conferred. The important rank, among human evils and wrongs, of the disappointment of expectation is shown in the fact that it constitutes the principal criminality of two such highly immoral acts as a breach of friendship and a breach of promise. Few hurts which human beings can sustain are greater, and none wound more, than when that on which they habitually and with full assurance relied fails them in the hour of need; and few wrongs are greater than this mere withholding of good; none excite more resentment, either in the person suffering or in a sympathizing spectator. The principle, therefore, of giving to each what they deserve, that is, good for good as well as evil for evil, is not only included within the idea of justice as we have defined it, but is a proper object of that intensity of sentiment which places the just human estimation above the simply expedient.

Most of the maxims of justice current in the world, and commonly appealed to in its transactions, are simply instrumental to carrying into effect the principles of justice which we have now spoken of. That a person is only responsible for what he has done voluntarily, or could voluntarily have avoided, that it is unjust to condemn any person unheard; that the punishment ought to be proportioned to the offense, and the like, are maxims intended to prevent the just principle of evil for evil from being perverted to the infliction of evil without that justification. The greater part of these common maxims have come into use from the practice of courts of justice, which have been naturally led to a more complete recognition and elaboration than was likely to suggest itself to others, of the rules necessary to enable them to fulfill their double function—of inflicting punishment when due, and of awarding to each person his right.

That first of judicial virtues, impartiality, is an obligation of justice, partly for the reason last mentioned, as being a necessary condition of the fulfillment of other obligations of justice. But this is not the only source of the exalted rank, among human obligations, of those maxims of equality and impartiality, which, both in popular estimation and in that of the most enlightened, are included among the precepts of justice. In one point of view, they may be considered as corollaries from the principles already laid down. If it is a duty to do to each according to his deserts, returning good for good, as well as repressing evil by evil, it necessarily follows that we should treat all equally well (when no higher duty forbids) who have deserved equally well of *us*, and that society should treat all equally well who have deserved equally well of *it*, that is, who have deserved equally well absolutely. This is the highest abstract standard of social and distributive justice, toward which all institutions and the efforts of all virtuous citizens should be made in the utmost possible degree to converge. But this great moral duty rests upon a still deeper foundation, being a direct emanation from the first principle of morals, and not a mere logical corollary from secondary or derivative doctrines. It is involved in the very meaning of utility, or the greatest happiness principle. That principle is a mere form of words without rational signification unless one person's happiness, supposed equal in degree (with the proper allowance made for kind), is counted for exactly as much as another's. Those conditions being supplied, Bentham's dictum "everybody to count for one, nobody for more than one," might be written under the principle of utility as an explanatory commentary.[11] The equal claim of everybody to happiness, in the estimation of the moralist and of the legislator, involves an equal claim to all the means of happiness except in so far as the inevitable conditions of human life and the general interest in which that of every individual is included set limits to the maxim; and those limits ought to be strictly construed. As every other maxim of justice, so this is by no means applied or held applicable universally; on the contrary, as I have already remarked, it bends to every person's ideas of social expediency. But in whatever case it is deemed applicable at all, it is held to be the dictate of justice. All persons are deemed to have a *right* to equality of treatment, except when some recognized social expediency requires the reverse. And hence all social inequalities which have ceased to be considered expedient assume the character, not of simple inexpediency, but of injustice, and appear so tyrannical that people are apt to wonder how they ever could have been tolerated—forgetful that they themselves, perhaps, tolerate other inequalities under an equally mistaken notion of expediency, the correction of which would make that which they approve seem quite as monstrous as what they have at last learned to condemn. The entire history of social improvement has been a series of transitions by which one custom or institution after another, from being a supposed primary necessity of social existence, has passed into the rank of a universally stigmatized injustice and tyranny. So it has been with the distinctions of slaves and freemen, nobles and serfs, patricians and plebeians; and so it will be, and in part already is, with the aristocracies of color, race, and sex.

It appears from what has been said that justice is a

11. This implication, in the first principle of the utilitarian scheme, of perfect impartiality between persons is regarded by Mr. Herbert Spencer (in his *Social Statics*) as a disproof of the pretensions of utility to be a sufficient guide to right; since (he says) the principle of utility presupposes the anterior principle that everybody has an equal right to happiness. It may be more correctly described as supposing that equal amounts of happiness are equally desirable, whether felt by the same or different persons. This, however, is not a *pre*supposition, not a premise needful to support the principle of utility, but the very principle itself; for what is the principle of utility if it be not that "happiness" and "desirable" are synonymous terms? If there is any anterior principle implied, it can be no other than this, that the truths of arithmetic are applicable to the valuation of happiness, as of all other measurable quantities.

(Mr. Herbert Spencer, in a private communication on the subject of the preceding note, objects to being considered an opponent of utilitarianism and states that he regards happiness as the ultimate end of morality; but deems that end only partially attainable by empirical generalizations from the observed results of conduct, and completely attainable only by deducing, from the laws of life and the conditions of existence, what kinds of action necessarily tend to produce happiness, and what kinds to produce unhappiness. With the exception of the word "necessarily," I have no dissent to express from this doctrine; and (omitting that word) I am not aware that any modern advocate of utilitarianism is of a different opinion. Bentham, certainly, to whom in the *Social Statics* Mr. Spencer particularly referred, is, least of all writers, chargeable with unwillingness to deduce the effect of actions on happiness from the laws of human nature and the universal conditions of human life. The common charge against him is of relying too exclusively upon such deductions and declining altogether to be bound by the generalizations from specific experience which Mr. Spencer thinks that utilitarians generally confine themselves to. My own opinion (and, as I collect, Mr. Spencer's) is that in ethics, as in all other branches of scientific study, the consilience of the results of both these processes, each corroborating and verifying the other, is requisite to give to any general proposition the kind and degree of evidence which constitutes scientific proof.)

name for certain moral requirements which, regarded collectively, stand higher in the scale of social utility, and are therefore of more paramount obligation, than any others, though particular cases may occur in which some other social duty is so important as to overrule any one of the general maxims of justice. Thus, to save a life, it may not only be allowable, but a duty, to steal or take by force the necessary food or medicine, or to kidnap and compel to officiate the only qualified medical practitioner. In such cases, as we do not call anything justice which is not a virtue, we usually say, not that justice must give way to some other moral principle, but that what is just in ordinary cases is, by reason of that other principle, not just in the particular case. By this useful accommodation of language, the character of indefeasibility attributed to justice is kept up, and we are saved from the necessity of maintaining that there can be laudable injustice.

The considerations which have not been adduced resolve, I conceive, the only real difficulty in the utilitarian theory of morals. It has always been evident that all cases of justice are also cases of expediency; the difference is in the peculiar sentiment which attaches to the former, as contradistinguished from the latter. If this characteristic sentiment has been sufficiently accounted for; if there is no necessity to assume for it any peculiarity of origin; if it is simply the natural feeling of resentment, moralized by being made co-extensive with the demands of social good; and if this feeling not only does but ought to exist in all the classes of cases to which the idea of justice corresponds—that idea no longer presents itself as a stumbling block to the utilitarian ethics. Justice remains the appropriate name for certain social utilities which are vastly more important, and therefore more absolute and imperative, than any others are as a class (though not more so than others may be in particular cases); and which, therefore, ought to be, as well as naturally are, guarded by a sentiment, not only different in degree, but also in kind; distinguished from the milder feeling which attaches to the mere idea of promoting human pleasure or convenience at once by the more definite nature of its commands and by the sterner character of its sanctions.

On Liberty

The grand, leading principle, towards which every argument unfolded in these pages directly converges, is the absolute and essential importance of human development in its richest diversity
—Wilhelm von Humboldt: *Sphere and Duties of Government.*[1]

To the beloved and deplored memory of her who was the inspirer, and in part the author, of all that is best in my writings—the friend and wife whose exalted sense of truth and right was my strongest incitement, and whose approbation was my chief reward—I dedicate this volume. Like all that I have written for many years, it belongs as much to her as to me; but the work as it stands has had, in a very insufficient degree, the inestimable advantage of her revision; some of the most important portions having been reserved for a more careful re-examination, which they are now never destined to receive. Were I but capable of interpreting to the world one half the great thoughts and noble feelings which are buried in her grave, I should be the medium of a greater benefit to it, than is ever likely to arise from anything that I can write, unprompted and unassisted by her all but unrivaled wisdom.

CHAPTER I

Introductory

. . . The object of this essay is to assert one very simple principle, as entitled to govern absolutely the dealings of society with the individual in the way of compulsion and control, whether the means used be physical force in the form of legal penalties or the moral coercion of public opinion. That principle is that the sole end for which mankind are warranted, individually or collectively, in interfering with the liberty of action of any of their number is self-protection. That the only purpose for which power can be rightfully exercised over any member of a civilized community, against his will, is to prevent harm to others. His own good, either physical or moral, is not a sufficient warrant. He cannot rightfully be compelled to do or forbear because it will be better for him to do so, because it will make him happier, because, in the opinions of others, to do so would be wise or even right. These are good reasons for remonstrating with him, or reasoning with him, or persuading him, or entreating him, but not for compelling him or visiting him with any evil in case he do otherwise. To justify that, the conduct from which it is desired to deter him must be calculated to produce evil to someone else. The only part of the conduct of anyone for which he is amenable to society is that which concerns others. In the part which merely concerns himself, his independence is, of right, absolute. Over himself, over his own body and mind, the individual is sovereign. . . .

This, then, is the appropriate region of human liberty. It comprises, first, the inward domain of consciousness, demanding liberty of conscience in the most comprehensive sense, liberty of thought and feeling, absolute freedom of opinion and sentiment on all subjects, practical or speculative, scientific, moral, or theological. The liberty of expressing and publishing opinions may seem to fall under a different principle, since it belongs to that part of the conduct of an individual which concerns other people, but, being almost of as much importance as the liberty of thought itself and resting in great part on the same reasons, is practically inseparable from it. Secondly, the principle requires liberty of tastes and pursuits, of framing the plan of our life to suit our own character, of doing as we like, subject to such consequences as may follow, without impediment from our fellow

1. [Wilhelm Freiherr von Humboldt (1767–1835), German statesman and philologist, was a liberal reformer and a founder of the University of Berlin.—S.M.C.]

creatures, so long as what we do does not harm them, even though they should think our conduct foolish, perverse, or wrong. Thirdly, from this liberty of each individual follows the liberty, within the same limits, of combination among individuals; freedom to unite for any purpose not involving harm to others: the persons combining being supposed to be of full age and not forced or deceived. . . .

It will be convenient for the argument if, instead of at once entering upon the general thesis, we confine ourselves in the first instance to a single branch of it on which the principle here stated is, if not fully, yet to a certain point, recognized by the current opinions. This one branch is the Liberty of Thought, from which it is impossible to separate the cognate liberty of speaking and of writing. Although these liberties, to some considerable amount, form part of the political morality of all countries which profess religious toleration and free institutions, the grounds, both philosophical and practical, on which they rest are perhaps not so familiar to the general mind, nor so thoroughly appreciated by many, even of the leaders of opinion, as might have been expected. Those grounds, when rightly understood, are of much wider application than to only one division of the subject, and a thorough consideration of this part of the question will be found the best introduction to the remainder. Those to whom nothing which I am about to say will be new may therefore, I hope, excuse me if on a subject which for now three centuries has been so often discussed I venture on one discussion more.

CHAPTER II

Of the Liberty of Thought and Discussion

The time, it is to be hoped, is gone by when any defense would be necessary of the "liberty of the press" as one of the securities against corrupt or tyrannical government. No argument, we may suppose, can now be needed against permitting a legislature or an executive, not identified in interest with the people, to prescribe opinions to them and determine what doctrines or what arguments they shall be allowed to hear. This aspect of the question, besides, has been so often and so triumphantly enforced by preceding writers that it needs not be specially insisted on in this place. Though the law of England, on the subject of the press, is as servile to this day as it was in the time of the Tudors, there is little danger of its being actually put in force against political discussion except during some temporary panic when fear of insurrection drives ministers and judges from their propriety; and, speaking generally, it is not, in constitutional countries, to be apprehended that the government, whether completely responsible to the people or not, will often attempt to control the expression of opinion, except when in doing so it makes itself the organ of the general intolerance of the public. Let us suppose, therefore, that the government is entirely at one with the people, and never thinks of exerting any power of coercion unless in agreement with what it conceives to be their voice. But I deny the right of the people to exercise such coercion, either by themselves or by their government. The power itself is illegitimate. The best government has no more title to it than the worst. It is as noxious, or more noxious, when exerted in accordance with public opinion than when in opposition to it. If all mankind minus one were of one opinion, and only one person were of the contrary opinion, mankind would be no more justified in silencing that one person than he, if he had the power, would be justified in silencing mankind. Were an opinion a personal possession of no value except to the owner, if to be obstructed in the enjoyment of it were simply a private injury, it would make some difference whether the injury was inflicted only on a few persons or on many. But the peculiar evil of silencing the expression of an opinion is that it is robbing the human race, posterity as well as the existing generation—those who dissent from the opinion, still more than those who hold it. If the opinion is right, they are deprived of the opportunity of exchanging error for truth; if wrong, they lose, what is almost as great a benefit, the clearer perception and livelier impression of truth produced by its collision with error.

It is necessary to consider separately these two hypotheses, each of which has a distinct branch of the argument corresponding to it. We can never be sure that the opinion we are endeavoring to stifle is a false opinion; and if we were sure, stifling it would be an evil still.

First, the opinion which it is attempted to suppress by authority may possibly be true. Those who desire to suppress it, of course, deny its truth; but they are not infallible. They have no authority to decide the question for all mankind and exclude every other person from the means of judging. To refuse a hearing to an opinion because they are sure that it is false is to assume that *their* certainty is the same thing as *absolute* certainty. All silencing of discussion is an assumption of infallibility. Its condemnation may be allowed to rest on this common argument, not the worse for being common.

Unfortunately for the good sense of mankind, the fact of their fallibility is far from carrying the weight in their practical judgment which is always allowed to it in theory; for while everyone well knows himself to be fallible, few think it necessary to take any precautions against their own fallibility, or admit the supposition that any opinion of which they feel very certain may be one of the examples of the error to which they acknowledge themselves to be liable. Absolute princes, or others who are accustomed to unlimited deference, usually feel this complete confidence in their own opinions on nearly all subjects. People more happily situated, who sometimes hear their opinions disputed and are not wholly unused to be set right when they are wrong, place the same unbounded reliance only on such of their opinions as are shared by all who surround them, or to whom they habitually defer; for in proportion to a man's want of confidence in his own solitary judgment does he usually repose, with implicit trust, on the infallibility of "the world" in general. And the world, to each individual, means the part of it with which he comes in contact: his party, his sect, his church, his class of society; the man may be called, by comparison, almost liberal and large-minded to whom it means anything so comprehensive as his own country or his own age. Nor is his faith in this collective authority at all shaken by his being aware that other ages, countries, sects, churches, classes, and parties have thought, and even now think, the exact reverse. He devolves upon his own world the responsibility of being in the right against the dissentient worlds of other people; and it never troubles him that mere accident has decided which of these numerous worlds is the object of his reliance, and that the same causes which make him a churchman in London would have made him a Buddhist or a Confucian in Peking. Yet it is as evident in itself, as any amount of argument can make it, that ages are no more infallible than individuals—every age having held many opinions which subsequent ages have deemed not only false but absurd; and it is as certain that many opinions, now general, will be rejected by future ages, as it is that many, once general, are rejected by the present.

The objection likely to be made to this argument would probably take some such form as the following. There is no greater assumption of infallibility in forbidding the propagation of error than in any other thing which is done by public authority on its own judgment and responsibility. Judgment is given to men that they may use it. Because it may be used erroneously, are men to be told that they ought not to use it at all? To prohibit what they think pernicious is not claiming exemption from error, but fulfilling the duty incumbent on them, although fallible, of acting on their conscientious conviction. If we were never to act on our opinions, because those opinions may be wrong, we should leave all our interests uncared for, and all our duties unperformed. An objection which applies to all conduct can be no valid objection to any conduct in particular. It is the duty of governments, and of individuals, to form the truest opinions they can; to form them carefully, and never impose them upon others unless they are quite sure of being right. But when they are sure (such reasoners may say), it is not conscientiousness but cowardice to shrink from acting on their opinions and allow doctrines which they honestly think dangerous to the welfare of mankind, either in this life or in another, to be scattered abroad without restraint, because other people, in less enlightened times, have persecuted opinions now believed to be true. Let us take care, it may be said, not to make the same mistake; but governments and nations have made mistakes in other things which are not denied to be fit subjects for the exercise of authority: they have laid on bad taxes, made unjust wars. Ought we therefore to lay on no taxes and, under whatever provocation, make no wars? Men and governments must act to the best of their ability. There is no such thing as absolute certainty, but there is assurance sufficient for the purposes of human life. We may, and must, assume our opinion to be true for the guidance of our own conduct; and it is assuming no more when we forbid bad men to pervert society by the propagation of opinions which we regard as false and pernicious.

I answer, that it is assuming very much more. There

is the greatest difference between presuming an opinion to be true because, with every opportunity for contesting it, it has not been refuted, and assuming its truth for the purpose of not permitting its refutation. Complete liberty of contradicting and disproving our opinion is the very condition which justifies us in assuming its truth for purposes of action; and on no other terms can a being with human faculties have any rational assurance of being right.

When we consider either the history of opinion or the ordinary conduct of human life, to what is it to be ascribed that the one and the other are no worse than they are? Not certainly to the inherent force of the human understanding, for on any matter not self-evident there are ninety-nine persons totally incapable of judging of it for one who is capable; and the capacity of the hundredth person is only comparative, for the majority of the eminent men of every past generation held many opinions now known to be erroneous, and did or approved numerous things which no one will now justify. Why is it, then, that there is on the whole a preponderance among mankind of rational opinions and rational conduct? If there really is this preponderance—which there must be unless human affairs are, and have always been, in an almost desperate state—it is owing to a quality of the human mind, the source of everything respectable in man either as an intellectual or as a moral being, namely, that his errors are corrigible. He is capable of rectifying his mistakes by discussion and experience. Not by experience alone. There must be discussion to show how experience is to be interpreted. Wrong opinions and practices gradually yield to fact and argument; but facts and arguments, to produce any effect on the mind, must be brought before it. Very few facts are able to tell their own story, without comments to bring out their meaning. The whole strength and value, then, of human judgment depending on the one property, that it can be set right when it is wrong, reliance can be placed on it only when the means of setting it right are kept constantly at hand. In the case of any person whose judgment is really deserving of confidence, how has it become so? Because he has kept his mind open to criticism of his opinions and conduct. Because it has been his practice to listen to all that could be said against him; to profit by as much of it as was just, and to expound to himself, and upon occasion to others, the fallacy of what was fallacious. Because he has felt that the only way in which a human being can make some approach to knowing the whole of a subject is by hearing what can be said about it by persons of every variety of opinion, and studying all modes in which it can be looked at by every character of mind. No wise man ever acquired his wisdom in any mode but this; nor is it in the nature of human intellect to become wise in any other manner. The steady habit of correcting and completing his own opinion by collating it with those of others, so far from causing doubt and hesitation in carrying it into practice, is the only stable foundation for a just reliance on it; for, being cognizant of all that can, at least obviously, be said against him, and having taken up his position against all gain-sayers—knowing that he has sought for objections and difficulties instead of avoiding them, and has shut out no light which can be thrown upon the subject from any quarter—he has a right to think his judgment better than that of any person, or any multitude, who have not gone through a similar process. . . .

In order more fully to illustrate the mischief of denying a hearing to opinions because we, in our own judgment, have condemned them, it will be desirable to fix down the discussion to a concrete case; and I choose, by preference, the cases which are least favorable to me—in which the argument against freedom of opinion, both on the score of truth and on that of utility, is considered the strongest. Let the opinions impugned be the belief in a God and in a future state, or any of the commonly received doctrines of morality. To fight the battle on such ground gives a great advantage to an unfair antagonist, since he will be sure to say (and many who have no desire to be unfair will say it internally), Are these the doctrines which you do not deem sufficiently certain to be taken under the protection of law? Is the belief in a God one of the opinions to feel sure of which you hold to be assuming infallibility? But I must be permitted to observe that it is not the feeling sure of a doctrine (be it what it may) which I call an assumption of infallibility. It is the undertaking to decide that question *for others*, without allowing them to hear what can be said on the contrary side. And I denounce and reprobate this pretension not the less if put forth on the side of my most solemn convictions. However positive anyone's persuasion may be, not only of the falsity but of the pernicious consequences—not only of the pernicious consequences, but (to adopt expressions which I altogether condemn) the immorality and impiety of an opinion—yet if, in pursuance of that private judgment, though backed by the public judgment of his country or his contemporaries, he prevents the opinion from being heard in its defense, he assumes infallibility. And so far from the assumption being less objectionable or less dangerous because the opinion is called immoral or impious, this is the case of all others in which it is most fatal. These are exactly the occasions on which the men of one generation commit those dreadful mistakes which excite the astonishment and horror of posterity. It is among such that we find the instances memorable in history, when the arm of the law has been employed to root out the best men and the noblest doctrines; with deplorable success as to the men, though some of the doctrines have survived to be (as if in mockery) invoked in defense of similar conduct toward those who dissent from *them*, or from their received interpretation.

Mankind can hardly be too often reminded that there was once a man called Socrates, between whom and the legal authorities and public opinion of his time there took place a memorable collision. Born in an age and country abounding in individual greatness, this man has been handed down to us by those who best knew both him and the age as the most virtuous man in it; while *we* know him as the head and prototype of all subsequent teachers of virtue, the source equally of the lofty inspiration of Plato and the judicious utilitarianism of Aristotle, "*i maestri di color che sanno*,"[2] the two headsprings of ethical as of all other philosophy. This acknowledged master of all the eminent thinkers who have since lived—whose fame, still growing after more than two thousand years, all but outweighs the whole remainder of the names which make his native city illustrious—was put to death by his countrymen, after a judicial conviction, for impiety and immorality. Impiety, in denying the gods recognized by the State; indeed, his accuser asserted (see the *Apologia*) that he believed in no gods at all. Immorality, in being, by his doctrines and instructions, a "corruptor of youth." Of these charges the tribunal, there is every ground for believing, honestly found him guilty, and condemned the man who probably of all then born had deserved best of mankind to be put to death as a criminal.

To pass from this to the only other instance of judicial iniquity, the mention of which, after the condemnation of Socrates, would not be an anticlimax: the event which took place on Calvary rather more than eighteen hundred years ago. The man who left on the memory of those who witnessed his life and conversation such an impression of his moral grandeur that eighteen subsequent centuries have done homage to him as the Almighty in person, was ignominiously put to death, as what? As a blasphemer. Men did not merely mistake their benefactor, they mistook him for the exact contrary of what he was and treated him as that prodigy of impiety which they themselves are now held to be for their treatment of him. The feelings with which mankind now regard these lamentable transactions, especially the later of the two, render them extremely unjust in their judgment of the unhappy actors. These were, to all appearance, not bad men—not worse than men commonly are, but rather the contrary; men who possessed in a full, or somewhat more than a full measure, the religious, moral, and patriotic feelings of their time and people: the very kind of men who, in all times, our own included, have every chance of passing through life blameless and respected. The high priest who rent his garments when the words were pronounced, which, according to all the ideas of his country, constituted the blackest guilt, was in all probability quite as sincere in his horror and indignation as the generality of respectable and pious men now are in the religious and moral sentiments they profess; and most of those who now shudder at his conduct, if they had lived in his time, and been born Jews, would have acted precisely as he did. Orthodox Christians who are tempted to think that those who stoned to death the first martyrs must have been worse men than they themselves are ought to remember that one of those persecutors was Saint Paul. . . .

Let us now pass to the second division of the argument, and dismissing the supposition that any of the received opinions may be false, let us assume them to be true and examine into the worth of the manner in which they are likely to be held when their truth is not freely and openly canvassed. However unwill-

2. [The master of them that know.]

ingly a person who has a strong opinion may admit the possibility that his opinion may be false, he ought to be moved by the consideration that, however true it may be, if it is not fully, frequently, and fearlessly discussed, it will be held as a dead dogma, not a living truth.

There is a class of persons (happily not quite so numerous as formerly) who think it enough if a person assents undoubtingly to what they think true, though he has no knowledge whatever of the grounds of the opinion and could not make a tenable defense of it against the most superficial objections. Such persons, if they can once get their creed taught from authority, naturally think that no good, and some harm, comes of its being allowed to be questioned. Where their influence prevails, they make it nearly impossible for the received opinion to be rejected wisely and considerately, though it may still be rejected rashly and ignorantly; for to shut out discussion entirely is seldom possible, and when it once gets in, beliefs not grounded on conviction are apt to give way before the slightest semblance of an argument. Waiving, however, this possibility—assuming that the true opinion abides in the mind, but abides as a prejudice, a belief independent of, and proof against, argument—this is not the way in which truth ought to be held by a rational being. This is not knowing the truth. Truth, thus held, is but one superstition the more, accidentally clinging to the words which enunciate a truth.

If the intellect and judgment of mankind ought to be cultivated, a thing which Protestants at least do not deny, on what can these faculties be more appropriately exercised by anyone than on the things which concern him so much that it is considered necessary for him to hold opinions on them? If the cultivation of the understanding consists in one thing more than in another, it is surely in learning the grounds of one's own opinions. Whatever people believe, on subjects on which it is of the first importance to believe rightly, they ought to be able to defend against at least the common objections. But, someone may say, "Let them be *taught* the grounds of their opinions. It does not follow that opinions must be merely parroted because they are never heard controverted. Persons who learn geometry do not simply commit the theorems to memory, but understand and learn likewise the demonstrations; and it would be absurd to say that they remain ignorant of the grounds of geometrical truths because they never hear anyone deny and attempt to disprove them." Undoubtedly: and such teaching suffices on a subject like mathematics, where there is nothing at all to be said on the wrong side of the question. The peculiarity of the evidence of mathematical truths is that all the argument is on one side. There are no objections, and no answers to objections. But on every subject on which difference of opinion is possible, the truth depends on a balance to be struck between two sets of conflicting reasons. Even in natural philosophy, there is always some other explanation possible of the same facts; some geocentric theory instead of heliocentric, some phlogiston instead of oxygen; and it has to be shown why that other theory cannot be the true one; and until this is shown, and until we know how it is shown, we do not understand the grounds of our opinion. But when we turn to subjects infinitely more complicated, to morals, religion, politics, social relations, and the business of life, three-fourths of the arguments for every disputed opinion consist in dispelling the appearance which favor some opinion different from it. The greatest orator, save one, of antiquity, has left it on record that he always studied his adversary's case with as great, if not still greater, intensity than even his own. What Cicero[3] practiced as the means of forensic success requires to be imitated by all who study any subject in order to arrive at the truth. He who knows only his own side of the case knows little of that. His reasons may be good, and no one may have been able to refute them. But if he is equally unable to refute the reasons on the opposite side, if he does not so much as know what they are, he has no ground for preferring either opinion. The rational position for him would be suspension of judgment, and unless he contents himself with that, he is either led by authority or adopts, like the generality of the world, the side to which he feels most inclination. Nor is it enough that he should hear the arguments of adversaries from his own teachers, presented as they state them, and accompanied by what they offer as refutations. That is not the way to do justice to the arguments or bring them into real contact with his own mind. He must be able to hear them from persons

3. [Regarding Cicero, see Locke's *Essay*, n.8.]

who actually believe them, who defend them in earnest and do their very utmost for them. He must know them in their most plausible and persuasive form; he must feel the whole force of the difficulty which the true view of the subject has to encounter and dispose of, else he will never really possess himself of the portion of truth which meets and removes that difficulty. Ninety-nine in a hundred of what are called educated men are in this condition, even of those who can argue fluently for their opinions. Their conclusion may be true, but it might be false for anything they know; they have never thrown themselves into the mental position of those who think differently from them, and considered what such persons may have to say; and, consequently, they do not, in any proper sense of the word, know the doctrine which they themselves profess. . . .

We have now recognized the necessity to the mental well-being of mankind (on which all their other well-being depends) of freedom of opinion, and freedom of the expression of opinion, on four distinct grounds, which we will now briefly recapitulate:

First, if any opinion is compelled to silence, that opinion may, for aught we can certainly know, be true. To deny this is to assume our own infallibility.

Secondly, though the silenced opinion be an error, it may, and very commonly does, contain a portion of truth; and since the general or prevailing opinion on any subject is rarely or never the whole truth, it is only by the collision of adverse opinions that the remainder of the truth has any chance of being supplied.

Thirdly, even if the received opinion be not only true, but the whole truth; unless it is suffered to be, and actually is, vigorously and earnestly contested, it will, by most of those who receive it, be held in the manner of a prejudice, with little comprehension or feeling of its rational grounds. And not only this, but, fourthly, the meaning of the doctrine itself will be in danger of being lost or enfeebled, and deprived of its vital effect on the character and conduct: the dogma becoming a mere formal profession, inefficacious for good, but cumbering the ground and preventing the growth of any real and heartfelt conviction from reason or personal experience.

Friedrich Nietzsche

Friedrich Nietzsche was born in 1844 in a small town in Prussia. He studied classical philology at the universities of Bonn and Leipzig, where he proved to be such an extraordinary student that, even without a completed doctoral thesis, he was appointed professor of classical philology at the University of Basel at the age of twenty-five. At Basel, he read Schopenhauer and Greek philosophy, and for a few years he was enthralled by the composer Richard Wagner. Somewhat shy and withdrawn by nature, Nietzsche was severely myopic and subject to migraine headaches. By 1879 his poor health led him to resign his professorship, and he spent the next ten years composing the works that make up his mature philosophy (five books, including *Twilight of the Idols* and *The Antichrist,* appeared in the last year of his productive life, 1888). At the age of forty-four he suffered a complete mental collapse that left him a helpless invalid until his death in 1900.

The key to Nietzsche's philosophy is his most famous one-liner, "God is dead." What this means is not that people are living more secular lives, but that all the traditional ideas of an "absolute" in Western civilization—ideas about a transcendent basis for finding direction and meaning in life—have collapsed, and there are no prospects of new absolutes arising in the future. So the term "God" in this remark refers not just to the deity of the Judeo-Christian tradition, but also to such god-terms as the Greek *cosmos,* the Enlightenment concept of Reason, and even our scientific idea of a law-governed nature.

Much of Nietzsche's thought is devoted to working out the consequences of this recognition of the loss of absolutes. If God is dead, then there is no way we can arrive at a "God's-eye view" of reality as it is in itself, independent of any perspective or interpretation. Nietzsche rejects the "doctrine of immaculate perception," the assumption that we can perceive things as they are in themselves. Instead, he holds that our beliefs about the world are always conditioned by our own point of view as specific sorts of creatures located in a particular place and time. This "perspectivism" in turn implies that we have no access to any timeless truths about our own essence as humans. It is pointless to try to find a "proper way to be human" or a fixed table of values that determines good or evil for all people at all times. In the end, it is up to us to create our own values in life. In Nietzsche's view, the ideal person is one who is freed from the old "craving for metaphysical comfort," one who understands that "truth" is nothing but "a mobile army of metaphors" that is always subject to revision.

Twilight of the Idols presents a vivid overview of Nietzsche's mature philosophy. A central aim of *Twilight* is to attack what Nietzsche sees as one of the chief enemies of life-affirmation in the West: the Platonic dream of an "other," better world—a world of transcendent Forms—beyond the sensory, material world in which we find ourselves. In Nietzsche's view, the belief in a "true world" distinct from our familiar material world arises because of Plato's fascination with reason and his distaste for our "animal" appetites and drives. To help shake us out of the unquestioning assumption that reason is the highest good for humans, Nietzsche employs a sort of thought-experiment about what might have motivated Platonism at its inception. Suppose it were the case, he suggests, that Socrates and Plato, far from embodying everything fine and noble about the Greeks, were in fact misfits and decadents who were unable to enjoy the sensuous, spontaneous life of the more "noble" Greeks described by Homer. On this supposition, their prejudice in favor of reason would be a form of sour grapes, a symptom of sickly, bitter minds that are incapable of fulfilling their natural, healthy drives. Rationalism would then be a symptom of decline and decadence, not a step toward the improvement of the human race.

Nietzsche toys with the idea that the Platonic glorification of reason results from a peculiarity of philosophers: their fear of change. Unable to stomach the uncertainties of a world of "becoming," philosophers turn away from the transient material objects that make up the actual world and instead focus on their own concepts of things. The fateful move comes when philosophers assume that their abstract concepts (for example, "being," "substance," "God") actually correspond to entities that exist in reality—things that are more real than the concrete, changing items in the material world we see around us.

The criticisms of Platonism carry consequences for all Western thought. Christianity, which Nietzsche calls "Platonism for the masses," reproduces Plato's "two-world" view in its distinction between heaven and earth. And even modern science presupposes Platonic dualism in its distinction between observable phenomena and underlying forces. These different conceptions of a distinction between "appearance" and "reality" are deposited in our language, and they make up a hardened "mythology" we pass along from generation to generation. Nietzsche's aim is to destabilize and undercut these assumptions. In his view, there is only *one* world—the world we find around us—and calling that world an "apparent" world just buys into the kind of invidious contrast that got Platonism going in the first place.

• • •

Valuable early works on Nietzsche include Arthur C. Danto, *Nietzsche as Philosopher* (New York: Macmillan, 1965) and Walter Kaufmann, *Nietzsche: Philosopher, Psychologist, Antichrist* (Princeton: Princeton University Press, 1974). Some especially helpful studies are Richard Schacht, *Nietzsche* (London: Routledge, 1983); Alexander Nehamas, *Nietzsche: Life as Literature* (Cambridge, Mass.: Harvard University Press, 1983); and Graham Parke, *Composing the Soul* (Chicago: University of Chicago Press, 1994). For Nietzsche's impact on postmodern movements, see David B. Allison, ed., *The New Nietzsche* (Cambridge, Mass.: MIT Press, 1985). Good collections of essays are Robert C. Solomon and Kathleen M. Higgins, eds., *Reading Nietzsche* (New York: Oxford University Press, 1988) and Bernd Magnus and Kathleen Higgins, eds., *The Cambridge Companion to Nietzsche* (Cambridge: Cambridge University Press, 1996).

Charles Guignon

Twilight of the Idols: Or, How to Philosophize with the Hammer

The Problem of Socrates

1

The wisest sages of all times have come to the same judgment about life: *it is good for nothing*. Always and everywhere we have heard the same sound escape their mouths—a sound full of diffidence, full of melancholy, full of fatigue with life, full of hostility to life. Even Socrates said, as he died, "Living—that means being sick a long time. I owe a rooster to the savior Asclepius."[1] Even Socrates had had enough.

What does that *demonstrate*? What does that *indicate*? In the past one would have said (oh, one has said it, and loud enough, especially our pessimists!): "Here there must be something true in any case! The *consensus sapientium* [agreement of the wise] demonstrates the truth." Shall we still speak this way today? *May* we do so? "Here there must be some *sickness* in any case"—that's *our* answer; these wisest sages of all times, one should first take a close look at them! Were they perhaps, all of them, no longer steady on their legs? Worn out? Shaky? *Décadents*? Does wisdom perhaps appear on Earth as a scavenger bird, excited by the scent of rotting meat?

2

In my own case this disrespectful thought—that the great sages are *declining types*—first occurred to me precisely in regards to an instance where learned and unlearned prejudice most strongly opposes it. I recognized Socrates and Plato as symptoms of decay, as instruments of the Greek dissolution, as pseudo-Greek, as anti-Greek (*Birth of Tragedy*, 1872). That *consensus sapientium*—this I grasped better and better—demonstrates least of all that they were right about what they agreed on. Rather, it demonstrates that they themselves, these wisest ones, were somehow in *physiological* agreement, so that they took the same negative stance toward life—and *had* to take it.

Judgments, value judgments about life, for or against, can in the final analysis never be true; they have value only as symptoms, they come into consideration only as symptoms—in themselves, such judgments are stupidities. One absolutely must reach out and try to grasp this astounding *finesse, that the value of life cannot be assessed*. Not by the living, since they are parties to the dispute—in fact, they are the objects of contention, and not the judges; not by the dead, for another reason. Thus, when philosophers see a problem in the *value* of life, this even amounts to an objection to them, a question mark attached to their wisdom, an unwisdom.—What? And all these great sages—are we saying they were not only *décadents*, but they were not even wise to begin with? But here I come back to the problem of Socrates.

3

Socrates belonged by origin to the lowest folk; Socrates was rabble. One knows, one can still see for oneself, how ugly he was. But ugliness, which in itself is an objection, was among the Greeks virtually a refutation. Was Socrates a Greek at all? Ugliness is often enough the expression of a blocked development, a development *hampered* by interbreeding. Otherwise, it comes to light as a development in

1. [Asclepius was the god of medicine. See Plato, *Phaedo* 118a.—R.P.]

decline. Forensic anthropologists tell us that the typical criminal is ugly: *monstrum in fronte, monstrum in animo* [monster in the face, monster in the soul]. But the criminal is a *décadent*. Was Socrates a typical criminal?—At any rate this would not clash with that well-known judgment of a physiognomist which sounded so offensive to Socrates' friends. A visitor who knew about faces, when he passed through Athens, said to Socrates' face that he *was* a *monstrum*—that he contained all bad vices and cravings within him. And Socrates simply answered: "You know me, sir!"

4

Socrates' *décadence* is signaled not only by the confessed depravity and anarchy of his instincts, but also by the overdevelopment of the logical and that *arthritic nastiness* that characterizes him. And let us not forget those auditory hallucinations which have been interpreted in religious terms as "Socrates' *daimonion* [divine sign]." Everything about him is exaggerated, *buffo*, a caricature; everything is at the same time covert, subliminal, ulterior.—I am trying to grasp from what idiosyncrasy that Socratic equation—reason = virtue = happiness—stems, the most bizarre equation that there is, and one which in particular has all the instincts of the older Hellenes against it.

5

With Socrates, Greek taste takes a turn in favor of dialectic. What is actually happening there? Primarily, a *noble* taste is thereby defeated; with dialectic, the rabble rises to the top. Before Socrates, dialectical manners were rejected in good society. They were taken to be bad manners, they were a compromising exposure. One warned the youth against them. And all such presentation of one's reasons was mistrusted. Respectable things, like respectable people, just don't carry their reasons around on their sleeves like that. It is improper to show your whole hand. Whatever has to get itself proved in advance is not worth much. Wherever authority is still considered good form, so that one does not "give reasons" but commands, the dialectician is a sort of clown. One laughs at him; one does not take him seriously.—Socrates was the clown who *succeeded in making people take him seriously*; what actually happened there?

6

Dialectic is chosen only as a last resort. It is well-known that it creates mistrust, that it is not very convincing. Nothing can be wiped away more easily than a dialectician's effect; this is proven by the experience of every gathering where people speak. It can only be a *last resort* deployed by those who have no other weapons. One needs to get one's rights by *force*; otherwise, one makes no use of it. This is why the Jews were dialecticians. Reynard the Fox was one. What? And Socrates was one too?

7

Is Socrates' irony an expression of revolt? Of the rabble's *ressentiment*?[2] Does he, as one of the oppressed, relish his own ferocity in the knife-thrusts of the syllogism? Does he take *revenge* on the nobles whom he fascinates? As dialectician, one has a merciless instrument at hand; one can play the tyrant with it; one compromises by conquering. The dialectician lays on his opponent the burden of proving that he is not an idiot. He infuriates, and at the same time paralyzes. The dialectician *disempowers* the intellect of his opponent.—What? Is dialectic just a form of *revenge* in Socrates?

8

I have made it understandable how Socrates could be repulsive. Now it is all the more necessary to explain why he was *fascinating*.—The fact that he discovered a new kind of *agon* [contest], that in this contest he served as the first fencing master for the noble circles of Athens, is the first point. He fascinated by stimulating the combative drive of the Hellenes: he introduced a variant into the wrestling match between young men and youths. Socrates was also a great *erotic*.

9

But Socrates surmised even more. He saw *past* his noble Athenians; he grasped that *his* case, his idiosyncratic case, was already not exceptional. The same kind of degeneration was silently preparing itself everywhere; the old Athens was coming to an end. And

2. [Resentful vengefulness. Nietzsche develops this concept at length in *On the Genealogy of Morals* (1887).]

Socrates understood that all the world had *need* of him—his means, his cure, his personal device for self-preservation. Everywhere, the instincts were in anarchy; everywhere, one was five steps away from excess; the *monstrum in animo* was the general threat. "The drives want to play the tyrant; a *counter-tyrant* who is stronger must be invented."

When that physiognomist had exposed to Socrates who he was, a cave of all bad cravings, the great ironist allowed himself another word that gives us the key to him. "That is true," he said, "but I became the master of them all." *How* did Socrates become master of *himself*? His case was at bottom only the extreme case, only the most striking example of what began at that time to be the general emergency: the fact that no one was master of himself any more, that the instincts were turning *against* each other. He was fascinating as this extreme case—his fearsome ugliness displayed him as such to every eye. He was even more fascinating, of course, as an answer, as a solution, as the semblance of a *cure* for this case.

10

When one finds it necessary to make a tyrant out of *reason*, as Socrates did, then there must be no small danger that something else should play the tyrant. Rationality was at that time surmised to be a *savior*; neither Socrates nor his "sick patients" were rational by free choice—it was *de rigueur*, it was their *final* means. The fanaticism with which all Greek speculation throws itself at rationality betrays a situation of emergency—they were in danger, they had to make *this* choice: either to be destroyed, or—to be *absurdly rational*.

The moralism of the Greek philosophers from Plato on is pathologically conditioned; likewise their assessment of dialectic. Reason = virtue = happiness simply means: one must imitate Socrates and produce a permanent *daylight* against the dark desires—the daylight of reason. One must be cunning, sharp, clear at all costs; every acquiescence to the instincts, to the unconscious, leads *downward*.

11

I have made it understandable how Socrates was fascinating: he appeared to be a doctor, a savior. Is it necessary to go on to point out the error which lay in his belief in "rationality at all costs"?—It is a self-deception on the part of philosophers and moralists to think that they can escape from *décadence* merely by making war against it. Such an escape is beyond their strength. What they choose as a means, as salvation, is itself just another expression of *décadence*—they *alter* its expression, they do not do away with it itself. Socrates was a misunderstanding; *the whole morality of betterment, that of Christianity included, was a misunderstanding.* The most glaring daylight, rationality at all costs, a life bright, cold, careful, aware, without instinct, in resistance to the instincts, was itself just a sickness, another sickness—and not at all a way back to "virtue," to "health," to happiness. To *have* to fight the instincts—that is the formula for *décadence*. As long as life *is ascending*, happiness is the same as instinct.

12

Did he himself still grasp that, this most cunning of all self-outwitters? Did he tell himself this in the end, in the *wisdom* of his courage in the face of death? Socrates *wanted* to die—not Athens, but *he* gave himself the poison cup, he forced Athens to give him the poison cup. "Socrates is no doctor," he said to himself softly, "death is the only doctor here . . . Socrates himself has just been sick for a long time. . . ."

"Reason" in Philosophy

1

You ask me what is idiosyncratic about philosophers? . . . There is, for instance, their lack of a sense of history, their hatred for the very notion of becoming, their Egyptianism. They think they are *honoring* a thing if they de-historicize it, see it *sub specie aeterni*[3]—if they make a mummy out of it. Everything that philosophers have handled, for thousands of years now, has been a conceptual mummy; nothing real escaped their hands alive. They kill and stuff whatever they worship, these gentlemen who idolize concepts; they endanger the life of whatever they worship. In their view, death, change, and age, like procreation

3. ["In its eternal aspect"—an expression used by Spinoza.]

and growth, are objections—refutations, even. That which is, does not *become*; that which becomes, *is* not.

Now, they all believe, desperately even, in that which *is*. But since they fail to get it into their grasp, they look for the reason why it withholds itself from them. "There must be an illusion, a trick, at work that prevents us from perceiving that which *is*; where's the trickster?"—"We've got the trickster!" they cry happily, "it's sensation! These senses, *which are so immoral anyway*, trick us about the *true* world. The moral is: free yourself from the senses' trickery, from becoming, from history, from the lie; history is nothing but belief in the senses, belief in the lie. The moral is: say No to everything that lends credence to the senses, to all the rest of humanity; all that is merely 'the masses.' Be a philosopher, be a mummy, portray monotono-theism with a gravedigger's pantomime!—And above all, away with the *body*, this pathetic *idée fixe* [pet idea] of the senses, afflicted with every logical error there is, refuted, even impossible—although it has the nerve to behave as if it were real!" . . .

2

I set aside with great respect the name of *Heraclitus*. While the rest of the mass of philosophers were rejecting the testimony of their senses, because they displayed plurality and change, he rejected the testimony of the senses because they displayed things as if they had duration and unity. Heraclitus did not do justice to the senses either. They do not lie either in the way the Eleatics[4] thought, or in the way that he thought—they do not lie at all. What we *make* of their testimony is what first introduces the lie—for instance, the lie of unity, the lie of thinghood, of substance, of duration. . . . "Reason" is what causes us to falsify the testimony of the senses. Insofar as the senses display becoming, passing away, and change, they do not lie. But Heraclitus will always be in the right for saying that being is an empty fiction. The "apparent" world is the only world; the "true world" is merely *added to it by a lie*.

4. [Followers of Parmenides of Elea (c. 475 B.C.), who asserted that that which is, is unchangeable, uniform, unitary, and indivisable. Becoming, as displayed by the senses, is this pure illusion or non-being.]

3

And what fine tools of observation we have in our senses! This nose, for instance, of which no philosopher has yet spoken with admiration and gratitude, is in fact the most delicate instrument at our disposal; it can register minimal differences in motion which even the spectroscope fails to register. The extent to which we possess science today is precisely the extent to which we have decided to *accept* the testimony of the senses—and learned to sharpen them, arm them, and think them through to their end. The rest is a miscarriage and not-yet-science—that is, metaphysics, theology, psychology, epistemology. *Or* it is formal science, a theory of signs, such as logic and that applied logic, mathematics. In these formal sciences, reality makes no appearance at all, not even as a problem; nor is there any hint of the question of what value such a convention of signs has in the first place.

4

The *other* idiosyncrasy of philosophers, which is no less dangerous, consists in confusing what is first with what is last. They posit what comes at the end—unfortunately, for it should never come at all!—the "highest concepts," that is, the most universal and emptiest concepts, the final wisp of evaporating reality—these they posit at the beginning *as* the beginning. This, again, just expresses their way of honoring something: the higher is not *permitted* to grow out of the lower, is not *permitted* to have grown at all.

The moral is: everything that is of the first rank must be *causa sui* [cause of itself]. Origination from something else counts as an objection that casts doubt on the value of what has so originated. All the supreme values are of the first rank; all the highest concepts—that which *is*, the unconditional, the good, the true, the perfect—all this cannot have become, and *must* consequently be *causa sui*. But all this cannot be at odds with itself either, cannot contradict itself. That's where they get their stupendous concept "God." The last, the thinnest, the emptiest concept is posited as the first, as a cause in itself, as *ens realissimum* [the most real being]. To think that humanity has had to take seriously the mental distortions of sickly webspinners!—And it has paid dearly for having done so!

5

Let us, finally, present the opposing way in which *we* (I politely say we) view the problem of error and illusion. It used to be that one took alteration, change, becoming in general as a proof of illusion, as a sign that something must be there, leading us astray. Today, in contrast, it is precisely to the extent that we are compelled by the prejudice of reason to posit unity, identity, duration, substance, cause, thinghood, being, that we see ourselves, as it were, entangled in error, *forced* into error—so sure are we, on the basis of a rigorous self-examination, that it is here that the error lies.

This case is just like the supposed motions of our great star. In that case, error has our eyes as its constant advocates, whereas in the first case, its advocate is our *language*. In its origin, language belongs to the time of the most rudimentary type of psychology; we encounter a crude set of fetishes when we pay attention to the basic presuppositions of the metaphysics of language—or, to put it plainly, *reason. Reason* sees actors and actions everywhere; it believes in the will as an absolute cause; it believes in the "I," in the I as a being, in the I as a substance, and *projects* its belief in the I-substance onto all things—that is how it first *creates* the concept "thing." Being is thought into things everywhere as a cause, is *imputed* to things; from the conception "I" there follows the derivative concept "being." At the beginning there stands the great and fatal error of thinking that the will is something that *acts*—that will is an *ability*. Today we know that it is merely a word.

Much, much later, in a world that was more enlightened by a thousandfold, philosophers were startled to become aware of their *certitude*, their subjective *certainty* in manipulating the categories of reason; they concluded that these categories could not come from experience—all experience stands in contradiction to them, after all. *So where did they come from?*—And in India, as in Greece, they made the same mistake: "We must already have been at home in a higher world"—instead of *in a far lower one*, which would have been the truth!—"we must have been divine, *since* we have reason!"

In fact, nothing up to now has been more naively persuasive than the error of being, as it was formulated by the Eleatics, for instance; after all, it has on its side every word, every sentence we speak! Even the opponents of the Eleatics fell prey to the seduction of their concept of being—among others, Democritus did so in inventing his *atom*. "Reason" in language: oh, what a tricky old woman she is! I'm afraid we're not rid of God because we still believe in grammar.

6

One will be thankful to me if I condense such an essential and new insight into four theses; I thus make it easier to understand, and I challenge you to argue against it.

First proposition. The grounds on which "this" world has been designated as apparent are, rather, grounds for its reality; *another* kind of reality is absolutely indemonstrable.

Second proposition. The distinguishing marks which one has given to the "true being" of things are the distinguishing marks of nonbeing, of *nothing*. The "true world" has been constructed by contradicting the actual world—this "true world" is in fact an apparent world, insofar as it is merely a *moral-optical* illusion.

Third proposition. It makes no sense whatsoever to tell fables about "another" world than this one, provided that the instinct to slander, trivialize, and look down upon life is not powerful in us; in that case, we *revenge* ourselves on life with the phantasmagorias of "another," "better" life.

Fourth proposition. To divide the world into a "true" and an "apparent" world, whether in the style of Christianity or in the style of Kant (a *sneaky* Christian to the end) is merely a sign of *décadence*—a symptom of *declining* life.—The fact that the artist prizes appearance over reality is no objection to this proposition. For "appearance" here means reality *once again*, but in the form of a selection, an emphasis, and a correction. Tragic artists are *not* pessimists—in fact, they say *Yes* to everything questionable and terrible itself; they are *Dionysian*.

How the "True World" Finally Became a Fiction

History of an Error

1. The true world, attainable for those who are wise, devout, virtuous—they live in it, *they are it.*

   (Oldest form of the idea, relatively clever, simple, convincing. Paraphrase of the assertion, "I, Plato, *am* the truth.")

2. The true world, unattainable for now, but promised to those who are wise, devout, virtuous ("to the sinner who does penance").

   (Progress of the idea: it becomes more refined, more devious, more mystifying—*it becomes woman*, it becomes Christian.)

3. The true world, unattainable, unprovable, unpromisable, but a consolation, an obligation, an imperative, merely by virtue of being thought.

   (The old sun basically, but glimpsed through fog and skepticism; the idea become sublime, pallid, Nordic, Königsbergian.[5])

4. The true world—unattainable? In any case, unattained. And if it is unattained, it is also *unknown*. Hence it is also not consoling, redeeming, obligating; to what could something unknown obligate us?

   (Grey dawn. First yawnings of reason. Rooster's crow of positivism.)

5. The "true world"—an idea that is useful for nothing anymore, no longer even obligating—an idea become useless, superfluous, *hence* a refuted idea; let us do away with it!

   (Bright day; breakfast; return of *bon sens* [good sense] and cheerfulness; Plato's blush; pandemonium of all free spirits.)

6. We have done away with the true world; what world is left over? The apparent one, maybe? . . . But no! *Along with the true world, we have also done away with the apparent!*

   (Midday; moment of the shortest shadow; end of the longest error; high point of humanity; INCIPIT ZARATHUSTRA [here begins Zarathustra].)

Morality as Anti-Nature

1

All passions have a time when they are merely fatal, when they drag their victim down with the heaviness of their stupidity—and a later, much later time when they marry the spirit, they "spiritualize" themselves. It used to be that on account of the stupidity in passion, one made war against passion itself; one conspired to destroy it. All the old moral monsters are of one mind on this point: "*il faut tuer les passions*" [the passions must be killed]. The best-known formula for this is in the New Testament, in that Sermon on the Mount in which, by the way, things are not contemplated *from a height* at all. For instance, there it is said with reference to sexuality, "if your eye offends you, pluck it out." Fortunately, no Christian acts according to this prescription.

To *destroy* the passions and desires, merely in order to protect oneself against their stupidity and the disagreeable consequences of their stupidity, seems to us today to be itself an acute form of stupidity. We no longer admire dentists who *pull out* teeth so that they won't hurt anymore. But on the other hand, it is only fair to concede that on the soil from which Christianity grew, the concept of "*spiritualizing* the passions" was simply inconceivable. After all, the early Church fought, as is known, *against* the "intellectuals," on behalf of those who were "poor in spirit"; how could one expect the Church to wage an intelligent war against passion? The Church fights passion by cutting it out, in every sense; its practice, its "therapy" is *castration*. It never asks, "How does one spiritualize, beautify, deify a desire?"—its discipline has always emphasized eradication—eradication of sensuality, pride, ambition to rule, covetousness, vengefulness. But ripping out the passions by the root means ripping out life by the root; the practice of the Church is *hostile to life*.

2

The same means—castration, eradication—is instinctively chosen in the struggle against a desire by those who are too weak-willed, too degenerate to moderate their own desire—by those natures who need La Trappe,[6] to use a metaphor (and not to use one), some ultimate declaration of war, an *abyss* between themselves and a passion. Radical means are indis-

5. [An allusion to Kant, who lived all his life in Königsberg, on the Baltic Sea. For Kant, it is impossible for us to know about "things in themselves"—including God, free will, and an immortal soul; however, rational morality obliges us to "postulate" such things.]

6. [The original abbey of the highly disciplined Trappist monks.]

pensable only for degenerates; to have a weak will, or, put more precisely, to be incapable of *not* reacting to a stimulus, is itself just another form of degeneration. Radical enmity, enmity to the death against sensuality, is always a symptom that repays reflection; it justifies one's suspicions about the general condition of one who goes to this type of extreme.

By the way, this enmity, this hatred reaches its peak only when such natures no longer have enough stamina even for the radical therapy, for the repudiation of their "devil." Survey the whole history of priests and philosophers, and artists too: the most poisonous words against the senses have come *not* from the impotent, *not* even from the ascetics, but from the impossible ascetics, from those who were in need of being ascetics.

3

The spiritualization of sensuality is known as *love*; it is a great triumph over Christianity. Another triumph is our spiritualization of *enmity*. It consists in a deep grasp of the value of having enemies; in short, our way of acting and drawing conclusions is the reverse of what it used to be. In every age, the Church wanted its enemies to be destroyed; we, we immoralists and anti-Christians, see our own advantage in the Church's continued existence. In the political sphere, too, enmity has now become more spiritual—much more clever, much more reflective, much more *considerate*. Almost every party grasps that its own interest, its own self-preservation, depends on the opposing party's not losing its strength. The same applies to politics on the large scale. Above all, a new creation, such as the new *Reich*,[7] needs enemies more than it needs friends; only in opposition does it feel that it is necessary, only in opposition does it *become* necessary.

We conduct ourselves no differently as regards the "inner enemy": here, too, we have spiritualized enmity; here, too, we have realized its *value*. One is *fruitful* only at the price of being rich in oppositions; one remains *young* only under the condition that the soul not slacken, not yearn for peace. Nothing has become more alien to us than that former object of desire, "peace of the soul," the *Christian* object of desire; nothing makes us less envious than the morality-cow and the fat contentment of good conscience. One has relinquished *great* life when one relinquishes war.

In many cases, of course, "peace of the soul" is just a misunderstanding—something *else* which simply does not know how to call itself by a more honest name. Without delay and without prejudice, here are a couple of cases. For instance, "peace of the soul" can be an animal richness, gently radiating into the moral (or the religious) realm. Or the beginning of fatigue, the first shadow cast by the evening, every sort of evening. Or a sign that the air is humid, that southern winds are on their way. Or unconscious thankfulness for good digestion (sometimes called "love of humanity"). Or the growing calm of the convalescent to whom all things taste new, and who is awaiting. . . . Or the condition that follows a powerful gratification of our dominant passion, the good feeling of a rare satisfaction. Or the senile feebleness of our will, our desires, our vices. Or laziness, convinced by vanity to dress itself up in morality. Or the arrival of a certainty, even a terrible certainty, after a long, suspenseful period of being tortured by uncertainty. Or the expression of ripeness and mastery in the midst of doing, creating, working, willing—unhurried breathing, the *attained* "freedom of the will". . . . *Twilight of the Idols*: who knows? Maybe this, too, is just a kind of "peace of the soul."

4

I shall put a principle into a formula. All naturalism in morality, that is, all *healthy* morality, is ruled by an instinct of life; some decree of life is fulfilled by a particular canon of "shall" and "shall not," some restriction and hostility on life's path is thereby shoved aside. *Anti-natural* morality—that is, almost every morality that has been taught, honored and preached up to now—turns, in contrast, precisely *against* the instincts of life; it is a sometimes stealthy, sometimes loud and bold *condemnation* of these instincts. By saying, "God looks into the heart," it says No to the lowest and highest desires of life, and takes God to be the *enemy of life*. The saint in whom God takes delight is the ideal eunuch. Life ends where the "kingdom of God" *begins*.

7. [The new German Empire, proclaimed by Bismarck in 1871.]

5

Once one has grasped the impiety of a revolt against life such as has become nearly sacrosanct in Christian morality, one has, fortunately, also grasped something else: the uselessness, illusiveness, absurdity, and *mendacity* of such a revolt. A condemnation of life by one who is alive is, in the end, just a symptom of a particular kind of life; the question of whether the condemnation is justified or unjustified has not been raised here at all. One would have to occupy a position *outside* life, and on the other hand, to know life as well as one who has lived it—as many, as all who have lived it—in order to be allowed even to touch upon the problem of the *value* of life. These are reasons enough to grasp that this problem is, for us, an inaccessible problem. When we speak of values, we speak under the inspiration and optics of life; life itself is forcing us to posit values, life itself is valuing by means of us, *when* we posit values.

It follows from this that even that *anti-nature of a morality* that takes God as the counter-concept and condemnation of life is itself just one of the value judgments of life.—A judgment of *which* life? Of *which* kind of life?—But I already gave the answer: of declining, weakened, tired, and condemned life. Morality as it has been understood up to now—as it was finally formulated once more by Schopenhauer, as "negation of the will to life"—is the *décadence-instinct* itself, making itself into an imperative. "*Perish!*" it says—it is the condemnation decreed by the condemned.

6

Finally, let us consider how naive it is in the first place to say, "Human beings *should* be such and such!" Reality shows us a captivating treasury of types, the exuberance of an evanescent play and alteration of forms. And some pathetic bystander of a moralist says to all this, "No! Human beings should be *different*"? He even knows *how* human beings should be, this sniveling bigot; he paints himself on the wall and pronounces, "*Ecce homo!*"[8]

But even if the moralist simply turns to the individual and says, "*You* should be such and such!" he does not stop making himself ridiculous. The individual is a slice of fate, both ahead and behind—one more law, one more necessity for everything that is coming and will be. To say to the individual, "change yourself," means wishing that everything should change itself, even retroactively. And there really have been consistent moralists; they wanted human beings to be different, namely virtuous, they wanted them made in their own image, namely as bigots. To this end, they *denied* the world! No small lunacy! No modest sort of immodesty!

Morality, insofar as it *condemns* on its own grounds, and *not* from the point of view of life's perspectives and objectives, is a specific error for which one should have no sympathy, an *idiosyncrasy of degenerates* which has done an unspeakable amount of harm! In contrast, we others, we immoralists, have opened our hearts wide to every form of understanding, comprehending, *approving*. We do not easily deny, we seek our honor in being those who *affirm*. Our eyes have been opened more and more to that economy that needs and knows how to use all that the holy craziness of the priest, the *sick* reason in the priest rejects—that economy in the law of life that draws its advantage even from the repulsive species of the bigot, the priest, the virtuous. *What* advantage?—But we ourselves, we immoralists, are the answer here.

The Four Great Errors

1

Error of confusing cause and effect

There is no error more dangerous than *confusing the effect with the cause*; I call it the genuine ruination of reason. Nevertheless, this error belongs among both the oldest and most contemporary customs of humanity; it has even been made sacred among us, it bears the names of "religion" and "morality." *Every* statement formulated by religion and morality contains it; priests and moral lawgivers are the ones who originated this ruination of reason.

I offer an example. Everyone knows the book of the famous Cornaro[9] in which he promotes his skimpy

8. ["Behold the man" (John 19:5); but also, "behold man," behold what it is to be human.]

9. [Luigi Cornaro (1475–1566) was a Venetian nobleman who wrote *Discourse on the Sober Life* (1558).]

diet as a prescription for a long, happy life—and a virtuous one. Few books have been read so widely; still today, in England, it is printed by the thousands of copies every year. I have no doubt that hardly any book (the Bible excepted, as is only fair) has done as much damage, has *shortened* as many lives as this curiosity which was so well-meaning. The reason: confusing effect and cause. The honorable Italian saw in his diet the *cause* of his long life, whereas in fact, the preconditions of his long life—extraordinary metabolic slowness, low expenditure of energy—were the cause of his skimpy diet. He was not at liberty to eat a little *or* a lot, his frugality was *not* "freely willed"; he got sick if he ate more. But for whoever is not a cold fish, not only does it do good, but it is necessary to eat *properly*. Scholars of *our* day, with their rapid expenditure of nervous energy, would destroy themselves if they followed Cornaro's regimen. *Crede experto* [believe the one with experience].

2

The most general formula that lies at the basis of every religion and morality is, "Do such and such, don't do such and such—that will make you happy! Or else. . . ." Every morality, every religion *is* this imperative; I call it the great original sin of reason, the *immortal unreason*. In my mouth, this formula changes into its opposite—*first* example of my "revaluation of all values": well-constituted people, "happy" ones, *must* do certain acts and instinctively shrink away from other acts; they import their characteristic physiological order into their relations to people and things. In a formula: their virtue is the *effect* of their happiness.

Long life and many offspring are *not* the reward of virtue; virtue itself is rather that slow metabolism that, among other things, also has a long life, many offspring, and, in short, *Cornarism* as its consequence. The Church and morality say, "A race, a people is destroyed by vice and luxury." My *reconstituted* reason says: when a people is perishing, physiologically degenerating, the *effects* of this are vice and luxury (that is, the need for ever stronger and ever more frequent stimuli, of the sort that is familiar to every exhausted nature). This young man becomes prematurely pale and flabby. His friends say: such and such a sickness is responsible for this. I say: the fact *that* he got sick, *that* he did not resist the sickness, was already the effect of an impoverished life, an inherited exhaustion. The newspaper reader says: this party is destroying itself by making such a mistake. My *higher* politics says: a party that makes such mistakes is over—it no longer has sure instincts.

Every mistake, in every sense, is the effect of degenerate instincts, of a disintegrated will; this virtually defines the *bad*. Everything *good* is instinct—and consequently is easy, necessary, free. Exertion is an objection; the *god* is typically different from the hero (in my language: *light* feet are the first attribute of godliness).

3

Error of a false causality

In every age we have believed that we know what a cause is. But where did we get our knowledge, or more precisely, our belief that we know about this? From the realm of the famous "internal facts," none of which has up to now proved to be factual. We believed that we ourselves were causal in the act of willing; there, at least, we thought that we were *catching causality in the act.*

Likewise, we never doubted that all the antecedents of an action, its causes, were to be sought in consciousness, and could be discovered there if we looked for them—discovered as "motives"; otherwise, one would not have been free *for* the action, responsible *for* it. Finally, who would have disputed the claim that a thought is caused? That the "I" causes the thought?—Of these three "interior facts" by which causality seemed to vouch for itself, the first and most convincing is the "fact" of *will as cause*; the conception of a consciousness ("mind") as cause, and still later of the "I" (the "subject") as cause were merely born later, after the will had firmly established causality as given, as an *empirical fact*.

In the meantime, we have thought better of this. Today we believe not a word of all that anymore. The "internal world" is full of optical illusions and false flashes; the will is one of them. The will no longer moves anything, and consequently no longer explains anything either; it merely accompanies events, and can even be absent. The so-called "motive": another error—just a surface phenomenon of consciousness, an accessory to the act, which rather conceals the antecedents of an act than represents them. And as for the "I"! That has become a fable, a fiction, a play on words; it has completely and utterly ceased to think, to feel, and to will! What is the consequence of this? There are no mental causes at all! The whole supposed empirical evidence for them has gone to the devil! *That's* the consequence!

And we had made a fine misuse of this "evidence"; we had *created* the world on that basis as a world of causes, a world of wills, a world of minds. The oldest and most long-standing psychology was at work here, and it did nothing else at all; all happening was for it a doing, all doing the effect of a willing; the world became for it a plurality of doers, a doer (a "subject") was imputed to all that happened. Human beings projected their three "internal facts," the objects of their firmest belief—will, mind, "I"—beyond themselves; they first derived the concept of being from the concept "I," they posited "things" as existing in their own image, according to their concept of the "I" as a cause. No wonder that they later rediscovered in things only *what they had put into them!*—The thing itself—to say it once again—the concept of a thing is a mere reflex of the belief in the "I" as a cause. And even your atom, my dear mechanists and physicists—how much error, how much rudimentary psychology remains in your atom!—Not to mention the "thing in itself," the *horrendum pudendum* [horrible, shameful thing] of the metaphysicians! The error of mind as cause confused with reality! And made into the measure of reality! And called *God!*

4

Error of imaginary causes

I begin from dreams: a particular sensation—for instance, the result of a distant cannon shot—subsequently has a cause imputed to it (often a whole little story in which precisely the dreamer is the protagonist). Meanwhile, the sensation persists in a kind of resonance; it waits, as it were, until the drive for causes allows it to come into the foreground—not as an accident anymore, but as "meaning." The cannon shot shows up in a *causal* way, in an apparent reversal of time. What is later, the motivation, is experienced first, often with a hundred particularities which flash by like lightning; the shot *follows.*—What has happened? The representations *generated* by a certain state of affairs were misunderstood as the cause of this state of affairs.

In fact, we do just the same thing when we are awake. Most of our common feelings—every sort of inhibition, pressure, tension, explosion in the play and counter-play of the organs, particularly including the state of our sympathetic nervous system—arouse our drive to find causes; we want to have a *reason* for finding ourselves in *such and such* a state—a bad state or a good state. It is never enough for us simply to ascertain the mere fact *that* we find ourselves in such and such a state; we admit this fact—become *conscious* of it—*if* we have given it some kind of motivation. Memory, which is activated in such cases without our knowing it, calls up earlier states of the same kind, and the causal interpretations that are rooted in them—but *not* their causation. To be sure, the belief that the representations, the accompanying occurrences in consciousness, were the causes is also called up by the memory. Thus we become *accustomed* to a particular interpretation of causes that in fact inhibits and even excludes an *investigation* of the cause.

5

A psychological explanation of this error

Tracing something unfamiliar back to something familiar alleviates us, calms us, pacifies us, and furthermore provides a feeling of power. The unfamiliar brings with it danger, unrest, and care; our first instinct is directed at *doing away with* these painful conditions. First principle: some explanation is better than none. Since at bottom it is only a matter of wanting to free oneself from oppressive representations, one is not exactly stringent about the means of freeing oneself from them; the first representation that serves to explain the unfamiliar as familiar is so beneficial that one "takes it to be true." Proof of *pleasure* ("strength") as criterion of truth.

The drive to find causes is thus conditioned and aroused by the feeling of fear. The "why?" should, whenever possible, not so much provide the cause for its own sake, but rather provide a *type of cause*—a calming, pacifying, alleviating cause. The fact that something already *familiar*, experienced, inscribed in memory, is posited as the cause, is the first consequence of this requirement. The new, the unexperienced, the alien, is excluded as a cause. Thus, not only is one type of explanation sought as the cause, but there is a type of explanation that is *singled out* and *preferred*, the type which does away with the feeling of the alien, new, and unexperienced, as quickly and as frequently as possible—the most *customary* explanations.

Consequence: one kind of cause-positing becomes more and more prevalent, concentrates itself into a system, and finally comes to the fore as *dominant*, that is, as simply *excluding* any *other* causes and explanations. The banker thinks right away about "business," the Christian about "sin," the girl about her love.

6

The entire realm of morality and religion belongs under this concept of imaginary causes

"Explanation" of the *unpleasant* common feelings. These feelings are brought about by beings that are our enemies (evil spirits—the most famous case—misunderstanding of hysterics as witches). They are brought about by unacceptable actions (the feeling of "sin," of "sinfulness," is imputed to a physiological unease—one always finds reasons to be dissatisfied with oneself). They are brought about as punishments, as payment for something that we ought not to have done, that we ought not to have *been*. (Impudently generalized by Schopenhauer into a statement in which morality appears as what it is, as something that really poisons and despises life: "every great pain, be it bodily or spiritual, expresses what we deserve, for it could not come to us if we did not deserve it."—*The World as Will and Representation*, II.) They are brought about as the effects of thoughtless actions that turned out badly (the emotions, the senses, are posited as a cause, as "responsible"; physiological crises are interpreted as "deserved" with the help of *other* crises).

"Explanation" of the *pleasant* common feelings. These feelings are brought about by trust in God. They are brought about by our awareness of good actions (the so-called "good conscience," a physiological condition that sometimes looks so similar to a good digestion that it might be confused with it). They are brought about by the successful outcome of our enterprises (naively false conclusion: the successful outcome of an enterprise does not at all create pleasant common feelings for a hypochondriac or a Pascal).[10] They are brought about by faith, love, hope—the Christian virtues.

In truth, all these supposed explanations are *subsequent* states and translations, so to speak, of feelings of pleasure or displeasure into a false dialect. One is in a state of hope *because* the basic physiological feeling is once again strong and rich; one trusts in God *because* the feeling of fullness and strength gives one calm. Morality and religion totally belong to the *psychology of error*: in every single case, cause and effect are confused, or truth is confused with the effect of what is *believed* to be true, or a state of consciousness is confused with the causation of this state.

7

Error of free will

Today we no longer have any sympathy for the concept of "free will." We know only too well what it is: the most disreputable of all the theologians' artifices, the aim of which is to make humanity "responsible" in the theologians' sense, that is, *to make it dependent on them.*—Here, I am simply offering the psychology of all making-responsible. Wherever responsibilities are sought, what tends to be doing the seeking is the instinct of *wanting to punish and rule.* One has stripped becoming of its innocence when some state of being-such-and-such is traced back to will, to intentions, to acts; the doctrine of the will was essentially invented for the purpose of punishment, that is, for the purpose of *wanting to find people guilty*. All the old psychology, the psychology of will, has its precondition in the fact that its originators, the priests in the elites of old communities, wanted to create a *right* for themselves to inflict punishments—or wanted to create a right for God to do so. Human beings were thought to be "free" so that they could be ruled, so that they could be punished—so that they could become *guilty*.

10. [In his *Pensées*, Blaise Pascal (1623–1662) stresses the fragility and wretchedness of human life.]

Consequently, every action *had* to be thought as willed, the origin of every action *had* to be thought to lie in consciousness (and thus the *most fundamental* act of counterfeiting *in psychologicis* [in psychological matters] was itself made into the principle of psychology). Today, when we have initiated the *reverse* movement, when we immoralists seek with all our strength to get the concepts of guilt and punishment back out of the world, and to purge psychology, history, nature, social institutions, and sanctions of these concepts, there is in our eyes no opposition more radical than that of the theologians, who, with the concept of the "moral order of the world," go on infecting the innocence of becoming by means of "punishment" and "guilt." Christianity is a metaphysics of the hangman.

8

What is the only doctrine that can be *ours*?—That nobody *gives* human beings their qualities, neither God, nor society, nor their parents and ancestors, nor *they themselves* (the nonsense of the last notion we have rejected was taught by Kant as "intelligible freedom," and perhaps already taught by Plato as well). *Nobody* is responsible for the fact that we are here at all, that we are constituted in such and such a way, that we are in these circumstances, in this environment. The fatality of our essence is not to be resolved by the fatality of all that was and that will be. We are *not* the consequence of a special intention, a will, a goal; we are *not* being used in an attempt to reach an "ideal of humanity," or an "ideal of happiness," or an "ideal of morality"—it is absurd to want to *divert* our essence towards some goal. *We* have invented the concept "goal"; in reality, goals are *absent*.

One is necessary, one is a piece of fate, one belongs to the whole, one *is* in the whole. There is nothing that could rule, measure, compare, judge our being, for that would mean ruling, measuring, comparing, and judging the whole—*but there is nothing outside the whole!*—That nobody is made responsible anymore, that no way of being may be traced back to a *causa prima* [first cause], that the world is not a unity either as sensorium or as "spirit," *this alone is the great liberation*—thus the *innocence* of becoming is restored.—The concept "God" was up to now the greatest *objection* against existence. We deny God, and in denying God we deny responsibility; only *thus* do we redeem the world.

What I Owe to the Ancients

1

In closing, a word about that world to which I have sought access, to which I have perhaps found a new access—the ancient world. My taste, which may be the opposite of a tolerant taste, is far, here too, from saying Yes to just anything; it does not like to say Yes at all, it prefers to say No, and what it likes best is to say nothing at all. . . . This applies to entire cultures, it applies to books—it also applies to places and landscapes.

Ultimately it is a very small number of ancient books that count in my life; the most famous are not among them. My feeling for style, for the epigram as a style, awoke almost instantly when I came into contact with Sallust. I have not forgotten the amazement of my honored teacher Corssen when he had to give the very first grade to the worst of his Latin students—I had finished in one blow. Concise, severe, founded on as much substance as possible, with a cold spite against the "beautiful word" and the "beautiful feeling"—I discovered myself in this. One will recognize in me, even in my *Zarathustra*, a very earnest ambition for the *Roman* style, for the "*aere perennius*"[11] in style.

It was no different upon my first contact with Horace. Even today I have never derived as much artistic delight from any poet as I got from the start from a Horatian Ode. In certain languages, what is attained here is not even *desirable*. This mosaic of words in which every word pours out its force as sound, as place, as concept to the right and to the left and over the whole, this minimum in the range and number of signs, this maximum in the energy of the signs which is thus achieved—all that is Roman, and, if one wishes to believe me, *noble par excellence*. All

11. [More lasting than bronze. "I have erected a monument more lasting than bronze" (i.e., my poetry): Horace, *Odes* III.30.]

remaining verse is, as compared to this, somewhat too popular—just emotional verbosity.

2

To the Greeks I owe no impressions that are comparably strong. And, to come right out and say it, they *cannot* be for us what the Romans are. One does not *learn* from the Greeks—their way is too alien, and also too fluid, to have an imperative effect, a "classical" effect. Who would ever have learned to write from a Greek! Who would ever have learned it *without* the Romans!

Please do not bring up Plato as an objection to me. In relation to Plato I am fundamentally a skeptic, and was always incapable of joining in the admiration for Plato the *artist* which is traditional among scholars. In this case, I ultimately have on my side the most refined arbiters of taste among the ancients themselves. As it seems to me, Plato mixes all the stylistic forms together; thus he is one of the *first décadents* in style. He has something similar on his conscience to what the Cynics[12] had, who invented the *satura Menippea*.[13] In order for the Platonic dialogue, this repulsively self-satisfied and childish kind of dialectic, to exert its charm, one must never have read good French authors—for instance, Fontenelle.[14] Plato is boring. Ultimately, my mistrust in the case of Plato reaches into the depths; I find him so divergent from all the fundamental instincts of the Hellenes, so overmoralized, such a Christian before his time—he already takes the concept "good" to be the highest concept—that in regards to the whole Plato phenomenon I would rather use the harsh expression "exalted swindle"—or if it sounds better, idealism—than any other. We have paid dearly for the fact that this Athenian went to school with the Egyptians (or with the Jews in Egypt? . . .). In the great disaster of Christianity, Plato is that ambiguity and fascination called the "ideal" which made it possible for the nobler natures of antiquity to misunderstand themselves and to step on the *bridge* that led to the "cross."—And how much Plato there still is in the concept "Church," in the structure, system, and practice of the Church!

My recreation, my predilection, my *cure* for all Platonism has always been *Thucydides*.[15] Thucydides and, perhaps, Machiavelli's[16] *Prince* are most closely related to me by their unconditional will to fabricate nothing and to see reason in *reality*—*not* in "reason," and still less in "morality." There is no cure more fundamental than Thucydides for the Greeks' miserable prettification of things into the ideal, a prettification which the "classically educated" youth brings with him into life as the reward for his school training. One must turn Thucydides over line by line and read his background thoughts as clearly as his words; there are few thinkers so rich in background thoughts. In him, the *culture of the sophists*, which means the *culture of the realists*, reaches its perfect expression—this invaluable movement in the midst of the Socratic schools' moralistic and idealistic swindle, which was then breaking out on every side. Greek philosophy as the *décadence* of Greek instinct; Thucydides as the great summation, the final appearance of that strong, strict, hard factuality that was a matter of instinct for the older Hellenes. *Courage* in the face of reality is, in the final analysis, the point of difference between natures such as Thucydides and Plato. Plato is a coward in the face of reality—*consequently* he flees into the ideal; Thucydides has control over *himself*—consequently he also has control over things.

3

Smelling out "beautiful souls" in the Greeks, "golden means" and other perfections, admiring in them, for instance, calm in grandeur, an ideal disposition, elevated simplicity—I was protected from this "elevated simplicity," which is in the end *niaiserie allemande* [German foolishness], by the psychologist in me. I saw their strongest instinct, the will to power; I saw them tremble before the boundless force of this drive;

12. [Regarding the Cynics, see Hume's *Treatise*, n.1.]

13. [Menippus the Cynic originated this genre, which expresses philosophical views in a humorous way, mixing verse and prose.]

14. [Regarding Bernard le Bovier de Fontenelle, see Hume's *Dialogues*, n.33.]

15. [Regarding Thucydides, see Hume's *Dialogues*, n.46.]

16. [Niccolò Machiavelli (1469–1527) was an Italian author and statesman whose best-known work, *The Prince*, describes how a ruler gains and maintains power.]

I saw all their institutions arise from rules of security, in order to make themselves safe in the face of each other's inner *explosives*. The immense internal tension then discharged itself in frightful and ruthless external hostility; the city-states ripped each other to shreds so that the citizens might, each of them, attain peace with themselves. It was necessary to be strong; danger was nearby—it lay in ambush everywhere. The wonderfully supple bodily character, the bold realism and immoralism that characterizes the Hellenes was a *necessity*, not their "nature." It was a consequence to begin with, it was not there from the start. And with their festivals and arts, they wanted nothing but to feel *superior*, to *show* that they were superior; these were means of glorifying themselves, and in certain circumstances, of making themselves frightening.

To judge the Greeks, in the German fashion, by their philosophers, to use, say, the simpleminded uprightness of the Socratic schools to elucidate *what* is essentially Hellenic—! After all, the philosophers are the *décadents* of the Greek world, the counter-movement against the old, noble taste (against the combative instinct, against the polis, against the value of the race, against the authority of tradition). The Socratic virtues were preached *because* the Greeks had lost them; excitable, fearful, inconstant comedians all of them, they had a couple of reasons too many to let morality be preached at them. Not that it was any help—but big words and attitudes suit *décadents* so well.

4

For the sake of understanding the older, the still rich and even overflowing Hellenic instinct, I was the first to take seriously that wonderful phenomenon that bears the name of Dionysus;[17] it is explainable only in terms of *too much* energy. Whoever investigated the Greeks—such as that deepest living connoisseur of their culture, Jacob Burckhardt of Basel[18]—knew right away that I had achieved something; Burckhardt included a special section on this phenomenon in his *Civilization of the Greeks*. If one wants to see the opposite, one should look at the almost amusing poverty of instinct of the German philologists when they come close to the Dionysian. The famous Lobeck,[19] in particular, who crept into this world of enigmas with the respectable self-assurance of a worm dried out between books, and convinced himself that being nauseatingly flippant and childish made him scientific—Lobeck made it known, sparing no expense on learned accoutrements, that there was really nothing to all these curiosities. Of course, the priests might have communicated to the participants in such orgies some things not devoid of value—for instance, that wine excites desire, that people can survive eating fruit under certain circumstances, that plants bloom in the spring and wither in the fall. As for the bewildering wealth of rites, symbols, and myths of orgiastic origin with which the ancient world was quite literally overgrown, Lobeck finds an opportunity here to increase his cleverness by another notch. "The Greeks," he says (*Aglaophamus* I, 672), "when they had nothing else to do, used to laugh, jump, and race around—or, since people sometimes have this desire too, they sat down, wept and wailed. *Others* then came along and sought some reason for this remarkable activity. And thus, as explanations of these customs, arose those countless sagas and myths. On the other hand, one believed that this *comical behavior* which now took place on festival days also necessarily belonged to the festivities, and took it to be an indispensable part of the worship."

That is despicable blather; one will not for a single moment take a Lobeck seriously. We are affected quite differently when we test the concept "Greek" that Winckelmann[20] and Goethe[21] developed, and find it incompatible with that element out of which grows Dionysian art—the orgy. In fact, I have no doubt that Goethe would have excluded anything of

17. [Dionysus was the Greek god of fertility and wine who came to symbolize divine creativity.]

18. [Jacob Burckhardt (1818–1897) was a noted Swiss cultural historian.]

19. [Christian August Lobeck (1781–1860) was a German classical scholar.]

20. [Johann Joachim Winckelmann (1717–1768) was a German classical archaeologist, art critic, and historian of ancient art.]

21. [Johann Wolfgang von Goethe (1749–1832), poet, dramatist, novelist, and scientist, was an intellectual titan of the modern world.]

the sort in principle from the possibilities of the Greek soul. *Consequently, Goethe did not understand the Greeks.* For only in the Dionysian mysteries, in the psychology of the Dionysian condition, does the *fundamental fact* of the Hellenic instinct express itself—its "will to life." *What* did the Hellene procure in these mysteries? *Eternal* life, the eternal recurrence of life; the future promised and made sacred in the past; the triumphant Yes to life beyond death and change; *true* life as collective survival through procreation, through the mysteries of sexuality. Thus, for the Greeks the *sexual* symbol was the ultimate revered symbol, the authentic, deep meaning in all ancient piety. Every element of the act of procreation, of pregnancy and birth, awoke the highest and most festive feelings. In the teachings of the mysteries, *pain* is declared holy; the "pangs of the childbearer" make pain in general holy—all becoming and growth, everything that vouches for the future *requires* pain. For there to be the eternal joy of creation, for the will to life to affirm itself eternally, there *must* also eternally be the "torment of the childbearer." . . . All this is signified by the name Dionysus; I know no higher symbolism than this *Greek* symbolism, the symbolism of the Dionysian rites. In them, the deepest instinct of life, the instinct for the future of life, for the eternity of life, is religiously experienced—the very way to life, procreation, as the *holy way*. It was Christianity, on the basis of its *ressentiment against* life, that first made something unclean out of sexuality; it threw *filth* on the beginning, on the precondition of our life.

5

The psychology of the orgy as an overflowing feeling of life and energy, within which even pain works as a stimulant, gave me the key to the concept of the *tragic* feeling, which was misunderstood as much by Aristotle as, especially, by our pessimists. Tragedy is so far from giving any evidence for the pessimism of the Hellenes in Schopenhauer's sense that it rather has to count as the decisive rejection of and *counter-authority* to such pessimism. Saying Yes to life even in its most strange and intractable problems, the will to life, celebrating its own inexhaustibility by *sacrificing* its highest types—*that* is what I called Dionysian, *that* is what I found as the bridge to the psychology of the *tragic* poet. *Not* in order to be released from terror and pity, not in order to purify oneself of a dangerous emotion through its vehement discharge—thus Aristotle understood it—but rather, beyond terror and pity, to *be* oneself the eternal joy of becoming, that joy that also includes in itself the *joy of destruction*. . . . And thus I touch again upon the spot from which I first set out—*The Birth of Tragedy* was my first revaluation of all values. Thus I take my stand again upon the ground from which grows my willing, my being *able*—I, the final follower of the philosopher Dionysus—I, the teacher of the eternal recurrence. . . .

Charles Sanders Peirce

Widely esteemed as America's most versatile and original philosopher, and renowned as the founder of pragmatism, Charles Sanders Peirce was born in Cambridge, Massachusetts in 1839. He was the second son of Benjamin Peirce, one of America's leading mathematicians, from whom he received much of his early education and acquired an intensely intellectual discipline. He was educated at Harvard College, graduating in 1859 and thereafter receiving the M.A. at Harvard in 1862, and the Sc.B. degree in chemistry, *summa cum laude*, in 1863. In 1861, he began work as a physical scientist with the U.S. Coast and Geodetic Survey, a relationship that continued intermittently until 1891.

Despite his brilliance and his pioneering contributions to metaphysics, the history and philosophy of science, the theory of signs, and the development of symbolic logic, Peirce never succeeded in gaining a permanent university position; the only extended teaching he did was on a logic lectureship at the Johns Hopkins University from 1879 to 1884.

In 1887 Peirce retired to Milford, Pennsylvania, where he spent the rest of his life in almost complete isolation, striving to complete a comprehensive work of philosophy. He never produced any systematic philosophical books, although he continued to labor on difficult theoretical problems and to write prolifically on specialized topics. He died in 1914, "a frustrated, isolated man, still working on his logic, without a publisher, with scarcely a disciple, unknown to the public at large" (*Dictionary of American Biography*).

Nevertheless, his fame and influence have continued to grow with the years, stimulated by the continuing study of the huge collection of manuscripts left at his death. The study of Peirce has indeed by now become a worldwide scholarly industry, ramifying into virtually every academic discipline.

The first of the papers to follow, "The Fixation of Belief," appeared in 1877. It presents Peirce's theory of inquiry. Doubt, for him, is not the mere absence of belief. Rather, it is "an uneasy and dissatisfied state from which we struggle to free ourselves and pass into the state of belief . . . a calm and satisfactory state which we do not wish to avoid, or to change to a belief in anything else." Belief is in the nature of habit, representing a regular association between our circumstances and our actions. Inquiry is, for Peirce, the struggle to overcome the irritation of doubt and to attain belief. Peirce compares four methods for the fixation of belief: the method of tenacity, the method of authority, the *a priori* method, and the method of science.

Tenacity is largely a matter of reiterating the belief in question and turning away from all contrary evidence. It is, however, he argues, ineffective, for when confronted with the contrary beliefs of others, our confidence in our own tenaciously held beliefs is shaken, unsettling our beliefs. The method of authority, essentially adoption of tenacity by a whole group using the group's institutions to enforce the preferred doctrines, is more effective than the previous method but is also ineffective, since no society can regulate all opinion within, nor prevent awareness of contrary opinions without. Again unsettlement ensues.

The *a priori* method rejects both the "willful adherence to a belief, and the arbitrary forcing of it upon others," allowing beliefs to form through the natural inclination to adopt whatever seems "agreeable to reason." This method assimilates inquiry to the development of taste, subject to pendulum swings and never reaching a stable agreement. Peirce considers, finally, the method of science, which settles opinion not by willfulness, force, or taste, but by reference to external permanencies with properties "independent of our opinions about them." It is the only method of the four that is self-corrective, allowing the possibility of errors in application corrigible by the very use of the method in question, whereas the pursuit of any of the other methods is necessarily correct by the method itself, so that errors cannot even be admitted, much less be open to correction.

Peirce's argument for the method of science is open to the charge that it is science itself that unsettles belief more rapidly than any of the other methods, holding all its theories to be provisional and subjecting all to the test of continuing experience. Indeed Peirce's essay seems to shift ground from considering the unsettlement of *beliefs* to the unsettlement of *methods*. He seems in the end to be arguing that because science is self-corrective, it is itself, as a method, capable of remaining firm while continuing to enable us to learn from experience.

"How to Make Our Ideas Clear" appeared in 1878. It applies his theory of inquiry to the development of what has been called his pragmatic maxim, as a method for the clarification of ideas. Since, as Peirce argues, the function of thought is to attain belief, the essence of which is "the establishment of a habit," we develop the meaning of an idea by determining "what habits it involves."

The pragmatic maxim, appearing at the end of Section II of the paper, thus reads: "Consider what effects, which might conceivably have practical bearings, we conceive the object of our conception to have. Then our conception of these effects is the whole of our conception of the object." An *effect with practical bearings* being, more precisely, a perceptible consequence contingent on our action, Peirce's idea is now to sum up all such action-contingent consequences of the object. Our conception of these consequences, he concludes, is our very conception of the object.

To clarify the notion of hardness, we are thus instructed not to seek some image of this property by introspection, nor to construct some abstract definition of it. Rather, we are to ask what perceptible effects habitually result from various operations upon hard things: A hard thing will, for example, "not be scratched by other substances," will make a noise if struck, will offer a certain resistance if pushed, and so on. The idea of hardness is then nothing more than the idea of these action-contingent affects. Moreover, in believing that an object is hard, we are set habitually to act toward it in accordance with its supposed trait of hardness, in pursuit of our purposes. Our belief in its hardness embodies a conditional prediction of its behavior, testable by the senses.

The meaning of an idea is, of course, independent of its truth; both false and true statements have meaning. But Peirce believes that the processes of inquiry, carried on by an open and ideal community of scientific investigators, continually weed out the false beliefs and in the long run converge on the true. In a celebrated passage he defines truth and reality in terms of such ultimate convergence: "The opinion which is fated to be ultimately agreed to by all who investigate is what we mean by the truth, and the object represented in this opinion is the real."

• • •

A biography of Peirce is available in Joseph Brent, *Charles Sanders Peirce: A Life* (Bloomington: Indiana University Press, 1993). Useful interpretive discussions of Peirce are Murray G. Murphey, *The Development of Peirce's Philosophy* (Cambridge, Mass.: Harvard University Press, 1961); W. B. Gallie, *Peirce and Pragmatism* (New York: Dover, 1966); and Peter Skagestad, *The Road of Inquiry: Charles Peirce's Pragmatic Realism* (New York: Columbia University Press, 1981). For a general discussion of Peirce as well as the other pragmatic philosophers, see H. S. Thayer, *Meaning and Action: A Critical History of Pragmatism* (Indianapolis: Bobbs-Merrill, 1968) and Israel Scheffler, *Four Pragmatists* (London: Routledge, 1974). A collection of critical articles on Peirce by the dean of American Peirce scholars is K. L. Ketner and C. Kloesel, eds., *Peirce, Semeiotic, and Pragmatism: Essays by Max H. Fisch* (Bloomington: Indiana University Press, 1986).

Israel Scheffler

The Fixation of Belief

I

Few persons care to study logic, because everybody conceives himself to be proficient enough in the art of reasoning already. But I observe that this satisfaction is limited to one's own ratiocination, and does not extend to that of other men.

We come to the full possession of our power of drawing inferences the last of all our faculties, for it is not so much a natural gift as a long and difficult art. The history of its practice would make a grand subject for a book. The mediæval schoolman, following the Romans, made logic the earliest of a boy's studies after grammar, as being very easy. So it was as they understood it. Its fundamental principle, according to them, was that all knowledge rests on either authority or reason; but that whatever is deduced by reason depends ultimately on a premise derived from authority. Accordingly, as soon as a boy was perfect in the syllogistic procedure, his intellectual kit of tools was held to be complete.

To Roger Bacon,[1] that remarkable mind who in the middle of the thirteenth century was almost a scientific man, the schoolmen's conception of reasoning appeared only an obstacle to truth. He saw that experience alone teaches anything—a proposition which to us seems easy to understand, because a distinct conception of experience has been handed down to us from former generations; which to him also seemed perfectly clear, because its difficulties had not yet unfolded themselves. Of all kinds of experience, the best, he thought, was interior illumination, which teaches many things about nature which the external senses could never discover, such as the transubstantiation of bread.

Four centuries later, the more celebrated Bacon,[2] in the first book of his *Novum Organum*, gave his clear account of experience as something which must be opened to verification and re-examination. But, superior as Lord Bacon's conception is to earlier notions, a modern reader who is not in awe of his grandiloquence is chiefly struck by the inadequacy of his view of scientific procedure. That we have only to make some crude experiments, to draw up briefs of the results in certain blank forms, to go through these by rule, checking off everything disproved and setting down the alternatives, and that thus in a few years physical science would be finished up—what an idea! "He wrote on science like a Lord Chancellor," indeed, as Harvey,[3] a genuine man of science, said.

The early scientists, Copernicus,[4] Tycho Brahe,[5] Kepler,[6] Galileo,[7] Harvey, and Gilbert,[8] had methods more like those of their modern brethren. Kepler undertook to draw a curve through the places of Mars; and his greatest service to science was in impressing on men's minds that this was the thing to be done if they wished to improve astronomy; that they were not to content themselves with inquiring whether one system of epicycles was better than another but that they were to sit down by the figures and find out what the curve, in truth, was. He accomplished this by his incomparable energy and courage, blundering along in the most inconceivable way (to us), from one irra-

Reprinted from *Popular Science Monthly*, 1878.

1. [The reference is to the English philosopher and scientist (c. 1214–1292).—S.M.C.]

2. [The reference is to the English philosopher and Lord Chancellor Francis Bacon (1561–1626).]

3. [The reference is to William Harvey (1578–1657), the English physician widely credited with laying the foundation of modern medicine.]

4. [Regarding Copernicus, see Hume's *Enquiry*, n.70.]

5. [The reference is to the Danish astronomer (1546–1601), who calculated the position of planets and stars.]

6. [The reference is to the German astronomer Johannes Kepler (1571–1630), whose three laws describe the revolution of the planets around the sun.]

7. [Regarding Galileo Galilei, see Hume's *Dialogues*, n.7.]

8. [The reference is to William Gilbert (1544–1603), the English scientist and physician, best known for his studies of electricity and magnetism.]

tional hypothesis to another, until, after trying twenty-two of these, he fell, by the mere exhaustion of his invention, upon the orbit which a mind well furnished with the weapons of modern logic would have tried almost at the outset.

In the same way, every work of science great enough to be remembered for a few generations affords some exemplification of the defective state of the art of reasoning of the time when it was written; and each chief step in science has been a lesson in logic. It was so when Lavoisier[9] and his contemporaries took up the study of Chemistry. The old chemist's maxim had been *Lege, lege, lege, labora, ora, et relege.*[10] Lavoisier's method was not to read and pray, not to dream that some long and complicated chemical process would have a certain effect, to put it into practice with dull patience, after its inevitable failure to dream that with some modification it would have another result, and to end by publishing the last dream as a fact: his way was to carry his mind into his laboratory, and to make of his alembics and cucurbits instruments of thought, giving a new conception of reasoning as something which was to be done with one's eyes open, by manipulating real things instead of words and fancies.

The Darwinian controversy is, in large part, a question of logic. Mr. Darwin[11] proposed to apply the statistical method to biology. The same thing has been done in a widely different branch of science, the theory of gases. Though unable to say what the movement of any particular molecule of gas would be on a certain hypothesis regarding the constitution of this class of bodies, Clausius[12] and Maxwell[13] were yet able, by the application of the doctrine of probabilities, to predict that in the long run such and such a proportion of the molecules would, under given circumstances, acquire such and such velocities; that there would take place, every second, such and such a number of collisions, etc.; and from these propositions they were able to deduce certain properties of gases, especially in regard to their heat-relations. In like manner, Darwin, while unable to say what the operation of variation and natural selection in every individual case will be, demonstrates that in the long run they will adapt animals to their circumstances. Whether or not existing animal forms are due to such action, or what position the theory ought to take, forms the subject of a discussion in which questions of fact and questions of logic are curiously interlaced.

II

The object of reasoning is to find out, from the consideration of what we already know, something else which we do not know. Consequently, reasoning is good if it be such as to give a true conclusion from true premises, and not otherwise. Thus, the question of validity is purely one of fact and not of thinking. A being the premises and B being the conclusion, the question is, whether these facts are really so related that if A is, B is. If so, the inference is valid; if not, not. It is not in the least the question whether, when the premises are accepted by the mind, we feel an impulse to accept the conclusion also. It is true that we do generally reason correctly by nature. But that is an accident; the true conclusion would remain true if we had no impulse to accept it; and the false one would remain false, though we could not resist the tendency to believe in it.

We are, doubtless, in the main logical animals, but we are not perfectly so. Most of us, for example, are naturally more sanguine and hopeful than logic would justify. We seem to be so constituted that in the absence of any facts to go upon we are happy and self-satisfied; so that the effect of experience is continually to counteract our hopes and aspirations. Yet a lifetime of the application of this corrective does not usually eradicate our sanguine disposition. Where hope is unchecked by any experience, it is likely that our optimism is extravagant. Logicality in regard to practical matters is the most useful quality

9. [The reference is to Antoine Laurent Lavoisier (1743–1794), a founder of modern chemistry.]

10. [Look, look, look, work, speak, and look again.]

11. [The reference is to the celebrated English naturalist Charles Darwin (1809–1882), who developed the theory of evolution.]

12. [The reference is to the German mathematical physicist Rudolf Julius Emanuel Clausius (1822–1888), a pioneer in the field of thermodynamics.]

13. [The reference is to the Scottish physicist James Clark Maxwell (1831–1879), who developed the theory of the electromagnetic field.]

an animal can possess, and might, therefore, result from the action of natural selection; but outside of these it is probably of more advantage to the animal to have his mind filled with pleasing and encouraging visions, independently of their truth; and thus, upon unpractical subjects, natural selection might occasion a fallacious tendency of thought.

That which determines us, from given premises, to draw one inference rather than another is some habit of mind, whether it be constitutional or acquired. The habit is good or otherwise, according as it produces true conclusions from true premises or not; and an inference is regarded as valid or not, without reference to the truth or falsity of its conclusion specially, but according as the habit which determines it is such as to produce true conclusions in general or not. The particular habit of mind which governs this or that inference may be formulated in a proposition whose truth depends on the validity of the inferences which the habit determines; and such a formula is called a *guiding principle* of inference. Suppose, for example, that we observe that a rotating disk of copper quickly comes to rest when placed between the poles of a magnet, and we infer that this will happen with every disk of copper. The guiding principle is that what is true of one piece of copper is true of another. Such a guiding principle with regard to copper would be much safer than with regard to many other substances—brass, for example.

A book might be written to signalize all the most important of these guiding principles of reasoning. It would probably be, we must confess, of no service to a person whose thought is directed wholly to practical subjects, and whose activity moves along thoroughly beaten paths. The problems which present themselves to such a mind are matters of routine which he has learned once for all to handle in learning his business. But let a man venture into an unfamiliar field, or where his results are not continually checked by experience, and all history shows that the most masculine intellect will ofttimes lose his orientation and waste his efforts in directions which bring him no nearer to his goal, or even carry him entirely astray. He is like a ship on the open sea, with no one on board who understands the rules of navigation. And in such a case some general study of the guiding principles of reasoning would be sure to be found useful.

The subject could hardly be treated, however, without being first limited; since almost any fact may serve as a guiding principle. But it so happens that there exists a division among facts, such that in one class are all those which are absolutely essential as guiding principles, while in the other are all those which have any other interest as objects of research. This division is between those which are necessarily taken for granted in asking whether a certain conclusion follows from certain premises, and those which are not implied in that question. A moment's thought will show that a variety of facts are already assumed when the logical question is first asked. It is implied, for instance, that there are such states of mind as doubt and belief—that a passage from one to the other is possible, the object of thought remaining the same, and that this transition is subject to some rules which all minds are alike bound by. As these are facts which we must already know before we can have any clear conception of reasoning at all, it cannot be supposed to be any longer of much interest to inquire into their truth or falsity. On the other hand, it is easy to believe that those rules of reasoning which are deduced from the very idea of the process are the ones which are the most essential; and, indeed, that so long as it conforms to these it will, at least, not lead to false conclusions from true premises. In point of fact, the importance of what may be deduced from the assumptions involved in the logical question turns out to be greater than might be supposed, and this for reasons which it is difficult to exhibit at the outset. The only one which I shall here mention is that conceptions which are really products of logical reflections, without being readily seen to be so, mingle with our ordinary thoughts, and are frequently the causes of great confusion. This is the case, for example, with the conception of quality. A quality as such is never an object of observation. We can see that a thing is blue or green, but the quality of being blue and the quality of being green are not things which we see; they are products of logical reflections. The truth is that common sense, or thought as it first emerges above the level of the narrowly practical, is deeply imbued with that bad logical quality to which the epithet *metaphysical* is commonly applied; and nothing can clear it up but a severe course of logic.

III

We generally know when we wish to ask a question and when we wish to pronounce a judgment, for there is a dissimilarity between the sensation of doubting and that of believing.

But this is not all which distinguishes doubt from belief. There is a practical difference. Our beliefs guide our desires and shape our actions. The Assassins, or followers of the Old Man of the Mountain, used to rush into death at his least command, because they believed that obedience to him would insure everlasting felicity. Had they doubted this, they would not have acted as they did. So it is with every belief, according to its degree. The feeling of believing is a more or less sure indication of there being established in our nature some habit which will determine our actions. Doubt never has such an effect.

Nor must we overlook a third point of difference. Doubt is an uneasy and dissatisfied state from which we struggle to free ourselves and pass into the state of belief; while the latter is a calm and satisfactory state which we do not wish to avoid, or to change to a belief in anything else. On the contrary, we cling tenaciously, not merely to believing, but to believing just what we do believe.

Thus, both doubt and belief have positive effects upon us, though very different ones. Belief does not make us act at once, but puts us into such a condition that we shall behave in a certain way, when the occasion arises. Doubt has not the least effect of this sort, but stimulates us to action until it is destroyed. This reminds us of the irritation of a nerve and the reflex action produced thereby; while for the analogue of belief, in the nervous system, we must look to what are called nervous associations—for example, to that habit of the nerves in consequence of which the smell of a peach will make the mouth water.

IV

The irritation of doubt causes a struggle to attain a state of belief. I shall term this struggle *inquiry*, though it must be admitted that this is sometimes not a very apt designation.

The irritation of doubt is the only immediate motive for the struggle to attain belief. It is certainly best for us that our beliefs should be such as may truly guide our actions so as to satisfy our desires; and this reflection will make us reject any belief which does not seem to have been so formed as to insure this result. But it will only do so by creating a doubt in the place of that belief. With the doubt, therefore, the struggle begins, and with the cessation of doubt it ends. Hence, the sole object of inquiry is the settlement of opinion. We may fancy that this is not enough for us, and that we seek not merely an opinion, but a true opinion. But put this fancy to the test, and it proves groundless; for as soon as a firm belief is reached we are entirely satisfied, whether the belief be false or true. And it is clear that nothing out of the sphere of our knowledge can be our object, for nothing which does not affect the mind can be a motive for a mental effort. The most that can be maintained is that we seek for a belief that we shall *think* to be true. But we think each one of our beliefs to be true, and, indeed, it is mere tautology to say so.

That the settlement of opinion is the sole end of inquiry is a very important proposition. It sweeps away, at once, various vague and erroneous conceptions of proof. A few of these may be noticed here.

1. Some philosophers have imagined that to start an inquiry it was only necessary to utter a question or set it down on paper, and have even recommended us to begin our studies with questioning everything! But the mere putting of a proposition into the interrogative form does not stimulate the mind to any struggle after belief. There must be a real and living doubt, and without all this, discussion is idle.

2. It is a very common idea that a demonstration must rest on some ultimate and absolutely indubitable propositions. These, according to one school, are first principles of a general nature; according to another, are first sensations. But, in point of fact, an inquiry, to have that completely satisfactory result called demonstration, has only to start with propositions perfectly free from all actual doubt. If the premises are not in fact doubted at all, they cannot be more satisfactory than they are.

3. Some people seem to love to argue a point after all the world is fully convinced of it. But no further advance can be made. When doubt ceases, mental action on the subject comes to an end; and, if it

did go on, it would be without a purpose, except that of self-criticism.

V

If the settlement of opinion is the sole object of inquiry, and if belief is of the nature of a habit, why should we not attain the desired end, by taking any answer to a question, which we may fancy, and constantly reiterating it to ourselves, dwelling on all which may conduce to that belief, and learning to turn with contempt and hatred from anything which might disturb it? This simple and direct method is really pursued by many men. I remember once being entreated not to read a certain newspaper lest it might change my opinion upon free-trade. "Lest I might be entrapped by its fallacies and misstatements" was the form of expression. "You are not," my friend said, "a special student of political economy. You might, therefore, easily be deceived by fallacious arguments upon the subject. You might, then, if you read this paper, be led to believe in protection. But you admit that free-trade is the true doctrine; and you do not wish to believe what is not true." I have often known this system to be deliberately adopted. Still oftener, the instinctive dislike of an undecided state of mind, exaggerated into a vague dread of doubt, makes men cling spasmodically to the views they already take. The man feels that if he only holds to his belief without wavering, it will be entirely satisfactory. Nor can it be denied that a steady and immovable faith yields great peace of mind. It may, indeed, give rise to inconveniences, as if a man should resolutely continue to believe that fire would not burn him, or that he would be eternally damned if he received his *ingesta* otherwise than through a stomach-pump. But then the man who adopts this method will not allow that its inconveniences are greater than its advantages. He will say, "I hold steadfastly to the truth and the truth is always wholesome." And in many cases it may very well be that the pleasure he derives from his calm faith overbalances any inconveniences resulting from its deceptive character. Thus, if it be true that death is annihilation, then the man who believes that he will certainly go straight to heaven when he dies, provided he have fulfilled certain simple observances in this life, has a cheap pleasure which will not be followed by the least disappointment. A similar consideration seems to have weight with many persons in religious topics, for we frequently hear it said, "Oh, I could not believe so-and-so, because I should be wretched if I did." When an ostrich buries its head in the sand as danger approaches, it very likely takes the happiest course. It hides the danger, and then calmly says there is no danger; and, if it feels perfectly sure there is none, why should it raise its head to see? A man may go through life, systematically keeping out of view all that might cause a change in his opinions, and if he only succeeds—basing his method, as he does, on two fundamental psychological laws—I do not see what can be said against his doing so. It would be an egotistical impertinence to object that his procedure is irrational, for that only amounts to saying that his method of settling belief is not ours. He does not propose to himself to be rational, and indeed, will often talk with scorn of man's weak and illusive reason. So let him think as he pleases.

But this method of fixing belief, which may be called the *method of tenacity*, will be unable to hold its ground in practice. The social impulse is against it. The man who adopts it will find that other men think differently from him, and it will be apt to occur to him in some saner moment that their opinions are quite as good as his own, and this will shake his confidence in his belief. This conception, that another man's thought or sentiment may be equivalent to one's own, is a distinctly new step, and a highly important one. It arises from an impulse too strong in man to be suppressed, without danger of destroying the human species. Unless we make ourselves hermits, we shall necessarily influence each other's opinions; so that the problem becomes how to fix belief, not in the individual merely, but in the community.

Let the will of the state act, then, instead of that of the individual. Let an institution be created which shall have for its object to keep correct doctrines before the attention of the people, to reiterate them perpetually, and to teach them to the young; having at the same time power to prevent contrary doctrines from being taught, advocated, or expressed. Let all possible causes of a change of mind be removed from men's apprehensions. Let them be kept ignorant, lest they should learn of some reason to think otherwise than they do. Let their passions be enlisted, so that they may regard private and unusual opinions with hatred and horror. Then, let all men who reject the established belief be terrified into silence. Let the people turn out and tar-and-feather such men, or let inquisitions be made into the manner of thinking of suspected persons, and, when they are found guilty of forbidden beliefs, let them be subjected to some signal punishment. When complete agreement could not otherwise be reached, a general massacre of all who have not thought in a certain way has proved a very effective means of settling opinion in a country. If the power to do this be wanting, let a list of opinions be drawn up, to which no man of the least independence of thought can assent, and let the faithful be required to accept all these propositions, in order to segregate them as radically as possible from the influence of the rest of the world.

This method has, from the earliest times, been one of the chief means of upholding correct theological and political doctrines, and of preserving their universal or catholic character. In Rome, especially, it has been practiced from the days of Numa Pompilius[14] to those of Pius Nonus.[15] This is the most perfect example in history; but wherever there is a priesthood—and no religion has been without one—this method has been more or less made use of. Wherever there is aristocracy, or a guild, or any association of a class of men whose interests depend or are supposed to depend on certain propositions, there will be inevitably found some traces of this natural product of social feeling. Cruelties always accompany this system; and when it is consistently carried out, they become atrocities of the most horrible kind in the eyes of any rational man. Nor should this occasion surprise, for the officer of a society does not feel justified in surrendering the interests of that society for the sake of mercy, as he might his own private interests. It is natural, therefore, that sympathy and fellowship should thus produce a most ruthless power.

In judging this method of fixing belief, which may be called the *method of authority*, we must, in the first place, allow its immeasurable mental and moral superiority to the method of tenacity. Its success is proportionally greater; and in fact it has over and over again worked the most majestic results. The mere structures of stone which it has caused to be put together—in Siam, for example, in Egypt, and in Europe—have many of them a sublimity hardly more than rivaled by the greatest works of nature. And, except the geological epochs, there are no periods of time so vast as those which are measured by some of these organized faiths. If we scrutinize the matter closely, we shall find that there has not been one of their creeds which has remained always the same; yet the change is so slow as to be imperceptible during one person's life, so that individual belief remains sensibly fixed. For the mass of mankind, then, there is perhaps no better method than this. If it is their highest impulse to be intellectual slaves, then slaves they ought to remain.

But no institution can undertake to regulate opinions upon every subject. Only the most important ones can be attended to, and on the rest men's minds must be left to the action of natural causes. This imperfection will be no source of weakness so long as men are in such a state of culture that one opinion does not influence another—that is, so long as they cannot put two and two together. But in the most priest-ridden states some individuals will be found who are raised above that condition. These men possess a wider sort of social feeling; they see that men in other countries and in other ages have held to very different doctrines from those which they themselves have been brought up to believe; and they cannot help seeing that it is the mere accident of their having been taught as they have, and of their having been surrounded with the manners and associations they have, that has caused them to believe as they do and not far differently. And their candor cannot resist the reflection that there is no reason to rate their own views at a higher value than those of other nations and other centuries; and this gives rise to doubts in their minds.

They will further perceive that such doubts as these must exist in their minds with reference to every belief which seems to be determined by the caprice either of themselves or of those who originated the popular opinions. The willful adherence to a belief, and the arbitrary forcing of it upon others, must, therefore,

14. [According to legend, Numa Pompilius was the king of Rome who succeeded its founder, Romulus.]

15. [The reference is to Pope Pius IX (1792–1878), the Italian whose pontificate (1846–1878) was the longest in history, during which he convened the First Vatican Council, whose principal work was the enunciation of papal infallibility.]

both be given up and a new method of settling opinions must be adopted, which shall not only produce an impulse to believe, but shall also decide what proposition it is which is to be believed. Let the action of natural preferences be unimpeded, then, and under their influence let men conversing together and regarding matters in different lights, gradually develop beliefs in harmony with natural causes. This method resembles that by which conceptions of art have been brought to maturity. The most perfect example of it is to be found in the history of metaphysical philosophy. Systems of this sort have not usually rested upon observed facts, at least not in any great degree. They have been chiefly adopted because their fundamental proposition seemed "agreeable to reason." This is an apt expression; it does not mean that which agrees with experience, but that which we find ourselves inclined to believe. Plato, for example, finds it agreeable to reason that the distances of the celestial spheres from one another should be proportional to the different lengths of strings which produce harmonious chords. Many philosophers have been led to their main conclusions by considerations like this; but this is the lowest and least developed form which the method takes, for it is clear that another man might find Kepler's theory, that the celestial spheres are proportional to the inscribed and circumscribed spheres of the different regular solids, more agreeable to *his* reason. But the shock of opinions will soon lead men to rest on preferences of a far more universal nature. Take, for example, the doctrine that man only acts selfishly—that is, from the consideration that acting one way will afford him more pleasure than acting in another. This rests on no fact in the world, but it has had a wide acceptance as being the only reasonable theory.

This method is far more intellectual and respectable from the point of view of reason than either of the others which we have noticed. But its failure has been the most manifest. It makes of inquiry something similar to the development of taste; but taste, unfortunately, is always more or less a matter of fashion, and accordingly, metaphysicians have never come to any fixed agreement, but the pendulum has swung backward and forward between a more material and a more spiritual philosophy, from the earliest times to the latest. And so from this, which has been called the *a priori method*, we are driven, in Lord Bacon's phrase, to a true induction. We have examined into this *a priori* method as something which promised to deliver our opinions from their accidental and capricious element. But development, while it is a process which eliminates the effect of some casual circumstances, only magnifies that of others. This method, therefore, does not differ in a very essential way from that of authority. The government may not have lifted its finger to influence my convictions; I may have been left outwardly quite free to choose, we will say, between monogamy and polygamy, and appealing to my conscience only, I may have concluded that the latter practice is in itself licentious. But when I come to see that the chief obstacle to the spread of Christianity among a people of as high culture as the Hindoos has been a conviction of the immorality of our way of treating women, I cannot help seeing that, though governments do not interfere, sentiments in their development will be very greatly determined by accidental causes. Now, there are some people, among whom I must suppose that my reader is to be found, who, when they see that any belief of theirs is determined by any circumstance extraneous to the facts, will from that moment not merely admit in words that that belief is doubtful, but will experience a real doubt of it, so that it ceases in some degree at least to be a belief.

To satisfy our doubts, therefore, it is necessary that a method should be found by which our beliefs may be caused by nothing human, but by some external permanency—by something upon which our thinking has no effect. Some mystics imagine that they have such a method in a private inspiration from on high. But that is only a form of the method of tenacity, in which the conception of truth as something public is not yet developed. Our external permanency would not be external, in our sense, if it was restricted in its influence to one individual. It must be something which affects, or might affect, every man. And, though these affections are necessarily as various as are individual conditions, yet the method must be such that the ultimate conclusion of every man shall be the same, or would be the same if inquiry were sufficiently persisted in. Such is the method of science. Its fundamental hypothesis, restated in more familiar language, is this: There are real things, whose characters are entirely independent of our opinions about them; those realities affect our senses according to regular laws, and, though our sensations are as different as our relations to the objects, yet, by taking advantage of the laws of perception, we can ascertain by reasoning how things really are, and any man, if he have sufficient experience and reason enough about it, will be led to the one true conclusion. The new conception here involved is that of reality. It may be asked how I know that there any realities. If this hypothesis is the sole support of my method of inquiry, my method of inquiry must not be used to support my hypothesis. The reply is this: (1) If investigation cannot be regarded as proving that there are real things, it at least does not lead to a contrary conclusion; but the method and the conception on which it is based remain ever in harmony. No doubts of the method, therefore, necessarily arise from its practice, as is the case with all the others. (2) The feeling which gives rise to any method of fixing belief is a dissatisfaction at two repugnant propositions. But here already is a vague concession that there is some *one* thing to which a proposition should conform. Nobody, therefore, can really doubt that there are realities, or, if he did, doubt would not be a source of dissatisfaction. The hypothesis, therefore, is one which every mind admits. So that the social impulse does not cause men to doubt it. (3) Everybody uses the scientific method about a great many things, and only ceases to use it when he does not know how to apply it. (4) Experience of the method has not led us to doubt it, but, on the contrary, scientific investigation has had the most wonderful triumphs in the way of settling opinion. These afford the explanation of my not doubting the method or the hypothesis which it supposes; and not having any doubt, nor believing that anybody else whom I could influence has, it would be the merest babble for me to say more about it. If there be anybody with a living doubt upon the subject, let him consider it.

To describe the method of scientific investigation is the object of this series of papers. At present I have only room to notice some points of contrast between it and other methods of fixing belief.

This is the only one of the four methods which presents any distinction of a right and a wrong way. If I adopt the method of tenacity and shut myself out from all influences, whatever I think necessary to doing this is necessary according to that method. So with the method of authority: the state may try to put down heresy by means which, from a scientific point of view, seem very ill-calculated to accomplish its purposes; but the only test *on that method* is what the state thinks, so that it cannot pursue the method wrongly. So with the *a priori* method. The very essence of it is to think as one is inclined to think. All metaphysicians will be sure to do that, however they may be inclined to judge each other to be perversely wrong. The Hegelian system recognizes every natural tendency of thought as logical, although it is certain to be abolished by countertendencies. Hegel thinks there is a regular system in the succession of these tendencies, in consequence of which, after drifting one way and the other for a long time, opinion will at last go right. And it is true that metaphysicians get the right ideas at last; Hegel's system of Nature represents tolerably the science of his day; and one may be sure that whatever scientific investigation has put out of doubt will presently receive *a priori* demonstration on the part of the metaphysicians. But with the scientific method the case is different. I may start with known and observed facts to proceed to the unknown; and yet the rules which I follow in doing so may not be such as investigation would approve. The test of whether I am truly following the method is not an immediate appeal to my feelings and purposes, but, on the contrary, itself involves the application of the method. Hence it is that bad reasoning as well as good reasoning is possible; and this fact is the foundation of the practical side of logic.

It is not to be supposed that the first three methods of settling opinion present no advantage whatever over the scientific method. On the contrary, each has some peculiar convenience of its own. The *a priori* method is distinguished for its comfortable conclusions. It is the nature of the process to adopt whatever belief we are inclined to, and there are certain flatteries to one's vanities which we all believe by nature, until we are awakened from our pleasing dream by rough facts. The method of authority will always govern the mass of mankind; and those who wield the various forms of organized force in the state will never be convinced that dangerous reasoning ought not to be suppressed in some way. If liberty of speech is to be untrammeled from the grosser forms of constraint, then uniformity of opinion will be secured by a moral terrorism to which the respectability of society will give its thorough approval. Following the method of authority is the path of peace. Certain non-conformities are permitted; certain others (considered unsafe) are forbidden. These are different in different countries and in different ages; but, wherever you are let it be known that you seriously hold a tabooed belief, and you may be perfectly sure of being treated with a cruelty no less brutal but more refined than hunting you like a wolf. Thus, the greatest intellectual benefactors of mankind have never dared, and dare not now, to utter the whole of their thought; and thus a shade of *prima facie* doubt is cast upon every proposition which is considered essential to the security of society. Singularly enough, the persecution does not all come from without; but a man torments himself and is oftentimes most distressed at finding himself believing propositions which he has been brought up to regard with aversion. The peaceful and sympathetic man will, therefore, find it hard to resist the temptation to submit his opinions to authority. But most of all I admire the method of tenacity for its strength, simplicity, and directness. Men who pursue it are distinguished for their decision of character, which becomes very easy with such a mental rule. They do not waste time in trying to make up their minds to what they want, but, fastening like lightning upon whatever alternative comes first, they hold to it to the end, whatever happens, without an instant's irresolution. This is one of the splendid qualities which generally accompany brilliant, unlasting success. It is impossible not to envy the man who can dismiss reason, although we know how it must turn out at last.

Such are the advantages which the other methods of settling opinions have over scientific investigation. A man should consider well of them; and then he should consider that, after all, he wishes his opinions to coincide with the fact, and that there is no reason why the results of those first three methods should do so. To bring about this effect is the prerogative of the method of science. Upon such considerations he has to make his choice—a choice which is far more than the adoption of any intellectual opinion, which is one of the ruling decisions of his life, to which when once made he is bound to adhere. The force of habit will sometimes cause a man to hold on to old beliefs after he is in a condition to see that they have no sound basis. But reflection upon the state of the case will overcome these habits, and he ought to allow reflection full weight. People sometimes shrink from doing this, having an idea that beliefs are wholesome which they cannot help feeling rest on nothing. But let such persons suppose an analogous though different case from their own. Let them ask themselves what they would say to a reformed Mussulman who should hesitate to give up his old notions in regard to the relations of the sexes; or to a reformed Catholic who should still shrink from the Bible. Would they not say that these persons ought to consider the matter fully, and clearly understand the new doctrine, and then ought to embrace it in its entirety? But, above all, let it be considered that what is more wholesome than any particular belief is integrity of belief; and that to avoid looking into the support of any belief from a fear that it may turn out rotten is quite as immoral as it is disadvantageous. The person who confesses that there is such a thing as truth, which is distinguished from falsehood simply by this, that if acted on it should, on full consideration, carry us to the point we aim at and not astray, and then, though convinced of this, dares not know the truth and seeks to avoid it, is in a sorry state of mind, indeed.

Yes, the other methods do have their merits: a clear logical conscience does cost something—just as any virtue, just as all that we cherish, costs us dear. But, we should not desire it to be otherwise. The genius of a man's logical method should be loved and reverenced as his bride, whom he has chosen from all the world. He need not condemn the others; on the contrary, he may honor them deeply, and in doing so he only honors her the more. But she is the one that he has chosen, and he knows that he was right in making that choice. And having made it, he will work and fight for her, and will not complain that there are blows to take, hoping that there may be as many and as hard to give, and will strive to be the worthy knight and champion of her from the blaze of whose splendors he draws his inspiration and his courage.

How to Make Our Ideas Clear

I

Whoever has looked into a modern treatise on logic of the common sort, will doubtless remember the two distinctions between *clear* and *obscure* conceptions, and between *distinct* and *confused* conceptions. They have lain in the books now for nigh two centuries, unimproved and unmodified, and are generally reckoned by logicians as among the gems of their doctrine.

A clear idea is defined as one which is so apprehended that it will be recognized wherever it is met with, and so that no other will be mistaken for it. If it fails of this clearness, it is said to be obscure.

This is rather a neat bit of philosophical terminology; yet, since it is clearness that they were defining, I wish the logicians had made their definition a little more plain. Never to fail to recognize an idea, and under no circumstances to mistake another for it, let it come in how recondite a form it may, would indeed imply such prodigious force and clearness of intellect as is seldom met with in this world. On the other hand, merely to have such an acquaintance with the idea as to have become familiar with it, and to have lost all hesitancy in recognizing it in ordinary cases, hardly seems to deserve the name of clearness of apprehension, since after all it only amounts to a subjective feeling of mastery which may be entirely mistaken. I take it, however, that when the logicians speak of "clearness," they mean nothing more than such a familiarity with an idea, since they regard the quality as but a small merit, which needs to be supplemented by another, which they call *distinctness*.

A distinct idea is defined as one which contains nothing which is not clear. This is technical language; by the *contents* of an idea logicians understand whatever is contained in its definition. So that an idea is *distinctly* apprehended, according to them, when we can give a precise definition of it, in abstract terms. Here the professional logicians leave the subject; and I would not have troubled the reader with what they have to say if it were not such a striking example of how they have been slumbering through ages of intellectual activity, listlessly disregarding the enginery of modern thought, and never dreaming of applying its lessons to the improvement of logic. It is easy to show that the doctrine that familiar use and abstract distinctness make the perfection of apprehension, has its only true place in philosophies which have long been extinct; and it is now time to formulate the method of attaining to a more perfect clearness of thought, such as we see and admire in the thinkers of our own time.

When Descartes set about the reconstruction of philosophy, his first step was to (theoretically) permit skepticism and to discard the practice of the schoolmen of looking to authority as the ultimate source of truth. That done, he sought a more natural fountain of true principles, and professed to find it in the human mind; thus passing, in the directest way, from the method of authority to that of apriority, as described in my first paper. Self-consciousness was to furnish us with our fundamental truths, and to decide what was agreeable to reason. But since, evidently, not all ideas are true, he was led to note, as the first condition of infallibility, that they must be clear. The distinction between an idea *seeming* clear and really being so, never occurred to him. Trusting to introspection, as he did, even for a knowledge of external things, why should he question its testimony in respect to the contents of our own minds? But then, I suppose, seeing men, who seemed to be quite clear and positive, holding opposite opinions upon fundamental principles, he was further led to say that clearness of ideas is not sufficient, but that they need also to be distinct, i.e., to have nothing unclear about them. What he probably meant by this (for he did not explain himself with precision) was that they must sustain the test of dialectical examination; that they must not only seem clear at the outset, but that discussion must never be able to bring to light points of obscurity connected with them.

Reprinted from *Popular Science Monthly*, 1878.

Such was the distinction of Descartes, and one sees that it was precisely on the level of his philosophy. It was somewhat developed by Leibniz. This great and singular genius was as remarkable for what he failed to see as for what he saw. That a piece of mechanism could not do work perpetually without being fed with power in some form, was a thing perfectly apparent to him; yet he did not understand that the machinery of the mind can only transform knowledge, but never originate it, unless it be fed with facts of observation. He thus missed the most essential point of the Cartesian philosophy, which is, that to accept propositions which seem perfectly evident to us is a thing which, whether it be logical or illogical, we cannot help doing. Instead of regarding the matter in this way, he sought to reduce the first principles of science to formulas which cannot be denied without self-contradiction, and was apparently unaware of the great difference between his position and that of Descartes. So he reverted to the old formalities of logic, and, above all, abstract definitions played a great part in his philosophy. It was quite natural, therefore, that on observing that the method of Descartes labored under the difficulty that we may seem to ourselves to have clear apprehensions of ideas which in truth are very hazy, no better remedy occurred to him than to require an abstract definition of every important term. Accordingly, in adopting the distinction of *clear* and *distinct* notions, he described the latter quality as the clear apprehension of everything contained in the definition; and the books have ever since copied his words. There is no danger that his chimerical scheme will ever again be overvalued. Nothing new can ever be learned by analyzing definitions. Nevertheless, our existing beliefs can be set in order by this process, and order is an essential element of intellectual economy, as of every other. It may be acknowledged, therefore, that the books are right in making familiarity with a notion the first step toward clearness of apprehension, and the defining of it the second. But in omitting all mention of any higher perspicuity of thought, they simply mirror a philosophy which was exploded a hundred years ago. That much-admired "ornament of logic"—the doctrine of clearness and distinctness—may be pretty enough, but it is high time to relegate to our cabinet of curiosities the antique *bijou*, and to wear about us something better adapted to modern uses.

The very first lesson that we have a right to demand that logic shall teach us is how to make our ideas clear; and a most important one it is, depreciated only by minds who stand in need of it. To know what we think, to be masters of our own meaning, will make a solid foundation for great and weighty thought. It is most easily learned by those whose ideas are meager and restricted; and far happier they than such as wallow helplessly in a rich mud of conceptions. A nation, it is true, may, in the course of generations, overcome the disadvantage of an excessive wealth of language and its natural concomitant, a vast, unfathomable deep of ideas. We may see it in history, slowly perfecting its literary forms, sloughing at length its metaphysics, and, by virtue of the untirable patience which is often a compensation, attaining great excellence in every branch of mental acquirement. The page of history is not yet unrolled which is to tell us whether such a people will or will not in the long run prevail over one whose ideas (like the words of their language) are few, but which possesses a wonderful mastery over those which it has. For an individual, however, there can be no question that a few clear ideas are worth more than many confused ones. A young man would hardly be persuaded to sacrifice the greater part of his thoughts to save the rest; and the muddled head is the least apt to see the necessity of such a sacrifice. Him we can usually only commiserate, as a person with a congenital defect. Time will help him, but intellectual maturity with regard to clearness comes rather late, an unfortunate arrangement of nature, inasmuch as clearness is of less use to a man settled in life, whose errors have in great measure had their effect, than it would be to one whose path lies before him. It is terrible to see how a single unclear idea, a single formula without meaning, lurking in a young man's head, will sometimes act like an obstruction of inert matter in an artery, hindering the nutrition of the brain, and condemning its victim to pine away in the fullness of his intellectual vigor and in the midst of intellectual plenty. Many a man has cherished for years as his hobby some vague shadow of an idea, too meaningless to be positively false; he has, nevertheless, passionately loved it, has made it his companion by day and by night, and has given to it his strength and his life, leaving all other occupations for its sake, and in short has lived with it and for it, until it has become, as it were, flesh of his flesh and bone of his bone; and then he has waked up some bright morning to find it gone, clean vanished away like the beautiful Melusina of the fable,[1] and the essence of his life gone with it. I have myself known such a man; and who can tell how many histories of circle-squarers, metaphysicians, astrologers, and what not, may not be told in the old German story?

II

The principles set forth in the first of these papers lead, at once, to a method of reaching a clearness of thought of a far higher grade than the "distinctness" of the logicians. We have there found that the action of thought is excited by the irritation of doubt, and ceases when belief is attained; so that the production of belief is the sole function of thought. All these words, however, are too strong for my purpose. It is as if I had described the phenomena as they appear under a mental microscope. Doubt and Belief, as the words are commonly employed, relate to religious or other grave discussions. But here I use them to designate the starting of any question, no matter how small or how great, and the resolution of it. If, for instance, in a horsecar, I pull out my purse and find a five-cent nickel and five coppers, I decide, while my hand is going to the purse, in which way I will pay my fare. To call such a question Doubt, and my decision Belief, is certainly to use words very disproportionate to the occasion. To speak of such a doubt as causing an irritation which needs to be appeased, suggests a temper which is uncomfortable to the verge of insanity. Yet, looking at the matter minutely, it must be admitted that, if there is the least hesitation as to whether I shall pay the five coppers or the nickel (as there will be sure to be, unless I act from some previously contracted habit in the matter), though irritation is too strong a word, yet I am excited to such small mental activity as may be necessary to deciding how I shall act. Most frequently doubts arise from some indecision, however momentary, in our action. Sometimes it is not so. I have, for example, to wait in a railway-station, and to pass the time I read the advertisements on the walls. I compare the advantages of different trains and different routes which I never expect to take, merely fancying myself to be in a state of hesitancy, because I am bored with having nothing to trouble me. Feigned hesitancy, whether feigned for mere amusement or with a lofty purpose, plays a great part in the production of scientific inquiry. However the doubt may originate, it stimulates the mind to an activity which may be slight or energetic, calm or turbulent. Images pass rapidly through consciousness, one incessantly melting into another, until at last, when all is over—it may be in a fraction of a second, in an hour, or after long years—we find ourselves decided as to how we should act under such circumstances as those which occasioned our hesitation. In other words, we have attained belief.

In this process we observe two sorts of elements of consciousness, the distinction between which may best be made clear by means of an illustration. In a piece of music there are the separate notes, and there is the air. A single tone may be prolonged for an hour or a day, and it exists as perfectly in each second of that time as in the whole taken together; so that, as long as it is sounding, it might be present to a sense from which everything in the past was as completely absent as the future itself. But it is different with the air, the performance of which occupies a certain time, during the portions of which only portions of it are played. It consists in an orderliness in the succession of sounds which strike the ear at different times; and to perceive it there must be some continuity of consciousness which makes the events of a lapse of time present to us. We certainly only perceive the air by hearing the separate notes; yet we cannot be said to directly hear it, for we hear only what is present at the instant, and an orderliness of succession cannot exist in an instant. These two sorts of objects, what we are *immediately* conscious of and what we are *mediately* conscious of, are found in all consciousness. Some elements (the sensations) are completely present at every instant so long as they last, while others (like thought) are actions having beginning, middle, and end, and consist in a congruence in the succession of sensations which flow through the mind. They cannot be immediately present to us, but must cover some portion of the past or future. Thought is a thread

1. [According to legend, Melusina, a fairy who changed into a serpent from the waist down every Saturday, married a mortal, made him promise not to visit her on that day, and, on his breaking that agreement, fled from him.—S.M.C.]

of melody running through the succession of our sensations.

We may add that just as a piece of music may be written in parts, each part having its own air, so various systems of relationship of succession subsist together between the same sensations. These different systems are distinguished by having different motives, ideas, or functions. Thought is only one such system; for its sole motive, idea, and function is to produce belief, and whatever does not concern that purpose belongs to some other system of relations. The action of thinking may incidentally have other results. It may serve to amuse us, for example, and among *dilettanti* it is not rare to find those who have so perverted thought to the purposes of pleasure that it seems to vex them to think that the questions upon which they delight to exercise it may ever get finally settled; and a positive discovery which takes a favorite subject out of the arena of literary debate is met with ill-concealed dislike. This disposition is the very debauchery of thought. But the soul and meaning of thought, abstracted from the other elements which accompany it, though it may be voluntarily thwarted, can never be made to direct itself toward anything but the production of belief. Thought in action has for its only possible motive the attainment of thought at rest; and whatever does not refer to belief is no part of the thought itself.

And what, then, is belief? It is the demi-cadence which closes a musical phrase in the symphony of our intellectual life. We have seen that it has just three properties: first, it is something that we are aware of; second, it appeases the irritation of doubt; and, third, it involves the establishment in our nature of a rule of action, or, say for short, a *habit*. As it appeases the irritation of doubt, which is the motive for thinking, thought relaxes, and comes to rest for a moment when belief is reached. But, since belief is a rule for action, the application of which involves further doubt and further thought, at the same time that it is a stopping-place, it is also a new starting-place for thought. That is why I have permitted myself to call it thought at rest, although thought is essentially an action. The *final* upshot of thinking is the exercise of volition, and of this thought no longer forms a part; but belief is only a stadium of mental action, an effect upon our nature due to thought, which will influence future thinking.

The essence of belief is the establishment of a habit, and different beliefs are distinguished by the different modes of action to which they give rise. If beliefs do not differ in this respect, if they appease the same doubt by producing the same rule of action, then no mere differences in the manner of consciousness of them can make them different beliefs, any more than playing a tune in different keys is playing different tunes. Imaginary distinctions are often drawn between beliefs which differ only in their mode of expression—the wrangling which ensues is real enough, however. To believe that any objects are arranged among themselves as in Fig. 1, and to believe

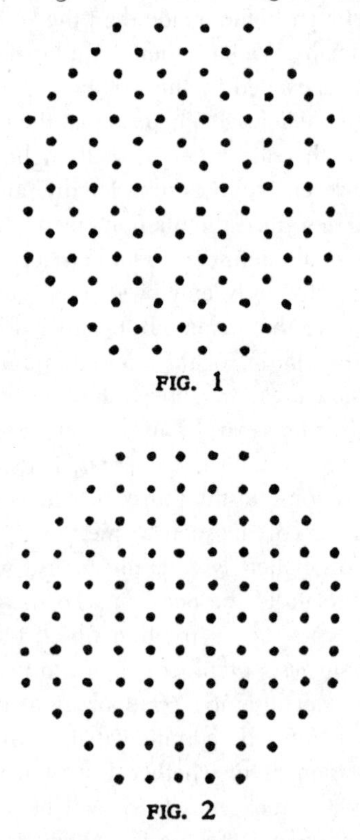

FIG. 1

FIG. 2

that they are arranged as in Fig. 2, are one and the same belief; yet it is conceivable that a man should assert one proposition and deny the other. Such false distinctions do as much harm as the confusion of beliefs really different, and are among the pitfalls of which we ought constantly to beware, especially when we are upon metaphysical ground. One singular deception of this sort, which often occurs, is to mistake the sensation produced by our own unclearness of thought for a character of the object we are thinking.

Instead of perceiving that the obscurity is purely subjective, we fancy that we contemplate a quality of the object which is essentially mysterious; and if our conception be afterward presented to us in a clear form we do not recognize it as the same, owing to the absence of the feeling of unintelligibility. So long as this deception lasts, it obviously puts an impassable barrier in the way of perspicuous thinking; so that it equally interests the opponents of rational thought to perpetuate it, and its adherents to guard against it.

Another such deception is to mistake a mere difference in the grammatical construction of two words for a distinction between the ideas they express. In this pedantic age, when the general mob of writers attend so much more to words than to things, this error is common enough. When I just said that thought is an *action*, and that it consists in a *relation*, although a person performs an action but not a relation, which can only be the result of an action, yet there was no inconsistency in what I said, but only a grammatical vagueness.

From all these sophisms we shall be perfectly safe so long as we reflect that the whole function of thought is to produce habits of action; and that whatever there is connected with a thought, but irrelevant to its purpose, is an accretion to it, but no part of it. If there be a unity among our sensations which has no reference to how we shall act on a given occasion, as when we listen to a piece of music, why, we do not call that thinking. To develop its meaning, we have, therefore, simply to determine what habits it produces, for what a thing means is simply what habits it involves. Now, the identity of a habit depends on how it might lead us to act, not merely under such circumstances as are likely to arise, but under such as might possibly occur, no matter how improbable they may be. What the habit is depends on *when* and *how* it causes us to act. As for the *when*, every stimulus to action is derived from perception; as for the *how*, every purpose of action is to produce some sensible result. Thus, we come down to what is tangible and practical as the root of every real distinction of thought, no matter how subtle it may be; and there is no distinction of meaning so fine as to consist in anything but a possible difference of practice.

To see what this principle leads to, consider in the light of it such a doctrine as that of transubstantiation. The Protestant churches generally hold that the elements of the sacrament are flesh and blood only in a tropical sense; they nourish our souls as meat and the juice of it would our bodies. But the Catholics maintain that they are literally just that, meat and blood; although they possess all the sensible qualities of wafer-cakes and diluted wine. But we can have no conception of wine except what may enter into a belief, either—

1. That this, that, or the other, is wine; or,

2. That wine possesses certain properties.

Such beliefs are nothing but self-notifications that we should, upon occasion, act in regard to such things as we believe to be wine according to the qualities which we believe wine to possess. The occasion of such action would be some sensible perception, the motive of it to produce some sensible result. Thus our action has exclusive reference to what affects the senses, our habit has the same bearing as our action, our belief the same as our habit, our conception the same as our belief; and we can consequently mean nothing by wine but what has certain effects, direct or indirect, upon our senses; and to talk of something as having all the sensible characters of wine, yet being in reality blood, is senseless jargon. Now, it is not my object to pursue the theological question; and having used it as a logical example I drop it, without caring to anticipate the theologian's reply. I only desire to point out how impossible it is that we should have an idea in our minds which relates to anything but conceived sensible effects of things. Our idea of anything *is* our idea of its sensible effects; and if we fancy that we have any other we deceive ourselves, and mistake a mere sensation accompanying the thought for a part of the thought itself. It is absurd to say that thought has any meaning unrelated to its only function. It is foolish for Catholics and Protestants to fancy themselves in disagreement about the elements of the sacrament, if they agree in regard to all their sensible effects, here or hereafter.

It appears, then, that the rule for attaining the third grade of clearness of apprehension is as follows: consider what effects, which might conceivably have practical bearings, we conceive the object of our conception to have. Then, our conception of these effects is the whole of our conception of the object.

III

Let us illustrate this rule by some examples; and, to begin with the simplest one possible, let us ask what we mean by calling a thing *hard*. Evidently that it will not be scratched by many other substances. The whole conception of this quality, as of every other, lies in its conceived effects. There is absolutely no difference between a hard thing and a soft thing so long as they are not brought to the test. Suppose, then, that a diamond could be crystallized in the midst of a cushion of soft cotton, and should remain there until it was finally burned up. Would it be false to say that that diamond was soft? This seems a foolish question, and would be so, in fact, except in the realm of logic. There such questions are often of the greatest utility as serving to bring logical principles into sharper relief than real discussions ever could. In studying logic we must not put them aside with hasty answers, but must consider them with attentive care, in order to make out the principles involved. We may, in the present case, modify our question, and ask what prevents us from saying that all hard bodies remain perfectly soft until they are touched, when their hardness increases with the pressure until they are scratched. Reflection will show that the reply is this: there would be no *falsity* in such modes of speech. They would involve a modification of our present usage of speech with regard to the words "hard" and "soft," but not of their meanings. For they represent no fact to be different from what it is; only they involve arrangements of facts which would be exceedingly maladroit. This leads us to remark that the question of what would occur under circumstances which do not actually arise is not a question of fact, but only of the most perspicuous arrangement of them. For example, the question of free-will and fate in its simplest form, stripped of verbiage, is something like this: I have done something of which I am ashamed; could I, by an effort of the will, have resisted the temptation, and done otherwise? The philosophical reply is that this is not a question of fact, but only of the [possible] arrangement of facts. Arranging them so as to exhibit what is particularly pertinent to my question—namely, that I ought to blame myself for having done wrong—it is perfectly true to say that, if I had willed to do otherwise than I did, I should have done otherwise. On the other hand, arranging the facts so as to exhibit another important consideration, it is equally true that when a temptation has once been allowed to work, it will, if it has a certain force, produce its effect, let me struggle how I may. There is no objection to a contradiction in what would result from a false supposition. The *reductio ad absurdum* consists in showing that contradictory results would follow from a hypothesis which is consequently judged to be false. Many questions are involved in the free-will discussion, and I am far from desiring to say that both sides are equally right. On the contrary, I am of opinion that one side [determinism] denies important facts, and that the other does not. But what I do say is that the above single question was the origin of the whole doubt; that, had it not been for this question, the controversy would never have arisen; and that this question is perfectly solved in the manner which I have indicated.

Let us next seek a clear idea of Weight. This is another very easy case. To say that a body is heavy means simply that, in the absence of opposing force, it will fall. This (neglecting certain specifications of how it will fall, etc., which exist in the mind of the physicist who uses the word) is evidently the whole conception of weight. It is a fair question whether some particular facts may not *account* for gravity; but what we mean by the force itself is completely involved in its effects.

This leads us to undertake an account of the idea of Force in general. This is the great conception which, developed in the early part of the seventeenth century from the rude idea of a cause, and, constantly improved upon since, has shown us how to explain all the changes of motion which bodies experience, and how to think about all physical phenomena; which has given birth to modern science, and changed the face of the globe; and which, aside from its more special uses, has played a principal part in directing the course of modern thought, and in furthering modern social development. It is, therefore, worth some pains to comprehend it. According to our rule, we must begin by asking what is the immediate use of thinking about force; and the answer is that we thus account for changes of motion. If bodies were left to themselves, without the intervention of forces, every motion would continue unchanged both in velocity and in direction. Furthermore, change of motion never takes place abruptly; if its direction is changed, it is always through a curve without angles; if its velocity alters, it is by degrees. The gradual changes which are constantly taking place are conceived by geometers to be compounded together according to the rules of the parallelogram of forces. If the reader does not already know what this is, he will find it, I hope, to his advantage to endeavor to follow the following explanation; but if mathematics are insupportable to him, pray let him skip three paragraphs rather than that we should part company here.

A *path* is a line whose beginning and end are distinguished. Two paths are considered to be equivalent, which, beginning at the same point, lead to the same point. Thus the two paths, *A B C D E* and *A F G H E* (Fig. 3), are equivalent. Paths which do *not* begin at the same point are considered to be equivalent, provided that, on moving either of them without turning it, but keeping it always parallel to its original position, [so that] when its beginning coincides with that of the other path, the ends also coincide. Paths are considered as geometrically added together, when one begins where the other ends; thus the path *A E* is conceived to be a sum of *A B*, *B C*, *C D*, and *D E*. In the parallelogram of Fig. 4 the diagonal *A C* is the sum of *A B* and *B C*; or, since *A D* is geometrically equivalent to *B C*, *A C* is the geometrical sum of *A B* and *A D*.

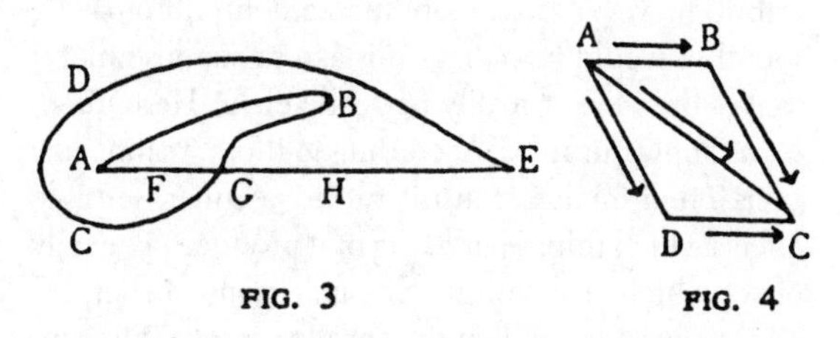

FIG. 3 FIG. 4

All this is purely conventional. It simply amounts to this: that we choose to call paths having the relations I have described equal or added. But, though it is a convention, it is a convention with a good reason. The rule for geometrical addition may be applied not only to paths, but to any other things which can be represented by paths. Now, as a path is determined by the varying direction and distance of the point which moves over it from the starting-point, it follows that anything which from its beginning to its end is determined by a varying direction and a varying magnitude is capable of being represented by a line. Accordingly, *velocities* may be represented by lines, for they have only directions and rates. The same thing is true of *accelerations*, or changes of velocities. This is evident enough in the case of velocities; and it becomes evident for accelerations if we consider that precisely what velocities are to positions—namely, states of change of them—that accelerations are to velocities.

The so-called "parallelogram of forces" is simply a rule for compounding accelerations. The rule is, to represent the accelerations by paths, and then to geometrically add the paths. The geometers, however, not only use the "parallelogram of forces" to compound different accelerations, but also to resolve one acceleration into a sum of several. Let *A B* (Fig. 5) be the path which represents a certain acceleration—say, such a change in the motion of a body that at the end of one second the body will, under the influence of that change, be in a position different from what it would have had if its motion had continued unchanged, such that a path equivalent to *A B* would lead from the latter position to the former. This acceleration may be considered as the sum of the accelerations represented by *A C* and *C B*. It may also be considered as the sum of the very different accelerations represented by *A D* and *D B*, where *A D* is almost the opposite of *A C*. And it is clear that there is an immense variety of ways in which *A B* might be resolved into the sum of two accelerations.

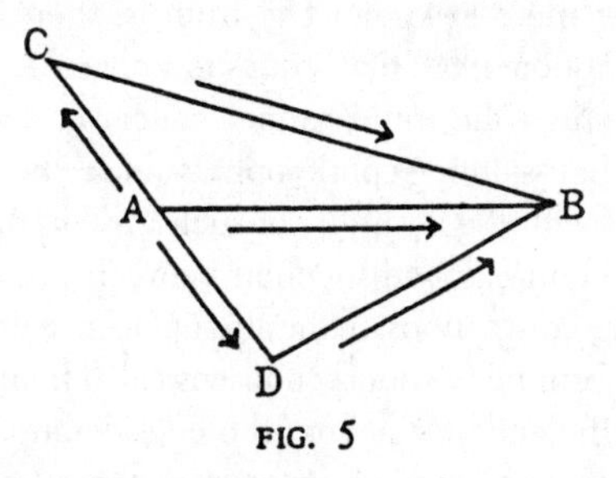

FIG. 5

After this tedious explanation, which I hope, in view of the extraordinary interest of the conception of force, may not have exhausted the reader's patience, we are prepared at last to state the grand fact which this conception embodies. This fact is that if the actual changes of motion which the different particles of bodies experience are each resolved in its appropriate way, each component acceleration is precisely such as is prescribed by a certain law of Nature, according to which bodies in the relative positions which the bodies in question actually have at the moment always receive certain accelerations, which, being compounded by geometrical addition, give the acceleration which the body actually experiences.

This is the only fact which the idea of force represents and whoever will take the trouble clearly to apprehend what this fact is perfectly comprehends what force is. Whether we ought to say that a force *is* an acceleration, or that it *causes* an acceleration, is a mere question of propriety of language, which has no more to do with our real meaning than the difference between the French idiom "*Il fait froid*" and its English equivalent "*It is cold.*" Yet it is surprising to see how this simple affair has muddled men's minds. In how many profound treatises is not force spoken of as a "mysterious entity," which seems to be only a way of confessing that the author despairs of ever getting a clear notion of what the word means! In a recent, admired work on *Analytic Mechanics*[2] it is stated that we understand precisely the effect of force, but what force itself is we do not understand! This is simply a self-contradiction. The idea which the word "force" excites in our minds has no other function than to affect our actions, and these actions can have no reference to force otherwise than through its effects. Consequently, if we know what the effects of force are, we are acquainted with every fact which is implied in saying that a force exists, and there is nothing more to know. The truth is, there is some vague notion afloat that a question may mean something which the mind cannot conceive; and when some hair-splitting philosophers have been confronted with the absurdity of such a view, they have invented an empty distinction between positive and negative conceptions, in the attempt to give their non-idea a form not obviously nonsensical. The nullity of it is sufficiently plain from the considerations given a few pages back; and, apart from those considerations, the quibbling character of the distinction must have struck every mind accustomed to real thinking.

IV

Let us now approach the subject of logic, and consider a conception which particularly concerns it, that of *reality*. Taking clearness in the sense of familiarity, no idea could be clearer than this. Every child uses it with perfect confidence, never dreaming that he does not understand it. As for clearness in its second grade, however, it would probably puzzle most men, even among those of a reflective turn of mind, to give an abstract definition of the real. Yet such a definition may perhaps be reached by considering the points of difference between reality and its opposite, fiction. A figment is a product of somebody's imagination; it has such characters as his thought impresses upon it. That those characters are independent of how you or I think is an external reality. There are, however, phenomena within our own minds, dependent upon our thought, which are at the same time real in the sense that we really think them. But though their characters depend on how we think, they do not depend on what we think those characters to be. Thus, a dream has a real existence as a mental phenomenon, if somebody has really dreamt it; that he dreamt so and so, does not depend on what anybody thinks was dreamt, but is completely independent of all opinion on the subject. On the other hand, considering, not the fact of dreaming, but the thing dreamt, it retains its peculiarities by virtue of no other fact than that it was dreamt to possess them. Thus we may define the real as that whose characters are independent of what anybody may think them to be.

But, however satisfactory such a definition may be found, it would be a great mistake to suppose that it makes the idea of reality perfectly clear. Here, then, let us apply our rules. According to them, reality, like every other quality, consists in the peculiar, sensible effects which things partaking of it produce. The only effect which real things have is to cause belief, for all the sensations which they excite emerge into consciousness in the form of beliefs. The question, therefore, is, how is true belief (or belief in the real) distinguished from false belief (or belief in fiction). Now, as we have seen in the former paper, the ideas of truth and falsehood, in their full development, appertain exclusively to the scientific method of settling opinion. A person who arbitrarily chooses the propositions which he will adopt can use the word truth only to emphasize the expression of his determination to hold on to his choice. Of course, the method of tenacity never prevailed exclusively; reason is too natural to men for that. But in the literature of the Dark Ages we find some fine examples of it. When

2. [The reference is to a book by the German physicist Gustav Robert Kirchhoff (1824–1887).]

Scotus Erigena[3] is commenting upon a poetical passage in which hellebore is spoken of as having caused the death of Socrates, he does not hesitate to inform the inquiring reader that Helleborus and Socrates were two eminent Greek philosophers, and that the latter having been overcome in argument by the former took the matter to heart and died of it! What sort of an idea of truth could a man have who could adopt and teach, without the qualification of a "perhaps," an opinion taken so entirely at random? The real spirit of Socrates, who I hope would have been delighted to have been "overcome in argument," because he would have learned something by it, is in curious contrast with the naïve idea of the glossist, for whom (as for the "born missionary" of today) discussion would seem to have been simply a struggle. When philosophy began to awake from its long slumber, and before theology completely dominated it, the practice seems to have been for each professor to seize upon any philosophical position he found unoccupied and which seemed a strong one, to intrench himself in it, and to sally forth from time to time to give battle to the others. Thus, even the scanty records we possess of those disputes enable us to make out a dozen or more opinions held by different teachers at one time concerning the question of nominalism and realism. Read the opening part of the *Historia Calamitatum* of Abélard,[4] who was certainly as philosophical as any of his contemporaries, and see the spirit of combat which it breathes. For him, the truth is simply his particular stronghold. When the method of authority prevailed, the truth meant little more than the Catholic faith. All the efforts of the scholastic doctors are directed toward harmonizing their faith in Aristotle and their faith in the Church, and one may search their ponderous folios through without finding an argument which goes any further. It is noticeable that where different faiths flourish side by side, renegades are looked upon with contempt even by the party whose belief they adopt; so completely has the idea of loyalty replaced that of truth-seeking. Since the time of Descartes, the defect in the conception of truth has been less apparent. Still, it will sometimes strike a scientific man that the philosophers have been less intent on finding out what the facts are than on inquiring what belief is most in harmony with their system. It is hard to convince a follower of the *a priori* method by adducing facts; but show him that an opinion he is defending is inconsistent with what he has laid down elsewhere, and he will be very apt to retract it. These minds do not seem to believe that disputation is ever to cease; they seem to think that the opinion which is natural for one man is not so for another, and that belief will, consequently, never be settled. In contenting themselves with fixing their own opinions by a method which would lead another man to a different result, they betray their feeble hold of the conception of what truth is.

On the other hand, all the followers of science are fully persuaded that the processes of investigation, if only pushed far enough, will give one certain solution to each question to which they can be applied. One man may investigate the velocity of light by studying the transits of Venus and the aberration of the stars; another by the oppositions of Mars and the eclipses of Jupiter's satellites; a third by the method of Fizeau;[5] a fourth by that of Foucault;[6] a fifth by the motions of the curves of Lissajous;[7] a sixth, a seventh, an eighth, and a ninth, may follow the different methods of comparing the measures of statical and dynamical electricity. They may at first obtain different results, but, as each perfects his method and his processes, the results will move steadily together toward a destined center. So with all scientific research. Different minds may set out with the most antagonistic views, but the progress of investigation carries them by a force outside of themselves to one and the same conclusion. This activity of thought by which we are carried, not where we wish, but to a foreordained goal, is like the operation of destiny. No modification of the point of view taken, no selection of other facts for study, no natural bent of mind even, can enable a man to escape the predestinate opinion. This great law is embodied in the conception of truth and reality. The

3. [The reference is to John Scotus Erigena (c. 810–c. 877), born in Ireland, a leading philosopher of his time.]

4. [The reference is to the French philosopher Peter Abelard (1079–1142).]

5. [The reference is to the French physicist Armand Hippolyte Louis Fizeau (1819–1896).]

6. [The reference is to the French physicist Jean Bernard Léon Foucault (1819–1868).]

7. [The reference is to the French physicist Jules Antoine Lissajous (1822–1880).]

opinion which is fated to be ultimately agreed to by all who investigate is what we mean by the truth, and the object represented in this opinion is the real. That is the way I would explain reality.

But it may be said that this view is directly opposed to the abstract definition which we have given of reality, inasmuch as it makes the characters of the real depend on what is ultimately thought about them. But the answer to this is that, on the one hand, reality is independent, not necessarily of thought in general, but only of what you or I or any finite number of men may think about it; and that, on the other hand, though the object of the final opinion depends on what that opinion is, yet what that opinion is does not depend on what you or I or any man thinks. Our perversity and that of others may indefinitely postpone the settlement of opinion; it might even conceivably cause an arbitrary proposition to be universally accepted as long as the human race should last. Yet even that would not change the nature of the belief, which alone could be the result of investigation carried sufficiently far; and if, after the extinction of our race, another should arise with faculties and disposition for investigation, that true opinion must be the one which they would ultimately come to. "Truth crushed to earth shall rise again," and the opinion which would finally result from investigation does not depend on how anybody may actually think. But the reality of that which is real does depend on the real fact that investigation is destined to lead, at last, if continued long enough, to a belief in it.

But I may be asked what I have to say to all the minute facts of history, forgotten never to be recovered, to the lost books of the ancients, to the buried secrets.

> Full many a gem of purest ray serene
> The dark, unfathomed caves of ocean bear;
> Full many a flower is born to blush unseen,
> And waste its sweetness on the desert air.[8]

Do these things not really exist because they are hopelessly beyond the reach of our knowledge? And then, after the universe is dead (according to the prediction of some scientists), and all life has ceased forever, will not the shock of atoms continue though there will be no mind to know it? To this I reply that, though in no possible state of knowledge can any number be great enough to express the relation between the amount of what rests unknown to the amount of the known, yet it is unphilosophical to suppose that, with regard to any given question (which has any clear meaning), investigation would not bring forth a solution of it, if it were carried far enough. Who would have said, a few years ago, that we could ever know of what substances stars are made whose light may have been longer in reaching us than the human race has existed? Who can be sure of what we shall not know in a few hundred years? Who can guess what would be the result of continuing the pursuit of science for ten thousand years, with the activity of the last hundred? And if it were to go on for a million, or a billion, or any number of years you please, how is it possible to say that there is any question which might not ultimately be solved?

But it may be objected, "Why make so much of these remote considerations, especially when it is your principle that only practical distinctions have a meaning?" Well, I must confess that it makes very little difference whether we say that a stone on the bottom of the ocean, in complete darkness, is brilliant or not—that is to say, that it *probably* makes no difference, remembering always that that stone *may* be fished up tomorrow. But that there are gems at the bottom of the sea, flowers in the untraveled desert, etc., are propositions which, like that about a diamond being hard when it is not pressed, concern much more the arrangement of our language than they do the meaning of our ideas.

It seems to me, however, that we have, by the application of our rule, reached so clear an apprehension of what we mean by reality, and of the fact which the idea rests on, that we should not, perhaps, be making a pretension so presumptuous as it would be singular, if we were to offer a metaphysical theory of existence for universal acceptance among those who employ the scientific method of fixing belief. However, as metaphysics is a subject much more curious than useful, the knowledge of which, like that of a sunken reef, serves chiefly to enable us to keep clear of it, I will not trouble the reader with any more Ontology at this moment. I have already been led

8. [The quotation is from "Elegy Written in a Country Churchyard," by the English poet Thomas Gray (1716–1771).]

much further into that path than I should have desired; and I have given the reader such a dose of mathematics, psychology, and all that is most abstruse, that I fear he may already have left me, and that what I am now writing is for the compositor and proofreader exclusively. I trusted to the importance of the subject. There is no royal road to logic, and really valuable ideas can only be had at the price of close attention. But I know that in the matter of ideas the public prefer the cheap and nasty; and in my next paper I am going to return to the easily intelligible, and not wander from it again. The reader who has been at the pains of wading through this paper shall be rewarded in the next one by seeing how beautifully what has been developed in this tedious way can be applied to the ascertainment of the rules of scientific reasoning.

We have, hitherto, not crossed the threshold of scientific logic. It is certainly important to know how to make our ideas clear, but they may be ever so clear without being true. How to make them so, we have next to study. How to give birth to those vital and procreative ideas which multiply into a thousand forms and diffuse themselves everywhere, advancing civilization and making the dignity of man, is an art not yet reduced to rules, but of the secret of which the history of science affords some hints.

William James

William James (1842–1910), brother of the novelist Henry James, was the eldest of five children. His father, Henry James, Sr., was a man of independent means who provided a rich but unconventional education for the children, sometimes in Europe and sometimes in the United States. For somewhat mysterious medical reasons, neither William nor Henry served in the Civil War, although their two younger brothers served with distinction. William found it difficult to decide on a career. He tried painting but found that he was not sufficiently talented. Also, he earned an M.D. but never practiced medicine. Instead, in 1873, he became an instructor of physiology at Harvard, where he remained until his retirement in 1907. He was America's leading psychologist, establishing both the first psychological laboratory and writing the leading textbook, *The Principles of Psychology*, and its abridged version, *Psychology: The Briefer Course*. He published his first paper in philosophy in 1878. Together with Charles Sanders Peirce, James is regarded as a founder of pragmatism, for reasons that he sets forth in the first paper to follow, "What Pragmatism Means." That paper was the second of eight public lectures delivered in the winter of 1906–1907 and published under the title *Pragmatism: A New Name for Some Old Ways of Thinking*. This particular lecture introduces all aspects of James' pragmatism.

As a young man, James suffered from a deep depression. He recovered when, stimulated by reading the French philosopher Charles Renouvier, he affirmed his belief in free will. For James, moral effort requires a belief in free will, a belief that the world needs to be and can be improved, and, for the utmost effort, a belief in a God who is on the side of good. But these are not beliefs that can be established by scientific methods; indeed, they cannot be established at all. However, since so much hangs on whether one has these beliefs, James defended one's right to them in the second paper to follow, "The Will to Believe." This paper, which also was first presented as a lecture, precedes "What Pragmatism Means" by ten years. It is, however, easily misunderstood without a clear understanding of James' pragmatic theory of truth.

What, then, is pragmatism? According to James, it is both a method for settling what would otherwise be interminable metaphysical disputes and a theory of truth. Pragmatism settles metaphysical disputes by clarifying the meaning of the concepts involved. It is interesting that James restates Peirce's maxim as "to develop a thought's meaning, we need only determine what conduct it is fitted to produce: that conduct is for us its sole significance," although James follows that statement with an almost verbatim quote of Peirce's formulation. In fact, James takes the maxim in a very wide sense, so that it does not eliminate, say, religious hypotheses but rather finds their point in the behavior they encourage.

Although pragmatism is a form of empiricism, it differs from earlier empiricisms, such as that of Hume, in three respects. (1) James does not regard the mind as a passive receptacle. We all bring to experience a set of concepts that have been developed by humans over the millennia, concepts such as space, time, cause, and thing. We may also bring to experience specialized concepts developed in the sciences, the arts, or religion. What we experience depends on these concepts as well as on the world, and, in turn, our experience may lead us to modify our concepts. (2) James held that we experience relations between things and their properties. He considered this to be the crucial difference between his empiricism and that of his predecessors. (3) For James "sensations" include not only the deliverances of the five senses but also feelings and emotions. Because the mind is not a passive receptacle, theories are not mere summaries of past experiences nor the deliverances of an a priori reason, but are *instruments*; they "become true just in so far as they help us to get into satisfactory relation with other parts of our experience."

What, then, is the pragmatist theory of truth? It is an attempt to clarify what is involved in the claim that truth is agreement with reality, which is itself a mere truism. Unlike other philosophers, pragmatists hold that there are many relations of agreement. Sometimes a mental image copies what one has just seen. But in almost all cases, belief leads to expectations of future experiences, and when these are not disappointed, or as long as these are not disappointed, we regard the belief as true. Since our existence in the world is precarious, true beliefs are of the utmost importance; they are good to believe. But that does *not* mean that they are pleasant to believe or are satisfying at the moment. We are not free to believe what we want. Our beliefs must harmonize with past experience; they must be logically coherent and prove themselves throughout the indefinite future. The latter is what James meant by saying that beliefs "become true."

James concluded "What Pragmatism Means" by applying it to his conception of God and to the contrasting conception of the Absolute of his Idealist colleagues. He held that a belief in his God—a God who, with our help, strives to make this a better world—would help us lead a better life, and that, therefore, it would be better for us to have that belief unless it clashes with other vital beliefs. That last proviso prevents us from believing whatever we like. But James has been accused of permitting, indeed encouraging, just that approach, an accusation based primarily on a careless reading of "The Will to Believe."

At times one has to believe "ahead of the evidence." If you do not trust a new acquaintance, your chance for a friendship will be lost forever. If you do not believe in a Jamesean deity, you will not have that maximum of moral energy. What characterizes the situations in question is that (a) the choice is momentous, and much hangs on it; (b) it is impossible to wait for further evidence—not choosing is to choose the other alternative; and (c) both alternatives are "live" for us, that is, we can see ourselves making either choice. In such cases, and only in such cases, James insists on our right to believe, that is, to choose. James himself exercised that right when he chose to believe in free will. Making that choice enabled him to emerge from a deep depression. Scientists exercise that right when they choose to devote themselves to a line of research, believing that the research will yield good results. Of course, beliefs so chosen are subject to the same verification/falsification processes as are all other beliefs.

• • •

The most readable introduction to James' philosophy is Jacques Barzun, *A Stroll with William James* (New York: Harper & Row, 1983). Gerald E. Myers, *William James: His Life and Thought* (New Haven: Yale University Press, 1986) is a massive, excellent study. Ruth Anna Putnam, ed., *The Cambridge Companion to William James* (Cambridge: Cambridge University Press, 1997) provides multiple perspectives on various aspects of James' philosophy.

Ruth Anna Putnam

What Pragmatism Means

Some years ago, being with a camping party in the mountains, I returned from a solitary ramble to find everyone engaged in a ferocious metaphysical dispute. The *corpus* of the dispute was a squirrel—a live squirrel supposed to be clinging to one side of a tree-trunk; while over against the tree's opposite side a human being was imagined to stand. This human witness tries to get sight of the squirrel by moving rapidly round the tree, but no matter how fast he goes, the squirrel moves as fast in the opposite direction, and always keeps the tree between himself and the man, so that never a glimpse of him is caught. The resultant metaphysical problem now is this: *Does the man go round the squirrel or not?* He goes round the tree, sure enough, and the squirrel is on the tree; but does he go round the squirrel? In the unlimited leisure of the wilderness, discussion had been worn threadbare. Everyone had taken sides, and was obstinate; and the numbers on both sides were even. Each side, when I appeared, therefore appealed to me to make it a majority. Mindful of the scholastic adage that whenever you meet a contradiction you must make a distinction, I immediately sought and found one, as follows: "Which party is right," I said, "depends on what you *practically mean* by 'going round' the squirrel. If you mean passing from the north of him to the east, then to the south, then to the west, and then to the north of him again, obviously the man does go round him, for he occupies these successive positions. But if on the contrary you mean being first in front of him, then on the right of him, then behind him, then on his left, and finally in front again, it is quite as obvious that the man fails to go round him, for by the compensating movements the squirrel makes, he keeps his belly turned towards the man all the time, and his back turned away. Make the distinction, and there is no occasion for any farther dispute. You are both right and both wrong according as you conceive the verb 'to go round' in one practical fashion or the other."

Altho one or two of the hotter disputants called my speech a shuffling evasion, saying they wanted no quibbling or scholastic hair-splitting, but meant just plain honest English 'round,' the majority seemed to think that the distinction had assuaged the dispute.

I tell this trivial anecdote because it is a peculiarly simple example of what I wish now to speak of as *the pragmatic method*. The pragmatic method is primarily a method of settling metaphysical disputes that otherwise might be interminable. Is the world one or many?—fated or free?—material or spiritual?—here are notions either of which may or may not hold good of the world; and disputes over such notions are unending. The pragmatic method in such cases is to try to interpret each notion by tracing its respective practical consequences. What difference would it practically make to anyone if this notion rather than that notion were true? If no practical difference whatever can be traced, then the alternatives mean practically the same thing, and all dispute is idle. Whenever a dispute is serious, we ought to be able to show some practical difference that must follow from one side or the other's being right.

A glance at the history of the idea will show you still better what pragmatism means. The term is derived from the same Greek word πράγμα,[1] meaning action, from which our words 'practice' and 'practical' come. It was first introduced into philosophy by Mr. Charles Peirce in 1878. In an article entitled 'How to Make Our Ideas Clear,' in the 'Popular Science

Reprinted from William James, *Pragmatism: A New Name for Some Old Ways of Thinking* (New York, 1907).

1. [Praxis.—S.M.C.]

Monthly' for January of that year[2] Mr. Peirce, after pointing out that our beliefs are really rules for action, said that, to develop a thought's meaning, we need only determine what conduct it is fitted to produce: that conduct is for us its sole significance. And the tangible fact at the root of all our thought-distinctions, however subtle, is that there is no one of them so fine as to consist in anything but a possible difference of practice. To attain perfect clearness in our thoughts of an object, then, we need only consider what conceivable effects of a practical kind the object may involve—what sensations we are to expect from it, and what reactions we must prepare. Our conception of these effects, whether immediate or remote, is then for us the whole of our conception of the object, so far as that conception has positive significance at all.

This is the principle of Peirce, the principle of pragmatism. It lay entirely unnoticed by anyone for twenty years, until I, in an address before Professor Howison's[3] philosophical union at the university of California, brought it forward again and made a special application of it to religion. By that date (1898) the times seemed ripe for its reception. The word 'pragmatism' spread, and at present it fairly spots the pages of the philosophic journals. On all hands we find the 'pragmatic movement' spoken of, sometimes with respect, sometimes with contumely, seldom with clear understanding. It is evident that the term applies itself conveniently to a number of tendencies that hitherto have lacked a collective name, and that it has 'come to stay.'

To take in the importance of Peirce's principle, one must get accustomed to applying it to concrete cases. I found a few years ago that Ostwald, the illustrious Leipzig chemist,[4] had been making perfectly distinct use of the principle of pragmatism in his lectures on the philosophy of science, tho he had not called it by that name.

"All realities influence our practice," he wrote me, "and that influence is their meaning for us. I am accustomed to put questions to my class in this way: In what respects would the world be different if this alternative or that were true? If I can find nothing that would become different, then the alternative has no sense."

That is, the rival views mean practically the same thing, and meaning, other than practical, there is for us none. Ostwald in a published lecture gives this example of what he means. Chemists have long wrangled over the inner constitution of certain bodies called 'tautomerous.' Their properties seemed equally consistent with the notion that an instable hydrogen atom oscillates inside of them, or that they are instable mixtures of two bodies. Controversy raged; but never was decided. "It would never have begun," says Ostwald, "if the combatants had asked themselves what particular experimental fact could have been made different by one or the other view being correct. For it would then have appeared that no difference of fact could possibly ensue; and the quarrel was as unreal as if, theorizing in primitive times about the raising of dough by yeast, one party should have invoked a 'brownie,' while another insisted on an 'elf' as the true cause of the phenomenon."[5]

It is astonishing to see how many philosophical disputes collapse into insignificance the moment you subject them to this simple test of tracing a concrete consequence. There can *be* no difference anywhere that doesn't *make* a difference elsewhere—no difference in abstract truth that doesn't express itself in a difference in concrete fact and in conduct consequent upon that fact, imposed on somebody, somehow, somewhere and somewhen. The whole function of philosophy ought to be to find out what definite difference it will make to you and me, at definite instants

2. Translated in the *Revue Philosophique* for January 1879 (vol. vii).

3. [The reference is to George Holmes Howison (1834–1916), head of the department of philosophy at the University of California at Berkeley.]

4. [The reference is to the German scientist Wilhelm Ostwald (1853–1932), who would win the 1909 Nobel Prize in Chemistry.]

5. "Theorie und Praxis," *Zeitsch, des Oesterreichischen Ingenieur u. Architecten-Vereines*, 1905, Nr. 4 u. 6. I find a still more radical pragmatism than Ostwald's in an address by Professor W. S. Franklin: "I think that the sickliest notion of physics, even if a student gets it, is that it is 'the science of masses, molecules and the ether.' And I think that the healthiest notion, even if a student does not wholly get it, is that physics is the science of the ways of taking hold of bodies and pushing them!" (*Science*, January 2, 1903.) [William Suddards Franklin (1863–1930) was an American physicist.]

of our life, if this world-formula or that world-formula be the true one.

There is absolutely nothing new in the pragmatic method. Socrates was an adept at it. Aristotle used it methodically. Locke, Berkeley and Hume made momentous contributions to truth by its means. Shadworth Hodgson[6] keeps insisting that realities are only what they are 'known-as.' But these forerunners of pragmatism used it in fragments: they were preluders only. Not until in our time has it generalized itself, become conscious of a universal mission, pretended to a conquering destiny. I believe in that destiny, and I hope I may end by inspiring you with my belief.

Pragmatism represents a perfectly familiar attitude in philosophy, the empiricist attitude, but it represents it, as it seems to me, both in a more radical and in a less objectionable form than it has ever yet assumed. A pragmatist turns his back resolutely and once for all upon a lot of inveterate habits dear to professional philosophers. He turns away from abstraction and insufficiency, from verbal solutions, from bad *a priori* reasons, from fixed principles, closed systems, and pretended absolutes and origins. He turns towards concreteness and adequacy, towards facts, towards action, and towards power. That means the empiricist temper regnant, and the rationalist temper sincerely given up. It means the open air and possibilities of nature, as against dogma, artificiality and the pretence of finality in truth.

At the same time it does not stand for any special results. It is a method only. But the general triumph of that method would mean an enormous change in what I called in my last lecture the 'temperament' of philosophy. Teachers of the ultra-rationalistic type would be frozen out, much as the courtier type is frozen out in republics, as the ultramontane type of priest is frozen out in protestant lands. Science and metaphysics would come much nearer together, would in fact work absolutely hand in hand.

Metaphysics has usually followed a very primitive kind of quest. You know how men have always hankered after unlawful magic, and you know what a great part, in magic, *words* have always played. If you have his name, or the formula of incantation that binds him, you can control the spirit, genie, afrite, or whatever the power may be. Solomon knew the names of all the spirits, and having their names, he held them subject to his will. So the universe has always appeared to the natural mind as a kind of enigma, of which the key must be sought in the shape of some illuminating or power-bringing word or name. That word names the universe's *principle*, and to possess it is, after a fashion, to possess the universe itself. 'God,' 'Matter,' 'Reason,' 'the Absolute,' 'Energy,' are so many solving names. You can rest when you have them. You are at the end of your metaphysical quest.

But if you follow the pragmatic method, you cannot look on any such word as closing your quest. You must bring out of each word its practical cash-value, set it at work within the stream of your experience. It appears less as a solution, then, than as a program for more work, and more particularly as an indication of the ways in which existing realities may be *changed*.

Theories thus become instruments, not answers to enigmas, in which we can rest. We don't lie back upon them, we move forward, and, on occasion, make nature over again by their aid. Pragmatism unstiffens all our theories, limbers them up and sets each one at work. Being nothing essentially new, it harmonizes with many ancient philosophic tendencies. It agrees with nominalism for instance, in always appealing to particulars; with utilitarianism in emphasizing practical aspects; with positivism in its disdain for verbal solutions, useless questions, and metaphysical abstractions.

All these, you see, are *anti-intellectualist* tendencies. Against rationalism as a pretension and a method, pragmatism is fully armed and militant. But, at the outset, at least, it stands for no particular results. It has no dogmas, and no doctrines save its method. As the young Italian pragmatist Papini has well said, it lies in the midst of our theories, like a corridor in a hotel. Innumerable chambers open out of it. In one you may find a man writing an atheistic volume; in the next someone on his knees praying for faith and strength; in a third a chemist investigating a body's properties. In a fourth a system of idealistic metaphysics is being excogitated; in a fifth the impossibility of metaphysics is being shown. But they all own the corridor, and all must pass through it if they want a practicable way of getting into or out of their respective rooms.

6. [The reference is to the English philosopher Shadworth Hollway Hodgson (1832–1912).]

No particular results then, so far, but only an attitude of orientation, is what the pragmatic method means. *The attitude of looking away from first things, principles, 'categories,' supposed necessities; and of looking toward last things, fruits, consequences, facts.*

So much for the pragmatic method! You may say that I have been praising it rather than explaining it to you, but I shall presently explain it abundantly enough by showing how it works on some familiar problems. Meanwhile the word pragmatism has come to be used in a still wider sense, as meaning also a certain *theory of truth*. I mean to give a whole lecture to the statement of that theory, after first paving the way, so I can be very brief now. But brevity is hard to follow, so I ask for your redoubled attention for a quarter of an hour. If much remains obscure, I hope to make it clearer in the later lectures.

One of the most successfully cultivated branches of philosophy in our time is what is called inductive logic, the study of the conditions under which our sciences have evolved. Writers on this subject have begun to show a singular unanimity as to what the laws of nature and elements of fact mean, when formulated by mathematicians, physicists and chemists. When the first mathematical, logical and natural uniformities, the first *laws*, were discovered, men were so carried away by the clearness, beauty and simplification that resulted, that they believed themselves to have deciphered authentically the eternal thoughts of the Almighty. His mind also thundered and reverberated in syllogisms. He also thought in conic sections, squares and roots and ratios, and geometrized like Euclid.[7] He made Kepler's[8] laws for the planets to follow; he made velocity increase proportionally to the time in falling bodies; he made the law of the sines for light to obey when refracted; he established the classes, orders, families and genera of plants and animals, and fixed the distances between them. He thought the archetypes of all things, and devised their variations; and when we rediscover any one of these his wondrous institutions, we seize his mind in its very literal intention.

But as the sciences have developed farther, the notion has gained ground that most, perhaps all, of our laws are only approximations. The laws themselves, moreover, have grown so numerous that there is no counting them; and so many rival formulations are proposed in all the branches of science that investigators have become accustomed to the notion that no theory is absolutely a transcript of reality, but that any one of them may from some point of view be useful. Their great use is to summarize old facts and to lead to new ones. They are only a man-made language, a conceptual shorthand, as someone calls them, in which we write our reports of nature; and languages, as is well known, tolerate much choice of expression and many dialects.

Thus human arbitrariness has driven divine necessity from scientific logic. If I mention the names of Sigwart,[9] Mach,[10] Ostwald, Pearson,[11] Milhaud,[12] Poincare,[13] Duhem,[14] Ruyssen,[15] those of you who are students will easily identify the tendency I speak of, and will think of additional names.

Riding now on the front of this wave of scientific logic Messrs. Schiller[16] and Dewey[17] appear with their pragmatistic account of what truth everywhere signifies. Everywhere, these teachers say, 'truth' in our

7. [Euclid was the fourth-century-B.C. Greek mathematician whose *Elements* contained the standard presentation of plane geometry.]

8. [Regarding Kepler, see Peirce, "The Fixation of Belief," n.6.]

9. [The reference is to the German logician Christoph Sigwart (1830–1904).]

10. [The reference is to the Austrian physicist and philosopher Ernst Mach (1838–1916).]

11. [The reference is to the English scientist Karl Pearson (1857–1936), who applied statistical methods to the study of biology.]

12. [The reference is to the French philosopher Gaston Samuel Milhaud (1858–1918).]

13. [The reference is to the French mathematician and physicist Jules Henri Poincaré (1854–1912).]

14. [The reference is to the French physicist, philosopher, and historian of science Pierre Duhem (1861–1916).]

15. [The reference is to the French philosopher Theodore Ruyssen (1868–1967).]

16. [The reference is to the British philosopher Ferdinand Canning Scott Schiller (1864–1937), who was professor of philosophy at Oxford University and then at the University of Southern California.]

17. [The reference is to John Dewey (1859–1952), the best-known American philosopher of the first half of the twentieth century.]

ideas and beliefs means the same thing that it means in science. It means, they say, nothing but this, *that ideas (which themselves are but parts of our experience) become true just in so far as they help us to get into satisfactory relation with other parts of our experience*, to summarize them and get about among them by conceptual short-cuts instead of following the interminable succession of particular phenomena. Any idea upon which we can ride, so to speak; any idea that will carry us prosperously from any one part of our experience to any other part, linking things satisfactorily, working securely, simplifying, saving labor; is true for just so much, true in so far forth, true *instrumentally*. This is the 'instrumental' view of truth taught so successfully at Chicago, the view that truth in our ideas means their power to 'work,' promulgated so brilliantly at Oxford.

Messrs. Dewey, Schiller and their allies, in reaching this general conception of all truth, have only followed the example of geologists, biologists and philologists. In the establishment of these other sciences, the successful stroke was always to take some simple process actually observable in operation—as denudation by weather, say, or variation from parental type, or change of dialect by incorporation of new words and pronunciations—and then to generalize it, making it apply to all times, and produce great results by summating its effects through the ages.

The observable process which Schiller and Dewey particularly singled out for generalization is the familiar one by which any individual settles into *new opinions*. The process here is always the same. The individual has a stock of old opinions already, but he meets a new experience that puts them to a strain. Somebody contradicts them; or in a reflective moment he discovers that they contradict each other; or he hears of facts with which they are incompatible; or desires arise in him which they cease to satisfy. The result is an inward trouble to which his mind till then had been a stranger, and from which he seeks to escape by modifying his previous mass of opinions. He saves as much of it as he can, for in this matter of belief we are all extreme conservatives. So he tries to change first this opinion, and then that (for they resist change very variously), until at last some new idea comes up which he can graft upon the ancient stock with a minimum of disturbance of the latter, some idea that mediates between the stock and the new experience and runs them into one another most felicitously and expediently.

This new idea is then adopted as the true one. It preserves the older stock of truths with a minimum of modification, stretching them just enough to make them admit the novelty, but conceiving that in ways as familiar as the case leaves possible. An *outrée* explanation, violating all our preconceptions, would never pass for a true account of a novelty. We should scratch round industriously till we found something less excentric. The most violent revolutions in an individual's beliefs leave most of his old order standing. Time and space, cause and effect, nature and history, and one's own biography remain untouched. New truth is always a go-between, a smoother-over of transitions. It marries old opinion to new fact so as ever to show a minimum of jolt, a maximum of continuity. We hold a theory true just in proportion to its success in solving this 'problem of maxima and minima.' But success in solving this problem is eminently a matter of approximation. We say this theory solves it on the whole more satisfactorily than that theory; but that means more satisfactorily to ourselves, and individuals will emphasize their points of satisfaction differently. To a certain degree, therefore, everything here is plastic.

The point I now urge you to observe particularly is the part played by the older truths. Failure to take account of it is the source of much of the unjust criticism leveled against pragmatism. Their influence is absolutely controlling. Loyalty to them is the first principle—in most cases it is the only principle; for by far the most usual way of handling phenomena so novel that they would make for a serious rearrangement of our preconceptions is to ignore them altogether, or to abuse those who bear witness for them.

You doubtless wish examples of this process of truth's growth, and the only trouble is their superabundance. The simplest case of new truth is of course the mere numerical addition of new kinds of facts, or of new single facts of old kinds, to our experience—an addition that involves no alteration in the old beliefs. Day follows day, and its contents are simply added. The new contents themselves are not true, they simply *come* and *are*. Truth is *what we say about* them, and when we say that they have come, truth is satisfied by the plain additive formula.

But often the day's contents oblige a rearrangement. If I should now utter piercing shrieks and act like a maniac on this platform, it would make many of you revise your ideas as to the probable worth of my philosophy. 'Radium' came the other day as part of the day's content, and seemed for a moment to contradict our ideas of the whole order of nature, that order having come to be identified with what is called the conservation of energy. The mere sight of radium paying heat away indefinitely out of its own pocket seemed to violate that conservation. What to think? If the radiations from it were nothing but an escape of unsuspected 'potential' energy, pre-existent inside of the atoms, the principle of conservation would be saved. The discovery of 'helium' as the radiation's outcome, opened a way to this belief. So Ramsay's[18] view is generally held to be true, because, altho it extends our old ideas of energy, it causes a minimum of alteration in their nature.

I need not multiply instances. A new opinion counts as 'true' just in proportion as it gratifies the individual's desire to assimilate the novel in his experience to his beliefs in stock. It must both lean on old truth and grasp new fact; and its success (as I said a moment ago) in doing this, is a matter for the individual's appreciation. When old truth grows, then, by new truth's addition, it is for subjective reasons. We are in the process and obey the reasons. That new idea is truest which performs most felicitously its function of satisfying our double urgency. It makes itself true, gets itself classed as true, by the way it works; grafting itself then upon the ancient body of truth, which thus grows much as a tree grows by the activity of a new layer of cambium.

Now Dewey and Schiller proceed to generalize this observation and to apply it to the most ancient parts of truth. They also once were plastic. They also were called true for human reasons. They also mediated between still earlier truths and what in those days were novel observations. Purely objective truth, truth in whose establishment the function of giving human satisfaction is marrying previous parts of experience with newer parts played no rôle whatever, is nowhere to be found. The reasons why we call things true is the reason why they *are* true, for 'to be true' *means* only to perform this marriage-function.

18. [The reference is to the Scottish chemist Sir William Ramsay, who would win the 1904 Nobel Prize in Chemistry.]

The trail of the human serpent is thus over everything. Truth independent; truth that we *find* merely; truth no longer malleable to human need; truth incorrigible, in a word; such truth exists indeed superabundantly—or is supposed to exist by rationalistically minded thinkers; but then it means only the dead heart of the living tree, and its being there means only that truth also has its paleontology and its 'prescription,' and may grow stiff with years of veteran service and petrified in men's regard by sheer antiquity. But how plastic even the oldest truths nevertheless really are has been vividly shown in our day by the transformation of logical and mathematical ideas, a transformation which seems even to be invading physics. The ancient formulas are reinterpreted as special expressions of much wider principles, principles that our ancestors never got a glimpse of in their present shape and formulation.

Mr. Schiller still gives to all this view of truth the name of 'Humanism,' but, for this doctrine too, the name of pragmatism seems fairly to be in the ascendant, so I will treat it under the name of pragmatism in these lectures.

Such then would be the scope of pragmatism—first, a method; and second, a genetic theory of what is meant by truth. And these two things must be our future topics.

What I have said of the theory of truth will, I am sure, have appeared obscure and unsatisfactory to most of you by reason of its brevity. I shall make amends for that hereafter. In a lecture on 'common sense' I shall try to show what I mean by truths grown petrified by antiquity. In another lecture I shall expatiate on the idea that our thoughts become true in proportion as they successfully exert their go-between function. In a third I shall show how hard it is to discriminate subjective from objective factors in Truth's development. You may not follow me wholly in these lectures; and if you do, you may not wholly agree with me. But you will, I know, regard me at least as serious, and treat my effort with respectful consideration.

You will probably be surprised to learn, then, that Messrs. Schiller's and Dewey's theories have suffered a hailstorm of contempt and ridicule. All rationalism has risen against them. In influential quarters Mr. Schiller, in particular, has been treated like an impudent schoolboy who deserves a spanking. I should not mention this, but for the fact that it throws so much sidelight upon that rationalistic temper to which I have opposed the temper of pragmatism. Pragmatism is uncomfortable away from facts. Rationalism is comfortable only in the presence of abstractions. This pragmatist talk about truths in the plural, about their utility and satisfactoriness, about the success with which they 'work,' etc., suggests to the typical intellectualist mind a sort of coarse lame second-rate makeshift article of truth. Such truths are not real truth. Such tests are merely subjective. As against this, objective truth must be something non-utilitarian, haughty, refined, remote, august, exalted. It must be an absolute correspondence of our thoughts with an equally absolute reality. It must be what we *ought* to think, unconditionally. The conditioned ways in which we *do* think are so much irrelevance and matter for psychology. Down with psychology, up with logic, in all this question!

See the exquisite contrast of the types of mind! The pragmatist clings to facts and concreteness, observes truth at its work in particular cases, and generalizes. Truth, for him, becomes a class-name for all sorts of definite working-values in experience. For the rationalist it remains a pure abstraction, to the bare name of which we must defer. When the pragmatist undertakes to show in detail just *why* we must defer, the rationalist is unable to recognize the concretes from which his own abstraction is taken. He accuses us of *denying* truth; whereas we have only sought to trace exactly why people follow it and always ought to follow it. Your typical ultra-abstractionist fairly shudders at concreteness: other things equal, he positively prefers the pale and spectral. If the two universes were offered, he would always choose the skinny outline rather than the rich thicket of reality. It is so much purer, clearer, nobler.

I hope that as these lectures go on, the concreteness and closeness to facts of the pragmatism which they advocate may be what approves itself to you as its most satisfactory peculiarity. It only follows here the example of the sister-sciences, interpreting the unobserved by the observed. It brings old and new harmoniously together. It converts the absolutely empty notion of a static relation of 'correspondence' (what that may mean we must ask later) between our minds and reality, into that of a rich and active commerce (that anyone may follow in detail and understand) between particular thoughts of ours, and the great universe of other experiences in which they play their parts and have their uses.

But enough of this at present? The justification of what I say must be postponed. I wish now to add a word in further explanation of the claim I made at our last meeting, that pragmatism may be a happy harmonizer of empiricist ways of thinking, with the more religious demands of human beings.

Men who are strongly of the fact-loving temperament, you may remember me to have said, are liable to be kept at a distance by the small sympathy with facts which that philosophy from the present-day fashion of idealism offers them. It is far too intellectualistic. Old fashioned theism was bad enough, with its notion of God as an exalted monarch, made up of a lot of unintelligible or preposterous 'attributes'; but, so long as it held strongly by the argument from design, it kept some touch with concrete realities. Since, however, darwinism has once for all displaced design from the minds of the 'scientific,' theism has lost that foothold; and some kind of an immanent or pantheistic deity working *in* things rather than above them is, if any, the kind recommended to our contemporary imagination. Aspirants to a philosophic religion turn, as a rule, more hopefully nowadays towards idealistic pantheism than towards the older dualistic theism, in spite of the fact that the latter still counts able defenders.

But, as I said in my first lecture, the brand of pantheism offered is hard for them to assimilate if they are lovers of facts, or empirically minded. It is the absolutistic brand, spurning the dust and reared upon pure logic. It keeps no connexion whatever with concreteness. Affirming the Absolute Mind, which is its substitute for God, to be the rational presupposition of all particulars of fact, whatever they may be, it remains supremely indifferent to what the particular facts in our world actually are. Be they what they may, the Absolute will father them. Like the sick lion in Esop's fable, all footprints lead into his den, but *nulla vestigia retrorsum*.[19] You cannot redescend into the world of particulars by the Absolute's aid, or deduce any necessary consequences of detail important

19. [No footprints return. Little is known about Aesop, the Greek author of fables.]

for your life from your idea of his nature. He gives you indeed the assurance that all is well with *Him*, and for his eternal way of thinking; but thereupon he leaves you to be finitely saved by your own temporal devices.

Far be it from me to deny the majesty of this conception, or its capacity to yield religious comfort to a most respectable class of minds. But from the human point of view, no one can pretend that it doesn't suffer from the faults of remoteness and abstractness. It is eminently a product of what I have ventured to call the rationalistic temper. It disdains empiricism's needs. It substitutes a pallid outline for the real world's richness. It is dapper; it is noble in the bad sense, in the sense in which to be noble is to be inapt for humble service. In this real world of sweat and dirt, it seems to me that when a view of things is 'noble,' that ought to count as a presumption against its truth, and as a philosophic disqualification. The prince of darkness may be a gentleman, as we are told he is, but whatever the God of earth and heaven is, he can surely be no gentleman. His menial services are needed in the dust of our human trials, even more than his dignity is needed in the empyrean.

Now pragmatism, devoted tho she be to facts, has no such materialistic bias as ordinary empiricism labors under. Moreover, she has no objection whatever to the realizing of abstractions, so long as you get about among particulars with their aid and they actually carry you somewhere. Interested in no conclusions but those which our minds and our experiences work out together, she has no *a priori* prejudices against theology. *If theological ideas prove to have a value for concrete life, they will be true, for pragmatism, in the sense of being good for so much. For how much more they are true, will depend entirely on their relations to the other truths that also have to be acknowledged.*

What I said just now about the Absolute of transcendental idealism is a case in point. First, I called it majestic and said it yielded religious comfort to a class of minds, and then I accused it of remoteness and sterility. But so far as it affords such comfort, it surely is not sterile; it has that amount of value; it performs a concrete function. As a good pragmatist, I myself ought to call the Absolute true 'in so far forth,' then; and I unhesitatingly now do so.

But what does *true in so far forth* mean in this case? To answer, we need only apply the pragmatic method. What do believers in the Absolute mean by saying that their belief affords them comfort? They mean that since in the Absolute finite evil is 'overruled' already, we may, therefore, whenever we wish, treat the temporal as if it were potentially the eternal, be sure that we can trust its outcome, and, without sin, dismiss our fear and drop the worry of our finite responsibility. In short, they mean that we have a right ever and anon to take a moral holiday, to let the world wag in its own way, feeling that its issues are in better hands than ours and are none of our business.

The universe is a system of which the individual members may relax their anxieties occasionally, in which the don't-care mood is also right for men, and moral holidays in order—that, if I mistake not, is part, at least, of what the Absolute is 'known-as,' that is the great difference in our particular experiences which his being true makes for us, that is part of his cash-value when he is pragmatically interpreted. Farther than that the ordinary lay-reader in philosophy who thinks favorably of absolute idealism does not venture to sharpen his conceptions. He can use the Absolute for so much, and so much is very precious. He is pained at hearing you speak incredulously of the Absolute, therefore, and disregards your criticisms because they deal with aspects of the conception that he fails to follow.

If the Absolute means this, and means no more than this, who can possibly deny the truth of it? To deny it would be to insist that men should never relax, and that holidays are never in order.

I am well aware how odd it must seem to some of you to hear me say that an idea is 'true' so long as to believe it is profitable to our lives. That it is *good*, for as much as it profits, you will gladly admit. If what we do by its aid is good, you will allow the idea itself to be good in so far forth, for we are the better for possessing it. But is it not a strange misuse of the word 'truth,' you will say, to call ideas also 'true' for this reason?

To answer this difficulty fully is impossible at this stage of my account. You touch here upon the very central point of Messrs. Schiller's, Dewey's and my own doctrine of truth, which I cannot discuss with detail until my sixth lecture. Let me now say only this, that truth is *one species of good*, and not, as is usually supposed, a category distinct from good, and co-ordinate with it. *The true is the name of whatever proves itself to be good in the way of belief and good, too, for definite, assignable reasons.* Surely you must admit this, that if there were *no* good for life in true ideas, or if the knowledge of them were positively disadvantageous and false ideas the only useful ones, then the current notion that truth is divine and precious, and its pursuit a duty, could never have grown up or become a dogma. In a world like that, our duty would be to *shun* truth, rather. But in this world, just as certain foods are not only agreeable to our taste, but good for our teeth, our stomach and our tissues; so certain ideas are not only agreeable to think about, or agreeable as supporting other ideas that we are fond of, but they are also helpful in life's practical struggles. If there be any life that it is really better we should lead, and if there be any idea which, if believed in, would help us to lead that life, then it would be really *better for us* to believe in that idea, *unless, indeed, belief in it incidentally clashed with other greater vital benefits.*

'What would be better for us to believe'! This sounds very like a definition of truth. It comes very near to saying 'what we *ought* to believe': and in *that* definition none of you would find any oddity. Ought we ever not to believe what it is *better for us* to believe? And can we then keep the notion of what is better for us and what is true for us, permanently apart?

Pragmatism says no, and I fully agree with her. Probably you also agree, so far as the abstract statement goes, but with a suspicion that if we practically did believe everything that made for good in our own personal lives, we should be found indulging all kinds of fancies about this world's affairs, and all kinds of sentimental superstitions about a world hereafter. Your suspicion here is undoubtedly well founded, and it is evident that something happens when you pass from the abstract to the concrete, that complicates the situation.

I said just now that what is better for us to believe is true *unless the belief incidentally clashes with some other vital benefit.* Now in real life what vital benefits is any particular belief of ours most liable to clash with? What indeed except the vital benefits yielded by *other beliefs* when these prove incompatible with the first ones? In other words, the greatest enemy of any one of our truths may be the rest of our truths. Truths have once for all this desperate instinct of self-preservation and of desire to extinguish whatever contradicts them. My belief in the Absolute, based on the good it does me, must run the gauntlet of all my other beliefs. Grant that it may be true in giving me a moral holiday. Nevertheless, as I conceive it,—and let me speak now confidentially, as it were, and merely in my own private person,—it clashes with other truths of mine whose benefits I hate to give up on its account. It happens to be associated with a kind of logic of which I am the enemy, I find that it entangles me in metaphysical paradoxes that are inacceptable, etc., etc. But as I have enough trouble in life already without adding the trouble of carrying these intellectual inconsistencies, I personally just give up the Absolute. I just *take* my moral holidays; or else as a professional philosopher, I try to justify them by some other principle.

If I could restrict my notion of the Absolute to its bare holiday-giving value, it wouldn't clash with my other truths. But we cannot easily thus restrict our hypotheses. They carry supernumerary features, and these it is that clash so. My disbelief in the Absolute means then disbelief in those other supernumerary features, for I fully believe in the legitimacy of taking moral holidays.

You see by this what I meant when I called pragmatism a mediator and reconciler and said, borrowing the word from Papini,[20] that she 'unstiffens' our theories. She has in fact no prejudices whatever, no obstructive dogmas, no rigid canons of what shall count as proof. She is completely genial. She will entertain any hypothesis, she will consider any evidence. It follows that in the religious field she is at a great advantage both over positivistic empiricism, with its anti-theological bias, and over religious rationalism, with its exclusive interest in the remote, the noble, the simple, and the abstract in the way of conception.

In short, she widens the field of search for God. Rationalism sticks to logic and the empyrean. Empiricism sticks to the external senses. Pragmatism is willing to take anything, to follow either logic or the senses, and to count the humblest and most personal experiences. She will count mystical experiences if they have practical consequences. She will take a

20. [The reference is to the Italian writer Giovanni Papini (1881–1956), who authored a book on pragmatism.]

God who lives in the very dirt of private fact—if that should seem a likely place to find him.

Her only test of probable truth is what works best in the way of leading us, what fits every part of life best and combines with the collectivity of experience's demands, nothing being omitted. If theological ideas should do this, if the notion of God, in particular, should prove to do it, how could pragmatism possibly deny God's existence? She could see no meaning in treating as 'not true' a notion that was pragmatically so successful. What other kind of truth could there be, for her, than all this agreement with concrete reality?

In my last lecture I shall return again to the relations of pragmatism with religion. But you see already how democratic she is. Her manners are as various and flexible, her resources as rich and endless, and her conclusions as friendly as those of mother nature.

The Will to Believe

In the recently published *Life* by Leslie Stephen[1] of his brother, Fitzjames,[2] there is an account of a school to which the latter went when he was a boy. The teacher, a certain Mr. Guest, used to converse with his pupils in this wise: "Gurney, what's the difference between justification and sanctification?—Stephen, prove the Omnipotence of God!" etc. In the midst of our Harvard freethinking and indifference we are prone to imagine that here at your good old orthodox College conversation continues to be somewhat upon this order; and to show you that we at Harvard have not lost all interest in these vital subjects, I have brought with me to-night something like a sermon on justification by faith to read to you—I mean an essay in justification *of* faith, a defence of our right to adopt a believing attitude in religious matters, in spite of the fact that our merely logical intellect may not have been coerced. "The Will to Believe," accordingly, is the title of my paper.

I have long defended to my own students the lawfulness of voluntarily adopted faith; but as soon as they have got well imbued with the logical spirit, they have as a rule refused to admit my contention to be lawful philosophically, even though in point of fact they were personally all the time chock-full of some faith or other themselves. I am all the while, however, so profoundly convinced that my own position is correct, that your invitation has seemed to me a good occasion to make my statements more clear. Perhaps your minds will be more open than those with which I have hitherto had to deal. I will be as little technical as I can, though I must begin by setting up some technical distinctions that will help us in the end.

An Address to the Philosophical Clubs of Yale and Brown Universities. Published in the *New World*, June 1896.

1. [The reference is to the English critic and philosopher Sir Leslie Stephen (1832–1904).—S.M.C.]

2. [The reference is to the English jurist and journalist Sir James Fitzjames Stephen (1829–1894).]

I

Let us give the name of *hypothesis* to anything that may be proposed to our belief; and just as the electricians speak of live and dead wires, let us speak of any hypothesis as either *live* or *dead*. A live hypothesis is one which appeals as a real possibility to him to whom it is proposed. If I ask you to believe in the Mahdi,[3] the notion makes no electric connection with your nature—it refuses to scintillate with any credibility at all. As an hypothesis it is completely dead. To an Arab, however (even if he be not one of the Mahdi's followers), the hypothesis is among the mind's possibilities: it is alive. This shows that deadness and liveness in an hypothesis are not intrinsic properties, but relations to the individual thinker. They are measured by his willingness to act. The maximum of liveness in an hypothesis means willingness to act irrevocably. Practically, that means belief; but there is some believing tendency wherever there is willingness to act at all.

Next, let us call the decision between two hypotheses an *option*. Options may be of several kinds. They may be—1, *living* or *dead*; 2, *forced* or *avoidable*; 3, *momentous* or *trivial*; and for our purposes we may call an option a *genuine* option when it is of the forced, living and momentous kind.

1. A living option is one in which both hypotheses are live ones. If I say to you: "Be a theosophist or be a mahomedan," it is probably a dead option, because for you neither hypothesis is likely to be alive. But if I say "Be an agnostic or be a Christian," it is otherwise: trained as you are, each hypothesis makes some appeal, however small, to your belief.

2. Next, if I say to you: "Choose between going out with your umbrella or without it," I do not offer you a genuine option, for it is not forced. You can easily avoid it by not going out at all. Similarly, if I say "Either love me or hate me," "Either call my theory true or call it false," your option is avoidable.

3. [The redeemer, according to Islam, who will come to bring justice on earth and establish universal Islam.]

You may remain indifferent to me, neither loving nor hating, and you may decline to offer any judgment as to my theory. But if I say "Either accept this truth or go without it," I put on you a forced option, for there is no standing place outside of the alternative. Every dilemma based on a complete logical disjunction, with no possibility of not choosing, is an option of this forced kind.

3. Finally, if I were Dr. Nansen[4] and proposed to you to join my North Pole expedition, your option would be momentous; for this would probably be your only similar opportunity, and your choice now would either exclude you from the North Pole sort of immortality altogether or put at least the chance of it into your hands. He who refuses to embrace a unique opportunity loses the prize as surely as if he tried and failed. *Per contra*,[5] the option is trivial when the opportunity is not unique, when the stake is insignificant, or when the decision is reversible if it later proves unwise. Such trivial options abound in the scientific life. A chemist finds an hypothesis live enough to spend a year in its verification: he believes in it to that extent. But if his experiments prove inconclusive either way, he is quit for his loss of time, no vital harm being done.

It will facilitate our discussion if we keep all these distinctions well in mind.

II

The next matter to consider is the actual psychology of human opinion. When we look at certain facts, it seems as if our passional and volitional nature lay at the root of all our convictions. When we look at others, it seems as if they could do nothing when the intellect had once said its say. Let us take the latter facts up first.

Does it not seem preposterous on the very face of it to talk of our opinions being modifiable at will? Can our will either help or hinder our intellect in its perceptions of truth? Can we, by just willing it, believe that Abraham Lincoln's existence is a myth, and that the portraits of him in *McClure's Magazine* are all of someone else? Can we, by any effort of our will, or by any strength of wish that it were true, believe ourselves well and about when we are roaring with rheumatism in bed, or feel certain that the sum of the two one-dollar bills in our pocket must be a hundred dollars? We can *say* any of these things, but we are absolutely impotent to believe them; and of just such things is the whole fabric of the truths that we do believe in made up—matters of fact, immediate or remote, as Hume said, and relations between ideas, which are either there or not there for us if we see them so, and which if not there cannot be put there by any action of our own.

In Pascal's[6] *Thoughts* there is a celebrated passage known in literature as Pascal's wager. In it he tries to force us into Christianity by reasoning as if our concern with truth resembled our concern with the stakes in a game of chance. Translated freely his words are these: You must either believe or not believe that God is—which will you do? Your human reason cannot say. A game is going on between you and the nature of things which at the day of judgment will bring out either heads or tails. Weigh what your gains and your losses would be if you should stake all you have on heads, or God's existence: If you win in such case, you gain eternal beatitude; if you lose, you lose nothing at all. If there were an infinity of chances, and only one for God in this wager, still you ought to stake your all on God; for though you surely risk a finite loss by this procedure, any finite loss is reasonable, even a certain one is reasonable, if there is but the possibility of infinite gain. Go, then, and take holy water, and have masses said; belief will come and stupefy your scruples—*Cela vous fera croire et vous abêtira*.[7] Why should you not? At bottom, what have you to lose?

You probably feel that when religious faith expresses itself thus, in the language of the gaming-table, it is put to its last trumps. Surely Pascal's own personal belief in masses and holy water had far other springs; and this celebrated page of his is but an argument for others, a last desperate snatch at a weapon against the hardness of the unbelieving heart. We feel that a faith in masses and holy water adopted

4. [The reference is to the Norwegian explorer Fridtjof Nansen (1861–1930).]

5. [In contrast (Latin translations are by William E. Mann).]

6. [The reference is to the French scientist and philosopher Blaise Pascal (1623–1662).]

7. [Even this will make you believe and deaden your acuity.]

willfully after such a mechanical calculation would lack the inner soul of faith's reality; and if we were ourselves in the place of the Deity, we should probably take particular pleasure in cutting off believers of this pattern from their infinite reward. It is evident that unless there be some pre-existing tendency to believe in masses and holy water, the option offered to the will by Pascal is not a living option. Certainly no Turk ever took to masses and holy water on its account; and even to us Protestants these means of salvation seem such foregone impossibilities that Pascal's logic, invoked for them specifically, leaves us unmoved. As well might the Mahdi write to us, saying "I am the Expected One whom God has created in his effulgence. You shall be infinitely happy if you confess me; otherwise you shall be cut off from the light of the sun. Weigh, then, your infinite gain if I am genuine against your finite sacrifice if I am not!" His logic would be that of Pascal; but he would vainly use it on us, for the hypothesis he offers us is dead. No tendency to act on it exists in us to any degree.

The talk of believing by our volition seems, then, from one point of view, simply silly. From another point of view it is worse than silly, it is vile. When one turns to the magnificent edifice of the physical sciences, and sees how it was reared; what thousands of disinterested moral lives of men lie buried in its mere foundations; what patience and postponement, what choking down of preference, what submission to the icy laws of outer fact are wrought into its very stones and mortar; how absolutely impersonal it stands in its vast augustness—then how besotted and contemptible seems every little sentimentalist who comes blowing his voluntary smoke-wreaths, and pretending to decide things from out of his private dream! Can we wonder if those bred in the rugged and manly school of science should feel like spewing such subjectivism out of their mouths? The whole system of loyalties which grow up in the schools of science go dead against its toleration; so that it is only natural that those who have caught the scientific fever should pass over to the opposite extreme, and write sometimes as if the incorruptibly truthful intellect ought positively to prefer bitterness and unacceptableness to the heart in its cup.

> "It fortifies my soul to know
> That, though I perish, Truth is so—"

sings Clough,[8] whilst Huxley[9] exclaims: "My only consolation lies in the reflection that, however bad our posterity may become, so long as they hold by the plain rule of not pretending to believe what they have no reason to believe because it may be to their advantage so to pretend [the word 'pretend' is surely here redundant], they will not have reached the lowest depths of immorality." And that delicious *enfant terrible*[10] Clifford[11] writes: "Belief is desecrated when given to unproved and unquestioned statements, for the solace and private pleasure of the believer . . . . Whoso would deserve well of his fellows in this matter will guard the purity of his belief with a very fanaticism of jealous care, lest at any time it should rest on an unworthy object, and catch a stain which can never be wiped away. . . . If [a] belief has been accepted on insufficient evidence [even though the belief be true, as Clifford on the same page explains], the pleasure is a stolen one. . . . It is sinful, because it is stolen in defiance of our duty to mankind. That duty is to guard ourselves from such beliefs as from a pestilence, which may shortly master our own body and then spread to the rest of the town. . . . It is wrong always, everywhere, and for anyone, to believe anything upon insufficient evidence."

III

All this strikes one as healthy, even when expressed, as by Clifford, with somewhat too much of robustious pathos in the voice. Free-will and simple wishing do seem, in the matter of our credences, to be only fifth wheels to the coach. Yet if anyone should thereupon assume that intellectual insight is what remains after wish and will and sentimental preference have taken wing, or that pure reason is what then settles our

8. [The reference is to the British poet Arthur Hugh Clough (1819–1861).]

9. [The reference is to the English biologist Thomas Henry Huxley (1825–1895), who was a leading exponent of the evolutionary theory of Charles Darwin, regarding whom see Peirce's "The Fixation of Belief," n.11.]

10. [One who is strikingly unorthodox.]

11. [The reference is to William Kingdom Clifford (1845–1879), the British philosopher and mathematician whose essay "The Ethics of Belief" defends the view that it is wrong to believe anything on insufficient evidence.]

opinions, he would fly quite as directly in the teeth of the facts.

It is only our already dead hypotheses that our willing nature is unable to bring to life again. But what has made them dead for us is for the most part a previous action of our willing nature of an antagonistic kind. When I say "willing nature," I do not mean only such deliberate volitions as may have set up habits of belief that we cannot now escape from—I mean all such factors of belief as fear and hope, prejudice and passion, imitation and partisanship, the circumpressure of our caste and set. As a matter of fact we find ourselves believing, we hardly know how or why. Mr. Balfour[12] gives the name of "authority" to all those influences, born of the intellectual climate, that make hypotheses possible or impossible for us, alive or dead. Here in this room, we all of us believe in molecules and the conservation of energy, in democracy and necessary progress, in Protestant Christianity and the duty of fighting for "the doctrine of the immortal Monroe,"[13] all for no reasons worthy of the name. We see into these matters with no more inner clearness, and probably with much less, than any disbeliever in them might possess. His unconventionality would probably have some grounds to show for its conclusions; but for us, not insight, but the *prestige* of the opinions, is what makes the spark shoot from them and light up our sleeping magazines of faith. Our reason is quite satisfied, in nine hundred and ninety-nine cases out of every thousand of us, if it can find a few arguments that will do to recite in case our credulity is criticized by someone else. Our faith is faith in someone else's faith, and in the greatest matters this is most the case. Our belief in truth itself, for instance, that there is a truth, and that our minds and it are made for each other—what is it but a passionate affirmation of desire, in which our social system backs us up? We want to have a truth; we want to believe that our experiments and studies and discussions must put us in a continually better and better position towards it; and on this line we agree to fight out our thinking lives. But if a pyrrhonistic sceptic asks us *how we know* all this, can our logic find a reply? No! Certainly it cannot. It is just one volition against another—we are willing to go in for life upon a trust or assumption which he, for his part, does not care to make.[14]

As a rule we disbelieve all facts and theories for which we have no use. Clifford's cosmic emotions find no use for Christian feelings. Huxley belabors the bishops because there is no use for sacerdotalism in his scheme of life. Newman,[15] on the contrary, goes over to Romanism, and finds all sorts of reasons good for staying there, because a priestly system is for him an organic need and delight. Why do so few "scientists" even look at the evidence for telepathy, so called? Because they think, as a leading biologist, now dead, once said to me, that even if such a thing were true, scientists ought to band together to keep it suppressed and concealed. It would undo the uniformity of Nature and all sorts of other things without which scientists cannot carry on their pursuits. But if this very man had been shown something which as a scientist he might *do* with telepathy, he might not only have examined the evidence, but even have found it good enough. This very law which the logicians would impose upon us—if I may give the name of logicians to those who would rule out our willing nature here—is based on nothing but their own natural wish to exclude all elements for which they, in their professional quality of logicians, can find no use.

Evidently, then, our non-intellectual nature does influence our convictions. There are passional tendencies and volitions which run before and others which come after belief, and it is only the latter that are too late for the fair; and they are not too late when the previous passional work has been already in their own direction. Pascal's argument, instead of being powerless, then seems a regular clincher, and is the last stroke needed to make our faith in masses and holy water complete. The state of things is evidently far from simple; and pure insight and logic, whatever

12. [The reference is to the British prime minister and philosopher Arthur James Balfour (1848–1930).]

13. [The reference is to James Monroe (1758–1831), fifth president of the United States, whose doctrine prohibited European colonization or intervention in the American continents.]

14. Compare the admirable page 310 in S. H. Hodgson's *Time and Space*, London, 1865.

15. [The reference is to the English writer John Henry Newman (1801–1890), who was ordained in the Church of England but later became a cardinal in the Roman Catholic Church.]

they might do ideally, are not the only things that really do produce our creeds.

IV

Our next duty, having recognized this mixed-up state of affairs, is to ask whether it be simply reprehensible and pathological, or whether, on the contrary, we must treat it as a normal element in making up our minds. The thesis I defend is, briefly stated, this: *Our passional nature not only lawfully may, but must, decide an option between propositions, whenever it is a genuine option that cannot by its nature be decided on intellectual grounds; for to say, under such circumstances, "Do not decide, but leave the question open," is itself a passional decision—just like deciding yes or no—and is attended with the same risk of losing the truth.* The thesis thus abstractly expressed will, I trust, soon become quite clear. But I must first indulge in a bit more of preliminary work.

V

It will be observed that for the purposes of this discussion we are on "dogmatic" ground—ground, I mean, which leaves systematic philosophical scepticism altogether out of account. The postulate that there is truth, and that it is the destiny of our minds to attain it, we are deliberately resolving to make, though the sceptic will not make it. We part company with him, therefore, absolutely, at this point. But the faith that truth exists, and that our minds can find it, may be held in two ways. We may talk of the *empiricist* way and of the *absolutist* way of believing in truth. The absolutists in this matter say that we not only can attain to knowing truth, but we can *know when* we have attained to knowing it; whilst the empiricists think that although we may attain it, we cannot infallibly know when. To *know* is one thing, and to know for certain *that* we know is another. One may hold to the first being possible without the second; hence the empiricists and the absolutists, although neither of them is a sceptic in the usual philosophic sense of the term, show very different degrees of dogmatism in their lives.

If we look at the history of opinions, we see that the empiricist tendency has largely prevailed in science, whilst in philosophy the absolutist tendency has had everything its own way. The characteristic sort of happiness, indeed, which philosophies yield has mainly consisted in the conviction felt by each successive school or system that by it bottom-certitude had been attained. "Other philosophies are collections of opinions, mostly false; *my* philosophy gives standing-ground forever"—who does not recognize in this the key-note of every system worthy of the name? A system, to be a system at all, must come as a *closed* system, reversible in this or that detail, perchance, but in its essential features never!

Scholastic orthodoxy, to which one must always go when one wishes to find perfectly clear statement, has beautifully elaborated this absolutist conviction in a doctrine which it calls that of "objective evidence." If, for example, I am unable to doubt that I now exist before you, that two is less than three, or that if all men are mortal then I am mortal too, it is because these things illumine my intellect irresistibly. The final ground of this objective evidence possessed by certain propositions is the *adæquatio intellectûs nostri cum re*.[16] The certitude it brings involves an *aptitudinem ad extorquendum certum assensum*[17] on the part of the truth envisaged, and on the side of the subject a *quietem in cognitione*,[18] when once the object is mentally received, that leaves no possibility of doubt behind; and in the whole transaction nothing operates but the *entitas ipsa*[19] of the object and the *entitas ipsa* of the mind. We slouchy modern thinkers dislike to talk in Latin—indeed, we dislike to talk in set terms at all; but at bottom our own state of mind is very much like this whenever we uncritically abandon ourselves: You believe in objective evidence, and I do. Of some things we feel that we are certain: we know, and we know that we do know. There is something that gives a click inside of us, a bell that strikes twelve, when the hands of our mental clock have swept the dial and meet over the meridian hour. The greatest empiricists among us are only empiricists on reflection: when left to their instincts, they dogmatize like infallible popes. When the Cliffords tell us how sinful it is to be Christians on such "insufficient evi-

16. [Our understanding achieving an equal footing with the thing.]

17. [Aptness for compelling doubt-free assent.]

18. [Cessation of inquiry.]

19. [Entity itself.]

dence," insufficiency is really the last thing they have in mind. For them the evidence is absolutely sufficient, only it makes the other way. They believe so completely in an anti-Christian order of the universe that there is no living option: Christianity is a dead hypothesis from the start.

VI

But now, since we are all such absolutists by instinct, what in our quality of students of philosophy ought we to do about the fact? Shall we espouse and indorse it? Or shall we treat it as a weakness of our nature from which we must free ourselves, if we can?

I sincerely believe that the latter course is the only one we can follow as reflective men. Objective evidence and certitude are doubtless very fine ideals to play with, but where on this moonlit and dream-visited planet are they found? I am, therefore, myself a complete empiricist so far as my theory of human knowledge goes. I live, to be sure, by the practical faith that we must go on experiencing and thinking over our experience, for only thus can our opinions grow more true; but to hold any one of them—I absolutely do not care which—as if it never could be re-interpretable or corrigible, I believe to be a tremendously mistaken attitude, and I think that the whole history of philosophy will bear me out. There is but one indefectibly certain truth, and that is the truth that pyrrhonistic scepticism itself leaves standing—the truth that the present phenomenon of consciousness exists. That, however, is the bare starting-point of knowledge, the mere admission of a stuff to be philosophized-about. The various philosophies are but so many attempts at expressing what this stuff really is. And if we repair to our libraries what disagreement do we discover! Where is a certainly true answer found? Apart from abstract propositions of comparison (such as two and two are the same as four), propositions which tell us nothing by themselves about concrete reality, we find no proposition ever regarded by anyone as evidently certain that has not either been called a falsehood, or at least had its truth sincerely questioned by someone else. The transcending of the axioms of geometry, not in play but in earnest, by certain of our contemporaries (As Zöllner[20] and Charles H. Hinton[21]), and the rejection of the whole aristotelian logic by the Hegelians, are striking instances in point.

No concrete test of what is really true has ever been agreed upon. Some make the criterion external to the moment of perception, putting it either in revelation, the *consensus gentium*,[22] the instincts of the heart, or the systematized experience of the race. Others make the perceptive moment its own test—Descartes, for instance, with his clear and distinct ideas guaranteed by the veracity of God; Reid[23] with his "common-sense"; and Kant with his forms of synthetic judgment *a priori*. The inconceivability of the opposite; the capacity to be verified by sense; the possession of complete organic unity or self-relation, realized when a thing is its own other—are standards which, in turn, have been used. The much lauded objective evidence is never triumphantly there; it is a mere aspiration or *Grenzbegriff*,[24] marking the infinitely remote ideal of our thinking life. To claim that certain truths now possess it, is simply to say that when you think them true and they *are* true, then their evidence is objective, otherwise it is not. But practically one's conviction that the evidence one goes by is of the real objective brand, is only one more subjective opinion added to the lot. For what a contradictory array of opinions have objective evidence and absolute certitude been claimed! The world is rational through and through—its existence is an ultimate brute fact; there is a personal God—a personal God is inconceivable; there is an extra-mental physical world immediately known—the mind can only know its own ideas; a moral imperative exists—obligation is only the resultant of desires; a permanent spiritual principle is in everyone—there are only shifting states of mind; there is an endless chain of causes—there is an absolute first cause; an eternal necessity—a freedom; a purpose—no purpose; a primal One—a primal Many; a universal continuity—an essential discontinuity in things; an

20. [The reference is to the German astrophysicist Johann Carl Friedrich Zöllner (1834–1882).]

21. [The reference is to the British mathematician Charles Howard Hinton (1853–1907).]

22. [Popular opinion.]

23. [The reference is to the Scottish philosopher Thomas Reid (1710–1796).]

24. [Limiting concept.]

infinity—no infinity. There is this—there is that; there is indeed nothing which someone has not thought absolutely true, whilst his neighbor deemed it absolutely false; and not an absolutist among them seems ever to have considered that the trouble may all the time be essential, and that the intellect, even with truth directly in its grasp, may have no infallible signal for knowing whether it be truth or no. When, indeed, one remembers that the most striking practical application to life of the doctrine of objective certitude has been the conscientious labors of the Holy Office of the Inquisition, one feels less tempted than ever to lend the doctrine a respectful ear.

But please observe, now, that when as empiricists we give up the doctrine of objective certitude, we do not thereby give up the quest or hope of truth itself. We still pin our faith on its existence, and still believe that we gain an ever better position towards it by systematically continuing to roll up experiences and think. Our great difference from the scholastic lies in the way we face. The strength of his system lies in the principles, the origin, the *terminus a quo*[25] of his thought; for us the strength is in the outcome, the upshot, the *terminus ad quem*.[26] Not where it comes from but what it leads to is to decide. It matters not to an empiricist from what quarter an hypothesis may come to him: he may have acquired it by fair means or by foul; passion may have whispered or accident suggested it; but if the total drift of thinking continues to confirm it, that is what he means by its being true.

VII

One more point, small but important, and our preliminaries are done. There are two ways of looking at our duty in the matter of opinion—ways entirely different, and yet ways about whose difference the theory of knowledge seems hitherto to have shown very little concern. *We must know the truth*; and *we must avoid error*—these are our first and great commandments as would-be knowers; but they are not two ways of stating an identical commandment, they are two separable laws. Although it may indeed happen that when we believe the truth A, we escape as an incidental consequence from believing the falsehood *B*, it hardly ever happens that by merely disbelieving *B* we necessarily believe A. We may in escaping *B* fall into believing other falsehoods, *C* or *D*, just as bad as *B*; or we may escape *B* by not believing anything at all, not even A.

Believe truth! Shun error!—these, we see, are two materially different laws; and by choosing between them we may end by colouring differently our whole intellectual life. We may regard the chase for truth as paramount, and the avoidance of error as secondary; or we may, on the other hand, treat the avoidance of error as more imperative, and let truth take its chance. Clifford, in the instructive passage which I have quoted, exhorts us to the latter course. Believe nothing, he tells us, keep your mind in suspense forever, rather than by closing it on insufficient evidence incur the awful risk of believing lies. You, on the other hand, may think that the risk of being in error is a very small matter when compared with the blessings of real knowledge, and be ready to be duped many times in your investigation rather than postpone indefinitely the chance of guessing true. I myself find it impossible to go with Clifford. We must remember that these feelings of our duty about either truth or error are in any case only expressions of our passional life. Biologically considered, our minds are as ready to grind out falsehood as veracity, and he who says "Better go without belief forever than believe a lie!" merely shows his own preponderant private horror of becoming a dupe. He may be critical of many of his desires and fears, but this fear he slavishly obeys. He cannot imagine anyone questioning its binding force. For my own part, I have also a horror of being duped; but I can believe that worse things than being duped may happen to a man in this world: so Clifford's exhortation has to my ears a thoroughly fantastic sound. It is like a general informing his soldiers that it is better to keep out of battle forever than to risk a single wound. Not so are victories either over enemies or over nature gained. Our errors are surely not such awfully solemn things. In a world where we are so certain to incur them in spite of all our caution, a certain lightness of heart seems healthier than this excessive nervousness on their behalf. At any rate, it seems the fittest thing for the empiricist philosopher.

25. [Departure point.]
26. [Destination point.]

VIII

And now, after all this introduction, let us go straight at our question. I have said, and now repeat it, that not only as a matter of fact do we find our passional nature influencing us in our opinions, but that there are some options between opinions in which this influence must be regarded both as an inevitable and as a lawful determinant of our choice.

I fear here that some of you my hearers will begin to scent danger, and lend an inhospitable ear. Two first steps of passion you have indeed had to admit as necessary—we must think so as to avoid dupery, and we must think so as to gain truth; but the surest path to those ideal consummations, you will probably consider, is from now onwards to take no farther passional step.

Well, of course I agree as far as the facts will allow. Wherever the option between losing truth and gaining it is not momentous, we can throw the chance of *gaining truth* away, and at any rate save ourselves from any chance of *believing falsehood*, by not making up our minds at all till objective evidence has come. In scientific questions, this is almost always the case; and even in human affairs in general, the need of acting is seldom so urgent that a false belief to act on is better than no belief at all. Law courts, indeed, have to decide on the best evidence attainable for the moment, because a judge's duty is to make law as well as to ascertain it, and (as a learned judge once said to me) few cases are worth spending much time over: the great thing is to have them decided on *any* acceptable principle, and got out of the way. But in our dealings with objective nature we obviously are recorders, not makers, of the truth; and decisions for the mere sake of deciding promptly and getting on to the next business would be wholly out of place. Throughout the breadth of physical nature facts are what they are quite independently of us, and seldom is there any such hurry about them that the risks of being duped by believing a premature theory need be faced. The questions here are always trivial options, the hypotheses are hardly living (at any rate not living for us spectators), the choice between believing truth or falsehood is seldom forced. The attitude of sceptical balance is therefore the absolutely wise one if we would escape mistakes. What difference, indeed, does it make to most of us whether we have or have not a theory of the Röntgen[27] rays, whether we believe or not in mind-stuff, or have a conviction about the causality of conscious states? It makes no difference. Such options are not forced on us. On every account it is better not to make them, but still keep weighing reasons *pro et contra*[28] with an indifferent hand.

I speak, of course, here of the purely judging mind. For purposes of discovery such indifference is to be less highly recommended, and science would be far less advanced than she is if the passionate desires of individuals to get their own faiths confirmed had been kept out of the game. See for example the sagacity which Spencer[29] and Weismann[30] now display. On the other hand, if you want an absolute duffer in an investigation, you must, after all, take the man who has no interest whatever in its results: he is the warranted incapable, the positive fool. The most useful investigator, because the most sensitive observer, is always he whose eager interest in one side of the question is balanced by an equally keen nervousness lest he become deceived.[31] Science has organized this nervousness into a regular *technique*, her so-called method of verification; and she has fallen so deeply in love with the method that one may even say she has ceased to care for truth by itself at all. It is only truth as technically verified that interests her. The truth of truths might come in merely affirmative form, and she would decline to touch it. Such truth as that, she might repeat with Clifford, would be stolen in defiance of her duty to mankind. Human passions, however, are stronger than technical rules. "Le coeur a ses raisons," as Pascal says, "que la raison ne connaît point";[32] and however indifferent to all but the bare rules of the game the umpire, the abstract intellect, may be, the concrete players who furnish him the

27. [The reference is to the German physicist Wilhelm Conrad Röntgen, discover of the X-ray, for which he received in 1901 the first Nobel Prize in Physics.]

28. [For and against.]

29. [The reference is to the English philosopher Herbert Spencer (1820–1903), a leading exponent of the theory of evolution.]

30. [The reference is to the German biologist August Weismann (1834–1914).]

31. Compare Wilfrid Ward's essay, "The Wish to Believe," in his *Witness to the Unseen* (Macmillan & Co., 1893).

32. [The heart has its reasons, which reason does not know.]

materials to judge of are usually, each one of them, in love with some pet "live hypothesis" of his own. Let us agree, however, that wherever there is no forced option, the dispassionately judicial intellect with no pet hypothesis, saving us, as it does, from dupery at any rate, ought to be our ideal.

The question next arises: Are there not somewhere forced options in our speculative questions, and can we (as men who may be interested at least as much in positively gaining truth as in merely escaping dupery) always wait with impunity till the coercive evidence shall have arrived? It seems *a priori* improbable that the truth should be so nicely adjusted to our needs and powers as that. In the great boarding-house of nature, the cakes and the butter and the syrup seldom come out so even and leave the plates so clean. Indeed, we should view them with scientific suspicion if they did.

IX

Moral questions immediately present themselves as questions whose solution cannot wait for sensible proof. A moral question is a question not of what sensibly exists, but of what is good, or would be good if it did exist. Science can tell us what exists; but to compare the *worths*, both of what exists and of what does not exist, we must consult not science, but what Pascal calls our heart. Science herself consults her heart when she lays it down that the infinite ascertainment of fact and correction of false belief are the supreme goods for man. Challenge the statement and science can only repeat it oracularly, or else prove it by showing that such ascertainment and correction bring man all sorts of other goods which man's heart in turn declares. The question of having moral beliefs at all or not having them is decided by our will. Are our moral preferences true or false, or are they only odd biological phenomena, making things good or bad for *us*, but in themselves indifferent? How can your pure intellect decide? If your heart does not *want* a world of moral reality, your head will assuredly never make you believe in one. Mephistophelian scepticism, indeed, will satisfy the head's play-instincts much better than any rigorous idealism can. Some men (even at the student age) are so naturally cool-hearted that the moralistic hypothesis never has for them any pungent life, and in their supercilious presence the hot young moralist always feels strangely ill at ease. The appearance of knowingness is on their side, of *naiveté* and gullibility on his. Yet, in the inarticulate heart of him, he clings to it that he is not a dupe, and that there is a realm in which (as Emerson[33] says) all their wit and intellectual superiority is no better than the cunning of a fox. Moral scepticism can no more be refuted or proved by logic than intellectual scepticism can. When we stick to it that there *is* truth (be it of either kind), we do so with our whole nature, and resolve to stand or fall by the results. The sceptic with his whole nature adopts the doubting attitude; but which of us is the wiser, Omniscience only knows.

Turn now from these wide questions of good to a certain class of questions of fact, questions concerning personal relations, states of mind between one man and another. *Do you like me or not?*—for example. Whether you do or not depends, in countless instances, on whether I meet you half-way, am willing to assume that you must like me, and show you trust and expectation. The previous faith on my part in your liking's existence is in such cases what makes your liking come. But if I stand aloof, and refuse to budge an inch until I have objective evidence, until you shall have done something apt, as the absolutists say, *ad extorquendum assensum meum*,[34] ten to one your liking never comes. How many women's hearts are vanquished by the mere sanguine insistence of some man that they *must* love him! he will not consent to the hypothesis that they cannot. The desire for a certain kind of truth here brings about that special truth's existence; and so it is in innumerable cases of other sorts. Who gains promotions, boons, appointments, but the man in whose life they are seen to play the part of live hypotheses, who discounts them, sacrifices other things for their sake before they have come, and takes risks for them in advance? His faith acts on the powers above him as a claim, and creates its own verification.

A social organism of any sort whatever, large or small, is what it is because each member proceeds to his own duty with a trust that the other members will simultaneously do theirs. Wherever a desired

33. [The reference is to the American poet and essayist Ralph Waldo Emerson (1803–1882).]

34. [For compelling my assent.]

result is achieved by the co-operation of many independent persons, its existence as a fact is a pure consequence of the precursive faith in one another of those immediately concerned. A government, an army, a commercial system, a ship, a college, an athletic team, all exist on this condition, without which not only is nothing achieved, but nothing is even attempted. A whole train of passengers (individually brave enough) will be looted by a few highwaymen, simply because the latter can count on one another, while each passenger fears that if he makes a movement of resistance, he will be shot before anyone else backs him up. If we believed that the whole car-full would rise at once with us, we should each severally rise, and train-robbing would never even be attempted. There are, then, cases where a fact cannot come at all unless a preliminary faith exists in it coming. *And where faith in a fact can help create the fact*, that would be an insane logic which should say that faith running ahead of scientific evidence is the "lowest kind of immorality" into which a thinking being can fall. Yet such is the logic by which our scientific absolutists pretend to regulate our lives!

X

In truths dependent on our personal action, then, faith based on desire is certainly a lawful and possibly an indispensable thing.

But now, it will be said, these are all childish human cases, and have nothing to do with great cosmical matter, like the question of religious faith. Let us then pass on to that. Religions differ so much in their accidents that in discussing the religious question we must make it very generic and broad. What then do we now mean by the religious hypothesis? Science says things are; morality says some things are better than other things; and religion says essentially two things.

First, she says that the best things are the more eternal things, the overlapping things, the things in the universe that throw the last stone, so to speak, and say the final word. "Perfection is eternal"—this phrase of Charles Secrétan[35] seems a good way of putting this first affirmation of religion, an affirmation which obviously cannot yet be verified scientifically at all.

35. [The reference is to the Swiss philosopher Charles Secrétan (1815–1895).]

The second affirmation of religion is that we are better off even now if we believe her first affirmation to be true.

Now let us consider what the logical elements of this situation are *in case the religious hypothesis in both its branches be really true*. (Of course, we must admit that possibility at the outset. If we are to discuss the question at all, it must involve a living option. If for any of you religion be a hypothesis that cannot, by any living possibility be true, then you need go no farther. I speak to the "saving remnant" alone.) So proceeding, we see, first, that religion offers itself as *a momentous* option. We are supposed to gain, even now, by our belief, and to lose by our non-belief, a certain vital good. Secondly, religion is a *forced* option, so far as that good goes. We cannot escape the issue by remaining sceptical and waiting for more light, because, although we do avoid error in that way *if religion be untrue*, we lose the good, *if it be true*, just as certainly as if we positively chose to disbelieve. It is as if a man should hesitate indefinitely to ask a certain woman to marry him because he was not perfectly sure that she would prove an angel after he brought her home. Would he not cut himself off from that particular angel-possibility as decisively as if he went and married someone else? Scepticism, then, is not avoidance of option; it is option of a certain particular kind of risk. *Better risk loss of truth than chance of error*—that is your faith-vetoer's exact position. He is actively playing his stake as much as the believer is; he is backing the field against the religious hypothesis, just as the believer is backing the religious hypothesis against the field. To preach scepticism to us as a duty until "sufficient evidence" for religion be found, is tantamount therefore to telling us, when in presence of the religious hypothesis, that to yield to our fear of its being error is wiser and better than to yield to our hope that it may be true. It is not intellect against all passions, then; it is only intellect with one passion laying down its law. And by what, forsooth, is the supreme wisdom of this passion warranted? Dupery for dupery, what proof is there that dupery through hope is so much worse than dupery through fear? I, for one, can see no proof; and I simply refuse obedience to the scientist's command to imitate his kind of option, in a case where my own stake is important enough to give me the right to choose my own form of risk. If religion be true and the evidence for it be still insufficient, I do not wish, by putting your extinguisher upon my nature (which feels to me as if it had after all some business in this matter), to forfeit my sole chance in life of getting upon the winning side—that chance depending, of course, on my willingness to run the risk of acting as if my passional need of taking the world religiously might be prophetic and right.

All this is on the supposition that it really may be prophetic and right, and that, even to us who are discussing the matter, religion is a live hypothesis which may be true. Now to most of us religion comes in a still farther way that makes a veto on our active faith even more illogical. The more perfect and more eternal aspect of the universe is represented in our religions as having personal form. The universe is no longer a mere *It* to us, but a *Thou*, if we are religious; and any relation that may be possible from person to person might be possible here. For instance, although in one sense we are passive portions of the universe, in another we show a curious autonomy, as if we were small active centers on our own account. We feel, too, as if the appeal of religion to us were made to our own active good-will, as if evidence might be forever withheld from us unless we met the hypothesis half-way. To take a trivial illustration: just as a man who in a company of gentlemen made no advances, asked a warrant for every concession, and believed no one's word without proof, would cut himself off by such churlishness from all the social rewards that a more trusting spirit would earn—so here, one who should shut himself up in snarling logicality and try to make the gods extort his recognition willy-nilly, or not get it at all, might cut himself off forever from his only opportunity of making the gods' acquaintance. This feeling, forced on us we know not whence, that by obstinately believing that there are gods (although not to do so would be so easy both for our logic and our life) we are doing the universe the deepest service we can, seems part of the living essence of the religious hypothesis. If the hypothesis *were* true in all its parts, including this one, then pure intellectualism, with its veto on our making willing advances, would be an absurdity; and some participation of our sympathetic nature would be logically required. I, therefore, for one, cannot see my way to accepting the agnostic rules for truth-seeking, or willfully agree to keep my willing nature out of the game. I cannot do so for this plain reason, that *a rule of thinking which would absolutely prevent me from acknowledging certain kinds of truth if those kinds of truth were really there, would be an irrational rule.* That for me is the long and short of the formal logic of the situation, no matter what the kinds of truth might materially be.

I confess I do not see how this logic can be escaped. But sad experience makes me fear that some of you may still shrink from radically saying with me, *in abstracto*, that we have the right to believe at our own risk any hypothesis that is live enough to tempt our will. I suspect, however, that if this is so, it is because you have got away from the abstract logical point of view altogether, and are thinking (perhaps without realizing it) of some particular religious hypothesis which for you is dead. The freedom to "believe what we will" you apply to the case of some patent superstition; and the faith you think of is the faith defined by the schoolboy when he said, "Faith is when you believe something that you know ain't true." I can only repeat that this is misapprehension. *In concreto*,[36] the freedom to believe can only cover living options which the intellect of the individual cannot by itself resolve; and living options never seem absurdities to him who has them to consider. When I look at the religious question as it really puts itself to concrete men, and when I think of all the possibilities which both practically and theoretically it involves, then this command that we shall put a stopper on our heart, instincts and courage, and *wait*—acting of course meanwhile more or less as if religion were *not* true[37]—

36. [In practice.]

37. Since belief is measured by action, he who forbids us to believe religion to be true, necessarily also forbids us to act as we should if we did believe it to be true. The whole defence of religious faith hangs upon action. If the action required or inspired by the religious hypothesis is in no way different from that dictated by the naturalistic hypothesis, then religious faith is a pure superfluity, better pruned away, and controversy about its legitimacy is a piece of idle trifling, unworthy of serious minds. I myself believe, of course, that the religious hypothesis gives to the world an expression which specifically determines our reactions, and makes them in a large part unlike what they might be on a purely naturalistic scheme of belief.

till doomsday, or till such time as our intellect and senses working together may have raked in evidence enough—this command, I say, seems to me the queerest idol ever manufactured in the philosophic cave. Were we scholastic absolutists, there might be more excuse. If we had an infallible intellect with its objective certitudes, we might feel ourselves disloyal to such a perfect organ of knowledge in not trusting to it exclusively, in not waiting for its releasing word. But if we are empiricists, if we believe that no bell in us tolls to let us know for certain when truth is in our grasp, then it seems a piece of idle fantasticality to preach so solemnly our duty of waiting for the bell. Indeed we *may* wait if we will—I hope you do not think that I am denying that—but if we do so, we do so at our peril as much as if we believed. In either case we *act*, taking our life in our hands. No one of us ought to issue vetoes to the other, nor should we bandy words of abuse. We ought, on the contrary, delicately and profoundly to respect one another's mental freedom—then only shall we bring about the intellectual republic; then only shall we have that spirit of inner tolerance without which all our outer tolerance is soulless, and which is empiricism's glory; then only shall we live and let live, in speculative as well as in practical things.

I began by a reference to Fitzjames Stephen; let me end by a quotation from him. "What do you think of yourself? What do you think of the world? . . . These are questions with which all must deal as it seems good to them. They are riddles of the Sphinx, and in some way or other we must deal with them. . . . In all important transactions of life we have to take a leap in the dark. . . . If we decide to leave the riddles unanswered, that is a choice. If we waver in our answer, that too is a choice; but whatever choice we make, we make it at our peril. If a man chooses to turn his back altogether on God and the future, no one can prevent him. No one can show beyond reasonable doubt that he is mistaken. If a man thinks otherwise, and acts as he thinks, I do not see how any one can prove that *he* is mistaken. Each must act as he thinks best, and if he is wrong so much the worse for him. We stand on a mountain pass in the midst of whirling snow and blinding mist, through which we get glimpses now and then of paths which may be deceptive. If we stand still, we shall be frozen to death. If we take the wrong road, we shall be dashed to pieces. We do not certainly know whether there is any right one. What must we do? 'Be strong and of a good courage.' Act for the best, hope for the best, and take what comes. . . . If death ends all, we cannot meet death better."[38]

38. *Liberty, Equality, Fraternity*, p. 353, 2d edition, London, 1874.

Bertrand Russell

Bertrand Russell (1872–1970) was one of the leading thinkers of the twentieth century. He was born into a prominent English family and inherited the title of Earl Russell from his brother. John Stuart Mill was his godfather. Russell received degrees in mathematics and philosophy from Cambridge University in 1893–1894, returning to Cambridge shortly afterward. He took up the project of showing that mathematics could be derived from logic; to this end, he collaborated with Alfred North Whitehead on the development of modern symbolic logic, which was an achievement of signal importance. At Cambridge, Russell was also closely associated with G. E. Moore and Ludwig Wittgenstein, themselves major twentieth-century philosophers.

Russell did not confine his activities to the academy. He was on familiar terms with many of the leading intellectuals and writers of his day, including D. H. Lawrence, Joseph Conrad, Virginia Woolf, and T. S. Eliot (who wrote a poem about him). Russell spent the period from 1938 to 1944 in the United States, where his liberal views about marriage and religion aroused controversy. Russell was an important and courageous public figure, who was willing to go to jail for what he believed in. He was tried and convicted for an article he wrote in opposition to Britain's role in World War I, and at age 88 he was arrested for his role in civil disobedience to promote nuclear disarmament.

Russell's philosophy combined the resources of modern logic with a staunch commitment to empiricism (the view that all knowledge of the world is derived from sense experience). Thus, Russell did much to set the pattern for the way philosophy has been done in English-speaking countries, and as it is practiced today. His contributions were honored with the award of a Nobel Prize for Literature in 1950.

Some of Russell's most important philosophical works are *The Philosophy of Leibniz* (1900), *The Principles of Mathematics* (1903), *Principia Mathematica* with Whitehead (1910–1913), *The Problems of Philosophy* (1912), *Introduction to Mathematical Philosophy* (1919), *The Analysis of Mind* (1921), *The Analysis of Matter* (1927), *An Inquiry into Meaning and Truth* (1940), and *Human Knowledge, Its Scope and Limits* (1948).

The Problems of Philosophy is an introduction to some central questions about the nature of knowledge and reality. In this book Russell undertakes to set out what the issues are, outlining his own views simply and briefly. (He pursues these matters much more fully in his other writings.) Russell's starting point is the natural supposition that what is real are physical objects, and that we gain knowledge about these things by perceiving them. This outlook is not wrong, but it needs to be examined and spelled out with care. For example, depending on where we are, the shape of a coin may look oval to you and circular to me. So, strictly speaking, you and I are experiencing different things: your experience confronts you with something oval, while my experience confronts me with something circular. Since one and the same thing can't be both oval and circular, the items we experience must be different from one another, and different from the coin as well. Russell calls these items "sense-data."

If experience informs us directly about our own sense-data, and not about physical objects, why should we suppose that there are any physical objects at all? Why not say that all there is, and all we know about, are our sense-data? A view like this one, which Russell calls "idealism," was adopted by Berkeley in the eighteenth century, and versions of idealism were prevalent in Britain when Russell came upon the philosophical scene. Russell presents some telling criticisms of the idealists' position. He also makes the positive point that our sense-data exhibit various patterns and regularities. A good explanation of the order in our sense-data is that they are caused by physical objects that exist independently of them. Russell's overthrow of idealism was a turning point in twentieth-century philosophy.

Although Russell maintains that we can have knowledge pertaining to physical objects as well as to sense-data, he distinguishes two different sorts of knowledge, namely *knowledge by acquaintance* and *knowledge by description*. The former is knowledge of *things*, the latter is knowledge of *truths*. All knowledge by description depends on or is derived from knowledge by acquaintance. Russell holds that we may know sense-data by acquaintance, since we experience them directly, but we know physical objects only by description. The scope of our acquaintance not only determines what we can know; it also sets the limits of what we can say or think. Russell writes, "Every proposition which we can understand must be composed wholly of constituents with which we are acquainted."

For Russell, philosophy begins with our ordinary beliefs and tries to clear away vagueness and confusion. Whatever insight we achieve is obtained by thinking as closely, precisely, and rigorously as we can, making use of the resources of logic and science. This conception of philosophy is itself among Russell's most significant and lasting contributions.

• • •

An excellent introduction is A. J. Ayer, *Russell* (New York: Viking Press, 1972). At a more advanced level are A. J. Ayer, *Russell and Moore: The Analytical Heritage* (Cambridge, Mass.: Harvard University Press, 1971); David Pears, *Bertrand Russell and the British Tradition in Philosophy* (New York: Random House, 1967); R. M. Sainsbury, *Russell* (London: Routledge and Kegan Paul, 1979); and Peter Hylton, *Russell, Idealism, and the Emergence of Analytical Philosophy* (New York: Oxford University Press, 1990). An important contemporary critique of the theory of sense-data is J. L. Austin, *Sense and Sensibilia* (excerpted in this volume).

Jonathan Vogel

The Problems of Philosophy

CHAPTER I

Appearance and Reality

Is there any knowledge in the world which is so certain that no reasonable man could doubt it? This question, which at first sight might not seem difficult, is really one of the most difficult that can be asked. When we have realized the obstacles in the way of a straightforward and confident answer, we shall be well launched on the study of philosophy—for philosophy is merely the attempt to answer such ultimate questions, not carelessly and dogmatically, as we do in ordinary life and even in the sciences, but critically, after exploring all that makes such questions puzzling, and after realizing all the vagueness and confusion that underlie our ordinary ideas.

In daily life, we assume as certain many things which, on a closer scrutiny, are found to be so full of apparent contradictions that only a great amount of thought enables us to know what it is that we really may believe. In the search for certainty, it is natural to begin with our present experiences, and in some sense, no doubt, knowledge is to be derived from them. But any statement as to what it is that our immediate experiences make us know is very likely to be wrong. It seems to me that I am now sitting in a chair, at a table of a certain shape, on which I see sheets of paper with writing or print. By turning my head I see out of the window buildings and clouds and the sun. I believe that the sun is about ninety-three million miles from the earth; that it is a hot globe many times bigger than the earth; that, owing to the earth's rotation, it rises every morning, and will continue to do so for an indefinite time in the future. I believe that, if any other normal person comes into my room, he will see the same chairs and tables and books and papers as I see, and that the table which I see is the same as the table which I feel pressing against my arm. All this seems to be so evident as to be hardly worth stating, except in answer to a man who doubts whether I know anything. Yet all this may be reasonably doubted, and all of it requires much careful discussion before we can be sure that we have stated it in a form that is wholly true.

To make our difficulties plain, let us concentrate attention on the table. To the eye it is oblong, brown and shiny, to the touch it is smooth and cool and hard; when I tap it, it gives out a wooden sound. Any one else who sees and feels and hears the table will agree with this description, so that it might seem as if no difficulty would arise; but as soon as we try to be more precise our troubles begin. Although I believe that the table is 'really' of the same colour all over, the parts that reflect the light look much brighter than the other parts, and some parts look white because of reflected light. I know that, if I move, the parts that reflect the light will be different, so that the apparent distribution of colours on the table will change. It follows that if several people are looking at the table at the same moment, no two of them will see exactly the same distribution of colours, because no two can see it from exactly the same point of view, and any change in the point of view makes some change in the way the light is reflected.

For most practical purposes these differences are unimportant, but to the painter they are all-important: the painter has to unlearn the habit of thinking that things seem to have the colour which common sense says they 'really' have, and to learn the habit of seeing things as they appear. Here we have already the beginning of one of the distinctions that cause most trouble in philosophy—the distinction between 'appearance' and 'reality', between what things seem to be and what they are. The painter wants to know what things seem to be, the practical man and the philosopher want to know what they are; but the philosopher's wish to know this is stronger than the practical man's, and is more troubled by knowledge as to the difficulties of answering the question.

To return to the table. It is evident from what we

Reprinted from *The Problems of Philosophy* by Bertrand Russell (1912) by permission of Oxford University Press.

have found, that there is no colour which preeminently appears to be *the* colour of the table, or even of any one particular part of the table—it appears to be of different colours from different points of view, and there is no reason for regarding some of these as more really its colour than others. And we know that even from a given point of view the colour will seem different by artificial light, or to a colour-blind man, or to a man wearing blue spectacles, while in the dark there will be no colour at all, though to touch and hearing the table will be unchanged. This colour is not something which is inherent in the table, but something depending upon the table and the spectator and the way the light falls on the table. When, in ordinary life, we speak of *the* colour of the table, we only mean the sort of colour which it will seem to have to a normal spectator from an ordinary point of view under usual conditions of light. But the other colours which appear under other conditions have just as good a right to be considered real; and therefore, to avoid favouritism, we are compelled to deny that, in itself, the table has any one particular colour.

The same thing applies to the texture. With the naked eye one can see the grain, but otherwise the table looks smooth and even. If we looked at it through a microscope, we should see roughnesses and hills and valleys, and all sorts of differences that are imperceptible to the naked eye. Which of these is the 'real' table? We are naturally tempted to say that what we see through the microscope is more real, but that in turn would be changed by a still more powerful microscope. If, then, we cannot trust what we see with the naked eye, why should we trust what we see through a microscope? Thus, again, the confidence in our senses with which we began deserts us.

The *shape* of the table is no better. We are all in the habit of judging as to the 'real' shapes of things, and we do this so unreflectingly that we come to think we actually see the real shapes. But, in fact, as we all have to learn if we try to draw, a given thing looks different in shape from every different point of view. If our table is 'really' rectangular, it will look, from almost all points of view, as if it had two acute angles and two obtuse angles. If opposite sides are parallel, they will look as if they converged to a point away from the spectator; if they are of equal length, they will look as if the nearer side were longer. All these things are not commonly noticed in looking at a table, because experience has taught us to construct the 'real' shape from the apparent shape, and the 'real' shape is what interests us as practical men. But the 'real' shape is not what we see; it is something inferred from what we see. And what we see is constantly changing in shape as we move about the room; so that here again the senses seem not to give us the truth about the table itself, but only about the appearance of the table.

Similar difficulties arise when we consider the sense of touch. It is true that the table always gives us a sensation of hardness, and we feel that it resists pressure. But the sensation we obtain depends upon how hard we press the table and also upon what part of the body we press with; thus the various sensations due to various pressures or various parts of the body cannot be supposed to reveal *directly* any definite property of the table, but at most to be *signs* of some property which perhaps *causes* all the sensations, but is not actually apparent in any of them. And the same applies still more obviously to the sounds which can be elicited by rapping the table.

Thus it becomes evident that the real table, if there is one, is not the same as what we immediately experience by sight or touch or hearing. The real table, if there is one, is not *immediately* known to us at all, but must be an inference from what is immediately known. Hence, two very difficult questions at once arise; namely, (1) Is there a real table at all? (2) If so, what sort of object can it be?

It will help us in considering these questions to have a few simple terms of which the meaning is definite and clear. Let us give the name of 'sense-data' to the things that are immediately known in sensation: such things as colours, sounds, smells, hardnesses, roughnesses, and so on. We shall give the name 'sensation' to the experience of being immediately aware of these things. Thus, whenever we see a colour, we have a sensation *of* colour, but the colour itself is a sense-datum, not a sensation. The colour is that *of* which we are immediately aware, and the awareness itself is the sensation. It is plain that if we are to know anything about the table, it must be by means of the sense-data—brown colour, oblong shape, smoothness, etc.—which we associate with the table; but, for the reasons which have been given, we cannot say that the table *is* the sense-data, or even that the sense-data are directly properties of the table.

Thus a problem arises as to the relation of the sense-data to the real table, supposing there is such a thing.

The real table, if it exists, we will call a 'physical object'. Thus we have to consider the relation of sense-data to physical objects. The collection of all physical objects is called 'matter'. Thus our two questions may be re-stated as follows: (1) Is there any such thing as matter? (2) If so, what is its nature?

The philosopher who first brought prominently forward the reasons for regarding the immediate objects of our senses as not existing independently of us was Bishop Berkeley (1685–1753). His *Three Dialogues between Hylas and Philonous, in Opposition to Sceptics and Atheists,* undertake to prove that there is no such thing as matter at all, and that the world consists of nothing but minds and their ideas. Hylas has hitherto believed in matter, but he is no match for Philonous, who mercilessly drives him into contradictions and paradoxes, and makes his own denial of matter seem, in the end, as if it were almost common sense. The arguments employed are of very different value: some are important and sound, others are confused or quibbling. But Berkeley retains the merit of having shown that the existence of matter is capable of being denied without absurdity, and that if there are any things that exist independently of us they cannot be the immediate objects of our sensations.

There are two different questions involved when we ask whether matter exists, and it is important to keep them clear. We commonly mean by 'matter' something which is opposed to 'mind', something which we think of as occupying space and as radically incapable of any sort of thought or consciousness. It is chiefly in this sense that Berkeley denies matter; that is to say, he does not deny that the sense-data which we commonly take as signs of the existence of the table are really signs of the existence of *something* independent of us, but he does deny that this something is non-mental, that it is neither mind nor ideas entertained by some mind. He admits that there must be something which continues to exist when we go out of the room or shut our eyes, and that what we call seeing the table does really give us reason for believing in something which persists even when we are not seeing it. But he thinks that this something cannot be radically different in nature from what we see, and cannot be independent of seeing altogether, though it must be independent of *our* seeing. He is thus led to regard the 'real' table as an idea in the mind of God. Such an idea has the required permanence and independence of ourselves, without being—as matter would otherwise be—something quite unknowable, in the sense that we can only infer it, and can never be directly and immediately aware of it.

Other philosophers since Berkeley have also held that, although the table does not depend for its existence upon being seen by me, it does depend upon being seen (or otherwise apprehended in sensation) by *some* mind—not necessarily the mind of God, but more often the whole collective mind of the universe. This they hold, as Berkeley does, chiefly because they think there can be nothing real—or at any rate nothing known to be real—except minds and their thoughts and feelings. We might state the argument by which they support their view in some such way as this: 'Whatever can be thought of is an idea in the mind of the person thinking of it; therefore nothing can be thought of except ideas in minds; therefore anything else is inconceivable, and what is inconceivable cannot exist.'

Such an argument, in my opinion, is fallacious; and of course those who advance it do not put it so shortly or so crudely. But whether valid or not, the argument has been very widely advanced in one form or another; and very many philosophers, perhaps a majority, have held that there is nothing real except minds and their ideas. Such philosophers are called 'idealists'. When they come to explaining matter, they either say, like Berkeley, that matter is really nothing but a collection of ideas, or they say, like Leibniz (1646–1716), that what appears as matter is really a collection of more or less rudimentary minds.

But these philosophers, though they deny matter as opposed to mind, nevertheless, in another sense, admit matter. It will be remembered that we asked two questions; namely, (1) Is there a real table at all? (2) If so, what sort of object can it be? Now both Berkeley and Leibniz admit that there is a real table, but Berkeley says it is certain ideas in the mind of God, and Leibniz says it is a colony of souls. Thus both of them answer our first question in the affirmative, and only diverge from the views of ordinary mortals in their answer to our second question. In fact, almost all philosophers seem to be agreed that there is a real table: they almost all agree that, however much our sense-data—colour, shape, smoothness, etc.—may depend upon us, yet their occurrence is a sign of something existing independently of us, something differing, perhaps, completely from our sense-data, and yet to be regarded as causing those sense-data whenever we are in a suitable relation to the real table.

Now obviously this point in which the philosophers are agreed—the view that there *is* a real table, whatever its nature may be—is vitally important, and it will be worth while to consider what reasons there are for accepting this view before we go on to the further question as to the nature of the real table. Our next chapter, therefore, will be concerned with the reasons for supposing that there is a real table at all.

Before we go farther it will be well to consider for a moment what it is that we have discovered so far. It has appeared that, if we take any common object of the sort that is supposed to be known by the senses, what the senses *immediately* tell us is not the truth about the object as it is apart from us, but only the truth about certain sense-data which, so far as we can see, depend upon the relations between us and the object. Thus what we directly see and feel is merely 'appearance', which we believe to be a sign of some 'reality' behind. But if the reality is not what appears, have we any means of knowing whether there is any reality at all? And if so, have we any means of finding out what it is like?

Such questions are bewildering, and it is difficult to know that even the strangest hypotheses may not be true. Thus our familiar table, which has roused but the slightest thoughts in us hitherto, has become a problem full of surprising possibilities. The one thing we know about it is that it is not what it seems. Beyond this modest result, so far, we have the most complete liberty of conjecture. Leibniz tells us it is a community of souls: Berkeley tells us it is an idea in the mind of God; sober science, scarcely less wonderful, tells us it is a vast collection of electric charges in violent motion.

Among these surprising possibilities, doubt suggests that perhaps there is no table at all. Philosophy, if it cannot *answer* so many questions as we could wish, has at least the power of *asking* questions which increase the interest of the world, and show the strangeness and wonder lying just below the surface even in the commonest things of daily life.

CHAPTER II

The Existence of Matter

In this chapter we have to ask ourselves whether, in any sense at all, there is such a thing as matter. Is there a table which has a certain intrinsic nature, and continues to exist when I am not looking, or is the table merely a product of my imagination, a dream-table in a very prolonged dream? This question is of the greatest importance. For if we cannot be sure of the independent existence of the objects, we cannot be sure of the independent existence of other people's bodies, and therefore still less of other people's minds, since we have no grounds for believing in their minds except such as are derived from observing their bodies. Thus if we cannot be sure of the independent existence of objects, we shall be left alone in a desert—it may be that the whole outer world is nothing but a dream, and that we alone exist. This is an uncomfortable possibility; but although it cannot be strictly *proved* to be false, there is not the slightest reason to suppose that it is true. In this chapter we have to see why this is the case.

Before we embark upon doubtful matters, let us try to find some more or less fixed point from which to start. Although we are doubting the physical existence of the table, we are not doubting the existence of the sense-data which made us think there was a table; we are not doubting that, while we look, a certain colour and shape appear to us, and while we press, a certain sensation of hardness is experienced by us. All this, which is psychological, we are not calling in question. In fact, whatever else may be doubtful, some at least of our immediate experiences seem absolutely certain.

Descartes (1596–1650), the founder of modern philosophy, invented a method which may still be used with profit—the method of systematic doubt. He determined that he would believe nothing which he did not see quite clearly and distinctly to be true. Whatever he could bring himself to doubt, he would doubt, until he saw reason for not doubting it. By applying this method he gradually became convinced that the only existence of which he could be *quite* certain was his own. He imagined a deceitful demon, who presented unreal things to his senses in a perpetual phantasmagoria; it might be very improbable that such a demon existed, but still it was possible, and therefore doubt concerning things perceived by the senses was possible.

But doubt concerning his own existence was not possible, for if he did not exist, no demon could deceive him. If he doubted, he must exist; if he had any experiences whatever, he must exist. Thus, his own existence was an absolute certainty to him. 'I think, therefore I am,' he said (*Cogito, ergo sum*); and on the basis of this certainty he set to work to build up again the world of knowledge which his doubt had laid in ruins. By inventing the method of doubt, and by showing that subjective things are the most certain, Descartes performed a great service to philosophy, and one which makes him still useful to all students of the subject.

But some care is needed in using Descartes' argument. '*I* think, therefore *I* am' says rather more than is strictly certain. It might seem as though we were quite sure of being the same person to-day as we were yesterday, and this is no doubt true in some sense. But the real Self is as hard to arrive at as the real table, and does not seem to have that absolute, convincing certainty that belongs to particular experiences. When I look at my table and see a certain brown colour, what is quite certain at once is not '*I* am seeing a brown colour', but rather, 'a brown colour is being seen'. This of course involves something (or somebody) which (or who) sees the brown colour; but it does not of itself involve that more or less permanent person whom we call 'I'. So far as immediate certainty goes, it might be that the something which sees the brown colour is quite momentary, and not the same as the something which has some different experience the next moment.

Thus it is our particular thoughts and feelings that have primitive certainty. And this applies to dreams and hallucinations as well as to normal perceptions: when we dream or see a ghost, we certainly do have the sensations we think we have, but for various reasons it is held that no physical object corresponds to these sensations. Thus the certainty of our knowledge of our own experiences does not have to be limited in any way to allow for exceptional cases. Here, therefore, we have, for what it is worth, a solid basis from which to begin our pursuit of knowledge.

The problem we have to consider is this: Granted that we are certain of our own sense-data, have we any reason for regarding them as signs of the existence of something else, which we can call the physical object? When we have enumerated all the sense-data which we should naturally regard as connected with the table, have we said all there is to say about the table, or is there still something else—something not a sense-datum, something which persists when we go out of the room? Common sense unhesitatingly answers that there is. What can be bought and sold and pushed about and have a cloth laid on it, and so on, cannot be a *mere* collection of sense-data. If the cloth completely hides the table, we shall derive no sense-data from the table, and therefore, if the table were merely sense-data, it would have ceased to exist, and the cloth would be suspended in empty air, resting, by a miracle, in the place where the table formerly was. This seems plainly absurd; but whoever wishes to become a philosopher must learn not to be frightened by absurdities.

One great reason why it is felt that we must secure a physical object in addition to the sense-data, is that we want the *same* object for different people. When ten people are sitting round a dinner-table, it seems preposterous to maintain that they are not seeing the same tablecloth, the same knives and forks and spoons and glasses. But the sense-data are private to each separate person; what is immediately present to the sight of one is not immediately present to the sight of another: they all see things from slightly different points of view, and therefore see them slightly differently. Thus, if there are to be public neutral objects, which can be in some sense known to many different people, there must be something over and above the private and particular sense-data which appear to various people. What reason, then, have we for believing that there are such public neutral objects?

The first answer that naturally occurs to one is that, although different people may see the table slightly differently, still they all see more or less similar things when they look at the table, and the variations in what they see follow the laws of perspective and reflection of light, so that it is easy to arrive at a permanent object underlying all the different people's sense-data. I bought my table from the former occupant of my room; I could not buy *his* sense-data, which died when he went away, but I could and did buy the confident expectation of more or less similar sense-data. Thus it is the fact that different people have similar sense-data, and that one person in a given place at different times has similar sense-data, which makes us suppose that over and above the sense-data there is a permanent public object which underlies or causes the sense-data of various people at various times.

Now in so far as the above considerations depend upon supposing that there are other people besides ourselves, they beg the very question at issue. Other people are represented to me by certain sense-data, such as the sight of them or the sound of their voices, and if I had no reason to believe that there were physical objects independent of my sense-data, I should have no reason to believe that other people exist except as part of my dream. Thus, when we are trying to show that there must be objects independent of our own sense-data, we cannot appeal to the testimony of other people, since this testimony itself consists of sense-data, and does not reveal other people's experiences unless our own sense-data are signs of things existing independently of us. We must therefore, if possible, find, in our own purely private experiences, characteristics which show, or tend to show, that there are in the world things other than ourselves and our private experiences.

In one sense it must be admitted that we can never *prove* the existence of things other than ourselves and our experiences. No logical absurdity results from the hypothesis that the world consists of myself and my thoughts and feelings and sensations, and that everything else is mere fancy. In dreams a very complicated world may seem to be present, and yet on waking we find it was a delusion; that is to say, we find that the sense-data in the dream do not appear to have corresponded with such physical objects as we should naturally infer from our sense-data. (It is true that, when the physical world is assumed, it is possible to find physical causes for the sense-data in dreams: a door banging, for instance, may cause us to dream of a naval engagement. But although, in this case, there is a physical *cause* for the sense-data, there is not a physical object *corresponding* to the sense-data in the way in which an actual naval battle would correspond.) There is no logical impossibility in the supposition that the whole of life is a dream, in which we ourselves create all the objects that come before us. But although this is not logically impossible, there is no reason whatever to suppose that it is true; and it is, in fact, a less simple hypothesis, viewed as a means of accounting for the facts of our own life, than the common-sense hypothesis that there really are objects independent of us, whose action on us causes our sensations.

The way in which simplicity comes in from supposing that there really are physical objects is easily seen. If the cat appears at one moment in one part of the room, and at another in another part, it is natural to suppose that it has moved from the one to the other, passing over a series of intermediate positions. But if it is merely a set of sense-data, it cannot have ever been in any place where I did not see it; thus we shall have to suppose that it did not exist at all while I was not looking, but suddenly sprang into being in a new place. If the cat exists whether I see it or not, we can understand from our own experience how it gets hungry between one meal and the next; but if it does not exist when I am not seeing it, it seems odd that appetite should grow during non-existence as fast as during existence. And if the cat consists only of sense-data, it cannot be *hungry*, since no hunger but my own can be a sense-datum to me. Thus the behaviour of the sense-data which represent the cat to me, though it seems quite natural when regarded as an expression of hunger, becomes utterly inexplicable when regarded as mere movements and changes of patches of colour, which are as incapable of hunger as a triangle is of playing football.

But the difficulty in the case of the cat is nothing compared to the difficulty in the case of human beings. When human beings speak—that is, when we hear certain noises which we associate with ideas, and simultaneously see certain motions of lips and expressions of face—it is very difficult to suppose that what we hear is not the expression of a thought, as we know it would be if we emitted the same sounds. Of course similar things happen in dreams, where we are mistaken as to the existence of other people. But dreams are more or less suggested by what we call waking life, and are capable of being more or less accounted for on scientific principles if we assume that there really is a physical world. Thus every principle of simplicity urges us to adopt the natural view, that there really are objects other than ourselves and our sense-data which have an existence not dependent upon our perceiving them.

Of course it is not by argument that we originally come by our belief in an independent external world.

We find this belief ready in ourselves as soon as we being to reflect: it is what may be called an *instinctive* belief. We should never have been led to question this belief but for the fact that, at any rate in the case of sight, it seems as if the sense-datum itself were instinctively believed to be the independent object, whereas argument shows that the object cannot be identical with the sense-datum. This discovery, however—which is not at all paradoxical in the case of taste and smell and sound, and only slightly so in the case of touch—leaves undiminished our instinctive belief that there *are* objects *corresponding* to our sense-data. Since this belief does not lead to any difficulties, but on the contrary tends to simplify and systematize our account of our experiences, there seems no good reason for rejecting it. We may therefore admit—though with a slight doubt derived from dreams—that the external world does really exist, and is not wholly dependent for its existence upon our continuing to perceive it.

The argument which has led us to this conclusion is doubtless less strong than we could wish, but it is typical of many philosophical arguments, and it is therefore worth while to consider briefly its general character and validity. All knowledge, we find, must be built up upon our instinctive beliefs, and if these are rejected, nothing is left. But among our instinctive beliefs some are much stronger than others, while many have, by habit and association, become entangled with other beliefs, not really instinctive, but falsely supposed to be part of what is believed instinctively.

Philosophy should show us the hierarchy of our instinctive beliefs, beginning with those we hold most strongly, and presenting each as much isolated and as free from irrelevant additions as possible. It should take care to show that, in the form in which they are finally set forth, our instinctive beliefs do not clash, but form a harmonious system. There can never be any reason for rejecting one instinctive belief except that it clashes with others; thus, if they are found to harmonize, the whole system becomes worthy of acceptance.

It is of course *possible* that all or any of our beliefs may be mistaken, and therefore all ought to be held with at least some slight element of doubt. But we cannot have *reason* to reject a belief except on the ground of some other belief. Hence, by organizing our instinctive beliefs and their consequences, by considering which among them is most possible, if necessary, to modify or abandon, we can arrive, on the basis of accepting as our sole data what we instinctively believe, at an orderly systematic organization of our knowledge, in which, though the *possibility* of error remains, its likelihood is diminished by the interrelation of the parts and by the critical scrutiny which has preceded acquiescence.

This function, at least, philosophy can perform. Most philosophers, rightly or wrongly, believe that philosophy can do much more than this—that it can give us knowledge, not otherwise attainable, concerning the universe as a whole, and concerning the nature of ultimate reality. Whether this be the case or not, the more modest function we have spoken of can certainly be performed by philosophy, and certainly suffices, for those who have once begun to doubt the adequacy of common sense, to justify the arduous and difficult labours that philosophical problems involve.

CHAPTER III

The Nature of Matter

In the preceding chapter we agreed, though without being able to find demonstrative reasons, that it is rational to believe that our sense-data—for example, those which we regard as associated with my table—are really signs of the existence of something independent of us and our perceptions. That is to say, over and above the sensations of colour, hardness, noise, and so on, which make up the appearance of the table to me, I assume that there is something else, *of* which these things are appearances. The colour ceases to exist if I shut my eyes, the sensation of hardness ceases to exist if I remove my arm from contact with the table, the sound ceases to exist if I cease to rap the table with my knuckles. But I do not believe that when all these things cease the table ceases. On the contrary, I believe that it is because the table exists continuously that all these sense-data will reappear when I open my eyes, replace my arm, and begin again to rap with my knuckles. The question we have to consider in this chapter is: What is the nature of this real table, which persists independently of my perception of it?

To this question physical science gives an answer,

somewhat incomplete it is true, and in part still very hypothetical, but yet deserving of respect so far as it goes. Physical science, more or less unconsciously, has drifted into the view that all natural phenomena ought to be reduced to motions. Light and heat and sound are all due to wave-motions, which travel from the body emitting them to the person who sees light or feels heat or hears sound. That which has the wave-motion is either aether or 'gross matter', but in either case is what the philosopher would call matter. The only properties which science assigns to it are position in space, and the power of motion according to the laws of motion. Science does not deny that it *may* have other properties; but if so, such other properties are not useful to the man of science, and in no way assist him in explaining the phenomena.

It is sometimes said that 'light *is* a form of wave-motion', but this is misleading, for the light which we immediately see, which we know directly by means of our senses, is *not* a form of wave-motion, but something quite different—something which we all know if we are not blind, though we cannot describe it so as to convey our knowledge to a man who is blind. A wave-motion, on the contrary, could quite well be described to a blind man, since he can acquire a knowledge of space by the sense of touch; and he can experience a wave-motion by a sea voyage almost as well as we can. But this, which a blind man can understand, is not what we mean by *light*: we mean by *light* just that which a blind man can never understand, and which we can never describe to him.

Now this something, which all of us who are not blind know, is not, according to science, really to be found in the outer world: it is something caused by the action of certain waves upon the eyes and nerves and brain of the person who sees the light. When it is said that light *is* waves, what is really meant is that waves are the physical cause of our sensations of light. But light itself, the thing which seeing people experience and blind people do not, is not supposed by science to form any part of the world that is independent of us and our senses. And very similar remarks would apply to other kinds of sensations.

It is not only colours and sounds and so on that are absent from the scientific world of matter, but also *space* as we get it through sight or touch. It is essential to science that its matter should be in *a* space, but the space in which it is cannot be exactly the space we see or feel. To begin with, space as we see it is not the same as space as we get it by the sense of touch; it is only by experience in infancy that we learn how to touch things we see, or how to get a sight of things which we feel touching us. But the space of science is neutral as between touch and sight; thus it cannot be either the space of touch or the space of sight.

Again, different people see the same object as of different shapes, according to their point of view. A circular coin, for example, though we should always *judge* it to be circular, will *look* oval unless we are straight in front of it. When we judge that it *is* circular, we are judging that it has a real shape which is not its apparent shape, but belongs to it intrinsically apart from its appearance. But this real shape, which is what concerns science, must be in a real space, not the same as anybody's *apparent* space. The real space is public, the apparent space is private to the percipient. In different people's *private* spaces the same object seems to have different shapes; thus the real space, in which it has its real shape, must be different from the private spaces. The space of science, therefore, though *connected* with the spaces we see and feel, is not identical with them, and the manner of its connexion requires investigation.

We agreed provisionally that physical objects cannot be quite like our sense-data, but may be regarded as *causing* our sensations. These physical objects are in the space of science, which we may call 'physical' space. It is important to notice that, if our sensations are to be caused by physical objects, there must be a physical space containing these objects and our sense-organs and nerves and brain. We get a sensation of touch from an object when we are in contact with it; that is to say, when some part of our body occupies a place in physical space quite close to the space occupied by the object. We see an object (roughly speaking) when no opaque body is between the object and our eyes in physical space. Similarly, we only hear or smell or taste an object when we are sufficiently near to it, or when it touches the tongue, or has some suitable position in physical space relatively to our body. We cannot begin to state what different sensations we shall derive from a given object under different circumstances unless we regard the object and our body as both in one physical space, for it is mainly the relative positions of the object and our body that determine what sensations we shall derive from the object.

Now our sense-data are situated in our private spaces, either the space of sight or the space of touch or such vaguer spaces as other senses may give us. If, as science and common sense assume, there is one public all-embracing physical space in which physical objects are, the relative positions of physical objects in physical space must more or less correspond to the relative positions of sense-data in our private spaces. There is no difficulty in supposing this to be the case. If we see on a road one house nearer to us than another, our other senses will bear out the view that it is nearer; for example, it will be reached sooner if we walk along the road. Other people will agree that the house which looks nearer to us is nearer; the ordnance map will take the same view; and thus everything points to a spatial relation between the houses corresponding to the relation between the sense-data which we see when we look at the houses. Thus we may assume that there is a physical space in which physical objects have spatial relations corresponding to those which the corresponding sense-data have in our private spaces. It is this physical space which is dealt with in geometry and assumed in physics and astronomy.

Assuming that there is physical space, and that it does thus correspond to private spaces, what can we know about it? We can know *only* what is required in order to secure the correspondence. That is to say, we can know nothing of what it is like in itself, but we can know the sort of arrangement of physical objects which results from their spatial relations. We can know, for example, that the earth and moon and sun are in one straight line during an eclipse, though we cannot know what a physical straight line is in itself, as we know the look of a straight line in our visual space. Thus we come to know much more about the *relations* of distances in physical space than about the distances themselves; we may know that one distance is greater than another, or that it is along the same straight line as the other, but we cannot have that immediate acquaintance with physical distances that we have with distances in our private spaces, or with colours or sounds or other sense-data. We can know all those things about physical space which a man born blind might know through other people about the space of sight; but the kind of things which a man born blind could never know about the space of sight we also cannot know about physical space. We can know the properties of the relations required to preserve the correspondence with sense-data, but we cannot know the nature of the terms between which the relations hold.

With regard to time, our *feeling* of duration or of the lapse of time is notoriously an unsafe guide as to the time that has elapsed by the clock. Times when we are bored or suffering pain pass slowly, times when we are agreeably occupied pass quickly, and times when we are sleeping pass almost as if they did not exist. Thus, in so far as time is constituted by duration, there is the same necessity for distinguishing a public and a private time as there was in the case of space. But in so far as time consists in an *order* of before and after, there is no need to make such a distinction; the time-order which events seem to have is, so far as we can see, the same as the time-order which they do have. At any rate no reason can be given for supposing that the two orders are not the same. The same is usually true of space: if a regiment of men are marching along a road, the *shape* of the regiment will look different from different points of view, but the men will appear arranged in the same *order* from all points of view. Hence we regard the *order* as true also in physical space, whereas the shape is only supposed to correspond to the physical space so far as is required for the preservation of the order.

In saying that the time-order which events *seem to have* is the same as the time-order which they *really have*, it is necessary to guard against a possible misunderstanding. It must not be supposed that the various states of different physical objects have the same time-order as the sense-data which constitute the perceptions of those objects. Considered as physical objects, the thunder and lightning are simultaneous; that is to say, the lightning is simultaneous with the disturbance of the air in the place where the disturbance begins, namely, where the lightning is. But the sense-datum which we call hearing the thunder does not take place until the disturbance of the air has travelled as far as to where we are. Similarly, it takes about eight minutes for the sun's light to reach us; thus, when we see the sun we are seeing the sun of eight minutes ago. So far as our sense-data afford evidence as to the physical sun they afford evidence as to the physical sun of eight minutes ago; if the physical sun had ceased to exist within the last eight minutes, that would make no difference to the sense-data which we call 'seeing the sun'. This affords a fresh illustration of the necessity of distinguishing between sense-data and physical objects.

What we have found as regards space is much the same as what we find in relation to the correspondence of the sense-data with their physical counterparts. If one object looks blue and another red, we may reasonably presume that there is some corresponding difference between the physical objects; if two objects both look blue, we may presume a corresponding similarity. But we cannot hope to be acquainted directly with the quality in the physical object which makes it look blue or red. Science tells us that this quality is a certain sort of wave-motion, and this sounds familiar, because we think of wave-motions in the space we see. But the wave-motions must really be in physical space, with which we have no direct acquaintance; thus the real wave-motions have not that familiarity which we might have supposed them to have. And what holds for colours is closely similar to what holds for other sense-data. Thus we find that, although the *relations* of physical objects have all sorts of knowable properties, derived from their correspondence with the relations of sense-data, the physical objects themselves remain unknown in their intrinsic nature, so far at least as can be discovered by means of the senses. The question remains whether there is any other method of discovering the intrinsic nature of physical objects.

The most natural, though not ultimately the most defensible, hypothesis to adopt in the first instance, at any rate as regards visual sense-data, would be that, though physical objects cannot, for the reasons we have been considering, be *exactly* like sense-data, yet they may be more or less like. According to this view, physical objects will, for example, really have colours, and we might, by good luck, see an object as of the colour it really is. The colour which an object seems to have at any given moment will in general be very similar, though not quite the same, from many different points of view; we might thus suppose the 'real' colour to be a sort of medium colour, intermediate between the various shades which appear from the different points of view.

Such a theory is perhaps not capable of being definitely refuted, but it can be shown to be groundless. To begin with, it is plain that the colour we see depends only upon the nature of the light-waves that strike the eye, and is therefore modified by the medium intervening between us and the object, as well as by the manner in which light is reflected from the object in the direction of the eye. The intervening air alters colours unless it is perfectly clear, and any strong reflection will alter them completely. Thus the colour we see is a result of the ray as it reaches the eye, and not simply a property of the object from which the ray comes. Hence, also, provided certain waves reach the eye, we shall see a certain colour, whether the object from which the waves start has any colour or not. Thus it is quite gratuitous to suppose that physical objects have colours, and therefore there is no justification for making such a supposition. Exactly similar arguments will apply to other sense-data.

It remains to ask whether there are any general philosophical arguments enabling us to say that, if matter is real, it *must* be of such and such a nature. As explained above, very many philosophers, perhaps most, have held that whatever is real must be in some sense mental, or at any rate that whatever we can know anything about must be in some sense mental. Such philosophers are called 'idealists'. Idealists tell us that what appears as matter is really something mental; namely, either (as Leibniz held) more or less rudimentary minds, or (as Berkeley contended) ideas in the minds which, as we should commonly say, 'perceive' the matter. Thus idealists deny the existence of matter as something intrinsically different from mind, though they do not deny that our sense-data are signs of something which exists independently of our private sensations. In the following chapter we shall consider briefly the reasons—in my opinion fallacious—which idealists advance in favour of their theory.

CHAPTER IV

Idealism

The word 'idealism' is used by different philosophers in somewhat different senses. We shall understand by it the doctrine that whatever exists, or at any rate whatever can be known to exist, must be in some sense mental. This doctrine, which is very widely held among philosophers, has several forms, and is advocated on several different grounds. The doctrine is so widely held, and so interesting in itself, that even the briefest survey of philosophy must give some account of it.

Those who are unaccustomed to philosophical speculation may be inclined to dismiss such a doctrine as obviously absurd. There is no doubt that common sense regards tables and chairs and the sun and moon and material objects generally as something radically different from minds and the contents of minds, and as having an existence which might continue if minds ceased. We think of matter as having existed long before there were any minds, and it is hard to think of it as a mere product of mental activity. But whether true or false, idealism is not to be dismissed as obviously absurd.

We have seen that, even if physical objects do have an independent existence, they must differ very widely from sense-data, and can only have a *correspondence* with sense-data, in the same sort of way in which a catalogue has a correspondence with the things catalogued. Hence common sense leaves us completely in the dark as to the true intrinsic nature of physical objects, and if there were good reason to regard them as mental, we could not legitimately reject this opinion merely because it strikes us as strange. The truth about physical objects *must* be strange. It *may* be unattainable, but if any philosopher believes that he has attained it, the fact that what he offers as the truth is strange ought not to be made a ground of objection to his opinion.

The grounds on which idealism is advocated are generally grounds derived from the theory of knowledge, that is to say, from a discussion of the conditions which things must satisfy in order that we may be able to know them. The first serious attempt to establish idealism on such grounds was that of Bishop Berkeley. He proved first, by arguments which were largely valid, that our sense-data cannot be supposed to have an existence independent of us, but must be, in part at least, 'in' the mind, in the sense that their existence would not continue if there were no seeing or hearing or touching or smelling or tasting. So far, his contention was almost certainly valid, even if some of his arguments were not so. But he went on to argue that sense-data were the only things of whose existence our perceptions could assure us, and that to be known is to be 'in' a mind, and therefore to be mental. Hence he concluded that nothing can ever be known except what is in some mind, and that whatever is known without being in my mind must be in some other mind.

In order to understand his argument, it is necessary to understand his use of the word 'idea'. He gives the name 'idea' to anything which is *immediately* known, as, for example, sense-data are known. Thus a particular colour which we see is an idea; so is a voice which we hear, and so on. But the term is not wholly confined to sense-data. There will also be things remembered or imagined, for with such things also we have immediate acquaintance at the moment of remembering or imaging. All such immediate data he calls 'ideas'.

He then proceeds to consider common objects, such as a tree, for instance. He shows that all we know immediately when we 'perceive' the tree consists of ideas in his sense of the word, and he argues that there is not the slightest ground for supposing that there is anything real about the tree except what is perceived. Its being, he says, consists in being perceived: in the Latin of the schoolmen its '*esse*' is '*percipi*'. He fully admits that the tree must continue to exist even when we shut our eyes or when no human being is near it. But this continued existence, he says, is due to the fact that God continues to perceive it; the 'real' tree, which corresponds to what we call the physical object, consists of ideas in the mind of God, ideas more or less like those we have when we see the tree, but differing in the fact that they are permanent in God's mind so long as the tree continues to exist. All our perceptions, according to him, consist in a partial participation in God's perceptions, and it is because of this participation that different people see more or less the same tree. Thus apart from minds and their ideas there is nothing in the world, nor is it possible that anything else should ever be known, since whatever is known is necessarily an idea.

There are in this argument a good many fallacies which have been important in the history of philosophy, and which it will be as well to bring to light. In the first place, there is a confusion engendered by the use of the word 'idea'. We think of an idea as essentially something *in* somebody's mind, and thus when we are told a tree consists entirely of ideas, it is natural to suppose that, if so, the tree must be entirely in minds. But the notion of being 'in' the mind is ambiguous. We speak of bearing a person in mind, not meaning that the person is in our minds, but that a thought of him is in our minds. When a man says that some business he had to arrange went clean out of his mind, he does not mean to imply that the business itself was ever in his mind, but only that a thought of the business was formerly in his mind, but afterwards ceased to be in his mind. And so when Berkeley says that the tree must be in our minds if we can know it, all that he really has a right to say is that a thought of the tree must be in our minds. To argue that the tree itself must be in our minds is like arguing that a person whom we bear in mind is himself in our minds. This confusion may seem too gross to have been really committed by any competent philosopher, but various attendant circumstances rendered it possible. In order to see how it was possible, we must go more deeply into the question as to the nature of ideas.

Before taking up the general question of the nature of ideas, we must disentangle two entirely separate questions which arise concerning sense-data and physical objects. We saw that, for various reasons of detail, Berkeley was right in treating the sense-data which constitute our perception of the tree as more or less subjective, in the sense that they depend upon us as much as upon the tree, and would not exist if the tree were not being perceived. But this is an entirely different point from the one by which Berkeley seeks to prove that whatever can be immediately known *must* be in a mind. For this purpose arguments of detail as to the dependence of sense-data upon us are useless. It is necessary to prove, generally, that by being known, things are shown to be mental. This is what Berkeley believes himself to have done. It is this question, and not our previous question as to the difference between sense-data and the physical object, that must now concern us.

Taking the word 'idea' in Berkeley's sense, there are two quite distinct things to be considered whenever an idea is before the mind. There is on the one hand the thing of which we are aware—say the colour of my table—and on the other hand the actual awareness itself, the mental act of apprehending the thing. The mental act is undoubtedly mental, but is there any reason to suppose that the thing apprehended is in any sense mental? Our previous arguments concerning the colour did not prove it to be mental; they only proved that its existence depends upon the relation of our sense organs to the physical object—in our case, the table. That is to say, they proved that a certain colour will exist, in a certain light, if a normal eye is placed at a certain point relatively to the table. They did not prove that the colour is in the mind of the percipient.

Berkeley's view, that obviously the colour *must* be in the mind, seems to depend for its plausibility upon confusing the thing apprehended with the act of apprehension. Either of these might be called an apprehension. Either of these might be called an 'idea'; probably either would have been called an idea by Berkeley. The act is undoubtedly in the mind; hence, when we are thinking of the act, we readily assent to the view that ideas must be in the mind. Then, forgetting that this was only true when ideas were taken as acts of apprehension, we transfer the proposition that 'ideas are in the mind' to ideas in the other sense, i.e., to the things apprehended by our acts of apprehension. Thus, by an unconscious equivocation, we arrive at the conclusion that whatever we can apprehend must be in our minds. This seems to be the true analysis of Berkeley's argument, and the ultimate fallacy upon which it rests.

This question of the distinction between act and object in our apprehending of things is vitally important, since our whole power of acquiring knowledge is bound up with it. The faculty of being acquainted with things other than itself is the main characteristic of a mind. Acquaintance with objects essentially consists in a relation between the mind and something other than the mind; it is this that constitutes the mind's power of knowing things. If we say that the things known must be in the mind, we are either unduly limiting the mind's power of knowing, or we are uttering a mere tautology. We are uttering a mere tautology if we mean by '*in* the mind' the same as by '*before* the mind', i.e., if we mean merely being apprehended by the mind. But if we mean this, we shall have to admit that what, *in this sense,* is in the mind, may nevertheless be not mental. Thus when we realize the nature of knowledge, Berkeley's argument is seen to be wrong in substance as well as in form, and his grounds for supposing that 'ideas'—i.e., the objects apprehended—must be mental, are found to have no validity whatever. Hence his grounds in favour of idealism may be dismissed. It remains to see whether there are any other grounds.

It is often said, as though it were a self-evident truism, that we cannot know that anything exists which we do not know. It is inferred that whatever can in any way be relevant to our experience must be at least capable of being known by us; whence it follows that if matter were essentially something with which we could not become acquainted, matter would be something which we could not know to exist, and which could have for us no importance whatever. It is generally also implied, for reasons which remain obscure, that what can have no importance for us cannot be real, and that therefore matter, if it is not composed of minds or of mental ideas, is impossible and a mere chimera.

To go into this argument fully at our present stage would be impossible, since it raises points requiring a considerable preliminary discussion; but certain reasons for rejecting the argument may be noticed at once. To begin at the end: there is no reason why what cannot have any *practical* importance for us should not be real. It is true that, if *theoretical* importance is included, everything real is of *some* importance to us, since, as persons desirous of knowing the truth about the universe, we have some interest in everything that the universe contains. But if this sort of interest is included, it is not the case that matter has no importance for us, provided it exists, even if we cannot know that it exists. We can, obviously, suspect that it may exist, and wonder whether it does; hence it is connected with our desire for knowledge, and has the importance of either satisfying or thwarting this desire.

Again, it is by no means a truism, and is in fact false, that we cannot know that anything exists which we do not know. The word 'know' is here used in two different senses. (1) In its first use it is applicable to the sort of knowledge which is opposed to error, the sense in which what we know is *true*, the sense which applies to our beliefs and convictions, i.e., to what are called *judgments*. In this sense of the word we know *that* something is the case. This sort of knowledge may be described as knowledge of *truths*. (2) In the second use of the word 'know' above, the word applies to our knowledge of *things*, which we may call *acquaintance*. This is the sense in which we know sense data. (The distinction involved is roughly that between *savoir* and *connaître* in French, or between *wissen* and *kennen* in German.)

Thus the statement which seemed like a truism becomes, when re-stated, the following: 'We can never truly judge that something with which we are not acquainted exists.' This is by no means a truism, but on the contrary a palpable falsehood. I have not the honour to be acquainted with the Emperor of China, but I truly judge that he exists. It may be said, of course, that I judge this because of other people's acquaintance with him. This, however, would be an irrelevant retort, since, if the principle were true, I could not know that any one else is acquainted with him. But further: there is no reason why I should not know of the existence of something with which *nobody* is acquainted. This point is important, and demands elucidation.

If I am acquainted with a thing which exists, my acquaintance gives me the knowledge that it exists. But it is not true that, conversely, whenever I can know that a thing of a certain sort exists, I or some one else must be acquainted with the thing. What happens, in cases where I have true judgement without acquaintance, is that the thing is known to me by *description*, and that, in virtue of some general principle, the existence of a thing answering to this description can be inferred from the existence of something with which I am acquainted. In order to understand this point fully, it will be well first to deal with the difference between knowledge by acquaintance and knowledge by description, and then to consider what knowledge of general principles, if any, has the same kind of certainty as our knowledge of the existence of our own experiences. These subjects will be dealt with in the following chapters.

CHAPTER V

Knowledge by Acquaintance and Knowledge by Description

In the preceding chapter we saw that there are two sorts of knowledge: knowledge of things, and knowledge of truths. In this chapter we shall be concerned exclusively with knowledge of things, of which in turn we shall have to distinguish two kinds. Knowledge of things, when it is of the kind we call knowledge by *acquaintance*, is essentially simpler than any knowledge of truths, and logically independent of knowledge of truths, though it would be rash to assume that human beings ever, in fact, have acquaintance with things without at the same time knowing some truth about them. Knowledge of things by *description*, on the contrary, always involves, as we shall find in the course of the present chapter, some knowledge of truths as its source and ground. But first of all we must make clear what we mean by 'acquaintance' and what we mean by 'description'.

We shall say that we have *acquaintance* with anything of which we are directly aware, without the intermediary of any process of inference or any knowledge of truths. Thus in the presence of my table I am acquainted with the sense-data that make up the appearance of my table—its colour, shape, hardness, smoothness, etc.; all these are things of which I am immediately conscious when I am seeing and touching my table. The particular shade of colour that I am seeing may have many things said about it—I may say that it is brown, that it is rather dark, and so on. But such statements, though they make me know truths *about* the colour, do not make me know the colour itself any better than I did before: so far as concerns knowledge of the colour itself, as opposed to knowledge of truths about it, I know the colour perfectly and completely when I see it, and no further knowledge of it itself is even theoretically possible. Thus the sense-data which make up the appearance of my table are things with which I have acquaintance, things immediately known to me just as they are.

My knowledge of the table as a physical object, on the contrary, is not direct knowledge. Such as it is, it is obtained through acquaintance with the sense-data that make up the appearance of the table. We have seen that it is possible, without absurdity, to doubt whether there is a table at all, whereas it is not possible to doubt the sense-data. My knowledge of the table is of the kind which we shall call 'knowledge by description'. The table is 'the physical object which causes such-and-such sense-data'. This *describes* the table by means of the sense-data. In order to know anything at all about the table, we must know truths connecting it with things with which we have acquaintance: we must know that 'such-and-such sense-data are caused by a physical object'. There is no state of mind in which we are directly aware of the table; all our knowledge of the table is really knowledge of *truths*, and the actual thing which is the table is not, strictly speaking, known to us at all. We know a description, and we know that there is just one object to which this description applies, though the object itself is not directly known to us. In such a case, we say that our knowledge of the object is knowledge by description.

All our knowledge, both knowledge of things and knowledge of truths, rests upon acquaintance as its foundation. It is therefore important to consider what kinds of things there are with which we have acquaintance.

Sense-data, as we have already seen, are among the things with which we are acquainted; in fact, they supply the most obvious and striking example of knowledge by acquaintance. But if they were the sole example, our knowledge would be very much more restricted than it is. We should only know what is now present to our senses: we could not know anything about the past—not even that there was a past—nor could we know any truths about our sense-data, for all knowledge of truths, as we shall show, demands acquaintance with things which are of an essentially different character from sense-data, the things which are sometimes called 'abstract ideas', but which we shall call 'universals'. We have therefore to consider acquaintance with other things besides sense-data if we are to obtain any tolerably adequate analysis of our knowledge.

The first extension beyond sense-data to be considered is acquaintance by *memory*. It is obvious that we often remember what we have seen or heard or had otherwise present to our senses, and that in such cases we are still immediately aware of what we remember, in spite of the fact that it appears as past and not as present. This immediate knowledge by memory is the source of all our knowledge concerning the past: without it, there could be no knowledge of the past by inference, since we should never know that there was anything past to be inferred.

The next extension to be considered is acquaintance by *introspection*. We are not only aware of things, but we are often aware of being aware of them. When I see the sun, I am often aware of my seeing the sun; thus 'my seeing the sun' is an object with which I have acquaintance. When I desire food, I may be aware of my desire for food; thus 'my desiring food' is an object with which I am acquainted. Similarly we may be aware of our feeling pleasure or pain, and generally of the events which happen in our minds. This kind of acquaintance, which may be called self-consciousness, is the source of all our knowledge of mental things. It is obvious that it is only what goes on in our own minds that can be thus known immediately. What goes on in the minds of others is known to us through our perception of their bodies, that is, through the sense-data in us which are associated with their bodies. But for our acquaintance with the contents of our own minds, we should be unable to imagine the minds of others, and therefore we could never arrive at the knowledge that they have minds. It seems natural to suppose that self-consciousness is one of the things that distinguish men from animals: animals, we may suppose, though they have acquaintance with sense-data, never become aware of this acquaintance. I do not mean that they *doubt* whether they exist, but that they have never become conscious of the fact that they have sensations and feelings, nor therefore of the fact that they, the subjects of their sensations and feelings, exist.

We have spoken of acquaintance with the contents of our minds as *self*-consciousness, but it is not, of course, consciousness of our *self*: it is consciousness of particular thoughts and feelings. The question whether we are also acquainted with our bare selves, as opposed to particular thoughts and feelings, is a very difficult one, upon which it would be rash to speak positively. When we try to look into ourselves we always seem to come upon some particular thought or feeling, and not upon the 'I' which has the thought or feeling. Nevertheless there are some reasons for thinking that we are acquainted with the 'I', though the acquaintance is hard to disentangle from other things. To make clear what sort of reason there is, let us consider for a moment what our acquaintance with particular thoughts really involves.

When I am acquainted with 'my seeing the sun', it seems plain that I am acquainted with two different things in relation to each other. On the one hand there is the sense-datum which represents the sun to me, on the other hand there is that which sees this sense-datum. All acquaintance, such as my acquaintance with the sense-datum which represents the sun, seems obviously a relation between the person acquainted and the object with which the person is acquainted. When a case of acquaintance is one with which I can be acquainted (as I am acquainted with my acquaintance with the sense-datum representing the sun), it is plain that the person acquainted is myself. Thus, when I am acquainted with my seeing the sun, the whole fact with which I am acquainted is 'Self-acquainted-with-sense-datum'.

Further, we know the truth 'I am acquainted with this sense-datum'. It is hard to see how we could know this truth, or even understand what is meant by it, unless we were acquainted with something which we call 'I'. It does not seem necessary to suppose that we are acquainted with a more or less permanent person, the same to-day as yesterday, but it does seem as though we must be acquainted with that thing, whatever its nature, which sees the sun and has acquaintance with sense-data. Thus, in some sense it would seem we must be acquainted with our Selves as opposed to our particular experiences. But the question is difficult, and complicated arguments can be adduced on either side. Hence, although acquaintance with ourselves seems *probably* to occur, it is not wise to assert that it undoubtedly does occur.

We may therefore sum up as follows what has been said concerning acquaintance with things that exist. We have acquaintance in sensation with the data of the outer senses, and in introspection with the data of what may be called the inner sense—thoughts, feelings, desires, etc.; we have acquaintance in memory with things which have been data either of the outer senses or of the inner sense. Further, it is probable, though not certain, that we have acquaintance with Self, as that which is aware of things or has desires towards things.

In addition to our acquaintance with particular existing things, we also have acquaintance with what we shall call *universals*, that is to say, general ideas, such as *whiteness*, *diversity*, *brotherhood*, and so on. Every complete sentence must contain at least one word which stands for a universal, since all verbs have a meaning which is universal. We shall return to universals later on . . . ; for the present, it is only necessary to guard against the supposition that whatever we can be acquainted with must be something particular and existent. Awareness of universals is called *conceiving*, and a universal of which we are aware is called a *concept*.

It will be seen that among the objects with which we are acquainted are not included physical objects (as opposed to sense-data), nor other people's minds. These things are known to us by what I call 'knowledge by description', which we must now consider.

By a 'description' I mean any phrase of the form 'a so-and-so' or 'the so-and-so'. A phrase of the form 'a so-and-so' I shall call an 'ambiguous' description; a phrase of the form 'the so-and-so' (in the singular) I shall call a 'definite' description. Thus 'a man' is an ambiguous description, and 'the man with the iron mask' is a definite description. There are various problems connected with ambiguous descriptions, but I pass them by, since they do not directly concern the matter we are discussing, which is the nature of our knowledge concerning objects in cases where we know that there is an object answering to a definite description, though we are not *acquainted* with any such object. This is a matter which is concerned exclusively with *definite* descriptions. I shall therefore, in the sequel, speak simply of 'descriptions' when I mean 'definite descriptions'. Thus a description will mean any phrase of the form 'the so-and-so' in the singular.

We shall say that an object is 'known by description' when we know that it is 'the so-and-so', i.e., when we know that there is one object, and no more, having a certain property; and it will generally be implied that we do not have knowledge of the same object by acquaintance. We know that the man with the iron mask existed, and many propositions are known about him; but we do not know who he was. We know that the candidate who gets the most votes will be elected, and in this case we are very likely also acquainted (in the only sense in which one can be acquainted with some one else) with the man who is, in fact, the candidate who will get most votes; but we do not know which of the candidates he is, i.e., we do not know any proposition of the form 'A is the candidate who will get most votes' where A is one of the candidates by name. We shall say that we have 'merely descriptive knowledge' of the so-and-so when, although we know that the so-and-so exists, and although we may possibly be acquainted with the object which is, in fact, the so-and-so, yet we do not know any proposition '*a* is the so-and-so', where *a* is something with which we are acquainted.

When we say 'the so-and-so exists', we mean that there is just one object which is the so-and-so. The proposition '*a* is the so-and-so' means that *a* has the property so-and-so, and nothing else has. 'Mr. A. is the Unionist candidate for this constituency' means 'Mr. A. is a Unionist candidate for this constituency, and no one else is'. 'The Unionist candidate for this constituency exists' means 'some one is a Unionist candidate for this constituency, and no one else is'. Thus, when we are acquainted with an object which is the so-and-so, we know that the so-and-so exists; but we may know that the so-and-so exists when we are not acquainted with any object which we know to be the so-and-so, and even when we are not acquainted with any object which, in fact, is the so-and-so.

Common words, even proper names, are usually really descriptions. That is to say, the thought in the mind of a person using a proper name correctly can generally only be expressed explicitly if we replace the proper name by a description. Moreover, the description required to express the thought will vary for different people, or for the same person at different times. The only thing constant (so long as the name is rightly used) is the object to which the name applies. But so long as this remains constant, the particular description involved usually makes no difference to the truth or falsehood of the proposition in which the name appears.

Let us take some illustrations. Suppose some statement made about Bismarck. Assuming that there is such a thing as direct acquaintance with oneself, Bismarck himself might have used his name directly to designate the particular person with whom he was acquainted. In this case, if he made a judgement about himself, he himself might be a constituent of the judgement. Here the proper name has the direct use which it always wishes to have, as simply standing for a certain object, and not for a description of the object. But if a person who knew Bismarck made a judgement about him, the case is different. What this person was acquainted with were certain sense-data which he connected (rightly, we will suppose) with Bismarck's body. His body, as a physical object, and still more his mind, were only known as the body and the mind connected with these sense-data. That is, they were known by description. It is, of course, very much a matter of chance which characteristics of a man's appearance will come into a friend's mind when he thinks of him; thus the description actually in the friend's mind is accidental. The essential point is that he knows that the various descriptions all apply to the same entity, in spite of not being acquainted with the entity in question.

When we, who did not know Bismarck, make a judgement about him, the description in our minds will probably be some more or less vague mass of historical knowledge—far more, in most cases, than is required to identify him. But, for the sake of illustration, let us assume that we think of him as 'the first Chancellor of the German Empire'. Here all the words are abstract except 'German'. The word 'German' will, again, have different meanings for different people. To some it will recall travels in Germany, to some the look of Germany on the map, and so on. But if we are to obtain a description which we know to be applicable, we shall be compelled, at some point, to bring in a reference to a particular with which we are acquainted. Such reference is involved in any mention of past, present, and future (as opposed to definite dates), or of here and there, or of what others have told us. Thus it would seem that, in some way or other, a description known to be applicable to a particular must involve some reference to a particular with which we are acquainted, if our knowledge about the thing described is not to be merely what follows *logically* from the description. For example, 'the most long-lived of men' is a description involving only universals, which must apply to some man, but we can make no judgements concerning this man which involve knowledge about him beyond what the description gives. If, however, we say, 'The first Chancellor of the German Empire was an astute diplomatist', we can only be assured of the truth of our judgement in virtue of something with which we are acquainted—usually a testimony heard or read. Apart from the information we convey to others, apart from the fact about the actual Bismarck, which gives importance to our judgement, the thought we really have contains the one or more particulars involved, and otherwise consists wholly of concepts.

All names of places—London, England, Europe, the Earth, the Solar System—similarly involve, when used, descriptions which start from some one or more particulars with which we are acquainted. I suspect that even the Universe, as considered by metaphysics, involves such a connexion with particulars. In logic, on the contrary, where we are concerned not merely with what does exist, but with whatever might or could exist or be, no reference to actual particulars is involved.

It would seem that, when we make a statement about something only known by description, we often *intend* to make our statement, not in the form involving the description, but about the actual thing described. That is to say, when we say anything about Bismarck, we should like, if we could, to make the judgement which Bismarck alone can make, namely, the judgment of which he himself is a constituent. In this we are necessarily defeated, since the actual Bismarck is unknown to us. But we know that there is an object B, called Bismarck, and that B was an astute diplomatist. We can thus *describe* the proposition we should like to affirm, namely, 'B was an astute diplomatist', where B is the object which was Bismarck. If we are describing Bismarck as 'the first Chancellor of the German Empire', the proposition we should like to affirm may be described as 'the proposition asserting, concerning the actual object which was the first Chancellor of the German Empire, that this object was an astute diplomatist'. What enables us to communicate in spite of the varying descriptions we employ is that we know there is a true proposition concerning the actual Bismarck, and that however we may vary the description (so long as the description is correct) the proposition described is still the same. This proposition, which is described and is known to be true, is what interests us; but we are not acquainted with the proposition itself, and do not know *it*, though we know it is true.

It will be seen that there are various stages in the removal from acquaintance with particulars: there is Bismarck to people who knew him; Bismarck to those who only know of him through history; the man with the iron mask; the longest-lived of men. These are progressively further removed from acquaintance with particulars; the first comes as near to acquaintance as is possible in regard to another person; in the second, we shall still be said to know 'who Bismarck was'; in the third, we do not know who was the man with the iron mask, though we can know many propositions about him which are not logically deducible from the fact that he wore an iron mask; in the fourth, finally, we know nothing beyond what is logically deducible from the definition of the man. There is a similar hierarchy in the region of universals. Many universals, like many particulars, are only known to us by description. But here, as in the case of particulars, knowledge concerning what is known by description is ultimately reducible to knowledge concerning what is known by acquaintance.

The fundamental principle in the analysis of propositions containing descriptions is this: *Every proposition which we can understand must be composed wholly of constituents with which we are acquainted.*

We shall not at this stage attempt to answer all the objections which may be urged against this fundamental principle. For the present, we shall merely point out that, in some way or other, it must be possible to meet these objections, for it is scarcely conceivable that we can make a judgement or entertain a supposition without knowing what it is that we are judging or supposing about. We must attach *some* meaning to the words we use, if we are to speak significantly and not utter mere noise; and the meaning we attach to our words must be something with which we are acquainted. Thus when, for example, we make a statement about Julius Caesar, it is plain that Julius Caesar himself is not before our minds, since we are not acquainted with him. We have in mind some *description* of Julius Caesar: 'the man who was assassinated on the Ides of March', 'the founder of the Roman Empire', or, perhaps, merely 'the man whose name was *Julius Caesar*'. (In this last description, *Julius Caesar* is a noise or shape with which we are acquainted.) Thus our statement does not mean quite what it seems to mean, but means something involving, instead of Julius Caesar, some description of him which is composed wholly of particulars and universals with which we are acquainted.

The chief importance of knowledge by description is that it enables us to pass beyond the limits of our private experience. In spite of the fact that we can only know truths which are wholly composed of terms which we have experienced in acquaintance, we can yet have knowledge by description of things which we have never experienced. In view of the very narrow range of our immediate experience, this result is vital, and until it is understood, much of our knowledge must remain mysterious and therefore, doubtful.

Edmund Husserl

Born in what is now the Czech Republic, Edmund Husserl (1859–1938) is the seminal figure in twentieth-century German and French philosophy. His philosophical approach, phenomenology, powerfully influenced such continental luminaries as Martin Heidegger, Jean-Paul Sartre, and Maurice Merleau-Ponty, and has increasingly come to influence important thinkers in the Anglo-American philosophical tradition. Early in his career, Husserl was predominantly concerned with the philosophies of mathematics and logic, but problems concerning the foundations of these disciplines drove him toward larger epistemological questions concerning all "objects of consciousness" ("logical" and "empirical"), thus giving rise to his renowned phenomenological approach. His most influential books include *Ideas Pertaining to a Pure Phenomenology and to a Phenomenological Psychology, Book I* (1913), or simply *Ideas I;* the *Cartesian Meditations* (1929), an expanded version of his *Paris Lectures;* and *The Crisis of the European Sciences and Transcendental Phenomenology,* which was published after his death in 1938.

Husserl's phenomenology is based on the desire to get back to "the things themselves"—namely, the way in which objects are immediately apprehended by consciousness. In certain respects, this approach sounds a good deal like empiricism, and, like the empiricists, Husserl not only believes that all knowledge is based on experience but also that the paradigmatic way in which knowledge is acquired is through perception. Husserl believes, nevertheless, that the empiricists fail to adequately attend to the essential features of the perceptual experience itself. As an initial matter, empiricism, at least as it has historically unfolded, gives methodological priority to language rather than experience. Moreover, he believes, even when empiricists attend to the experience itself, they tend to falsify it by focusing solely on the image produced by the object perceived instead of the way in which the object is necessarily experienced by consciousness. For the empiricists, the "sensory data" that comprises the object of which we have an image (for example, its color, shape, and texture) is all that is experienced, but this fails to take into account that this sensory data is actually experienced as a particular object. When I see the cover of a book in the distance, for example, my experience is of a book, even if the sensory data that comprises this perception does not actually warrant this conclusion. Perception thus sketches a "horizon of expectations" in which the experience goes beyond the sensory data, and only based on ensuing perceptions (that is, on further inspection) can I confirm whether I have perceived an actual book—or, as Husserl articulates it, whether my ensuing perceptions "fulfill" the "unfulfilled" or "empty" aspects that augmented my prior perceptual experience. This attribution of empty aspects to experience suggests that, like the rationalists (and in contrast to Locke's notion of the mind as a "blank slate"), Husserl believes that the mind is active in constituting the world of its experience.

According to Husserl, the fundamental feature of consciousness is that it is "intentional," or marked by "intentionality." This means not only that consciousness is always consciousness of something (i.e., that it is always about some object) but also that the mind actively, although typically unconsciously, "intends" the objects of its experience. Thus, when I see the book cover in the distance, and absent other disconfirming perceptions, I simply take it to be the case that a book is there. "Intending" an object as a particular object therefore involves a complex interplay of presence and absence, of fulfilled and unfulfilled aspects: given the necessarily perspectival nature of all perception, all objects are presented to consciousness as mere "profiles." Moreover, what enables me to intend a particular object, notwithstanding the fact that the perceptions I have of it at any given time may not be sufficiently fulfilled for this identification, is that experience itself unfolds in time. For Husserl, consciousness is essentially temporal in nature, as "before," "now," and "after" interpenetrate one another. My horizon of expectations with respect to an object is formed by prior perceptions and can be continually modified by futures ones. What Husserl calls "retentions" (past perceptions that form the ground of my horizon of expectations) and "protentions" (expected perceptions in the immediate future based on past perceptions) are constantly changing, as I am continuously confronted with new sensory data within the perpetual stream of "nows." So, too, consciousness constantly synthesizes the perceptual states that make up this perpetual stream of "nows"—that is, it ties together conscious states over time to give rise to a unified sense of experience that I can identify as my own.

Ultimately, Husserl is concerned with providing indubitable foundations for our experience rather than simply examining it from the "natural" or "ordinary" standpoint. Like Descartes, he wants to ensure the truth of our perceptions to pave the way for a rigorous science (combating skepticism), and, like Descartes, he believes that the only way to do this is to call into question all knowledge of the world and return to the one thing that cannot be called into question: the ego. Going beyond Descartes, however, Husserl argues that the ego is not a substance to be contrasted with matter nor is the ego an "inside" whose task it is to link up with a world that is (mistakenly) viewed as an "outside." What's more, the ego that cannot be called into question is not the empirical ego or self that we ordinarily associate with persons (that is, the qualities that we ordinarily use to describe someone) but is a "transcendental" ego, which is the ultimate ground of subjectivity and, as such for Husserl, the ultimate ground of truth and knowledge. The transcendental ego can never be the object of experience like the empirical ego but (like Kant's transcendental ego) is the condition for the possibility of any experience: it is, therefore, the transcendental ego, pure consciousness or consciousness *as such* that synthesizes our experiences over time. To get to indubitable knowledge, which for Husserl is knowledge that is necessary for any experiencing consciousness, various so-called reductions are needed, the most crucial of which is the phenomenological reduction or *epoché*. With the phenomenological reduction, we bracket or put out of play "the natural attitude," with all its biases, and attend to the object of consciousness as it purely presents itself to consciousness. This step furnishes the foundation on which our more elaborate constitutions of the world (including the natural sciences) are based.

• • •

Good introductions to Husserl's phenomenology are Maurice Nathanson, *Husserl: Philosopher of Infinite Tasks* (Evanston: Northwestern University Press, 1973) and Robert Sokolowski, *Introduction to Phenomenology* (Cambridge: Cambridge University Press, 2000). A thorough introduction to Husserl's *Cartesian Meditations* (the expanded version of the *Paris Lectures*) is A. D. Smith, *Husserl and the Cartesian Meditations* (London: Routledge, 2003). A more advanced approach to Husserl's thought is David Bell, *Husserl* (London: Routledge & Kegan Paul, 1991). A more advanced topical discussion of the central themes in Husserl's thought is Barry Smith and David Woodruff Smith, eds., *The Cambridge Companion to Husserl* (Cambridge: Cambridge University Press, 1995).

David Sherman

Paris Lectures

I am filled with joy at the opportunity to talk about the new phenomenology at this most venerable place of French learning, and for very special reasons.[1] No philosopher of the past has affected the sense of phenomenology as decisively as René Descartes, France's greatest thinker. Phenomenology must honor him as its genuine patriarch. It must be said explicitly that the study of Descartes' *Meditations* has influenced directly the formation of the developing phenomenology and given it its present form, to such an extent that phenomenology might almost be called a new, a twentieth century, Cartesianism.

Under these circumstances I may have advance assurance of your interest, especially if I start with those themes in the *Meditationes de prima philosophia*[2] which are timeless, and if through them I point out the transformations and new concepts which give birth to what is characteristic of the phenomenological method and its problems.

Every beginner in philosophy is familiar with the remarkable train of thought in the *Meditations*. Their goal, as we remember, is a complete reform of philosophy, including all the sciences, since the latter are merely dependent members of the one universal body of knowledge which is philosophy. Only through systematic unity can the sciences achieve genuine rationality, which, as they have developed so far, is missing. What is needed is a radical reconstruction which will *satisfy* the ideal of philosophy as being the *universal unity of knowledge* by means of a unitary and *absolutely rational foundation*. Descartes carries out the demand for reconstruction in terms of a subjectively oriented philosophy. This subjective turn is carried out in two steps.

First, anyone who seriously considers becoming a philosopher must once in his life withdraw into himself and then, from within attempt to destroy and rebuild all previous learning. Philosophy is the supremely personal affair of the one who philosophizes. It is the question of *his sapientia universalis*, the aspiration of *his* knowledge for the universal. In particular, the philosopher's quest is for truly scientific knowledge, knowledge for which he can assume—from the very beginning and in every subsequent step—complete responsibility by using *his* own absolutely self-evident justifications. I can become a genuine philosopher only by freely choosing to focus my life on this goal. Once I am thus committed and have accordingly chosen to begin with total poverty and destruction, my first problem is to discover an absolutely secure starting point and rules of procedure, when, in actual fact, I lack any support from the existing disciplines. Consequently, the Cartesian meditations must not be viewed as the private affair of the philosopher Descartes, but as the necessary prototype for the meditations of any beginning philosopher whatsoever.

When we now turn our attention to the content of the *Meditations*, a content which appears rather strange to us today, we notice immediately a *return to the philosophizing ego* in a second and deeper sense. It is the familiar and epoch-making return to the ego as subject of his pure *cogitationes*.[3] It is the ego which, while it suspends all beliefs about the reality of the world on the grounds that these are not indubitable, discovers itself as the only apodictically certain being.

The ego is engaged, first of all, in philosophizing that is seriously solipsistic. He looks for apodictically certain and yet purely subjective procedures through which an objective external world can be deduced. Descartes does this in a well-known manner. He first infers both the existence and *veracitas*[4] of God. Then,

Reprinted from *Paris Lectures*, translated by P. Koestenbaum (The Hague, Netherlands: Martinus Nijhoff, 1964), by permission of the publisher.

1. [The Paris lectures were delivered at the Sorbonne.—S.M.C.]

2. [Meditations on First Philosophy.]

3. [Thoughts.]

4. [Truthfulness.]

through their mediation, he deduces objective reality as a dualism of substances. In this way he reaches the objective ground of knowledge and the particular sciences themselves as well. All his inferences are based on immanent principles, i.e., principles which are innate to the Ego.

So much for Descartes. We now ask, is it really worthwhile to hunt critically for the eternal significance of these thoughts? Can these infuse life into our age?

Doubt is raised, in any event, by the fact that the positive sciences, for which the meditations were to have served as absolutely rational foundation, have paid so very little attention to them. Nonetheless, and despite the brilliant development experienced by the sciences over the last three centuries, they feel themselves today seriously limited by the obscurity of their foundations. But it scarcely occurs to them to refer to the Cartesian meditations for the reformulation of their foundations.

On the other hand, serious consideration must be given to the fact that the meditations constitute an altogether unique and epochal event in the history of philosophy, specifically because of their return to the *ego cogito*.[5] As a matter of fact, Descartes inaugurates a completely new type of philosophy. Philosophy, with its style now changed altogether, experiences a radical conversion from naive objectivism to *transcendental subjectivism*. This subjectivism strives toward a pure end-form through efforts that are constantly renewed yet always remain unsatisfactory. Might it not be that this continuing tendency has eternal significance? Perhaps it is a vast task assigned to us by history itself, invoking our collective cooperation.

The splintering of contemporary philosophy and its aimless activity make us pause. Must this situation not be traced back to the fact that the motivations from which Descartes' meditations emanate have lost their original vitality? Is it not true that the only fruitful renaissance is one which reawakens these meditations, not in order to accept them, but to reveal the profound truth in the radicalism of a return to the *ego cogito* with the external values that reside therein?

In any case, this is the path that led to transcendental phenomenology.

5. [Thinking self.]

Let us now pursue this path together. In true Cartesian fashion, we shall become philosophers meditating in a radical sense, with, of course, frequent and critical modifications of the older Cartesian meditations. What was merely germinal in them must be freely developed here.

We thus begin, everyone for himself and in himself, with the decision to disregard all our present knowledge. We do not give up Descartes' guiding goal of an absolute foundation for knowledge. At the beginning, however, to presuppose even the possibility of that goal would be prejudice. We are satisfied to discover the goal and nature of science by submerging ourselves in scientific activity. It is the spirit of science to count nothing as really scientific which cannot be fully justified by the evidence. In other words, science demands proof by *reference to the things and facts themselves, as these are given in actual experience and intuition*. Thus guided, we, the beginning philosophers make it a rule to judge only by the evidence. Also, the evidence itself must be subjected to critical verification, and that on the basis, of course, of further available evidence. Since from the beginning we have disregarded the sciences, we operate within our prescientific life, which is likewise filled with immediate and mediate evidences. This, and nothing else, is first given to us.

Herein arises our first question. Can we find evidence that is both immediate and apodictic? Can we find evidence that is primitive, in the sense that it must by necessity precede all other evidence?

As we meditate on this question one thing does, in fact, emerge as both prior to all evidence and as apodictic. It is the existence of the world. All science refers to the world, and before that, our ordinary life already makes reference to it. *That the being of the world precedes everything is* so *obvious* that no one thinks to articulate it in a sentence. Our experience of the world is continuous, incessant, and unquestionable. But is it true that this experiential evidence, even though taken for granted, is really apodictic and primary to all other evidence? We will have to deny both. Is it not the case that occasionally something manifests itself as a sensory illusion? Has not the coherent and unified totality of our experience been at times debased as a mere dream? We will ignore Descartes' attempt to prove that, notwithstanding the fact of its being constantly experienced, the world's nonbeing can be conceived. His proof is carried out by a much too superficial criticism of sensory experience. We will keep this much: experiential evidence that is to serve as radical foundation for knowledge needs, above all, a critique of its validity and range. It cannot be accepted as apodictic without question and qualification. Therefore, merely to disregard all knowledge and to treat the sciences as prejudices is not enough. Even the experience of the world as the true universal ground of knowledge becomes an unacceptably naive belief. We can no longer accept the reality of the world as a fact to be for taken for granted. *It is a hypothesis that needs verification.*

Does there remain a ground of being? Do we still have a basis for all judgments and evidences, a basis on which a universal philosophy can rest apodictically? Is not "world" the name for the totality of all that is? Might it not turn out that the world is not the truly ultimate basis for judgment, but instead that its existence presupposes a prior ground of being?

Here, specifically following Descartes, we make the great shift which, properly carried out, leads to *transcendental subjectivity*. This is the shift to the *ego cogito*, as the apodictically certain and *last basis for judgment* upon which all radical philosophy must be grounded.

Let us consider: as radically meditating philosophers we now have neither knowledge that is valid for us nor a world that exists for us. We can no longer say that the world is real—a belief that is natural enough in our ordinary experience—; instead, it merely makes a claim to reality. This skepticism also applies to other selves, so that we rightly should not speak communicatively, that is, in the plural. Other people and animals are, of course, given to me only through sensory experience. Since I have questioned the validity of the latter I cannot avail myself of it here. With the loss of other minds I lose, of course, all forms of sociability and culture. In short, the entire concrete world ceases to have reality for me and becomes instead mere appearance, However, whatever may be the veracity of the claim to being made by phenomena, whether they represent reality or appearance, phenomena in themselves cannot be disregarded as mere "nothing." On the contrary, it is precisely the phenomena themselves which, without exception, render possible for me the very existence of both reality and appearance. Again, I may freely abstain from entertaining any belief about experience—which I did. This simply means that I refuse to assert the reality of the world. Nonetheless, we must be careful to realize that this epistemological abstention is still what it is: it includes the whole stream of experienced life and all its particulars, the appearances of objects, other people, cultural situations, etc. Nothing changes, except that I no longer accept the world simply as real; I no longer judge regarding the distinction between reality and appearance. I must similarly abstain from any other of my opinions, judgments, and valuations about the world, since these likewise assume the reality of the world, But for these, as for other phenomena, epistemological abstention does not mean their disappearance, at least not as pure phenomena.

This ubiquitous detachment from any point of view regarding the objective world we term the *phenomenological epoché*. It is the methodology through which I come to understand myself as that ego and life of consciousness in which and through which the entire objective world exists for me, and is for me precisely as it is, Everything in the world, all spatio-temporal being, exists for me because I experience it, because I perceive it, remember it, think of it in any way, judge it, value it, desire it, etc. It is well known that Descartes designates all this by the term *cogito*. For me the world is nothing other than what I am aware of and what appears valid in such *cogitations. The whole meaning and reality of the world rests exclusively on such cogitationes.* My entire worldly life takes its course within these. I cannot live, experience, think, value, and act in any world which is not in some sense in me, and derives its meaning and truth from me. If I place myself above that entire life and if I abstain from any commitment about reality, specifically one which accepts the world as existing, and if I view that life exclusively as consciousness *of* the world, then I reveal myself as the pure ego with its pure stream of *cogitationes*.

I certainly do not discover myself as one item among others in the world, since I have altogether suspended judgment about the world. I am not the ego of an individual man. I am the ego in whose stream of consciousness the world itself—including myself as an object in it, a man who exists in the world—first acquires meaning and reality.

We have reached a dangerous point. It seems simple indeed to understand the pure ego with its *cogitationes* by following Descartes. And yet it is as if we were on the brink of a precipice, where the ability to step calmly and surely decides between philosophic life and philosophic death. Descartes was thoroughly sincere in his desire to be radical and presuppositionless. However, we know through recent researches—particularly the fine and penetrating work of Messrs. Gilson[6] and Koyré[7]—that a great deal of Scholasticism is hidden in Descartes' meditations as unarticulated prejudice. But this is not all. We must above all avoid the prejudices, hardly noticed by us, which derive from our emphasis on the mathematically oriented natural sciences. These prejudices make it appear as if the phrase *ego cogito* refers to an apodictic and primitive axiom, one which, in conjunction with others to be derived from it, provides the foundation for a deductive and universal science, a science *ordine geometrico*.[8] In relation to this we must under no circumstances take for granted that, with our apodictic and pure ego, we have salvaged a small corner of the world as the single indubitable fact about the world which can be utilized by the philosophizing ego. It is not true that all that now remains to be done is to infer the rest of the world through correct deductive procedures according to principles that are innate to the ego.

Unfortunately, Descartes commits this error, in the apparently insignificant yet fateful transformation of the ego to a *substantia cogitans*,[9] to an independent human *animus*,[10] which then becomes the point of departure for conclusions by means of the principle of causality. In short, this is the transformation which made Descartes the father of the rather absurd transcendental realism. We will keep aloof from all this if we remain true to radicalism in our self-examination and with it to the principle of pure intuition. We must regard nothing as veridical except the pure immediacy and givenness in the field of the *ego cogito* which the *epoché*[11] has opened up to us. In other words, we must not make assertions about that which we do not ourselves *see*. In these matters Descartes was deficient. It so happens that he stands before the greatest of all discoveries—in a sense he has already made it—yet fails to see its true significance, that of transcendental subjectivity. He does not pass through the gateway that leads into genuine transcendental philosophy.

The independent *epoché* with regard to the nature of the world as it appears and is real to me—that is, "real" to the previous and natural point of view—discloses the greatest and most magnificent of all facts: I and my life remain—in my sense of reality—untouched by whichever way we decide the issue of whether the world is or is not. To say, in my natural existence, "I am, I think, I live," means that I am one human being among others in the world, that I am related to nature through my physical body, and that in this body my *cogitationes*, perceptions, memories, judgments, etc. are incorporated as psycho-physical facts. Conceived in this way, I, we, humans, and animals are subject-matter for the objective sciences, that is, for biology, anthropology, and zoology, and also for psychology. The life of the psyche, which is the subject-matter of all psychology, is understood only as the psychic life in the world. The methodology of a purified Cartesianism demands of me, the one who philosophizes, the phenomenological *epoché*. The *epoché* eliminates as worldly facts from my field of judgment both the reality of the objective world in general and the sciences of the world. *Consequently, for me there exists no "I" and there are no psychic actions, that is, psychic phenomena in the psychological sense.* To myself I do not exist as a human being, [nor] do my *cogitationes* exist as components of a psychophysical world. But through all this I have discovered my true self. I have discovered that I alone am the pure ego, with pure existence and pure capacities (for example, the obvious capacity to abstain from judging). Through this ego alone does *the being of the world*, and, for that matter, any being whatsoever, make sense *to me* and has possible validity, The

6. [The reference is to Étienne Henri Gilson (1884–1978), the French philosopher and historian, who was a leader of the Roman Catholic neo-Thomist movement.]

7. [The reference is to Alexandre Koyré (1892–1964), a Russian historian of science, who taught for many years at the Sorbonne.]

8. [On the order of geometry.]

9. [Thinking substance.]

10. [Mind.]

11. [Suspension of belief.]

world—whose conceivable nonbeing does not extinguish my pure being but rather presupposes it—is termed *transcendent*, whereas my pure being or my pure ego is termed *transcendental*. Through the phenomenological *epoché* the natural human ego, specifically my own, is reduced to the transcendental ego. This is the meaning of the phenomenological reduction.

Further steps are needed so that what has been developed up to this point can be adequately applied. What is the philosophic use of the transcendental ego? To be sure, for me, the one who philosophizes, it obviously precedes, in an epistemological sense, all objective reality. In a way, it is the basis for all objective knowledge, be it good or bad, But does the fact that the transcendental ego precedes and presupposes all objective knowledge mean also that it is an epistemological ground in the ordinary sense? The thought is tempting. All realistic theories are guilty of it. But the temptation to look in the transcendental subjectivity for premises guaranteeing the existence of the subjective world evanesces once we realize that all arguments, considered in themselves, exist already in transcendental subjectivity itself. Furthermore, all proofs for the world have their criteria set in the world just as it is given and justified in experience. However, these considerations must not be construed as a rejection of the great Cartesian idea that the ultimate basis for objective science and the reality of the objective world is to be sought in transcendental subjectivity. Otherwise—our criticisms aside—we would not be true to Descartes' method of meditation. However, the Cartesian discovery of the ego may perhaps open up a *new concept of foundation, namely, a transcendental foundation*.

In point of fact, instead of using the *ego cogito* merely as an apodictic proposition and as an absolutely primitive premise, we notice that the phenomenological *epoché* has uncovered for us (or for me, the one who philosophizes), through the apodictic *I am*, a new kind and an endless sphere of being. This is the sphere of a new kind of experience: transcendental experience. And herewith also arises the possibility of both transcendental epistemology and transcendental science.

A most extraordinary epistemological situation is disclosed here. The phenomenological *epoché* reduces me to my transcendental and pure ego. I am, thus, at least *prima facie*, in a certain sense *solus ipse*,[12] but not in the ordinary sense, in which one might say that a man survived a universal holocaust in a world which itself remained unaffected. Once I have banished from my sphere of judgments the world, as one which receives its being from me and within me, then I, as the transcendental ego which is prior to the world, am *the sole source and object capable of judgment*. And now I am supposed to develop an unheard-of and unique science, since it is one that is created exclusively by and inside my transcendental subjectivity! Furthermore, this science is meant to apply, at least at the outset, to my transcendental subjectivity alone. It thus becomes a transcendental-solipsistic science. It is therefore not the *ego cogito*, but a science about the ego—a pure *egology*—which becomes the ultimate foundation of philosophy in the Cartesian sense of a universal science, and which must provide at least the cornerstone for its absolute foundation. In actual fact this science exists already as the lowest transcendental phenomenology. And I mean the lowest, not the fully developed phenomenology, because to the latter, of course, belongs the further development from transcendental solipsism to transcendental intersubjectivity.

To make all this intelligible it is first necessary to do what was neglected by Descartes, namely, to describe the endless field of the ego's transcendental experience itself. His own experience, as is well known, and especially when he judged it to be apodictic, plays a role in the philosophy of Descartes. But he neglected to describe the ego in the full concretion of its transcendental being and life, nor did he regard it as an unlimited work-project to be pursued systematically. It is an insight central to a philosopher that, by introducing the transcendental reduction, he can reflect truthfully on his *cogitationes* and on their pure phenomenological content. In this way he can uncover all aspects of his transcendental being with respect to both his transcendental-temporal life and also his capabilities. We are clearly dealing with a train of thought parallel to what the world-centered psychologist calls inner experience or experience of the self.

One thing of the greatest, even decisive, impor-

12. [A self alone.]

tance remains. One cannot lightly dismiss the fact—even Descartes has so remarked on occasion—that the *epoché* changes nothing in the world. All experience is still his experience, all consciousness, still his consciousness. The expression *ego cogito* must be expanded by one term. Every *cogito* contains a meaning: its *cogitatum.* The experience of a house, as I experience it, and ignoring theories of perception, is precisely an experience of this and only this house, a house which appears in such-and-such a way, and has certain specific determinations when seen from the side, from near-by, and from afar. Similarly, a clear or a vague recollection is the recollection of a vaguely or clearly apprehended house. Even the most erroneous judgment means a judgment about such-and-such factual content, and so on. *The essence of consciousness, in which I live as my own self, is the so-called intentionality.* Consciousness is always consciousness of something. The nature of consciousness includes, as modes of being, presentations, probabilities, and non-being, and also the modes of appearance, goodness, and value, etc. Phenomenological experience as reflection must avoid any interpretative constructions. Its descriptions must reflect accurately the concrete contents of experience, precisely as these are experienced.

To interpret consciousness as a complex of sense data and then to bring forth gestalt-like qualities out of these—which are subsequently equated with the totality—is a sensualist invention. This interpretation is a basic error even from the worldly and psychological perspective, and much more so from the transcendental point of view. It is true that in the process of phenomenological analyses sense data do occur, and something is, in fact, disclosed about them. But what phenomenological analysis fails to find as primary is the "perception of an external world." The honest description of the unadulterated data of experience must disclose what appears first of all, i.e., the *cogito.* For example, we must describe closely the perception of a house in terms of what it means as object and its modes of appearing. The same applies to all forms of consciousness.

When phenomenology examines objects of consciousness—regardless of what kind, whether real or ideal—it deals with these exclusively as objects of the immediate consciousness. The description—which attempts to grasp the concrete and rich phenomena of the *cogitationes*—must constantly glance back from the side of the object to the side of consciousness and pursue the general existing connections. For example, if I consider the perception of a hexahedron, then I notice in pure reflection that the hexahedron is given as a continuous and unitary object together with a many-formed and determinate manifold of modes of appearance. It is the same hexahedron, the same appearance, regardless of whether viewed from this side or that one, from this or that perspective, from close or from afar, with greater or with lesser distinctness and determinateness. Nonetheless, if we see any hexahedral surface, any edge or corner, any spot of color, in short, any aspect of the objective sense, then we notice the same thing in every case: it is the unity of a manifold with constantly changing modes of appearance, a unity of its particular perspectives and of the particular differentiations of the subjective here and there. If we look uncritically we find a color that is always identical and unchanging. But if we reflect on the mode in which it appears we recognize that the color is nothing other, nor can it be thought as anything other, than that which presents itself now as this and now as that shade of color. Unity is always unity of representations, which is the representation of the spontaneous presentation of color or the presentation of an edge. . . .

Intentional analysis is thus something altogether different from analysis in the ordinary sense. The life of consciousness is neither a mere aggregate of data, nor a heap of psychic atoms, nor a whole composed of elements united through gestalt-like qualities. This is true also of pure introspective psychology, as a parallel to transcendental phenomenology. *Intentional analysis is the disclosure of the actualities and potentialities in which objects constitute themselves as perceptual units.* Furthermore, all perceptual analysis takes place in the transition from real events to the intentional horizons suggested by them.

This late insight prescribes to phenomenological analysis and description an altogether new methodology, It is a methodology which goes into action whenever objects and meanings, questions about being, questions about possibilities, questions of origin, and questions of right are to be considered seriously. Every intentional analysis reaches beyond the immediately and actually given events of the immanent sphere, and in such a way that the analysis discloses potentialities—which are now given actually and whose horizons have been sketched—and brings out manifold aspects of new experiences in which are made manifest what earlier was meant only implicitly and in this way was already present intentionally. When I see a hexahedron I say, in reality and in truth I see it only from one side. It is nonetheless evident that what I now experience is in reality more. The perception includes a nonsensory belief through which the visible side can be understood to be a mere side in the first place. But how does this belief, that there is more, disclose itself? How does it become obvious that I mean more? It occurs through the transition to a synthetic sequence of possible perceptions, perceptions I would have—as indeed I can—were I to walk around the object. Phenomenology always explains meanings, that is, intentionality, by producing these sense-fulfilling syntheses. The tremendous task placed on description is to expound the universal structure of transcendental consciousness in its reference to and creation of meanings. . . .

The conceptual fixation of an intentional object-class leads, in intentional researches, as one soon recognizes, to an organization or order. In other words, transcendental subjectivity is not a chaos of intentional experiences, but it is a unity through synthesis. It is a many-levelled synthesis in which always new classes and individuals are constituted. However, every object expresses a *rule structured within transcendental subjectivity*. . . .

An object exists for me; that is to say, it has reality for me in consciousness. But this reality is reality for me only as long as I believe that I can confirm it. By this I mean that I must be able to provide usable procedures, that is, procedures which run through automatically, and other evidences, which lead me then to the object itself and through which I realize the object as being *truly there*. The same holds when my awareness of the object is a matter of experience, that is, when my awareness tells me that the object itself is already there, that the object is seen. This act of seeing, in turn, points to further seeing, that is, it points to the possibility of confirmation. Finally, it points to the fact that what has already once been realized as being can nonetheless be restored, again and again, to its previous condition of progressive confirmation.

Think about the tremendous importance of this remark, considering that we are on an egological foundation. We can see, from this ultimate point of view, that existence and essence have for us, in reality and truth, no other meaning than that of possible confirmation. Furthermore, these confirmation-procedures and their accessibility belong to me as transcendental subjectivity and make sense only as such.

True being, therefore, whether real or ideal, *has significance only as a particular correlate of my own intentionality*, actual or potential. Of course, this is not true of an isolated *cogito*. For example, the being of a real thing is not the mere *cogito* of an isolated perception that I now have. But the perception and its intentionally given object call to my attention, by virtue of the presumed horizon, an endless and open-system of *possible* perceptions, perceptions which are not invented but which are motivated from within my intentional existence, and which can lose their presumed validity only when conflicting experience eliminates it. These possible perceptions are necessarily presupposed as *my* possibilities, ones which I can bring about—provided I am not hindered—by approaching the object, looking around it, etc.

Needless to say, the foregoing has been stated very crudely. Extremely far-reaching and complex intentional analyses are needed in order to explain the structure of these possibilities as they relate to the specific horizons belonging to every individual class of objects, and to clarify therewith the meaning of actual being. At the outset only one fact is evident and guides me, namely, that I accept as being only that which presents itself to me as being, and that all conceivable justification of it lies within my own self and is determined in my immediate and mediate intentionality, in which any other meaning of being is also to be determined.

Jean-Paul Sartre

Born in Paris in 1905, Jean-Paul Sartre spent a number of years after graduating from the École Normale Supérieure teaching in *lycées* (roughly equivalent to high schools). His study of phenomenology in Berlin in 1933–1934 led to his early works, *Nausea, Transcendence of the Ego,* and his greatest work, *Being and Nothingness* (1943). His 1945 lecture, "The Humanism of Existentialism" (published in 1946), contributed to the worldwide vogue of existentialism in the fifties and sixties. Sartre also wrote novels and plays, including *No Exit, The Age of Reason, The Wall,* and *The Flies,* and for many years he edited *Les Temps Modernes,* the most influential literary journal in France. One of the greatest intellectuals in French history, he was mourned in the streets of Paris by tens of thousands of people when he died in 1980.

"The Humanism of Existentialism" was a popular lecture designed to answer critics and present a rough outline of Sartre's views. In response to charges that existentialism paints a dreary picture of human existence, Sartre claims that this philosophy is the most humanistic of all, for it starts out from a description of how things appear to us prior to reflection and theorizing, and it rejects the idea that there is any transcendent basis for values or truth to which humans must submit themselves. This is part of what it means to say that "subjectivity" is the starting point: we have no choice but to begin with a phenomenological account of how things present themselves to us in our ordinary experience.

Sartre defines existentialism as the view that, for humans, "existence precedes essence." This succinct formula is best understood by contrasting it with "essentialism," the view that, for any type of thing in the world, there is an essence (e.g., a Platonic Form) that determines in advance what things of that type are and what they ought to be. Sartre diagnoses essentialism by suggesting that such a view only makes sense if people assume that there is a Creator who has created things in the world in a way similar to that in which human artisans create tools. In other words, essentialism assumes that, just as craftspersons have a concept of what a tool should be before they create it, so God also has a plan for creation and has created things with particular ideas about what things should be. It would follow, then, that whatever exists is derived from, and should strive to be like, the essences that existed in the mind of God before creation.

Existentialism, in Sartre's definition, holds the exact opposite view. If "God is dead" (as Nietzsche claimed) and there are no transcendent Absolutes that determine what things are and ought to be, then for one type of entity at least, for humans, existence precedes essence. This means that humans first exist—they just show up one day; they are there, involved in the world and trying to accomplish something—and only afterward do they create their own identity (or essence) through what they do. If there is no essence or human nature given in advance, it follows that humans are self-creating beings: they make themselves in the course of living out their lives. In this sense, you *are* what you *do*—you fashion your own identity through the choices you make as an agent in the world. For example, if you generally run away whenever you are faced with a frightening situation, then you are making yourself into a coward. Being a coward is something you are choosing for yourself, though you are probably quite unaware that you are doing so. Since each of us creates a configuration of possibilities for ourselves in the choices we make in our lives, Sartre can say that we are nothing other than the "ensemble" of our actions over a lifetime.

If there is no pregiven human nature that determines in advance how we act, then we are free in the sense that we are the ultimate causes of our actions. To say that we are free is not to say that environmental and genetic factors have no influence on what we are and do. Sartre insists that, as living organisms in the causal order of the world, we are *en soi* or "in itself," as much a part of the causal order as a lectern or a cauliflower. But he holds that, as self-conscious—as *pour soi* or "for itself"—we can become aware of these causal factors and reflect on them, and through this reflection we can decide what these factors mean to us and interfere with their influence if we wish. In this respect, we always "surpass" or "transcend" our causal conditioning: we can step back from the causal context in which we find ourselves and redefine it through our choices. We are therefore fully responsible for everything we do.

On what basis do we make our choices? Sartre argues that there is no basis for choice. Ethical principles are always too general and broad to provide guidance in dealing with concrete moral dilemmas. Moreover, our ethical principles are just as much a matter of free choice as the actions themselves. If we turn to an advisor, we usually know in advance what they will say, so that choosing an advisor is choosing the advice. Even our feelings can't be a guide, because as a rule we don't know how we really feel about things until after we have acted. In the end, making a choice comes down to just taking a leap in one direction rather than another. You just "invent" or "create," in the same way a painter might decide to splash a little red in the corner of a painting. There are no rules or directives that compel us to act in one way rather than another. We are alone, with neither excuses behind us nor justifications before us.

"The Humanism of Existentialism" tries to respond to charges that existentialism undermines ethics by leaving individuals with no basis for deliberation or choice in deciding how to act. Though Sartre's reasoning is not easy to follow here, he seems to be saying that, since phenomenology shows that the individual is only an instance of the human, with no morally relevant differences from other humans, one should see that, in making choices, one is always choosing for all humans. Sartre here seems to be looking for something like Kant's "principle of universalizability." In choosing to act in a specific way, I commit myself to the position that all people should act, or are entitled to act, in the same way. This attempt to save ethics has been subjected to some powerful criticisms over the years, and the jury is still out on whether existentialism makes room for ethics.

• • •

A clear summary and criticism of Sartre is found in Richard Bernstein, *Praxis and Action* (Philadelphia: University of Pennsylvania Press, 1971). Good studies dealing with the topics of freedom and ethics are Thomas C. Anderson, *Sartre's Two Ethics: From Authenticity to Integral Humanity* (La Salle, Ill.: Open Court, 1993); David Detmer, *Freedom as a Value: A Critique of the Ethical Theory of Jean-Paul Sartre* (La Salle, Ill.: Open Court, 1988); and Thomas Busch, *The Power of Consciousness and the Force of Circumstances in Sartre's Philosophy* (Bloomington: Indiana University Press, 1990).

Charles Guignon

The Humanism of Existentialism

I should like on this occasion to defend existentialism against some charges which have been brought against it.

First, it has been charged with inviting people to remain in a kind of desperate quietism because, since no solutions are possible, we should have to consider action in this world as quite impossible. We should then end up in a philosophy of contemplation; and since contemplation is a luxury, we come in the end to a bourgeois philosophy. The communists in particular have made these charges.

On the other hand, we have been charged with dwelling on human degradation, with pointing up everywhere the sordid, shady, and slimy, and neglecting the gracious and beautiful, the bright side of human nature; for example, according to Mlle. Mercier, a Catholic critic, with forgetting the smile of the child. Both sides charge us with having ignored human solidarity, with considering man as an isolated being. The communists say that the main reason for this is that we take pure subjectivity, the *Cartesian I think*, as our starting point; in other words, the moment in which man becomes fully aware of what it means to him to be an isolated being; as a result, we are unable to return to a state of solidarity with the men who are not ourselves, a state which we can never reach in the *cogito*.

From the Christian standpoint, we are charged with denying the reality and seriousness of human undertakings, since, if we reject God's commandments and the eternal verities, there no longer remains anything but pure caprice, with everyone permitted to do as he pleases and incapable, from his own point of view, of condemning the points of view and acts of others.

I shall try today to answer these different charges. Many people are going to be surprised at what is said here about humanism. We shall try to see in what sense it is to be understood. In any case, what can be said from the very beginning is that by existentialism we mean a doctrine which makes human life possible and, in addition, declares that every truth and every action implies a human setting and a human subjectivity.

As is generally known, the basic charge against us is that we put the emphasis on the dark side of human life. Someone recently told me of a lady who, when she let slip a vulgar word in a moment of irritation, excused herself by saying, "I guess I'm becoming an existentialist." Consequently, existentialism is regarded as something ugly; that is why we are said to be naturalists; and if we are, it is rather surprising that in this day and age we cause so much more alarm and scandal than does naturalism, properly so called. The kind of person who can take in his stride such a novel as Zola's *The Earth*[1] is disgusted as soon as he starts reading an existentialist novel; the kind of person who is resigned to the wisdom of the ages—which is pretty sad—finds us even sadder. Yet, what can be more disillusioning than saying "true charity begins at home" or "a scoundrel will always return evil for good?"

We know the commonplace remarks made when this subject comes up, remarks which always add up to the same thing: we shouldn't struggle against the powers-that-be; we shouldn't resist authority; we shouldn't try to rise above our station; any action which doesn't conform to authority is romantic; any effort not based on past experience is doomed to failure; experience shows that man's bent is always toward trouble, that there must be a strong hand to hold him in check, if not, there will be anarchy. There are still people who go on mumbling these melancholy old saws, the people who say, "It's only human!" whenever a more or less repugnant act is pointed out to them, the people who glut themselves

1. [The reference is to the French novelist Émile Zola (1840–1902).—S.M.C.]

on *chansons réalistes*; these are the people who accuse existentialism of being too gloomy; and to such an extent that I wonder whether they are complaining about it, not for its pessimism, but much rather its optimism. Can it be that what really scares them in the doctrine I shall try to present here is that it leaves to man a possibility of choice? To answer this question, we must re-examine it on a strictly philosophical plane. What is meant by the term *existentialism?*

Most people who use the word would be rather embarrassed if they had to explain it, since, now that the word is all the rage, even the work of a musician or painter is being called existentialist. A gossip columnist in *Clartés* signs himself *The Existentialist*, so that by this time the word has been so stretched and has taken on so broad a meaning, that it no longer means anything at all. It seems that for want of an advance-guard doctrine analogous to surrealism, the kind of people who are eager for scandal and flurry turn to this philosophy which in other respects does not at all serve their purposes in this sphere.

Actually, it is the least scandalous, the most austere of doctrines. It is intended strictly for specialists and philosophers. Yet it can be defined easily. What complicates matters is that there are two kinds of existentialist; first, those who are Christian, among whom I would include Jaspers[2] and Gabriel Marcel,[3] both Catholic; and on the other hand the atheistic existentialists, among whom I class Heidegger,[4] and then the French existentialists and myself. What they have in common is that they think that existence precedes essence, or, if you prefer, that subjectivity must be the starting point.

Just what does that mean? Let us consider some object that is manufactured, for example, a book or a paper-cutter: here is an object which has been made by an artisan whose inspiration came from a concept. He referred to the concept of what a paper-cutter is and likewise to a known method of production, which is part of the concept, something which is, by and large, a routine. Thus, the paper-cutter is at once an object produced in a certain way and, on the other hand, one having a specific use; and one cannot postulate a man who produces a paper-cutter but does not know what it is used for. Therefore, let us say that, for the paper-cutter, essence—that is, the ensemble of both the production routines and the properties which enable it to be both produced and defined—precedes existence. Thus, the presence of the paper-cutter or book in front of me is determined. Therefore, we have here a technical view of the world whereby it can be said that production precedes existence.

When we conceive God as the Creator, He is generally thought of as a superior sort of artisan. Whatever doctrine we may be considering, whether one like that of Descartes or that of Leibniz, we always grant that will more or less follows understanding or, at the very least, accompanies it, and that when God creates He knows exactly what He is creating. Thus, the concept of man in the mind of God is comparable to the concept of paper-cutter in the mind of the manufacturer, and, following certain techniques and a conception, God produces man, just as the artisan, following a definition and a technique, makes a paper-cutter. Thus, the individual man is the realization of a certain concept in the divine intelligence.

In the eighteenth century, the atheism of the *philosophes* discarded the idea of God, but not so much for the notion that essence precedes existence. To a certain extent, this idea is found everywhere; we find it in Diderot,[5] in Voltaire,[6] and even in Kant. Man has a human nature; this human nature, which is the concept of the human, is found in all men, which means that each man is a particular example of a universal concept, man. In Kant, the result of this universality is that the wild-man, the natural man, as well as the bourgeois, are circumscribed by the same definition and have the same basic qualities. Thus, here too the essence of man precedes the historical existence that we find in nature.

Atheistic existentialism, which I represent, is more coherent. It states that if God does not exist, there is at least one being in whom existence precedes essence, a

2. [The reference is to the German philosopher Karl Jaspers (1883–1969).]

3. [The reference is to the French philosopher and dramatist (1889–1973).]

4. [The reference is to the German philosopher Martin Heidegger (1889–1976).]

5. [The reference is to the French philosopher, playwright, and critic Denis Diderot (1713–1784).]

6. [The reference is to the influential French philosopher, historian, writer, and critic François Marie Arouet de Voltaire (1694–1778).]

being who exists before he can be defined by any concept, and that this being is man, or, as Heidegger says, human reality. What is meant here by saying that existence precedes essence? It means that, first of all, man exists, turns up, appears on the scene, and, only afterwards, defines himself. If man, as the existentialist conceives him, is indefinable, it is because at first he is nothing. Only afterward will he be something, and he himself will have made what he will be. Thus, there is no human nature, since there is no God to conceive it. Not only is man what he conceives himself to be, but he is also only what he wills himself to be after this thrust toward existence.

Man is nothing else but what he makes of himself. Such is the first principle of existentialism. It is also what is called subjectivity, the name we are labeled with when charges are brought against us. But what do we mean by this, if not that man has a greater dignity than a stone or table? For we mean that man first exists, that is, that man first of all is the being who hurls himself toward a future and who is conscious of imagining himself as being in the future. Man is at the start a plan which is aware of itself, rather than a patch of moss, a piece of garbage, or a cauliflower; nothing exists prior to this plan; there is nothing in heaven; man will be what he will have planned to be. Not what he will want to be. Because by the word "will" we generally mean a conscious decision, which is subsequent to what we have already made of ourselves. I may want to belong to a political party, write a book, get married; but all that is only a manifestation of an earlier, more spontaneous choice that is called "will." But if existence really does precede essence, man is responsible for what he is. Thus, existentialism's first move is to make every man aware of what he is and to make the full responsibility of his existence rest on him. And when we say that a man is responsible for himself, we do not only mean that he is responsible for his own individuality, but that he is responsible for all men.

The word subjectivism has two meanings, and our opponents play on the two. Subjectivism means, on the one hand, that an individual chooses and makes himself; and, on the other, that it is impossible for man to transcend human subjectivity. The second of these is the essential meaning of existentialism. When we say that man chooses his own self, we mean that every one of us does likewise; but we also mean by that that in making this choice he also chooses all men. In fact, in creating the man that we want to be, there is not a single one of our acts which does not at the same time create an image of man as we think he ought to be. To choose to be this or that is to affirm at the same time the value of what we choose, because we can never choose evil. We always choose the good, and nothing can be good for us without being good for all.

If, on the other hand, existence precedes essence, and if we grant that we exist and fashion our image at one and the same time, the image is valid for everybody and for our whole age. Thus, our responsibility is much greater than we might have supposed, because it involves all mankind. If I am a workingman and choose to join a Christian trade-union rather than be a communist, and if by being a member I want to show that the best thing for man is resignation, that the kingdom of man is not of this world, I am not only involving my own case—I want to be resigned for everyone. As a result, my action has involved all humanity. To take a more individual matter, if I want to marry, to have children; even if this marriage depends solely on my own circumstances or passion or wish, I am involving all humanity in monogamy and not merely myself. Therefore, I am responsible for myself and for everyone else. I am creating a certain image of man of my own choosing. In choosing myself, I choose man.

This helps us understand what the actual content is of such rather grandiloquent words as anguish, forlornness, despair. As you will see, it's all quite simple.

First, what is meant by anguish? The existentialists say at once that man is anguish. What that means is this: the man who involves himself and who realizes that he is not only the person he chooses to be, but also a lawmaker who is, at the same time, choosing all mankind as well as himself, cannot help escape the feeling of his total and deep responsibility. Of course, there are many people who are not anxious; but we claim that they are hiding their anxiety, that they are fleeing from it. Certainly, many people believe that when they do something, they themselves are the only ones involved, and when someone says to them, "What if everyone acted that way?" they shrug their shoulders and answer, "Everyone doesn't act that way." But really, one should always ask himself, "What would happen if everybody looked at things that way?" There is no escaping this disturbing thought except by a kind of double-dealing. A man who lies and makes excuses for himself by saying "not everybody does that," is someone with an uneasy conscience, because the act of lying implies that a universal value is conferred upon the lie.

Anguish is evident even when it conceals itself. This is the anguish that Kierkegaard called the anguish of Abraham. You know the story: an angel has ordered Abraham to sacrifice his son; if it really were an angel who has come and said, "You are Abraham, you shall sacrifice your son," everything would be all right. But everyone might first wonder, "Is it really an angel, and am I really Abraham? What proof do I have?"

There was a madwoman who had hallucinations; someone used to speak to her on the telephone and give her orders. Her doctor asked her, "Who is it who talks to you?" She answered, "He says it's God." What proof did she really have that it was God? If an angel comes to me, what proof is there that it's an angel? And if I hear voices, what proof is there that they come from heaven and not from hell, or from the subconscious, or a pathological condition? What proves that they are addressed to me? What proof is there that I have been appointed to impose my choice and my conception of man on humanity? I'll never find any proof or sign to convince me of that. If a voice addresses me, it is always for me to decide that this is the angel's voice; if I consider that such an act is a good one, it is I who will choose to say that it is good rather than bad.

Now, I'm not being singled out as an Abraham, and yet at every moment I'm obliged to perform exemplary acts. For every man, everything happens as if all mankind had its eyes fixed on him and were guiding itself by what he does. And every man ought to say to himself, "Am I really the kind of man who has the right to act in such a way that humanity might guide itself by my actions?" And if he does not say that to himself, he is masking his anguish.

There is no question here of the kind of anguish which would lead to quietism, to inaction. It is a matter of a simple sort of anguish that anybody who has had responsibilities is familiar with. For example, when a military officer takes the responsibility for an attack and sends a certain number of men to death, he chooses to do so, and in the main he alone makes the choice. Doubtless, orders come from above, but they are too broad; he interprets them, and on this interpretation depend the lives of ten or fourteen or twenty men. In making a decision he cannot help having a certain anguish. All leaders know this anguish. That doesn't keep them from acting; on the contrary, it is the very condition of their action. For it implies that they envisage a number of possibilities, and when they choose one, they realize that it has value only because it is chosen. We shall see that this kind of anguish, which is the kind that existentialism describes, is explained, in addition, by a direct responsibility to the other men whom it involves. It is not a curtain separating us from action, but is part of action itself.

When we speak of forlornness, a term Heidegger was fond of, we mean only that God does not exist and that we have to face all the consequences of this. The existentialist is strongly opposed to a certain kind of secular ethics which would like to abolish God with the least possible expense. About 1880, some French teachers tried to set up a secular ethics which went something like this: God is a useless and costly hypothesis; we are discarding it; but, meanwhile, in order for there to be an ethics, a society, a civilization, it is essential that certain values be taken seriously and that they be considered as having an a priori existence. It must be obligatory, a priori, to be honest, not to lie, not to beat your wife, to have children, etc., etc. So we're going to try a little device which will make it possible to show that values exist all the same, inscribed in a heaven of ideas, though otherwise God does not exist. In other words—and this, I believe, is the tendency of everything called reformism in France—nothing will be changed if God does not exist. We shall find ourselves with the same norms of honesty, progress, and humanism, and we shall have made of God an outdated hypothesis which will peacefully die off by itself.

The existentialist, on the contrary, thinks it very distressing that God does not exist, because all possibility of finding values in a heaven of ideas disappears along with Him; there can no longer be an a priori Good, since there is no infinite and perfect consciousness to think it. Nowhere is it written that the Good exists, that we must be honest, that we must not lie; because the fact is we are on a plane where there are only men. Dostoyevsky said, "If God didn't exist, everything would be possible." That is the very starting point of existentialism. Indeed, everything is permissible if God does not exist, and as a result man is forlorn, because neither within him nor without does he find anything to cling to. He can't start making excuses for himself.

If existence really does precede essence, there is no explaining things away by reference to a fixed and given human nature. In other words, there is no determinism, man is free, man is freedom. On the other hand, if God does not exist, we find no values or commands to turn to which legitimize our conduct. So, in the bright realm of values, we have no excuse behind us, nor justification before us. We are alone, with no excuses.

That is the idea I shall try to convey when I say that man is condemned to be free. Condemned, because he did not create himself, yet, in other respects is free; because, once thrown into the world, he is responsible for everything he does. The existentialist does not believe in the power of passion. He will never agree that a sweeping passion is a ravaging torrent which fatally leads a man to certain acts and is therefore an excuse. He thinks that man is responsible for his passion.

The existentialist does not think that man is going to help himself by finding in the world some omen by which to orient himself. Because he thinks that man will interpret the omen to suit himself. Therefore, he thinks that man, with no support and no aid, is condemned every moment to invent man. Ponge,[7] in a very fine article, has said, "Man is the future of man." That's exactly it. But if it is taken to mean that this future is recorded in heaven, that God sees it, then it is false, because it would really no longer be a future. If it is taken to mean that, whatever a man may be, there is a future to be forged, a virgin future before him, then this remark is sound. But then we are forlorn.

To give you an example which will enable you to understand forlornness better, I shall cite the case of one of my students who came to see me under the following circumstances: his father was on bad terms with his mother, and, moreover, was inclined to be a collaborationist; his older brother had been killed in the German offensive of 1940, and the young man, with somewhat immature but generous feelings, wanted to avenge him. His mother lived alone with him, very much upset by the half-treason of her husband and the death of her older son; the boy was her only consolation.

The boy was faced with the choice of leaving for England and joining the Free French Forces—that is, leaving his mother behind—or remaining with his mother and helping her to carry on. He was fully aware that the woman lived only for him and that his going-off—perhaps his death—would plunge her into despair. He was also aware that every act that he did for his mother's sake was a sure thing, in the sense that it was helping her to carry on, whereas every effort he made toward going off and fighting was an uncertain move which might run aground and prove completely useless; for example, on his way to England he might, while passing through Spain, be detained indefinitely in a Spanish camp; he might reach England or Algiers and be stuck in an office at a desk job. As a result, he was faced with two very different kinds of action: one, concrete, immediate, but concerning only one individual; the other concerned an incomparably vaster group, a national collectivity, but for that very reason was dubious, and might be interrupted en route. And, at the same time, he was wavering between two kinds of ethics. On the one hand, an ethics of sympathy, of personal devotion; on the other, a broader ethics, but one whose efficacy was more dubious. He had to choose between the two.

Who could help him choose? Christian doctrine? No. Christian doctrine says, "Be charitable, love your neighbor, take the more rugged path, etc., etc." But which is the more rugged path? Whom should he love as a brother? The fighting man or his mother? Which does the greater good, the vague act of fighting in a group, or the concrete one of helping a particular human being to go on living? Who can decide a priori? Nobody. No book of ethics can tell him. The Kantian ethics says, "Never treat any person as a means, but as an end." Very well, if I stay with my mother, I'll treat her as an end and not as a means; but by virtue of this very fact, I'm running the risk of treating the people around me who are fighting, as means; and, conversely, if I go to join those who are fighting, I'll be treating them as an end, and, by doing that, I run the risk of treating my mother as a means.

7. [The reference is to the French essayist and poet Francis Ponge (1899–1988).]

If values are vague, and if they are always too broad for the concrete and specific case that we are considering, the only thing left for us is to trust our instincts. That's what this young man tried to do; and when I saw him, he said, "In the end, feeling is what counts. I ought to choose whichever pushes me in one direction. If I feel that I love my mother enough to sacrifice everything else for her—my desire for vengeance, for action, for adventure—then I'll stay with her. If, on the contrary, I feel that my love for my mother isn't enough, I'll leave."

But how is the value of a feeling determined? What gives his feeling for his mother value? Precisely the fact that he remained with her. I may say that I like so-and-so well enough to sacrifice a certain amount of money for him, but I may say so only if I've done it. I may say "I love my mother well enough to remain with her" if I have remained with her. The only way to determine the value of this affection is, precisely, to perform an act which confirms and defines it. But, since I require this affection to justify my act, I find myself caught in a vicious circle.

On the other hand, Gide[8] has well said that a mock feeling and a true feeling are almost indistinguishable; to decide that I love my mother and will remain with her, or to remain with her by putting on an act, amount somewhat to the same thing. In other words, the feeling is formed by the acts one performs; so, I cannot refer to it in order to act upon it. Which means that I can neither seek within myself the true condition which will impel me to act, nor apply to a system of ethics for concepts which will permit me to act. You will say, "At least, he did go to a teacher for advice." But if you seek advice from a priest, for example, you have chosen this priest; you already knew, more or less, just about what advice he was going to give you. In other words, choosing your adviser is involving yourself. The proof of this is that if you are a Christian, you will say, "Consult a priest." But some priests are collaborating, some are just marking time, some are resisting. Which to choose? If the young man chooses a priest who is resisting or collaborating, he has already decided on the kind of advice he's going to get. Therefore, in coming to see me he knew the answer I was going to give him, and I had only one answer to give: "You're free, choose, that is, invent." No general ethics can show you what is to be done; there are no omens in the world. The Catholics will reply, "But there are." Granted—but, in any case, I myself choose the meaning they have.

When I was a prisoner, I knew a rather remarkable young man who was a Jesuit. He had entered the Jesuit order in the following way: he had had a number of very bad breaks; in childhood, his father died, leaving him in poverty, and he was a scholarship student at a religious institution where he was constantly made to feel that he was being kept out of charity; then, he failed to get any of the honors and distinctions that children like; later on, at about eighteen, he bungled a love affair; finally, at twenty-two, he failed in military training, a childish enough matter, but it was the last straw.

This young fellow might well have felt that he had botched everything. It was a sign of something, but of what? He might have taken refuge in bitterness or despair. But he very wisely looked upon all this as a sign that he was not made for secular triumphs, and that only the triumphs of religion, holiness, and faith were open to him. He saw the hand of God in all this, and so he entered the order. Who can help seeing that he alone decided what the sign meant?

Some other interpretation might have been drawn from this series of setbacks; for example, that he might have done better to turn carpenter or revolutionist. Therefore, he is fully responsible for the interpretation. Forlornness implies that we ourselves choose our being. Forlornness and anguish go together.

As for despair, the term has a very simple meaning. It means that we shall confine ourselves to reckoning only with what depends upon our will, or on the ensemble of probabilities which make our action possible. When we want something, we always have to reckon with probabilities. I may be counting on the arrival of a friend. The friend is coming by rail or streetcar; this supposes that the train will arrive on schedule, or that the street-car will not jump the track. I am left in the realm of possibility; but possibilities are to be reckoned with only to the point where my action comports with the ensemble of these possibilities, and no further. The moment the possibilities I am considering are not rigorously involved by my action, I ought to disengage myself from them, because no God, no scheme, can adapt the world and

8. [The reference is to the French writer André Gide (1869–1951).]

its possibilities to my will. When Descartes said, "Conquer yourself rather than the world," he meant essentially the same thing.

The Marxists to whom I have spoken reply, "You can rely on the support of others in your action, which obviously has certain limits because you're not going to live forever. That means: rely on both what others are doing elsewhere to help you, in China, in Russia, and what they will do later on, after your death, to carry on the action and lead it to its fulfillment, which will be the revolution. You even *have* to rely upon that, otherwise you're immoral." I reply at once that I will always rely on fellow-fighters insofar as these comrades are involved with me in a common struggle, in the unity of a party or a group in which I can more or less make my weight felt; that is, one whose ranks I am in as a fighter and whose movements I am aware of at every moment. In such a situation, relying on the unity and will of the party is exactly like counting on the fact that the train will arrive on time or that the car won't jump the track. But, given that man is free and that there is no human nature for me to depend on, I cannot count on men whom I do not know by relying on human goodness or man's concern for the good of society. I don't know what will become of the Russian revolution; I may make an example of it to the extent that at the present time it is apparent that the proletariat plays a part in Russia that it plays in no other nation. But I can't swear that this will inevitably lead to a triumph of the proletariat. I've got to limit myself to what I see.

Given that men are free and that tomorrow they will freely decide what man will be, I cannot be sure that, after my death, fellow-fighters will carry on my work to bring it to its maximum perfection. Tomorrow, after my death, some men may decide to set up Fascism, and the others may be cowardly and muddled enough to let them do it. Fascism will then be the human reality, so much the worse for us.

Actually, things will be as man will have decided they are to be. Does that mean that I should abandon myself to quietism? No. First, I should involve myself; then, act on the old saw, "Nothing ventured, nothing gained." Nor does it mean that I shouldn't belong to a party, but rather that I shall have no illusions and shall do what I can. For example, suppose I ask myself, "Will socialization, as such, ever come about?" I know nothing about it. All I know is that I'm going to do everything in my power to bring it about. Beyond that, I can't count on anything. Quietism is the attitude of people who say, "Let others do what I can't do." The doctrine I am presenting is the very opposite of quietism, since it declares, "There is no reality except in action." Moreover, it goes further, since it adds, "Man is nothing else than his plan; he exists only to the extent that he fulfills himself; he is therefore nothing else than the ensemble of his acts, nothing else than his life."

According to this, we can understand why our doctrine horrifies certain people. Because often the only way they can bear their wretchedness is to think, "Circumstances have been against me. What I've been and done doesn't show my true worth. To be sure, I've had no great love, no great friendship, but that's because I haven't met a man or woman who was worthy. The books I've written haven't been very good because I haven't had the proper leisure. I haven't had children to devote myself to because I didn't find a man with whom I could have spent my life. So there remains within me, unused and quite viable, a host of propensities, inclinations, possibilities, that one wouldn't guess from the mere series of things I've done."

Now, for the existentialist there is really no love other than one which manifests itself in a person's being in love. There is no genius other than one which is expressed in works of art; the genius of Proust[9] is the sum of Proust's works; the genius of Racine[10] is his series of tragedies. Outside of that, there is nothing. Why say that Racine could have written another tragedy, when he didn't write it? A man is involved in life, leaves his impress on it, and outside of that there is nothing. To be sure, this may seem a harsh thought to someone whose life hasn't been a success. But, on the other hand, it prompts people to understand that reality alone is what counts, that dreams, expectations, and hopes warrant no more than to define a man as a disappointed dream, as miscarried hopes, as vain expectations. In other words, to define him negatively and not positively. However,

9. [The reference is to the French novelist Marcel Proust (1871–1922), a leading figure in twentieth-century literature.]

10. [The reference is to the French dramatist Jean Racine (1639–1699).]

when we say, "You are nothing else than your life," that does not imply that the artist will be judged solely on the basis of his works of art; a thousand other things will contribute toward summing him up. What we mean is that a man is nothing else than a series of undertakings, that he is the sum, the organization, the ensemble of the relationships which make up these undertakings.

When all is said and done, what we are accused of, at bottom, is not our pessimism, but an optimistic toughness. If people throw up to us our works of fiction in which we write about people who are soft, weak, cowardly, and sometimes even downright bad, it's not because these people are soft, weak, cowardly, or bad; because if we were to say, as Zola did, that they are that way because of heredity, the workings of environment, society, because of biological or psychological determinism, people would be reassured. They would say, "Well, that's what we're like, no one can do anything about it." But when the existentialist writes about a coward, he says that this coward is responsible for his cowardice. He's not like that because he has a cowardly heart or lung or brain; he's not like that on account of his physiological makeup; but he's like that because he has made himself a coward by his acts. There's no such thing as a cowardly constitution; there are nervous constitutions; there is poor blood, as the common people say, or strong constitutions. But the man whose blood is poor is not a coward on that account, for what makes cowardice is the act of renouncing or yielding. A constitution is not an act; the coward is defined on the basis of the acts he performs. People feel, in a vague sort of way, that this coward we're talking about is guilty of being a coward, and the thought frightens them. What people would like is that a coward or a hero be born that way.

One of the complaints most frequently made about *The Ways of Freedom*[11] can be summed up as follows: "After all, these people are so spineless, how are you going to make heroes out of them?" This objection almost makes me laugh, for it assumes that people are born heroes. That's what people really want to think. If you're born cowardly, you may set your mind perfectly at rest; there's nothing you can do about it; you'll be cowardly all your life, whatever you may do. If you're born a hero, you may set your mind just as much at rest; you'll be a hero all your life; you'll drink like a hero and eat like a hero. What the existentialist says is that the coward makes himself cowardly, that the hero makes himself heroic. There's always a possibility for the coward not to be cowardly any more and for the hero to stop being heroic. What counts is total involvement; some one particular action or set of circumstances is not total involvement.

Thus, I think we have answered a number of the charges concerning existentialism. You see that it cannot be taken for a philosophy of quietism, since it defines man in terms of action; nor for a pessimistic description of man—there is no doctrine more optimistic, since man's destiny is within himself; nor for an attempt to discourage man from acting, since it tells him that the only hope is in his acting and that action is the only thing that enables a man to live. Consequently, we are dealing here with an ethics of action and involvement.

Nevertheless, on the basis of a few notions like these, we are still charged with immuring man in his private subjectivity. There again we're very much misunderstood. Subjectivity of the individual is indeed our point of departure, and this for strictly philosophic reasons. Not because we are bourgeois, but because we want a doctrine based on truth and not a lot of fine theories, full of hope but with no real basis. There can be no other truth to take off from than this: *I think; therefore, I exist.* There we have the absolute truth of consciousness becoming aware of itself. Every theory which takes man out of the moment in which he becomes aware of himself is, at its very beginning, a theory which confounds truth, for outside the Cartesian *cogito*, all views are only probable, and a doctrine of probability which is not bound to a truth dissolves into thin air. In order to describe the probable, you must have a firm hold on the true. Therefore, before there can be any truth whatsoever, there must be an absolute truth; and this one is simple and easily arrived at; it's on everyone's doorstep; it's a matter of grasping it directly.

Secondly, this theory is the only one which gives man dignity, the only one which does not reduce him to an object. The effect of all materialism is to treat all men, including the one philosophizing, as

11. [The reference is to Sartre's trilogy of novels, *The Age of Reason*, *The Reprieve*, and the subsequently published *Troubled Sleep*.]

objects, that is, as an ensemble of determined reactions in no way distinguished from the ensemble of qualities and phenomena which constitute a table or a chair or a stone. We definitely wish to establish the human realm as an ensemble of values distinct from the material realm. But the subjectivity that we have thus arrived at, and which we have claimed to be truth, is not a strictly individual subjectivity, for we have demonstrated that one discovers in the *cogito* not only himself, but others as well.

The philosophies of Descartes and Kant to the contrary, through the *I think* we reach our own self in the presence of others, and the others are just as real to us as our own self. Thus, the man who becomes aware of himself through the *cogito* also perceives all others, and he perceives them as the condition of his own existence. He realizes that he cannot be anything (in the sense that we say that someone is witty or nasty or jealous) unless others recognize it as such. In order to get any truth about myself, I must have contact with another person. The other is indispensable to my own existence, as well as my knowledge about myself. This being so, in discovering my inner being I discover the other person at the same time, like a freedom placed in front of me which thinks and wills only for or against me. Hence, let us at once announce the discovery of a world which we shall call intersubjectivity; this is the world in which man decides what he is and what others are.

Besides, if it is impossible to find in every man some universal essence which would be human nature, yet there does exist a universal human condition. It's not by chance that today's thinkers speak more readily of man's condition than of his nature. By condition they mean, more or less definitely, the a priori limits which outline man's fundamental situation in the universe. Historical situations vary; a man may be born a slave in a pagan society or a feudal lord or a proletarian. What does not vary is the necessity for him to exist in the world, to be at work there, to be there in the midst of other people, and to be mortal there. The limits are neither subjective nor objective, or, rather, they have an objective and a subjective side. Objective because they are to be found everywhere and are recognizable everywhere; subjective because they are *lived* and are nothing if man does not live them, that is, freely determine his existence with reference to them. And though the configurations may differ, at least none of them are completely strange to me, because they all appear as attempts either to pass beyond these limits or recede from them or deny them or adapt to them. Consequently, every configuration, however individual it may be, has a universal value.

Every configuration, even the Chinese, the Indian, or the Negro, can be understood by a Westerner. "Can be understood" means that by virtue of a situation that he can imagine, a European of 1945 can, in like manner, push himself to his limits and reconstitute within himself the configuration of the Chinese, the Indian, or the African. Every configuration has universality in the sense that every configuration can be understood by every man. This does not at all mean that this configuration defines man forever, but that it can be met with again. There is always a way to understand the idiot, the child, the savage, the foreigner, provided one has the necessary information.

In this sense we may say that there is a universality of man; but it is not given, it is perpetually being made. I build the universal in choosing myself; I build it in understanding the configuration of every other man, whatever age he might have lived in. This absoluteness of choice does not do away with the relativeness of each epoch. At heart, what existentialism shows is the connection between the absolute character of free involvement, by virtue of which every man realizes himself in realizing a type of mankind, an involvement always comprehensible in any age whatsoever and by any person whosoever, and the relativeness of the cultural ensemble which may result from such a choice; it must be stressed that the relativity of Cartesianism and the absolute character of Cartesian involvement go together. In this sense, you may, if you like, say that each of us performs an absolute act in breathing, eating, sleeping, or behaving in any way whatever. There is no difference between being free, like a configuration, like an existence which chooses its essence, and being absolute. There is no difference between being an absolute temporarily localized, that is, localized in history, and being universally comprehensible.

This does not entirely settle the objection to subjectivism. In fact, the objection still takes several forms. First, there is the following: we are told, "So you're able to do anything, no matter what!" This is expressed in various ways. First we are accused of anarchy; then they say, "You're unable to pass judgment on others, because there's no reason to prefer one configuration to another"; finally they tell us, "Everything is arbitrary in this choosing of yours. You take something from one pocket and pretend you're putting it into the other."

These three objections aren't very serious. Take the first objection. "You're able to do anything, no matter what" is not to the point. In one sense choice is possible, but what is not possible is not to choose. I can always choose, but I ought to know that if I do not choose, I am still choosing. Though this may seem purely formal, it is highly important for keeping fantasy and caprice within bounds. If it is true that in facing a situation, for example, one in which, as a person capable of having sexual relations, of having children, I am obliged to choose an attitude, and if I in any way assume responsibility for a choice which, in involving myself, also involves all mankind, this has nothing to do with caprice, even if no a priori value determines my choice.

If anybody thinks that he recognizes here Gide's theory of the arbitrary act, he fails to see the enormous difference between this doctrine and Gide's. Gide does not know what a situation is. He acts out of pure caprice. For us, on the contrary, man is in an organized situation in which he himself is involved. Through his choice, he involves all mankind, and he cannot avoid making a choice; either he will remain chaste, or he will marry without having children, or he will marry and have children; anyhow, whatever he may do, it is impossible for him not to take full responsibility for the way he handles this problem. Doubtless, he chooses without referring to preestablished values, but it is unfair to accuse him of caprice. Instead, let us say that moral choice is to be compared to the making of a work of art. And before going any further, let it be said at once that we are not dealing here with an aesthetic ethics, because our opponents are so dishonest that they even accuse us of that. The example I've chosen is a comparison only.

Having said that, may I ask whether anyone has ever accused an artist who has painted a picture of not having drawn his inspiration from rules set up a priori? Has anyone ever asked, "What painting ought he to make?" It is clearly understood that there is no definite painting to be made, that the artist is engaged in the making of his painting, and that the painting to be made is precisely the painting he will have made. It is clearly understood that there are no a priori aesthetic values, but that there are values which appear subsequently in the coherence of the painting, in the correspondence between what the artist intended and the result. Nobody can tell what the painting of tomorrow will be like. Painting can be judged only after it has once been made. What connection does that have with ethics? We are in the same creative situation. We never say that a work of art is arbitrary. When we speak of a canvas of Picasso[12] we never say that it is arbitrary; we understand quite well that he was making himself what he is at the very time he was painting, that the ensemble of his work is embodied in his life.

The same holds on the ethical plane. What art and ethics have in common is that we have creation and invention in both cases. We cannot decide a priori what there is to be done. I think that I pointed that out quite sufficiently when I mentioned the case of the student who came to see me, and who might have applied to all the ethical systems, Kantian or otherwise, without getting any sort of guidance. He was obliged to devise his law himself. Never let it be said by us that this man—who, taking affection, individual action, and kind-heartedness toward a specific person as his ethical first principle, chooses to remain with his mother, or who, preferring to make a sacrifice, chooses to go to England—has made an arbitrary choice. Man makes himself. He isn't ready made at the start. In choosing his ethics, he makes himself, and force of circumstances is such that he cannot abstain from choosing one. We define man only in relationship to involvement. It is therefore absurd to charge us with arbitrariness of choice.

In the second place, it is said that we are unable to pass judgment on others. In a way this is true, and in another way, false. It is true in this sense, that, whenever a man sanely and sincerely involves himself and chooses his configuration, it is impossible for him to prefer another configuration, regardless of what his own may be in other respects. It is true in this sense, that we do not believe in progress. Progress is betterment. Man is always the same. The situation confronting him varies. Choice always remains a

12. [The reference is to the renowned Spanish artist Pablo Picasso (1881–1973).]

choice in a situation. The problem has not changed since the time one could choose between those for and those against slavery, for example, at the time of the Civil War, and the present time, when one can side with the Maquis Resistance Party, or with the Communists.

But, nevertheless, one can still pass judgment, for, as I have said, one makes a choice in relationship to others. First, one can judge (and this is perhaps not a judgment of value, but a logical judgment) that certain choices are based on error and others on truth. If we have defined man's situation as a free choice, with no excuses and no recourse, every man who takes refuge behind the excuse of his passions, every man who sets up a determinism, is a dishonest man.

The objection may be raised, "But why mayn't he choose himself dishonestly?" I reply that I am not obliged to pass moral judgment on him, but that I do define his dishonesty as an error. One cannot help considering the truth of the matter. Dishonesty is obviously a falsehood because it belies the complete freedom of involvement. On the same grounds, I maintain that there is also dishonesty if I choose to state that certain values exist prior to me; it is sélf-contradictory for me to want them and at the same time state that they are imposed on me. Suppose someone says to me, "What if I want to be dishonest?" I'll answer, "There's no reason for you not to be, but I'm saying that that's what you are, and that the strictly coherent attitude is that of honesty."

Besides, I can bring moral judgment to bear. When I declare that freedom in every concrete circumstance can have no other aim than to want itself, if man has once become aware that in his forlornness he imposes values, he can no longer want but one thing, and that is freedom, as the basis of all values. That doesn't mean that he wants it in the abstract. It means simply that the ultimate meaning of the acts of honest men is the quest for freedom as such. A man who belongs to a communist or revolutionary union wants concrete goals; these goals imply an abstract desire for freedom; but this freedom is wanted in something concrete. We want freedom for freedom's sake and in every particular circumstance. And in wanting freedom we discover that it depends entirely on the freedom of others, and that the freedom of others depends on ours. Of course, freedom as the definition of man does not depend on others, but as soon as there is involvement, I am obliged to want others to have freedom at the same time that I want my own freedom. I can take freedom as my goal only if I take that of others as a goal as well. Consequently, when, in all honesty, I've recognized that man is a being in whom existence precedes essence, that he is a free being who, in various circumstances, can want only his freedom, I have at the same time recognized that I can want only the freedom of others.

Therefore, in the name of this will for freedom, which freedom itself implies, I may pass judgment on those who seek to hide from themselves the complete arbitrariness and the complete freedom of their existence. Those who hide their complete freedom from themselves out of a spirit of seriousness or by means of deterministic excuses, I shall call cowards; those who try to show that their existence was necessary, when it is the very contingency of man's appearance on earth, I shall call stinkers. But cowards or stinkers can be judged only from a strictly unbiased point of view.

Therefore though the content of ethics is variable, a certain form of it is universal. Kant says that freedom desires both itself and the freedom of others. Granted. But he believes that the formal and the universal are enough to constitute an ethics. We, on the other hand, think that principles which are too abstract run aground in trying to decide action. Once again, take the case of the student. In the name of what, in the name of what great moral maxim do you think he could have decided, in perfect peace of mind, to abandon his mother or to stay with her? There is no way of judging. The content is always concrete and thereby unforeseeable; there is always the element of invention. The one thing that counts is knowing whether the inventing that has been done, has been done in the name of freedom.

For example, let us look at the following two cases. You will see to what extent they correspond, yet differ. Take *The Mill on the Floss*.[13] We find a certain young girl, Maggie Tulliver, who is an embodiment of the value of passion and who is aware of it. She is in love with a young man, Stephen, who is engaged to an

13. [The reference is to a novel by the remarkable Englishwoman, born Mary Ann Evans (1819–1880), who, writing under the pseudonym George Eliot, became one of the nineteenth century's leading literary figures.]

insignificant young girl. This Maggie Tulliver, instead of heedlessly preferring her own happiness, chooses, in the name of human solidarity, to sacrifice herself and give up the man she loves. On the other hand, Sanseverina, in *The Charterhouse of Parma*,[14] believing that passion is man's true value, would say that a great love deserves sacrifices; that it is to be preferred to the banality of the conjugal love that would tie Stephen to the young ninny he had to marry. She would choose to sacrifice the girl and fulfill her happiness; and, as Stendahl shows, she is even ready to sacrifice herself for the sake of passion, if this life demands it. Here we are in the presence of two strictly opposed moralities. I claim that they are much the same thing; in both cases what has been set up as the goal is freedom.

You can imagine two highly similar attitudes: one girl prefers to renounce her love out of resignation; another prefers to disregard the prior attachment of the man she loves out of sexual desire. On the surface these two actions resemble those we've just described. However, they are completely different. Sanseverina's attitude is much nearer that of Maggie Tulliver, one of heedless rapacity.

Thus, you see that the second charge is true and, at the same time, false. One may choose anything if it is on the grounds of free involvement.

The third objection is the following: "You take something from one pocket and put it into the other. That is, fundamentally, values aren't serious, since you choose them." My answer to this is that I'm quite vexed that that's the way it is; but if I've discarded God the Father, there has to be someone to invent values. You've got to take things as they are. Moreover, to say that we invent values means nothing else but this: life has no meaning a priori. Before you come alive, life is nothing; it's up to you to give it a meaning, and value is nothing else but the meaning that you choose. In that way, you see, there is a possibility of creating a human community.

I've been reproached for asking whether existentialism is humanistic. It's been said, "But you said in *Nausea* that the humanists were all wrong. You made fun of a certain kind of humanist. Why come back to it now?" Actually, the word humanism has two very different meanings. By humanism one can mean a theory which takes man as an end and as a higher value. Humanism in this sense can be found in Cocteau's tale *Around the World in Eighty Hours*[15] when a character, because he is flying over some mountains in an airplane, declares, "Man is simply amazing." That means that I, who did not build the airplanes, shall personally benefit from these particular inventions, and that I, as man, shall personally consider myself responsible for, and honored by, acts of a few particular men. This would imply that we ascribe a value to man on the basis of the highest deeds of certain men. This humanism is absurd, because only the dog or the horse would be able to make such an over-all judgment about man, which they are careful not to do, at least to my knowledge.

But it cannot be granted that a man may make a judgment about man. Existentialism spares him from any such judgment. The existentialist will never consider man as an end because he is always in the making. Nor should we believe that there is a mankind to which we might set up a cult in the manner of Auguste Comte.[16] The cult of mankind ends in the self-enclosed humanism of Comte, and, let it be said, of fascism. This kind of humanism we can do without.

But there is another meaning of humanism. Fundamentally it is this: man is constantly outside of himself; in projecting himself, in losing himself outside of himself, he makes for man's existing; and, on the other hand, it is by pursuing transcendent goals that he is able to exist; man, being this state of passing-beyond, and seizing upon things only as they bear upon this passing-beyond, is at the heart, at the center of this passing-beyond. There is no universe other than a human universe, the universe of human subjectivity. This connection between transcendency, as a constituent element of man—not in the sense that God is transcendent, but in the sense of passing beyond—and subjectivity, in the sense that man is

14. [The reference is to the influential novel by the French author Marie Henri Beyle (1783–1842), who used the pseudonym Stendhal.]

15. [The reference is to the French writer Jean Cocteau (1889–1963).]

16. [The reference is to the French philosopher and social theorist Auguste Comte (1798–1857), whose study of the nature of social change led to the development of the field of sociology.]

not closed in on himself but is always present in a human universe, is what we call existentialism humanism. Humanism, because we remind man that there is no law-maker other than himself, and that in his forlornness he will decide by himself; because we point out that man will fulfill himself as man, not in turning toward himself, but in seeking outside of himself a goal which is just this liberation, just this particular fulfillment.

From these few reflections it is evident that nothing is more unjust than the objections that have been raised against us. Existentialism is nothing else than an attempt to draw all the consequences of a coherent atheistic position. It isn't trying to plunge man into despair at all. But if one calls every attitude of unbelief despair, like the Christians, then the word is not being used in its original sense. Existentialism isn't so atheistic that it wears itself out showing that God doesn't exist. Rather, it declares that even if God did exist, that would change nothing. There you've got our point of view. Not that we believe that God exists, but we think that the problem of His existence is not the issue. In this sense existentialism is optimistic, a doctrine of action, and it is plain dishonesty for Christians to make no distinction between their own despair and ours and then to call us despairing.

Ludwig Wittgenstein

Ludwig Wittgenstein (1889–1951) was born in Vienna, where his parents were leading patrons of the arts. He showed an early talent for mechanics, which led to his studying engineering in Berlin and Manchester, England. His interests began to shift to mathematics and the foundations of mathematics, leading him to go in 1912 to Cambridge University to meet Bertrand Russell, who became his mentor. Wittgenstein's studies at Cambridge ended with the onset of World War I. He enlisted in the Austrian army and was noted for his courage in war. During his time at the front he completed his first great philosophical work, the *Tractatus Logico-Philosophicus.* In 1918 he was taken prisoner and sent to a prisoner-of-war camp in Italy, from which he managed to smuggle out to Russell a copy of the *Tractatus.*

Published in English in 1922, the *Tractatus* aims to show that language must have a certain structure if it is to represent reality. Language "pictures" reality by mimicking its structure. Like all pictures, a sentence-picture shows how things stand in the world. Sentences that do not represent possible states of affairs—including ethical statements, philosophical discourse, and religious theses—may be important to our lives but are nonetheless nonsensical.

Having completed the *Tractatus,* Wittgenstein believed that nothing more remained to be said in philosophy, and so he turned to other occupations, designing a mansion for his sister, and working as a gardener and then as a school teacher. Urged by friends, he returned to Cambridge in 1929 and submitted the *Tractatus* for his Ph.D. thesis. He was immediately made a fellow at Trinity College. Though he published nothing after the *Tractatus,* the next twenty years were a time of tremendous philosophical output in the form of lectures and manuscript writing. His lectures of 1932–1933, circulated as *The Blue and Brown Books,* contain many of the problems and ideas fully developed in the *Philosophical Investigations.* The *Blue Book* initiates a critique of the *Tractatus* theory of language, while the *Brown Book* introduces the language-game as a device to explore the limits of the imaginable. Wittgenstein's concerns with meaning, the limits of meaningfulness, nonsense, and necessity remained throughout his life at the heart of his philosophical inquiries. The *Philosophical Investigations,* published posthumously in 1953, gives his mature treatment of these issues. Wittgenstein worked virtually up until the day of his death, and his final efforts, directed toward issues of knowledge and certainty, were published as *On Certainty.*

The *Philosophical Investigations* is primarily a critical examination of theories of language and mind that have dominated Western philosophy since Descartes. Wittgenstein aims to show that viewing language as representational of reality or mind as an arena of special powers of knowing are profound mistakes resulting from conceptual confusions and fallacious arguments.

His most distinctive device is the language-game (1–18), either a primitive form of language "in which one can command a clear view of the aim and functioning of the words" (5) or "the whole, consisting of language and the actions into which it is woven" (7). Understood either way the language-game resists assimilation to the representationalist theory of language.

His criticism of that theory is first directed against the idea that what fixes the meaning of a word is the object that the word names (28–38). Wittgenstein demonstrates the diverse ways in which words are used, many of which have nothing to do with naming objects, and he constructs compelling arguments to show that naming cannot fix meanings because it always presupposes some "stage-setting" before it can be correctly interpreted. He concludes that uses of language have no single essence but display the variety of a family resemblance (65–68).

Meaning is a matter of the rule-governed character of language (139–242). Rules determine correct application of words. So the meaning of an expression is not given by naming some object but by use in accord with a rule. As Wittgenstein puts it, a rule determines what it is to go on in the same way or how one *ought* to act.

His paradigmatic case of following a rule focuses on the natural numbers—1, 2, 3, 4. . . . Can we explain how one ought to continue this arithmetic sequence? Wittgenstein critiques all attempted solutions to this problem: no one can show why it is correct to continue one way rather than another, for any method of projection can itself be multiply interpreted. "This was our paradox: no course of action could be determined by a rule, because every course of action can be made out to accord with the rule" (202). He concludes that rule-following requires a background of acting routinely, nonreflectively, and cooperatively.

He turns next to the Cartesian theory of mind, according to which mental episodes are marked by immediacy, transparency, and privacy. In seeking to put to rest the idea that mental acts have these extraordinary powers, he focuses on the heart of the Cartesian theory of mind, the idea that mental states are private. Wittgenstein takes pain as his paradigmatic mental state, for it is supposed to be intrinsically knowable, immediately given, and wholly private.

The foundation for Wittgenstein's critique of the Cartesian theory of mind is the so-called private language argument (243–304). It has two components. The first, which is illustrated by a private diary in which an individual marks an S every time S is sensed, shows that the distinction between one sensation and a different one cannot be maintained if sensations are private. The second component maintains that objects are irrelevant to our linguistic practice. Here Wittgenstein imagines a game in which each player has a box with a beetle inside it, but no one can look inside another's box. Wittgenstein concludes that instead of making the private object what matters most, as Cartesians do, we should recognize that living beings, not inner private states or public behaviors, are the medium of mental life. In coming to accept that we act as a matter of course (without rules) and relate to others and ourselves as living human beings, we accept the obvious and so find our way out of the "fly-bottle" (309).

• • •

A definitive biography of Wittgenstein is Ray Monk, *Ludwig Wittgenstein: The Duty of Genius* (New York: Free Press, 1990). A clear introduction to the *Tractatus* and the *Philosophical Investigations* is Anthony Kenny, *Wittgenstein* (Cambridge, Mass.: Harvard University Press, 1973). Two introductions to the *Investigations* are Marie McGinn, *Wittgenstein and the Philosophical Investigations* (London: Routledge, 1997) and Norman Malcolm, *Wittgenstein: Nothing Is Hidden* (Oxford: Basil Blackwell, 1986). More advanced treatments are Robert Fogelin, *Wittgenstein,* second edition (London, Routledge & Kegan Paul, 1987) and P. M. S. Hacker, *Insight and Illusion,* second edition (Oxford: Clarendon Press, 1986). A collection of incisive essays is Meredith Williams, ed., *Wittgenstein's Philosophical Investigations: Critical Essays* (Lanham, Md.: Rowman & Littlefield, 2007).

Meredith Williams

Philosophical Investigations

1. "Cum ipsi (majores homines) appellabant rem aliquam, et cum secundum eam vocem corpus ad aliquid movenant, videbam, et tenebam hoc ab eis vocari rem illam, quod sonabant, cum eam vellent ostendere. Hoc autem eos velle ex motu corporis aperiebatur: tamquam verbis naturalibus omnium gentium, quae fiunt voltu et nutu oculorum, ceterorumque membrorum actu, et sonitu vocis indicante affectionem animi in petendis, habendis, rejiciendis, fugiendisve rebus. Ita verba in variis sententiis locis suis posita, et crebo audita, quarum rerum signa essent, paulatim clligebam, measque jam voluntates, edomito in eis signis ore, per haec enuntiabam." (Augustine, *Confessions*, I. 8.)[1]

These words, it seems to me, give us a particular picture of the essence of human language. It is this: the individual words in language name objects—sentences are combinations of such names.—In this picture of langage we find the roots of the following idea: Every word has a meaning. This meaning is correlated with the word. It is the object for which the word stands.

Augustine does not speak of there being any difference between kinds of word. If you describe the learning of language in this way you are, I believe, thinking primarily of nouns like "table", "chair", "bread", and of people's names, and only secondarily of the names of certain actions and properties; and of the remaining kinds of word as something that will take care of itself.

Now think of the following use of langage: I send someone shopping. I give him a slip marked "five red apples". He takes the slip to the shopkeeper, who opens the drawer marked "apples"; then he looks up the word "red" in a table and finds a colour sample opposite it; then he says the series of cardinal numbers—I assume that he knows them by heart—up to the word "five" and for each number he taks an apple of the same colour as the sample out of the drawer.—It is in this and similar ways that one operates with words.—"But how does he know where and how he is to look up the word 'red' and what he is to do with the word 'five'?"—Well, I assume that he *acts* as I have described. Explanations come to an end somewhere.—But what is the meaning of the word "five"?—No such thing was in question here, only how the word "five" is used.

2. That philosophical concept of meaning has its place in a primitice idea of the way language functions. But one can also say that it is the idea of a language more primitive than ours.

Let us imagine a language for which the description given by Augustine is right. The language is meant to serve for communication between a builder A and an assisstant B. A is building with building-stones: there are blacks, pillars, slabs and beams. B has to pass the stones, and that in the order in which A needs them. For this purpose they use a language consisting of the words "block", "pillar", "slab", "beam". A calls them out;—B brings the stone which he has learnt to bring at such-and-such a call.—Conceive this as a complete primitive language.

3. Augustine, we might say, does describe a system of communication; only not everything that we call language is this system. And one has to say this in many cases where the question arises "Is this an appropriate description or not?" The answer is: "Yes, it is appropriate, but only for this narrowly circum-

Reprinted from Ludwig Wittgenstein, *Philosophical Investigations*. Translated by G.E.M. Anscombe (Oxford: Blackwell Publishing, 1953), by permission of John Wiley and Sons.

1. ["When they (my elders) named some object, and accordingly moved towards something, I saw this and I grasped that the thing was called by the sound they uttered when they meant to point it out. Their intention was shown by their bodily movements, as it were the natural language of all peoples: the expression of the face, the play of th eyes, the movement of other parts of the body, and the tone of voice which expresses our state of mind in seeking, having, rejecting, or avoiding something. Thus, as I heard words repeatedly used in their proper places in various sentences, I gradually learnt to understand what objects they signified; and after I had trained my mouth to form these signs, I used them to express my own desires." —G.E.M.A.]

scribed region, not for the whole of what you were claiming to describe."

It is as if someone were to say: "A game consists in moving objects about on a surface according to certain rules . . ."—and we replied: You seem to be thinking of board-games, but there are others. You can make your definition correct by expressly restricting it to those games.

4. Imagine a script in which the letters were used to stand for sounds, and also as signs of emphasis and punctuation. (A script can be conceived as a language for describing sound-patterns.) Now imagine someone interpreting that script as if there were simply a correspondence of letters to sounds and as if the letters had not also completely different functions. Augustine's conception of language is like such an over-simple conception of the script.

5. If we look at the example in §1, we may perhaps get an inkling how much this general notion of the meaning of a word surrounds the working of language with a haze which makes clear vision impossible. It disperses the fog to study the phenomena of language in primitive kinds of application in which one can command a clear view of the aim and functioning of the words.

A child uses such primitive forms of language when it learns to talk. Here the teaching of language is not explanation, but training.

6. We could imagine that the language of §2 was the *whole* language of A and B; even the whole language of a tribe. The children are brought up to perform *these* actions, to use *these* words as they do so, and to react in *this* way to the words of others.

An important part of the training will consist in the teacher's pointing to the objects, directing the child's attention to them, and at the same time uttering a word; for instance, the word "slab" as he points to that shape. (I do not want to call this "ostensive definition", because the child cannot as yet *ask* what the name is. I will call it "ostensive teaching of words".——I say that it will form an important part of the training, because it is so with human beings; not because it could not be imagined otherwise.) This ostensive teaching of words can be said to establish an association between the word and the thing. But what does this mean? Well, it can mean various things; but one very likely thinks first of all that a picture of the object comes before the child's mind when it hears the word. But now, if this does happen—is it the purpose of the word?—Yes, it *can* be the purpose.—I can imagine such a use of words (of series of sounds). (Uttering a word is like striking a note on the keyboard of the imagination.) But in the language of §2 it is *not* the purpose of the words to evoke images. (It may, of course, be discovered that that helps to attain the actual purpose.)

But if the ostensive teaching has this effect,—am I to say that it effects an understanding of the word? Don't you understand the call "Slab!" if you act upon it in such-and-such a way?—Doubtless the ostensive teaching helped to bring this about; but only together with a particular training. With different training the same ostensive teaching of these words would have effected a quite different understanding.

"I set the brake up by connecting up rod and lever."—Yes, given the whole of the rest of the mechanism. Only in conjunction with that is it a brake-lever, and separated from its support it is not even a lever; it may be anything, or nothing.

7. In the practice of the use of language (2) one party calls out the words, the other acts on them. In instruction in the language the following process will occur: the learner *names* the objects; that is, he utters the word when the teacher points to the stone.—And there will be this still simpler exercise: the pupil repeats the words after the teacher——both of these being processes resembling language.

We can also think of the whole process of using words in (2) as one of those games by means of which children learn their native language. I will call these games "language-games" and will sometimes speak of a primitive language as a language-game.

And the processes of naming the stones and of repeating words after someone might also be called language-games. Think of much of the use of words in games like ring-a-ring-a-roses.

I shall also call the whole, consisting of language and the actions into which it is woven, the "language-game".

8. Let us now look at an expansion of language (2). Besides the four words "block", "pillar", etc., let it contain a series of words used as the shopkeeper in (1) used the numerals (it can be the series of letters of the alphabet); further, let there be two words, which may as well be "there" and "this" (because this roughly indicates their purpose), that are used in connexion

with a pointing gesture; and finally a number of colour samples. A gives an order like: "d—slab—there". At the same time he shews the assistant a colour sample, and when he says "there" he points to a place on the building site. From the stock of slabs B takes one for each letter of the alphabet up do "d", of the same colour as the sample, and brings them to the place indicated by A.—On other occasions A gives the order "this—there". At "this" he points to a building-stone. And so on.

9. When a child learns this language, it has to learn the series of 'numerals' a, b, c, . . . by heart. And it has to learn their use.—Will this training include ostensive teaching of the words?—Well, people will, for example, point to slabs and count: "a, b, c slabs".—Something more like the ostensive teaching of the words "block", "pillar", etc. would be the ostensive teaching of the numerals that serve not to count but to refer to groups of objects that can be taken in at a glance. Children do learn the use of the first five or six cardinal numerals in this way.

Are "there" and "this" also taught ostensively?—Imagine how one might perhaps teach their use. One will point to places and things—but in this case the pointing occurs in the *use* of the words too and not merely in learning the use.—

10. Now what do the words of this language *signify?*—What is supposed to show what they signify, if not the kind of use they have? And we have already described that. So we are asking for the expression "This word signifies *this*" to be made a part of the description. In other words the description ought to take the form: "The word . . . signifies . . .".

Of course, one can reduce the description of the use of the word "slab" to the statement that this word signifies this object. This will be done when, for example, it is merely a matter of removing the mistaken idea that the word "slab" refers to the shape of building-stone that we in fact call a "block"—but the kind of '*referring*' this is, that is to say the use of these words for the rest, is already known.

Equally one can say that the signs "a", "b", etc. signify numbers; when for example this removes the mistaken idea that "a", "b", "c", play the part actually played in language by "block", "slab", "pillar". And one can also say that "c" means this number and not that one; when for example this serves to explain that the letters are to be used in the order a, b, c, d, etc. and not in the order a, b, d, c.

But assimilating the descriptions of the uses of words in this way cannot make the uses themselves any more like one another. For, as we see, they are absolutely unlike.

11. Think of the tools in a tool-box: there is a hammer, pliers, a saw, a screw-driver, a rule, a glue-pot, glue, nails and screws.—The functions of words are as diverse as the functions of these objects. (And in both cases there are similarities.)

Of course, what confuses us is the uniform appearance of words when we hear them spoken or meet them in script and print. For their *application* is not presented to us so clearly. Especially when we are doing philosophy!

12. It is like looking into the cabin of a locomotive. We see handles all looking more or less alike. (Naturally, since they are all suppposed to be handled.) But one is the handle of a crank which can be moved continuously (it regulates the opening of a valve); another is the handle of a switch, which has only two effective positions, it is either off or on; a third is the handle of a brake-lever, the harder one pulls on it, the harder it brakes; a fourth, the handle of a pump: it has an effect only so long as it is moved to and fro.

13. When we say: "Every word in language signifies something" we have so far said *nothing whatever*; unless we have explained exactly *what* distinction we wish to make. (It might be, of course, that we wanted to distinguish the words of language (8) from words 'without meaning' such as occur in Lewis Carroll's poems, or words like "Lilliburlero" in songs.)

14. Imagine someone's saying: "*All* tools serve to modify something. Thus the hammer modifies the position of the nail, the saw the shape of the board, and so on."—And what is modified by the rule, the glue-pot, the nails?—"Our knowledge of a thing's length, the temperature of the glue, and the solidity of the box."——Would anything be gained by this assimilation of expressions?—

15. The word "to signify" is perhaps used in the most straightforward way when the object signified is marked with the sign. Suppose that the tools A uses in building bear certain marks. When A shows his assistant such a mark, he brings the tool that has that mark on it.

It is in this and more or less similar ways that a name means and is given to a thing.—It will often prove useful in philosophy to say to ourselves: naming something is like attaching a label to a thing.

16. What about the colour samples that A shows to B: are they part of the *language*? Well, it is as you please. They do not belong among the words; yet when I say to someone: "Pronounce the word 'the'", you will count the second "the" as part of the sentence. Yet it has a role just like that of a colour-sample in language-game (8); that is, it is a sample of what the other is meant to say.

It is most natural, and causes least confusion, to reckon the samples among the instruments of the language. . . .

17. It will be possible to say: In language (8) we have different *kinds of word.* For the functions of the word "slab" and the word "block" are more alike than those of "slab" and "d". But how we group words into kinds will depend on the aim of the classification,—and on our own inclination.

Think of the different points of view from which one can classify tools or chessmen.

18. Do not be troubled by the fact that languages (2) and (8) consist only of orders. If you want to say that this shows them to be incomplete, ask yourself whether our language is complete;—whether it was so before the symbolism of chemistry and the notation of the infinitesimal calculus were incorporated in it; for these are, so to speak, suburbs of our language. (And how many houses or streets does it take before a town begins to be a town?) Our language can be seen as an ancient city: a maze of little streets and squares, of old and new houses, and of houses with additions from various periods; and this surrounded by a multitude of new boroughs with straight regular streets and uniform houses.

28. Now one can ostensively define a proper name, the name of a colour, the name of a material, a numeral, the name of a point of the compass and so on. The definition of the number two, "That is called 'two'"—pointing to two nuts—is perfectly exact.—But how can two be defined like that? The person one gives the definition to doesn't know what one wants to call "two"; he will suppose that "two" is the name given to *this* group of nuts!——He *may* suppose this; but perhaps he does not. He might make the opposite mistake; when I want to assign a name to this group of nuts, he might understand it as a numeral. And he might equally well take the name of a person, of which I give an ostensive definition, as that of a colour, of a race, or even of a point of the compass. That is to say: an ostensive definition can be variously interpreted in *every* case.

29. Perhaps you say: two can only be ostensively defined in *this* way: "This *number* is called 'two'". For the word "number" here shows what place in language, in grammar, we assign to the word. But this means that the word "number" must be explained before the ostensive definition can be understood.—The word "number" in the definition does indeed show this place; does show the post at which we station the word. And we can prevent misunderstandings by saying: "This *colour* is called so-and-so", "This *length* is called so-and-so", and so on. That is to say: misunderstandings are sometimes averted in this way. But is there only *one* way of taking the word "colour" or "length"?—Well, they just need defining.—Defining, then, by means of other words! And what about the last definition in this chain? (Do not say: "There isn't a 'last' definition". That is just as if you chose to say: "There isn't a last house in this road; one can always build an additional one".)

Whether the word "number" is necessary in the ostensive definition depends on whether without it the other person takes the definition otherwise than I wish. And that will depend on the circumstances under which it is given, and on the person I give it to.

And how he 'takes' the definition is seen in the use that he makes of the word defined.

30. So one might say: the ostensive definition explains the use—the meaning—of the word when the overall role of the word in language is clear. Thus if I know that someone means to explain a colour-word to me the ostensive definition "That is called 'sepia'" will help me to understand the word.—And you can say this, so long as you do not forget that all sorts of problems attach to the words "to know" or "to be clear".

One has already to know (or be able to do) something in order to be capable of asking a thing's name. But what does one have to know?[2]

2. Could one define the word "red" by pointing to something that was *not red*? That would be as if one were supposed to explain the word "modest" to someone whose English

31. When one shows someone the king in chess and says: "This is the king", this does not tell him the use of this piece—unless he already knows the rules of the game up to this last point: the shape of the king. You could imagine his having learnt the rules of the game without ever having been shown an actual piece. The shape of the chessman corresponds here to the sound or shape of a word.

One can also imagine someone's having learnt the game without ever learning or formulating rules. He might have learnt quite simple board-games first, by watching, and have progressed to more and more complicated ones. He too might be given the explanation "This is the king",—if, for instance, he were being shown chessmen of a shape he was not used to. This explanation again only tells him the use of the piece because, as we might say, the place for it was already prepared. Or even: we shall only say that it tells him the use, if the place is already prepared. And in this case it is so, not because the person to whom we give the explanation already knows rules, but because in another sense he is already master of a game.

Consider this further case: I am explaining chess to someone; and I begin by pointing to a chessman and saying: "This is the king; it can move like this, . . . and so on."—In this case we shall say: the words "This is the king" (or "This is called the 'king'") are a definition only if the learner already 'knows what a piece in a game is'. That is, if he has already played other games, or has watched other people playing 'and understood'—*and similar things*. Further, only under these conditions will he be able to ask relevantly in the course of learning the game: "What do you call this?"—that is, this piece in a game.

We may say: only someone who already knows how to do something with it can significantly ask a name.

And we can imagine the person who is asked replying: "Settle the name yourself"—and now the one who asked would have to manage everything for himself.

32. Someone coming into a strange country will sometimes learn the language of the inhabitants from ostensive definitions that they give him; and he will often have to *guess* the meaing of these definitions; and will guess sometimes right, sometimes wrong.

And now, I think, we can say: Augustine describes the learning of human language as if the child came into a strange country and did not understand the language of the country; that is, as if it already had a language, only not this one. Or again: as if the child could already *think*, only not yet speak. And "think" would here mean something like "talk to itself".

33. Suppose, however, someone were to object: "It is not true that you must already be master of a language in order to understand an ostensive defintion: all you need—of course!—is to know or guess that the person giving the explanation is pointing to. That is, whether for example to the shape of the object, or to its colour, or to its number, and so on." —And what does 'pointing to the shape', 'pointing to the colour' consist in? Point to a piece of paper.—And now point to its shape—now to its colour—now to its number (that sounds queer).—How did you do it?—You will say that you 'meant' a different thing each time you pointed. And if I ask how that is done, you will say you concentrated your attention on the colour, the shape, etc. But I ask again: how is *that* done?

Suppose someone points to a vase and says "Look at that marvellous blue—the shape isn't the point."—Or: "Look at the marvellous shape—the colour doesn't matter." Without doubt you will do something *different* when you act upon these two invitations. But do you always do the *same* thing when you direct your attention to the colour? Imagine various different cases. To indicate a few:

"Is this blue the same as the blue over there? Do you see any difference?"—

You are mixing paint and you say "It's hard to get the blue of this sky."

"It's turning fine, you can already see blue sky again."

"Look what different effects these two blues have."

"Do you see the blue book over there? Bring it here."

---

was weak, and one pointed to an arrogant man and said "That man is *not* modest". That it is ambiguous is no argument against such a method of definition. Any definition can be misunderstood.

But it might well be asked: are we still to call this "definition"?—For, of course, even if it has the same practical consequences, the same *effect* on the learner, it plays a different part in the calculus from what we ordinarily call "ostensive definition" of the word "red".

"This blue signal-light means . . . ."

"What's this blue called?—Is it 'indigo'?"

You sometimes attend to the colour by putting your hand up to keep the outline from view; or by not looking at the outline of the thing; sometimes by staring at the object and trying to remember where you saw that colour before.

You attend to the shape, sometimes by tracing it, sometimes by screwing up your eyes so as not to see the colour clearly, and in many other ways. I want to say: This is the sort of thing that happens *while* one 'directs one's attention to this or that'. But it isn't these things by themselves that make us say someone is attending to the shape, the colour, and so on. Just as a move in chess doesn't consist simply in moving a piece in such-and-such a way on the board—nor yet in one's thoughts and feelings as one makes the move: but in the circumstances that we call "playing a game of chess", "solving a chess problem", and so on.

34. But suppose someone said: "I always do the same thing when I attend to the shape: my eye follows the outline and I feel . . . ." And suppose this person to give someone else the ostensive definition "That is called a 'circle'", pointing to a circular object and having all these experiences—cannot his hearer still interpret the definition differently, even though he sees the other's eyes following the outline, and even though he feels what the other feels? That is to say: this 'interpretation' may also consist in how he now makes use of the word; in what he points to, for example, when told: "Point to a circle".—For neither the expression "to intend the definition in such-and-such a way" nor the expression "to interpret the definition in such-and-such a way" stands for a process which accompanies the giving and hearing of the definition.

35. There are, of course, what can be called "characteristic experiences" of pointing to (e.g.) the shape. For example, following the outline with one's finger or with one's eyes as one points.—But *this* does not happen in all cases in which I 'mean the shape', and no more does any other one characteristic process occur in all these cases.—Besides, even if something of the sort did recur in all cases, it would still depend on the circumstances—that is, on what happened before and after the pointing—whether we should say "He pointed to the shape and not to the colour".

For the words "to point to the shape", "to mean the shape", and so on, are not used in the same way as *these*: "to point to this book (not to that one), "to point to the chair, not to the table", and so on.—Only think how differently we *learn* the use of the words "to point to this thing", "to point to that thing", and on the other hand "to point to the colour, not the shape", "to mean the colour", and so on.

To repeat: in certain cases, especially when one points 'to the shape' or 'to the number' there are characteristic experiences and ways of pointing—'characteristic' because they recur often (not always) when shape or number are 'meant'. But do you also know of an experience characteristic of pointing to a piece in a game *as a piece in a game*? All the same one can say: "I meant that this *piece* is called the 'king', not this particular bit of wood I am pointing to". (Recognizing, wishing, remembering, etc.)[3]

36. And we do here what we do in a host of similar cases: because we cannot specify any *one* bodily action which we call pointing to the shape (as opposed, for example, to the colour), we say that a *spiritual* [mental, intellectual] activity corresponds to these words.

Where our language suggests a body and there is none: there, we should like to say, is a *spirit*.

37. What is the relation between name and thing named?—Well, what *is* it? Look at lanaguage-game (2) or at another one: there you can see the sort of thing this relation consists in. This relation may also consist, among many other things, in the fact that hearing the name calls before our mind the picture of what is named; and is also consists, among other things, in the name's being written on the thing named or being pronounced when that thing is pointed at.

38. But what, for example, is the word "this" the name of in language-game (8) or the word "that" in the ostensive definition "that is called . . . ."?—If you do not want to produce confusion you will do best not to call these words names at all.—Yet, strange to

3. What is it to *mean* the words "*That* is blue" at one time as a statement about the object one is pointing to—at another as an explanation of the word "blue"? Well, in the second case one really means "That is called 'blue'".—Then can one at one time mean the word "is" as "is called" and the word "blue" as "'blue'", and another time mean "is" really as "is"? . . .

say, the word "this" has been called the only *genuine* name; so that anything else we call a name was one only in an inexact, approximate sense.

This queer conception springs from a tendency to sublime the logic of our language—as one might put it. The proper answer to it is: we call very different things "names"; the word "name" is used to characterize many different kinds of use of a word, related to one another in many different ways;—but the kind of use that "this" has is not among them.

It is quite true that, in giving an ostensive definition for instance, we often point to the object named and say the name. And similarly, in giving an ostensive definition for instance, we say the word "this" while pointing to a thing. And also the word "this" and a name often occupy the same position in a sentence. But it is precisely characteristic of a name that it is defined by means of the demonstrative expression "That is N" (or "That is called 'N'"). But do we also give the definitions: "That is called 'this'", or "This is called 'this'"?

This is connected with the conception of naming as, so to speak, an occult process. Naming appears as a *queer* connexion of a word with an object.—And you really get such a queer connexion when the philosopher tries to bring out *the* relation between name and thing by staring at an object in front of him and repeating a name or even the word "this" innumerable times. For philosophical problems arise when language *goes on holiday*. And *here* we may indeed fancy naming to be some remarkable act of mind, as it were a baptism of an object. And we can also say the word "this" *to* the object, as it were *address* the object as "this"—a queer use of this word, which doubtless only occurs in doing philosophy.

65. Here we come up against the great question that lies behind all these considerations.—For someone might object against me: "You take the easy way out! You talk about all sorts of language-games, but have nowhere said what the essence of a language-game, and hence of language, is: what is common to all these activities, and what makes them into language or parts of language. So you let yourself off the very part of the investigation that once gave you yourself most headache, the part about the *general form of propositions* and of language."

And this is true.—Instead of producing something common to all that we call language, I am saying that these phenomena have no one thing in common which makes us use the same word for all,—but that they are *related* to one another in many different ways. And it is because of this relationship, or these relationships, that we call them all "language". I will try to explain this.

66. Consider for example the proceedings that we call "games". I mean board-games, card-games, ball-games, Olympic games, and so on. What is common to them all?—Don't say: "There *must* be something common, or they would not be called 'games'"—but *look and see* whether there is anything common to all.—For if you look at them you will not see something common to all.—For if you look at them you will not see something that is common to *all*, but similarities, relationships, and a whole series of them at that. To repeat: don't think, but look!—Look for example at board-games, with their multifarious relationships. Now pass to card-games; here you find many correspondences with the first group, but many common features drop out, and others appear. When we pass next to ball-games, much that is common is retained, but much is lost.—Are they all 'amusing'? Compare chess with noughts and crosses. Or is there always winning and losing, or competition between players? Think of patience. In ball games there is winning and losing; but when a child throws his ball at the wall and catches it again, this feature has disappeared. Look at the parts played by skill and luck; and at the difference between skill in chess and skill in tennis. Think now of games like ring-a-ring-a-roses; here is the element of amusement, but how many other characteristic features have disappeared! And we can go through the many, many other groups of games in the same way; can see how similarities crop up and disappear.

And the result of this examination is: we see a complicated network of similarities overlapping and criss-crossing: sometimes overall similarities, sometimes similarities of detail.

67. I can think of no better expression to characterize these similarities than "family resemblances"; for the various resemblances between members of a family: build, features, colour of eyes, gait, temperament, etc. etc. overlap and criss-cross in the same way.—And I shall say: 'games' form a family.

And for instance the kinds of number form a family in the same way. Why do we call something a "number"? Well, perhaps because it has a—direct—relationship with several things that have hitherto been called number; and this can be said to give it an indirect relationship to other things we call the same name. And we extend our concept of number as in spinning a thread we twist fibre on fibre. And the strength of the thread does not reside in the fact that some one fibre runs through its whole length, but in the overlapping of many fibres.

But if someone wish to say: "There is something common to all these constructions—namely the disjunction of all their common properties"—I should reply: Now you are only playing with words. One might as well say: "Something runs through the whole thread—namely the continuous overlapping of those fibres".

68. "All right: the concept of number is defined for you as the logical sum of these individual interrelated concepts: cardinal numbers, rational numbers, real numbers, etc.; and in the same way the concept of a game as the logical sum of a corresponding set of sub-concepts."—It need not be so. For I *can* give the concept 'number' rigid limits in this way, that is, use the word "number" for a rigidly limited concept, but I can also use it so that the extension of the concept is *not* closed by a frontier. And this is how we do use the word "game". For how is the concept of a game bounded? What still counts as a game and what no longer does? Can you give the boundary? No. You can *draw* one; for none has so far been drawn. (But that never troubled you before when you used the word "game".)

"But then the use of the word is unregulated, the 'game' we play with it is unregulated."—It is not everywhere circumscribed by rules; but no more are there any rules for how high one throws the ball in tennis, or how hard; yet tennis is a game for all that and has rules too.

139. When someone says the word "cube" to me, for example, I know what it means. But can the whole *use* of the word come before my mind, when I *understand* it in this way?

Well, but on the other hand isn't the meaning of the word also determined by this use? And can't these ways of determining meaning conflict? Can what we grasp *in a flash* accord with a use, fit or fail to fit it? And how can what is present to us in an instant, what comes before our mind in an instant, fit a *use*?

What really comes before our mind when we *understand* a word?—Isn't it something like a picture? Can't it *be* a picture?

Well, suppose that a picture does come before your mind when you hear the word "cube", say the drawing of a cube. In what sense can this picture fit or fail to fit a use of the word "cube"?—Perhaps you say: "It's quite simple;—if that picture occurs to me and I point to a triangular prism for instance, and say it is a cube, then this use of the word doesn't fit the picture."—But doesn't it fit? I have purposely so chosen the example that it is quite easy to imagine a *method of projection* according to which the picture does fit after all.[4]

The picture of the cube did indeed *suggest* a certain use to us, but it was possible for me to use it differently.

140. Then what sort of mistake did I make; was it what we should like to express by saying: I should have thought the picture forced a particular use on me? How could I think that? What *did* I think? Is there such a thing as a picture, or something like a picture, that forces a particular application on us; so that my mistake lay in confusing one picture with another?—For we might also be inclined to express ourselves like this; we are at most under a psychological, not a logical, compulsion. And now it looks quite as if we knew of two kinds of case.

What was the effect of my argument? It called our attention to (reminded us of) the fact that there are other processes, besides the one we originally thought of, which we should sometimes be prepared to call "applying the picture of a cube". So our 'belief that the picture forced a particular application upon us' consisted in the fact that only the one case and no other occurred to us. "There is another solution as well" means there is something else that I am also prepared to call a "solution"; to which I am prepared to apply such-and-such a picture, such-and-such an analogy, and so on.

What is essential is to see that the same thing can come before our minds when we hear the word and

4. . . . I see a picture; it represents an old man walking up a steep path leaning on a stick.—How? Might it not have looked just the same if he had been sliding downhill in that position? Perhaps a Martian would describe the picture so. I do not need to explain why *we* do not describe it so.

the application still be different. Has it the *same* meaning both times? I think we shall say not.

141. Suppose, however, that not merely the picture of the cube, but also the method of projection comes before our mind?——How am I to imagine this?—Perhaps I see before me a schema showing the method of projection: say a picture of two cubes connected by lines of projection.—But does this really get me any further? Can't I now imagine different applications of this schema too?——Well, yes, but then can't an *application come before my mind?*—It can: only we need to get clearer about our application of *this* expression. Suppose I explain various methods of projection to someone so that he may go on to apply them; let us ask ourselves when we should say that *the* method that I intend comes before his mind.

Now clearly we accept two different kinds of criteria for this: on the one hand the picture (of whatever kind) that at some time or other comes before his mind; on the other, the application which—in the course of time—he makes of what he imagines. (And can't it be clearly seen here that it is absolutely inessential for the picture to exist in his imagination rather than as a drawing or model in front of him; or again as something that he himself constructs as a model?)

Can there be a collision between picture and application? There can, inasmuch as the picture makes us expect a different use, because people in general apply *this* picture like *this*.

I want to say: we have here a *normal* case, and abnormal cases.

142. It is only in normal cases that the use of a word is clearly prescribed; we know, are in no doubt, what to say in this or that case. The more abnormal the case, the more doubtful it becomes what we are to say. And if things were quite different from what they actually are——if there were for instance no characteristic expression of pain, of fear, of joy; if rule became exception and exception rule; or if both became phenomena of roughly equal frequency——this would make our normal language-games lose their point.—The procedure of putting a lump of cheese on a balance and fixing the price by the turn of the scale would lose its point if it frequently happened for such lumps to suddenly grow or shrink for no obvious reason. This remark will become clearer when we discuss such things as the relation of expression to feeling, and similar topics.[5]

143. Let us now examine the following kind of language-game: when A gives an order B has to write down series of signs according to a certain formation rule.

The first of these series is meant to be that of the natural numbers in decimal notation.—How does he get to understand this notation?—First of all series of numbers will be written down for him and he will be required to copy them. (Do not balk at the expression "series of numbers"; it is not being used wrongly here.) And here already there is a normal and an abnormal learner's reaction.—At first perhaps we guide his hand in writing out the series 0 to 9; but then the *possibility of getting him to understand* will depend on his going on to write it down independently.—And here we can imagine, e.g., that he does copy the figures independently, but not in the right order: he writes sometimes one sometimes another at random. And then communication stops at *that* point.—Or again, he makes '*mistakes*' in the order.—The difference between this and the first case will of course be one of frequency.—Or he makes a *systematic* mistake; for example, he copies every other number, or he copies the series 0, 1, 2, 3, 4, 5, ... like this: 1, 0, 3, 2, 5, 4, ... Here we shall almost be tempted to say that he has understood *wrong*.

Notice, however, that there is no sharp distinction between a random mistake and a systematic one. That is, between what you are inclined to call "random" and what "systematic".

Perhaps it is possible to wean him from the systematic mistake (as from a bad habit). Or perhaps one accepts his way of copying and tries to teach him ours as an offshoot, a variant of his.—And here too our pupil's capacity to learn may come to an end.

151. But there is also *this* use of the word "to know"; we say "Now I know!"—and similarly "Now I can do it!" and "Now I understand!"

Let us imagine the following example: A writes series of numbers down; B watches him and tries to find a law for the sequence of numbers. If he succeeds

5. What we have to mention in order to explain the significance, I mean the importance, of a concept, are often extremely general facts of nature: such facts as are hardly ever mentioned because of their great generality.

he exclaims: "Now I can go on!"—So this capacity, this understanding, is something that makes its appearance in a moment. So let us try and see what it is that makes its appearance here.—A has written down the numbers 1, 5, 11, 19, 29; at this point B says he knows how to go on. What happened here? Various things may have happened; for example, while A was slowly putting one number after another, B was occupied with trying various algebraic formulae on the numbers which had been written down. After A had written the number 19 B tried the formula $a_n = n^2 + n - 1$; and the next number confirmed his hypothesis.

179. Let us return to our case (151). It is clear that we should not say B had the right to say the words "Now I know how to go on", just because he thought of the formula—unless experience showed that there was a connexion between thinking of the formula—saying it, writing it down—and actually continuing the series. And obviously such a connexion does exist.—And now one might think that the sentence "I can go on" meant "I have experience which I know empirically to lead to the continuation of the series." But does B mean that when he says he can go on? Does that sentence come to his mind, or is he ready to produce it in explanation of what he meant?

No. The words "Now I know how to go on" were correctly used when he thought of the formula: that is, given such circumstances as that he had learnt algebra, had used such formulae before.—But that does not mean that his statement is only short for a description of all the circumstances which constitute the scene for our language-game.—Think how we learn to use the expressions "Now I know how to go on", "Now I can go on" and others; in what family of language-games we learn their use.

We can also imagine the case where nothing at all occurred in B's mind except that he suddenly said, "Now I know how to go on"—perhaps with a feeling of relief; and that he did in fact go on working out the series without using the formula. And in this case too we should say—in certain circumstances—that he did know how to go on.

180. *This is how these words are used.* It would be quite misleading, in this last case, for instance, to call the words a "description of a mental state".—One might rather call them a "signal"; and we judge whether it was rightly employed by what he goes on to do.

185. Let us return to our example (143). Now—judged by the usual criteria—the pupil has mastered the series of natural numbers. Next we teach him to write down other series of cardinal numbers and get him to the point of writing down series of the form

0, n, 2n, 3n, etc.

at an order of the form "+n"; so at the order "+1" he writes down the series of natural numbers.—Let us suppose we have done exercises and given him tests up to 1000.

Now we get the pupil to continue a series (say +2) beyond 1000—and he writes 1000, 1004, 1008, 1012.

We say to him: "Look what you've done!"—He doesn't understand. We say: "You were meant to add *two*: look how you began the series!"—He answers: "Yes, isn't it right? I thought that was how I was *meant* to do it."—Or suppose he pointed to the series and said: "But I went on in the same way."—It would now be no use to say: "But can't you see .... ?"—and repeat the old examples and explanations.—In such a case we might say, perhaps: It comes natural to this person to understand our order with our explanations as *we* should understand the order: "Add 2 up to 1000, 4 up to 2000, 6 up to 3000 and so on."

Such a case would present similarities with one in which a person naturally reacted to the gesture of pointing with the hand by looking in the direction of the line from finger-tip to wrist, not from wrist to finger-tip.

186. "What you are saying, then, comes to this: a new insight—intuition—is needed at every step to carry out the order '+n' correctly."—To carry it out correctly! How is it decided what is the right step to take at any particular stage?—"The right step is the one that accords with the order—as it was *meant*."—So when you gave the order +2 you meant that he was to write 1002 after 1000—and did you also mean that he should write 1868 after 1866, and 100036 after 100034, and so on—an infinite number of such propositions?—"No: what I meant was, that he should write the next but one number after *every* number that he wrote; and from this all those propositions follow in turn."—But that is just what is in question: what, at any stage, does follow from that sentence. Or, again, what, at any stage we are to call "being in accord" with that sentence (and with the *mean*-ing

you then put into the sentence—whatever that may have consisted in). It would almost be more correct to say, not that an intuition was needed at every stage, but that a new decision was needed at every stage.

191. "It is as if we could grasp the whole use of the word in a flash." Like *what* e.g.?—Can't the use—in a certain sense—be grasped in a flash? And in *what* sense can it not?—The point is, that it is as if we could 'grasp it in a flash' in yet another and much more direct sense than that.—But have you a model for this? No. It is just that this expression suggests itself to us. As the result of the crossing of different pictures.

192. You have no model of this superlative fact, but you are seduced into using a super-expression. (It might be called a philosophical superlative.)

193. The machine as symbolizing its action: the action of a machine—I might say at first—seems to be there in it from the start. What does that mean?—If we know the machine, everything else, that is its movement, seems to be already completely determined.

We talk as if these parts could only move in this way, as if they could not do anything else. How is this—do we forget the possibility of their bending, breaking off, melting, and so on? Yes; in many cases we don't think of that at all. We use a machine, or the drawing of a machine, to symbolize a particular action of the machine. For instance, we give someone such a drawing and assume that he will derive the movement of the parts from it. (Just as we can give someone a number by telling him that it is the twenty-fifth in the series 1, 4, 9, 16, ...)

"The machine's action seems to be in it from the start" means: we are inclined to compare the future movements of the machine in their definiteness to objects which are already lying in a drawer and which we then take out.—But we do not say this kind of thing when we are concerned with predicting the actual behaviour of a machine. Then we do not in general forget the possibility of a distortion of the parts and so on.—We *do* talk like that, however, when we are wondering at the way we can use a machine to symbolize a given way of moving—since it can also move in quite *different* ways.

We might say that a machine, or the picture of it, is the first of a series of pictures which we have learnt to derive from this one.

But when we reflect that the machine could also have moved differently it may look as if the way it moves must be contained in the machine-as-symbol far more determinately than in the actual machine. As if it were not enough for the movements in question to be empirically determined in advance, but they had to be really—in a mysterious sense—already *present*. And it is quite true: the movement of the machine-as-symbol is predetermined in a different sense from that in which the movement of any given actual machine is predetermined.

197. "It's as if we could grasp the whole use of a word in a flash."—And that is just what we say we do. That is to say: we sometimes describe what we do in these words. But there is nothing astonishing, nothing queer, about what happens. It becomes queer when we are led to think that the future development must in some way already be present in the act of grasping the use and yet isn't present.—For we say that there isn't any doubt that we understand the word, and on the other hand its meaning lies in its use. There is no doubt that I now want to play chess, but chess is the game it is in virtue of all its rules (and so on). Don't I know, then, which game I want to play until I *have* played it? or are all the rules contained in my act of intending? Is it experience that tells me that this sort of game is the usual consequence of such an act of intending? so is it impossible for me to be certain what I am intending to do? And if that is nonsense—what kind of super-strong connexion exists between the act of intending and the thing intended?——Where is the connexion effected between the sense of the expression "Let's play a game of chess" and all the rules of the game?—Well, in the list of rules of the game, in the teaching of it, in the day-to-day practice of playing.

198. "But how can a rule show me what I have to do at *this* point? Whatever I do is, on some interpretation, in accord with the rule."—That is not what we ought to say, but rather: any interpretation still hangs in the air along with what it interprets, and cannot give it any support. Interpretations by themselves do not determine meaning.

"Then can whatever I do be brought into accord with the rule?"—Let me ask this: what has the expression of a rule—say a sign-post—got to do with my actions? What sort of connexion is there here?—Well, perhaps this one: I have been trained to react to this sign in a particular way, and now I do so react to it.

But that is only to give a causal connexion; to tell how it has come about that we now go by the sign-post; not what this going-by-the-sign really consists in. On the contrary; I have further indicated that a person goes by a sign-post only in so far as there exists a regular use of sign-posts, a custom.

201. This was our paradox: no course of action could be determined by a rule, because every course of action can be made out to accord with the rule. The answer was: if everything can be made out to accord with the rule, then it can also be made out to conflict with it. And so there would be neither accord nor conflict here.

It can be seen that there is a misunderstanding here from the mere fact that in the course of our argument we give on interpretation after another; as if each one contented us at least for a moment, until we thought of yet another standing behind it. What this shows is that there is a way of grasping a rule which is *not* an *interpretation*, but which is exhibited in what we call "obeying the rule" and "going against it" in actual cases.

Hence there is an inclination to say: every action according to the rule is an interpretation. But we ought to restrict the term "interpretation" to the substitution of one expression of the rule for another.

217. "How am I able to obey a rule?"—if this is not a question about causes, then it is about the justification for my following the rule in the way I do.

If I have exhausted the justifications I have reached bedrock, and my spade is turned. Then I am inclined to say: "This is simply what I do."

(Remember that we sometimes demand definitions for the sake not of their content, but of their form. Our requirement is an architectural one; the definition a kind of ornamental coping that supports nothing.)

218. Whence comes the idea that the beginning of a series is a visible section of rails invisibly laid to infinity? Well, we might imagine rails instead of a rule. And infinitely long rails correspond to the unlimited application of a rule.

219. "All the steps are really already taken" means: I no longer have any choice. The rule, once stamped with a particular meaning, traces the lines along which it is to be followed through the whole of space.—But if something of this sort really were the case, how would it help?

No; my description only made sense if it was to be understood symbolically.—I should have said: *This is how it strikes me.*

When I obey a rule, I do not choose.

I obey the rule *blindly*.

241. "So you are saying that human agreement decides what is true and what is false?"—It is what human beings *say* that is true and false; and they agree in the *language* they use. That is not agreement in opinions but in form of life.

242. If language is to be a means of communication there must be agreement not only in definitions but also (queer as this may sound) in judgments. This seems to abolish logic, but does not do so.—It is one thing to describe methods of measurement, and another to obtain and state results of measurement. But what we call "measuring" is partly determined by a certain constancy in results of measurement.

243. A human being can encourage himself, give himself orders, obey, blame and punish himself; he can ask himself a question and answer it. We could even imagine human beings who spoke only in monologue; who accompanied their activities by talking to themselves.—An explorer who watched them and listened to their talk might succeed in translating their language into ours. (This would enable him to predict these people's actions correctly, for he also hears them making resolutions and decisions.)

But could we also imagine a language in which a person could write down or give vocal expression to his inner experiences—his feelings, moods, and the rest—for his private use?—Well, can't we do so in our ordinary language?—But that is not what I mean. The individual words of this language are to refer to what can only be known to the person speaking; to his immediate private sensations. So another person cannot understand the language.

257. "What would it be like if human beings showed no outward signs of pain (did not groan, grimace, etc.)? Then it would be impossible to teach a child the use of the word 'tooth-ache'."—Well, let's assume the child is a genius and itself invents a name for the sensation!—But then, of course, he couldn't make himself understood when he used the word.—So does he understand the name, without being able to explain its meaning to anyone?—But what does it mean to say that he has 'named his pain'?—How has he done this naming of pain?! And whatever he did, what was its purpose?—When one says "He gave a

name to his sensation" one forgets that a great deal of stage-setting in the language is presupposed if the mere act of naming is to make sense. And when we speak of someone's having given a name to pain, what is presupposed is the existence of the grammar of the word "pain"; it shows the post where the new word is stationed.

258. Let us imagine the following case. I want to keep a diary about the recurrence of a certain sensation. To this end I associate it with the sign "S" and write this sign in a calendar for every day on which I have the sensation.——I will remark first of all that a definition of the sign cannot be formulated.—But still I can give myself a kind of ostensive definition.—How? Can I point to the sensation? Not in the ordinary sense. But I speak, or write the sign down, and at the same time I concentrate my attention on the sensation—and so, as it were, point to it inwardly.—But what is this ceremony for? for that is all it seems to be! A definition surely serves to establish the meaning of a sign.—Well, that is done precisely by the concentrating of my attention; for in this way I impress on myself the connexion between the sign and the sensation.—But "I impress it on myself" can only mean: this process brings it about that I remember the connexion *right* in the future. But in the present case I have no criterion of correctness. One would like to say: whatever is going to seem right to me is right. And that only means that here we can't talk about 'right'.

259. Are the rules of the private language *impressions* of rules?—The balance on which impressions are weighed is not the *impression* of a balance.

260. "Well, I *believe* that this is the sensation S again."—Perhaps you *believe* that you believe it!

Then did the man who made the entry in the calendar make a note of *nothing whatever*?—Don't consider it a matter of course that a person is making a note of something when he makes a mark—say in a calendar. For a note has a function, and this "S" so far has none.

(One can talk to oneself.—If a person speaks when no one else is present, does that mean he is speaking to himself?)

261. What reason have we for calling "S" the sign for a *sensation*? For "sensation" is a word of our common language, not of one intelligible to me alone. So the use of this word stands in need of a justification which everybody understands.—And it would not help either to say that it need not be a *sensation*; that when he writes "S", he has *something*—and that is all that can be said. "Has" and "something" also belong to our common language.—So in the end when one is doing philosophy one gets to the point where one would like just to emit an inarticulate sound.—But such a sound is an expression only as it occurs in a particular language-game, which should now be described.

265. Let us imagine a table (something like a dictionary) that exists only in our imagination. A dictionary can be used to justify the translation of a word X by a word Y. But are we also to call it a justification if such a table is to be looked up only in the imagination?—"Well, yes; then it is a subjective justification."—But justification consists in appealing to something independent.—"But surely I can appeal from one memory to another. For example, I don't know if I have remembered the time of departure of a train right and to check it I call to mind how a page of the time-table looked. Isn't it the same here?"—No; for this process has got to produce a memory which is actually *correct*. If the mental image of the time-table could not itself be *tested* for correctness, how could it confirm the correctness of the first memory? (As if someone were to buy several copies of the morning paper to assure himself that what it said was true.)

Looking up a table in the imagination is no more looking up a table than the image of the result of an imagined experiment is the result of an experiment.

273. What am I to say about the word "red"?—that it means something 'confronting us all' and that everyone should really have another word, besides this one, to mean his *own* sensation of red? Or is it like this: the word "red" means something known to everyone; and in addition, for each person, it means something known only to him? (Or perhaps rather: it *refers* to something known only to him.)

274. Of course, saying that the word "red" "refers to" instead of "means" something private does not help us in the least to grasp its function; but it is the more psychologically apt expression for a particular experience in doing philosophy. It is as if when I uttered the word I cast a sidelong glance at the private sensation, as it were in order to say to myself: I know all right what I mean by it.

281. "But doesn't what you say come to this: that there is no pain, for example, without *pain-behaviour*?"—It comes to this: only of a living human being and what resembles (behaves like) a living human being can one say: it has sensations; it sees; is blind; hears; is deaf; is conscious or unconscious.

282. "But in a fairy tale the pot too can see and hear!" (Certainly; but it *can* also talk.)

"But the fairy tale only invents what is not the case: it does not talk *nonsense*."—It is not as simple as that. Is it false or nonsensical to say that a pot talks? Have we a clear picture of the circumstances in which we should say of a pot that it talked? (Even a nonsense-poem is not nonsense in the same way as the babbling of a child.)

We do indeed say of an inanimate thing that it is in pain: when playing with dolls for example. But this use of the concept of pain is a secondary one. Imagine a case in which people ascribed pain *only* to inanimate things; pitied *only* dolls! (When children play at trains their game is connected with their knowledge of trains. It would nevertheless be possible for the children of a tribe unacquainted with trains to learn this game from others, and to play it without knowing that it was copied from anything. One might say that the game did not make the same *sense* to them as to us.)

283. What gives us *so much as the idea* that living beings, things, can feel?

Is it that my education has led me to it by drawing my attention to feelings in myself, and now I transfer the idea to objects outside myself? That I recognize that there is something there (in me) which I can call "pain" without getting into conflict with the way other people use this word?—I do not transfer my idea to stones, plants, etc.

Couldn't I imagine having frightful pains and turning to stone while they lasted? Well, how do I know, if I shut my eyes, whether I have not turned into a stone? And if that has happened, in what sense will *the stone* have the pains? In what sense will they be ascribable to the stone? And why need the pain have a bearer at all here?!

And can one say of the stone that it has a soul and *that* is what has the pain? What has a soul, or pain, to do with a stone?

Only of what behaves like a human being can one say that it *has* pains.

For one has to say it of a body, or, if you like of a soul which some body *has*. And how can a body *have* a soul?

284. Look at a stone and imagine it having sensations.—One says to onself: How could one so much as get the idea of ascribing a *sensation* to a *thing*? One might as well ascribe it to a number!—And now look at a wriggling fly and at once these difficulties vanish and pain seems able to get a foothold here, where before everything was, so to speak, too smooth for it.

And so, too, a corpse seems to us quite inaccessible to pain.—Our attitude to what is alive and to what is dead, is not the same. All our reactions are different.—If anyone says: "That cannot simply come from the fact that a living thing moves about in such-and-such a way and a dead one not", then I want to intimate to him that this is a case of the transition 'from quantity to quality'.

293. If I say of myself that it is only from my own case that I know what the word "pain" means—must I not say the same of other people too? And how can I generalize the *one* case so irresponsibly?

Now someone tells me that *he* knows what pain is only from his own case!——Suppose everyone had a box with something in it: we call it a "beetle". No one can look into anyone else's box, and everyone says he knows what a beetle is only by looking at *his* beetle.—Here it would be quite possible for everyone to have something different in his box. One might even imagine such a thing constantly changing.—But suppose the word "beetle" had a use in these people's language?—If so it would not be used as the name of a thing. The thing in the box has no place in the language-game at all; not even as a *something*: for the box might even be empty.—No, one can 'divide through' by the thing in the box; it cancels out, whatever it is.

That is to say: if we construe the grammar of the expression of sensation on the model of 'object and designation' the object drops out of consideration as irrelevant.

304. "But you will surely admit that there is a difference between pain-behaviour accompanied by pain and pain-behaviour without any pain?"—Admit it? What greater difference could there be?—"And yet you again and again reach the conclusion that the sensation itself is a *nothing*."—Not at all. It is not

a *something*, but not a *nothing* either! The conclusion was only that a nothing would serve just as well as a something about which nothing could be said. We have only rejected the grammar which tries to force itself on us here.

The paradox disappears only if we make a radical break with the idea that language always functions in one way, always serves the same purpose: to convey thoughts—which may be about houses, pains, good and evil, or anything else you please.

309. What is your aim in philosophy?—To show the fly the way out of the fly-bottle.

J. L. Austin

John Langshaw Austin was born in 1911 and died unexpectedly in 1960, a few weeks short of his forty-ninth birthday. Although he was one of the most influential English philosophers of his generation, he did not publish a great deal during his lifetime. *Sense and Sensibilia*, the book from which selections are printed here, was put together after his death from notes for a course of lectures that he gave regularly at Oxford between 1947 and 1959.

He attended Balliol College, Oxford, emerging with a first-class degree in "Greats" (Oxford's mixture of classics and philosophy). He was then elected, after examination, to a fellowship at All Souls College, a position he held for two years before becoming a fellow and tutor of Magdalen. In 1952, he became White's Professor of Moral Philosophy, holding the chair until his death. Austin's only break from academic life came during World War II, in which he served with great distinction as an intelligence officer. His contributions to the planning for the D-Day landings are said to have saved many Allied lives.

The emergence of "Oxford philosophy," as it became known, involved a profound change in the way that philosophy was conceived. Whereas Bertrand Russell had made the revolutionary advances in mathematical logic the starting point for philosophy, the Oxford school, under the leadership of Austin, turned to ordinary language for insight into philosophical problems. Among so-called "ordinary language" philosophers, Austin stands out for his interest in the details of ordinary ways of talking. His exceptional ear for nuance and flair for vivid examples lend his philosophical writings an altogether distinctive character.

Austin's qualities are clearly displayed in *Sense and Sensibilia*, a no-holds-barred attack on the sense-data theory of perception. This theory is a version of the view, held by the classic British empiricists (Locke, Berkeley, and Hume), and taken over by Russell, that we are never "directly" aware of objects in our surroundings but only of our "ideas," "perceptions," or, as Russell called them, "sense-data." This account of perception appears to raise a serious skeptical problem, for if all we immediately know are our own perceptions, how can we determine the real nature of external objects? Indeed, how can we know that there is an external world at all? Russell thought that Berkeley's solution—that objects are just collections of ideas—could be made precise and rigorous with the aid of modern logic. Objects, Russell said, are "logical constructions out of sense-data." By this he meant that any statements about a material object could in principle be translated into (or perhaps, in Russell's case, it would be better to say "replaced by") a logically complex statement about sense-data. This epistemological/metaphysical theory, which became known as "phenomenalism," was widely held by those philosophers who identified themselves with the empiricist tradition.

An important objection to phenomenalism is that the promised translations of talk about material objects into talk about sense-data cannot be given. But Austin levels a deeper objection. His target is the "argument from illusion," the source of the view that we are always aware ("directly" or "immediately") only of our own sense-data. Theories like phenomenalism seem needed only if we have already made this critical concession.

The argument from illusion begins by pointing out that some perceptual experiences are "veridical" whereas others are "delusive." In a veridical experience, I am aware of an object that appears to me as it really is; for example, I see a round penny that looks round. In a delusive experience, the object may look other than as it really is; if the penny is tilted to my line of sight, it will appear elliptical. In extreme cases of delusive perception (the drunkard's pink rats), there may be no object there at all. Nevertheless, in the case of the penny viewed aslant, there is something elliptical present to consciousness. (Why else would I say that the penny looks elliptical?) Even the drunkard experiences pinkness. But the pinkness that the drunkard experiences cannot belong to a material object, for no object is really there. The pinkness must therefore belong to something else: a sense-datum. However, it would be implausible to hold that we are generally aware of sense-data, except when objects happen to present their true appearances; and in any case, there is no intrinsic qualitative difference between delusive and veridical experiences. The conclusion is reached that we are always aware (directly, anyway) of our own sense-data. Knowledge of material objects depends on some kind of inference from experiential data.

According to Austin, the argument from illusion is a family of arguments, every member of which is a farrago of fallacies, largely verbal. The "arguments" are driven by bogus dichotomies involving ill-explained technical terms (sense-data versus material objects, "veridical" versus "delusive" perception); misunderstandings and oversimplifications of certain crucial words ("appears," "real," etc.); obsessive concentration on hackneyed and tendentiously described examples (the straight stick that looks bent when half-immersed in water); failures to make necessary distinctions (illusions versus delusions); and implausible and ill-grounded empirical claims (dreams are qualitatively indistinguishable from waking experience). Austin exposes these fallacies by paying close attention to how we actually talk about the things we see and how we perceive (and misperceive) them. His investigation reveals that our ordinary ways of talking and thinking are powerful and nuanced, involving none of the simple dichotomies or confusions that drive the argument from illusion.

Austin does not suppose that ordinary language is sacrosanct. Rather, his view is that ordinary language is much more subtle than the "blinkering philosophical English" spoken by sense-data theorists. Since ordinary language has evolved over a long time to deal with an enormous range of practical contingencies, distinctions that have survived are likely to be worth making. In this respect, his attitude has some affinities with American Pragmatism.

• • •

A. J. Ayer responds to Austin's attack on sense-data in "Has Austin Refuted Sense-Data?" in K. T. Fann, ed., *Symposium on J. L. Austin* (New York: Humanities Press, 1969). See also Jonathan Bennett, "Real," in the same volume. Whether Austin's "ordinary language" method really gets to grips with philosophical skepticism is interestingly discussed by Barry Stroud in *The Significance of Philosophical Scepticism* (Oxford: Oxford University Press, 1984). Mark Kaplan defends Austin's method against Stroud's criticisms in "To What Must an Epistemology Be True?" *Philosophy and Phenomenological Research* 61 (September 2000). For a comprehensive account of Austin's philosophical work, see Geoffrey Warnock, *J. L. Austin* (London and New York: Routledge, 1991).

Michael Williams

Sense and Sensibilia

I

In these lectures I am going to discuss some current doctrines (perhaps, by now, not so current as they once were) about sense-perception. We shall not, I fear, get so far as to decide about the truth or falsity of these doctrines; but in fact that is a question that really *can't* be decided, since it turns out that they all bite off more than they can chew. I shall take as chief stalking-horse in the discussion Professor A. J. Ayer's *The Foundations of Empirical Knowledge*;[1] but I shall mention also Professor H. H. Price's *Perception*,[2] and, later on, G. J. Warnock's book on Berkeley.[3] I find in these texts a good deal to criticize, but I choose them for their merits and not for their deficiencies; they seem to me to provide the best available expositions of the approved reasons for holding theories which are at least as old as Heraclitus[4]—more full, coherent, and terminologically exact than you find, for example, in Descartes or Berkeley. No doubt the authors of these books no longer hold the theories expounded in them, or at any rate wouldn't now expound them in just the same form. But at least they did hold them not very long ago; and of course very numerous great philosophers have held these theories, and have propounded other doctrines resulting from them. The authors I have chosen to discuss may differ from each other over certain refinements, which we shall eventually take note of—they appear to differ, for example, as to whether their central distinction is between two 'languages' or between two classes of entities—but I believe that they agree with each other, and with their predecessors, in all their major (and mostly unnoticed) assumptions.

Ideally, I suppose, a discussion of this sort ought to begin with the very earliest texts; but in this case that course is ruled out by their no longer being extant. The doctrines we shall be discussing—unlike, for example, doctrines about 'universals'—were already quite ancient in Plato's time.

The general doctrine, generally stated, goes like this: we never see or otherwise perceive (or 'sense'), or anyhow we never *directly* perceive or sense, material objects (or material things), but only sense-data (or our own ideas, impressions, sensa, sense-perceptions, percepts, &c.).

One might well want to ask how seriously this doctrine is intended, just how strictly and literally the philosophers who propound it mean their words to be taken. But I think we had better not worry about this question for the present. It is, as a matter of fact, not at all easy to answer, for, strange though the doctrine looks, we are sometimes told to take it easy—really it's just what we've all believed all along. (There's the bit where you say it and the bit where you take it back.) In any case it is clear that the doctrine is thought *worth stating*, and equally there is no doubt that people find it disturbing; so at least we can begin with the assurance that it deserves serious attention.

My general opinion about this doctrine is that it is a typically *scholastic* view, attributable, first, to an obsession with a few particular words, the uses of which are over-simplified, not really understood or carefully studied or correctly described; and second, to an obsession with a few (and nearly always the same) half-studied 'facts.' (I say 'scholastic,' but I might just as well have said 'philosophical'; over-simplification, schematization, and constant obsessive repetition of the same small range of jejune 'examples' are not only not peculiar to this case, but far too common to be dismissed as an occasional weakness of philosophers.) The fact is, as I shall try to make clear, that our ordinary words are much

1. Macmillan, 1940.

2. Methuen, 1932.

3. Penguin Books, 1953.

4. [Regarding Heraclitus, see Aristotle, *Metaphysics*, n.8.—S.M.C.]

subtler in their uses, and mark many more distinctions, than philosophers have realized; and that the facts of perception, as discovered by, for instance, psychologists but also as noted by common mortals, are much more diverse and complicated than has been allowed for. It is essential, here as elsewhere, to abandon old habits of *Gleichschaltung*, the deeply ingrained worship of tidy-looking dichotomies.

I am *not*, then—and this is a point to be clear about from the beginning—going to maintain that we ought to be 'realists,' to embrace, that is, the doctrine that we *do* perceive material things (or objects). This doctrine would be no less scholastic and erroneous than its antithesis. The question, do we perceive material things or sense-data, no doubt looks very simple—*too* simple—but is entirely misleading (cp. Thales'[5] similarly vast and over-simple question, what the world is made of). One of the most important points to grasp is that these two terms, 'sense-data' and 'material things,' live by taking in each other's washing—what is spurious is not one term of the pair, but the antithesis itself.[6] There is no *one* kind of thing that we 'perceive' but many *different* kinds, the number being reducible if at all by scientific investigation and not by philosophy: pens are in many ways though not in all ways unlike rainbows, which are in many ways though not in all ways unlike after-images, which in turn are in many ways but not in all ways unlike pictures on the cinema-screen—and so on, without assignable limit. So we are *not* to look for an answer to the question, what kind of thing we perceive. What we have above all to do is, negatively, to rid ourselves of such illusions as 'the argument from illusion'—an 'argument' which those (e.g., Berkeley, Hume, Russell, Ayer) who have been most adept at working it, most fully masters of a certain special, happy style of blinkering philosophical English, have all themselves felt to be somehow spurious. There is no simple way of doing this—partly because, as we shall see, there is no simple 'argument.' It is a matter of unpicking, one by one, a mass of seductive (mainly verbal) fallacies, of exposing a wide variety of concealed motives—an operation which leaves us, in a sense, just where we began.

In a sense—but actually we may hope to learn something positive in the way of a technique for dissolving philosophical worries (*some* kinds of philosophical worry, not the whole of philosophy); and also something about the meanings of some English words ('reality,' 'seems,' 'looks,' &c.) which, besides being philosophically very slippery, are in their own right interesting. Besides, there is nothing so plain boring as the constant repetition of assertions that are not true, and sometimes not even faintly sensible; if we can reduce this a bit, it will be all to the good.

II

Let us have a look, then, at the very beginning of Ayer's *Foundations*—the bottom, one might perhaps call it, of the garden path. In these paragraphs[7] we already seem to see the plain man, here under the implausible aspect of Ayer himself, dribbling briskly into position in front of his own goal, and squaring up to encompass his own destruction.

> It does not normally occur to us that there is any need for us to justify our belief in the existence of material things. At the present moment, for example, I have no doubt whatsoever that I really am perceiving the familiar objects, the chairs and table, the pictures and books and flowers with which my room is furnished; and I am therefore satisfied that they exist. I recognize indeed that people are sometimes deceived by their senses, but this does not lead me to suspect that my own sense-perceptions cannot in general be trusted, or even that they may be deceiving me now. And this is not, I believe, an exceptional attitude. I believe that, in practice, most people agree with John Locke that 'the certainty of things existing *in rerum natura*, when we have the testimony of our senses for it, is not only as great as our frame can attain to, but as our condition needs.'
>
> When, however, one turns to the writings of those philosophers who have recently concerned themselves with the subject of perception, one may begin to wonder whether this matter is quite so simple. It is true that they do, in general, allow that our belief

5. [Regarding Thales, see Aristotle, *Metaphysics*, n.3.]

6. The case of 'universal' and 'particular,' or 'individual,' is similar in some respects, though of course not in all. In philosophy it is often good policy, where one member of a putative pair falls under suspicion, to view the more innocent-seeming party suspiciously as well.

7. Ayer, op. cit., pp. 1–2.

> in the existence of material things is well founded; some of them, indeed, would say that there were occasions on which we knew for certain the truth of such propositions as 'this is a cigarette' or 'this is a pen.' But even so they are not, for the most part, prepared to admit that such objects as pens or cigarettes are ever directly perceived. What, in their opinion, we directly perceive is always an object of a different kind from these; one to which it is now customary to give the name of 'sense-datum.'

Now in this passage some sort of contrast is drawn between what we (or the ordinary man) believe (or believes), and what philosophers, at least 'for the most part,' believe or are 'prepared to admit.' We must look at both sides of this contrast, and with particular care at what is assumed in, and implied by, what is actually said. The ordinary man's side, then, first.

1. It is clearly implied, first of all, that the ordinary man believes that he perceives material things. Now this, at least if it is taken to mean that he would *say* that he perceives material things, is surely wrong straight off; for 'material thing' is not an expression which the ordinary man would use—nor, probably, is 'perceive.' Presumably, though, the expression 'material thing' is here put forward, not as what the ordinary man would *say*, but as designating in a general way the *class* of things of which the ordinary man both believes and from time to time says that he perceives particular instances. But then we have to ask, of course, what this class comprises. We are given, as examples, 'familiar objects'—chairs, tables, pictures, books, flowers, pens, cigarettes; the expression 'material thing' is not here (or anywhere else in Ayer's text) further defined.[8] But *does* the ordinary man believe that what he perceives is (always) something like furniture, or like these other 'familiar objects'—moderate-sized specimens of dry goods? We may think, for instance, of people, people's voices, rivers, mountains, flames, rainbows, shadows, pictures on the screen at the cinema, pictures in books or hung on walls, vapours, gases—all of which people say that they see or (in some cases) hear or smell, i.e., 'perceive.' Are these all 'material things'? If not, exactly which are not, and exactly why? No answer is vouchsafed. The trouble is that the expression 'material thing' is functioning *already*, from the very beginning, simply as a foil for 'sense-datum'; it is not here given, and is never given, any other role to play, and apart from this consideration it would surely never have occurred to anybody to try to represent as some single *kind of things* the things which the ordinary man says that he 'perceives.'

2. Further, it seems to be also implied *(a)* that when the ordinary man believes that he is not perceiving material things, he believes he is being deceived by his senses; and *(b)* that when he believes he is being deceived by his senses, he believes that he is not perceiving material things. But both of these are wrong. An ordinary man who saw, for example, a rainbow would not, if persuaded that a rainbow is not a material thing, at once conclude that his senses were deceiving him; nor, when for instance he knows that the ship at sea on a clear day is much farther away than it looks, does he conclude that he is not seeing a material thing (still less that he *is* seeing an immaterial ship). That is to say, there is no more a simple contrast between what the ordinary man believes when all is well (that he is 'perceiving material things') and when something is amiss (that his 'senses are deceiving him' and he is *not* 'perceiving material things') than there is between what he believes that he perceives ('material things') and what philosophers for their part are prepared to admit, whatever that may be. The ground is already being prepared for *two* bogus dichotomies.

3. Next, is it not rather delicately hinted in this passage that the plain man is really a bit naïve?[9] It 'does not normally occur' to him that his belief in 'the existence of material things' needs justifying—but perhaps it *ought* to occur to him. He has 'no doubt whatsoever' that he really perceives chairs and tables—but perhaps he ought to have a doubt or two and not be so easily 'satisfied.' That people are sometimes deceived by their senses 'does not lead him to suspect' that all may not be well—but perhaps a more reflective person *would* be led to suspect.

8. Compare Price's list on p. 1 of *Perception*—'chairs and tables, cats and rocks'—though he complicates matters by adding 'water' and 'the earth.' See also p. 280, on 'physical objects,' 'visuo-tactual solids.'

9. Price, op. cit., p. 26, says that he *is* naïve, though it is not, it seems, certain that he is actually a Naïve Realist.

Though ostensibly the plain man's position is here just being described, a little quiet undermining is already being effected by these turns of phrase.

4. But, perhaps more importantly, it is also implied, even taken for granted, that there is *room* for doubt and suspicion, whether or not the plain man feels any. The quotation from Locke, with which most people are said to agree, in fact contains a strong *suggestio falsi*.[10] It suggests that when, for instance, I look at a chair a few yards in front of me in broad daylight, my view is that I have (*only*) as much certainty as I need and can get that there is a chair and that I see it. But in fact the plain man would regard doubt in such a case, not as far-fetched or over-refined or somehow unpractical, but as plain *nonsense*; he would say, quite correctly, 'Well, if that's not seeing a real chair then *I don't know what is*.' Moreover, though the plain man's alleged belief that his 'sense-perceptions' can 'in general' or 'now' be trusted is implicitly contrasted with the philosophers' view, it turns out that the philosophers' view is not just that his sense-perceptions *can't* be trusted 'now,' or 'in general,' or as often as he thinks; for apparently philosophers 'for the most part' really maintain that what the plain man believes to be the case is really *never* the case—'what, in their opinion, we directly perceive is *always* an object of a different kind.' The philosopher is not really going to argue that things go wrong more often than the unwary plain man supposes, but that in some sense or some way he is wrong all the time. So it is misleading to hint, not only that there is always room for doubt, but that the philosophers' dissent from the plain man is just a matter of degree; it is really not *that* kind of disagreement at all.

5. Consider next what is said here about deception. We recognize, it is said, that 'people are sometimes deceived by their senses,' though we think that, in general, our 'sense-perceptions' can 'be trusted.'

Now first, though the phrase 'deceived by our senses' is a common metaphor, it *is* a metaphor; and this is worth noting, for in what follows the same metaphor is frequently taken up by the expression 'veridical' and taken very seriously. In fact, of course, our senses are dumb—though Descartes and others speak of 'the testimony of the senses,' our senses do not *tell* us anything, true or false. The case is made much worse here by the unexplained introduction of a quite new creation, our 'sense-perceptions.' These entities, which of course don't really figure at all in the plain man's language or among his beliefs, are brought in with the implication that whenever we 'perceive' there is an *intermediate* entity *always* present and *informing* us about something *else*—the question is, can we or can't we trust what it says? Is it 'veridical'? But of course to state the case in this way is simply to soften up the plain man's alleged views for the subsequent treatment; it is preparing the way for, by practically attributing to *him*, the so-called philosophers' view.

Next, it is important to remember that talk of deception only *makes sense* against a background of general non-deception. (You can't fool all of the people all of the time.) It must be possible to *recognize* a case of deception by checking the odd case against more normal ones. If I say, 'Our petrol-gauge sometimes deceives us,' I am understood: though usually what it indicates squares with what we have in the tank, sometimes it doesn't—it sometimes points to two gallons when the tank turns out to be nearly empty. But suppose I say, 'Our crystal ball sometimes deceives us': this is puzzling, because really we haven't the least idea what the 'normal' case—*not* being deceived by our crystal ball—would actually be.

The cases, again, in which a plain man might say he was 'deceived by his senses' are not at all common. In particular, he would *not* say this when confronted with ordinary cases of perspective, with ordinary mirror-images, or with dreams; in fact, when he dreams, looks down the long straight road, or at his face in the mirror, he is not, or at least is hardly ever, *deceived* at all. This is worth remembering in view of another strong *suggestio falsi*—namely, that when the philosopher cites as cases of 'illusion' all these and many other very common phenomena, he is either simply mentioning cases which the plain man already concedes as cases of 'deception by the senses,' or at any rate is only extending a bit what he would readily concede. In fact this is very far indeed from being the case.

And even so—even though the plain man certainly does not accept anything like so *many* cases as cases

10. [Misleading implication.]

of being 'deceived by his senses' as philosophers seem to—it would certainly be quite wrong to suggest that he regards all the cases he *does* accept as being of just the same kind. The battle is, in fact, half lost already if this suggestion is tolerated. Sometimes the plain man would prefer to say that his senses were deceived rather than that he was deceived by his senses—the quickness of the hand deceives the eye, &c. But there is actually a great multiplicity of cases here, at least at the edges of which it is no doubt uncertain (and it would be typically scholastic to try to decide) just which are and which are not cases where the metaphor of being 'deceived by the senses' would naturally be employed. But surely even the plainest of men would want to distinguish *(a)* cases where the *sense-organ* is deranged or abnormal or in some way or other not functioning properly; *(b)* cases where the *medium*—or more generally, the conditions—of perception are in some way abnormal or off-colour; and *(c)* cases where a wrong inference is made or a wrong construction is put on things, e.g. on some sound that he hears. (Of course these cases do not exclude each other.) And then again there are the quite common cases of misreadings, mishearings, Freudian over-sights, &c., which don't seem to belong properly under any of these headings. That is to say, once again there is no neat and simple dichotomy between things going right and things going wrong; things may go wrong, as we really all know quite well, in lots of *different* ways—which don't have to be, and must not be assumed to be, classifiable in any general fashion.

Finally, to repeat here a point we've already mentioned, of course the plain man does *not* suppose that all the cases in which he is 'deceived by his senses' are alike in the particular respect that, in those cases, he is not 'perceiving material things,' or *is* perceiving something not real or not material. Looking at the Müller-Lyer diagram (in which, of two lines of equal length, one looks longer than the other), or at a distant village on a very clear day across a valley, is a very different kettle of fish from seeing a ghost or from having D.T.s and seeing pink rats. And when the plain man sees on the stage the Headless Woman, what he sees (and this *is* what he sees, whether he knows it or not) is not something 'unreal' or 'immaterial,' but a woman against a dark background with her head in a black bag. If the trick is well done, he doesn't (because it's deliberately made very difficult for him) properly size up what he sees, or see *what* it is; but to say this is far from concluding that he sees something *else*.

In conclusion, then, there is less than no reason to swallow the suggestions *either* that what the plain man believes that he perceives most of the time constitutes a *kind* of things (*sc.* 'material objects'), *or* that he can be said to recognize any other single *kind* of cases in which he is 'deceived.'[11] Now let us consider what it is that is said about philosophers.

Philosophers, it is said, 'are not, for the most part, prepared to admit that such objects as pens or cigarettes are ever directly perceived.' Now of course what brings us up short here is the word 'directly'—a great favourite among philosophers, but actually one of the less conspicuous snakes in the linguistic grass. We have here, in fact, a typical case of a word, which already has a very special use, being gradually stretched, without caution or definition or any limit, until it becomes, first perhaps obscurely metaphorical, but ultimately meaningless. One can't abuse ordinary language without paying for it.[12]

1. First of all, it is essential to realize that here the notion of perceiving *in*directly wears the trousers—'directly' takes whatever sense it has from the contrast with its opposite:[13] while 'indirectly' itself *(a)* has a use only in special cases, and also *(b)* has *different*

11. I am not denying that cases in which things go wrong *could* be lumped together under some single name. A single name might in itself be innocent enough, provided its use was not taken to imply either *(a)* that the cases were all alike, or *(b)* that they were all in certain ways alike. What matters is that the facts should not be pre-judged and (therefore) neglected.

12. Especially if one abuses it without realizing what one is doing. Consider the trouble caused by unwitting stretching of the word 'sign,' so as to yield—apparently—the conclusion that, when the cheese is in front of our noses, we see *signs* of cheese.

13. Compare, in this respect, 'real,' 'proper,' 'free,' and plenty of others. 'It's real'—what exactly are you saying it isn't? 'I wish we had a proper stair-carpet'—what are you complaining of in the one you've got? (That it's *im*proper?) 'Is he free?'—well, what have you in mind that he might be instead? In prison? Tied up in prison? Committed to a prior engagement?

uses in different cases—though that doesn't mean, of course, that there is not a good reason why we should use the same word. We might, for example, contrast the man who saw the procession directly with the man who saw it *through a periscope*; or we might contrast the place from which you can watch the door directly with the place from which you can see it only *in the mirror*. *Perhaps* we might contrast seeing you directly with seeing, say, your shadow on the blind; and *perhaps* we might contrast hearing the music directly with hearing it relayed outside the concert-hall. However, these last two cases suggest two further points.

2. The first of these points is that the notion of not perceiving 'directly' seems most at home where, as with the periscope and the mirror, it retains its link with the notion of a kink in *direction*. It seems that we must not be looking *straight at* the object in question. For this reason seeing your shadow on the blind is a doubtful case; and seeing you, for instance, through binoculars or spectacles is certainly not a case of seeing you *indirectly* at all. For such cases as these last we have quite distinct contrasts and different expressions—'with the naked eye' as opposed to 'with a telescope,' 'with unaided vision' as opposed to 'with glasses on.' (These expressions, in fact, are much more firmly established in ordinary use than 'directly' is.)

3. And the other point is that, partly no doubt for the above reason, the notion of indirect perception is not naturally at home with senses other than sight. With the other senses there is nothing quite analogous with the 'line of vision.' The most natural sense of 'hearing indirectly,' of course, is that of being *told* something by an intermediary—a quite different matter. But do I hear a shout indirectly, when I hear the echo? If I touch you with a barge-pole, do I touch you indirectly? Or if you offer me a pig in a poke, might I feel the pig indirectly—*through* the poke? And what smelling indirectly might be I have simply no idea. For this reason alone there seems to be something badly wrong with the question, 'Do we perceive things directly or not?,' where perceiving is evidently intended to cover the employment of *any* of the senses.

4. But it is, of course, for other reasons too extremely doubtful how far the notion of perceiving indirectly could or should be extended. Does it, or should it, covet the telephone, for instance? Or television? Or radar? Have we moved too far in these cases from the original metaphor? They at any rate satisfy what seems to be a necessary condition—namely, concurrent existence and concomitant variation as between what is perceived in the straightforward way (the sounds in the receiver, the picture and the blips on the screen) and the candidate for what we might be prepared to describe as being perceived indirectly. And this condition fairly clearly rules out as cases of indirect perception seeing photographs (which statically record scenes from the past) and seeing films (which, though not static, are not seen contemporaneously with the events thus recorded). Certainly, there *is* a line to be drawn somewhere. It is certain, for instance, that we should not be prepared to speak of indirect perception in *every* case in which we see something from which the existence (or occurrence) of something else can be inferred; we should *not* say we see the guns indirectly, if we see in the distance only the flashes of guns.

5. Rather differently, if we are to be seriously inclined to speak of something as being perceived indirectly, it seems that it has to be the kind of thing which we (sometimes at least) just perceive, or could perceive, or which—like the backs of our own heads—others could perceive. For otherwise we don't want to say that we perceive the thing *at all*, even indirectly. No doubt there are complications here (raised, perhaps, by the electron microscope, for example, about which I know little or nothing). But it seems clear that, in general, we should want to distinguish between seeing indirectly, e.g. in a mirror, what we might have just *seen*, and seeing signs (or effects), e.g. in a Wilson cloud-chamber, of something not itself perceptible at all. It would at least not come naturally to speak of the latter as a case of perceiving something indirectly.

6. And one final point. For reasons not very obscure, we always prefer in practice what might be called the *cash-value* expression to the 'indirect' metaphor. If I were to report that I see enemy ships indirectly, I should merely provoke the question what exactly I mean. 'I mean that I can see these blips on the radar screen'—'Well, why didn't you say so then?' (Compare 'I can see an unreal duck.'—'What on earth do you mean?' 'It's a decoy duck'—'Ah, I see, Why didn't you say so at once?') That is, there is seldom if ever any particular point in actually saying

'indirectly' (or 'unreal'); the expression can cover too many rather different cases to be *just* what is wanted in any particular case.

Thus, it is quite plain that the philosophers' use of 'directly perceive,' whatever it may be, is not the ordinary, or any familiar, use; for in *that* use it is not only false but simply absurd to say that such objects as pens or cigarettes are never perceived directly. But we are given no explanation or definition of this new use[14]—on the contrary, it is glibly trotted out as if we were all quite familiar with it already. It is clear, too, that the philosophers' use, whatever it may be, offends against several of the canons just mentioned above—no restrictions whatever seem to be envisaged to any special circumstances or to any of the senses in particular, and moreover it seems that what we are to be said to perceive indirectly is *never*—is not the kind of thing which ever *could* be—perceived directly.

All this lends poignancy to the question Ayer himself asks, a few lines below the passage we have been considering: 'Why may we not say that we are directly aware of material things?' The answer, he says, is provided 'by what is known as the argument from illusion'; and this is what we must next consider. Just possibly the answer may help us to understand the question.

III

The primary purpose of the argument from illusion is to induce people to accept 'sense-data' as the proper and correct answer to the question what they perceive on certain *abnormal, exceptional* occasions; but in fact it is usually followed up with another bit of argument intended to establish that they *always* perceive sense-data. Well, what is the argument?

In Ayer's statement[15] it runs as follows. It is 'based on the fact that material things may present different appearances to different observers, or to the same observer in different conditions, and that the character of these appearances is to some extent causally determined by the state of the conditions and the observer.' As illustrations of this alleged fact Ayer proceeds to cite perspective ('a coin which looks circular from one point of view may look elliptical from another'); refraction ('a stick which normally appears straight looks bent when it is seen in water'); changes in colour-vision produced by drugs ('such as mescal'); mirror-images; double vision; hallucination; apparent variations in tastes; variations in felt warmth ('according as the hand that is feeling it is itself hot or cold'); variations in felt bulk ('a coin seems larger when it is placed on the tongue than when it is held in the palm of the hand'); and the oft-cited fact that 'people who have had limbs amputated may still continue to feel pain in them.'

He then selects three of these instances for detailed treatment. First, refraction—the stick which normally 'appears straight' but 'looks bent' when seen in water. He makes the 'assumptions' *(a)* that the stick does not *really change its shape* when it is placed in water, and *(b)* that it *cannot be* both crooked and straight.[16] He then concludes ('it follows') that 'at least one of the *visual appearances* of the stick is *delusive*.' Nevertheless, even when 'what we see is not the *real quality* of a *material thing*, it is supposed that we are still seeing something'—and this something is to be called a 'sense-datum.' A sense-datum is to be 'the object of which we are *directly* aware, in perception, if it is not *part* of any *material thing*.' (The italics are mine throughout this and the next two paragraphs.)

Next, mirages. A man who sees a mirage, he says, is 'not perceiving any material thing; for the oasis which he thinks he is perceiving *does not exist*.' But 'his *experience* is not an experience of nothing'; thus 'it is said that he is experiencing sense-data, which are similar in character to what he would be experiencing if he were seeing a real oasis, but are delusive in the sense that *the material thing which they appear to present* is not *really there*.'

Lastly, reflections. When I look at myself in a mirror 'my body *appears to be* some distance behind the glass'; but it cannot actually be in two places at once; thus, my perceptions in this case 'cannot all be *veridical*.' But I do see *something*; and if 'there

14. Ayer takes note of this, rather belatedly, on pp. 60–61.

15. Ayer, op. cit., pp. 3–5.

16. It is not only strange, but also important, that Ayer calls these 'assumptions.' Later on he is going to take seriously the notion of denying at least one of them, which he could hardly do if he had recognized them here as the plain and incontestable facts that they are.

really is no such material thing as my body in the place where it appears to be, what is it that I am seeing?' Answer—a sense-datum. Ayer adds that 'the same conclusion may be reached by taking any other of my examples.'

Now I want to call attention, first of all, to the name of this argument—the 'argument from *illusion*,' and to the fact that it is produced as establishing the conclusion that some at least of our 'perceptions' are *delusive*. For in this there are two clear implications—*(a)* that all the cases cited in the argument are cases of *illusions*; and *(b)* that *illusion* and *delusion* are the same thing. But both of these implications, of course, are quite wrong; and it is by no means unimportant to point this out, for, as we shall see, the argument trades on confusion at just this point.

What, then, would be some genuine examples of illusion? (The fact is that hardly any of the cases cited by Ayer is, at any rate without stretching things, a case of illusion at all.) Well, first, there are some quite clear cases of *optical* illusion—for instance the case we mentioned earlier in which, of two lines of equal length, one is made to look longer than the other. Then again there are illusions produced by professional 'illusionists,' conjurors—for instance the Headless Woman on the stage, who is made to look headless, or the ventriloquist's dummy which is made to appear to be talking. Rather different—not (usually) produced on purpose—is the case where wheels rotating rapidly enough in one direction may look as if they were rotating quite slowly in the opposite direction. Delusions, on the other hand, are something altogether different form this. Typical cases would be delusions of persecution, delusions of grandeur. These are primarily a matter of grossly disordered beliefs (and so, probably, behaviour) and may well have nothing in particular to do with perception.[17] But I think we might also say that the patient who sees pink rats has (suffers from) delusions—particularly, no doubt, if, as would probably be the case, he is not clearly aware that his pink rats aren't real rats.[18]

The most important differences here are that the term 'an illusion' (in a perceptual context) does not suggest that something totally unreal is *conjured up*—on the contrary, there just is the arrangement of lines and arrows on the page, the woman on the stage with her head in a black bag, the rotating wheels; whereas the term 'delusion' *does* suggest something totally unreal, not really there at all. (The convictions of the man who has delusions of persecution can be *completely* without foundation.) For this reason delusions are a much more serious matter—something is really wrong, and what's more, wrong *with* the person who has them. But when I see an optical illusion, however well it comes off, there is nothing wrong with me personally, the illusion is not a little (or a large) peculiarity or idiosyncrasy of my own; it is quite public, anyone can see it, and in many cases standard procedures can be laid down for producing it. Furthermore, if we are not actually to be taken in, we need to be *on our guard*; but it is no use to tell the sufferer from delusions to be on his guard. He needs to be cured.

Why is it that we tend—if we do—to confuse illusions with delusions? Well, partly, no doubt the terms are often used loosely. But there is also the point that people may have, without making this explicit, different views or theories about the facts of some cases. Take the case of seeing a ghost, for example. It is not generally known, or agreed, what seeing ghosts *is*. Some people think of seeing ghosts as a case of something being conjured up, perhaps by the disordered nervous system of the victim; so in their view seeing ghosts is a case of delusion. But other people have the idea that what is called seeing ghosts is a case of being taken in by shadows, perhaps, or reflections, or a trick of the light—that is, they assimilate the case in their minds to illusion. In this way, seeing ghosts, for example, may come to be labelled sometimes as 'delusion,' sometimes as 'illusion'; and it may not be noticed that it makes a difference which label we use. Rather, similarly, there seem to be different doctrines in the field as to what mirages are. Some seem to take a mirage to be a vision conjured up by the crazed brain of the thirsty and exhausted traveller (delusion), while in other accounts it is a case of atmospheric refraction, whereby something below the horizon is made to appear above it (illusion). (Ayer, you may remember, takes the delusion view, although he cites it along with the rest as a case of illusion.

17. The latter point holds, of course, for *some* uses of 'illusion' too; there are the illusions which some people (are said to) lose as they grow older and wiser.

18. Cp. the white rabbit in the play called *Harvey*.

He says not that the oasis appears to be where it is not, but roundly that 'it does not exist.')

The way in which the 'argument from illusion' positively trades on not distinguishing illusions from delusions is, I think, this. So long as it is being suggested that the cases paraded for our attention are cases of *illusion*, there is the implication (from the ordinary use of the word) that there really is something there that we perceive. But then, when these cases begin to be quietly called delusive, there comes in the very different suggestion of something being conjured up, something unreal or at any rate 'immaterial.' These two implications taken together may then subtly insinuate that in the cases cited there really is something that we are perceiving, but that this is an immaterial something; and this insinuation even if not conclusive by itself, is certainly well calculated to edge us a little closer towards just the position where the sense-datum theorist wants to have us.

So much, then—though certainly there could be a good deal more—about the differences between illusions and delusions and the reasons for not obscuring them. Now let us look briefly at some of the other cases Ayer lists. Reflections, for instance. No doubt you *can* produce illusions with mirrors, suitably disposed. But is just *any* case of seeing something in a mirror an illusion, as he implies? Quite obviously not. For seeing things in mirrors is a perfectly *normal* occurrence, completely familiar, and there is usually no question of anyone being taken in. No doubt, if you're an infant or an aborigine and have never come across a mirror before, you may be pretty baffled, and even visibly perturbed, when you do. But is that a reason why the rest of us should speak of illusion here? And just the same goes for the phenomena of perspective—again, one *can* play tricks with perspective, but in the ordinary case there is no question of illusion. That a round coin should 'look elliptical' (in one sense) from some points of view is exactly what we expect and what we normally find; indeed, we should be badly put out if we ever found this not to be so. Refraction again—the stick that looks bent in water—is far too familiar a case to be properly called a case of illusion. We may perhaps be prepared to agree that the stick looks bent; but then we can see that it's partly submerged in water, so that is exactly how we should expect it to look.

It is important to realize here how familiarity, so to speak, takes the edge off illusion. Is the cinema a case of illusion? Well, just possibly the first man who ever saw moving pictures may have felt inclined to say that here was a case off illusion. But in fact it's pretty unlikely that even he, even momentarily, was actually taken in; and by now the whole thing is so ordinary a part of our lives that it never occurs to us even to raise the question. One might as well ask whether producing a photograph is producing an illusion—which would plainly be just silly.

Then we must not overlook, in all this talk about illusions and delusions, that there are plenty of more or less unusual cases, not yet mentioned, which certainly aren't either. Suppose that a proof-reader makes a mistake—he fails to notice that what ought to be 'causal' is printed as 'casual'; does he have a delusion? Or is there an illusion before him? Neither, of course; he simply *misreads*. Seeing after-images, too, though not a particularly frequent occurrence and not just an ordinary case of seeing, is neither seeing illusions nor having delusions. And what about dreams? Does the dreamer see illusions? Does he have delusions? Neither; dreams are *dreams*.

Let us turn for a moment to what Price has to say about illusions. He produces,[19] by way of saying 'what the term "illusion" means,' the following 'provisional definition': 'An illusory sense-datum of sight or touch is a sense-datum which is such that we tend to take it to be part of the surface of a material object, but if we take it so we are wrong.' It is by no means clear, of course, what this dictum itself means; but still, it seems fairly clear that the definition doesn't actually fit all the cases of illusion. Consider the two lines again. Is there anything here which we tend to take, wrongly, to be part of the surface of a material object? It doesn't seem so. We just see the two lines, we don't think or even tend to think that we see anything else, we aren't even raising the question whether anything is or isn't 'part of the surface' of—what, anyway? the lines? the page?—the trouble is just that one line looks longer than the other, though it isn't. Nor surely, in the case of the Headless Woman, is it a question whether anything is or isn't part of her surface; the trouble is just that she looks as if she had no head.

It is noteworthy, of course, that, before he even

19. *Perception*, p. 27.

begins to consider the 'argument from illusion,' Price has already incorporated in this 'definition' the idea that in such cases there is something to be seen *in addition to* the ordinary things—which is part of what the argument is commonly used, and not uncommonly taken, to *prove*. But this idea surely has no place in an attempt to say what 'illusion' *means*. It comes in again, improperly I think, in his account of perspective (which incidentally he also cites as a species of illusion)—'a distant hillside which is full of protuberances, and slopes upwards at quite a gentle angle, will appear flat and vertical. . . . This means that the sense-datum, the colour-expanse which we sense, actually *is* flat and vertical.' But why should we accept this account of the matter? Why should we say that there is *anything* we see which *is* flat and vertical, though not 'part of the surface' of any material object? To speak thus is to assimilate all such cases to cases of delusion, where there *is* something not 'part of any material thing.' But we have already discussed the undesirability of this assimilation.

Next, let us have a look at the account Ayer himself gives of some at least of the cases he cites. (In fairness we must remember here that Ayer has a number of quite substantial reservations of his own about the merits and efficacy of the argument from illusion, so that it is not easy to tell just how seriously he intends his exposition of it to be taken; but this is a point we shall come back to.)

First, then, the familiar case of the stick in water. Of this case Ayer says *(a)* that since the stick looks bent but is straight, 'at least one of the visual appearances of the stick is *delusive*'; and *(b)* that 'what we see [directly anyway] is not the real quality of [a few lines later, not part of] a material thing.' Well now: does the stick 'look bent' to begin with? I think we can agree that it does, we have no better way of describing it. But of course it does *not* look *exactly* like a bent stick, a bent stick out of water—at most, it may be said to look rather like a bent stick partly immersed *in* water. After all, we can't help seeing the water the stick is partly immersed in. So exactly what in this case is supposed to be *delusive*? What is wrong, what is even faintly surprising, in the idea of a stick's being straight but looking bent sometimes? Does anyone suppose that if something is straight, then it jolly well has to *look* straight at all times and in all circumstances? Obviously no one seriously supposes this. So what mess are we supposed to get into here, what is the difficulty? For of course it has to be suggested that there *is* a difficulty—a difficulty, furthermore, which calls for a pretty radical solution, the introduction of sense-data. But what is the problem we are invited to solve in this way?

Well, we are told, in this case you are seeing *something*; and what is this something 'if it is not part of any material thing'? But this question is, really, completely mad. The straight part of the stick, the bit not under water, is presumably part of a material thing; don't we see that? And what about the bit *under* water?—we can see that too. We can see, come to that, the water itself. In fact what we see is *a stick partly immersed in water*; and it is particularly extraordinary that this should appear to be called in question—that a question should be raised about *what* we are seeing—since this, after all, is simply the description of the situation with which we started. It was, that is to say, agreed at the start that we were looking at a stick, a 'material thing,' part of which was under water. If, to take a rather different case, a church were cunningly camouflaged so that it looked like a barn, how could any serious question be raised about what we see when we look at it? We see, of course, *a church* that now *looks like a barn*. We do *not* see an immaterial barn, an immaterial church, or an immaterial anything else. And what in this case could seriously tempt us to say that we do?

Notice, incidentally, that in Ayer's description of the stick-in-water case, which is supposed to be prior to the drawing of any philosophical conclusions, there has already crept in the unheralded but important expression 'visual appearances'—it is, of course, ultimately to be suggested that all we *ever* get when we see is a visual appearance (whatever that may be).

Consider next the case of my reflection in a mirror. My body, Ayer says, 'appears to be some distance behind the glass'; but as it's in front, it can't really be behind the glass. So what am I seeing? A sense-datum. What about this? Well, once again, although there is no objection to saying that my body 'appears to be some distance behind the glass,' in saying this we must remember what sort of situation we are dealing with. It does not 'appear to be' there in a way which might tempt me (though it might tempt a baby or a savage) to go round the back and look for it, and be astonished when this enterprise proved a failure.

(To say that A is *in* B doesn't always mean that if you open B you will find A, just as to say that A is *on* B doesn't always mean that you could pick it off—consider 'I saw my face in the mirror,' 'There's a pain in my toe,' 'I heard him on the radio,' 'I saw the image on the screen,' &c. Seeing something in a mirror is not like seeing a bun in a shop-window.) But does it follow that, since my body is not actually located behind the mirror, I am not seeing a material thing? Plainly not. For one thing, I can see the mirror (nearly always anyway). I can see my own body 'indirectly,' *sc.* in the mirror. I can also see the reflection of my own body or, as some would say, a mirror-image. And a mirror-image (if we choose this answer) is not a 'sense-datum'; it can be photographed, seen by any number of people, and so on. (Of course there is no question here of either illusion or delusion.) And if the question is pressed, what actually *is* some distance, five feet say, behind the mirror, the answer is, not a sense-datum, but some region of the adjoining room.

The mirage case—at least if we take the view, as Ayer does, that the oasis the traveler thinks he can see 'does not exist'—is significantly more amenable to the treatment it is given. For here we are supposing the man to be genuinely deluded, he is *not* 'seeing a material thing.'[20] We don't actually have to say, however, even here that he is 'experiencing sense-data'; for though, as Ayer says above, 'it is convenient to give a name' to what he is experiencing, the fact is that it already has a name—a *mirage*. Again, we should be wise not to accept too readily the statement that what he is experiencing is '*similar in character* to what he would be experiencing if he were seeing a real oasis.' For is it at all likely, really, to be very similar? And, looking ahead, if we were to concede this point we should find the concession being used against us at a later stage—namely, at the stage where we shall be invited to agree that we see sense-data always, in normal cases too.

V

I want now to take up again the philosophical argument as it is set out in the texts we are discussing. As I mentioned earlier, the argument from illusion is intended primarily to persuade us that, in certain exceptional, abnormal situations, what we perceive—directly anyway—is a sense-datum; but then there comes a second stage, in which we are to be brought to agree that what we (directly) perceive is *always* a sense-datum, even in the normal, unexceptional case. It is this second stage of the argument that we must now examine.

Ayer expounds the argument thus.[21] There is, he says, 'no intrinsic difference in kind between those of our perceptions that are veridical in their presentation of material things and those that are delusive. When I look at a straight stick, which is refracted in water and so appears crooked, my experience is qualitatively the same as if I were looking at a stick that really was crooked. . . .' If, however, 'when our perceptions were delusive, we were always perceiving something of a different kind from what we perceived when they were veridical, we should expect our experience to be qualitatively different in the two cases. We should expect to be able to tell from the intrinsic character of a perception whether it was a perception of a sense-datum or of a material thing. But this is not possible. . . .' Price's exposition of this point,[22] to which Ayer refers us, is in fact not perfectly analogous; for Price has already somehow reached the conclusion that we are always aware of sense-data, and here is trying to establish only that we cannot distinguish *normal* sense-data, as 'parts of the surfaces of material things,' from *abnormal* ones, not 'parts of the surfaces of material things.' However, the argument used is much the same: 'the abnormal crooked sense-datum of a straight stick standing in water is qualitatively indistinguishable from a normal sense-datum of a crooked stick'; but 'is it not incredible that two entities so similar in all these qualities should really be so utterly different: that the one should be a real constituent of a material object, wholly independent of the observer's mind and organism, while the other is merely the fleeting product of his cerebral process?'

It is argued further, both by Ayer and Price, that 'even in the case of veridical perceptions we are not

20. Not even 'indirectly,' no such thing is 'presented.' Doesn't this seem to make the case, though more amenable, a good deal less useful to the philosopher? It's hard to see how normal cases could be said to be *very like* this.

21. Ayer, op. cit., pp. 5–9.

22. *Perception*, p. 31.

directly aware of material things' [or *apud*[23] Price, that our sense-data are not parts of the surfaces of material things] for the reason that 'veridical and delusive perceptions may form a continuous series. Thus, if I gradually approach an object from a distance I may begin by having a series of perceptions which are delusive in the sense that the object appears to be smaller than it really is. Let us assume that this series terminates in a veridical perception.[24] Then the difference in quality between this perception and its immediate predecessor will be of the same order as the difference between any two delusive perceptions that are next to one another in the series. . . .' But 'these are differences of degree and not of kind. But this, it is argued, is not what we should expect if the veridical perception were a perception of an object of a different sort, a material thing as opposed to a sense-datum. Does not the fact that veridical and delusive perceptions shade into one another in the way that is indicated by these examples show that the objects that are perceived in either case are generically the same? And from this it would follow, if it was acknowledged that the delusive perceptions were perceptions of sense-data, that what we directly experience was always a sense-datum and never a material thing.' As Price puts it, 'it seems most extraordinary that there should be a total difference of nature where there is only an infinitesimal difference of quality.'[25]

Well, what are we to make of the arguments thus set before us?

1. It is pretty obvious, for a start, that the terms in which the argument is stated by Ayer are grossly tendentious. Price, you remember, is not producing the argument as a proof that we are always aware of sense-data; in his view that question has already been settled, and he conceives himself to be faced here only with the question whether any sense-data are 'parts of the surfaces of material objects.' But in Ayer's exposition the argument *is* put forward as a ground for the conclusion that what we are (directly) aware of in perception is always a sense-datum; and if so, it seems a rather serious defect that this conclusion is practically assumed from the very first sentence of the statement of the argument itself. In that sentence Ayer uses, not indeed for the first time, the term 'perceptions' (which incidentally has never been defined or explained), and takes it for granted, here and throughout, that there is at any rate some kind of entities of which we are aware in absolutely all cases—namely, 'perceptions,' delusive or veridical. But of course, if one has already been induced to swallow the idea that every case, whether 'delusive' or 'veridical,' supplies us with 'perceptions,' one is only too easily going to be made to feel that it would be straining at a gnat not to swallow sense-data in an equally comprehensive style. But in fact one has not even been told what 'perceptions' *are*; and the assumption of their ubiquity has been slipped in without any explanation or argument whatever. But if those to whom the argument is ostensibly addressed were not thus made to concede the essential point from the beginning, would the statement of the argument be quite such plain sailing?

2. Of course we shall also want to enter a protest against the argument's bland assumption of a simple dichotomy between 'veridical and delusive experiences.' There is, as we have already seen, *no* justification at all *either* for lumping all so-called 'delusive' experiences together, *or* for lumping together all so-called 'veridical' experiences. But again, could the argument run quite so smoothly without this assumption? It would certainly—and this, incidentally, would be all to the good—take rather longer to state.

3. But now let us look at what the argument actually says. It begins, you will remember, with an alleged statement of fact—namely, that 'there is no intrinsic difference in kind between those of our perceptions that are veridical in their presentation of material things and those that are delusive' (Ayer), that 'there is no qualitative difference between normal sense-data as such and abnormal sense-data as such' (Price). Now, waiving so far as possible the numerous obscurities in and objections to this manner of speaking, let us ask whether what is being alleged here is actually true. Is it the case that 'delusive and veridical experiences' are not 'qualitatively different'? Well, at least it

23. [In the words of.]

24. But what, we may ask, does this assumption amount to? From what distance *does* an object, a cricket-ball say, 'look the size that it really is'? Six feet? Twenty feet?

25. I omit from consideration a further argument cited by both Price and Ayer, which makes play with the 'causal dependence' of our 'perceptions' upon the conditions of observation and our own 'physiological and psychological states.'

seems perfectly extraordinary to say so in this sweeping way. Consider a few examples. I may have the experience (dubbed 'delusive' presumably) of dreaming that I am being presented to the Pope. Could it be seriously suggested that having this dream is 'qualitatively indistinguishable' from *actually being* presented to the Pope? Quite obviously not. After all, we have the phrase 'a dream-like quality'; some waking experiences are said to have this dream-like quality, and some artists and writers occasionally try to impart it, usually with scant success, to their works. But of course, if the fact here alleged *were* a fact, the phrase would be perfectly meaningless, because applicable to everything. If dreams were not 'qualitatively' different from waking experiences, then *every* waking experience would be like a dream; the dream-like quality would be, not difficult to capture, but impossible to avoid.[26] It is true, to repeat, that dreams are *narrated* in the same terms as waking experiences: these terms, after all, are the best terms we have; but it would be wildly wrong to conclude from this that what is narrated in the two cases is *exactly alike*. When we are hit on the head we sometimes say that we 'see stars'; but for all that, seeing stars when you are hit on the head is *not* 'qualitatively' indistinguishable from seeing stars when you look at the sky.

Again, it is simply not true to say that seeing a bright green after-image against a white wall is exactly like seeing a bright green patch actually on the wall; or that seeing a white wall through blue spectacles is exactly like seeing a blue wall; or that seeing pink rats in D.T.s is exactly like really seeing pink rats; or (once again) that seeing a stick refracted in water is exactly like seeing a bent stick. In all these cases we may *say* the same things ('It looks blue,' 'It looks bent,' &c.), but this is no reason at all for denying the obvious fact that the 'experiences' are *different*.

4. Next, one may well wish at least to ask for the credentials of a curious general principle on which both Ayer and Price seem to rely,[27] to the effect that, if two things are not 'generically the same,' the same 'in nature,' then they can't be alike, or even very nearly alike. If it were true, Ayer says, that from time to time we perceived things of two different kinds, then 'we should expect' them to be qualitatively different. But why on earth should we?—particularly if, as he suggests would be the case, we never actually found such a thing to be true. It is not at all easy to discuss this point sensibly, because of the initial absurdity in the hypothesis that we perceive just *two* kinds of things. But if, for example, I had never seen a mirror, but were told *(a)* that in mirrors one sees reflections of things, and *(b)* that reflections of things are not 'generically the same' as things, is there any reason why I should forthwith *expect* there to be some whacking big 'qualitative' difference between seeing things and seeing their reflections? Plainly not; if I were prudent, I should simply wait and see what seeing reflections was like. If I am told that a lemon is generically different from a piece of soap, do I 'expect' that no piece of soap could look just like a lemon? Why should I?

(It is worth noting that Price helps the argument along at this point by a bold stroke of rhetoric: how *could* two entities be 'qualitatively indistinguishable,' he asks, if one is a 'real constituent of a material object,' the other '*a fleeting product of his cerebral processes*'? But how in fact are we supposed to have been persuaded that sense-data are *ever* fleeting products of cerebral processes? Does this colourful description fit, for instance, the reflection of my face in a mirror?)

5. Another erroneous principle which the argument here seems to rely on is this: that it *must* be the case that 'delusive and veridical experiences' are not (as such) 'qualitatively' or 'intrinsically' distinguishable—for if they were distinguishable, we should never be 'deluded.' But of course this is not so. From the fact that I am sometimes 'deluded,' mistaken, taken in through failing to distinguish A from B, it does not follow at all that A and B must be *indistinguishable*. Perhaps I should have noticed the difference if I had been more careful or attentive; perhaps I am just bad at distinguishing things of this sort (e.g. vintages); perhaps, again, I have never learned to discriminate between them, or haven't had much practice at it. As Ayer observes, probably truly, 'a child who had not learned that refraction was a means of distortion would naturally believe that the stick really was crooked as he saw it'; but how is the fact that an uninstructed child probably would not

26. This is part, no doubt *only* part, of the absurdity in Descartes' toying with the notion that the whole of our experience might be a dream.

27. Ayer in fact expresses qualms later: see p. 12.

discriminate between *being refracted* and *being crooked* supposed to establish the allegation that there *is* no 'qualitative' difference between the two cases? What sort of reception would I be likely to get from a professional tea-taster, if I were to say to him, 'But there can't be any difference between the flavours of these two brands of tea, for I regularly fail to distinguish between them'? Again, when 'the quickness of the hand deceives the eye,' it is not that what the hand is really doing is *exactly like* what we are tricked into thinking it is doing, but simply that it is *impossible to tell* what it is really doing. In this case it may be true that we can't distinguish, and not merely that we don't; but even this doesn't mean that the two cases are exactly alike.

I do not, of course, wish to deny that there may be cases in which 'delusive and veridical experiences' really are 'qualitatively indistinguishable'; but I certainly do wish to deny *(a)* that such cases are anything like as *common* as both Ayer and Price seem to suppose, and *(b)* that there *have* to be such cases to accommodate the undoubted fact that we are sometimes 'deceived by our senses.' We are not, after all, quasi-infallible beings, who can be taken in only where the avoidance of mistake is completely impossible. But if we are prepared to admit that there may be, even that there are, *some* cases in which 'delusive and veridical perceptions' really are indistinguishable, does this admission require us to drag in, or even to let in, sense-data? No. For even if we were to make the prior admission (which we have so far found no reason to make) that in the 'abnormal' cases we perceive sense-data, we should not be obliged to extend this admission to the 'normal' cases too. For why on earth should it *not* be the case that, in some few instances, perceiving one sort of thing is exactly like perceiving another?

6. There is a further quite general difficulty in assessing the force of this argument, which we (in common with the authors of our texts) have slurred over so far. The question which Ayer invites us to consider is whether two classes of 'perceptions,' the veridical and the delusive, are or are not 'qualitatively different,' 'intrinsically different in kind'; but how are we supposed to set about even considering this question, when we are not told what 'a perception' *is*? In particular, how many of the circumstances of a situation, as these would ordinarily be stated, are supposed to be included in 'the perception'? For example, to take the stick in water again: it is a feature of this case that part of the stick is under water, and water, of course, is not invisible; is the water, then, part of 'the perception'? It is difficult to conceive of any grounds for denying that it is; but *if* it is, surely this is a perfectly obvious respect in which 'the perception' differs from, is distinguishable from, the 'perception' we have when we look at a bent stick *not* in water. There is a sense, perhaps, in which the presence or absence of water is not the *main thing* in this case—we are supposed to be addressing ourselves primarily to questions about the stick. But in fact, as a great quantity of psychological investigation has shown, discrimination between one thing and another very frequently depends on such more or less extraneous concomitants of the main thing, even when such concomitants are not consciously taken note of. As I said, we are told nothing of what 'a perception' is; but could any defensible account, if such an account were offered, completely exclude all these highly significant attendant circumstances? And if they *were* excluded—in some more or less arbitrary way—how much interest or importance would be left in the contention that 'delusive' and 'veridical' perceptions are indistinguishable? Inevitably, if you rule out the respects in which A and B differ, you may expect to be left with respects in which they are alike.

I conclude, then, that this part of the philosophical argument involves (though not in every case equally essentially) *(a)* acceptance of a quite bogus dichotomy of all 'perceptions' into two groups, the 'delusive' and the 'veridical'—to say nothing of the unexplained introduction of 'perceptions' themselves; *(b)* an implicit but grotesque exaggeration of the *frequency* of 'delusive perceptions'; *(c)* a further grotesque exaggeration of the *similarity* between 'delusive' perceptions and 'veridical' ones; *(d)* the erroneous suggestion that there *must* be such similarity, or even qualitative *identity*; *(e)* the acceptance of the pretty gratuitous idea that things 'generically different' could not be qualitatively alike; and *(f)*—which is really a corollary of *(c)* and *(a)*—the gratuitous neglect of those more or less subsidiary features which often make possible the discrimination of situations which, in other *broad* respects, may be roughly alike. These seem to be rather serious deficiencies.